FIRST SUPPLEMENT

A BENEDICTINE BIBLIOGRAPHY

A
BENEDICTINE BIBLIOGRAPHY

An Author-Subject Union List

Compiled for the Library Science Section
of the American Benedictine Academy

by

OLIVER L. KAPSNER, O.S.B.

First Supplement

Author and Subject Part

THE LITURGICAL PRESS

ST. JOHN'S ABBEY   COLLEGEVILLE   MINNESOTA

1982

American Benedictine Academy. Library Science Studies, No. 1

The publication of this Supplement to *A Benedictine Bibliography* has been made possible through grants from the Grotto Foundation, St. Paul, Minnesota; the Chadwick Foundation, Minneapolis, Minnesota; the I. A. O'Shaughnessey Foundation, St. Paul, Minnesota; the Harold J. and Marie O'Brien Slawik Foundation, St. Paul, Minnesota; Volkmuth Printers, Inc., St. Cloud, Minnesota; and St. John's Abbey, Collegeville, Minnesota.

Library of Congress Cataloging in Publication Data

Kapsner, Oliver Leonard, 1902–
  A Benedictine bibliography.

  Includes index.
  1. Benedictines – Bibliography – Union lists.
2. Catalogs, Union – United States. I. American
Benedictine Academy. Library Science Section.
II. Title.
Z7840.B3K33 Suppl. [BX3002.2] 016.271'1 81-20790
ISBN 0-8146-1258-X   AACR2

CONTENTS

INTRODUCTION

When the idea of a Benedictine bibliography was first conceived in 1948 at the meeting of the Library Science Section of the American Benedictine Academy, the bibliography was to develop from a union card catalog. Since the editor for the contemplated bibliography was from St. John's Abbey, Collegeville, Minnesota, it was logical that the catalog would be assembled in that abbey's library. After the publication of *A Benedictine Bibliography* in two volumes in 1962, the cooperating Benedictine libraries continued to send their contributions in the form of cards periodically to St. John's.

The American Benedictine libraries which possessed the major book collections faithfully continued to send their card contributions since 1962. Some other libraries needed a little prodding, but the general response and cooperation was very good, so much so that enough material had collected since 1962 as to make the publication of this Supplement possible. Another factor which encouraged the publication of a Supplement was the excellent reviews which the published work received, as well as the favorable comments from libraries and users of the publication, and, last but not least, its inclusion in the ninth edition (1976) of *Reference Books for Libraries*.

Like the original publication the Supplement again consists of an Author Part (books by Benedictine authors on any subject) and a Subject Part (books on Benedictine topics by any author – about 40 percent of the subject material is by non-Benedictine writers).

The editor encountered a problem which did not occur when preparing the original work, namely, the frequent change of personal names (monks and nuns) from religious to baptismal name, a practice which began about 1965. There were also changes of corporate names, mostly in the case of recently-founded abbeys and convents but also for some older congregations.

Some readers may wonder why the date of death was not supplied for most Benedictine writers born between 1860 and 1900. Such dates were not readily available, information which is normally supplied in the directory for the entire Benedictine Order, published every five years, known as *SS. Patriarchae Benedicti Familiae Confoederatae, Catalogus Monasteriorum*. Because of the havoc created by World War II, this directory was not published for the scheduled years 1940 and 1945, and subsequent editions did not include the dates of death for recently deceased members until the 1965 issue. As a result, the gap from 1935 to 1960 for gathering such information will be there forever. A necrologium or list of recently deceased members in the first issues published after the war was not included because not only older monks died but there were also many military casualties among younger monks. Information as to where and when they died could not be readily supplied.

The Supplement contains three types of literature: (1) books published during the years 1962–81, (2) books published before 1962 any time during the five centuries since the invention of printing in 1454 (the oldest printed book in this Supplement is dated 1477), (3) manuscripts or books written by hand before the invention of printing (such manuscripts, almost always on microfilm, in the Supplement date from the eighth to the seventeenth century).

A new feature in this Supplement is the inclusion of a good deal of Benedictine items culled from precious microfilmed manuscript material which has been collecting at St. John's Abbey since 1965. Such material requires a special filing arrangement in some instances, namely, for voluminous Benedictine writers in the Author Part, such as, Alcuin, Anselm of Canterbury, Bede the Venerable, Pope Gregory the Great, Engelbert of Admont, Rupert of Deutz, etc., and in the Subject Part under commentaries of the Rule of St. Benedict and for the principal liturgical books, such as Breviarium, Missale, etc. In such instances the usually extensive manuscript items are filed ahead of all printed works, the arrangement preferred by scholars. Where there are only a few items under an author's name, the manuscript and printed items are simply interfiled.

Microfilmed manuscript items are treated in this manner: After the title of the book follows the symbol "MS," meaning manuscript. Then follows the name of the library which owns the manuscript, together with the current codex number by which the manuscript is identified in the respective library. In a separate line follows the location of the film, which is always MnCH (Hill Monastic Manuscript Library, St. John's Abbey and University, Collegeville, Minn.), with or without another number. If it is with a number, e.g., MnCH proj. no. 2643, this is the project number or order in which the manuscript was filmed by the microfilm team. It is also the order in which the films are filed in the vault at MnCH. If the location symbol is merely MnCH, that is, without any number, the film was acquired from the respective European library on a commercial basis. Such films are filed separately in MnCH under country and library.

Under new publications are also included theses or dissertations, published or unpublished, done by Benedictine students since 1962. These are of special interest because they indicate at which universities, American or foreign, studies were pursued and the varied topics selected for the dissertations. Interest is also growing that non-Benedictine students in American universities are selecting Benedictine topics for dissertations, evidence for which can be seen here in the Subject Part.

It is also desirable that Festschriften, mélanges, symposiums, workshops, congresses, and similar collective publications should be analyzed and cataloged for inclusion in this bibliography. As such material, often the work of scholars, is not listed in periodical indexes, it is somewhat difficult to know and to locate. This Supplement includes analytics from a number of such collective publications, as many as were supplied by the cooperating libraries.

Serials (periodicals and monograph series) are again listed separately at the end of the Author Part. The listing is limited to new serials first published since 1961 and to older serials which had not been reported previously.

Another new feature is the inclusion of several Benedictine groups which for seven or eight centuries have been functioning as distinct Orders under their own names but which recently have joined the large Benedictine Federation. This applies to both the Author Part and the Subject Part, where books by and about them are included, though on a somewhat limited scale because of the short time since the changes were made. Three such groups (the Camaldolese, the Olivetans, and the Sylvestrines) now have at least one foundation in the United States, which are listed under Cooperating Libraries in California, Louisiana, and Michigan.

As in the case of the original publication of *A Benedictine Bibliography,* this Supplement would not have been possible without the contributions of the Benedictine cooperating libraries. Hence, the editor again extends a hearty thanks to all of them for their goodwill and continued cooperation. It is hoped that their cooperation will make another supplement possible, perhaps by A.D. 2000. And to the abbots of St. John's Abbey, the librarians, the American Benedictine Academy, and the entire Order of St. Benedict in this country are indebted for allowing a member of the St. John's community to devote part of his time to compiling and preparing this Supplement for publication. The era since 1962 covers the complete reign of one abbot at St. John's, the tail end of another, and the beginning of still another, namely, Baldwin Dworschak, O.S.B. (1950–71), John Eidenschink, O.S.B. (1971–79) and Jerome Theisen, O.S.B. (1979–). Abbots, like all human beings, come and go, but it is precisely the institution of the abbot as a steady helmsman that has kept the Benedictine ship sailing safely through calm and turbulent seas for over fourteen centuries.

This Supplement was scheduled for publication in 1980. When publication was delayed, occasioned by seeking financial assistance from foundations, several hundred new Benedictine items were inserted in both the Author and the Subject Part. This in turn necessitated adding the letters *a, b, c,* etc. to already used numbers. In one instance, where a new heading was introduced in the Subject Part, namely, for the 1980 sesquimillennium celebration, a long list of interesting commemorative publications was added, which in turn necessitated the use of a good part of the alphabet under one number (300 in the Subject Part).

Oliver L. Kapsner, O.S.B.

COOPERATING LIBRARIES

Below are listed the various Benedictine institutions in the United States, Puerto Rico, Canada, Mexico, and the Bahamas which cooperated in the compilation of this Supplement, together with their symbols. The system is based on *Symbols Used in the Union Catalog of the Library of Congress* (8th ed., 1960).

Alabama

ACu	Sacred Heart Convent, Box 317, Cullman, 35055
AStb	St. Bernard Abbey, St. Bernard, 35138

Arizona

AzTu	Benedictine Convent of Perpetual Adoration, 800 N. Country Club, Tucson, 85716
AzSd	Holy Trinity Monastery, Box 298, St. David, 85630

Arkansas

ArFsS	St. Scholastica Convent, Box 3099, Fort Smith, 72901
ArJH	Holy Angels' Convent, 223 E. Jackson Ave., Jonesboro, 72401
ArSu	New Subiaco Abbey, Subiaco, 72865

Bahamas

BNS	St. Augustine's Priory, Box N3940, Nassau

California

CGlS	St. Lucy's Priory, 19045 E. Sierra Madre, Glendora, 91740
COce	St. Charles Priory, Oceanside, 92054
CPoW	Woodside Priory, 302 Portola Rd., Portola Valley, 94025
CVal	St. Andrew's Priory, Valyermo, 93563
CSan	Benedictine Convent of Perpetual Adoration, 3888 Paducah Dr., San Diego, 92177
CSun	Holy Spirit Convent, 9725 Pigeon Pass Rd., Sunnymead, 92388
CBig	Immaculate Heart of Mary Hermitage, New Camaldoli, Big Sur, 93920

Canada

CaBMi	Westminster Abbey, Mission City, British Columbia, V2V 4J2
CaMWSb	St. Benedict's Priory, 225 Masters Ave., R.R. 1, Winnipeg, Manitoba R3C 2E4
CaQStB	Abbaye de Saint-Benoît-du-Lac, Brome County, Quebec, J0B 2M0
CaQMo	Abbaye du Mont-de-la-Redémption, Mont-Laurier, Quebec, J9L 1J9
CaQJo	Abbaye Notre-Dame-de-la-Paix, 490 nord, Rue Saint-Charles Borromée, Joliette, Quebec, J6E 4R7
CaQStM	Abbaye Sainte-Marie des Deux-Montagnes, 2803 Chemin d'Oka, Sainte-Marthe-sur-le-Lac, Quebec, J0N 1P0
CaSMu	St. Peter's Abbey, Muenster, Saskatchewan, S0K 2Y0

Colorado

CoCoH	Holy Cross Abbey, Canon City, 81212
CoCsB	Benet Hill Priory, 2555 Chelton Rd., Colorado Springs, 80909
CoBo	Convent of St. Walburga, 6717 S. Boulder Rd., Boulder, 80303

Connecticut
CtBeR   Regina Laudis Monastery, Bethlehem, 06751

District of Columbia
DStAA   St. Anselm's Abbey, S. Dakota Ave. and 14th St., N.E., Washington, 20017

Florida
FSanH   Holy Name Priory, San Antonio, Pasco County, 33576
FStL   St. Leo Abbey, St. Leo, Pasco County, 33574

Georgia
GASa   Benedictine Priory, 6502 Seawright Dr., Savannah, 31406

Idaho
IdCoS   St. Gertrude's Convent, Cottonwood, 83522

Illinois
IAurM   Marmion Abbey, Butterfield Road, Aurora, 60504
ICSS   St. Scholastica's Priory, 7430 Ridge Blvd., Chicago, 60645
ILSH   Sacred Heart Convent, 1910 Maple Ave., Lisle, 60532
ILSP   St. Procopius Abbey, Lisle, 60532
INauS   St. Mary's Priory, Nauvoo, 62354
IPeS   St. Bede Abbey, Peru, 61354
IOaF   Our Lady of Sorrows Convent, 5900 W. 147 St., Oak Forest, 60452

Indiana
InFer   Convent of the Immaculate Conception, Ferdinand, 47532
InStme   St. Meinrad Archabbey, St. Meinrad, 47577
InBe   Our Lady of Grace Convent, 1402 Southern Ave., Beech Grove, 46107
InInS   St. Maur Priory, 4545 Northwestern Ave., Indianapolis, 46208

Kansas
KAM   Mount St. Scholastica Convent, 801 8th St., Atchison, 66002
KAS   St. Benedict's Abbey, Atchison, 66002

Kentucky
KyCovS   St. Walburg's Convent, 2500 Amsterdam Rd., Covington, 41016
KySu   St. Mark's Priory, South Union, 42283
KyTr   Gethsemani Abbey, Trappist, 40073

Louisiana
LCov   St. Scholastica's Convent, 509 Asia St., Covington, 70433
LRam   St. Gertrude's Monastery, Ramsay, 70433
LStB   St. Joseph's Abbey, St. Benedict, 70457
LLa   Our Lady of Mount Olivet Monastery, 4029 Ave. G., Lake Charles, 70601

Maryland
MdRi   St. Gertrude Priory, Ridgely, 21660

Massachusetts
MGl   Glastonbury Abbey, Hingham, 02043

Mexico
MxCu   Monasterio Benedictino Nuestra Señora de la Resurreción, Cuernavaca, Morelos
MxMGM   Misioneras Guadalupanas de Cristo Rey, O.S.B., Villa de Guadalupe, Allende 37, Mexico 14 (D.F.)

MxMT   Monasterio Benedictino del Tepeyac, Apartado postal 345, Tlalnepantla, Estado de Mexico

MxMC   St. Benedict's Convent, Colonnia Linda Vista, 850 Rio Bamba, Mexico 14 (D.F.)

Michigan

MiOx   St. Benedict's Monastery, 2711 E. Drahner Rd., Oxford, 28051

Minnesota

MnCS   St. John's Abbey, Collegeville, 56321

MnCH   Hill Monastic Manuscript Library, St. John's University, Collegeville, 56321

MnCRM   Mount St. Benedict Convent, Summit Ave., Crookston, 56716

MnDuS   St. Scholastica Priory, Kenwood Ave., Duluth, 55811

MnStj   St. Benedict's Convent, St. Joseph, 56374

MnSSP   St. Paul's Priory, 2675 Larpenteur Ave., St. Paul, 55109

Missouri

MoSaB   Benedictine Convent of Perpetual Adoration, 8300 Morganford Rd., St. Louis, 63123

MoCl   Benedictine Convent of Perpetual Adoration, Clyde, 64432

MoCo   Conception Abbey, Conception, 64433

MoSaP   Priory of St. Mary and St. Louis, 500 S. Mason Rd., St. Louis, 63141

MoKB   Benedictine Convent of Perpetual Adoration, Pasco and Meyer Blvd., Kansas City, 64131

MoPe   St. Pius X Monastery, Pevely, 63070

MoCol   Our Lady of Peace Convent, 1511 Wilson St., Columbia, 65201

Nebraska

NbElm   Mount Michael Abbey, Elkorn, 68022

NbNo   Immaculata Convent, 300 N. 18th St., Norfolk, 68701

New Hampshire

NhMSA   St. Anselm's Abbey, Manchester, 03102

New Jersey

NjEliS   St. Walburga Convent, 851 N. Broad St., Elizabeth, 07208

NjMoS   St. Mary's Abbey, Box 347, Morristown, 07960

NjNN   Newark Abbey, 526 High St., Newark, 07102

NjNeS   St. Paul's Abbey, Newton, 07860

New Mexico

NmP   Our Lady of Guadalupe Abbey, Pecos, 87552

New York

NPi   Mount Savior Monastery, Pine City, 14871

North Carolina

NcBe   Belmont Abbey, Belmont, 28012

North Dakota

NdBel   Queen of Peace Priory, 701 Roller, Belcourt, 58316

NdBiA   Annunciation Priory, Apple Creek Rd., Bismarck, 58501

NdRiS   Sacred Heart Priory, Richardton, 58652

NdRiA   Assumption Abbey, Richardton, 58652

Ohio

OClSta   St. Andrew's Abbey, 2900 East Blvd., Cleveland, 44104

OWaQ   Queen of Heaven Convent, 8640 Squires Lane N.E., Warren, 44484

Oklahoma

OkShg	St. Gregory's Abbey, Shawnee, 74801
OkTu	St. Joseph Convent, 2200 S. Lewis, Tulsa, 74114
OkOs	St. Benedict's Convent, 1132 N.E. 32nd St., Oklahoma City, 73118

Oregon

OrMta	Queen of Angels Priory, Mt. Angel, 97362
OrStb	Mount Angel Abbey, St. Benedict, 97373

Pennsylvania

PBut	Holy Trinity Monastery, Butler, 16001
PErS	St. Benedict's Convent, 6101 E. Lake Rd., Erie, 16511
PLatS	St. Vincent Archabbey, Latrobe, 15650
PPiSM	Mount St. Mary Convent, 4530 Perryville Ave., Pittsburgh, 15229
PSaS	St. Joseph Convent, 303 Church St., St. Marys, Elk Co., 15857
PGrS	St. Emma's Convent, 1001 Harvey St., Greensburg, 15601

Puerto Rico

PuHu	Monasterio San Antonio Abad, Box 215, Humacao

Rhode Island

RPorP	Abbey of St. Gregory, Cory's Lane, Portsmouth, 02871

South Dakota

SdMar	Blue Cloud Abbey, Marvin, 57251
SdRa	St. Martin's Priory of the Black Hills, R.R. 4, Box 253, Rapid City, 57701
SdYa	Sacred Heart Convent, 1101 W. 5th St., Yankton, 57087
SdWa	Mother of God Priory, Watertown, 57201

Texas

TxCor	Corpus Christi Abbey, Box A-38-A, Sandia, 78383
TxBo	St. Scholastica's Convent, Boerne, 78006

Vermont

VtWes	Priory of St. Gabriel the Archangel, Weston, 05161

Virginia

ViBris	St. Benedict's Convent, 9535 Linton Hall Rd., Bristow, 22013

Washington

WaOSM	St. Martin's Abbey, Olympia, 98503
WaOSP	St. Placid Priory, 4600 Martin Way, Olympia, 98506

Wisconsin

WBenH	Holy Family Convent, Benet Lake, 53102
WBenS	St. Benedict's Abbey, Benet Lake, 53102
WEStb	St. Bede's Priory, Box 66, Eau Claire, 54701
WFif	King of Martyrs Monastery, Fifield, 54524
WFox	St. Benedict's Priory, Box 5070, Fox Bluff, 53705

MANUSCRIPT SOURCES

In 1965 St. John's Abbey launched a project to photograph and preserve on microfilm medieval manuscripts preserved in European Benedictine abbeys which have never been dissolved and which have enjoyed an unbroken existence since they were founded during the early or later Middle Ages. These abbeys possess precious manuscripts, which for the most part were written in the respective abbeys. Due to the success of the project, the work was extended to include all medieval religious Orders (notably the Cistercians, Augustinian Canons, and Premonstratensians). Still later state libraries and private libraries were included, as most of the manuscript material in such libraries was obtained from religious houses which were at some time dissolved. All the microfilming done in Austria and Spain is the product of a special microfilm team whose first director was the editor of *A Benedictine Bibliography*. Then, in the 1970s, some select microfilms were also obtained from other countries.

All this microfilm material is collected and made available to scholars for study purposes in one center at St. John's Abbey. The Benedictine items in this microfilm collection, which constitute only a very small portion of the entire collection, are included in this Supplement. The location of such items in the Supplement is signified by the symbol MnCH, which stands for Hill Monastic Manuscript Library, Collegeville, Minnesota.

Below is a list of all the abbeys and libraries where microfilming was done or from which copies of microfilms were obtained.

Austria

Admont. Benediktinerabtei
Altenburg. Benediktinerabtei
Fiecht. Benediktinerabtei
Göttweig. Benediktinerabtei
Graz. Universitätsbibliothek
Heiligenkreuz. Cistercienserabtei
Herzogenburg. Augustinerchorherrenstift
Innsbruck. Universitätsbibliothek
Klagenfurt. Bischöfliche Bibliothek.
Klagenfurt. Kärtner Landesarchiv.
Klagenfurt. Studienbibliothek
Klosterneuburg. Augustinerchorherrenstift
Kremsmünster. Benediktinerabtei
Kreuzenstein. Burg
Lambach. Benediktinerabtei
Lilienfeld. Cistercienserabtei
Linz. Bundesstaatliche Studienbibliothek
Linz. Oberösterreichisches Landesmuseum Bibliothek
Linz. Oberösterreichisches Landesarchiv
Maria Saal. Archiv des Collegialstiftes
Mehrerau. Cistercienserabtei
Melk. Benediktinerabtei

Michaelbeuern. Benediktinerabtei
Rein. Cistercienserabtei
Salzburg. Nonnberg (Benediktinerinnenabtei)
Salzburg. Sankt Peter (Benediktinerabtei)
Salzburg. Universitätsbibliothek
Sankt Florian. Augustinerchorherrenstift
Sankt Paul im Lavanttal. Benediktinerabtei
Sankt Pölten. Diözesanbibliothek
Schlägl. Prämonstratenserabtei
Schlierbach. Cistercienserabtei
Seitenstetten. Benediktinerabtei
Stams. Cistercienserabtei
Vienna. Dominikanerkloster
Vienna. Haus-, Hof- und Staatsarchiv
Vienna. Mechitaristenkongregation
Vienna. Oesterreichische Nationalbibliothek
Vienna. Schottenstift (Benediktinerabtei)
Vorau. Augustinerchorherrenstift
Wilhering. Cistercienserabtei
Zwettl. Cistercienserabtei

England

Hereford. Cathedral Library
Lincoln. Cathedral Library
London. British Museum
London. Lambeth Palace
Oxford. Bodleian Library
Salisbury. Cathedral Library
Winchester. Winchester College

France

Paris. Abbaye de Sainte-Marie
Paris. Bibliothèque Nationale
Rouen. Bibliothèque Municipale

Germany

Karlsruhe. Badische Landesbibliothek
Munich. Bayerische Staatsbibliothek
Stuttgart. Württembergische Landesbibliothek
Trier. Stadtbibliothek

Hungary

Budapest. Szecheny Library of the National Museum

Italy

Cava. Badia della SS. Trinità
Novacella (Neustift). Augustinerchorherrenkloster
Subiaco. Badia di S. Scholastica
Torino. Biblioteca Nazionale Universitaria

Malta

Mdina. Cathedral Museum

Spain

Barcelona. Archivo Capitular de la Catedral
Barcelona. Sant Pere de les Puel-les
Gerona. Archivo Capitular
Gerona. La Colegiata de San Félix
Huesca. Archivo de la Catedral

Madrid.   Real Academia de la Historia
Montserrat.   Biblioteca del Monasterio (O.S.B.)
Pamplona.   Archivo General de Navarra
Pamplona.   Biblioteca de la Catedral
Perelada.   Palacio Perelada
Poblet.   Monasterio de Santa Maria (Cistercian)
Seo de Urgel. Archivo de la Catedral
Silos.   Monasterio de Sto. Domingo (O.S.B.)
Tarazona.   Archivo de la Catedral
Tarragona.   Archivo Historico Archidiocesano
Toledo.   Biblioteca del Cabildo
Tortosa.   Archivo de la Catedral
Vallbona.   Monasterio de Sta. Maria (Cistercian)
Vich.   Archivo Capitular
Vich.   Museo Capitular
Zaragoza.   Biblioteca Capitular

Switzerland

Einsiedeln.   Benediktinerabtei
Sankt Gallen.   Stiftsbibliothek (formerly Benedictine)
Zürich.   Zentralbibliothek

United States

Durham, N.C.   Duke University Library
Latrobe, Pa.   St. Vincent Archabbey

Vatican City

Biblioteca Apostolica Vaticano

AUTHOR PART

1 **Abbas;** la figura dell' abate nel pensiero di S. Benedetto. Sorrento, Monastero di S. Paolo [1960?]
49 p. 23 cm.
PLatS

2 **Abbas Panormitanus.**
Lectura in lib. I-V Decretalium. MS. Gerona, Spain, Archivo Capitular, codex 21, b, 2–10. Folio. Saec. 15.
Microfilm: MnCH proj. no. 30,965

3 **L'Abbaye bénédictine de Fécamp;** ouvrage scientifique du XIIIe centenaire, 658-1958. Fécamp, L. Durand, 1959–61.
3 v. illus., plates. 25 cm.
– – Addenda & errata, index & tables. [Fécamp, L. Durand, 1963] 165 p.
CaQStB; KAS, MoCo, MnCS; NcBe; PLatS

4 **L'Abbaye de Maredsous;** guide illustrè. [Maredsous, Belgique] 1923.
96 p. illus.
MoCo

5 **Abbaye du Bec-Hellouin;** journées Anselmiennes, 7-12 juillet, 1959, retour du bienheureux Herluin. [Beauvais, l'Imprimerie Centrale Administrative, 1960]
68 p. illus.
MoCo

6 **Abbé bénédictin.**
Homélies pour notre temps, par un abbé bénédictin. [Ligugé, France, L'Abbaye Saint Martin, 1969]
112 p. 22 cm. (Lettre de Liguté, no. 139. Supplément)
KAS

7 **The Abbey of Monte Cassino;** an illustrated guide. [Printed in Italy by Alteroca-Terni, 196?]
44 p. chiefly col. illus. 21 cm.
MnCS

8 **Abbo, Saint, abbot of Fleury,** 945 (ca.)–1004.
Life of St. Edmund.
(*In* Three lives of English saints, ed. by Michael Winterbottom. Toronto, 1972)
Texts in Latin.
PLatS

9 **Abbo, monk of St. Germain,** ca. 850–ca. 923.
Abbonis Bella parisiacae urbis.
(*In* Poetae latini aevi carolini . . . Recensuit Paulus de Winterfeld . . . t. IV, fasc. I (1899), p. [72]–[122]
Monumenta Germaniae historica . . . Poetarum latinorum medii aevi, t. IV, fasc. I.
KAS (microfilm)

10 Abbonis de bellis Parisiacae urbis libri III.
(*In* Monumenta Germaniae historica. Scriptores. Stuttgart, 1963. t. 2, p. 776–805)
MnCS; PLatS

11 **Abélard, Pierre,** 1079-1142.
[Selections]
The everlasting Sabbath (O quanta qualia).
(*In* Donahoe, D. J. Early Christian hymns. New York, 1908. v. 1, p. 157–164)
PLatS

12 [Carmina]
(*In* Fourcher, J. P. Florilège de la poésie sacrée. Paris, 1961. p. 165–170)
PLatS

13 Dialogus. Incipit: Aspiciebam in visu noctis. MS. Vienna, Nationalbibliothek, codex 819, f. 1r–59v. Quarto. Saec. 13.
Microfilm: MnCH proj. no. 14,133

14 Epistola contra calumnias objectorum capitulorum. MS. Vienna, Nationalbibliothek, codex 998, f.151r–151v. Folio. Saec. 13.
Microfilm: MnCH proj. no. 998

15 Haereses seu 18 capitula a S. Bernardo ad Innocentium II missa. Ms. Vienna, Nationalbibliothek, codex 998, f.173r–173v. Folio. Saec. 13.
Microfilm: MnCH proj. no. 14,308

16 [Historia calamitatum. English]
An open letter: Abelard to a friend.
(*In* University library of autobiography. New York, 1918. v. 3, p. 39–53)
PLatS

17 O quanta qualia. [English translation]
(*In* Heaven; an anthology. New York, 1935. p. 29)
PLatS

18 Versus in laudem sanctae crucis. Inc.: Quam venerabilis, impreciabilis hic ades o crux. Vienna, Nationalbibliothek, codex 143, f. 12r. Folio. Saec. 13.
Microfilm: MnCH proj. no. 13,512

Abhishiktananda. *See* Le Saux, Henri.

19 **An account of the church and priory of Saint Mary Magdalene,** Davington, in the County of Kent. Faversham, Frederick W. Monk, 1852.
24 p. engr. front. 22 cm.
KAS

20 **Achatius, Frater, O.S.B.**
Liber syntaxis latinae. MS. Benediktinerabtei St. Peter, Salzburg, Austria, codex b.IV.35a. 139 f. Quarto. Saec. 16.
Microfilm: MnCH proj. no. 10,419

21 **Ad Sanctum Stephanum 969-1969;**

Festgabe zur Tausendjahr-Feier von St. Stephan in Augsburg. [Hrsg. von Egino Weidenhiller, O.S.B., Anton Uhl [und] Bernhard Weishaar, O.S.B.] Eigenverlag St. Stephan, Augsburg, 1969.
v,317 p. illus. 24 cm.
InStme; KAS; PLatS

21a **Adalard, Saint, abbot of Corbie,** d. 826.
Consuetudines Corbeienses. The customs of Corbie. A translation by Charles W. Jones of the directives of Adalhard of Corbie (753–826).
(*In* Horn, Walter W. The plan of St. Gall . . . 1979. vol. III, p. 91–128)
MnCS; PLatS

Adalboldus. *See* Adelboldus.

22 **Adam de Saint Victor,** d. 1192.
Sämtliche Sequenzen, lateinisch und deutsch. [2. Aufl.]. München, Kösel-Verlag [1955].
390 p. 20 cm.
Einführung und Formgetreue Uebertragung von Franz Wellner.
InStme; MnCS

23 **Adam of Eynsham,** fl. 1196–1232.
The life of St. Hugh of Lincoln. Edited by Decima L. Douie and Hugh Farmer. London, New York, Nelson [1961].
v. maps. 23 cm. (Medieval texts)
English and Latin.
KAS; MnCS; NcBe

24 **Adam of Perseigne,** d. 1221.
The letters of Adam of Perseigne. Translated by Grace Perigo. Introduction by Thomas Merton. Kalamazoo, Mich., Cistercian Publications [1976].
NcBe

25 **Adams, Alfons M.**
Am Dienste des Kreuzes; Erinnerungen aus meinem Missionsleben in Deutsch-Ostafrika. St. Ottilien, Post Türkenfeld (Oberbayern), 1899.
xiv, 154 p. illus. 27 cm.
InStme

26 **Adelboldus, bp. of Maastricht,** d. ca. 1027.
Vita Heinrici II imperatoris auctore Adalboldo, edente D. G. Waitz.
(*In* Monumenta Germaniae historica. Scriptores. Stuttgart, 1963. t. 4, p. 679–695)
MnCS; PLatS

Ademarus, monk of St. Cybard, 988–1034.
27 Chroniques de Saint-Martial de Limoges, pub. d'après les manuscrits originaux pour la Société de l'histoire de France par H. Duplès-Agier. Paris, V. J. Renounard, 1874.

lxxii, 429 p. 24 cm. (Société de l'histoire de France. Publications in octavo, 167)
KAS; MnCS

28 Ademari historiarum libri III, edente D. C. Waitz.
(*In* Monumenta Germaniae historica. Scriptores. Stuttgart, 1963, t. 4, p. 106–108)
MnCS; PLatS

Admont, Austria (Benedictine abbey).
29 Album Admontense; seu, Catalogus religiosorum Ordinis S.P. Benedicti in Abbatia Admontensis Superioris Stiriae anno jubilaeo 1874 viventium et ab anno 1674 pie defunctorum. Graecii, sumptibus Abbatiae Admont, 1874.
161 p. 24 cm.
InStme; MnCS; PLatS

30 Album Admontense; seu, Catalogus religiosorum Ordinis S.P.N. Benedicti in Abbatia originali conceptae . . . anno domini 1901 viventium et ab anno 1891 pie defunctorum. Graecii, Abbatia Admont, 1901.
81 p. 23 cm.
MnCS

31 [Catalog of manuscripts in Stift Admont] Austria.
396 p. 29 cm.
Manuscript. Xeroxed by University Microfilms, Ann Arbor, Mich., 1968.
MnCS

32 Catalogus antiquissimi monasterii Admontensis Ordinis S. Benedicti in Superiori Stiria, fundati anno 1045, conditi anno 1074. Vindobonae, Typis Congregationis Mechitˑristicae.
v. size varies.
PLatS

33 Documenta monasterii Admontensis (23 Urkunden Abschriften, saec. 12–15). MS. Benediktinerabtei Admont, Austria, codex 462a. 13 f. Folio. Saec. 15.
Microfilm: MnCH proj. no. 9513

34 Necrologium Admontense. MS. Benediktinerabtei Admont, Austria, codex 184, f. 189r–228v. Folio. Saec. 12.
Microfilm: MnCH proj. no. 9273

35 Necrologium Admontensis monasterii. MS. Benediktinerabtei Admont, Austria, codex 686a. 12 f. Octavo. Saec. 12–13.
Microfilm: MnCH proj. no. 9721

36 Schematismus der Benediktiner von Admont. [Admont, Benediktinerstift] 19___.
v. 23 cm.
InStme (1954); MnCS

37 **Ado, Saint, abp. of Vienne,** 800(ca.)–875.
Ex Adonis archiepiscopi Viennensis chronico usque ad a. 869.

(*In* Monumenta Germaniae historica. Scriptores. Stuttgart, 1963. t. 2, p. 315–326)
MnCS; PLatS

Adrevaldus, monk of Fleury, d. ca. 878.
38   Historia translationis S. Benedicti (abbreviated). MS. Abtei Kremsmünster, Austria, codex 95, f. 211r–212v. Quarto. Saec. 15.
Microfilm: MnCH proj. no. 88
39   Translatio S. Benedicti abbatis. MS. Abtei Kremsmünster, Austria, codex 34, f.170r–175r. Folio. Saec. 13.
Microfilm: MnCH proj. no. 34

Adso, abbot of Montier-en-Der, d. 992.
40   Adso Dervensis De ortu et tempore Antichristi; necnon et tractatus qui ab eo dependunt, edidit D. Verhelst. Turnholti, Typographi Brepols, 1976.
ix, 185 p. 26 cm. (Corpus christianorum. Continuatio mediaevalis, 45)
InStme; PLatS
41   Ex miraculis S. Mansueti auctore Adsone.
(*In* Monumenta Germaniae historica. Scriptores. Stuttgart, 1963. t. 4, p. 509–514)
MnCS; PLatS

42   **Aedilvulfus,** f. 803.
De abbatibus. Edited by A. Campbell. Oxford, Clarendon Press, 1967.
xlix, 72 p. 19 cm.
PLatS

43   **Aelfric, Saint, abp. of Canterbury,** d. 1006.
Three rare monuments of antiquitie . . . Aelfricus, Arch-bishop of Canterburie, an Englishman, his sermon on the Sacrament . . . Translated and compacted by M. William Guild. Aberdene, Printed by E. Raban for D. Melvill, 1624.
Aelfric's sermon is from an edition of Aelfric's works by Matthew Parker.
Short-title catalogue no. 12492 (carton 1174)
MnCS

Aelfric, abbot of Eynsham, ca. 955– ca. 1025.
44   Aelfric's first series of Catholic homilies; British Museum, Royal 7 C.XII, fols.4–218. Edited by Norman Eliason and Peter Clemoes. Copenhagen, Rosenkilde and Bagger, 1966.
37 p., 4–218 leaves. 38 cm. (Early English manuscripts in facsimile, v. 13)
MnCS; PLatS
45   Homilies of Aelfric: a supplementary collection, being twenty-one full homilies of his middle and later career for the most part not previously edited with some shorter pieces mainly passages added to the second and third series. Edited from all the known manuscripts with introduction, notes, Latin sources and a glossary by John C. Pope. London, New York, Oxford U.P. for the Early English Text Society, 1967–
v. facsims. 23 dm. (Early English Text Society. Publications. Original series, no. 259, v. 1: 84/-)
InStme; PLatS

46   The homilies of the Anglo-Saxon church. The first part, containing the Sermones catholici, or Homilies of Aelfric. In the original Anglo-Saxon, with an English version, by Benjamin Thorpe. London, Printed for the Aelfric Society, 1944–46.
2 v. 22 cm.
KAS
47   Life of St. Ethelwold.
(*In* Three lives of English saints, compiled by Michael Winterbottom. Toronto, Pontifical Institute of Mediaeval Studies [1972])
PLatS
48   Aelfric's homily on the Epiphany of the Lord. Copyright Thomas C. Wright (n.p.), 1929.
16 p. 32 cm.
MnCS (Archives)
49   Aelfric's lives of saints; being a set of sermons of saints' days formerly observed by the English Church, ed. from British Museum Cott. Ms. Julius E. VII, with various readings from other manuscripts, by the Rev. Walter W. Skeat . . . London, Published for the Early English Text Society, by the Oxford University Press, 1966.
2 v. 22 cm.
Reprint of the 1881–1900 edition.
PLatS
50   The old English version of the Heptateuch, Aelfric's treatise on the Old and New Testament and his Preface to Genesis, edited together with a reprint of "A Saxon treatise concerning the Old and New Testament: now first published in print with English of our times by William L'Isle of Wilburgham (1623)" and the Vulgate text of the Heptateuch, by S. J. Crawford . . . [London], Published for Early English Text Society by the Oxford University Press [1969].
ix, 460 p. facsims. 23 cm.
Originally published in 1922.
PLatS

Aethelwold, Saint, bp. of Winchester, 908–984.

51   Die angelsächsischen Prosabearbeitungen der Benediktinerregel. Hrsg. von Arnold Schröer. 2. Aufl., mit einem Anhang von Helmut Gneuss. Darmstadt, Wissenschaftliche Buchgesellschaft, 1964.
xliv, 284 [i.e., 224] p. 22 cm.
The translation is attributed to St. Aethelwold.
MnCS

52   Regularis concordia.
(*In* Gjerlow, Lilli. Adoratio crucis, the Regularis concordia and the Decreta Lanfranci. Manuscript studies in the early medieval church of Norway. [Oslo] Norwegian Universities Press, 1961.
176 p. 25 cm.
PLatS

53   Aethelwold's translation of the Regula Sancti Benedicti and its Latin exemplar, by Mechthild Gretsch.
(*In* Anglo-Saxon England 3. Cambridge Univ. Press, 1974. p. 125–151)
PLatS

Afflighem, Belgium (Benedictine abbey).
54   Het heilig doopsel; tekst en verklaring von de monniken van de Abdij Affligem. Hekelgem, Liturgisch Propagandawerk [1953].
46 p. 17 cm.
MnCS

55   Het heilig vormsel; tekst en verklaring van de monniken van de Abdij Affligem. Hekelgem, Liturgisch Propagandawerk [1953].
29 p. 17 cm.
MnCS

56   De heilige bisschopswijding; tekst en verklaring van de monniken van de Abdij Affligem. Hekelgem, Liturgisch Propagandawerk [1954].
46 p. 17 cm.
MnCS

57   De heilige wijdingen; tekst en verklaring van de Abdij Affligem. Hekelgem, Liturgisch Propagandawerk [1954].
63 p. 17 cm.
MnCS

58   **Agius, monk of Corvey,** fl. 870.
Agii vita et obitus Hathumodae a. 840–874.
(*In* Monumenta Germaniae historica. Scriptores. Stuttgart, 1963. t. 4, p. 165–189)
MnCS; PLatS

59   **Agius, Ambrose,** 1890–
The problem of Mary's holiness in the first Christian centuries.

(*In* Mariological Society of America. Marian studies, v. 14 (1963), p. 41–61)
PLatS

60   **Ahlbrecht, Ansgar,** 1922–
Tod und Unsterblichkeit in der evangelischen Theologie der Gegenwart. Paderborn, Verlag Bonifatius-Druckerei [1944].
154 p. 24 cm. (Konfessionskundliche und kontroverstheoligische Studien, Bd. X)
MnCS

Aicher, Otto, 1628–1705
61   Epitome chronologica historiae sacrae & profanae, ab orbe condito usque ad Christi ortum. Cui praefixa est brevis isagoge seu introductio ad historiam . . . Coloniae, sumpt. & typis Wilhelmi Metternich, 1706.
[6], 16, 166, [17] p. 21 cm. (*His* Opera)
InStme

62   Epitome chronologica historiae sacrae & ecclesiasticae, a Christo nato ad restitutum Occidentis imperium per Leonem III. pont. rom . . . Coloniae, sumpt. et typis Wilhelmi Metternich, 1706.
2 v. 21 cm. (*His* Opera)
InStme

63   Infantia, et adolescentia Romae; sive, Ortus, et progressus Romani Imperii. Annexis legibus regiis, consularibus, ac decemviralibus, una cum fastis Romanorum antiquis. [Salisburgi] 1693.
[24], 202, 80 p. geneal. tables. 14 cm.
InStme; PLatS

Alameda, Julian, 1897–
64   Las iglesias de oriente y su unión con Roma. Buenos Aires, P. P. Benedictinos Villanueva, 1929–1930.
2 v. 19 cm.
InStme

65   San Benito. Prólogo de Justo Perez de Urbel. 2. ed. [Madrid] Escelicer [1951].
199 p. 19 cm. (Coleccion piscis, 21)
KAS

66   **Alanus, abbot of Tewkesbury,** d. 1201–02.
Alani . . . Tewkesberiensis Scripta quae extant. E codicibus manuscriptis edita ab I. A. Giles. New York, B. Franklin [1967].
xi, 60 p. 23 cm. (Publications of the Caxton Society, 6)
Reprint of the edition published in Oxford in 1846.
PLatS

Albareda, Anselm Maria, 1892–1966.
67   L'Abat Oliba, fundador de Montserrat (971?–1046). [Barcelona] Abadia de Montserrat, 1972.
359 p. plates.
MnStj

68   Bibie manoscritte e bibbie stampate nel

quattrocento dell'antica biblioteca de Monserrato, note bibliografiche.
(*In* Studi di bibliografia e di storia in onore di T. De Marinis. p. 1–16)
PLatS

69   Historia de Montserrat. 5. ed. rev. a cura de Josep Massot i Muntaner. Montserrat, Abadia, 1972.
320 p. plates, 23 cm.
InStme; MnCS

70   Historia de Montserrat. 6. ed., revisada i ampliada per Josep Massot i Muntaner. Publicacions de l'Abadia de Montserrat, 1977.
331 p. col. plates, 24 cm. (Biblioteca "Abat Oliba," 12)
MnCS

71   Miscellania. Montserrat, 1962.
2 v. (Analecta Montserratensia, IX–X)
NcBe

72   Sant Ignasi a Montserrat. Monestir de Montserrat, 1935.
248 p. 24 cm.
MnCS; WBenS

73   Gli scritti del Cardinale Mercati. Articolo apparso su "L'Osservatore Romano" preceduto da "Appunti biografici." Biblioteca Apostolica Vaticana, 1957.
44 p. front (port) 18 cm.
MnCS

74   (2dary) Kapsner, Oliver. A Benedictine bibliography . . . With a foreword by Anselmo M. Cardinal Albareda, O.S.B., Prefect, Vatican Library, 1936–1962. Collegeville, Minn., St. John's Abbey Press, 1962.
MnCS; PLatS; etc., etc.

75   (2dary) Llibre d'amoretes atribuit a un ermita de Montserrat del segle XIVe. Monestir de Montserrat, 1930.
Introducció signed: Dom Anselm M. Albareda.
MnCS

76   (2dary) Montserrat (Benedictine abbey). Biblioteca. [Catalog of manuscripts].
3 v. 29 cm.
Handwritten. Xeroxed by University Microfilms, Ann Arbor, Mich., 1973.
Manuscripts 1–72 were covered by Anselm Albareda in Analecta Montserratensia, 1917, v. 1, p. 3–99.
MnCS

77   (2dary) Tavole e indici generali dei primi cento volumi di "Studi e testi." Città del Vaticano, Biblioteca Apostolica Vaticana, 1942.
xxiii, 182 p. 26 cm. (Studi e testi, 100)
"Introduzione" signed: Anselmo M.

Albareda.
PLatS

78   **Albelda, Spain. San Martin (Benedictine monastery).**
Cartulario de Albelda. [por] Antonio Ubeto Arteta. Valencia [Graficas Bautista, 1960.
203 p. 17 cm. (Textos medievales, 1)
PLatS

Albericus, monk of Monte Cassino, Cardinal, 1008–1088?

79   Liber de barbarismo et soloecismo et tropo et schemate. MS. Cistercienserabtei Lilienfeld, Austria, codex 98, f. 91v–111v. Quarto. Saec. 12.
Microfilm: MnCH proj. no. 4396

80   De barberismo et solocismo, tropo et scemate. MS. Cistercienserabtei Heiligenkreuz, Austria, codex 257, f. 103r–123v. Folio. Saec. 13.
Microfilm: MnCH proj. no. 4796

81   Rationes dictandi [et] De dictamine.
(*In* Rockinger, Ludwig. Briefsteller und Formelbücher des eilften bis vierzehnten Jahrhunderts. New York, 1961. v. 1, p. 1–46)
PLatS

82   La vision d'Alberic.
(*In* Marchand, Jean, tr. L'autre monde au Moyen Age: voyages et visions. Paris, E. de Boccard, 1940)
MnCS

83   (2dary) Willard, Henry M. The use of classics in the Flores rhetorici of Alberic of Monte Cassino. [Boston] Houghton Mifflin Co. [1929])
MnCS

84   **Albers, Bruno,** 1866–1941.
Manuale di propedeutica storica. Roma, Federico Pustet, 1909.
xi, 286 p. 23 cm.

85   **Albuinus, monk of Gorze.**
De antichristo, quomodo nasci debeat. MS. Vienna, Nationalbibliothek, codex 861, f. 2r–7v. Octavo. Saec. 12.
Microfilm: MnCH proj. no. 14,172

86   **Album Einsidlense;** seu, Catalogus religiosorum monasterii B.V.M. Einsidlensis Ordinis S. Benedicti Pagi Suitensis in Helvetia ad annum a Christo nato 1876 necnon pie defunctorum ab anno 1800. Einsidlae, C. et N. Benziger, 1876.
152 p. 22 cm.
NdRi; PLatS

Alcuin, 735–804.
Manuscript copies.

87   [Opera]
Epistola ad Aquilam; Epistola altera; De

hoc quod dicit apostolus ad Corinthos; Quaestio ubi ad Epheseos apostolus loquitur; De epistola ad Titum; Epistolae variae (13); Epistola ad Candidum Romam abeuntem; Carolus Magnus, rex, Epistola ad Alcuinum. MS. Vienna, Nationalbibliothek, codex 795. 204 f. Saec. 10.
Microfilm: MnCH proj. no. 14,139

88   [Opera]
Praefatio in librum de S. Trinitate; Confessio de S. Trinitate; Quaestiones de S. Trinitate; De ratione animae; Instructio, seu de virtutibus et vitiis; Libri tres de S. Trinitate. MS. Vienna, Nationalbibliothek, codex 794, f. 42v–96r. Quarto. Saec. 12.
Microfilm: MnCH proj. no. 14,110

89   [Opera]
De fide S. Trinitatis; De Trinitate ad Fredegisum quaestiones; De ratione animae liber ad Eulaliam virginem; Doctrina de fide. MS. Universitätsbibliothek Graz, codex 724, f. 241v–272r. Folio. Saec. 13.
Microfilm: MnCH proj. no. 26,829

90   [Opera]
Carmen–Inc.: O vos, est aetas iuvenes quibus apta legendo; Dialecta; Carmen–Inc.: Qui rogo civiles cupiat congnoscere mores; Rhetorica; Arithmetica; Musica; Astrologia. MS. Vienna, Nationalbibliothek, codex 2269, f. 1r–8v. Folio. Saec. 13.
Microfilm: MnCH proj. no. 20,324

91   [Opera]
Isagoge, seu Dialectica modo dialogi inter imperatorem Karolum Magnum et ipsum; Rhetorica; Arithmetica; Musica; Astrologia; Apophthegmata veterum philosophorum. MS. Vienna, Nationalbibliothek, codex 5271. 44 f. Folio. Saec. 16.
Microfilm: MnCH proj. no. 18,446

92   Ad pueros S. Martini de confessione puerorum. MS. Vienna, Nationalbibliothek, codex 458, f. 168r–175r. Folio. Saec. 10.
Microfilm: MnCH proj. no. 13,785

93   Albini ad Sigulfum presb. in quaestiones libri Geneseos. MS. Lambeth Palace Library, London, codex 148, f. 120–150. Quarto. Saec. 12.
Microfilm: MnCH

94   Alcuinus ad Guidonem. MS. Lambeth Palace Library, London, codex 378, f. 1–14. Quarto. Saec. 13.
Microfilm: MnCH

95   Carmina. MS. Vienna, Nationalbibliothek, codex 808, f. 225v–234v. Quarto. Saec. 10.
Microfilm: MnCH proj. no. 14,126

96   Collectio homiliarum et sermonum. MS. Augustinerchorherrenstift Klosterneuburg, Austria, codex 50. 327 f. Folio. Saec. 14.
Microfilm: MnCH proj. no. 5020

97   De adventu antichristi. MS. Vienna, Nationalbibliothek, codex 923, f. 193r–194v. Folio. Saec. 14.
Microfilm: MnCH proj. no. 14,237

98   De divinis officiis (fragmentum). MS. Vienna, Nationalbibliothek, codex 983. 6 f. Folio. Saec. 11.
Microfilm: MnCH proj. no. 14,289

99   De fide S. Trinitatis libri tres. MS. Salisbury, England, Cathedral Library, codex 165, f. 122–151. Quarto. Saec. 12.
Microfilm: MnCH

100 De fide S. Trinitatis. MS. Vienna, Nationalbibliothek, codex 1012, f. 122v–128v. Folio. Saec. 12.
Microfilm: MnCH proj. no. 14,330

101 De imagine Dei. MS. Vienna, Nationalbibliothek, codex 458, f. 175r–179r. Folio. Saec. 10.
Microfilm: MnCH proj. no. 13,785

102 De psalmorum usu. MS. Prämonstratenserabtei Schlägl, Austria, codex 97, f. 8r–8v. Folio. Saec. 15.
Microfilm: MnCH proj. no. 2956

103 De Trinitate. MS. Vienna, Nationalbibliothek, codex 827, f. 135r–202r. Quarto. Saec. 11.
Microfilm: MnCH proj. no. 14,123

104 De Trinitate. MS. Subiaco, Italy (Benedictine abbey), codex 118. 54 f. Quarto. Saec. 11.
Microfilm: MnCH

105 De Trinitate. MS. Vienna, Nationalbibliothek, codex 4760, f. 1r–33v. Quarto. Saec. 15.
Microfilm: MnCH proj. no. 14,451

106 Opusculum de vitiis et virtutibus. MS. Vich, Spain, Archivo Capitular, codex 46, f. 1r–21r. Quarto. Saec. 12.
Microfilm: MnCH proj. no. 31,196

107 Dialogi duo de rhetorica et dialectica. MS. Vienna, Nationalbibliothek, codex 2484. 68 f. Quarto. Saec. 9.
Microfilm: MnCH proj. no. 15,793

108 Dialogus de rhetorica et de virtutibus. MS. Vienna, Nationalbibliothek, codex 160, f. 50r–70v. Quarto. Saec. 13.
Microfilm: MnCH proj. no. 13,506

109 Carolini Magni et Alcuini magistri ejus Dialogus de rhethoricae virtutibus. MS. Benediktinerabtei Göttweig, Austria, codex 107, f., f. 27r–41v. Folio. Saec. 12.
Microfilm: MnCH proj. no. 3387

110 Dicta in Genes. I, 26. MS. Prämonstratenserabtei Schlägl, Austria, codex 3, f. 6r–7r. Quarto. Saec. 12–13.
Microfilm: MnCH proj. no. 3068

111 Dictatus seu Epistola ad Karolum Magnum de ordinandis piis praedicatoribus. MS. Vienna, Nationalbibliothek, codex 458, f. 186r–189v. Folio. Saec. 10.
Microfilm: MnCH proj. no. 13,785

112 Disputatio de dialectica. MS. Vienna, Nationalbibliothek, codex 223, f. 18r–30v. Quarto. Saec. 11.
Microfilm: MnCH proj. no. 13,580

113 Disputatio de vera philosophia. Finis deest. MS. Vienna, Nationalbibliothek, codex 2404, f. 8v. Folio. Saec. 9.
Microfilm: MnCH proj. no. 15,723

114 Disputatio de vera phylosophia Albini magistri. MS. Augustinerchorherrenstift St. Florian, Austria, codex III, 222, B, f. 128v–171v. Octavo. Saec. 10.
Microfilm: MnCH proj. no. 2246

115 Disputatio Pippini cum Albino. MS. Vienna, Nationalbibliothek, codex 808, f. 221v–225v. Quarto. Saec. 10.
Microfilm: MnCH proj. no. 14,126

116 Disputatio puerorum. MS. Vienna, Nationalbibliothek, codex 966, f. 6r–24r. Folio. Saec. 10.
Microfilm: MnCH proj. no. 14,277

117 Disputationes de dialectica (fragmenta). MS. Vienna, Nationalbibliothek, codex 160, f. 50r. Quarto. Saec. 15.
Microfilm: MnCH proj. no. 13,506

118 Duo poemata. MS. Vienna, Nationalbibliothek, codex 1190, f. 16r–16v. Folio. Saec. 9.
Microfilm: MnCH proj. no. 14,540

119 Epistolae. MS. Vienna, Nationalbibliothek, codex 808, f. 101r–221v. Quarto. Saec. 10.
Microfilm: MnCH proj. no. 14,126

120 Epistola ad Arnonem archiepiscopum Salisburgensem. MS. Vienna, Nationalbibliothek, codex 458, f. 81v–86v. Folio. Saec. 10.
Microfilm: MnCH proj. no. 13,785

121 Epistola ad Arnonem archiepiscopum Salisburgensem de natura et personis divinis. MS. Vienna, Nationalbibliothek, codex 966, f. 33v–34r. Folio. Saec. 10.
Microfilm: MnCH proj. no. 14,277

122 Epistola Albyni sive Alcuyni monachi ad Karolum et alios. MS. Lambeth Palace Library, London, codex 218, f. 91– Quarto. Saec. 12.
Microfilm: MnCH

123 Epistola ad Karolum Magnum. MS. Vienna, Nationalbibliothek, codex 966, f. 24r–26r. Folio. Saec. 10.
Microfilm: MnCH proj. no. 14,277

124 Epistola ad Carolum imperatorem. MS. Vienna, Nationalbibliothek, codex 1012, f. 121v–122v. Folio. Saec. 12.
Microfilm: MnCH proj. no. 14,330

125 Epistola ad Karolum regem de Septuagesima, Sexagesima et Quinquagesima. MS. Augustinerchorherrenstift Klosterneuburg, Austria, codex 1023, f. 65r–66v. Quarto. Saec. 13.
Microfilm: MnCH proj. no. 6022

126 Epistola ad Eulalium de animae ratione. MS. Salisbury, England, Cathedral Library, codex 165, f. 157–162. Quarto. Saec. 12.
Microfilm: MnCH

127 Epistola Albini ad Fredegisum. Interrogationes Fredegisi et responsiones Albini. MS. Salisbury, England, Cathedral Library, codex 165, f. 153v–156. Quarto. Saec. 12.
Microfilm: MnCH

128 Epistola ad Fredegisum et quaestiones de Trinitate. MS. Vienna, Nationalbibliothek, codex 4760, f. 33v–36v. Quarto. Saec. 15.
Microfilm: MnCH proj. no. 14,451

129 Epistola Albini ad Heribertum episcopum Coloniensem. MS. Cistercienserabtei Wilhering, Austria, codex IX, 132, f. 79r–81r. Octavo. Saec. 13.
Microfilm: MnCH proj. no. 2911

130 Epistola ad Singulphum. MS. Vienna, Nationalbibliothek, codex 1060, f. 1r. Quarto. Saec. 12.
Microfilm: MnCH proj. no. 14,373

131 Expositio super Ecclesiasten. MS. Benediktinerabtei Kremsmünster, Austria, codex 32, f. 52v–94v. Folio. Saec. 12.
Microfilm: MnCH proj. no. 32

132 Expositio in librum Ecclesiasten. MS. Benediktinerabtei Göttweig, Austria, codex 429, f. 4r–42v. Quarto. Saec. 15.
Microfilm: MnCH proj. no. 3693

133 Expositio super Ecclesiasten. MS. Benediktinerabtei Göttweig, Austria, codex 430a, f. 7r–42v. Quarto. Saec. 15.
Microfilm: MnCH proj. no. 3689

134 In loca obscuriora libri Genesis. MS. Cistercienserabtei Lilienfeld, Austria, codex 132, f. 142r–180r. Folio. Saec. 14.
Microfilm: MnCH proj. no. 4433

135 Explanatio libri Levitici. MS. Benediktinerabtei Admont, Austria, codex 174. Folio. Saec. 13.
Microfilm: MnCH proj. no. 9262

136   Expositio in psalmos graduales. MS. Vienna, Nationalbibliothek, codex 458, f. 143r–168r. Folio. Saec. 10.
Microfilm: MnCH proj. no. 13,785

137   Expositio in psalmos poenitentiales. MS. Vienna, Nationalbibliothek, codex 458, f. 86v–114r. Folio. Saec. 10.
Microfilm: MnCH proj. no. 13,785

138   Homelia in die natali s. Vedasti pontificis. MS. Vienna, Nationalbibliothek, codex 550, f. 109r–112r. Quarto. Saec. 10.
Microfilm: MnCH proj. no. 13,870

139   Homelia in nativitatem Beatae Mariae Virginis. MS. Vienna, Nationalbibliothek, codex 4873, f. 167r–169v. Folio. Saec. 14.
Microfilm: MnCH proj. no. 18,029

140   Hymnus in s. Vedastum. Versus in s. Vedastum. MS. Vienna, Nationalbibliothek, codex 550, f. 112r–113v. Quarto. Saec. 10.
Microfilm: MnCH proj. no. 13,870

141   Albinus ad Fredegisum. Interrogationes et responsiones de Sancta Trinitate. MS. Cistercienserabtei Zwettl, Austria, codex 363, f. 66v–70r. Octavo. Saec. 12.
Microfilm: MnCH proj. no. 6961

142   Interrogationes et responsiones in Genesin. MS. Augustinerchorherrenstift Vorau, Austria, codex 187, f. 96r–103r. Octavo. Saec. 12–13.
Microfilm: MnCH proj. no. 7182

143   Liber de Sancta Trinitate. MS. Benediktinerabtei Melk, Austria, codex 1869, f. 90r–108r. Folio. Saec. 15.
Microfilm: MnCH proj. no. 2166

144   Liber de usu psalmorum. MS. Augustinerchorherrenstift Klosterneuburg, Austria, codex 20, f. 1v–2r. Folio. Saec. 12.
Microfilm: MnCH proj. no. 4988

145   Liber de usu psalmorum. MS. Augustinerchorherrenstift Vorau, Austria, codex 215, f. 187v–188r.
Microfilm: MnCH proj. no. 7204

146   Liber de virtutibus et vitiis. MS. Vienna, Nationalbibliothek, codex 956, f. 123v–141r. Folio. Saec. 11.
Microfilm: MnCH proj. no. 14,274

147   Oratio de Summa Trinitate, MS. Dominikanerkloster, Vienna, codex 30, f. 2r–3r. Quarto. Saec. 15.
Microfilm: MnCH proj. no. 8822

148   Propositiones. MS. Vienna, Nationalbibliothek, codex 891, f. 4v–27v. Octavo. Saec. 10.
Microfilm: MnCH proj. no. 14,199

149   Quaestiones de litteris et libris. MS. Vich, Spain, Archivo Capitular, codex 39. Folio. Saec. 11.
Microfilm: MnCH proj. no. 31,163

150   Quaestiones in Genesin. MS. Vienna, Nationalbibliothek, codex 1029, f. 241v–267r. Quarto. Saec. 11.
Microfilm: MnCH proj. no. 14,336

151   Quaestiones in Genesin. MS. Cistercienserabtei Zwettl, Austria, codex 239, f. 85r–112v. Quarto. Saec. 12.
Microfilm: MnCH proj. no. 6839

152   Quaestiones super Genesin. MS. Cistercienserabtei Lilienfeld, Austria, codex 101, f. 95v–124v. Quarto. Saec. 14.
Microfilm: MnCH proj. no. 4390

153   Super Genesin "obscurae inquisitiones." Finis deest. MS. Vienna, Nationalbibliothek, codex 1060, f. 1r–34v. Quarto. Saec. 12.
Microfilm: MnCH proj. no. 14,373

154   Quaestiones in Genesim ad Sigulfum. MS. Benediktinerabtei St. Peter, Salzburg, codex b.VI.20, f. 66r–89v. Quarto. Saec. 15.
Microfilm: MnCH proj. no. 10,489

155   Sermo ad pueros S. Martini de confessione peccatorum. MS. Cistercienserabtei Wilhering, Austria, codex IC, 121, f. 32v–41v. Octavo. Saec. 12.
Microfilm: MnCH proj. no. 2891

156   Super Genesim obscurae inquisitiones et utiles explicationes. MS. Cistercienserabtei Heiligenkreuz, Austria, codex 212, f. 91r–135r. Folio Saec. 12.
Microfilm: MnCH proj. no. 4752

157   Super septem psalmos. MS. Cistercienserabtei Wilhering, Austria, codex IX,121, f. 1r–32r. Octavo. Saec. 12.
Microfilm: MnCH proj. no. 2891

158   Super Vetus Testamentum MS. Benediktinerabtei Admont, Austria, codex 174. 204 f. Folio. Saec. 13.
Microfilm: MnCH proj. no. 9262

159   Symbolum fidei. MS. Salisbury, England, Cathedral Library, codex 165, f. 152v. Quarto. Saec. 12.
Microfilm: MnCH

160   Versus duo in abbatem Radonem. MS. Vienna, Nationalbibliothek, codex 550, f. 112r. Quarto. Saec. 10.
Microfilm: MnCH proj. no. 13,870

Alcuin, 735–804
Printed works

161   Alkuin-Briefe und andere Traktate. Im Auftrage des Salzburger Erzbischofs Arnum 799 zu einem Sammelband vereinigt. Codex Vindobonensis 795 der Oesterreichischen Nationalbibliothek Faksimileausgabe. Einführung Franz Unterkircher. Graz, Austria, Akademische

Druck u. Verlagsanstalt, 1969.

41, 205 p. 28 cm. (Codices selecti, photo-typice impressi, v. 20)

Introduction in German, Facsimile in Latin.

PLatS

162 [Carmina]

(*In* Foucher, J. P. Florilège de la poésie sacrée. Paris, 1961. p. 107–112).

PLatS

163 Un opuscolo inedito di Alcuino [De con-versorum acceptione opusculum]. Edidit Carmelo Ottaviano.

(*In* Aevum, anno II (1928), p. 3–16)

MnCS

164 The rhetoric of Alcuin & Charlemagne. A translation with an introduction, the Latin text and notes by Wilbur Samuel Howell. New York, Russell & Russell, 1965 [c. 1941].

ix, 175 p. 22 cm.

"Disputatio de rhetorica et de virtutibus sapientissimi regis Karali et Albini magistri" is the formal title of the work . . ."

InStme; PLatS

165 Son well-beloved; six poems by Alcuin. Translated by the Benedictines of Stan-brook. Worcester, Stanbrook Abbey Press, 1967.

viii, 9 p. 21 cm.

PLatS

166 Two Alcuin letter-books. Edited by Colin Chase from the British Museum MS. Cot-ton Vespasian A XIV. Toronto. Published for the Centre for Medieval Studies by the Pontifical Institute of Mediaeval Studies [1975]

[4], 84 p. 22 cm. (Toronto medieval Latin texts, 5)

Text in Latin.

PLatS

167 (2dary) Foliot, Gilbert, Bp. of London. Expositio in Canticum Canticorum, una cum Compendio Alcuini. Nunc primum e Bibliotheca Regia in lucem prodiit, opera & studio Patricii Junii . . . Londini, Ex Typographio Regio, 1638.

Special title page for Alcuini Compen-dium in Canticum Canticorum.

MnCS (microfilm)

Aldhelm, Saint, bp. of Sherborne, 640?–709.

168 Opera. Edidit Rudolfus Ehwald. Adiec-tae sunt tabulae V. [Berlin-Charlotten-burg, Weidmannsche Verlagsbuchhand-lung] 1961.

xxiv, 765 p. facsims. 27 cm. (Monumenta Germaniae historica. Auctores antiquis-simi, t. 15)

Reprint of Berlin ediiton of 1919.

MnCS; PLatS

168a Aldhelm: the prose works. Translated by Michael Lapidge & Michael Herren. Ipswich [England], D. S. Brewer; Totowa, N.J., Roman & Littlefield, 1979.

vi, 210 p. 23 cm.

KAS

169 De virginibus, cum glossis theodiscis (German). MS. Vienna, Nationalbibliothek, codex 969, f. 1r–46v. Folio. Saec. 10.

Microfilm: MnCH proj. no. 14,278

170 De virginitate. MS. Exeter, England, Cathedral Library, codex P 1 xvii, f. 1–102. Octavo. Saec. 13.

Microfilm: MnCH

171 Liber de laude virginitatis. MS. Salis-bury, England, Cathedral Library, codex 38. 81 f. Quarto. Saec. 11.

Microfilm: MnCH

172 Metra de S. Benedicto abbate. MS. Bene-diktinerabtei Melk, Austria, codex 1087, f. 57–58. Duodecimo. Saec. 15.

Microfilm: MnCH proj. no. 1842

173 Poeme de octo principalibus vitiis. MS. Vienna, Nationalbibliothek, codex 969, f. 46v–55r. Folio. Saec. 10.

174 **Alexander, abbot of Jumièges,** d. 1213.

Distinctio bonorum verborum de manna in significatione Verbi Dei. A letter on Filius hominis. MS. Lambeth Palace Library, London, codex 36, f. 1–93. Oc-tavo. Saec. 13.

Microfilm: MnCH

175 **Alfanus, abp. of Salerno,** d. 1085.

La leggenda di S. Nicola di Mira in un'ode di Alfano Cassinese. Edidit Anselmo Lentini, O.S.B.

(*In* Mélanges Eugene Tisserant, v. 2, p. 333–343)

PLatS

Alfonso de San Vitores, ca. 1600–1660

176 Ceremonial monastico, conforme al Breviario y Misal, que la santidad de Paulo V. concedio a todos los que militan debajo de santa regla . . . di San Benito . . . Siendo general el reverendisimo padre maestro fr. Alonso de San Victores . . . Reimpresso por orden del capitulo general, celebrado en 1773 . . . Madrid, en la Im-prenta de Pedro Marin, 1774.

[15], 900 p. music. 22 cm.

KAS

177 El sol del occidente, n. glorioso padre S. Benito, principe de todos los monges, patriarca de las religiones todas. Commen-tarios sobre su santa regla [v. 1]. Madrid,

Gregorio Rodriguez, 1645.
[40], 490 p. [51] p. 29 cm.
KAS

177a **Allanson, Peter,** 1804–1876.
A history of the English Benedictine
Congregation, 1558–1850. Microfiche edi-
tion. Bicester, Oxon: OMP and Micromedia
Ltd., c 1978.
2 v. (98 fiche. 148 x 105 mm.) 17 cm.
The original edition of 14 volumes is in
copperplate script.
Introduction and guide to the micro-
fiches, compiled by Placid Spearritt and
Bernard Green. ii, 29 p. 21 cm.
PLatS

178 **Allen, Cuthbert Edmund,** 1906–1977,
comp.
The slavery question as seen in the
Freedman's Journal and the Baltimore
Catholic Mirror, 1850–1865.
Photostatic copies of newspaper clip-
pings.
NcBe

Allodi, Leone, 1841–1914.
179 Inventario dei manoscritti della biblioteca di Subiaco. Forli, Casa Editrice Luigi
Bordandini, 1891.
74 p. 29 cm.
MnCS

180 Il regesto Sublancese del secolo XI,
pubblicato dalla Reale società romana di
storia patria a cura di L. Allodi e G. Levi
. . . Roma, nella sede della Società, 1885.
xx p., 277 p. facsims. 36 cm.
PLatS

181 (ed) The founders of the New Devotion;
being the lives of Gerard Groote, Floren-
tius Radewin and their followers. Translated into English by J. P. Arthur. [Trans-
lation revised by Fr. Leo Almond, O.S.B.].
London, K. Paul, Trench, Trübner & Co.,
1905.
xlvii, 266 p.
ILSP

182 **Alonso de Santa Maria.**
Vida, regla, y exercicios de nuestro
glorioso padre S. Benito.
(*In* Gregory I, Saint, Pope. Leteras
apostolicas . . . n. 3. Barcelona, 1633)
MnCS

183 **Alpertus, monk of St. Symphorien,
Metz,** fl. 1020.
Alperti opera: De episcopis Mettensibus
libellus. De diversitate temporum libri II.
(*In* Monumenta Germaniae historica.
Scriptores. Stuttgart, 1963. t. 4, p.
696–723)
MnCS; PLatS

Altenburg, Austria (Benedictine abbey).
184 Catalogus bibliothecae monasterii Altenburgensis noviter erectae sub auspiciis Rmi
Dni Mauri abbatis, continens libros tam in
cellis quam in bibliotheca existentes. Anno
1679. Auch einige spätere Nachträge. MS.
Benediktinerabtei Altenburg, Austria,
codex AB 5 Bb 78. 57 f. Quarto. Saec. 17
(1679).
Microfilm: MnCH proj. no. 6574

185 Catalogus librorum bibliothecae Altenburgensis, de anno 1668. (Verzeichnet nur
einige Werke). MS. Benediktinerabtei
Altenburg, Austria, codex AB 13 F 31, f.
64r–65v.
Microfilm: MnCH proj. no. 6514

186 Catalogus librorum bibliothecae monasterii ad S. Lambertum Altenburgi, per
Lambert Wenin, O.S.B., MS. Benediktinerabtei Altenburg, Austria, codex AB 15 A
2/1. 297 p. Folio. Saec. 19 (1864).
Microfilm: MnCH proj. no. 6591

187 Catalogus religiosorum patrum et
fratrum monasterii ad S. Lambertum in
Altenburg Austriae Inferioris Ordinis S.
Benedicti . . . Vindobonae, Typis Congregationis Mechitharisticae.
v. 23 cm.
PLatS

188 Necrologium monasterii Altenburgensis.
Cum indice eorum monasteriorum, quae
cum nostro fraternitatem contraxerunt.
MS. Benediktinerabtei Altenburg, codex
AB 7 D 14. 97 f. Folio. Saec. 17 (1623).
Microfilm: MnCH proj. no. 6593

189 Necrologium monasterii Altenburgensis
. . . renovatum anno salutis 1843, iterum
renovatum 1902. MS. Benediktinerabtei
Altenburg, Austria, codex AB 7 D 16. 186
f. Folio. Saec. 19.
Microfilm: MnCH proj. no. 6582

190 Personal-Catalog der Stiftsbibliothek zu
Altenburg, per Lambert Wenin, O.S.B.,
MS. Benediktinerabtei Altenburg, Austria,
codex AB 15 A 2/2. 279 p. Folio. Saec. 19
(1864).
Microfilm: MnCH proj. no. 6592

191 Repertorium et succincta series
diplomatum, documentorum, instrumentorum, actionum contentiosarum, et
scriptorum omnium, quae in Archivis antiquissimi monasterii Altenburgensis
asservantur, per Placidus Wöss, O.S.B.,
MS. Benediktinerabtei Altenburg, Austria,
codex AB 7 D 1. 388 p. Folio. Saec. 18
(1757).
Microfilm: MnCH proj. no. 6587

192 **Amadeo, Fausto,** 1837–1919.

Vita di S. Benedetto, ab., patriarca dei monaci d'occidente. 2. ed. Fabriano, "Gentile," 1921.

    263 p. plates, 20 cm.

    MnCS

193   **Amalarius abbas.**

De officiis divinis. MS. Hereford, England, Cathedral Library, codex 0 5 iv. 192 f. Quarto. Saec. 12.

    Microfilm: MnCH

Amato di Monte Cassino, bp., 11th cent.

194   Il poeme di Amato su S. Pietro apostolo [a cura di] Anselmo Lentini. Montecassino, 1958–59.

    2 v. 25 cm. (Miscellanea Cassinese a cura dei monaci di Montecassino, 30, 31)

    MnCS; PLatS

195   L'ystoire de li Normani, et la Chronique de Robert Viscart par Aimé, moine du Mont-Cassin. Publiées pour la première fois, d'après un manuscrit françois inédit du xiii. siècle, appartenant à la Bibliothèque royale, pour la Sociéte de l'histoire de France, par m. Champollion-Figeac. Paris, chez Jules Renouard, 1835. Johnson Reprint, 1965.

    viii, cvij, 370 p.

    MnCS

196   Die Historia sicula des Anonymus Vaticanus [Amato di Monte Cassino? Disputed] und des Gaufredus [Gioffredo] Malaterra. Ein Beitrag zur Quellenkunde für die Geschichte Unteritaliens und Siziliens im 11. Jahrhundert, von Alex Heskel. Kiel, Druck der Carl Boldt'schen Hof-Buchdruckerei in Rostock, 1891.

    100 p. 22 cm.

    Thesis (Ph.D.)–Universität Kiel.

    MnCS

American Benedictine Academy.

197   Christians in conversation [papers]. With a preface by Peter W. Bartholome. Westminster, Md., Newman Press, 1962.

    x, 112 p. 21 cm.

    "A colloquy between American Catholics and Protestants . . . held at St. John's Abbey, Collegeville, Minnesota, on 1, 2, 3 December, 1960."

    "Organized by the American Benedictine Academy."

    MnCS

197a [Constitution]. [Chicago, St. Procopius Priory, 1947].

    15 p.

    NcBe

198   Constitution. 1965. [Submitted to the Council at the meeting of January 5, 1965, held at Mount Michael Abbey, Elkhorn,

Nebr. American Benedictine Academy, 1965.

    15 p. 23 cm.

    KAS; PLatS

199   A Jewish colloquy; a project of the National Conference of Christians and Jews and the American Benedictine Academy, Saint Vincent Archabbey, Latrobe, Pa., January 25–28, 1965. [Latrobe, Pa., The Archabbey Press, 1965].

    4 leaves, 16 cm.

    PLatS

American Benedictine Academy. Library Science Section.

200   A Benedictine bibliography; an author-subject union list. Compiled for the Library Science Section of the American Benedictine Academy, by Oliver L. Kapsner, O.S.B. . . . Collegeville, Minn., St. John's Abbey Press, 1962.

    2 v. 27 cm.

    ACu; etc. etc.

201   Science material in the library. Prepared by Sister M. Kenneth Scheessele, O.S.B., and Sister Mary Walter Goebel, O.S.B.

    23 p. 28 cm.

    PLatS

202   **Amico, Vito Maria,** 1663–1743.

Sicilia sacra disquisitionibus et notitiis illustrata . . . di Rocco Pirri . . . Accessere additiones & notitiae abbatiarum Ordinis Sancti Benedicti, Cisterciensium, & aliae, quae desiderabantur, auctore P. domino Vito Maria Amico . . . Panormi, apud haeredes Petri Coppulae, 1733.

    2 v. 35 cm.

    KAS

203   **Amis du vieux Corbie.**

La tresors de l'Abbaye royale Saint-Pierre de Corbie. Amiens, Musée de Picordie, 1962.

    51 p. plates, 20 cm.

    MnCS

204   **Amon, Stephan,** 1913–

Klösterliches Leben.

(*In* Die Benediktinerabtei Münsterschwarzach. Vier-Türme-Verlag, 1965. p. 66–73)

    PLatS

205   **Ampleforth Abbey, England.**

Novena to Saint Benedict. 2d ed. Ampleforth, Malton, n.d.

    unpaged.

    AStb

206   **Anastasius, Bibliothecarius,** d. 866.

Passio sancti Petri patriarchae Alexandrini, Anastasio bibliothecario interprete (incompletum). MS. Augustinerchorher-

renstift Klosterneuburg, Austria, codex
248. f. 112r–115r.
Microfilm: MnCH proj. no. 5214

207 **Anciaux, Paul.**
The ecclesial dimension of penance.
(*In* Taylor, Michael J., comp. The
mystery of sin and forgiveness. 1971. p.
155–165)
PLatS

208 **Andechs, Bavaria (Benedictine abbey).**
Catalogus codicum manu scriptorum
Bibliothecae Regiae Monacensis, num.
3001–3132 ex coenobio S. Nicolai in monte
sancto Andechs. Monachii, sumptibus
Bibliothecae Regiae, 1894.
MnCH

209 **Andert, Mary Roger, Sister,** 1926–
Selected factors associated with the
presence of physicians on hospital boards
of trustees.
157 leaves, 28 cm.
Thesis (M.A.)–University of Iowa, 1971.
Typescript.
MnStj (Archives)

210 **Andreas, monk of Fleury,** 11th cent.
Vie de Gauzlin abbé de Fleury. Vita
Gauzlini abbatis Floriacensis monasterii.
Texte édité, traduit et annoté par Robert-
Henri Bautier et Gillette Labory. Paris,
Editions du Centre National de la Re-
cherche Scientifique, 1969.
234 p. 25 cm. (Sources d'histoire
médiévale, 2)
Latin and French on opposite pages.
InStme; MnCS; PLatS

211 **Andreas, abbot of Michelsberg,** 1450–
1502.
Der Catalogus sanctorum Ordinis Sancti
Benedicti des Abtes Andreas von Michels-
berg [hrsg.] von Joseph Fassbinder. Bonn,
Carl Georgi, 1910.
136 p. 22 cm.
Diss.–Rheinische Friedrich-Wilhelms-
Universität zu Bonn.
InStme; MnCS

Andreas de Escobar. *See* Escobar,
Andrés de.

Andreas Hispanus. *See* Escobar, Andrés
de.

212 **Andreotti, Stanislaus,** 1924–
Subiaco, culla dell'Ordine Benedettino,
sede della prima tipografia italiana.
Subiaco, 1965.
108 p. illus.
MoCo

213 **Angela, Sister M.**
God and a mouse; a festival of reflective
jubilation. San Diego, Calif., Benedictine

Sisters [c 1972]
12 p. illus. 16 cm.
CaMWiSb

214 **Angelomontana; Blätter aus der
Geschichte von Engelberg.** Jubiläums-
gabe für Abt Leodegar II. Hangartner,
1914.
500 p.
MoCo

Angelomus, monk of Juxeuil, d. ca. 855.
215 Commentarius in Cantica Canticorum,
cum prologo ad Lotharium imperatorem.
MS. Cistercienserabtei Lilienfeld, Austria,
codex 160, f. 133r–143v. Quarto. Saec. 12.
Microfilm: MnCH proj. no. 4524

216 Expositio super Genesin. MS. Cistercienserabtei Zwettl, Austria, codex 89, f.
102v–146v. Folio. Saec. 12.
Microfilm: MnCH proj. no. 6683

217 Expositio super Regum (III). MS. Cistercienserabtei Zwettl, Austria, codex 89,
f. 147r–194r. Folio. Saec. 12.
Microfilm: MnCH proj. no. 6683

218 **Angerer, Joachim,** 1934–
Die Bräuche der Abtei Tegernsee unter
Abt Kaspar Ayndorfer (1426–1461), ver-
bunden mit einer textkritischen Edition
der Consuetudines Tegernseenses von P.
Joachim Angerer, O.S.B. [Roma, 1968]
xv, 362 p. 25 cm.
Diss.–Pontificium Athenaeum S.
Anselmi de Urbe.
KAS
Also available: Augsburg, Kommissions-
verlag Winfried-Werk, 1968.
MnCS; PLatS

Angilbertus, Saint, abbot of St. Riquier,
d. 814.
219 Carmen de Karolo Magno.
(*In* Monumenta Germaniae historica.
Scriptores. Stuttgart, 1963. t. 2, p.
391–403).
MnCS; PLatS

220 [Carmina]
(*In* Foucher, J. P. Florilège de la poésie
sacrée. Paris. 1961. p. 113–118)
PLatS

221 Carmina minora Pauli Diaconi, Paulini,
Angilberti . . .
(*In* Poetae latini aevi carolini. Recensuit
Karolus Strecker. Berolini, 1880. t. IV,
fasc. II/III (1923). Supplementa, p.
911–943)
KAS; MnCS; PLatS

222 Epistolae tres. MS. Vienna, National-
bibliothek, codex 795, f. 197v–199r.
Quarto. Saec. 10.
Microfilm: MnCH proj. no. 14,139

223   Angilbert's ritual order for Saint-Riquier [with Latin text].
(*In* Bishop, Edmund. Liturgica historica. Oxford, 1918. p. 314–332)
PLatS

224   **Annales Bertiniani.**
(*In* Monumenta Germaniae historica. Scriptores. Stuttgart, 1963. t. 1, p. 419–515)
MnCS; PLatS

225   **Annales Bertiniani.**
Chronicon de Normannorum gestis in Francia a.820–911.
(*In* Monumenta Germaniae historica. Scriptores. Stuttgart, 1963. t. 1, p. 532–536)
"Wertlos: aus Annales bertin. und vedast. entnommen."–Potthast.
MnCS; PLatS

226   **Annales Cestrienses;** or, Chronicle of the Abbey of St. Werburg at Chester. Edited with an introduction, translation, and notes by Richard Copley Christie. [London], Printed for The Record Society, 1887.
xxxii, 152 p. 22 cm.
PLatS

227   **Annales Corbeienses.**
Annales Corbeienses a.658–1148.
(*In* Monumenta Germaniae historica. Scriptores. Stuttgart, 1963. t. 3, p. 1–18)
MnCS; PLatS

Annales Cremifanenses. *See* Kremsmünster, Austria (Benedictine abbey). Annales.

Annales Fuldenses.
228   Annales Fuldenses. Part. 1–4. Explicit: consternati pariter discesserunt. MS. Vienna, Nationalbibliothek, codex 615. 80 f. Octavo. Saec. 12.
Microfilm: MnCH proj. no. 13,935

229   Annales Fuldenses a.680–901.
(*In* Monumenta Germaniae historica. Scriptores. Stuttgart, 1963. t. 1, p. 337–415)
MnCS; PLatS

230   Annales Fuldenses antiqui, a.651–838.
(*In* Monumenta Germaniae historica. Scriptores. Stuttgart, 1963. t. 3, p. 116–117)
MnCS; PLatS

231   Petri Bibliothecarii Historia Francorum abbreviata a.680–898.
(*In* Monumenta Germaniae historica. Scriptores. Stuttgart, 1963. t. 1, p. 416–418)
"Wertloses Excerpt der Annales Fuldenses."–Potthast.
MnCS; PLatS

232   **Annales Hildesheimenses.**
Annales Hildesheimenses ab O.C.–1137.
(*In* Monumenta Germaniae historica. Scriptores. Stuttgart, 1963. t. 3, p. 22–116)
MnCH; PLatS

233   **Annales Lambacenses.** MS. Vienna, Nationalbibliothek, codex 3415, f. 140r–150r. Folio. Saec. 15.
Microfilm: MnCH proj. no. 20,379

234   **Annales Laubacenses.**
(*In* Monumenta Germaniae historica. Scriptores. Stuttgart, 1963. t. 1, p. 3–18, 52–55)
MnCS; PLatS

Annales Laurissenses. *See* Lorsch, Germany (Benedictine abbey). Annales.

Annales Mellicenses. *See* Melk, Austria (Benedictine abbey). Annales.

235   **Annales Quedlinburgenses.**
Annales Quedlinburgenses ab O.C.–1025.
(*In* Monumenta Germaniae historica. Scriptores. Stuttgart, 1963. t. 3, p. 22–90)
MnCS; PLatS

236   **Annales Vedastini.**
Annales Vedastini a.877–900.
(*In* Monumenta Germaniae historica. Scriptores. Stuttgart, 1963. t. 1, p. 516–531)
MnCS; PLatS

Annunciation Priory, Bismarck, N.D.
237   Mary, prototype of every witnessing Christian. Bismarck, N.D., Annunciation Priory, Feast of the Annunciation, 1968.
unpaged.
MnStj (Archives)

238   A study of the role of the Sisters of Annunciation Priory regarding their participation in Bismarck diocesan institutions of education, 1964–65 to 1968–69. Bismarck, 1969.
43 p.
MnStj (Archives)

239   **Anonymus Benedictinus.**
Liber de poenitentia et confessione. MS. Benediktinerabtei Kremsmünster, Austria, codex 105, f. 1r–13r. Saec. 13.
Microfilm: MnCH proj. no. 369

240   **Anonymus Benedictinus.**
Tractatulus abbreviatus de cognitione ipsius. MS. Benediktinerabtei Melk, Austria, codex 1653, f. 111r–132r. Sextodecimo. Saec. 15.
Microfilm: MnCH proj. no. 2011

241   **Anonymus Benedictinus Bohemus.**
Malogranatum, seu, De statu incipientium, proficientium et perfectorum. MS. Benediktinerabtei Melk, Austria, codex 68.

188 f. Folio. Saec. 15.
Microfilm: MnCH proj. no. 1199

242 **Anonymus Gottwicensis.**
Cujusdem in monasterio Gottwicensi
commorantis, ad N cellararium ejusdem
monasterii epistola, de peccato originali.
MS. Benediktinerabtei Melk, Austria,
codex 853, f. 142v–145. Quarto. Saec. 15.
Microfilm: MnCH proj. no. 1676

242a **Anonymus Mellicensis.**
De fundatoribus nostri monasterii
Mellicensis. MS. Benediktinerabtei Melk,
Austria, codex 937, f. 143–146. Folio.
Saec. 15.
Microfilm: MnCH proj. no. 1744

243 **Anonymus Mellicensis.**
De scriptoribus ecclesiasticis. MS. Benediktinerabtei Admont, Austria, codex 443,
f. 128v–144v. Quarto. Saec. 12.
Microfilm: MnCH proj. no. 9504

244 **Anonymus Mellicensis.**
Monachus quidam Mellicensis respondet
ad dubia de psalterio. MS. Vienna, Schot-
tenstift, codex 352, f. 218v–219v. Folio.
Saec. 14.
Microfilm: MnCH proj. no. 4199

245 **Anonymus Mellicensis, 12th cent.**
Anonymus Mellicensis saeculo XII.
clarus de scriptoribus ecclesiasticis, nuper
primum in lucem editus, et notulis chrono-
logico-criticis illustratus a Bernardo Pez,
O.S.B.
(*In* Johann Albert Fabricius. Bibliotheca
ecclesiastica. Hants., England, Gregg
Press, 1967. p. 141–160)
Reprint of 1718 edition.
PLatS

246 **Anonymus Mellicensis, fl. 1429.**
Collectio ascetico-theologica-moralis.
MS. Benediktinerabtei Melk, Austria,
codex 189, p. 397–407. Duodecimo. Saec.
15.
Microfilm: MnCH proj. no. 1227

247 **Anonymus Mellicensis, fl. 1429.**
Excerpta ex Summa misteriorum. MS.
Benediktinerabtei Melk, Austria, codex
1829, f. 92v–140r. Duodecimo. Saec. 15.
Microfilm: MnCH proj. no. 2139

248 **Anonymus Mellicensis, fl. 1429.**
Excerpta ex Summa sacrificiorum. MS.
Benediktinerabtei Melk, Austria, codex
1829, f. 7r–91v. Duodecimo. Saec. 15.
Microfilm: MnCH proj. no. 2139

249 **Anonymus Mellicensis, fl. 1431.**
Tractatus de peccatis mortalibus et
venialibus. MS. Benediktinerabtei Melk,
Austria, codex 1471, f. 95r–160v. Duo-
decimo. Saec. 15.
Microfilm: MnCH proj. no. 1939

250 **Anonymus Mellicensis, f. 1441.**
Vitae ss. Patrum. Incipit: De abbate
Johanne. MS. Benediktinerabtei Melk,
Austria, codex 1739, p. 53–137. Duo-
decimo. Saec. 15.
Microfilm: MnCH proj. no. 2049

251 **Anonymus Mellicensis, fl. ca. 1445.**
Diversissima excerpta ex Nicolao de
Dinkelspihl, S. Bernardo, Ioanne Nider,
Ioanne Gerson, Gregorio, Ioanne de Spira,
aliisque quam plurimis. MS. Benedik-
tinerabtei Melk, Austria, codex 1843, f.
72r–360v. Duodecimo. Saec. 15.
Microfilm: MnCH proj. no. 2153

252 **Anonymus Mellicensis, fl. ca. 1450.**
Notitiae breves de officio Missae. MS.
Benediktinerabtei Melk, Austria, codex
1829, f. 146r–148r. Duodecimo. Saec. 15.
Microfilm: MnCH proj. no. 2139

253 **Anonymus Mellicensis, fl. 1450.**
Sermones de tempore et festis per an-
num. MS. Benediktinerabtei Melk,
Austria, codex 955, f. 1r–230r. Quarto.
Saec. 15.
Microfilm: MnCH proj. no. 1765

254 **Anonymus Mellicensis, fl. 1460.**
Excerpta ex variis S. Bernardi operibus
vitam monasticam concernentia. MS.
Benediktinerabtei Melk, Austria, codex
866, f. 90v–103r. Quarto. Saec. 15.
Microfilm: MnCH proj. no. 1684

255 **Anonymus Mellicensis, fl. 1460.**
Expositio brevis librorum Veteris Testa-
menti a libro Genesi usque ad librum Iob in-
clusive. MS. Benediktinerabtei Melk,
Austria, codex 1802, f. 158r–202v. Quarto.
Saec. 15.
Microfilm: MnCH proj. no. 2118

256 **Anonymus Mellicensis, fl. 1460.**
Expositio 27 capitulorum Regulae S.
Benedicti. MS. Benediktinerabtei Melk,
Austria, codex 1381, p. 535–595. Duo-
decimo. Saec. 15.
Microfilm: MnCH proj. no. 1904

257 **Anonymus Mellicensis, fl. 15th cent.**
De 39 generibus metrorum in Boetii
libro: De consolatione philosophiae. MS.
Benediktinerabtei Melk, Austria, codex
1916, p. 62. Quarto. Saec. 15.
Microfilm: MnCH proj. no. 2201

258 **Anonymus Mellicensis, fl. 15th cent.**
Expositio in cap. 49 Regulae S. Bene-
dicti. MS. Benediktinerabtei Melk,
Austria, codex 1381, p. 233–267. Duo-
decimo. Saec. 15.
Microfilm: MnCH proj. no. 1904

259 **Anonymus Mellicensis, fl. 15th cent.**
Modus confitendi sacramentaliter. MS.

Benediktinerabtei Melk, Austria, codex 1719, f. 205v–208v. Octavo. Saec. 15.
Microfilm: MnCH proj. no. 2040

260 **Anonymus Mellicensis,** fl. 15th cent.
Syntagma rerum ascetico-moralium. MS. Benediktinerabtei Melk, Austria, codex 1095, f. 248v–287v. Duodecimo. Saec. 15.
Microfilm: MnCH proj. no. 1849

261 **Anonymus Mellicensis,** fl. 15th cent.
Tractatus de modo inungendi fratrem infirmum. MS. Benediktinerabtei Melk, Austria, codex 960, p. 1–24. Quarto. Saec. 15.
Microfilm: MnCH proj. no. 1775

262 **Anonymus Mellicensis,** fl. 15th cent.
Tractatus de necessitate poenitentiae, ex tractatu Nicolai de Dinkelspihl, ejusdem argumenti. MS. Benediktinerabtei Melk, Austria, codex 1095, f. 315r–357v. Duodecimo. Saec. 15.
Microfilm: MnCH proj. no. 1849

263 **Anonymus Monachus Benedictinus.**
Tractatus de poenitentia et tentationibus cujusdam juvenis monachi. MS. Benediktinerabtei Melk, Austria, codex 651, f. 55r–88v. Quarto. Saec. 15.
Microfilm: MnCH proj. no. 1529

264 **Ansegisus, Saint, abbot of Fontenelle,** d. 833.
Capitularia. MS. Cistercienserabtei Heiligenkreuz, Austria, codex 217, f. 205r–266v. Folio. Saec. 10.
Microfilm: MnCH proj. no. 4866

Anselm, Saint, abp. of Canterbury, 1033–1109.
Manuscript copies.

265 [Opera]
Epistolae; De beatitudine coelestis patriae; Admonitio morienti; De similitudinibus; Monologion; Proslogion; De libertate arbitrii. MS. Lambeth Palace Library, London, codex 59. 278 f. Quarto. Saec. 12.
Microfilm: MnCH

266 [Opera]
Epistola ad Lanfrancum; Proslogion; Contra insipientem; De incarnatione Verbi; Cur Deus homo; De conceptu virginali; De concordia trium questionum predestinationis et gratie Dei cum libero arbitrio; Unde malum (Si malum nihil est); Meditatio redemptionis humanae; Liber de grammatico; Tractatus tres pertinentes ad studium. MS. Lambeth Palace Library, London, codex 224. 213 f. Quarto. Saec. 12.
Microfilm: MnCH

267 [Opera]

Monologion; Proslogion; De libertate arbitrii; De veritate; De casu diaboli; De incarnacione Verbi; Cur Deus homo; De conceptu virginali; De processione Spiritus Sancti; De sacrificio azymi; De sacramentis ecclesiae; Sentencia ex libro Proslogion; Pro insipiente; Contra insipientem; De concordia; De similitudinibus. MS. Exeter, England, Cathedral Library, codex P 2 i. 210 fl. Octavo. Saec. 13.
Microfilm: MnCH

268 [Opera]
Dialogus de libero arbitrio. Liber de casu diaboli; Tractatus de concordia praescientiae et praedestinationis nec non gratiae Dei cum libero arbitrio; Epistola de tribus Waleramni quaestionibus et praefatio de azymo et fermentato; Epistola de sacramentorum diversitate ad Waleramnum episcopum. MS. Benediktinerabtei Göttweig, Austria, codex 60 b, f. 1r–37r. Folio. Saec. 13.
Microfilm: MnCH

269 [Opera]
Cur Deus homo; De cognitione vitae; De veritate; De libero arbitrio; De casu diaboli; De conceptu virginali et de originali peccato; De incarnatione Verbi ad Urbanum papam; De processione Spiritus Sancti contra Graecos. MS. Cistercienserabtei Lilienfeld, Austria, codex 139, f. 113r–240r. Folio. Saec. 13.
Microfilm: MnCH proj. no. 4437

270 [Opera]
Tractatus de veritate; De libero arbitrio; De conceptu virginali et originali peccato; Monologion; De casu diaboli; De processione S. Spiritus; De sacrificio azimi et fermentati; De sacramentis ecclesiae; De concordia praescientiae predestinationis gratiae Dei et liberi arbitrii; Cur Deus homo; De incarnatione Verbi; Proslogion; Contra insipientem. MS. Lambeth Palace Library, London, codex 151, f. 117–179. Quarto. Saec. 13.
Microfilm: MnCH

271 [Opera]
De conceptu virginali; Monologion; Proslogion; Contra insipientem. MS. Lambeth Palace Library, London, codex 356, f. 192–220. Quarto. Saec. 13–14.
Microfilm: MnCH

272 [Opera]
Cur Deus homo; De conceptu virginali et peccato originali; De processione Spiritus Sancti; De sacramentis; De incarnatione; De concordia praescientiae et praedestinationis cum libero arbitrio. MS. Vienna, Nationalbibliothek, codex 785, f. 98r–124r.

Folio. Saec. 13.
Microfilm: MnCH proj. no. 14,111

273 [Opera]
Cur Deus homo; Tractatus de cognitione vitae (pseud?); Tractatus de veritate; Tractatus de libero arbitrio; Liber de casu diaboli; Tractatus de conceptu virginali et de originali peccato; Liber de incarnatione Verbi; Tractatus de processione Spiritus Sancti contra Graecos. MS. Cistercienserabtei Zwettl, Austria, codex 221, f. 2r–127r. Quarto. Saec. 13.
Microfilm: MnCH proj. no. 6821

274 [Opera]
Tractatus de concordia praescientiae et praedestinationis et gratiae Dei cum libero arbitrio; Monologion; Proslogion; Liber apologeticus contra Gaunilonem; Liber de veritate; Liber de libero arbitrio; Liber de casu diaboli; Liber de fide Trinitatis et de incarnatione Verbi; Liber de conceptu virginali et peccato originali; Liber de processione Spiritus Sancti contra Graecos; Cur Deus homo; Liber de similitudinibus; S. Anselmus in extasi positus. MS. Benediktinerabtei Göttweig, Austria, codex 131. 132 f. Folio. Saec. 14.
Microfilm: MnCH proj. no. 3408

275 [Opera]
MS. Universitätsbibliothek Graz, Austria, codex 739. 205 f. Folio. Saec. 14.
Microfilm: MnCH proj. no. 26,840

276 [Opera]
Libri de libero arbitrio; De casu diaboli; De incarnatione Verbi; De peccato originali et de conceptu virginali; De processione Spiritus Sancti, Cur Deus homo; De similitudinibus et divisione voluntatis. MS. Augustinerchorherrenstift Herzogenburg, Austria, codex 28, f. 69r–144v. Folio. Saec. 14–15.
Microfilm: MnCH proj. no. 3193

277 [Opera]
De praescientia et libero arbitrio; De praedestinatione et libero arbitrio; De gratia et libero arbitrio; Monologion; Proslogion; Obiectio insipientis, auctore Gaunilone monacho; Responsio contra insipientem; De veritate; De libertate arbitrii; De casu diaboli; Epistola de incarnatione; De conceptu virginali et peccato originali; De processione Spiritus Sancti contra Graecos; Cur Deus homo; De similitudinibus. MS. Universitätsbibliothek Innsbruck, codex 564, f. 88r–196v. Folio. Saec. 14.
Microfilm: MnCH proj. no. 28,541

278 [Opera]
Liber de similitudinibus rerum (excerpta); Liber de praedestionatione, gratia et libero arbitrio (excerpta); Epistola ad novitium Lanzenem, monachum Cluniacensem (excerptum); De vita ipsius; Liber de veritate (excerptum); De libero arbitrio (excerptum); Liber de casu diaboli (excerptum); Liber de processione Spiritus Sancti (excerptum); Epistola ad Lanfrancum in Monologio (excerptum); Monologium de divinitatis essentia (excerptum); Cur Deus homo (libri duo). MS. Augustinerchorherrenstift Klosterneuburg, Austria, codex 798, f. 113r–170v. Quarto. Saec. 14.
Microfilm: MnCH proj. no. 5785

279 [Opera]
Meditatio super psalmum: Miserere; Similitudines; Liber de mensuratione crucis (pseudo); Liber de conceptu virginali; Cur Deus homo (libri duo); Liber de incarnatione Verbi Dei. MS. Augustinerchorherrenstift Klosterneuburg, Austria, codex 799, f. 1r–186v. Quarto. Saec. 14.
Microfilm: MnCH proj. no. 5784

280 [Opera]
Monologion; Proslogium; Cur Deus homo; De incarnatione Verbi; De peccato originali; De processione Spiritus Sancti; De concordia praescientiae et praedestinationis et gratiae dei cum libero arbitrio; Prologus in libros tres; de veritate, de libertate arbitrii, de casu diaboli (sequuntur libri ipsi); De grammatico; De similitudinibus; Disputatio pro insipiente et contra respondentem pro insipiente; Epistolae septem. MS. Vienna, Nationalbibliothek, codex 747, f. 1r–145r. Folio. Saec. 14.
Microfilm: MnCH proj. no. 14,063

281 [Opera]
Monologion; Proslogion; Liber de incarnatione; Cur Deus homo; Liber de conceptu viriginali et de peccato originali; Liber de concordia praescientiae, praedestinationis et gratiae Dei cum libero arbitrio; Tractatus de casu diaboli. MS. Cistercienserabtei Zwettl, Austria, codex 154, f. 108v–182r. Folio. Saec. 15.
Microfilm: MnCH proj. no. 6748

282 [Selections]
Ex dictis ejus. MS. Augustinerchorherrenstift St. Florian, Austria, codex XI, 255, f. 79r–81r. Quarto. Saec. 15.
Microfilm: MnCH proj. no. 2489

283 [Selections]
Flores: exhortatio ad secretum contemplationis. MS. Dominikanerkloster, Vienna, codex 234, f. 221r–225v. Quarto. Saec. 14.
Microfilm: MnCH proj. no. 9016

284 [Selections]
Flores Anselmi. MS. Lincoln Cathedral Library, England, codex 33, f. 267–273. Quarto. Saec. 15.
Microfilm: MnCH

285 [Selections]
Flores. MS. Cistercienserabtei Wilhering, Austria, codex IX, 101, f. 141r–144v. Quarto. Saec. 15.
Microfilm: MnCH proj. no. 2876

286 [Selections]
Opuscula varia SS. Patrum (S. Augustinus, Bernardus, Anselmus, etc.). MS. Burg Kreuzenstein, Austria, codex 5663. 138 f. Folio. Saec. 15.
Microfilm: MnCH proj. no. 9071

287 [Selections]
Oratio ad S. Crucem; Passio Domini, sicut eam Beata Virgo S. Anselmo revelavit; De ultimis temporibus et Antichristo; Liber meditationum seu orationum (38 capitula). MS. Cistercienserabtei Lilienfeld, Austria, codex 144, f. 62v–69v. Folio. Saec. 13.
Microfilm: MnCH proj. no. 4513

288 [Selections]
S. Anselmus: Sammlung von Tractaten. MS. Universitätsbibliothek Innsbruck, codex 254, f. 2r–177r. Folio. Saec. 13.
Microfilm: MnCH proj. no. 28,285

289 [Selections]
S. Anselmus: Varia. MS. Toledo, Spain, Biblioteca del Cabildo, codex 15, 7, f. 13r–99v. Folio. Saec. 14.
Microfilm: MnCH proj. no. 33,120

290 Admonitio morienti et de peccatis suis nimium formidanti. MS. Prämonstratenserabtei Schlägl, Austria, codex 97, f. 8r. Folio. Saec. 15.
Microfilm: MnCH proj. no. 2956

291 Aliquae regulae Anselmo. MS. Augustinerchorherrenstift St. Florian, Austria, codex XI, 126, f. 27r–28r. Folio. Saec. 14.
Microfilm: MnCH proj. no. 2390

292 Carmen de contemptu mundi. MS. Benediktinerabtei Admont, Austria, codex 829a, f. 153v–164r. Quarto. Saec. 17.
Microfilm: MnCH proj. no. 9858

293 Carmen de contemptu vitae. MS. Benediktinerabtei Admont, Austria, codex 833, f. 279v–282v. Quarto. Saec. 17.
Microfilm: MnCH proj. no. 9827

294 Contemplatio de passione Domini. MS. Vienna, Nationalbibliothek, codex 4072, f. 37r–43v. Octavo. Saec. 15 (1499).
Microfilm: MnCH proj. no. 17,271

295 Cur Deus homo. MS. Benediktinerabtei St. Peter, Salzburg, codex a.V.32, f. 2r–42v. Octavo. Saec. 11–12.
Microfilm: MnCH proj. no. 10,063

296 Cur Deus homo. MS. Exeter, England, Cathedral Library, codex P 1 i, f. 135–157. Quarto. Saec. 12.
Microfilm: MnCH

297 Cur Deus homo. Liber secundus. MS. Universitätsbibliothek Graz, codex 171, f. 2r–43r. Quarto. Saec. 12.
Microfilm: MnCH proj. no. 26,102

298 Cur Deus homo. MS. Universitätsbibliothek Graz, codex 1545, f. 1v–72v. Octavo. Saec. 12.
Microfilm: MnCH proj. no. 26,483

299 Cur Deus homo. Tantummodo prologus et index. MS. Augustinerchorherrenstift St. Florian, Austria, codex XI, 250, f. 64r–64v. Folio. Saec. 12.
Microfilm: MnCH proj. no. 2483

300 Cur Deus homo. MS. Vienna, Nationalbibliothek, codex 691, f. 1r–25v. Folio. Saec. 12.
Microfilm: MnCH proj. no. 14,017

301 Cur Deus homo. MS. Vienna, Nationalbibliothek, codex 1019, f. 1r–37v. Folio. Saec. 12.
Microfilm: MnCH proj. no. 14,332

302 Cur Deus homo. MS. Benediktinerabtei Admont, Austria, codex 725, f. 19r–34v. Quarto. Saec. 13.
Microfilm: MnCH proj. no. 9764

303 Cur Deus homo. MS. Cistercienserabtei Heiligenkreuz, Austria, codex 256, f. 1r–48v. Folio. Saec. 13.
Microfilm: MnCH proj. no. 4794

304 Cur Deus homo. MS. Augustinerchorrenstift Vorau, Austria, codex 335, f. 86r–112v. Quarto. Saec. 13–14.
Microfilm: MnCH proj. no. 7305

305 Cur Deus homo. MS. Augustinerchorrenstift Klosterneuburg, Austria, codex 248, f. 87r–112r. Folio. Saec. 14.
Microfilm: MnCH proj. no. 5214

306 Cur Deus homo. MS. Lambeth Palace Library, London, codex 180, f. 91–116. Quarto. Saec. 14.
Microfilm: MnCH

307 Cur Deus homo. MS. Dominikanerkloster, Vienna, codex 110, f. 1r–33r. Folio. Saec. 14.
Microfilm: MnCH proj. no. 8911

308 Cur Deus homo. MS. Vienna, Nationalbibliothek, codex 902, f. 1r–76r. Duodecimo. Saec. 14.
Microfilm: MnCH proj. no. 14,211

309 Cur Deus homo. MS. Subiaco, Italy (Benedictine abbey), codex 299. Saec. 14.
Microfilm: MnCH

310   Cur Deus homo. MS. Toledo, Spain, Biblioteca del Cabildo, codex 15, 6, f. 1r–27r. Folio. Saec. 14?
Microfilm: MnCH proj. no. 33,119

311   Cur Deus homo. MS. Benediktinerabtei Melk, Austria, codex 336, f. 315–355. Folio. Saec. 15.
Microfilm: MnCH proj. no. 1344

312   Cur Deus homo. MS. Benediktinerabtei St. Paul, Austria, codex 192/4, pars XII. Folio. Saec. 15.
Microfilm: MnCH proj. no. 12,436

313   Cur Deus homo. MS. Benediktinerabtei Seitenstetten, Austria, codex 123, f. 153r–171v. Folio. Saec. 15.
Microfilm: MnCH proj. no. 936

314   Cur Deus homo. MS. Vienna, Nationalbibliothek, codex 1473, f. 100v–131r. Folio. Saec. 15 (1402).
Microfilm: MnCH proj. no. 14,820

315   Cur Deus homo. MS. Vienna, Nationalbibliothek, codex 4434, f. 140v–161v. Folio. Saec. 15.
Microfilm: MnCH proj. no. 17,621

316   De amissione virginitatis planctus. MS. Augustinerchorherrenstift St. Florian, Austria, codex XI, 57, f. 12r–15r. Quarto. Saec. 14.
Microfilm: MnCH proj. no. 2313

317   De Antichristo. MS. Vienna, Schottenstift, codex 297, f. 196r–197r. Folio. Saec. 15.
Microfilm: MnCH proj. no. 4189

318   De casu diaboli. MS. Cava, Italy (Benedictine abbey), codex 54. 14 f. Folio. Saec. 12.
Microfilm: MnCH

319   De conceptu virginali et originali peccato. MS. Vienna, Nationalbibliothek, codex 1070, f. 1r–14v. Quarto. Saec. 13.
Microfilm: MnCH proj. no. 14,377

320   De conceptione b. virginis Dei genitricis. MS. Lambeth Palace Library, London, codex 52. f. 205v–206. Octavo. Saec. 14.
Microfilm: MnCH

321   De conceptione Sanctae Mariae Virginis epistola. MS. Vienna, Nationalbibliothek, codex 4876, f. 166r–171r. Folio. Saec. 15.
Microfilm: MnCH proj. no. 18,051

322   De conceptu virginali et originali peccato. MS. Subiaco, Italy (Benedictine abbey), codex 299. Saec. 14.
Microfilm: MnCH

323   De concordia praescientiae (excerpta). MS. Vienna, Nationalbibliothek, codex 533, f. 78v–80v. Quarto. Saec. 14.
Microfilm: MnCH proj. no. 13,874

324   De divinis scripturis. MS. Universitätsbibliothek Innsbruck, Austria, codex 396, f. 64v–93v. Octavo. Saec. 13.
Microfilm: MnCH proj. no. 28,399

325   De incarnatione Filii. MS. Benediktinerabtei Fiecht, Austria, codex 15, f. 139r–147r. Octavo. Saec. ?
Microfilm: MnCH proj. no. 28,792

326   De interrogandis in hora mortis. MS. Vienna, Nationalbibliothek, codex 965, f. 39v–40r. Folio. Saec. 14.
Microfilm: MnCH proj. no. 14,265

327   De libero arbitrio. MS. Benediktinerabtei Fiecht, Austria, codex 15, f. 133r–139r. Octavo. Saec. ?
Microfilm: MnCH proj. no. 28,792

328   De libero arbitrio. MS. Toledo, Spain, Biblioteca del Cabildo, codex 15, 7, f. 1r–8v. Folio. Saec. 14.
Microfilm: MnCH proj. no. 33,120

329   De libero arbitrio. MS. Vienna, Nationalbibliothek, codex 4684, f. 1r–13v. Quarto. Saec. 15.
Microfilm: MnCH proj. no. 17,868

330   De libero arbitrio. MS. Vienna, Nationalbibliothek, codex 14,225, f. 179r–191v. Folio. Saec. 15.
Microfilm: MnCH proj. no. 20,197

331   De mensuratione crucis. MS. Vienna, Nationalbibliothek, codex 4684, f. 26r–31r. Quarto. Saec. 15.
Microfilm: MnCH proj. no. 17,868

332   De mensuratione crucis. MS. Vienna, Nationalbibliothek, codex 4822, f. 118r–121v. Folio. Saec. 15.
Microfilm: MnCH proj. no. 17,991

333   De passione Domini, et Dialogus B.M.V. MS. Universitätsbibliothek Graz, codex 1434, f. 64v–66v. Octavo. Saec. 14.
Microfilm: MnCH proj. no. 26,422

334   De passione Domini. MS. Augustinerchorherrenstift Herzogenburg, Austria, codex 14, f. 210r–213v. Quarto. Saec. 14–15.
Microfilm: MnCH proj. no. 3227

335   De passione Domini. MS. Universitätsbibliothek Innsbruck, Austria, codex 415, f. 175r–195r. Octavo. Saec. 14–15.
Microfilm: MnCH proj. no. 28,415

336   De passione Domini. MS. Universitätsbibliothek Graz, Austria, codex 1569, f. 92v–104r. Octavo. Saec. 15.
Microfilm: MnCH proj. no. 26,496

337   De passione Domini. MS. Augustinerchorrenstift Klosterneuburg, Austria, codex 1121, f. 79v–92r. Octavo. Saec. 15.
Microfilm: MnCH proj. no. 6100

338 De passione Domini. MS. Benediktinerabtei, St. Paul im Lavanttal, Austria,
codex 22/4, pars III. Quarto. Saec. 15.
Microfilm: MnCH proj. no. 12,462

339 De passione Dominica. MS. Cistercienserabtei Wilhering, Austria, codex IX, 101,
f. 219v–226v. Quarto. Saec. 15.
Microfilm: MnCH proj. no. 2876

340 De passione Domini. MS. Vienna, Na-
tionalbibliothek, codex 3841, f. 176v–181r.
Octavo. Saec. 15.
Microfilm: MnCH proj. no. 17,081

341 De planctu Beatae Virginis. MS. Cistercienserabtei Lilienfeld, Austria, codex 35,
f. 10v–12v. Quarto. Saec. 13.
Microfilm: MnCH proj. no. 4343

342 De planctu Beatae Virginis. MS. Benediktinerabtei Kremsmünster, Austria,
codex 124, f. 58v–62v. Saec. 14.
Microfilm: MnCH proj. no. 115

343 De planctu Beatae Virginis. MS. Benediktinerabtei Lambach, Austria, codex
chartaceus 79, f. 92v–193v. Saec. 14.
Microfilm: MnCH proj. no. 501

344 De planctu beatae Mariae Virginis. Incipit: Fugientibus discipulis. MS. Benediktinerabtei Melk, Austria, codex 1096, f.
520–530. Duodecimo. Saec. 15.
Microfilm: MnCH proj. no. 1851

345 De processione Spiritus Sancti. MS.
Toledo, Spain, Biblioteca del Cabildo,
codex 15, 6, f. 27r–39v. Folio. Saec. 14?
Microfilm: MnCH proj. no. 33,119

346 De salvatione generis humani. MS. Vienna, Nationalbibliothek, codex 3841, f.
164v–176v. Octavo. Saec. 15.
Microfilm: MnCH proj. no. 17,081

347 Similitudines. MS. Hereford, England,
Cathedral Library, codex P 5 ix, f. 2v–19r.
Quarto. Saec. 13–14.
Microfilm: MnCH

348 De similitudinibus. MS. Lambeth Palace
Library, London, codex 353, f. 1–79.
Quarto. Saec. 13.
Microfilm: MnCH

349 Tractatus de similitudinibus. MS. Benediktinerabtei Admont, Austria, codex 433,
f. 177r–219v. Quarto. Saec. 14.
Microfilm: MnCH proj. no. 9493

350 De similitudinibus. MS. Lambeth Palace
Library, London, codex 180, f. 117–171.
Quarto. Saec. 14.
Microfilm: MnCH

351 De similitudinibus. MS. Benediktinerab-
tei Fiecht, Austria, codex 172, f. 1r–26r.
Folio. Saec. 15.
Microfilm: MnCH proj. no. 28,852

352 De similitudinibus. MS. Benediktinerab-
tei Melk, Austria, codex 321, f. 173v–200v.
Folio. Saec. 15.
Microfilm: MnCH proj. no. 1330

353 De similitudinibus. MS. Vienna, Nation-
albibliothek, codex 14,523, f. 223r–286r.
Quarto. Saec. 15.
Microfilm: MnCH proj. no. 20,229

354 De timore judicii, et de spe quae est in
Deum. MS. Benediktinerabtei Melk,
Austria, codex 1089, f. 554–578. Duode-
cimo. Saec. 15.
Microfilm: MnCH proj. no. 1840

355 Dialogus inter S. Anselmum et Beatam
Mariam Virginem de passione Domini. MS.
Augustinerchorherrenstift Vorau, Austria,
codex 334, f. 38v–41v. Quarto. Saec. 13.
Microfilm: MnCH proj. no. 7308

356 Dialogus inter S. Anselmum et Beatam
Mariam Virginem de passione Domini. MS.
Augustinerchorherrenstift Vorau, Austria,
codex 401, f. 9r–13v. Octavo. Saec. 13.
Microfilm: MnCH proj. no. 7370

357 Dialogus S. Anselmi et Beatae Mariae
Virginis de passione Dominica. MS. Cistercienserabtei Heiligenkreuz, Austria, codex
107, f. 108v–111r. Folio. Saec. 14.
Microfilm: MnCH proj. no. 4676

358 Dialogus de passione. MS. Cistercienserabtei Heiligenkreuz, Austria, codex
316, f. 72r–74v. Quarto. Saec. 14.
Microfilm: MnCH proj. no. 4854

359 Dialogus sanctissimae Mariae et Anselmi
de passione Domini. MS. Augustinerchorherrenstift Klosterneuburg, Austria,
codex 940, f. 212r–218r. Quarto. Saec. 14.
Microfilm: MnCH proj. no. 5927

360 Dialogus inter S. Anselmum et Matrem
Dei de passione Christi. MS. Vienna, Na-
tionalbibliothek, codex 898, f. 127r–140v.
Octavo. Saec. 14–15.
Microfilm: MnCH proj. no. 14,215

361 Dialogus cum Beata Maria Virgine de
passione Domini. MS. Benediktinerabtei
Admont, Austria, codex 194, f. 157r–161r.
Folio. Saec. 14–15.
Microfilm: MnCH proj. no. 9281

362 Dialogus de passione Domini. MS. Benediktinerabtei Admont, Austria, codex 777,
f. 48r–248v. Octavo. Saec. 15.
Microfilm: MnCH proj. no. 9811

363 Dialogus Beatae Mariae Virginis cum S.
Anselmo, de passione Domini. MS. Benediktinerabtei Göttweig, Austria, codex
296b, f. 103r–107r. Folio. Saec. 15.
Microfilm: MnCH proj. no. 3965

364 Dialogus inter Sanctum Anselmum et
Matrem Dei de passione. MS. Benedik-

tinerabtei Kremsmünster, Austria, codex
75, f. 97r–1014. Saec. 15.
Microfilm: MnCH proj. no. 69

365   Interrogationes Anshelmi ad Mariam de
passione filii eius Domini Nostri Jesu
Christi. MS. Cistercienserabtei
Neukloster, Wienerneustadt, Austria,
codex D 20, f. 101r–109v. Octavo. Saec. 15.
Microfilm: MnCH proj. no. 4952

366   Dialogus de dolore Beatae Mariae Vir-
ginis. MS. Prämonstratenserabtei Schlägl,
Austria, codex 202, f. 418v–422r. Folio.
Saec. 15.
Microfilm: MnCH proj. no. 3054

367   Dialogus Beatae Mariae et Anselmi de
passione Domini. MS. Benediktinerabtei
Seitenstetten, Austria, codex 126, f. 38v–
40v. Folio. Saec. 15.
Microfilm: MnCH proj. no. 939

368   Dialogus Beatae Virginis Mariae et b.
Anselmi de passione Domini. MS. Benediktinerabtei Seitenstetten, Austria, codex
289, f. 170r–174v. Quarto. Saec. 14–15.
Microfilm: MnCH proj. no. 1097

369   Dialogus cum Beata Maria Virgine de
passione Domini nostri. MS. Vienna, Nationalbibliothek, codex 14,894, f.
209v–213v. Quarto. Saec. 15.
Microfilm: MnCH proj. no. 20,279

370   Dialogus inter S. Anselmum et BMV de
passione Domini. MS. Augustinerchorherrenstift Vorau, Austria, codex 86, f. 124v–
128v. Folio. Saec. 15.
Microfilm: MnCH proj. no. 7094

371   Dialogus de libero arbitrio. MS. Vienna,
Nationalbibliothek, codex 1070, f. 15r–21v.
Quarto. Saec. 13.
Microfilm: MnCH proj. no. 14,377

372   Doctrina qualiter moribundus sit interro-
gandus. MS. Vienna, Nationalbibliothek,
codex 4724, f. 216v–262r. Quarto. Saec.
14.
Microfilm: MnCH proj. no. 17,889

373   Elucidarium super quaedam quaestiun-
culas condiscipulorum (finis deest). MS.
Vienna, Nationalbibliothek, codex 757, f.
147r–176v. Folio. Saec. 12.
Microfilm: MnCH proj. no. 14,077

374   Elucidarium. MS. Augustinerchorherrenstift St. Florian, Austria, codex XI,
649, f. 58r–104r. Quarto. Saec. 14.
Microfilm: MnCH proj. no. 2757

375   Elucidarium de diversis dubiis. MS.
Augustinerchorherrenstift St. Florian,
Austria, codex XI, 71, f. 49r–68v. Folio.
Saec. 14.
Microfilm: MnCH proj. no. 2328

376   Epistola beati Anselmi ad B. monachum.
MS. Salisbury, England, Cathedral
Library, codex 55, f. 137. Quarto. Saec. 14.
Microfilm: MnCH

377   [Epistolae]
Letter of Archbishop Anselm to William
(Giffard) bishop of Winchester. Letter of
King Henry to Anselm. MS. Hereford,
England, Cathedral Library, codex P 1 iii,
fly-leaf. Saec. 12.
Microfilm: MnCH

378   Epistola de diversitate sacramentorum.
MS. Cistercienserabtei Rein, Austria,
codex 67, f. 54v–55r. Folio. Saec. 15.
Microfilm: MnCH proj. no. 7471

379   Epistola de incarnatione Verbi. MS.
Universitätsbibliothek Graz, codex 1545, f.
73r–94v. Octavo. Saec. 12.
Microfilm: MnCH proj. no. 26,483

380   Epistola de sacramentis ecclesiae ad
Menburgensem episcopum. MS. Benediktinerabtei Melk, Austria, codex 1869, f.
241r–242r. Folio. Saec. 15.
Microfilm: MnCH proj. no. 2166

381   Epistola de sacrificio fermenti et azymi.
MS. Benediktinerabtei Melk, Austria,
codex 1869, f. 238v–241r. Folio. Saec. 15.
Microfilm: MnCH proj. no. 2166

382   Ex verbis beati Anselmi: Adoramus te
Christe rex Israel. MS. Benediktinerabtei
Melk, Austria, codex 791, f. 38v. Quarto.
Saec. 15.
Microfilm: MnCH proj. no. 1629

383   Exhortatio ad timorem. Germanice. MS.
Benediktinerabtei Melk, Austria, codex
1389, f. 188–197. Duodecimo. Saec. 15.
Microfilm: MnCH proj. no. 1911

384   Exhortatio ad timorem. MS. Benediktinerabtei Melk, Austria, codex 1478, f.
197–200. Duodecimo. Saec. 15.
Microfilm: MnCH proj. no. 1945

385   Exhortatio ad timorem. MS. Benediktinerabtei Melk, Austria, codex 1577, p.
141–143. Duodecimo. Saec. 15.
Microfilm: MnCH proj. no. 1974

386   Exhortatio ad timorem. MS. Benediktinerabtei Melk, Austria, codex 1743, p.
407–410. Duodecimo. Saec. 15.
Microfilm: MnCH proj. no. 2053

387   Exhortationes pro bona vita. MS.
Vienna, Nationalbibliothek, codex 4334, f.
1r–7v. Octavo. Saec. 15.
Microfilm: MnCH proj. no. 17,503

388   Explanationes in cantica. Benediktinerabtei Admont, Austria, codex 255. 138
f. Folio. Saec. 12.
Microfilm: MnCH proj. no. 9342

389   Homilia super: Intravit Jesus in quoddam castellum. MS. Augustinerchorherrenstift St. Florian, Austria, codex XI, 17,
f. 147v–151r. Folio. Saec. 13.
Microfilm: MnCH proj. no. 2272

390   Homiliae de assumptione b. Mariae Virginis. MS. Benediktinerabtei Melk,
Austria, codex 2, f. 433–439. Folio. Saec.
15.
Microfilm: MnCH proj. no. 1121

391   Homilia in evangelium Lucae X, 38. MS.
Vienna, Nationalbibliothek, codex 982, f.
95r–97r. Folio. Saec. 12.

392   Hymnus ad Beatam Mariam Virginem,
cum neumis in campo aperto. MS. Augustinerchorrenstift Klosterneuburg,
Austria, codex 793, f. 1r. Quarto. Saec. 12.
Microfilm: MnCH proj. no. 5783

393   Lamentatio amissae castitatis. MS. Cis-
tercienserabtei Wilhering, Austria, codex
IX, 101, f. 205v–207r. Quarto. Saec. 15.
Microfilm: MnCH proj. no. 2876

394   Lectiones de conceptione Beatae Mariae
Virginis. MS. Augustinerchorherrenstift
St. Florian, Austria, codex XI, 125, f.
194r–196v. Folio. Saec. 14.
Microfilm: MnCH proj. no. 2390

395   Lectura super Psalterium. MS. Benediktinerabtei Admont, Austria, codex 597.
165 f. Quarto. Saec. 13.
Microfilm: MnCH proj. no. 9643

396   Liber de conceptu virginali. MS. Universitätsbibliothek Graz, Austria, codex
169, f. 62r–64v. Quarto. Saec. 12.
Microfilm: MnCH proj. no. 26,107

397   Liber de conceptu virginali et peccato
originali. MS. Benediktinerabtei Göttweig,
Austria, codex 119, f. 17v–29r. Folio. Saec.
13.
Microfilm: MnCH proj. no. 3398

398   Liber de conceptu virginali. MS. Benediktinerabtei Seitenstetten, Austria, codex
257, f. 27r–35v. Folio. Saec. 15.
Microfilm: MnCH proj. no. 1062

399   Liber de laudibus Beatae Mariae Virginis
(Speculum Beatae Mariae Virginis). MS.
Cistercienserabtei Zwettl, Austria, codex
135, f. 2r–17v. Octavo. Saec. 13.
Microfilm: MnCH proj. no. 6727

400   Liber de libero arbitrio. MS. Cistercienserabtei Heiligenkreuz, Austria, codex
256, f. 90r–100r. Folio. Saec. 12.
Microfilm: MnCH proj. no. 4794

401   Liber de miseria. MS. Benediktinerabtei
Melk, Austria, codex 1554, f. 221v–224v.
Duodecimo. Saec. 15.
Microfilm: MnCH proj. no. 1953

402   Liber de quaerendo Deum. MS. Benediktinerabtei St. Peter, Salzburg, codex
a.I.18, f. 1r–22r. Duodecimo. Saec. 14–15.
Microfilm: MnCH proj. no. 9888

403   Tractatus de similitudinibus. MS.
Hereford, England, Cathedral Library,
codex 0 1 ii, f. 117v–130. Quarto. Saec. 13.
Microfilm: MnCH

404   Liber de similitudinibus. MS. Augustinerchorherrenstift St. Florian, Austria,
codex XI, 303, f. 197v–204v. Folio. Saec.
14.
Microfilm: MnCH proj. no. 2532

405   Liber de similitudinibus. MS. Dominikanerkloster, Vienna, codex 234, f.
23r–52r. Quarto. Saec. 14.
Microfilm: MnCH proj. no. 9016

406   Liber de similitutinibus. MS. Cistercienserabtei Zwettl, Austria, codex 290, f.
?17r–239r. Quarto. Saec. 14.
Microfilm: MnCH proj. no. 6886

407   Liber de similitutinibus. MS. Benediktinerabtei Melk, Austria, codex 544, f.
172r–206r. Folio. Saec. 15.
Microfilm: MnCH proj. no. 1466

408   Liber de veritate sub dialogo editus. MS.
Vienna, Nationalbibliothek, codex 984, f.
32r–42r. Folio. Saec. 13.
Microfilm: MnCH proj. no. 14,290

409   Liber "quod Deus homo." MS. Benediktinerabtei Melk, Austria, codex 6, f. 136v–
168v. Folio. Saec. 13.
Microfilm: MnCH proj. no. 1130

410   Libri duo contra Wicbertum et sequaces
ejus. MS. Benediktinerabtei Admont,
Austria, codex 162, f. 197v–206v. Folio.
Saec. 12.
Microfilm: MnCH proj. no. 9249

411   Libri tres de fide Sanctae Trinitatis et de
incarnatione Christi. MS. Cistercienserabtei Zwettl, Austria, codex 363, f. 33r–64v.
Octavo. Saec. 12.
Microfilm: MnCH proj. no. 6961

412   Lucidarius libellus bonus. MS. Cistercienserabtei Wilhering, Austria, codex IX,
83, f. 195v–220v. Quarto. Saec. 15.
Microfilm: MnCH proj. no. 2857

413   Meditationes et orationes. MS. Benediktinerabtei Admont, Austria, codex 289.
193 f. Folio. Saec. 12.
Microfilm: MnCH proj. no. 9383

414   Meditationes duae. Metrice. Incipit: a) O
lumen verum quo lux est facta dierum; b)
Ut iocundus cervus undas estuans
desiderat. MS. Cistercienserabtei Heiligenkreuz, Austria, codex 108, f.
101r–101v. Folio. Saec. 12.
Microfilm: MnCH proj. no. 4652

415 Meditationes. MS. Augustinerchorherrenstift Klosterneuburg, Austria, codex
798, f. 3r–78r. Quarto. Saec. 12.
Microfilm: MnCH proj. no. 5801

416 Meditationes. MS. Cistercienserabtei
Zwettl, Austria, codex 225, f. 97r–146v.
Quarto. Saec. 12.
Microfilm: MnCH proj. no. 6829

417 Meditationes (et orationes). MS. Vienna,
Schottenstift, codex 201, f. 2r–31v.
Quarto. Saec. 13–14.
Microfilm: MnCH proj. no. 4144

418 Meditationes et orationes. MS. Cistercienserabtei Zwettl, Austria, codex 260, f.
107r–141v. Quarto. Saec. 13.
Microfilm: MnCH proj. no. 6858

419 Meditationes et orationes. MS. Augustinerchorherrenstift Klosterneuburg,
Austria, codex 796, f. 1r–41v. Folio. Saec.
14.
Microfilm: MnCH proj. no. 5786

420 Meditationes; Meditatio de occulta
Christi virtute; Meditatio de periculis hujus
vitae. MS. Augustinerchorherrenstift
Klosterneuburg, Austria, codex 1121, f.
30r–60r. Octavo. Saec. 14.
Microfilm: MnCH proj. no. 6100

421 Orationes et Meditationes. MS. Toledo,
Spain, Biblioteca del Cabildo, codex 15, 5.
198 f. Folio. Saec. 14?
Microfilm: MnCH proj. no. 33,118

422 Meditationes. MS. Lambeth Palace
Library, London, codex 194, f. 57–102.
Microfilm: MnCH

423 Meditationes et orationes. MS. Cistercienserabtei Rein, Austria, codex 49, f.
2r–28r. Quarto. Saec. 15.
Microfilm: MnCH proj. no. 7446

424 Meditationes et orationes. MS. Benediktinerabtei St. Peter, Salzburg, Austria,
codex b.IX.29, f. 165r–206r. Folio. Saec.
15.
Microfilm: MnCH proj. no. 10,589

425 Meditationes. MS. Vienna, Nationalbib-
liothek, codex 4308, f. 187r.–192v. Quarto.
Saec. 15.
Microfilm: MnCH proj. no. 17,469

426 Meditationes et orationes excerptae. MS.
Vienna, Nationalbibliothek, codex 4560, f.
59r–122r. Octavo. Saec. 15 (1479).
Microfilm: MnCH proj. no. 17,732

427 Meditationes. MS. Vienna, Schottenstift,
codex 63, f. 1r–58v. Quarto. Saec. 15.
Microfilm: MnCH proj. no. 3985

428 Meditationes et orationes. MS. Subiaco,
Italy (Benedictine abbey), codex 282. Saec.
15.
Microfilm: MnCH

429 [Meditationes. German]
Excerpta ex libello Meditationum. Ger-
manice. MS. Benediktinerabtei Melk,
Austria, codex 1389, f. 174–188.
Duodecimo. Saec. 15.
Microfilm: MnCH proj. no. 1911

430 [Meditationes. German]
Hie hebt sich an das puech sand An-
shelms gepet und meditiern. MS. Benediktinerabtei Melk, Austria, codex 235, f.
81r–1204. Folio. Saec. 15.
Microfilm: MnCH proj. no. 1277

431 [Meditationes. German]
Gebet und Betrachtung Anshelmi. MS.
Benediktinerabtei Melk, Austria, codex
1001. 113 f. Quarto. Saec. 15.
Microfilm: MnCH proj. no. 1793

432 Meditatio ad excitandum timorem. Incipit: Terret me vita mea. MS. Cistercienserabtei Heiligenkreuz, Austria, codex
133, f. 126v–127v. Folio. Saec. 12.
Microfilm: MnCH proj. no. 4678

433 Meditatio ad excitandum timorem. MS.
Vienna, Nationalbibliothek, codex 965, f.
133r–133v. Folio. Saec. 14.
Microfilm: MnCH proj. no. 14,265

434 Meditatio ad excitandum timorem. MS.
Salisbury, England, Cathedral Library,
codex 13, f. 163–164. Octavo. Saec. 14.
Microfilm: MnCH

435 Meditatio ad excitandum timorem. MS.
Diöcesanbibliothek St. Pölten, Austria,
codex 99, f. 119v–134. Octavo. Saec. 14.
Microfilm: MnCH proj. no. 6339

436 Meditatio de morte Christi. MS. Vienna,
Schottenstift, codex 245, f. 143v–146v.
Folio. Saec. 15.
Microfilm: MnCH proj. no. 3903

437 Meditatio de reparatione lapsi hominis.
MS. Benediktinerabtei Melk, Austria,
codex 1869, f. 195r–197r. Folio. Saec. 15.
Microfilm: MnCH proj. no. 2166

438 Meditatio. Incipit: Terret me vita mea.
MS. Vienna, Schottenstift, codex 328, f.
340v–344r. Octavo. Saec. 15.
Microfilm: MnCH proj. no. 4091

439 Meditatio et gratiarum actio. MS. Vienna, Nationalbibliothek, codex 4115, f.
66r–67r. Octavo. Saec. 15.
Microfilm: MnCH proj. no. 17,311

440 Meditatio super psalmum "Miserere."
MS. Vienna, Nationalbibliothek, codex
3616, f. 192r–226r. Quarto. Saec. 15.
Microfilm: MnCH proj. no. 16,809

441 Monologium de divinitatis essentia. MS.
Benediktinerabtei Seitenstetten, Austria,
codex 123, f. 133r–148r. Folio. Saec.
14–15.
Microfilm: MnCH proj. no. 936

442 Monologion. MS. Benediktinerabtei Melk, Austria, codex 1869, f. 251v–266v. Folio. Saec. 15.
Microfilm: MnCH proj. no. 2166

443 Moralitates in Paralipomena. MS. Vienna, Nationalbibliothek, codex 1197, f. 58r–75r. Folio. Saec. 13.
Microfilm: MnCH proj. no. 14,547

444 Opus de beatitudine. MS. Benediktinerabtei Admont, Austria, codex 240, f. 215–218. Folio. Saec. 13.
Microfilm: MnCH proj. no. 9325

445 Oratio ad Christum. MS. Vienna, Nationalbibliothek, codex 4081, f. 1r–2v. Octavo. Saec. 15.
Microfilm: MnCH proj. no. 17,413

446 Oratio ad S. Mariam. Germanice. MS. Augustinerchorherrenstift Klosterneuburg, Austria, codex 1036, f. 14v–31v. Quarto. Saec. 14.
Microfilm: MnCH proj. no. 6011

447 Oratio ad S. Mariam Magdalenam; Oratio pro desidero lacrimarum; Meditatio ad concitandum timorem. MS. Augustinerchorherrenstift Vorau, Austria, codex 82, f. 180r–206r. Duodecimo. Saec. 15.
Microfilm: MnCH proj. no. 7087

448 Orationes compositae a S. Ambrosio, Anselmo, Petro Damiani et Berengario. MS. Cistercienserabtei Heiligenkreuz, Austria, codex 262, f. 111r–134v. Quarto. Saec. 12.
Microfilm: MnCH proj. no. 4802

449 Orationes: Meditacio ad concitandum timorem Domini; Deploratio virginitatis male amissae; Orationes ad S. Paulum, Nicolaum, de passione Domini, ad Deum patrem omnipotentem; Excitatio animae christianae ad meditandum de reparacione sua vera; Orationes ad dominum Iesus Christum, ad sanctam crucem, ad sumendum Corpus Domini nostri Iesu Christi; Apologium sacerdotis. MS. Benediktinerabtei Lambach, Austria, codex chartaceus 339, f. 1r–41r. Saec. 15.
Microfilm: MnCH proj. no. 708

450 Orationes. MS. Augustinerchorherrenstift Vorau, Austria, codex 80, f. 186v–246r. Duodecimo. Saec. 15.
Microfilm: MnCH proj. no. 7083

451 Orationes de Beata Virgine Maria (septem orationes). MS. Cistercienserabtei Lilienfeld, Austria, codex 144, f. 70v–71v. Folio. Saec. 13.
Microfilm: MnCH proj. no. 4513

452 Orationes de Beata Maria Virgine. MS. Vienna, Nationalbibliothek, codex 3841, f. 181v–201r. Octavo. Saec. 15.
Microfilm: MnCH proj. no. 17,081

453 Orationes duae. Incipit: Terret me vita mea. MS. Prämonstratenserabtei Schlägl, Austria, codex 24, f. 7r–10v. Sextodecimo. Saec. 14.
Microfilm: MnCH proj. no. 3131

454 Orationes precatoriae. MS. Cistercienserabtei Lilienfeld, Austria, codex 31. f. 1r–56r. Quarto. Saec. 14.
Microfilm: MnCH proj. no. 4341

455 Orationes precatoriae, maxime ad B. Virginem Mariam. MS. Benediktinerabtei Melk, Austria, codex 2, f. 173–185. Folio. Saec. 15.
Microfilm: MnCH proj. no. 1121

456 Passionis dominicae misericordia. MS. Tortosa, Spain, Archivo de la Catedral, codex 110, f. 132v–136r. Quarto. Saec. 14.
Microfilm: MnCH proj. no. 30,680

457 Planctus de compassione Beatae Virginis Mariae. MS. Augustinerchorherrenstift St. Florian, Austria, codex XI, 57, f. 177r–178v. Quarto. Saec. 14.
Microfilm: MnCH proj. no. 2313

458 Planctus de passione. MS. Universitätsbibliothek Graz, Austria, codex 611, f. 9r–12v. Folio. Saec. 15.
Microfilm: MnCH proj. no. 26,754

459 Planctus ad Beatam Mariam Virginem. MS. Studienbibliothek, Klagenfurt, Austria, codex cart. 90, f. 54v–59r. Quarto. Saec. 15.
Microfilm: MnCH proj. no. 13,072

460 Planctus Mariae. MS. Vienna, Nationalbibliothek, codex 15,040, f. 129v–136r. Quarto. Saec. 15.
Microfilm: MnCH proj. no. 20,456

461 Postilla super psalmum mei deus. MS. Dominikanerkloster, Vienna, codex 81, f. 10v–22v. Folio. Saec. 15.
Microfilm: MnCH proj. no. 8883

462 Prologus in librum Imago mundi. MS. Vienna, Nationalbibliothek, codex 113, f. 89r–90v. Folio. Saec. 13.
Microfilm: MnCH proj. no. 13,473

463 Proslogion. MS. Universitätsbibliothek Graz, Austria, codex 737, f. 114v–120v. Folio. Saec. 12.
Microfilm: MnCH proj. no. 26,870

464 Proslogion. MS. Cistercienserabtei Heiligenkreuz, Austria, codex 133, f. 119r–125v. Folio. Saec. 12.
Microfilm: MnCH proj. no. 4678

465 Proslogion. MS. Bundesstattliche Studienbibliothek, Linz, Austria, codex 45, f. 97v–107v. Quarto. Saec. 12.
Microfilm: MnCH proj. no. 27,857

466 Proslogion. MS. Augustinerchorherrenstift Vorau, Austria, codex 190, f.

99r–108r. Octavo. Saec. 13.
Microfilm: MnCH proj. no. 7185

467   Proslogion (in codice: Soliloquium). MS.
Benediktinerabtei Göttweig, Austria,
codex 78, b, f. 38v–42v. Folio. Saec. 14.
Microfilm: MnCH proj. no. 3363

468   Proslogion. MS. Augustinerchorherrenstift Herzogenburg, Austria, codex 103, f.
56v–64v. Quarto. Saec. 14.
Microfilm: MnCH proj. no. 3261

469   Proslogion. MS. Augustinerchorherrenstift Klosterneuburg, Austria, codex 1121,
f. 60v–74v. Octavo. Saec. 14.
Microfilm: MnCH proj. no. 1121

470   Proslogion. MS. Cistercienserabtei
Lilienfeld, Austria, codex 137, f. 148r–
152v. Folio. Saec. 14.
Microfilm: MnCH proj. no. 4435

471   Proslogion, cum prologo. MS. Vienna,
Nationalbibliothek, codex 965, f.
125r–133r. Folio. Saec. 14.
Microfilm: MnCH proj. no. 14,265

472   Proslogion. MS. Augustinerchorherrenstift St. Florian, Austria, codex XI, 57, f.
175v–176v. Quarto. Saec. 14.
Microfilm: MnCH proj. no. 2313

473   Proslogion. MS. Augustinerchorherrenstift St. Florian, Austria, codex XI, 285, f.
160r–169v. Quarto. Saec. 14.
Microfilm: MnCH proj. no. 2522

474   Proslogion. MS. Diezösanbibliothek St.
Pölten, Austria, codex 99, f. 105r–119v.
Octavo. Saec. 14.
Microfilm: MnCH proj. no. 6339

475   Proslogium, cap. 24–25. MS. Prämonstratenserabtei Schlägl, Austria, codex 28,
41v–43r. Octavo. Saec. 14.
Microfilm: MnCH proj. no. 3093

476   Prologus in Proslogion. MS. Benediktinerabtei Lambach, Austria, codex chartaceus 339, f. 17v–23v. Saec. 15.
Microfilm: MnCH proj. no. 708

477   Proslogion. MS. Benedictinerabtei Melk,
Austria, codex 1869, f. 233v–238v. Folio.
Saec. 15.
Microfilm: MnCH proj. no. 2166

478   Proslogion. MS. Benediktinerabtei St.
Paul im Lavanttal, Austria, codex 327/4, f.
20v–33r. Octavo. Saec. 15.
Microfilm: MnCH proj. no. 12,555

479   Proslogion, seu Colloquium de Dei existentia. MS. Benediktinerabtei Seitenstetten, Austria, codex 123, f. 148r–153r.
Folio. Saec. 15.
Microfilm: MnCH proj. no. 936

480   Proslogion. MS. Vienna, Nationalbibliothek, codex 1473, f. 70v–77v. Folio. Saec.
15 (1402).

Microfilm: MnCH proj. no. 14,820

481   Prooemium in proslogion. MS. Vienna,
Nationalbibliothek, codex 4409, f.
107r–113v. Folio. Saec. 15.
Microfilm: MnCH proj. no. 17,612

482   Quaestio de concordia gratiae et liberi arbitrii. MS. Vienna, Nationalbibliothek,
codex 1070, f. 21v–30v. Quarto. Saec. 13.
Microfilm: MnCH proj. no. 14,377

483   Responsio contra insipientem. MS. Benediktinerabtei Melk, Austria, codex 1869, f.
197v–200v. Folio. Saec. 15.
Microfilm: MnCH proj. no. 2166

484   Scriptum super Miserere. Alias Hugo de
S. Victore. MS. Augustinerchorherrenstift
St. Florian, Austria, codex XI, 126, f.
56r–69r. Folio. Saec. 14.
Microfilm: MnCH proj. no. 2390

485   Sententiae. Incipit: Principium et causa
omnium Deus. MS. Cistercienserabtei
Heiligenkreuz, Austria, codex 236, f.
42r–85v. Folio. Saec. 12.
Microfilm: MnCH proj. no. 4776

486   Sentencie a magistro Anselmo collecta.
MS. Benediktinerabtei Kremsmünster,
Austria, codex 289, f. 126r–191v. Saec. 14.
Microfilm: MnCH proj. no. 274

487   Sententia Anselmi archiepiscopi de motione altaris. MS. Hereford, England,
Cathedral Library, codex 0 1 vi, f. 43.
Quarto. Saec. 12.
Microfilm: MnCH

488   Sermo de conceptione B.M.V. MS. Universitätsbibliothek Graz, Austria, codex
1239, f. 94r–96r. Quarto. Saec. 14.
Microfilm: MnCH proj. no. 26,349

489   Sermo de conceptione Beatae Mariae
Virginis. MS. Benediktinerabtei Göttweig,
Austria, codex 483, f. 3r–7v. Quarto. Saec.
15.
Microfilm: MnCH proj. no. 3738

490   Sermo de conceptione Mariae. MS. Studienbibliothek, Klagenfurt, Austria, codex
cart. 85, f. 156v–158v. Quarto. Saec. 15
(1476).
Microfilm: MnCH proj. no. 13,067

491   Sermo de conceptione Mariae Virginis.
MS. Vienna, Schottenstift, codex 318, f.
1v–5v. Quarto. Saec. 15.
Microfilm: MnCH proj. no. 4080

492   Sermo de duobus beatitudinibus et
duobus miseriis. MS. Exeter, England,
Cathedral Library, codex P 1 vi, f.
141–145. Quarto. Saec. 12.
Microfilm: MnCH

493   Sermones de Beata Maria Virgine. MS.
Benediktinerabtei Admont, Austria, codex
275, f. 43r–74v. Folio. Saec. 13.
Microfilm: MnCH proj. no. 9356

494 Libellus qui vocatur Sigillum Mariae, cum prologo (mutilus). MS. Vienna, Nationalbibliothek, codex 4038, f. 26r–27r. Quarto. Saec. 15.
Microfilm: MnCH proj. no. 17,235

495 Soliloquium. MS. Benediktinerabtei St. Peter, Salzburg, codex a.III.18, f. 173r–177v. Octavo. Saec. 15.
Microfilm: MnCH proj. no. 9960

496 Speculum animae in passionem Christi. MS. Vienna, Nationalbibliothek, codex 3598, f. 148r–158v. Quarto. Saec. 15.
Microfilm: MnCH proj. no. 16,813

497 Stimulus dilectionis. MS. Benediktinerabtei St. Peter, Salzburg, codex b.IX.29, f. 206v–212r. Folio. Saec. 15.
Microfilm: MnCH proj. no. 10,589

498 Tractatus contra Graecos de processione Spiritus Sancti. MS. Benediktinerabtei Melk, Austria, codex 1869, f. 242r–251v. Folio. Saec. 15.
Microfilm: MnCH proj. no. 2166

499 Tractatus de aeterna beatitudine et meritis electorum. MS. Benediktinerabtei Melk, Austria, codex 1869, f. 191v–195r. Folio. Saec. 15.
Microfilm: MnCH proj. no. 2166

500 Tractatus de casu diaboli. MS. Benediktinerabtei Melk, Austria, codex 1869, f. 201v–211v. Folio. Saec. 15.
Microfilm: MnCH proj. no. 2166

501 Tractatus de conceptu virginali. MS. Benediktinerabtei Admont, Austria, codex 201, f. 59v–68r. Folio. Saec. 15.
Microfilm: MnCH proj. no. 9288

502 De tribus quaestionibus (i.e., Tractatus de concordia praescientiae et praedestinationis etc.). MS. Cistercienserabtei Heiligenkreuz, Austria, codex 256, f. 100v–120v. Folio. Saec. 12.
Microfilm: MnCH proj. no. 4794

503 Tractatus de concordia praescientiae et praedestinationis et gratiae cum libero arbitrio. MS. Augustinerchorherrenstift Herzogenburg, Austria, codex 28, f. 1r–57v. Folio. Saec. 14–15.
Microfilm: MnCH proj. no. 3193

504 Tractatus de concordia praescientiae, predestionationis et liberi arbitrii. MS. Benediktinerabtei Seitenstetten, Austria, codex 257, f. 35v–46v. Folio. Saec. 15.
Microfilm: MnCH proj. no. 1062

505 Tractatus de mensuratione crucis. MS. Augustinerchorherrenstift St. Florian, Austria, codex XI, 163, f. 159r–174r. Duodecimo. Saec. 15.
Microfilm: MnCH proj. no. 2431

506 Tractatus de mensuratione crucis docens qualiter perfectio attingatur ex doctrina Christi. MS. Augustinerchorherrenstift St. Florian, codex XI, 167, f. 102r–119r. Duodecimo. Saec. 15.
Microfilm: MnCH proj. no. 2434

507 Tractatus de passione Domini. MS. Vienna, Nationalbibliothek, codex 475, f. 213v–215v. Folio. Saec. 15.
Microfilm: MnCH proj. no. 13,808

508 Tractatus de passione Domini. MS. Vienna, Nationalbibliothek, codex 4241, f. 130r–134v. Folio. Saec. 14.
Microfilm: MnCH proj. no. 17,426

509 Tractatus de peccato originali et de conceptu virginali. MS. Benediktinerabtei Melk, Austria, codex 1869, f. 218r–225r. Folio. Saec. 15.
Microfilm: MnCH proj. no. 2166

510 Tractatus de processione Spiritus Sancti contra Graecos. MS. Benediktinerabtei Göttweig, Austria, codex 119, f. 2r–17v. Folio. Saec. 13.
Microfilm: MnCH proj. no. 3398

511 Tractatus de veritate. MS. Benediktinerabtei Melk, Austria, codex 1869, f. 211v–218r. Folio. Saec. 15.
Microfilm: MnCH proj. no. 2166

512 Tractatus in evangelio de assumptione Sanctae Mariae. MS. Salisbury, England, Cathedral Library, codex 55, f. 136v. Quarto. Saec. 14.
Microfilm: MnCH

513 Super miserum conditionem hominis peccatoris. MS. Benediktinerabtei Melk, Austria, codex 386, f. 50r–51v. Folio. Saec. 14.
Microfilm: MnCH proj. no. 1373

514 Verba super miseram conditionem hominis peccatoris. MS. Augustinerchorherrenstift Klosterneuburg, Austria, codex 576, f. 139r–141r. Folio. Saec. 15.

515 Von liebchosung der seil in Christo Iesu. MS. Benediktinerabtei Melk, Austria, codex 1762, f. 104r–118v. Duodecimo. Saec. 15.

Anselm, Saint, abp. of Canterbury, 1033–1109.
Printed works.

516 Opera. Nürnberg, Caspar Hochfeder, 1491. 177 folia.
Vita Anselmi que communiter legitur. Duo libri Cur Deus homo contra gentiles. Liber unus de incarnatione Verbi. De conceptu virginali et peccato originali. Declaratio cuiusdam de eodem. Proslogion. Monologion. Liber unus de processione Spiritus Sancti. Dyalogus de casu dyaboli.

Pro insipiente. Contra insipientem. De diversitate sacramentorum. De fermento et azimo. Expositiones membrorum et actuum Dei et vestimentorum. De voluntate. De concordia prescientiae et praedestinationis et gratiae Dei cum libero arbitrio. De liber arbitrio. De veritate. De similitudinibus. De mensuratione crucis. Meditationes magnae Anselmi. Meditatio cuisudam de redemptione generis humani. De passione Domini. Speculum evangelici sermonis. Homelia Intravit Jesus in quoddam castellum. Epistolae sancti Anselmi. De imagine mundi.

MnCS (microfilm)

517   Opuscula beati Anselmi archiepiscopi Cantuarensis Ordinis Sancti Benedicti. [Basel, Joh. Amerbach, ca. 1497]

[208] leaves. 22 cm.

References: HC 1136; GW 2033; Stillwell A 672.

PLatS

518   [Opera]

Omnia D. Anselmi cantuareiensis archiepiscopi, theologorum omnium sui temporis facile principis opuscula. Cum luculensissimis eiusdem in aliquot evangelia enarrationibus, Antonij Democharis Ressonaei industria nunc primum restituta. Catalogum omnium pagina quinta demonstrat. Venetijs, ad signum Spei, 1547.

[8], 230, 159 leaves. 22 cm.

Text on both sides of leaves in double columns.

InStme; KAS

519   [Opera. English]

Anselm of Canterbury. Edited and translated by Jasper Hopkins and Herbert Richardson. Toronto, New York, Edwin Mellen Press [c 1974–

v. 23 cm.

". . . will make available in translation the complete treatises of Anselm."–Dust jacket.

PLatS

Anselm, Saint.

[Selections]

519a   Memorials of St. Anselm. Edited by R. W. Southern and F. S. Schmitt, O.S.B. London, Published for the British Academy by the Oxford University Press, 1969.

viii, 370 p. 26 cm. (Auctores Britannici Medii Aevi, 1)

Latin texts.

InStme; MnCS

520   [Selections. English]

O God, the sire of faithful ones (Deus Pater credentium). Incarnate God, thou Word Divine (Qui Deus homo diceris). Virgin of virgins, Mary mild (Maria virgo virginum). Sweet Christ be with us (Esto Christe propitius).

(*In* Donahoe, D. J. Early Christian hymns. New York, 1911. v. 2, p. 87–94)

PLatS

521   [Selections. English]

Basic writings: Proslogium; Monologium; Gaunilou's On behalf of the fool; Cur Deus homo. Translated by S. W. Deane, with an introduction by Charles Hartshorne. 2nd ed. La Salle, Ill., Open Court Pub. Co., 1962.

19, xxxv, 288 p. 22 cm.

InStme; PLatS

522   [Selections. French]

Saint Anselme: textes choisies [traduits et présentés par la R. M. Marie Pascal Dickson, O.S.B.]. Précédés de La vie de Saint Anselme du Bec, tirée des récits de son biographe Eadmer [par R. M. Isabelle de Jouffroy d'Abbens, O.S.B.]. Namur, Belgique, Editions du Soleil Levant [1961].

189 p. 19 cm. (Les Ecrits des saints)

PLatS

523   Cur Deus homo, by St. Anselm; to which is added a selection from his letters. London, Griffith, Farran, Okeden & Welsh [1891].

xxviii, 244 p. 13 cm. (The Ancient and modern library of theological literature).

Translator unknown.

"Life of St. Anselm," p. xi–xxv, signed R. C.

KAS

524   [Cur Deus homo]

Pourquoi Dieu s'est fait homme. Text latin, introduction, bibliographie, traduction et notes de René Roques. Paris, Editions du Cerf, 1963.

525 p. 21 cm. (Sources chrétiennes, no. 91)

InStme; MnCS; PLatS

525   [Cur Deus homo. English]

Why God became man, and The Virgin conception and original sin, by Anselm of Canterbury. Translation, introduction, and notes by Joseph M. Colleran. Albany, N.Y., Magi Books [c 1969].

viii, 245 p. 21 cm.

InStme

526   The De grammatico of St. Anselm; The theory of paronymy, by Desmond P. Henry. [Notre Dame, Ind.], University of Notre Dame Press, 1964.

xiii, 169 p. 24 cm. (University of Notre Dame. Publications in mediaeval studies, 18)

KAS

527 Dialogus de passione Jesu Christi et B. Mariae Virginis. [Strassburg, printer of the 1483 Jordanus de Quedlinburg (Georg Husner) 1496?].
6 leaves. Quarto.
PLatS

528 [Epistolae. English]
St. Anselm's letters to Lanfranc; a translation, with an introduction and commentary by Rev. Anselm Pedrizetti, O.S.B.
82 p. 28 cm.
Thesis (M.A.)–Catholic University of America, Washington, D.C., 1961.
MnCS

529 [Meditationes]
Meditationes S. Augustini et S. Bernardi aliorumque sanctorum antiquorum Patrum . . . Includes the Meditationes of St. Anselm . . . Lugduni, apud A. Gryphium, 1587.
853 p.
PLatS (microfilm)

530 [Meditationes. French]
Méditations et prières de Saint Anselme; traduites par D. A. Castel . . . Introduction par D. A. Wilmart . . . Paris, P. Lethielleux, 1923.
lxii, 240 p. 18 cm. (Collection "Pax", v.xi)
KAS; MnCS

531 Memorials of St. Anselm. Edited by R. W. Southern and F. S. Schmitt, O.S.B. London, Published for the British Academy by the Oxford University Press, 1969.
viii, 370 p. 26 cm. (Auctores Britannici Medii Aevi, 1)
InStme

532 [Proslogion. English]
Proslogium; Monologium; An appendix in behalf of the fool by Gaunilon; and Cur Deus homo. Translated from the Latin by Sidney Norton Deane, with an introduction, bibliography, and reprints of the opinions of leading philosophers and writers on the ontological argument. Reprint edition. La Salle, Ill., Open Court Pub. Co., 1961.
xxxv, 288 p. 20 cm. (Open Court classics, P54)
InStme; NcBe (1910)

533 [Proslogion. English]
St. Anselm's Proslogion. With, A reply on behalf of the fool, by Gaunilo, and the author's reply to Gaunilo. Translated with an introduction and philosophical commentary, by M. J. Charlesworth. Oxford Clarendon Press, 1965.
vi, 196 p. 23 cm.
The texts are in Latin and English.
InStme; PLatS

534 [Proslogion. English]
Proslogion. With a reply on behalf of the fool by Gaunilo and the author's reply.
(*In* Great ideas today. 1969. p. 318–343)
PLatS

535 [Proslogion. German]
Proslogion. Untersuchungen lateinisch-deutsche Ausgabe von P. Franciscus Salesius Schmitt, O.S.B. [Stuttgart], Friedrich Frommann Verlag [1962].
159 p. 21 cm.
PLatS

536 [Proslogion. Italian]
Il Proslogion, le Orazioni e le Meditazioni. Introduzione e testo latino di Franciscus Sal. Schmitt O.S.B. Traduzione italiana di Giuseppe Sandri. Padova, CEDAM, 1959.
293 p. 25 cm.
PLatS

537 Psalterium beatae Mariae V.
(*In* Analecta hymnica Medii Aevi. New York, 1961. v. 35, p. 254–262)
PLatS; MnCS

538 Truth, freedom, and evil; three philosophical dialogues. Edited and translated by Jasper Hopkins & Herbert Richardson. New York, Harper & Row [1967].
196 p. 21 cm. (Harper torchbooks. The Cathedral library, TB 317)
InStme; PLatS

539 (2dary) Josephus ab Expectatione, O.S.B. Systema theologicum ad mentem S. Anselmi archiepiscopi . . . Elaboratum studio, & cura R.P. AC M . . . Conimbricae, Ex Architypographia Academico-Regia, 1765.
4 v. 22 cm.
PLatS (v. 1)

540 **Anselmus, abbot of Gembloux,** 12th cent.
Continuatio chronici Sigeberti Gemblacensis.
(*In* Patrologiae cursus completus. Scriptores latini. Series secunda. Tomus 160, col. 239–258. Lutetiae Parisiorum, 1854)
MnCS; PLatS

541 **Anselmus, bp. of Lucca,** d. 1086.
Collectio canonum. MS. Universitätsbibliothek Graz, Austria, codex 351, f. 5v–198r. Folio. Saec. 12.
Microfilm: MnCH proj. no. 26,277

542 **Anselmus, abbot of Nonantula.**
Vita Anselmi abbatis Nonantula.
(*In* Monumenta Germaniae historica. Scriptores rerum Langobardicarum et Italicarum. p. 566–573. Berolini, 1878)
MnCS; PLatS

543 **Ansgar, Saint, abp. of Hamburg and Bremen,** 801–865.
Anskarii vita s. Willehad episcopi Bremensis.
(*In* Monumenta Germaniae historica. Scriptores. Stuttgart, 1963. t. 2, p. 378–390)
MnCS; PLatS

544 **Antin, Paul,** 1902–
Recueil sur saint Jérome. Bruxelles, Latomus, 1968.
474 p. 26 cm. (Collection Latomus, v. 95)
InStme

545 Saint Jérome.
(*In* Théologie de la vie monastique, p. [191]–199)
PLatS

546 (ed) Jérome, Saint. Sur Jonas. Introduction, texte latin, traduction et notes de Dom Paul Antin, O.S.B. Paris, Les Editions du Cerf, 1956.
135 p. (Sources chrétiennes, no. 43)
MnCS; NcBe; PLatS

547 (tr) Jérome, Saint. La vie monastique selon saint Jérome. (Ligugé, Abbaye Saint-Martin, 1970].
37 p. 21 cm.
On cover: Traduction par Dom Paul Antin, O.S.B.
KAS

548 **Argaiz, Gregorio de,** d. 1683.
Población eclesiastica de Espana y noticia de sus primeras honras, hallada en los escritos de S. Gregorio, obispo de Granada, y el Chronicon de Hauberto . . . Madrid, M. Sanchez, 1667–
v. 30 cm.
MnCS

549 La soledad lavrzada, por San Benito y svs hijos, en las igelesias de Espana y teatro monastico de la provincia Cartaginense . . . Madrid, por Bernardo de Herbada, 1675.
7 v. 29 cm.
MnCS (v. 1)

550 **Armellini, Mariano,** 1662–1737.
Additiones et correctiones Bibliothecae benedictino-casinensis, alias S. Justinae Pataviae. Fulginei, typis Pompei Campana Impressoris Episcopalis, 1735.
96, 19 p. 31 cm.
MnCS

551 Appendix de quibusdam aliis per Italiam Ordinis S. Benedicti congregationum scriptoribus, episcopis, virisque sanctitate illustribus. Fulginei, typis Pompeii Campana Impressoris Cameralis, 1736.
76 p. 31 cm.
Includes: Camaldulese, Celestines, Cis-

tercians, Olivetans, Sylvestrines, Vallumbrosians.
MnCS

552 Catalogi tres episcoporvm, reformatorvm, et virorvm sanctitate illvstrivm e congregatione Casinensi alias s. Justinae patavinae. Assisii, ex typographia A. Sgariglia, 1733–34.
3 v. in 1. 32 cm.
KAS (microfilm); PLatS (microfilm)

553 Lezioni di archeologia cristiana. Opera postuma. Roma, Tip. della pace di F. Cuggiani, 1898.
xxix, 653 p. 24 cm.
KAS

554 **Armstrong, Anthony,** 1935–. Philippe de la Trinité. What is redemption? Translated from the French by Anthony Armstrong. New York, Hawthorn Books [1961]. 151 p. 21 cm. (Twentieth-century encyclopedia of Catholicism, v. 25)
Translation of: La rédemption par le sang.
InStme; ILSP; KAS; MnStj; MnCS; NdRi

Arnoldstein, Austria (Benedictine abbey).

555 Urbar (1334, 1352, 1430). Latine et germanice. MS. Kärtner Landesarchiv, Klagenfurt, Austria, codex GV 6/9. 24 f. Quarto. Saec. 14–15.
Microfilm: MnCH proj. no. 12,816

556 Urbar und Kopialbuch. MS. Museum der Stadt Villach, Austria, codex C 858. 124 f. Quarto. Saec. 16 (1519).
Microfilm: MnCH proj. no. 12,928

557 Urbarium des Gotteshauses und Untertanen. MS. Kärtner Landesarchiv, Klagenfurt, Austria. Allgemeine Handscriftensammlung 720. 81 f. Saec. 16 (1526).
Microfilm: MnCH proj. no. 12,875

558 **Arnoldus, monk of St. Emmeram, Regensburg,** 11th cent.
Ex Arnoldi libris de S. Emmerammo, edente D. G. Waitz.
(*In* Monumenta Germaniae historica. Scriptores. Stuttgart, 1963. t. 4, p. 543–574)
PLatS

559 **Arnulph, Saint, bp. of Metz,** d. ca. 640.
Genealogia S. Arnulfi. MS. Vienna, Nationalbibliothek, codex 473, f. 169v–170v. Quarto. Saec. 9.
Microfilm: MnCH proj. no. 13,820

560 **Arras, France. St. Vaast (Benedictine abbey).**
The monastic Ordinale of St. Vedast's Abbey, Arras. Arras, Bibliothèque municipale, MS. 230 (907), of the beginning of the 14th century. Edited with introduction,

notes and indexes by Louis Brou, O.S.B. [London] 1957.
2 v. facsim. 23 cm. (Henry Bradshaw Society. [Publications] v. 86–87)
InStme

561 **Artz, Jean Marie, Sister.**
Even God took seven days – a practicum thesis: formation of religious education teachers based on self-awareness.
Thesis (MRE) – Seattle University, 1975.
NdRiS

562 **Arx, Ildephonsus von,** 1755–1783.
Abbates monasterii Augiensis, edende D. Ildephonso ab Arx.
(*In* Monumenta Germaniae historica. Scriptores. Stuttgart, 1963. t. 2, p. 37–39)
MnCS; PLatS

563 Rhythmi de S. Otmaro, edente D. Ildephonso ab Arx.
(*In* Monumenta Germaniae historica. Scriptores. Stuttgart, 1963. t. 2, p. 54–58)
MnCS; PLatS

564 Scriptores rerum Sangallensium, edente D. Ildephonso ab Arx.
(*In* Monumenta Germaniae historica. Scriptores. Stuttgart, 1963. t. 2, p. 1–183)
MnCS; PLatS

565 Vita sancti Galli hucusque inedita, edente D. Ildephonso ab Arx.
(*In* Monumenta Germaniae historica. Scriptores. Stuttgart, 1963, t. 2, p. 1–21)
MnCS; PLatS

Ashworth, Henry, 1914–
566 Practical commentaries on some prayers of the Missal.
(*In* Murray, Placid, ed. Studies in pastoral liturgy. Dublin, 1967. v. 3, p. 74–115)
PLatS

567 The Psalter collects of Pseudo-Jerome and Cassiodorus. Manchester, England, John Rylands Library [c 1963].
Reprinted from Bulletin of the John Rylands Library, v. 45, no. 2, March, 1963.
MoCo

568 A word in season; an anthology of readings from the Fathers for general use . . . Dublin, Talbot Press, 1973–
v. 22 cm.
MoCo; NcBe

569 **Aspach, Bavaria (Benedictine abbey).**
Catalogus codicum manu scriptorum Bibliothecae Regiae Monacensis. num. 3201–3261 ex coenobio Ordinis S. Benedicti Aspacensi. Monachii, sumptibus Bibliothecae Regiae, 1894.
MnCH

570 **Assenmacher, Hugh,** 1933–
A place called Subiaco; a history of the

Benedictine monks in Arkansas. Little Rock, Rose Publishing Company, 1977.
486 p. illus. 23 cm.
InStme; KAS; MnCS; MoCo; NcBe; PLatS

Atlas O.S.B. *See* Muller, Jean Pierre. Atlas O.S.B.

571 **Atsch, Lancelot,** 1909–
Loose-leaf college freshmen religion textbook. Collegeville, Minn., St. John's Abbey, 1949.
196 p. illus. 28 cm.
Multilithed.
MnCS

572 **Attel, Bavaria (Benedictine abbey).**
Catalogus codicum manu scriptorum Bibliothecae Regiae Monacensis, num. 3301–3348, ex bibliotheca monasterii Ordinis S. Benedicti in Attel. Monachii, sumptibus Bibliothecae Regiae, 1894.
MnCH

573 Ordo judiciarius. Rechtsbuch des Stiftes Attel. MS. Vienna, Haus-, Hof- und Staatsarchiv, codex W 953. 69 f. Saec. 15.
Microfilm: MnCH proj. no. 23,622

Auer, Albert, 1891–
574 Grundlage der Ethik des Dialektischen Materialismus.
(*In* Perennitas; Beiträge . . . P. Thomas Michels, O.S.B., zum 70. Geburtstag. Münster, 1963. p. 656–673)
PLatS

575 Reformation aus dem Ewigen. Salzburg, Müller [c 1955].
191 p. (Reihe Wort und Antwort, Bd. 13)
MoCo

576 **Auer, Alfons,** 1891–
Open to the world; an analysis of lay spirituality. Translated by Dennis Doherty and Carmel Callaghan. Baltimore, Helicon Press [1966].
337 p. 22 cm.
Translation of: Weltoffener Christ.
PLatS

577 **Augsburg, Bavaria. St. Stephan (Benedictine abbey).**
Ad sanctum Stephanum 969–1969. Festgabe zur Tausendjahr-Feier von St. Stephan in Augsburg. [Hrsg. für die Abtei St. Stephan von Dr. P. Egino Weidenhiller, O.S.B., Dr. Anton Uhl [und] P. Bernhard Weisshaar, O.S.B. Augsburg, Eigenverlag St. Stephan, 1969].
317 p. illus. 24 cm.
InStme; KAS; PLatS

578 **Augsburg, Bavaria, St. Ulrich und Afra (Benedictine abbey).**
Catalogus codicum manu scriptorum Bibliothecae Regiae Monacensis, num.

4301–4432, ex bibliotheca monasterii S. Ulrici Augustae Vindelicorum. Monachii, sumptibus Bibliothecae Regiae, 1894.
MnCH

579   Notitia historico-literaria de codicibvs manvscriptis in bibliotheca liberi ac imperialis monasterii Ordinis S. Benedicti ad SS. Vdalricvm et Afram Avgvstae extantibus. Congessit P. Placidvs Bravn . . . Avgvstae Vindelicorvm, svmptibvs fratrvm Veith, 1791–96.
6 pts. in 2 vols.
PLatS (microfilm)

580   **Augustin, Pius,** 1934–
Religious freedom in church and state; a study in doctrinal development. Baltimore, Helicon [1966].
328 p. 21 cm.
AStb; ILSP; InStme; MnCS; PLatS

581   **Augustinus de Obernalb, abbot of Melk**
Flores parvi ex omnibus operibus Aristotelis. MS. Benediktinerabtei Melk, Austria, codex 1834, f. 1r–96v. Duodecimo. Saec. 15.
Microfilm: MnCH proj. no. 2142

582   **Aurelianus,** fl. 9th cent.
Aureliani Reomensis musica disciplina. Edidit Lawrence Gushee. [Rome], American Institute of Musicology, 1975.
167 p. facsims. 24 cm. (Corpus scriptorum de musica, 21)
PLatS

Autpertus, Ambrosius, abbot of San Vincenzo al Volturno, d. 778?

583   Ambrosii Autperti opera. Cura et studio Roberti Weber, O.S.B. Turnholti, Typographi Brepols, 1975–
v. 26 cm. (Corpus Christianorum. Continuatio mediaevalis, 27)
InStme; MnCS; PLatS

584   Sermo de cupidate. MS. Vienna, Nationalbibliothek, codex 1010, f. 23v–35r. Folio. Saec. 11.
Microfilm: MnCH proj. no. 14,320

Ava, member of Göttweig Abbey of Benedictine nuns. d. 1127.

585   Deutsche Gedichte des XI. und XII. Jahrhunderts. Aufgefunden im Regulierten Chorherrenstifte zu Vorau in der Steiermark (codex 276) und zum ersten Male mit einer Einleitung und Anmerkungen hrsg. von Joseph Diemer. Wien, Wilhelm Braumüller, 1849.
lxii, 384, 117 p. 26 cm.
Frau Ava was the author of a number of these early German poems.
MnCS

586   Gedichte der Ava.
(*In* Die deutschen Gedichte der Vorauer

Handschrift (Kodex 276). Faksimile Ausgabe. Graz, 1958. II. Teil, p. 115–125).
MnCS

587   Das Leben Jesu. Der Antichrist. Das jüngste Gericht. MS. Augustinerchorherrenstift Vorau, Austria, codex 276, f. 115v–125r. Folio. Saec. 12.
Microfilm: MnCH proj. no. 7254

588   **Avagliano, Faustino,** 1941–
I regesti dell'archivio di Monte Cassino. Roma [M. Pisani] 1964–
v. illus. 25 cm.
Editor: v. 9– Tommaso Leccisotti, O.S.B., e Faustino Avagliano, O.S.B.
KAS; MnCS; PLatS

Aveling, Hugh, 1917–

589   The Catholic recusants of the West Riding of Yorkshire, 1558–1790.
(*In* Proceedings of the Leeds Philosophical and Literary Society. Literary and historical section, vol. X, part VI, p. 191–306)
InStme; MnCS; PLatS

590   Nothern Catholics; the Catholic recusants of the North Riding of Yorkshire, 1558–1790. London, G. Chapman, 1966.
477 p. illus. 23 cm. (Studies in theology and church history)
InStme

591   Post-Reformation Catholicism in East Yorkshire, 1558–1790. Micklegate, East Yorkshire, Local History Society, 1960.
70 p. map. 21 cm. (E.Y. local history series, no. 11)
MnCS; PLatS

592   The Recusancy papers of the Meynell Family of North Kilvington, North Riding of Yorks, 1596–1676.
xl p. (Catholic Record Society, London. Miscellanea)
PLatS

593   Westminster Abbey – the beginning to 1474.
(*In* Carpenter, E. F., ed. A house of kings; the history of Westminster Abbey. 1966. p. 3–84)
PLatS

594   (ed) Reynolds, E. E. Miscellanea. London, Catholic Record Society, 1964.
xl, 214 p. 23 cm.
MnCS

595   (ed) Robert Joseph, O.S.B. The letter book of Robert Joseph, monk-scholar of Evesham and Gloucester College, Oxford 1530–33. Edited by Hugh Aveling and W. A. Pantin. Oxford, At the Clarendon Press for the Oxford Historical Society, 1967.

lv, 300 p. 23 dm. (Oxford Historical Society. New series, v. 19)
PLatS

596 **Avery, Raymond,** 1919–
A guide to the sacred art in Saint John's Abbey church. [Collegeville, Minn., St. John's Abbey, 1969?]
24 p. 28 cm.
Typescript.

597 **Axtman, Boniface J.,** 1908–
Educational work of the Benedictine Order in the Philippines.
xxiv, 228 leaves, 28 cm.
Thesis (M.A.)–University of Santo Tomas, Manila, 1941.
Typescript.
MnCS (Archives)

598 **Axtmann, Carol, Sister.**
Prayer: the core of religion.
Thesis (M.A.)–Mount Angel Seminary, 1978.
Typescript.
NdRiS

Ayglier, Bernard, abbot of Monte Cassino, d. 1282.

599 Expositio Regulae S.P. Benedicti. MS. Benediktinerabtei Göttweig, Austria, codex 422. 236 f. Folio. Saec. 14.
Microfilm: MnCH proj. no. 3681

600 Expositio Regulae S. Benedicti. MS. Vienna, Nationalbibliothek, codex 2220, f. 33r–196r. Quarto. Saec. 14.
Microfilm: MnCH proj. no. 15,508

601 Expositio Regulae S. Benedicti. MS. Benediktinerabtei Admont, Austria, codex 76. 95 f. Folio. Saec. 15.
Microfilm: MnCH proj. no. 9177

602 Expositio Regulae S. Benedicti. MS. Benediktinerabtei Admont, Austria, codex 349, f. 24r–28v. Folio. Saec. 15.
Microfilm: MnCH proj. no. 9424

603 In Regulam S. Benedicti expositiones. MS. Universitätsbibliothek Graz, Austria, codex 899. 191 f. Quarto. Saec. 15.
Microfilm: MnCH proj. no. 26,969

604 In Regulam S. Benedicti expositiones. MS. Universitätsbibliothek Graz, Austria, codex 992, f. 1r–124r. Quarto. Saec. 15.
Microfilm: MnCh proj. no. 27,054

605 Expositio Regulae S. Benedicti. MS. Benediktinerabtei Kremsmünster, Austria, codex 57. Saec. 15.
Microfilm: MnCH proj. no. 57

606 Expositio in Regulam S. Benedicti. MS. Benediktinerabtei Lambach, Austria, codex chartaceus 308. 270 f. Saec. 15.
Microfilm: MnCH proj. no. 682

607 Expositio in Regulam S. Benedicti. MS. Cistercienserabtei Lilienfeld, Austria, codex 69. 225 f. Quarto. Saec. 15.
Microfilm: MnCH proj. no. 4519

608 Expositio Regula S. Benedicti. MS. Benediktinerabtei Melk, Austria, codex 625, f. 21r–197v. Quarto. Saec. 15.
Microfilm: MnCH proj. no. 1512

609 Expositio Regulae S. Benedicti. MS. Benediktinerabtei Melk, Austria, codex 1804. 241 f. Quarto. Saec. 15.
Microfilm: MnCH proj. no. 2117

610 Expositio Regulae S. Benedicti. MS. Benediktinerabtei Melk, Austria, codex 1914. 176 f. Quarto. Saec. 15.
Microfilm: MnCH proj. no. 2197

611 Expositio Regulae S. Benedicti. MS. Benediktinerabtei St. Peter, Salzburg, codex b. XII. 1, f. 1r–214v. Folio. Saec. 15.
Microfilm: MnCH proj. no. 10,674

612 Commentarius in Regulam S. Benedicti. MS. Benediktinerabtei Seitenstetten, Austria, codex 147. 337 f. Quarto. Saec. 15.
Microfilm: MnCH proj. no. 958

613 Expositio Regulae S. Benedicti. MS. Cistercienserabtei Stams, Tirol, codex 55. 335 f. Quarto. Saec. 15.
Microfilm: MnCH proj. no. 15

614 Expositio Regulae beati Benedicti. MS. Subiaco, Italy (Benedictine abbey), codex 88. 97 f. Quarto. Saec. 14.
Microfilm: MnCH

615 Commentarius in Regulam S. Benedicti. MS. Vienna, Nationalbibliothek, codex 3838, f. 1r–182r. Octavo. Saec. 15.
Microfilm: MnCH proj. no. 17,085

616 Expositio Regulae S. Benedicti. MS. Vienna, Schottenstift, codex 307, f. 23v–191r. Folio. Saec. 15.
Microfilm: MnCH proj. no. 4177

617 Expositio Regulae S. Benedicti. MS. Vienna, Schottenstift, codex 400, f. 37r–276r. Octavo. Saec. 15.
Microfilm: MnCH proj. no. 3916

618 Explanationes Regulae S. Benedicti. MS. Cistercienserabtei Zwettl, Austria, codex 219. 155 f. Quarto. Saec. 15.
Microfilm: MnCH proj. no. 6811

619 Excerptum. Incipit: Domo consistere pedibus suis. MS. Benediktinerabtei Melk, Austria, codex 1241, f. 252r–257r. Quarto. Saec. 15.
Microfilm: MnCH proj. no. 1885

620 Prologus in expositionem suam Regulae S. Benedicti. MS. Benediktinerabtei Admont, Austria, codex 430, f. 126r–126v. Quarto. Saec. 14.
Microfilm: MnCH proj. no. 9461

621 Speculum monachorum beati Benedicti. MS. Benediktinerabtei Kremsmünster, Austria, codex 179, f. 174r–210 r. Saec. 14.
Microfilm: MnCH proj. no. 168

622 Speculum monachorum. MS. Universitätsbibliothek Graz, Austria, codex 992, f. 135r–1684. Quarto. Saec. 15.
Microfilm: MnCH proj. no. 27,054

623 Speculum monachorum. MS. Benediktinerabtei Kremsmünster, Austria, codex 95. Saec. 15.
Microfilm: MnCH proj. no. 88

624 Quaestio supra Regulam beati Benedicti, quam ponit in libello suo, quem vocat Speculum monachorum. MS. Benediktinerabtei Lambach, codex chartaceus 103, f. 114r–117v. Saec. 15.
Microfilm: MnCH proj. no. 524

625 Quaestio ex eius opere: Speculum monachorum. MS. Benediktinerabtei Lambach, Austria, codex chartaceus 177, f. 151v–152v. Saec. 15.
Microfilm: MnCH proj. no. 589

626 Quaestio super Regula beati Benedicti quam in libello suo vocat Speculum monachorum. MS. Benediktinerabtei Lambach, Austria, codex chartaceus 333, f. 254v–259r. Saec. 15.
Microfilm: MnCH proj. no. 704

627 Quaestio super Regulam beati Benedicti quam ponit in libello quem vocat Speculum monachorum. MS. Benediktinerabtei Lambach, Austria, codex chartaceus 431, f. 265r–286v. Saec. 15.
Microfilm: MnCH proj. no. 721

628 Speculum Regulae monachorum beati Benedicti, abbatis, cum commentario Petri Boerii. MS. Benediktinerabtei Melk, Austria, codex 3, f. 123r–167r. Folio. Saec. 14.
Microfilm: MnCH proj. no. 2124

629 Quaestio super Regula beati Benedicti, quam proponit in libello suo, quem vocat Speculum monachorum. MS. Benediktinerabtei Melk, Austria, codex 94, f. 241–251. Duodecimo. Saec. 15.
Microfilm: MnCH proj. no. 1171

630 Speculum monachorum. MS. Benediktinerabtei Melk, Austria, codex 787, f. 88r–124r. Quarto. Saec. 15.
Microfilm: MnCH proj. no. 1623

631 Speculum Regulae monachorum beati Benedicti abbatis. MS. Benediktinerabtei Melk, Austria, codex 979, f. 64r–112v. Quarto. Saec. 15.
Microfilm: MnCH proj. no. 1790

632 Tractatus, qui appellatur Speculum monachorum. MS. Benediktinerabtei Melk, Austria, codex 866, f. 20r–70v. Quarto. Saec. 15.
Microfilm: MnCH proj. no. 1684

633 Speculum monachorum. MS. Benediktinerabtei Melk, Austria, codex 1554, f. 139v–142v. Duodecimo. Saec. 15.

634 Quaestio super Regula S. Benedicti, quem possit in libello suo Speculum monachorum. Benediktinerabtei St. Peter, Salzburg, codex a.III.15, f. 184r–193r. Octavo. Saec. 15.
Microfilm: MnCH proj. no. 9954

635 Quaestio super Regula beati Benedicti in libello "Speculum peccatorum." MS. Benediktinerabtei St. Peter, Salzburg, codex b.IX.20, f. 71r–75r. Folio. Saec. 15.

636 Opus tripartitum, quod vulgo vocatur Speculum monachorum. MS. Vienna, Nationalbibliothek, codex 5135, f. 115r–142r. Folio. Saec. 15.
Microfilm: MnCH proj. no. 18,301

637 Speculum Bernardi abbatis Casinensis de his ad que in professione obligator monachus.
(*In* Gregory I, Pope. Secundus dyalogorom liber . . . Venecia, 1505. p 84–191)
MnCS

638 Quaestiones variae de vita monastica (incompl.). MS. Benediktinerabtei Altenburg, Austria, codex AB 13 B 9, f. 110r–125v. Quarto. Saec. 17.
Microfilm: MnCH proj. no. 6498

639 (2dary) Epistola S. Thomae Aquinatis ad Bernardum abbatem Casinensem propria manu conscripta, nunc primum e tabulario Casinensi in lucem prolata opera et studio monachorum O.S.B. Typis Montis Casini, 1875.
xxiv p. facsims. 41 cm.
InStme

640 **Aymard, Odilon,** 1927–
Touraine roman [par] Odilon Aymard [et al.]. Photos inédites de R. G. Phelipeaux. Traduction anglaise de Pamela Clarke. Traduction allemande de Albert Delfosse. [La Pierre-qui-Vire (Yonne)] Zodiaque, 1957.
255 p. illus., col. plates. 23 cm. (La Nuit des temps, 6)
InStme

641 **Aymard, Paul.**
Un homme nommé Benoît. [Paris] Desclée De Brouwer [1977].
217 p. illus. 26 cm.
All the miniatures are taken from Codex la . Vaticanus 1202 (9th century).
MnCS

642 **Ayndorffer, Kaspar,** 15th cent.
Die Bräuche der Abtei Tegernsee unter
Abt Kaspar Ayndorffer (1426–1461) . . .
von Joachim Angerer, O.S.B. Ottobeuren;
Kommissionsverlag Winfried-Werk,
Augsburg, 1968.
xv, 362 p. 25 cm.
PLatS

643 **Azcárate, Andrés,** 1891–
Misal diario para América, en latin y
castellano . . . Buenos Aires, Liturgica
Argentina [1945].
lxxix, 1861, 163 p. illus. 17 cm.
KAS

Babo, Bede, 1900–
644 Jesus, Mary, and Joseph, daily Missal;
the official prayers of the Catholic Church
arranged for participation in the Mass.
Under the editorial supervision of Bede
Babo [and others]. New York, Benziger
Bros. [c 1962].
1408 p. illus. 17 cm.
MnCS

644a Morning and evening prayers of the
Divine Office: lauds, vespers and compline
for the entire year from the Roman
Breviary [edited by Bede Babo, O.S.B.].
New York, Benziger, 1965.
lxix, 846, 4 p. 18 cm.
PLatS

645 Parish ritual, designed to aid parish
priests in the regular exercise of the
pastoral ministry . . . Edited by Rev.
Frederick R. McManus, in association with
Rev. Bede Babo, O.S.B. New York, Benziger Brothers [1962].
v, 314, 8 p. 20 cm.
Latin and English.
PLatS

646 The Roman Breviary; an approved
English translation complete in one volume
from the official text of the Breviarium
Romanum authorized by the Holy See.
[Edited by Bede Babo. Translations of the
prayers by Christine Mohrmann]. New
York, Benziger Brothers, [1964].
various pagings (1 vol.) 19 cm.
InStme; MnCS

647 **Bacchini, Benedetto,** 1651–1721.
Dell'istoria del monastero di S. Bene-
detto di Polirone nello stato di Mantoua.
Modona, Capponi, 1696.
[28], 244, [11], 110, [5] p. 22 cm.
KAS

Bachofen, Charles Augustine, 1872–
1943.
648 A commentary on the new Code of canon
law, by Rev. P. Chas. Augustine, O.S.B.
4th ed. St. Louis, B. Herder, 1921–25.

8 v. 19 cm.
InStme; NeBe

649 Der Mons Aventinus zu Rom und die
Benediktiner Klöster auf demselben.
(*In* Studien und Mittheilungen aus dem
Benediktinerorden. Jahrg. 18 (1897), p.
663–669; 19 (1898), p. 69–78, 303–310,
460–476, 648–661).
Offprint.
53 p. 21 cm.
KAS

650 Summa iuris matrimonialis, quam
tradidit . . . Augustinus Bachofen, O.S.B.
Roma, Tipolitografia C. Speranza [1908].
573 p. 25 cm.
MnCS

651 **Back, Benedetta, Sister.**
Chronicles of the Olivetan Benedictine
Nuns (1344–1939). Oxford, Oxonian Press
[1939?].
163 p. 19 cm.
InStme

652 **The Bahamas Catholic mission hymnal.**
[Compiled . . . for the use in the vicari-
ate apostolic of the Bahamas]. [Nassau,
1955 ca.].
176 p. 23 cm.
MnCS

Baij, Maria Cäcilia, 1694–1766.
653 Das Innenleben Jesu, geoffenbart der
Maria Cäcilia Baij, hrsg. von Odo
Staudinger. Aus dem Italienischen über-
tragen von Ferdinand Kröpfl. Innsbruck-
Hungerburg, Katholische Legion, 1935.
9 pts in 2 vols., illus. 17 cm.
InStme

654 . . . 2. Aufl. Innsbruck, P. Maier, 1958.
954 p. 23 cm.
InStme; KySu

655 Das Leben des heiligen Josef; mit einem
Geleitwort von Odo Staudinger. Deutsch
von Ferdinand Kröpfl. Innsbruck-
Hungerburg, F. Reisinger, 1939.
291 p. 22 cm.
InStme

656 Offenbarungen des göttlichen Heilandes
über das selige Hinscheiden des heiligen
Joseph. Hrsg. von Dr. Walter Disler. Freiburg im Breisgau, Herder, 1922.
107 p.
NcBe; OrMta

657 Patron of the dying; the sickness and
death of St. Joseph. Translated from the
German edition by Placidus Kempf. North
Royalton, Ohio, Prayer and Penance Publications, 1973.
48 p. 21 cm.
InStme

658   Vita del glorioso patriarca San Giuseppe, manifestata da Gesù Cristo alla serva di dio. Viterbo, G. Agnesotti, 1921.
606 p. 19 cm.
At head of title: Sac. Pietro Bergamaschi.
MnCS

659   Vita di S. Giovanni Battista, manifestata da Gesù alla sua serva . . . Viterbo, Stab. Tip. G. Agnesotti, 1922.
424 p. 20 cm.
At head of title: Sac. Dott. Pietro Bergamaschi.
MnCS

Bailey, Ralph Robert, 1911–

660   Mass of the Holy Spirit & closing of the cloister, St. Vincent Archabbey, July 20, 1967. Music composed by: Archabbot Rembert Weakland, O.S.B., Ildephonse Wortman, O.S.B., [and] Ralph Bailey, O.S.B. Archabbey Press, 1967.
13 leaves, 23 cm.
PLatS

661   The sound of Christmas, as sung by the Madrigal Singers of Savannah. Directed by Fr. Ralph Bailey, O.S.B. [Phonodisc]. Richland Custom Recording, Columbia, S.C. Stereophonic RCR-351.
2 s. 12 in. 33⅓ rpm. microgroove.
PLatS

662   **Baillie, Alexander.**
A true information of the unhallowed of spring, progresse and impoisoned fruits of our Scottish Calvinian Gospel. [Menston, Yorkshire, England] Scolar Press, 1972.
[16], 225 p. 21 cm. (English recusant literature, 1558–1640, v. 95)
Facsimile reprint of 1628 edition.
PLatS

663   **Baillie, Bernard,** 1683–1735, ed.
Pez, Bernhard: Bibliotheca ascetica antiquo-nova . . . Ratisbonae, sumptibus Joannis Conradii Peezii, 1723–40.
12 v. 16 cm.
Vols. 11–12 edited, with preface, by B. Baillie.
KAS; PLatS

Bainbridge, Gregory, 1913–

664   (tr) Boros, Ladislaus, S.J. The moment of truth; mysterium mortis. London, Burns & Oates [1965].
x, 201 p. 23 cm.
American edition has title: The mystery of death.
PLatS

665   (tr) Boros, Ladislaus, S.J. The mystery of death. New York, Herder and Herder [1965].
x, 201 p. 21 cm.

Translation of Mysterium mortis: der Mensch in der letzen Entscheidung.
ILSP; KAS; PLatS

666   **Baker, Aelred,** 1932–
Messalianism: the monastic heresy.
(*In* Monastic studies, v. 10, p. 135–141)
PLatS

Baker, Augustine, 1575–1641.

667   Acts and affections for mental prayer. Adapted from [Father Baker's] Sancta sophia, 1656, by Dom B. Weld-Blundell. St. Louis, Herder [1925?]
149 p. 17 cm.
MnCS

668   Apostolatvs Benedictinorvm in Anglia, sive Disceptatio historica, de antiqvitate ordinis congregationisqve monachorvm nigrorvm S. Benedicti in regno Angliae . . . Dvaci, ex officina Lavrentii Kellami, 1626.
22, 248, 222, 254 p.
MnCS (microfilm); PLatS

669   Sancta sophia; or, Directions for the prayer of contemplation & c. Extracted out of more than XL treatises written by the late Ven. Father F. Augustin Baker . . . by the R. F. Serenus Cressy . . . Doway, John Platte and Thomas Fievet, anno D.MDCLVII.
2 v. 16 cm.
PLatS

670   [Sancta sophia]
Holy wisdom; or, Directions for the prayer of contemplation. With an introduction by Dom Gerard Sitwell, O.S.B. London, Burns & Oates [1964].
xxvi, 497 p. 21 cm.
MoCo; NdRi

671   [Sancta sophia]
Holy wisdom; or, Directions for the prayer of contemplation, by Augustine Baker. The digest made by Serenus Cressy from the treatises of Fr. Baker, first published under the title Sancta sophia in 1657. With an introduction by Gerard Sitwell. Wheathamstead, Hertfordshire, Anthony Clark Books [1972].
xxvi, 497 p. 20 cm.
KAS

672   Self-discipline and holiness; the teaching of Ven Augustine Baker thereon from Sancta Sophia, by Dom B. Weld-Blundell. London, Methuen [1931].
xx, 154 p. 19 cm.
MnCS

673   (ed) Collins, Henry. The Divine cloud. With notes and a preface by Father Augustin Baker, O.S.B. London, Thomas Richardson and Son, 1871.

274 p. 17 cm.
KySu

674 **Baldwin, Armand Jean,** 1917–
A history of economic thought. Latrobe, Pa., Archabbey Press, 1963.
210 leaves, 28 cm.
PLatS

675 **Balthasar, monk of Mondsee.**
Rotula des Benediktiners Balthasar von Mondsee. MS. Linz, Austria, Bundestaatliche Studienbibliothek, codex 560. 8 f. Quarto. Saec. 16.
Microfilm: MnCH proj. no. 28,026

676 **Balthasar, Basilius,** 1709–1776.
Alveare historicum ex variis flosculis collectum. Sive, cl. historiae ex variis authoribus amoeno stylo, et selecta phrasi elaboratae. S. Galli, Typis principalis Monasterij, 1751.
[16], 454, [42] p. 17 cm.
PLatS

677 **Bamberg, Germany. St. Michael (Benedictine abbey).**
Urkunden-Copien des Benediktiner-Stiftes St. Michael in Bamberg. MS. Benediktinerabtei St. Paul im Lavanttal, Austria, codex 35/2. 170 f. Quarto. Saec. 18.
Microfilm: MnCH proj. no. 11,770

678 **Banz, Romuald,** 1866–
Kurze Geschichte der Stiftsschule Einsiedeln . . . Einsiedeln, Eberle, Kälin [1948].
160 p. 24 p., illus. 21 cm.
"Eine Festgabe zu der vor 100 Jahren erfolgten Einführung des Lyzeums."
InStme; NdRi

Bar, Catherine de. See Mechtilde de Saint-Sacrement.

Baraut, Cebrià, 1917–
679 Les cantigues d'Alfons el Savi e el primitiu Liber miraculorum de Nostra Dona de Montserrat. Barcelona, Institut d'Estudis Catalans, 1949–1950.
92 p. 24 cm.
"Extret d'Estudis romànics. LI."
MnCS

680 Les fonts franciscanes dels escrits de Garsias de Cisneros.
(In Miscellània Anselm. M. Albareda. v. 1 (1962), p. 65–78. Analecta Montserratensia, v. 9)
PLatS

681 (ed) Cisneros, Garsias de. Obras completas. Abadia de Montserrat, 1965.
2 v. plates, 25 cm.
InStme; MnCS; PLatS

682 (ed) Joachim, O. Cist., abbot of Fiore. Un tratado inédito de Joaquin de Fiore: De

vita sancti Benedicti et De officio divino secundum eius doctrinam. Barcelona, Biblioteca Balmes, 1953.
90 p. 24 cm.
MnCS

683 **Barbo, Ludovico,** 1381–1443.
De initiis congregationis Cassinensis historia brevis. MS. Subiato, Italy (Benedictine abbey), codex 159. 42 f. Octavo. Saec. 15.
Microfilm: MnCH

Barbosa, Marcos, 1915–
684 Sacred art.
(In Baraúna, Guilherme, ed. The liturgy of Vatican II; a symposium. 1966. v. 2, p. 249–291)
PLatS

685 (2dary) Rosenbauer, Stefan. O Mosteiro de Sao Bento de Rio de Janeiro. Fotografias de Stefan Rosenbauer e Hugo Rodrigo Octavio. Prefácio de D. Marcos Barbosa, O.S.B. Rio de Janeiro, Livraria Agir editore, 1955.
[9] p. 64 plates (part col) 30 cm.
PLatS

Barcelona, Spain. Sant Pere de les Puelles (abbey of Benedictine nuns).
686 Adminstracio. MS. 41 vols. Legajo 9–50. Folio.
Microfilm: MnCH proj. no. 34,614

687 Beneficis. MS. 2 vols. Folio. Legajo 5–6.
Microfilm: MnCH proj. no. 34,610–34,611

688 Capbreus de Abadesses, 1356–1382. MS. 5 vols. Abadesses, 1–20. Folio. Saec. 14.
Microfilm: MnCH proj. no. 34,327–34,331

689 Cartas de professio. MS. Carp. 5. 164 f.
Microfilm: MnCH proj. no. 34,314

690 Causas pias, 1617–1694. MS. 672 f. Quarto. Saec. 17.
Microfilm: MnCH proj. no. 34,593

691 Llibres de les Abadesses, 1390–1478. MS. 46 vols. Abadessas, 21–246. Folio.
Microfilm: MnCH proj. no. 34,332–34,379

692 Llibres de les Abadesses, 1500–1626. MS. 4 vols. Abadesses, 247–254. Folio.
Microfilm: MnCH proj. no. 34,679–34,683

693 Llibres de datas (pra. major i menor), 1703–1865. MS. 3 vols. Datas, 1–21. Quarto.
Microfilm: MnCH proj. no. 34,586–34,588

694 Llibres dels dominis y sensos que lo R. Monastir de St. Pere de las Puellas, te y deu rebrer sobre dincas situadas en lo

terme de Mataro y en altres circumbeins. MS. 4 vols. Mataro, 1–4.
Microfilm: MnCH proj. no. 34,566–34,569

695   Llibres de visites, 1572–1716. MS. 459 f. Folio.
Microfilm: MnCH proj. no. 34,581

696   Privilegis de las ayguas y altres papers faents al Monastir de St. Pere de la Puellas. MS. Concessions, 2–93 f. Folio. Saec. 19.
Microfilm: MnCH proj. no. 34,565

697   **Barcos, Martin de,** 1600–1678.
Correspondance de Martin de Barcos, abbé de Saint-Cyran, avec les abbesses de Port-Royal et les principaux personnages de groupe Janséniste. Thèse (LL.D., Paris) par Lucien Goldmann. Paris, Presses Universitaires de France, 1956.
629 p. 23 cm.
MnCS

Barrett, Michael, 1848–1924.

698   A calendar of Scottish saints. 2d ed. Fort Augustus, Abbey Press, 1919.
195 p. 17 cm.
MnCS

699   The pre-Reformation Church of Scotland. London, Catholic Truth Society, 1906.
31 p. 18 cm.
MnCS

700   **Barrion, Caridad, Sister.**
Religious life of the laity in eighteenth-century Philippines as reflected in the decrees of the Council of Manila of 1771 and the Synod of Calasiao of 1773. Manila, Philippines, University of Santo Tomas Press, 1961.
v, 105 p. 23 cm.
PLatS

Barry, Colman James, 1921–

701   American nuncio; Cardinal Aloisius Muench. Collegeville, Minn., Saint John's University Press, 1969.
xii, 379 p. illus. 25 cm.
InStme; KAS; MnCS; MnStj; MoCo; PLatS; NcBe

702   Boniface Wimmer, pioneer of the American Benedictines.
Offprint from The Catholic Historical Review, v. XLI, no. 3, October, 1955, p. 272–296.
MnCS

703   Geburtswehen einer Nation; Peter Paul Cahensly und die Einbürgung der katholischen deutschen Auswander in Kirche und Nation der Vereinigten Staaten von Amerika. [Recklingshausen-Hamburg] Paulus Verlag [1971].

389 p. 22 cm.
Translation of: The Catholic Church and German Americans. Translated by Dr. Karl und Grete Borgmann.
MnCS

704   The great carrying-place.
(*In* Yzermans, V. A., ed. Catholic origins of Minnesota. St. Cloud, Minn., 1961. p. 38–48)
PLatS; MnCS

705   Readings in church history. Westminster, Md., Newman Press [1960–65].
3 v. 24 cm.
CaMWiSb; InStme; KySu; ILSP; KAS; NcBe; MnStj; MnCS; PLatS

706   Upon these rocks; Catholics in the Bahamas. Collegeville, Minn., St. John's Abbey Press [1973].
ix, 582 p. illus. 24 cm.
AStb; NcBe; InStme; PLatS; OkShG; MoCo; MnCS; MnStj

706a   Worship and work; Saint John's Abbey and University, 1856–1980. Collegeville, Minn., The Liturgical Press, 1980.
526 p. plates. maps. 24 cm. (American Benedictine Academy. Historical studies: [Abbeys and convents] no. 2)
p. 343–414: Epilogue, 1956–1980.
MnCS

707   (ed) Satolli, Francesco. Tour of His Eminence Cardinal Francesco Satolli, pro-apostolic delegate, through the United States (of the North) from 12 February to 13 March 1896. Edited by Colman J. Barry, O.S.B.
27–94 p. 23 cm.
PLatS

707a   **Barsenbach, Dunstan,** 1909–
The coolie bishop; the life story of Dom Bernard Regno, O.S.B., bishop of Kandy, Sri Lanka. [Kandy, Sri Lanka (Ceylon), Bravi Press, 1979].
90 p. plates. 22 cm.
MnCS

708   **Barth, Bernhard,** 1887–, tr.
Thomas Aquinas, Saint. Summa theologica III, 6072: Die Sakramente. Taufe und Firmung. [Uebersetzung von P. Bernhard Barth, O.S.B., und P. Burkhard Neunheuser? . . . Salzburg, A. Pustet, 1935].
24, 579 p. 20 cm. (Die deutsche Thomas-Ausgabe, 29. Bd.)
PLatS

709   **Barth, Pudentiana, Sister.**
Der heiligen Hildegard von Bingen Reigen der Tugenden: Ordo virtutum; ein Singspiel, . . . hrsg. von der Abtei Sankt

Hildegard, Eibingen im Rheingau. Berlin, Sankt Augustinusverlag, 1927.

135 p. illus. (music) diagrs. 24 cm.

"Den Text dieser Ausgabe besorgte d. Maura Böckeler, den musikalischen Teil d. Pudentiana Barth . . . Chorfrauen der Abtei Sankt Hildegard."

MnCS

710 **Barthel, Dominic,** 1865–1930.

Manuale alumnorum; a collection of prayers, devotions and formulas used at the theological and preparatory seminaries of St. Meinrad. St. Meinrad Abbey Print, 1898.

151 p. 13 cm.

InStme

Bartscherer, Aegidius, 1730–1799.

711 Tyrocinium benedictinum; sive, Manuductio ad perfectionem evangelicam, in commodum novitiorum Congregationis Benedictino-Bavaricae & Sacra Scriptura, ss. Patribus, conciliis ac solidioris asceseos magistris collecta . . . et anno 1788 iussu reverendissimi Capituli Generalis in synopse redacta.

184 p. 22 cm.

Manuscript, "finitum 1834."

MnCS

712 Tyrocinium religiosum; or, School of religious perfection based upon the Holy Rule of St. Benedict by Giles Bartscherer, abbot. Rev. and translated from the Latin by Vincent Huber, O.S.B. 8th ed. [Peru, Ill., St. Bede Abbey, 1948 c 1896].

xv, 333 p. 16 cm.

KAS

713 **Bas, Anselm.**

De arte diplomatica. MS. Benediktinerabtei St. Paul im Lavanttal, Austria, codex 280/2. 4 vols. Quarto. Saec. 18.

Microfilm: MnCH proj. no. 12,126; 12,128; 12,130; 12,131.

Basilius Valentinus, 15th cent.

714 Fr. B. V. . . . chymische Schriften . . . zum ersten Mahl zusammen gedruckt . . . un in zwey Theile verfasset. Hamburg, 1677.

2 v. illus. (woodcuts) 16 cm.

Edited by W.S.L.

PLatS

715 Traktat von dem grossen Stein der Uralten. MS. Kärtner Landesarchiv, Klagenfurt, Austria, codex GV 7/1, p. 305–422. Folio. Saec. 18.

Microfilm: MnCH proj. no. 12,843

716 Tripus aureus Michaelis Majeri, hoc est, Tres tractatus chimici selectissimi, nempe Basilii Valentini . . . una cum XII. clavibus & appendice.

(*In* Museum hermeticum reformatum et amplificatum . . . Francofurti, 1678. p. 373–432)

PLatS (microfilm)

717 Tripvs avrevs, hoc est, tres tractatvs chymici selectissimi, nempe I. Basilii Valentini, Benedictini Ordinis monachi, Germani, practica vna cum 12 clavibus & appendice . . . Francofvrti, ex chalcographia Pauli Iacobi, impensis Ovgae Iennis, 1618.

MnCS (microfilm)

718 (2dary) Kerckring, Theodore. Commentarius in currum triumphalem antimonii Basilii Valentini, a se latinitate donatum. Amstelodami, sumptibus Andreae Frisi, 1671.

12 leaves, 342 p., 9 leaves. 16 cm.

PLatS

719 **Bastide, Philippe,** 1620–1690.

D. Joannis Mabillonii . . . Praefationes in Acta sanctorum Ordinis Sancti Benedicti . . . Accedit in hac editione Philippi Bastide . . . dissertatio de antiqua Ordinis Sancti Benedicti terra Gallias propagatione. Venetiis, apud Sebastianum Coleti, 1740.

652 p.

PLatS (microfilm)

720 **Bastien, Pierre,** 1886–1940.

Compendium privilegiorum congregationis Cassinensis [Schema]. n.p., n.d.

115 p. 25 cm.

Xerox copy.

PLatS

Batlle, Columba, 1926–

721 Die Adhorationes sanctorum patrum (Verba seniorum) im lateinischen Mittelalter; Ueberlieferung, Fortleben und Wirkung. Münster Westfalen, Aschendorff [1972].

xix, 340 p. 23 cm. (Beiträge zur Geschichte des alten Mönchtums und des Benediktinerordens, Heft 31)

MnCS; PLatS

722 L'antiga versió catalana de la Vita Pauli monachi del ms. Montserrat 810.

(*In* Miscellània Anselm M. Albareda. vol. 1 (1962) p. 297–324. Analecta Montserratensia, v. 9)

PLatS

723 (ed) Pelagius I, Pope. Epistulae quae supersunt. Collexit, notulis historicis adornavit Pius M. Gassó. Ad fidem codicum recensuit, praefatione et indicibus instruxit Columba M. Battle. [Abbatia Montisserrati] 1956.

cxiv, 260 p. 26 cm. (Scripta et documenta, 8)

KAS

Batt, Anthony, d. 1651.
724   A poore mans mite. [Menston, York-shire, England, The Scolar Press, 1973]
68 p. 19 cm. (English recusant literature, 1558–1640, v. 133)
Facsimile reprint of 1639 edition.
PLatS

724a   A three-fold mirrour of mans vanitie and miserie [the first written by that learned and Religious Father, John Trithemius, Monke of the holy Order of S. Benet, and Abbot of Spanhem. The two others by Catholicke authors unknown: faithfully Englished by the R. Father Antonie Batt, Monke of the holy Order aforesaid, of the Congregation of England]. London, The Scolar Press, 1978.
[6], 364 p. 20 cm. (English recusant literature, 1558–1640, f. 386)
Facsimile reprint of the 1633 edition.
PLatS

725   (tr) Augustine, Saint. A heavenly treasure of comfortable meditations and prayers [written by S. Augustin] . . . faithfully translated into English by the R. F. Antony Batt . . . [London] The Scolar Press, 1975.
[42], 256, 121, 110 p. 19 cm. (English recusant literature, 1558–1640, v. 256)
Facsimile reprint of 1621 edition.
PLatS

726   (tr) Bernard of Clairvaux, Saint. A hive of sacred honiecombes . . . translated into English by Anthonie Batt, O.S.B. . . . [London] The Scolar Press, 1974.
605 [39] p. 20 cm. (English recusant literature, 1558–1640, v. 194)
Facsimile reprint of 1631 edition.
PLatS

727   **Battle Abbey, England.**
Chronicon Monasterii de Bello. Nunc primum typis mandatum . . . Londini, impensis Societatis, 1846.
xi, 203 p. 23 cm. (Anglia christiana)
InStme; KAS

728   **Batzill, Hartmann,** 1887–
Mente et corde psallite; contenuto dei Salmi per l'uso del divino ufficio. 2. ed. Roma, Societá Apostolato Stampa [1944].
95 p. 15 cm.
KAS

729   **Baudot, Jules Léon,** 1857–1929.
Martyrologie romain . . . Traduction française par Dom J. Baudot, O.S.B., et Dom F. Gilbert, O.S.B. . . . Nouvelle édition, revisée, annotée et rendue conforme a l'édition officielle de 1930 . . . Paris, A. Tralin [1931].

687 p. 23 cm.
InStme

729a   **Bauer, Petrus,** 1912–
Die Benediktinerabtei Plankstetten in Geschichte und Gegenwart. Plankstetten/ Oberpfalz, Benediktinerabtei, 1979.
139 p. 80 plates (part col.), folded map, 23 cm.
MnCS

Bauerreiss, Romuald, 1893–
730   Basileus tes doxes; ein frühes eucharistisches Bild und seine Auswirkung.
(In Pro mundi vita; Festschrift zum Eucharistischen Weltkongress, 1960. München, 1960. p. 44–48)
PLatS

731   Der heilige Berg Andechs. 2. Aufl. München, Schnell und Stein, 1972.
47 p. illus. 22 cm.
MnCS

732   Kirchengeschichte Bayerns. 2. neubearb. u. erweiterte Aufl. [St. Ottilien, Eos Verlag der Erzabtei St. Ottilien [1958–   ]
v. plates, maps, 25 cm.
KAS; MnCS; PLatS

733   Das "Lebenszeichen"; Studien zur Frühgeschichte des griechischen Kreuzes und zur Ikonographie des frühen Kirchenportals. München, Birkenverlag, 1961.
xi, 67 p. illus. 24 cm. (Veröffentlichungen der [neue Folge der Abhandlungen der] Bayerischen Benediktinerakademie. B. I. [Regarded as Bd. VII of Abhandlungen])
InStme; KAS; MnCS; PLatS

734   Stefanskult und frühe Bischofsstadt. München, Abtei St. Bonifaz, 1963.
66 p. illus. 24 cm. (Veröffentlichungen der [neue Folge der Abhandlungen der] Bayerischen Benediktinerakademie. Bd. II. [Regarded as Bd. VIII of the Abhandlungen])
InStme; MnCS; PLatS

735   Vescovi bavaresi nell'Italia seteentrionale tra le fine del X secolo e l'inizio dell XI.
(In Vescovi e diocesi in Italia nel medioevo, p. [157]–160)
PLatS

736   **Bauldry, Michael.**
Manvale sacrarvm caeremoniarvm, iuxta ritvm romanvm. Ad vsum omnium ecclesiarum, tam saecularium, quam regularium. Parisiis, apud Ioannem Billaine, 1637.
[36], 634 p. 17 cm.
PLatS

737   **Bauman, Mark Maurice,** 1932–
(tr) Casel, Odo. The commemoration of the Lord in the early Christian liturgy;

basic notions of the Canon. [Translated by Mark Bauman. 1964].
iii, 53 p. 29 cm.
Translation of: Das Gedächtnis des Herrn in der altchrislichen Liturgie. 6. Aufl., 1922.
KAS

738 **Baumstein, Paschal,** 1950–
A full life, an integrated life: the Benedictine monks of Belmont Abbey. [Gastonia, N.C., Commercial Printers, 1978].
16 p.
NcBe

Baur, Benedikt, 1877–1963.
739 Beseligende Beicht; Belehrungen, Betrachtungen und Gebete für den öfteren Empfang des heiligen Busssakramentes. Freiburg im Breisgau, Herder, 1922.
299 p. 16 cm.
IdCoS; MnCS

740 Frequent confession, its place in the spiritual life. Translated from the 9th German edition by Patrict [sic] C. Barry, S.J. New York, St. Paul Publications [1960].
217 p. 19 cm.
Translation of: Die häufige Beicht.
ILSP; KAS; MnCS; MnStj; PLatS

741 John Chrysostom and his time. Translated by Sr. M. Gonzaga. Westminster, Md., Newman Press [c 1959–1960].
2 v. 23 cm.
Translation of: Der heilige Johannes Chrysostomus und seine Zeit.
ILSP; KAS; MoCo; NcBe

742 Kardinal Ildefons Schuster; ein Lebensbild. Mödling bei Wien, St. Gabriel-Verlag [1961].
103 p. illus. 19 cm.
InStme

743 Kein Mass kennt die Liebe; das Leben der Dienerin Gottes Schwester Ulrika Nisch von Hegne aus der Kongregation der Barmherzigen Schwestern vom Heiligen Kreuz, Mutterhaus Ingenbohl (Schweiz) . . . Konstanz/Bodensee, Merk & Co. [1963].
240 p. port.
NdRi

744 Love knows no measure; a life of the servant of God, Sister Ulrika Nisch, of Hegne . . . of the Congregation of the Sisters of Mercy of the Holy Cross . . . Edited by Father Eckhardt, O.S.B. [Konstanz/Bodensee, Merk & Co., c 1968].
208 p. plates, facsims. 19 cm.
MnCS

745 Sed luz!; meditaciones liturgicas para los domingos y ferias del año eclesiático.

Tradución del alemán por los padres Justo Pérez de Urbel y Enrique Diez, O.S.B. 4. ed. Barcelona, Editorial Herder, 1946.
3 v. 16 cm.
MnCS

746 Werde Licht! Liturgische Betrachtungen an den Sonn- und Wochentagen des Kirchenjahres. 5. Aufl. Freiburg i.B., Herder [1938–40].
3 v. 16 cm.
PLatS

747 **Bavaria benedictina.** Sonderausgabe der Zeitschrift "Bayerland." München [1961?].
68 p. illus. 30 cm.
PLatS

748 **Bavoz, Thérèse de, abbess,** 1768–1838.
Lettres de Madame Thérèse de Bavoz, première abbesse de Pradines, fondatrice de la Congrégation Bénédictine du Saint Coeur de Marie. Abbaye de Pradines, 1942.
307 p.
CaStB

749 **Bayne, William Wilfrid,** 1893–
The heraldic art of Rev. Dom William Wilfrid Bayne, O.S.B., Ch.L.J. [South Pasadena, Calif., American Society of Heraldry, 1967].
39 p. illus., coats of arms, port. 28 cm.
MnCS

750 **Beattie, Gordon,** 1941–
The Benedictine yearbook . . . A guide to the abbeys, priories, parishes, and schools of the monks and nuns of the Order of St. Benedict in the British Isles and their foundations abroad. Warrington, Lancashire, St. Alban's Priory.
v. illus. 19 cm. annual.
Editors: 1970– Gordon Beattie.
KAS; NcBe

751 **Beaudoin, Lambert,** 1873–1960.
Une oeuvre monastique pour l'union des églises. Louvain, Abbaye du Mont-César [1925?].
32 p. 18 cm.

752 **Beaudran, Abbot.**
Geistliche Schriften / Abts Beaudran. Augsburg, N. Doll, 1790–
v. 18 cm.
InStme (v. 7–10, 1797–99)

753 **Beaulieu Abbey, England.**
The Beaulieu cartulary. Edited by S. F. Hockey, with an introduction by P. D. A. Harvey and S. F. Heckey. Southampton, University Press, 1974.
lxix, 281 p. 25 cm. (Southampton records series, vol. xvii)
MnCS

754 **Beaunier, Benedictine monk,** fl. 1726.
Recueil historique, chronologique, et topographique, des archevêchez, evêchez, abbayes et prieurez de France, tant d'hommes, que de filles, de nomination et collation royale . . . le tout distribué par dioceses, par ordre alphabetique, & enrichi di 18 cartes geographiques, avec les armes des archevêques . . . par Dom Beavnier . . . Paris, A. X. R. Mesnier, 1726.
2 v. illus. (coats of arms), maps. 27 cm.
CtBeR; KAS; MnCS; PLatS

Bec, France (Benedictine abbey).
755 The Bec Missal. Edited by Anselm Hughes. [London, Henry Bradshaw Society, 1963].
xv, 302 p. 23 cm. (Henry Bradshaw Society. Publications, v. 94)
InStme; PLatS

756 Consuetudines Beccenses. Edidit Marie Pascal Dickson. Siegburg, apud F. Schmitt, 1967.
xc, 419 p. 26 cm. (Corpus consuetudinum monasticarum, 4)
InStme; KAS

757 Problems of authority; the papers read at an Anglo-French symposium held at the Abbey of Notre-Dame du Bec, in April 1961 . . . Edited by John Murray Todd. Baltimore, Helicon Press [1962].
PLatS

Beck, Edmund, 1902–
758 (ed and tr) Ephraem Syrus, Saint. Hymnen contra haereses, hrsg. [und übersetzt] von Edmund Beck. Louvain, L. Durbecq, 1957.
2 v. 23 cm. (Corpus scriptorum Christianorum orientalium, v. 169–170. Scriptores Syri, t. 76–77)
InStme

758a (ed and tr) Ephraem Syrus, Saint. Carmina Nisibena, hrsg. von Edmund Beck. Louvain, Secretariat du Corpus SCO, 1961–63.
4 v. 25 cm. (Corpus scriptorum Christianorum orientalium, v. 218–19, 240–41. Scriptores Syri, t. 92–93, 102–103)
InStme

758b (ed) Hymnen auf Abraham Kidunaya und Julianos Saba, hrsg. von Edmund Beck. Louvain, Secretariat du Corpus SCO, 1972.
2 v. 25 cm. (Corpus Scriptorum Christianorum Orientalium, v. 322–323. Scriptores Syri, t. 140–141)
InStme

758c (ed and tr) Ephraem Syrus, Saint. Hymnen de fide, hrsg. [und übersetzt] von Edmund Beck. Louvain, L. Durbecq, 1955.

2 v. 25 cm. (Corpus scriptorum Christianorum orientalium, v. 154–155. Scriptores Syri, t. 73–74)
InStme

759 (ed and tr) Ephraem Syrus, Saint. Hymnen de ecclesia . . . Louvain, Secretariat du Corpus SCO, 1960.
2 v. 23 cm. (Corpus scriptorum Christianorum orientalium, v. 198–199. Scriptores Syri, t. 84–85)
InStme

760 (ed and tr) Ephraem Syrus, Saint. Hymnen de ieiunio . . . Louvain, Secretariat du Corpus SCO, 1964.
2 v. 23 cm. (Corpus scriptorum Christianorum orientalium, v. 246–247. Scriptores Syri, t. 106–107)
InStme

760a (ed and tr) Ephraem Syrus, Saint. Hymnen de nativitate (Epiphania), hrsg. [und übersetzt] von Edmund Beck. Louvain, Secretariat du Corpus SCO, 1959.
2 v. 25 cm. (Corpus scriptorum Christianorum orientalium, v. 186–187. Scriptores Syri, t. 82–83)
InStme

761 (ed and tr) Ephraem Syrus, Saint. Hymnen de paradiso und Contra Julianum . . . Louvain, Secretariat du Corpus SCO, 1957.
2 v. 23 cm. (Corpus scriptorum Christianorum orientalium, v. 174–175. Scriptores Syri, t. 78–79)
InStme

762 (ed and tr) Ephraem Syrus, Saint. Hymi en de virginitate . . . Louvain, Secretariat du Corpus SCO, 1962.
2 v. 25 cm. (Corpus scriptorum Christianorum orientalium, v. 223–224. Scriptores Syri, t. 94–95)
InStme

762a (ed and tr) Nachträge zu Ephraem Syrus, hrsg. [und übersetzt] von Edmund Beck. Louvain, Secretariat du Corpus SCO, 1975.
2 v. 25 cm. (Corpus scriptorum Christianorum orientalium, v. 363–364. Scriptores Syri, t. 159–160)
InStme

762b (ed) Ephräms Polemik gegen Mani und die Manichäer im Rahmen der Zeitgenössischen griechischen Polemik und der des Augustinus. Louvain, Secretariat du Corpus SCO, 1978.
vii, 178 p. 25 cm. (Corpus scriptorum Christianorum orientalium, v. 391. Subsidia, t. 55)
InStme

763 (ed and tr) Ephraem Syrus, Saint. Paschahymnen (De azymis, de crucifixione, de resurrectione) . . . Louvain, Secretariat du Corpus SCO, 1964.
2 v. 23 cm. (Corpus scriptorum Christianorum orientalium, v. 248–249. Scriptores Syri, t. 108–109)
InStme

763a (ed and tr) Ephraem Syrus, Saint. Sermo de Domino Nostro, hrsg. [und übersetzt] von Edmund Beck. Louvain, Secretariat du Corpus SCO, 1966.
2 v. 25 cm. (Corpus scriptorum Christianorum orientalium. Scriptores Syri, t. 116–117)
InStme

763b (ed) Ephraem Syrus, Saint. Sermones, hrsg. von Edmund Beck. Louvain, Secretariat du Corpus SCO, 1970–73.
8 v. 25 cm. (Corpus scriptorum Christianorum orientalium, 305–06, 311–12, 320–21, 334–35. Scriptores Syri, 130–31, 134–35, 138–39, 148–49)
InStme

764 (ed and tr) Ephraem Syrus, Saint. Sermones de fide, . . . Louvain, Secretariat du Corpus SCO, 1961.
2 v. 23 cm. (Corpus scriptorum Christianorum orientalium, v. 212–213. Scriptores Syri, t. 88–89)
InStme

765 **Becker, Bruno,** 1907–
The new order of Mass; an introduction and commentary by J. Martin Patino . . . Translated by Bruno Becker, O.S.B. Institutio generalis Missalis Romani translated by the monks of Mount Angel Abbey. Collegeville, Minn., The Liturgical Press [1970].
301 p. 18 cm.
InStme; MdRi; MnCS; PLatS

765a **Becker, Jane F., Sister.**
Change in counselor's and client's definition of the problem as a function of the counseling process.
76 p.
Thesis (M.A.)–St. Louis University, 1971.
Manuscript.
InFer

766 **Becker, Johanna, Sister,** 1921–
Karatsu techniques: fabrication and firing.
(*In* International Symposium on Japanese ceramics. [Papers published at] Seattle Art Museum, Seattle, Wash., Sept. 11–13, 1972. p. 66–71)
MnStj (Archives)

Becker, Petrus, 1914–
767 Initia consuetudinis Benedictinae: consuetudines saeculi octavi et noni. Cooperantibus D. Petro Becker, O.S.B. [et al.]. Siegburg, F. Schmitt, 1963.
cxxiii, 626 p. 26 cm. (Corpus consuetudinum monasticarum, t. I)
InStme; PLatS

768 Das monastische Reformprogram des Johannes Rode, Abtes von St. Matthias in Trier; ein darstellender Kommentar zu seinen Consuetudines. Münster, Aschendorff [1970].
xix, 218 p. 25 cm. (Beiträge zur Geschichte des alten Mönchtums und des Benediktinerordens, Heft 30)
InStme; MnCS; PLatS

769 Consuetudines et observantiae monasteriorum Sancti Mathiae et Sancti Maximini Treverensium ab Iohanne Rode abbate conscriptae. Edidit Petrus Becker, O.S.B. Siegburg, apud Franciscum Schmitt, 1968.
lxx, 320 p. 26 cm. (Corpus consuetudinum monasticarum, t. 5)
InStme; KAS; PLatS

770 **Beckman, Martin,** 1930–
Maccabees. Translated by Martin Beckman, O.S.B. Conception, Mo., Conception Abbey [1962].
38 p. 21 cm. (Saint Andrew Bible commentary, 18)
PLatS

771 **Becquet, Jean,** 1917–
L'Abbaye d'Henin-Lietard; introduction historique, chartes et documents (XIIe–XVIe s.). Paris, P. Lethielleux, 1965.
144 p. maps, 24 cm. (Bibliothèque d'histoire et d'archéologie chrétiennes).
French or Latin.
InStme; KAS; PLatS

772 Abbayes et prieures de l'ancienne France; recueil historique des archevéches, evéches, abbayes et prieures de France . . . Ligugé, France, Abbaye Saint-Martin, 1970–75).
535 p. illus., maps
MoCo

773 Les chanoines reguliers en Limousin aux XIe et XIIe siècles.
(*In* La vita commune del clero nei secoli XI e XII. 1962. v. 2, p. 107–109)
PLatS

774 Scriptores Ordinis Grandimontensis. Recensuit Johannes Becquet, O.S.B. Turnholti, Brepols, 1968.
xiii, 628 p. 26 cm. (Corpus christianorum. Continuatio mediaevalis, 8)
InStme; KAS; MnCS; PLatS

775   Constitutiones canonicorum regularium
Ordinis Arroasiensis. Edidit Ludovicus
Milis, auxilium praestante Johanne Bec-
quet, O.S.B. Turnholti, Typographi
Brepols, 1970.
   lxxiii, 352 p. 26 cm. (Corpus christiano-
rum. Continuatio mediaevalis, 20)
   PLatS

Becquet, Thomas, 1896–
776   Easter.
   (*In* Stages of experience; the year in the
Church. Baltimore, 1965. p. 52–68)
   PLatS

777   Missal for young Catholics. Glen Rock,
N.J., Paulist Press [c 1963].
   224 p. illus. 15 cm.
   MnCS

778   (2dary) Ghéon, Henri. The way of the
cross. Translated by Frank de Jonge, with
a foreword by Thomas Becquet. 2d ed.
Westminster, Dacre Press, 1952.
   56 p. 18 cm.
   InStme

Bede the Venerable, Saint, 673–735
   Manuscript copies
779   [Opera]
   Super Parabolas Salomonis; Expositio in
librum Tobiae; Epistola ad Nothelmum de
triginta quaestionibus; Expositio super
canticum Abacuc; Expositio de templo
Salomonis. MS. Lambeth Palace Library,
London, codex 191, f. 1–146. Quarto. Saec.
12.
   Microfilm: MnCH
780   [Opera]
   Catalogus operum Bedae ab ipso com-
positus. MS. Augustinerchorherrenstift
St. Florian, Austria, codex XI, 247, f.
168r–168v. Folio. Saec. 12.
   Microfilm: MnCH proj. no. 2478
781   [Opera]
   De natura rerum; Liber de temporibus,
horis et momentis; Liber de temporibus;
De sole, luna et stellis; De natura rerum et
temporum ratione. MS. Cistercienserabtei
Zwettl, Austria, codex 296, f. 3r–102r.
Folio. Saec. 12.
   Microfilm: MnCH proj. no. 6889
782   [Selections]
   Extracts from Augustine, Jerome,
Gregory, Bede. . . . MS. Hereford,
England, Cathedral Library, codex 0 1 xii,
f. 35–74. Octavo. Saec. 12.
   Microfilm: MnCH
783   [Selections]
   Opuscula aliquot. MS. Benediktinerabtei
Admont, Austria, codex 111. 76 f. Folio.
Saec. 11.
   Microfilm: MnCH proj. no. 9209

784   Allegorica expositio super Parabolas
Salomonis. MS. Augustinerchorherrenstift
Klosterneuburg, Austria, codex 759, f.
1r–68v. Folio. Saec. 11.
   Microfilm: MnCH proj. no. 5746
785   Canon chronicus temporum usque ad annum 5199. MS. Vienna, Nationalbibliothek,
codex 3359, f. 162v–163v. Folio. Saec. 15
(1462).
   Microfilm: MnCH proj. no. 16,586
786   Chronica de sex mundi aetatibus, continuata ab Hermanno et Bertholdo. MS.
Vienna, Nationalbibliothek, codex 3399, f.
2r–260r. Folio. Saec. 16.
   Microfilm: MnCH proj. no. 16,639
787   Chronicon. MS. Vienna, Nationalbibliothek, codex 580, f. 168v–171f. Quarto.
Saec. 11.
   Microfilm: MnCH proj. no. 13,911
   Commentarius. *See* Expositio.
788   Computus sive de ratione temporum.
MS. Vienna, Nationalbibliothek, codex
12,600, f. 42r–135v. Folio. Saec. 13.
   Microfilm: MnCH proj. no. 19,993
789   Contemplatione de passione Domini. MS.
Maria Saal, Austria, codex 19, f. 259–263v.
Quarto. Saec. 15.
   Microfilm: MnCH proj. no. 13,343
790   Cordialis, seu Liber quatuor novis-
simorum. MS. Vienna, Nationalbibliothek,
codex 3896, f. 1r–36r. Folio. Saec. 15.
   Microfilm: MnCH proj. no. 17,097
791   De constellationibus. MS. Vienna, Nationalbibliothek, codex 5415, f. 246r–259v.
Folio. Saec. 15.
   Microfilm: MnCH proj. no. 18,595
792   De indigitatione, cum figuris calamo ex-
aratis. MS. Vienna, Nationalbibliothek,
codex 12600, f. 22r–23r. Folio. Saec. 12.
   Microfilm: MnCH proj. no. 19,993
793   De locis sanctis. MS. Vienna, Nationalbibliothek, codex 580, f. 10r–19v. Quarto.
Saec. 11.
   Microfilm: MnCH proj. no. 13,911
794   De locis sanctis libellus. MS. Cistercienserabtei Rein, Austria, codex 20, f. 1v–47v.
Octavo. Saec. 12.
   Microfilm: MnCH proj. no. 7447
795   De muliere forti. MS. Vienna, Nationalbibliothek, codex 1040, f. 65v–71v. Quarto.
Saec. 12.
   Microfilm: MnCH proj. no. 14,354
796   De natura rerum. MS. Vienna, Nationalbibliothek, codex 387, f. 130v–156v. Folio.
Saec. 9.
   Microfilm: MnCH proj. no. 17,564
797   De natura rerum. MS. Vienna, Nationalbibliothek, codex 522, f. 3r–29r. Quarto.

Saec. 10.
Microfilm: MnCH proj. no. 13,852

798 De natura rerum. MS. Benediktinerabtei Melk, Austria, codex 348, f. 1–17. Folio. Saec. 12.
Microfilm: MnCH proj. no. 1355

799 De notitia artis metricae. MS. Tortosa, Spain, Archivo de la Catedral, codex 161, f. 2r–38v. Octavo. Saec. 12.
Microfilm: MnCH proj. no. 30,729

800 De nominibus propriis in Actis Apostolorum. MS. Vienna, Nationalbibliothek, codex 934, f. 153r–155v. Folio. Saec. 9.
Microfilm: MnCH proj. no. 14,251

801 De numerorum divisione libellus. MS. Bischöfliche Bibliothek, Klagenfurt, Austria, codex XXIX d 3, f. 33r–35v. Quarto. Saec. 12.
Microfilm: MnCH proj. no. 13,168

802 De quatuor modis Sacrae Scripturae. MS. Prämonstratenserabtei Schlägl, Austria, codex 97, f. 164r–164v. Folio. Saec. 15.
Microfilm: MnCH proj. no. 2956

803 De ratione temporum (fragmenta). Permultas glossae iricae inter lineas et in marginibus adscriptae sunt. MS. Vienna, Nationalbibliothek, codex 5209. 4 f. Quarto. Saec. 9–10.
Microfilm: MnCH proj. no. 20,524

804 De remediis peccatorum. MS. Cistercienserabtei Heiligenkreuz, Austria, codex 217, f. 45r–54v. Folio. Saec. 10.
Microfilm: MnCH proj. no. 4866

805 De schematibus et tropis Sacrae Scripturae. MS. Vienna, Nationalbibliothek, codex 114, f. 17r–24v. Folio. Saec. 10.
Microfilm: MnCH proj. no. 13,475

806 De tabernaculo Domini et vasis eius ac vestibus sacerdotum libri tres. MS. Cistercienserabtei Heiligenkreuz, Austria, codex 225, f. 1r–66v. Folio. Saec. 12.
Microfilm: MnCH proj. no. 4765

807 De tabernaculo Domini et vasis eius et vestibus sacerdotum. MS. Cistercienserabtei Lilienfeld, Austria, codex 83. 102 f. Quarto. Saec. 13.
Microfilm: MnCH proj. no. 4384

808 De tabernaculo Domini et vasis ejus ac vestibus sacerdotum. MS. Benediktinerabtei Melk, Austria, codex 1869, f. 109r–165r. Folio. Saec. 15.
Microfilm: MnCH proj. no. 2166

809 De temporibus. MS. Cava, Italy (Benedictine abbey). codex 3, f. 1–97. Folio. Saec. 11.
Microfilm: MnCH

810 De temporibus. MS. Benediktinerabtei Melk, Austria, codex 348, f. 17–30. Folio. Saec. 12.
Microfilm: MnCH proj. no. 1355

811 De temporum ratione. MS. Universitätsbibliothek Graz, Austria, codex 297, f. 9v–111v. Folio. Saec. 12.
Mcirofilm: MnCH proj. no. 26,209

812 Descriptio Terrae Sanctae. MS. Benediktinerabtei St. Paul im Lavanttal, Austria, codex r1/3, pars III. Folio. Saec. 15.
Microfilm: MnCH proj. no. 12,148

813 Ephemerida de feria de luna et his quae ad lunam pertinent. MS. Vienna, Nationalbibliothek, codex 12600, f. 31v–41v. Folio. Saec. 13.
Microfilm: MnCH proj. no. 19,993

814 Epistola ad Nothelmum, de quibusdam quaestionibus quae exponit in libro Regum. MS. Vienna, Nationalbibliothek, codex 716, f. 111r–121v. Folio. Saec. 12.
Microfilm: MnCH proj. no. 14,035
Commentarius and Expositio are interfiled.

815 Expositiones biblicae: In Epistolas catholicas; In Apocalypsin Joannis Apostoli; Super Tobiam; In Actus apostolorum; Alia expositio in Actus apostolorum. MS. Benediktinerabtei Altenburg, Austria, codex AB 14 D 15. 270 p. Saec. 12.
Microfilm: MnCH proj. no. 6360

816 Expositio in Acta apostolorum. MS. Vienna, Nationalbibliothek, codex 934, f. 128r–153r. Folio. Saec. 9.
Microfilm: MnCH proj. no. 14,251

817 Super Actus apostolorum. MS. Vienna, Nationalbibliothek, codex 2206, f. 18r–24v. Quarto. Saec. 12.
Microfilm: MnCH proj. no. 15,552

818 Expositio in Actus apostolorum et Apocalypsim. MS. Benediktinerabtei Admont, Austria, codex 246. 183 f. Saec. 12.
Microfilm: MnCH proj. no. 9326

819 Expositio in Actus apostolorum. MS. Cistercienserabtei Heiligenkreuz, Austria, codex 237, f. 1r–56v. Folio. Saec. 12.
Microfilm: MnCH proj. no. 4780

820 Super Actus apostolorum. MS. Benediktinerabtei Melk, Austria, codex 1908, f. 1r–34v. Folio. Saec. 15.
Microfilm: MnCH proj. no. 2191

821 Expositio in Actus apostolorum. MS. Benediktinerabtei St. Peter, Salzburg, codex a.V.38. 98 f. Octavo. Saec. 10 (f. 1–79) et 15.
Microfilm: MnCH proj. no. 10,064

822 Expositio in Actus apostolorum. MS. Toledo, Spain, Biblioteca del Cabildo,

codex 15,15, f. 132v–162v.
Microfilm: MnCH proj. no. 33,124

823   Super Actus apostolorum. MS. Vienna, Nationalbibliothek, codex 3870, f. 3r–25v. Folio. Saec. 15 (1467).
Microfilm: MnCH proj. no. 17,065

824   Expositio in Apocalypsin. MS. Vienna, Nationalbibliothek, codex 934, f. 88r–127r. Folio. Saec. 9.
Microfilm: MnCH proj. no. 14,251

825   Expositio super Apocalysim. MS. Lambeth Palace Library, London, codex 149, f. 1–95. Quarto. Saec. 10.
Microfilm: MnCH

826   Expositio in Apocalypsin. MS. Vienna, Nationalbibliothek, codex 994, f. 1r–74v. Folio. Saec. 10.
Microfilm: MnCH proj. no. 14,300

827   Expositio super Apocalypsin. MS. Cistercienserabtei Heiligenkreuz, Austria, codex 52, f. 70r–111r. Folio. Saec. 12–13.
Microfilm: MnCH proj. no. 12–13

828   Expositio in Apocalypsim libri tres. MS. Benediktinerabtei Melk, Austria, codex 573, f. 1–98. Folio. Saec. 13.
Microfilm: MnCH proj. no. 1478

829   Expositio in Apocalypsim. MS. Benediktinerabtei Admont, Austria, codex 766, f. 134r–173v. Octavo. Saec. 14.
Microfilm: MnCH proj. no. 9803

830   Expositio in Cantica Canticorum. Libri V. MS. Benediktinerabtei Göttweig, Austria, codex 37, f. 1r–79r. Folio. Saec. 12.
Microfilm: MnCH proj. no. 3319

831   In Cantica Canticorum. MS. Lincoln Cathedral Library, codex 165. 97 p. Quarto. Saec. 12.
Microfilm: MnCH

832   Expositio in Cantica Canticorum. MS. Cistercienserabtei Heiligenkreuz, Austria, codex 234, f. 92r–109v. Folio. Saec. 13.
Microfilm: MnCH proj. no. 4779

833   Expositio in Cantica Canticorum. MS. Cistercienserabtei Zwettl, Austria, codex 101, f. 1r–92v. Folio. Saec. 13.
Microfilm: MnCH proj. no. 6687

834   Super Cantica Canticorum. MS. Universitätsbibliothek Innsbruck, Austria, codex 701. 71 f. Octavo. Saec. 14.
Microfilm: MnCH proj. no. 28,626

835   In Cantica. MS. Benediktinerabtei Melk, Austria, codex 133, f. 169–200. Folio. Saec. 15.
Microfilm: MnCH proj. no. 1200

836   Expositio in Ecclesiasten. MS. Cistercienserabtei Heiligenkreuz, Austria, codex 234, f. 62v–92r. Folio. Saec. 13.
Microfilm: MnCH proj. no. 4779

837   Expositio in epistolas canonicas. MS. Benediktinerabtei Admont, Austria, codex 370. 197 f. Folio. Saec. 11.
Microfilm: MnCH proj. no. 9436

838   Super VII epistolis canonicis. MS. Pamplona, Spain, Biblioteca de la Catedral, codex 13. Quarto. Saec. 11–12.
Microfilm: MnCH proj. no. 34,788

839   Expositio in epistolas beati Iacobi, Petri, Ioannis et Judae. MS. Cistercienserabtei Heiligenkreuz, Austria, codex 52, f. 2v–70r. Folio. Saec. 12–13.
Microfilm: MnCH proj. no. 4583

840   Expositio super septem canonicas seu catholicas epistolas. MS. Cistercienserabtei Rein, Austria, codex 46, f. 1r–84r. Quarto. Saec. 12.
Microfilm: MnCH proj. no. 7443

841   Expositio in septem epistolas canonicas. MS. Benediktinerabtei St. Peter, Salzburg, codex a.IX.29, p. 1–159. Folio. Saec. 12.
Microfilm: MnCH proj. no. 10,224

842   Expositio super septem epistolas canonicas. MS. Augustinerchorherrenstift Klosterneuburg, Austria, codex 246, f. 1r–80r. Folio. Saec. 12.
Microfilm: MnCH proj. no. 5219

843   Expositio in epistolas canonicas, et Tractatus de regimine principum. MS. Benediktinerabtei Admont, Austria, codex 320. 176 f. Folio. Saec. 14.
Microfilm: MnCH proj. no. 29,593

844   Expositio in epistolas canonicas. MS. Benediktinerabtei Melk, Austria, codex 249. 47 f. Folio. Saec. 15.
Microfilm: MnCH proj. no. 1285

845   Expositio in Epistolas canonicas. MS. Vienna, Nationalbibliothek, codex 4795, f. 227v–281v. Folio. Saec. 15.
Microfilm: MnCH proj. no. 17,928

846   Expositio in Jacobi epistolam canonicam. MS. Vienna, Nationalbibliothek, codex 1066. 135 f. Quarto. Saec. 13.
Microfilm: MnCH proj. no. 14,367

847   In Ecclesiasten. MS. Benediktinerabtei Melk, Austria, codex 133, f. 119–168. Folio. Saec. 15.
Microfilm: MnCH proj. no. 1200

848   Expositio in librum Esdrae. MS. Benediktinerabtei St. Peter, Salzburg, codex a.IX.29, p. 160–327. Folio. Saec. 12.
Microfilm: MnCH proj. no. 10,224

849   Expositio allegorica in Esdram et Nehemiam. MS. Benediktinerabtei Admont, Austria, codex 245, f. 1r–95v. Folio. Saec. 12.
Microfilm: MnCH proj. no. 9327

850 Expositio allegorica in Esdram et Nehemiam prophetas. MS. Cistercienserabtei Heiligenkreuz, Austria, codex 202. 131 f. Folio. Saec. 12.
Microfilm: MnCH proj. no. 4743

851 Expositio allegorica in Ezram et Nehemiam. MS. Cistercienserabtei Rein, Austria, codex 46, f. 84r–198v. Quarto. Saec. 12.
Microfilm: MnCH proj. no. 7443

852 Expositio in Esdram et Nehemiam. MS. Vienna, Nationalbibliothek, codex 741, f. 1v–69v. Folio. Saec. 12.
Microfilm: MnCH proj. no. 14,066

853 Expositio libri Geneseos ad Accam episcopum. MS. Lambeth Palace Library, London, codex 148, f. 1–119. Quarto. Saec. 12.
Microfilm: MnCH

854 Commentarius in Lucam. MS. Benediktinerabtei Admont, Austria, codex 109. 150 f. Folio. Saec. 12.
Microfilm: MnCH proj. no. 9208

855 Expositio in evangelium secundum S. Lucae. MS. Universitätsbibliothek Graz, Austria, codex 383. 150 f. Folio. Saec. 12.
Microfilm: MnCH proj. no. 26,321

856 Expositio in evangelium Lucae apostoli. MS. Cistercienserabtei Heiligenkreuz, Austria, codex 169. 155 f. Folio. Saec. 12.
Microfilm: MnCH proj. no. 4710

857 Expositio in evangelium S. Lucae. MS. Augustinerchorherrenstift Klosterneuburg, Austria, codex 242, f. 1r–157v. Folio. Saec. 12.
Microfilm: MnCH proj. no. 5213

858 Commentarius in Lucam. MS. Salisbury, England, Cathedral Library, codex 37. 154 f. Quarto.
Microfilm: MnCH

859 Expositio in Lucam. MS. Benediktinerabtei St. Peter, Salzburg, codex a.X.3, p. 7–341. Folio. Saec. 10.
Microfilm: MnCH proj. no. 10,219

860 [Commentarium in evangelium S. Lucae] Evangelium S. Lucae, cum commentariis Bedae Venerabilis et S. Ambrosii in margine et notis interlinearibus. MS. Benediktinerabtei St. Paul im Lavanttal, Austria, codex 27/1. 195 f. Quarto. Saec. 12–13.
Microfilm: MnCH proj. no. 11,680

861 Expositio super Lucam. MS. Subiaco, Italy (Benedictine abbey), codex 15. 176 f. Quarto. Saec. 11.
Microfilm: MnCH

862 Expositio evangelii S. Lucae. MS. Vienna, Nationalbibliothek, codex 657. 188 f. Folio. Saec. 10.
Microfilm: MnCH proj. no. 13,990

863 Expositio in evangelium Lucae. MS. Vienna, Nationalbibliothek, codex 915. 164 f. Folio. Saec. 14.
Microfilm: MnCH proj. no. 14,224

864 Commentarius in Lucam et Johannem. MS. Vienna, Nationalbibliothek, codex 997, f. 1r–84v. Folio. Saec. 10.
Microfilm: MnCH proj. no. 14,303

865 Commentarius in Marcum. MS. Benediktinerabtei Admont, Austria, codex 244. 135 f. Folio. Saec. 12.
Microfilm: MnCH proj. no. 9329

866 Commentarius in Evangelium Sancti Marci. MS. Barcelona, Spain, Archivo de la Catedral. 119 f. Folio.
Microfilm: MnCH proj. no. 30,298

867 Expositio in evangelium secundum Marcum. MS. Cistercienserabtei Heiligenkreuz, Austria, codex 142. 141 f. Folio. Saec. 12.
Microfilm: MnCH proj. no. 4686

868 Expositio evangelii S. Marci. MS. Augustinerchorherrenstift Klosterneuburg, Austria, codex 247. 115 f. Folio. Saec. 13.
Microfilm: MnCH proj. no. 5221

869 Expositio Marci evangilistae. MS. Lambeth Palace Library, London, codex 147, f. 61–159.
Microfilm: MnCH

870 Expositio in Marci evangelium. MS. Vienna, Nationalbibliothek, codex 767. 198 f. Folio. Saec. 9.
Microfilm: MnCH proj. no. 14,078

871 Commentarius super Matthaeum. MS. Benediktinerabtei Admont, Austria, codex 561. 147 f. Quarto. Saec. 12.
Microfilm: MnCH proj. no. 9603

872 Expositio de operibus sex dierum. MS. Vienna, Nationalbibliothek, codex 1004, f. 1v–174. Folio. Saec. 13.
Microfilm: MnCH proj. no. 14,310

873 Expositio de natura rerum. MS. Augustinerchorherrenstift Klosterneuburg, Austria, codex 685, f. 1v–8v. Folio. Saec. 12.
Microfilm: MnCH proj. no. 5666

874 Expositio in Parabolas Salomonis. MS. Rouen, France. Bibliothèque municipale, codex A 275 (526). 143 f.
Microfilm: MnCH

875 In Parabolas Salomonis. MS. Benediktinerabtei Lambach, Austria, codex membranaceus 101, f. 1r–108v. Quarto. Saec. 12.
Microfilm: MnCH proj. no. 804

876 Expositio super Parabolas Salomonis. MS. Lambeth Palace Library, London,

codex 147, f. 1–60. Quarto. Saec. 12.
Microfilm: MnCH

877   Expositiones super Parbolas Salomonis, Ecclesiasten et Cantica canticorum. MS. Benediktinerabtei Altenburg, Austria, codex AB 13 A 4, f. 1r–69r. Quarto. Saec. 13.
Microfilm: MnCH proj. no. 6364

878   Expositio in Parabolas Salomonis. MS. Cistercienserabtei Heiligenkreuz, Austria, codex 234, f. 1r–63v. Folio. Saec. 13.
Microfilm: MnCH proj. no. 4779

879   Commentarium in Proverbia Salomonis. MS. Benediktinerabtei Admont, Austria, codex 357, f. 59r–139v. Folio. Saec. 12.
Microfilm: MnCH proj. no. 9413

880   In Proverbia Salomonis. MS. Benediktinerabtei Melk, Austria, codex 133, f. 1–118. Folio. Saec. 15.
Microfilm: MnCH proj. no. 1200

881   In Proverbia Salomonis libri tres. MS. Cistercienserabtei Rein, Austria, codex 38, f. 1v–60r. Quarto. Saec. 12.
Microfilm: MnCH proj. no. 7435

882   In Proverbia Salomonis libri tres. MS. Cistercienserabtei Rein, Austria, codex 41, f. 1r–105r. Quarto. Saec. 14.
Microfilm: MnCH proj. no. 7439

883   Tractatus in Proverbia Salomonis. MS. Benediktinerabtei St. Peter, Salzburg, codex a.VIII.18, f. 1v–86v. Quarto. Saec. 12.
Microfilm: MnCH proj. no. 10,186

884   Commentarius in Salomonis Proverbia, Ecclesiasten, et Canticum canticorum. MS. Vienna, Nationalbibliothek, codex 718. 69 f. Folio. Saec. 14.
Microfilm: MnCH proj. no. 14,041

885   Expositio Psalterii. MS. Cistercienserabtei Heiligenkreuz, Austria, codex 29. 156 f. Folio. Saec. 12.
Microfilm: MnCH proj. no. 4572

886   Expositio Psalterii. MS. Cistercienserabtei Heiligenkreuz, Austria, codex 54. 134 f. Folio. Saec. 12.

887   Expositio in libros Regum. MS. Vienna, Nationalbibliothek, codex 685, f. 179v–189v. Folio. Saec. 12.
Microfilm: MnCH proj. no. 14,007

888   Expositio de tabernaculo et vasis ejus ac vestibus sacerdotum libri tres. MS. Benediktinerabtei St. Peter, Salzburg, codex a.VII.4. 128 f. Quarto. Saec. 9.
Microfilm: MnCH proj. no. 10,130

889   Tractatus de tabernaculo, vestis et vestibus sacerdotalibus. MS. Benediktinerabtei Admont, Austria, codex 348, f. 8v–98r. Folio. Saec. 12.
Microfilm: MnCH proj. no. 9419

890   Expositio de tabernaculo et vasis eius ac vestibus sacerdotum, libri tres. MS. Augustinerchorherrenstift Klosterneuburg, Austria, codex 245, f. 1r–69v. Folio. Saec. 12.
Microfilm: MnCH proj. no. 5218

891   Expositio de tabernaculo Domini et vasis ejus ac vestibus sacerdotum. MS. Vienna, Nationalbibliothek, codex 749. 79 f. Folio. Saec. 12.
Microfilm: MnCH proj. no. 14,086

892   Explanatio in Tobiam. MS. Benediktinerabtei Admont, Austria, codex 348, f. 1r–8r. Folio. Saec. 12.
Microfilm: MnCH proj. no. 9419

893   Expositio super Tobiam. MS. Benediktinerabtei Melk, Austria, codex 1915, f. 37v–42r. Quarto. Saec. 15.
Microfilm: MnCH proj. no. 2199

894   Expositio super librum Tobias. MS. Cistercienserabtei Rein, Austria, codex 46, f. 198v–209v. Quarto. Saec. 12.
Microfilm: MnCH proj. no. 7443

895   Expositio in Tobiam. MS. Salisbury, England, Cathedral Library, codex 169, f. 81v–91. Octavo. Saec. 12.
Microfilm: MnCH

896   Expositio in librum Tobiae. MS. Benediktinerabtei St. Peter, Salzburg, codex a.IX.29, p. 328–344. Folio. Saec. 12.
Microfilm: MnCH proj. no. 10,224

897   Expositio in Tobiam. MS. Vienna, Nationalbibliothek, codex 741, f. 184v–191v. Folio. Saec. 12.
Microfilm: MnCH proj. no. 14,066

898   Expositio in tria opera Salomonis: Parabolae, Ecclesiastes et Cantica canticorum. MS. Cistercienserabtei Zwettl, Austria, codex 269, f. 2r–114v. Quarto. Saec. 12.
Microfilm: MnCH proj. no. 6969

899   Figurae. MS. Vienna, Nationalbibliothek, codex 3250, f. 22r–29v. Quarto. Saec. 15.
Microfilm: MnCH proj. no. 16,472

900   [Historia ecclesiastica. Anglo-Saxon]
The Leningrad Bede; an eighth-century manuscript of the Venerable Bede's Historia ecclesiastica gentis Anglorum in the Public Library, Leningrad. Edited by O. Arngart. Copenhagen, Rosenkilde and Bagger, 1952.
35 p. fascim (161 leaves) 32 cm. (Early English manuscripts in facsimile, v. 2)
MnCS; PLatS

901   [Historia ecclesiastica. Anglo-Saxon]
The Moore Bede; an eighth-century manuscript of the Venerable Bede's

Historia ecclesiastica gentis Anglorum in Cambridge University Library (Kk.5.16). Edited by Peter Hunter Blair with contribution by Roger A. B. Mynors. [Copenhagen, Rosenkilde and Bagger, 1959] 37 p., facsim. (129 leaves) 35 cm. (Early English manuscripts in facisimile, v. 9) MnCS; PLatS

902 Historia ecclesiastica gentis Anglorum. MS. Vienna, Nationalbibliothek, codex 443. 81 f. Saec. 11.
Microfilm: MnCH proj. no. 13,777

903 Historia ecclesiastica gentis Anglorum. MS. Benediktinerabtei Admont, Austria, codex 325, f. 14–80v. Folio. Saec. 12.
Microfilm: MnCH proj. no. 9404

904 Historia ecclesiastica gentis Anglorum. MS. Cistercienserabtei Heiligenkreuz, Austria, codex 145, f. 1r–141v. Folio. Saec. 12.
Microfilm: MnCH proj. no. 4687

905 Historia ecclesiastica gentis Anglorum. MS. Hereford, England, Cathedral Library, codex P 5 i, f. 29–150. Quarto. Saec. 12.
Microfilm: MnCH

906 Historia ecclesiastica gentis Anglorum. Libri quinque. Cistercienserabtei Rein, Austria, codex 59. 157 f. Folio. Saec. 12.
Microfilm: MnCH proj. no. 9843

907 Historia gentis Anglorum. MS. Augustinerchorherrenstift St. Florian, Austria, codex XI, 247, f. 1r–167v. Folio. Saec. 12.
Microfilm: MnCH proj. no. 2478

908 Breviarium Historiae Anglorum Ven. Bedae. MS. Augustinerchorherrenstift St. Florian, Austria, codex XI, 247, f. 166r–168r. Folio. Saec. 12.
Microfilm: MnCH proj. no. 2478

909 Historia ecclesiastica gentis Anglorum. MS. Vienna, Nationalbibliothek, codex 532, f. 32r–47v. Quarto. Saec. 12.
Microfilm: MnCH proj. no. 13,861

910 Historia ecclesiastica gentis Anglorum. MS. Cistercienserabtei Zwettl, Austria, codex 106, f. 1r–93v. et 109r (in tegumento). Folio. Saec. 12.
Microfilm: MnCH proj. no. 6694

911 Historia ecclesiastica gentis Anglorum. MS. Benediktinerabtei Admont, Austria, codex 552, f. 1r–156v. Quarto. Saec. 13.
Microfilm: MnCH proj. no. 9596

912 Historia ecclesiastica gentis Anglorum. MS. Vienna, Nationalbibliothek, codex 429. 95 f. Folio. Saec. 13.
Microfilm: MnCH proj. no. 13,761

913 Historia Anglorum et ecclesiastica. MS. Vienna, Nationalbibliothek, codex 3157, f. 1r–181r. Folio. Saec. 15.
Microfilm: MnCH proj. no. 3157

914 Historia ecclesiastica gentis Anglorum. MS. Vienna, Nationalbibliothek, codex 3178, f. 1r–101v. Folio. Saec. 15 (1469).
Microfilm: MnCH proj. no. 16,425

915 Historia ecclesiastica gentis Anglorum. MS. Vienna, Nationalbibliothek, codex 13707, f. 72r–136v. Folio. Saec. 15.
Microfilm: MnCH proj. no. 20,144
Homiliae and Sermones are interfiled

916 Homiliae. MS. Lincoln, England, Cathedral Library, codex 182. 196 f. Octavo. Saec. 10–11.
Microfilm: MnCH

917 Homiliae (S. Beda, Augustinus, etc.). MS. Benediktinerabtei Admont, Austria, codex 65. Folio. Saec. 11.
Microfilm: MnCH proj. no. 9161

918 Homiliae (74). MS. Hereford, England, Cathedral Library, codex 0 7 iv. 239 f. Folio. Saec. 12.
Microfilm: MnCH

919 Sermones Fulgentii, Ambrosii . . . venerabilis Bedae . . . MS. Hereford, England, Cathedral Library, codex P 8 vii. 178 f. Quarto. Saec. 12.
Microfilm: MnCH

920 Quattuor omelie venerabilis Bedae presbyteri: 1. Exordium nobis nostrae redemptionis; 2. Lectio quam audivimus; 3. Quia temporalem; 4. Mediator Dei. MS. Hereford, England, Cathedral Library, codex 0 8 iii, f. 136–153. Folio. Saec. 12.
Microfilm: MnCH

921 Homiliae (excerpta). MS. Vienna, Nationalbibliothek, codex 660, f. 149r–155v. Folio. Saec. 12.
Microfilm: MnCH proj. no. 13,991

922 Homiliae duae. a) Incipit: Quae impossibilia sunt apud homines. b) Incipit: Audivimus ex lectione evangelica fratres. MS. Cistercienserabtei Heiligenkreuz, Austria, codex 300, f. 77v–82r. Quarto. Saec. 13.
Microfilm: MnCH proj. no. 4840

923 Homiliae (16). MS. Benediktinerabtei Kremsmünster, Austria, codex 336. 298 f. Saec. 14 et 15.
Microfilm: MnCH proj. no. 335

924 Homiliae aliquot. MS. Augustinerchorherrenstift St. Florian, Austria, codex XI, 97, f. 254r–262r. Folio. Saec. 14.
Microfilm: MnCH proj. no. 2357

925 Homiliae. MS. Vienna, Nationalbibliothek, codex series nova 12,782. Folio. Saec. 14.
Microfilm: MnCH proj. no. 25,138

926   Sermones ex ss. Patribus (S. Ambrosius . . . Beda Venerabilis . . .) MS. Benediktinerabtei Melk, Austria, codex 330, f. 507–606. Folio. Saec. 15.
Microfilm: MnCH proj. no. 1337

927   Sermones ex ss. Patribus (S. Augustinus, Beda Venerabilis . . .). MS. Benediktinerabtei Melk, Austria, codex 425, f. 71r–291v. Folio. Saec. 15.
Microfilm: MnCH proj. no. 1393

928   Homilia. Incipit: Liber generacionis Jesu. MS. Cistercienserabtei Wilhering, Austria, codex IX, 7, f. 18r–20v. Folio. Saec. 15.
Microfilm: MnCH proj. no. 2784

929   Homilia in feriam secundam post dominicam palmarum in illud Joannis: Proximum erat pascha Judaeorum. Homilia in Coena Domini. MS. Benediktinerabtei Melk, Austria, codex 6, f. 133v–136v. Folio. Saec. 13.
Microfilm: MnCH proj. no. 1130

930   Homilia in Ioannis: Proximum erat Pascha. Homilia in Coena Domini. MS. Benediktinerabtei Melk, Austria, codex 135, f. 241–244. Folio. Saec. 15.
Microfilm: MnCH proj. no. 1202

931   Homilia in litania maiore secundum Bedam Venerabilem et Rabanum Maurum. MS. Augustinerchorherrenstift Klosterneuburg, Austria, codex 242, f. 157v–159r.
Microfilm: MnCH proj. no. 5213

932   SS. Bedae, Augustini et Hieronymi homiliae in illud: Extollens vocem quaedam mulier. MS. Benediktinerabtei Melk, Austria, codex 2, f. 443–450. Folio. Saec. 15.
Microfilm: MnCH proj. no. 1121

933   Sermo in vigilia assumptionis sanctae Mariae. MS. Cistercienserabtei Wilhering, Austria, codex IX, 110, f. 77v–78v. Quarto. Saec. 13.
Microfilm: MnCH proj. no. 2886

934   Sermo super Magnificat. MS. Benediktinerabtei Melk, Austria, codex 2, f. 143–150. Folio. Saec. 15.
Microfilm: MnCH proj. no. 1121

935   Homilia super Matth. I, l. MS. Benediktinerabtei Göttweig, Austria, codex 130, a, f. 76r–78r. Folio. Saec. 14.
Microfilm: MnCH proj. no. 3407

936   Sermo super: Missus est. MS. Benediktinerabtei Lambach, Austria, codex chartaceus 312, f. 102v–105r. Saec. 15.
Microfilm: MnCH proj. no. 683

937   Hymnus de universis Dei operibus. MS. Augustinerchorherrenstift Klosterneu-

burg, Austria, codex 809, f. 102r. Quarto. Saec. 12.
Microfilm: MnCH proj. no. 5799

938   In fine libelli Historiae ecclesiasticae personam suam, vitae ordinem, studiumque suum auctor commemorat nec non aetatis tempora. MS. Augustinerchorherrenstift Klosterneuburg, Austria, codex 787, f. 181r–182r. Folio. Saec. 12.
Microfilm: MnCH proj. no. 5764

939   Interpretationes nominum hebraicorum. MS. Cistercienserabtei Rein, Austria, codex 3, f. 533r–572v. Duodecimo. Saec. 13.
Microfilm: MnCH proj. no. 7402

940   Interpretatio hebraicorum et graecorum nominum in Sacra Scriptura. MS. Benediktinerabtei St. Peter, Salzburg, codex a.V.39, 62 f. Octavo. Saec. 13.
Microfilm: MnCH proj. no. 10,079

941   Interpretationes nominum hebraicorum. MS. Benediktinerabtei Melk, Austria, codex 348, f. 49–164. Folio. Saec. 14.
Microfilm: MnCH proj. no. 1355

942   Interpretationes nominum hebraeorum, seu eorum in latinum sermonem translatio. MS. Benediktinerabtei Seitenstetten, Austria, codex 122, f. 208r–255v. Folio. Saec. 15.
Microfilm: MnCH proj. no. 934

943   Libellus de locis sanctis. MS. Benediktinerabtei Admont, Austria, codex 256, f. 119r–127v. Folio. Saec. 12.
Microfilm: MnCH proj. no. 9341

944   Libellus de loquella digitorum. MS. Benediktinerabtei Melk, Austria, codex 412, f. 62–65. Folio. Saec. 9.
Microfilm: MnCH proj. no. 1957

945   Libellus de temporibus. MS. Benediktinerabtei Melk, Austria, codex 412, f. 16–26. Folio. Saec. 9.
Microfilm: MnCH proj. no. 1957

946   Libellus in opusculum de tractatione actionis Missarum sanctorum patrum Cypriani, Ambrosii . . . Bedae . . . MS. Cistercienserabtei Heiligenkreuz, Austria, codex 193. 116 f. Folio. Saec. 13.
Microfilm: MnCH proj. no. 4731

947   Liber de natura rerum. MS. Benediktinerabtei Melk, Austria, codex 412, f. 1–16. Folio. Saec. 9.
Microfilm: MnCH proj. no. 1957

948   Liber de natura rerum. MS. Universitätsbibliothek Graz, Austria, codex 297, f. 1r–9v. Folio. Saec. 12.

949   Liber de schematis et tropis Sacrae Scripturae (excerpta). MS. Augustiner-

chorherrenstift Klosterneuburg, Austria, codex 345, f. 1v–2r. Folio. Saec. 12.
Microfilm: MnCH proj. no. 5319

950   Liber de temporibus. MS. Augustinerchorherrenstift Klosterneuburg, Austria, codex 685, f. 14v–64v. Folio. Saec. 12.
Microfilm: MnCH proj. no. 5666

951   Liber secundus de temporibus, horis et momentis. MS. Augustinerchorherrenstift Klosterneuburg, Austria, codex 685, f. 8v–13v. Folio. Saec. 12.
Microfilm: MnCH proj. no. 5666

952   Liber de temporum ratione. MS. Benediktinerabtei Melk, Austria, codex 348, f. 31–48. Folio. Saec. 12.
Microfilm: MnCH proj. no. 1355

953   Liber de titulis psalmorum. MS. Cistercienserabtei Rein, Austria, codex 74, f. 140v–171r. Folio. Saec. 12.
Microfilm: MnCH proj. no. 7472

954   Liber de trimoda temporum ratione. MS. Benediktinerabtei Melk, Austria, codex 412, f. 65–191. Folio. Saec. 9.
Microfilm: MnCH proj. no. 1957

955   Liber generacionis Iesu Christi. MS. Benediktinerabtei Lambach, Austria, codex chartaceus 283, f. 121r–126r. Saec. 15.
Microfilm: MnCH proj. no. 659

956   Libri duo expositionis de domo Salomonis, cum praefatione. MS. Benediktinerabtei Göttweig, Austria, codex 37, f. 121r–155v. Folio. Saec. 12.
Microfilm: MnCH proj. no. 3319

957   Martyrologium (fragmentum) Bedae Venerabili tributum. MS. Vienna, Nationalbibliothek, codex 751, 188r. Folio. Saec. 10.
Microfilm: MnCH proj. no. 14,091

958   Martyrologium. Linz, Austria, Bundesstaatliche Studienbibliothek, codex 258. 140 f. Folio. Saec. 12.
Microfilm: MnCH proj. no. 27,893

959   Oratio de septis ultimis verbis Domini. MS. Benediktinerabtei Admont, Austria, codex 748, f. 101r–141r. Octavo. Saec. 13.
Microfilm: MnCH proj. no. 9784

960   Oratio de septem verbis Domini. MS. Benediktinerabtei St. Peter, Salzburg, codex b.I.31, f. 209r–310r. Octavo. Saec. 14–15.
Microfilm: MnCH proj. no. 10,302

961   Oratio de septem verbis Domini. MS. Benediktinerabtei St. Peter, Salzburg, codex b.V.15, f. 252r–253r. Quarto. Saec. 15.
Microfilm: MnCH proj. no. 10,445

962   Oratio. Incipit: Domine Iesu Christe. MS. Benediktinerabtei Melk, Austria, codex 1743, p. 288–289. Duodecimo. Saec. 15.
Microfilm: MnCH proj. no. 2053

963   Orationes formatae ex dictis Evangeliorum. MS. Benediktinerabtei St. Peter, Salzburg, codex b.XII.26, f. 2r–8v. Folio. Saec. 15.
Microfilm: MnCH proj. no. 10,697

964   Orationes ex dictis evangeliorum formatae. MS. Bischöfliche Bibliothek, Klagenfurt, Austria, codex XXX c 22, f. 71r–92r. Quarto. Saec. 15 (1415).
Microfilm: MnCH proj. no. 13,248

965   Poema. Incipit: Nobilibus quondam fueras constructa patronis. MS. Vienna, Nationalbibliothek, codex 754, f. 100r. Folio. Saec. 12.
Microfilm: MnCH proj. no. 14,081

966   Poenitentiale. MS. Vienna, Nationalbibliothek, codex 2223, f. 17r–22v. Quarto. Saec. 9–10.
Microfilm: MnCH proj. no. 15,569

967   Praefatio in librum de temporum ratione. MS. Benediktinerabtei Melk, Austria, codex 412, f. 59–60. Folio. Saec. 9.
Microfilm: MnCH proj. no. 1957

968   Retractatio in Actus Apostolorum. MS. Cistercienserabtei Heiligenkreuz, Austria, codex 237, f. 63r–98v. Folio. Saec. 12.
Microfilm: MnCH proj. no. 4780

969   Retractatio, seu altera expositio Actuum Apostolorum. MS. Benediktinerabtei Melk, Austria, codex 1908, f. 32v–51v. Folio. Saec. 15.
Microfilm: MnCH proj. no. 2191

Sermones. *See* Homiliae.

970   Tractatus de situ urbis Jerusalem. MS. Augustinerchorherrenstift Klosterneuburg, Austria, codex 787, f. 170r–181r. Folio. Saec. 12.
Microfilm: MnCH proj. no. 5764

971   Versiculi de die judicii. MS. Salisbury, England, Cathedral Library, codex 168, f. 85v. Octavo. Saec. 12.
Microfilm: MnCH

972   Versus. Incipit: Ramis incumbe sic vives more columbe. MS. Cistercienserabtei Heiligenkreuz, Austria, codex 203, f. 1r. Folio. Saec. 13.
Microfilm: MnCH proj. no. 4744

973   Versus. Incipit: Ramis incumbe, sic vives more columbae. MS. Cistercienserabtei Lilienfeld, Austria, codex 132, f. 180v. Folio. Saec. 14.
Microfilm: MnCH proj. no. 4433

974 Visio Drictelini. MS. Vienna, National-
bibliothek, codex 815, f. 72r–74v. Quarto.
Saec. 12.
Microfilm: MnCH proj. no. 14,146

Bede the Venerable, Saint, 673–735
Printed works

975 [Opera]
Venerabilis Bedae . . . Opera theologica, moralia, historica, philosophica,
mathematica & rhetorica, quotquot hucusque haberi potuerunt omnia . . . Hac
postrema editione diligenter recognita,
sedulo correcta, & divisa in tomos VIII
. . . Coloniae Agrippinae, apud IW.
Friessem, 1688.
8 v. in 7., illus. (incl. music), diagrs. 42
cm.
InStme

976 Opera. Turnholti, Typographri Brepols,
1955–
v. 26 cm. (Corpus Christianorum. Series
latina, v. 120, 122)
InStme; MnCS; NdRi

977 Opera didascalica. Turnholti, Typographi Brepols, 1975–77.
2 v. 26 cm. (Corpus Christianorum.
Series latina, v. 123A–B)
InStme; PLatS

978 Venerabilis Bedae opera historica. Ad
fidem codicum manuscriptorum resensuit
Josephus Stevenson . . . Londini, sumptibus Societatis, 1841.
2 v. facsims. (col.) 23 cm. [English
Historical Society. Publications]
PLatS

979 Baedae opera historica, with an English
translation by J. E. King. London, W.
Heinemann; Cambridge, Mass., 1934–
1962.
2 v. 17 cm. (The Loeb classical library.
[Latin authors])
KAS; MnCS

980 Opera homiletica. Opera rhythmica.
Turnholti, Typographi Brepols, 1955.
xxi, 473 p. 26 cm. (Corpus Chris-
tianorum. Series latina, 122. Bedae
Venerabilis Opera, pars III–IV)
ILSP; PLatS

981 Abacvs atqve vetvstissima, vetervm
latinorum per digitos manusq; numerandi
(quinetiam loquendi) consuetudo, ex Beda
cum picturis & imaginibus . . . a Io. Auen-
tino edita. [Ratispone, apud I. Khol, 1532].
[21] p.
PLatS (microfilm)

982 Anecdota Bedae, Lanfranci, et aliorum.
Inedited tracts, letters, poems &c. of
Venerable Bede, Lanfranc, Tatwin, and
others, by the Rev. Dr. Giles. New York, B.
Franklin [1957].
xviii, 344 p. 23 cm. ([Publications of the
Caxton Society, 12)
Burt Franklin research & source works
series, #154.
Reprint of the edition published in Lon-
don in 1851.
PLatS

983 Axiomata philosophica venerabilis Bedae
. . . ex Aristotele et aliis praestantibvs
philosophis diligenter collecta . . . Londini, apud Richardum Yardley & Petrum
Short, impensis Richardi Oliff, 1592.
Short-title catalogue no. 1777.
PLatS (microfilm)

984 Chronica maiora ad a. 725. Chronica
minora ad a. 703. Accedunt: I. Interpola-
tiones cod. Parisini nuper empt. 1615. II.
Interpolationes cod. Monacensis 246. III.
Auctaria quaedam chronicorum
Bedanorum maiorum. IV. Continuatio
Chronicorum Bedanorum minorum Ca-
rolingica prima. V. Generationum
regnorumque laterculus Bedanus cum con-
tinuatione Carolingica altera. Edidit
Theodorus Mommsen.
(*In* Monumenta Germaniae historica.
Auctores antiquissimi. Berlin, 1961. t. 13,
p. 223–354)
Reprint of Berlin edition of 1898.
MnCS; PLatS

985 De locis sanctis. [Incipit libellus Bedae
Venerabilis de locis sanctis, quem de opus-
culis maiorum abbreviando composuit)
(*In* Itineraria et alia geographica. Turn-
holdi, Brepols, 1965. v. 1, p. [245]–280.
Corpus Christianorum. Series latina, v.
175)
PLatS

986 De tabernaculo; De templo; In Ezram et
Neemiam. Cura et studio D. Hurst, O.S.B.
Turnholti, Brepols, 1969.
v, 417 p. 26 cm. (Corpus Christianorum.
Series latina, 119a. Bedae opera. Pars II,
2a).
PLatS

987 Historia ecclesiastica gentis Anglorum.
Historia abbatum (Uyremuthensium et
Gyruuensium] et Epistola ad Ecgberctum,
cum Epistola Bonifacii ad Cudberthum,
cura Georgii H. Moberly. Oxonii, Clarendon Press, 1869.
xxviii, 442 p. 20 cm.
MnCS

988 Venerabilis Baedae Historia ecclesiastica
gentis Anglorum, Historia abbatum et
Epistola ad Ecberctum, cum Epistola
Bonifacii ad Cuthberthum. Cura Georgii H.

Moberly. Oxonii, e Typographeo Clarendo-niano, MDCCCLXXXI.
    xxviii, 442 p. 20 cm.
    PLatS

989   [Historia ecclesiastica. Anglo-Saxon]
The Old English version of Bede's Eccle-siastical history of the English people. Edited with a translation and introduction by Thomas Miller. London, published for the Early English Text Society by the Oxford U.P. [1959–1963].
    2 v. in 4. 22 cm. (Early English Text Society. Original series, 95, 96, 110, 111)
    Reprint of the 1890–1898 edition.
    PLatS

990   The ecclesiastical history of the English nation, written by the Venerable Bede. London, J. M. Dent and Co., 1903.
    392 p. 16 cm. (The Temple classics)
    Edited by L. Cecil Nane, with brief bio-graphical notice and notes.
    InStme; KAS

991   The ecclesiastical history of the English nation, by the Venerable Bede. London, J. M. Dent; New York, E. P. Dutton [1930?].
    xxxiv, 370 p. 17 cm. (Everyman's library. History [479])
    Introduction by Vida D. Scudder.
    InStme

992   Bede's ecclesiastical history of the English nation. Introduction by Dom David Knowles. London, J. M. Dent; New York, E. P. Dutton [1954, 1910].
    xxiii, 382 p. 19 cm. (Everyman's library, no. 479)
    PLatS

993   A history of the English church and people / Bede. Translated and with an introduction by Leo Sherley-Price. Baltimore, Md., Penguin Books [1965].
    341 p. 18 cm. (Penguin classics, L42)
    InStme

994   The Venerable Bede's Ecclesiastical history of England. Also the Anglo-Saxon chronicle. Edited by J. A. Giles. 2d ed. London, H. G. Bohn, 1849. [New York, AMS Press, 1971].
    xliv, 515 p. 23 cm. (Bohn's antiquarian library)
    MnCS

995   The history of the church of Englande . . . [translated out of Latin into English by Thomas Stapleton]. [Menston, Yorkshire, England], The Scolar Press, 1973.
    [14], 192, [6] leaves, 21 cm. (English recusant literature, 1558–1640, v. 162)
    Facsimile reprint of the 1565 edition.
    PLatS

996   Home. [English translation]
    (*In* Heaven; an anthology. New York, 1935. p. 54–55)
    PLatS

997   Libri quatuor in principium Genesis usque ad nativitatem Isaac et eiectionem Ismahelis adnotationum. Cura et studio Ch. W. Jones. Turnholti, Typographi Brepols, 1967.
    xii, 269 p. 26 cm. (Corpus Christianorum. Series latina, 118a. Bedae Opera, pars II: Opera exegetica, 1)
    PLatS

998   In Lucae evangelium expositio. In Marci evangelium expositio. Cura et studio D. Hurst O.S.B. Turnholti, Typographi Brepols, 1960.
    vii, 682 p. 26 cm. (Corpus Christianorum. Series latina, 120. Bedae Venerabilis opera, pars II: Opera exegetica, 3)
    MnCS; PLatS

999   In primam partem Samuhelis libri III. In Regum librum XXX quaestiones. Cura et studio D. Hurst, O.S.B. Turnholti, Typographi Brepols, 1962.
    vi, 343 p. 26 cm. (Corpus Christianorum. Series latina, 119. Bedae opera, pars II: Opera exegetica, 2)
    MnCS; PLatS

1000   A critical edition of Bede's Vita Felicis, by Thomas William Mackay. [Stanford, Calif.] 1971 [c 1972].
    cc, 223 leaves.
    Thesis (Ph.D.)–Stanford University.
    MnCS (microfilm)

1001   [Vita sancti Cuthberti]
Two lives of Saint Cuthbert; a life by an anonymous monk of Lindisfarne and Bede's Prose life. Texts, translation, and notes by Bertram Colgrave. New York, Greenwood Press [1969].
    xiii, 375 p. 23 cm.
    "Reprinted from a copy in the collections of the New York Public Library, Astor, Lenox and Tilden Foundations."
    Latin and English on opposite pages.
    InStme; MoCo

1002   [Vita sancti Cuthberti]
Bede: Life of Cuthbert.
    (*In* Lives of the saints [pt. 2]. Translated with an introduction by J. F. Webb. Baltimore, Penguin Books [1965])
    PLatS

Bedos de Celles, François, 1706–1779.

1003   L'art du facteur d'orgues. Faksimile-Nachdruck hrsg. von Christhard Mahrenholz. Kassel, Bärenreiter, 1963–66.
    4 v. in 3. illus. 29 cm.
    MnCS

1004   The organ-builder. Translated by Charles Ferguson. Raleigh, N.C., The Sunbury, 1977.
2 v. 46 cm. (v. 1: Text. v. 2: Plates [part folded])
PLatS; MnCS

1005   **Beeke, Radulf van der,** d. 1403.
Radulph decani tungrensis Expositio missae. Romae, In Collegio Pontificio S. Anselmi, 1948.
44 p. 19 cm. (Textus breviores de sacrificio missae agentes, ad usum seminariorum edidit Philippus Oppenheim, fasc. 1)
ILSP

Beekman, Andreas, 1888–
1006   Het leven van de heilige Benedictus in het licht van zijn tijd, 480–547. Deutekom, Heiloo, 1950.
209 p. plates, 25 cm.
PLatS

1007   Verschijningen van Maria in West-Europa, 1491–1953. Heiloo, S. Deutekom, 1959.
189 p. 20 cm.
MnCS; PLatS

1008   **Beerli, Willibald,** 1885–
Mariastein; seine Geschichte, sein Heiligtum, seine Gäste, seine Ablässe und Gottesdienste. [Mariastein], Im Selbstverlag, 1935.
63 p. plates, 18 cm.
InStme

Behrendt, Roland, 1901–
1009   Abbot John Trithemius (1462–1516), monk and humanist.
Reprint from: Revue Bénédictine, t. 84 (1974), p. 212–229.
This is a review article of three recent books: Johannes Trithemius, von Arnold Klaus (Würzburg, 1971); Des Abtes Johannes Trithemius Chronik des Klosters Sponheim, von C. Velten (Kreuznach, 1969); Grandeur et adversité de Jean Trithème, par P. Chacornac (Paris, 1963).
MnCS

1010   Abbot John Trithemius; a spiritual writer of the fifteenth century.
22, [6] leaves, 28 cm.
Reproduced from typed copy.
MnCS; PLatS

1011   The consecration of virgins; conferences to Benedictine Sisters. Collegeville, Minn., St. John's Abbey, 1964.
198 leaves, front. 28 cm.
Multilithed.
MnCS; MnStj; PLatS

1012   Conversatio morum, the second vow of the Rule of St. Benedict; a résumé of opinions. Collegeville, Minn., St. John's Abbey, 1962.
66 leaves, 28 cm.
Multilithed.
MnCS; MnStj; PLatS

1013   Fifteenth-century Tegernsee revisited.
Sunderdruck aus: Regulae Benedicti studia, v. 3/4 (1974–75), p. 125–131.
This is a review article of: Tegernsee und die deutsche Geistesgeschichte im 15. Jahrhundert, von P. Virgil Redlich, O.S.B., (München, 1931. Reprint: Aalen, 1974).
MnCS

1014   Monastic Manuscript Library.
(In Tjurunga; an Australasian Benedictine review, October, 1976, p. 61–64)
MnCS

1015   Templum Domini; the dedication of a church in patristic thought.
53 p. front. 28 cm.
Multigraphed, 1961.
MnCS

1016   (tr) Puniet, Pierre de. Benedictine spirituality. Translated by Roland Behrendt, O.S.B. Collegeville, Minn., St. John's Abbey, 1965.
57 p. 28 cm.
Multigraphed.
MnCS; MnStj; PLatS

1017   (tr) Trithemius, Johannes. In praise of scribes. De laude scriptorum. Edited with introduction by Klaus Arnold. Translated by Roland Behrendt. Lawrence, Kans., Coronado Press, 1974.
viii, 111 p. illus. 22 cm.
MnCS; MnStj; PLatS

1018   **Behrman, Peter,** 1896–
Centennial of St. Meinrad, town and parish, from 1861 to 1961. [St. Meinrad, Ind.], 1961].
57 p. illus. 27 cm.
InStme

1019   **Behrman, Peter,** 1896–
The story of St. Meinrad Abbey; an historical sketch. [St. Meinrad, Ind., The Grail, 1929].
(In The Grail, vol. 10 (1929), p. 487–516 & 522)
InStme; PLatS

Békés, Gellért, 1915–
1020   L'umanesimo moderno e l'Immacolata.
(In Virgo Immaculata; actus Congressus Mariologici-Mariani, 1954, v. 13, p. 141–151)
PLatS

1021   Unitatis redintegratio, 1964–1974; the impact of the decree on ecumenism, edited by Gerard Bekes and Vilmos Vajta. Roma, Editrice Anselmiana, 1977.

176 p. 24 cm. (Studia Anselmiana, v. 71)
InStme; PLatS

1022 **Belhomme, Humbert,** 1653–1727.
Historia Mediani in monte Vosago monasterii Ordinis Sancti Benedicti ex congregatione sanctorum Vitoni et Hidulfi. Argenterati, sumptibus J. R. Dulsseckeri, 1724.
[6], 467 p. 26 cm.
KAS

Belmont Abbey, Belmont, N.C.
1023 My Catholic companion; a handbook of daily devotions with the new simplified Missal. Revised according to the new code of rubrics . . . Gastonia, N.C. Good Will Publishers [1961].
493 p. col. plates, 17 cm.
MnCS

1024 To him who knocks it shall be opened. [A preview of the newly renovated Belmont Abbey Cathedral, 1964].
unpaged.
NcBe

1025 Saint Walburga's manual; prefaced by a short sketch of the saint's life, by a member of the Benedictine Order. Belmont, N.C., Belmont Abbey Press, 1913.
69 p.
NcBe

1026 (2dary) Burton, Katherine. The birth of Christ . . . Sponsored by the Benedictine monks of Belmont Abbey. Garden City, N.Y., The Catholic Know-Your-Bible Program [1958].
64 p. illus., plates 21 cm.
MnCS

Belmont Abbey College, Belmont, N.C.
1027 Annual catalogue of the officers and students of Belmont Abbey College, Belmont, N.C. 1913–
Belmont Abbey College was until November 27, 1913, St. Mary's College.
NcBe

1028 Belmont Abbey College alumni directory, 1978–
NcBe

1029 Belmont Review; published monthly during the school year by the faculty and students of Belmont College. February 1915–June, 1917.
NcBe

1030 Report of the institutional self-study, Belmont Abbey College, March, 1968.
220 p.
NcBe

1031 Self-study report, Belmont Abbey College, 1977.
347 p.
NcBe

1032 **Beltrame Quattrocchi, Paolino,** 1909–
Questo sconcertante evangelo; ultime conferenze zpirituali del Padro Don Paolino Beltrame Quattrocchi, O.S.B., prima del "gran silenzo." Sorrento, Monasteri di S. Paulo [1963].
316 p. illus. 21 cm.
PLatS

1033 **Bender, Edwin Paul,** 1910–1952.
Benedictine hospitality.
v, 32 leaves, 28 cm.
Thesis (B.A.) – St. Vincent College, Latrobe, Pa., 1933.
Typescript.
PLatS

1034 **I Benedettini nelle valli del Maceratese;** atti del II Convegno del Centro di studi storici Maceratesi (9 ottobre 1966). Ravenna, A. Longo, 1967.
281 p. plates, 25 cm. (Studi Maceratesi, 2)
MnCS

Benedict, Saint, abbot of Monte Cassino, 480–547.
1035 Verba S. Patris Benedicti, reperta in fine Regulae, quam ipse propriis manibus conscripsit, et S. Mauro, cum eum ad Gallias mitteret, tradidit. MS. Benediktinerabtei Melk, Austria, codex 1083, f. 525–538. Duodecimo. Saec. 15.
Microfilm: MnCH proj. no. 1846

1036 Epilogus S. P. Benedicti in suam Regulam, traditus S. Mauro in Galliam profisciscenti. MS. Benediktinerabtei St. Peter, Salzburg, a.IV.23, f. 48r–52r. Octavo. Saec. 15.
Microfilm: MnCH proj. no. 10,016
Regula S. Benedicti. See Subject Part, nos. 386–615.

Benedict, Saint, of Aniane, d. 821.
1037 An interlinear Old English rendering of the Epitome of Benedict of Aniane. By Arthur S. Napier.
(In The Old English version of the enlarged rule of Chrodegang together with the Latin original. London, 1916)
KAS

1038 Regula sancti Benedicti abbatis Anianensis, sive Collectio capitularis (818/819?). Recensuit J. Semmler.
(In Corpus consuetudinum monasticarum. Siegburg, 1963. t. 1, p. 501–536)
PLatS

1039 Tractatus asceticus. MS. Monasterio benedictino de Montserrat, Spain, codex 824, f. 74r–84v. Octavo. Saec. 15.
Microfilm: MnCH proj. no. 30,086

1040 **Benedict, abbot of Peterborough,** d. 1193.

Benedicti Abbatis Petriburgensis de vita et miraculis S. Thomae Cantuar. The life and miracles of Saint Thomas of Canterbury, by the Rev. Dr. Giles. New York, B. Franklin [1967].
281 p. 23 cm. (Burt Franklin research & source works series, no. 154)
Reprint of the 1850 edition.
Text in Latin, preface in English.
PLatS

1041   Gesta regis Henrici secundi Benedicti abbatis. The chronicle of the reigns of Henry II and Richard I, A.D. 1169–1192, known commonly under the name of Benedict of Peterborough. Edited from the Cotton mss. by William Stubbs . . . London, 1867.
(Great Britain. Public Record Office. Rerum britannicarum medii aevi scriptores . . . no. 49)
ILSP

1041a   **A Benedictine book of song:** a centenary collection of hymns for seasons, feasts, and rites of the Church; eucharistic music; responsorial songs. By the Benedictines for parish and responsorial songs. Collegeville, Minn., The Liturgical Press [1980].
2 v. music. 20 cm. & 30 cm.
MnCS

Benedictine College, Atchison, Kans.
See also St. Benedict's College, Atchison, Kans.

1042   Benedictine College catalog, 1971–72– Atchison, Kansas, 1971–
v. illus. 26 cm. (Benedictine College bulletin, v. 1– 1971)
KAS

1043   Benedictine College Ravens, 1971–72– [Basketball]. Atchison, Kans., 1971–
v. illus. 22 cm.
Previous title: Benedictine College basketball.
KAS

1044   Benedictine College report to the Commission on Institutions of Higher Education of the North Central Association of Colleges and Secondary Schools. Atchison, Kans., Benedictine College, 1972.
115, 10 leaves. 28 cm.
KAS

Benedictine Convent of Perpetual Adoration, Clyde, Mo.
1045   Anbetungsbuch, vorzüglich geeignet für das 40stündige Gebet sowie ein vollständiges Gebetbuch. Clyde, Mo., Benediktiner Kloster, 1911.
703 p. 15 cm.
MoCo

1046   Behold I come; the life of the Benedictine Sisters of Perpetual Adoration, Clyde, Mo., Benedictine Convent of Perpetual Adoration, 1961.
64 p. illus. 23 cm.
KAS

1047   Daily companion for Secular Oblates of St. Benedict. St. Meinrad, Ind., Grail Publications [1963].
100 p. 15 cm.
MnCS
Originally published by Benedictine Convent of Perpetual Adoration, Clyde, Mo.

1048   St. Benedict, the branching tree. [Clyde, Mo.]
64 p.
MnStj (Archives)

1049   (tr) Meschler, Moritz. The life of Our Lord Jesus Christ, the Son of God, in meditations . . . Translated from the fourth edition of the German original by a Benedictine of the Perpetual Adoration. St. Louis, Herder, 1909.
2 v. plates, 20 cm.
MnCS

1050   (tr) The Monastic Breviary, according to the Holy Rule of our most holy father Benedict. For private instruction and benefit of the Benedictine Sisters of Perpetual Adoration, Clyde, Mo., 1940–42.
5 v. 22 cm.
ILSP

1051   **Benedictine Institute, Kansas City, Mo.**
Secular Benedictine Institute: Constitution. [Kansas City, Mo., Benedictine Institute Press, 1968].
36 p. 23 cm.
KAS

Benedictines of Stanbrook Abbey. *See* Stanbrook Abbey, England.
Benedictine Sisters. Congregations. St. Benedict.
1052   Adaptations of the Rule of Saint Benedict [for the Congregation of Saint Benedict, 1968].
ix, 42 p. 22 cm.
Mimeographed
MnStj (Archives)

1053   Federation of St. Benedict: A chronicle. [Bismarck, Annunciation Priory, 1975].
various paging. 28 cm.
A compilation of the histories of each priory in the Congregation.
MnStj (Archives)

1054   [Constitution]
Adaptations of the Rule of Saint Benedict and Constitution of the Congregation

of Saint Benedict. Adopted by the Seventh General Chapter, 1969 . . . Duluth, Minn., St. Scholastica Priory Press, 1970.
viii, 68 p. 22 cm.
MnStj (Archives)

1055 [Constitution]
Declarations on the Rule of our Holy Father Benedict and Constitutions of the Congregation of St. Benedict, St. Joseph, Minn., 1958.
107 p. 19 cm.
MnCS; MnStj (Archives)

1056 Directory [of the] Congregation of St. Benedict. 1948– [St. Joseph, Minn.]
Published irregularly.
MnStj (Archives)

1057 Federation documents: due process document [and] visitation guidelines. St. Joseph, Minn., Office of the Federation of St. Benedict, St. Benedict's Convent, 1975.
9, 13 p. 22 cm.
MnStj (Archives)

1058 Necrology: Federation of St. Benedict. St. Joseph, Minn., 1976.
13 p. 22 cm.
MnStj (Archives)

1059 **Benedictine Sisters. Congregations. St. Gertrude the Great.**
Listen; testament of the Federation of Saint Gertrude according to the Rule of Saint Benedict. Richardton, N.D., Assumption Abbey, 1976.
47 p.
MoCo

1060 **Benedictine Sisters. Congregations. St. Scholastica.**
Declarations and Rule of our Holy Father St. Benedict and constitutions of the Congregation of St. Scholastica. [Atchison, Kans.] Abbey Student Press, 1953.
91 p.
MdRi

1061 **Benedictine Sisters. Diocese of Richmond, Va.**
Statutes and community exercises of the Benedictine Sisters in the Diocese of Richmond, Va. Approved September 30, 1920 . . .
p. 133–292.
Bound with: The Holy Rule of our Most Holy Father, Saint Benedict.
NcBe

Benedictine Sisters of Perpetual Adoration, Clyde, Mo.

1062 100 years for You; the story of the Benedictine Sisters of Perpetual Adoration. St. Louis, Mo., 1973.

32 p. illus.
MoCo

1063 The proper and the common of the saints of the Monastic Breviary according to the Holy Rule of our Most Holy Father Benedict. For private instruction and benefit of the Benedictine Sisters of Perpetual Adoration. Clyde, Mo., 1942.
604, 215 p. 22 cm.
Multigraphed.
MnCS

Benedictine yearbook. *See* Benedictines. Congregations. English.

1064 **Benedictines.**
Instructiones [i.e., monastic rubrics– 19th cent.]. St. Vincent College Library, Latrobe, Pa. Mss. 15.
li leaves, 20 cm.
PLatS

Benedictines. Congregations. American Cassinese.

1065 Decreta capituli generalis VIII, diebus 9, 10 et 11 decembris 1884 celebrati, jussu Archiabbatis et Praesidis edita. Typis Abbatiae, S. Vincentii, Pa., 1885.
4 p. 23 cm.
PLatS

1066 Acts and decrees of the 34th General Chapter, St. Martin's Abbey, Olympia, Washington, 27–30 August, 1962. [Collegeville, Minn., St. John's Abbey Press, 1962].
28 p. 19 cm.
MnCS; PLatS

1067 Acts and decrees of the 35th General Chapter, American Cassinese Congregation, Order of Saint Benedict. Lisle, Ill., Saint Procopius Abbey, 1965.
31 p. 19 cm.
MnCS

1068 De Capitulo Generali. [Atchison, Kans., Abbey Student, St. Benedict's College, 1896].
[19] p. 24 cm.
PLatS

1069 [Constitution]
Constitutiones et statuta Congregationis Benedictino-Americanae sub invocatione Angelorum Custodum constitutae. [19th cent.]. MS. St. Vincent College Library, Latrobe, Pa. Miss. 15.
71 p. 20 cm.
PLatS

1070 [Constitution]
Emendationes constitutionum provisoriae (juxta rescriptum Abbatis Primatis de die 8 Septembris 1918, mandatae) ab Abbate Praeside et abbatibus visitatoribus

propositae, quae vim habent a S.C. de Religiosis confirmatae sint.
8 p. 23 cm.
PLatS

1071   [Constitution]
Declarationes in Regulam s.p.n. Benedicti et Statuta Congregationis Americano-Cassinensis. [Latrobe, Pa., Archabbey Press, 1947 [i.e., 1962].
64 p. 19 cm.
Reprint of 1947 edition.
KAS; PLatS

1072   [Constitution]
Documents of the American Cassinese Congregation [O.S.B.], IV: Juridic elements.
n.p., 1969.
28 p. 22 cm.
KAS; MnCS

1073   Documents of the American Cassinese Federation, IV: Juridic elements. n.p., 1971.
30 p. 22 cm.
KAS; MnCS; PLatS

1074   American-Cassinese Federation: Juridic elements. n.p., 1974.
22 p. 21 cm.
MnCS

1075   [Constitution]
Documents of the American Cassinese Federation, IV: Juridic elements. n.p., 1977.
24 p. 22 cm.
KAS; MnCS

1076   Guidelines for visitation in the American-Cassinese Federation; approved by the 38th Ordinary General Chapter, 1974. [Peru, Ill., St. Bede Abbey Press, 1974].
27 p. 21 cm.
MnCS

1077   Renew and create; a statement of the American-Cassinese Benedictine monastic life, thirty-sixth general chapter, second session, June 1969. n.p., 1969.
78 p. 18 cm.
AStb; KAS; MnCS; MdRi; MnStj

1078   Rite of monastic profession according to the Ritual of the American-Cassinese Congregation of the Order of St. Benedict. Collegeville, Minn., St. John's Abbey Press, 1953.
iv, 32 p. 15 cm.
MnCS

1079   **Benedictines. Congregations. American-Cassinese. General Chapter.**
Conspectus actorum ac omnium decretorum, quae a I. usque ad novissimum, quod est Cap. Gen. VI., condita sunt, atque hucusque in tota Congrega-

tione Americo-Casinensi, O.S.B., ex omnium reverendissimorum abbatum auctoritate observanda sunt. Jussu Revmi D. D. Bonifacii, abbatis et praesidis, ex Abb. Sti. Vincentii, conf., Pennsylv. [Typis Joannis Murphy et Soc.], Baltimore, 1878.
26 p. 23 cm.
PLatS

1080   Recessus III. capituli generalis in Abbatia S. Vincentii diebus 17. 18. 19. Augusti 1867 celebrati. Typis Abbatiae S. Vincentii, Pa., 1867.
4 p. 23 cm.
PLatS

1081   **Benedictines. Congregations. Annunciation B.V.M.**
Ordo divini officii recitandi sacrique peragendi juxta kalendarium Congregationis Belgicae Annuntiationis B.M.V. Ord. S. Benedicti . . . [Mechliniae, H. Dessain].
MnCS

Benedictines. Congregations. Austrian.

1082   Catalogi monachorum et monialium O.S.B.: S. Petri, Salzburg; S. Michaelis, Burae; B.V.M., Lambach; SS. Cordis, Innsbruck; Nonnberg in Salzburg; St. Hemma in Gurk; Saben in Tirol. n.p., n.p., 1913.
[113]–165 p. 14 cm.
In the Austrian Congregation since 1930.
MnCS

1083   Catalogus monachorum Congregationis Austro-Benedictinae sub invocatione B.V.M. Deiparae sine labe originali conceptae. St. Pölten, Pressvereins-Druckeri Ges.
MnCS

1084   Constitutiones Congregationis Austriacae Ordinis S. Benedicti. MS. Universitätsbibliothek Innsbruck, Austria, codex 687. 82 f. Quarto. Saec. 16.
Microfilm: MnCH proj. no. 28,614

1085   Diarium Congregationis Austriae Superioris Ordinis divi patris Benedicti, una cum adiunctis ss. meditationibus. MS. Benediktinerabtei Kremsmünster, Austria, codex novus 578. 107 p. Saec. 17 (1622).
Microfilm: MnCH proj. no. 418

1086   Directorium officii divini Ord. SS. Patris Benedicti specialiter monasteriis ad S. Petrum Salzburgi, Michaelburano, Lambacensi, Lambertino, Congregationis Austriacae, ac sanctimonialium Nonnbergensi et Sabionensi . . . Salzburgi, A. Pustet.
MnCS

1087   Statuta in Capitulo Ordinis, quod auctoritate Eminentissimi D. D. Visitoris

Apostolici diebus 5. 6. 7. et 8. Junii 1859 in monasterio S. Petri Salisburgi celebratum est, condita pro Congregatione Benedictina sub patrocinio B. Mariae V. sine labe conceptae. Salisburgi, ex Typographia Duyleana, 1859.

[38] p. 22 cm.

PLatS

1088 Mitteilungen der Oesterreichischen Benediktinerkongregation, Nr. 5, Dezember 1971.

26 p. 30 cm.

Multigraphed.

MnCS

Benedictines. Congregations. Bavarian.

1089 Directorium pro monasteriis et ecclesiis Congregationis Benedictinae Bavaricae et pro monialium O.S.B. in Bavaria monasteriis ad annum . . . Ratisbon, Fr. Pustet.

MnCS

1090 Satzungen der Bayerischen Benediktiner-Kongregation von dem hl. Schutzengeln . . . Auszug für Laienbrüder und Oblaten. Augsburg, Mühlberger, 1922.

56 p.

AStb; MnCS

Benedictines. Congregations. Belgian.

See Benedictines. Congregations. Annunciation B.V.M.

1091 **Benedictines. Congregations. Beuronese.**

Constitutiones Congregationis Beuronensis, continentes Declarationes in Regulam Sancti Benedicti et Statuta Congregationis. Beuron, typis Sancti Martini de Beuron, 1959.

104 p. 17 cm.

1092 **Benedictines. Congregations. Bursfeld.**

Die Generalkapitels-Rezesse der Bursfelder Kongregation, von Paul Volk. Siegburg, Respublica-Verlag, 1955–1959.

3 v. 25 cm.

Text of the Rezesse in Latin.

InStme; KAS; MnCS; PLatS

Benedictines. Congregations. Cassinese.

1093 Cérémonial de la bénédiction d'un abbé bénédictin del la Congrégation du Mont Cassin. Albi, Apprentis-Orphelins, 1896.

30 p. 21 cm.

French and Latin in parallel columns.

KAS

1094 [Constitution]

Constitutiones Congregationis Cassinensis. MS. Benediktinerabtei Admont, Austria, codex 829r, f. 201r–278v. Quarto. Saec. 17.

Microfilm: MnCH proj. no. 9858

1095 [Constitution]

Regvla sancti patris Benedicti. Cum declarationibus & constitutionibus editis a patribus Congregationis Casinensis . . . Mogvntiae, Balthasar Lippius, 1603.

187, 173 p. 18 cm.

MnCS

1096 [Constitution]

Regvla s.p. Benedicti, cum declarationibus & constitutionibus Congregationis Montis Cassini, alias S. Iustina de Padua. Hvic secvndae editioni accessere bullae romanorum pontificum . . . Parisiis, apud Ambrosium & Hieronymvm Drovart, 1604.

187, [52], 173, [26], 170, [12] p.

KyTr; MnCS (microfilm); PLatS (microfilm)

1097 [Constitution]

Decreta et constitutiones quae de praecepto legi debent in publico refectorio in monasteriis Congregationis Cassinensis . . . Cavae Tyrrhenorum, ex Tipographia Pauli Fenoglio, 1889.

48 p. 21 cm.

PLatS

Benedictines. Congregations. Cassinese of the Primitive Observance. *See* Benedictines. Congregations. Subiaco.

Benedictines. Congregations. English.

1098 The Benedictine yearbook; a guide to the abbeys, priories, parishes, monks and nuns of the English Congregation of the Order of Saint Benedict. York, Ampleforth Abbey, 1967–

Previously published under title: The Benedict almanac.

KAS; MnCS; MoCo; PLatS

1099 Constitutiones Congregationis Anglicanae Ordinis Sancti Benedicti. Parisiis, typis Michaelis Lambert, 1784.

xi, 271, lxiii p. 18 cm.

InStme; KAS

1100 Directorium, formularium, et ritualis compendium Congregationos Anglicanae O.S.B. Anneci, typis J. Nierat, 1901.

95 p. 22 cm.

KAS

1101 A form for receiving a person into confraternity with the English Benedictine Congregation. [Menston, Yorkshire, England, The Scolar Press, 1973].

1 leaf, 40 x 29 cm., folded to 21 x 15 cm. (English recusant literature, 1558–1640, v. 162)

Facsimile reprint of the 1625? edition.

Bound with: Bede, the Venerable: The history of the church of Englande. 1973.

PLatS

1102 (2dary) A statement on Benedictine life adopted by the Congress of Abbots held in Rome in September, 1967, and translated into English by monks and nuns of the E.B.C. [St. Benedict, Or.] Printed for private circulation at Mount Angel Abbey, 1968.
32 p. 20 cm.
MnCS

Benedictines. Congregations. Federation of the Americas. *See* Benedictines. Congregations. Swiss-American.

Benedictines. Congregations. French. *See* Benedictines. Congregations. Solesmes.

1103 **Benedictines. Congregations. Portuguese. Province of Brazil.**
Primeiras constituições de Ordem de São Bento na Província de Brasil, 1596. Salvador, Bahia [Brasil], 1977.
22 p. 21 cm.
At head of title: José Lohr Endres, O.S.B.
Offprint from: Universitas, no. 17 (1977), p. 105–126.

Benedictines, Congregations. Santa Justina.

1104 Bullae de la Congregatio de St. Justina de Padua. MS. Monasterio benedictino de Montserrat, Spain, codex 827. 87 f. Octavo. Saec. 15.
Microfilm: MnCH proj. no. 30,088

1105 Constitutiones regularis observantiae Congregationis Cassinensis O.S.B. seu Sanctae Iustinae. MS. Monasterio benedictino de Montserrat, Spain, codex 35. 61 f. Quarto. Saec. 16.
Microfilm: MnCH proj. no. 29,988

Benedictines. Congregations. St. Maur.

1106 Regula s. p. Benedicti, cum declarationibus, Congregationis Sancti Mauri, Jussu et authoritate capituli generalis eiusdem Congregationis. n.p., 1701.
[8], 29b, [49] p. 20 cm.
KAS

1107 Mémorial du XIVe centenaire de l'Abbaye de Saint-Germain-des-Prés; recueil de travaux sur le monastère et la Congrégation de Saint-Maur, publié avec le concours du Centre National de la Recherche Scientifique. Paris, Libraire philosophique J. Vrin, 1959.
x, 350 p. maps, 25 cm.
InStme

1108 Nouveau traité de diplomatique où l'on examine les fondemens de cet art: on etablit des regles sur le discernement des titres, et l'on expose historiquement les caractères des bulles pontificales et des diplomes . . . par deux religieux Bénédictins de la Congrégation de S. Maur. Paris, Guillaume Desprez, 1750–65.
6 v. fold. plates, 27 cm.
Attributed to C. F. Toustain and R. F. Tassin.
MnCS

1109 Tractatus asceticus de felicitate religiosi ab officiis liberi atque obligationis et salutis suae studiosi. Per quemdam Benedictinum ex Congregatione S. Mauri Parisiis gallico idiomate conscriptus, modo ab alio ejusdem Ordinis in Monasterio Benedictino-Burano professo latinitate donatus. Ratisonae, Io. Gastl, 1737.
283 p. 16 cm.
MnCS

1110 **Benedictines. Congregations. Sankt Ottilien.**
Directorium sive Ordo divini officii recitandi sacrique peragendi juxta ritum romano-monasticum ad usum monachorum Ordinis Sancti Benedicti Congregationis Ottiliensis pro Missionibus exteris . . . Typis Archiabbatiae Ss. Cordis Jesu ad S. Ottiliam.
MnCS; PLatS

1111 **Benedictines. Congregations. Saint Vanne et Saint Hydulphe.**
Matricula religiosorum professorum clericorum et sacerdotum Congregationis Sanctorum Vitoni et Hydulphi (1604–1789). Nouvelle ed. rev. et traduite par Gilbert Cherest. Paris, P. Lethielleux, 1963.
xvi, 76 p. 25 cm.
InStme; KAS; MnCS; PLatS

1112 **Benedictines. Congregations. Solesmes.**
Messes propres de la Congrégation de Saint-Pierre de Solesmes. Paris, Abbaye Sainte-Marie [1948].
195 p. 15 cm.

Benedictines. Congregations. Spanish.

1113 Constitucions de la congregacio del SS. patriarca S. Benet de la Provincia de Terragona Cesaraugustana, y Navarra, y reformadas en lo Capitol General del any 1662. MS. Monasterio benedictino de Montserrat, Spain, codex 694. 103 f. Quarto. Saec. 17.
Microfilm: MnCH proj. no. 30,033

1114 Constitucions de la congregacio claustral Terraconesa benedictina. MS. Monasterio benedictino de Montserrat, Spain, codex 695. 118 p. Quarto. Saec. 18.
Microfilm: MnCH proj. no. 30,032

1115 Constituciones de la congregacion de nuestro glorioso padre San Benito de España, è Inglaterra. Avgmentadas, y

añadidas con las nuevas difiniciones, que desde el año de 1610 hasta el de 1701 han sido establecidas y aprobadas en diversos capitulos . . . Impressas en Madrid a costa de la congregacion, en la oficina de la viuda de Melchor Alvarez. Añno de 1706.
[8], 48 p.
KAS (microfilm)

1116   Ordinacions et Constituciones per als monastirs de les religioses del Orde de Sant Benet de la Provincia de Terragona. MS. Barcelona, Spain, Sant Pere de les Puel-les, Constituciones, 1–31. 3 vols. Quarto. Saec. 17.
Microfilm: MnCH proj. no. 34,677

Benedictines. Congregations. Subiaco.
1117   Costituzioni dei monaci benedettini Cassinesi della Primitiva Osservanza. MS. Monasterio benedictino de Montserrat, Spain, codex 645. 50 p. Quarto. Saec. 19 (1868).
Microfilm: MnCH proj. no. 30,031

1118   Constitutiones et declarationes Congr. Sublacensis O.S.B. a capitula generali an. 1967 ad experimentum approbatae. [Garcelona, Grafficae Marina, 1967].
69 p. 20 cm.
MnCS

1119   Ephemerides Congregationis Casinensis a Primaeva Observantia Ordinis Sancti Benedicti. v. 1–   1905–   Sublaci, excuderunt Monachi Proto-Coenobii.
MnCS

1120   Ordo operis Dei persolvendi sacrique peragendi juxta ritum monasticum . . . Congregationis Casinensis a P.O. Sublaci, typis Proto-Coenobii.
v. 19 cm.
MnCS

1121   **Benedictines. Congregations. Subiaco. English Province.**
Choir ceremonial of the English Province of the Cassinese Congregation, O.P. Ramsgate, The Monastery Press, 1949.
86 p. 19 cm.
InStme; NdRi

1122   **Benedictines. Congregations. Subiaco. Italian Province.**
I monasteri italiani della Congregazione Sublacense (1843–1972); saggi storici nel primo centenario della Congregazione. Parma, Scuola Tipografica Benedettina, 1972.
616 p. illus., ports. 24 cm.
KAS

Benedictines. Congregations. Swiss.
1123   Benediktinische Lebensform; Satzungen der Schweizerischen Benediktinerkongre-

gation. Approbiert ad experimentum vom Kongregations-Kapitel, 1970.
92 p. 24 cm.
MnCS

1124   Constitutiones Congregationis Benedictinorum Suevicae approbatae et receptae in conventu rev. dominorum abbatum die 6 Oct. 1671 in monasterio Ochsenhusano celebrato. Descriptae 1740. MS. Universitätsbibliothek Innsbruck, codex 964. 113 f. Quarto. Saec. 18 (1740).
Microfilm: MnCH proj. no. 28,723

1125   Directorium seu cantvs et responsoria in processionibus ordinariis per annum, et exequiis defunctorum una cum tono Missalis, et Psalterii. Juxta Rituale, & Missale Romanum pro uniformitate Helveto-Benedictinae Congregationis anno 1639 revisum, & approbatum. Nunc primum juxta originale fideliter typis excusum . . . opera R. P. Valentini Molitoris. In Monasterio S. Galli, per Adolphus Josephum Ebell, 1692.
311 p. 19 cm.
MnCS

Benedictines. Congregations. Swiss-American.
1126   Declarations on the Holy Rule and Constitutions of the Swiss-American Congregation, O.S.B., under the title of the Immaculate Conception of the Blessed Virgin Mary. By order of the General Chapter, October, 1935, translated from the Latin original as approved by the Sacred Congregation for Religious, September 9, 1924. Conception, Mo., Conception Abbey, Altar and Home Press, 1938.
102 p. 16 cm.
InStme

1127   [Constitution]
Covenant of peace, including the Rule of Benedict, and a Declaration on Benedictine monastic life, and the Constitution for the monasteries of the Benedictine Federation of the Americas adopted by the General Chapter, October 12–28, 1969, St. Benedict, La., St. Joseph Abbey.
[6], 58 p. 22 cm.
MdRi; MnStj; NcBe; PLatS; ViBris

1128   Covenant of peace; a declaration on Benedictine monastic life for the monasteries of the Benedictine Federation of the Americas. Adopted by the General Chapter of 1975, St. Meinrad Abbey, St. Meinrad, Ind. Conception, Mo., Conception Abbey [n.d.].
38 p. 21 cm.
InStme

1128a   Covenant of peace; the Constitution for the monasteries of the Swiss-American Federation adopted by the General Chapter October 12–18, 1969, and revised by the General Chapters of 1972, 1975, 1978 and edited under the directions of the 1978 General Chapter. Conception, Mo., Conception Abbey, 1978.
    45 p.
    MoCo

1129   Lectures of the Monastic Institute. St. Benedict, La., St. Joseph Abbey, 1973–
    MoCo

1130   Minutes of the meeting of the "New Document" Subcommittee of the Central Renewal Committee of the Swiss-American Congregation, O.S.B., held at St. Pius X Monastery, Pevely, Mo., August 18–23, 1968, in the form of an edited transcription of the taped discussions. Pevely, Mo., 1968.
    5 parts (various pagings)
    MoCo

1131   The official minutes of the Special General Chapter of Renewal of the Benedictine Federation of the Americas held at St. Joseph Abbey, St. Benedict, La., Oct. 12–28, 1969.
    64 p.
    MoCo

1132   Ordo divini officii recitandi sacrique peragendi juxta ritum Roman-Monasticum in ecclesiis et oratoriis Congregationis Helveto-Americano, O.S.B. . . . 1885–
    Includes directory of members.
    InStme; PLatS

1133   Ritual of monastic profession for the Benedictine Federation of the Americas [1978?].
    4 parts.
    MoCo

Benedictines. Congregations. Valladolid.

1134   Bulas de la Congregacion benedictine de San Benito el Real de Valladolid. MS. Monasterio benedictino de Montserrat, Spain, codex 616. 58 f. Folio. Saec. (1503).
    Microfilm: MnCH proj. no. 30,028

1135   Caerimonial de la Congregatio de Valladolid. MS. Monasterio benedictino de Montserrat, Spain, codex 831, f. 1r–159r. Octavo. Saec. 17.
    Microfilm: MnCH proj. no. 30,090

1136   Ceremonial monastico, conforme al Breviario, 7 Misal, que la santidad de Paulo V concedió à todos los que militan debajo de la santa Regla de . . . San Benito. Con los usos, y costumbres loables de la Congregacion de España. Nuevamente dis-

puesto por el capitulo general, que se celebró en el año de 1633 . . . Madrid, en la Imprenta de Pedro Marin, 1774.
    [15], 900 p. music. 22 cm.
    KAS

1137   Constituciones de la Congregacion de Sant Benito de Valladolid. Additiones capituli generali anni 1550 ad Constitutiones Cong. Vallisolentanae. MS. Monasterio benedictino de Montserrat, Spain, codex 982. 401 f. Quarto. Saec. 16.
    Microfilm: MnCH proj. no. 30,113

1138   **Benedictines. Congress of Abbots, Rome,** 1967.
    A statement on Benedictine life adopted by the Congress of Abbots held in Rome in September 1967, and translated into English by monks and nuns of the E.B.C. [St. Benedict, Or.], Printed for private circulation at Mount Angel Abbey, 1968.
    32 p. 20 cm.
    KAS; MdRi; MnCS; MoCo; MnStj; NcBe; PLatS

1139   **Benedictines. Congress of Abbots,** 1970.
    Acta Congressus abbatum ac priorum conventualium congregationum confoederatarum OSB. Romae, Abbatia S. Anselmi, 1970.
    132 p.
    MoCo

1140   **Benedictines. Congress of Abbots,** 1973.
    Acta Congressus abbatum ac priorum conventualium congregationum confoederatarum O.S.B. in aedibus S. Anselmi de Urbe celebrati 1973 a die 19 Sept. ad diem 3 Oct. Romae, Secretaria Abbatis Primatis O.S.B. [1975].
    144 p. 24 cm.
    Manuscripti instar.
    MnCS

1141   **Les Bénédictines de la rue monsieur;** histoire et vocation d'une chapelle. Paris, Editions F. X. Le Roux, 1950.
    271 p.
    MoCo

1142   **The Benedictines of Thanet,** 1856–1931 . . . Ramsgate, England, Monastery Press, 1931.
    66 p. plates, ports. 22 cm.
    KAS; MoCo; NdRi

1143   **The Benedictines: the liberal tradition** [motion picture]. New York, Columbia Broadcasting System, Inc., CBS News, n.d.
    1 motion picture ad bw 16mm. (Look up and live)
    MnCS

Benedictines throughout the world. *See* Muller, Jean Pierre.

1144 **Benedictus, monk of St. Andrew on Mount Soracte,** fl. ca. 1000.
Benedicti Sancti Andreae monachi chronicon a.c. 360–973.
(*In* Monumenta Germaniae historica. Scriptores. Stuttgart, 1963. t. 3, p. 695–722)
PLatS; MnCS

1145 **Benedictus de Bavaria, monk of Melk,** 15th cent.
Memoriale seu epistola ad Laurentium abbatem Gottwicensem de vita sua et monachorum in Monasterio Sublacensi, scripta circa 1471. MS. Benediktinerabtei Melk, Austria, codex 91, on inside cover. Duodecimo. Saec. 15.
Microfilm: MnCH proj. no. 1170

Benediktbeuern, Bavaria (Benedictine abbey).

1146 Carmina Burana. Faksimile-Ausgabe der Carmina Burana und der Fragmenta Burana (Clm 4660 und 4660a) der Bayerischen Staatsbibliothek in München . . . Hrsg. von Bernhard Bischoff. München, Prestel-Verlag, 1967.
2 v. facsims. 25 cm.
MnCS

1147 Catalogus codicum manu scriptorum Bibliothecae Regiae Monacensis, num. 4501–5046 ex bibl. Benedictoburana. Monachii, sumptibus Bibliothecae Regiae, 1894.
MnCH

1148 Chronicon Benedictoburanum, in quo ex incunabilis, vicissitudinibus, decrementis, incrementis monasterii, actis abbatum et aliorum virorum historia Germaniae, a saeculo Christi VIII usque ad saeculum XVIII . . . Opus posthumum . . . curante p. Alphonso Haidenfeld. Sumptibus Monasterii Benedictoburani, 1751–53.
2 v. illus. 34 cm.
KAS

1149 **Das Benediktiner-Stift St. Peter;** kurze Geschichte und Beschreibung des Stiftes und seiner Sehenswürdigkeiten, von einem Mitgliede des Stiftes. Salzburg, im Selbstverlage des Stiftes, 1908.
38 p. plates, 17 cm.
KAS

1150 **Die Benediktinerklöster in Baden-Württemberg,** bearb, von Franz Quarthal . . . Augsburg, Verlag Winfried-Werk [in Kommission], 1975.
845 p. illus (part col), maps, 25 cm. (Germania Benedictina, Bd. 5)
MnCS

1151 **Benediktinische Lebensform;** Satzungen der Schweizerischen Benediktinerkon-gregation. Approbiert ad experimentum vom Kongregationskapitel, 1970.
92 p.
MoCo

Benet Lake, Wis. Holy Family Convent. *See* Holy Family Convent, Benet Lake, Wis.

1152 **Benevento, Italy. Santa Sophia (Benedictine convent).**
Annales Beneventani a. 788–1130.
(*In* Monumenta Germaniae historica. Scriptores. Stuttgart, 1963. t. 3, p. 173–185)
MnCS; PLatS

Benoist d'Azy, Paul, 1909–

1153 À travers la Bible; meditations sur l'Ecriture. Paris, Fleurus [1958–].
v. 22 cm. (Action Féconde)
PLatS

1154 L'Eglise et notre vie chrétienne. Paris, Editions Fleurus, 1958.
156 p. 22 cm. (Action Féconde)
PLatS

1155 Une Journée avec le Maitre; retraites du mois pour religieuses. Paris, Editions Fleurus [1956–1960].
3 v. 22 cm.
MnCS

1156 **Benoît, Paul,** 1893–
[Elevations for organ on modal themes]
Fifty elevations for organ on modal themes. New York, J. Fischer [1948].
66 p. 31 cm.
MnCS

1157 **Benoît, Pierre,** 1906–
Dix-septième dimanche après la Pentecôte . . . [Bruges], Biblica [1963].
106 p. 21 cm. (Assemblées du Seigneur, 71)
PLatS

1158 **Benz, Suitbert,** 1927–
Der Rotulus von Ravenna. Nach seiner Herkunft und seiner Bedeutung für Liturgiegeschichte kritisch untersucht . . . Münster i.W., Aschendorff [1967].
xxiii, 372 p. 24 cm. (Liturgiewissenschaftliche Quellen und Forschungen)
InStme; MnCS; PLatS

1159 **Berau, Germany (abbey of Benedictine nuns).**
Constitutionen des Fürstabtes Martin II von St. Blasien für das Nonnenkloster zu Berau. MS. Benediktinerabtei St. Paul im Lavanttal, Austria, codex 222/2. 97 p. Folio. Saec. 18.
Microfilm: MnCH proj. no. 11,988

Berchmans Zwilling, Sister. *See* Zwilling, Berchmans, Sister.

Berchorius, Petrus. *See* Bersuire, Pierre.

1160 **Bérengier, Theophile,** 1827–1897.
Historical sketch of western monachism.
[St. John's Abbey] n.d.
various pagings, 28 cm.
Typescript.
Translation and adaptation made by
Rev. Basil Stegman, O.S.B.
MnCS

1161 **Berger, Placidus,** 1933–
Religiöses Brauchtum im Umkreis der
Sterbeliturgie in Deutschland. Münster,
Regensburg, 1966.
151 p. 23 cm. (Forschungen zur Volks-
kunde, Heft 41)
MnCS

1162 **Berger, Victorin,** 1855–1914.
Wahrheit ohne Dichtung; ein Religions-
buch für gebildete Laien . . . Admont,
Selbstverlage des Verfassers, 1903.
94 p. 20 cm.
MnCS

1163 **Berger, Wilibald,** 1886–1969.
Die Wiener Schotten. Wien, Bergland
Verlag [1962].
71 p. illus. 18 cm. (Oesterreich-Reihe, Bd.
179–181)
MnCS

Berlière, Ursmer, 1861–1932.

1164 Benedictine asceticism, from its origin to
the end of the 12th century . . . Translated by an anonymous author at Benet
Lake Abbey, 1927.
248 p. 28 cm.
Typescript.
MoCo

1165 Les chapitres généraux de l'Ordre de
Saint-Benoît dans la province de Cologne-
Trèves. Bruxelles, Librairie Kiessling et
Cie, 1900–1901.
2 v. 22 cm.
KAS

1166 Les origines de Cîteaux et l'Ordre
bénédictin au XIIe siècle. Louvain, C.
Peeters, 1901.
66 p. 25 cm.
KAS

1167 Lettres des moines d'Afflighem aux
Bénédictins de Saint-Maur, 1642–1672.
Anvers, J. Van Hille-De Backer, 1913.
102–226 p. 23 cm.
Extrait des Annales de l'Académie
royale d'Archéologie de Belgique. Sér. 6,
tom. 5, livr. 2)
KAS

1168 L'ordre monastique, des origines au XIIe
siècle. 2. ed. Paris, Desclée, 1921.
276 p.
MoCo

1169 Les terres & seigneuries de Maredsous
et de Maharenne. Maredsous, Abbaye de
Saint Benoît, 1920.
142 p. plates, 26 cm.
MnCS

1170 (ed) Bulletin d'histoire bénédictine.
He was editor 1901–1925.
CaQStb; KAS; MnCS; PLatS

1171 (ed) Wilhelm, Henry. Nouveau supplé-
ment à l'Histoire littéraire de la Congré-
gation de Saint-Maur. Notes de Henry
Wilhelm, pub. et complétées par Dom
Ursmer Berlière, O.S.B. . . . Paris, A.
Picard, 1908–1932.
3 v. illus. 25 cm.
InStme

1172 **Bernaldus, monk of St. Blasien im
Schwarzwald.**
Apologeticae rationes contra schismati-
corum objectiones: de lege excommunica-
tionis, de vitandis excommunitatis . . .
MS. Benediktinerabtei St. Paul im Lavan-
thal, Austria, codex 24/1. 30 f. Quarto.
Saec. 12.
Microfilm: MnCH proj. no. 11,684

Bernard von Baching, 15th cent.

1173 Epistola contra illicitum carnium esum
monachorum Ordinis S. Benedicti. MS.
Benediktinerabtei Melk, Austria, codex
960, f. 351–390, 404. Quarto. Saec. 15.
Microfilm: MnCH proj. no. 1775

1174 Epistola seu tractatus contra illicitum
carnium esum monachorum O.S.B. MS.
Vienna, Nationalbibliothek, codex 3595, f.
142r–179v. Quarto. Saec. 15.
Microfilm: MnCH proj. no. 16,821

1175 Lamentationes et treni super excidio ac
desolatione conversationis et vitae
monasticae. MS. Benediktinerabtei Melk,
Austria, codex 960, f. 390–403. Quarto.
Saec. 15.
Microfilm: MnCH proj. no. 1775

1176 Opus insigne de spiritualibus sentimen-
tis. MS. Benediktinerabtei Melk, Austria,
codex 773. 405 p. Quarto. Saec. 15.
Microfilm: MnCH proj. no. 1614

1177 Tractatus aureus de tribulatione. MS.
Benediktinerabtei Melk, Austria, codex
648, f. 186r–199v. Quarto. Saec. 15.
Microfilm: MnCH proj. no. 1528

Bernardus I, abbot of Monte Cassino.
See Ayglier, Bernard.

1178 **Bernardus Iterii,** 1163–1225.
Chronicon b. Iterii, armarii monasterii S.
Martialis.
(*In* Chroniques de Saint-Martial de
Limoges . . . Paris, 1974)
KAS

1179 **Bernardus Morlanensis, monk of Cluny,**
fl. 1140.
Bernardi Cluniacensis carmine De Trinitate et de fide catholica . . . Recensuit Katarina Halvarson. Stockholm, Almquist & Wiksell [1963].
160 p. 25 cm.
MnCS; PLatS

1180 **Bernardus Noricus,** fl. 1290–1326.
[Opera]
De ordine episcoporum Laureacensium. De ordine ducum Bawarie sive regum. De origine ducum Austrie. De kathologo abbatum. Narracio de ecclesia Chremsmünster. Epistola de consuetudine regulari. Decretales pro ecclesia Chremsmuenster in causa Manegoldi abbatis. Epistola de cessione abbacie. Diplomata et epistolae novem quae ecclesiam Laurencensem vel Pataviensem concernunt. Legenda de S. Agapito martire. Sermo de S. Agapito martire. Constitutiones monachorum. MS. Benediktinerabtei Kremsmünster, Austria, codex Schatzkasten 3, f. 1r–152v. Saec. 13 et 14.
Microfilm: MnCH proj. no. 382

1181 **Bernhard, Ludger,** 1912–
Athos, Berg der Verklärung. Text von P. Chrysostomus Dalm und P. Ludger Bernhard. [Offenburg, Baden], Burda [1959].
228 p. illus. 31 cm.
MnCS; PLatS

1182 **Bernhard, Ludger,** 1912–
Zu Klemens' von Alexandrien Stromateon III 82, 6; eine quellenkritische Studie.
(*In* Perennitas; Beiträge . . . P. Thomas Michels, O.S.B., zum Geburtstag. Münster, 1963. p. 11–18)
PLatS

1183 **Bernhardus Mellicensis.**
De beato Godhalmo peregrino, cujus ossa in monasterio Mellicensi quiescunt. MS. Vienna, Nationalbibliothek, codex 3256, f. 10v–12v. Quarto. Saec. 16.
Microfilm: MnCH proj. no. 16,505

Berning, Nivelle, Sister, 1916–
1184 Comparative histology of the thymus and adrenal glands in normal infants and infant victims of sudden and unexplained death.
40 p.
Thesis (M.S.)–Marquette University, 1962.
MnStj (Archives)

1185 Effect of beef spleen extract on mitosis in the small intestine of the mouse [by] John C. Fardon, John E. Prince and Sister Nivelle Berning.

Reprinted from: Cancer Research, v. 8, no. 11, Nov., 1948.
MnStj (Archives)

Berno von Reichenau, d. 1048.
1186 Die Briefe des Abtes Bern von Reichenau [von Franz-Josef Schmale]. Stuttgart, W. Kohlhammer [1961].
vii, 78 p. 24 cm.
German or Latin
MnCS

1187 De monochordo mensurando. MS. Vienna, Nationalbibliothek, codex 51, f. 52v–55r. Folio. Saec. 12.
Microfilm: MnCH proj. no. 13,416

1188 Epistola ad Aribonem archiepiscopum Moguntinum, de modo celebrandi adventum Domini, quando Nativitas in feriam secundam incidit. MS. Vienna, Nationalbibliothek, codex 701, f. 138v–140v. Folio. Saec. 12.
Microfilm: MnCH proj. no. 14,027

1189 Initium tonarii. Incipit: Omnis igitur regularis monochordi constitutio. MS. Vienna, Nationalbibliothek, codex 2502, f. 37v–38v. Octavo. Saec. 12.
Microfilm: MnCH proj. no. 15,815

1190 Liber de musica, qui inscribitur Tonarius. MS. Benediktinerabtei Melk, Austria, codex 950, f. 113r–126v. Quarto. Saec. 14.
Microfilm: MnCH proj. no. 1747

1191 Musica s. prologus in tonarium. MS. Vienna, Nationalbibliothek, codex 51, f. 49r–52v. Folio. Saec. 12.
Microfilm: MnCH proj. no. 13,416

1192 Tonarius. MS. Benediktinerabtei St. Paul im Lavanttal, Austria, codex 110/6. 9 f. Quarto. Saec. 11.
Microfilm: MnCH proj. no. 12,701

1193 Tonarius. MS. Vienna, Nationalbibliothek, codex 51, f. 62v–70v. Folio. Saec. 12.
Microfilm: MnCH proj. no. 13,416

1194 Vita S. Udalrici episcopi. MS. Cistercienserabtei Rein, Austria, codex 36, f. 239r–255r. Quarto. Saec. 15.
Microfilm: MnCH proj. no. 7432

1195 Vita S. Udalrici episcopi Augustani. MS. Vienna, Schottenstift, codex 210, f. 1r–38r. Quarto. Saec. 14.
Microfilm: MnCH proj. no. 3907

1196 Vita S. Ulrici. MS. Vienna, Nationalbibliothek, codex 573, f. 26r–107r. Quarto. Saec. 12.
Microfilm: MnCH proj. no. 13,904

1197 Vita S. Udalrici episcopi Augustani. MS. Vienna, Nationalbibliothek, codex 4028, f. 12r–27v. Quarto. Saec. 15.
Microfilm: MnCH proj. no. 17,310

1198   Vita S. Meginradi, ex antiquissimis manu scriptis membranis nostrae bibliothecae sumta, anonymo quidem, sed, meo iudicio, Bernone auctore.
       (*In* Hartmann, Christopher. Annales heremi Dei Parae Matris monasterii in Helvetia. Friburgi Brisg., 1612. 8 p. apud finem)
       InStme; PLatS

1198a **Berres, Peregrin Jerome,** 1930–
       Easter Vigil slide packets. Collegeville, Minn., The Liturgical Press, 1979.
       80 slides.
       MnCS

       Bersuire, Pierre, 1290 (ca.)–1362.
1199   Reductorium morale, liber XV.
       (*In* Metamorphosis ouidiana moraliter a Magistro Thoma Walleys anglico . . . Utrecht, 1960–62. 189 leaves. 33 cm.)
       PLatS

1200   Repertorium. MS. Benediktinerabtei Michaelbeuern, Austria, codex cart. 5–8. 4 vols. Folio. Saec. 14–15.
       Microfilm: MnCH proj. no. 11,508–11,511

1201   **Bertaud, Emile,** 1909–
       Spiritualité de l'action; à l'école de Monsieur Vincent. Textes recueillis par Dom René-Jean Hesbert et Dom Emile Bertaud. Paris, Editions Alsatia [1960].
       204 p. illus. 19 cm.

       Bertharius, Saint, abbot of Monte Cassino.
1202   Homilia in laudem S. Scholasticae. MS. Benediktinerabtei St. Peter, Salzburg, codex a.VI.46, f. 78r–79r. Quarto. Saec. 15.
       Microfilm: MnCH proj. no. 10,119

1203   Sermo de Sancta Scholastica. MS. Benediktinerabtei Melk, Austria, codex 1386, f. 31v–59v. Duodecimo. Saec. 15.
       Microfilm: MnCH proj. no. 1908

1204   **Besange, Hieronymus,** 1726–1781.
       Exercitationes religiosae singvlis diebvs, hebdomadis, et mensibvs, assvmendae ex S. Scriptvra, ss. patribvs, aliisqve probatissimis scriptoribvs collectae . . . Styrae, Gregorius Menhardt, 1757.
       [28], 216, 464, [24] p. 21 cm.
       KAS; MnCS

       Besse, Jean Martial Léon, 1861–1920.
1205   Le Cardinal Pie; sa vie, son action religieuse et sociale. Paris, P. J. Béduchaud, 1903.
       xi, 168 p. 19 cm.
       MnCS

1206   Les fondateurs de la Congrégation de Saint-Maur. Lille, H. Morel, 1902.
       36 p.

       Extrait de la Revue des sciences ecclésiastiques.
       NcBe

1207   (2dary) Beaunier, Benedictine monk, fl. 1726. Abbayes et prieurés de l'ancienne France . . . Paris, 1905–
       CtBeR; KAS; MnCS

1208   **Bessler, Willibrord,** 1875–1926.
       Aufsatzfreuden; Winke und Wege beim Aufsatzschreiben Freuden zu erlegen. Donauworth, Ludwig Auer, n.d.
       301 p. 20 cm.
       PSaS

1209   **Beste, Ulric,** 1885–1976.
       Introductio in Codicem, quam in usum et utilitatem scholas et cleri ad promptam expeditamque canonum interpretationem paravit et edidit R. P. Udalricus Beste. Editio 5. Neapoli, M. D'Auria, 1961.
       1117 p. 24 cm.
       InStme; MnCS

1210   **Beste, Ulric,** 1885–1976.
       Dictionarium morale et canonicum, ed. Pietro Palazzini. Romae, Officium Libri Catholici, 1962–
       Rev. mus P. Udalricus Beste O.S.B. is listed among the "cooperatores" in volume one and contributed articles to the dictionary.
       PLatS

1210a De privilegiis Ord S. Benedicti.
       168 p. 28 cm. Cum indice.
       Typescript, 1922.
       MnCS (Archives)

       Betschart, Ildefons, 1903–1959.
1211   Salzburg und Einsiedeln; das Kräftespiel zweier Kulturzentren. Einsiedeln, J. & K. Eberle, 1951.
       100 p. 21 cm.
       InStme

1212   Das Wesen der Strafe; Untersuchungen über Sein und Wert der Strafe in phänomenologischer und aristotelischthomistischer Schau. Einsiedeln, Benziger [1940].
       143 p. 23 cm.
       InStme

1213   (2dary) Herbrich, Elisabeth, ed. Der Mensch als Persönlichkeit und Problem. 1963.
       MnCS

1214   **Bettencourt, Estevao Tavares,** 1919–
       The reformed divine office, a font of spiritual life.
       (*In* Barauna, Guilherme, ed. The liturgy of Vatican II; a symposium. 1966. p. 187–208)
       PLatS

Beuron, Germany (Benedictine abbey).

1215　Aus der Geschichte der lateinischen Bibel. Freiburg i.B., Herder, 1957–
　　　v. (various sizes) 32, 35 cm. (Vetus Latina. Ergänzende Schriftenreihe)
　　　MnCS; KAS; PLatS

1216　Beuron: 1863–1963. Festschrift zum 100-jährigen Bestehen der Erzabtei St. Martin. Beuron (Hohenzollern), Beuroner Kunstverlag [1963]
　　　566 p. plates (part col.) 24 cm.
　　　KAS; MnCS; MoCo; NbElm; PLatS

1217　Messantiphonar; die Psalmen und Antiphonen des römischen Messbuches für gemeinschaftliche deutsche Messfeiern. Hrsg. von Benediktinern der Erzabtei Beuron. Freiburg, Herder [1953]
　　　640 p. 16 cm.
　　　MnCS

1218　Muster Beuroner Bilder, ein- und mehrfarbig. Beuron (Hohenzollern), Verlag der Kunstschule, n.d.
　　　39 p. mounted col. pictures, 18 cm.
　　　MnCS

1219　Schott: Messbuch der heiligen Kirche, mit liturgischen Erklärungen und kurzen Lebensbeschreibungen der Heiligen. Neubearbeitet von Mönchen der Erzabtei Beuron. Jubiläums-Auflage, 1884–1934. Freiburg i.B., Herder [1934].
　　　xii, 68–998, [202], xx, 76 p. illus., music. 16 cm.
　　　MnCS

1220　Spicilegium palimpsestorum; arte photographica paratum per S. Benedicti monachos Archiabbatiae Beuronensis. 1– Beuronae; Lipsiae, apud O. Harrassowitz, 1913–
　　　v. facsims., plates, 39 cm.
　　　PLatS

1221　Das Tagzeitenbuch des monastischen Breviers (Diurnale monasticum) im Anschluss an die Messbücher von Anselm Schott, O.S.B., hrsg. von der Erzabtei Beuron. 2. Auflage. Regensburg, Verlag Friedrich Pustet, 1949.
　　　36, 1670 p. 16 cm.
　　　Latin and German on facing columns.
　　　MnCS

1222　Die XIV Stationen des heiligen Kreuzwegs, nach Composition der Malerschüler des Klosters Beuron. Mit einleitendem und erklärendem Text von Paul Keppler. 2. Aufl. Freiburg im Breisgau, Herder, 1892.
　　　14 plates, 34 x 41 cm.
　　　KAS

1223　(ed) Die Regel des hl. Benedikt. Hrsg. von der Erzabtei Beuron. [10. Aufl.].

Beuron, Hohenzollern, Beuroner Kunstverlag [1965]
　　　137 p. 17 cm.
　　　PLatS

1223a　Regel des hl. Benedict. Hrsg. von der Erzabtei Beuron. 11. Aufl. Beuron, Kunstverlag, 1977.
　　　143 p.
　　　MnCS

1224　(2dary) Fischer, Bonifatius. Vetus Latina Institut der Erzabtei Beuron. Bericht 3. Beuron/Hohenzollern, 1969.
　　　31 p. 21 cm.
　　　MnCS; PLatS

1225　(2dary) Leben und Regel des heiligen Vaters Benediktus. Mit 75 Illustrationen nach Compositionen der Beuroner Kunstschule. 2. Aufl. Prag, Abtei Emaus, 1902.
　　　214 p. illus., plates, 22 cm.
　　　MnCS

1226　(tr) Das Römische Martyrologium. Uebersetzt von den Benediktinern der Erzabtei Beuron. 3. neubearb. Aufl. Regensburg, R. Pustet [1962]
　　　395 p. 21 cm.
　　　KAS

1227　**Bévenot, Hugh Gaston,** 1891–1936.
　　　(tr) Grandmaison, Fernand de. Twenty cures at Lourdes, medically discussed. Authorized translation by Hugo G. Bevenot, O.S.B., and Luke Izard, O.S.B. . . . St. Louis, Herder [1912?]
　　　xix, 272 p. 20 cm.
　　　NdRi; PLatS

1228　**Bévenot, Laurence,** 1901–
　　　Music in worship.
　　　(*In* Crichton, James D., ed. The liturgy and the future. 1966. p. 151–163)
　　　PLatS

1229　**Beverley Minster, England.**
　　　Memorials of Beverley minster; the chapter act book of the collegiate church of S. John of Beverley, A.D. 1285–1347, with illustrative documents and introduction by Arthur Francis Leach . . . Durham [England], Pub. for the Society by Andrews & Co., 1898–1903.
　　　2 v. 23 cm. (The publications of the Surtees Society, vol. XCVIII, CVIII)
　　　MnCS

Biggs, Anselm Gordon, 1914–

1230　The Benedictine life. Belmont, N.C., 1969.
　　　unpaged
　　　NcBe

1231　The Benedictine life. Revised. Belmont, N.C., Belmont Abbey, 1974.

19 p.
NcBe

1232 Don Diego Gelmirez, first archbishop of Compostela; his life as revealed in the Historia Compostellana.
138 p.
Thesis (M.A.)–Catholic University of America, 1946.
NcBe

Bihlmeyer, Hildebrand, 1873–1924.

1233 An heiliger Stätte; berühmte Wallfahrtsorte und Heiligtümer der katholischen Welt in Wort und Bild . . . Berlin, Sankt Augustinus-Verlag, 1924.
200 p.
NcBe

1234 Das Messbuch der heiligen Kirche, lateinisch und deutsch . . . Vollständige Neubearbeitung durch Mönche der Erzbtei Beuron, auf Grund des neuen Missale Romanum, hrsg. von Pius Bihlmeyer, O.S.B. 23. Aufl. Freiburg i.B., St. Louis, Herder [1922].
60, 832, 220 p. illus. 15 cm.
MnCS; NcBe

1235 **Billet, Bernard,** 1919–
Croissance de Lourdes et vocation de Bernadette, 30 aout 1862–1 3 juillet 1866, avec deux dossiers annexes par . . . René Laurentin . . . Lourdes Oeuvre de la Grotte [1966].
560 p. illus. 26 cm.
MnCS

1236 **Birkle, Suitbertus,** 1876–1926.
Der Choral das Ideal der kathol. Kirchenmusik. Graz, "Styria," 1906.
xii, 327 p. music. 20 cm.
InStme

1237 **Biroat, Jacques,** d. 1666.
The eucharistic life of Jesus Christ. Translated from the 5th ed. (Paris, 1676) by Edward G. Varnish, with an introduction by Rev. Arthur Tooth . . . London, Swan Sonnenschein, Lowrey & Co. [1886?]
xxxi, 232 p. 23 cm.
InStme

Birt, Henry Norbert, 1861–1919.

1238 "In the net," or, Advertisement by libel. London, Catholic Truth Society, 1906.
24 p. 18 cm.
MnCS

1239 The line of cleavage under Elizabeth. London, Catholic Truth Society, 1929.
38 p. 19 cm.
PLatS

1240 The Roman Breviary. London, Catholic Truth Society [1914].
16 p. 19 cm.
KAS

1241 **Bischof, Margo, Sister,** 1934–
The value of business offerings in the college preparatory high school.
24 p.
Thesis (M.A.)–Catholic University of America, 1969.
Typescript.
MnStj (Archives)

1242 **Blaes, Arnold,** 1927–
The origin, symbolism, and purpose of the canonical hours . . . With introduction by Dom Patrick Cummins . . . Conception, Mo., Conception Abbey Press [c 1956].
50 p. 21 cm.
KAS

Blaschkewitz, Joannes Chrysostomus, 1915–

1243 Die Glaubenswelt der orthodoxen Kirche [von] Bernhard Schultze [und] Johannes Chrysostomus. Salzburg, O. Müller [1961].
253 p. 18 cm. (Reihe-Wort und Antwort, Bd. 26)
PLatS

1244 Die Katholische Kirche und die Orthodoxie. Recklinghausen, Paulus Verlag [1960].
28 p. 16 cm. (Dass alle eins seien)
MnCS

1245 Kirchengeschichte Russlands der neuesten Zeit [von] Johannes Chrysostomus. München, A. Pustet [1965–].
v. ports. 22 cm. (Sammlung Wissenschaft und Gegenwart)
PLatS

1246 Die "Pomorskie Otvety" als Denkmal der Anschauungen der Russischen Altgläubigen gegen Ende des 1. Viertels des XVIII. Jahrhunderts. Roma, Pont. Institutum Orientalium Studiorum, 1957.
209 p. 24 cm. (Orientalia Christiana analecta, 148)
InStme

Blecker, Michael, 1931–

1247 Medieval monastic conspiracies and contemporary parallels [phonotape-cassette]. Collegeville, 1973.
1 cassette.
Address delivered at St. John's University Colloquium December 10, 1973. Response by Alfred Deutsch, O.S.B.
MnCS

1248 The two laws and Benedictine monasticism; a study in Benedictine government, 1198–1216.
Thesis (Ph.D.)–University of Wisconsin, 1964.
327 p. 22 cm.
MnCS; NcBe

1249 **Blenkner, Louis,** 1922–
The theological structure of "Pearl."
New York, Fordham University, 1968.
43–75 p.
Reprint of article in Traditio.
MnStj

Blois, Louis de, 1506–1566.
1250 Favus mellis, composita verba, Prov. 16,
24. Sive sententiae mellifluae, ex omnibus
operibus venerabilis Ludovici Blosii, abbatis Laetiensis Ord. S. Bened. collectae
. . . opere P. Philippi Jacobi Steyrer,
ejusdem ordinis . . . n.p., Johannes Conradus Wohler, 1742.
[46], 446, [16] p. 17 cm.
KAS; InStme; MnCS; MoCo

1251 Institutio spiritualis, das ist, Geistliche
ler und unterweisung allen denen so
begeren volkomen zu werden. In Teutsch
gebracht durch Philippum Dobreiner von
Türschenreuth, 1564. MS. Vienna, Nationalbibliothek, codex 11727. 160 f.
Octavo. Saec. 16.
Microfilm: MnCH proj. no. 19,848

1252 Institvtio spiritvalis, non parvm vtilis iis,
qvi ad vitae perfectionem contendunt:
itemq Exercitium piarum precationum. Accessit Apologia pro D. Ioanne Thaulero,
vnacum breui Regula tyronis spiritualis.
Lovanii, A. M. Bergagne, 1553.
14 leaves, 122 [i.e. 244] p. 16 cm.
First edition.
KAS

1253 Speculum monachorum a Dacryano Ordinis Sancti Benedicti abbate conscriptum.
Antehac nusquam excusum. Louanij,
venundantur a B. Grauio, 1538.
[53] p. 20 cm.
KAS; PLatS

1254 Speculum monachorum a Dacryano Ordinis S. Benedicti abbate conscriptum,
multo quam antea, in hac secunda aedi-
tione castigatius. Louanij, ex officina
Bartholomei Gravij, 1549.
[110] p. 14 cm.
KAS

Blois, Louis de, 1506–1566.
1255 Trost für Kleinmüthige. Neu in's
Deutsche übersetzt von einem katholischen
Geistlichen. Regensburg, G. J. Manz, 1857.
225 p.
NdRi

1256 (2dary) Nakateni, Wilhelm, S.J. Coeleste
palmetum ad ubertatem et sacras delicias
excultum . . . Plurimis novis iisque lectis-
simis sanctorum Patrum et . . . L. Blosii
obsitum floribus pietatis. Ed. 4a. Mechliniae, H. Dessain, 1859.

776 p. 15 cm.
MnCS

1257 **Blue Cloud Abbey, Marvin, S.D.**
A Benedictine beginning in Dakota; the
Blue Cloud community's twenty-fifth year.
Blue Cloud Mission Press, 1975.
unpaged, illus.
MoCo

1258 **Blundell, Odo,** 1868–
The Catholic highlands of Scotland.
Edinburgh, Sands & Co., 1909–1917.
2 v. illus. 19 cm.
InStme

1259 **Blyth Priory, England.**
The cartulary of Blyth Priory. Edited by
R. T. Timson . . . London, Her Majesty's
Stationery Office, 1973.
647 p. (Royal Commission on Historical
Manuscripts, no. 17)
NcBe; MnCS

1260 **Bobbio, Italy (Benedictine abbey).**
Epigrammata Bobiensis edidit Wolfgang
Speyer . . . Lipsiae, Teubner, 1963.
xvii, 105 p. facsims 21 cm. (Bib. scrip.
graec. et rom. Teub. From Vatican Library
Latin ms. 2836)
MnCS; PLatS

1261 **Boberek, Aurelius,** 1930–
The liturgy and spiritual growth.
(*In* North American Liturgical Week,
22nd, 1961, p. 97–105)
PLatS

1262 **Bobo, Sebastiano,** 1922–
Orientamento teologico-spirituale dello
studio dell'A.T. nelle recente rinascita
biblica.
(*In* Problemi e orientamenti di spirituala
monastica, biblica, e liturgica, p. [93]–120)
PLatS

1263 **Böck, Michael von.**
Die sieben freien Künste im eilften Jahrhundert. Donauwörth, C. Veith, 1847.
88 p. 19 cm.
KAS

Bodine, Bernadette, Sister.
1264 Development of biochemistry activities
and laboratory experiences for nursing
students based on clinical cases using the
guided design approach.
Thesis (Ph.D.)–University of Northern
Colorado, 1978.
Typescript.
NdRiS

1265 Ethylene production in flax and its rela-
tionship in disease resistence.
Thesis (M.S.)–North Dakota State
University, 1968.
Typescript.
NdRiS

1266 **Boehm, Clement, Sister,** 1904–
The art of practicing. Miami, Whitford
Publications [1957].
4 p.
Address given at a meeting of the Inter-
national Piano Teachers Association in
New York City, August, 1957.
MnStj (Archives)

1267 **Boer, Nicolass,** 1908–
Leeken Breviertj. Roermond-Maaseik, J.
J. Romen [1937?].
437 p. music, 14 cm.
MnCS

Boerius, Petrus. *See* Bohier, Pierre.

1268 **Boerste, M. Aquina, Sister.**
Constructive school discipline in the
elementary grades.
Thesis – University of Notre Dame, 1934.
InFer

1269 **Bogaert, Pierre.**
Apocalypse de Baruch. Introduction,
traduction du Syriaque et commentaire
[par] Pierre Bogaert. Paris, Editions du
Cerf, 1969.
2 v. 20 cm. (Sources chrétiennes, 144,
145)
InStme; MnCS; PLatS

Bogler, Theodor, 1897–1968.

1270 Benedikt und Ignatius: Maria Laach als
Collegium maximum der Gesellschaft Jesu,
1863– , 1872–1892. Maria Laach,
Verlag Ars Liturgica, 1963.
112 p. ports. 23 cm. (Liturgie und
Mönchtum. Laacher Hefte. Heft 32)
MnCS

1271 Beten und Arbeiten; aus Geschichte und
Gegenwart benediktinischen Lebens.
Maria Laach, Verlag Ars Liturgica, 1961)
105 p. plates, 23 cm. (Liturgie und
Mönchtum. Laacher Hefte. Heft 22)
MnCS

1272 Christliche Kunst als Verkündigung.
Maria Laach, Verlag Ars Liturgica, 1953.
112 p. plates, 23 cm. (Liturgie und
Mönchtum. Laacher Heft. 3. Folge. Heft
XIII)
MnCS

1273 Deutsche Liturgie? Sind wir auf dem
Weg dahin? Maria Laach, Verlag Ars
Liturgica, 1967.
130 p. 22 cm. (Liturgie und Mönchtum.
Laacher Hefte. Heft 40)
PLatS

1274 Die Engel in der Welt von heute. Maria
Laach, Verlag Ars Liturgica, 1960.
140 p. plates, 23 cm. (Liturgie und
Mönchtum. Laacher Hefte. Heft XXI)
2. erweiterte Auflage.
MnCS

1275 Erneuerung der Liturgie: Schwierig-
keiten – Wünsche – Vorschläge. Maria
Laach, Verlag Ars Liturgica, 1954.
120 p. plates, 23 cm. (Liturgie und
Mönchtum. Laacher Hefte. 3. Folge. Heft
XIV)
MnCS

1276 Eucharistiefeiern in der Christenheit.
Maria Laach, Verlag Ars Liturgica, 1960.
136 p. plates, 23 cm. (Liturgie und
Mönchtum. Laacher Hefte. Heft 26)
MnCS

1277 Die Familie, Gotteswerk und Menschen-
mühen. Maria Laach, Verlag Ars Liturgica, 1958.
102 p. plates, 23 cm. (Liturgie und
Mönchtum. Laacher Hefte. Heft XXIII)
MnCS

1278 Die Frau im Heil. Maria Laach, Verlag
Ars Liturgica, 1962.
99 p. plates, 23 cm. (Liturgie und Mönchtum. Laacher Hefte. Heft 30)
MnCS; PLatS

1279 Frauen im Bannkreis Christi. Maria
Laach, Verlag Ars Liturgica, 1964.
96 p. plates, 23 cm. (Liturgie und Mönchtum. Laacher Hefte. Heft 35)
MnCS; PLatS

1280 Frömmigkeit. Maria Laach, Verlag Ars
Liturgica, 1960.
159 p. plates, 23 cm. (Liturgie und
Mönchtum. Laacher Hefte. Heft 27)
MnCS

1281 Ist der Mensch von heute noch liturgie-
fähig? Ergebnisse einer Umfrage. Maria
Laach, Verlag Ars Liturgica, 1966.
128 p. plates, 23 cm. (Liturgie und
Mönchtum. Laacher Hefte. Heft 38)
MnCS; PLatS

1282 Kirchenmusik in der Gegenwart. Maria
Laach, Verlag Ars Liturgica, 1956.
111 p. plates, 23 cm. (Liturgie und
Mönchtum. Laacher Hefte. 3. Folge. Heft
XVIII)
MnCS

1283 Leben aus der Taufe [Abt Basilius Ebel
zum 25. Jahrestag seiner äbtlichen Weihe
dargebracht]. Maria Laach, Verlag Ars
Liturgica, 1963–64.
216 p. plates, 23 cm. (Liturgie und
Mönchtum, Laacher Hefte. Heft 33/34)
MnCS

1284 Liturgische Haltung und soziale
Wirklichkeit. Maria Laach, Verlag Ars
Liturgica, 1956.
110 p. plates, 23 cm. (Liturgie und
Mönchtum. Laacher Hefte. Heft XIX)
MnCS

1285   Maria in Liturgie und Lehrwort. Maria Laach, Verlag Ars Liturgica, 1954.
 111 p. plates, 23 cm. (Liturgie und Mönchtum. Laacher Hefte. 3. Folge. Heft XV)
 MnCS

1286   Maria Laach; Vergangenheit und Gegenwart der Abtei am Laacher See. 4., neubearb. Aufl. München, Schnell & Steiner, 1961.
 48 p. illus. 24 cm. (Die Grossen Kunstführer, Bd. 12)
 PLatS

1287   . . . 9. Aufl. München, Schnell & Steiner, 1975.
 26 p. plates, 24 cm.
 MnCS

1288   Maria Laach Abbey. English translation by Margaret Senft-Howie and Radbert Kohlhas. 4th ed. Munich, Zurich, Verlag Schnell & Steiner, 1970.
 14 p. illus. 17 cm.
 PLatS

1289   Der Mensch vor dem Worte Gottes. Maria Laach, Verlag Ars Liturgica, 1953.
 122 p. plates, 23 cm. (Liturgie und Mönchtum. Laacher Hefte. 3. Folge. Heft XII)

1290   Das Menschenbild im Jahr der Kirche; aus Imago Dei gesammelte Aufsätze zur Frage des christlichen Menschenbildes. Düsseldorf, Bastion-Verlag, 1948.
 44 p. 17 cm.
 MnCS

1291   Mönchisches Leben und liturgischer Dienst. Maria Laach, Verlag Ars Liturgica, 1958.
 125 p. 23 cm. (Liturgie und Mönchtum. Laacher Hefte. Heft XXII)
 MnCS

1292   Mönchtum in der Entscheidung. Maria Laach, Verlag Ars Liturgica, 1952.
 110 p. plates, 23 cm. (Liturgie und Mönchtum, Laacher Hefte. Heft XI)
 MnCS

1293   Mönchtum-Aergernis oder Botschaft? Maria Laach, Verlag Ars Liturgica, 1968.
 176 p. 22 cm. (Liturgie und Mönchtum. Laacher Hefte. Heft 43)

1294   Münster am See; Landschaft, Kunst, Kultur, Geschichte, Gegenwart. Ein Laacher Lese- und Bilderbuch. [2. Aufl.] [Honnef/Rhein] H. Peters [1956]
 233 p. illus. 19 cm.

1295   Muttersprache.
 (*In* Sakrale Sprache und kultischer Gesang. p. 31–36)
 PLatS

1296   Nachfolge Christ in Bibel, Liturgie und Spiritualität. Maria Laach, Verlag Ars Liturgica, 1962.
 95 p. plates, 23 cm. (Liturgie und Mönchtum. Laacher Hefte. Heft 31)
 MnCS

1297   Oesterliches Heilsmysterium; das Paschamysterium – Grundmotiv der Liturgie-Konstitution. Maria Laach, Verlag Ars Liturgica, 1965.
 105 p. plates, 23 cm. (Liturgie und Mönchtum. Laacher Hefte. Heft 36)
 MnCS; PLatS

1298   Ostern – Fest der Auferstehung heute. Maria Laach, Verlag Ars Liturgica, 1968.
 116 p. illus. 22 cm.
 PLatS

1299   Das Paschamysterium auf Elfenbeinplaketten des frühen Mittelalters.
 (*In* Osterliches Heilsmysterium, p. 88–104. Liturgie und Mönchtum, Heft 36)
 PLatS

1300   Priestertum und Mönchtum. Maria Laach, Verlag Ars Liturgica, 1961.
 119 p. plates, 23 cm. (Liturgie und Mönchtum. Laacher Hefte. Heft 29)
 MnCS

1301   Das Sakrale im Widerspruch. Maria Laach, Verlag Ars Liturgica, 1967.
 148 p. 22 cm. (Liturgie und Mönchtum. Laacher Hefte. Heft 41)
 PLatS

1302   Sakrale Sprache und kultischer Gesang. Maria Laach, Verlag Ars Liturgica, 1965.
 130 p. plates, 23 cm. (Liturgie und Mönchtum. Laacher Hefte. Heft 37)
 MnCS

1303   Sechs Miniaturen zum Kirchenjahr. Maria Laach, Verlag Ars Liturgica, n.d.
 6 illustrations with introduction.
 MnStj

1304   Spiel und Feier; ihre Gestaltung aus dem Geist der Liturgie. Maria Laach, Verlag Ars Liturgica, 1955.
 112 p. plates, 23 cm. (Liturgie und Mönchtum. Laacher Hefte. 3. Folge. Heft XVI)
 MnCS

1305   Suche den Frieden und jage ihm nach. Recklinghausen, Paulus Verlag [1964].
 350 p. 22 cm.
 PLatS

1306   Symbole. [Limburg an der Lahn], Ars Liturgica, 1962.
 64 p. illus. 18 cm. (Von christlichen Sein und Leben, 5)
 MnCS; PLatS

1307   Tod und Leben; von den letzten Dingen. Maria Laach, Verlag Ars Liturgica, 1959.

126 p. illus. 23 cm. (Liturgie und Mönch-tum. Laacher Hefte. Heft 25)
MnCS

1308   Weg-Wahrheit – Leben: Meditationen. Maria Laach, Verlag Ars Liturgica, 1960.
700 p. 18 cm. (Von christlichen Sein und Leben, 1)
PLatS

1309   Weihnachten heute; das Weinachtsfest in der pluralistischen Gesellschaft. Maria Laach, Verlag Ars Liturgica, 1966.
120 p. plates, 23 cm. (Liturgie und Mönchtum. Heft 39)
MnCS; PLatS

1310   (ed) Alle Kirchen Gesäng und Gebeet des gantzen Jars von der heiligen Christen-lichen Kirchen angenommen/und bissher in löblichen brauch erhalten/Vom Introit der Mess biss auff die Complent. Darneben die benedeyung der Liecht/der Palm/des Deürs/des Osterstocks/der Tauff/und der Kreiitter. Faksimile-Ausgabe. In Verbin-dung mit R. Bellm, hrsg. von Theodor Bogler. Maria Laach, Verlag Ars Litur-gica, 1964.
147 p., 355 leaves, 224 leaves, illus., fac-sims. 17 cm.
Special title page: Deutsches Messbuch von M. Christophorus Flurheym. 1529.
MnCS; PLatS

Bohier, Pierre, bp. of Orvieto, 14th cent.

1311   Regula S. Patris Benedicti, cum com-mentario Petri Boerii. MS. Benedik-tinerabtei Melk, Austria, codex 3, f. 1r–71v. Folio. Saec. 14.
Microfilm: MnCH proj. no. 2124

1312   Commentarium in Regulam S. Benedicti. MS. Subiaco, Italy (Benedictine abbey), codex 61. 340 f. Quarto. Saec. 14.
Microfilm: MnCH

1313   Commentum Regulae S. Benedicti. MS. Vienna, Schottenstift, codex 356, f. 3r–242v. Folio. Saec. 15.
Microfilm: MnCH proj. no. 4206

1314   Commentarius in Speculum monachorum Bernardi Cassinensis ad Nar-bonensem episcopum. MS. Vienna, Na-tionalbibliothek, codex 5135, f. 144r–191r. Folio. Saec. 15.
Microfilm: MnCH proj. no. 18,301

1315   Commentarius in Speculum Regulae monachorum b. Ben. abb. MS. Benedik-tinerabtei Fiecht, codex 213, f. 137v–158r.
Microfilm: MnCH proj. no. 28,855

1316   Commentarius super Constitutionibus O.S.B. MS. Benediktinerabtei Fiecht, Austria, codex 213, f. 1r–114r. Folio. Saec. 14/15.
Microfilm: MnCH proj. no. 28,855

1317   Glosela ex Petro Boerii, excerpta in Regulam b. patris Benedicti. MS. Benedik-tinerabtei Melk, Austria, codex 436, f. 29r–63b. Folio. Saec. 15.
Microfilm: MnCH proj. no. 1406

1318   Privilegium concessum capitulo provin-ciali monachorum nigrorum provinciae Narboensis, cum commentario Petri Boerii. MS. Benediktinerabtei Melk, Austria, codex 3, f. 117v–120v. Folio. Saec. 14.
Microfilm: MnCH proj. no. 2124

1319   **Boland, Paschal**, 1912–1979.
In praise of Mary. St. Meinrad, Ind., Grail Publications, 1955.
InFer

1320   **Bollmann, Henry J.**, 1915–
The validity of the time of death by the insect fauna found on cadavers.
86 p.
Thesis (M.S.) – Catholic University of America, 1951.
NcBe

1321   **Bolton, Bernard Basil.**
The Rule of Saint Benedict for monasteries. A translation by Dom Ber-nard Basil Bolton, O.S.B. Newport, Gwent, England, R. H. Johns Ltd [1969]
81 p. 18 cm.
MoCo; PLatS

Bomm, Urban, 1901–

1322   Gottesdienstliches Wort bei den Exe-quien für Vater Abt Basilius Eben. Maria Laach, 1968.
3 p. 21 cm. (In viam pacis. Nr. 58)
MnCS

1323   Lateinisch-deutsches Volksmessbuch; das vollständige römische Messbuch für alle Tage des Jahres. Mit Erklärungen und einem Choralanhang von Urbanus Bomm. Einsiedeln, Benziger [1956].
lv, 1744, 80, [20] p. music, 17 cm.
MnCS

Bonazzi, Benedetto, 1840–1915.

1324   Il giubileo papale di Leone XIII. La prov-videnza e la vigoria sovrunana dei ponte-fici; poche parole ai monaci, al clero, ai giovani educandi e al popolo . . . Salerno, Jovane, 1902.
24 p. 25 cm.
MnCS

1325   Poche parole pronunziate per la santa memoria di d. Michele Morcaldi OSB, abate ordinario della SS. Trinita dei Tirreni, nella Chiesa di S. Ferdinando in Napoli il XIII marzo MCCCCXCIV. Napoli, R. Tipo-grafia Francesco Giannini, 1894.
20 p. 20 cm.
PLatS

1326 **Bondonnet, Jean,** 1594-1664.
Les vies des evesqves du Mans restitvées et corrigées, avec plvsievrs belles remarqves svr la chronologie. Paris, Edme Martin, 1641.
740, 388 p. tables, 23 cm.
MnCS

Boniface, Saint, abp. of Mainz, 680-755.
1327 Epistola ad Cudbertum.
(*In* Bede the Venerable. Historia ecclesiastica gentis Anglorum . . . cum Epistola Bonifacii ad Cudberthum, cura Georgii H. Moberly. Oxonii, Clarendon Press, 1869. Reissued 1881. xxviii, 442 p.)
MnCS; PLatS

1328 The English correspondence of Saint Boniface: being for the most part letters exchanged between the apostle of the Germans and his English friends, translated and edited with an introductory sketch of the saint's life by Edward Kylie. New York, Cooper Square Publishers, 1966.
xiv, 212 p. 17 cm. (The Medieval Library)
PLatS

1329 S. Bonifatii et Lulli Epistolae. Edidit E. Dümmler.
(*In* Monumenta Germaniae historica. Epistolae. Berlin, 1957. t. 3, p. 215-433)
Reprint of Berlin edition of 1892.
PLatS

1330 Sancti Bonifacii epistolae. Codex Vindobonensis 751 der Oesterreichischen Nationalbibliothek. Faksimile-Ausgabe der Wiener Handschrift der Briefe des heiligen Bonifatius. Einführung Franz Unterkircher. Graz, Austria, Akedemische Druck u. Verlagsanstalt, 1971.
38 p. 77 p. of plates, 35 cm. (Codices selecti, Phototypice, v. 24)
PLatS

1331 [Epistolae. German]
Briefe des Bonifatius. Willibalds Leben des Bonifatius. Nebst einigen zeitgenössischen Dokumenten. Unter Benützung der Uebersetzungen von M. Tangl und Ph.H. Külb neu bearb. von Reinhold Rau. Darmstadt, Wissenschaftliche Buchgessellschaft, 1968.
535 p. 23 cm. (Ausgewählte Quellen zur deutschen Geschichte des Mittelalters, Bd. IVb)
MnCS

1332 **Bonstetten, Albertus von.**
Gesta monasterii Einsiedelensis. MS. Benediktinerabtei St. Paul im Lavanttal, Austria, codex 8/2, part II. Folio. Saec. 16.
Microfilm: MnCH proj. no. 11,741

1333 **Book of prayer for personal use;** a short breviary abridged and simplified by monks of St. John's Abbey from the Liturgia horarum. Wholly revised fourth edition.
Collegeville, Minn. Saint John's Abbey Press, 1975.
1823 p. 18 cm.
MnCS

1334 **Boon, Amand,** 1898-
Pachomiana latina: Règle et épitres de S. Pachome, épitre de S. Théodore . . . édité par Amand Boon. Louvain, Bureaux de la Revue, 1932.
lix, 209 p. 22 cm. (Bibliothèque de la Revue d'histoire ecclésiastique, fasc. 7)
InStme

Boppert, Konrad, 1750-1811.
1335 Liber sacerdotalis; seu, Scutum fidei ad usus quotidianos sacerdotum. Editio belgica. Bruxellis, H. Goemaere, 1855-56.
6 v. 15 cm.
KAS; PLatS

1336 Scutum fidei ad usus quodidianos sacerdotum. Ed. 3. Lutetiae Parisiorum, Julien, Lanier et Socii, 1853-55.
12 v. in 6, 18 cm.
KAS; PLatS

1337 **Borghini, Vincenzo,** 1515-1580.
Discorsi di Vincenzo Borghini con le annotazioni di Domenico Maria Manni. Milano, dalla Società tipografica de Classici Italiani, 1808-09.
4 v. 20 cm.
PLatS

1338 **Borlenghi, Federico.**
Elementi di canto corale che possono servire anche d'iniziamento al canto figurato. Parma, dalla Tipografia Reale, 1857.
54 p. 25 cm.
PLatS

Bornert, René, 1931-
1339 Les Commentaires byzantins de la divine liturgie du VIIe au XVe siècle . . . Paris, Institut français d'études byzantines, 1966.
293 p. 25 cm. (Archives de l'Orient chrétien, 9)
InStme; PLatS

1340 Deuxième dimanche de Carême . . . [Bruges], Biblica [1963]
107 p. 21 cm. (Assemblées du Seigneur, 28)
PLatS

1341 Fête de la Pentecôte . . . [Bruges], Biblica [1963]
114 p. 21 cm. (Assemblées du Seigneur, 51)
PLatS

1342 (ed) Cabasilas, Nicolas. Explication de la divine liturgie. Traduction et notes de Séverien Salaville. 2. éd., munie du texte

grec, rev. et augm. par René . . . Paris, Editions du Cerf, 1967.
405 p. 20 cm. (Sources chrétiennes, no. 4 bis)
InStme; MnCS

1343   **Böser, Fidelis,** 1876–
Der rhythmische Vortrag des gregorianischen Chorals. Zum Gebrauch bei Instruktionskursen und zum Selbstunterricht. Düsseldorf, L. Schwann, 1910.
31 p. illus. (music) 22 cm.
PLatS

Botte, Bernard, 1893–
1344   Les anaphores syriennes orientales.
(*In* Eucharistiens d'Orient et d'Occident. Paris, 1970. v. 2, p. 7–24)
PLatS

1345   The Church at prayer: introduction to the liturgy . . . Translators: Robert Fisher and others. Editors of the English edition: Austin Flannery [and] Vincent Ryan. New York, Desclée Co., 1968–
v. illus. 22 cm.
InStme; PLatS

1346   Collegial character of the priesthood and the episcopate [translated by Ruth Dowd, R.S.C.J.]
(*In* The Church and ecumenism . . . v. 4, p. 177–184)
PLatS

1347   Collegiate character of the presbyterate and episcopate.
(*In* The Sacrament of holy orders . . . London, 1962. p. 75–97)
PLatS

1348   Le concile et les conciles; contribution à l'histoire de la vie conciliaire de l'Eglise . . . Chevetogne, 1960.
xix, 348 p. 23 cm.
KySu; MnCS

1349   Le Dimanche [par] Dom Botte [et al]. Paris, Editions du Cerf, 1965.
184 p. 21 cm. (Lex orandi, 39)
PLatS

1350   Les dénominations du dimanche dans la tradition chrétienne.
(*In* Le Dimanche . . . Paris, 1965. p. 7–28)
PLatS

1351   L'église en prière; introduction à la liturgie [par] A. G. Martimort avec la collaboration de R. Béraudy, B. Botte [et al]. Paris, Desclée et cie [1961].
xv, 916 p. 23 cm.
PLatS

1352   Eucharisties d'Orient et Occident; semaine liturgique de l'Institut Saint-Serge [par] B. Botte [et al]. Paris, Editions du Cerf, 1970.

2 v. 20 cm. (Lex orandi, no. 46–47)
PLatS

1353   Holy orders in the ordination prayers.
(*In* The sacrament of holy orders . . . London, 1962. p. 5–23)
PLatS

1354   Le mouvement liturgique; témoignage et souvenirs. Paris, Desclée [1973]
211 p. illus. 22 cm.
InStme

1355   Oikonomia; quelques emplois spécifiquement chrétiens.
(*In* Corona gratiarum; miscellanea patristica . . . Brugge, 1975. v. 1, p. 3–9)
PLatS

1356   Les origines de la noël et de l'epiphanie; étude historique. Louvain, Abbaye du Mont César, 1932.
105 p. 24 cm.
CaQMo; CaQStB; MoCo; KAS; InStme

1357   Les prière des heures [par] Monseigneur Cassien [Joannes Cassianus] [et] Bernard Botte. Paris, Editions du Cerf, 1963.
334 p. 21 cm. (Lex orandi, 35)
InStme; MnCS; PLatS

1358   La sputation, antique rite baptismal?
(*In* Mélanges offerts à Mademoiselle Christine Mohrmann. Utrecht, 1963. p. 196–201)
PLatS

1359   (ed and tr) Ambrose, Saint. Des sacrements. Des mystères. Texte établi, traduit et annoté par dom Bernard Botte. Nouv. éd. rev. et a ugm. de l'explication du symbole. Paris, Editions du Cerf, 1961.
128, 138 p. 21 cm. (Sources chrétiennes [25 bis])
MnCS; NcBe
Latin and French text on opposite pages numbered in duplicate.

1360   (ed) Hippolytus, Saint. La tradition apostolique de Saint Hippolyte. Essai de reconstitution par Dom Bernard Botte, O.S.B. Münster Westf., Aschendorff [1963].
xliv, 112 p. 25 cm. (Liturgiewissenschaftliche Quellen und Forschungen, Heft 39)
Text (Latin and French) of Traditio apostolica.
InStme; MnCS; PLatS

1361   (tr) Le Nouveau Testament. Traduction nouvelle d'après le texte grec par Dom Bernard Botte, O.S.B. Turnhout, Brepols [1944]
MnCS

1362   **Botte, Xavier,** 1907–
(tr) Laan, Joannes van der. Le nombre plastique; quinze leçons sur l'ordinnance

architectionique. Traduit du manuscrit hollandais par Dom Xavier Botte. Leiden, E. J. Brill, 1960.
  xvi, 135 p. diagrs. 24 cm.
  PLatS

Botz, Paschal Robert, 1905–
1363 Benedictine poverty (workshop paper given at Sacred Heart Convent, Yankton, S.D., 1962).
  38 p. 28 cm.
  Typescript.
  MnCS (Archives)

1364 Benedictine theology (paper at Novice Mistresses Workshop at Villa St. Scholastica, Duluth, Minn., 1955)
  16 p. 28 cm.
  Multilithed.
  MnCS (Archives)

1365 Blessed old age. Collegeville, Minn., The Liturgical Press [c 1961].
  23 p. 14 cm. (Popular liturgical library)
  MnCS

1366 Characteristics of Benedictine education.
  (*In* The National Benedictine Education Association: Bulletin, v. 22 (1939), p. 54–63)
  MnCS

1367 The Holy Rule [of St. Benedict] in the modern world.
  (*In* St. Joseph magazine, v. 48 (1947), p. 30–33)
  MnCS

1368 Meaning of the altar.
  Reprinted from Sponsa Regis, Feb., 1956, p. 3–12.
  MnCS

1369 A new secular spiritual order (Spiritual Union of the Diocese of Saint Cloud). [Collegeville, Minn., St. John's Abbey, 1968]
  17 p. 28 cm.
  Multilithed.
  MnCS

1370 The prayer of Christ.
  10 p. 28 cm.
  Multilithed.
  MnCS (Archives)

1371 Prayer of faith.
  52 p. 28 cm.
  Typescript.
  MnCS (Archives)

1372 Runways to God; the psalms as prayer. Collegeville, Minn., The Liturgical Press [1979].
  xiii, 345 p. 20 cm.
  MnCS

1373 Sisters in the Church today.
  13 p. 28 cm.
  Multilithed.
  MnCS (Archives)

1374 The spiritual direction of professed brothers.
  (*In* Report of the Benedictine Brother Instructors' Convention, St. Meinrad Abbey, St. Meinrad, Ind., June 9–11, 1942. p. 102–122)
  MnCS

1375 Thanksgiving after Holy Communion. Collegeville, Minn., The Liturgical Press, 1959.
  16 p. 15 cm.
  MnCS

1376 The traditional way of Benedictine prayer (paper at Novice Mistresses Workshop, Clyde, Mo., 1953)
  27 p. 28 cm.
  Multilithed.
  MnCS (Archives)

1377 [Magazine and workshop articles]
  Contributed articles for the Benedictine Review, Orate Fratres (Worship), Sponsa Regis (Sisters Today), St. Joseph's Magazine, The Wanderer, St. Cloud Visitor, and Benedictines. Also papers at workshops conducted at various Benedictine abbeys and convents. Also symposium articles at National Liturgical Week and Maritime Week.

1378 (ed) Kreuter, Joseph. The way of victimhood in the Sacred Heart. [Edited by Fr. Paschal Botz, O.S.B.] Collegeville, Minn., St. John's Abbey Press, 1951.
  47 p. 18 cm.
  MnCS

1379 (ed) A Short breviary for religious and the laity. Collegeville, Minn., The Liturgical Press, 1941.
  viii, 766 p. 16 cm.
  Father Paschal Botz was co-editor.
  MnCS

1380 **Bouaké, Ivory Coast. Monastère Ste Marie.**
  Les religions africaines traditionnelles. Paris, Editions du Seuil [1965].
  201 p. 21 cm.
  "Recontres internationales organisées par le Centre culturel du monastère bénédictin de Bouaké."
  InStme

1381 **Bouange, Guillaume Marie Frédéric,** 1814–1884.
  Saint Géraud d'Aurillac et son illustre abbaye. Aurillac, L. Bonnet-Picut, 1881.
  2 v. 22 cm.
  KAS

Bougis, Simon, 1630–1714.
1382 Betrachtungen vor die Novizen, dan vor junge geistliche Professen, wie auch vor alle die sich annoch auf den Weeg der

Reinigung befinden. Vorhero in französischer Sprach beschrieben . . . anjetzo aber in das Teutsche Ubersetzt von Frau Maria Josepha Walburg . . . des Klosters Nonnberg. MS. Benediktinerinnenabtei Nonnberg, Salzburg, codex 28 D 9. 500 p. Folio. Saec. 18 (1762).
  Microfilm: MnCH proj. no. 10,969

1383   Meditations pour les novices, et les jeunes profes. et pour toutes sortes de personnes, qui sont encore dans la vie purgative. Paris, Antoine Vuarin, 1684.
  [40], 467 p. 25 cm.
  KAS

1384   **Bouley, Allan,** 1936–
  (tr) Tournay, Raymond, O.P. Introduction to Les Psaumes. Translated by Allan Bouley, O.S.B. . . . [and] Lawrence DeMong, O.S.B. [Collegeville, Minn.] n.d.
  75 p. 28 cm.
  Mimeographed.
  MnCS

Boultwood, Alban, 1911–
1385   Alive to God; meditations for everyman. Baltimore, Helicon [1964].
  180 p. 23 cm. (Benedictine studies, 7)
  InStme; PLatS; MoCo; MnCS; MnStj; KAS; ViBris; NdRi

1386   Into his splendid light. With a foreword by Eugene J. McCarthy. New York, Sheed and Ward [1968].
  xiii, 238 p. 22 cm. (American Benedictine Academy studies)
  InFer; KAS; MnCS; InStme; MoCo; NdRi; MnStj; ViBris

1387   **Bourassé, Jean Jacques,** 1813–1872.
  Abbayes et monastères; histoire, monuments, souvenirs et ruines . . . Illustrations par Clerget, Lancelot et Karl Girarde Gararardet. Tours, A. Mame et fils, 1870.
  590 p. plates, 25 cm.
  KAS

1388   **Bourbourg, France. Notre Dame (Benedictine abbey).**
  Un cartulaire de l'abbaye de N.-D. de Bourbourg, recueilli et dressé par Ignace du Coussemaker . . . Lille, Impr. V. Ducoulombier, 1882–91.
  3 v. in 1. 26 cm.
  KAS

1389   **Bourget, Jean,** 1724–1776.
  The history of the royal abbey of Bec near Rouen in Normandy . . . Translated from the French [by J. Nichols]. London, J. Nichols, 1779.
  viii, 140 p. paltes, 18 cm.
  KAM; KAS

1390   **Bouton, André,** 1914–
  Vigile de Noël. [Bruges], Biblica [1962].
  111 p. 21 cm. (Assemblées du Seigneur, 8)
  PLatS

Bouveret, Switzerland. Saint-Benoît de Port-Valais (Benedictine abbey).
1391   Colophons de manuscrits occidentaux des origines au XVI. siècle. [Par les] Bénédictins du Bouveret. Fribourg, Suisse, Editions Universitaires, 1965–
  v. 22 cm. (Spicilegii Friburgensis subsidia, v. 2–   )
  InStme; MnCS (v. 1–5, A–O, 1965–76); PLatS

1392   La Règle de saint Benoit. Le Bouveret, Prieuré Saint-Benoit de Port-Valais, 1961.
  257 p. 12 cm.
  KAS

Bouvilliers, Adelard, 1887–1950.
1393   Dictionnaire des Bouvier. Belmont, Caroline du nord [1947].
  486 p. 26 cm.
  French and/or English.
  Only vol. 1 was published.
  NcBe; PLatS

1394   [Essays from various issues of "Laudate," "Pax" and "The Placidian."
  2 v.
  NcBe

1395   Léon Boëllmann (1862–1897); a short biography and analysis of his organ works. Boston, McLaughlin & Reilly Co., 1924.
  p. 33–42
  From "Laudate," March, 1924.
  NcBe

1396   Organ and chant aesthetics I. Boston, McLaughlin & Reilly [1937?]
  1 vol.
  Reprint of a series of articles which appeared during 1934–1937 in "The Cecilia."
  NcBe

1397   An outlook on the sixty years of the Solesmes School of Music. Washington, D.C., Benedictine Foundation [192-?]
  p. 152–161.
  From the "Placidian."
  NcBe

1398   **Boval, Marcel,** 1898–
  De culte perpetuel et universal de Marie. (*In* Maria et Ecclesia; acta Congressus Mariologici-mariani in civitate Lourdes, anno 1958 celebrati, vol. 14, p. 169–175)
  PLatS

Bovo, Sabastiano, 1922–
1399   Problemi e orientamenti di spiritualità monastica, biblica et liturgica. Roma, Edizione Paoline [1961].
  790 p. 18 cm.

At head of title: C. Vagaggini, S. Bovo [etc]
MnCS

1400 (ed) Höpfl, Hildebrand. Introductio specialis in Vetus Testamentum. Editio sexta quam curavit P. Sebastianus Bovo, O.S.B. Neapoli, M. D'Auria, 1963.
xxviii, 701 p. 22 cm.
MnCS; PLatS

1401 **Bowes, David William.**
The effect of ultrasonic radiation upon the internal organs of the tropical fish Lebistes reticulatus (Peters).
36 p. plates.
Thesis–Catholic University of America, 1952.
AStb

Bowler, Hugh, 1894–
1402 Recusant roll, no. 2 (1593–94). An abstract in English with an explanatory introduction by Dom Hugh Bowler. [London], Catholic Record Society, 1965.
cxvii, 273 p. facsim. 23 cm. (Catholic Record Society. Publications, v. 57)
PLatS

1403 Recusant roll, no. 3 (1594–1595), and Recusant roll no. 4 (1595–1596). An abstract, in English by Dom Hugh Bowler. [London], Catholic Record Society [1970].
xiii, 294 p. 23 cm. (Catholic Record Society. Publications, v. 61)
PLatS

1404 **Boxgrove Priory, England.**
Chartulary of the Priory of Boxgrove. Lewes, Published by the Society [1960].
xlviii, 229 p. tables, 22 cm. (Sussex Record Society. [Publications] v. 59)
PLatS

1405 **Bracco, Leone,** 1847–1918.
Histoire de l'Ordre de S. Benoît.
(*In* Analecta juris pontificii, 1876, v. 15, col. 513–546, 641–654)
AStb

1406 **Bradley, Bede J.,** 1909–1971.
The speech philosophy of John Henry Cardinal Newman.
iv, 122 leaves, 28 cm.
Thesis (M.A.)–State University of Iowa, 1941.
Typescript.
KAS

1407 **Bradley, Benedict Francis,** 1867–1945.
St. Benedict of Nursia; address delivered in the Catholic Hour, August 10, 1930.
(*In* Connell, F. J. Four religious founders. Washington, 1931. p. 13–23)
PLatS

1408 **Bradley, Paul John.**
My Catholic devotions. Gastonia, N.C., Good Will Publishers [c 1955].
unpaged.
NcBe

Brandes, Karl, 1810–1867.
1409 Aus einer merkwürdigen Reise. Stans, Hans von Matt, 1920.
40 p. 23 cm.
Sonderabdruck aus: Schweizer Rundschau, XX (1919)
InStme

1410 Leben und Wirken des heiligen Meinrad für seine Zeit und für die Nachwelt; eine Festschrift zur tausendjährigen Jubelfeier des Bendiktiner-Klosters Maria-Einsiedeln. Einsiedeln, New-York, K. u. N. Benziger, 1861.
xx, 244 p. plates, 23 cm.
InStme; MoCo; NdRi; PLatS

1411 Ueber den Werth der Arbeit für den Studirenden; Vortrag an die Zöglinge der Lehranstalt von Einsiedeln bei Anlass der geistlichen Uebungen. Einsiedeln und New-York, K. u. N. Benziger, 1856.
30 p. 23 cm.
PLatS

1412 **Brandi, Antonio,** 1846–1892.
Guido Aretino, monaco di S. Benedetto; della sua vita, del suo tempo e dei suoi scritti . . . Firenze, Arte della Stampa, 1882.
480 p. illus. (music), facsim. 23 cm.
PLatS

1413 **Brandlmeier, Rupert,** 1926–
Abba, Vater–Gib mir ein Wort! Uebersicht über das schriftstellerische Wirken von Abt Emmanuel [von] Ansgar Ahlbrecht und Rupert Brandlmeier.
(*In* Hören sein Wort; Festgabe für Abt Emmanuel M. Heufelder zum 70. Geburtstag. Niederaltaich, 1968. p. 167–188)
PLatS

1414 **Brandstetter, Ildephonse Charles,** 1870–1945.
A visit to T'ai Shan.
(*In* Catholic University of Peking. Bulletin, no. 6 (1929), p. 93–118)
PLatS

1415 **Brang, Marie, Sister,** 1917–
The effectiveness of a developmental reading program for the ninth grade.
47 p.
Research paper (M.Ed.)–Marquette University, 1963.
Typescript.
MnStj (Archives)

1416 **Brannigan, Renée, Sister.**
An extrinsic-intrinsic analysis of the

rhetoric of inspector James McLaughlin in the Rosebud Land Cession Council Agreement in 1906–1907.
Thesis (M.A.)–University of North Dakota.
Typescript.
NdRiS

Braso, Gabriel M., 1912–
1417   Liturgie et vie spirituelle. Tr. de l'espagnol par Mgr. P. Jobit et P. Chevalier. [Paris], Desclée [1964]
384 p. 19 cm.
MnCS

1418   Liturgy and spirituality. Translated by Leonard Doyle. [2d ed.]. Collegeville, Minn., The Liturgical Press [c 1971].
xxi, 297 p.
CaMWiSb; MnStj

1419   Sentier de vie au seuil de notre conversion; conferences sur la Règle de saint Benoît. Abbaye de Bellefontaine, 1974.
196 p. 21 cm. (Vie monastique, no. 2)
InStme

Braulik, Georg Peter, 1941–
1420   Cölestin Wolfsgruber, O.S.B., Hofprediger und Professor für Kirchengeschichte (1848–1924). Wien, Herder, 1968.
121 p. 23 cm. (Wiener Beiträge zur Theologie, Bd. 19)
MnCS

1421   Deutsches Psalterium für Sonntage und Wochentage des Kirchenjahres. Zusammengestellt von Georg Braulik, O.S.B., Notker Füglister, O.S.B. . . . [Vier-Türme-Verlag, Abtei Münsterschwarzach, 1969]
430 p. 18 cm.
Erläuterungen, p. 419–430, von Georg Braulik, O.S.B.
MnCS

1421a   Die Mittel deuterononomischer Rhetorik erhoben aus Deuteronomium 4, 1–40. Rome, Biblical Institute Press, 1978.
xi, 171 p. 24 cm. (Analecta biblica, 68)
PLatS

1422   **Braun, Heinrich,** 1732–1792.
Akademische Rede von der Kunst zu denken als dem Grunde der wahren Beredsamkeit, welche an dem höchsterfreulichen Namesfeste Seiner Churfürstlichen Durchleucht in Baiern den 14 October, 1765, gehalten worden. München, Johann Friedrich Ott, 1765.
9 leaves, 20 cm.
PLatS

1423   **Braun, Heinrich Suso,** 1930–
Die Sakramente. Innsbruck, Tyrolia Verlag, 1960.

409 p. 19 cm. (Radiopredigten, VII)
MnCS

1424   **Braun, Hugh.**
English abbeys. London, Faber and Faber Ltd, [1971].
299 p. 32 plates, 23 cm.
KAS

1425   **Braun, Joan Mary, Sister.**
St. Catherine's Monastery Church, Mount Sinai: literary sources from the fourth through the nineteenth centuries.
viii, 343 leaves, illus. 21 cm.
Thesis (Ph.D)–University of Michigan, 1973.
Abstracted in Dissertation abstracts international, v. 34 (1974), no. 8, p. 5215-A–5216-A.
MnDuS; MnCS

1426   **Braun, Placidus Ignatius,** 1756–1829.
Notitia historico-literaria de codicibus manuscriptis in bibliotheca liberi ac imperialis monasterii Ordinis S. Benedicti ad SS. Udalricum et Afram Augustae extantibus. Augustae Vindelicorum, sumptibus Fratrum Veith, 1791–96.
2 v. in 6 parts.
PLatS (microfilm)

1427   **Braun, Rosemary, Sister.**
Ten interludes for communion on Gregorian themes.
10 p. illus. (music)
Thesis (M.A.)–University of Notre Dame, 1960.
InFer

1428   **Braunmüller, Benedikt,** 1825–
Universaller Charakter des Benediktiner-Ordens.
(*In* Studien und Mittheilungen O.S.B., v. 1 (1880), p. [29]–)
AStb

1429   **Braunweiler, Germany (Benedictine abbey).**
Annales Brunwilarenses a. 1000–1125.
(*In* Monumenta Germaniae historica. Scriptores. Stuttgart, 1963. t. 1, p. 99–101)
MnCS; PLatS

Brechter, Heinrich Suso, 1910–
1430   Beurons Beitrag zur Gründung von St. Ottilien.
(*In* Beuron, 1863–1963; Festschrift . . . Beuron, 1963. p. 231–267)
PLatS

1431   Das zweite Vatikanische Konzil. Dokumente und Kommentare . . . hrsg. von H. S. Brechter [et al]. Freiburg, Herder, 1966–68.
3 v. 27 cm.
MnCS; PLatS

1432 **Breen, Columba.**
Vernacular translations of Scripture.
(*In* Murray, Placid, ed. Studies in
pastoral liturgy. Dublin, 1967. v. 3, p.
154–162)
PLatS

1433 **Breen, Dunstan,** 1841–1911.
189; or, The Church of old England pro-
tests. London, Catholic Truth Society,
1903.
16 p. 17 cm.
MnCS

1434 **Breitschopf, Robert,** 1866–
Einfache und kurze Predigten auf die
Feste des Herrn sowie der heiligsten Jung-
frau Maria und der Heiligen, mit einem
Anhange von Gelegenheitsreden . . . 2.
verb. Aufl. Regensburg, G. J. Manz, 1913.
viii, 396 p. 22 cm.
KAS

Brennan, Maynard James, 1921–
1435 Compact handbook of college composition. Boston, Heath, 1964.
xv, 140 p. illus. 20 cm.
NcBe; PLatS

1436 Faculty handbook [of St. Vincent Col-
lege]. Foreword by Maynard J. Brennan.
1966.
41 p. map, charts, 26 cm.
PLatS

Brennan, Robert John, 1898–1964.
1437 Golden jubilee, Benedictine High School,
1911–1961. Centennial, Benedictine
Fathers in Richmond, Va., 1861–1961.
[Richmond, 1961].
[10] p. 28 cm.
NcBe; PLatS

1438 A professional course in education in the
seminary curriculum.
67 p.
Thesis (M.A.)–University of Notre
Dame, 1929.
NcBe

1439 **Brennell, Anselma, Sister.**
St. Bonaventure.
(*In* Walsh, James, S.J. Spirituality
through the centuries . . . 1964. p. 171–
180)
PLatS

Brenner, Henry, 1881–1967.
1440 The bread of life; a few thoughts for the
more worthy and profitable reception of
the Most Blessed Sacrament of the Altar.
n.p., n.d.
72 p. 15 cm.
Mimeographed.
InStme

1441 429 outlines in brief. St. Meinrad, Ind.,
Author, n.d.

79 p. 25 cm.
Mimeographed.
MnCS; PLatS

1442 Library of current Catholic thought,
comprising 3300 articles and narratives
taken from . . . the Catholic press . . . St.
Meinrad, Ind., 1933–1945.
24 v. 25 cm.
InStme; MnCS; OrStb (1942–45)

1443 The Master's directions. St. Meinrad,
Ind., The author, 1959.
ix, 125 p. 19 cm.
PLatS

1444 Narratives drawn from the Catholic
press. St. Meinrad, Ind. [The author,
19–].
v. 25 cm.
Mimeographed.
InStme; KAS; MnCS; PLatS; NcBe (v.
1–5)

1445 Sermon brevities; 700 short paragraphs
containing in concise and simple form a
condensation of the chief spiritual ideas
called for in pastoral dissertations of the
present day . . . St. Meinrad, Ind., The
author [19–].
88 p. 25 cm.
Mimeographed.
KAS; MnCS

1446 Short discourses (numbered 1 to 285). St.
Meinrad, Ind., The author [19–].
76, 74, 77, 69, 74 leaves, 25 cm.
Mimeographed.
KAS; MnCS

1447 **Brentano, Maria Rafaela, Sister.**
Wie Gott mich rief; mein Weg vom Pro-
testantismus in die Schule St. Benedikts. 4.
Aufl. Freiburg i.B., Herder [1929]
ix, 339 p. 21 cm.
First published 1925.
PLatS

Bresnahan, William, 1913–1974.
1448 Community retreat, 1956. [Collegeville,
Minn., St. John's Abbey, 1956]
44 p. 28 cm.
Typescript.
MnCS

1449 The concept of martyrdom according to
St. Augustine, bishop of Hippo.
101 p. 28 cm.
Thesis (M.A.)–Creighton University,
1965.
MoCo

1450 **Breul, Jacques,** 1528–1614.
Regvla sancti patris Benedicti. Cum
declarationibus & constitutionibus editis a
patribus Congregationis Casinensis . . .
Quid lucis huic nouae editioni F. Iacobus du

Brevl . . . sequens pagella docebit. Mogvntiae, Balthasar Lippius, 1603.
　187, 173 p. 18 cm.
　MnCS

Breviarium. Benedictine. *See* Subject Part, nos. 1110–1210

Breviarium. Cistercian. *See* Subject Part, nos. 4893–4916

Breviarium Fuldense. *See* Cornelius, F. Fuldense.

Brevnov, Czechoslovakia (Benedictine abbey).

1451　Catalogus religiosorum sub Regula s.p. Benedicti in archisterio Brevnoviensi et monasterio Braunaviensi atque extra eadem militantium, anno domini MDCCCLXXX . . . Praemissa brevis memoria monasteriorum S. Ordinis Benedictini in Bohemia et series abbatum Brevnoveno-Braunaviensium. [Pragae] 1885.
　23 p. 23 cm.
　ILSP; KAS; MnCS

1452　Memoria abbatum et fratrum monasteriorum Brevnoviensis et Braunensis Ord. S.P. Benedicti in Domino defunctorum. Sumptibus monasteriorum, 1888.
　87 p. 23 cm.
　PLatS

Bridge, Gerard, 1873–1950.

1453　Clerical alumni supplement [for St. Vincent College journal], June, 1908.
　11 p. 23 cm.
　MnCS

1454　Sixty selections from Shakespeare. 2d ed. Latrobe, Pa., Latrobe Printing & Publishing Co. [c 1907].
　158 p. 23 cm.
　PLatS

1455　**Briestensky, Gabriel Nicolas,** 1918–
　Saint Benedict Church, Baltimore, Md. [Diamond jubilee]. South Hackensack, N.J., Custombook, 1968.
　28 p. illus. 27 cm.
　PLatS

1456　**Brisson, Paschal,** 1926–1980.
　Current issues in the treatment of alcoholism.
　87 p. 28 cm.
　Research report for M.A.–Southern Illinois University, 1975.
　MnCS

1457　**Britt, Matthew,** 1872–1055.
　The hymns of the Breviary and Missal, edited with introduction and notes by Dom Matthew Britt, O.S.B. . . . Revised edition with latest hymns. New York, Benziger Bros. [1953].
　xxxvi, 416 p. 23 cm.

Without music.
　PLatS; WBenS

1458　**Brodner, Martin,** 1915–
　The action of the Mass. Rev. ed. Muenster, Sask., St. Peter's Press [1960].
　32 p. 15 cm.
　CaSMu; MnCS

1458a　**Broekaert, Jean Damascene,** 1915–
　Bibliographie de la Règle de Saint Benoît. Editions latines et traductions imprimées de 1489 à 1929. Description diplomatique 1239 numeros. Roma, Editrice Anselmiana [1980].
　2 v. 24 cm. (Studia Anselmiana, 77–78)
　InStme; KAS; MnCS; PLatS

1459　**Bronder, Joseph,** 1942–
　The Saint Vincent Community Camerata. Vols I–III, 1973–75. [Phonodisc]. Greensburg, Pa., Grubb Associates Recording.
　Each vol. 2 s. 12 in. 33⅓ rpm. Stereo.
　Joseph Bronder, O.S.B., music director.
　Recorded in the Crypt of the St. Vincent Archabbey Basilica, Latrobe, Pa.
　PLatS

1460　**Brooke, Odo,** 1919–1971.
　William of St. Thierry.
　(*In* Walsh, James, S.J. Spirituality through the centuries . . . [1964] p. 121–131)
　PLatS

1460a　Studies in monastic theology. Kalamazoo, Mich., Cistercian Publications, 1980.
　xv, 274 p. 22 cm. (Cistercian studies series, no. 37)
　InStme

1461　**Brou, Alexandre,** 1862–1947.
　Saint Augustine of Canterbury and his companions. From the French. London, Art and Book Co.; New York, Benziger, 1897.
　xiii, 188 p. illus. 20 cm.
　KAS

Brou, Louis, 1898–1961.

1462　Antifonario visigótico mozárabe de la catedral de León. Edición del texto, notas, y indices, por Dom Louis Brou . . . Barcelona-Madrid, 1959.
　xviii, 636 p. 25 cm. (Monumenta Hispaniae sacra. Series liturgica, vol. V, 1)
　InStme; MnCS

1463　Deux mauvaises lectures du Chanoine Ortiz dans l'édition du Bréviaire mozarabe de Ximénès: Lauda, Capitula.
　(*In* Miscelánea en homenaje a Monseñor Higinio Anglés. Barcelona, 1958–61. v. 1, p. 175–202)
　PLatS

1464 Les oraisons des dimanches après la pentecôte; commentaire liturgique. Bruges, Abbaye de Saint-André, 1959.
132 p. 24 cm. (Paroisse et liturgie. Collection du pastorale liturgique, no. 38)
InStme; MoCo; PLatS

1465 Les oraisons dominicales. Deuxieme serie, De l'Avent à la Trinité. Bruges, Apostolat liturgique, 1960.
139 p. 24 cm. (Paroisse et liturgie, n. 50)
PLatS

1466 **Brouwer, Augustine de,** 1907–
(tr) Renckens, H., S.J. La Bible et les origines du monde: Quand Israël regarde le Passé a propos de la Genèse 1–3. Traduit du néerlandais et adapté par A. de Brouwer, O.S.B. [Tournai], Desclée [c 1964].
198 p. 21 cm.
Translation of: Israëls visie op het verleden.
PLatS

Bruges, Belgium. Abbaye de Saint-André.

1467 Abbaye de Saint-André. n.d.
35 p. chiefly illus. 18 cm.
PLatS

1468 Assemblées du Seigneur; catéchèse des dimanches et des fêtes [par les moines bénédictins de l'Abbaye de Saint-André]. [Bruges], Biblica [1961–　].
v. 21 cm.
MnCS; PLatS

1469 Bible Missal. Prepared by a commission of St. Andrew's Abbey. Bruges, Biblica, 1962.
1535 p.
NcBe

1470 La Biblia, pao a paso. Madrid, Editorial Marova, 1960–
v. 21 cm. (Colecciön Biblia y vida)
MnCS

1471 Chronica monasterii Sancti Andreae juxta Brugas Ordinis Sancti Benedicti ab Arnulpho Goethals conscriptanunc primum accurate e codice Bibliothecae Brugensis erta edidit W. H. Weale. Brugis, apud Edw. Gailliard, 1868.
xxii, 228 p. coats of arms, 30 cm.
KAS

1472 Chronique de l'Abbaye de Saint-André, traduite pour la première fois d'après le manuscrit de la Bibliothèque de Bruges; suivie de Mélanges historiques et littéraires, par Octave Delepierre. Bruges, Imprimerie de Vandecasteele-Werbrouck, 1839.
340 p. 22 cm.
InStme

1473 La Messe solennele. Lophem les-Bruges, Abbaye de St. André, n.d.
35 postcards, 9 x 15 cm.
MnCS

1474 The new Saint Andrew Bible Missal. Prepared by a Missal commission of Saint Andrew's Abbey. New edition, containing the complete Psalter and the Mass prayers and readings approved by the bishops of the United States. New York, Benziger Brothers [1966].
xiv, 1478 p. 17 cm.
InStme

1475 Nôtre catéchèse; collection de pastorale catéchètique. [Bruges], Biblica, 1966–
v. plates, 22 cm.
MnCS

1476 Pas à pas avec la Bible. 2. éd. [Bruges], Biblica, 1964–
v. 22 cm. (Publications de St. André)
MnCS

1477 Pour chanter l'office; guide practique. [Bruges, Abbaye de S. André, 196-].
89 p. 28 cm.

1478 Saint Andrew Bible commentary. Conception, Mo., Conception Abbey Press [1960–1963].
30 pamphlets, 21 cm.
Originally published in French under the title: Pas à pas avec la Bible.
InStme; MnCS

1479 Saint Andrew Bible Missal. Prepared by a Missal Commission of St. Andrew's Abbey. Bruges, Biblica; [New York, DDB Publishers, 1963].
xvi, 1535 p. col. plates, 16 cm.
MnCS; PLatS

1480 Saint Andrew daily Missal, with Vespers for Sundays and feasts, by Dom Gaspar Lefebvre, O.S.B., and the monks of St. Andrew's Abbey. Bruges, Biblica; [New York, DDB Publishers, 1962].
xlviii, 2041 p. illus., music, 17 cm.
"Proper feasts kept in the dioceses of the United States of America": p. 1925–2022.
PLatS

1481 Saint Andrew Sunday Missal; Masses for Sundays and principal feasts of the ecclesiastical year, by Dom Gaspar Lefebvre, O.S.B., and the monks of St. Andrew's Abbey. Bruges, Biblica; [New York, DDB Publishers, 1962].
xxxii, 816 p. illus. 15 cm.
"Feasts proper to the dioceses of the United States of America": p. 801–813.
PLatS

1482 **Brunet, Albin,** 1862–
(ed) Mombrizio, Bonino. Sanctuarium seu Vitae sanctorum. Novam hanc edi-

tionem curaverunt duo monachi Soles-
menses . . . Parisiis, apud Albertum Font-
moing, 1910.
2 v. 28 cm.
Preface signed: Fr. A. Brunet.
KAS; NcBe; PLatS

1483 **Brunner, Luitpold,** 1823–1881.
(ed) Möhner, Reginald. Reise des P.
Reginbald Möhner, Benedictiners von St.
Ulrich in Augsburg, als Feldcaplans bei
den . . . deutschen Regimentern in die
Niederlande im Jahre 1651 . . . hrsg. von
Dr. P. L. Brunner. Augsburg, F. Butsch
Sohn, 1872.
118 p. 25 cm.
KAS

Bruno, Saint, bp. of Segni, 1048–1123.
1484 Opera in duos tomos distributa aucta et
adnotationibus illustrata . . . Romae,
Typographio Joannis Zempel, 1789–1791.
2 v. 37 cm.
MnCS

1485 Sententiarum libri. MS. Cava, Italy
(Benedictine abbey), codex 6, p. 87–176.
Quarto. Saec. 12.
Microfilm: MnCH

1486 **Brussels, Belgium.** Our Blessed Lady
the Perpetuall Virgin Mary (Abbey of
Benedictine Nuns).
Statvtes compyled for the better observation of the holy rvle of the Most Gloriovs
Father and Patriarch S. Benedict con-
firmed by the ordinary authoritie of the
Right Honorable and Reuer Father in Chr.
the Lo. Matthias Hovivs Archbishop of
Macklin and Primate of the Netherlands
&c as alsoe by authority from the Pope His
Holynesse delegated to him, and by delivered to the English religious vvoemen of
the Monastery of Our Blessed Lady the
Perpetuall Virgin Mary in Bruxelles and to
all their succesours. Gant, Printed by I.
Dooms [1632].
in 3 parts.
Short-title catalogue no. 17552 (carton
1027).
MnCS (microfilm)

Bruyère, Cécile, Abbess, 1845–1909.
1487 Leben aus dem Gebet. Aus dem Französischen übertragen von Lucilla Wewer,
Benediktinerin der Abtei St. Hildegard,
Eibingen. Düsseldorf, Patmos-Verlag
[1953].
264 p. 22 cm.
PLatS

1488 La vie spirituelle et l'oraison d'aprés la
Sainte Ecriture et la tradition monastique.
Nouvelle édition. Solesme (Sarthe), Ab-
baye Saint-Pierre [1960].

xvii, 424 p. 19 cm.
InStme

1489 In spiritu et veritate . . . [La Ferté-
Bernard, impr. R. Bellanger et fils, 1966.
190 p. 19 cm.
Includes a selection of texts by Cécile
Bruyère.
InStme

Bruyne, Donatien de, 1871–1935.
1490 Incerti auctoris Testimonia de Patre et
Filio et Spiritu Sancto, cura et studio D. de
Bruyne.
(*In* Florilegia biblica Africana saec. V.
Turnholti, 1961. p. 224–260)
CaQStB

1491 (ed) Augustine, Saint, bp. of Hippo.
Quaestionum in Heptateuchum libri VII
. . . [cura et studio D. de Bruyne]. Turnholti, Typographi Brepols, 1958.
xviii, lxxxi, 503 p. 25 cm.

Bryce, Mary Charles, Sister.
1492 Come let us eat; preparing for First
Communion. [New York, Herder and
Herder, 1964].
64 p. illus. 21 cm.
MnCS; MoCo; OkShG; PLatS

1493 First Communion. A parent-teacher
manual for "Come let us eat." [New York],
Herder and Herder [1964]
125 p. illus.
MoCo; OkShG

1494 Prayer in school.
(*In* Jesus Christ reforms His Church . . .
26th annual North American Liturgical
Week, 1965, p. 230–237)
PLatS

1495 The preparation of the Christian teacher.
(*In* The renewal of Christian education
. . . 24th annual North American
Liturgical Week, 1963, p. 198–202)
PLatS

1496 Teaching music before Mass.
(*In* Worship in the city of man. 27th
North American Liturgical Week, 1966, p.
186–193)
PLatS

Bucelin, Gabriel, 1599–1681.
1497 Annales benedictini quibus potiora
monachorium [sic] eiusdem ordinis merita
ad compendium referuntur. Aug. Vindel.,
typis Ioannis Praetori, 1656.
[6], 260, 238, [14] p. 35 cm.
KAS; MnCS (microfilm); PLatS
(microfilm)

1498 Germania sacra. Augustae Vindel., typis
Joannis Praetorii, 1655.
3 v. 34 cm.
KAS

1499   Kurzer Inhalt des Lebens des heiligisten
unnd wunderbarlieben Vaters unnd Patriarchen Benedicti. Verteitschter abgeschrieben durch P. Maximinum Rolandinum, O.S.B. MS. Benediktinerinnenabtei
Nonnberg, Salzburg, codex 23 B 23. 211 f.
Quarto. Saec. 17.
    Microfilm: MnCH proj. no. 17

1500   Menologium benedictinum sanctorum,
beatorum atque illustrium ejusdem ordinis
virorum. Veldkirchii, apud Henricum
Bilium, 1655.
    [65], 895, [28] p. 35 cm.
    KAS; MnCS (microfilm); NdRi; PLatS
(microfilm)

1501   Sacrarium benedictinum, in quo magnus
ss. reliquiarum thesaurus describitur. n.p.,
1656.
    33 [i.e. 35] p. 35 cm.
    KAS

1502   (ed) Gerardus Belga, O.S.B. Opuscula,
vere aurea ac divina ad monachos. Excusum primum Augustae Vindelicorum
anno MDCXXXII. Opera a R. P. Gabrielis
Butzlini, deinde Bruxellis . . . secundo impressa. [Brussels], typis Francisci
Foppens, MDCLXXIII.
    401 p. 14 cm.
    PLatS

1503   **Bucelin, Gabriel,** fl. 1890.
    Uebersicht der Mönchsabteien des
Benediktiner-Ordens in Deutschland,
Oesterreich, der Schweiz bis zum Anfange
dieses Jahrhunderts [19. Jahrh.].
    (*In* Archivalische Zeitschrift. Neue
Folge, 2. Bd., p. 188–288)
    KAS; MnCS (Xerox copy)

Bucher, Zeno Richard, 1907–
1504   Das Problem der Materie in der
modernen Atomphysik; Versuch einer
philosophischen Deutung. Missionsverlag
St. Ottilien, 1939.
    vi, 175 p. 24 cm.
    Thesis–Collegio di Sant'Anselmo,
Roma.
    MnCS; PLatS

1505   Die Teleologie der Natur bei Aristoteles
(Physik B).
    (*In* Sapientiae procerum amore;
mélanges médiévistes offerts à Dom Jean-
Pierre Müller . . . Roma, 1974. p. [1]–20)
    PLatS

1506   **Buck, Peter Damian,** 1871–
    Zweihundert Jahre geologische
Forschertätigkeit im Kanton Schwyz. Einsiedeln, Benziger & Co., 1936.
    44 p. 23 cm.
    PLatS

1507   **Buckfast Abbey, England.**
    In Memoriam: Abbot Vonier, 1875–1938.
[Buckfast Abbey Publications, 1939].
    56 p. illus. 25 cm.
    Special number of the Buckfast Abbey
Chronicle, v. 9, no. 1, 1939.
    InStme

1508   **Buenner, Denys,** 1887–
    Madame de Bavoz, abbesse de Pradines
de l'Ordre de Saint-Benoît (1768–1838)
. . . Paris, E. Vitte [1961].
    xxi, 573 p. plates, 26 cm.
    CaQStB; MnCS; PLatS

1509   **Bugmann, Kuno,** 1909–
    Einsiedeln; die Stiftskirche. 2. Ausgabe.
München, Verlag Schnell & Steiner, 1971.
    22 p. illus. 17 cm.
    MnCS

1510   **Bulffer, Gervase,** 1714–1792.
    Negotiator evangelicus, das ist: Evange-
lischer Kauffmann . . . oder, Kurtze
Predigen . . . Augspurg, Johann Baptista
Burckhard, 1767–1760.
    8 v. 19 cm.
    KAS; MoCo

1511   **Bullarium Vallumbrosanum,** sive Tabula
chronologica in qua continentur bullae
illorum pontificum qui eumdem ordinem
privilegiis decorarunt. Florentiae, typis
Dominici Ambrosii Verdi, 1729.
    134, 8 p.
    MnCS (microfilm)

1512   **Buonafede, Appiano,** 1716–1793.
    Della restaurazione di ogni filosofia ne'
secoli XVI, XVII e XVIII, di Agatopisto
Cromaziano . . . Venezia, Stamperia
Graziosi, 1785–89.
    3 v.
    PLatS (microfilm)

1513   **Burbach, Jude,** 1927–
    The centennial of St. Patrick's Church,
1866–1966. Atchison, Kans., [1966].
    21 p. illus. 22 cm.
    KAS

Burbach, Maur, 1914–
1514   Annual community retreat, June 7–11,
1954. [Collegeville, Minn., St. John's
Abbey, 1954].
    30 p. 28 cm.
    Typescript.
    MnCS

1515   The Bible, marriage and worship.
    (*In* North American Liturgical Week,
22nd, 1961, p. 52–58)
    InFer; PLatS

1516   Bible prayer book; a book of prayers and
meditations taken from Sacred Scripture
for every day of the year . . . New York,
Regina Press [1967].

xiv, 732 p. 16 cm.
MnCS; MnStj; MoCo

1517   The book of Catholic worship.
Washington, D.C., The Liturgical Conference [c 1966].
xxii, 807 p. 22 cm.
PLatS

1518   The convergence of liturgy and theology.
(*In* McManus, F. R., ed. The revival of
the liturgy. New York, 1963. p. 33–41)
PLatS

1519   The Divine Office; sacrifice of praise.
Offprint from: The homiletic and
pastoral review, 1964, p. 36–40)
PLatS

1520   The Eucharist makes the people of God.
(*In* Jesus Christ reforms His Church . . .
26th annual North American Liturgical
Week, 1965, p. 95–102)
PLatS

1521   The normal school of sanctity. St. Louis,
Pio Decimo Press, n.d.
24 p. 17 cm.
PLatS

1522   The person in the Church.
(*In* The challenge of the council . . . 25th
annual North American Liturgical Week,
1964, p. 9–19)
PLatS

1523   The priest and the renewed liturgy [by]
Maur Burbach [and others]. New York, J.
F. Wagner, 1964.
71 p.
NcBe

1524   **Burckhardt, Stephan,** 16th cent.
Codices manuscripti bibliothecae Mellicensis. Collegit Frater Stephanus Burckhardus anno Domini 1517.
3 v. 28 cm.
Handwritten.
MnCS (Xerox copy)

Buresh, Vitus Aloysius, 1923–
1525   (tr.) Ekert, Frantisek. St. Procopius,
abbot of Sázava. [Chicago, Benedictine
Abbey Press, 1961]
ILSP

1526   (tr) Kadlec, Jaroslav. Saint Procopius,
guardian of the Cyrilo-Methodian legacy.
[Cleveland, Micro Photo Division, Bell &
Howell Co. 1964].
331 p. illus. 23 cm.
Photocopy of typescript reproduced by
duopage process.
ILSP; PLatS

1527   **Burge, Anselm,** 1846–1929.
Acts of the Apostles. London, Burns &
Oates, 1910.

2 v. maps, 18 cm. (Scripture manuals for
Catholic schools [v. 5–6])
MnCS

Burger, Bertilla, Sister.
1528   Christian symbols and their interpretations. Terre Haute, Ind., Indiana State
Univ., 1958.
37 p. illus.
InFer

1529   European tour; diary of highlights. Ferdinand, Ind., 1972.
27 p.
InFer

Burger, Honorius.
1530   Abschrift mehrerer älteren das Stift
Altenburg betreffenden Urkenden mit
Veränderung mancher veralteten
Ausdrücke im verständlichere, deren
Originale sich im Archiv des Stiftes
befinden. 234 Urkunden. MS. Benedik-
tinerabtei Altenburg, Austria, codex AB 7
D r. 152 p. Folio. Saec. 19 (1825).
Microfilm: MnCH proj. no. 6583

1531   Geschichtliche-zusammengestellter
Auszug aus dem in dem Archiv des Stiftes
Altenburg vorhandenen Urkunden. MS.
Benediktinerabtei Altenburg, Austria,
codex AB 6 C 42. 2 vols. Quarto. Saec. 19
(1846).
Microfilm: MnCH proj. no. 6585

1532   Kurzer Inhalt der im Archiv des
Benediktiner Stiftes St. Lambrecht zu
Altenburg in Oesterreich verhandenen
Urkunden und Schriften. Cum indice. MS.
Benediktinerabtei Altenburg, Austria,
codex AB 6 C 40–41. 2 vols. Quarto. Saec.
19 (1824).
Microfilm: MnCH proj. no. 6579–6580

1533   Repertorium über die im Archiv des
Stiftes St. Lambert zu Altenburg sich vor-
findenen Urkunden und Schriften. Alpha-
betisch angelegt nach Ortschaften, Sach-
gebieten, Personennamen. MS. Benediktinerabtei Altenburg, Austria, codex AB 7
D 3. 71 f. Folio. Saec. 19 (1864).
Microfilm: MnCH proj. no. 6588

1534   Urkundenbuch, oder buchstäbliche
Abschriften aller älteren im Archiv des
Stiftes Altenburg vorhandenen Urkunden.
1. Bd. MS. Benediktinerabtei Altenburg,
Austria, codex AB 6 C 40. 501 p. Quarto.
Saec. 19 (1846–47).
Microfilm: MnCH proj. no. 6578

1535   **Burger, Imelda, Sister.**
An investigation of the doctrine of the
divine adoption in the early religious training of the child.
66 p.

Thesis–Catholic University of America, 1954.

InFer

1536 **Burgos i Valle, Pedro de.**
Compendio breve de exercisios espiri-tuales.
(*In* Regla del bienaventurado San Benito . . . n. 6. Valladolid, 1599)
MnCS

1537 **Burns, Mirella, Sister,** 1906–
An American phase in the life of Prince Alexander von Hohenlohe, 1794–1849.
viii, 114 p.
Thesis (M.A.)–Catholic University of America, 1938.
Typescript.
MnStj (Archives)

Bury St. Edmunds Abbey, England.

1538 The chronicle of Bury St. Edmunds, 1212–1301. Edited with introd., notes, and translation by Antonia Gransden. London, Nelson, 1964.
xiv, 164, 187 p. 23 cm. (Medieval texts)
IlSP; InStme; KAS; MnCS; NdRi

1539 The customary of the Benedictine Abbey of Bury St. Edmunds in Suffolk (from Harleian MS. 1005 in the British Museum) edited by Antonia Gransden. London, Henry Bradshaw Society, 1973.
xlii, 142 p. 23 cm. (Henry Bradshaw Society [Publications] v. 99)
MnCS

1540 The kalendar of Abbot Samson of Bury St. Edmunds and related documents, edited for the Royal Historical Society by R. H. C. Davis. London, Offices of the Royal Historical Society, 1954.
ix, 200 p. maps, 22 cm. (Camden third series, v. 84)
InStme; KAS; MnCS; PLatS

1541 **Bütler, Anselm,** 1925–
Die Seinslehre des hl. Anselm von Canterbury. Ingenbohl (Schweiz), Theodosius Druckerei, 1959.
112 p. 21 cm.
Diss. (Ph.D)–Fribourg.
MnCS; PLatS

Butler, Basil Christopher, 1902–

1542 Christians in a new era. [Maryknoll, N.Y.], Maryknoll Publications [1969].
102 p. 22 cm.
InStme; MnCS

1543 The Church and the Bible. Baltimore, Helicon Press [1960]
v, 111 p. 19 cm.
InFer; InStme; KAS; MnCS; MoCo; NcBe; PLatS

1544 Dlaczego Chrystus? Paris, Editions du Dialogue [1971]

144 p. 21 cm.
MnCS

1545 The ecumenical aspect.
(*In* Coulson, John. Theology and the university; an ecumenical investigation, p. 13–22)
PLatS

1546 John Chapman.
(*In* Davis, Charles. English spiritual writers. New York, 1962. p. 182–202)
InFer; PLatS

1547 The idea of the Church. Baltimore, Helicon Press [1963]
xvi, 236 p. 23 cm.
ICSS; ILSP; InStme; MnCS; MnStj; MdRi; MoCo

1548 The object of faith according to St. Paul's Epistles.
(*In* Studiorum Paulinorum Congressus Internationalis Catholicus, 1961. v. 1, p. 15–30)
PLatS

1549 Prayer; an adventure in living. London, Darton, Longman & Todd [1966].
ix, 118 p. 19 cm. (Libra books)
NcBe; PLatS

1550 Prayer in practice. Baltimore, Helicon Press [1961]
x, 118 p. 19 cm. (Benedictine studies, v. 3)
ICSS; InStme; ILSP; KAS; MnCS; MnStj; NcBe; PLatS

1551 Searchings; essays and studies. [London], G. Chapman [c 1974]
272 p. 23 cm.
KAS; PLatS

1552 Spirit and institution in the New Testa-ment. London, A. R. Mowbray [1961]
33 p. 22 cm. (Contemporary studies in theology, 3)
InStme; KAS; MnCS; PLatS

1553 The theology of Vatican II. London, Dar-ton, Longman & Todd [1967]
194 p. 21 cm. (The Sarum lectures, 1966)
InStme; MoCo

1554 Teologia soboru Watykańskiego drugiego. Paris, Editions du Dialogue, 1971.
213 p. 21 cm.
MnCS

1555 A time to speak. Tenby Wells, England, Fowler Wright Books, 1972.
[6], 209 p. 22 cm.
InStme; KAS; MoCo

1556 A time to speak. Southend-on-Sea [England], Mayhew-McCrimmon [c 1973]
209 p. 21 cm.
InStme; MnCS

1557   Why Christ. [London, Darton, Longman & Todd, c 1960]
viii, 164 p. 19 cm. (A Libra book)
MnCS

1558   (ed) Butler, Edward Cuthbert. The Vatican Council, 1869–1870, based on Bishop Ullathorne's letters. Edited by Christopher Butler. Westminster, Md., Newman Press, 1962.
510 p. 20 cm.
InStme; MnCS; PLatS

1559   (2dary) Vatican Council, 2d, 1961–64. De ecclesia; the Constitution on the Church of Vatican Council II proclaimed by Pope Paul VI, November 21, 1964. Edited by Edward H. Peters. Forward by Basil C. Butler . . . [Study club ed.]. Glen Rock, N.J., Paulist Press [1965].
192 p. 18 cm. (Deus books)
PLatS

Butler, Christopher. *See* Butler, Basil Christopher.

Butler, Edward Cuthbert, 1858–1934.
1560   Christmas in Australia, 1834. Christmas in Rome, 1859.
(*In* Clonmore, Wm. A Christian's Christmas. London, 1939. p. 235–236)
PLatS

1561   Mabillon. [Downside Abbey, England, 1893]
[116]–132 p. 22 cm.
"Reprinted from the Downside review, 1893."
PLatS

1562   The Vatican Council, 1869–1870, based on Bishop Ullathorne's letters. Edited by Christopher Butler. Westminster, Md., Newman Press, 1962.
510 p. 20 cm.
InStme; KAS; MnCS; MnStj; NcBe; NdRi; MoCo; PLatS

1563   Western mysticism: the teaching of Augustine, Gregory and Bernard on contemplation and the contemplative life. 3rd ed. with Afterthoughts, and a new foreword by Professor David Knowles. London, Constable, 1967.
lxxii, 242 p. 23 cm.
PLatS

1563a   **Butters, Jude C.,** 1851–
Confidence in God as a theme in the theologies of H. Richard Niebuhr and James M. Gustafson; a comparative study.
v, 116 leaves. 28 cm.
Thesis (M.A.)–Indiana University, 1979.
InStme

Cabrol, Fernand, 1855–1937.
1564   The Epiphany, and its octave.

(*In* Clonmore, Wm. A Christian's Christmas. London, 1939. p. 211–218)
PLatS

1565   The Latin liturgy: the Roman Missal, the Holy Eucharist in the liturgy.
(*In* Lattey, Cuthbert. Catholic faith in the Holy Eucharist. Cambridge, 1928. p. 127–154)
PLatS

1566   The liturgy of Christmas.
(*In* Clonmore, Wm. A Christian's Christmas. London, 1939. p. 100–107)
PLatS

1567   Le livre de la prière antique. 4. éd. Paris, Oudin, 1910.
xv, 591 p. 19 cm.
MnCS

1568   Penance.
(*In* Lattey, Cuthbert, ed. Six sacraments . . 1929. p. 131–162)
PLatS

1569   Holy Week; the complete offices of Holy Week in Latin and English. A new explanatory edition by the Right Rev. Abbot Cabrol, O.S.B. 4th ed. New York, P. J. Kenedy and Sons [1933].
376 p. illus. 15 cm.
Sine cantu.
MnCS

1570   (ed) Monumenta ecclesiae liturgica, ediderunt et curaverunt Ferdinandus Cabrol [et] Henricus Leclercq. Paris, F. Didot, 1890–1912.
Only vols. 1, 5–6 were published.
InStme; KAS; MnCS

1571   **Cacciamani, Giuseppe M., O.S.B.Cam.**
Atlante storico-geografico dei Benedettini d'Italia. Roma, Edizioni Paolini, 1967.
284 p. maps. 18 cm. (Universa, 24)
MnCS

1572   **Cadden, John Paul,** 1913–
The historiography of the American Catholic Church: 1785–1943. Washington, Catholic University of America Press, 1944.
xi, 122 p. 23 cm.
Thesis (S.T.D.)–Catholic University of America.
PLatS

1573   **Caffrey, Cletus Bernard,** 1932–
Behavior patterns and personality characteristics as related to prevalence rates of coronary heart disease in Trappist and Benedictine monks.
v, 99 leaves, 28 cm.
Thesis (Ph.D)–Catholic University of America, 1966.

Typescript.
PLatS

Caigney, Mayeul Pierre de, 1862–1939.
1574   Commentaire ascétique du Magnificat, par un Bénédictin. Bruges, Ch. Beyaert [1933].
295 p. 20 cm.
MnCS

1575   De gemino probabilismo licito; dissertatio critico-practica exarata conciliationis gratia. Brugis, Desclée, De Brouwer, 1901.
124 p. 23 cm.
KAS

Calmet, Augustin, 1672–1757.
1576   Brevis chronologia; sev, Rationarium temporum ecclesiasticae ac civilis historiae, a mondo condito ad annum Christi MDCCXXXIV. Argentorati, J. R. Dulssecker, 1734.
10, 369 p.
PLatS (microfilm)

1577   Commentarium literale in omnes ac singulos tum Veteris cum Novi Testamenti libros . . . E gallico in latinum sermonem translatum. Augustae Vindelicorum, sumptibus Philippi ac Martini Veith, 1734.
8 v. in 5.
NcBe

1578   Dictionarium historicum, criticum, chronologicum, geographicum, et literale Sacrae Scripturae, cum figuris antiquitates judaicas repraesentantibus . . . E gallico in latinum translatum, & nonihil expurgatum ab R.P.D.Jo. Dominico Mansi. Venetiis, apud Sebastianum Coleti, 1726.
2 v. illus., maps, 35 cm.
MnCS

1579   Calmet's Dictionary of the Holy Bible: historical, critical, geographical and etymological . . . now rev., corr., and augm . . . under the direction of C. Taylor. 3d ed. London, Printed by Charles Taylor, 1814.
4 v.
NcBe

1580   Calmet's Dictionary of the Holy Bible, by the late Mr. Charles Taylor, with the fragments incorporated. The whole condensed and arranged in alphabetical order, with numerous additions. Illustrated with maps and engravings on wood. 2d ed. London, Holdsworth and Ball, 1832.
951, [13] p. illus. 27 cm.
KAS

1581   Histoire de l'Abbaye de Senones. Manuscrit inédit de Dom Calmet, publié dans le Bulletin de la Société Philomatique Vosgienne et par tirage à part, avec une préface, des notes et quelques détails sur le réunion de la Principauté de Salm à la France, par F. Dinago, avocat à Saint-Dié. Saint-Dié, Typographie et Lithographie L. Humbert [1879].
439 p. illus.
CaQStB

1582   Histoire ecclésiastique et civile de Lorraine, qui comprend ce qui s'est passé de plus mémorable dans l'archeveché de Trèves, & dans les évechés de Metz, Toul & Verdun, depuis l'entrée de Jules César dans les Gaules, jusqu'à la mort de Charles V, duc de Lorraine, arrivée en 1690 . . . Nancy, J. B. Cusson, 1728.
3 v. plates, maps, 39 cm.
KAS

1583   Notice de la Lorraine, qui comprend les duchés de Bar et de Luxembourg, l'electorat de Trèves, les trois évechés (Metz, Toul et Verdun), l'histoire par ordre alphabétique des villes, bourgs, villages, des abayes, des prieurés, des chapitres et des principaux établissements sacrés ou civils, des camps romains, de chateaux, des palais royaux des anciens rois d'Austrasie, des antiquités remarquables qui se voient en chaque lieu. Nouvelle édition. Luneville, chez Creusat, 1835–36.
2 v.
CaQStB

1584   **Caloen, Gerard van,** 1853–1932.
Dom Maur Wolter et les origines de la Congregation Bénédictine de Beuron. Bruges-Lille, Desclée, 1891.
132 p. 19 cm.
CaQStL; CtBeR; MnCS

Camara, Helder, 1909–
1585   The desert is fertile. Translated by Dinah Livingstone. Maryknoll, N.Y., Orbis Books, 1974.
vi, 61 p. illus. 21 cm.
InStme

1586   Race against time. Translated [from the French] by Della Couling. Denville, N.J., Dimension Books [1971].
136 p.
Translation of: Pour arriver à temps.
NcBe

1587   Spiral of violence. Translated [from the French] by Della Couling. Denville, N.J., Dimension Books [1971].
83 p.
NcBe

Camm, Bede, 1864–1942.
1588   The Anglican Benedictines of Caldey. New York, America Press, 1913.
14 p.

Reprinted from Catholic mind.
AStb

1589   De l'anglicanisme au monachisme; journal d'étapes d'un converti. Traduit de l'anglais par Charles Grolleau. Paris, Desclée, De Brouwer, 1930.
112 p. 19 cm. (Collection "Pax," v. 32)
CaQMo; CaWStB; KAS

1590   Caldey and St. Bride's.
(Catholic mind, 1913, no. 7)
AStb

1591   Some Devonshire screens and the saints represented on their panels; with numerous original illustrations. York [England], Ampleforth Abbey, 1906.
52 p. illus 23 cm.
KAS

1592   William Cardinal Allen, founder of the seminaries. London, R. & T. Washbourne, 1914.
xii, 194 p. 17 cm.
NcBe

1593   **Campbell, Immaculata, Sister.**
A survey of library resources available to adult Catholic readers in the city of Covington.
Thesis (M.S.L.S.)–Catholic University of America, 1963.
Typescript.
KyCovS

1594   **Campbell, Stephanie, Sister.**
Chosen for peace; the history of the Benedictine Sisters of Elizabeth, New Jersey. [Paterson, N.J., St. Anthony Guild Press, 1968]
246 p. illus. 24 cm.
ICSS; MdRi; MnCS; ViBris

1595   **Cannon, Lawrence, Sister.**
Christo-centric character of the Rule of St. Benedict.
Thesis (M.A.)–St. John's University, 1963.
Typescript.
KyCovS

Canterbury, England. Christ Church Priory.

1596   Accounts of Christ Church, Canterbury. MS. Lambeth Palace Library, London, codex 243. 224 f. Quarto. Saec. 14.
Microfilm: MnCH

1597   Cartae regiarum in thesauraro archiepiscopi inventarum. MS. Lambeth Palace Library, London, codex 1212. 201 f. Quarto. Saec. 13–14.
Microfilm: MnCH

1598   Martyrolgy etc. MS. Lambeth Palace Library, London, codex 20. 250 f. Octavo. Saec. 16.
Microfilm: MnCH

Capelle, Bernard, 1884–1961.

1599   Fondements scripturaires de l'angelologie liturgique.
(In Sacra pagina; miscellanea biblica Congressus Internationalis Catholici de re biblica. Gembloux, 1959. v. 2, p. 456–464)
PLatS

1600   Les liturgies "basiliennes" et saint Basile.
(In Doresse, Jean. Un témoin archaique de la liturgie de S. Basile. Louvain, 1960. p. 45–74)
InStme; PLatS

1601   Liturgique et non-liturgique. 2d ed. Louvain, Abbaye du Mont Cesar [1938].
17 p. 22 cm. (La liturgie catholique, no. 5)
MnCS

1602   A new light on the Mass. Translated by a monk of Glenstal. Dublin, Clonmore & Reynolds [1952].
61 p.
NdRi

1603   A new light on the Mass. London, Burns, Oates and Washbourne, 1961.
66 p.
MoCo

1604   Um das Wesens-Verständnis der Messe. Aus dem Französischen übertragen von Dr. Hans Krömler. Salzburg, St. Peter, Verlag Rupertswerk [1949].
72 p. 23 cm. (In viam salutis, v. 2)
InStme; NdRi

1605   (ed) An early Euchologium; the Der-Balizeh papyrus, enlarged and reedited by C. H. Roberts and B. Capelle. Louvain, Bureaux du Muséon, 1949.
69 p. facsims 27 cm.
InStme

1606   **Capesius, Andrew J.,** d. 1960.
Nomina monachorum quae continentur in Album Benedictum. St. Bernard, Ala., n.d.
Typescript.
AStb

Cappuyns, Maieul, 1901–

1607   Jean Scot Erigene; sa vie, son oeuvre, sa pensée. Louvain, Abbaye du Mont Cesar; Paris, Desclée, de Brouwer, 1933.
xxiii, 410 p. 26 cm.
InStme; MnCS; PLatS

1608   Lexique de la Regula Magistri. Steenbrugis, in Abbatia S. Petri, 1964.
209 p. 24 cm. (Instrumenta patristica, VI)
InStme; KAS; MoCo; MnCS; PLatS

Capra, Ramiro M., O.S.B.Oliv., 1903–

1609   Monte Oliveto Maggiore. Monza, Società Anonima, 1939.
142 p. illus. 20 cm.
InStme

1610   Monte Oliveto Maggiore. Seregno (Milano), Maschile S. Giuseppe, 1954.
143 p. plates, 21 cm.
MnCS

1611   **Caraccioli, Antonius, abbot of St. Victor, Marseille.**
Epistola consolatoria ad parentem in morte primogeniti. MS. Cava, Italy (Benedictine abbey, codex 65. 55 f. Octavo. Saec. 16.
Microfilm: MnCH

1612   **Caralt, Ambròs,** 1904–
L'Escolania de Montserrat. Abadia de Montserrat, 1955.
221 p. illus. 22 cm.
CaQStB; MnCS

1613   **Caravita, Andrea,** d. 1875.
I codici e le arti a Monte Cassino. Monte Cassino, Tipi della Badia, 1870.
3 v.
MoCo

Cardine, Eugène, 1905–

1614   Is Gregorian chant measured music; a critique of the book by J.W.A. Vollaerts, Rhythmic proportions in early medieval ecclesiastical chant, Leiden, Brill, 1958. Translated with a foreword by A. Dean. Solesmes, Abbaye Saint-Pierre, 1964.
69 p. 21 cm.
KAS; NcBe

1615   Première année de chant grégorien. Rome, Institut Pontifical de Musique Sacrée, 1975.
68 p. music, 25 cm.
InStme

1616   **Carl, Hildalita, Sister.**
Kansas history as seen in the works of Margaret Hill McCarter. Seneca, Kans., The Courier-Tribune Press, 1938.
xiii, 123 p. 20 cm.
KAM; KAS; MnCS

1617   **Carletta, Sister.**
Unison Mass for parish use. By Sister M. Carletta, O.S.B., and Rev. Jerome Coller, O.S.B. Collegeville, Minn., The Liturgical Press, 1960.
[8] p. 19 cm.
MnCS; PLatS

1618   **Carlevaris, Angela, Sister.**
(ed) Hildegardis Scivias. Edidit Adelgundis Führkötter, collaborante Angela Carlevaris. Turnholti, Brepols, 1978.
2 v. illus. 25 cm.
InStme

1619   **Carluccio, Gerard Majella,** 1916–
The gifts of the Holy Ghost according to St. Gregory the Great. Newton, N.J., Little Flower Monastery [1945].

45 p. 25 cm.
Extract from dissertation.

Carnot, Maurus, 1865–

1620   Die Geschichte des Jörg Jenatsch. Einsiedeln, Benziger, n.d.
260 p. 19 cm.
PLatS

1621   Wo die Bündertannen rauschen; Erzählungen. Einsiedeln, Benziger & Co., n.d.
250 p. 19 cm.
KAS; PLatS

1622   **Carosi, Paolo,** 1914–
Cerreto Laziale. Presso Bernardino Carosi, Cerreto Laziale, 1955.
126 p. plates, 18 cm.
InStme

1623   **Carré, Remi,** 1706–1780(?).
Recueil curieux & édifiant, sur les cloches de l'église, avec les cérémonies de leur bénédiction, à l'occasion de celle qui fui faite à Paris le jeudi 3 juin 1756 à l'Abbaye de Penthemont, sous le gouvernement de Madame de Bethisy . . . Cologne, 1757.
104 p. 17 cm.
MnCH (Plante)

Cartier, Germanus, d. 1749.

1624   Biblia Sacra vulgatae editiones . . . recognita . . . sub directione P. Germani Cartier. Constantiae, sumptibus Jacobi Friderici Bez, 1770.
4 v. 37 cm.
InStme; PLatS

1625   Psalmodiae ecclesiasticae elucidatio . . . Germani Cartier. Denuo edidit Josephus Schneider. Ratisonae, G. J. Manz, 1871.
xx, 396 p. 17 cm.
InStme; PLatS

Cary-Elwes, Columba, 1903–

1626   Monastic renewal. [New York], Herder and Herder [1967].
256 p. 22 cm.
CaMWiSb; InStme; MnCS; PLatS; OkShG; NcBe; MoCo; MdRi; MnStj; InFer; ViBris

1627   The problem of reunion in England. Garrison, N.Y., Graymoor [1951].
unpaged. 22 cm. (Unity studies, no. 6)
"Reprint from Unitas."
InFer; InStme

1628   Drawings at the Second Vatican Council. [New York, Macmillan, 1963?].
vii, 52 plates, 22 cm.
MnCS; PLatS

Casel, Odo, 1886–1949.

1629   Altchristlicher Kult und Antike.
(*In* Mysterium; gesammelte Arbeiten Laacher Mönche. Münster, 1926. p. 9–28)
PLatS

1630   Benedikt von Nursia als Pneumatiker.
(*In* Heilige Ueberlieferung. Münster, 1938. p. 96–123)
PLatS

1631   Das christliche Opfermysterium; zur Morphologie und Theologie des eucharistischen Hochgebetes. [Graz], Verlag Styria [1968].
lv, 719 p. 22 cm.
Hrsg. von P. Viktor Warnach, O.S.B.
KAS; MnCS

1632   The commemoration of the Lord in the early Christian liturgy; basic notions of the Canon. [Translated by Mark Bauman. 1964].
Typescript.
Translation of: Das Gedächtnis des Herrn in der altchristlichen Liturgie. 6th ed.
KAS

1633   De philosophorum graecorum silentio mystico. Giessen, A. Töpelmann, 1919. [Nachdruck 1967].
166 p. 23 cm.
Published in part as the author's inaugural dissertation, Bonn, 1919.
MnCS; PLatS

1634   Faites ceci en memoire de moi. Traduit de l'allemand par J. C. Didier. Paris, Editions du Cerf, 1962.
184 p. 21 cm. (Lex orandi, 34)
Translation of: Das Mysteriengedächtnis der Messliturgie im Lichte der Tradition.
InStme; MnCS; PLatS

1635   La fete de paques dans l'église des Pères. Traduit de l'allemand par J. C. Didier. Paris, Editions du Cerf, 1963.
155 p. 20 cm. (Lex orandi, 37)
Translation of: Art und Sinn der ältesten christlichen Osterfeier.
KAS; MoCo; PLatS

1636   Die grosse Mysteriennacht.
(*In* Oesterliches Heilsmysterium, p. 68–81)
PLatS

1637   Die Messe als heilige Mysterienhandlung.
(*In* Mysterium; gesammelte Arbeiten Laacher Mönche. Münster, 1926. p. 29–52)
PLatS

1638   Le mystère du culte dans le Christianisme; richesse du mystère du Christ. Traduction de Dom J. Hild et A. Liefooghe. [2. éd.]. Paris, Editions du Cerf, 1964.
331 p. 21 cm. (Lex orandi, 38)
Translation of: Das christliche Kultmysterium.
PLatS

1639   Le mystère de l'Eglise. Textes tirés des écrits et conférences de Dom Odo Casel, choisis, groupés et présentés par madame Théophora Schneider, moniale de l'Abbaye Sainte-Croix de Herstelle. Traduit de l'allemand par Dom P. Schaller et l'abbé G. Blin. [Tours], Mame [1965].
370 p. 22 cm.
PLatS

1640   Mysterium der Ekklesia; von der Gemeinschaft aller Erlösten in Christus Jesus. Aus Schriften und Vorträgen [ausgewählt und eingeleitet von Theophora Schneider, mit einem Vorwort versehen von Burkhard Neunheuser]. Mainz, M. Grünewald [1961].
427 p. 21 cm.
InStme

1641   The mystery of Christian worship, and other writings. Edited by Burkhard Neunheuser, with a preface by Charles Davis. Westminster, Md., Newman Press [1962].
xvii, 212 p. 22 cm.
Translation of: Das christliche Kultmysterium. 4th ed.
ILSP; InStme; MnCS; OkSh; PLatS; NcBe; MnStj

1642   Vom Spiegel als Symbol. Aus nachgelassenen Schriften zusammengestellt von Julia Plat. Maria Laach, Ars liturgica, 1961.
62 p. 18 cm.
PLatS

1643   Zur Idee der liturgischen Festfeier.
(*In* Mysterium; gesammelte Arbeiten Laacher Mönche. Münster, 1926. p. 53–61)
PLatS

1644   **Casey, Noah Joseph,** 1949–
Martin B. Hellriegel, liturgist.
iv, 54 leaves, 29 cm.
Thesis (M.A.)–Indiana University, 1978.
InStme

Casey, Teresita, Sister.

1645   Character formation through biography.
Thesis (Lib. Sc.)–Catholic University of America, 1933.
Typescript.
KyCovS

1646   Latin hymns as literature.
Thesis (M.A.)–Xavier University, 1927.
Typescript.
KyCovS

Caspar I, abbot of St. Blasien im Schwarzwald.

1647   Liber originum monasterii S. Blasii Hercyneae Silvae. MS. Benediktinerabtei St. Paul im Lavanttal, Austria, codex 98/2. 475 p. Folio. Saec. 16.
Microfilm: MnCH proj. no. 11,884

1648   Relatio de prima inhabitatione Silvae
Nigrae et aedificatione monasterii S.
Blasii. MS. Benediktinerabtei St. Paul im
Lavanttal, Austria, codex 74/1. Folio.
Saec. 16.
Microfilm: MnCH proj. no. 11,731

1649 **Caspar von Altenburg.**
Cantilene germanica cum notis musicis.
MS. Vienna, Nationalbibliothek, codex
4015, f. 119r. Quarto. Saec. 15.
Microfilm: MnCH proj. no. 17,215

1650 **Castaniza, Juan de,** d. 1599.
Vida de la prodigiosa virgen Santa Gertrudis la Magna . . . sacada de los cinco
libros intitulados: Insinuación de la piedad
divina . . . Madrid, Blas Roman, 1782.
396 p. 21 cm.
MnCS

Castelli, Benedetto, 1577–1644.
1651   Della misura dell'acque correnti. Roma,
nella Stamparia Camerale, 1628.
59 p. diagrs. 22 cm.
Massachusetts Institute of Technology;
John Crerar Library, Chicago.

1652   Risposta alle oppositzioni del s. Lodovico
delle Colombe e del s. Vinzensio di Grazia,
contro trattato del sig. Galileo Galilei, delle
cose che stanno su l'acqua, ò che in quelle si
muovono. Firenze, appresso Cosimo
Giunti, MDCXV.
319 [i.e. 335] p. 23 cm.
Library of Congress; University of
Michigan.

1653 **Catalogue of the nuns and convents of
holy Order of St. Benedict in the
United States.** [Beatty, Pa.], St. Vincent's Abbey, 1879.
69 p. 22 cm.
KAS; PLatS

Catholic University of Peking.
1654   From provisional to final registration.
(*In* Catholic University of Peking.
Bulletin, no. 8 (1931), p. 103–130).
PLatS

1655   The promoters of the library of the
Catholic University of Peking, Peking,
China. n.p., n.d.
26 p. 18 cm.
Published ca. 1927.
PLatS

Cava, Italy (Benedictine abbey).
1656   Annales Cavenses. MS. Cava, Italy
(Benedictine abbey), codex 3, f. 97–131.
Folio. Saec. 11.
Microfilm: MnCH

1657   Annales Cavenses a. 569–1315.
(*In* Monumenta Germaniae historica.
Scriptores. Stuttgart, 1963. t. 3, p.
185–197)

MnCS; PLatS

1658   La badia della SS. Trinità di Cava; cenni
storici. Badia di Cava, 1942.
90 p. plates, 22 cm.
MnCS

1659   Codex diplomaticus Cavensis, nunc
primum in lucem editus, curantibus DD.
Michaele Morcaldi . . . Neapoli, P. Piazzi,
1873–93.
8 v. illus., Facsims. 32 cm.
KAS (v. 1–5); PLatS (v. 6)

1660   Propria sanctorum pro Cathedrali Ecclesia SS. Trinitatis Cavae Tyrrenorum.
[Cava dei Tirreni, Stab. Tip. del Popolo,
n.d.]
95 p. 19 cm.
Published ca. 1800.
PLatS

1661 **Cavelti, Sigisbert,** 1885–1918.
Grundriss der Philosophie. Engelberg,
1914–
v. 23 cm.
Reproduced from typed copy.
PLatS

1662 **Cecilia, Sister.**
The parish burns "Red," by Martin Car-
rabine, S.J., and Sister M. Cecilia, O.S.B.
(Queen's Work pamphlets, 248)
PLatS

Celesia, Pietro Geremia Michelangelo,
1814–1904.
1663   La caduta e la redenzione secondo la
rivelazione et la filosofia . . . Roma, Tipografia Salviucci, 1864.
19 p. 23 cm.
PLatS

1664   Il giudeo ed il gentile al cospetto del
Cristo . . . Roma, Tipografia Salviucci,
1864.
19 p. 23 cm.
PLatS

1665   La infallibilitate R. Pontificis . . .
Augustae Taurinorum, Julius Speirani et
Filii, 1870.
17 p. 23 cm.
PLatS

1666   Il magistero della Chiesa Cattolica in ordine alla civiltà dei popoli . . . Roma, Tipografia Salviucci, 1863.
29 p. 23 cm.
PLatS

1667   Pel XIV centenario del patriarca S.
Benedetto . . . Palermo, C. Tamburello,
1880.
25 p. 21 cm.
KAS

1668 **Celestines (Benedictines).**
Constitvtiones monachorvm Ordinis S.
Benedicti Congregationis Coelestinorvm

SS. mi Dni. Nri. Urbani PP. VIII iussu recognitae, et eiusdem auctoritate approbatae et confirmatae. Romae, apud Haered. Bartholomei Zanetti, 1627.
288, xli, 11, [21] p.
KAS (microfilm); MnCS (microfilm); PLatS (microfilm)

1669 **The Centenary of St. Gregory the Great at Downside,** with the three sermons preached on the occasion . . . Downside, St. Gregory's Monastery, 1890.
56 p. 23 cm.
PLatS

1670 **Center for Slav Culture, St. Procopius College, Isle, Ill.**
Czech-American Catholics, 1850–1920 [by Joseph Cada]. Lisle, Ill., 1964.
124 p. 19 cm.
KAS

1671 **Cerda, Joseph de la,** d. 1645.
In sacram Iudith historiam commentarius litteralis & moralis . . . Editio novissima. Lugduni, sumptibus Laurentii Anisson, 1663.
2 v. 35 cm.
MnCS; PLatS

1672 **Casi, Innocenzo,** d. 1704.
Tractatus de antiquis romanorum ritibus . . . Bononiae, typis Petri Mariae de Montibus, 1698.
117 p. 14 cm.
KAS

1673 **Cestello, Bosco David,** 1920–1961.
The University of Pittsburgh and the crisis of our age.
9 p. 28 cm.
PLatS

1674 **Cham, Switzerland. Schwestern-Institut Heiligkreuz.**
Hundert Jahre Schwestern-Institut Heiligkreuz Cham. [Cham], hrsg. von der Institut-Leitung, 1962.
231 p. illus. 25 cm.
PLatS

1675 **Chang, Cornelius Patrick,** 1931–
Doctrine of the mutual indwelling of God and man according to St. John the Evangelist.
iv, 34 leaves, 28 cm.
Thesis (M.A.)–St. Vincent College, Latrobe, Pa., 1962.
Typescript.
PLatS

Chapman, John, 1865–1933.
1676 The Byzantine Schism.
(*In* Lattey, Cuthbert. The Church; papers from the Summer School of Catholic Studies held at Cambridge, 1927. p. 240–271)
PLatS

1677 The Holy Eucharist in the pre-Nicene Church.
(*In* Lattey, Cuthbert. Catholic faith in the Holy Eucharist; papers from the Summer School of Catholic Studies held at Cambridge, 1922. 3d. ed. Cambridge, 1928. p. 16–41)
PLatS

1678 John the Presbyter, and the Fourth Gospel. Oxford, Clarendon Press, 1911.
10 p. 23 cm.
NcBe

1679 Studies on early Papacy. Port Washington, N.Y., Kennikat Press [1971].
238 p. 22 cm.
Reprint of the 1928 edition.
MnCS

Charlier, Célestin, 1911–
1680 Cassiodore, Pélage et les origines de la Vulgate Paulinienne.
(*In* Studiorum Paulinorum Congressus Internationalis Catholicus, 1961. v. 2, p. 461–470)
PLatS

1681 The Christian approach to the Bible. Translated from the French by Hubert J. Richards and Brendan Peters. Westminster, Md., Newman Press, 1963.
298 p.
InFer

1682 La lecture chrètienne de la Bible. [6. éd.]. Maredsous (Belgium), Editions de Maredsous, 1957.
xiii, 316 p. 21 cm.
KAS

1683 **Charvin, Gaston,** 1887–
(ed) Statuts, chapitres généraux et visites de l'Ordre de Cluny, avec un avant-propos et des notes par G. Charvin. Paris, Editions E. de Boccard, 1965–
v. 28 cm.
InStme; MnCS; MoCo; KAS; PLatS

Chaussy, Ives, 1912–
1684 L'Abbaye d'Amenèches-Argentan et Sainte Opportune; sa vie et son culte . . . Paris, P. Lethielleux, 1970.
480 p. plates, 24 cm.
MnCS; PLatS

1685 Les Bénédictins anglais réfugiés en France au xvii siècle (1611–1669). Paris, F. Lethielleux, 1967.
xxiv, 255 p. plates, 24 cm.
InStme; KAS; MnCS; MoCo; PLatS

1686 Une paroisse bretonne: Lennon. Quimper, Librairie Saint-Corentin, 1953.
203 p. illus. 24 cm.
MnCS

1687 **Chertsey Abbey, England.**
Chertsey Abbey cartularies; volume II,
part I–II, being the second portion of the
Cartulary in the Public Record Office . . .
Frome and London, Surrey Record Soci-
ety, 1958–63.
2 v. 26 cm.
PLatS

1688 **Cherubini, Angelo Maria,** fl. 1633–1637.
Magnum bullarium romanum, a Beato
Leone Magno usque S.P.N. Benedictum
XIV. Opus absolutissimum Laertii
Cherubini . . . a D. Angelo Maria
Cherubino monacho Cassinensi . . . il-
lustratum & auctum. Editio novissima.
Luxemburgi, Henricus-Albertus Gosse,
1742.
6 v. in 5. 42 cm.
InStme

1689 **Chevallier, Philippe,** 1884–
(ed) Dionysiaca; recueil donnant l'ensem-
ble des traductions latines des ouvrages at-
tribues au Denys de l'Aréopage . . .
[Paris], Desclée, de Brouwer [1937].
2 v. 30 cm.
Edited by Ph. Chevallier (see p. xcvi)
PLatS

1690 **Chevetogne, Belgium (Benedictine
priory).**
Ordre de la sainte et divine liturgie telle
au'on la célèbre dans le grande église et
sur la Sainte Montagne. [Amay, Prieuré
Bénédictin, 1935?]
64 p.
ILSP

1691 **Chiari, Isidoro, bp. of Foligno,** 1495–
1555.
Isidori Clarii Brixiani, monachi Casinensis, ad eos qui a communi ecclesiae sententia discessere, adhortatio ad concordiam.
Lutetia Parisiorum, per Nicolaum Diutem
[1540?].
unpaged, 17 cm.
MnCS

1692 **Chicago, Ill. St. Paul's Church.**
Pfarrbote der St. Paulus Gemeinde;
Monatschrift für Familie und Haus.
Februar, 1905.
16 p. 20 cm.
KAS

1693 **Chiemsee (Frauenchiemsee), Bavaria
(abbey of Benedictine nuns).**
Die Künstlerchronik von Frauenchiemsee. Hrsg. von Karl Raupp und Franz
Wolter. München, F. Bruckmann [1918].
141 p. plates (part col.) 25 cm.
MnCS

1694 **Chifflet, Philippe,** 1597–1657.
(ed) Sacrosancti et oecumenici concilii
Tridentini . . . canones et decreta. Quod

in hac editione praestitum sit, sequens
Philippi Chifflettii, abbatis Balernnensis
. . . praefatio indicabit. Lugduni, 1864.
ILSP

1695 **Chittister, Jean, Sister.**
Climb along the cutting edge; an
analysis of change in religious life . . .
New York, Paulist Press, c. 1977.
xiv, 304 p. 23 cm.
InFer; InStme; ICSS; MnCS; MnStj;
MoCo; MdRi; ViBris

1696 **Chopiney, George,** 1921–
Les Psaumes, ces inconnus. Paris, Editions du Cedre, 1955.
47 p.
MoCo

1697 **Christophorus, abbot of Millstat.**
Rubricae de vita monastica. MS. Benediktinerabtei St. Peter, Salzburg, codex
b.III.10, f. 191r–199r. Quarto. Saec. 15.
Microfilm: MnCH proj. no. 10,359

1698 **Chronicon Angliae Petriburgense.**
Interum post Sparkium cum cod. isto
contulit J. A. Giles. New York, B.
Franklin [1967].
xiii, 180 p. 23 cm. (Publications of the
Caxton Society, 154)
"Originally published . . . 1845"
PLatS

Chronicon Gotwicense. *See* Bessel,
Johann Georg. Chronicon Gotwicense.

1699 **Chronicon Mellicense,** prima manu scriptum anno 1126 (teste pagina 125), varie
glossatum et recentiorum manibus interpolatum, deinde glossatum usque ad
annum 1564. MS. Benediktinerabtei
Melk, Austria, codex 391, p. 45–166.
Folio. Saec. 12–16.
Microfilm: MnCH proj. no. 2009

1700 **Chronica Ordinis S. Benedicti.** Tomus
secundus: centuria secunda. MS. Vienna, Schottenstift, codex 613. 22 f.
Quarto. Saec. 17.
Microfilm: MnCH proj. no. 4269

1701 **Chronicon Petroburgense.** Nunc primum
typis mandatum, curante Thoma Stapleton. Londini, 1849.
(Camden Society. Publications, 47)
ILSP

1702 **Chronik der Benediktiner-Abtei St.
Georgenberg,** nun Fiecht, in Tirol.
Verfasst von einem Mitgliede dieser
Abtei. Innsbruck, Wagner'schen Uni-
versitäts-Buchhandlung, 1874.
352 p. plates, 21 cm.
KAS; MnCS

Chupungco, Anscar J., 1939–
1703 The cosmic elements in Christian Pass-
over. Roma, Editrice Anselmiana, 1977.

119 p. 25 cm. (Studia Anselmiana, 72)
InStme; KAS

1704   An essay on symbolism and liturgical celebration.
(*In* Symbolisme et theologie. Sacramentum 2. Roma, 1974. Studia Anselmiana, v. 64, p. [173]–193)
PLatS

1705   **Chutis, Gervase Alexander,** 1904–
The development of international action against narcotics.
96 p.
Thesis (M.A.)–University of Notre Dame, 1935.
Typescript.
PLatS

Cisneros, Garcias de, 1455–1510.

1706   Obras completas. Abadia de Montserrat, 1965.
2 v. 25 cm. (Scripta et documenta, 15, 16)
InStme; KAS; MnCS; PLatS

1707   Constituciones de los Monges Hermitanos de la Montaña de Montserrate. MS. Monasterio benedictino de Montserrat, Spain, codex 835, f. 121–159. Quarto. Saec. 17.
Microfilm: MnCH proj. no. 30,092

1708   Constituciones de los Padres Hermitanos de la Montaña de Montserrate. MS. Monasterio benedictino de Montserrat, Spain, codex 55. 80 f. Quarto. Saec. 18.
Microfilm: MnCH proj. no. 29,998

1709   Exercitia spiritualia, sive Secundum viam purgativam, illuminativam & unitivam orandi & meditandi methodus . . . ante unum alterumve seculum conscripta, ad facilem usum a Matthaeo Weiss [O.S.B.] digesta. Salisburgi, typis Christophori Katzenbergeri, 1634.
237 p. 13 cm.
MnCS

1710   **Cisneros, Juan de.**
Origen de la Congregacion de la Observancia de S. Benito de Espana y sus monasterios capitulares. MS. Monasterio benedictino de Montserrat, Spain, codex 846. 135 f. Quarto. Saec. 17 (1645).
Microfilm: MnCH proj. no. 30,098

1711   **Clair, Romain,** 1928–
Les filles d'Hautecombe dans l'Empire latin de Constantinople.
(*In* Analecta Sacri Ordinis Cisterciensis, v. 17, p. 261–277)
PLatS

1712   **Clauss, Benedicta, Sister.**
The first one-hundred years; commemorative pageant for the centennial of the Sisters of St. Benedict, Ferdinand, Indiana, 1967.
27 p. illus.
InFer

Clément, Jean Marie, 1904–

1713   Initia patrum latinorum, collegit ordinavitque J.-M. Clement. Turnholti, Brepols, 1971.
190 p. 26 cm. (Corpus christianorum [Series latina])
InStme; PLatS

1714   (ed) Facundus, Bp. of Hermiane, 6th cent. Opera omnia. Ediderunt Johannes-Maria Clement, O.S.B., et Rolandus Vander Plaetse. Turnholti, Brepols, 1974.
xxxv, 519 p. 26 cm. (Corpus christianorum. Series latina, v. 90A)
PLatS

1715   (2dary) La Règle du Maitre . . . Paris, 1964–65. 3 vols. Partial contents: v. 3: Concordance verbale du text critique conforme a l'orthographe du manuscrit Par. lat. 12205 per Jean-Marie Clément . . .
MnCS; PLatS

1716   **Clements, David J.,** 1926–
Built on a firm foundation; Standing Rock Centenary, 1873–1973. Fort Yates, N.D., Catholic Indian Mission, 1973.
96 p. illus.
MoCo

1717   **Clinch, Columban,** 1903–1968.
The problem of employment relief in France during the revolutionary eighteenth century.
xxxvi, 398 p. 28 cm.
Thesis (Ph.D.)–University of Kansas, 1949.
Typescript.
KAS

1718   **Closs, Lothar,** 1924–
Sittlicher Relativismus und Schelers Wertethik. St. Ottilien, Eos Verlag, 1955.
110 p.
ILSP

1719   **Clougherty, Francis Xavier,** 1895–
The publications of the Catholic University of Peking.
(*In* Catholic University of Peking. Bulletin, no. 6 (1929), p. 67–92)
PLatS

1720   **Cluniacs.**
Statuts, chapitres généraux et visites de l'Ordre de Cluny, par Dom. G. Charvin . . . Paris, E. de Boccard, 1965–
v. 28 cm.
French or Latin.
InStme; KAS; MnCS; PLatS

1721 **Cluny, France (Benedictine abbey).**
Recueil des chartes de l'Abbaye de Cluny, formé par Auguste Bernard, complété et publié par Alexandre Bruel . . . Paris, Imprimerie nationale, 1876–1903.
6 v. plates, facsims. 27 x 22 cm.
KAS; MnCS

Cody, Aelred, 1932–
1722 Heavenly sanctuary and liturgy in the Epistle to the Hebrews; the achievements of salvation in the Epistle's perspectives. St. Meinrad, Ind., Grail Publications, 1960.
xiii, 227 p. 23 cm.
Thesis–University of Ottawa.
InStme; KAS; MnCS; MoCo; OkShG

1723 A history of Old Testament priesthood. Rome, Pontifical Biblical Institute, 1969.
xxvii, 216 p. 24 cm. (Analecta biblica, 35)
InStme; MoCo; PLatS

1724 **Coebergh, Charles,** 1898–
Testimonia orationis christianae antiquioris. Turnholti, Brepols, 1977.
xxxvii, 217 p. 26 cm. (Corpus christianorum. Continuatio mediaevalis, 47)
PLatS

1725 **Coelestinus, abbot of St. Emmeram,** 1631–1691.
Ratisbona monastica. Klösterliches Regensburg . . . Regensburg, J. V. Rädlmayer, 1752.
[24], 620, [15] p. 22 cm.
KAS

1726 **Coelho, Antonio,** 1892–
Cours de liturgie romaine. Traduit par Dom Gaspar Lefebvre. Premier volume: Liturgie fondamentale. Lophem-lez-Bruges, Apostolat liturgique, 1928.
376 p. 21 cm.
CaQStB; KAS

1727 **Coffin, Lorane, Sister.**
The Benedictine community; a reinterpretation. Divine Word International Centre, 1971.
19 p.
InFer

Coggin, Walter A., 1916–
1728 The role of the will in personality development.
228 p.
Thesis (Ph.D.)–Catholic University of America, 1954.
Typescript.
NcBe

1729 The role of the will in personality development. Washington, D.C., Catholic University of America Press, 1954.
vii, 42 p. 23 cm. (Catholic University of America. Philosophical studies, no. 154. Abstract series, no. 10)

MnCS; NcBe

1730 **Coldingham Priory, England.**
The correspondence, inventories, account rolls, and law proceedings, of the Priory of Coldingham. London, J. B. Nichols and Son, 1841.
xvii, 259, cxxxvi p. illus., facsims. 23 cm. (Publications of the Surtees Society, v. 12)
MnCS

1731 **Cole, Edwin,** 1938–
A study of interpersonal trust in a group and its relation to the amount and type of communication and leadership-role behavior within that group.
91 p.
Thesis (M.A.)–University of Kansas, 1969.
MoCo

Coleman, Bernard, Sister, 1890–1975.
1732 Masinaigans: the little book. A biography of Monsignor Joseph F. Buh, Slovenian missionary in America, 1864–1922 . . . Saint Paul, Minn., North Central Pub. Co., 1972.
x, 368 p. illus. 25 cm.
InStme; MnCS

1733 Ojibwa myths and legends . . . Minneapolis, Ross and Haines, 1962.
135 p. illus. 23 cm.
MnCS

1734 **Colgan, Quentin,** 1942–
Perception, expression and the painter in Merleau-Penty.
133 p. 28 cm.
Thesis (M.A.)–St. Louis University, 1974.
Typescript.
InStme

College of St. Benedict, St. Joseph, Minn.
1735 Facula [yearbook]. 1–21, 1939–1959.
MnStj (Archives)

1736 Master Planning Committee. Directions for the future. June 15, 1971.
106 p. illus., charts, tables, 22.32 cm.
MnCS

1737 Office of Planning and Program Development. Retention-attrition, freshmen of 1971–72.
31 p.
MnStj (Archives)

1738 Office of Planning and Program Development. Retention-attrition study of the freshmen class of 1972–73.
42 p.
MnStj (Archives)

Coller, Jerome Thomas, 1929–
1739 Concerto for piano and winds.
2 parts.

Thesis (D.M.A.)—Cornell University, 1971.
Typescript.
MnCS (Archives)

1740   Understanding 20th-century music [Phonotape cassette]. Collegeville, Minn., St. John's University, 1974.
1 cassette, 2 sides.
Recorded at SJU April 27, 1974—Parents' Day.
MnCS

1741   Unison Mass for parish use, by Sister M. Carletta and Jerome Coller, O.S.B. Collegeville, Minn., The Liturgical Press, 1960.
11 p. music 24.28 cm.
MnCS; PLatS

1742   Our parish prays and sings: organ accompaniment . . . [compiled] by Irvin Udulutsch, O.F.M.Cap. [and] Jerome Coller, O.S.B. Collegeville, Minn., The Liturgical Press [c 1959].
x, 222 p. music, 24/29 cm.
MnCS

1743   (tr) Reichgauer, Eduard. Union in God through the Body of Christ . . . Translated by Jerome Coller, O.S.B. Collegeville, Minn., The Liturgical Press, 1959.
InStme; KySu; MnCS

1744   **Collins, Mary Dennis, Sister.**
Liturgical prayer; the spiritual life of the Christian.
(*In* Experiments in community. 28th North American Liturgical Week, 1967, p. 113–119)
PLatS

1745   **Collins, Mary L., Sister.**
Presidential prayer in the liturgy: proclamation and confession of the Christian mystery.
iii, 211 leaves, 28 cm.
Thesis (Ph.D.)—Catholic University of America, 1967.
KAM

1746   **Collopy, Andrea, Sister.**
The Crescent-Villa Community: the bicentennial celebration, 1776–1976.
48 p. illus. 9 x 12 cm.
Lithographed.
KyCovS

Colombás, Garcia, 1920–
1747   The ancient concept of the monastic life. Translated by a nun of Mt. St. Mary's Abbey, Wrentham, Mass.
(*In* Monastic studies 2, p. 65–117)
PLatS

1748   El concepto de monje y vida monástica hasta fines del siglo V. Abadia de Montserrat, 1959.

[257]–342 p. 24 cm.
(*In* Studia monastica, vol. 1, fasc. 2)
MnCS

1749   La confirmació de la conraria de la mare de Déu de Montserrat.
(*In* Analecta Montserratensis, v. 10, p. 55–63)
PLatS

1750   Historia de la fundación de tres cátedras de teología en la Universidad de Salamanca (1692).
90 p. 24 cm.
Extracta de: Hispania sacra, vol. 13.
MnCS

1751   Origenes y primer desarrollo del Colegio de San Vicente de Salamanca.
74 p. 27 cm.
Extract from unidentified periodical, p. 257–330.
MnCS

1752   Paradis et vie angélique; le sens eschatologique de la vocation chrétienne. Traduit de l'espagnol par Dom Suitbert Caron. Paris, Éditions du Cerf, 1961.
289 p. 20 cm.
MnCS; MoCo; PLatS

1753   La primera edición de las constituciones de la Congregación Benedictina de Valladolid.
8 p. facsims. 28 cm.
MnCS

1753a   La Regla de San Benito; introducción y comentario por García M. Colombás, O.S.B. Traducción y notas por Inaki Arranguren, O. Cist. Madrid, Biblioteca de Autores Cristianos, 1979.
xxiii, 510 p. 20 cm.
PLatS

1754   **Combe, Pierre,** 1913–
Histoire de la restauration du chant grégorien d'après des documents inédits. Abbaye de Solesmes, 1969.
476 p. plates, 22 cm.
KAS

1755   **Compendium asceseos Benedictinae.**
Posonii, Typis Haeredum Belnayanorum, 1852.
115 p. 21 cm.
Preface signed at S. Monte Pannoniae.
KAS

Compte, Efrem M., 1926–
1756   Guillem de Miers, abat de Sant Pau de Roma, i la seva obra litúrgico-monàstica [by] Alexander Oliver and Efrem Compte.
(*In* Liturgica, 2: Cardinal I. A. Schuster im memoriam, 1958. v. 2, p. 299–345)
PLatS

1757   Els necrologis antics de Sant Cugat del Valles.

(*In* Analecta Montserratensia, v. 10, p. [131]–164)
PLatS

Conception Abbey, Conception, Mo.

1758   Centennial photo album, 1873–1973.
4 v. illus.
MoCo; MnStj (Archives)

1759   The Holy Rule of Saint Benedict as lived by the monks of Conception Abbey, Conception, Missouri. [Conception, Mo., 1961].
[48] p. illus. 22 x 28 cm.
Consists of illustrations accompanied by quotations from the Rule of St. Benedict.
MnCS; MoCo; PLatS

1760   Religious books . . . 1975.
64 p. 20 cm.
List of religious books compiled by the library staff of Conception Abbey and Seminary.
InStme

1761   Second Passion Sunday, or Palm Sunday. Translated and arranged especially for lay participation, with commentary and musical notation by the monks of Conception Abbey. Conception Abbey Press [1956].
48 p. 21 cm.
KAS; PLatS

1762   The solemn Evening Mass [Holy Thursday]. Translated and arranged especially for lay participation, with commentary and musical notation, by the monks of Conception Abbey. Conception Abbey Press [1956].
32 p. 21 cm.
PLatS

1763   To the memory of the first Benedictine pope, St. Gregory the Great, on the occasion of the thirteenth centennial of his death, 604–1904, by a Benedictine of Conception Abbey. Conception, Mo. [1904?].
unpaged. 20 cm.
MnCS

1764   Tower topics (periodical). 1967–
InFer; MoCo

1765   **Conception Seminary College, Conception, Mo.**
Conception news. 1–   1974–
InFer; MoCo

1766   **Conference of American Prioresses.**
Newsletter. 1976–
InFer; MnStj

1767   **Conference of American Prioresses,** Norfolk, Nebr., March 7, 1975.
Upon this tradition; a statement of monastic values in the lives of American Benedictine sisters. Erie, Pa., Benet Press, 1975.

[8] p.
CaMWiSb; MnStj

1768   **Conference of American Benedictine Prioresses,** Madison, Wis., March 5, 1978.
Of time made holy; a statement on the Liturgy of the Hours in the lives of American Benedictine Sisters. Erie, Pa., Benet Press, 1978.
[12] p.
MnStj

1769   **Congrès international du IXe centenaire** de l'arrivée d'Anselme au Bec. Bec-Hellouin, Abbaye Notre-Dame du Bec, 1959.
636 p. 25 cm. (Spicilegium Beccense, v. 1)
CaQStB; KAS

Congress of Abbots. *See* Benedictines. Congress of Abbots.

Conley, Kieran, 1927–1966.

1770   Common prayer and worship in an ecumenical age.
(*In* The challenge of the Council . . . 25th annual North American Liturgical Week, 1964. p. 112–121)
PLatS

1771   The liturgical dimensions of scriptural and theological studies.
(*In* Catholic Theological Society of America. Proceedings, 1965. p. 1–9)
PLatS

1772   Procreation and the person.
(*In* Contraception and holiness, the Catholic predicament, ed. by Thomas D. Roberts, p. 61–71)
InFer; PLatS

1773   A theology of wisdom; a study in St. Thomas. Dubuque, Ia., Priory Press [1963].
xiii, 171 p. 23 cm.
InFer; InStme; MnCS; MoCo; PLatS

Connolly, Richard Hugh, 1873–1948.

1774   The De sacramentis. Oxford, Alden, 1942.
31 p.
MoCo

1775   The so-called Egyptian church order and derived documents. Cambridge [England], University Press, 1916; [Nendeln, Kraus reprint, 1967].
xiv, 197 p. 24 cm.
InStme; MnCS

1776   Some dates and documents for the early history of our house [Downside Abbey], I: Our establishment as a community at Douay. Printed for private circulation, 1930.
69 p. 26 cm.

No more published.
PLatS

1777   (ed) Giwargis, Metropolitan of Arbela, d. 987? Anonymi auctoris Expositio officiorum ecclesiae, Georgio Arbelensi vulgo adscripta. Edidit [et interpreatus est] R. H. Connolly. Parisiis, E. Typographeo Reipublicae, 1911–15.
       4 v. 25 cm. (Corpus scriptorum christianorum orientalium, v. 64, 71–72, 76)
       Syriac and Latin.
       InStme; MnCS; PLatS

1778   (tr) Narsei, 413 (ca)–503. The liturgical homilies of Narsei, translated into English with an introduction by R. H. Connolly . . . Cambridge, University Press, 1909; [Nendeln, Kraus reprint, 1967]
       lxxvi, 176 p. 21 cm.
       InStme

1778a **Conradus, monk of Hirsau,** d. 1190.
       Dialogus de mundi contemptu vel amore, attribué à Conrad d'Hirsau. Extraits de Allocutio ad Deum et du De veritatis inquisitione. Textes inédits introduits par R. Bultot. Louvain, Nauwelaerts, 1966.
       90 p. 25 cm.
       MnCS

1779   **Conradus, monk of Jumiéges.**
       Matutinale Beatae Mariae Virginis. MS. Augustinerchorherrenstift Klosterneuburg, Austria, codex 583. 226 f. Folio. Saec. 14.
       Microfilm: MnCH proj. no. 5560

       Conradus, abbot of Obernburg.
1780   Tractatus de indulgensiis, maxime monasterio Mellicensi et capellas ad S. Georgium prope Weitneck concessis a papis, archiepiscopis et episcopis. MS. Benediktinerabtei Melk, Austria, codex 1381, f. 661–681. Duodecimo. Saec. 15.
       Microfilm: MnCH proj. no. 1904

1781   Tractatus, utrum omnia quae continet regularis institutio sint praecepta. MS. Benediktinerabtei Melk, Austria, codex 1381, f. 645–   . Duodecimo. Saec. 15.
       Microfilm: MnCH proj. no. 1904

1782   **Conradus, monk of Scheyern,** d. 1241.
       Chronicon Schirense, saeculo XIII conscriptum, P. F. Stephano abbate, additionibus quibusdam, notisque auctum, & an. MDCXXIII publicae luci datum; Ioannis Aventini Chronicon Schirense nova hac editione ad praesens usque tempus perductum, accurante Georgio Christiano Ioannis. Argentorati, Dulsseckerus, 1616.
       [20], 236 p. plates, 20 cm.
       MnCS; PLatS

1783   **Conradus de Geissenfeld,** fl. 1460.
       Commentarius interlinearis in epistolam canonicam beati Iacobi apostoli, et in primam et alteram S. Petri apostoli epistolam. MS. Benediktinerabtei Melk, Austria, codex 1793, f. 180r–195r. Quarto. Saec. 15.
       Microfilm: MnCH proj. no. 2100

1784   **Consider your call;** a theology of monastic life by Daniel Rees and other members of the English Benedictine Congregation. Foreword by Cardinal Basil Hume. London, SPCK, 1978.
       xx, 447 p. 22 cm.
       InStme; MnCS; MnStj; PLatS

1785   **Constantinus, abbot of St. Symphorien, Mets,** d. 1024.
       Vita Adalberonis II Mettensis episcopi, auctore Constantino abbate.
       (*In* Monumenta Germaniae historia. Scriptores. Stuttgart, 1963. t. 4, p. 658–672)
       MnCS; PLatS

1786   **Constitutio monachorum nigrorum** (approbata a Benedicto papa). MS. Benediktinerabtei Kremsmünster, Austria, codex sine numero. 332 p. Saec. 15.
       Microfilm: MnCH proj. no. 430

1787   **Constitutiones iuxta Regulam sanctissimi** et Deo acceptissimi patris nostri Benedicti et reformationem (Mellicensem) anno 1419 et 1421 habitam. MS. Benediktinerabtei Kremsmünster, Austria, codex sine numero. 99 f. Saec. 1 & (1606).
       Microfilm: MnCH proj. no. 429

1788   **Consuetudines Benedictinae variae** (saec. XI–saec. XIV) publici juris fecit Giles Constable, Siegburg, apud Franciscum Schmitt Sucess., 1975.
       395 p. 26 cm. (Corpus consuetudinum monasticarum, t. 6)
       PLatS

       Contat, Jérome Joachim Le. *See* Le Contat, Jérome Joachim.

       Convent of the Immaculate Conception, Ferdinand, Ind.
1789   Christ yesterday . . . today . . . forever: centennial. Sisters of St. Benedict, Convent of the Immaculate Conception, Ferdinand, Ind., 1867–1967.
       unpaged, chiefly illus. 28 cm.
       InFer; InStme; MnStj (Archives); PLatS

1790   The Dove. 1-   1974-
       InFer

1791   Ferdinand Benedictine Missions– Coban, Guatemala. Earthquake of 1976.
       20 2 x 2" color slides
       InFer (Archives)

1792 Ferdinand Benedictine Missions – Convento Reina de la Paz, Coban, Guatemala, 1978.
20 2 x 2" color slides, and cassette tape (30 min.)
InFer (Archives)

1793 Ferdinand Benedictine Sisters – Peru missions.
80 color slides 2 x 2"
InFer (Archives)

1794 Hermanas Misioneras OSB – Hands minding other suffering brethren (Mission appeal letters of Ferdinand Benedictine Sisters in the Diocese of Coban, Guatemala, 1965–)
InFer (Archives)

1795 In-Formation. 1– 1970–
Bi-weekly.
InFer

1796 Newsletter of Ferdinand Benedictine Sisters working in Morropon and Santo Domingo, Piura, Peru. Published occasionally (3–6 issues per yr.), 1970–
InFer

1797 Properties of Convent of the Immaculate Conception, Ferdinand, Indiana, 1974–
50 color slides 2 x 2"
InFer (Archives)

1798 Reach out; a statement of purpose and guidelines adopted for a period of one year by the Ferdinand Benedictines, Sept. 1971–Sept. 1972.
56 p. illus.
InFer

1799 Reach out; a statement of the philosophy of the Benedictine Sisters of Ferdinand, Indiana, composed . . . under the leadership . . . of the Renewal Committee in 1971, and revised in 1972 and 1973.
80 p. illus.
InFer

1800 Specification of materials to be furnished and labor to be performed in the erection of a chapel, together with additions and alterations to Convent of the Immaculate Conception, located at Ferdinand, Indiana . . . 1915.
85 p.
InFer (Archives)

1801 **Cooney, Cyprian,** 1929–
Understanding the new theology. Milwaukee, Bruce Pub. Co. [1969]
xii, 193 p. 22 cm.
InStme; MnStj; OkShG

Corbie, France. Saint-Pierre (Benedictine abbey).

1802 Corbie, abbaye royale, volume du XIIIe centenaire. Lille, Facultés Catholiques

[1963].
444 p. illus. 24 cm.
InStme

1803 Studia Corbeiensia edidit Karl August Eckhardt. Bibliotheca rerum historicarum Corbeiensia; traditiones Corbeienses; rotula Corbeiensis; chronicon Corbeiense et fasti Corbeienses. Aalen, Scientia Verlag, 1970.
2 v. 24 cm.
MnCS

1804 **Corias, Spain (Benedictine abbey).**
Cartulari del monestir de Corias. MS. Monasterio benedictino de Montserrat, Spain, codex 787. 101 f. Quarto. Saec. 13.
Microfilm: MnCH proj. no. 30,065

Corner, David Gregor, 1585–1648.

1805 Feriae Paschales: sive, Commentarii ascetici de descensu ad inferos, & resurrectione D. N. Jesu Christi, ex Sacris Literis, sanctis Patribus . . . concinnati. Viennae, Typis Gregorii Gelbhaar, 1639.
[8], 517, [5] p. 16 cm.
KAS

1806 Nucleus catholicae devotionis. MS. Benediktinerabtei St. Peter, Salzburg, codex b.II.41. 228 f. Octavo. Saec. 17.
Microfilm: MnCH proj. no. 10,346

1807 **Corpus Christi Abbey, Sandia, Tex.**
Texas Benedictine Bulletin. 1– 1970–
InFer; TxCor

1808 **Corpus consuetudinum monasticarum.**
t. 1– Siegburg, F. Schmitt, 1963–
v. 26 cm.
"Cura Pontificii Athenaei Sancti Anselmi de Urbe."
Editor: 1963– K. Hallinger.
AStb; InStme; KAS; MnCS; MoCo; PLatS

1808a **Corrigan, Felicitas, Sister, tr.**
Dreuille, Mayeul de, O.S.B.
From East to West: man in search of the absolute. Bangalore, India, Theological Publications in India [1972?]
207 p. 22 cm.
Translated by Dame Felicitas Corrigan, O.S.B.
PLatS

1809 **Costalta, Josephus.**
In divum Benedictum elogia. Romae, Fabius de Falco, 1665.
[16], 210, [4] p. 20 cm.
Text is versified.
KAS

1810 **Costello, Maurice,** 1900–1952.
De origine animae humanae.
62 leaves. 28 cm.
Thesis (Ph.D.) – St. Vincent Seminary, Latrobe, Pa., 1925.

Typescript.
PLatS

Cousin Patrice, 1905–
1811   Les moines de St-Riquier sous la réforme mauriste et devant la Révolution.
(*In* Saint-Riquier; études . . . 1962. v. 1, p. 175–196)
PLatS

1812   La psalmodie chorale dans la Règle de Saint Colomban.
(*In* Mélanges colombaniens. Paris, 1950. p. 179–191)
PLatS

1813   Les relations de saint Anselme avec Cluny.
(*In* Spicilegium Beccense. 1959. v. 1, p. 439–454)
PLatS

Coustant, Pierre, 1654–1721.
1814   (ed) Epistolae romanorum pontificum, et quae ad eos scriptae sunt a S. Clemente usque ad Innocentium III . . . Studio et labore Petri Coustant. Tomus 1, ab anno Christi 67 ad annum 440. Parisiis, apud L. D. Delatour, 1721; Farnborough, Hants., England, Gregg Press, 1967.
c 1, 1280, 124 columns 34 cm.
No more published?
InStme; PLatS

1815   Epistolae romanorum pontificum genuinae et quae ad eos scriptae sunt a S. Hilaro usque ad Pelagium II [ex schedis clar. Petri Coustantii aliisque editis, adhibitis praestantissimis codicibus Italiae et Germaniae] recensuit et edidit Andreas Thiel. Tomus I. Hildesheim, Georg Olms, 1974.
xl, 1018 p. 25 cm.
Facsimile reprint of the 1867–68 edition.
No more published.
PLatS

1815a   **Coustant, Pierre,** 1654–1721.
Vindiciae manuscriptorum codicum a R. P. Bartolomeo Germon impugnatorum. Paris, 1706.
306 p.
Catholic University of America; Yale Univ.

1816   **Covington, Ken. St. Joseph's Church.**
St. Joseph's Church, Covington, Kentucky, 1855–1970 . . . one hundred and fifteen years of service to God and man. n.p., 1970.
16 p. illus. 21 cm.
PLatS

Craighead, Meinrad, Sister, 1936–
1816a   The mother's birds; images for a death and birth. Worcester, Stanbrook Abbey

Press, 1976.
[41] p. illus. 24 cm.
PLatS

1816b   The sign of the tree. London, Artists House, 1979.
192 p. 72 plates. 25 x 27 cm.
MnCS

1817   **Cramer, Winfrid,** 1933–
Die Engelvorstellungen bei Ephräm dem Syrer. Roma, Pont. Institutum Orientalium Studiorum, 1965.
xx, 197 p. 24 cm. (Orientalia christiana analecta, 173)
InStme

1818   **Cranenburgh, Henri van,** 1915–
La vie latine de Saint Pachome, traduite du grec par Denus le Petit. Edition critique par H. van Cranenburgh, O.S.B. Bruxelles, Société des Bollandistes, 1969.
238 p. 25 cm. (Subsidia hagiographica, n. 46)
MnCS; PLatS

1819   **Cremer, Drutmar,** 1930–
Oeffne meine Augen; Bildmeditationen zur Christussäule Bernwards von Hildesheim. [Würzburg] Echter Verlag [1974]
58 p. illus.
MoCo

1820   **Cremer, John,** 14th cent.
Tripvs avrevs, hoc est, tres tractatvs . . . III. Cremeri cvivsdam abbatis Westmonasteriensis Angli Testamentum, hactenus nondum publicatum . . . opera & studio Michaelis Maieri. Francofvrti, ex chalcographia Pauli Iacobi, 1618.
PLatS (microfilm)

1821   **Cremer, John,** 14th cent.
[Testamentum]
Musaeum hermeticum reformatum et amplificatum . . . XIII (p. 533–544): Cremeri cujusdam abbatis Westmonasteriensis Angli Testamentum, in diversarum nationum gratiam editi & figuris cupro affabre incis ornati. Francofurti, apud Hermannum à Sande, 1678.
PLatS (microfilm)

Cressy, Serenus, 1605–1674.
1822   Exomologesis; or, A faithfvll narration of the occasion and motives of the conversion unto Catholique vnity of Hvgh-Pavlin de Cressy, lately deane of Laghlin & c. in Ireland, and prebend of Windsore in England. Printed at Paris, 1647.
[24], 655 p. 15 cm.
PLatS

1823   Roman-Catholick doctrines on novelties; or, An answer to Dr. Pierce's court-sermon, miscalled The primitive rule of

reformation. By S.C. a Roman-Catholick. [Paris?] 1663.
[14], 322, [6] p. 16 cm.
PLatS

1824 **La Cripta de S. Benedetto in Norcia.**
[Valle di Pompei, Scuola tipografica pontificia pei figli dei carcerati fondata da Bartolo Longo, 1913]
23 p. illus. 31 cm.
InStme

Crispin, Gilbert. *See* Gilbert, abbot of Westminster.

1825 **Crusellas, Francisco de.**
Nueva historia del santuario y monasterio de Nuestra Senora de Montserrat. MS. Monasterio benedictino de Montserrat, Spain, codex 643. 265 p. Folio. Saec. 19.
Microfilm: MnCH proj. no. 30,030

1826 **Cuernavaca, Morelos, Mexico.** Monasterio de Nuestra Señora de la Resurrección. Una escuela de servicio del Señor. [1951]
61 p. illus.
NcBe

1827 **Cullinan, Thomas,** 1935–
Eucharist and politics. London, Catholic Institute for International Relations [1947?]
12 p. 21 cm. (Justice papers, no. 2)
KAS

1827a Mine and thine, ours and theirs: an anthology on ownership in the Christian tradition. London, Catholic Truth Society, 1979.
50 p. 19 cm.
PLatS

1828 **Cummins, Patrick,** 1880–1968.
The Psalms; a version in the original rhythm. Conception, Mo., Dom Patrick Cummins, O.S.B. [1950]
154 p.
Private printing in ditto form.
MoCo

1829 **Curiel, Fausto.**
Vida del Ven. H. José de San Benito, religioso de Montserrat. MS. Monasterio benedictino de Montserrat, Spain, codex 1178. 35 f. Octavo. Saec. 20.
Microfilm: MnCH proj. no. 30,157

1830 **Curran, Mary Carole, Sister.**
Personality in relation to attitudes toward prolonging life.
vi, 177 leaves.
Thesis – University of Nebraska.
SdYa

Cuthbert, monk of Jarrow, fl. ca. 735.
1831 De obitu Bedae Venerabilis presbiteri. MS. Augustinerchorherrenstift Kloster-

neuburg, Austria, codex 787, f. 182r–184v. Folio. Saec. 12.
Microfilm: MnCH proj. no. 5764

1832 Obitus S. Bedae Venerabilis. MS. Benediktinerabtei Göttweig, Austria, codex 54, f. 12r–12v. Folio. Saec. 12.
Microfilm: MnCH proj. no. 3342

1833 Epistola ad Chuninum de transitu Bedae Venerabilis. MS. Vienna, Nationalbibliothek, codex 12761, f. 122r–123r. Quarto. Saec. 15.
Microfilm: MnCH proj. no. 14,454

1834 **Czinár, Mór Pál,** 1787–1875.
Monasteriologiae regni Hungariae libri duo, totidem tomis comprehensi. Recognovit, ad fidem fontium revocavit et auxit Maurus Czinár. Vindobonae & Strigonii, Carolus Sartori, 1869.
2 v. 29 cm.
MnCS

1835 **Dahlheimer, Cosmas Raymond,** 1906–
A study of Demosthenes' policy and opposing trends.
101 p. 28 cm.
Thesis (M.A.) – State University of Iowa, 1947.
Multigraphed
MnCS

Dahm, Chrysostomus, 1912–
1836 Athos, Berg der Verklärung. [Offenburg, Baden], Burda, 1959.
228 p. illus. 31 cm.
InStme; MnCS; PLatS

1837 Die Kirche im Osten; Macht und Pracht der Patriarchen. Offenburg, Baden, Burda-Verlag, 1964–
v. illus. 31 cm.
PLatS

1838 **Daily companion for Oblates of St. Benedict.** [4th rev. ed.]. St. Meinrad, Ind., Abbey Press [c 1960]
96 p. 16 cm.
KAS

1839 **Daily companion for Secular Oblates of St. Benedict,** St. Meinrad, Ind., Grail Publication [1963]
100 p. 15 cm.
Originally published by Benedictine Convent of Perpetual Adoration, Clyde, Mo.
MnCS

1840 **Daily companion for Oblates of St. Benedict.** 5th rev. ed. St. Meinrad, Ind., Abbey Press, 1974.
141 p. illus. 16 cm.
InStme; MdRi

1841 **Dalbec, Eucharista, Sister.**
Creative thinking potential at the college level; identification and growth, relationi-

ships with traditional criteria (I.Q., G.P.A., G.R.E.), faculty and peer perceptions.
91 p.
Thesis (M.A.)–University of Minnesota, 1966.
MnDuS

1842 **Dalmau, Barnabe M.,** 1944–
La aplicacion de la instruccion "Renovationis causam" en el ambito monastico.
(*In* Semana de Estudios monasticos, 14th, Silos, Spain, 1973. p. 369–375)
PLatS

1843 **Daly, Simeon,** 1922–
The selection of materials in the field of Sacred Scripture in the Major Seminary library with a list of recommended titles.
ii, 62 numbered leaves, 28 cm.
Thesis (M.S.)–Catholic University of America, 1951.
InStme

1844 **Damen, Cornelius Ignatius,** 1922–
Geschiedenes van den Benediktijnenkloosters in de provincie Gronigen. Asen, Netherlands, Van Gorcum, 1972.
256 p. 24 cm.
MnCS

1845 **Dammertz, Viktor,** 1929–
Das Verfassungsrecht der benediktinischen Mönchkongregationen in Geschichte und Gegenwart. Erzabtei St. Ottilien, Eos Verlag, 1963.
xxiv, 276 p. 25 cm.
KAS; MnCS; PLatS

1846 **Danzer, Beda,** 1881–
Der Missionsgedanke auf der Kanzel . . . Missions-Verlag St. Ottilien, 1927.
273 p. 21 cm.
InStme

1847 **Danzl, Arthur,** 1898–1975.
Concerning the loop of the folium of Descartes and its rectification. n.p., n.d.
[6] p. diagrs. 22 x 29 cm.
MnCS

D'Aoust, Henry Jean Jacques, 1924–
1848 The energetics of love.
(*In* Francoeur, R. T. The world of Teilhard. Baltimore, 1961. p. 146–155)
PLatS

1849 God-seeking, the essence of monastic life according to St. Benedict.
iv, 43 p. 28 cm.
Thesis (M.A.)–St. Vincent College, Latrobe, Pa., 1960.
Typescript.
PLatS

1850 **Darby, Wilfrid,** 1857–1928.
The Gospel according to St. Luke. London, Burns & Oates, 1914.

296 p. 18 cm.
MnCS

1851 **Darham, Rose, Sister,** 1894–
Letters to Ann. New York, J. F. Wagner [c 1964]
155 p. 21 cm.
InFer; MnCS

1852 **Darley, Etienne.**
Les Acta Salvatoris; un évangile de la Passion & de la Résurrection et une mission apostolique en Aquitaine, suivis d'une traduction de la version anglosaxonne. Paris, A. Picard, 1913.
51 p. 26 cm.
PLatS

1853 **Darricau, Ildefonse,** 1886–
L'Abbaye de Belloc, 1875–1955. Urt, Editions Ezkila [1957]
viii, 104 p. plates, 23 cm.
KAS

1854 **Dartein, Gustav de,** 1837–1913.
(tr) Peltre, Hugues, O.Praem. Vie latine inédite de Sainte Odile . . . Avec traduction et notes de Dom G. de Dartein, O.S.B. Rixheim (Alsace), Léon, Schmitt, 1913.
lxxxix, 143 p. 25 cm.
MnCS

1855 **Dashian, Jacobus, O.S.B.Mech.**
Catalog der armenischen Handschriften in der Mechitaristen-Bibliothek in Wien, von Jacobus Dashian (v. 1) und Hamazasp Oskian (v. 2). Wien, Mechitaristen-Buchdruckerei, 1895–1963.
2 v. plates, 30 cm.
MnCS

David, Lucien, 1875–1955.
1856 Les grandes abbayes d'Occident. Lille, Desclée [1907?]
473 p. illus. 30 cm.
CaQStB; MnCS

1857 Méthode de chant grégorien et petit Solfège selon l'édition Vaticane. Grenoble, Librairie St-Grégoire, 1942.
72 p. 24 cm.
InStme

1858 Le rythme verbal et musical dans le chant romain. Les Editions de l'Université d'Ottawa, 1933.
104 p. 27 cm.
InStme; MoCo

1859 (ed) Revue du chant grégorien.
Dom Lucien David was the chief contributor for vols. 27–44, 1892–1944.
CaQSt; PLatS

Davis, Cyprian, 1930–
1860 A challenge for today; the problem of contemplative community at the end of the eighteenth century.

(*In* Contemplative community. Washington, 1972. p. 171–184)
PLatS

1861   The familia at Cluny in the eleventh and twelfth centuries.
xxiv, 155, 60 leaves, illus. 26 cm.
Thesis – Université Catholique de Louvain, 1963.
Typescript.
InStme

1862   The familia at Cluny, 900–1350. Louvain, C. Davis, 1977.
2 v. 27 cm.
Thesis (Ph.D) – Université Catholique de Louvain.
Xerographed.
InStme

1863   **Davril, Anselm,** 1922–
Consuetudines Floriacenses saeculi tertii decimi, edidit D. Anselmus Davril, O.S.B. Siegburg, F. Schmitt, 1976.
lxxxix, 507 p. facsim. 26 cm. (Corpus consuetudinum monasticarum, t. 9)
InStme; MnCS; PLatS

1864   **De origine status monastici tractatus.**
Cui additur in appendice brevis dilucidatio epistolae apostolicae nuperrime directae ad monasteria O.S.B. in Austria. Auctore quodam benedictino-professo in Austria. Augustae Vindel., M. Huttler, 1889.
24 p. 23 cm.
PLatS

1865   **De viris illustribus monasterii S. Galli libri tres.** Anno Domini 1606. MS. Vienna, Schottenstift, codex 616. 177 f. Quarto. Saec. 17.
Microfilm: MnCH proj. no. 4276

1866   **Dealy, Bonaventure, Sister.**
Catholic schools in Scotland.
305 p.
Thesis (Ph.D.) – Catholic University of America, 1945.
MoCo; SdYa

Dean, Aldhelm, 1903–
1867   (tr) Barthélemy, Dominique, O.P. God and his image . . . Translated from the French by Dom Aldhelm Dean. London, Dublin, G. Chapman, 1966.
xix, 199 p. 23 cm.
InStme; PLatS

1868   (tr) Gasnier, Henri Michel, O.P. The Psalms, school of spirituality. Translated by Dom Aldhelm Dean. St. Louis, Herder [1962]
160 p. 19 cm.
NcBe; PLatS

1869   (tr) Herbin, Pierre. We die unto the Lord . . . Translated by Aldhelm Dean, O.S.B.

London, Challoner, 1960.
132 p. 19 cm.
Translation of: Maladie et mort du chrétien.
KAS; PLatS

1870   (tr) Rétif, André. The Catholic spirit. Translated from the French by Dom Aldhelm Dean. New York, Hawthorn Books [1959]
126 p.
NcBe

1871   (tr) Tardif, Henri. The sacraments are ours. Translated by Dom Aldhelm Dean. London, Challoner Publications, 1956.
v, 89 p. 1956.
Translation of: Christiani populi sacramenta.
MnCS; PLatS

1872   **Debes, Dunstan William,** 1911–
St. Mary's Church, Bolivar, Pennsylvania, 1850–1961. [1961]
24 p. illus., ports. 31 cm.
PLatS

Debuyst, Frederic, 1922–
1873   Architecture modern et celebration chrétienne. [Bruges], Biblica, 1966.
63 p. illus. 22 cm.
PLatS

1874   Bénédictins pas morts.
(*In* Art d'Eglise, no. 142, 1968. p. 129–131)
PLatS

1875   Feast days and festive occasions. Translated by John Drury.
(*In* The gift of joy . . . Concilium: theology in the age of renewal: Spirituality, v. 39, p. 7–16)
PLatS

1876   Modern architecture and Christian celebration. London, Lutterworth Press [1968?]
80 p. illus. 22 cm.
Translated from the French.
InStme; PLatS

Dechanet, Jean Marie, 1906–
1877   Christian yoga. [Translation by Roland Hindmarsh]. New York, Harper [1960]
196 p. illus. 22 cm.
Translation of: La voie du silence.
InStme; ILSP; MoCo; NdRi; NcBe; OkShG

1878   The Christology of Saint Bernard.
(*In* Cistercian studies v. 2 (1961), p. 37–51)
PLatS

1879   John Scotus Erigena.
(*In* Walsh, James, S.J. Spirituality through the centuries . . . 1964. p. 83–96)
PLatS

1880   The sources of Saint Bernard's philosophical thought.
(*In* Cistercian studies, v. 1 (1961), p. 55–80)
PLatS

1881   William of St. Thierry; the man and his work. Translated by Richard Strachan. Spencer, Mass., Cistercian Publications, 1972.
x, 172 p. 23 cm.
MnCS; NcBe; PLatS

1882   Yoga in ten lessons. New York, Harper & Row, 1971 [c. 1965]
174 p. illus. 21 cm.
InFer; InStme; MnCS; MnStj; PLatS

1883   (ed) Cuillaume de Saint Thierry. Exposé sur le Cantique des Cantiques. Texte latin, introduction et notes de M. J. Dechanet, O.S.B. Traduction française de M. Dumontier, O.C.S.O. Paris, Editions du Cerf, 1962.
418 p. 20 cm. (Sources chrétiennes, 82)
InStme; MnCS; PLatS

1884   (ed) Guillaume de Saint-Thierry. The works of William of St. Thierry. Shannon, Ireland; Spencer, Mass., Cistercian Publications, 1971–
PLatS

1885   **Decker, Aegid,** 1906–
Stift Seitenstetten, Benediktinerabtei. München, Schnell & Steiner, 1957.
15 p. 17 cm. (Kunstführer Nr. 662)
PLatS

1886   **Defarges, Beninge,** 1904–
Histoire petite chronique de Vézelay.
(*In* Bourgogne romane, par Jean Baudry et al. La Pierre-qui-Vire, 1962. p. 209–211)
PLatS

Defensor, monk of Ligugé, 7th cent.

1887   Liber scintillarum. MS. Augustinerchorherrenstift Klosterneuburg, Austria, codex 838, f. 1v–96r. Quarto. Saec. 12.
Microfilm: MnCH proj. no. 5830

1888   Liber scintillarum (excerpta). MS. Vienna, Nationalbibliothek, codex 1059, f. 39r–48v. Quarto. Saec. 12.
Microfilm: MnCH proj. no. 14,371

1889   Liber scintillarum. MS. Augustinerchorherrenstift Klosterneuburg, Austria, codex 244, f. 1r–58r. Folio. Saec. 13.
Microfilm: MnCH proj. no. 5216

1890   Scintillarius. MS. Linz, Bundesstaatliche Studienbibliothek, codex 9, f. 140r–155r. Quarto. Saec. 14.
Microfilm: MnCH proj. no. 27,894

1891   Liber scintillarum. MS. Benediktinerabtei Göttweig, Austria, codex 245b, f. 158r–193v. Folio. Saec. 15.
Microfilm: MnCH proj. no. 3510

1892   Liber scintillarum. MS. Augustinerchorherrenstift Klosterneuburg, Austria, codex 941, f. 138r–234r. Quarto. Saec. 15.
Microfilm: MnCH proj. no. 5935

1893   Defensor's Liber scintillarum, with an interlinear Anglo-Saxon version made early in the eleventh century, ed. with introduction and glossary from the Royal ms. 7 C IV in the British Museum by E. W. Rhodes . . . London, Trübner and Co., 1889.
xvi, 250 p. 23 cm. (Early English Text Society. [Original series] 93)
KAS

1894   Liber scintillarum quam recensuit Henricus M. Rochais. Turnholti, Brepols, 1957.
xxxi, 689 p. 26 cm. (Corpus christianorum. Series latina, 117)
InStme

1895   Livre d'étincelles. Texte latin, traduction et notes de H. M. Rochais, O.S.B. Paris, Editions du Cerf, 1961–62.
2 v. 21 cm. (Sources chrétiennes, 77, 86)
InStme; MnCS; PLatS

1896   **Deininger, Franziskus,** 1893–
Johannes Sinnich; der Kampf der Löwener Universität gegen den Laximus. Düsseldorf, L. Schwann [1928?]
77 p. 22 cm.
MnCS

1897   **De Jean, Hilary,** 1895–1947.
Suggested modifications in high school courses of religion as determined by an analysis of current Catholic publications.
37 leaves, 21 cm.
Thesis (M.A.) – University of Notre Dame, 1927.
Typescript.
InFer; InStme

Dekkers, Eligius, 1915–

1898   Un cas de critique historique à St-Riquier; les reliques de St Mauguille.
(*In* Saint-Riquier; études . . . Abbaye de Saint-Riquier, 1962. v. 1, p. 59–67)
PLatS

1899   Corona gratiarum; miscellanea patristica, historica et liturgica Eligio Dekkers, O.S.B., XII lustra complenti oblata. Brugge, Sint Pietersabdej, 1975.
2 v. illus. 26 cm. (Instrumenta patristica, 10–11)
InStme; MnCS

1900   Monastic life today: some suggestions. Translated by James McMurray.
(*In* Monastic studies, v. 4, p. 55–60)
PLatS

1901   Propheteia – praefatio.
(*In* Mélanges offerts à Mademoiselle

Christine Mohrmann. Utrecht, 1963. p. 190–195)
PLatS

1902 **Delatte, Paul,** 1848–1937.
De lettere di S. Paolo; inquadrate nell' ambiente storico deglii Atti degli Apostoli. Traduzione autorizzata dal francese del sacerdote Giovanni Montali. Torino, Società Editrice Internazionale [1935–36]
2 v. illus. 23 cm.
InStme

1902a Contempler l'invisible. Editions de l'Abbaye de Solesmes, c 1965, 1974.
135 p. 18 cm.
A retreat preached to the nuns of Solesmes in 1889.
InStme

1902b Retraite avec Dom Delatte; textes recueillis et présentés par un moine de Solesmes. Editions de l'Abbaye de Solesmes [1941], 1974.
93 p. 18 cm.
InStme

1902c Vivre à Dieu; notes inédites sur la vie spirituelle . . . choisies et présentés par Lucian Regnault. Editions de l'Abbaye de Solesmes, 1973.
205 p. 20 cm.
"Texte abrégé des conférences prononcées par l'auteur au noviciat de Solesmes en 1899."
InStme

Delforge, Thomas, 1906–
1903 Columba Marmion, serviteur de Dieu. Turnhout, Brepols, 1963.
[82] p. 18 cm.
MnCS; PLatS

1904 Columba Marmion, servant of God. Translated by Richard L. Stewart. St. Louis, B. Herder Book Co. [c. 1965]
viii, 71 p. 19 cm.
InStme; KAS; MnCS; PLatS

1905 (ed) Marmion, Columba. The English letters of Abbot Marmion. [Edited by Gisbert Ghysens, O.S.B. and Thomas Delforge, O.S.B. . . . Baltimore, Helicon Press [1962]
xvi, 228 p. 23 cm. (Benedictine studies, v. 4)
PLatS

1906 **Della Marra, Luigi Taddeo,** 1859–
El Collegio Sant Anselmo in Roma e il Cardinal Dusmet. Catania, C. Galatola, 1901.
107 p. 27 cm.
MnCS; PLatS

1907 **Del Marmol, Boniface,** 1874–
Marie Corédemptrice. Eadmer enseignat-il que Marie rachetante fut rachetée?

(*In* Virgo Immaculata; actus Congressus Mariologici-Mariani, 1954, v. 5, p. 194–201)
PLatS

1908 **De Lorenzi, Lorenzo,** 1930–
I sinottici, gli atti et le epistole cattoliche nella spiritualità degli ultimi trent'anni.
(*In* Problemi e orientamenti di spiritualità monastica . . . Roma, 1961. p. 121–198)
MnCS; PLatS

Denis, Paul, 1873–1918.
1909 Nouvelles de Rome; recueillies . . . Paris, Picard et Fils, 1913–
v. 24 cm.
MnCS

1910 (ed) Mabillon, Jean. Seize lettres de Dom Mabillon. Ligugé, E. Aubin, 1909.
44 p.
NcBe

1911 **Desager, Luc,** 1929–
Lettre inédite du Patriarche Copte Jean XI au Papa Nicolas V (1450).
(*In* Mélanges Eugéne Tisserant, v. 2, p. 41–53)
PLatS

Deshusses, Jean, 1906–
1912 (ed) Amadeus, Saint, bp. of Lausanne. Huit homélies Mariales . . . Texte latin établi par Dom Jean Deshusses, O.S.B. . . . Paris, Editions du Cerf, 1960.
240 p. 20 cm. (Sources chrétiennes, 72)
InStme; PLatS

1913 (ed) Le Sacramentaire grégorien, ses principales formes d'après les plus anciens manuscrits. Edition comparative [par] Jean Deshusses. Fribourg, Editions universitaires, 1971–
v. 26 cm. (Spicilegium Friburgense, v. 16,)
InStme; MNS; PLatS

Desing, Anselm, 1699–1773.
1914 Juris naturae larva, detracta compluribus libris sub titulo juris naturae prodeuntibus . . . a.p. Anselmo Desing. Monachii, J. U. Gastl, 1753.
3 v. 34 cm.
InStme

1915 Opes sacerdotii num respublicae noxiae? Ex rerum natura, sana politica, et communi sensu generis humani examinatum a p. A. Desing. Ratisbonae, Joannis Gastl, 1753.
[26], 388, [18] p. 22 cm.
InStme

1916 **Le désir de Dieu.** [Par] un moine bénédictin. Genève, Claude Martingay, 1970.
141 p. 18 cm.
PLatS

1917 **Deutsch, Alcuin,** 1877–1951.
Animadversiones in philosophiam P.
Salvatoris Tongiorgi S.J.
109 leaves, 28 cm.
Thesis (Ph.D.)–Collegio Sant'Anselmo,
Rome, 1903.
Typescript.
MnCS (Archives)

Deutsch, Alfred Henry, 1914–
1918 Bruised reeds and other stories. Collegeville, Minn., Saint John's University Press
[1971]
213 p. illus. 23 cm.
InStme; KAS; MnCS; MnStj; NcBe;
PLatS

1919 Education for the priesthood at Saint
John's [Phonotape-cassette]. Collegeville,
1974.
1 cassette
MnCS

1919a Still full of sap, still green. Collegeville,
Minn., The Liturgical Press [1979].
130 p. 22 cm.
MnCS; InStme

1920 **Devauz, Eloi,** 1923–
Le maitre de Chaource. Preface de S.E.
Mgr. Julien le Couëdic, evéque de Troyes.
Texte de Dom Eloi Devau O.S.B. Photos
inédites de R. G. Phelipeaux et P.
Belzeaux. [Paris, Braun, 1956]
93 p. (chiefly illus.) 26 cm.
PLatS

1921 **Dewig, Mary Boniface, Sister.**
Study of the Benedictine convent
libraries in the United States in view of
establishing a library for a newly-founded
Benedictine convent.
58 p. map, tables.
Diss. (M.A.)–Rosary College, River
Forest, Ill., 1959
InFer

1922 **Dialogus duorum monachorum Cluniacensis et Cisterciensis.** MS. Cistercienserabtei Zwettl, Austria, codex 380,
f. 78r–1284. Octavo. Saec. 12.
Microfilm: MnCH proj. no. 6977

1923 **Diaz, Romuald,** 1914–
Dom Bonaventura Ubach, l'homme, el
monjo, el biblista . . . Barcelona, Editorial
Aedos [1962]
252 p. plates, 22 cm.
MnCS

1924 **Diaz, Rosendo.**
La confirmacion en la vida del cristiano.
[Santiago de Chile], Ediciones Paulinas
[1965]
183 p. 17 cm.
PLatS

Dickson, Marie Pascal.
1925 Consuedines Beccenses. Siegburg, apud
Franciscum Schmitt, 1967.
xv, 419 p. 26 cm. (Corpus consuetudinum
monasticarum, 4)
InStme; PLatS

1926 (ed and tr) Anselm, Saint. Textes
choisies [traduits et présentés par la R. M.
Marie Pascal Dickson, O.S.B.]. Namur,
Editions du Soleil Levant [1961]
189 p. 19 cm.
PLatS

1927 **Didicus Andreas.**
Lumen confessorum. MS. Cistercienserabtei Zwettl, Austria, codex 90, f.
220v–253v. Folio. Saec. 14.
Microfilm: MnCH proj. no. 6681

1928 **Dietricus, monk of Hersfeld.**
Narratio de illatione S. Benedicti ab-
batis. MS. Benediktinerabtei Admont,
Austria, codex 529, f. 139r–145v. Quarto.
Saec. 13.
Microfilm: MnCH proj. no. 9583

Diekmann, Godfrey Leo, 1908–
1929 Come, let us worship. Baltimore, Helicon
Press [1961]
180 p. 23 cm. (Benedictine studies, vol.
12)
CaMWiSb; InStj; MdRi; NcBe; ILSP;
PLatS; CaQStB; InStme; MoCo; KAS;
MnCS; InFer; ViBris

1930 The Eucharist makes the people of God.
(*In* Jesus Christ reforms His Church.
26th annual North American Liturgical
Week, 1965, p. 102–113)
PLatS

1931 Factors that unite us: Catholic.
(*In* Christians in conversation. West-
minster, Md., 1962. p. 81–112)
PLatS

1932 Feast of St. Zephyrinus, pope and mar-
tyr, August 26.
(*In* The challenge of the Council . . .
25th annual North American Liturgical
Week, 1964. p. 267–270)
PLatS

1933 First-born from the dead.
(*In* The kingdom come . . . 23rd annual
North American Liturgical Week, 1962. p.
16–28)
PLatS

1934 The full sign of the Eucharist.
(*In* The challenge of the Council . . .
25th annual North American Liturgical
Week, 1964, p. 86–94)
PLatS

1935 Liturgy in the life and apostolate of the
religious.

(*In* Religious life in the Church today . . . Notre Dame, Ind., 1962. p. 131-   )
InFer

1936   Mary, the model of our worship.
(*In* North American Liturgical Week. 21st, 1960. p. 61–66)
PLatS

1937   Personal prayer and the liturgy. London, G. Chapman, 1969.
63 p. 22 cm.
MdRi; MnCS; PLatS

1938   The place of liturgical worship.
(*In* The Church and the liturgy, p. 67–107. Concilium theology in the age of renewal: Liturgy, vol. 2)
PLatS

1939   The primary apostolate.
(*In* Ward, Leo R. The American apostolate. Westminster, Md., 1952. p. 29–46)
InFer

1940   The reformed liturgy and the Eucharist.
(*In* Liturgical Conference, 1965. Church architecture, the shape of reform. p. 35–51)
MnCS; PLatS

1941   Sacramental life–the mystery shared.
(*In* The renewal of Christian education. 24th annual North American Liturgical Week, 1963. p. 35–43)
PLatS

1942   A theological history of penance (Phono-tape cassette). Kansas City, Mo., National Catholic Reporter, 1975.
1 cassette 2s
MnCS

1943   To worship in spirit and truth (Phono-tape cassette). Collegeville, Minn., St. John's University, 1978.
6 tapes. 60 min. each 1 7/8 ips.
InStme

1944   Two approaches to understanding the sacraments.
(*In* Sullivan, C. Stephen. Readings in sacramental theology. Englewood Cliffs, N.J., 1964. p. 1–17)
InFer

1945   (ed) The Book of Catholic worship. Washington, D.C., The Liturgical Conference [c 1966].
xxii, 907 p. 22 cm.
PLatS

Diepen, Heeman Michel, 1908–
1946   Douze dialogues de christologie ancienne, Roma, Herder, 1960.
247 p. 21 cm.
CaQStB; InStme; MnCS; MoCo; PLatS

1947   L'esprit du Coeur de Jésus.
(*In* Cor Jesu; commentationes in . . .

"Haurietis aquas." Roma, 1959. v. 1, p. 151–189)
PLatS

1948   **Diethrich, Cecil Gerald,** 1933–
Conversion electron spectra: a line shape analysis for permanent magnet spectrographs.
ix, 111 p. illus. 28 cm.
Thesis (Ph.D.)–University of Michigan, 1967.
Typescript.
PLatS

1949   **Dietl, Gregorius,** d. 1690.
Pharmacopoea sacramentalis, hoc est, Tractatus de sacramentis tum in genere, tum in specie. Ratisponae, Typis Christophori Fischeri, 1674.
[6], 447, p. 21 cm.
PLatS

1950   **Diez Ramos, Gergorio,** 1927–
Obras completas de San Bernardo. Edición española preparada por el Rvd. P. Gregorio Diez Ramos, O.S.B. Madrid, Biblioteca de Autores Cristianos, 1953–
v. 20 cm.
MnCS

1951   **Dilworth, Mark.**
The Scots in Franconia; a century of monastic life. Totowa, N.J., Rowman and Littlefield [1974]
301 p. illus. 23 cm.
InStme; KAS

1952   **Dingjan, François.**
Discretio. Les origines patristiques et monastiques de la doctrine sur la prudence chez Saint Thomas d'Aquin. Assen, Van Gorcum & Comp., 1967.
272 p. 23 cm.
InStme; KAS; PLatS

1953   **Dion, Jean,** 1927–
Les Sentences des Pères du désert. Les apophtegmes des Pères (recension de Pélage et Jean). Introduction de L. Regnault. Traduction de J. Dion et G. Gury. Sarthe, Abbaye Saint-Pierre de Solesmes [1966].
312 p. 21 cm.
InStme

1954   **Directory of religious orders,** congregations and societies of Great Britain and Ireland. Glasgow, J. S. Burns & Sons.
v. 19 cm. biennial
KAS

Dittberner, Arnold, 1907–
1955   Let the sun shine. Collegeville, Minn., The Liturgical Press, 1974.
xiv, 94 p. illus. 22 cm.
MdRi; MnCS; MnStj; MoCo

1956   What they're saying about the 1920's in America (Phonotape-cassette). Collegeville, Minn., 1974.
1 cassette
MnCS

1957   **Dobmayer, Marianus,** 1753–1805.
Systema theologiae catholicae. Opus posthumum cura et studio Theodori Pantaleonis Senestrey . . . editum. Solisbaci, Typis Seidelianis, 1807–1819.
8 v. 20 cm.
InStme; PLatS

Diurnale. *See* Subject Part, nos. 1254–1287

1958   **Döbrentei, Beda,** 1912–
Christ-Mensch; Radiopredigten. Wien, Herder, 1952.
354 p. 20 cm.
MnCS

1959   **Doc, Jean, bp.,** d. 1560.
Homiliae sev enarrationes in Evangelia dominicalia totius anni necnon & festa occurrentia, per Ioannem Docaevm episcopum Laudunensem. Antverpiae, In sedibus Ioannis Steelsii, 1561.
401 p. 18 cm.
PLatS

Docherty, Jerome, 1904–1975.
1960   The splendor of Christian marriage [Phonotape cassette]. Marshfield, Wis., Wanderer Forum Recordings, 1973.
7 cassettes 14 sides.
MnCS

1961   Verbum salutis; the word of salvation. St. Joseph, Minn., College of St. Benedict, n.d.
various pagings, 28 cm.
Mimeographed
MnCS

Doens, Irenaeus, 1907–
1962   Aeltere Zeugnisse über den Diakon aus den Oestlichen Kirchen.
(*In* Rahner, Karl. Diaconia in Christo, p. 31–56)
PLatS

1963   Der Diakonat in den griechischen und slavischen Kirchen.
(*In* Rahner, Karl. Diaconia in Christo, p. 136–177)
PLatS

1964   Die Weiheriten des Diakons in den nicht-byzantinischen Ostkirche.
(*In* Rahner, Karl. Diaconia in Christo, p. 62–75)
PLatS

1965   Der Weiheritus des Diakons in der Ostkirche des Byzantinischen Ritus.

(*In* Rahner, Karl. Diaconia in Christo, p. 57–61)
PLatS

1966   De Heilige Liturgie van onze H. Vader Joannes Chrysostomus. Inleiding en vertaling door Dom Irenaeus Doens. Derde Druk. Chevetogne, Iconographie Paters Benediktijnen, 1950.
xxxi, 59 p. 18 cm.
MnCS

Doherty, Dennis, 1932–
1967   Marriage instructions; a guide for priests, by Charles Riker [and] Rev. Dennis Doherty, O.S.B. [St. Meinrad, Ind., Marriage, 1965]
63 p. 28 cm.
MnCS

1968   The sexual doctrine of Cardinal Cajetan. Regensburg, Friedrich Pustet, 1966.
xvii, 372 p. 22 cm.
InStme; MoCo; PLatS

1969   (tr) Auer, Alfons. Open to the world . . . Baltimore, Helicon Press [1966]
337 p. 22 cm.
Translation of Weltoffener Christ.
ILSP; InStme; PLatS

Dold, Alban, 1882–1960.
1970   Ein Hymnus abecedarius auf Christus. Aus Codex Einsiedlensis 27 (1125) mitgeteilt von Alban Dold . . . Beuron, Beuroner Kunstverlag, 1959.
viii, 23 p. facsims. 23 cm. (Texte und Arbeiten. I.Abt., Heft 51)
InStme; MnCS

1971   Das irische Palimpsestsakramentar im CLM 14429 der Staatsbibliothek München. Entziffert und hrsg. von Alban Dold, O.S.B., und Leo Eizenhöfer, O.S.B. . . . Beuron, Beuroner Kunstverlag, 1964.
xxv, 128, 212 p. facsims. 23 cm. (Texte und Arbeiten . . . Heft 53–54)
InStme; MnCS; PLatS

1972   Das Sakramentar von Jena (Bud. M.F. 366 der Universitäts-Bibliothek). In beratender Verbindung mit Alban Dold OSB und Virgil Fiala, O.S.B., hrsg. von Klaus Gamber . . . Beuron, Beuroner Kunstverlag, 1962)
126 p. facsim. 23 cm. (Texte und Arbeiten, Heft 52)
PLatS

Dollard, Jerome Robert, 1941–
1973   Ethics and international relations in the Realist School of International Relations and the teachings of Vatican II and Pope Paul VI; a critical comparison.
470 p.
Thesis (Ph.D.)–Catholic University of America, 1974.
NcBe

1974   The religious life as a sign of the eschatological nature of the Church.
137 p.
Thesis (M.A.) – Catholic University of America, n.d.
NcBe

Domeier, Renée, Sister, 1933–
1975   The lyric poetry of St. John of the Cross.
33 p.
Thesis (M.A.) – University of Michigan, 1964.
Typescript.
MnStj (Archives)

1976   The parable of the prodigal son in the theater of Tirso de Molina.
304 p.
Thesis (Ph.D) – University of Michigan, 1970.
Typescript.
MnStj (Archives)

1977   **Domenichetti, Basilio, C.V.U.O.S.B.**
Guida storica illustrata di Vallombrosa. 3. ed. Firenze, Faggio Vallombrosano [1929].
208 p. illus. 16 cm.
MnCS

Dooley, Brendan John, 1910–
1978   The life of Newman up till his conversion. Belmont Abbey, N.C., n.d.
Privately printed.
NcBe

1979   Strike at Hatch Hosiery Mill, unlawful and unjustified. Belmont Abbey, 1934.
various pagings.
Thesis (M.A.)
NcBe

1980   **Doppelfeld, Basilius,** 1943–
Mönchtum und kirchlicher Heilsdienst; Entstehung und Entwicklung des nordamerikanischen Benediktinertums im 19. Jahrhundert. Münsterschwarzach, Vier-Türme-Verlag, 1974.
xx, 381 p. 21 cm. (Münsterschwarzacher Studien, Bd. 22)
Originally presented as the author's thesis, Würzburg.
InStme; KAS; MnCS; MoCo; PLatS

Doris, Sebastian Thomas, 1904–
1981   Belmont Abbey. [Belmont, N.C., 1949]
5 p.
NcBe

1982   Belmont Abbey; its history and educational influence.
68 p.
Thesis (M.A.) – Catholic University of America, 1933.
NcBe

1983   Belmont Abbey; its origin, development and present status. Belmont, N.C., 1971.
112 p.
Typescript.
NcBe

1984   **Dority, Hippolytus,** 1920–
[Book of hymns]. [Collegeville, Minn., St. John's Abbey, 196-]
66 p. music, 14 cm.
MnCS

1985   **Dörr, Lambert,** 1936–
Die Abtei Münsterschwarzach in Vergangenheit und Gegenwart.
(*In* Die Benediktinerabtei Münsterschwarzach. Vier-Türme-Verlag, 1965. p. 13–63)
PLatS

1986   **Dorsi, Jacobus.**
Philosophia secundum mentem Thomae Aquinatis. MS. Benediktinerabtei Fiecht, codex 84. 211 & 233 f. Quarto. Saec. 18?
Microfilm: MnCH proj. no. 28,863

1987   **Douai Abbey, England.**
Bible services. [Woolhampton, Douai Abbey, 1965]
32 p. 20 cm.
"Text by monks of Douai Abbey"
MnCS

1988   **Dougherty, Denis Donald,** 1929–
Differential acceptance of normative values among adolescents in Missouri schools.
505 p.
Thesis – University of Missouri, 1964.
MoCo

1989   **Dover Priory, England.**
Register of Dover Priory. MS. Lambeth Palace Library, London, codex 241. 262 f. Quarto. Saec. 14.
Microfilm: MnCH

Dowdall, Joseph, 1927–
1990   The Eucharist and the New Testament.
(*In* Conference of practical liturgy. London, 1965. p. 17–36)
PLatS

1991   The liturgy of the dead.
(*In* Murray, Placid, ed. Studies in pastoral liturgy. Maynooth, 1961. v. 1, p. 79–91)
PLatS

1992   Preaching and the liturgy.
(*In* Drury, Ronan. Preaching. New York, 1962. p. 26–40)
PLatS

1993   A study of the rite of baptism.
(*In* Murray, Placid, ed. Studies in pastoral liturgy. Maynooth, 1961. v. 1, p. 62–78)
PLatS

1994   **Dowling, Dolores, Sister.**
The legend of the shepherd. Illustrated by De Grazia. St. Louis, Mo., Benedictine Sisters [1973]
[30] p. col. illus. 22 cm.
Poetry.
InFer; CaMWiSb; ICSS; MnCS; MnStj; MdRi

1995   **Downside Abbey, England.**
A guide to the Church of Saint Gregory the Great, Downside Abbey near Bath. [11th ed.] Bath, Downside Abbey [1960]
27 p. plates, 18 cm.
KAS; MnCS

1996   **Downside Symposium Group. London Branch.**
Theology in modern education; a creative encounter, edited by Laurence Bright. London, Darton, Longman & Todd, 1965.
vii, 96 p. 23 cm.
Five papers delivered at a conference held on 10–12 April 1964 at the University of Leicester, and organized by the London Branch of the Downside Symposium Group.
InStme; PLatS

1997   **Doyere, Pierre,** 1890–
The need for accountancy.
(*In* Ple, Albert. Poverty. The Newman Press, 1956. p. 244–248)
InFer

1998   Saint Benoît Labre, ermite pèlerin, 1748–1783. Paris, Editions de Cerf, 1964.
88 p. 21 cm.
MnCS; PLatS

1999   **Doyle, Francis Cuthbert,** 1842–1932.
The prophecy of Simeon.
(*In* Sermons for the times. New York, 1913. v. 2, p. 92–99)
PLatS

2000   **Doyle, Mary Edith, Sister.**
The teaching of St. Thomas on the multiplicity of the literal senses of Scripture.
139 p.
Thesis (M.A.) – Providence College, 1957.
Typescript.
MdRi

Drayna, Elvan, Sister, 1914–
2001   Casper Cebulla family. St. Paul, 1970
unpaged, illus.
MnStj (Archives)

2002   Drayna family. St. Paul, 1970
unpaged, illus.
MnStj (Archives)

2003   **Dreher, Ansgar,** 1912–
Zur Beuroner Kunst.
(*In* Beuron, 1863–1963; Festschrift . . . Beuron, 1963. p. 358–394)
PLatS

Dreuille, Mayeul de, 1920–
2004   Monks yesterday and today. [Dasarahalli, Bangalore], St. Paul Publications [1972].
121 p. 19 cm. (Seekers of God, 1)
CaMWiSb; MoCo; PLatS

2004a   From East to West: man in search of the absolute. Bangalore, India, Theological Publications in India [197?]
207 p. 22 cm.
Translated by Dame Felicitas Corrigan, O.S.B.
PLatS

2005   St. Benedict life and miracles by St. Gregory the Great; and, An introduction to his Rule by Dom Mayeul de Dreuille. [Dasarahalli, Bangalore], St. Paul Publications [1972].
180 p. 19 cm. (Seekers of God, 2)
MoCo; PLatS

Dript, Lorenz von, 1633–1686.
2006   Antidecalogus theologico-politicus reformatus . . . Coloniae, sumptibus Joannis Hessii, 1672.
602 [11] p. 14 cm.
KAS

2007   Specvlvm archidiaconale; sive, Praxis officij & visitationis archidiaconalis . . . Nevhvsii, Imprimebat Joannes Todt, 1676.
[12], 240 p. 13 cm.
KAS

2008   Virgo Lavretana commentariis illustrata, sive compendiosa explicatio Litaniarum Lavretanarum . . . Neuhusii, imprimebat Joannes Todt, 1673.
[18], 530 p. 15 cm.
KAS

2009   **Droste, Benedicta, Sister.**
"Celebrare" in der römischen Liturgiesprache; eine Liturgie-theologische Untersuchung. München, Max Haeber Verlag, 1963.
xii, 197 p. 25 cm.
Inaug.-Diss. – München.
InStme; MnCS

2010   **Drübeck, Germany (abbey of Benedictine nuns).**
Urkundenbuch des in der Graftschaft Wernigerode belegenen Klosters Drübeck, vom Jahr 877–1594. Bearbeitet . . . von Ed. Jacobs . . . Halle, Buchhandlung des Waisenhauses, 1874.
xxxviii, 344 p. plates, facims. 23 cm.
KAS

Dubois, Jacques, 1919–
2011   Une sanctuaire monastique au Moyenage: Saint-Fiacre-en-Brie. Genève, Librairie Droz, 1976.
371 p. 22 cm.
MnCS

2012 Le Martyrologe d'Usuard. Texte et commentaire par Jacques Dubois, O.S.B. Bruxelles, Société des Bollandistes, 1965.
444 p. 25 cm. (Subsidia hagiographica, no. 40)

Du Bourg, Antoine, 1838–1918.
2013 Saint Odon (879–942). 2. éd. Paris, Victor Lecoffre, 1905.
xii, 214 p. 18 cm.
CaQStB; CaQStE; MnCS

2014 Nouveau supplément à l'Histoire littéraire de la Congrégation de Saint-Maur; notes de Henry Wilhelm, pub. et complétées par Dom Ursmer Berlière, O.S.B., avec la collaboration de D. Antoine Dubourg, O.S.B., et de A.M.P. Ingold. Paris, A. Picard, 1908–1932.
3 v. illus. 25 cm.
InStme

Dudik, Beda Franziskus, 1815–1890.
2015 Geschichte des Benediktiner-Stiftes Raygern im Markgrafthum Mähren . . . Brünn, Carl Winiker, 1849–68.
2 v. illus. 23 cm.
KAS; MnCS (v. 1)

Dudine, Mary Frederica, Sister.
2016 The castle on the hill; centennial history of the Convent of the Immaculate Conception, Ferdinand, Indiana, 1867–1967. Milwaukee, Bruce Pub. Co., 1967.
xvi, 330 p. illus. 24 cm. (American Benedictine Academy. Historical studies, no. 5)
KAS; InStme; InFer; MdRi; MoCo; PLatS

Duerr, Gregory, 1937–
2017 Mount Angel Abbey. St. Benedict, Or., 1973.
64 p. illus. 28 cm.

Duesberg, Hilaire, 1888–
2018 Antidote à la mort. Editions de Maredsous, 1962.
113 p. 21 cm.
PLatS
2019 Aspects bibliques du mystère de la Messe. Paris, Editions Alsatia [c 1962].
93 p. 19 cm.
MnCS
2020 Le Psautier des malades. Editions de Maredsous [1952?]
237 p. 21 cm.
CaQStB; MnCS
2021 Silence, culture et civilisation.
(*In* Mémorial de l'année Martinienne, 1960–1961. Paris, 1962. p. 223–234)
PLatS

Duesing, Lucian, 1916–
2022 Annual community retreat notes June 6–10, 1960. [Collegeville, Minn., St. John's Abbey, 1960]

34 p. 28 cm.
Typescript.
MnCS

Duin, Adelbert van, 1915–
2023 De impedimento impotentiae psychicae in iure canonico. Romae, Pontificium Athenaeum Lateranense, 1954.
61 p. 25 cm.
MnCS

Duman, Maximilian George, 1906–
2024 (tr) L'Heritier de Brutelle, Charles Louis. Sertum anglicum; [seu Plantae rariores quae in hortis juxta Londonum, imprimis in horto regio Kewensi excoluntur ab anno 1786 ad annum 1787 observatae]. Facsimile [of 1788 edition] with critical studies and a translation. [Edited by George H. M. Lawrence. Translated by Maximilian Duman, O.S.B., Leopold Krul, O.S.B., and Rembert Weakland, O.S.B.]. Pittsburgh, Hunt Botanical Library, 1963.
xciii, 36 p. 34 plates, 31 cm. (Hunt facsimile series, no. 1)
PLatS

Dumas, Antoine, 1915–
2025 (tr) Amadeus, Saint. Huit homélies Mariales . . . Traduction par Dom Antoine Dumas, O.S.B. Paris, Editions du Cerf, 1960.
InStme; PLatS
2026 (ed) Blaise, Albert. Le Vocabulaire latin des principaux thèmes liturgiques. Ouvrage revu par Dom Antoine Dumas, O.S.B. Turnhout, Brepols, 1966.
MnCS
2027 (ed & tr) Des hommes en quiête de Dieu: la Règle de Saint Benoît. Introduction, traduction et notes par Antoine Dumas, O.S.B. Paris, Editions du Cerf [1967]
CaQMo; MoCo; PLatS
2028 (ed & tr) La Règle de Saint Benoît. [Traduction, introduction et notes par Antoine Dumas, O.S.B. Haute-Provence, Editions Robert Morel, 1961]
MnCS; PLatS
2029 (tr) La Règle de Saint Benoît. 2d ed. [Traduction du Antoine Dumas]. [Paris], Editions du Cerf, 1977.
MoCo

Dumm, Demetrius Robert, 1923–
2030 The Biblical foundations of prayer. Reprint from: The American Benedictine review, v. 23 (1973), p. 181–204)
PLatS
2031 The decree on revelation and Catholic education.
(*In* Workshop on Vatican Council II: its challenge to education. Catholic University of America, 1966. p. 81–91)
PLatS

2032   An introduction to the liturgy. Latrobe, Pa., St. Vincent Seminary, 1961.
21 leaves, 28 cm.
Multilithed.
PLatS

2033   An introduction to the New Testament. Latrobe, Pa., St. Vincent Archabbey, 1965.
iii, 78 p. 28 cm.
PLatS

2034   Jesus of Nazareth. [Woodcuts by Irwin Zagar, text by Father Demetrius]. Latrobe, Pa., Archabbey Press [1962]
[16] double leaves, 7 woodcuts, 33 cm.
PLatS

2035   The theological basis of virginity according to St. Jerome. Latrobe, Pa., St. Vincent Archabbey, 1961.
ix, 167 p. 23 cm.
Thesis (S.T.D.)—Pontificium Athenaeum Anselmianum, Rome.
InStme; KAS; PLatS

2036   Tobit, Judith, Esther [commentary].
(*In* The Jerome Biblical commentary . . . 1968. p. 620–632)
PLatS

2037   Tobit; Judith; The rest of the chapters of the Book of Esther which are found neither in the Hebrew nor in the Syriac.
(*In* The New English Bible with the Apocrypha. New York, 1976. p. 53–96 [of the Apocrypha])
PLatS

2038   **Dumont, Pierre,** 1901–
(ed) Papadopoulos, Chrysostomos. L'Union de l'Orient avec Rome; une controversé recente . . . Roma, Pont. Institutum Orientalium Studiorum, 1930.
156 p. 24 cm. (Orientalia christiana, 60)
At head of title: Hieromoine Pierre.
InStme; MnCS

2039   (tr) Trempelas, Panagiotes Nikolaou. Dogmatique de l'Eglise orthodoxe catholique. Traduction française par Pierre Dumont, O.S.B. Editions de Chevetogne [1966–68].
3 v. 22 cm.
InStme

Dunegan, Bertrand Howard, 1930–
2040   Beachcomber's guide to Golden Isles. [Private printing, 1969]
35 p. illus. 22 cm.
PLatS

2041   Beachcombing on Hilton Head Island; a guide to marine life prevalent in the waters of the sea islands of South Carolina and Georgia with 127 illustrations . . . Hilton Head Island, S.C., Hilton Head Island Pub. Co., 1970.

68 p. illus. 18 cm.
PLatS

2042   Belief in the guardian angels sent to individual men according to the early Church Fathers.
34 leaves, 28 cm.
Thesis (M.A.)—St. Vincent College, Latrobe, Pa., 1959.
Typescript.
PLatS

2043   **Dungalus, recluse of St. Denis,** 9th cent.
Dungali Scotti Epistolae.
(*In* Monumenta Germaniae historica. Epistolae. Berolini, 1895. t. IV, p. 568–585)
InStme; MnCS

2044   **Dunne, Lambert,** 1907–
Retreat 1941. n.p.
71 p. 28 cm.
Typescript.
MnCS

2045   **Dunstan, Saint, abp. of Canterbury,** d. 988.
Saint Dunstan's classbook from Glastonbury (Codex Biblioth. Bodleianae Oxon. auct. F. 4/32). Introduction by R. W. Hunt. Amsterdam, North-Holland Publishing Co., 1961.
xvii facsims. 31 cm. (Umbrae codicum occidentalium . . . IV)
MnCS

Dupont, Jacques, 1915–
2046   Les Béatitudes. Nouv. éd. entièrement refondue. Bruges, Abbaye de Saint-André, 1958–
v. 24 cm.
InStme; KAS; PLatS

2047   Les Béatitudes. Reimpression de la seconde édition. Paris, J. Gabalda, 1969–
v. 25 cm.
PLatS

2048   Fête de la Sainte Famille, présentée par J. Dupont, Th. Maertens [et al]. [Bruges], Biblica [1961]
111 p. 21 cm.
PLatS

2049   Le discours de Milet; testament pastoral de Saint Paul (Actes 20, 18–36). Paris, Editions du Cerf, 1962.
407 p. 23 cm.
InStme; MnCS; PLatS

2050   Etudes sur les Actes des Apôtres. Paris, Editions du Cerf, 1967.
573 p. 23 cm.
InStme; PLatS

2051   Mariage et divorce dans l'Evangile; Matthieu 19, 3–12 et parallèles. [Bruges], Abbaye de Saint-André, 1959.

239 p. 24 cm.
CaQStB; InStme; MnCS

2052 The meal at Emmaus.
(*In* The Eucharist in the New Testament; a symposium [by] J. Delorme . . . p. 105–124)
PLatS

2052a The salvation of the gentiles; essays on the Acts of the Apostles. Translated by John R. Keating. New York, Paulist Press, 1979.
163 p. 21 cm.
InStme

2053 Les sources du Livre des Actes; état de la question. [Bruges], Desclée de Brouwer, 1960.
168 p. 22 cm.
InStme; KAS; MnCS; PLatS

2054 The sources of the Acts. [English translation by Kathleen Pond.] New York, Herder and Herder [1964]
180 p. 23 cm.
InFer; InStme; MnCS; MoCo; PLatS

2055 "Soyez parfaits" (Mt., VI, 48). "Soyez miséricordieux" (Lc., VI, 36).
(*In* Sacra pagina; miscellanea biblica Congressus Internationalis Catholici de re biblica. Gembloux, 1959. v. 2, p. 150–162)
PLatS

2056 Les tentations de Jésus au désert. [Paris], Desclée de Brouwer [1968]
152 p. 22 cm.
InStme

2057 "This is my Body . . . This is my Blood."
(*In* Tartre, Raymond, ed. The Eucharist today. New York, 1967. p. 13–28)
PLatS

2058 Die Versuchungen Jesu in der Wüste. Stuttgart, Verlag Katholisches Bibelwerk [1969].
132 p. 21 cm.
Translation of: Les tentations de Jésus au désert.
MnCS

2059 (tr) Les Actes des Apôtres. Traduction et notes de Dom J. Dupont, O.S.B. Paris, Editions du Cerf, 1958.
CaQStB; KySu; InStme; MnCS; PLatS

2060 (2dary) Jésus aux origines de la christologie, par J. Dupont [et al.]. Louvain, Leuven University Press, 1975.
375 p. 25 cm.
English, French, or German.
InStme

2061 **Dupriez, Edouard,** 1903–
La pauvreté monastique.
(*In* Le message des moines à notre temps. Paris, 1958. p. 195–206)
PLatS

2062 Que sont donc les Bénédictins? [Belley, Imprimerie du Bugey, 1956?]
16 p. plates, 18 cm.
MnCS

2063 **Duratschek, Claudia, Sister.**
Under the shadow of His wings; history of Sacred Heart Convent of Benedictine Sisters, Yankton, South Dakota, 1880–1970. Aberdeen, S.D., North Plains Press, 1971.
368 p. illus. 24 cm.
InStme; MnCS; MoCo

2064 **Durdevic, Ignjat,** 1675–1737.
D. Paulus Apostolus in mari, quod nunc Venetus Sinus dicitur, naufragus, et Melitae Dalmatensis insulae post naufragium hospes . . . Venetiis, apud Christophroum Zane, 1730.
311 p. illus., maps, 24 cm.
MnCS

Durham Cathedral, England.
2065 Liber vitae Ecclesiae Dunelmensis. A collotype facsimile of the original manuscript, with introductory essays and notes . . . Durham, Pub. for the Society by Andrews & Co., 1923.
v. 23 cm. (Publications of the Surtees Society . . . vol. cxxxvi)
MnCS

2066 The obituary role of William Ebchester and John Burnby, priors of Durham, with notices of similar records preserved at Durham, from the year 1233 downwards . . . Durham, Pub. for the Society by G. Andrews, 1856.
xxxv, 135 p. illus. 23 cm. (Publications of the Surtees Society . . . vol. xxxi)
MnCS

Durken, Daniel Donald, 1929–
2066a Blow the trumpet at the new moon; a Sisters Today jubilee. Edited by Daniel Durken, O.S.B. Collegeville, Minn., The Liturgical Press, 1979.
x, 470 p. 24 cm.
MnCS

2066b Marching thru Exodus. Collegeville, Minn., The Liturgical Press, 1979.
Cassette (6 hrs.)
MnCS; InStme

2066c Sin, salvation and the Spirit; commemorating the fiftieth year of The Liturgical Press. Collegeville, Minn., The Liturgical Press, 1979.
xiv, 368 p. 23 cm.
MnCS; InStme

2067 **Du Roy, Olivier,** 1933–
Moines aujourd'hui; une experience de réforme institutionnelle. Paris, Epi [1972].
403 p. 24 cm.
InStme; MnCS

2068 **Dusault, Jean Paul,** 1650–1724.
Entretiens avec Jésus-Christ dans le trés
S. Sacrement de l'autel . . . Toulouse, Aux
dépens de J. Guillemette, 1737.
480 p.
NcBe

2069 **Dusmet, Giuseppe Benedetto,** 1818–
1894.
S. Benedetto e il mese di maggio; lettera
di Monsignor Arcivescovo di Catania ai
suoi diocesani. [Monte Cassino, 1880].
11 p. 23 cm.
PLatS

2070 **Dussler, Georg,** 1893–
Geschichte der Ettaler Bergstrasse. [3.
Aufl.]
(*In* Ettaler Mandl. Jahrg. 51/24 (1971–
72), p. 73–170)
KAS

2071 **Dux, Victor L.,** 1903–
What the world needs. [Boston], St. Paul
Editions [1968]
192 p. 22 cm.
InStme; NcBe

2072 **Dworschak, Baldwin Wilfred,** 1907–
Benedictine education.
15 p. 23 cm. (College of Saint Benedict,
Saint Joseph, Minn. Mother Benedicta
Riepp memorial lectureship. First annual
lecture, 1963)
MnCS; MnStj (Archives)

Eadmer, ca. 1060–1124.

2073 De laude Mariae Virginis. MS. Benediktinerabtei Melk, Austria, codex 452, f.
24v–36v. Folio. Saec. 15.
Microfilm: MnCH proj. no. 1419

2074 Ecrits spirituels d'Elmer de Cantorbéry,
par Dom Jean Leclercq, O.S.B.
(*In* Analecta monastica, 2. ser. 1953. p.
45–117. Studia Anselmiana, fasc. 31)
PLatS

2075 Historia novorum. MS. Lambeth Palace
Library, London, codex 175. 199 f. Quarto.
Saec. 16.
Microfilm: MnCH

2076 Historiae novorum sive sui saeculi libri
VI . . . In lucem ex Bibliotheca Cottoniana
emisit Ioannes Aeldenvs, & notas porro adjecit & spicilegium. Londoni, Typis & impensis G. Stanesbeij, ex officinis R.
Meighen & T. Dew, 1623.
MnCS (microfilm)

2077 Eadmer's History of recent events in
England. Historia novorum in Anglia.
Translated from the Latin by Geoffrey
Bosanquet, with a foreword by R. W.
Souther. London, Cresset Press [1964].
xv, 240 p. 22 cm.
NcBe; PLatS

2078 Liber de similitudinibus. MS. Augusti-
nerchorherrenstift Klosterneuburg,
Austria, codex 251, f. 124r–128r. Folio.
Saec. 14.
Microfilm: MnCH proj. no. 5212

2079 De similitudinibus. MS. Augustinerchorherrenstift Klosterneuburg, Austria,
codex 1123, f. 6v–66r. Octavo. Saec. 15.
Microfilm: MnCH proj. no. 6122

2080 The life of St. Anselm, archbishop of
Canterbury. Edited with introduction,
notes, and translation by R. W. Southern.
London, New York, T. Nelson [1962]
xxxvi, 171, 179 p. 23 cm. (Medieval texts)
NcBe; InStme; NdRi; ILSP; PLatS;
KAS; MnCS

2081 Vita beati Anselmi, archiepiscopi Can-
tuariensis. MS. Benediktinerabtei Melk,
Austria, codex 1869, f. 166r–191v. Folio.
Saec. 15.
Microfilm: MnCH proj. no. 2166

2082 La vie de saint Anselme du Bec, tirée des
récits de son biographe Eadmer [par R. M.
Isabelle de Jouffroy d'Abbans, O.S.B.]
(*In* Saint Anselm: Textes choisiers . . .
Namur, Belgique, Editions du Soleil Le-
vant [1961]
PLatS

Earls, John Patrick, 1935–

2083 Organ accompaniment to A Short
Breviary (including hymns in the Franciscan edition). Collegeville, Minn., The Liturgical Press [1973?]
127 p. 20 x 28 cm.
MnCS

2084 (tr) Arrondo, E., C.SS.R. The eucharistic
liturgy in song and dialog . . . Englished
by Claude Earls. Collegeville, Minn., The
Liturgical Press [1964]
33 p. music, 18 cm.
MnCS

Ebel, Basilius, 1896–

2085 Das Bild des guten Hirten im 22. Psalm
nach Erklärungen der Kirchenväter.
Sonderdruck aus Festschrift für Bischof
Dr. Albert Stohr. Mainz [1959?], p. 48–57)
MnCS; PLatS

2086 Musik der römischen Messliturgie.
(*In* Internationaler Kongress für Kirchenmusik, 4th., Cologne, 1961. p.
163–202)
PLatS

2087 **Eberhardus, monk of Zwiefalt.**
Chronologia vitae et gestorum Jesu
Christi. MS. Augustinerchorherrenstift
Klosterneuburg, Austria, codex 415, f.
297r–299r. Folio. Saec. 15.
Microfilm: MnCH proj. no. 5385

2088 **Eberl, Martin.**
Wallfahrt Ettal. Ettal, Kunstverlag Ettal [1941]
44 p. plates, 16 cm.
MnCS

Eberle, Luke, 1910–
2089 (tr) Hunkeler, Leodegar. It began with Benedict . . . St. Benedict, Or., Benedictine Press [1973].
Translation of: Vom Mönchtum des heiligen Benedikt.
InStme; PLatS
2090 (tr) The Rule of the Master. Regula magistri. Translated by Luke Eberle. Kalamazoo, Mich., Cistercian Publications, 1977.
291 p. 23 cm.
ICSS; InStme; MnCS; MoCo; NcBe
2091 (tr) Villiger, Anselm. The foundation of Mount Angel Abbey as recorded in the diary of the founding abbot Anselm Villiger of Engelberg, January, 1881, to December, 1900.
57 p.
Typescript.
MoCo

2092 **Ebersberg, Bavaria (Benedictine abbey).**
Catalogus codicum manu scriptorum Bibliothecae Regiae Monacensis: Codices Ebersbergenses num. 5801–6059. Monachii, sumptibus Bibliotecae Regiae, 1873. Unveränderter Nachdruck, Otto Harrassowitz, Wiesbaden, 1968.
MnCH

2093 **Echternach, Luxemburg (Benedictine abbey).**
The Golden Gospels of Echternach, Codex aureus Epternacensis. Text based on the German by Peter Metz. [Rendered into English by Ise Schrier and Peter Gorge]. New York, Praeger [1957]
96 p. illus., 106 facsims. 34 cm.
ILSP; InStme

Eckebert, abbot of Schönau, d. 1184.
2094 Contra Catharos. MS. Universität Salzburg, codex M I 41. 68 f. Quarto. Saec. 12–13.
Microfilm: MnCH proj. no. 10,992
2095 Liber contra Kataros. MS. Cistercienserabtei Heiligenkreuz, Austria, codex 308. 77 f. Quarto. Saec. 13.
Microfilm: MnCH proj. no. 4844
2096 De obitu S. Elisabethae Schönaugiensis. MS. Vienna, Nationalbibliothek, codex 488, f. 47v–170r. Quarto. Saec. 13.
Microfilm: MnCH proj. no. 13,822
2097 Poema. Incipit: Jesum nulla tibi mea mens oblivio tollat. MS. Vienna, National-

bibliothek, codex 878, f. 125r–129v. Quarto. Saec. 12.
Microfilm: MnCH proj. no. 14,192
2098 Soliloquium. MS. Universitätsbibliothek Graz, Austria, codex 347, f. 135r–137v. Folio. Saec. 15.
Microfilm: MnCH proj. no. 26,270
2099 Soliloquium. MS. Universitätsbibliothek Graz, Austria, codex 1124, f. 171r–182r. Octavo. Saec. 16.
Microfilm: MnCH proj. no. 26,305
2100 Stimulus amoris. MS. Augustinerchorherrenstift Vorau, Austria, codex 304, f. 147v–151v.
Microfilm: MnCH proj. no. 7277
2101 Stimulus caritatis in dominum Jesus Christum. MS. Benediktinerabtei St. Peter, Salzburg, codex a.II.13, f. 65r–79r. Octavo. Saec. 14.
Microfilm: MnCH proj. no. 9907
2102 Stimulus caritatis. MS. Benediktinerabtei St. Peter, Salzburg, codex a.III.18, f. 221r–242v. Octavo. Saec. 15.
Microfilm: MnCH proj no. 9960
2103 Stimulus caritatis in Jesum Christum. MS. Benediktinerabtei St. Peter, Salzburg, codex a.VII.27, f. 90r–98v. Quarto. Saec. 15.
Microfilm: MnCH proj. no. 10,156
2104 **Ecker, Gerald Robert,** 1927–1969.
A descriptive catalog of the Carolingian manuscripts in Conception Abbey Library.
67 p. 29 cm.
Thesis (M.A.L.S.)–Rosary College, River Forest, Ill., 1955.
Typescript.
MnCS; MoCo

Eckhardt, Maternus, 1911–
2105 Der Bruder im Beuroner Kloster.
(*In* Beuron, 1863–1963; Festschrift . . . 1963. p. 473–485)
PLatS
2106 The Cross is our salvation; a life of the servant of God, Ulrika Nisch, Sister of the Holy Cross, Hegne (Constance), Germany. Konstanz, Merk & Co. [1964]
95 p.
NdRi
2107 (tr) Baur, Benedikt. Love knows no measure; a life of the servant of God, Sister Ulrika Nisch . . . [Konstanz, Mark & Co., 1968]
208 p. plates, 19 cm.
MnCS

2108 **The Ecumenical Institute, Belmont, N.C.**
Seminar on abortion. The proceedings of a dialogue between Catholics and Baptists

sponsored by the Bishops' Committee for Ecumenical and Interreligious Affairs and The Ecumenical Institute of Wake Forest University and Belmont Abbey College, November 10–12, 1975. Edited by Claude U. Broach. [Belmont, N.C., Belmont Abbey, 1975].
85 p.
NcBe

2109   Issues of Church and State. The proceedings of a dialogue between Catholics and Baptists sponsored by the Bishops' Committee for Ecumenical and Interreligious Affairs and The Ecumenical Institute of Wake Forest University and Belmont Abbey College, November 3–5, 1976. Edited by Claude U. Broach. [Belmont, N.C., Belmont Abbey, 1976]
96 p.
NcBe

2109a **Edelbrock, Alexius,** 1843–1908.
Die Benediktiner in Minnesota [1856–1867].
96 leaves, 32 cm.
Manuscript. Written 1882.
MnCS (Archives)

2109b   The Benedictines in Minnesota [1856–1867].
95 leaves, 32 cm.
Translated from the German by Eugene Bode, O.S.B.
Manuscript
MnCS (Archives)

2110   **Edie, Callistus James,** 1927–
The philosophy of Etienne Gilson.
3 v. 28 cm.
Thesis (Ph.D.)– Université catholique de Louvain, 1958.
MnCS

Edmer. *See* Eadmer.

2111   **Edmonds, Columba,** 1861–
Irish monks in Europe.
(*In* Dunn, Joseph. Glories of Ireland. 1914. p. 20–32)
AStb

Effinger, Konrad Maria, 1800–
2112   Officium ecclesiasticum; vollständiges katholisches Gebetbuch, lateinisch und deutsch . . . 2. Aufl. Einsiedeln, New York, Gebr. Benziger 1872.
572 p. 14 cm.
PLatS

2113   Vade mecum, sive Libellus precum ad usum praecipue juventutis studiosae accommodatus. Editio altera augmentata. Einsiedeln, C. & N. Benziger, 1856.
viii, 632 p. illus. 12 cm.
MnCS

2114   (ed) Libri quattuor de Immitatione Christi. Cum appendice precationum. Collegit et edidit P. Conradus Maria Effinger, O.S.B. Einsiedeln, Neo-Eboraci, C. et N. Benziger, 1878.
320 p. illus. 10 cm.
PLatS

Egbert, abbot of Schönau. *See* Eckebert, abbot of Schönau.

2115   **Egger, Felix,** 1659–1720.
Idea Ordinis hierarchico-Benedictini; sive, Brevis delineatio exhibens principatum, clericatum, scientiam, actionem & antiquitatem Ordinis Sancti Benedicti . . . Constantiae, typis Leonardi Parcus, 1715–21.
3 v. 17 cm.
KAS (v. 1); MoCo (v. 2); PLatS (v. 1–2)

Eginhard. *See* Einhard.

2116   **Egli, Beat,** 1930–
Der vierzehnte Psalm im Prolog der Regal des heiligen Benedikt; eine patrologischmonastische Studie. Sarnen, Buchdruckerei Louis Ehrli, 1962.
xi, 134 p. diagrs. 22 cm.
Beilage zum Jahresbericht des Kollegiums Sarnen 1961–62.
MnCS

2117   **Eichhorn, Ambrosius.**
Ascesis Benedictino-Blasiana succincta methodo tradita. MS. Benediktinerabtei St. Paul im Lavanttal, Austria, codex 85/6. 66 f. Folio. Saec. 18.
Microfilm: MnCH proj. no. 12,631

Eichstätt, Germany. Abtei St. Walburg.
2118   Benediktinerinnen-Abtei St. Walburg, Eichstätt. Wasserburg am Inn, Joseph Käser, n.d. [post 1914]
unpaged, views, 9 x 15 cm.
MnCS

2119   Unsere Klosterheimat, Abtei St. Walburg, Eichstätt.
16 p.
MnStj (Archives)

2120   Die Wallfahrtskirche der hl. Walburga zu Eichstätt. 2. neub. Aufl. Eichstätt, Brönner & Daentler, 1951.
23 p.
MnStj (Archives)

2121   **Eickhoff, Mary Dominic, Sister,** 1919–
Behavior of parents of hospitalized children as perceived and dealt with by a selected group of nursing students in a three-year school of nursing.
63 p.
Thesis (M.S.)–Catholic University of America, 1960.
MnStj (Archives)

2122 **Eigil, abbot of Fulda,** d. 822.
Eigilis vita s. Sturmi abbatis Fuldensis.
(*In* Monumenta Germaniae historica.
Scriptores. Stuttgart, 1963. t. 2, p.
365–377)
MnCS; PLatS
Einhard, 779 (ca.)–840.
2123 Annales (fragmentum). MS. Vienna, Nationalbibliothek, codex 473, f. 152v–169r.
Quarto. Saec. 9.
Microfilm: MnCH proj. no. 13,820
2124 Annales et Annales Laurissenses. MS.
Vienna, Nationalbibliothek, codex 610, f.
15r–56v. Octavo. Saec. 14.
Microfilm: MnCH proj. no. 13,959
2125 Epitaphium Karoli Magni. MS. Vienna,
Nationalbibliothek, codex 969, f. 55v.
Folio. Saec. 10.
Microfilm: MnCH proj. no. 14,278
2126 [Epistolae]
Weinckens, Johannes. Vir fama super
aethera notus Eginhartus . . . In fine adjectae sunt ejusdem Eginharti epistolae, in
Germania hactenus praelo nunquam subjectae. Francofurti ad Moenum, impensis
Joannis Philippi Andreae, 1714.
[16], 127 p. 33 cm.
MnCS
2127 Vita Karoli Magni (fragmentum). MS.
Vienna, Nationalbibliothek, codex 473, f.
144r–151v. Quarto. Saec. 9.
Microfilm: MnCH proj. no. 13,820
2128 Vita Karoli Magni. MS. Vienna, Nationalbibliothek, codex 529, f. 1r–13v.
Quarto. Saec. 9.
Microfilm: MnCH proj. no. 13,875
2129 Vita Caroli Magni. MS. Vienna, Nationalbibliothek, codex 510, f, 31r–55r.
Quarto. Saec. 10.
Microfilm: MnCH proj. no. 13,845
2130 Vita Caroli Magni. MS. Vienna, Nationalbibliothek, codex 182, f. 69r–82v.
Folio. Saec. 12.
Microfilm: MnCH proj. no. 13,538
2131 Vita Karoli Magni. MS. Vienna, Nationalbibliothek, codex 532, f. 48r–57r.
Quarto. Saec. 12.
2132 Vita Caroli Magni. MS. Salisbury,
England, Cathedral Library, codex 80, f.
189–197. Quarto. Saec. 13.
Microfilm: MnCH
2133 Vita Caroli Magni. MS. Vienna, Nationalbibliothek, codex 400, f. 40v–51r.
Folio. Saec. 13.
Microfilm: MnCH proj. no. 13,732
2134 Vita Caroli Magni. MS. Vienna, Nationalbibliothek, codex 639, f. 1v–31v. Octavo. Saec. 13.
Microfilm: MnCH proj. no. 13,961

2135 Vita Caroli Magni. MS. Vienna, Nationalbibliothek, codex 610, f. 1v–15r. Octavo. Saec. 14.
Microfilm: MnCH proj. no. 13,959
2136 Vita Caroli Magni, cui subjecti sunt versus Gerwardi bibliothecarii. MS. Vienna,
Nationalbibliothek, codex 3126, f. 43v–50r.
Folio. Saec. 15.
Microfilm: MnCH proj. no. 16,431
2137 Vita Caroli Magni. MS. Vienna, Nationalbibliothek, codex 427, f. 125r–132r.
Folio. Saec. 16.
Microfilm: MnCH proj. no. 13,755
2138 Einhardi Vita Karoli imperatoris.
(*In* Monumenta Germaniae historica.
Scriptores. Stuttgart, 1963. t. 2, p. 426–463)
MnCS; PLatS
2139 [Vita Karoli Magni. English]
Early lives of Charlemagne, by Eginhard
& the Monk of St. Gall. Translated and
edited by A. J. Grant. New York, Cooper
Square Publishers, 1966.
xxv, 179 p. 17 cm. (The Medieval
Library)
PLatS
Einsiedeln, Switzerland (Benedictine abbey).
2140 Annales Einsidlenses.
(*In* Monumenta Germaniae historica.
Scriptores. Stuttgart, 1963. t. 3, p. 137–149)
MnCS; PLatS
2141 Catalogus religiosorum monast. B.M.V.
Einsidlensis Ordinis S. Benedicti . . . Einsidlae, Typis Salesii Benziger.
v. 16 cm.
PLatS
2142 Dreyfacher Ehrenkranz St. Meinradi;
das ist, Einsidlische in drey Theil verfasste
Chronik . . . Einsiedlen, Meinrad Eberlin,
1728.
2 v. illus. 17 cm.
InStme
2143 Der Einsiedler aus'm finstern Wald (Abbey chronicle from 1888–1909)
InStme
2144 Einsidlische in drey theil verfasste
Chronik . . . Neue Auflage. Einsidlen,
Johann Eberhard Kälin, 1752.
673 p. illus. 18 cm.
InStme
2145 Die Regesten der Benedictiner-Abtei
Einsiedeln. Bearb. von Gallus Morel. Chur,
G. Hitz, 1848.
[10], 98 p. 30 cm.
KAS
2146 Sankt Meinrad. Zum elften Zentenarium
seines Todes, 1861–1961, hrsg. von Bene-

diktinern des Klosters Maria Einsiedln. Einsiedeln, Benziger Verlag, 1961.

    126 p. 26 plates. 23 cm.

    InStme; MoCo; PLatS

Einsiedeln, Switzerland (Benedictine abbey). Bibliothek.

2147 Das Blockbuch von Sankt Meinrad und seinen Mördern und vom Ursprung von Einsiedeln. Farbige Faksimile-Ausgabe zum elften Zentenar des Heiligen, 861–1961. Mit einer Einleitung von Leo Helbling. Einsiedeln, Benziger, 1961.

    35 p. 64 col. illus.

    InStme; MnCS; PLatS

2148 Ein Hymnus abecedarius auf Christus. Aus Codex Einsiedlensis 27 (1125) mitgeteilt von Alban Dold. Mit einem Wort der Einführung von Benedikt Reetz. Beuron, Beuroner Kunstverlag, 1959.

    viii, 23 p. facsims. 23 cm. (Texte und Arbeiten. 1. Abt., Hft. 51)

    InStme

2149 Stiftsbibliothek Einsiedeln: Handschriften aus schweizerischen Benediktinerklöstern, 8.–18. Jahrhundert. Ausstellung, Juni–November 1971.

    unpaged, 21 cm.

    MnCS

2150 **Einsiedeln, Switzerland (Benedictine abbey). Stiftsschule.**

    Jahresbericht der Stiftsschule Einsiedeln für das Studienjahr . . . Einsiedeln, Benziger & Co. [1840–

    v. illus., ports, 21 cm.

    InStme; MnCS; PLatS

2151 **Einsiedler, Josef Maria,** 1870–1950.

    De Tertulliani adversus Judaeos libro. Augustae Vindelicorum, typis Ph. J. Pfeifferi, 1897.

    44 p. 21 cm. (Programma Gymnasii Augustani et St. Stephani, MDCCCXCVII)

2152 **Eisenman, Victoria, Sister.**

    An exploratory study to investigate the values of literature as experienced by elementary and parochial school children and teachers in the Diocese of Covington.

    Thesis (Ph.D.)–St. Louis University, 1962.

    Typescript.

    KyCovS

2153 **Eisvogl, Weremund,** 1687–1761

    Concordia animae benedictinae cum Deo; seu, Reflexiones asceticae in singulos anni dies super acta, praecipuas virtutes, & mirabilem vitam sanctorum ex Ordine magni monachorum patriarche s. p. Benedicti . . . Augustae Vindelicorum, Joannes Stötter, 1723.

    2 v. 17 cm.

    KAS; KySu (v. 1); MnCS

Eizenhöfer, Leo, 1907–

2154 Horae resurrectionis in einem Benediktinerinnengebetbuch des 16. Jahrhunderts in Darmstadt.

    (*In* Corona gratiarum; miscellanea patristica . . . Eligio Dekkers . . . oblata. Brugge, 1975. v. 2, p. 71–97)

    PLatS

2155 Das irische Palimpsestsakramentar im CLM 14429 der Staatsbibliothek München. Entziffert und hrsg. von Alban Dold, O.S.B., und Leo Eizenhöfer, O.S.B. . . . Beuron, Beuroner Kunstverlag, 1964.

    xxv, 128, 212 p. facsims. 23 cm. (Texte und Arbeiten . . . Heft 53–54)

    InStme; PLatS

2156 Die liturgischen Handschriften des Hessischen Landes- und Hochschulbibliothek Darmstadt, beschrieben von Leo Eizenhoefer und Herman Knaus. Wiesbaden, Otto Harrassowitz, 1968.

    382 p. 23 cm.

    MnCS

Ekkebert, abbot of Schönau. *See* Eckebert, abbot of Schönau.

Ekkebertus, monk of Hirschfeld. *See* Egbert, monk of Hirschfeld.

Ekkehardus, abbot of Aura, fl. 1100.

2157 Chronicon, incipiens ab origine Francorum (fragmentum). MS. Vienna, Nationalbibliothek, codex 460. 25 f. Quarto. Saec. 12.

    Microfilm: MnCH proj. no. 13,800

2158 Chronicon universalis, usque ad historiam Francorum. MS. Vienna, Nationalbibliothek, codex 486. 159 f. Quarto. Saec. 12.

    Microfilm: MnCH proj. no. 13,816

2159 **Ekkehardus I, monk of St. Gall,** d. 973.

    Das Waltharilied und die Waldere Bruchstüke. Uebertraggen, eingeleitet und erläutert von Felix Genzmer. Stuttgart, Reclam [1957]

    54 p. 16 cm.

    MnCS

Ekkehardus IV, monk of St. Gall, ca. 980–1060.

2160 Casuum S. Galli continuatio I.

    (*In* Monumenta Germaniae historica. Scriptores. Stuttgart, 1963. t. 2, p. 74–147)

    MnCS; PLatS

2161 Der Liber benedictionum Ekkeharts IV., nebst den kleinen Dichtungen aus dem Codex Sangallensis 393. Zum ersten Mal vollständig hrsg. und erläutert von Johannes Egli. St. Gallen, Fehrische Buchhandlung, 1909.

    li, 439 p. facsims. 24 cm.

    MnCS

2162 **Electio Hugonis. English.**
The chronicle of the election of Hugh, abbot of Bury St. Edmunds and later bishop of Ely. Edited and translated by R. M. Thomson. Oxford, Clarendon Press, 1974.
li, 208 p. 23 cm. (Oxford medieval texts)
PLatS

Elizabeth, Saint, of Schönau, 1129 (ca)–1164.

2163 Visio beatae Elisabethae Schönaugiensis de S. Ursula et undecim millibus virginum. MS. Vienna, Nationalbibliothek, codex 426, f. 10v–22v. Folio. Saec. 15.
Microfilm: MnCH proj. no. 13,768

2164 Visiones S. Elisabethae ancillae Christi in Schönaugia. De obitu S. Elisabethae Schönaugiensis. MS. Vienna, Nationalbibliothek, codex 428, f. 47v–170r. Quarto. Saec. 13.
Microfilm: MnCH proj. no. 13,822

Ellspermann, Gerard Leo, 1914–

2165 The vocabulary of Livy, book XXIX.
x, 54 leaves. 28 cm.
Thesis (M.A.)–Catholic University of America, 1942.
Typescript.
InFer; InStme

2166 (tr) Zürcher, Johannes Chrysostomus. Man of God–Brother Meinrad Eugster. Einsiedeln, Benziger [1976]
InStme

Elsensohn, Alfreda, Sister, 1897–

2167 History of St. Gertrude's Convent, Cottonwood, Idaho; a short historical sketch: 78 years of service, 1884–1962, 53 years at Cottonwood, 1909–1962. [Cottonwood, Id., Cottonwood Chronicle Print 1962]
22 p. illus.
MnStj (Archives); IdCos

2168 Idaho Chinese lore. Caldwell, Id., Caxton Printers [c 1970]
121 p. illus. 23 cm.
IdCos

2169 **Emonds, Hilarius,** 1905–
Der topos der militia spiritualis in der antiken Philosophie.
(*In* Heilige Ueberlieferung. Münster, 1938. p. 21–50)
PLatS

2170 **Ename, Belgium. Saint-Sauveur (Benedictine abbey).**
De onuitgegeven oorkonden van de Sint-Salvatorsabdij te Aname voor 1200, door Ludo Milis. Brussel, Paleis der Academien, 1965.
L, 88 p. 32 cm.
MnCS

Encalcat, France (Benedictine abbey).

2171 Livre d'heures, latin-français. Dourgne-Tarn, Editions de l'Abbaye d'Encalcat, 1952.
xlvii, 1487 p. 18 cm.
CaQStB; MnCS

2172 Office of Our Lady. [Compiled by the Benedictine monks of Encalcat, France. Translated from the French]. London, Darton, Longman & Todd [1962]
2 v. 17 cm.
PLatS

2173 Présence d'En Calcat. 1– 1964–
MnCS

Endres, José Lohr, 1904–

2174 Catálogo dos bispos, gerais, provinciais, abades e mais cargos da Ordem de S. Bento do Brasil, 1582–1975. Salvador, Bahia [Brazil], Mosteiro de S. Bento, 1976.
510 p. 28 cm.
MnCS

2175 Primeiras constituçioes da Ordem de Sao Bento na Provincia do Brasil, 1596. Salvador, Bahia, 1977.
[22] p. 21 cm.
MnCS

2176 **Engberding, Hieronymus,** 1899–
Maria in der Frömmigkeit der östlichen Liturgien.
(*In* Sträter, Paul. Katholische Marienkunde. v. 1 (1962), p. 119–136)
PLatS

Engel, Ludwig, 1634–1674.

2177 Collegium universi juris canonici; antehac juxta triplex juris objectum partitum, nunc vero servato ordine Decretalium accuratius translatum, et indice copioso locupletatum, omnibus tam in foro quam in scholis apprime utile ac necessarium . . . Salisburgi, typis Joan. Jos. Mayr, 1712.
[11] 1254, [39] p. 21 cm.
KAS

2178 . . . Ed. 7. prioribus longe accuratior . . . Venetiis, apud Josephum Bettinelli, 1733.
2 v. 35 cm.
KAS

2179 . . . Ed. 9 . . . Beneventi, prostat Venetiis, in Typographia Balleoniana, 1760.
[8], 478 p. 39 cm.
KAS

2180 . . . Ed. 10, cui accessit ejusdem authoris Tractatus de privilegiis monasteriorum. Salisburgi, Joan. Bapt. Mayr, 1766.
2 v.
KAS

2181 Manuale parochorum, de obligationibus, functionibus et juribus parochialibus, quod

nuper disputationi publicae exhibitum nunc rebus quamplurimis auctum denuo in lucem edit P. Ludovicus Engel . . . Salisburgi, Joan. Bapt. Mayr, 1662.
382 p. 13 cm.
InStme

2182 Manuale parochorum, de plerisque functionibus & obligationibus ad parochios, parochos, & parochianos attinentibus . . . [Beneventi, prostat Venetiis, in typographia Balleoniana, 1760]
120 p. 39 cm.
KAS

2183 Tractatus de privilegiis et juribus monasteriorum ex jure communi deductus nunc sexta vice impressus et adnotationibus auctus. Salisburgi, Joan. Bapt. Mayr, 1712.
72 leaves. 21 cm.
KAS

2184 **Engel, Peter,** 1856–1921.
Bird notes, by Lambert Thelen, O.S.B., and Peter Engel, O.S.B.
[26] p. 20 cm.
The notes are about birds observed in the vicinity of St. John's about 1895 to 1903.
MnCS (Archives)

Engelberg, Switzerland (Benedictine abbey).

2185 Versuch einer urkundlichen Darstellung des reichsfreien Stiftes Engelberg, St. Benedikten-Ordens in der Schweiz, zwölftes und dreizehntes Jahrhundert . . . Luzern, Räber, 1846.
iv, 122 p. illus. 22 cm.
InStme; KAS; PLatS

2186 Catalogus codicum manu scriptorum qui asservantur in Bibliotheca monasterii O.S.B. Engelbergensis in Helvetia. Edidit Benedictus Gottwald. [Friburgi Brisgoviae, Typis Herderianis, 1891]
xvi, 327 p. 28 cm.
InStme; MnCS; PLatS

Engelbert, abbot of Admont, ca. 1250–1331.
Manuscript copies.

2187 [Opera]
Quaestiones de trinitate personarum et aliae dodecim theologicae; Tractatulus de miraculis Christi; Tractatus de fascinatione; Tractatus de libero arbitrio; Tractatus de quaestionibus super antiphonam: Cum rex gloriae. MS. Augustinerchorherrenstift Klosterneuburg, Austria, codex 306, f. 131v–231v. Folio. Saec. 14.
Microfilm: MnCH proj. no. 5274

2188 [Opera]
Tractatus de gratia Salvatoris et justitia damnationis humanae; Tractatus de quaestionibus super antiphonam: Cum rex

gloriae; Sermones ad antiphonas adventus; Tractatus de gratiis et virtutibus Beatae Mariae Virginis (incompl.). MS. Augustinerchorherrenstift Klosterneuburg, Austria, codex 512, f. 247r–307r. Folio. Saec. 14.
Microfilm: MnCH proj. no. 5480

2189 [Selections]
Opera quaedam. MS. Benediktinerabtei Admont, Austria, codex 181. 90 f. Folio. Saec. 14.
Microfilm: MnCH proj. no. 9275

2190 [Selections]
Tractatus varii. Tractatus de vita et moribus beatae Virginis. MS. Monasterio benedictino de Montserrat, Spain, codex 816. Quarto. Saec. 14–15.
Microfilm: MnCH proj. no. 30,081

2191 Commentum super Magnificat. MS. Augustinerchorherrenstift Klosterneuburg, Austria, codex 584, f. 99v–120v. Folio. Saec. 14.
Microfilm: MnCH proj. no. 5561

2192 De consilio vitae. MS. Benediktinerabtei Admont, Austria, codex 509, f. 63r–64v. Quarto. Saec. 13.
Microfilm: MnCH proj. no. 9558

2193 De XII quaestionibus specialibus. MS. Benediktinerabtei Kremsmünster, Austria, codex 138, f. 146–148r.
Microfilm: MnCH proj. no. 127

2194 De gratia salvationis et justitia damnationis humanae. MS. Benediktinerabtei Admont, Austria, codex 140, f. 69r–75v. Folio. Saec. 15.
Microfilm: MnCH proj. no. 9229

2195 De gratiis et virtutibus Beatae Virginis Mariae. MS. Benediktinerabtei Admont, Austria, codex 140, f. 98v–113v. Folio. Saec. 15.
Microfilm: MnCH proj. no. 9229

2196 De naturis animalium. MS. Benediktinerabtei Admont, Austria, codex 547, f. 82r–120v. Quarto. Saec. 14.
Microfilm: MnCH proj. no. 9584

2197 De ortu et fine imperii Romani. MS. Benediktinerabtei Admont, Austria, codex 600, f. 59r–92v. Quarto. Saec. 14.
Microfilm: MnCH proj. no. 9637

2198 De ortu et statu et fine Romani imperii. MS. Augustinerchorherrenstift Klosterneuburg, Austria, codex 833, f. 380r–410v. Quarto. Saec. 15.
Microfilm: MnCH proj. no. 5823

2199 De passione Domini et mysterio crucis. MS. Universitätsbibliothek Graz, Austria, codex 481, f. 1r–48r. Folio. Saec. 14.
Microfilm: MnCH proj. no. 26,657

2200 De regimine principum. MS. Benediktinerabtei Admont, Austria, codex 551. 52 f. Quarto. Saec. 14.
Microfilm: MnCH proj. no. 9601

2201 De regimine principum. MS. Benediktinerabtei Admont, Austria, codex 665. 123 f. Quarto. Saec. 15.
Microfilm: MnCH proj. no. 9699

2202 De regimine principum. MS. Studienbibliothek, Klagenfurt, Austria, codex cart. 171, f. 132r–200e. Folio. Saec. 15.
Microfilm: MnCH proj. no. 13,142

2203 De statu animarum post mortem. MS. Benediktinerabtei Admont, Austria, codex 837. 45 f. Quarto. Saec. 17.
Microfilm: MnCH proj. no. 9844

2204 De summo bono hominis in hac vita. MS. Cistercienserabtei Rein, Austria, codex 60, f. 111r–120v. Folio. Saec. 15.
Microfilm: MnCH proj. no. 7456

2205 Dialogus concupiscentiae et rationis. MS. Benediktinerabtei Admont, Austria, codex 492, f. 49r–53v. Folio. Saec. 14.
Microfilm: MnCH proj. no. 9545

2206 Dialogus concupscentiae et rationis de bonis moribus. MS. Augustinerchorherrenstift Klosterneuburg, Austria, codex 428, f. 172r–176v. Folio. Saec. 15
Microfilm: MnCH proj. no. 5402

2207 Dialogus concupiscentiae et rationis de bonis moribus. MS. Augustinerchorherrenstift Klosterneuburg, Austria, codex 934, f. 120r–131v. Quarto. Saec. 14.
Microfilm: MnCH proj. no. 5923

2208 Duodecim quaestiones. MS. Vienna, Schottenstift, codex 314, f. 208r–212r. Quarto. Saec. 15.
Microfilm: MnCH proj. no. 3983

2209 Epistola ad magistrum Ulricum, scholasticum Viennensem (de studiis et scriptis suis). MS. Cistercienserabtei Rein, Austria, codex 60, f. 139v–141r. Folio. Saec. 15.
Microfilm: MnCH proj. no. 7456

2210 Expositio antiphonae: Cum rex gloriae. MS. Benediktinerabtei Melk, Austria, codex 907, f. 152v–156v. Quarto. Saec. 15.
Microfilm: MnCH proj. no. 1643

2211 Expositio super antiphonam: Cum rex gloriae. MS. Cistercienserabtei Rein, Austria, codex 18, f. 57v–60r. Quarto. Saec. 14.
Microfilm: MnCH proj. no. 7417

2212 Expositio super antiphonam: Cum rex gloriae. MS. Cistercienserabtei Rein, Austria, codex 60, f. 109v–111r. Folio. Saec. 15.
Microfilm: MnCH proj. no. 7456

2213 Super: Cum rex gloriae Christe. MS. Vienna, Schottenstift, codex 314, f. 148r–152r. Quarto. Saec. 15.
Microfilm: MnCH proj. no. 3983

2214 Expositio in evangelium: In principio erat Verbum. MS. Cistercienserabtei Rein, Austria, codex 60, f. 65v–92r. Folio. Saec. 15.
Microfilm: MnCH proj. no. 7456

2215 Expositio super psalmum 118. MS. Benediktinerabtei Admont, Austria, codex 96. 226 f. Folio. Saec. 14.
Microfilm: MnCH proj. no. 9193

2216 Expositio super psalmum 118. MS. Benediktinerabtei Admont, Austria, codex 97. 319 f. Folio. Saec. 14.
Microfilm: MnCH proj. no. 9203

2217 Expositio continua super psalmum "Beati immaculati" per totum usque "ad dominum cum tribularer." MS. Augustinerchorherrenstift Klosterneuburg, Austria, codex 12, f. 1r–233r. Folio. Saec. 14.
Microfilm: MnCH proj. no. 4989

2218 Expositio super psalmum: Beati immaculati in via (118). MS. Benediktinerabtei Lambach, Austria, codex chartaceus 3, 287 f. Saec. 15.
Microfilm: MnCH proj. no. 435

2219 Expositio super psalmum CXVIII. MS. Benediktinerabtei St. Paul im Lavanttal, Austria, codex 147/4, pars II. Folio. Saec. 15 (1473).
Microfilm: MnCH proj. no. 12,395

2220 In antiphonam: Tu rex gloriae. MS. Benediktinerabtei Melk, Austria, codex 664, f. 6v–10v. Quarto. Saec. 14.
Microfilm: MnCH proj. no. 1534

2221 Libellus duodecim quaestionum. MS. Cistercienserabtei Rein, Austria, codex 60, f. 137v–139v. Folio. Saec. 15.
Microfilm: MnCH proj. no. 7456

2222 Liber de regimine principum, cum indice capitulorum praemisso et prologo. MS. Vienna, Nationalbibliothek, codex 5158. 117 f. Quarto. Saec. 15 (1495)
Microfilm: MnCH proj. no. 18,335

2223 Liber de summo bono hominis in hac vita. MS. Vienna, Schottenstift, codex 314, f. 152r–176v. Quarto. Saec. 15.
Microfilm: MnCH proj. no. 3983

2224 Meditatio articulorum passionis Domini. MS. Augustinerchorherrenstift Vorau, Austria, codex 166, f. 126r–126v. Quarto. Saec. 15.
Microfilm: MnCH proj. no. 7161

2225 Orationes ad Dei genetricem Mariam. MS. Benediktinerabtei St. Peter, Salzburg,

codex b.VII.10, f. 171r–186v. Octavo. Saec. 15.
Microfilm: MnCH proj. no. 10,516

2226 Orationes ad dominum Jesum. MS. Benediktinerabtei St. Peter, Salzburg, codex b.VII.10, f. 158r–170v. Octavo. Saec. 15.
Microfilm: MnCH proj. no. 10,516

2227 Psalterium de Beata Maria Virgine. MS. Benediktinerabtei St. Peter, Salzburg, codex b.VII.10, f. 1874–200r. Octavo. Saec. 15.
Microfilm: MnCH proj. no. 10,516

2228 Quaestiones de trinitate personarum divinarum. MS. Benediktinerabtei Kremsmünster, Austria, codex 138, f. 144r–146v.
Microfilm: MnCH proj. no. 127

2229 Quaestiones de trinitate personarum divinarum. MS. Benediktinerabtei Lambach, Austria, codex chartaceus 337, f. 61r–66r. Saec. 14.
Microfilm: MnCH proj. no. 706

2230 Resolutio quaestionis: Utrum deus adhuc incarnatus fuisset. MS. Benediktinerabtei Admont, Austria, codex 532. 43 f. Quarto. Saec. 14.
Microfilm: MnCH proj. no. 9591

2231 Sermo de sancto Jacobo. MS. Augustinerchorherrenstift Klosterneuburg, Austria, codex 564 A, f. 35v–36r. Folio. Saec. 14.
Microfilm: MnCH proj. no. 5542

2232 Speculum virtutum. MS. Vienna, Nationalbibliothek, codex 2435. 90 f. Quarto. Saec. 14.
Microfilm: MnCH proj. no. 15,749

2233 Speculum virtutum moralium. Incipit: Quod regimen vite humane versatur cura. MS. Hereford, England, Cathedral Library, codex 0 6 ii, apud finem. Quarto. Saec. 15.
Microfilm: MnCH

2234 Speculum virtutum moralium. MS. Vienna, Schottenstift, codex 30, f. 1r–128v. Folio. Saec. 15.
Microfilm: MnCH proj. no. 3880

2235 Summa de regimine principum. MS. Cistercienserabtei Rein, Austria, codex 18, f. 60v–89v. Quarto. Saec. 14.
Microfilm: MnCH proj. no. 7417

2236 Summa de regimine principum. MS. Benediktinerabtei Melk, Austria, codex 824, f. 97v– . Folio. Saec. 15.
Microfilm: MnCH proj. no. 2224

2237 Super antiphonas duodecim. MS. Benediktinerabtei Admont, Austria, codex 600, f. 9r–58v. Quarto. Saec. 14.
Microfilm: MnCH proj. no. 9637

2238 Super Magnificat. MS. Vienna, Schottenstift, codex 314, f. 121r–148r. Quarto. Saec. 15.
Microfilm: MnCH proj. no. 3983

2239 Tabulae quaedam astronomicae, cum canonibus et perspectiva. MS. Vienna, Nationalbibliothek, codex 2325. 100 f. Folio. Saec. 141.
Microfilm: MnCH proj. no. 15,647

2240 Tractatus de dignitate Virginis Mariae. MS. Vienna, Schottenstift, codex 290, f. 139r–225v. Folio. Saec. 15.
Microfilm: MnCH proj. no. 4127

2241 Tractatus de fascinacione. MS. Benediktinerabtei Kremsmünster, Austria, codex 138, f. 150r–162r. Saec. 14.
Microfilm: MnCH proj. no. 127

2242 Tractatus de fascinatione. MS. Benediktinerabtei Lambach, Austria, codex chartaceus 337, f. 67r–81v. Saec. 14.
Microfilm: MnCH proj. no. 706

2243 Tractatus de fascinatione. MS. Cistercienserabtei Wilhering, Austria, codex IX, 38, f. 257v–268v. Folio. Saec. 14–15.
Microfilm: MnCH proj. no. 2819

2244 Tractatus de fascinatione. MS. Benediktinerabtei Melk, Austria, codex 648, f. 210r–224r. Quarto. Saec. 15.
Microfilm: MnCH proj. no. 1528

2245 Tractatus de fascinatione. MS. Cistercienserabtei Rein, Austria, codex 60, f. 126v–135v. Folio. Saec. 15.
Microfilm: MnCH proj. no. 7456

2246 Tractatus de gratia salvationis. MS. Benediktinerabtei Admont, Austria, codex 600, f. 173r–196v. Quarto. Saec. 14.
Microfilm: MnCH proj. no. 9637

2247 Tractatus de gratia salvationis et justitia damnationis. MS. Cistercienserabtei Rein, Austria, codex 18, f. 54r–57v. Quarto. Saec. 14.
Microfilm: MnCH proj. no. 7417

2248 Tractatus de gratiis et virtutibus B.V.M. MS. Benediktinerabtei Kremsmünster, Austria, codex 153, f. 114r–203r.
Microfilm: MnCH proj. no. 142

2249 Tractatus de libero arbitrio. MS. Cistercienserabtei Rein, Austria, codex 60, f. 120v–126r. Folio. Saec. 15.
Microfilm: MnCH proj. no. 7456

2250 Tractatus de libero arbitrio. MS. Vienna, Schottenstift, codex 314, f. 176r–189v. Quarto. Saec. 15.
Microfilm: MnCH proj. no. 3983

2251 Tractatus de miraculis Christi. MS. Benediktinerabtei Admont, Austria, codex 398, f. 22r–46v. Quarto. Saec. 14.
Microfilm: MnCH proj. no. 9474

2252 Tractatus de miraculis Christi. MS. Benediktinerabtei Admont, Austria, codex 600, f. 93r–129v. Quarto. Saec. 14.
Microfilm: MnCH proj. no. 9637

2253 Tractatus de miraculis Christi. MS. Benediktinerabtei Kremsmünster, Austria, codex 52, f. 169r–180r. Saec. 15.
Microfilm: MnCH proj. no. 52

2254 Tractatus de miraculis Christi. MS. Benediktinerabtei Kremsmünster, Austria, codex 138, f. 124v–144r. Saec. 14.
Microfilm: MnCH proj. no. 127

2255 Tractatus de miraculis Christi. MS. Benediktinerabtei Kremsmünster, Austria, codex 52, f. 198v–200v. Saec. 15.
Microfilm: MnCH proj. no. 52

2256 Tractatus de miraculis Christi. MS. Benediktinerabtei Lambach, Austria, codex chart. 337, f. 41r–60v. Saec. 14.
Microfilm: MnCH proj. no. 706

2257 Tractatus de miraculis Christi. MS. Cistercienserabtei Rein, Austria, codex 60, f. 51v–65v. Folio. Saec. 15.
Microfilm: MnCH proj. no. 7456

2258 Tractatus de musica. MS. Benediktinerabtei Admont, Austria, codex 397, f. 1r–47v. Quarto. Saec. 14.
Microfilm: MnCH proj. no. 9471

2259 Tractatus de officiis et abusionibus eorum. MS. Benediktinerabtei Admont, Austria, codex 600, f. 1r–8v. Quarto. Saec. 14.
Microfilm: MnCH proj. no. 9637

2260 Tractatus de ortu et fine Romani imperii. MS. Vienna, Nationalbibliothek, codex 572. 34 f. Quarto. Saec. 14.
Microfilm: MnCH proj. no. 13,906

2261 Tractatus de ortu et statu et fine imperii Romani. MS. Benediktinerabtei Melk, Austria, codex 1560, f. 147r–175r. Duodecimo. Saec. 15.
Microfilm: MnCH proj. no. 2225

2262 Tractatus de ortu et statu et fine imperii Romani. MS. Cistercienserabtei Zwettl, Austria, codex 269, f. 184v–200r. Quarto. Saec. 12.
Microfilm: MnCH proj. no. 6869

2263 Tractatus de passione Domini et de mysterio crucis. MS. Benediktinerabtei Admont, Austria, codex 499. 63 f. Folio. Saec. 14.
Microfilm: MnCH proj. no. 9560

2264 Tractatus de passione Domini et de mysterio crucis. MS. Benediktinerabtei Admont, Austria, codex 290. 145 f. Folio. Saec. 14.
Microfilm: MnCH proj. no. 9384

2265 Tractatus de passione Domini et de mysterio sanctae crucis. MS. Benediktinerabtei Admont, Austria, codex 395. 63 f. Quarto. Saec. 14.
Microfilm: MnCH proj. no. 9468

2266 Tractatus de passione Domini secundum Matthaeum. MS. Benediktinerabtei Admont, Austria, codex 397, f. 48r–59v. Quarto. Saec. 14.
Microfilm: MnCH proj. no. 9471

2267 Tractatus de passione Domini et mysterio sanctae crucis. MS. Benediktinerabtei Admont, Austria, codex 699. 123 f. Octavo. Saec. 14.
Microfilm: MnCH proj. no. 9731

2268 Tractatus de passione Domini secundum Matthaeum. MS. Benediktinerabtei Admont, Austria, codex 704, f. 43r–50v. Quarto. Saec. 14.
Microfilm: MnCH proj. no. 9748

2269 Tractatus de passione Domini secundum Matthaeum. MS. Benediktinerabtei Admont, Austria, codex 147, f. 24r–283v. Folio. Saec. 15.
Microfilm: MnCH proj. no. 9231

2270 Tractatus de passione Domini et de misterio sancte crucis. MS. Benediktinerabtei Kremsmünster, Austria, codex 153, f. 13r–75v.
Microfilm: MnCH proj. no. 142

2271 Tractatus de passione Domini et de mysteriis s. crucis. MS. Benediktinerabtei St. Paul im Lavanttal, Austria, codex 94/4, pars II. Folio. Saec. 15.
Microfilm: MnCH proj. no. 12,338

2272 Tractatus de providentia Christi. MS. Benediktinerabtei Admont, Austria, codex 600, f. 130r–169v. Quarto. Saec. 14.

2273 Tractatus de providentia Dei. MS. Benediktinerabtei Admont, Austria, codex 398, f. 1r–21v. Quarto. Saec. 14.
Microfilm: MnCH proj. no. 9474

2274 Tractatus de restitutione generis humani ad gratiam et gloriam per meritum mortis Christi. MS. Cistercienserabtei Rein, Austria, codex 60, f. 1r–51v. Folio. Saec. 15.
Microfilm: MnCH proj. no. 7456

2275 Tractatus de vita et virtutibus Beatae Mariae Virginis. MS. Benediktinerabtei Admont, Austria, codex 396. 75 f. Quarto. Saec. 14.
Microfilm: MnCH proj. no. 9469

2276 Tractatus de vita et virtutibus Beatae Mariae Virginis. MS. Benediktinerabtei Admont, Austria, codex 489. 175 f. Folio. Saec. 15.
Microfilm: MnCH proj. no. 9536

2277 Tractatus de vita et virtutibus B.V.M. MS. Benediktinerabtei Lambach, Austria, codex 283, f. 1r–199. Saec. 15.
Microfilm: MnCH proj. no. 659

2278 Tractatus metricus de consilio vitae. MS. Benediktinerabtei Admont, Austria, codex 405, f. 45r–48v. Quarto. Saec. 14.
Microfilm: MnCH proj. no. 9478

2279 Tractatus metricus de consilo vivendi. MS. Benediktinerabtei Admont, Austria, codex 492, f. 47v–48v. Folio. Saec. 14.
Microfilm: MnCH proj. no. 9545

2280 Tractatus super antiphonam: Cum rex gloriae. MS. Benediktinerabtei Admont, Austria, codex 140, f. 76r–98r. Folio. Saec. 15.
Microfilm: MnCH proj. no. 9229

2281 Tractatus super antiphonam: Rex gloriae. MS. Benediktinerabtei St. Paul im Lavanttal, Austria, codex 74/3, f. 73v–76v. Quarto. Saec. 15.
Microfilm: MnCH proj. no. 12,167

2282 Dicta super antiphona "O" in adventu. MS. Augustinerchorherrenstift Klosterneuburg, Austria, codex 12, f. 233v–251v. Folio. Saec. 14.
Microfilm: MnCH proj. no. 4989

2283 Dicta super antiphona "O" in adventu. MS. Cistercienserabtei Zwettl, Austria, codex 56 f. 63r–79v. Folio. Saec. 13.
Microfilm: MnCH proj. no. 6651

2284 Tractatus super antiphonas "O" in adventu. MS. Augustinerchorherrenstift Klosterneuburg, Austria, codex 372, f. 239v–268r. Folio. Saec. 14.
Microfilm: MnCH proj. no. 5344

2285 Expositio in antiphonas "O" in adventu. MS. Augustinerchorherrenstift Klosterneuburg, Austria, codex 584, f. 1r–22v. Folio. Saec. 14.
Microfilm: MnCH proj. no. 5561

2286 Tractatus super evangelium: In principio erat Verbum. MS. Benediktinerabtei Admont, Austria, codex 397, f. 69v–75v. Quarto. Saec. 14.
Microfilm: MnCH proj. no. 9471

2287 Tractatus, utrum homines ante diluvium tam longo tempore vixerint, sicut legitur in libro Genesis. MS. Cistercienserabtei Zwettl, Austria, codex 269, f. 138r–153v. Quarto. Saec. 13.
Microfilm: MnCH proj. no. 6869

2288 Tractatus, utrum sapienti competat ducere uxorem. MS. Cistercienserabtei Zwettl, Austria, codex 269, f. 176v–184r. Quarto. Saec. 13.
Microfilm: MnCH proj. no. 6869

Engelbert, abbot of Admont, ca. 1250–1331.
Printed works.

2289 De ortu et fine Romani imperij liber. Cum Gasparis Brvschii poetae laureati praefatione . . . Basileae, per Joannem Operinum, 1553.
165 p. 16 cm.
MnCS

2290 Letter of Abbot Engelbert of Admont to Master Ulrich of Vienna. [Edited by George B. Fowler]. Louvain, Abbaye du Mont Cesar, 1962.
"Extrait des: Recherches de théologie ancienne et médiévale, t. 29 (1962), p. 298–306"
PLatS

2291 Psalterium de D. N. Iesu Christo. Psalterium Beatae Mariae V.
(*In* Analecta hymnica Medii Aevi. New York, 1961. v. 35, p. 79–90, 123–136)
MnCS; PLatS

2292 **Engelbert, Pius,** 1936–
Smaragdi abbatis Expositio in Regulam S. Benedicti/ediderunt Alfredus Spannagel [et] Pius Engelbert, O.S.B. Siegburg, F. Schmitt, 1974.
lxxxiv, 394 p. facsims. 26 cm. (Corpus consuetudinum monasticarum, t. 8)
InStme; MnCS; PLatS

Engelmann, Ursmar, 1909–

2293 Christus am Kreuz; romanische Kruzifixe zwischen Bodensee und Donau. Beuron, Beuroner Kunstverlag [1966]
[70] p. illus. (part col.) 23 cm.
PLatS

2294 Hundert Jahre Bibliothek Beuron.
(*In* Beuron, 1863–1963; Festschrift . . . Beuron, 1963. p. 395–440)
PLatS

2295 Wurzel Jesse; Buchmalerei des frühen 13. Jahrhunderts. Beuron, Beuroner Kunstverlag [1960]
76 p. col. plates, 19 x 17 cm.
PLatS

2296 (tr) Der heilige Pirmin und sein Missionsbüchlein (Dicta Abbatis Pirmii). Eingeleitet und ins Deutsche übertragen von Ursmar Engelmann, O.S.B. Konstanz, Jan Thorecke Verlag [c 1959].
99 p. illus., plates, facsim. 18 cm.
MnCS

2297 **Enout, Joao Ev. de Oliveiro,** 1917–
Regra de São Bento, tradução e notas de D.João Ev. de Ribeiro Enout, O.S.B. . . . Salvador, Bahia, Impresso na Tip Beneditina LTDA., 1958.
123 p. 20 cm.
KAS

2298 **Enshoff, Dominikus,** 1868–
Die Benediktiner-Mission in Korea. Post
Geltendorf, Oberbayern, Missions-Verlag
St. Ottilien, 1909.
15 p. 22 cm.
KAS; MnCS

2299 **Erbacher, Rhabanus,** 1937–
Deutsches Antiphonale . . . [Hrsg. von
P. Godehard Joppich, O.S.B. [und] P.
Rhabanus Erbacher, O.S.B. Abtei Mün-
sterschwarzach [1972]
2 v. illus. 22 cm.
InStme

2300 **Erceg, David F.,** 1942–
1969 pictorial directory – Church of St.
Bernard, St. Paul, Minn. [Hollywood,
Calif., J. Frank & Son, Inc., 1969]
unpaged, illus. 28 cm.
MnCS

2301 **Erchanbertus,** 9th cent.
Erchanberti Breviarium regum Francorum, inde a saeculo quinto usque ad a.
827. Monachi Augiensis continuatio a. 840-
881.
(*In* Monumenta Germaniae historica.
Scriptores. Stuttgart, 1963. t. 2, p. 327–
330)
MnCS; PLatS

2302 **Erchempertus, monk of Monte Cassino,**
9th cent.
Erchemperti historia Langobardorum a.
774–889.
(*In* Monumenta Germaniae historica.
Scriptores. Stuttgart, 1963. t. 3, p. 240–
264)
MnCS; PLatS

Erchenfridus, abbot of Melk.
2303 Legenda de S. Colomanno martyre. MS.
Vienna, Nationalbibliothek, codex 3256, f.
1r–5v. Quarto. Saec. 16.
Microfilm: MnCH proj. no. 16,505

2304 Passio beati Colomanni martyris. MS.
Augustinerchorherrenstift Klosterneu-
burg, Austria, codex 580, f. 253r–255v.
Folio. Saec. 13.
Microfilm: MnCH proj. no. 5556

2305 Passio beati Colomanni martyris. MS.
Augustinerchorherrenstift Klosterneu-
burg, Austria, codex 634, f. 108r–110r.
Folio. Saec. 14.
Microfilm: MnCH proj. no. 5614

2306 Vita sancti Colomanni martyris. MS.
Augustinerchorherrenstift Klosterneu-
burg, Austria, codex 239, f. 129v–133v.
Folio. Saec. 13.
Microfilm: MnCH proj. no. 5210

2307 **Erfurt, Germany. St. Peter (Benedictine
abbey).**

Chronicon Erfordiense (ab initio
mutilum). MS. Vienna, Nationalbibliothek,
codex 3375. 26 f. Folio. Saec. 15.
Microfilm: MnCH proj. no. 16,733

2308 **Erhard, Caspar,** 1665–1729.
Des christlichen Hauss-Buchs oder
grossen Leben Christi anderer Theil, von
dem bittern Leyden unsers Erlösers . . .
Augspurg, Sebastien Eysenhart, 1753.
3 v. in 1. 21 cm.
MnCS

2309 . . . Christliche Hausbuch, oder das
grosse Leben Christi, mit ausführlichen
kräftigen und andächtigen Betrachtungen
. . . 30. neu. verb. Aufl. von Simon Buch-
felner. Augsburg, Matth. Rieger, 1845.
2 v. in 1. illus. 23 cm.
InStme

2310 . . . Nueste, sehr verb. Aufl. Regensburg, G. J. Manx, 1865.
3 v. in 1. 23 cm.
MnCS

2311 **Erhard, Thomas Aquinas,** 1675–1743.
Biblia Sacra vulgatae editionis auctori-
tate Sixti V. et Clementis VIII. pont. max.
recognita, summariis & notis theologicis,
historicis, et chronologicis illustrata studio
P. Thomae Aq. Erhard Ord. S. Benedicti
. . . Editio 5. Augustae Vindelicorum,
Typis Antonii Maximiliani Heiss, 1737.
2 v. 39 cm.
InStme; PLatS

2312 . . . Editio 6. Augspurg und Würzburg,
1748.
2 v. in 1.
MnCS; PLatS

2313 . . . Grätz und Inspruck, Philipp Jacob
Veith und Wolff, 1749.
2 v. in 1. 39 cm.
InStme

2314 Libri quatuor de Imitatione Christi . . .
ad commodiorem usum in versis distributi,
una cum novis concordantiis studio
Thomae Aq. Erhard O.S.B. Augustae Vindelicorum, Strötter, 1724.
280, 493, 182 p. 17 cm.
MnCS; MnStj; PLatS

2315 **Erhardus de Lomptz.**
Expositio in psalmum 12. MS. Benediktinerabtei St. Peter, Salzburg, codex
a.V.2., f. 2r–34v. Octavo. Saec. 15.
Microfilm: MnCH proj. no. 10,045

2316 **Erickson, Edgar John,** 1925–
Metaphysical transcendentality.
55 leaves, 28 cm.
Thesis (M.A.) – St. Vincent College,
Latrobe, Pa., 1950.
Typescript.
PLatS

2317 **Ermin, Saint, abbot of Lobbes,** d. 737.
La plus ancienne vie de S. Ursmer;
poème acrostiche inédit de S. Ermin, son
successeur [par] Dom Germain Morin,
O.S.B. Bruxelles, Imprimerie Polleunis et
Ceuterick, 1904.
[315–319] p. 25 cm.
"Extraite des Analecta Bollandiana, t.
23."
PLatS

2318 **Ermoldus Nigellus,** 9th cent.
Ermoldi Nigelli carmina.
(*In* Monumenta Germaniae historica.
Scriptores. Stuttgart, 1963. t. 2, p.
464–523)
MnCS; PLatS

2319 **Ernetti, Pallegrino Maria,** 1925–
(ed) Cassianus, Joannes. Instituzioni dei
cenobiti e rimedi contro gli otto vizi
capitali. Introducione, traduzione, annotazioni di D. Pellegrino Maria Ernetti . . .
Praglia, [Badia Benedettina, 1957–]
v. 20 cm. (Scritti monastici, n. 20–
Serie ascetico-mistica, n. 14–)
MnCS; PLatS

2320 **Eschle, Laurentius,** 1866–
Unsere Liebe Frau im Stein, in Wort,
und Bild; Geschichte der Wallfahrt und des
Klosters Mariastein. Solothurn (Schweiz),
Verlag der Buch und Kunstdruckerei
Union, 1896.
204 p. illus. 19 cm.

Escobar, Andrés de, d. ca. 1431.
2321 Gubernaculum conciliorum per dominum
Andream episcopum Magorensem. MS.
Vienna, Schottenstift, codex 30, f.
270r–328r. Folio. Saec. 15.
Microfilm: MnCH proj. no. 3880

2322 Gubernaculum conciliorum. MS. Vienna,
Schottenstift, codex 4138, f. 217r–262r.
Folio. Saec. 15.
Microfilm: MnCH proj. no. 17,328

2323 Lumen confessorum. MS. Benediktinerabtei St. Paul im Lavanttal, Austria,
codex 241/4, pars III. Quarto. Saec. 14
(1435)
Microfilm: MnCH proj. no. 12,478

2324 Lumen confessorum. MS. Benediktinerabtei St. Paul im Lavanttal, Austria,
codex 133/4, pars III. Folio. Saec. 15.
Microfilm: MnCH proj. no. 12,372

2325 Lumen confessorum. MS. Prämonstratenserabtei Schlägl, Austria, codex 99, f.
384r–425v. Folio. Saec. 15.
Microfilm: MnCH proj. no. 3044

2326 Lumen confessorum, vel Modus confitendi. MS. Vienna, Schottenstift, codex 51,
f. 167r–202r. Folio. Saec. 15.
Microfilm: MnCH proj. no. 3942

2327 Lumen confessorum. MS. Vienna, Na-
tionalbibliothek, codex 4212, f. 247r–300v.
Folio. Saec. 15.
Microfilm: MnCH proj. no. 4212

2328 Lumen confessorum. MS. Vienna, Na-
tionalbibliothek, codex 4463, f. 1r–44r.
Folio. Saec. 15.
Microfilm: MnCH proj. no. 17,643

2329 Modus confitendi. MS. Vienna, Na-
tionalbibliothek, codex 13048, f. 1r–11v.
Quarto. Saec. 15.
Microfilm: MnCH proj. no. 20,059

2330 Modus confitendi omnibus christifideli-
bus multum utilis. [Cologne, H. Quentell,
ca. 1495]
[6] leaves. 19 cm.
PLatS

2331 Poenitentiales casus papales. MS. Studienbibliothek, Klagenfurt, Austria, codex
cart. 101, f. 241r–263v. Quarto. Saec. 15.
Microfilm: MnCH proj. no. 13,082

2332 Recensus 36 errorum Graecorum. MS.
Vienna, Nationalbibliothek, codex 4139, f.
25v–26r. Folio. Saec. 15.
Microfilm: MnCH proj. no. 17,339

2333 Tractatus, qui vocatur Regula deci-
marum. MS. Benediktinerabtei Altenburg,
Austria, codex AB 13 A 15, f. 128v–141v.
Folio. Saec. 15.
Microfilm: MnCH proj. no. 6427

2334 Tractatus de regula decimarum. MS.
Universitätsbibliothek Graz, Austria,
codex 230, f. 1r–14v. Folio. Saec. 15
(1456).
Microfilm: MnCH proj. no. 26,145

2335 Tractatus de decimis. MS. Universitätsbibliothek Graz, Austria, codex 497, f.
335r–351r. Folio. Saec. 15.
Microfilm: MnCH proj. no. 26,664

2336 Regula decimarum. MS. Studienbibliothek, Klagenfurt, Austria, codex cart. 66,
f. 185r–231v. Quarto. Saec. 15.
Microfilm: MnCH proj. no. 13,047

2337 Regula decimarum. MS. Studienbibliothek, Klagenfurt, Austria, codex cart. 70,
f. 1r–24v. Quarto. Saec. 15 (1466).
Microfilm: MnCH proj. no. 13,051

2338 Regula decimarum pro presbyteris om-
nium ecclesiarum. MS. Benediktinerabtei
Melk, Austria, codex 531, f. 45r–60v.
Folio. Saec. 15.
Microfilm: MnCH proj. no. 1447

2339 Tractatus, qui vocatur "Regula decima-
rum." MS. Benediktinerabtei St. Paul im
Lavanttal, Austria, codex 133/4, pars IV.
Folio. Saec. 15.
Microfilm: MnCH proj. no. 12,372

2340   Tractatus, qui dicitur Regula decimarum. MS. Prämonstratenserabtei Schlägl, Austria, codex 133, f. 99r–122v. Quarto. Saec. 15.
Microfilm: MnCH proj. no. 3070

2341   Regula decimarum in duodecim conclusionibus. MS. Vienna, Nationalbibliothek, codex 3601, f. 65v–90v. Quarto. Saec. 15.
Microfilm: MnCH proj. no. 16,817

2342   Regula decimarum. MS. Vienna, Nationalbibliothek, codex 3778, f. 352r–366v. Folio. Saec. 15 (1458).
Microfilm: MnCH proj. no. 16,988

2343   Tractatus qui vocatur Regula decimarum. MS. Vienna, Nationalbibliothek, codex 3746, f. 144r–153v. Folio. Saec. 15.
Microfilm: MnCH proj. no. 14,442

2344   Regula decimarum. MS. Vienna, Nationalbibliothek, codex 3792, f. 85r–112r. Quarto. Saec. 15.
Microfilm: MnCH proj. no. 17,012

2345   Tractatus de decimis. MS. Vienna, Nationalbibliothek, codex 3906, f. 274r–304v. Folio. Saec. 15.
Microfilm: MnCH proj. no. 17,101

2346   De decimis, primitiis et oblationibus. MS. Vienna, Nationalbibliothek, codex 4180, f. 193v–208r. Folio. Saec. 15.
Microfilm: MnCH proj. no. 14,432

2347   Tractatus de septem vitiis capitalibus. MS. Vienna, Schottenstift, codex 51, f. 203r–246r. Folio. Saec. 15.
Microfilm: MnCH proj. no. 3942

2348   **Espenmiler, Edmundus.**
Olla pauperum, sive Omnis generis dicta et facta ordine alphabetico collecta. MS. Benediktinerabtei St. Paul im Lavanttal, Austria, codex 314/4. 180 f. Quarto. Saec. 17 (1679).
Microfilm: MnCH proj. no. 12,514

2349   **L'Esprit de Cluny;** testes clunisiens. [La Pierre-qui-Vire (Yonne)], Zodiaque, 1963.
195 p. illus. 26 cm.
KAS

Essai historique sur l'Abbaye de Solesmes. *See* Guéranger, Prosper.

2350   **Esser, Ignatius,** 1890–1973.
The Fatima Week sermons . . . with an introduction, "The story of Fatima Week in St. Meinrad," by the Right Rev. Ignatius Esser, O.S.B. . . . St. Meinrad, Ind., Grail [1949].
168 p. 22 cm.
InStme

Esterl, Franz, 1781–1848.

2351   Bibliotheca Salisburgensis, i.e. Verzeichnis aller Schriftsteller, die entweder geborne Salzburger waren oder einige Zeit in Salzburg gelebte haben oder über Salzburg geschrieben haben oder deren Werke in Salzburg sind im Druck erschienen. MS. Benediktinerabtei St. Peter, Salzburg, codex b.XI.20. 1123 p. Folio. Saec. 19.
Microfilm: MnCH proj. no. 10,669

2352   Chronik des adeligen Benediktiner-Frauen-Stiftes Nonnberg in Salzburg, vom Entstehen desselben bis zum Jahre 1840 aus den Quellen bearbeitet von P. Franz Esterl, aus dem Stifte St. Peter. Salzburg, Franz Xaver Duyle, 1841.
xii, 267 p. 18 cm.
MnCS

2353   **Ettenheimmünster, Germany (Benedictine abbey).**
Catalogus librorum ab arte typographica inventa usque ad annum 1517 impressorum et olim in monasterio Ettenheimmünster asservatorum. MS. Vienna, Nationalbibliothek, codex 9737z4. 20 f. Saec. 16.
Microfilm: MnCH proj. no. 19,348

2354   **Ettinger, David.**
Tractatus juridicus de potestate ordinis, ad librum I. Decretalium a titulo XI usque ad tit. XXII . . . praeside P. Fransico Schmier, O.S.B. . . . Publice defendum suscepit D.F. David Ettinger, O.S.B. . . . Salisburgi, typis Joan. J. Mayr [1713].
[14], 202, [67] p. 20 cm.
PLatS

2355   Eulogium (historiarum sive temporis): Chronicon ab orbe condito usque ad annum Domini M.CCC.LXVI a monacho quodam Malmesburiensi exaratum. Accedunt continuationes duae . . . Edited by Frank Scott Haydon . . . London, 1858–63.
3 v. (Gt. Brit. Public Record Office. Rerum britannicarum medii aevi scriptores)
ILSP

2356   **Exercices de pieté sur la Règle de saint Benoist,** avec des examens fort étendus, & tres utiles auz personnes qui veulent en prendre l'esprit. Retraite de dix jours. Paris, chez Theodore Huguet, 1697.
[53], 211, [5] p. 17 cm.
KAS

2357   **Explication de la Règle de S. Benoist,** addressés à un monastère où l'on suit la mitigation, en quoi elle consiste, & à quoi la Règle oblige. Paris, Pierre Witte, 1738.
602 p. 17 cm.
Manuscript English translation by Pirmin Koumly, O.S.B., of St. Benedict's Abbey, Atchison, Kans.
KAS

2358 **Exposition du millennaire de Saint-Laurent de Liège:** église, abbaye, hôpital militaire. Cloitres de la cathédrale, 23 septembre–23 octobre 1968, Liège. [Liège, Belgique, Cathédrale, 1968]
58 p. plates (part col) 26 cm.
MnCS

Eynsham Abbey, England.
2359 The customary of the Benedictine abbey of Eynsham in Oxfordshire, edited by Antonia Grandsen. Siegburg, F. Schmitt, 1963.
245 p. 26 cm. (Corpus consuetudinum monasticarum, t. 2)
InStme; KAS; NdRi; PLatS

2360 Eynsham cartulary. Edited by the Rev. H. E. Salter . . . [Oxford], Printed for the Oxford Historical Society, 1907–08.
2 v. plates, facsims. 22 cm. (Oxford Historical Society, v. 49, 51)
PLatS

2361 **Faessler, Franz,** 1911–
(tr) Die Regel des heiligen Benedictus, übertragen von P. Franz Faessler, O.S.B., eingeleitet von Leodegar Hunkeler, Abt von Engelberg.
(*In* Balthasar, H. U. von. Die grossen Ordensregeln. 1961. p. 173–260)
PLatS

2362 **Faita, Johannes,** d. 1395.
Manipvlvs exemplorvm, qvi Magni specvli est tomvs secvndvs, virtvtvm vitiorvmqve serie digestvs. Editus nunc primum in lucem e belgicis mss. tribus perantiquis . . . opera & studio D. Maximiliani Thivlaine religiosi Vedastini. Editio altera priore longe castigatior. Dvaci, ex officina Baltazaris Belleri, 1615.
[24], 414 p. 21 cm.
PLatS

2363 **Falk, Conrad,** 1916–
The fourth way of St. Thomas.
122 p.
Thesis–Collegio di Sant'Anselmo, Rome.
MoCo

2364 **Fallon, Clarisse, Sister.**
Share our joy, 1874–1974. Nauvoo, Ill., St. Mary's Priory, 1974.
48 p. illus.
MoCo

2365 **Fals, Mary James, Sister.**
Honor and honra in the poem of "The Cid."
56 p.
Thesis (M.A.)–Catholic University of America, 1963.
InFer

Farmer, Hugh, 1923–
2366 The monk of Farne.
(*In* Walsh, James. Pre-Reformation English spirituality. New York, 1965. p. 145–157)
PLatS

2367 Stephen of Sawley.
(*In* Walsh, James. Pre-Reformation English spirituality. New York, 1965. p. 93–103)
PLatS

2368 (ed) Adam of Eynsham. The life of St. Hugh of Lincoln. Edited by Decima L. Douie and Hugh Farmer. London, New York, Nelson [1961–
v. maps. 23 cm. (Medieval texts)
ILSP; InStme; KAS; MnCS; NdRi; PLatS

2369 (ed) Whiterig, John. The monk of Farne; the meditations of a fourteenth-century monk, edited and introduced by Hugh Farmer. Translated by a Benedictine of Stanbrook. Baltimore, Helicon Press [1961]
vii, 155 p. illus. 22 cm. (The Benedictine studies [1])
CaMWiSb; InStme; MnCS; MnStj; MoCo

2370 **Farrelly, Mark John,** 1927–
Predestination, grace, and free will. Westminster, Md., Newman Press, 1964.
XIV, 317 p. 24 cm.
Originally written as the author's thesis, Catholic University of America.
InFer; InStme; MnCS; KAS; MoCo; NcBe; PLatS

2371 **Farrington, Hugh,** 1912–
The altar and the home.
(*In* Proceedings of the liturgical week held for priests at St. Benedict's Abbey, Atchison, Kans., May 8–11, 1944. p. 66–76)
PLatS

2372 **Fasbender, Veronica, Sister.**
Pollen grain morphology and its taxonomic significance in the amherstieae, gynonetreae, and sclerolobieae, with special reference to American genera.
Thesis (Ph.D)–St. Louis, 1959.
SdYa

2373 **Fassero, Jonathan,** 1950–
The effect of the joint pastoral on the religious future of George Tyrrell.
iv, 75 leaves. 28 cm.
Thesis (M.A.)–Indiana University, 1977.
InStme

2374 **Faust, Ulrich,** 1935–
Bernhard's "Liber de gratia et libero arbitrio"; Bedeutung, Quellen und Einfluss.

(*In* Analecta monastica, 6. ser. 1962. p. 35–51. Studia Anselmiana, fasc. 50)
PLatS

Faustus, monk of Monte Cassino.

2375 Vita s. Mauri abbatis. MS. Cistercienserabtei Rein, Austria, codex 85, f. 156r–187v. Folio. Saec. 12.
Microfilm: MnCH proj. no. 7486

2376 Vita Mauri abbatis auctore Fausto monacho. MS. Benediktinerabtei Kremsmünster, Austria, codex 27, f. 182r–202r. Saec. 14.
Microfilm: MnCH proj. no. 27

2377 Vita S. Mauri abbatis Glannafolii. MS. Benediktinerabtei Melk, Austria, codex 909, f. 164r–183v.
Microfilm: MnCH proj. no. 1727

2378 Vitae patrum et sanctorum Mauri, Mariae Aegyptiacae, S. Antonii Aegyptiaci, Sanctae Paulae, S. Pachomii, Simeonis, Julii et Juliani. MS. Vienna, Nationalbibliothek, codex 442. 134 f. Folio. Saec. 14.
Microfilm: MnCH proj. no. 13,774

Fayta, Johannes. *See* Faita, Johannes.

2379 **Feder, Martha, Sister.**
The liturgy celebration of the mystery of grace.
Thesis (M.A.)–St. John's University, Collegeville, Minn., 1963.
Typescript.
KyCovS

2380 **Feeney, Florence, Sister.**
The convent library.
(*In* Martin, David. Catholic library practice. University of Portland Press, 1947. p. 121–138)
InFer

Feijóo y Montenegro, Benito Jerónimo, 1676–1764.

2381 Obras escogidas. Madrid, 1952–61.
4 v. 26 cm.
NdRi; PLatS

2382 Teatro crítico universal. Selección, prólogo y notas de Augustin Millares Carlo. Madrid, Espasa-Calpe [1951–   ]
v. 18 cm.
NdRi; InStme

2383 **Feistritzer, Emily, Sister.**
Giant steps through science, by Sister Christopher Bertke and Sister Emily Feistritzer. Covington, Ky., Lithographed, 1970.
256 p. illus.
KyCovS

2384 **Feldhohn, Sophronia, Sister.**
Sihe, da bin ich; das Zeugnis heiliger Väter und Mönche von der letzten Stunde.

Herausgegeben, eingeleitet und übersetzt von Sophronia Feldhohn, O.S.B. Düsseldorf, Patmos-Verlag [1964]
233 p. 20 cm. (Alte Quellen neuer Kraft)
MnCS

Feligonde, Jean de, 1908–

2385 L'armure du chrètien; exposé complet de la religion chrétienne à l'usage des curés et catéchistes, des séminaristes . . . Paris, Editions du Levain, 1957–
v. illus. 19 cm.
MnCS

2386 Conversations pastorales par Dom Jean de Feligonde, Hadelin Van Erck and Thierey Maertens.
(*In* Paroisse et liturgie . . . no. 8, p. 17–51)
PLatS

2387 La paroisse de l'Hay les Roses et les Oblats de Saint Benoît.
(*In* Paroisse et liturgie . . . no. 8, p. 7–16)
PLatS

2388 The religious community and the apostolic necessity for common action.
(*In* Communal life, p. 166–194)
PLatS

Felix, Richard, 1890–1973.

2389 Commentary on the Apostles Creed. Kansas City, Mo., Benedictine Institute Press [1968?–   ]
404 p. 17 cm.
InStme; KAS

2390 What about the Bible? Conception, Mo., Altar and Home Press, [1936]
27 p. 18 cm.
MnCS; PLatS

2391 **Fellin, Jo Ann, Sister.**
An historical and comparative study concerned with the unsolvability of the word problem for groups.
207 leaves, 28 cm.
Thesis (Ph.D.)–University of Illinois at Urbana-Champaign, 1970.
Typescript.
KAM

Fellner, Felix, 1874–1963.

2392 Abbot Boniface and his monks. [Latrobe, Pa., St. Vincent Archabbey, 1956]
731 leaves, 36 cm.
Mimeographed.
MnCS; MoCo; PLatS

2393 Abbot Boniface Wimmer and his monks. Latrobe, Pa., St. Vincent Archabbey, 1957.
64 p. 23 cm.
The first six chapters in printed form of the projected book.
PLatS

2394   The development of Freemasonry (1666–1751).
14 leaves, 28 cm.
Reproduced from typed copy.
PLatS

2395   History of Benedictine education. Latrobe, Pa., St. Vincent College [1939]
Reprint from National Benedictine Educational Association bulletin, v. 22 (1939), p. 25–42.
PLatS

2396   A short bibliography of ecclesiastical history. [Latrobe, Pa., St. Vincent Archabbey, 1923]
10 leaves, 28 cm.
Typescript.
PLatS

2397   **Fernández de la Cuesta, Ismael,** 1939–
El "Breviarium Gothicum" de Silos (Archivo monástico, ms. 6). Madrid-Barcelona, 1965.
126 p. 26 cm.
MnCS; PLatS

Férotin, Marius, 1855–1914.
2398   Le Liber mozarabicus sacramentorum et les manuscrits mozarabes. Paris, Firmin-Didot, 1912.
xci p., 1096 col., facsims. 32 cm. (Monumenta ecclesia liturgica, v. 6)
CaQStB; InStme

2399   Le Liber ordinum en usage dans l'église visigothique et mozarabe d'Espagne du cinquième au onzième siècle . . . Paris, Firmin-Didot, 1904.
xiv p., 800 col. facsims. 32 cm. (Monumenta ecclesiae liturgica, v. 5)
InStme

Ferrari, Guy, 1924–1965.
2400   The basilica of Saints John and Paul on the Caelian Hill after the restoration and archaeological explorations promoted by his eminence, Francis Cardinal Spellman, archbishop of New York and cardinal titular of the Basilica. Rome, 1958.
147 p. illus., plates, plans, 20 cm.
InStme

2401   Early Roman monasteries; an historical and topographical study of the monasteries and convents at Rome from the V through the X centuries. Rome, 1956.
3 v. plans, 28 cm.
Typescript.
Contents: v. 1. Text – v. 2. Notes. – v. 3. Plans
InStme

2402   Early Roman monasteries; notes for the history of the monasteries and convents at Rome from the V through the X centuries.

Città del Vaticano, Pontificio Istituto di Archeologia Cristiana, 1957.
xxxvii, 455 p. plans (part fold.) 26 cm. (Studi di antichità cristiana, 23)
InStme; MoCo

2403   (ed) Vatican. Biblioteca Vaticana. Catalogo delle publicazioni periodiche esistenti in varie biblioteche de Rome e Firenze. Pubblicato con la collaborazione dell'Unione Internazionale degli Istituti di Archeologia, Storia e Storia dell'Arte in Roma. Città del Vaticano, 1955.
xiii, 495 p. 26 cm.
Foreword signed: Guy Ferrari, O.S.B.
PLatS

2404   (ed) Vatican. Biblioteca Vaticano. Museo Sacro. The gold-glass collection of the Vatican Library; with additional catalogues of other gold-glass collections, edited by Guy Ferrari. Città del Vaticano, Biblioteca Apostolica Vaticana, 1959.
xii, 82 p. 38 plates (part col.) 42 cm.
InStme

2405   **Festschrift Abt Dr. Raphael, Molitor, O.S.B.** zum 30 jährigen Jubiläum seiner äbtlichen Würde. Gewidmet von seinen Mönchen. [Beuron] 1936.
53 p. 24 cm.
KAS; PLatS

2406   **Festschrift zum 600 jährigen Weihejubiläum** der Klosterkirche Ettal. [Ettal, Buch-Kunstverlag, 1970].
251 p. illus. 24 cm.
MnCS; NcBe

Festugière, Maurice, 1870–
2407   La liturgie catholique devant la conscience moderne et contemporaine. Abbaye de Maredsous [1914].
Extrait de la Revue thomiste, 1914, p. 143–178.
PLatS

2408   Misère et miséricorde; sermon de charité, prononcé en l'église des rr. pp. Carmes de Bruxelles . . . Abbaye de Maredsous, Belgique, 1913.
73 p. 14 cm.
CaQStB; InStme; KySu

2409   **Feuling, Daniel Martin,** 1882–1947.
Katholische Glaubenslehre; Einführung in das theologische Leben für weitere Kreise. 4. Aufl. O. Müller [1951, c1937]
xxvii, 964 p. 20 cm.
KAS

2410   **Feyerabend, Maurus,** 1754–1818.
Des ehemaligen Reichsstiftes Ottenbeuren sämmtliche Jahrbücher, in Verbindung mit der allgemeinen Reichs- und der besondern Geschichte Schwabens diplomatisch,

kritisch, und chronologisch bearbeitet . . . Ottenbeuren, Joh. Bapt. Ganser, 1813–16.
4 v. chart. 21 cm.
KAS; MnCS

Fiala, Virgil, 1911–

2411   Ein Jahrhundert Beuroner Geschichte.
(*In* Beuron, 1863–1963; Festschrift . . . Beuron, 1963. p. 39–230)
InFer; PLatS; MnCS; InStme

2412   Les prières d'acceptation de l'offrande et le genre littéraire du canon romain.
(*In* Eucharisties d'Orient et d'Occident. Paris, 1970. v. 1, p. 117–133)
PLatS

2413   Das Sakramentar von Jena (Bud. M.F. 366 der Universitäts-Bibliothek). In beratender Verbindung mit Alban Dold, O.S.B., und Virgil Fiala, O.S.B., hrsg. von Klaus Gamber . . . Beuron, Beuroner Kunstverlag, 1962.
126 p. 23 cm. (Texte und Arbeiten, Heft 52)
PLatS

Fiecht, Tyrol (Benedictine abbey).

2414   Gebräuche bei Tisch und im Chor in St. Georgen-Fiecht. MS. Benediktinerabtei Fiecht, codex 15a. 4 f. Quarto. Saec. 15.
Microfilm: MnCH proj. no. 28,828

2415   Manuscript catalog of St. Georgen-Fiecht.
Xerographed by University Microfilm, Ann Arbor, Mich., 1973.
unpaged, 25 cm.
MnCS

2416   Scripta ascetica pro novitiis Monasterii S. Josephi in Fiecht, O.S.B. MS. Benediktinerabtei Fiecht, codex 87. 377 f. Quarto. Saec. 18.
Microfilm: MnCH proj. no. 28,796

2417   Statuta regularia pro Monsterio S. Josephi ad pedem M.S.G., OSB. MS. Benediktinerabtei Fiecht, Austria, codex 86. 383 f. Quarto. Saec. 18.
Microfilm: MnCH proj. no. 28,865

2418   Verzeichnis der Bibliothek des Stiftes Fiecht im Jahre 1817 zurückgegebenen Bücher und Landkarten. Verzeichnis eines Theiles der Bibliothek des Klosters Fiecht. MS. Universitätsbibliothek Innsbruck, Austria, codex 983 & 983b. Saec. 18 & 19.
Microfilm: MnCH proj. no. 28,736

Field, Anne, Sister.

2419   From darkness to light. Ann Arbor, Mich., Servant Books, 1978.
210 p. 21 cm.
InStme

2419a   (tr) Leo I, Pope. The binding of the strong man; the teaching of St. Leo the

Great in a modern version by Ann Field, O.S.B. Ann Arbor, Mich., Word of Life [c 1976].
113 p.
MoCo

Figueras, Cesáreo M., 1924–

2420   Acerca del rito de la profesión monástica medieval "ad succurrendum."
(*In* Liturgica, 2: Cardinal I. A. Schuster in memoriam, 1958. v. 2, p. 359–400)
PLatS

2421   Una donació modal a Sant Cugat i Oblació d'infanta a Catalunya al segle XII.
(*In* Analecta Montserratensis, v. 10, p. 165–176)
PLatS

Filguerira, Domenec.

2422   La autoridad explicada y sostenida. MS. Monasterio benedictino de Montserrat, Spain, codex 391. 486 p. Quarto. Saec. 18.
Microfilm: MnCH proj. no. 30,021

2423   Compendio de la historia del santuario y monasterio de Monserrate de Cataluna. MS. Monasterio benedictino de Montserrat, Spain, codex 29. 615 p. Quarto. Saec. 19.
Microfilm: MnCH proj. no. 30,085

2424   **Filippetto, Pio, 1907–**
Il discorso sulla povertá e sul lavoro in S. Bonaventura.
(*In* Sapientiae procerum amore . . . Roma, 1974. p. 211–224)
PLatS

2425   **Finis, Kathleen, Sister.**
Gregorian chant for high school students.
70 p. illus.
Thesis – Indiana University, 1963
InFer

2426   **Fink, Augustinus.**
Fragmenta Diarii quando Romae in Collegio Teutonico morabatur anni 1666–69. MS. Benediktinerabtei St. Paul im Lavanttal, Austria, codex 6/5. 63 f. Octavo. Saec. 17.
Microfilm: MnCH proj. no. 12,655

2427   **Fink, Louis Maria, 1834–1904.**
A catechism of the Catholic religion, preparatory to First Holy Communion . . . Kansas City, Kans., Bishop's Chancery, 1895.
156 p. 18 cm. (St. Benedict's catechism, no. II)
KAS

2428   A catechism of the Catholic religion preparatory to First Holy Communion . . . Atchison, Kans., Abbey Student Press, 1930 [c 1915]

32 p. 14 cm. (Bishop Fink's Catechism, no. I)
KAS

Fink, Wilhelm, 1899–

2429   Abt Benedikt Braumüller von Metten.
(*In* Bayerische Benediktinerakademie. Jahresericht, 1925)
MnCS; AStb

2430   Kloster Metten. [2. neubearb. Aufl.] München, Schnell & Steiner, 1957.
17 p. illus. 17 cm.
MnCS

Fischer, Anselm, fl. 1706.

2431   Conversatio externa religiosa; seu, Modus pie, et religiose vivendi in communitate, & societate hominum. Constantiae, J. C. Wohler, 1711.
[16], 530, [16] p. 16 cm.
KAS; MnCS

2432   Specus Sancti Benedicti; seu, Solitudo sacra, in quam religiosa anima se recipit, ut ubidem eo liberius sola cum solo Deo agat. Augustae Vindelicorum, Joannes Conradus Wohler, 1708.
170 p. 13 cm.
MnCS

2433   Tractatus asceticus de tribus votis religiosis. Ed. 2. Augustae Vindelicorum, Casp. Bencard, 1724.
[16], 523, [13] p. 16 cm.
KAS; PLatS

2434   Vita interna cum Deo; seu, Doctrina ascetica, quomodo religiosos debeat sibi, & mundo mori, ut uni vivat Deo. Augustae Vindel., J. M. Labart, 1708.
[24], 562, [13] p. 14 cm.
KAS; MnCS

Fischer, Bonifatius, 1915–

2435   Bibelausgaben des frühen Mittalalters.
(*In* La Bibbia nell'alto medioevo, p. 519–600)
PLatS

2435a   Novae concordantiae Bibliorum Sacrorum iuxta Vulgatam versionem critice editam. Stuttgart, Friedrich Frommann Verlag, 1977.
5 v. 32 cm.
MnCS

2436   Ein neuer Zeuge zum westlichen Text der Apostelgeschichte.
(*In* Biblical and patristic studies, in memory of Robert P. Casey, p. 33–63)
PLatS

2437   Verzeichnis der Sigel für Kirchenschriftsteller. 2. Aufl. Freiburg, Herder, 1963.
527 p. 25 cm. (Vetus latina; die Reste der altlateinischen Bibel, 1, 1)
First published 1949.
MnCS; PLatS

2438   **Fischer, Leander,** 1904–
Der klösterliche Grundbesitz, 1863–1963.
(*In* Beuron, 1863–1963; Festschrift . . . Beuron, 1963. p. 486–520)
PLatS

Fischer, Pius, 1902–

2439   Der Barokmaler, Johann Jakob Zeiller und sein Ettaler Werk. München, Verlag Herold [1964]
135 p. illus. 30 cm.
PLatS

2440   Die französische Uebersetzung des Pseudo-Turpin nach dem Codex Gallicus 52 (München). Wertheim a.M., E. Beckstein, 1931.
109 p. 21 cm.
Inaug. Diss. – Würzburg.
KAS

2441   **Fitzpatrick, Patricia, Sister.**
With gladdened hearts we celebrate our first fifty years, 1919–1969: Sisters of St. Benedict of Crookston, Mount St. Benedict Priory, Crookston, Minnesota. [St. Paul, Minn., North Central Pub. Co., 1970]
60 p. illus. 22 x 28 cm.
LSTB; ICCS; KAS: MnCS; PLatS

2442   **Flading, Agatho John,** 1900–1969.
Nitrogen trichloride with indene and cyclopropane.
15 leaves, 28 cm.
Thesis (M.S.) – State University of Iowa, 1932.
Typescript.
KAS

2443   **Flaherty, Etienne, Sister,** 1922–
The effect of time-expansion on listening comprehension of high school students in second-year French classes.
159 p.
Thesis (Ph.D.) – Ohio State University, 1975.
Typescript.
MnStj (Archives)

2444   **Flanagan, Mary Callista, Sister.**
Jesuit education in the Archdiocese of Cincinnati in the past one hundred years.
Thesis (M.A.) – University of Notre Dame, 1939.
Typescript.
KyCovS

Flavigny-sur-Moselle, France. Abbaye de Saint-Eustase.

2445   Annales Flaviniacenses et Lausonenses.
(*In* Monumenta Germaniae historica. Scriptores. Stuttgart, 1963. t. 3, p. 150–152)
MnCS; PLatS

2446   Histoire de l'Abbaye bénédictine de Saint-Eustase (966–1924) . . . par les religieuses de la Communauté. Nancy, Société d'impressions typographiques, 1924.
xvi, 175 p.
KAS; LStB

2447   **Flicoteaux, Emmanuel,** 1882–1956.
The splendor of Pentecost. Translated from the French by Mary Louise Helmer. Baltimore, Helicon Press, 1961.
112 p. 23 cm.
InFer; KAS; InStme; PkShG; PLatS

2448   **Flodoard, of Reims,** 894–966.
Flodoardi annales a. 919–966. Continuatio a. 966–978.
(*In* Monumenta Germaniae historica. Scriptores. Stuttgart, 1963. t. 3, p. 363–408)
MnCS; PLatS

Flood, Edmund, 1931–
2449   Evidence for God. New York, Paulist Press [1972].
v, 55 p. 17 cm.
PLatS

2450   From Advent to Lent; the Sunday Epistles and Gospels. London, Darton, Longman & Todd [c 1965].
124 p. 19 cm.
MnCS; PLatS

2451   In memory of me; God's plan for men: present in history, made active in the Eucharist. New York, Sheed and Ward [1963].
117 p. 22 cm.
First published in 1962 under title: No small plan.
InFer; CaMWiSb; MoCo; MnCS; InStme; PLatS

2452   Jesus and His contemporaries. Glen Rock, N.J., Paulist Press [1968].
v, 85 p. 18 cm.
KAS; MnCS; MnStj

2453   Lent and Easter; the Sunday Epistles and Gospels. London, Darton, Longman & Todd [c 1966].
125 p. 19 cm.
MnCS

2454   No small plan; God's friendship for man: effected in history, made effective in the Eucharist. London, Darton, Longman & Todd [1962].
177 p. 22 cm.
InStme; KAS; MnCS

2455   The Orthodox, their relations with Rome [by] Joseph Gill and Edmund Flood. With study-club questions. Glen Rock, N.J., Paulist Press [1964].
46 p. 18 cm.
KAS; MnCS

2456   Parables of Jesus. New York, Paulist Press [1971].
64 p. 17 cm.
MnCS; MnStj

2457   The resurrection. New York, Paulist Press [1973].
v, 55 p. 17 cm.
PLatS

2458   Where we stand [a series of books for Christian education]. [General editors: Rev. Edmund Flood, O.S.B., and Paul Olsen]. London, Darton, Longman & Todd, 1964–
v. 19 cm.
MnCS; PLatS

Flood, Peter, 1898–
2459   The dissolution of marriage; non-consummation as a ground for annulment or dissolution of marriage, a study of English civil and church law compared with the canon law. London, Burns & Oates [1962].
viii, 129 p. 23 cm.
MnCS; PLatS

2460   The priest in practice; preaching and some other priestly duties. Westminster, Md., Newman Press [1962].
164 p. 20 cm.
ILSP; InStme; KAS; MnCS; MoCo; PLatS

2461   (ed) Cahiers Laënnec. New problems in medical ethics. Edited in English by Peter Flood . . . Westminster, Md., Newman Press, 1953–
NcBe; InFer

Florence, of Worcester, d. 1118.
2462   Chronicorum chronicon. MS. Lambeth Palace Library, London, codex 42. 155 f. Octavo. Saec. 12.
Microfilm: MnCH

2463   Florentii Wigorniensis monachi Chronicon ex chronicis, ab adventu Hengesti et Horsi in Britanniam usque ad annum M.C.XVII., cui accesserunt continuationes duae, quarum una ad annum M.CC.XCI., altera, nunc primum typis vulgata, ad annum M.CCXCV. perducat. Ad fidem codicum manuscriptorum edidit, brevique adnotatione passim illustravit Benjamin Thorpe . . . Londini, sumptibus Societatis, 1848–49. Faduz, Kraus reprint, 1964.
2 v. 22 cm. [English Historical Society Publications]
BNS; MnCS; PLatS

2464   **Folcuinus, abbot of Lobbes,** d. ca. 990.
Folcuini Gesta abbatum Lobiensium a. 637–970.

(*In* Monumenta Germaniae historica.
Scriptores. Stuttgart, 1963. t. 4, p. 52–74)
MnCS; PLatS

Folengo, Giambattista, 1490–1559.

2465   In canonicas apostolorvm epistolas, d.
videlicet Jacobi unam, d. Petri duas, ac d.
Joannis primam commentarii. Lvgdvni,
apvd Seb. Gryphivm, 1555.
532 p. 18 cm.
KAS

2466   In Psalterivm Dauidis . . . commentarij,
summa fide . . . ex ipsa hebraica ueritate
confecti & absoluti . . . Basilileae, per
Mich. Isingrinium [1549 or 1557]
[6], 449, [10] leaves, 35 cm.
KAS

2467   **Foley, Wilfrid,** 1891–1968.
. . . Patrick N. Lynch, Catholic bishop
and Confederate statesman.
Thesis (M.A.)–University of Notre
Dame, 1930.
NcBe

2468   **Folger, Herbert,** 1909–
Swikersperch; Beittträge zur Geschichte
Schwiklbergs und das Landkreises Volsho-
fen in Niederbayern. Abtei Schwiklberg,
1954.
119 p., 10 plates, 25 cm.
KAS; MnCS; NdRi; PLatS

2469   **Foliot, Gilbert, bp. of London,** 1107
(ca.)–1187.
The letters and charters of Gilbert
Foliot, Abbot of Gloucester (1139–48),
Bishop of Hereford (1148–63), and London
(1163–87): an edition projected by the late
Z. N. Brooke and completed by Dom
Adrian Morey and C. N. L. Brooke. Lon-
don, Cambridge U.P., 1967.
liv, 576 p. plates. 25 cm.
PLatS

Ford, Hugh Edmund, 1851–1930.

2470   Notes on the origin and early development of the restored English Benedictine
Congregation, 1600–1661, from contemporary documents. [Downside, 1887]
[16], 78 p. 24 cm.
NdRi; PLatS

2471   Some remarks on the question: To whom
belongs what is acquired by the religious
missionary in England? Yeovil, Printed by
the Western Chronicle Company [1888].
12 p. 23 cm.
PLatS

2472   **Fornaroli, Gerardo,** 1883–
Christi agere vices.
(*In* Abbas; la figura dell'abate nel pen-
siero di S. Benedetto. 1960. p. 18–19)
PLatS

2473   **Forner, Miquel.**
Summa theologiae moralis. MS. Monasterio benedictino de Montserrat, Spain,
codex 32. 276 f. Quarto. Saec. 16.
Microfilm: MnCH proj. no. 29,985

Forster, Anselm, 1935–

2474   Gesetz und Evangelium bei Girolamo
Seripando. Paderborn, Verlag Bonifacius-
Druckerei [1963].
159 p. 23 cm.
MnCS

2475   (ed) Seripando, Girolamo, 1493–1563. De
iustitia et libertate christiana. Hrsg. von
Anselm Forster, O.S.B. Münster, Westfalen, Aschendorffsche Verlagsbuchhandlung, 1969.
xxii, 130 p. 25 cm. (Corpus catholicorum
. . . 30)
MnCS; PLatS

2476   **Forster, Olivia, Sister,** 1924–
Benedictinism; its place in Japan.
12 p.
Mimeographed.
MnStj (Archives)

2477   **Forstner, Dorothea, Sister.**
Die Welt der Symbole. Mit 124 graphi-
schen D arstellungen von Oswald Haller.
Innsbruck, Tyrolia Verlag [1961].
670 p. illus. 21 cm.
MnCS

**Fort Augustus, Scotland. St. Benedict's
Abbey.** *See* St. Benedict's Abbey, Fort
Augustus, Scotland.

2478   **Fournier, Alphonse Marie,** 1852–
Notices sur les saints médicins. Solesmes, Imprimerie Saint-Pierre, 1893.
246 p.
St. John's Seminary, Brighton, Mass.

2479   **Fournier, Denis,** 1934–
Assumption Abbey, Richardton, N.D.
[1965?].
32 p. illus. 23 cm.
PLatS

Foyo, Bernardo.

2480   Catecismo benedictino, en donde se explican por menor los exercicios en que se
debe coupar un monge de la Congregacion
de San Benito de Valladolid. MS. Monasterio benedictino de Montserrat, Spain,
codex 23. 350 p. Quarto. Saec. 18 (1793).
Microfilm: MnCH proj. no. 29,986

2481   Idea de un benedictino que vive segun el
espiritu de su Regla. MS. Monasterio
benedictino de Montserrat, Spain, codex
30 & 31. 19 & 166 f. Quarto. Saec. 18.
Microfilm: MnCH proj. no. 29,984 &
29,987

2482   **Franchère, Lucille Corinne, Sister.**
(tr) Bossuet, Jacques Benigne. Selections from Meditations on the Gospel. Translated by Lucille Corinne Franchère. Chicago, H. Regnery Co., 1962.
2 v. 21 cm.
InStme

2483   **Franchville, Mary Noël, Sister.**
An experimental study of the effectiveness of reenforcing developmental lessons in reading with tape recordings.
87 p. illus., graphs.
Master's dissertation.
InFer

2484   **François, Augustin,** 1888–
Comment je présente la Messe à mes paroissiens. Bruges, Apostolate liturgique, 1955.
28 p.
MoCo

2485   **François, Jean,** 1722–1791.
Bibliothèque genérale des écrivains de l'Ordre de Saint Benoît, 1777–1778. Louvain, Bibliothèque S.J., 1961.
4 v. 27 cm.
"Reproduction anastatique accompagnée d'une note liminaire sur les bibliographies bénédictines."
ILSP; InStme; MoCo; NdRi; CaQStb

Frank, Hieronymus, 1901–
2486   Ambrosius und die Büsseraussöhnung im Mailand; ein Betrag zur Geschichte der mailändischen Gründonnerstagsliturgie.
(*In* Heilige Ueberlieferung. Münster, 1938. p. 136–173)
PLatS

2487   Ecce advenit dominator Dominus; Alter und Wanderung eines römischen Epiphaniemotivs.
(*In* Perennitas; Beiträge . . . P. Thomas Michels, O.S.B., zum 70. Geburtstag. Münster, 1963. p. 136–154)
PLatS

Franks, Gabriel, 1927–
2488   The ethical theory of George Edward Moore. New Subiaco, Ark., Subiaco Press, 1961.
57 p.
Excerpt from doctoral dissertation, Pontifical Institute of St. Anselm, Rome.
MoCo

2489   USA. Mainz, Matthias-Grünewald-Verlag [c 1965].
212 p. tables, 21 cm.
MnCS

2490   (tr) Riet, Georges van. Thomistic epistemology . . . St. Louis, 1963–65.
2 v. 24 cm.
InStme; NcBe; PLatS

2491   **Franquesa, Adalberto M.,** 1908–
El Ritual tarraconense.
(*In* Liturgica, 2: Cardinal I. A. Schuster in memoriam. 1958. v. 2, p. 249–298)
PLatS

2492   **Fransen, Irenaeus,** 1921–
Les scribes inspirés. Introduction aux livres Sapeientiaux de la Bible: Proverbes, Job, Ecclésiaste, Sagesse, Ecclésiastique. [Par] H. Duesberg et I. Fransen. Edition remaniée. Editions de Maredsous [1966].
936 p. 23 cm.
PLatS

Frederick Mary Dominic, Sister.
2493   A brief historical sketch of Marian Heights Academy (Ferdinand, Ind.)
24 p. illus.
Research paper – Indiana State University, 1973.
Typescript.
InFer

2494   An interpretive study of Milton's Samson Agonistes in view of the Renaissance concept of self-knowledge. Washington, D.C., Catholic University of America, 1964.
50 p.
InFer

2495   Christ yesterday – today – forever – 1867–1967; centennial brochure of the Sisters of St. Benedict, Convent of the Immaculate Conception, Ferdinand, Ind., 1967.
InFer

2496   **Frey, Cornelia, Sister.**
A study of the family. Terre Haute, Ind., Indiana State Teachers College, 1938.
24 p.
InFer

2497   **Freising, Bavaria (Benedictine abbey).**
Catalogus codicum manu scriptorum Bibliothecae Regiae Monacensis: Codices Frisingenses num. 6201–6832. Monachii, sumptibus Bibliothecae Regiae, 1873. Unveränderter Nachdruck, Otto Harrassowitz, Wiesbaden, 1968.
MnCH

2498   **Frey, Alfons.**
Commentarius in Apocalypsim S. Joannis Bapt. MS. Benediktinerabtei St. Paul im Lavanttal, Austria, codex 97/2, pars IX. Folio. Saec. 18.
Microfilm: MnCH proj. no. 11,870

Freyberger, Udalricus, fl. 1660.
2499   Commentarius in organum sive logicam Aristotelis. MS. Universität Salzburg, codex M I 303. 403 f. Quarto. Saec. 17 (1644).
Microfilm: MnCH proj. no. 11,078

2500   Tractatus controversiatici de verbo dei scripto et non scripto, item de ecclesia. MS. Benediktinerabtei St. Peter im Lavanttal, Austria, codex b.II.22. 607 p. Octavo. Saec. 17.
Microfilm: MnCH proj. no. 10,327

2501   **Frias, Juan Crisostomo de.**
Cursus philosophiae tam realis quam mentalis juxta mentem parentis nostri Anselmi et angelici praeceptoris. MS. Monasterio benedictino de Montserrat, Spain, codex 699. 303 f. Quarto. Saec. 18.
Microfilm: MnCH proj. no. 30,034

Frickel, Michael, 1921–
2502   Deus totus ubique simul; Untersuchungen zur allgemeinen Gottgegenwart im Rahmen der Gotteslehre Gregors des Grossen. Freiburg, Verlag Herder, 1956.
xvi, 148 p. 24 cm.
InStme

2503   (ed) Hörer und Predigt; ein Tagungsbericht, hrsg. von Otto Wehner und Michel Frickel, O.S.B. Würzburg [IBM – Staz, Gugel] 1960.
433 p. 21 cm.
InStme

2504   (ed) Sprache und Predigt; ein Tagungsbericht. Würzburg [IBM – Sats und Offset-Druck Gugel], 1963.
264 p. 21 cm.
InStme

2505   **Frieders, Fabian,** 1919–
The effect of thiouren and phenylthiouren on growth and pigmentation of several species of fish.
li, 22 leaves, illus. 28 cm.
Thesis (M.S.)–Catholic University of America, 1949.
Typescript.
InStme

2506   **Friesenegger, Maurus,** 1590–1655.
Tagebuch aus dem 30 jährigen Krieg. Nach einer Handschrift im Kloster Andechs mit Vorwort, Anmerkungen und Register hrsg. von P. Willibald Mathäser. [München], Südeutscher Verlag [1974].
MnCS

2507   **Frigge, Mariella, Sister.**
2 Cor 3:18. Transformation into the image of Christ as ministry of the new covenant.
93 p.
Thesis (M.A.)–Washington Theological Union, Silver Spring, Md., 1978.
SdYa

2508   **Fritz, Bernard,** 1880–1960.
(tr) Kalt, Edmund. Herder's commentary on the Psalms. Translated by Bernard

Fritz. Westminster, Md., Newman Press, 1961.
xxii, 559 p. 24 cm.
MnStj; ICCSS; MoCo; ILSP; PLatS; KAS; InStme; NdRi; MnCS

2509   **Froger, Jacques,** 1909–
La critique des textes et son automatisation. Paris, Dunod, 1968.
xxii, 280 p. illus., facsims. 22 cm.
InStme

2510   **Fruth, Alban,** 1913–
Church of St. Martin, St. Martin, Minnesota. [Chicago, C.D. Stampley Enterprise, 1973].
unpaged, ports. 28 cm.
MnCS

2511   **Fry, Timothy Paul,** 1915–
A study of the Ludus Conventriae with special reference to the doctrine of the redemption.
xii, 497 leaves, 28 cm.
Thesis (Ph.D.)–University of North Carolina, Chapel Hill, 1948.
Typescript.
KAS

2511a   (ed) RB 1980: the Rule of St. Benedict in Latin and English. Editor: Timothy Fry, O.S.B. Collegeville, Minn., The Liturgical Press [1981].
xxxvi, 627 p. 23 cm.
MnCS

2511b   (ed) American Benedictine Review. Published quarterly by the American Benedictine Academy. 1–   1950–
Editor: 1968–

Fu jên ta hsüch, Peking. *See* Catholic University of Peking.

2512   **Fuchs, Michaela, Sister,** 1913–
Suggestive procedures for integrating speech with subjects taught in the fourth grade.
223 p.
Thesis (M.A.)–Marquette University, 1939.
Typescript.
MnStj (Archives)

Fuerst, Bartholomew, 1919–
2513   A reading course in Greek. St. Meinrad, Ind., A Grail Publication, 1965–
v. illus. 22 cm.
InStme

2514   Seminarian's reading list. College list. Rev. ed. St. Meinrad, Ind., Abbey Press, 1962.
63 p. 20 cm.
InStme

2515   Seminarian's reading list. Theology list. Rev. ed. St. Meinrad, Ind., Abbey Press, 1964.

54 p. 19 cm.
PLatS

Füglister, Notker, 1931–

2516 Die Heilsbedeutung des Pascha. München, Kösel-Verlag, 1963.
309 p. 25 cm.
InStme

2517 Das Psalmengebet. München, Kösel-Verlag [c 1965].
168 p. 19 cm.
KAS; MnCS

2518 **Führkötter, Adelgundis, Sister.**
(ed) Hildegard, Saint. Hildegardis Scivias/edidit Adelgundis Fuhrkötter . . . Turnholti, Brepols, 1978.
2 v. illus., facsims. 25 cm. (Corpus christianorum . . . 43–43A)
InStme

Fulda, Germany (Benedictine abbey).

2519 Codex diplomaticus Fuldensis, hrsg. von Ernst Friedrich Johann Dronke. Neudruck der Ausgabe 1850. Aalen, O. Zeller, 1962.
437, 77 p. 27 cm.
MnCS

2520 Nachtrag zu dem fünften Capitel der Fürstlich-Hochstifft Fuldischen festgegründeten Information . . . Fulda, 1743.
166 p. 31 cm.
MnCS

2521 Traditiones et antiquitates Fuldenses. Hrsg. [von] Ernst Friedr. Joh. Dronke. Neudruck der Ausgabe 1844. Osnabrück, Zeller, 1966.
xvi, 244 p. 27 cm.
PLatS

2522 Urkundenbuch des Klosters Fulda. Bearbeitet von Edmund E. Stengel. Marburg, N.G., Elwert Verlag, 1958–
v. 24 cm.
PLatS

2523 **Fullman, Christopher Edward,** 1918–
The energetics of love [by] Christopher E. Fullman, O.S.B., and Henry J. J. d'Aoust, O.S.B.
(*In* Francoeur, R.T. The world of Teilhard. Baltimore, 1961. p. 146–155)
PLatS

2524 **Fultz, Norma J., Sister.**
Introduction to multimedia. 2d ed. revised. Muncie, Ind., Educational Resources, Ball State University, 1976.
Sound-slide set. 143 slides, script.
InFer

2525 **Fuxhoffer, Damian,** 1741–1814.
Monasteriologiae regni Hungariae libri duo . . . Recognovit, ad fidem fontium recovavit et auxit Maurus Szinár. Vindobonae & Strigonii, Carolus Sartori, 1869.

2 v. 29 cm.
KAS

Gaetano, Constantino, 1560–1650.

2526 Pro Ioanne Gersen . . . librorum De imitatione Christore auctore. Concertatio priori editione auctior. Accessit apologetica eiusdem responsio pro hoc ipso librorum auctore adversus Heribertum Rosvueydum [S.J.]. n.p., 1618.
unpaged, 15 cm.
MnCS

2527 Sanctor. trium episcopor. relig. bened. luminum Isidori Hispalens., Ildefonsi Tolet., Gregorii card. Ost. vitae, et actiones. Romae, apud Jacobum Mascardum, 1606.
156 p. 24 cm.
MnCS

2528 **Gai, Jean Baptiste,** 1898–
Corse, ile de beauté. [Paris], Arthaud [1961].
193 p. plates (part col.) 24 cm.
MnCS

Gaillard, Louis, 1899–

2529 Le cardinal de Richelieu, abbé commendataire de St-Riquier (24 mars 1628–4 décembre 1642).
(*In* Saint-Requier; études . . . Abbaye de Saint-Riquier, 1962. v. 1, p. 138–147)
PLatS

2530 Corbie, abbaye royale; volume du XIIIe centenaire. Lille, Facultés catholiques, 1963)
444 p. 24 cm.
MnCS

2531 Les débuts de la restauration grégorienne à Solesmes. Roma, Associazione italiana Santa Cecilia [195-?]
32 p. 24 cm.
MnCS; PLatS

2532 Quelques réflexions sur les premières formes de la musique sacrée. Roma, Associazione italiana Santa Cecilia [195-?]
40 p. 24 cm.
MnCS; PLatS

2533 **Gales, Leo Lawrence,** 1905–
Love and suffering for hospital and home. Conception, Mo., Conception Abbey Press, 1958.
64 p. 16 cm.
KAS

2534 **Gallia monastica:** tableaux et cartes de dépendances monastiques/publiés sous la direction de J. F. Lemarignier. Paris, A. et J. Picard, 1974–
v. 28 cm.
KAS

2535   **Gallick, Gerard R.,** 1943–
Communication in the philosophy of Karl
Jaspers.
v, 26 p. 28 cm.
Typescript.
PLatS

2536   **Gallivan, Ricarda, Sister.**
Shades in the fabric; excerpts from the
Nauvoo Benedictine story. Nauvoo, Ill.,
1970.
96 p. 28 cm.
Mimeographed.
ICSS; MnStj; MoCo

2537   **Gallois, Geneviève, Sister,** 1888–1962.
L'Album de Mère Geneviève Gallois,
présenté par Marcelle Auclair.
(*In* Les Moniales. Paris, Desclée de
Brouwer [1966])
MnCS; MnStj

Gallus, abbot of Reichenau.
2538   Malogranatum lib. I et II, cum indice.
MS. Benediktinerabtei Lambach, Austria,
codex chart. 184. 180 f. Saec. 15.
Microfilm: MnCH proj. no. 592

2539   Malogranatum lib I et II. MS. Benediktinerabtei Lambach, Austria, codex chart.
185. 238 f. Saec. 15.
Microfilm: MnCH proj. no. 593

Gams, Pius Bonifacius, 1816–1892.
2540   Series episcoporum Ecclesiae catholicae.
Graz, Akademische Druck u. Verlagsan-
stalt, 1957.
963 p. 27 cm.
"Unveränderter Abdruck der 1873 . . .
Ausgabe."
InStme

2541   Zur Geschichte der spanischen Staatsin-
quisition. Regensburg, G. J. Manz, 1878.
96 p. 23 cm.
KAS; MnCS; PLatS

Gander, Martin, 1855–1916.
2542   Die Bakterien. 2., verm. u. verb. Aufl.
Einsiedeln, New York, Benziger, 1910.
viii, 173 p. illus. 17 cm.
PLatS

2543   Somatologie; oder, Lehre vom mensch-
lichen Körper. Einsiedeln, Eberle, Kälin,
1891.
112 p.
NdRi

2543a   **Gannon, M. Teresita, Sister.**
Proverbs worth remembering. [Pitts-
burgh, 1977].
[47] leaves, chiefly col. illus., 19 x 30 cm.
Manuscript.
PLatS

2544   **Gardi, Jacopo,** d. 1585.
Historia divina l'uno e l'altro mondo.
Fiorenza, appresso Bartolomeo Sermar-

tell, MDLXXI.
23 leaves, 541 p. 22 cm.
PLatS

2545   **Gardner, Annella, Sister.**
Study of the graduates of St. Leo's High
School, Minot, N.D., from 1943–58.
Thesis (M.A.)–St. Thomas College, St.
Paul, Minn., 1961.
Typescript.
NdRiS

2546   **Garrido Bonaño, Manuel,** 1925–
Curso de liturgia romana . . . Madrid,
Biblioteca de Autores Cristianos, 1961.
751 p. 21 cm.
MnCS

Garsten, Austria (Benedictine abbey).
2547   Catalogus venerabilis coetus Benedictini
Garstensis. MS. Benediktinerabtei St. Paul
im Lavanttal, Austria, codex 10/5, pars II.
Folio. Saec. 18.
Microfilm: MnCH proj. no. 12,656

2548   Chronicon monasterii Garstensis in
Austria. MS. Vienna, Nationalbibliothek,
codex 340, 4 f. Folio. Saec. 12 & 13.
Microfilm: MnCH proj. no. 13,693

Gasquet, Francis Aidan, 1846–1929.
2549   Address delivered by the abbot of Downside at the conventual chapter, September
18, 1907, on the principles that should
guide the community in view of calls to
undertake new external works. [Letch-
worth, Arden Press, n.d.].
12 p. 23 cm.
KAS

2550   Ancestral prayers. [Preface by Cardinal
Gasquet]. Springfield, Ill., Templegate
Publishers [1976]
63 p. illus.
NcBe

2551   The Bosworth Psalter; an account of a
manuscript formerly belonging to O.
Turville-Petre esq. of Bosworth Hall, now
Addit. MS. 37517 at the British Museum.
By Abbot Gasquet and Edmund Bishop
. . . London, G. Bell, 1908.
189 p. facims. 26 cm.
PLatS

2552   Christian democracy in pre-Reformation
time. London, Catholic Truth Society,
1899.
16 p. 17 cm.
MnCS; NdRi

2553   Codex Vercellensis iamdudum ab iroco et
bianchino. Roma, Pustet, 1914. (Collectanea biblica latina, v. 3)
MoCo

2554   Hampshire recusants; a story of their
troubles in the time of Queen Elizabeth.
London, John Hodges, n.d.

58 p. 23 cm.
PLatS

2555   The layman in the pre-Reformation parish. London, Catholic Truth Society, n.d.
39 p.
KAS; NcBe

2556   A little book of prayers from Old English sources. Edited by F. Aidan Gasquet. London, Catholic Truth Society, 1900.
viii, 53 p. 15 cm.
InStme

2557   The making of St. Alban's Shrine. [n.p., n.d.]
8 p. illus. 21 cm.
A paper read before the Guild of SS. Gregory and Luke at St. Alban's.
KAS; PLatS

2558   The mission of St. Augustine; its import for Englishmen and Catholics today. London, Catholic Truth Society [1897].
32 p. 19 cm.
KAS

2559   The Order of the Visitation; its spirit and its growth in England. London, Burns & Oates; New York, Benziger Brothers, n.d.
57 p. 17 cm.
MoCo; NcBe

2560   The question of Anglican ordinations. Notre Dame, Ind., Ave Maria Press [1907].
52 p. 18 cm.
KAS; NcBe; NdRi; PkTB; PLatS

2561   Religio religiosi; objecte i fine de la vida religiosa. Versio catalana de la 3. ed. anglesa per Dom Placid M.a Feliu. Montserrat, 1927.
223 p. 18 cm.
MnCS

2562   Saggio storico della costituzione monastica. Versione dall'inglese. Roma, Tipografia Vaticana, 1896.
72 p. 21 cm.
KAS

2563   A short history of the Catholic Church in England. New and rev. ed. London, Catholic Truth Society, 1928.
123 p.
NcBe

2564   Sketches of mediaeval monastic life, III: the scriptorium. Yeovil [England], Printed by the Western Chronicle Co. [1892].
12 p. 22 cm.
Offprint from Downside review, v. 11 (1892).
KAS

2565   Two dinners at Wells in the 15th century. Yeovil [England], Printed by the Western Chronicle Co., 1896.

16 p. 22 cm.
Reprinted from the Downside review.
KAS

2566   (2dary) The nun's rule, being the Ancren riwle modernised by James Morton, with introduction by Abbot Gasquet. New York, Cooper Square Publishers, 1966.
xxvii, 339 p. illus. 17 cm. (The Medieval Library)
InStme

2567   **Gassner, Gabriel,** 1894–
Rabanus Maurus; Vortrag gehalten 1956 in einer Feierstunde in Eltville, anlässlich der elfhundertsten Wiederkehr des Todestages des heiligen Rabanus Maurus. [Eltville, Druckerei Seb. Wolf, 1956].
16 p. 22 cm.
PLatS

2568   **Gatterer, Christophorus.**
Methodus aetatis codicum definiensus (excerptum: tabulae sex). MS. Benediktinerabtei St. Paul im Lavanttal, Austria, codex 10/5, pars I. Folio. Saec. 18.
Microfilm: MnCH proj. no. 12,656

Gavaler, Campion, 1929–

2569   Die Homilie als Teil der Messe.
(*In* Sonderdruck aus Liturgisches Jahrbuch, 15 Jahr., 1965, p. 103–107)
PLatS

2570   Theology of the sermon as part of the Mass.
Offprint from Worship, v. 38 (1964), p. 201–207)
PLatS

2571   **Gebl, Benedikt.**
Kurtzer Bericht aller in St. Blasischen Archiv sich befindenen Acten und Actitäten. MS. Benediktinerabtei St. Paul im Lavanttal, Austria, codex 51/2. 5 vols. Folio. Saec. 17.
Microfilm: MnCH proj. no. 11,772; 11,776; 11,778; 11,781; 11,783

2572   **Gebhart, Emile,** 1839–1908.
Autour d'une tiare. Paris, Crès et cie, 1914.
261 p.
NcBe

2573   **Geiger, Eduard Ephraem.**
Der Psalter Salomo's. Hrsg. und erklärt von P. Eduard Ephraem Geiger. Augsburg, J. Wolffischen Buchhandlung, 1871.
vi, 166 p. 23 cm.
InStme

2574   **Geiser, Georgius.**
Privilegia Ordinis S. Benedicti, quaestionibus theologico-juridicis illustrata. MS. Benediktinerabtei Altenburg, Austria, codex AB 13 F 37. 149 f. Quarto. Saec. 17.
Microfilm: MnCH proj. no. 6536

Gelasius II, Pope. *See also* Popes, 1118–1119 (Gelasius II)

Gelasius II, Pope, d. 1119.

2575   Quae opuscula vel qui libri inter apocryphos computandi. MS. Benediktinerabtei Melk, Austria, codex 1562, f. 140r–141r. Duodecimo. Saec. 15.
Microfilm: MnCH proj. no. 1967

2576   De opusculis sanctorum Patrum, qui in ecclesia catholica recipuntur. MS. Benediktinerabtei Melk, Austria, codex 1562, f. 139v–140r. Duodecimo. Saec. 15.
Microfilm: MnCH proj. no. 1967

2577   **Genebrard, Gilbert,** 1537–1597.
Chronographiae libri qvatvor . . . Parisiis, apud Martinum Ivvenem, 1580.
[20], 568, [30] p. 35 cm.
PLatS

Geraets, David, 1935–

2578   Baptism of suffering. Pecos, N.M., Dove Publications [c 1970].
43 p.
MoCo

2579   Jesus beads. Pecos, N.M., Dove Publications, 1972.
76 p. 18 cm.
CaMWiSb; MoCo; PLatS

2580   The role of music in the missionary catechetical apostolate. Benet Lake, Wis., 1968.
68 p.
MoCo

Gerarda, Sister.

2581   A case study of the implementation of differentiated staffing in an urban Manitoba school. Winnipeg, Man., 1974.
iii, 148 p. 28 cm.
CaMWiSb

2582   A study of teacher's attitudes towards parental volunteers in the classroom and their relationships to professional role orientation and situational job security.
xi, 140 p. 28 cm.
Thesis–Ottawa University, 1976.
CaMWiSb

Gerardus, Belga.

2583   Mancipatvs Deiparae quo augustissimae coelitum imperatricis diligens servulus ad obsequium placitumque eiusdem quotidiana servitij praxi pie instituitur, authore Gerardo Belga benedictino, opera r.p.f. Gabrielis Bucelini . . . Amisii, Gregorius Waibl, 1659.
[12], 274 p. 10 cm.
KAS

2584   Opuscula, vere aurea ac divina ad monachos. Excusum primum Augustae Vindelicorum anno MDCXXXII, opera a R. P. Gabrielis Butzlini, deinde Bruxellis . . . secundo impressa. [Brussels], typis Francisci Foppens, MDCLXXIII.
401 p. 14 cm.
PLatS

2585   Sapienti pauca; sive, Meditationes in verbis breves, longae in sensu, ad singulos anni dies. Ex piis opusculis Gerardi Belgae . . . traductae per P. Maximilianum d'Agaro . . . Monachii & Pedeponti, sumptibus Joannis Gastl, 1750.
[14], 424 p. 17 cm.
KAS; MnCS

Gerbert of Aurilac. *See* Sylvester II, pope.

Gerbert, Martin, 1720–1793.

2586   Apparatus ad eruditionem theologicam, institutioni tironum congregationis S. Blasii, O.S.B., in Silva Nigra destinatus. Augustae Vindelic., sumptibus Ignatii Wagner, 1754.
[18], 211, [12] p. 18 cm.
PLatS

2587   De cantu et musica sacra a prima ecclesiae aetate usque ad praesens tempus. Hrsg. und mit Registern versehen von Othmar Wessely. Graz, Akademische Druck- und Verlagsanstalt, 1968.
2 v. illus. 25 cm.
MnCS; PLatS

2588   De ratione exercitiorum scholasticorum, praecipue disputationum cum inter Catholicos, tum contra haereticos in rebus fidei. Litteris San-Blasianis, 1758.
151 p. 17 cm.
MnCS

2589   De recto et perverso usu theologiae scholasticae. Litteris San Blasianis, 1758.
204 p. 17 cm.
MnCS; PLatS (microfilm)

2590   Exhortationes, 1769–1792. MS. Benediktinerabtei St. Paul im Lavanttal, Austria, codex 182/2. 399 f. Folio. Saec. 18.
Microfilm: MnCH proj. no. 11,967

2591   Iter alemannicvm, accedit italicvm et gallicvm. Editio secunda, revisa & correcta . . . [Abbatia S. Blasii in Silva Nigra], typis San-Blasianis, 1773.
533, [15] p. 19 cm.
KAS; PLatS (microfilm)

2592   Lumina et proposita ex sacris exercitiis. MS. Benediktinerabtei St. Paul im Lavanttal, Austria, codex 31/6, pars II. Quarto. Saec. 18.
Microfilm: MnCH proj. no. 12,591

2593   Principia theologiae liturgicae quoad divinum officium, Dei cultum, et sanctorum. Typis princ. Monast. S. Blasii, 1759.
[35], 452, [14] p. 19 cm.
PLatS

2594   Vetus liturgia Alemannica disquisitionibus praeviis, notis, et observationibus illustrata, . . . Typis San Blasianis, 1776. Reprograrischer Nachdruck, Hildesheim, Olms, 1967.
2 v. 23 cm.
PLatS

2595   (tr) Praxis Regulae SS. Patris Benedicti. E gallico in latinum sermonem transtulit P.M.G., O.S.B. Typis princ. Monasterii S. Blasii, 1757.
[20], 248 p. 17 cm.
InStme; MoCo

2596   **Germain, Aiden Henry,** 1896–1946.
Ecclesiastical jurisdiction in the Catholic Church in England (1559–1685).
116, iv leaves.
Thesis (S.T.L.) – Catholic University of America, 1927.
Typescript.
MnCS (Archives)

2597   **Germania monastica:** Klosterverzeichnis der deutschen Benediktiner und Cisterzienser. Neu hrsg. von der Bayerischen Benediktiner-Akademie. Augsburg, Winfried-Werk, 1967.
185 p. 21 cm.
Reprint of edition hrsg. von Stift St. Peter, Salzburg, 1917.
KAS; PLatS

2598   **Gerrer, Gregory,** 1867–1946.
Catalogue of the Wightman Memorial Art Gallery in the library of the University of Notre Dame. Notre Dame, Ind., n.d.
181 p. plates, 24 cm.
MnCS

2599   **Gerritzen, François,** 1912–
Le sens et l'origine de l'EN XRISTOI paulinien.
(*In* Studiorum Paulinorum Congressus Internationalis Catholicus 1961. v. 2, p. 311–322)
PLatS

Gersen, Giovanni, abbot of Vercelli, 14th cent.
2600   De imitatione Christi / vulgo Thomas à Kempis, Joannis Gersen . . . Glacii, M. Erich, n.d.
412, [12] p. 13 cm.
InStme

2601   (2dary) Gaetano, Constantino. Pro Ioanne Gersen . . . librorum de imitatione Christi auctore. Concertatio priori editione auctior. Accessit apologetica eiusdem responsio pro hoc ipso librorum auctore adversus Heribertum Rosvueydum [S.J.]. n.p. 1618.
unpaged, 15 cm.
MnCS

2602   **Gerstenberg, Miriam Thomas, Sister.**
A study of the marital status and attitudes of parents of retarded children in a private residential school of Maryland.
82 p.
Thesis (M.A.) – Cardinal Stritch College, Milwaukee, Wis., 1967.
Typescript.
MdRi

Gertken, Cecile, Sister.
2603   Chant accompaniment simplified. Collegeville, Minn., The Liturgical Press, 1960.
15 p. music, 24 x 28 cm.
MnCS

2604   Christian heritage chants; English text seasonal chants [and] organ accompaniment. Sisters of Saint Benedict, St. Joseph, Minn. [1978].
2 parts. 20 & 28 cm.
MnCS; MnStj

2605   Divine Office: English text fitted to Gregorian chant. Huntsville, Utah, Holy Trinity Abbey, 1977–78.
various parts
MnCS; MnStj

2606   Gradual: English text fitted to Gregorian chant. Huntsville, Utah, Holy Trinity Abbey, 1977–78.
MnCS; MnStj

2607   Hymns: English text fitted to Gregorian chant. Huntsville, Utah, Holy Trinity Abbey, 1977.
MnCS; MnStj

2608   Kyriale: Masses I, X, XV, XVI, XVII. English text. Organ accompaniment by Sister Cecile Gertken, O.S.B. Sisters of St. Benedict, St. Joseph, Minn., 1978.
MnCS; MnStj

2609   The Psalms arranged for recitation and chant. Sisters of St. Benedict, St. Joseph, Minn., 1977.
unpaged, 20 cm.
MnCS; MnStj

2610   **Gertken, Severin James,** 1881–1960.
The whole Christ; the five principal allegories in Holy Writ which tell us something about the relation of the members of the Church to Christ. Muenster, Sask., Canada, St. Peter's Press, 1961.
31 p. 15 cm.
CaSMu; MnCS

Gertrude, Saint, the Great, 1256–1302.
2611   Oeuvres spirituelles [de] Gertrude d'Helfta. Texte latin, introduction, traduction et notes par Jacques Hourlier et Albert Schmitt. Paris, Editions du Cerf, 1967–

v. 21 cm. (Sources chrétiennes, 127, 139)
InStme; PLatS

2612 Les exercices de Sainte Gertrude. Introduction, traduction et notes par Albert Schmitt. Paris, Librairie Plon [1943]
xiv, 236 p. 18 cm.
PLatS

2613 Gertrudenbuch; oder, Geistliche Uebungen der hl. Jungfrau, Gertrud der Grossen . . . und Sammlung täglicher Gebete. Nach dem lateinischen Originaltext von P. Maurus Wolter. Schaffhausen, Fr. Hurter, 1864.
xli, 378 p. 15 cm.
InStme

2614 . . . 6. Aufl. München, G. J. Manz, 1902.
xxxix, 395 p. 16 cm.
KAS

2615 [Legatus divinae pietatis]
Exercitia diversa [ex libris insinuationum divinae pietatis] . . . divae Gertrudis abbatissae Elpedianae . . . [n.p., 1655?]
[14] p. 35 cm.
KAS

2616 [Legatus divinae pietatis. German]
Der hl. Gertrud der Grossen Gesandter der göttlichen Liebe. Nach der Ausgabe der Benediktiner von Solesmes übersetat von Johannes Weissbrodt. 12. Aufl. Freiburg, Verlag Herder, 1954.
xv, 637 p. 16 cm.
MnCS

2617 O Beata Trinitas; the prayers of St. Gertrude and St. Mechtilde. Translated by Rev. John Gray. St. Louis, Mo., B. Herder [1927].
141 p. 18 cm.
KAS; MoCo; OkTB

2618 Philosophia coelestis, tradita ab aeterna Sapientia, id est,. doctrinae salutares dictatae a Magistro et Sponso coelesti, Christo Jesu, dilectae suae discipulae et sponsae S. Gertrudi virgini; ex libro suo Insinuationis d. pietatis collectae, extractae et in ordinem dispositae . . . per R. P. Simonem Huebmann, O.S.B. Salisburgi, Joan. Bapt. Mayr [1672?].
758 p. illus. 16 cm.
InStme

2619 Preces Gertrudianae; sive, Vera et sincera medulla devotissimarum precum, potissimum ab ipso Christo dictarum, et per Spiritum S. revelatarum, ex mellifluis divinisque revelationibus beatissimarum virginum et sororum Gertrudis et Mechtildis . . . Coloniae Agrippinae, apud Jean. Wilhelmum Friessem, 1679.

[32], 333, [12] p. illus. 12 cm.
PLatS

2620 Preces Gertrudianae . . . Juxta exemplar Coloniae editum apud, Wilhelmum Frissem, anno 1573. Gandavi, S. et H. Van der Schelden [1855].
254 p. 11 cm.
PLatS

2621 Preces Gertrudianae: Prayers of St. Gertrude and St. Mechtilde of the Order of St. Benedict. New York, D. & J. Sadlier, n.d.
288 p. 12 cm.
KAS

2622 Prières dites de Sainte Gertrude, ou vrai esprit des prières que Jésus-Christ lui-même a révélées, pour la plupart à sainte Gertrude et à sainte Mechthilde . . . Traduites per le R.P.A. Denis de la Compagnie de Jésus . . . 3. ed. Paris, H. Casterman, 1858.
444 p. 13 cm.
MnCS

2623 Revelationes, cum tabula alphabetica subsequenti. MS. Vienna, Nationalbibliothek, codex 4224, f. 83r–282v. Folio. Saec. 15.
Microfilm: MnCH proj. no. 17,388

2624 The life and revelations of Saint Gertrude, virgin and abbess, of the Order of St. Benedict. New edition. Westminster, Md., Christian Classics Inc., 1975.
xiv, 570 p. 18 cm.
Facsimile reprint of an earlier edition, probably 1890.
PLatS

2625 **Gesta abbatum Fontanellensium usque ad a. 833. Appendix annorum 834–850.**
(*In* Monumenta Germaniae historica. Scriptores. Stuttgart, 1963. t. 2, p. 270–304)
MnCS; PLatS

2626 **Geyer, Kenneth Albert,** 1927–
Interpretative directions in the piano music of Claude Debussy.
83 p.
Thesis–Catholic University of America, 1964.
NcBe

2627 **Ghent, Belgium. Saint-Pierre (Benedictine abbey).**
Liber traditionum sancti Petri blandiniensis, publié per Arnold Fayen. Gand, F. Meyer-Van Loo, 1906.
xii, 809 p. facsims. 26 cm.
MnCS

2627a **Ghislenghien, Belgium (abbey of Benedictine nuns).**
Inventaire des archives de l'abbaye de Ghislenghien, par Daniel van Overstrae-

ten. Bruxelles, Archives Generales du Royaume, 1976.
496 p. 24 cm.
MnCS

2628 **Gibson, Jean, Sister,** 1930–
The correlation of x-ray radiation (2-12A) with microwave radiation (10.7 cm) from the non-flaring sun.
117 p.
Thesis (Ph.D)–University of Iowa, 1969. Typescript.
MnStj (Archives)

Gilbert, abbot of Westminster, d. 1114.

2629 Altercatio Synagogae et Ecclesiae, seu Disputatio Judaei et Christiani de fide christiana. MS. Vienna, Nationalbibliothek, codex 13824. 21 f. Quarto. Saec. 13.
Microfilm: MnCH proj. no. 20,151

2630 Disputatio Judaei cum Christiano. MS. Augustinerchorherrenstift Klosterneuburg, Austria, codex 826, f. 57r–82v. Quarto. Saec. 14.
Microfilm: MnCH proj. no. 5807

2631 Disputatio Judei et Christiani et anonymi auctoris disputationis Judei et Christiani continuatio Gisleberti Crispini. Ad fidem codicum recensuit, prolegomenis notisque instruxit B. Blumenkranz. Ultraiecti/ Antverpiae, in Aedibus Spectrum, 1926.
82 p. 23 cm. (Stromata patristica et mediaevalia, 3)
PLatS

2632 Jüdische Verteidigungsschrift. Incipit: Quia christiani te dicunt litteris eruditum . . . MS. Studienbibliothek, Klagenfurt, Austria, codex perg. 7, f. 46r–47v. Octavo. Saec. 12.
Microfilm: MnCH proj. no. 12,943

Gillet, Robert, 1913–

2633 Spititualité et place du moine dans l'Eglise selon Saint Grégoire le grand.
(*In* Théologie de la vie monastique, p. 323–351)
PLatS

2634 (ed) Gregory I, Pope. Morales sur Job. 2. ed. revue et corrigée. Paris, Editions du Cerf, 1975–
v. 20 cm. (Sources chrétiennes, 32 bis)
PLatS

2635 **Gindele, Corbinian,** 1901–
Beurons Choralgesang.
(*In* Beuron, 1863–1963; Festschrift . . . Beuron, 1963. p. 308–336)
PLatS

2636 **Ginter, Anselm,** 1930–
Married couples retreats.
(*In* Baillargeon, Anatole, ed. Handbook for special preaching. 1965. p. 103–122)
PLatS

Gislebertus, abbot of Westminster. *See* Gilbert, abbot of Westminster.

2636a **Giustiniani, Paolo, O.S.B.Cam.,** 1476–1528.
Trattati, lettere e frammenti dai manoscritti originali dell'Archivio dei Camaldolesi di Monte Corona nell'Eremo di Frascati. A cura di Eugenio Massa. Roma, Edizioni di Storia e Letteratura, 1967–
v. 35 cm.
Contents: v. 1 (1967): Descrizione analitica dai manoscritti; v. 2 (1974): I primi trattati dell'amore di Dio.
MnCS

2637 **Glastonbury Abbey, Hingham, Mass.**
Tower tidings. 1–   1978–
InFer; MGl

Gleink, Austria (Benedictine abbey)

2638 Annalen von Gleink, 1125–1694. MS. Linz, Austria. Oberösterreichische Landesarchiv. Stiftsarchiv Gleink, Hs. 2. 140 f. Saec. 12–17.
Microfilm: MnCH proj. no. 27,652

2639 Kopialbuch von Gleink, 1125–1615. MS. Linz, Austria. Oberösterreichische Landesarchiv. Stiftsarchiv Gleink, Hs. 4. 245 f. Saec. 12–17.
Microfilm: MnCH proj. no. 27,649

2640 Urbar des Stiftes Gleink, 1310 & 1437–1441. MS. Linz, Austria. Oberösterreichische Landesarchiv. Stiftsarchiv Gleink, Hs. 11 & 11a. 35 & 77 f. Saec. 14 & 15.
Microfilm: MnCH proj. no. 27,662

Godefridus I, abbot of Admont.

2641 Sermones in dominicas et festa. MS. Benediktinerabtei Admont, Austria, codex 62. 180 f. Folio. Saec. 12.
Microfilm: MnCH proj. no. 9159

2642 Sermones. MS. Universitätsbibliothek Graz, codex 1432, f. 11r–21v. Octavo. Saec. 11.
Microfilm: MnCH proj. no. 26,416

2643 Homiliae in festa. MS. Benediktinerabtei Admont, Austria, codex 58. 176 f. Folio. Saec. 12.
Microfilm: MnCH proj. no. 9156

2644 Sermones de tempore et de sanctis. MS. Augustinerchorherrenstift Vorau, Austria, codex 193, f. 1r–68v. Octavo. Saec. 12.
Microfilm: MnCH proj. no. 7188

2645 Sermones de tempore. MS. Universitätsbibliothek Innsbruck, Austria, codex 374. 126 f. Octavo. Saec. 13.
Microfilm: MnCH proj. no. 28,382

Godescalcus, monk of Orbais, ca. 805–868.

2646 [Carmina]

(*In* Foucher, J. P. Florilège de la poésie sacrée. Paris, 1961. p. 137–142)
PLatS

2647   Carmina minora Pauli Diaconi . . . Godescalci . . .
(*In* Poetae latini aevi carolini. Berolini, 1880–   t. IV, fasc. II/III (1923). Supplementa, p. 911–943)
MnCS; PLatS

2648   **Godstow, England (abbey of Benedictine nuns).**
The English register of Godstow nunnery, near Oxford, written about 1450. Edited, with an introduction, by Andrew Clark. London, Pub. for the Early English Text Society by K. Paul, Trench, Trübner & Co., 1911.
cxiiii, 722 p. 23 cm.
PLatS

2648a **Goeb, Cuthbert,** 1893–1973.
[Ordinarium Missae. Zulu)
Umasethule offeramus. Izincwadi ze nkonzo ya Makolwa (Popular Liturgical Library) incwajana y ngqukithi ye misa of his letters to the abbots of Metten taken from the collection-in-book-form, archives of St. Vincent . . .
168 p. plates, 12 cm.
MnCS

Goebel, Mary Walter, Sister.
2649   Physical geography of Dubois County, Indiana.
105 p. illus., graphs, maps.
Thesis – University of Notre Dame, 1971.
InFer

2650   Science material in the library. Prepared by Sister M. Kenneth Scheessele, O.S.B., and Sister Mary Walter Goebel, O.S.B. (American Benedictine Academy. Library Science Section)
InFer

2651   **Goeke, Lillian, Sister.**
Analysis of circulation of classroom motion pictures in Catholic Film Centers, 1958–59.
Thesis (M.S.L.S.) – Catholic University of America, 1960.
Typescript.
KyCovS

2652   **Goetz, Rhabanus,** 1880–1966.
Archabbot Boniface Wimmer; catalogue ngu Cuthbert Goeb, O.S.B. 11 Isibuya yalungiswa. Printed in Czechoslovakia, 1932.
19 leaves. 29 cm.
Typescript, 1964.
PLatS

2653   **Goldstain, Jacques,** 1924–
Le monde des Psaumes. Paris, Editions de La Source [1964].
412 p. 19 cm.
MnCS

2654   **Gollowitz, Dominikus,** 1761–1809.
Pastoraltheologie. Zuerst bearbeitet von Dominicus Gollowitz, nun vielfach umgearbeitet und hrsg. . . . 7. Aufl. Regensburg, G. J. Manz, 1855–
v. 21 cm.
InStme

2655   **Gordianus monachus.**
Passio S. Placidi et sociorum ejus. MS. Vienna, Nationalbibliothek, codex 4031, f. 168r–172v. Quarto. Saec. 15.
Microfilm: MnCH proj. no. 17,222

2656   **Gordon, Andreas,** 1712–1751.
Philosophia utilis et jucunda . . . Pedeponti prope Ratisbonam, Joannes Gastl, 1745.
3 v. 17 cm.
MnCS

2657   **Gordon, Paul,** 1912–
(ed) Bulletin inter-monastéres pour les jeunes Eglises. Vanves, France. 1– 1965–
MnCS

2658   **Gosbertus, abbot of St. Gall,** 9th cent.
Gozberti diaconi continuatio libri II de miraculis s. Galli, per Walafridum emendata.
(*In* Monumenta Germaniae historica. Scriptores. Stuttgart, 1963. t. 2, p. 21–31)
MnCS; PLatS

2659   **Göss, Austria (abbey of Benedictine nuns).**
Urbarium parthenonis Goessensis in Styria, O.S.B., jussu abbatissae Annae e gente Herberstorf concinnatum anno 1459. MS. Vienna, Nationalbibliothek, codex 2788. 217 f. Folio. Saec. 15 (1459).
Microfilm: MnCH proj. no. 16,039

Göttweig, Austria (Benedictine abbey).
2660   Annales Gottwicenses. Chronici olim Gottwici conscripti fragmentum. MS. Benediktinerabtei Göttweig, Austria, codex 180. 9f. Quarto. Saec. 12–13.
Microfilm: MnCH proj. no. 3487

2661   Catalogus religiosorum Ordinis S. P. Benedicti in monasterio Gottwicensi Inferioris Austriae viventium. Cremisae, sumptibus Abbatiae Gottwicensis.
v. 22 cm.
PLatS

2662   Der heilige Altmann, Bischof von Passau; sein Leben und sein Werk. Festschrift zur 900-Jahr-Feier 1965. [Abtei Göttweig, 1965]

2663   Necrologium ut Denisius vult in Gallia inchoatum, in monasterio Gotwicensi continuatum. MS. Vienna, Nationalbibliothek, codex 684, f. 143r–144v. Folio. Saec. 12.
Microfilm: MnCH proj. no. 14,002

2664   Das Saal-Buch des Benedictiner-Stiftes Göttweig. Mit Erläuterungen und einem diplomatischen Anhange von Wilhelm Karlin. Wien, Hof- und Staatsdruckerei, 1855. Unveränderter Nachdruck, Graz, 1964.
xii, 440 p. facsim. 23 cm. (Fontes rerum Austriacarum. 2. Abt. Diplomataria et acta, Bd. 8)
MnCS; PLatS

2665   Die Traditionsbücher des Benediktinerstiftes Göttweig, bearb. von Dr. Adalbert Fr. Fuchs. Wien und Leipzig, Hölder-Pichler-Tempsky, 1931.
704 p. facsim. 24 cm. (Fontes rerum Austriacarum . . . 2. Abt.: Diplomataria et acta. 69. Bd.)
MnCS

Göttweig, Austria (Benedictine abbey). Stiftsbibliothek.

2666   Manuscripten-Catalog der Stiftsbibliothek zu Göttweig. n.d.
3 v. 27 cm.
Handwritten. Xeroxed by University Microfilms, Ann Arbor, Mich., 1966.
MnCS

2667   Die typographischen Incunabeln der Stiftsbibliothek zu Göttweig verzeichnet und beschrieben.
unpaged, 28 cm.
Handwritten (1939). Xeroxed by University Microfilms, Ann Arbor, Mich., 1966.
MnCS

2668   Pelagius' expositions of thirteen Epistles of St. Paul, by Alexander Souter. Cambridge, University Press, 1922–1931. [Nendeln, Kraus Reprint, 1967].
3 v. 24 cm.
Part III includes "Göttweig ms. 36 (old number G 23).
InStme

Göttweig, Austria (Benedictine abbey). Graphisches Kabinett.

2669   Ausstellung [1. bis] des Graphischen Kabinettes des Stiftes. Leitung und Gestaltung, P. Emmeram Ritter, O.S.B. [Abtei Göttweig, 1960?–]
v. plates, 21 cm.
MnCS

2670   Oesterreich, Habsburg, Europa. Graphische Dokumentation zur Geschichte Oesterreichs v. Hubertusburg (1763) bis Königsgrätz (1866). Leitung und Gestaltung: Emmeram Ritter in Zusammenbearbeitung mit Adolfine Treiber. [Stift Göttweig, 1970]
96 p. 16 leaves of illus., ports. 21 cm. (*Its* Ausstellung, 15)
MnCS

2671   Peter Paul Rubens-Stecherkreis. Elfte Austellung . . . Leitung und Gestaltung P. Emmeram Ritter, O.S.B. Stift Göttweig, 1968.
28 p. plates, 21 cm.
MnCS

2672   **Götz, Franz Sales,** 1884–1944.
Maurus Xaverius Herbst, Abt von Plankstetten; ein Lebensbild aus dem 18. Jahrhundert. 2., verb. Aufl., hrsg. von Bonifatius M. Schumacher, O.S.B. Würzburg, Echter-Verlag [1957].
87 p. illus. 19 cm.
NdRi; OKShG; PLatS

2673   **Götz, Wunibald,** 1869–
Abt Dr. Benedikt Braunmüller; ein Lebensbild. [Landshut, Jos. Thomann'schen, 1901].
38 p. 21 cm.
KAS

2674   **Gowan, Olivia, Sister,** 1888–1977.
The development of professional nursing at the Catholic University of America 1932–1958; relationships to the national scene . . . Duluth, College of St. Scholastica, Dept. of Nursing, 1967.
xvii, 248 p. illus. 28 cm.
MnCS; MnDuS

2675   **Grabert, Colman,** 1939–
The unity and distinction of bishops according to Ep. 14 of Leo the Great; an historico-philological commentary.
2 v. 28 cm.
Thesis (S.T.L.)–Pont. Athenaeum Sancti Anselmi, Rome, 1967.
Typescript.
InStme

Grabner, Donald, 1928–

2676   Galatians and Romans. Conception, Mo., Conception Abbey. [1960]
55 p. 21 cm. (Saint Andrew Bible commentary, 20)
KySu; PLatS

2677   Jeremiah and Baruch. Conception, Mo., Conception Abbey [1961]
79 p. 21 cm. (Saint Andrew Bible commentary, 4)
KySu; PLatS

2678   Lamentations. Conception, Mo., Conception Abbey [1962]
54–64 p. 21 cm. (Saint Andrew Bible Commentary, 12)
PLatS

2679 Saint John. Conception, Mo., Conception Abbey [1961]
83 p. 21 cm. (Saint Andrew Bible commentary, 30)
PLatS

Graf, Ernest, 1879–1962.
2680 Christmas in Bethlehem today.
(*In* Clonmore, Wm. A Christian's Christmas. London, 1939. p. 193–198)
PLatS

2681 The holy man of Ars, Saint John Baptist Vianney. St. Meinrad, Ind., Grail Publications [1955].
[4], 40 p. 16 cm.
KAS; MnCS

2682 On prayer. Bristol, The Burleigh Press [1945].
40 p. 21 cm.
MnCS

Graf, Thomas Aquinas, 1902–
2683 The Benedictine spirit. Translated from the German by Very Rev. Martin Pollard, O.S.B. Benet Lake, Wis., Our Faith Press [195-?]
40 p.
NcBe; WBenS

Graham, Aelred, 1907–
2684 Contemplative Christianity; an approach to the realities of religion. New York, Seabury Press [1974].
x, 131 p. 22 cm.
InStme; PLatS

2685 Conversations: Christian and Buddhist; encounters in Japan. New York, Harcourt, Brace & World [1968].
xvi, 206 p. 21 cm.
InStme; MoCo

2686 The end of religion; autobiographical explorations. New York, Harcourt, Brace, Jovanovich [1971].
xii, 292 p. 21 cm.
InStme; MnStj; NcBe

2687 Zen Catholicism; a suggestion. New York, Harcourt, Brace & World [1963].
xxv, 228 p. 21 cm.
CaMWiSb; ILSP; InStme; MnCS; MnStj; MoCo; PLatS

Grammont, Paul, O.S.B.Oliv., 1911–
2688 The authority of the indwelling Word [by] Dom Paul Gramont and Dom Philibert Zobel.
(*In* Todd, J. M., ed. Problems of authority. Baltimore, 1962. p. 79–103)
ILSP; PLatS

2689 Liturgy and contemplation.
(*In* Sheppard, Lancelot. True worship. Baltimore, 1963. p. 83–97)
InFer; PLatS

2690 **Granata, Onofrio,** 1799–1878.
Per l'apertura della sacra visita editto e lettere pastorale. Napoli, dalla Stamperia del Vaglio, 1852.
25 p. 22 cm.
InStme

Granfield, David, 1922–
2691 Domestic relations; civil and canon law, by Philip A. Ryan and David Granfield. Brooklyn, Foundation Press, 1963.
580 p. 27 cm.
PLatS

2692 Legal aspects of family relations.
(*In* D'Agostino, A. A. Family, church and community. 1965. p. 44–49)
PLatS

2693 **Granfield, Patrick,** 1930–
Theologians at work. New York, Macmillan [1967].
xxvi, 262 p. 21 cm.
Interviews with sixteen contemporary theologians.
InFer; InStme; MoCo; NcBe; PLatS

2694 **Graser, Rudolf,** 1728–1787.
Praktische Beredsamkeit der christlichen Kanzel, in Regeln, Exempeln, und vollständigen Mustern . . . Augsburg, Matthäus Rieger, 1769.
xl, 702 p. 22 cm.
KAS

Gratianus, the canonist, 12th cent.
2695 Concordia discordantium canonum. MS. Salisbury, England, Cathedral Library, codex 26. 190 f. Octavo. Saec. 13. Imperfect copy.
Microfilm: MnCH

2696 Concordantia discordantium canonum seu decretum. MS. Cistercienserabtei Rein, Austria, codex 86. 274 f. Folio. Saec. 14.
Microfilm: MnCH proj. no. 7488

2697 Decretum (pars secunda et tertia). Aliquot ex Codice Justinianeo. MS. Benediktinerabtei Admont, Austria, codex 43. 342 f. Folio. Saec. 12.
Microfilm: MnCH proj. no. 9136

2698 Decretum. MS. Benediktinerabtei Admont, Austria, codex 23. 296 p. Folio. Saec. 12.
Microfilm: MnCH proj. no. 9120

2699 Decretum cum glossa. MS. Benediktinerabtei Admont, Austria, codex 389. 105 f. Quarto. Saec. 12.
Microfilm: MnCH proj. no. 9463

2700 Decretum. MS. Lambeth Palace Library, London, codex 449. 355 f. Octavo. Saec. 12.
Microfilm: MnCH

2701 Decretum. MS. Benediktinerabtei St. Paul im Lavanttal, Austria, codex 25/1. 272 f. Folio. Saec. 12.
Microfilm: MnCH proj. no. 11,687

2702 Decretum, sive Concordantia discordantium canonum. MS. Benediktinerabtei St. Peter, Salzburg, codex a.XI.9. 316 f. Folio. Saec. 12.
Microfilm: MnCH proj. no. 10,269

2703 Decretum accurtatum. MS. Augustinerchorherrenstift Vorau, Austria, codex 376, f. 6r–61v. Quarto. Saec. 12.
Microfilm: MnCH proj. no. 7342

2704 Decretum glossatum. MS. Benediktinerabtei Admont, Austria, codex 35. 326 f. Folio. Saec. 13.
Microfilm: MnCH proj. no. 9127

2705 Justiniani Corpus juris. Gratiani Decretum. MS. Benediktinerabtei Admont, Austria, codex 48. 316 f. Folio. Saec. 13.
Microfilm: MnCH proj. no. 9138

2706 Decretum cum glossa Bartholomaei Brixiensis. MS. Universitätsbibliothek Graz, Austria, codex 52. 278 f. Folio. Saec. 13.
Microfilm: MnCH proj. no. 25,989

2707 Decretum cum glossis. MS. Universitätsbibliothek Graz, Austria, codex 71. 172 f. Folio. Saec. 13.
Microfilm: MnCH proj. no. 26,009

2708 Decretum cum glossis. MS. Universitätsbibliothek Graz, Austria, codex 80. 295 f. Folio. Saec. 13.
Microfilm: MnCH proj. no. 26,020

2709 Decretum cum glossis Bartholomaeus Avogrado Brixiensis. MS. Augustinerchorherrenstift Klosterneuburg, Austria, codex 87. 260 f. Folio. Saec. 13.
Microfilm: MnCH proj. no. 5058

2710 Decretum cum glossis Bartholomaei Avogadro Brixiensis. MS. Augustinerchorherrenstift Klosterneuburg, Austria, codex 101. 102 f. Folio. Saec. 13.
Microfilm: MnCH proj. no. 5075

2711 Decretum. MS. Lincoln Cathedral Library, England, codex 137. 207 f. Quarto. Saec. 13.
Microfilm: MnCH

2712 Decretum. MS. Cistercienserabtei Heiligenkreuz, Austria, codex 44. 300 f. Folio. Saec. 13.
Microfilm: MnCH proj. no. 4592

2713 Decretales iuris canonicis. MS. Universisätsbibliothek Innsbruck, Austria, codex 90. 277 f. Folio. Saec. 13.
Microfilm: MnCH proj. no. 28,173

2714 Decretales. MS. Madrid, Spain, Real Academia de la Historia, codex 6. 371 f. Folio. Saec. 13.
Microfilm: MnCH proj. no. 34,862

2715 Decretales. Madrid, Spain, Real Academia de la Historia, codex 67. 311 f. Folio. Saec. 13.
Microfilm: MnCH proj. no. 34,925

2716 Decretum cum apparatu. MS. Seo de Urgel, Spain, Archivo de la Catedral, codex 2009, 209 f. Folio. Saec. 13.
Microfilm: MnCH proj. no. 31,402

2717 Decretum, cum breve commentario. MS. Tortosa, Spain, Archivo de la Catedral, codex 70. 164 f. Quarto. Saec. 13.
Microfilm: MnCH proj. no. 30,643

2718 Decretum. MS. Tortosa, Spain, Archivo de la Catedral, codex 239. 403 f. Folio. Saec. 13/14.
Microfilm: MnCH proj. no. 30,806

2719 Decretum. Pars secunda et pars tertia (de consecratione). MS. Vienna, Nationalbibliothek, codex 1758, f. 131v–222r. Sestodecimo. Saec. 13–14.
Microfilm: MnCH proj. no. 15,065

2720 Decretum. Pars secunda, cum glossa ad Causam II. usque ad Causae XI. quaestionem primam. MS. Vienna, Nationalbibliothek, codex 2061. 172 f. Folio. Saec. 13.
Microfilm: MnCH proj. no. 15,365

2721 Decretum (excerptum). Incipit: Omnia quaecunque vultis. MS. Vienna, Nationalbibliothek, codex 2183, f. 1r–86r. Folio. Saec. 13.
Microfilm: MnCH proj. no. 15,486

2722 Epitome Decreti Gratiani. MS. Vienna, Nationalbibliothek, codex 2221, f. 62v–120v. Quarto. Saec. 13.
Microfilm: MnCH proj. no. 15,506

2723 Exceptiones decretorum Gratiani. MS. Augustinerchorherrenstift Vorau, Austria, codex 184. 193 f. Quarto. Saec. 13.
Microfilm: MnCH proj. no. 7179

2724 Quaedam excerpta de libro magistri Gratiani. Incipit: Humanum genus duobus regitur. MS. Cistercienserabtei Zwettl, Austria, codex 285, f. 116v–147v. Quarto. Saec. 13.
Microfilm: MnCH proj. no. 6863

2725 Decretum cum glossa Bartholomaei (Joannis) Brixiensis. MS. Benediktinerabtei Admont, Austria, codex 9. 294 f. Folio. Saec. 14.
Microfilm: MnCH proj. no, 9103

2726 Decretum (con la recension laurenciana de la glosa ordinaria de Bertolome de Brescia). MS. Gerona, Spain, La Colegiata de San Felix, codex 26. 290 f. Folio. Saec. 14.
Microfilm: MnCH proj. no. 31,056

2727   Registrum in Decretum Gratiani et in libros Decretalium. MS. Universitätsbibliothek Graz, Austria, codex 72, f. 233r–242r. Folio. Saec. 14.
Microfilm: MnCH proj. no. 25,011

2728   Decretum. MS. Cistercienserabtei Heiligenkreuz, Austria, codex 43. 339 f. Folio. Saec. 14.
Microfilm: MnCH proj. no. 4589

2729   Decretum cum apparatu. MS. Hereford, England, Cathedral Library, codex P 9 ii. 396 f. Folio. Saec. 14.
Microfilm: MnCH

2730   Decretum Gratiani cum apparatu Bartholomei Brixiensis. MS. Linz, Austria, Bundestaatliche Studienbibliothek, codex 257. 156 f. Folio. Saec. 14.
Microfilm: MnCH proj. no. 27,902

2731   Decretum, cum apparatu. MS. Cistercienserabtei Lilienfeld, Austria, codex 222. 268 f. Folio. Saec. 14.
Microfilm: MnCH proj. no. 4500

2732   Decretum, cum apparatu. Accedit glossa Bartholomaei Brixiensis. MS. Cistercienserabtei Lilienfeld, Austria, codex 223. 244 f. Folio. Saec. 14.

2733   Decretum cum prohemio et glossa. MS. Benediktinerabtei St. Peter, Salzburg, codex a.XII.9. 256 f. Folio. Saec. 14.
Microfilm: MnCH proj. no. 10,732

2734   Decretum Gratiani cum glossis Joannis, quas supplevit in multis Bartholomaeus Brixiensis. MS. Benediktinerabtei St. Paul im Lavanttal, Austria, codex 3/3. 322 f. Folio. Saec. 14.
Microfilm: MnCH proj. no. 12,034

2735   Decretum, cum glossis Bartholomei Brixiensis. MS. Seo de Urgel, Spain, Archivo de la Catedral, codex 2008. 226 f. Folio. Saec. 14.
Microfilm: MnCH proj. no. 31,401

2736   Decretum. MS. Subiaco, Italy (Benedictine abbey), codex 33. Folio. Saec. 14.
Microfilm: MnCH

2737   Decreta, cum glossa Bartholomaei Brixiensis. MS. Tarazona, Spain, Archivo de la Catedral, codex 93. 379 f. Folio. Saec. 14.
Microfilm: MnCH proj. no. 32,672

2738   Decreta, cum glosaa. MS. Tarazona, Spain, Archivo de la Catedral, codex 120. 258 f. Folio. Saec. 14/15.
Microfilm: MnCH proj. no. 32,699

2739   Decretales. MS. Toledo, Spain, Biblioteca del Cabildo, codex 4, 1. 372 f. Folio. Saec. 14.
Microfilm: MnCH proj. no. 32,841

2740   Decretales. MS. Toledo, Spain, Biblioteca del Cabildo, codex 4, 2. 331 f. Folio.

Saec. 14.
Microfilm: MnCH proj. no. 32,842

2741   Decretum cum glossa Bartholomaei Brixiensis. MS. Tortosa, Spain, Archivo de la Catedral, codex 3. 292 f. Folio. Saec. 14.
Microfilm: MnCH proj. no. 30,577

2742   Decretum, cum glossa. MS. Vich, Spain, Archivo Capitular, codex 135. 346 f. Folio. Saec. 14.
Microfilm: MnCH proj. no. 31,106

2743   Decretum, cum glossa. MS. Vienna, Nationalbibliothek, codex 2082. 242 f. Folio. Saec. 14.
Microfilm: MnCH proj. no. 15,398

2744   Decretum, cum glossa Bartholomaei Brixiensis. MS. Vienna, Nationalbibliothek, codex 2070. 310 f. Folio. Saec. 14.
Microfilm: MnCH proj. no. 15,392

2745   Decretum, cum glossa Bartholomaei Brixiensis, usque ad Partis II. causam 12, quaestionem 5. MS. Vienna, Nationalbibliothek, codex 2069. 214 f. Folio. Saec. 14.
Microfilm: MnCH proj. no. 15,401

2746   Decretum (excerptum, cum indice). MS. Vienna, Nationalbibliothek, codex 2185, f. 1r–193r. Folio. Saec. 14.
Microfilm: MnCH proj. no. 15,499

2747   Decretum, cum apparatu Johannis Teutonici et additionibus Bartholomaei Brixiensis. MS. Vienna, Nationalbibliothek, series nova codex 2640. 280 f. Folio. Saec. 14.
Microfilm: MnCH proj. no. 20,891

2748   Decretum, cum glossis Bartholomaei Brixiensis. MS. Cistercienserabtei Zwettl, Austria, codex 12. 349 f. Folio. Saec. 14.
Microfilm: MnCH proj. no. 6598

2749   Decretum. MS. Madrid, Spain, Real Academia de la Historia, codex 15. 121 f. Folio. Saec. 15.
Microfilm: MnCH proj. no. 34,871

2750   Decretum. Pars secunda: liber de causis (excerpta). MS. Benediktinerabtei St. Peter, Salzburg, codex z.VII.41, f. 8r–13v. Folio. Saec. 15.
Microfilm: MnCH proj. no. 10,154

2751   Liber distinctionum decreti Gratiani. MS. Benediktinerabtei St. Paul im Lavanttal, Austria, codex 173/4. 158 f. Folio. Saec. 15.
Microfilm: MnCH proj. no. 12,409

2752   Excerpta decretorum Gratiani, cum prologo. MS. Prämonstratenserabtei Schlägl, Austria, codex 220, f. 1r–345r. (f.1b–19r: Register). Sestodecimo. Saec. 15.
Microfilm: MnCH proj. no. 3140

2753   Decretum, cum glossa et apparatu. MS. Vienna, Nationalbibliothek, codex 2057, f.

26r–353v. Folio. Saec. 15.
Microfilm: MnCH proj. no. 15,384

2754 Decretum epitomatum et metrice compositum. MS. Vienna, Nationalbibliothek, codex 4268, f. 206r–220v. Quarto. Saec. 15.
Microfilm: MnCH proj. no. 17,459

2755 Breviarium Decreti, praemisso registro. MS. Vienna, Nationalbibliothek, codex 5404, f. 1r–222r. Folio. Saec. 15.
Microfilm: MnCH proj. no. 18,570

2756 Epitome decreti Gratiani et totius libri decretorum pleniorem intelligentiam. MS. Vienna, Nationalbibliothek, codex 4268, f. 194r–204r. Quarto. Saec. 15.
Microfilm: MnCH proj. no. 17,459

2757 Epitome metrica causarum Decreti Gratiani. MS. Vienna, Nationalbibliothek, codex 4533, f. 144r–147r. Quarto. Saec. 15 (1428).
Microfilm: MnCH proj. no. 17,717

2758 Index alphabeticus in Decretum Gratiani. MS. Vienna, Nationalbibliothek, codex 4522, f. 1r–21r. Quarto. Saec. 15 (1423).
Microfilm: MnCH proj. no. 17,712

2759 Decretum, seu Concordantia discordantium canonum. Venetiae, Nicolaus Jenson, 1474.
389 leaves, illus. Folio.
Microfilm: MnCH proj. no. 7609

Gredt, Joseph, 1863–1940.

2760 Elementa philosophiae aristotelico-thomisticae. Ed. 13., recognita et aucta ab Euchario Zenzen, O.S.B. Barcinone; Neo Eboraci, Herder, 1961.
2 v. 24 cm.
KAS; MoCo; NcBe; PLatS

2760a Rational psychology. [Translated] by Thomas M. Marpes.
93 p.
Thesis (B.A.)–St. Vincent College, Latrobe, Pa., 1947.
PLatS

Green, Andrew, 1865–1950.

2761 Libretto of The chancellor prize; a school operetta in three acts. Male characters. Atchison, Kans., Abbey Student Press, St. Benedict's College, 1918.
28 p. 18 cm.
KAS; PLatS

2762 The proper of the Mass set to Gregorian themes by Rev. Andrew Green and Rev. Herman J. Koch. [Kansas City, Kans.], 1946.
137 p. music, 24 cm.
MnCS

2763 (ed) Hohe, Joseph. Laudate, choir manual, originally compiled by the Rev.

Joseph Hohe; completely revised by Rev. Herman J. Koch and Rev. Andrew Green. [Kansas City, Kans.], 1942.
viii, 256 p. 17 cm.
KAS

2764 **Green, Augustine Gregory,** 1868–
The eucharistic hour; meditations and exercises for the monthly hour of the People's Eucharistic League. New York, Kenedy [1919?].
159 p. 17 cm.
KySu; MnCS

2765 **Green, Peter Mathias,** 1926–
Density of population as a regulating factor in the reproductive potential of sigmodon hispidus.
viii, 101 p. 28 cm.
Thesis (Ph.D.)–Oklahoma State University, 1964.
Typescript.
OkShG

Grégoire, Reginald, 1935–

2766 Bruno de Segni, exégète médiéval et théologien monastique. Spoleto, 1965.
445 p. 21 cm.
MnCS

2767 Les homéliaires du Moyen Age. Inventaire at analyse des manuscrits. Roma, Herder, 1966.
264 p. 26 cm.
InStme; KAS; MnCS; PLatS

2768 La pratique des conseils évangeliques à Cluny.
(*In* Semana de estudios monasticos, 14th, Silos, Spain, 1973. p. 75–101)
PLatS

2769 Prières liturgiques médiévales en l'honneur de Saint Benoit, de Sainte Scholastique et de Saint Maur.
(*In* Analecta monastica, 7. sér., 1965. p. 1–85. Studia Anselmiana, fasc. 54)
PLatS

2769a **Gregorio di Catino, monk of Farfa,** fl. 1000.
Il regesto di Farfa di Gregorio di Catino, pubblicato da I. Giorgi e U. Balzani. Roma, Presso la Società, 1878–83, 1914.
5 v. 36 cm. (Biblioteca della R. Società Romana di storia patria)
Vol. 1 is 1914 reprint.
MnCS

Gregory I, the Great, Saint, Pope, 540 (ca.)–604. *See also* Popes, 590–604 Gregory I).
Manuscript copies.

2770 [Selections]
Liber Flos moralium dictus. MS. Augustinerchorherrenstift Klosterneuburg,

Austria, codex 1078, f. 9r–95r. Quarto. Saec. 11.
Microfilm: MnCH proj. no. 6068

2771 [Selections]
Extracts from Augustine, Jerome, Gregory, Bede . . . MS. Hereford, England, Cathedral Library, codex 0 1 xii, f. 35–74. Octavo. Saec. 12.
Microfilm: MnCH

2772 Excerpta de diversis dictis beati Gregorii papae super Bibliam. MS. Cistercienserabtei Zwettl, Austria, codex 223. 217 f. Quarto. Saec. 12.
Microfilm: MnCH proj. no. 6827

2773 [Selections]
Anonymi vitae ex S. Gregorii homiliis et libris Dialogorum. MS. Benediktinerabtei Melk, Austria, codex 1739, p. 251–280. Duodecimo. Saec. 13.
Microfilm: MnCH proj. no. 2049

2774 [Selections]
Collectaneum ex dictis S. Gregorii Magni de vitiis capitalibus vel de confessione. MS. Augustinerchorherrenstift Vorau, Austria, codex 399, f. 1r–26v. Octavo. Saec. 13.
Microfilm: MnCH proj. no. 7361

2775 [Selections]
Excerpta. MS. Vienna, Nationalbibliothek, codex 1488, f. 26v–48r. Folio. Saec. 13.
Microfilm: MnCH proj. no. 14,834

2776 [Selections]
Flores beati Gregorii. MS. Benediktinerabtei Kremsmünster, Austria, codex 277, f. 133r–142v. Saec. 14.
Microfilm: MnCH proj. no. 261

2777 [Selections]
Excerpta ex libris S. Gregorii papae. MS. Cistercienserabtei Lilienfeld, Austria, codex 87, f. 1r–84r. Quarto. Saec. 14.
Microfilm: MnCH proj. no. 4386

2778 [Selections]
Flores de diversis libris excerpti. MS. Universitätsbibliothek Innsbruck, Austria, codex 389, f. 1r–207v. Octavo. Saec. 14.
Microfilm: MnCH proj. no. 28,407

2779 [Selections]
Insignis collectio sententiarum praecipuorum ex operibus S. Gregorii Magni, maxime libris Moralium, Senecae philosophi et poetae, et Tulli libris tribus Rhetoricorum. MS. Benediktinerabtei Melk, Austria, codex 1414. 264. p. Octavo. Saec. 14.
Microfilm: MnCH proj. no. 1936

2780 [Selections]
Flores. MS. Dominikanerkloster, Vienna, codex 234, f. 144v–177r. Quarto. Saec. 14.
Microfilm: MnCH proj. no. 9016

2781 Auctoritates beati Gregorii papae ex ejus Moralibus sumptae. MS. Vienna, Nationalbibliothek, codex 4064, f. 252r–264v. Octavo. Saec. 15.
Microfilm: MnCH proj. no. 17,260

2782 Auctoritates biblicae expositae per B. Gregorium in suis operibusordinatae per libros et capitula. MS. Cistercienserabtei Heiligenkreuz, Austria, codex 296, f. 1r–16v. Quarto. Saec. 14.
Microfilm: MnCH proj. no. 4833

2783 Carmen de vita Benedicti abbatis. Incipit: Puer petens heremum sancte Benedicte. MS. Benediktinerabtei Melk, Austria, codex 1087, f. 62–66. Duodecimo. Saec. 15.
Microfilm: MnCH proj. no. 1842

2784 Collatio de S. Gregorio papa. Incipit: In nomine . . . negociamini dum venio. MS. Vienna, Schottenstift, codex 153, f. 103r–109v. Octavo. Saec. 15.
Microfilm: MnCH proj. no. 4079

2785 Concordia testimoniorum Scripturae. MS. Vienna, Nationalbibliothek, codex 1008, f. 140r–154v. Folio. Saec. 11.
Microfilm: MnCH proj. no. 14,318

2786 Contemplationum libri septem. MS. Cava, Italy (Benedictine abbey), codex 29. 369 f. Quarto. Saec. 13.
Microfilm: MnCH

2787 De abusionibus saeculi (excerptum). MS. Augustinerchorherrenstift Vorau, Austria, codex 336, f. 242v–243r. Quarto. Saec. 12.
Microfilm: MnCH proj. no. 7304

2788 De conflictu vitiorum et virtutum. MS. Vienna, Nationalbibliothek, codex 1147, f. 49v–69v. Octavo. Saec. 12.
Microfilm: MnCH proj. no. 14,531

2789 De cottidiana communione. MS. Benediktinerabtei Lambach, Austria, codex chart. 333, f. 170r–170v. Saec. 15.
Microfilm: MnCH proj. no. 704

2790 De cottidiana communione. MS. Benediktinerabtei Lambach, Austria, codex chart. 435, f. 215v–216v. Saec. 15.
Microfilm: MnCH proj. no. 725

2791 De curiositate. MS. Benediktinerabtei Melk, Austria, codex 1843, f. 70v–71v. Duodecimo. Saec. 15.
Microfilm: MnCH proj. no. 2153

2792 De judicio poenitentiae. MS. Vienna, Nationalbibliothek, codex 2223, f. 41r–44r. Quarto. Saec. 9–10.
Microfilm: MnCH proj. no. 15,569

2793 De juramentis episcoporum. MS. Salisbury, England, Cathedral Library, codex 157, f. 151v. Octavo. Saec. 11.
Microfilm: MnCH

2794   De obedientia. MS. Cistercienserabtei Zwettl, Austria, codex 338, f. 76r–77r. Quarto. Saec. 12.
Microfilm: MnCH proj. no. 6954

2795   De praelatis et subditis. MS. Vienna, Nationalbibliothek, codex 1032, f. 1v. Quarto. Saec. 9.
Microfilm: MnCH proj. no. 14,341

2796   De reparatione lapsi. MS. Benediktinerabtei St. Peter, Salzburg, codex b.IX.13, f. 195r–196r. Folio. Saec. 15.
Microfilm: MnCH proj. no. 10,572

2797   De visione divinae essentiae. MS. Benediktinerabtei St. Peter, Salzburg, codex a.IV.15, f. 94r–95v. Octavo. Saec. 12.
Microfilm: MnCH proj. no. 9996

2798   De vitis Patrum qui dicitur Paradisus. MS. Hereford, England, Cathedral Library, codex 0 1 iii, f. 69–117. Quarto. Saec. 13.
Microfilm: MnCH

2799   Dialogi MS. Lambeth Palace Library, London, codex 204, f. 1–119. Quarto. Saec. 10–11.
Microfilm: MnCH

2800   Dialogi. MS. Salisbury, England, Cathedral Library, codex 96. 111 f. Quarto. Saec. 10.
Microfilm: MnCH

2801   Dialogi. MS. Silos, Spain. Archivo del Monasterio de Sto. Domingo. MS. 2. 159 f. Quarto. Saec. 10.
Microfilm: MnCH proj. no. 33,687

2802   Dialogorum libri quatuor de vita et miraculis patrum italicorum. MS. Cistercienserabtei Rein, Austria, codex 57. 140 f. Saec. 11(?).
Microfilm: MnCH proj. no. 7455

2803   Dialogorum libri quatuor. MS. Benediktinerabtei St. Peter, Salzburg, codex a.VIII.28, f. 1r–154a. Folio. Saec. 11.
Microfilm: MnCH proj. no. 10,191

2804   Dialogorum libri quatuor. MS. Vich, Spain, Archivo Capitular, codex 38. 171 f. Quarto. Saec. 11.
Microfilm: MnCH proj. no. 31,190

2805   Dialogorum libri. MS. Vich, Spain, Archivo Capitular, codex 39. Folio. Saec. 11.
Microfilm: MnCH proj. no. 31,163

2806   Dialogorum de vita et miraculis patrum italicorum libri quatuor. MS. Benediktinerabtei Admont, Austria, codex 274. 154 f. Folio. Saec. 12.
Microfilm: MnCH proj. no. 9357

2807   Dialogi. MS. Benediktinerabtei Göttweig, Austria, codex 109, f. 10r–133v. Folio. Saec. 12.
Microfilm: MnCH proj. no. 3388

2808   Dialogorum libri IV. MS. Universitätsbibliothek Graz, Austria, codex 183, f. 1r–82r. Quarto. Saec. 12.
Microfilm: MnCH proj. no. 26,111

2809   Dialogorum livri IV. MS. Universitätsbibliothek Graz, Austria, codex 933. 122 f. Quarto. Saec. 12.
Microfilm: MnCH proj. no. 27,024

2810   Dialogi de vitis patrum italicorum. MS. Hereford, England, Cathedral Library, codex 0 1 x. 99 f. Quarto. Saec. 12.
Microfilm: MnCH

2811   Liber dialogorum. MS. Universitätsbibliothek Innsbruck, Austria, codex 464. 174 f. Quarto. Saec. 12.

2812   Dialogorum liber. MS. Augustinerchorherrenstift Klosterneuburg, Austria, codex 235. 115 f. Folio. Saec. 12.
Microfilm: MnCH proj. no. 5207

2813   Dialogus. Incipit: Quadam die, quorundam secularium nimius depressus. MS. Augustinerchorherrenstift Klosterneuburg, Austria, codex 794, f. 1r–79v. Quarto. Saec. 12.
Microfilm: MnCH proj. no. 5788

2814   Dialogi. MS. Linz, Bundesstaatliche Studienbibliothek, codex 276. 135 f. Quarto. Saec. 12.
Microfilm: MnCH proj. no. 27,905

2815   Liber dialogorum. MS. Augustinerchorherrenstift Neustift, Südtirol, codex 495. 202 f. Quarto. Saec. 12.
Microfilm: MnCH proj. no. 29,689

2816   Dialogi. MS. Salisbury, England, Cathedral Library, codex 95. 118 f Quarto. Saec. 12. Imperfect copy.
Microfilm: MnCH

2817   Liber dialogorum. MS. Tortosa, Spain, Archivo de la Catedral, codex 233, f. 1r–88v. Folio. Saec. 12.
Microfilm: MnCH proj. no. 30,800

2818   Dialogi. Libri quatuor. MS. Vienna, Nationalbibliothek, codex 802. 119 f. Quarto. Saec. 12.
Microfilm: MnCH proj. no. 14,136

2819   Dialogi. MS. Vienna, Nationalbibbliothek, codex 979, f. 56r–135r. Folio. Saec. 12.
Microfilm: MnCH proj. no. 14,288

2820   Dialogi. MS. Cistercienserabtei Zwettl, Austria, codex 263. 101 f. Quarto. Saec. 12.
Microfilm: MnCH proj. no. 6861

2821   Dialogi (incompletum). Incipit: De quodam abbate. MS. Benediktinerabtei Altenburg, Austria, codex AB 13 A 8, f. 87r–94v. Quarto. Saec. 13.
Microfilm: MnCH proj. no. 6376

2822 Dialogorum libri quatuor. MS. Cistercienserabtei Heiligenkreuz, Austria, codex 64, f. 1r–94v. Folio. Saec. 13.
Microfilm: MnCH proj. no. 4610

2823 Dialogorum libri quatuor MS. Benediktinerabtei Kremsmünster, Austria, codex 24. 115 f. Quarto. Saec. 13.
Microfilm: MnCH proj. no. 24

2824 Dialogorum libri quatuor. MS. Benediktinerabtei Kremsmünster, Austria, codex 335, f. 2v–88r. Saec. 13 vel 14.
Microfilm: MnCH proj. no. 424

2825 Dialogi. MS. Augustinerchorherrenstift St. Florian, Austria, codex XI, 77, f. 1r–98r. Folio. Saec. 13.
Microfilm: MnCH proj. no. 2335

2826 Libri quatuor dialogorum. MS. Prämonstratenserabtei Schlägl, Austria, codex 8, f. 1v–95v. Quarto. Saec. 13.
Microfilm: MnCH proj. no. 3059

2827 Dialogi. MS. Toledo, Spain, Biblioteca del Cabildo, codex 9, 10. 139 f. Quarto. Saec. 13.
Microfilm: MnCH proj. no. 32,981

2828 Dialogi. Libri quatuor. MS. Vienna, Nationalbibliothek, codex 803, f. 76r–167v. Quarto. Saec. 13.
Microfilm: MnCH proj. no. 14,150

2829 Dialogorum libri quatuor. MS. Vienna, Schottenstift, codex 208, f. 1r–145r. Folio. Saec. 13.
Microfilm: MnCH proj. no. 3899

2830 Dialogorum libri IV. MS. Subiaco, Italy (Benedictine abbey), codex 74. 210 f. Folio. Saec. 13.
Microfilm: MnCH

2831 Dialogorum libri quatuor. MS. Benediktinerabtei Göttweig, Austria, codex 129, f. 1r–45r. Folio. Saec. 14.
Microfilm: MnCH proj. no. 3404

2832 Dialogorum libri IV. MS. Universitätsbibliothek Graz, Austria, codex 536, f. 1r–68v. Folio. Saec. 14.
Microfilm: MnCH proj. no. 26,675

2833 Liber dialogorum. MS. Universitätsbibliothek Innsbruck, Austria, codex 225, f. 181r–244r. Folio. Saec. 14.
Microfilm: MnCH proj. no. 28,260

2834 Dialogorum liber. MS. Augustinerchorherrenstift Klosterneuburg, Austria, codex 234, f. 1r–74r. Folio. Saec. 14.
Microfilm: MnCH proj. no. 5205

2835 Liber dialogorum. MS. Augustinerchorherrenstift Klosterneuburg, Austria, codex 233, f. 1r–46r. Folio. Saec. 15.
Microfilm: MnCH proj. no. 5202

2836 Dialogi. MS. Benediktinerabtei Melk, Austria, codex 342. 151 f. Folio. Saec. 14.
Microfilm: MnCH proj. no. 1343

2837 Dialogi. MS. Augustinerchorherrenstift St. Florian, Austria, codex XI, 69. f. 1r–55v. Folio. Saec. 14.
Microfilm: MnCH proj. no. 2326

2838 Dialogi. MS. Augustinerchorherrenstift St. Florian, Austria, codex XI, 78, f. 1r–69r. Folio. Saec. 14.
Microfilm: MnCH proj. no. 2336

2839 Dialogi. MS. Benediktinerabtei St. Paul im Lavanttal, Austria, codex 150/4. 101 f. Folio. Saec. 14 (1371).
Microfilm: MnCH proj. no. 12,393

2840 Dialogi et Homiliae. MS. Tarazona, Spain, Archivo de la Catedral, codex 51. 240 f. Folio. Saec. 14.
Microfilm: MnCH proj. no. 32,630

2841 Libri quatuor dialogorum. MS. Vienna, Schottenstift, codex 352, f. 115r–173r. Folio. Saec. 14.
Microfilm: MnCH proj. no. 4199

2842 Dialogi. MS. Vienna, Nationalbibliothek, codex 3994, f. 1r–67v. Folio. Saec. 14.
Microfilm: MnCH proj. no. 17,194

2843 Dialogorum libri quatuor. MS. Benediktinerabtei Admont, Austria, codex 208, f. 246r–292v. Folio. Saec. 15.
Microfilm: MnCH proj. no. 9291

2844 Libri quatuor dialogorum. MS. Benediktinerabtei Göttweig, Austria, codex 455a. 136 f. Quarto. Saec. 15.
Microfilm: MnCH proj. no. 3713

2845 Liber dialogorum. MS. Universitätsbibliothek Innsbruck, Austria, codex 137. 113 f. Folio. Saec. 15.
Microfilm: MnCH proj. no. 28,216

2846 Dialogorum libri IV. MS. Universitätsbibliothek Innsbruck, Austria, codex 4, f. 1r–58v. Folio. Saec. 15.
Microfilm: MnCH proj. no. 28,748

2847 Dialogi. MS. Benediktinerabtei Lambach, Austria, codex membr. 55, f. 1r–123v. Folio. Saec. 15.
Microfilm: MnCH proj. no. 786

2848 Dialogorum libri IV. MS. Benediktinerabtei Lambach, Austria, codex chart. 173, f. 203r–266v. Saec. 15.
Microfilm: MnCH proj. no. 585

2849 Dialogi, lib. I, 1–10; lib II; lib III, 14–21. MS. Benediktinerabtei Lambach, Austria, codex chart. 452, f. 162r–190r. Duodecimo. Saec. 15.
Microfilm: MnCH proj. no. 741

2850 Libri quatuor dialogorum. MS. Benediktinerabtei Melk, Austria, codex 563, f. 124–320. Folio. Saec. 15.
Microfilm: MnCH proj. no. 1465

2851 Dialogorum liber I, III et IV. MS. Benediktinerabtei Melk, Austria, codex 189, f.

1–227. Duodecimo. Saec. 15.
Microfilm: MnCH proj. no. 1227

2852 Duo libri Dialogorum. MS. Benediktinerabtei Melk, Austria, codex 957, f. 1–48. Quarto. Saec. 15.
Microfilm: MnCH proj. no. 1768

2853 Dialogi. MS. Augustinerchorherrenkloster Neustift, Südtirol, codex 83, f. 1r–52r. Quarto. Saec. 15 (1440).
Microfilm: MnCH proj. no. 29,665

2854 Liber dialogorum. MS. Augustinerchorherrenkloster Neustift, Südtirol, codex 165, f. 1r–42r. Quarto. Saec. 15.
Microfilm: MnCH proj. no. 29,655

2855 Libri quatuor dialogorum. MS. Benediktinerabtei Seitenstetten, Austria, codex 246, 107 f. Folio. Saec. 15.
Microfilm: MnCH proj. no. 1051

2856 Quatuor libri dialogorum. MS. Benediktinerabtei Seitenstetten, Austria, codex 272, f. 44v–106v. Folio. Saec. 15.
Microfilm: MnCH proj. no. 1083

2857 Dialogi. MS. Toledo, Spain, Biblioteca del Cabildo, codex 9, 11. 152 f. Quarto. Saec. 15.
Microfilm: MnCH proj. no. 32,982

2858 Dialogi. MS. Augustinerchorherrenstift St. Florian, Austria, codex XI, 72, f. 1r–85r. Folio. Saec. 15.
Microfilm: MnCH proj. no. 2329

2859 Dialogi. MS. Augustinerchorherrenstift St. Florian, Austria, codex XI, 133, f. 119r–194r. Folio. Saec. 15.
Microfilm: MnCH proj. no. 2399

2860 Dialogi. MS. Benediktinerabtei St. Paul im Lavanttal, Austria, codex 92/4, f. 141r–213r. Folio. Saec. 15.
Microfilm: MnCH proj. no. 12,322

2861 Dialogi. MS. Benediktinerabtei St. Paul im Lavanttal, Austria, codex 144/4, pars II. Folio. Saec. 15.
Microfilm: MnCH proj. no. 12,388

2862 Libri quatuor dialogorum. MS. PrämonstratenserabteiSchlägl, Austria, codex 204, f. 1r–82v. Folio. Saec. 15.
Microfilm: MnCH proj. no. 3057

2863 Dialogi. MS. Vienna, Nationalbibliothek, codex 933. 177 f. Folio. Saec. 15.
Microfilm: MnCH proj. no. 14,246

2864 Dialogi. MS. Vienna, Nationalbibliothek, codex 972. 64 f. Folio. Saec. 15.
Microfilm: MnCH proj. no. 14,283

2865 Dialogi. MS. Vienna, Nationalbibliothek, codex 2843, f. 118r–179v. Folio. Saec. 15.
Microfilm: MnCH proj. no. 16,078

2866 Dialogi. MS. Vienna, Nationalbibliothek, codex 4382, f. 72r–131v. Folio. Saec. 15.
Microfilm: MnCH proj. no. 17,572

2867 Libri quatuor dialogorum. MS. Vienna, Schottenstift, codex 296, f. 52r–114r. Folio. Saec. 15.
Microfilm: MnCH proj. no. 4185

2868 Dialogi. Lingua germanica. MS. Universitätsbibliothek Innsbruck, Austria, codex 65, f. 1r–96r. Folio. Saec. 15.
Microfilm: MnCH proj. no. 28,146

2869 [Dialogi. German]
Libri quatuor dialogorum in linguam germanicam, versi a Johanne de Spira. MS. Benediktinerabtei Melk, Austria, codex 570, f. 1r–11r. Folio. Saec. 15.
Microfilm: MnCH proj. no. 1475

2870 [Dialogi. German]
Sand Gregori des Pabsts der stat zu Rom dy puecher der szwayerred. MS. Benediktinerabtei Melk, Austria, codex 220, f. 156v–237v. Folio. Saec. 15.
Microfilm: MnCH proj. no. 1261

2871 Dialogi, in linguam germanicam translati. MS. Vienna, Nationalbibliothek, codex 2672, f. 1r–85v. Folio. Saec. 15 (1453).
Microfilm: MnCH proj. no. 15,941

2872 Dialogi. Germanice. MS. Vienna, Nationalbibliothek, codex 3026, f. 75r–110r. Octavo. Saec. 15.
Microfilm: MnCH proj. no. 16,290

2873 Dialogi. Germanice. MS. Benediktinerinnenabtei Nonnberg, Salzburg, codex 28 D 8, f. 124r–232v. Folio. Saec. 15 (1459).
Microfilm: MnCH proj. no. 10,970

2874 Dialogorum libri. Germanice. MS. Benediktinerabtei St. Peter, Salzburg, codex b.VIII.31, f. 1r–120r. Folio. Saec. 15.
Microfilm: MnCH proj. no. 10,562

2875 [Dialogi. German]
Dialogorum moralium libri, in linguam germanicam translati. Finis deest. MS. Vienna, Nationalbibliothek, codex 12532. 226 f. Quarto. Saec. 15.
Microfilm: MnCH proj. no. 19,941

2876 [Dialogi. Old Slavonic]
De vitis et miraculis patrum italicorum deque animarum aeternitate dialogorum libri quatuor. Palaeoslavonice, dialecta bulgarica, litteris cyrillicis. MS. Vienna, Nationalbibliothek, codex slavonicus 22. 378 f. Folio.
Microfilm: MnCH proj. no. 24,145

2877 [Dialogi. Spanish]
Dialogo, romanzado por F. Gonzalo de Ocana. MS. Madrid, Spain, Real Academia de la Historia, codex 59, f. 1–93. Folio. Saec. 15.
Microfilm: MnCH proj. no. 34,915

2878 [Dialogi. Liber I. German]
Das erst buch der tzwier rede sand Gregorii des babstes der stat zu Rom. Opus

pertingit usque ad capitis noni initium. MS. Benediktinerabtei Melk, Austria, codex 1004, f. 108r–123v. Octavo. Saec. 15.
Microfilm: MnCH proj. no. 1797
Dialogi. Liber II. *See his* Vita s. Benedicti.

2879   Dialogi. Liber quartus. MS. Universitätsbibliothek Innsbruck, Austria, codex 357, f. 1r–42v. Octavo. Saec. 12.
Microfilm: MnCH proj. no. 28,392

2880   Dialogi. Liber quartus. MS. Vienna, Nationalbibliothek, codex 1057, f. 142v–158v. Quarto. Saec. 13.
Microfilm: MnCH proj. no. 14,357

2881   Dialogi. Liber quartus (fragmentum). MS. Benediktinerabtei Altenburg, Austria, codex AB 14 C 18, f. 309r–310v. Folio. Saec. 15.
Microfilm: MnCH proj. no. 6411

2882   Excerpta ex libro quarto Dialogorum. MS. Benediktinerabtei Melk, Austria, codex 625, f. 1r–5v. Quarto. Saec. 15.
Microfilm: MnCH proj. no. 1512

2883   [Dialogi. Liber IV. Armenian]
Vierte Buch der Dialog, übersetzt (into Armenian) von Nerses Lambronatsi. MS. Vienna, Mechitaristenkongregation, codex 33. 20 f. Quarto. 1852 (Abschrift).
Microfilm: MnCH proj. no. 7636

2884   [Dialogi. Liber IV. German]
Dialogi. Liber quartus. Germanice. MS. Benediktinerabtei Altenburg, Austria, codex AB 15 B 2, f. 162r–190r. Folio. Saec. 15.
Microfilm: MnCH proj. no. 6424

2885   Ecloga de Moralibus in Job. MS. Vienna, Nationalbibliothek, codex 921. 250 f. Folio. Saec. 9.
Microfilm: MnCH proj. no. 14,231

2886   [Epistolae]
Registrum epistolarum (a Gregorio ipso ordinatum). MS. Benediktinerabtei Admont, Austria, codex 40. 182 f. Folio. Saec. 11.
Microfilm: MnCH proj. no. 9132

2887   Epistolae nonnullae. MS. Benediktinerabtei Göttweig, Austria, codex 108, f. 131r–138r. Quarto. Saec. 12.
Microfilm: MnCH proj. no. 3390

2888   Epistolae. MS. Cistercienserabtei Heiligenkreuz, Austria, codex 230, f. 159r–168v. Folio. Saec. 12.
Microfilm: MnCH proj. no. 4763

2889   Epistolae sex. MS. Vienna, Nationalbibliothek, codex 469, f. 113v–120v. Folio. Saec. 12.
Microfilm: MnCH proj. no. 13,805

2890   Epistolarum libri XIV. MS. Salisbury, England, Cathedral Library, codex 94. 157 f. Quarto. Saec. 12.
Microfilm: MnCH

2891   Epistolae: ad Theodoricum et Theodebertum reges Francorum; ad Palladium presbyterum; ad Joannem abbatem; ad Cononem Lirensem abbatem; ad Brunichildem Francorum reginam; ad Maximianum episcopum Syracusanum; ad Theotistam patriciam. MS. Augustinerchorherrenstift Klosterneuburg, Austria, codex 703, f. 81v–146r. Folio. Saec. 12.
Microfilm: MnCH proj. no. 5682

2892   Epistolae. MS. Universitätsbibliothek Innsbruck, Austria, codex 234, f. 17r–24v. Folio. Saec. 14.
Microfilm: MnCH proj. no. 28,272

2893   Epistolae nonnullae. MS. Augustinerchorherrenstift Klosterneuburg, Austria, codex 236, f. 48r–86r. Folio. Saec. 14.
Microfilm: MnCH proj. no. 6204

2894   Epistolae sex. MS. Vienna, Nationalbibliothek, codex 414, f. 139r–147v. Folio. Saec. 14.
Microfilm: MnCH proj. no. 13,739

2895   Epistola ad Palladium. MS. Cava, Italy (Benedictine abbey), codex 6, f. 44v–45r. Quarto. Saec. 11.
Microfilm: MnCH

2896   Epistola ad Castorium episcopum Ariminensem. MS. Budapest, Hungary, Orszagos Szechenyi Könyvtar (Szecheny Library of the National Museum, codex 328, f. 64–65).
Microfilm: MnCH

2897   Epistola ad Reccardum regem Visigothorum, cum aliis collectis sententiis beati Gregorii. MS. Augustinchorherrenstift St. Florian, Austria, codex CI, 82, f. 5r–54r. Quarto. Saec. 12–13.
Microfilm: MnCH proj. no. 2339

2898   Ad Secundinum inclusum epistola. MS. Vienna, Nationalbibliothek, codex 1029, f. 227r–229v. Quarto. Saec. 11.
Microfilm: MnCH proj. no. 14,336

2899   De epistola beati Gregorii directa ad Secundinum dei servo (sic) de lapsu. MS. Salisbury, England, Cathedral Library, codex 9, f. 66v. Octavo. Saec. 12.
Microfilm: MnCH

2900   Epistola omnibus episcopis Angliae. MS. Lambeth Palace Library, London, codex 482, f. 41–42. Octavo. Saec. 15.
Microfilm: MnCH

2901   Ex septimo libro super illud: Et inventum vana profertis. MS. Benediktinerabtei

St. Peter, Salzburg, codex a.III.14, f. 213v–215v. Octavo. Saec. 15.
Microfilm: MnCH proj. no. 9952
Expositiones, Homiliae and Sermones are interfiled.

2902   [Homiliae. Index]
Index homiliarum Gregorii papae I. MS. Benediktinerabtei St. Peter, Salzburg, codex b.II.42, f. 245r–246r. Octavo. Saec. 16.
Microfilm: MnCH proj. no. 10,342

2903   Homiliae 40 de diversis lectionibus evangelii. MS. Benediktinerabtei Admont, Austria, codex 56. 177 f. Folio. Saec. 12.
Microfilm: MnCH proj. no. 9142

2904   Sermones de sanctis et festis. MS. Benediktinerabtei Altenburg, Austria, codex AB 13 C 1, f. 2r–86v. Quarto. Saec. 12.
Microfilm: MnCH proj. no. 6362

2905   Sermones Fulgentii, Ambrosii . . . beati Gregorii . . . MS. Hereford, England, Cathedral Library, codex P 8 vii. 178 f. Quarto. Saec. 12.
Microfilm: MnCH

2906   [Homiliae]
Gregorii sancti evangelii secundum Lucam quadraginta lectiones. MS. Hereford, England, Cathedral Library, codex 0 8 iii, f. 1–135. Folio. Saec. 12.
Microfilm: MnCH

2907   Homiliae quaedam. MS. Lambeth Palace Library, London, codex 345, f. 9–96. Quarto. Saec. 12–13.
Microfilm: MnCH

2908   Homiliae XL in evangelia. MS. Subiaco, Italy (Benedictine abbey), codex 252. 104 f. Quarto. Saec. 12.
Microfilm: MnCH

2908a   Homiliae. MS. Tortosa, Spain, Archivo de la Catedral, codex 106, f. 1r–106r. Quarto. Saec. 12.
Microfilm: MnCH proj. no. 30,676

2909   Homiliae. MS. Tortosa, Spain, Archivo de la Catedral, codex 223. 157 f. Quarto. Saec. 12–13.
Microfilm: MnCH proj. no. 30,789

2910   Homilae in evangelia. MS. Augustinerchorherrenstift Vorau, Austria, codex 336, f. 1r–242v. Quarto. Saec. 12.
Microfilm: MnCH proj. no. 7304

2911   Homiliae (40) in evangelia. MS. Vienna, Nationalbibliothek, codex 660, f. 1r–136r. Folio. Saec. 12.
Microfilm: MnCH proj. no. 13,991

2912   XL homiliae in evangelia. MS. Universitätsbibliothek Graz, Austria, codex 294, f. 1r–227v. Quarto. Saec. 13.
Microfilm: MnCH proj. no. 26,197

2913   Fragmenta ex homiliis et diversis sermonibus. MS. Cistercienserabtei Heiligenkreuz, Austria, codex 297, f. 42r–49v. Quarto. Saec. 13.
Microfilm: MnCH proj. no. 4837

2914   Homiliae XL in evangelia. MS. Hereford, England, Cathedral Library, codex 0 3 ix, f. 1–113. Quarto. Saec. 13.
Microfilm: MnCH

2915   Homiliae in evangelia. MS. Lambeth Palace Library, London, codex 96, f. 113–131. Quarto. Saec. 13.
Microfilm: MnCH

2916   Homiliae quadraginta in evangelia. MS. Benediktinerabtei Melk, Austria, codex 6, f. 1–127. Folio. Saec. 13.
Microfilm: MnCH proj. no. 1130

2917   Homiliae quadraginta in evangelia. MS. Benediktinerabtei Melk, Austria, codex 448, f. 1v–56v. Folio. Saec. 13.
Microfilm: MnCH proj. no. 1415

2918   Homiliae super evangelia. MS. Augustinerchorherrenstift St. Florian, Austria, codex XI, 17, f. 78r–142r. Folio. Saec. 13.
Microfilm: MnCH proj. no. 2272

2919   Homiliae. MS. Vienna, Nationalbibliothek, codex 1082, f. 107r–194v. Quarto. Saec. 13.
Microfilm: MnCH proj. no. 14,395

2920   Homiliae 40 de diversis lectionibus evangelii. MS. Benediktinerabtei Admont, Austria, codex 74. 95 f. Saec. 14.
Microfilm: MnCH proj. no. 9171

2921   Homiliae de diversis lectionibus evangelii. MS. Benediktinerabtei Admont, Austria, codex 319, f. 269r–307v. Folio. Saec. 14–15.
Microfilm: MnCH proj. no. 9390

2922   Homiliae in evangelia. MS. Benediktinerabtei Altenburg, Austria, codex AB 13 A 7, f. 1v–64v. Quarto. Saec. 14.
Microfilm: MnCH proj. no. 6382

2923   Homiliae 40. MS. Benediktinerabtei Göttweig, Austria, codex 130a, f. 62r–74r. Folio. Saec. 14.
Microfilm: MnCH proj. no. 3407

2924   Homiliae . . . super 50 omelias ex evangeliis et totidem lectionibus . . . MS. Augustinerchorherrenstift Herzogenburg, Austria, codex 52, f. 144r–207r. Folio. Saec. 14.
Microfilm: MnCH proj. no. 3205

2925   Homiliae in evangelia, 1–37. MS. Augustinerchorherrenstift Klosterneuburg, Austria, codex 241, f. 1r et 4r–145r. Folio. Saec. 14.
Microfilm: MnCH proj. no. 5211

2926   Homiliae in evangelia, I–X. MS. Augustinerchorherrenstift Klosterneuburg,

Austria, codex 489, f. 106r–126v. Folio. Saec. 14–15.
Microfilm: MnCH proj. no. 5477

2927 Omelie (40) Gregorii cum aliquibus aliis omeliis aliorum doctorum. MS. Benediktinerabtei Kremsmünster, Austria, codex 242, f. 1r–146r. Folio. Saec. 14.
Microfilm: MnCH proj. no. 14.

2928 Quadraginta omelie a beato Gregorio papa exposite. MS. Benediktinerabtei Kremsmünster, Austria, codex 239, f. 2r–144r. Saec. 14.
Microfilm: MnCH proj. no. 226

2929 Homiliae. MS. Cistercienserabtei Schlierbach, Austria, codex 6. 136 f. Folio. Saec. 14.
Microfilm: MnCH proj. no. 28,069

2930 Forty homilies of Gregory the Great, in two books (in Latin). MS. Salisbury, England, Cathedral Library, codex 55, f. 137–186. Quarto. Saec. 14.
Microfilm: MnCH

2931 Sermones. MS. Vienna, Nationalbibliothek, codex 732, f. 117r–178v. Folio. Saec. 14.
Microfilm: MnCH proj. no. 14,056

2932 Homiliae. MS. Vienna, Nationalbibliothek, codex 1427, f. 43r–99r. Folio. Saec. 14.
Microfilm: MnCH proj. no. 14,773

2933 Homiliae. MS. Vienna, Schottenstift, codex 299, f. 1r–145r. Folio. Saec. 14.
Microfilm: MnCH proj. no. 4188

2934 Homiliae. MS. Benediktinerabtei Admont, Austria, codex 206, f. 1r–74v. Folio. Saec. 15.
Microfilm: MnCH proj. no. 9296

2935 Homiliae XL. MS. Benediktinerabtei Göttweig, Austria, codex 247a, f. 1r–87r. Folio. Saec. 15.
Microfilm: MnCH proj. no. 3517

2936 XL homiliae in evangelia. MS. Universitätsbibliothek Graz, Austria, codex 985, f. 97r–217r. Quarto. Saec. 15.
Microfilm: MnCH proj. no. 27,050

2937 Homiliae in evangelia. MS. Cistercienserabtei Heiligenkreuz, Austria, codex 109. 149 f. Folio. Saec. 15.
Microfilm: MnCH proj. no. 4653

2938 Tractatus ex omeliis beati Gregorii. MS. Hereford, England, Cathedral Library, codex O 6 vii, f. 271–273. Quarto. Saec. 15.
Microfilm: MnCH

2939 Liber homeliarium. Incipit: Inter sacra missarum sollemnia . . . 40 lectiones exposui. MS. Klagenfurt, Austria, Studienbibliothek, codex cart. 48, f. 17r–69r. Folio. Saec. 15.
Microfilm: MnCH proj. no. 13,031

2940 Homiliae nonnullae. MS. Benediktinerabtei Lambach, Austria, codex chart. 102. Saec. 15.
Microfilm: MnCH proj. no. 523

2941 Homiliae 40 in evangelia. MS. Benediktinerabtei Melk, Austria, codex 135, f. 73–230. Folio. Saec. 15.
Microfilm: MnCH proj. no. 1202

2942 Homiliae 40 in evangelia. MS. Benediktinerabtei Melk, Austria, codex 336, f. 1–169. Folio. Saec. 15.
Microfilm: MnCH proj. no. 1344

2943 Homiliarius. Est compendium homiliarum S. Gregorii in evangelia. MS. Benediktinerabtei Melk, Austria, codex 615, f. 629–722. Quarto. Saec. 15.
Microfilm: MnCH proj. no. 1504

2944 Homilia 17. super evangelia. MS. Benediktinerabtei Melk, Austria, codex 1405, f. 33v–35v. Duodecimo. Saec. 15.
Microfilm: MnCH proj. no. 1926

2945 Homiliae quadraginta in evangelia. MS. Prämonstratenserabtei Schlägl, Austria, codex 86, f. 1r–108r. Folio. Saec. 15.
Microfilm: MnCH proj. no. 3061

2946 Homiliae in evangelia. MS. Toledo, Spain, Biblioteca del Cabildo, codex 11, 11. 65 f. Folio. Saec. 15.
Microfilm: MnCH proj. no. 33,039

2947 Homiliae quadraginta. MS. Vienna, Nationalbibliothek, codex 4172, f. 2v–76v. Folio. Saec. 15.
Microfilm: MnCH proj. no. 17,401

2948 Homiliae, quibus epistola Gregorii ad episcopum Taurominitanum praemissa est. MS. Vienna, Nationalbibliothek, codex 4358, f. 175r–270r. Folio. Saec. 15.
Microfilm: MnCH proj. no. 17,533

2949 Homiliae quadraginta super evangelia. MS. Vienna, Nationalbibliothek, codex 4411, f. 367v–482r. Folio. Saec. 15.
Microfilm: MnCH proj. no. 17,603

2950 Homiliarium in evangelia. MS. Vienna, Nationalbibliothek, codex 3987. 113 f. Folio. Saec. 15.
Microfilm: MnCH proj. no. 17,195

2951 Homiliae quadraginta. MS. Vienna, Nationalbibliothek, codex 4434, f. 2r–85r. Folio. Saec. 15.
Microfilm: MnCH proj. no. 17,621

2952 Homiliae quadraginta. MS. Vienna, Nationalbibliothek, codex 4456, f. 81v–187r. Folio. Saec. 15.
Microfilm: MnCH proj. no. 4456

2953 Homiliae in evangelia. MS. Vienna, Schottenstift, codex 25. 133 f. Folio. Saec. 15.
Microfilm: MnCH proj. no. 3874

2954 Homiliae. MS. Vienna, Schottenstift, codex 374, f. 263r–370v. Folio. Saec. 15.
Microfilm: MnCH proj. no. 4220

2955 Homiliae. MS. Cistercienserabtei Zwettl, Austria, codex 150, f. 1r–95r. Folio. Saec. 15.
Microfilm: MnCH proj. no. 6740

2956 Homilia ad populum habita in basilica S. Mariae, die sancto Paschae. MS. Vienna, Nationalbibliothek, codex 1190, f. 2v–3v. Folio. Saec. 9.
Microfilm: MnCH proj. no. 14,540

2957 Ex homelia de angelis. MS. Universitätsbibliothek Graz, Austria, codex 234. f. 243. Quarto. Saec. 13.
Microfilm: MnCH proj. no. 26,154

2958 Homilia de conversione Mariae Magdalenae. MS. Benediktinerabtei Kremsmünster, Austria, codex 97, f. 104r–106v. Saec. 14.
Microfilm: MnCH proj. no. 90

2959 Homilia de negligentia praelatorum in illud "Designavit." MS. Vienna, Nationalbibliothek, codex 4946, f. 135r–138v. Quarto. Saec. 15 (1481)
Microfilm: MnCH proj. no. 18,123

2960 Homiliae de tempore et de sanctis. MS. Cistercienserabtei Zwettl, Austria, codex 91. 117 f. Folio. Saec. 12.
Microfilm: MnCH proj. no. 6641

2961 Liber sextus in Cantica Canticorum, excerptus ex variis opusculis S. Gregorii papae. MS. Benediktinerabtei Göttweig, Austria, codex 37, f. 79v.–120v. Folio. Saec. 12.
Microfilm: MnCH proj. no. 3319

2962 Expositio in Cantica Canticorum. MS. Linz, Austria, Bundesstaatliche Studienbibliothek, codex 36, f. 91r–131r. Folio. Saec. 12.
Microfilm: MnCH proj. no. 27,901

2963 Super Cantica Canticorum. MS. Benediktinerabtei St. Peter, Salzburg, codex a.VII.8. 65 f. Quarto. Saec. 12.
Microfilm: MnCH proj. no. 10,144

2964 Expositio in Cantica Canticorum. MS. Cistercienserabtei Zwettl, Austria, codex 308, f. 1r–91v. Quarto. Saec. 12.
Microfilm: MnCH proj. no. 6887

2965 Expositio super Cantica Canticorum. MS. Universitätsbibliothek Innsbruck, Austria, codex 257, f. 92v–138v. Folio. Saec. 13.
Microfilm: MnCH proj. no. 28,286

2966 Super Cantica Canticorum. MS. Toledo, Spain, Biblioteca del Cabildo, codex 9, 7. 88 f. Octavo. Saec. 13.
Microfilm: MnCH proj. no. 32,978

2967 Expositio super Canticum Canticorum. MS. Augustinerchorherrenstift Vorau, Austria, codex 334, f. 68v–76r. Quarto. Saec. 13.
Microfilm: MnCH proj. no. 7308

2968 Liber sextus in Cantici Canticorum collationem. MS. Cistercienserabtei Zwettl, Austria, codex 101, f. 92v–99v. Folio. Saec. 13.
Microfilm: MnCH proj. no. 6687

2969 Relacio de Cantico Canticorum. MS. Benediktinerabtei Kremsmünster, Austria, codex 37, f. 1r–10v. Saec. 14.
Microfilm: MnCH proj. no. 37

2970 Expositio super Cantica Canticorum. MS. Benediktinerabtei Kremsmünster, Austria, codex 37, 10v–42r. Saec. 14.
Microfilm: MnCH proj. no. 37

2971 Expositio super Cantica Canticorum. MS. Benediktinerabtei Melk, Austria, codex 1237, f. 1r–56r. Quarto. Saec. 14.
Microfilm: MnCH proj. no. 1878

2972 Revelatio et expositio super Cantica Canticorum. MS. Augustinerchorherrenstift St. Florian, Austria, codex XI, 32, f. 228r–243v. Octavo. Saec. 14.
Microfilm: MnCH proj. no. 2291

2973 Super Cantica Canticorum. MS. Augustinerchorherrenstift St. Florian, Austria, codex XI, 80, f. 64r–79v. Folio. Saec. 14.
Microfilm: MnCH proj. no. 2338

2974 Expositio Cantici Canticorum. MS. Subiaco, Italy (Benedictine abbey), codex 229. 69 f. Saec. 14 (1398).
Microfilm: MnCH

2975 Super Canticum Canticorum. MS. Vienna, Nationalbibliothek, codex 905, f. 106r–131v. Folio. Saec. 14.
Microfilm: MnCH proj. no. 14,219

2976 Expositio super cantica. MS. Vienna, Nationalbibliothek, codex 4241, f. 52r–87v. Folio. Saec. 14.
Microfilm: MnCH proj. no. 17,426

2977 Expositio canticorum. MS. Cistercienserabtei Wilhering, Austria, codex IX, 25, f. 121r–152v. Folio. Saec. 14.
Microfilm: MnCH proj. no. 2801

2978 De Cantica Canticorum, etc. MS. Toledo, Spain, Biblioteca del Cabildo, codex 9, 8. 126 f. Duodecimo. Saec. 15.
Microfilm: MnCH proj. no. 32,979

2979 Expositio super Cantica Canticorum. MS. Cistercienserabtei Lilienfeld, Austria, codex 106, f. 118r–148v. Quarto. Saec. 15.
Microfilm: MnCH proj. no. 4405

2980 Expositio super Cantica Canticorum. MS. Subiaco, Italy (Benedictine abbey),

codex 282. 56 f. Palimsesti. Quarto. Saec. 15 (1418).
Microfilm: MnCH

2981 Expositio super Cantica Canticorum. MS. Vienna, Nationalbibliothek, codex 4413, f. 181r–226r. Folio. Saec. 15.
Microfilm: MnCH proj. no. 17,608

2982 Homilia super: Cum appropinquantes ad Jesus publicani et peccatores. MS. Benediktinerabtei Kremsmünster, Austria, codex 97, f. 109v–111v. Saec. 14.
Microfilm: MnCH proj. no. 90

2983 Homiliae in dominicas. MS. Benediktinerabtei Admont, Austria, codex 63. 198 f. Folio. Saec. 12.
Microfilm: MnCH proj. no. 9160

2984 Homiliae dominicales et festivales. MS. Benediktinerabtei Admont, Austria, codex 455. 126 f. Folio. Saec. 12.
Microfilm: MnCH proj. no. 9512

2985 Homilia habita ad episcopos in fontes Lateranensium. MS. Augustinerchorherrenstift Klosterneuburg, Austria, codex 464b, f. 299v–305r. Folio. Saec. 14.
Microfilm: MnCH proj. no. 5448

2986 Homilia in evangelium: Designavit Jesus et alios septuaginta duos. MS. Salzburg, Diöcesanseminar, codex Cm 221, f. 67–72. Quarto. Saec. 13.
Microfilm: MnCH proj. no. 11,648

2987 Homiliae in Ezechielem prophetam. MS. Madrid, Spain, Real Academia de la Historia, codex 38. 218 f. Folio. Saec. 9.
Microfilm: MnCH proj. no. 34,894

2988 Expositiones in Ezechielem prophetam. MS. Benediktinerabtei St. Peter, Salzburg, codex a.VII.3. 293 f. Quarto. Saec. 9 & 11.
Microfilm: MnCH proj. no. 10,134

2989 Homiliae in Ezechielem prophetam. MS. Vienna, Nationalbibliothek, codex 970. 133 f. Folio. Saec. 9.
Microfilm: MnCH proj. no. 14,280

2990 Homilia super Ezechielem (excerpta). MS. Vienna, Nationalbibliothek, codex 1003, f. 44r–144r. Folio. Saec. 9.
Microfilm: MnCH proj. no. 14,296

2991 Homilia nona in Ezechielem (fragmentum). MS. Vienna, Nationalbibliothek, codex 966, f. 27v–28r. Folio. Saec. 10.
Microfilm: MnCH proj. no. 14,277

2992 Homiliae in Ezechielem. MS. Benediktinerabtei Admont, Austria, codex 224. 166 f. Folio. Saec. 11.
Microfilm: MnCH proj. no. 9309

2993 Homiliae super Ezechielem prophetam. MS. Lambeth Palace Library, London, codex 96, f. 1–112. Quarto. Saec. 11.
Microfilm: MnCH

2994 Homiliae in Ezechielem. MS. Benediktinerabtei Admont, Austria, codex 276. 154 f. Folio. Saec. 12.
Microfilm: MnCH proj. no. 9360

2995 Homiliae in Ezechielem prophetam. Benediktinerabtei Göttweig, Austria, codex 45, f. 2r–149v. Folio. Saec. 12.
Microfilm: MnCH proj. no. 3332

2996 Homiliarium in Ezechielem prophetam. MS. Universitätsbibliothek Graz, Austria, codex 184. 200 f. Quarto. Saec. 12.
Microfilm: MnCH proj. no. 26,076

2997 Homiliae in Ezechielem. MS. Universitätsbibliothek Graz, Austria, codex 237. 182 f. Quarto. Saec. 12.
Microfilm: MnCH proj. no. 26,167

2998 Homiliae super Ezechielem XXIII–XXIV. MS. Cistercienserabtei Heiligenkreuz, Austria, codex 211, f. 102r–132v. Folio. Saec. 12–13.
Microfilm: MnCH proj. no. 4751

2999 Homiliae in Ezechielem. MS. Cistercienserabtei Heiligenkreuz, Austria, codex 195, f. 1v–115r. Folio. Saec. 12.
Microfilm: MnCH proj. no. 4737

3000 Homiliae in Ezechielem prophetam. Liber secundus. MS. Cistercienserabtei Heiligenkreuz, Austria, codex 205, f. 1r–85v. Folio. Saec. 12.
Microfilm: MnCH proj. no. 4745

3001 Homiliae super Ezechielem prophetam. MS. Hereford, England, Cathedral Library, codex P 6 i. 176 f. Quarto. Saec. 12.
Microfilm: MnCH

3002 Expositio super Ezechielem. MS. Augustinerchorherrenstift Klosterneuburg, Austria, codex 792. 93 f. Quarto. Saec. 12.
Microfilm: MnCH proj. no. 5781

3003 Homilia in Ezekielem. MS. Lincoln Cathedral Library, England, codex 89. Saec. 12.
Microfilm: MnCH

3004 Homiliae in Ezechielem prophetam. MS. Lambeth Palace Library, London, codex 144, f. 166–305. Octavo. Saec. 12.
Microfilm: MnCH

3005 Homilia super Ezechielem. MS. Lambath Palace Library, London, codex 240. 162 f. Quarto. Saec. 12.
Microfilm: MnCH

3006 Homiliae in Ezechielem. MS. Vich, Spain, Archivo Capitular, codex 25. 182 f. Folio. Saec. 12.
Microfilm: MnCH proj. no. 31,138

3007 Expositio super Ezechielem. MS. Nationalbibliothek, Vienna, codex 853. 125 f. Quarto. Saec. 12.
Microfilm: MnCH proj. no. 14,171

3008 Homiliae in Ezechielem. MS. Vienna, Nationalbibliothek, codex 937. 217 f. Folio. Saec. 12.
Microfilm: MnCH proj. no. 14,248

3009 Expositio super Ezechielem. MS. Vienna, Nationalbibliothek, codex 4413, f. 1r–172r. Folio. Saec. 12.
Microfilm: MnCH proj. no. 17,608

3010 Expositio super Ezechielem. MS. Cistercienserabtei Zwettl, Austria, codex 102, f. 2r–148v. Folio. Saec. 12.
Microfilm: MnCH proj. no. 6692

3011 Homiliae in Ezechielem. MS. Benediktinerabtei Admont, Austria, codex 121. 140 f. Folio. Saec. 13.
Microfilm: MnCH proj. no. 9219

3012 Super Ezechielem. MS. Universitätsbibliothek Graz, Austria, codex 521. 183 f. Folio. Saec. 13.
Microfilm: MnCH proj. no. 26,732

3013 Homiliarium in Ezechielem libri duo. MS. Benediktinerabtei Kremsmünster, Austria, codex 333, f. 1r–95v. Saec. 13.
Microfilm: MnCH proj. no. 333

3014 Super Ezechielem. MS. Benediktinerabtei Lambach, Austria, codex membr. 110. 59 f. Saec. 13.
Microfilm: MnCH proj. no. 807

3015 Homiliae (numero 22) in tria priora capita et finem Ezechielis prophetae. MS. Cistercienserabtei Lilienfeld, Austria, codex 42, f. 14–117v. Quarto. Saec. 13.
Microfilm: MnCH proj. no. 4352

3016 Homiliae quadraginta in Ezechielem prophetam. MS. Benediktinerabtei Melk, Austria, codex 448, f. 57r–101v. Folio. Saec. 13.
Microfilm: MnCH proj. no. 1415

3017 In Ezechielem prophetam. MS. Toledo, Spain, Biblioteca del Cabildo, codex 9, 6. 97 f. Quarto. Saec. 13.
Microfilm: MnCH proj. no. 32,977

3018 Super Ezechielem prophetam. MS. Toledo, Spain, Biblioteca del Cabildo, codex 11, 6. 104 f. Folio. Saec. 13.
Microfilm: MnCH proj. no. 33,034

3019 In Ezequielem prophetam. Item, Homiliae XL in evangelia. MS. Barcelona, Spain, Archivo de la Catedral, codex 9. 196 f. Folio. Saec. 14?
Microfilm: MnCH proj. no. 30,280

3020 Expositio in Ezechielem prophetam (10 homiliae). MS. Madrid, Spain, Real Academia de la Historia, codex 23, f. 40–167. Folio. Saec. 14.
Microfilm: MnCH proj. no. 34,879

3021 Expositio super Ezechielem prophetam. MS. Benediktinerabtei Melk, Austria,

codex 1269. 383 f. Duodecimo. Saec. 14.
Microfilm: MnCH proj. no. 1894

3022 Homeliae in Ezechielem. MS. Subiaco, Italy (Benedictine abbey), codex 106. 104 f. Quarto. Saec. 14.
Microfilm: MnCH

3023 Homiliae in Ezechielem. MS. Tarazona, Spain, Archivo de la Catedral, codex 38. 143 f. Folio. Saec. 14.
Microfilm: MnCH proj. no. 32,617

3024 Homiliae in Ezechielem prophetam. MS. Toledo, Spain, Biblioteca del Cabildo, codex 9, 5. 127 f. Folio. Saec. 14.
Microfilm: MnCH proj. no. 32,976

3025 Super Ezechielem. MS. Toledo, Spain, Biblioteca del Cabildo, codex 11, 7. 235 f. Folio. Saec. 14.
Microfilm: MnCH proj. no. 33,035

3026 Super Ezechielem. MS. Vienna, Nationalbibliothek, codex 905, f. 1r–106r. Folio. Saec. 14.
Microfilm: MnCH proj. no. 14,219

3027 Homiliae super Ezechielem. MS. Universitätsbibliothek Innsbruck, Austria, codex 98, f. 2r–126r. Folio. Saec. 15.
Microfilm: MnCH proj. no. 28,182

3028 Commentarium super Ezechielem. MS. Benediktinerabtei St. Paul im Lavanttal, Austria, codex 16/4, pars I. Folio. Saec. 15.
Microfilm: MnCH proj. no. 12,250

3029 Homiliae in Ezechielem prophetam. Libri duo. MS. Prämonstratenserabtei Schlägl, Austria, codex 66, f. 1r–145v. Folio. Saec. 15.
Microfilm: MnCH proj. no. 3035

3030 Super Ezechielem et Dialogi. MS. Toledo, Spain, Biblioteca del Cabildo, codex 11, 8. 250 f. Folio. Saec. 15.
Microfilm: MnCH proj. no. 35,036

3031 Homiliae in Ezechielem prophetam. MS. Vienna, Nationalbibliothek, codex 3980, f. 1r–130r. Folio. Saec. 15.
Microfilm: MnCH proj. no. 17,196

3032 Expositiones et homiliae super Ezechielem. MS. Vienna, Nationalbibliothek, codex 4232, f. 1r–81r. Folio. Saec. 15.
Microfilm: MnCH proj. no. 17,427

3033 Homiliae in Ezechielem. MS. Vienna, Nationalbibliothek, codex 4610, f. 1r–142r. Folio. Saec. 15.
Microfilm: MnCH proj. no. 17,788

3034 Homiliae super Ezechielem. MS. Vienna, Nationalbibliothek, codex 13670, f. 1r–221r. Quarto. Saec. 15 (1423).
Microfilm: MnCH proj. no. 20,114

3035 Sermo de officio sacerdotum. MS. Vienna, Nationalbibliothek, codex 4947, f. 149r–154r. Quarto. Saec. 15.
Microfilm: MnCH proj. no. 14,472

3036   Sermo de ordinibus angelorum. MS. Universitätsbibliothek Innsbruck, Austria, codex 357, f. 53v–64v. Octavo. Saec. 12.
Microfilm: MnCH proj. no. 28,392

3037   Homiliae in Lucam, a XXI ad XL. MS. Barcelona, Spain, Archivo de la Catedral, codex 120. 315 f. Folio. Saec.?
Microfilm: MnCH proj. no. 30,389

3038   Homiliae (40) super Matthaeum. MS. Diöcesanbibliothek St. Pölten, Austria, codex 32, f. 1r–111v. Folio. Saec. 15.
. Microfilm: MnCH proj. no. 6272

3039   Expositiones in Parabolas, Ecclesiasten, Sapientiam, Josue, Judices, Reges, Numeros, Exodum, Jesum Syrach. MS. Tortosa, Spain, Archivo de la Catedral, codex 103. 112 f. Octavo. Saec. 12.
Microfilm: MnCH proj. no. 30,673

3040   Super septem psalmos poenitentiales. MS. Toledo, Spain, Biblioteca del Cabildo, codex 11, 9. 176 f. Folio. Saec. 15.
Microfilm: MnCH proj. no. 33,037

3041   Super septem psalmos poenitentiales. MS. Toledo, Spain, Biblioteca del Cabildo, codex 11, 10. 67 f. Folio. Saec. 15.
Microfilm: MnCH proj. no. 33,038

3042   Expositio in primum librum Regum. MS. Cava, Italy (Benedictine abbey), codex 9. 269 f. Folio. Saec. 11–12
Microfilm: MnCH

3043   Expositio in libris Sapientialibus (Proverbia, Ecclesiastes, Sapientia et Ecclesiasticus). MS. Cava, Italy (Benedictine abbey), codex 6, f. 50–80. Quarto. Saec. 11.
Microfilm: MnCH

3044   Expositio in S. Scripturam. MS. Cava, Italy (Benedictine abbey), codex 11, f. 1–122. Folio. Saec. 12.
Microfilm: MnCH

3045   Expositio super Trenos. MS. Universitätsbibliothek Innsbruck, Austria, codex 98, f. 126v–139r.
Microfilm: MnCH proj. no. 28,182

3046   Homilia in vigilia nativitatis Domini. MS. Vienna, Nationalbibliothek, codex 1255, f. 43r–43v. Folio. Saec. 14.
Microfilm: MnCH proj. no. 14,599

3047   Sermo super: Consumpta est caro ejus a suppliciis. MS. Benediktinerabtei St. Peter, Salzburg, codex b.V.39, f. 144r–153v. Quarto. Saec. 15.
Microfilm: MnCH proj. no. 10,461

3048   Sermo super: Ipse est rex super. MS. Benediktinerabtei St. Peter, Salzburg, codex b.V.39, f. 159r–165r. Quarto. Saec. 15.
Microfilm: MnCH proj. no. 10,461

3049   Homilia versibus latinis. Incipit: Christicole miseri. MS. Vienna, Nationalbibliothek, codex 898, f. 49v–50r. Octavo. Saec. 14–15.
Microfilm: MnCH proj. no. 14,215

3050   Illuminatio animae, ex libris Moralium. MS. Madrid, Spain, Real Academia de la Historia, codex 86. 268 f. Folio. Saec. 14.
Microfilm: MnCH proj. no. 34,942

3051   Legenda de S. Scholastica. MS. Benediktinerabtei St. Peter, Salzburg, codex a.VI.46, f. 79r–87v. Quarto. Saec. 15.
Microfilm: MnCH proj. no. 10,119

3052   Libellus de conflictu viciorum atque virtutum. MS. Salisbury, England, Cathedral Library, codex 97, f. 74–77. Quarto. Saec. 13.
Microfilm: MnCH

3053   Libellus in opusculum de tractatione actionis Missarum sanctorum patrum Cypriani, Ambrosii, Gregorii . . . MS. Cistercienserabtei Heiligenkreuz, Austria, codex 193. 116 f. Folio. Saec. 13.
Microfilm: MnCH proj. no. 4731

3054   Liber de conflictu vitiorum et virtutum. MS. Vienna, Schottenstift, codex 187, f. 64r–69v. Octavo. Saec. 14.
Microfilm: MnCH proj. no. 4089

3055   [Moralia in Job. Index]
Registrum super libros Moralium Gregorii Magni, factum in monasterio Lambacensi. MS. Benediktinerabtei Göttweig, Austria, codex 465a, f. 2r–80v. Quarto. Saec. 15.
Microfilm: MnCH proj. no. 3720

3056   Libri morales in Job. MS. Vich, Spain, Archivo Capitular, codex 26. 302 f. Folio. Saec. 10–11.
Microfilm: MnCH proj. no. 31,104

3057   Moralia in Job. Lib. 6–10. MS. Benediktinerabtei Admont, Austria, codex 374. 154 f. Folio. Saec. 11.
Microfilm: MnCH proj. no. 9440

3058   Moralia in Job. Lib. 17–22. MS. Benediktinerabtei Admont, Austria, codex 375. 139 f. Folio. Saec. 11.
Microfilm: MnCH proj. no. 9444

3059   Moralia in Job. Lib. 24–27. MS. Benediktinerabtei Admont, Austria, codex 378. 132 f. Folio. Saec. 11.
Microfilm: MnCH proj. no. 9446

3060   Moralia in Job. Lib. 6–10. MS. Benediktinerabtei Admont, Austria, codex 391. 130 f. Quarto. Saec. 11.
Microfilm: MnCH proj. no. 9467

3061   Moralia in Job. Lib. 1–6. MS. Benediktinerabtei Admont, Austria, codex 555. 200 f. Quarto. Saec. 11.
Microfilm: MnCH proj. no. 9598

3062 Expositio in librum Job. MS. Barcelona, Spain, Archivo de la Catedral, codex 102. 448 f. Folio. Saec. 11.
Microfilm: MnCH proj. no. 30,372

3063 Moralia in Job. Pars IV. MS. Cava, Italy (Benedictine abbey), codex 7, f. 1–136. Folio. Saec. 11.
Microfilm: MnCH

3064 Moralia in Job. Lib. XXVIII usque ad finem. MS. Benediktinerabtei Göttweig, Austria, codex 31, f. 2r–207v. Folio. Saec. 11.
Microfilm: MnCH proj. no. 3329

3065 Moralia in Job. MS. Madrid, Spain, Real Academia de la Historia, codex 5. 181 f. Folio. Saec. 11.
Microfilm: MnCH proj. no. 34,861

3066 Moralia in Job. MS. Benediktinerabtei St. Peter, Salzburg, codex a.X.24–27. 6 vols. Folio. Saec. 11.
Microfilm: MnCH proj. no. 10,226; 10,229; 10,257; 10,258; 10,259; 10,261

3067 Moralia in Job. Liber XXIII. MS. Subiaco, Italy (Benedictine abbey), codex 5. Folio. Saec. 11.
Microfilm: MnCH

3068 Moralia in Job. Lib. 17–35. MS. Vienna, Nationalbibliothek, codex 677. 305 f. Folio. Saec. 11.
Microfilm: MnCH proj. no. 14,001

3069 Compendium Moralium in Job. MS. Vienna, Nationalbibliothek, codex 860. 157 f. Quarto. Saec. 11.
Microfilm: MnCH proj. no. 14,170

3070 Moralia in Job. Lib. 28– MS. Benediktinerabtei Admont, Austria, codex 171. 184 f. Folio. Saec. 12.
Microfilm: MnCH proj. no. 9256

3071 Moralia in Job. Lib. 28–35. MS. Benediktinerabtei Admont, Austria, codex 258. 212 f. Folio. Saec. 12.
Microfilm: MnCH proj. no. 9336

3072 Moralia in Job. Lib. 11–16. MS. Benediktinerabtei Admont, Austria, codex 262. 121 f. Folio. Saec. 12.
Microfilm: MnCH proj. no. 9345

3073 Moralia in Job. Lib. 1–5. MS. Benediktinerabtei Admont, Austria, codex 279. 136 f. Folio. Saec. 12.
Microfilm: MnCH proj. no. 9359

3074 Moralia in Job. Lib. 11–15. MS. Benediktinerabtei Admont, Austria, codex 477. 106 f. Folio. Saec. 12.

3075 Moralia in Job. Lib. 17–22. MS. Benediktinerabtei Admont, Austria, codex 293. 149 f. Quarto. Saec. 12.
Microfilm: MnCH proj. no. 9400

3076 Moralia in Job. Lib. 24–27. MS. Benediktinerabtei Admont, Austria, codex 476. 125 f. Folio. Saec. 12.
Microfilm: MnCH proj. no. 9534

3077 Moralia in Job. Lib. XVII–XXII. MS. Benediktinerabtei Göttweig, Austria, codex 46. 123 f. Folio. Saec. 12.
Microfilm: MnCH proj. no. 3334

3078 Moralia in Job. Lib. 1–22. MS. Universitätsbibliothek Graz, Austria, codex 148. 2 vols. Folio. Saec. 13.
Microfilm: MnCH proj. no. 26,066; 26,083

3079 Moralia in Job. Lib. 23–35. MS. Universitätsbibliothek Graz, Austria, codex 380. 219 f. Folio. Saec. 12.
Microfilm: MnCH proj. no. 26,313

3080 Moralia in Job. MS. Hereford, England, Cathedral Library, codex O 5 v. 323 f. Quarto. Saec. 12.
Microfilm: MnCH

3081 Moralia in Job. MS. Hereford, England, Cathedral Library, codex P 6 xi. 208 f. Quarto. Saec. 12.
Microfilm: MnCH

3082 Moralia in Job. Lib. 6–35. MS. Augustinerchorherrenstift Klosterneuburg, Austria, codex 231, 232, 237. Folio. Saec. 12.
Microfilm: MnCH proj. no. 5200, 5203, 5206

3083 Moralia in Job. Lib. XI–XXII. MS. Benediktinerabtei Kremsmünster, Austria, codex 331. 239 f. Saec. 12.
Microfilm: MnCH proj. no. 327

3084 Moralia in Job. Lib. XXIII–XXXV. MS. Benediktinerabtei Kremsmünster, Austria, codex 332. 286 f. Saec. 12.
Microfilm: MnCH proj. no. 329

3085 Moralia in Job. Lib. 1–32. MS. Benediktinerabtei Lambach, Austria, cod. membr. 44–49. 6 vols. Saec. 12.
Microfilm: MnCH proj. no. 778–783

3086 Moralia in Job. Lib. I–III. MS. Lincoln Cathedral Library, England, cod. 74–76. Quarto. Saec. 12.
Microfilm: MnCH

3087 Moralia in Job (excerpta). MS. Lincoln Cathedral Library, England, codex 196. 178 f. Octavo. Saec. 12.
Microfilm: MnCH

3088 Moralia in Job. Pars I et II. MS. Linz, Austria, Bundesstaatliche Studienbibliothek. codex 127 et 95. 151 et 122 f. Folio. Saec. 12.
Microfilm: MnCH proj. no. 27,945 & 27, 949

3089   Moralia in Job. MS. Lambeth Palace Library, London, codex 56. 236 f. Quarto. Saec. 12.
Microfilm: MnCH

3090   Moralia in Job. Lib. 6–10, MS. Lambeth Palace Library, London, codex 109. 50 f. Quarto. Saec. 12.
Microfilm: MnCH

3091   Moralia in Job. Lib. 11–22. MS. Lambeth Palace Library, London, codex 152. 226 f. Quarto. Saec. 12.
Microfilm: MnCH

3092   Expositio in librum Job. MS. Madrid, Spain, Real Academia de la Historia, codex 1. 240 f. Folio. Saec. 12–13.
Microfilm: MnCH proj. no. 34,857

3093   Moralia in Job. Pars I–IV, VI,1. MS. Augustinerchorherrenstift St. Florian, Austria, codex XI,14,t.1–5. 5 vols. Folio. Saec. 12.
Microfilm: MnCH proj. no. 2263–2267

3094   Moralia in Job. MS. Toledo, Spain, Biblioteca del Cabildo, codex 11,4. Folio. Saec. 12?
Microfilm: MnCH proj. no. 33,609

3095   Moralia in Job. Lib. 11–22. MS. Tortosa, Spain, Archivo de la Catedral, codex 30. 198 f. Folio. Saec. 12.
Microfilm: MnCH proj. no. 30,603

3096   Moralia in Job. Lib. 1–22. MS. Vienna, Nationalbibliothek, codex 673–674. 2 vols. Folio. Saec. 12.
Microfilm: MnCH proj. no. 14,009 & 14,012

3097   Moralia in Job. Lib. 23–35. Vienna, Nationalbibliothek, cod. 675–676. 2 vols. Folio. Saec. 12.
Microfilm: MnCH proj. no. 13,998–99

3098   Moralia in Job. Pars II, lib. 6, et pars III. MS. Vienna, Nationalbibliothek, codex 696. 210 f. Folio. Saec. 12.
Microfilm: MnCH proj. no. 14,022

3099   Moralia in Job. Lib. 27–35. MS. Vienna, Nationalbibliothek, codex 697. 169 f. Folio. Saec. 12.
Microfilm: MnCH proj. no. 14,021

3100   Moralia in Job. Lib. 1–10. MS. Augustinerchorherrenstift Vorau, Austria, codex 4/1. 274 f. Folio. Saec. 12.
Microfilm: MnCH proj. no. 7039

3101   Moralia in Job. Lib. 11–22. MS. Augustinerchorherrenstift Vorau, Austria, codex 4/2. 238 f. Folio. Saec. 12.
Microfilm: MnCH proj. no. 7392

3102   Moralia in Job. Lib. 23–27. MS. Augustinerchorherrenstift Vorau, Austria, codex 341. 129 f. Quarto. Saec. 12.
Microfilm: MnCH proj. no. 7312

3103   Moralia in Job. Lib. 23–35. MS. Cistercienserabtei Zwettl, Austria, codex 22, f. 2v–180r. Folio. Saec. 12.
Microfilm: MnCH proj. no. 6616

3104   Moralia in Job. Lib. 11–22. MS. Cistercienserabtei Zwettl, Austria, codex 44, f. 2v–195r. Folio. Saec. 12.
Microfilm: MnCH proj. no. 6637

3105   Moralia in Job. Pars IV. MS. Cava, Italy (Benedictine abbey), codex 10. 180 f. Folio. Saec. 13.
Microfilm: MnCH

3106   Moralia in Job. Pars II. MS. Cava, Italy (Benedictine abbey), codex 8. 227 f. Folio. Saec. 13.
Microfilm: MnCH

3107   Moralia in Job. Lib. 1–22. MS. Universitätsbibliothek Graz, Austria, codex 414. 413 f. Folio. Saec. 13.
Microfilm: MnCH proj. no. 27,131

3108   [Moralia in Job]
Alcuini [Adalberti] Speculum (an anthology from the Moralia of Gregory). MS. Hereford, England, Cathedral Library, codex 0 2 xi. 170 f. Quarto. Saec. 13.
Microfilm: MnCH

3109   Moralia in Job. Lib 27–35. MS. Cistercienserabtei Heiligenkreuz, Austria, codex 37, f. 2v–156v. Folio. Saec. 13.
Microfilm: MnCH proj. no. 4582

3110   Moralia in Job. Lib. 6–16. MS. Cistercienserabtei Heiligenkreuz, Austria, codex 46, f. 1r–164v. Folio. Saec. 13.
Microfilm: MnCH proj. no. 4599

3111   Moralia in Job. Lib. 1–5. MS. Cistercienserabtei Heiligenkreuz, Austria, codex 146. 118 f. Folio. Saec. 13.
Microfilm: MnCH proj. no. 4690

3112   Moralia in Job. Lib. 1–5. MS. Augustinerchorherrenstift Klosterneuburg, Austria, codex 239, f. 14–126v. Folio. Saec. 13.
Microfilm: MnCH proj. no. 5210

3113   Moralia in Job. Lib. 6–10. MS. Benediktinerabtei Kremsmünster, Austria, codex 330, f. 123r–260r. Saec. 13.
Microfilm: MnCH proj. no. 324

3114   Explanatio moralis in Job. 5 vols. MS. Cistercienserabtei Lilienfeld, Austria, cod. 141, 162, 163, 168, 246. Folio. Saec. 13.
Microfilm: MnCH proj. no. 4439, 4454, 4456, 4461, 4504

3115   Moralia in Job. Lib. I–V. MS. Benediktinerabtei Melk, Austria, codex 241. 124 f. Folio. Saec. 13.
Microfilm: MnCH proj. no. 1275

3116   Moralia in Job. Lib. XVII–XXII. MS. Benediktinerabtei Melk, Austria, codex

438. Folio. Saec. 13.
Microfilm: MnCH proj. no. 1404

3117 Moralia in Job. Pars ultima, nempe lib. 28–35. MS. Benediktinerabtei Melk, Austria, codex 1864. 135 f. Folio. Saec. 13.
Microfilm: MnCH proj. no. 2159

3118 Moralia in Job. Lib. 11–16. MS. Vienna, Nationalbibliothek, codex 711. 86 f. Folio. Saec. 13.
Microfilm: MnCH proj. no. 14,029

3119 Moralia in Job. Lib. 26–35. MS. Benediktinerabtei Admont, Austria, codex 169. 209 f. Folio. Saec. 14.
Microfilm: MnCH proj. no. 9252

3120 Moralia in Job. Lib. 23– MS. Benediktinerabtei Admont, Austria, codex 170. 255 f. Folio. Saec. 14.
Microfilm: MnCH proj. no. 9254

3121 [Moralia in Job. Index]
Indices duo super libros (1–35) Moralium sancti Gregorii. MS. Benediktinerabtei Altenburg, Austria, codex AB 15 B 11, f. 90r–158r. Folio. Saec. 14.
Microfilm: MnCH proj. no. 6403

3122 Moralia in Job. Lib. 1–5. MS. Universitätsbibliothek Graz, Austria, codex 478. 133 f. Folio. Saec. 14.
Microfilm: MnCH proj. no. 26,643

3123 Moralia in Job. Lib. 19–35. MS. Augustinerchorherrenstift Klosterneuburg, Austria, codex 238. 219 f. Folio. Saec. 14.
Microfilm: MnCH proj. no. 5208

3124 Moralia in Job. Lib. 1–18. MS. Augustinerchorherrenstift Klosterneuburg, Austria, codex 240. 246 f. Folio. Saec. 14.
Microfilm: MnCH proj. no. 5209

3125 Moralia in Job. MS. Salisbury, England, Cathedral Library, codex 33. 497 f. Quarto. Saec. 14.
Microfilm: MnCH

3126 Moralia in Job. MS. Subiaco, Italy (Benedictine abbey), codex 40. 396 f. Folio. Saec. 14.
Microfilm: MnCH

3127 Moralia in Job. MS. Subiaco, Italy (Benedictine abbey), codex 291. 142 & 144 f. Octavo. Saec. 14.
Microfilm: MnCH

3128 Moralium libri in librum Job. MS. Tarazona, Spain, Archivo de la Catedral, codex 108. 320 f. Folio. Saec. 14.
Microfilm: MnCH proj. no. 32,687

3129 Moralia in Job. MS. Toledo, Spain, Biblioteca del Cabildo, codex 9,12. 442 f. Folio. Saec. 14.
Microfilm: MnCH proj. no. 32,983

3130 Moralia in Job. Lib. 4–6. MS. Universitätsbibliothek Innsbruck, Austria, codex

104. 308 f. Folio. Saec. 15.
Microfilm: MnCH proj. no. 28,184

3131 Moralia in Job. Lib. 1–35. MS. Benediktinerabtei Lambach, Austria, codex chart. 158–159. 2 vols. Saec. 15.
Microfilm: MnCH proj. no. 575–576

3132 Moralia in Job. Lib. 6–10. MS. Benediktinerabtei Melk, Austria, codex 26. 141 f. Folio. Saec. 15.
Microfilm: MnCH proj. no. 1131

3133 Moralia in Job. Libri XXXV. MS. Benediktinerabtei Melk, Austria, codex 317. 582 f. Folio. Saec. 15.
Microfilm: MnCH proj. no. 1325

3134 Moralia in Job. Lib. XI–XVI. MS. Benediktinerabtei Melk, Austria, codex 455. 126 f. Saec. 15.
Microfilm: MnCH proj. no. 1421

3135 Moralia in Job. Lib. XXIII–XXVII. MS. Benediktinerabtei Melk, Austria, codex 465. 92 f. Folio. Saec. 15.
Microfilm: MnCH proj. no. 1430

3136 Moralia in Job. Lib. 35. Incipit: Sed quia ad ostendandam virtutem obedientiae. MS. Benediktinerabtei St. Peter, Salzburg, codex b.V.39, f. 165r–168r. Quarto. Saec. 15.
Microfilm: MnCH proj. no. 10,461

3137 Moralia in Job. Lib. 24–35. MS. Benediktinerabtei St. Paul im Lavanttal, Austria, codex 144/4, pars I. Folio. Saec. 15.
Microfilm: MnCH proj. no. 12,388

3138 Moralia in Job. MS. Benediktinerabtei St. Paul im Lavanttal, Austria, codex 148/4. 423 f. Folio. Saec. 15 (1447).
Microfilm: MnCH proj. no. 12,397

3139 Moralia sive Expositio in librum Job. Vol. I–II. MS. Prämonstratenserabtei Schlägl, Austria, codex 174 & 176. 264 & 285 f. Folio. Saec. 15.
Microfilm: MnCH proj. no. 2949 & 2951

3140 Moralia sive Expositio in librum Job. MS. Benediktinerabtei Seitenstetten, Austria, codex 175 & 176. 235 & 308 f. Folio. Saec. 15.
Microfilm: MnCH proj. no. 985 & 987

3141 Moralia in Job. Tortosa, Spain, Archivo de la Catedral, codex 146. 346 f. Folio. Saec. 15.
Microfilm: MnCH proj. no. 30,715

3142 Moralia in Job. Lib. 1–18, cum indice duplici, alphabetico et chronologico. MS. Vienna, Nationalbibliothek, codex 3941. 316 f. Folio. Saec. 15.
Microfilm: MnCH proj. no. 17,151

3143 Moralia in Job. Lib. 1–16. MS. Vienna, Nationalbibliothek, codex 3958. 242 f. Folio. Saec. 15.
Microfilm: MnCH proj. no. 17,186

3144   Moralia in Job. Lib. 1–28, cum indice. MS. Vienna, Nationalbibliothek, codex 4170. 357 f. Folio. Saec. 15.
Microfilm: MnCH proj. no. 17,357

3145   Moralia in Job. MS. Vienna, Schottenstift, cod. 26–27. 2 vols. Folio. Saec. 15.
Microfilm: MnCH proj. no. 3875 & 3877

3146   Moralia in Job. Lib. 1–35 (2 vols.). MS. Cistercienserabtei Neukloster, Wiener-Neustadt, Austria, codex B 17 & B 18. 221 & 257 f. Folio. Saec. 15.
Microfilm: MnCH proj. no. 4938 & 4939

3147   Oratio ad plebem de mortalitate. MS. Augustinerchorherrenstift Vorau, Austria, codex 336, f. 94r–95r. Quarto. Saec. 12.
Microfilm: MnCH proj. no. 7304

3148   Orationes et excerptum. MS. Vienna, Schottenstift, codex 405, f. 249r–250v. Octavo. Saec. 15.
Microfilm: MnCH proj. no. 4148

3149   Proverbia ex Gregorii Moralia in Job. MS. Vienna, Nationalbibliothek, codex 1054, f. 24v–25r. Quarto. Saec. 12.
Microfilm: MnCH proj. no. 14,368

3150   Quaedam proverbiorum loca explanata. MS. Vienna, Nationalbibliothek, codex 792, f. 9r–13r. Quarto. Saec. 12.
Microfilm: MnCH proj. no. 14,114

3151   Regaredo regi Visigothorum. MS. Cistercienserabtei Zwettl, Austria, codex 237, f. 28r–32v. Quarto. Saec. 12.
Microfilm: MnCH proj. no. 6837

3152   Regula pastoralis. MS. Augustinerchorherrenstift St. Florian, Austria, codex III, 222,B, f.2r–123r. Octavo. Saec. 9.
Microfilm: MnCH proj. no. 2246

3153   Regula pastoralis. Cap. II. MS. Vienna, Nationalbibliothek, codex 949. 115 f. Folio. Saec. 10
Microfilm: MnCH proj. no. 14,276

3154   Regulae pastoralis liber. MS. Cava, Italy (Benedictine abbey), codex 6, f.1–44. Quarto. Saec. 11.
Microfilm: MnCH

3155   Liber pastoralis. MS. Benediktinerabtei Göttweig, Austria, codex 83a. 104 f. Quarto. Saec. 11.
Microfilm: MnCH proj. no. 3364

3156   Liber pastoralis. MS. Barcelona, Spain, Archivo de la Catedral, codex 29. 66 f. Saec. 12?
Microfilm: MnCH proj. no. 38,299

3157   Liber pastoralis. MS. Benediktinerabtei Göttweig, Austria, codex 99, f.1r–77v. Folio. Saec. 12.
Microfilm: MnCH proj. no. 3379

3158   Liber pastoralis curae. MS. Cistercienserabtei Heiligenkreuz, Austria, codex 231. 113 f. Folio. Saec. 12.
Microfilm: MnCH proj. no. 4774

3159   Liber pastoralis curae. MS. Cistercienserabtei Heiligenkreuz, Austria, codex 287. 61 f. Octavo. Saec. 12.
Microfilm: MnCH proj. no. 4830

3160   Regula pastoralis. MS. Klagenfurt, Austria, Studienbibliothek, codex perg. 32. 76 f. Octavo. Saec. 12–13.
Microfilm: MnCH proj. no. 12,971

3161   Liber regulae pastoralis. MS. Augustinerchorherrenstift Klosterneuburg, Austria, codex 793, f.1v–90v. Quarto. Saec. 12.
Microfilm: MnCH proj. no. 5783

3162   Liber pastoralis curae. MS. Lambeth Palace Library, London, codex 218, f.3v–88v. Quarto. Saec. 12.
Microfilm: MnCH

3163   Liber de cura pastorali, scriptus ad Johannem episcopum. MS. Benediktinerabtei Melk, Austria, codex 252. 83 f. Folio. Saec. 12.
Microfilm: MnCH proj. no. 1286

3164   Regula pastoralis. MS. Vienna, Nationalbibliothek, codex 772, f.1r–88r. Folio. Saec. 12.
Microfilm: MnCH proj. no. 14,093

3165   Liber curae pastoralis. MS. Vienna, Nationalbibliothek, codex 786. 82 f. Folio. Saec. 12.
Microfilm: MnCH proj. no. 14,102

3166   Liber de cura pastorali. Finis deest. MS. Vienna, Nationalbibliothek, codex 796. 110 f. Quarto. Saec. 12.
Microfilm: MnCH proj. no. 14,147

3167   Regula pastoralis. MS. Vienna, Nationalbibliothek, codex 3599, f.16r–107r. Quarto. Saec. 12.
Microfilm: MnCH proj. no. 20,832

3168   Liber regulae pastoralis. MS. Augustinerchorherrenstift Vorau, Austria, codex 169, f.1r–89r. Quarto. Saec. 12.
Microfilm: MnCH proj. no. 7168

3169   Regula pastoralis. Titulus octavus: Dum de cavendis perversis. MS. Cistercienserabtei Zwettl, Austria, codex 265, f.1r–39r. Quarto. Saec. 12.
Microfilm: MnCH proj. no. 6863

3170   Liber curae pastoralis. MS. Cistercienserabtei Zwettl, Austria, codex 293, f.40v–137v. Quarto. Saec. 12.
Microfilm: MnCH proj. no. 6890

3171   Cura pastoralis (excerpta). MS. Benediktinerabtei Admont, Austria, codex 510, f.96r–117v. Quarto. Saec. 13.
Microfilm: MnCH proj. no. 9559

3172 Cura pastoralis. MS. Benediktinerabtei Admont, Austria, codex 515. 95 f. Quarto. Saec. 13.
Microfilm: MnCH proj. no. 9564

3173 Regula pastoralis. MS. Universitätsbibliothek Innsbruck, Austria, codex 278, f.2r–103b. Quarto. Saec. 13.
Microfilm: MnCH proj. no. 28,306

3174 Liber regulae pastoralis. MS. Augustinerchorherrenstift Klosterneuburg, Austria, codex 791, f.1r–89v. Quarto. Saec. 13.
Microfilm: MnCH proj. no. 5782

3175 Regula pastoralis. MS. Hereford, England, Cathedral Library, codex 0 1 iii, f.3–68. Quarto. Saec. 13.
Microfilm: MnCH

3176 Liber regulae pastoralis. MS. Salzburg, Diöcesanseminar, codex CM 221, f.1–66. Quarto. Saec. 13.
Microfilm: MnCH proj. no. 11,648

3177 Pastoral et Secreta theologiae. MS. Toledo, Spain, Biblioteca del Cabildo, codex 9,9. 110 f. Folio. Saec. 13.
Microfilm: MnCH proj. no. 32,980

3178 Pastorale. MS. Vienna, Nationalbibliothek, codex 822. 125 f. Quarto. Saec. 13.
Microfilm: MnCH proj. no. 14,131

3179 Regula pastoralis. MS. Vienna, Nationalbibliothek, codex 803, f.1r–67r. Quarto. Saec. 13.
Microfilm: MnCH proj. no. 14,150

3180 Cura pastoralis. MS. Vienna, Nationalbibliothek, codex 839. 90 f. Quarto. Saec. 13.
Microfilm: MnCH proj. no. 14,149

3181 Cura pastoralis. MS. Benediktinerabtei Admont, Austria, codex 346, f.146r–180v. Folio. Saec. 14.
Microfilm: MnCH proj. no. 9422

3182 Regulae pastoralis liber. MS. Universitätsbibliothek Graz, Austria, codex 245, f.1r–44r. Folio. Saec. 14.
Microfilm: MnCH proj. no. 26,169

3183 Liber pastoralis curae. MS. Universitätsbibliothek Graz, Austria, codex 911. 114 f. Quarto. Saec. 14.
Microfilm: MnCH proj. no. 26,982

3184 Liber pastoralis curae. MS. Augustinerchorherrenstift Herzogenburg, Austria, codex 52, f. 207v–240v. Folio. Saec. 14.
Microfilm: MnCH proj. no. 3206

3185 Liber pastoralis. MS. Benediktinerabtei Kremsmünster, Austria, codex 138, f. 1r–46r. Saec. 14.
Microfilm: MnCH proj. no. 127

3186 Regulae pastoralis liber. MS. Benediktinerabtei Kremsmünster, Austria, codex

335, f.88r–155r. Saec. 13 vel 14.
Microfilm: MnCH proj. no. 424

3187 De cura pastorali. MS. Benediktinerabtei Lambach, Austria, codex membr. 80, f.2r–63v. Quarto. Saec. 14.
Microfilm: MnCH proj. no. 794

3188 Regula pastoralis. MS. Benediktinerabtei Lambach, Austria, codex chart. 337, f.142r–142v.
Microfilm: MnCH proj. no. 706

3189 Regula pastoralis. MS. Lambeth Palace Library, London, codex 144, f.1–32. Quarto. Saec. 14.
Microfilm: MnCH

3190 Liber pastoralis regulae. MS. Benediktinerabtei St. Peter, Salzburg, codex a.VII.16. 85 f. Quarto. Saec. 14.
Microfilm: MnCH proj. no. 10,149

3191 Regula pastoralis. MS. Augustinerchorherrenstift St. Florian, Austria, codex XI,54, f.1v–69v. Quarto. Saec. 14.
Microfilm: MnCH proj. no. 2310

3192 Regula pastoralis. MS. Augustinerchorherrenstift St. Florian, Austria, codex XI,55. f.1r–64v. Quarto. Saec. 14.
Microfilm: MnCH proj. no. 2311

3193 Regula pastoralis. MS. Subiaco, Italy (Benedictine abbey), codex 299. Saec. 14.

3194 Pastorales. MS. Tarazona, Spain, Archivo de la Catedral, codex 103, f.73r–104r. Folio. Saec. 14.
Microfilm: MnCH proj. no. 32,682

3195 Regula pastoralis. MS. Vienna, Nationalbibliothek, codex 1026, f.1r–36r. Quarto. Saec. 14.
Microfilm: MnCH proj. no. 14,322

3196 Liber regulae pastoralis. MS. Vienna, Nationalbibliothek, codex 1065, f.1v–92r. Folio. Saec. 14.
Microfilm: MnCH proj. no. 14,375

3197 Cura pastoralis. MS. Vienna, Nationalbibliothek, codex 4241, f.1r–43v. Folio. Saec. 14.
Microfilm: MnCH proj. no. 17,426

3198 Regula pastoralis scripta ad Ioannem episcopum. MS. Vienna, Schottenstift, codex 196, f.1r–117r. Quarto. Saec. 14.
Microfilm: MnCH proj. no. 3900

3199 Liber pastoralis curae. MS. Vienna, Schottenstift, codex 352, f. 175r–218r. Folio. Saec. 14.
Microfilm: MnCH proj. no. 4199

3200 Liber regulae pastoralis. MS. Augustinerchorherrenstift Vorau, Austria, codex 148, f.165v–192v. Folio. Saec. 14.
Microfilm: MnCH proj. no. 7143

3201 Liber regulae pastoralis. MS. Augustinerchorherrenstift Vorau, Austria, codex 215, f.98v–143v. Quarto. Saec. 14.
Microfilm: MnCH proj. no. 7204

3202 Regulae pastoralis liber. MS. Cava, Italy (Benedictine abbey), codex 56. 93 f. Quarto. Saec. 15.
Microfilm: MnCH

3203 Liber pastoralis. MS. Benediktinerabtei Göttweig, Austria, codex 245a, f.1r–44v. Folio. Saec. 15.
Microfilm: MnCH proj. no. 3511

3204 Liber pastoralis curae. MS. Universitätsbibliothek Graz, Austria, codex 923 & 1353. 71 & 89 f. Quarto. Saec. 15.
Microfilm: MnCH proj. no. 26,991

3205 Regula pastoralis ad Johannem episcopum. MS. Universitätsbibliothek Innsbruck, Austria, codex 456, f. 141r–188v. Folio. Saec. 15.
Microfilm: MnCH proj. no. 28,455

3206 Cura pastoralis. MS. Linz, Austria, Bundestaatliche Studienbibliothek, codex 40, f.1r–54v. Folio. Saec. 15.
Microfilm: MnCH proj. no. 27,929

3207 Liber pastoralis. MS. Madrid, Spain, Real Academia de la Historia, codex 96, 42 f. Folio. Saec. 15.
Microfilm: MnCH proj. no. 34,952

3208 Regula pastoralis. Mancat initium. MS. Maria Saal, Austria, codex 10, f.1r–68v. Folio. Saec. 15.
Microfilm: MnCH proj. no. 13,353

3209 Liber regulae pastoralis. MS. Benediktinerabtei Melk, Austria, codex 135, f.1–71. Folio. Saec. 15.
Microfilm: MnCH proj. no. 1202

3210 Liber regulae pastoralis. MS. Benediktinerabtei Melk, Austria, codex 336, f.169–257. Folio. Saec. 15.
Microfilm: MnCH proj. no. 1344

3211 Liber regulae pastoralis. MS. Benediktinerabtei Melk, Austria, codex 563, f.1–123. Folio. Saec. 15.
Microfilm: MnCH proj. no. 1465

3212 Regula pastoralis. MS. Monasterio benedictino de Montserrat, Spain, codex 864. Quarto. Saec. 15.
Microfilm: MnCH proj. no. 30,108

3213 Pastorale. MS. Cistercienserabtei Neukloster, Wiener-Neustadt, Austria, codex D 20, f.1r–43b. Octavo. Saec. 15.
Microfilm: MnCH proj. no. 4952

3214 Liber pastoralis. MS. Benediktinerabtei St. Peter, Salzburg, codex b.VIII.20, f.126r–160v. Folio. Saec. 15.
Microfilm: MnCH proj. no. 10,551

3215 Liber curae pastoralis. Sermones diversarum materiarum et adhortationes. MS. Universitätsbibliothek Salzburg, Austria, codex M II 102. 169 f. Folio. Saec. 15.
Microfilm: MnCH proj. no. 11,185

3216 Liber curae pastoralis. Universitätsbibliothek Salzburg, Austria, codex M II 121. 95 f. Quarto. Saec. 15.
Microfilm: MnCH proj. no. 11,207

3217 Pastorale ad Joannem episcopum. MS. Benediktinerabtei St. Paul im Lavanttal, Austria, codex 63/4, pars II. Folio. Saec. 15.
Microfilm: MnCH proj. no. 12,301

3218 Liber scriptus ad Joannem episcopum de officio pastoris. MS. Prämonstratenserabtei Schlägl, Austria, codex 66, f.146r–204v. Folio. Saec. 15.
Microfilm: MnCH proj. no. 3035

3219 Liber de cura pastorali. MS. Benediktinerabtei Seitenstetten, Austria, codex 272, f.1r–44v. Folio. Saec. 15.
Microfilm: MnCH proj. no. 1083

3220 Liber de cura pastorali. MS. Benediktinerabtei Seitenstetten, Austria, codex 264. 63 f. Folio. Saec. 15.
Microfilm: MnCH proj. no. 1067

3221 Cura pastoralis. MS. Vienna, Nationalbibliothek, codex 4260, f.2r–40r. Folio. Saec. 15.
Microfilm: MnCH proj. no. 17,451

3222 Cura pastoralis. MS. Vienna, Nationalbibliothek, codex 4406, f.268r–305r. Folio. Saec. 15.
Microfilm: MnCH proj. no. 17,587

3223 Cura pastoralis. MS. Vienna, Nationalbibliothek, codex 4434, f.86r–128v. Folio. Saec. 15.
Microfilm: MnCH proj. no. 17,621

3224 Liber regulae pastoralis. MS. Augustinerchorherrenstift Vorau, Austria, codex 86, f.231v–281v. Folio. Saec. 15.

3225 Liber regulae pastoralis. MS. Augustinerchorherrenstift Vorau, Austria, codex 379, f.37r–118r. Quarto. Saec. 15.
Microfilm: MnCH proj. no. 7346

3226 Regula pastoralis. MS. Cistercienserabtei Wilhering, Austria, codex IX,32, f.12r–52v. Folio. Saec. 15.
Microfilm: MnCH proj. no. 2806

3227 Liber pastoralis. MS. Cistercienserabtei Zwettl, Austria, codex 154, f.1r–29r. Folio. Saec. 15.
Microfilm: MnCH proj. no. 6748

3228 Sacramentarium. MS. Vienna, Nationalbibliothek, codex 1815, f.15v–198v. Folio. Saec. 9.
Microfilm: MnCH proj. no. 15,137

3229 Liber sacramentorum. MS. Vienna, Nationalbibliothek, codex 1022. 113 f. Quarto. Saec. 11.
Microfilm: MnCH proj. no. 14,337

3230 Liber sacramentorum. MS. Vienna, Nationalbibliothek, codex 1845, f.75v–275r. Quarto. Saec. 11.
Microfilm: MnCH proj. no. 15,167
Sermones. *See* Homiliae.

3231 Liber qui vocatur Speculum. MS. Salisbury, England, Cathedral Library, codex 101, f.65–148. Quarto. Saec. 10.
Microfilm: MnCH

3232 Liber qui speculationum vocatur (excerpta from Augustine, Gregory . . .). MS. Hereford, England, Cathedral Library, codex 0 2 vii, f.126v–143. Quarto. Saec. 12.
Microfilm: MnCH

3233 Speculum peccatoris. MS. Benediktinerabtei Altenburg, Austria, codex AB 13 F 4. Octavo. Saec. 15.
Microfilm: MnCH proj. no. 6430

3234 Speculum peccatoris. MS. Benediktinerabtei St. Peter, Salzburg, codex a.III.35, f.268v–275v. Octavo. Saec. 15.
Microfilm: MnCH proj. no. 9972

3235 Symbolum de fide Sanctae Trinitatis. MS. Benediktinerabtei St. Peter, Salzburg, codex a.XI.12, f.1r–39r. Folio. Saec. 15.
Microfilm: MnCH proj. no. 10,715

3236 Tabula de auctoritatibus Bibliae in libris Gregorii expositis. MS. Hereford, England, Cathedral Library, codex P 3 xii, f.68–104. Octavo. Saec. 13–14.
Microfilm: MnCH

3237 Tabula exhibens locos S. Scripturae, quos et quo loco S. Gregorius in libris moralium, in homiliis super evangelia et super Ezechielem et in pastoralibus libris exponit. MS. Augustinerchorherrenstift Klosterneuburg, Austria, codex 391, f.294v–317r. Folio. Saec. 15.
Microfilm: MnCH proj. no. 5363

3238 Tractatus de reparatione lapsi (excerpta). MS. Vienna, Nationalbibliothek, codex 1322, f.68v–71r. Quarto. Saec. 10.
Microfilm: MnCH proj. no. 14,688

3239 Tractatus super septem psalmis poenitentialibus. MS. Vienna, Schottenstift, codex 63, f.59r–152v. Quarto. Saec. 15.
Microfilm: MnCH proj. no. 3985

3240 Versus. Incipit: Virgo parens hac luce deumque virumque. MS. Vienna, Nationalbibliothek, codex 143, f.13v–14r. Folio. Saec. 13.
Microfilm: MnCH proj. no. 13,512

3241 Versus psalmorum a Gregorio M. in homiliis suis explanati. MS. Benediktinerabtei Admont, Austria, codex 735, f.1r–64v. Octavo. Saec. 12.
Microfilm: MnCH proj. no. 9775

3242 [Vita s. Benedicti]
Liber secundus Dialogorum. MS. Benediktinerabtei Melk, Austria, codex 321, f.116r–133v. Folio. Saec. 15.
Microfilm: MnCH proj. no. 1330

3243 [Vita S. Benedicti]
Dialogorum liber secundus. MS. Benediktinerabtei Admont, Austria, codex 829, f.279r–301v. Quarto. Saec. 17.
Microfilm: MnCH proj. no. 9858

3244 Memoriale vitae sancti Benedicti ex secundo libro Dialogorum. MS. Vienna, Schottenstift, codex 405, f.244r–245r.
Microfilm: MnCH proj. no. 4148

3245 [Vita s. Benedicti. German]
Dialogorum liber secundus. Germanice. MS. Benediktinerabtei Melk, Austria, codex 1752, f.177r–235v. Duodecimo. Saec. 15.
Microfilm: MnCH proj. no. 2063

3246 [Vita s. Benedicti. German]
Dialogi. Liber secundus. Germanice. MS. Vienna, Nationalbibliothek, codex 2968, f.125r–167v. Quarto. Saec. 15.
Microfilm: MnCH proj. no. 16,212

3247 [Vita s. Benedicti. German]
Dialogorum liber secundus. Germanice. MS. Cistercienserabtei Lilienfeld, Austria, codex 21, f.1r–60v. Duodecimo. Saec. 16.
Microfilm: MnCH proj. no. 4331
Gregory I, the Great.
Printed works.

3248 [Selections. English]
The works of the days (Lucis Creator optime) [and 18 other hymns].
(*In* Donahoe, D. J. Early Christian hymns. New York, 1908. v. 1, p. 87–108)
PLatS

3249 [De approbatione Regulae S. Benedicti]
Leteras apostólicas . . . en aprobación de la Regla del glorioso Padre San Benito . . . Barcelona, Estevan Liberòs, 1633.
The "aprobación" is the first item in the book.
MnCS

3250 Aprobación y confirmación de esta Santa Regla por nuestro Padre San Gregorio el Grande.
(*In* Regla de le gran patriarcha S. Benito . . . Madrid, Antonio Sanz, 1746)
The "aprobación" is the first item in the book.
MnCS

3251   Dialogorum libri IV. [Italian]. Modena, Domenico Roccociola, 1481.
[67] leaves.
PLatS (microfilm)

3252   Dialogorum libri quatuor. [Italian]. Venice, Andreas Torresanus, 1487.
[101] leaves.
PLatS (microfilm)

3253   [Dialogi. English]
The dialogvues of S. Gregorie, svrnamed the Greate . . . devided into fower bookes. Wherein he intreateth of the lives and miracles of the saintes in Italie, and of the eternitie of mens soules . . . Translated into our English tongue by P. W. [Philip Woodward]. Paris, 1608.
MnCS (microfilm)

3254   [Dialogi. English]
Saint Benedict, by Saint Gregory the great; being a new translation of the Second Book of the Dialogues, by Abbot Justin McCann . . . [2d ed]. Worcester, Stanbrook Abbey Press [1951].
iv, 72 p. 19 cm.
KAS

3255   [Dialogi. English]
The Dialogues of Gregory the Great. Book two: Saint Benedict. Translated with an introduction and notes, by Myra L. Uhlfelder. Indianapolis, Bobbs-Merrill [1967]. xxiv, 49 p. 20 cm.
MnCS

3256   [Dialogi. French]
Dialogues de saint Grégoire et Règle de saint Benoît. Extraits traduits par E. de Solms. La Pierre-qui-Vire, Zodiaque, 1965.
199 p. 72 plates (part col.) 26 cm.
MnCS
Dialogi. Liber secundus. *See* his Vita s. Benedicti.

3257   [Epistolae]
Gregorii I papae Registrum epistolarum. Ediderunt Paulus Dwald et Ludovicus M. Hartmann. Editio secunda lucis ope expressa. Berolini, apud Weidmannes, 1957.
2 v. 30 cm. (Monumenta Germaniae historica. Epistolae, t. 1–2)
PLatS; MnCS

3258   [Epistolae. German]
Des heiligen Pabstes und Kirchenlehrers Gregorius des Grossen sämmtliche Briefe, vom September der IX indiktion, oder des Jahres 590, bis auf den Hornung der VIII Indiktion, oder des Sterbejahres 604. Uebersetzt von Maurus Fayerabend, Benediktiner. Kemptem, Joseph Kösel, 1807–09.
6 v. 22 cm.
MnCS; PLatS

3259   Sancti Gregorii Magni Expositiones: in Canticum canticorum, in librum primum Regum. Recensuit Patricius Verbraken. Turnholti, Brepols, 1963.
xi, 637 p. 25 cm. (Corpus Christianorum. Saries latina, 144)
InStme; MnCS; NdRi; PLatS

3260   [Homiliae in Evangelia. French]
Homélie pour les dimanches du cycle de Paques, choisies et traduites par René Wasselynck . . . Namur, Editions du Soleil Levant, 1963.
175 p. 17 cm.
PLatS

3261   Homiliae in Hiezechihelem prophetam. Cura et studio Marcus Adriaen. Turnholti, Brepols, 1971.
xxi, 461 p. 26 cm. (Corpus Christianorum. Series latina, 142)
PLatS

3262   [Moralia in Job]
Egloga quam scripsit Lathcen, filius Baith, De moralibus Iob quas Gregorius fecit. Cura et studio M. Adriaen. Turnholti, Brepols, 1969.
ix, 373 p. 26 cm. (Corpus Christianorum. Series latina, 145)
InStme

3262a   Moralia in Job, cura et studio Marci Adriaen. Turnholti, Brepols, 1979–
v. 26 cm. (Corpus Christianorum. Series latina, 143
PLatS; InStme

3263   Morales sur Job/Grégoire le Grand. Paris, Editions du Cerf, 1974–
v. 20 cm. (Sources chrétiennes, 32 bis   )
Text in Latin and French.
InStme; PLatS

3264   Parables of the Gospel. [Translated by Nora Burke]. Dublin, Chicago, Scepter [1960].
169 p. 19 cm.
PLatS

3265   [Regula pastoralis]
Liber cure pastoralis beati Gregorii pape. [Cologne, Conrad Winters de Homborch] 1482.
[108] leaves, 21 cm.
KAM; PLatS

3266   Pastorale sancti Gregorii. [Colophon: Impressum Rome per magistrum Ioannem Besicken alemanum expensis Iacobi de Mazochis, 1506].
[54] leaves, 28 cm.
PLatS

3267   Cura pastoralis, omnibus animarum pastoribus summe utilis et necessaria. Opera Matthiae, abbatis Admontensis, in

hanc formam recusa. Monaci, apud Raphaelem Sadelerum, 1622.
625 p. 13 cm.
MnCS; MoCo

3268 The Regula pastoralis of Saint Gregory the Great. Collegeville, Minn., Saint John's University, 1953.
33 p. 28 cm.
Text wholly in Latin.
Multigraphed.
MnCS

3269 [Regula pastoralis. Anglo-Saxon]
The pastoral care; King Alfred's translation of St. Gregory's Regula pastoralis. Ms. Hatton 20 in the Bodleian Library at Oxford, MS. Cotton Tiberius B.XI in the British Museum . . . Edited by N. R. Ker. Copenhagen, Rosenkilde and Bagger, 1956.
25, [5] p. facsim., [14] p. 36 cm. (Early English manuscripts in facsimile, v. 6)
InStme

3270 [Regula pastoralis. Anglo-Saxon]
King Alfred's West-Saxon version of Gregory's Pastoral care. Edited by Henry Sweet. London, Oxford Univ. Press [1958, 1871].
2 v. 22 cm. (Early English Text Society. Original series, no. 45, 50)
KAM; KAS; PLatS

3271 [Regula pastoralis. French]
Le Pastoral de Saint Grégoire le Grand. Du ministère et des devoirs des pasteurs. Traduction nouvelle par P. Antoine de Marsili. Paris, André Pralard, 1694.
370 p. 14 cm.
CaQStB

3272 [Vita s. Benedicti]
Secundus dyalogorum liber beati Gregorij pape de vita ac miraculis beatissimi Benedicti . . . [Venicia, L. A. de Giunta, 1505].
191 p. plates, 11 cm.
KyTr; MnCS

3273 [Vita s. Benedicti]
Regula & vita beatissimi patris Benedicti cum miraculis a beato Gregorio IX [i.e. I] papa conscripta. London, W. de Worde, 1512?].
Short-title catalogue no. 12,351.
MnCS (microfilm)

3274 [Vita s. Benedicti]
Regvla sancti patris Benedicti . . . Adiecta vita eiusdem s. patris . . . Mogvntiae, Balthasar Lippius, 1603.
187, 173 p. 18 cm.
MnCS

3275 [Vita s. Benedicti]
Vita s.s. patris Benedicti . . . Coloniae, Joannis Leonard, 1684.
InStme (defective copy: p. 1–28 only)

3276 [Vita s. Benedicti]
S.P.N. Benedicti Regula et vita . . . Viennae, sumptibus Ignatii Coldhann, MDCCXCV.
280 p. 14 cm.
PLatS

3277 [Vita s. Benedicti. English]
Saint Benedict, by Saint Gregory the Great. Being a new translation of the second book of the Dialogues, by Dom Justin McCann. Rugby [England], Princethorpe Priory, 1941.
60 p. 19 cm.
PLatS

3278 [Vita s. Benedicti. English]
St. Benedict life and miracles by St. Gregory the Great; and, An introduction to his Rule, by Dom Mayeul de Dreuille. [Dasarahalli, Bangalore], St. Paul Publications [1972].
180 p. 19 cm. (Seekers of God, 2)
CaMWiSb; MoCo; PLatS

3279 [Vita s. Benedicti. English]
The second booke of the dialogues of S. Gregorie the Greate . . . containinge the life and miracles of our Holie Father S. Benedict . . . translated into the Englishe tonge by C.F., priest & monke of the same order . . . [London] The Scolar Press, 1976.
[4], 108, 130, 63 p. 19 cm. (English recusant literature, 1588–1660, vol. 294)
Facsimile reprint of 1638 edition.
PLatS; MnCS

3280 [Vita s. Benedicti. English]
The life of S. Benet abbot, taken out of the Dialogues of S. Gregory.
(*In* Maffei, Giovanni Pietro, S.J. Fuga saeculi . . . London, Scolar Press, 1977)
Facsimile reprint of the 1632 edition. English recusant literature, 1558–1640, v. 345, p. 236–258.
PLatS

3281 [Vita s. Benedicti. French]
Saint Benoît. Textes choisies . . . Vie de saint Benoît. Traduit et présentés par Dom Antoine Dumas, O.S.B. Namur, Editions du Soleil Levant [1958].
183 p. 18 cm.
MnCS

3282 [Vita s. Benedicti. French]
La vie et la Règle de Saint Benoît . . . Traduction de Mère Elisabeth de Solms. [Paris], Desclée de Brouwer [1965].
319 p.
MnStj

3283   [Vita s. Benedicti. Slovak]
Zivot a Regula sv. otca Benedikta. Poslo-
vencil najdp. Gregor K. Vaniscak, O.S.B.
Cleveland, Ohio, vydali Slovenski Benedik-
tini, 1933.
139 p. 23 cm.
ILSH; ILSP; KAS; MnCS; OClSta

3284   [Vita s. Benedicti. Spanish]
Regla . . . y Vida santissima y grandes
milagros de S. Benito que San Gregorio
Magno dexo escrita en Latin. Valladolid,
Juan Godinez de Millis, 1599.
MnCS

3285   [Vita s. Benedicti. Spanish]
Vida de San Benito, patriarca de los
monjes. Versión castellana del Bruno
Avila. 3. ed. Beunos Aires, Editorial San
Benito, 1956.
100 p. 19 cm.
KAS

Gregory VII, Saint, Pope. *See also*
Popes, 1073–1085 (Gregory VII)

3286   Epistola ad Wratislaum Bohemiae
ducem. MS. Prämonstratenserabtei
Schlägl, Austria, codex 152, f. 1r. Folio.
Saec. 15.
Microfilm: MnCH proj. no. 3040

3287   Sermo de S. Catharina. MS. Benediktinerabtei Göttweig, Austria, codex 326,
f.281r–282v. Folio. Saec. 15.
Microfilm: MnCH proj. no. 3594

3288   **Gregory XVI, Pope,** 1765–1846.
Il trionfo della Santa Sede e della Chiesa
contro gli assalti de' novatori respinti e
combattuti colle stesse loro armi. Opera di
D. Mauro Cappellari. Roma, Stamp. Pagli-
arini, 1799.
xxiii, 453 p.
PLatS (microfilm)

Grell, Mary, Sister, 1912–
3289   Heredity; an introduction to genetics.
19 p.
Typescript, 1959.
MnStj (Archives)

3290   A study with the ultracentrifuge of the
mechanism of death in frozen cells.
ii, 42 p. illus.
Thesis (M.A.)–St. Louis University,
1937.
Typescript.
MnStj

3291   **Grénaud, Georges,** 1903–
Dom Guéranger et le project de bulle
"Quemadmodum Ecclesia" pur la définition
de l'Immaculée Conception.
(*In* Virgo Immaculata; acta Congressus
Mariologici-Mariani, 1954, v.2, p. 337–386)
PLatS

3292   **Gresnigt, Adalbert,** 1877–1956.
Reflections on Chinese architecture.
(*In* Catholic University of Peking.
Bulletin, no. 8 (1931), p. 3–26)
PLatS

Gribomont, Jean, 1920–
3293   Conscience philologique chez les scribes
du haut moyen age.
(*In* La Bibbia nell'alto medioevo, p.
601–630. Settimane di studio del Centro
italiano di studi sull'alto medioevo, 10)
PLatS

3294   L'influence du monachisme oriental sur
Sulpice Sévère.
(*In* Saint Martin et son temps. Romae,
1961. p. 135–150. Studia Anselmiana, 46)
PLatS

3295   Le Paulinisme de saint Basile.
(*In* Studiorum Paulinorum Congressus
Internationalis Catholicus, 1961. v.2, p.
480–490. Analecta biblica, 18)
PLatS

3296   Saint Basile.
(*In* Théologie de la vie monastique, p.
99–113)
PLatS

3297   Il salterio di Rufino. Edizione critica a
cura di Francesca Merlo. Commento da
Jean Gribomont. Roma, Abbazie San
Girolamo, 1972.
xi, 207 p. 26 cm. (Collectanea biblica
latina, v. 14)
KAS

3298   (2dary) Rupert, abbot of Deutz. Les
oeuvres du Saint-Esprit. Introd. et notes
par Jean Gribomont, O.S.B. . . . Paris,
Editions du Cerf, 1967–
v. 20 cm. (Sources chrétiennes, n. 131)
InStme; PLatS

3299   **Grienmelt, Lambert.**
Annus columbinus historico-moralis. Das
ist: Jahr-lauff dess H. Geists . . . Dillin-
gen, J. C. Bencard, 1709.
[16], 626 p. 20 cm.
The publication is a lives of the saints.
PLatS

Griffiths, Bede, 1906–
3300   Christ in India; essays towards a Hindu-
Christian dialogue. New York, Scribner
[1977].
249 p. illus. 22 cm.
First published in 1966 under title: Christian Ashram.

3301   The golden string. Garden City, N.Y.,
Doubleday [1964, c1954].
187 p. 18 cm. (Image Books, D173)
KAS

3302 John Cassian.
(*In* Walsh, James. Spirituality through the centuries. 1964. p. 25–41)
PLatS

3303 The meeting of East and West.
(*In* Derrick, Christopher. Light of revelation and non-Christians. New York, 1965. p. 13–38)
InFer

3304 Monastic life in India today.
(*In* Monastic studies, v. 4, p. 117–160)
PLatS

3305 Return to the center. Springfield, Ill., Templegate [1976].
154 p. 22 cm.
CaMWiSb; InFer; MoCo

3306 **Grill, Maria Regis, Sister,** 1901–
Coelestin Steiglehner, letzter Fürstabt von St. Emmeram zu Regensburg. München, Bayerische Benediktinerakademie, 1937.
xiv, 131 p. plates, 25 cm.
KAS

3307 **Grillo, Angelo.**
Lettere . . . nuovamente raccolte dal Sig. Pietro Petracci . . . Venetia, Gio. Battista Ciotti, 1612.
2 v. illus. 20 cm.
PLatS

3308 **Groll, Ignatius Albert,** 1884–1934.
Bethlehem; drama in four acts, by Gilbert J. Straub, O.S.B. Music by the Rev. Ignatius Groll, O.S.B. [Pittsburgh, St. Joseph's Protectory Print, 1944].
31 p. 23 cm.
PLatS; KAS

3309 **Gropp, Ignaz,** 1695–1758.
Collectio novissima scriptorvm et rervm Wircebvrgensivm a saecvlo XVI. XVII. et XVIII. hactenvs gestarvm . . . Francofvrti, ex Officina Weidmanniana, 1741–50.
4 v. illus. 35 cm.

3310 **Gros, Irénée,** 1908–
La mort. [Paris], Desclée, de Brouwer [1954].
186 p. 20 cm.
PLatS

3311 **Gruber, Benno.**
XXIV antiphonae Marianae, nimirum VI Alma, VI Ave, VI Regina, VI Salve Regina, a 4 vocibus ordinariis, concinentibus 2 violinis et organo obligatis. Augustae Vindelicorum, Joan. Jac. Lotter, 1793.
10 pts. in portfolio. 33 cm.
PLatS

3312 **Grünewald, Marzellin,** 1932–
Benediktinische Arbeit.

(*In* Die Benediktinerabtei Münsterschwarzach. Vier-Türme-Verlag, 1965. p. 76–85)
PLatS

3313 **Grüssau, Germany (Benedictine abbey).**
Chronicon Silesiae, seu potius Annales Grussavienses 1230–1306. MS. Vienna, Nationalbibliothek, codex 509, f. 1r–1v. Quarto. Saec. 14.
Microfilm: MnCH proj. no. 13,847

3314 **Gruwe, Luke,** 1849–1940.
Gründungs und Entwicklungsgeschichte der St. Meinrads-Abtei in Nordamerika.
Offprint from: Studien und Mitteilungen zur Geschichte des Benediktinerordens und seiner Zweige. Neu Folge, Jhrg. 5(1915), Heft II, p. 1–32.
InStme; KAS; MnCS; PLatS

3315 **G'Sell, Amandus,** 1887–
Die Vita des Erzbischofs Arnold von Mainz (1153–1160) auf ihre Echtheit geprüft.
Sonderabdruck aus dem Neuen Archiv für ältere deutsche Geschichtskunde, Bd. 43, Heft 1 u. 2. p. 29–85, 319–379.
MnCS

3316 **Gualterus, abbot of Montier-en-Der,** 12th cent.
Walteri abbatis Dervensis Epistolae. The letters of Walter, abbot of Dervy. New first published from a MS. preserved in the library of St. John's College, Oxford, by C. Messiter. New York, B. Franklin [1967].
148 p. 23 cm. (Publications of the Caxton Society, 10)
KAS; PLatS

3317 **Guarda Geywitz, Gabriel,** 1928–
La implantación del monacato en Hispanoamérica, siglos XV–XIX. Universidad Católica de Chile, 1973.
103 p. illus. 25 cm.
MnCS

Guepin, Alphonse, 1836–1917.

3318 Un apôtre de l'union des Eglises au XVIIe siècle: Saint Josaphat et l'Eglise greco-slave en Pologne et en Russie. Paris, H. Oudin, 1898.
2 v. 21 cm.
CaBMi; CaQStB; MnCS

3319 Saint Josaphat, archevéque de Polach, martyr de l'unité catholique (1613) et l'Eglise grecque unie en Pologne. Poitiers, Oudin, 1874.
CtBeR; MoCo

Guéranger, Prosper, 1806–1875.

3320 Antwort auf die letzten Einwürfe gegen die Erklärung der Unfehlarbeit des Papstes . . . Mainz, Franz Kirchheim, 1870.

32 p. 22 cm.

InStme

3321 De la monarchie pontificale à propos du livre de Mgr. l'Evêque de Sura. 3. ed. Paris, V. Palmé, 1870.

xi, 311 p. 23 cm.

InStme; KAS

3322 Défense de l'Eglise romaine contre les accusations du R. P. Graty. 2. ed. Paris, V. Palmé, 1870.

42 p. 23 cm.

CaQStB; KAS

3323 Deuxième défense de l'Eglise romaine contre les accusations du R. P. Graty. Paris, V. Palmé, 1870.

67 p. 23 cm.

KAS

3324 L'Eglise; ou, La société de la louange divine. Solesmes, 1875.

32 p.

CaQStB

3325 Essai historique sur l'Abbaye de Solesmes, suivi de la description de l'église abbatiale, avec l'explication des monuments qu'elle renferme. Le Mans, Fleuriot, 1846.

vii, 131 p. 23 cm.

PLatS

3326 The history of Christmas. The mystery of Christmas.

(*In* Clonmore, Wm. A Christian's Christmas. London, 1939. p. 85–99)

PLatS

3327 Nouvelle defense des institutions liturgiques. Paris, Le Mans, 1846.

3 pts.

MoCo

Gufl, Veremund, 1705–1761.

3328 Demonstratio jurium status ecclesastici circa temporalia ex principiis juris naturae potissimum deducta. n.p., 1757.

350, 479 p. 21 cm.

MnCS

3329 Philosophia scholastica universa. Ratisbonae, typis & sumptibus Christiani Theophili Seiffarti, 1750–1753.

4 vols.

PLatS (microfilm)

3330 **Guibert de Nogent,** 1053(ca.)–1124.

Self and society in medieval France; the memoirs of Abbot Guibert of Nogent. Edited with an introd. and notes by John F. Benton. The translation of C. C. Swinton Bland revised by the editor. New York, Harper & Row [1970].

260 p. illus. 21 cm.

Translation of: De vita sua.

InStme

3331 **Guibertus, abbot of Gembloux,** 12th cent.

Destructio vel potius combustio monasterii Gemblacensis a.1037. MS. Vienna, Nationalbibliothek, codex 3469, f.21r–24v. Quarto. Saec. 15.

Microfilm: MnCH proj. no. 20,398

Guido Aretinus. *See* Guido d'Arezzo.

Guido de Arezzo, ca.990–ca.1050.

3332 De arte musica. MS. Vienna, Nationalbibliothek, codex 787, f.69r–70v. Folio. Saec. 12.

Microfilm: MnCH proj. no. 14,101

3333 Epistola ad Michaelem monachum: De ignoto cantu (fragmentum). MS. Vienna, Nationalbibliothek, codex 2502, f.25r–26r. Octavo. Saec. 12.

Microfilm: MnCH proj. no. 15,815

3334 Micrologus de disciplina artis musicae. MS. Vienna, Nationalbibliothek, codex 51, f.35r–44v. Folio. Saec. 12.

Microfilm: MnCH proj. no. 13,416

3335 Micrologus. Cap. 1–15. MS. Vienna, Nationalbibliothek, codex 2502, f.19v–24r, et f.26r (capitulum ultimum). Octavo. Saec. 12.

Microfilm: MnCH proj. no. 15,815

3336 Micrologus de musica. Regulae musicae rhythmicae. Regula musicae de ignoto cantu. MS. Vienna, Nationalbibliothek, codex 2503, f.1r–37r. Octavo. Saec. 13.

Microfilm: MnCH proj. no. 15,818

3337 Regulae de ignoto cantu. MS. Vienna, Nationalbibliothek, codex 51, f.43r–44r. Folio. Saec. 12.

Microfilm: MnCH proj. no. 13,416

3338 Regulae musicae rythmicae. MS. Vienna, Nationalbibliothek, codex 51, f.41v–43r. Folio. Saec. 12.

Microfilm: MnCH proj. no. 13,416

3339 Tractatus de ignoto cantu. MS. Vienna, Nationalbibliothek, codex 51, f.44r–45r. Folio. Saec. 12.

Microfilm: MnCH proj. no. 13,416

Guilielmus, abbot of Hirsau, d. 1091.

3340 Constitutiones Hirsaugienses. MS. Vienna, Schottenstift, codex 194, 134 f. Folio. Saec. 15.

Microfilm: MnCH proj. no. 4061

3341 Consuetudines regularis vitae. MS. Benediktinerabtei Kremsmünster, Austria, codex 99a. 133 f. Saec. 12.

Microfilm: MnCH proj. no. 95

Guilielmus, abbas S. Theodorici prope Remos. *See* Guillaume de Saint-Thierry.

Guillaume de Saint-Thierry, 1085(ca.)–1148?

3342 The works of William of St. Thierry. Shannon, Ireland, or, Spencer, Mass., Cistercian Publications, 1971–

v. 23 cm. (Cistercian Fathers series, v. 3, 6, 9, 12)
NcBe; PLatS

3343 La contemplation de Dieu. Introduction, texte latin et traduction de Jacques Hourlier. 2. ed. Paris, Editions du Cerf, 1977.
160 p. illus. 20 cm.
InStme

3344 On contemplating God. Translated by Sr. Penelope. Shannon, Ireland, Irish Univ. Press, 1971.
199 p.
InFer

3345 The enigma of faith. Translated, with an introduction and notes, by John D. Anderson. Washington, Consortium Press, 1974.
vii, 122 p. 23 cm.
KAS

3346 Epistola ad fratres de Monte Dei. MS. Vienna, Nationalbibliothek, codex 4259, f.109r–127r. Folio. Saec. 15.
Microfilm: MnCH proj. no. 17,450

3347 Exposé sur le Cantique des Cantiques. Texte latin, introduction et notes de J. M. Dechanet, O.S.B. Traduction française de M. Dumontier, O.C.S.O. Paris, Editions du Cerf, 1962.
418 p. 20 cm. (Sources chrétiennes, 82)
PLatS

3348 Exposition on the Song of Songs. Translated by Mother Columba Hart, O.S.B., introduction by J. M. Déchanet, O.S.B. Spencer, Mass., Cistercian Publications, 1970.
xlviii, 169 p. 22 cm.
PLatS

3349 In Cantici Canticorum priora duo capita brevis commentatio ex S. Bernardi sermonibus contexta. MS. Prämonstratenserabtei Schlägl, Austria, codex 4, f.63v–80r. Folio. Saec. 12–13.
Microfilm: MnCH proj. no. 3073

3350 Tractatus de sacramento Corporis et Sanguinis Christi. MS. Benediktinerabtei Melk, Austria, codex 136, f.212r–222v. Folio. Saec. 15.
Microfilm: MnCH proj. no. 2112

3351 **Gumpp, Ignatius, O.S.B.**
Compendium discursus canonici de mensaprivilegiata abbatis et conventus monasterii S. Blasii. MS. Benediktinerabtei St. Paul im Lavanttal, Austria, codex 260/2. 180 p. Folio. Saec. 18.
Microfilm: MnCH proj. no. 12,094

3352 **Gundackerus, abbot of Seitenstetten.**
Memoriale fundationis. MS. Benediktinerabtei Seitenstetten, Austria, codex

208, f.267r–269v. Folio. Saec. 15.
Microfilm: MnCH proj. no. 1013

3353 **Gundry, JoAnn, Sister.**
The effect of guidance activities on the self-concept of primary grade children.
Thesis (M.A.)–University of North Dakota, 1977.
Typescript.
NdRiS

Günthör, Anselm, 1911–
3354 Kommentar zur Enzyklika Humanae vitae. Freiburg, Seelsorge-Verlag [1969].
159 p. 21 cm.
MnCS

3355 Kritische Bemerkungen zu neuen Theorien über Ehe und eheliche Hingabe.
Sonderdruck aus der Tübinger Theologischen Quartalschrift, 144. Jahrgang (1964), p. 316–350.
MnCS

3356 Die Predigt; theoretische und praktische theologische Wegweisung. Freiburg, Herder [1963].
x, 278 p. 23 cm.
InStme; PLatS

3357 Riflessioni sui problema della regolazione delle nascite. Lezioni tenute nella Pontificia Università Lateranense, febbraio-maggio 1968. Roma, 1968.
99 p. 23 cm.
Pro manuscripto.
MnCS

3358 Zum derzeitigen Stand moraltheologischer Diskussion über Ehefragen.
Estratto da "Seminarium", n.2, 1965, p. 347–363.
MnCS

3359 **Gustin, Arno,** 1906–
St. John's University, Collegeville, Minn. Registrar, St. John's University [1961?].
unpaged, illus., ports., panorama, plan, 28 cm.
MnCS

3360 **Guzzolini, Sylvestro,** 1177–1267.
The life of Blessed Bonfil, bishop and confessor of Christ.
(*In* The saints of the Benedictine Order of Montefano, by Andrew Jacobi. Clifton, N.J., 1972)
InStme

3361 **H., C.**
Die Staats-Kirchengesetze im Lichte der kathol. Wahrheit und ihrer Folgen, dargestellt von P.C.H., O.S.B. Salzburg, Verlag der Zaunrith'schen Buchdruckerei, 1874.
32 p. 20 cm.
PLatS

Haacke, Rhaban, 1912–

3362   Programme zur bildenden Kunst in den
Schriften Ruperts von Deutz. Siegburg,
Respublica-Verlag, 1974.
63 p. 23 plates, 24 cm.
MnCS

3363   Rupert von Deutz zur Frage: Cur Deus
homo?
(*In* Corona gratiarum; miscellanea
patristica . . . Eligio Dekkers . . . oblata.
Brugge, 1975. v. 2, p. 143–159)
PLatS

3364   (ed) Rupert of Deutz. Commentaria in
Canticum Canticorum, edidit Hrabanus
Haacke. Turnholti, Brepols, 1974.
lx, 192 p. 26 cm. (Corpus Christianorum.
Continuatio Mediaevalis, 26)
MnCS; PLatS

3365   (ed) Rupert of Deutz. Commentaria in
Evangelium sancti Johannis. Edidit
Rhabanus Haacke, O.S.B. Turnholti,
Brepols, 1969.
xv, 831 p. 26 cm. (Corpus Christianorum.
Continuatio mediaevalis, 9)
InStme; MnCS; PLatS

3365a   (ed) Rupert of Deutz. De gloria et honore
filii hominis super Mattheum. Edidit
Hrabanus Haacke, O.S.B. Turnholti,
Brepols, 1979.
xxi, 456 p. 26 cm. (Corpus Christianorum. Continuatio Mediaevalis, 29)
PLatS

3366   (ed) Rupert of Deutz. De Sancta Trinitate et operibus eius. Edidit Hrabanus
Haacke. Turnholti, Brepols, 1971–
v. 26 cm. (Corpus Christianorum. Continuatio mediaevalis, 21, 22, 23, 24)
InStme; PLatS

3367   (ed) Rupert of Deutz. De victoria Verbi
Dei. Hrsg. von Rhaban Haacke. Weimar,
Hermann Böhlaus Nachfolger, 1970.
lix, 474 p. illus. 22 cm. (Monumenta Germaniae historica. Quellen zur Geistesgeschichte des Mittelalters, Bd. 5)
PLatS

3368   (ed) Rupert of Deutz. Liber de divinis officiis. Edidit Hrabanus Haache, O.S.B.
Turnholti, Brepols, 1967.
lvii, 477 p. 25 cm. (Corpus Christianorum. Continuatio mediaevalis, 7)
InStme; MnCS

3369   **Haas, Adalbero,** 1881–
Glaube; Farbenzeichnungen zum
Einheits-Katechismus. Würzburg, Haas &
Co. [1928].
22, 2 col. charts. 33 cm.
ILSP

3370   **Haas, Odo,** 1931–
Paulus der Missionar; Ziel, Grundsätze
und Methoden der Missionstätigkeit des
Apostels Paulus nach seinen eigenen
Assagen. Münsterschwarzach, Vier-Türme
-Verlag, 1971.
ix, 132 p. 18 cm. (Münsterschwarzacher
Studien, Bd. 11)
MnCS

3371   **Hacker, Leopold.**
Zwei Fliegen auf einen Schlag; ein Licht-
lein für unsere Zeit. Wien, C. Sartori,
1872.
26 p. 18 cm.
PLatS

Haeften, Benedictus Jacobus van, 1588–
1648.

3372   De heyr-baene des cruys, seer ver-
maeckelyck om lesen . . . in't Latijn
beschreven door . . . Benedictus
Haeftenus . . . in het Nederduytsch ver-
taelt door P. Petrus Mallants, Carthuyser.
Antwerpen, Jacobus Woons, 1693.
440 p. illus.
NdRi

3373   Jerzem Schuel, das ist: Das abgewandten
von Got Herzen zu denselben Wieder-
fierung unnd Unverweisung. Zu Deutsch
verseat durch F. Vitus Gadolt, O.S.B. MS.
Benediktinerinnenabtei Nonnberg,
Salzburg, codex 23 D 16. 707 p. Quarto.
Saec. 17 (1652).
Microfilm: MnCH proj. no. 10,885

3374   Panis quotidianvs, sive sacrarvm medita-
tionvm in singvlos anni dies distribvtarvm,
libri sex . . . ex variis aucthoribus collecti
a R.D.B.H.P.A. Antverpiae, apud Hieronymvm Verdvssivm, 1634.
[72], 359, [3], 433, [3], 432 p. 15 cm.
KAS

3375   Regia via crucis. Coloniae, apud Joannem Carolum Munich, 1673.
[36], 341, [29] p. illus. 12 cm.
KAS

3376   Regia via crucis. Antverpiae, ex Officina
viduae Henrici Verdussen, 1728.
404, [22] p. 18 cm.
KAS; NdRi

3377   S. Benedictusillustratus; sive, Disquisi-
tionum monasticarum libri XII, quibus S.
P. Benedicti Regula & religiosorum rituum
antiquitates varie dilucidantur . . . Antverpiae, apud Petrum Bellerum, 1644.
203, lx, 1103 p. 35 cm.
Xeroxed by University Microfilms, Ann
Arbor, Mich., 1963.
KAS

3378   Schola cordis; sive, Aversi a Deo cordis
ad eumdem reductio, et instructio. Antver-

piae, apud Ioannem Mervsivm et Hieronimvm Verdvssivm, 1635.
[32], 631, [25] p. illus. 16 cm.
KAS

3379   . . . Antverpiae, apud Hieronymvm et Ioan. Bapt. Verdvssen, 1663.
[28], 553, [22] p. illus. 16 cm.
KAS

3380   Venatio sacra, sive de arte quaerendi Deum, libri XII. Antverpiae, apud Jacobum Meursium, 1650.
[24], 578 [49] p. 31 cm.
KAS

3381   **Haeringshauser, Sigismund.**
Catalogus librorum bibliothecae Mellicensis, Hic catalogus renovatus est iussu Reverendissimi Dni Gaspari abbatis Mellicensis, anno 1605. MS. Benediktinerabtei Melk, Austria, codex 1629. 3 vols.
Microfilm: MnCH proj. no. 2003, 2004, 2006

3382   **Hafner, Wolfgang,** 1922–
Der St. Galler Klosterplan im Lichte von Hildemars Regelkommentar.
(*In* Duft, Johannes. Studien zum St. Galler Klosterplan, 1962. p. 177–192)
PLatS

3383   **Hagan, Harry,** 1947–
An analysis of 1 Samuel 12 and its place within the traditions.
101 leaves, 28 cm.
Thesis (M.A.)–Indiana University, 1975.
Typescript.
InStme

3383a   **Hagarty, Paul Leonard, Bp.,** 1909–
The right to life of the unborn; pastoral letter on abortion. Nassau, Bahamas, Bishop's Office, 1980.
17 p. illus. 20 cm.
BNS; MnCS

        Hagemeyer, Oda.
3384   Ich bin Christ; frühchristliche Martyrerakten. Uebertragen und erläutert von Oda Hagemeyer, O.S.B. Düsseldorf, Patmos-Verlag [1961].
261 p. 20 cm.
MnCS; PLatS

3385   Säben, ein stiller Blickwinkel europäischer Geschichte. Bozen, Verlagsanstalt Athesia [1968].
86 p. illus. 20 cm.
PLatS

3386   **Haid, Leo Michael,** 1849–1924.
Major John André; an historical drama in five acts. Belmont, N.C., Belmont Abbey Press, 1913.
64 p.
NcBe

Haimo, bishop of Halberstadt, d. 853.

3387   Abbreviatio ecclesiasticae historiae. MS. Benediktinerabtei Melk, Austria, codex 1838, f.1r–60r. Duodecimo. Saec. 15.
Microfilm: MnCH proj. no. 2148

3388   Christianarum rerum memoria, i.e. abbreviatio ecclesiasticae historiae. MS. Vienna, Nationalbibliothek, codex 3262, f.1r–36r. Quarto. Saec. 15.
Microfilm: MnCH proj. no. 16,481

3389   Commentarius in Apocalypsin. MS. Vienna, Nationalbibliothek, codex 956, f.74r–83r. Folio. Saec. 11.
Microfilm: MnCH proj. no. 14,274

3390   Expositio super Apocalypsin. MS. Benediktinerabtei Göttweig, Austria, codex 48. 248 f. Folio. Saec. 12.
Microfilm: MnCH proj. no. 3337

3391   Explanatio in Apocalypsin. MS. Cistercienserabtei Lilienfeld, Austria, codex 160, f.1r–132v. Quarto. Saec. 13.
Microfilm: MnCH proj. no. 4524

3392   Expositio super Apocalypsin S. Joannis apostoli. MS. Cistercienserabtei Rein, Austria, codex 64, f.1v–179r. Folio. Saec. 12.
Microfilm: MnCH proj. no. 7463

3393   Expositio super Apocalypsin. MS. Cistercienserabtei Zwettl, Austria, codex 41, f.75v–200r. Folio. Saec. 12.
Microfilm: MnCH proj. no. 6634

3394   Commentarium in Apocalypsin. MS. Linz, Studienbibliothek, codex 22, f.1r–151v. Folio. Saec. 13.
Microfilm: MnCH proj. no. 27,973

3395   Expositio in Apokalypsin Johannis. MS. Universitätsbibliothek Innsbruck, Austria, codex 250, f.1r–143r. Folio. Saec. 14.
Microfilm: MnCH proj. no. 28,281

3396   Expositio super Apocalypsin MS. Klagenfurt, Austria, Studienbibliothek, codex cart. 125. 178 f. Folio. Saec. 14 (1388).
Microfilm: MnCH proj. no. 13,108

3397   Expositio in Apocalypsin. MS. Vienna, Nationalbibliothek, codex 4840, f.1r–123v. Folio. Saec. 14.
Microfilm: MnCH proj. no. 18,017

3398   Expositio in Apocalypsin. MS. Benediktinerabtei Göttweig, Austria, codex 233. 103 f. Folio. Saec. 15.
Microfilm: MnCH proj. no. 3501

3399   Glossa super Apocalypsin. MS. Augustinerchorherrenstift Klosterneuburg, Austria, codex 316, f.145r–253r. Folio. Saec. 15.
Microfilm: MnCH proj. no. 5289

3400   Expositio super Apocalypsim. MS. Benediktinerabtei Melk, Austria, codex 573, f.99–362. Folio. Saec. 15.
Microfilm: MnCH proj. no. 1478

3401   Expositio super Apocalypsim. MS. Cistercienserabtei Stams, Tirol, codex 54, f.72v–177r.
Microfilm: MnCH proj. no. 29,844

3402   Expositio in Apocalypsim. MS. Vienna, Nationalbibliothek, codex 3784, f.1r–135v. Folio. Saec. 15.
Microfilm: MnCH proj. no. 16,985

3403   Commentarius in Cantica Canticorum. MS. Universitätsbibliothek Graz, Austria, codex 591, f.145r–172v. Folio. Saec. 14.
Microfilm: MnCH proj. no. 26,730

3404   Expositio super Epistolas Pauli. MS. Universitätsbibliothek Graz, Austria, codex 406. 2 vols. Folio. Saec. 11.
Microfilm: MnCH proj. no. 26,587

3405   Commentarii in omnes Pauli Epistolas. MS. Klagenfurt, Austria, Studienbibliothek, codex cart. 24, 367 f. Folio. Saec. 14.
Microfilm: MnCH proj. no. 13,011

3406   Super Epistolas Pauli. MS. Augustinerchorherrenstift Klosterneuburg, Austria, codex 248, f.1v–288r. Folio. Saec. 12.
Microfilm: MnCH proj. no. 5214

3407   Commentarium in beati Pauli Epistolas. MS. Linz, Austria, Studienbibliothek, codex 98. 233 f. Folio. Saec. 12.
Microfilm: MnCH proj. no. 28,010

3408   Commentarium in Epistolas S. Pauli. MS. Lincoln Cathedral Library, England, codex 171. 244 f. Quarto. Saec. 12.
Microfilm: MnCH

3409   Espositio super Epistolas et Evangelia per circulum anni. MS. Vienna, Nationalbibliothek, codex 919. 294 f. Folio. Saec. 12.
Microfilm: MnCH proj. no. 14,242

3410   Commentarius in Pauli Epistolas. MS. Vienna, Nationalbibliothek, codex 1549. 169 f. Folio. Saec. 12.
Microfilm: MnCH proj. no. 14,892

3411   Commentarius in Epistolas S. Pauli. MS. Benediktinerabtei Admont, Austria, codex 160. 295 f. Folio. Saec. 13.
Microfilm: MnCH proj. no. 9278

3412   Commentarium in Epistolas Pauli ad Romanos et ad Hebraeos. MS. Klagenfurt, Austria, Studienbibliothek, codex cart. 155, f.1r–100r. Folio. Saec. 14.
Microfilm: MnCH proj. no. 1

3413   Expositio Heumonis super aliquas Epistolas Pauli. MS. Benediktinerabtei

Kremsmünster, Austria, codex 300, f.24v–32v. Saec. 14.
Microfilm: MnCH proj. no. 286

3414   Commentarius in Epistolas S. Pauli. MS. Vienna, Nationalbibliothek, codex 944. 248 f. Folio. Saec. 14.
Microfilm: MnCH proj. no. 14,268

3415   Expositio super Epistolas S. Pauli. MS. Benediktinerabtei Melk, Austria, codex 1801, f.4r–12v. Quarto. Saec. 15.
Microfilm: MnCH proj. no. 2116

3416   Sermones dominicales super Epistolas S. Pauli. MS. Benediktinerabtei St. Paul im Lavanttal, Austria, codex 105/4, pars I. Folio. Saec. 15.
Microfilm: MnCH proj. no. 12,343

3417   Commentarium super omnes Epistolas S. Pauli. MS. St. Pölten, Austria, Diöcesanbibliothek, codex 4. 416 f. Folio. Saec. 15.
Microfilm: MnCH proj. no. 6248

3418   Commentarius in S. Pauli Epistolas. MS. Vienna, Nationalbibliothek, codex 4795, f.1v–226v. Folio. Saec. 15.
Microfilm: MnCH proj. no. 17,928

3419   Homiliae. MS. Universitätsbibliothek Salzburg, codex M II 174. 101 f. Folio. Saec. 11.
Microfilm: MnCH proj. no. 11,242

3420   Homiliae. MS. Benediktinerabtei Admont, Austria, codex 108. 136 f. Folio. Saec. 12.
Microfilm: MnCH proj. no. 9207

3421   Homiliae per circulum anni ex diversis libris collectae. MS. Cistercienserabtei Zwettl, Austria, codex 21, f.2r–158v. Folio. Saec. 12.
Microfilm: MnCH proj. no. 6614

3422   Memoria christianarum rerum, i.e. Abbreviatio historiae ecclesiasticae libri X. MS. Benediktinerabtei Melk, Austria, codex 1092, f.143r–197v. Duodecimo. Saec. 15.
Microfilm: MnCH proj. no. 1845

3423   Quaestiones excerptae ex Haimo et Augustino. MS. Benediktinerabtei St. Peter, Salzburg, codex b.I.27, f.325r–336r. Octavo. Saec. 15.
Microfilm: MnCH proj. no. 10,299

3424   Dicta Haymonis de sanctis (Sermones de sanctis). MS. Universitätsbibliothek Innsbruck, Austria, codex 457, f.1r–71v. Quarto. Saec. 14.
Microfilm: MnCH proj. no. 28,454

3425   Super canones. MS. Benediktinerabtei Admont, Austria, codex 764. 33 f. Octavo. Saec. 12.
Microfilm: MnCH proj. no. 9802

3426 In omnes Psalmos pia brevis ac dilucida explanatio, quam ille veluti spiritualis apicula ex omnium veterum hortis ac pratis florentissimus decerpsit, quo simplicibus & occupatis esset parata saluberrimi mellis copia. Aeditio secunda. Coloniae, 1532.
798 p.
NcBe

3427 **Haiss, Emmanuel,** 1896–
Cathedral of Our Lady of Ettal. Ettal Abbey, n.d.
31 p. illus. 17 cm.
PLatS

3428 **Hale, Robert, O.S.B.Cam.**
Christ and the universe; Teilhard de Chardin and the cosmos. Chicago, Franciscan Herald Press [1973].
125 p.
MoCo

Hall, Jeremy, Sister, 1918–
3429 The full stature of Christ: the ecclesiology of Virgil Michel. A golden anniversary edition, 1926–1976. Collegeville, Minn., The Liturgical Press, 1976.
xix, 234 p. 24 cm.
InStme; MdRi; MnCS; MnStj; MoCo; KAS

3430 Meditations on the "O" antiphons, by a Sister of Saint Benedict. St. Joseph, Minn., Sisters of St. Benedict, 1962–1968.
7 v. illus.
InFer; MnStj (Archives)

3431 A Thomistic theory of social control.
55 p.
Thesis (M.A.)–Catholic University of America, 1951.
Typescript.
MnStj (Archives)

Hallinger, Kassius, 1911–
3432 Der Barberinus Latinus 477.
(*In* Sapientiae procerum amore; mélanges médiévistes offerts à Dom Jean-Pierre Müller . . . Roma, 1974. p. 21–64)
PLatS

3433 Initia consuetudinis benedictinae; consuetudines saeculi octavia et noni . . . Siegburg, F. Schmidt, 1963.
cxxiii, 626 p. 26 cm. (Corpus consuetudinum monasticarum, t.1)
InStme; KAS; NdRi; PLatS

3434 Regula Benedicti 64 und die Wahlgewohnheiten des 6.-12. Jahrhunderts.
(*In* Latinität und alte Kirche; Festschrift für Rudolf Hanslik zum 70. Geburtstag. Wien, 1977. p. 109–130)
MnCS

3435 Zur geistigen Welt der Anfänge Klunys.
(*In* Richter, Helmut, ed. Cluny; Beiträge zu Gestalt und Wirkung der Cluniazenisi-

schen Reform. Darmstadt, 1975. p. 91–124)
MnCS

3436 (ed) Corpus consuetudinum monasticarum, cura Pontificii Athenaei Sancti Anselmi de Urbe editum. Publici iuris fecit Kassius Hallinger, O.S.B. Siegburg, apud Franciscum Schmitt, 1962–
v. 26 cm.
AStb; InStme; KAS; MoCo; NcBe; MnCS; PLatS

3437 **Halloran, Briant James,** 1919–
Saint Gregory I – a Benedictine.
43 leaves, 28 cm.
Typescript.
PLatS

3438 **Hamel, Raoul,** 1903–
La vie liturgique; Messes du dimanche. Saint-Benoît-du-Lac [Canada], 1946.
392 p. 19 cm.
CaQMo; CaQStB; KAS; NElmM

Hammenstede, Albert, 1876–1955.
3439 Die Friedensmission des Königtums Christi . . . Münster i.W., Aschendorff, 1927.
32 p. 21 cm.
MnCS

3440 Die Liturgie als Erlebnis. 4. u. 6., verb. Aufl. Freiburg i.B., Herder, 1922.
xi, 98 p. 17 cm.
First published 1919.
KAS; NcBe; PLatS

3441 Retreat conferences, 1936.
134 p. 27 cm.
Typescript.
This text presents two retreats; the first has ten conferences, the second is incomplete, breaking off near the end of the seventh conference.
KAS; PLatS (155 p.)

3441a The religious life. 1938.
15, 15, 12, 11, 8 leaves. 28 cm.
Typescript.
Contents: Retreat conferences.– Religious life in the early Church (until the ninth century).– Religious life in the Catholic Church (from the ninth to the twentieth century).– The liturgy and art.– The Eucharist (the Antepast of the "Beata visio")
PLatS

3442 **Haneburg, Daniel Bonifacius von,** 1816–1876.
E. Renan's Leben Jesu, beleuchtet von Dr. Daniel Bonifacius Haneburg. Regensburg, Georg Joseph Manz, 1864.
91 p. 21 cm.
InStme

3443 **Hansen, Regina, Sister.**
The "atmospherical medium"; a study of the romantic milieu in Hawthorne's major fiction.
190 p.
Thesis (Ph.D.)–Marquette University, 1972.
MnCS (microfilm)

3444 **Hantsch, Hugo,** 1895–
Reich und Kirche von Karl dem Grossen bis zum Investiturstreit.
(*In* Der heilige Altmann, Bischof von Passau. Göttweig, 1965. p. 8–15)
PLatS

3445 **Hardebeck, Helen, Sister.**
Development of a model for designing programs of tutorial interaction among language learners.
Thesis (Ph.D.)–University of Texas, Austin, 1976.
TxB

3446 **Harmeling, Deborah, Sister.**
The story of Covington's Monte Cassino Chapel. Thomas More College, 1969.
51 p. 28 cm.
Typescript.
KyCovS

3447 **Harrison, Genevieve, Sister.**
Where there was need; a history of the Chicago Benedictine Sisters from 1861 to 1965.
234 p. illus. 29 cm.
Xeroxed.
ICSS

3448 **Hartmann, abbot of St. Gall,** d. ca.924.
Ex Hartmanni vita S. Wilboradae.
(*In* Monumenta Germaniae historica. Scriptores. Stuttgart, 1963. t.4, p. 352–457)
MnCS; PLatS

3449 **Hartmann, Christopher,** d. 1637.
Annales heremi Dei Parae Matris monasterii in Helvetio Ordinis S. Benedicti antiqvitate, religione . . . Friburgi Brisgoviae, ex Typographio Archiducali, 1612.
[8], 478, [60] p. engrs. 33 cm.
InStme; KAS; MoCo; PLatS

Hathorn, Raban, 1916–
3450 Annual community retreat notes June 8–12, 1959. [Collegeville, Minn., St. John's Abbey].
20 p. 28 cm.
Typescript.
MnCS

3451 Marriage; an interfaith guide for all couples. Edited by Raban Hathorn, O.S.B., William H. Genné [and] Mordecai L. Brill. New York, Association Press [1970].

253 p. 21 cm.
InStme

3452 The relation between the English literary lyric and musical composition in post-Renaissance development.
iv, 64 leaves, 28 cm.
Thesis (M.A.)–Catholic University of America.
Typescript.
InStme

Hau, Johannes, 1899–
3453 Die Erzbruderschaft des hl. Matthias in Geschichte und Gegenwart . . . Trier, Paulinus-Druckerei [1936].
50 p. 23 cm.
MnCS

3454 Die Heiligen von St. Matthias in ihrer Verehrung. n.p., Saarbrücker Druckerei, 1933.
142 p. illus. 20 cm.
MnCS

Haunstinger, Nepomuk, 1756–1798.
3455 Süddeutsche Klöster vor hundert Jahren; Reisetagebuch des P. Nepomuk Haunstinger . . . Hrsg. . . . von P. Gabriel Meier. Köln, M. P. Bachem, 1889.
xv, 114 p. 22 cm.
KAS; MnCS; PLatS

3456 **Hausmann, Daniel, Sister.**
Role of the president in American four-year liberal arts colleges conducted by the Benedictine Sisters.
199 p., tables.
Typescript, Washington, D.C., 1963.
InFer; MnStj

Häussling, Angelus, 1932–
3457 The celebration of the Eucharist, by Karl Rahner and Angelus Häussling. [Translated by W. J. O'Hara]. New York, Herder and Herder [1968].
x, 132 p. 21 cm.
Translation of: Die vielen Messen und das eine Opfer.
InStme

3457a Das Buch der Benediktregel in der Abtei Maria Laach; eine kleine Austellung im Benediktus-Jahr 1980. Maria Laach, 1980.
43 p. 21 cm.
MnCH

3458 Mönchskonvent und Eucharistiefeier; eine Studie über die Messe in der abendländischen Klosterliturgie des frühen Mittelalters und zur Geschichte der Messhäufigkeit. Münster i.W., Aschendorff [1973].
xiv, 380 p. 23 cm.
InStme

3459 Die vielen Messen und das eine Opfer; eine Untersuchung über die rechte Norm der Messhäufigkeit [von] Karl Rahner und Angelus Häussling. 2., überarb. und erw. Aufl. Freiburg, Basel, Wien, Herder [1966].
144 p. 22 cm.
MnCS

3460 **Hauthaler, Willibald Kasper,** 1843–1922.
Die dem heiligen Rupertus, Apostel von Bayern, geweihten Kirchen und Kapellen. Salzburg, Verlag der f. e. Consistorial-Kanzlei, 1885.
31 p. fold. map, 20 cm.
KAS

3461 **Hautecombe, France. Saint Pierre-de-Curtille (Benedictine abbey).**
Saint Benoît et ses fils; textes bénédictins traduits par les moines d'Hautecombe. Introduction et notes par Dom M. F. Lacan. Préface de Daniel-Rops . . . Paris, Fayard [1961].
412 p. 18 cm.
MnCS; PLatS

Havener, Ivan, 1943–
3462 The credal formulae of the New Testament: a history of the scholarly research and a contribution to the on-going study. München, n.p., 1976.
x, 587 p. 21 cm.
Thesis (S.T.D.) – Ludwig-Maximilians Universität, München.
MnCS; MoCo

3462a Spiritual Reading of Scripture. Collegeville, Minn., The Liturgical Press, 1979.
24 p. 20 cm.
MnCS

3463 **Haverkamp, Albert,** 1893–
The solemn glorification of God through parish community singing.
(*In* Proceedings of the liturgical week held for priests at St. Benedict's Abbey, Atchison, Kans., May 8–11, 1944. p. 5–12)
PLatS

Hawkins, Denis John Bernard, 1906–
3464 Christian ethics. New York, Hawthorn Books [1963].
122 p. (The twentieth-century encyclopedia of Catholicism)
NcBe

3465 Crucial problems of modern philosophy. [Notre Dame, Ind.], University of Notre Dame Press, 1962.
158 p.
NcBe

3466 **Hayden, Jerome,** 1902–
Religion and psychiatry; a historical perspective. [Boston?], Marsalin Institute, 1967.

xv, 48 p. 22 cm.
InStme

Hayes, Bernard, 1871–1926.
3467 Ascension Day.
(*In* Sermons for the times by noted preachers of our own day. New York, 1913. v. 2, p. 253–260)
PLatS

3468 Charity – true and false.
(*In* Sermons for the times by noted preachers of our own day. New York, 1913. v. 1, p. 368–377)
PLatS

3469 Faith and hope in Christ.
(*In* Sermons for the times by noted preachers of our own day. New York, 1913. v. 2, p. 121–127)
PLatS

3470 The love of Jesus.
(*In* Sermons for the times by noted preachers of our own day. New York, 1913. v. 1, p. 318–325)
PLatS

3471 The right way of praying.
(*In* Sermons for the times by noted preachers of our own day. New York, 1913. v. 1, p. 246–253)
PLatS

3472 The teaching of penance.
(*In* Sermons for the times by noted preachers of our own day. New York, 1913. v. 2, p. 192–199)
PLatS

3473 **Haymarus monachus.**
De statu Terrae Sanctae. MS. Universitätsbibliothek Graz, Austria, codex 290, f. 6r–11v. Folio. Saec. 12.
Microfilm: MnCH proj. no. 26,215

Haymo, bp. of Halberstadt. *See* Haimo, bp. of Halberstadt.

3474 **Hays, Alice Marie, Sister.**
A song in the pines; the history of Benet Hill Community. Erie, Pa., 1973.
177 p. illus.
ICSS; KAM; MdRi; MnStj; CoCsB

3475 **Healy, Sylvester,** 1891–
The plans of the new university building.
(*In* Catholic University of Peking. Bulletin, no. 6(1929), p. 3–12)
PLatS

Hébert Desroquettes, Jean, 1887–
3476 Gregorian musical values. Cincinnati, Ralph Jusko Publications, 1943 (1961?).
xiv, 71 p. music, 23 cm.
MnCS

3477 Gregorian musical values. London, Chappell; Cincinnati, R. Jusko Publications, 1963.

vii, 72 p. music, 24 cm.
PLatS

3478 **Hecht, Laurenz,** 1800–1871.
Vollständiger Bericht über die wunder-
bare Bekehrung des jungen Israeliten
Maria Alphons Ratisbonae zu Rom im
Januar 1842 . . . Einleitung von P.
Laurenz Hecht. 2. Aufl. Einsiedeln, Ben-
ziger, 1843.
xx, 192 p. illus. 17 cm.
InStme

3479 **Heck, Theodore,** 1901–
The formation and present status of the
course of studies in the major seminary. 62
leaves, 28 cm.
Thesis (M.A.)–Catholic University of
America, 1933.
Typescript.
InStme

Hedley, John Cuthbert, 1837–1915.
3480 Faith; a pastoral letter (Lent, 1908), by
the bishop of Newport. London, Catholic
Truth Society, 1908.
16 p. 18 cm.
MnCS

3481 Heaven.
(*In* Heaven; an anthology. New York,
1935. p. 37–44)
InFer; PLatS

3482 The light of the Holy Spirit in the world.
Herefore, W. Prosser [1873?].
3 pts. in 1 v. 19 cm.
KAS

3483 The monasticism of St. Gregory the
Great.
(*In* The Centenary of St. Gregory the
Great at Downside. Downside, 1890. p.
29–40)
PLatS

3484 New work and old ways; a sermon
preached at the opening of the monastery
and college of St. Benedict, at Fort
Augustus, on August 26, 1880. London,
Burns & Oates, 1880.
32 p. 23 cm.
KAS

3485 The saints of Ireland. Dublin, M. H. Gill,
1933.
13 p. 19 cm.
KAS

3486 Wisdom from above, set forth in sermons. London, Sands & Co., 1934.
272 p.
MoCo; NdBiA

3487 **Heer, Gall,** 1897–
Aus der Vergangenheit von Kloster und
Tal Engelberg, 1120–1970. Verlag Bene-
diktinerkloster Engelberg [1975].

554 p.
MoCo

3488 **Heer, Rusten.**
Commentarius super Regulam S. Bene-
dicti. MS. Benediktinerabtei St. Paul im
Lavanttal, Austria, codex 230/2, pars I.
Folio. Saec. 18.
Microfilm: MnCH proj. no. 12,055

3489 **Hegglin, Benno,** 1884–
Der benediktinische Abt in rechts-
geschichtlicher Entwicklung und
geltenden Kirchenrecht. St. Ottilien, Eos
Verlag, 1961.
xxiv, 227 p. 24 cm.
InStme; KAS; MnCS; NcBe; NdRi;
PLatS

3490 **Heidlage, Rebecca, Sister.**
Characteristics of college student
volunteers involved in the Atchison Community Center Tutorial program.
vi, 73 leaves. 28 cm.
Thesis (M.S. in Ed.)–University of Kansas, 1973.
Typescript.
KAM

Heidt, William George, 1913–
3491 The Book of the Apocalypse. Introduction and commentary by William G. Heidt,
O.S.B. Collegeville, Minn., The Liturgical
Press [1962].
128 p. 20 cm. (New Testament reading
guide, 14)
MnCS; PLatS

3491a Canticle of canticles and the Book of
Wisdom. Collegeville, Minn., Human Life
Center, 1979.
MnCS

3492 Genesis 1:1-11: 32. Introduction and
commentary. Collegeville, Minn.,
The Liturgical Press [1967].
88 p. 20 cm. (Old Testament reading
guide, 9)
MnCS; PLatS

3493 Inspiration, canonicity, texts, versions,
hermeneutics–a general introduction to
Sacred Scripture. Collegeville, Minn.,
The Liturgical Press [1970].
124 p. 20 cm. (Old-New Testament
reading guide, v. 31)
MnCS; PLatS

3494 The major Old Testament theme. Collegeville, Minn., The Liturgical Press
[1968].
68 p. 20 cm. (Old Testament reading
guide, 30)
MnCS; PLatS

3494a A short breviary for religious and the
laity. 3rd ed [of Complete edition]. Collegeville, Minn., The Liturgical Press, 1962.

1568 p. plates, music. 16 cm. (Popular liturgical library)
KAS; MnCS; NcBe

3495 **Heigl, Gotthard,** 1834–1912.
Die weltlichen Oblaten des hl. Benedictus; historische Skizze. Brünn, Druck der Benedictiner Buchdruckeri, 1889.
24, 5 p. 23 cm.
KAS; PLatS

3496 **Das Heiligtum Mariä-Heimgang auf dem Berge Sion;** Festschrift zur Kirchweihe am 10. April 1910. Prag, Verlag der St. Benedikts-Stimmen, Abtei Emaus, 1910.
xcviii p. 16 plates, 23 cm.
NdRi; PLatS

Heiming, Odilo, 1898–
3497 Die altmailändische Heiligenvigil.
(*In* Heilige Ueberlieferung. Münster, 1938. p. 174–192)
PLatS

3498 Corpus Ambrosiano-Liturgicum.
Münster i.W., Aschendorff, 1968–
v. facsims. 26 cm.
InStme; MnCS

3499 **Heimling, Leander.**
Catalogus manuscriptorum bibliothecae Altenburgensis. Anno 1924. MS. Benediktinerabtei Altenburg, Austria, codex AB 5 Bb 79. 50 p. Quarto. Saec. 20 (1924).
Microfilm: MnCH proj. no. 6576

Heimo. *See* Haimo.

3500 **Hein, Kenneth.**
Eucharist and excommunication; a study in early Christian doctrine and discipline. Bern, Herbert Lang; Frankfurt/M., Peter Lang, 1973.
xiii, 491 p. 21 cm. (European university papers. Series 23: Theology, v. 19)
InStme

3501 **Heindl, Emmeram,** 1854–1917.
Der heilige Berg Andechs in seiner Geschichte, seinen Merkwürdigkeiten und Heiligthümern. München, Lentner, 1895.
xv, 19 6 p. illus. 24 cm.
AStb; InStme

Heinrich von Melk, 12th cent.
3502 Der sogenannte Heinrich von Melk. Nach R. Heinzels Ausgabe von 1867 neu hrsg. von Richard Kienast. Heidelberg, Carl Winter Universitätsverlag, 1946.
80 p. 18 cm.
Middle High German poetry.
MnCS

3503 Henricus. Von des todes gehügende. Carmen. MS. Vienna, Nationalbibliothek, codex 2696, f.83r–89v. Folio. Saec. 14.
Microfilm: MnCH proj. no. 15,949

3504 **Heinricus, abbot of Breitenau,** d. ca. 1170.
Des Abtes Heinrich zu Bretanau Passio (inedita) S. Thimonis . . . von Dr. Nolte. Wien, Karl Gerold's Sohn, 1876.
8 p. 23 cm.
MnCS

3505 **Heinz, Gerard,** 1864–1946.
St. Benedict's Parish, Atchison, Kansas; an historical sketch, 1858–1908. Atchison, Kans., Abbey Student Press, St. Benedict's College, [1908?].
[38] leaves. illus., ports. 26 cm.
KAM; KAS

3506 **Heitmann, Adalhard,** 1907–
Imitatio Dei; die ethische Nachahmung Gottes nach der Väterlehre der zwei ersten Jahrhunderte. Romae, Herder, 1940.
Xeroxed copy, University Microfilms, Ann Arbor, Mich.
InStme

Helbling, Leo, 1901–
3507 Das Blockbuch von Sankt Meinrad und seinen Mördern und vom Ursprung von Einsiedeln. Farbige Faksimile-Ausgabe zum elften Zentenar des Heiligen, 861–1961. Mit einer Einleitung von Leo Helbling. Einsiedeln, Benziger, 1961.
35 p. facims. [64] p.
InStme

3508 Die "Exhortationes in Regulam sancti Benedicti" des Einsiedler Abtes Augustin Reding.
(*In* Studien aus dem Gebiete von Kirche und Kultur. Paderborn, 1930. p. 87–127).
PLatS

3509 Sankt Meinrad zum elften Zentenarium seines Todes, 861–1961. Hrsg. von Benediktinern des Klosters Maria Einsiedeln. Einsiedeln, Benziger, 1961.
126 p. illus. 22 cm.
Preface signed: Leo Helbling, O.S.B.
InStme

3510 **Helgaldus, monk of Fleury,** d.ca.1048.
Vie de Robert le Pieux; Epitoma vitae regis Roterti Pii [par] Helgaud de Fleury. Texte édité, traduit et annoté par Robert-Henri Bautier et Gillette Labory . . . Paris, Centre National de la Recherche Scientifique, 1965.
165 p. plates, 25 cm.
InStme; MnCS; PLatS

3511 **Hellman, Mary Carol, Sister.**
Survey of church music in the Diocese of Covington, Kentucky.
Thesis (M.M.)–Catholic University of America, 1971.
Typescript.
KyCovS

3512 **Helmecke, Drutmar,** 1912–
Die theologische Schule der Beuroner
Kongregation.
(*In* Beuron, 1863–1963; Festschrift . . .
Beuron, 1963. p. 441–472)
PLatS

3513 **Helmling, Leander,** 1863–1929.
Die Urkunden des königlichen Stiftes
Emaus in Prag aus den Jahren 1415 bis
1885. Prag, J. G. Calvesche, 1914.
376 p. 24 cm.
MnCS

3514 **Hemmauer, Aemilianus,** 1691–1755.
Historischer Entwurff der im Jahr tau-
send siben hundert ein und dreysieg,
tausendjährlichen Obern Alten Aich . . .
Straubing, Cassian Betz, 1731.
[10], 628 p. 20 cm.
KAS; PLatS

3515 **Hemptinne, Jean de,** 1876–1958.
Dom Pie de Hemptinne, 1880–1907,
moine de l'Abbaye de Maredsous. 10. ed.
Editions de Maredsous [1963].
ix, 282 p. 18 cm.
MnCS

3516 **Henggeler, Rudolf,** 1890–1971.
Helvetia sacra. Reihenfolge der kirch-
lichen Obern und Oberinnen in den schwei-
zerischen Bistümern, Kollegiatstiften und
Klöstern . . . Zug, Verlag Eberhard Kalt-
Sender, 1961–
v. 25 cm.
InStme

3517 Helvetia sacra. Begründer: Rudolf Henggeler. Hrsg. von Albert Bruckner. Bern,
Francke, 1972–
v. maps, 24 cm.
InStme

3518 Die Rosenkranz-Bruderschaft in Einsiedeln.
(*In* Sträter, Paul. Katholische Marienkunde. v. 3 (1952), p. 226–246)
PLatS

3519 Das Stift Einsiedeln und die französische
Revolution . . . Einsiedeln, Einsiedler
Anzeiger, 1924.
160 p. 21 cm.
KAS

3520 **Henricus de S. Gallen.**
Expositiones a variis scriptoribus col-
lectae de passione Jesu Christi. Germanice.
Vienna, Nationalbibliothek, codex 12,546,
f.99r–139r. Quarto. Saec. 15.
Microfilm: MnCH proj. no. 14,452

3521 **Henry, Mary Donna, Sister.**
A selected annotated bibliography of
Catholic short stories of thematic value for
high school students.

Thesis (M.S.L.S.)–Catholic University
of America, 1962.
Typescript.
KyCovS

3522 **Heredia, Antonio de,** fl. 1680.
Vidas de santos, bienaventvrados, y personas venerables de la sagrada religion de
n.p.s. Benito . . . Madrid, M. Alvarez,
1683–85.
4 v. 32 cm.
MnCS (v.1–3 microfilm); PLatS (v.4)

Hergott, Marquard. *See* Herrgott,
Marquard.

3523 **Hering, Roseanne, Sister.**
A comparative study of the achievement
in arithmetic of the 4th grade pupils taught
by two different methods.
Thesis (M.A.)–Marquette University,
1962.
Typescript.
KyCovS

3524 **Hermann, Basilius,** 1883–
Verborgene Heilige des griechischen
Ostens. Kevelaer, Jos. Thum, 1931.
244 p. 19 cm.
InStme

3525 **Hermann, Friedrich,** 1913–
St. Peter, Salzburg, geschichtlicher
Ueberblick. 8. Aufl. Salzburg, Verlag St.
Peter, 1967.
23 p. 27 cm.
PLatS

3526 **Hermannus, abbot of Niederaltaich,**
1201–1275.
Chronicon Hermanni abbatis Altaichae
inferioribus, cum continuatione Heinrici
Steronis, ejusdem monasterii monachi, et
fratrum Udalrici et Welling monachorum
ad SS. Udalricum et Afram. MS. Benediktinerabtei Seitenstetten, Austria, codex
13, f.206r–307r. Folio. Saec. 14.
Microfilm: MnCH proj. no. 848

Hermannus Contractus, 1013–1054.
3527 [Selections]
Vesper hymn to the Virgin (Alma
Redemptoris mater). A Vesper psalm
(Salve Regina). Vesper hymn (Ave Regina
caelorum).
(*In* Donahoe, D. J. Early Christian
hymns. New York, 1908. v. 1, p. 151–156)
PLatS

3528 Chronicon. MS. Benediktinerabtei Gött-
weig, Austria, codex 110a, f.44r–83v.
Folio. Saec. 12.
Microfilm: MnCH proj. no. 3393

3529 Chronicon a Christo natu usque ad annum 1159, cum Annalibus Mellicensibus.

MS. Vienna, Nationalbibliothek, codex 427, f.42r–71v. Folio. Saec. 12.
Microfilm: MnCH proj. no. 13,755

3530 Chronicon Hermanni Augiensis, abbreviatum a monacho San Gallensi, ab anno Christi 1 usque ad annum 1075. MS. Vienna, Nationalbibliothek, codex 352, f. 26v–39v. Folio. Saec. 13.
Microfilm: MnCH proj. no. 13,683

3531 Annales Claustro-Neoburgenses et Chronicon Salisburgense alias Chronicon Hermanni Contracti cum continuatione Weichhardi de Polheim. MS. Vienna, Nationalbibliothek, codex 9533. 120 f. Folio. Saec. 17.
Microfilm: MnCH proj. no. 19,250

3532 Herimanni Augiensis Chronicon; Hermann von Reichenau Chronik.
(*In* Quellen des 9 und 11 Jahrhunderts zur Geschichte der hamburgischen Kirche und des Reiches, p. 613–707)
Latin and German.
PLatS

3533 Liber de mensura Astrolabii. MS. Benediktinerabtei St. Peter, Salzburg, codex a.VI.32, f.94r–96v. Octavo. Saec. 11–12.
Microfilm: MnCH proj. no. 10,063

3534 Sermones de sanctis per circulum anni. MS. Vienna, Nationalbibliothek, codex 1329. 100 f. Quarto. Saec. 14.
Microfilm: MnCH proj. no. 14,682

3535 **Herrad von Landsberg, abbess of Hohenburg,** d. 1195.
Hortus deliciarum (Garden of delights). Commentary and notes by A. Straub and G. Keller. Edited and translated [from the French] by Aristide D. Caratzas. New Rochelle, N.Y., Caratzas Brothers, 1977.
xxxii, 250 p. illus. (facsim.) 41 cm.
MnCS; PLatS

Herrgott, Marquard, 1694–1762.
3536 Ad historiam S. Blasii. MS. Benediktinerabtei St. Paul im Lavanttal, Austria, codex 195/2. 2 vols. Folio. Saec. 18.
Microfilm: MnCH proj. no. 12,013 & 12,015

3537 Collectanea pro historia augustae domus Austriacae. MS. Benediktinerabtei St. Paul im Lavanttal, Austria, codex 57/2–58/2. 5 vols. Folio. Saec. 18.
Microfilm: MnCH proj. no. 11,807; 11,813–15; 11,822; 11,857

3538 Collectanea pro nummotheca augustae domus Austriacae. MS. Benediktinerabtei St. Paul im Lavanttal, Austria, codex 58/2. 283 f. Folio. Saec. 18.
Microfilm: MnCH proj. no. 11,814

3539 Diaria über seine Wiener-Geschäften de annis 1728–1730. MS. Benediktinerabtei St. Paul im Lavanttal, Austria, codex 166/2. 2 vols. Folio. Saec. 18.
Microfilm: MnCH proj. no. 11,960 & 11,965

3540 Diplomata monasterii S. Blasii concernantia ab annis 1093–1236. MS. Benediktinerabtei St. Paul im Lavanttal, codex 60/2. 396 f. Folio. Saec. 18.
Microfilm: MnCH proj. no. 11,812

3541 Libellus precatoris ad S. Blasianum . . . translatus ex lingua latina in linguam hebraicam opera F. Marquardi Herrgott et F. Theodorici Seiz. MS. Benediktinerabtei St. Paul im Lavanttal, Austria, codex 73/6. 63 f. Octavo. Saec. 18 (1721).
Microfilm: MnCH proj. no. 12,616

3542 Monasticon San-Blasianum. MS. Benediktinerabtei St. Paul im Lavanttal, Austria, codex 196/2. 361 f. Folio. Saec. 18.
Microfilm: MnCH proj. no. 12,028

3543 Monumenta. MS. Benediktinerabtei St. Paul im Lavanttal, Austria, codex 59/2. 6 vols. Folio. Saec. 18.
Microfilm: MnCH proj. no. 11,801; 11,804; 11,806; 11,807; 11,808; 11,809; 11,811.

3544 Orationes Romae habitae, etc. MS. Benediktinerabtei St. Paul im Lavanttal, Austria, codex 291/2. 441 p. Quarto. Saec. 18 (1716).
Microfilm: MnCH proj. no. 12,129

3545 **Hertlein, Siegfried Oswald,** 1931–
Christentum und Mission im Urteil der neoafrikanischen Prosaliteratur. Münsterschwarzach, Vier-Türme-Verlag [1962].
xxiii, 216 p. 21 cm.
PLatS

3546 **Herveus, monk of Bourg-Dieu,** 1080(ca.)–1150.
Commentarium in Jesiam prophetam, cum praefatione Isidori Hispalensis. MS. Augustinerchorherrenstift Klosterneuburg, Austria, codex 166. 243 f. Folio. Saec. 12.
Microfilm: MnCH proj. no. 5131

Herwegen, Ildefons, 1874–1946.
3547 De apostolatu liturgico. Ad manuscripti instar typis mandatum.
11 p. 29 cm.
MnCS

3548 Germanische Rechtssymbolik in der römischen Liturgie. Sonderausgabe . . . Darmstadt, Wissenschaftliche Buchgesellschaft, 1962. 38 p. 19 cm.
MnCS

3549   The Holy Rule of our holy father Saint Benedict; lectures given in the Liturgical Academy of Maria Laach 1935–36. Compiled from notes taken by several auditors of his course.
311 p. 29 cm.
Multigraphed.
MnCS; PLatS

3550   Das Pactum des hl. Fruktuosus von Brara; ein Beitrag zur Geschichte des suevisch-westgothischen Mönchtums und seines Rechtes. Mit einem Vorwort des Herausgebers. Stuttgart, F. Enke, 1907; Amsterdam, P. Schippers, 1965.
x, 84 p. 23 cm.
PLatS

3551   Väterspruch und Mönchsregel. 2., unveränderte Aufl. hrsg. und durch einen Vortrag ergänst von Emmanuel v. Severus, O.S.B. Münster i.W., Aschendorff, 1977.
InStme; MoCo; NcBe

Hesbert, René Jean, 1899–
3552   Les compositions rythmiques en l'honneur de Saint Colomban.
(*In* Mélanges colombaniens. Paris, 1950. p. 327–358)
PLatS

3553   Les manuscrits musicaux de Jumièges. Macon, Protat frères, 1954.
102 p. 100 plates (facsims.) 33 cm. (Monumentamusicae sacrae, 2)
InStme; PLatS

3554   Spiritualité de l'action; à l'école de Monsieur Vincent . . . Paris, Editions Alsatia [1960].
204 p. illus. 19 cm.
MnCS; PLatS

3555   (ed) Corpus antiphonalium officii . . . Roma, Herder, 1963–
InStme; MnCS; PLatS

3556   (ed) Mabillon, Jean. Science et sainteté; l'étude dans la vie monastique. Textes recueillis et présentés par Dom René-Jean Hesbert. Paris, Editions Alsatia [1958]
CaQStB; InStme; PLatS

3557   (ed) Martin, Claude. Conférences ascétiques . . . Texte publié avec préface et notes d'après le ms. Paris, B.N. fr. 17105 par Dom René Jean Hesbert. Paris, Editions Alsatia, 1956–57.
2 vols. 20 cm.
CaQStB; PLatS

3558   (ed) Le Prosaire d'Aix-la-Chapelle. Manuscrit 13 du Chapitre d'Aix-la-Chapelle (XIIIe siècle, début). Rouen, Imprimerie Rouennaise, 1961.
105 p. 99 facsims., music. 32 cm.

3559   **Hess, Ignaz,** 1871–1963.
Die Kunst im Kloster Engelberg. Schriften zur Heimatkunde von Engelberg, 1946.
136 p. illus.
MoCo

3560   **Hess, Luke,** 1867–1941.
New Subiaco Abbey; a retrospect on the occasion of the silver jubilee of Abbot Ignatius Conrad, O.S.B., 1917. With an appendix by Vincent Orth, O.S.B.
12 p. illus. 25 cm.
ArSu; InStme; KAS

3561   **Hess, Salesius,** 1899–
Das Kloster Banz in seinen Beziehungen zu den Hochstiften Bamberg und Würzburg under Abt Johannes Burckhard . . . St. Ottilien, Missionsdruckerei, 1935.
xii, 101 p. 23 cm.
KAS

Hettich, Blaise, 1924–
3562   Prayer starters for every day, 1971. With the Mass year guide. St. Meinrad, Ind., Abbey Press [1970].
80 p. 15 cm.
InStme; MnCS

3563   Sex in your marriage; everything for the Christian family. St. Meinrad, Ind., Abbey Press, 1964.
63 p.
InFer

3564   **Heuch, Andreas, monk of Melk.**
Excerpta ex Chronica Mellicensi de fundatione et aliis ejusdem monasterii, MS. Benediktinerabtei Melk, Austria, codex 1917,1, f.91v–97r. Quarto. Saec. 15.
Microfilm: MnCH proj. no. 2202

Heufelder, Emmanuel Maria, 1898–
3565   Die Fackel des Vertrauens und der Liebe weiterreichen! Erwägungen über die Ansprache Papst Johannes XXIII am 8 Dezember 1962 an die Konzilväter. Meitingen bei Augsburg, Kyrios-Verlag [1963].
22 p. 18 cm.
MnCS

3566   In the hope of His coming; studies in Christian unity. Translated by Otto M. Knab. Notre Dame, Ind., Fides Publishers [1964].
261 p. 21 cm.
InFer; InStme; KAS; MnCS; MoCo; PLatS

3567   Konzil und Einigung der Christenheit. Recklinghausen, Paulus Verlag [1961].
28 p. 17 cm.
MnCS

3568   A new Pentecost. Translated by Gregory J. Roettger. Collegeville, Minn., The Liturgical Press, 1976.

67 p. 18 cm.
MnCS; MoCo

3569   Niederalteich; Benediktinerabtei und Basilika. 10. erweiterte Farbausgabe. München, Schnell & Steiner, 1972.
18 p. illus., col. plates, 17 cm.
MnCS

3570   Der Ruf zur Einheit. Recklinghausen, Paulus Verlag [1962].
24 p. 16 cm.
MnCS

3571   The Spirit prays in us: reflections on Romans 8:26-27. Translated by Gregory J. Roettger. Collegeville, Minn., The Liturgical Press, 1976.
48 p. 18 cm.
MnCS; MoCo

3572   St. Benedikt von Nursia und die Kirche. (*In* Daniélous, Jean, ed. Sentire Ecclesiam. Freiburg, 1961. p. 176–184)
PLatS

3573   Weite des Herzens; Meditationen über den Geist der Benediktusregel. Regensburg, F. Pustet [1971].
125 p. 19 cm.
InStme; MoCo

3574   **Heufler, Adalbertus.**
Disputationes de praecipuis controversiis christianae fidei adversus nostri temporis haereticos traditae ab Adalberto Heufler benedictino Admontensi . . . quas excepit Fr. Aemilianus Stockhamer, O.S.B., ad S. Petrum Salisb. anno 1668. MS. Benediktinerabtei St. Peter, Salzburg, codex f.III.19. 135 p. Quarto. Saec. 17.
Microfilm: MnCH proj. no. 10,370

Hickey, Regis Francis, 1917–
3575   A comparison of English, history and religion/theology grades at St. Benedict's College.
iii, 31 leaves, 30 cm.
Thesis (M.S.)–Kansas State Teachers College, Emporia, 1971.
Typescript.
KAS

3576   Kansas monks in Brazil. v. 1–4, 1962–1971. Atchison, Kans., St. Benedict's Abbey.
Editor: Regis Hickey, O.S.B.
KAS

3577   **Hiedl, Augustin.**
Die Pseudo-Augustinische Schrift "De spiritu et anima" in den frühwerken Alberts des Grossen.
(*In* Sapientiae procerum amore; mélanges médiévistes offerts à Dom Jean-Pierre Müller . . . Roma, 1974, p. 91–121)
PLatS; MnCS

3578   **Hieronymus de Mondsee.**
Opuscula. MS. Benediktinerabtei Lambach, Austria, codex chart. 472. 186 f. Duodecimo. Saec. 15.
Microfilm: MnCH proj. no. 751

3579   **Hieronymus de Werdea,** d. 1475.
Psalterium de D. N. Iesu Christo.
(*In* Analecta hymnica Medii Aevi. New York, 1961. v. 35, p. 64–78)
PLatS

Highbaugh, Assunta, Sister.
3580   An analysis of the teacher-education programs of the Benedictine Sisters in the United States. Washington, Catholic University of America, 1961.
xi, 189 p. map, tables. 23 cm.
InFer; InStme; KAS; MnCS; PLatS

3581   Study of the cause of the drop-outs in the Catholic secondary schools of Indianapolis, 1945–1954.
Thesis (M.A.)–Catholic University of America, 1957.
Typescript.
InFer

Hildebertus, abp. of Tours, 1056?–1133.
3582   [Selections]
Address to God the Father (Alpha et Omega magne Deus). The faithful soul (Tutur inane nescit amare).
(*In* Donahoe, D. J. Early Christian hymns. New York, v. 2, p. 99–102)

3583   Carmen: Cur Deus homo. Incipit: Ade peccatum. MS. Augustinerchorherrenstift Klosterneuburg, Austria, codex 248. f.112r.
Microfilm: MnCH proj. no. 5214

3584   De Corpore et Sanguine Christi. MS. Benediktinerabtei St. Peter, Salzburg, codex a.VI.28, f.37v–38v. Octavo. Saec. 12.
Microfilm: MnCH proj. no. 10,099

3585   De expositione Missae. Metrice. MS. Benediktinerabtei St. Peter, Salzburg, codex a.VI.28, f.32v–37v. Octavo. Saec. 12.
Microfilm: MnCH proj. no. 10,099

3586   De vita S. Mariae Egyptiacae. MS. Benediktinerabtei St. Peter, Salzburg, codex a.VI.28, f.39v–46v. Octavo. Saec. 12.
Microfilm: MnCH proj. no. 10,099

3587   Epigrammata undecim. MS. Vienna, Nationalbibliothek, codex 814, f.153r–153v. Quarto. Saec. 14.
Microfilm: MnCH proj. no. 14,120

3588   Epistolae. MS. Toledo, Spain. Biblioteca del Cabildo, codex 10,10. 25 f. Quarto. Saec. 13.
Microfilm: MnCH proj. no. 33,018

3589   Epistolae 70. MS. Vienna, National-
bibliothek, codex 160, f.1r–40v. Quarto.
Saec. 13.
Microfilm: MnCH proj. no. 13,506

3590   Epitaphium Senecae. MS. Vienna, Na-
tionalbibliothek, codex 174, f.12v. Folio.
Saec. 14.
Microfilm: MnCH proj. no. 13,530

3591   Fabulae. MS. Vienna, Nationalbibliothek, codex 303, f. 12v–22v. Octavo. Saec.
14.
Microfilm: MnCH proj. no. 13,646

3592   The hymn of Hildebert and other
mediaeval hymns, with translations by
Erastus C. Benedict. A new and enlarged
edition. New York, Anson D. F. Randolph
& Co., 1868.
xiii, 143 p. 19 cm.
Latin and English on opposite pages.
PLatS

3593   Mohamedes. MS. Vienna, Nationalbibliothek, codex 303, f.52r–64r. Octavo. Saec.
14.
Microfilm: MnCH proj. no. 13,646

3594   Versus de Missa. MS. Universitätsbiblio-
thek Graz, Austria, codex 820, f.48r–52v.
Quarto. Saec. 12.
Microfilm: MnCH proj. no. 26,925

3595   Versus de Sacra Scriptura. MS. Cistercienserabtei Lilienfeld, Austria, codex 124,
f.109r–111v. Folio. Saec. 14.
Microfilm: MnCH proj. no. 4425

Hildebrand (Pope Gregory VII). *See*
Gregory VII, Pope.

Hildegard, Saint, 1098?–1179.

3596   [Carmina]
(*In* Foucher, J. P. Florilège de poésie
sacrée. Paris, 1961. p. 190–192)
PLatS

3597   Divina revelatio. MS. Benediktinerabtei
Melk, Austria, codex 1554, f.143v–144r.
Duodecimo. Saec. 15.
Microfilm: MnCH proj. no. 1953

3598   Epistolae (166). MS. Vienna, Nationalbibliothek, codex 881. 119 f. Quarto. Saec.
13.
Microfilm: MnCH proj. no. 14,193

3599   Epistolae. MS. Vienna, Nationalbibliothek, codex 963, f.42v–151r. Folio. Saec.
13.
Microfilm: MnCH proj. no. 14,263

3600   Epistolae: Ad clericos sacerdotalis of-
ficii; Ad S. Bernhardum Claravallensem;
Ad congregationem puellarum suarum;
Gunthero episcopo Spirensi (finis deest).
MS. Vienna, Nationalbibliothek, codex
1016, f.116r–121v. Folio. Saec. 13.
Microfilm: MnCH proj. no. 14,321

3601   Epistolae duae de haeresibus praesertim
Wiclefistarum Coloniensium. MS. Vienna,
Nationalbibliothek, codex 4761, f.26v–28v.
Quarto. Saec. 15.
Microfilm: MnCH proj. no. 17,952

3602   Epistola ad clericos Colonienses. MS.
Vienna, Nationalbibliothek, codex 4948,
f.150v–152r. Quarto. Saec. 15.
Microfilm: MnCH proj. no. 14,457

3603   Excerpta ex operibus ejus. MS. Benediktinerabtei St. Peter, Salzburg, codex
b.IV.39, f.106v–127r. Quarto. Saec. 15.
Microfilm: MnCH proj. no. 10,426

3604   Explicatio Regulae S. Benedicti. MS.
Vienna, Nationalbibliothek, codex 3702,
f.228r–236v. Folio. Saec. 15.
Microfilm: MnCH proj. no. 16,913

3605   Heilkunde; das Buch von dem Grund und
Wesen und der Heilung der Kranken-
heiten. Nach den Quellen übersetzt und
erläutert von Henirich Schipperges. Salzburg, Otto Müller Verlag [1957].
332 p. 23 cm.
MnCS

3605a   [Liber simplicis medicinae]
Naturkunde; das Buch von dem inneren
Wesen der verschiedenen Naturen in der
Schöpfung. Nach den Quellen übersetzt
und erläutert von Peter Riethe. Salzburg,
O. Müller [1959].
176 p. 24 cm.
MnCS

3606   Liber vitae meritorum. MS. Vienna, Na-
tionalbibliothek, codex 1016, f. 1v–108v.
Folio. Saec. 13.
Microfilm: MnCH proj. no. 14,321

3607   Prophetia S. Hildegardis contra mendi-
cantes. MS. Benediktinerabtei Kremsmünster, Austria, codex 94, f.78v–79r.
Saec. 15.
Microfilm: MnCH proj. no. 87

3608   Responsiones super quaestiones. MS.
Vienna, Nationalbibliothek, codex 1016,
f.108v–115v. Folio. Saec. 13.
Microfilm: MnCH proj. no. 14,321

3609   Revelationes, et quidam a lib 3. visione
11. MS. Vienna, Nationalbibliothek, codex
4500. 37 f. Quarto. Saec. 15.
Microfilm: MnCH proj. no. 17,676

3610   Revelationes. Germanice. MS. Vienna,
Nationalbibliothek, codex 2739, f.167v–
169r. Quarto. Saec. 14.
Microfilm: MnCH proj. no. 16,021

3611   Hildegardis Scivias. Edidit Adelgundis
Fuhrkötter, collaborante Angela
Carlevaris. Turnholti, Brepols, 1978.
2 v. illus., facsims. (part col.) 25 cm. (Corpus Christianorum. Continuatio mediaevalis, 43–43A)
InStme

3612 Speculum futuroum temporum. MS. Vienna, Nationalbibliothek, codex 4919, f.61r–83v. Quarto. Saec. 15.
Microfilm: MnCH proj. no. 18,102

3613 Tractatus de morte. Germanice. MS. Vienna, Nationalbibliothek, codex 2739, f.195v–200r. Quarto. Saec. 14.
Microfilm: MnCH proj. no. 16,021

3614 Visio. MS. Augustinerchorherrenstift Klosterneuburg, Austria, codex 809, f.101v. Quarto. Saec. 12.
Microfilm: MnCH proj. no. 5799

3615 Visio. MS. Cistercienserabtei Zwettl, Austria, codex 386, f.176v. Octavo. Saec. 12.
Microfilm: MnCH proj. no. 6978

3616 Visio. MS. Augustinerchorherrenstift Klosterneuburg, Austria, codex 840, f.4v–26r. Quarto. Saec. 13.
Microfilm: MnCH proj. no. 5833

3617 Visio. MS. Incipit: Et iterum audivi vocem de celo. Vienna, Nationalbibliothek, codex 963, f.155r–161r. Folio. Saec. 13.
Microfilm: MnCH proj. no. 14,263

3618 Visio de venerabili sacramento. MS. Cistercienserabtei Lilienfeld, Austria, codex 137, f.1v–16v. Folio. Saec. 14.
Microfilm: MnCH proj. no. 4435

3619 Visio Hiltigardis. Incipit: Vidi ab aquilone bestiae quinque. Vienna, Nationalbibliothek, codex 363, f. 222v. Folio. Saec. 14.
Microfilm: MnCH proj. no. 13,706

3620 Vita S. Ruperti confessoris. MS. Vienna, Nationalbibliothek, codex 963, f.151r–155r. Folio. Saec. 13.
Microfilm: MnCH proj. no. 14,263

Hildemar, monk of Civate, fl. 833.

3621 Epistola de ratione legendi. MS. Cistercienserabtei Heiligenkreuz, Austria, codex 30, f.118v–188v. Folio. Saec. 13.
Microfilm: MnCH proj. no. 4574

3622 Expositio Regulae [S. Benedicti] ab Hildemaro tradita et nunc primum typis mandata. Ratisbonae, Neo-Eboraci, F. Pustet, 1880.
xv, 657 p. 22 cm.
ILSP; KAS; NcBe; PLatS

3623 Tractatus in Regulam S. Benedicti. MS. Benediktinerabtei Melk, Austria, codex 1808. 270 f. Folio. Saec. 13.
Microfilm: MnCH proj. no. 2075

3624 Tractatus in Regulam S. Benedicti. MS. Benediktinerabtei St. Peter, Salzburg, codex a.X.14, f.1r–159r. Folio. Saec. 14.
Microfilm: MnCH proj. no. 10,241

3625 Nota ex tractatu et expositione Regulae S. Benedicti in capitulo de abbate. MS. Vienna, Schottenstift, codex 177, f.344r–369v. Octavo. Saec. 15.
Microfilm: MnCH proj. no. 3910

Hilger, Inez, Sister, 1891–1977.

3626 The Ainu: a vanishing people. 1968.
56 p.
Typescript.
MnStj (Archives)

3627 The Ainu of Japan.
(*In* National Geographic Society research reports. Abstracts and reviews of research . . . during the year 1964. Washington, D.C., 1969, p. 91–103)
MnStj (Archives)

3628 The Ainu then and now; a photographic essay.
87 p.
Manuscript.
MnStj (Archives)

3629 Araucanian customs; an afternoon with an Araucanian family on the coastal range of Chile, by Sister M. Inez Hilger and Margaret Mondloch.
"Extrait du Journal de la Société des Américanistes. t. 55(1966), p. 201–220."
MnStj (Archives)

3630 The Araucanian weaver, by Sister M. Inez Hilger and Margaret Mondloch.
(*In* Boletin del Museo Nacional de Historio Natural, Santiago. t. 30(1967), p. 291–298).
MnStj (Archives)

3631 Chippewa interpretations of natural phenomena.
Reprinted from: The Scientific Monthly, f. 45(1937), p. 178–179.
MnStj (Archives)

3632 Culture and human behavior; an address delivered to the assembly of students at the Japan Women's University, Tokyo.
(*In* Mainichi Daily News, Tokyo, Feb. 3 & 4, 1963)
MnStj (Archives)

3633 An enlarged Ainu bibliography.
20 p.
Typescript.
MnStj (Archives)

3634 An ethnographic field method.
(*In* Spencer, Robert E., ed. Method and perspective anthropology. Minneapolis, 1954. p. 25–42)
MnStj (Archives)

3635 Ethnological field study of the beliefs, customs, and traditions in the development, rearing, and training of the Araucanian Indian child in Chile.
Reprint from: Year Book of the American Philosophical Society, 1952, p. 260–270.
MnStj (Archives)

3636   Field guide to the ethnological study of child life. New Haven, Human Relations Area Files Press, 1960.
xvi, 55 leaves (Behavior science field guides, v. 1)
MnStj

3637   . . . 2d rev. and augm. edition. New Haven, 1966.
80 p.
MnStj (Archives)

3638   Grandmothers' stories from many parts of the world.
139 p.
Manuscript.
MnStj (Archives)

3639   Huenun Namku; an Araucanian Indian of the Andes remembers the past, by M. Inez Hilger, with the assistance of Margaret A. Mondloch. Preface by Margaret Mead. Norman, University of Oklahoma Press [1966].
xxiv, 128 p. illus., map, 24 cm. (The Civilization of the American Indian series [84])
KAS; MnStj

3640   Japan's "Sky people," the vanishing Ainu.
Reprinted from National Geographic Magazine, Feb., 1967, p. 268–296.
MnStj (Archives)

3641   Letters and documents of Bishop Baraga extant in the Chippewa country.
(In Records of the American Catholic Historical Society, v. 47(1936), p. 292–302)
MnStj (Archives)

3642   Menomini child life.
"Extrait du Journal de la Société des Américanistes, n.s., t. 40(1951), p. 163–172"
MnStj (Archives)

3643   Mysterious "sky people": Japan's dwindling Ainu.
(In Vanishing peoples of the earth. Washington, D.C., National Geographic Society, 1968. p. 92–113)
MnStj (Archives)

3644   Notes on Cheyenne child life.
Reprinted from American anthropologist, v. 48(1946), p. 60–69.
MnStj (Archives)

3645   Notes on Crow culture.
Reprinted from: Baessler-Archiv Beiträge zur Völkerkunde, n.f., Bd. 18 (1970), p. 253–294.
MnStj (Archives)

3646   Performance of Ainu and Japanese six-year-olds on the Goodenough-Harris Drawing Test [by] Sister M. Inez Hilger, William G. Klett and Charles G. Watson.

Reprinted from Perceptual and motor skills, v. 12(1976), p. 435–438.
MnStj (Archives)

3647   Rock paintings in Argentina, by M. Inez Hilger and Margaret Mondloch.
Reprinted from Anthropos, Bd. 57 (1962), p. 514–523.
MnStj (Archives)

3648   Some early customs of the Menomini Indians.
"Extrait du Journal de la Société des Américanistes, n.s., t. 49(1960), p. 45–68)
MnStj (Archives)

3649   Some phases of Chippewa material culture.
Reprinted from Anthropos, Bd. 32 (1937), p. 780–782.
MnStj (Archives)

3650   A source list in ethnobotany.
Reprinted from New York Folklore Quarterly, March, 1972, p. 61–78.
MnStj (Archives)

3651   Together with the Ainu; a vanishing people, by M. Inez Hilger, with the assistance of Chiye Sano and Midori Yamaha. Norman, University of Oklahoma Press [1971].
xxi, 223 p. illus., map, ports. 26 cm.
MnCS; MnStj; OkShG

3652   Una araucana de los Andes.
(In: Notas del Centro de Estudios Antropologicos, Universidad de Chile, no. 4 (1960), p. 5–17)
MnStj (Archives)

3653   (ed) Hilger, Frederick William. Die Reise nach Americka (aus einem alten Tagebuch).
(In Zeitschrift für Kulturaustausch, v. 20(1970), p. 33–36)
MnStj (Archives)

3654   **Hilger, Mary Ione, Sister.**
The first Sioux nun: Sister Marie-Josephine Nebraska, 1859–1894. Illustrator: Mary Michael Kaliher. Milwaukee, Bruce Pub. Co., [1963].
157 p. illus. 22 cm.
MnCS; MnStj; MoCo

3655   **Hill, Mary Karen, Sister.**
The status of the music specialist in the Catholic elementary school of Evansville, Indiana.
66 p. illus., tables.
Thesis (M.A.)—Catholic University of America, 1969.
InFer

Hill, Lawrence Henry, 1937–
3656   The Carolingian and Renaissance scripts and the early Roman type.

13 [3] leaves, 28 cm.

Paper delivered at the meeting of the Library Science Section of the American Benedictine Academy, August 12, 1969.

Typescript.

PLatS

3657 . . . Revised.

20, A-23 leaves, 28 cm.

Typescript.

PLatS

3658 A history of manuscript production in medieval monasteries.

11 leaves, 28 cm.

Typescript.

PLatS

Hill, Thomas, 1564–1644.

3659 A plaine path-way to heaven. Meditacions or spirituall discourses and illuminations upon the gospells of all the yeare, for every daie of the weeke, on the text of the gospells. Composed and sett forther by Thomas Buckland [pseud] of the most venerable and holie Order of Sainct Benedict. [London] the Scolar Press, 1976.

878 p. 19 cm. (English recusant literature, 1558–1640, v. 324)

Facsimile reprint of the 1634 edition.

PLatS

3660 A plaine path-way to heaven . . . the second part [composed and set forth by Thomas Buckland [pseud] of the most venerable Order of S. Benedict]. [London] The Scolar Press, 1976.

1269 p. 19 cm. (English recusant literature, 1558–1640, v. 325)

Facsimile reprint of the 1637 edition.

PLatS

3661 A quartron of reasons of Catholike religion, with as many briefe reasons of refusal. [Menston, Yorkshire, Eng., Scolar Press, 1972].

187 p. 21 cm. (English recusant literature, 1558–1640, v. 98)

Facsimile reprint of the 1600 edition.

PLatS

3662 **Hill Monastic Manuscript Library, Collegeville, Minn.**

Publications.

Here are listed, in alphabetical order, all the publications of the Hill Monastic Manuscript Library.

Arbesmann, Rudolph, O.S.A.

The Regula beati Augustini and its manuscript tradition (Medieval and Renaissance studies, no. 3, Dec. 1970)

Archives of the Cathedral of Malta. Misc. 32A: 1313–1529.

The study and text of an eighteenth-century index of transcripts, by John Az-

zopardi. Malta, 1977.

Catalogs of manuscripts in Austrian monasteries. 1970.

A catalogue of Ethiopian manuscripts microfilmed for the Ethiopian Manuscript Microfilm Library. I: Project numbers 1–300, by William F. Macomber (1975). II. Project numbers 301–700, by William F. Macomber (1976). III. Project numbers 701–1100, by William F. Macomber (1978). IV. Project numbers 1101–1500, by Getatchew Haile (1978).

Catalogue of manuscripts in the Bibliothek der Phil.-Theol. Hochschule der Diözese Linz, by Julian G. Plante (1976).

Catalogue of manuscripts in the Library of Stift Reichersberg, by Julian G. Plante (1973).

Checklist of manuscripts microfilmed for the Hill Monastic Library. Vol. I: Austrian monasteries (and other manuscript collections in Austria), by Julian G. Plante. Part 1 (1967), Part 2 (1974). Vol. II: Spain. Part I, by Julian G. Plante, with comprehensive index by Donald Yates (1978).

Descriptive inventories of manuscript collections microfilmed for the Hill Monastic Library. I. Austria. Fasc. 1: Geras, Güssing, Neukloster, Salzburg, Schlierbach, Schwaz, Wilten, described and analyzed by Donald Yates (1978). 177 mss. Fasc. 2: Fiecht, by Donald Yates (1979). 188 mss. Fasc. 3: Herzogenburg, by Hope Mayo (1979). 138 mss.

Fowler, George Bingham.

A medieval thinker confronts modern perplexities: Engelbert, abbot of Admont, ca. 1250–1331 (Medieval and Renaissance studies, no. 4, Nov. 16, 1971).

Handlist of the ecclesiastical archives of the Malta Cathedral Museum Mdina. I: The Episcopal and Pro-Vicarial Archives, by Rev. John Azzopardi (1975).

Kristeller, Paul Oscar.

The contributions of religious orders in Renaissance thought and learning (Medieval and Renaissance studies, no. 1, Oct. 15, 1968).

Kuttner, Stephan.

Glossators and commentators of the two laws; problems and achievements in manuscript research (Medieval and Renaissance studies, no. 6, April 4, 1974). Unpublished.

Progress report of the Monastic Manuscript Microfilm Project (on overseas operations). I-V, 1964–68, by Oliver

Kapsner, O.S.B.; VI–VIII, 1970–78, by Julian G. Plante.

Plante, Julian G.
The Monastic Manuscript Microfilm Library; its purpose and progress. Text by Julian G. Plante. Designed by Frank Kacmarcik. Collegeville, Minn., Monastic Manuscript Microfilm Library, 1970.
[24] p. illus. (part col.) 23 x 28 cm.

Prete, Sesto.
Observations on the history of textual criticism in the Medieval and Renaissance periods (Medieval and Renaissance studies, no. 2, Nov. 3, 1969).

Quain, Edwin A., S.J.
Paleography, manuscripts and librarians (Medieval and Renaissance studies, no. 7 (Nov. 15, 1974).

Translatio studii; manuscript and library studies honoring Oliver L. Kapsner, O.S.B. Edited by Julian G. Plante (1973).

Trithemius, Johannes.
In praise of scribes (De laude scriptorum). Edited with introduction by Klaus Arnold and translated by Roland Behrendt, O.S.B. (1974).

Weitzmann, Kurt.
Illustrated manuscripts at St. Catherine's Monastery on Mount Sinai (Medieval and Renaissance studies, no. 5, Oct. 31, 1972).

Hilpisch, Stephanus, 1894–
3663 Benediktus; Leben und Werk [von] Leonard von Matt [und] Stephan Hilpisch. Würzburg, Echter Verlag [1960].
225 p. 190 illus. 25 cm.
KAS; MnCS

3664 Chorgebet und Frömmigkeit im Spätmittelalter.
(*In* Heilige Ueberlieferung. Münster, 1938. p. 263–284)
PLatS

3665 Die Feier der Karwoche in der Abtei Fulda zu Beginn des 17. Jahrhunderts.
(*In* Perennita; Beiträge . . . P. Thomas Michels, O.S.B., zum 70. Geburtstag. Münster, 1963. p. 189–196)
PLatS

3666 Klosterleben, Mönchsleben. [3. neu bearb. Aufl.]. Maria Laach, Ars Liturgica [1963].
55 p. illus. 17 cm.
KAS; NdRi

3667 Saint Benedict, by Leonard von Matt and Dom Stephan Hilpisch. Translated from the German by Ernest Graf, O.S.B. Chicago, Regnery, 1961.
226 p. 190 plates, 25 cm.

CaMWiSb; ILSP; InStme; MnCS; MoCo; NdRi; PLatS

Hincmarus, abp. of Rheims, d. 882.
3668 Hincmari, archiepiscopi Remensis, Annales a.820–911.
(*In* Monumenta Germaniae historica. Scriptores. Stuttgart, 1963. t. 1, p. 455–515)
MnCS; PLatS

3669 Les annales de Saint-Bertin . . . Pars 3. Ab anno 861 usque ad annum 882, auctore Hincmaro, Remensi archiepiscopo . . . Paris, Mme Ve J. Renouard, 1871.
KAS

3670 De cavendis vitiis, de virtutibus Christi imitandis et exercendis. MS. Benediktinerabtei St. Peter, Salzburg, codex a.VII.34, f.52v–135r. Quarto. Saec. 11.
Microfilm: MnCS proj. no. 10,165

3671 Epistola ad Carolum Calvum. MS. Augustinerchorherrenstift St. Florian, Austria, codex XI, 82, f.1r–5r. Quarto. Saec. 12–13.
Microfilm: MnCH proj. no. 2339

3672 Epistola ad Karolum regem. MS. Benediktinerabtei St. Peter, Salzburg, codex a.VII.34, f.43v–49v. Quarto. Saec. 11.
Microfilm: MnCH proj. no. 10,165

3673 Epistola seu tractatus ad Carolum Calvum. MS. Vienna, Nationalbibliothek, codex 628, f.1r–100r. Octavo. Saec. 11.
Microfilm: MnCH proj. no. 13,956

3674 Epistola ad Karolum regem de cavendis vitiis. MS. Vienna, Nationalbibliothek, codex 1040, f.1r–45r. Quarto. Saec. 12.
Microfilm: MnCH proj. no. 14,354

3675 Epistola ad Carolum imperatorem. MS. Cistercienserabtei Zwettl, Austria, codex 237, f.28r–32v. Quarto. Saec. 13.
Microfilm: MnCH proj. no. 6837

3676 Vita S. Remigii. MS. Benediktinerabtei Admont, Austria, codex 677, f.36r–92v. Quarto. Saec. 12.
Microfilm: MnCH proj. no. 9709

3677 Vita S. Remigii. MS. Benediktinerabtei Admont, Austria, codex 708, f.50v–111v. Quarto. Saec. 12.
Microfilm: MnCH proj. no. 9750

3678 Vita sancti Remigii. MS. Benediktinerabtei Göttweig, Austria, codex 110a, f.1r–28v. Folio. Saec. 12.
Microfilm: MnCH proj. no. 3393

3679 Vita S. Remigii. MS. Cistercienserabtei Heiligenkreuz, Austria, codex 145, f.142r–173r. Folio. Saec. 12.
Microfilm: MnCH proj. no. 4687

3680 Vita S. Remigii. MS. Cistercienserabtei Rein, Austria, codex 69, f.1r–27r. Folio.

Saec. 13.
Microfilm: MnCH proj. no. 7465

3681 **Hindel, Richard,** 1922–
The effect of novocaine and testosterone upon the neurosecretory phenomena in Xiprophorous Helleri Heckel.
24 leaves. illus. 28 cm.
Thesis (M.S.) – Catholic University of America, 1961.
Typescript.
InStme

3682 **Hindery, Roderick,** 1931–
The disinterested love of God according to Eusebius Amort, C.R.L. (1692–1775). Romae, Academia Alfonsiana, 1962.
79 p.
MoCo

Hintemeyer, Felix, 1862–1924.

3683 Patricia; or, The unknown martyr. A drama in four acts. Baltimore and New York, John Murphy, 1906.
58 p.
NcBe

3684 Pontia: the daughter of Pilate. A drama in four acts. 2d ed. Baltimore, J. Murphy, 1906.
52 p.
NcBe

3685 A reply to a Gaston Co. preacher [N.C.] Beatty, Pa., St. Vincent Abbey, 189–?].
16 p. 24 cm.
KAS

3686 Walburga, or, From darkness to light. A drama in four acts, by V. Rev. F. Felix, O.S.B. Baltimore, J. Murphy [1906].
65 p.
NcBe

3687 **Hintler, Anselm.**
Chronicon novissimum antiqui monasterii ad S. Petrum Salisburgi, ab anno 582 usque ad 1782. MS. Benediktinerabtei St. Peter, Salzburg, codex b.XII.17. 20, 756, 490 p. Folio. Saec. 18.
Microfilm: MnCH proj. no. 10,691

3688 **Hirsau, Germany (Benedictine abbey).**
Consuetudines Hirsaugienses. MS. Benediktinerabtei Admont, Austria, codex 518. 136 f. Quarto. Saec. 12.
Microfilm: MnCH proj. no. 9563

3688a **His Holy Hill; a pageant.** Centenary, St. Walburg Convent, Covington, Ky. (phonodisc).
4 s. 12" 33⅓ rpm.
KyCovS

Hockey, Frederick, 1906–

3689 The account-book of Beaulieu Abbey. Edited for the Royal Historical Society by S. F. Hockey. Offices of the Royal Historical Society, University College, London, 1975.
348 p. 24 cm.
MnCS

3690 Beaulieu, King John's abbey; a history of Beaulieu Abbey, Hampshire, 1204–1538. Pioneer Publications Ltd. [1976].
xiv, 251 p. illus. 22 cm.
MnCS

3691 Quarr Abbey and its lands, 1132–1631. Leicester, Leicester U.P., 1970.
xxii, 320 p. maps, 23 cm.
MnCS

3692 (tr) Führkötter, Adelgundis. The miniatures from the book Scivias: Know the ways – of St. Hildegard of Bingen . . . [English version by Fr. Hockey]. Turnout, Brepols, 1977.
32 p. 32 leaves of facsims. 28 cm.
MnCS

3693 **Hoeck, Johannes,** 1902–
Nikolaos-Nektarios von Otranto, Abt von Casole; Beiträge zur Geschichte der ostwestlichen Beziehungen unter Innozenz III. und Friedrich II., von Johannes M. Hoeck und Raimund J. Loenertz. Ettal, Buch-Kunstverlag, 1965.
265 p. facsims. 26 cm.
PLatS

Hoehn, Mary Sharen, Sister.

3694 Come in; the life of Father Richard Voight. Ferdinand, Ind., Sisters of St. Benedict [n.d.].
89 p. port. 18 cm.
InFer; CaMWiSb

3695 The death of Pope John Paul I, and other poems (16).
15 p. 28 cm.
Typescript.
InFer

3696 Saint Anselm.
Thesis (M.A.) – Benedictine Institute of Sacred Theology, St. John's University, Collegeville, Minn., 1962.
15 p. 28 cm.
Typescript.
InFer

3697 **Hoffman, Corita, Sister.**
Survey of leadership qualities of the principals in selected Benedictine elementary schools.
106 p. 28 cm.
Thesis (M.A.) – Marquette University, 1969.
InFer

Hoffmann, Alexius, 1863–1940.

3698 Autobiography.
10 vols. (ca. 100 p. each)
Typescript.

MnCS(Archives)
3699   Benedictine abbeys.
179 p. 20 cm.
Typescript.
MnCS(Archives)
3700   Clippings of articles which appeared in newspapers and in The Record.
MnCS(Archives)
3701   [Dictionary of religious terms and events]
181 p. 30 cm.
Typescript.
MnCS(Archives)
3702   A history of St. Martin's Parish, St. Martin, Minn., written on the occasion of the diamond jubilee, June 11–13, 1933. St. Paul, Wanderer Printing Co. [1933].
33 p. illus., ports. 22 cm.
KySu; MnCS
3702a   Literarische Tätigkeit der Patres der St. Joannis Abtei zu Collegeville in Minnesota, U.S.A. Prepared for the Catholic Exposition in Cologne, 1928.
9 p. 30 cm.
Typescript.
MnCS(Archives)
3703   Natural history of Collegeville, Minn.
124 p. 24 cm.
Manuscript. Written 1926.
MnCS(Archives)
3704   Verse or worse (poems) composed by Alexius Hoffmann, O.S.B.
84 p. 20 cm.
Typescript.
MnCS(Archives)
3705   (tr) The Benedictines in Brazil. Translated by Alexius Hoffmann, O.S.B.
Translation of: L'Ordre de S. Benoît au Brézil (in Revue bénédictine, v. 15(1898), p. 414–425)
Typescript.
MnCS(Archives)
3706   (2dary) Cicero, Marcus Tullius, Oratio pro Archia poeta, cum notis analyticis R. P. Martini Du Cygne, S.J. Adjumenta adjecit A. H. Collegeville, Minn., 1901.
16 p. 19 cm.
MnCS

Hofmeister, Philipp, 1888–
3707   Das Beichtrecht der männlichen und weiblichen Ordensleute. München, K. Zink, 1954.
vii, 277 p. 24 cm.
InStme
3708   Mitra und Stab der wirklichen Prälaten ohne bischöflichen Charakter. Stuttgart, F. Enke, 1928.
x, 132 p. 23 cm.
ILSP; PLatS

Hohenbaum van der Meer, Moritz, 1718–1795.
3709   Collectanea ad historiam episcopatus Genevensis. MS. Benediktinerabtei St. Paul im Lavanttal, Austria, codex 239/2. 368 p. Folio. Saec. 18.
Microfilm: MnCH proj. no. 12,066
3710   Ethica religiosa ascetico-theologica, qua obligationes religiosorum quoad vota & s. Regulam media ac tutissima via pertractantur publicae disputationi proposita. Lucernae, typis Henrici Ignatii Nicomedis Hautt, 1747.
[14], 509, [25] p. 18 cm.
KAS; MoCo
3711   Historia episcopatus Sedunensis. MS. Benediktinerabtei St. Paul im Lavanttal, Austria, codex 243/2. 400 f. Folio. Saec. 18.
Microfilm: MnCH proj. no. 11,989

Hohenlohe-Schillingsfürst, Constantin, 1864–
3712   Gründe der Schadenersatzpflicht in Recht und Moral. Regensburg, F. Pustet, 1914.
v, 208 p. 21 cm.
InStme; MnCS; MoCo

Hohn, Albert, 1911–
3713   Die Orgeln in der ehemaligen Abteikirche von Schwarzach.
(In Tschira, Arnold. Die ehemalige Benediktinerabtei Schwarzach. Karlsruhe, 1977. p. 65–72)
MnCS

Hollermann, Ephrem, Sister, 1942–
3714   Berakah: the stance of contemplative prayer.
23 p. 28 cm.
Research paper (M.A.)–St. John's University, 1974.
Typescript.
MnStj(Archives)
3715   Liturgy of the Word and Good Friday.
30 p. 28 cm.
Research paper (M.A.)–St. John's University, 1975.
Typescript.
MnStj(Archives)
3716   Psalmic typology in the Book of Revelation.
27 p.
Research paper (M.A.)–St. John's University, 1974.
Typescript.
MnStj(Archives)

Holme Eden Abbey, Carlisle, England.
3717   (tr) Leclercq, Jean. The spirituality of the Middle Ages. [Translated from the French

by the Benedictines of Holme Eden Abbey, Carlisle]. London, Burns & Oates, 1968.
x, 602 p. 23 cm.
MnCS

3718 **Holmes, Jerome,** 1885–
Thoughts on prayer. London, Campion Press [1960].
62 p. 19 cm.
KySu; MoCo

3719 **Holthaus, Mary Joachim, Sister.**
Music in the liturgy; its role: handmaid or ornament? [Phonotape cassette]. Kansas City, Mo., National Catholic Reporter, 1974.
1 cassette 2 sides.
MnCS

Holy Family Convent, Benet Lake, Wis.

3720 Benet Center news. 1974–1978.
Changed name to: Listen.
InFer: WBenH

3721 [Benet Lake breviary manuals] 1955–
v. various sizes.
Multigraphed.
MnCS; WBenH

3722 **Holy Spirit Convent, Sunnymead, Calif.**
The Benedictine roadrunner. 1975–
InFer; CSun

3723 **Holy Trinity Monastery, Butler, Pa.**
The Byzantine Mass. Pittsburgh, Pa., Benedictine Fathers of the Byzantine Rite, Holy Trinity Monastery, 1957.
19 p. 22 cm.
English text of the Divine Liturgy of St. John Chrysostom.
PLatS; PBut

3724 **Holzherr, Georg,** 1927–
Regula Ferioli; ein Beitrag zur Entstehungsgeschichte und zur Sinndeutung der Benediktinerregel. Einsiedeln, Benziger Verlag [1961].
212 p. 21 cm.
InStme; KAS; MnCS; NdRi; PLatS

3724a Die Benediktsregel; eine Anleitung zu christlichem Leben. Der vollständige Text der Regel übersetzt und erklärt von Georg Holzherr, Abt von Einsiedeln. [Einsiedeln] Benziger Verlag [1980].
370 p. map, 22 cm.
MnCS

3725 **Hombach, Raphael,** 1905–
Psalterium monasticum per quatuor hebdomadas distributum. Maria Laach, n.d.
2 v. 21 cm.
Manuscripti instar.
MnCS

3726 **Homélies pour notre temps,** par un abbé bénédictin. [Ligugé, Abbaye Saint Martin, 1969].

112 p. 22 cm.
KAS

Honorius Augustodunensis, fl. 1106–1135.

3727 Libelli IV honorii Augustodunensis presbyteri De luminatibus ecclesiae, sive De scriptoribus ecclesiasticis.
(*In* Johann Albert Fabricius, Bibliotheca ecclesiastica. Hants, England, 1967. p. 73–92)
PLatS

3728 (2dary) Beinert, Wolfgang. Die Kirche – Gottes Heil in der Welt. Die Lehre von der Kirche nach den Schriften des Rupert von Deutz, Honorius Augustodunensis und Gerhoch von Reichersberg . . . Münster, 1973)
PLatS

3829 **Hoolihan, Christopher.**
The phonetic and phonemic approach to the solution of phonological problems; a critical analysis, with special reference to French.
vii, 78 leaves. 29 cm.
Thesis (M.A.)–Catholic University of America, 1952.
Typescript.
InStme

Höpfl, Hildebrand, 1872–1934.

3730 Introductio specialis in Novum Testamentum. Editio sexta quam paravit Adalbertus Metzinger. Neapoli; Romae, 1962.
xxvii, 581 p.
ILSP

3731 Introductio specialis in Vetus Testamentum. Editio sexta quam curavit P. Sebastianus Bovo, O.S.B. Neapoli, M. d'Auria, 1963.
xxviii, 701 p. 22 cm.
MoCo; PLatS

3732 Introductionis in sacros utriusque Testamenti libros compendium. Ed. 6. Neapoli, M. d'Auria, 1963.
3 v. 22 cm.
KAS

Hoppenbrouwers, Henricus, 1913–

3733 Commodien, poète chrétien.
(*In* Graecitas et latinitas Christianorum primaeva supplementa, n. 2, p. 47–88)
PLatS

3734 Conversatio; une étude sémasiologique.
(*In* Graecitas et latinitas Christianorum primaeva supplementa, n. 1, p. 45–95)
PLatS

3735 Recherches sur la terminologie du martyre de Tertullien à Lactance. Nijmegen, Dekker & van de Vegt, 1961.

xv, 217 p. 24 cm. (Latinitas Christianorum, fasc. 15)
PLatS

3736   (ed) Athanasius, Saint. La plus ancienne
version latine de la vie de S. Antoine.
Etude critique textuelle par H. Hoppenbrouwers, O.S.B. Nijmegen, Dekker & van
de Vegt, 1960.
xiii, 220 p. 24 cm. (Latinitas Christianorum primaeva, fasc. 14)
InStme

3737   **Horne, Ethelbert,** 1857–1952.
Relics of popery. London, Catholic Truth
Society, [1946].
19 p. 18 cm.
MnCS; PLatS

Hortig, Johann Nepomuk, 1774–1847.

3738   Reisen zu Wasser und zu Land, mit
etwelchen Abhängseln und Eintreuungen.
Sulzbach, J. E. Seidel, 1835.
236 p. 14 cm.
MnCS

3739   Wunderbare Begebenheiten des Blasius
Berneiter und seiner Gefährten. Zusammengestellt von Johann Nariscus [pseud.].
Sulzbach, in der J. E. v. Seidelschen Buchhandlung, 1837.
400 p. 14 cm.
MnCS

3740   **Horvath, Achilleo,** 1925–
Exegesis patrum de Phil 2, 5–8 ejusque
momentum. Excerptum ex dissertatione
ad lauream in facultate theologica Pontificii Athenaei S. Anselmi de Urbe asse-
quendam conscripta. Collegeville, Minn.,
1956.
71 p. 28 cm.
MnCS

3741   **Hoschette, Luke, Sister.**
A procedural manual for hospital
business offices.
107 p.
Thesis (M.B.A.)–University of Notre
Dame, 1960.
MnStj

Hoschette, Rosemary, Sister, 1929–

3742   An inquiry into the feasibility of having
the same person hold the position of dis-
ciplinarian and counselor in a school.
45 p. 28 cm.
Research paper (M.A.)–College of St.
Thomas, St. Paul, Minn.
Typescript.
MnStj(Archives)

3743   A study of high school students' attitudes
toward learning and scholastic marks.
33 p. 28 cm.
Research paper (M.A.)–College of St.
Thomas, St. Paul, Minn.

Typescript.
MnStj(Archives)

3744   Thomistic philosophy and its implications
in education.
22 p. 28 cm.
Research paper (M.A.)–College of St.
Thomas, St. Paul, Minn.
Typescript.
MnStj(Archives)

Hoste, Anselm, 1930–

3745   Bibliotheca Aelrediana; a survey of the
manuscripts, old catalogues, editions and
studies concerning St. Aelred of Rievaulx.
Steenbrugis, Abbatia Sancti Petri, 1962.
206 p. facsims. 25 cm. (Instrumenta
patristica, 2)
InStme; KAS; MnCS; PLatS

3746   (ed) Aelred, Saint. Opera omnia.
Ediderunt A. Hoste, O.S.B. et C. H.
Talbot. Turnholti, Brepols, 1971.
xviii, 766 p. 26 cm. (Corpus Christiano-
rum. Continuatio mediaevalis, 1)
PLatS

3747   (ed) Chromatius, Saint. Opera quae
supersunt. Cura et studio A. Hoste.
(*In* Corpus Christinaorum. Series latina,
v. 9, p. 371–447)
PLatS

3748   (ed) Aelred, Saint. Quand Jésus eut
douze ans. Introduction et texte critique de
Dom Anselme Hoste, O.S.B. . . . Paris,
Cerf, 1958.
132 p. 20 cm.
InStme; MnCS; PLatS

3749   (ed) Hegemonius. Adversus haereses.
Cura et studio A. Hoste.
(*In* Corpus Christianorum. Series latina,
vol. IX, p. 325–329)
PLatS

3750   (ed) Isaac, O. Cist., abbot of Stella.
Sermons. Text et introduction critique par
Anselm Hoste . . . Paris, Editions du
Cerf, 1967–
v. 20 cm.
InStme; PLatS

3751   (ed) Isaac Judaeus. Isacis Iudaei quae
supersunt. Cura et studio A. Hoste.
(*In* Corpus Christianorum. Series latina,
vol. IX, p. 331–348)
PLatS

Hourlier, Jacques, 1910–

3752   L'âge classique, 1140–1378: les religieux.
Paris, Editions Cujas [1974].
567 p.
NcBe

3753   Das Kloster des hl. Odilo. Cluny und der
Begriff des religiösen Ordens.
(*In* Richter, Helmut, ed. Cluny; Beiträge
zu Gestalt und Wirkung der Cluniazensis-

chen Reform. Darmstadt, 1975. p. 1–21, 50–59)
MnCS

3754 Le monastère de saint Odilon.
(*In* Analecta monastica, 6.sér. 1962. p. 5–21. Studia Anselmiana, fasc. 50)
PLatS

3755 Saint Odilon, abbé de Cluny. Publications Universitaires de Louvain, 1964.
234 p. 25 cm.
InStme; KAS; MnCS

3756 (ed) Gertrude, Saint. Oeuvres spirituelles. Texte latin, introduction, traduction et notes par Jacques Hourlier et Albert Schmitt. Paris, Editions du Cerf, 1967–
v. 21 cm.
InStme; PLatS

3757 (ed) Guillaume de Saint-Thierry. La contemplation de Dieu. Introduction, texte latin et traduction de Jacques Hourlier. 2. ed. Paris, Editions du Cerf, 1977.
160 p. 20 cm.
InStme

3758 **Houtman, Mary Immaculata, Sister.**
A study of some of the concepts applicable to business education in St. Benedict's Rule for monasteries.
117 p. 28 cm.
Thesis (M.A.)–Catholic University of America, 1962.
Typescript.
MdRi

Houtryve, Idesbald van, 1886–1964.

3759 Ami de Dieu et des hommes. 2. ed. Gembloux (Belgium), J. Duculot, 1952.
379 p. 21 cm.
InStme

3760 La devotion humble et généreuse selon S. François de Sales. Editions de l'Abbaye du Mont César [Belgique] 1946.
191 p. 19 cm.
CaQStB; InStme

3761 Dom Robert de Kerchov d'Exaerde, premier abbé du Mont-César, 1846–1899–1942. Louvain, Editions du Mont-César, 1950.
87 p. illus., plates, 18 cm.
KAS; MnCS; NdRi

3762 Nello spirito di Cristo. Tradotta dal francese dalle Benedettine del Monasteri di S. Paolo di Sorrento . . . [Firenze], Libreria Editrice Fiorentina [1942].
86 p. 20 cm.
MnCS

3763 Via vitae. Bruxelles, Action Catholique, 1926.
2 v. 20 cm.
CaQStB; InStme

3764 La vie dans la paix. Bruxelles, Action Catholique, 1927.
3 v. 20 cm.
CaQStB; InStme

3765 La vie dans la paix. 8. ed. Louvain, Editions du Mont-Cesar [1946].
2 v. 18 cm.
InStme

3766 La vierge des pauvres. 3. ed. Banneaux, Editions Caritas, 1947.
190 p.
MoCo

3767 La vierge des pauvres. 4. ed. Louvain, Mont César [1958].
171 p. plates, 18 cm.
InStme; MnCS

3768 **Howard, Brice John,** 1929–
Abbey and University Church of Saint John the Baptist, Collegeville, Minn. [Text by the Reverend Fathers Ronald Roloff and Brice Howard, O.S.B. . .] [Collegeville, Minn., St. John's Abbey, 1961].
[40] p. illus. 31 cm.
Church dedication brochure, August 24, 1961.
KAS; MnCS; PLatS

Hrabanus Maurus, Abp., 784?–856.
Manuscripts copies

3769 Commentaria in Genesin. Libri quatuor. MS. Benediktinerabtei Göttweig, Austria, codex 47. 147 f. Folio. Saec. 12.
Microfilm: MnCH proj. no. 3335

3770 Commentarius in libros Judith et Esther. MS. Vienna, Nationalbibliothek, codex 741, f.140r–184v. Folio. Saec. 12.
Microfilm: MnCH proj. no. 14,066

3771 Super libros Machabaeorum. MS. Toledo, Spain, Biblioteca del Cabildo, codex 10,o. 191 f. Folio. Saec. 13.
Microfilm: MnCH proj. no. 33,011

3772 Commentarium in librum Numerum. MS. Cistercienserabtei Zwettl, Austria, codex 73, f.2r–94r. Folio. Saec. 12.
Microfilm: MnCH proj. no. 6671

3773 De benedictionibus filiorum Jacob. MS. Vienna, Nationalbibliothek, codex 956, f.84r–94v. Folio. Saec. 11.
Microfilm: MnCH proj. no. 14,274

3774 De gravibus mortalibus peccatis ac criminibus eorumque poenitudine ac satisfactione, adjecto indice. MS. Vienna, Nationalbibliothek, codex 1595, f.48r–86v. Quarto. Saec. 12.
Microfilm: MnCH proj. no. 14,965

3775 De inventione linguarum. MS. Vienna, Nationalbibliothek, codex 1609, f.2r–3v. Octavo. Saec. 10.
Microfilm: MnCH proj. no. 14,933

3776   De inventione linguarum. MS. Vienna, Nationalbibliothek, codex 1010, f.90r–90v. Folio. Saec. 11.
Microfilm: MnCH proj. no. 14,320

3777   De laudibus sanctae crucis. MS. Vienna, Nationalbibliothek, codex 911. 55 f. Folio. Saec. 9.
Microfilm: MnCH proj. no. 14,238

3778   De laudibus sanctae crucis. MS. Vienna, Nationalbibliothek, codex 652. 47 f. Folio. Saec. 9.
Microfilm: MnCH proj. no. 20,330

3779   De laudibus sanctae crucis. MS. Vienna, Nationalbibliothek, codex 908. 109 f. Folio. Saec. 10.
Microfilm: MnCH proj. no. 14,226

3780   De laudibus s. crucis. MS. Benediktinerabtei Admont, Austria, codex 219. 41 f. Folio. Saec. 13.
Microfilm: MnCH proj. no. 29,594

3781   De laudibus crucis. MS. Vienna, Nationalbibliothek, codex 1355, f.167r–168v. Quarto. Saec. 14–15.
Microfilm: MnCH proj. no. 14,712

3782   De laudibus s. crucis. Universitätsbibliothek Graz, Austria, codex 19. 16 f. Folio. Saec. 15.
Microfilm: MnCH proj. no. 25,985

3783   De laude sanctae crucis. MS. Benediktinerabtei Melk, Austria, codex 358, 30 f. Folio. Saec. 15.
Microfilm: MnCH proj. no. 1361

3784   De laude sanctae crucis libri duo. MS. Benediktinerabtei St. Peter, Salzburg, codex a.XII.4. 82 p. Folio. Saec. 15.
Microfilm: MnCH proj. no. 10,715

3785   De mysterio sanctae crucis. MS. Cistercienserabtei Zwettl, Austria, codex 86, f.1r–41r. Folio. Saec. 12.
Microfilm: MnCH proj. no. 6677

3786   De principalibus vitiis et virtutibus. MS. Vienna, Nationalbibliothek, codex 956, f.1v–19r. Folio. Saec. 11.
Microfilm: MnCH proj. no. 14,274

3787   De sacramentis divinis et sacris ordinibus, nec non de vestimentibus sacerdotalibus ad Thiotmarum (capitula 38). MS. Vienna, Nationalbibliothek, codex 1073. 98 f. Quarto. Saec. 10.
Microfilm: MnCH proj. no. 14,376

3788   De sacramentis, i.e. Institutio clericorum. MS. Vienna, Nationalbibliothek, codex 1050, f.1v–40r. Octavo. Saec. 12.
Microfilm: MnCH proj. no. 14,372

3789   De virtutibus et vitiis. MS. Vienna, Nationalbibliothek, codex 842. 80 f. Quarto. Saec. 9.
Microfilm: MnCH proj. no. 14,162

3790   Epistola ad Heribaldum Alcedronensis ecclesiae episcopum. MS. Cistercienserabtei Heiligenkreuz, Austria, codex 217, f.63r–93v. Folio. Seac. 10.
Microfilm: MnCH proj. no. 4866

3791   Epistola ad Humbertum episcopum. MS. Cistercienserabtei Heiligenkreuz, Austria, codex 217, f.101r–106r. Folio. Saec. 10.
Microfilm: MnCH proj. no. 4866

3792   Epistola ad Isanbertum. MS. Vienna, Nationalbibliothek, codex 966, f.26r–26v. Folio. Saec. 10.
Microfilm: MnCH proj. no. 14,277

3793   Epistola ad Regibaldum chorepiscopum. MS. Cistercienserabtei Heiligenkreuz, Austria, codex 217, f.94r–101r. Folio. Saec. 10.
Microfilm: MnCH proj. no. 4866

3794   Epistola ad Virdunensem episcopum. MS. Vienna, Nationalbibliothek, codex 956, f.110v–113v. Folio. Saec. 11.
Microfilm: MnCH proj. no. 14,274

3795   Excerpta liturgici argumenti, ex operibus Hrabani Mauri et Amalarii. MS. Vienna, Nationalbibliothek, codex 914, f.68r–74r. Folio. Saec. 10.
Microfilm: MnCH proj. no. 14,239

3796   Exodus glossatus per Rabanum et alios. MS. Exeter, England, Cathedral Library, codex 0 6 ix. 125 f. Quarto. Saec. 12.
Microfilm: MnCH

3797   Expositio super Exodum. MS. Cistercienserabtei Zwettl, Austria, codex 95, f.32v–72v. Folio. Saec. 12.
Microfilm: MnCH proj. no. 6699

3798   Expositio super Exodum. MS. Linz, Austria, Studienbibliothek, codex 41, f. 129r–158r. Folio. Saec. 13.
Microfilm: MnCH proj. no. 27,995

3799   Liber Genesis glossatus. MS. Hereford, England, Cathedral Library, codex 0 5 1. 93 f. Quarto. Saec. 12.
Microfilm: MnCH

3800   Expositio in Job. MS. Benediktinerabtei Melk, Austria, codex 148, f.1r–119v. Quarto. Saec. 18.
Microfilm: MnCH proj. no. 1209

3801   Expositio super Lamentationes Jeremiae. MS. Universitätsbibliothek Graz, Austria, codex 1046. 78 f. Quarto. Saec. 12.
Microfilm: MnCH proj. no. 27,090

3802   Expositio in Lamentationem Jeremiae. MS. Augustinerchorherrenstift Klosterneuburg, Austria, codex 214, f.97r–127r. Folio. Saec. 12.
Microfilm: MnCH proj. no. 5186

3803　Super Lamentationes Hieremiae prophetae. MS. Universitätsbibliothek Graz, Austria, codex 1540, f.89v–140r. Octavo. Saec. 13.
Microfilm: MnCH proj. no. 26,468

3804　In Lamentationes Jeremiae. MS. Universitätsbibliothek Graz, Austria, codex 1055, f.121r–168r. Quarto. Saec. 14.
Microfilm: MnCH proj. no. 27,107

3805　Expositio in Macchabaeos. MS. Vienna, Nationalbibliothek, codex 741, f.69v–139r. Folio. Saec. 12.
Microfilm: MnCH proj. no. 14,066

3806　Machabaeorum libri duo, cum glossa Hrabani Mauri. MS. Augustinerchorherrenstift Klosterneuburg, Austria, codex 250. 80 f. Folio. Saec. 13.
Microfilm: MnCH proj. no. 5223

3807　Expositiones in evangelium Matthaei, et quidem lib. 5–8. MS. Vienna, Nationalbibliothek, codex 988. 319 f. Folio. Saec. 10.
Microfilm: MnCH proj. no. 14,293

3808　Expositiones in evangelium Matthaei. MS. Vienna, Nationalbibliothek, codex 991. 343 f. Folio. Saec. 10.
Microfilm: MnCH proj. no. 14,302

3809　Homilia de libro generationis Matthaei apostoli. MS. Vienna, Nationalbibliothek, codex 701, f.141r–142v. Folio. Saec. 12.
Microfilm: MnCH proj. no. 14,027

3810　Super Matthaeum. MS. Vienna, Nationalbibliothek, codex 925, f.1r–91v. Folio. Saec. 13.
Microfilm: MnCH proj. no. 14,235

3811　Expositio in libros Regum. MS. Benediktinerabtei Admont, Austria, codex 176. 176 f. Folio. Saec. 12.
Microfilm: MnCH proj. no. 9265

3812　Commentarius in libros Regum. MS. Vienna, Nationalbibliothek, codex 1000. 234 f. Folio. Saec. 12.
Microfilm: MnCH proj. no. 14,305

3813　Commentarii in libros Regum. Finis deest. MS. Vienna, Nationalbibliothek, codex 941, f.89r–188v. Folio. Saec. 15.
Microfilm: MnCH proj. no. 14,250

3814　Glossarium latino-theodiscum [Latin-German (teutsch)]. MS. Vienna, Nationalbibliothek, codex 162, f.10r–43r. Quarto. Saec. 9.
Microfilm: MnCH proj. no. 13,520

3815　Homilia in litania maiore secundum Bedam Venerabilem et Rabanum Maurum. MS. Augustinerchorherrenstift Klosterneuburg, Austria, codex 242, f.157v–159r.
Microfilm: MnCH proj. no. 5213

3816　Liber contra eos, qui repugnant institutis beati patris Benedicti. MS. Benediktiner-

abtei Göttweig, Austria, codex 54, f.1r–11v. Folio. Saec. 12.
Microfilm: MnCH proj. no. 3342

3817　Opusculum contra eos qui repugnant institutis beati patris Benedicti. MS. Benediktinerabtei Göttweig, Austria, codex 3559a. 13 f. Folio. Saec. 15.
Microfilm: MnCH proj. no. 3559

3718　Opusculum contra eos qui repugnant institutis b. p. Benedicti. MS. Benediktinerabtei Melk, Austria, codex 1915, f.66r–77v. Quarto. Saec. 15.
Microfilm: MnCH proj. no. 2199

3819　Responsum ad quaestionem theologicam. MS. Vienna, Nationalbibliothek, codex 956, f.113v–115r. Folio. Saec. 11.
Microfilm: MnCH proj. no. 14,274

Hrabanus Maurus, Abp., 784?–856.
Printed works.

3820　[Selections]
Vesper hymn for All Saints (Placare Christe servulis) [and 7 other hymns].
(*In* Donahoe, D. J. Early Christian hymns. New York, 1908. v. 1, p. 127–138)
PLatS

3821　[Carmina]
(*In* Foucher, J. P. Florilège de la poésie sacrée. Paris, 1961. p. 133–136)
PLatS

3822　De institutione clericorum libri tres. Textum recensuit, adnotationibus criticis et exegeticis illustravit, introductionem atque indicem addidit Aloisius Knoepfler. Monachii, sumptibus Librariae Lentnerianae, 1900.
xxix, 300 p. 22 cm.
PLatS

3823　De institutione clericorum. Part 3 translated into English.
(*In* Kohake, C.P. The life and educational writings of Rabanus Maurus. Thesis, Cornell University, 1948. Typescript)
KAS

3824　Liber de laudibus sanctae crucis. Vollständige Faksimile-Ausgabe des Codex Vindobonensis 652 der Oesterreichischen Nationalbibliothek, Wien. Graz, Akademische Druck- u. Verlagsanstalt, 1972.
47 leaves, illus. 43 cm. (Codices selecti, v. 33)
PLatS

3825　Epistola ad Heribaldum episcopum Antissiodorensem.
(*In* Regino, abbot of Prüm. Libri duo de ecclesiasticis disciplinis . . . Parisiis, 1671. Apud finem)
658 p.
PLatS (microfilm)

3826   Discourse on the Bodie and Blood of Christ.
(*In* Guild, William, ed. Three rare monuments of antiquitie . . . Aberdene, D. Melvill, 1624. Apud finem)
MnCS (microfilm)

Hrotsvit, of Gandersheim, b. ca. 935.
3827   [Opera]
Comediae sex in emulationem Terentii: Prima Gallicanus, Secunda Dulcicius, Tercia Callimachus, Quarta Abraham, Quinta Paffnucius, Sexta Fides et Spes. Octo sacrae hystorie versu hexametro et penthametro: Hystoria beate Maria virginis, Hystoria sancti Pelagii, Hystoria conversionis sancti Theophili, Hystoria Proterii et sancti Basilii, Hystoria passionis sancti Dynoisii, Hystoria passionis sanctae Agnetis. Panegiricus versu hexamaetro in laudem et gesta Oddonis magni primi in Germania imperatoris. Herimbergae, 1501. Augustinerchorherrenstift, Austria, codex typicus 301.
163 p.
Microfilm: MnCH proj. no. 7375

3828   Werke in deutscher Uebertragung mit einem Beitrag zur frühmittelalterlichen Dichtung von H. Homeyer. München, Verlag F. Schöningh, [1973]
342 p. 24 cm.
MnCS; PLatS

3829   Hrotsuithae carmina.
(*In* Monumenta Germaniae historica. Scriptores. Stuttgart, 1963, t. 4, p. 303–335)
Contents: Carmen de primordiis coenobii Gandersheimensis. Carmen de gestis Oddonis I imperatoris.
PLatS; MnCS

3830   Comoedias sex ad fidem codicis Emmeranensis typis expressas edidit, praefationem poetriae et eius epistolam ad quosdam sapientes huius libri fautores praemisit, versuculos quosdam Hrotsvithae, nondum antea editae, eodem ex codice iis adiunsit J. Bendixen. Lubecae, impensis Librariae Dittmerianae, 1857.
xix, 152 p. 14 cm.
PLatS

3831   Maria; Sapientia (fragmentum). MS. Klagenfurt, Austria, Studienbibliothek, codex perg. 44. 4 f. Octavo. Saec. 11.
Microfilm: MnCH proj. no. 12,888

3832   The non-dramatic works of Hrosvitha; text, translation, and commentary . . . by Sister M. Gonsalva Wiegand, O.S.B. St. Louis, 1936.
xxiv, 273 p. 24 cm.

Thesis (Ph.D.)–St. Louis University.
PLatS

3833   Poésies latines de Rosvith . . . Traduction libre en vers français . . . per Vignon Rétif de la Bretonne. Paris, Napoléon Chaix, 1854.
404 p. 25 cm.
MnCS

3834   Théatre de Hrotsvitha . . . traduit pour la première fois en français, avec le texte latin, revu sur le manuscrit de Munich. Précédé d'une introduction et suivi de notes par Charles Magnin. Paris, Benjamin Duprat, 1945.
lxiv, 481 p. illus. 22 cm.
Latin and French on facing pages.
MnCS

3835   **Huber, Albert,** 1907–
1000 Jahre Pferdezucht Kloster Einsiedeln; geschichtliche Studie von der Klostergründung bis zur Gegenwart. 2. Aufl. Einsiedeln, EDE-Verlag [1963].
39 p. plates, 24 cm.
InStme

Huber, Michael, 1874–
3836   Die "Vita illustrata Sancti Benedicti" in Handschriften und Kupferstichen.
Offprint from Studien und Mitteilungen zur Geschichte des Benediktiner-Ordens . . . Bd. 48(1930) p. 4–82
KAS

3837   (ed) Joannes monachus. Liber de miraculis. Heidelberg, Carl Winter, 1913.
xxxi, 144 p. 20 cm.
MnCS; PLatS

3838   **Hübl, Albert,** 1867–1931.
Catalogus codicum manu scriptorum qui in bibliotheca monasterii B.M.V. ad Scotos Vindobonae servantur. Vindobonae, Guil. Braumüller, 1899.
x, 609 p. 25 cm.
MnCS; PLatS

3839   **Hübscher, Ignatius.**
De imagine Dei in homine viatore sec. doctrinam S. Thomae Aquinatis. Lovanii, F. Ceuterick, 1932.
viii, 114 p. 26 cm.
InStme

Hucbald, monk of St. Armand, d. 930.
3840   Carmen de laude calvorum ad Carolum imperatorem calvum. MS. Vienna, Nationalbibliothek, codex 3192, f.171r–176r. Quarto. Saec. 15.
Microfilm: MnCH proj. no. 16,436

3841   De musica (fragmentum). MS. Vienna, Nationalbibliothek, codex 55, f.208v. Folio. Saec. 10.
Microfilm: MnCH proj. no. 13,420

3842   Musica Euchiriadis, et Euchiriades: scholia de arte musica. MS. Vienna, Nationalbibliothek, codex 44, f.168r–208v. Folio. Saec. 10.
Microfilm: MnCH proj. no. 13,420

3843   Ex vita s. Lebuini auctore Hucbaldo Einonensi.
(*In* Monumenta Germaniae historica. Scriptores. Stuttgart, 1963. t. 2, p. 360–364)
MnCS; PLatS

3844   **Huck, Gabriel.**
The Bible service, by Gabriel Huck, O.S.B., and Geoffrey Wood, S.A. Washington, D.C. Liturgical Conference [c 1964].
64 p.
MoCo

3845   **Hueber, Philibert,** 16th cent.
Farrago memorandorum monasterii Mellicensis ex variis antiquis manuscriptis in hunc librum congesta, anno 1594 per P. Philibertum Hueber. MS. Benediktinerabtei Melk, Austria, codex 1362. 711 p. Quarto. Saec. 17.
Microfilm: MnCH proj. no. 1900

3846   **Huebsch, Rosemary, Sister,** 1928–
Spelling a pleasant and satisfying experience.
83 p.
Colloquium paper (M.A.)–University of Minnesota, 1962.
Typescript.
MnStj (Archives)

3847   **Huemer, Blasius,** 1886–1923.
Verzeichnis der deutschen Cistercienserinnenklöster.
(*In* Germania monastica. Augsburg, 1967. p. 139–185)
PLatS

3848   **Huerre, Denis,** 1915–
The monk, the guest and God. Translated by a monk of Mount Saviour.
(*In* Monastic studies, v. 10, p. 49–54)
PLatS

Hugbald. *See* Hucbald.

Hugger, Pirmin, 1939–
3849   Leitgedanken zum Psalmengebet des "Neuen Offiziums." Münsterschwarzach, Vier-Türme-Verlag [196-?]
iii, 69 p. 21 cm.
InStme

3850   Die Missions geschichte der Benediktinerkongregation von St. Ottilien.
(*In* Die Benediktinerabtei Münsterschwarzach. Vier-Thürme-Verlag, 1965. p. 88–117)
PLatS

Hughes, Anselm, 1889–
3851   Ars nova and the Renaissance, 1300–1540. New York, 1950.
ILSP

3852   Early medieval music, up to 1300. New York, 1954.
ILSP

3853   Septuagesima: reminiscences of the Plainsong & Mediaeval Music Society, and of other things, personal and musical. Westminster [England], Plainsong & Mediaeval Music Society, 1959.
77 p. 22 cm.
InStme

3854   (ed) Bannister, Henry Marriott. Anglo-French sequelae . . . [Farnborough, England, Gregg Press, 1966]
142 p. music. 23 cm.
InStme; KAS

3855   (ed) The Bec Missal. Edited by Anselm Hughes. [London, Henry Bradshaw Society] 1963.
xv, 302 p. 23 cm.

3856   (ed) The Portiforium of Saint Wulstan (Corpus Christi College, Cambridge, Ms. 391). Edited by Dom Anselm Hughes. Leighton Buzzard, England, Henry Bradshaw Society, 1958–60.
2 v. 23 cm.
MnCS; MoCo

Hugo, abbot of Venosa. *See* Ugo, abbot of Venosa.

3857   **Hugo Pictavinus,** 12th cent.
Histoire du Monastère de la Madeleine par Hugues de Poitiers . . . Traduit du Latin en français par François Guizot, présenté et annoté par François Vogade. La Charité-sur-Loire, Imprimerie Bernadat, 1969.
273 p. 19 cm.
PLatS

Human Life Center, St. John's University, Collegeville, Minn. *See* St. John's University, Collegeville, Minn. Human Life Center.

Hume, George Basil, 1923–
3858   Searching for God. New York, Paulist Press [c 1977]
InFer; MdRi; MnCS; ViBris

3858a   Cardinal Hume speaks to the Church of England Synod. London, Catholic Truth Society, 1978.
11 p. 17 cm. (Catholic Truth Society pamphlets. S 328 [v. 3])
PLatS

3859   **Hundstorfer, Rudolf,** 1900–
Das Stift unterm Hakenkreuz, Wels, Druck- und Verlagsanstalt Welsermühl [1961?]

93 p. plates, 24 cm.
MnCS

3860 **Hundtriser, Benedict,** 1718–1770.
Antidotum quotidianum contra morbos animae . . . Augustae Vind., Jos. Wolff, 1765.
[32], 836, [11] p. 18 cm.
KAS

Hunkeler, Leodegar, 1889–1956.
3861 Benediktinerstift Engelberg. 3. Aufl. München, Schnell & Steiner, 1968.
14 p. illus. 17 cm.
MnCS

3862 Clemens Brentanos religiöser Entwicklungsgang; eine psychologische Studie. Sarnen, L. Ehrli, 1915.
163 p. 24 cm.
PLatS

3863 The historical development of Benedictine monasticism. [Mt. Angel, Or., 1951].
122 p. 28 cm.
A translation from the German.
Mimeographed.
KAS; WaOSM

3864 It began with Benedict. The Benedictines: their background, their founder, their history, their life, their contributions to Church and world. Translated by Luke Eberle, O.S.B. St. Benedict, Or., Benedictine Press [c 1973].
80 p. illus. 22 cm.
Translation of "Vom Mönchtum des heiligen Benedikt."
InFer; InStme; MnStj; PLatS

3865 Uebersicht über die geschichtliche Entwicklung des benediktinischen Mönchtums. [Engelberg, Benediktiner Abtei, 1946]
200 p.
Class lectures for novices, privately printed.
MoCo

Hunt, Ignatius, 1920–
3866 The Bible and the liturgy. Glen Rock, N.J., Paulist Press [1963]
30 p. 19 cm.
KAS

3867 God's call to worship; biblical background.
(*In* North American Liturgical Week, 21st, 1960. p. 8–13)
PLatS

3868 The history of Israel. Conception, Mo., Conception Abbey [1960]
45 p. 21 cm. (Saint Andrew Bible commentary, 1)
KySu; PLatS

3869 Recent Melkizedek study.
(*In* McKenzie, J. L., ed. The Bible in current Catholic thought. New York, 1962. p. 21–33)
ILSP

3870 Understanding the Bible. New York, Sheed and Ward [1962]
xiv, 207 p. 21 cm.
CaMWiSb; InFer; MnStj; NcBe; InStme; ILSP; NdRi; MoCo; PLatS; OkShG; MnCS

3871 The world of the patriarchs. Englewood Cliffs, N.J., Prentice-Hall [1967]
xiii, 176 p. 22 cm.
InFer; ICSS; InStme; KAS; MnStj; NcBe; PLatS

3872 (ed) The Books of Joshua and Judges; introduction and commentary by Ignatius Hunt, O.S.B. Collegeville, Minn., The Liturgical Press [1965]
125 p. map, 20 cm. (Old Testament reading guide, 5)
MnCS; PLatS

3873 (tr) Joshua and Judges. Conception, Mo., Conception Abbey [1961]
47 p. 21 cm. (Saint Andrew Bible commentary, 6)
PLatS

3874 (tr) Ruth. Conception, Mo., Conception Abbey [1963]
36–41 p. 21 cm. (Saint Andrew Bible commentary, 11)
PLatS

3875 **Huot, François.**
L'Ordinaire de Sion. Etude sur sa transmission manuscrits, son cadre historique et sa liturgie. Fribourg, Editions universitaires, 1973.
800 p. map, plates, 26 cm. (Spicilegium Friburgense, v. 18)
MnCS

3876 **Hurry, Jamieson Boyd,** 1857–1930.
In honor of Hugh de Boves and Hugh Cook Farrington, first and last abbots of Reading. [Reading, England, E. Poynder and Son], 1911.
33 p. 21 cm.
KAS

Hurst, David, 1916–
3877 (ed) Bede the Venerable. Opera homiletica. Opera rhythmica. Turnholti, Brepols, 1955.
xxi, 473 p. 26 cm. (Corpus Christianorum. Series latina, 122)
ILSP; PLatS

3878 (ed) Bede the Venerable. De tabernaculo; De templo; In Ezram et Neemiam. Cura et studio D. Hurst, O.S.B. Turnholti, Brepols, 1969.

v, 417 p. 26 cm. (Corpus Christianorum. Series latina, 119a)
ILSP; PLatS

3879   (ed) Bede the Venerable. In Lucae evangelium expositio. In Marci evangelium expositio. Cura et studio D. Hurst, O.S.B. Turnholti, Brepols, 1960.
vii, 682 p. 26 cm. (Corpus Christianorum. Series latina, 120)
ILSP; PLatS

3880   (ed) Bede the Venerable. In primam partem Samuhelis libri III. In Regum librum XXX quaestiones. Cura et studio D. Hurst, O.S.B. Turnholti, Brepols, 1962.
vi, 343 p. 26 cm. (Corpus Christianorum. Series latina, 119)
ILSP; PLatS

3881   **Hurt, Anselm,** 1932–
Before the deluge [by] Sebastian Moore, O.S.B., and Anselm Hurt, O.S.B. New York, Newman Press [1968]
124 p. 23 cm.
KAS; MnCS

3882   **Hutschenreiter, Johann Baptista.**
Azarias fidelis Tobiae in via spiritualium exercitiorum per octiduum in comitem datus . . . Pedeponti, Joannes Gastl, 1741.
[46], 495, [20] p. 17 cm.
InStme; KAS

Huyghebaert, Nicolas, 1912–
3883   La consécration de l'église abbatiale de Saint-Pierre de Gand (975) et les reliques de Saint Bertulfe de Renty.
(*In* Corona gratiarum; miscellanea . . . Eligio Dekkers . . . oblata. Brugge, Sint Pietersabdij, 1975. v. 2, p. 129–141)
PLatS

3884   Les documents nécrologiques. Turnholt, Brepols, 1972.
75 p. 24 cm.
MnCS

3885   Stella Maris; notes sur la devotion mariale à l'Abbaye de Saint-André. [Bruges], Abbaye de Saint André, 1955.
51 p. illus. 22 cm.
InStme

3886   **Huynes, Jean,** 17th cent.
Historie générale de l'Abbaye du Mont St. Michel su péril de le mer. Publiée pour le première fois avec une introduction et des notes par E. de Robillard de Beaurepaire. Rouen, A. Le Brument, 1872–73.
2. v. 24 cm.
KAS; PLatS

Hyde Abbey, Winchester, England.
3887   Liber monasterii de Hyda; comprising a chronicle of the affairs of England, from the settlement of the Saxons to the reign of King Cnut, and a chartulary of the Abbey

of Hyde, in Hampshire, 455–1023, A.D. Edited by Edward Edwards . . . London, 1866.
(Gt. Brit. Public Record Office. Rerum britannicarum medii aevi scriptores, no. 45)
ILSP

3888   Liber vitae: register and martyrology of New Minster and Hyde Abbey, Winchester. Edited by Walter de Gray Birch. London, Simpkin & Co., 1892.
xcvi, 335 p. 23 cm. (Hampshire Record Society. [Publications], v. 5)
PLatS

3889   The Missal of the New Minster, Winchester (Le Havre, Bibliothèque municipale, ms. 330). Edited by D. H. Turner. [London] 1962.
xxviii, 238 p. 24 cm. (Henry Bradshaw Society. [Publications], v. 93)
KAS; MnCS; PLatS

3890   **Ibscher, Fortunat,** 1879–1964.
Ecce Agnus Dei! Die Einführung in die Liturgie der hl. Messe in der Volksschule . . . Regensburg, G. J. Manz, 1930.
48 p. 19 cm.
MnCS

3891   **Iburg, Germany (Benedictine abbey).**
Annalium Iburgensium fragmenta. Bruchstücke von Annalen des Klosters Iburg. Nach einer Handschrift des zwölften Jahrhunderts zum erstenmale hrsg. von Ludwig Perger. Münster, F. Regensberg, 1857.
21 p. 23 cm.
PLatS

3892   **Igers, Jane, Sister,** 1931–
On finding the inverse of a matrix.
79 p. 28 cm.
Thesis (M.S.)–University of North Dakota, 1965.
Typescript.
MnStj (Archives)

Ildephonsus ab Arx. *See* Arx, Ildephonsus von.

3893   **Ill, Innocenz,** 17th cent.
Iter ad astra. Apparentia, errantia, inerrantia in coelo aëreo, planetario, sidereo . . . Altdórffij ad Vineas, apud Joannem Adamum Hercknerum, 1687.
207 p. 16 cm.
MnCS

3894   **Illatio sanctissimi patris nostri Benedicti.** MS. Benediktinerabtei Kremsmünster, Austria, codex 34, f.175v–176r. Saec. 13.
Microfilm: MnCH proj. no. 34

3895   **Index alphabeticus monasteriorum O.S.B.** cum inscriptione epistolarum et

telegraphica, tabulis geographicis quibus indicantur situs monasteriorum auctus. Ex Catalogo familiarum confoederatarum O.S.B. desumptum. Romae, 1950– v. 24 cm.
MnCS; PLatS

Inguanez, Mauro, 1877–1955.
3896   Codicum Casinensium manuscriptorum catalogus cura et studio monachorum S. Benedicti archicoenobii Montis Casini . . . [Romae, Typographia Pontificia Instituti Pii IX], 1915–1941.
3 v. 31 cm.
Vol. 2 & 3 recensuit Maurus Inguanez, O.S.B.
InStme; MnCS; NcBe; PLatS

3897   S. Beda Venerabilis, ab B. Capelle, M. Inguanez [et] Beda Thum. Romae, Herder, 1936.
71 p. 25 cm. (Studia Anselmiana, fasc. 6)
InStme; PLatS

3898   **Initia consuetudinis Benedictinae;** consuetudines saeculi octavi et noni. Cooperantibus D. Petro Becker, O.S.B. [et al] publici iuris fecit Kassius Hallinger, O.S.B. Siegburg, F. Schmitt, 1963.
cxxiii, 626 p. 26 cm. (Corpus consuetudinum monasticarum, t. 1)
InStme; PLatS

3899   **International Congress on the Rule of St. Benedict,** lst, Rome, 1971.
Erster Internationaler Regula Benedicti-Kongress. First International Congress on the Rule of St. Benedict . . . Roma, 4–9. 10. 1971. Hildesheim, Verlag H. A. Gerstenberg, 1972.
[4], 337 p. 25 cm. (Regulae Benedicti studia, Bd. 1)
PLatS

3900   **International Congress on the Rule of St. Benedict,** 2nd, Maria Laach, 1975.
Zweiter Internationaler Regula Benedicti-Kongress. Second International Congress on the Rule of St. Benedict . . . Maria Laach, 15–20. 9. 1975. Hildesheim, Gerstenberg Verlag, 1977.
448 p. illus. 25 cm. (Regulae Benedicti studia, v. 5)
KAS; PLatS

3901   **International Ecumenical Colloquim,** Sant'Anselmo, Rome, 1974.
Unitatis redintegratio, 1964–1974; impact of the decree on ecumenism. Edited by Gerard Békés, O.S.B. and Vilmos Vajta. Roma, Editrice Anselmiana, 1977.
176 p. 25 cm. (Studia Anselmiana, 71)
PLatS

Ioannes. *See* Joannes; Johannes.

Irimbertus, abbot of Admont, d. 1176.
3902   Expositio in Cantica Canticorum. MS. Benediktinerabtei Admont, Austria, codex 530. 53 f. Quarto. Saec. 12.
Microfilm: MnCH proj. no. 9589

3903   Commentarius allegoricus in selecta loca Cantica Canticorum. MS. Benediktinerabtei Admont, Austria, codex 682, f. 96r–110v. Octavo. Saec. 12.
Microfilm: MnCH proj. no. 9715

3904   Expositio in libros Josue, Judicum et Ruth. MS. Benediktinerabtei Admont, Austria, codex 17. 221 f. Folio. Saec. 13.
Microfilm: MnCH proj. no. 9106

3905   Commentarius in libros Judicum. MS. Benediktinerabtei Admont, Austria, codex 650, f.25r–54v. Octavo. Saec. 12.
Microfilm: MnCH proj. no. 9691

3906   Expositio in libros Judicum. MS. Benediktinerabtei Admont, Austria, codex 682, f.30r–59v. Octavo. Saec. 12.
Microfilm: MnCH proj. no. 9715

3907   Expositio super librum Judicum, cap. 19–21. MS. Augustinerchorherrenstift Vorau, Austria, codex 193, v. 157r–185r. Octavo. Saec. 12.
Microfilm: MnCH proj. no. 7188

3908   Expositio in libros Regum. MS. Benediktinerabtei Admont, Austria, codex 682, f.69r–90v. Octavo. Saec. 12.
Microfilm: MnCH proj. no. 9715

3909   Expositio in quatuor libros Regum. MS. Benediktinerabtei Admont, Austria, codex 16. 342 f. Folio. Saec. 13.
Microfilm: MnCH proj. no. 9117

3910   Commentarius in Ruth. MS. Benediktinerabtei Admont, Austria, codex 650, f.1r–24v. Octavo. Saec. 12.
Microfilm: MnCH proj. no. 9691

3911   Expositio in librum Ruth. MS. Benediktinerabtei Admont, Austria, codex 682, f.1r–29v. Octavo. Saec. 12.
Microfilm: MnCH proj. no. 9715

3912   Expositio super librum Ruth. MS. Augustinerchorherrenstift Vorau, Austria, codex 193, f.186r–214v.
Microfilm: MnCH proj. no. 7188

3913   **Iso, monk of St. Gall,** ca. 840–871.
Ysonis de miraculis s. Otmari libri II.
(*In* Monumenta Germaniae historica. Scriptores. Stuttgart, 1963. t. 2, p. 47–54)
MnCS; PLatS

Jacob, Carolus, 17th cent.
3914   Comentarii in philosophiam Aristotelis. MS. Universität Salzburg, codex M I 251. 368 f. Octavo. Saec. 17(1625–26).
Microfilm: MnCH proj. no. 11,063

3915 Commentarium in Organum Aristotelis. MS. Universität Salzburg, codex M I 206. 253 f. Quarto. Saec. 17(1624). Microfilm: MnCH proj. no. 11,050

3916 Tractatus de jure et justitia ex IIa IIae S. Thomas traditus. MS. Universität Salzburg, codex M I 299. 352 f. Quarto. Saec. 17(1650). Microfilm: MnCH proj. no. 11,077

3917 **Jacob, Clément,** 1906– L'art et la grâce. Paris, Editions Nouvelles [1946]. 72 p. 19 cm. CaQStB; InStme

3918 **Jacob, Karl, of Andechs,** d. 1661. De actibus humanis disputatio in theologia morali. Munich, ex Typographeo Nicolai Henrici, 1619. 35 p. MnCS (microfilm)

3919 **Jacobi, Andrew, O.S.B.Sylv.** The saints of the Benedictine Order of Montefano. Clifton, N.J., Holy Face Monastery [c 1972] 268 p. illus. 21 cm. CaMWiSb; InFer; ICSS; InStme; KAS; MnCS; MnStj; NcBe; MoCo; MdRi

3920 **Jacutius, Matthaeus,** d. 1764. Syntagma quo adparentis Magno Constantino crucis historia complexa est universa, ac suis ita ab omnibus non priscis modo, quam nuperrimis osoribus vindicata, tempori suo et loco restituta, ceteris tandem gestae rei monumentis illustratur. Roma, A. Rotilus, 1755. cxxx p. 26 cm. PLatS

Jäger, Moritz, 1911–
3921 Schwester Gertrud Leupi, 1825–1904; Gründerin der drei Benediktinerinnenklöster: Maria Rickenbach, Yankton, Marienburg. [Freiburg, Schweiz], Kanisius Verlag [1974]. 200 p. plates, ports. 19 cm. MnCS

3922 Sister Gertrude Leupi, 1825–1904. Translated by Alexander J. Luetkemeyer. 188 p. Typescript. MoCo

Jais, Aegidius, 1750–1822.
3923 Bemerkungen über die Seelsorge, besonders auf dem Lande. 2., mit vom Verfasser selbst noch revidirten und hinterlassenen Verbesserungen und Zusatzen vermehrte Ausgabe. Salzburg, Franz Xaver Duyle, 1828. 332 p. 18 cm.

3924 Guter Same für ein gutes Erdreich; ein Lehr- und Gebetbuch für gut gesinnte Christen . . . 3., verb. u. verm. Ausgabe. Markt Weiler, Johann Jakob Blank, 1795. 382 p. 17 cm. MnCS

3925 Handbuch des Seelsorgers für Amt und Leben. Neue, erw. Ausgabe der Bemerkungen über die Seelsorge. Paderborn, F. Schöningh, 1870. 2 v. 19 cm. InStme

Jaki, Stanley L., 1924–
3926 Brain, mind, and computers. New York, Herder and Herder [1969]. 267 p. 22 cm. MoCo; PLatS

3926a And on this rock; the witness of one land and two covenants. Notre Dame, Ind., Ave Maria Press, c 1978. 125 p. NcBe

3926b Culture and science; two lectures delivered at Assumption University, Windsor, Canada, on February 26 and 28, 1975. [Windsor, Ont.], University of Windsor Press [1975]. 52 p. NcBe

3926c The Milky Way; an elusive road for science. New York, Science History Publications [1975, c 1972]. 352 p. NcBe

3926d Planets and planetarians; a history of theories of the origin of planetary systems. New York, Wiley, c 1977. 266 p. illus. 25 cm. "A Halsted Press Book." PLatS

3926e The relevance of physics. Chicago, University of Chicago Press, [1966]. 604 p. NcBe

3927 Science and creation: from eternal cycles to an oscillating universe. New York, Science History Publications [1974]. viii, 367 p. 25 cm. MnCS; PLatS

3928 **James, Augustine,** 1883– The story of Downside Abbey church. Stratton on the Foss, Downside Abbey [1961]. 115 p. illus., plan. 22 cm. InStme; KAS; MnCS; MoCo; PLatS

Jamin, Nicolas, 1711–1782.
3929 Pensées théologiques, relatives aux erreurs du temps. Paris, chez Humblot, 1769.

370 p.
NcBe

3930　. . . 6. éd., rev. & corr. Bruxelles, J. s'Tertevens, 1778.
519 p.
NcBe

3931　. . . Paris, Landriot, 1789.
xxiii, 374 p. 17 cm.
KAS

3932　Placidus an Maclovien; Abhandlung über die Scrupeln, oder Gewissens-Aengsten. Aus dem Französischen ins Teutsche übersetzt . . . Constanz, Martin Wagner, 1778.
302 p. 17 cm.
Translation of: Placide à Maclovie, sur les scruples.
InStme

3933　Theologische Gedanken in Absicht auf die Irrthümer dieses Zeit. Aus dem Französischen übersetzt . . . Mannheim, Akademischen Schriften, 1770.
xxx, xviii, 512 p. 17 cm.
InStme

3934　Trattato della lettura cristiana, in cui si espongono le regole piu acconcie a guidare i fedeli nella scelta de' libri, ed a loro rendergli utile . . . Trasportate in italiano da D. Carlo Budardi . . . Fulgino, Giovanni Tomassini, 1785.
xxiii, 275 p. 19 cm.
MnCS

3935　**Janecko, Benedict,** 1938–
Consulting ghosts in the Old Testament. [Rome], Collegio di Sant'Anselmo, 1969.
35 leaves, 28 cm.
Typescript.
PLatS

3936　**Jankowski, Augustyn,** 1916–
Listy wiezienne swietego Pawla: do Filipian, do Kolosan, do Filemona, do Efezjan . . . Poznan, Pallottinum, 1962.
592 p. 25 cm.
PLatS

Janssens, Henri Laurent, 1855–1925.

3937　L'arte della scuola benedettina di Beuron. Milano, Società Amici dell'Arte Cristiana [1913].
25 p. illus. 39 cm.
AStb; MnCS

3938　La confirmation – exposé dogmatiques, historique et liturgique. Lille, Desclée, 1888.
325 p.
CaQStB

3939　La Grève; drame en un acte et en vers. Lille, Desclée, 1891.
29 p.
CaQStB

3940　Hermeneutica sacra. 4. ed. Taurini, Marietti, 1920.
420 p.
MoCo

3941　Tractatus de Deo uno. Friburgi Brisgoviae, Herder, 1900.
2 v. 24 cm.
PLatS

Jean Marie, Sister.

3942　He knows how you feel. Liguori, Mo., Liguorian Pamphlets and Books [1971].
87 p. illus. 18 cm.
InStme; MnCS; MoCo

3943　Years of sunshine, days of rain. Westminster, Md., Newman Press, 1966.
145 p. illus., 22 cm.
ICSS; InFer; InStme; MnStj

Jean-Nesmy, Claude. *See* Surchamp, Claude.

3944　**Jebb, Philip,** 1932–
Religious education: drift or decision? [London], Darton, Longman & Todd [1968].
viii, 275 p. 22 cm.
InStme

3945　**Jellouschek, Carl Johann,** 1877–
Die Lehre von Marias Empfängnis bei den ältesten Theologen der Wiener Universität.
(*In* Virgo Immaculata; actus Congressus Mariologici-Mariani, 1954, v. 14, p. 1–34)
PLatS

3946　**Jensen, Joseph,** 1924–
God's word to Israel. Boston, Allyn and Bacon [1968].
xix, 314 p. illus., maps. 22 cm.
InFer; InStme; NcBe; PLatS

3947　. . . Collegeville, Minn., The Liturgical Press [1975].
314 p. illus. 22 cm.
MnCS

3948　The use of tôrâ by Isaiah; his debate with the wisdom tradition. Washington, Catholic Biblical Association of America, 1973.
ix, 156 p. 26 cm.
InStme; MnCS; MoCo; PLatS

Jerome, Father. *See* Wisniewski, Jerome Joseph.

3949　**Jerusalem. Dormition Abbey.**
Jerusalem: die heilige Stadt und Umgebung; Rundschau vom Turm der Dormitio. [Fest und Erinnerungsgabe der Benediktiner vom Berge Sion zur Vollendung und Einweihung der Kirche Mariae-Heimgang am 10. April des Jahres 1910 . . . [Jerusalem, 1910].
Panorama (8 fold. plates) 23 x 30 cm.

Includes an account of "Die deutsche Sionskirche zu Jerusalem."
InStme; MnCS; PLatS

Joachim, abbot of Fiore, 1132(ca.)–1202.

3950 Vaticinia pontificum. MS. Vienna, Nationalbibliothek, codex 412. 31 f. Folio. Saec. 15.
Microfilm: MnCH proj. no. 13,753

3951 Vaticinia sive prophetiae abbatis Joachimi et Anselmi episcopi marsicani, cum imaginibus . . . Una cum praefatione et adnotationibus Paschalini Regiselmi. Venetiis, apud Hieronymum Porrum, 1589. Reprint: Leipzig, Zentralantiquariat, 1972.
[140] p. illus. 19 cm.
MnCS

3952 **Joannes O.S.B.**
Fasciculus myrrhae. MS. Benediktinerabtei Kremsmünster, Austria, codex 218, f.1r–53. Saec. 14.
Microfilm: MnCH proj. no. 207

Joannes, abbas.
3953 Excerpta ex tractatu Iohannis Abbatis de professione monachorum. MS. Benediktinerabtei Melk, Austria, codex 663, f.139r–159v. Quarto. Saec. 15.
Microfilm: MnCH proj. no. 1533

3954 Expositio super professione monachorum. MS. Benediktinerabtei Melk, Austria, codex 1386, f.60r–140r. Duodecimo. Saec. 15.
Microfilm: MnCH proj. no. 1908

3955 Poema morale. Incipit: Ardua virtutum faciles cape lector ad usum. MS. Vienna, Nationalbibliothek, codex 693, f.151v–154v.
Microfilm: MnCH proj. no. 14,024

3956 Tractatus tripartitus de professione monachorum. MS. Benediktinerabtei Melk, Austria, codex 1717, f.119–222. Octavo. Saec. 14.
Microfilm: MnCH proj. no. 2038

3957 Tractatus tripartitus de professione monachorum. MS. Benediktinerabtei Melk, Austria, codex 1267, f.128r–153v. Octavo. Saec. 15.
Microfilm: MnCH proj. no. 1892

Joannes, monk of Abbeville.
3958 Homiliae in omnes dominicas per annum. MS. Cistercienserabtei Lilienfeld, Austria, codex 167. 225 f. Folio. Saec. 14.
Microfilm: MnCH proj. no. 4459

3959 Postilla, seu Summa sermonum in epistolas et evangelia. MS. Benediktinerabtei Melk, Austria, codex 941. 208 f. Folio. Saec. 14.
Microfilm: MnCH proj. no. 1752

3960 Sermones de tempore. MS. Cistercienserabtei Heiligenkreuz, Austria, codex 125. 137 f. Folio. Saec. 13.
Microfilm: MnCH proj. no. 4674

3961 **Joannes, abbot of St. Arnould, Metz,** d. 983.
Vita Iohannis abbatis Corziensis auctore Iohanne abbate S. Arnulfi.
(*In* Monumenta Germaniae historica. Scriptores. Stuttgart, 1963. t. 4, p. 335–377)
MnCS; PLatS

3962 **Joannes Canaparius,** d. 1004.
Vita S. Alberti episcopi auctore Iohanne Canapario.
(*In* Monumenta Germaniae historica. Scriptores. Stuttgart, 1963. t. 4, p. 581–595)
MnCS; PLatS

Joannes Castellensis. *See* Johannes von Kastl.

3963 **Joannes de Garsonibus.**
Carmen philosophicum. MS. Benediktinerabtei Göttweig, Austria, codex 143a, f.117v–118r. Folio. Saec. 14.
Microfilm: MnCH proj. no. 3412

3964 **Joannes de Gmunden.**
Artificium conficiendi calendarium (continet calendarium, tractatus de aureo numero, de signis lunae et solis cum tabulis). MS. Benediktinerabtei St. Peter, Salzburg, codex a.V.21. 23 f. Octavo. Saec. 15(1439).
Microfilm: MnCH proj. no. 10,054

3965 **Joannes de Ochsenhausen, abbot of Schottenstift, Vienna.**
Tres epistolae Ioannis de Ochsenhausen abbatis Scotensis (1428–1466) ad episcopum Pataviensem datae. MS. Vienna, Schottenstift, codex 111, f. 238v.
Microfilm: MnCH proj. no. 3970

Joannes de Spira, d.ca. 1456.
3966 Apologia. Tractatus, utrum monachus, qui contra praeceptum praelati sui comedit carnes, peccet mortaliter, adversus cujusdam monachi objectiones. MS. Benediktinerabtei Melk, Austria, codex 1566. f.107r–127v. Duodecimo. Saec. 15.
Microfilm: MnCH proj. no. 1966

3967 Axiomata, collecta ex libris juris canonici. MS. Benediktinerabtei Melk, Austria, codex 1400, p. 155–160. Duodecimo. Saec. 15.
Microfilm: MnCH proj. no. 1934

3968 Epistola ad Decanum. Epistola ad fratrem . . . MS. Benediktinerabtei Melk, Austria, codex 793, f.181r–183v. Quarto. Saec. 15.
Microfilm: MnCH proj. no. 1634

3969   Excerpta ex summa Magistri Gwilhelmi medici Plancentini, quam conservationis et curationis vocat cap. 192 de doloribus iuncturarum et podagrae. MS. Benediktinerabtei Melk, Austria, codex 323–329. Quarto. Saec. 15.
Microfilm: MnCH proj. no. 1617

3970   Excerpta ex tractatu Magistri Ioannis Nieder de eremitis et anachoretis. MS. Benediktinerabtei Melk, Austria, codex 1833, f.161r–167r. Duodecimo. Saec. 15.
Microfilm: MnCH proj. no. 2141

3971   Excerpta et tractatu Magistri Theodorici de proprietate religiosorum. MS. Benediktinerabtei Melk, Austria, codex 900, f.56r–62r. Quarto. Saec. 15.
Microfilm: MnCH proj. no. 1720

3972   Expositio orationis dominicae. Germanice. MS. Benediktinerabtei Melk, Austria, codex 570, f.135r–136r. Folio. Saec. 15.
Microfilm: MnCH proj. no. 1475

3973   Expositio prologi Regulae S. Benedicti, et ejusdem capitum 1, 2 et 68. MS. Benediktinerabtei Melk, Austria, codex 1833, f.1r–160v. Duodecimo. Saec. 15.
Microfilm: MnCH proj. no. 2141

3974   Expositio salutationis angelicae. Germanice. MS. Benediktinerabtei Melk, Austria, codex 570, f.136r–140r. Folio. Saec. 15.
Microfilm: MnCH proj. no. 1475

3975   Expositio super capitulo 33 Regulae S. Benedicti. MS. Benediktinerabtei Melk, Austria, codex 911, f.3r–32r. Quarto. Saec. 15.
Microfilm: MnCH proj. no. 1729

3976   Farrago materiarum ascetico-moralium ex diversis patribus et auctoribus collecta. MS. Benediktinerabtei Melk, Austria, codex 1400, p. 179–231. Duodecimo. Saec. 15.
Microfilm: MnCH proj. no. 1934

3977   Farrago quaestionum et resolutionum canonico-theologico-moralium. MS. Benediktinerabtei Melk, Austria, codex 1400, p. 114–154. Duodecimo. Saec. 15.
Microfilm: MnCH proj. no. 1934

3978   Quaedam dicta de castitate, et ejus speciebus. MS. Benediktinerabtei Melk, Austria, codex 663, f.175r–242v. Quarto. Saec. 15.
Microfilm: MnCH proj. no. 1533

3979   Quaestiones, utrum monachis Ordinis s. Benedicti sanis uti liceat carnibus. MS. Benediktinerabtei Melk, Austria, codex 1241, f.1r–54v. Quarto. Saec. 15.
Microfilm: MnCH proj. no. 1885

3980   Refutatio objectionum contra tractatum, utrum monachus, qui contra praeceptum praelati carnes comedit mortaliter. MS. Benediktinerabtei Melk, Austria, codex 1400, p. 161–178, 240–246. Duodecimo. Saec. 15.
Microfilm: MnCH proj. no. 1934

3981   Sermo de Coena Domini. MS. Benediktinerabtei Melk, Austria, codex 793, f.136r–139v. Quarto. Saec. 15.
Microfilm: MnCH proj. no. 1634

3982   Sermo de iustificatione a peccatis et profectu in virtutibus. MS. Benediktinerabtei Melk, Austria, codex 911, f.230r–239v. Quarto. Saec. 15.
Microfilm: MnCH proj. no. 1729

3983   Sermo de observatione monasticorum votorum. MS. Benediktinerabtei Melk, Austria, codex 793, f.184r–185v. Quarto. Saec. 15.
Microfilm: MnCH proj. no. 1634

3984   Sermo de observatione votorum monasticorum. MS. Benediktinerabtei Melk, Austria, codex 911, f.219r–221v. Quarto. Saec. 15.
Microfilm: MnCH proj. no. 1729

3985   Sermo de vita religiosa. Benediktinerabtei Melk, Austria, codex 911, f.240r–243r. Quarto. Saec. 15.
Microfilm: MnCH proj. no. 1729

3986   Sermo in illud Lucae: Nemo mittens manum ad aratrum. MS. Benediktinerabtei Melk, Austria, codex 793, f.186r–187v. Quarto. Saec. 15.
Microfilm: MnCH proj. no. 1634

3987   Sermo in illud Matthaei: Ecce nos reliquimus omnia. MS. Benediktinerabtei Melk, Austria, codex 793, f.244r–247r. Quarto. Saec. 15.
Microfilm: MnCH proj. no. 1634

3988   Sermo in illud ad Romanos: Hora est jam nos de somno surgere. MS. Benediktinerabtei Melk, Austria, codex 793, f.247v–249v. Quarto. Saec. 15.
Microfilm: MnCH proj. no. 1634

3989   Sermo in illud Rom. 2: Hora est iam nos de somno surgere. MS. Benediktinerabtei Melk, Austria, codex 911, f.214r–217r. Quarto. Saec. 15.
Microfilm: MnCH proj. no. 1729

3990   Sermo in principio reformationis. MS. Benediktinerabtei Melk, Austria, codex 911, f.208r–213v. Quarto. Saec. 15.
Microfilm: MnCH proj. no. 1729

3991   Sermo super illud Lucae 9: Nemo mittens manum suam ad aratrum. MS. Benediktinerabtei Melk, Austria, codex 911, f.222r–224r. Quarto. Saec. 15.
Microfilm: MnCH proj. no. 1729

3992 Sylloge quaestionum de proprietate et paupertate religiosorum. MS. Benediktinerabtei Melk, Austria, codex 900, f.280r–286v. Quarto. Saec. 15.
Microfilm: MnCH proj. no. 1720

3993 Sylloge quaestionum regularium ex S. Thoma. MS. Benediktinerabtei Melk, Austria, codex 900, f.310r–313v. Quarto. Saec. 15.
Microfilm: MnCH proj. no. 1720

3994 Tractatus alius de proprietate monachorum. MS. Benediktinerabtei Melk, Austria, codex 793, f.293v–311v. Quarto. Saec. 15.
Microfilm: MnCH proj. no. 1634

3995 Tractatus amplius et subtilis de praeceptis decalogi. MS. Benediktinerabtei Melk, Austria, codex 1400, p. 248–415. Duodecimo. Saec. 15.
Microfilm: MnCH proj. no. 1934

3996 Tractatus de communitate. MS. Benediktinerabtei Melk, Austria, codex 911, f.54v–60v. Quarto. Saec. 15.
Microfilm: MnCH proj. no. 1729

3997 Tractatus de distinctione juris naturalis. MS. Benediktinerabtei Melk, Austria, codex 1400, p. 232–239. Duodecimo. Saec. 15.
Microfilm: MnCH proj. no. 1934

3998 Tractatus de esu carnium. MS. Benediktinerabtei Melk, Austria, codex 761, f.1r–47r. Quarto. Saec. 15.
Microfilm: MnCH proj. no. 1609

3999 Tractatus de illis S. Benedicti Regulae cap. VII verbis: Ergo his omnibus humilitatis gradibus. MS. Benediktinerabtei Melk, Austria, codex 900, f.140r–180v. Quarto. Saec. 15.
Microfilm: MnCH proj. no. 1720

4000 Tractatus de oratione. Germanice. MS. Benediktinerabtei Melk, Austria, codex 1084, f.242–246. Duodecimo. Saec. 15.
Microfilm: MnCH proj. no. 1839

4001 Tractatus de proprietate monachorum. MS. Benediktinerabtei Melk, Austria, codex 911, f.32r–54v. Quarto. Saec. 15.
Microfilm: MnCH proj. no. 1729

4002 Tractatus de rebus ecclesiae non alienandis. MS. Benediktinerabtei Melk, Austria, codex 900, f.62v–65v.
Microfilm: MnCH proj. no. 1720

4003 Tractatus de vitio proprietatis monachorum in caput 33 Regulae S. Benedicti. MS. Benediktinerabtei Melk, Austria, codex 793, f.265r–293v. Quarto. Saec. 15.
Microfilm: MnCH proj. no. 1634

4004 Tractatus in caput 33 et 34 Regulae S. Benedicti, et in caput 13 Regulae S. Augus-

tini, cum variis quaestionibus de proprietate et communitate monasticorum bonorum. MS. Benediktinerabtei Melk, Austria, codex 793, f.247v–249v. Quarto. Saec. 151.
Microfilm: MnCH proj. no. 1634

4005 Tractatus, utrum monachus frangens jejunium regulare peccet minus vel aeque, sicut si frangeret jejunium ecclesiae. MS. Benediktinerabtei Melk, Austria, codex 1400, p. 105–113. Duodecimo. Saec. 15.
Microfilm: MnCH proj. no. 1934

4006 Tractatus, utrum monachus qui contra praeceptum praelati sui comedit carnes, peccet mortaliter. MS. Benediktinerabtei Melk, Austria, codex 1400, p. 1–104. Duodecimo. Saec. 15.
Microfilm: MnCH proj. no. 1934

4007 **Joannes de Spiz,** fl.1451.
Carmina, tractus theologici varii, et tractatuli, numero 44. Benediktinerabtei Melk, Austria, codex 1776. 317 f. Duodecimo. Saec. 15.
Microfilm: MnCH proj. no. 2082

Joannes de Weilheim. *See* Schlitpacher, Johann.

Joannes Diaconus, f. 880.

4008 Vita S. Gregorii Magni. MS. Benediktinerabtei Göttweig, Austria, codex 108, f.1r–130v. Quarto. Saec. 12.
Microfilm: MnCH proj. no. 3390

4009 Vita Gregorii Magni. MS. Universitätsbibliothek Graz, Austria, codex 799, 134 f. Quarto. Saec. 12.
Microfilm: MnCH proj. no. 26,899

4010 De vita S. Gregorii papae. MS. Universitätsbibliothek Graz, Austria, codex 793, f.67r–181r. Quarto. Saec. 12.
Microfilm: MnCH proj. no. 26,901

4011 Vita sancti Gregorii. MS. Augustinerchorherrenstift Klosterneuburg, Austria, codex 703, f.1r–137v. Folio. Saec. 12.
Microfilm: MnCH proj. no. 5682

4012 Vita sancti Gregorii papae. MS. Cistercienserabtei Heiligenkreuz, Austria, codex 230, f.1r–159r. Folio. Saec. 12.
Microfilm: MnCH proj. no. 4763

4013 Vita s. Gregorii papae. MS. Vienna, Nationalbibliothek, codex 469, f.1r–113r. Folio. Saec. 12.
Microfilm: MnCH proj. no. 13,805

4014 Vita s. Gregorii papae. MS. Cistercienserabtei Zwettl, Austria, codex 280. 145 f. Folio. Saec. 12.
Microfilm: MnCH proj. no. 6884

4015 Vita Gregorii papae. MS. Linz, Austria, Studienbibliothek, codex 7. 143 f. Quarto. Saec. 13.
Microfilm: MnCH proj. no. 27,872

4016   Vita Gregorii papae. Quatuor libri. Mancant liber primus et secundus. MS. Cistercienserabtei Lilienfeld, Austria, codex 94,
f.1r–64r. Quarto. Saec. 14.
Microfilm: MnCH proj. no. 4399

4017   Vita sancti Gregorii. MS. Augustinerchorherrenstift Klosterneuburg, Austria,
codex 236, f.1r–81r. Folio. Saec. 14.
Microfilm: MnCH proj. no. 5204

4018   Vita s. Gregorii Magni papae. MS. Vienna, Nationalbibliothek, codex 414, f.1r–
138v. Folio. Saec. 14.
Microfilm: MnCH proj. no. 13,739

4019   De vita et gestis beatissimi Gregorii
papae. MS. Vienna, Nationalbibliothek,
codex series nova 12,776. 213 f. Folio.
Saec. 15.
Microfilm: MnCH proj. no. 25,134

4020   S. Gregorii Magni papae primi vita a
Ioanne Diacono scripta libris quattuor.
(*In* Gregory I, pope. Opera. Parisiis,
MDCV. v. 1, col. 1–128)
PLatS

4021   Versiculi de Cena Cypriani.
[*In* Poetae latini aevi carolini . . .
Berolini, 1880–   t.IV, fasc.II/III (1923)]
. . . . Microfiche. Slangenburg, St.
Willibrordsabdij [196-]
PLatS (microfiche)

4022   **Joannes monachus.**
Apparatus in sextum librum Decre-
talium. MS. Benediktinerabtei Admont,
Austria, codex 20. 83 f. Folio. Saec. 14.

4023   **Joao, dos Prazeros,** fl. 17th cent.
O Principe dos patriarcas S. Bento . . .
sua vida discursada en emprezas politicas e
predicaveis . . . [Lisboa, 1683–1690]
2 v. illus. 30 cm.
KAS (v. 1)

Jocelin de Brakelond, fl. 1200.

4024   Monastic and social life in the twelfth
century, as exemplified in the Chronicles of
Jocelin of Brakelond, from A.D.
MCLXXIII to MCCII. Translated, with
notes, introduction, & c. by T. E. Tomlins.
London, Whitaker and Co., 1844.
xii, 52 p. 23 cm.
InStme; MoCo

4025   (2dary) Koenig, Clara. Englisches Klosterleben im 12. Jahrhundert, auf Grund
der Chronik des Jocelinus de Brakelonda.
Jena, Frommannsche Buchhandlung,
1928.
vii, 98 p. 23 cm.
MnCS

4026   **Johannes, abbot of Gorze,** fl. 960–974.
Johannes Gorziensis de miraculis ss. Glo-
desindis et Gorgonii.

(*In* Monumenta Germaniae historica.
Scriptores. Stuttgart, 1963. t. 4, p. 235–
247)
MnCS; PLatS

Johannes, monk of Lambach.

4027   Collecta ex diversis authoribus de fraterna correccione. Tractatus de virtutibus.
Tractatus, utrum omnia praecepta dicalogi
sunt de lege naturae . . . MS. Benediktinerabtei Lambach, Austria, codex chart.
258, f.1r–14v, 17r–49v. Saec. 15.
Microfilm: MnCH proj. no. 642

4028   Commentarius in epistolam II Pauli ad
Corinthios. MS. Benediktinerabtei Lambach, Austria, codex chart. 132,
f.217r–277r. Saec. 15.
Microfilm: MnCH proj. no. 549

4029   Commentarius in Genesin. MS. Benediktinerabtei Lambach, Austria, codex chart.
132, f.60r–216r. Saec. 15.
Microfilm: MnCH proj. no. 549

4030   Conceptum sermonis. Notata quaedam
super cap. 48 et 49 Regulae S. Benedicti.
MS. Benediktinerabtei Lambach, Austria,
codex chart. 262, f.224r–233v. Saec. 15.
Microfilm: MnCH proj. no. 646

4031   Expositio epistolae II Hieronomi ad
Paulinum et prologi in Genesin. MS. Benediktinerabtei Lambach, Austria, codex
chart. 132, f.14r–54r. Saec. 15.
Microfilm: MnCH proj. no. 549

4032   Extensior lectura super librum II. Sententiarum. MS. Benediktinerabtei Lambach, Austria, codex chart. 263,
f.26r–207v. Saec. 15.
Microfilm: MnCH proj. no. 644

4033   Lectura super lib. II. Sentenciarum, cap.
1–29. MS. Benediktinerabtei Lambach,
Austria, codex chart. 155. 376 f. Saec. 15.
Microfilm: MnCH proj. no. 572

4034   Ioannes prof. Lambacensis, dein abbas
ad Scotas Vieniae: Sermones de tempore.
MS. Benediktinerabtei Lambach, Austria,
codex chart. 345, f.5r–270v. Saec. 15.
Microfilm: MnCH proj. no. 714

4035   Tractatus de virtutibus theologicis. Finitum anno Domini 1460. Benediktinerabtei
Lambach, Austria, codex chart. 85, f.295r–
328v.
Microfilm: MnCH proj. no. 507

4036   **Johannes, monk of Morigny.**
Liber apparitionum et visionum Beatae
Virginis Mariae, seu Liber florum coelestis
doctrinae. MS. Benediktinerabtei Seiten-
stetten, Austria, codex 273. 67 f. Folio.
Saec. 14–15.
Microfilm: MnCH proj. no. 1085

Johannes, monachus Salzburgensis.

4037 Alphabetum aureum (Das guldine ABC). MS. Vienna, Nationalbibliothek, codex 3741, f.11r–13v. Folio. Saec.15(1469).
Microfilm: MnCH proj. no. 16,956

4038 Carmen in honorem Beatae Virginis Mariae. Germanice. MS. Augustinerchorherrenstift Klosterneuburg, Austria, codex 725, f.209v. Folio. Saec. 15.
Microfilm: MnCH proj. no. 5707

4039 Hymnus: Christus, qui lux es. Germanice. MS. Augustinerchorherrenstift Klosterneuburg, Austria, codex 782, f.226v. Quarto. Saec. 14.
Microfilm: MnCH proj. no. 5743

4040 Sequentiae et hymni ecclesiastici germanice versi, cum notis musicis. MS. Vienna, Nationalbibliothek, codex 4696, f.107r–188v. Quarto. Saec. 15.
Microfilm: MnCH proj. no. 17,870

Johannes, monk of Sankt Lambrecht.

4041 Super passione. MS. Vienna, Nationalbibliothek, codex 1563, f.190r–250v. Folio. Saec. 15.
Microfilm: MnCH proj. no. 14,895

4042 Tractatus de passione Domini. MS. Benediktinerabtei Admont, Austria, codex 629, f.29r–178v. Quarto. Saec. 15.
Microfilm: MnCH proj. no. 9670

Johannes von Kastl, 15th cent.

4043 Expositio in Regulam s. Benedicti. MS. Benediktinerabtei St. Peter, Salzburg, codex b.XII.23–25. 3 vols. Folio. Saec. 15.
Microfilm: MnCH proj. no. 10,707

4044 Glossae in Regulam S. Benedicti. MS. Vienna, Nationalbibliothek, codex 3702, f.1r–226r et 342r–356v (index). Folio. Saec. 15.
Microfilm: MnCH proj. no. 16,913

4045 Libri duo in Regulam S. Benedicti, cum indice alphabetico rerum praemisso. MS. Vienna, Nationalbibliothek, codex 3663. 180 f. Folio. Saec. 15.
Microfilm: MnCH proj. no. 16,884

4046 Unpublished theological writings of Johannes Castellensis [edited by] Clemens Stroick. Ottawa, University of Ottawa Press, 1964.
ix, 200 p. 24 cm. (Université d'Ottawa. Publications seriées, 73)
InStme

4047 **Johner, Dominicus,** 1874–1955.
Wort und Ton im Choral; ein Beitrag zur Aesthetik des gregorianischen Gesanges. 2. Aufl. Leipzig, Breitkopf & Härtel Musikverlag, 1953.
xv, 482 p. illus. (music), plates, diagrs. 26 cm.
InStme; PLatS

Johnson, Earl, 1930–

4048 The freedom of the sons of God.
(*In* The challenge of the Council . . . 25th annual North American Liturgical Week, 1964. p. 247–252)
PLatS

4049 The liturgy, where man is confronted by God's word.
(*In* Jesus Christ reforms His Church . . . 26th annual North American Liturgical Week, 1965. p. 174–180)
PLatS

4050 The place of Holy Baptism.
(*In* The challenge of the Council . . . 25th annual North American Liturgical Week, 1964. p. 160–164)
PLatS

4051 The Psalm piety of Cardinal Newman as revealed in his Christian interpretation of the Psalter. Trier, 1960.
xi, 61 p. 21 cm.
Excerpt of thesis–Theological Faculty of Trier, 1960.
InStme; MoCo

4052 Wisdom and Canticle of Canticles. Conception, Mo., Conception Abbey [1962].
40 p. 21 cm. (Saint Andrew Bible commentary, 17)
PLatS

4053 **Johnston, Henry Joseph,** d. 1723.
A vindication of the Bishop of Condom's Exposition of the doctrine of the Catholic Church. In answer to a book entitled, An exposition of the doctrine of the Church of England . . . London, Printed by Henry Hills, 1686.
122 p. 20 cm.
PLatS

4054 **Joliette, Canada (Quebec).** Abbaye de Notre-Dame-de-la-Paix.
Manuel des Oblats et Oblates de saint Benoit . . . Mont-Laurier, P.Q. Canada, Editions de Moniales Bénédictines [1977].
96 p. illus. 16 cm.
CaQJo

4055 **Jones, James,** 1924–
De voto stabilitatis in jure benedictino vigenti.
xvii, 106 p. 27 cm.
Thesis (J.C.D.)–Pontificium Institutum Utriusque Juris, Rome, 1955.
MoCo

4056 **Jones, Susanna, Sister.**
The American Benedictine Sister; a historical profile.
13 p.
InFer

Joppich, Godehard, 1932–
4057   Deutsches Antiphonale . . . [hrsg. von
P. Godehard Joseph, O.S.B. [und] P.
Rhabanus Erbacher, O.S.B. Abtei
Münsterschwarzach [1972].
2 v. illus. 22 cm.
InStme
4058   Salus carnis: eine Untersuchung in der
Theologie des hl. Irenäus von Lyon.
Münsterschwarzach, Vier-Türme-Verlag,
1965.
xii, 145 p. 21 cm.
InStme
4059   **Jordan, Placidus Max,** 1895–1977.
The divine dimension; Christian reflections on a credible faith. [Dublin], Gill and
Macmillan [1970].
xii, 195 p. 21 cm.
MnCS
Josep de Sant Benet, 1654–1723.
4060   Opera omnia, tum latino, tum hispano
sermone conscripta. Matriti, L. F. Ma-
jados, 1731.
428 p.
MnCS (microfilm)
4061   Opera omnia, tum latino, tum hispano
sermone conscripta. Ed. 4. Matriti,
Haeredes Francisci del Hierro, 1738.
[52], 428, [4] p. port. 30 cm.
KAS; MnCS
4062   Vida del v. fra Josep de Sant Benet,
religiòs llec del real monestir de Santa
Maria de Montserrat de Catalunya, excrita
de la seva pròpria mà. Monestir de Montserrat, 1930.
186 p. port. 17 cm.
PLatS
4063   **Josephus ab Expectatione.**
Systema theologicum ad mentem S.
Anselmi archiepiscopi . . . elaboratum
studio, & cura R. P. ac M. Fr. Josephi ab
Expectatione . . . Conimbricae, ex Architypographia Academico-Regia, 1765.
4 v. 22 cm.
PLatS (v.1)
4064   **Journées oecuméniques,** Chevetogne,
1961.
L'infaillibilité de l'Eglise . . . Editions de
Chevetogne [1963].
266 p. 22 cm.
InStme
4065   **The Jubilee book of the Benedictines of
Nashdom,** 1914–1964. London, The
Faith Press, 1964.
86 p. plates, 21 cm.
MnCS; PLatS
4066   **Juettner, Leora, Sister,** 1932–
A program of in-service education in the
language arts area for several rural
schools.

46 p. 28 cm.
Thesis (M.S.)–University of Dayton,
1969.
Typescript.
MnStj(Archives)
4067   **Juglar, Jean,** 1896–
Mass and Office in the common life.
(*In* Communal life. Westminster, Md.,
1957. p. 107–138)
InFer; PLatS
Julian of Norwich, 1343–1443.
4068   The revelations of divine love of Julian of
Norwich. Translated by James Walsh, S.J.
London, Burns & Oates [1961].
xix, 210 p. 21 cm.
PLatS
4069   Showings. Translated from the critical
text with an introduction by Edmund Col-
ledte and James Walsh. Preface by Jean
Leclercq, O.S.B. New York, Paulist Press
[1978].
369 p. (The Classics of western spirituality)
NcBe
4070   **Julianus, monk of Vézelay,** 12th cent.
Sermons. Introduction, texte latin,
traduction et notes per Damien Vorreux.
Paris. Editions du Cerf, 1972.
2 v. 20 cm. (Sources chrétiennes, 192–
193)
InStme
4071   **Jumièges, France. Saint Pierre (Benedictine abbey).**
Les manuscrits musicaux de Jumièges
[ed. par] René Jean Hesbert, O.S.B.
Macon, Protat Frères, 1954. (Monumenta
musicae sacrae, 2)
InStme
Jüngt, Thomas Aquinas, 1883–
4072   Leben des Dieners Gottes, Bruder Meinrad Eugster, Benediktiner aus dem Stifte
Maria-Einsiedeln. [3., neu durchgesehene
Aufl]. Einsiedeln, Benziger Verlag [1955].
207 p. illus. 20 cm.
InStme
4073   Der Weg zur Seelenreife; Lesungen und
Erwägungen über das Demutskapitel des
heiligen Benedikt. Missionsverlag St. Otti-
lien, 1928.
189 p. illus. 19 cm.
InStme
4074   **Jungwirth, Augustin,** 1876–
Catalog of manuscripts, Universitätsbib-
liothek, Salzburg.
8 v.
Handwritten.
Xeroxed by University Microfilms, Ann
Arbor, Mich., 1968.
MnCS

4075 **Kalberer, Augustine,** 1918–
Lives of the saints; daily readings. Chicago, Franciscan Herald Press [c1975].
470 p. illus.
MoCo

4076 **Kalff, Athanasius Walter,** 1904–
Ps.-Hieronymi De septem ordinibus ecclesiae. [Würzburg? 1935?]
viii, 82 p. 23 cm.
Inaug.-Diss. – Würzburg.
MnCS

Kälin, Bernard, 1887–1962.
4077 Einführung in die Ethik. 3. Aufl., umgearbeitet von Dr. Raphael Fäh, O.S.B. Sarnen, Slebstverlag Benediktinerkollegium, 1962.
xv, 396 p. 25 cm.
MnCS; PLatS

4078 Einführung in die Logik, Ontologie, Kosmologie, Psychologie, Kriteriologie, Theodizee. 5. Aufl., bearb. von Dr. P. Raphael Fäh, O.S.B. Sarnen, Selbstverlag Benediktinerkollegium, 1957.
xi, 464 p. 25 cm.
PLatS

4079 Die Erkenntnislehre des hl. Augustinus. Sarnen, Buch- und Kunstdruckerei Louis Ehrli, 1921.
85 p. 24 cm.
InStme

4080 **Kalinowski, Kathleen, Sister,** 1926–
Discussion of natural monopoly; a new approach.
57 p. 28 cm.
Thesis (M.A.) – Marquette University, 1963.
Typescript.
MnStj(Archives)

4081 **Kansas City, Kans. St. Benedict's Church.**
Fifty years of Catholic life in St. Benedict's Parish, Kansas City, Kansas. Golden jubilee celebration, 1902–1952. [Kansas City, Kans., 1952].
23 p. illus., ports. 28 cm.
KAS

Kapsner, Celestine Charles, 1892–1973.
4082 Kapsner family tre, 1874–1974. Prepared by Celestine Kapsner and Oliver Kapsner. Centenary edition. Collegeville, Minn., St. John's Abbey, 1974.
65 leaves, 28 cm.
MnCS; PLatS

4083 Kopka family tree. Prepared over the years by Celestine Kapsner and Oliver Kapsner. Collegeville, Minn., St. John's Abbey, 1973.
24 leaves, 28 cm.
MnCS

4083a The angels, our God-given companions and servants. Rockford, Ill., Tan Books and Publishers, 1974.
48 p. 18 cm.
First published by St. John's Abbey Press, Collegeville, Minn., 1945.
MnCS

4084 (tr) Vogl, Karl. Begone Satan! A soul-stirring account of diabolical possession . . . Translated by Rev. Celestine Kapsner, O.S.B. New Haven, Conn., Theotokia Press [1945].
48 p. illus. 21 cm.
Foreword by Virgil Michel, O.S.B.
Translation of: Gibt's heute noch Teufel?
InStme; MnCS; PLatS

4085 . . . . Rockford, Ill., Tan Books and Publishers [1973]
48 p. 21 cm.
Reprint of the New Haven, Conn., edition of 1945. First published by St. John's Abbey, Collegeville, Minn., 1935.
MnCS; PLatS

Kapsner, Oliver Leonard, 1902–
4086 A Benedictine bibliography; an author-subject union list. Compiled for the Library Science Section of the American Benedictine Academy. With a foreword by Anselmo M. Cardinal Albareda. 2d ed. Collegeville, Minn., St. John's Abbey Press, 1962.
2 v. 27 cm. (American Benedictine Academy. Library science studies, no. 1)
ACu; etc.

4087 Benedictine subject headings and classification schedule. 2d ed., enlarged. Collegeville, Minn., St. John's University Library, 1964.
iv, 38 p. 29 cm.
Multilithed.
ACu; etc.

4088 The Benedictines in Brazil.
Offprint from: The American Benedictine review, v. 28 (1977), p. 113–132.
MnCS; PLatS

4089 Catholic subject headings; a list designed for use with Library of Congress Subject headings or the Sears List of subject headings. 5th ed., with an appendix on names of saints. Collegeville, Minn., St. John's Abbey Press, 1963.
xxiii, 488 p. 29 cm.
"Under the auspices of the Catholic Library Association."
ACu; etc.

4090 Kapsner family tree. Prepared over the years by Rev. Celestine Kapsner, O.S.B., and Rev. Oliver Kapsner, O.S.B. Cen-

tenary edition, 1874–1974. Collegeville, Minn., St. John's Abbey, 1974.
65 leaves, 28 cm.
MnCS; PLatS

4091   Kopka family tree. Prepared over the years by Rev. Celestine Kapsner, O.S.B., and Rev. Oliver Kapsner, O.S.B. Collegeville, Minn., St. John's Abbey, 1973.
22 leaves. 28 cm.

4092   Monastic Manuscript Microfilm Project; progress reports I–V, 1964–1968. Collegeville, Minn., St. John's Abbey, 1964–1968.
5 pts., 28 cm.
InStme; KAS; MnCS; NcBe; PLatS

4093   Theological subject headings for a Catholic library. Collegeville, Minn., St. John's Abbey Library, 1941.
v, 88 p. 32 cm.
Mimeographed.
MnCS

4094   (2dary) International Federation of Library Associations. List of uniform titles for liturgical works of the Latin rites of the Catholic Church. London, IFLA Committee on Cataloging, 1975.
x, 17 p. 30 cm.
Based in part on A Manual of cataloging practice for Catholic author and title entries, by Oliver Kapsner, O.S.B.
MnCS

4094a   (ed) The Oblate; a monthly leaflet devoted to the interests of the Oblates of the Order of St. Benedict, St. John's Abbey, Collegeville, Minn. 1–   1927–
Editor: vol. 1, 1927–28.
MnCS

4095   **Kaspar, Adelhard,** 1902–
Die Quellen zur Geschichte der Abtei Münsterschwarzach am Main . . . München, Kommissionsverlag R. Oldenbourg, 1930.
xii, 86 p. 23 cm.
KAS

Kathol, Quentin, 1936–

4096   Pastoral Epistles and Hebrews. Conception, Mo., Conception Abbey [1962].
45 p. 21 cm. (Saint Andrew Bible commentary, 25)
PLatS

4097   Proverbs and Ecclesiasticus. Conception, Mo., Conception Abbey [1963].
56 p. 21 cm. (Saint Andrew Bible commentary, 15)
PLatS

4098   **Katzner, John,** 1851–1930.
Articles in: The Minnesota Horticulturist.
v. 35(1907), p. 139: Annual report of the Vice-President.

v. 35(1907), p. 441: Experiment work at Collegeville.
v. 36(1908), p. 190: The farmer's orchard.
v. 37(1909), p. 45: Annual report of Collegeville Trial Station.
v. 37(1909), p. 242: Midsummer report.
v. 38(1910), p. 31: A theory of pear growing.
v. 38(1910), p. 43: Report of Collegeville Trial Station.
v. 38(1910), p. 214: My pear theory.
v. 39(1911), p. 44: Report of Collegeville Trial Station.
v. 39(1911), p. 253: Midsummer report.
v. 40(1912), p. 99: Annual report.
v. 40(1912), p. 255: Midsummer report.
v. 40(1912), p. 377: My pear experiment up to date.
v. 41(1913), p. 59: Annual report of Collegeville Trial Station.
v. 41(1913), p. 266: Midsummer report.
v. 41(1913), p. 317: Pears are coming.
v. 42–46(1914–1918): Two reports each year.
MnCS (Archives)

4099   **Kaufman, Philip,** 1911–
Bases for a theology of preaching in Luther's "Lectures on Romans, 1515–16." Saint John's University, Collegeville, Minn., 1966.
xvi, 98 leaves. 28 cm.
Thesis (M.A.) – St. John's University, Collegeville, Minn., 1966.
Multigraphed.
MnCS

4100   **Kaufungen, Germany (Benedictine abbey).**
Urkundenbuch des Klosters Kaufungen in Hessen. Im Auftrage des Historischen Vereines der Diöcese Fulda bearb. u. hrsg. von Hermann von Roques . . . Cassel, Max Siering, 1900–02.
2 v. 25 cm.
KAS; MnCS

4101   **Kavanagh, Aidan,** 1929–
The concept of eucharistic memorial in the canon revisions of Thomas Cranmer, archbishop of Canterbury, 1533–1556. St. Meinrad, Ind., Abbey Press, 1964.
xxix, 231 p. 23 cm.
Diss. – Theological Faculty, Trier.
InStme; MnCS

4102   The shape of baptism; the rite of Christian initiation. New York, Pueblo, c 1978.
xv, 224 p. illus. 22 cm.
InStme

4103   The tradition of Judaeo-Christian worship: our debt to each other.

(*In* Scharper, Philip. Torah and Gospel. New York, 1966. p. 47–59)
InStme; PLatS

4104 **Kavanaugh, Mary Charlotte, Sister.**
A critical evaluation of audio-visual aids in teaching religion in the elementary school.
122 p. tables.
Diss. (M.A.)–Catholic University of America, 1951.
InFer

Keck, Johann, 1400–1450.

4105 Aliqua de anima et potentiis ejus. MS. Benediktinerabtei Melk, Austria, codex 1384, f.309v–317v. Duodecimo. Saec. 15.
Microfilm: MnCH proj. no. 1906

4106 Apologia pro tractatu "Ecclesiasticus unitor." MS. Vienna, Nationalbibliothek, codex 4937, f.198v–200v. Quarto. Saec. 15.
Microfilm: MnCH proj. no. 18,139

4107 Chronologia a creatione mundi usque ad Christum natum (fragmentum). MS. Benediktinerabtei Melk, Austria, codex 959, f. 185v. Quarto. Saec. 15.
Microfilm: MnCH proj. no. 1762

4108 Commentaria in Regulam sancti Benedicti. MS. Dominikanerkloster, Vienna, codex 207, f.2r–222v. Folio. Saec. 15.
Microfilm: MnCH proj. no. 9009

4109 De annis a creatione mundi usque ad Christi nativitatem. MS. Benediktinerabtei Melk, Austria, codex 1653, f.181v. Sextodecimo. Saec. 15.
Microfilm: MnCH proj. no. 2011

4110 De floribus temporum Veteris Testamenti excriptio (excerptum). MS. Benediktinerabtei Melk, Austria, codex 1561, p. 1–5. Duodecimo. Saec. 15.
Microfilm: MnCH proj. no. 1962

4111 De intervallo. MS. Benediktinerabtei Melk, Austria, codex 907, f.114r–117r. Quarto. Saec. 15.
Microfilm: MnCH proj. no. 1725

4112 Decaperotision ad Canonicos Undersdorfenses. MS. Benediktinerabtei Melk, Austria, codex 907, f.97r–114r. Quarto. Saec. 15.
Microfilm: MnCH proj. no. 1725

4113 Ecclesiasticus unitor, sive Tractatus contra Concilium Basileense. MS. Vienna, Nationalbibliothek, codex 4957, f.82r–87v. Quarto. Saec. 15.
Microfilm: MnCH proj. no. 18,139

4114 Epistola ad Ioannem Schlitpacher. MS. Benediktinerabtei Melk, Austria, codex 662, f.13r–15v. Quarto. Saec. 15.
Microfilm: MnCH proj. no. 1532

4115 Flores chronicorum Veteris Testamenti. MS. Benediktinerabtei Melk, Austria, codex 873, f.315–337. Quarto. Saec. 15.
Microfilm: MnCH proj. no. 1694

4116 Responsiones ad decem quaestiones sibi a praeposito Undersdorfensi exhibitae. MS. Vienna, Nationalbibliothek, codex 3248, f.190v–204r.
Microfilm: MnCH proj. no. 16,463

4117 Sermo in Concilio. MS. Benediktinerabtei Melk, Austria, codex 916, f.118r–127v. Quarto. Saec. 15.
MnCH proj. no. 1734

4118 Sermones. MS. Benediktinerabtei Melk, Austria, codex 907, f.130v–222v. Quarto. Saec. 15.
Microfilm: MnCH proj. no. 1725

4119 Tractatus brevis de Concilio Basileensi. Vienna, Nationalbibliothek, codex 3473, f.103r–112v. Quarto. Saec. 15.
Microfilm: MnCH proj. no. 16,698

4120 Tractatus de cautela praedicandi. MS. Benediktinerabtei Melk, Austria, codex 907, f.117r–117v. Quarto. Saec. 15.
Microfilm: MnCH proj. no. 1725

4121 Tractatus de observantia statutorum Regulae S. Benedicti. MS. Vienna, Schottenstift, codex 405, f.1r–50r. Octavo. Saec. 15.
Microfilm: MnCH proj. no. 4148

4123 Tractatus de sacro Basiliensi Concilio. MS. Vienna, Nationalbibliothek, codex 3473, f.75r–102r. Quarto. Saec. 15.
Microfilm: MnCH proj. no. 16,698

4124 Tractatus finalis commentariorum super Regula S. Benedicti de obligatione statutorum regularium. MS. Benediktinerabtei Göttweig, Austria, codex 375, f.164r–173v. Folio. Saec. 15.
Microfilm: MnCH proj. no. 3643

4125 Tractatus finalis commentariorum super Regula S. Benedicti de obligatione statutorum regularium. MS. Benediktinerabtei Melk, Austria, codex 1405, f.171r–189v. Duodecimo. Saec. 15.
Microfilm: MnCH proj. no. 1926

4126 Tractatus finalis commentariorum supra Regula S. Benedicti de obligatione statutorum regularium. MS. Vienna, Schottenstift, codex 356, f.243r–366v. Folio. Saec. 15.
Microfilm: MnCH proj. no. 4206

4127 Tractatus in facto Basileensi Concilio si in depositione olim Eugenii potuit errare. MS. Benediktinerabtei Melk, Austria, codex 741,1, f.117v–139v. Quarto. Saec. 15.
Microfilm: MnCH proj. no. 1602

4128   Tractatus pro Concilio Basileensi. MS.
Vienna, Nationalbibliothek, codex 3957,
f.45r–70r. Quarto. Saec. 15.
Microfilm: MnCH proj. no. 18,139

4129   Vallis salinarum, de fossione salis. MS.
Benediktinerabtei Melk, Austria, codex
907, f.117v–130r. Quarto. Saec. 15.
Microfilm: MnCH proj. no. 1725

4130   **Keckeisen, Bead,** 1895–
Missal quotidiano completo em latim e
português, com o proprio do Brasil adiçao a
Editora Beneditina, Salvador, Bahia
[1962].
1057, [237] p. 17 cm.
PLatS

4131   **Keefe, Ambrose John,** 1937–
A critical evaluation of the indexing of
the religious periodical literature of Bel-
mont College Library, Belmont, N.C.
[1966].
Research paper (M.A.)–University of
North Carolina.
NcBe

4132   **Keiblinger, Ignaz Franz,** 1797–1869.
Geschichte des Benedictiner-Stiftes Melk
in Niederöstereich, seiner Besitzungen und
Umgebung. Wien, Fr. Beck, 1851–1869.
2 v. plates, 24 cm.
KAS (v.1)

4133   **Kellenbenz, Eugene,** 1917–
Music for various liturgical rites, . . .
Music supplement to the Roman Ritual,
new English translation . . . 1964. Milwaukee, Bruce [1965].
64 p. music, 28 cm.
MnCS

4134   **Keller, Dominic Joseph,** 1902–1978.
Syllabus for development of western
music. Collegeville, Minn., St. John's University, 1971.
29 p. 28 cm.
Multilithed.
MnCS(Archives)

4135   **Keller, Ludwig,** 1849–1915.
Johann von Staupitz und die Anfänge
der Reformation. Nieuwkoop, B. de Graaf,
1967.
xii, 436 p. 22 cm.
Nachdruck der Ausgabe Leipzig, 1888.
PLatS

Keller, Mary Louis, Sister.
4136   An analytical cumulative index to The
Messenger, official newspaper of the
Diocese of Covington, for the years 1945
through 1959.
228 p. 28 cm.
Thesis (M.S.L.S.)–Catholic University
of America, 1964.

Typescript.
KyCovS

4137   Leaders in the early history of the
Church in Kentucky.
62 p. 28 cm.
Thesis (B.A.)–Villa Madonna College,
1945.
Typescript.
KyCovS

Kellner, Altman, 1902–
4138   Professbuch des Stiftes Kremsmünster.
Sumptibus Monasterii Cremifanensis,
1968.
629 p. 25 cm.
InStme

4139   Stift Kremsmünster, Benediktinerabtei
in Oberösterreich. [3. Aufl. München,
Verlag Schnell & Steiner, 1967].
[23] p. plates, 17 cm.
PLatS

Kelly, Columba, 1930–
4140   The cursive torculus design in the Codex
St. Gall 359 and its rhythmical significance; a paleographical and semiological
study. [St. Meinrad, Ind., Abbey Press,
1964].
xiii, 546 p. facsims., music, tables, 23 cm.
Thesis–Pontifical Institute of Sacred
Music, Rome.
InStme; PLatS

4141   The organ.
(*In* Liturgical Conference, 1966. Har-
mony and discord, an open forum on
church music. Advance papers . . . p.
75–79)
PLatS

4142   The Sung Mass for feast days; music for
the proper texts for all first and second
class feasts, the entire common of the
saints . . . [Cincinnati, World Library of
Sacred Music, 1966].
vii, 237 p. music. 23 cm.
InStme

4143   **Kelly, James William,** 1915–
The Faust legend in music. Evanston,
Ill., 1960.
v, 213 leaves, illus., music, 28 cm.
Thesis–Northwestern University.
ILSP; InStme; MnCS; MoCo; MdRi;
NcBe; PLatS

4144   **Kelsch, Emmanuel,** 1910–
(ed) Freshmen inklings: themes,
dialogues, letters, tall tales by the
members of the English class of 1937–38.
Collegeville, Minn., St. John's Preparatory
College, 1938.
147 leaves, ports. 30 cm.
Mimeographed.
MnCS

Kemmer, Alfons, 1911–
4145   Christ in the Rule of St. Benedict.
       (*In* Monastic studies, v. 3, p. 87–98)
       PLatS

4146   (tr) Cassianus, Joannes. Weisheit der
       Wüste; Auswahl und Uebertragung von P.
       Alfons Kemmer, O.S.B. Einsiedeln, Ben-
       ziger [1948].
       199 p. 20 cm.
       MnCS

4147   **Kempf, Gilmary, Sister,** 1933–
       Community dimensions in sacramental
       preparation.
       75 p.
       Thesis (M.A.)–Mundelein College, 1974.
       Typescript.
       MnStj(Archives)

       Kempf, Placidus, 1895–1978.
4148   The authentic image of the priest, as pro-
       jected by Papal documents from Leo XIII
       to Paul VI and arranged as points for daily
       reflection. St. Meinrad, Ind., Abbey Press,
       1970.
       170 p. 18 cm.
       InFer; InStme; KAS; MnCS; NcBe

4149   This is your mother; the authentic image
       of Mary as projected by Papal documents
       and arranged as points of daily reflection.
       St. Meinrad, Ind., Abbey Press, 1972.
       ix, 229 p. 18 cm.
       InStme; KAS; MnCS

4150   Under Mary's mantle; a brief sketch of
       St. Mary's Parish, Lanesville, Indiana, dur-
       ing the 125 years of its growth from a tiny
       seed into a giant tree. [Printed by Abbey
       Press, St. Meinrad, Ind., 1968]
       36 p. illus. 24 cm.
       InStme

4151   **Kemph, Nicolaus.**
       Tractatus de proponentibus religionis in-
       gressum. MS. Benediktinerabtei Melk,
       Austria, codex 878, f.178r–295v. Quarto.
       Saec. 15.
       Microfilm: MnCH proj. no. 1695

4152   **Kennedy, Timothy,** 1922–
       A study of eucharistic chalices.
       ii, 23 leaves, illus., 28 cm.
       Thesis (B.F.A.)–Washington Univer-
       sity, St. Louis, Mo., 1950.
       MnCS

4153   **Kercher, Mary Victor, Sister.**
       Phraseology of Sancho compared to
       modern Spanish equivalents.
       91 p. 28 cm.
       Thesis (M.A.)–Catholic University of
       America, 1958.
       Typescript.
       InFer

4154   **Kerkhoff, Radbert,** 1908–
       Beiträge zur Lehre des unablässigen
       Betens im Neuen Testament. [Roma], Pon-
       tificium Institutum Academicum S.
       Anselmi de Urbe [1951].
       64 p. 21 cm.
       Excerpted from thesis (S.T.D.).
       MnCS

       Kerkvoorde, Augustin, 1913–
4155   Erneuerung der niederen Weihen?
       (*In* Rahner, Karl, ed. Diaconia in Christo,
       p. 575–620)
       PLatS

4156   Le mouvement théologique dans le
       monde contemporain: liturgie, dogme,
       philosophie, exégès, par A. Kerkvoorde et
       O. Rousseau. Paris, Beauchesne [1969–]
       v. 27 cm.
       MnCS

4157   Où en est le problème du diaconat.
       Bruges, Editions de l'Apostolat Litur-
       gique, 1961.
       91 p. 24 cm.
       PLatS

4158   Die Theologie des Diakonatis.
       (*In* Rahner, Karl, ed. Diaconia in Christo,
       p. 220–284)
       PLatS

4159   **Kessinger, David Robert,** 1932–
       An analytical subject and author index to
       the National Catholic Reporter for the
       period October 28, 1964, through October
       20, 1965.
       160 p.
       Thesis (M.S.L.S.)–Catholic University
       of America, 1972.
       NcBe

       Kessler, Verona, Sister.
4160   The effects of the laic laws of 1901 and
       1904 on the Benedictines in France.
       428 p.
       Thesis (Ph.D.)–University of Notre
       Dame.
       SdYa

4161   The suppression of the Benedictine
       Order in France during the Revolution.
       184 p.
       Thesis (M.A.)–Creighton University,
       Omaha, Neb., 1957.
       SdYa

       Kettenaker, Paul.
4162   Schriften: Kurze Nachrichten de scrip-
       toribus San-Blasianis, de fatis bibliothecae
       San-Blasianae, de sacris reliquiis ad S. Bla-
       sianum, de bibliotheca ad S. Paulum. MS.
       Benediktinerabtei St. Paul im Lavanttal,
       Austria, codex 86/6. 129 f. Folio. Saec.
       18–19.
       Microfilm: MnCH proj. no. 12,628

4163   Tractatus de disciplina monastica San-
Blasiana. MS. Benediktinerabtei St. Paul
im Lavanttal, Austria, codex 224/2. 3 vols.
Folio. Saec. 18.
Microfilm: MnCH proj. no. 12,052–53, &
12,075

4164   **Khamm, Korbinian,** 1645–1730.
Hierarchia augustana chronologica
tripartita in partem cathedralem, collegia-
lem, et regularem . . . Augustae, Joan.
Mich. Labhart, 1709–19.
5 v. 21 cm.
KAS(v.3); MnCS(v.1); PLatS(v.1–2)

4165   **Kholperger, Agapitus.**
Sacris s. Bibliis vox una varias res signi-
ficans eruta tum S. Scripturae studio eis,
tum vero vel maxime verbi divini praeconi-
bus utilis ac necessaria. MS. Benediktinerabtei Kremsmünster, Austria, codex
297. 503 p. Saec. 17.
Microfilm: MnCH proj. no. 282

4166   **Kiefer, Odo,** 1932–
Die Hirtenrede; Analyse und Deutung
von Joh. 10, 1–18. Stuttgart, Verlag
Katholisches Bibelwerk [1967].
92 p. 21 cm.
MnCS

4167   **Kiem, Martin,** 1829–1903.
Das Benediktinerstift Muri-Gries 1845–
1895 . . . Sarnen [Schweiz], J. Müller,
1895.
47 p. 23 cm.
KAS

4168   **Kienle, Ambrosius,** 1852–1905.
Théorie et pratique de chant grégorien
. . . Traduit de l'allemand par Dom
Laurent Janssens. 2. ed. Tournay, Desclée,
Lefebvre & cie, 1895.
viii, 191, 83 p. music. 22 cm.
Translation of: Choralschule.
PLatS

4169   **Kiess, Matthew Martin,** 1900–1979.
The Jacobsen reaction and certain ethyl-
tetramethyl benzemes.
129 leaves, 28 cm.
Thesis (Ph.D.)–University of Minnesota,
1938.
Typescript.
MnCS (Archives)

4170   **Kimpfler, Gregorius,** d. 1693.
Tractatus theologico-moralis, in Decem
Decalogi & quinque Ecclesiae Praecepta
. . . Ratisbonae, Joan. Aegidius Raith,
1708.
[16], 502, [12] p. illus. 20 cm.
InStme

4171   **Kleczewski, Kieran Russell,** 1950–
The origins of Christianity in Edessa; a
study of hypotheses and sources.

iii, 96 leaves. 29 cm.
Thesis (M.A.)–Indiana University, 1978.
InStme

Klein, Laurentius, 1928–

4172   Das Amt der Einheit; Grundlegendes zur
Theologie des Bischofsamtes. Stuttgart,
Schwabenverlag [1964].
311 p. 21 cm.
MnCS

4173   Evangelisch-lutherische Beichte; Lehre
und Praxis. Paderborn, Verlag Bonifacius-
Druckerei [1961].
269 p. 23 cm.
MnCS; MoCo; PLatS

4174   Ueber Wesen und Gestalt der Kirche; ein
katholisch-evangelischer Briefwechsel
[von] Laurentius Klein [und] Peter Mein-
hold. [Freiburg im Breisgau, Herder,
1963].
123 p. 18 cm.

4175   **Kleiner, Rafael,** 1931–
Feiern des Gottesvolk; eine Einführung
in die Liturgie für jeden. Klosterneuburger
Buch- und Kunstverlag [1967].
239 p. 20 cm.
MnCS

4176   **Kleppel, Placid,** 1897–
A bibliography of North Carolina poetry.
Belmont, N.C., Abbey Press, 1934.
15 p.
NcBe

Klimisch, Mary Jane, Sister.

4177   A cumulative index of Gregorian chant
sources. Yankton, S.D., Boller Printing,
1975.
SdYa

4178   The music of the lamentations; historical
and analytical aspects.
Thesis (Ph.D.)–Washington University,
St. Louis, Mo., 1971.
SdYa

4179   The one bride; the Church and conse-
crated virginity. New York, Sheed and
Ward [1965].
xviii, 235 p. 24 cm.
CaMWiSb; InFer; ICSS; InStme; KAS;
MnCS; MnStj; MoCo; PLatS; SdYa

4180   Sacred music resource center project
progress report: a cumulative index of
Gregorian chant sources. Yankton, S. D.,
Mount Marty College, 1971–
v. 21 cm.
MnCS

Kline, Omer Urban, 1923–

4181   The public address of James Cardinal
Gibbons as a Catholic spokesman on social
issues in America.
ix, 466 leaves, 29 cm.

Thesis (Ed.D)–Teachers College, Columbia University, 1963.
Typescript.
PLatS

4182 St. Vincent Brewery once center of controversy.
Photocopied from: The Latrobe Bulletin, v. 74, June 25, 1976, p. 36.
PLatS

4183 **Klingenberg, Joseph Marie, Sister.**
The direct product of matrices.
Thesis (M.S.)–Marquette Univeristy, 1962.
Typescript.
KyCovS

4184 **Klotz, Petrus Karl,** 1878–1968.
Amerre Krusztus járt, szentföldi utirajz.
Az ötödik német kindást forditotta Frater Peregrinus, O.P. Budapest, A "Credo." Kiadása, 1927.
132 p. 18 cm.
Translation of: Was ich unter Palmen fand.
PLatS

4185 **Knaebel, Bonaventure,** 1918–
Concept of the absolute in projective geometry.
25 leaves, 28 cm.
Thesis (M.S.)–Catholic University of America, 1946.
Typescript.
InStme

Knowles, David, 1896–1974.
4186 Archbishop Thomas Becket: a character study.
(*In* his: The historian and character. Cambridge, 1963. p. 98–128)
PLatS

4186a Authority. London, Catholic Truth Society, 1969.
20 p. 17 cm. (Catholic Truth Society pamphlets. Do 416 [v.4])
PLatS

4187 Bare ruined choirs; the dissolution of the English monasteries. Cambridge [England], New York, Cambridge University Press, 1976.
329 p. illus., 25 cm.
Abridged edition of: The religious orders in England, v. 3: The Tudor age.
InStme

4188 The Benedictines; a digest for moderns . . . St. Leo, Fla., Abbey Press, 1962.
xi, 50 p. 18 cm.
AStb; McBe; KAS; PLatS; InStme; OkShG; MoCo; MnCS; InFer; MnStj; CaMWiSb

4189 Cardinal Gasquet as an historian.
(*In* his: The historian and character. Cambridge, 1963. p. 240–263)
PLatS

4190 The case of St. William of York.
(*In* his: The historian and character. Cambridge, 1963. p. 76–97)
PLatS

4191 The censured opinions of Uthred of Boldon.
(*In* his: The historian and character. Cambridge, 1963. p. 129–170)
PLatS

4192 Christian monasticism. New York, McGraw-Hill [1969].
253 p. illus. 19 cm.
InFer; CaMWiSb; ICSS; KAS; MnCS; PLatS; NcBe; MnStj; ViBris

4193 Cistercians and Cluniacs; the controversy between St. Bernard and Peter the Venerable.
(*In* his: The historian and character. Cambridge, 1963. p. 50–75)
PLatS

4194 The Cluniacs in England.
(*In* Williams, Schafer. The Gregorian epoch. Boston, 1964. p. 37–41)
PLatS

4195 Edward Cuthbert Butler, 1858–1934.
(*In* his: The historian and character. Cambridge, 1963. p. 264–362)
PLatS

4196 The English bishops, 1070–1532.
(*In* Medieval studies presented to Aubrey Gwynn, S.J. p. 283–296)
PLatS

4197 The English mystical tradition. New York, Harper [1961].
197 p. 22 cm.
MnCS; MnStj; KAS; CaQStB; ILSP; InStme

4198 The episcopal colleagues of Archbishop Thomas Becket. Cambridge [England], University Press, 1970.
190 p. (Ford lectures, 1949)
"First edition 1951. Reprinted with corrections 1970."
NcBe

4199 The evolution of medieval thought. Baltimore, Helicon Press [1962].
ix, 356 p. 23 cm.
InFer; ILSP; NdRi; PLatS; NcBe

4200 Father Augustine Baker.
(*In* Davis, Charles. English spiritual writers. New York, 1961. p. 97–111)
InFer; PLatS

4201 From Pachomius to Ignatius; a study in the constitutional history of the religious

orders. New York, Oxford University Press, 1966.
98 p. 19 cm. (The Sarum lectures, 1964–65)
MnCS; NcBe; PLatS

4202   Great historical enterprises. London, Royal Historical Society, 1958–61.
4 v. 20 cm.
ILSP; InStme; MnCS; MnStj; NcBe; KAS; MoCo; NdRi; PLatS

4203   The heads of religious houses, England and Wales, 940–1215 . . . Cambridge [England], University Press, 1972.
xlviii, 277 p. 24 cm.
MnCS; NcBe

4204   The historian and character, and other essays . . . Cambridge [England], University Press, 1963.
xxix, 387 p. 22 cm.
ILSP; InStme; KAS; MnCS; MnStj; NcBe; PLatS; OkShG

4205   The last abbot of Wigmore.
(In his: The historian and character. Cambridge, 1963. p. 171–178)
PLatS

4206   Medieval religious houses, England and Wales. New York, St. Martin's Press, 1972.
xv, 565 p. fold. maps, 24 cm.
InStme; PLatS

4207   The Middle Ages. By David Knowles with Dimitri Obolensky. New York, McGraw-Hill [c 1968].
519 p. illus. 23 cm.
NcBe; PLatS

4207a   Le Moyen Age. Traduit de l'anglais par Laurent Jezéquel, avec la collaboration d'André Crépin. Paris, Editions du Seuil, 1968.
620 p. illus. 20 cm. (Nouvelle histoire de l'Eglise, 2)
InStme

4208   The monastic buildings of England.
(In his: The historian and character. Cambridge, 1963, p. 179–212)
PLatS

4209   The monastic order in England; a history of its development from the times of St. Dunstan to the Fourth Lateran Council, 940–1216. 2d ed. Cambridge [England], University Press, 1963.
xxi, 780 p. diagrs. 26 cm.
InFer; InStme; KAS; MnCS; MdRi; PLatS

4210   The nature of mysticism. New York, Hawthorn Books [1966].
140 p. 21 cm. (Twentieth-century encyclopedia of Catholicism, v. 38)
ILSP; MdRi; PLatS

4210a   Peter has spoken; the encyclical without ambiguity. London, Catholic Truth Society, 1968.
11 p. 17 cm. (Catholic Truth Society pamphlets. Do 413 [v. 4])
PLatS

4211   St. Benedict.
(In Walsh, James, S.J. Spirituality through the centuries. 1964. p. 57–71)
PLatS

4212   St. Bernard of Clairvaux: 1090–1153.
(In his: The historian and character. Cambridge, 1963. p. 31–47)
PLatS

4213   Saints and scholars; twenty-five medieval portraits. Cambridge [England], University Press, 1962.
207 p. illus. 21 cm.
MdRi; MnStj; NdRi; KAS; PLatS

4214   Thomas Becket. Stanford, Calif., Stanford University Press, 1971.
xi, 183 p. illus. 23 cm.
KAS; MnCS; NcBe

4215   What is mysticism? London, Burns & Oates [1967].
140 p. 22 cm.
PLatS

4216   (2dary) Butler, Edward Cuthbert. Western mysticism. 3rd ed., with Afterthoughts and a new foreword by Professor David Knowles. London, Constable, 1967.
lxxii, 242 p. 23 cm.
PLatS

4217   (ed) The Christian centuries; a new history of the Catholic Church. [New York, McGraw-Hill, 1964–]
v. illus., maps, 23 cm.
PLatS

4218   (ed) Downside Review.
David Knowles was editor of v. 35–57, 1936–1958.

4219   (ed) Decreta Lanfranci monachis Canturariensibus transmissa. Edidit David Knowles. Siegburg, apud Franciscum Schmitt, 1967.
xliii, 149 p. 26 cm. (Corpus consuetudinum monasticarum, 3)
Introduction in English, text in Latin.
PLatS

4220   **Kocarnik, Wenceslaus,** 1845–1912.
Rehole Sv. Otce Benedikta, do cestiny prelozil a opsal P. Wenceslav Kocarnĭk, O.S.B. Plzen, Nebr., 1885.
111 p. 19 cm.
Manuscript.
MnCS

4221   **Koch, Imelda, Sister.**
By the power of the vine; history of the Missionary Benedictine Sisters in the United States: 1922–1952.

118 p. 28 cm.
Thesis (M.A.)–St. John's University, Collegeville, Minn., 1964.
Typescript.
MnStj(Archives); NbMo

4222 **Kodell, Jerome,** 1940–
Responding to the Word; a biblical spirituality. New York, Alba House, c 1978.
xiii, 128 p. 21 cm.
InFer; MnCS; MnStj; MoCo; InStme; PLatS

4223 **Koenig, Robert,** d. 1713.
Principia juris canonici ex libro I & II Decretalium Gregorii IX. . . . Salisburgi, Joan. Bapt. Mayr, 1697.
4 v. 21 cm.
KAS (v.1–2)

4224 **Kögel, Raphael,** 1882–
Die photographie historischer Dokumente nebst den Grundzügen der Reproduktionsverfahren, wissenschaftlich und praktisch dargestellt. Leipzig, Harrassowitz 1914; Nendeln, Kraus Reprint, 1968.
119 p. illus. 23 cm.
PLatS

Kohake, Cletus Paul, 1915–
4225 Co-operative campus living.
Offprint from: The Catholic educational review, v. 61(1963), p. 37–51
KAS

4226 The life and educational writings of Rabanus Maurus.
188, 183 leaves. illus. 27 cm.
Thesis–Cornell University, 1948.
Contains English translation of part 3 of De institutione clericorum.
Typescript.
KAS

Köhler, Theodor Wolfram, 1936–
4227 Der Begriff der Einheit und ihr ontologisches Prinzip nach dem Sentenzenkommentar des Jakob von Metz, O.P. Romae, Herder, 1971.
xxxiii, 540 p. 25 cm. (Studia Anselmiana, 58)
KAS; PLatS

4228 Sapientiae procerum amore: mélanges médiévistes offerts à Dom Jean-Pierre Müller, O.S.B., à l'occasion de son 70éme anniversaire. Edités par Theodor Wolfram Köhler. Roma, Editrice Anselmiana [1975].
xvii, 514 p. 25 cm. (Studia Anselmiana, 63)
InStme; MnCS; PLatS

4229 Zur Kognitionspsychologischen Erforschung symbolischen Denkens–die Untersuchungen Jean Plagets.
(*In* Symbolisme et theologie. Sacramentum 2. Roma, 1974. p. 45–69)
PLatS

4230 **Kohlhaas, Radbert,** 1923–
(ed) Bar Hebraeus, 1226–1286. Jakobitische Sakramententheologie im 13. Jahrhundert; der Liturgiekommentar des Gregorius Barheraeus, erstmals hrsg. und erläutert von Radbert Kohlhaas. Münster, Aschendorff [1959].
xii, 118 p. 25 cm.
InStme; MnCS; PLatS

4231 **Kolb, Aegidius,** 1923–
Ottobeuren; Festschrift zur 1200-Jahrfeier der Abtei. Augsburg, Winfried-Werk, 1964.
416 p. 24 cm.
MnCS

4232 **Koller, Ludwig,** 1882–
Stift Göttweig, Benediktinerabtei in Niederösterreich . . . 5. neubearb. Aufl. München, Verlag Schnell & Steiner, 1967.
15 p. illus. 17 cm. (Kunstführer Nr. 645)
PLatS

4233 **Komechak, Michael,** 1932–
The seven positive canons of criticism applied to architectural masterpieces. [Lisle, Ill.] 1954.
various pagings, mounted plates, 29 cm.
ILSP

4234 **Koneberg, Hermann,** 1837–1891.
Das Kirchenjahr in Bildern. Augsburg, M. Huttler, 1892.
27 p. illus. 27 cm.
InStme

4235 **Königsdorfer, Cölestin,** 1756–1840.
Geschichte des Klosters zum. Heil Kreutz in Donauwörth. Donauwörth, Sebastian Sedlmayr, 1819–29.
3 v. in 4, 22 cm.
KAS

4236 **Kopp, Fridolin,** 1691–1757.
Acta fundationis Murensis monasterij. [Typis monasterij Murensis, 1750].
98 p. 25 cm.
KAS

4237 **Kopp, Ignatius.**
Breve chronicon monasterii S. Blasii. MS. Benediktinerabtei St. Paul im Lavanttal, Austria, codex 32/6. 24 f. Folio. Saec. 17.
Microfilm: MnCH proj. no. 12,692

4238 **Kornides, Marcian,** 1913–
Sacred Heart Church, Jeannette, Pennsylvania; golden jubilee, 1924–1974. Parish founded, 1889. Present church erected 1924.
unpaged, chiefly illus., 24 cm.
PLatS

4239 **Kort, Barbara, Sister,** 1939–
A plan for improving the reading program at St. Mary's School.

52 p. 28 cm.
Research paper (M.A.)–University of Minnesota, 1973.
Typescript.
MnStj(Archives)

4240 **Korvin-Krasinski, Cyrill von,** 1905–
Die kosmische Uebs als Kult- und Zeitmitte; ein Beitrag zum Problem "Kulteidos und Geschichte".
(*In* Perennitas; Beiträge . . . P. Thomas Michels, O.S.B., zum 70. Geburtstag. Münster, 1963. p. 471–497)
PLatS

4241 **Kotter, Bonifaz,** 1912–
Die Ueberlieferung der Pege Gnoseos des hl. Johannes von Damaskos. Ettal, Buch-Kunstverlag, 1959.
243 p. 25 cm.
InStme; MnCS; PLatS

4242 **Kraft, Katherine, Sister,** 1938–
Hebrew meals of the Old Testament; a preparation for the Eucharist.
iv, 79 p. 28 cm.
Thesis (M.A.)–St. John's University, 1969.
Typescript.
MnStj(Archives)

Kramer, Maurus, 1900–
4243 Abteikirche, Fiecht, Tirol. [Salzburg, Rupertuswerk, 1959].
[23] p. illus. 17 cm.
MnCS; PLatS

4244 Geschichte der Benediktinerabtei St. Georgen-Fiecht bei Schwaz in Tirol. Fiecht, 1954.
67 p. illus. 19 cm.
MnCS; PLatS

4245 **Kranz, Marie, Sister.**
A semantic analysis of the verbs denoting speech in the Anglo-Saxon poem Daniel.
205 p.
Thesis (Ph.D.)–Catholic University of America, 1972.
SdYa

4246 **Kranz, Rosaria, Sister.**
A comparative study of small hospitals in the South Dakota region.
238 p.
Thesis (D.P.H.)–John Hopkins University School of Hygiene and Public Health, 1973.
SdYa

4247 **Kraus, Johann Baptist,** 1700–1762.
Liber probationum; sive, Bullae summorum pontificum, diplomata imperatorum et regum . . . quae ad historiam . . . S. Emmerami Ratisbonae maxime

spectant. Ratisbonae, J. V. Raedlmayer, 1752.
[28], 563, [16] p. 22 cm.
KAS

Krause, Adalbert, 1901–1979.
4248 Admont und das Gesäuse in Geschichte und Sage. 2. Aufl. [Linz], Oberösterreichischer Landesverlag [1954].
144 p. illus. 21 cm.
MnCS

4249 Das Blasiusmünster in Admont. Linz, Oberösterreichischer Landesverlag [n.d.].
40, [12] p. 22 plates, 17 cm.
PLatS

4250 Das Dreigestirn: Altmann, Gebhard und Adalbero.
(*In* Der heilige Altmann, Bischof von Passau. Göttweig, 1965. p. 39–47)
PLatS

4251 Die Krippenkunst des Steirischen Bildhauers Josef Thaddäus Stammel im Stifte Admont. [Wien, Oesterreichische Staatsdruckerei] 1962.
27 p. illus (part col.) 17 cm.
PLatS; MnCS

4252 St. Hemma. Mödling bei Wien, Missionsdruckerei St. Gabriel, 1948.
47 p. illus. 21 cm.
MnCS; NdRi

4253 Die Stiftsbibliothek in Admont. 6 Aufl. Linz, Oberösterreichischer Landesverlag [n.d.].
47 p. 17 cm.
MnCS; PLatS

4254 . . . 7., verb. Aufl. Linz, Oberösterreichischer Landesverlag [1969].
45 p. illus. 17 cm.
MnCS

4255 **Krebs, Anselm, Sister.**
Education for leisure.
52 p.
Thesis–University of Notre Dame, 1941.
InFer

Kremsmünster, Austria (Benedictine abbey).
4256 Annales Cremifanenses. Initium deest. MS. Vienna, Nationalbibliothek, codex 375, 58 f. Folio. Saec. 12–13.
Microfilm: MnCH proj. no. 13,702

4257 Annales monasterii Cremifanensis. MS. Vienna, Nationalbibliothek, codex 3399, f.386r–401r. Folio. Saec. 16.
Microfilm: MnCH proj. no. 16,639

4258 Catalogus librorum manuscriptorum antiquorum qui inventi fuerunt in Bibliotheca Cremifanensi anno 1631 (geschrieben von P. Matthias Pierbaumer). MS. Benediktinerabtei Kremsmünster, Austria, codex novus 421. 64 p. Saec. 17.

Microfilm: MnCH proj. no. 403

4259 Catalogus religiosorum Ordinis S. P. Benedicti in monasterio Cremifanensi vulgo Kremsmünster Superioris Austriae viventium . . .

v. 22 cm.

PLatS

4260 Kremsmünster Kalendarius. MS. Benediktinerabtei Kremsmünster, Austria, codex sine numero. 12 f. Saec. 15.

Microfilm: MnCH proj. no. 432

4261 Kremsmünster heute. Text: Patres von Kremsmünster. Fotos: Erich Widder.

13 p. illus. 30 cm.

PLatS

4262 Liber de ordinatione officiorum monasticorum tam in choro quam in monasterio. MS. Benediktinerabtei Kremsmünster, Austria, codex 321a. 83 f. Saec. 14.

Microfilm: MnCH proj. no. 431

4263 Necrologium II Cremifanense. MS. Benediktinerabtei Kremsmünster, Austria, codex Schatzkammer 5, f.1r–46v. Saec. 13.

Microfilm: MnCH proj. no. 384

4264 Professbuch des Stiftes Kremsmünster, von Altman Kellner. Sumptibus Monasterii Cremifanensis, 1968.

629 p. 25 cm.

InStme

4265 Rubricae Cremifanenses. Rubrica continens in se dispositionem fratrum chori Chremiphanensis monasterii quatenus ea concernit libris a maioribus nobis relictis 1594. MS. Benediktinerabtei Kremsmünster, Austria, codex 103. 177 f. Saec. 16.

Microfilm: MnCH proj. no. 96

4266 Schematismus der Benediktiner von Kremsmünster, 1965. [Wels, OÖ, Landesverlag.]

56 p. 21 cm.

MnCS

Kremsmünster, Austria (Benedictine abbey). Stiftsbibliothek.

4267 Catalogus codicum manuscriptorum. Auszug aus dem Katalog des P. Hugo Schmid. Neue codices 1–1361.

2 v. 25 cm.

Handwritten. Xeroxed by University Microfilms, Ann Arbor, Mich., 1965.

MnCS

4268 Codices im Schatzkasten. [Compilation traced to Hugo Schmid, O.S.B.].

unpaged.

Handwritten. Xeroxed by University Microfilms, Ann Arbor, Mich., 1965.

MnCS

4269 Catalogus codicum manuscriptorum in bibliotheca Cremifanensis . . . asservatorum. In memoriam anni a fundato monasterio MC. jubilaei edidit P. Hugo Schmid.

2 v. (the first volume is printed, Lintii, prostat in Libraria Ebenhoechiana, 1877; the second volume is handwritten)

Xeroxed by University Microfilms, Ann Arbor, Mich., 1965.

MnCS

4269a Codex Millenarius Maior. Faksimile-Ausgabe im Originalformat des Codex cremifanensis cim. 1 des Benediktinerstifts Kremsmünster. Kommentar von Willibrord Neumüller u. Kurt Holter. Graz, Akademische Verlagsanstalt, 1974.

39, vi p. [398] leaves (facsims.), 34 cm. (Codices selecti phototypice impressi, 45)

The codex dates from about the year 800.

Both the text and the commentary contain illustrations in color.

MnCS

4270 Die Wiegendrucke des Stiftes Kremsmünster. Hrsg. von der Stiftsbibliothek . . . Linz/Donau, H. Muck, 1947.

279 p. plates. 24 cm.

Vorwort signed: P. Willibrord Neumüller, Stiftsbibliothekar.

MnCS

4271 **Krenner, Amandus,** fl. 17th cent.

Compendium disciplinae monasticae e sanctorum patrum regulis et sententiis contextum. Salisburgi, Joan. Bapt. Mayr, 1678.

[6], 152 p. 16 cm.

KAS

4272 **Kreuzer, Ildefons,** 1932–

Die Wiedererrichtung der Benediktinerabtei Scheyern . . . [n.p.] 1961.

175 leaves, mounted photos, 30 cm.

Mimeographed.

KAS

4273 **Krez, Albert,** 1643–1713.

Paradigmata practica recollectionis asceticae triduanae, nec non et renovationis votorum religiosorum . . . Altdorfii, ad Vineas, Jo. Adam Hercknerus, 1696.

362 p. 16 cm.

InStme; MnCS

4274 **Kriedler, Ildephonse,** 1888–

The fostering of religious vocations for the brotherhood.

99 leaves, 28 cm.

Thesis (M.A.)–University of Notre Dame, 1933.

Typescript.

InStme

Krinetzki, Leo, 1922–

4275 Der Bund Gottes mit den Menschen nach dem Alten und Neuen Testament. Düsseldorf, Patmos-Verlag [1963].
128 p. 19 cm.
PLatS

4276 Das Hohe Lied; Kommentar zu Gestalt und Kerygma eines alttestamentlichen Liebesliedes. Düsseldorf, Patmos-Verlag [1964].
324 p. 25 cm.
MnCS; PLatS

4277 Die Liebe hört nie auf; die Botschaft des Hohen Liedes heute. Stuttgart, Verlag Katholisches Bibelwerk [1964].
184 p. 21 cm.
PLatS

4278 **Kroening, Mary Christa, Sister.**
A catechesis of the creation and paradise accounts.
197 leaves. 28 cm.
Thesis (M.A.)–St. John's University, Collegeville, Minn., 1972.
Typescript.
MnDuS

4279 **Krohe, Severin,** 1856–1932.
Liturgische Predigten über die wichtigsten kirchlichen Segnungen und Weihungen. Wien, H. Kirsch, 1894.
xii, 692 p. 23 cm.
KAM; NdRi

4280 **Kropff, Martinus,** 1701–1779.
Bibliotheca Mellicensis; sev, Vitae et scripta inde a sexcentis et eo amplivs annis Benedictinorvm Mellicensivm auctore Martino Kropff, qvi etiam catalogvm selectorvm nonnvllorvm manvscriptorvm addidit, et hic primvm ex bibliotheca mss. Mellicensi publicae lvci commisit. [Vindobnae, svmptibus Ioannis Pavli Kravs, 1747].
24, 683, [14], 14 p. 24 cm.
Xeroxed by University Microfilms International, Ann Arbor, Mich., 1978.
ILSP; MnCS (microfilm & xeroxed copy)

Krumpelmann, Cosmas, 1895–1970.

4281 In this sign thou shalt conquer; an appreciation of the work of Mother d'Youville and her daughters, the Grey Nuns. Muenster, Sask., St. Peter's Press, 1944.
18 p. illus. 18 cm.
CaSMu; MnCS; NdRi

4282 On wings of love; an appreciation of the Little Flower–Saint Thérèse of the Child Jesus. Muenster, Sask., St. Peter's Press [1943].
48 p. illus. 18 cm.
CaSmu; MnCS; NdRi

4283 **Kuebelbeck, Mary Rachel, Sister,** 1939–
Body temperature, perineal healing, involution, and breast engorgement among postpartum mothers.
viii, 21 p. 28 cm.
Thesis (M.S.)–University of Utah, 1974.
Typescript.
MnStj(Archives)

4284 **Kuhn, Albert,** 1839–1929.
Die Kirche; ihr Bau, ihre Austattung, ihre Restauration. Mit 144 Abbildungen. 2. Aufl. Einsiedeln, Benziger, 1917.
140 p. illus. 19 cm.
InStme

4285 **Kuhn, Kaspar,** 1819–1906.
Geschichts-Kalender; oder, Tägliche Erinnerungen aus der Welt und Kirchen, Kunst und Literatur-Geschichte. 2., verb. und stark verm. Aufl. Regensburg, G. J. Manz, 1892.
2 v. 24 cm.
KAS

4286 **Kunz, Madeleine, Sister.**
American Catholic opinion on feminism; a study of the periodical literature.
Thesis (M.A.)–Catholic University of America, 1946.
Typescript.
TxB

4287 **Kurth, Goedefroid Joseph François,** 1847–1916.
Saint Boniface, 680–755. Paris, V. Lecoffre, 1902.
iv, 195 p. 19 cm.
KAS

Kurtz, Gregor, fl. 18th cent.

4288 Accessus ad sacrificium altaris et recessus per totum annum quotidie. Bambergae, J. G. Lochner, 1748.
300 p.
NdRi

4289 Die wahre Heiligkeit eines geistlichtugendsamen Wandels in anmuthig und auserlesenen Betrachtungen. Bamberg, Joh. Georg Lochner, 1750.
[10], 604, [34] p. 18 cm.
KAS

4289a **Kwatera, Michael, O.S.B.,** 1950–
A critique of Vatican II's directives regarding the hagiographical readings in the Liturgy of the Hours. Notre Dame, Ind., Department of Theology, 1980.
v, 199 leaves, 28 cm.
Thesis (M.A.)–University of Notre Dame.
Multilithed.
MnCS

4290 **Laan, Joannes van der,** 1904–
Le nombre plastique; quinz leçons sur
l'ordonnance archetectonique. Traduit du
manuscrit hollandais per Dom Xavier
Botte. Leiden, E. J. Brill, 1960.
xvi, 135 p. diagrs. 24 cm.
PLatS

4291 **Labhardt, Theobaldus.**
Quae de Iudaeorum origine judicaverint
veteres . . . Augustae Vindelicorum, P. J.
Pfeiffer, 1881.
46 p. 23 cm.
Dissertatio inauguralis.
InStme

4292 **Lablond, Germain,** 1923–
Fils de lumière; l'inhabitation person-
nelle et spéciele du Saint Esprit en notre
âme selon saint Thomas d'Aquin et saint
Jean de la Croix. Saint-Léger-Vauban
(Yonne), Les Press Monastique, 1961.
374 p. 21 cm.
MnCS

4293 **LaBud, Verona, Sister.**
Masinaigans; the little book. A biography
of Monsignor Joseph F. Buh, Slovenian
missionary in America, 1864-1922 [by]
Sister Bernard Coleman [and] Sister
Verona LaBud. Saint Paul, Minn., North
Central Pub. Co., 1972.
x, 368 p. illus. 25 cm.
InStme; MnCS

4294 **Lacerte, Henry,** 1933–
The nature of canon law according to
Suarez. Ottawa, University of Ottawa
Press, 1964.
186 p. 25 cm.
Thesis – University of Ottawa.
InStme; KAS; PLatS

4295 **Lafitau, Pierre François,** 1685-1764.
Auserlesene und sehr eindringende
Fasten-Predigen . . . Augsburg, Matthäus
Rieger, 1757.
532 p. 22 cm.
InStme

Lafont, Ghislain, 1928–
4296 L'Eglise en marche [par] J. Le Guillou,
O.P., et Ghislain Lafont, O.S.B. [Paris,
Desclée de Brouwer [1964].
223 p. 19 cm.
PLatS

4297 Structures et méthode dans la Somme
théologique de saint Thomas d'Aquin.
[Bruges], Desclée de Brouwer [1961].
512 p. 22 cm.
KAS; MoCo

4298 **La Loyèye, France (abbey of Benedictine nuns).**
Tobie et son temps, par A. Renou . . . et
les Bénédictines de La Loyère. Paris, Les

Editions de l'Ecole [1961].
155 p. illus. 22 cm.
MnCS

Lambach, Austria (Benedictine abbey).
4299 De summis vitae regularis conditionibus.
Brevis disquisitio, auctore presbytero
Benedictino monasterii Lambacensis
capitulari. Viennae, G. Braumülleri, 1860.
[4], 83 p. 19 cm.
KAS

4300 Necrologium Lambacense. MS. Benediktinerabtei Lambach, Austria, codex membr. 131, f.153r–166v. Quarto. Saec. 12.
Microfilm: MnCH proj. no. 816

4301 900 Jahre Lambach; eine Festgabe.
[Lambach, Benediktinern des Stiftes,
1956].
31 p. 37 plates, 19 cm.
MnCS; NdRi; PLatS

4302 Handschriften-Katalog Lambach. [Com-
piled by Petrus Resch, O.S.B., late 18th
century.]
2 v. 28 cm.
Handwritten. Xeroxed by University
Microfilms, Ann Arbor, Mich., 1965.
MnCS

4303 **Lambert, Bernard,** 1931–
Bibliotheca Hieronymiana manuscripta;
la tradition manuscrite des oeuvres de
saint Jerome. Steenbrugis, in Abbatia S.
Petri, 1969–1972.
4 v. in 7. 25 cm. (Instrumenta patristica,
4)
InStme; KAS; PLatS

Lambert von Hersfeld, d. 1088?
4304 Annalen. Neu übersetzt von Adolf
Schmidt, erläutert von Wolfgang Dietrich
Fritz. Darmstadt, Wissenschaftliche Buchgesellschaft, 1962.
xxi, 448 p. 23 cm.
MnCS

4305 Lamberti annalium pars prior ab O.C. –
1039.
(*In* Monumenta Germaniae historica.
Scriptores. Stuttgart, 1963. t.3, p.22–102)
MnCS; PLatS

4306 **Lambertus, monk of Deutz,** fl. 1040.
Vita Heriberti archiepiscopi Coloniensis
auctore Lantberto.
(*In* Monumenta Germaniae historica.
Scriptores. Stuttgart, 1963. t. 4, p. 739–
753)
MnCS; PLatS

Lambot, Cyrille, 1900–
4307 Le "Message" de Beauraing.
(*In* Virgo Immaculata; actus Congressus
Mariologici-Mariani, 1954, v. 16, p. 152–
163)
PLatS

4308   (ed) Augustine, Saint. Sermones de Vetere Testamento . . . recensuit Cyrillus Lambot, O.S.B. Turnholti, Brepols, 1961.
xxxv, 658 p. 26 cm. (Corpus Christianorum. Series latina, 41)
CaQStB; ILSP; InStme; MnCS; PLatS

4309   (ed) Ratramnus, monk of Corbie. Liber de anima ad Odonem Bellovacensem. Texte inedit, publie par d. C. Lambot, O.S.B. Namur, Editions Godenne [1952].
158 p. 26 cm. (Analecta mediaevalia Namurcensia, 2)
PLatS

4310   **Lancelot, Claude,** 1615?–1695.
Narrative of a tour taken in the year 1667 to la Grande Chartreuse and Alet . . . London, printed for J. and A. Arch, Cornhill, 1813.
xxiv, 261 p. 22 cm.
KAS

4311   **Lancellotti, Secondo, O.S.B.Oliv.**
Historiae Olivetanae, auctore D. Secundo Lancellotto Perusino abbate Olivetano, libri duo. Venetiis, ex Typographia Gueriliana, 1623.
[24], 360 p. 22 cm.
InStme

4312   **Landesdorfer, Simon,** 1880–
Die Kultur der Babylonier und Assyrier. Kempten, Jos. Kösel, 1913.
238 p.
NdRi

4313   **Landévenec, France (Benedictine abbey).**
Cartulaire de l'Abbaye de Landévenec, publié pour la Société archéologique du Finistère, par Arthur de la Borderie . . . Rennes, Impr. de C. Catel et Cie, 1888.
xi, 218 p. 25 cm.
Latin text. No more published.
MnCS

Lanfranc, abp. of Canterbury, 1005?–1089.
Manuscript items

4314   Antidotarium. MS. Vienna, Nationalbibliothek, codex 2466, f.124r–128r. Quarto. Saec. 14.
Microfilm: MnCH proj. no. 15,751

4315   Controversia contra Berengarium. MS. Benediktinerabtei St. Paul im Lavanttal, Austria, codex 30/1. Quarto. Saec. 12–13.
Microfilm: MnCH proj. no. 11,688

4316   De Corpore et Sanguine Domini contra Berengarium. MS. Benediktinerabtei Admont, Austria, codex 443, f.59r–84v. Quarto. Saec. 12.
Microfilm: MnCH proj. no. 9504

4317   De Corpore et Sanguine Domini. MS. Universitätsbibliothek Graz, Austria, codex 975, f.42r–52v. Quarto. Saec. 13.
Microfilm: MnCH proj. no. 27,036

4318   De eucharistia. MS. Benediktinerabtei St. Peter, Salzburg, codex a.V.32, f.114r–132v. Octavo. Saec. 12.
Microfilm: MnCH proj. no. 10,063

4319   Disputatio de Corpore et Sanguine Domini adversus Berengarium Turensem. MS. Augustinerchorherrenstift Klosterneuburg, Austria, codex 253, f.159v–163r. Folio. Saec. 12.
Microfilm: MnCH proj. no. 253

4320   Liber de Corpore et Sanguine Domini (incompletum). MS. Augustinerchorherrenstift Klosterneuburg, Austria, codex 218, f.142r–144v. Folio. Saec. 12.
Microfilm: MnCH proj. no. 5181

4321   Scriptum contra Berengarium. MS. Vienna, Nationalbibliothek, codex 864, f.57r–87v. Quarto. Saec. 11.
Microfilm: MnCH proj. no. 14,190

4322   Contra Berengarium. MS. Vienna, Nationalbibliothek, codex 878, f.33r–61v. Quarto. Saec. 12.
Microfilm: MnCH proj. no. 14,192

4323   Scriptum . . . contra Berengarii circa sacramentum eucharistiae haereticam pravitatem. MS. Benediktinerabtei Melk, Austria, codex 984, f.134r–149v. Quarto. Saec. 15.
Microfilm: MnCH proj. no. 1777

4324   Tractatus contra errores Berengarii de Corpore Christi. MS. Augustinerchorrenstift Vorau, Austria, codex 412, f.149r–162r. Octavo. Saec. 14.
Microfilm: MnCH proj. no. 7388

Lanfranc, abp. of Canterbury.
Printed works

4325   Anecdota Bedae, Lanfranci, et aliorum. Inedited tracts, letters, poems, &c, of Venerable Bede, Lanfranc, Tatwin and others. By the Rev. Dr. Giles. London, D.Nutt, 1851. Reprint: New York, Burt Franklin, 1967.
xviii, 314 p. 23 cm. (Publications of the Caxton Society)
MnCS

4326   Decreta Lanfranci monachis Cantuariensibus transmissa. Edidit David Knowles. Siegburg, apud F. Schmidt, 1967.
xlii, 149 p. 26 cm. (Corpus consuetudinum monasticarum, t. 3)
InStme; KAS; PLatS

4327   [Decreta]
Adoratio crucis, the Regularis concordia and the Decreta Lanfranci. Manuscript

studies in the early medieval church of Norway [by] Lilli Gjerlow. [Oslo], Norwegian Universities Press, 1961.
176 p. 25 cm.
PLatS

4327a The letters of Lanfranc, archbishop of Canterbury. Edited and translated by the late Helen Clover and Margaret Gibson. Oxford, Clarendon Press, 1979.
xvi, 204 p. 22 cm.

Lang, Hugo, 1892–
4328 Augustinus das Jenie des Herzens. München, Gesellschaft für christliche Kunst [1930?].
52 p. illus.
KAS

4329 Eucharistic teachings of St. Augustine.
(*In* Pro mundi vita; Festschrift zum Eucharistischen Weltkongress, 1960. München, 1960. p. 44–48)
PLatS

4330 Die Grösse kleiner Dinge; Kurzpredigten. München, M. Hueber, 1954.
64 p. 18 cm.
KAS

4331 München [by Leonhard Lenk, Hugo Lang, et al.]. München, Bayerland Verlag [196-].
89 p. illus. 30 cm.
KAS

4332 Das Problem der Qualität in der Kunst.
(*In* Perennitas; Beiträge . . . P. Thomas Michels, O.S.B., zum 70. Geburtstag. Münster, 1963. p. 363–370)
PLatS

4333 **Lang, Michael,** 1645–1718.
Arbor frugifera ex eremo, sive Meditationes sacrae in quadragesima de passione Domini, et dominicas anni . . . Joan. Henricus Ebersbach, 1705.
154, 202 p. 15 cm.
MnCS

4334 **Lang, Odo,** 1938–
Das Commune sanctorum in den Missale-Handschriften und vortridentinischen Drucken der Stiftsbibliothek Einsiedeln . . . Ottobeuren, Kommissionsverlag Winfried-Werk, 1970.
xvii, 145 p. 25 cm.
MnCS; PLatS

4335 **Langan, Damasus,** 1917–
Indian policy of the United States Army, Military Division of Missouri, 1865–1871.
iv, 80 leaves, 28 cm.
Thesis (M.A.)–Catholic University of America, 1950.
Typescript.
InStme

4336 **La Noue, Bertrand E.,** 1927–
Analysis of the factors which affect the investment decision; a case study.
216 leaves, illus. 29 cm.
Digest of thesis (Ph.D)–St. Louis University, 1968.
KAS

4337 **Lanslots, Ildephonse,** 1859–1931.
What must I believe? or, The Creed. (*From* St. Thomas, op. sel. I). Belmont, N.C., Belmont Abbey Press, 1924.
69 p.
NcBe

Lantpertus, monk of Deutz. *See* Lambertus, Monk of Deutz.

Laporte, Jean, 1905–
4338 Compléments à l'étude chronologique de la liste abbatiale de St-Riquier.
(*In* Saint-Riquier; études . . . Abbaye de Saint-Riquier, 1962. v. 1, p. 197–200)
PLatS

4339 Histoire et vie monastiques. Paris. P. Lethielleux, 1966.
820 p. illus. 24 cm.
MnCS; PLatS

4340 Quelques documents sur Fécamp au temps d'Henri de Sully (1140–1189).
(*In* Analecta monastica, 6. sér. 1962. p. 23–33)
PLatS

4341 Saint Anselme et l'ordre monastique.
(*In* Spicilegium Beccense. 1959. v. 1, p. 455–476)
PLatS

4342 Sources de la biographie de Saint Colomban.
(*In* Mélanges colombaniens. Paris, 1950. p. 75–90)
PLatS

4343 (ed) Columban, Saint. Le pénitentiel. Introduction et édition critique par Jean Laporte. Tournai, New York, Desclée [1958].
111 p. 21 cm.
InStme

4344 **Larson, Paula, Sister.**
Influence of patient status and health condition on nurse perceptions of patient characteristics.
Thesis (M.S.)–University of Wisconsin, 1975.
Typescript.
NdRiS

4345 **Larson, Valentin.**
Murenulae aureae vermiculatae argento. Guldene Spangen mit Silber durchzogen . . . Augspurg, M. Veith, 1716.
400 p.
NdRi

4346 **Laurence, of Durham,** d. 1154.
Dialogi Laurentii Dunelmensis monachi
ac prioris. Durham [England], Pub. for the
Society by Andrews and Co., 1880.
xxxviii, 92 p. 23 cm.
Edited by James Raine.
MnCS

4347 **Laurentius, abp. of Amalfi,** d. 1048.
Opera/Laurentius monachus Casinensis
[deinde] archiepiscopus Amalfitanus.
Hrsg. von Francis Newton. Weimar, H.
Böhlaus Nachfolger, 1973.
viii, 97 p. 23 cm. (Monumenta Germaniae
historica. Die deutschen Geschichtsquellen
des Mittelalters, Bd. 7)
MnCS; PLatS

4348 **Lautz, Boniface,** 1935–
The doctrine of the communion of saints
in Anglican theology, 1833–1963. Ottawa,
University of Ottawa Press, 1967.
x, 200 p. 25 cm.
MoCo; PLatS

4349 **Lavin, Aaron,** 1950–
Formal psychology and the psychology
of religion; issues and the study of motiva-
tion.
56 p.
Thesis (M.A.)–Catholic University of
America, 1975.
MoCo

Lawrence, Emeric Anthony, 1908–
4350 Each month with Christ; insights into
the liturgy of the months. Baltimore,
Helicon Press, 1961.
116 p. 23 cm.
InFer; InStme; KAS; MdRi; MnCS;
MoCo; PLatS

4350a Becoming a mature Christian. Collegeville, Minn., The Liturgical Press, 1979.
xiv, 198 p. 22 cm.
MnCS

4351 Homilies for the year and prayers for the
faithful. Collegeville, Minn., The Liturgical
Press [1965].
xv, 327 p. 22 cm.
CaMWiSb; MnCS; MnStj; MoCo; NcBe;
PLatS

4352 A new meditating the Gospels. Collegeville, Minn., The Liturgical Press, 1977.
xvi, 418 p. 20 cm.
InStme; MnCS; MnStj

4353 The Savior's healing; sermons on the
rites of penance and the anointing of the
sick. Collegeville, Minn., The Liturgical
Press, 1974.
38 p. 22 cm.
MdRi; MnCS; KAS

4354 Understanding our neighbor's faith. Collegeville, Minn., The Liturgical Press
[1975].
281 p. 20 cm.
MnCS; MoCo; KAS

4355 **Lawrence, Lucille, Sister,** 1926–
Virginity as charism.
67 p. 28 cm.
Thesis (M.A.)–St. John's University,
Collegeville, Minn., 1968.
Typescript.
MnStj(Archives)

4356 **Lawrence, Neal,** 1908–
Soul's inner sparkle; moments of Waka
sensations (English poetry in the Japanese
form of tanka or waka). Tokyo, Eichosha
Publishing Co., 1978.
MnCS

4357 **Leander von Feldorf, monk of Melk.**
Versus de viris ecclesiasticis. MS. Benediktinerabtei Melk, Austria, codex 1761,
p. 423. Duodecimo. Saec. 15.
Microfilm: MnCH proj. no. 2083

Lèbe, Léon, 1898–
4358 (ed and tr) Basil, Saint. Les Règles
monastiques. Editions de Maredsous,
1969.
367 p. 20 cm.
InStme; MoCo

4359 (ed and tr) Basil, Saint. Les Règles
morales et portrait du chrétien. Editions
de Maredous, 1969.
199 p. 20 cm.
InStme; MoCo

4360 **Ledesma, Martin de.**
Le Virgen da Monserrata (drama). MS.
Monasterio benedictino de Montserrat,
Spain, codex 47. 109 f. Octavo. Saec.
17(1632).
Microfilm: MnCH proj. no. 29,992

Leben und Wirken des hl. Meinrad. *See*
Brandes, Karl.

Leblond, Germain, 1923–
4361 Fils de lumiere. L'inhabitation personelle
et speciele du Saint-Esprit en notre âme
selon saint Thomas d'Aquin et saint Jean
de la Croix. Abbaye Sainte-Marie de la
Pierre-qui-Vire, 1961.
374 p. 21 cm.
InStme; PLatS

4362 Soleil de justice; présence permanente
du Christ en glorie à notre âme par les
sacrements. Abbaye Sainte-Marie de La
Pierre-qui-Vire, 1961.
261 p. 21 cm.
InStme; MnCS; PLatS

Le Bouveret, Switzerland. *See* Bouveret,
Switzerland.

Leccisotti, Tommaso Domenico, 1895–

4362a Il Cardinale Schuster. Milano [Scuola Tipografica S. Benedetto] 1969.
2 v. plates, 24 cm.
MnCS

4363 Casinensium Ordines antiquiores (saec. VIII-med.IX).
(*In* Corpus consuetudinum monasticarum. Siegburg, 1963. t. 1, p. 93–175)
PLatS

4363a Il cardinale Dusmet. Catania, O.V.E., 1962.
xix, 684 p. 33 plates. 24 cm.
PLatS

4364 Documenti per la storia del Monastero di S. Benedetto in Norcia.
(*In* Analecta monastica, 7. sér., 1965. p. 175–228)
PLatS

4365 Documenti vaticani per la storia de Montecassino. Montecassino, 1952–
v. 26 cm. (Miscellanea cassinese . . . 28   )
MnCS

4366 Montecassino. 4. ed. Badia di Montecassino, 1963.
294 p. illus., ports. 23 cm.
PLatS

4367 Montecassino. 5. ed. Badia di Montecassino, 1967.
328, [17] p. illus. 24 cm.
PLatS

4368 Montecassino. 7. ed. Badia di Montecassino, 1975.
346 p. illus., plates, 22 cm.
MnCS

4369 Montecassino; sein Leben und seine Ausbreitung. Aus dem Italienischen übersetzt von H. R. Balmer-Basilius. Basel, Thomas Morus Verlag [1949].
239 p. plates, 23 cm.
MnCS

4370 Note in margine all'edizione dei Regesti di Clemente V.
(*In* Melanges Eugene Tisserant, v. 5, p. 15–45)
PLatS

4371 S. Tommaso d'Aquino e Montecassino. Badia di Montecassino, 1965.
[60] p. 8 facsims., 27 cm. (Miscellanea Cassinense . . . 32)
PLatS

4372 (ed) I Regesti dell'archivio [di Montecassino]. Roma, [M. Pisani], 1964–
v. illus. 25 cm. (Ministero dell'Interno Pubblicazioni degli Archivi de Stato, 54, 56, 58, 60, 64, 78, 79, 81   )

Editor: v. 1–8: Tommaso Leccisotti, O.S.B.; v. 9– Tommaso Leccisotti, O.S.B. e Faustino Avagliano, O.S.B.
KAS; MnCS; NcBe; PLatS

Leclercq, Henri, 1869–1945.

4373 Comment le Christianisme fut envisagé dans l'empire romain. Bruges, Desclée, 1901.
40 p. 25 cm.
KAS

4374 Saint-Benoît-sur-Loire: les reliques, le monastère, l'èglise. Paris, Letouzey, 1925.
159 p. illus. 19 cm.
MnCS; NcBe

4374a Saint Gall.
168 cols., illus., facsims. 28 cm.
(*In* Dictionnaire d'archéologie chrétienne et de l'liturgie, t. 6, col. 80–248)
Includes: Le plan de Saint Gall [with folded illus. of plan], col. 86–106.
MnCS; PLatS

4375 Saint Jérôme. Louvain, Em. Warny, 1927.
174 p. 20 cm.
PLatS

Leclercq, Jean, 1911–

4376 Alone with God. [Translated by Elizabeth McCabe from the French]. New York, Farrar, Straus and Cudahy [1961].
xxvii, 209 p. 21 cm.
Translation of: Seul avec Dieu.
MnCS; MnStj; MdRi; ILSP; OkShG; NdRi; MoCo; KAS; NcBe; PLatS; InFer; CaMWiSb

4377 Ancien sermon monastique dans le manuscrit Palat. Lat. 295.
(*In* Mélanges Eugéne Tisserant, v. 6, p. 577–582)
PLatS

4378 Aspects du monachisme, hier et aujourd'hui. Paris, Editions de la Source, 1968.
367 p. 19 cm.
MnCS

4379 Aspects of monasticism. Translated by Mary Dodd. Kalamazoo, Mich., Cistercian Publications, 1978.
343 p. 22 cm.
InStme; KAS; MnCS; NcBe; ViBris

4380 L'authenticite de l'epitre 462 de S. Bernard "Ad noviter conversos".
(*In* Sapientiae procerum amore; Mélanges . . . à Dom Jean-Pierre Müller . . . Roma, 1974. p. 81–96)
PLatS

4381 Aux sources de la spiritualité occidentale; étapes et constantes. Paris, Editions du Cerf, 1964.

317 p. 21 cm.
InStme; KAS; MnCS; PLatS

4382　Benedictine rule and active presence in the world. Translated by Louis Merton, O.C.S.O.
(*In* Monastic studies, no. 2(1964), p. 51–63)
PLatS

4383　Bernard of Clairvaux and the Cistercian spirit. Translated by Claire Lavoie. Kalamazoo, Mich., Cistercian Publications, 1976.
163, [14] p. 23 cm.
InStme; MnCS; MoCo; NcBe; PLatS; ViBris

4384　The Bible and the Gregorian reform.
(*In* Historical investigations; Concilium theology in the age of renewal. v. 17, p. 63–77)
PLatS

4385　Bibliography of the works of Jean Leclercq.
(*In* Bernard of Clairvaux: studies presented to Dom Jean Leclercq. Washington, 1973. p. 215–264)
PLatS

4386　Caratteristiche della spiritualità monastica.
(*In* Problemi e orientamenti di spiritualità monastica, biblica e liturgica, p. 327–336)
PLatS

4387　Chances de la spiritualité occidentale. Paris, Editions du Cerf, 1966.
xii, 383 p. 19 cm.
InStme; MnCS; PLatS

4388　Le cloître est-il un paradis?
(*In* Le message des moines à notre temps, mélanges offerts à Dom Alexis, abbé de Boquen. Paris, 1958. p. 141–160)
PLatS

4389　Contemplative life. Translated by Elizabeth Funder. Kalamazoo, Mich., Cistercian Publications, 1978.
ix, 193 p. 22 cm.
Translation of: Vie religieuse et vie contemplative.
InStme; KAS; MnCS; MoCo; NcBe; ViBris

4390　Cultura umanistica e desiderio di Dio; studio sulla letteratura monastica del Medio Evo. [Firenze], Sansoni [1965].
viii, 386 p. 24 cm.
Translation of: L'amour des lettres et le desir de Dieu.
PLatS

4391　Le défi de la vie contemplative. Gembloux, J. Duculot, 1970.

374 p. 19 cm.
InStme; KAS; MnCS

4392　Documents sur les "fugitifs."
(*In* Analecta monastica, 7. sér., 1965. p. 87–145)
PLatS

4393　L'Ecriture Sainte dans l'hagiographie monastique du haut Moyen Age.
(*In* Le Bibbia nell'alto medioevo, p. 103–128)
PLatS

4394　Etudes sur le vocabulaire monastique du Moyen Age. Romae, Orbis Catholicus, Herder, 1961.
viii, 176 p. 25 cm. (Studia Anselmiana, 48)
InStme; KAS; MnCS; PLatS

4395　Evangelio y cultura en la historia del compromiso en la vida religiosa.
(*In* Los consejos evangelicos en la tradicion monastica. Silos, 1975. p. 327–342)
PLatS

4396　Guerric of Igny and the monastic school.
(*In* Cistercian studies, v. 2(1961), p. 53–61)
PLatS

4397　Initiation aux auteurs monastiques du Moyen Age; l'amour des lettres et le désir de Dieu. 2. ed. corrigée. Paris, Editions du Cerf, 1963 [c1957].
271 p. illus. 22 cm.
InStme

4398　The intentions of the founders of the Cistercian Order.
(*In* The Cistercian spirit; a symposium in memory of Thomas Merton. Spencer, Mass., 1970. p. 88–133)
PLatS

4399　"Ioculator et saltator": S. Bernard et l'image du jongleur dans les manuscrits.
(*In* Translatio studii; manuscript and library sutdies honoring Oliver L. Kapsner. Collegeville, Minn., 1973. p. 124–148)
MnCS; PLatS

4400　"Lectulus"; variazioni su un tema biblico nella tradizione monastica.
(*In* Vagaggini, Cypriano. Bibbia e spiritualità. Roma, 1967. p. 417–436)
MnCS

4400a　Libérez les prisonniers; du bon larron à Jean XXIII. Paris, Editions du Cerf, 1976.
166 p.
MnCS

4401　The life of perfection; points of view on the essence of the religious state. Translated by Leonard J. Doyle. Collegeville, Minn., The Liturgical Press [1961].
125 p. 22 cm.

Translation of: La vie parfaite.
InStme; KAS; MnCS; MnStj; MoCo;
MdRi; NcBe; ViBris

4402 La liturgie et les paradoxes chrétiens.
Paris, Editions du Cerf, 1963.
305 p. 19 cm.
InStme; KAS; MnCS; PLatS

4403 Liturgie et monastères. Etudes, par E.
Dekkers, Cl. Jean Nesmy, J. Leclercq . . .
[Bruges], Publications de Saint-André,
1966–
v. 22 cm.
KAS

4404 Liturgy and contemplation. Translated
by Stephen P. Manning, S.M.
(*In* Monastic studies, v. 10, p. 71–86)
PLatS

4405 The love of learning and the desire for
God; a study of monastic culture. Trans-
lated by Catharine Misrahi. New York,
Fordham University Press, 1961.
x, 415 p.
Translation of: L'amour des lettres et le
désir de Dieu.
InFer; MnStj; ViBris

4406 . . . . New York, New American Library
[1962].
336 p. 18 cm. (Mentor Omega book,
MT432)
InStme; KAS; NcBe

4407 . . . . 2d rev. ed. New York, Fordham
University Press [1974, 1977].
viii, 397 p. 20 cm.
MnCS

4408 Moines et moniales, ont-ils un avenir?
Bruxelles, Editions Lumen Vitae [1971].
263 p. 19 cm.
MnCS

4409 Le monachisme Clunisien.
(*In* Théologie de la vie monastique, p.
447–457)
PLatS

4410 Le monachisme du haut Moyen Age
(VIII-X siècles).
(*In* Théologie de la vie monastique, p.
437–445)
PLatS

4411 Monasticism and St. Benedict.
(*In* Monastic studies. Berryville, Va.
v. 1(1963), p. 9–23)
PLatS

4411a Monks and love in twelfth-century
France; psycho-historical essays. Oxford,
Clarendon Press; New York, Oxford Uni-
versity Press, 1979.
x, 146 p. 23 cm.
InStme

4412 Nouveau visage de Bernard de Clairvaux; approches psycho-historiques. Paris,
Editions du Cerf, 1976.
181 p. 20 cm.
MnCS

4413 Otia monastica; études sur le vocabulaire
de la contemplation au Moyen Age.
Romae, Herder, 1963.
viii, 185 p. 25 cm. (Studia Anselmiana,
51)
InStme; KAS; MnCS; PLatS

4414 Pour l'histoire des traités de s. Bernard.
(*In* Analecta Sacri Ordinis Cisterciensis.
v. 15(1959), p. 56–78)
PLatS

4415 Present-day problems in monasticism.
(*In* Meeting of the Monastic Superiors in
the Far East, Bangkok, Thailand, 1969.
Notre Dame, Ind., 1970. p. 23–44)
PLatS

4416 The priesthood for monks. Translated by
monks of Caldey Abbey.
(*In* Monastic studies, v. 3, p. 53–85)
PLatS

4417 Problemi e orientamenti di spiritualità
monastica, biblica et liturgica. Roma, Edizione Paoline [1961].
790 p. 18 cm.
At head of title: C. Vagaggini, S. Bovo
. . . J. Leclercq.
MnCS; MoCo

4418 Recueil d'études sur Saint Bernard et ses
écrits. Roma, Edizioni di Storia e Letteratura, 1962–66.
2 v.
KAS; MnCS; PLatS

4419 Regola benedettina e presenza nel
mondo.
(*In* La bonifica benedettina, p. 15–25)
PLatS

4420 The role of monastic spirituality critically
discussed.
(*In* Protestants and Catholics on the
spiritual life, ed. by Michael Marx, O.S.B.
Collegeville, Minn., 1965. p. 20–33)
PLatS

4421 Le Sacré-Coeur dans la tradition
bénédictine au Moyen Age.
(*In* Cor Jesu; commentationes in . . .
"Haurietis aquas." Roma, 1959. v. 2,
p. 1–28)
PLatS

4422 Saint Bernard and the monastic theology
of the twelfth century.
(*In* Cistercian studies, v. 1(1961), p.
1–18)
PLatS

4423   St. Bernard et l'esprit cistercien. Paris, Editions du Seuil, 1966.
192 p. illus. 18 cm.
MnCS; PLatS

4424   Saint Bernard in our times; a lecture delivered before an open meeting of the Stubbs Society on February 28, 1973, in the Upper Library of Christ Church, Oxford. Translated by Garth L. Fowden. Oxford, Stubbs Society [1973].
19 p. 24 cm.
MnCS

4425   S. Martin dans l'hagiographie monastique du Moyen Age.
(*In* Saint Martin et son temps. Romae, 1961. p. 175–187. Studia Anselmiana, 46)
KAS; InStme; PLatS

4426   Saint Pierre Damien, ermite et homme d'Eglise. Roma, Edizioni di Storia e Letteratura, 1960.
283 p. 26 cm.
KAS; MnCS; PLatS

4427   A sociological approach to the history of a religious order.
(*In* The Cistercian spirit; a symposium in memory of Thomas Merton. Spencer, Mass., 1970. p. 134–143)
PLatS

4428   La spiritualité des chanoines réguliers.
(*In* La vita comune del clero nei secoli XI e XII. 1962. p. 117–135)
PLatS

4429   La spiritualité du Moyen Age [par] Jean Leclercq, François Vandenbroucke [et] Louis Bouyer. [Paris], Aubier, 1961.
718 p. 22 cm.
CaQStB; InStme; KAS; MnCS; PLatS

4430   Spiritualité et culture à Cluny.
(*In* Spiritualité cluniacense. Todi, 1960. p. 101–152)
PLatS

4431   The spirituality of the Middle Ages, by Jean Leclercq, François Vandenbroucke [and] Louis Boyer. London, Burns & Oates [1968].
602 p. 23 cm.
InStme; MnCS

4432   Un témoignage sur l'influence de Grégoire VII dans la réforme canoniale.
(*In* Borino, G. B. Studi gregoriani. Roma, 1959–61. v. 6, p. 173–228)
PLatS

4433   Témoins de la spiritualité occidentale. Paris, Editions de Cerf, 1965.
409 p. 19 cm.
InStme; KAS; PLatS

4434   Textes et manuscrits Cisterciens à la bibliothèque vaticane.

(*In* Analecta Sacri Ordinis Cisterciensis. v. 15(1959), p. 79–103)
PLatS

4435   Textes et manuscrits Cisterciens dans diverses bibliothèques.
(*In* Analecta Sacri Ordinis Cisterciensis. v. 18(1962), p. 121–134)
PLatS

4436   Textes sur la vocation et la formation des moines au Moyen Age.
(*In* Corona gratiarum; miscellanea . . . Eligio Dekkers . . . oblata. Brugge, 1975. p. 169–194)
PLatS

4437   Theology and prayer; Father Cyril Gaul Memorial Lecture delivered at Saint Meinrad Seminary, September 23, 1962. [St. Meinrad, Ind., St. Meinrad Essays, 1963].
23 p. 23 cm.
InStme; MnCS; MoCo; PLatS

4438   Tradition; a door to the present. Translated by Basil De Pinto, O.S.B.
(*In* Monastic studies. v. 4, p. 1–15)
PLatS

4439   Un traité sur la "Profession des abbés" au XIIe siècle.
(*In* Analecta monastica, 6. sér., 1962. p. 177–191)
PLatS

4440   La vie et la prière des chevaliers de Santiago d'après leur règle primitive.
(*In* Liturgica, 2: Cardinal I. A. Schuster in memoriam. 1958. v. 2, p. 347–357)
PLatS

4441   Vie religieuse et vie contemplative. Paris, P. Lethielleux [1969].
273 p. 19 cm.
InStme; MnCS; MoCo; NcBe

4442   Zeiterfahrung und Zeitbegriff im Spätmittelalter.
(*In* Antiqui und moderni . . . hrsg. von Albert Zimmermann. Berlin, 1974. p. 1–20)
PLatS

4443   Zur Geschichte des Lebens in Cluny.
(*In* Cluny; Beiträge zu Gestalt und Wirkung der Cluniazensischen Reform, hrsg. von Helmut Richter. Darmstadt, 1975. p. 254–318)
MnCS

4444   **Le Contat, Jérôme Joachim,** 1607–1690.
Conférences ou exhortations monastiques pour tous les dimanches de l'année. Paris, Pierre de Bats, 1692.
[205], 661 p. 25 cm.
First published 1671.
PLatS

4445 Dioptra politices religiosae. Hoc est, Exercitia spiritualia decem dierum . . . gallicè proposita ab adm. r.p.d. Joachimo le Contat . . . latinitate donata à r.p. Francisco Mezger. Salisburgi, Joan.Bapt. Mayr, 1694.
    [80], 870 p. 17 cm.
    KAS; MnCS

4446 Exercitia spiritualia pro X diebus, religiosis Ord. D. Benedicti propria . . . Gallice conscripta . . . latinitate donata a Francisco Mezger, O.S.B. [Salisburgi], Joan. Bapt. Mayr, 1645.
    627 p. 13 cm.
    MnCS

4447 Succintae meditationes christianae pro dominicis, ferijs & praecipuae festis totius anni in IV partes divisae. Gallice compositae . . . latinitate donatae à r.p. Francisco Mezger. [Salisburgi], Joan. Bapt. Mayr [1695–96].
    4 v. in 5. 14 cm.
    InStme; KAS (v.4)

Lectiones in jure canonico. Abbatiae St. Vincentii. *See* Kaeder, Maurus.

4448 **Ledergerber, Ildephons,** 1872–
    Lukian und die altattische Komödie. Einsiedeln, Benziger, 1905.
    vii, 136 p. 24 cm.
    Inaug.-Diss. – Freiburg in der Schweiz.
    InStme

Lefebvre, Gaspar, 1880–196-

4449 Avec le Christ, avec l'Eglise, nous disons la Messe. Missel quotidien de formule moderne presenté par Dom Lefebvre . . . Paris, Editions Ouvrières [1947].
    384 p. illus., music. 17 cm.
    MnCS

4450 Daily Missal with vespers for Sundays and feasts. Bruges, Belgium, St. Andrew's Abbey; St. Paul, Minn., E. M. Lohmann Co. [1924].
    xxxvi, 1918, 34 p. illus. 16 cm.
    InStme; KAS

4451 Daily Missal with vespers for Sundays and feasts. Bruges, Abbey of St. André; St. Paul, Minn., E. M. Lohmann Co. [1934].
    xxxvi, 1980, 63, vi, 42, 34 p. illus. 16 cm.
    InStme

4452 Devotion to the Precious Blood in relationship to the "Mystery of Christ" and its application in the Mass centered liturgy.
    (*In* Proceedings of the Second Precious Blood Study Week, 1960. p. 83–109)
    PLatS

4453 Grammaire du latin liturgique. Lille, Gachie et Aula, 1919; Saint André-les-Bruges, 1923–

    v. 22 cm.
    MnCS (v. 1 & 4)

4454 The liturgical year in colour-pictures. Explanations by Dom Gaspar Lefebvre. Illustrations by Joseph Speybrouck. Bruges, Belgium, Liturgical Apostolate, Abbey of St. André [1955].
    unpaged, col. illus., 39 cm.
    InStme

4455 Liturgie et action catholique. Abbaye St. André les-Bruges, Apostolat Liturgique [1938].
    44 p. 17 cm.
    MnCS; PSaS

4456 Manuel de liturgie; livre du maître. Paris, Société Liturgique, 1934–
    v. 20 cm.
    MnCS

4457 Messale romano. Testo latino completo e traduzione italiana di S. Bertola e G. Destefani. Commento di D. G. Lefebvre, O.S.B. Torino, R. Berruti & C. [1936].
    xxxi, 2089 p. 16 cm.
    InStme (1936); MnCS (1958)

4458 Messe de communion des enfants . . . Paris, Société Liturgique [1927].
    32 p. illus. 16 cm.
    MnCS

4459 Misal diario y vesperal . . . Traduccion castellana y adaptacion del rdo P. German Prado. Desclée de Brouwer [1958].
    2149, 80, 47 p. illus. 16 cm.
    MnCS

4460 Missel quotidien et Vesperal . . . Lophem-lez-Bruges, Abbaye de St. André [1922].
    xxxiv, 2056 p. illus., music, 16 cm.
    PLatS

4461 Missel quotidien pour enfants de 5 à 11 ans . . . Bruges, Filles de l'Eglise, n.d.
    655, 28 p. illus. 15 cm.
    MnCS

4462 The new liturgy of Holy Week. Supplement to the Saint Andrew Daily Missal . . . Bruges, Liturgical Apostolate [1956].
    154 p. illus. 16 cm.
    MnCS

4463 Saint Andrew Daily Missal. Bruges, Liturgical Apostolate [1937].
    xxxviii, 980, 177 p. illus. 16 cm.
    InStme; MnCS

4464 Saint Andrew Daily Missal. Saint Paul, Minn., E. M. Lohmann Co. [1949].
    xxiv, 1129 [i.e. 1169] p. illus. 17 cm.
    Latin text.
    InStme (1949 & 1953)

4465 Saint Andrew Daily Missal. Pocket edition. Bruges, Liturgical Apostolate [1955].

4 v. illus. 14 cm.
MnCS

4466   Saint Andrew Daily Missal. Bruges,
Liturgical Apostolate; Saint Paul, Minn.,
E. M. Lohmann Co. [1956].
1149 p. illus. 17 cm.
InStme (1956 & 1962); MnCS (1960)

4467   Saint Andrew daily Missal, with Vespers
for Sundays and feasts, by Dom Gaspar
Lefebvre, O.S.B., and the monks of St.
Andrew's Abbey. Bruges, Biblica; [New
York, DDB Publishers, 1962].
xlviii, 2041 p. illus., music. 17 cm.
"Proper feasts kept in the dioceses of the
United States of America": p. 1925–2022.
InStme; KAS; MnCS; PLatS

4468   Saint Andrew junior daily Missal by Dom
Gaspar Lefebvre, O.S.B. Adapted by
Canon Gray. Illustrated by Marc Amsens.
Bruges, Biblica [1957].
576 p. illus. 15 cm.
MnCS

4469   Saint Andrew Sunday Missal; Masses for
Sundays and principal feasts of the eccle-
siastical year, by Dom Gaspar Lefebvre,
O.S.B., and the monks of St. Andrew's
Abbey. Bruges, Belgium, Biblica; [New
York, DDB Publishers, 1962].
xxxii, 816 p. illus. 15 cm.
"Feasts proper to the dioceses of the
United States of America": p. 801–813.
MnCS

4470   La saint Messe et la sainte communion.
Bruges, Apostolat Liturgique [1937].
39 p. illus. 14 cm.
MnCS

Lefebvre, Georges, 1908–
4471   Les chemins du ciel. Paris, Desclée de
Brouwer, 1963.
167 p. 16 cm.
PLatS

4472   Courage to pray [by] Metropolitan Anthony and Georges Lefebvre. Translated
[from the French] by Dinah Livingstone.
London, Darton, Longman and Todd,
1973.
123 p. 18 cm.
Translation of: La prière.
ICSS; MnCS

4473   . . . Tenbury Wells, England, Fowler
Wright [1973].
122 p. 18 cm.
CaMWiSb; KAS

4474   La foi dans les oeuvres. [Bruges],
Desclée de Brouwer [1962].
177 p. 16 cm.
PLatS

4474a   God present. Translated by John Otto, in
collaboration with Marie Philip Haley,
Mary Virginia Micka. Minneapolis, Minn.,
Winston Press, 1979.
109 p. 22 cm.
Translation of Dieu présent.
KAS; MnCS

4475   The mystery of God's love. New York,
Sheed & Ward [1961].
ix, 146 p. 21 cm.
Translation of: Le mystère de la divine
charité.
InFer; InStme; MnCS; MnStj; MoCo;
NcBe; OkShG; PLatS

4476   Prière pure et pureté du coeur d'aprés
saint Grégoire le Grand et saint Jean de la
Croix. Nouv. éd. rev. et augm. [Bruges],
Desclée de Brouwer [1959].
157 p. 17 cm.
First published 1953.
MnCS; PLatS

4477   Simplicity, the heart of prayer. New
York, Paulist Press [c 1975].
73 p.
MnStj; MoCo

4478   L'unité, mystère de vue, Paris-Bruges,
Desclée de Brouwer [c 1964].
104 p. 16 cm.
PLatS

4479   Vie et prière. [8. éd.]. [Bruges], Desclée
de Brouwer [1960].
169 p. 17 cm.
First published 1958.
PLatS

4480   The well-springs of prayer. [Translated
by Kathleen Pond]. New York, Desclée
Co., 1961.
79 p. 19 cm.
Translation of: La grâce de la prière.
CaMWiSb; InStme; KAS; MnCS; MnStj;
OkShG; PLatS

4481   **Legipont, Oliver,** 1698–1758.
Monasticon Moguntiacum; sive, Succincta veterum monasteriorum in Arch-
Episcopatu Moguntini, vicinisque locis,
partim extantium, partim suppressorum
. . . notitia. [Pragae], typis Joannis Julii
Gerzabek, 1746.
[32], 80 p. 16 cm.
KAS

Leloir, Louis, 1911–
4482   Bibliography of the works of Jean
Leclercq.
(*In* Bernard of Clairvaux: studies presented to Dom Jean Leclercq. Washington,
1973. p. 217–264)
PLatS

4483 Le Diatessarion de Tatien et son commentaire par Ephrem.
(*In* La venue du Messie. p. 243–260)
PLatS

4484 Divergences entre l'original Syriaque et la version Arménienne du Commentaire d'Ephrem sur le Diatessaron.
(*In* Mélanges Eugene Tisserant, v. 2, p. 303–331)
PLatS

4485 Doctrines et méthodes de S. Ephrem d'après son Commentaire et l'Evangile concordant (original syriaque et version armenienne). Louvain, Secrétariat du Corpus SCO, 1961.
viii, 71 p. 23 cm. (Corpus scriptorum Christianorum orientalium, v. 220)
InStme

4486 Saint Ephrem, moine et pasteur.
(*In* Théologie de la vie monastique, p. 85–97)
PLatS

4487 Symbolisme et parallélisme chez Ephrem.
(*In* a la recontre de Dieu: mémorial Albert Gelin. Le Puy, 1961. p. 363–372)
PLatS

4488 Le temoignage d'Ephrem sur le Diatessaron. Louvain, Secrétariat du Corpus SCO, 1962.
xx, 259 p. 23 cm. (Corpus scriptorum Christianorum orientalium, v. 227)
InStme

4489 Towards a more prayerful liturgy. [Translated by a monk of Our Lady of Guadalupe Abbey].
(*In* Monastic studies, v. 3, p. 99–118)
PLatS

4490 (ed & tr) Ephraem Syrus. Commentaire de l'Evangile concordant. Version arménienne. Editée [et traduite] par Louis Leloir. Louvain, L. Durbecq, 1953–54.
2 v. 25 cm. (Corpus scriptorum Christianorum orientalium, v. 137, 145)
PLatS

4491 (ed & tr) Ephraem Syrus. Commentaire de l'Evangile concordant. Texte syriaque (manuscrit Chester Beatty 709). Edité et traduit par Louis Leloir, O.S.B. Dublin, Hodges Figgis, 1963.
xiv, 261 p. 26 cm. (Chester Beatty monographs, no. 8)
InStme; PLatS

4492 (ed & tr) Ephraem Syrus. Commentaire de l'Evangile concordant ou Diatessaron. Traduit du syriaque et de l'arménien. Introduction, traduction et notes par Louis Leloir. Paris, Editions du Cerf, 1966.
438 p. 20 cm. (Sources Chrétiennes, 121)
PLatS

4493 (ed) Ephraem Syrus. L'Evangile d'Ephrem d'après les oeuvres éditées. Recueil des textes par Louis Leloir. Louvain, Secrétariat du Corpus SCO, 1958.
viii, 157 p. 26 cm. (Corpus scriptorum Christianorum orientalium, v. 180)
PLatS

4494 (ed) Paterica armenica à P. P. Mechitaristis edita (1955), nunc latine reddita à Louis Leloir. Louvain, Secrétariat du Corpus SCO, 1974–76.
4 v. 25 cm. (Corpus Scriptorum Christianorum Orientalium, v. 353, 361, 371, 379)
PLatS

4495 **Le Mans, France. Saint Victeur (Benedictine priory).**
Cartulaire de Saint-Victeur au Mans, prieuré de l'Abbaye du Mont-Saint-Michel (994–1400). . . . Paris, A. Picard, 1895.
xv, 255 p. 26 cm.
PLatS

4496 **Le Mans, France. Saint Vincent (Benedictine abbey).**
Liber controversiarum sancti Vincentii cenomannensis, ou Second cartulaire de l'abbaye de Saint-Vincent du Mans . . . Paris, C. Klinksieck [1968].
434 p. 24 cm.
MnCS

Lemarié, Joseph, 1917–
4497 Le Bréviaire de Ripoll, Paris, B.N. lat. 742; étude sur sa composition et ses textes inédits. [Montserrat], Abadia de Montserrat, 1965.
xiii, 233 p. facsims. 25 cm.
InStme; KAS

4498 Fragment d'un nouveau sermon inédit de Chromace d'Aquilée.
(*In* Corona gratiarum; miscellanea . . . Eligio Dekkers . . . oblata. Brugge, 1975. v. 1, p. 201–209)
PLatS

4499 La manifestation du Seigneur; la liturgie de Noël et de l'Epiphanie. Paris, Editions du Cerf, 1957.
537 p. 21 cm.
CaQStB; MnCS; PLatS

4500 Le sanctoral de Saint-Michel de Cuxa d'après le manuscrit Perpignam B.M. 2)
(*In* Liturgica, 3: Cardinal I. A. Schuster in memoriam. Montisserrati, 1966, p. 85–100)
PLatS

4501 **Lemcke, Peter Henry,** 1796–1882.
Haudegen Gottes: das Leben d. P. H. Lemke, 1796–1882, von ihm selbst erzählt. Kommentirt und hrsg. von Willibald

Mathäser, O.S.B. Würzburg, Echter-Verlag, 1971.
305 p. 21 cm.
InStme; KAS; MnStj; PLatS

4502 **Lemercier, Grégoire,** 1912–
Dialogues avec le Christ; moines en psychanalyse. Paris, Grasset [1966].
286 p. 21 cm.
PLatS

4503 **Le Moyne, Jean,** 1924–
Les Sadducéens. Paris, J. Gabalda, 1972.
464 p. 25 cm.
PLatS

4504 **Lenertz, Anne, Sister.**
Administration of secondary schools.
Thesis (M.A.)–College of St. Thomas, St. Paul, Minn., 1962.
Typescript.
NdRiS

4505 **Lenoble, André,** 1859–
La médaille de saint Benoît. Ligugé, Abbaye Saint-Martin [193?].
63 p. 16 cm.
KAS

Lentini, Anselmo, 1901–
4506 La leggenda di S. Nicola di Mira in un'ode di Alfano Cassinese.
(*In* Mélanges Eugene Tisserant, v. 2, p. 333–343)
PLatS

4507 Vita e missione sociale di S. Benedetto.
(*In* La bonifica Benedettina, p. 195–199)
PLatS

4508 (ed) Amato di Monte Cassino. Il poema di Amato su S. Pietro apostolo [a cura di Anselmo Lentini]. Montecassino, 1958–59.
2 v. 25 cm. (Miscellanea Cassinese 30–31)
MnCS; PLatS

4509 **Lenton Priory, England.**
Lenton Priory estate accounts, 1296 to 1298. Edited by F. B. Stitt. Nottingham, Printed for the Thornton Society by Derry & Sons, 1959.
xlix, 51 p. 22 cm. (Thornton Society record series, v. 19)
PLatS

4510 **Lenz, Desiderius,** 1832–1928.
Zur Aesthetik der Beuroner Schule. 2. Aufl. Beuron, Verlag der Beuroner Kunstschule, 1927.
50 p. 16 cm.
InStme

4511 **Leo, abbot of Saint Bonifacio et Alessio, Rome,** fl. 995.
Leonis abbatis et legati ad Hugonem et Rotbertum reges epistola.
(*In* Monumenta Germaniae historica. Scriptores. Stuttgart, 1963, t.3, p. 686–690)
MnCS; PLatS

Leo Marsicanus, bp. of Ostia, d. 1115?
4512 Chronica sacri monasterii Casinensis, continuatore Petro diacono eiusdem coenobii monacho, ex manu scriptis codicibus summa cura . . . primus evulgat d. Angelus de Nuce. Lutetiae Parisiorum, ex Officina Ludovici Billaine, 1668.
19 leaves, 577, 72 p. 36 cm.
ILSP; InStme; KAS (microfilm); PLatS (microfilm)

4513 Translatio S. Clementis, auctore Leone Ostiensi. E codice Pragensi Capituli Metropolitano no. XXIII, fol. 147–150 collato Vaticano lat. 9668, fol. 10–11.
(*In* Meyvaert, Paul. Trois énigmes cyrillo-méthodiennes de la "Legende italique." Bruxelles, 1955. p. 455–461)
PLatS

4514 **Leonard, D. L.**
Manuel pratique du fervent religieux. Traduit de l'allemand sur la cinquième edition par D. Athanase Vincart, moine de l'Abbaye de Maredsous. Abbaye de Maredsous, 1912.
874 p.
CaQStB

4515 **Leonard, Ludger,** 1852–1925.
The Benedictine lay brother; a manual of instruction and devotion for the use of Brothers and Sisters of the Order of St. Benedict. Adapted from the German . . . by a monk of Fort Augustus. Fort-Augustus [Scotland], Abbey Press, 1888.
iv, 319 p. 15 cm.
InStme; PSaS; WaOSM

Leonard, Sebastian, 1931–
4516 The opposition of Francis I to the Council of Trent, 1535 to 1545.
v, 143 leaves, 29 cm.
Thesis (M.A.)–Georgetown University, Washington, D.C., 1962.
Typescript.
InStme

4517 The relations between Great Britain and the Papal States, 1792–1817.
x, 398 leaves. 27 cm.
Thesis–Merton College, Oxford, 1968.
Typescript.
InStme

4518 **Leonardus de Burkhausen, monk of Melk.**
Tractatus de cura infirmorum et morientium. MS. Benediktinerabtei Melk, Austria, codex 76, f.1r–127v. Octavo. Saec. 15.
Microfilm: MnCH proj. no. 1157

Leroy, Julien, 1916–
4519   La réforme studite.
(*In* Il monachesimo orientale; atti del
Convegno di studi orientali. Roma, 1958. p.
181–214).
PLatS
4520   Saint Théodore Studite.
(*In* Théologie de la vie monastique, p.
423–436)
PLatS
4521   Studitisches Mönchtum; Spiritualität
und Lebensform . . . Graz, Verlag Styria
[1969].
116 p. 19 cm.
InStme; PLatS
Le Saux, Henri, 1910–
4522   A Benedictine Ashram. By Abbé J. Monchanin, S.A.M., and Dom Henri Le Saux,
O.S.B. [Rev. ed.]. Douglas, Times Press
[c 1964].
91 p. illus. 22 cm.
MoCo; NcBe; PLatS
4523   Die Eremiten von Saccidânanda; ein
Versuch zur christlichen Integration der
monastischen Ueberlieferung Indiens.
Salzburg, Otto Müller Verlag [1962]
314 p. 18 cm.
At head of title: Jules Monchanin
S.A.M. – Henri Le Saux, O.S.B.
MnCS
4524   Ermites du Saccidânanda; un essai d'intégration chrétienne de la tradition
monastique de l'Inde. [Par] J. Monchanin,
S.A.M. [et] Henri Le Saux, O.S.B. 2. ed.
Tournai, Casterman, 1957.
204 p. 22 cm.
CaQStB; InStme; KAS; PLatS
4525   Guru and disciple [by] Abhishiktananda,
Henri Le Saux. Translated [from the
French] by Heather Sanderman. Foreword
by Kenneth Leech. London, S.P.C.K.,
1974.
xiii, 176 p. 21 cm.
Translation of: Gnânânanda et une
messe aux sources du Gange.
InStme; KAS
4526   Prayer [by] Abhishiktananda. Philadelphia, Westminster Press [1973, c 1967].
81 p. 19 cm.
InStme; KAS; MnStj; MoCo
4527   La rencontre de l'Hindouisme et du
Christianisme. Paris, Editions du Seuil,
1966.
237 p. 20 cm.
PLatS
4528   **Letschert, Joseph,** 1925–
Scheppend denken in de liturgie.
[Brugge], Desclée de Brouwer [1960].
220 p. 20 cm.
MnCS; PLatS

4529   **Leuringer, Nicolaus, abbot of Melk.**
Formula de practica regularis observantia. MS. Benediktinerabtei Melk, Austria,
codex 662, f.21r–30r. Quarto. Saec. 15.
Microfilm: MnCH proj. no. 1532
Leutner, Coelestin, 1685–1759.
4530   Coelum christianum: in quo vita, doctrina, passio D.N. Jesu Christi . . . pia
meditatione expensa proponuntur. Londini, Burns, Oates et Soc., 1871.
vii, [105] p. 18 cm.
KAS
4531   Leben, Lehr, und Leyden Jesu Christi
unseres Welt-Heylands. Augspurg, Verlag
Franz Anton Strötters, 1735.
[208] p. 16 cm.
KAS
4532   **Leveque, Louis,** 1830–1901.
S. Grégoire le Grand et l' Ordre Bénédictin. Paris, P. Lethielleux [1910?].
xxxi, 330 p. 21 cm.
KAS
L'Huillier, Albert, 1852–1928.
4533   Le patriarche saint Benoît. Bruxelles,
Action catholique, 1923.
[4], iv, 295 p. 20 cm.
KAS; NcBe
4534   Saint Thomas de Canterbéry. Paris, V.
Palmé, 1891–92.
2 v. illus. 25 cm.
CaQStE; KAS
4535   **Lialine, Clement,** 1901–
Eastern and western monasticism.
(*In* Monastic studies. Berryville, Va.
v. 1(1963), p. 58–83)
PLatS
4536   **Lidl, Bernhard.**
Acta de erectione, confoederatione et
visitatione academiae et universitatis Salisburgensis. Item de fundatione peregrinationis Plaiensis, Colleggi nobilium et missionis benedictinae Schwarcensis,
1617–1773. Gesammelt von Abt Bernhard
Lidl (von Mondsee). MS. Linz, Austria,
Oberösterreiches Landesarchiv. Stiftsarchiv Mondsee, Hs. 7. 811 f. Saec. 17–18.
Microfilm: MnCH proj. no. 27,595
Lieb, Christopher, fl. ca. 1471.
4537   Legendae sanctorum. Martius-Aprilis.
MS. Benediktinerabtei Melk, Austria,
codex 97. 281 f. Folio. Saec. 15.
Microfilm: MnCH proj. no. 1174
4538   Legendarium. Pars II: Majus Junius.
MS. Benediktinerabtei Melk, Austria,
codex 492. 291 f. Folio. Saec. 15.
Microfilm: MnCH proj. no. 1429
4539   Legendae sanctorum. Julius-Augustus.
MS. Benediktinerabtei Melk, Austria,
codex 101. 355 f. Folio. Saec. 15.
Microfilm: MnCH proj. no. 1181

4540   Legendarium. September–October. MS.
Benediktinerabtei Melk, Austria, codex 16.
348 f. Folio. Saec. 15.
Microfilm: MnCH proj. no. 1136

4541   **Liébana, Spain. Santo Toribio (Benedic-
tine abbey).**
Cartulario de Santo Toribio de Liébana.
Edición y estudio por Luis Sánchez Belda.
Madrid, 1948.
508 p. plates, 25 cm.
MnCS

4542   **Liebardus monachus.**
Horreum formicae, i.e. Lexikon voca-
bulorum significationes explanans. MS.
Benediktinerabtei St. Peter, Salzburg,
codex a.VII.21. 366 f. Quarto. Saec. 14.
Microfilm: MnCH proj. no. 10,146

Lierheimer, Bernard Maria, 1826–1900.
4543   Der Fastenprediger; ein sechsfacher
Cyklus von Predigten für die heilige
Fastenzeit. Regensburg, G. J. Manz, 1890–
v. 22 cm.
PLatS

4544   Gnade und Sakramente; Kanzelvorträge.
Regensburg, G. J. Manz, 1887.
xxiv, 459 p. 22 cm.
FStL; KAS

4545   **Lies, Eric,** 1919–
A critical study of Part III of Whately's
Rhetoric.
57 leaves, 29 cm.
Thesis (M.A.)–Catholic University of
America, 1952.
Typescript.
InStme

4546   **Limoges, France. Saint-Martial (Bene-
dictine abbey).**
Prosarium Lemovicense. Die Prosen der
Abtei St. Martial zu Limoges. Hrsg. von
Guido Maria Dreves, S.J. New York and
London, Johnson Reprint Corporation,
1961.
282 p. 21 cm. (Analecta hymnica Medii
Aevi, 7)
Reprint of Leipzig edition of 1889.
PLatS

Lindner, Pirmin, 1848–1912.
4547   Die Aebte und Mönche der Benediktiner-
Abtei Tegernsee von den ältesten Zeiten
bis jzu ihrem Aussterben (1861) und ihr
literarischer Nachlass. München, Histor.
Verein von Oberbayern, 1897–98.
2 v. 25 cm.
KAS

4548   Professbuch der Benediktiner-Abtei St.
Peter in Salzburg (1419–1856). Salzburg,
Buchdruckerei Ringlschwendtner &
Rathmayr, 1906.
328 p. 24 cm.
KAS; MnCS

4549   Verzeichnis der deutschen Benedik-
tinerabteien vom 7. - 20. Jahrhundert.
(*In* Germania monastica. Augsburg,
1967. p. 1–50)
PLatS

4550   **Lipari, Anselmo,** 1944–
Dottrina spirituale teologico-symbolica
in Anselm Stolz, O.S.B. Palermo, Edizioni
O Theologos, 1975.
93 p. 25 cm.
PLatS

4551   **Liturgie et monastères.** Etudes, par E.
Dekkers [et al.]. [Bruges], Biblica, 1966–
v. 22 cm.
KAS

Liutholdus, monk of Mondsee, 12th cent.
4552   Passionale et Vitae patrum. MS. Vienna,
Nationalbibliothek, codex 444. 365 f. Folio.
Saec. 12.
Microfilm: MnCH proj. no. 13,781

4553   Sermones octo. MS. Vienna, Nationalbibliothek, codex 1755. 56 f. Octavo. Saec.
13.
Microfilm: MnCH proj. no. 15,100

4554   **Llopart, Estanislau M.,** 1915–
Les fórmules de la confirmació en el Pon-
tifical romà.
(*In* Liturgica, 2: Cardinal I. A. Schuster
in memoriam. 1958. p. 121–180)
PLatS

Lobbes, Belgium (Benedictine abbey).
4555   Annales Laubacenses.
(*In* Monumenta Germaniae historica.
Scriptores. Stuttgart, 1963. t. 1, p. 3–18,
52–55.
MnCS; PLatS

4556   Annales Laubienses a.418–1054. Con-
tinuatio a.1055–1505.
(*In* Monumenta Germaniae historica.
Scriptores. Stuttgart, 1963. t. 4, p. 9–28)
MnCS; PLatS

4557   Annalium Lobiensium fragmentum.
(*In* Monumenta Germaniae historica.
Scriptores. Stuttgart, 1963. t. 2, p. 192–
211)
MnCS; PLatS

4558   **Loehr, Philip Joseph,** 1917–
Inland terminals threaten small towns. If
the elevators go, can the small towns sur-
vive? Muenster, Sask., St. Peter's Abbey
[1975].
14 p. illus. 22 cm.
MnCS

4559   **Löhr, Aemiliana, Sister,** 1896–
Das Herrenjahr; das Mysterium Christi
im Jahreskreis der Kirche. [5. verb. Aufl.].
Regensburg, F. Pustet [1955].
2 v. 20 cm.
PLatS

Löhrer, Magnus, 1928–
4560 Mysterium salutis; Grundriss heilsgeschichtlicher Dogmatik. Hrsg. von Johannes Feiner und Magnus Löhrer. Einsiedeln, Benziger, 1965–
5 v. 24 cm.
PLatS
4561 Was heisst Wiederkunft Christi? Analyse und Thesen: Paul Schütz. Stellungnahmen: Magnus Löhrer [et al.]. Freiburg, Herder [1972].
95 p. 20 cm.
InStme
4562 **Lojendio, Luis Maria de.**
Castille romane [par] Abundio Rodriguez [et] Luis-Maria de Lojendio. [La Pierre-qui-Vire (Yonne)] Zodiaque, 1966–
v. illus. 23 cm.
InStme
4563 **London, England. Tyburn Convent.**
(tr) Marmion, Columba. The structure of God's plan; being the first part of Christ the life of the soul. Translated from the French by a nun of Tyburn Convent. St. Louis, B. Herder Book Co., 1962.
160 p. 19 cm.
CaMWiSb; KAS; MnCS; PLatS
4564 **London. Vita et Pax Convent School.**
Children's Advent and Christmas, written and illustrated by Vita et Pax, Benedictine Nuns of Cockfosters. Baltimore, Helicon [1966].
unpaged, col. illus. 21 cm.
MnCS
4565 **Long, Camillus Thomas,** 1903–1966.
Freshman panorama. [Latrobe, Pa., St. Vincent College Preparatory] 1961.
[2], 318, [8] leaves, 25 cm.
Multilithed.
PLatS
Longchamp, Nigel. *See* Wireker, Nigellus.
4566 **Longen, Leonarda, Sister.**
Manual for calligraphy. Conception, Mo., Conception Abbey Press, 1964.
44 p. illus.
MoCo; SdYa
4567 **Lopez de Sirez, Melchior.**
In exercitatorium vitae spiritualis.
(*In* Regla del bienaventurado San Benito . . . n. 4. Valladolid, 1599.)
MnCS
4568 **Lopez, Bernardo,** 1901–
The policy of the United Nations toward the Franco regime from 1945–1949.
vi, p. 132, vi leaves, ports. 28 cm.
Thesis (M.A.)–St. Vincent College, Latrobe, Pa., 1949.
Typescript.
PLatS

Lorsch, Germany (Benedictine abbey).
4569 Annales Laurissenses. MS. Vienna, Nationalbibliothek, codex 473, f.116–143v. Quarto. Saec. 9.
Microfilm: MnCH proj. no. 13,820
4570 Annales Laureshamenses (fragmentum). MS. Vienna, Nationalbibliothek, codex 515, f.1r–5r. Quarto. Saec. 9.
Microfilm: MnCH proj. no. 13,851
4571 Annales Laurissenses (fragmentum). MS. Vienna, Nationalbibliothek, codex 334. 1 f. Quarto. Saec. 10.
Microfilm: MnCH proj. no. 13,697
4572 Annales breves Laurishaimenses ab anno 703 usque ad annum 803. MS. Benediktinerabtei St. Paul im Lavanttal, Austria, codex 8/1. 8 f. Folio. Saec. 10.
Microfilm: MnCH proj. no. 11,675
4573 Annales Laurissenses. MS. Vienna, Nationalbibliothek, codex 612, f.1v–73v. Quarto. Saec. 12.
Microfilm: MnCH proj. no. 13,984
4574 Annales Eginhardi et Annales Laurissenses. MS. Vienna, Nationalbibliothek, codex 610, f.5r–56v. Octavo. Saec. 14.
Microfilm: MnCH proj. no. 13,959
4575 Annales Laureshamenses.
(*In* Monumenta Germaniae historica. Scriptores. Stuttgart, 1963. t. 1, p. 22–39)
MnCS; PLatS
4576 Annales Laurissenses et Einhardi a.741–923.
(*In* Monumenta Germaniae historica. Scriptores. Stuttgart, 1963. t. 1, p. 124–218)
MnCS; PLatS
4577 Annales Laurissenses minores a. 680–817.
(*In* Monumenta Germaniae historica. Scriptores. Stuttgart, 1963. t. 1, p. 112–218)
MnCS; PLatS
4578 [Annales Laureshamenses]
Codex Vindobonensis 515 der Oesterreichischen Nationalbibliothek, Facsimileausgabe. Einführung und Transkription [von] Franz Unterkircher. Graz, Akademische Druck u. Verlagsanstalt, 1967.
48 p. 8 leaves of facsimiles. 28 cm.
(Codices selecti phototypice impressi, v. 15)
PLatS
Lortie, Jeanne Marie, Sister.
4579 Gracious living. Duluth, Minn., The Priory Press, 1974.
180 p. illus. 23 cm.
CaMWiSb; MnDuS

4580   Mary, our sister. Duluth, Minn., The Priory Press, 1975.
198 p.
InFer; MdRi; MnDuS

4581   Music appreciation for the elementary schools, grades 1-6. Cincinnati, Willis Music Co., 1962.
81 p.
MnDuS

4582   Music appreciation for high school, grades 10-12. Cincinnati, Willis Music Co., 1964.
240 p.
MnDuS

4583   Music appreciation for junior high school, grades 7-9. Cincinnati, Willis Music Co., 1963.
68 p.
MnDuS

Lott, Roger Richard, 1922–
4584   Anthology of sports poems. Nashville, Tenn., George Peabody College.
54 p.
AStb

4585   A bibliographic manual in botany for the high school student. Nashville, Tenn., 1957.
55 p.
AStb

4586   Eugene O'Neill and the frustrated personality.
19 p.
AStb

4587   Notes on moral theology.
2 v. 28 cm.
Typescript.
AStb

4588   Sampling American ballads. Nashville, Tenn., George Peabody College.
80 p.
AStb

Lottin, Odon, 1880–1965.
4589   L'âme du culte; la vertu de religion d'après S. Thomas d'Aquin. Louvain, Abbaye du Mont-César, 1920.
87 p. 18 cm.
MnCS

4590   Aristote et la connexion des vertus morales.
(*In* Autour d'Aristote. Louvain, 1955. p. 343–366)
PLatS

4591   Etudes de morale; histoire et doctrine. Gembloux, J. Duculit, 1961.
365 p. 26 cm.
CaQStB; InStme; MnCS; PLatS

4592   Une tradition spéciale du texte des "Sententiae divinae paginae."

(*In* Studia mediaevalia in honorem Raymundi Josephi Martin. Brugis, 1948. p. 147–169)
PLatS

Louis, Conrad, 1914–
4593   Psalms; lectures given 1973–74 to Sisters of St. Benedict of Ferdinand and Beech Grove at St. Martin Convent, Siberia, Indiana.
6 tapes (8 hrs.)
InFer(Archives)

4594   Saint Paul: Paul and the crucified. Lectures given Feb. 9, 1975, to Benedictine Sisters of Beech Grove and Ferdinand at Siberia, Indiana.
3 tapes (3 hrs.)
InFer(Archives)

4595   Scripture study: commentary on readings of the Lectionary for Cycles A, B and C, given weekly at Convent of the Immaculate Conception, Ferdinand, Indiana, 1976–78.
20, 20 and 25 tapes (30, 30 and 35 hrs.)
InFer(Archives)

Louismet, Savinian, 1858–1926.
4596   Wahre und falsche Mystik. Mit Genehmigung des Autors übersetzt nach der 2. Auflage des Englischen von P. Chrysostomus Schmid. St. Ottilien, Missions-Verlag, 1920.
193 p.
NcBe

Louvain, Belgium. Mont-César (Benedictine abbey).
4597   Petite bibliothèque liturgique. Louvain, Abbaye de Mont César, Bureau Liturgique [1937].
17 p. 17 cm.
MnCS

Lu, Pierre Célestin, 1870–1949.
4598   The relations of the Church with the nation and with society in China.
(*In* Catholic University of Peking. Bulletin, no. 7(1930–, p. 31–36)
PLatS

Ludwig, Beda, 1871–
4599   Tugendschule Gemma Golganis, Dienerin Gottes und stigmatisierten Jungfrau von Lucca. 4. u. 5. verb. Aufl. Baden Schulbrüder.
544 p. illus.
MoCo

Luecke, Janemarie, Sister.
4599a   The rape of the Sabine women: poems. Fort Lauderdale, Fla., Wake-Brook House, 1978.
88 p. 22 cm.
KAS; MnCS

4599b Measuring Old English rhythm; an application of the principles of Gregorian chant rhythm to the meter of "Beowulf." Madison, Wis., University of Wisconsin Press, 1978.
viii, 158 p. music. 25 cm.
MnCS; PLatS

Luetkemeyer, Alexander John, 1923–
4600 Catholic political organization in France 1830–1850.
Thesis – St. Louis University.
112 p.
MoCo

4601 Don Luigi Sturzo and the Italian Popular Party.
352 p.
Digest of doctoral dissertation, St. Louis University, 1962.
MoCo

4602 American Catholicism, 1945–72.
246 p.
Manuscript.
MoCo

4603 Outline of history of American Catholicism.
179 p.
Manuscript, 1968.
MoCo

4604 (tr) Jäger, Moritz. Sister Gertrude Leupi, 1825–1904. Translated by Alexander J. Luetkemeyer.
188 p.
Typescript, 1974.
MoCo

4605 **Luetmer, Nora,** 1921–1974.
The history of Catholic education in the present Diocese of St. Cloud, Minnesota, 1855–1965.
555 leaves, 29 cm.
Thesis (Ph.D.) – University of Minnesota, 1970.
Typescript.
MnCS; MnStj

4606 **Luffield Priory, England.**
Luffield Priory charters . . . Edited, with an introduction, by G. R. Elvey. Oxford, Northamptonshire Record Society, 1968–
v. plates, facsims. 25 cm.
MnCS

Lugano, Placido, 1876–1947.
4607 La Congregazione Camaldolese degli eremiti di Montecorona dalle origini ai nostri tempi . . . Frascati, Sacra Eremo Tuscolano, 1908.
543 p. 26 cm.
KAS

4608 L'Italia benedettina. Roma, F. Ferrari, 1929.
xix, 618 p. illus. 20 cm.
MnCS

4609 Il Messalino Romano per i fedeli a cura del P. D. Placido T. Lugano. 2. ed. con eucologio o manuale di preghiere. Città del Vaticano [1958].
xlvii, 1554, 198 p. 15 cm.
MnCS

4610 I processi inediti per Francesca Bussa dei Ponziani (Santa Francesca Romano) 1440–1453. Città del Vaticano, Biblioteca Apostolica Vaticana, 1945.
xl, 345 p. 26 cm. (Studi e testi, 120)
CaQStB; PLatS

4611 **Luitholdus, monk of Mondsee.**
Epitaphia tria in Chunradum abbatem Lunaelacensem anno 1145 interfectum. MS. Vienna, Nationalbibliothek, codex 849, f. 132v. Quarto. Saec. 12.
Microfilm: MnCH proj. no. 14,168

4612 **Lullus, Saint, abp. of Mainz,** d. 787.
S. Bonifatii et Lulli Epistolae. Edidit E. Dümmler.
(*In* Monumenta Germaniae historica. Epistolae. Berlin, 1957. t. 3, p. 215–433)
Reprint of Berlin edition of 1892.
InStme; MnCS; PLatS

4613 **Lumper, Gottfried,** 1747–1800.
Historia theologico-critica de vita, scriptis, atque doctrina sanctorum patrum, aliorumque scriptorum ecclesiasticorum trium primorum saeculorum . . . Augustae Vindelicorum, Matthaeus Rieger, 1783–99.
13 v. 20 cm.
KAS; MnCS

4614 **Luna, Joaquim Grangeiro de,** 1881–
The Benedictine Congregation of Brazil in general. Translated by Dom Otho Sullivan, O.S.B. 1966.
[3], 43 leaves. 28 cm.
Typescript.
KAM

Lupus Servatus, abbot of Ferrières, 9th cent.
4615 Opera. Stephanvs Balvzivs Tutelensis in unum collegit, epistolas ad fidem vetustissimi codicis emendavit, notisque illustravit. Parisiis, F. Muguet, 1664.
535 p. 18 cm.
MnCS

4616 The Letters of Lupus of Ferrières. Translated, with an introduction and notes, by Graydon W. Regenos. The Hague, M. Nijhoff, 1966.
xii, 160 p. 24 cm.
InStme

Lutterotti, Nikolaus, 1892–

4617   Abt Bernardus Rosa von Grüssau. Nach Notizien P. Nikolaus v. Lutterotti bearbeitet und hrsg. durch Ambrosius Rose, O.S.B. Stuttgart, Brentanoverlag, 1960.
128 p. plates, 22 cm.
MnCS; PLatS

4618   Abtei Grüssau; ein Führer. Grüssau in Schlesien, Verlag für Liturgik, 1930.
67 p. plates, 18 cm.
MnCS

4619   Altgrüssauer Klostergeschichten. Breslau, Verlag des Katholischen Sonntagsblattes, 1927.
59 p. 19 cm.
InStme

4620   **Luz, Columban,** 1713–1778.
Nothwendige Wissenschafft geistlicher Ordens-Personen, sonderheitlich derjenigen welche unter der Regul des grossen heiligen Ertz-Patriarchen Benedicti streiten . . . Constantz und Ulm, Joh. Fridr. Baum, 1751.
[44], 514 p. 21 cm.
InStme; KAS

Lydgate, John, 1370?–1451?
Manuscript items.

4621   [Opera]
The Mass; Litany in verse; Prayer in old age; Goode counselle; Steadfastness; To the Virgin; Life of the Virgin. MS. Lambeth Palace Library, London, codex 344. 99 f. Quarto. Saec. 15.
Microfilm: MnCH

4622   Minor poems. MS. Lincoln Cathedral Library, England, codex 129. 89 f. Octavo. Saec. 15.
Microfilm: MnCH

4623   Bochas' Fall of princes. MS. Lambeth Palace Library, London, codex 256. 180 f. Quarto. Saec. 15.
Microfilm: MnCH

4624   Siege of Thebes. MS. Lambeth Palace Library, London, codex 742. 68 f. Quarto. Saec. 15.
Microfilm: MnCH

Printed works.

4625   Le assemble de dyeus. London, W. de Worde, 1500?
MnCS (microfilm)

4626   The assemble of goddes. London, W. de Worde, n.d.
MnCS (microfilm)

4627   The assembly of the gods. London? n.d.
Colophon: Emprynted by Richards Pynson.
MnCS (microfilm)

4628   The assembly of the gods. London, W. de Worde, 1498.
MnCS (microfilm)

4629   The assembly of gods: or, The accord of reason and sensuality in the fear of death. Ed. from the mss. with introduction, notes, index of persons and places, and glossary by Oscar Lovell Triggs. London, K. Paul, Trench, Trübner & Co., 1896.
lxxvi, 166 pl. 22 cm. (Early English Text Society. Extra series, LXIX)
MnCS

4630   The childe of Bristow, a poem of John Ludgate. Edited from the original ms. in the British Museum, by Clarence Hopper. [Westminster], Printed for the Camden Society, 1859.
27 p. 21 cm. (Camden miscellany, v. 4, pt. 4)
KAS; MnCS

4631   The chorle and the birde. Westminster, W. Caxton, 1477?
MnCS (microfilm)

4632   The tale of the chorle & the byrd. London, R. Pinson, 1493.
MnCS (microfilm)

4633   Here begynneth the chorle and the byrde. [London, W. de Worde, 1520].
MnCS (microfilm)

4634   Here foloweth: the Churle and the byrde. [Canterbury, 1550?]
MnCS (microfilm)

4635   The churle and the byrde. [London, 156-?]
MnCS (microfilm)

4636   The courte of sapyence. [London, W. de Worde, 1510]
MnCS (microfilm)

4637   Here begynneth the cronycle of all ỹ kỹges names that haue reygned in Englande syth the conquest of Wyllyâ Conquerour. And sheweth ỹdayes of theyr coronacyon, and of theyr byrthe. [London, 1530].
Colophon: Jmprynted by me Wnkyn de Worde, dwellynge in London . . .
MnCS (microfilm)

4638   De curia sapiencie. Westminster, W. Caston, 1480.
MnCS (microfilm)

4639   [Fall of princes]
Here begynnethe the boke calledde John bochas descriuinge the falle of princis, princessis & other nobles, traslated ito Englissh by John Ludgate. London, R. Pynson, 1494.
MnCS (microfilm)

4640   [Fall of princes]
Here begynneth the boke of Johan Bochas discryuing the fall of prînces, princesses and other nobles. Translated into Englysshe by John Lydgate monke of Bury . . . [London, Pynson, 1527]
MnCS (microfilm)

4641   This present boke called the Gouernaunce of kynges and prync . . . [London], Imprynted by R. Prynson, 1511.
Translated by John Lydgate (Secretum secretorum).
MnCS (microfilm)

4642   Gouernayle of helthe. Medicina stomachi. London, W. Caxton, 1489.
MnCS (microfilm)

4643   The hors, the shepe & the ghoos. Westminster, W. Caxton, 1477? Second edition.
MnCS (microfilm)

4644   The horse the ghoos & the sheep. Westminster, W. Caxton, 1477?
First edition.
MnCS (microfilm)

4645   The horse / the sheep / and the ghoos. Westminster, W. de Worde, 1500.
MnCS (microfilm)

4646   Here foloweth the Interpretaciô of the names of goddes and goddesses / as is rehersed in this treatyse folowynge as poets wryte. [London, 1529?].
MnCS (microfilm)

4647   The life and death of Hector. One, and the first of the most puissant, valiant, and renowned monarches of the world . . . London, Printed by T. Purfoot, 1614.
Modernized and abridged by Thomas Heywood, from Lydgate's "Troy-book," a version of Guido delle Colonne.
MnCS (Microfilm)

4648   A critical edition of John Lydgate's Life of Our Lady, by Joseph A. Lauritis, general editor . . . Pittsburgh, Duquesne University, 1961.
742 p. (Duquesne studies. Philological series, 2)
NcBe; ILSP; PLatS

4649   The lyf of our lady. Westminster, W. Caston, 1484.
MnCS (microfilm)

4650   The lyfe of our lady. London, R. Redman, 1531.
MnCS (microfilm)

4651   Here begynnethe the glorious lyfe and passion of saint Albon prothomartyr of Englande/and also the lyfe and passion of saint Amphabel whiche converted saint Albon to the fayth of Christe. [St. Albans, J. Hertford, 1534].
MnCS (microfilm)

4652   The life of Saint Alban and Saint Amphibal. Edited by J. E. van der Westhuizen. Leiden, Brill, 1974.
327 p. 24 cm.
English or Latin.
MnCS; PLatS

4653   The loue and complayntes betwene Mars and Venus. [Westmoster, Pnpryntyde for I. Notarii, 1500?]
MnCS (microfilm)

4654   Here begynnys the mayng or disport of Chaucer. [Edinburgh], W. Chepman, 1508].
MnCS (microfilm)

4655   Lydgate's minor poems. The two nightingale poems (A.D. 1446). Edited from the mss. with introduction, notes, and glossary by Otto Glauning. London, K. Paul, Trench, Trübner & Co., 1900.
xlvi, 84 p. 22 cm. (Early English Text Society. Extra series, LXXX)
MnCS

4656   The minor poems of John Lydgate. Edited from all available mss., with an attempt to establish the Lydgate canon, by Henry Noble MacCracken . . . [London, Early English Text Society, 1961].
vii [379]-847 p. 23 cm. (Early English Text Society. Original series, 192)
"First published 1934, reprinted 1961."
PLatS

4657   Poems: with an introduction, notes, and glossary by John Norton-Smith. Oxford, Clarendon P., 1966.
xvi, 202 p. 19 cm. (Clarendon medieval and Tudor series)
KAS

4658   The proverbes of Lydgate. [London, W. de Worde, 1515?]
Colophon: Here endeth the proverbes of Lydgate upon the fall of prynces . . .
MnCS (microfilm)

4659   The hystorye / sege and destruccyon of Troye. [London, 1513].
MnCS (microfilm)

4660   Stana puer ad mensam. Westminster, W. Caxton, 1477?
MnCS (microfilm)

4661   The storye of Thebes. London, W. de Worde, 1500?
MnCS (microfilm)

4662   Here begynneth the temple of glas. [Westminster, Wynkyn de Worde, n.d.]
MnCS (microfilm)

4663   The temple of glas. Westminster, W. Caxton, 1477?
MnCS (microfilm)

4664   The temple of glas. London, W. de Worde, 1500?
MnCS (microfilm)

4665   This boke called the Têmple of glasse is in many places amended / and late diligently imprynted. [London, 1530?]
MnCS (microfilm)

4666   Here begynneth the testamênt of John Lydgate monke of Berry, which he made hymselfe by his lyfe dayes. [London, R. Pynson, 1515?]
MnCS (microfilm)

4667   Here begynneth A treatyse of the smyth whych that forged hym a new dame. [London, 156-].
MnCS (microfilm)

4668   Verses on the seven virtues. London? 1500?
Attributed to John Lydgate.
MnCS (microfilm)

4669   The vertue of y masse. [London, W. de Worde, n.d.]
MnCS (microfilm)

4670   The tragedies, gathered by Ihon Bochas, of all such princes as fell from theyr estates tyroughe the mutability of fortune . . . Translated into Englysh by Iohn Lidgate . . . Imprinted at London, by John Wayland [1554?]
MnCS (microfilm)

4671   A treatise excellent and compêdious, shewing . . . the falles of sondry most notable princes . . . First ocompylled in Latin by . . . Bocatius . . . and sence that tyme translated into our English . . . by Dan John Lidgate . . . now newly imprynted . . . In aedibus Richardi Tottelli . . . [London, 1554].
MnCS (microfilm)

4672   The workes of Geffrey Chaucer, newly printed . . . with the siege and destruccion of the worthy citee of Thebes, compiled by John Lidgate . . . [London, 1561]
MnCS (microfilm)

4673   (tr) Guillaume de Deguilleville, 14th cent. The book of the pylgremage of the sowle late translated out of Frensshe into Englysshe [by John Lydgate]. [Westemestre, W. Caxton, 1483].
MnCS (microfilm)

Lynch, Claire, Sister, 1898–

4674   The story of St. Gertrude's Convent, Shakopee, Minnesota, 1862–1880.
28, [8] p. illus.
Privately printed.
MnSSP; MnStj(Archives)

4675   The Shakopee story: episodes in oppression.

Reprint from: Benedictines, v. 31, p. 6–15, 35–37, 58–63.
MnSSP

4675a   The leaven. St. Paul, Minn., St. Paul's Priory [1980].
71 p. ports., facsims. 22 cm.
MnSSP; MnStj

4676   **M., H. W., comp.**
A short explanation & history of the medal or cross of Saint Benedict, with a list of indulgences and conditions for gaining them, and the form for blessing the medal. London, R. & T. Washbourne, 1907.
15 p.
NcBe

Mabillon, Jean, 1632–1707.

4677   De liturgia Gallicana libri III . . . Parisiis, apud Montalant, 1729.
17, 477, [21] p. 26 cm.
ILSP

4678   Mabillon outlines a "Ratio studiorum" for Maurist clerics and scholars. Translated by Rev. Bernard S. Sause, O.S.B.
Reprint from: Benedictine Review, 1962, p. 31–40.
PLatS

4679   Ouvrages posthumes de D. Jean Mabillon et de D. Thierri Ruinart . . . Paris, 1724. Republished by Gregg Press Ltd., 1967.
InStme; PLatS

4680   Seize lettres de Dom Mabillon [ed. par Dom Paul Denis]. Ligugé (Vienne), Imprimerie E. Aubin, 1909.
44 p.
NcBe

4681   Caeremoniale romanum of Agostino Patrizi Piccolomini. The first edition, Venice 1516, to which is appended Patrizi's original preface, rediscovered by Jean Mabillon and published by him in the second volume of his Museum italicum, Lutetia Parisiorum, 1689. Republished in 1965 by Gregg Press, Ridgewood, N.J.
clxii p. 28 cm.
MnCS

McCaffrey, Edmund Fairbanks, 1933–

4682   The concept of war and self-defense in the papal statements of Pius XII: 1945–1958.
81 p. 28 cm.
Thesis (M.A.)–Catholic University of America, 1963.
Typescript.
NcBe

4683   The relevance of systems theories to the analysis of international politics.
229 p. 28 cm.
Thesis (Ph.D.)–Catholic University of America, 1969.

Typescript.
NcBe

4684 **McAndrews, Dunstan,** 1906–
Father Joseph Kundek: 1810–1857. A
missionary priest of the Diocese of Vin-
cennes.
vi, 118 leaves, 28 cm.
Thesis (M.A.)–De Paul University,
Chicago, 1936.
Typescript.
InStme

McCann, Justin, 1882–1959.
4685 Ampleforth Abbey and College; a short
history. [3rd ed.]. Ampleforth Abbey,
York, 1953.
24 p. 19 cm.
KAS

4686 . . . . 4th ed. Ampleforth Abbey, York,
1964.
24 p. 19 cm.
PLatS

4687 The early history of the Benedictine
medal.
Reprint from Ampleforth Journal, v. 38
(1933), p. 83–94.
NcBe

4688 The Rule of St. Benedict in Latin and
English. Edited and translated by Abbot
Justin McCann. London, Sheed and Ward,
1972.
214 p.
InFer

4689 (ed) The cloud of unknowing, together
with The epistle of privy counsel, by an
English mystic of the XIVth century.
Edited by Abbot Justin McCann. Springfield, Ill., Templegate [1964].
xvi, 142 p. 17 cm.
InStme; MnCS

4690 **McCormack, Eric David,** 1911–1963.
Frederick Matthias Alexander and John
Dewey: a neglected influence.
260 p. 28 cm.
Thesis (Ph.D.)–University of Toronto,
1958.
Typescript.
PLatS

McDonnell, Kilian, 1921–
4691 The baptism in the Holy Spirit as an
ecumenical problem; two essays relating
the baptism in the Holy Spirit to sacramental life [by] Kilian McDonnell, O.S.B.,
and Arnold Bittlinger. Notre Dame, Ind.,
Charismatic Renewal Services [1972].
53 p. 19 cm.
MnCS

4692 Catholic Pentecostalism: problems in
evaluation. [Pecos, N.M., Dove Publications, 1970].

58 p. 18 cm.
PLatS

4693 The charismatic renewal and
ecumenism. New York, Paulist Press,
1978.
125 p. 20 cm.
MnCS

4694 Charismatic renewal and the Churches.
New York, Seabury Press, 1976.
x, 202 p. 24 cm.
MnCS

4695 The Holy Spirit and power; the Catholic
charismatic renewal. Garden City, N.Y.,
Doubleday & Co., 1975.
186 p. 21 cm.
InStme; MnCS; NcBe

4696 John Calvin, the Church, and the
eucharist. Princeton, N.J., Princeton University Press, 1967.
ix, 410 p. 21 cm.
A revision and expansion of the author's
thesis, Treves.
InStme; KAS; MnCS; OkShG; PLatS

4697 Problems and perspectives; an epilogue.
(*In* Protestants and Catholics on the
spiritual life. Collegeville, Minn., 1965. p.
97–106)
PLatS

4697a Presence, power, praise: documents on
the charismatic renewal. Collegeville,
Minn., The Liturgical Press, 1980.
3 v. 22 cm.
MnCS

4698 **McKenna, Mary Bonaventure, Sister.**
Successful devices in teaching Latin.
Portland, Me., J. Weston Walch, 1959.
ii, 205 p. illus. 28 cm.
InStme; KAM; KAS

McKinney, Mary Benet, Sister.
4699 Shared decision-making; a manual for
local school boards, pastors and principals.
Archdiocese of Chicago School Board,
1972.
44 p. illus.
ICSS

4700 Shared decision-making revisited; guidelines for parish school boards, principals,
and pastors. Archdiocese of Chicago
School Office, 1977.
93 p. illus.
ICSS

4701 **McLaughlin, James Bede Benedict,**
1866–
Catechism theology. London, New York,
Longmans, Green and Co., 1922.
vi, 115 p. 19 cm.
KAS; OrStb

4702 **McLaughlin, Raymond, Sister,** 1897–
Religious education and the state;
democracy finds a way. Washington,
Catholic University of America Press
[1967].
ix, 439 p. 22 cm.
KAM; KAS; MnCS; PLatS

4702a The liberty of choice: freedom and justice
in education. Collegeville, Minn., The
Liturgical Press [1979].
viii, 176 p. 23 cm.
KAS; MnCS

4703 **McMullen, John,** 1940–
A guide to the Christian Indians of the
Upper Plains (an annotated, selective
bibliography) . . . Marvin, S.D., Blue Cloud
Abbey, 1969.
60 p. 28 cm.
Multigraphed.
MnCS; MoCo; SdMar

4704 **McNamara, Kathleen, Sister.**
Women of vision; the Theresian story,
1961–1969. The Theresians of America,
1972.
xvi p. 188 p. illus.
ICSS

4705 **McSorley, Aidan,** 1941–
An analysis of ANSCR.
Thesis (M.S.L.S.)–Catholic University
of America.
60 p.
MoCo

4706 **Madonna Day School, Memphis,
Tenn.**
Newsletter. v. 1– 1969– Quar-
terly.
InFer

4707 **Madres Benedictinas, Coban, Alta Vera-
paz, Guatemala.**
Cablegram from Coban (newsletter
published quarterly). v. 1– 1970–
InFer

4708 **Maeder, Michael,** 1938–
Church as people; a study of election.
Collegeville, Minn., St. John's University
Press [1968].
xii, 60 p. 23 cm.
InStme; MnCS; PLatS

Maertens, Thierry, 1921–
4709 The advancing dignity of woman in the
Bible. Translated by Sandra Dibbs. De
Pere, Wis., St. Norbert Abbey Press,
1969.
241 p. 19 cm.
Translation of: La promotion de la
femme dans la Bible.
MnCS

4710 L'assemblée chrétienne de la théologie
biblique à pastorale du XX siècle. [Bruges],
Publications de Saint André, 1964.
154 p. 22 cm.
MnCS; PLatS

4711 Assembly for Christ; from biblical
theology to pastoral theology in the twentieth century. London, Darton, Longman
& Todd, 1970.
[5], 153 p. 23 cm.
MnCS

4712 Au coeur de notre pastorale: La Semaine
Sainte. 2. ed. rev. et augm. Bruges, Apostolat Liturgique, 1956.
158 p. 24 cm.
CaQStB; MnCS; MoCo; PLatS

4713 Bible themes–a source book. Bruges,
Biblica [c. 1964].
2 v. 22 cm.
Translation of the 4th rev. ed. of Fichier
biblique.
InStme; CaMWisb

4714 The breath and spirit of God. Translated
by Robert J. Olsen and Albert J. LaMothe,
Jr. Notre Dame, Ind., Fides Publishers
[1964].
166 p. 21 cm.
InFer; MnCS; MnStj; PLatS; KAS

4715 Carême: catéchuménat pour notre temps
[par Thierry Maertens et al.]. Bruges, Abbaye de Saint André, 1958.
72 p. 24 cm.
MnCS

4716 C'est fête en l'honneur de Yahvé.
[Bruges], Desclée de Brouwer [1961].
223 p. 20 cm.
KAS; MnCS; MoSo; PLatS

4717 La Constitution de Vatican II sur la liturgie, [par Thierry Maertens et al.]. [Bruges],
Biblica, 1964.
43 p. 24 cm.
KAS; PLatS

4718 Contemporary prayer . . . Thierry
Maertens [et al.]. Notre Dame, Ind., Fides
Pub. [1974].
2 v. 20 cm.
"Translated by Jerome J. DuCharme."
InStme

4719 Conversations pastorales par Dom Jean
de Feligonde, Hadelin Van Erck et Thierry
Maertens.
(*In* Paroisse et liturgie, no. 8, p. 17–51)
PLatS

4720 Dieu-Père au catéchisme, par Th.
Maertens [et al.]. Bruges, Editions de
l'Apostolat Liturgique, 1960.
63 p. illus.
MnCS

4721   Doctrine et pastorale de la liturgie de la mort. Bruges, Abbaye de Saint-André, 1957.
135 p. 24 cm.
CaQAtB; MnCS; MoCo; PLatS

4722   L'éducation du sens du péché au catéchisme, par Th. Maertens [et al.]. [Bruges], Biblica, 1962.
72 p. 22 cm.
MnCS

4723   L'Eglise Jérusalem au catéchisme, par Th. Maertens [et al.]. Bruges, Editions de l'Apostolat Liturgique, 1961.
72 p. illus. 22 cm.
MnCS

4724   Faut-il encore une liturgie? Liturgie, religion et foi . . . Th. Maertens [et al.]. Paris, Editions du Centurion, 1968.
176 p. 21 cm.
MnCS

4725   A feast in honor of Yahweh. Translated by Kathryn Sullivan . . . Notre Dame, Ind., Fides Publishers [1965].
245 p. 21 cm.
Translation of: C'est fête en l'honneur de Yahvé.
CaMWiSb; ICSS; MnCS; MnStj; KAS; MoCo; PLatS

4726   Fichier biblique, sous la direction de Dom Thierry Maertens. 3. éd. entierement refondue. Bruges, Apostolat Liturgique, 1961–
v. 15x24 cm.
InStme

4727   Der Geist des Herrn erfüllt den Erdkreis. Das Wirken des Gottesgeistes nach dem Zeugnis der Heiligen Schrift. Düsseldorf, Patmos-Verlag [1959].
115 p. 19 cm.
Translation of: Le souffle et l'Esprit de Dieu, and L'Esprit qui donne la vie.
MnCS

4728   Guide for the Christian assembly; a background book of the Mass . . . [Translated by monks of Valyermo]. Notre Dame, Ind., Fides Publishers [1967–1972].
8 v. 21 cm.
Translation of: Guide de l'Assemblée chrétienne.
InFer; InStme; ILSP; KAS; MnCS; MnStj; NcBe; PLatS

4729   Histoire et pastoral du rituel du catéchuménat et du baptême. Bruges. Biblica, 1962.
351 p. 23 cm.
InStme; MnCS; PLatS

4730   Liturgie et monde d'aujourd'hui, [par] Pierre Jadot, Thierry Maertens [et] Louis Retif. [Bruges], Biblica, 1966.

101 p. 21 cm.
MnCS; PLatS

4731   La nouvelle célébration liturgique et ses implications, [par] R. Gantoy et Th. Maertens. [Bruges], Biblica, 1965.
155 p. 22 cm.
PLatS

4732   Les oraisons du Missel de l'Assemblée chrétienne; textes du temporal et concordances [par] Thierry Maertens et Monique Herbecq. [Bruges], Biblia, 1964.
249 p. 22 cm.
MnCS; PLatS

4733   Pastorale de la Messe à la lumiere de la tradition. 2. éd. entièrement refondue. [Bruges], Biblica, 1964.
211 p. 21 cm.
MnCS; PLatS

4734   Pastorale liturgique de l'Avent et du Carême. 3. éd. rev. et augm. [Bruges], Biblica, 1962.
183 p. 24 cm.
PLatS

4735   Les petits groupes et l'avenir de l'Eglise. [Paris], Editions du Centurion [1971].
202 p. 20 cm.
MnCS

4736   Points chauds: recherches [par] J. Th. Maertens [et al.]. Bruxelles, Editions Foyer Notre-Dame [1969].
2 v. 17 cm.
MnCS

4737   Pour un renouveau des prières de prône [par] J. B. Molin et Th. Maertens. Bruges, Editions de l'Apostolat Liturgique, 1961.
181 p. 24 cm.
PLatS

4738   Pour une meilleure intelligence du canon de la Messe. Bruges, Apostolat Liturgique, 1959.
115 p. 23 cm.
MnCS; PLatS

4739   La promotion de la femme dans la Bible; ses applications au mariage et su ministère. [Tournai, Paris], Casterman, 1967.
230 p. 18 cm.
MnCS; PLatS

4740   Les risques de plafonnement du mouvement liturgique. Bruges, Editions de l'Apostolat Liturgique, 1961.
71 p. 24 cm.
MnCS; PLatS

4741   Le souffle et l'Esprit de Dieu. [Bruges], Desclée de Brouwer [1959].
144 p. 20 cm.
CaQStB; MnCS; MoSo; PLatS

4742   The spirit of God in Scripture. Baltimore, Helicon [1966].
128 p. 18 cm.
InStme; MnCS; MnStj; PLatS; CaMWiSb

4743   Die Sterbeliturgie der katholischen Kirche; Glaubenslehre und Seelsorge. Paderborn, Verlag Bonifacius-Druckerei, 1959.
165 p. 21 cm.
Translation of: Doctrine et pastorale de la liturgie de la mort.
MnCS

4744   Le thème "lumière-ténèbres" au catéchisme [par] Th. Maertens [et al.]. [Bruges], Biblica, 1962.
101 p. illus. 22 cm.
MnCS

4745   Les thèmes du pasteur et de la route au catéchisme [par] Th. Maertens [et al.]. Bruges, Editions de l'Apostolat Liturgique, 1961.
117 p. diagrs. 22 cm.
MnCS

4746   Le thème du sacrifice au catéchisme [par] Th. Maertens [et al.]. [Bruges], Biblica, 1962.
69 p. illus. 22 cm.
MnCS

4747   **Maerz, Angelus,** 1731–1784.
Angelus contra Michaelem; seu, Crisis apologetica adversus . . . Michaelis [i.e. Michael Kuen] praeposoti Wengensis ulmae abbatiae Lateranensis &c. Joannem de Canabaco . . . in favorem Joannis Gersenii abbatis Vercellensis, O.S.B., concepta. Frisingae, P. L. Böck, 1761.
79 p. 17 cm.
PLatS

4748   **Magarini, Cornelio,** 1605–1681.
Bullarium Casinense, seu Constitutiones summorum pontificum, imperatorum, regum, principium, & decretat sacrarum congregationum pro Congregatione Casinensi, caeterisque regularibus cum eadem directe vel indirecte participantibus . . . Venetiis, typis Omnibenij Ferretti, 1650–70.
2 v.
KAS (microfilm)

Magrassi, Mariano, 1930–
4749   Problemi e orientamenti di spiritualità monastica, biblica, et liturgica. Roma, Edizione Paoline [1961].
790 p. 18 cm.
At head of title: C. Vagaggini . . . M. Magrassi . . .
MnCS

4750   Teologia e storia nel pensiero di Ruperto di Deutz. Roma, apud Pontificiam Universitatem Urbanianam de Propaganda Fide [1960].
290 p. 25 cm.
MnCS

4751   **Maguire, Kevin.**
The dreamer not the dream [by] Sebastian Moore and Kevin Maguire. New York, Newman Press [1970].
159 p. 21 cm.
Prose and poems.
InStme; PLatS

4752   **Maher, Paul R.,** 1925–
The dualism of Paul Elmer More; a historico-critical study of an American humanist. Latrobe, Pa., St. Vincent Archabbey, 1961.
xvi, 221 p. 23 cm.
Thesis   (Ph.D.) – Collegio   di Sant'Anselmo, Rome.
PLatS

4753   **Maier, Marinus,** 1936–
Früher Georgskult im Altbayerischen Raum. München, Bayerische Benediktinerakademie, 1965.
62 p. 24 cm.
InStme; MnCS

4754   **Maiers, Mary Gerald, Sister.**
A study of extraordinary means in religion to the aged, the critically ill, and the dying.
118 p. 28 cm.
Thesis (M.A.) – Montana State University, 1971.
Typescript.
MnStj

Maihew, Edward, 1570–1625.
4755   A paradise of prayers and meditations. [Menston, Yorkshire, England], Scolar Press, 1973.
[63], 603 p. 20 cm. (English recusant literature, 1558–1640, v. 132)
MnCS; PLatS

4756   A treatise of the groundes of the old and newe religion. [Menston, Yorkshire, England], Scolar Press, 1973.
232 p. 23 cm. (English recusant literature, 1558–1640, v. 124)
Facsimile reprint of the 1608 edition.
MnCS; PLatS

4757   **Maillefer, Elie,** fl. 1740.
The life of John Baptist de La Salle, priest, doctor, former canon of the Cathedral of Rheims, and founder of the Brothers of the Christian Schools. Translated by Didymus John. Winona, Minn., St. Mary's College Press, 1963.
179 p. illus. 22 cm.
PLatS

Malerich, Anne, Sister, 1926–
4758   Plans for the implementation of the enrichment of ninth and tenth grade mathematics in Cathedral High School, St. Cloud, Minn.
153 p. 28 cm.
Thesis (M.S.)–University of Dayton, 1963.
Typescript.
MnStj(Archives)

4759   Whether the philosophy of mathematics as a science of formal systems refutes the Thomistic theory of first principles of human knowledge.
70 p. 28 cm.
A speculative research paper–University of Dayton, 1963.
Xeroxed.
MnStj(Archives)

4760   **Mallersdorf, Bavaria (Benedictine abbey).**
Catalogus codicum manuscriptorum Bibliothecae Regiae Monacensis: Codices n. 8121–8160 ex bibliotheca monasterii Ord.S. Benedicti in Mallersdorf. Monachii, sumptibus Bibliothecae Regiae, 1874. Unveränderter Nachdruck, Otto Harrassowitz, Wiesbaden, 1968.
MnCH

4761   **Malloy, Kristin, Sister,** 1922–
Dante and the streetcars.
(*In* A seal upon my heart, ed. by G. L. Kane. Milwaukee, 1957, p. 118–125)
MnStj(Archives)

Malone, Edward Eugene, 1904–
4762   Conception: a history of the first century of the Conception colony, 1858–1958; a history of the first century of Conception Abbey, 1873–1973; a history of New Engelberg College, Conception College, and the Immaculate Conception Seminary, 1886–1971. Omaha, Nebr., Interstate Printing Co. [1971].
223 p. illus. 30 cm. (Benedictine studies)
AStb; InStme; KAS; MnCS; MoCo; NcBe; PLatS

4763   Father Lukas Etlin, O.S.B., apostle of the Eucharist; a short biography compiled from original sources. Clyde, Mo., Benedictine Convent of Perpetual Adoration, 1961.
64 p. illus. 23 cm.
KAS; MoCo

4764   The monk and the martyr; the monk as the successor of the martyr. Washington, Catholic University of America Press, 1950.
157 p.
NcBe

4765   Of monks and men . . . Elkhorn, Nebr., The Michaeleen Press [1964?].
vi, 134 p. illus. 22 cm.
InStme; KAS; MnCS; MnStj; MoCo

4766   An offering to God and the Catholic Church; the centennial history of St. Mary's Parish, Carrollton, Missouri. Marceline, Mo., Walsworth Pub. Co., 1972.
96 p. illus.
MoCo

4767   William Dean Howells's passion for Tolstoy.
66 p. 28 cm.
Thesis (M.A.)–University of Notre Dame, 1933.
Typescript.
MoCo

4768   **Mancone, Ambrogio,** 1915–
I documenti Cassinesi del secolo X con formule in volgare. [Roma], Istituto poligrafico dello Stato [1960].
16 p. 4 facsims. 61 cm.
KAS; MnCS; PLatS

4769   **Mandabach, Priscilla, Sister.**
Suggested aids in teaching the mentally retarded child.
53 p. 28 cm.
Thesis–University of Notre Dame, 1940.
Typescript.
InFer

4770   **Mannhart, Johannes Baptist.**
Geschichtliche Darstellung der Auflösung von St. Blasien. MS. Benediktinerabtei St. Paul im Lavanttal, Austria, codex 34/6. 118 f. Folio. Saec. 18 (1797–1807).
Microfilm: MnCH proj. no. 12,594

Mannock, John, 1677–1764.
4771   The poor man's catechism; or, The Christian doctrine explained. With short admonitions. Baltimore, Kelly, Hedian & Piet, 1859.
276 p. 17 cm.
InStme

4772   . . . . with suitable admonitions. A new edition, revised and corrected. With a memoir of the author. London, C. Dolman [n.d.].
338 p. 15 cm.
InStme

4773   **Manser, Anselm,** 1876–1951.
Christkönigszüge im römischen und benediktinischen Adventgottesdienst.
(*In* Heilige Ueberlieferung. Münster, 1938. p. 124–135)
PLatS

4774   **Mansini, Guy,** 1950–
The understanding of the experience of God according to Karl Rahner and Bernard Lonergan.

ix, 143 leaves, 28 cm.
Thesis (M.A.)–Indiana University, 1976.
Typescript.
InStme

4775 **Manternach, Bonifatius.**
Sprüche der Väter, Hrsg. und übersetzt von Pater Bonifatius Manternach. Graz, Verlag Styria [1963].
258 p. illus. 20 cm.
PLatS

4776 **Manuale Casinense** (Cod. Ottob. lat. 145) [hrsg. von] Klaus Gamber, Sieghild Rehle. Regensburg, Pustet, 1977.
172 p. 22 cm.
Instme; PLatS

Manuk, Peter. *See* Mechitar of Sebaste.

Marechaux, Bernard, O.S.B. Oliv.
4777 Saint Benoit; sa vie, sa Règle, sa doctrine spirituelle. 12me éd. Paris, G. Beauchesne, 1918.
viii, 194 p.
ILSP; KAS

4778 Vita del beato Bernardo Tolomei, fondatore della Congrezatione di N. S. di Monte Oliveto dell'Ordine di S. Bendetto . . . Robigo, Istituto Padano di Arti Grafiche, 1948.
360 p. 18 cm.
PLatS

Maredsous, Belgium (Benedictine abbey).
4779 Ecole abbatiale de Maredsous: 1881–1931. [Bruges, Desclée, 1931?]
125 p. illus. 23 cm.
InStme; MnCS

4780 La Sainte Bible; version nouvelle d'après les textes originaux par les moines de Maredsous. Editions de Maredsous [1956].
xlv, 1578 p. maps, 22 cm.
InStme; KAS

4781 **Margaret Mary, Sister.**
My divine song book; the author of its song is the Holy Spirit. [Crookston, Minn., Sisters of St. Benedict, the Mount Press, 1951].
64 p. illus. 21 cm.
MnCS; MnCrM

Maria Laach, Germany (Benedictine abbey).
4782 Abt Basilius Ebel, 1896–1968. n.p., n.d.
17 p. port. 21 cm.
MnCS

4783 Maria in der Kirche; Väterwort und Gotteslob. Regensburg, Fr. Pustet [1955].
118 p. plates, 21 cm.
MnCS; NElmM

4784 Münster am See; ein Lesebuch. Herausgeber: Die Mönche der Abtei Maria Laach. Bonn, Götz Schwippert Verlag [1948].

242 p. illus. 19 cm.
InStme; NdRi

4785 P. Theodor Bogler, 1897–1968. n.p., n.d.
15 p. port. 21 cm.
MnCS

4786 Vom christlichen Sein und Leben. Maria Laach, Ars Liturgica, 1960–
v. 18 cm.
MnCS

Marian Heights Academy, Ferdinand, Ind.
4787 Marian Heights news. 1974–
InFer

4788 Pax (yearbook). 1– 1937–
InFer

4789 Stella maris, 1933–1969. Publication of Academy of the Immaculate Conception, Ferdinand, Indiana, name changed in 1970 to Marian Heights Academy.
InFer

4790 **Marianus, Thomas.**
Commentarius in summam theologiae. MS. Universität Salzburg, codex M I 280. 699 f. Quarto. Saec. 17(1622–24)
Microfilm: MnCH proj. no. 11,081

4791 **Marie Jean, Sister.**
He knows how you feel. Liguori, Mo., Liguorian Books [c 1971].
87 p. illus. 18 cm.
CaMWiSB

4792 **Marie Yvonne, Mère.**
Edouard Herrit et Dieu. [Tournai], Casterman, 1965.
141 p. 20 cm.
MnCS

Marmion, Columba, 1858–1923.
4793 [Christ dans ses mystères. Spanish]
Jesucristo en sus misterios; conferencias espirituales. [Santiago, Imprenta Chile, 1919?]
518 p. 18 cm.
MnCS

4794 [Le Christ vie de l'âme. English]
Christ the life of the soul; spiritual conferences. Translated from the French by a nun of Tyburn Convent . . . 11th ed. London, Sands & Co. [1963].
380 p. 22 cm.
KAS; PLatS

4795 [Consécration à la Trinitè. Spanish]
La Trinidad en nuestra vida espiritual . . . Version del original frances por el R. P. Agustin S. Ruiz, O.S.B. Bilbao, Coleccion "Spiritus" Desclée, 1952.
318 p. 18 cm.
MnCS

4796 The English letters of Abbot Marmion, 1858–1923. [Edited by Gisbert Ghysens,

O.S.B., and Thomas Delforge, O.S.B.].
Baltimore, Helicon Press [1962].
xvi, 228 p. 23 cm. (Benedictine studies, v. 4)

CaMWiSB; ILSP; KAS; MnCS; MoCo; PLatS; NdRi; InStme; PkShG; NcBe; MnStj; ViBris

4797   Fire of love; an anthology of Abbot Marmion's published writings on the Holy Spirit, by Charles Dollen. St. Louis, Herder [1964].
124 p. 23 cm.
KAS; MnCS; MoCo; PLatS

4798   Growth in Christ; being the second part of Christ the life of the soul. Translated from the French by a nun of Tyburn Convent. St. Louis, B. Herder Book Co. [1962].
160 p. 19 cm.
CaMWiSB; MnCS

4799   Marmion meditorials; thoughts from Abbot Marmion for each day of the ecclesiastical year, based on the Sunday Mass texts as found in books by Abbot Marmion . . . Edited by a monk of Marmion Abbey, Aurora, Ill., for the purpose of furthering the cause of beatification of the Servant of God, Dom Columba Marmion, O.S.B. [Aurora, Ill., Marmion Abbey, 1962].
65 p. 28 cm.
Multigraphed.
MnCS

4800   The mysteries of the rosary. Translated by the monks of Marmion Abbey. Aurora, Ill., Marmion Abbey [1958].
21 p. 16 cm.
KAS

4801   [Sponsa Verbi. Spanish]
Sponsa Verbi, la virgen consagrada al Señor; conferencias espirituales. Versión e introducción por Don Roberto Grau . . . 2. ed. española. [Monasterio de Montserrat, 1941].
154 p. 18 cm.
KAS

4803   The structure of God's plan; being the first part of Christ the life of the soul. Translated from the French by a nun of Tyburn Convent. St. Louis, B. Herder Book Co., [1962].
160 p. 19 cm.
KAS; MnCS; PLatS

4804   A thought a day. Edited by a monk of Marmion Abbey. St. Meinrad, Ind., Abbey Press [c1964].
95 p.
MoCo

4805   **Marmion Abbey, Aurora, Ill.**
Abbot Columba Marmion. By the monks of Marmion Abbey, Aurora, Illinois, on the centenary of [his] birth . . . Benet Lake, Wis., Our Faith Press [1958].
30 p. 12 cm.
KAS

4806   **Marmion Military Academy, Aurora, Ill.**
Marmion.   1956–   Monthly.
InFer

4807   **Marmoutier, France (Benedictine abbey).**
Cartulaire de Marmoutier pur le Vendômois, publié sous les auspices de la Société archéologique du Vendômois par M. le Trémault. Paris, A. Picard & fils, 1893.
xxxii, 509 p. illus. 25 cm.
KAS

Marot, Hilaire, 1920–
4808   The primacy and the decentralization of the early Church. Translated by Theodore L. Westow.
(*In* Historical problems of Church renewal, p. 15–28)
PLatS

4809   Unité de l'Eglise et diversité géographique aux premiers siècles.
(*In* Congar, M. J. L'episcopat et l'église universelle. Paris, 1962. p. 565–590)
PLatS

Marra, Luigi Taddeo della. *See* Della Marra, Luigi Taddeo.

4810   **Marre, Jean de,** 1436–1521.
Enchiridion sacerdotale concinnatum ad salutarem eruditionem christifidelium. [Paris, J. Badius Ascensius, 1519].
72 leaves, 20 cm.
PLatS

4811   **Marrier, Martin,** 1572–1644.
Monasterii regalis S. Martini de Campis Paris ordinis cluniacensis historia. Parisiis, apud Sebastianum Cramoisy, 1637.
[14], 576 p. illus. (engr.), 23 cm.
KAS

4812   **Marron, Vincent,** 1935–
The ecumenical development of theology.
(*In* Lash, Nicholas, ed. Doctrinal development and Christian unity. 1967. p. 63–83)
InFer; PLatS

4813   **Mars, Noël,** 1512–1602.
Histoire du royal monastère de Saint-Lomer de Blois de l'Ordre de Saint-Benoist, recueillie fidellement des vieilles chartes du mesme monastère 1646 . . . Blois, Imprimerie J. Marchand, 1869.
472 p. 27 cm.
MnCS

4814   **Marsili, Salvatore,** 1910–
The Mass, Paschal mystery and mystery of the Church.

(*In* Barauna, Guilherme, ed. The liturgy of Vatican II; a symposium. 1966. v. 2, p. 3–25)
PLatS

Martène, Edmond, 1654–1739.

4815   De antiquis ecclesiae ritibus libri tres . . . Editio novissima ab eodem auctore tertiam ultra partem aucta, et novis uberrimis indicibus locupletata. Basani Venetiis, apud Remondini, 1788.
4 v. 39 cm.
KAS

4816   Correspondance . . . avec le baron G. de Grassier . . . publiée par Léon Halkin. Bruxelles, Société Belge de Librairie, 1898.
294 p. 25 cm.
MnCS

4817   Voyage litteraire de deux religieux bénédictins de la Congregation de Saint Maur. Westmead, England, Gregg International Publishers, 1969.
2 v. illus. 27 cm.
By Edmond Martène and Ursin Durand.
Photocopy of the 1717 edition.
MnCS

4818   **Martin, abbot of St. Peter, Salzburg.**
Chronik des Abtes Martin von St. Peter in Salzburg, MS. Universitätsbibliothek Salzburg, Archivium HS A 9. 549 p. Quarto. Saec. 17(1606).
Microfilm: MnCH proj. no. 11,366

Martin, Claude, 1619–1696.

4819   Conduite pour la retraite du mois. 7. éd. Paris, chez Imbert de Bats, 1700.
130 p.
CaQStB

4820   Praxis Regulae ss. patris Benedicti. E. gallico in latinum sermonem transtulit P.M.G., O.S.B. Typis princ. Monasterii S. Blasii, 1757.
[20], 248, [4] p. 17 cm.
InStme; MoCo

4821   **Martin, Louis.**
La vie de S. Martin; 76 dessins actuels du Frère Louis de Liguge sur un texte ancien. [Paris, Club du livre chrétien, 1960].
unpaged, illus. 20 cm.
CaQStb; KAS

4822   **Martini, Galen.**
The heart's slow race; a farewell to the land. Poems and photographs. St. Cloud, Minn., North Star Press, 1976.
ix, 37 p. illus. 23 cm.
MnCS; MnStj

4823   **Martinus, monk of Melk.**
Formularius scriptus et collectus in Basilea tempore Concilii per Dominum Martinum, monachum Mellicensem. MS.

Benediktinerabtei Melk, Austria, codex 1946. 206 f. Quarto. Saec. 15.
Microfilm: MnCH proj. no. 2218

Martinus, abbot of Schottenstift, Vienna.

4824   Caeremonialia. MS. Vienna, Nationalbibliothek, codex 4970, f.8v–18v. Quarto. Saec. 15.
Microfilm: MnCH proj. no. 18,143

4825   Quodlibetarium (dialogus theologicoasceticus). MS. Benediktinerabtei St. Peter, Salzburg, codex a.VI.46, f.35v–50v. Quarto. Saec. 15.
Microfilm: MnCH proj. no. 10,119

4826   Magister Martinus olim abbas Scotorum Viennae: Senatorium per modum dialogi scriptum. MS. Benediktinerabtei Melk, Austria, codex 139, f.185r–217r. Folio. Saec. 15.
Microfilm: MnCH proj. no. 1205

4827   Senatorium, sive Dialogum historicum inter senem et juvenem. MS. Benediktinerabtei St. Peter, Salzburg, codex a.VI.46, f.1r–45v.
Microfilm: MnCH proj. no. 10,119

4828   Sermo in visitatione monasteriorum O.S.B. in provincia Salisburgensi. MS. Vienna, Nationalbibliothek, codex 4969, f.103–108v. Quarto. Saec. 15.
Microfilm: MnCH proj. no. 18,141

Marx, Michael, 1913–

4829   The altar of the Sacrifice banquet.
(*In* The challenge of the Council . . . 25th annual North American Liturgical Week, 1964. p. 155–160)
PLatS

4830   Protestants and Catholics on the spiritual life. Collegeville, Minn., The Liturgical Press [1965].
viii, 106 p. 23 cm.
Reprint from Worship magazine, Dec. 1965.
InFer; InStme; MnCS; MoCo; PLatS

Marx, Paul, 1920–

4831   Abortion international. Collegeville, Minn., The Liturgical Press, 1978.
17 p. 14 cm.
MnCS

4832   The death peddlers; war on the unborn. Collegeville, Minn., St. John's University Press [1971].
xvi, 191 p. 19 cm.
InStme; KAS; MnCS; MnStj; NcBe; MoCo; PLatS

4833   [The death peddlers. Japanese]
Printed in Japan, 1972.
274 p. 19 cm.
Title and text in Japanese. Translation of Japanese title: Unborn right.
MnCS

4834 Death without dignity: killing for mercy. Collegeville, Minn., The Liturgical Press [1975].
46 p. 18 cm.
MdRi; MnCS; MnStj

4835 Los mercaderas de la muerte; guerra a los niños por nacer. [Centro de Integración de Guatemala, 1972].
215 p. 22 cm.
Translation of: The death peddlers.
MnCS

4836 (2dary) A reader in natural family planning; report on international conferences. No. 1, second edition. Collegeville, Minn., The Human Life Center, St. John's University, 1978.
171 p. col. plates, ports., diagrs. 25 cm.
Introductory notes by Father Paul Marx, O.S.B.
Printed by Sata International Printing Co., Tokyo.
MnCS

4837 **Mary Anthony, Sister.**
Christian life in the mystery of the Church.
(*In* Society of Catholic College Teachers of Sacred Doctrine. Proceedings of 9th annual convention, 1963. p. 53–77)
PLatS

4838 **Mason, Mary Elizabeth, Sister.**
Active life and contemplative life; a study of the concepts from Plato to the present. Milwaukee, Marquette University Press, 1961.
xi, 137 p. 23 cm.
InStme; KAS; MnCS; MoCo; MnStj; PLatS

4839 **Massot i Muntaner, Josep,** 1941–
(ed) Albareda, Anselmo. Historia de Montserrat. 6. ed., revisada i ampliada per Josep Massot i Muntaner. Publicacions de l'Abadia de Montserrat, 1977.
331 p. 24 cm.
MnCS

Mathäser, Willibald, 1901–1978.
4840 Erzabt Wimmer im Spiegel seiner Briefe.
(*In* Studien und Mitteilungen zur Geschichte des Benediktiner-Ordens. 60. Jahrgang, 1946, p. 234–302)
PLatS

4841 König Ludwig I von Bayern und die Gründung der ersten bayerischen Benediktinerabtei in Amerika.
(*In* Studien und Mitteilungen zur Geschichte des Benediktiner-Ordens, Bd. 43(1925), p. 123–182)
PLatS

4842 (ed) Friesenegger, Maurus. Tagebuch aus dem 30jährigen Krieg. Nach einer Handschrift im Kloster Andechs mit Vorwort, Anmerkungen und Register hrsg. von P. Willibald Mathäser. [München], Süddeutscher Verlag [1974].
MnCS

4843 (ed) Lemcke, Peter Henry. Haudegen Gottes . . . Kommentiert u. hrsg. von Willibald Mathäser. Würzburg, Echter-Verlag [in Kommission], 1971.
305 p. 21 cm.
InStme; KAS; PLatS

4844 **Mathou, Hugues,** 1622–1705.
De vera Sernonum origine christiana, adversus Johannis de Launoy . . . criticae observationes &c. dissertatio . . . Parisiis, apus Simonem Langronne, 1687.
373, 276 p. 25 cm.
MnCS

4845 **Matoso, José.**
L'Abbaye de Pendorada des origines à 1160. Coimbra, 1962.
xv, 194 p. maps, 25 cm.
InStme

4846 **Mattei-Cerasoli, Leone,** 1880–1949.
Codices Gavensis. [Arpino, Società Tipografica Arpinate] 1935–
v. 30 cm.
MnCS

4847 **Mattingly, Basil,** 1921–
(ed) Thomas Aquinas, Saint. De principiis naturae of St. Thomas Aquinas; critical edition [edited by] Basil Mattingly, O.S.B.
125, 46, 179 p. 28 cm.
Thesis – University of Notre Dame, 1957.
Typescript.
InStme

4848 **Maur Hill School, Atchison, Kans., Alumni.**
[Lenten meditations. Atchison, Kans., 1962?]
40 p. 18 cm.
"Maur Hill alumni priests were asked to write a meditation . . ."–p. 1.
Mimeographed.
KAS

4849 **Maurer, Helen, Sister.**
Independent arias of Antonio Vivaldi in FOA 28.
263 p. illus.
Thesis (Ph.D.)–Indiana University.
InFer

4850 **Maurer, Mary Damian, Sister.**
Basic guide to a well balanced diet. Ferdinand, Ind.
53, xxxiii p.
Mimeographed.
InFer

Maus, Mary Gertrude, Sister, 1902–
4851   A critical study of the poetry in Spirit,
1934–1943.
iii, 78 p. 29 cm.
Thesis (M.A.)–Marquette University,
1943.
MnStj

4852   Mary, our Mother.
32 p. 28 cm.
Thesis (M.A.)–Benedictine Institute of
Sacred Theology, Collegeville, Minn.,
1963.
Typescript.
MnStj(Archives)

4853   **Maus, Scholastica, Sister.**
A study of the effect of instruction in
library science on eighth grade students.
161 p. graphs, figures, tables, 29 cm.
Thesis (M.A.)–College of St. Thomas,
St. Paul, Minn., 1959.
Typescript.
MnSSP

4854   **Mayer, Augustinus,** 1911–
Das Gottesbild im Menschen nach
Clemens von Alexandrien. Roma, Herder,
1942.
viii, 99 p. 25 cm. (Studia Anselmiana, 15)
InStme

4855   **Mayer, Heinrich Suso,** 1890–
Beuroner Bibliographie; Schriftsteller
und Künstler während der ersten hundert
Jahre des Benediktinerklosters Beuron,
1863–1963. Beuron, Hohenzollern, 1963.
196 p. 23 cm.
KAM; KAS; MnCS; NdRi; PkShG;
PLatS

4856   **Mayr, Beda,** 1742–1794.
Predigten über den Catechismus für das
Landvolk auf alle Sonn- und Festtage des
Jahres. Augsburg, Matthäus Rieger, 1777.
2 v. 19 cm.
MnCS

4857   **Mayr, Theodor Johann,** 1886–
Studien zu dem Paschale Carmen des
christlichen Dichters Sedulius. Augsburg,
Ph. J. Pfeiffer, 1916.
96 p. 20 cm.
Inaug.-Diss.–München.
MnCS

Mayr, Werigand, 1901–
4858   Benediktinerabtei Michaelbeuern bei
Salzburg. München, Schneel & Steiner,
1958.
15 p. illus. 17 cm.
PLatS

4859   Catalogus manuscriptorum qui in Bibliotheca monasterii Burae ad S. Michaelem
asservantur. 1950.
unpaged, 22 cm.

Xeroxed by University Microfilms, Ann
Arbor, Mich., 1968.
MnCS

4860   **Mysterle, Sigismundus.**
Historia civitatis Augustensis. Chronik
der Augspurger. MS. Benediktinerabtei
St. Paul im Lavanttal, Austria, codex
158/4. 189 f. Saec. 15(1437).
Microfilm: MnCH proj. no. 12,403

4861   **Meagher, Luanne, Sister,** 1901–
Beginning anew–St. Paul's Priory,
1948–1973. [St. Paul, North Central Publishing Co., 1973].
12 p. illus. 23 cm.
MnCS; MnStj(Archives)

Mechitar, of Sebaste, 1676–1749.
4862   Auslese von den Worten, Lehren und
Erklärungen der Heiligen Schrift, auch
von den Werken des Abtes Mechithar. MS.
Vienna, Mechitaristenkongregation, codex
1187. 27 f. & 319 p. Octavo. Saec. 19.
Text in Armenian.
Microfilm: MnCH proj. no. 8714

4863   Einleitung zur Redekunst Mechithar von
Sebaste. MS. Vienna, Mechitaristenkon-
gregation, codex 1204. 144 p. Octavo.
Saec. 18(1769).
Microfilm: MnCH proj. no. 8712

4864   Hymnen. MS. Vienna, Mechitaristenkongregation, codex 1228. 60 f. Octavo. Saec.
19.
Microfilm: MnCH proj. no. 8733

4865   Rhetorik. MS. Vienna, Mechitaristen-
kongregation, codex 748. 81 f. Quarto.
Saec. 18.
Microfilm: MnCH proj. no. 8321

4866   Theologie (Dogmatik, Zusammensetzung
aus seinen Vorlesungen). MS. Vienna,
Mechitaristenkongregation, codex 728.
742 f. Quarto. Saec. 19(1836).
Microfilm: MnCH proj. no. 8287

4867   Uebung des frommen Lebens. Armenian. MS. Vienna, Mechitaristenkongregation, codex 1212, p. 76–159. Octavo. Saec.
18(1793).
Microfilm: MnCH proj. no. 8723

Mechtild of Magdeburg, ca. 1212–
ca. 1282.
4868   Liber specialis gratiae. MS. Universitätsbibliothek Graz, Austria, codex 1082, f.2r–
86v. Quarto. Saec. 14.
Microfilm: MnCH proj. no. 27,093

4869   Liber spiritualis gratiae (excerptae). MS.
Benediktinerabtei St. Peter, Salzburg,
codex b.V.18, f.183r–225v. Quarto. Saec.
15.
Microfilm: MnCH proj. no. 10,449

Mechtilde, Saint, 1241-1299.
4870 Liber gratiae spiritualis visionum et revelationum beatae Mechtildis virginis devotissimae, ad fidelium instructionem. Venetiis, 1558.
163 leaves. 16 cm.
KAS

4871 Preces Gertrudianae; sive, Vera et sincera medulla precum potissimum ex Revelationibus bb. Gertrudis et Mechtildis excerptarum. Editio nova, accurate recognita et emendata a monacho Ordinis S. Benedicti Congregationis Beuronis. Friburgi Brisg., Herder, 1903.
xviii, 275 p. 15 cm.
PLatS

4872 Prières dites de Sainte Gertrude, ou Vrai esprit des prières qui Jésus-Christ lui-même a révélées, pour la plupart à saint Gertrude et à sainte Mechtilde . . . Traduites par le R.P.A. Denis de la Compagnie de Jesus . . . 3. êd. Paris, H. Casterman, 1858.
444 p. 13 cm.
MnCS

4873 Revelationes, cum indice praecedente et tabula alphabetica rerum subjuncta. MS. Vienna, Nationalbibliothek, codex 4224, f.2r-82v. Folio. Saec. 15.
Microfilm: MnCH proj. no. 17,388

4874 The true prayers of St. Gertrude and St. Mechtilde. Translated by the Rev. John Gray. [2d ed.]. London, Sheed & Ward [1928].
141 p. 18 cm.
InStme

4875 Visiones venerabilie Mechtildis. MS. Vienna, Nationalbibliothek, codex 12,865. 180 f. Octavo. Saec. 15.
Microfilm: MnCH proj. no. 25,218

4876 Vita sanctae Mechtildis, seu Visiones ejusdem et intitulatur Liber spiritualis gratiae. MS. Vienna, Nationalbibliothek, codex 13795, f.2r-77v. Quarto. Saec. 15(1451).
Microfilm: MnCH proj. no. 20,141

4877 **Mechtilde de Saint-Sacrement, Mère,** 1614-1698.
Lettres inédites. Rouen, Bénédictines du Saint-Sacrement, 1976.
428 p. illus. 22 cm.
MnCS

Meer de Walcheren, Petrus Balthazar Albertus van der, 1880-
4878 Journal d'un converti. Traduit du néerlandais par l'auteur. Introduction de Lêon Bloy. [Bruges], Desclée, De Brouwer [1962].
265 p. 20 cm.
KySu; PLatS

4879 Recontres: Léon Bloy, Raïssa Maritain, Christine et Pieterke. Traduit de néerlandais par dom Walter Willems, O.S.B. [Bruges], Desclée, De Brouwer [1961].
180 p. ports. 20 cm.
Translation of: Allis is liefde.
PLatS

4880 **Maginhardus, of Fulda,** d. 888.
Translatio s. Alexandri auctoribus Ruodolfo et Meginharto.
(*In* Monumenta Germaniae historica. Scriptores. Stuttgart, 1963. t. 2, p. 673-681)
MnCS; PLatS

4881 **Mehlmann, Johann Evangelist,** 1914-
Der "Name" Gottes im Alten Testament. Rom, Pontificium Athenaeum Anselmianum, 1956.
108 p. 25 cm.
Thesis – Pontificium Athenaeum S. Anselmi de Urbe.
KAS

Meier, Gabriel, 1845-1924.
4882 Catalogus codicum manu scriptorum qui in bibliotheca monasterii Einsidlensis O.S.B. servantur. Einsidlae, sumptibus Monasterii, 1899-
v. 28 cm.
NdRi; PLatS; MnCH

4883 Heinrich von Ligerz, Bibliothekar von Einsiedeln im 14. Jahrhundert. Leipzig, Harrassowitz, 1968.
68 p. 24 cm. (Zentralblatt für Bibliothekswesen. Beiheft 17)
PLatS

4884 **Meinberg, Cloud Herman,** 1914-
An outline history of sacred art. Collegeville, Minn., The University Press [1959].
260 p. illus. 28 cm.
Mimeographed.
MnCS

4885 **Meinrad, Saint. Legend.**
Das Blockbuch von Sankt Meinrad und seinen Mördern und vom Ursprung von Einsiedeln; farbige Faksimile-Ausgabe zum elften Zentenar des Heiligen, 861-1961. Mit einer Einleitung von Leo Helbling. Einsiedeln, Benziger Verlag, 1961.
35, [64] p. col. illus. 19 cm.
Facsimile of the Einsiedeln manuscript.
Issued in portfolio.
InStme; MnCS; PLatS

Melk, Austria (Benedictine abbey).
4886 Acta electionis abbatis Mellicensis 1480. Bulla confirmationis anni jubilaei . . . 1474. MS. Benediktinerabtei Melk,

Austria, codex 131, f.362v–368r. Folio. Saec. 15.
Microfilm: MnCH proj. no. 1197

4887　Annales Mellicenses, Cremifanenses et Lamacenses annorum 1177–1348 complectens. MS. Vienna, Nationalbibliothek, codex 373, f.1r–7v. Folio. Saec. 12–14.
Microfilm: MnCH proj. no. 13,704

4888　Annales Mellicenses, 1075–1308. MS. Vienna, Nationalbibliothek, codex 352, f.39v–65v, 72v. Folio. Saec. 13.
Microfilm: MnCH proj. no. 13,683

4889　Annales Mellicenses, cum continuatione Claustroneoburgensi et Sancrucensi, quarum ultima usque ad annum 1310 pertinet. MS. Vienna, Nationalbibliothek, codex 539, f.34v–105v. Quarto. Saec. 12 et 14.
Microfilm: MnCH proj. no. 13,866

4890　Annales Mellicenses, cum continuatione Claustroneoburgensi et Sancrucensi. MS. Vienna, Nationalbibliothek, codex 5382, f.26v–70r. Folio. Saec. 15.
Microfilm: MnCH proj. no. 18,550

4891　Breviarium caeremoniarium monasterii Mellicensis. MS. Benediktinerabtei Fiecht, Austria, codex 184. Quarto. Saec. 15.
Microfilm: MnCH proj. no. 28,828

4892　Brevis historia reformationis monasterii Mellicensis, anno 1418 factae. MS. Benediktinerabtei Melk, Austria, codex 46, f.318–323. Folio. Saec. 15.
Microfilm: MnCH proj. no. 1149

4893　Catalogus religiosorum Ordinis S. P. Benedicti in monasterio Mellicensi viventium . . .
v. 23 cm.
MnCS; PLatS

4894　Copia litterae compromissariorum, ad Dominum Legatum missa, in causa confirmationis Domini Ludovici abbatis electi Mellicensis 1474. Copia litterae Prioris ac Conventus Mellicensis . . . 1474. Copia litterae missae ad Imperialem Majestatem in facto electionis 1474 . . . MS. Benediktinerabtei Melk, Austria, codex 131, f.237v–239v. Folio. Saec. 15.
Microfilm: MnCH proj. no. 1197

4895　Epistolae abbatum (Mellicensis, Lambacensis, etc.) et episcoporum, formae, intimationes, resolutiones, supplicationes, commendationes, petitiones monasticae. MS. Benediktinerabtei Melk, Austria, codex 778, f.48v–305v. Quarto. Saec. 15.
Microfilm: MnCH proj. no. 1618

4896　Festa abbatis, prioris, et hebdomadarii, quibus annexa sunt Agenda pro defunctis, in monasterio Mellicensi. MS. Benedik-

tinerabtei Seitenstetten, Austria, codex 88, f.200r–209v. Octavo. Saec. 15.
Microfilm: MnCH proj. no. 897

4897　Flores chronicarum Austriacarum. Descriptum anno 1613 in monasterio Mellicensi. MS. Benediktinerabtei Melk, Austria, codex 1842, p. 319–380. Duodecimo. Saec. 16.
Microfilm: MnCH proj. no. 2152

4898　Legenda seu memoriale scriptum de portione ligni salutiferae crucis, quae in praesenti nostro Mellicensi monasterio sub laminis aureis habetur. Littera Rudolphi quarti de hac sancta cruce. MS. Benediktinerabtei Melk, Austria, codex 1398, f.225v–236v. Duodecimo. Saec. 15.
Microfilm: MnCH proj. no. 1920

4899　Prologus in breviarium caeremoniarum Mellicensium ducatus Austriae. MS. Benediktinerabtei Fiecht, Austria, codex 60. 101 f. Folio. Saec. 15.
Microfilm: MnCH proj. no. 28,833

4900　Quaedam excerpta ex memorialibus monasterii Mellicensis circa 1418. MS. Benediktinerabtei Melk, Austria, codex 1842, p. 243–292 (p. 293–302 vacant. p. 304–315: Index rerum). Duodecimo. Saec. 16.
Microfilm: MnCH proj. no. 2152

4901　Statuta Domini Ludovici abbatis Mellicensis et Seniorum. Ioannis abbatis Mellicensis Statuta de fratribus conversis. Ordinatio domini abbatis Leonardi pro fratribus conversis in lotione vestium servanda. MS. Benediktinerabtei Seitenstetten, Austria, codex 88, f.232r–236r. Octavo. Saec. 15.
Microfilm: MnCH proj. no. 897

4902　Statuta Mellicensia: Nic. de Mazzen coeremonias regularis observantiae monachis Mellicensibus anno 1418 datae. MS. Benediktinerabtei Seitenstetten, Austria, codex 94, f.14–200v. Duodecimo. Saec. 15.
Microfilm: MnCH proj. no. 905

4903　Statuta monasterii Mellicensis. MS. Benediktinerabtei Altenburg, Austria, codex AB 13 B 9, f.1r–97v. Quarto. Saec. 17.
Microfilm: MnCH proj. no. 6498

4904　Statuta Mellicensia. MS. Benediktinerabtei Melk, Austria, codex 1252. 119 f. Quarto. Saec. 17(1617).
Microfilm: MnCH proj. no. 1888

4905　Statuta Mellicensia. MS. Benediktinerabtei Melk, Austria, codex 1253. 106 f. Quarto. Saec. 17(1604).
Microfilm: MnCH proj. no. 1889

Melk, Austria (Benedictine abbey). Bibliothek.

4906 Aeltester Bibliothekskatalog (15. Jahrhundert). MS. Benediktinerabtei Melk, Austria, codex 1898. 2 vols. Folio. Saec. 15.
Microfilm: MnCH proj. no. 2222

4907 Catalogus codicum manu scriptorum qui in bibliotheca Monasterii Mellicensis O.S.B. servantur. In memoriam anni ab introductis in hoc monasterium Benedictinis octingentesimi a Monasterio Mellicensi editus. Vindobonae, Alfredus Hoelder, 1889.
3 vols. 6 suppl. 21 & 27 cm.
Facisimile of manuscripts.
MnCS

4908 Catalogus librorum bibliothecae Mellicensis, per Sigismundum Haeringshauser. Hic catalogus renovatus est iussu Reverendissimi Dmi Gaspari abbatis Mellicensis, anno 1605. Continet circa 2000 opera sub litteris A-N (classification symbols). MS. Benediktinerabtei Melk, Austria, codex 1629. 3 vols.(82, 58, 54 f.). Quarto. Saec. 17.
Microfilm: MnCH proj. no. 2003, 2005, 2006

4909 Codices manuscripti Bibliothecae Mellicensis. Collegit Frater Stephanus Burckhardus anno Domini 1517.
3 vols. 28 cm.
Handwritten.
Xeroxed by University Microfilms, Ann Arbor, Mich., 1972.
Contents: v. 1, Shelflist (arranged by classification letters) lists the full contents of the collection; v. 2, Subject part, alphabetical; v. 3, Author part, alphabetical.
MnCH

4910 A fifteenth-century modus scribendi from the Abbey of Melk, Cambridge [England], Printed at the University Press, 1940.
xxiv, 31 p. 23 cm.
MnCS

4911 Ichonographia de bene ordinanda ornandaque bibliotheca Mellicensi ac praecipue de conficiendo duplici catalogo . . . 1751. MS. Benediktinerabtei Melk, Austria, codex 1906. 15 f. Quarto. Saec. 18.
Microfilm: MnCH proj. no. 2223

4912 Registrum omnium librorum Biblothecae Mellicensis, et quidem triplex: primo opera auctorum quorum nomina inotuerunt, secundo materiae quarum authores ignorantur, tertio singulorum voluminum (shelflist). MS. Benediktinerabtei Melk, Austria, codex 874. 227 f. Quarto. Saec. 15(1483).
Microfilm: MnCH proj. no. 1692

4913 Ordinatio librorum Bibliothecae Mellicensis anno 1483 facta. MS. Benediktinerabtei Melk, Austria, codex 1075, f.2-93. Duodecimo. Saec. 15.
Microfilm: MnCH proj. no. 1833

4914 **Melk, Austria (Benedictine abbey). Gymnasium.**
[Brochure. No title]
Eigentümer, Herausgeber und Verleger: Konvikt des Stiftes Melk am öffentlichen Stiftsgymnasium. Verantwortlicher Schriftleiter: Johannes Schüttengruber, O.S.B. n.p. n.d. [ca. 1964].
16 p. illus (part col.) plans, 21 x 23 cm.
MnCS

Melnar, Joannes.

4915 Collectanea quorundam generum carminum usitatiorum ex diversis autoribus. MS. Benediktinerabtei St. Peter, Salzburg, codex b.VI.40, f.271r–299r. Quarto. Saec. 17.
Microfilm: MnCH proj. no. 10,506

4916 Promptuarium animae, in quo continentur variae praecationes in dies singulos. MS. Benediktinerabtei St. Peter, Salzburg, codex b.I.40. 276 f. Duodecimo. Saec. 17(1612).
Microfilm: MnCH proj. no. 10,362

4917 Technopaenion (introductio in grammaticum, poeticam, musicam artem) 1613. MS. Benediktinerabtei St. Peter, Salzburg, codex b.VI.40, f.1r–252r. Quarto. Saec. 17.
Microfilm: MnCH proj. no. 10,506

4918 **Memoriale visitationis Mellicensis anno 1451 institutus.** MS. Benediktinerabtei Seitenstetten, Austria, codex 88, f.210r–231v. Octavo. Saec. 15.
Microfilm: MnCH proj. no. 897

4919 **Menardus monachus.**
Compendiosa Sacrae Scripturae notitia. MS. Benediktinerabtei Kremsmünster, Austria, codex 50, f.270r–275r. Saec. 15.
Microfilm: MnCH proj. no. 50

Mengwasser, Herman Peter, 1885–1936.

4920 Argumenta latino sermone scripta iuvenibus nostris litterarum studiosis ad imitandum proposita. Lisle, Illinois, ex Typographia Abbatiae S. Procopii [1925].
31 p. 20 cm.
FStL; KAS; KySu

4921 Commentarius in oden primam Quinti Horatii Flacci ad Maecenatem complectens paraphrasim quum brevem tum uberiorem, adornatus adnotationibus grammaticis, etymologicis, historicis, geographicis,

mythologicis. Atchison, Kans., ex Typographia Collegii S. Benedicti [1921].
14 p. 21 cm.
KAS

4922 Commentarius in satiram primam Quinti Horatii Flacci complectens paraphrasim brevem, adornatus adnotationibus grammaticis, etymologicis, historicis, geographicis. [Atchison, Kans., St. Benedict Abbey] 1921.
28 p. 21 cm.
PLatS

4923 **Menzel, Beda Franz,** 1904–
Abt Franz Stephan Rautenstrauch von Brevnov-Braunau: Herkunft, Umwelt und Wirkungskreis. Königstein/Ts., Königsteiner Institut für Kirchen- und Geistesgeschichte der Sudetenländer, 1969.
284 p. illus. 24 cm.
KAS; MnCS; MoCo; NcBe

Mercier, Gérard, 1912–
4924 La liturgie, culte de l'Eglise: sa nature, son excellence, ses principes fondamentaux, ses éléments constitutifs. Mulhouse, Salvator, 1961.
347 p. 19 cm.
MnCS

4925 Le testament des novices; les prescriptions du droit canonique et les formalites du droit civil. Romae, Officium Libri Catholici, 1963.
xviii, 207 p. 25 cm.
PLatS

4926 **Mercier, James,** 1864–1935.
Short spiritual treatises on some fundamental truths. Written for the Sisters of St. Gertrude's Community, Cottonwood, Idaho. n.p., 1927 (1917).
138, 187 p. 23 cm.
MnCS

4927 **Merendino, Pius,** 1931–
Paschale sacramentum; eine Untersuchung über die Osterkatechese des hl. Athanasius von Alexandrien in ihrer Beziehung zu den frühchristlichen exegetisch-theologischen Ueberlieferungen. Münster in Westf., Aschendorff, [1965].
xv, 94 p. 26 cm.

4928 **Merki, Hubert,** 1913–
Vox patrum; lateinische Texte christlicher Väter, ausgewählt von Hubert Merki und Oskar Wyss. [Einsiedeln], Benziger Verlag [1960].
149 p. 20 cm.
MnCS; PLatS

4929 **Merkle, Coelestin,** 1927–
Das hundertste Jahr; zur Hundertjahrfeier der Benediktiner in Beuron,

1963. Hrsg. von P. Coelestin Merkle. [Beuron], Beuroner Kunstverlag [1962].
159 p. illus., plates, ports. 20 x 21 cm.
MnCS; PLatS

4930 **Mershman, Francis,** 1852–1916.
Notes for dogmatic theology, compiled by P. Francis, O.S.B. [Collegeville, Minn., St. John's Abbey, 1894?].
152 p. 20 cm.
MnCS(Archives)

4931 **Meske, Jutta.**
Die sieben Worte Marias. [Würzburg, Arena-Verlag] 1963.
141 p.
MnStj

4932 **Metellus, of Tegernsee,** fl. 1160.
Die Quirinalien des Metellus von Tegernsee; Untersuchungen zur Dichtkunst und kritische Textausgabe, von Peter Christian Jacobsen. Leiden, E. J. Brill, 1965.
416 p. 25 cm. (Mittellateinische Studien und Texte, Bd. 1)
MnCS

Metten, Bavaria (Benedictine abbey).
4933 Annales Mettenses (a.687–930).
(*In* Monumenta Germaniae historica. Scriptores. Stuttgart, 1963. t. 4, p. 314–336)
PLatS

4934 Catalogus codicum manu scriptorum Bibliothecae Regiae Monacensis: Codices 8201–8258 ex monasterio Ord. S. Benedicti in Metten. Monachii, sumptibus Bibliothecae Regiae, 1874. Unveränderter Nachdruck, Otto Harrassowitz, Wiesbaden, 1968.
MnCH

4935 Proprium Mettense, sive Supplementum Breviarii Benedictino-monastici pro choro Mettenensi, editum auctoritate . . . Gregorii I., abbatis Monasterii Metten. Landishuti, typis Jos. Thomann, 1856.
240 p. 19 cm.
MnCS

4936 **Metz, France. Saint-Vincent (Benedictine abbey).**
(*In* Monumenta Germaniae historica. Scriptores. Stuttgart, 1963. t. 3, p. 155–160)
MnCS; PLatS

4937 **Metzger, Paul.**
Mercurius logicus; seu, Relationes novissimae de dictis & gestis in orbe intellectuali, expositae luci ac certamini publico . . . sub praesidio P. Pauli Metzger . . . stabit Odilo Recher . . . Viennae, typis Joannis Jacobi Kuerner, 1671.
82 p. 13 cm.
PLatS

4938 **Metzger, Witmar,** 1930–
Der Organongedanke in der Christologie
der griechischen Kirchenväter; seine
Herkunft aus der griechischen Philosophie
und seine Bedeutung bei den Vätern bis
Eusebius von Cäsarea. Münsterschwar-
zach [Vier-Türme-Verlag] 1968.
xxiv, 258 p. 23 cm.
Diss.–Pont. Athenaeum S. Anselmi,
Roma.
InStme

4939 **Metzinger, Adalbert,** 1910–
(ed) Höpfl, Hildebrand. Introductio
specialis in Novum Testamentum. Editio
sexta quam curavit Adalbertus Metzinger.
Neapoli, Romae, 1962.
xxvii, 581 p.
ILSP

4940 **Mexico (City). Colegio de Tepeyac.**
Labor (yearbook). 1960–
v. illus., ports. 29 cm.
MnCS

Meyenschein, Benedikt.
4941 Stella Benedictina; sive, Regula sanctissimi patris nostri Benedicti, in gratiam
tyronum religiosorum breviore commentario illustrata. Hildesii, typis Wilh.
Theodori Schlegel, 1725.
[12], 296 p. 14 cm.
KAS

4942 Stella Benedictina quinque radii corusca:
quorum primus exhibet Regulam . . .
Benedicti cum breviore commentario; alte
vitam ejusdem . . . ; tertius diurnum
monasticum; quartus exercitia heb-
domadalia; quintus menstrua & annua & c.
Hildesii, typis Wilh. Theod. Schlegel
[1729].
755, [10] p. 14 cm.
KAS

4943 **Meyer, Benedict.**
(tr & ed) Clichtove, Josse van. Libellus de
laude monasticae religionis. The text
translated with an introduction and notes
by Rev. Benedict Meyer, O.S.B.
xxxiii, 113 leaves, 28 cm.
Thesis–Catholic University of America,
1957.
InStme

Meyer, Boniface, 1934–
4944 Monastic themes in ancient Eastern
religions.
(*In* Monastic studies, v. 3, p. 197–220)
PLatS

4945 Presbyterian worship–an American
recovery.
(*In* Yearbook of liturgical studies, v.
6(1965), p. 97–115)
PLatS

4946 **Meyerpeter, Raymond Joseph,** 1892–
The Messias of Klopstock's epic.
107 p. 28 cm.
Thesis (M.A.)–Washington University,
St. Louis, Mo., 1937.
Typescript.
MoCo

4947 **Meyers, Cyrilla, Sister.**
Chopin: pianist and composer.
46 p.
Thesis–University of Notre Dame, 1923.
Typescript.
InFer

Meyvaert, Paul, 1921–
4948 Autour de Léon d'Ostie et de sa "Translatio S. Clementis."
Reprint from Analecta Bollandiana,
t. 74(1956), p. 189–240.
PLatS

4949 Bede and Gregory the Great. [Printed by
J. & P. Bealls, Newcastle upon Tyne,
1964].
26 p. 22 cm.
PLatS

4950 Trois énigmes cyrillo-méthodiennes de la
"Légende italique" résolues grâce à un
document inédit.
Reprint from Analaecta Bollandiana,
t. 73–(1955), p. 375–461.
PLatS

4951 **Mezger, Franz,** 1632–1701.
Exercitatorium religiosae perfectionis,
sive Exercitia spiritualia iis maxime ac-
comodata qui e tyrocinio ad s. profes-
sionem in religione sancti patris nostri
Benedicti aspirant. MS. Benediktinerabtei
St. Peter, Salzburg, codex b.II.32. 200 f.
Octavo. Saec. 17.
Microfilm: MnCH proj. no. 10,341

4952 **Mezger, Paul,** 1637–1702.
Specula Marianae devotionis, sive
Sacrae allocutiones de mediis Marianae
pietatis . . . Salisburgi, Joan. Bapt. Mayr,
1677.
[8], 331, [19] p. 16 cm.
KAS

4953 **Mezler, Thomas.**
Manuale practicum novitiorum Zwifal-
tensium. MS. Benediktinerabtei St. Paul
im Lavanttal, Austria, codex 65/6. 187 f.
Octavo. Saec. 17(1646).
Microfilm: MnCH proj. no. 12,609

**Michaelbeuern, Austria (Benedictine
abbey).**
4954 Catalogus manuscriptorum qui in Bibliotheca monasterii Burae ad S. Michaelem
asservantur. P. Werigand Mayr, O.S.B.,
1950.
unpaged, 22 cm.

Xeroxed by University Microfilms, Ann Arbor, Mich., 1968.
MnCH

4955   Rotula anno 1526. Unter Abt Wolfgang von Michaelbeuren (1518–1531). MS. Benediktinerabtei Michaelbeuren, Austria, codex perg. 14.
Microfilm: MnCH proj. no. 11,613.

4956   **Michaelfeld, Germany (Benedictine abbey).**
Tyrocinium pro novitiis. MS. Benediktinerabtei Fiecht, Austria, codex 126A. 4 copies (105, 158, 181, 193 f.). Quarto. Saec. 18.
Microfilm: MnCH proj. no. 28,824

4957   **Michel, Bede Eugene,** 1909–
Studies as the dehydration of aromatic amino alcohols.
18 p. 21 cm.
Abstract of thesis (Ph.D.)–University of Notre Dame, 1939.
MnCS (Archives)

Michel, Virgil George, 1890–1938.
4958   Liturgical index . . . arranged–as here –by Sister Jane Marie, O.P., Marywood, Grand Rapids, Mich. n.p., n.d.
82 p. 27 cm.
Typescript.
MnCS

4959   Philosophy of human conduct; a study of ethics on the basis of theism. Minneapolis, Minn., Burgess Pub. Co., c 1936.
138 leaves, 28 cm.
Mimeoprinted.
KAS; MnCS

4960   Purpose and duty of ownership according to Thomas Aquinas. St. Louis, Central Bureau, 1936.
18 p. 17 cm.
KAS; MnCS

Michels, Aloysius, 1913–
4961   Political principles of John Dryden.
50 leaves, 28 cm.
Thesis (M.A.)–University of Minnesota, 1942.
Typescript.
MnCS(Archives)

4962   **Michels, Charitas, Sister.**
Rückblick und Ausschau (1920–1962). Freiburg-Günterstal, St. Lioba, 1962.
23 p. 21 cm.
"Fastenkonferenz 1962–Priorin Charitas Michels"
MnCS

Michels, Thomas Aquinas, 1892–
4963   Aevum christianum; Salzburger Beiträge zur Religions- und Geistesgeschichte des Abendlandes. Unter Mit-

wirkung von P. Beda Thum hrsg. von P. Thomas Michels. Münster, Aschendorff.
This is a monograph series.
v. 21 cm.
MnCS

4964   Laudatio, gehalten zur Feier des 80. Geburtstages von Albert Servaes im Grossratssaal zu Luzern am 20. April 1963. n.p., n.d.
8 p. 23 cm.
MnCS

4965   Heuresis; Festschrift für Andreas Rohracher, 25 Jahre Erzbischof von Salzburg. Hrsg. von Thomas Michels. Salzburg, Otto Müller Verlag [1969].
362 p. 24 cm.
MnCS

4966   Sarmenta: gesammelte Studien von Thomas Michels. Anlässlich seines 80. Geburtstages hrsg. von Norbert Brox u. Ansgar Pau, O.S.B. Münster i.W., Aschendorff [1972].
xiii, 241 p. illus. 25 cm.
English, French, German or Latin.
Includes a bibliography of the author's works, p. vii–xiii.
InStme

4967   **Middendorf, Ann, Sister.**
A critical analysis of the facilities in northern Kentucky for the mentally retarded.
Thesis–Cardinal Strich College, Milwaukee.
KyCovS

4968   **Millénaire monastique du Mont Saint-Michel . . .** mélanges commémoratifs. Paris, P. Lethielleux, 1966–
NcBe (vols. 1 & 2)

Miller, Athanasius, 1881–1963.
4969   Das Buch Judith. Uebersetzt und erlkärt von Athanasius Miller, O.S.B. Bonn, P. Hanstein, 1940.
viii, 124 p. 25 cm.
PLatS

4970   Das Buch Tobias. Uebersetzt und erlkärt von Athanasius Miller, O.S.B. Bonn, P. Hanstein, 1940.
xi, 116 p. 25 cm.
PLatS

4971   Miscellanea biblica et orientalia. Romae, Herder, 1951.
511 p. (Studia Anselmiana)
MoCo

4972   The Psalms; an introduction to their history, spirit and liturgical use.
125 p. 28 cm.
Translation of 5th–8th German edition of 1924.
Typescript.
MoCo; OrMta

4973 I Salmi; introduzione alla loro storia, spirito ed uso liturgico. Unica versione autorizzate dal tedesco di una Clarissa del monastero di Fiesole. Torino, Società editrice internazionale [1924].
237 p. 21 cm.
KAS; PLatS

Millstatt, Austria (Benedictine abbey).
4974 Archivregister. MS. Klagenfurt, Austria, Kärntner Landesarchiv, codex GV 2/36. 307 p. Folio. Saec. 17.
Microfilm: MnCH proj. no. 12,753

4975 Chronik von Millstatt, 772–1776 (latine). Summa residii parochialium ecclesiarum et filialium Millestadii. MS. Klagenfurt, Austria, Kärntner Landesarchiv, codex GV 10/24. 14 f. Quarto. Saec. 18.
Microfilm: MnCH proj. no. 12,871

4976 Diplomatarium monasterii Milstatensis in Carinthia a 12. usque ad 16. saeculum. MS. Vienna, Nationalbibliothek, codex 14177. 474 f. Folio. Saec. 15–17.
Microfilm: MnCH proj. no. 20,195

4977 Etlicher der Stift Millstatt zu corporierten Kyrchen und pfarn in Kärnten Einkommen. MS. Klagenfurt, Austria, Kärntner Landesarchiv, Allgemeine Handschriftensammlung 2280. 135 f.
Microfilm: MnCH proj. no. 12,916

4978 Millstätter Genesis und Physiologus Handschrift. Vollständige Facsimileausgabe der Sammelhandschrift 6/19 des Geschichtsvereines für Kärnten im Kärntner Landesarchiv, Klagenfurt. Einführung und Kodikologische Beschreibung von A. Kracher. Graz, Akademische Druck- u. Verlagsanstalt, 1967.
167 leaves (facsim), 52, [18] p. illus. 22 cm. (Codices selecti, phototypice impressi, col. 10)
PLatS

4979 Millstätter Sündenklage. Mittelhochdeutsch. MS. Klagenfurt, Austria, Kärntner Landesarchiv, codex GV 6/19, f. 154v–164v. Octavo. Saec. 12.
Microfilm: MnCH proj. no. 12,848

4980 Pantaiding-Buch, 1503–1671. MS. Klagenfurt, Austria, Kärntner Landesarchiv, codex GV 2/23. 302 f. Folio. Saec. 16–17.
Microfilm: MnCH proj. no. 12,732

4981 Registratur über die fürnehmen brieflichen Urkunden welche noch im 1598 Jar zu Müllstatt gefunden . . . und anderswo. Klagenfurt, Austria, Kärntner Landesarchiv, codex GV 2/17–19. 3 vols. Folio. Saec. 16–17.
Microfilm: MnCH proj. no. 12,726–27

4982 Sammlung von Kanzelakten des Stiftes Millstadt in Kärnten. 1. u. 3. Bd. MS. Vienna, Haus-, Hof- und Staatsarchiv, codex 456. Folio. Saec. 16.
Microfilm: MnCH proj. no. 23,573 & 23,608

4983 Urbarium. MS. Klagenfurt, Austria, Kärntner Landesarchiv, Allgemeine Handschriftensammlung 533. 210 f. Saec. 16(1571).
Microfilm: MnCH proj. no. 12,910

4984 Urbarium. MS. Klagenfurt, Austria, Kärntner Landesarchiv, Allgemeine Handschriftensammlung 542. 631 f. Saec. 16(1599).
Microfilm: MnCH proj. no. 12,907

4985 Urbarium. MS. Klagenfurt, Austria, Kärntner Landesarchiv, Allgemeine Handschriftensammlung 541. 643 f. Saec. 16(1598–1599).
Microfilm: MnCH proj. no. 12,905

4986 Urbar des Stiftes. MS. Klagenfurt, Austria, Kärntner Landesarchiv, Allgemeine Handschriftensammlung 1467. 305 f. Saec. 16(1598).
Microfilm: MnCH proj. no. 12,912

4987 Urkunden und Briefprotokoll. MS. Klagenfurt, Austria, Kärntner Landesarchiv, Allgemeine Handschriftensammlung 456. Saec. 17(1638–1661).
Microfilm: MnCH proj. no. 12,902

4988 **Minton, Virginia, Sister.**
The role of the consecrated virgin in the mystical body.
iv, 57 leaves. 28 cm.
Thesis (M.A.)–St. John's University, Collegeville, Minn., 1965.
Typescript.
KAM

4989 **Miscellània Anselm M. Albareda.** Abadia de Montserrat, 1962.
v. plates, 25 cm.
PLatS

Missale. Benedictine. *See* Subject Part, n. 1371–1424.

Mitchell, Carla, Sister.
4990 What life! A short autobiographical sketch of a Benedictine Sister of Convent of the Immaculate Conception, Ferdinand, Indiana. 1976.
42 p. 28 cm.
Typescript.
InFer

4991 Dear folks at home . . . St. Benedict College, Ferdinand, Indiana, 1965.
80 p.
Letters, mimeographed.
InFer

4992   Vivid sense impressions in the novels of
François Mauriac.
104 leaves, 28 cm.
Thesis (M.A.)–University of Nebraska,
1964.
Typescript.
InFer

4993   The people's part in the sung Mass.
58 p. 28 cm.
Thesis (M.Mus.)–University of Notre
Dame, 1958.
Typescript.
InFer

Mitchell, Nathan Dennis, 1943–

4994   Christians at prayer. Notre Dame, Ind.,
University of Notre Dame Press [1977].
160 p.
NcBe

4994a   Christain initiation [by] Andrew Ciferni
and Nathan Mitchell. (Phonotape-cassette).
Kansas City, Mo., National Catholic
Reporter, 1978.
1 tape (c. 60 min.) 1 7/8 ips.
InStme

4994b   Church, eucharist, and liturgical reform
at Mercersburg, 1843–1857.
iii, 659 leaves. 28 cm.
Thesis–University of Notre Dame, 1978.
InStme

4995   The Coptic Gnostic Gospel of Philip and
its sacramental system; an inquiry into the
relation between baptism and anointing.
90 leaves, 28 cm.
Thesis (M.A.)–Indiana University, 1971.
InStme

4995a   Does church music have a future?
(Phonotape-cassette). Kansas City, Mo.,
National Catholic Reporter, 1976.
1 tape (c. 60 min.) 1 7/8 ips.
InStme

4995b   Go forth and witness. (Phonotape-
cassette). Kansas City, Mo., National
Catholic Reporter, 1978.
1 tape. (c. 60 min.) 1 7/8 ips.
InStme

4996   In search of penance today [phonotape-
cassette]. Kansas City, Mo., National
Catholic Reporter, 1975.
1 cassette 2s
MnCS; InStme

4996a   Rites of exorcism in the Christian initiation of adults. (Phonotape-cassette). Kansas City, Mo., National Catholic Reporter,
1978.
1 tape (c. 60 min.) 1 7/8 ips.
InStme

4996b   Table and eucharist. (Phonotape-
cassette). Kansas City, Mo., National
Catholic Reporter, 1977.

1 tape (c. 60 min.) 1 7/8 ips.
InStme

**Mittarelli, Giovanni Benedetto,
O.S.B.Cam., 1707–1777.**

4997   Annales Camaldulenses Ordinis Sancti
Benedicti, quibus plura interferuntur tam
ceteras italico-monasticas res, tum
historiam ecclesiasticam remque diplomaticam illustrantia . . . Venetiis, Jo. Bapt.
Pasquali, 1755–73.
9 v. illus. 39 cm.
KAS; MnCS; PLatS

4998   Bibliotheca codicum manuscriptorum
monasterii S. Michaelis Venetiarum prope
Muranum una cum appendice librorum impressorum seculi XV. Opus posthumum
. . . Venetiis, ex Typographia Fentana,
1779.
xxiv, 1257 col.
PLatS(microfilm)

Mitterer, Sigisbert, 1891–

4999   Bavaria benedictina. Sonderausgabe der
Zeitschrift "Bayerland." München [1961?].
68 p. illus. 30 cm.
Includes 13 articles by Abt Sigisbert Mit-
terer [et al.]
PLatS

5000   1200 Jahre Kloster Schäftlarn,
762–1962; Blätter zum Gedächtnis. Hrsg.
von Dr. Sigisbert Mitterer, O.S.B., Abt
von Schäftlarn. Im Selbstverlag der Abtei,
1962.
171 p. plates, 25 cm.
InStme; MnCS; MoCo; NdRi; PLatS

5001   **Mittler, Mauritius, 1921–**
Miracula sancti Annonis. Hrsg. von
Mauritius Mittler. Siegburg, Republica-
Verlag, 1966–1968.
3 v. 24 cm.
KAS; MnCS

5002   **Mittler, Placidus, 1928–**
Melodieuntersuchung zu den dorischen
Hymnen der lateinischen Liturgie im Mit-
telalter. Siegburg, Republica-Verlag,
1965.
144 p. music. 24 cm.
Inaug.-Diss.–Bonn.
KAS; PLatS

5003   **Mocciaro, Bernardo, 1904–**
A d. Guglielmo Placenti, O.S.B., priore
conventuale di S. Martino delle Scale nel
suo primo giubileo sacerdotale. S. Martino
delle Scale, 1961.
80 p. plates, ports. 30 cm.
MnCS

Mocquereau, André, 1849–1930.

5004   Causerie sur les signes rythmiques et
leur utilité. [Tournai], Desclée et cie [n.d.].
24 p. 19 cm.
CaQStB; InStme

5005 De la clivis épisématique dans les manuscrits de Saint-Gall.
(*In* Mélanges offerts à M. Emile Chatelain. Paris, 1910. p. 508–530)
PLatS

5006 Rules for psalmody. Adapted from the rev. 2d ed. of the Petit traité de psalmodie by the Benedictines of Solesmes. Rome, Desclée, Lefebvre & Co., 1904.
32 p. music, 17 cm.
Signed on p. 32: D. André Mocquereau.
InStme

5007 **Moeller, Edmond Eugène,** 1909–
Corpus benedictionum pontificalium. Edité avec une étude, un index scripturaire et liturgique et un index verborum par Dom Edmond (Eugène) Moeller. Turnholti, Brepols, 1971–79.
4 v. 25 cm. (Corpus Christianorum. Series latina, 162, 162A, 162B, 162C)
InStme; KAS; MnCS; PLatS

Mohlberg, Kumibert, 1878–1963.

5008 Das Fränkische Sacramentarium Gelasianum in alamannischer Ueberlieferung . . . Nachtrag Sonderdruck aus der 3. verb. Aufl. zur Ergänzung der 1939 erschienen 2. Aufl. Münster, Westfalen, Aschendorffsche Verlagsbuchhandlung [c 1971].
[285]–357 p. 24 cm.
PLatS

5009 Liber sacramentorum Romanae Aeclesiae ordinis anni circuli (Cod. Vat. Reg. lat.316/Paris, Bibl. Nat. 7193,41/56 – Sacramentarium gelasianum). In Verbindung mit Leo Eizenhöfer und Petrus Siffrin, hrsg. von Leo Cunibert Mohlberg. Roma, Herder, 1960.
xliv, 314 p. facsims. 26 cm.
InStme; ILSP; KAS

5010 Meditazioni sulla santa Messa. Roma, Herder, 1955.
16 p. 22 cm.
KAS

5011 Missale gothicum (Vat. Reg. lat. 317), hrsg. von Leo Cunibert Mohlberg, O.S.B. Roma, Casa editrice Herder, 1961.
xxxii, 141 p. plates 24 cm. (Rerum ecclesiasticarum documenta . . . Series maior; Fontes.V)
InStme; KAS; MnCS; PLatS

5012 Mittelalterliche Handschriften. Zürich [Buchdruckerei Berichthaus], 1951–1952.
3 v. in 1, 27 cm. (Katalog der Handschriften der Zentralbibliothek Zürich. I)
InStme; MnCS; PLatS

5013 **Möhner, Reginbald,** d. 1672.
Reise des P. Reginbald Möhner, Benedictiners von St. Ulrich in Augsburg, als Feldcaplans bei den . . . deutschen Regimentern in die Niederlande im Jahre 1651 . . . hrsg. von Dr. P. L. Brunner. Augsburg, F. Butsch Sohn, 1872.
118 p. 25 cm.
KAS

5014 **Mohr, Charles Henry,** 1863–1931.
Supplement to the Handbuch für die Laienbrüder. St. Leo Abbey, Fla. [1930].
15 p.
ArStb

Moissac, France (Benedictine abbey).

5015 Chronicon Moissiacense a saeculo quarto usque ad a. 818 et 840.
(*In* Monumenta Germaniae historica. Scriptores. Stuttgart, 1963. t. 1, p. 280–313)
MnCS; PLatS

5016 Hymnarius Moissiacensis. Das Hymnar der Abtei Moissac im 10. Jahrhundert, nach einer Handschrift der Rossiana . . . Hrsg. Von Guido Maria Dreves, S.J. New York and London, Johnson Reprint Corporation, 1961.
174 p. 21 cm. (Analecta hymnica Medii aevi, 2)
Reprint of Leipzig edition of 1888.
PLatS

5017 **Molesme, France (Benedictine abbey).**
Cartulaires de l'Abbaye de Molesme, ancien diocèse de Langres, 916–1250 . . . Publié . . . par Jacques Laurent. Paris, A. Picard, 1907–11.
2 v. maps, facsims., 31 cm.
PLatS

5018 **Molitor, Jacob,** fl. 1626.
De verbo Dei incarnato. Salzburg, typis Gregorii Kyrneri, 1626.
iv, 22 p.
Diss. – University of Salzburg, 1626.
MnCS (microfilm)

5019 **Molitor, Raphael,** 1873–1948.
De privilegiis Cassinensium brevis relatio. Monasterii Guestfalorum, Aschendorff, 1917.
v, 44 p. 23 cm.
Manuscripti instar.
NdRi; NElmM(microfilm); PLatS

5020 **Molitor, Valentinus.**
Directorium seu cantus et responsoria in processionibus ordinariis per annum . . . In Monasterio S. Galli, per Adolphum Josephum Ebell, 1692.
311 p. 19 cm.
MnCS; NdRi

5021 **Monachus Bardeneiensis.**
The collections of a monk of Bardney: a dismembered Rowlinson manuscript. By Richard W. Hunt.

(*In* Mediaeval and renaissance studies, v. 5, p. 28–42)

PLatS

5022 **Monachus Mellicensis.**
Responsio ad apologiam (Ecclesiasticus unitor) Johannis Beck. MS. Vienna, Nationalbibliothek, codex 4957, f.95r–97v. Quarto. Saec. 15.
Microfilm: MnCH proj. no. 18,139

Monachus Sangallensis.
5023 De gestis Karoli Magni. MS. Vienna, Nationalbibliothek, codex 532, f.57r–79r. Quarto. Saec. 12.
Microfilm: MnCH proj. no. 13,861

5024 Vita et facta Caroli Magni. MS. Vienna, Nationalbibliothek, codex 610, f.56r–81v. Octavo. Saec. 14.
Microfilm: MnCH proj. no. 13,959

5025 **Le Monastére de Chevetogne;** notice historique et informations. 2. ed. Chevetogne [1962].
65 p. 17 cm.
KAS

Monastic Manuscript Microfilm Library, Collegeville, Minn. *See* Hill Monastic Manuscript Library, Collegeville, Minn.

5025a **Monasticon Belge.** Liège, Centre de Recherches d'Histoire Religieuse, 1955–
Contents: Tome I: Namur, 1961–62. 2 v.
Tome II: Liège, 1955–62. 3 v.
Tome III: Flandre Occidentale, 1960–78. 4 v.
Tome IV: Brabant, 1964–72. 6 v.
Tome V: Luxembourg, 1975. 1 v.
Tome VI: Limbourg, 1976. 1 v.
Tome VII: Flandre Orientale, 1977–79. 3 v.
MnCS

Mondsee, Austria (Benedictine abbey).
5026 Acta de erectione confoederatione et visitatione academiae et universitatis Salisburgensis. Item de fundatione peregrinationis Plainensis, Collegii nobilium et missionis benedictinae Schwarcnensis, 1617–1773. Gesammelt von Abt Bernhard Lidl. MS. Linz, Austria, Oberösterreiches Landesarchiv, Stiftsarchiv Mondsee, Ms. 7. 811 f. Saec. 17–18.
Microfilm: MnCH proj. no. 27,595

5027 Aufschreibungen über die Wirtschaftsführung des Klosters. Speisenfolge für Konvent und für das übrige Klosterpersonal besonders an Festtagen. MS. Linz, Austria, Oberösterreichisches Landesarchiv. Stiftsarchiv Mondsee, Hs. 35. 85 f. Saec. 16(1538).
Microfilm: MnCH proj. no. 27,591

5028 Briefprotokoll des Klosters Mondsee, 1486–1504. MS. Linz, Austria, Oberösterreichisches Landesarchiv, Stiftsarchiv Mondsee, Hs. 171. 284 f. Saec. 15–16.
Microfilm: MnCH proj. no. 27,609

5029 Chronicon Lunaelacense juxta seriem abbatum trina rerum memorabilium genera recensens . . . Pedepontani, sumptibus Joannis Gastl, 1748.
[15], 487 p. illus. 20 cm.
KAS; PLatS

5030 Glossae Lunaelacenses theodiscae. MS. Vienna, Nationalbibliothek, codex 2723. 135 f. Quarto. Saec. 10.
Microfilm: MnCH proj. no. 16,025

5031 Glossae Lunaelacenses theodiscae et latinae. MS. Vienna, Nationalbibliothek, codex 2732. 191 f. Quarto. Saec. 10.
Microfilm: MnCH proj. no. 16,023

5032 Katalog über sammentliche Manuskripten des (1786–1787) aufgelassenen Klosters Mondsee in Oesterreich ob der Enns. MS. Vienna, Nationalbibliothek, codex series nova 2162. 74 f. Folio. Saec. 18(1787–1790).
Microfilm: MnCH proj. no. 20,643

5033 Kopialbuch des Klosters Mondsee. Urkundenabschriften von 1184–1521. MS. Linz, Austria, Oberösterreichisches Landesarchiv, Stiftsarchiv Mondsee, Hs. 1. 145 f. Saec. 12–16.
Microfilm: MnCH proj. no. 27,585

5034 Litterae abbatis et conventus monasterii Lunaelacensis ad Ulricum episcopum Pataviensem d.d. 27.Maii 1466. MS. Vienna, Nationalbibliothek, codex 4969, f.27r–28v. Quarto. Saec. 15.
Microfilm: MnCH proj. no. 18,141

5035 Mantissa chronici Lunae-lacensis bipartita . . . Pedepontani, sumptibus Joannis Gastl, 1749.
[8], 416 p. 20 cm.
"Catalogum manuscriptorum Lunaelacensium, ab aerae christianae saeculo IX ad XVI proponit."–p. 350–416.
KAS; PLatS

5036 Professbuch des Klosters Mondsee, 1384–1783. MS. Linz, Austria, Oberösterreichisches Landesarchiv, Stiftsarchiv Mondsee, Hs. 2. 194 f. Saec. 14–18.
Microfilm: MnCH proj. no. 27,599

5037 Kloster Mondseeisches Stiftsbuch, 1533–1537. MS. Linz, Austria, Oberösterreichisches Landesarchiv, Stiftsarchiv Mondsee, Hs. 84. 153 f. Saec. 16.
Microfilm: MnCH proj. no. 27,587

5038 Stiftsbuch des Klosters Mondsee, 1547–1560. MS. Linz, Austria, Oberösterreichis-

ches Landesarchiv, Stiftsarchiv Mondsee, Hs. 86. 152 f. Saec. 16.
Microfilm: MnCH proj. no. 27,588

5039 Stiftungsbuch des Spitales Mondsee A & B. MS. Linz, Austria, Oberösterreichisches Landesarchiv, Stiftsarchiv Mondsee, Hs. 283 & 284. 143 & 65 f. Saec. 16–17.
Microfilm: MnCH proj. no. 27,605 & 27,607

5040 Urbar über die in Bayern gelegenen Untertanen des Klosters Mondsee. MS. Linz, Austria, Oberösterreichisches Landesarchiv, Stiftsarchiv Mondsee, Hs. 114. 61 f. Saec. 16.
Microfilm: MnCH proj. no. 27,598

Mongelli, Giovanni, 1915–
5041 L'archivio dell'abbazia di Montevergine. Roma [La Galluzza] 1962.
181 p. 24 cm.
PLatS

5042 I codici dell'abbazia di Montevergine. Montevergine, Edizioni del Santuario [1959].
53 p. 24 cm.
MnCS

5043 Storia di Montevergine e della Congregazione Verginiana. [Napoli], Administrazione provinciale di Avellino, 1965.
2 v. 25 cm.
KAS

5044 **Les Moniales.** [Préface de Jean Guitton, introduction de Louis Chaigne]. Paris, Desclée de Brouwer [1966].
various pagings, illus. 23 x 27 cm.
Contents: L'Album de Mère Geneviève Gallois (1888–1962), présenté par Marcelle Auclair. – Chronique de Saint Louis du Temple, rédigée par Carmen Bernos de Gasztold avec la collaboration de René Rancoeur.
MnStj

5045 **Les Moniales bénédictines de Mont-Laurier.** Mont-Laurier, Province de Québec, Canada, Abbaye du Mont-de-la-Rêdemption [1977].
46 p. front (map), illus. 32 cm.
CaQMo; MnCS

5046 **Moniales et sorores vel oblatae regulares O.S.B.** Desumptum ex Catalogo familiarum confoederatarum O.S.B. [Romae]
v. 24 cm.
Published periodically.
MnCS; PLatS

5047 **Los monjes y los estudios;** IV semanas de estudios monasticos. Abadia de Poblet, 1963.
501 p.
MoCo

5048 **Monk of Malmesbury.**
The life of Edward the Second, by the so-called Monk of Malmesbury. Translated from the Latin with introduction and notes by N. Denholm-Young. London and New York, T. Nelson [1957].
xxviii, 145, [146]–150 p. 23 cm.
Latin and English on opposite pages.
PLatS

Monnoyeur, Jean Baptiste, 1879–
5049 L'argument de Mabillon contre Thomas à Kempis, auteur de l'Imitation. 3. éd. Ligugé, Abbaye Saint-Martin [n.d.]
46 p. 24 cm.
"Extrait de la Revue Mabillon."
First published 1930.
PLatS

5050 L'essentiel de la liturgie. Ligugé, Abbaye Saint-Martin [1926]. ·
115, 36 p. illus. 15 cm.
MnCS

5051 La Messe dialoguée en l'honneur du Christ-Roi. Ligugé, Abbaye Saint-Martin, 1927.
47 p. illus. 16 cm.
MnCS

Montboissier, Pierre de. See Petrus Venerabilis.

Mont-de-la-Rédemption, Abbaye du, Mont-Laurier, Canada (Quebec). See Mont-Laurier, Canada (Quebec). Abbaye de Mont-de-la-Rédemption.

Monte Cassino (Benedictine abbey).
5052 Catalogo degli incunabuli di Montecassino. Badia di Montecassino, 1929.
58 p. 25 cm.
KAS; PLatS

5053 Chronica Sancti Benedicti.
(*In* Monumenta Germaniae historica. Scriptores. Stuttgart, 1963. t. 3, p. 197–213)
MnCS; PLatS

5054 Chronicon Casinense a. 568–867.
(*In* Monumenta Germaniae historica. Scriptores. Stuttgart, 1963. t. 3, p. 222–230)
MnCS; PLatS

5055 Codicum Casinensium manuscriptorum catalogus cura e studio monachorum S. Benedicti archicoenobii Montis Casini . . . [Romae, ex Typographia Pontificia Instituti Pii IX], 1915–1941.
3 v. 31 cm.
InStme; MnCS; NcBe; PLatS

5056 I documenti Cassinesi del secolo X con formule in volgare, a cura di Ambrogio Mancone. [Roma] Istituto poligrafico dello Stato, Libreria dello Stato [1960].
16 p. 4 facsims. 61 cm.
KAS; MnCS; PLatS

5057   Eredità perennis: D. Martino Matronola nuovo abate di Monte Cassino. [S. Elia Fiumerapido, Industria Grafica Casinate, 1971].
79 p. illus.(part col.) 24 cm.
"Bolletino diocesano, numero speciale."
KAS

5058   Montecassino vedute dell'esterno.
18 postcards in folder, 9 cm.
MnCS

5059   Monumenta litterarum ad consecrationem turris sanctissimi p. Benedicti pertinentia . . . Typis Montis Casini [1880].
[32] p. 24 cm.
KAS; PLatS

5060   Pacis nuntius: Paolo VI a Montecassino, 24 ottobre 1964. Abbazzia di Montecassino [1965].
143 p. plates (part col.) 29 cm.
InStme; KAS; MnCS; PLatS

5061   La paleografia artistica nei codici Cassinesi applicata ai lavori industriali. [Monte Cassino], Litografie di Montecassino, 1910.
[2] p. 20 plates in portfolio, 34 cm.
Half-title: Disegni ricavati dai codici corali di scrittura gotica.
MnCS

5062   Paleografia artistica di Montecassino. Litografia di Montecassino, 1876–84.
7 pts. in 1 vol., plates, facsims. 38 cm.
Edited by Oderisio Piscitelli Taeggi.
MnCS

5063   Synodus Casinensis. Romae, [apud Gulielmum Faciottum], 1592.
[30], 214, [9] p. 18 cm.
PLatS

5064   (ed) Dante Alighieri. Il codice Cassinese della Divina commedia, per la prima volta letteralmente messo a stampa per cura dei monaci Benedettini della Badia di Monte Cassino. Tipografia di Monte Cassino, 1865.
lv, 592 p. illus., facsims. 37 cm.
InStme

5065   (ed) Sereno, Bartolomeo, 16th cent. Commentari della Guerra di Cipro e della lega dei principi cristiani contro il Turco . . . ora per la prima volta pubblicati da ms. autografo con note e documenti per cura de' monaci della Badia Cassinese. Monte Cassino, 1845–
v. 25 cm.
MnCS

5066   (ed) Thomas Aquinas, Saint. Epistola S. Thomae Aquinatis ad Bernardum abbatem Cassinensem propria manu conscripta, nunc primum e tabulario Casinensi in lucem prolata opera et studio monachorum O.S.B. Typis Montis Cassini, 1875.

xxiv p. facsims. 41 cm.
InStme

Monte Cassino (Benedictine abbey). Archivio.

5067   I regesti dell'archivio [di Monte Cassino]. Roma, [M. Pisani], 1964–
v. illus. 25 cm. (Ministero dell'Interno Pubblicazioni degli Archivi di Stato, 54, 56, 58, 60, 64, 70, 78, 79, 81   )
Editor: v. 1–8, Tommaso Leccisotti, O.S.B.; v. 9– Tommaso Leccisotti, O.S.B., e Faustino Avagliano, O.S.B.
KAS; MnCS; NcBe; PLatS

Montfaucon, Bernard de, 1655–1741.

5068   The antiquities of Italy; being the travels of . . . Bernard de Montfaucon, from Paris through Italy, in the years 1698 and 1699 . . . Made English from the Paris edition of the Latin original. The 2d edition, revised throughout, with large improvements, and corrections, communicated by the author to the editor John Henley. London, Printed by D. L. for J. Darby, 1725.
xxviii, 331 p.
ILSP

5068a   Bibliotheca bibliothecarum manuscriptorum nova: ubi, quae innumeris pene manuscriptorum bibliothecis continentur, ad quodvis literaturae genus spectantia & notatu digna, describuntur & indicantur. Parisiis, apud Briasson, 1739.
2 v. 40 cm.
MnCS

5069   Bibliotheca bibliothecarum manuscriptorum nova . . . Parisiis, apud Briasson, 1739.
2 v. 40 cm.
PLatS (microfilm)

5070   Les manuscrits de la reine de Suède au Vatican; réédition du catalogue de Montfaucon et cotes actuelles. Città del Vaticano, Biblioteca apostolica vaticana, 1964.
133 p. 26 cm. (Studi e testi, 238)
MnCS

Mont-Laurier, Canada (Quebec). Abbaye de Mont-de-la-Rédemption.

5071   Manuel des oblats et oblates de Saint Benoit de l'Abbaye du Mont-de-la-Rédemption du Mont-Laurier. Mont-Laurier, Editions de Moniales Bénédictines [1976].
96 p. illus. 16 cm.
CaQMo; MnCS

Montserrat, Spain (Benedictine abbey).

5072   L'abat Marcet; resum biogràfic fisonomia espiritual, oracio fúnebre. Montserrat, 1951.

60 p. plates, 18 cm.
MnCS

5073 Album de Montserrat; amb text intro-
ductiu a sis llengüos. 164 vistes. Abadia de
Montserrat, n.d.
150 p. illus. 19 x 25 cm.
MnCS

5074 Catalogo de los bienhechores de Montserrate acado de los originales del archivo,
1637. MS. Monasterio benedictino de
Montserrat, Spain, Archivo, codex A/II.
178 p. Folio. Saec. 17.
Microfilm: MnCH proj. no. 30,164

5075 Ceremonial de Montserrat. MS. Monasterio benedictino de Montserrat, Spain,
codex 46 & 74. 242 p. Octavo. Saec. 16.
Microfilm: MnCH proj. no. 29,991

5076 Constituciones del monasterio de Mont-
serrat. MS. Monasterio benedictino de
Montserrat, Spain, codex 39. 90 f. Quarto.
Saec. 16.
Microfilm: MnCH proj. no. 29,989

5077 Die Drehem- und Djoha-texte im Kloster
Montserrat (Barcelona) in Autographie
und mit systematischen Wörterverzeich-
nissen hrsg. von Dr. Nikolaus Schneider.
Roma, Pontificio Instituto Biblico, 1932.
88, 122 p. facsims. 28 cm.
MnCS

5078 Himnari e salms dels fidels. Lletra dels
himnes: D. Hildebrand M. Miret: versió del
text original dels salms: D. Guiu M. Camps;
musica: D. Ireneu M. Segarra. Monestir de
Montserrat, 1964.
108 p. music, 20 cm.
MnCS

5079 Indice artistico de Montserrat. Abadia de
Montserrat, 1956.
45 p. 21 cm.
CaQStB; MnCS

5100 La liturgia en Montserrat. Abadia de
Montserrat, 1957.
57 p. plates, 20 cm.
MnCS

5101 Litúrgica; Cardinali I. A. Schuster in
memoriam. [Abbatia Montisserati] 1956–
v. 26 cm. (Scripta et documenta. 7, 10)
CaQStB; MnCS; PLatS (v. 3)

5102 Los mártires de Montserrat; trabajos
premiados y resena de la fiesta celebrada
con motivo del concurso Montserratino
Regina martyrum. Barcelona, La Hormiga
de Oro, 1952.
94 p. illus. 17 cm.
MnCS

5103 Studia monastica. v. 1–   1959–
Abadia de Montserrat.
v. 25 cm.
InStme; KAS; MnCS; PLatS

5104 Vetlla de santa Maria. Abadia du Montserrat, 1956.
93 p. music, 17 cm.
MnCS

5105 La vida monastica i sacerdotal a Montserrat. Abadia de Montserrat, 1956.
32 p. illus. 20 cm.
MnCS

5106 Visioni attuali sulla vita monastica.
Montserrat, 1966.
315 p. 19 cm.
MnCS

5107 Vistas de Montserrat. [Abadia du Montserrat, 1898].
unpaged, illus. 28 x 36 cm.
MnCS

5108 What Montserrat is. 4th ed. Montserrat
Abbey, 1964.
45 p. plates, 20 cm.
English translation by Roderic Bright.
MnCS; PLatS

**Montserrat, Spain (Benedictine abbey).
Biblioteca.**

5109 Catàleg dels incunables de la Biblioteca
de Montserrat. [Abadia de Montserrat]
1955.
xviii, 322 p. 12 facsims. 26 cm.
MnCS

5110 [Catalog of manuscripts].
3 v. 29 cm.
Handwritten.
Xeroxed by University Microfilms, Ann
Arbor, Mich., 1973.
MnCS

5111 Els manuscrits litúrgics de la Biblioteca
de Montserrat. Monastir de Montserrat,
1969.
211 p. 25 cm.
MnCS

5112 Manual de l'Escolà de Montserrat. Monastir de Montserrat, 1932.
379 p. music, 15 cm.
MnCS

5113 **Monumenta litterarum ad consecrationem** turris sanctissimi p. Benedicti
pertinentia et ad conventum revdorum
dd. abbatum in archicoenobio Montis
Casini habitum sacro Pentecostes festo
anno MCCCCLXXX. Typis Montis
Casini [n.d.]
[24], 8 p. 23 cm.
PLatS

5114 **Monumenta Mettensia.**
(*In* Monumenta Boica. Edidit Acad.
Scientiar. Elect. Boica. Monachii, 1771, v.
11, p. 341–518)
KAS; PLatS

Moore, Sebastian, 1917–

5115   Before the deluge [by] Sebastian Moore, O.S.B., and Anselm Hurt, O.S.B. New York, Newman Press [1968].
124 p. 23 cm.
ICSS; InFer; KAS; MnCS; MnStj; ViBris; CaMWiSb

5116   The crucified Jesus is no stranger. New York, Seabury Press, 1977.
xii, 116 p. 22 cm.
ICSS; KAS; MnStj; ViBris

5117   The dreamer not the dream [by] Sebastian Moore and Kevin Maguire. New York, Newman Press [1970].
159 p. 21 cm.
Prose and poems.
InStme; KAS; PLatS

5118   The experience of prayer [by] Sebastian Moore and Kevin Maguire, with an introduction by Peter Harvey. London, Darton, Longman & Todd [1969].
130 p.
KAS; CaMWiSb

5119   God is a new language. Westminster, Md., Newman Press [1967].
184 p. 20 cm.
CaMWiSb; InFer; InStme; KAM; KAS; MnStj; MoCo; ViBris

5120   No exit. Glen Rock, N.J., Newman Press [1968].
151 p. 21 cm.
ICSS; InStme; MnStj

5121   The work of the intellect.
(*In* Todd, J. M. Work. 1960. p. 182–210)
PLatS

Moore, Thomas Verner, 1877–1969.

5122   The home and its inner spiritual life; a treatise on the mental hygiene of the home, by a Carthusian of Miraflores. Westminster, Md., Newman Press, 1952.
viii, 256 p. 21 cm.
PLatS

5123   Human and animal intelligence.
(*In* Scientific aspects of the race problem. Washington, 1941. p. 93–158)
PLatS

Moragas, Beda M., 1924–

5124   La Misa, sintesis de la vida cristiana. Abadia de Montserrat, 1961.
146 p. 20 cm.
MnCS

5125   Transcripció musical de dos himnes.
(*In* Miscelánea en homehaje a Monseñor Higinio Anglés. Barcelona, 1958–61. p. 591–598)
PLatS

5126   **Moral, Tomás,** 1938–
Monasterios. Pamplona, Bibliotecas y Cultura Popular, 197-.

31 p. illus. 22 cm.
MnCS

Morandus Cluniacensis.

5127   Dyalogus metricum inter sanctum Bernhardum et Morandum abbatem. MS. Vienna, Schottenstift, codex 192, f.1v. Folio. Saec. 15.
Microfilm: MnCH proj. no. 4059

5128   Dyalogus visionis sancti Bernhardi cum Morando. MS. Vienna, Schottenstift, codex 191, f.152r. Quarto. Saec. 15.
Microfilm: MnCH proj. no. 4057

5129   **Morant, Adelrich,** 1915–
Die philosophisch-theologische Bildung in den Priesterseminarien Schwarz-Afrikas; aktuelle Fragen der Priesterbilding mit besonderer Berücksichtigung Kameruns. Schöneck, Beckenried, 1959.
xxi, 263 p. 23 cm.
MnCS; PLatS

5130   **Morcaldi, Michael,** 1818–1894.
Synopsis historico-diplomatica monasterii et tabularii Cavensis quae codici diplomatico Cavensi proxime edendo praefatur. Neapoli, Petrus Piazzi, 1873.
75 p. 32 cm.
InStme

Morel, Gall, 1803–1872.

5131   Eremus sacra, die heilige Wüste [Erinnerung an Maria-Einsiedeln]. [Einsiedeln, New York, Gebr. Benziger, 1885]
[16] leaves, illus. 19 x 26 cm.
InStme; MoCo

5132   Die Regesten der Benedictiner-Abtei Einsiedeln. Bearb. von Gallus Morel. Chur, G. Hitz, 1848.
[10], 93 p. 30 cm.
KAS

5133   **Morel, Robert,** 1653–1731.
Meditations sur la Règle de s. Benoit pour tous les jours de l'année. Lophem-lez-Bruges, Charles Beyaert, 1923.
xvi, 443 p. 21 cm.
Reprint of the Paris edition of 1717.
KAS

5134   **Moretti, Emmanuella, Abbess.**
L'oblato benedettino; lineamenti di spiritualità. [Parma, Scuola tipografica benedettina, 1969].
30 p. plates, 22 cm.
MnCS

5135   **Morey, Adrian,** 1904–
Gilbert Foliot and his letters [by] Dom Adrian Morey and C.N.L. Brooke. Cambridge [England], University Press, 1965.
xv, 312 p. 23 cm.
InStme; KAM; NdRi; PLatS

5135a David Knowles; a memoir. London, Darton, Longman & Todd, 1979.
viii, 166 p. 23 cm.
InStme

5136 **Morgan, Michael Thomas,** 1914–
Contribution to the flora of Cullman County, Ala. Washington, Catholic University of America, 1942.
114 p.
AStb

5137 **Morgand, Claude,** 1923–
Monumenta aevi Anianensis (saec. VIII fin.-IX med.). Recunsuerunt D. C. Morgand, O.S.B. [et al.].
(*In* Corpus consuetudinum monasticarum. Siegburg, 1963. t. 1, p. 176–422)
PLatS

Morin, Germain, 1861–1946.
5138 Un écrivain inconnu du XIe siècle: Walter, moine de Nonnecourt, puis de Vézelay.
"Extrait de la Revue bénédictine, t. 22(1905), p. 165–180)"
PLatS

5139 Un giorno nella casa di S. Benedetto. Badia di Montecassino, 1928.
139 p. plates, 19 cm.
PLatS

5140 Le Te Deum, type anonyme d'anophore latine préhistorique?
"Extrait de la Revue bénédictine," 1907. p. 180–223)
CaQStB; CtBer; PLatS

Mork, Wulstan, 1916–
5141 The biblical meaning of man. Milwaukee, Bruce Pub. Co. [1967].
xi, 168 p. 22 cm.
CaMWiSb; ICSS; InStme; KAS; MnStj; MoCo; PLatS

5142 Led by the spirit; a primer of sacramental theology. Milwaukee, Bruce Pub. Co. [1965].
ix, 181 p. 22 cm.
ICSS; MdRi; KAS; InStme; MnCS; MoCo; PLatS

5143 Moreau spirituality. Notre Dame, Ind., Sisters of the Holy Cross [c 1973].
251 p.
MoCo

5144 A synthesis of the spiritual life. Milwaukee, Bruce Pub. Co. [1962]
283 p. 18 cm.
CaMWiSb; InFer; ICSS; InStme; MnCS; MnStj; NdRi; MoCo; PkShG; PLatS

Morlino, Paschal, 1938–
5145 A bibliography on Christian ecumenism. [Latrobe, Pa., St. Vincent Archabbey, 1968].

18 leaves, 28 cm.
Typescript.
PLatS

5146 Evaluation of periodicals on Christian ecumenism. [Latrobe, Pa., St. Vincent Archabbey, 1969].
18 leaves, 28 cm.
Typescript.
PLatS

5147 The Pharisees. [Latrobe, Pa., St. Vincent Archabbey, 1969].
38 p. 28 cm.
Typescript.
PLatS

5148 **Mornacchi, Nicola,** 1916–
Aspetti della vita commune presso i canonici regolari Mortariensi in Genova.
(*In* La vita comune del clero nei secoli XI e XII. 1962. v. 2, p. 154–162)
PLatS

Morthorst, Edmund, 1916–1975.
5149 The stranger in a city parish; a study of the adjustment of newcomers in an urban area to parish life and activities.
80 leaves, 28 cm.
Thesis (M.S.)–Catholic University of America, 1944.
Typescript.
InStme

5150 Roger Ascham; his influence on the development of the English vernacular.
iv, 80 leaves, 28 cm.
Thesis (M.A.)–Catholic University of America, 1938.
Typescript.
InStme

5151 **Mossong, John Emmanuel,** 1901–
Love's sorrowful journey; a way of the cross. Composed by John E. Mossong, O.S.B., and Rev. Bernard Strasser, O.S.B. Spalding, Nebr., Bopp Pub. Co. [1959].
[205] p. 13 cm.
KySu; PLatS

Mount Angel Abbey, St. Benedict, Or.
5152 The Psalms, by the monks of Mount Angel Abbey [translated from the Hebrew by Bonaventure Zerr, O.S.B.]. Rev. edition. St. Benedict, Or., Mount Angel Abbey, 1975.
xii, 274 p. 22 cm.
MnCS

5153 Reflections. 1– 1974–
InFer; OrStb

5154 **Mount Angel College, Mount Angel, Or.**
Silver jubilee, 1887–1912.
44 p. illus., ports. 27 cm.
MnCS; OrMta

5155 **Mount Michael Abbey, Elkhorn, Nebr.**
Michaeleen. 1955–
InFer; NbElm

5156 **Mount St. Benedict Priory, Crookston, Minn.**
With gladdened hearts we celebrate our first fifty years, 1919–1969 . . . [St. Paul, Minn., North Central Pub. Co., 1970]
60 p. illus., ports. 22 x 28 cm.
KAS; MnCS; MnStj; MoCo; PLatS

5157 **Mount Saint Mary's Convent, Pittsburgh, Pa.**
Benedictine Sisters of Pittsburgh, 1870–1970. [Pittsburgh, Pa., 1970]
45 p. chiefly illus. 28 cm.
InFer; PLatS; PPiSM

Mount St. Scholastica College, Atchison, Kans. *See also* Benedictine College, Atchison, Kans.

5158 Dedication of Feeney Memorial Library . . . November 17, 1962.
[18] p. 23 cm.
KAM; PLatS

5159 A report on teacher education at Mount St. Scholastica and St. Benedict's Colleges. Submitted to the National Council for Accreditation of Teacher Education. 1969.
x, 247 leaves, tables, chart. 28 cm.
KAS

Mount St. Scholastica Convent, Atchison, Kans.

5160 ABC–Atchison Benedictine Community News. 1971–76. Quarterly.
InFer; KAM

5161 Special dedication in remembrance of the golden jubilee of profession [of] Rev. Mother Mildred Knoebber, O.S.B., 1918–1968.
[48] p.
MnStj(Archives)

Mount Savior Monastery, Pine City, N.Y.

5162 Chronicle. 1967–   Quarterly.
InFer; NPi

5163 Monastic studies. no. 1–   1963–
Monograph series.
CaMWiSb; InFer; NPi; PLatS; ViBris

5164 Psalterium monasticum ad experimentum novo ordine dispositum. Elmira, N.Y., Mount Savior Monastery [196?]
172 p. 21 cm.
MnCS; PLatS; NPi

5165 (tr) Garrone, Gabriel, How to pray the Psalms. Translated by the Benedictine monks of Mount Savior Monastery, Elmira, New York. Notre Dame, Ind., Fides Pub. [1965].
118 p. 19 cm.
MnCS; NPi

5166 **Mouzon, France (Benedictine abbey).**
Annales Mosomagenses a.969–1452.
(*In* Monumenta Germaniae historica. Scriptores. Stuttgart, 1963. t. 3, p. 160–166)
MnCS; PLatS

5166a **Muehlenbein, Wibora, Sister.**
Benedictine mission to China. St. Joseph, Minn., St. Benedict's Convent, 1980.
35 p. illus. 22 cm.
MnCS; MnStj

Mueller, Joseph, 1868–

5167 The Church of Rome in the United States; a defense against bigotry. [Charlotte, N.C., Printed by Observer Printing House] 1913.
34 p.
NcBe

5168 Via salutis; or, Various methods of the exercise of the Way of the Cross. New York, Christian Press Association Pub. Co., 1903.
245 p.
NcBe

5169 **Muff, Peter Cölestin,** 1852–1924.
Die Hausfrau nach Gottes Herzen; Gedenkblätter und Gebete den Bräuten und Frauen des katholischen Volkes gewidmet. Einsiedeln, Benziger [1908].
736 p. plates (part col.) 12 cm.
MnCS

5170 **Muhovich, Michaeleen, Sister.**
A study of the relationship of endogenous bacterial flora to pneumonia.
107 p.
Thesis (M.A.)–Virginia Commonwealth University, 1973.
SdYa

5171 **Muller, Deodat,** fl. 1750.
Spiritus sanctissimi patris nostri Benedicti omnium justorum spiritu pleni . . . ex sacra ipsius Regula & vita . . . Tugii, Joan.Casp. Miltensperger, 1753.
4 v. 17 cm.
InStme; KAS; MnCS

5172 **Müller, Gallus,** 17th cent.
Animae devotae requies, sive Piae meditationes et considerationes in dominicas, et festa praecipua sanctorum per annum . . . Typis Einsidlensibus, 1669.
298, 397 p. 16 cm.
MnCS

5173 **Müller, Gregor,** 1920–
Die Wahlhaftigkeitspflicht und die Problematik der Lüge; ein Längsschnitt durch die Moraltheologie und Ethik unter besonderer Berücksichtigung der Tugendlehre

des Thomas von Aquin und der modernen
Lösungsversuche. Freiburg, Herder, 1962.
xxiv, 359 p. 23 cm.
PLatS

Müller, Iso, 1901–

5174 Die Altar-Tituli des Klosterplanes.
(*In* Duft, Johannes. Studien zum St.
Galler Klosterplan. 1962. p. 129–176)
PLatS

5175 Die Fürstabtei Disentis im ausgehenden
18. Jahrhundert. Münster, Westf., Aschendorff [1963].
viii, 247 p. 25 cm.
InStme; KAS; PLatS

5176 Geschichte der Abtei Disentis von den
Anfängen bis zur Gegenwart. Einsiedeln,
Benziger, 1971.
276 p. maps, 8 plates. 25 cm.
KAS; MnCS

5177 Geschichte des Klosters Müstair, von
den Anfängen bis zur Gegenwart. Disentis,
Disentina-Verlag, 1978.
288 p.
MnCS

5178 St. Adalgott (m. 1160), ein Schüler des
hl. Bernhard und Reformbischof von Chur.
(*In* Analecta Sacri Ordinis Cisterciensis.
v. 16(1960), p. 92–119)
PLatS

Muller, Jean Pierre, 1904–

5179 Atlas O.S.B: Benedictinorum per orbem
praesentia; Benedictines throughout the
world; [etc.]. Prima editio. Romae, Editiones Anselmianae, 1973.
2 v. maps. 22 cm. (v. 2: 32 cm.)
Contents: I. Index monasteriorum. II.
Tabulae geographicae.
InStme; KAS; MnCS; MoCo; PLatS;
ViBris

5180 (ed) Jean de Paris, O.P. Commentaire
sur les Sentences. Reportation, livre I-II
Edition critique par Jean-Pierre Muller,
O.S.B. Romae, Herder, 1961.
2 v. 25 cm. (Studia Anselmiana, 47, 62)
InStme; PLatS

5181 **Müller, Romanus.**
Commentarius in beati Pauli primam
epistolam ad Corinthios et Philippenses.
MS. Universitätsbibliothek Salzburg,
codex M I 307. 208 f. Octavo. Saec. 17.
Microfilm: MnCH proj. no. 11,111

5182 **Münchsmünster, Germany (Benedictine
abbey).**
Die Traditionen, Urkunden und Urbare
des Klosters Mönchsmünster. Bearb. von
Matthias Thiel und Odilo Engels. München, Beck, 1961.
73, 442 p. plates, 25 cm.
German or Latin.
PLatS

5183 **Munding, Emmanuel,** 1882–1960.
Der Untergang von Montecassino. 3.
unveränderte Aufl. Beuroner Kunstverlag,
1954.
45 p. 17 cm.
First published 1951.
PLatS

Mundó, Anscari, 1923–

5184 Adnotationes in antiquissimam Ordinem
Romanum Feriae V in Cena Domini
noviter editum.
(*In* Liturgica, 2: Cardinal I. A. Schuster
in memoriam. 1908. v. 2, p. 181–216)
PLatS

5185 Entorn de la carta de l'abat Oliba a Arnau Mir de Tost.
(*In* Miscellània Anselm M. Albareda.
v. 1(1962), p. 207–216)
PLatS

5186 El Proser-Troper Montserrat 73.
(*In* Liturgica, 3: Cardinal I. A. Schuster
in memoriam. Montisserrati, 1966. p. 101–
142)
PLatS

5187 **Muos, Beatus.**
De jure advocattiae tutelaris antiquissimi, liberi ac exempti monasterii Rhenoviensis . . . in Helvetia tractatus historico-
juridicus . . . publicae discussioni expo-
suerunt praeside P. Beato Muos . . . pp.
Januarius Dangel, Benedictus Kahé,
Maurus Werner, Sebastianus Greutter
O.S.B. . . . Lucernae, Typis H.I.N. Hautt,
1748.
[10], 145, [22] p. 21 cm.
PLatS

Murga, Pedro de, f. 1666.

5188 Opera canonica et moralia. Lucernae,
Iohan. Böttiger, 1684.
2 v. 35 cm.
KAS

5189 Quaestiones pastorales, seu de iure, et
potestate parochi unitarum ecclesiarum
. . . Addita . . . Disquisitione canonica &
regulari de iure & potestate prioris conven-
tualis . . . Lugduni, Joan. Couronneau,
1657.
[16], 292, 214, [81] p. 23 cm.
KAS

Muri-Gries, Itlay (Benedictine abbey).

5190 Catalogus monachorum O.S.B. Benedicti
exempti monasterii Muro-Griesensis congregationis Helveticae editus ad jubilaeum
aureum professionis Reverendissimi et Illustrissimi domini Abbatis Ambrosii II,
1904. Bulsani, A. Auer, 1904.
27 p. plates, 22 cm.
MnCS; PLatS

5191   Gedenk-Blatt zum 50. jährigen Priester-jubiläum seiner Gnaden des Hochwst. Herrn Prälaten Abt Ambrosius II. 5. September 1906. [Bozen, Alois Auer] 1906.
14 p. port. 22 cm.
MnCS

Murphy, Joseph Francis, 1910–
5192   Historic Sacred Heart Mission. [n.p., n.d.]
[20] p. illus. 23 cm.
PLatS

5193   The monastic centers of the Order of St. Benedict in Oklahoma.
iv, 65 p. 28 cm.
Thesis – University of Oklahoma, 1968.
OkShG

5194   Potawatomi Indians of the West: origins of the Citizen Band.
x, 522 p. maps. 28 cm.
Thesis (Ph.D.) – University of Oklahoma, 1961.
OkShG

5195   Tenacious monks: the Oklahoma Bene-dictines, 1875–1975 – Indian missionaries, Catholic founders, educators, agricul-turists. Shawnee, Okla., Benedictine Color Press [1974].
x, 465 p. illus. 24 cm.
InStme; KAS; MnCS; MoCo; NcBe; PLatS

5196   **Murphy, Malachy,** 1919–1978.
Wang Mang "The Usurper": social reform or Watergate in ancient China [phonotape cassette]. Collegeville, 1974.
1 cassette
Recorded at St. John's University, May 11, 1974: Alumni College Day.
MnCS

Murray, Gregory, 1905–
5197   Accentual cadences in Gregorian chant. Bath, Downside Abbey [1958].
12 p. illus.(music) 23 cm.
PLatS

5198   The choral chants of the Mass. [Exeter], Burleigh Press [n.d.].
35 p.
InFer

5199   Gregorian chant according to the manu-scripts. London, L. J. Cary [1963].
97 p. illus. 24 cm.
– – – Musical supplement. 1963. 31 p.
InStme; KAS; MnCS; MoCo; PLatS

5200   Gregorian rhythm in the Gregorian cen-turies; the literary evidence. Bath, Down-side Abbey [1957].
25 p. music. 23 cm.
PLatS

5201   Plainsong rhythm; the editorial methods of Solesmes. [Exeter, Printed at Catholic Record Press, 1956].
18 p. music. 22 cm.
PLatS

5202   **Murray, Jeannette, Sister.**
A critical synthesis of community at-titudes with specific focus on the accept-ance and provisions made for retarded children in the State of Maryland.
56 p. 28 cm.
Thesis (M.A.) – Cardinal Stritch College, Milwaukee, 1962.
Typescript.
MdRi

5203   **Murray, Mary Teresa Gertrude, Sister.**
Vocational guidance in Catholic second-ary schools; a study of development and present status. New York, Columbia Uni-versity, Teachers College, 1938.
163 p. 24 cm.
MnCS

Murray, Placid, 1918–
5204   The canon of the Mass; a study and a new translation. 2d ed. Maynooth, The Furrow Trust [1961].
18 p. 21 cm.
MnCS; PLatS

5205   Christ in our midst.
(*In* Studies in pastoral liturgy. Dublin, 1967. v. 3, p. 163–180)
PLatS

5206   Contemporary church music.
(*In* Prayer and community, ed. by Her-man Schmidt. New York, 1970. p. 147–149)
PLatS

5207   The graces of the Eucharist; studies in the Post-communions of the Missal.
(*In* Studies in pastoral liturgy. 1961. p. 117–131)
PLatS

5208   The history and meaning of the Canon.
(*In* Studies in pastoral liturgy. May-nooth, 1961. v. 1, p. 101–116)
PLatS

5209   The liturgical history of extreme unction.
(*In* Studies in pastoral liturgy. Maynooth, 1963. v. 2, p. 18–38)
PLatS

5210   Liturgical piety according to Mediator Dei.
(*In* Studies in pastoral liturgy. May-nooth, 1961. v. 1, p. 132–139)
PLatS

5211   The Passion of Christ. And The Chris-tian risen life in the texts of Holy Week.
(*In* Studies in pastoral liturgy. May-nooth, 1961. p. 140–151)
PLatS

5212 Principles of participation [in the Mass].
(*In* Studies in pastoral liturgy. Maynooth, 1963. v. 2, p. 92–106)
PLatS

5213 A study of the Secrets of the Missal.
(*In* Studies in pastoral liturgy. Maynooth, 1963. v. 2, p. 154–167)
PLatS

5214 (ed) Newman the Oratorian; his unpublished Oratory papers. Edited with an introductory study on the continuity between his Anglican and his Catholic ministry, by Placid Murray. Dublin, Gill and Macmillan [1969].
xxv, 500 p. 23 cm.
Thesis–Pontificio Ateneo S. Anselmo, Rome.
InStme; PLatS

Murrman, Warren Daniel, 1938–
5215 Lanfranc of Bec.
44 leaves. 28 cm.
Thesis (M.A.)–St. Vincent College.
Typescript.
PLatS

5216 The significance of the human nature of Christ and the sacraments for salvation according to William Estius. Latrobe, Pa., St. Vincent Archabbey Press, c 1970.
xvi, 259 p. 23 cm.
Thesis (S.T.D.)–Ludwig-Maximilian Universität, München, 1967.
PLatS

Murtha, Ronin John, 1930–
5217 The Catholic parochial schools and the New York Constitutional Convention of 1894.
91 p. 28 cm.
Thesis (M.A.)–Columbia University, 1960.
Typescript.
PLatS

5218 The life of the Most Reverend Ambrose Maréchal, third archbishop of Baltimore, 1768–1828.
ix, 317 p. 28 cm.
Thesis (Ph.D.)–Catholic University of America, 1965.
Typescript.
PLatS

5219 **Mussoni, Albert, 1837–**
De origine status monastici tractatus . . . Augustae Vindelicorum, M. Huttler, 1889.
24 p. 23 cm.
KAS; PLatS

5220 **Muth, Placidus.**
Ueber den Einfluss des königlichen Benedictiner Stiftes auf dem Petersberge zu Erfurt auf die erste Urbarmachung der hiesigen Gegenden durch Ackerbau und Viehzucht . . . Erfurt, Beyer und Maring, 1798.
[165]–208 p. 22 cm.
Separate from f. Akademie nützlicher Wissenschaften zu Erfurt, 2. November 1797.
KAS

5221 **Nack, Karl Alois, 1751–1828.**
Reichsstift Neresheim; eine kurze Geschichte dieser Benediktinerabtei in Schwaben . . . Neresheim, Bernard Kaelin, 1792.
144 p. 20 cm.
KAS

Naisl, Aemilianus, 1670–1743.
5222 Lineae asceticae; sive, Meditationes quotidianae secundum tres vias, purgativam, illuminativam & unitivam, conformiter sacrae Regulae . . . Benedicti . . . Dillingae, J. C. Bencard, 1715.
v. 16 cm.
KAS(v. 1); MnCS(v. 2–3)

5223 Scintillae asceticae ad excitandum et fovendum spiritum . . . Monachii, Joan. Gastel, 1752.
[30], 240 p. 17 cm.
KAS; PLatS

5224 Speculum cleri utrisque tam saecularis quam regularis, in quo . . . via perfectionis . . . demonstratur . . . Coloniae Agrippinae, Joan. Werner Van der Poll, 1734–35.
4 v. 21 cm.
KAS

5225 **Naples, Italy. San Severino (Benedictine abbey).**
Hymnarius Severinianus. Das Hymnar der Abtei S. Severin in Neapel. Hrsg. von Guido Maria Dreves, S.J. New York and London, Johnson Reprint Corporation, 1961.
143 p. 21 cm. (Analecta hymnica Medii Aevi, 14a)
PLatS
Reprint of Leipzig edition of 1893.
PLatS

5226 **Nardin, Giuseppe.**
Il movimento d'unione tra i religiosi. Roma, Commentarium pro Religiosis, 1961.
399 p. 25 cm.
PLatS

Nariscus, Johannes, pseud. *See* Hortig, Johann Nepomuk.

5227 **Nashdom Abbey, Burnham, England.**
The jubilee book of the Benedictines of Nashdom, 1914–1964. London, Faith Press, [1964].

86 p. illus. 22 cm.
InStme

Nathe, Margretta, Sister, 1913–

5228   Common prayers for Christian unity. [Translated from the German by Sister Margretta Nathe]. Garrison, N.Y., Graymoor Friars.
24 p.
MnStj(Archives)

5229   (tr) Ernst, Siegfried. Man – the greatest of miracles; an answer to the sexual counter-revolution. Translated by Sister Margretta Nathe and Mary Rosera Joyce. Collegeville, Minn., The Liturgical Press [1976].
xvii, 172 p.
MnStj(Archives)

5230   (tr) Frank, Karl Borromaus. Fundamental questions on ecclesiastical art. Translated by Sister M. Margretta Nathe, O.S.B. Collegeville, Minn., The Liturgical Press [1962].
104 p. 21 cm.
KAS; MnCS; MnStj; MoCo; PLatS

5231   **Negrelos, Portugal. Mosteiro de Singeverga (Benedictine abbey).**
Regra do glorioso patriarca S. Bento. Traduzida do latim e anotada pelos monges de Singeverga. Mosteiro de Singeverga, 1951.
xv, 188 p. 16 cm.
MnCS

5232   **Necrologium Congregationis Benedictinae Bavaricae,** 1836–1950. Monachii, 1950.
110 p.
AStb

5233   **Neft, Nivard, Sister,** 1922–
Chemistry of antimycin A.
x, 91 p. 28 cm.
Thesis (Ph.D.) – Utah State University, 1971.
Typescript.
MnStj(Archives)

Neugart, Trudpert.

5234   Ad historiam episcopatus Constantiensis. MS. Benediktinerabtei St. Paul im Lavanttal, Austria, codex 83/6. 735 p. Folio. Saec. 18.
Microfilm: MnCH proj. no. 12,665

5235   Auszüge aus dem Viktringer-Urkundenbuch. MS. Benediktinerabtei St. Paul im Lavanttal, Austria, codex 889/0. 283 p. Folio. Saec. 18.
Microfilm: MnCH proj. no. 12,669

5236   Episcopatus Lavantinus. MS. Benediktinerabtei St. Paul im Lavanttal, Austria, codex 889/0. 723 p. Folio. Saec. 18.
Microfilm: MnCH proj. no. 12,674

Neuman, Matthias L., 1941–

5237   The imagination in theology; some contemporary American and British perspectives. Rome, Pontificium Athenaeum Anselmianum [1976].
ix, 112 p. 23 cm.
Thesis (Ph.D.) – Sant'Anselmo, Rome – an excerpt.
InStme

5237a   Directory of Benedictine resource personnel for North America. [St. Meinrad, Ind., St. Meinrad Archabbey, 1981].
[x, 200 leaves] 21 cm. (American Benedictine Academy. Research studies, 1)
InStme; MnCS

5238   Self-identity, symbol, and imagination; some implications of their interaction for Christian sacramental theology.
(*In* Symbolisme et théologie. Sacramentum 2. Roma, 1974. p. 91–123)
PLatS

Neumüller, Willibrord, 1909–1978.

5239   Bernardus Noricus von Kremsmünster. Weis [Austria], Verlag "Weisermühl," 1947.
167 p. 24 cm.
MnCS; PLatS

5240   Der Codex Millenarius, von Willibrord Neumüller [und] Kurt Holter. Graz, In Kommission bei H. Böhlaus Nachf. [1959].
195 p. illus. 31 cm.
MnCS

5240a   Codex Millenarius Maior. Faksimile-Ausgabe im Originalformat des Codex cremifanensis cim. 1. Kommentar von Willibrord Neumüller u. Kurt Holter. Graz, Akademische Verlagsanstalt, 1974.
39, vi p. [398] leaves (facsims.) 34 cm. (Codices selecti phototypice impressi, 45)
MnCS

5240b   Das Gründungsjahr Kremsmünster.
(*In* Cremifanum 777–1977; Festschrift . . . Linz, 1977. p. 7–15)
MnCS

5241   Markus und der Löwe; die Evangelisten und ihre Symbole im Codex Millenarius. Mit einer Einführung von Willibrord Neumüller, O.S.B., und Kurt Holter. Graz, Akedemische Druck- u. Verlagsanstalt, 1977.
[16] p. 8 col. plates (facsims) 30 cm.
MnCS; PLatS

5242   Die mittelalterlichen Bibliotheksverzeichnisse des Stiftes Kremsmünster, von P. Willibrord Neumüller und Kurt Holter. Linz, Verlag des Amtes der o.-ö. Landesregierung, 1950.
69 p. 26 cm.
MnCS

5243 Die Wiegendrucke des Stiftes Kremsmünster. Linz/Donau, H. Muck, 1947.
  279 p. plates, 24 cm.
  Vorwort signed: Dr. P. Willibrord Neumüller, Stiftsbibliothekar.
  MnCS

5244 Zur Benediktinerreform des heiligen Altmann (Die Vita Altmanni in ihrem Wert als monastische Quelle).
  (*In* Der heilige Altmann, Bischof von Passau. Göttweig, 1965. p. 16–22)
  PLatS

Neunheuser, Burkhard, 1903–
5245 Baptême et confirmation. Traduit de l'allemand. Paris, Editions du Cerf, 1966.
  249 p. 23 cm.
  PLatS

5246 Baptism and confirmation. Translated by John Jay Hughes. [New York], Herder and Herder [1964].
  x, 251 p. 22 cm.
  CaMWiSb; MnCS; MnStj; NcBe; ILSP; NdRi; KAS; InStme; MoCo; PLatS

5247 Il canone nella concelebrazione.
  (*In* Liturgia eucaristica: teologica, storia e pastorale. Torino, 1966. p. 117–128)
  PLatS

5248 The Catechumenate.
  (*In* Barauna, Guilherme, ed. The liturgy of Vatican II. 1966. v. 2, p. 163–188)
  PLatS

5249 L'Eucharistie: I. au moyen âge et à l'époque moderne. Traduit de l'allemand par A. Liefooghe. Paris, Du Cerf, 1966.
  149 p. 23 cm.
  PLatS

5250 Eucharistie im Mittelalter und Neuzeit. Freiburg, Herder, 1963.
  69 p. 27 cm.
  InStme; MnCS

5251 Der Gestaltwandel liturgischer Frömmigkeit; Grundsätzliches zur geistesgeschichtlichen Deutung.
  (*In* Perennitas; Beiträge . . . P. Thomas Michels, O.S.B., zum 70. Geburtstag. Münster, 1963. p. 160–181)
  PLatS

5252 Mysterium Paschale.
  (*In* Liturgie und Mönchtum, Laacher Hefte, 36. p. 12–33)
  PLatS

5253 Storia della liturgia attraverse le epoche culturali. Roma, Edizioni Liturgiche, 1977.
  144 p. 24 cm.
  InStme

5254 (ed) Casel, Odo. Das christliche Kult Mysterium. 4. durchgesehene und erweiterte Aufl., hrsg. von P. Burkhard Neunheuser, O.S.B. Regensburg, F. Pustet, 1960.
  243 p. 23 cm.
  PLatS

5255 (ed) Casel, Odo. The mystery of Christian worship, and other writings. Edited by Burkhard Neunheuser. Westminster, Md., Newman Press [1962].
  212 p. 22 cm.
  MnCS

5256 (ed) Opfer Christi und Opfer der Kirche . . . Düsseldorf, Patmos-Verlag [1960].
  151 p. 24 cm.
  MnCS

5257 (tr) Thomas Aquinas, Saint. [Summa theologica] III, 60–72: Die Sakramente. Taufe und Firmung. [Uebersetzung von P. Bernhard Barth, O.S.B., und P. Burkhard Neunheuser], Salzburg, A. Pustet, 1935.
  24, 579 p. 20 cm. (Die deutsche Thomas-Ausgabe, 29. Bd)
  PLatS

5258 (tr) Thomas Aquinas, Saint. [Summa theologica] III, 84–90 [und] Supplement, 1–16: Das Sakrament der Busse. Kommentiert von Burkhard Neunheuser, O.S.B. Graz, Verlag Styria, 1962.
  16, 652 p. 20 cm. (Die deutsche Thomas-Ausgabe, 31. Bd.)
  ILSP; InStme; PLatS

5259 **Neut, Edouard,** 1890–
  Moines et apotres . . . Louvain, Museum Lessianum [1926].
  32 p. 16 cm.
  InStme

Neužil, Procopius, 1861–1946.
5260 Mluvnice pro české akoly v Americe, Dil l . . . Chicago, Nákl. tiskárny českých Benediktinu [188-].
  44 p. 16 cm.
  ILSP

5261 Svaty Benedikt, ucitel, apostol a vudce. Chicago, Tiskarny Ceskych Benediktinu [1932].
  224 p. illus. 19 cm.
  MnCS

5262 **Neville, Eileen, Sister.**
  The function of the concept of organic unity in the writings of John Ruskin between 1857 and 1870.
  433 p.
  Thesis (Ph.D.)–St. Louis University, 1958.
  SdYa

5263 **New Subiaco Abbey, Subiaco, Ark.**
  The Abbey message. 1– 1952–
  Bi-annual.
  InFer; ArSu

Newark, N.J., St. Mary's Church.

5264 Andenken an das goldene Jubilaeum der Sankt Marien Kirche, Newark, N. J., 1907. 56 p. illus., ports. 26 cm.
PLatS

5265 Official souvenir of St. Mary's Parish for the golden jubilee. [Newark, 1907]. [18] p. ports. 23 cm.
PLatS

5266 **Newark Abbey, Newark, N. J.**
Saint Mary, my every day Missal and heritage . . . by the monks of St. Mary's Abbey, Newark, N.J., Boston, Benziger Bros. [1948]. 36, 1340 p. illus. 17 cm.
MnCS; NcBe

5267 **Ngoc-Hoang, Marie-Joseph.**
Toward a Vietnamese monasticism.
(*In* Meeting of the Monastic Superiors in the Far East, Bangkok, Thailand, 1968. A new charter for monasticism. Notre Dame, 1970. p. 199–211)
PLatS

5268 **Nicolaus de Dulcano.**
Ars planae musicae, et alia ad musicam pertinentia. MS. Benediktinerabtei Melk, Austria, codex 1099, f.103– Duodecimo. Saec. 15.
Microfilm: MnCH proj. no. 1853

5269 **Nicolaus de Görlitz, monk of Melk.**
Sermones. MS. Benediktinerabtei Melk, Austria, codex 1090. 505 p. Octavo. Saec. 15.
Microfilm: MnCH proj. no. 1844

Nicolaus de Tudeschis.

5270 Glossa Clementinarum. MS. Vienna, Schottenstift, codex 134, f.221r–273v. Folio. Saec. 15.
Microfilm: MnCH proj. no. 3934

5371 Lectura in librum primum Decretalium. MS. Vienna, Schottenstift, codex 2. 320 f. Folio. Saec. 15.
Microfilm: MnCH proj. no. 3851

5272 Lectura in librum secundum Decretalium. MS. Vienna, Schottenstift, codex 3. 413 f. Folio. Saec. 15.
Microfilm: MnCH proj. no. 3853

5273 Lectura in librum tertium Decretalium. MS. Vienna, Schottenstift, codex 4. 305 f. Folio. Saec. 15.
Microfilm: MnCH proj. no. 3852

5274 Recollectae. MS. Schottenstift, codex 9. 196 f. Folio. Saec. 15.
Microfilm: MnCH proj. no. 3857

5275 Super secundo Decretalium. Pars prima. MS. Vienna, Schottenstift, codex 77. 440 f. Folio. Saec. 15.
Microfilm: MnCH proj. no. 3925

Nikolaus von Matzen, abbot of Melk, d. 1425.

5276 Praxis Regulae s. p. Benedicti in sacro loco Specus. MS. Benediktinerabtei Melk, Austria, codex 866, f.1r–13v. Quarto. Saec. 15.
Microfilm: MnCH proj. no. 1684

5277 Practica observantia regularum. MS. Benediktinerabtei Melk, Austria, codex 1094, f.157v–173v. Duodecimo. Saec. 15.
Microfilm: MnCH proj. no. 1847

5278 **Nichols, John,** 1745–1826.
Some account of the alien priories, and of such lands as they are known to have possessed in England and Wales . . . London, J. Nichols, MDCCCLXXIX.
2 v. plates, 19 cm.
KAS

Nicholson, David, 1919–

5279 The interpretation and style of Gregorian chant. Toledo, Gregorian Institute of America [1956].
21 p. music, 22 cm.
MnCS; OrStb

5280 Vernacular and music in the missions. Cincinnati, World Library of Sacred Music [1962].
63 p. 21 cm.
Includes melodies.
MnCS; MoCo; PLatS; InStme

Niederaltaich, Bavaria (Benedictine abbey).

5281 Catalogus codicum manu scriptorum Bibliothecae Regiae Monacensis: Codices 9475–9493 ex monasterio Niederaltaich. Monachii, sumptibus Bibliothecae Regiae, 1874. Unveränderter Nachdruck, Otto Harrassowitz, Wiesbaden, 1968.
MnCH

5282 Erbe und Sendung. [Hrsg. von den Mönchen der Abtei Niederaltaich]. [Stuttgart, Hauchler-Druckhaus, 1963].
13 leaves, [26] p. illus. 15 cm.
PLatS

5283 Hören sein Wort; Festabe für Abt Emmanuel M. Heufelder zum 70. Geburtstag. Hrsg. von der Abtei Niederaltaich. Niederaltaich, Dreiberg-Verlag, 1968.
188 p. port. 23 cm.
PLatS

Niederaltaich, Bavaria (Benedictine abbey). Oekumenisches Institut.

5284 Ehe unter dem Kreuz; ökumenisches Wort für konfessionsverschiedene Braut- und Ehepaare . . . Regensburg, F. Pustet [1967].
130 p. 19 cm.
InStme

5285 Kult und Kontemplation in Ost und West . . . Hrsg. vom Oekumenischen Institut der Abtei Niederaltaich. Regensburg, F. Pustet [1967].
167 p. 19 cm.
InStme

5286 Una sancta; Zeitschrift für ökumenische Begegnung. Jahrg. 1– 1946– Quarterly.
KAS

5287 **Niederberger, Basilius,** 1893–
Die Logoslehre des hl. Cyril von Jerusalem . . . Paderborn, F. Schöningh, 1923.
xii, 127 p. 24 cm.
KAS

5288 **Nierengarten, Ruth, Sister,** 1925–
The relationship of social rank urbanization and segregation to auto theft in the city of St. Louis.
25 p. 28 cm.
Thesis (M.A.)–St. Louis University, 1961.
Typescript.
MnStj(Archives)

Nithard, abbot of St. Riquier, d. 844?
5289 Histoire des fils de Louis le Pieux, édités et traduite par Ph. Lauer. Paris, H. Champion, 1926.
xx, 172 p. 19 cm.
Latin and French on opposite pages.
MnDuS; PLatS

5290 Nithardi historiarum libri IIII.
(*In* Monumenta Germaniae historica. Scriptores. Stuttgart, 1963. t. 2, p. 649–672)
MnCS; PLatS

5291 **Nivelles, Belgium (abbey of Benedictine nuns).**
Cartulaire de Nivelles. Extrait des archives communales de Nivelles transcrit et annoté par Joseph Buisseret et Edgar de Prelle de la Nieppe. Nivelles, Ch. Guignardé, 1892.
119 p. 25 cm.
KAS

Nocent, Adrian, 1913–
5292 L'avenir de la liturgie. Paris, Editions Universitaires [1961].
197 p. 20 cm.
MnCS

5293 Célébrer Jésus Christ; l'année liturgique. Paris, J. P. Delarge [1975–77].
7 v. 20 cm.
MnCS

5294 Contemplar sa gloire: Avent, Noël, Epiphanie. Paris, Ed. Universitaires [1960].
228 p. 21 cm.
CaQStB; PLatS

5295 De libris liturgicis liturgiae romanae. [Roma], Institutum Pontificum Liturgicum Anselmianum, 1967–68.
152 p. 23 cm.
InStme

5296 Dictionary of the Council. Edited by J. Deretz and A. Nocent, O.S.B. Washington, Corpus Books [1968].
506 p. 24 cm.
Slightly abridged translation of Synopse des textes conciliaires.
MnCS; NcBe; PLatS

5297 The future of the liturgy. [Translated by Irene Uribe]. [New York], Herder and Herder [1963].
215 p. 21 cm.
InFer; NcBe; PLatS; KAS; NdRi; MoCo; MnCS

5298 The liturgical year. Translated by Matthew J. O'Connell. Collegeville, Minn., The Liturgical Press [1977].
4 v. 20 cm.
Translation of: Célébrer Jésus-Christ; l'année liturgique.
InFer; CaMWiSb; MdRi; InStme; KAS; MnCS; NcBe; MnStj

5299 The parts of the Mass.
(*In* Barauna, Guilherme, ed. The liturgy of Vatican II. 1966. v. 2, p. 27–61)
PLatS

5300 The prayer of the faithful.
(*In* Barauna, Guilherme, ed. The liturgy of Vatican II. 1966. v. 2, p. 83–106)
PLatS

5301 **Nogent le Rotrou, France. Saint Denis (Benedictine abbey).**
Saint-Denis de Nogent-Le-Rotrou, 1031–1789. Vannes, Lafolye, 1895.
cxxiv, 345 p. illus. 25 cm.
KAS

5302 **Nolan, Kieran,** 1933–
The immortality of the soul and the resurrection of the body according to Giles of Rome: a historical study of a 13th-century theological problem. Roma, Studium Theologicum Augustianum, 1967.
xxii, 146 p. 23 cm.
Author's thesis–Ludwig-Maximilian University, Munich, 1962.
KAS; MnCS; PLatS

Nolle, Lambert, 1864–
5303 All Souls.'
(*In* Sermons for the times, by noted preachers of our own day. New York, 1913. v. 1, p. 7–13)
PLatS

5304 The fruits of the Holy Ghost.
(*In* Sermons for the times, by noted preachers of our own day. New York,

1913. v. 1, p. 381–386)
PLatS

5305   What is the Eucharist? London, Catholic
Truth Society, 1937.
32 p. 13 cm.
MnCS

**5305a Nonnemielen, Belgium (abbey of Bene-
dictine nuns).**
Regestenlist der Oorkonden van de
Benediktinessenabdij te Nonnemielen-bij-
Sint-Truiden, door J. Martens, A. Zoete.
Brussel, Algemeen Rijksarchief, 1971.
vii, 251 p. 30 cm.
MnCS

5305b Noreen, Gladys Ruth, Sister.
Notes and comments on the Rule of Saint
Benedict. San Diego, Calif., Benedictine
Sisters [1979].
[7], 178 p. 22 cm.
KAS; MnCS; MoCo

5306   **Norwich Priory, England.**
The charters of Norwich Cathedral
Priory. Edited by Barbara Dodwell. Lon-
don, J. W. Ruddock & Sons, 1974–
v. plates, 25 cm.
MnCS

Notes on the origin . . . of the restored
English Benedictine Congregation. *See*
Ford, Hugh Edmund.

Notker, Balbulus, ca. 840–912.

5307   [Selections]
The alleluiatic sequence (Cantemus
cuncti). Hymn for the Nativity (Natus ante
saecula). Hymn for Christmastide (Grates
nunc omnes).
(*In* Donahoe, D. J. Early Christian
hymns. New York, 1908–11. v. 1, p. 139–
140; v. 2, p. 73–74)
PLatS

5308   [Carmina]
(*In* Foucher, J. P. Florilege de la poésie
sacrée. Paris, 1961. p. 143–151)
PLatS

5309   De illustribus viris, qui ex intentione
Sacras Scripturas exponebant. MS. Vienna, Nationalbibliothek, codex 766,
v. 61v–67r. Folio. Saec. 12.
Microfilm: MnCH proj. no. 14,083

5310   De viris illustribus. MS. Cistercienserabtei Zwettl, Austria, codex 328, f.145v–
152v. Quarto. Saec. 13.
Microfilm: MnCH proj. no. 6938

5311   Epistola ad cancellarium Liutwardum
(fragmentum). MS. Vienna, Nationalbibliothek, codex 1609, f.64r. Octavo. Saec. 10.
Microfim: MnCH proj. no. 14,933

5312   Liber de gestis Caroli Magni. MS. Salisbury, England, Cathedral Library, codex
80, f.198–241. Quarto. Saec. 13.
Microfilm: MnCH

5313   [Gesta Karoli Magni]
Early lives of Charlemagne, by Eginhard
& the Monk of St. Gall. Translated and
edited by A. J. Grant. New York, Cooper
Square Publishers, 1966.
xxv, 179 p. 17 cm.
PLatS

5314   Liber de interpretibus Divinarum Scrip-
turarum. MS. Augustinerchorherrenstift
Klosterneuburg, Austria, codex 1037,
f.39r–44r. Quarto. Saec. 12.
Microfilm: MnCH proj. no. 6013

5315   Notkeri poetae (Balbuli) Liber hymnorum, latine et theotisce. Editio minor.
Accedunt Melodiae V. Notkers des
Dichters (des Stammlers) Hymnenbuch, lateinisch und deutsch, hrsg. von Wolfram
von den Steinen. Kleine Ausgabe, ver-
mehrt um 5 Melodien, hrsg. von Günter
Birkner. Bern, Francke Verlag [1960].
94 p. music. 23 cm.
Latin and German on opposite pages.
PLatS

5316   Liturgische Prosen erster Epoche aus
den Sequenzenschulen des Abendlandes,
insbesondere die dem Notkerus Balbulus
zugeschriebenen . . . neu hrsg. von
Clemens Blume, S.J., und Henry Bannister. New York and London, Johnson
Reprint Corporation, 1961.
xxx, 414 p. 21 cm. (Analecta hymnica
Medii Aevi, 53)
PLatS

5317   Notatio: Cenobitae sunt Galli de illustri-
but viris . . . MS. Augustinerchorherrenstift Klosterneuburg, Austria, codex 1037,
f.39r. Quarto. Saec. 12.
Microfilm: MnCH proj. no. 6013

5318   Sequentia in natalitiis SS. Petri et Pauli.
MS. Prämonstratenserabtei Schlägl,
Austria, codex 3, f.1r. Quarto. Saec.
12–13.
Microfilm: MnCH proj. no. 3068

5319   Sequentiae. MS. Vienna, Nationalbibliothek, codex 4977, f.8r–54r. Quarto. Saec.
15.
Microfilm: MnCH proj. no. 18,157

5320   Taten Kaiser Karls des Grossen. Hrsg.
von Hans F. Haefele. Berlin, Weidmannsche Verlagsbuchhandlung, 1962.
lvi, 127 p. 23 cm. (Monumenta Germaniae historica. Scriptores rerum
germanicarum. Nova series, t. 12)
MnCS; PLatS

**Notre-Dame-de-la-Paix, Joliette,
Canada.** *See* Joliette, Canada. Abbaye
de Notre-Dame-de-la-Paix.

Novelli, Leandro, 1909–
5321   Il coro intagliato della Basilica di S. Maria del Monte di Cesena. Cesena, Edizioni Badia S. Maria del Monte [n.d.].
43 p. plates, 32 cm.
MnCS

5322   Costituzioni della chiesa Bolognese emanate nel sinodo diocesano del 1310 al tempo del vescovo Uberto. Bononiae, Institutum Gratianum, 1962.
450–552 p. 24 cm.
MnCS

5323   Ex voto del Santuario della Madonna del Monte diCesena. [Forli, Società tip. forlivese, 1961]
187 p. 214 plates (21 col.) 32 cm.
KAS; MnCS; MnStj; PLatS

5324   **Novena en honor del glorioso patriarca San Benito,** sequida de un triduo en honor de Santa Escolastica. Mexico, D.F., Padres Benedictinos, 1959.
46 p. 15 cm.
KAS; MxMT

5325   **The Novice manual;** a collection of prayers and instructions for novices of the Order of St. Benedict. 3d rev. ed. St. Meinrad, Ind., St. Meinrad Abbey, 1927.
285 p. 15 cm.
InStme

5326   **Nowell, Mary Irene, Sister.**
Der arme Heinrich, by Hartmann von Aue and Gerhart Hauptmann.
81 leaves, 28 cm.
Thesis (M.A.)–Catholic University of America, 1964.
Typescript.
MnCS

Nuestra Señora de la Resurrección, Cuernavaca, Mexico. *See* Cuernavaca, Mexico. Monasterio de Neustra Señora de la Resurrección.

Nun of Stanbrook. *See* Stanbrook Abbey.

Nun of Tyburn Convent. *See* London, England. Tyburn Convent.

5327   **Nuremberg, Germany. St. Aegidius (Benedictine abbey).**
Excerpta consuetudinum observantiae regularis monasterii Nurnbergensis conventus Ordinis S. Benedicti. MS. Benediktinerabtei Melk, Austria, codex 639, f.247r–249v. Quarto. Saec. 15.
Microfilm: MnCH proj. no. 1524

5328   **Nuxoll, M. Ildephonse, Sister,** 1906–
Idaho Benedictine; St. Gertrude's Convent, Cottonwood, Idaho. [Cottonwood, Idaho, St. Gertrude's Convent, 1974].
71 p. illus., map.
InFer; MoCo

5329   **Oberaltaich, Bavaria (Benedictine abbey).**
Catalogus codicum manu scriptorum Bibliothecae Regiae Monacensis: Codices 9501–9841 ex mon. Oberaltaich. Monachii, sumptibus Bibliothecae Regiae, 1874. Unveränderter Nachdruck, Otto Harrassowitz, Wiesbaden, 1968.
MnCH

5330   **Oberascher, Maurus,** d. 1697.
Ara coeli, seu Memoria mirabilium de augustissimo Missae sacrificio speculative & practice concinnata . . . Salisburgi, Joan. Bapt. Mayr, 1669.
[10], 236 p. 14 cm.
KAS

5331   **Oberembt, Doris, Sister.**
A study of the relationship between physiological reactions of listeners and their attitudes toward stuttering.
Thesis (M.A.)–University of South Dakota, 1964.
52 p.
SdYa

5332   **Oberhauser, Benedikt,** 1719–1786.
Manuale selectiorum conciliorum, et canonum aliorumque rerum memorabiliorum . . . Salzburg, Orphanotrophium, 1776.
440 p.
AStb

5333   **Obermeier, Mildred, Sister.**
Some Catholic writers of Kentucky.
66 leaves, 28 cm.
Thesis (Lib. Sc.)–Catholic University of America, 1936.
Typescript.
KyCovS

5334   **Oberndorffer, Coelestinus,** 1724–1765.
Theologia dogmatico-historico-scholastica ad usum inclyti et episcopalis lycei Frisingeneis. Frisingae, Philippus Ludovicus Böck, 1762–80.
12 v. 18 cm.
KAS(v.1–8); NcBe(v.1–7)

5335   **O'Brien, Columban,** 1922–
A summer pilgrimage 1970. St. Meinrad, Ind., 1970.
45 p.
InFer

Oddo, abbot of Cluny, *See* Odo, Saint, abbot of Cluny.

Odilo, Saint, abbot of Cluny, ca. 962–1048.
5336   Epitaphium domnae Adalheidae Augustae. MS. Vienna, Nationalbibliothek, codex 622, f.3v–26r. Octavo. Saec. 11.
Microfilm: MnCH proj. no. 13,968

5337 Epitaphium Adalheidae imperatricis auctore Odilone.
(*In* Monumenta Germaniae historica. Scriptores. Stuttgart, 1963. t. 4, p. 633–649)
MnCS; PLatS

5338 Lebensbeschreibung der Kaiserin Adelheid.
(*In* Festschrift zur Jahrtausendfeier der Kaiserkrönung Ottos des Grossen. Graz, 1962–   , v. 2)
MnCS; PLatS

5339 Epitaphium maximi Ottonis Augusti imperatoris. MS. Vienna, Nationalbibliothek, codex 622, f.1v–3r. Octavo. Saec. 11.
Microfilm: MnCH proj. no. 13,968

5340 Vita sancti Zosimi abbatis, seu sanctae Mariae Aegyptiacae. MS. Vienna, Nationalbibliothek, codex 622, f.26v–61v. Octavo. Saec. 11.
Microfilm: MnCH proj. no. 13,968

5341 (2dary) Les saints abbés de Cluny. Textes choisis, traduits et présentés par Raymond Oursel. Namur, Editions du Soleil Levant [1960].
100 p. 17 cm.
PLatS

Odington, Walter, d.ca. 1330.

5342 De speculatione musicae, part VI, translated by Jay A. Huff. [n.p.], American Institute of Musicology, 1973.
40 p. music. 25 cm. (Musicological studies & documents, 31)
PLatS

Odo, monk of Asta, fl. ca. 1120

5343 Expositio super Apocalypsim Ioannis evang. MS. Subiaco, Italy (Benedictine abbey), codex 90. Quarto. Saec. 13.
Microfilm: MnCH

5344 Super Psalmos. MS. Lambeth Palace Library, London, codex 219. 118 f. Quarto. Saec. 12.
Microfilm: MnCH

Odo, bp. of Beauvais, 801–881.

5345 (2dary) Ratramnus, monk of Corbie. Liber de anima ad Odonem Bellovacensem. Texte inedit, publié par d. C. Lambot, O.S.B. Namur, Editions Godenne [1952].
158 p. 26 cm.
PLatS

Odo, Saint, abbot of Cluny, 779(ca.)–942.

5346 Dialogus de musica. MS. Vienna, Nationalbibliothek, codex 51, f.45v–48v. Folio. Saec. 12.
Microfilm: MnCH proj. no. 13,416

5347 Dialogus de arte musica. Quomodo organistrum construatur et de fistulis. Regulae super abacum. Regulae de rhyth-

mimachia. MS. Vienna, Nationalbibliothek, codex 2503, f.37r–57v. Octavo. Saec. 13.
Microfilm: MnCH proj. no. 15,818

5348 Hymn for St. Mary Magdalene (Summi parentis unice).
(*In* Donahoe, D. J. Early Christian hymns. New York, 1908. v. 1, p. 143–146)
PLatS

Odo, abbot of Glandfeuil.

5349 Sermo de festo S. Bernardi. MS. Vienna, Nationalbibliothek, codex 445, f.69v–75v. Folio. Saec. 12.
Microfilm: MnCH proj. no. 13,782

Odo de Deuil, abbot of Saint Denis, d.ca. 1162.

5350 De profectione Ludovici VII in orientem. The journey of Louis VII to the East. Edited, with an English translation, by Virginia Gingerick Berry. New York, Norton [1965, c 1948].
xliv, 154 p. maps, 21 cm.

Odorannus, monk of St. Pierre-le-Vir, d. 1046.

5351 Opera omnia. Textes édités, traduits et annotés par Robert Henri Bautier et Monique Gilles, et pour la partie musicologique, par Marie-Elisabeth Duchez et Michel Huglo. Paris, Editions du Centre National de la Recherche Scientifique, 1972.
321 p. 25 cm.
PLatS

Oer, Sebastian von, 1845–1925.

5352 Handbuch für Oblaten des hl. Vaters Benediktus. Beuron, 1898.
v, 150 p. 16 cm.
InStme

5353 Kommet und kostet! Kommunionbuch. 4. u. 5. Aufl. Freiburg i.B., Herder [1921].
634 p. 13 cm.
MnCS

5354 Unsere Schwächen. 9. Aufl. Freiburg i.B., Herder [1910].
viii, 286 p. 17 cm.
PLatS

Oesterreich, Thomas, 1872–1943.

5355 A general introduction to the books of the Bible; an outline. Belmont, N.C., Belmont Abbey Press [1918].
56 p.
NcBe

Oesterle, Gerard, 1879–1963.

5356 Beuron und die Anfänge des Studienkollegs St. Anselm in Rom.
(*In* Beuron, 1863–1963; Festschrift . . . p. 268–280)
PLatS

5356a Das päpstliche Eigengesetz für die Benediktinische Konfoederation. Sonderdruck:
Benediktinische Monatschrift, Jhg. 28
(1952), p. 353–363.
KAS; MnCS

5357 De potestate abbatum dispensandi ab irregularitatibus.
(*In* Liturgica, 2: Cardinal I. A. Schuster
in memoriam. 1958. v. 2, p. 465–481)
PLatS

Oetgen, Jerome J., 1946–
5358 Background to Chaucer's treatment of
free will and necessity.
iii, 75 leaves, 28 cm.
Thesis – University of North Carolina,
1971.
PLatS

5359 Benedictines in Georgia. Latrobe, Pa.,
St. Vincent Archabbey [1967?]
13 p. illus. 29 cm.
Published as no. 12 of Confluence; intra-
monastic communications.
PLatS

5360 **Ogerius, Abbot.**
Sermones de verbis Domini in coena.
MS. Benediktinerabtei Lambach, Austria,
codex chart. 115, f.185r–208v. Saec. 15.
Microfilm: MnCH proj. no. 535

O'Hare, Kieran.
5361 Corinthians. Conception, Mo., Conception Abbey [1963].
52 p. 21 cm. (Saint Andrew Bible commentary, 21)
PLatS

5362 The Epistles of John and the Apocalypse.
Conception, Mo., Conception Abbey
[1962].
38 p. 21 cm. (Saint Andrew Bible commentary, 29)
PLatS

5363 Samuel. Conception, Mo., Conception
Abbey [1963].
30 p. 21 cm. (Saint Andrew Bible commentary, 7)
PLatS

Ohem, Gallus.
5364 Chronicon Augiae divitis (Reichenau).
MS. Benediktinerabtei St. Paul im Lavanttal, Austria, codex 8/2, part I. Folio. Saec.
16.
Microfilm: MnCH proj. no. 11,741

5365 Chronik des Klosters Reichenau. Mit
coloriten Wappen. MS. Benediktinerabtei
St. Paul im Lavanttal, Austria, codex 11/2.
254 f. Quarto. Saec. 15.
Microfilm: MnCH proj. no. 11,746

Ohligschlager, Maurus, 1895–
5366 An investigation of the teaching of
liturgy in Catholic high schools.

49 leaves, 28 cm.
Thesis (M.A.) – University of Notre
Dame, 1929.
Typescript.
InFer; InStme

5367 Why monastic life? Fundamentals re-
examined.
99 leaves, 29 cm.
Typescript.
InStme

Ohlmeyer, Albert, 1905–
5368 Biblische Volksschriften der Abtei Neuburg. Karlsruhe, Badenin Verlag [1950–
v. 16 cm.
MnCS

5369 Elias, Fürst der Propheten. Freiburg
i.B., Herder [1962].
222 p. 20 cm.
MnCS

5369a (tr) Die Regel des Magister oder die
Regel der heiligen Väter. [Münsterschwar-
zach, Vier-Türme-Verlag, 1974].
159 p. 30 cm.
Als Manuskript gedruckt.
MnCS

Ohm, Thomas, 1892–
5370 Ex contemplatione loqui: gesammelte
Aufsätze. Münster, Aschendorff [1961].
468 p. 24 cm.
MnCS

5371 Die Gebetsgebärden der Völker und das
Christentum. Leiden, Brill, 1948.
xvi, 471 p. illus. 25 cm.
InStme

5372 Die kultischen Elemente in den afri-
kanischen Stammesreligionen.
(*In* Schmaus, Michael, ed. Der Kult und
der heutige Mensch. München, 1961.
p. 107–113)
PLatS

5373 Machet zu Jüngern alle Völker. Freiburg
i.B., Erich Wewel Verlag, 1962.
927 p. 23 cm.
MnCS; PLatS

5374 Mohammedaner und Katholiken. [Mün-
chen], Kösel Verlag [1961].
86 p. 20 cm.
MnCS; PLatS

5375 Wichtige Daten der Missionsgeschichte;
eine Zeittafel. 2., erweiterte und verb.
Aufl. Münster i.W., Aschendorff [1961].
290 p. 19 cm.
PLatS

Oka, Maria Beda, Sister, 1938–
5376 The Elizabethan persecution as reflected
in Evelyn Waugh's "Edmund Campion," by
Oka Yumiko.
62 p. 28 cm.
Typescript.
MnStj(Archives)

5377   (tr) Dazai, Osam. Asa morning. Translated by David J. Brudnoy and Oka Yumiko.
       (*In* Monumenta Nipponica, v. 24, p. 519–522)
       MnStj(Archives)

5378   (tr) Dazai, Osam. Mother Haha. Translated by David J. Brudnoy and Oka Yumiko.
       (*In* Monumenta Nipponica, v. 24, p. 327–335)
       MnStj(Archives)

5379   **Old Testament reading guide.** Collegeville, Minn., The Liturgical Press [1960–79].
       32 v. maps, 20 cm.
       Text and commentaries.
       KAS; MnCS

5380   **Oliba, abbot of Ripoll,** d. 1020.
       Signos e indicois en la portada de Ripoll. olibae abbatis carmina quae exstant de rebus monasterii Rivipullensis edidit A. M. Mundo. Abat Oliba: poemes entorn de Ripoll, traduccio de Jaume Medina. Barcelona, Fundación Juan March, 1976.
       68 p. plates, 22 cm.
       MnCS

5381   **Olinda, Brazil. São Bento (Benedictine abbey).**
       As escolas superiores de agricultura e medicina-veterinaria, Sao Bento, Pernambuco, 1913–1923. [Friburgo em Brisgau (Allemanha), Tipographia de Herder & Cia, 1923].
       [5] p. 20 plates (40 illus.) 32 cm.
       PLatS

       Olivar, Alexandre, 1919–

5382   Catalog dels manuscrits de la biblioteca del monestir de Montserrat. Monestir de Montserrat, 1977.
       xxiv, 562 p. 25 cm. (Scripta et documenta, 25)
       InStme; MnCS

5383   La duración de la predicación antiqua.
       (*In* Liturgica, 3: Cardinal I. A. Schuster in memoriam. Montisserrati, 1966. p. 143–184)
       PLatS

5384   Guillem de Miers, abat de Sant Pau de Roma, i la seva obra litúrgico-monàstica.
       (*In* Liturgica, 2: Cardinal I. A. Schuster in memoriam. 1958. p. 299–345)
       PLatS

5385   Els manuscrits litúrgics de la biblioteca de Montserrat. Monestir de Montserrat, 1969.
       211 p. 25 cm. (Scripta et documenta, 18)
       InStme; KAS; MnCS

5387   Sacramentarium Rivipullense, por Alejandro Olivar. Madrid-Barcelone, 1964.
       301 p. 25 cm. (Monumenta Hispania sacra. Series liturgica, v. 7)
       InStme; PLatS

5388   Los sermones de San Pedro Crisólogo; estudio crítico. Abadia de Montserrat, 1962.
       533 p. 25 cm. (Scripta et documenta, 13)
       InStme; KAS; MnCS

       O'Meara, Shaun, 1931–

5389   Report on first meeting of Asian Benedictine and Trappist superiors, Bangkok, Thailand, December, 1968.
       8 p. 28 cm.
       Mimeographed.
       MnStj(Archives)

5390   Benedictine meeting in Korea, April, 1970.
       10 p. 28 cm.
       Mimeographed.
       MnStj(Archives)

5391   Report on Asian monastic meeting, Bangalore, India, October 14–23, 1973.
       10 p. 28 cm.
       Mimeographed.
       MnStj(Archives)

5392   **O'Neill, Hugh Thomas,** 1894–
       The rates of reduction of some aromatic nitro compounds. [Washington, Catholic University of America, 1930].
       31 p. 23 cm.
       Thesis – Catholic University of America.
       InStme

5393   **Oost, Gregorius van,** 1924–
       De hora celebrationis sacrificii Missae.
       (*In* Liturgica, 2: Cardinal I. A. Schuster in memoriam. 1958. v. 2, p. 401–464)
       PLatS

       Oppenheim, Philipp, 1899–1949.

5394   Christi persona et opus secundum textus liturgiae sacrae. [Roma], Typis Polyglottis Vaticanis, 1935.
       37 p. 24 cm.
       Reprint from Ephemerides liturgicae, a. 1935–36.
       KAS

5395   Maria in der lateinischen Liturgie.
       (*In* Sträter, Paul. Katholische Marienkunde. v. 1(1962), 3.Aufl., p. 183–267)
       PLatS

       Orchard, Bernard, 1910–

5396   Matthew, Luke & Mark. [2d ed.]. Manchester [England], Koinonia Press [1977].
       151 p.
       NcBe

5397   A new Catholic commentary on Holy Scripture. Editorial committee: Bernard Orchard, O.S.B., Reginald C. Fuller [and others]. [2d ed.]. [London], Nelson [1969].
       xix, 1377 p. maps, 26 cm.
       MnCS; PLatS

5398 **Ordericus Vitalis,** 1075–1143?
The ecclesiastical history of Orderic
Vitalis. Edited and translated with intro-
duction and notes by Marjorie Chibnall.
Oxford, Clarendon Press, 1969–
v. 23 cm. (Oxford medieval texts)
PLatS

5399 **Ordinationes et doctrinae pro fratribus
minoribus** (extractatum de constitutione
Mellicensi?). MS. Benediktinerabtei
Kremsmünster, Austria, codex 20,
f.18r–29v. Saec. 15.
Microfilm: MnCH proj. no. 20

5400 **Ordinationes quaedam divinum officium
O.S.B. spectantes.** MS. Benediktinerabtei Kremsmünster, Austria, codex 20,
f.12–172. Saec. 15.
Microfilm: MnCH proj. no. 20

5401 **Origines Murensis monasterii in Helvetiis atque adeo Europa universa celeberrimi Ordinis S. Benedicti . . .**
Spirembergii, in Bibliopolio Brucknausenio, 1618.
[6], 65, [5] p. fold. chart. 24 cm.
KAS

5402 **Ortega, Petri de.**
Exercitium et devotiones. MS. Monasterio benedictino de Montserrat, Spain,
codex 50. 128 f. Octavo. Saec. 17.
Microfilm: MnCH proj. no. 29,993

Osbern, monk of Gloucester.
5403 Liber vocabularius latinus. MS. Augustinerchorherrenstift Klosterneuburg,
Austria, codex 1092. 57 f. Quarto. Saec.
13.
Microfilm: MnCH proj. no. 6101

5404 Panormia sive linguae latinae dictionarium sive vocabulorum derivationes. MS.
Hereford, England, Cathedral Library,
codex P 5 v. 172 f. Quarto. Saec. 12–13.
Microfilm: MnCH

5405 **Osgniach, Augustine John,** 1891–1975.
The philosophic roots of law and order; a
commentary of Christian thought. New
York, Exposition Press [1970]
336 p. 22 cm.
KAS; MnCS; NcBe; OkShG

5406 **Oskian, Hamazasp, O.S.B.Mech.**
Catalog der armenischen Handschriften
in der Mechitaristen-Bibliothek zu Wien,
von Jacobus Dashian (vol. 1) und
Hamazasp Oskian (vol. 2). Wien, Mechitaristen-Buchdruckerei, 1895–1963.
2 v. plates, 30 cm.
MnCS

5407 **Oslaender, Bonifazio,** 1836–1904.
Charitas; letters inaugurale al clero e al
popolo della Abbazia di S. Paolo di Roma
nella Quaresima dell'anno 1896. Roma,
Tipografia della pace di Filippo Cuggiani,
1896.
31 p. 23 cm.
PLatS

Oslender, Frowin, 1902–1960.
5408 (ed) Hampe, Johann Christoph. Paulus:
zwölf farbige Bilder aus dem 9. bis 13.
Jahrhundert, erläutert von Johann
Christoph Hampe. [Hrsg. von Frowin
Oslender, O.S.B.]. Hamburg, Friedrich
Wittig Verlag [1960].
14 [25] p. plates (col.) 21 cm. (Frühmit-
telalterliche Buchmalerei)
MnCS

5409 (ed) Krönig, Wolfgang. Engel: zwölf farbige Miniaturen aus dem frühen Mittelalter, erläuert von Wolfgang Krönig. [Hrsg.
von Frowin Oslender]. Hamburg, F. Wittig
[1957].
15 p. 12 col. plates, 21 cm. (Frühmit-
telalterliche Buchmalerei)
KAS

5410 (ed) Michels, Thomas Aquinas. Parabeln
Christi; zwölf farbige Bilder aus frühmittelalterlichen Handschriften. [Hrsg. von
Frowin Oslender]. Hamburg, F. Wittig
[1959].
16 [24] p. 12 col. plates, 21 cm. (Frühmit-
telalterliche Buchmalerei)
MnCS

5411 (ed) Nyssen, Wilhelm. Eucharistie; zwölf
farbige Bilder aus dem 6. bis 11. Jahrhundert, erläutert von Wilhelm Nyssen. [Hrsg.
von Pater Dr. Frowin Oslender, O.S.B.].
Hamburg, Friedrich Wittig Verlag [1960].
unpaged. col. plates, 21 cm. (Frühmit-
telalterliche Buchmalerei)
MnCS

5412 (ed) Wenger, Paul Wilhelm. Irische
Miniaturen; zwölf farbige Bilder aus Hand-
schriften irischer Mönche, erläutert von
Paul Wilhelm Wenger. [Hrsg. von Pater
Dr. Frowin Oslender, O.S.B.]. Hamburg,
Friedrich Wittig Verlag [1957].
unpaged, col. plates 21 cm. (Frühmit-
telalterliche Buchmalerei)
MnCS

Ossiach, Austria (Benedictine abbey).
5413 Annales Ossiacenses von Abt Zacharias
Gröblacher (1587–1593). Latine et ger-
manice. MS. Klagenfurt, Austria, Kärtner
Landesarchiv, codex GV 2/32. 154 f. Folio.
Saec. 16–18.
Microfilm: MnCH proj. no. 12,747

5414 Ossiacher Aebtebuch. Colorierte Por-
träts. MS. Museum der Stadt Villach,
codex G. 827. 131 f. Folio. Saec. 17.
Microfilm: MnCH proj. no. 12,970

5415   Stiftsregister. MS. Klagenfurt, Austria, Kärtner Landesarchiv, Allgemeine Handschriftensammlung 1154. 251 f. Saec. 17.
Microfilm: MnCH proj. no. 12,911

5416   **Ossino, Angelo,** 1932–
A study in the history of writing and the preservation of books, from the clay tablets to the Renaissance.
123 p.
A paper submitted to the Graduate School of Rosary College, Chicago, 1960.
MoCo

5417   **Ostojić, Ivan.**
Benediktinci u Hrvatskoj i ostalim nasim krajevima. Split, 1963–65.
3 v. illus., maps, 25 cm.
ILSP; InFer; KAS; MoCo; NcBe

Otfridus, monk of Weissenburg.

5418   Liber evangeliarum. MS. Vienna, Nationalbibliothek, codex 913. 376 f. Folio. Saec. 18. Abschrift der Freisinger Handschrift ex saec. 10 (jetzt in München).
Microfilm: MnCH proj. no. 14,808

5419   Poema germanicum de vita Jesu Christi (Liber evangeliorum theotisce conscriptus). MS. Vienna, Nationalbibliothek, codex 2687. 194 f. Quarto. Saec. 9.
Microfilm: MnCH proj. no. 15,935

Othlo, monk of St. Emmeram, Regensburg.

5420   Vita S. Wolfgangi episcopi. Finis deest. MS. Vienna, Nationalbibliothek, codex 818, f.107r–116v. Quarto. Saec. 12.
Microfilm: MnCH proj. no. 14,152

5421   Vita S. Wolfgangi. MS. Universitätsbibliothek Graz, Austria, codex 964, f.286r–294r. Quarto. Saec. 15.
Microfilm: MnCH proj. no. 27,027

5422   Vita S. Wolfgangi episcopi, edente D. G. Waitz.
(*In* Monumenta Germaniae historica. Scriptores. Stuttgart, 1963. t. 4, p. 521–542)
MnCS; PLatS

Ottobeuren, Germany (Benedictine abbey).

5423   Die mittelalterlichen Handschriften in der Abtei Ottobeuren: Kurzverzeichnis [von] Hermann Hauke. Wiesbaden, Otto Harrassowitz, 1974.
122 p. 28 cm.
MnCS

5424   Uttinburra 764–1964; 1200 Jahre Benediktinerabtei Ottobeuren. n.p. n.d.
portfolio, plates (part col.) 55 cm.
MnCS

5425   **Oudenbourg, Belgium (Benedictine abbey).**
Chronique du monastère d'Oudenbourg, de l'Ordre de s. Benoit, publiée pour la première fois d'après un manuscrit du XVe siècle, par l'abbé F. van de Putte. Gand, Impr. et lith. de C. Annoot-Braeckman, 1843.
6, xi, 133 p. 31 cm.
KAS

Our Lady of Grace Convent, Beech Grove, Ind.

5426   The Christ in me recognizes the Christ in you. Beech Grove, Ind., Sisters of St. Benedict, 1975.
72 p.
InFer; InBeG

5427   Encounter.   1–   1961–
InFer; InBeG

5428   Mary-go-round.   1978–
InFer; InBeG

5429   **Our Lady of Guadalupe Abbey, Pecos, N.M.**
The Pecos Benedictine. 1974–
InFer; NmP

5430   **Our Lady of Peace Convent, Columbia, Mo.**
Shalom sharing.   1–   1975–
InFer; MoCol

Oury, Guy Marie, 1929–

5431   Ce que croyait Benoit. [Paris] Mame [1974].
165 p. 18 cm.
CaQMo; MnCS

5431a   Histoire de l'Eglise. Solesmes, [Abbaye Saint-Pierre], 1978.
300 p. 23 cm.
MnCS

5432   Marie, mère de l'Eglise, dans l'année liturgique. Paris, Editions Alsatia, 1966.
208 p. 18 cm.
PLatS

5433   L'Ordre de Saint Benoît. [Paris, les Nouvelles Editions Latines, n.d.].
31 p. 19 cm.
PLatS

5433a   St. Benedict, blessed by God. Translated by Rev. John A. Otto. Collegeville, Minn., The Liturgical Press [1980].
vi, 90 p. 20 cm.
Translation of: Ce que croyait Benoît.
KAS; MnCS

5434   Sainte Opportune, sa vie et ses reliques.
(*In* Chaussy, Yves. L'abbaye d'Almenèches-Argentan. Paris, 1970. p. 221–236)
PLatS

5435   (tr) Les Sentences des Pères du désert. Les Apophtegmes des Pères . . . Traduction de J. Dion et G. Oury. Sarthe, Abbaye Saint-Pierre de Solesmes [1966].
312 p. 21 cm.
InStme

5436 **Oviedo, Spain. San Vicente (Benedictine abbey)**
Colección diplomática del Monasterio de San Vincente de Oviedo (años 781–1200). Estudio y transcripción por Pedro Floriano Llorente. Oviedo, Instituto de Estudios Asturianos, 1968–
v. 24 cm.
MnCS

Pachler, Amandus, fl. 17th cent.
5437 Antiquitates memorabiles Salisburgenses, ex manuscriptis collectae anno 1659. MS. Benediktinerabtei St. Peter, Salzburg, codex a.XII.6. 326 p. Folio. Saec. 17.
Microfilm: MnCH proj. no. 10,268

5438 Compendium in quosdam libros Aristotelis. Dictata ab P. Amando Pachler anno 1652 et 53, scripta ab Joanne Marquardo Mezger. MS. Benediktinerabtei St. Peter, Salzburg, codex a.III.31. 354 p. Octavo. Saec. 17.
Microfilm: MnCH proj. no. 9994

5439 Devotiones hebdomadales quibus amabilis trias Jesus, Maria et Joseph speciali affectu in suis cultoribus coli et honorari possunt. MS. Benediktinerabtei St. Peter, Salzburg, codex b.II.44. 67 p. (secunda vice). Octavo. Saec. 17.
Microfilm: MnCH proj. no. 10,363

5440 Domus cordis decem diebus aedificata, sive Sancta et spiritualia decem dierum exercitiis accommodata secundum ordinem trium viarum. MS. Benediktinerabtei St. Peter, Salzburg, codex a.III.22. 369 p. Octavo. Saec. 17(1650).
Microfilm: MnCH proj. no. 9964

5441 Domus cordis decem diebus aedificata, sive, Spiritualia exercitia accommodata secundum ordinem trium viarum purgativae, illuminativae, et unitivae. MS. Benediktinerabtei St. Peter, Salzburg, codex a.IV.24. 304 f. Octavo. Saec. 17.
Microfilm: MnCH proj. no. 10,015

5442 Exercitia pietatis erga augustissimam coelorum principem Virginam Mariam. MS. Benediktinerabtei St. Peter, Salzburg, codex a.IV.3, f.1–66 (secunda vice). Octavo. Saec. 17.
Microfilm: MnCH proj. no. 9991

5443 Intentiones sanctae quibus asceta spiritualis tota die Deo intendere et animam suam spiritualibus delitiis omni momento recreare poterit. MS. Benediktinerabtei St. Peter, Salzburg, codex a.III.27. 376 f. Octavo. Saec. 17(1650).
Microfilm: MnCH proj. no. 9976

5444 Libellus sanctorum per totum annum. MS. Benediktinerabtei St. Peter, Salzburg, codex a.IV.3, f.1–78. Octavo. Saec. 17(1650).
Microfilm: MnCH proj. no. 9991

5445 Sancti per annum. MS. Benediktinerabtei St. Peter, Salzburg, codex b.II.44. 235 p. Octavo. Saec. 17.
Microfilm: MnCH proj. no. 10,363

Pacis nuntius. *See* Monte Cassino (Benedictine abbey). Pacis nuntius.

Pail, Leander, 1894–1954.
5446 History of the foundation of the Catholic University of Peking.
unpaged, 20 cm.
Entirely in Chinese.
MnCS

Palacios, Mariano, 1927–
5447 El monasterio de Santo Domingo de Silos. Leon, Editorial Everst [1973].
64 p. illus. 26 cm.
MnCS

Palmer, Jerome, 1904–
5448 History of the rite of solemn profession in the Order of St. Benedict.
iii, 164 leaves, 28 cm.
Thesis (M.A.)–Catholic University of America, 1962.
Typescript.
InStme

5449 How to give a talk. St. Meinrad, Ind., Abbey Press, 1972.
64 p. 18 cm.
InStme

5450 Our Lady returns to Egypt. [San Bernardino, Cal., Culligan Book Co., 1969].
64 p. illus. 22 cm.
InFer; InStme

Palmer, Robert.
5451 The Rule of the Master. An English translation by Robert Palmer, O.S.B., of Mount Angel Abbey, 1968.
129, 47 p. 28 cm.
Typescript.
MoCo

Palmieri, Gregorio, 1828–1918.
5452 Introito ed esiti di Papa Niccolò III (1279–1280). Antichissimo documento di lingua italiana tratto dall'archivio Vaticano, corredato di due pagine in eliotipia, degl'indici alfabetici geografico e onomastico e di copiose note. Roma, Tipografia Vaticana, 1889.
xxxvii, 127 p. facsims. 26 cm.
MnCS

5453 (ed) Garampi, Giuseppe. Viagio in Germania, Baviera, Svizzera, Olanda e Francia compiuto negli anni 1761-1763 . . . Edizione condotta sul codice inedito esistente nell' archivio Vaticano . . . per Gregorio

Palmieri. Roma, Tipografia Vaticana, 1889.
xxii, 328 p. 27 cm.
InStme; MnCS

Pannonhalma, Hungary (Benedictine abbey).
5454   Compendium asceseos Benedictinae. Posonii, typis Haeredum Belnayanorum, 1852.
115 p. 21 cm.
Preface signed at S. Monte Pannoniae.
KAS

5455   Schematismus religiosorum Ordinis S. Benedicti de Sacro Monte Pannoniae ad annum . . . Coloczae, typis Antonii Malatin, 1896–
v. 23 cm.
MnCS (1896–1914); PLatS

5456   **Pansini, Jude,** 1930–
"El Pilar," a plantation microcosm of Guatemalan ethnicity.
346 p. illus.
Thesis (Ph.D.)–University of Rochester, N.Y., 1977.
MoCo

Pantoni, Angelo, 1905–
5457   Una venduta Vaticana di Montecassino nei suoi rapporti con le raffigurazioni e descrizioni coeve delle'abbazia.
(*In* Mélanges Eugéne Tisserant, v. 5, p. 171–182)
PLatS

5458   La vicende della basilica di Montecassino attraverso la documentazione archeologica. Introduzione e appendice di Tommaso Leccisotti. Montecassino [1973].
225 p. plates (part col.), diagrs. 26 cm.
(Miscellanea Cassinese . . . 36)
MnCS

Paris, Matthew, 1200–1259.
5459   Appendix ad Rogeri de Wendover Flores historiarum: in qua lectionum varietas additionesque, quibus chronicon istud ampliavit et instruxit Matthaeus Parisiensis. Londini, sumptibus Societatis, 1844.
xvi, 327 p. 23 cm. [English Historical Society Publications]
Vaduz, Kraus Reprint, 1964.
PLatS

5460   Historia major juxta exemplar Londinense 1640 verbatim recusa, et cum Rogeri Wendoveri, Willielmi Rishangeri, authorisque majori minorique historiis . . . fideliter collata . . . Editore Willielmo Wats . . . Londini, impensis A. Mearne . . . 1682–1684.
[35], 861, [111], 961–1175, [33] p. 37 cm.

Vitae and additamenta have separate title pages, with imprints 1682 and 1683, respectively.
KAS

5461   **Paris, France. St. Germain-des-Prés (Benedictine abbey).**
Nécrologe de la Congrégation de Saint-Maur décédés à l'Abbaye de Saint-Germain-des-Prés. Publié avec introduction, suppléments et appendices par m. l'abbé J. B. Vanel. Paris, H. Champion, 1896.
lxiii, 412 p. 29 cm.
MnCS

5462   **Paris, France. Saint-Louis-du-Temple (abbey of Benedictine nuns).**
Great Saint Benedict as told to little ones, by B. Temple. [Montreal, Les Ateliers St.-Grégoire, 1947].
21 p. illus. 18 cm.
MnCS

Parry, David, 1908–
5463   Benedictine heritage. Ramsgate, The Monastery Press, 1961.
44 p. 19 cm.
MnCS; NdRi; PLatS

5463a   Households of God; the Rule of St. Benedict with explanations for monks and laypeople today. London, Darton, Longman & Todd, 1980.
xxiv, 199 p. 22 cm.
KAS; NcBe

5463b   Households of God; the Rule of St. Benedict with explanations for monks and laypeople today. Kalamazoo, Cistercian Publications [1980].
199 p. (Cistercian studies series, no. 39)
NcBe

5464   Monastic century; St. Augustine's Abbey, Ramsgate, 1861–1961. [Tenbury Wells, England], Fowler Wright Books [1965].
142 p. illus., ports. 23 cm.
InStme; KAS; MnCS; NcBe; PLatS

5464a   Not mad, most noble Festus; essays on the renewal movement. London, Darton, Longman & Todd [1978].
[vi], 103 p. 22 cm.
KAS

5465   Scholastic century; St. Augustine's Abbey School, Ramsgate, 1865–1965. [Tenbury Wells, England], F. Wright Books [1965].
101 p. illus., ports. 23 cm.
InStme; KAS; MnCS; PLatS

5466   This promise is for you; spiritual renewal and the charismatic movement. New York, Paulist Press, 1977.
vii, 147 p. 19 cm.
InFer; InStme; MnCS; MdRi; KAS

5467 **Pascek, Bonaventure,** 1932–
Property updated; a study of doctrine.
47 leaves, 28 cm.
Thesis (M.A.)–St. Vincent College,
Latrobe, Pa., 1966.
Typescript.
PLatS

**Paschasius Radbertus, Saint, abbot of
Corbie,** d. ca. 860.
Manuscript items.

5468 Collatio monachorum. MS. Winchester
College, England, codex 18, pt. 2. 200 f.
folio. Saec. 12.
Microfilm: MnCH

5469 Liber de Corpore et Sanguine Domini.
MS. Benediktinerabtei St. Peter, Salzburg,
codex a.VI.15, f.33r–76r. Quarto. Saec. 11.
Microfilm: MnCH proj. no. 10,077

5470 De Corpore et Sanguine Domini. MS.
Benediktinerabtei St. Paul im Lavanttal,
Austria, codex 13/1, f.66r–70v. Quarto.
Saec. 11–12.
Microfilm: MnCH proj. no. 11,668

5471 Liber de Corpore et Sanguine Christi.
MS. Vienna, Nationalbibliothek, codex
864, f.1r–54r. Quarto. Saec. 11.
Microfilm: MnCH proj. no. 14,190

5472 Tractatus de Corpore et Sanguine
Christi. MS. Benediktinerabtei Admont,
Austria, codex 662, f.35r–141v. Quarto.
Saec. 12.
Microfilm: MnCH proj. no. 9700

5473 Liber de Corpore et Sanguine Domini.
MS. Universitätsbibliothek Graz, Austria,
codex 171, f.75r–118v. Quarto. Saec. 12.
Microfilm: MnCH proj. no. 26,102

5474 De Corpore et Sanguine Christi. MS.
Cistercienserabtei Heiligenkreuz, Austria,
codex 215, f.117r–163r. Folio. Saec. 12.
Microfilm: MnCH proj. no. 4755

5475 Liber de Corpore et Sanguine Christi.
MS. Linz, Austria. Bundesstaatliche Stu-
dienbibliothek, codex 138, f.1r–43v.
Quarto. Saec. 12.
Microfilm: MnCH proj. no. 27,864

5476 De sacramento eucharistiae. MS. Salisbury, England, Cathedral Library, codex
130, f.1–33. Quarto. Saec. 12.
Microfilm: MnCH

5477 Versus de Corpore et Sanguine Domini.
MS. Vienna, Nationalbibliothek, codex
863, f.51v–52r.
Octavo. Saec. 12.
Microfilm: MnCH proj. no. 14,177

5478 De Corpore et Sanguine Domini (excerpta). MS. Vienna, Nationalbibliothek,
codex 982, f.71v–76r. Folio. Saec. 12.
Microfilm: MnCH proj. no. 14,292

5479 Liber de Corpore et Sanguine Domini.
MS. Augustinerchorherrenstift Vorau,
Austria, codex 335, f.114r–142r. Quarto.
Saec. 13–14.
Microfilm: MnCH proj. no. 7305

5480 De sacramento Corporis et Sanguinis
Christi. MS. Augustinerchorherrenstift
Klosterneuburg, Austria, codex 817,
f.4r–32v. Quarto. Saec. 14.
Microfilm: MnCH proj. no. 5798

5481 Liber de Corpore et Sanguine Christi.
MS. Subiaco, Italy (Benedictine abbey),
codex 299. Saec. 14.
Microfilm: MnCH

5482 Liber de Corpore et Sanguine Domini.
MS. Vienna, Nationalbibliothek, codex
863, f.140v–141v.
Microfilm: MnCH proj. no. 14,177

5483 Epistola ad Rupertum Placidum. MS.
Vienna, Nationalbibliothek, codex 863,
f.52r–140r. Octavo. Saec. 12.
Microfilm: MnCH proj. no. 14,177

5484 In Lamentationibus Hieremiae votorum
libri quinque. MS. Winchester College,
England, codex 5. 126 f. Quarto. Saec.
11–12.
Microfilm: MnCH

Printed works

5485 Charlemagne's cousins; contemporary
lives of Adalard and Wala. Translated,
with introduction, notes, by Allen
Cabaniss. Syracuse University Press
[1967].
vii, 266 p. 24 cm.
InStme; PLatS

5486 Der Pseudo-Hieronymus Brief IX
"Cogitis me"; ein erster Marianischer Traktat des Mittelalters von Paschasius Radbert. Hrsg. von Albert Ripberger.
Freiburg, Schweiz, Universitätsverlag,
1962.
xiv, 150 p. 26 cm. (Spicilegium Friburgense, v. 9)
PLatS

5487 De Corpore et sanguine Domini, cum appendice Epistola ad Fredugardum. Cura et
studio Bedae Paulus, O.S.B. Trunholti,
Brepols, 1969.
lvii, 250 p. 25 cm. (Corpus Christianorum. Continuatio mediaevalis, 16)
InStme; KAS; PLatS

5488 Vita s.Adalhardi abbatis Corbeiensis et
vita Walae abbatis Corbeiensis.
(*In* Monumenta Germaniae historica.
Scriptores. Stuttgart, 1963. t. 2, p. 524–
569)
MnCS; PLatS

5489 **Passio Herasmi monachi.** Benediktinerabtei Kremsmünster, Austria, codex 7, f.129r–137r. Saec. 13.
Microfilm: MnCH proj. no. 7

Passelecq, Paul, 1909–
5490 Criez-le sur les toits . . . 2. éd. Bruges, Beyaert [1966].
505 p. 19 cm.
MnCS

5491 Du neuf et du vieux . . . 2. éd. Bruges, Ch. Beyaert [1964].
362 p. 19 cm.
MnCS

5492 L'Evangile parlé. 3. éd. Editions de Maredsous [1966].
188 p. 20 cm.
MnCS

5493 Guide to the Bible, by the Monks of Maredsous. Translated from the French by Gerda R. Blumenthal, with a preface by John M. T. Barton. Springfield, Ill., Templegate [1958].
92 p. illus. 18 cm.
Translation of Guide biblique.
KAS

5494 Panorama biblique; exposition sur la Bible. Panneaux décoratifs exécutes par Roger Duterme. 3. éd. Editions de Maredsous [1954].
31 p. illus. 22 cm.
CaQStB; PLatS

5495 Préjugés des catholiques contre la lecture de la Bible. Editions de Maredsous [1954].
46 p. 19 cm.
CaQStB; CaQStM; PLatS

5496 Sous le marteau de la parole (Jérêmie, 23:29). Editions de Maredsous [1968].
307 p. 20 cm.
MnCS

Paulus, monk of Altenburg.
5497 Expositiones super libros S. Scripturae: Job, Parabolas, Ecclesiasten, Cantica canticorum, Sapientia, Ecclesiasticum, Treni, Apocalypsin, Epistolas S. Jacobi, Petri, Joannis, Judae, XII Prophetae. MS. Benediktinerabtei Altenburg, Austria, codex AB 13 F 23, f.1r–137v. Octavo. Saec. 14.
Microfilm: MnCH proj. no. 6383

5498 Sermones de tempore; Sermones de caritate et praeceptis. MS. Benediktinerabtei Altenburg, Austria, codex AB 13 F 23, f.139r–194v. Octavo. Saec. 14.
Microfilm: MnCH proj. no. 6383

Paulus Diaconus, 720(ca.)–797?
Manuscript copies
5499 De gestis Longobardorum. MS. Salisbury, England, Cathedral Library, codex 80, f.132–188. Quarto. Saec. 13.
Microfilm: MnCH

5500 De gestis Romanorum libri XII (fragmentum). Incipit: . . . maximi se in acquam suffocavit. MS. Universitätsbibliothek Salzburg, codex M II 280. 1 f. Octavo. Saec. 15.
Microfilm: MnCH proj. no. 11,388

5501 Eutropius et Paulus Diaconus: Historia romana. MS. Benediktinerabtei Kremsmünster, Austria, codex 36, f.177r–252v. Saec. 12.
Microfilm: MnCH proj. no. 36

5502 Excerpta e Pompejo Festo De verborum significatione, libri 1–9. MS. Vienna, Nationalbibliothek, codex 142. 104 f. Quarto. Saec. 10.
Microfilm: MnCH proj. no. 13,495

5503 Excerpta e Pompejo Festo De verborum significatione. Libri 19. MS. Vienna, Nationalbibliothek, codex 250. 121 f. Quarto. Saec. 15.
Microfilm: MnCH proj. no. 13,587

5504 Historiae Langobardorum. Libri sex. MS. Vienna, Nationalbibliothek, codex 237. 105 f. Quarto. Saec. 11.
Microfilm: MnCH proj. no. 13,596

5505 Historia Langobardorum. Libri sex. MS. Vienna, Nationalbibliothek, codex 182, f.1r–69v. Folio. Saec. 12.
Microfilm: MnCH proj. no. 13,538

5506 Historia Langobardorum. Finis deest. MS. Vienna, Nationalbibliothek, codex 406, f.27v–81v. Folio. Saec. 12.
Microfilm: MnCH proj. no. 13,742

5507 Historia Langobardorum. MS. Vienna, Nationalbibliothek, codex 443, f.89r–130r. Folio. Saec. 12.
Microfilm: MnCH proj. no. 13,777

5508 Historia miscella. Lib. 1–16. MS. Vienna, Nationalbibliothek, codex 583, f.1r–82r. Quarto. Saec. 10.
Microfilm: MnCH proj. no. 13,925

5509 Historia miscella. MS. Salisbury, England, Cathedral Library, codex 80, f.1–16. Quarto. Saec. 12.
Microfilm: MnCH

5510 Historia miscella. Lib. 1–16. MS. Vienna, Nationalbibliothek, codex 239. 84 f. Quarto. Saec. 12.
Microfilm: MnCH proj. no. 13,588

5511 Historia miscella, cum continuatione Landulphi. MS. Vienna, Nationalbibliothek, codex 57, f.1r–185r. Folio. Saec. 13.
Microfilm: MnCH proj. no. 13,423

5512 Historia miscella et Historia Langobardorum. MS. Vienna, Nationalbibliothek, codex 104. 106 f. Folio. Saec. 14.
Microfilm: MnCH proj. no. 13,467

5513 Homiliarium iussu Caroli Magni a Paulo Diacono digestum. Pars aestivalis. MS. Universitätsbibliothek Graz, Vienna, codex 697. 267 f. Folio. Saec. 11.
Microfilm: MnCH proj. no. 26,818

5514 Legenda de S. Scholastica virgine (?). MS. Benediktinerabtei St. Peter, Salzburg, codex a.VI.46, f.73r–78r. Quarto. Saec. 15.
Microfilm: MnCH proj. no. 10,119

Printed works
5515 [Selections]
Vesper hymn to St. John the Baptist (Ut queant laxis). Hymn for matins (Antra deserti). Hymn for lauds (O nimis felix).
(*In* Donahoe, D. J. Early Christian hymns. New York, 1908. v. 1, p. 113–118)
PLatS

5516 [Carmina]
(*In* Foucher, J. P. Florilège de la poésie sacrée. Paris, 1961. p. 119–123)
PLatS

5517 [Carmina minora Pauli Diaconi(?), Paulini, Angilberti . . .
(*In* Monumenta Germaniae historica. Poetae latini aevi carolini. t. IV, p. 911–943)
MnCS; PLatS

5518 [Carmina]
Die Gedichte des Paulus Diaconus. Kritische und erklärende Ausgabe von Karl Neff. München, C.H. Beck, 1908.
xx, 231 p. 25 cm.
PLatS

5519 Epistolae variorum Carolo Magno regnante scriptae.
(*In* Monumenta Germaniae historica. Epistolae. t. IV, p. 494–567)
MnCS; PLatS

5520 Pauli Warnefridi liber de episcopis Mettensibus.
(*In* Monumenta Germaniae historica. Scriptores. Stuttgart, 1963. t. 2, p. 260–270)
MnCS; PLatS

5520a **Paur, Roman,** 1939–
Saint John's directory. Prepared by Roman Paur, O.S.B., [and others]. Collegeville, Minn., St. John's University, Center for Human Resources, 1980.
49 p. ports. 28 cm.
MnCS

5521 **Pawlowsky, Sigismund,** 1916–
Die biblischen Grundlagen der Regula Benedicti. Wien, Herder, 1965.
122 p. 23 cm. (Wiener Beiträge zur Theologie, 9)
InStme; KAS; MnCS; MoCo; PLatS

5522 **Pedrizetti, Anselm Raymond,** 1930–
(tr & ed) Anselm, Saint. St. Anselm's letters to Lanfranc; a translation, with an introduction and commentary by Rev. Anselm Pedrizetti, O.S.B.
82 p. 28 cm.
Thesis (M.A.)–Catholic University of America, 1961.
Typescript.
MnCS

5523 **Pedrosa, Juan de,** 16th cent.
Responsio ad doctissimas et prudentissimas sacrosanctae Congr. Sacrorvm Ritvvm oppositiones contra processvm fvlminatum super martyrio 200 monachorum, qui in persecutione arabica, apud Caradignam passi sunt. n.p., n.d.
29 p. 13 cm.
MnCS

5524 **Peichl, Hermann,** 1887–1966.
Der Tag des Herrn; die Heiligung des Sonntags im Wandel der Zeit. Hrsg. von Hermann Peichl . . . unter Mitwirkung von Walter Kornfeld [et al.] Wien, Verlag Herder [1958].
156 p. 25 cm. (Studien der Wiener Katholischen Akademie, 3. Bd.)
MnCS; PLatS

5525 **Peifer, Claude,** 1927–
Feature review of Problemi e orientamenti di spiritualità monastica, biblica & liturgica [di] C. Vagaggini [et al.].
(*In* Monastic studies, no. 2(1964), p. 137–165)
PLatS

5526 The first and second epistles of St. Paul to the Crointhians; introduction and commentary. Collegeville, Minn., The Liturgical Press [1960].
111 p. 20 cm. (New Testament reading guide, 8)
ILSP; KySu; MnCS; PLatS

5527 Monastic spirituality. New York, Sheed and Ward [1966].
xvii, 555 p. 24 cm.
CaMWiSb; CaQMo; ICSS; InStme; InFer; KAS; MnCS; MdRi; MnStj; MoCo; NcBe; PLatS; ViBris

5528 **Peking, China. Benedictine sisters.**
The art of Chinese cooking, by the Benedictine sisters of Peking. Rutland, Vt., Charles E. Tuttle Co., n.d.
94 p.
AStb

Peking, China. Catholic University. *See* Catholic University of Peking.

5529 **Pelagius, Voester.**
Vinculum charitatis, seu Designatio historica monasteriorum et collegiorum, quae

cum monasterio S. Blasii confoederata sunt et fuerunt. MS. Benediktinerabtei St. Paul im Lavanttal, Austria, codex 200/2. 139 p. Folio. Saec. 18.
Microfilm: MnCH proj. no. 12,032

5530 **Peleman, Albert,** 1924–
Der Benediktiner, Simpert Schwarzhueber (1727–1795), Professor in Salzburg, als Moraltheologe . . . Regensburg, Fr. Pustet, 1961.
196 p. 22 cm.
InStme; MnCS; PLatS

5531 **Peña, La, Spain. San Juan (Benedictine abbey).**
Cartulario de San Juan de la Peña. [Por.] Antonio Ubieto Arteta. Valencia, 1962–
v. 17 cm.
PLatS

Penco, Gregorio, 1926–
5532 Estensione e diffusione della bonifica benedettina.
(*In* La bonifica benedettina, p. 51–84)
PLatS

5533 S. Benedicti Regula. Introduzione, testo, apparati, traduzione e commento a cura di Gregorio Penco, O.S.B. Firenze, "La Nuova Italia" editrice [1958].
cviii, 281 p. 17 cm.
ILSP; MoCo; PLatS

5534 Storia del monachesimo in Italia, dalle origini alla fine del Medio Evo. [Roma], Edizioni Paoline [1961].
601 p. plates, 22 cm.
InStme; KAS; MnCS; MoCo; PLatS

5535 Storia del monachesimo in Italia nell'epoca moderna. Roma, Edizioni Paoline, 1969.
429 p. plates, 22 cm.
KAS; MoCo

5536 Il tema dell'Esodo nella spiritualità monastica.
(*In* Vagaggini, Cypriano. Biblia e spiritualità. Roma, 1967. p. 331–378)
PLatS

5537 La vita monastica in Italia all'epoca di S. Martino di Tours.
(*In* Saint Martin et son temps. Romae, 1961. p. 67–83)
PLatS

5538 **Pendleton, Arthur James,** 1930–
A thermodynamic study of basic dye sorption on chemically modified cotton.
92 p.
Thesis (Ph.D.)–Clemson University, 1972.
NcBe

5539 **Un Pensiero dei santi benedettini per ciascun giorno dell'anno.** Traduzione

dal francese. Prato, Tip. Contrucci e comp., 1887.
[128] p. 12 cm.
Translation of: Une Pensée des saints bénédictins pour chaque jour de l'année. 1882.
PLatS

5540 **Pepi, Ruperto,** 1887–
L'Abbazia de Santa Giustina in Padova; storia e arte. Padova, Edizioni Monaci Benedettini, 1966.
203 p. illus.(part col.) 17 cm.
InStme; MnCS; PLatS

5541 **Peregrinus, Pater [pseud.].**
Im Glanz der Morgensonne. Clyde, Mo., Benedictine Convent of Perpetual Adoration [n.d.].
62 p. 16 cm.
MnCS

5542 **Perennitas: Beiträge zur christlichen Archäologie und Kunst,** zur Geschichte der Literatur . . . P. Thomas Michels, O.S.B., zum 70. Geburtstag. Hrsg. von Hugo Rahner, S.J., und Emmanuel von Severus, O.S.B. Münster, Aschendorff [1963].
xxiii, 734 p. 25 cm.
PLatS

Perez, Antonio, 1559–1637.
5543 Commentaria oder Grundtliche Auslegung über die Regul des hl. Benedikt . . . verteutscht von P. Bonifacio Schneidt, O.S.B. MS. Benediktinerinnenabtei Nonnberg, Salzburg, codex 28 D 7-8a. 2 vols. Folio. Saec. 17.
Microfilm: MnCH proj. no. 10,967

5544 Commentarie in Regvlam ss. p. Benedicti. Coloniae Agrippinae, apud Bernardum Gualteri [1625?].
[16], 963, [87] p. 19 cm.
KAS

5545 **Perez, Eugene,** 1910–
Benedictine items, featuring articles on St. Benedict, St. Scholastica, Monte Cassino, Subiaco, Benedictine oblates, liturgy, Benedictine foundations in Western Aust. New Norcia, The Abbey Press, 1953.
76 p. illus., plates, 18 cm.
InFer; MnCS

5545a Kalumburu: the Benedictine Mission and the Aborigines, 1908–1975. Kalumburu, West Australia, Kalumburu Benedictine Mission, 1977.
173 p. 8 leaves of plates, illus. 23 cm.
KAS

Pérez de Urbel, Justo, 1895–
5546 El compromiso monastico en la España de la reconquista.

(*In* Semaña de Estudios monasticos, 14th, Silos, Spain, 1973. p. 57–73)
PLatS

5547   Los manuscritos del real monasterio de Santo Domingo de Silos, por Walter Muir Whitehall, jr., y Justo Pérez de Urbel, O.S.B. Madrid, Tipografia de la "Revista de archivos," 1930.
85 p. XI facsims. 24 cm.
MnCS; PLatS

5548   Le monachisme en Espagne au temps de saint Martin.
(*In* Saint Martin et son temps. Romae, 1961. p. 45–66)
PLatS

5549   Origen de los himnos mozárabes. Bordeaux, Feret et fils, 1926.
94 p. 25 cm.
InStme; WFif

5550   Los Vascos en el nacimiento de Castilla; conferencia pronunciada en el salon de actos del hotel Carlton el dia 16 de febrero de 1945.
29 p. 22 cm.
MnCS

5551   (ed) Historia Silense. Edición, crítica e introducción por Justo Pérez de Urbel y Atilano González Ruiz-Zorrilla. Madrid, 1959.
235 p. 25 cm.
InStme

5552   (ed) Yepes, Antonio de. Crónica general de la Orden de San Benito. Estudio preliminar y edición por Justo Pérez de Urbel. Madrid, Ediciones Atlas, 1959–60.
3 v. 25 cm.
MnCS; PLatS

Perion, Joachim, 1499?–1559.

5553   De optimo genere interpretandi commentarij. Parisiis, apud Joannem Lodoicum Tiletanum, 1540.
229 p.
PLatS(microfilm)

5554   De Romanorvm et Graecorvm magistratibvs libri tres . . . Parisiis, in officina Caroli Perier, 1560.
5 p., 51 numb. leaves [6] p. 21 cm.
PLatS

5555   De sanctorvm virorum, qui patriarchae ab Ecclesia appellantur, rebus gestis ac vitis. Lutetiae, ex officina Michaelis Vascosani, 1555.
131 leaves, 23 cm.
MnCS; PLatS

5556   Dialectica libri tres. Lvgdvni, apud Godefridum & Marcellum Beringos, 1551.
346 p. 17 cm.
PLatS

5557   Pro Aristotele in Petrum Ramum orationes II. Eiusdem De dialectica liber I. Parisiis, apud Ioannem Lodoicum Tiletanum, 1543.
MnCS(microfilm)

Pernety, Antoine Joseph, 1716–1801.

5558   Dictionnaire portatif de peinture, sculpture et gravure . . . Paris, chez Onfroy, 1781.
NcBe (v. 1 & 2)

5559   Treatise on the great art; a system of physics according to hermetic philosophy and theory and practice of the magisterium . . . edited by Edouard Blitz. Boston, Occult Pub. Co., 1898.
255 p. illus. 24 cm.
KAS

5560   **Perrot, Claudius,** 1803–1881.
Geistliches Morgenbrod für christliche Seelen im Kloster und Weltstande . . . 2. Aufl. New York, Gebrüder Benziger, 1869.
2 v. 18 cm.
IDCoS; InStme

5561   **Perugia, Italy. San Pietro (Benedictine abbey).**
Liber contractuum (1331–32) dell'Abbazia benedettina de San Pietro in Perugia. A cura di Don Costanzo Tabarelli, O.S.B., con introduzione di Giuseppe Mira. Perugia, Deputazione di Storia Patria per l'Umbria, 1967.
xi, 568 p. 26 cm.
PLatS

Peter Damian, Saint, 1007?–1072.
Manuscripts.

5562   [Opera]
Disputatio de horis canonicis; Regula heremitica a Petro Damiano descripta; Opusculum de ordine vitae heremiticae et facultatibus heremi; Sermo fratribus heremitanis de Spiritu Sancto; Sermo de vitio linguae; Sermo de spirituali certamine; Liber Gomorrianus. MS. Augustinerchorherrenstift Klosterneuburg, Austria, codex 331, f.175r–222v. Folio. Saec. 15.
Microfilm: MnCH proj. no. 5302

5563   Opera. MS. Benediktinerabtei Melk, Austria, codex 732, f.1r–216v. Folio. Saec. 15.
Microfilm: MnCH proj. no. 1585

5564   [Opera]
De contemptu huius seculi ad Albizonem heremitam et Petrum cenobitum. Liber de perfectione religiosorum. Liber qui appellatur Dominus vobiscum. Regula heremitica a Petro Damiani potius exponendo quam percipiendo descripta. De ordine vitae heremiticae. Sermones tres. Invectio in episcopum monachos ad saeculum revo-

cantem. Epistolae (numero ca. 40). MS. Vienna, Schottenstift, codex 29, f.169r–357v. Folio. Saec. 15.
Microfilm: MnCH proj. no. 3879

5565 Opuscula, epistolae, sermones. MS. Universitätsbibliothek Graz, Austria, codex 573. 438 f. Folio. Saec. 15(1404).
Microfilm: MnCH proj. no. 26,297

5566 Opuscula aliquot. MS. Augustinerchorherrenstift St. Florian, Austria, codex XI,166, f.160v–181v. et 269v–270r. Duodecimo. Saec. 15.
Microfilm: MnCH proj. no. 2435

5567 Opuscula et Epistolae. MS. Linz, Austria, Bundesstattliche Studienbibliothek, codex 281. 148 f. Folio. Saec. 14.
Microfilm: MnCH proj. no. 27,966

5568 Antilogus contra Iudaeos ad Honestum virum clarrisimum. MS. Augustinerchorherrenstift Klosterneuburg, Austria, codex 194, f.242r–247v. Folio. Saec. 15.
Microfilm: MnCH proj. no. 5163

5569 Antilogus contra Judaeos. Epilogus contra Judaeos. MS. Benediktinerabtei Melk, Austria, codex 141, f.70r–87r. Folio. Saec. 15.
Microfilm: MnCH proj. no. 1207

5570 Apologeticum de contemptu huius seculi (ad Albizonem eremitam et Petrum monachum). MS. Augustinerchorherrenstift Klosterneuburg, Austria, codex 194, f.268v–279v. Folio. Saec. 15.
Microfilm: MnCH proj. no. 5163

5571 Contra Graecos, qui negant Spiritum Sanctum procedere a Filio. MS. Vienna, Nationalbibliothek, codex 2177, f.79r–84v. Folio. Saec. 12.
Microfilm: MnCH proj. no. 15,503

5572 De abdicatione episcopatus. MS. Cistercienserabtei Heiligenkreuz, Austria, codex 227, f.30v–42v. Folio. Saec. 12–13.
Microfilm: MnCH proj. no. 4768

5573 Tractatus de solitaria vita. MS. Universitätsbibliothek Innsbruck, Austria, codex 313, f.54v–57r. Quarto. Saec. 13–14.
Microfilm: MnCH proj. no. 28,334

5574 De laude solitariae vitae. MS. Universitätsbibliothek Graz, Austria, codex 1239, f.102r–103v. Quarto. Saec. 14.
Microfilm: MnCH proj. no. 26,349

5575 De laude vitae solitariae. MS. Universitätsbibliothek Innsbruck, Austria, codex 415, f.153r–172r. Octavo. Saec. 14–15.
Microfilm: MnCH proj. no. 28,415

5576 De narratione. MS. Lincoln Cathedral Library, England, codex 23, f.252v–266. Quarto. Saec. 15.
Microfilm: MnCH

5577 Dialogus qui appellatur Gratissimus. MS. Vienna, Nationalbibliothek, codex 2177, f.91r–122v. Folio. Saec. 12.
Microfilm: MnCH proj. no. 15,503

5578 Duo sermones de Johanne apostolo. MS. Universitätsbibliothek Graz, Austria, codex 282, f.1r–9v. Folio. Saec. 12.
Microfilm: MnCH proj. no. 26,218

5579 Epistolae et alia opera. MS. Vienna, Nationalbibliothek, codex 722, f.9r–72v. Folio. Saec. 13.
Microfilm: MnCH proj. no. 14,050

5580 Ex ejus epistola qui intitulatur Antilogus contra Iudaeos. MS. Vienna, Schottenstift, codex 98, f.183r–184r. Folio. Saec. 15.
Microfilm: MnCH proj. no. 3955

5581 Epistola contra simoniacas ad Alexandrum papam. MS. Benediktinerabtei Admont, Austria, codex 162, f.166r–197r. Folio. Saec. 12.
Microfilm: MnCH proj. no. 9249

5582 Epistola de resignatione episcopatus. MS. Benediktinerabtei Admont, Austria, codex 352, f.81v–92v. Folio. Saec. 12.
Microfilm: MnCH proj. no. 9421

5583 Epistola supplicatoria pro obtinenda licentia ad muneris episcopalis resignationem. MS. Cistercienserabtei Rein, Austria, codex 23, f.24v–45r. Quarto. Saec. 12.
Microfilm: MnCH proj. no. 7420

5584 Liber, qui appelatur "Dominus vobiscum" ad Leonem eremitam. MS. Augustinerchorherrenstift Klosterneuburg, Austria, codex 373B, f.218v–228r. Folio. Saec. 15.
Microfilm: MnCH proj. no. 5340

5585 Liber ad Leonem inclusum, qui liber appellatur Dominus vobiscum. MS. Benediktinerabtei Melk, Austria, codex 141, f.87v–96v. Folio. Saec. 15.
Microfilm: MnCH proj. no. 1207

5586 Liber qui dicitur Gratissimus. MS. Benediktinerabtei Kremsmünster, Austria, codex 27, f.129r–179r.
Microfilm: MnCH proj. no. 27

5587 Liber, qui appellatur "Gratissimus" ad Henricum archiepiscopum Ravannatensem. MS. Augustinerchorherrenstift Klosterneuburg, Austria, codex 194, f.253r–268v. Folio. Saec. 15.
Microfilm: MnCH proj. no. 5163

5588 Liber qui dicitur Gratissimus, qui de his est compositus qui gratis sunt a symoniacis ordinati. MS. Benediktinerabtei Melk, Austria, codex 993, f.25r–87v. Quarto. Saec. 15.
Microfilm: MnCH proj. no. 1807

5589 Liber de privilegio Romanae Ecclesiae. MS. Benediktinerabtei Göttweig, Austria, codex 143a, f.120r–124r. Folio. Saec. 14.
Microfilm: MnCH proj. no. 3412

5590 Litterae, sermones et preces. MS. Vienna, Nationalbibliothek, codex 698. 236 f. Folio. Saec. 15.
Microfilm: MnCH proj. no. 14,020

5591 Opusculum apologeticum, de contemptu mundi. MS. Benediktinerabtei Melk, Austria, codex 993, f.88r–127r. Quarto. Saec. 15.
Microfilm: MnCH proj. no. 1807

5592 Opusculum de perfectione monachorum. MS. Benediktinerabtei Melk, Austria, codex 993, f.1r–24v. Quarto. Saec. 15.
Microfilm: MnCH proj. no. 1807

5593 Orationes ad Patrem, Filium et Spiritum S. MS. Benediktinerabtei Melk, Austria, codex 1546, f.309r–315v. Octavo. Saec. 15.
Microfilm: MnCH proj. no. 1949

5594 Orationes compositae a S. Ambrosio, Anselmo, Petro Damiani et Berengario. MS. Cistercienserabtei Heiligenkreuz, Austria, codex 262, f.111r–134v. Quarto. Saec. 12.
Microfilm: MnCH proj. no. 4802

5595 Orationes. Germanice. MS. Augustinerchorherrenstift Klosterneuburg, Austria, codex 1036, f.1r–14v. Quarto. Saec. 14.
Microfilm: MnCH proj. no. 6011

5596 Ritmi de omnibus ordinibus. MS. Benediktinerabtei St. Peter, Salzburg, codex a.VI.11, f.245v–247r. Quarto. Saec. 14–15.
Microfilm: MnCH proj. no. 10,090

5597 Sermones. MS. Augustinerchorherrenstift Vorau, Austria, codex 309, f.141v–167v. Folio. Saec. 12.
Microfilm: MnCH proj. no. 7282

5598 Sermo de commendatione vitae heremiticae. MS. Benediktinerabtei Melk, Austria, codex 737, f.138r–140r. Folio. Saec. 15.
Microfilm: MnCH proj. no. 1590

5599 Sermo de commendatione vitae solitariae. MS. Benediktinerabtei Melk, Austria, codex 878, f.170r–174v. Quarto. Saec. 15.
Microfilm: MnCH proj. no. 1695

5600 Sermo de spirituali certamine. MS. Benediktinerabtei Melk, Austria, codex 993, f.137v–142r. Quarto. Saec. 15.
Microfilm: MnCH proj. no. 1807

5601 Sermo de vitio linguae. MS. Benediktinerabtei Melk, Austria, codex 993, f.131r–137v. Quarto. Saec. 15.
Microfilm: MnCH proj. no. 1807

5602 Sermo fratribus Ieremi de Spiritu Sancto. MS. Benediktinerabtei Melk, Austria, codex 993, f.127r–131r. Quarto. Saec. 15.
Microfilm: MnCH proj. no. 1807

5603 Sermones 182 de ss. Patribus (S. Bernardus, Petrus Damianus, S. Fulgentius . . . MS. Benediktinerabtei Melk, Austria, codex 325. 395 f. Folio. Saec. 15.
Microfilm: MnCH proj. no. 1334

5604 Sermones de tempore et sanctis. MS. Cistercienserabtei Lilienfeld, Austria, codex 40, f.1r–92r. Quarto. Saec. 13.
Microfilm: MnCH proj. no. 4350

5605 Tractatus de solitaria vita. MS. Benediktinerabtei Melk, Austria, codex 319, f.215r–224v. Folio. Saec. 15.
Microfilm: MnCH proj. no. 1329

5606 Tractatus de suffragiis mortuorum. MS. Vienna, Nationalbibliothek, codex 4686, f.22v–25v. Quarto. Saec. 15.
Microfilm: MnCH proj. no. 17,868

5607 Tractatus de vita heremitica. MS. Benediktinerabtei Melk, Austria, codex 1405, f.11r–13v. Duodecimo. Saec. 15.
Microfilm: MnCH proj. no. 1926

5608 Versus de simoniacis. MS. Benediktinerabtei Göttweig, Austria, codex 143a, f.118v. Folio. Saec. 14.
Microfilm: MnCH proj. no. 3412

5609 Versus de symoniacis. MS. Augustinerchorherrenstift Klosterneuburg, Austria, codex 194, f.247v. Folio. Saec. 15.
Microfilm: MnCH proj. no. 5163

Peter Damian, Saint.
Printed works
5610 [Selections]
On the day of death (Gravi me terrore pulsas). Hymn for the Easter season (Paschalis festi gaudium). To St. Paul (Paule doctor egregie).
(*In* Donahoe, D. J. Early Christian hymns. New York, 1911. v. 2, p. 79–86)
PLatS

5611 [Carmina]
(*In* Fourcher, J. P. Florilège de la poésie sacrée. Paris, 1961. p. 162–164)
PLatS

5612 Dictum mirabile de hora mortis.
(*In* Meditationes S. Augustini et S. Bernardi aliorumque sanctorum antiquorum patrum . . . Lugduni, apud A. Gryphium, 1587)
PLatS (microfilm)

5613 Lettere e discorsi, a cura di Mons. Adamo Pasini. Siena, Edizioni Cantagalli [1956].
350 p. 19 cm. (I Classici cristiani)
PLatS

5614 Lettre sur la toute-puissance divine. Introduction, texte critique, traduction et notes par André Cantin, Paris, Du Cerf, 1972.
502 p. 20 cm. (Sources chrétiennes, 191)
PLatS

5615 Medulla operum omnium beati Petri Damiani . . . collecta & in quinque libros distributa a Benedictino S. Petri in Silva Nigra . . . Friburgi Brisgoviae, typis Joannis Andreae Satron, 1777.
14, xviii, 613, 11 p. ports. 20 cm.
KAS

5616 L'Opera poetica di S. Pier Damiani; descrizione dei manoscritti, edizione del testo, esame prosodico-metrico, discussione delle questioni d'autenticità, a cura di Margareta Lokrantz. Stockholm, Almquist & Wiksell [1964].
258 p. illus., facsims. 25 cm.
PLatS

5617 Selected writings on the spiritual life, translated with an introduction by Patricia McNulty. London, Faber and Faber [1959].
187 p. 21 cm.
PLatS

5618 La vita di S. Domenico, confessore, detto il Loricato, eremita benedettino di S. Croce del Fonte Avellano; tratta dagli scritti di S. Pier-Damiano. Raccolta, ed illustrata da Ottavio Turchi. Roma, Andonio de'Rossi, 1749.
200 p. 25 cm.
MnCS

5619 Ex Petri Damiani vita S. Romualdi, edente D. G. Waitz.
(*In* Monumenta Germaniae historica. Scriptores. Stuttgart, 1963. t. 4, p. 846–854)
MnCS; PLatS

5620 A wonderfull and worthy saying of blessed S. Peter Damian, monke of the holy order of S. Bennet, cardinal of Ostia, concerning the day of deathe. [London], The Scolar Press, 1975.
[6] p. 19 cm. (English recusant literature, 1558–1640, v. 256)
PLatS

Peterborough Abbey, England.
5621 Carte nativorum; a Peterborough Abbey cartulary of the fourteenth century. Edited by C.N.L. Brooke and M. M. Postan. Oxford, Printed for the Northhamptonshire Record Society by V. Ridler at the University Press, 1960.
lxv, 261 p. geneal. tables. 26 cm.
KAS

5622 Peterborough Consuetudinary, part III. MS. Lambeth Palace Library, London, codex 198b. 293 f. Quarto. Saec. 14.
Microfilm: MnCH

5623 **Peters, Richarda, Sister,** 1895–1972.
A study of the problems of 355 high school boys and girls as revealed by an adjustment questionnaire.
79 p. 28 cm.
Thesis (M.A.)–University of Notre Dame, 1933.
Typescript.
MnStj(Archives)

5624 **Petitdidier, Matthieu,** 1659–1727.
Dissertation historique et theologique, dans la quelle on examine quel a été le sentiment du Concile de Constance, & des principaux theologiens qui y ont assisté, sur l'autorité des papes & sur leur infaillibilité . . . Luxembourg, André Chevalier, 1725.
284 p. 17 cm.
MnCS

5625 **Petrus II, abbot of Göttweig.**
Epistola de anno 1405. MS. Benediktinerabtei Göttweig, Austria, codex 270b, f. 313v. Folio. Saec. 15.
Microfilm: MnCH proj. no. 3450

5626 **Petrus, monk of Lambach.**
Memoriale capitulorum Regule Sancti Benedicti. MS. Benediktinerabtei Lambach, Austria, codex chart. 435, f.101v–104r. Saec. 15.
Microfilm: MnCH proj. no. 725

5627 **Petrus, ex Ordine Coelestinorum,** inquisitor haereticae pravitatis.
Processus contra Waldenses in Austria. MS. Benediktinerabtei Seitenstetten, Austria, codex 188, f.1r–62r. Quarto. Saec. 15.
Microfilm: MnCH proj. no. 989

5628 **Petrus, abbot of Reichenau.**
Verse de morte Christi, de cella, de bibliotheca, de lectore mense . . . MS. Benediktinerabtei Lambach, Austria, codex chart. 435, f.48r–48v. Saec. 15.
Microfilm: MnCH proj. no. 15

Petrus, bp. of Orvieto. *See* Bohier, Pierre.

5629 **Petrus, abbot of St. Peter, Salzburg.**
Briefbuch des Abtes Petrus, 1455–1465. MS. Benediktinerabtei St. Peter, Salzburg, Archivium Hs. A 26. 110 f. Quarto. Saec. 15.
Microfilm: MnCH proj. no. 10,764

5630 **Petrus Cellensis, bp. of Chartres,** 1115–1183.
L'Ecole du cloitre; introduction, texte critique, traduction et notes par Gerard de Martel. Paris, Les Editions du Cerf, 1977.

351 p. (Sources chrétiennes, v. 240)
MoCo; MnCS

5631 **Petrus de Arbona, monk of Admont.**
Catalogus librorum bibliothecae Admontensis. MS. Benediktinerabtei Admont, Austria, codex 589. 30 f. Quarto. Saec. 14(1370).
Microfilm: MnCH proj. no. 9619

Petrus Diaconus, monk of Monte Cassino, d.1140.

5632 Archisterii, de viris illustribus Casinensis opusculum. Ex celeberrima bibliotheca Barberina depromitum.
(*In* Fabricius, Johann Albert. Bibliotheca ecclesiastica. Hants, England, Gregg Press, 1967, p. 161–202) Reprint of 1718 edition.
PLatS; MnCS

5632a Ortus et vita iustorum Cenobii Casinensis. Edited from the autograph ms. and with a commentary by R. H. Rodgers. Berkeley, University of California Press, 1972.
lx, 216 p. facsims. 24 cm.
InStme; KAS; MnCS

Petrus Venerabilis, abbot of Cluny, 1092(ca.)–1156.

5632b Selected letters of Peter the Venerable. Edited by Janet Martin in collaboration with Giles Constable. Toronto, Published for the Centre for Medieval Studies by the Pontifical Institute of Mediaeval Studies [1974].
[3], 107 p. 22 cm.
Text in Latin.
PLatS

5632c Epistola ad sanctum Bernhardum super improperatione rigoris ordinis sui non servati. MS. Vienna, Schottenstift, codex 152, f.3r–25v. Octavo. Saec. 15.
Microfilm: MnCH proj. no. 4071

5632d Contra Petrobrusianos hereticos. Cura et studio James Fearns. Turnholti, Brepols, 1968.
xviii, 179 p. 26 cm. (Corpus Christianorum. Continuatio mediaevalis, 10)
InStme; PLatS

5632e The letters of Peter the Venerable. Edited, with an introduction and notes by Giles Constable. Cambridge, Harvard University Press, 1967.
2 v. 25 cm. (Harvard historical studies, 78)
InStme; KAS; MoCo

5632f Sermo de quodcumque sancto cujus reliquiae sunt praesentes. MS. Benediktinerabtei Melk, Austria, codex 791, f.252v–267v. Quarto. Saec. 15.
Microfilm: MnCH proj. no. 1629

Petrus von Rosenheim, 1380(ca.)–1433.

5632g Avisationes pro patre Stephano de Riettental, dum in causa reformationis mitteretur ad Seittensteten. MS. Benediktinerabtei Melk, Austria, codex 1094, f.275r–276v. Duodecimo. Saec. 15.
Microfilm: MnCH proj. no. 1847

5632h Biblia (metrice). MS. Benediktinerabtei Melk, Austria, codex 83. 140 f. Octavo. Saec. 15.
Microfilm: MnCH proj. no. 1166

5632i Biblia metrica. MS. Benediktinerabtei St. Peter, Salzburg, codex b.X.2. 58 f. Folio. Saec. 15.
Microfilm: MnCH proj. no. 10,608

5632j Canon in Regulam S. Benedicti. Metrice. MS. Vienna, Nationalbibliothek, codex 4117, f.33v–36v. Sextodecimo. Saec. 16.
Microfilm: MnCH proj. no. 17,296

5633 De esu carnium in Regula S. Benedicti prohibito (excerpta ex notatis). MS. Benediktinerabtei Melk, Austria, codex 959, f.207r–207v. Quarto. Saec. 15.
Microfilm: MnCH proj. no. 1762

5634 Memoriale capitulorum Regulae Sancti Benedicti. MS. Benediktinerabtei Kremsmünster, Austria, codex 268, f.140r–144v. Saec. 15.
Microfilm: MnCH proj. no. 252

5635 Memoriale capitulorum Regulae S. Benedicti. MS. Benediktinerabtei Melk, Austria, codex 614, f.67v–70v. Quarto. Saec. 15.
Microfilm: MnCH proj. no. 1503

5636 Memoriale roseum S. Scripturae. MS. Benediktinerabtei Melk, Austria, codex 88, f.64–171. Octavo. Saec. 15.
Microfilm: MnCH proj. no. 1162

5637 Memoriale roseum Sacrae Scripturae. MS. Benediktinerabtei Seitenstetten, Austria, codex 279. 60 f. Quarto. Saec. 15.
Microfilm: MnCH proj. no. 1089

5638 Metra biblica. MS. Benediktinerabtei Melk, Austria, codex 614, f.1r–67r. Quarto. Saec. 15.
Microfilm: MnCH proj. no. 1503

5639 Metra in laudem Leonardi episcopi Paviensis. MS. Benediktinerabtei Melk, Austria, codex 662, f.14r–18v. Quarto. Saec. 15.
Microfilm: MnCH proj. no. 1532

5640 Nota de esu carnium. MS. Vienna, Schottenstift, codex 4245, f.212r–213r. Folio. Saec. 15.
Microfilm: MnCH proj. no. 4245

5641 Opus super totam Bibliam. MS. Subiaco, Italy (Benedictine abbey), codex 277 Octavo. Saec. 15 (1438).
Microfilm: MnCH proj. no. 277

5642   Quatuor evangelia versu elegiaco reddita. MS. Benediktinerabtei Melk, Austria, codex 1830, f.281r–288v. Duodecimo. Saec. 15.
Microfilm: MnCH proj. no. 2138

5643   Roseum memoriale divinorum eloquiorum. MS. Universitätsbibliothek Graz, Austria, codex 100, f.1r–12r. Folio. Saec. 15.
Microfilm: MnCH proj. no. 26,032

5644   Roseum memoriale divinorum eloquiorum metricum, cum prologo prosaico. MS. Vienna, Nationalbibliothek, codex 3570, f.28v–77v.
Microfilm: MnCH proj. no. 16,791

5645   Roseum memoriale metrice conscriptum in totam Bibliam. MS. Benediktinerabtei St. Peter, Salzburg, codex a.III.11, f.1r–87v. Octavo. Saec. 16.
Microfilm: MnCH proj. no. 9953

5646   Scriptum Petri de Rosenheim de Sacro Specu ad monasterium Mellicense translati. MS. Benediktinerabtei Melk, Austria, codex 1396, f.235r–236r. Duodecimo. Saec. 15.
Microfilm: MnCH proj. no. 1918

5647   Versus de medicina. MS. Benediktinerabtei Melk, Austria, codex 1153, f.39r–40v. Quarto. Saec. 15.
Microfilm: MnCH proj. no. 1862

5648   Versus memoriales de Bibliis, cum prologo prosaico. MS. Vienna, Nationalbibliothek, codex 3750, f.302v–303r. Folio. Saec. 15.
Microfilm: MnCH proj. no. 16,959

5649   Versus de vita S. Benedicti. MS. Benediktinerabtei Melk, Austria, codex 1153, f.36r–38v. Quarto. Saec. 15.
Microfilm: MnCH proj. no. 1862

5650   Vita metrica S. Benedicti. MS. Benediktinerabtei Melk, Austria, codex 1646, f.4r–10v. Sextodecimo, Saec. 15.
Microfilm: MnCH proj. no. 1996

5651   Vita S. Benedicti, metrice compillata. MS. Benediktinerabtei Melk, Austria codex 880, f.91–98. Quarto. Saec. 15.
Microfilm: MnCH proj. no. 1697

5652   Metra super vita s. patris Benedicti. MS. Benediktinerabtei Lambach, Austria, codex chart. 453, f.257r–265v. Saec. 15.
Microfilm: MnCH proj. no. 740

5653   **Peuger, Leonard,** b. ca. 1400.
Deutsche Uebersetzungen von biblischen cantica und anderen lateinischen Gebete. MS. Benediktinerabtei Melk, Austria, codex 808. 120 f. Quarto. Saec. 15.
Microfilm: MnCH proj. no. 1644

Pez, Bernard, 1683–1735.
5654   Bibliotheca ascetica antiquo-nova. Farnborough (Hants), Gregg, 1967.
12 v. in 3, 32 cm.
Facsimile reprint of Ratisbon edition of 1723–24.
InStme; PLatS

5655   Collecta in bibliotheca S. Dorotheana Vindobonae 1715. MS. Benediktinerabtei Melk, Austria, codex 910. 92 f. Quarto. Saec. 18.
Microfilm: MnCH proj. no. 1728

5656   Liber de miraculis sanctae Dei genitricis Mariae. Published at Vienna in 1731 by Bernard Pez, O.S.B. Reprinted for the first time by Thomas Frederick Crane . . . Ithaca, Cornell University, 1925.
xxvi, 117, 38 p. 24 cm.
ILSP; InStme; MnCS; NdRi

5657   (ed) Anonymus Mellicensis saeculo XII clarus de scriptoribus ecclesiasticis, nuper primum in lucem editus, et notulis chronologico-criticis illustratus a Bernardo Pez, O.S.B.
(*In* Fabricius, Joh. A. Bibliotheca ecclesiastica. Hants, England, Gregg Press, 1967. p. 141–160. Reprint of 1718 edition)
PLatS

5658   **Phalèse, Hubert,** d. 1638.
(ed) Hugo de Sancto Charo. Sacrorum Bibliorum Vulgatae editionis concordantiae . . . nunc denuo variis locis expurgatae, ac locupletatae cura et studio Huberti Phalesii. Viennae, typis A. Strauss, 1825.
[6], 771 p. 35 cm.
KAS

Pfaller, Louis Lawrence, 1923–
5659   The Catholic Church in western North Dakota, 1738–1960; a history of the Diocese of Bismarck written on the occasion of its golden jubilee year. [Mandan, N.D., Crescent Printing Co.] 1960.
159 p. illus., maps, 21 cm.
KAS; NdRi

5660   Diocese of Bismarck.
(*In* Catholic heritage in Minnesota, North Dakota, South Dakota. 1964. p. 208–224)
MnCS; NdRi

5661   Father De Smet in Dakota. Richardton, N.D., Assumption Abbey Press, 1962.
79 p. illus. 23 cm.
ILSP; InStme; KAS; MnCS; MnStj; MoCo; NdRi; PLatS; OkShG

5662   Guide to the microfilm edition of the Major James McLaughlin papers. Richardton, N.D., Assumption College, 1969.
23 p.
MoCo; NdRi

5662a James McLaughlin; the man with an Indian heart. New York, Vantage Press, 1978.
xvi, 440 p. illus., maps. 21 cm.
InStme; NdRi

5663 Sermon treasury; the filing and indexing of sermons and sermon material. Richardton, N. D., Assumption Abbey Press [1963].
94 p. 23 cm.
First published 1961.
InStme; KAS; MnCS; NdRi; PLatS

5664 **Pfättisch, Ioannes Maria,** 1877–
Der Einfluss Platos auf die Theologie Justins des Märtyrers . . . Paderborn, F. Schöningh, 1910.
viii, 199 p. 24 cm.
KAS

5665 **Pfiester, Emeric James,** 1921–
Saint Bede Church, Bovard, Pennsylvania, 1915–1965.
36 p. illus., ports. 22 cm.
PLatS

5666 **Pfister, Bonifaz,** 1915–
Geschichte der Abtei Niederaltaich 741–1971 . . . Ottobeuren, Bayerische Benediktinerakadamie, 1972.
516 p. illus. 25 cm.
InStme; KAS; MnCS; NcBe; PLatS

5667 **Pfundstein, Hugo,** 1908–
Marianisches Wien; eine Geschichte der Marienverehrung in Wien. Wien, Bergland Verlag [1963].
197 p. illus. 19 cm.
KAS; MnCS

5668 **Pichery, Eugène,** 1883–
(ed & tr) Cassianus, Joannes. Conférences. Introduction, texte latin, traduction et notes par Dom E. Pichery. Paris, Editions du Cerf, 1955–59.
3 v. 21 cm. (Sources chrétiennes, 42, 54, 64)
InStme; PLatS

5669 **Pichler, Virgil, abbot of St. Peter, Salzburg.**
Schreiben an das Benediktiner Kloster Göss, 1497, und an das Benediktiner Kloster St. Georgen am Langsee, 1496. MS. Benediktinerabtei St. Peter, Salzburg, codex b.V.20, f.52r–61r. Quarto. Saec. 15.
Microfilm: MnCH proj. no. 10,453

5670 **Piel, Alain.**
Les moines dans l'Eglise; textes des souverains pontifes recueillis et présentés par Dom Alain Piel. Paris, Editions du Cerf, 1964.
206 p.
KAS; InStme; PLatS

5671 **Pierami, Benedetto, O.S.B.Val.**
The life of the servant of God, Pius X . . . Turin, Rome, Casa Editrice Marietti, 1928.
214 p.
NcBe

5672 **Pierbaumer, Matthias.**
Catalogus librorum manuscriptorum antiquorum qui inventi fuerunt in Bibliotheca Cremifanensi anno 1631. MS. Benediktinerabtei Kremsmünster, Austria, codex novus 421. 64 p. Saec. 17.
Microfilm: MnCH proj. no. 403

Pierre de Celle. *See* Petrus Cellensis.

5673 **Pierre-qui-Vire, France (Benedictine abbey).**
Saint Bernard, homme d'Eglise. 2. éd. [Paris], Desclée De Brouwer [1953].
259 p. 20 cm.
PLatS

Pinell, Jordi, 1921–
5674 La benedicció del ciri pasqual i els seus textos.
(*In* Liturgica, 2: Cardinal I. A. Schuster in memoriam. 1958. v. 2, p. 1–119)
PLatS

5675 Las horas vigiliares del oficio monacal hispánico.
(*In* Liturgica, 3: Cardinal I. A. Schuster in memoriam. 1966. p. 197–340)
PLatS

5676 Il mistero della pasqua in melitone di Sardi. Roma, Pontificio Istituto Liturgico, 1970.
81 p. 23 cm.
InStme

5677 Liber orationum psalmographus; colectas de salmos del antique rito hispánico. Recomposición y edición critica por Dom Jorge Pinell. Barcelona, Instituto F. Enrique Florez, 1972.
299, 287 p. 25 cm.
Text in Latin or Spanish.
InStme

5678 Las oraciones del Salterio per annum en el nuevo libro de la liturgia de las horas. Roma, Edizioni Liturgiche, 1974.
99 p. 24 cm.
InStme

Piolin, Paul Leo, 1817–1892.
5679 Histoire de l'Eglise du Mans. Paris, Julien Lanier, 1851–1863.
6 v. 23 cm.
KAS

5680 Testament spiritual d'un benedictin.
(*In* Analecta juris pontificii, v. 17(1878), p. 897–910)
AStb

Pirmin, Saint, d. 753.

5681 Der heilige Pirmin und sein Missionsbüchlein [Dicta abbatis Pirminii]. Eingeleitet und ins Deutsche übertragen von
Ursmer Engelmann, O.S.B. Konstanz, Jan
Thorbecke Verlag [1959].
99 p. illus. 18 cm.
MnCS

5682 Die Heimat des hl. Pirmin, des Apostels
der Alamannen, hrsg. von Gallus Jecker,
O.S.B. Münster in Westf., Aschendorff,
1927.
xv, 192 p. 25 cm.
Text and study of "Dicta abbatis Pirminii, de singulis libris canoncis scarap-
sus."
InStme

5683 **Piscicelli Taeggi, Oderisio.**
La paleografia artistica nei codici Cassinesi applicata ai lavori industriali. [Monte
Cassino], Litografia di Montecassino,
1910.
[2] p. 20 plates in portfolio, 34 cm.
MnCS

Pitra, Jean Baptiste, 1812–1889.

5684 Analecta sacra et classica spicilegio
Solesmensi parata. Parisiis, apud Roger et
Chernowitz Bibliopolas, 1876–1891.
8 v. facsims. 28 cm.
InStme (v. 2–5, 7–8); MnCS; PLatS (v. 3)

5685 Analecta sacra et classica spicilegio
Solesmensi. Parisiis, apud Roger et Chernowitz Bibliopolas; 1888–91. [Farn-
borough, Hants., Gregg Press, 1966].
2 v. 25 cm.
Forms the 2d series of his Analecta.
PLatS

5686 Analecta novissima spicilegi Solesmensis
altera continuatio. Roma, Typis Tuscula-
nis, 1885–88 [Farnborough, Hants., Gregg
Press, 1967].
2 v. 25 cm.
Forms the 3rd series of his Analecta.
PLatS

5687 The Latin Heptateuch, published piece-
meal by the French printer William Morel
(1560) and the French Benedictines E.
Martène (1733) and J. B. Pitra (1852–88)
critically reviewed [by] John E. B. Mahor.
London, C. J. Clay and Sons, 1889.
lxxiv, 268 p. 23 cm.
MnCS

5688 Spicilegium Solesmense, complectens
sanctorum patrum scriptorumque ecclesiasticorum anecdota hactenus opera selecta e graecis orientaliusque et latinis
codicibus. Graz, Akademische Druck- und
Verlagsanstalt, 1962–.
4 v. 25 cm.

Reprint of Paris edition of 1852–58.
PLatS

5689 (ed) Hildegard, Saint. Analecta Sanctae
Hildegardis opera spicilegio Solesmensi
parata [par] J. B. Pitra. typis Sacri Montis
Casinensis, 1882.
xxiii, 614 p. 28 cm.
CaQStB; PLatS

5689a **Plank, Benedikt,** 1912–
Geschichte der Abtei St. Lambrecht;
Festschrift zur 900. Wiederkehr des
Todestages des Gründers Markward v. Ep-
penstein, 1076–1976. Stift St. Lambrecht,
1976.
107 p. plates (some col.) 23 cm.
InStme

5690 **Plattner, Maurus,** 1854–1910.
Der Unbefleckten Ruhmeskranz; eine
Jubelgabe für das fünfzigste Jahr seit der
Definition des Glaubenssatzes von der
unbefleckten Empfängnis Mariä. Graz und
Leipzig, U. Moser, 1904.
vi, 170 p. 22 cm.
KAS

5691 **Placidus, prior of Nonantula.**
De honore ecclesiae. MS. Vienna, Na-
tionalbibliothek, codex 2235, f.1v–57v.
Quarto. Saec. 12.
Microfilm: MnCH proj. no. 15,551

Planckh, Bernardinus.

5692 Eclogae, afflictiones, aliaque carminum
genera a patribus professoriis Ord. S.
Benedicti Salisburgi composita et a P. Bernardino Planckh collecta et conscripta
anno 1629. MS. Prämonstratenserabtei
Schlägl, Austria, codex sine numero,
f.1r–35r. Octavo. Saec. 17.
Microfilm: MnCH proj. no. 3161

5693 Fasciculus carminum, collectus et con-
scriptus a P. Bernardino Planckh Ord. D.
Benedicti, monacho Garstensi, 1630. MS.
Prämonstratenserabtei Schlägl, Austria,
codex sine numero, f.36r–144v. Octavo.
Saec. 17.
Microfilm: MnCH proj. no. 3161

5694 **Plantenberg, Dunstan, Sister,** 1926–
Factors influencing digestion in the black
bullhead, ictalurus melas (Rafinesque).
v, 36 p. 28 cm.
Thesis (M.S.)–Marquette University,
1961.
Typescript.
MnStj(Archives)

5695 **Plautius, Caspar, abbot of Seitenstetten,** fl. 1621.
Nova typis transacta navigatio. Novi Orbis Indiae Occidentalis admodvm reveren-
disimorvm pp. ac ff. referendissimi ac illustrissimi Domini, Dn. Bvelli Cataloni ab-

batis Montisserrati, & in vniversam Americam, sive novum orbem Sacrae Sedis Apostolicae Romanae a Latere Legati, vicarij, ac patriarchae; sociorumq. monachorum ex Ordine S.P.N. Benedicti ad supra dicti Novi Mundi barbaras gentes Christi s. evangelium praedicandi gratis delegatorum sacerdotum dimissi per S.D.D. Papam Alexandrum VI anno Christi 1492. Nunc primvm e varijs scriptoribus in vnum collecta & figuris ornata. Avthore Venerando Fr. Don Honorio Philopono Ordinis S. Benedicti monacho. n.p., 1621.
3, 101 p. 18 plates, 29 cm.
KAS

5696 **Polding, John Bede,** abp., 1794–1877.
The eye of faith; the pastoral letters of John Bede Polding. Editors: Gregory Haines, Sister Mary Gregory Forster, F. Brophy. Foreword by Cardinal Sir James Freeman. Lowden Publishing Co., Kilmore, Victoria, Australia; Books Australia, Norwalk, Connecticut, 1978.
xvi, 430 p. plates, ports. 22 cm.
MnCS

5697 **Pomerleau, Marianne, Sister,** 1893–1968.
Bossuet ascétique, disciple des mystiques, Saint Augustin, Saint Grégoire le Grand et Saint Bernard.
179 p. 28 cm.
Thesis (M.A.)–University of Minnesota, 1929.
Typescript.
MnStj(Archives)

5698 **Poncet, Maurice.**
Nouveaux éclaicissemens sur l'origine et le Pentateuque des Samaritains, par un religieux bénédictin de la Congrégation de S. Maur. Paris, Jean-Luc Noyon, 1760.
xvi, 259 p.
CaQAtB

5699 **Pons, Blaise,** 1922–
Saint Benoît. Illustrations de Robert Rigot. Paris, Éditions Fleurus, 1956.
[48] p. 164 illus. 27 cm.
MnCS; PLatS

Pontoise, France. Saint Martin (Benedictine abbey).
5700 Chartrier de l'Abbaye de Saint-Martin de Pontoise publié d'après les documents inédits par J. Depoin. Pontoise, Société Historique du Vexin, 1911.
72 p. 29 cm.
MnCS

5701 Tables du cartulaire de l'Abbaye Saint-Martin de Pontoise. Annexes et appendices exclus. Pontoise, Bureaux de la Société Historique, 1969.

55 p. tables, 24 cm.
MnCS

5702 **Poole, Mary Jo, Sister.**
Self as content in teacher education.
194 p. 28 cm.
Thesis (Ed.D.)–University of Cincinnati, 1975.
Typescript.
KyCovS

Popes, 590–604 (Gregory I).
5703 Constitutiones. MS. Vienna, Nationalbibliothek, codex 1318, f.186r–192r. Quarto. Saec. 14.
Microfilm: MnCH proj. no. 14,672

5704 Decreta aliquot, et Capitularia. MS. Vienna, Nationalbibliothek, codex 2171, f.30r–31v. Folio. Saec. 9.
Microfilm: MnCH proj. no. 15,470

5705 Decretales. MS. Augustinerchorherrenstift, Herzogenburg, Austria, codex 72, f.1r–221r. Octavo. Saec. 15.
Microfilm: MnCH proj. no. 3241

5706 Decretum de resurrectione. MS. Vienna, Nationalbibliothek, codex 914, f.33r. Folio. Saec. 10.
Microfilm: MnCH proj. no. 14,239

5707 Epistolae. MS. Vienna, Nationalbibliothek, codex 934, f.55v–87v. Folio. Saec. 9.
Microfilm: MnCH proj. no. 14,251

5708 Epistolae. MS. Vienna, Nationalbibliothek, codex 4372, f.1r–104v. Folio. Saec. 14.
Microfilm: MnCH proj. no. 17,577

5709 Epistolae aliquot. Vienna, Nationalbibliothek, codex 4530, f.141r–150v. Quarto. Saec. 14(1393).
Microfilm: MnCH proj. no. 17,710

5710 Epistola ad episcopum Carnotensem. MS. Vienna, Nationalbibliothek, codex 2221, f.192r–194r. Quarto. Saec. 13.
Microfilm: MnCH proj. no. 15,506

Popes, 1073–1085 (Gregory VII).
5711 Decretalium libri quinque, cum glossa et adnotationibus. MS. Benediktinerabtei St. Peter, Salzburg, codex a.XII.2, f.8r–317v. Folio. Saec. 14.
Microfilm: MnCH proj. no. 10,731

5712 Epistolae seu bullae tres. MS. Benediktinerabtei Kremsmünster, Austria, codex 27, f.202v–203v. Saec. 14.
Microfilm: MnCH proj. no. 27

5713 Epistolae quatuor. MS. Vienna, Nationalbibliothek, codex 4902, f.97r–98v. Quarto. Saec. 15.
Microfilm: MnCH proj. no. 18,068

5714 The Epistolae Vagantes of Pope Gregory VII. Edited and translated by H.E.J. Cowdrey. Oxford, Clarendon Press, 1972.

xxxi, 175 p. 23 cm. (Oxford medieval texts)
Latin and English on facing pages.
PLatS

5715 Registrum. MS. Lincoln Cathedral Library, England. codex 4. 216 f. Quarto. Saec. 12.
Microfilm: MnCH

5716 Registrum. MS. Lambeth Palace Library, London, codex 64. 189 f. Quarto. Saec. 12.
Microfilm: MnCH

5717 Registrum (excerpta). MS. Lambeth Palace Library, London, codex 345, f.98–226. Quarto. Saec. 13.
Microfilm: MnCH

5718 Registrum. MS. Benediktinerabtei Melk, Austria, codex 21. 182 f. Folio. Saec. 15.
Microfilm: MnCH proj. no. 1125

5719 Registrum epistolarum. MS. Benediktinerabtei Kremsmünster, Austria, codex 334, f.1v–204v. Saec. 14.
Microfilm: MnCH proj. no. 332

5720 Registrum epistolarum. MS. Benediktinerabtei Lambach, Austria, codex chart. 45, f.1r–288v. Saec. 15.
Microfilm: MnCH proj. no. 467

5721 **Popes,** 1088–1099 (Urban II).
Bulla de falsa translatione sanctissimi patris nostri Benedicti abbatis. MS. Vienna, Dominikanerkloster, codex 207, f.223v–224r. Folio. Saec. 15.
Microfilm: MnCH proj. no. 9009

5722 **Popes,** 1118–1119 (Gelasius II).
Breve ad clerum Galliae. MS. Vienna, Nationalbibliothek, codex 445, f.1r. Folio. Saec. 12.
Microfilm: MnCH proj. no. 13,782

5723 **Popular Liturgical Library,** 1926–1976, golden anniversary catalog. Collegeville, Minn., The Liturgical Press [1976].
77 p. illus. (part col.) 28 cm.
"1926–1976, come, let us reminisce . . . p. 2–6."
MnCS; PLatS

5724 **Poras, Grégoire,** 1912–
Répertoire topo-bibliographique des abbayes et prieurés, par Dom L. H. Cottineau (v. 1–2). Vol. 3 préparé par Dom Grégoire Poras, O.S.B. Macon, Protat Frères, 1935–1970.
3 v. 29 cm.
MnCS; PLatS

5725 **Porcel, Olegario M.,** 1914–
La doctrina monastica de san Gregorio Magno y la "Regula monachorum." Washington, Catholic University of America Press, 1951.
xii, 226 p. 23 cm.

Thesis (S.T.D.)–Catholic University of America.
MnCS; MoCo; NdRiA; PLatS

5726 **Porter, Jerome,** d. 1632.
The flowers of the lives of the most renowned saints. Idley, Scolar Press, 1975.
[40], 611 p. illus. 21 cm. (English recusant literature, 1558–1640, v. 239)
MnCS; PLatS

5727 **Portraits of Benedictine saints.** Biographical sketch under each engraving, n.p., n.d.
273 leaves of engravings. 20 cm.
Title page wanting.
Portraits in alphabetical sequence.
PLatS

5728 **Portsmouth Abbey School, Portsmouth, R.I.**
Fiftieth anniversary, 1926–1976.
96 p. illus.
MoCo; RPorP

5729 **Pothier, Joseph,** 1835–1923.
Revue du chant grégorien. 1–44, 1892–1940. Grenoble [France].
44 v. 25 cm.
Dom Joseph Pothier was the chief contributor for vols. 1–26.
MnCS; PLatS

Potho of Prüfening.
5730 Liber de miraculis sanctae Dei genitricis Mariae. Published at Vienna in 1731 by Bernard Pez, O.S.B. Reprinted for the first time by Thomas Frederick Crane . . . with an introduction and notes and a bibliography of the writings of T. F. Crane. Ithaca, N.Y., Cornell University, 1925.
xvii, 117, 42 p. 24 cm.
InStme

5731 Miracula XLII Beatae Virginis Mariae. MS. Benediktinerabtei Göttweig, Austria, codex 176. 55 f. Quarto. Saec. 13.
Microfilm: MnCH proj. no. 13.

5733 **Pouchet, Robert.**
La rectitudo chez Saint Anselme; un itinéraire augustinien de l'ame à Dieu. Paris, Etudes Augustiniennes, 1964.
330 p. 25 cm.
InStme; PLatS; MnCS

Poulet, Charles, 1887–1950.
5734 Guelfes et Gibelins. Bruxelles, Vromant, 1922.
2 v. 19 cm.
InStme; NcBe

5735 Histoire de l'Eglise. 18. éd. rev. et augm. Paris, Beauchesne, 1943.
2 v. in 4, 20 cm.
InStme

5736   Histoire de l'Eglise. Nouvelle édition revue et mise à jour par dom Louis Gaillard, O.S.B. Paris, Beauchesne, 1959–62.
3 v. 23 cm.
PLatS

5737   **Pour chanter l'office; guide practique.**
[Bruges, Abbaye de S. André, 196-].
89 p. 28 cm.
KAS

Prado, Germán, 1891–
5738   Historia del Rito Mozárabe y Toledano. Burgos, Espana, Abadía de Santo Domingo de Silos, 1928.
121 p. illus., plates. 25 cm.
InStme

5739   Madre Soledad. [Madrid], Siervas de Maria [1953].
469 p. illus. 21 cm.
KAS

5740   Misal diario y vesperal, por Gaspar Lefebvre . . . Traduccion castellana y adaptacion del P. Germán Prado. Desclée de Brouwer [1958].
2149, 80, 47 p. illus. 16 cm.
MnCS

5741   Textos ineditos de la liturgia mozárabe: rito solemne de la iniciación cristiana, consecratión de las iglesias, unción de los enfermos. Transcription y comentarios por Germán Prado, O.S.B. Madrid [Establimento tipografico de J. Góngora] 1926.
200 p. 18 cm.
MnCS; WFif

Prager, Mirjam, Sister.
5742   Israel in the parables. [Translated by J. M. Oesterreicher].
(*In* The Bridge . . . v. 4. New York, 1962. p. 44–88)
PLatS

5743   (tr) Lossky, Vladimir. Die mystische Theologie der morgenländischen Kirche. Uebersetzt von Mirjam Prager, O.S.B. Graz, Verlag Styria [1961].
317 p. 20 cm.
PLatS

5744   **Praglia, Italy (Benedictine abbey).**
Modo di assistere alla santa Messa secondo lo spirito della liturgia. 4. ed. Padova, Tip. Pontificia Antoniana, 1921.
93 p. 15 cm.
MnCS

5745   **Prangnell, Dunstan,** 1897–
The chronicle of William of Byholte (1310–1320). An account of the legal system known as frankpledge. Edited by Dom Dunstan Prangnell, O.S.B. Ramsgate, Monastery Press [1967].
25 p. 22 cm.
PLatS

Presinger, Rupert, 1688–1741.
5746   Benedictinus mortem quotidie ante oculos suspectam habens ac per solicitam omni hora actuum vitae custodiam ad eam se disponens . . . Salisburgi, J. J. Mayr, 1739.
130 p. 14 cm.
InStme

5747   Sacerdos benedictinus ad Sacrae Regulae normam, et praecipue juxta exempla ac doctrinas summi sacerdotis Christi Jesu efformatus. [Tegernsee], typis monasterii Tegernseensis, 1720.
76 p. 14 cm.
KAS

5748   **Preske, Matthew,** 1896–1976.
The teaching of liturgy; a need in the curriculum of the Catholic high school.
ii, 39 leaves, 28 cm.
Thesis (M.A.) – University of Notre Dame, 1928.
Typescript.
InStme

Preston, Thomas, 1563–1640.
5749   Ad sanctissimum Dominum Paulum Quintum humillima supplicatio, cui adiungitur appendix. [Menston, Yorkshire] Scolar Press, 1971.
94, 262 p. 21 cm. (English recusant literature, 1558–1640, v. 65)
PLatS

5750   Appendix ad disputationem theologicam de juramento fidelitatis. [Menston, Yorkshire], Scolar Press, 1970.
284 p. 19 cm. (English recusant literature, 1558–1640, v. 51)
Original edition 1616.
PLatS

5751   A cleare, sincere, and modest confutation. [London] The Scolar Press, 1974.
[30], 294, 94 p. 21 cm. (English recusant literature, 1558–1640, v. 223)
Facsimile reprint of 1616 edition.
PLatS

5752   A copy of the decree [wherein two books of Roger Widdrington [pseud] an English Catholick are condemned, and the author commanded to purge himselfe: and a copy of the purgation which the same Roger Widdrington sent to his Holiness Pope Paul the fift. Translated out of Latine into English by the author . . . London, The Scolar Press, 1977].
67 p. 20 cm. (English recusant literature, 1558–1640, v. 337)
Facsimile reprint of 1614 edition.
PLatS

5753   Discussio discussionis [decreti magni Concilii Lateranensis, adversus Leonardum Lessium, S.J. . . . in qua omnia argumenta, quae idemmet Lessius pro Papali potestate principes deponendi ex jure canonico, & decretis Conciliorum, atq: Pontificum, aliisque incommodis adducit, dilucide examinantur, & refutantur . . . a Rogero Widdringtono. London] The Scolar Press, 1976.

[37], 461 p. 21 cm. (English recusant literature, 1558–1640, v. 292)

Facsimile reprint of 1618 edition.

PLatS

5754   A new-yeares gift for English Catholikes. [Menston, Yorkshire] Scolar Press, 1973.

[30], 208 p. 20 cm. (English recusant literature, 1558–1640, f. 130)

Facsimile reprint of 1620 edition.

PLatS

5755   Roger Widdringtons last rejoynder [to Mr. Thomas Fitz-Herberts reply concerning the Oath of Allegiance, and the popes power to depose princes . . . London] The Scolar Press, 1976.

[30], 645 p. 27 cm. (English recusant literature, 1558–1640, v. 280)

Facsimile reprint of 1619 edition.

PLatS

5756   Rogeri Widdringtoni . . . responsio apologetica. [Menston, Yorkshire] The Scolar Press, 1973.

various pagings. 19 cm. (English recusant literature, 1558–1640, v. 161)

Facsimile reprint of 1612 edition.

PLatS

5757   **Primus, Colette, Sister,** 1933–

A study of the acquisition and use of periodicals in the elementary school.

53 p. 28 cm.

Thesis (M.S.)–St. Cloud State College, 1970.

Mimeographed.

MnStj(Archives)

5758   **Primus, Idamarie, Sister,** 1923–

A study of the guidance services in selected Catholic high schools of Illinois, Iowa, Minnesota and Wisconsin.

110 p. 28 cm.

Thesis (M.A.)–College of St. Thomas, 1960.

Typescript.

MnStj(Archives)

Prinknash Abbey, England.

5759   The Benedictine Oblate's manual. Edited by a monk of Prinknash Priory, Gloucester. [Gloucester, 1928].

240 p. 18 cm.

PLatS

5760   The Church and the people. 1–   1939–

InFer

5761   **Prüfening, Bavaria (Benedictine abbey).**

Catalogus codicum manu scriptorum Bibliothecae Regiae Monacensis: Codices 12004–12054 ex monasterio in Prüfening sive Prüfling. Monachii, sumptibus Bibliothecae Regiae, 1876. Unveränderter Nachdruck, Otto Harrassowitz, Wiesbaden, 1968.

MnCS

5762   **Pueroni, Domenico, O.S.B.Oliv.,** fl. 1660.

Iter coeli per semitas viae purgativae, illuminativae, ac unitivae. Romae, typis Ignatij de Lazaris, 1666.

[8], 769 p. 22 cm.

Treats mainly, in spite of title, of novitiate training and mental prayer.

KAS

5763   **Puigdavra, Ioseph.**

Regla del gran padre San Benito. Llave maestra del Paraiso, y Paraiso benedictino, en que abrevió las excelencias de su s. patriarca Regla y religión. Ioseph Puigdoura, O.S.B., ed. Barcelona, Rafael Fugueró, 1712.

MnCS

5764   **Pujol, David,** 1894–

Musica instrumental . . . Transcripció, revisió i anotació de dom David Pujol, monjo de Montserrat. Monestir de Montserrat, 1934–

v. 34x28 cm.

MnCS

Puniet, Pierre de, 1877–1941.

5765   Benedictine spirituality. Translated by Roland Behrendt, O.S.B. Collegeville, Minn., St. John's Abbey, 1965.

57 p. 28 cm.

Multigraphed.

AStb; KAS; MnCS; MnStj; MoCo; PLatS

5766   La liturgie de la Messe; ses origines et son histoire. 2. éd., rev. et corr. Avignon, Aubanel Fils Aîné, 1930.

259 p. 19 cm.

CaQStB; CaQStM; InStme

5767   **Purchardus, monk of Reichenau,** fl. ca. 1000.

Carmen de gestis Witigowonis abbatis Augiensis.

(*In* Monumenta Germaniae historica. Scriptores. Stuttgart, 1963. t. 4, p. 621–632)

MnCS; PLatS

Putrer, Modestus

5768   Comentarii in epistolas S. Pauli ad Hebraeos, Philippenses et Colossenses. MS. Benediktinerabtei Admont, Austria, codex 791. 53 f. Quarto. Saec. 16.

Microfilm: MnCH proj. no. 9828

5769   Inventarium auctoritatum Bibliae. MS. Benediktinerabtei Admont, Austria, codex 856. 128 f. Octavo. Saec. 16.
Microfilm: MnCH proj. no. 9859

Puy, Le, France. *See* Le Puy, France.

5770   **Quatrième dimanche de carême,** présenté par R. Bornert [et al.]. Paris, Du Cerf [1966].
110 p. 21 cm. (Assemblées du Seigneur, 32)
PLatS

5771   **XIV [quattuordecimo] centenario de San Benito;** exposicion historica de la Orden Benedictina nacional. Madrid, 1948.
70 p. illus., plates.
MoCo

5772   **Queen of Peace Priory, Belcourt, N.D.**
Par-Take [periodical].
InFer (1974–75); NdBel

Raasch, Juana, Sister, 1927–1974.
5773   A bibliography for Benedictine renewal, with excerpts.
38 p. 28 cm.
Mimeographed.
MoCo

5774   The character of the Mexican Indians as described by some sixteenth-century Spanish writers.
56 p. 28 cm.
Thesis (M.A.)–University of Illinois, 1951.
Typescript.
MnStj(Archives)

Rabanus Maurus. *See* Hrabanus Maurus.

Räber, Ludwig, 1912–
5775   Images d'Einsiedeln. 8. éd., rev. et corr. Einsiedeln, Benziger [1966].
33 p. illus., 64 plates, 17 cm.
Traduction française: Dom Germain Varin.
MnCS

5776   Our Lady of hermits: guide-book. Einsiedeln, Benziger & Co. [1961].
40 p. illus.
MoCo

5777   Ständerat Räber; ein Leben im Dienst der Heimat, 1872–1934. Mit einem Nachwort von Philip Etter. Einsiedeln, Benziger [1950].
324 p. illus. 22 cm.
InStme

5778   **Rader, Rosemary, Sister,** 1931–
The role of celibacy in the origin and development of Christian heterosexual friendship.
Thesis–Stanford University, 1977.
MnSSP

Radó, Polikárp, 1899–
5779   Enchiridion liturgiae pastoralis, seu Synthesis theologiae sacramentalis. Archiabbatia S. Martini de S. Monte Pannoniae, 1959.
48 p.
NcBe

5780   Enchiridion liturgicum, complectens theologiae sacramentalis et dogmata et leges iuxta novum codicem rubricarum. Romae, Herder, 1961.
2 v. 25 cm.
CaQStB; ILSP; InStme; KAS; MnCS; MoCo; PLatS

5781   Esztergomi könyvtárak liturgikus kéziratai. [Pannonhalma, 1941].
58 p. 29 cm.
MnCS

5782   Libri liturgici manuscripti bibliothecarum Hungariae et limitropharum regionum . . . 1 Budapest, Akadémiai Kiadé, 1973.
639 p. 25 cm.
MnCS

5783   Répertoire hymologique des manuscrits liturgiques dans les bibliothèques publiques de Hongrie. Budapest, Magyar Nemzeti Múzeum Orsz. Széchény Könyvtára [1945].
59 p. 25 cm.
PLatS

Radulphus, monk of St-Germer-de-Flay.
5784   Commentarius in Leviticum (libri decem posteriores). MS. Vienna, Nationalbibliothek, codex 679, f.1v–204r. Folio. Saec. 13.
Microfilm: MnCH proj. no. 14,000

5785   Commentarius super Leviticum. MS. Vienna, Nationalbibliothek, codex 909, f.2v–232r. Folio. Saec. 13.
Microfilm: MnCH proj. no. 14,221

5786   Commentarius in Leviticum. Prima pars (lib. 1–10). Vienna, Nationalbibliothek, codex 936. 186 f. Folio. Saec. 13.
Microfilm: MnCH proj. no. 14,244

Radziwill, Benedikt, 1842–
5787   Festrede zum fünfzigjährigen Bischofs-Jubiläum Seiner Heiligkeit Papst Leo XIII, gehalten im Grossen Museumssaale zu Heidelberg am 19. Febr. 1893. Freiburg i.B., Herder, 1893.
31 p. 21 cm.
PLatS

5788   Die kirchliche Autorität und das moderne Bewusstsein. Breslau, G. P. Aderholz, 1872.
xxi, 664 p. 22 cm.
InStme

Rajrad, Czechoslovakia (Benedictine abbey).

5789 Catalogus religiosorum Ordinis S. P. Benedicti abb. in antiquissimo monasterio Rajhradensi.
v. 14 cm.
MnCS (1900–1914); PLatS

5790 Directorium divini officii celebrandi sacrique peragendi in usum monachorum O.S.P. Benedicti Abbatiae Raihradiensis in Moravia. Brunae, Typis et sumptibus Ordinis.
v. 16 cm. Published annually.
KAS; PLatS

5791 **Ramsey Abbey, England.**
The Liber Gersumarum of Ramsey Abbey; a calendar and index of B. L. Harley MS. 445, by Edwin Brezette Dewindt. Toronto, Pontifical Institute of Mediaeval Studies, 1976.
445 p. 24 cm.
PLatS

5792 **Ranbeck, Aegidius,** 1608–1692.
Parasceve mortalitatis humanae, sive, necessaria preparatio, qua imprimis senes & qui lethali morbo correpti sunt ad mortem feliciter obeundam utilissime instituuntur. Ingolstadii, Joh. Philippus Zinck, 1676.
210, [12] p. 13 cm.
KAS

Ranek, Jeanne, Sister.
5793 Social factors in the posthospital adjustment of mental patients.
129 p.
Thesis – University of Notre Dame, 1972.
SdYa

5794 Research report of the 1972–73 Sacred Heart Convent survey team, Yankton, So. Dak.
63 p.
SdYa

5797 **Rapf, Cölestin Roman,** 1907–
Die Bibliothek der Benediktinerabtei Unserer Lieben Frau zu den Schotten in Wien.
(*In* Translatio studii; manuscript and library studies honoring Oliver L. Kapsner. 1973. p. 4–35)
AStb, etc.

Rapid City, S.D. St. Martin's Convent.
See St. Martin's Convent, Rapid City, S.D.

5798 **Rapp, Urban,** 1915–
Das Mysterienbild. Münsterschwarzach, Vier-Türme-Verlag [1952].
161 p. 24 plates, 25 cm.

Issued as thesis, Würzburg, 1950, under title: Kultbild und Mysterienbild im Abendland.
InStme

5799 **Rast, Timotheus,** 1923–
Von der Beichte zum Sakrament der Busse . . . Düsseldorf, Patmos [1965].
269 p. 21 cm.
PLatS

Ratherius, bp. of Verona, ca. 890–974.
5800 Opera minora, edidit Petrus L. D. Reid. Turnholti, Brepols, 1976.
xxxvi, 322 p. 26 cm. (Corpus Christianorum. Continuatio mediaevalis, 46)
PLatS

5801 Sermones Ratherii episcopi Veronensis. [ed. Benny R. Reese. Worcester [Mass.], Holy Cross College, 1969.
132 p. 24 cm.
MnCS

Ratpert, monk of St. Gall, d. ca. 890.
5802 Casus S. Galli.
(*In* Monumenta Germaniae historica. Scriptores. Stuttgart, 1963. t. 2, p. 59–74)
MnCS; PLatS

5803 (2dary) Stotz, Peter. Ardus spes mundi; Studien zu latenischen Gedichten aus Sankt Gallen. Bern, H. Lang, 1972.
265 p. 23 cm.
MnCS

Ratramnus, monk of Corbie, d. ca. 868.
5804 The boke of Barthran priest intreatinge of the bodye and bloude of Christ wryten to greate Charles the Emperooure/and set forth vii.C yeares ago, and imprinted an. dni. M.D.XLVIII. Colophon: London, Thomas Raynolde.
MnCS (film)

5805 Liber de anima ad Odonem Bellovacensem. Texte inédit, publié par d. C. Lambot, O.S.B. Namur, Editions Godenne [1952].
158 p. 26 cm. (Analecta mediaevalia Namurcensia, 2)
PLatS

5806 De Corpore et Sanguine Domini ad Carolum Calvum. MS. Benediktinerabtei Admont, Austria, codex 654, f.207r–249v. Quarto. Saec. 12.
Microfilm: MnCH proj. no. 9694

5807 Liber ad Karolum regem de Corpore et Sanguine Domini. MS. Benediktinerabtei Göttweig, Austria, codex 54, f.21v–27v. Folio. Saec. 12.
Microfilm: MnCH proj. no. 3342

5808 De Corpore et Sanguine Domini. MS. Universitätsbibliothek Graz, Austria, codex 171, f.51r–66r. Quarto. Saec. 12.
Microfilm: MnCH proj. no. 26,102

5809 Liber ad Karolum regem de Corpore et Sanguine Domini. MS. Benediktinerabtei Göttweig, Austria, codex 3553, f. 79v–84v. Folio. Saec. 15.
Microfilm: MnCH proj. no. 3553

5810 [De Corpore et Sanguine Domini]
Guild, William. Three rare monuments of antiquitie; or, Bertram (Ratramnus), priest, a French-man, of the bodie and blood of Christ . . . Aberdene, 1624.
MnCS

5811 **Rauber, Placidus.**
Tyrocinium boni rhetoris. MS. Benediktinerabtei St. Peter, Salzburg, codex b.VI.38, f.1r–174r. Octavo. Saec. 17(1628).
Microfilm: MnCH proj. no. 10,494

Rauen, Rose, Sister.
5812 Embedding topological spaces in topological semigroups.
Thesis (Ph.D.)–St. Louis University, 1959.
KyCovS

5813 Reduced, binary quadratic forms having odd, negative discriminants.
Thesis (M.S.)–St. Louis University, 1955.
KyCovS

Raulin, Jean, 1443–1514.
5814 Doctrinale mortis. Parrhisijs, Johannes Parvus [1518].
[10], 134 leaves. 23 cm.
PLatS

5815 Itinerarium paradisi . . . complectens sermones de penitentia et eius partibus. Parisius, Johannes Parvus [1518].
[8], 151 p. 23 cm.
PLatS

5816 Opus sermonum de adventu. Parisius, Johannes Parvus [1516].
[10], 188 leaves. 23 cm.
PLatS

5817 Sermones dominicales. Adiecti sunt multi sermones, in variis Universitatis Parisiensis processionibus proclamati. Adiecta insuper in fine questio vesperiarum. Antverpiae, apud Koannem Keerbergium, 1612.
491 p. 20 cm.
MnCS

5818 **Raus, Karl,** 1904–
Einführung in den Ordo Divini Officii, 1961. [Salzburg, DruckhausNonntal, 1961].
56 p. 14 cm.
MnCS

5819 **Rausch, Sheila, Sister,** 1926–
Mary Russell Mitford and regional realism.
188 p. 28 cm.

Thesis (Ph.D.)–University of Minnesota, 1968.
Typescript.
MnStj(Archives)

5820 **Raynal, Paul Wilfrid,** 1830–1904.
The Imitation of Christ, as written by Thomas à Kempis. Translated by Richard Whitford. Reedited into modern English by Wilfrid Raynal, O.S.B., 1872. Springfield, Ill., Templegate [1964?].
xii, 283 p. 15 cm.
MnCS

Rebiser, Simon.
5821 Aristotelis octo libri physicorum commentariis illustrati et Aristotelis quatuor libri meteorum. MS. Universitätsbibliothek Salzburg, codex M I 328. 283 f. Quarto. Saec. 17(1648–49).
Microfilm: MnCH proj. no. 11,092

5822 Organum Aristotelis commentariis illustratum. MS. Universitätsbibliothek Salzburg, codex M I 321. 279 f. Quarto. Saec. 17(1647).
Microfilm: MnCH proj. no. 11,086

Recheis, Athanasius, 1926–
5823 Angels; spirits, magnificent and mighty. Translated by Rev. John A. Otto. Collegeville, Minn., The Liturgical Press [1976].
76 p. 18 cm.
Translation of: Die Engel sind mächtige Geister.
MdRi; MnCS; MoCo

5824 Engel, Tod und Seelenreise; das Wirken der Geister beim Heimgang des Menschen in der Lehre der Alexandrinischen und Kappadokischen Väter. Roma, Edizioni di Storia e Letteratura [1958].
222 p. 26 cm.
MnCS; WFif

5825 **Reding, Augustinus,** 1625–1692.
Theologiae scholaticae in [Summa theologica] Divi Thomae ad normam theologorum Salisburgensium . . . Typis Monasterii Einsidelensis, per Jacobum Ammon, 1667–1687.
11 v. 35 cm.
Publishers vary.
InStme

5826 **Redler, Placidus.**
Commentarius in quinque libros Decretalium Gregorii IX. Benediktinerabtei St. Peter, Salzburg, codex b.VI.32. 550 p. Octavo. Saec. 17(1633).
Microfilm: MnCH proj. no. 10,503

5827 **Redlich, Virgil,** 1890–1970.
Tegernsee und die deutsche Geistesgeschichte im 15. Jahrhundert. Aelen, Scientia Verlag, 1974.
268 p. 23 cm.

5828 **Redon, France. Saint Saveur (Benedictine abbey).**
Cartulaire de l'Abbaye de Redon en Bretagne, publié, par M. Aurélien de Courson . . . Paris, Imprimeriale Impériale, 1863.
cccxcv, 760 p. 30 cm.
KAS

5829 **Reed, James,** 1897–1965.
Some practical projects in the liturgical method of religious education.
44 leaves, 28 cm.
Thesis (M.A.)–University of Notre Dame, 1929.
Typescript.
InStme

5830 **Rees, Daniel,** 1931–
Consider your call; a theology of monastic life [by] Daniel Rees and other members of the English Benedictine Congregation. London, SPCK, 1978.
xx, 447 p. 22 cm.
InStme; MnCS; MnStj; NcBe; ViBris; PLatS

Reetz, Benedikt, 1897–
5831 Christus; die grosse Frage. Graz, Steirische Verlagsanstalt [1946].
46 p. 21 cm.
MnCS; PLatS

5832 Die monastischen Grundprinzipien nach Erzabt Dr. Maurus Wolter.
(*In* Beuron, 1863–1963; Festschrift . . . Beuron, 1963. p. 19–38)
PLatS

5833 Ostern–der königliche Tag. Wien, Herder, 1946.
viii, 172 p. 21 cm.
PLatS

Regensburg, Bavaria. St. Emmeram (Benedictine abbey).
5834 Annales Sancti Emmerammi Ratisbonensis.
(*In* Monumenta Germaniae historica. Scriptores. Stuttgart, 1963. t. 1, p. 91–94)
MnCS; PLatS

5835 Catalogus codicum manu scriptorum Bibliothecae Regiae Monacensis: Codices 14000–15028 ex bibliotheca monasterii Ord. S. Benedicti ad S. Emmeramum Ratisbonensis. Monachii, sumptibus Bibliothecae Regiae, 1876. Unveränderter Nachdruck, Otto Harrassowitz, Wiesbaden, 1968.
MnCH

5836 **Reger, Ambrose Anthony,** 1872–1938.
The secular oblates of St. Benedict. St. Bernard Abbey [1932].
38 p.
AStb

5836a How Johnny was baptized; a narrative with a lesson. Corbin, Ky., Sacred Heart Church [1912].
[34] p. 15 cm.
KAS

Regino, abbot of Prüm, d. 915.
5837 Annales, non tam de augustorum vitis quam aliorum Germanorum gestis et docte et compendiose disserentes, ante sexingentos fere annos editi. [Colophon: Moguntiae, in aedibus Ioannis Schoeffer, 1521].
12, 58 leaves.
PLatS

5838 Chronicon. MS. Augustinerchorherrenstift Klosterneuburg, Austria, codex 741, f.108r–202v. Folio. Saec. 12.
Microfilm: MnCH proj. no. 5725

5839 Chronicon, cum continuatione usque ad annum 967. MS. Vienna, Nationalbibliothek, codex 538. 124 f. Quarto. Saec. 13.
Microfilm: MnCH proj. no. 13,855

5840 Chronicon. MS. Vienna, Nationalbibliothek, codex 639, f.32r–187v. Octavo. Saec. 15.
Microfilm: MnCH proj. no. 13,961

5841 Chronicon. MS. Vienna, Nationalbibliothek, codex 3522, f.168r–280r. Quarto. Saec. 15.
Microfilm: MnCH proj. no. 16,734

5842 Chronicon. Duo libri: 1. De Romanorum gestis. 2. De Francorum regibus (ex codice monasterii Augiae Divitis) lex alemannica. MS. Benediktinerabtei St. Paul im Lavanttal, Austria, codex 81/2. 177, (100) p. Folio. Saec. 18.
Microfilm: MnCH proj. no. 11,850

5843 Reginonis chronicon a.1–906.
(*In* Monumenta Germaniae historica. Scriptores. Stuttgart, 1963. t. 1, p. 537–629)
MnCS; PLatS

5844 De ecclesiasticis disciplinis et religione christiana. MS. Vienna, Nationalbibliothek, codex 694, f.20r–168v. Folio. Saec. 11.
Microfilm: MnCH proj. no. 14,018

5845 Libri duo de ecclesiasticis disciplinis & religione christiana. Stephanus Baluzius . . . ad fidem vetustissimi codicis emendavit, nunc primum in Gallia edidit, & notis illustravit . . . Parisiis, Franciscus Muguet, 1671.
[38], 658, [27] p.
PLatS (microfilm)

5846 Libri duo de ecclesiasticis disciplinis. Viennae, Joan. Thomas Trattern, 1765.
537 p. 23 cm.
MnCS

5847 Libri duo de synodalibus causis et disciplinis ecclesiasticis . . . ex diversis sanctorum patrum conciliis atque decretis collecti. Ad optimum codd. fidem recensuit adnotationem duplicem adjecit F.G.A. Wasserschleben. Lipsiae, Guil. Engelmann, 1840. Graz, Akademisch Druck- u. Verlagsanstalt, 1964.
xxvi, 526 p. 19 cm.
PLatS

5848 **Reglas de urbanidad que de a sus monjes,** el patriarca San Benito, en la aprobada por la Iglesia. Manresa, Imprenta de Roca S. Muguel, 1876.
87 p. 14 cm.
MnCS

Regnault, Lucien, 1924–
5849 Les Sentences des Pères du désert; nouveau recueil. Apophtegmes inédits ou peu connus rassemblés et présentés par L. Regnault, traduits par les moines des Solesmes. Abbaye Saint-Pierre-de-Solesmes [1970].
337 p. 21 cm.
InStme

5850 Théologie de la vie monastique selon Barsanuphe et Dorothée (Vie siècle).
(*In* Théologie de la vie monastique, p. 315–322)
PLatS

5851 (ed) Dorotheus, of Gaza, Saint. Oeuvres spirituelles. Introduction, texte grec, traduction et notes par Dom L. Regnault et Dom J. de Préville. Paris, Cerf, 1963.
575 p. 20 cm. (Sources chrétiennes, 92)
InStme; MnCS; PLatS

5851a (tr) Barsanuphius, Saint, 6th cent. Barsanuphe et Jean de Gaza: correspondance/recueil complet traduit du grec par Lucien Regnault et Philippe Lemaire our du géorgien par Bernard Cuttier. Abbaye Saint-Pierre de Solesmes, 1972.
547 p. 21 cm.
InStme

Regner, Renata, Sister.
5852 Carmen Peralta & Aseneta, a lay apostle (1914–1937).
(*In* Herbst, Winfrid. Real life stories. St. Nazianz, Wis., 1943. p. 33–46)
PLatS

5853 Lily Tanedo, a saintly girl of our times (1920–1938).
(*In* Herbst, Winfrid. Real life stories. St. Nazianz, 1943. p. 88–90)
PLatS

5854 **Regulae Benedicti studia.** Annuarium internationale, in connection with Rudolf Hanslik [et al.]. Hildesheim, H. A. Gerstenberg, 1972–

v. 25 cm.
Text in French, German or Italian.
MnCS; InStme; PLatS

5855 **Regulae Benedicti studia.** Supplementa, in connection with Rudolf Hanslik [et al.]. Hildesheim, H. A. Gerstenberg, 1974–
v. 22 cm.
InStme; MnCS; PLatS

5856 **Reichhart, Gottfried,** 1821–
Beiträge zur Incunabelnkunde. Eingeleitet von O. Hartwig. Leipzig, Harrassowitz, 1895; Nendeln, Kraus Reprint, 1968.
xviii, 464 p. 24 cm. (Zentralblatt für Bibliothekswesen, Beiheft 14)
PLatS

5857 **Reichlin von Meldegg, Regintrudis, Sister,** d. 1943.
Stift Nonnberg zu Salzburg im Wandel der Zeiten . . . Salzburg, Anton Pustet [1953].
88 p. plates, 21 cm.
MnCS

5858 **Reilly, Mary Paul, Sister.**
An inquiry into the nature of faith. Thesis (M.A.)–St. John's University, Collegeville, Minn., 1964.
102 p. 28 cm.
Typescript.
ICSS

5859 **Reimer, Jakob,** 1877–1958.
Jakobus Reimer; Briefe, Dichtungen, Ansprachen. Ausgewählt, zusammengestellt, bearbeitet von Agnes Kolbinger. Graz, Universitätsbuchdruckerei Styria, 1963.
60 p. illus. 24 cm.
InStme

Reis, Benita, Sister.
5860 A study of the personality differences of women in religious community structure.
45 p. 28 cm.
Thesis (M.A.)–Xavier University, 1967.
Typescript.
KyCovS

5861 Virgin; icon of the Kingdom of God.
56 p. 28 cm.
Thesis (M.A. in Sacred Studies)–St. John's University, Collegeville, Minn., 1968.
Typescript.
KyCovS

5862 **Reischl, Marcellin,** 1697–1763.
Enchiridium teutonis catholici, aliarum sectarum falsitatem, religionis suae veritatem, nec non politicum dilectae patriae suae systema, aliaque utilissima edocti . . . Augustae Vind., Math. Rieger, 1759.
140 p. 14 cm.
MnCS

5863 **Reiten, Paula, Sister,** 1924–
A critical study of *The River*.
176 p. 28 cm.
Thesis (Ph.D.)–Columbia University,
1970.
Typescript.
MnStj(Archives)

5864 **Réjalot, Thierry,** 1869–
Inventaire des lettres publiées des Béné-
dictins de la Congrégation de Saint-Maur.
[Ligugé, Abbaye Saint Martin, 1933–43]
344 p. 25 cm.
KAS

5865 **Le Religieux mourant;** ou, Préparation
à la mort pour les personnes religieuses
. . . par un religieux bénédictin de la
Congregation de Saint Maur. Avignon,
Charles Giroud, 1736.
4 v. 17 cm.
PLatS

5866 **Reller, Giles, Sister,** 1917–
Social studies of the United States made
more meaningful through the use of audio-
visual aids in the fifth grade.
v, 252 p. 28 cm.
Thesis (M.A.)–University of Minnesota,
1961.
Typescript.
MnStj(Archives)

**Rembert, Saint, abp. of Hamburg and
Bremen,** d. 888.

5867 Vita S. Anscharii primi archiepiscopi
Hamburgensis, conscripta a S. Rimberto
ejus successore, ex codice olim monasterii
Corbeiensis, nunc vero S. Germani Pratensis. MS. Vienna, Nationalbibliothek, codex
9372*, f. 1r–51v. Quarto. Saec. 17.
Microfilm: MnCH proj. no. 19,305

5868 Vita s. Anskarii, edita a D.C.F. Dahl-
mann.
(*In* Monumenta Germaniae historica.
Scriptores. Stuttgart, 1963. t. 2, p. 683–
725)
MnCS; PLatS

5869 Rimberti vita Anskari. Rimbert, Ansgars
Leben.
(*In* Quellen des 9. und 11. Jahrhunderts
zur Geschichte der Hamburgischen Kirche
und des Reiches, p. 613–707)
PLatS

Remigius, of Auxerre, 9th cent.

5870 Commentarium in psalmos. MS. Cistercienserabtei Lilienfeld, Austria, codex 193.
345 f. Folio. Saec. 14.
Microfilm: MnCH proj. no. 4490

5871 Commentum Remegii super Sedulium
(on the Carmen Paschale). MS. Salisbury,
England, Cathedral Library, codex 134. 53
f. Quarto. Saec. 12.
Microfilm: MnCH

5872 **Remiremont, France (Benedictine
abbey).**
Liber memorialis von Remiremont,
Bearb. von Eduard Hlawitschka, Karl
Schmid und Gerd Tellenbach. [Dublin/
Zürich, 1970.
2 v. 30 cm. (Monumenta Germaniae his-
torica. Libri memoriales, t. I)
InStme; MnCS; PLatS

5873 **Renajdin, Paulo.**
Assumptio B. Mariae Virginis. Romae,
Marietti, 1932.
184 p.
MoCo

Renaudin, Paul, 1864–

5874 Die Definierbarkeit der Himmelfahrt
Mariä; eine theologische Studie. Ueber-
setzt von einem deutschen Benedictiner.
Hrsg. von J. Ev. Kleiser. Freiburg
(Schweiz), Canisiusdruckerei, 1904.
159 p. 23 cm.
KAS

5875 Le role de l'Ordre de Saint-Benoît dans
l'Eglise et la société civile. Orne, Montligeon, 1925.
218 p.
AStb

5876 Saint Benoit dans la chaire française:
panégyriques par Bossuet, évêque de
Meaux (1627–1704), Fléchier, évêque de
Nimes (1632–1710), Massillon, évêque de
Clermont (1663–1742). Besançon, Jacques
et Demontrond, 1932.
80 p. 19 cm.
KAS

5877 **Rendle, Alfred Barton,** 1865–1938.
The classification of flowering plants.
Cambridge [England], University Press,
1956.
2 v. illus. 22 cm.
InStme

Renew and create. *See* Benedictines.
Congregations. American-Cassinese.

5878 **Rettenacher, Paul.**
Geschichte von St. Blasien. MS. Benediktinerabtei St. Paul, Austria, codex 34/2.
215 p. Quarto. Saec. 18.
Microfilm: MnCH proj. no. 11,756

Renner, Emmanuel, Sister, 1926–

5879 The historical thought of Frederic
Ozanam. Washington, Catholic University
of America Press, 1959.
86 p.
Thesis (Ph.D.)–Catholic University of
America.
MnStj(Archives)

5880 The relationship of Peter the Venerable
and Bernard of Clairvaux.
47 p. 28 cm.

Research paper (M.A.)—University of Minnesota, 1955.
Typescript.
MnStj(Archives)

5881 The services performed by nuns from 300 to 1600 A.D.
58, [5] p. 28 cm.
Research paper (M.A.)—University of Minnesota, 1955.
Typescript.
MnStj (Archives)

5882 **Renner, Frumentius,** 1908–
Der fünfarmige Leuchter . . . Sankt Ottilien, Eos Verlag, 1971.
2 v. illus. 24 cm.
MnCS

5883 **Renner, Maranatha, Sister,** 1931–
Considerations related to directing Benedictines in their prayer.
63, [12] p. 28 cm.
IRF project—St. Louis University, 1978.
Typescript.
MnStj(Archives)

5884 **Renoux, Athanasius,** 1925–
L'anaphore arménienne de Saint Grégoire l'Illuminateur.
(*In* Eucharisties d'Orient et d'Occident. Paris, 1970. v. 2, p. 83–108)
PLatS

5885 **Renz, Placidus,** d. 1748.
Philosophia ad mentem angelici doctoris divi Thomae Aquinatis . . . 2. ed. rev. & aucta. Altdorffii ad Vineas, Jo. Ben. Herckner, 1714.
3 vols.
PLatS (microfilm)

5886 **Resch, Petrus,** 1723–1789.
Handschriften-Katalog Lambach.
2 v. 28 cm.
Handwritten.
Xeroxed by University Microfilms, Ann Arbor, Mich., 1966.
MnCS

5887 **Rettenbacher, Simon,** 1634–1706.
Consilia sapientiae; seu, Epitome axiomatum Salomonis necessariorum ad vitam prudenter instituendam/cum axiomatum illorum considerationibus ex gallico in latinum sermonem traducta a Simone Rettenbacher. Lincij, J. M. Feichtinger, 1733.
2 v. 16 cm.
InStme

5888 **Rettger, Emmeran Aloysius,** 1912–
Pontifical requiem at the faldstool.
vi, 56 leaves, 28 cm.
Thesis (M.A.)—St. Vincent College, Latrobe, Pa., 1949.
Typescript.
PLatS

5889 (ed) Stehle, Aurelius. Manual of episcopal ceremonies . . . Revised by Rev. Emmeran A. Rettger, O.S.B. 5th ed. Latrobe, Pa., Archabbey Press, 1961.
2 v. 24 cm.
PLatS

5890 **Reyner, Clement,** 1589–1651.
A treatise of indulgence. [Menston, Yorkshire], Scolar Press, 1973.
258, [13] p. 20 cm. (English recusant literature, 1558–1640, v. 139)
Facsimile reprint of the 1623 edition.
PLatS

Reynolds, Bede, 1892–

5891 Draw your strength from the Lord. Canfield, Ohio, Alba Books, 1976.
154 p. illus. 18 cm.
CaMWiSb; InFer

5892 How come—my faith; some words about the meaning of the world. Canfield, Ohio, Alba Books, 1974.
176 p. 18 cm.
CaMWiSb; InFer

5893 Let's mend the mess. Canfield, Ohio, Alba Books, 1975.
xiii, 221 p. 18 cm.
CaMWiSb

5894 Project sainthood your business; God's reason for the universe. Canfield, Ohio, Alba Books, 1975.
177 p. illus. 18 cm.
CaMWiSb; InFer

5895 A rebel from riches; the autobiography of an unpremeditated monk. San Bernardino, Cal., Culligan Publications [1970?].
v, 183 p. illus. 22 cm.
InStme

5896 A rebel from riches . . . Canfield, Ohio, Alba Books [1975].
150 p. illus., 11 leaves of plates, 18 cm.
CaMWiSb; InFer; KAS; MoCo

Rhabanus Maurus. *See* Hrabanus Maurus.

5897 **Rheinau, Switzerland (Benedictine abbey).**
Chartularium Rhenoviense. MS. Benediktinerabtei St. Paul im Lavanttal, Austria, codex 35/2. 318 p. Quarto. Saec. 18.
Microfilm: MnCH proj. no. 11,769

5898 **Rheinwald, J.**
L'Abbaye et la Ville de Wissembourg, avec quelques châteaux-forts de la Basse-Alsace et du Palatinat; monographie historique. Wissembourg, Fr. Wentzel fils, 1863.
xix, 509 p. 22 cm.
KAS

5899 **Richalmus, abbas de Speciosa Valle (Schöntal).**
Visitationes seu revelationes. MS. Universitätsbibliothek Innsbruck, Austria, codex 36, f.166r-195v. Folio. Saec. 14.
Microfilm: MnCH proj. no. 28,127

Richard of Devizes, fl. 1191.
5900 The chronicle of Richard of Devizes on the time of King Richard the First. Edited by John T. Appleby. London, New York, T. Nelson [1963].
xxvi, 106, 84, 84, 85-106 p. 23 cm.
English and Latin. Opposite pages numbered in duplicate.
PLatS

5901 Chronicon Ricardi Divisiensis de rebus gestis Ricardi Primi regis Angliae. Nunc primum typis mandatum, curante Josepho Stevenson. Londini, 1838.
viii, [3], 88 p. 23 cm. [English Historical Society. Publications]
PLatS

5902 **Richard of Wallingford,** d. 1336.
An edition of his writings with introductions, English translation and commentary by J. D. North. Oxford, Clarendon Press, 1976.
3 v. diagrs. 24 cm.
MnCS

5903 **Richardson, M. Monathan, Sister.**
A selected and annotated bibliography of the Chicanos (Mexican-Americans) of the Southwest.
iii, 54 leaves, 28 cm.
Thesis (M.S.L.S.)—Catholic University of America, 1970.
Typewritten.
KAM

Richardus Cluniacensis.
5904 De consonantia Veteris et Novi Testamenti. MS. Benediktinerabtei St. Peter, Salzburg, codex b.VIII.28, f.2r-111r. Folio. Saec. 15.
Microfilm: MnCH proj. no. 10,559

5905 Dictum de peccatis delectionis et consensis. MS. Benediktinerabtei St. Peter, Salsburg, codex b.X.26, f.219r-220v. Folio. Saec. 15.
Microfilm: MnCH proj. no. 10,624

5906 Sermones ascetici. MS. Benediktinerabtei St. Peter, Salzburg, codex b.VIII.28, f.112r-124r. Folio. Saec. 15.
Microfilm: MnCH proj. no. 10,559

5906a **Richardus Pictaviensis, monk of Cluny,** 12th cent.
Some poems attributed to Richard of Cluny.

(*In* Medieval learning and literature; essays presented to Richard W. Hunt. Oxford, 1976. p. 181-199)
MnCS

5907 **Richerus, monk of Saint-Remi, Reims,** 10th cent.
Richeri historiarum libri IIII, a. 884-995.
(*In* Monumenta Germaniae historica. Scriptores. Stuttgart, 1963. t. 3, p. 561-657)
MnCS; PLatS

5908 **Rickenbach, Heinrich,** 1831-1911.
The sanctuary of the Tower of S. Benedict. Translated, revised and completed by Dom Bede Camm, O.S.B. Monte Cassino, Abbey Press, 1895.
67 p. illus. 18 cm.
MnCS

Riedinger, Utto, 1924-
5909 Petros der Walker von Antiocheia als Verfasser der pseudo-dionysischen Schriften.
(*In* Festschrift für Albert Auer, O.S.B. . . . 1961-62, p. 135-156)
PLatS

5910 Tharreitai theou ta mysteria; ein Beitrag des Pseudo-Kaisarios zu den Symbola des Firmicus Maternus.
(*In* Perennitas; Beiträge . . . P. Thomas Michels, O.S.B., zum 70. Geburtstag. Münster, 1963. p. 19-24)
PLatS

5911 **Riehl, Agatha, Sister.**
The reaction mechanism of the chronic acid oxidation of cyclohexanone.
154 p. 28 cm.
Thesis (Ph.D.)—Catholic University of America, 1966.
Typescript.
MnDuS

5912 **Riesenhuber, Martin,** 1876-1933.
Die kirchliche Barockkunst in Oesterreich. Wien, Herder, 1924.
vi, 670 p. illus., incl. 208 plates, 24 cm.
InStme; NdRi

Ringholz, Odilo Emil Adolf, 1852-1929.
5913 Anselm von Schwanden, Abt des Stiftes U.L.F. zu Einsiedeln. Mit urkundlichen und artistischen Beilagen. [n.p., n.d.]
100-148 p. 23 cm.
InStme

5914 Geschichte des Benediktinerinenklosters zu Allen Heiligen in der Au bei Einsiedeln. Einsiedeln, Benziger; New York, Benziger Brothers, 1909.
142 p. illus. 19 cm.
InStme

5915 Geschichte des fürstlichen Benediktiner-
stiftes U.L.F. zu Einsiedeln unter Abt
Johannes I. von Schwanden, 1298-1327
. . . [n.p., 1890?].
[129]-394 p. 22 cm.
InStme

5916 Die Schindellegi im Kanton Schwyz welt-
lich und kirchlich dargestellt . . . Verlag
des Kirchenbau-Vereines Schindellegi
(Kanton Schwyz), 1906.
39 p. illus. 21 cm.
InStme

5917 Zum Gnadenquell: in der Meinradszell.
Eine Anleitung für die Wallfahrt nach
Maria-Einsiedeln. Einsiedeln, Benziger
[1912].
174 p. illus. 13 cm.
InStme; LStB

5918 (ed) Brandes, Karl. Aus einer merkwür-
digen Reise [hrsg.] von Odilo Ringholz.
Stans, Hans von Matt & Co., 1920.
40 p. port. 23 cm.
An extract from the journal of a journey
from April 9th to May 1st, 1867, by Karl
Brandes.
InStme

Rippinger, Joel, 1948–
5919 From old world to new; the origins and
development of St. Meinrad and Conception Abbeys in the nineteenth century.
1976.
75 p. 28 cm.
Typescript.
MoCo

5920 Some historical determinants of
American Benedictine monasticism: 1846-
1900.
38 p. 28 cm.
Thesis (B.S.T.) – Pontificium Athanaeum
Anselmianum, Rome, 1974.
Typescript.
MoCo

5921 **Riss, Bruno,** 1829-1900.
First beginnings of St. John's Abbey.
(Monthly installments in: The St. John's
University Record, vols. 2-3 (1889-91)
MnCS(Archives)

Ritter, Emmeram, 1927–
5922 Stift Göttweig, Benediktinerabtei in Niederösterreich [von Ludwig Koller, O.S.B.,
und Emmeram Ritter, O.S.B.] 5. neubearb.
Aufl. München, Verlag Schnell und
Steiner, 1967.
15 p. illus. 17 cm. (Kunstführer Nr. 645
von 1956)
PLatS

5923 Ausstellung [1. bis   ] des Graphischen
Kabinettes des Stiftes [Göttweig]. Leitung

und Gestaltung, P. Emmeram Ritter,
O.S.B. [Stift Göttweig, 1960?-   ]
v. plates, 21 cm.
MnCS

5924 Peter Paul Rubens-Stecherkreis. Elfte
Ausstellung . . . Leitung und Gestaltung
P. Emmeram Ritter, O.S.B. Stift Gött-
weig, 1968.
MnCS

5925 **Ritter, Gallus,** 1865–
Das heilige Mirakel; ein Spiel vom Gna-
denwunder zu Deggendorf. Musik von
Simon Breu. [Deggendorf] Abtei Metten,
1925.
94 p. 17 cm.
KAS

5926 **Ritzer, Korbinian,** 1908–
Formen, Riten und religiöses Brauchtum
der Eheschliessung in den christlichen Kirchen des ersten Jahrtausends. Münster
Westf., Aschendorff [1962].
xliii, 392 p. 25 cm.
InStme; MnCS; PLatS

5927 **Rizelius, Bertholdus,** 1721-1792.
Sancta et beata Austria; seu, Acta et
vitae sanctorum eorum qui . . . eam quam
nunc appellamus Austriam regionem olim
illustrarunt . . . Augustae Vind., Joan.
Daniel Hertzius, 1750.
[40], 234, [18] p. engravings, 34 cm.
MnCS

Robert, abbot of Shrewsbury, d. 1167.
5928 The admirable life of Saint VVenefride,
virgin, martyr, abbesse. Written in Latin
about 500 yeares ago, by Robert, monke
and priour of Shrewsbury . . . now translated into English, out of a very ancient
and authenticall manuscript, for the
edification and comfort of Catholikes, by
I.F. of the Society of Iesus [John Falconer].
[St. Omer?] 1635.
[32], 275, [11] p. 14 cm.
Facsimile reprint: London, The Scolar
Press, 1976. (English recusant literature,
1558-1640, v. 319)
PLatS

5929 **Roberts, Augustine.**
Centered on Christ; an introduction to
monastic profession. [Azul], 1975.
124 p. 28 cm.
Typescript.
NcBe

Rochais, Henri Marie, 1920–
5930 Enquête sur les sermons divers et les
sentences de Saint Bernard. Rome, Editiones Cistercienses, 1962.
183 p. 27 cm.
PLatS

5931   Inédits bernardins dans le manuscrit
Harvard 185.
(*In* Analecta monastica. 6. sér. 1962. p.
53–175)
PLatS

5932   (tr & ed) Defensor, monk of Ligugé.
Livre d'etincells (Liber scintillarum). Introduction, texte, traduction et notes de H. M.
Rochais. Paris, Editions de Cerf, 1961–62.
2 v. 20 cm. (Sources chrétiennes, no. 77
& 86)
InStme; MnCS; PLatS

Rode, Joannes, ca.1385–1439.
5933   Consuetudines et observantiae monasteriorum Sancti Mathiae et Sancti Maximini Treverensium. Siegburg, F. Schmitt,
1968.
lxx, 320 p. 26 cm. (Corpus consuetudinum monasticarum, v. 5)
InStme; KAS; PLatS

5934   [Consuetudines et observantiae monas-
teriorum]
Das monastische Reformprogramm des
Johannes Rode Abtes von St. Matthias in
Trier; ein darstellender Kommentar zu
seinen Consuetudines von Petrus Becker,
O.S.B. Münster Westf., Aschendorff
[1970].
xix, 218 p. 25 cm. (Beiträge zur
Geschichte des alten Mönchtums und des
Benediktinerordens, Heft 30)
MnCS

5935   Statuta pro monialibus Ordinis S. Bene-
dicti. Germanice. MS. Benediktinerabtei
Göttweig, Austria, codex 499, f.1r–24v.
Quarto. Saec. 15.
Microfilm: MnCH proj. no. 3754

5936   **Rodgers, Kieran Joseph,** 1920–
Devotion to Mary in Benedictine com-
munities.
47 leaves, 28 cm.
Thesis (B.A.)–St. Vincent College,
Latrobe, Pa., 1943.
Typescript.
PLatS

5937   **Rodrigues, Teresa, Sister.**
A Christian's prayer book: poems,
psalms, and prayers for the church's year,
edited by Peter Coughlan, Ronald C. D.
Jasper, Teresa Rodrigues. Chicago, Franciscan Herald Press [1972].
x, 374 p. 18 cm.
InStme

5938   **Rodriguez, Abundio,** 1931–
Castille romane. [La Pierre-qui-Vire
(Yonne)] Zodiaque, 1966–
v. illus. (part col.) 23 cm.
InStme

5939   **Rodulphus Glaber,** d.ca. 1050.
Ex Rodulfi Glabri vita S. Willelmi Di-
vionensis.
(*In* Monumenta Germaniae historica.
Scriptores. Stuttgart, 1963. t. 4, p. 655–
658)
MnCS; PLatS

5940   **Roesle, Maximilian,** 1908–
Begegnung der Christen; Studien
evangelischer und katholischer Theologen,
hrsg. von Maximilian Roesle und Oscar
Cullmann. 2. Aufl. Stuttgart, Evangelisches Verlagswerk [1960].
695 p. 24 cm.
PLatS

Roettger, Gregory John, 1907–
5941   Benedictine missionary method.
Reprint from Social justice review, v.
43(1950), p. 149–153).
PLatS

5942   Liturgy 31 class notes, first semester
1947–48.
62 p. 36 cm.
Mimeographed.
MnCS

5943   Liturgy 32 class notes [1949?].
36 p. 36 cm.
Mimeographed.
MnCS

5944   (tr) Guardini, Romano. The focus of
freedom. Translated by Gregory Roettger.
Baltimore, Helicon [1966].
160 p. 22 cm.
InStme; MnCS; PLatS

5945   (tr) Guerry, Emile Maurice. The popes
and world government. Translated by
Gregory J. Roettger. Baltimore, Helicon
[1964].
254 p. 23 cm.
ILSP; InStme; MnCS; NcBe

5946   (tr) Hanssler, Bernhard. The Church and
God's people. Translated by Gregory
Roettger. Baltimore, Helicon [1963].
192 p. 23 cm.
InStme; MnCS; MnStj; MoCo; PLatS

5947   (tr) Heufelder, Emmanuel. A new Pentecost. Translated by Gregory J. Roettger.
Collegeville, Minn., The Liturgical Press,
1976.
67 p. 18 cm.
MnCS

5948   (tr) Heufelder, Emmanuel. The Spirit
prays in us; reflections on Romans 8:26-27.
Translated by Gregory J. Roettger. Collegeville, Minn., The Liturgical Press,
1976.
MnCS

5949   (tr) Neuhäusler, Engelbert. The sacred
way; biblical meditations on the Passion of

Christ. Translated by Gregory J. Roettger. Baltimore, Helicon Press, 1960.
128 p. 21 cm.
InStme; NdRi; PLatS

5950 (tr) Schwarzbauer, Engelhart. Forgiveness of sins in current Catholic practice. Translated by Abbot Gregory J. Roettger, O.S.B. Collegeville, Minn., The Liturgical Press, 1976.
46 p. 18 cm.
MnCS

5951 (tr) Tillmann, Fritz. The Master calls; a handbook of Christian living. Translated by Gregory J. Roettger. Baltimore, Helicon Press, 1960.
355 p. 24 cm.
InFer; KAS; MnCS; MnStj; NdRi; PLatS

5952 **Roettlin, Georg.**
Disputatio philosophica de iis quae potissimum in octo Physicorum libris Aristotelicis attinguntur. Salzburg, Gregorius Kyrenerus typographicus aulicus, 1620.
62 p.
Diss. – University of Salzburg.
MnCS (microfilm)

5953 **Roger, of Wendover,** d. 1236.
Chronica; sive, Flores historiarum. Nunc primum edidit Henricus O. Coxe. Londini, sumptibus Societatis, 1841–42.
4 v. 23 cm. (English Historical Society. Publications)
BNS; ILSP

5954 _____ **Vaduz, Kraus Reprint,** 1964.
4 v. 23 cm.
PLatS

Rohner, Beat, 1836–1891.
5955 Die rechtlichen Wirkungen der Exkummunikation. Luzern, Gebr. Räber, 1872.
29 p. 22 cm.
InStme

5956 The Salve Regina.
(*In* The American sixth reader for Catholic schools. Boston, 1931. p. 5–8)
PLatS

5957 **Rolandinus, Maximinus.**
Kurzer Inhalt des Lebens des heiligsten unnd wunderbarlieben Vaters unnd Patriarchen Benedicti. Verteitschter abgeschrieben durch P. Maximinum Rolandinum, O.S.B. MS. Benediktinerinnenabtei Nonnberg, Salzburg, codex 23 B 23. 211 f. Quarto. Saec. 17.
Microfilm: MnCH proj. no. 10,843

5958 **Rollin, Bertrand,** 1926–
Commentaire de la Règle de Saint Benoît. Dourgne, Abbaye d'En Calcat, 1978.
xxii, 160 p. 30 cm.
MnCS

5959 **Roloff, Ronald William,** 1922–
Abbey and University Church of Saint John the Baptist, Collegeville, Minnesota. [Text by the Reverend Fathers Ronald Roloff and Brice Howard, O.S.B. Photography by Mr. Shin Koyama].
[40] p. illus., diagrs. 31 cm.
Church dedication brochure, August 24, 1961.
CaQStB; KAS; MnCS; PLatS

5960 **Romainmôtier, France (Benedictine abbey).**
Liber cartularis S. Petri principis apostolorum monasterii Romanensis; Bibliothèque cantonale et universitaire Lausanne MS. 5011. Einleitung von Albert Bruckner. Amsterdam, North-Holland Publishing Company, 1962.
xx p. facsim (29 p.) 31 cm.
MnCS; PLatS

Rome (City). Collegio di Sant'Anselmo.
5961 Corpus consuetudinum monasticarum, cura Pontificii Athenaei Sancti Anselmi de Urbe editum. Publici iuris fecit Kassius Hallinger, O.S.B. Sieburg, apud Franciscum Schmitt, 1962–
v. 26 cm.
MnCS; PLatS

5962 Kalendarium lectionum, 1953–
KAS; PLatS

5963 Liber annualis.
v. 21 cm.
KAS (1970–72)

5964 Liber usuum et manuale chori Collegii Internationalis S. Anselmi de Urbe. 19____.
32 p. 18 cm.
KAS

5965 Ordo anni academici.
Title varies: Liber annualis.
KAS (1970–72)

5965a Ordo et ratio studiorum Collegii Internationalis S. Anselmo de Urbe. Sublaci, typis Proto-Coenobii, 1920.
28 p. 19 cm.
KAS

5966 Res scholasticae apud Benedictinos in S. Anselmi de Urbe Collegio actae. Fasciculus I- 1896-.
PLatS

5967 Statuta in Internationali Benedictinorum Collegio Sancti Anselmi de Urbe observanda.
Publisher varies: Sublaci, Romae.
KAS (1962); MnCS (1920, 1939); OrStb (1939); PLatS (1939)

5968 **Rome (City). Collegio di Sant'Anselmo.**
Facultas philosophica.
Miscellanea philosophica r.p. Josepho Gredt, O.S.B., completis LXXV annis

oblata cura Facultatis Philosophicae . . .
Romae, Herder, 1938.
294 p. 25 cm. (Studia Anselmiana, fasc.
VII–VIII)
InStme; MnCS

Rome (City). S. Benedetto (abbey of Benedictine nuns).
5969   Life of St. Mechtildis. Printed at the
Vatican Press, Rome, 1899.
295 p. 20 cm.
KAM

5970   Saint Benedict and Grottaferrata. Rome,
n.p., 1895.
56 p. 20 cm.
MnCS

Rome (City). S. Girolamo (Benedictine abbey).
5971   Biblia Sacra vulgatae editionis, Sixti V
. . . iussu recognita et Clementis VIII auctoritate edita. Editio emendatissima apparatu critico instructa cura et studio monachorum Abbatiae Pontificae Sancti
Hieronymi in Urbe, Ordinis Sancti Benedicti. [Torino], Marietti, 1959.
xiv, 1238 p. plates (incl. facsims.), maps,
25 cm.
InStme; MnCS; PLatS

5972   _____ [Torino], Marietti [1965].
xiv, 124 p. 25 cm.
MnCS

5973   Catalogue des microfilms de la Vulgate
de Saint Jérôme. Roma, Abbazia di S.
Girolamo [n.d.].
unpaged, 28 cm.
Xeroxed copy of manuscript.
MnCS

5974   **Rome (City). S. Paolo fuori le Mura.**
Patriarcale basilica di S. Paolo, Roma.
Serie di 18 cartoline. [Roma, Grimaldi &
Mercandetti, n.d.].
18 postcards in folder, 10 cm.
MnCS

5975   **Rome (City). Tor de' Specchi (convent of Benedictine Oblate sisters).**
Fatti memorabili della vita di Santa
Francesca Romana tratti dalle pitture
murali del convento . . . 1440–1940.
[Roma, Tipografia Marviana 1940?].
unpaged, illus. 21 cm.
MnCS

5976   **Romero, Mary Jane, Sister.**
Seeking; a paraphrase of the Rule of
Saint Benedict with commentary. College-
ville, Minn., The Liturgical Press [c 1972].
xiv, 67 p. 20 cm.
The book is an adaptation of the Rule of
St. Benedict for Benedictine sisters.
CaMWiSb; InStme; KAS; MnCS; MnStj;
MdRi; MoCo; PLatS; ViBris

Rooney, Marcel, 1917–
5977   Acts of the Apostles. Conception, Mo.,
Conception Abbey [1963].
52 p. 21 cm. (Saint Andrew Bible commentary, 27)
PLatS

5978   The evolution of the complexus of recon-
ciliation as seen through certain official
liturgical books of the medieval period.
86 p. 28 cm.
Thesis–Pontifical Liturgical Institute,
Rome, 1975.
Typescript.
MoCo

5979   The sacred music for solo voice and ac-
companiment of Giovanni Battista
Fergusio, six motets and Magnificat; a
transcription and commentary.
87 p. illus.
Thesis (M.A.Music)–University of
Rochester, 1971.
MoCo

5980   St. Luke. Conception, Mo., Conception
Abbey [1961].
83 p. 21 cm. (Saint Andrew Bible commentary, 24)
PLatS

5981   A theology for architecture; an analysis
of the theological principles applicable to
church building in the postconciliar
renewal.
275 p. 28 cm.
Thesis (S.T.D.)–Pontificium Athenaeum
Anselmianum, 1976.
Typescript.
MoCo

5982   **Rosano, Italy. S. Maria (abbey of Benedictine nuns).**
La Regola. Introduzione, versione e commento della Bendettine de S. Maria di
Rosano. 2. ed. Siena, Cantagalli, 1974.
313 p. 18 cm.
MnCS

5983   **Rösch, Johannes.**
Acta, et res praeclare gestae, item electio
et confirmatio Abbatis Caspari II, 1571–
1592. MS. Benediktinerabtei St. Paul im
Lavanttal, Austria, codex 125/2. 289 p.
Folio. Saec. 16.
Microfilm: MnCH proj. no. 11,892

Rose, Ambrosius, 1911–
5984   Abt Bernardus Rosa von Grüssau. Nach
Notizien P. Nikolaus v. Lutterotti bearbeitet und hrsg. durch Ambrosius Rose,
O.S.B. Stuttgart, Brentanoverlag, 1960.
128 p. plates, ports. 22 cm.
MnCS; PLatS

5985   Grüssauer Gedenkbuch, in Verbindung
mit Freunden und Mönchen der Abtei

Grüssau herausgegeben. Stuttgart, Brentanoverlag [1949].
199 p. plates, 21 cm.
MnCS

Rosenheim, Petrus von. *See* Petrus von Rosenheim.

5986 **Rösle, Maximilian,** 1908–
Begegnung der Christen; Studien evangelischer und katholischer Theologen, hrsg. von M. Roesle und Oscar Cullman. [2. Aufl.]. Stuttgart, Evangelisches Verlagswerk [1960].
695 p. 24 cm.
MnCS

5987 **Rösner, Ferdinand,** 1709–1778.
Bitteres Leiden; Oberammergau Passionsspiel. Text von 1750, verfasst von Pater Ferdinand Rösner, O.S.B. Hrsg. von Otto Mausser. Leipzig, K. W. Hiersemann, 1934.
xxiv, 267 p. 24 cm.
MnCS

5988 **Rose, Maurus,** 1666–1706.
Annales monasterii S. Clementis in Iburg, collectore Mauro abbate. Die Iburger Klosterannalen des Abts Maurus Rost. Im Auftrage des Historischen Vereins hrsg. von C. Stüve. Osnabrück, Rackhorst, 1895.
xx, 173, 173, 174–308 p. plates. 25 cm.
Latin and German texts on opposite pages, numbered in duplicate.
KAS; MnCS

5989 **Rotalde, Esteban de.**
Sermones. MS. Monasterio benedictino de Montserrat, Spain, codex 291. 398 f. Quarto. Saec. 17–18.
Microfilm: MnCH proj. no. 30,017

Roth, Benno, 1903–
5990 Beschlagnahme und Enteignung der Benediktinerabtei Seckau in Obersteiermark am 8. April 1940 durch die Gestapo. [Seckau] 1965.
106 p. 21 cm.
PLatS

5991 Seckau; Erbe und Auftrag. Ein Gang durch seine Geschichte, Kunst und Kultur. Wien, Bergland Verlag [1960].
78 p. illus. 18 cm.
KAS

5992 _____ **3. wesentlich umgearb.,** neubebilderte Aufl. München, Schnell & Steiner [1965].
47 p. illus. 24 cm.
PLatS

5993 **Roth, Owen Harold,** 1915–
Laboratory manual for comparative anatomy. Latrobe, Pa., St. Vincent College, 1956.

134 p. illus. 28 cm.
Mimeographed.
PLatS

5994 **Rothenhäusler, Konrad,** 1840–
Die Abteien und Stifte des Herzogthums Württemberg im Zeitalter der Reformation. Stuttgart, Deutsches Volksblatt, 1886.
xvi, 268 p. 23 cm.
KAS

Rothenhäusler, Matthäus, 1874–1958.
5995 Die Regel des heiligen Benedikt, ausgewëhlt und übertragen von Matthäus Rothenhäusler. Paderborn, F. Schöningh, 1923.
72 p. 20 cm.
InStme

5996 Zur asketischen Lehrschrift des Diadochos von Photike.
(*In* Heilige Ueberlieferung. Münster, 1938. p. 86–95)
PLatS

5997 **Rott am Inn, Bavaria (Benedictine abbey).**
Catalogus codicum manu scriptorum Bibliothecae Regiae Monacensis: Codices 15501–16633 monasterii Ord. S. Benedicti in Rot ad Oenum. Monachii, sumptibus Bibliothecae Regiae, 1878. Unveränderter Nachdruck, Otto Harrassowitz, Wiesbaden, 1969.
MnCH

5998 **Rouen, France. Saint-Ouen (Benedictine abbey).**
Chronique des Abbés de Saint-Ouen de Rouen publiée pour la première fois . . . par Francisque Michel. Rouen, E. Frère, 1840.
vii, 98 p. 22 cm.
KAS

Rouillard, Philippe, 1926–
5999 Dictionnaire des saints de tous les jours établi et présenté par Dom Philippe Rouillard, O.S.B., suivi d'une étude sur les miracles par Pierre Teilhard de Chardin, S.J. [Paris], Robert Morel [1963].
415 p. 14 cm.
PLatS

6000 Quelques symboles pénitentiels.
(*In* Symbolisme et théologie. Sacramentum 2. Roma, 1974. p. 215–228)
PLatS

Rousseau, Olivier, 1898–
6001 Le Concile et les Conciles; contribution à l'histoire de la vie conciliaire de l'Eglise [par] B. Botte [et al.]. Chevetogne], Editions de Chevetogne, 1960.
xix, 348 p. 23 cm.
KAS; MnCS; PLatS

6002 La doctrine du ministère épiscopal et ses vicissitudes dans l'Eglise d'Occident.
(*In* Congar, M. J. L'épiscopat et l'Eglise universelle. Paris, 1962. p. 279–308)
PLatS

6003 L'Eglise en prière; introduction à la liturgie. Avec la collaboration de R. Béraudy, B. Botte [et al.]. Paris, Desclée & cie [1961].
xv, 916 p. 23 cm.
PLatS

6004 L'expérience oecoménique de monastère de Chevetogne.
(*In* Le Guillou, Joseph. Découverte de l'oecuménisme. Paris, 1961. p. 222–227)
PLatS

6005 The idea of the kingship of Christ. Translated by Kathyrn Sullivan, R.S.C.J.
(*In* Who is Jesus of Nazareth? p. 129–143)
PLatS

6006 L'infaillibilité de l'Eglise; Journées oecuménique de Chevetogne, 25–29 septembre 1961. Editions de Chevetogne [1963].
266 p. 22 cm.
At head of title: O. Rousseau [et al.]
InStme

6007 Le mouvement théologique dans le monde contemporain; liturgie, dogme, philosophie, exégèse, par A. Kerkvoorde et O. Rousseau. Paris, Beauchesne [1969–].
v. 27 cm.
MnCS

6008 Priesthood and monasticiem.
(*In* The sacrament of holy orders . . . London, 1962. p. 168–180)
PLatS

6009 Retrospect.
(*In* Romeau, L. V. Ecumenical experiences. Westminster, Md., 1965. p. 118–128)
PLatS

6010 Le rôle important du monachisme dans l'Eglise d'Orient.
(*In* Il monachesimo orientale; atti del Convegno di studi orientali. Roma, 1958. p. 33–55)
PLatS

6011 La vraie valeur de l'épiscopat dans l'Eglise d'après d'importants documents de 1875.
(*In* Congar, M. J. L'épiscopat et l'épiscopat universelle. Paris, 1962. p. 709–738)
PLatS

6012 (ed) Origenes. Homélies sur le Cantique des cantiques. Introduction, traduction et notes d'Olivier Rousseau. 2. éd. Paris, Editions du Cerf, 1966.
160 p. 20 cm. (Sources chrétiennes, no. 37)
InStme

6013 **Roy, Albertus van,** 1888–
Affligem, Roem van ons land. Leuven, Davidsfonds, 1953.
228 p.
MoCo

Rudbertus de Salzburg.
6014 Collatio in visitatione monasterii Admontensis anno 1462. MS. Vienna, Nationalbibliothek, codex 4969, f.74r–81v. Quarto. Saec. 15.
Microfilm: MnCH proj. no. 18,141

6015 Sermo ad monachos die S. Valentini. MS. Vienna, Nationalbibliothek, codex 4969, f. 98r–102v. Quarto. Saec. 15.
Microfilm: MnCH proj. no. 18,141

6016 Historia hierosolymitana, seu Gesta de Hieriusalem. MS. Vienna, Nationalbibliothek, codex 427, f.2r–41r. Folio. Saec. 12.
Microfilm: MnCH proj. no. 13,755

6017 Historia hierosolymitana. MS. Vienna, Nationalbibliothek, codex 3497, f.1r–59v. Quarto. Saec. 15.
Microfilm: MnCH proj. no. 16,707

Rudloff, Leo, 1902–
6018 The emergence of an indigenous culture in Israel: problems and hopes.
(*In* Derrick, Christopher. Light of revelation and non-Christians. New York, 1965. p. 113–124)
InFer

6019 Theology for the laity. Translated from the German by monks of St. John's Abbey. Collegeville, Minn., 1937.
93 p. 30 cm.
Mimeographed.
MnCS (Archives)

6020 **Rudolf, of Fulda,** d. 865.
Translatio s. Alexandri, auctoribus Ruodolfo et Meginharto.
(*In* Monumenta Germaniae historica. Scriptores. Stuttgart, 1963. t. 2, p. 673–681)
PLatS

Rugerus, called also Theophilus. *See* Theophilus, called also Rugerus.

6021 **Ruhland, Anna Rose, Sister.**
Relationship of the nutrient composition of meals served to food actually consumed by nursing home residents on a five-meal-a-day plan.
Thesis (M.S.)–North Dakota State University, 1975.
Typescript.
NdRiS

6022 **Ruhstaller, Rupert,** 1917–
Methodologische Untersuchungen über
den Bau des griechischen Satzes, auf der
Grundlage von Aischylos' Agamemnon;
eine strukturlinguistische Forschung.
[Einsiedeln, Benziger, 1968].
368 p. 21 cm.
Diss. – Universität Freiburg in der
Schweiz, 1959.
InStme

Ruinart, Thierry, 1657–1709.
6023 Abregé de la vie de Dom Jean Mabillon,
prêtre & religieux bénédictin de la Congregation de Saint-Maur. Paris, chez la
veuve François Muguet, 1709.
436 p. 17 cm.
CtBeR; InStme

6024 Historia persecutionis vandalicae in duas
partes distincta . . . Venetiis, typis
Josephi Bettinelli, 1732.
334 p. 24 cm.
MnCS

6025 Ouvrages posthumes de d. Jean Mabillon
et de d. Thierri Ruinart, bénédictins de la
Congrégation de Saint Maur . . . par D.
Vincent Thuillier . . . Paris, 1724. [Repub-
lished by Gregg Press Ltd., 1967].
3 v. 25 cm.
InStme; PLatS

Ruiz, Augustín S. [pseud].
6026 Abadia de Santo Domingo de Silos: el
abad santo, el claustro románico, la vida
benedictina. [Burgos, 1960].
102 p. plates, 24 cm.
MnCS

6027 Los exclaustrados de Silos, una "com-
midad" fuera de su monasterio.
(*In* Semana de estudios monasticos,
14th, 1973. p. 247–277)
PLatS

6028 **Ruiz de Valladolid, Francisco.**
Canones, sive regulae quae ad divinae
Scripturae intelligentiam plurimum con-
fuerunt; cum suis explanationibus, ex
Dionysio Areopagita, Origene, Hilario, etc
excerpta. Nunc denuo . . . aucta. Franco-
furti, apud D. Zachariam Palthenium,
MDCXI.
[14], 253 p. 17 cm.
PLatS

6029 **Ruotger, of Cologne,** fl. 968.
Vita Brunonis auctore Ruotgero.
(*In* Monumenta Germaniae historica.
Scriptores. Stuttgart, 1963. t. 4, p. 252–
275)
PLatS

Rupert, abbot of Deutz, 1070(ca.)–1129.
Manuscript copies

6030 [Opera]
Tractatus in librum Numeri. Commen-
tarium in Deuteronomium. Commentarium
in librum Josuae. Commentarium in librum
Judicum. Commentarium in librum Ruth.
MS. Augustinerchorherrenstift Kloster-
neuburg, Austria, codex 253, f.7r–137r.
Folio. Saec. 12.
Microfilm: MnCH proj. no. 5224

6031 [Selections]
Rupertus Tuitiensis, et Anonimi diversi.
MS. Tarazona, Spain, Archivo de la Cate-
dral, codex 47. 142 f. Folio. Saec. 14.
Microfilm: MnCH proj. no. 32,626

6032 Annulus, seu Dialogi de sacramentis
fidei. MS. Benediktinerabtei Admont,
Austria, codex 517. 40 f. Quarto. Saec. 12.
Microfilm: MnCH proj. no. 9569

6033 Annulus fidei, seu Dialogus Saraceni et
Judaei de sacramentis fidei. MS. Vienna,
Nationalbibliothek, codex 1420, f.171r–
175r. Folio. Saec. 12.
Microfilm: MnCH proj. no. 14,767

6034 Annulus sive dialogi inter Christianum et
Judaeum. MS. Benediktinerabtei Admont,
Austria, codex 443, f.19r–58v. Quarto.
Saec. 12.
Microfilm: MnCH proj. no. 9504

6035 Annulus sive dialogus inter Christianum
et Judaeum. MS. Universitätsbibliothek
Graz, Austria, codex 975, f.26v–42r.
Quarto. Saec. 13.
Microfilm: MnCH proj. no. 27,036
"Commentarius" and "Expositio" are in-
terfiled.

6036 Expositio in Apocalypsim. MS. Cistercienserabtei Heiligenkreuz, Austria, codex
83, 181 f. Folio. Saec. 12.
Microfilm: MnCH proj. no. 4629

6037 Expositio in Apocalypsin. MS. Augus-
tinerchorherrenstift Klosterneuburg,
Austria, codex 254. 240 f. Folio. Saec. 12.
Microfilm: MnCH proj. no. 5220

6038 Commentarius in Apocalypsim, libri 12.
MS. Benediktinerabtei St. Peter, Salzburg,
codex a.VIII.6. 492 f. Folio. Saec. 12–13.
Microfilm: MnCH proj. no. 10,174

6039 Commentarius in Apocalypsin. MS.
Vienna, Nationalbibliothek, codex 723. 238
f. Folio. Saec. 13.
Microfilm: MnCH proj. no. 14,032

6040 Commentarius super Cantica canticorum. MS. Benediktinerabtei Admont,
Austria, codex 549. 124 f. Quarto. Saec.
12.
Microfilm: MnCH proj. no. 9662

6041 Explanatio in Cantica canticorum (libri
VII de incarnatione Domini). MS. Benedik-

tinerabtei Göttweig, Austria, codex 49. 113 f. Folio. Saec. 12.
Microfilm: MnCH proj. no. 3830

6042   Expositio super Canticum canticorum. MS. Augustinerchorherrenstift Klosterneuburg, Austria, codex 1122. 170 f. Quarto. Saec. 12.
Microfilm: MnCH proj. no. 6092

6043   Expositio magistri Rudberti super Canticum canticorum. MS. Benediktinerabtei Kremsmünster, Austria, codex 29, f.44r–150v. Saec. 12.
Microfilm: MnCH proj. no. 29

6044   Super Canticum canticorum. MS. Benediktinerabtei St. Peter, Salzburg, codex a.VI.12. 150 f. Quarto. Saec. 12.
Microfilm: MnCH proj. no. 10,084

6045   Expositio super Canticum canticorum. MS. Vienna, Nationalbibliothek, codex 757, f.40v–127v. Folio. Saec. 12.
Microfilm: MnCH proj. no. 14,077

6046   Expositio in Canticum canticorum. MS. Vienna, Nationalbibliothek, codex 1054, f.3r–24v. Quarto. Saec. 12.
Microfilm: MnCH proj. no. 14,368

6047   Expositio super Cantica Canticorum. MS. Cistercienserabtei Wilhering, Austria, codex IX,41. 80 f. Folio. Saec. 12.
Microfilm: MnCH proj. no. 2816

6048   In Cantica canticorum. MS. Universitätsbibliothek Graz, Austria, codex 1047, f.20r–56r. Quarto. Saec. 13.
Microfilm: MnCH proj. no. 27,126

6049   Commentarius in Cantica canticorum. MS. Linz, Austria, Bundesstaatliche Studienbibliothek, codex 10, f.115v–178v. Folio. Saec. 13.
Microfilm: MnCH proj. no. 27,874

6050   Expositio in Cantica canticorum. MS. Benediktinerabtei Melk, Austria, codex 1231. 90 f. Octavo. Saec. 13.
Microfilm: MnCH proj. no. 1876

6051   Libri septem in Canticum canticorum. MS. Vienna, Nationalbibliothek, codex 1743, f.1r–82r. Octavo. Saec. 13.
Microfilm: MnCH proj. no. 15,080

6052   Expositio super Cantica. Vienna, Nationalbibliothek, codex series nova 3607, f.44v–151v. Quarto. Saec. 13.
Microfilm: MnCH proj. no. 20,874

6053   Expositio in Cantica canticorum. MS. Cistercienserabtei Zwettl, Austria, codex 262, f.3r–86r. Quarto. Saec. 13.
Microfilm: MnCH proj. no. 6860

6054   In Cantica canticorum libri septem. MS. Benediktinerabtei Göttweig, Austria, codex 263, f.87r–170r. Folio. Saec. 15.
Microfilm: MnCH proj. no. 3698

6055   Expositio in Exodum et Leviticum. MS. Cistercienserabtei Rein, Austria, codex 84, f.1v–136v. Folio. Saec. 12.
Microfilm: MnCH proj. no. 7484

6056   Expositio in Exodum; Expositio in Leviticum. MS. Augustinerchorherrenstift Klosterneuburg, Austria, codex 255. 155 f. Folio. Saec. 15.
Microfilm: MnCH proj. no. 5226

6057   Commentarium in Genesin. MS. Augustinerchorherrenstift Klosterneuburg, Austria, codex 260. 175 f. Folio. Saec. 12.
Microfilm: MnCH proj. no. 5231

6058   Expositio super Genesin. MS. Cistercienserabtei Heiligenkreuz, Austria, codex 82, f.1r–150r. Folio. Saec. 13.
Microfilm: MnCH proj. no. 4627

6059   Expositio super Genesin. MS. Linz, Austria, Bundesstaatliche Studienbibliothek, codex 41, f.1r–128v. Folio. Saec. 13.
Microfilm: MnCH proj. no. 27,995

6060   Commentarium in prophetas: Isaiam, Ieremiam, Ezechielem, Danielem. Commentarium in quatuor evangelia. MS. Augustinerchorherrenstift Klosterneuburg, Austria, codex 258. 144 f. Folio. Saec. 12.
Microfilm: MnCH proj. no. 5230

6061   Commentarius in Joannem. MS. Vienna, Nationalbibliothek, codex 110. 129 f. Folio. Saec. 12.
Microfilm: MnCH proj. no. 9211

6062   Commentarium in evangelium Joannis apostoli et evangelistae. MS. Augustinerchorherrenstift Klosterneuburg, Austria, codex 256. 158 f. Folio. Saec. 12.
Microfilm: MnCH proj. no. 5227

6063   Commentarium in evangelium Joannis apostoli et evangelistae. Liber octavus. MS. Chorherrenstift Klosterneuburg, Austria, codex 257. 138 f. Folio. Saec. 12.
Microfilm: MnCH proj. no. 5228

6064   Expositio in Matthaeum. MS. Cistercienserabtei Heiligenkreuz, Austria, codex 104. 170 f. Folio. Saec. 13.
Microfilm: MnCH proj. no. 4649

6065   Commentarius in Oseam prophetam. MS. Benediktinerabtei Admont, Austria, codex 107. 95 f. Folio. Saec. 12.
Microfilm: MnCH proj. no. 9205

6066   Commentarius in Oseam, Johel, Amos et Abdiam. MS. Benediktinerabtei Admont, Austria, codex 158. 199 f. Folio. Saec. 12.
Microfilm: MnCH proj. no. 9246

6067   Explanatio in Osee, Johelem, Amos et Abdiam prophetas. MS. Cistercienserabtei Heiligenkreuz, Austria, codex 98. 190 f. Folio. Saec. 12.
Microfilm: MnCH proj. no. 4638

6068 Commentarius super Pentateuchum et Josuam. MS. Benediktinerabtei Admont, Austria, codex 159. 184 f. Folio. Saec. 12.
Microfilm: MnCH proj. no. 9245

6069 Commentarium in Pentateuchum, Josue, Judicum et Regum libros. MS. Universitätsbibliothek Graz, Austria, codex 401. 261 f. Folio. Saec. 13.
Microfilm: MnCH proj. no. 26,572

6070 Commentarii in quatuor Prophetas majores et volumen Evangelistarum. MS. Vienna, Nationalbibliothek, codex 702. 176 v. Folio. Saec. 12.
Microfilm: MnCH proj. no. 14,026

6071 Expositiones in Prophetas Majores. MS. Vienna, Nationalbibliothek, codex 1015. 209 f. Folio. Saec. 13.
Microfilm: MnCH proj. no. 14,311

6072 Commentarius in Prophetas Minores: Jonas usque ad Malachiam. MS. Benediktinerabtei Admont, Austria, codex 229. 224 f. Folio. Saec. 12.
Microfilm: MnCH proj. no. 9316

6073 Super VII Prophetas Minores ultimos. MS. Universitätsbibliothek Graz, Austria, codex 136. Folio. Saec. 12.
Microfilm: MnCH proj. no. 26,073

6074 Super XII Prophetas. MS. Universitätsbibliothek Graz, Austria, codex 373. 209 f. Folio. Saec. 12.
Microfilm: MnCH proj. no. 26,320

6075 Commentarium in Prophetas Minores. MS. Augustinerchorherrenstift Klosterneuburg, Austria, codex 259. 211 f. Folio. Saec. 12.
Microfilm: MnCH proj. no. 5229

6076 Super duodecim Prophetas. MS. Vienna, Nationalbibliothek, codex 727. 225 f. Folio. Saec. 12.
Microfilm: MnCH proj. no. 14,046

6077 Commentarius in duodecim Prophetas Minores. MS. Benediktinerabtei St. Peter, Salzburg, codex a.X.21. Folio. Saec. 13.
Microfilm: MnCH proj. no. 10,255

6078 Commentarium in Prophetas Minores (excerpta). MS. Augustinerchorherrenstift Klosterneuburg, Austria, codex 1116, f.101r–109r. Quarto. Saec. 17.
Microfilm: MnCH proj. no. 6118

6079 Commentarius in libros Regum. MS. Benediktinerabtei Admont, Austria, codex 237. 138 f. Folio. Saec. 12.
Microfilm: MnCH proj. no. 9322

6080 Commentarius super Vetus Testamentum. MS. Benediktinerabtei St. Peter, Salzburg, codex a.XI.1. 470 p. Folio. Saec. 12.
Microfilm: MnCH proj. no. 10,264

6081 De officiis divinis per anni circulum libri duodecim. MS. Augustinerchorherrenstift Klosterneuburg, Austria, codex 252, f.1r–215r. Folio. Saec. 12.
Microfilm: MnCH proj. no. 5217

6082 De divinis officiis. MS. Universitätsbibliothek Graz, Austria, codex 736. 144 f. Folio. Saec. 12.
Microfilm: MnCH proj. no. 26,850

6083 De divinis officiis. MS. Vienna, Nationalbibliothek, codex 913. 196 f. Folio. Saec. 12.
Microfilm: MnCH proj. no. 14,225

6084 De divinis officiis. MS. Benediktinerabtei Göttweig, Austria, codex 1112. 202 f. Saec. 13.
Microfilm: MnCH proj. no. 3802

6085 De ecclesiasticis officiis. MS. Lincoln Cathedral Library, England, codex 77. Saec. 13.
Microfilm: MnCH

6086 Opusculum de divinis officiis per circulum anni (liber XII deest). MS. Vienna, Nationalbibliothek, codex 1568. 188 f. Folio. Saec. 13.
Microfilm: MnCH proj. no. 14,901

6087 Rupertus Tuitiensis, Hugo a Sancto Victore et alii: De divinis officiis. MS. Tarazona, Spain, Archivo de la Catedral, codex 62. 238 f. Quarto. Saec. 14.
Microfilm: MnCH proj. no. 32,641

6088 De gloria et honore filii hominis. MS. Vienna, Nationalbibliothek, codex 938. 107 f. Folio. Saec. 13.
Microfilm: MnCH proj. no. 14,252

6089 De glorificatione Trinitatis et processione Spiritus Sancti, cum Epistola ad papam Honorium II. MS. Vienna, Nationalbibliothek, codex 716, f.1v–99r. Folio. Saec. 12.
Microfilm: MnCH proj. no. 14,035

6090 De meditatione mortis. MS. Benediktinerabtei Admont, Austria, codex 443, f.1r–18v. Quarto. Saec. 12.
Microfilm: MnCH proj. no. 9504

6091 De meditatione mortis (excerpta). MS. Vienna, Nationalbibliothek, codex 998, f.152r–170v. Folio. Saec. 13.
Microfilm: MnCH proj. no. 14,308

6092 De victoria Verbi Dei. MS. Benediktinerabtei St. Peter, Salzburg, codex a.IX.3, f.1v–103r. Folio. Saec. 11.
Microfilm: MnCH proj. no. 10,207

6093 De victoria Verbi Dei. MS. Cistercienserabtei Heiligenkreuz, Austria, codex 113. 160 f. Folio. Saec. 12.
Microfilm: MnCH proj. no. 4656

6094 De victoria Verbi Dei. MS. Vienna, Nationalbibliothek, codex 738, f.1r–139v. Folio. Saec. 12.
Microfilm: MnCH proj. no. 14,062

6095 De victoria Verbi Dei. Libri 13. MS. Vienna, Nationalbibliothek, codex 1420, f.1r–139r. Folio. Saec. 12.
Microfilm: MnCH proj. no. 14,767

6096 De victoria Verbi Dei. Libri 13. MS. Vienna, Nationalbibliothek, codex 1547. 150 f. Folio. Saec. 12.
Microfilm: MnCH proj. no. 14,880

6097 De victoria Verbi Dei. MS. Cistercienserabtei Zwettl, Austria, codex 51, f.124r–235v. Folio. Saec. 12.

6098 De victoria Verbi Dei, libri XIII. MS. Universitätsbibliothek Graz, Austria, codex 292. 135 f. Folio. Saec. 13.
Microfilm: MnCH proj. no. 26,206

6099 De victoria Verbi Dei. MS. Linz, Austria, Bundesstaatliche Studienbibliothek, codex 99. 138 f. Folio. Saec. 13.
Microfilm: MnCH proj. no. 27,942

6100 De victoria Verbi Dei. MS. Vienna, Nationalbibliothek, codex 929, f.1v–104v. Folio. Saec. 14.
Microfilm: MnCH proj. no. 14,227

6101 De victoria Verbi Dei. MS. Universitätsbibliothek Salzburg, codex M II 336. 195 f. Folio. Saec. 15.
Microfilm: MnCH proj. no. 11,346

6102 Dialogus Christiani et Judaei. MS. Augustinerchorherrenstift Klosterneuburg, Austria, codex 714, f.141v–177v. Folio. Saec. 12.
Microfilm: MnCH proj. no. 5697
Expositio. See his Commentarius.

6103 Liber de victoria Dei (excerptum). MS. Benediktinerabtei St. Peter, Salzburg, codex a.VI.7, f.380v–381r. Quarto. Saec. 15.

6104 Libri XIII de victoria Dei. MS. Benediktinerabtei Seitenstetten, Austria, codex 104. Folio. Saec. 15.
Microfilm: MnCH proj. no. 917

6105 Liber cantici de incarnatione Domini. MS. Vienna, Nationalbibliothek, codex series nova 3606. 80 f. Quarto. Saec. 12.
Microfilm: MnCH proj. no. 20,813

6106 Liber quartus operis super quaedam capitula Regulae S. Benedicti. MS. Vienna, Nationalbibliothek, codex 2235, f.66r–70v. Quarto. Saec. 12.
Microfilm: MnCH proj. no. 15,551

6107 Sermones de tempore. MS. Benediktinerabtei Admont, Austria, codex 598. 119 f. Quarto. Saec. 13.
Microfilm: MnCH proj. no. 9647

6108 Summa de adventu Domini et de aliis festis per circulum anni. MS. Vienna, Nationalbibliothek, codex 1604, f.2v–87v. Quarto. Saec. 13.
Microfilm: MnCH proj. no. 14,927

6109 Tractatus subtilis de Corpore Domini (forse pseudo). MS. Cistercienserabtei Heiligenkreuz, Austria, codex 215, f.87v–90v. Folio. Saec. 12.
Microfilm: MnCH proj. no. 4755

Rupert, abbot of Deutz.
Printed works

6110 Opera. Editio veneta novissima. Venetiis, 1748.
4 v.
NcBe

6111 Commentaria in Canticum canticorum, edidit Hrabanus Haacke. Turnholti, Brepols, 1974.
lx, 192 p. 26 cm. (Corpus Christianorum. Continuatio mediaevalis, 26)
MnCS; PLatS

6112 Commentaria in Evangelium Sancti Johannis . . . edidit Hrabanus Haacke, O.S.B. Turnholti, Brepols, 1969.
xv, 831 p. illus. 25 cm. (Corpus Christianorum. Continuatio mediaevalis, 9)
InStme; MnCS; PLatS

6113 Opera duo: In Matthaeum de gloria & honore Filij Hominis lib. xiii; De glorificatione Trinitatis & processione Spiritus Sancti lib. ix. Coloniae [impensis Arnoldi Birckman, MDXLI].
xlxvii, cxcv p. 31 cm.
MnCS

6113a De gloria et honore filii hominis super Mattheum, edidit Hrabanus Haacke, O.S.B. Turnholti, Brepols, 1979.
xxi, 456 p. 26 cm. (Corpus Christianorum. Continuatio Mediaevalis, 29)
MnCS; PLatS; InStme

6114 De Sancta Trinitate et operibus eius, edidit Hrabanus Haacke. Turnholti, Brepols, 1971–72.
4 v. 25 cm. (Corpus Christianorum. Continuatio mediaevalis, 21–24)
InStme; MnCS; PLatS

6115 De victoria Verbi Dei. Hrsg. von Hraban Haacke. Weimar, Hermann Böhlaus Nachfolger, 1970.
lix, 474 p. illus. 22 cm. (Monumenta Germaniae historica. Quellen zur Geistesgeschichte des Mittelalters, Bd. 5)
PLatS

6116 Liber de divinis officiis edidit Hrabanus Haacke, O.S.B. Turnholti, Brepols, 1967.
lxii, 477 p. plates (col.) 25 cm. (Corpus Christianorum. Continuatio mediaevalis, 7)
InStme; KAS; MnCS

6117 Les oeuvres du Saint-Esprit. Introduction et notes par Jean Gribomont, O.S.B. Texte établi et traduit par Elisabeth de Solms, O.S.B. Paris, Editions du Cerf, 1967–
v. 20 cm. (Sources chrétiennes, n. 131. Série des textes monastiques d'Occident, no. 21)
InStme; PLatS

6118 Vita Heriberti. Kritische Edition mit Kommentar und Untersuchungen von Peter Dinter. Bonn, Ludwig Röhrscheid Verlag, 1976.
146 p. 24 cm.
MnCS

6119 (2dary) Die Kirche–Gottes Heil in der Welt; die Lehre von der Kirche nach den Schriften des Rupert von Deutz, Honorius Augustodunensis und Gerhoch von Reichersberg . . . von Wolfgang Beinert. Münster, Aschendorff, 1973.
xvi, 464 p. 23 cm.
PLatS

6120 **Rupert, abbot of St. Peter, Salzburg.**
Briefbuch des Abtes Rupert, 1467–1472. MS. Benediktinerabtei St. Peter, Salzburg, Archivium HS A 27. 238 f. Saec. 15.
Microfilm: MnCH proj. no. 10,863

6121 **Rupertus, abbot of Göttweig, Austria.**
Vita sancti Altmanni. MS. Vienna, Schottenstift, codex 231, f.140r–156r. Quarto. Saec. 15.
Microfilm: MnCH proj. no. 3897

Rupertus, abbot of Limburg an der Haart.
6122 Sermones. MS. Vienna, Nationalbibliothek, codex 917. 21 c. Folio. Saec. 12.
Microfilm: MnCH proj. no. 14,241

6123 Sermones de tempore. MS. Benediktinerabtei Lambach, Austria, codex chart. 171, f.148r–258v. Saec. 15.
Microfilm: MnCH proj. no. 583

Rupertus, monachus Remensis.
6124 Historia Hierosolemitana. MS. Linz, Bundesstaatliche Studienbibliothek, codex 251, f.1r–56r. Folio. Saec. 14.
Microfilm: MnCH proj. no. 27,915

6125 Historia Hierosolymitana, libri octo. MS. Benediktinerabtei St. Peter, Salzburg, codex b.IX.28, f.84r–124v. Folio. Saec. 15.
Microfilm: MnCH proj. no. 10,600

Rupertus Tuitiensis. *See* Rupert of Deutz.
6126 **Ruppert, Fidelis,** 1938–
Das pachomianische Mönchtum und die Anfänge klösterlichen Gehorsams. Münsterschwarzach, Vier-Türme-Verlag, 1971.
xxx, 466 p. 21 cm.
MnCS; PLatS

6127 **Rupprecht, Melvin Clarence,** 1915–1974.
Happiness in the making.
vi, 95 leaves, 28 cm.
Thesis (M.A.)–St. Vincent College, Latrobe, Pa., 1942.
Typescript.
PLatS

6127a Saint Vincent Archabbey Church.
63 leaves. 28 cm.
Thesis (B.A.), Saint Vincent College, Latrobe, Pa., 1938.
Typescript.
PLatS

6128 **Rupprecht, Placidus,** 1890–
Der Mittler und sein Heilswerk; Sacrificium Mediatoris. Eine Opferstudie auf Grund einer eingehenden Untersuchung der Aeusserungen des hl. Thomas von Aquin. Freiburg i.B., Herder, 1934.
164 p. 24 cm.
MnCS; NdRi

6129 **Russell, Ralph,** 1903–
In this world; the sacraments and the lay apostolate . . . London, Darton, Longman & Todd [1962].
viii, 51 p. 25 cm.
KAS; MnCS; PLatS

Rust, Renée, Sister.
6130 Comprehensive project: Spirituality of liturgy.
Thesis (M.A.)–University of Dayton, 1974.
KyCovS

6131 The sounds around: poetry. Hicksville, N.Y., Exposition Press [1976].
64 p. illus. 24 cm.
InFer; KyCovS; MnCS

6132 **Rutherford, Anselm.**
Acts for mental prayer. London, Darton, Longman & Todd [1921, 1961].
88 p.
MoCo

Rutledge, Denys, 1906–
6133 The complete monk; vocation of the monastic order. London, Routledge & K. Paul, 1966.
xii, 363 p. 16 plates, 23 cm.
InStme; MoCo; PLatS

6134 Cosmic theology; the ecclesiastical hierarchy of pseudo-Denys: an introduction. London, Routledge and K. Paul [1964].
xi, 212 p. 23 cm.
InFer; OkShG; PLatS

6135 In search of a yogi. New York, Farrar, Straus [1963].
321 p. 22 cm.
ILSP; InStme; KAS; MnCS; MoCo; PLatS

6136 **Ryan, Kevin,** 1916–
The vetatron; an induction electron acce-
lerator.
66 leaves, illus. 29 cm.
Typescript.
InStme

Ryan, Vincent, 1930–
6137 Every Sunday an Easter Sunday.
(*In* Murray, Placid. Studies in pastoral
theology. Dublin, 1967. v. 3, p. 181–194)
PLatS

6138 (ed) Mortimort, Aimé Georges. The
Church at prayer . . . Shannon, Ireland,
1968.
PLatS

Ryelandt, Idesbald, 1878–
6139 The life of grace. Translated by Dom M.
Dillon, O.S.B. Dublin, Clonmore &
Reynolds [1964].
142 p. 19 cm.
KAS; MnCS; MnStj; NcBe; PLatS

6140 Pour mieux communier; la Messe et la
vie intérieure, la Communion unie à la
Messe, les effets vivifiant de l'Eucharistie.
Abbaye de Maredsous, Belgique, 1927.
47 p. 19 cm.
MnCS; PLatS

6141 Les richesses de la grâce baptismale.
[Bruges], Desclée [1961].
207 p. 20 cm.
MnCS

6142 Union with Christ: Benedictine and
liturgical spirituality . . . Translated by
Dom Matthew Dillon. Dublin, Clonmore &
Reynolds; London, Burns & Oates, 1966.
175 p. 19 cm.
InFer; InStme; KAS; MdRi; MnCS;
MnStj; PLatS

6143 **Rylance, Cyril,** 1880–
One body in Jesus Christ. London,
Catholic Truth Society [1955].
47 p. 19 cm.
KAS

6144 **Sacred Heart Convent, Lisle, Ill.**
Lisle Benedictine women today
(periodical). 1–   1978–
InFer; ILSH

6145 **Sacred Heart Convent, Yankton, S. D.**
Encounter (periodical). 1–   1965–
InFer; SdYa

6146 **Il Sacro Speco di Subiaco.** [n.p., n.d.]
32 plates, 20 x 26 cm.
PLatS

6147 **Sacro Speco Subiaco.** Benedettini di
Subiaco, 1968.
72 p. illus., plates (col.)
Text in French and English.
InFer

Saelinger, Irmina, Sister.
6148 The challenge; centennial history of
Benedictine Sisters, St. Walburg Convent,
Covington, Kentucky, 1959.
34 p. illus. 28 cm.
Privately printed.
KyCovS

6149 Retrospect and vista; the first fifty years
of Thomas More College, formerly Villa
Madonna College. Wendling Printing Co.,
1971.
86 p. illus., 5.9 cm.
KyCovS; MoCo

6150 **Saenz, Pablo,** 1926–
Dialogo del silencio; monjes en la iglesia
de hoy. Buenos Aires, Latino America
Libros, 1967.
169 p. 20 cm.
PLatS

6151 **Sáenz de Aguirre, José,** 1630–1699.
De virtutibus et vitiis disputationes
ethicae . . . Romae, ex Typographia Antonii de Rubeis, 1697.
[24], 602, [12] p. 37 cm.
KAS

Saint. *See also* entries beginning with
Sainte.
San.
Sankt.
Santa.
Santo.
Sao.
Sint.

6152 **St. Alban's Abbey, England.**
St. Alban's Chronicle. MS. Lambeth
Palace Library, London, codex 6. 258 f. Oc-
tavo. Saec. 15.
Microfilm: MnCH

**Saint-Amand-les-Eaux, France (Bene-
dictine abbey).**
6153 Annales Sancti Amandi.
(*In* Monumenta Germaniae historica.
Scriptores. Stuttgart, 1963. t. 1, p. 3–14)
MnCS; PLatS

6154 Sacramentarium Gelasianum mixtum
von Saint-Amand [von] Sieghild Rehle, mit
einer sakramentargeschichtlichen Einführung von Klaus Gambet . . . Regensburg,
Fr. Pustet [1973].
142 p. 22 cm.
PLatS

Saint-André, Bruges. *See* Bruges, Belgium. Abbaye de Saint-André.

6155 **St. Andrew's Priory, Valyermo, Calif.**
(tr) Maertens, Thierry. Guide for the
Christian assembly . . . [Translated by
monks of Valyermo]. Notre Dame, Ind.,
Fides Publishers [1967–72].

7 v. 21 cm.
ILSP; InStme; KAS; NcBe; PLatS

6156 **St. Ann's Indian Mission, Belcourt, N. D.**
Bells of St. Ann (periodical). 1–
InFer

6157 **St. Anselm's Abbey, Washington, D.C.**
Biography and bibliography, no. 1. St. Anselm's Abbey, Washington, D.C. [1964].
43 p. 23 cm.
KAM; MnStj; PLatS

St. Anselm's College, Manchester, N. H.
6158 The Crier (periodical). 1969–
InFer; NhSMA

6159 In a great tradition: St. Anselm's College, Manchester. [1958].
[16] p. illus., ports., plan, 28 cm.
PLatS; NhSMA

6160 **St. Augustine's Abbey, Canterbury, England.**
Tractatus diversi. MS. Lambeth Palace Library, London, codex 1213. 176 f. Quarto. Saec. 13.
Microfilm: MnCH

St. Augustine's Abbey, Ramsgate, England.
6161 The book of saints; a dictionary of servants of God canonized by the Catholic Church, compiled by the Benedictine monks of St. Augustine's Abbey, Ramsgate. 5th ed. London, Black, 1966.
xii, 740 p. 23 cm.
MnCS; PLatS

6162 University education under the guidance of the Church; or, Monastic studies. By a monk of St. Augustine's, Ramsgate. London, R. Washbourne, 1873.
120 p. 21 cm.
KAS; MnCS; PLatS

6163 **St. Benedict's, Rome.** [Rome] Vatican Press, 1896.
16 p. front. 20 cm.
KAS

St. Benedict's Abbey, Atchison, Kans.
6164 Christ has a family in Atchison. [Atchison, Kans., Abbey Student Press, 1961?].
[14] p. chiefly illus. 27 cm.
KAS

6165 Community prayers. Atchison, Kans., [Abbey Student Press, 1965].
43 p. 13 cm.
KAS

6166 Community prayers, Latin and English. Printed as manuscript for the use of the Brothers of St. Benedict's Abbey, Atchison, Kans. [Abbey Student Press, 1953?].
68 p. 12 cm.
KAS; PLatS

6167 A new monastery, St. Benedict's Abbey, Atchison, Kansas [1927].
19 p. illus. 18 cm.
Contains artist's conception of monastery and church.
KAS

6168 Prime and Compline of the monastic breviary. Printed as manuscript for the use of the Benedictine Brothers of St. Benedict's Abbey, Atchison, Kans. [Abbey Student Press] 1960.
44 p. 24 cm.
KAS; MnCS

6169 St. Benedict's, Atchison, Kansas [an album]. 1919.
unpaged, plates, 15 x 21 cm.
MnCS

St. Benedict's Abbey, Benet Lake, Wis.
6170 Benet Lake news and views (periodical). 1950–
InFer: WBenS

6171 The interpretation of the Rule of St. Benedict for the monks of St. Benedict's Abbey, Benet Lake, Wisconsin. [196-].
25 p.
MoCo; WBens

St. Benedict's College, Atchison, Kans.
See also Benedictine College, Atchison, Kans.

St. Benedict's College, Atchison, Kans.
6172 Corvus corax (periodical). v. 1–
1960–
KAS

6173 Course of instruction. [Atchison, Kans., Abbey Student Print, 1894].
17 p. 22 cm.
KAS

6174 Faculty handbook; statement of policy, constitution and by-laws, functions of officers. Atchison, Kans,. St. Benedict's College [1940].
23 p. 23 cm.

6175 _____ 2d completely revised edition. 1962.
unpaged, 29 cm.
Reproduced from typescript.
KAS

6176 A master plan for campus development; a cooperative project supported by St. Benedict's College . . . Coordinated and administered by Eastern Regional Center, Educational Facilities Laboratories . . . [Stanford] School of Education, Stanford University, 1963.
[6], 62 leaves, fold. plan, 28 cm.
KAS

6177 Profile of a college. Atchison [1960?].
unpaged, illus. (part fold.) ports. 27 cm.
MnCS

6178   Russian area studies; a list of acquisitions by St. Benedict's College Library, 1969–70. Atchison, Kans., 1970.
       45 p. 28 cm.
       Mimeographed.
       KAS

6179   St. Benedict's scholasticate. U.I.O.G.D. Upward and onward. [Abbey Student Press, 1913?].
       22 p. illus. 18 cm.
       KAS

6180   **St. Benedict's Convent, Erie, Pa.**
       Sisters of Saint Benedict, Erie, Pa., 1856–1931. [Erie, Pa., 1931].
       36 p. illus., ports. 32 cm.
       PLatS

St. Benedict's Convent, St. Joseph, Minn.

6181   Book of customs of St. Benedict's Priory of the Congregation of St. Benedict. St. Joseph, Minn., 1949.
       33 p. 19 cm.
       MnStj(Archives)

6182   Constitutions for the Sisters of the Order of St. Benedict of St. Benedict's Convent. St. Cloud, Minn., W. P. Remer, Ptr., 1887.
       51 p. 13 cm.
       MnStj(Archives)

6183   Constitutions for the Sisters of the Order of St. Benedict, of St. Benedict's Convent, St. Joseph, Minnesota. St. Paul, Wanderer Print, 1888.
       49 p. 15 cm.
       MnStj(Archives)

6184   Directory [of St. Benedict's Convent]. 1972.
       108 p. illus., 29 cm.
       MnStj(Archives)

6185   Golden jubilee profession of vows according to the rite used by the Sisters of Saint Benedict. Adapted from the "Caeremoniale monasticum" (First ed. 1875) of the American Cassinese Congregation of the Order of Saint Benedict. St. Joseph, Minn., St. Benedict's Convent, 1937.
       18 p. 15 cm.
       MnStj(Archives)

6186   Manual of prayers, St. Benedict's Convent, St. Joseph, Minnesota. St. Cloud, Minn., North Star Ptg. Co., 1922.
       58 p. 13 cm.
       In German and English.
       MnStj(Archives)

6187   Meditations on the O antiphons, by a Sister of St. Benedict [Jeremy Hall]. St. Joseph, Minn., Sisters of St. Benedict, 1962.
       ICSS; MdRi; MnCS; MnStj

6188   Monastic table prayers, Convent of Saint Benedict, Saint Joseph, Minnesota. [St. Benedict's Press] 1951.
       59 p. 12 cm.
       MnStj(Archives)

6189   Practical maxims and offices at the Court of Jesus to be drawn at Christmastide. St. Joseph, Minn., St. Benedict's Press [1940].
       112 p. 10 cm.
       MnStj(Archives)

6190   Seekers of God. St. Joseph, Minn., Convent of St. Benedict [1957?]
       [32] p. illus. 21 cm.
       MnStj; PLatS

6191   Table manners; booklet prepared for the Sister Formation Program of Saint Benedict's Convent, Saint Joseph, Minnesota. 1965.
       12 p. 14 x 22 cm.
       MnStj(Archives)

Saint-Benoît de Port Valais, Bouveret, Switzerland. *See* Bouveret, Switzerland. Saint-Benoît de Port-Valais.

Saint-Benoît-du-Lac, Canada (Quebec).

6192   Abbaye Saint-Benoît-du-Lac. [L'Abbaye de la Pierre-qui-Vire] 1962.
       63 p. illus. 23 cm.
       KAS; MnCS; PLatS

6193   Rythmique grégorienne. [Lake Memphremagog, Benedictine monks of St. Benoît-du-lac, Canada] n.d.
       20 p. 22 cm.
       MnCS

6194   Rythmique grégorienne, par les moines de Saint-Benoît-du-Lac: Guide du professeur. [n.p., n.d.].
       102 p. illus. 28 cm.
       Mimeographed.
       InStme

6195   **Saint Benoît et ses fils.** Textes bénédictins traduits par les moines d'Hautecombe. Introduction et notes par M. F. Lacan. Préface de Daniel-Rops. Paris, A. Fayard [1961].
       vii, 412 p. 19 cm. (Textes pour l'histoire sacrée)
       CaQStB; KAS

Saint-Benoît-sur-Loire. France (Benedictine abbey).

6196   Consuetudines Floriacenses saeculi tertii decimi, edidit D. Anselmus Davril, O.S.B. Siegburg, F. Schmitt, 1976.
       lxxxix, 507 p. facsim. 26 cm. (Corpus consuetudinum monasticarum, v. 9)
       PLatS

6197   Dialogues de saint Grégoire et Règle de saint Benoît. Extraits traduits par E. de Solms. La Pierre-qui-Vire, Zodiaque. 1965.

199 p. 72 plates (part col.) 26 cm.
MnCS

6198 **St. Charles Priory, Oceanside, Calif.**
Benet Hill news (periodical). 1961–
InFer; COce

St. Gall, Switzerland (Benedictine abbey).
6199 Annales Sangallenses.
(*In* Monumenta Germaniae historica. Scriptores. Stuttgart, 1963. t. 1, p. 63–65, 69–85)
MnCS; PLatS

6200 Libri confraternitatum Sancti Galli augiensis faboriensis. Edidit Paulus Piper. Berolini, apud Weidmannos, 1884.
vii, 550 p. 28 cm. (Monumenta Germaniae historica . . .)
MnCS

6201 Monachi Sangallensis de gestis Karoli M. libri II.
(*In* Monumenta Germaniae historica. Scriptores. Stuttgart, 1963. t. 2, p. 726–763)
MnCS; PLatS

6202 Das Professbuch der Abtei St. Gallen. St. Gallen Stiftsarchiv cod. class. I. cist. C.3.B.56. Phototypische Wiedergabe mit Einführung und einem Anhang von Paul M. Krieg. Augsburg, Benno Filser Verlag, 1931.
36 p. facsims. 33 cm. (Codices liturgici e vaticanis praesertim delecti phototypice expressi, v. 2)
InStme; MnCS

6203 Versus sangallenses. [Edidit Karl Strecker].
(*In* Poetae latini aevi carolini . . . Berolini. t. IV(1923). [Supplementa] p. 1091–1112)
MnCS

St. Gall, Switzerland. Stiftsbibliothek.
6204 Verzeichniss der Handschriften der Stiftsbibliothek von St. Gallen. Hrsg. auf Veranstaltung und mit Unterstützung des Kath. Administrationsrathes des Kantons St. Gallen. Halle, Verlag der Buchhandlung des Waisenhauses, 1875.
xii, 650 p. 24 cm.

6205 **St. Gall, Switzerland. Stiftsbibliothek. Mss. (350).**
Ein St. Galler Sakrament-Fragment (cod. Sangall. no. 350) als Nachtrag zum fränkischen Sacramentarium Gelasium . . . hrsg. von Dr. Georg Manz. Münster i.W., Aschendorff, 1939.
xv, 92 p. 26 cm.
MnCS

6206 **St. Gall, Switzerland. Stiftsbibliothek. Mss. (359).**
Das Quilisma im Codex 359 der Stiftsbibliothek St. Gallen, erhellt durch das Zeugniss der codices: Einsiedeln 121, Bamberg lit. 6, Leon 239 und Chartres 47. Eine paläographisch-semiologische Studie von Walter Wiesli. Immensee, Schweiz, Verlag Missionshaus Bethlehem [1966].
xiii, 90 p. music, diagrs. 21 cm.
MnCS

6207 **St. Gall, Switzerland. Stiftsbibliothek. Mss. (381).**
Sylloga codicis sangallensis CCCLXXXI.
(*In* Poetae latini aevi carolini . . . Berolini . . . t. IV(1899), p. 315–349)
KAS(microfilm); MnCS

6208 **St. Gall, Switzerland. Stiftsbibliothek. Mss. (841).**
Lateinische und deutsch-lateinische proverbia aus der Galler Handschrift 841. Text und Kommentar von Josef Georg Bregenzer. Zürich, Juris-Verlag, 1972.
173 p. 23 cm.
MnCS

6209 **St. Gall, Switzerland. Stiftsbibliothek. Mss. (908).**
Getilgte Paulus- und Psalmentexte unter getilgten ambrosianischen Liturgiestücken aus Cod. sangall. 908 . . . hrsg. und bearb. von P. Alban Dold, O.S.B. Beuron, Verlag der Kunstschule der Erzabtei, 1928.
52 p. 11 facsims. 24 cm. (Texte und Arbeiten . . . Beuron. 1. Abt., Heft 14)
MnCS

6210 **St. Gall, Switzerland. Stiftsbibliothek. Mss. (912).**
Eine Palimpseststudie (St. Gallen 912), von Paul J. G. Lehmann. München, Verlag der Bayerischen Akademie der Wissenschaften, 1931.
45 p. 6 facsims. 23 cm.
MnCSS

6211 **St. Gall, Switzerland. Stiftsbibliothek. Mss. (916).**
Die althochdeutsche Benediktinerregel des Cod. Sang. 916. Hrsg. von Ursula Daab. Tübingen, M. Niemeyer, 1959.
304 p. 19 cm. (Altdeutsche Textbibliothek, Nr. 50)
KAM; PLatS

6211a **St. Gall, Switzerland. Stiftsbibliothek. Mss. (1092).**
Der karolingische Klosterplan von St. Gallen (Schweiz). The Carolingian plan of St. Gall Abbey (Switzerland). Facsimile-Wiedergabe in acht Farben, mit einer Monographie: Der St. Galler Klosterplan, von Hans Reinhardt. St. Gallen, Kommis-

sionsverlag der Fehr'schen Buchhandlung, 1952.

41 p. illus. and portfolio (fold. col. plan, 116 x 81 cm.) 31 cm. (Neujahrsblatt, hrsg. vom Historischen-Verein des Kantons S. Gallen)

Issued in case with title on mounted label.

MnCS; PLatS

6212 **St. Gregory's Abbey, Three Rivers, Mich.**
Abbey letter (periodical). 1947(?)–
MnCS

St. John's Abbey, Collegeville, Minn.

6213 Abbey and University church of Saint John the Baptist. Collegeville, Minn., 1961.
47 p. illus. 23 cm.
MnCS

6214 American Benedictine foundations (portfolio). [Collegeville, Minn., The Scriptorium, 1960].
44 x 29 cm.
Includes abbeys and convents.
MnCS

6215 Book of prayer for personal use; a short breviary abridged and simplified by monks of St. John's Abbey from the Liturgia horarum, wholly revised fourth edition, 1975. Collegeville, Minn., Saint John's Abbey Press [1975].
1823 p. 18 cm.
MnCS

6216 Book of sacred song; a selection of hymns, songs, chants from contemporary and folk sources and the Church's heritage of sacred music. 6th ed. Collegeville, Minn., The Liturgical Press, 1977.
482 p. music. 20 cm.
Originally published in 1959 under the title: Our parish prays and sings.
MnCS

6217 Christians in conversation. With a preface by Peter W. Bartholome. Westminster, Md., Newman Press, 1962.
x, 112 p. 21 cm.
"A colloquy between American Catholics and Protestants . . . held at St. John's Abbey, Collegeville, Minn., on 1, 2, 3 December, 1960."
"Organized by the American Benedictine Academy."
MnCS

6218 Confrere [monthly publication for the monastic community]. v. 1–   1963–
MnCS

6219 The eucharistic liturgy; the rite of blessing an abbot. The blessing of John A. Eidenschink, O.S.B., abbot of Saint John's Abbey, Collegeville, Minnesota [in] Saint John's Abbey Church, Friday, October fifteenth 1971.
26 p. music, 34 cm.
MnCS

6220 The Hours of the Divine Office in English and Latin; a bilingual edition of the Roman Breviary text, together with introductory notes and rubrics in English only. Prepared by the staff of The Liturgical Press. Collegeville, Minn., The Liturgical Press [1963–64].
3 v. 19 cm.
MnCS; PLatS

6221 Mary, the throne of wisdom; dedication of a sacred image [in the] Abbey and University Church of Saint John the Baptist, Collegeville, Minnesota (24 October 1963).
unpaged, illus. 26 cm.
MnCS

6222 The monks of St. John's [a directory, 1967].
103 p. ports. 28 cm.
MnCS; MnStj(Archives)

6223 Oblate library catalog, July, 1958.
70 p. 23 cm.
MnCS

6224 Our parish prays and sings; Sunday Mass book. Collegeville, Minn., The Liturgical Press [1967].
1055 p. col. plates, music, 18 cm.
MnCS

6225 Our parish prays and sings hymnbook; a service book for liturgical worship. Collegeville, Minn., The Liturgical Press [1970].
32, 351 p. music. 20 cm.
MnCS

6226 Symposium one: on monastic poverty, by and for members of St. John's only. [Collegeville, Minn., St. John's Abbey, 1971].
142 leaves, 28 cm.
MnCS

6227 Symposium three: on work. [Collegeville, Minn., St. John's Abbey, 1973?].
81 p. 28 cm.
MnCS

6228 To praise the living God [brochures and publications collected from various sources and bound into one volume – all connected with St. John's Abbey Church].
various pagings, illus., plates, 31 cm.
MnCS

6229 **St. John's Abbey, Collegeville, Minn., Brothers' Library.**
Catalog of Brothers' Library.
24 p. 30 cm.
Lists 845 books numerically as they stand on the shelves.

Handwritten.
MnCS(Archives)

St. John's Abbey, Collegeville, Minn. Clerics' Liturgical Study Club.

6230   Papers delivered by the members . . . from June 20, 1933, to _____.
Multigraphed.
MnCS

6231   Minutes, June 20, 1933–Sept. 18, 1938.
67 p. 24 cm.
Manuscript.
MnCS

6232   **St. John's Abbey, Collegeville, Minn. Novitiate.**
Fratres nostri in pace dormientes. Prepared by the novices of 1954, 1955 and 1956.
229 p. ports, 28 cm.
Typescript.
MnCS(Archives)

St. John's University, Collegeville, Minn.

6233   Alumni directory, Saint John's University, Collegeville, Minnesota, 1971.
688, [17] p. ports. 21 cm.
MnCS

6234   Saint John's University alumni directory, 1978.
xviii, 422 p. plates, 23 cm.
MnCS

6235   Calendar, published daily by the Office of Communications.
MnCS

6236   College life; a manual for students. St. John's University Press, 1894.
168 p.
MnCS; MnStj

6237   Community. Weekly newsletter published by the Saint John's University Office of Communications. Spring, 1969–
MnCS

6238   Encounter with artists #10: selected works by the joint art faculty of St. John's University/College of Saint Benedict. [St. Paul, Minn.], Minnesota Museum of Art, 1973.
16 p. illus. 18 x 26 cm.
MnCS

6239   Institutional data, Saint John's University, Collegeville, Minn., December 1, 1968.
122 p. tables, 29 cm.
Multigraphed.
MnCS

6240   Institutional profile, Saint John's University, Collegeville, Minn., September 1, 1968.
97 p. 29 cm.

Multigraphed.
MnCS

6241   The Off-Campus Record. v. 1–7, 1961–1968.
Superseded 1968 by St. John's Magazine.
MnCS

6242   Priest and religious alumni, St. John's University, 1856–1963. Collegeville, Minn. [The Alumni Office, 1963].
38 p. 22 cm.
MnCS

6243   St. John's Magazine. Published quarterly by the Office of Communications, St. John's University, v. 8–   1968–
Supersedes The Off-Campus Record.
MnCS

6243a   Saints [yearbook of] College of St. Benedict/St. John's University, 1977–
Supersedes The Sagatagan.
MnCS

6244   Souvenir (photo album) of St. John's University, 1907.
[30] p. 12 x 20 cm.
MnCS(Archives)

6245   **St. John's University, Collegeville, Minn. Campus Ministry Office.**
Student volunteer program. [1968]
12 p. 20 cm.
MnCS

6246   **St. John's University, Collegeville, Minn. Faculty Library Committee.**
Statement of library aids relative to a comprehensive plan. [1953]
11 leaves, 28 cm.
Hectographed.
MnCS(Archives)

6247   **St. John's University, Collegeville, Minn. Graduate School.**
Religious Education Planning Team: Summer study team report, 1975.
78 p. 30 cm.
MnCS

St. John's University, Collegeville, Minn. Hill Monastic Manuscript Library. *See* Hill Monastic Manuscript Library.

6248   **St. John's University, Collegeville, Minn. The Human Life Center.**
A reader in natural family planning; report on international conferences. No. 1, second edition. Collegeville, Minn., The Human Life Center, St. John's University, 1978.
171 p. col. plates, ports., diagrs. 25 cm.
Printed by Sata International Printing Co., Tokyo.
MnCS

St. John's University, Collegeville, Minn. Library.

6249   Dedication [of] Saint John's University Library, Collegeville, Minnesota, May, 1966.
[21] p. 31 cm.
MnCS; PLatS

6250   The Kritzeck collection, an exhibit, on the occasion of the dedication of Saint John's Abbey and University Library, Collegeville, Minnesota, May 7, 1966.
[6] p. illus. 23 x 11 cm.
MnCS

6251   The library of Saint John's University. Collegeville, Minn. [1966].
[21] p. illus.(10 plats), 21 x 27 cm.
MnCS

6252   **St. John's University. School of Divinity.**
[Bulletin, 1975?]
20 p. illus. 28 cm.
MnCS

6253   **St. John's University. School of Theology.**
Quarterletter. 1978(?)–
MnCS

6254   **St. Joseph, Minn. St. Joseph's Church.**
[Album of] St. Joseph's Parish, St. Joseph, Minn., 1977.
[30] leaves, col. plates, 21 cm.
MnCS

6255   **St. Joseph, Minn. St. Joseph's Church.**
A centennial of consecration, St. Joseph Church, St. Joseph, Minn., June 29, 1971.
unpaged, ports.
MnStj(Archives)

St. Joseph's Convent, St. Marys, Pa.

6256   For God a seed is cast, for God it grows; centennial pageant. St. Marys, Pa., 1952.
45 p.
InFer; PSaS

6257   The Newslites (periodical). 1960–
InFer(1975–   ); PSaS

St. Leo Abbey, St. Leo, Fla.

6258   Florida Benedictines; newsletter of Saint Leo Abbey. v. 1–   1978–
FStL

6259   St. Leo chronicle-reporter (periodical).
InFer (1961–63)

St. Leo College, St. Leo, Fla.

6260   The golden legend of Saint Leo College. St. Leo, Fla., 1962.
72 p. illus. 31 cm.
PLatS; FStL

6261   Invitation to learning; Florida's Catholic college of distinction. [St. Leo, Fla., 1964]
24 p. illus., ports., plan, 29 cm.
PLatS; FStL

6262   The library world of St. Leo College. Weekly.
InFer (1968–70); FStL

6263   **St. Mark's Monastery, South Union, Ky.**
St. Mark's Chronicle. 1977–
InFer; KySu

6264   **Saint Martin et son temps.** Mémorial du XVIe centenaire des débuts de monachisme en Gaule, 361–1961. Romae, Herder, 1961.
vii, 263 p. 25 cm. (Studia Anselmiana, fasc. 46)
InStme; KAS; PLatS

6265   **St. Martin, Minn. St. Martin's Church.**
Dedication and blessing of the Church of St. Martin, St. Martin, Minn., July 11, 1971.
36 p. illus.
MnStj(Archives)

6266   **St. Martin's Abbey, Olympia, Wash.**
St. Martin's News. 1–   1954–
InFer; WaOSM

6267   **St. Martin's Priory, Rapid City, S.D.**
Saint Martin's of the Black Hills. Commemorating the dedication and diamond jubilee, St. Martin's Convent and Academy, Rapid City, South Dakota, conducted by the Sisters of St. Benedict, dedicated May 8th, 1963.
unpaged, illus., ports. 27 cm.
MnCS

St. Mary's Abbey, Morristown, N.J.

6268   Blessing of Saint Mary's Abbey, Morristown, New Jersey, and Mass of thanksgiving, July 16, 1966.
unpaged, illus., music. 27 cm.
NjMoS; PLatS

6269   Delbarton today (periodical). 1971–73.
InFer; NjMoS

6270   Saint Mary's Abbey church. [Printed by Monastery of Our Lady of the Rosary, Summit, N.J., 1970].
7 p. illus. 27 cm.
NjMoS; PLatS

St. Mary's Abbey, Newark, N.J.
See Newark Abbey, Newark, N.J.

6271   **St. Mary's Abbey, West Malling, Kent, England.**
The life of the venerable man Gunduld, bishop of Rochester. Translated into English by the nuns of Malling Abbey. [West Malling, Kent, printed at St. Mary's Abbey, 1968].
[8], V, 76 p. 19 cm.
KAS

6272   **St. Mary's Abbey, Winchester, England.**
An ancient manuscript of the eighth or ninth century: formerly belonging to St.

Mary's Abbey, or Nunnaminster, Winchester. Edited by Walter de Gray Birch. London, Simplin & Marshall, 1889.
162 p. illus. 23 cm.
InStme

6273 **St. Mary's Abbey, York, England.**
The chronicle of St. Mary's Abbey, York, from Bodley ms. 39, edited by H.H.E. Craster and M. E. Thornton. London, B. Quaritch, 1934.
xiii, 154 p. 23 cm. (Publications of the Surtees Society, v. 148)
MnCS

6274 **St. Mary's College, Gaston County, N.C.**
Catalogue of the officers and students of St. Mary's College, Gaston County, N.C. Wheeling, W.Va., James F. Carroll, 1879–1913.
St. Mary's College changed to Belmont Abbey College, Belmont, N.C.
NcBe

St. Mary's Priory, Nauvoo, Ill.
6275 Nauvoo–Benedictine self-study. Committee reports.
5 v.
MnStj(Archives); INauS

6276 Waters of promise: 1874–1974. Nauvoo, Ill., Sisters of St. Benedict, 1974.
48 p. illus (Centennial picture-book)
InFer; INauS

St. Maur Theological Center, Indianapolis, Ind.
6277 Arrow (periodical). 1976–   Quarterly.
InFer; InInS

6278 The City of God (periodical). 1–   1979–
InFer; InInS

St. Meinrad Archabbey, St. Meinrad, Ind.
6279 Benedictine Brother Instructors' Convention, June 9–11, 1942. Report.
MnCS; InStme

6280 The Benedictine junior brother. St. Meinrad, Ind. [1934].
unpaged, illus.
AStb

6281 Daily companion for Oblates of St. Benedict. [4th rev. ed.]. St. Meinrad, Ind., Abbey Press [c 1960].
96 p. 16 cm.
KAS

6282 The lessons of the temporal cycle and the principal feasts of the sanctoral cycle according to the monastic Breviary. Compiled and adapted for the office of the Brothers of St. Meinrad's Abbey . . . 1940.
941, 1v p. 18 cm.
InStme

6283 The Liturgy of the Hours . . . St. Meinrad, Ind., St. Meinrad Archabbey [1974].
2 v. music, 23 cm.
These books are somewhat similar to the former Antiphonarium.
InStme

6284 The Mass year 1945–1970.
Superseded by: My daily visitor.
InFer

6284a Musical settings for the new prefaces of the Roman Rite. Prepared by the Benedictine monks of St. Meinrad Archabbey. St. Meinrad, Ind., Abbey Press, 1972.
59 p.
NcBe

6285 Resonance (periodical). 1–8, 1966–1975.
InFer

6286 St. Meinrad Newletter. 1–   1957–
InFer

6287 St. Rita's Letter. 1–4, 1925–1928.
InFer

6288 **St. Meinrad Archabbey, St. Meinrad, Ind. Library.**
Handbook, Archabbey Library, St. Meinrad, Ind. [1964].
[15] p. 22 cm.
PLatS; InStme

St. Meinrad School of Theology, St. Meinrad, Ind.
6289 Doing theology. 1969–1972.
InFer

6290 Ministry to the Hispano-American . . . St. Meinrad, 1975.
InFer

St. Meinrad Seminary, St. Meinrad, Ind.
6291 Alumni directory, 1863–1975.
158 p.
InFer; InStme

6292 Campus chatter (periodical). 1957–
InFer

6293 **St. Michael's Mount, Cornwall, England.**
The cartulary of St. Michael's Mount (Hatfield House MS. no. 315). Edited with an introduction by P. L. Hull. Torquay, Printed for the Society of The Devonshire Press, 1962.
xxx, 77 p. 24 cm.
PLatS

Saint Michel, Verdun, France. See Verdun, France. Saint Michel.

St. Neot's Priory, Eynesbury, England. See Eynesbury, England. St. Neot's Priory.

Saint-Omer, France. Saint-Bertin (Benedictine abbey).

6294   Cartulaire de l'Abbaye de Saint-Bertin, publié par M. Guérard. Paris, Imprimerie royal, 1840.
    xcvii, 487 p. 28 cm.
    KAS; PLatS

6295   Le polyptyque de l'Abbaye de Saint-Bertin (844–859). Edition critique et commentaire par François-Louis Ganshof, avec la collaboration de Françoise Godding-Ganshof [et] Antoine De Smet. Paris, Imprimerie Nationale, 1975.
    xii, 145 p. maps, 30 cm.
    MnCS

6296   **St. Paul's Indian Mission, Marty, S.D.**
    Little bronzed angel (periodical). 1967–
    InFer

6297   **The Saint Paul's Jarrow Project** for the restoration and protection of the monastic site, home of the Venerable Bede. [Prepared by Redheads & Associates Ltd., New Castle upon Tyne and London. Printed in England by R. Ward & Sons Ltd., Newcastle upon Tyne, 1971?]
    10 p. illus. 21 cm.
    PLatS

6298   **St. Pius X. Monastery, Pevely, Mo.**
    Peace (periodical)
    InFer (1968–   )

6299   **Saint-Pons, France (Benedictine abbey).**
    Chartrier de l'Abbaye de Saint-Pons, hors le murs de Nice, publié par ordre de S.A.S. le prince Albert Ier, par le comte E. Cais de Pierlas; continué et augmenté d'une étude et de table par Gustave Saige. [Monaco], Impr. de Monaco, 1903.
    xxxii, 549 p. 29 cm.
    MnCS

St. Procopius Abbey, Lisle, Ill.
6300   The abbatial blessing of Rt. Rev. Thomas Havlik, 6th abbot of St. Procopius Abbey, conferred by Most Rev. Romeo Blanchette, June 1, 1971.
    38 p.
    ILSP

6301   Abbey organ dedication, May 21, 1973.
    6 p.
    ILSP

6302   Blessing and dedication of St. Procopius Abbey church and monastery, June 10, 1970.
    62 p.
    ILSP

6303   Home (periodical). 1948–   Weekly.
    InFer; ILSP

6304   News quarterly. 1969–
    InFer (1974–   ); ILSP

6305   The ordination of the Most Reverend Daniel W. Kucera, O.S.B., as titular bishop of Natchez and auxiliary bishop of Joliet, July 21, 1977.
    40 p.
    ILSP

6306   Unionistic Congress. Proceedings . . . 1956–
    v. 23 cm.
    ILSP; MnCS

St. Procopius College, Lisle, Ill. *See also* Illinois Benedictine College, Lisle, Ill.

6307   **St. Procopius College, Lisle, Ill.**
    Annual report of the President.
    KAS

6308   **Saint-Riquier;** études concernant l'Abbaye depuis le huitième siècle jusqu'à la Revolution. [Introduction par Clovis Brunel]. Abbaye de Saint-Riquier, Somme, [1962?–].
    v. 22 cm.
    InStme; PLatS

Saint Saveur, Redon, France. *See* Redon, France. Saint Saveur.

6309   **St. Scholastica Convent, Fort Smith, Ark.**
    Horizons (periodical). 1–   1971–
    InFer; ArFsS

6310   **St. Scholastica High, Chicago, Ill.**
    Thrust (periodical). 1971–
    InFer

St. Scholastica Priory, Chicago, Ill.
6311   Archives newsletter. v. 1–   1978–
    InFer; ICSS

6312   Community in the Spirit; government handbook. 1972.
    34 p.
    Mimeographed.
    ICSS

6313   Community in the Spirit . . . Revision, 1977.
    45 p.
    Mimeographed.
    ICSS

St. Scholastica Priory, Duluth, Minn.
6314   The English Matins of the monastic Breviary according to the Holy Rule of our most holy Father Benedict. For private use of the Benedictine Sisters of Villa St. Scholastica, Duluth, Minn. 1959.
    4 v. 22 cm.
    MnCS; MnDuS

6315   Swinger of birches, 1892–1967. Rejoice with us in peace and love . . . as we celebrate the 75th jubilee of the Benedictine Sisters of Scholastica Priory . . .
    [40] p. illus.
    MnStj; MnDuS

6316   **Saint-Sébastien d'Aignes prés Nantes,** par l'abbé A.R. [Vannes, Imprimerie Lafolye, 1897].

131 p. 25 cm.
KAS

6317 St. Swithun's Priory, Winchester, England.
Compotus rools of the obedientiaries of St. Swithun's Priory, Winchester, from the Winchester Cathedral archives. Transcribed and edited, with an introduction on the organisation of a convent, by G. W. Kitchin. London, Simpkin & Co., 1892.
xiv, 540 p. plans, 23 cm.
InStme

St. Vincent Archabbey, Latrobe, Pa.

6318   The Archabbey directory. Latrobe, Pa., Sept. 1964.
13 p. 23 cm.
Mimeographed.
PLatS

6319   Benedictine confluence (periodical). 1969–
InFer; PLatS

6320   **The Benedictine rite of solemn** profession. Latrobe, Pa., St. Vincent Archabbey, 1938.
[33] p. 2 plates, 23 cm.
Includes an explanation of vows and of the habit and text of the ceremony.
PLatS

6321   Handbuch für die Laienbrüder des Benedictiner Ordens. Beatty, Pa., Archabbey Press, 1918.
[2], xiv, 221 p. 15 cm.
KAS; NcBe; PLatS

6322   Holy Thursday Concelebrated Mass, April 15, 1965, St. Vincent Archabbey Basilica.
[12] p. 22 cm.
PLatS

6323   Holy Week music. By the monks of St. Vincent Archabbey, Latrobe, Pa. Pittsburgh, Pa., Volkwein [1967].
48 p. music. 27 cm.
PLatS

6324   A Jewish colloquy. A project of the National Conference of Christians and Jews and the American Benedictine Academy. Saint Vincent Archabbey, Latrobe, Pa., January 25–28, 1965.
4 leaves, 16 cm.
PLatS

6325   Laymen's retreats, fiftieth anniversary, 1913–1963. Latrobe, Pa., St. Vincent College [1963].
[40] p. illus., ports. 29 cm.
PLatS

6326   Lay retreats, sixtieth anniversary, 1913–1973. Latrobe, Pa., St. Vincent College [1973].

unpaged, illus., ports. 23 cm.
PLatS

6327   Manual for Benedictine Oblates. Edited by monks of St. Vincent Archabbey [4th ed.]. Latrobe, Pa., Saint Vincent Archabbey Press [1962].
139 p. illus. 18 cm.
InStme; MnCS; PLatS

6328   Der Messdiener; oder, Anleitung dem Priester bei der heiligen Messe, Austheilung der heiligen Communion, u.s.w., zu dienen. [Beatty, Pa], Abtei St. Vincenz, 1876.
146 p. 12 cm.
"Compiled by the Benedictine Fathers of St. Vincent's Monastery."–Approbation of the bishop.
KAS

6329   Records, 1846–1966. 1 ft.
In St. Vincent College & Archabbey Libraries (Latrobe, Pa.)
Correspondence, charters, bylaws, minutes, and other documents, relating to St. Vincent Archabbey and St. Vincent College.
PLatS

6330   Regulae genuflectendi, standi, sedendi in choro et a circumstantibus tempore Missae Solemnis. Latrobe, Pa., Typis Archiabbatiae S. Vincentii, 1931.
8 p. 14 cm.
PLatS

6331   The rite of solemn Benedictine profession. Latrobe, Pa., Saint Vincent Archabbey, 1937.
23 p. 22 cm.
PLatS

6332   **St. Vincent Archabbey, Latrobe, Pa. Library.**
[Catalogue]
18 v. in 28. 32 cm.
This is a classified subject catalog, begun about 1900 and continued to about 1940. The entries are all in longhand. There is a corresponding author catalog on cards, first in longhand, later typed. The author cards and the books on the shelves carried the call numbers assigned to each book in the classified book catalog. Call numbers were devised according to a threefold distinction, namely: first, the broad class indicated by a Roman number; then the breakdown by size (F for folios, Q for quartos, O for octavos, D for duodecimos); then arabic numbers assigned consecutively as books were entered under the second breakdown. Example: VIII 0, 1080 means: book no. 1080 among the octavos shelved under Historia Ecclesiastica (VIII).
PLatS

St. Vincent College, Latrobe, Pa.

6333   The government and the individual. Seminar given by Thomas Cornell, Rev. Campion Gavaler, O.S.B. [and] George Baurouth. St. Vincent College, Latrobe, November 9, 1967.
2 reels (7 in.) 2¾ IPS.
PLatS

6334   Hawks versus the doves; the war in Vietnam. Seminar held at St. Vincent College, Latrobe, March 12, 1968.
2 reels (7 in.) 3¾ IPS
PLatS

6335   Saint Vincent College, Latrobe, Pennsylvania [1964] (Descriptive brochure of the school).
16 p. 22 cm.
PLatS

6336   St. Vincent College alumni newsletter.
1-   1955–
PLatS

6337   Study week on Communism, October 4, 1966, Latrobe, St. Vincent College.
6 reels (7 in.) 7½ and 3¾ IPS.
PLatS

6338   Study week on Negritude, March 6–9, 1967. Latrobe, St. Vincent College.
3 reels (7 in.) ¾ IPS
PLatS

6339   Summa doctrinae christianae in usum alumnorum humanioribus studiis operam dantium in Collegio S. Vincentii. Ed. altera. Typis Archiabbatiae S. Vincentii, Pa., 1899.
128 p.
NdRi

6340   **St. Vincent College, Latrobe, Pa. Alumni Association.**
Alumni directory 1965. St. Vincent College, Latrobe, Pa., 1965.
172 p. illus., maps, 23 cm.

St. Vincent College, Latrobe, Pa. Library.

6341   A library for St. Vincent; aims, plans, building. 1955.
[3], 29, [4] p. drawings, 28 cm.
Typescript.
PLatS

6342   The dedication of the Saint Vincent Archabbey and College Library, April 17, 1958.
[20] p. illus., ports. 29 cm.
PLatS

6343   **St. Vincent College, Latrobe, Pa. Music Department.**
Verzeichniss aller Instrumenten u. Musikalien im Kloster St. Vincenti.
[37] p. 32 cm.

Manuscript catalog and inventory in book form, apparently prepared by Joseph Maurice Schwab. Earliest entry is 1849, latest 1859.
Classed arrangement: Messen. Cantica et Choral. Offertorien und Graduale. Predigtlieder und Tantum ergo. Vespern. Litaneien. Nicht kirchliche Musikalien. Piano Forte.
PLatS

6344   **St. Vincent College, Latrobe, Pa. Women's Auxiliary.**
The Women's Auxiliary of St. Vincent College; a short history of the organization together with its constitution and by-laws as submitted for adoption in March, 1944.
14 p. 21 cm.

6345   **The Saint Vincent Community Camerata.**
Phonodisc for 1973, 1974 and 1975. Greensburg, Grubb Associates Recording. Each year: 2 s. 12 in. 33⅓ rpm. Stereo.
PLatS

St. Vincent Seminary, Latrobe, Pa.

6346   Prospectus. Published by the St. Thomas L. & D. Society of St. Vincent Seminary, Pennsylvania. [Beatty, Pa.] St. Vincent Abbey Print., 1891.
32 p. 24 cm.
The St. Thomas Literary and Dialectic Society was organized in 1885.
The Prospectus was prepared with a view to publishing the St. Vincent College Journal.
PLatS

6347   Regulae et monita pro alumnis Seminarii ad Montem Sancti Vincentii. Typis Archiabbatiae St. Vincentii, Pa., 1912.
34 p. 15 cm.
PLatS

St. Walburg's Convent, Covington, Ky.

6348   The challenge; centennial 1859–1959, Benedictine Sisters, S. Walburg Convent, Covington, Kentucky, 1959.
unpaged, illus. 28 cm.
KyCovS; PLatS; PSAS

6349   Constitutions of St. Walburg's Monastery of Benedictine Sisters of Covington. Covington, Ky., 1890.
136 p. 15 cm.
KyCovS; NdRi; PLatS

6350   **Saint-Wandrille, France (Benedictine abbey).**
Revue de chant grégorien. 1–44, 1892–1940.
CaQStB; PLatS

6351   **Sala, Torello, O.S.B.V., 1815–1891.**
Dizionario storico biografico di scrittori, letterati ed artisti del l'Ordine di Vallom-

brosa. Firenze, Tipografia dell'Istituto Gualandi Sordomuti [1929].

2 v. 21 cm.

MnCS

6352 **Salm-Reifferscheidt, Edeltraut zu, Sister.**

Sankt Hildegard, die grosse Jungfrau und Seherin . . . Paderborn, F. Schöningh, 1904.

156 p. plates, 19 cm.

IdCoC; MnCS

Salmon, Pierre, 1896–

6353 L'abbé dans la tradition monastique . . . [Paris] Sirey [1962].

168 p. 20 cm.

KAS; MnCS; PLatS

6354 The abbot in monastic tradition . . . Translated by Claire Lavoie. Washington, Cistercian Publications, Consortium Press, 1972.

xv, 160 p. 23 cm.

InFer; InStme; KAS; MnCS; MoCo; NcBe; PLatS; ViBris

6355 L'ascèse monastique dans les lettres de saint Anselme de Canterbury.

(*In* Spicilegium Beccense. 1959. v. 1, p. 509–520)

PLatS

6356 Un Bréviaire-Missel du XIe siècle; le manuscrit Vatican latin 7018.

(*In* Mélanges Eugéne Tisserant, v. 7, p. 327–343)

PLatS

6357 The Breviary through the centuries. Translated by Sister David Mary. Collegeville, Minn., The Liturgical Press [1962].

103 p. 24 cm.

Translation of: L'office divin.

CaMWiSb; InFer; InStme; MnCS; MnStj; Kas; MoCo; PLatS

6358 Le Lectionnaire de Luxeuil et ses attaches colombaniennes.

(*In* Mélanges colombaniens. Paris, 1950. p. 247–255)

PLatS

6359 Les manuscrits liturgiques latin de la Bibliothéque Vaticane. Città del Vaticano, Biblioteca Apostolica Vaticana, 1968–

v. 25 cm. (Studi e testi, 251, 253, 260)

InStme; PLatS

6360 Mitra und Stab; die Pontifikalinsignien im römischen Ritus. Mainz, Matthias-Grünewald-Verlag [1960].

112 p. plates, 23 cm.

6361 Monastic asceticism and the origins of Citeaux.

(*In* Monastic studies, v. 3, p. 119–138)

Translated by a monk of Gethsemani Abbey, Trappist, Ky.

PLatS

6362 L'Office divin au Moyen Age; histoire de la formation du Bréviaire du IXe au XVIe siècle. Paris, Editions du Cerf, 1967.

199 p. 20 cm.

PLatS

6363 Les origines de la prière des heures d'après le témoignage de Tertullien et de saint Cyprien.

(*In* Mélanges offerts à Mademoiselle Christine Mohrmann. Utrecht, 1963. p. 202–212)

PLatS

6364 Le texte biblique des lectionnaires Mérovingiens.

(*In* La Bibbia nell'alto medioevo. p. 491–517)

PLatS

6365 Testimonia orationis christianae antiquioris. Turnholti, Brepols, 1977.

xxxviii, 217 p. 26 cm. (Corpus Christianorum. Continuatio mediaevalis, 47)

PLatS

Salomo III, bp. of Constance, 860 (ca.)–919.

6366 Salomonis et Waldrammi Carmina.

(*In* Poetae latini aevi carolino. Berolini . . . t. IV(1899) p. 296–314)

KAS(microfilm); MnCS; PLatS

6367 Das Formelbuch des Bischofs Salomo III von Konstanz, aus dem neunten Jahrhundert. Hrsg. und erläutert von Ernst Dümmler. Osnabrück, Otto Zeller, 1964.

xxxvii, 184 p. 24 cm.

Neudruck der Ausgabe 1857.

MnCS

6368 **Salvado, Rosendo,** 1814–1900.

Memorie storiche dell'Australia, particolarmente della missione benedettina di Nuova Norci e degli usu e costumi degli Australiani. Roma, S. Congregazione de Propaganda Fide, 1851.

xii, 388 p. map, 23 cm.

KAS; PLatS

6369 **Salvini, Alphonso.**

Manuale precum sancti Joannis Gualberti. Romae, S. Pauli, 1933.

97 p.

MoCo

Salzburg, Austria. Nonnberg (abbey of Benedictine nuns).

6370 Catalogus codicum manu scriptorum Bibliothecae Regiae Monacensis: Codices 15902–15920 monasterii S. Erentrudis Salisb. Nunbergensis. Monachii, sumptibus Bibliothecae Regiae, 1878. Unveränderter

Nachdruck, Otto Harrassowitz, Wiesbaden, 1969.

MnCH

6371   Chronik des adeligen Benediktiner-Frauen-Stiftes Nonnberg in Salzburg; vom Entstehen desselben bis zum Jahre 1840 aus den Quellen bearbeitet von P. Franz Esterl, aus dem Stifte St. Peter. Salzburg, Franz Xaver Duyle, 1841.

xii, 267 p. 18 cm.

MnCS

6372   Nonnberger Faltstuhl und Hirtenstab vom Jahre 1242. Hrsg. von der Benediktinerabtei Nonnberg in Salzburg. Salzburg, Anton Pustet [n.d.].

32 p. plates, 21 cm.

MnCS

6373   Stift Nonnberg zu Salzburg im Wandel der Zeiten; nach Aufzeichnungen der langjährigen Archivarin Frau M. Regintrudis Reichlin von Meldegg, gest. 1943. Salzburg, Anton Pustet [1953].

88 p. plates, 21 cm.

MnCS

Salzburg, Austria. Sankt Peter (Benedictine abbey).

6374   Antiphonar der Erzabtei St. Peter in Salzburg (Codex Vindobonensis s.n. 2700). Graz, Akademische Druck u. Verlagsanstalt, 1969–1973.

845 p. (issued in 4 parts), illus. 45 cm. (Codices selecti, phototypice impressi, v. 21)

PLatS

6375   Auszug der neuesten Chronick des alten Benediktiner Klosters zu St. Peter in Salzburg . . . Salzburg, Joh. Jos. Mayer, 1782.

2 v. illus.(woodcuts) 20 cm.

KAS

6376   Catalogus religiosorum Ordinis S. P. Benedicti in antiquissimo monasterio ad S. Petrum Salisburgi viventium . . . [Published periodically]

v. size varies.

PLatS

6377   Collectio litterarum abbatum S. Petri Salisburgi: Georgius I, 1435 . . . Latine et germanice. MS. Benediktinerabtei St. Peter, Salzburg, codex b.VII.18a. 735 f. Folio. Saec. 15–16.

Microfilm: MnCH proj. no. 10,621

6378   Kopialbuch von St. Peter in Salzburg. Germanice. MS. Benediktinerabtei St. Peter, Salzburg, Archivium Hs. B 572. 89 f. Quarto. Saec. 14–15.

Microfilm: MnCH proj. no. 11,361

6379   Libellus mortuorum abbatum, fratrum et sororum S. Petri in Salisburga. MS. Benediktinerabtei St. Peter, Salzburg, Archi-

vium Hs. A 247. Octavo. Saec. 16 (1560–1597).

Microfilm: MnCH proj. no. 10,772

6380   Necrologium S. Ruperti Salisburgensis ecclesiae. MS. Benediktinerabtei St. Peter, Salzburg, codex a.IX.7. 78 f. Saec. 11–14.

Microfilm: MnCH proj. no. 10,213

6381   Rotula von St. Peter in Salzburg, 1.März bis 10.Nov., 1503. MS. Benediktinerabtei St. Peter, Salzburg, Archivium A 563/1.

Microfilm: MnCH proj. no. 11,363

6382   Rotula von St. Peter in Salzburg, Jan.–Mai, 1624. MS. Benediktinerabtei St. Peter, Salzburg, Archivium A 563/3.

Microfilm: MnCH proj. no. 11,365

6383   Schulordnung und Schulgesetz von St. Peter in Salzburg: 1575, 1577, 1615. MS. Universitätsbibliothek Salzburg, codex M III 81. 21 f. Folio. Saec. 16–17.

Microfilm: MnCH proj. no. 11,488

6384   Stift- und Anlaitlibelle aller Aemter 1345–1427. MS. Benediktinerabtei St. Peter, Salzburg, Archivium HS B 1223a. 916 f. Folio. Saec. 14–15.

Microfilm: MnCH proj. no. 11,413

6385   Urbar von St. Peter in Salzburg: Teilurbar Oblei, Kalendarium und Urbar 1404, Urbar 1371, "liber quartus decimus urbariorum". MS. Benediktinerabtei St. Peter, Salzburg, Archivium Hs B 120. 70 f. Folio. Saec. 14.

Microfilm: MnCH proj. no. 11,360

6386   Gesamturbar von St. Peter in Salzburg. MS. Benediktinerabtei St. Peter, Salzburg, Archivium HS B 5. 138 f. Folio. Saec. 14.

Microfilm: MnCH proj. no. 11,362

6387   Gesamturbar von St. Peter in Salzburg: "Liber primus urbariorum" "2". MS. Benediktinerabtei St. Peter, Salzburg, Archivium HS B 7. 106 f. Folio. Saec. 15.

Microfilm: MnCH proj. no. 11,359

6388   Gesamturbar von St. Peter in Salzburg: "liber secundus" ca. 1230. MS. Benediktinerabtei St. Peter, Salzburg, Archivium HS B 1. 16 f. Quarto. Saec. 13.

Microfilm: MnCH proj. no. 11,370

6389   Gesamturbar von St. Peter in Salzburg: "liber tercius" 1272–ca.1280. MS. Benediktinerabtei St. Peter, Salzburg, Archivium HS B 3. 16 f. Quarto. Saec. 13.

Microfilm: MnCH proj. no. 11,368

6390   Gesamturbar von St. Peter: Liber quartus ca. 1272. MS. Benediktinerabtei St. Peter, Salzburg, Archivium HS B2. 40 f. Quarto. Saec. 13.

Microfilm: MnCH proj. no. 11,402

6391   Catalogus manuscriptorum cartaceorum in Bibliotheca monasterii ad S. Petrum

Salisburgi extantium (443 codices). MS. Benediktinerabtei St. Peter, Salzburg, codex b.XIV.38. 116, 50 p. Folio. Saec. 18. Microfilm: MnCH proj. no. 10,668

6392   Catalogus manuscriptorum membraneorum in Bibliotheca monasterii ad S. Petrum extantium (453 codices). MS. Benediktinerabtei St. Peter, Salzburg, codex b.XIV.39. 168, 46 p. Folio. Saec. 18. Microfilm: MnCH proj. no. 10,666

6393   [Catalog of manuscripts in Stift St. Peter, Salzburg, Austria. n.d.]
        5 v. 19 cm.
        Handwritten.
        Xeroxed 1969 by University Microfilms, Ann Arbor, Mich.

6394   Catalogus codicum manu scriptorum Bibliothecae Regiae Monacensis: Codices n.15951–15965 Salisburgenses S. Petri. Monachii, sumptibus Bibliothecae Regiae, 1878. Unveränderter Nachdruck, Otto Harrassowitz, Wiesbaden, 1969.
        MnCH

6395   Catalogus librorum editorum ab anno 1500–1600 in bibliotheca antiqua et quidem secundum materiam (18 divisiones) institutus. MS. Benediktinerabtei St. Peter, Salzburg, codex b.XIV.1. 607 p. Folio. Saec. 18.
        Microfilm: MnCH proj. no. 10,672

6395a   **Salzburg, Austria. St. Peter (Benedictine abbey). Archiv. Mss. (A 1).**
        Das Verbrüderungsbuch von St. Peter in Salzburg; vollständige Faksimile-Ausgabe im Originalformat der Handschrift A l aus dem Archiv von St. Peter in Salzburg. Einführung: Karl Forstner. Graz, Akademische Druck- u. Verlagsanstalt, 1974.
        36 p. 39 leaves (facsim.) 40 cm. (Codices selecti phototypice impressi, LI)
        MnCS

6395b   **Salzburg, Austria. Sankt Peter Kolleg.**
        Zur Erinnerung an die Weihe des Benediktiner Kolleges. [Salzburg, Zaurithsche Buchdruckerei, 1926].
        35 p. illus., ports. 30 cm.
        KAS

6396   **Salzgeber, Joachim.**
        Die Klöster Einsiedeln und St. Gallen im Barockzeitalter; historisch-soziologische Studie. Münster i.W., Aschendorff [1967].
        xix, 232 p. 26 cm.
        InStme; KAS; MnCS; PLatS

6397   **Samay, Sebastian,** 1926–
        Reason revisited; the philosophy of Karl Jaspers. [Notre Dame, Ind., University of Notre Dame Press [1971].

xviii, 300 p. 23 cm.
MnCS; NcBe; OkShG; PLatS

San Juan de la Peña, Spain. See Peña, La, Spain. San Juan.

San Lazzaro, Venice, Italy. See Venice, Italy. San Lazzaro.

6398   **Sandeman, Frideswide.**
        Regulae Benedicti studia; annuarium internationale. In Verbindung mit Rudolf Hanslik . . . Frideswide Sandwman, O.S.B. . . . hrsg. von Bernd Jaspert . . . Hildesheim, Verlag Dr. H. A. Gerstenberg, 1972–
        MnCS

Sangrinus, Angelus.

6399   Carminum, de pietate in Deum, divosque, libri III. Recens ab authore recogniti, & castigati, christiano lectori cum suavissimi, tum utilissimi. Venetiis, apud Franciscum Franciscium Senensem, 1570.
        [4], 315 leaves. illus. 23 cm.
        InStme

6400   Speculum et exemplar Christicolarum; vita beatissimi patris Benedicti monachorum patriarchae . . . Romae [ex Typographia Bartholomaei Bonfadini] 1587.
        [14], 246 p. illus. 23 cm.
        InStme; KAS; PLatS

Sankt Andreas, Sarnen, Switzerland. See Sarnen, Switzerland. Sankt Andreas.

Sankt Blasien im Schwarzwald, Germany (Benedictine abbey).

6401   Calendarium cum necrologio monasterii S. Blasii sub abbate Gaspari I. scriptum. MS. Benediktinerabtei St. Paul im Lavanttal, Austria, codex 73/1. 65 f. Folio. Saec. 16.
        Microfilm: MnCH proj. no. 11,714

6402   Catalogus codicum manuscriptorum ex monasteriis S. Blasii in Nigra Silva et Hospitalis ad Pyrhum montem in Austria nunc in monast.S. Pauli in Carinthia.
        [113], 30 p. 29 cm.
        Handwritten.
        Xeroxed by University Microfilms, Ann Arbor, Mich., 1969.
        MnCS

6403   Catalogus numismatum imperialium Romanorum gazophylacii S. Blasii. MS. Benediktinerabtei St. Paul im Lavanttal, Austria, codex 84/6. 518 p. Folio. Saec. 18(1782–84).
        Microfilm: MnCH proj. no. 12,627

6404   Catalogus über die von St. Blasien im Schwarzwalde, nach St. Paul im Lavanttale übertragenen Urkunden. Archiv St. Paul. Saec. 19.

Handwritten.
Xeroxed by University Microfilms, Ann Arbor, Mich., 1969.
MnCS

6405 Codex diplomaticus, oder Copyen-Buch enthältend die Briefe und Urkunden aller S. Blasischen Aemter. Scriptum sub Heinrico IV. abbate. MS. Benediktinerabtei St. Paul im Lavanttal, Austria, codex 46/1. [20], 569 p. Folio. Saec. 14.
Microfilm: MnCH proj. no. 11,705

6406 Constitutiones monasticae pro religiosis fratribus principalis et imperalis Monasterii et Congregationis S. Blasii in Silva Nigra . . . adprobatae anno 1784. MS. Benediktinerabtei St. Paul im Lavanttal, Austria, codex 70/6. 53 p. Folio. Saec. 18.
Microfilm: MnCH proj. no. 12,611

6407 Constitutiones Monasterii et Congregationis S. Blasii. MS. Benediktinerabtei St. Paul im Lavanttal, Austria, codex 221/2. 361 f. Folio. Saec. 18.
Microfilm: MnCH proj. no. 12,024

6408 Diarium monasterii S. Blasii in Silva Nigra de annos 1650-1657. MS. Benediktinerabtei St. Paul im Lavanttal, Austria, codex 154/2 et 155/2. 327 et 110 f. Folio. Saec. 17.
Microfilm: MnCH proj. no. 11,924

6409 Diplomata Helvetica pro monasterio S. Blasii de annos 1200-1402. Benediktinerabtei St. Paul im Lavanttal, Austria, codex 102/2. 303 f. Folio. Saec. 17.
Microfilm: MnCH proj. no. 11,874

6410 Gesänge zu den Festen. MS. Benediktinerabtei St. Paul im Lavanttal, Austria, codex 145/6. 250 f. Octavo. Saec. 18.
Microfilm: MnCH proj. no. 12,634

6411 Kopien-Buch enthältend die von Kaisern, Königen und Erzherzogen erhaltenen Privilegie und Gnadenbriefe 1545, fortgesettzt bis 1613. MS. Benediktinerabtei St. Paul im Lavanttal, Austria, codex 103/2. 129 f. Folio. Saec. 16.
Microfilm: MnCH proj. no. 11,876

6412 Kopien-Buch enthältend die päpstlichen und bischöflichen Briefe und Privilegie de annis 1100-1505. MS. Benediktinerabtei St. Paul im Lavanttal, Austria, codex 99/2. 68 f. Folio. Saec. 16.
Microfilm: MnCH proj. no. 11,872

6413 Kopien-Buch enthältend die Privilegie ss. pontificum, legatorum et episcoporum saec. XI-XVI. MS. Benediktinerabtei St. Paul im Lavanttal, Austria, codex 100/2. 441 p. Folio. Saec. 18.
Microfilm: MnCH proj. no. 11,873

6414 Liber annalium scriptus sub abbate S. Blasii Casparo I., continens calendarium cum inscriptione anniversariorum. MS. Benediktinerabtei St. Paul im Lavanttal, Austria, codex 89/1. 63 f. Folio. Saec. 16.
Microfilm: MnCH proj. no. 11,825

6415 Liber copiarum omnium privilegiorum, immunitatum, tratiarum, etc. ab imperatoribus, regibus, archiducibus Austriae abbatibus et monsaterio S. Blasii concessorum ab Ottone II. usque ad Carolum VI. MS. Benediktinerabtei St. Paul im Lavanttal, Austria, codex 19/6. 717 p. Folio. Saec. 18.
Microfilm: MnCH proj. no. 12,583

6416 Monumenta typographica in bibliotheca San-Blasiana. MS. Benediktinerabtei St. Paul im Lavanttal, Austria, codex 122/6. 261 f. Folio. Saec. 18.
Microfilm: MnCH proj. no. 12,621

6417 Necrologium abbatum et fundatorum atque benefactorum monasterii S. Blasii, . . . 1595. MS. Benediktinerabtei St. Paul im Lavanttal, Austria, Urkunden St. Blasien 130. 22 f. Folio. Saec. 16.
Microfilm: MnCH proj. no. 12,382

6418 Necrologium monasterii S. Blasii ex cod. bibliothecae Vindobonensi saeculi XII. MS. Benediktinerabtei St. Paul im Lavanttal, Austria, codex 94/2, pars V. Folio. Saec. 18.
Microfilm: MnCH proj. no. 11,867

6419 Necrologium San-Blasianum de annis 964-1638. MS. Benediktinerabtei St. Paul im Lavanttal, Austria, codex 210/2, pars I. Folio. Saec. 18.
Microfilm: MnCH proj. no. 12,033

6420 Necrologium San-Blasianum ab annis 1597-1800. MS. Benediktinerabtei St. Paul im Lavanttal, Austria, codex 123/2. 138 f. Folio. Saec. 18.
Microfilm: MnCH proj. no. 11,898

6421 Nomina patrum et fratrum Congregationis S. Blasii 1669-1698 et seq. MS. Benediktinerabtei St. Paul im Lavanttal, Austria, codex 257/2. 2 vols. Duodecimo. Saec. 17.
Microfilm: MnCH proj. no. 12,108-09

6422 Ordo visitandi patres monasterii S. Blasii in Silva Nigra extra conventum degentes. MS. Benediktinerabtei St. Paul im Lavanttal, Austria, codex 67/6. 32 f. Octavo. Saec. 17(1694).
Microfilm: MnCH proj. no. 12,613

6423 Privilegia summorum pontificum et episcoporum pro monasterio S. Blasii de annis 1046-1698. MS. Benediktinerabtei St. Paul im Lavanttal, Austria, codex 101/2. 371 f. Folio. Saec. 18.
Microfim: MnCH proj. no. 11,879

6424 Professurkunden aus St. Blasien im Schwarzwald, 1517–1676. MS. Benediktinerabtei St. Paul im Lavanttal, Austria, codex 62/6. 168 f. Quarto. Saec. 16–17.
Microfilm: MnCH proj. no. 12,601

6425 Statuta monastica. MS. Benediktinerabtei St. Paul im Lavanttal, Austria, codex 68/6. 123 f. Folio. Saec. 17–18.
Microfilm: MnCH proj. no. 12,596

Sankt Emmeram, Regensburg. *See* Regensburg, Germany. Sankt Emmeram.

Sankt Georgen am Langsee, Austria (abbey of Benedictine nuns)

6426 Kopialbuch. Latine et germanice. MS. Klagenfurt, Austria, Kärntner Landesarchiv, codex GV 2/28. 163 f. Folio. Saec. 18.
Microfilm: MnCH proj. no. 12,735

6427 Regesten. Germanice. Nach einem Kopialbuch. MS. Klagenfurt, Austria, Kärntner Landesarchiv, codex GV 9/35, 22 f. Folio. Saec. 19.
Microfilm: MnCH proj. no. 12,868

6428 Urbar, MS. Klagenfurt, Austria, Kärntner Landesarchiv, codex GV 2/18. 91 f. Folio. Saec. 15–17.
Microfilm: MnCH proj. no. 12,746

6429 Verzeichnis der für die Hofbibliothek ausgewählten Urkunden des Stiftes St. Georgen am Langsee. MS. Kärntner Landesarchiv, Klagenfurt, Austria, codex GV 9/36. 22 f. Folio. Saec. 19.
Microfilm: MnCH proj. no. 12,869

6430 Verzeichnis von Urkunden des Stiftes St. Georgen a. L. Germanice. MS. Klagenfurt, Austria, Kärntner Landesarchiv, codex GV 9/37. 26 f. Folio. Saec. 16(1515).
Microfilm: MnCH proj. no. 12,867

Sankt Georgenberg, Austria. *See* Fiecht, Austria.

Sankt Lambert, Altenburg, Austria. *See* Altenburg, Austria.

Sankt Lambrecht, Austria (Benedictine abbey).

6431 Die beiden ältesten Todtenbücher des Benedictinerstiftes St. Lambrecht in Obersteierm. Mitgetheilt von Mathias Pangerl. Wien, Kaiserlich-Königliche Hof- und Staatsdruckerei, 1869.
345 p. 24 cm.
KAS

6432 Catalogus religiosorum Ordinis S. P. Benedicti antiquissimi monasterii ad S. Lambertum in Styria Superiori . . .
v. 27 cm.
PLatS

6433 Necrologium vetustius monasterii S. Lamberti. MS. Universitätsbibliothek Graz, Austria, codex 325, f.106r–137r. Folio. Saec. 12.
Microfilm: MnCH proj. no. 26,219

6434 Necrologium recentius monasterii S. Lamberti. MS. Universitätsbibliothek Graz, Austria, codex 391, f.44v–74v. Folio. Saec. 15.
Microfilm: MnCH proj. no. 26,575

Sankt Matthias, Trier, Germany. *See* Trier, Germany. Sankt Matthias.

Sankt Paul im Lavanttal, Austria (Benedictine abbey).

6435 Album Benedictino-San-Paulense, in quo monachi S. Pauli ad novitiatum et professionem admissorum . . . nomina, aetates, patriae describuntur. MS. Benediktinerabtei St. Paul, Austria, codex 32/0. 224 f. Folio. Saec. 17(1682).
Microfilm: MnCH proj. no. 12,660

6436 Archivum. MS.Benediktinerabtei St. Paul im Lavanttal, Austria, codex 16/0. 12 vols. Folio. Saec. 17.
Microfilm: MnCH proj. no. 12,622–

6437 Archivum, registratum per Hieronymum abbatem anno 1618. Benediktinerabtei St. Paul im Lavanttal, Austria, codex 17/0. 103 f. Folio. Saec. 17.
Microfilm: MnCH proj. no. 12,650

6438 Catalogus d. d. religiosorum Ordinis S. Benedicti monasterii ad S. Paulum in dioecesi Gurcensi et valle Lavantina Carinthiae. Clagenfurti, Typis Joannis & Friderici Leon.
v. 22 cm.
PLatS

6439 Catalogus librorum in bibliotheca monasterii S. Pauli. MS. Benediktinerabtei St. Paul im Lavanttal, Austria, codex 18/0. 51 f. Folio. Saec. 17(1684).
Microfilm: MnCH proj. no. 12,654

6440 Directorium cultus divini et disciplinae monasticae in monasterio S. Pauli . . . auctore Hieronymo abbate. MS. Benediktinerabtei St. Paul im Lavanttal, Austria, codex 28/0. 359 p. Folio. Saec. 17(1624).
Microfilm: MnCH proj. no. 12,640

6441 Index archivii monasterii S. Pauli noviter compilatus ab Alberto abbate S. Pauli. MS. Benediktinerabtei St. Paul im Lavanttal, Austria, codex 19/0. 523 f. Folio. Saec. 17(1686).
Microfilm: MnCH proj. no. 12,678

6442 Liber fundatorum, fundationum benefactorumque monasterii S. Pauli, conscriptus circa a.d. 1210 auctore Udalrico abbate S. Pauli. MS. Benediktinerabtei St. Paul im Lavanttal, Austria, codex 2/0. 25 f. Folio. Saec. 13.
Microfilm: MnCH proj. no. 12,522

6443   Uebergangsinventar der Religiosen Fondsherrschaft an die Benediktiner von Spital am Pyhrn, 1809. MS. Klagenfurt, Austria, Kärntner Landesarchiv, Allgemeine Handschriftensammlung 359. 388 f. Saec. 19.
Microfilm: MnCH proj. no. 12,923

6444   Urkunden-Copien. MS. Benediktinerabtei St. Paul im Lavanttal, Austria, codex 61/2. 12 vols. Folio. Saec. 18.
Microfilm: MnCH proj. no. 11,816–

6445   Urkunden von St. Paul. Nr. 1–1650. MS. Benediktinerabtei St. Paul im Lavanttal, Austria, Urkunden.
Microfilm: MnCH proj. no. 12,423–27

Sant Cugat, Vallès, Spain. *See* Vallès, Spain. Sant Cugat.

6446   **Santa Cruz de la Serós, Spain (Benedictine convent).**
Cartulario de Santa Cruz de la Serós [por] Antonio Ubieto Arteta. Valencia, 1966.
[127] p. 22 cm. (Textos medievales, 19)
PLatS

Santa Maria, Tremiti, Italy. *See* Tremiti, Italy. Santa Maria.

Santo Domingo, Silos, Spain. *See* Silos, Spain. Santo Domingo.

Santo Toribio, Liébana, Spain. *See* Liébana, Spain. Santo Toribio.

6447   **Sao Paulo, Brazil. Mosteiro de S. Bento.**
Sterbechronik des hochwürdigsten Herrn Abtes Dom Miguel Kruse, O.S.B. 1929.
36 p. 23 cm.
MnCS; NdRi

6448   **Sao Paulo, Brazil. Santa Maria (abbey of Benedictine nuns).**
The blessing of the first Abbess of Santa Maria in S. Paulo.
27 p.
MnStj(Archives)

6449   **Sapp, Mary John, Sister.**
Resident satisfaction in Saint Benedict Nursing Home, San Antonio, Texas.
Thesis (M.S.)–Trinity University, San Antonio, Tex., 1972.
Typescript.
TxB

6450   **Sarach, Rupert,** 1943–
Festschrift zum 600jährigen Weihejubiläum der Klosterkirche Ettal. Ettal, Buch-Kunstverlag, 1970.
251 p. illus. 24 cm.
MnCS

6451   **Sarnen, Switzerland. St. Andreas (Benedictine convent).**
Catalog des Benedictinerinnen-Klosters St. Andreas in Sarnen (Obwalden) und

seiner Filiale in Amerika. Sarnen, Druck von Jos. Müller, 1888.
12 p. 16 cm.
PLatS

6452   **Sartore, Placidus,** d. 1809.
Ueber die Flucht und Rückkehr der Kirchenhirten, veranlasset durch die französische Staatsumwälzung zu Ende des achtzehnten Jahrhunderts mit steter Rücksicht auf die gallikanische Kirche. Augsburg, N. Doll, 1804.
3 v. 20 cm.
InStme

Sartory, Thomas Aquinas, 1925–
6453   Die Eucharistie im Verständnis der Konfessionen. Recklinghausen, Paulus Verlag [1961].
463 p. 21 cm.
InStme; MnCS; MoCo

6454   Gespräch zwischen den Konfessionen [von] Hans Asmussen [und] Thomas Sartory. [Frankfurt am Main], Fischer Bücherei [1959].
223 p. 18 cm.
MnCS

6455   Mut zur Katholizität; geistliche und theologische Erwägungen zur Einigung der Christen. Salzburg, Otto Müller Verlag [1962].
475 p. 21 cm.
MnCS

6456   A new interpretation of faith. Translated by Martha Schmidt. Westminster, Md., Newman Press [1968].
94 p. 21 cm.
InStme

6457   The oecumenical movement and the unity of the Church. Translated by Hilda C. Graef. Westminster, Md., Newman Press, 1963.
xx, 290 p. 23 cm.
InFer; InStme; KAS; MnCS; MoCo; PLatS

6458   Um die Einheit im Glauben. Recklinghausen, Paulus Verlag [1962].
32 p. 16 cm.
MnCS

6459   **Sasse, Margaret, Sister.**
The Eucharist, sign and source of Christian community.
14 p. 28 cm.
Paper for M.S., St. John's University, Collegeville, Minn., 1977.
Typescript.

6460   **Sattler, Magnus.**
Kurze Geschichte der Benedictiner-Abtei von Altdorf. Strassburg, E. Bauer, 1887.
280 p. illus. 22 cm.
InStme

6461   (ed) Jocham, Magnus. Memoiren eines Obskuranten; eine Selbstbiographie von Dr. Magnus Jocham . . . Nach dem Tode des Verfassers hrsg. von P. Magnus Sattler, O.S.B. Kempten, Jos. Kösel, 1896.
vi, 851 p. illus. 19 cm.
InStme

6462   **Sauer, Marion, Sister,** 1929–
A study of 100 medication errors in a 300-bed general hospital to discover kinds and causes of these errors.
55 p. 28 cm.
Thesis (M.S.)–Saint Louis University, 1961.
Typescript.
MnStj(Archives)

6463   **Sauer, Walter.**
Die Wappen der Wiener Schotten, von Ales Zelenka und Walter Sauer, O.S.B. Wien, Schottenstift, 1971.
40 p. illus. 20 cm.
MnCS

Sause, Bernard Austin, 1901–1975.

6464   The church year and home life. Atchison, Abbey Student Press, 1941.
MdRi

6465   How the general decree (March 23, 1955) of the Sacred Congregation of Rites on the simplification of rubrics affects the Benedictines of the American Cassinese Congregation. Complete text translated, with brief commentary. [Atchison, Kans., 1955].
34 leaves, 28 cm.
KAS

6466   The rite of monastic profession. [Atchison, Kans., St. Benedict's Abbey, 1962].
Reprint from; Benedictine review, v. 18(1962), p. 20–52)
KAS; MoCo; PLatS

6467   Some liturgical means for fostering faith within the parish.
(*In* Proceedings of the liturgical week held for priests at St. Benedict's Abbey, Atchison, Kansas, May 8–11, 1944. p. 30–39)
PLatS

6468   (ed) Constitution of the Congregation of the Sisters of Saint Joseph of Concordia. [n.p., 1940?].
2 v. 28 cm.
Latin and English manuscript in separate volumes.
Drawn up and translated by Bernard Sause, O.S.B.
KAS

6469   (ed and tr) Wolter, Maurus. The principles of monasticism. Translated, edited, and annotated by Bernard A. Sause, O.S.B. St. Louis, Herder, 1962.

xx, 789 p. 24 cm.
ILSP; InStme; MnCS; MnStj; PLatS

Sauter, Benedikt, 1835–1908.

6470   Lenten sermons. From the German . . . by J. F. Timmins. 4th ed. New York, F. Pustet [1897].
43 p. 23 cm.
PLatS

6471   Die Sonntagsschule des Herrn; oder, Die Sonn- und Feiertagsevangelien des Kirchenjahrs. 2., verb. Aufl. Freiburg i.B., Herder, 1909–11.
2 v. 20 cm.
NdRi; PLatS

6472   **Savannah. Ga. Sacred Heart Priory.**
Dedication: Sacred Heart Priory and Benedictine Military School, April 30, 1964.
unpaged.
NcBe

6473   **Savaton, Augustin,** 1878–
Valeurs fondamentales du monachisme. [Paris], Mame, [1962].
138 p. 18 cm.
MnCS; MoCo; PLatS

Schaaf, Anselm, 1884–1977.

6474   Ascetical theology outline. St. Meinrad, Ind., St. Meinrad Seminary [1941?]
260 p. 28 cm.
Privately printed.
InStme; MnCS; PLatS

6475   Ascetical (mystical) theology outlines. 191 outlines. Compiled by V. Rev. Anselm Schaaf, O.S.B. St. Meinrad, Ind., Grail Publication [1954].
2 v. 28 cm.
InStme; KAS; KySu

6476   Pastoral guide for marriage instructions. [St. Meinrad, Ind., Grail, 1963].
vii, 28 p. 28 cm.
InStme; MoCo

6477   The Psalms; a brief introduction and exegesis. [St. Meinrad, Ind.], Abbey Press, 1919.
88 columns, 28 cm.
InStme; KySu

6478   The Psalms; an explanation of Psalms 1 & 2 according to the interpretation of the Fathers and later Catholic authorities. St. Meinrad, Ind., Abbey Press [c 1922].
144 cols. 27 cm.
InStme; KySu; PLatS

6479   **Schäfer, Bernhard.**
Beuroner Benedictiner-Congregation, 50 Jähriges Jubiläum. Hechingen. Press-Verein, 1913.
19 p.
AStb

6480 **Schäftlarn, Bavaria (Benedictine abbey).**
Catalogus codicum manu scriptorum Bibliothecae Regiae Monacensis: Codices 17001–17320 ex monasterio in Scheftlarn. Monachii, sumptibus Bibliothecae Regiae, 1878. Unveränderter Nachdruck Otto Harrassowitz, Wiesbaden, 1969.
MnCH

6481 **Schamel, Johann Martin.**
Historische Beschreibung des vormahls berümten Benedictiner-Klosters zu Memleben in Thüringen . . . Naumburg, Joh. Chr. Martini, 1729.
[93]–188 p. 21 cm.
KAS

6482 **Schappler, Norbert,** 1926–
Summation of the replies to a questionnaire on the Catholic major seminary library. River Forest, Ill., Rosary College, Department of Library Science, 1954.
15 p. 2 appendices.
MoCo

6483 **Schapperger, Desiderius,** d. 1698.
Speculum theologicum, circa varia praeceptorum genera, selectis, ac perutilibus illustratum quaestionibus, et in alma archiepiscopali Universitate Salisburgensi praeside P. Desiderio Schapperger . . . publico certamini expositum a p. Aegidio Pemesperger, Ord. S. Bened. Salisburgi, Joan. Bapt. Mayr, 1663.
404 p. 13 cm.
PLatS

6484 **Schaut, Quentin Lemar,** 1900–
Chaucer's pardoner and indulgences. (*In* Greyfriar lectures, 1961. p. 25–39)
PLatS

6485 **Scheessele, Mary Kenneth, Sister.**
Handbook of archival policies and procedures; brief history and listing of major collections of the archives of the Sisters of St. Benedict, Convent of the Immaculate Conception, Ferdinand, Indiana.
25 p. 28 cm.
Typescript.
InFer

6486 Science material in the library. Prepared by Sister M. Kenneth Scheessele, O.S.B., and Sister Mary Walter Goebel, O.S.B.
23 p. 28 cm.
Paper given at the meeting of the Library Science Section of the American Benedictine Academy.
PLatS

6487 Sisters of St. Benedict, Marian Heights Academy, Ferdinand, Indiana, SISWA award 1975–76. An American bicentennial project.
33 p. 28 cm.

Consists of 11 biographical sketches.
Typescript.
InFer

6488 Sisters of St. Benedict, St. Joseph Hospital, Huntingburg, Indiana, SISWA award, 1975–1976. An American bicentennial project.
33 p. 28 cm.
Consists of biographical sketches of 13 women.
Typescript.
InFer

6489 Sisters of St. Benedict, Convent of the Immaculate Conception, Ferdinand, Indiana, SISWA award 1975–1976. An American bicentennial project.
130 p. 28 cm.
Consists of 57 biographical sketches.
Typescript.
InFer

6490 Special classification schedule for 200's in a Catholic library. Adaptation of the Dewey 200's (religion) done for the library of the Convent of the Immacualte Conception, Ferdinand, Indiana, by Sister Mary Kenneth Scheessele and Sister Angela Sasse, O.S.B.
14 p. 28 cm.
Typescript.
InFer

6491 **Scheiwiler, Iso,** 1912–
Die religiöse Erziehung des ausserehelichen Kindes nach schweizerischen Privatrecht. Wil, J. Meyerhans, 1959.
xiv, 152 p. 24 cm.
Diss. – Freiburg, Schweiz.
MnCS; PLatS

6492 **Scheiwiller, Otmar,** 1884–
Das "reiche" Kloster Einsiedeln; ein offenes Wort ans Schweizervolk, Einsiedeln, Meinrad-Verlag, 1949.
48 p. 21 cm.
MnCS

6493 **Scheller, LaVerne, Sister.**
Life in a German and American culture; a biographical sketch of Sister Maria Goeltl, O.S.B.
14 p. 28 cm.
A graduate research paper, University of Evansville, Ind., 1977.
Typescript.
InFer

Schenk, Theresita, Sister, 1920–
6494 Antiphons and responsories for the Liturgy of the Hours. Musical arrangement by Sister Theresita Schenk, O.S.B., at the Convent of the Immaculate Conception, Ferdinand, Ind. 1969–
InFer

6495 Mass in honor of Mary Immaculate. Composed by Sister Theresita Schenk, O.S.B. 1975.
Score of 4 pages, for unison voices.
InFer

6496 **Schenker, Lukas,** 1937–
Das Benediktinerkloster Beinwil im 12. und 13. Jahrhundert . . . Solothurn, Gassmann, 1973.
157 p. 23 cm.
Thesis–Universität Fribourg, 1971.
MnCS

Schenkl, Maurus, 1749–1816.
6497 Institutiones juris ecclesiastici Germaniae imprimis, et Bavariae accommodatae. Coloniae, Jon. Georg Schmitz, 1815.
2 v. 19 cm.
PLatS

6498 Theologiae pastoralis systema. De novo recognitum emendatum atque adauctum a Joan. Georgio Wesselack. Ed. 4. Ratisbonae, G. J. Manz, 1859.
xii, 440 p. 22 cm.
KAS; OrStb; PLatS

6499 **Scherer, Michael Emilio,** 1889–
Ein grosser Benediktiner, Abt Michael Kruse von São Paulo (1864–1929). München, Bayer. Benediktinerakademie, 1963.
180 p. illus., plates, ports. 24 cm.
MnCS; NdRi; PLatS

Scheyern, Bavaria (Benedictine abbey)
6500 Catalogus codicum manu scriptorum Bibliothecae Regiae Monacensis: Codices 17401–17524 monasterii Schirensis (B. Mariae in comitatu Scheyern). Monachii, sumptibus Bibliothecae Regiae, 1878. Unveränderter Nachdruck Otto Harrassowitz, Wiesbaden, 1969.
MnCH

6501 Die Schriften des Johannes von Damaskos. Hrsg. vom Byzantinischen Institut der Abtei Scheyern. Berlin, W. de Gruyter, 1969–
v. 24 cm. (Patristische Texte und Studien, Bd. 7, 12)
InStme; PLatS

6502 **Scheyven, Daniel,** 1909–
La confirmation, doctrine et pastorale. Par B. Luykx et D. Scheyven. Bruges, Abbaye de Saint-André, 1958.
72 p. 24 cm.
PLatS

6503 **Schidler, Stephen,** 1923–
In the beginning it was something like this at Blue Cloud Abbey; or, The Blue Cloud blues. [The author] 1978.
251 p. illus. 28 cm.

A chronicle of the early years (1950–1963) of Blue Cloud Abbey, Marvin, South Dakota.
InStme

6504 **Schieber, Joachim,** 1919–
Father James Power and the Reading Colony from Reading, Pennsylvania, to Conception, Missouri.
v, 87 p. 28 cm.
Thesis–Catholic University of America, 1953.
MoCo

6505 **Schildenberger, Johannes,** 1896–
Literarische Arten der Geschichtsschreibung im Alten Testament. Einsiedeln, Benziger Verlag [1964].
67 p. 21 cm.
MnCS

Schirber, Martin Edward, 1907–
6506 The Bahama missions.
Reprint from: The American Benedictine review, v. 9(1958).
MnCS

6507 An overall economic development plan for Sherburne County, Minnesota. Elk River, Minn., Sherburne County Agricultural Extension Service Office, 1968.
104 p. map, tables, 28 cm.
Multilithed.
MnCS

6508 Scoreboard; a history of athletics of Saint John's University, Collegeville, Minnesota. Written and compiled by Dunstan Tucker, O.S.B., and Martin Schirber, O.S.B. Collegeville, Minn., St. John's University Press [c 1979].
444 p. illus. 20 cm.
MnCS

6509 What's happening to the dollar? [Phonotape-cassette]. Collegeville, 1974.
1 cassette
Recorded at St. John's University, May 11, 1974: Alumni College Day.
MnCS

6510 **Schirmann, Coelestin.**
Tractatus de Deo uno. MS. Benediktinerabtei St. Paul im Lavanttal, Austria, codex 304/4. 129 f. Quarto. Saec. 18(1762).
Microfilm: MnCH proj. no. 12,552

6511 **Schirmer, Loretta, Sister.**
A resume of the literature related to factors affecting the tenderness of certain beef muscles, by D. L. Harrison, Rosemary [and] Sister Loretta Schirmer. Manhattan, Kans., Ag. Experiment Station, 1959.
80 p. 28 cm.
KAS

6512 **Schlibnig, Bruno.**
Philosophia rationalis, seu Logica Aristotelico-thomistica. MS. Universitätsbibliothek Salzburg, codex M I 302. 359 f.
Quarto. Saec. 17 (1685).
Microfilm: MnCH proj. no. 11,082

6513 **Schlimm, Chrysostom Vincent,** 1934–
The syntax of the cases and prepositions in Seneca, Epistulae morales xxx–xlvii.
xii, 90 p. 28 cm.
Thesis (M.A.)–Catholic University of America, 1964.
Typescript.
PLatS

Schlitpacher, Joannes, 1403–1482.

6514 Abbreviatio vitae S. Benedicti excerpta ex II. Dialogorum. Metrice. MS. Benediktinerabtei Melk, Austria, codex 662, f.139r–140v. Quarto. Saec. 15.
Microfilm: MnCH proj. no. 1532

6515 Articuli propositi tempore tentatae reformationis monasterii Gottwicensis, anno 1450. MS. Benediktinerabtei Göttweig, Austria, codex 496b, f.1r–8r. Quarto. Saec. 15.
Microfilm: MnCH proj. no. 3748

6516 Avizatio praelatorum. MS. Benediktinerabtei Melk, Austria, codex 1653, f.143r–147v. Sextodecimo. Saec. 15.
Microfilm: MnCH proj. no. 2011

6517 Biblia metrica. MS. Benediktinerabtei Melk, Austria, codex 1558, f.160r–200r. Duodecimo. Saec. 15.
Microfilm: MnCH proj. no. 1960

6518 Biblia metrica, i.e., universa Sacra Scriptura versibus hexametris comprehensa. MS. Benediktinerabtei Melk, Austria, codex 267, f.1–230. Octavo. Saec. 15.
Microfilm: MnCH proj. no. 1295

6519 Biblia metrica, cum prologo. MS. Vienna, Nationalbibliothek, codex 3570, f.1r–28r. Octavo. Saec. 15.
Microfilm: MnCH proj. no. 16,791

6520 Breve carmen hexametro versu in laudem professorum quorundam Universitatis Viennis. MS. Benediktinerabtei Melk, Austria, codex 662, f.105r. Quarto. Saec. 15.
Microfilm: MnCH proj. no. 1532

6521 Brevis collectura de principalibus punctis philosophiae naturalis, 1469. MS. Benediktinerabtei Melk, Austria, codex 91, f.181–192. Duodecimo. Saec. 15.
Microfilm: MnCH proj. no. 1170

6522 Brevis praeparatio sacerdotis ad Missam. MS. Benediktinerabtei Melk, Austria, codex 1093, f.409–416. Duodecimo. Saec. 15.
Microfilm: MnCH proj. no. 1846.

6523 Brevis praeparatio sacerdotis celebrare volentis Missam. MS. Benediktinerabtei Melk, Austria, codex 1650, f.244v–252r. Sextodecimo. Saec. 15.
Microfilm: MnCH proj. no. 1999

6524 [Carmina]
Carmen in honorem beatae Mariae Virginis. Carmen pro laude virginis gloriosae. Carmen de S. Barbara virgine et martyre. Oratio de Sancta Anna. Alia de Sancta Maria. MS. Benediktinerabtei Melk, Austria, codex 1391, f.484–489. Duodecimo. Saec. 15.
Microfilm: MnCH proj. no. 1912

6525 Carmen. Incipit: Omnem diphtongum. MS. Benediktinerabtei Melk, Austria, codex 1221, f.279–   Sextodecimo. Saec. 15.
Microfilm: MnCH proj. no. 1869

6526 Carmen acrostichum versu hexametro in laudem Ladislai regis Bohemiae, ducis Austriae. MS. Benediktinerabtei Melk, Austria, codex 662, f.153v. Quarto. Saec. 15.
Microfilm: MnCH proj. no. 1532

6527 Carmen versibus 14 distans, in laudem doctorum suo tempore virorum. MS. Benediktinerabtei Melk, Austria, codex 662, f.141r. Quarto. Saec. 15.
Microfilm: MnCH proj. no. 1532

6528 Carta visitatorum monasterii S. Petri. MS. Benediktinerabtei St. Peter, Salzburg, codex b.XI.19, f.30r–36v. Folio. Saec. 15.
Microfilm: MnCH proj. no. 10,671

6529 Claviger Psalterii. MS. Benediktinerabtei Melk, Austria, codex 960, f.45–122. Quarto. Saec. 15.
Microfilm: MnCH proj. no. 1775

6530 Claviger Psalterii. MS. Benediktinerabtei Melk, Austria, codex 1381, f.1–235. Duodecimo. Saec. 15.
Microfilm: MnCH proj. no. 1904

6531 Collatio in Ascensione Domini. MS. Benediktinerabtei Melk, Austria, codex 1561, p.416–425. Duodecimo. Saec. 15.
Microfilm: MnCH proj. no. 1962

6532 Collatio in Coena Domini, anno 1473. MS. Benediktinerabtei Melk, Austria, codex 1075, f.308–313. Duodecimo. Saec. 15.
Microfilm: MnCH proj. no. 1833

6533 Collatio in Coena Domini. MS. Benediktinerabtei Melk, Austria, codex 1561, p. 396–404. Duodecimo. Saec. 15.
Microfilm: MnCH proj. no. 1962

6534 Collatio in die Corporis Christi. MS. Benediktinerabtei Melk, Austria, codex 1075, f.287–299. Duodecimo. Saec. 15.
Microfilm: MnCH proj. no. 1833

6535 Collatio in die Paschae. MS. Benediktinerabtei Melk, Austria, codex 1561, p. 408–415. Duodecimo. Saec. 15.
Microfilm: MnCH proj. no. 1962

6536 Collatio in festo Pentecostes, anno 1470. MS. Benediktinerabtei Melk, Austria, codex 1075, f.337–344. Duodecimo. Saec. 15.
Microfilm: MnCH proj. no. 1833

6537 Collatio in festo Purificationis S. Mariae virginis, anno 1474. MS. Benediktinerabtei Melk, Austria, codex 1075, f.301–308. Duodecimo. Saec. 15.
Microfilm: MnCH proj. no. 1833

6538 Collatio facta Gotwici 1468. MS. Benediktinerabtei Melk, Austria, codex 1075, f.345–350. Duodecimo. Saec. 15.
Microfilm: MnCH proj. no. 1833

6539 Collatio seu sermo in capite jejunii. MS. Benediktinerabtei Melk, Austria, codex 1839, f.39r–46v. Duodecimo. Saec. 15.
Microfilm: MnCH proj. no. 2149

6540 Collectio ascetico-theologica ex diversis auctoribus. MS. Benediktinerabtei Melk, Austria, codex 1561, p.426–433. Duodecimo. Saec. 15.
Microfilm: MnCH proj. no. 1962

6541 Commentarius in Regulam S. Benedicti. MS. Benediktinerabtei Lambach, Austria, codex chart. 253. 335 f. Saec. 15.
Microfilm: MnCH proj. no. 634

6542 Commentarius in Regulam S. Benedicti, cum indice rerum praemisso. MS. Vienna, Nationalbibliothek, codex 3813. 477 f. Quarto. Saec. 15.

6543 Commentarium in universam Regulam S. Benedicti. MS. Benediktinerabtei Melk, Austria, codex 1394. 322 f. Duodecimo. Saec. 15.
Microfilm: MnCH proj. no. 1916

6544 Compendium commentarii Nicolai de Dinkelspihl in quartum Sententiarum. MS. Benediktinerabtei Melk, Austria, codex 540, f.1–270. Folio. Saec. 15.
Microfilm: MnCH proj. no. 1446

6545 Compendium de Missa. MS. Vienna, Nationalbibliothek, codex 3651, f.116r–117v. Octavo. Saec. 15.
Microfilm: MnCH proj. no. 16,906

6546 Compendium de Missa. MS. Benediktinerabtei St. Peter, Salzburg, codex a.III.33, f.10v–14r. Octavo. Saec. 15.
Microfilm: MnCH proj. no. 9972

6547 Compendium elucidationum theologiae mysticae Marquardi Sprenger. MS. Benediktinerabtei Melk, Austria, codex 896, f.201r–210r. Quarto. Saec. 15.
Microfilm: MnCH proj. no. 1715

6548 Compendium humanae salvationis. MS. Benediktinerabtei Melk, Austria, codex 662, f.95v–103r. Quarto. Saec. 15.
Microfilm: MnCH proj. no. 1532

6549 Compendium librorum novem reductorii moralis Petri Berthorii de Pictavia. MS. Benediktinerabtei Melk, Austria, codex 1561, p. 336–395. Duodecimo. Saec. 15.
Microfilm: MnCH proj. no. 1962

6550 Compendium librorum quindecim de Trinitate sancti Augustini. MS. Benediktinerabtei Melk, Austria, codex 1561, p. 272–335. Duodecimo. Saec. 15.
Microfilm: MnCH proj. no. 1962

6551 Compendium metricum speculi humanae salvationis. MS. Benediktinerabtei Melk, Austria, codex 1839, f.2r–10r. Duodecimo. Saec. 15.
Microfilm: MnCH proj. no. 2149

6552 Confessiones et privilegia. MS. Benediktinerabtei St. Peter, Salzburg, codex b.XI.19, f.36v–38r. Folio. Saec. 15.
Microfilm: MnCH proj. no. 10,671

6553 Copia brevis pro danda charta, monasteriis visitandis et visitatis anno 1452. MS. Benediktinerabtei Melk, Austria, codex 896, f.IIr. Quarto. Saec. 15.
Microfilm: MnCH proj. no. 1715

6554 Copia chartae ejusmodi vulgaris pro monialibus Ord. S. Benedicti dandae. Germanice. MS. Benediktinerabtei Melk, Austria, codex 896, f.IVr. Quarto. Saec. 15.
Microfilm: MnCH proj. no. 1715

6555 De contemplatione. MS. Benediktinerabtei Melk, Austria, codex 1561, p. 252–271. Duodecimo. Saec. 15.
Microfilm: MnCH proj. no. 1962

6556 De esu carnium. MS. Vienna, Nationalbibliothek, codex 3548, f.1r–2r. Octavo. Saec. 15.
Microfilm: MnCH proj. no. 16,770

6557 De esu carnium. MS. Benediktinerabtei St. Peter, Salzburg, codex b.XI. 19, f.26v–28v. Folio. Saec. 15.
Microfilm: MnCH proj. no. 10,671

6558 De expositione somnii Nabuchodonosor de statua Danielis 2. MS. Vienna, Schottenstift, codex 121, f.404r. Folio. Saec. 15.
Microfilm: MnCH proj. no. 3981

6559 De gaudiis coelestis mercedis. MS. Benediktinerabtei Melk, Austria, codex 1561, p. 217–220. Duodecimo. Saec. 15.
Microfilm: MnCH proj. no. 1962

6560 De ieiunio regulari. MS. Vienna, Schottenstift, codex 237, f.140v–141v. Quarto. Saec. 15.
Microfilm: MnCH proj. no. 4143

6561   De quantitatibus syllabarum et de figuris grammaticalibus. MS. Benediktinerabtei Melk, Austria, codex 1221, f.271r–279r., etiam f.253v–260. Sextodecimo. Saec. 15.
Microfilm: MnCH proj. no. 1869

6562   De reformatione monasterii Mellicensi anno 1418. MS. Benediktinerabtei Melk, Austria, codex 91, f.311–312. Duodecimo. Saec. 15.
Microfilm: MnCH proj. no. 1170

6563   Descriptio summorum pontificum, cardinalium, patriarcharum, archiespiscoporum, episcoporum, canonistorum, qui in conventu Nürnbergensi ad S. Egidium depicti sunt. MS. Benediktinerabtei Melk, Austria, codex 1763, f.211r–220v. Duodecimo. Saec. 15.
Microfilm: MnCH proj. no. 2072

6564   Descriptiones titulorum quinque librorum Decretalium. MS. Benediktinerabtei Melk, Austria, codex 1763, f.205r–210r. Duodecimo. Saec. 15.
Microfilm: MnCH proj. no. 2072

6565   Duae epistolae ad Ioannem de Werth. MS. Benediktinerabtei Melk, Austria, codex 662, f.189v. Quarto. Saec. 15.
Microfilm: MnCH proj. no. 1532

6566   Duodecim remedia contra tentationes hujus temporis tradita a quodam experto. MS. Benediktinerabtei Melk, Austria, codex 1081, f.371–384. Duodecimo. Saec. 15.
Microfilm: MnCH proj. no. 1835

6567   Epigramma in laudem sui saeculi eruditorum virorum, videlicet Schaumbergii . . . MS. Benediktinerabtei Melk, Austria, codex 619, f.266r. Quarto. Saec. 15.
Microfilm: MnCH proj. no. 1508

6568   Epistola ad Bernardum de Kreyburg de modo reformandi et dispensandi cum monialibus Ordinis S. Benedicti dioecesis Salisburgensis. MS. Benediktinerabtei Melk, Austria, codex 896, f.196v. Quarto. Saec. 15.
Microfilm: MnCH proj. no. 1715

6569   Epistola ad Bernardum de Kreyburg de non adhibendis formulis deorum in scriptis christianorum. MS. Benediktinerabtei Melk, Austria, codex 896, f.199r–200r. Quarto. Saec. 15.
Microfilm: MnCH proj. no. 1715

6570   Epistola ad Nicolaum de Cusa, pro mitiganda bulla visitationis monasteriorum. MS. Benediktinerabtei Melk, Austria, codex 1093, f.431–432. Duodecim. Saec. 15.
Microfilm: MnCH proj. no. 1846

6571   Epistola apologetica ad Hieronymum de Werdea. Excerpta ex excusatorio contra Hieronymum de Werdea. Benediktinerabtei Melk, Austria, codex 91, f.319–324. Duodecimo. Saec. 15.
Microfilm: MnCH proj. no. 1170

6572   Epistola apologetica ad Udalricum, priorem Tegernseensem, adversus Hieronymi de Werdeae epistolam. MS. Benediktinerabtei Melk, Austria, codex 1560, f.218r–218v. Duodecimo. Saec. 15.
Microfilm: MnCH proj. no. 2225

6573   Epistola critica contra Apologiam unitoris ecclesiastici a Keckio editam. MS. Benediktinerabtei Melk, Austria, codex 662, f.183v–184r. Quarto. Saec. 15.
Microfilm: MnCH proj. no. 1532

6574   Excerpta ex libris sapientalibus. MS. Benediktinerabtei Melk, Austria, codex 1839, f.135v–152v. Duodecimo. Saec. 15.
Microfilm: MnCH proj. no. 2149

6575   Excerpta ex Novo Testamento. MS. Benediktinerabtei Melk, Austria, codex 1839, f.67r–135r. Duodecimo. Saec. 15.
Microfilm: MnCH proj. no. 2149

6576   Excerpta ex sermonibus Nicolai de Dinkelspihl. MS. Benediktinerabtei Melk, Austria, codex 653, f.165r–243r. Quarto. Saec. 15.
Microfilm: MnCH proj. no. 1530

6577   Excerpta ex tractatu bipartito edito (a Richardo a S. Victore) pro Christianorum confirmatione contra oppositiones Judaeorum et Judaizantium. MS. Benediktinerabtei Melk, Austria, codex 1560, f.132v–146v. Duodecimo. Saec. 15.
Microfilm: MnCH proj. no. 2225

6578   Excerpta super quarto Sententiarum. MS. Benediktinerabtei Melk, Austria, codex 406, f.1r–71v. Folio. Saec. 15.
Microfilm: MnCH proj. no. 1380

6579   Excerptum ex opusculo de floribus temporum Veteris Testamenti fratris Ioannis Zeck. MS. Benediktinerabtei Melk, Austria, codex 648, f.184v–185v. Quarto. Saec. 15.
Microfilm: MnCH proj. no. 1528

6580   Expositio amplissima Regulae S. Benedicti. MS. Benediktinerabtei Melk, Austria, codex 1578. Duodecimo. Saec. 15. 334 p.
Microfilm: MnCH proj. no. 1973

6581   Expositio metrica super oratione dominica. MS. Benediktinerabtei Melk, Austria, codex 662, f.39r–41v. Quarto. Saec. 15.
Microfilm: MnCH proj. no. 1532

6582   Expositio Regulae S. Benedicti. MS. Benediktinerabtei Melk, Austria, codex 1075, f.162–294. Duodecimo. Saec. 15.
Microfilm: MnCH proj. no. 1833

6583 Expositio super Pater noster. MS. Benediktinerabtei Melk, Austria, codex 1081, f.465–474. Duodecimo. Saec. 15.
Microfilm: MnCH proj. no. 1835

6584 Extractio Bibliorum. MS. Benediktinerabtei Melk, Austria, codex 1761, p. 429–458. Duodecimo. Saec. 15.
Microfilm: MnCH proj. no. 2083

6585 Extractiones Bibliorum, seu Succincti commentarii in universam Scripturam. MS. Benediktinerabtei Melk, Austria, codex 298, f.15v–451v. Folio. Saec. 15.
Microfilm: MnCH proj. no. 1317

6586 Forma de modo procedenti in visitatione monasteriorum. MS. Benediktinerabtei Melk, Austria, codex 959, f.189v–191r. Quarto. Saec. 15.
Microfilm: MnCH proj. no. 1762

6587 Formula metrica de christiana puerorum institutione, cum glossa interlineari. MS. Benediktinerabtei Melk, Austria, codex 1393, 316 f. Octavo. Saec. 15.
Microfilm: MnCH proj. no. 1915

6588 Formula vitae christianae. MS. Benediktinerabtei Melk, Austria, codex 1089, f.622–624. Duodecimo. Saec. 15.
Microfilm: MnCH proj. no. 1840

6589 Fragmentum Bibliae. MS. Benediktinerabtei Melk, Austria, codex 662, f.44r–87r. Quarto. Saec. 15.
Microfilm: MnCH proj. no. 1532

6590 Fragmentum Bibliae, vel Memoriale Bibliae alphabeticum, vel Biblia metrica. MS. Benediktinerabtei Melk, Austria, codex 298, f.2r–15v. Folio. Saec. 15.
Microfilm: MnCH proj. no. 1317

6591 Gemma Bibliae, hoc est, universa Biblia compendio versibus hexametris reddita. MS. Benediktinerabtei Melk, Austria, codex 662, f.142r–153v. Quarto. Saec. 15.
Microfilm: MnCH proj. no. 1532

6592 Gemma Bibliorum. MS. Benediktinerabtei Göttweig, Austria, codex 428. 311 f. Quarto. Saec. 15.
Microfilm: MnCH proj. no. 3688

6593 Glossa in universum Novum Testamentum. MS. Benediktinerabtei Melk, Austria, codex 850. 497 f. Quarto. Saec. 15.
Microfilm: MnCH proj. no. 1675

6594 Glossa litteralis totius Psalterii. MS. Benediktinerabtei Melk, Austria, codex 960, f.123–305. Quarto. Saec. 15.
Microfilm: MnCH proj. no. 1775

6595 Iudicium de tractatu Bernardi de Baching contra illicitum esum carnium. MS. Benediktinerabtei Melk, Austria, codex 960, f.405–406. Quarto. Saec. 15.
Microfilm: MnCH proj. no. 1775

6596 Liber de antiquis philosophis. MS. Benediktinerabtei Göttweig, Austria, codex 2434. 18 f. Folio. Saec. 15.
Microfilm: MnCH proj. no. 3508

6597 Liber Theobaldi de naturis animalium versu elegiaco in compendium missum. MS. Benediktinerabtei Melk, Austria, codex 662, f.103v–104r. Quarto. Saec. 15.
Microfilm: MnCH proj. no. 1532

6598 Libri a Ioanne Schlitpacher Viennae ad gradum magisterii auditi. MS. Benediktinerabtei Melk, Austria, codex 873. f.339. Quarto. Saec. 15.
Microfilm: MnCH proj. no. 1694

6599 Libri Sententiarum versibus hexametris redditi. MS. Benediktinerabtei Melk, Austria, codex 662, f.105v–139r. Quarto. Saec. 15.
Microfilm: MnCH proj. no. 1532

6600 Manuale viaticum super Regulam S. Benedicti. MS. Benediktinerabtei Melk, Austria, codex 1404, f.41–623. Duodecimo. Saec. 15.
Microfilm: MnCH proj. no. 1923

6601 Manuale viaticum super Regulam S. Benedicti. MS. Benediktinerabtei St. Peter, Salzburg, codex b.X.28. 186 f. Folio. Saec. 15.
Microfilm: MnCH proj. no. 10,625

6602 Materiale Psalterii. MS. Benediktinerabtei Melk, Austria, codex 1763, f.201r–204v. Duodecimo. Saec. 15.
Microfilm: MnCH proj. no. 2072

6603 Memoriale breve Regulae S. Benedicti. Memoriale vitae S. Benedicti. Salutatio alphabetica et mystica de beata Virgine Maria. MS. Benediktinerabtei Melk, Austria, codex 1405, f.1r–1v. Duodecimo. Saec. 15.
Microfilm: MnCH proj. no. 1926

6604 Memoriale breve vitae S. Benedicti. MS. Benediktinerabtei Melk, Austria, codex 662, f.140v–141r. Quarto. Saec. 15.
Microfilm: MnCH proj. no. 1532

6605 Memoriale in Regulam S. Benedicti. Metrice. MS. Vienna, Nationalbibliothek, codex 4117, f.37r–38r. Sextodecimo. Saec. 16.
Microfilm: MnCH proj. no. 17,296

6606 Memoriale in Regulam S. Benedicti. MS. Benediktinerabtei Melk, Austria, codex 1558, f.202r–203v. Duodecimo. Saec. 15.
Microfilm: MnCH proj. no. 1960

6607 Memoriale librorum Sententiarum. MS. Benediktinerabtei Melk, Austria, codex 662, f.89v–95v. Quarto. Saec. 15.
Microfilm: MnCH proj. no. 1532

6608   Memoriale metricum ad Regulam S. Benedicti. MS. Benediktinerabtei Melk, Austria, codex 1758, f.279v–281r. Duodecimo. Saec. 15.
Microfilm: MnCH proj. no. 2069

6609   Memoriale metricum legendae S. Benedicti. MS. Vienna, Schottenstift, codex 391, f.6r–6v. Folio. Saec. 15.
Microfilm: MnCH proj. no. 4245

6610   Memoriale metricum Regulae S. Benedicti. MS. Vienna, Schottenstift, codex 237, f.3r–3v. Quarto. Saec. 15.
Microfilm: MnCH proj. no. 4143

6611   Memoriale metricum majus et amplius trium librorum Senteniarum. MS. Benediktinerabtei Melk, Austria, codex 1821, p. 433–450. Folio. Saec. 15.
Microfilm: MnCH proj. no. 2131

6612   Memoriale metricum quatuor librorum Sententiarum. MS. Benediktinerabtei Melk, Austria, codex 121, apud finem codicis. Folio. Saec. 15.
Microfilm: MnCH proj. no. 1191

6613   Memoriale minus metri cum quatuor librorum Sententiarum. MS. Benediktinerabtei Melk, Austria, codex 527, f.1r–1v. Folio. Saec. 15.
Microfilm: MnCH proj. no. 1441

6614   Memoriale viaticum Regulae S. Benedicti. MS. Vienna, Schottenstift, codex 237, f.3r–140r. Quarto. Saec. 15.
Microfilm: MnCH proj. no. 4143

6615   Metra ad Iodocum Weiler de Heilbrunna. MS. Benediktinerabtei Melk, Austria, codex 662, f.1r. Quarto. Saec. 15.
Microfilm: MnCH proj. no. 1532

6616   Notulae in Hieronymi de Werdea epistolam. MS. Benediktinerabtei Melk, Austria, codex 1560, f.197r–197v et 206. Duodecimo. Saec. 15.
Microfilm: MnCH proj. no. 2225

6617   Opus metricum in Bibliam, quod dicitur Fragmentum Bibliae. MS. Benediktinerabtei Melk, Austria, codex 1652, f.309r–324v. Sextodecimo. Saec. 15.
Microfilm: MnCH proj. no. 2008

6618   Ordines militantes sub Regula S. Benedicti. MS. Benediktinerabtei Melk, Austria, codex 1396, f.237r Duodecimo. Saec. 15.
Microfilm: MnCH proj. no. 1918

6619   Postilla super Regulam S. Patris Benedicti. MS. Benediktinerabtei Melk, Austria, codex 753. Quarto. Saec. 15.
Microfilm: MnCH proj. no. 1600

6620   Postilla textualis super Regula S. Augustini. MS. Benediktinerabtei Melk, Austria, codex 1839, f.52v–66v. Duodecimo. Saec. 15.
Microfilm: MnCH proj. no. 2149

6621   Prefaciuncula in Fragmentum Bibliae. MS. Benediktinerabtei Lambach, Austria, codex chart. 338, f.113v–144r. Saec. 15.
Microfilm: MnCH proj. no. 707

6622   Prima epistola adversus Ioannis Keckii Tegernsensis Unitorem ecclesiasticum. MS. Benediktinerabtei Melk, Austria, codex 662, f.181r. Quarto. Saec. 15.
Microfilm: MnCH proj. no. 1532

6623   Psalterium, cum glossa marginali et interlineari. Orationes variae. MS. Benediktinerabtei Melk, codex 1390. [12], 175, [19] f. Duodecimo. Saec. 15.
Microfilm: MnCH proj. no. 1913

6624   Regula S. Benedicti, germanice, cum commentario. MS. Benediktinerabtei Melk, Austria, codex 278, p. 119–140. Duodecimo. Saec. 15.
Microfilm: MnCH proj. no. 2110

6625   Regula S. Benedicti metrice. MS. Benediktinerabtei Melk, Austria, codex 1087, f.51–55. Duodecimo. Saec. 15.
Microfilm: MnCH proj. no. 1842

6626   Remedia metrica contra tentationes. MS. Benediktinerabtei Melk, Austria, codex 662, f.43v. Quarto. Saec. 15.
Microfilm: MnCH proj. no. 1532

6627   Resolutio quaestionis, utrum monachis S. Benedicti sanis et fortibus esus carnium sit constitutione Benedicti XII concessus. MS. Benediktinerabtei Melk, Austria, codex 1404, f.1–40. Duodecimo. Saec. 15.
Microfilm: MnCH proj. no. 1923

6628   Sermo ad populum factus. Incipit: Ego sum ostium. MS. Benediktinerabtei Melk, Austria, codex 1075, f.314–328. Duodecimo. Saec. 15.
Microfilm: MnCH proj. no. 1833

6629   Sermo de adventu Domini. MS. Benediktinerabtei Melk, Austria, codex 1839, f.31r–38v. Duodecimo. Saec. 15.
Microfilm: MnCH proj. no. 2149

6630   Sermo de observatione quadragesimae. MS. Benediktinerabtei Melk, Austria, codex 91, f.305–310. Duodecimo. Saec. 15.
Microfilm: MnCH proj. no. 1170

6631   Sermo de purificatione beatae Virginis Mariae. MS. Benediktinerabtei Melk, Austria, codex 1560, f.199–200, 203r–204v. Duodecimo. Saec. 15.
Microfilm: MnCH proj. no. 2225

6632   Sermo de ultima coena. MS. Benediktinerabtei Melk, Austria, codex 1560, f.201r–202v. Duodecimo. Saec. 15.
Microfilm: MnCH proj. no. 2225

6633 Sermo dictus 1466. Incipit: Vocabis nomen ejus Iesum. MS. Benediktinerabtei Melk, Austria, codex 1075, f.328–331. Duodecimo. Saec. 15.
Microfilm: MnCH proj. no. 1833

6634 Sermo in Ascensione Domini super illud: Ascendes in altum. MS. Benediktinerabtei Melk, Austria, codex 662, f.190r–192r. Quarto. Saec. 15.
Microfilm: MnCH proj. no. 1532

6635 Sermo in ascensione Domini super illud: Assumptus est in coelum. MS. Benediktinerabtei Melk, Austria, codex 662, f.192r–193v. Quarto. Saec. 15.
Microfilm: MnCH proj. no. 1532

6636 Sermo in Coena Domini, Augustae Vindelicorum 1441 dictus. MS. Benediktinerabtei Melk, Austria, codex 1839, f.47r–50v. Duodecimo. Saec. 15.
Microfilm: MnCH proj. no. 2149

6637 Sermo in Coena Domini,. de passione Domini nostri. MS. Benediktinerabtei Melk, Austria, codex 1566, f.202r–229v. Duodecimo. Saec. 15.
Microfilm: MnCH proj. no. 1966

6638 Sermo in Parasceve de passione Domini. MS. Benediktinerabtei Melk, Austria, codex 1839, f.22r–30r. Duodecimo. Saec. 15.
Microfilm: MnCH proj. no. 2149

6639 Sermo in vigilia Nativitatis Domini 1466. Sermo de Pentecoste. MS. Benediktinerabtei Melk, Austria, codex 91, f.107–125. Duodecimo. Saec. 15.
Microfilm: MnCH proj. no. 1170

6640 Summula de continentia regulari. MS. Benediktinerabtei Melk, Austria, codex 1396, f.237v–242v. Duodecimo. Saec. 15.
Microfilm: MnCH proj. no. 1918

6641 Summula de continentia regulari S. Benedicti. MS. Benediktinerabtei Melk, Austria, codex 959, f.182r–185v. Quarto. Saec. 15.
Microfilm: MnCH proj. no. 1762

6642 Summula metrica Regulae S. Benedicti. MS. Benediktinerabtei Melk, Austria, codex 959, f.a. Quarto. Saec. 15.
Microfilm: MnCH proj. no. 1762

6643 Summarium de continentia Bibliae. MS. Benediktinerabtei Melk, Austria, codex 1396, f.1r–192r. Duodecimo. Saec. 15.
Microfilm: MnCH proj. no. 1918

6644 Super libros octo partiales Topicorum. MS. Benediktinerabtei Melk, Austria, codex 1395, f.708–758. Duodecimo. Saec. 15.
Microfilm: MnCH proj. no. 1917

6645 Syntagma rerum phisicarum. MS. Benediktinerabtei Melk, Austria, codex 1395, f. 506–673. Duodecimo. Saec. 15.
Microfilm: MnCH proj. no. 1917

6646 Tractatulus compendiosissima de quantitate sillabarum. MS. Benediktinerabtei Melk, Austria, codex 1652, f. 342v–428v. Sextodecimo. Saec. 15.
Microfilm: MnCH proj. no. 2008

6647 Tractatulus de immaculata conceptione beatae Mariae Virginis. MS. Benediktinerabtei Melk, Austria, codex 1560, f.239v–240v. Duodecimo. Saec. 15.
Microfilm: MnCH proj. no. 2225

6648 Tractatulus de Sancta Trinitate, ex libris Richardi de S. Victore succincte collectus. MS. Benediktinerabtei Melk, Austria, codex 1561, p. 220–252. Duodecimo. Saec. 15.
Microfilm: MnCH proj. no. 1962

6649 Tractatus brevis de continentia singulorum psalmorum. MS. Benediktinerabtei Melk, Austria, codex 960, f.424. Quarto. Saec. 15.
Microfilm: MnCH proj. no. 1775

6650 Tractatus brevis de quatuor Missae partibus. MS. Benediktinerabtei Melk, Austria, codex 1560, f.59v–60v. Duodecimo. Saec. 15.
Microfilm: MnCH proj. no. 2225

6651 Tractatus de annis ab exitu filiorum Israel de Aegypto usque ad annum quartum regni Salamonis. MS. Benediktinerabtei Melk, Austria, codex 1763. f.210v. Duodecimo. Saec. 15.
Microfilm: MnCH proj. no. 2072

6652 Tractatus de casibus, in quibus prelatus monasticus esset deponendus. MS. Benediktinerabtei Melk, Austria, codex 959, f.189r–189v. Quarto. Saec. 15.
Microfilm: MnCH proj. no. 1762

6653 Tractatus de duratione et annis ab urbe condito usque ad Christum. MS. Benediktinerabtei Melk, Austria, codex 648, f.184r. Quarto. Saec. 15.
Microfilm: MnCH proj. no. 1528

6654 Tractatus de quantitatibus sillabarum, excerptum ex doctrinali, cum glossa. MS. Benediktinerabtei Melk, Austria, codex 1094, f.1r–24r. Duodecimo. Saec. 15.
Microfilm: MnCH proj. no. 1847

6655 Tractatus de triplici modo eligendi abbatem. MS. Benediktinerabtei Melk, Austria, codex 959, f.186r–189v. Quarto. Saec. 15.
Microfilm: MnCH proj. no. 1762

6656 Tractatus logicales gemini de suppositionibus terminorum et de consequentiis.

MS. Benediktinerabtei Melk, Austria, codex 958, f.506–551. Quarto. Saec. 15.
Microfilm: MnCH proj. no. 1770

6657   Tractatus metricus de quantitate syllabarum et figuris grammaticalibus. MS. Benediktinerabtei Melk, Austria, codex 662, f.32r–38v. Quarto. Saec. 15.
Microfilm: MnCH proj. no. 1532

6658   Versus breves de dominica oratione. MS. Benediktinerabtei Melk, Austria, codex 662, f.42v–43r. Quarto. Saec. 15.
Microfilm: MnCH proj. no. 1532

6659   Versus memoriales librorum Sententiarum. MS. Benediktinerabtei Melk, Austria, codex 1086, f.23–32. Duodecimo. Saec. 15.
Microfilm: MnCH proj. no. 1848

6660   Versus quos fecit Regi Ladislao posthumo pro memoria. MS. Benediktinerabtei Melk, Austria, codex 1086, f.53. Duodecimo. Saec. 15.
Microfilm: MnCH proj. no. 1848

6661   Versus super totam Bibliam, et fere quaelibet dictio comprehendit unum capitulum. MS. Benediktinerabtei Melk, Austria, codex 1793, f.235v–253r. Quarto. Saec. 15.
Microfilm: MnCH proj. no. 2100

6662   Versus viginti duo de tonis musicis. MS. Benediktinerabtei Melk, Austria, codex 662, f.104v. Quarto. Saec. 15.
Microfilm: MnCH proj. no. 1532

6663   Vita S. Benedicti metrica. MS. Benediktinerabtei Melk, Austria, codex 1404, f.623–624. Duodecimo. Saec. 15.
Microfilm: MnCH proj. no. 1923

Schmelz, Damian Vincent, 1932–
6664   A graphical analysis of the size-class structure of Indiana forests.
189 leaves, maps, tables, diagrs. 28 cm.
Thesis (M.S.)–Purdue University, 1964.
Typescript.
InStme

6665   Methodological approaches in the analysis of Indiana old-growth forests.
xii, 199 leaves. illus.(part col.) 28 cm.
Thesis (Ph.D.)–Purdue University, 1969.
Typescript.
InStme

6666   Natural areas in Indiana and their preservation [by] Alton A. Lindsey, Damian V. Schmelz [and] Stanley A. Nichols. The report of the Indiana Natural Areas Survey. Lafayette, Purdue University, 1969.
xi, 594 p. illus., maps, 24 cm.
InStme

Schmid, Hugo, 1840–1900.
6667   Catalogus codicum manuscriptorum in bibliotheca Cremifanensis . . . asservatorum. In memoriam anni a fundato monasterio MC. jubilaei edidit P. Hugo Schmid. 1877.
2 v. 24 cm.
Handwritten.
Xeroxed by University Microfilms, Ann Arbor, Mich., 1965.
MnCS

6668   Bibliotheca Cremifanensis: Catalogus codicum manuscriptorum . . . Neue Codices 1–1361.
Handwritten.
Xeroxed by University Microfilms, Ann Arbor, Mich., 1965.
MnCS

6669   Bibliotheca Cremifanensis: Codices im Schatzkasten.
Handwritten.
Xeroxed by University Microfilms, Ann Arbor, Mich., 1965.
MnCS

Schmid, Placidus, 1856–1932.
6670   Gems of prayers and devotion; a prayer book for all. By a Benedictine Father in Conception, Mo. [n.p., c 1888].
xii, 436 p. 12 cm.
KAS

6671   _____ New edition. St. Louis, Mo., B. Herder, 1896.
386 p. 11 cm.
PLatS

6672   A prayer book for Catholics, with an optional Sunday and holyday Missal. Chicago, Daleiden [c 1931].
xvi, 579 p. illus. 14 cm.
KAS; MoCo

Schmidfeld, Hugo.
6673   Acta Murensia integrae fidei restituta, sive Gesta et fundatio monasterii Murensis, a scriniis monasterii Engelbergensis educat. MS. Benediktinerabtei St. Paul im Lavanttal, Austria, codex 76/2. 2 vols. Folio. Saec. 18.
Microfilm: MnCH proj. no. 11,852 & 11,858

6674   Conspectus diatribae de duobus Reginbertis, fundatoribus monasterii S. Blasii. MS. Benediktinerabtei St. Paul im Lavanttal, Austria, codex 25/2. 74 f. Quarto. Saec. 18.
Microfilm: MnCH proj. no. 11,755

6675   Donati Calci propinomium evangelicum translatum in linguam latinam. MS. Benediktinerabtei St. Paul im Lavanttal, Austria, codex 44/2. 259 f. Folio. Saec. 18.
Microfilm: MnCH proj. no. 11,779

6676 **Schmidt, Mary, Sister.**
An account of the independent French painters from 1840-1900.
22 p.
Thesis (M.A.)–Indiana State Teachers College, Terre Haute, 1954.
InFer

Schmiedeler, Edgar, 1892-1963.
6677 The Association of the Holy Family. Washington, Family Life Section, Social Action Dept., N.C.W.C. [Atchison, Kans., Abbey Student Press, 193–?].
16 p. 18 cm.
KAS; MnCS; OkTB

6678 Christian marriage; a study of the sacrament of matrimony and of Christian family life . . . Wichita, Kans., Catholic Bookshop, 1956.
72 p. 23 cm.
KAS

6679 Christian marriage and the family. Washington, D.C., Family Life Section, Social Action Department, N.C.W.C., 1932.
56 p. 19 cm.
"Reprinted from Catholic Action, January and July, 1932."
KAS

6680 The Family Life Bureau.
19 p. 26 cm.
Offprint from American Benedictine Review, f. 9(1958–59), p. 41-57.
KAS

6681 Looking toward marriage; [a modern text for the high school student]. Washington, Family Life Bureau, National Catholic Welfare Conference [1960]
90 p. 22 cm.
KAS

6682 The program of the Catholic Conference on Family Life. Huntington, Ind., Our Sunday Visitor [n.d.].
30 p. 15 cm.
MnCS

6683 Towards a better family life; problems and programs of action. Washington [1946].
102 p. 19 cm.
Preface signed: Rev. Edgar Schmiedeler, O.S.B.
PLatS

6684 Vanishing homesteads. New York, published for the Social Action Dept., National Catholic Welfare Conference, by the Paulist Press [1941].
32 p. 18 cm.
KAS; PLatS

6685 **Schmieder Pius,** 1839-1918.
Die Benediktiner-Ordensreform des 13. und 14. Jahrhunderts . . . Linz, J. Feichtinger, 1867.
60 p. 22 cm.
KAS; MnCS; PLatS

6686 **Schmier, Franz,** 1680-1728.
Tractatus juridicus de potestate ordinis, ad librum I. Decretalium, a titulo XI usque ad tit. XXII . . . praeside P. Francisco Schmier, O.S.B. . . . una cum Parergis ex universo jure. Publice defendendum suscepit D.F. David Ettinger, O.S.B. Salisburgi, Joan. J. Mayr [1713].
[14], 202, [67] p. 20 cm.
PLatS

6687 **Schmitt, Albert,** 1894-
Die Neubelebung des Klostergedankens in der Anglikanischen Kirche.
(*In* Universitas; Dienst an Wahrheit und Leben. Mainz, 1960. v. 2, p. 126–136)
PLatS

6688 **Schmitt, Albert,** 1908-
(ed & tr) Oeuvres spirituelles [par] Gertrude d'Helfta. Texte latin, introduction, traduction et notes per Jacques Hourlier et Albert Schmitt. Paris, Editions du Cerf, 1967.
v. 20 cm. (Sources chrétiennes, 127)
InStme; PLatS

Schmitt, Franciscus Salesius, 1894-
6689 Analecta Anselmiana; Untersuchungen über Person und Werk Anselms von Canterbury . . . hrsg. von F. S. Schmitt. Frankfurt/Main, Minerva, 1969-
v. 24 cm.
InStme

6690 Sola ratione; Anselm-Studien für Pater Dr. n.c. Franciscus Salesius Schmitt, O.S.B., zum 75. Geburtstag am 20. Dez. 1969. (In Verbindung mit B. Geyer und A. Hufnagel hrsg. von Helmut K. Kohlenberger). Stuttgart-Bad-Cannstatt., Frommann, 1970.
236 p. 22 cm.

6691 Die wissenschaftliche Methode in "Cur Deus homo."
(*In* Spicilegium Beccense. 1959. v. 1, p. 349-57)
PLatS

6692 (ed) Memorials of St. Anselm. Edited by R. W. Southern and F. S. Schmitt, O.S.B. London, Published for the British Academy by the Oxford University Press, 1969.
viii, 370 p. 26 cm. (Auctores Britannici Medii aevi, 1)
InStme

6693   (tr) Anselm von Canterbury: Proslogion. Untersuchungen, lateinisch-deutsche Ausgabe von P. Franciscus Salesius Schmitt, O.S.B. [Stuttgart], Friedrich Frommann Verlag [1962].
159 p. 21 cm.
MnCS; PLatS

6694   **Schmitt, Jerome, Sister.**
The struggle of the expressionists against human mechanization.
72 p.
Thesis (M.A.)–Marquette University, Milwaukee, 1962.
SdYa

Schmitt, Rosina, Sister, 1935–
6695   Augustine on the unity of man.
96 p. 28 cm.
Thesis (M.A.)–Saint Louis University, 1966.
Typescript.
MnStj(Archives)

6696   The end of evolution in Pierce's cosmology.
v. 158 leaves. 28 cm.
Thesis (Ph.D.)–St. Louis University, 1978.
MnStj

6697   **Schmitz, Edward Matthias,** 1893–
Kansas Poems. 1967.
39 p. 29 cm.
Typescript.
KAS

Schmitz, Philibert, 1888–1963.
6698   Benedicti Regula; texte latin, traduction et concordance par D. Ph. Schmitz. Etude sur la langue de S. Benoît par Ch. Mohrmann. 3. éd. Maredsous, 1962.
xli, 306 p. 18 cm.
MnCS

6699   History of the Order of Saint Benedict. Translation by Rev. Cosmas W. Krumpelmann, O.S.B., St. Peter's Abbey, Muenster, Canada, 1951.
7 v. in 14.
Typescript.
MoCo

6700   La liturgie de Cluny.
(*In* Spiritualità cluniacense. Todi, 1960. p. 83–100)
PLatS

6701   (ed) Bulletin d'histoire bénédictine.
Ph. Schmitz was editor: 1925–1963.
CaQStB; KAS; MnCS; PLatS

Schmitz, Thomas, ca. 1691–1758.
6702   Medulla juris canonici secundum titulos in quinque libris Decretalium Gregorii P. IX contentos digesta . . . Coloniae Agrippinae, ex Officina Noetheniana, 1740.

3 v. 21 cm.
KAS

6703   Theologiae scholasticae ad mentem S. Thomas Aquinatis . . . Coloniae Agrippinae, apud Haeredes Thomae Von Collen & Josephum Huisch, 1734.
3 v.
NcBe

Schneeweis, Magdalena, Schwester.
6704   Allerlei Gebete. MS. Benediktinerinnenabtei Nonnberg, Salzburg, codex 23 A 6. Duodecimo. Saec. 17(1612).
Microfilm: MnCH proj. no. 10,802

6705   Schöne christliche katholische Gebete zu Gott und seiner gebenedeiten Müetter, wie man sij morgens und abents, auch auf alle Tage der gantzen Wochen lobenn und ehren solle. MS. Benediktinerinnenabtei Nonnberg, Salzburg, codex 23 A 5. Duodecimo. Saec. 17(1612).
Microfilm: MnCH proj. no. 10,800

6706   **Schnell, Anselm,** d. 1751.
Cursus theologiae polemicae abbreviatus . . . Augustae Vindelicorum, Joan. J. Mauracher, 1744.
2 vols.
PLatS(microfilm)

6707   **Schneppenheim, Werner,** 1875–1956.
Fundamentals of Catholic pedagogy. [Collegeville, Minn., St. John's Abbey, n.d.].
516 leaves, 30 cm.
Mimeographed.
MnCS(Archives)

Schnitzhofer, Urban, 1887–
6708   (tr) Steidle, Basilius. The Rule of St. Benedict, with an introduction . . . translated with a few brief annotations by Urban J. Schnitzhofer, O.S.B. [Beuron, Beuroner Kunstverlag, 1952].
x, 307 p.
InStme; MnCS

6709   _____ Canon City, Colorado, Holy Cross Abbey [1967?].
x, 307 p. 19 cm.
MnStj; PLatS

6710   **Schnur, Mary Alice, Sister.**
Some significant trends of modern religious art.
49 p.
Thesis (M.A.)–Indiana State Teachers College, Terre Haute, Ind., 1955.
Typescript.
InFer

Schoenbechler, Roger Robert, 1900–
6711   Book of prayer for personal use; a short breviary abridged and simplified by monks of St. John's Abbey from the Liturgia

horarum . . . Collegeville, Minn., Saint John's Abbey Press, 1975.
1823 p. 18 cm.
The hymns (about 200) were translated by Roger Schoenbechler, O.S.B.
MnCS

6712   Book of psalms; an interpretative version in measured rhythm. Large print edition for easy reading. Collegeville, Minn., The Liturgical Press [1978].
x, 408 p. 18 cm.
MnCS; MoCo

6713   The book of wisdom; an interpretative version in measured rhythm. Collegeville, Minn., The Liturgical Press [1975].
128 p. 18 cm.
ICSS; MdRi; MnCS; MnStj

6714   **Scholliner, Hermann,** 1722–1795.
Observationes ad quaedam Henricorum II., III. & IV. Germ. reggg. & imppp. aliaque diplomata. Ingolstadii, Joh. Wilh. Krüll, 1790.
23 p. 20 cm.
PLatS

6715   **Schons, Johann Joseph,** 1887–
Führer zum Himmel; vollständiges Gebet- und Erbauungsbuch für katholische Christen. [München, 1928].
365 p. 12 cm.
PLatS

Schorsch, Dolores, Sister, 1896–
6716   Early history of the Church (filmstrips). Research and reading scripts by Sister M. Dolores Schorsch, O.S.B., in collaboration with Reverend Fidelis Buck, S.J. Encyclopedia Britannica Films, 1961.
8 filmstrips (color)
Reading scripts.
ICSS

6717   Jesu-Maria course in religion, by Alexander P. Schorsch, C.M., and Sister M. Dolores Schorsch, O.S.B. Archdiocese of Chicago School Board, 1954–1963.
9 v. guidebook (paper)
9 v. workbook, illus.(paper)
ICSS

Schott, Anselm, 1843–1896.
6718   Messbuch der heiligen Kirche, mit liturgischen Erklärungen und kurzen Lebensbeschreibung der Heiligen. Neubearbeitet von Mönchen der Erzabtei Beuron. [37]. Jubiläums-Auflage, 1884 bis 1934. Freiburg i.B., Herder [1934].
xii, 68–998, [202], xx, 76 p. illus., music, 16 cm.
MnCS

6719   Das Tagzeitenbuch des monastischen Breviers (Diurnale monasticum) im Anschluss an die Messbücher von Anselm Schott, O.S.B., hrsg. von der Erzabtei Beuron. 2. Aufl. Regensburg, Fr. Pustet, 1949.
36, 1670 p. 16 cm.
Latin and German on facing columns.
MnCS

Schottenstift, Vienna. *See* Vienna, Austria. Schottenstift.

Schram, Dominikus, 1722–1797.
6720   Compendium theologiae dogmaticae, scholasticae, et moralis methodo scientifico propositum. Augustae Vindelicorum, Matth. Rieger, 1768.
3 v. 19 cm.
InStme

6721   Institutiones theologiae mysticae ad usum directorum animarum, ex S. Scriptura, concillis, ss. patribus, mysticis primariis, ac theologicis rationiniis adornatae. Nova editio. Parisiis, L. Baldeveck, 1868.
2 v. 22 cm.
InStme

6722   **Schramb, Anselm.**
Chronicon Mellicense, seu Annales monasterii Mellicensis . . . Viennae Austriae, typis Joannis Georgii Schlegel, 1702.
[16], 980, [25] p. illus. fold. plans, 32 cm.
InStme

Schramm, Gregory John, 1898–1974.
6723   The laying of the corner stone.
(*In* Catholic University of Peking. Bulletin, no. 7(1930), p. 19–30)
PLatS

6724   A periodic table of emotional phases. [Newark, N.J., St. Mary's Abbey, 1936].
[12] p. 23 cm.
Reprint from: The journal of abnormal and social psychology, v. 31(1936), p. 87–98)
PLatS

6725   **Schreger, Odilo,** 1697–1774.
Studiosus Jovialis; seu Auxilia ad jocose, & honeste discurrendum, in gratiam & usum studiosorum juvenum, aliorumque litteratorum virorum, honesta recreationis amantium . . . Editio secunda ab auctore aucta. Monachii et Pedeponti, J. Gastl, 1751.
[8], 840 p. 17 cm.
KAS

6726   **Schreifels, Ferdinand,** 1910–
History of St. Joseph's Church, Moorhead, Minn. 1954.
unpaged, illus., ports. 25 cm.
KAS; MnCS

6727   **Schreiner, Chrysostom,** 1859–1928.
Glimpses of four continents [by] C. S.

17 installments in: The St. John's University Record, vols. 3–4 (1891–92).
MnCS

Schroll, Beda, 1823–1892.

6728   Necrologium des Benediktinerstiftes St. Paul im Lavanttale.
(*In* Archiv für vaterländische Geschichte und Topographie. Klagenfurt. 10. Jahrg. (1866), p. 33–240)
KAS

6729   Regesten aus Leben-Urkunden des Benediktiner-Stiftes St. Paul vom XVI bis XVIII Jahrhunderte.
(*In* Archiv für vaterländische Geschichte und Topographie. Klagenfurt. 12. Jahrg. (1872), p. 71–137)
KAS

6730   Urkendenbuch des Benedictiner-Stiftes St. Paul in Kärnten. Hrsg. von Beda, Schroll O.S.B. Wien, Karl Gerold's Sohn, 1876. Reproduced, University Microfilms, Ann Arbor, Mich. [1968].
594 p. 23 cm. (Fontes rerum austriacarum, 39)
MnCS

6731   **Schuermans, Marie-Philippe, Sister.**
Parole de Dieu et rite sacramental; étude critique des anciennes de communion néotestamentaires. Bruxelles, Editions de Lumen Vitae, 1963.
178 p. 23 cm.
PLatS

Schuette, Dorothy, Sister.

6732   The correlation of the monetary value of employee benefit programs with the importance of the benefit to the employee.
45 p. 28 cm.
Thesis (M.A.)–Xavier University, Cincinnati, 1971.
Typescript.
KyCovS

6733   Evaluation of the 2 + 3 patient meal system. Internal research, Good Samaritan Hospital, Cincinnati, 1978.
45 p. 28 cm.
Typescript.
KyCovS

Schulte, Raphael, 1926–

6734   Kirche und Kult.
(*In* Holböck, F. Mysterium Kirche in der Sicht der theologischen Disciplinen. p. 713–813)
PLatS

6735   Theologie und Heilsgeschehen. Essen, Ludgerus-Verlag [1969].
102 p. 21 cm.
InStme

Schultheis, Miriam, Sister.

6736   A guidebook for bibliotherapy. Glenview, Ill., Psychotechnics [1972].
138 p. 23 cm.
InFer

6737   Happiness is humanism; a tribute to Sister Fridian, O.S.F. Fort Wayne, Ind., St. Francis Print Shop, 1972.
141 p. illus.
InFer

6738   **Schultz, Blaine K.,** 1933–
Ten overtures of William Boyce.
v, 84 p. music, 29 cm.
Thesis (M.M.)–University of Wisconsin, 1966.
KAS

6739   **Schulz, Anselm,** 1931–
Nachfolgen und Nachahmen; Studien über das Verhältnis der neutestamentlichen Jüngerschaft zur urchristlichen Vorbildethik. München, Kösel, 1962.
348 p. 25 cm.
Diss.–Munich, 1959.
MnCS

6740   **Schülz, Christian,** 1938–
Deus absconditus, Deus manifestus; die Lehre Hugos von St. Viktor über die Offenbarung Gottes. Romae, Herder, 1967.
xxv, 398 p. 25 cm. (Studia Anselmiana, 56)
PLatS

Schumacher, Laurian, Sister, 1926–

6741   A guide for a course in piano pedagogy.
35 p. 28 cm.
Research paper (M.A.)–University of Minnesota, 1971.
Typescript.
MnStj(Archives)

6742   The Kodaly-Richards method and the Pestalozzian "Object lesson."
23, [12] p. 28 cm.
Research paper (M.A.)–University of Minnesota, 1971.
Typescript.
MnStj(Archives)

6743   The place of Schubert's Wanderer Fantasy in nineteenth-century romanticism.
23 p. 28 cm.
Research paper (M.A.)–University of Minnesota, 1971.
Typescript.
MnStj(Archives)

Schumacher, Mario, Sister, 1938–

6744   A comparative study of Verdi's operas: Luisa Miller & La Traviata.
55 p. 28 cm.
Research paper (M.A.)–University of Minnesota, 1976.

Typescript.
MnStj(Archives)

6745   A model for staffing a senior high music program; special emphasis on the characteristics of faculty members individually and in a group.
41 p. 28 cm.
Research paper (M.A.) – University of Minnesota, 1976.
Typescript.
MnStj(Archives)

6746   Women composers in nineteenth-century Germany.
60 p. 28 cm.
Research paper (M.A.) – University of Minnesota, 1976.
Typescript.
MnStj(Archives)

Schuster, Ildefonso, 1880–1954.

6747   Historical notes on St. Benedict's Rule for monks. Translated by Leonard J. Doyle. Hamden, Conn., Shoe String Press, 1962.
102 p. 22 cm.
ILSP; InStme; MnCS; MoCo; NdRi; PLatS

6748   I quattro cardini della pietà cristiana; lettera pastorale per la santa quaresima nell'anno santo MCML. Milano, Tip. Pont. Ed. Arciv. S. Giuseppe [1950].
12 p. 24 cm.
MnCS

6749   Le sacre stazioni quaresimali secondo l'ordine del Messale romano . . . Roma, Tip. Pol. Vaticana, 1915.
135 p. 16 cm.
MnCS

6750   Les saintes stations du carême selon l'ordre du Missel romain . . . Rome, Imprimerie Polyglotte, 1922.
146 p. 15 cm.
KAS

6751   Scritti del Card. A. Ildefonso Schuster. A cura di Giulio Oggioni. Venegono Inferiore (Varese), La Scuola Cattolica [1959].
535 p. 25 cm.
PLatS

6752   Gli ultimi tempi di un regime. Milano, "La Via" [1946].
186 p. 24 cm.
PLatS

Schuster, Mary Faith, Sister.
The meaning of the mountain; a history of the first century at Mount St. Scholastica. Baltimore, Helicon [1963].
329 p. illus. 22 cm. (Benedictine studies, 6)

6753

AStb; CaMWiSb; ICSS; ILSP; InStme; InFer; MnCS; MnStj; KAS; MoCo; PLatS

6754   **Schüttengruber, Johannes,** 1935–
[Brochure about Stiftsgymnasium Melk]. Eigentümer, Herausgeber und Verleger: Konvikt des Stiftes Melk am öffentlichen Stiftsgymnasium. Verantwortlicher Schriftleiter: Johannes Schüttengruber, O.S.B. [1967?]
16 p. illus.(part col.), plans, 21x23 cm.
MnCS

6755   **Schütz, Christian.**
Deus absconditus, Deus manifestus; die Lehre Hugos von St. Viktor über die Offenbarung Gottes. Romae, Herder, 1967.
xxv, 398 p. 25 cm. (Studia Anselmiana, 56)
InStme; KAS

6756   **Schuver, Ursula Maria, Sister.**
De reus op de Sint-Jorisberg; flitsen uit het leven van de grote metropoliet Graaf Andreas Szeptyckyj van Galicië. Rotterdam, N. V. Uitgeverij de Forel [1959].
456 p. plates, ports. 20 cm.
PLatS

6757   **Schwab, Barbara Ann, Sister.**
Reverence: the passiontide's *anaw* (poor).
Thesis (M.A.) – St. John's University, Collegeville, Minn., 1964.
Typescript.
NdRiS

6758   **Schwab, Franz,** 1855–
P. Aegyd Everaard von Raitenau, 1605–1675, Benedictiner von Kremsmünster, Mathematiker, Mechaniker und Architekt . . . Salzburg, Buchdruckerei Oberndorfer & Cie., 1898.
105 p. plates, 24 cm.
KAS

Schwab, Marianus.

6759   Commentarius in materiam de angelis. MS. Universitätsbibliothek Salzburg, codex M I 322, f.1–99. Quarto. Saec. 17(1652).
Microfilm: MnCH proj. no. 11,084

6760   Materia de Deo uno et trino commentariis illustrata. MS. Universitätsbibliothek Salzburg, codex M I 323. 496 f. Quarto. Saec. 17(1650–52).
Microfilm: MnCH proj. no. 11,087

6761   Tractatus in materiam de actibus humanis ex Ima IIdae Summa S. Thomae Aq. MS. Universitätsbibliothek Salzburg, codex M I 322, f.100–227. Quarto. Saec. 17(1652).
Microfilm: MnCH proj. no. 11,084

6762   Tractatus in materiam de vitiis et peccatis ex Ima IIdae Summa S. Thomae Aq.

MS. Universitätsbibliothek Salzburg, codex M I 322, f.228–452. Quarto. Saec. 17(1652).
Microfilm: MnCH proj. no. 11,084

Schwäble, M., pseud. *See* Miller, Athanasius.

Schwank, Benedikt, 1923–
6763 Der erste Brief des Apostels Petrus, erläutert von Benedikt Schwank, O.S.B. Düsseldorf, Patmos-Verlag [1963].
143 p. 20 cm.
MnCS; MoCo

6764 Pseudo-Augustini Solutiones diversarum quaestionum ab haereticis obiectarum.
(*In* Florilegia biblica africana saec. V. Turnholti, 1961. p. 135–223)
CaQStB

6765 Pseudo-Vigilii Thapsensis opus Contra Varimadum, cura et studio B. Schwank.
(*In* Florilegia biblica africana saec. V. Turnholti, p. I–XV, 1–134)
CaQStB

6766 **Schwarzhüber, Simpert,** 1727–1795.
Praktisch-katholisches Religionshandbuch für nachdenkende Christen. Prage, 1785–86.
4 v. 20 cm.
KAS; MnCS

Schwegler, Theodor, 1877–
6767 Familie, Gesellschaft und Wirtschaft nach dem mosaischen Gesetz und den Propheten. Einsiedeln, Benziger, 1935.
87 p.
MoCo

6768 Geschichte der katholischen Kirche in der Schweiz von den Anfängen bis auf die Gegenwart. 2., umgearb. u. verm. Aufl. Stans, Verlag Josef von Matt [1943].
426 p. 25 cm.
PLatS

6769 **Schweighofer, Gregor,** 1910–
Die Handschriften des Stiftes Altenburg. 1956.
129 p. 28 cm.
Typescript.
Xeroxed by University Microfilms, Ann Arbor, Mich., 1967.
MnCS

6770 **Scheninger, Florian.**
Peri tes auypodesias Jesou Chrustiy hypothesis (Ob der Heiland Schuhe getragen hat). Laus S.Laurentii ex ss. patribus. Verschiedene Sachen ("Versuche"). Sammlung verschiedene Advent-Lieder. MS. Benediktinerabtei Fiecht, codex 262, 262a, 262b N.S. 145, 87, 10, 147, 15 f. Quarto. Saec. 19.
Microfilm: MnCH proj. no. 28,830

6771 **Schwind, Gallus,** 1894–
Beuroner Glocken einst und jetzt.
(*In* Beuron, 1863–1963; Festschrift . . . Beuron, 1963. p. 521–544)
PLatS

6772 **Schwindt, Helen, Sister.**
The improvement of teachers through faculty meetings.
Thesis (M.A.)–University of Dayton, Ohio, 1970.
Typescript.
NdRiS

Schyz, Pontianus.
6773 Politia Helvetiae triumphalis, hoc est, Forma regiminis Helvetici ex monarchia, aristocratia, democratia perfectissima oratorie deducta . . . Lucernae, typis Annae Felicitatis Hauttin, anno MDCCIII.
[10], 19 p.
PLatS

6774 Spes immortalitate plena, seu Animae humanae immortalitas. [Stuttgart], apud Wolfgang Mauritium Endter, 1712.
295 p. 16 cm.
MnCS

6775 Romanum imperium doctum per imperium charitatis . . . [Stuttgart], Impensis auctoris, 1712.
328 p. 16 cm.
MnCS

6776 **Scipio, Marcus Antonius.**
Elogia abbatum sacri monasterii Casinensis . . . Neapoli, apud Octavium Beltranum, 1630.
248 p. 29 cm.
InStme

6777 **Score, Clement J.,** 1912–
The teaching of speech in the minor seminary.
75 leaves, 28 cm.
Thesis (M.A.)–Catholic University of America, Washington, D.C., 1942.
Typescript.
InStme

6778 **Scott, Patricia, Sister.**
Social science dimensions; guide for elementary schools. Department of Education Diocese of Covington, Ky., 1969.
137 p. 28 cm.
Lithographed.
KyCovS

Sczygielski, Stanislas. *see* Szczgielski, Stanislas.

Seasoltz, Robert Kevin, 1930–
6780 Devotions and other uses of the Church.
(*In* Liturgical Conference. 1965. p. 61–68)
PLatS

6781   The house of God; sacred art and church architecture. [New York], Herder and Herder, [1963].
272 p. diagrs. 21 cm.
ILSP; InFer; MnCS; NdRi

6782   The new liturgy; a documentation, 1903–1965. [New York], Herder and Herder, [1966].
xlvii, 707 p. 23 cm.
ILSP; MoCo; MnStj; KAS; PLatS

6782a   New liturgy, new laws. Collegeville, Minn., The Liturgical Press [1980].
vi, 257 p. 20 cm.
MnCS

6783   The people of God at prayer (Phonotape-cassette). Collegeville, Minn., St. John's University, 1978.
4 tapes. 90 min. each. 1 7/8 ips.
InStme

6784   **Sebastian, Irmine, Sister.**
Hroswitha, tenth-century nun-poetess.
14 p. 28 cm.
Thesis – University of Notre Dame, 1940.
Typescript.
InFer

Seeauer, Beda, 1716–1785.

6785   Chronicon novissimum antiqui monasterii ad S. Petrum Salisburgi, ab anno 582 usque ad 1782. Anselm Hintler, O.S.B., et Beda Seeauer, O.S.B. MS. Benediktinerabtei St. Peter, Salzburg, codex b XII 17. 20, 796, 490 p. Folio. Saec. 18.
Microfilm: MnCH proj. no. 10,691

6786   Concionator catechetico-moralis in duas partes divisus . . . Augspurg und Innsprug, Joseph Wolff, 1756.
2 v. 34 cm.
InStme

6787   Geistliche Liebs-Gedancken von dem hochwürdigen Sacrament des Altars . . . Augsburg, Matth. Wolff, 1744.
348 p. 17 cm.
KAS

6788   Liber professionis in monasterio ad S. Petrum Salisburgi ab anno 1419–1817. MS. Benediktinerabtei St. Peter, Salzburg, Archivum Hs. A 98. 900 p. Folio. Saec. 18–19.
Microfilm: MnCH proj. no. 10,755

6789   Novendialia exercitia pro septem festis principalioribus Beatissimae Virginis Mariae . . . Augustae Vindel., Mathias Wolff, 1743.
[20], 659, [21] p. 17 cm.
KAS; MnCS

6790   **Seemann, Michael,** 1934–
Heilsgeschehen und Gottesdienst; die Lehre Peter Brunners in katholischer Sicht . . . Paderborn, Verlag Bonifacius-Druckerei [1966].
xiv, 215 p. 24 cm.
MnCS

6791   **Seeon, Bavaria (Benedictine abbey).**
Catalogus codicum manu scriptorum Bibliothecae Regiae Monacensis: Codices 17701–17730 ex monasterio in Seon. Monachii, sumptibus Bibliothecae Regiae, 1878. Unveränderter Nachdruck Otto Harrassowitz, Wiesbaden, 1969.
MnCH

Seidel, George Joseph, 1932–

6792   A contemporary approach to classical metaphysics. Apple-Century-Crofts [1969].
126 p.
MoCo

6793   The crisis of creativity. Notre Dame, Ind., University of Notre Dame [1966].
ix, 182 p. 22 cm.
ILSP

6794   Martin Heidegger and the pre-Socratics; an introduction to his thought. Lincoln, Nebr., University of Nebraska Press [1964].
x, 169 p. 22 cm.
InStme; KAS; MnCS; MoCo; OkShG; PLatS

6795   **Seiler, Joachim,** d. 1688.
Geistliches Präservativ / Das ist: Vier und zwanzig nutzliche Betracht- und Uebungen . . . Einsiedeln, Joh. H. Ebersbach, 1708.
71 p. 16 cm.
MnCS

6796   **Seilhac, Lazare de.**
L'utilisation par S. Césaire d'Arles de la Règle de S. Augustin; étude de terminologie et de doctrine monastiques. Roma, Editrice Anselmiana, 1974.
350 p. 24 cm. (Studia Anselmiana, 62)
KAS; MoCo; PLatS

Seitenstetten, Austria (Benedictine abbey).

6797   Libellus precatorius, summa elegantia scriptus . . . MS. Benediktinerabtei Seitenstetten, Austria, codex 95. 201 f. Saec. 14.
Microfilm: MnCH proj. no. 907

6798   Oeffentliches Stiftsgymnasium Seitenstetten, 1814–1964. [Im Selbstverlag des Stiftes, 1964].
63 p. illus., ports, maps. 21 cm.
PLatS

6799   Urkundenbuch des Benediktiner-Stiftes Seitenstetten, von p. Isidor Raab. Wien, A. Holzhausen, 1870.

iv, 421 p. 24 cm. (Fontes rerum austriacarum, 2. Abt., 33 Bd)
KAS

Seitenstetten, Austria (Benedictine abbey). Bibliothek.
6800   Catalogus codicum manuscriptorum
bibliothecae Seitenstettensis.
2 v. 28 cm.
Handwritten.
Xeroxed by University Microfilms, Ann
Arbor, Mich., 1966.
MnCS

6801   De Plutarchi codice manuscripto Seiten-
stettensi scripsit Carolus Theodorus
Michaëlis. Berlin, R. Gaertners
Verlagsbuchhandlung, 1885.
27 p. 17 cm.
Xeroxed by University Microfilms, Ann
Arbor, Mich., 1966.
MnCS

6802   Der Seitenstettener Commentariolus
historicus über Burindans Verhältnis zu
Johanna von Navarra. [Linz, Jos. Feich-
tingers Erben, 1917].
20 p. 21 cm.
MnCS

6803   **Séjourné, Paul,** 1886–
L'Ordinaire de S. Martin d'Utrecht.
Utrecht, Dekker en van de Vegt, 1919–21.
243, 38 p. tables. 30 cm.
MnCS

6804   **Selle, Paulinus Jerome,** 1914–
Building construction at St. Vincent
[1789–1936].
vi, 84 leaves, 29 cm.
Thesis (B.A.)–St. Vincent College,
Latrobe, Pa., 1936.
Typescript.
PLatS

6805   **Semaña de Estudios Monasticos.** 4th,
Poblet, 1963.
Los monjes y los estudios. [Poblet],
Abadia de Poblet, 1963.
501 p. 25 cm.
In English, French and Spanish.
KAS

6806   **Semaña de Estudios Monasticos,** 14th,
Silos, Spain, 1973.
Los consejos evangelicos en la tradicion
monastica. [Silos], Abadia di Silos, 1975.
422 p. 24 cm.
PLatS

Senger, Basilius, 1920–
6807   Ansgar, Mönch und Apostel des
Nordens. Dülmen i.W., A. Laumann,
[1964].
80 p. plates, 19 cm.
MnCS

6808   Das Buch von Jesus Christus; eine Bil-
derbibel für die Familie. Düsseldorf,
Patmos-Verlag [1962].
89 p. illus.
MnStj

6809   Leienliturgik. Kevelaer, Rheinland, But-
zon & Bercker, 1962.
258 p. 19 cm.
MnCS; PLatS

6810   Sankt Benedikt; Prophet und Vater
vieler Völker. Essen, Fredebeul & Koenen
[1963].
168 p. 19 cm.
KAS; MnCS; PLatS

6811   **Senging, Martin, monk of Melk.**
Compendium primae et secundae partis
Speculi historialis Vincentii Bellovacensis.
MS. Benediktinerabtei Melk, Austria,
codex 1741, p. 5–830. Duodecimo. Saec. 15.
Microfilm: MnCH proj. no. 2052

6812   **Sens, France. Sainte-Colombe (Bene-
dictine abbey).**
Annales Sanctae Columbae Senonensis
a. 708–1218.
(*In* Monumenta Germaniae historica.
Scriptores. Stuttgart, 1963. t. 1, p. 102–
109)
MnCS; PLatS

6813   **Serna, Clemente de la,** 1946–
El voto de clausura en la Congregación
de Valladolid.
(*In* Semana de Estudios monasticos,
14th, Silos, 1973. p. 149–182)
PLatS

Serrano, Luciano, 1879–1944.
6814   La liga de Lepanto entre España,
Venecia y la Santa Sede (1570–1573) . . .
Madrid, Imprenta de Archivos, 1918–19.
2 v. 26 cm.
PLatS

6815   El obispado de Burgos y Castilla primitiva desde el siglo V al XIII. Madrid [Insti-
tuto de Valencia], 1935–36.
3 v. plates, maps, 24 cm.
PLatS

6816   El real monasterio de Santo Domingo de
Silos (Burgos); su historia y tesoro artistico. Burgos, Hijos de S. Rodrigues [1926?].
196 p. 18 cm.
CaQStB; MnCS

Severus, Emmanuel von, 1908–
6817   Der Herr ist wahrhaft auferstanden;
sechs Ansprachen über Christi Leiden, Tod
und Auferstehung. Maria Laach, Ars
Liturgica [1960].
69 p. 18 cm.
PLatS

6818   "Silvestrem tenui musam meditaris
avena"; zur Bedeutung der Wörter

mediatio und meditari beim Kirchenlehrer Ambrosius.

(*In* Perennitas; Beiträge . . . P. Thomas Michels zum 70. Geburtstag. Münster, 1963. p. 25–31)

PLatS

6819 Und ist Mensch geworden; geistliches Wort zur Geburt Erscheinung des Herrn. Maria Laach, Ars Liturgica [1961].

88 p. 18 cm.

PLatS

6820 Was haltet ihr von der Kirche? Die Frage des Abtes Ildefons Herwegen an seine und unsere Zeit . . . Münster, Aschendorff [1976].

36 p. 23 cm.

InStme; MnCS; PLatS

6821 (ed & tr) Cassianus, Joannes. Das Glutgebet; zwei Unterredungen aus der sketischen Wüste. Aus dem Lateinischen des Johannes Kassianus ausgewählt, übertragen und kurz erläutert von Emmanuel von Severus. Düsseldorf, Patmos-Verlag [1966].

115 p. 20 cm.

InStme

Sfondrati, Celestino, 1644–1696.

6822 Ethicae religiosae & religiosi ethici . . . Monasterii S. Galli, 1793.

244, 217 p. 17 cm.

MnCS

6823 Quindena Mariana, sive XV orationes ad sodales quondam Marianos dictae. Typis principalis Monasterii S. Galli, 1744.

277 p. 16 cm.

6824 **Shanahan, Mary Margaret, Sister.**

Out of time, out of place; Henry Gregory and the Benedictine Order in colonial Australia. Canberra, Australian National University Press, 1970.

187 p.

MoCo

6825 **Sharkey, Mary Giles, Sister.**

The De regimine claustralium of Abbot Johannes Trithemius; a study of his sources and method of composition.

73 p. 29 cm.

Thesis (M.A.)–Fordham University, New York City, 1964.

Mimeographed.

MnCS

6825a **Sharum, Elizabeth Louise, Sister.**

Write the vision down; a history of St. Scholastica Convent, Fort Smith, Arkansas, 1879–1979. Fort Smith, American Print. & Lithographing Co., 1979.

xii, 175 p. illus. 23 cm.

InStme; NcBe

Shaughnessy, Patrick, 1907–

6826 (tr) Gaiani, Vito. For a better religious life. Staten Island, N.Y., Alba House, 1963.

212 p. 21 cm.

InFer; PLatS; InStme

6827 (tr) Häring, Bernhard. The liberty of the children of God. Staten Island, N.Y., Alba House [1966].

135 p. 19 cm.

InStme; NeBe

6828 **Shaw, Mario W.,** 1929–

Studies in revelation and the Bible. Catholic Seminary Foundation of Indianapolis, c 1971.

iii, 92 p. 23 cm.

PLatS

6829 **Sheppard, Vincent Francis,** 1919–

Thomistic principles in training for American citizenship.

53 p. 28 cm.

Thesis (M.A.)–Catholic University of America, Washington, D.C., 1947.

Typescript.

AStb

Sherwood, Polycarp, 1912–1969.

6830 "Alleluia": papers of Polycarp Sherwood, O.S.B.

(*In* Resonance, vol. 5(1970), p. 1–80)

KAS

6831 Constantinople II et Constantinople III [par] F. X. Murphy, C. SS. R., [et] P. Sherwood, O.S.B. Paris, Editions de l'Orante [1974].

358 p. illus. 20 cm.

PLatS

6832 The doctrine of St. Maximus the Confessor on the nature of man. Washington, D.C., 1946.

57 leaves, 28 cm.

Typescript.

InStme

6833 Le fonds patriarcal de la bibliotheque manuscrite de Charfet.

(*In* L'Orient Syrien, vol. 2(1957), p. 93–107)

MnCS

6834 Maximus and Origenism. Arke kai telos. München, 1958.

27 p. 24 cm. (Berichte zum XI. Internationalen Byzantinisten-Kongress, München, 1958. III, 1)

InStme

6835 The unity of the churches of God. Baltimore, Helicon [1963].

227 p. 23 cm.

CaMWiSb; InStme; MnCS; MoCo; NcBe; PLatS

6836   (ed & tr) Sergius of Reshayna Mimro do Serge de Resayna sur la vie spirituelle. [Edité et traduit par Dom Polycarpe Sherwood. Vernon (Eure), France, 1960–61]. [84] p. cm.
Extracted and collected from issues of "L'Orient Syrien," v. 5(1960) and v. 6(1961).
InStme

Shoniker, Fintan Raymond, 1914–
6837   A Benedictine bibliography – now a reality.
Reprint from American Benedictine review, v. 13(1962), p. 610–615.
PLatS

6838   Incunabula from the Rare Book Collection of St. Vincent Archabbey and College Library, shown in an exhibit on the occasion of a visit by the Pittsburgh Bibliophiles . . . September 11, 1965.
7 leaves. 28 cm.
PLatS

6839   Library study, Benedictine Military School, Savannah, Georgia, 1967; and, Library study, Benedictine Priory, Savannah, Gerogia, 1967.
18, 7 leaves, 28 cm.
Multilithed.
PLatS

6840   St. Vincent College Library, Latrobe, Pa. (Introductory statement by the librarian & library dimensions). 1963.
4 p. 28 cm.
Typescript.
PLatS

6841   St. Vincent College Library.
(In Library Buildings and Equipment Institute, University of Maryland. Guidelines for library planners. 1960. p. 50–53)
PLatS

6841a   A service marking the dedication of a plaque in memory of Mr. and Mrs. Roy Arthur Hunt; sermon on the occasion of the dedication, June 20, 1976, by Rev. Fintan R. Shoniker, O.S.B.
4 leaves. 28 cm.
Typescript.
PLatS

6842   Statement of the library, January, 1963.
4 p. 28 cm.
Reproduced from typed page.
PLatS

6843   A study of the Abbey Library, St. Benedict's College, Atchison, Kansas. Made on the occasion of a visit, February 21–23, 1968.
25 leaves, 28 cm.
Typescript.
PLatS

6844   **Sidler, Wilhelm,** 1842–
Zur Entwicklungsgeschichte der modernen Meteorologie. Einsiedeln, New York, Benziger, 1877.
24, 29 p. illus. 28 cm.
PLatS

6845   **Siebenand, Alcuin,** 1933–
Recent popes and the press; a study of fifty-six pronouncements on the print media by Pope Pius XII and Pope John XXIII . . .
98, [73] leaves, 28 cm.
Research paper for M.A. – University of Wisconsin, 1963.
MnCS

6846   **Siffrin, Petrus,** 1888–
Missale gothicum (Vat. Reg. lat. 317). Roma, Herder, 1961.
174 p. 21 cm.
ILSP; InStme; PLatS

Sigebertus, monk of Gembloux, d. 1112.
6847   [Carmina]
(In Foucher, J. P. Florilège de la poésie sacrée. Paris, 1961. p. 211–213)
PLatS

6848   Liber Sigeberti Gemblacensis monachi De scriptoribus ecclesiasticis.
(In Fabricius, Johann A. Bibliotheca. p. 93–116)
PLatS

6849   Vita Deoderici episcopi Mettensis auctore Sigeberto Gemblacensi.
(In Monumenta Germaniae historica. Scriptores. Stuttgart, 1963. t. 4, p. 461–483)
PLatS

6850   Vita S. Wicberti. MS. Vienna, Nationalbibliothek, codex 3469, f.2r–14v. Quarto. Saec. 15.
Microfilm: MnCH proj. no. 20,398

6851   Vitae S. Guiberti et Maclovii. MS. Vienna, Nationalbibliothek, codex 490, f.1v–30v. Quarto. Saec. 12.
Microfilm: MnCH proj. no. 13,827

6852   **Sigehardus.**
Distinctiones Decreti. MS. Vienna, Nationalbibliothek, codex 2166. 72 f. Folio. Saec. 14.
Microfilm: MnCH proj. no. 15,482

Silos, Spain. Santo Domingo (Benedictine abbey).
6853   El "Breviarium Gothicum" de Silos (Archivo monastico, ms. 6) por Ismael Fernández de la Cuesta, O.S.B. Madrid-Barcelona, 1965.
125 p. 26 cm. (Monumenta Hispaniae sacra. Serie liturgica, v. 8)
PLatS

6854 Los manuscritos del real monasterio de Santo Domingo de Silos, por Walter Muir Whitehill, jr., y Justo Pérez de Urbel, O.S.B. Madrid, Tipografia de la "Revista de archivos," 1930.
85 p. XI facsims. 24 cm.
MnCS

6855 Novena a santa Gertrudis la magna. Nueva ed. Burgos, Centro Católico, 1912.
39 p. 14 cm.
MnCS

6856 Novena en honor del glorioso patriarca San Benito. Seguida de un triduo en honor de Santa Escolástica. 6. ed. Burgos, Abadia Benedictina de Santo Domingo de Silos, 1944.
46 p. plates, 14 cm.
MnCS

Silva-Nigra, Clemente Maria de, 1903–
6857 Frei Bernardo de Sâo Bento, o arquiteto seiscentista do Rio di Janeiro. Salvador, Bahia, Tip. Beneditina, 1950.
120, 27 p. illus., 50 plates, 33 cm.
MnCS

6858 Frei Domingos da Conceiçáo, o escultor seiscentista do Rio de Janeiro. Salvador, Bahia, Tipografia Beneditina, 1950.
42, 20 p. 70 plates, 33 cm.
MnCS

6859 Frei Ricardo do Pilar, o pintor seiscentista do Rio do Rio de Janeiro. Salvador, Bahia, Tipografia Beneditina, 1950.
98 p. 24 plates. 32 cm.
MnCS

6860 **Silvius, Peter.**
Vita S. Guilelmi eremitae et confessoris nec non primicerii Ordinis Guilielmitarum. MS. Benediktinerabtei St. Paul im Lavanttal, Austria, codex 31/2. 138 f. Octavo. Saec. 17.
Microfilm: MnCH proj. no. 11,757

6861 **Simeon, monk of Durham,** fl. 1130.
Symeonis Dunelmensis Opera et collectanea. Vol. I. Durham [Eng.], Pub. for the Society by Andrews and Co., 1868.
lxxxi, 301 p. 23 cm. (Publications of the Surtees Society . . . v. 51)
MnCS

6862 **Simonis, Raphaela.**
Deo gratias et Mariae; thanks be to God and Mary [an autobiographical memoir by] Mother Superior M. Raphaela Simonis, O.S.B. New York, Vantage Press [1973].
x, 122 p. 21 cm.
InFer; MoCo; PLatS

6863 **Sinder, Clemens.**
Collectio decretorum et constitutionum Pontificum Romanorum. MS. Benediktinerabtei St. Paul im Lavanttal, Austria,

codex 12/2. 364 p. Quarto. Saec. 16(1504, 1505, 1507).
Microfilm: MnCH proj. no. 11,751

Singeverga, Mosteiro de, Negrelos, Portugal. See Negrelos, Portugal. Mosteiro de Singeverga.

6864 **Sinhuber, Edmund, abbas.**
Gallus cantans et increpans, seu 107 sermones ascetici . . . in capitulo habiti. MS. Benediktinerabtei St. Peter, Salzburg, codex a.IX.36. 107, 55, 162 p. Folio. Saec. 17.
Microfilm: MnCH proj. no. 10,232

6865 **Siresa, Spain. San Pedro (Benedictine abbey).**
Cartulario de Siresa [edited by] Antonio Ubieto Arteta. Valencia, [Gráficas Bautista] 1960.
51 p. 17 cm.
PLatS

Sitwell, Gerard, 1906–
6866 Benet Canfield.
(*In* Walsh, James, ed. Pre-Reformation English spirituality. New York, 1965. p. 240–251)
PLatS

6867 The Cloud of unknowing.
(*In* Davis, Charles. English spiritual writers. New York, 1961. p. 41–50)
PLatS; InFer

6868 Spiritual writers of the Middle Ages. New York, Hawthorn Books [1961].
144 p. 21 cm.
ILSP; InStme; KAS; MnCS; MnStj; KAS; MoCo; NdRi; NcBe; OkShG; PSaS

6869 Walter Hilton.
(*In* Davis, Charles. English spiritual writers. New York, 1961. p. 30–40)
PLatS

6870 **Slangenburg, Netherlands. Sint Willibrordsmunster (Benedictine abbey).**
Microlibrary, Slangenburg Abbey, Doetinchem, Holland, 1978.
196 p. 12x20 cm.
This is a catalog of titles available on microfiches from Slangenburg Abbey.
Contents: Periodicals; Collections; Bibliographia; Exegesis; Historia ecclesiastica; Islamitica; Jus ecclesiasticum; Liturgia; Monastica; Oecomenica; Patristica; Theologia.
MnCH

Smaragdus, abbot of St. Mihiel, fl. 809–819.
Manuscript copies
6871 Admonitiones Smaragdi aliorumque patrum. MS. Universitätsbibliothek Graz,

Austria, codex 214. 146 f. Quarto. Saec. 14.
Microfilm: MnCH proj. no. 26,148

6872   Carmen in Regulam S. Benedicti. MS. Benediktinerabtei Melk, Austria, codex 3, f. 72r. Folio. Saec. 14.
Microfilm: MnCH proj. no. 2124

6873   Collectiones epistolarum et evangeliorum de tempore et de sanctis. MS. Benediktinerabtei St. Peter, Salzburg, codex a.IX.28. 490 p. Folio. Saec. 10.
Microfilm: MnCH proj. no. 10,227

6874   De diversis virtutibus. MS. Lambeth Palace Library, London, codex 373, f.1–33. Quarto. Saec. 12.
Microfilm: MnCH

6875   De diversis virtutibus. MS. Benediktinerabtei Kremsmünster, Austria, codex 128, f.235r–319v. Saec. 13.
Microfilm: MnCH proj. no. 118

6876   De diversis virtutibus. MS. Augustinerchorherrenstift St. Florian, Austria, codex XI, 77,f.98v–156v. Folio. Saec. 13.
Microfilm: MnCH proj. no. 2335

6877   Diadema monachorum. MS. Salisbury, England, Cathedral Library, codex 12, f.1–55. Octavo. Saec. 12.
Microfilm: MnCH

6878   Diadema monachorum. MS. Benediktinerabtei Admont, Austria, codex 331, f.94r–160v. Folio. Saec. 13.
Microfilm: MnCH proj. no. 9408

6879   Diadema monachorum. MS. Prämonstratenserabtei Schlägl, Austria, codex 8, f.96r–156v. Quarto. Saec. 13.
Microfilm: MnCH proj. no. 3059

6880   Diadema monachorum. MS. Subiaco, Italy (Benedictine abbey), codex 92. Quarto. Saec. 13.
Microfilm: MnCH

6881   Diadema monachorum. MS. Lambeth Palace Library, London, codex 180, f.43–88. Quarto. Saec. 14.
Microfilm: MnCH

6882   Diadema monachorum. MS. Madrid, Spain, Real Academia de la Historia, codex 75. 121 f. Quarto. Saec. 14.
Microfilm: MnCH proj. no. 34,933

6883   Diadema monachorum, sive De diversis virtutibus. Prämonstratenserabtei Schlägl, Austria, codex 47, f.80v–94v. Folio. Saec. 14–15.
Microfilm: MnCH proj. no. 2996

6884   Diadema monachorum. MS. Subiaco, Italy (Benedictine abbey), codex 139. Octavo. Saec. 14.
Microfilm: MnCH

6885   Diadema monachorum. MS. Benediktinerabtei Admont, Austria, codex 525. 78 f. Quarto. Saec. 15.
Microfilm: MnCH proj. no. 9577

6886   Diadema monachorum, seu Libellus de diversis virtutibus. Benediktinerabtei Melk, Austria, codex 737, f.104r–138r. Folio. Saec. 15.
Microfilm: MnCH proj. no. 1590

6887   Diadema monachorum. MS. Benediktinerabtei St. Paul im Lavanttal, Austria, codex 60/4, f.51r–81r. Folio. Saec. 15.
Microfilm: MnCH proj. no. 12,291

6888   Diadema monachorum. MS. Subiaco, Italy (Benedictine abbey), codex 314. 297 f. Octavo. Saec. 15.
Microfilm: MnCH

6889   Diadema monachorum. MS. Benediktinerabtei Admont, Austria, codex 833, f.1r–120v.
Microfilm: MnCH proj. no. 9827

6890   Expositio in Regulam S. Benedicti. MS. Kornik, Poland, Bibliotheka Kornicka, codex F 1 (3). Saec. 9.
Microfilm: MnCH

6891   Expositio Regulae s.p.n. Benedicti. MS. Silos, Spain, Archivo del Monasterio de Sto. Domingo, Ms. 1. 282 f. Folio. Saec. 9–10.
Microfilm: MnCH proj. no. 33,686

6892   Liber de diversis virtutibus. MS. Winchester College, England, codex 18. 252 f. Folio. Saec. 12.
Microfilm: MnCH

6893   Libellus de diversis virtutibus, dictus etiam Diadema monachorum. MS. Vienna, Nationalbibliothek, codex 1580, f.1v–57v. Quarto. Saec. 12.
Microfilm: MnCH proj. no. 14,907

6894   Libellus de diversis virtutibus, dictus etiam Diadema monachorum. MS. Vienna, Nationalbibliothek, codex 1582, f.1r–63v. Quarto. Saec. 12.
Microfilm: MnCH proj. no. 14,963

6895   Versus in Regulam S. Benedicti. MS. Universitätsbibliothek Graz, Austria, codex 2194, f.86r–87r. Quarto. Saec. 14–15.
Microfilm: MnCH proj. no. 26,374

6896   Versus super Regulam S. Benedicti. MS. Benediktinerabtei Melk, Austria, codex 1214, f.74v–76v. Sextodecimo. Saec. 15.
Microfilm: MnCH proj. no. 1865

6897   Via regia. MS. Vienna, Nationalbibliothek, codex 956, f.162v–190v. Folio. Saec. 11.
Microfilm: MnCH proj. no. 14,274

6898 Via regia, seu De educandis regum filiis, cum indice et prologo. MS. Vienna, Nationalbibliothek, codex 2336. 34 f. Folio. Saec. 15.
Microfilm: MnCH proj. no. 15,689

Smaragdus, abbot of St. Mihiel, fl. 809–819.
Printed works
6899 Expositio in Regulam S. Benedicti / ediderunt Alfredus Spannagel [et] Pius Engelbert, O.S.B. Siegburg, F. Schmitt, 1974.
lxxxiv, 394 p. 26 cm. (Corpus consuetudinum monasticarum, t. 8)
InStme; MnCS; PLatS

6899a Diadema monachorum, opus plane aureum . . . nunc vero hactenus impressum [etc.] [Paris] Joannes Parvus & Iodocus Badius [1532].
[8], 103 leaves. 16 cm.
Imprint from colophon.
Edited with a prefatory epistle by Joannes Joannellus Basauerianus.
KAS

6900 Summaria in Evangelia et Epistolas (ut vocant) dominicales & festivas, per totum annum in ecclesijs legi consuetas, quae pijs cum lectoribus tum verbi divini concionatoribus brevium commentariorum loco haberi possint, e luculentissimis S. Smaragdi abbatis lucubrationibus desumpta. n.p., 1536.
unpaged, 16 cm.
MnCS

6901 **Smith, Ermin Richard,** 1917–
Mental prayer in Benedictinism.
37 leaves, 28 cm.
Thesis (M.A.)–St. Vincent College, Latrobe, Pa., 1945.
Typescript.
PLatS

Smith, Joseph Oswald, 1854–1924.
6902 Meditations for the Holy Hour. [Ampleforth Abbey, England, 1917].
84 p. 19 cm.
PLatS

6903 Meditations on the Passion of Our Lord. 2d ed. London, Burns, Oates & Washbourne, 1922.
192 p. 19 cm.
First published 1915.
InFer; NcBe; OrMta; PLatS

6904 The Ordinary of the Mass, the food of prayer; a series of meditations and prayers. London, Burns, Oates, & Washbourne [1912].
421, viii p. 19 cm.
KAS; PLatS

Sneed, Richard Joseph, 1929–
6905 The biblical renewal and its bearing on catechetics.
(In Hofinger, J. Pastoral catechetics, p. 16–32)
PLatS

6906 The mystery foreshadowed in Israel.
(In The renewal of Christian education . . . 24th annual North American Liturgical Week, 1963, p. 9–16).
PLatS

Snow, Benedict, 1838–1907.
6907 The Church and labour. Christian aspects of the labour question. Fair treatment for honest work.
(In The Catholic Church and labour. London, Catholic Truth Society, 1908)
MnCS; NdRi

6908 Dreams; a paper read to the Maryport Literary and Scientific Society on March 11, 1890. [Yeovil, Printed by the Western Chronicle Company, Limited, n.d.]
21 p. 23 cm.
PLatS

6909 Glastonbury. Yeovil, Printed by the Western Chronicle Company, Limited [n.d.].
27 p. illus., plates, plan. 23 cm.
PLatS

6910 The home and Church of St. Gregory the Great. Yeovil, Printed by the Western Chronicle Company, Limited, 1890.
24 p. plates, 23 cm.
PLatS

6911 Pius IX; his early life to the return from Gaëta. Liverpool, Rockliff Brothers, 1877.
74 p. 20 cm.
PLatS

Solà, Ferran M., 1899–
6912 Gloria nostra; oda als martirs de Montserrat. Barcelona, Libreria La Hormiga de Oro, 1959.
52 p. illus. 21 cm.
MnCS

6913 Vesperal monástico de Montserrat. Texto latino-castellano, introducción y notas por F. S., O.S.B. Monasterio de Montserrat, 1947.
728 p. 17 cm.
MnCS

6914 **Sohler, Rogatia, Sister,** 1902–
Plant extracts as inhibitors of amylase and other enzyme systems.
110 p. 28 cm.
Thesis (M.D.)–Institutum Divi Thomae, 1956.
Typescript.
MnStj (Archives)

Solesmes, France (Benedictine abbey).

6915   Cantus Passionis Domini Nostri Jesu Christi secundum Matthaeum, Marcum, Lucam et Joannem ex editione Vaticana adamussim excerptus et rhythmicis signis a Solesmensibus monachis diligenter ornatus. Paris, Tornaci, Romae, Desclée et Socii, 1935.

    3 v. music. 35 cm.
    NdRi; PLatS

6916   Dominica Palmarum ad Missam et horas, cum cantu gregoriano ex editione Vaticana adamussim excerpto et rhythmicis signis a Solesmensibus monachis diligenter ornato. Parisiis, Desclée & Socii [1930].

    102 p. 20 cm.
    NdRi; OClSta; PLatS

6917   Der Einfluss des tonischen Accentes auf die melodische und rhythmische Struktur der gregorianischen Psalmodie. Von den Benediktinern zu Solesmes. Vergleichende Tabellen zwischen der Version der Manuskripte und der Version der Ausgabe von Regensburg. [Uebersetzt von P. Bohn]. Freiburg i.B., Herder, 1894.

    vi, 69 p. illus.(music) 31 cm.
    PLatS

6918   Graduale sacrosanctae Romanae Ecclesiae de tempore et de sanctis SS. D. N. Pii X. pontificis maximi jussu restitutum et editum ad exemplar editionis typicae concinnatum et rhythmicis signis a Solesmensibus monachis diligenter ornatum. Parisiis, Desclée, 1961.

    xxvii, 658, [149], 159, 182, (42) p. 21 cm.
    PLatS

6919   A manual of Gregorian chant, compiled from the Solesmes books and from ancient manuscripts. Rome-Tournai, Desclée, Lefebvre & Co., 1903.

    xxii, 394 p. 18 cm.
    PLatS

6920   The new office of Holy Week with Gregorian chant and rhythmic signs of the Benedictines of Solesmes. Modern notation. Paris, Desclée, 1962.

    218 p. music. 18 cm.
    MnCS

6921   La notation musicale des chants liturgiques latins. Présentée par les moines de Solesmes. [Solesmes, Abbaye de Saint-Pierre, 1963].

    [38] p. facsim.(39 p.) map, 32 cm.
    MnCS; PLatS

6922   Office and ceremonies for Holy Saturday and the Easter Vigil according to the newly-restored rite. Plainsong with the rhythmic signs of the Benedictines of Solesmes. Paris, Desclée, 1952.

    44 p. music. 19 cm.
    KAS

6923   A primer of plainsong with practical exercises, according to the Solesmes method (Editions with and without rhythmic signs). Tournai, Desclée, Lefebvre & Co., 1906.

    110 p. music, 16 cm.
    MnCS

6924   (ed) Guéranger, Prosper. L'année liturgique. Edition nouv., rev. & mise à jour par les moines de Solesmes. Tournai, Desclée, 1948–52.

    5 v. 18 cm.
    PLatS

6925   **Solesmes, France. Abbaye Sainte-Cécile.**

    In spiritu et veritate. [La Ferté-Bernard, impr. R. Bellanger et fils, 1966].

    190 p. 19 cm.
    InStme

Solesmes Congregation. See Benedictines. Congregations. Solesmes.

Solms, Elisabeth de, Sister.

6926   (tr) Baldwin, Abp. of Canterbury. Le sacrement de l'autel [par] Baudouin de Ford . . . traduction française par E. de Solms, O.S.B. Paris, Editions du Cerf, 1963.

    2 v. 21 cm. (Sources chrétiennes, no. 93–94)
    InStme; PLatS

6927   (tr) Bernard of Clairvaux, Saint. Lettres choisies . . . Traduction de E. de Solms, O.S.B. Namur, Belgique, Les Editions du Soleil Levant [1962].

    192 p. 17 cm. (Collection Ecrits des saints)
    PLatS

6928   (tr) Bernard of Clairvaux, Saint. Saint Bernard: Textes choisis et présentés par Dom Jean Leclercq. Traduction de E. de Solms. Namur, Editions du Soleil Levant, 1958.

    191 p. 18 cm. (Les Ecrits des saints)
    PLatS

6929   (tr) Rupert, Abbot of Deutz. Les oeuvres du Saint-Esprit . . . Texte établi et traduit par Elisabeth de Solms, O.S.B. Paris, Editions du Cerf, 1967–

    v. 20 cm. (Sources chrétiennes, n. 131),
    InStme; PLatS

6930   **Soltner, Louis.**

    Solesmes & Dom Guéranger, 1805–1975. Saint-Pierre de Solesmes, 1974.

    177 p. 48 leaves of plates, illus. 24 cm.
    InStme

6931 **Some European Benedictine abbeys** as seen by one American monk. St. Leo, Fla., St. Leo Abbey Press, 1964.
92 p.
NcBe

6932 **Sonnenburg, Austria (abbey of Benedictine nuns).**
Die ältesten Urbare des Benediktinerinnenstiftes Sonnenburg im Pustertal, hrsg. von Karl Wolfsgruber. Wien, Graz, Böhlau in Kommission, 1968.
lxxix, 147 p. facsims. 25 cm.
MnCS

Sorg, Rembert, 1908–
6933 Ecumenic Psalm 87; original form and two rereadings, with an appendix on Psalm 110,3. Fifield, Wis., King of Martyrs Priory, 1969.
xvi, 83 p. 23 cm.
InStme; PLatS

6934 Habaqquq III and Selah. Fifield, Wis., King of Martyrs Priory, 1968.
vii, 81 p. illus. 24 cm.
InStme; PLatS

6935 Meditating like a dove; an essay on silence and meditation. St. Louis, Pio Decimo Press, 1961.
32 p. 22x28 cm.
ILSP; MnCS; MoCo; PLatS

6936 Religion at King of Martyrs: Credo in Spiritum Sanctum. Fifield, Wis., King of Martyrs Priory, 1963.
30 p. 23 cm.
MnCS; PLatS

6937 **Soukup, Cuthbert Gregory,** 1914–
Hymns through the year [by Cuthbert Soukup and Camillus Talafous. Collegeville, Minn., St. John's University, n.d.]
[24] p. 21 cm.
MnCS

6938 **South Greensburg, Pa. St. Bruno's Church.**
St. Bruno's School, dedicated November 11, 1956, South Greensburg, Pa.
[26] p. illus., ports. 29 cm.
PLatS

6939 **Souvenir of the silver jubilee of St. Peter's Colony,** 1903–1928. Zum Andenken an das silberne Jubiläum der St. Peter's Kolonie. [Muenster, Sask., St. Peter's Press, 1929].
[48] p. illus. 28 cm.
CaSMu; NcBe; PLatS

6940 **Spahr, Gebhard,** 1913–
Kreuz und Blut Christi in der Kunst Weingartens; eine ikonographische Studie. Konstanz, Jan Thorbecke Verlag [1962].
136 p. plates, 23 cm.
MnCS

Spayd, Mary Carmel, Sister.
6941 Survey of insurance carried by religious motherhouses of Sisters and by schools and hospitals operated by Sisters.
85 p. tables, 28 cm.
Thesis (M.A.) – University of Notre Dame, 1959.
InFer

6942 A case study of the accounting procedures of the business and dietary departments of a small hospital.
81 p. illus., tables, 28 cm.
Thesis – University of Notre Dame, 1962.
InFer

6942a **Spearritt, Placid,** 1933–
(ed) Allanson, Peter, O.S.B. A history of the English Benedictine Congregation, 1558–1850. Introduction and guide compiled by Placid Spearritt and Bernard Green. Bicester, Oxon, OMP and Micromedia Ltd., c 1978.
PLatS

6943 **Speck. Carolus.**
De potestate iudiciali in monasteriis monachorum Ordinis S. Benedicti usque ad Benedictum XII. Roma, Pontificia Università Lateranense, 1963.
xiv, 67 p. 25 cm.
MoCo; PLatS

6944 **Speculum Regulae monachorum b. Bened. abbatis.** MS. Benediktinerabtei Fiecht, Austria, codex 213, f.120r–137r. Folio. Saec. 14–15.
Microfilm: MnCH proj. no. 28,855

6945 **Spicilegium Beccense;** ouvrage publié avec le concours du Centre National de la Recherche Scientifique. Paris, J. Vrin, 1959–
v. facsims. 25 cm.
CaQStB; MnCS; MoCo; PLatS

Spies, Placidus, fl. 17th cent.
6946 Praxis catechistica; oder, Nutzliches Gespräch zwischen einem Vater und Sohn. Item: zwischen einen Catholisch- und Uncatholischen. Constantz, David Hautt, 1683.
[12], 464 [4] p. 13 cm.
KAS

6947 Praxis catechistica, das ist: Einfältiges und nutzliches Gespräch zwischen einem Vater und Sohn von dem rechten Glauben und christlicher catholischer Lehr. Augsburg, Reith, 1757.
378 p. 15 cm.
MnCS; PLatS

6948 **Spilker, Reginhard,** 1910–
Die Busspraxis in der Regel des hl. Benedikt; Untersuchung über die altmonastische Busspraxis und ihr Verhältnis zur

altkirchlichen Bussdisziplin. [Romae] S. Anselmo [1936?].

[281]– 339, 12-[39] p. 22 cm.

Diss.–Pontificium Institutum S. Anselmi de Urbe.

Vita.

InStme

6949 **Spitz, Andreas,** d. 1811.
Dissertatio historico-ecclesiastica: num attenta historica ecclesiae universali, ac speciatim attentis Germanorum factis, et decretis Basileensibus a canonistis Germaniae defendi valeat sententia, quae infallibalitatem Romani Pontificis, ejusque superioritatem supra Concilium Oecumenicum adstruit . . . praeside Andrea Spits, O.S.B. . . . eruditorum tentamini exponit . . . Wilhelmus Henr. Franc. Vischers ex Kalkar, Cliviaco-Borussus, ad diem XXXI Martii 1787 in acroaterio majore Bonnensi. Bonnae, typis Joan. Frid. Abshoven, 1787.
76 p. 19 cm.
PLatS

6950 **Spitzmesser, Norbert,** 1892–1962.
The Benedictine ideal vs. modern ills; a suggestion to modern psychologists and educators.
48 leaves, 28 cm.
Thesis (M.A.)–University of Notre Dame, 1929.
Typescript.
InStme

6951 **Spreitzenhofer, Ernest,** 1859–
Die historischen Voraussetzungen der Regel des hl. Benedict von Nursia. Wien, 1895.
93 p. 23 cm.
FStL; KAS; MnCS

6952 **Stadlmayer, Alphonsus.**
Tractatus in materiam de legibus. Tractatus in materiam de gratia Dei ex Ia IIae Summae S. Thomae Aquinatis. Tractatus de fide, spe et charitate ex IIa IIae Summae S. Thomae. MS. Universitätsbibliothek Salzburg, codex M I 329. 594 f. Quarto. Saec. 17(1649–51).
Microfilm: MnCH proj. no. 11,093

Staerk, Antonius, 1871–
6953 Le Père Jean de Cronstadt, archiprétre de l'Eglise Russe. Pau, G. Lesgher-Moutoné, 1902.
xv, 158 p. 19 cm.
InStme

6954 Les manuscrits latins du Ve au XIIIe siècle conservés à la bibliothèque impériale de Saint-Pétersbourg. New York, Georg Olms Verlag, 1976.
2 v. 142 facsims. 25 cm.
MnCS

First published by F. Krois, Saint-Petersbourg, 1910.
MnCS

6955 **Stainhauser, Johann.**
Lebensbeschreibung der Erzbischöfe von Salzburg Michael und Georg von Kienburg. MS. Benediktinerabtei St. Peter, Salzburg, codex b.XI.65. 34 f. Folio. Saec. 17(1612).
Microfilm: MnCH proj. no. 10,684

Stanbrook Abbey, England.
6956 Aelfric of Eynsham. By a Benedictine of Stanbrook Abbey.
(*In* Davis, Charles. English spiritual writers. New York, 1961. p. 1–17)
InFer; PLatS

6957 Dame Julian of Norwich. By a Benedictine of Stanbrook Abbey.
(*In* Davis, Charles. English spiritual writers. New York, 1961. p. 51–65)
PLatS; InFer

6958 Frances Xavier Cabrini, the saint of the emigrants. By a Benedictine of Stanbrook Abbey. London, Burns, Oates, & Washbourne [1944].
vii, 195 p. 19 cm.
AStb

6959 Letters from the saints. Arranged and selected by a Benedictine of Stanbrook Abbey. With illustrations by Vivian Berger. New York, Hawthorn Books [1964].
ix, 302 p. illus., facsims. 22 cm.
AStb; MnCS; MnStj; OkStG; PLatS

6960 The Stanbrook Abbey Press; ninety-two years of its history written and illustrated by the Benedictines of Stanbrook. Worcester, Stanbrook Abbey Press, 1970.
xiv, 180 p. illus. 23 cm.
MnCS; PLatS

6961 Unless the grain die: Saint Augustine of Hippo, Saint Ignatius of Antioch. [Translated from the Latin & Greek texts by the Benedictines of Stanbrook]. Worcester, Stanbrook Abbey Press, 1961.
18 p. 30 cm.
"Handset in spectrum, decorations by Margaret Adams, printed at the Stanbrook Abbey Press, bound by George Percival & Rigby Graham."
PLatS

6962 (tr) Alcuin. Son well-beloved; six poems by Alcuin. Translated by the Benedictines of Stanbrook. Worcester, Stanbrook Abbey Press, 1967.
viii, 9 p. 21 cm.
PLatS

6963 (ed) Benedict, Saint, Abbot of Monte Cassino. Sancti Benedicti Regula monas-

teriorum. [Worcester] Stanbrook, MCMXXX.
PLatS

6964 (tr) A Capuchin chronicle. New York, Benziger, 1931.
xv, 198 p. 18 cm.
"Translated and abridged from the original Italian by a Benedictine of Stanbrook Abbey."
InStme

6965 (tr) Elisabeth de la Trinité, Sister. Reminiscences of Sister Elizabeth of the Trinity, servant of God, discalced Carmelite of Dijon. Translated by a Benedictine of Stanbrook Abbey. Westminster, Md., Newman Press, 1952.
xi, 265 p. 22 cm.
MnCS

6966 (tr) Whiterig, John, d.1371. The monk of Farne; the meditations of a fourteenth-century monk, edited and introduced by Hugh Farmer. Translated by a Benedictine of Stanbrook. [1st American edition]. Baltimore, Helicon Press [1961].
vii, 155 p. illus. 22 cm. (Benedictine studies [1])
MnCS

6967 **Stapleton, Fridswide, Sister.**
The history of the Benedictines of St. Mary's Priory, Princethorpe. Hinckley, S. Walker, 1930.
xvi, 165 p. plates, 22 cm.
KAS; NdRi

6968 **Stark, Matthew,** 1937–
The office of abbot.
(*In* Monastic studies, v. 10, p. 165–179)
PLatS

6969 **Statham, Denis Patrick,** 1919–
St. Thomas and the senses of Sacred Scripture in the Summa theologiae and the In psalmos Davidis expositio. Rome (private printing), 1955.
xii, 97 p. 23 cm.
Part of thesis – Pontificium Institutum "Angelicum" de Urbe.
OkShG

6970 **Stavelot, Belgium (Benedictine abbey).**
Recueil des chartes de l'Abbaye de Stavelot-Malmedy, publié par Jos. Halkin et C. G. Roland. Bruxelles, Kiessling et cie, 1909–30.
2 v. 30 cm.
MnCS

6971 **Stead, Julian,** 1926–
Liturgy and the separated Christians.
(*In* North American Liturgical Week, 21st, Pittsburgh, Pa., 1960. p. 113–121)
PLatS

6972 **Stegbuecher, Joachim.**
Vorbereitung auf die heilige Profess: geistliche Uebungen auf 6 Tag aussgethailet . . . MS. Benediktinerinnenabtei Nonnberg, Salzburg, codex 23 E 33. 188 f. Octavo. Saec. 17(1604).
Microfilm: MnCH proj. no. 10,935

Stegmann, Basil August, 1893–1981.

6973 Life in the Spirit.
(*In* Dooley, L. M. Further discourses on the Holy Ghost. New York, 1945. p. 31–40)
PLatS

6974 Mission of monasticism. [194–?].
15 p. 28 cm.
Multigraphed.
MnCS

Stehle, Aurelius, 1877–1930.

6975 Manual of episcopal ceremonies, based on the Caeremoniale episcoporum, decrees of the Sacred Congregation of Rites and approved authors. Revised by Rev. Emmeran A. Rettger, O.S.B. 5th ed. Latrobe, Pa., Archabbey Press, 1961.
2 v. 24 cm.
KAS; MoCo; NcBe; PLatS

6976 Systematic exercises in Latin syntax, especially adapted to Englmann's Latin grammar (7th American ed.). 3d rev. ed. Beatty, Pa., St. Vincent Archabey, 1911.
286 p. 23 cm.
KAS

Steidle, Basilius, 1903–

6977 Die Benediktusregel, lateinisch-deutsch. Hrsg. von P. Basilius Steidle, O.S.B. Beuron, Beuroner Kunstverlag [1963].
229 p. 19 cm.
MnCS; PLatS

6977a Die Benedictus-Regel. Lateinisch-deutsch. Hrsg. von Basilius Steidle. 2. überarbeitete Aufl. Beuron, Kunstverlag, 1975.
211 p.
MnCS

6978 The Rule of St. Benedict, with an introduction, a new translation of the Rule and a commentary, all reviewed in the light of an earlier monasticism. Translated with a few brief annotations by Urban J. Schnitzhoffer, O.S.B. [Beuron, Beuroner Kunstverlag, 1952].
x, 307 p. 19 cm.
InStme; MdRi; MoCo; MnCS

6979 ———— Canon City, Colorado, Holy Cross Abbey [1967].
x, 307 p. 19 cm.
ICSS; MnStj; NcBe; PLatS

Stein, Benjamin John, 1910–

6980 Microfilm record for a time capsule to be placed above the cornerstone of the abbey church. Filmed by Recordak Corporation, February 16, 1959.

Positive (Reduction 12-1). Negative in Abbey Archives.

MnCS

6981   Muggli family record. 3d ed. Collegeville, Minn., St. John's Abbey, 1961.

90 p. tables, 18 cm.

MnCS; NdRi

Stein, Ernest von.

6982   De conatibus haereticorum Germaniae saeculis 16. et 17. doctrinas suas adulterinas Ecclesiae Graecorum Schismaticae imponendi. [Beatty, Pa.] St. Vincent Abbey Print [1890?].

8 p. 23 cm.

PLatS

6983   Predigt auf das Fest des allerheiligsten Erlösers (Dom. III. Julii) gehalten in der Kirche der Redemptoristen zum allerheiligsten Erlösers in New York am 19. Juli 1891. [n.p., n.d.]

10 p. 22 cm.

PLatS

Steindl-Rast, David, 1926–

6984   The biblical view of the cosmos; myth, symbol, and ritual.

(*In* Cosmic piety; modern man and the meaning of the universe. p. 15–59)

PLatS

6985   Exposure: key to Thomas Merton's Asian Journal?

(*In* Monastic studies, v. 10, p. 181–204)

PLatS

6986   Why a man becomes a monk. [Mount Saviour Monastery, 196-?]

[15] p. 26 cm.

KAS

Steiner, Urban James, 1932–

6987   Benedictine libraries yesterday and today.

42 p. 29 cm.

Thesis (M.A.) – University of Illinois, Urbana, Ill., 1960.

Multigraphed.

MnCS

6988   Contemporary theology; a reading guide. Collegeville, Minn., The Liturgical Press [1965].

vi, 111 p. 23 cm.

KAS; MnCS; MnStj; PLatS

Stengel, Carl, 1581–1663.

6989   Christianae pietatis in VII operibus misericordiae corporalis spectanda & Legenda proposita. Augustae Vindel. [apud Saram Mangiam, viduam] 1622.

152 p. illus. 18 cm.

KAS

6990   Gazophylacium sacrarum cogitationum in festis totius anni, orandi, meditandi, concionandi, materiam ministrantium. Ingolstadij, apud Gregorium Haelinum, 1645.

[14], 326, [8] p. 13 cm.

KAS

6991   Imagines sanctorum Ordinis S. Benedicti tabellis aereis expressae, cum eulogiis eorundem vitis. [Augsburg, Mon. SS. Udalricae & Afrae] 1625.

180, [3] p., incl. 86 full-page engravings, 20 cm.

MnCS; MoCo

6992   Josephus, hoc est, sanctissimi educatoris Christi Dom. Deiq. nostri in terris apparentis, ac aeternae Virginis Mariae sponsi vitae historia, compendio, quantum potuit, adumbrata ex fide dignioribus auctoribus collecta. Monaci, R. Sadeler, 1616.

278, [10] p. 13 cm.

KAS

6993   Optica praelatorum et pastorum, qua inprimis apostolica eorundem vita & mores, officium ac regimen, pastoralis denique cura & potestas . . . proponitur. Coloniae Agrippinae, Joan. Schlebusch, 1684.

[8], 384, [8] p. 21 cm.

KAS

6994   Thuribulum aureum in quo thymiama suavissimi odoris Deo offertur, id est, de VII horis canoncis syntagma. Augustae Vindelicorum, [apud Saram Mangiam] 1622.

4, 131 p. 17 cm.

KAS; PLatS

Stephan, John, 1886–

6995   Buckfast Abbey; historical guide. S. Devon, Buckfast Abbey [1923].

112 p. illus.

MoCo

6996   Historical guide to Buckfast Abbey. New and revised. Devon, Buckfast Abbey [1955].

48 p. illus.

MoCo

6997   A history of Buckfast Abbey from 1018 to 1968. Bristol, The Burleigh Press [1970].

ix, 372 p. illus. 22 cm.

KAS; MoCo; PLatS

Stephanus de Spanberg, abbot of Melk, d. 1453.

6998   Epistolae quatuor ad Johannem Schlitpacher. MS. Benediktinerabtei Melk, Austria, codex 662, f.186r–188r. Quarto. Saec. 15.

Microfilm: MnCH proj. no. 1532

6999   Lectura in epistolam primam S. Pauli ad Timotheum. MS. Benediktinerabtei Melk,

Austria, codex 120, f.151r–162v. Folio. Saec. 15.

Microfilm: MnCH proj. no. 1190

7000 Lectura in librum Ecclesiastici. MS. Benediktinerabtei Melk, Austria, codex 120, f.1r–150r. Folio. Saec. 15.

Microfilm: MnCH proj. no. 1190

7001 Sermo de passione Domini. MS. Benediktinerabtei Melk, Austria, codex 775, f.143r–149r. Quarto. Saec. 15.

Microfilm: MnCH proj. no. 1615

Stevens, Gregory, 1926–1964.

7002 Grace: the kingdom of the Father.

(*In* Fortman, Edmund. The theology of man and grace, 1966. p. 23–26)

PLatS

7003 The life of grace. Englewood Cliffs, N.J., Prentice-Hall, 1963.

viii, 118 p. 24 cm.

ILSP; InStme; KAS; MnCS; MnStj; MoCo; NcBe; OKShG; PLatS

7004 The new life.

(*In* Fortman, Edmund. The theology of man and grace, 1966. p. 49–53)

PLatS

Stifft, Wolfgangus.

7005 Cursus philosophicus, seu Commentarius in universam Aristotelis philosophiam. MS. Benediktinerabtei Altenburg, Austria, codex AB 14 A 13. 555 p. Quarto. Saec. 17(1690–91).

Microfilm: MnCH proj. no. 6542

7006 Manuductio ad logicam, sive Summarium dialecticum praeparando ad logicam studios accomatum. MS. Benediktinerabtei Altenburg, Austria, codex AB 14 A 13. 128 p. Quarto. Saec. 17 (1690–91).

Microfilm: MnCH proj. no. 6542

Stimmen aus Rom. *See* Rome (City). S. Paolo fuori le Mura.

Stock, Augustine, 1920–

7007 Counting the cost; New Testament teaching on discipleship. Collegeville, Minn., The Liturgical Press, 1977.

MdRi; MoCo

7008 Jonah. Conception, Mo., Conception Abbey [1963].

58–63 p. 21 cm. (Saint Andrew Bible commentary, 11)

PLatS

7009 Kingdom of heaven; the good tidings of the Gospel. [New York], Herder and Herder [1964].

191 p. 21 cm.

ICSS; KAS; MnCS; MnStj; MoCo; NdRi; OkShG; PLatS

7010 Lamb of God; the promise and fulfillment of salvation. [New York], Herder and Herder [1963].

175 p. 21 cm.

CaMWiSb; ICSS; MnCS; MnStj; MoSo; InStme; NcBe; PLatS

7011 Meaning and prophecy and Isaiah. Conception, Mo., Conception Abbey [1962].

79 p. 21 cm. (Saint Andrew Bible commentary, 3)

PLatS

7012 The New Testament. Conception, Mo., Conception Abbey [1960].

80 p. 21 cm. (Saint Andrew Bible commentary, 19)

KySu; PLatS

7013 The Psalms. Conception, Mo., Conception Abbey [1961].

2 pts. 21 cm. (Saint Andrew Bible commentary, 13, 14)

KySu; PLatS

7014 Saint Matthew. Conception, Mo., Conception Abbey [1960].

120 p. 21 cm. (Saint Andrew Bible commentary, 28)

KySu; PLatS

7015 The smaller Prophecies. Conception, Mo., Conception Abbey [1960].

79 p. 21 cm. (Saint Andrew Bible commentary, 2)

KySu; PLatS

7016 The way in the wilderness; Exodus, wilderness, and Moses in the Old Testament and New. Collegeville, Minn., The Liturgical Press [1969].

xii, 156 p. 23 cm.

MnCS; MnStj; MoCo; NdRi; PLatS

Stockhamer, Aemilianus.

7017 Disputationes de praecipuis controversiis christianae fidei adversus nostri temporis haereticos traditae ab Adalberto Heufler benedictino Admontensi . . . quas excepit Fr. Aemilianus Stockhamer, O.S.B., ad S. Petrum Salisb. anno 1668. MS. Benediktinerabtei St. Peter, Salzburg, codex b.III.19. 135 p. Quarto. Saec. 17.

Microfilm: MnCH proj. no. 10,370

Stöcklin, Ulrich, d. 1443.

7018 Psalteria Wessofontana. Ulrich Stöcklins von Rottach, Abt zu Wessobrunn, 1438–1443, siebenzehn Reimpsalterien, hrsg. von Guido Maria Dreves, S.J. New York and London, Johnson Reprint Corporation, 1961.

248 p. 21 cm. (Analecta hymnica Medii Aevi, 38)

PLatS

7019 Ulrich Stöcklins von Rottach Reimgebete und Leselieder, hrsg. von Guido Maria Dreves, S.J. New York and London, Johnson Reprint Corporation, 1961.

204 p. 21 cm. (Analecta hymnica Medii Aevi, 6)
Reprint of Leipzig edition of 1889.
PLatS

Stoeckle, Bernard, 1927–

7020 Amor carnis – abusus amoris; das Verständnis von der Konkupiszenz bei Bernhard von Clairvaux und Aelred von Rieval.
(*In* Analecta monastica, 7. ser., 1965. p. 148–174)
PLatS

7020a Concise dictionary of Christian ethics, edited by Bernhard Stoeckle, with contributions by J. Dominian [et al.]. New York, Seabury Press, c 1979.
x, 285 p. 24 cm.
PLatS

7021 Gratia supponit naturam; Geschichte und Analyse eines theologischen Axioms . . . Romae, Herder, 1962.
xxiv, 407 p. 25 cm. (Studia Anselmiana, 49)
InStme; PLatS

Stollenmayer, Pankraz, 1889–

7022 Das Grab Herzog Tassilos III, von Bayern. [n.p., n.d.].
66 p. illus. 24 cm.
MnCS

7023 Der Tassilokelch. Wels, Druck der Buch- und Kunstdruckerei "Welsermühl" [1949?].
109 p. illus. 24 cm.
MnCS

7024 Tassilo-Leuchter – Tassilo Zepter. Wels, Druck- und Verlagsanstalt Welsermühl [1959?].
72 p. illus. 24 cm.
MnCS

Stolz, Anselm, 1900–1942.

7025 Die Mittlerin aller Gnaden.
(*In* Sträter, Paul. Katholische Marienkunde, v. 2 (1962), p. 241–271)
PLatS

7026 (2dary) Thomas Aquinas, Saint. [Summa theologica] I, 14–26: Gottes Leben, sein Erkennen und Wollen . . . Einleitung und Kommentar von P. Anselm Stolz, O.S.B. Salzburg, A. Pustet, 1934.
16, 439 p. 20 cm. (Die deutsche Thomas-Ausgabe, 2. Bd.)
PLatS

Strange, Marcian, 1925–

7027 The books of Amos, Osee & Michea, with a commentary by Marcian Strange, O.S.B. New York, Paulist Press [1961].
96 p. illus. 23 cm. (Pamphlet Bible series, v. 26)
KySu; PLatS

7028 Job and Qoheleth. Introduction and commentary by Marcian Strange, O.S.B. Collegeville, Minn., The Liturgical Press [1968].
56 p. 20 cm. (Old Testament reading guide, v. 27)
MnCS; PLatS

7029 The question of moderation in Eccl. 7:15-18.
ix, 138 leaves, 28 cm.
Thesis – Catholic University of America, Washington, D.C., 1969.
Typescript.
InStme

7030 **Strasser, Bernard,** 1895–
The dews of Tabor. New York, Exposition Press, 1960.
207 p.
InFer

Strebl, Benedikt.

7031 Nuclei Nucleatoris . . . Andreae Coppensteinii (Quos ipse ex Bessace enucleavit). Conciones de tempore et de sanctis. MS. Benediktinerabtei Altenburg, Austria, codex AB 13 E 18. 484 p. Quarto. Saec. 17.
Microfilm: MnCH proj. no. 6502

7032 Sonntagspredigten: Advent bis Trinitas. MS. Benediktinerabtei Altenburg, Austria, codex AB 13 E 20. Quarto. Saec. 17.
Microfilm: MnCH proj. no. 6499

7033 Sonntagspredigten: 1. Sonntag nach Trinitatis bis letzten Sonntag nach Trinitatis. MS. Benediktinerabtei Altenburg, Austria, codex AB 13 E 22. Quarto. Saec. 17.
Microfilm: MnCH proj. no. 6497

7034 Variarum concionum quodlibitum, das ist, Mancherlay Predigten. MS. Benediktinerabtei Altenburg, Austria, codex AB 13 E 19. Quarto. Saec. 17.
Microfilm: MnCH proj. no. 6500

7035 **Strittmatter, Anselm,** 1894–
Notes on Leo Tuscus' translation of the Liturgy of St. John Chrysostom.
(*In* Didascaliae; studies in honor of Anselm M. Albareda. New York, 1961. p. 409–424)
PLatS

7036 **Strittmatter, Blase Raymond,** 1905–
De motu locali ejusque causa.
64 leaves, 29 cm.
Thesis (Ph.D.) – Collegio di Sant'Anselmo, Rome, 1930.
Typescript.
PLatS

7037 **Strotmann, Théodore,** 1911–
L'évêque dans la tradition orientale.
(*In* Congar, M. J. L'épiscopat et l'église universelle. Paris, 1962. p. 309–328)
PLatS

Stuckenschneider, Placid, 1926–
7038   (illus.) Beaumont, Jeanne. Growing up in Christ . . . Illustrated by Brother Placid, O.S.B. Collegeville, Minn., The Liturgical Press [1967].
139 p. illus., plates, 29 cm.
MnCS

7039   (illus.) Liesel, Nikolaus. The eucharistic liturgies of the Eastern Churches . . . Art and layout: Brother Placid, O.S.B. Collegeville, Minn., The Liturgical Press [1963].
310 p. illlus. 32 cm.
KAS; MnCS; PLatS

7040   (illus.) Sunday Mass book . . . Illustrated by Brother Placid, O.S.B. Collegeville, Minn., The Liturgical Press [1963].
MnCS

7041 **Studer, Basilius,** 1925–
Soteriologie in der Schrift und Patristik. Freiburg i.B., Herder, 1978.
vii, 225 p. 26 cm.
InStme

7042 **Studzinski, Raymond,** 1943–
John Wyclif and the sacrament of penance.
xxii, 208 leaves. 28 cm.
Thesis (Ph.D.)–Fordham University, New York, 1977.
InStme

7043 **Sturm, Dalph D.,** 1927–
Chesterton's ideas on education.
85 p.
Thesis (M.A.)–University of Ottawa, 1954.
MoCo

7044 **Subercaseaux Errázuriz, Pedro,** 1880–1956.
Memorias. Santiago de Chile, Editorial del Pacifico [1962].
270 p. illus. 19 cm.
MnCS

Subiaco, Italy (Benedictine abbey).
7045   Nocturnale secundum consuetudinem monasteriorum Sublacensis et Sacri Specus. MS. St. Vincent College Library, Latrobe, Pa., ms. 13. 336 f. Octavo. Saec. 15.
PLatS

7046   Il Sacro Speco di Subiaco. LII vedute. Ediz. del Monastero del Sacro Speco, n.d.
52 plates, 26x20 cm.
MnCS

7047   Sacro Speco, Subiaco. Benedettini di Subiaco, 1968.
71 p. illus., plates, 17 cm.
French and English.
MnCS

7048   St. Scholastica's Abbey; an historical and artistic guide, edited by the Benedictine Fathers. Roma, Casa Editrice Lozzi [1971].
46 p. illus. (part col.) 18 cm.
MnCS

7049 **Sulger, Arsenius,** 17th cent.
Vita divi Benedicti, monachorum patriarchae. Colore didactico renovata. [St. Gall, Switzerland], typis Monasterij S. Galli, 1691.
259, 29, 27, 124 p. 12 cm.
MnCS

7050 **Sullivan, Bede, Sister.**
Movies; universal language, film study in high school. Notre Dame, Ind., Fides Publishers, 1967.
xv, 160 p. 22 cm.
KAM; KAS; InStme; MnStj; MoCo

7050a   Movies: universal language; film study in high school. Notre Dame, Ind., Fides Publishers, 1970 (c 1967).
xvi, 168 p. 18 cm. (Fides DOME edition)
This edition includes new material and some modifications.
KAM; MnCS

7051 **Sullivan, Otho Leo,** 1902–1978.
The obligation of self development.
69 p. 28 cm.
Thesis (M.A.)–University of Notre Dame, 1951.
Typescript.
KAS

7052 **Sullivan, Terence James,** 1930–
Statistical variation in the use of core tract and area average in the construction of Shevky-Bell indices for the analysis of parish localities.
v, 87 p. 28 cm.
Thesis (M.A.)–Fordham University, 1960.
KAS

7053 **Sullivan, Walter,** 1905–1958.
Reflections on the Holy Rule. St. Meinrad, Ind., Abbey Press [1974].
72 p. 23 cm.
InStme; KAS; NcBe; ViBris

Suñol, Gregório María, 1879–1946.
7054   Metodo completo di canto gregoriano, con un'appendice per il canto ambrosiano, secondo la scuola di Solesmes. 3. ed. aumentata e riveduta. Roma, Desclée e cie, 1952.
viii, 227 p. 22 cm.
PLatS

7055   Paleografia literària latina. Abadia de Montserrat [Spain], 1925.
44 p. 26 cm.
PLatS

7056 **Super, Dolores, Sister,** 1930–
Music performance in American higher
education, 1850–1951.
179 p. 28 cm.
Thesis (Ed.D.)– University of Michigan,
1970.
MnStj(Archives)

7057 **Supplementum ad Ordinem,** continens
Calendarium O.S.B. necnon textus novos
pro Divino Officio explendo. Collegeville, Minn., Typis Abbatiae Sancti
Joannis Baptistae, 1962.
xvi, 76 p. 15 cm.
PLatS

7058 **Surchamp, Angelico,** 1924–
St. Aignan-sur-Cher [par] L'abbé Pierre
Renoux et Dom Angelico Surchamp.
Pierre-qui-vire (Yvonne), Presses Monas-
tiques, [196–].
87 p. illus. 23 cm.
KAS

Surchamp, Claude, 1920–
7059 L'amour du Christ [par] dom Claude
Jean-Nesmy [pseud.] . . . [Paris], Desclée,
De Brouwer, [1959].
352 p. 20 cm.
CaQStB; KAS; NcBe; PLatS

7060 Conscience and confession, by Dom
Claude Jean-Nesmy [pseud.]. Translated
by Malachy Carroll. Chicago, Franciscan
Herald Press [1965].
xvii, 22 p. 21 cm.
MnCS; PLatS

7061 La joie de la pénitence. Paris, Editions
du Cerf, 1968.
160 p. 18 cm.
MnCS; PLatS

7062 Liturgie et monastères. Etudes. Par E.
Dekkers, Cl. Jean Nesmy, J. Leclercq . . .
[Bruges], Publications de Saint-André,
1966–
v. 22 cm.
KAS

7063 Living the liturgy, by Claude Jean-
Nesmy, O.S.B. Staten Island, Alba House
[1966].
216 p. 22 cm.
Translation of Pratique de la liturgie.
Translated by Norah Smaridge.
InFer; MdRi; MnCS; MnStj; NcBe;
OkShG; PLatS

7064 Pourquoi se confesser aujourd'hui?
[Paris], Desclée De Brouwer, 1968.
157 p. 18 cm.
PLatS

7065 Pratique de la confession. [Bruges],
Desclée [1963].
309 p. plates, 19 cm.
MnCS; PLatS

7066 Pratique de la liturgie. [Bruges], Desclée
[1964].
106 p. 19 cm.
PLatS

7067 Pratique de la Messe [par] Dom Claude
Jean Nesmy [pseud]. [Paris], Desclée
[1965].
265, [39] p. illus. 20 cm.
PLatS

7068 6,000,000 de morts. Paris, Desclée De
Brouwer [1964].
87 p. 18 cm.
PLatS

7069 Spiritualité de l'année liturgique. [Paris],
Desclée De Brouwer [1957–62].
3 v. 20 cm.
MnCS; PLatS

7070 Spiritualité de la Pentecôte. Paris,
Desclée De Brouwer [1960].
317 p. 20 cm.
MnCS; PLatS

7071 Spiritualité de Noël. Paris, Desclée De
Brouwer [1960].
334 p. 20 cm.
CaQStB; MnCS; PLatS

7072 Spiritualité pascale. [2. éd. revu par Dom
Germain Leblond, O.S.B.]. Paris, Desclée
De Brouwer [1957].
285 p. 20 cm.
PLatS

7073 **Sweeney, James Norbert,** 1821–1883.
Lectures on the oecumenical council,
delivered in the church of St. John the
Evangelist, Bath. London, Catholic Publishing Company, 1870.
vii, 248 p. 22 cm.
KAS

Sweinshaupt, Rudegerus. *See* Swyneshed, Roger.

Swisshelm, Germain, 1934–
7074 Un analisis detallado de la fonologia del
Quechua de Huaraz. Huaraz, Peru, 1971.
ii, 211 p. 28 cm.
InStme

7075 Un diccionario del Quechua de Huaraz:
Quechua-Castellano, Castellano-Quechua.
Huaraz, Peru, 1972.
lxxxv, 399 p. 28 cm.
InStme

7076 Quechua del Callejon de Huaylas . . .
Huaraz, Peru, Priorato de San Benito
[1974].
v. 28 cm.
InStme

7077 Salterio del Breviario monastico. Lima,
Peru, Parroquia de San Juan de Luri-
ganche, 1969.
368 p.
InFer

7078   Ritual Quechia. Para el uso en la Diócesis de Huaraz. Huaraz, Peru, Priorato di San Benito, 1973.
    258 p. 21 cm.
    Text in Spanish and Quechua.
    Edited and translated by Germain Swisshelm, O.S.B.
    InStme

Sylvester II, Pope, d. 1003.

7079   De rationali et ratione. MS. Vienna, Nationalbibliothek, codex 766, f.67r–73r. Folio. Saec. 12.
    Microfilm: MnCH proj. no. 14,083

7080   De sacramento Corporis et Sanguinis Domini. MS. Benediktinerabtei Göttweig, Austria, codex 285, f.74v–79r. Folio. Saec. 15.
    Microfilm: MnCH proj. no. 3553

7081   Epistola ad Adelbodum de causa diversitatis arearum in Trigono Aequilatero. MS. Benediktinerabtei St. Peter, Salzburg, codex a.V.7, f.105r–106r. Octavo. Saec. 12–13.
    Microfilm: MnCH proj. no. 10,031

7082   Geometria cum glossa. MS. Benediktinerabtei St. Peter, Salzburg, codex a.V.7, f.39v–101r. Octavo. Saec. 12–13.
    Microfilm: MnCH proj. no. 10,031

7083   The letters of Gerbert, with his papal privileges as Sylvester II. Translated with an introduction by Harriet Pratt Lattin. New York, Columbia University Press, 1961.
    x, 412 p. illus. 24 cm.
    PLatS

7084   Liber de rationali et ratione ad Ottonem III imperatorem. MS. Benediktinerabtei Admont, Austria, codex 247, f.161r–169r. Folio. Saec. 12.
    Microfilm: MnCH proj. no. 9331

7085   Opera mathematica (872–1003). Accedunt aliorum opera ad Gerberti libellos aestimandos intelligendosque necessaria per septem appendices distributa. Collegit . . . figuris illustravit Nicolaus Bubnov. Hildesheim, Georg Olms Verlagsbuchhandlung, 1963.
    cxix, 620 p. illus. 24 cm.
    Reprint of Berlin edition of 1899.
    PLatS

7086   Oratio habita in Concilio Mosomensi. MS. Vienna, Nationalbibliothek, codex 766, f.73r–74v. Folio. Saec. 12.
    Microfilm: MnCH proj. no. 14,083

7087   Sermo de informatione episcoporum. MS. Benediktinerabtei St. Peter, Salzburg, codex a.VI.30, f.46r–53v. Quarto. Saec. 11–12.
    Microfilm: MnCH proj. no. 10,098

7088   **Swyneshed, Roger,** d. 1365.
    Rudegerus Sweinshaupt: Expositio super textus de obligatoriis. MS. Vienna, Dominikanerkloster, codex 160(130), f.109v–122v. Saec. 14.
    Microfilm: MnCH proj. no. 8963

7089   **Szalay, Jeromos,** 1896–
    Rassembler ce que l'on a dispersé. Paris, Imprimerie Doris, 1914–
    v. 21 cm.
    PLatS (v. 1, pt. 2)

Szczygielski, Stanislas, 1616–1687.

7090   Aquila polono-benedictina in qua, beatorum & illustrium virorum elogia . . . exordia & progressus Ordinis d. p. Benedicti per Poloniam . . . describuntur. Cracoviae, Haeredes Francisci Casari, 1663.
    [8], 367, [20] p.
    KAS

7090a Pharus benedictina universum orbem irradicans, sive, Vita s.p.n. Benedicti abbatis, eiusque sanctissimae Regulae et ordinis utilitas . . . Crac, ex Offic. Schedellana, 1669.
    [16], 232 p. 21 cm.
    KAS

7091   **Tabarelli, Costanzo,** 1920–
    Liber contractuum (1331–32) dell'Abbazia Benedettina di San Pietro in Perugia. Perugia [Italia], Deputazione di Storia Patria per l'Umbria, 1967.
    xi, 568 p. 26 cm.
    PLatS

7092   **Talafous, Donald,** 1926–
    Readings in science and spirit, edited by Camillus D. Talafous. Englewood Cliffs, N.J., Prentice-Hall [1966].
    xi, 271 p. 22 cm.
    InStme; KAS; MnCS; PLatS

Tamburini de Marradio, Ascanio, fl. 1640.

7093   De iure abbatissarum et monialium; sive, Praxis gubernandi moniales . . . Editio emendata & aucta. Lugduni, sumptibus Laurentii Anisson, 1668.
    [16], 220, [31], 80, 36 p. 37 cm.
    KAS

7094   De iure abbatum, et aliorum praelatorum, tam regularium quam saecularium . . . Lugdini, Haered. G. Boissat & L. Anisson, 1640.
    3 v. 37 cm.
    KAS

Tan, Celaine, Sister, 1939–

7095   (tr) Carothers, Merlin R. Chan-meide liliang. Translated by Celaine Tan. Taichung, Taiwan, Kuang-chi, 1978.
    179 p.

Translation of: Power in praise.
MnStj(Archives)

7096   (tr) Hinnebusch, Paul. Hsian-shen yu ch'ong-pai. Translated by Tan Biy-huey. Taichung, Taiwan, Kuang-chi, 1975.
94 p.
Translation of: Religious life; a living liturgy.
MnStj(Archives)

7097   (tr) Hollings, Michael. Chang Hsiang chuo-you. Translated by Sr. Celaine Tan, O.S.B. Taichung, Taiwan, Kuang-chi, 1969.
133 p.
Translation of: I will be there.
MnStj(Archives)

7098   (tr) Poslusney, V. Ké-mu de Duan Dao. Translated by Sr. Celaine Tan, O.S.B. Taichung, Taiwan, Kuang-chi, 1978.
104 p.
Translation of: The prayer of love; the art of aspiration.
MnStj(Archives)

7099   (tr) Storey, William George. Chan song Shang-chu. Translated by Sister Celaine Tan. Taipei, Taiwan, Hua-ming, 1976.
194 p.
Translation of: Praise Him! A prayer book for today's Christian.
MnStj(Archives)

7100   **Tanner, Konrad,** 1752–1825.
Die Rückkehr des Sünders zu Gott . . . 2. Aufl. Augsburg, N. Doll, 1829.
x, 487 p. 18 cm.
KAS

Tasch, Alcuin William, 1892–
7101   Formal organization of the Benedictine Society of Westmoreland County and the St. Vincent College, Latrobe, Pennsylvania. [Latrobe, Pa., St. Vincent College] 1950.
v, 123 leaves, 28 cm.
Mimeographed.
PLatS

7102   Religious constitutions and institutional control.
274 leaves, 28 cm.
Thesis (Ph.D.)–University of Chicago, 1953.
Typescript.
PLatS

7103   **Tassi, Ildefonso,** 1914–
Ludovico Barbo (1381–1443). Roma, Storia e Letteratura, 1952.
xvi, 179 p. 26 cm.
InStme; KAS; MnCS

Tassin, René Prosper, 1697–1777.
7104   Histoire littéraire de la Congrégation de Saint-Maur, Ordre de S. Benoit, où l'on trouve la vie & les travaux des auteurs qu'elle a produits, depuis son origine en 1618 jusqu'à present: avec les titres, l'énumeration, l'analyse, les diférentes éditions des livres qu'ils ont donnés au public, & le jugement manuscrits, composés par des Bénédictines du même corps. Bruxelles, Paris, chez Humblot, 1770.
xxviii, 800, [28] p. 26x20 cm.
KAS; MnCS; PLatS(microfilm)

7104a   Supplement à l'Histoire littéraire de la Congrégation de Saint-Maur . . . par Ulysse L. L. Robert. Paris, A. Picard, 1881.
98 p. 28x22 cm.
Library of Congress

Tasto, Maria, Sister.
7105   A critical study of four nineteenth-century actors' interpretations of Iago.
169 p. 28 cm.
Thesis–University of Dayton, 1968.
Typescript.
InFer

7106   Vespers; its origin and development.
51 p. 28 cm.
Thesis (M.A.)–St. John's University, Collegeville, Minn., 1972.
Typescript.
InFer

Tate, Judith, Sister.
7107   Religious women in the modern world. New York, Herder and Herder [1970].
x, 102 p. 21 cm.
InFer

7108   Sisters for the world. New York, Herder and Herder [1966].
141 p. 21 cm.
ICSS; InFer; InStme; MnStj; MoCo; OkShG

Tatwin, abp. of Canterbury, d. 734.
7109   Tatvini Opera omnia. Variae collectiones aenigmatum Merovingicae aetatis. Anonymus. De dubiis nominibus. Turnholti, Brepols, 1968.
2 v. 25 cm.
KAS; PLatS

7110   **Taxster, John de,** d. 1265?
The chronicle of Bury St. Edmunds, 1212–1301. Edited with introd., notes, and translation by Antonia Gradsden. [London; Camden, N.J.] Nelson [1964].
xlv, 164, 164, [165]–187 p. 23 cm. (Medieval texts)
English and Latin on opposite pages, numbered in duplicate.
Probably written by John de Taxter and two other unknown monks. cf. p.xvii.
InStme

7111 **Taylor, Finnian Daniel,** 1945–
Augustine of Hippo's notion and use of the Apocrypha.
x, 307 leaves. 28 cm.
Thesis (Ph.D.)–University of Notre Dame, 1978.
Typescript.
ILSP

Tedeschi, Niccolò de, 1385–1445.
7112 Abbatis Panormitani Commentaria in primum (-quintum) Decretalium librum . . . et Interpretationem ad Clementinas epistolas . . . Venetiis, apud Iuntas, 1588–1592.
9 v. 42 cm.
KAS

7113 Abbatis Panormitani Consilia, tractatus, quaestiones et practica . . . Venetiis, [apud Guerraeos fratres et socios], 1578.
[318] f. 38 cm.
KAS(microfilm); PLatS(microfilm)

7113a **Tegeder, Vincent George,** 1910–
St. John's Abbey, Collegeville, Minnesota [a photographic directory of the monks of Saint John's Abbey, comprising the monastic community of January 1, 1980 . . . Published by the Saint John's Abbey Archives, Fr. Vincent Tegeder, O.S.B., archivist].
106 p. illus., ports. 22x28 cm.
MnCS

7113b Guide to the holdings [of] the archives, Saint John's Abbey and University, Collegeville, Minnesota, December 1, 1980.
10 p. 22 cm.
MnCS

Tegels, Aelred Hilary, 1922–
7114 The reformed liturgy and the other sacraments.
(*In* Liturgical Conference, 1965. p. 52–60)
PLatS

7115 Relevance; the present liturgical reform.
(*In* North American Liturgical Week, 26th, 1965. p. 14–21)
PLatS

7116 Virginity in the liturgy.
(*In* Marian studies, vol. 13 (1962), p. 99–121)
PLatS

7117 **Tegernsee, Bavaria (Benedictine abbey).**
Catalogus codicum manu scriptorum Bibliothecae Regiae Monacensis: Codices 18001–20212 ex monasterio in Tegernsee. Monachii, sumptibus Bibliothecae Regiae, 1878. Unveränderter Nachdruck Otto Harrassowitz, Wiesbaden, 1969.
MnCH

7118 **Tell, Isidoro,** 1910–
Praglia. 1960.
[32] p. illus. 17 cm.
PLatS

Temple, B. *See* Paris. Saint-Louis-du-Temple (abbey of Benedictine nuns)

Theis, Lawrence, 1871–1952.
7119 Historical sketch of St. Charles Church, Troy, Kansas, on the occasion of the golden jubilee, 1881–1931.
28 p. illus., 23 cm.
KAS

7120 History of St. Patrick's Parish, commemorating the diamond jubilee, 1857–1937. Atchison, Kans. [1937?].
47 p. illus., ports. 24 cm.
KAS

7121 **Theisen, Dianne, Sister,** 1926–
The use of video tape in in-service training for the purpose of improvement of instruction.
98 p. 28 cm.
Thesis (M.A.)–University of Minnesota, 1968.
Typescript.
MnStj(Archives)

Theisen, Jerome, 1930–
7122 Mass liturgy and the Council of Trent. Collegeville, Minn., St. John's University Press, 1965.
x, 169 p. 23 cm.
InStme; MnCS; PLatS

7123 Saint Peter the Mass liturgist according to the Council of Trent.
(*In* Archivum historiae pontificiae, v. 5 (1967), p. 345–354)
MnCS

7124 The ultimate church and the promise of salvation. Collegeville, Minn., St. John's University Press, 1976.
xx, 198 p. 24 cm.
KAS; MnCS; MoCo

7125 **Theisen, Romaine, Sister,** 1922–
A survey and appraisal of the student councils in the Catholic secondary schools of Wisconsin.
xi, 251 p. 28 cm.
Thesis (M.A.)–College of St. Thomas, St. Paul, Minn., 1961.
Typescript.
MnStj(Archives)

Theisen, Wilfred Robert, 1929–
7125a Liber de visu: the Greco-Latin translation of Euclid's Optics. Toronto, Canada, Pontifical Institute of Mediaeval Studies.
Offprint from: Mediaeval studies, v. 41(1979), p. 44–105.
MnCS

7125b   The Hill Monastic Manuscript Library—
an update.
Photocopy from Manuscripta, vol.
32(1980), p. 109–114.
MnCH

7125c   Sacred art at St. John's Abbey. Editors:
Wilfred Theisen, O.S.B., Mark Twomey.
[Collegeville, Minn., The Liturgical Press,
1980].
[32] p. illus. 26 cm.
MnCS

7126   **Thelen, Lambert,** 1874–1900.
Bird notes, by Lambert Thelen, O.S.B.,
and Peter Engel, O.S.B.
[26] p. 20 cm.
The notes are on birds observed in the
vicinity of St. John's, about 1895 to 1903.
MnCS(Archives)

7127   **Theobaldus Episcopus.**
Physiologus, edited with introduction,
critical apparatus, translation and commentary by P. T. Eden. Leiden und Köln,
E. J. Brill, 1972.
viii, 82 p. 25 cm.
PLatS

Theodomar, abbot of Monte Cassino.

7128   Epistola ad Carolum Magnum, cui
Regulam et instructiones monasticas
tradit. MS. Benediktinerabtei St. Peter,
Salzburg, codex a.VIII.18, f.87r–88v.
Quarto. Saec. 12.
Microfilm: MnCH proj. no. 10,186

7129   Epistola ad Carolum Magnum de observantia monasterii sui. MS. Benediktinerabtei Admont, Austria, codex 860, f.1r–11r.
Octavo. Saec. 17.
Microfilm: MnCH proj. no. 9872

7130   Epistola ad Karolum imperatorem. MS.
Benediktinerabtei St. Peter, Salzburg,
codex b.V.38, f.160v–163r.
Microfilm: MnCH proj. no. 10,474

7131   Epistola congregationis S. Benedicti ad
Karolum regem Francorum de privatis
eorum moribus. Benediktinerabtei St.
Peter, Salzburg, codex a.III.5, f.179r–
183r. Octavo. Saec. 15.
Microfilm: MnCH proj. no. 9950

7132   **Theodulfus, bp. of Orleons,** d. 821.
Paraenesis ad iudices. Nunc secundo
edita et ex VC locis plurimis emendata,
opera Geverharti Elmenhorsti. Leiden, J.
Marci, 1618.
48 p. 18 cm.
PLatS

7133   **Theofridus, abbot of Echternach,** d.
1110.
(2dary) Lampen, Willibrord. Thiofried
van Echternach en zijn Vita S. Liutwini.

'S-Hertogenbosch, Teulings Uitgevers-
Maatschappij, 1936.
xxxvii, 57 p. 27 cm.
MnCS

Theophilus, called also Rugerus, fl.ca.
1100.

7134   On divers arts; the treatise of
Theophilus. Translated from the medieval
Latin with introd. and notes by John G.
Hawthorne and Cyril Stanley Smith.
[Chicago, University of Chicago Press
[1963].
xxxv, 216 p. illus. 25 cm.
Translation of: Diversarum artium
schedula.
PLatS

7135   The various arts. Translated from the
Latin, with introd. and notes by C. R.
Dodwell. London, New York, T. Nelson
[1961].
lxxvi, 171, 171, [172]–178 p. 22 cm.
Latin and English on opposite pages.
NdRi; PLatS

7136   **Thesaurus Liturgiae horarum monasticae**/edidit Secretarius Abbatis
Primatis O.S.B. Romae, 1977.
viii, 562 p. 29 cm.
InStme; MnCS; MoCo

Theuner, Mary Domitilla, Sister.

7137   The quadratic law of reciprocity.
Thesis (M.S.)—Catholic University of
America, Washington, D.C., 1923.
Typescript.
KyCovS

7138   On the number and reality of the self
symmetric quadrilaterals in and circum-
scribed to the triangular symmetric ra-
tional quartic.
Thesis (Ph.D.)—Catholic University of
America, Washington, D.C., 1932.
Typescript.
KyCovS

7139   **Thibaut, Raymond,** 1877–
Columba Marmion, ein Meister des
Lebens in Christ. [Deutsche Uebertragung
durch P. Ignatius Rollenmüller, O.S.B.].
Ettal, Buch-Kunstverlag [1954].
532 p. 20 cm.
MnCS

Thiel, Matthias, 1894–

7140   Die Traditionen, Urkunden und Urbare
des Klosters Weltenburg. München, Beck,
1958.
64, 443 p. plates, 25 cm.
PLatS

7141   Die Traditionen, Urkunden und Urbare
des Klosters Münchsmünster. München,
Beck, 1961.

73, 442 p. plates, 25 cm.
PLatS

7142 **Thiele, Augustinus.**
Echternach und Himmerod; Beispiele benediktinischer und zisterziensischer Wirtschaftsführung, G. Fischer, 1964.
186 p. facsims. 24 cm.
MnCS; PLatS

7143 **Thierhaupten, Bavaria (Benedictine abbey).**
Catalogus codicum manu scriptorum Bibliothecae Regiae Monacensis: Codices 21001–21121 ex monasterio in Thierhaupten. Monachii, sumptibus Bibliothecae Regiae, 1878. Unveränderter Nachdruck Otto Harrassowitz, Wiesbaden, 1969.
MnCH

Thimmesh, Hilary Donald, 1928–
7144 A synoptic reading of central themes in Piers Plowman.
292 p. 28 cm.
Thesis (Ph.D.) – Cornell University, 1963.
MnCS

7145 Anthony and Cleopatra: The nobleness of life is to do thus, Milton Friedman [Phonotape-cassette]. Collegeville, 1974.
1 cassette.
Address delivered at St. John's University Faculty Colloquium, March 25, 1974. With questions.
MnCS

7146 **Thiroux, Jean Evangéliste,** 1663–1731.
Histoire abrégée de l'Abbaye de Saint-Florentin de Bonneval . . . Chateaudun, H. Lecesne, 1875; Paris, Dumoulin, 1876.
clxxi, 258 p. 25 cm.
KAS(1875); InStme(1876); MnCS(1976)

7147 **Thissen, Gretta, Sister.**
An inquiry into problems and practices of articulation in the ninth grades of two selected secondary schools.
Thesis (M.A.) – College of St. Thomas, St. Paul, Minn., 1959.
Typescript.
MnSSP

7148 **Thomas, abbot of Lambach.**
Epistola Thomas abbatis Lambacensis ad Canonicum S. Floriani Wolfgangum Kerspeken, ejusque responsio. MS. Augustinerchorherrenstift St. Florian, Austria, codex XI,89, f.237v. Folio. Saec. 15.
Microfilm: MnCH proj. no. 2347

Thomas, abbot of Vercelli.
7149 Commentum super quattuor libros beati Dyonisii. MS. Hereford, England, Cathedral Library, codex P 5 x, f.80r–124. Quarto. Saec. 13.
Microfilm: MnCH

7150 Expositio super Canticum canticorum (incompletum). MS. Augustinerchorherrenstift Klosterneuburg, Austria, codex 765. 166 f. Quarto. Saec. 12.
Microfilm: MnCH proj. no. 5745

7151 Expositio ad Canticum canticorum. MS. Augustinerchorherrenstift Klosterneuburg, Austria, codex 18, f.1r–131v. Folio. Saec. 15.
Microfilm: MnCH proj. no. 4992

7152 Super Cantica canticorum. MS. Benediktinerabtei Melk, Austria, codex 672, f.234r–329r. Quarto. Saec. 15.
Microfilm: MnCH proj. no. 1539

Thomas de Paden, monk of Melk, fl.ca. 1475.
7153 Carmen de passione Christi. MS. Benediktinerabtei Melk, Austria, codex 1602, p. 251–257. Duodecimo. Saec. 15.
Microfilm: MnCH proj. no. 1992

7154 Commentariolus in Lamentationes Ieremiae. Germanice. MS. Benediktinerabtei Melk, Austria, codex 774, f.96r–118v. Quarto. Saec. 15.
Microfilm: MnCH proj. no. 1613

7155 Concio in conversione S. Pauli. Germanice. MS. Benediktinerabtei Melk, Austria, codex 774, f.119r–124v. Quarto. Saec. 15.
Microfilm: MnCH proj. no. 1613

7156 Oratio precatoria ad beatam Virginem Mariam. MS. Benediktinerabtei Melk, Austria, codex 1602, p. 294–295. Duodecimo. Saec. 15.
Microfilm: MnCH proj. no. 1992

7157 Sacrae canciones de praecipuis Passionis dominicae. MS. Benediktinerabtei Melk, Austria, codex 1602, p. 236–242. Duodecimo. Saec. 15.
Microfilm: MnCH proj. no. 1992

7158 Tractatus de oratione. Germanice. MS. Benediktinerabtei Melk, Austria, codex 1602, p. 378–385. Duodecimo. Saec. 15.
Microfilm: MnCH proj. no. 1992

7159 Variae preces. Germanice. MS. Benediktinerabtei Melk, Austria, codex 1602, p. 369–377. Duodecimo. Saec. 15.
Microfilm: MnCH proj. no. 1992.

Thuente, Adelard Walter, 1910–1962.
7160 Some quantitative aspects of phototropism in plants.
37 p. charts. 28 cm.
Thesis (M.S.) – University of Illinois, Urbana, 1940.
Mimeographed.
MnCS

7161 An evaluation of the statolith theory of georeception in plants.

118 p. 20 plates, 28 cm.
Thesis (Ph.D.)–University of Illinois.
Mimeographed.
MnCS

7162 **Thuillier, Vincent,** 1685–1736.
Ouvrages posthumes de D. Jean Mabillon
et de D. Thierri Ruinart . . . [London,
Gregg Press Ltd., 1967].
3 v. 25 cm.
Reprint of Paris edition of 1724.
InStme; PLatS

7163 **Thum, Beda,** 1901–
Versuch über die Quantität im Anschluss
zu die Theorie der Wellenfelder.
(*In* Festschrift für Albert Auer, O.S.B.
1962. p. 319–350)
PLatS

7164 **Thun, Georg,** d. 1526.
Das Lehenbuch des Abtes Georgius Thun
zu Saalfeld, 1497–1526. Hrsg. von Ernst
Koch. Jena, Gustav Fischer, 1913.
lxxx, 335 p. 22 cm.
MnCS

7165 **Tiefenthal, Franz Sales,** 1840–1917.
Novum commentarium in Psalmos mere
messianicos, cum duobus psalmis introduc-
toriis. Parisiis, Lethielleux, 1912.
268 p. 25 cm.
InStme

Tierney, Mark, 1925–
7166 Advent. Notre Dame, Ind., Ave Maria
Press [c 1959].
32 p. 16 cm.
MnCS

7167 Correspondence between J. H. Newman
and Archbishop Leahy on the sale of University Church, Dublin, 1857–1864.
(*In* Collectanea Hibernica, nos. 6–7, p.
245–263)
PLatS

7168 The Council and the Mass. Dublin, Clonmore & Reynolds; London, Burns & Oates
[1965].
152 p. 20 cm.
InStme; MnCS; PLatS

7169 The Council and the Mass [1st American
edition]. Wilkes-Barre, Pa., Dimension
Books [1965].
128 p.
InFer; NcBe

7170 Dr. Croke, the Irish bishops and the
Parnell crisis, 18 Nov. 1890–21 April 1891.
(*In* Collectanea Hibernica, no. 11 (1968),
p. 111–148)
PLatS

7171 The use of commentary in Holy Week.
(*In* Murray, Placid, ed. Studies in
pastoral liturgy. Maynooth, 1961. v. 1, p.
264–266)
PLatS

7172 **Tissot, Gabriel,** 1886–1964.
L'Abbaye Notre-Dame d'Argentan de
1830 à nos jours.
(*In* Chaussy, Yves. L'Abbaye
d'Almenèches-Argentan. Paris, 1970.
p. 173–217)
PLatS

Tkacik, Arnold, 1919–
7173 Ezekiel.
(*In* The Jerome biblical commentary.
1968. p. 344–365)
PLatS

7174 The prophetic element in worship.
(*In* North American Liturgical Week,
22nd, 1961. p. 235–246)
PLatS

7175 (ed) The New English Bible with the
Apocrypha . . . Arnold J. Tkacik, Apocry-
pha editor. New York, Oxford University
Press, 1976.
various pagings, 24 cm.
PLatS

Tobella, Antonius M., 1892–
7176 Cronologia dels Capítols de la congregació claustral Tarraconense i Cesaraugustana (primera part: 1219–1661).
(*In* Analecta Montserratensia, v. 10, p.
221–298)
PLatS

7177 Documents del primer segle de la congregació claustral Tarraconense.
(*In* Analecta Montserratensia, v. 10, p.
339–455)
PLatS

7178 **Toigno, Mary Angela, Sister,** 1941–
God and a mouse; a festival of reflective
jubilation. Words by Sister M. Angela,
O.S.B. Illustrated by [Ted] De Grazia. San
Diego, Calif., Benedictine sisters [c 1972].
12, [19] leaves, illus. 16 cm.
MoCo; PLatS

7179 **Toner, Jerome Lorraine,** 1899–
Abbatial power.
Reprinted from The Jurist, v. 22 (1962),
p. 81–89)
NcBe

7180 **Toon, Mark,** 1925–
The philosophy of procreation; the
generative power of man according to St.
Thomas Aquinas.
iv, 64 leaves, 28 cm.
Thesis (M.A.)–Catholic University of
America, Washington, D.C., 1952.
Typescript.
InStme

7181 **Tord, Joannes de.**
Disputationes scholasticae in octo libros
Physicorum. MS. Monasterio benedictino

de Montserrat, Spain, codex 338. 251 p.
Quarto. Saec. 18(1739).
Microfilm: MnCH proj. no. 30,019

7181a **Tornare alle fonti;** il primo convegno
delle abbadesse e priore benedettine in
Italia, 24–29 ottobre 1966. [Sorrento,
Italia, Monastero di S. Paolo, 1966].
283 p. 22 cm.
MnCS

Tosti, Luigi, 1811–1897.

7182   La contessa Matilde e i romani pontifici.
Roma, Tip. della Camera dei Deputati,
1887.
xvi, 403 p. 23 cm.
KAS

7183   Prolegomeni alla storia universale della
Chiesa. Roma, L. Pasqualucci, 1888.
xix, 481 p. 22 cm.
KAS

7184   S. Benedetto al Parlamento Nazionale.
Napoli, Gaetano Gioja, 1861.
30 p. 25 cm.
KAS; PLatS

7185   Scritti vari. Roma, Tip. della Camera dei
Deputati, 1886–1890.
2 v. 22 cm.
KAS; AStb

7186   Storia dell'origine dello scisma greco.
Roma, L. Pasqualucci, 1888.
xv, 515 p. 22 cm.
KAS

7187   (tr) Sallustius Crispus, C. La congiura di
Catilina e la Guerra di Giugurta, volgariz-
zate da Luigi Tosti. Roma, L. Pasqualucci,
1888.
vii, 279 p. 22 cm.
KAS; PLatS

Totzke, Irenäus, 1932–

7188   Die katholischen Ostkirchen. Recklinghausen, Paulus Verlag [1960].
20 p. 16 cm.
MnCS

7189   Der theologische Dialog mit der Ortho-
doxie; Möglichkeiten nach den
Dokumenten des II. Vatikanums.
(*In* Hören Sein Wort; Festgabe für Abt
Emmanuel M. Heufelder . . . 1968. p.
105–116)
PLatS

7190   Unsere Verpflichtung gegenüber der ost-
kirchlichen Musik.
(*In* Internationaler Kongress für Kirchenmusik, 4th, Cologne, 1961. p.
161–163)
PLatS

**Tournai, Belgium. Saint-Martin (Bene-
dictine abbey).**

7191   Chartes de l'Abbaye de Saint-Martin de
Tournai, recueillies & publiées par Armand

d'Herbomez. Bruxelles, Hayes, impr.,
1898–1901.
2 v. 31 cm.
MnCS

7192   Comptes et documents de l'Abbaye de
Saint-Martin de Tournai sous l'administra-
tion des gardiens royaux (1312–1355) par
Albert d'Haenens. Bruxelles, Palais des
Académies, 1962.
882 p. facsims. 22 cm.
PLatS

7193 **Trafoyer, Ambrose,** 1891–
Das Kloster Gries (Bolzano). Bolzano,
Vogelweider, 1927.
269 p. illus.
MoCo

7194 **Tragan, Pius-Ramon,** 1928–
(ed) Segni e sacramenti nel Vangelo di
Giovanni. Roma, 1977.
253 p. 24 cm. (Studia Anselmiana, 66)
English, French, Italian, or Spanish.
InStme; PLatS

7195 **Tranfaglia, Anselmo,** 1889–
Montevergine e la Congregazione Verginiana. 2. ed. riveduta e aggiornata. Montevergine, Edizioni del Santuario, 1960.
[72] p. 23 cm.
PLatS

7196 **Translatio studii;** manuscript and library
studies honoring Oliver L. Kapsner,
O.S.B. Edited by Julian G. Plante.
Collegeville, Minn., Published for the
Monastic Manuscript Microfilm Library
by St. John's University Press, [College-
ville, Minn.], 1973.
xiv, 288 p., plates (part col.) 24 cm.
Contributions in English, French, German, or Spanish.
MnCS; NcBe; PLatS

7197 **Traunkirchen, Austria (abbey of Bene-
dictine nuns).**
Urbar des Klosters Traunkirchen, 1347.
MS. Linz, Austria, Oberösterreichisches
Landesarchiv, Stiftsarchiv Traunkirchen,
Hs. 4. 76 f. Quarto. Saec. 14.
Microfilm: MnCH proj. no. 27,756

7198 **Traversarius, Ambrosius, O.S.B.Cam.,**
1376–1439.
Ambrosii Traversarii generalis
Camaldulensium aliorumque ad ipsum, et
ad alios de eodem Ambrosio, latinae epistolae. Bologna, Forni editore, 1968.
2 v. 26 cm.
Includes title page of original edition of
1759.
MnCS

7199 **Trelo, Virgil John,** 1930–
The critical realism of Roy Wood Sellars.
Lisle, Ill., St. Procopius College, 1966.
ILSP

7200   **Tremiti, Italy. Santa Maria (Benedictine abbey).**
Codice diplomatico del monastero benedettino di S. Maria di Tremiti (1005–1237). A cura di Armando Petrucci. Roma, Istituto storico italiano, 1960.
3 v. plates (facsims.) 26 cm.
PLatS

Trethowan, Illtyd, 1907–
7201   The absolute and the atonement. London, George Allen & Unwin; New York, Humanities Press [1971].
289 p. 23 cm.
NcBe; PLatS

7202   Absolute value; a study in Christian theism. London, Allen & Unwin; New York, Humanities Press [1970].
255 p. 22 cm.
InStme; PLatS

7203   The basis of belief. New York, Hawthorn Books, [1961].
142 p. 21 cm. (Twentieth-century encyclopedia of Catholicism, v. 13)
InStme; KAS; MdRi; MnCS; MnStj; MoCo; ILSP; NcBe; PLatS; PSaS

7204   Mysticism and theology; an essay in Christian metaphysics. [London], G. Chapman, 1975.
x, 163 p. 23 cm.
InStme

7205   Natural theology and its relation to poetry.
(*In* Coulson, John. Theology and the university, p. 193–207)
PLatS

7206   A theological bombshell.
(*In* Baum, Gregory. The future of belief debate. New York, 1967, p. 13–17)
PLatS

7207   What is the liturgy?
9 p. 21 cm.
Reprinted from: Music and liturgy, 1942.
MnCS

7208   (ed) Hilton, Walter, d. 1396. The scale of perfection. Abridged and presented by Illtyd Trethowan. St. Meinrad, Ind., Abbey Press, 1975.
x, 148 p. 21 cm.
InFer; InStme; MnStj; MoCo

7209   **Tricalet, Pierre Joseph,** 1696–1762.
Bibliotheca manualis ecclesiae patrum, presbyter Petrus Ios. Tricaletius gallice edidit, Eudoxius Philenius latinitate donavit, notisque illustravit. Editio 2da emendatior. Romae, P. Marietti, 1871–72.
5 v. 23 cm.
KAS

Trier, Germany. St. Matthias (Benedictine abbey).
7210   Führer durch die Basilika des hl. Apostels Matthias zu Trier. Trier, Druck der Paulinus-Druckerei, n.d.
64 p. illus. 11x14 cm.
MnCS

7211   Manuale spirituale seu Exercitia religiosa respective quotidiana omnibus sine exceptione Regulam s.p. Benedicti professis . . . Coloniae & Francofurti, Pütz, 1771.
313 p. 14 cm.
MnCS

Trithemius, Johannes, 1462–1516.
Manuscript copies.
7212   Allgemeiner Schlüssel der Geheimnissen. Ein Werklein des Trithemius. Germanice. MS. Benediktinerabtei Melk, Austria, codex 1013, f.44r–52r. Quarto. Saec. 17.
Microfilm: MnCH proj. no. 1804

7213   De vita spirituali monachorum. MS. Subiaco, Italy (Benedictine abbey), codex 274. 308 f. Saec. 17.
Microfilm: MnCH

7214   Excerpta varia ex libris chronicis Trithemii, cum glossa Stabii, insertis epistolis Trithemii ad Maximilianum I imperatorem. MS. Vienna, Nationalbibliothek, codex 9045. 33 f. Folio. Saec. 16.
Microfilm: MnCH proj. no. 19,236

7215   Liber octo quaestio num ad Maximilianum I. caesarem directus, qui videtur ab auctore ipso exaratus. MS. Vienna, Nationalbibliothek, codex 11716. 112 f. Octavo. Saec. 16.
Microfilm: MnCH proj. no. 19,851

7216   Oratio de utilitate celebrationis capituli annalis habita in Reinhartzborn anno 1499. MS. Vienna, Nationalbibliothek, codex 5172. 17 f. Octavo. Saec. 16.
Microfilm: MnCH proj. no. 18,324

7217   Polygraphia. MS. Vienna, Nationalbibliothek, codex 3308. 251 f. Folio. Saec. 16.
Microfilm: MnCH proj. no. 20,367

7218   Praefatio in librum de steganographia. MS. Benediktinerabtei St. Paul im Lavanttal, Austria, codex 179/4, pars VI. Folio. Saec. 18.
Microfilm: MnCH proj. no. 12,408

Trithemius, Johannes, 1462–1516.
Printed works.
7219   Carmelitana bibliotheca, sive Illustrium aliquot Carmelitanae religionis scriptorum, & eorum operum catalogus . . . Florentiae, apud Georgium Marescottum, 1593.
KAS; PLatS (microfilm)

7220 Chronik des Klosters Sponheim. Wortgetreue Uebersetzung nach den in Würzburg und Madrid vorliegenden Handschriften, unter Benützung der jüngeren Druckausgabe von Freher, Frankfurt, 1601. (Chronikon Spanheimense, Deutsch, 1024–1509). Bad Kreuznach, Selbstverlag Carl Velten [Herausgeber] 1969.
263 p. illus. 24 cm.
MnCS

7221 Eyn schone Cronica vö Erstem vrsprück ün vfwachsen der Fräcken, wie sie in Deutsch Landt komen. Auch von dheren Kunig, Hertzogen . . . herümlichsten Kriegs vnd andern Tugentlichen vbungen . . . Newlichst durch . . . Jacoben Schenck . . . in Deütsch gezogen. [Johans Eckharten, 1522].
120 p. 30 cm.
MnCS

7221a Compendium sive breviarium primi voluminis annalium sive historiarum de origine regum et gentis Francorum. Mainz, Johann Schoeffer, 1515.
MnCS

7222 De laude scriptorum. Zum Lobe der Schreiber. Eingeleitet, hrsg. und übersetzt von Klaus Arnold. Würzburg, Freunde Mainfrankischer Kunst und Geschichte, 1973.
111 p. plates, 20 cm.
MnCS

7223 In praise of scribes. De laude scriptorum. Edited with introduction by Klaus Arnold. Translated by Roland Behrendt, O.S.B. Lawrence, Kans., Coronado Press, 1974.
viii, 111 p. illus. 22 cm.
Latin and English.
InStme; KAS; MnCS; MnStj; PLatS

7224 In praise of scribes. De laude scriptorum. Translated by Elizabeth Bryson Bongie. Edited with an introduction by Michael S. Batts. Vancouver, Alcuin Society, 1977.
xi, 47 p. 29 cm.
MnCS

7225 De laudibus Carmelitanae religionis liber . . . centesimo post anno diligenter recognitus brevique apologia defensus, per R. P. Petrum Lucium Belgam . . . Florentiae, apud Georgium Marescottum, 1593.
4 p. 25 leaves.
KAS; KAS(microfilm); MnCS(microfilm); PLatS(microfilm)

7226 De proprietate monachorum. [Oratio de cura pastorali. Paris, Marnef, n.d.].
[32] leaves, woodcut, 15 cm.
PLatS

7227 Liber de ecclesiasticis scriptoribus. (*In* Fabricius, Johann. Bibliotheca ecclesiastica. 1967. Reprint of 1718 edition)
MnCS; PLatS

7228 The lyfe of Barthram pryeste. (*In* Ratramnus, Monk of Corbie. The boke of Barthram priest. London, M.D.XLIX)
MnCS(microfilm)

7229 Polygraphiae libri sex. Accessit clavis polygraphiae liber unus, eodem authore . . . additae sunt etiam aliquot locorum explicationes . . . Coloniae, Ioannes Birckmannus, 1571.
554 p. 16 cm.
MnCS

7230 Die Prunkreden des Abtes Johannes Trithemius. Sarnen, Louis Ehrli, 1934.
2 v. in 1, 24 cm.
MnCS

7231 Sermones et exhortationes, quorum sermonum duo sunt libri: primus vocatur Omeliarum, secundus Sermonum. [Argenti, impressi sunt per Joannem Nooblouch, 1516].
74 leaves, 28 cm.
PLatS

7231a A three-fold mirrour of mans vanitie and miserie: 1633/Johann von Tritheim. Manston, York, Scolar Press, 1978.
various pagings, 19 cm. (English recusant literature, 1558–1648, v. 386)
MnCS

7231b A three-fold mirrovr of man's vanitie and miserie. The first written by that learned and religious father, Iohn Trithemivs. The two others by Catholicke authors vnknowen: faithfully Englished by the R. Father Antonie Butt. Doway, Printed by L. Kellam, 1633.
Imperfect: p. 275–283 lacking.
MnCS(microfilm)

7232 Tractatulus de proprietariis monachis. [Paris, Marnef, n.d.].
[8] leaves, 15 cm.
PLatS

True, Isaac David, 1937–

7233 Digest; the unity of Hume's ethics.
111 p.
Thesis (M.A.)–St. Louis University, 1968.
MoCo

7234 Kings. Conception, Mo., Conception Abbey, [1963].
31–68 p. 21 cm. (Saint Andrew Bible commentary, 7)
PLatS

7235   Whitehead on truth.
236 p. illus.
Thesis (Ph.D.)–St. Louis University, 1972.
MoCo

Tschudi, Aegidius.
7236   Collectanea de monsaterio Wetingense. MS. Benediktinerabtei St. Paul im Lavanttal, Austria, codex 28/6. 53 f. Folio. Saec. 18(1733).
Microfilm: MnCH proj. no. 12,699

7237   Chronicon Helveticum ab annis 1472–1499. MS. Benediktinerabtei St. Paul im Lavanttal, Austria, codex 84/2. 2 vols. Folio. Saec. 17.
Microfilm: MnCH proj. no. 11,846 & 11,849

7238   Chronicon secundum Evangelia A.D. 1–63 propria manu scriptum. MS. Benediktinerabtei St. Paul im Lavanttal, Austria, codex 82/2. 354 p. Folio. Saec. 17.
Microfilm: MnCH proj. no. 11,848

7239   Fundatio et acta monasterii Murensis. MS. Benediktinerabtei St. Paul im Lavanttal, Austria, codex 8/2, pars III. Folio. Saec. 16.
Microfilm: MnCH proj. no. 11,741

7240   Scripta varia. MS. Benediktinerabtei St. Paul im Lavanttal, Austria, codex 85/2. 2 vols. Folio. Saec. 17.
Microfilm: MnCH proj. no. 11,856 & 11,871

Tschudy, Raimund, 1914–
7241   Les Bénédictins. Paris, Editions Saint-Paul [1963].
271 p. plates, 18 cm.
PLatS

7242   Die Benediktiner. Freiburg in der Schweiz, Paulusverlag [1960].
281 p. plates, 18 cm.
KAS; MnCS; MoCo; PLatS

7243   Die Mutter. Munich, Ars Sacra, 1963.
31 p. 19 cm.
PLatS

Tucker, Dunstan, 1898–
7244   Baseball notes. n.p., n.d.
15 p. 28 cm.
Multigraphed.
MnCS

7245   The influence of the Church's liturgy on the Divine Comedy; a study in Dante sources.
Typescript.
MnCS

7246   Institutional data, Saint John's University, Collegeville, Minn., 1968.
iv, 122 p. 28 cm.
Multilithed.
MnCS

7247   Jonathan Swift's religious beliefs.
various paginations, 28 cm.
Thesis (M.A.)–University of Minnesota, 1930.
Typescript.
MnCS(Archives)

7248   Scoreboard; a history of athletics of Saint John's University, Collegeville, Minnesota. Written and compiled by Dunstan Tucker, O.S.B., and Martin Schirber, O.S.B. Collegeville, Minn., St. John's University Press [c. 1979].
xii, 444 p. illus. 22 cm.
MnCS

Tunink, Wilfrid, 1920–
7249   Jesus is Lord. Garden City, N.Y., Doubleday & Co., 1979.
164 p. 20 cm.
MnCS; KAS; PLatS

7250   Vision of peace; a study of Benedictine monastic life. New York, Farrar, Straus & Co. [1963].
xiv, 332 p. 22 cm.
AStb; CaMWiSb; InFer; InStme; ILSP; KAS; MnCS; MnStj; MoCo; NdRi; NcBe; PLatS; ViBris

Turbessi, Giuseppe, 1912–
7251   Ascetismo e monachesimo in S. Benedetto. Roma, Editrice Studium [1965].
220 p. 17 cm.
MnCS; MoCo; PLatS

7252   Ascetismo e monachesimo prebenedettino. Roma, Editrice Studium [1961].
217 p. 17 cm.
InStme

7253   Quaerere Deum; il tema della "ricerca di Dio" nell'ambiente ellenistico e giudaico, contemparaneo al N.T.
(*In* Studiorum Paulinorum Congressus Internationalis Catholicis 1961, v. 2, p. 383–398)
PLatS

7254   Regole monastiche antiche. Roma, Editrice Studium, 1974.
487 p. 19 cm.
InStme

7255   **Tutbury Priory, England.**
The cartulary of Tutbury Priory. Edited, with an introduction, by Avrom Saltman. [London], Her Majesty's Stationery Office, 1962.
289 p. 25 cm.
PLatS

Tuto, abbot of Theres.
7256   Opusculum de praeconiis S. Felicitatis. MS. Benediktinerabtei Admont, Austria, codex 763, f.1r–67v. Octavo. Saec. 12.
Microfilm: MnCH proj. no. 9799

7257 Sermones tres cum epistola in natalem et laudem S. Felicitatis et filiorum ejus. MS. Benediktinerabtei Admont, Austria, codex 763, f.68r–98v. Octavo. Saec. 12.
Microfilm: MnCH proj. no. 9799

7258 **Tuttle, Mary Jean, Sister.**
A study of the Psalms of praise in selected musical settings from Hebrew chant through the romantic period.
Thesis (M.Ed. in Music)–University of North Dakota, 1972.
Typescript.
MnDuS

7259 **Tvedten, Benet,** 1936–
An American Indian anthology. [Marvin, S.D., Blue Cloud Abbey, [c 1971].
72 p. 21 cm.
Prose and poetry.
InFer; MnCS; SdMar

Tyburn Convent, London. *See* London. Tyburn Convent.

7260 **Tyniec, Poland (Benedictine abbey).**
Codex diplomaticus monasterii Tynecensis. Kodeks dyplomatyczny Klasztoru Tynieckiego. Wydali Dr. Wojciech Ketrzyński i Dr. Stanislaw Smolka. Lwowie, 1875.
2 v. 29 cm.
KAS

7261 **Udalricus, prior Cellae in Nigra Silva.**
De disciplinis novitiorum. MS. Vienna, Nationalbibliothek, codex 1671. 48 f. Octavo. Saec. 12.
Microfilm: MnCH proj. no. 15,070

7262 **Udalricus, prior Tegernseensis.**
Epistolae duae. MS. Benediktinerabtei Melk, Austria, codex 1094, f.246r–248v. Duodecimo. Saec. 15.
Microfilm: MnCH proj. no. 1847

Udalscalcus, abbot of St. Ulric and Afra, Augsburg, d. 1151.

7263 Vita Adalberonis episcopi Augustani. MS. Vienna, Nationalbibliothek, codex 573, f.1r–9r. Quarto. Saec. 12.
Microfilm: MnCH proj. no. 13,904

7264 Vita S. Conradi episcopi Constantiensis. MS. Vienna, Nationalbibliothek, codex 573, f.107v–125v. Quarto. Saec. 12.
Microfilm: MnCH proj. no. 13,904

7265 Vita Chounradi episcopi Constantiensis.
(*In* Monumenta Germaniae historica. Scriptores. Stuttgart, 1963. t. 4, p. 429–436)
MnCS; PLatS

7266 **Uffing, monk of Werden,** fl. 980.
Ex Uffingi Werthinensis vita s. Idae.
(*In* Monumenta Germaniae historica. Scriptores. Stuttgart, 1963. t. 2, p. 569–576)
MnCS; PLatS

7267 **Ugo, abbot of Venosa,** 12th cent.
Vitae ss. Alferii, Leonis, Petri et Constabilis, abbatum Cavensium. MS. Cava, Italy (Benedictine abbey), codex 24. 37 f. Folio. Saec. 13(1295).
Microfilm: MnCH

7268 **Ujlaki, John Joseph,** 1891–
Exegesis [by] P. John and P. Justin. [Latrobe, Pa., St. Vincent Archabbey] 1954.
various pagings, 29 cm.
Mimeographed lectures.
PLatS

Ullathorne, William Bernard, 1806–1889.

7269 The Catholic mission in Australasia. Liverpool, Printed by Rocklif & Duckworth, 1937. [Adelaide, Library Board of South Australia, 1963].
v, 58 p. 17 cm.
PLatS

7270 Ecclesiastical discourses. London, Burns and Oates, 1876.
viii, 322 p. 20 cm.
KAS; KySu; MnSSP; MoCo

7271 The holy mountain of La Salette. 9th ed., with illustrations and appendix. Altamont, La Salette Press [1942].
188 p. plates, 18 cm.
PLatS

7272 Three lectures on the conventual life. London, Catholic Truth Societh, 1910.
96 p.
MoCo

7273 (2dary) Butler, Edward Cuthbert. The Vatican Council, 1869–1870, based on Bishop Ullathorne's letters. Edited by Christopher Butler. Westminster, Md., Newman Press, 1962.
510 p. 20 cm.
InStme; MnCS; PLatS

7274 **Ussermann, Aemilian.**
Canones et regulae de disciplina monastica loco collationum legendi. MS. Benediktinerabtei St. Paul im Lavanttal, Austria, codex 220/2. 144 p. Saec. 18.
Microfilm: MnCH proj. no. 12,038

Usuard, monk of St-Germain-des-Prés, d. ca. 875.

7275 Martyrologium. MS. Benediktinerabtei Admont, Austria, codex 184, f.2v–54v. Folio. Saec. 11–12.
Microfilm: MnCH proj. no. 9273

7276 Martyrologium. MS. Benediktinerabtei Admont, Austria, codex 567, f.1r–44r. Quarto. Saec. 12.
Microfilm: MnCH proj. no. 9610

7277   Martyrologium. MS. Universitätsbibliothek Graz, Austria, codex 325, f.12r–43v. Folio. Saec. 12.
Microfilm: MnCH proj. no. 26,219

7278   Martirologium Usuardi. MS. Vich, Spain, Museo Episcopal, codex 207. 23 f. Quarto. Saec. 14.
Microfilm: MnCH proj. no. 31,254

7279   Martyrologium secundum Bedam, Hieronymum et Usuardum. Incipit: Notandum quod licet multi. Vienna, Nationalbibliothek, codex 4977, f.54v–117v.
Microfilm: MnCH proj. no. 18,157

7280   Le martyrologe d'Usuard. Texte et commentaire par Jacques Dubois, O.S.B. Bruxelles, Société des Bollandistes, 1965.
444 p. facsim. 25 cm. (Subsidia hagiographica, no. 40)
InStme; MnCS; PLatS

Uva, Benedetto dell', b. 1530?
7281   Il Doroteo. Firenze, Bartolomeo Sermatelli, 1582.
17 p. 22 cm.
MnCS

7282   Il pensier della morte. Firenze, Bartolomeo Sermatelli, 1582.
[5], 40 p. 22 cm.
MnCS

7283   Le vergini prudenti. Firenze, Bartolomeo Sermatelli, 1582.
[6], 198 p. 22 cm.
MnCS

Vagaggini, Cipriano, 1909–
7284   The bishop and the liturgy. [Translated by Philip Perfetti].
(*In* The Church and the liturgy, p. 7–24)
PLatS

7285   Bibbia e spiritualità. [Roma] Edizioni Paoline [1967].
655 p. 18 cm.
MnCS

7286   Le canon de la Messe et la réforme liturgique. Traduit par A. M. Roguet et Ph. Rouillard. Paris, Editions du Cerf, 1967.
199 p. 20 cm. (Lex orandi, 41)
InStme

7287   The Canon of the Mass and liturgical reform. Translation editor: Peter Coughlan. Staten Island, N.Y., Alba House [1967].
200 p. 23 cm.
InFer; InStme; MnCS; MnStj; MoCo; NcBe; PLatS

7288   Il canone della Messa e la riforma liturgica; problemi e progetti. Torino-Leumann, Elle di Ci [1966].
MnCS; PLatS

7289   La constitution de Vatican II sur la liturgie, par Thierry Maertens et Cyprien Vagaggini. [Bruges], Biblica, 1964.
43 p. 24 cm.
KAS; PLatS

7290   La dévotion au Sacré-Coeur chez Sainte Mechtilde et Sainte Gertrude.
(*In* Cor Jesu; commentationes in . . . "Haurietis aquas." Roma, 1959. v. 2, p. 29–48)
PLatS

7291   The flesh, instrument of salvation; a theology of the human body. Staten Island, N.Y., Alba House [1969].
152 p. 22 cm.
Translation of: Caro salutis est cardo.
InStme; MnCS; NcBe; PLatS

7292   Fundamental ideas of the Constitution.
(*In* Baraúna, Guilherme, ed. The liturgy of Vatican II; a symposium. 1966. v. 1, p. 95–129)
PLatS

7293   General norms for the reform and fostering of the liturgy.
(*In* Ephemerides liturgicae. The commentary on the Constitution and on the Instruction on the sacred liturgy. New York, 1965. p. 62–134)
PLatS

7294   La hantise des "rationes necessariae" de saint Anselme dans la théologie des processions trinitaires de saint Thomas.
(*In* Spicilegium Becceense. 1959. v. 1, p. 103–140)
PLatS

7295   Initiation théologique à la liturgie. Adapté de l'italien par Dom Philippe Rouillard. Bruges, Apostolat liturgique, 1959–1963.
2 v. 22 cm.
Vol. 2 adapté de l'italien par Dom Robert Gantoy, O.S.B.
CaQStB; InStme; MnCS; MoCo; PLatS

7296   Liturgia e pensiero teologico recente; inaugurazione del Pontificio Istituto Liturgico. Roma, Pontificio Ateneo Anselmiano, 1961.
78 p. ports. 24 cm.
InStme; MnCS; OkShG; PLatS

7297   Patriarchi orientali cattolici e dispense matrimoniali . . . Roma, Pont. Institutum Orientalium Studiorum, 1959.
xii, 254 p. 24 cm.
InStme; MnCS; PLatS

7298   La preghiera nella Bibbia e nella tradizonne patristica e monastica [di] C. Vagaggini, G. Penco. [Roma] Edizioni Paoline [1964].

1012 p. 19 cm.
KAS; MnCS; PLatS

7299 Prospetto di un saggio su simbolismo e linguaggio teologico.
(*In* Symbolisme et theologie. Studia Anselmiana, v. 64(1974), p. 297–307)
PLatS

7300 Tesi per un approccio filosofico gnose-logico della conoscenza simbolica sulla base dei principi essenziali della gnoseologia Tomistia.
(*In* Symbolisme et theologie. Studia Anselmiana, v. 64(1974) p. 125–135)
PLatS

7301 Theological dimensions of the liturgy; a general treatise on the theology of the liturgy. Translated by Leonard J. Doyle and W. A. Jurgens. Collegeville, Minn., The Liturgical Press [1976].
xxix, 996 p. 24 cm.
InFer; InStme; MnCS; MnStj; NcBe; PLatS

7302 (ed) Problemi e orientamenti di spirit-ualità monastica, biblica e liturgica [per] C. Vagaggini [et al.]. Roma, Edizioni Paoline [1961].
590 p. 18 cm.
InStme; MnCS; MoCo

7303 **Vagaggini, Giovanni,** 1894–
Bibbia e spiritualità con particolare riferimento ai salmi. Roma, Coletti [1964].
239 p. 18 cm.
PLatS

Valentinus, Basilius. *See* Basilius Valentinus.

7304 **Vallés, Spain. Sant Cugat (Benedictine abbey).**
Cartulario de "Sant Cugat" del Vallés, editado por José Rius. Barcelona [Sobs. de Lopez Robert & cía.] 1945–
v. 25 cm.
MnCS

Valyermo, Calif. St. Andrew's Priory. *See* St. Andrew's Priory, Valyermo, Calif.

Vandenbroucke, François, 1912–1971.

7305 Communion under both species and con-celebration.
(*In* Baraúna, Guilherme, ed. The liturgy of Vatican II; a symposium. 1966. v. 2, p. 107–118)
PLatS

7306 Die diakonische Aufgabe im Ordenstand.
(*In* Rahner, Karl, ed. Diaconia in Christo, p. 389–397)
PLatS

7307 Initiation liturgique. Paris, Beauchesne [1964].

159 p. 18 cm.
InStme; PLatS

7308 Liturgical initiation. Translated by Kathryn Sullivan. With study-club questions. Glen Rock, N.J., Paulist Press [1965].
127 p. 18 cm.
MnCS; MoCo; PLatS

7309 Moines: pourquoi? Théologie critique du monachisme. Paris, P. Lethielleux [1967].
252 p. 19 cm.
InStme; KAS; PLatS

7310 La morale monastique du XIe au XVe siècle. Louvain, Editions Nauwelaerts, 1966.
209 p. 25 cm.
InStme; MnCS; MoCo; PLatS

7311 Les Psaumes, le Christ, et nous. 2. éd., revue et complétée. Louvain, Abbaye du Mont César, 1965.
103 p. 19 cm.
MnCS; PLatS

7312 La spiritualité du Moyen Age [par] Jean Leclercq, François Vandenbroucke [et] Louis Bouyer. [Paris] Aubier, 1961.
718 p. 23 cm.
InStme; MnCS

7313 The spirituality of the Middle Ages, by Jean Leclercq, François Vandenbroucke [and] Louis Bouyer. London, Burns & Oates [1968].
x, 602 p. 23 cm.
InStme; MnCS

7314 Why monks? Translated by Leon Brockman. Washington, D.C., Cistercian Publications, 1972.
xvi, 185 p. 23 cm. (Cistercian studies series, no. 17)
ICSS; InFer; InStme; KAS; MnCS; MdRi; MoCo; NcBe; PLatS; ViBris

7315 (ed) Rolle, Richard, of Hampole, 1290–1349. Le Chant d'amour (Melos amoris) . . . Introduction et notes par François Vandenbroucke, O.S.B. Paris, Editions du Cerf, 1971.
2 v. 20 cm. (Sources chrétiennes, no. 168–69)
InStme; MnCS; PLatS

7316 **Van der Heijden, Joannes B.,** 1919–
L'Eglise orientale de Chevetogne: archi-tecture, décoration, symbolisme. Cheve-togne [Belgique] Les Editions de Cheve-togne, 1962.
64 p. illus. 12 fold. diagrs. 14 cm.
KAS

Vandeur, Eugène, 1875–

7317 Living the Lord's prayer. Translated by M. Angeline Bouchard. St. Louis, Herder, [1961].

102 p. 21 cm.
Translation of: L'abandon à Dieu voie de la paix.
InFer; InStme; KAS; MnCS; MdRi; MoCo; NcBe; PLatS

7318 **Vanmackelberg, Maurice,** 1921–
L'orgue de l'église abbatiale de Saint-Riquier.
(*In* Saint-Riquier; études . . . 1962. v. 1, p. 155–174)
PLatS

Van Zeller, Hubert, 1905–

7319 Approach to spirituality. London, Sheed and Ward [1974, c 1970].
ix, 150 p. 22 cm.
PLatS

7320 Benedictine life at Minster Abbey. [Exeter, Catholic Records Press] n.d.
23 p. plates, 12 cm.
MnCS

7321 The Benedictine nun; her story and aim. Baltimore, Helicon [1965].
271 p. 22 cm.
CaMWiSb; ICSS: InStme; MdRi; KAS; MnCS; MnStj; MoCo; PLatS; ViBris

7322 The book of beginnings. Springfield, Ill., Templegate, [1975].
124 p.
InFer; ICSS

7323 Considerations. Springfield, Ill., Templegate [1973].
127 p. 24 cm.
ICSS; InFer; InStme; MdRi; MoCo; ViBris

7324 Cracks in the curia, or, Brother Choleric rides again, by Brother Choleric [pseud.]. London and New York, Sheed and Ward [1972].
unpaged, illus. 23 cm.
InStme

7325 The current of spirituality. Springfield, Ill., Templegate [1970].
170 p. 18 cm.
CaMWiSb; InStme; KAS; MdRi; MnCS; NcBe; ViBris

7326 Death in other words; a presentation for beginners. Springfield, Ill., Templegate [1963].
96 p. 20 cm.
ICSS; InFer; InStme; MnSt; MoCo; NcBe; MnStj; NdRi; PLatS; ViBris

7327 Famine of the spirit. Springfield, Ill., Templegate, [1964].
194 p.
MnStj

7328 First person singular. London, J. Murray, [1970].
207 p. 21 cm.
MnCS; MnStj

7329 The Gospel in other words; a presentation for beginners. Springfield, Ill., Templegate [1965].
127 p. 20 cm.
InFer; InStme; MnCS; MnStj; MdRi; NcBe

7330 Ideas for prayer; 200 suggestions. Springfield, Ill., Templegate [1966].
156 p. 24 cm.
ICSS; InFer; InStme; KAS; MnCS; MnStj; MoCo; OkShG; PLatS

7331 Last cracks in legendary cloisters, by Brother Choleric [pseud.]. London, Sheed and Ward [1960].
unpaged, illus. 22 cm.
MnCS; NcBe

7332 Leave your life alone. London, Sheed and Ward [1972].
128 p. 22 cm.
MdRi; NcBe; PLatS; ViBris

7333 Leave your life alone. Springfield, Ill., Templegate, [1972].
128 p.
ICSS; InFer

7334 Letters to a soul. London, Sheed and Ward [1975].
122 p. 21 cm.
InFer; PLatS; CaMWiSb

7335 The Mass in other words; a presentation for beginners. Springfield, Ill., Templegate [1965].
90 p. 20 cm.
CaMWiSb; InFer; InStme; MdRi; MnCS; MnStj; MoCo; NcBe; OkShG; ViBris

7336 Moments of light. Springfield, Ill., Templegate [1963].
xi, 196 p. 17 cm.
CaMWiSb

7337 More ideas for prayer; 200 suggestions. Springfield, Ill., Templegate [1967].
160 p. 24 cm.
InFer; InStme; ICSS; KAS; MnCS; MnStj; PLatS

7338 One foot in the cradle; an autobiography. New York, Holt, Rinehart and Winston [1966].
xi, 282 p. illus., ports. 22 cm.
InFer; InStme; MnCS; MnStj; MoCo; NcBe; PLatS; ViBris

7339 The other kingdom; a book of comfort. Springfield, Ill., Templegate [1969].
123 p.
MdRi; MoCo

7340 Our Lady in other words; a presentation for beginners. Springfield, Ill., Templegate [1963].
92 p. 20 cm.
Meditative essays on the Hail Mary.
ICSS; InFer; InStme; MdRi; MoCo; PLatS

7341   Posthumous cracks in the cloisters, by Brother Choleric [pseud.]. London, New York, Sheed and Ward [1962].
    unpaged, illus. 22 cm.
    MnCS; NcBe

7342   Prayer in other words; a presentation for beginners. Springfield, Ill., Templegate [1963].
    94 p. 20 cm.
    ICSS; InFer; InStme; MnCS; MnStj; NdRi; PLatS

7343   Prier en travaillant. Livre d'heures pour les femmes de ce temps. Traduit de l'anglais par Anne Barrault Theims. Paris, Spes [1958].
    183 p. 19 cm.
    Translation of: Praying while you work.
    KAS

7344   The Psalms in other words; a presentation for beginners. Springfield, Ill., Templegate [1964].
    94 p. 20 cm.
    InFer; InStme; MdRi; MnCS; MnStj; KAS; NcBe; PLatS; ViBris

7345   Sanctity in other words; a presentation for beginners. Springfield, Ill., Templegate [1963].
    94 p. 20 cm.
    CaMWiSb; ICSS; InFer; InStme; MdRi; MnCS; MnStj; NcBe; PLatS; ViBris

7346   Suffering in other words; a presentation for beginners. Springfield, Ill., Templegate [1964].
    96 p. 20 cm.
    InFer; InStme; KAS; MnCS; NcBe

7347   We live with our eyes open. Garden City, N.Y., Doubleday [1963].
    152 p. 18 cm.
    CaMWiSb; KAS; NcBe

7348   We sing while there's voice left. Garden City, N.Y., Doubleday, [1964].
    155 p.
    CaMWiSb

7349   We work while the light lasts. Garden City, N.Y., Doubleday [1962].
    160 p. 18 cm.
    CaMWiSb

7350   The will of God in other words; a presentation for beginners. Springfield, Ill., Templegate [1964].
    124 p. 20 cm.
    CaMWiSb; ICSS; InFer; InStme; MdRi; MnCS; MnStj; MoCo; NdRi; PkShG; PLatS

7351   (illus.) Coulson, John. Logic for lunatics; a fabulous primer with illustrations by Brother Choleric. London, Sheed and Ward, [1960].

162 p. 23 cm.
    MnCS

7352   **Vascelli, Francesco Maria.**
    Dialogo dove secondo la vera nozione della sustanza si dimostra qual sia l'origine, l'essenza, e la natura de' corpi, ed in nuova maniera si spiega i loro fenomeni. Venezia, Domenico Battifoco, 1769.
    167 p. 26 cm.
    MnCS

Vasconcelos, Bernardo de, 1902–1932.
7353   Sed de luz y pas. [Traducción y notas del P. Germán Prado, O.S.B.]. Bilbao, Desclée de Brouwer, 1959.
    154 p. front. (port) 19 cm.
    MnCS

7354   Your Mass. [Translated from the Portuguese]. Dublin, Chicago, Scepter [1960].
    138 p. 19 cm.
    Translation of: A Missa e a vida interior.
    InStme; KAS; MnCS; PLatS

7355   **Venice, Italy. San Lazzaro (Mechitarist Benedictine abbey).**
    Armenian miniature paintings of the monastic library at San Lazzaro [by Mesrop Janashian. English version of the text by Bernard Grebanier]. Venice [Armenian Press, San Lazzaro, 1966–   ].
    v. chiefly col. facsims. 46 cm.
    PLatS

Verbraken, Patrick, 1926–
7356   The beginnings of the Church; the first Christian centuries. Translated by Vivienne Healy. Dublin, Gill; New York, Paulist Press [1968].
    xii, 171 p. 18 cm.
    InStme; PLatS
    Translation of: Naissance et essor de l'Eglise.

7357   Etudes critiques sur les sermons authentiques de Saint Augustin. Steenbrugie, Abbatia S. Petri, 1976.
    265 p. 25 cm.
    PLatS

7358   Oraisons sur les cent cinquante Psaumes. Texte latin et traduction française de trois séries de collectes psalmiques. Paris, Editions du Cerf, 1967.
    343 p. 20 cm.
    InStme; MnCS

7359   (ed) Gregory I, Pope. Expositiones in Canticum canticorum [et] in librum primum Regum. Recensuit Patricius Verbraken. Turnholti, Brepols, 1963.
    xi, 637 p. 25 cm. (Corpus Christianorum. Series latina, 144)
    ILSP; InStme; MnCS; PLatS

7360 **Vercelli, Italy. San Stefano (Benedictine abbey).**
Abbatis Vercellensis extractio super librum S. Dionysii de angelica hierarchia . . . de ecclesiastica hierarchia . . . de divinis nominibus . . . de mystica theologia . . . ad Titum pontificem. MS. Benediktinerabtei Melk, Austria, codex 896, f.11r–160v. Quarto. Saec. 15.
Microfilm: MnCH proj. no. 1715

7361 **Verdun, France. Saint-Michel (Benedictine abbey).**
Chronicon S. Michaelis in pago Virdunensi a. 722–1034, edente D. Georgio Waitz.
(*In* Monumenta Germaniae historica. Scriptores. Stuttgart, 1963. t. 4, p. 78–86)
PLatS

Verheul, Ambrosius, 1916–
7362 De Beata Maria Virgine in liturgia romana.
(*In* Maria et Ecclesia. 1958. p. 25–46)
PLatS

7363 "Christo signati"; farde pastorale sur la confirmation [par] P. Anciaus [et] A. Verheul [et] J. Rabau. Malines, Comité de Pastorale Liturgique de l'Archidiocèse [1954].
64 p. 21 cm.
CaQStB; MnCS

7364 De Dienst van het woord in synagoge en christendom.
(*In* Corona gratiarum . . . 's Gravenhage, 1975. v. 2, p. 3–49)
PLatS

7365 Einführung in die Liturgie; zur Theologie des Gottesdienstes. Wien, Herder [1964].
275 p. 20 cm.
PLatS

7366 Het Paasmysterie in kerkelijke vroomheid en viering; een bezinningsboekje voor priester en leek. Roermond en Maaseik, J. J. Romen [1957].
141 p. 19 cm.
MnCS

7367 **Verkamp, Gabriel,** 1900–
De divina providentia secundum Commentarium S. Thomae in librum Job.
90 leaves. 28 cm.
Thesis (S.T.D.)–Collegio di Sant' Anselmo, Rome, 1931.
Typescript.
InStme

Verostko, Roman Joseph, 1929–
7368 [Catalog of exhibit] Westmoreland County, Museum of Art, Greensburg, Pa., April 2 through May 2, 1965.

[16] p. plates, 18 cm.
PLatS

7369 Saint Vincent monastery. Latrobe, Pa., Archabbey Press, 1967.
[16] leaves, plates, 24 cm.
PLatS

7370 **Veselenak, Stephen,** 1925–
Bibliography [of] the Byzantine (Ruthenian) Rite of the Catholic Church in east Central Europe and North America. Butler, Pa., Holy Trinity Monastery.
23 leaves, 28 cm.
Typescript.
PLatS

7371 **Veth, Martin,** 1874–1944.
The medal of Saint Benedict. [Atchison, Kans., Abbey Student Press, c 1961].
40 p. illus. 15 cm.
KAS

7372 **Vézelay, France (Benedictine abbey).**
Monumenta Vizeliacensis: textes relatifs à l'histoire de l'Abbaye de Vézelay, édites par R.B.C. Huygens. Turnholti, Brepols, 1976.
xli, 686 p. facsims. 25 cm.
InStme

7373 **Viboldone, Italy (abbey of Benedictine nuns).**
Galateo monastico. Viboldone, Scuola tipografica San Benedetto [1960].
xv, 205 p. 19 cm.
PLatS

7374 **Viechter, Bernardus.**
Alveare. Pars I: Miscellanea ascetica. Pars II: Miscellanea moralia. Pars III: Miscellanea historica. MS. Benediktinerabtei St. Peter, Salzburg, codex a.IS.27–29. 434, 458, 481 p. Folio. Saec. 18.
Microfilm: MnCH proj. no. 10,252–54

Vienna, Austria. Mechitharisten-Kongregation.
7375 Catalog der Armenischen Handschriften in der Mechitharisten-Bibliothek zu Wien, von P. Jacobus Dashian and P. Hamazasp Oskian. Wien, Mechitharisten-Buchdruckerei, 1895–1963.
2 v. 30 cm.
The entries are listed in Armenian and German.
MnCS

7376 Festschrift aus Anlass der Hundertjahrfeier des Neubaues des Mutterhauses der Mechitharisten in Wien, 1837–1937. Wien, Mechitharisten-Buchdruckerei, 1937.
8 p. 46 plates, 25 cm.
MnCS

7377 Huschardzen; Festschrift aus Anlass des 100-jährigen Bestandes der Mechitharisten-Kongregation in Wien (1811–1911) und

des 25. Jahrgangs der philologischen Monatschrift "Handes amsorya" . . . Wien, Mechitharisten-Kongregation, 1911 [i.e. 1912].
    435 p. illus. 32 cm.
    Edited by P. N. Akinian.
    MnCS

7378   Die illuminierten armenischen Handschriften der Mechitaristen-Congregation in Wien. Wien, 1976.
    250 p. incl. 80 col. plates, 30 cm.
    At head of title: Heide & Helmut Buschhausen unter Mithilfe von Eva Zimmermann.
    MnCS

7379   Nuovo dizionario italiano-francese-armenoturco, compilato sui migliori vocabolarii di queste quattro lingue dai padri della Congregazione Mechitaristica. Vienna, Tipografia dei PP. Mechitaristi, 1846.
    1120 p. 25 cm.
    MnCS

7380   Rule of our holy father, Benedict, translated by the disciples of their great father Mechitar. Vienna, in the monastery under the tutelage of the Holy Mother of God, 1842.
    [12], 138, [6] p. 14 cm.
    In Armenian language and script.
    MnCS

Vienna, Austria. Schottenstift (Benedictine abbey).
7381   Catalogus religiosorum Ordinis S. P. Benedicti in monsaterio B.M.V. ad Scotos degentium, anno domini . . .
    v. 21 cm.
    MnCS(1903–1921); PLatS

7382   Inventarium ecclesiae Beatae Mariae Virginis ad Scotos Viennae ex anno 1650 et sqq. regnante Petro Heister abbate. MS. Vienna, Schottenstift, codex 534. 173 f. Folio. Saec. 17.
    Microfilm: MnCH proj. no. 4295

Vienna, Austria, Schottenstift (Benedictine abbey). Bibliothek.
7383   Catalogus bibliothecae monasterii Scotensis. Pertinet usque ad annum fere 1740. MS. Vienna, Schottenstift, codex 530. 504 f. Folio. Saec. 18.
    Microfilm: MnCH proj. no. 4293

7384   Catalogus bibliothecae monasterii Scotensis. Pertinet usque ad annum 1750. MS. Vienna, Schottenstift, codex 532. 32 f. Folio. Saec. 18.
    Microfilm: MnCH proj. no. 4291

7385   Catalogus bibliothecae monasterii Scotensis. Pertinet usque ad annum fer

1750. MS. Vienna, Schottenstift, codex 531. 640 f. Folio. Saec. 18.
    Microfilm: MnCH proj. no. 4287

7386   Catalogus codicum manu scriptorum qui in bibliotheca monasterii B.M.V. ad Scotos Vindobonae servantur. Ex mandato Ernesti Hauswirth edidit Albertus Hüble, O.S.B. Wiesbaden, Martin Sändig [1970].
    x, 609 p. 21 cm.
    Reprint of 1899 edition, Vindobonae, Guilelmus Braumüller.
    PLatS (1970); MnCS (1899)

7387   **Vierholz, Carlmann,** 1658–1745.
    Ascesis illuminata; sive, Lumina practica ex meditatione vitae Christi hausta . . . Viennae et Francofurti, P. C. Monath, 1734.
    4 v. 17 cm.
    KAS

7388   **Vila, Benito.**
    Arpa de David (commentari als salms). MS. Monasterio benedictino de Montserrat, Spain, codex 9. 202 f. Folio. Saec. 17.
    Microfilm: MnCH proj. no. 29,981

7389   **Villiers, Pierre de,** 1648–1728.
    Verités satiriques en dialogues. Paris, chez Jacques Etienne, 1725.
    ix, 441 p. 17 cm.
    Also ascribed to L. Bordelon. – cf. Barbier, Dict. des ouvrages annon., t. IV(1879), p. 946.
    PLatS

7390   **Villiger, Anselm,** 1824–1901.
    The founding of Mount Angel Abbey as recorded in the diary of the founding Abbot Anselm Villiger of Engelberg, January, 1881, to December, 1900. Translation, 1974.
    57 p. 28 cm.
    Typescript.
    MoCo

7391   **Vischl, Gotthard.**
    Disquisitiones in universam philosophiam Aristotelico-Thomisticam. Salisburgi, Joan. Bapt. Mayr, 1707.
    PLatS(microfilm)

7392   **Vita beati Emmerammi.** MS. Benediktinerabtei Kremsmünster, Austria, codex 7, f.166v–189v. Saec. 13.
    Microfilm: MnCH proj. no. 7

7393   **Vita et actus beati Corbiniani.** MS. Benedidktinerabtei Kremsmünster, Austria, codex 7, f.137r–166v. Saec. 13.
    Microfilm: MnCH proj. no. 7

7394   **Vita et Regula ss. p. Benedicti una cum expositione Regulae a Hildemaro tradita.** Ratisbonae, Neo-Eboraci, F. Pustet, 1880.

xi, 76, xxix, 74, xv, 658 p. 22 cm.
ILSP; InStme; KAS; PLatS

7395 **Vita Gundulphi.**
The life of the venerable man, Gundulf, bishop of Rochester; translated into English by the nuns of Malling Abbey. [West Malling, Kent, printed at St. Mary's Abbey, 1968].
[8], v, 76 p. 19 cm.
KAS

7396 **Vitry, Ermin,** 1884–1960.
Being at ease with the Liber Usualis. [n.p.] c 1951.
179 p. illus., music, 28 cm.
InStme; MoCo

7397 **Vogt, Gabriel,** 1912–
Der selige Egbert, Abt von Münsterschwarzach, 1046–1076; Persönlichkeit und Werk des fränkisches Reformabtes . . . [Münsterschwarzach, Vier-Türme-Verlag, 1976].
83 p. illus. 20 cm.
MnCS

Vogüe, Adalbert du, 1924–
7398 Autour de Saint Benoît: la Règle en son temps et dans le notre. Begrolles en Mauges, Abbaye de Bellefontaine, 1975.
158 p. plates, 21 cm.
InStme

7399 La communauté et l'abbé dans la Règle de saint Benoît. [Bruges] Desclée, De Brouwer [1961].
559 p. 21 cm.
InStme; MnCS; MoCo; NcBe; PLatS

7399a Community and abbot in the Rule of Saint Benedict. Translated by Charles Philippi, monk of New Camaldoli. Kalamazoo, Mich., Cistercian Publications, 1979.
256 p. 20 cm. (Cistercian studies series, no. 5/1)
MnCS; NcBe; PLatS; InStme

7400 Conferences on the Benedictine rule and life (Phonotape-cassette). St. Meinrad, Ind., St. Meinrad Archabbey, 1977.
9 tapes (c. 45 min. each side) 1 7/8 ips.
InStme

7401 Les conseils evangeliques chez le Maitre et Saint Benoit.
(*In* Semana de Estudios Monasticos, 14th, Silos, Spain, 1973 . . . p. 13–27)
PLatS

7402 Monachisme et Eglise dans la pensée de Cassien.
(*In* Théologie de la vie monastique, p. 213–240)
PLatS

7403 Monasticism and the Church in the writings of Cassian. [Translated by a nun of Holy Cross Abbey, Stapehill, England].
(*In* Monastic Studies, v. 3, p. 19–51)
PLatS

7404 La Règle de Saint Benoît. Paris, Editions du Cerf, 1971–72.
6 v. 20 cm. (Sources chrétiennes, n. 181–186)
Contents: v. 1–2, Latin text and French translation; v. 3, Instruments pour l'étude de la tradition manuscrite, par Jean Neufville; v. 4–6, Commentaire historique et critique par Adalbert de Vogüe.
CaQMo; KAS; InStme; MnCS; MnStj; MoCo; PLatS

7404a La Règle de saint Benoit, VIII: Commentaire doctrinal et spiritual. Paris, Editions du Cerf, 1977.
496 p. 20 cm.
MnCS; InStme

7405 Sur le texte des Dialogues de saint Grégoire le Grand.
(*In* Latinität und alte Kirche; Festschrift für Rudolf Hanslik zum 70. Geburtstag. Wien, 1977. p. 326–335)
PLatS

7406 (ed & tr) Regula Magistri. La Règla du Maître. Introduction, texte, tradition et notes par Adalbert de Vogüe. Paris, Editions du Cerf, 1964–65.
3 v. 20 cm. (Sources chrétiennes, 105–07)
InStme; MnCS; PLatS

7407 **Voici Montserrat:** une montagne, un sanctuaire, un monastère . . . 5. éd. [Montserrat] Publicacions de l'Abadia de Montserrat, 1967.
74 p. plates, 20 cm.
PLatS

Volk, Paulus, 1889–
7408 Abt Johannes Trithemius.
Sonderabdruck aus: Rheinische Vierteljahrs-Blätter. Jahrg. 27(1962), p. 37–49)
KAS; MnCS

7409 Die Bursfelder Missalien.
(*In* Liturgica, 3: Cardinal I. A. Schuster in memoriam. Montisserrati, 1966, p. 185–196)
PLatS

7410 Zur Geschichte des Bursfelder Breviers. [Beuron] 1928.
97 p. 21 cm.
MoCo; PLatS

7411 **Vollmann, Benedikt,** 1913–
Studien zum Priszillianismus; die Forschung, die Quellen, der 15te Brief Papst Leos des Grossen. St. Ottilien, Eos Verlag, 1965.

xxiv, 175 p. diagrs. 24 cm.
MnCS; PLatS

7412 **Von Raczeck, Eucharis.**
Im Heiligthum unserer Lieben Frau von
Varensell. Paderborn, Bonifacius-Druckerei [1956?].
72 p. illus. 21 cm.

Vooght, Paul de, 1900–
7413 L'héresie de Jean Huss . . . Louvain,
Bibliothèque de l'Université, 1960.
494 p. 25 cm.
InStme; MnCS; PLatS

7414 Hussiana. Louvain, Publications universitaires de Louvain, 1960.
vii, 450 p. 25 cm.
InStme; PLatS

7415 Les pouvoirs du concile et l'autorité du
Pape au Concile de Constance. Le decret
Haec sancta synodus du 6 avril 1415. Paris,
Editions du Cerf, 1965.
198 p. 23 cm.
PLatS

7416 **Voss, Gerhard,** 1935–
Die Christologie der Lukanischen Schriften in Grundzügen. Paris, Desclée [1965].
219 p. 22 cm.
MnCS

Voth, Agnes, Sister.
7417 Green olive branch. Chicago, Franciscan
Herald Press [1973].
xii, 351 p. illus. 21 cm.
InFer; InStme; KAS; MoCo

7418 (tr) Weibel, Johann Eugen. The Catholic
missions of north-east Arkansas,
1867–1893. Translated from the German
by Sister M. Agnes Voth, O.S.B. Printed
by Arkansas State University Press, 1967.
109 p. 23 cm.
InStme; KAS; MoCo

7419 (tr) Weibel, Johann Eugen. Forty years
missionary in Arkansas. Translation [by]
Sister M. Agnes, O.S.B. [Jonesboro, Ark.,
Holy Angels Convent] 1968.
252 p. illus. 23 cm.
InFer; InStme

7420 **Vromen, Franciscus,** 1918–
(tr. & ed.) Leo I, Pope. Preken voor het
liturgisch jaar. Vertaald en ingeleid door
Dom F. Vromen, O.S.B. Oosterhout, Sint
Paulusabdij, 1960–61.
4 v. 20 cm.
MnCS; PLatS

7421 **Wack, Dunstan John,** 1916–
The image of God in psychotherapy: a
study of cases.
(*In* Godin, André. From cry to word; con-
tributions towards a psychology of prayer.
Brussels, 1968. p. 95–100)
KAS

7422 **Wagner, Benedikt,** 1929–
Der Religionsfonds versteigert eine alte
Stiftsbibliothek.
(*In* Translatio studii . . . Collegeville,
Minn., 1973. p. 235–243)
MnCS; PLatS

7423 **Wagner, Mary Anthony, Sister,** 1916–
The Christian assembly.
(*In* Hargrove, K.T. On the other side.
New York, 1967. p. 67–77)
MnStj(Archives)

Wahl, Thomas Peter, 1931–
7424 The books of Judith and Esther. Introduction and commentary. Collegeville,
Minn., The Liturgical Press [1971].
99 p. 20 cm. (Old Testament reading
guide, v. 25)
MnCS; PLatS

7425 How Jesus came. [St. Paul, Minn.,
North Central Pub. Co., 1959].
unpaged, illus. 25 cm.
MnCS

7426 Saint John's University Library index to
biblical journals, edited by Thomas Peter
Wahl – Established by Raymond Breun.
Collegeville, Minn., St. John's University
Press, 1971.
531 leaves, 24 cm.
Computer print-out.
MnCS

7427 **Waibel, Maurus.**
Alchymia magna, seu Supellex alchymica
in qua continentur processus pro lapide
philosophorum et particulares pro
metallorum particulari melioratione. MS.
Vienna, Nationalbibliothek, codex 11469,
f.1r–259r. Folio. Saec. 17.
Microfilm: MnCH proj. no. 19,802

Walafrid Strabo, 807–849.
Manuscript copies.
7428 Expositio super Canticum canticorum.
MS. Augustinerchorherrenstift Kloster-
neuburg, Austria, codex 788, f.1r–54v.
Folio. Saec. 13.
Microfilm: MnCH proj. no. 5769

7429 Liber Danielis prophetae, cum glossa ordinaria Walafridi Strabi et interlineari
Anselmi Laudunensis. MS. Augustinerchorherrenstift Klosterneuburg, Austria,
codex 249. 39 f. Folio. Saec. 13.
Microfilm: MnCH proj. no. 5222

7430 Expositio in Deuteronomium. MS. Vienna, Nationalbibliothek, codex 1042,
f.179v–205v. Quarto. Saec. 10.
Microfilm: MnCH proj. no. 14,356

7431 S. Pauli epistolae, cum glossa ordinaria
Walafridi Strabi et interlineari Anselmi
Laudunensis. MS. Augustinerchorher-

renstift Klosterneuburg, Austria, codex 153. 234 f. Folio. Saec. 13.

7432   Epistolae catholicae cum glossa ordinaria Walafridi Strabi et interlineari Anselmi Laudunensis. MS. Augustiner-chorherrenstift Klosterneuburg, Austria, codex 190, f.1r–75r. Folio. Saec. 13.
Microfilm: MnCH proj. no. 5157

7433   Expositio super Exodus, Leviticus, Numeri et Deuteronomium. MS. Linz, Austria, Bundesstaatliche Studienbibliothek, codex 97, f.41v–161v. Folio. Saec. 12.
Microfilm: MnCH proj. no. 27,941

7434   Expositio super Genesin. MS. Vienna, Nationalbibliothek, codex 1042, f.1v–52r. Quarto. Saec. 10.
Microfilm: MnCH proj. no. 14,356

7435   Libri Iosue, Iudicum, Regum glossati (Walafridus Strabo, Anselmus de Lucca). MS. Cistercienserabtei Lilienfeld, Austria, codex 175. 445 f. Folio. Saec. 14.
Microfilm: MnCH proj. no. 4478

7436   Isaias prophetia, cum Walafridi Strabonis glossa ordinaria et Anselmi Laudunensis glossa interlineari. MS. Universitätsbibliothek Graz, Austria, codex 170. 165 f. Quarto. Saec. 13.
Microfilm: MnCH proj. no. 26,092

7437   Expositio super Leviticum. MS. Vienna, Nationalbibliothek, codex 1042, f.115v–151r. Quarto. Saec. 10.
Microfilm: MnCH proj. no. 14,356

7438   Expositio in Leviticum. MS. Cistercienserabtei Zwettl, Austria, codex 95, f.72v–100r. Folio. Saec. 12.
Microfilm: MnCH proj. no. 6699

7439   S. Lucae evangelium cum Walafridi Strabonis glossa ordinaria et Anselmi Laudunensis glossa interlineari. MS. Universitätsbibliothek Graz, Vienna, codex 260. 149 f. Folio. Saec. 13.
Microfilm: MnCH proj. no. 26,279

7440   Evangelium S. Marci et prologus Sedulii Scoti, cum glossa ordinaria Walafridi Strabi et interlineari Anselmi Laudunensis. MS. Augustinerchorherrenstift Klosterneuburg, Austria, codex 183. 64 f. Folio. Saec. 12.
Microfilm: MnCH proj. no. 5152

7441   Evangelium S. Matthaei cum prologo Sedulii Scoti et glossa ordinaria Walafridi Strabi et interlineari Anselmi Laudunensis. MS. Augustinerchorherrenstift Klosterneuburg, Austria, codex 198, f.146r–245r. Folio. Saec. 14.
Microfilm: MnCH proj. no. 5169

7442   Expositio in librum Numeri. MS. Vienna, Nationalbibliothek, codex 1042, f.151r–

179v. Quarto. Saec. 10.
Microfilm: MnCH proj. no. 14,356

7443   Expositio in librum Numeri. MS. Cistercienserabtei Zwettl, Austria, codex 95, f.100r–120r. Folio. Saec. 12.
Microfilm: MnCH proj. no. 6699

7444   Glossa ordinaria in S. Scripturam. MS. Benediktinerabtei Admont, Austria, codex 426, f.19r–112v. Quarto. Saec. 12.
Microfilm: MnCH proj. no. 9484

7445   Glossa ordinaria in S. Scripturam. MS. Benediktinerabtei Admont, Austria, codex 508. 112 f. Quarto. Saec. 12.
Microfilm: MnCH proj. no. 9555

7446   Glossa ordinaria (Walafridi Strabi) et interlinearis (Anselmi Laudunensis) super Matthaeum et Marcum (cum prologis Sedulii Scoti). MS. Augustinerchorherrenstift Klosterneuburg, Austria, codex 180. 195 f. Folio. Saec. 14.
Microfilm: MnCH proj. no. 5149

7447   Glossa ordinaria. MS. Monasterio benedictino de Montserrat, Spain, codex 3. 123 f. Folio. Saec. 14.
Microfilm: MnCH proj. no. 29,975

7448   Libellus de exordiis et incrementis quarundam in observationibus ecclesiasticis rerum. MS. Vienna, Nationalbibliothek, codex 914, f.36r–65v. Folio. Saec. 10.
Microfilm: MnCH proj. no. 14,239

7449   Vita et miracula S. Galli. Libri duo. MS. Vienna, Nationalbibliothek, codex 357, f.244v–271r. Folio. Saec. 10.
Microfilm: MnCH proj. no. 13,688

7450   Vita S Galli. Vienna, Nationalbibliothek, codex 520, f.1v–77r. Quarto. Saec. 11.
Microfilm: MnCH proj. no. 13,858

7451   Sermo de S. Gallo, ex ejusdem auctoris Vita S. Galli. MS. Vienna, Nationalbibliothek, codex 694, f.4r–5v. Folio. Saec. 11.
Microfilm: MnCH proj. no. 14,018

7452   Vita S. Galli. MS. Benediktinerabtei Admont, Austria, codex 673. 72 f. Quarto. Saec. 12.
Microfilm: MnCH proj. no. 9707

7453   De vita beati Galli. MS. Benediktinerabtei Kremsmünster, Austria, codex 126, f.266r–325v. Saec. 12.
Microfilm: MnCH proj. no. 119

7454   Vita S. Galli. MS. Benediktinerabtei Melk, Austria, codex 1248, f.1v–48r. Octavo. Saec. 12.
Microfilm: MnCH proj. no. 1879

7455   Vita S. Galli. Cistercienserabtei Heiligenkreuz, Austria, codex 282, f.1r–66v. Quarto. Saec. 13.
Microfilm: MnCH proj. no. 4821

7456 Vita et actus sancti Galli abbatis. MS. Cistercienserabtei Wilhering, Austria, codex IX,47. 24 f. Folio. Saec. 14. Microfilm: MnCH proj. no. 2823

7457 Vita et miracula S. Galli abbatis. MS. Vienna, Nationalbibliothek, codex series nova 2458, f.168v–196v. Octavo. Saec. 14. Microfilm: MnCH proj. no. 20,683

7458 Vita sancti Othmari, cum praefatione Ioannis episcopi Constantiensis. MS. Benediktinerabtei Göttweig, Austria, codex 110a, f.29r–42v. Folio. Saec. 12. Microfilm: MnCH proj. no. 3393

7459 Vita S. Otmari. MS. Benediktinerabtei Kremsmünster, Austria, codex 126, f.325v–336v. Saec. 12. Microfilm: MnCH proj. no. 119

7460 Vita S. Othmari abbatis. MS. Cistercienserabtei Heiligenkreuz, Austria, codex 282, f.67r–72v. Quarto. Saec. 13. Microfilm: MnCH proj. no. 4821

7461 Vita S. Walpurgis virginis. MS. Cistercienserabtei Heiligenkreuz, Austria, codex 282, f.73r–82v. Quarto. Saec. 13. Microfilm: MnCH proj. no. 4821

Walafrid Strabo.
Printed works.

7462 A Christmas hymn (Lumen inclytum refulget).
(*In* Donahoe, D. J. Early Christian hymns. New York, 1911. v. 2, p. 95–98)
PLatS

7463 Hortulus. Translated by Raef Payne. Commentary by Wilfrid Blunt. Pittsburgh, Hunt Botanical Library, 1966.
xi, 91 p. ilus., facsims. 27 cm. (The Hunt facsimile series, no. 2)
Facsims. of the leaves 30–39 of Codex Vaticanus Latinus Reginae no. 469, followed by transcription and translation.
PLatS

7464 Vita sancti Otmari abbatis Sangallensis.
(*In* Monumenta Germaniae historica. Scriptores. Stuttgart, 1963. t. 2, p. 41–47)
MnCS; PLatS

7465 (ed.) Gosbertus, abbot of St. Gall. Gozberti diaconi continuatio libri II de miraculis s. Galli, per Walafridum emendata.
(*In* Monumenta Germaniae historica. Scriptores. Stuttgart, 1963. t. 2, p. 21–31)
MnCS; PLatS

7466 **Walcher, Bernhard,** 1893–
Beiträge zur Geschichte der bayerischen Abtswahlen mit besonderer Berücksichtigung der Benediktinerklöster. München, Kommissionsverlag R. Oldenbourg, 1930.
xi, 79 p. 23 cm.
KAS; NdRi

7467 **Walker, William,** 1903–
Dissertatio historico-dogmatica doctrinae venerabilis Petri Cluniacensis de Beata Dei Genitrice.
v. 99 leaves. 31 cm.
Thesis (S.T.D.)–Collegio di Sant' Anselmo, Rome, 1931.
Typescript.
InStme

Wallace, Wilfrid, 1838–1896.

7468 Circumcision.
(*In* Holy Name Society. Sermons on the Holy Name. Somerset, Ohio, 1921. p. 119–124)
PLatS

7469 The coming of Christ.
(*In* Sermons for the times, by noted preachers of our own day. New York, 1913. v. 2, p. 56–59)
PLatS

7470 **Wallbaum, Amanda, Sister.**
Exploration of art in the basic readers at the primary level, factors to which children respond positively.
iii, 25 p. 28 cm.
Thesis (M.A.)–Ball State University, Muncie, Ind., 1969.
InFer

Wallis, Patricia, Sister, 1930–

7471 The elementary school principal and the administration and supervision of the first-year teacher in the St. Cloud area.
54 p.
Thesis (M.S.)–St. Cloud State College, 1974.
MnStj(Archives)

7472 A study to compare the differences in background of elementary students with curriculum theology.
156 p. 28 cm.
Field study (Specialist Degree)–St. Cloud State University, 1977.
Typescript.
MnStj(Archives)

7473 **Walsh, Joachim,** 1912–
The Roman military system.
107 leaves, illus. 28 cm.
Thesis (M.A.)–University of Notre Dame, 1942.
Typescript.
InStme

7474 **Walsingham, Thomas,** fl. 1360–1420.
De archana deorum. Edited by Robert A. van Kluyve. Durham, N.C., Duke University Press, 1968.
xxii, 227 p. facsims. 28 cm.
PLatS

7475 **Walter, Silja (Sr. M. Hedwig).**
Das Kloster am Rande der Stadt. Zürich,
Verlag der Arche [1971].
86 p. illus. 20 cm.
MnCS

7476 **Walzer, Raphael,** 1888–
Beuroner Rundfunksstunden. Kunstverlag Beuron, 1931.
35 p. 16 cm.
FStL; KAS

Wansbrough, Henry, 1934–
7477 Event and interpretation. London,
Sheed & Ward [1973].
147 p. 20 cm.
PLatS

7478 The passion. [Slough], St. Paul Publications [c 1972].
111 p. 20 cm. (Scripture for meditations,
7)
KAS

7479 Theology in St. Paul. Notre Dame, Ind.,
Fides Publishers [1970].
96 p. 18 cm.
InStme; KAS; MnCS; MnStj

7479a **Ward, Daniel J.,** 1944–
Readings, cases, materials in canon law,
by Jordan F. Hite, T.O.R., Gennaro J.
Sesto, S.D.B., Daniel J. Ward, O.S.B. Collegeville, Minn., The Liturgical Press,
1980.
xiv, 368 p. 20 cm.
MnCS

Warnach, Viktor, 1909–1970.
7480 Das Wirken des Pneuma in den Gläubi-
gen nach Paulus.
(*In* Pro veritate; ein theologischer
Dialog. Münster, 1963. p. 156–202)
PLatS

7481 Wort und Wirklichkeit bei Anselm von
Canterbury.
(*In* Festschrift für Albert Auer, O.S.B.
1962. p. 157–176)
PLatS

7482 Zur Theologie des Gebetes bei Nilus von
Ankyra.
(*In* Perennitas; Beiträge . . . P. Thomas
Michels, O.S.B., zum 70. Geburtstag.
Münster, 1963. p. 65–90)
PLatS

7483 (ed) Casel, Odo. Das christliche Opfermysterium. Zur Morphologie und Theologie
des eucharistischen Hochgebetes. Hrsg.
von Viktor Warnach. Graz, Styria Verlag,
1968.
lv, 719 p. 21 cm.
KAS; MnCS

Washington, D.C. St. Anselm's Abbey.
See St. Anselm's Abbey, Washington,
D.C.

7484 **Wathen, Ambrose G.,** 1931–
Silence; the meaning of silence in the
Rule of St. Benedict. Washington, Cister-
cian Publications, 1973.
xviii, 240 p. illus. 23 cm.
CaMWiSb; InStme; MnCS; MnStj;
MoCo; NcBe; PLatS; ViBris

Watkin, Aelred, 1918–
7485 The enemies of love. New York, P. J.
Kenedy [1962].
118 p. 20 cm.
NcBe

7486 St. Aelred of Rievaulx.
(*In* Walsh, James, Pre-Reformation
English spirituality. New York, 1965.
p. 56–66)
PLatS

7487 **Watrin, Benno,** 1895–
St. Benedict's Mission, White Earth,
Minn., 1878–1978. [White Earth, Minn.,
1978].
[28] p. illus., ports. 20 cm.
MnCS

7488 **Watson, Frances, Sister.**
An analytical study of the social relation-
ships within the familia institutions of the
Prairie Potawatomi.
176 leaves. maps, tables, 28 cm.
Thesis (M.A.)–Marquette University,
Milwaukee, Wis., 1967.
Typescript.
KAM

Watson, Harold Mark, 1924–
7489 Claudel's immortal heroes; a choice of
deaths. New Brunswick, N.J., Rutgers
University Press [1971].
xiii, 199 p. 24 cm.
KAS

7490 The theme of death in three plays of Paul
Claudel.
v, 212 p. 28 cm.
Thesis – University of Colorado, 1965.
Typescript.
KAS

7491 **Watson, Simone, Sister.**
The cult of Our Lady of Guadalupe; a
historical study. Collegeville, Minn.,
The Liturgical Press [1964].
87 p. illus. 24 cm.
InFer; InStme; MnCS; MnStj; MoCo;
PLatS

7492 **Watzl, Hermann, S.O.Cist.,** 1902–
Die Summa dictaminis prosayci des
Codex 220 Sancrucensis, ein bisher unbe-
kanntes Opus des Gutolf von Heiligen-
kreuz.
Sonderdruck aus: Jahrbuch für
Landeskunde von Niederösterreich, Jg.
71–73, p. 40–68.
MnCH

7493 **Weakland, Rembert George,** 1927–
El abad como padre espiritual.
(*In* Cuadernos monasticos, v. 11(1976), p. 37–42)
"Conferencia pronunciada en el II Encuentro de Superiores Monasticos de Asia, Bangalore, India, octubre de 1973."
PLatS

7494 L'abate in una società democratica.
(*In* Vita monastica, n. 99(1969), p. 206–214)
PLatS

7495 The Abbot as spiritual father.
Offprint from: Cistercian studies, no. 2 & 3 (1974), p. 231–238.
PLatS

7496 The Abbot in a democratic society.
Offprint from: Cistercian studies, no. 4, 1969, p. 95–100.
PLatS

7497 Actualité de la pensée de Saint Benoît dans le monde d'aujourd'hui.
(*In* Lettre de l'Abbaye Saint-Martin, Liguié, n. 131(1968), p. 5–11)
PLatS

7498 Aportación a la iglesia de la vida monastica femenina hoy.
(*In* Cuadernos monasticos. Año XI(1976), p. 285–293)
"Conferencia a las abadesas españolas, mayo de 1976"
PLatS

7499 Aportación . . . al tema: Pluralismo monastico.
(*In* Cuadernos monasticos, Año X (1975), p. 395–396)
PLatS

7500 Aspects litteraires et musicaux de l'usage de la langue vernaculaire.
(*In* Lettre de l'Abbaye Saint-Martin, Liguié, Mars-Avril, 1967, p. 3–6)
PLatS

7501 Attualità del pensiero benedettino.
(*In* La Scala, anno 22(1968), p. 217–224)
PLatS

7502 Aus dem Leben der Kirche; Krise und Erneuerung des Mönchtums heute.
Sonderdruck aus: Geist und Leben, Heft 47(1974), p. 299–313)
PLatS

7503 Authority in religious life.
(*In* Religious life today, by John Coventry, S.J. [and others]. Tenbury Wells, England [n.d.], p. 16–36)
PLatS; KAS

7504 The beginnings of troping.
(*In* The Musical quarterly, v. 44(1958), p. 477–488)
PLatS

7505 Benedictine oblation: without distinction.
(*In* The Saint Vincent oblate, v. 16(1960), p. 3–4)
PLatS

7506 Cercare Dio.
(*In* Monastica (Roma), anno 18(1977), p. 38–41)
PLatS

7507 The church composer and the liturgical challenge.
(*In* Leonard, W.J., ed. Liturgy for the people; essays in honor of Gerald Ellard, S.J. Milwaukee, 1963, p. 132–146)
PLatS

7508 Collegiality and the educator.
(*In* Mission Secretariat, Washington, D.C. Revolution in missionary thinking; a symposium. 1966. p. 129–136)
PLatS

7509 La comunidad en la tradición monastica.
(*In* Cuadernos monasticos, año 11(1976), p. 131–143)
Translation of: Community; the monastic tradition (American Benedictine Review, v. 26, Sept., 1975)
PLatS

7510 Community; the monastic tradition.
(*In* The American Benedictine review, v. 26(1975), p. 233–250)
PLatS

7511 Community – the monastic tradition.
(*In* Life in the spirit; lectures read at a Conference for Anglican Religious at St. John's College, York, July, 1974, p. 27–33)
PLatS

7512 The compositions of Hucbald.
Extract from: Etudes grégoriennes, v. 3(1959), p. 155–162.
PLatS

7513 Conclusions of the Bangkok Conference; Final remarks by Dom Rembert Weakland, O.S.B.
(*In* Meeting of the Monastic Superiors in the Far East, Bangkok, Thailand, 1968. A New charter for monasticism; proceedings. Notre Dame, Ind., 1970, p. 267–269)
PLatS

7514 Conférence de Père Abbé Primat aux abbesses, jeudi matin – 2 mai [n.p., n.d.].
11 p. 30 cm.
PLatS

7515 Conférence du Rme Père Abbé Primat Dom Rembert Weakland, 22 juillet 1972.
(*In* A.I.M. Bulletin, no. 15(1973), p. 10–22. Secretariat de l'Aide à l'Implantation Monastique)
PLatS

7516 Conférence du Père Abbé Primat: Monachisme et evangélisation.
(*In* Notre Dame de Tournay, no. 126(1975), p. 11–19)
"Cette conférence donnée aux moniales de Dourgne . . ."
PLatS

7517 Creativity and the spirit.
(*In* The Ampleforth journal, v. 78(1973), p. 60–68)
PLatS

7518 Crisi e rinnovamento del monachesimo oggi (un bilancio de 10 anni).
(*In* Ora et labora (Milano), v. 30(1975), p. 99–115)
"Conferenza tenuta in una sessione dell'Accademia "Paolo" a Zurigo sulla vita degli ordini religiosi oggi, 23–24 marzo 1974."
PLatS

7519 Le culte dans un monde sécularisé.
(*In* Paroisse et liturgie, n. 6(1968), p. 483–491)
PLatS

7520 Il culto in un mondo secolarizzato.
(*In* Revista liturgica, anno 55(1968), p. 645–655)
PLatS

7521 The Divine Office and contemporary man.
(*In* Worship, v. 43(1969), p. 214–218)
PLatS

7522 Discorso de apertura.
(*In* San Benedetto; rivista degli oblati benedettini d'Italia, anno 12(1968), p. 196–199)
PLatS

7523 Discurso de apertura del congreso.
(*In* Cuadernos monasticos, año 9(1974), p. 485–492)
PLatS

7524 El drama liturgico en la Edad Media.
(*In* Revista musical Chilena, año 15(1961), p. 52–60)
PLatS

7525 Echos: the Church in the United States after the Council. Translated from the Italian by Slavko Kovacic. Translated from the Serbo-Croatian by Rev. Ludwig Capon. Latrobe, Pa., n.d.
11 leaves. 28 cm.
Typescript.
Translation of: Odjeci: Crkva u Sjedinjenim drzavama poslije Koncila.
PLatS

7526 Elementi essenziali della vocazione monastica benedettina.
(*In* Inter Fratres, v. 25(1976), p. 1–6)

"Conferenza tenuta . . . nel Monastero di S. Silvestro (Fabriano), il 9 giugno 1975"
PLatS

7527 The essential elements of the Benedictine monastic vocation. Summary of a conference held . . . at St. Sylvester's Monastery (Fabriano), June 9, 1975.
(*In* Inter Fratres, v. 25(1976), p. 6–8)
PLatS

7528 Eröffnungsrede von Abt-Primas Rembert G. Weakland, O.S.B., zum Abtekongress am 19 September 1973).
(*In* Erbe und Auftrag, 49. Jahrgang, 1973. Sonderdruck Heft 6, p. 448–455)
PLatS

7529 Evangelizzazione e vita contemplativa.
(*In* Ora et labora, v. 29(1974), p. 99–108)
PLatS

7530 Evangelización y vida contemplativa.
(*In* Cuadernos monasticos, año 10(1974), p. 79–87)
PLatS

7531 Final remarks of the Abbot Primate; Opening speech of the Abbot Primate [at the Asian Monastic Congress, Bangalore, India, October, 1973].
Offprint from: Cistercian studies, nos. 2 & 3, 1974, p. 320–327.
PLatS

7532 Gregorian chant.
(*In* Hays, William, ed. Twentieth-century views on music history. New York, 1972. p. 24–35)
"Reprinted from the New Catholic Encyclopedia, v. 6, p. 756–761."
PLatS

7533 Growth through authority.
Extract from: Tjurunga; an Australasian Benedictine review, no. 14(1977), p. 75–92)
PLatS

7534 Der heutige Mensch und das Chorofficium.
Offprint from: Erbe und Auftrag, 44. Jahrgang (1968), p. 443–449.
PLatS

7535 L'Homme d'aujourd'hui et l'Office Divin.
(*In* La Maison-Dieu, n. 95(1968), p. 66–74)
PLatS

7536 Interior debate, exterior uniformity; the Abbot Primate's response at the Synod of Bishops.
Extract from: The Ampleforth journal, v. 75(1970), p. 210–212.
PLatS

7537 [Intervention des Pères]: Déclaration de Dom Rembert G. Weakland.

(*In* Rythmes de monde; le bulletin des missions (Bruges), v. 19(1971), p. 190–191)
PLatS

7538 Krisis en vernieuwing bij de monniken van onze tijd; een balans over de lastate tien jaar.
(*In* Monastieke informatie (Brugge), n. 40(1975), p. 149–171)
PLatS

7539 La lenceridad.
(*In* Cuadernos monasticos, año 11(1975), p. 179–183)
PLatS
"Originally appeared in Lettre de Ligugé, n. 131."

7540 La liturgia in una chiesa che cambia.
Estratto da: Orientamenti pastorali, no. 6(1969), p. 593–600.
PLatS

7541 Mass of the Holy Spirit & closing of the cloister, St. Vincent Archabbey, July 20, 1967. Music composed by Archabbot Rembert Weakland, O.S.B., Ildephonse Wortman, O.S.B. [and] Ralph Bailey, O.S.B. Archabbey Press, 1967.
13 leaves. 23 cm.
PLatS

7542 Monastic renewal.
(*In* New Blackfriars, v. 46(1965), p. 511–516)
PLatS

7543 El monacato en el mundo de hoy.
(*In* Cuadernos monasticos, v. 23(1972), p. 19–30)
PLatS

7544 Music and the Constitution on the liturgy.
(*In* Liturgical arts, v. 33(1964), p. 7–11)
PLatS

7545 Music as art in liturgy.
(*In* Worship, v. 41(1967), p. 5–15)
PLatS

7546 Music and liturgy in evolution.
(*In* Liturgical arts, v. 35(1967), p. 114–117)
PLatS

7547 La musica nella liturgia dopo il Concilio.
(*In* Revista liturgica, v. 59(1972), p. 208–213)
PLatS

7548 Musica sacra.
Estratto dal: Dizionario del Concilio Ecumenico Vaticano Secondo. Roma, 1969. cols. 1505–1513)
PLatS

7549 The new liturgy and the music educator.
(*In* Musart, v. 17(1965), p. 8–)
PLatS

7550 Nuevos horizontes; apertura del II Encuentro Monastico Latino Americano (Bogota), July 22, 1975.
(*In* Cuadernos monasticos, año 10(1975), p. 381–387)
PLatS

7551 Nouveaus horizons; message du Père Abbé Primat pour l'ouverture de la Seconde "Recontre" Monastique d'Amerique Latine, Bogota, July 22, 1975.
(*In* A.I.M. Bulletin, n. 19(1975), p. 13–21)
PLatS

7552 Obedience to the Abbot and the community in the monastery.
Offprint from: Cistercian studies, no. 5(1970), p. 309–316)
PLatS

7553 Odjeci: Crkva u Sjedinjenim drzavama poslije Koncila.
(*In* Crkva u Svijetu. Codina Z (1975), p. 249–254)
PLatS

7554 Omelia del Rev.mo Padre Abate Primate Remberto Weakland durante la concelebrazione del 130 abati benedettini riuniti a Roma per il Congresso della Confederazione O.S.B., 23 settèmbre 1973.
(*In* La Gruccia, 1973, p. 22–25)
PLatS

7555 Omelia per la domenica III dopo Pasqua.
(*In* San Benedetto; rivista degli oblati benedettini d'Italia, anno 12(1968), p. 212–)
PLatS

7556 Omelia . . . 21 marzo, 1976, Domenica III di Quaresima (Giov. 2: 13–25).
(*In* La Gruccia; bolletino dei monaci benedettini de Vallombrosa (Firenze), n. 7–8(1976), p. 103–106)
PLatS

7557 Palabras pronunciada per el Rvmo. Padre Abad Primado en el acto de clausura del Encuentro monastico latino-americano, el 29 de julio de 1972.
(*In* Cuadernos monasticos, v. 23(1972), p. 259–263)
PLatS

7558 The performance of Ambrosian chant in the 12th century.
(*In* LaRue, Jan, ed. Aspects of medieval and renaissance music; a birthday offering to Gustave Reese. 1966. p. 856–866)
PLatS

7559 Preface to monastic growth: Africa, Asia, Latin America, Oceania.
(*In* A.I.M. Bulletin, special issue, 1970, p. 1–3. Secretariat de l'Aide à l'Implantation Monastique)
PLatS

7560   Problemi attuali di vita monastica.
(*In* Ora et labora, anno 26(1971), p. 99–107)
PLatS

7561   Die Psalmen im Rahmen des Offiziums.
(*In* Erbe und Auftrag, 45. Jahrgang (1969), p. 96–102)
PLatS

7562   Recent trends in Catholic church music.
(*In* Liturgical arts, v. 33(1965), p. 32–33)
PLatS

7563   Le renouveau liturgique: perspectives d'avenir.
(*In* Communautés et liturgies, v. 57(1975), p. 85–87)
PLatS

7564   La "Re-sacralisation" du monde.
(*In* Lettre de Ligugé, n. 141(1970), p. 12–21)
PLatS

7565   The response of the Brother to the demands of the Church today.
(*In* Brothers Newsletter (West Springfield, Maine), v. 16(1974–75), p. 12–17)
PLatS

7566   La riforma monastica del B. Bernardo Tolomei.
(*In* L'Ulivo, n.s., anno III(1973), p. 34–36)
PLatS

7567   The rhythmic modes and medieval Latin drama.
Offprint from: Journal of the American Musicological Society, v. 14(1961), p. 131–146.
PLatS

7568   The "Sacred" and liturgical renewal.
(*In* Worship (Collegeville, Minn.), v. 49(1975), p. 512–529)
". . . Abbot Weakland's edited text of the Second Annual Dom Thomas Werner Moore Lecture . . . 27 September 1975, at the Catholic University of America."
PLatS

7569   St. Benedikt – Schutzherr Europas.
(*In* Benediktus-Bote, 44. Jahrgang(1974), p. 146–148)
PLatS

7570   La simplicité bénédictine.
(*In* Présence d'En Calcat, v. 43(1974), p. 97–99)

7571   La simplicidad benedictina.
(*In* Cuadernos monasticos, año 10(1975), p. 271–273)
Translation of: La simplicité bénédictine.
PLatS

7572   Situation, attitudes, and hurdles.
(*In* Sacred music, v. 93(1966), p. 53–58)
PLatS

7573   Some observations on the development of the English sung Mass.
(*In* Sacred music, v. 93(1966), p. 4–8)
PLatS

7574   Unexplored areas of music education.
(*In* Musart, v. 13(1960), p. 6–   )
PLatS

7575   The state of the Confederation; inaugural speech, 1970 Congress of Abbots, O.S.B.
(*In* Cistercian studies, v. 6(1971), p. 91–103)
PLatS

7576   Lo studio sacro nella parola dell'Abate Primate.
(*In* Colloqui monastici, III(1970), p. 65–67)
PLatS

7577   The sung Mass and its problems.
(*In* Jesus Christ reforms His Church . . . 26th annual North American Liturgical Week, 1965, p. 238–244)
PLatS

7578   The task of a liturgical musician.
(*In* Origins; NC documentary service, v. 7(1978), p. 685–688)
PLatS

7579   The theory and practice of music in the Carolingian cloisters; a lecture to the Medieval Faculty Seminar at Columbia University, March 11, 1958.
20 leaves. 21 cm.
Typescript.
PLatS

7580   La virtù della perseveranza.
(*In* Potenza e carità di Dio, anno VI(1969), p. 7–8)
PLatS

7581   (2dary) Brzic, Zarko, Benediktinski Primas kos nas.
(*In* Veritas; revija Sv. Antuna Padovanskoga. Broj 9(1975), p. 12–13)
PLatS

7582   (2dary) Brzic, Zarko. The Benedictine Primate with us; interview with Abbot Primate Rembert G. Weakland, O.S.B. Translated from Serbo-Croatian by Rev. Ludwig Cepon. Latrobe, Pa., n.d.
8 leaves, 28 cm.
Typescript.
Translation of: Benediktinski Primas kos nas.
PLatS

7583   (2dary) Mönche in Afrika gefragt; Kontinente-Interview mit Dom Rembert Weakland, Abtprimas des Benediktinerordens, Rom.
(*In* Kontinente, 7.Jg.(1972), p. 8–10)
PLatS

7584 (2dary) Abbot contends U.S. Church lags behind revival in religion [Interview with Abbot Primate Rembert G. Weakland, O.S.B.].
(*In* National Catholic Reporter, October 31, 1975, p. 1–2)
PLatS

7585 (2dary) Liturgy: medium or message? Desmond O'Grady interviews Abbot Primate Rembert Weakland, O.S.B.
(*In* U.S. Catholic and jubilee, v. 35(1970), p. 21–25)
PLatS

7586 (2dary) Thesaurus Liturgiae horarum monasticae. Romae, Badia Primeziale Sant' Anselmo, 1977.
viii, 562 p. 30 cm.
Praefatio by Rembertus Weakland, O.S.B., Abbas Primas.
MnCS

Weaver, Cyprian Victor, 1945–
7587 The development of tools and art in human evolution; independent study in anthropology. [Collegeville, Minn., St. John's University, 1968]
76 p. illus. 28 cm.
Privately printed.
MnCS

7588 The fossil evidence of himinid evolution. [An independent study for the January Interim Program of St. John's University, Collegeville, Minn.].
86 p. illus. 28 cm.
Published privately, 1968.
MnCS

Weber, Emeric, Sister, 1914–
7589 The responsibilities of the school.
70 p. 28 cm.
Thesis (M.E.)–College of St. Thomas, St. Paul, Minn., 1959.
Typescript.
MnStj(Archives)

Weber, Robert, 1904–
7590 Exemplar pro revisione psalterii gallicani. [n.p., n.d.]
unpaged, 29 cm.
MnCS

7591 (ed) Autpertus, Ambrosius. Opera. Cura et studio Roberti Weber, O.S.B. Turnholti, Brepols, 1975–
v. 26 cm. (Corpus Christianorum. Continuatio mediaevallis, 27
InStme; PLatS

7592 (ed) Cyprian, Saint. Opera. Edidit R. Weber. Turnholti, Brepols, 1972–
v. 26 cm. (Corpus Christianorum. Series latina, 3)
KAS

7593 (ed) Psalterii secundum Vulgatam Bibliorum versionem nova recensio . . . cura et studio Roberti Weber monachi Claravallensis edita. Clervau (Luxembourg), Abbaye S. Maurice et S. Maur, 1961.
192 p. 25 cm.
ILSP; InStme; MnCS; MoCo; NcBe; PLatS

Weber, Wunibald, 1907–1961.
7594 Die Benediktiner-Abtei auf dem Michaelsberg zu Siegburg. Siegburg, Verlag Michaelsberg [n.d.].
20 p. illus. 20 cm.
MnCS

7595 Michaelsberg; Geschichte einer 900 jährigen Abtei. Siegburg, im Selbstverlag der Abtei, 1953.
64 p. 21 cm.
KAS; NdRi

Wehrmeister, Cyrillus, 1969–
7596 Mutterherz; ein Sonnenstrahl für jedermann. Missionsverlag St. Ottilien, Oberbayern [1918].
63 p. 14 cm.
MnCS

Weibel, Johann Eugen, 1853–
7597 The Catholic missions of north-east Arkansas, 1867–1893. Translated by Sister M. Agnes Voth, O.S.B. Arkansas State Univ. Press, 1967.
109 p. 23 cm.
InFer; KAS

7598 Forty years a missionary in Arkansas. Translation [by] Sister M. Agnes. [St. Meinrad, Ind., Abbey Press] 1968.
252 p. 23 cm.
InFer; InStme; KAS; MoCo

Weidenhiller, Egino, 1930–
7599 Ad Sanctum Stephanum 969–1969. Festgabe zur Tausendjahr-Feier von St. Stephan in Augsburg. [Hrsg. von Egino Weidenhiller, Anton Uhl, Berhard Weisshaar. Wemding, G. Appl, 1969].
[4], 322 p. illus., plates, 24x23 cm.
InStme; KAS; PLatS

Weihenstephan, Bavaria (Benedictine abbey).
7600 Catalogus codicum manu scriptorum Bibliothecae Regiae Monacensis; Codices 21501–21725 ex bibliotheca monasterii in Weihenstephan. Monachii, sumptibus Bibliothecae Regiae, 1871. Unveränderter Nachdruck Otto Harrassowitz, Wiesbaden, 1969.
MnCH

Weinckens, Johannes, d. 1734.
7601 Navarchia Seligenstadiana, seu Fundatio antiquissimae & regalis abbatiae Seligen-

stadiensis . . . Francofurti ad Moenum, typis Joannis Philippi Andreae, 1714.
[12], 140 p. illus. 33 cm.
KAS

7602   Vir fama super aethera notus Eginhartus, quondam Caroli Magni cancellarius . . . illustratus et contra quosdam authores vindicatus . . . Francofurti ad Moenum, impensis Joannis Philippi Andreae, 1714.
[16], 127 p. illus. 33 cm.
KAS

Weingarten, Germany (Benedictine abbey).

7603   Annales Weingartenses.
(*In* Monumenta Germaniae historica. Scriptores. Stuttgart, 1963. t. 1, p. 64–67)
MnCS; PLatS

7604   Die Handschriften des Klosters Weingarten, von Karl Löffler. Unter Beihilfe von Dr. Scherer-Fulda. Leipzig, Harrassowitz, 1912. Nendeln, Kraus Reprint, 1968.
iv, 185 p. 24 cm.
PLatS

Weiss, Thomas.

7605   Agilbertus. Tragoedia. MS. Vienna, Schottenstift, codex 637. 50 f. Quarto. Saec. 17.
Microfilm: MnCH proj. no. 4278

7606   Anastasius perditus. Ludus dramaticus. MS. Vienna, Schottenstift, codex 638, f.14–69r. Quarto. Saec. 17.
Microfilm: MnCH proj. no. 4280

7607   Conradus ultimus dux Sveuorum. Ludus dramaticus. MS. Vienna, Schottenstift, codex 640. 63 f. Quarto. Saec. 17.
Microfilm: MnCH proj. no. 4282

7608   **Weissenberger, Paul,** 1902–
Die Anfänge des Hohenstaufenklosters Lorch bei Schwäbisch-Gmünd.
(*In* Perennitas; Beiträge . . . P. Thomas Michels, O.S.B., zum 70. Geburtstag. Münster, 1963. p. 246–273)
PLatS

7609   **Weixer, Melchior.**
Fontilegium sacrum, sive Fundatio . . . monasterii S. Georgi Ord. s. Benedicti vulgo Prifling dicti prope Ratisponam . . . Ingolstadii, Gregorius Haenlin, 1627.
[16], 312 p. 28 cm.
KAS

7610   **Wellnhofer, Simon,** 1904–
Ettal; seine Entstehung, Geschichte und Kunst. Buch-Kunstverlag Ettal [n.d.].
80 p. plates, 17 cm.
MnCS; MnStj

7611   **Welsonius, Phalesius.**
Viridarium sacrarum meditationum . . . Ratisbonae, Joan Leopold Montag, 1735.

980 p. 17 cm.
MnCS

Wenin, Lambert.

7612   Catalogus librorum bibliothecae monasterii ad S. Lambertum Altenburgi. MS. Benediktinerabtei Altenburg, Austria, codex AB 15 A 2/1. 297 p. Folio. Saec. 19(1864).
Microfilm: MnCH proj. no. 6591

7613   Personal-Catalog der Stiftsbibliothek zu Altenburg. MS. Benediktinerabtei Altenburg, Austria, codex AB 15 A 2/2. 279 p. Folio. Saec. 19(1864).
Microfilm: MnCH proj. no. 6592

Wenninger, Magnus Joseph, 1919–

7614   The concept of number according to St. Albert and Roger Bacon.
83 leaves, 28 cm.
Thesis (M.A.)–University of Ottawa, 1948.
Typescript.
MnCS (Archives)

7615   Polyhedron models. Cambridge [England], University Press [1975].
xii, 208 p. illus. 26 cm.
MnCS; BNS

7616   Moderni miogogrannikov (Russian translation of Polyhedron models). Moskva, "Mir," 1976
236 p.
BNS; MnCS

7617   Polyhedron models for the classroom. Washington, National Council of Teachers of Mathematics [1966].
iii, 43 p. illus. 23 cm.
BNS; MnCS

7618   Polyhedron models for the classroom. 2nd ed. Reston, Virginia, National Council of Teachers of Mathematics, 1975.
viii, 43 p. 14 plates, 23 cm.
BNS; MnCS

7619   **Wenstrup, Edward Joseph,** 1894–
Male biparentalism and reciprocal crosses in habrobracon.
31 leaves, 28 cm.
Thesis (Ph.D.)–University of Pennsylvania, 1931.
Typescript.
PLatS

7620   **Wenzl, Alphonsus,** 1660–1743.
Controversiae selectae ex universa theologia scholastica . . . Ratisbonae, J. C. Peezil, 1723–1726.
4 v. 35 cm.
InStme

7621   **Werden, Germany (Benedictine abbey).**
Septendialis recollectio, septem Spiritus Sancti donis accommodata . . . auctore et collectore Abbatiae Werdinensis professo

sacerdote . . . Coloniae Agrippinae, apud Franciscum Metternich, 1722.
　528 p. 18 cm.
　MnCS

7622 **Wessobrun, Bavaria (Benedictine abbey).**
Catalogus codicum manu scriptorum Bibliothecae Regiae Monacensis: Codices 22001–22129 ex monasterio S. Benedicti in Wessobrun. Monachii, sumptibus Bibliothecae Regiae, 1871. Unveränderter Nachdruck Otto Harrassowitz, Wiesbaden, 1969.
　MnCH

Westkaemper, Remberta, Sister, 1890–
7623 On the occurrence, distribution and periodicity of some Minnesota algae.
　43 p. 28 cm.
　Thesis (M.S.)–University of Minnesota, 1922.
　Typescript.
　MnStj(Archives)

7624 The vitamin content of some marine algae.
　46 p. 28 cm.
　Thesis (Ph.D.)–University of Minnesota, 1929.
　Typescript.
　MnStj (Archives)

7625 **Wettinus, monk of Reichenau,** fl. ca. 824.
Visio. MS. Cistercienserabtei Rein, Austria, codex 51, f.141r–151v. Quarto. Saec. 12.
　Microfilm: MnCH proj. no. 7449

Weygant, Noemi, Sister.
7626 Ask rain from the Lord. Collegeville, Minn., The Liturgical Press, c 1974.
　94 p. illus. 21 cm.
　InStme; MdRi; MnDuS

7627 Green ghetto. Poetry: Herbert F. Brokering. Photography: Noemi Weygant, O.S.B. Collegeville, Minn., Saint John's University Press [c 1972].
　78 p. illus. 27 cm.
　MnCS; MnDuS; MoCo

7628 In a promise. Text by Herbert F. Brokering. Photos by Noemi Weygant. Minneapolis, Augsburg Publishing House, 1968.
　unpaged, illus. 32 cm.
　MnDuS

7629 In due season, by Herbert F. Brokering. Photos by Sister Noemi. Minneapolis, Augsburg Publishing House, 1966.
　unpaged, illus., 32 cm.
　MnDuS

7630 In the rustling grass, by Herbert F. Brokering. Photos by Sister Noemi. Minneapolis, Augsburg Publishing House, 1964.

　63 p. illus. 32 cm.
　MnDuS; MnStj

7631 It's autumn. Text and photos by Noemi Weygant. Philadelphia, Westminster Press, 1968.
　63 p. col. illus. 27 cm.
　Poems.
　MnCS; MnDuS; MnStj

7632 It's spring. Text and photographs by Noemi Weygant. Philadelphia, Westminster Press. 1968.
　68 p. col. illus. 27 cm.
A collection of poems, illustrated with color photographs, about the coming of spring and its effects upon the plants and animals of the woodland.
　MnCS; MnDuS; MnStj

7633 It's summer. Text and photographs by Sister Noemi Weygant. Philadelphia, Westminster Press [1970].
　63 p. col. illus. 27 cm.
Poems and accompanying color photographs present the plants and animals of the summer woods.
　MnCS; MnDuS

7634 It's winter. Text and photographs by Noemi Weygant. Philadelphia, Westminster Press [1969].
　63 p. col. illus. 27 cm.
Poems and accompanying color photographs present many aspects of winter during a winter of ice and snow.
　MnCS; MnDuS

7635 Lift up your hearts. Poetry [by] Herbert F. Brokering. Photography: Noemi Weygant. Collegeville, Minn., The Liturgical Press [1966].
　ix, 50 p. col. illus. 27 cm.
　MnCS; MnDuS; MnStj; MoCo; InStme

7636 More than a dream; poetry by Herbert F. Brokering. Photography: Noemi Weygant. Collegeville, Minn., Saint John's University Press, 1972.
　78 p. illus. 27 cm.
　MnDuS; MoCo

7637 **Whitby Abbey, England.**
Cartularium abbathiae de Whiteby, Ordinis S. Benedicti, fundatae anno MLXXVIII. Durham [England], 1879–81.
　2 v. 23 cm. (Publications of the Surtees Society, v. 69, 72)
　InStme; MnCS

7638 **Whiterig, John,** d. 1371.
The monk of Farne; the meditations of a fourteenth-century monk, edited and introduced by Hugh Farmer. Translated by a Benedictine of Stanbrook. Baltimore, Helicon Press [1961].

vii, 155 p. illus. 22 cm. (The Benedictine studies, 1)

InFer; InStme; KAS; MnCS; MnStj; NcBe

7639 **Whitney, Pa. St. Cecilia Church.**
Diamond jubilee [of] St. Cecilia Parish, November 20, 1966.
[32] p. illus. 23 cm.
PLatS

7640 **Wiblingen, Germany (Benedictine abbey).**
Ceremoniae secundum morem monasterii Wiblingenses. MS. Benediktinerabtei Melk, Austria, codex 639, f.250r–251r. Quarto. Saec. 15.
Microfilm: MnCH proj. no. 1524

Wichner, Jakob, 1825–1903.
7641 [Catalog of manuscripts in Stift Admont, Austria].
396 p. 29 cm.
Handwritten.
Xeroxed by University Microfilms, Ann Arbor, Mich., 1968.
MnCS

7642 Geschichte des Benediktiner-Stiftes Admont. Graz, Vereins-Buchdruckerei, 1874–1880.
4 v. 24 cm.
InStme; MnCS (v. 1–2)

Widdrington, Roger, pseud. *See* Preston, Thomas.

7643 **Widricus, abbot of St. Ghislain,** fl. 1065.
1065.
Vita S. Gerardi episcopi Tullensis, edente D. G. Waitz.
(*In* Monumenta Germaniae historica. Scriptores. Stuttgart, 1963, t. 4, p. 485–520)
MnCS; PLatS

7644 **Widukind, monk of Corvey,** fl. 970.
Widukindi Res gestae Saxonicae a. 919–973, edente D. Georgio Waitz.
(*In* Monumenta Germaniae historica. Scriptores. Stuttgart, 1963. t. 3, p. 408–467)
MnCS; PLatS

7645 **Wiegand, Gonsalva, Sister.**
The non-dramatic works of Hrosvitha; text, translation, and commentary . . . by Sister M. Gonsalva Wiegand, O.S.B.
xxiv, 273 p 24 cm.
Thesis (Ph.D.)–St. Louis University, 1936.
PLatS

7646 **Wieland, Otmar,** 1937–
Gertrud von Helfta ein botte der götlichen miltekeit. Ottobeuren, Kommissionsverlag Winfried-Werk, 1973.

xviii, 254 p. 24 cm.
PLatS

7647 **Wiest, Veneranda, Sister,** 1908–
Honorat Kolb, Abt von Seon, 1603–1670. München, Selbstverlag der Bayerischen Benediktinerakademie, 1937.
xx, 139 p. 25 cm.
KAS

7648 **Wild, Moira, Sister,** 1939–
Introduction to a uniform system of financial accounting in the Catholic elementary schools of the Diocese of St. Cloud.
232 p. 28 cm.
Thesis (Specialist in Administration)–University of Minnesota, 1970.
Typescript.
MnStj(Archives)

Wilhelmus, abbot of Hirsau, d. 1091.
7649 Willehelmi Hirsaugensis musica, edidit Denis Harbinson. [Rome], American Institute of Musicology, 1975.
92 p. illus. 26 cm.
PLatS

7650 Philosophicarum et astronomicarum institutionum Guilielmi Hirsaugiensis olim abbatis, libri tres . . . Basileae, Henricus Petrus, 1531.
77 p.
PLatS (microfilm)

7651 **Willems, Luke,** 1885–
Scito cur; Latin moods and tenses in theory and practice. Ramsgate [England], Monastery Press [1937].
223 p. 24 cm.
InStme; KAS; MnCS

Willeram, abbot of Ebersberg, d. 1085.
7652 Expositio super Cantica canticorum. MS. Benediktinerabtei Kremsmünster, Austria, codex 32, f.95r–176r. Saec. 12.
Microfilm: MnCH proj. no. 32

7653 Poemata latina. MS. Benediktinerabtei Kremsmünster, Austria, codex 32, f.176v–185r. Saec. 12.
Microfilm: MnCH proj. no. 32

7654 The "Expositio in Cantica canticorum" . . . A critical edition [by] Erminnie Hollis Bartelmez. Philadelphia, American Philosophical Society, 1967.
xxviii, 573 p. illus., facsims. 31 cm.
PLatS

7655 **William of Hoo,** fl. 1280–1294.
The letter-book of William of Hoo, sacrist of Bury St. Edmunds, 1280–1294. Edited by Antonia Gransden. [Ipswich] Suffolk Records Society, 1963.
166 p. 25 cm.
PLatS

William of Malesbury, d. 1143?

7656   Gesta regum Anglorum, atque Historia novella. Ad fidem codicum manuscriptorum recensuit Thomas Duffus Hardy. Londini, 1840. Vaduz, Kraus Reprint, 1964.
     2 v. 23 cm. [English Historical Society. Publications]
     ILSP; PLatS

7657   On the antiquity of Glastonbury.
     (*In* Robinson, Joseph A. Somerset historical essays. London, Oxford University Press, 1921)
     PLatS

7658   **Williams, Raphael.**
     The immateriality and immortality of the soul.
     (*In* Man: papers read at the summer school of Catholic Studies, Cambridge. London, 1938. p. 13–34)
     InFer

Willibald, Presbyter, 8th cent.

7659   Vita s. Bonifacii. MS. Vienna, Nationalbibliothek, codex 474, f.179r–210r. Folio. Saec. 11.
     Microfilm: MnCH proj. no. 13,819

7660   Vita s. Bonifacii. MS. Benediktinerabtei Admont, Austria, codex 654, f.146r–182v. Quarto. Saec. 12.
     Microfilm: MnCH proj. no. 9694

7661   Vita s. Bonifacii archiespiscopi auctore Willibaldo presbytero.
     (*In* Monumenta Germaniae historica. Scriptores. Stuttgart, 1963. t. 2, p. 331–359)
     MnCS; PLatS

7662   [Vita s. Bonifacii]
     Briefe des Bonifatius. Willibalds Leben des Bonifatius . . . neu bearb. von Reinhold Rau. Darmstadt, Wissenschaftliche Buchgessellschaft, 1968.
     535 p. 23 cm.
     MnCS

7663   **Willson, Dominic,** 1879–
     Plainsong for schools; Masses and occasional chants. New York, J. Fischer, 1943–51.
     2 v. 16 cm.
     InStme

Wilmart, André, 1876–1941.

7664   Auteurs spirituels et textes dévots du Moyen Age latin; études d'histoire littéraire. Paris, Bloud et Gay, 1932. Paris, Etudes augustiniennes, 1971.
     628 p. 25 cm.
     InStme; PLatS

7665   Le genis du rit romain. Paris, Librairie de l'art catholique, 1920.

103 p.
     MoCo

7666   Le Lectionnaire d'Alcuin. Roma, Ephemerides Liturgicae, 1937. 137–197 p. 25 cm.
     "Excerptum ex Ephemerides Liturgicae A. H., a. 1937.
     InStme

7667   Lettres de jeunesse et lettres d'amitie. Editées par G. De Luca et M. L. Baud avec notes biographiques. Roma, Edizioni di Storia e letteratura, 1963.
     xxvi, 172, vi p. plates, 26 cm.
     KAS; PLatS

7668   **Wilson, Debora, Sister,** 1936–
     Benedictine higher education and the development of American higher education. Ann Arbor, Mich., University Microfilms, 1969.
     xvi, 335 p. 22 cm.
     Thesis (Ph.D.)–University of Michigan, 1969.
     InFer; InStme; PLatS

7669   **Wimmer, Boniface,** 1809–1887.
     Correspondence, 1846–1887. 10 ft.
     In St. Vincent College and Archabbey Libraries (Latrobe, Pa.).
     Contents: 11 letters (1883–87) to the Rev. Wolfgang Amberger, of Regensburg, Germany, concerning the history of St. Vincent Archabbey; 14 letters (1846–68) to the Ludwig-Missionsverein, Munich; 11 letters (1847–55) to Karl August von Reisach, Archbishop of Munich; correspondence with the Catholic hierarchy and Benedictines in the U.S.; and 11 letters from Ludwig I, King of Bavaria.
     PLatS

7670   **Wimmer, Florian,** 1816–
     Anleitung zur Erforschung und Beschreibung der kirchlichen Kunstdenkmäler. In 2. Aufl. mit Illustrationen vermehrt und hrsg. von D. Mathias Hiptmair. Linz, Haslinger, 1892.
     xiv, 152 p. illus. 25 cm.
     InStme; KAS

7671   **Wimmer Simplicius,** 1844–1905.
     Kurze Geschichte der Benedictiner-Abtei St. Ludwig am See, jetzt St. John's-Abtei in Minnesota (Nord-Amerika).
     (*In* Studien und Mitteilungen aus dem Benedictiner-Orden, II. Jahrgang(1881), 2.Bd., p. 266–281, & III. Jhg.(1882), 1.Bd., p. 42–65.)
     MnCS; PLatS

7672   **Winance, Eleutherius,** 1909–
     [Philosophy notes]. Collegeville, Minn., St. John's University, n.d..
     3 vols. 29 cm.

Multilithed.
MnCS

Winandy, Jacques, 1907–

7673　Autour de la naissance de Jésus; accomplissement et prophétie. Paris, Editions du Cerf, 1970.
　　115 p. 18 cm.
　　InStme

7674　Benedictine spirituality.
　　(*In* Gautier, Jean, ed. Some schools of Catholic spirituality. New York, 1959. p. 17–48)
　　InFer

7675　Le Cantique des cantiques; poème d'amour mué en écrit de sagesse. [Tournai], Casterman, 1960.
　　174 p. 22 cm.
　　PLatS

7676　L'idée de fuite du monde.
　　(*In* Le message des moines à notre temps. Paris, 1958. p. 95–104)
　　PLatS

Winchester, England. St. Swithun's Priory. *See* St. Swithun's Priory, Winchester, England.

7677　**Winidharius, monk of St. Gall,** 8th cent.
　　Ein neues Winitharfragment mit liturgischen Texten.
　　(*In* Neue St. Galler vorhieronymianische Prophetenfragmente . . . Beuron, 1955)
　　InStme; MnCS; PLatS

Winston, Colleen, Sister.

7678　The communication process in Archdiocesan Offices of Communication: two studies and a generalized tool.
　　Thesis (M.A.)–University of Dayton, 1976.
　　Typescript.
　　KyCovS

7679　A journey in the spirit: Benedictines in the Americas. Slide-tape program commissioned by the Presidents of the American Benedictine Federations of North America, completed 1969.
　　KyCovS

7680　The sounds around; poetry by Renée Rust. Photography by Colleen Winston. Hicksville, N.Y., Exposition Press [1976].
　　64 p. illus. 24 cm.
　　InFer; KyCovS; MnCS

7681　Spectroscopic study of larval hemolymph in two populations of chironomus plumosus.
　　Thesis (M.S.)–St. Mary's College, Winona, Minn., 1971.
　　Typescript.
　　KyCovS

7682　Who Benedictines say they are; content analysis and some interpretation on replies from 54 monasteries of men and women in response to the request: Name the six major characteristics that describe your community. Submitted to the Presidents of the American Benedictine Federations of North America.
　　6 p. 28 cm.
　　KyCovS

Wintersig, Athanasius, 1900–

7683　Die Psalmen als Gebet der Kirche. Düsseldorf, L. Schwann [1926].
　　58 p. 18 cm.
　　MnCS

7684　Sie Selbstdarstellung der heiligen Kirche in ihrer Liturgie.
　　(*In* Mysterium; gesammelte Arbeiten Laacher Mönche. Münster, 1926. p. 79–104)
　　PLatS

Winzen, Damasus, 1901–1971.

7685　The biblical aspect of the ecumenical approach to non-Christian cultures.
　　(*In* Derrick, Christopher. Light of revelation and non-Christians. New York, 1965. p. 125–138)
　　InFer

7686　Conferences on the Prologue to the Rule. Pine City, N.Y., Mount Saviour Monastery, 1976.
　　20 p.
　　MoCo

7687　Conference on the reception of guests.
　　(*In* Monastic studies, v. 10, p. 55–63)
　　PLatS

7688　Introduction to the Psalms and commentary on Psalm 1. [Pine City, N.Y., Mount Saviour Monastery, 1975].
　　11 p. 24 cm.
　　MoCo; PLatS

7689　On the psalms of Compline; commentaries on Psalm 4, Psalm 90 and Psalm 133. [Pine City, N.Y., Mount Saviour, 1975].
　　12 p. 24 cm.
　　MoCo; PLatS

7690　Pathways in Scripture. Introduction by Jean Leclercq. Ann Arbor, Servant Books, 1976.
　　320 p. 21 cm.
　　InStme; MoCo

7691　The spiritual basis of Catholicism.
　　(*In* Dooley, L. M. Further discourses on the Holy Ghost. New York, 1945. p. 41–50)
　　PLatS

Wion, Arnold, 1554–1610?

7692　Brieve dechiaratione dell'arbore monastico benedittino, intitolato Legno della vita, cavata di i cinque libri dechiara-

tivi di detto arbore. Venetia, G. Angelieri, 1594.
144 p. 15 cm.
KAS

7693 Lignum vitae, continens fundatoris S. P. Benedicti, dilatorum et restauratorum ac aliorum insignium virorum nomina et gesta. MS. Benediktinerabtei St. Peter, Salzburg, codex a.III.16. 92 f. Octavo. Saec. 17(1645).
Microfilm: MnCH proj. no. 9961

Wireker, Nigellus, ca.1130–ca.1200.
7694 The book of Daun Burnel the ass: Nigellus Wireker's Speculum stultorum. Translated with an introduction and notes by Graydon W. Regenos. Austin, University of Texas Press [c 1959].
165 p. illus. 24 cm.
MnCS

7695 A mirror of fools; the book of Burnel the ass, by Nigel Longchamp. Translated from the Latin by J. H. Mozley. With illus. by Eve Graham, and a preface by Paul E. Beichner. [Notre Dame, Ind.], University of Notre Dame Press [1963].
xvi, 143 p. illus. 21 cm.
Translation of: Speculum stultorum.
InFer; InStme; MoCo; NcBe; PLatS

7696 Nigel de Longchamps: Speculum stultorum. Edited, with an introduction and notes, by John H. Mozley and Robert R. Raymo. Berkeley, University of California Press, 1960.
191 p. illus., facsim. 24 cm.
InStme

7697 **Wirth, Augustine,** 1828–1901.
New and old (sermons); a monthly repertory of Catholic pulpit eloquence embracing two sermons for each Sunday and Holy Day of obligation of the ecclesiastical year. Elizabeth, N.J. [1885].
8 v. 23 cm.
Vol. 2 has imprint: New York, H. Bartsch [c 1885].
Vols. 4–8 have imprint: Newark, N.J., St. Mary's Abbey [n.d.]
KAS

7698 **Wirtner, Modestus,** 1861–1948.
A preliminary list of the hemiptera of western Pennsylvania. [Beatty, Pa., St. Vincent Archabbey, 1904].
"Reprinted from Annals of the Carnegie Museum, vol. III, 1904, p. 183–232"
PLatS

7699 **Wirz, Corbinian,** 1875–1929.
Die heilige Eucharistie und ihre Verherrlichung in der Kunst. M. Gladbach, B. Kühlen [1913].

79 p. illus. 26 cm.
InStme; KAS; MoCo

7700 **Wischler, Johannes.**
Tractatus de esu carnis monachorum S. Benedicti. MS. Benediktinerabtei Kremsmünster, Austria, codex 111, f.229r–301v. Saec. 15.
Microfilm: MnCH proj. no. 103

7701 **Wisniewski, Jerome Joseph,** 1885–
Early Celts in America. St. Leo, Fla., Abbey Press, 1962.
49 p. 20 cm.
FStL; PLatS

7702 El Inca, by Father Jerome. St. Leo, Fla., Abbey Press, 1965.
33 p. facsims. 20 cm.
PLatS; FStL

7703 Juan Ponce de León. St. Leo, Fla., Abbey Press, 1962.
61 p. ports., map. 20 cm.
FStL; PLatS

7704 Saint Augustine in 1835, by Father Jerome. St. Leo, Fla., Abbey Press, 1964.
29 p. plates, 20 cm.
MnCS; FStL

7705 Tokens. Cedar Rapids, Ia., The Torch Press, 1927.
[32] p. 20 cm.
MnCS; FStL

7706 The Vatican and the Southern Confederacy, by Father Jerome. St. Leo, Fla., Abbey Press, 1962.
39 p. illus. 20 cm.
FStL; PLatS

7707 **Wissman, Melchior,** 1938–
Esther, Judith and Tobit. Conception, Mo., Conception Abbey [1963].
57 p. 21 cm. (Saint Andrew Bible commentary, 11)
PLatS

7708 **Woerdemann, Jude,** 1917–
The transfer of the Easter trope Quem quaeritis in sepulchro to its position before the Te Deum in Easter Matins.
iv, 42 leaves. 28 cm.
Thesis (M.A.)–Catholic University of America, 1945.
Typescript.
InStme

7709 **Woffenschmid, Adam.**
Thesurus devotionis omnibus pietatem colentibus cum religiosis tum sacerdotibus et aliis quibuscumque vere catholicis valde utilis. MS. Benediktinerabtei St. Paul im Lavanttal, Austria, codex 16/2. 436 f. Quarto. Saec. 16(1581).
Microfilm: MnCH proj. no. 11,737

Wokurka, Annerose, Sister, 1911–1970.

7710   An attitude scale for measuring the effectiveness of an oral reading.
68 p. 28 cm.
Thesis (M.A.) – University of Minnesota, 1934.
Typescript.
MnStj(Archives)

7711   The evolving image of a Benedictine.
78 p. 28 cm.
Thesis (M.A.) – St. John's University, 1965.
Typescript.
MnStj(Archives)

7712   **Wolfgang, Saint,** 924–994.
Epistola Wolfgangi episcopi ad quemdam sacerdotem in causa sponsalium. MS. Benediktinerabtei Kremsmünster, Austria, codex 40, f.262v. Saec. 16.
Microfilm: MnCH proj. no. 40

Wolking, Teresa, Sister.

7713   Archive holdings of St. Walburg Convent of Benedictine Sisters of Covington, Kentucky, 1859–
Typescript 1980.
KyCovS

7714   The Crescent-Villa Community: the Bicentennial celebration, 1776–1976.
48 p. illus. 28 cm.
Lithographed.
KyCovS

Wolter, Maurus, 1825–1900.

7715   The principles of monasticism. Translated, edited, and annotated by Bernard A. Sause. St. Louis, Herder, 1962.
xx, 789 p. 24 cm.
CaMWiSb; ILSP; InFer; InStme; KAS; MdRi; MnCS; MnStj; MoCo; NcBe; OkShG; PLatS; ViBris

7716   The Roman catacombs. Translated by H. S. Butterfield. London, Thomas Richardson, 1867.
160 p.
MoCo

Wonisch, Othmar, 1884–

7717   Erinnerungsblätter an die Jubiläums- und Krönungsfeierlichkeiten in Mariazell in den Jahren 1907 und 1908. St. Lambrecht [Austria], Selbstverlag des Benediktinerstiftes St. Lambrecht, 1909.
119 p. illus., 23 cm.
MnCS

7718   Die Gründung der Benediktinerinnenabtei Säben. Innsbruck, Universitätsverlag Wagner, 1938.
iv, 75 p. 25 cm.
MnCS

7719   Mariazell. München, Verlag Schnell & Steiner [1957].
46 p. illus. 24 cm.
PLatS

7720   **Woodside Priory, Portola Valley, Calif.**
The plan for Woodside Priory, a new preparatory school for boys in the San Francisco Peninsula, an establishment of the Order of St. Benedict, 1958.
[15] p. illus., plan, 29 cm.
PLatS

Worcester Priory, England.

7721   The cartulary of Worcester Cathedral Priory (register I). Edited by R. R. Darlington. London, The Pipe Roll Society, 1968.
lxx, 373 p. facsims. 25 cm.
InStme

7722   Compotus rolls of the Priory of Worcester of the XIVth and XVth centuries, transcribed and edited by Sidney Graves Hamilton. Oxford, James Parker and Co., 1910.
xxv, 93, 49–64 p. 28 cm.
MnCS

7723   **Ein Wort für und über Religion** und Offenbarung dem heutigen Zeitgeist geswidmet. Von einem alten Benediktiner des vormaligen Stiftes St. Georgen in Villingen. Einsiedeln, Benziger Und Söhne, 1822.
67 p. 23 cm.
PLatS

Wortman, Ildephonse, 1918–

7724   Gregorian chant. [St. Vincent Archabbey, Latrobe, Pa., n.d.]
48 p. 28 cm.
Typescript.
PLatS

7725   Larger rhythmic, melodic, dynamic analysis of text, incise, period. Latrobe, Pa., Saint Vincent Archabbey [n.d.].
48 leaves, music. 28 cm.
Typescript.
PLatS

7726   Modality. [St. Vincent Archabbey, Latrobe, Pa., n.d.]
38 leaves, 28 cm.
Typescript.
PLatS

7727   Orations, epistles, gospels and other chants at the altar. [St. Vincent Archabbey, Latrobe, Pa., n.d.]
50 leaves, 28 cm.
Typescript.
PLatS

7728   Principles of choir recitation. [St. Vincent Archabbey, Latrobe, Pa., n.d.]
19 leaves, 28 cm.
Typescript.
PLatS

7729 Principles of English choir recitation. [St. Vincent Archabbey, Latrobe, Pa., n.d.] 14 leaves, 28 cm. Typescript. PLatS

7730 Psalmody. [St. Vincent Archabbey, Latrobe, Pa., n.d.] 38 leaves, music. 28 cm. At head of title: Gregorian chant. Typescript. PLatS

7731 Rhythm and Rhythmic considerations; Rhythmic interval study; Rhythm and melodic groups. [St. Vincent Archabbey, Latrobe, Pa., n.d.] ix, 25, 8 leaves. 28 cm. Typescript. PLatS

7732 Trope, sequence, organum, medieval motet, the vertical and horizontal broadening of Gregorian chant. [Saint Vincent Archabbey, Latrobe, Pa., n.d.] 7 leaves, 28 cm. Typescript. Published later in Benedictine Review. PLatS

7733 **Wöss, Placidus.** Repertorium et succincta series diplomatum, documentorum, instrumentorum, actionum cententiosarum, et scriptorum omnium, quae in Archivio antiquitissimi monasterii Altenburgensis asservantur. MS. Benediktinerabtei Altenburg, Austria, codex AB 7 D 1. 388 p. Folio. Saec. 18(1757). Microfilm: MnCH proj. no. 6587

7734 **Wright, Ralph,** 1938– Ripples of stillness [poems]. Boston, St. Paul Editions, c 1978. 77 p. illus.(col.) 22 cm. KAS

Wülberz, Stanislaus.
7735 Analecta ad historiam Blasianam. MS. Benediktinerabtei St. Paul im Lavanttal, Austria, codex 192/2. 8 vols. Folio. Saec. 18. Microfilm: MnCH proj. no. 11,980–

7736 Analecta San-Blasiana. MS. Benediktinerabtei St. Paul im Lavanttal, Austria, codex 187/2. 111 f. Folio. Saec. 18. Microfilm: MnCH proj. no. 11,983

7737 Codex probationum ad historiam Blasianam. MS. Benediktinerabtei St. Paul im Lavanttal, Austria, codex 191/2. 4 vols. Folio. Saec. 18. Microfilm: MnCH proj. no. 11,977–

7738 Epitome omnium rerum, quae ad notitiam domesticam monasterii S. Blasii facere possunt usque ad annum 1749. MS. Benediktinerabtei St. Paul im Lavanttal, Austria, codex 186/2. 2 vols. Folio. Saec. 18. Microfilm: MnCH proj. no. 11,969 & 11,971

7739 **Wundrak, Salome, Sister.** The values of visual aids in the teaching of the social studies in the elementary school. 39 p. 28 cm. Thesis – University of Notre Dame, 1940. Typescript. InFer

7740 **Yaiser, Hildebrand,** 1901– [Introduction to Catholic liturgy. Tokyo, Japan, 1944?] 240 p. illus., 18 cm. Entire text in Japanese.

7741 **Yannic, Thomas d'Aquin,** 1906– La guerre. [Paris], Desclée, De Brouwer [1953]. 215 p. 20 cm. PLatS

Yepes, Antonio de, 1554–1618.
7742 Chronicon generale Ordinis S. Benedicti. Hispanice conditum, a Thoma Weiss lingua romana donavit auxitque. Coloniae, Constantinus Münich, 1648. 2 v. 31 cm. The first two of the 7 vol. Spanish work published 1609–1621. KAS

7743 Compendium compendiosissimum ex Chronico. (In Bucelin, Gabriel. Annales benedictini. Augustae Vindel., 1656. p. 158–190) KAS

7744 La coronica general de la Orden de San Benito . . . Valladolid, Francisco Fernandez de Cordova, 1609–1621. 7 v. 30 cm. MnCS; PLatS(microfilm)

7745 Crónica general de la Orden de San Benito. Estudio preliminar y edición por Fray Justo Pérez de Urbel, O.S.B. Madrid, 1959–60. 3 v. 26 cm. (Biblioteca de autores españoles, t. 123–125) MnCS; PLatS

7746 **Yochum, Lucy, Sister.** St. Benedict and the Benedictines on postage stamps. [10] p. illus. 30 cm. The article appeared in The Cross Chronicle, vols. 13–14, 1961–62. A set of slides goes with the article. PLatS

7747 **Youngwood, Pa. Holy Cross Church.**
Holy Cross Church dedication, April 21,
1963.
63 p. illus., ports. 29 cm.
PLatS

7748 **Yunker, Judy, Sister.**
A syllabus for the humanities on the
senior school level; a studio-historical ap-
proach.
97 p.
Thesis (M.A.)—Indiana State University,
Terre Haute, Ind., 1974.
InFer

7749 **Zähringer, Damasas,** 1899–
Der Beitrag Beurons zur liturgischen
Erneurung.
(*In* Beuron, 1863–1963; Festschrift . . .
Beuron, 1963. p. 337–357)
PLatS

Zallwein, Gregorius, 1712–1766.
7750 Collectiones juris ecclesiastici antiqui et
novi a primordiis ecclesiae usque ad decretum Gratiani . . . Salisburgi, Joan. Jos.
Mayer [1760].
143 p. 23 cm.
PLatS

7751 Principia juris ecclesiastici universalis &
particularis Germaniae. Ed. 2. Augustae,
J. Wolff, 1781.
4 v. 20 cm.
KAS; MoCo

7752 **Zapf, Georg Wilhelm,** 1747–1810.
Reisen in einige Klöster Schwabens,
durch den Schwarzwald und in die
Schweiz. Im Jahr 1781 . . . Erlangen, J. J.
Palm, 1786.
260 p. 13 plates, 25 cm.
KAS

Zedinek, Wilhelm Felix, 1898–
7753 Das alte Göttweig.
(*In* Der heilige Altmann, Bischof von
Passau. Göttweig, 1965. p. 58–84)
PLatS

7754 Altmanns Lebenslauf.
(*In* Der heilige Altmann, Bischof von
Passau. Göttweig, 1965. p. 119–128)
PLatS

7755 Die Göttweiger Stiftsbibliothek, ihr
Werden und Wachsen, ihre Kostbarkeiten.
9 p.
Lecture delivered in Passau, March 23,
1964.
MnCS (microfilm)

Zelli-Jacobuzi, Leopoldo, 1818–1895.
7756 Che negato il miracolo è distrutta la base
logica del sopranaturale; dissertazione
letta nell'Accademia di religione cattolica
nella tornata dei 17 maggio 1866. Roma,
Tipografia Salviucci, 1866.

51 p. 23 cm.
PLatS

7757 Del sacrifizio di Gesù eucaristico sugli
altari; lettera pastorale . . . Roma, Tipografia della pace di Filippo Cuggiani, 1895.
23 p. 23 cm.
PLatS

7758 **Zenzen, Eucharius,** 1903–
(ed) Gredt, Joseph. Elementa philosophiae aristotelico-thomisticae. Ed. 13
recognita et aucta ab Eucharío Zenzen,
O.S.B. Friburgi Brisgoviae, Neo Eboraci,
Herder, 1961.
2 v. 24 cm.
PLatS

Zerda, José de la. *See* Cerda, José de la.

7759 **Ziegelbauer, Magnoald,** 1689–1750.
Centifolium Camaldulense; sive, Notitia
scriptorum Camaldulensium . . . Venetiis,
J. B. Albrizzi, 1750.
[8], 96 p. 40 cm.
KAS; MnCS

7759a Historia rei literariae Ordinis S. Benedicti, in IV partes distributum . . . recensuit, auxit, jurisque publici fecit r.p. Oli-
verius Legipontius, O.S.B. Augustae
Vind., M. Veith, 1754.
4 v. 38 cm.
Republished 1967 by Gregg Press
Limited, Farnborough, Hants, England.
MnCH
Microfich cards are also available since
1980 from Gregg International, Farnborough, England.

7760 **Zimmer, Alard, Sister.**
The solution of some linear diophantine
equations.
42 p.
Thesis (M.S.)—Boston College, 1960.
MnStj

7761 **Zimmermann, Gerd,** 1939–
Ordensleben und Lebensstandard; die
Cura corporis in den Ordensvorschriften
des abendländischen Hochmittalalters.
Münster i.W., Aschendorff, 1973.
2 v. 23 cm.
MnCS

Zimmermann, Odo John, 1906–
7762 Early Christian Latin poetry. Collegeville, Minn., St. John's University,
1956.
60 p. 28 cm. Mimeographed.
MnCS

7763 Medieval Latin poetry: lyrics, hymns, se-
quences, 800–1300. Collegeville, Minn., St.
John's University, 1953.
87 p. 28 cm. Mimeographed.
MnCS

7764 **Zingeler, Karl Theodor,** 1845–
Geschichte des Klosters Beuron im
Donauthale. Sigmaringen, M. Liehner,
1890.
271 p. 22 cm.
KAS

7765 **Zingg, Thaddäus,** 1903–
Die erneuerte Einsiedler Barockfassade
. . . Einsiedeln, Benziger, 1957.
78, viii, 16 p. illus., plates. 22 cm.
InStme

7766 **Zünd, Canisius,** 1903–
Neue Forschungsergebnisse auf dem
Gebiete der Hörtheorien. Einsiedeln, Ben-
ziger, 1944.
32 p. illus. 20 cm.
PLatS

7767 **Zupancic, Reginald,** 1905–
Stift Melk, Benediktinerabtei in
Niederösterreich. München, Schnell &
Steiner, 1966.
15 p. illus. 17 cm.
PLatS

Zürcher, Johannes Chrysostomus, 1921–
7768   Mann Gottes – Bruder Meinrad Eugster,
Benediktiner von Maria Einsiedeln. Stift
Einsiedeln, Verlag des Vizepostulators
[1965].
135 p. illus. (part col.) 27 cm.
InStme; KAS; MnCS

7769   Man of God – Brother Meinrad Eugster.
[Translated by Gerard Ellspermann,
O.S.B.]. Einsiedeln, Benziger [1976].
135 p. illus. 26 cm.
InFer; InStme; MoCo

BENEDICTINE SERIALS

Here are listed new serials (periodicals or monograph serials), that is, either new publications which began since 1961 or older serials which had not been listed in the 1962 edition of *A Benedictine Bibliography.*

As in the first list, only serials edited and/or published by Benedictines are included. But since 1962 the term "Benedictine" has been expanded to include three groups which formerly were independent bodies but recently joined the larger Benedictine Federation and now constitute a Congregation. These three groups are the Camaldolese, the Olivetans, and the Sylvestrines. All three have recently made one or more foundations in the United States. For each group at least one periodical is included. The Cistercians, however, continue as a separate body. Their periodicals are listed in the Subject Part under Cistercians—Periodicals, specifically nos. 4991–5002.

Here are listed only scholarly or general serials. Local newsletters of abbeys, convents, and schools are listed under the name of the respective institution in the Author Part.

7770 **ABC (Atchison Benedictine Community) News.** Atchison, Kans. Mount St. Scholastica Convent. 1– 1969–
KAM; InFer

7771 **A.I.M. (Aide inter-monastères pour les jeunes Eglises.** Formerly: Aide à l'implantation monastique).
Bulletin. n. 1– 1964– Published twice a year, in English and French. Paris & Vanves, France.
MnCS; MoCl; MoCo (n. 9–); ViBris (n. 16–)

7772 **Am Tisch des Wortes.** Stuttgart, Verlag Katholisches Bibelwerk. Hft. 1–
1965– Register zu den Heften 1–20. New series begins in 1969 with numbering 101–.
MnCS

7773 **American Benedictine Academy.** Library science studies. 1– 1962–
InStme; KAS; MnCS; PLatS
Monograph series.
The following has been published to date:
No. 1. Kapsner, Oliver L. A Benedictine bibliography. Collegeville, Minn., St. John's Abbey Press, 1962. 2 vols. 27 cm.

7773a **American Benedictine Academy. Research studies.** 1– 1981–
The following number has been published to date:
No. 1. Neuman, Matthias. A directory of Benedictine personnel for North America. St. Meinrad, Ind., St. Meinrad Archabbey. x, 200 p. 21 cm.
InStme; MnCS

7774 **American Benedictine Academy.** Studies in ascetical theology. 1– 1962–

Monograph series.
InStme; KAS; MnCS; PLatS
The following has been published to date:
No. 1. Wolter, Maurus, O.S.B. The principles of monasticism. Translated, edited, and annotated by Bernard A. Sause, O.S.B. St. Louis, Herder [1962]. xx, 789 p. 24 cm.

7775 **Bayerische Benediktiner-Akademie.** Veröffentlichungen. Bd. 1– 1961–
Neue Folge of its Abhandlungen.
Monograph series.
KAS; MnCS; PLatS

7776 **Beiträge zur Geschichte des alten Mönchtums und des Benediktinerordens.** Supplementband. Münster, Aschendorff. 1– 1938–
MoCo; PLatS

7777 **Benedictine confluence.** Latrobe, Pa. St. Vincent Archabbey. 1– 1968–
InFer; InStme; KAS; MoCo; PLatS

7778 **Benedictines. Atchison, Kans.** v. 21, no. 1– Fall, 1966– Continues Benedictine review.
ILSP; InFer; InStme; KAM; KAS; MoCo; MnCS; PLatS

7779 **The Bible today;** a periodical promoting popular appreciation of the Word of God. Collegeville, Minn., The Liturgical Press. 1– 1962–
InFer; InStme; KAM; MnCS; MoCo; PLatS; KAS

7780 **Bibliotheca Montisfani (Fabriano).** 1975–
MiOx

7781 **Bulletin de Saint Martin et de Saint Benoît.** Ligugé (Vienne), E. Aubin. v. 1–   1891–
InStme; MnCS; KAS

7782 **Bulletin inter-monastères pour les jeunes Eglises.** Vanves, France. 1–1965–   Editor: Dom Paul Gordon, O.S.B.
Published twice a year, in English and French.
MnCS

7783 **CSC News (Conception Seminary College).** 1–   1973–
MoCo

7784 **Collection "Pax";** ascèse, mystique et histoire monastiquées et bénédictines. Abbaye de Maredsous. 1–
PLatS

7785 **Communautés et liturgies (Abbaye de Saint-André).** Bi-monthly. Continues Paroisse et liturgie.
InStme (v. 57–   1975–   )

7786 **Corpus consuetudinum monasticarum,** cura Pontificii Athenaei Sancti Anselme de Urbe editum. Siegburg, apud Franciscum Schmitt. t. 1–   1962–
Monograph serial.
Editor: Kassius Hallinger, O.S.B.
AStb; InStme; KAS; MnCS; MoCo; NcBe; PLatS

7787 **Cuadernos monásticos;** revista trimestral auspiciada por la conferencia de communidades monasticas del Cono Sur. 1–1966–
InStme (1–   )

7788 **The Douai magazine;** quidquid agunt homines Duacenses. Douai Abbey.
AStB

7789 **Écoute.** Sainte-Marie de la Pierre qui Vire. 1–
MnCS

7790 **Église que chante.** 1–   1967–
Irregular.
InStme (1–   )

7791 **Ephemerides Congregationis Casinensis a Primaeva Observantia Ordinis Sancti Benedicti.** Sublaci. v. 1–1905–
MnCS

7792 **Etudes des Oblats.** Abbayes de Paris et Clervaux. 1–
MnCS

7793 **The Gregorian review;** studies in sacred chant and liturgy. v. 1–v. 5, no. 6, Jan. 1954–Dec. 1958.
English language edition of the Revue grégorienne.
Bulletin of the School of Solesmes.
InStme; MnCS; MoCo; PLatS

7794 **Inter fratres** (Detroit–Rome). 1950–
A Sylvestrine publication.
MiOx

7795 **Jucunda laudatio;** rassegne gregoriana. Rivista trimestrale dei PP. Benedictini. Venezia, S. Giorgio Maggiore. 1–1963–
InStme; MnCS; PLatS

7796 **Kansas monks. Atchison, Kans., St. Benedict's Abbey.** 1–   1972–   Bi-monthly.
KAM; KAS

7797 **Kansas monks in Brazil.** v. 1–4, Oct. 1962–Dec. 1971.
KAM; KAS

7798 **Kloster Kronik;** the newsletter of St. Canute Priory, Vedbaek, Denmark. v. 1–12, 1963–66.
MoCo (1–12)

7799 **Laudate;** the quarterly magazine of the Benedictine [Anglican] community at Nashdom Abbey, Burnham, Buckinghamshire [England]. v. 1–   1923–
AStb; InStme

7800 **Little messenger (Conception College).** Conception, Mo. 1–3, 1894–1898?
MoCo

7801 **Liturgia;** revista benedictina. Burgos, Abadía de Santo Domingo de Silos. Año 1–   1946–
KAS

7802 **Liturgia e vida.** Rio De Janeiro, Instituto Pio X. v. 1–   1954–
KAS

7803 **Maria Einsiedeln;** benediktinische Monatschrift. v. 1–   1895–   Title varies: 1896–1935, Mariengrüsse aus Einsiedeln.
InStme; KAS

7804 **Marriage and family living.** St. Meinrad, Ind. v. 1–   1919–   Title varies: v. 1–41 as Grail; v. 42–55 as Marriage.
InStme; MoCo

7805 **Monastic studies.** Mount Saviour Monastery, Pine City, N. Y. 1–   1963–
Monograph series.
InStme; MnCS; PLatS

7806 **Morning star (Conception College).** Conception, Mo. 1–41, 1905–52.
MoCo

7807 **Münsterschwarzacher Studien.** Hrsg. von Missionsbenediktinern der Abtei Münsterschwarzach. Monograph series.
MnCS

7808 **One in Christ.** Monks of Cockfosters, London. 1–   1965–   Continues Eastern Churches quarterly, & incorporates Ecumenical notes.
MoCo; OrStb

7809 **Pax;** quaderni mensili di vita benedettina. Sorrento, Monasterio di San Paolo. v. 1–1932–
MnCS

7810 **Pax Orienti;** St. Benedict's China mission news. Sisters of St. Benedict, St. Joseph, Minn. 1–13, 1949–1962.
Superseded in 1963 by St. Benedict's missions.
MnStj(Archives)

7811 **Il Pilastrello.** Lendinara, Rovigo. 1916–
An Olivetan publication.
LLa

7812 **Quarry.** College of St. Benedict, St. Joseph, Minn. 1–42, 1914–1968.
Title varies: College days, v. 1–5, 1914–25; St. Benedict's quarterly, v. 1–38, 1926–1964; Quarry, v. 39–42, 1965–1968.
MnStj(Archives)

7813 **Recherches et bulletin de théologie ancienne et médiévale.** Louvain, Abbaye du Mont César. 1–   1929–
InStme; PLatS

7814 **Regulae Benedicti studia;** annuarium internationale. v. 1–   1972–
ILSP; InStme; MnCS; OrStb; PLatS

7815 **Res scholasticae apud Benedictinos** in S. Anselmi de Urbe Collegio actus. Fasciculus I–   1896–
PLatS

7816 **Resonance.** St. Meinrad, Ind., St. Meinrad School of Theology. 1965–1975. Supersedes St. Meinrad essays.
ILSP; InStme; KAM; KAS; MoCo

7817 **Revue Mabillon.** Les éditions de la Revue Mabillon: Moines et monastères. v. 1–1905–
Monograph series.
InStme; MnCS; KAS

7818 **St. Benedict's missions** (Sisters of St. Benedict, St. Joesph, Minn). 1–13, 1963–1975.
Supersedes Pax Orienti.
MnStj

7819 **St. Procopius Abbey news quarterly.** 1.–
ILSP

7820 **St. Meinrads Raben.** Einsiedeln, Switzerland. 1–   1911–
NdRi (1–7); InStme (15, 38–42, 48–49, 52–53, 65)

7821 **Scriptorium;** a student publication of St. Benedict's College, Atchison, Kans. 1–15, 1955–1968.

Superseded by Loomings, Fall, 1968.
KAM; KAS

7822 **Seckauer Hefte.** 1–   1932–
MnCS

7823 **Siegburger Studien.** 1–   1960–
KAS

7824 **Sisters Today;** to explore the role of the religious women in the Church of our time. 21–   1950–
Continues Sponsa Regis.
InFer; INauS; etc., etc.

7825 **Spirit and Life** (Benedict Convent of Perpetual Adoration, Clyde, Mo.). 1965–
Continues Tabernacle and Purgatory (1–60).
MoCo

7826 **Spirituels bénédictins du grand siècle;** collection de textes publiée sous la direction de Dom. R. J. Hesbert. Paris, Editions Alsatia. 1958(?)–
PLatS

7827 **Tjurunga;** an Australasian Benedictine review. Benedictine Abbey, New Norcia, Australia. 1–   1971–   Index: no. 1–12 (1971–1977).
MnCS; InStme; KAS; PLatS; MoCo

7828 **L'Ulivo.** Abbazia di Monteoliveto Maggiore, Siena. 1974–
LLa

7829 **Una Sancta;** Zeitschrift für ökumenische Begegnung. Jahrg. 1–   1946–
Under the direction of the Benedictines of Niederaltaich.
InStme; KAS; PLatS

7830 **La Vetta di Picciano (Matera, Italy).** 1974–
An Olivetan publication.
LLa

7831 **La Vie bénédictine.** Supplement au Bulletin paroissial liturgique. Abbaye de Saint-André-lez-Bruges. 1–   1921–
InStme (3, 7–10, 12–57, 59–62)

7832 **Vita monastica (Firenze, Camaldoli).** 1956–
Continues: Camaldoli, 1947–1955.
KAS; MoCo

7833 **Yermo;** cuadernos da historia & de espiritualidad monásticas. Madrid, Santa Maria del Paular. v. 1–   1963–
_____Suplemento bibliografico. 1–1964–
KAS; MoCo

SUBJECT PART

INTRODUCTION

The Subject Part of *A Benedictine Bibliography* lists all works about Benedictines and their activities throughout the fourteen hundred years of the Order. It thus includes works by Benedictine writers as well as works by non-Benedictine writers. A Benedictine writer is always characterized by the "O.S.B." following his name. The strength of contributions by non-Benedictine writers in this Subject Part is in the large historical sector, in particular histories and other studies of abbeys (chapters XI–XII) and Benedictine biographies (chapters XIII–XIV), though there are also contributions in other areas, such as linguistic studies of the Rule of St. Benedict, Benedictine economy, art, libraries, scriptoria, etc. There is an alphabetical index of non-Benedictine writers at the end, intended especially for the convenience of the cooperating libraries, namely, to enable them to check at a glance which titles by such authors have already been reported to this union list and where their impact fell.

The Subject Part is presented in the nature of a classified list, which is the type of arrangement cherished by scholars. Its scheme can be seen and studied in the table of contents. There is also an alphabetical subject index, where the vast complexity of subject matter is minutely scrutinized and where references are made to any specialized topic of Benedictine interest, which readers wish to locate quickly.

As to scope, any publication about the Order of St. Benedict, its history, and its activities is included. The table of contents gives a graphic picture of the full scope of the Subject Part in this bibliography. In chapter XVIII, which deals with other Orders following the Benedictine Rule, only general works about these independent Orders are included in this project. However, since the publication of the original edition of this bibliography in 1962, three independent Orders have joined the general Benedictine confederation, namely, the Camaldolese, the Olivetans, and the Sylvestrines. Hence, not only general works about these former independent Orders are included in this Supplement but also works about their individual abbeys, though not extensively in this short period. These three branches now also have foundations in the United States, as listed under "Cooperating Libraries." About the Cistercian Order, both of the common observance and of the strict observance (Trappists), only general works are included in this Supplement, as was also the procedure in the 1962 edition. The Cistercians are in the process of publishing a bibliography for their Order, which will in itself be a fairly extensive project.

A unique feature of the subject matter in this Supplement is its inclusion of manuscript material (books written before the invention of printing). This material is on microfilm, assembled from European libraries from 1965 through 1979. In areas where there is much manuscript material, the manuscript items (indicated by "MS") are always filed ahead of printed works, specifically under such topics as: Rule of St. Benedict (under texts of the Rule and under commentaries) and under certain liturgical books (Antiphonarium, Breviarium, Diurnale, Graduale, Missale, Psalterium), as that is the desired approach for scholars. Under headings where there are only a few manuscripts, the manuscript items are interfiled alphabetically with printed works. The microfilmed medieval manuscripts include what is considered the oldest basic text of the Rule of St. Benedict, namely, the St. Gall Codex 914 from the ninth century. Among printed copies of the Rule is included the first printed edition (on microfilm), published in Venice in 1489.

CONTENTS

I. Order of St. Benedict

II. St. Benedict

III. Rule of St. Benedict

IV. Benedictine Constitutions

V. Benedictine Asceticism

VI. Benedictine Liturgy

Contents

VII. Special Topics

VIII. Benedictine History

Contents

IX. Benedictine History: By Locality

X. Benedictine History: Congregations

XI. Benedictine History: Abbeys—Collective

XII. Benedictine History: Individual Abbeys

XIII. Benedictine History: Collective Biography

XIV. Benedictine History: Individual Biography

XV. Benedictine Brothers

XVI. Benedictine Oblates

XVII. Benedictine Nuns and Sisters

XVIII. Other Orders Following the Rule of St. Benedict

422   Contents

Indexes

I. ORDER OF ST. BENEDICT

1. GENERAL WORKS

1 **Adnotationes chronologicae de S. Benedicto** . . . Speculum monasteriorum Ordinis Sancti Benedicti ca. anno 1417 (numerantur 6600 monasteria). MS. Vienna, Schottenstift, codex 208, f.145r-145v. Folio. Saec. 15.
Microfilm: MnCH proj. no. 3899

2 **Benedict XV, Pope.**
Holy Father blesses Benedictine Order; allocution of Pope Benedict XV to the Abbot-Presidents of the Benedictine Order, May 19, 1920. [n.p., 1920].
[4] p. 17 cm.
KAS

3 **Benedictines. Congress of Abbots, Rome,** 1967.
A statement on Benedictine life adopted by the Congress of Abbots held in Rome in September, 1967, and translated into English by monks and nuns of the E.B.C. [English Benedictine Congregation]. Printed for private circulation at Mount Angel Abbey, St. Benedict, Or., 1968.
32 p. 20 cm.
KAS; MdRi; MnCS; MoCo; PLatS

3a **Benedettini.**
(*In* Dizionario degli Istituti di Perfezione. Roma, 1973. vol. 1, col. 1197-1351)
MnCS

4 **Besse, Jean Martial Léon, O.S.B.**
Donde vengano i monaci? Studio storico. Traduzione italiana sulla seconda edizione francese. Roma, Desclée, Lefebvre, 1904.
62 p. 20 cm.
KAS; MnCS

5 **Biggs, Anselm Gordon, O.S.B.**
The Benedictine life. Revised. Belmont, N.C., 1974.
19 p.
NcBe

6 **Bogler, Theodor, O.S.B.**
Beten und Arbeiten, aus Geschichte und Gegenwart benediktinischen Lebens. Maria Laach, Verlag Ars Liturgica, 1961.
105 p. plates, 23 cm.
MnCS

7 **Botz, Paschal Robert, O.S.B.**
Benedictine theology (Novice Mistresses Workshop at Villa St. Scholastica, Duluth, Minn., 1955).
16 p. 28 cm.
Multilithed.
MnCS (Archives)

8 **Braunmüller, Benedict, O.S.B.**
Universaller Charakter des Benediktiner-Ordens.

(*In* Studien und Mitteilungen des Benediktinerordens, v. 1(1880), 1. Heft, p. 29-52; 2. Heft, p. 3-26)
AStb; MnCS

9 **Brooke, Christopher N. L.**
The formation of the traditional monasticism.
(*In* his The monastic world, 1000-1300. New York, 1974. p. 41-58)
PLatS

10 **Bullae summorum pontificum** (Gregorius IX, Nicolaus IV, Benedictus XII, Innocentius III, Clemens V) pro reformatione et observantia Reguale. MS. Benediktinerabtei Admont, Austria, codex 829a, f.105r-150v. Quarto. Saec. 17.
Microfilm: MnCH proj. no. 9859

11 **Caffrey, Cletus Bernard, O.S.B.**
Behavior patterns and personality characteristics as related to prevalence rates of coronary heart disease in Trappist and Benedictine monks.
99 leaves, 28 cm.
Thesis (Ph.D.) – Catholic University of America, Washington, D.C., 1966.
PLatS

12 **Caldwell, Mark Stuart.**
Ideological and institutional reflections of the Benedictine ideal in sixteenth-century Hutterites; a study in ecclesiastical ecology.
238 p.
Thesis – Southern Baptist Theological Seminary, 1969.
Xerographic reprint, University Microfilms, Ann Arbor, Mich., 1976.
NcBe

13 **Callahan, Thomas.**
The Black Monks and "The anarchy."
vii, 258 leaves. 28 cm.
Thesis (Ph.D.) – University of Connecticut, 1972.
MnCS (microfilm)

14 **Caramuel Lobkowitz, Juan.**
Theologia regularis, hoc est, in ss. Basili, Augustini, Benedicti, Francisci, &c, regulas commentarii. Venetiis, apud Iuntas et Hertz, 1651.
2 v. 24 cm.
KAS

15 **Cary-Elwes, Columba, O.S.B.**
Monastic renewal. [New York], Herder and Herder [1967].
256 p. 22 cm.
PLatS

15a **Consider your call:** a theology of monastic life / Daniel Rees and other members of the English Benedictine Congregation. London, SPCK, 1978.
xx, 447 p. 22 cm.
InStme; MnCS; PLatS

16 **Daly, Lowrie John.**
Benedictine monasticism; its formation and development through the 12th century. New York, Sheed and Ward [1965].
xv, 375 p. 22 cm.
InFer; NcBe

17 **De dignitate et magnificentia Ordinis S. Benedicti.** MS. Benediktinerabtei Melk, Austria, codex 1087, f.1-43. Duodecimo. Saec. 15.
Microfilm: MnCH proj. no. 1842

18 **De parentela S. Benedicti,** de ordinibus sub ejus regula militantibus, de summis pontificibus, cardinalibus etc. sanctis ex Ordine S. Benedicti. MS. Benediktinerabtei Melk, Austria, codex 1560. f.177r–188v. Duodecimo. Saec. 15.
Microfilm: MnCH proj. no. 2225

19 **Dekkers, Eligius, O.S.B.**
Monastic life today: some suggestions. Translated by James McMurry.
(*In* Monastic studies, v. 4, p. 55-60)
PLatS

20 **Dirks, Walter.**
Die Antwort der Mönche. [Frankfurt am Main], Frankfurter Hefte [1952].
236 p. 22 cm.
MnCS

21 **Dreuille, Mayeul de, O.S.B.**
Monks yesterday and today. [Dasarshalli, Bangalore] St. Paul Publications [1972].
121 p. 19 cm.
PLatS

22 **Dupriez, Edouard, O.S.B.**
Que sont donc les Bénédictins? Belley, Imprimerie du Bugey [1956?].
16 p. 18 cm.
MnCS

23 **Enumerantur ordines,** qui sub regulis ss. Benedicti, Francisci, Augustini militant, et describuntur vestimenta monastica. MS. Vienna, Schottenstift, codex 356, f.372v–373v. Folio. Saec. 16.
Microfilm: MnCH proj. no. 4206

24 **Enumerationes ordinum** . . . qui sub regulis S. Augustini, S. Benedicti et S. Francisci militent. MS. Benediktinerabtei Göttweig, Austria, codex 375, f.173v–174r. Folio. Saec. 15.
Microfilm: MnCH proj. no. 3643

25 **Una escuela de servicio del Señor.** Cuernavaca [Mexico], Monasterio de Nuestra Señora de la Resurreccion, 1951.
61 p. illus.
NcBe

26 **Excerpta super Ordinem et Regulam S. Benedicti.** MS. Benediktinerabtei Melk, Austria, codex 1075, f.543-635. Duodecimo. Saec. 15.
Microfilm: MnCH proj. no. 1833

27 **Graf, Thomas Aquinas, O.S.B.**
The Benedictine spirit. [Translated from the German by Very Rev. Martin Pollard, O.S.B.]. Benet Lake, Wis., Our Faith Press [195-?].
40 p. 20 cm.
Reprint from The Benedictine review, v. 1, 1950.
NcBe; WBenS

28 **Gury, Guy-Marie, O.S.B.**
Ce que croyait Benoît. [n.p.], Mame [1974].
165 p. 18 cm.
CaQMo

29 **Harnack, Adolf von.**
Das Mönchtum; seine Ideale und seine Geschichte. 8. bis 10. Auflage. Giessen, Töppelmann, 1921.
64 p. 21 cm.
PLatS

30 **Hautecombe, France. Saint Pierre-de-Curtille (Benedictine abbey).**
Saint Benoît et ses fils; textes bénédictins traduit par les moines d'Hautecombe. Paris, Fayard [1961].
412 p. 18 cm.
Mr CS

31 **Hunkeler, Leodegar, O.S.B.**
It began with Benedict. The Benedictines: their background, their founder, their history, their life, their contributions to Church and world. Translated by Luke Eberle, O.S.B. St. Benedict, Or., Benedictine Press [c 1973].
80 p. illus. 22 cm.
Translation of: Vom Mönchtum des heiligen Benedikt.
InStme; PLatS

32 **Jameson, Anna Brownell.**
Legends of the monastic orders, as represented in the fine arts. Boston, Ticknor and Fields, 1866.
489 p.
pp. 1-64: The early Benedictines; St. Benedict.
FStL

33 **Knowles, David, O.S.B.**
The Benedictines; a digest for moderns. Introduction by Marion R. Bowman,

O.S.B. Saint Leo, Fla., The Abbey Press, 1962.
xi, 50 p. 18 cm.
InStme; FLa

34 **Meeting of the Monastic Superiors in the Far East, Bangkok, Thailand,** 1968.
A new charter for monasticism; proceedings. Notre Dame, Ind., University of Notre Dame Press, 1970.
xv, 335 p. 24 cm.
Includes articles by Rembert Weakland, O.S.B., Jean Leclercq, O.S.B., and Marie-Joseph Ngoc-Hoang, O.S.B.
KAS

35 **Mönchtum—Aergernis oder Botschaft?**
Gesammelte Aufsätze hrsg. von Theodor Bogler, O.S.B. Maria Laach, Verlag Ars Liturgica, 1968.
176 p. 22 cm.
PLatS

36 **Neut, Edouard, O.S.B.**
Moines et apotres. Louvain, Museum Lessianum [1926].
32 p. 16 cm.
InStme

37 **Ordinationes et reformationes** pro bono regimine monachorum nigrorum Ordinis S. Benedicti. MS. Vienna, National-bibliothek, codex 2218. 54 f. Quarto. Saec. 14.
Microfilm: MnCH proj. no. 15,543

38 **Oury, Guy, O.S.B.**
L'Ordre de Saint Benoit. [Paris], Les Nouvelles editions latines, n.d.].
31 p. 19 cm.
PLatS

39 **Parry, David, 1908-**
Benedictine heritage. Ramsgate [England], The Monastery Press, 1961.
44 p. 19 cm.
PLatS

40 **Paul VI, Pope.**
The Benedictine ideal; address of Pope Paul VI to the abbots and priors of the Benedictine Congregation, September 23, 1977.
(*In* The Pope speaks, v. 22 (1977), p. 329–331)
MnCS

41 **Penco, Gregorio, O.S.B.**
Estensione e diffusione della bonifica benedettina.
(*In* La Bonifica benedettina, p. 51-84)
PLatS

42 **Popes** (1305-1314). Clement V.
De statu monachorum et canonicorum regularium capitulum tricesimum. MS.

Benediktinerabtei Kremsmünster, Austria, codex 111, f.311-316r. Saec. 15.
Microfilm: MnCH proj. no. 103

43 **Popes** (1335-1342). Benedict XII.
Declaraciones Benedicti XII super con-stitutionibus monachorum nigrorum. MS. Benediktinerabtei Lambach, Austria, codex chart. 255. 55 f. Saec. 16.
Microfilm: MnCH proj. no. 650

44 **Raasch, Juana, Sister, O.S.B.**
A bibliography for Benedictine renewal, with excerpts. Under the auspices of the Library Science Section of the American Benedictine Academy, July 20, 1967.
38 p. 28 cm.
Typescript.
MoCo; MnStj (Archives)

45 **Reformatio nigrorum** monachorum monasterii Ordinis S. Benedicti edita in concilio Basiliensi per R. P. ejusdam or-dinis. MS. Benediktinerabtei Göttweig, Austria, codex 496c. 8 f. Quarto. Saec. 15.
Microfilm: MnCH proj. no. 3748

46 **Reformatio Ordinis S. Benedicti** edita in Concilio Basiliensi. MS. Benediktin-erabtei Michaelbeuern, Austria, codex cart. 97, f.2v–8v. Quarto. Saec. 15.
Microfilm: MnCH proj. no. 11,577

47 **Regulae et constitutiones O.S.B.** novellae. MS. Vienna, Na-tionalbibliothek, codex 4970, f.95r-102v. Quarto. Saec. 15.
Microfilm: MnCH proj. no. 18,143

47a **Saint Benedict and the Benedictine life,** by a monk of Ampleforth.
London, Catholic Truth Society [n.d.].
20 p. 16 cm. (Catholic Truth Society pamphlets, B 475 [v. 7])
PLatS

48 **Santos, Manuel dos.**
Analysis benedictina. Conclue por documentos e razoens verdadeiras, que a sagrada, e augusta Ordem de S. Bento he a princeza das religioens e a mais antiga com precedencia a todas... Madrid, Francisco del Hierro, 1732.
[16], 234, 16 p. 30 cm.
KAS

49 **Savaton, Augustin, O.S.B.**
Valeurs fondamentales du monachisme. [Paris], Mame, [1962].
138 p. 18 cm.
MnCS; MoCo; PLatS

50 **Schlitpacher, Johannes, O.S.B.**
Ordines militantes sub Regula s. Benedicti. MS. Benediktinerabtei Melk, Austria, codex 1396, f.237r. Duodecimo. Saec. 15.
Microfilm: MnCH proj. no. 1918

51 **Schola divini servitii.** MS. Benediktinerabtei Melk, Austria, codex 1075, p. 527–542. Duodecimo. Saec. 15.
Microfilm: MnCH proj. no. 1075

52 **Sczygielski, Stanislaus, O.S.B.**
Pharus benedictine universum orbem irradicans, sive, Vita s.p.n. Benedicti abbatis eiusque sanctissimae regulae et ordinis utilitas, ac monachorum de orbe merita gloriosa . . . Crae, ex offic. Schedellana, 1669.
[15], 232 p. 21 cm.
KAS

53 **Sedgwick, Henry Dwight.**
Pro vita monastica; an essay in defense of the contemplative virtues. Boston, The Atlantic Monthly Press, 1923.
164 p.
NcBe

54 **Semana de Estudios Monasticos, 14th, Silos, Spain, 1973.**
Los consejos evangelicos en la tradicion monastica. Abadia de Silos, 1975.
422 p. 24 cm.
PLatS

55 **Staley, Austin, O.S.B.**
Saint Benedict and the American Benedict; a Benedictine perspective on American fatherhood. Morristown, N.J., Delbarton School [196-?]
24 p. 24 cm.
KAS

56 **Statuta monachorum nigrorum** in Concilio Narbonensis provinciae edita et a Gregorio IX approbata (fragmentum). MS. Benediktinerabtei Melk, Austria, codex 959, f.193v. Quarto. Saec. 15.
Microfilm: MnCH proj. no. 1762

57 **Statuta monachorum** Ordinis S. Benedicti. MS. Linz, Austria, Bundesstaatliche Studienbibliothek, codex 77, f.92r–98r. Folio. Saec. 14.
Microfilm: MnCH proj. no. 27,930

58 **Statuta seu reformatio disciplinae monasticae.** MS. Benediktinerabtei Admont, Austria, codex 829a, f.164v-200v. Quarto. Saec. 17.
Microfilm: MnCH proj. no. 9858

59 **Tschudy, Raimond, O.S.B.**
Die Benediktiner. Freiburg in der Schweiz, Paulusverlag [1960].
281 p. 18 cm.
KAS; MnCS; MoCo; PLatS

60 **Vandenbroucke, François, O.S.B.**
Moines: pourquoi? Théologie critique du monachisme. Paris, P. Lethielleux [1967].
252 p. 19 cm.
InStme; KAS; PLatS

61 **Vandenbroucke, François, O.S.B.**
Why monks? Translated by Leon Brockman. Washington, Cistercian Publications, 1972.
xvi, 185 p. 23 cm.
MdRi; MnCS; MoCo; NcBe

62 **Visioni attuali sulla vita monastica.**
Montserrat, 1966.
315 p. 19 cm.
InStme

63 **Weakland, Rembert George, O.S.B.**
Actualité de la pensée de Saint Benoit dans le monde d'aujourd'hui.
(*In* Lettre de l'Abbaye Saint-Martin, Ligugé, n. 131(1968), p. 5-11)
PLatS

64 **Weakland, Rembert George, O.S.B.**
Benedictine optimism.
(*In* The Saint Vincent Oblate, v. 15(1960), p. 1–2)
PLatS

65 **Weakland, Rembert George, O.S.B.**
Eröffungsrede vom Abt-Primas Rembert G. Weakland O.S.B., zum Aebtekongress am 19 September 1973
(*In* Erbe und Auftrag, 49. Jahrg.(1973), p. 448-455)
PLatS

66 **Weakland, Rembert George, O.S.B.**
Monastic renewal.
Reprint from: New Blackfriars, v. 46(1965), p. 511-516)
PLatS

67 **Weakland, Rembert George, O.S.B.**
Problemi attuali di vita monastica.
(*In* Ora et labora, anno 26(1971), p. 99-107)
PLatS

68 **Weakland, Rembert George, O.S.B.**
La simplicité bénédictine.
(*In* Présence d'En Calcat, v. 43(1974), p. 97-99)
PLatS

69 **Wokurka, Annerose, Sister, O.S.B.**
The evolving image of a Benedictine.
78 p. 28 cm.
Thesis (M.A.)–St. John's University, Collegeville, Minn., 1965.
Typescript.
MnStj(Archives)

70 **Zarnecki, George.**
The monastic achievement. New York, McGraw-Hill, 1972.
144 p. illus. 22 cm.
KAS

2. APOSTOLATE

71 **Battaglia, Dante.**
S. Benedetto di Norcia; l'apostolo sociale

e i suoi discepoli. Subiaco, Tipografia dei Monasteri, 1928.
134 p. plates, 21 cm.
MnCS

72 **Doppelfeld, Basilius, O.S.B.**
Mönchtum und kirchlicher Heilsdienst; Enstehung und Entwicklung des nordamerikanischen Benediktinertums im 19. Jahrhundert. Münsterschwarzach, Vier-Türme-Verlag, 1974.
xx, 381 p. 21 cm.
InStme; MnCS; PLatS

73 **Gasquet, Francis Aidan, O.S.B.**
Address delivered by the abbot of Downside at the conventual chapter, September 18, 1907, on the principles that should guide the community in view of calls to undertake new external works. [Letchworth, Arden Press, n.d.].
12 p. 23 cm.
KAS

74 **Grünewald, Marzellin, O.S.B.**
Benediktinsche Arbeit.
(*In* Die Benediktinerabtei Münsterschwarzach. Vier-Türme-Verlag, 1965. p. 76–85)
PLatS

75 **Hamilton, Adam, O.S.B.**
De apostolatu Ordinis S. Benedicti, seu De vitae apostolicae cum monastica ad normam traditionis benedictinae concordia disquisitio historica. Albi, Imprimerie des Apprentis-Orphelins, 1900.
30 p. 21 cm.
MnCS

76 **Hänni, Rupert, O.S.B.**
Die Mission des Benediktinerordens, und das geistige Leben in Muri . . . Sarnen, Louis Ehrli, 1927.
64 p. 25 cm.
MnCS

77 **Renaudin, Paul, O.S.B.**
Le role de l'Ordre de Saint-Benoît dans l'Eglise et la société civile. Orne, De Mentligeon, 1925.
218 p.
AStb

78 **Rutledge, Denys, O.S.B.**
The complete monk: vocation of the monastic order. London, Routledge & K. Paul, 1966.
xii, 363 p. plates, 23 cm.
InStme; MoCo; PLatS

79 **Saint-Benoît-du-Lac, Canada (Benedictine abbey).**
Les Bénédictins et leurs oeuvres. [Abbaye de Saint-Benoît-du-Lac, 1919?].
45 p. 21 cm.
MnCS

79a **Symposium on the apostolates of St. John's:** the parish apostolate, the University apostolate, the Preparatory School apostolate, The Liturgical Press apostolate, the mission apostolate, the chaplaincy, manual labor.
(*In* The Scriptorium [St. John's Abbey], vol. 22(1980), p. 62-97)
MnCS

80 **Vicaire, Marie Humbert, O.P.**
L'imitation des apotres: moines, chanoines et mendicants (IV.–XIII. siècles). Paris, Cerf, 1963.
90 p. 19 cm.
MnCS

3. BIBLIOGRAPHY

81 **Kapsner, Oliver Leonard, O.S.B.**
A Benedictine bibliography; an author-subject union list. Compiled for the Library Science Section of the American Benedictine Academy. 2nd ed. Collegeville, Minn., St. John's Abbey Press, 1962.
2 v. 27 cm. (American Benedictine Academy. Library science studies, no. 1)
ACu; etc.

82 **Mayer, Heinrich Suso, O.S.B.**
Beuroner Bibliographie; Schriftsteller und Künstler während der ersten hundert Jahre des Benediktinerklosters Beuron, 1863-1963. Beuron, Hohenzollern, 1963.
196 p. 23 cm.
KAS; MnCS; NdRi; OKShG; PLatS

82a **Oxford, England. University.** Bodleian Library.
The Benedictines and the book; an exhibition to commemorate the fifteenth centenary of the birth of St. Benedict, A.D. 480-1980. Bodleian Library, Oxford [1980].
viii, 68 p. 20 cm.
MnCS

83 **Panzer, Georg Wolfgang Franz.**
Annales typographici ab artis inventae origine ad annum MD . . . Norimbergae, J. E. Zeh, 1793–97. Reprint: Hildesheim, G. Olms, 1964.
5 v. 25x21 cm.
PLatS

84 **Rouse, Richard H.**
Serial bibliographies for medieval studies. Berkeley, Univ. of California Press, 1969.
xiii, 150 p. 23 cm.
MnCS

85 **St. Anselm Abbey, Washington, D.C.**
Biography and bibliography. No. 1-1964-
PLatS

86 **Tassin, René Prosper, O.S.B.**
Histoire littéraire de la Congrégation de
Saint-Maur, Ordre de S. Benoît, où l'on
trouve la vie & les travaux des auteurs
qu'elle a produits depuis son origine en
1618 jusqu'à présent. Bruxelles, Paris,
chez Humblot, 1770.
xxviii, 800 p.
KAS (microfilm); PLatS (microfilm)

4. CANON LAW

87 **Bastien, Pierre, O.S.B.**
Compendium privilegiorum Congrega-
tionis Cassinensis [Schema]. [Roma, n.d.]
115 p. 25 cm.
Multigraphed.
PLatS

88 **Blume, Karl.**
Abbatia; ein Beitrag zur Geschichte der
kirchlichen Rechtesfrage. Stuttgart, F.
Enke, 1914.
xiv, 118 p. 23 cm. (Kirchenrechtliche
Abhandlungen, 83, Heft)
MnCS

89 **Engel, Ludwig, O.S.B.**
Tractatus de privilegiis et juribus
monasteriorum ex jure communi deductus,
nunc sexta vice impressus et adnotationibus auctus. Salisburgi, Joan. Bapt. Mayr,
1712.
72 p. 21 cm.
KAS

90 **Dammertz, Viktor, O.S.B.**
Das Verfassungsrecht der benediktinischen Mönchskongregationen in Geschichte und Gegenwart. Erzabtei St.
Ottilien, Eos Verlag, 1963.
xxiv, 276 p. 25 cm.
KAS; MnCS; PLatS

91 **Fabiani, Luigi.**
La terra di S. Benedetto; studio storico-
giuridico sul l'Abbazia di Montecassino
dall'VIII al XIII secolo. Badia di
Montecassino, 1968.
2 v. plates, 26 cm. (Miscellanea
cassinese, 33-34)
KAS

92 **Figuerás, Caesarius, O.S.B.**
De impedimentis admissionis in
religionem usque ad decretum Gratiani.
In Abbatia Montserrati, 1957.
xxv, 184 p. 25 cm.
KAS

93 **Molitor, Raphael, O.S.B.**
De privilegiis Cassinensium brevis
relatio. Monasterii Guestfalorum, e
Typographeo Aschendorffiano, 1917.
v, 44 p. 23 cm.
PLatS

94 **Murga, Petrus de, O.S.B.**
Quaestiones pastorales, seu de iure et
potestate parochi unitarum ecclesiarum . . .
addita . . . de iure & potestate prioris con-
ventualis . . . Lugduni, sumptis Ioanis
Couronneau, 1657.
[16], 282, 214, [81] p. 23 cm.
KAS

95 **Speck, Carolus, O.S.B.**
De potestate iudiciali in monasteriis
monachorum Ordinis S. Benedicti usque ad
Benedictum XII. Roma, Pontificia Università Lateranense, 1963.
xiv, 67 p. 25 cm.
PLatS

5. CARE OF THE SICK

96 **Anonymus Mellicensis,** fl. 15th cent.
Tractatus de modo inungendi fratrem
infirmum. MS. Benediktinerabtei Melk,
Austria, codex 960, p.1-24. Quarto. Saec.
15.
Microfilm: MnCH proj. no. 1775

97 **De fratribus morituris inungendis,** com-
municandis et custodiendis. MS. Benediktinerabtei Melk, Austria, codex 1774,
p. 21–61. Duodecimo. Saec. 15.
Microfilm: MnCH proj. no. 2089

98 **Leonardus de Burkhausen, monk of
Melk.**
Tractatus de cura infirmorum et morien-
tium. MS. Benediktinerabtei Melk,
Austria, codex 76, f.1r-127v. Octavo. Saec.
15.
Microfilm: MnCH proj. no. 1157

6. COMMEMORATION OF THE DECEASED

99 **Ebner, Adalbert.**
Die klösterlichen Gebets-Verbrüderun-
gen bis zum Ausgange des karolingischen
Zeitalters. Regensburg, New York, Fr.
Pustet, 1890.
viii, 158 p. 22 cm.
MnCS

7. COMMON LIFE

100 **Berliere, Ursmer, O.S.B.**
La familia dans les monastères bénédictins de Moyen Age. [Bruxelles, M. Lamer-
tin, 1931].
123 p. 26 cm.
MnCS

101 **Fischer, Anselm, O.S.B.**
Conversatio externa religiosa; seu,
Modus pie & religiose vivendi in communitate & societate hominum. Constantiae, J. C. Wolder, 1711.

[16], 530, [16] p. 16 cm.
KAS; MnCS

102 **Joannes de Spira, O.S.B.**
Tractatus de communitate. MS. Benediktinerabtei Melk, Austria, codex 911, f.54v-60v. Quarto. Saec. 15. Microfilm: MnCH proj. no. 1729

102a **Vogüé Adalbert de, O.S.B.**
Community and abbot in the Rule of Saint Benedict. Translated by Charles Philippi, O.S.B. Kalamazoo, Mich., Cistercian Publication, 1978-
v. 23 cm. (Cistercian studies series, no. 5/1)
MnCS; PLatS

103 **Weakland, Rembert George, O.S.B.**
Community: the monastic tradition.
(*In* The American Benedictine review, v. 26(1975), p. 233-250)
PLatS

104 **Zimmermann, Gerd.**
Ordensleben und Lebensstandard; die Cura corporis in den Ordensvorschriften des abendländischen Hochmittelalters. Münster in Westfalen, Aschendorff, 1973.
577 p. 23 cm.
MnCS

8. CONFEDERATION

105 **Mayer, Heinrich Suso, O.S.B.**
Die Benediktinische Konföderation. Quellen (im Originaltext und in deutscher Uebersetzung) zu Geschichte und geltendem Recht der Benediktinischen Konföderation. Beuron, Beuroner Kunstverlag [1957].
168 p. 18 cm.
InStme

106 **Moulin, Leo.**
L'Ordre de Saint-Benoit et les problemes du federalisme.
(*In* his: Le monde vivent des religieux. Paris, 1964. p. 218-242)
MnCS

106a **Oesterle, Gerard, O.S.B.**
Das päpstliche Eigengesetz für die Benediktinische Konfoederation.
Sonderdruck: Benediktinische Monatschrift, Jhg. 28 (1952), p. 353-363.
KAS; MnCS

107 **Weakland, Rembert George, O.S.B.**
The state of the Confederation; inaugural address [at the] 1970 Congress of Abbots O.S.B.
(*In* Cistercian studies, v. 6(1971), p. 91-103)
PLatS

9. CONGRESSES

108 **Benedictines. Congress of Abbots, Rome, 1967.**
A statement of Benedictine life adopted by the Congress of Abbots held in Rome in September 1967 and translated into English by monks and nuns of the E.B.C. [English Benedictine Congregation]. Printed for private circulation at Mount Angel Abbey, 1968.
32 p. 20 cm.
KAS; MdRi; MnCS; MoCo; PLatS

109 **Benedictines. Congress of Abbots, Rome, 1975.**
Acta Congressi abbatum ac priorum conventualium congregationum confoederatarum O.S.B. in aedibus S. Anselmi de urbe celebrati 1973 a die 19 Sept. ad diem 3 Oct. Manuscripti instar. Romae, Secretaria Abbatis Primatis, O.S.B. [1975].
144 p. 24 cm.
MnCS

110 **International Congress on the Rule of St. Benedict, 1st, Rome, 1971.**
Erster Internationaler Regula Benedicti Kongress. First International Congress on the Rule of St. Benedict. Premier Congrès International sur la Règle de S. Benoît, Roma, 4-9. 10. 1971. Hildesheim Verlag H. A. Gerstenberg, 1972.
[4], 337 p. 25 cm. (Regulae Benedicti Studia. Annuarium Internationale, Bd. 1)
PLatS

111 **International Congress on the Rule of St. Benedict, 2nd, Maria Laach, 1975.**
Zweiter Internationaler Regula Benedicti Kongress. Second International Congress on the Rule of St. Benedict . . . Maria Laach, 15-20. 9. 1975. [Proceedings, edited by Berndt Jaspert [and] Eugene Manning]] Hildesheim, Gerstenberger Verlag, 1977.
448 p. illus. 25 cm. (Regulae Benedicti Studia, v. 5)
KAS

111a **Tornare alle fonti;** il primo convegno delle abbadesse e priore benedettine in Italia, 24-29 ottobre 1966. [Sorrento, Italia, Monastero di S. Paolo, 1966].
283 p. 22 cm.
MnCS

10. CONTROVERSIAL LITERATURE

112 **Alciati, Andrea,** 1492-1550.
Tractatus contra vitam monasticam, cui accedit Sylloge epistolarum . . . quae variam doctrinam continent, nec non vetera aliquot testamenta seculo XIII . . . Hagaecomitum, G. Block, 1740.

[22], 387, [7] p. 24 cm.
InStme

113 **Mohler, James A.**
The heresy of monasticism; the Christian
monks, types and anti-types. An historical
survey. Staten Island, N.Y., Alba House
[1971].
xviii, 263 p. illus., maps. 22 cm.
InFer; InStme; NcBe

11. COSTUME

114 **Bonanni, Filippo, S.J.**
Histoire du clergé seculier et regulier . . .
avec des figures qui representent les dif-
ferens habillemens de ces ordres & congregations. Nouvelle édition . . . Amsterdam, Pierre Brunel, 1716.
4 v. plates, 16 cm.
KAS

115 **Bonanni, Filippo, S.J.**
Ordinum religiosorum in Ecclesia
militanti catalogus, eorumque indumenta
in iconibus expressa. Romae, De Rossi,
1706-41.
4 v.
AStb

116 **Quod variis coloribus utantur** in Ordine
S. Benedicti, et de viris praeclaris. MS.
Benediktinerabtei Melk, Austria, codex
1087, f.61-62. Duodecimo. Saec. 16.
Microfilm: MnCH proj. no. 1842

12. CUSTOMS

See also chapter VI, L: Customaries

117 **Gougaud, Louis, O.S.B.**
Anciennes coutumes claustrales. Abbaye
Saint-Martin de Ligugé, France, 1930.
121 p. 19 cm.
CaQStB; MnCS

118 **Hallinger, Kassius, O.S.B.**
Corpus consuetudinum monasticarum,
cura Pontificii Athenaei Sancti Anselmi de
Urbe editum. Sieburg, apud Franciscum
Schmitt, 1962-
v. 26 cm.
MnCS; PLatS; InStme; KAS

118a **Ordo qualiter agendum** sit monachis in
monasteriis constitutis et sub regula
patris Benedicti degentibus. Ms. Budapest National Sychény Library, codex
329, f. 65v-109v. Octavo. Saec. 11-12.
Microfilm: MnCH

119 **Schäfer, Thomas, O.S.B.**
Die Fusswaschung im monastischen
Brauchtum und in der lateinischen
Liturgie. Beuron, Beuroner Kunstverlag,
1956.

xi, 119 p. 23 cm.
MnCS

13. DIET

120 **Bernard von Baching, O.S.B.**
Epistola contra illicitum carnium esum
monachorum Ordinis S. Benedicti. MS.
Benediktinerabtei Melk, Austria, codex
960, f.351-390. Quarto. Saec. 15.
Microfilm: MnCH proj. no. 1775

121 **Bernard von Baching, O.S.B.**
Epistola seu tractatus contra illicitum
carnium esum monachorum O.S.B. MS.
Vienna, Nationalbibliothek, codex 3595,
f.142r-179v. Quarto. Saec. 15.
Microfilm: MnCH proj. no. 16,821

122 **De esu carnium (declarationes ad con-**
stitutiones nigrorum monachorum).
MS. Vienna, Schottenstift, codex 152,
f. 139v-141v. Octavo. Saec. 15.
Microfilm: MnCH proj. no. 4071

123 **De esu et abstinentia carnium mona-**
chorum. MS. Benediktinerabtei Melk,
Austria, codex 1088, f.433-439. Duodecimo. Saec. 15.
Microfilm: MnCH proj. no. 1850

124 **Joannes de Palomar.**
De non esu carnium monachorum. MS.
Benediktinerabtei Melk, Austria, codex
663, f.96r-101v. Quarto. Saec. 15.
Microfilm: MnCH proj. no. 1533

125 **Joannes de Palomar.**
Tractatus de esu carnium monachorum
Ordinis S. Benedicti ad Ioannem, abbatem
Scotorum Viennae. MS. Benediktinerabtei
Melk, Austria, codex 1739, p. 229-319.
Duodecimo. Saec. 13.
Microfilm: MnCH proj. no. 2049

126 **Joannes de Spira, O.S.B.**
Apologia. Tractatus, utrum monachus,
qui contra praeceptum praelati sui comedit
carnes, peccet mortaliter, adversus cujusdam monachi objectiones. MS.
Benediktinerabtei Melk, Austria, codex
1566, f.107r-127v. Duodecimo. Saec. 15.
Microfilm: MnCH proj. no. 1966

127 **Joannes de Spira, O.S.B.**
Quaestiones, utrum monachis Ordinis S.
Benedicti sanis uti liceat carnibus. MS.
Benediktinerabtei Melk, Austria, codex
1241, f.14-15v. Quarto. Saec. 15.
Microfilm: MnCH proj. no. 1885

128 **Joannes de Spira, O.S.B.**
Tractatus de esu carnium. MS.
Benediktinerabtei Melk, Austria, codex
761, f.1r-47r. Quarto. Saec. 15.
Microfilm: MnCH proj. no. 1609

129 **Joannes de Spira, O.S.B.**
Tractatus, utrum monachus qui contra praeceptum praelati sui comedit carnes, peccet mortaliter. MS. Benediktinerabtei Melk, Austria, codex 1400, p. 1–104. Duodecimo. Saec. 15.
Microfilm: MnCH proj. no. 1934

130 **Nicolaus de Dinkelsbühl.**
Tractatus de abstinentia a carnibus monachorum Ordinis Sancti Benedicti. MS. Vienna, Schottenstift, codex 152, f.130r-138v. Octavo. Saec. 15.
Microfilm: MnCH proj. no. 4071

131 **Petrus von Rosenhaim, O.S.B.**
De esu carnium in Regula S. Benedicti prohibito (excerpta ex notatis). MS. Benediktinerabtei Melk, Austria, codex 959, f.207r-207v. Quarto. Saec. 15.
Microfilm: MnCH proj. no. 1762

132 **Schlitpacher, Johannes, O.S.B.**
De esu carnium. MS. Vienna, National-bibliothek, codex 4970, f.19r-20r. Quarto. Saec. 15.
Microfilm: MnCH proj. no. 18,143

133 **Schlitpacher, Johannes, O.S.B.**
Iudicium de tractatu Bernardi de Baching contra illicitum esum carnium. MS. Benediktinerabtei Melk, Austria, codex 960, f.405-406. Quarto. Saec. 15.
Microfilm: MnCH proj. no. 1775

134 **Schlitpacher, Johannes, O.S.B.**
Resolutio quaestionis, utrum monachis S. Benedicti sanis et fortibus esus carnium sit constitutione Benedicti XII concessus. MS. Benediktinerabtei Melk, Austria, codex 1404, f.1-40. Duodecimo. Saec. 15.
Microfilm: MnCH proj. no. 1923

135 **Tractatus de abstinentia a carnibus monachorum Ordinis Sancti Benedicti.**
MS. Benediktinerabtei St. Peter, Salzburg, codex bXII.1, f.270r–281r. Folio. Saec. 15.
Microfilm: MnCH proj. no. 10,674

136 **Tractatus de eo an monachis S. Benedicti esus carnium licitus sit.** MS. Vienna, Nationalbibliothek, codex 4912, f.1r-4r. Quarto. Saec. 15.
Microfilm: MnCH proj. no. 18,099

137 **Tractatus de esu carnium.** Incipit: Propter instantiam quorumdam abbatum O.S.B. MS. Benediktinerabtei Melk, Austria, codex 993, f.230r-277v. Quarto. Saec. 15.
Microfilm: MnCH proj. no. 1807

138 **Utrum monachus existens** fortis et validus de licentia sui abbatis possit comedere carnes. MS. Benediktinerabtei

Melk, Austria, codex 1652, f.146v–149r. Sextodecimo. Saec. 15.
Microfilm: MnCH proj. no. 2008

139 **Wischler, Johannes, O.S.B.**
Tractatus de esu carnis monachorum S. Benedicti. MS. Benediktinerabtei Kremsmünster, Austria, codex 111, f.229r-301v. Saec. 15.
Microfilm: MnCH proj. no. 103

14. DIRECTORIES

140 **Admont, Austria (Benedictine abbey).**
Schematismus der Benediktiner von Admont. 19–
MnCS

141 **Almanach bénédictin.** Paris, A. -J. Corierre, 1910.
80 p.
AStb

142 **The Benedictine yearbook** . . . A guide to the abbeys, priories, parishes, and schools of the monks and nuns of the Order of St. Benedict in the British Isles and their foundations abroad.
KAS

143 **Benedictines. Congregations. St. Joseph.**
Catalogi monachorum et monialium O.S.B.: S. Petri, Salzburg; S. Michaelis, Burae; B.M.V., Lambach; SS. Cordis, Innsbruck; Nonnberg i Salzburg; St. Hemma i Gurk; Säben i Tirol. 1913.
MnCS

144 **Göttweig, Austria (Benedictine abbey).**
Catalogus religiosorum Ordinis S. P. Benedicti in monasterio Gottwicensi Inferioris Austriae viventium.
PLatS

145 **Index alphabeticus monasteriorum O.S.B.** cum inscriptione epistolarum et telegraphica, tabulis geographicis quibus indicantur situs monasteriorum auctus. Ex Catalogo familiarum confoederatarum O.S.B. desumptum. [Romae] 1950-
InStme; MnCS; PLatS

146 **Monte Cassino, Italy (Benedictine abbey).**
Ordo divini officii recitandi sacrique peragendi juxta ritum Breviarii et Missalis monastici in cathedrali basilica Montis Casini servandus anno Domini . . .
PLatS

147 **Muller, Jean Pierre, O.S.B.**
Atlas O.S.B.: Benedictinorum per orbem praesentia; Benedictines throughout the world; [etc.]. Prima editio. Romae, Editiones Anselmianae, 1973.

2 v. maps. 22 cm. (v. 2 32 cm.)
MnCS; PLatS

148 **Pannonhalma, Hungary (Benedictine abbey)**
Schematismus venerabilis cleri regularis Ordinis S. Benedicti archi-abbatiae Sancti Martini in sacro Monte Pannoniae nullius dioeceseos . . .
MnCS(1896-1914); PLatS

149 **Rajrad, Czechoslovakia (Benedictine abbey).**
Catalogus religiosorum Ordinis S. Benedicti abb. in antiquissimo monasterio Rajhradensi.
MnCS(1900-1914); PLatS

150 **Sankt Paul im Lavantthal, Austria (Benedictine abbey).**
Catalogus d. d. religiosorum Ordinis S. Benedicti monasterii ad S. Paulum in dioecesi Gurcensi et Valle Lavantina Carinthiae. S.
PLatS

151 **Seeauer, Beda, O.S.B.**
Liber professionis in monasterio ad S. Petrum Salisburgi ab anno 1419-1817. MS. Benediktinerabtei St. Peter, Salzburg, Archivum HS. A 98. 900 p. Folio. Saec. 18-19.
Microfilm: MnCH proj. no. 10,755

15. DORMITIO

152 **Leclercq, Jean, O.S.B.**
"Lectulus"; variazioni su un tema biblico nella tradizione monastica.
(*In* Vagaggini, Cypriano. Bibbia e spiritualità. Roma, 1967. p. 417-436)
MnCS

16. DRAMA

153 **Kuhn, Kaspar, O.S.B.**
Silach; oder, Die Stiftung des Klosters Ottobeuren. Historisches Ritterspiel mit Gesang in 4 Aufzügen. Kempten, Jos. Kösel, 1877.
103 p. 16 cm.

17. ECONOMIC POLICY

154 **Chibnall, Marjorie.**
The English lands of the Abbey of Bec. Oxford, Clarendon Press [1968, 1946].
vi, 164 p. maps, 23 cm.
MnCS; NcBe

155 **Constable, Giles.**
Monastic tithes from their origins in the twelfth century. Cambridge [England], University Press, 1964.
xxi, 346 p. 23 cm.
MnCS; NcBe

156 **Fastlinger, Max.**
Die wirtschaftliche Bedeutung der Bayerischen Klöster in der Zeit der Agilulfinger. Freiburg i.B., Herder Verlagshandlung, 1903.
xii, 182 p. 24 cm.
InStme; MnCS

157 **Garcia de Cortazar.**
El dominio del monasterio de San Millán de la Cogolle (siglos X a XIII). Salamanca, 1969.
371 p. illus. 25 cm.
MnCS

157a **Kuchenbuch, Ludolf.**
Bäuerliche Gesellschaft und Klosterherrschaft im 9. Jahrhundert; Studien und Sozialstruktur der Familia der Abtei Prüm. Wiesbaden Franz Steiner Verlag, 1978.
xv, 443 p. facsim., maps, 23 cm.
MnCS

158 **Müller, Walter.**
Landsatzung und Landmandat der Fürstabtei St. Gallen . . . 15. bus 18. Jahrhundert. St. Gallen, Fehr, 1971.
xx, 340 p. 23 cm.
MnCS

159 **Platt, Colin.**
The monastic grange in medieval England. New York, Fordham University Press, 1969.
272 p. illus. 23 cm.
MnCS; PLatS

160 **Saint-Bertin, France (Benedictine abbey).**
Le polytyque de l'Abbaye de Saint-Martin (844-859). Edition critique et commentaire par François Louis Ganshof . . . Paris, Imprimerie Nationale, 1975.
xii, 145 p. fold. maps, 30 cm.
MnCS

160a **Schuller, Helga.**
Dos – praebenda – peculium [der weiblichen Kongregationen des Mittelalters].
(*In* Festschrift Friedrich Hausmann. Graz, 1977. p. 453-487)
The article covers abbeys of nuns (Benedictine, Cistercian, Augustinian and Premonstratensian) in southern Germany, Austria and Switzerland.
MnCS

161 **Stuckert, Howard M.**
Corrodies in the English monasteries; a study in English social history of the Middle Ages. Philadelphia, 1923.
54 p. 24 cm.
Thesis (Ph.D.) – University of Pennsylvania, 1923.
MnCS

162 **Thiele, Augustinus.**
Echternach und Himmerod; Beispiele benediktinischer und zisterziensischer Wirtschaftsführung im 12. und 13. Jahrhundert. Stuttgart, F. Fischer, 1964.
186 p. 24 cm.
MnCS

18. ETIQUETTE

163 **Reglas de urbanidad** que da á sus monjes el patriarca San Benito en la aprobada por la Iglesia. Manresa, S. Miguel, 1876.
87 p. 14 cm.
MnCS

19. FICTION

164 **Allmendiger, Karl.**
Der Klostersturm; geschichtliche Erzählung aus St. Gallens Vergangenheit von Felix Nabor [pseud.]. St. Gallen, Jos. Zehnder, 1923.
160 p. 22 cm.
MnCS

165 **Balneum monachorum,** sive, Satyra in monasticos. Incipit: Phoebe sator lucis mundique et jambicum ad furem. MS. Vienna, Nationalbibliothek, codex 9819. 31 f. Quarto. Saec. 16.
Microfilm: MnCH proj. no. 19,367

166 **Carr, Philippa.**
The miracle at St. Bruno's. New York, G. P. Putnam, 1972.
InFer

167 **Deutsch, Alfred Henry, O.S.B.**
Bruised reeds and other stories. Collegeville, Minn., St. John's University Press [c 1971].
213 p. illus. 22 cm.
MnCS; PLatS

168 **Hure, Anne.**
The two nuns. Translated from the French by Emma Crawfurd. New York, Sheed and Ward, 1964.
220 p. 21 cm.
InFer

169 **Vercel, Roger.**
Tides of Mont St. Michel. Translated from the French by Warre Bradley Wells. New York, Random House, 1938.
305 p. 21 cm.
MnCS

170 **White, Helen Constance.**
To the end of the world. New York, Macmillan Co., 1939.
675 p. 21 cm.
The book describes conditions at Cluny at the outbreak of the French Revolution.
AStb

20. GOVERNMENT

171 **Gasquet, Francis Aidan, O.S.B.**
A sketch of monastic constitutional history.
(*In* Montalembert, Charles de. The monks of the West. London, 1896. v. 1, p. vii–lvi)
MnCS; PLatS

172 **Grossi, Paolo.**
Le abbazie benedettine nell'alto medioevo italiano; struttura giuridica, amminstrazion e giurisdizione. Firenze, Felice Le Monnier, 1957.
xxix, 168 p. 26 cm.
InStme

173 **Jassmeier, Joachim.**
Das Mitbestimmungsrecht der Untergebenen in den älteren Männerordensverbänden. Munich, K. Zink, 1954.
x, 301 p. 24 cm.
MnCS

174 **Knowles, David, O.S.B.**
From Pachomius to Ignatius; a study of the constitutional history of the religious orders. Oxford, 1966.
98 p. 20 cm. (Serum lectures, 1964-65)
MnCS

175 **Some European Benedictine abbeys** as seen by one American monk. Saint Leo, Fla., Saint Leo Abbey Press, 1964.
92 p. 24 cm.
PLatS

176 **Valous, Guy de.**
Le domaine de l'Abbaye de Cluny aux X. et XI. siècles: formation – organisation – administration. Paris, Librairie Ancienne Edouard Champion, 1923.
190 p.
NcBe

179 **Vogüe, Adalbert de, O.S.B.**
La communité et l'abbé dans la Regula de Saint Benoît. Paris, Desclée, De Brouwer [1961].
559 p. 21 cm.
InStme; MnCS; MoCo; NcBe; PLatS

21. HOLY ORDERS

180 **Bogler, Theodor, O.S.B.**
Priestertum und Mönchtum. Maria Laach, Verlag Ars Liturgica, 1961.
119 p. illus. 23 cm.
MnCS

181 **Epistola de admissione monachorum** ad officium sacerdotale. MS. Benediktinerabtei Kremsmünster, Austria, codex 334, f.112r–134. Saec. 15.
Microfilm: MnCH proj. no. 344

182 **Frank, Hieronymus, O.S.B.**
Die Klosterbischöfe des Frankenreiches.
Münster i.W., Aschendorff, 1932.
189 p. 25 cm.
MnCS

183 **Leclercq, Jean, O.S.B.**
The priesthood for monks.
(*In* Monastic studies, v. 3, p. 53-85)
Translated by monks of Caldey Abbey.
PLatS

184 **Nussbaum, Otto.**
Kloster, Priestermönch und
Privatmesse; ihr Verhältnis im Westen
von den Anfängen bis zum hohen Mittelalter. Bonn, P. Hanstein, 1961.
286 p. 25 cm.
MnCS

185 **Presinger, Rupert, O.S.B.**
Sacerdos benedictinus ad Sacrae
Regulae normam, et praecipue juxta
exempla ac doctrinas summi sacerdotis
Christi Jesu efformatus. Typis Monasterii
Tegernseensis, 1720.
76 p. 14 cm.
KAS

186 **Rousseau, Olivier, O.S.B.**
Priesthood and monasticism.
(*In* The sacrament of holy orders; some
papers ... at the Centre de pastoral liturgi-
que, 1955. London, 1962. p. 168-180)
PLatS

187 **Vanucci, Ildebrando, O.S.B.**
Il sacerdote e la spiritualità e la benedet-
tina.
(*In* Rome (City). Pontificia Università
Gregoriana. Il sacerdote e la spiritualità.
1946. p. 1-24)
MnCS; PLatS

188 **La vida monastica i sacerdotal a Montserrat.** Abadia de Montserrat, 1956.
32 p. illus. 20 cm.
MnCS

22. HOSPITALITY

189 **Bender, Edwin Paul, O.S.B.**
Benedictine hospitality.
Thesis (B.A.)–St. Vincent College,
Latrobe, Pa., 1933.
Typescript.
PLatS

190 **Huerre, Denis, O.S.B.**
The monk, the guest and God.
Translated by a monk of Mount Saviour.
(*In* Monastic studies, v. 10, p. 49-54)
PLatS

191 **Willmes, Peter.**
Der Herrscher "Adventus" im Kloster
des Frühmittelalters. München, Wilhelm
Fink Verlag, 1976.

205 p. 24 cm.
MnCS

192 **Winzen, Damasus, O.S.B.**
Conference on the reception of guests.
(*In* Monastic studies, v. 10, p. 55-63)
PLatS

23. ICONOGRAPHY

See also chapter II,3: Benedict,
Saint–Art.

193 **Portraits of Benedictine saints.**
Biographical sketch under engravings.
[n.p., n.d.].
273 leaves of engravings. 20 cm.
Portraits in alphabetical sequence.
PLatS

194 **Stengel, Carl, O.S.B.**
Imagines sanctorum Ordinis S. Benedicti
tabellis aereis expressae, cum eulogiis
eorundem vitis. [Augsburg], Mon.SS.
Udalricae & Afra], 1625.
180 p., incl. 86 full-page engravings.
20 cm.
MnCS

24. OBITUARIES

195 **Admont, Austria (Benedictine abbey).**
Necrologium Admontense. MS.
Benediktinerabtei Admont, Austria, codex
184, f.189r–228v. Folio. Saec. 12.
Microfilm: MnCH proj. no. 9273

196 **Altenburg, Austria (Benedictine abbey).**
Necrologium monasterii Altenburgensis.
Cum indice eorum monasteriorum, quae
cum nostro fraternitatem contraxerunt.
MS. Benediktinerabtei Altenburg, Austria,
codex AB 7 D 14. 97 f. Folio. Saec. 17.
Microfilm: MnCH proj. no. 6593

197 **Altenburg, Austria (Benedictine abbey).**
Necrologium monasterii Altenburgensis
. . . renovatum anno salutis 1843, iterum
renovatum 1902. MS. Benediktinerabtei
Altenburg, Austria, codex AB 7 D 16.
186 f. Folio. Saec. 19.
Microfilm: MnCH proj. no. 6582

198 **Balthasar, monk of Mondsee.**
Rotula des Benediktiners Baltasar von
Mondsee. MS. Linz, Austria,
Bundesstaatliche Studienbibliothek, codex
500. 8 f. Quarto. Saec. 16.
Microfilm: MnCH proj. no. 28,026

199 **Durham Cathedral, England.**
The obituary roll of William Ebchester
and John Burnby, priors of Durham.
Durham, G. Andrews, 1856.
xxxv, 135 p. 23 cm. (Publications of the
Surtees Society, vol. xxxi)
MnCS

200 **Eckhardt, Karl August, ed.**
Studia Corbeiensia: bibliotheca rerum historicarum . . . rotula Corbeiensis . . . Aalen, Scientia Verlag, 1970.
MnCS

201 **Göttweig, Austria (Benedictine abbey).**
Necrologium ut Denisius vult in Gallia inchoatum, in monasterio Gotwicensi continuatum. MS. Vienna, Nationalbibliothek, codex 684, f.143r-144v. Folio. Saec. 12.
Microfilm: MnCH proj. no. 14,002

202 **Huyghebeert, Nicolas, O.S.B.**
Les documents necrologiques. Turnhout, Brepols, 1972.
75 p. 24 cm.
MnCS

203 **Kremsmünster, Austria (Benedictine abbey).**
Necrologium II Cremifanense. MS. Benediktinerabtei Kremsmünster, Austria, codex Schatzkammer 5, f.1r-46v. Saec. 13.
Microfilm: MnCH proj. no. 384

204 **Lambach, Austria, (Benedictine abbey).**
Necrologium Lambacense. MS. Benediktinerabtei Lambach, Austria, codex membr. 131, f.153r–166v. Quarto. Saec. 12.
Microfilm: MnCH proj. no. 816

205 **Michaelbeuern, Austria (Benedictine abbey).**
Rotula anno 1526. Unter Abt Wolfgang von Michaelbeuern (1518-1531). MS. Benediktinerabtei Michaelbeuern, Austria, codex perg. 14.
Microfilm: MnCH proj. no. 11,613

206 **Necrologium Congregationis benedictinae bavaricae,** 1836-1950. Monachii, 1950.
110 p.
AStb

207 **Necrologium Mariae-Cellense.** MS. Benediktinerabtei Melk, Austria, codex 836, f.113r-138v. Quarto. Saec. 13.
Microfilm: MnCH proj. no. 1664

208 **Necrologium San-Blasianum de annis** 964-1638. Necrologium de Göss et Admont in Styria. Necrologium San-Petrense et Lambacense. MS. Benediktinerabtei St. Paul im Lavantthal, Austria, codex 210/2, pars I, VI, VIII. Folio. Saec. 18.
Microfilm: MnCH proj. no. 12,033

209 **Paris. St. Germain-des-Prés (Benedictine abbey).**
Nécrologe de la Congrégation de Saint-Maur. Publié avec introduction, suppléments et appendices par m. l'abbé J-B. Vanel. Paris, H. Champion, 1896.

lxiii, 412 p. 29 cm.
MnCS

210 **Rotula.** MS. Benediktinerinnenabtei Nonnberg, Salzburg, Archivium. Saec. 16(1508).
Microfilm: MnCH proj. no. 10,962

211 **Rotulus funebris Pauli Pirmisser abbatis Seitenstettensis** (m. 1477) aliorumque confratrum defunctorum, sex membranaceis ex foliis palman latis, et in longum consatis, confectus, qui per Superioram Austriam, Bavariam, Tyrolim, Sueviam, Franconiam, Thuringiam, Hassiam, ad diversorum ordinum monasteria, e quibus plura id temporis in alienis sunt manibus, circumlatus fuerat. MS. Benediktinerabtei Seitenstetten, Austria, codex 305, Saec. 15(1477).
Microfilm: MnCH proj. no. 1117

212 **Salzburg, Austria. St. Peter (Benedictine abbey).**
Libellus mortuorum abbatum, fratrum et sororum S. Petri in Salisburga. MS. Benediktinerabtei St. Peter, Salzburg, Archivium HS. A 247. Octavo. Saec. 16(1560-1597).
Microfilm: MnCH proj. no. 10,772

213 **Salzburg, Austria. St. Peter (Benedictine abbey).**
Rotula von St. Peter in Salzburg, 1. März bis 10.Nov.1503. MS. Benediktinerabtei St. Peter, Salzburg, Archivium A 563/1.
Microfilm: MnCH proj. no. 11,363

214 **Salzburg, Austria. St. Peter (Benedictine abbey).**
Rotula von St. Peter in Salzburg, Jan.-Mai, 1624. MS. Benediktinerabtei St. Peter, Salzburg, Archivium A 563/3.

215 **St. Blasien im Schwarzwald, Germany (Benedictine abbey).**
Calendarium cum necrologio monasterii S. Blasii sub abbate Gaspari I. scriptum. MS. Benediktinerabtei St. Paul im Lavantthal, Austria, codex 73/1. 65 f. Folio. Saec. 16(1567).
Microfilm: MnCH proj. no. 11,714

216 **St. Blasien im Schwarzwald, Germany (Benedictine abbey).**
Necrologium abbatum et fundatorum atque benefactorum Monasterii S. Blasii, approbatum a Cardinale Andrea episcopo Constantiensi, anno 1595. MS. Benediktinerabtei St. Paul im Lavantthal, Austria, Urkunden St. Blasien 130. 22 f. Folio. Saec. 16.
Microfilm: MnCH proj. no. 12,382

217 **St. Blasien im Schwarzwald, Germany (Benedictine abbey).**
Necrologium monasterii S. Blasii ex

cod. bibliothecae Vindobonensi saeculi XII. MS. Benediktinerabtei St. Paul im Lavantthal, Austria, codex 94/2, pars V. Folio. Saec. 18.
Microfilm: MnCH proj. no. 11,867

218 **St. Blasien im Schwarzwald, Germany (Benedictine abbey).**
Necrologium San-Blasianum de annis 964-1638. MS. Benediktinerabtei St. Paul im Lavantthal, Austria, codex 210/2, pars I. Folio. Saec. 18.
Microfilm: MnCH proj. no. 12,033

219 **St. Blasien im Schwarzwald, Germany (Benedictine abbey).**
Necrologium San-Blasianum ab annis 1597-1800. MS. Benediktinerabtei St. Paul im Lavantthal, Austria, codex 123/2. 138 f. Folio. Saec. 18.
Microfilm: MnCH proj. no. 11,698

220 **Sankt Lambrecht, Austria (Benedictine abbey).**
Necrologium vetustius monasterii S. Lamberti. MS. Universitätsbibliothek Graz, Austria, codex 325, f.106r-137r. Folio. Saec. 12.
Microfilm: MnCH proj. no. 26,219

221 **Sankt Lambrecht, Austria (Benedictine abbey).**
Necrologium recentius monasterii S. Lamberti. MS. Universitätsbibliothek Graz, Austria, codex 391, f.44v-74v. Folio. Saec. 15.
Microfilm: MnCH proj. no. 26,575

222 **Schroll, Beda, O.S.B.**
Necrologium des Benedictinerstiftes St. Paul im Lavantthal.
(*In* Archiv für vaterländische Geschichte und Topographie (Klagenfurt), 10. Jahrg.(1866), p. 33-240)
KAS

25. PENAL CODE

223 **Clement VI, Pope.**
Bulla de suspensione poenarum Benedictinarum. MS. Benediktinerabtei Melk, Austria, codex 3, f.167v. Folio. Saec. 14.
Microfilm: MnCH proj. no. 2124

224 **Commentarius in caput** 23 Regulae s. Benedicti: de correctione fraterna. MS. Benediktinerabtei Melk, Austria, codex 619, f.103r-108v. Quarto. Saec. 15.
Microfilm: MnCH proj. no. 1508

26. PERIODICALS

Here are listed periodicals which are wholly or for the most part Benedictine in substance.

225 **Benedictines.** v. 21- [1966-] Atchison, Kans. Mount St. Scholastica.
Continues Benedictine review.
KAM; KAS; MnCS

226 **Regulae Benedicti Studia.** v. 1- [1972-] Hildesheim, H. A. Gerstenberg.
InStme; MnCS; PLatS

227 **Tjurunga;** an Australasian Benedictine review. Benedictine Abbey, New Norsia, Australia. 1971-
MnCS; MoCo

27. POETRY

228 **Carmina de S. Benedicto,** de Ordine S. Benedicti, de Regula S. Benedicti, de vita S. Benedicti. MS. Benediktinerabtei Michaelbeuern, Austria, codex cart. 107, f.307v-320r. Quarto. Saec. 15.
Microfilm: MnCH proj. no. 11,593

229 **De Ordine Sancti Benedicti.** Metrice. MS. Benediktinerabtei Lambach, Austria, codex chart. 435, f.104v-105v. Saec. 15.
Microfilm: MnCH proj. no. 725

230 **Meissburger, Gerhard.**
Grundlagen zum Verständnis der deutschen Mönchsdichtung im 11. und 12. Jahrhundert. München, W. Fink, 1970.
331 p. 23 cm.
MnCS

231 **Regulae vivendi pro monachis.** Metrice. MS. Benediktinerabtei St. Peter, Salzburg, codex b.I.27, f.1r-94. Octavo. Saec. 15.
Microfilm: MnCH proj. no. 10,299

232 **Relatio de Ordine S. Benedicti.** Metrice. Benediktinerabtei St. Peter, Salzburg, codex a.VII.18, f.155v-156r. Quarto. Saec. 15.
Microfilm: MnCH proj. no. 10,142

233 **Scheuten, Paul.**
Das Mönchtum in der altfranzösischen Profandichtung (12.-14. Jahrhundert). Münster in Westfalen, Aschendorff, 1921.
xx, 124 p. 23 cm.
MnCS

234 **Versus rhythmici de Ordine S. Benedicti.** MS. Benediktinerabtei Melk, Austria, codex 1086, f.178-181. Duodecimo. Saec. 15.
Microfilm: MnCH proj. no. 1848

28. PRAYER CONFRATERNITIES

234a **Das Verbrüderungsbuch von St. Peter in Salzburg;** vollständige Faksimile-Ausgabe im Originalformat der Handschrift A 1 aus dem Archiv von St. Peter in Salzburg. Einführung: Karl Forstner.

Graz, Akademische Druck- u. Verlagsanstalt, 1974.
36 p. 39 leaves (facsim.) 40 cm. (Codices selecti phototypice impressi, LI)
MnCS

234b **Libri confraternitatum Sancti Galli,** Agiensis, Fabariensis. Edidit Paulus Piper. Berolini, apud Weidmannum, 1884.
vii, 550 p. 30 cm. (Monumenta Germaniae historica)
MnCS; PLatS

29. PRIVILEGES, ECCLESIASTICAL

235 **Anton, Hans Hubert.**
Studien zu den Klosterprivilegen der Päpste im frühen Mittelalter, unterbesonderer Berücksichtigung der Privilegierung von St. Maurice d'Agaune. Berlin, New York, Walter De Gruyter, 1975.
x, 172 p. 24 cm.
MnCS

235a **Beste, Ulric, O.S.B.**
De privilegiis Ord. 'S. Benedicti.
168 p. 28 cm. Cum indice.
Typescript, 1922.
MnCS(Archives)

236 **Constitutiones vel actus summorum pontificum,** ex quibus privilegia enerrata desumpta sunt. Monasterii Guestfalorum, Aschendorff, 1918.
13 leaves, 23 cm.
PLatS

236a **De privilegiis Cassinensium brevis relatio.** Monasterii Guestfalorum, e Typographeo Ascneodrffiano, 1917.
vii, 44 p. 24 cm.
Constitutiones vel actus summorum pontificum, ex quibus privilegia enarrata desumpta sunt. 1918. 14 p.
MnCS(Archives)

237 **Geiser, Georgius.**
Privilegia Ordinis S. Benedicti, quaestionibus theologico-juridicis illustrata. MS. Benediktinerabtei Altenburg, Austria, codex AB 13 F 37. 149 f. Quarto. Saec. 17.
Microfilm: MnCH proj. no. 6536

237a **Hirsch, Hans.**
Die Klosterimmunität seit dem Investiturstreit. Weimar, H. Böhlau, 1913.
viii, 229 p. 22 cm.
Reprinted with Nachwort by Heinrich Büttner, 1967.
MnCS

238 **Privilegia Congregationis S. Justinae** de Padua seu Cassinensis olim concessa et ad aetatis nostrae indigentia selecta et accommodata, synodoque reverendorum abbatum O.S.B. mense octobri 1925

celebratae proposita. Romae, ex Typographia "Campitell," 1925.
21 p. 28 cm.
MnCS (Archives)

239 **Schreiber, Georg.**
Kurie und Kloster im 12. Jahrhundert; Studien zur Privilegierung. Stuttgart, F. Enke, 1910.
2 vols. 23 cm.
MnCS

30. VISITATION

240 **Bernardus de Kreyburg.**
Epistola ad visitatores monasteriorum Ordinis S. Benedicti, per provinciam Salzburgensem. MS. Benediktinerabtei Melk, Austria, codex 896, f.195v-196r. Quarto. Saec. 15.
Microfilm: MnCH proj. no. 1715

241 **Brevis pro danda charta** (id est instructione) monasteriis visitandis. MS. Benediktinerabtei Melk, Austria, codex 959, f.194r–197v. Quarto. Saec. 15.
Microfilm: MnCH proj. no. 1762

242 **De officiis visitatorum monasteriorum.**
MS. Benediktinerabtei Melk, Austria, codex 1093, f.421-427. Duodecimo. Saec. 15.
Microfilm: MnCH proj. no. 1846

243 **De visitationibus monasteriorum paraenetica quaedam,** bullae, etc. MS. Benediktinerabtei Melk, Austria, codex 1087, f.152-175. Duodecimo. Saec. 15.
Microfilm: MnCH proj. no. 1842

244 **Dubia circa Regulam S. Benedicti** resoluta ab abbate S. Sabinae per Germaniam delegato super reformatione O.S.B. MS. Benediktinerabtei Admont, Austria, codex 860, f.94r-118v. Octavo. Saec. 17.
Microfilm: MnCH proj. no. 9872

245 **Guidelines for visitation in the American-Cassinese Federation,** approved by the 39th Ordinary General Chapter, 1974 [Peru, Ill., St. Bede Abbey Press, 1974].
27 p. 21 cm.
MnCS

246 **Ludovicus, patriarcha Aquleensis.**
Epistola ad Conradum, monachum Mellicensem, qua eum ad visitandum et reformandum monasterium Obernburgense invitat. MS. Benediktinerabtei Melk, Austria, codex 896, f.VIIIr. Quarto. Saec. 15.
Microfilm: MnCH proj. no. 1715

246a **Mandatum Leonardi episcopi dioecesis Pataviensis . . .** de visitatione et refor-

matione Ordinis S. Benedicti. MS.
Vienna, Schottenstift, codex 152, f.163r–
163v. Octavo. Saec. 15.
Microfilm: MnCH proj. no. 4071

246b **Martinus, abbot of Schottenstift, Vienna.**
Sermo in visitatione monasteriorum
O.S.B. in provincia Salisburgensi. MS.
Vienna, Nationalbibliothek, codex 4969,
f.103r-108v. Quarto. Saec. 15.
Microfilm: MnCH proj. no. 18,141

246c **Memoriale visitationis Mellicensis anno**
1451 institutus. MS. Benediktinerabtei
Seitenstetten, Austria, codex 88, f.210r-
231v. Octavo. Saec. 15.
Microfilm: MnCH proj. no. 897

246d **Modus visitandi monasteria.** MS. Benediktinerabtei Melk, Austria, codex 785,
f.162r-177v. Quarto. Saec. 15.
Microfilm: MnCH proj. no. 1627

246e **Modus visitandi monasteria.** Modus
agendorum in visitatione facta inquisitione. MS. Vienna, Schottenstift, codex
4071, f.185r-203v. Octavo. Saec. 15.
Microfilm: MnCH proj. no. 4071

246f **Quaedam interrogatoria in visitationibus monasteriorum fienda.** MS. Benediktinerabtei Melk, Austria, codex 911,
f. 324r–335r. Quarto. Saec. 15.
Microfilm: MnCH proj. no. 1729

247 **St. Blasien im Schwarzwald, Germany
(Benedictine abbey).**
Ordo visitandi patres monasterii S. Blasii
in Silva Nigra extra conventum degentes.
MS. Benediktinerabtei St. Paul im Lavant-
thal, Austria, codex 67/6. 32 f. Octavo.
Saec. 17.
Microfilm: MnCH proj. no. 12,613

248 **Schlitbacher, Johannes, O.S.B.**
Carta visitatorum monasterii S. Petri.
MS. Benediktinerabtei St. Peter, Salzburg,
codex b.XI.19. f.30r-36v. Folio. Saec. 15.
Microfilm: MnCH proj. no. 10,671

249 **Schlitbacher, Johannes, O.S.B.**
Epistola ad Nicolaum de Cusa, pro
mitiganda bulla visitationis monasteri-
orum. MS. Benediktinerabtei Melk,
Austria, codex 1093, f.431–432.
Duodecimo. Saec. 15.
Microfilm: MnCH proj. no. 1846

250 **Schlitbacher, Johannes, O.S.B.**
Forma de modo precedendi in visitatione
monasteriorum. MS. Benediktinerabtei
Melk, Austria, codex 959, f.189v-191r.
Quarto. Saec. 15.
Microfilm: MnCH proj. no. 1762

251 **Summa faciendae visitationis in monasteriis S. Benedicti.** Collatiuncula
facienda tempore visitationis. Alia
exhortatio tempore visitationis. MS.
Benediktinerabtei Melk, Austria, codex
1754, p. 1-21. Duodecimo. Saec. 15.
Microfilm: MnCH proj. no. 2066

31. VOCATION

252 **Leclercq, Jean, O.S.B.**
Moines et moniales, ont-ils un avenir?
Bruxelles, Editions Lumen Vitae [1971].
263 p. 19 cm.
MnCS

253 **Steindl-Rast, David, O.S.B.**
Why a man becomes a monk, by David,
monk of Mt. Saviour. [n.p., 196-?]
[15] p. 26 cm.
KAS

II. ST. BENEDICT

1. GENERAL WORKS

254 **Alameda, Julian, O.S.B.**
San Benito. Prólogo de Justo Perez de Urbel. 2. ed. [Madrid] Escelicer [1961].
199 p. 19 cm.
KAS

255 **Aymard, Paul, O.S.B.**
Un homme nommé Benoît. [Paris] Desclée, De Brouwer [1977].
217 illus. 26 cm.
MnCS

256 **Casel, Odo, O.S.B.**
Benedikt von Nursia als Pneumatiker.
(*In* Heilige Ueberlieferung. Münster, 1938. p. 96-123)
PLatS

257 **Chronica Sancti Benedicti Casinensis.**
(*In* Monumenta Germaniae historica. Scriptores rerum Longobardicarum et Italicarum. Berlin, 1878. p. 467-489)
MnCS

258 **Christophe, Jacques.**
Saint Benoît par mont et par vaux. Paris, Spes [c 1969].
158 p.
MoCo

259 **Delisle, Léopold Victor.**
Le livre de Jean de Stavelot sur Saint Benoît. Paris, Imp. Nationale, 1908.
35 p. plate, 28 cm.
MnCS

260 **De origine et parentela S. Benedicti abbatis.** MS. Benediktinerabtei St. Peter, Salzburg, codex b.IV.11, f.203v-205r. Octavo. Saec. 15-16.
Microfilm: MnCH proj. no. 10,393

261 **Epistola et miraculum beatissimi Benedicti ad s. Remigium,** episcopum Remensem. MS. Benediktinerabtei Melk, Austria, codex 525, f.272v. Folio. Saec. 15.
Microfilm: MnCH proj. no. 1472

262 **Flavius, Brother, C.S.C.**
Melody in their hearts; a story of Saint Benedict. Notre Dame, Ind., Dujarie Press [1961].
92 p. illus.
MoCo

263 **Heufelder, Emmanuel Maria, O.S.B.**
St. Benedikt von Nursia und die Kirche.
(*In* Daniélou, Jean. Sentire Ecclesiam. Freiburg i.B., 1961. p. 176-184)
PLatS

264 **Hrabanus Maurus, O.S.B.**
Liber contra eos, qui repugnant institutis beati patris Benedicti. MS. Benediktiner-

abtei Göttweig, Austria, codex 54, f.1r-11v. Folio. Saec. 12.
Microfilm: MnCH proj. no. 3342

265 **Hrabanus Maurus, O.S.B.**
Opusculum contra eos qui repugnant institutis b. p. Benedicti. MS. Benediktinerabtei Melk, Austria, codex 1915, f.66r-77v. Quarto. Saec. 15.
Microfilm: MnCH proj. no. 2199

266 **Joachim, O. Cist., abbot of Fiore.**
De vita sancti Benedicti et de Officio Divino secundum eius doctrinam. Barcelona, Biblioteca Balmes, 1953.
90 p. 24 cm.
MnCS

267 **João, dos Prazeres, O.S.B.**
O principe dos patriarcas S. Bento. [Lisboa, 1683–1690].
KAS (v. 1)

268 **Knowles, David, O.S.B.**
St. Benedict.
(*In* Walsh, James, S.J. Spirituality through the centuries. 1964. p. 57-71)
PLatS

269 **Leccisotti, Thomas, O.S.B.**
Documenti per la storia del Monastero di S. Benedetto in Norcia.
(*In* Analecta monastica, 7. ser. 1965. p. 175–228)
PLatS

270 **Leclercq, Jean, O.S.B.**
Aux sources de la spiritualité occidentale. Paris, Editions du Cerf, 1964.
317 p. 21 cm.
PLatS

271 **Leclercq, Jean, O.S.B.**
Monasticism and St. Benedict.
(*In* Monastic studies. Berryville, Va., v. 1(1963), p. 9–23)
PLatS

272 **Lentini, Anselmo, O.S.B.**
Vita e missione sociale di S. Benedetto.
(*In* La bonifica benedettina. p. 195-199)
PLatS

273 **Marechaux, Bernard, O.S.B.Oliv.**
Saint Benoît; sa Règle, sa doctrine spirituelle. 12. éd. Paris, G. Beauchesne, 1918.
viii, 194 p.
ILSP; KAS

274 **Matt, Leonard von.**
Saint Benedict [by] Leonard von Matt and Stephen Hilpisch. Translated from the German by Ernest Graf. Chicago, H. Regnery, 1961.
226 p. illus. 25 cm.
CaMWiSb; ILSP; InStme; MnCS; MoCo; NdRi; PLatS

275 **Meyenschein, Benedikt, O.S.B.**
Stella benedictina quinque radii corusca: quorum primus exhibet Regulam . . . Benedicti cum breviore commentario; alte vitam ejusdem . . . Hildesii, Wilh. Theod. Schlegel [1729].
755, [10] p. 14 cm.
KAS

276 **Meyvaert Paul.**
Benedict, Gregory, Bede and others. London, Variorum Reprints, 1977.
388 p. illus. 24 cm.
Reprint of 16 studies published between 1955 and 1976. English or French.
InStme

277 **Miserey, Marie de.**
Saint Benedict. Translated by Julie Kernan. New York, Macmillan, 1962.
112 p. 18 cm.
MdRi; MoCo; NdRi

278 **Neuzil, Procopius Charles, O.S.B.**
Svaty Benedikt, ucitel, apostol a vudce. Chicago, Ill., Tiskarny Ceskych Benedictinu [1932].
224 p. illus. 19 cm.
MnCS

279 **Nigg, Walter.**
Benedikt und seine Regel.
(*In* his: Von Heiligen und Gottesnarren. Freiburg, 1960)
PLatS

280 **Ortus s. Benedicti.** MS. Benediktinerabtei Michaelbeuern, Austria, codex cart. 107, f.305r-306r. Quarto. Saec. 15.
Microfilm: MnCH proj. no. 11,593

281 **Ortus s. Benedicti abbatis.** MS. Vienna, Nationalbibliothek, codex 4119, f.106v-108v. Sextodecimo. Saec. 16.
Microfilm: MnCH proj. no. 14,429

282 **Ortus s. Benedicti.** Incipit: Justinianus imperator. MS. Vienna, Nationalbibliothek, codex 11698, f.1r-4r. Octavo. Saec. 17.
Microfilm: MnCH proj. no. 19,856

283 **Paul VI, Pope.**
Beata pacis visio. Montecassino, Bollettino Diocesano, 1964.
InFer

284 **Paul VI, Pope.**
The address of His Holiness Paul VI at the Abbey of Montecassino: Brief proclaiming St. Benedict patron of Europe.
(*In* Pax; the quarterly review of the Benedictines of Prinknash, v. 54, p. 151–180)
PLatS

285 **Paul VI, Pope.**
Discorso di S.S. Paolo VI, dal Cenobio di Montecassino, in occasione della consacra-zione della ricostruita basilica, e proclamazione de S. Benedetto a patrono di Europa. [Roma, Tip. Scopel, 1964 or 65?].
[9] p. 20 cm.
KAS

286 **Praeconia et laudes S. Benedicti.** MS. Benediktinerabtei Melk, Austria, codex 1087, f.59-61. Duodecimo. Saec. 15.
Microfilm: MnCH proj. no. 1842

287 **Regla de el gran patriarcha S. Benito, nuevamente traducida.** Madrid, Josef Herrera Batanero, 1791.
248 p. illus. 15 cm.
Xerographic copy.
Contents: 1. Aprobación y confirmación . . . por San Gregorio el Grande. 2. Regla . . . 3. Résumen de las excelencias de el-gran patriarca S. Benito, de su Santa Regla, y sagrada religión . . .
MnCS

287a **Renaudin, Paul, O.S.B.**
Saint Benoît dans la chaire française: panégyriques par Bossuet, évêque de Meaux, Fléchier, évêque de Nimes, Massillon, évêque de Clermont. Besançon, Jacques et Demontrond, 1932.
80 p. 19 cm.
KAS

288 **Saint Benedict and the Benedictine life,** by a monk of Ampleforth.
London, Catholic Truth Society [n.d.].
20 p. 16 cm. (Catholic Truth Society pamphlets, B 475 [v. 7].
PLatS

289 **Senger, Basilius,** 1920-
Sankt Benedikt; Prophet und Vater vieler Völker. Essen, Fredebeutl & Koenen [1963].
168 p. 19 cm.
KAS; MnCS; PLatS

290 **Sermo amplius de insignibus seu armis gentilitiis** s. p. Benedicti eorumque morali interpretatione. MS. Benediktinerabtei Melk, Austria, codex 525, f.268r-272r. Folio. Saec. 15.
Microfilm: MnCH proj. no. 1472

291 **Staley, Austin, O.S.B.**
Saint Benedict and the American Benedict; a Benedictine perspective on American fatherhood. Morristown, N.J., Delbarton School [196-].
24 p. 24 cm.
KAS; PLatS

292 **Sulger, Arsenius, O.S.B.**
Vita divi Benedicti, monachorum patriarchae. Colore didactico renovata. [St. Gall, Switzerland] typis Monasterij S. Galli, 1691.
259 p. 12 cm.
MnCS

293 **Tractätlein von der Verehrung des heiligen Vater Benedikt.** MS. Benediktinerinnenabtei Nonnberg, Salzburg, codex 23 E 16. 405 p. Octavo. Saec. 17(1660). Microfilm: MnCH proj. no. 10,924

294 **Turbessi, Giuseppe, O.S.B.**
Ascetismo e monachesimo in S. Benedetto. Roma, Editrice Studium [1965].
220 p. 17 cm.
PLatS

295 **Vogüé, Adalbert de, O.S.B.**
Autour de Saint Benoît; la Régle en son temps et dans le nôtre. Begrolles en Mauges, Abbaye de Bellefontaine, 1975.
158 p. 21 cm.
InStme

296 **Weakland, Rembert George, O.S.B.**
S. Benedetto, patrona d'Europa.
(*In* Il Sacro Speco, luglio-agosto, 1970, p. 105-106)
PLatS

2. ANNIVERSARIES

a. 1880

297 **Celesia, Pietro Geremia Michaelangelo, O.S.B.**
Pel XIV centenario del patriarca S. Benedetto ricordi storici. Palermo, C. Tamburello, 1880.
25 p. 21 cm.
"Estratto dalla Sicilia Cattolica."
KAS

298 **Monte Cassino, Italy (Benedictine abbey).**
Monumenta litterarum ad consecrationem turris sanctissimi p. Benedicti pertinentia et ad conventum rev. morum dd. abbatum in archicoenobio Montis Casini habitum sacro Pentecostes festo, anno 1880. Typis Montis Casini [1880?].
32 p. 24 cm.
KAS; PLatS

299 **Tosti, Luigi, O.S.B.**
Scritti vari. Roma, Tip. della Camera dei Deputati, 1886-1890.
2 v. 22 cm.
KAS

b. 1947

300 **XIV centenario di San Benito;** exposicion historica de la Orden Benedictine en la Biblioteca Nacional. Catalogo. Madrid, 1948.
70 p. illus., plates.
MoCo

c. 1980

300a **American Benedictine Review.**
Sesquimillenium of St. Benedict–480.
The March, 1980, issue (vol. 31, no. 1) is devoted entirely to honor the 1500th year of the birth of St. Benedict, with articles by seven scholars on Benedictine life and history. 152 p.
MnCS

300b **Benedictines (periodical). Atchison, Kans.**
Themes in the Rule of St. Benedict: North America, 1980. Anniversary issue, 480–1980, vol. XXXV, 2, 1980, Fall–Winter.
200 p. plates, 24 cm.
This special issue consists of 13 articles, mostly by Benedictine Sisters.
KAM; MnCS

300c **Die Benediktregel in Bayern:** Ausstellung der Bayerischen Staatsbibliothek, 29 November 1980–10 Januar 1981. München [Bayerische Staatsbibliothek] 1980.
79 p. 16 plates (part col.) 22 cm.
MnCS

300d **Cistercium; revista monastica.**
XV centenario del nacimiento de San Benito. [Anniversary issue, 480–1980], año XXXII, no. 158, Julio–Dicèmbre, 1980, p. 251–505.
This "num. extraordinario" consists of ten articles written for the occasion.
MnCS

300e **Einsiedeln, Switzerland** (Benedictine Abbey). Bibliothek, Secundum Regulam S. Benedicti; Austellung von Handschriften 8./17.Jh. zum Gedenkjahr des Hl. Benedikt, 480–1980. Einsiedeln, 1980.
[24] p. 20 cm.
MnCS

300f **Farmer, Hugh, O.S.B., ed.**
Benedict's disciples; a commemorative volume of the fifteeth centenary of the birth of Saint Benedict. Leominster, Herefordshire, England, 1980.
x, 368 p. 4 plates, 2 maps.
MnCS

300g **Hacia una relectura de la Regla de San Benito;** XVII Semana de Estudios Monasticos (XV centenario del nacimiento de San Benito, 480-1980). Abadia de Silos, 1980.
476 p. 23 cm. (Studia Silensia, VII)
MnCS

300h **Häusling, Angelus A., O.S.B.**
Das Buch der Benediktregel in der Abtei Maria Laach; eine kleine Ausstellung im

Benediktus-Jahr 1980. Maria Laach, 1980.
43 p. 21 cm.
Als Manuskript gedruckt.
MnCH

300i **London, England. British Library.**
The Benedictines in Britain. [London]
The British Library [1980].
111 p. 60 illus. (mostly facsims.), 4 col.
plates, 23 cm. (British Library series no. 3)
A publication issued by the British
Library in conjunction with an exhibition
of the same title held in the King's Library,
July 11 to November 30, 1980.
Contents: 1. A rule for beginners; 2. A
school of the Lord's service; 3. The work of
God; 4. Guests; 5. Benedictine libraries and
writers; 6. Dissolution; 7. Rebirth; 8. List
of 128 exhibits.
MnCS

300j **Moines au present, année Saint Benoît,**
1980.
(*In* Communautés et liturgies [1979].
p. 377–488)
MoCo

300k **Olmert, Michael.**
Scholars celebrate 1,500 years of
Benedictine vision.
(*In* Smithsonian, June, 1980, p. 80–87)
MnCS

300l **Ora et labora;** revista beneditina de
liturgia & pastoral (Singeverga, Portugal).
Bento de Nursia, padroeiro de Europa.
[Anniversary issue, 480–1980], ano XXVI,
no. 3–4, Julho–Dez., 1980, p. 153–320.
This special issue consists of nine articles
written for the occasion.
MnCS

300m**Oxford, England. University. Bodleian
Library.**
The Benedictines and the book; an exhibition to commemorate the fifteenth
centenary of the birth of St. Benedict,
A.D., 480-1980. Oxford, Bodleian Library
[1980].
viii, 68 p. 20 cm.
MnCS

300n **Plante, Julian G.**
Saint Benedict, Patron of All Europe;
public lecture, commemorating the fifteen-
hundreth anniversary of St. Benedict, at
the University of Kansas, Lawrence. Sponsored by the KU Mediaeval Society and the
Dept. of History–3 April 1980.
21 p. 28 cm.
Photocopy of typescript.
MnCH

300o **XV Centenario della nascita de S. Benedetto,** 480-1980: "Ora et labora." Testi-
monianze Benedettine nella Biblioteca

Apostolica Vaticana. Città del Vaticano,
Biblioteca Apostolica Vaticana, 1980.
xiii, 91 p. 24 col. plates.
MnCS

300p **San Benedetto agli uomini d'oggi;**
miscellanea di studi per il XV centenario
della nascita di San Benedetto (Benedictina, anno 28, 1981, numerico unico)
KAS; MnCS

300q **La Vie Spirituelle (periodical).**
Benoît moine. [Anniversary issue, 480–
1980], 62e année, no. 639, Juillet–Août,
1980, p. 484-671.
This special issue consists of ⌣ight articles written for the occasion.
MnCS

3. ART

301 **Aymard, Paul, O.S.B.**
Un homme nommé Benoît. [Paris]
Desclée De Brouwer [1977].
217 p. illus. 26 cm.
The miniatures in color are all taken
from Codex lat. Vaticanus 1202 (9th cen-
tury).
MnCS

302 **Carli, Enzo.**
L'Abbazia di Monteoliveto. Milano, Elec-
ta Editrice, 1962.
185 p. 98 plates (part col.) 30 cm.
Most of the plates portray the life of St.
Benedict.
MnCS

303 **Effigies S. Benedicti,** Mauri et Placidi.
MS. Benediktinerstift St. Peter,
Salzburg, codex b.VI.51, f. 10r. Quarto.
Saec. 16.
Microfilm: MnCH proj. no. 10,505.

304 **La cripta di S. Benedetto in Norcia.**
[Valle di Pompei, Scuola tipografica
pontificia pei figli dei carcerati fondata
da Bartolo Longo, 1913].
23 p. illus. 31 cm.
InStme

305 **Gregorius et miracula sanctissimi patris
Benedicti** . . . Romae, sumptu Paullini
Arnolfini Lucen., 1596.
51 plates, 41 cm.
KAS; MnCS

306 **Huber, Michael, O.S.B.**
Die "Vita illustrata Sancti Benedicti" in
Handschriften und Kupferstichen.
(*In* Studien und Mitteilungen zur
Geschichte des Benediktiner-Ordens und
seiner Zweige. Bd. 48(1930), p. 4-82,
433–440)
Offprint.
KAS

307 **Pons, Blaise, O.S.B.**
Saint Benoît. Illustrations de Robert
Rigot. Paris, Editions Fleurus, 1956.
48 p. 164 illus. 27 cm.
MnCS; PLatS

308 **Vita sancti patris Benedicti imaginibus**
(101) depicta. MS. Vienna, Schottenstift,
codex 173. 14 f. Folio. Saec. 15.
Microfilm: MnCH proj. no. 4044

4. BIOGRAPHY

309 **Beekman, Andreas, O.S.B.**
Het leven van de heilige Benedictus in
het licht van zijn tijd, 480-547. Deutekom,
Heiloo, 1950.
209 p. plates, 25 cm.
PLatS

310 **Bucelin, Gabriel, O.S.B.**
Kurzer Inhalt des Lebens des heiligsten
und wunderbarlieben Vaters und Patriarchen Benedicti. Verteitschter abgeschrieben durch P. Maximinum Rolandinum, O.S.B. MS. Benediktinerinnenabtei
Nonnberg, Salzburg, codex 23 B 23. 211 f.
Quarto. Saec. 17.
Microfilm: MnCH proj. no. 10,843

311 **Compendium vitae S. Benedicti,** item
quaedem de origine vitae religiosae. MS.
Benediktinerabtei Melk, Austria, codex
1560, f. 131v-132r. Duodecimo. Saec. 15.
Microfilm: MnCH proj. no. 2225

312 **Gregory I, Pope.**
[Vita s. Benedicti]
Dialogorum liber secundus.
For editions and translations of this
work see under Gregory I, Pope, "Vita s.
Benedicti" in the Author Part.

313 **Leben des hl. Benedict.** MS. Benediktinerinnenabtei Nonnberg, Salzburg, codex
23 C 3, f.88r-156v. Quarto. Saec. 16.
Microfilm: MnCH proj. no. 10,844

314 **Massini, Carlo.**
Compendio della vita di S. Benedetto,
abate, patriarca dei monaci d'occidente . . .
estratta delle opere del P. D. Carlo Massini
. . . Tipografia di Monte Cassino, 1899.
37 p. 16 cm.
KAS

315 **Navrátil, Jan Sarkander, O.S.B.**
Zivot Sv. Otce Benedikta, reholnictva na
západe patriarchy a zákonodárce . . .
Brune, Dkoly B.S.P., 1880.
347 p. 17 cm.
MnCS

316 **Primm, Orrin, C.S.C.**
The mountain of God; a life of St.
Benedict. Illustrated by Leslie Johnson.
Valatie, N.Y., Holy Cross Press, 1965.

104 p. illus. (Saints who changed history
series)
MoCo

317 **Salvi, Guglielmo.**
San Benedetto, "Il Padre dell'Europa."
Subiaco, Tipografia dei Monasteri, 1948.
428 p. illus. 22 cm.
PLatS

318 **Senger, Basilius, O.S.B.**
Sankt Benedikt; Prophet und Vater
vieler Völker. Essen, Fredebeul & Koenen
[1963].
168 p. illus. 19 cm.
MnCS

319 **Sulger, Arsenius, O.S.B.**
Vita divi Benedicti, monachorum patriarchae. Colore didactico renovata. [St. Gall,
Switzerland] typis Monasterij S. Galli,
1691.
259 p. 12 cm.
MnCS

320 **Ueber das Leben und Orden des hl.** Mann
Gottes Benedicti. MS. Benediktinerabtei
St. Peter, Salzburg, codex b.VII.2, f.74r-
183v. Quarto. Saec. 17.
Microfilm: MnCH proj. no. 10,511

321 **La vie et la Règle de Saint Benoît.**
[Dirigée par les moines de la Pierre-qui-
Vire de préparé par la R. M. Elisabeth de
Solms]. [Bruges] Desclée, De Brouwer
[1965].
319 p. 17 cm.
PLatS

322 **Vie populaire de Saint Benoît.** [Abbaye
de Saint Benoît, Maredsous, 1949].
71 p.
CaQStB

5. DRAMA

323 **College of St. Benedict, St. Joseph,
Minn.**
So let your light shine; annual pageant.
[Text by Angeline Dufner].
Reprint from Saint Benedict's Quarterly,
June 1957.
MnCS

6. FICTION

324 **Christophe, Jacques.**
Saint Benoît par monts et par vaux.
[Paris, Spes, 1969].
158 p. 18 cm.
MnCS

7. INFLUENCE

325 **Battaglia, Dante.**
S. Benedetto di Norcia; l'apostolo sociale
e i suoi discepoli. Subiaco, Tipografia dei
Monasteri, 1928.

134 p. plates, 21 cm.
MnCS

326 **Lentini, Anselmo, O.S.B.**
Vita e missione sociale di S. Benedetto.
(*In* La Bonifica benedettina, p. 195-199)
PLatS

8. JUVENILE LITERATURE

327 **Paris. Saint-Louis-du-Temple (abbey of Benedictine nuns).**
Great Saint Benedict as told to little ones, by B. Temple. [Montreal, Les Ateliers St.-Grégoire, 1947].
21 p. illus. 18 cm.
MnCS

328 **Willett, Franciscus, Brother, C.S.C.**
The mountain of God; a life of St. Benedict [by] Orrin Primm. Illustrated by Leslie Johnson. Valatie, N.Y., Holy Cross Press, 1965.
104 p. illus. 23 cm.
MnCS

9. MIRACLES

329 **Erzählung mehrerer Wunderthaten des hl.** Benedikt. MS. Benediktinerabtei St. Peter, Salzburg, codex b.VII.2, f.184r-218r. Quarto. Saec. 17.
Microfilm: MnCH proj. no. 10,511

330 **Gregory I, Pope, Saint.**
Life and miracles of St. Benedict.
For editions and translations of this work see under Gregory I, Pope, "Vita S. Benedicti" in the Author Part.

331 **Miraculum ex Legenda Henricii imperatoris de apparitione S. Benedicti.** MS. Benediktinerabtei Göttweig, Austria, codex 375, f.175r. Folio. Saec. 15.
Microfilm: MnCH proj. no. 3643

10. NOVENAS

332 **Ampleforth Abbey, England.**
Novena to Saint Benedict. 2nd ed. Malton, Ampleforth, n.d.
unpaged.
AStb

333 **Novena en honor del glorioso patriarca San Benito,** seguida de un triduo en honor de Santa Escolastica. Mexico, D.F., Padres Benedictinos, 1959.
46 p. 15 cm.
KAS

334 **Novena en honor del glorioso patriarca San Benito.** Seguida de un triduo en honor de Santa Escolástica. 6. ed. Burgos, Abadia Benedictina de Santo Domingo de Silos, 1944.
46 p. plates. 14 cm.
MnCS

335 **Novena en honor del gloriosoo patriarca San Benito,** sequida de un triduo en honor de Santa Escolastica y den Santa Gertrudis. 5. ed. Buenos Aires, Padres Benedictinos, 1945.
76 p. 14 cm.
MnCS

11. POETRY

336 **Aldhelm, Saint.**
Metra de s. Benedicto abbate. MS. Benediktinerabtei Melk, Austria, codex 1087, f.57-58. Duodecimo. Saec. 15.
Microfilm: MnCH proj. no. 1842

337 **Carmen ad S. Benedictum.** MS. Benediktinerabtei Melk, Austria, codex 1646, f. 243r. Sextodecimo. Saec. 15.
Microfilm: MnCH proj. no. 1996

338 **Carmen de S. Benedicto et est tractum de secundo libro dialogorum S. Gregorii papae.** MS. Benediktinerabtei St. Peter, Salzburg, codex b.VIII.16, f. 247r-248r. Folio. Saec. 15.
Microfilm: MnCH proj. no. 10,541

339 **Carmen de vita Benedicti abbatis.** Incipit: Puer petens heremum sancte Benedicte. MS. Benediktinerabtei Melk, Austria, codex 1087. f.62-64. Duodecimo. Saec. 15.
Microfilm: MnCH proj. no. 1842

340 **Carmen de vita S. Benedicti.**MS. Benediktinerabtei Michaelbeuern, Austria, codex cart. 107, f.329r–330r. Quarto. Saec. 15.
Microfilm: MnCH proj. no. 11,593

341 **Carmina in honorem S. Benedicti.** MS. Benediktinerabtei St. Peter, Salzburg, codex b.VI.51, f.107r-111v. Quarto. Saec. 16.
Microfilm: MnCH proj. no. 10,505

342 **Costalta, Josephus, O.S.B.**
In divum Benedictum elogia. Romae, Fabius de Falco, 1665.
[16], 210, [4] p. 20 cm.
KAS; MnCS; PLatS

343 **Hymnus de sancto Benedicto.** Incipit: Preclarum tate tibi vir sine fine beate. MS. Benediktinerabtei Altenburg, Austria, codex AB 13 A 22, p. 212–214. Folio. Saec. 12.
Microfilm: MnCH proj. no. 6361

344 **Hymnus de S. Benedicto.** MS. Benediktinerabtei Michaelbeuern, Austria, codex cart. 113, f.159r-159v. Octavo. Saec. 16.
Microfilm: MnCH proj. no. 11,612

345 **Hymnus in S. Benedictum.** Incipit: Mortis invicte Criste vernalis Benedicte. MS.

Benediktinerabtei St. Peter, Salzburg, codex b.VI.7, f.309r.
Microfilm: MnCH proj. no. 10,466

346 **Martinelli, Thoma Angelico, O.P.**
Sanctissimi viri Benedicti abbatis monachorum in oris occiduis patriarchae acta latinis carminibus exornata. Parmae, ex Imperiali Typographeo. 1808.
92 p. 23 cm.
MnCS

347 **Metra de progenie et vita S. Benedicti.**
MS. Benediktinerabtei Melk, Austria, codex 1087, f.58-59. Duodecimo. Saec. 15.
Microfilm: MnCH proj. no. 1842

348 **Metra de vita S. Benedicti.** Incipit: Confratri dulci Simoni. MS. Vienna, Nationalbibliothek, codex 4117, f.29r-33v. Sextodecimo. Saec. 16.
Microfilm: MnCH proj. no. 17,296

349 **Petrus de Rosenheim, O.S.B.**
Versus de vita S. Benedicti. MS. Benediktinerabtei Melk, Austria, codex 1153, f.36r-38v. Quarto. Saec. 15.
Microfilm: MnCH proj. no. 1862
For other manuscript copies of this item see under Petrus von Rosenheim in the Author Part.

350 **Schlitpacher, Johannes, O.S.B.**
Memoriale breve vitae S. Benedicti. MS. Benediktinerabtei Melk, Austria, codex 662, f.140v-141r. Quarto. Saec. 15.
Microfilm: MnCH proj. no. 1532

351 **Versus de S. Benedicto.** Incipit: Vas reparat Benedictus. Benediktinerabtei Melk, Austria, codex 673, f.284v. Quarto. Saec. 15.
Microfilm: MnCH proj. no. 1540

352 **Vita patris nostri Benedicti sub brevibus metris comprehensa.** MS. Benediktinerabtei Kremsmünster, Austria, codex 268, f.39r-43v. Saec. 15.
Microfilm: MnCH proj. no. 252

353 **Vita sancti Benedicti.** Metrice. MS. Benediktinerabtei Lambach, Austria, codex chart. 453, f.59r-59v. Saec. 15.
Microfilm: MnCH proj. no. 740

354 **Vita S. Benedicti picta metrice,** scripta 1444. MS. Benediktinerabtei Melk, Austria, codex 1087, f.43-50. Duodecimo. Saec. 15.
Microfilm: MnCH proj. no. 1087

12. POPULAR DEVOTIONS

355 **Dusmet, Giuseppe Benedetto, O.S.B.**
S. Benedetto e il mese di maggio; lettera di Monsignor Arcivescovo di Catania ai suoi diocesani. [Monte Cassino, 1880].

11 p. 23 cm.
PLatS

13. PRAYER BOOKS

356 **Grégoire, Reginald, O.S.B.**
Prières liturgiques médiévales en l'honneur de Saint Benoît, de Sainte Scolastique et de Saint Maur.
(*In* Analecta monastica, 7. sér., 1965. p. 1-85)
PLatS

357 **Morrall, John Alphonsus Maria, O.S.B.**
A manual of devotions to our holy father Saint Benedict, abbot and patriarch of the western monks; to his sister Saint Scholastica, virgin & abbess, and to all saints of his holy order. London, Catholic Publishing & Bookselling Co., 1861.
235 p. illus. 16 cm.
InStme

358 **Oratio de S. Benedicto.** MS. Benediktinerabtei Melk, Austria, codex 1557, f. 152v. Duodecimo. Saec. 15.
Microfilm: MnCH proj. no. 1955

359 **Oratio s. patris Benedicti.** Incipit: Dignari mihi Domine. MS. Benediktinerabtei Melk, Austria, codex 791, f.179v. Quarto. Saec. 15.
Microfilm: MnCH proj. no. 1629

360 **Studerus, Leopold, O.S.B.**
Benediktus-Büchlein; oder, Regel- und Gebetbüchlein für Verehrer und Oblaten des hl. Benediktus . . . Einsiedeln, Benziger, 1904.
256 p. illus. 11 cm.
IdCoS; MnCS

14. RELICS

361 **Brettes, Ferdinand.**
Catena Floriacensis de existentia corporis Sancti Benedicti in Galliis . . . Paris, Victor Palmé, 1880.
284 p. 24 cm.
MnCS

361a **Meyvaert, Paul.**
L'invention des reliques Cassiniennes de Saint Benoît en 1484.
50 p. 24 cm.
(*In* his: Benedict, Gregory, Bede and others. London, 1977)
InStme; MnCS

15. SERMONS

362 **Bradley, Benedict Francis, O.S.B.**
St. Benedict of Nursia; address delivered in the Catholic Hour, August 10, 1930.
(*In* Connell, F. J. Four religious founders. Washington, 1931. p. 13-23)
PLatS

363 **Guerric, of Igny, O.C.S.O.**
     Two sermons for the Feast of St.
     Benedict.
     (*In* Monastic studies, v. 3, p. 1-17)
     Edited, translated and annotated by
     monks of Mount St. Bernard Abbey,
     England.
     PLatS

364 **Petrus, bishop of Ostia.**
     Sermo in vigilia s.p.n. Benedicti. MS.
     Benediktinerabtei Göttweig, Austria,
     codex 375, f.176r-178v. Folio Saec. 15.
     Microfilm: MnCH proj. no. 3643

365 **Pius XII, Pope.**
     Sermon by Pope Pius XII on St.
     Benedict. [Delivered at] Basilica of St.
     Paul, Rome, September 18, 1947. [St.
     Meinrad, Ind., Grail, 1947?].
     7 p. 19 cm.
     KAS

366 **Sermo de S. Benedicto.** MS. Benediktin-
     erabtei Admont, Austria, codex 328, f.
     74r. Folio. Saec. 13.
     Microfilm: MnCH proj. no. 9405

367 **Sermo de S. Benedicto.** Incipit: Ingredere
     Benedicte domum. MS. Vienna, Nation-
     albibliothek, codex 3714, f.166r-168r.
     Folio. Saec. 15.
     Microfilm: MnCH proj. no. 16,936

368 **Sermo de S. Benedicto.** Incipit: Dedit illi.
     MS. Vienna, Nationalbibliothek, codex
     5135, f.250r-258v. Folio. Saec. 15.
     Microfilm: MnCH proj. no. 18,301

369 **Sermo in festo S. Benedicti.** Incipit:
     Sancti estote. MS. Cava, Italy (Benedic-
     tine abbey), codex 6, f.46. Quarto. Saec.
     11.
     Microfilm: MnCH

370 **Sermo in honorem S. Benedicti** super
     illud Eccl. 24: In multitudine electorum.
     MS. Benediktinerabtei Melk, Austria,
     codex 840, f.83v-84r. Quarto. Saec. 14.
     Microfilm: MnCH proj. no. 1668

16. TOMB

371 **De inventione corporis S. Benedict.** MS.
     Benediktinerabtei Altenburg, Austria,
     codex Ab 6 0 5, f.180v-181v. Quarto.
     Saec. 15(1411)
     Microfilm: MnCH proj. no. 6396

371a **Leccisotti, Tommaso, O.S.B.**
     Il sepolcro de S. Benedetto.
     (*In* his: Montecassino. 7. ed. Badia di
     Montecassino, 1975)
     MnCS

371b **Meyvaert, Paul.**
     Peter the Deacon and the tomb of St.
     Benedict.

     70 p. 23 cm.
     (*In* his: Benedict, Gregory, Bede and
     others. London, 1977)
     Reprint from: Revue bénédictine,
     65(1955).
     MnCS

17. TRANSLATION

372 **Adrevaldus, monk of Fleury.**
     Translatio s. Benedicti abbatis. MS.
     Benediktinerabtei Kremsmünster,
     Austria, codex 34, f.170r-175r. Folio. Saec.
     13.
     Microfilm: MnCH proj. no. 34

373 **Adrevaldus, monk of Fleury.**
     Historia translationis S. Benedicti (ab-
     breviated). MS. Benediktinerabtei Krem-
     smünster, Austria, codex 95, f.211r-212v.
     Quarto. Saec. 15.
     Microfilm: MnCH proj. no. 88

374 **Bulla,** ne festum translationis S. Benedicti
     celebretur. MS. Benediktinerabtei Melk,
     Austria, codex 1088, f.371-374. Duode-
     cimo. Saec. 15.
     Microfilm: MnCH proj. no. 1850

375 **De illacione S. Benedicti abbatis** (frag-
     mentum), V idus Iulii. MS. Benediktiner-
     abtei Kremsmünster, Austria, codex
     270. Saec. 15.
     Microfilm: MnCH proj. no. 254

376 **De translatione S. Benedicti abbatis.**
     MS. Benediktinerabtei St. Peter,
     Salzburg, codex a.VI.46, f.88r-90r.
     Quarto. Saec. 15.
     Microfilm: MnCH proj. no. 10,119

377 **Dietricus, monk of Hersfeld.**
     Narratio de illatione S. Benedicti ab-
     batis. MS. Benediktinerabtei Admont,
     Austria. codex 529, f.139r-145v. Quarto.
     Saec. 13.
     Microfilm: MnCH proj. no. 9583

378 **Illatio sanctissimi patris nostri Bene-
     dicti.** MS. Benediktinerabtei Krem-
     smünster, Austria, codex 34, f.175v-
     176r. Saec. 13.
     Microfilm: MnCH proj. no. 34

379 **Notabile de falsa** translatione corporum
     S. Benedicti et ipsius sororis Scholasti-
     cae. MS. Vienna, Nationalbibliothek,
     codex 12761, f.178v. Quarto. Saec. 15.
     Microfilm: MnCH proj. no. 14,454

380 **Notitia de falsa** translatione s.p.n. Ben-
     edicti. Incipit: Zacharius papa. MS. Ben-
     ediktinerabtei Göttweig, Austria, codex
     375, f.175r. Folio. Saec. 15.
     Microfilm: MnCH proj. no. 3643

381 **Popes,** 1088-1099 (Urban II)
Bulla de falsa translatione sanctissimi patris nostri Benedicti abbatis. MS. Vienna. Dominikanerkloster, codex 207, f.223r.-224r. Folio. Saec. 15.
Microfilm: MnCH proj. no. 9009

382 **Popes,** 1088-1099 (Urban II)
Bulla de falsa translatione sanctissimi patris nostri Benedicti abbatis. Dat. 1092. MS. Benediktinerabtei Göttweig, Austria, codex 375, f.175r. Folio. Saec. 15.
Microfilm: MnCH proj. no. 3643

383 **Regla del bienaventurado San Benito . . .** [and] Trasladando el cuerpo de San Benito del Monte Casino al Monasterio Floricense, sucedieron estos milagros. Valladolid, Juan Godinez de Millis, 1599. MnCS

384 **Sermo in translatione** beati Benedicti abbatis. MS. Cistercienserabtei Heiligenkreuz, Austria, codex 103, f.116v-119v. Folio. Saec. 12.
Microfilm: MnCH proj. no. 4648

385 **Sermones duo** de translatione S. Benedicti. MS. Cistercienserabtei Zwettl, Austria, codex 238, f.117r-120r.
Microfilm: MnCH proj. no. 6838

III. RULE OF ST. BENEDICT

A. TEXTS OF THE RULE

1. Manuscripts

For works about manuscript Rules *see* below, n. 784-788

Manscript copies of the Rule are filed by language, and under each language by centuries, and under each century by place name, e.g., Admont, Einsiedeln. Melk, Montserrat, Subiaco, etc.

a. Latin

Latin saec. 8

386 Regula s. Benedicti. MS. Munich, Germany, Bayerische Staatsbibliothek, codex lat. 19,408. Saec. 8 exeunte.
Microfilm: MnCH

Latin saec. 8

387 The Rule of St. Benedictine [Latin], Oxford, Bodleian Library, Hatton 48. Edited by D. H. Farmer. [Facsimile]. Copenhagen, Rosenkilde and Bagger, 1968.
29 p. 77 leaves, 37 cm. (Early English manuscripts in facsimile, v. 15)
Distributed in the United States by Johns Hopkins Press, Baltimore.
MnCS; PLatS

Latin saec. 8-9

388 Regula s. Benedicti. MS. Stiftsbibliothek von St. Gallen, Switzerland, codex 914, p. 1-172. Quarto. Saec. 8-9.
Microfilm: MnCH

Latin saec. 9

389 Regula s. Benedicti. MS. Einsiedeln, Switzerland, Benediktinerabtei, codex 236. Saec. 9.
Microfilm: MnCH

Latin saec. 9

390 Regula s. Benedicti. MS. Fulda, Germany, codex D 3.
Microfilm: MnCH

Latin Saec. 9

391 Regula s. Benedicti. MS. Karlsruhe, Germany, Badische Landesbibliothek, codex CXXVIII. Saec. 9.
Microfilm: MnCH

Latin saec. 9

392 Regula Magistri et Regula s. Benedicti. MS. Munich, Germany, Bayerische Staatsbibliothek, codex lat. 28,118. Saec. 9.
Microfilm: MnCH

Latin saec. 9

393 Regula s. Benedicti. MS. Paris, Bibliothèque Nationale, codex lat. 4209.
Microfilm: MnCH

Latin saec. 9

394 Regula sancti Benedicti. MS. Paris, Bibliothèque Nationale, codex lat. 13,745.
Microfilm: MnCH

Latin saec. 9

395 Regula s. Benedicti cum versione interlineari germanica. MS. Stiftsbibliothek St. Gallen, Switzerland, codex 916, p. 2-159. Octavo. Saec. 9.
Microfilm: MnCH

Latin saec. 9

396 Regula s. Benedicti. MS. Turin, Italy, codex G VII 18. Saec. 9.
This is the copy from Bobbio.
Microfilm: MnCH

Latin saec. 9

397 Regula s. Benedicti. MS. Trier, Germany, Stadtbibliothek, codex 1245. Saec. 9.
Microfilm: MnCH

Latin saec. 9-10

398 Regula s. Benedicti. MS. Zürich, Switzerland, Zentralbibliothek, codex Rh. hist. 28, f.4v-46r. Saec. 9-10.
Microfilm: MnCH

Latin saec. 10

399 Regula s. Benedicti. MS. London, British Museum, codex add. 30,055. Saec. 10.
Microfilm: MnCH

Latin saec. 10

400 Regula s. Benedicti, cum annexis solitis. MS. Vienna, Nationalbibliothek, codex 2232, f.2v-61v. Octavo. Saec. 10.
Microfilm: MnCH proj. no. 15,585

Latin saec. 10

401 Regula s. Benedicti. MS. Zürich, Switzerland, Zentralbibliothek, codex Rhenanus 111. Saec. 10.
Microfilm: MnCH

Latin saec. 11-12

402 Regula s. Benedicti. MS. Benediktinerabtei Admont, Austria, codex 184, f.55r-110v. Folio. Saec. 11-12.
Microfilm: MnCH proj. no. 9273

Saec. 11-12

402a S. Benedicti Regula. MS. Budapest National Schényi Library, codex 329, f.3v-594v. Octavo. Saec. 11–12.
Microfilm: MnCH

Latin saec. 11-12

403 Regula s. Benedicti. MS. Benediktinerabtei Melk, Austria, codex 1942(947.R24), f. 83r-135v. Quarto. Saec. 11-12.
Microfilm: MnCH proj. no. 2221

Latin saec. 12

404 Regula s. Benedicti. Cum pulchris initialibus. MS. Benediktinerabtei Admont,

Austria, codex 567, f.47r-86v. Quarto. Saec. 12.
Microfilm: MnCH proj. no. 9610
Latin saec. 12

405 Benedicti Regula monachorum. MS. Universitätsbibliothek Graz, Austria, codex 325, f.44r-77v. Folio. Saec. 12.
Microfilm: MnCH proj. no. 26,219
Latin saec. 12

406 Regula s. Benedicti. MS. Klagenfurt, Austria. Kärntner Landesarchiv, codex GV 6/36, f.49v-84r. Quarto. Saec. 12.
Microfilm: MnCH proj. no. 12,835
Latin saec. 12

407 Regula s. Benedicti, cum glossis. MS. Benediktinerabtei Lambach, Austria, codex membr. cxxxi, f.97r-152v. Quarto. Saec. 12.
Microfilm: MnCH proj. no. 816
Latin saec. 12

408 Regula sancti Benedicti. Prologum Simplicii monachi abrasum restituit manus saec. XV. Finis deest. MS. Benediktinerabtei Melk, Austria, codex 552, (189. D26), f.5r-43v. Folio. Saec. 12.
Microfilm: MnCH proj. no. 1454
Latin saec. 12

409 Regula s. Benedicti. MS. Poppi, Italy. Biblioteca Communale Rilliana, codex 63. Saec. 12.
Microfilm: MnCH
Latin saec. 12

410 Regula s. Benedicti. MS. Vienna, Nationalbibliothek, codex 2182, f.1r-31v. Folio. Saec. 12.
Microfilm: MnCH proj. no. 15,502
Latin saec. 12

411 Regula sancti Benedicti abbatis (a Simplicio eius discipulo edita). Cum pulchris initialibus. MS. Cistercienserabtei Zwettl, Austria, codex 84, f.123r-185r. Folio. Saec. 12.
Microfilm: MnCH proj. no. 6803
Latin saec. 12-13

412 Regula s. Benedicti. MS. Benediktinerabtei St. Paul im Lavantthal, Austria, codex 31/1 (25.4.18). 124 f. Quarto. Saec. 12-13.
Microfilm: MnCH proj. no. 11,685
Latin saec. 12-13

413 Regula s. Benedicti. MS. Torino, Italy. Biblioteca Nazionale Universitaria, codex G.V. 38.
Microfilm: MnCH
Latin saec. 13

414 Regula s. Benedicti. MS. Benediktinerabtei Altenburg, Austria, codex AB 13 F 1, f. 1r-57r. Duodecimo. Saec. 13.
Microfilm: MnCH proj. no. 6372

Latin saec. 13

415 Regula s. Benedicti. MS. Cava, Italy (Benedictine abbey), codex 19, f.213-254. Octavo. Saec. 13(1280).
Microfilm: MnCH
Latin saec. 13

416 Benedicti Regula monachorum. MS. Universitätsbibliothek Graz, Austria, codex 1630, f.1r-19r. Duodecimo. Saec. 13.
Microfilm: MnCH proj. no. 26,546
Latin saec. 13

417 Regula s. Benedicti. MS. Cistercienserabtei Heiligenkreuz, Austria, codex 131, f. 104r-130r. Folio. Saec. 13.
Microfilm: MnCH proj. no. 4675
Latin saec. 13

418 Regula s. Benedicti. MS. Cistercienseratei Heiligenkreuz, Austria, codex 159, f.58r-106v. Folio. Saec. 13.
Microfilm: MnCH proj. no. 4702
Latin saec. 13

419 Regula s. Benedicti. MS. Innsbruck, Austria, Tiroler Landesmuseum Ferdinandeum, codex F.B. 1110. Saec. 13?
Microfilm: MnCH proj. no. 29,722
Latin saec. 13

420 Regula s. patris Benedicti. Cum prologo Simplicii monachi. MS. Benediktinerabtei Melk, Austria, codex 836 (1708), f. 70r-112v. Quarto. Saec. 13.
Microfilm: MnCH proj. no. 1664
Latin saec. 13

421 Benedicti Regula monachorum. MS. Toledo, Spain, Biblioteca del Cabildo, codex 25,5. 50 f. 15 cm. Saec. 13.
Microfilm: MnCH proj. no. 33,326
Latin saec. 14

422 Regula s. Benedicti. Benediktinerabtei Admont, Austria, codex 430, f.127r-158v. Quarto. Saec. 14.
Microfilm: MnCH proj. no. 9461
Latin saec. 14

423 Benedicti Regula monachorum. Universitätsbibliothek Graz, Austria, codex 418, f.94r-114v. Folio. Saec. 14.
Microfilm: MnCH proj. no. 26,582
Latin saec. 14

424 S. Benedicti Regula monachorum. Universitätsbibliothek Graz, Austria, codex 1011, f.1r-28v. Quarto. Saec. 14.
Microfilm: MnCH proj. no. 27,077
Latin saec. 14

425 Regula s. Benedicti. MS. Linz, Austria, Bundesstaatliche Studienbibliothek, codex 706, f.1r-8r. Quarto. Saec. 14.
Microfilm: MnCH proj. no. 28,041
Latin saec. 14

426 Regula s. patris Benedicti, cum commentario Petri Boerii. MS. Benediktinerabtei

Melk, Austria, codex 3 (149.C27), f.1r-71v. Folio. Saec. 14.
Microfilm: MnCH proj. no. 2124
Latin saec. 14

427   S. Benedicti Regula. MS. Benediktinerabtei Melk, Austria, codex 88 (119.B89), f. 1-24. Octavo. Saec. 14.
Microfilm: MnCH proj. no. 1162
Latin saec. 14

428   Benedicti Regula monachorum. MS. Monasterio benedictino de Montserrat, Spain, codex 824, f.1r-52v. Octavo. Saec. 14.
Microfilm: MnCH proj. no. 30,086
Latin saec. 14

429   Regula s. Benedicti. MS. Monasterio benedictino de Montserrat, Spain, codex 847. 62 f. Quarto. Saec. 14.
Microfilm: MnCH proj. no. 30,097
Latin saec. 14

430   Regula di S. Benedetto (latine), con versione italiana. MS. Perugia, Italy, Badia di San pietro, codex 17. Sec. XIV.
Microfilm: MnCH
Latin saec. 14

431   Regula s. Benedicti. MS. St. Vincent College Library, Latrobe, Pa. Mss. 14. 111 f. 22 cm. Saec. 14.
PLatS
Latin saec. 14

432   Regula s. Benedicti abbatis. MS. Cistercienserabtei Schlierbach, Austria, codex 7, f.116r-171r. Folio. Saec. 14.
Microfilm: MnCH proj. no. 28,073
Latin saec. 14

433   Regula s. Benedicti, cum notis Petri episcopi Urbevetani. MS. Subiaco, Italy (Benedictine abbey), codex XIII(14). 179 f. Folio. Saec. 14(1337).
Microfilm: MnCH
Latin saec. 14

434   Regula s. Benedicti, cap. 28-73. MS. Subiaco, Italy (Benedictine abbey), codex cviii (111). 126 f. Quarto. Saec. 14.
Microfilm: MnCH
Latin saec. 14

435   S. Benedicti Regula monachorum. MS. Vich, Spain, Museo Episcopal, codex 150. Folio. Saec. 14.
Microfilm: MnCH proj. no. 31,255
Latin saec. 14

436   Regula s. Benedicti. MS. Vienna, Nationalbibliothek, codex 417, f.150r-218v. Folio. Saec. 14.
Microfilm: MnCH proj. no. 13,741
Latin saec. 14

437   Regula s. Benedicti. MS. Vienna, Nationalbibliothek, codex 2174, f.1r-24v. Folio. Saec. 14.
Microfilm; MnCH proj. no. 15,491

Latin saec. 14

438   Regula s. Benedicti. MS. Vienna, Nationalbibliothek, codex 2220a, f.1r-32r. Quarto. Saec. 14.
Microfilm: MnCH proj. no. 15,508
Latin saec. 14-15

439   Regula s. Benedicti. MS. Vienna, Schottenstift, codex 178, f.1r-45r. Octavo. Saec. 14-15.
Microfilm: MnCH proj. no. 4102
Latin Saec. 14

440   Regula s. Benedicti. MS. Cistercienserabtei Zwettl, Austria, codex 141, f.1r-37v. Duodecimo. Saec. 14.
Microfilm: MnCH proj. no. 6745
Latin saec. 15

441   Regula s. Benedicti. MS. Benediktinerabtei Admont, Austria, codex 581, f.1r-34v. Quarto. Saec. 15.
Microfilm: MnCH proj. no. 9632
Latin saec. 15

442   Regula s. Benedicti. Apud finem: 1446 scripsi in Lambaco. MS. Benediktinerabtei Admont, Austria, codex 873, f.2r-59v. Duodecimo. Saec. 15.
Microfilm: MnCH proj. no. 9866
Latin saec. 15

443   Regula s. Benedicti. MS. Benediktinerabtei Altenburg, Austria, codex AB 6 C 5, f. 114r-180r. Quarto. Saec. 15(1411).
Microfilm: MnCH proj. no. 6396
Latin saec. 15.

444   Regula s. Benedicti. MS. Durham, N.C., Duke University Library, codex latinus Dukianus 116. Vellum. Germany, ca. 1400.
Microfilm: MnCH
Latin saec. 15

445   Regula s. Benedicti. MS. Benediktinerabtei Göttweig, Austria, codex 498, f.2r-126v. Quarto. Saec. 15.
Microfilm: MnCH proj. no. 3751
Latin saec. 15

446   Instituta seu Regula s. Benedicti abbatis cum aliquibus notabilibus, quae concernunt vitam regularem. MS. Universitätsbibliothek Graz, Austria, codex 1615. 175 f. Octavo. Saec. 15.
Microfilm: MnCH proj. no. 26,552
Latin saec. 15

447   Benedicti Regula monachorum. MS. Universitätsbibliothek Graz, Austria, codex 202, f.86r-114v. Quarto. Saec. 15.
Microfilm: MnCH proj. no. 26,119
Latin saec. 15

448   Benedicti Regula monachorum. MS. Universitätsbibliothek Graz, Austria, codex 391, f.1r-19r. Folio. Saec. 15.
Microfilm: MnCH proj. no. 26,575

Latin saec. 15

449 Regula s. Benedicti. MS. Klagenfurt, Austria, Studienbibliothek, codex cart. 11, f. 1r-35v. Octavo. Saec. 15.
Microfilm: MnCH proj. no. 13,007

Latin saec. 15

450 S. Benedicti Regula. Benediktinerabtei Kremsmünster, Austria, codex 268, f.2r-39r. Saec. 15.
Microfilm: MnCH proj. no. 252

Latin saec. 15

451 Regula s. patris Benedicti. Benediktinerabtei Kremsmünster, Austria, codex 384, f. 2r-80v. Saec. 15.
Microfilm: MnCH proj. no. 363

Latin saec. 15

452 Regula s. p. Benedicti. Benediktinerabtei Kremsmünster, Austria, codex 395, f.1r-152v. Saec. 15.
Microfilm: MnCH proj. no. 375

Latin saec. 15

453 Regula beati Benedicti abbatis. Benediktinerabtei Kremsmünster, Austria, codex 402, f.1r-45v. Saec. 15.
Microfilm: MnCH proj. no. 401

Latin saec. 15

454 Regula s.p.n. Benedicti. Benediktinerabtei Kremsmünster, Austria, codex 411. 146 f. Saec. 15.
Microfilm: MnCH proj. no. 405

Latin saec. 15

455 Regula S. Benedicti. MS. Benediktinerabtei Lambach, Austria, codex chart. 435, f.109r-171v. Saec. 15.
Microfilm: MnCH proj. no. 725

Latin saec. 15

456 Regula beati Benedicti abbatis. Benediktinerabtei Lambach, Austria, codex chart. 452, f.113v-157v. Duodecimo. Saec. 15.
Microfilm: MnCH proj. no. 741

Latin saec. 15

457 Regula s. Benedicti. MS. Benediktinerabtei Lambach, Austria, codex membr. cliv. 36 f. Quarto. Saec. 15.
Microfilm: MnCH proj. no. 831

Latin saec. 15

458 Regula s. Benedicti. MS. Cistercienserabtei Mehrerau, Tirol, Austria, codex C 14, f.289r-378r. Folio. Saec. 15.
Microfilm: MnCH proj. no. 29,894

Latin saec. 15

459 Regula s. Benedicti a Simplicio ejus discipulo edita. Incipit: Qui levi jugo Christi. MS. Benediktinerabtei Melk, Austria, codex 321(624.L49), f.75r-93v. Folio. Saec. 15.
Microfilm: MnCH proj. no. 1330

Latin saec 15

460 S. Benedicti Regula. MS. Benediktinerabtei Melk, Austria, codex 436 (144.C22), f. 4r-25r. Folio. Saec. 15.
Microfilm: MnCH proj. no. 1406

Latin saec. 15

461 Regula s. Benedicti. MS. Benediktinerabtei Melk, Austria, codex 748 (954.R33), f.2r-23r. Quarto. Saec. 15.
Microfilm: MnCH proj. no. 1597

Latin saec. 15

462 Regula s. Benedicti secundum veram litteram manibus dicti patris scripta. MS. Benediktinerabtei Melk, Austria, codex 787 (757), f.55v-88r. Quarto. Saec. 15.
Microfilm: MnCH proj. no. 1623

Latin saec. 15

463 Regula s.p. Benedicti. MS. Benediktinerabtei Melk, Austria, codex 918 (835.P24), f. 1r-29r. Quarto. Saec. 15.
Microfilm: MnCH proj. no. 1736

Latin saec. 15

464 Ex Regula s. patris Benedicti. Incipit: Ausculta o fili. MS. Benediktinerabtei Melk, Austria, codex 1093 (423.H41), f.475-520. Duodecimo. Saec. 15.
Microfilm: MnCH proj. no. 1846

Latin saec. 15

465 Regula s. Benedicti. MS. Benediktinerabtei Melk, Austria, codex 1214 (1777,1761), f. 1r-47r. Sextodecimo. Saec. 15.
Microfilm: MnCH proj. no. 1865

Latin saec. 15

466 Regula s. Benedicti. Latine et germanice. MS. Benediktinerabtei Melk, Austria, codex 1582 (285.E76), p. 1–282. Octavo. Saec. 15.
Microfilm: MnCH proj. no. 1979

Latin saec. 15

467 Regula s. Benedicti. MS. Benediktinerabtei Melk, Austria, codex 1648 (660.L90), f. 13r-64r. Sextodecimo. Saec. 15.
Microfilm: MnCH proj. no. 1998

Latin saec. 15

468 Regula s. Benedicti. MS. Benediktinerabtei Melk, Austria, codex 1716 (104.B74), f. 1r-49v. Octavo. Saec. 15.
Microfilm: MnCH proj. no. 2032

Latin saec. 15

469 Regula s. Benedicti. MS. Benediktinerabtei Melk, Austria, codex 1764, p. 283–364. Duodecimo. Saec. 15.
Microfilm: MnCH proj. no. 2074

Latin saec. 15

470 Kalendarium benedictinum cum Regula s. Benedicti. MS. Monasterio benedictino de Montserrat, Spain, codex 54. 117 f. Duodecimo. Saec. 15.
Microfilm: MnCH proj. no. 29,997

Latin saec. 15

471 Regula s. Benedicti (prima pars). MS. Augustinerchorherrenstift St. Florian, Austria, codex XI,164, f.372r-278v. Duodecimo. Saec. 15.
Microfilm: MnCH proj. no. 2432

Latin saec. 15

472 Regula s. Benedicti. MS. Benediktinerabtei St. Peter, Salzburg, codex a.I.11, f.2r-55r. Duodecimo. Saec. 15.
Microfilm: MnCH proj. no. 9881

Latin saec. 15

473 Regula sancti Benedicti. MS. Benediktinerabtei St. Peter, Salzburg, codex a.I.3., f. 11v-101v. Duodecimo. Saec. 15.
Microfilm: MnCH proj. no. 9875

Latin saec. 15

474 Regula s. Benedicti. MS. Benediktinerabtei St. Peter, Salzburg, codex b.V.15, f. 177r-215r. Quarto. Saec. 15.
Microfilm: MnCH proj. no. 10,445

Latin saec. 15

475 Regula s. Benedicti. MS. Benediktinerabtei St. Paul im Lavantthal, Austria, codex 60/6. 73 f. Folio. Saec. 15(1499).
Microfilm: MnCH proj. no. 12,593

Latin saec. 15

476 Regula s. Benedicti. MS. Benediktinerabtei St. Paul im Lavantthal, Austria, codex 227/4, pars I. Quarto. Saec. 15.
Microfilm: MnCH proj. no. 12,466

Latin saec. 15

477 Regulaas. Benedicti. MS. Vienna, Nationalbibliothek, codex 2014, f.92r-145v. Sextodecimo. Saec. 15.
Microfilm: MnCH proj. no. 15,322

Latin saec. 15

478 Regula s. Benedicti. MS. Vienna, Nationalbibliothek, codex 2247, f.1r-88v. Duodecimo. Saec. 15.
Microfilm: MnCH proj. no. 15,541

Latin saec. 15

479 Regula s. Benedicti. MS. Vienna, Nationalbibliothek, codex 2248, f.3r-103r. Duodecimo. Saec. 15.
Microfilm: MnCH proj. no. 15,543

Latin saec. 15

480 Regula s. Benedicti. Latine et gallice. MS. Vienna, Nationalbibliothek, codex 2655, f.1r-102v. Quarto. Saec. 15(1455).
Microfilm: MnCH proj. no. 15,909

Latin saec. 15

481 Regula s. Benedicti. MS. Vienna, Nationalbibliothek, codex 3839, f.1r-56v. Octavo. Saec. 15.
Microfilm: MnCH proj. no. 17,084

Latin saec. 15

482 Regula s. Benedicti. MS. Vienna, Nationalbibliothek, codex 4108, f.16v-77v. Octavo. Saec. 15.
Microfilm: MnCH proj. no. 17,291

Latin saec. 15

483 Regula s. Benedicti. MS. Vienna, Schottenstift, codex 400, f.1r-36v. Octavo. Saec. 15.
Microfilm: MnCH proj. no. 3916

Latin saec. 15

484 Regula s. Benedicti. MS. Vienna, Schottenstift, codex 307, f.1r-23r. Folio. Saec. 15.
Microfilm: MnCH proj. no. 4177

Latin saec. 15

485 Regula s. Benedicti. MS. Augustinerchorherrenstift Vorau, Austria, codex 146, f. 275r-300r. Folio. Saec. 15.
Microfilm: MnCH proj. no. 7147

Latin saec. 15

486 Regula s. Benedicti. MS. Cistercienserabtei Neukloster, Wiener-Neustadt, Austria, codex C 11. 48 f. Quarto. Saec. 15.
Microfilm: MnCH proj. no. 4970

Latin saec. 15

487 Regula s. Benedicti. MS. Benediktinerabtei Seitenstetten, Austria, codex 321, f.36r-145v. Duodecimo. Saec. 15.
Microfilm: MnCH proj. no. 1114

Latin saec. 16

488 Regula beatissimi Benedicti abbatis. Benediktinerabtei Kremsmünster, Austria, codex 401. 151 f. Saec. 16.
Microfilm: MnCH proj. no. 392

Latin saec. 16

489 Regula b. Benedicti abbreviata. MS. Lambeth Palace Library, London, codex 20, f.145-156. Octavo. Saec. 16.
Microfilm: MnCH

Latin saec. 16

490 Regla de San Benito (latine). MS. Monasterio benedictino de Montserrat, Spain, codex 40, 59 f. Quarto. Saec. 16.
Microfilm: MnCH proj. no. 29,990

Latin saec. 16

491 Regla de San Benito (latine). MS. Monasterio benedictino de Montserrat, Spain, codex 41. 201 f. Octavo. Saec. 16.
Microfilm: MnCH proj. no. 29,990

Latin saec. 16

492 Regla de Sant Benet (latine). MS. Monasterio benedictino de Montserrat, Spain, codex 67. Octavo. Saec. 16.
Microfilm: MnCH proj. no. 30,002

Latin saec. 16

493 Regula s. Benedicti. MS. Vienna, Schottenstift, codex 578, f.1v-20r. Octavo. Saec. 16.
Microfilm: MnCH proj no. 4272

Latin saec. 17

494 S. Benedicti Regula (latine et catalane).
MS. Monasterio benedictino de Montserrat, Spain, codex 42. 90 f. Octavo. Saec.
17.
Microfilm: MnCH proj. no. 29,900

Latin saec. 17

495 S. Benedicti Regula monachorum. MS.
Monasterio benedictino de Montserrat,
Spain, codex 831, f.9r-87v. Octavo. Saec.
17.
Microfilm: MnCH proj. no. 30,090

Latin saec. 17

496 Regla de Sant Benet (latine). MS. Monasterio benedictino de Montserrat, Spain,
codex 1165. 70 f. Octavo. Saec. 17.
Microfilm: MnCH proj. no. 30,155

Latin saec. 17

497 Regula s. Benedicti. MS. Cistercienserabtei Neukloster, Wiener-Neustadt, Austria, codex A 8 b. 64 p. Saec. 17.
Microfilm: MnCH proj. no. 4943

Latin saec. 17

498 Regula s. Benedicti (Maurist Congregation
1645). MS. Paris, France, Abbaye de
Sainte-Marie. Saec. 17.
Microfilm: MnCH

Latin saec. 18

499 Regula s. Benedicti, cum versione interlineari germanica. Copy of a 10th-11th
century Zwiefalten manuscript which is
lost. MS. Benediktinerabtei Melk, Austria, codex 148 (1074), f.204r-317r.
Quarto. Saec. 18.
Microfilm: MnCH proj. no. 1209

Latin saec. 18

500 Regula s. Benedicti . . . a rel. mon. huj. fr.
prof. nova scribendi methodo perfecta
anno Domini 1763. MS. Vienna, Schottenstift, codex 740. 60 f. Folio. Saec. 18.
Microfilm: MnCH proj. no. 4294

Latin saec. 19

501 Regula s. p. Benedicti cum declarationibus
ab exempta Congregatione Benedictino-
Bavarica sub titulo SS. Angel. Custod.
MS. St. Vincent College Library,
Latrobe, Pa., Mss. 15. 132 p. 20 cm.
Saec. 19.
Title page signed: P. Coelestinus
Englbrecht.
PLatS

b. Anglo-Saxon

Anglo-Saxon saec. 11

502 Regula s. Benedicti. MS. Cambridge, Eng-
land, Corpus Christi College, codex 57.
Saec. 11.
Microfilm: MnCH

Anglo-Saxon saec. 11

503 Regula s. Benedicti. MS. London, British
Museum, codex Cotton Tit. A.IV. Saec.
11.
Microfilm: MnCH

c. Armenian

504 Regula s. Benedicti in lingua Armeniana
(25 capitula). MS. Mechtaristenkongre-
gation, Vienna, codex 307. 20 f. Saec. 18
(1794).
Microfilm: MnCH proj. no. 7895

d. Catalan

505 S. Benedicti Regula (en llati e catala). MS.
Monasterio benedictino de Montserrat,
Spain, codex 42. 90 f. Octavo. Saec. 17.
Microfilm: MnCH: proj. no. 29,900

e. Croation (Old Croation)

506 Stara Hrvatska Regula Svetoga
Benedikta.
(In Ostojic, Ivan. Benediktinci u Hrvatskoj i ostalim nasim krajevinia. Split,
1963-65. v. 3, p. 361-533)
Croation and Latin texts in parallel columns, with complete photographic
reproduction of the fourteenth-century
glagolithic Ms.
KAS; PLatS

ea. Dutch

506a Coun, Theo.
De oudste middelnederlandse vertaling
van de Regula S. Benedicti. With a general
introduction in English. Mit einer allgemeinen Einleitung auf Deutsch.
Hildesheim, Gerstenberg Verlag, 1980.
xxiv, 617 p. facsims. 21 cm. (Regulae
Benedicti studia. Supplementa, 8)
Latin text and Dutch translation on opposite pages, p. 242–407.
MnCS

f. French

507 Regula s. Benedicti. Latine et gallice. MS.
Vienna, Nationalbibliothek, codex 2655,
f.1r-102v. Quarto. Saec. 15(1455).
Microfilm: MnCH proj. no. 15,909

g. German

German saec. 9

508 Regula S. Benedicti saec. IX cum notis
interlinearibus teutonicis. MS. Stiftsbibliothek St. Gallen, Switzerland, codex
914, p. 1-172. Quarto. Saec. 9.

The quaint interlinear German gloss is traceable to the early ninth century.
MnCH

German saec. 12

509 A Middle High German Benedictine Rule: MS. 4486a Germanisches Nationalmuseum Nürnberg. Commentary, edition, glossary [by Mary C. Sullivan]. Hildesheim, Gerstenberg, 1976. 17 leaves (16 of plates), 324 p. 22 cm.
PLatS

German saec. 14

510 Regula s. Benedicti. Germanice. Incipit: Hore sun maisters gebot. MS. Benediktinerabtei Admont, Austria, codex 624. 47 f. Quarto. Saec. 14.
Microfilm: MnCH proj. no. 9665

German saec. 14

511 Benedictinerregel, verdeutscht von Leonhart Sattler, Abt von Raitenhaslach. MS. Bayerische Staatsbibliothek, Munich, codex germ. 153. 73 f. Saec. 14.
Microfilm: MnCH

German saec. 14

512 Benediktinerregel. Deutsch. MS. Bayerische Staatsbibliothek, Munich, codex germ. 91. 36 f. Saec. 14.
Microfilm: MnCH

German saec. 14

513 Benediktinerregal. Deutsch. MS. Bayerische Staatsbibliothek, Munich, codex germ. 36. 56 f. Saec. 14(1388).
Microfilm: MnCH

German saec. 15

514 Regula s. Benedicti. Germanice. Incipit: O sun hör fleyssikleich. Uebersetzer: Johannes de Spira, Mellicensis. MS. Benediktinerabtei Admont, Austria, codex 757, f.31r-147v. Octavo. Saec. 15.
Microfilm: MnCH proj. no. 9795

German saec. 15

515 Regula s. Benedicti. Germanice, pro monialibus. MS. Benediktinerabtei Göttweig, Austria, codex 499, f.25r-74v. Quarto. Saec. 15.
Microfilm: MnCH proj. no. 3754

German saec. 15

516 S. Benedikts Regel. MS. Benediktinerabtei Kremsmünster, Austria, codex 285, f.1r-163v. Saec. 15.
Microfilm: MnCH proj. no. 270

German saec. 15

517 Regel sandt Benedicti. MS. Benediktinerabtei Kremsmünster, Austria, codex 393, f.2r-54v. Saec. 15.
Microfilm: MnCH proj. no. 374

German saec. 15

518 Regula s. Benedicti (germanice) cum glossis. MS. Benediktinerabtei Lambach, Austria, codex chart. 229. 122f. Saec. 15.
Microfilm: MnCH proj. no. 617

German saec. 15

519 Regula s. Benedicti (germanice) cum commentario (a Joanne Schlitpacher). MS. Benediktinerabtei Melk, Austria, codex 278 (1934), p. 119-140. Duodecimo. Saec. 15.
Microfilm: MnCH proj. no. 2110

German saec. 15

520 S. Benedicti Regula Germanice, interprete Joanne de Spira. MS. Benediktinerabtei Melk, Austria, codex 570 (140.C18), f.114v-135r. Folio. Saec. 15.
Microfilm: MnCH proj. no. 1475

German saec. 15

521 Sand Benedicten Regel. Incipit: O sun hör fleissikleich die gepott des maisters. MS. Benediktinerabtei Melk, Austria, codex 575 (407.H19), f.49-81. Folio. Saec. 15.
Microfilm: MnCH proj. no. 1479

German saec. 15

522 Regula s. Benedicti. Germanice. MS. Benediktinerabtei Melk, Austria, codex 1794 (786.o22), f.1r-30r. Quarto. Saec. 15.
Microfilm: MnCH proj. no. 2102

German saec. 15

523 Regel des hl. Benedikt. Incipit: O erhor sun dy gepott deines maister. MS. Benediktinerinnenabtei Nonnberg, Salzburg, codex 28 A 10, f.43r-118v. Octavo. Saec. 15.
Microfilm: MnCH proj. no. 10,955

German saec. 15

524 Regula S. Benedicti. Germanice. Incipit: Hör sun dye gepot deines maisters. MS. Benediktinerabtei St. Peter, Salzburg, codex b.IV.5, f.97r-136r. Quarto. Saec. 15.
Microfilm: MnCH proj. no. 10,390

German saec. 15

525 Regula s. Benedicti. Germanice. MS. Benediktinerabtei St. Peter, Salzburg, codex b.V.25. 54 f. Saec. 15.
Microfilm: MnCH proj. no. 10,477

German saec. 15

526 Regula s. Benedicti. Germanice. MS. St. Pölten, Austria, Diöcesanbibliothek, codex 119. 72 f. Octavo. Saec. 15(1437).
Microfilm: MnCH proj. no. 6358

German saec. 15

526a Eine Mittelhochdeutsche Benediktinerregel: Hs. 1256/587 (Anfang 15. Jh) Stadtbibliothek Trier. Edition, mittelhochdeutsch-lateinisches Glossar / Edda Petri. Hildesheim, Gerstenberg, 1978.

viii, 367 p. 8 plates (facsims.) 22 cm. (Regulae Benedicti studia: Supplementa, Bd. 6)
MnCS; PLatS
German saec. 15

527 Regula s. Benedicti (germanice) cum commentario et registro. MS. Vienna, Nationalbibliothek, codex 2968, f.1r-124r. Quarto. Saec. 15.
Microfilm: MnCH proj. no. 16,212
German saec. 15

528 Regula s. Benedicti. Germanice. MS. Vienna, Nationalbibliothek, codex 12911, f. 182v-197v. Octavo. Saec. 15.
Microfilm: MnCH proj. no. 20,028
German saec. 15

529 Regula s. Benedicti. Germanice. Incipit: Erhorsch und lern o sun. MS. Cistercienserabtei Wilhering, Austria, codex IX,14, f.1r-48v. Folio. Saec. 15.
Microfilm: MnCH proj. no. 2791
German saec. 16

530 Regula s. Benedicti. Germanice. Incipit: Hör sun die gepot deines maisters. MS. Benediktinerabtei Admont, Austria, codex 538. 62 f. Quarto. Saec. 16.
Microfilm: MnCH proj. no. 9595
German saec. 16

531 Regula s. Benedicti. Germanice. Incipit: Hor, o Tochter, die gepot deines Maysters. MS. Benediktinerabtei Altenburg, Austria, codex AB 6 C 6, f.119r-156v. Folio. Saec. 16.
"Diez Puech ist auss geschriben . . . in das Frawn Chloster zw Göttweich . . . 1505."
Microfilm: MnCH proj. no. 6400
German saec. 16

532 Regula s. Benedicti. Germanice. MS. Cistercienserabtei Lilienfeld, Austria, codex 21, f.61r-124v. Duodecimo. Saec. 16.
Microfilm: MnCH proj. no. 4331
German saec. 16

533 Regula s. Benedicti. Germanice. Incipit: Mein kind, merck auff die gebott deines Maisters. MS. Benediktinnerinenabtei Nonnberg, Salzburg, codex 23 C 3, f.1r-77v. Quarto. Saec. 16.
Microfilm: MnCH proj. no. 10,844
German saec. 16

533a Regula S. Benedicti saec. IX cum versione interlineari germanica saec. XVI. MS. Stiftsbibliothek St. Gallen, Switzerland, codex 916, p. 2-159. Octavo.
MnCH
German saec. 16

534 Regula s. Benedicti. Germanice. Benediktinerabtei St. Peter, Salzburg, codex b.X.7, f.5r-127r. Folio. Saec. 16.
Microfilm: MnCH proj. no. 10,598

German saec. 17

535 Regula s. Benedicti. Lingua germanica. MS. Benediktinerabtei St. Paul im Lavantthal, Austria, codex 910/0, III. Folio. Saec. 17.
Microfilm: MnCH proj. no. 12,646
German saec. 17

536 Regula s. Benedicti. Germanice. MS. Benediktinerabtei St. Peter, Salzburg, codex b.VII.2, f.1r-73r. Quarto. Saec. 17.
Microfilm: MnCH proj. no. 10,511
German saec. 18

537 Regula s. Benedicti, cum versione interlineari germanica. MS. Benediktinerabtei Melk, Austria, codex 148 (1074), f. 204r-317r). Quarto. Saec. 18.
Microfilm: MnCH proj. no. 1209

h. Italian

538 Regola di s. Benedetto (latine) con versione italiana. MS. Perugia, Italy, Badia di San Pietro, codex 17. Saec. 14.
Microfilm: MnCH

539 Regula s. Benedicti (italice), in Monasterio S. Conceptionis B.M.V. in Campo Mario servanda. MS. Toledo, Spain, Biblioteca del Cabildo, codex 25,7. 81 f. Quarto. Saec. 16?
Microfilm: MnCH proj. no. 33,327

i. Spanish

540 Regula monachorum s. Benedicti. Lingua Castellana. MS. Silos, Spain, Archivo del Monasterio de Sto. Domingo, Ms. 13. 59 f. Quarto. Saec. 14.
Microfilm: MnCH proj. no. 33,695

2. Printed Editions

Here are listed printed texts of the Rule. For works about printed editions of the Rule see under History of the Rule of St. Benedict, chapter III, B,9.

The references to Albareda are to Anselmo M. Albareda's *Bibliografia de la Regla Benedictina* (published at Monserrat, 1930).

a. Latin

Latin 1489

541 Regula s. Benedicti. Venetiae, 1489. Universitätsbibliothek Salzburg, codex M I 72, f.14-82. (The Regula is bound into a codex of manuscript material).
This is the first printed edition of the Rule of St. Benedict.
Albareda 1; Ges. Kat. der Wiegendrucke 3828; Hain 2772
Microfilm: MnCH proj. no. 10,981

Latin 1500

542 Regula b. patris Benedicti, ab Dunstano diligenter recognita. [Paris] Venundatur ab Iodoco Badio Ascensio [1500?].
[4], 100 leaves.
Hain 2771; Albareda 17; Ges. Kat. der Wiegendrucke 3831
PLatS

Latin 1505

543 Secundus dyalogorum liber beati Gregorij pape de vita et miraculis beatissimi Benedicti. Eiusdem almi patris nostri Benedicti Regula. [Venecia, L.A. de Giunta, 1505].
The Regula is p. [41]-83.
Albareda 26.
MnCS

Latin 1520

544 Regula sanctissimi patris nostri Benedicti, cum declarationibus editis a patribus Congregationis Casinensis pro directione et conservatione regularis observantiae & salubris regiminis dictae Congregationis. [Opus impressum Florentiae, 1520].
92 leaves.
Albareda 45.
Microfilm: MnCH proj. no. 10,663

Latin 1572

545 In Regulam divi patris Benedicti declarationes et constitutiones PP. Ordinis Camaldulensis. Florentiae, apud Bartholomaeum Sermatellium, 1572.
[32], 334 p. 17 cm.
The Rule is given in sections, with declarations following each section.
Albareda 79.
KAS

Latin 1595

546 Regula s. Benedicti, cvm constitvtionibvs Eremitarvm s. Romvaldi, Ordinis Camaldulensis. Venetiis, apud Matthaeum Valentinum, 1595.
[16], 285 p. 16 cm.
Albareda 118.
PLatS

Latin 1604

547 Regvla sancti patris Benedicti. cum declarationibus & constitutionibus editis a patribus Congregationis Casinensis . . . Mogvntiae, Balthasar Lippius, 1604.
187, 173 p. 18 cm.
Albareda 136.
MnCS

Latin 1684

548 Regula s. p. Benedicti. Coloniae, sumptibus Joannis Leonard Bibliopolae Bruxellensis, 1684.
74, 61 p.
NcBe

Latin 1701

549 Regula s. p. Benedicti, cum declarationibus Congregationis Sancti Mauri. [n.p.,] 1701.
[8], 296, [49] p. 20 cm.
Albareda 415.
KAS

Latin 1795

550 S. P. N. Benedicti Regula et vita . . . Viennae, typis & sumptibus Ignatii Goldhann, anno MDCCXCV.
280 p. 14 cm.
Albareda 557.
PLatS

Latin 1937

551 The Holy Rule of our most holy father Saint Benedict. Edited by the Benedictines of St. Meinrad Abbey. St. Meinrad, Ind., The Abbey Press, 1937.
110 p. 18 cm.
KAS

Latin 1956

552 Regla del gran padre y patriarca San Benito. 4. ed. Burgos: Abadia de Santo Domingo de Silos, 1956.
190 p. 10 cm.
KAS

Latin 1960

553 The Rule of Saint Benedict, in Latin and English, edited & translated by Justin McCann. London, Burnes Oates, 1960.
xxiv, 214 p. 20 cm.
First published 1952.
InFer; NcBe

Latin 1960

553a Benedicti Regula. Recensuit Rudolphus Hanslik. Vindobonae, Hoelder-Pichler-Tempsky, 1960.
lxxiv, 376 p. 24 cm. (Corpus ecclesiasticorum latinorum, v. 75)
MnCS; PLatS

Latin 1962

554 Benedicti Regula; text latin, traduction et concordance par D. Ph. Schmitz. Etude sur la langue de S. Benoit par Ch. Mohrmann. 3. ed. Maredsous, 1962.
xii, 306 p. 18 cm.
MnCS

Latin 1962

555 Regula monasteriorum. Westmalle [Belgium], 1962.
vi, 132 p. 12 cm.
InStme

Latin 1963

556 Die Benediktusregel, lateinisch-deutsch. Hrsg. von P. Basilius Steidle, O.S.B. Beuron, Beuroner Kunstverlag [c 1963].
229 p. 19 cm.
KAS; MnCS; PLatS

Latin 1968

556a San Benito, su vida y su Regla. Dirección e introducciones del padre Dom Garcia M. Colombás, versiones del padre Dom Leon M. Sansegundo, comentarios y notas del padre Dom Odilon M. Cunill. 2. ed. Madrid, Biblioteca de Autores Cristianos, 1968.
xx, 789 p. 20 cm.
Text of Regula (Latin and Spanish), p. 263–720.
MnCS

Latin 1972

557 Règle de saint Benoît. Introduction, traduction, et notes par Adalbert de Vogüé. Texte établi et présenté par Jean Neufville. Paris, Editions du Cerf, 1972.
3 v. 20 cm. (Série des textes monastiques, no. 34-36. Sources chrétiennes, no. 181-183)
Latin text and French translation of the Rule.
CaQMo; InStme; KAS; MnCS; PLatS

Latin 1975

557a Regula monasteriorum Sancti Benedicti abbatis. Rosano, Italy, Monastero S. Maria, 1975.
246 p.
Latin and Italian.
MnCS

Latin 1975

557b Die Benedictus-Regel. Lateinisch-deutsch. Hrsg. von Basilius Steidle. 2. überarbeitete Aufl. Beuron, Kunstverlag, 1975.
211 p.
MnCS

Latin 1977

557c Benedicti Regula. Recensuit Rudolphus Hanslik. Editio altera emendata. Vindobonae, Hoelder-Pichler-Tempsky, 1977.
lxix, 375 p. 23 cm. (Corpus ecclesiasticorum latinorum, v. 75)
MnCS; PLatS

Latin 1978

557d Dei Winteney-Version der Regula S. Benedicti, hrsg. von Arnold Schröer. Nachdruck des mittelenglischen und lateinischen Textes nach der ersten Auflage (1888) mit einem Anhang von Mechtild Gretsch. Tübingen, Max Niemeyer, 1978.
xxviii, 193 p. facsim. 24 cm.
InStme; MnCS

Latin 1979

557e La Regla de San Benito. Introducción y comentario por García M. Colombás, monje benedictino, traducción y notas por Iñaki Araguren, monje cisterciense. Madrid, Biblioteca de Autores Cristianos, 1979.

xxiii, 510 p. 20 cm.
Text of Regula (Latin and Spanish), p. 65-190.
MnCS

Latin 1980

558 Règle de Saint Benoît. Texte latin, version française par H. Rochais. Introduction et notes par E. Manning. Edition centenaire. Rochefort, Belgium. Les Editions La Documentation Cistercienne, 1980.
xlii, 236 p. 22 cm.
KAS; MnCS

Latin 1981

558a RB 1980: The Rule of St. Benedict in Latin and English with notes. Editor: Timothy Fry, O.S.B. Collegeville, Minn., The Liturgical Press [1981].
xxxvi, 627 p. 23 cm.
MnCS

b. Armenian

559 Rule of our holy father, Benedict, translated by the disciples of their great father, Mechitar. Vienna, in the Monastery under the Tutelage of the Holy Mother of God, 1842.
[12], 138, [6] p. 14 cm.
Title page and text in Armenian.
MnCS; PLatS

ba. Briton

559a Reoleun ar Venech. Louannec, Itron Varia Keresperzh, 1974.
75 p. dactyl.
MnCS

c. Chinese

560 [Regula sancti Benedicti. Chinese translation].
(In Straelen, Henricus van. Mountains of peace. Tokyo, 1956. p. 363-443)
InStme

d. Czech

561 Rehole Sv. Otce Benedikta, do cestiny prelozil a opsal P. Wenceslav Kocarník, O.S.B. Pilzen, Nebr., 1883.
111 p. 19 cm.
Handwritten.
MnCS

da. Danish

561a "Luister"; Grandgedachten von de Regel van St. Benedictus. 2. ed. Berkel-Enshot [Denmark], Abbaye de Koningsoord, 1974.
43 p.
MnCS

db. Dutch

561b Die Middelnederlandse vergaling van de
     Regula sancti Benedicti.
     3 v. in 1.
     Katholische Univ. te Leuven Faculteit
     van de Wijabegerte en de Letteren, 1976.
     MnCS

e. English

Middle English

562 Die Winteney-Version der Regula S. Bene-
    dicti, hrsg. von Arnold Schröer. Nach-
    druck des mittelenglischen und lateinis-
    chen Textes nach der ersten Auflage
    [1888] mit einem Anhang von Mechthild
    Gretsch. Tübingen, Max Niemeyer,
    1978.
    xxviii, 193 p. facsim. 24 cm.
    InStme; MnCS

English 1516

562a Here begynneth the Rule of seynt Benet.
     [London, R. Pynson, 1516?].
     Albareda 41.
     MnCS(microfilm)

English 1632

563 The Rvle of the Most Blissed Father Saint
    Benedict . . . Gant, printed by I. Dooms
    [1632].
    Short-title catalogue no. 1860.
    Albareda 248?
    KAS(microfilm); MnCS(microfilm)

English 1632

564 The rule of the most blissed Father Saint
    Benedict [with] Statutes compyled for
    the better observation of the Holy Rule
    of the most glorious Father and Patri-
    arch S. Benedict. [London, The Scolar
    Press, 1976].
    [6], 103, 61, 75, 30 p. 23 cm. (English
    recusant literature, 1558–1640, v. 278).
    MnCS; PLatS

English 1638

565 The second book of the Dialogves of S.
    Gregorie the Greate, the first pope of
    that name, containinge the life and mira-
    cles of ovr holie father S. Benedict. To
    which is adcoined the Rule of the same
    holie Patriarche translated into Englishe
    tonge by C. F. priest & monke of the
    same order. Printed ann. 1638.
    110, 130 p.
    Albareda 245.
    Yale University Library

English 1638

566 The second booke of the dialogves of S.
    Gregorie the Greate . . . containinge the
    life and miracles of ovr holie Father S.
    Benedict. To which is adcoined The Rule
    of the same holie Patriarche . . . origin-

ally published 1638. Ilkley, The Scolar
Press, 1976.
[11], 108, [5], 130, [10], 62 p. 19 cm. (Eng-
lish recusant literature, 1558–1640, v. 294)
Facsimile reprint of the 1638 edition.
MnCS

English 1921

567 The Holy Rule of our most holy father
    Saint Benedict. Belmont, N.C., Belmont
    Abbey Press, 1921.
    127 p. 14 cm.
    KyCovS; NcBe

English 1948

568 Rule for monasteries, tr. from the Latin by
    Leonard J. Doyle. Collegeville, Minn.,
    The Liturgical Press [c 1948].
    viii, 100 p. 14 cm.
    KAS; MnCS

English 1960

569 The Rule of Saint Benedict, in Latin and
    English, edited & translated by Justin
    McCann. London, Burnes Oates [1960].
    xxiv, 214 p. 20 cm. (The Orchard books)
    NcBe

English 1963

570 The Rule of St. Benedict, published for the
    first time in Australia, with a translation
    by Richard (John) Crotty. [Nedlands,
    West Australia] The University of West-
    ern Australia Press, 1963.
    viii, 91 p. 22 cm.
    Latin and English on opposite pages.
    CaQStB; KAS; PLatS

English 1967

571 The Rule of St. Benedict. With an introduc-
    tion, new translation of the Rule and a
    commentary, all reviewed in the light of
    an earlier monasticism . . . by Urban J.
    Schnitzhofer, O.S.B. Canon City Colo.,
    Holy Cross Abbey [1967?].
    x, 307 p. 19 cm.
    InStme; KAS; PLatS

English 1968

572 The Holy Rule of St. Benedict, Abbot, with
    prolegomena from Book I of excerpts
    from the saints. St. Charles House, 1968.
    48 p.
    MdRi

English 1969

573 The Rule of Saint Benedict for monaste-
    ries. A translation by Dom Bernard Basil
    Bolton, O.S.B. Newport, Gwent, Eng-
    land, R. J. Johns [1969].
    81 p.
    MoCo; PLatS

English 1975

574 The Holy Rule of our most holy father,
    Saint Benedict. Edited by the Benedic-

tine monks of St. Meinrad Archabbey. St. Meinrad, Ind., Abbey Press, 1975.
xii, 95 p. 22 cm.
InStme; MdRi ; PLatS

English 1975

575 The Rule of St. Benedict. Translated, with introduction and notes by Anthony C. Meisel and M. L. del Mastro. Garden City, N.Y., Image Books, 1975.
117 p. 18 cm.
InFer; KAS; MdRi; MnStj

English 1980

575a Households of God; the Rule of St. Benedict with explanations for monks and lay-people today. [Translation and commentary by] David Parry, O.S.B. Kalamazoo, Cistercian Publications [1980].
199 p. (Cistercian studies series, no. 39)
NcBe

English 1981

575b RB 1980: the Rule of St. Benedict in Latin and English with notes. Editor: Timothy Fry, O.S.B. Collegeville, Minn., The Liturgical Press [1981].
xxxvi, 627 p. 23 cm.
MnCS

f. French

Norman French

576 The Rule of St. Benedict, a Norman prose version. Edited by Ruth J. Dean and M. Dominica Legge. Oxford, Published for the Society for the Study of Mediaeval Languages and Literature, 1964.
xxx, 111 p. facsim. 25 cm. (Medium Aevum monographs, VII)
InStme; KAS; MnCS; PLatS

French 1666

577 Règle et statvts des religievses de l'Ordre S. Benoist, réformées par R.P.M. Estienne Poncher. Paris, chez Florentin Lambert, 1666.
[66], 388 p.
Albareda 320.
NcBe

French 1950

578 La Règle de Saint Benoît, traduite et annotée par Dom Augustin Savaton. Wisques, Pas-de-Calais, Abbaye Saint-Paul; Lille, S.I.L.I.C. [1950].
179 p. 20 cm.
PLatS

French 1961

579 La Règle de saint Benoit. Le Bouveret, Prieuré Saint-Benoît de Port-Valais, 1961.
257 p. 12 cm.
KAS

French 1961

580 La Règle de saint Benoît [Trad., introd. et notes par Antoine Dumas, O.S.B.]. Le Jas du Revest-Saint-Martin, R. Morel, 1961.
283 p. 14x20 cm.
KAS; PLatS

French 1962

581 Benedicti Regula; texte latin, traduction et concordance par D. Ph. Schmitz. Etude sur la langue de S. Benoît par Ch. Mohrmann. 3. éd. Maredsous, 1962.
xli, 306 p. 18 cm.
MnCS

French 1965

582 Dialogues de saint Grégoire et Règle de saint Benoît. Extraits traduits par E. de Solms. La Pierre-qui-Vire, Zodiaque, 1965.
199 p. 72 plates (part col.) 26 cm.
MnCS

French 1965

583 La vie et la Règle de saint Benoît. [Dirigée par les moines de la Pierre-qui-Vire et préparé par la R.M. Elisabeth de Solms]. Bruges, Desclée de Brouwer [c 1965].
319, [7] p. 17 cm.
PLatS

French 1967

584 Des hommes en quête de Dieu: la Règle de saint Benoît. Introduction et notes par Antoine Dumas, O.S.B. Paris, Editions du Cerf [1967].
181 p. 18 cm.
CaQMo; MoCo; PLatS

French 1972

585 La Règle de saint Benoît. Introd., traduction, et notes par Adalbert de Vogüé. Paris, Editions du Cerf, 1972.
3 v. 20 cm. (Sources chrétiennes, no. 181-183)
CaQMo; InStme; KAS; MnCS; PLatS

French 1977

586 La Règle de saint Benoît. [Tr. par Antoine Dumas, O.S.B.]. 2. éd. [Paris], Editions du Cerf, 1977.
153 p.
MoCo

French 1980

587 Règle de Saint Benoît. Texte latin, version française par H. Rochais. Introduction et notes par E. Manning. Edition centenaire. Rochefort, Belgium, Les Editions La Documentation Cistercienne, 1980.
xlii, 236 p. 22 cm.
KAS; MnCS

g. German

For Old High German and Middle High German *see also* under Manuscripts, nos. 428-429.

1. Old High German, 800-1100

588 Die althochdeutsche Benediktinerregel des Cod. Sang. 916, hrsg. von Ursula Daab. Tübingen, M. Niemeyer, 1959.
304 p. (Altdeutsche Textbibliothek, Nr. 50)
KAS; PLatS

589 Daab, Ursula.
Studien zur althochdeutschen Benediktinerregel. [Wiesbaden] M. Sändig [1973].
93 p. 23 cm.
Reprint of the 1929 edition.
PLatS

2. Middle High German, 1100-1350

590 A Middle High German Benedictine Rule: MS. 448a Germanisches Nationalmuseum Nürnberg. Commentary, edition, glossary [edited by] Mary C. Sullivan. Hildesheim, H. G. Gerstenberg, 1976.
324 p. 16 leaves of plates, facsims., 22 cm. (Regulae Benedicti studia: Supplementa, Bd. 4)
Originally presented as the editor's thesis, University of Pennsylvania, 1973.
MnCS

591 Eine mittelhochdeutsche Benediktinerregel: Hs. 1256/587 (Aufang 15. Jh.) Stadtbibliothek Trier. Edition, lateinisch-mittelhochdeutsches Glossar, mittelhochdeutsch-lateinisches Glossar. Hildesheim, Gerstenberg Verlag, 1978.
viii, 8 facsims. 267 p. 22 cm.
At head of title: Edda Petri.
MnCS

592 Schmidt, Konrad.
Vier deutsche Benediktinerregeln aus dem späten Mittelalter, nach den Handschriften hrsg. und mit Einleitungen und einem lateinisch-deutschen Glossar versehen. Berlin, 1969.
viii, 345 p. 21 cm.
Diss. – Technische Universität, Berlin.
MnCS

3. Modern German

German 15th cent.
592a MS. Archabbey Beuron no. 39; a late east Middle Netherlandic version of the Benedictine Rule edited with philological and textual-critical commentary by Philip E. Weber. Ann Arbor, Mich., University Microfilms, 1973.

ix, 280 p. facsim. 20 cm.
Diss. (Ph.D.) – Bryn Maur.
MnCS

German 1684
593 Regvla s. p. Benedicti. Coloniae, Joannis Leonard, 1684.
74 p. 10 cm.
Albareda 366
InStme

German 1961
594 Die Regel des heiligen Benedikt, übersetzt und kurz erklärt von Dr. P. Eugen Pfiffner. Einsiedeln / Zürich, Benziger Verlag, 1961.
181 p. 19 cm.
MnCS

German 1963
595 Die Benediktusregel, lateinisch-deutsch. Hrsg. von P. Basilius Steidle, O.S.B. Beuron, Beuroner Kunstverlag [1963].
229 p. 19 cm.
MnCS; KAS; PLatS

German 1965
596 Die Regel des hl. Benedikt. Hrsg. von der Erzabtei Beuron. 10. Aufl. Beuron, Beuroner Kunstverlag [1965].
137 p. 17 cm.
PLatS

German 1975
596a Die Benedictus-Regel. Lateinisch-deutsch. Hrsg. von Basilius Steidle. 2. überarbeitete Aufl. Beuron, Kunstverlag, 1975.
211 p.
MnCS

German 1977
596b Regel des hl. Benedict. Hrsg. von der Erzabtei Beuron. 11. Aufl. Beuron, Kunstverlag, 1977.
143 p.
MnCS

German 1977
596c Benediktusregel. Auszug und freie Uebersetzung ins Deutsche. St. Ottilien, Eos-Verlag, 1977.
107 p.
MnCS

h. Italian

Italian 1501
597 Questa sie la Regula del gloriosissimo confessore miser sancto Benedeto vulgarizata. [Venecia, L.A. di Giunta, 1501].
103 p. plate, 11 cm.
Albareda 21.
KyTr; MnCS

Italian 1866
598 Regola del padre San Benedetto sopra un testo italiano del cinquecento ad uso delle

monache che vivono sotto la detta Regola ed osservanza Cassinese ... 2. ed. Roma, Tipografia Salviucci, 1866.
282 p. 23 cm.
Albareda 633.
KAS

Italian 1928

599 Regola di s. Benedetto abate, patriarca dei monaci. Subiaco, Tipografia dei monasteri, 1928.
viii, 136 p.
Albareda 865.
ILSP

Italian 1974

600 La Regola. Introduzione, versione e commento delle Benedettine di S. Maria di Rosano. 2. ed. Siena, Cantagalli, 1974.
313 p. 18 cm.
MnCS

Italian 1975

600a Regula monasteriorum Sancti Benedicti abbatis. Rosano, Monasterio S. Maria, 1975.
246 p.
Latin and Italian.
MnCS

i. Japanese

601 Regula monasteriorum (Japanese title: Rule of the monasteries of Saint Benedict). [Translator: Van Straelen. Tokyo, L. Enderly, agent for Herder, 1958].
87 p. 22 cm.
Japanese text only.
CaQStB; MnCS

j. Korean

602 [The Rule of St. Benedict, translated into Korean]. Benedictine Abbey Waegwan, Kyong-buk, South Korea, 1962.
[8], 116 p. front. (port.) 14 cm.
Title page and text in Korean.
MnCS

603 [The Rule of St. Benedict, translated into Korean]. 4th edition. Benedictine Abbey Waegwan, Kyong-buk, South Korea, 1974.
[4], 122 p. front. (facsim.) 15 cm.
Title page and text in Korean.
MnCS

k. Portuguese

Portuguese 1632

604 Regra do glorioso patriarcha S. Bento tirada de latim em lingoagem portuguese por industria de rev. p. fr. Thomas do Socorro. Coimbra, Nicolas Carvalho, 1632.

47 p. 19 x 27 cm.
Photo-reproduction. Chicago, Newberry Library, 1961?
Albareda 227.
KAS

Portuguese 1937

605 Regra do S. Bento, traduzida de latim por D. Crisostomo d'Aguiar. [Porto?], Cucuiäes, 1937.
189 p. 14 cm.
MnCS

Portuguese 1951

606 Regra do glorioso patriarca S. Bento. Traduzida do latim e anotada pelos monges de Singeverga. Edicöes "Ora & Labora," 1951.
xv, 116 p. 18 cm.
CaQStB; MnCS; PLatS

Portuguese 1958

607 Regra do Sao Bento, traduçao e notas di D. Joao Ev. de O. Ribeiro Enout, O.S.B. Salvador-Bahia, impresso na Tip Beneditina LTDA., 1958.
123 p. 20 cm.
KAS

l. Spanish

Spanish 1599

608 Regla del bienaventurado San Benito [incomplete at beginning]. Valladolid, Juan Godínez de Millis, 1599.
55 p.
Xerographic copy.
Albareda 129.
MnCS

Spanish 16 –

608a Regla del gran patriarcha San Benito. n.p., n.d.
312 p. 7 cm.
Title page and first four pages are missing.
p. 249-312: Several chapters about St. Benedict, the Regula, and the Order of St. Benedict.
MnCH (microfilm)

Spanish 1633

608b Regla, vida, y milagros de nuestro glorioso p. S. Benito patriarcha de todas las ordenes monasticas. Barcelona, Lorenco Deu, 1633.
123 p. 7 cm.
Albareda 231.
MnCH (microfilm)

Spanish 1663

608c Vida, milagros, transito, translacion, y Santa Regla de nuestro gloriosisimo padre San Benito abad, princips, y patriarca de los ordenes monaches y militares

. . . Zaragosa, Pedro Lanaja y Lannares, 1663.
144, 152 p. 14 cm.
MnCH (microfilm)

Spanish 1693
608d Regla monachorum. Madrid, Melchior Alvares, 1693.
242 p. 10 cm.
MnCH (microfilm)

Spanish 1725
609 Regla de el gran patriarcha S. Benito. Nuevamenta traducida. Madrid, Lorenço Francisco Mojados, 1725.
256 p. 15 cm.
Xerographic copy.
MnCS

Spanish 1746
610 Regla de el gran patriarcha S. Benito. Madrid, Antonio Sanz, 1746.
Xerographic copy.
MnCS

Spanish 1752
610a Regla de monges que escribio el patriarca de todas S. Benito, nuevamente traducida en lengua vulgar. Ldon de Francia, Tournes Hermans, 1752.
229, 44 p. 8 cm.
Albareda 498.
MnCH (microfilm)

Spanish 1762
611 Regla de el gran patriarcha S. Benito. Madrid, por Andrès Ortega, 1762.
248 p. 6 cm.
Albareda 513.
MnStj(Archives)

Spanish 1791
612 Regla de el gran patriarcha S. Benito, nuevamente traducida. Madrid, Josef Herrera Batanero, 1791.
248 p. illus. 15 cm.
Xerographic copy.
Albareda 553.
MnCS

Spanish 1837
612a Regla monachorum. Valladolid, Plazuela Vieja, 1837.
MnCH (microfilm)

Spanish 1876
613 Regla del gran patriarca San Benito. Barcelona, Heredero de H. Pablo Riera, 1876.
238 p. 16 cm.
Xerographic copy.
Albareda 648.
MnCS

Spanish 1949
614 Regla de monjes; versión castellana con una introducción y breves comentarios por el R. P. Bruno Avila, O.S.B. 3. ed.

Buenos Aires, Editorial Benedictina [1947].
203 p. 20 cm.
KAS

Spanish 1968
614a San Benito, su vida y su Regla. Dirección e introducciones del padre Dom García M. Colombás, versiones del padre Dom Leon M. Sansegundo, comentarios y notas del padre Dom Odilon M. Cunill. 2. ed. Madrid, Biblioteca de Autores Cristianos, 1968.
xx, 789 p. 20 cm.
Text of Regula (Latin and Spanish), p. 263-720.
MnCS

Spanish 1973
615 Regla del gran padre y patriarca San Benito. 6. ed. Burgos, Abadia de Santo Domingo de Silos, 1973.
186 p. front. 11 cm.
MnCS; PLatS

Spanish 1979
615a La Regla de San Benito. Introducción y comentario por García M. Colombás, monje benedictino, traducción y notas por Iñaki Araguren, monje cisterciense. Madrid, Biblioteca de Autores Cristianos, 1979.
xxiii, 510 p. 20 cm.
Text of Regula (Latin and Spanish), p. 65-190.
MnCS

B. ABOUT THE RULE

1. General Works

a. Manuscripts

616 **Canon in Regulam s. Benedicti.** MS. Universitätsbibliothek Graz, Austria, codex 1609, f.300r-302r. Octavo. Saec. 15.
Microfilm: MnCH proj. no. 26,509

617 **Canon in Regulam s. Benedicti.** MS. Benediktinerabtei St. Peter, Salzburg, codex b.V.15, f.215r-223r. Quarto. Saec. 15.
Microfilm: MnCH proj. no. 10,445

618 **De praeceptis Regulae s. Benedicti.** MS. Universitätsbibliothek Graz, Austria, codex 992, f.130r-133v. Quarto. Saec. 15.
Microfilm: MnCH proj. no. 27,054

619 **De Regula s. Benedicti** ejusque divisione. MS. Benediktinerabtei Melk, Austria, codex 1075, f.647-661. Duodecimo. Saec. 15.
Microfilm: MnCH proj. no. 1833

620 **Ad Regulae sancti Benedicti** singula capita phraeses commodae. MS. Cister-

cienserabtei Heiligenkreuz, Austria, codex 567, f.3r-45v. Quarto. Saec. 17. Microfilm: MnCH proj. no. 4934

621 **Keck, Johann, O.S.B.**
Tractatus de observantia statutorum Regulae s. Benedicti. MS. Vienna, Schottenstift, codex 405, f.1r-50r. Octavo. Saec. 15.
Microfilm: MnCH proj. no. 4148

622 **Memoriale capitulorum** Regulae s. Benedicti. MS. Benediktinerabtei Melk, Austria, codex 1214, f.69r-72v. Sextodecimo. Saec. 15.
Microfilm: MnCH proj. no. 1865

623 **Memoriale in Regulam s. Benedicti.** MS. Benediktinerabtei Lambach, Austria, codex chart. 453, f.254r-256v. Saec. 15.
Microfilm: MnCH proj. no. 740

624 **Memoriale in Regulam s. Benedicti.** MS. Benediktinerabtei St. Peter, Salzburg, codex b.II.1, f.122r-123v. Duodecimo. Saec. 15.
Microfilm: MnCH proj. no. 10,313

625 **Notabilia varia,** loci e Regula s. Benedicti, etc. MS. Vienna, Nationalbibliothek, codex 3792, f.304r-312r. Quarto. Saec. 15.
Microfilm: MnCH proj. no. 17,012

626 **Notabiliora capitula Regulae** s. Benedicti magis valentia pro instructione novitiorum. MS. Vienna, Nationalbibliothek, codex 4554, f.1r-39v. Octavo. Saec. 15.
Microfilm: MnCH proj. no. 17,731

627 **Petrus de Rosenheim, O.S.B.**
Memoriale capitulorum Regulae s. Benedicti. MS. Benediktinerabtei Melk, Austria, codex 614, f.67v-70v. Quarto. Saec. 15.
Microfilm: MnCH proj. no. 1503
For other manuscript copies of this work see under Petrus von Rosenheim in Author Part.

628 **Praxis in Regulam s. Benedicti.** MS. Vienna, Schottenstift, codex 405, f.121r-139v. Octavo. Saec. 15.
Microfilm: MnCH proj. no. 4148

629 **Quaedam tuitiones** pro observantia Regulae s. Benedicti. MS. Benediktinerabtei Melk, Austria, codex 1802, f.203r-214r. Quarto. Saec. 16.
Microfilm: MnCH proj. no. 2118

630 **Quaestiones theologicae varii argumenti,** v.g., de confessione, de Corpore Christi, de Regula s. Benedicti, etc. MS. Vienna, Schottenstift, codex 177, f.158r-369v. Octavo. Saec. 15.
Microfilm: MnCH proj. no. 3910

631 **Rodriguez, Antonio Rodriguez, O.Cist.**
Antiguidad de le Regla del gran patriarca s. Benito dentro de España vindicada contra Cayetano Cenni. MS. Monasterio benedictino de Montserrat, Spain, codex 1012. 163 f. Octavo. Saec. 19.
Microfilm: MnCH proj. no. 30,123

632 **Signationes capitulorum Regulae** s. Benedicti secundum alphabetum. MS. Benediktinerabtei Melk, Austria, codex 1075, f.880-882. Duodecimo. Saec. 15.
Microfilm: MnCH proj. no. 1833

633 **Summula Regulae s. Benedicti.** MS. Benediktinerabtei Melk, Austria, codex 1087, f.54-56. Duodecimo. Saec. 15.
Microfilm: MnCH proj. no. 1842

634 **Torquemada, Juan, O.P.**
Commendatio Regulae sanctissimi patris Benedicti. MS. Benediktinerabtei Melk, Austria, codex 939, f.193r-193v. Folio. Saec. 14.
Microfilm: MnCH proj. no. 1748

635 **Utrum omnia in Regula** s. Benedicti sint in praecepto. MS. Benediktinerabtei Melk, Austria, codex 1933, f.121v-131v. Quarto. Saec. 15.
Microfilm: MnCH proj. no. 2213

b. Printed Works

636 **Albareda, Anselm M., O.S.B.**
Bibliografia de la Regla Benedictina. Monastir de Montserrat, MCMXXXIII. xviii, 660 p. illus. 28 cm.
Contents: p. 5–21, Fonts utilitzades; p. 22–28, Estat actual de la bibliografia de la Regla; p. 29–45, Literatura ascetica inspirada en la Regla Benedictina; p. 46–63, Escrits estampats junt amb la Santa Regla; p. 64–115, El text; p. 115–176, Les versions; p. 177–194, Edicions destinades a monges; p. 195–286, Remarques tipografiques; p. 287–634, Recensions; p. 635–643, Epileg; p. 647–656, Indexs.
InStme; KAS; MnCS; PLatS

636a **Bernard de Clairvaux, Saint.**
Elimatvm ad Regvlam Benedictinam scholion, qvod inscribitur Liber de praecepto et dispensatione, omnes qvaestiones morales, qvae in monastico foro ventilantvr solide, acvte et benigne resolvens . . . Recognitum illustratum, dilucidatum a Ioanne Caramvel Lobkowitz. Lovanii, apud Everardum de Witte, 1643.
[8], 254, [24] p. 20 cm.
KAS

637 **Bieler, Ludwig.**
     Miscella Benedictina (Bemerkungen zum
     Text der Benediktinerregel).
     (*In* Latinität und alte kirche; Festschrift
     für Rudolf Hanslik zum 70. Geburtstag.
     Wien, 1977. p. 36-38)
     MnCS; PLatS

638 **Botz, Paschal Robert, O.S.B.**
     The Holy Rule [of St. Benedict] in the
     modern world . . .
     (*In* St. Joseph magazine, v. 48(1947),
     p. 30-33)
     MnCS

639 **Braso, Gabriel, O.S.B.**
     Sentier de vie au seuil de notre conver-
     sion; conferences sur la Règle de saint
     Benoît. Abbaye de Bellefontaine, 1974.
     196 p. 21 cm.
     InStme

640 **Brooke, Christopher N. L.**
     The Rule of St. Benedict.
     (*In* his: The monastic world 1000-1300.
     New York, 1974, p. 33-40)
     PLatS

641 **Cannon, Mary Lawrence, Sister, O.S.B.**
     Christo-centric character of the Rule of
     St. Benedict.
     Thesis (M.A.)–St. John's University,
     Collegeville, Minn., 1963.
     KyCovS

642 **Conception Abbey, Conception, Mo.**
     The Holy Rule of Saint Benedict as lived
     by the monks of Conception Abbey, Con-
     ception, Missouri. [Conception, Mo., 1961].
     [48] p. illus. 21x28 cm.
     MnCS

643 **Deseille, Placide.**
     Regards sur la tradition monastique. Ab-
     baye de Bellefontaine, 1974.
     222p. 21 cm.
     InStme

644 **Dreuille, Mayeul de, O.S.B.**
     St. Benedict life and miracles by St.
     Gregory the Great; and, An introduction to
     his Rule by Dom Mayeul de Dreuille.
     [Dasarahalli, Bangalore] St. Paul Publica-
     tions [1972].
     180 p. 19 cm.
     PLatS

645 **Dudine, Charles, O.S.B.**
     Educational psychology and the Rule of
     St. Benedict; a comparative study.
     63 leaves, 28 cm.
     Thesis (M.A.)–University of Notre
     Dame, 1929.
     Typescript.
     InStme

646 **Gretsch, Mechthild.**
     Aethelwold's translation of the Regula
     sancti Benedicti and its Latin exemplar.
     (*In* Anglo-Saxon England 3. Edited by
     Peter Clemoes. Cambridge, 1874. p.
     125-151)
     PLatS

646a **Hacia una relectura** de la Regla de San
     Benito; XVII Semana de Estudios
     Monasticos (XV centenario del nacimien-
     to de San Benito, 480–1980).
     Abadia de Silos, 1980.
     476 p. 23 cm. (Studia Silensia, VI)
     MnCS

647 **Helbling, Leo, O.S.B.**
     Die "Exhortationes in Regulam sancti
     Benedicti" des Einsiedler Abtes Augustin
     Reding.
     (*In* Studien aus dem Gebiete von Kirche
     und Kultur. Paderborn, 1930. p. 87-127)
     PLatS

648 **Jaspert, Bernd.**
     Die Regula Benedicti - Regula Magistri-
     Kontroverse. Hildesheim, H. A. Gersten-
     berg, 1975.
     xxii, 519 p. 22 cm. (Regula Benedicti
     studia. Supplementa, Bd. 3)
     MnCS; PLatS

649 **Kasch, Elisabeth.**
     Das liturgische Vokabular der frühen la-
     teinischen Mönchsregeln. Hildesheim,
     Gerstenberg Verlag, 1974.
     xv, 403 p. 22 cm.
     MnCS

650 **Kemmer, Alfons, O.S.B.**
     Christ in the Rule of St. Benedict.
     (*In* Monastic studies, v. 3, p. 87-98)
     PLatS

651 **Knowles, David, O.S.B.**
     Great historical enterprises: Problems in
     monastic history. London, New York,
     Nelson [1964].
     viii, 231 p. 23 cm.
     PLatS

652 **Leclercq, Jean, O.S.B.**
     Regola benedettina e presenza nel mon-
     do.
     (*In* La Bonifica benedettina, p. 15-25)
     PLatS

653 **Linage Conde, Antonio.**
     Una regla monastica riojana feminina
     des siglo X: el "Libellus a Regula sancti
     Benedicti subtractatus." Salamanca,
     Universidad, 1973.
     xiii, 142 p. facsims. 26 cm.
     MnCS

653a **RB 1980:** the Rule of St. Benedict in Latin
     and English with notes. Editor: Timothy

Fry, O.S.B. Collegeville, Minn., The Liturgical Press [1981].
xxxvi, 627 p. 23 cm.
Contents: p. 3–112, Historical orientation; p. 113–151, The Rule in history; p. 156–297, Latin and English text, with patristic sources and notes; p. 301–493, Longer expositions of monastic topics: Monk, Cenobite, Nun, Abbot, Liturgy, Discipline, Profession, Scripture in the Rule, Rule of Benedict and Rule of the Master; p. 497–612, Classified reference resources; p. 613–627, Indexes.
InStme; KAS; MnCS; PLatS

654 **La Règle de saint Benoît.** [Laval, France, Abbaye Cistercienne, 1973].
220 p. illus., charts, 31 cm.
InStme

655 **Regulae Benedicti studia.** Annuarium internationale, in connection with Rudolf Hanslik [et al.]. Hildesheim, H. A. Gerstenberg, 1972–
v. 25 cm.
Contributions in various languages.
InStme; MnCS; PLatS

655a **Roberts, Augustine, O.C.S.O.**
Centered on Christ. Still River, Mass., St. Bede's Publications, 1979.
x, 169 p. 23 cm.
PLatS

656 **St. Benedict's Abbey, Benet Lake, Wis.**
The interpretation of the Rule of St. Benedict for the monks of St. Benedict's Abbey, Benet Lake, Wisconsin. [Benet Lake, Wis., St. Benedict's Abbey, 196-?]
25 p.
MoCo

657 **Sczielski, Stanislaus, O.S.B.**
Catechismus monasticus; sive, Regulae s. Benedicti synopsis analytica in gratiam religiosorum omnium sub eadem sacra Regula militantium. Nunc denuo typis recusa. Bambergae, Wolfgangus Mauritius, 1713.
148 p. 17 cm.
KAS

658 **Sullivan, Walter, O.S.B.**
Reflections on the Holy Rule. St. Meinrad, Ind., Abbey Press [1974].
72 p. 23 cm.
InStme

659 **Vogüé, Adalbert de, O.S.B.**
Autour de saint Benoît: la Règle en son temps et dans le notre. Abbaye de Bellefontaine, 1975.
158 p., plates, 21 cm.
InStme

660 **Vogüé, Adalbert de, O.S.B.**
Conferences on the Benedictine Rule and life (Phonotape-cassette). St. Meinrad, Ind., St. Meinrad Archabbey, 1977.
9 tapes (c. 45 min. each side) 1 7/8 ips.
InStme

661 **Vogüé, Adalbert de, O.S.B.**
Les conseils evangéliques chez le Maitre et saint Benoît.
(*In* Semana de Estudios monasticos, 14th, Silos, Spain, 1973. Silos, 1975. p. 13-27)
PLatS

662 **Widhalm, Gloria Maria.**
Die rhetorischen Elemente in der Regula Benedicti. Hildesheim, Gerstenberg, 1974.
264 p. 22 cm. (Regulae Benedicti studia. Supplementa, Bd. 2)
InStme; MnCS; PLatS

2. Art.

663 **Regula s. Benedicti.** Cum pulchris initialibus. MS. Benediktinerabtei Admont, Austria, codex 567, f.47r-86v. Quarto. Saec. 12.
Microfilm: MnCH proj. no. 9610

3. Biblical Quotations

664 **Pawlowsky, Sigismund, O.S.B.**
Die biblischen Grundlagen der Regula Benedicti. Wien, Herder [1965].
122 p. 23 cm. (Wiener Beiträge zur Theologie, Bd. 9)
InStme; KAS; MnCS; PLatS

4. Bibliography

665 **Die Benediktregel in Bayern:** Ausstellung der Bayerischen Staatsbibliothek, 29. November 1980–10. Januar 1981. München [Bayerische Staatsbibliothek] 1980.
79 p. 16 plates (part col.) 22 cm.
MnCS

666 **Broekaert, Jean D., O.S.B.**
Bibliographie de la Règle de saint Benoît. Editions latines et traductions imprimées de 1489 à 1929: 1239 numeros. Roma, Editrice Anselmiana, 1980.
2 v. 24 cm. (Studia Anselmiana, 77-78)
InStme; KAS; MnCS; PLatS

666a **Kapsner, Oliver Leonard, O.S.B.**
Texts of the Rule.
(*In* his A Benedictine bibliography. Collegeville, Minn., 1962. v. 2, p. 31-64)
ACu; etc.

666b **Regulae Benedicti studia.** Annuarium internationale, in connection with Rudolf

Hanslik [et al.]. Hildesheim, H. A. Gerstenberg, 1972-
v. 25 cm.
InStme; MnCS; PLatS

5. Commentaries

a. Manuscripts

667 **Adnotationes de Regulae s. Benedicti,** capp. 21-31. MS. Vienna, Schottenstift, codex 153, f.348v-350r. Octavo. Saec. 15.
Microfilm: MnCH proj. no. 4079

668 **Anonymus Mellicensis.**
Expositio 27 capitulorum Regulae s. Benedicti. MS. Benediktinerabtei Melk, Austria, codex 1381, p. 535-595. Duodecimo. Saec. 15.
Microfilm: MnCH proj. no. 1904

669 **Auslegung oder eine kurze** Mainung über die Regel des hl. Benedikt. MS. Benediktinerinnenabtei Nonnberg, Salzburg, codex 23 B 15. 162 p. Quarto. Saec. 16.
Microfilm: MnCH proj. no. 10,884

670 **Auslegung oder ein kürce** der maynung über dye Regel des heiligen Benedict. MS. Benediktinerinnenabtei Nonnberg, Salzburg, codex 28 D 3, f.1r-80r. Folio. Saec. 15(1490).
Microfilm: MnCH proj. no. 10,956

671 **Auslegung oder kurtze** Mannung über dye Regel des hl. Vaters Benedikt. MS. Benediktinerinnenabtei Nonnberg, Salzburg, codex 23 B 13. 140 f. Saec. 16(1551).
Microfilm: MnCH proj. no. 10,833

672 **Auslegung der Regel** des hl. Benedikt (cap. 1-20). MS. Benediktinerinnenabtei Nonnberg, Salzburg, codex 23 D 15. Octavo. Saec. 17 (1645).
Microfilm: MnCH proj. no. 10,895

673 **Auslegung der Regel** des hl. Benedikt. MS. Benediktinerabtei St. Peter, Salzburg, codex a.VI.6, f.5v-125v. Quarto. Saec. 15.
Microfilm: MnCH proj no. 10,082

674 **Auslegung der Regel** des hl. Benedikt. Incipit: Eye ir allerliebsten brüder MS. Benediktinerabtei St. Peter, Salzburg, codex z.VIII.13. 18 f. Quarto. Saec. 15.
Microfilm: MnCH proj. no. 10,200

675 **Auslegung der Regel S. Benedikt.** MS. Benediktinerabtei St. Peter, Salzburg, codex b.III.11, f.1r-140r. Quarto. Saec. 15.
Microfilm: MnCH proj. no. 10,358

676 **Auslegung oder kurze** Ermanung über die Regel des hl. Benedikt. MS. Benedik-

tinerabtei St. Peter, Salzburg, codex a.VIII.13. 87 f. Folio. Saec. 15.
Microfilm: MnCH proj. no. 10,185

677 **Ayglier, Bernard, O.S.B.**
Expositio Regulae s.p. Benedicti. MS. Benediktinerabtei Göttweig, Austria, codex 422. 236 f. Folio. Saec. 14.
Microfilm: MnCH proj. no. 3681
For other manuscript copies of this work, see under Ayglier, Bernard, in Author Part.

678 **Bernard, Saint.**
Incipit epistola libri de praecepto et dispensatione editi per beatum Bernhardum super Regula almifici Benedicti. MS. Benediktinerabtei Melk, Austria, codex 866, f.72v-89v. Quarto. Saec. 15.
Microfilm: MnCH proj. no. 1684

679 **Bernard, Saint.**
Instrucciones a su hermana Humbelina sobre la santa Regla. MS. Vallbona de las Monjas, Spain, codex 6. 94 f. Saec. 13.
Microfilm: MnCH proj. no. 30,550

680 **Bernard, Saint.**
Liber de praecepto et dispensatione super Regula almifici Benedicti abbatis. MS. Vienna, Schottenstift, codex 240, f.64r-86v. Quarto. Saec. 15.
Microfilm: MnCH proj. no. 4152

681 **Bohier, Pierre.**
Exposicio super Regula sancti Benedicti abbatis. MS. Benediktinerabtei Lambach, Austria, codex chart. 330. 244 f. Saec. 15.
Microfilm: MnCH proj. no. 692

682 **Bohier, Pierre.**
Regula s. Benedicti, cum commentario Petri Boerii, MS. Benediktinerabtei Melk, Austria, codex 3, f.1r-71v. Folio. Saec. 14.
Microfilm: MnCH proj. no. 2124

683 **Bohier, Pierre.**
Commentum Regulae s. Benedicti. MS. Vienna, Schottenstift, codex 356, f.3r-242v. Folio. Saec. 15.
Microfilm: MnCH proj. no. 4206

684 **Commentarium in Regulam s. Benedicti.**
MS. Subiaco, Italy (Benedictine abbey), codex 61. 340 f. Quarto. Saec. 14.
Microfilm: MnCH

685 **Commentarius historico-moralis in** Regulam s. Benedicti . . . S. Blasii 1746. MS. Benediktineratei St. Paul im Lavantthal, Austria, codex 50/6, pars I. Folio. Saec. 18.
Microfilm: MnCH proj. no. 12,598

686 **Commentarius in Regulam Benedicti.**
MS. Universitätsbibliothek Graz, Austria, codex 202, f.1r-67r. Quarto. Saec. 15.
Microfilm: MnCH proj. no. 26,119

687 **Commentarius in Regulam** monachorum s. Benedicti. MS. Madrid, Spain, Real Academia de la Historia, codex 42. 92 f. Saec. 9.
Microfilm: MnCH proj. no. 34, 918

688 **Commentarius in Regulam s. Benedicti,** cap. 32-73. Lingua castellana. MS. Monasterio benedictino de Montserrat, Spain, codex 888. 258 p. Quarto. Saec. 18.
Microfilm: MnCH proj. no. 20,106

689 **Commentarius in Regulam s. Benedicti.** MS. Vienna, Nationalbibliothek, codex 3621-3622. 2 vol. Quarto. Saec. 16.
Microfilm: MnCH proj. no. 16,832 & 20,413

690 **Commentarius in Regulam s. Benedicti.** MS. Vienna, Nationalbibliothek, codex 3624–3625. 2 vols. Quarto. Saec. 16.
Microfilm: MnCH proj. no. 16,833 & 16,837

691 **Commentarius in Regulam s. p. Benedicti.** MS. Benediktinerabtei Fiecht, Austria, codex 126 B. 120 f. Quarto.
Microfilm: MnCH proj. no. 28,795

692 **Compendium pro dubiis** aut expositionum difficultate in Regula s. Benedicti resolvendis. MS. Universitätsbibliothek Salzburg, codex M I 72, f.83-193. Duodecimo. Saec. 15.
Microfilm: MnCH proj. no. 10,981

693 **Declarationes in Regulam s. Benedicti.** MS. Klagenfurt, Austria, Kärntner Landesarchiv, codex GV 7/12. 26 f. Folio. Saec. 17.
Microfilm: MnCH proj. no. 12,845

694 **Declarationes Regulae s. Benedicti.** MS. Benediktinerabtei Admont, Austria, codex 829a, f.19r-64v. Quarto. Saec. 17.
Microfilm: MnCH proj. no. 9858

695 **Erklärung der Regel des hl. Benedikt.** MS. Benediktinerinnenabtei Nonnberg, Salzburg, codex 23 C 9. 107 f. Quarto. Saec. 15.
Microfilm: MnCH proj. no. 10,852

696 **Explanatio in Regulam s. Benedicti** per quaestiones diversas in ordine ad commodiorem praxim pie facta . . . in monasterio S. Crucis conscripta anno 1732. MS. Cistercienserabtei Heiligenkreuz, Austria, codex 510. 172 f. Quarto. Saec. 18.
Microfilm: MnCH proj. no. 4909

697 **Explanatio Regulae beati Benedicti** anno Domini 1420 in coenobio Cassinensi collecta. MS. Subiaco, Italy (Benedictine abbey), codex 165. Saec. 15.
Microfilm: MnCH

698 **Expanatio Regulae s. Benedicti** per quaestiones pie facta. MS. Cistercienser-

abtei Heiligenkreuz, Austria, codex 468, f.1r-106v. Quarto. Saec. 17.
Microfilm: MnCH proj. no. 4897

699 **Expositio in Regulam Benedicti.** MS. Universitätsbibliothek Graz, Austria, codex 418, f.114v-169v. Folio. Saec. 14.
Microfilm: MnCH proj. no. 26,582

700 **Expositiones in Regulam s. Benedicti.** MS. Universitätsbibliothek Graz, Austria, codex 706, f.1r-55v. Folio. Saec. 15.
Microfilm: MnCH proj. no. 26,807

701 **Expositio in Regulam s. Benedicti,** cum glossis interlineareis. Benediktinerabtei Kremsmünster, Austria, codex 20, f.30r-268r. Saec. 15.
Microfilm: MnCH proj. no. 20

702 **Expositio in Regulam s. Benedicti.** MS. Benediktinerabtei St. Peter, Salzburg, codex b.II.43. 56 f. Octavo. Saec. 15.
Microfilm: MnCH proj. no. 10,344

703 **Expositio quorumdam capitulorum** Regulae s. Benedicti. Ab initio et in fine mutila. MS. Vienna, Nationalbibliothek, codex 3548, f.156r-175v. Octavo. Saec. 15.
Microfilm: MnCH proj. no. 16,770

704 **Expositio Regulae s. Benedicti.** Incipit: Quamvis beatissimi patris nostri Benedicti Regula. MS. Benediktinerabtei Melk, Austria, codex 1241, f.240r-250r. Quarto. Saec. 15.
Microfilm: MnCH proj. no. 1885

705 **Expositio 27 capitulorum** Regulae s. Benedicti. MS. Benediktinerabtei Melk, Austria, codex 1381, f.535-595. Duodecimo. Saec. 15.
Microfilm: MnCH proj. no. 1904

706 **Fragmenta commentariorum in Regulam** s. Benedicti. Incipit: et virga rebus miraculosis. MS. Vienna, Nationalbibliothek, codex 3792, f.280r-301r. Quarto. Saec. 15.
Microfilm: MnCH proj. no. 17,012

707 **Glossa super Regulam s. Benedicti.** Cum initialibus coloratis. MS. Benediktinerabtei Michaelbeuern, Austria, codex cart. 50. 404 f. Folio. Saec. 15.
Microfilm: MnCH proj. no. 11,545

708 **Heer, Rusten, O.S.B.**
Commentarius super Regulam s. Benedicti. MS. Benediktinerabtei St. Paul im Lavantthal, Austria, codex 230/2, pars I. Folio. Saec. 18.
Microfilm: MnCH proj. no. 12,055

709 **Hildegard, Saint.**
Explicatio Regulae s. Benedicti. MS. Vienna, Nationalbibliothek, codex 3702, f.228r-236v. Folio. Saec. 15.
Microfilm: MnCH proj. no. 16,913

710 **Hildemar.**
Expositio Regulae s. Benedicti. MS. Cistercienserabtei Heiligenkreuz, Austria, codex 30, f.1r-118r. Folio. Saec. 13.
Microfilm: MnCH proj. no. 4574

711 **Hildemar.**
Tractatus in Regulam s. Benedicti. MS. Benediktinerabtei Melk, Austria, codex 1808. 270 f. Folio. Saec. 13.
Microfilm: MnCH proj. no. 2075

712 **Hildemar.**
Tractatus in Regulam s. Benedicti. MS. Benediktinerabtei St. Peter, Salzburg, codex c.X.14, f.1r-159r. Folio. Saec. 14.
Microfilm: MnCH proj. no. 10,241

713 **Joannes Castellensis.**
Expositio in Regulam s. Benedicti. MS. Benediktinerabtei St. Peter, Salzburg, codex b.XII.23-25. 3 vols. Folio. Saec. 15.
Microfilm: MnCH proj. no. 10,707

714 **Joannes Castellensis.**
Glossae in Regulam s. Benedicti. MS. Vienna, Nationalbibliothek, codex 3702, f.1r-226r. et 342r-356v(index). Folio. Saec. 15.
Microfilm: MnCH proj. no. 16,913

715 **Joannes Castellensis.**
Libri duo in Regulam s. Benedicti, cum indice alphabetico rerum praemisso. MS. Vienna, Nationalbibliothek, codex 3663. 180 f. Folio. Saec. 15.
Microfilm: MnCH proj. no. 16,884

716 **Joannes de Spira, O.S.B.**
Expositio prologi Regulae s. Benedicti, et ejusdem capitum 1, 2, et 68. MS. Benediktinerabtei Melk, Austria, codex 1833, f.1r-160v. Duodecimo. Saec. 15.
Microfilm: MnCH proj. no. 2141

717 **Keck, Johannes, O.S.B.**
Commentaria in Regulam sancti Benedicti. MS. Vienna, Dominikanerkloster, codex 207, f.2r-222v. Folio. Saec. 15.
Microfilm: MnCH proj. no. 9009

718 **Keck, Johannes, O.S.B.**
Tractatus de observantia statutorum Regulae s. Benedicti. MS. Vienna, Schottenstift, codex 405, f.1r-50r. Octavo. Saec. 15.
Microfilm: MnCH proj. no. 4148

719 **Keck, Johannes, O.S.B.**
Tractatus finalis commentariorum super Regula s. Benedicti de obligatione statutorum regularium. MS. Benediktinerabtei Göttweig, Austria, codex 375, f.164v-173v. Folio Saec. 15.
Microfilm: MnCH proj. no. 3643

720 **Keck, Johannes, O.S.B.**
Tractatus finalis commentariorum supra Regula s. Benedicti de obligatione statutorum regularium. MS. Vienna, Schottenstift, codex 356, f.243r-366v. Folio. Saec. 15.
Microfilm: MnCH proj. no. 4206

721 **Keck, Johannes, O.S.B.**
Tractatus singularis commentariorum super Regula s. Benedicti de obligatione statutorum regularium. MS. Benediktinerabtei Melk, Austria, codex 959, f.173r-181v. Quarto. Saec. 15.
Microfilm: MnCH proj. no. 1762.

722 **Kurze Anmerkungen über** die Regel des hl. Benedikt (cap. 1-73). MS. Benediktinerinnenabtei Nonnberg, Salzburg, codex 23 E 32. 155 f. Octavo. Saec. 17.
Microfilm: MnCH proj. no. 10,905

723 **Lampertinae constitutiones super** Regulam s. Benedicti. MS. Benediktinerabtei Admont, Austria, codex 829a, f.65r-104v. Quarto. Saec. 17.
Microfilm: MnCH proj. no. 9858

724 **Meditation und Auslegung** der Regel des hl. Benedikt. MS. Benediktinerinnenabtei Nonnberg, Salzburg, codex 23 E 28. 215 p. Octavo. Saec. 17.
Microfilm: MnCH proj. no. 10,937

725 **Nikolaus von Matzen, abbot of Melk.**
Praxis Regulae s. p. Benedicti in sacro loco Specus. MS. Benediktinerabtei Melk, Austria, codex 866, f.1r-13v. Quarto. Saec. 15.
Microfilm: MnCH proj. no. 1684

726 **Notae et observationes** in Regulam s. Benedicti. MS. Benediktinerabtei St. Paul im Lavantthal, Austria, codex 33/2. 93, 18 p. Octavo. Saec. 18.
Microfilm: MnCH proj. no. 11,761

727 **Perez, Antonio, O.S.B.**
Commentaria oder Grindtliche Auslegung über die Regul des hl. Benedikt . . . Durch gaystliche Exhortationes vorgetragen verteutscht . . . von P. Bonifacio Schneidt, O.S.B. MS. Benediktinerinnenabtei Nonnberg, Salzburg, codex 28 D 7-8a. 2 vols. Folio. Saec. 17.
Microfilm: MnCH proj. no. 10,967

728 **Platiques sobre la Regla** de Sant Benet i altres oracions de la vita monastica. MS. Monasterio benedictino de Montserrat, Spain. codex 1135-1136. 2 vols. Quarto. Saec. 18.
Microfilm: MnCH proj. no. 30,154

729 **Responsio cujusdam fratris O.S.B.** super consultatione "Utrum quilibet Regulam s. Benedicti profitens . . . peccet mortal-

iter in omni transgressione cujuscunque in eadam Regula contenti." MS. Vienna, Nationalbibliothek, codex 3595, f.131r-141v. Quarto. Saec. 15.
Microfilm: MnCH proj. no. 16,821

730 **Schlitpacher, Johannes, O.S.B.**
Commentarius in Regulam s. Benedicti. MS. Benediktinerabtei Lambach, Austria, codex chart. 253. 335 f. Saec. 15.
Microfilm: MnCH proj. no. 634
For other copies of this work see under Schlitpacher, Johannes in Author Part.

731 **Siebenbürger, Johannes.**
Ueber die Regel des hl. Benedikt; Einführung in den Geist derselben durch Fragen und Antworten. MS. Cistercienserabtei Heiligenkreuz, Austria, codex 556. 279 f. Quarto. Saec. 17.
Microfilm: MnCH proj. no. 4921

732 **Smaragdus, abbot of St. Mihiel.**
Expositio in Regulam s. Benedicti. MS. Kornik, Poland, Bibliotheka Kornicka, codex F 1 (3). Saec. 9.
Microfilm: MnCH

733 **Smaragdus, abbot of St. Mihiel.**
Expositio Regulae s.p.n. Benedicti. MS. Silos, Spain, Archivo del Monasterio de Sto. Domingo, Ms. 1. 282 f. Folio. Saec. 9-10.
Microfilm: MnCH proj. no. 33,686

734 **Speculum Regulae monachorum** b. Benedicti abbatis. MS. Benediktinerabtei Fiecht, Austria, codex 213, f.120r-137r. Folio. Saec. 14-15.
Microfilm: MnCH proj. no. 28,855

735 **Stephanus Parisiensis.** Expositio in Regulam s. Benedicti. MS. Benediktinerabtei Melk, Austria, codex 285, 180 f. Folio. Saec. 15.
Microfilm: MnCH proj. no. 1309

736 **Teuzonis expositio super Regula** s. Benedicti. MS. Benediktinerabtei Melk, Austria, codex 673, f.156r-277v. Quarto. Saec. 15.
Microfilm: MnCH proj. no. 1540

737 **Torquemada, Juan de, O.P.**
Expositio Regulae s. Benedicti. MS. Benediktinerabtei Göttweig, Austria, codex 375, f.2r-164r. Folio. Saec. 15.
Microfilm: MnCH proj. no. 3643

738 **Torquemada, Juan de, O.P.**
Expositio super Regulam s. Benedicti. MS. Benediktinerabtei Lambach, Austria, codex chart. 154. 246 f. Saec. 15.
Microfilm: MnCH proj. no. 571

739 **Torquemada, Juan de, O.P.**
Expositio Regulae s. Benedicti. MS. Benediktinerabtei Melk, Austria, codex 854. 247 f. Quarto. Saec. 15.
. Microfilm: MnCH proj. no. 1682

740 **Torquemada, Juan de, O.P.**
Prohemium in expositionem Regulae s. Benedicti. MS. Benediktinerabtei Melk, Austria, codex 959, f.1r-172v. Quarto. Saec. 15.
Microfilm: MnCH proj. no. 1762

741 **Torquemada, Juan de, O.P.**
Expositio Regulae s. Benedicti. MS. Perugia, Italy, Badia di San Pietro, codex 30. Saec. 15.
Microfilm: MnCH

742 **Torquemada, Juan de, O.P.**
Expositio in Regulam s. Benedicti. MS. Benediktinerabtei St. Peter, Salzburg, codex b.VIII.16, f.2r-246r. Folio. Saec. 15.
Microfilm: MnCH proj. no. 10,541

743 **Torquemada, Juan de, O.P.**
Erklärung einiger Capitel der Regel des hl. Benedikt. MS. Benediktinerinnenabtei Nonnberg, Salzburg, codex 23 b 22. 466 f. Quarto. Saec. 17.
Microfilm: MnCH proj. no. 10,842

744 **Torquemada, Juan de, O.P.**
Expositio super Regulam beatissimi patris Benedicti. MS. Universitätsbibliothek Graz, Austria, Incunabula 9773. 160 f. Folio. 1491.
Microfilm: MnCH proj. no. 27,128

745 **Tractatus de Regula s. Benedicti.** MS. Vienna, Schottenstift, codex 153, f.357r-364v. Octavo. Saec. 15.
Microfilm: MnCH proj. no. 4079

746 **Weybeckh, Kilianus.**
Expositio Regulae s. Benedicti, potissimum a commentariis Johannis de Turrecremata sed etiam ex aliorum scriptis collecta anno 1529. MS. Vienna, Nationalbibliothek, codex 11849. 488 f. Folio. Saec. 16.
Microfilm: MnCH proj. no. 19,923

b. Printed Works

747 **Alfonso de San Vitores, O.S.B.**
El sol del occidente, n. glorioso padre s. Benito . . . Commentarios sobre sv santa Regla. Madrid, Gregorio Rodriguez, 1945-48.
2 v. 29 cm.
KAS (v. 1)

748 **Barsotti, Divo.**
"Ascolta o figlio . . ."; commento spirituale al prologo della Regola di s. Benedetto. [Firenze] Libreria Editrice Fiorentina [1965].
249 p. 21 cm.
PLatS

749 **Caramuel Lobkowitz, Juan.**
Theologia regvlaris, hoc est, in ss. Basili, Avgvstini, Benedicti, Francisci, &c,

regvlas commentarii . . . Venetiis, apud Iuntas et Hertz, 1651.

2 v. 24 cm.

KyTr; KAS

749a Columbás, García, O.S.B.

La Regla de San Benito; introducción y comentario por García, O.S.B. Traducción y notas por Inaki Aranguren, O.Cist. Madrid, Biblioteca de Autores Cristianos, 1979.

xxiii, 510 p. 20 cm. (Biblioteca de Autores Cristianos, 406)

PLatS; MnCS

750 Explication de la Règle de s. Benoît, addressée à un monastère où l'on suit la mitigation, en quoi elle consiste, & à quoi la Règle oblige. Paris, Pierre Witte 1738.

602 p. 17 cm.

KAS

KAS also has a handwritten English translation by Pirmin Koumly, O.S.B., of St. Benedict's Abbey, Atchison, Kans.

751 Goutagny, Etienne, O.Cist.

Commentaire de la Règle de saint Benoît. 2. éd. Abbaye Notre-Dame des Dombes, 1978.

xiii, 514 p. 30 cm.

MnCS

752 Herwegen, Ildefons, O.S.B.

Väterspruch und Mönchsregel. Hrsg. und durch einen Vortrag, Was heisst ekklesiastikos monaxein heute? ergänzt von Emmanuel v. Severus. 2. unveränderte Aufl. Münster, Aschendorff, 1977.

50 p. 23 cm.

InStme

753 Hildemar.

Expositio Regulae [s. Benedicti] ab Hildemaro tradita. Ratisbonae, Neo-Eboraci, F. Pustet, 1880.

xv, 658 p. 22 cm.

ILSP; KAS; MnCS; PLatS

754 Luz, Columban, O.S.B.

Nothwendige Wissenschafft für geistlicher Ordens-persohenen sonderheitlich derjenigen welche unter der Regul des grossen heiligen Erzpatriarchen Benedicti streiten. Constanz und Ulm, J. F. Gaum, 1751.

[42], 514, [10] p. 21 cm.

InStme; KAS

755 Meyenschein, Benedikt, O.S.B.

Stella benedictina; sive, Regula sanctissimi patris nostri Benedicti in gratiam tyronum religiosorum breviore commentario illustrata. Hildesii, typis Wilh. Theodori Schlegel, 1725.

[12], 296 p. 14 cm.

KAS

756 Meyenschein, Benedikt, O.S.B.

Stella benedictina quinque radii corusca: quorum primus exhibet Regulam . . . Benedicti cum breviore commentario . . . Hildesii, typis Wilh. Theod Schlegel [1729].

755, [10] p. 14 cm.

KAS

756a Noreen, Gladys Ruth, Sister, O.S.B.

Notes and comments on the Rule of Saint Benedict. San Diego, Calif., Benedictine Sisters [1979].

178 p. 22 cm.

KAS; MoCo

756b Parry, David, O.S.B.

Households of God; the Rule of St. Benedict with explanations for monks and lay-people today. Kalamazoo, Cistercian Publications [1980].

199 p. (Cistercian studies series, no. 39)

NcBe

757 Philippe, Marie Dominique, O.P.

Analyse théologique de la Règle de saint Benoît. Paris, La Colombe [1961].

174 p. 18 cm.

CaQMo; KAS; MoCo

758 Presinger, Rupert, O.S.B.

Sacerdos benedictinus ad Sacrae Regulae normam, et praecipue juxta exempla ac doctrinas summi sacerdotis Christi Jesu efformatus. [Tegernsee] typis Monasterii Tegernseensis, 1720.

76 p. 14 cm.

KAS

759 Rollin, Bertrand, O.S.B.

Commentaire de la Règle de saint Benoît. Dourgne, Abbaye d'En Calcat, 1978.

xxii, 160 p. 30 cm.

MnCS

760 Romero, Mary Jane, Sister, O.S.B.

Seeking; a paraphrase of the Rule of St. Benedict with commentary. Collegeville, Minn., The Liturgical Press [1972].

xiv, 67 p. 20 cm.

InStme; KAS; MdRi; MnCS; PLatS

761 Rosano, Italy. S. Maria (abbey of Benedictine nuns).

La Regola. Introduzione, versione e commento delle Benedettine di S. Maria di Rosano. 2. ed. Siena, Cantagalli, 1974.

313 p. 18 cm.

MnCS

762 Schimperna, Umberto, S.O.Cist.

S. Benedetto padre e maestro. Tipografia dell'Abbazia di Casamari (Frosinone), 1961.

390 p.

CaQStB

763 **Sharkey, Mary Giles, Sister, O.S.B.**
The De regimine claustralium of Abbot Johannes Trithemius: a study of his sources and method of composition.
73 p. 28 cm.
Thesis – Fordham University, New York, 1934.
Mimeographed.
MnCS

764 **Smaragdus, abbot of St. Mihiel.**
Smaragdi abbatis Expositio in Regulam s. Benedicti ediderunt Alfredus Spannagel, Pius Engelbert, O.S.B. Siegburg, F. Schmitt, 1974.
lxxxiv, 394 p. (Corpus consuetudinum monasticarum, f. 8)
InStme; MnCS; PLatS

765 **Steidle, Basilius, O.S.B.**
The Rule of St. Benedict. With an introduction, new translation of the Rule and a commentary, all reviewed in the light of an earlier monasticism. Translated with a few brief annotations by Urban J. Schnitzhofer, O.S.B. Canon City, Col., Holy Cross Abbey [1967?].
x, 307 p. 19 cm.
InStme; MnCS; PLatS

766 **Turbessi, Giuseppi, O.S.B.**
Ascetismo e monachesimo in s. Benedetto. Roma, Editrice Studium [1965].
220 p. 17 cm.
MnCS

767 **Viboldone, Italy (abbey of Benedictine nuns).**
Galateo monastico. Viboldone, Scuola tipografico San Benedetto [1960].
xv, 205 p. 19 cm.
PLatS

768 **Vogüé, Adalbert de, O.S.B.**
La communauté et l'abbé dans al Règle de saint Benoît. [Paris] Desclée de Brouwer [1961].
552 p. 20 cm.
MnCS; MoCo

768a **Vogüé, Adalbert de, O.S.B.**
Community and abbot in the Rule of Saint Benedict. Translated by Charles Philippi, O.S.B. Kalamazoo, Mich., Cistercian Publications, 1978-
v. 23 cm. (Cistercian studies series, no. 5/1
PLatS; MnCS

769 **Vogüé, Adalbert de, O.S.B.**
La Règle de saint Benoît . . . commentaire historique et critique . . . Paris, Editions du Cerf, 1971.
3 v. 20 cm. (Sources chrétiennes, v. 184-186)
CaQMo; InStme; KAS; MnCS; PLatS

6. Concordances

770 **Index capitum et concordantiae** in Regulam s. Benedicti. MS. Benediktinerabtei Melk, Austria, codex 3, f.72r-75v. Folio. Saec. 14.
Microfilm: MnCH proj. no. 2124

771 **Köbler, Gerhard.**
Verzeichnis der Uebersetzungsgleichungen der althochdeutschen Benediktinerregel. Göttingen, Zürich, Frankfurt, Musterschmidt [1970].
107 p. 21 cm.
MnCS

7. Criticism and Interpretation

772 **Kemmer, Alfons, O.S.B.**
Christ in the Rule of St. Benedict.
(*In* Monastic studies, v. 3, p. 87-98)
PLatS

773 **Philippe, Marie Dominique, O.P.**
Analyse théologique de la Règle de saint Benoît. Paris, La Colombe [1961].
174 p. 18 cm.
MnCS

774 **Spreitzenhofer, Ernst, O.S.B.**
Die historischen Voraussetzungen der Regel des hl. Benedikt von Nursia (nach den Quellen). Wien, 1895.
91 p. 22 cm.
Separat-Abdruck aus dem Jahres-Bericht des k.k. Schottengymnasiums in Wien.
MnCS

8. Criticism: Textual

775 **Hanslik, Rudolf.**
Textkritische und sprachliche Bemerkungen zu Stellen der Regula Benedicti.
(*In* Corona gratiarum: miscellanea . . . Eligio Dekkers . . . oblata. Bruges, Sint Pietersabdij, 1975. vol. 1, p. 229-235)
InStme; MnCS

775a **Kasch, Elisabeth.**
Das liturgische Vokabular der frühen lateinischen Mönchsregeln. Hildesheim, H. A. Gerstenberg, 1974.
xv, 403 p. 22 cm. (Regulae Benedicti studia. Supplementa Bd. 1)
PLatS

776 **Mohrmann, Christine.**
Etude sur la langue de S. Benoît.
(*In* Benedicti Regula; text latin, traduction et concordance par D. Ph. Schmitz. Maredsous, 1962)
MnCS

777 **Widhalm, Gloria-Maria.**
Die rhetorischeen Elemente in der
Regula Benedicti. Hildesheim, H. A.
Gerstenberg, 1974.
[4], 264 p. 22 cm. (Regula Benedicti
studia. Supplementa, Bd. 2)
InStme; MnCS; PLatS

9. History

778 **Holzherr, Georg, O.S.B.**
Regula Ferioli; ein Beitrag zur
Enstehungsgeschichte und zur Sinndeutung der Benediktinerregel. Einsiedeln, Benziger Verlag [1961].
212 p. 21 cm.
MnCS

779 **Spreitzenhofer, Ernst, O.S.B.**
Die historischen Voraussetzungen der
Regel des hl. Benedict von Nursia (nach
den Quellen). Wien, 1895.
Separat-Abdruck aus dem Jahres-
Bericht des k.k. Schottengymnasius in
Wien)
MnCS

10. Indices

780 **Benedicti Regula.** Recensuit Rudolphus
Hanslik. Vindobonae, Hoelder-Pichler-
Tempsky, 1960.
lxxiv, 376 p. 24 cm. (Corpus scriptorum
ecclesiasticorum latinorum, v. 75)
Includes an extensive linguistic index.
MnCS; PLatS

781 **Vocabula pro Regula s. Benedicti.** Pars
secunda. MS. Universitätsbibliothek
Graz, codex 202, f.67v-85v. Quarto.
Saec. 15.
Microfilm: MnCH proj. no. 26,119

11. Influence

782 **Deanesly, Margaret.**
Augustine of Canterbury. [London]
Nelson [1964].
167 p. 22 cm.
PLatS

783 **Leclercq, Jean, O.S.B.**
Regola benedettina e presenza nel mon-
do.
(*In* La Bonifica benedettina, p. 15-25)
PLatS

12. Manuscripts

784 **Daab, Ursula.**
Die althochdeutsche Benediktinerregel
des Cod. Sang. 916. Tübingen, M.
Niemeyer, 1959.

304 p. 19 cm. (Altdeutsche Textbibliothek, Nr. 50)
KAM; PLatS

785 **Daab, Ursula.**
Studien zur althochdeutschen Benedik-
tinerregel. [Wiesbaden] M. Sändig [1973].
93 p. 23 cm.
Reprint of the 1929 edition.
PLatS

786 **Farmer, D. H., ed.**
The Rule of St. Benedict: Oxford,
Bodleian Library, Hatton 48. Edited by D.
H. Farmer. Copenhagen, Rosenkilde and
Bagger, 1968.
29 p. 77 leaves (facsims.) 37 cm. (Early
English manuscripts in facsimile, v. 15)
MnCS; PLatS

787 **Gretsch, Mechthild.**
Die Regula sancti Benedicti in England
und ihre altenglische Uebersetzung. München, Fink, 1973.
viii, 406 p. 22 cm. (Texte und Untersuchungen zur englischen Philologie, Bd. 2)
InStme; MnCS; PLatS

788 **Petri, Edda.**
Eine mittelhochdeutsche Benediktinerregel: Hs. 1256/587 (Anfang 15 Jh.) Stadtbibliothek Trier. Hildesheim, Gerstenberg
Verlag, 1978.
viii, 8 facsims. 267 p. 22 cm.
MnCS

789 **Schröer, Arnold.**
Die angelsächsischen Prosabearbeitngen
der Benediktinerregel. 2. Aufl. Darmstadt,
Wissenschaftliche Buchgesellschaft, 1964.
xliv, 284 (i.e., 224) p. 22 cm. (Bibliothek
der angelsächisischen Prosa, 2. Bd.)
MnCS

790 **Stara hrvatska Regula Svetoga Benedikta.**
Text in Croatian and Latin in parallel columns: p. 369–427. Facsimile of the original
Croatian Glagolithic: p. 433-533.
(*In* Ostojic, Ivan. Benediktinci u Hrat-
skok i Ostalim Nasim Krajevima. 1963.
v. 3, p. 361-533)
KAS; PLatS

791 **Sullivan, Mary C.**
A Middle High German Benedictine
Rule: MS. 4486a Germanisches Na-
tionalmuseum Nürnberg. Commentary,
edition, glossary by Mary C. Sullivan.
Hildesheim, Gerstenberg, 1976.
17 leaves (inc. 16 plates), 324 p. 22 cm.
(Regulae Benedicti studia. Supplementa,
Bd. 4)
PLatS

792 **Webber, Philip.**
MS. Archabbey Beuron no. 39: a late
east middle Netherlandic version of the

Benedictine Rule, edited with philological and textural-critical commentary.
ix, 280 p. facsim.
Thesis (Ph.D.) – Bryn Maur College.
Xerographic copy from University Microfilms, Ann Arbor, Mich.
MnCS

13. Meditations

793 **Bernigaud, Sinforien, O.C.S.O.**
La Regla de San Benito meditada. Traducido por Sor Teresa del Sacramento [O.Cist]. Burgos, El Monte Carmelo, 1953.
844 p. 19 cm.
KAS; MnCS

794 **Bernigaud, Sinforien, O.C.S.O.**
La Règle de St. Benoit méditée, par Dom Symphorien. Nevers, Mazeron Frères, 1909.
825 p.
ILSP

795 **Exercices de pieté** sur la Règle de saint Benoît, avec des examens fort étendus, & trés utiles aux personnes qui veulent en prendre l'esprit. Retraite de dix jours. Paris, chez Theodore Muguet, 1697.
[53], 211, [5] p. 17 cm.
KAS

796 **Heufelder, Emmanuel Maria, O.S.B.**
Weite des Herzens; Meditationen über den Geist der Benediktusregel. Regensburg, R. Pustet [1971].
125 p. 19 cm.
InStme; MnCS; PLatS

LeContat, Jerome Joachim, O.S.B.
797 Dioptra politices religiosae. Hoc est, Exercitia spiritualia decem dierum . . . praecipue Regula Smi. P. Benedicti . . . Satinitate donata a R. P. Francisco Merger [O.S.B.]. Salisburgi, Joan. Bapt. Mayr, 1694.
870 p. 15 cm.

Morel, Robert, O.S.B.
798 Meditations sur la Règle de s. Benoît pour tous les jours de l'année. Lophem-les-Bruges, Charles Beyaert, 1923.
xvi, 443 p. 21 cm.
Reprint of the Paris edition of 1717.
KAS

14. Papal Approbation

799 **Léteras apostólicas de San Gregorio Papa** . . . en aprobación de la Regla del glorioso Padre S. Benito . . . Barcelona, Estevan Liberòs, 1633.
Xerographic copy.
MnCS

800 **Regla de el gran Patriarcha S. Benito,** nuevamente traducida . . . 1. Aprobación y confirmación por San Gregorio el Grande. Madrid, Josef Herrera Batanero, 1791.
Xerographic copy.
MnCS

15. Paraphrases

801 **Romero, Mary Jane, Sister, O.S.B.**
Seeking; a paraphrase of the Rule of St. Benedict with commentary. Collegeville, Minn., The Liturgical Press [1972].
xiv, 67 p. illus. 20 cm.
InStme; MnCS; MnStj; PLatS

16. Sources

802 **Pawlowsky, Sigismund, O.S.B.**
Die biblischen Grundlagen der Regula Benedicti. Wien, Herder [1965].
122 p. 23 cm. (Wiener Beiträge zur Theologie, 9)
PLatS

17. Versions

803 **Betz, Werner.**
Deutsch und Lateinisch; die Lehnbildungen der althochdeutschen Benediktinerregel. 2. Aufl. Bonn, H. Bouvier, 1965.
227 p. 21 cm.
PLatS

804 **Daab, Ursula.**
Studien zur althochdeutschen Benediktinerregel. [Wiesbaden] M. Sändig [1973].
93 p. 23 cm.
PLatS

805 **Gretsch, Mechtild.**
Die Regula sancti Benedicti in England und ihre altenglische Uebersetzung. München, Fink, 1973.
viii, 406 p. 22 cm. (Texte und Untersuchungen zur englischen Philologie, Bd. 2)
InStme; MnCS; PLatS

806 **The Rule of St. Benedict.** A Norman prose version, edited by Ruth J. Dean and M. Dominica Legge. Oxford, Published for the Society for the Study of Mediaeval languages and literature by Basil Blackwell, 1964)
xxx, 111 p. 25 cm. (Medium Aevum monographs, 7)
PLatS

807 **Sullivan, Mary C.**
A Middle High German Benedictine Rule: MS 4486a Germanisches Nationalmuseum Nürnberg. Commentary, edition,

glossary [by] Mary C. Sullivan. Hildesheim, Gerstenberg, 1976.

17 leaves (16 plates), 324 p. 22 cm. (Regulae Benedicti Studia. Supplementa, Bd. 4)

PLatS

18. Versions: Metrical

808 **Memoriale Regulae sancti Benedicti.** Metrice. MS. Benediktinerabtei Lambach, Austria, codex chart. 338, f.202v-204r. Saec. 15.
Microfilm: MnCH proj. no. 707

809 **Petrus von Rosenheim, O.S.B.** Canon in Regulam s. Benedicti. Metrice. MS. Vienna, Nationalbibliothek, codex 4117, f.33v-36v. Sextodecimo. Saec. 16.
Microfilm: MnCH proj. no. 17,296

810 **Schlitpacher, Johannes, O.S.B.** Memoriale in Regulam s. Benedicti. Metrice. MS. Vienna, Nationalbibliothek, codex 4117, f.37r-38r. Sextodecimo. Saec. 16.
Microfilm: MnCH proj. no. 17,296
For other manuscript copies of this item, see under Schlitpacher, Johannes, in Author Part.

811 **Smaragdus, abbot of St. Mihiel.** Carmen in Regulam s. Benedicti. MS. Benediktinerabtei Melk, Austria, codex 3, f. 72r. Folio. Saec. 14.
Microfilm: MnCH proj. no. 2124

812 **Smaragdus, abbot of St. Mihiel.** Versus in Regulam s. Benedicti. MS. Universitätsbibliothek Graz, Austria, codex 2194, f.86r-87r. Quarto. Saec. 14-15.
Microfilm: MnCH proj. no. 26,374

813 **Summa metrica totius** Regulae s. Benedicti. MS. Benediktinerabtei Melk, Austria, codex 88, f.172-173. Saec. 15.
Microfilm: MnCH proj. no. 1162

19. Parts of the Rule
Prologue

814 **Egli, Beat, O.S.B.** Der vierzehnte Psalm im Prolog der Regel des Heiligen Benedikt; eine patrologisch-monastische Studie. Sarnen, Buchdruckerei Louis Ehrli, 1962.
xi, 134 p. diagrs. 22 cm.
Beilage zum Jahresbericht des Kollegiums Sarnen 1961/62.
MnCS

815 **Winzen, Damasus, O.S.B.** Conferences on the prologue of the Rule. Pine City, N.Y., Mount Saviour Monastery, 1976.

20 p.
MoCo

Chapter 1: De generibus monachorum

816 **Brevis expositio caput I.** Regulae s. Benedicti. MS. Benediktinerabtei Melk, Austria, codex 793, f.381r-381v. Quarto. Saec. 15.
Microfilm: MnCH proj. no. 1634

817 **De quatuor monachis.** MS. Benediktinerabtei Melk, Austria, codex 1086, f.227-244. Duodecimo. Saec. 15.
Microfilm: MnCH proj. no. 1848

Chapter 2: Qualis debeat esse abbas

818 **Hildemar.** Nota ex tractatu et expositione Regulae s. Benedicti in capitulo de Abbate. MS. Vienna, Schottenstift, codex 177, f.344r-369v. Octavo. Saec. 15.
Microfilm: MnCH proj. no. 3910

Chapter 4: Instrumenta bonorum operum

819 **Finckeneis, Basilius, O.S.B.** Instrumenta virtutum seu bonorum operum, id est: septuaginta selectissima virtutum & bonorum operum genera, a s.p. Benedicto conscripta & praescripta in Sacrae Regulae cap. IV . . . Viennae, typis Joannis Jacobi Mann, 1691.
4 v. 16 cm.
KAS

Chapter 5: De obedientia

820 **Ein capitel von dem gehorsam** [nach der Regel Sand Benedicten]. MS. Benediktinerabtei Kremsmünster, Austria, codex 285, f.175r-179r. Saec. 15.
Microfilm: MnCH proj. no. 270

Chapter 7: De humilitate

821 **Bernard, Saint.** Tractatus de duodecim gradibus humilitatis. MS. Benediktinerabtei Melk, Austria, codex 663, f.160r-173r. Quarto. Saec. 15.
Microfilm: MnCH proj. no. 1533

822 **Bernard, Saint.** Tractatus de gradibus humilitatis. MS. Hereford, England, Cathedral Library, codex P 3 xii, f.142-151. Octavo. Saec. 13-14.
Microfilm: MnCH

823 **De humilitatis gradibus.** MS. Benediktinerabtei Melk, Austria, codex 1648, f.131r-135v.
Microfilm: MnCH proj. no. 1998

824 **Die Demut nach der Lehre** des hl. Benediktus. Freiburg, Herder, 1911.
165 p.
MoCo

825 **Duodecim gradus humilitatis.** MS. Benediktinerabtei Melk, Austria, codex 979,
f.311r. Quarto. Saec. 15.
Microfilm: MnCH proj. no. 1790

826 **Joannes de Spira, O.S.B.**
Tractatus de illis s. Benedicti Regulae
cap.VII verbis: Ergo his omnibus
humilitatis gradibus. MS. Benediktinerabtei Melk, Austria, codex 900, f.140r-
180v. Quarto. Saec. 15.
Microfilm: MnCH proj. no. 1720

827 **Versus de duodecim humilitatis gradibus.** MS. Benediktinerabtei Melk, Austria, codex 1214, f.76v-77r. Sextodecimo.
Saec. 15.
Microfilm: MnCH proj. no. 1865

828 **Versus de duodecim gradibus humili-
tatis.** MS. Benediktinerabtei St. Peter,
Salzburg, codex a.I.11, f.138v-139r.
Duodecimo. Saec. 15.
Microfilm: MnCH proj. no. 9881

Chapter 23: Qualis debeat esse modus excommunicationis

829 **Commentarius in caput** 23 Regulae s.
Benedicti. MS. Benediktinerabtei Melk,
Austria, codex 619, f.103r-108v. Quarto.
Saec. 15.
Microfilm: MnCH proj. no. 1508

Chapter 33: Si quid debeant monachi proprium habere

830 **Joannes de Spira, O.S.B.**
Tractatus de vitio proprietatis
monachorum in caput 33 Regulae s.
Benedicti. MS. Benediktinerabtei Melk,
Austria, codex 793, f.265r-293v. Quarto.
Saec. 15.
Microfilm: MnCH proj. no. 1634

Chapter 36: De infirmis fratribus

831 **Regula s. Benedicti,** cap. 36: Von Aus-
wartung der Kranken. MS. Augustinerchorherrenstift Klosterneuburg, codex
1155, f.20v. Octavo. Saec. 15.
Microfilm: MnCH proj. no. 6167

Chapter 42: Ut post completorium nemo loquatur

832 **Wathen, Ambrose G., O.S.B.**
Silence; the meaning of silence in the
Rule of St. Benedict. Washington, Cister-
cian Publications, 1973.
xviii, 240 p. 23 cm.
InStme; MnCS; PLatS

Chapter 49: De quadragesimae observatione

833 **Anonymus Mellicensis,** 15th cent.
Expositio in cap. 49 Regulae s. Benedic-
ti MS. Benediktinerabtei Melk, Austria,
codex 1381, p. 233-267. Duodecimo.
Saec. 15.
Microfilm: MnCH proj. no. 1904

Chapter 58, 17: Conversatio morum

834 **Hoppenbrouwers, Henricus, O.S.B.**
Conversatio; une étude sémasiologique.
(*In* Graecitas et latinitas Christianorum
primaeva. Supplementa, n. 1, p. 45, 95)
PLatS

Chapter 59: De filiis nobilium vel pauperum

835 **Expositio brevis capitis** 59 Regulae s.
Benedicti (forsan Ruperti Tuitiensis).
MS. Vienna, Nationalbibliothek, codex
2235, f.66r-70v. Quarto. Saec. 12.
Microfilm: MnCH proj. no. 15,551

Chapter 60: De sacerdotibus, qui in monasterio habitare voluerint

836 **De monacho faciendo ex electo saeculari.**
MS. Benediktinerabtei Kremsmünster,
Austria, codex novus 109, f.50v-61r.
Saec. 16.
Microfilm: MnCH proj. no. 396

Chapter 64: De ordinando abbatis

837 **Hallinger, Kassius, O.S.B.**
Regula Benedicti 64 und die Wahlge-
wohnheiten des 5.-12. Jahrhunderts.
(*In* Latinität und alte Kirche; Festschrift
für Rudolf Hanslik zum 70. Geburtstag.
Wien, 1977. p. 109-130)
MnCS; PLatS

Chapter 68: Ut in monasterio non praesumat alter alium defendere

838 **Joannes de Spira, O.S.B.**
Expositio in cap. 68 Regulae s. Benedic-
ti. MS. Benediktinerabtei Lambach,
Austria, codex chart. 254, f.262v-267v.
Saec. 15.
Microfilm: MnCH proj. no. 636

IV. BENEDICTINE CONSTITUTIONS

1. GENERAL WORKS

839 **Albers, Bruno**
Untersuchungen zu den ältesten Mönchsgewohnheiten; ein Beitrag zur Benediktiner-ordensgeschichte des X.–XII Jahrhunderts. München, J. J. Lentner, 1905.
xii, 132 p.
KAS

840 **Bohier, Pierre.**
Commentarius super Constitutionibus O.S.B. MS. Benediktinerabtei Fiecht, Austria, codex 213, f.1r-114r. Folio. Saec. 14/15.
Microfilm: MnCH proj. no. 28,855

841 **Constitutio monachorum nigrorum** (approbata a Benedicto papa). MS. Benediktinerabtei Kremsmünster, Austria, codex sine numero. 332 p. Saec. 15.
Microfilm: MnCH proj. no. 430

842 **Constitutiones iuxta Regulam** sanctissimi et Deo acceptissimi patris nostri Benedicti et reformationem (Mellicensem) anno 1419 et 1421 habitam. MS. Benediktinerabtei Kremsmünster, Austria, codex sine numero. 99 f. Saec. 17(1606).
Microfilm: MnCH proj. no. 429

843 **Constitutiones monachorum Ordinis** S. Benedicti Congregationis Coelestinorum SS. Dnj. Nri. Urbani PP. VIII iussu recognitae et eiusdem auctoritate approbatae et confirmatae. Romae, apud Haered. Bartholomei Zanetti, 1627.

288, xli, [3], 11, [21] p.
MnCS(microfilm); PLatS(microfilm)

844 **Constitutiones Regulae s. Benedicti.**
MS. Madrid, Spain, Real Academia de la Historia, codex 50. 41 f. Folio. Saec. 13.
Microfilm: MnCH proj. no. 34,906

845 **Dammertz, Viktor, O.S.B.**
Das Verfassungsrecht der benediktinischen Mönchskongregationen in Geschichte und Gegenwart. St. Ottilien, Eosverlag der Erzabtei, 1963.
xxiv, 276 p. 24 cm.
MnCS

846 **Knowles, David, O.S.B.**
From Pachomius to Ignatius; a study of the constitutional history of the religious orders. Oxford, 1966.
98 p. 20 cm.
Sarum lectures, 1964-65.
MnCS; NcBe; PLatS

2. CONGREGATIONS AND ABBEYS

The Constitutions of the various Benedictine Congregations are listed under the name of each Congregation in the Author Part, e.g., "Benedictines. Congregations. American-Cassinese. Constitution."

The Constitution of an independent house is listed under its name in the Author Part.

For the Constitutions of Benedictine Sisters, see the directive in chapter 17, 4.

V. BENEDICTINE ASCETICISM

See also commentaries on the Rule of St. Benedict in chapter 3 and Benedictine Liturgy (chapter 6).

1. GENERAL WORKS

847 **Alfonso de San Vitores, O.S.B.**
El sol del occidente, n. glorioso padre S. Benito, principe de todos los monges . . . Commentarios sobre su Santa Regla. Madrid, Gregorio Rodriguez, 1645-48.
2 v. 29 cm.
KAS(v. 1)

848 **Benedictines. Congregations. American-Cassinese.**
Renew and create; a statement on the American-Cassinese Benedictine monastic life. Thirty-sixth General Chapter, second session, June, 1969.
78 p. 18 cm.
MnCS; KAS; AStb

849 **Anonymus Mellicensis, fl.** 1460.
Excerpta ex variis S. Bernardi operibus vitam monasticam concernentia. MS. Benediktinerabtei Melk, Austria, codex 866, f.90v-103r. Quarto. Saec. 15.
Microfilm: MnCH proj. no. 1684

850 **Ayglier, Bernard, abbot of Monte Cassino.**
Speculum monachorum beati Benedicti. MS. Benediktinerabtei Kremsmünster, Austria, codex 179, f.174r–210r. Saec. 14.
Microfilm: MnCH proj. no. 168
For other manuscript copies of this work, see under Ayglier, Bernard, in the Author Part.

851 **Benedictines. Congregations. Swiss-American.**
Lectures on the Monastic Institute. St. Benedict, La., St. Joseph Abbey, 1973–
MoCo (1973, 1974, 1976, 1977)

852 **Das benediktinische ewige Directorium.**
Verdeutscht. 4. Teil: Regel. MS. Benediktinerinnenabtei Nonnberg, Salzburg, codex 23 C 27. 424 p. Quarto. Saec. 17.
Microfilm: MnCH proj. no. 10,869

853 **Berliere, Ursmer, O.S.B.**
Benedictine asceticism, from its origin to the end of the 12th century. Translated by a monk of Benet Lake Abbey, Benet Lake, Wis., 1927.
248 p. 28 cm.
Typescript.
MoCo

854 **Bernard von Paching, O.S.B.**
Lamentationes et treni super excidio ac desolatione conversationis et vitae monasticae. MS. Benediktinerabtei Melk, Austria, codex 960, f.390-403. Quarto. Saec. 15.
Microfilm: MnCH proj. no. 1775

855 **Blois, Louis de, O.S.B.**
Favus mellis . . . sive, Sententiae mellifluae, omnibus operibus venerabilis Ludovici Blosii collectae, & . . . in singulos anni dies bipartito ordine distributae, opera P. Philippi Jacobi Steyrer . . . [n.p.] sumptibus Johannis Conradi Wohler, 1742.
[48], 446, [16] p. 17 cm.
KAS

856 **Bogler, Theodor, O.S.B.**
Beten und Arbeiten aus Geschichte und Gegenwart benediktinischen Lebens. Maria Laach, Verlag Ars Liturgica, 1961.
105 p. plates, 23 cm.
MnCS

857 **Bogler, Theodor, O.S.B.**
Suche den Frieden und jage ihm nach. Recklinghausen, Paulus Verlag [1964].
350 p. 22 cm.
PLatS

858 **Braso, Gabriel, O.S.B.**
Sentier de vie au seuil de notre conversion; conferences sur la Règle de saint Benoît. Abbaye de Bellefontaine, 1974.
196 p. 21 cm.
InStme

858a **Bynum, Caroline Walker.**
Docere verbo et exemplo; an aspect of twelfth-century spirituality. [Missoula, Mont.] Scholars Press [1979].
xvii, 226 p. 23 cm.
Includes such Benedictine writers as: Rupert of Deutz, Abelard, Petrus Diaconus, Hildegard of Bingen, Pierre de Celle, Smaragdus, etc.
MnCS

859 **Cary-Elwes, Columba, O.S.B.**
Monastic renewal. [New York], Herder and Herder [1967].
256 p. 22 cm.
MnCS

860 **Charmans, Bruon, O.S.B.**
Enchiridion pietatis benedictinae, in quo exhibentur duodecim exercitia monastica, ad Regulam, caeremonias, statuta, & observantias Ordinis S. Benedicti Congreg. Bursfeldensis digesta. Coloniae, apud Constantinum Minich, 1661.
[24], 577 p. 13 cm.
KAS; MnCS

861 **Christophorus, abbot of Millstat.**
Rubricae de vita monastica. MS. Benediktinerabtei St. Peter, Salzburg,

codex b.III.10, f.191r-199r. Quarto. Saec. 15.

Microfilm: MnCH proj. no. 10,359

862 **Clichtove, Josse van.**
Judoci Clichtovei Libellus de laude monasticae religionis. The text translated with an introduction and notes by Rev. Benedict Meyer, O.S.B.
xxxiii, 113 leaves, 28 cm.
Thesis–Catholic University of America, Washington, D.C., 1957.
InStme

863 **Compendium asceseos Benedictinae.**
Posonii, typis haeredum Belnayanorum, 1852.
115 p. 21 cm.
Preface signed at S. Monte Pannoniae.
KAS

864 **Conception Abbey, Conception, Mo.**
The Holy Rule of Saint Benedict as lived by the monks of Conception Abbey, Conception, Missouri. [Conception, Mo., 1961].
[48] p. illus. 22x28 cm.
MnCS; MoCo; PLatS

865 **D'Aoust, Henry Jean Jacques, O.S.B.**
God-seeking, the essence of monastic life according to St. Benedict.
iv, 43 p. 28 cm.
Thesis (M.A.)–St. Vincent College, Latrobe, Pa., 1960.
Typescript.
PLatS

866 **Deseille, Placide.**
L'échelle de Jacob et la vision de Dieu: spiritualité monastique. Aubazine, Monastère de la Transfiguration [1974].
128 p. 21 cm.
InStme

867 **Du Roy, Olivier, O.S.B.**
Moines aujourd'hui; une expérience de réforme institutionelle. Paris, Epi [1972].
403 p. 24 cm.
InStme; MnCS

868 **Eichhorn, Ambrosius, O.S.B.**
Ascesis Benedictino-Blasiana succincta methodo tradita. MS. Benediktinerabtei St. Paul im Lavantthal, Austria, codex 84/6. 66 f. Folio. Saec. 18.
Microfilm: MnCH proj. no. 12,631

869 **Eisvogl, Weremund, O.S.B.**
Concordia animae benedictinae cum Deo; seu, Reflexiones asceticae in singulos anni dies . . . Augustae Vindelicorum, Joannes Stötter, 1723.
2 v. 17 cm.
KAS

870 **Finckeneis, Basilius, O.S.B.**
Instrumenta virtutum seu bonorum operum, id est: septuaginta selectissima

virtutum & bonorum operum genera a s. p. Benedicto conscripta & praescripta in Sacrae Regulae cap. IV. Viennae, Joannes Jacobus Mann, 1691.
4 v. 16 cm.
KAS

871 **Fischer, Anselm, O.S.B.**
Vita interna cum Deo; seu, Doctrina ascetica, quomodo religiosus debeat sibi & mundo mori, ut uni vivat Deo. Augustae, J. M. Labhart, 1780.
[24], 562, [13] p. 14 cm.
KAS

872 **Fiske, Adele M.**
Friends and friendship in the monastic tradition. Cuernavaca, Mexico, Centro Intercultural de Documentación, 1970.
1 v.(various pagings) 24 cm.
Collected articles.
MnCS

873 **Foyo, Bernardo, O.S.B.**
Catecismo benedictino, en donde se explican por menor los exercicios en que se debe compar un monge de la Congregacion de San Benito de Valladolid. MS. Monasterio benedictino de Montserrat, Spain, codex, 23. 350 p. Quarto. Saec. 18(1793).
Microfilm: MnCH proj. no. 29,986

874 **Foyo, Bernardo, O.S.B.**
Idea de un benedictino que vive segun el espiritu de su Regla. MS. Monasterio benedictino de Montserrat, Spain, codex 30 & 31, 19 & 166 f. Quarto. Saec. 18.
Microfilm: MnCH proj. no. 29,984 & 29,987

875 **Gautier, Jean, ed.**
Some schools of Catholic spirituality. New York, Desclee, 1959.
384 p.
InFer

876 **Geistlicher Weg zu Gott** nach der Regel des hl. Benedikt. MS. Benediktinerinnenabtei Nonnberg, Salzburg, codex 23 C 24. 815 p. Quarto. Saec. 16.
Microfilm: MnCH proj. no. 10,864

877 **Gougaud, Louis, O.S.B.**
Dévotions et pratiques ascetiques de Moyen Age. Paris, Desclée, De Brouwer, 1925.
236 p. 19 cm.
CaQStB; MnCS; PLatS

878 **Gougaud, Louis, O.S.B.**
Devotional and ascetic practices in the Middle Ages. English translation prepared by G. C. Bateman. London, Burns, Oates & Washbourne [1927].
xiii, 237 p. 19 cm.
MnCS

879 **Guéranger, Prosper, O.S.B.**
Notions sur la vie religieuse & monastique. Tours, Maison Mame, 1950.
134 p.
AStb

880 **Hume, Basil, O.S.B.**
Searching for God. New York, Paulist Press, 1977.
192 p. 18 cm.
MdRi; MnCS

881 **Krenner, Amandus, O.S.B.**
Compendium desciplinae monasticae e sanctorum patrum regulis et sententiis contextum. Salisburgi, Joan. Bapt. Mayr, 1678.
[6], 152 p. 16 cm.
KAS

882 **Krez, Albert, O.S.B.**
Paradigmata practica recollectionis asceticas triduanae, nec non et renovationis votorum religiosorum . . . Altdorffii ad Vineas, Jo. Adam Harcknarus, 1696.
362 p. 16 cm.
InStme; MnCS

883 **Lambach, Austria (Benedictine abbey).**
De summis vitae regularis conditionibus brevis disquisitio, auctore presbytero benedictino Monasterii Lambacensis capitulari. Viennae, G. Braumüller, 1860.
[4], 83 p. 19 cm.

884 **Leclercq, Jean, O.S.B.**
Aspects of monasticism. Translated by Mary Dodd. Kalamazoo, Cistercian Publications, 1978.
343 p. 22 cm.
InStme

885 **Leclercq, Jean, O.S.B.**
Benedictine rule and active presence in the world. Translated by Louis Merton, O.C.S.O.
(*In* Monastic studies, no. 2(1964), p. 51-63)
PLatS

886 **Leclercq, Jean, O.S.B.**
Caratteristiche della spiritualità monastica.
(*In* Problemi e orientmenti di spiritualità . . . p. 327-336)
PLatS

887 **Leclercq, Jean, O.S.B.**
Contemplative life. Translated by Elizabeth Funder. Kalamazoo, Mich., Cistercian Publications, 1978.
ix, 193 p. 22 cm.
InStme

888 **Leclercq, Jean, O.S.B.**
The love of learning and the desire for God; a study of monastic culture. 2d rev.

ed. Translated by Catharine Misrahi. New York, Fordham University Press [1974].
viii, 397 p. 20 cm.
MnCS

889 **Leclercq, Jean, O.S.B.**
The role of monastic spirituality critically discussed.
(*In* Protestants and Catholics on the spiritual life. Edited by Michael Marx, O.S.B. Collegeville, Minn., 1965. p. 20-33)
PLatS

890 **Magrassi, Mariano, O.S.B.**
La spiritualità del secolo XII benedettino attraverso gli studi degli ultimi tempi.
(*In* Problemi e orientamenti de spiritualità monastica . . . p. 235-293)
PLatS

891 **Marechaux, Bernard, O.S.B.Oliv.**
Saint Benoît; sa vie, sa Règle, sa doctrine spirituelle. 12me éd. Paris, G. Beauchesne, 1918.
viii, 195 p.
ILSP; KAS

892 **Melanges,** publiés par les abbayes bénédictines de la Congrégation belge à l'occasion du XIVe centenaire de la fondation du Mont-Cassin, 529-1929. Abbayes de Maredsous, Mont-César, St. André, 1929.
270 p. plates, 26 cm.
KAS

893 **Merton, Thomas, O.C.S.O.**
Spiritual direction and meditation. Collegeville, Minn., The Liturgical Press 1960.
99 p.
InFer

894 **Le Message des moines à notre temps;** mélanges offerts à Dom Alexis, abbé de Boquen, à l'occasion de son jubilé sacerdotal . . . Paris, A. Fayard [1958].
387 p. illus. 22 cm.
KAS

895 **Mezger, Franz, O.S.B.**
Exercitatorium religiosae perfectionis, sive Exercitia spiritualia iis maxime accomodata qui e tyrocinio ad s. professionem in religione sancti patris nostri Benedicti aspirant. MS. Benediktinerabtei St. Peter, Salzburg, codex b.II.32. 200 f. Octavo. Saec. 17.
Microfilm: MnCH proj. no. 10,341

896 **Monte Cassino, Italy (Benedictine abbey).**
Eredità perennis: D. Martino Matronola nuovo abate di Monte Cassino. [S. Elia Fiumerapido, Industria Grafica Casinate, 1971].
79 p. illus. 24 cm.
KAS

897 **Ohligslager, Maurus, O.S.B.**
Why monastic life? Fundamentals reex-
amined. [Saint Meinrad, Ind.].
99 leaves. 29 cm.
Typescript.
InStme

898 **Ordo ad monachum faciendum . . .** Forma
profitendi sub Regula s. Benedicti . . .
Quae sunt instrumenta bonorum
operum. MS. Universitätsbibliothek
Graz, Austria, codex 391, f.20r-78v.
Folio. Saec. 15.
Microfilm: MnCH proj. no. 26,575

899 **Peifer, Claude J., O.S.B.**
Monastic spirituality. New York, Sheed
and Ward [1966].
xvii, 555 p. 24 cm.
CaQMo; InStme; KAS; MnCS; MoCo;
PLatS;

900 **Penco, Gregorio, O.S.B.**
Il tema dell'Esodo nella spiritualità
monastica.
(*In* Vagaggini, Cypriano. Bibbia e
spiritualità. Roma, 1967. p. 331-378)
MnCS

901 **Peter Damian, Saint.**
Opusculum de perfectione monachorum.
MS. Benediktinerabtei Melk, Austria,
codex 993, f.1r-24r. Quarto. Saec. 15.
Microfilm: MnCH proj. no. 1807

902 **Petrus Cellensis, bp. of Chartres.**
L'école du cloitre; introduction, texte
critique, traduction et notes par Gerard de
Martel. Paris, Éditions du Cerf, 1977.
531 p. (Sources chrétiennes, v. 240)
MoCo

903 **Pieuses et devotes conceptions** contenan-
tes le discernement de l'esprit de la Regle
du glorieux patriarche sainct Benoist.
Par un des plus excellents esprit de ce
temps. Paris, chez Denys Bechet, 1639.
[4], 182, [5] p. 15 cm.
KAS

904 **Piolin, Paul, O.S.B.**
Testament spiritual d'un Benedictin.
(*In* Analecta juris pontificii, v. 17(1878),
p. 897-910)
AStb

905 **Presinger, Rupert, O.S.B.**
Benedictinus mortem quotidie ante
oculos suspectam habens ac per solicitam
omni hora actuum vitae custodiam ad eam
se disponens. Salisburgi, J. J. Mayr, 1739.
130 p. 14 cm.
InStme

906 **Puniet, Pierre de, O.S.B.**
Benedictine spirituality. Translated by
Roland Behrendt, O.S.B. Collegeville,
Minn., St. John's Abbey, 1965.

57 p. 28 cm.
Multigraphed.
AStb; KAS; MnCS; PLatS

907 **Rebstock, Bonaventura, O.S.B.**
La scuola del Signore; guida della vita
benedettina. Versione a cure delle
Monache Benedettine Sorrento. Sorrento
[Tipografia delle Benedettine 1958].
[8], 150 p. 12 cm.
PLatS

908 **Rees, Daniel, O.S.B.**
Consider your call; a theology of
monastic life [by] Daniel Rees and other
members of the English Benedictine Congregation. London, SPCK, 1978.
xx, 447 p. 22 cm.
InStme; MnCS; MnStj

909 **Riccardi, Placido, O.S.B.**
Discorsi monastici del servo di Dio
Placido Riccardi. Prefazione del Ildefonso
Schuster, [Padova] Badia di Praglia, 1928.
xiv, 83 p. 20 cm. (Serie ascetico-mistica,
n. 8)
InStme

910 **Ryelandt, Idesbald, O.S.B.**
Union with Christ: Benedictines and
liturgical spirituality. [Translated from the
French by Dom Matthew Dillon]. Wilkes-
Barre, Pa., Dimension Books [1966].
195 p. 21 cm.
InStme; KAS; MnCS

911 **Schlitpacher, Johannes, O.S.B.**
Summula de continentia regulari s.
Benedicti. MS. Benediktinerabtei Melk,
Austria, codex 959, f.182r-185v. Quarto.
Saec. 15.
Microfilm: MnCH proj. no. 1762

912 **Semana de estudios monasticos,** 14th,
Silos, Spain, 1973.
Los consejos evangelicos in la tradicion
monastica. Abadia de Silos, 1975.
422 p. 24 cm.
PLatS

913 **Sinhuber, Edmund, abbas.**
Gallus cantans et increpans, seu 107 ser-
mones ascetici . . . in capitulo habiti. MS.
Benediktinerabtei St. Peter, Salzburg,
codex a.IX.36. 107, 55, 162 p. Folio.
Saec. 17.
Microfilm: MnCH proj. no. 10,232

914 **Smaragdus, abbot of St. Mihiel.**
Diadema monachorum. MS. Benediktinerabtei Admont, Austria, codex 331, f.94r-
160v. Folio. Saec. 13.
Microfilm: MnCH proj. no. 9408
For other manuscript copies of this work
see under Smaragdus in Author Part.

915 **Smith, Ermin Richard, O.S.B.**
Mental prayer in Benedictinism.
37 leaves. 28 cm.
Thesis (M.A.)–St. Vincent College,
Latrobe, Pa., 1945.
Typescript.
PLatS

916 **Spilker, Reginhard, O.S.B.**
Die Busspraxis in der Regel des hl.
Benedikt . . . [Romae] S. Anselmo [1936?].
281–339, 12–39 p. 22 cm.
Diss. (S.T.D.)–Collegio di Sant'Anselmo, Roma.
InStme

917 **Steindl-Rast, David, O.S.B.**
Why a man becomes a monk, by David,
monk of Mt. Saviour. [n.p., 196-?]
[15] p. 26 cm.
KAS

918 **Strittmatter, Blase Raymond, O.S.B.**
School of the Lord's service.
[46]-57 p. 20 cm.
Excerpt from The St. Vincent Alumnus.
PLatS

919 **Summula de continentia regulari.** Incipit:
Discernere et noscere, quid in Regula s.
Benedicti vim habeat praecepti. MS.
Benediktinerabtei Melk, Austria,
codex 673, f.278r-284r. Quarto. Saec. 15.
Microfilm: MnCH proj. no. 1540

920 **Théologie de la vie monastique;** études
sur la tradition patristique. [Paris]
Aubier, [1961].
571 p. 23 cm.
MoCo; PLatS

921 **Thornton, Martin, Father (Anglican).**
English spirituality; an outline of
ascetical theology according to the English
pastoral tradition. London, S.P.C.K.,
1963.
xv, 330 p. 23 cm.
PLatS

922 **Tractatus ascetici praecipue pro monachis.** MS. Benediktinerabtei St. Peter,
Salzburg, codex b.II.9, f.1r-26r. Octavo.
Saec. 16.
Microfilm: MnCH proj. no. 10,317

923 **Trithemius, Johannes, O.S.B.**
De vita spirituali monachorum. MS.
Subiaco, Italy (Benedictine abbey),
codex 280. 308 f. Saec. 17.
Microfilm: MnCH

924 **Tunink, Wilfrid, O.S.B.**
Vision of peace; a study of Benedictine
monastic life. New York, Farrar, Straus,
1963.
xiv, 332 p. 22 cm.
ILSP; InStme; KAS; MnCS; MoCo;
NdRi; NcBe; OkShG; PLatS; MdRi

925 **Turbessi, Giuseppe, O.S.B.**
Ascetismo e monachesimo in S. Benedetto. Roma, Editrice Studium [1965].
220 p. 17 cm.
MnCS; PLatS

926 **Ussermann, Aemilian, O.S.B.**
Canones et regulae de disciplina
monastica loco collationum legendi. MS.
Benediktinerabtei St. Paul im Lavantthal,
Austria, codex 220/2. 144 p. Saec. 18.
Microfilm: MnCH proj. no. 12,038

927 **Vagaggini, Cipriano, O.S.B.**
La preghiera nella Bibbia e nella tradizione patristica e monastica. [Roma], Edizioni Paoline [1964].
1014 p. 19 cm.
KAS; PLatS

928 **Viboldone, Italy (abbey of Benedictine
nuns).**
Galateo monastico. Viboldone, Scuola
tipografico San Benedetto [1960].
xv, 205 p. 19 cm.
PLatS

929 **Visioni attuali sulla vita monastica.**
Montserrat [Spain], 1966.
315 p.
MoCo

930 **Vogüé, Adalbert de, O.S.B.**
Conferences on the Benedictine Rule and
life. (Phonotape-cassette). St. Meinrad,
Ind., St. Meinrad Archabbey, 1977.
9 tapes (c. 45 min. each side) 1 7/8 ips.
InStme

931 **Vogüé, Adalbert de, O.S.B.**
Les conseils évangeliques chez le Maitre
et Saint Benoît.
(*In* Semana de Estudios Monasticos,
14th, Silos, 1973. p. 13-17)
PLatS

932 **Von zweien sachen** die eyn munich seinen
orden lustlich machent. MS. Benediktinerabtei Melk, Austria, codex 1382,
f.223r-229r. Duodecimo. Saec. 15.
Microfilm: MnCH proj. no. 1905

933 **Winandy, Jacques, O.S.B.**
Benedictine spirituality.
(*In* Gautier, Jean. Some schools of
Catholic spirituality. New York, 1959.
p. 17-48)
InFer

934 **Wolter, Maurus, O.S.B.**
The principles of monasticism.
Translated, edited and annotated by Bernard A. Sause. St. Louis, Herder, 1962.
xx, 789 p. 24 cm. (American Benedictine
Academy. Studies in ascetical theology,
no. 1)
ILSP; InStme; KAS; MnCS; MoCo;
OkShG; PLatS

2. CLAUSURA

935 **Serna, Clemente de la, O.S.B.**
El voto de clausura en la Congregacion
de Valladolid.
(*In* Semana de estudios monasticos,
14th, Silos, Spain, 1973. p. 149-182)
PLatS

936 **Sharkey, Mary Giles, Sister, O.S.B.**
The De regimine claustralium of Abbot
Johannes Trithemius; a study of his
sources and method of composition.
73 p. 29 cm.
Thesis (M.A.)–Fordham University,
New York, 1964.
MnCS

3. CONVERSATIO MORUM

937 **Hoppenbrouwers, Henricus, O.S.B.**
Conversatio; une étude sémasiologique.
(*In* Graecitas et latinitas christianorum
primaeva. Supplementa, n. 1, p. 45-95)
PLatS

938 **Joannes de Spira, O.S.B.**
Sermo in principio reformationis. MS.
Benediktinerabtei Melk, Austria, codex
911, f.208r-213v. Quarto. Saec. 15.
Microfilm: MnCH proj. no. 1729

4. DIVINE OFFICE

939 **Baumstark, Anton.**
Nocturna laus; Typen frühchristlicher
Vigilienfeier und ihr Fortleben vor allem
im römischen und monastischen Ritus.
Münster, Aschendorff, 1957.
viii, 240 p. 25 cm.
MnCS

940 **Das Benediktiner-Officium;** ein altenglisches Brevier aus dem 11. Jahrhundert. Ein Beitrag zur Wulfstanfrage, von
Emil Feiler. Heidelberg, C. Winter's
Universitätsbuchhandlung, 1901; Amsterdam, Sweta & Zeitlinger, 1966.
81 p. 23 cm. (Anglistische Forschungen,
Heft 4)
Pages 1-49 issued also as the editor's Inaug.-Diss., Heidelberg.
PLatS

941 **Franxman, Justine, Sister, O.S.B.**
Monastic prayer in the Rule of St.
Benedict.
Thesis (M.A.)–St. John's University,
Collegeville, Minn., 1969.
KyCovS

942 **Hilpisch, Stephanus, O.S.B.**
Chorgebet und Frömmigkeit im Spätmit-
telalter.
(*In* Heilige Ueberlieferung. Münster,
1938. p. 263-284)
PLatS

943 **Joachim, O.Cist., abbot of Fiore.**
De vita sancti Benedicti et de Officio
Divino secundum eius doctrinam.
Barcelona, Biblioteca Balmes, 1953.
90 p. 24 cm.
MnCS

944 **Manuale Casinense** (Cod. Ottob. lat. 145)
hrsg. von Klaus Gamber, Sieghild Rehle.
Regensburg, Pustet, 1977.
172 p. 22 cm. (Textus patristici et
liturgici, facs. 13)
Contents: Ordo officii per hebdomadam.
Hymnarium. Cantica. Lectiones. Litaniae
per hebdomadam. Rituale monasticum.
Collectarium.
InStme; PLatS

945 **Pour chanter l'office;** guide practique.
[Bruges, Abbaye de S. André, 196-?].
89 p. 28 cm.
KAS

946 **Rome (City). Collegio di Sant'Anselmo.**
Liber usuum et manuale chori Collegii
Internationalis S. Anselmi de Urbe.
32 p. 18 cm.
MnCS

947 **Salmon, Pierre, O.S.B.**
The Breviary through the centuries.
Translated by Sister David Mary. Collegeville, Minn., The Liturgical Press
[1962].
163 p. 14 cm.
"Authorized English version of L'Office
divin."
InStme; KAS; MnCS; MoCo; PLatS

948 **Salmon, Pierre, O.S.B.**
L'Office divin; histoire de la formation du
Bréviaire. Paris, Editions du Cerf, 1959.
252 p. 20 cm. (Lex orandi, 27)
InStme; KAS; MnCS; PLatS

949 **Salmon, Pierre, O.S.B.**
L'Office divin au Moyen Age; histoire de
la formation du Breviaire du IX. au XVI.
siècle. Paris, Editions du Cerf, 1967.
199 p. 20 cm. (Lex orandi, 43)

950 **Thesaurus liturgiae horarum monasticae**
[edidit Secretariatus Abbatis Primatis
O.S.B.].
Romae [Tipografica "Liberit"] 1977.
viii, 562 p. 28 cm.
PLatS

951 **Weakland, Rembert George, O.S.B.**
Der heutige Mensch und das Chorof-
fizium.
Offprint from: Erbe und Auftrag, Heft 6,
44. Jahrgang, 1968, p. 443-449.
PLatS

5. FASTING

952 **Joannes de Spira, O.S.B.**
Utrum monachus frangens jejunium regulare peccat minus, vel aeque, sicut si franget jejunium ecclesiae. MS. Benediktinerabtei Melk, Austria, codex 1386, f.198r-203v. Duodecimo. Saec. 15.
Microfilm: MnCH proj. no. 1908
Etiam codex 1400, p. 105-113. Duodecimo. Saec. 15.
Microfilm: MnCH proj. no. 1934

953 **Schlitpacher, Johannes, O.S.B.**
De ieiunio regulari. MS. Vienna, Schottenstift, codex 237, f.140v-141v. Quarto. Saec. 15.
Microfilm: MnCH proj. no. 4143

6. HUMILITY

See also III. Rule of St. Benedict, chapter 7.

954 **De humilitate.** MS. Cistercienserabtei Zwettl, Austria, codex 319, f.75r-76r. Quarto. Saec. 14.
Microfilm: MnCH proj. no. 6915

955 **Duodecim gradus humilitatis.** 29 p.
Bound with: Sulger, Arsenius. Vita divi Benedicti. Typis Monasterij S. Galli, 1691.
MnCS

956 **Joannes de Spira, O.S.B.**
Tractatus de illis s. Benedicti Regulae cap.VII verbis: Ergo his omnibus humilitatibus gradibus. MS. Benediktinerabtei Melk, Austria, codex 900, f.140r-180v. Quarto. Saec. 15.
Microfilm: MnCH proj. no. 1720

957 **Jüngt, Thomas Aquinas, O.S.B.**
Der Weg zur Seelenreife; Lesungen und Erwägungen über das Demutskapitel des heiligen Benedikt. Missionsverlag St. Ottilien, 1928.
189 p. illus. 19 cm.
InStme

7. INVESTITURE AND PROFESSION

958 **Ayglier, Bernard, O.S.B.**
Speculum Bernardi abbatis Casinensis de his ad que in professione obligatur monachus.
(*In* Gregory I, Pope. Secundus dyalogorum liber. Venecia, L. A. de Giunta, 1605. p. 89–191)
MnCS

959 **Benedictines. Congregations. American-Cassinese.**
Rite of monastic profession according to the Ritual of the American-Cassinese Congregation of the Order of St. Benedict. Col-

legeville, Minn., St. John's Abbey Press, 1953.
iv, 32 p. 15 cm.
MnCS

960 **Benedictines. Congregations. Swiss American.**
Ritual of monastic profession for the Benedictine Federation of the Americas [1978?].
4 parts.
MoCo

961 **Figuerás, Cesáreo, O.S.A.**
Acerca del rito de la profesión monástica medieval "ad succurrendum."
(*In* Liturgica, 2: Cardinal I. A. Schuster in memoriam. 1958. v. 2, p. 359-400)
PLatS

962 **Forma professionis fratrum** in monasterio Lunaelacensi (Mondsee) anni 1435. MS. Vienna, Nationalbibliothek, codex 641, f.14-18v. Ocatvo. Saec. 15.
Microfilm: MnCH proj. no. 13,965

963 **Formula profitendi Regula s. Benedicti.** MS. Benediktinerabtei Melk, Austria, codex 979, f.234r-235r. Quarto. Saec. 15.
Microfilm: MnCH proj. no. 1790

964 **Joannes, abbas.**
Excerpta ex tractatu Ioannis abbatis de professione monachorum. MS. Benediktinerabtei Melk, Austria, codex 663, f.139r-159v. Quarto. Saec. 15.
Microfilm: MnCH proj. no. 1533

965 **Joannes, abbas.**
Expositio super professione monachorum. MS. Benediktinerabtei Melk, Austria, codex 1386, f.60r-140r. Duodecimo. Saec. 15.
Microfilm: MnCH proj. no. 1908

966 **Joannes, abbas.**
Tractatus de professione monachorum (excerpta). Vienna, Nationalbibliothek, codex 3815, f.91v-113v. Quarto. Saec. 15.
Microfilm: MnCH proj. no. 14,427

967 **Joannes, abbas.**
Tractatus tripertitus de professione monachorum. MS. Benediktinerabtei Melk, Austria, codex 1267, f.129r-153v. Octavo. Saec. 15.
Microfilm: MnCH proj. no. 1892
Etiam codex 1717, f.119-222. Octavo. Saec. 14.
Microfilm: MnCH proj. no. 2038

968 **K. K. Hofdekrete an Fürstabt Martin II** (Gerbert) von St. Blasien im Schwarzwald und Acten betreffend des zur Ablegung der klösterlichen Professionen bestimmte Alter der Novizen de annis 1772-1791. MS. Benediktinerabtei St.

Paul im Lavantthal, Austria, codex 225/2. 419 f. Folio. Saec. 18.
Microfilm: MnCH proj. no. 12,071

969 **Leclercq, Jean, O.S.B.**
Un traité sur la "Profession des abbés" au XIIe siècle.
(*In* Analecta monastica, 6. ser., 1962, p. 177-191)
PLatS

970 **Migazzi, Cardinal.**
Schreiben an die Kaiserin Maria Theresia wegen der Bestimmung von einem Alter von 24 Jahren bei Zulassung zur Ordensprofess. MS. Benediktinerabtei St. Paul im Lavantthal, Austria, codex 306/4. 42 f. Quarto. Saec. 18.
Microfilm: MnCH proj. no. 12,551

971 **Ordo induendi novitios.** MS. Benediktinerabtei Altenburg, Austria, codex AB 13 F 14, f.95r-97v. Octavo. Saec. 17(1604).
Microfilm: MnCH proj. no. 6494

972 **Palmer, Jerome, O.S.B.**
History of the rite of solemn profession in the Order of St. Benedict.
iii, 164 leaves, 28 cm.
Thesis (M.A.)–Catholic University of America, Washington, D.C., 1962.
Typescript.
InStme; MnCS

973 **Ritus conferendi sacrum** Benedictinae religionis habitum juxta consuetudinem Monasterii S. Blasii in Silva Nigra. MS. Benediktinerabtei St. Paul im Lavantthal, Austria, codex 129/6. 20 f. Quarto. Saec. 18(1744).
Microfilm: MnCH proj. no. 12,686

974 **Ritus professionis monasticae.** MS. Benediktinerabtei Admont, Austria, codex 829a, f.151r-153r. Quarto. Saec. 17.
Microfilm: MnCH proj. no. 9858

975 **Roberts, Augustine.**
Centered on Christ; an introduction to monastic profession.
124 p. 28 cm.
Typescript, 1975.
MoCo; NcBe

976 **St. Bede's Abbey, Peru, Ill.**
Translation and explanation of the rite of Benedictine solemn profession, prepared by the monks of St. Bede's Abbey, Peru, Illinois [1949].
30 p. 28 cm.
MnCS

977 **St. Vincent Archabbey, Latrobe, Pa.**
The rite of solemn Benedictine profession. Latrobe, Pa., Saint Vincent Archabbey, 1937.

23 p. 22 cm.
PLatS

978 **St. Vincent Archabbey, Latrobe, Pa.**
The Benedictine rite of solemn profession. Latrobe, Pa., St. Vincent Archabbey, 1938.
[33] p. 23 cm.
Includes an explanation of the vows and of the habit and text of the ceremony.
PLatS

979 **Sause, Bernard Austin, O.S.B.**
The rite of monastic profession. [Atchison, Kans., St. Benedict's Abbey, 1962].
Offprint from American Benedictine review, v. 18(1962), p. 20-52.
KAS; MoCo; PLatS

980 **Tractatus de professione monachorum.**
MS. Benediktinerabtei Lambach, Austria, codex membr. 126, f.102r-137v. Quarto. Saec. 13.
Microfilm: MnCH proj. no. 812

981 **Tractatus de professione monachorum** (H. Gerson, G. Peralsus). MS. Benediktinerabtei St. Peter, Salzburg, codex b.IX.20, f.145v-173v. Folio. Saec. 15.
Microfilm: MnCH proj. no. 10,583

8. MEDITATIONS

982 **Bougis, Simon, O.S.B.**
Betrachtungen vor die Novizen, dan for junge geistliche Professen . . . in das Teutsche übersetzt von Frau Maria Josepha Walburg . . . des Klosters Nonnberg. MS. Benediktinerinnenabtei Nonnberg, Salzburg, codex 28 D 9. 500 p. Folio. Saec. 18(1762).
Microfilm: MnCH proj. no. 10,969

983 **Bougis, Simon, O.S.B.**
Meditations pour tous les jours de l'anné . . . 4me ed. rev. & corr. Paris, François Muguet, 1708.
[12], 720, [12] p. 25 cm.
KAS

984 **Eisvogl, Weremund, O.S.B.**
Concordia animae benedictinae cum Deo; seu, Reflexiones asceticae in singulos anni dies . . . Augustae Vindelicorum, Joannes Stötter, 1723.
2 v. 17 cm.
KySu(v. 1); KAS; MnCS

985 **Fischer, Anselm, O.S.B.**
Specus sancti Benedicti, seu, Solitudo sacra, in quam religiosa anima se recipit, ut ubidem eo liberius sola cum solo Deo agat. Augustae Vindelicorum. Joannes Conradus Wohler, 1708.
170 p. 13 cm.
MnCS

986 **Hutschenreiter, Johann Baptist, O.S.B.**
Azarias fidelis Tobiae in via spiritualium excercitiorum per octiduum in comitem datus; seu, Exercitia octiduana . . . omnibus religiosis . . . praecipue autem Regulam a. patriarchae Benedicti professis accomodata. Pedeponti, Joannes Gastl, 1741.
[46], 495, [20] p. 17 cm.
InStme; KAS

987 **Manuale spirituale;** seu, Exercitia religiosa respective quotidiana omnibus sine exceptione Regulam s. p. Benedicti professis . . . Coloniae et Francofurti, Joan. Mich. Jos. Pütz, 1771.
[24], 513, [11] p. 15 cm.
KAS; MnCS

988 **Müller, Deodat, O.S.B.**
Spiritus sanctissimi patris nostri Benedicti . . . omnibus quidem religiosis, sed maxime monachis sub ejusdem almi patris Regula militantibus propositus a monacho Ordinis S. Benedicti Congreg. B.V.M. sine labe Conceptae. 1753.
4 v. 17 cm.
InStme; MnCS

989 **Presinger, Rupert, O.S.B.**
Ascesis benedictina, seu varia opuscula ascetica juxta mentem et spiritum Regulae s. p. Benedicti exposita ad praeparandum, exculendum, & perficiendum spiritum vere religiosum . . . Augustae Vindel., Joseph Wolff, 1757.
549 p. 20 cm.

9. NOVITIATE

990 **Fiecht, Austria (Benedictine abbey).**
Scripta ascetica pro novitiis Monasterii S. Josephi ni Fiecht O.S.B. MS. Benediktinerabtei Fiecht, codex 87, 377 f. Quarto. Saec. 18.
Microfilm: MnCH proj. no. 28,796

991 **Formula novitiorum in religione.** MS. Benediktinerabtei Lambach, Austria, codex membr. 126, f.1r-10v. Quarto. Saec. 13.
Microfilm: MnCH proj. no. 812

992 **Formula novitiorum (decem capitula).**
Incipit: Desiderasti a me karissime. MS. Cistercienserabtei Zwettl, Austria, codex 319, f.65v-75r. Quarto. Saec. 14.
Microfilm: MnCH proj. no. 6915

993 **Formula noviciorum.** Incipit: Primo considerare debes quare veneris . . . MS. Hereford, England, Cathedral Library, codex O 6 vii, f.1-107. Quarto. Saec. 15.
Microfilm: MnCH

994 **Gute Lehren für einen Novizen.** MS. Benediktinerinnenabtei Nonnberg, Salzburg, codex 23 E 14. 54 f. Octavo. Saec. 15-16.
Microfilm: MnCH proj. no. 10,952

995 **Mezler, Thomas, O.S.B.**
Manuale practicum novitiorum Zwifaltensium. MS. Benediktinerabtei St. Paul im Lavantthal, codex 65/6. 187 f. Octavo. Saec. 17(1646).
Microfilm: MnCH proj. no. 12,609

996 **Michaelfeld, Germany (Benedictine abbey).**
Tyrocinium pro novitiis. MS. Benediktinerabtei Fiecht, Austria, codex 1264 A. 4 copies. 105, 158, 181 & 193 f. Quarto. Saec. 18.
Microfilm: MnCH proj. no. 28,824

997 **Modus,** qualiter novitii post annum probationis profiteantur. MS. Benediktinerabtei Altenburg, Austria, codex AB 13 A 10, f. 33r-39v. Quarto. Saec. 15.
Microfilm: MnCH proj. no. 6401

998 **Regulae vitae religiosae pro novitiis.**
MS. Benediktinerabtei St. Paul im Lavantthal, Austria, codex 313/4. 88 f. Quarto. Saec. 17.
Microfilm: MnCH proj. no. 12,542

999 **St. Blasien im Schwarzwald, Germany (Benedictine abbey).**
Regulae universaliores a candidatis et novitiis observandae. MS. Benediktinerabtei St. Paul im Lavantthal, Austria, codex 51/6. 280 p. Folio. Saec. 17.
Microfilm: MnCH proj. no. 12,584

1000 **Tractatus de magistro novitiorum.**
Incipit: Oportet ipsum magistrum. MS. Benediktinerabtei Admont, Austria, codex 860, f.32r-40v. Octavo. Saec. 17.
Microfilm: MnCH proj. no. 9872

1001 **Tractatus magistri Hugonis** de institucione noviciorum. MS. Benediktinerabtei Lambach, Austria, codex chart. 435, f.49r-90r. Saec. 15.
Microfilm: MnCH proj. no. 725

1002 **Udalricus, prior Cellae in Nigra Silva.**
De disciplinis novitiorum. MS. Nationalbibliothek, codex 1671. 48 f. Octavo. Saec. 12.

10. OBEDIENCE

1003 **Lehre vom Gehorsam** und von der Bekehrung des Sünders. MS. Benediktinerabtei St. Peter, Salzburg, codex a.VI.6, f.126r-133r. Quarto. Saec. 15.
Microfilm: MnCH proj. no. 10,082

1004 **Weakland, Rembert George, O.S.B.**
Obedience to the abbot and the community in the monastery.
Offprint from: Cistercian studies, no. 5, p. 309-316.
PLatS

11. POVERTY

1005 **Botz, Paschal Robert, O.S.B.**
Benedictine poverty (workshop paper given at Sacred Heart Convent, Yankton, South Dakota, 1962).
38 p. 28 cm.
Typescript.
MnCS(Archives)

1006 **Ein churdze unterweisung** von der aigenschafft über das xxxiii Capitel der Regel sand Benedicten. Benediktinerabtei Kremsmünster, Austria, codex 285, f.163v-175r. Saec. 15.
Microfilm: MnCH proj. no. 270

1007 **De paupertate religiosorum servanda,** sive proprietate. MS. Benediktinerabtei Melk, Austria, codex 1933, f.119v-121v. Quarto. Saec. 15.
Microfilm: MnCH proj. no. 2213

1008 **Joannes de Spira, O.S.B.**
Expositio super capitulo 33 Regulae s. Benedicti. MS. Benediktinerabtei Melk, Austria, codex 911, f.3r-32r. Quarto. Saec. 15.
Microfilm: MnCH proj. no. 1729

1009 **Joannes de Spira, O.S.B.**
Excerpta ex tractatu Magistri Theodorici de proprietate religiosorum. MS. Benediktinerabtei Melk, Austria, codex 900, f.56r-62r. Quarto. Saec. 15.
Microfilm: MnCH proj. no. 1720

1010 **Joannes de Spira, O.S.B.**
Sylloge quaestionum de proprietate et paupertate religiosorum. MS. Benediktinerabtei Melk, Austria, codex 900, f.280r-286v. Saec. 15.
Microfilm: MnCH proj. no. 1720

1011 **Joannes de Spira, O.S.B.**
Tractatus alius de proprietate monachorum. MS. Benediktinerabtei Melk, Austria, codex 793, f.293v-311v. Quarto. Saec. 15.
Microfilm: MnCH proj. no. 1634

1012 **Joannes de Spira, O.S.B.**
Tractatus de proprietate monachorum. MS. Benediktinerabtei Melk, Austria, codex 911, f.32r-54v. Quarto. Saec. 15.
Microfilm: MnCH proj. no. 1729

1013 **Joannes de Spira, O.S.B.**
Tractatus de vitio proprietatis monachorum in caput 33 Regulae s.

Benedicti. MS. Benediktinerabtei Melk, Austria, codex 793, f.265r-293v. Quarto. Saec. 15.
Microfilm: MnCH proj. no. 1634

1014 **Liber contra vitium proprietatis,** qui potest intitulari: Pauper monachus. MS. Benediktinerabtei Melk, Austria, codex 1241, f.165r-193v. Quarto. Saec. 15.
Microfilm: MnCH proj. no. 1885

1015 **St. John's Abbey, Collegeville, Minn.**
Symposium one: On monastic poverty, by and for members of St. John's only. [Collegeville, Minn., St. John's Abbey, 1971].
142 leaves. 28 cm.
MnCS

1016 **Sermones de paupertate et proprietate religiosorum.** Germanice. MS. Benediktinerabtei Lambach, Austria, codex chart. 255, f.15v-133r. Saec. 15.
Microfilm: MnCH proj. no. 638

1017 **Trithemius, Johannes, O.S.B.**
De proprietate monachorum. [Oratio de cura pastorali. Paris, Marnef, n.d.]
[32] leaves. 15 cm.
Copinger 5880.
PLatS

1018 **Trithemius, Johannes, O.S.B.**
Tractatulus de proprietariis monachis. [Paris, Marnef, n.d.].
8 leaves. 15 cm.
PLatS

1019 **Vom Eigentum der Mönche.** MS. Benediktinerabtei St. Peter, Salzburg, codex b.III.11, f.145r-168v. Quarto. Saec. 15.
Microfilm: MnCH proj. no. 10,358

1020 **Von der Eigenschaft der Mönche.** Incipit: Sand Benedict redt in seiner Regel. MS. Benediktinerabtei St. Peter, Salzburg, codex a.IV.23, f.142r-153r. Octavo. Saec. 15.
Microfilm: MnCH proj. no. 10,016

12. PRAYER

See also chapter V, 4: Divine Office; and chapter VI: Liturgy.

1021 **Botz, Paschal Robert, O.S.B**
The traditional way of Benedictine prayer (paper at Novice Mistresses Workshop, Clyde, Missouri, 1953).
27 p. 28 cm.
Multilithed.
MnCS (Archives)

1022 **Franxman, Justina, Sister, O.S.B.**
Monastic prayer in the Rule of St. Benedict.

Thesis (M.A.)–St. John's University, Collegeville, Minn., 1969.
KyCovS

1023 **Joannes de Spira, O.S.B.**
Tractatus de oratione. Germanice. MS. Benediktinerabtei Melk, Austria codex 1084, f.242-246v. Duodecimo. Saec. 15.
Microfilm: MnCH proj. no. 1839

1024 **Renner, Maranatha, Sister, O.S.B.**
Considerations related to directing Benedictines in their prayer.
63, [12] p. 28 cm.
IRF project–St. Louis University, 1978.
Typescript.
MnStj(Archives)

1025 **Vagaggini, Cypriano, O.S.B.**
La preghiera nella Bibbia e nella tradizione patristica e monastica [di] C. Vagaggini [et al.]. [Roma] Edizioni Paoline [1964].
1012 p. 18 cm.
MnCS

13. PRAYER BOOKS

1026 **Morrall, Alphonsus M. J., O.S.B.**
A manual of devotions to our holy father Saint Benedict, abbot and patriarch of the western monks; to sister Saint Scholastica, virgin & abbess, and to all saints of his holy order. London, Catholic Publishing & Bookselling Co., 1861.
235 p. illus. 16 cm.
InStme; KAS; PLatS

1027 **Preces diversae.** [Collegeville, Minn.], typis Abbatiae S. Joannis, 1896.
64 p. 14 cm.
MnCS

1028 **St. Benedict's College, Atchison Kans.**
The student's daily prayer. Atchison, Kans., St. Benedict's College [1926].
30 p. 13 cm.
KAS

1029 **Via crucis Salvatoris nostri, Iesu Christi,** in XIV stationes partita . . . pro usu specialiter religiosi Ord. S. Benedicti . . . [Sankt Blasien, Ger.]. Typis prin. Monast. S. Blasii, 1767.
64 p. 17 cm.
KAS

14. RETREATS

1030 **Krez, Albert, O.S.B.**
Paradigmata practica recollectionis asceticae triduanae . . . In usum & commodum regularium omnium Ordinis SS. P. Benedicti selecta & collecta. Altdorffi ad Vineas, apud Joannem Adamum Hercknerum, 1696.

362 p. 16 cm.
MnCS

1031 **Le Contat, Jerome Joachim, O.S.B.**
Exercitia spiritualia pro X diebus, religiosis Ord. D. Benedicti propria . . . Gallice conscripta . . . latinitate donata a Francisco Mezger, O.S.B. [Salisburgi], Joan. Bapt. Mayr, 1645.
627 p. 13 cm.
MnCS

1032 **Octiduana spiritus benedictini recollectio;** sive, Exercitia juxta mentem ss. patris Benedicti pro usu omnium monachorum, sed maxime sub Regula ejusdem almi patris militantium compilata a monacho dicti s. ordinis congregationis B. V. Mariae sone labe conceptae. Lucernae, typis Henrici Ignatii Nicodemis Hautt, 1754.
[16], 312, [5] p. 18 cm.
KAS

15. SILENCE

1033 **Saenz, Pablo, O.S.B.**
Dialogo del silencio; monjes en la iglesia de hoy. Buenos Aires, Latino America Libros, 1967.
169 p. 20 cm.
PLatS

1034 **Wathen, Ambrose G., O.S.B.**
Silence; the meaning of silence in the Rule of St. Benedict. Washington, Cistercian Publications, 1973.
xviii, 240 illus. 23 cm. (Cistercian studies, series, no. 22)
Originally presented as the author's thesis, St. Paul University, Ottawa.
InStme; MnCS; MoCo; NcBe; PLatS

16. STABILITY

1035 **Endress, Richard.**
The enduring vision; stability and change in an American Benedictine monastery. Ann Arbor, Mich., 1974.
2 vols.
MnCS

1036 **Jones, James, O.S.B.**
De voto stabilitatis in jure benedictino vigenti.
xvii, 106 p. 28 cm.
Thesis (J.C.D.)–Pontificium Institutum Utriusque Juris, Roma, 1955.
Typescript.
MoCo

1037 **Raasch, Juana, Sister, O.S.B.**
Benedictine stability.
8 p. 28 cm.

Typescript, 1968.
MnStj(Archives)

17. VOWS

1038 **Faré, André.**
Les voeux monastiques et leurs effets
civils dans l'ancien droit et le droit
moderne. Paris, Arthur Rousseau, editeur,
1902.
218 p. 28 cm.
Thése pour le doctorat, Université de
Paris, 1902.
MnCS

1039 **Fischer, Anselm, O.S.B.**
Tractatus asceticus de tribus votis
religiosis. Ed. 2. Augustae Vindel., Joan.
Casp. Bencard, 1724.
[16], 523, [13] p. 16 cm.
KAS; PLatS

1040 **Gay, Charles Louis.**
The religious life and the vows.
Translated from the French by O.S.B.,
with an introduction by the Rev. William T.
Gordon. London, Burns & Oates, 1898.
viii, 276 p. 19 cm.
Translation of chapters 9-11 of the
author's De la vie et des virtus chrétiennes.
KAS

1041 **Henricus de Coesfeld.**
Tractatus de tribus votis monasticis. MS.
Benediktinerabtei Melk, Austria, codex
900, f.184r-251v. Quarto. Saec. 15.
Microfilm: MnCH proj. no. 1720

1042 **Joannes de Spira, O.S.B.**
Sermo de observatione monasticorum
votorum. MS. Benediktinerabtei Melk,
Austria, codex 793, f.184r-185v. Quarto.
Saec. 15.
Microfilm: MnCH proj. no. 1634
Etiam codex 911, f.219r-221v. Quarto.
Saec. 15.
Microfilm: MnCH proj. no. 1729

1043 **Joannes de Spira, O.S.B.**
Quaedam dicta de castitate, et ejus
speciebus. MS. Benediktinerabtei Melk,
Austria, codex 663, f.175r-242v. Quarto.
Saec. 15.
Microfilm: MnCH proj. no. 1533

1044 **Joannes de Spira, O.S.B.**
Sermo in illus Mathaei: Ecce nos reli-
quimus omnia. MS. Benediktinerabtei
Melk, Austria, codex 793, f.244r-247r.
Quarto. Saec. 16.
Microfilm: MnCH proj. no. 1634

1045 **Steele, Francisca Maria.**
Benedictines under solemn vows.
(*In* her Monasteries and religious houses
of Great Britain and Ireland. 1903.
p. 26-37)
AStb

VI. BENEDICTINE LITURGY

1. GENERAL WORKS

1046 **Baumstark, Anton.**
Nocturna laus; Typen frühchristlicher Vigilienfeier und ihr Fortleben vor allem im römischen und monastischen Ritus. Münster i.W., Aschendorff, 1957.
viii, 240 p. 25 cm.
MnCS

1047 **Cantus secundum modum monasterii Sublacensis. MS.** Benediktinerabtei Michaelbeuern, Austria, codex cart. 86, f.212r-224v. Quarto. Saec. 15.
Microfilm: MnCH proj. no. 11,578

1048 **Congregatio Sacrorum Rituum.**
Praecipua notanda in codice rubricarum a S. Rit. Congr. publicato 15 aug. 1960 et, pro ritu monastico O.S.B. approbato 5 nov. 1960. Iussu Rev.mi D.D. Abbatis Primatis edita. Mechliniae, H. Dessain, 1960.
36 p. 17 cm.
PLatS

1049 **Corpus consuetudinum monasticarum.**
t. 1-   1963-
Cura Pontificii Athenaei Sancti Anselmi de Urbe.
Editor: 1963-   K. Hallinger, O.S.B.
AStb; InStme; KAS; MnCS; MoCo; PLatS

1050 **Dekkers, Eligius, O.S.B.**
Les anciens moines cultivaient-ils la liturgie?
(*In* Vom christlichen Mysterium; gesammelte Arbeiten zum Gedächtnis von Odo Casel, O.S.B. Düsseldorf, 1951. p. 97-114)
MnCS

1051 **Häussling, Angelus, O.S.B.**
Mönchskonvent und Eucharistiefeier; eine Studie über die Messe in der abendländischen Klosterliturgie des frühen Mittelalters und zur Geschichte der Messhäufigkeit. Münster, Westfalen, Aschendorff [1973].
xiv, 380 p. 23 cm. (Liturgiewissenschaftliche Quellen und Forschungen, Heft 58)
InStme

1052 **Hilpisch, Stephanus, O.S.B.**
Chorgebet und Frömmigkeit im Spätmittelalter.
(*In* Heilige Ueberlieferung. Münster, 1938. p. 263-284)
PLatS

1053 **Kasch, Elisabeth.**
Das liturgische Vokabular der frühen lateinischen Mönchsregeln. Hildesheim, Gerstenberg, 1974.

xv, 403 p. 22 cm. (Regulae Benedicti studia. Supplementa, Bd. 1)
MnCS

1054 **King, Archdale Arthur.**
Liturgies of the religious orders. London, New York, Longmans, Green, 1955.
xii, 431 p. illus. 23 cm.
MnCS

1055 **Liturgie et monastères.** Etudes. Par E. Dekkers, Cl. Jean Nesmy, J. Leclercq . . . [Bruges] Publications de Saint-André, 1966-
v. 22 cm.
KAS

1056 **Manser, Anselm, O.S.B.**
Christkönigszüge im römischen und benediktinischen Adventgottesdienst.
(*In* Heilige Ueberlieferung. Münster, 1938. p. 124-135)
PLatS

1057 **Martin, Jean Baptiste.**
Bibliographie liturgique de l'Ordre de Saint Benoît.
(*In* Revue Mabillon, v. 11(1921) p. 47-59, 125-129; v. 12(1922) p. 181-188; v. 13 (1923), p. 188-197; v. 14(1924), p. 96-107; etc.
MnCS; PLatS

1058 **Montserrat, Spain (Benedictine abbey).**
La liturgia en Montserrat. Abadia de Montserrat, 1957.
57 p. plates, 20 cm.
MnCS

1059 **Ordo Sacros Libros legendi** tam in officio divino quam in refectorio. MS. Benediktinerabtei Seitenstetten, Austria, codex 297, f.10v-21v. Quarto. Saec. 15.
Microfilm: MnCH proj. no. 1074

1060 **Ryelandt, Idesbald, O.S.B.**
Union with Christ; Benedictine and liturgical spirituality. [Translated from the French by Matthew Dillon, O.S.B.]. Wilkes-Barre, Pa., Dimension Books [1966].
175 p. 22 cm.

1061 **Salmon, Pierre, O.S.B.**
The Breviary through the centuries. Translated by Sister David Mary. Collegeville, Minn., The Liturgical Press [1962].
163 p. 24 cm.

1062 **Salmon, Pierre, O.S.B.**
L'église en prière; introduction à la liturgie. Avec la collaboration de R. Béraudy, B. Botte [et al.]. Paris, Desclée & cie [1961].

xv, 916 p. 23 cm.
PLatS

1062a **Salmon, Pierre, O.S.B.**
Analecta liturgica; extrait des
manuscrits liturgiques de la Bibliothèque
Vaticane. Città del Vaticano, Biblioteca
Apostolica Vaticana, 1974.
352 p. (Studi e testi, 273)
Includes manuscripts which came from
Benedictine abbeys: Monte Cassino,
Subiaco, Farfa, Tegernsee, Winchester,
etc.
MnCS

1063 **Sause, Bernard Austin, O.S.B.**
How the general Decree (March 23,
1955) of the Sacred Congregation of Rites
on the simplification of rubrics affects the
Benedictines of the American Cassinese
Congregation. Complete text translated,
with a brief commentary. [Atchison, Kans.,
1955].
34 leaves, 28 cm.
KAS

1064 **Schmitz, Philibert, O.S.B.**
La liturgie de Cluny.
(*In* Spiritualità cluniacense. Todi, 1960.
p. 83-100)
PLatS

1065 **Stengel, Carl, O.S.B.**
Thuribulum aureum . . . id est, de VII
horis canonicis syntagma. Augustae
Vindel., apud Saram Mangiam, 1622.
131 p. 17 cm.
KAS

1066 **Thesaurus liturgiae horarum monasti-
cae.** [Edidit Secretariatus Abatis
Primatis, O.S.B.]. Romae, [Tipografica
"Leberit"] 1977.
viii, 562 p. 28 cm.
PLatS

1067 **Volk, Paulus, O.S.B.**
Die Busfelder Missalien.
(*In* Liturgica, 3: Cardinal I. A. Schuster
in memoriam. Montisserati, 1966.
p. 185–196)
PLatS

2. LITURGICAL BOOKS

a. Antiphonarium

1. Manuscripts

(arranged by century)

1068 Antiphonarium (fragmentum), cum
neumis. MS. Benediktinerabtei Melk,
Austria, codex 1698. 101 f. Octavo.
Saec. 10?
Microfilm: MnCH proj. no. 2119

1069 Antiphonarium benedictinum. Pars
hiemalis. MS. Universitätsbibliothek
Graz, Austria, codex 258. 176 f. Folio.
Saec. 12.
Microfilm: MnCH proj. no. 26,188

1070 Antiphonarium monasticum. MS. Silos,
Spain, Archivo del monasterio de Sto.
Domingo, Ms. 9. 396 f. Quarto.
Saec. 12-13.
Microfilm: MnCH proj. no. 33,691

1071 Antiphonarium benedictinum. MS.
Universitätsbibliothek Graz, Austria,
codex 211. 159 f. Quarto. Saec. 13.
Microfilm: MnCH proj. no. 26,149

1072 Antiphonarium cum notis musicis.
Benediktinerabtei Kremsmünster, Aus-
tria, codex 31, f.3r-71v. Quarto. Saec. 13.
Microfilm: MnCH proj. no. 31

1073 Antiphonarium benedictinum. Pars
hiemalis et aestiva. MS. Universitätsbibliothek Graz, Austria, codex 29 & 30.
2 vols. Folio. Saec. 14.
Microfilm: MnCH proj. no. 26,075 &
26,057

1074 Antiphonarium et Graduale ad usum
monasterii Ordinis Sancti Benedicti in
Domo Petri (Petershausen). 2 vols. MS.
Benediktinerabtei Göttweig, Austria,
codex 7-8. Folio. Saec. 15.
Microfilm: MnCH proj. no. 3313 & 3315

1075 Antiphonarium benedictinum. MS.
Universitätsbibliothek Graz, Austria,
codex 116. 247 f. Folio. Saec. 15.
Microfilm: MnCH proj. no. 26,038

1076 Antiphonale (cum notis musicis recent.).
Benediktinerabtei Kremsmünster, Aus-
tria, codex 190. 292 f. Saec. 15.
Microfilm: MnCH proj. no. 178

1077 Antiphonar aus Stift Mondsee. MS. Linz,
Austria, Oberösterreichise Landes-
museum Bibliothek, codex 2. 360 f.
Folio. Saec. 15(1464).
Microfilm: MnCH proj. no. 28,101

1078 Antiphonarium. MS. Benediktinerabtei
Melk, Austria, codex 756. 251 f. Quarto.
Saec. 15.
Microfilm: MnCH proj. no. 1601

1079 Antiphonarium. MS. Benediktinerabtei
Michaelbeuern, Austria, codex cart. 3-4.
2 vols. Folio. Saec. 15.
Microfilm: MnCH proj. no. 11,496 &
11,505

1080 Antiphonarium diurnum monastico-
Castiliniense. MS. Monasterio benedictino de Montserrat, Spain, codex 837.
155 f. Quarto. Saec. 15.

1081 Antiphonarium, cum notis musicis. MS.
Benediktinerinnenabtei Nonnberg,

Salzburg, 359 p. Folio. Saec. 15. Codex sine numero.
Microfilm: MnCH proj. no. 10,971

1082 Antiphonale. MS. Benediktinerinnenabtei Nonnberg, Salzburg, codex 23 A 11. 320 f. Octavo. Saec. 15-16.
Microfilm: MnCH proj. no. 10,790

1083 Antiphonarium cum notis musicis. MS. Benediktinerabti St. Paul im Lavantthal, Austria, codex 213/4. 2 vols. Quarto. Saec. 15.
Microfilm: MnCH proj. no. 12,449

1084 Antiphonarium benedictinum, cum notis musicis. MS. Prämonstratenserabtei Schlägl, Austria, codex sine numero. Duodecimo. Saec. 15.
Microfilm: MnCH proj. no. 3154

1085 Antiphonae ad vesperas, Responsoria, Psalmi, Hymni, nec non Kyrie eleison, Gloria pro festis diversis, additis notis musicis. MS. Benediktinerabtei Seitenstetten, Austria, codex 148. 26 f. Quarto. Saec. 15.
Microfilm: MnCH proj. no. 960

1086 Antiphonarium monasterii Seitenstettensis. Incipit proprium sanctorum secundum consuetudines monasterii Seitenstetten. MS. Benediktinerabtei Seitenstetten, Austria, codex 120. 219 f. Folio. Saec. 15.
Microfilm: MnCH proj. no. 933

1087 Antiphonarius. MS. Barcelona, Spain, Sant Pere de les Puel-les, Cantoral, 2. Saec. 16(1599).
Microfilm: MnCH proj. no. 34,667

1088 Antiphonarium pro solemnioribus festis. MS. Benediktinerabtei Lambach, Austria, codex membr. 163. 72 f. Quarto. Saec. 16.
Microfilm: MnCH proj. no. 834

1089 Antiphonarium. Textus latine, rubricae germanice. MS. Benediktinerinnenabtei Nonnberg, Salzburg, codex 23 B 2. 200 f. Quarto. Saec. 16.
Microfilm: MnCH proj. no. 10,825

1090 Antiphonarium et Lectionarium a Septuagesima usque Pascha. MS. Benediktinerinnenabtei Nonnberg, Austria, codex 23 C 18. 240 f. Quarto. Saec. 16(1566).
Microfilm: MnCH proj. no. 10,860

1091 Antiphonarium, sine neumis. MS. Benediktinerabtei Seitenstetten, Austria, codex 308. 134 f. Quarto. Saec. 16.
Microfilm: MnCH proj. no. 1108

1092 Antiphonale Admontense. MS. Benediktinerabtei Admont, Austria, codex 323. 131 f. Folio. Saec. 17.
Microfilm: MnCH proj. no. 9403

1093 Antiphonale benedictinum [a] Leo Haid. MS. 246, xlii, [5] p. 20 cm. Saec. 19(1865).
KAS

2. Printed Editions

1094 Antiphonale monasticum pro diurnis horis juxta vota rr. dd. abbatum congregationum confoederatarum Ordinis Sancti Benedicti a Solesmensibus monachis restitutum. Parisiis, Desclée et Socii, 1934.
2 v. 21 cm.
InStme

1095 Corpus antiphonalium officii, editum a Renato-Joanne Hesbert. Roma, Herder, 1963–
v. facsims. 28 cm. (Rerum ecclesiasticarum documenta. Ser. maior. Fontes 7)
KAS (v. 1-3)
v. 2: Manuscripti "Cursus monasticus".

1096 Antiphonar der Erzabtei St. Peter in Salzburg (Codex Vindobonensis series nova 2700). Graz, Akademische Druck u. Verlagsanstalt, 1969-1973.
845 p. (issued in 4 parts), illus. 45 cm. (Codices selecti, phototypice impressi, v. 21)
PLatS

1097 Das Antiphonar von St. Peter. Vollständige Faksimile-Ausgabe im Originalformat des Codex Vindobonensis series nova 2700 der Oesterreichischen Nationalbibliothek: *Kommentarband.* Franz Unterkircher, kodikologische und liturgiegeschichtliche Einleitung. Otto Demus, kunstgeschichtliche Analyse mit 93 Abbildungen. Graz, Akademische Druck- u. Verlagsanstalt, 1974.
304, [70] p. plates 28 cm. (Codices selecti phototypice impressi, v. 21*)
PLatS

1098 Divine Office (antiphonal): English text fitted to Gregorian chant by Sister Cecile Gertken, O.S.B. Huntsville, Ut., Holy Trinity Abbey, 1977–78.
MnCS; MnStj

b. Antiphonarium Missae

1099 Antiphonale Missarum sextuplex, édité par dom René-Jean Hesbert . . . D'après le Graduel de Monza et les Antiphonaires de Rheinau, du Mont-Blandin, de Compiègne, de Corbie et de Senlis. Rome, Herder, 1967.
cxxvi, 256 p. facsims. 31x23 cm.

"Reimpression de la première édition
publiée 1935."
KAS

c. Benedictionale

1100 Agenda et benedictionale (Agenda ad
usum fratrum Cremifanensium). MS.
Benediktinerabtei Kremsmünster, Austria, codex 383. 51 f. Saec. 15.
Microfilm: MnCH proj. no. 361

1101 Benedictiones matutinales per totum
annum tam de tempore quam de sanctis
ob commodiorem usum in hanc formulam
conscriptae 1585. MS. Vienna, Schottenstift, codex 576. 35 f. Octavo. Saec. 16.
Microfilm: MnCH proj. no. 4288

d. Blessing of an Abbess

1102 Missa de benedictione abbatissae. MS.
Barcelona, Spain. Archivo de la Cate-
dral, codex 135. 29 f. Folio. Saec?
Microfilm: MnCH proj. no. 30,403

1103 Ordo benedictionis abbatis et abbatissae.
Editio typica. Typis Polyglottis Vaticanis, 1970.
30 p. 24 cm.
PLatS

e. Blessing of an Abbot

1104 Benedictio abbatis. MS. Klagenfurt,
Austria, Bischöfliche Bibliothek,
codex XXX e 2, f.1v-3r. Octavo. Saec. 16.
Microfilm: MnCH proj. no. 13,261

1105 The bestowing of the abbatial blessing on
the Right Reverend Thomas Hartman,
O.S.B., coadjutor abbot of St. Benedict's
Abbey, Atchison, Kansas, Sept. 5, 1962.
60, [4] p. ports., music. 25 cm.
Latin and English in parallel columns.
KAS

1106 Cérémonial de la bénédiction d'un abbé
bénédiction de la Congrégation du Mont
Cassin. Albi, Apprentis-Orphelins, 1896.
30 p. 21 cm.
Latin and French in parallel columns.
KAS

1107 Prières et cérémonies pour la bénédiction
d'un abbé selon le Pontifical Romain.
Pairs, Desclée [1928?].
MnCS
Latin and French in parallel columns.

1108 Ordo benedictionis abbatis et abbatissae.
Editio typica. Typis Polyglottis Vaticanis, 1970.
30 p. 24 cm.
PLatS

f. Blessing of a Cuculla

1109 Benedictio cucullae, vel vestimentorum pro
pueris vel devotis saecularibus.
(*In* Regla del gran patriarca San Benito
. . . n. 4. Barcelona, Heredero de H.
Pablo Riera, 1876)
Xerographic copy.
MnCS

g. Breviarium: Latin
1. Manuscripts

(arranged by century)

1110 Breviarium monasticum. MS. Huesca,
Spain, Archivo de la Catedral, codex 2.
194 f. Folio. Saec. 11.
Microfilm: MnCH proj. no. 31,555

1111 Breviarium, cum neumis. MS. Benediktinerabtei Michaelbeuern, Austria, codex
perg. 6. 178 f. Quarto. Saec. 11.
Microfilm: MnCH proj. no. 11,622

1112 Breviarium cum neumis: Vesperale,
Orationale, Hymnale, Nocturnale et
Matutinale. MS. Benediktinerabtei St.
Peter, Salzburg, codex a.V.24. 328 f.
Octavo. Saec. 11-12.
Microfilm: MnCH proj. no. 10,047

1113 Horae diurnae et nocturnae (Rituale
antiquissimum). MS. Silos, Spain,
Archivo del Monasterio de Sto. Domingo, Ms. 7. 141 f. Quarto. Saec. 11.
Microfilm: MnCH proj. no. 33,689

1114 Breviarium, Missale et Rituale. MS.
Monesterio di Montserrat, Spain,
codex 72. 181 f..
MnCS (microfiche)

1115 Breviarium monasticum sine psalmis. MS.
Benediktinerabtei St. Paul im Lavantthal, Austria, codex 33/1. 303 f. Duodecimo. Saec. 12-13.
Microfilm: MnCH proj. no. 11,694

1116 Breviarium. Scriptura longobardica. MS.
Vienna, Nationalbibliothek, codex 1106.
145 f. Quarto. Saec. 12.
Microfilm: MnCH proj. no. 14,392

1117 Breviarium monasticum. MS. Cava, Italy
(Benedictine abbey), codex 27-28. 2 vols.
Folio. Saec. 13.
Microfilm: MnCH

1118 Breviarium benedictinum. MS. Universitätsbibliothek Graz, Austria, codex
134. 548 f. Folio. Saec. 13.
Microfilm: MnCH proj. no. 25,055

1119 Breviarium monasticum (fou compost per
a l'ús del priorat cluniaceno de Vergy).
MS. Monasterio benedictino de Mont-
serrat, Spain, codex 36. 434 f. Octavo.
Saec. 13/14.
Microfilm: MnCH proj. no. 30,162

1120 Breviarium benedictinum, cum calendario.
MS. Benediktinerabtei St. Peter,
Salzburg, codex a.VI.40. 459 f. Octavo.
Saec. 13-14.
Microfilm: MnCH proj. no. 10,107

1121 Breviarium, cum calendario. MS. Benedik-
tinerabtei St. Paul im Lavantthal,
Austria, codex 41/1. 304 f. Duodecimo.
Saec. 13-14.
Microfilm: MnCH proj. no. 12,520

1122 Breviarium monasticum dioecesis cuisdam
Bohemiae. MS. Vienna, Schottenstift,
codex 161. 350 f. Quarto. Saec. 13.
Microfilm: MnCH proj. no. 4005

1123 Breviarium benedictinum. MS. Benediktin-
erabtei Admont, Austria, codex 6. 462 f.
Folio. Saec. 14.
Microfilm: MnCH proj. no. 9099

1124 Breviarium benedictinum. Pars hiemalis.
MS. Universitätsbibliothek Graz, Aus-
tria, codex 843. 383 f. Quarto. Saec. 14.
Microfilm: MnCH proj. no. 26,947

1125 Breviarium benedictinum. MS. Universitätsbibliothek Graz, Austria, codex
1527. 242 f. Octavo. Saec. 14.
Microfilm: MnCH proj. no. 26,479

1126 Breviarium benedictinum, cum calendario.
MS. Klagenfurt, Austria, Studien-
bibliothek, codex perg. 40. 466 f.
Octavo. Saec. 14.
Microfilm: MnCH proj. no. 12,975

1127 Breviarium benedictinum. MS. Benediktinerabtei St. Peter, Salzburg, codex
a.IV.10. 274 f. Octavo. Saec. 14.
Microfilm: MnCH proj. no. 9990

1128 Breviarium monasticum, sine Psalterio.
MS. Benediktinerabtei St. Paul im
Lavantthal, Austria, codex 50/1. 514 f.
Quarto. Saec. 14-15.
Microfilm: MnCH proj. no. 11,712

1129 Breviarium monastico-benedictinum. MS.
Benediktinerabtei Seitenstetten, Austria, codex 287. 367 f. Quarto. Saec.
14-15.
Microfilm: MnCH proj. no. 1098

1130 Breviarium monasticum benedictinorum
Mellicensium, cum calendario. MS.
Vienna, Nationalbibliothek, codex 1935.
491 f. Quarto. Saec. 14-15.
Microfilm: MnCH proj. no. 15,217

1131 Breviarium monasticum Lunaelacense
(Mondsee). MS. Vienna, National-
bibliothek, codex 1968. 221 f. Octavo.
Saec. 14.
Microfilm: MnCH proj. no. 15,283

1132 Breviarium monasticum, cum calendario.
In fine mutilum. Vienna, Nationalbibliothek, codex 2016. 274 f. Sextodecimo. Saec. 14.
Microfilm: MnCH proj. no. 15,325

1133 Breviarium, uti videtur in usum mona-
sterii Lunaelacensis conscriptum, et
quidam pars prima. MS. Vienna,
Nationalbibliothek, codex 3817. 349 f.
Quarto. Saec. 14.
Microfilm: MnCH proj. no. 17,013

1134 Breviarium in usum monasterii Lunaelacensis. MS. Vienna, Nationalbibliothek,
codex 3849. 198 f. Octavo. Saec. 15.
Microfilm: MnCH proj. no. 17,140

1135 Breviarium benedictinum Congregationis
S. Justinae. MS. Benediktinerabtei
Admont, Austria, codex 746a. 563 p.
Octavo. Saec. 15.
Microfilm: MnCH proj. no. 9766

1136 Breviarium benedictinum. MS. Benediktinerabtei Altenburg, Austria, codex AB
13 F 22. Octavo. Saec. 15(1448).
Microfilm: MnCH proj. no. 6426

1137 Breviarium Benedictinum Gottwicense.
MS. Benediktinerabtei Göttweig, Aus-
tria, codex 437. 515 f. Octavo. Saec. 15.
Microfilm: MnCH proj. no. 3697

1138 Breviarium benedictinum. MS. Benediktinerabtei Göttweig, Austria, codex 438,
f.1r-366v. Octavo. Saec. 15.
Microfilm: MnCH proj. no. 3696

1139 Breviarium benedictinum. Pars aestiva.
MS. Universitätsbibliothek Graz,
Austria, codex 1521. 429 f. Octavo.
Saec. 15.
Microfilm: MnCH proj. no. 26,446

1140 Breviarium divini officii secundum modum
monasterii Mellicensis. MS. Benediktinerabtei Kremsmünster, Austria,
codex 150, f.3r-74v. Saec. 15.
Microfilm: MnCH proj. no. 139

1141 Breviarium monasticum O.S.B. MS.
Benediktinerabtei Kremsmünster, Aus-
tria, codex 170a. 337 f. Saec. 15.
Microfilm: MnCH proj. no. 162

1142 Breviarium per totum annum secundum
usum ecclesie Cremifanensis. MS.
Benediktinerabtei Kremsmünster, Austria, codex 392. 588 f. Saec. 15.
Microfilm: MnCH proj. no. 380

1143 Breviarium secundum consuetudinem
monachorum sive specus S. Benedicti
(S. Zeno in Verona). MS. Benediktinerabtei Kremsmünster, Austria, codex 60.
396 f. Saec. 15.
Microfilm: MnCH proj. no. 420

1144 Breviarium Lambacense (die erste Hälfte
fehlt). MS. Benediktinerabtei Lambach,
Austria, codex chart. 224. 98 f. Saec. 15.
Microfilm: MnCH proj. no. 615

1145 Breviarium monasticum. MS. Lincoln Cathedral Library, England, codex 112. 259 f. Octavo. Saec. 15.
Microfilm: MnCH

1146 Breviarium divini officii secundum modum monasterii Mellicensis. MS. Benediktinerabtei Melk, Austria, codex 290. 110 f. Quarto. Saec. 15.
Microfilm: MnCH proj. no. 1314

1147 Breviarium Mellicense. MS. Benediktinerabtei Melk, Austria, codex 272. 213 f. Octavo. Saec. 15.
Microfilm: MnCH proj. no. 1299

1148 Breviarium Mellicense. MS. Benediktinerabtei Melk, Austria, codex 1556. 406 p. Duodecimo. Saec. 15.
Microfilm: MnCH proj. no. 1959

1149 Breviarium Mellicense. MS. Benediktinerabtei Melk, Austria, codex 1772. xv, 729 f. Octavo. Saec. 15.
Microfilm: MnCH proj. no. 2086

1150 Ordo Breviarii per anni circulum secundum consuetudinem monasterii Mellicensis. MS. Benediktinerabtei Melk, Austria, codex 186. 289 f. Octavo. Saec. 15.
Microfilm: MnCH proj. no. 1236

1151 Ordo Breviarii secundum rubricum Romanum juxta modum et consuetudinem monasterii Mellicensis. MS. Benediktinerabtei Melk, Austria, codex 1579, f.1-344 (secunda pars). Octavo. Saec. 15(1469).
Microfilm: MnCH proj. no. 1978

1152 Breviarium cum calendario. MS. Benediktinerabtei St. Peter, Salzburg, codex a.I.10. 348 f. Duodecimo. Saec. 15.
Microfilm: MnCH proj. no. 9880

1153 Psalterium Davidis secundum ordinem. Breviarium psalterii. Hymni per annum. MS. Benediktinerabtei St. Peter, Salzburg, codex a.IV.7. 154 f. Octavo. Saec. 15.
Microfilm: MnCH proj. no. 9982

1154 Breviarium pro monialibus. MS. Benediktinerabtei St. Peter, Salzburg, codex a.IV.17. 196 f. Octavo. Saec. 15.
Microfilm: MnCH proj. no. 9988

1155 Breviarium benedictinum. MS. Benediktinerabtei St. Peter, Salzburg, codex b.II.31. 290 f. Octavo. Saec. 15-16.
Microfilm: MnCH proj. no. 10,335

1156 Breviarium benedictinum, cum calendario. MS. Benediktinerabtei St. Peter, Salzburg, codex b.VII.9. 271, 281, 141 f. Octavo. Saec. 15-16.
Microfilm: MnCH proj. no. 15-16

1157 Breviarium benedictinum. MS. Benediktinerabtei St. Paul im Lavantthal. Austria, codex 106/3. 676 f. Duodecimo. Saec. 15(1477).
Microfilm: MnCH proj. no. 12,194

1158 Breviarium. MS. Benediktinerabtei St. Paul im Lavantthal, Austria, codex 320/4. 8 vols. Octavo. Saec. 15.
Microfilm: MnCH proj. no. 12,502-

1159 Breviarium romano-benedictinum. MS. Benediktinerabtei Seitenstetten, Austria, codex 92. 410 f. Duodecimo. Saec. 15.
Microfilm: MnCH proj. no. 904

1160 Breviarium benedictinum. MS. Benediktinerabtei Seitenstetten, Austria, codex 128. 160 f. Folio. Saec. 15.
Microfilm: MnCH proj. no. 941

1161 Breviarium pro officio chori et quidem monasterii Ordinis S. Benedicti probabiliter Papiensis, Sancti Juventii, praecedente calendario. MS. Vienna, Nationalbibliothek, codex 1896. 526 f. Quarto. Saec. 15.
Microfilm: MnCH proj. no. 15,193

1162 Breviarium, cum calendario, computo, tabula signorum lunae, etc., in usum monasterii Lunaelacensis scriptum. MS. Vienna, Nationalbibliothek, codex 1914. 406 f. Octavo. Saec. 15(1477).
Microfilm: MnCH proj. no. 15,207

1163 Breviarium monasticum "secundum ordinem Romanum, in quo antiquae legendae et ceremoniae habentur." MS. Vienna, Nationalbibliothek, codex 1919. 466 f. Octavo. Saec. 15.
Microfilm: MnCH proj. no. 15,216

1164 Breviarium benedictinum monasterii Opatovicensis (Oppatowitz, Bohemia). MS. Vienna, Nationalbibliothek, codex 1962. 352 f. Octavo. Saec. 15.
Microfilm: MnCH proj. no. 15,268

1165 Breviarium monasticum Lunaelacense (Mondsee), cum officio proprio S. Wolfgangi. MS. Vienna, Nationalbibliothek, codex 1975. 472 f. Octavo. Saec. 15.
Microfilm: MnCH proj. no. 16,262

1166 Breviarium cum calendario, Diurnale, Psalterio et Officiis mortuorum et sanctorum anno 1473 usui monasterii Beatae Mariae Virginis Coelestinorum Parisiensium dicatum. MS. Vienna, Nationalbibliothek, codex 2019. 406 f. Sextodecimo. Saec. 15.
Microfilm: MnCH proj. no. 15,331

1167 Breviarium Lunaelacense, cum calendario praemisso. MS. Vienna, Nationalbibliothek, codex 3546. 350 f. Octavo. Saec. 15.
Microfilm: MnCH proj. no. 16,787

1168 Breviarium, cum calendario. praemisso officio proprio S. Wolfgangi. Pars aestivalis et autumnalis. MS. Vienna, Nationalbibliothek, codex 3840. 403 f. Octavo. Saec. 15.
Microfilm: MnCH proj. no. 17,037

1169 Breviarium monasticum, cum calendario, cum versibus germanicis cuique mensi adscriptis. MS. Vienna, Nationalbibliothek, codex 4005. 532 f. Quarto. Saec. 15.
Microfilm: MnCH proj. no. 17,202

1170 Breviarium in usum monasterii Lunaelacensis. Hymni instructi sunt notis musicis. MS. Vienna, Nationalbibliothek, codex 4076. 222 f. Octavo. Saec. 15.
Microfilm: MnCH proj. no. 17,268

1171 Breviarium antiquum, cum calendario. MS. Vienna, Nationalbibliothek, codex 4474. 454 f. Folio. Saec. 15(1458).
Microfilm: MnCH proj. no. 17,657

1172 Breviarium, cum calendario secundum consuetudinem monachorum S. Benedicti in Mondsee. MS. Vienna, Nationalbibliothek, codex 4566. 294 f. Octavo. Saec. 15(1477).
Microfilm: MnCH proj. no. 17,719

1173 Breviarium Mellicense. MS. Vienna, Schottenstift, codex 148. 418 f. Octavo. Saec. 15.
Microfilm: MnCH proj. no. 3999

1174 Breviarium Mellicense. MS. Vienna, Schottenstift, codex 333. 279 f. Octavo. Saec. 15.
Microfilm: MnCH proj. no. 4011

1175 Breviarium benedictinum ad usum monasterii S. Lamberti. Pars hiemalis. MS. Universitätsbibliothek Graz, Austria, codex 108. 436 f. Folio. Saec. 16(1510).
Microfilm: MnCH proj. no. 26,025

1176 Breviarium benedictinum. Pars aestivalis. MS. Universitätsbibliothek Graz, Austria, codex 56. 544 f. Folio. Saec. 16.
Microfilm: MnCH proj. no. 25,976

1177 Ordinarium seu Breviarium secundum Mellicensium reformationem observandum (de tempore, de sanctis et de communi). Benediktinerabtei Lambach, Austria, codex chart. 163. Saec. 16.
Microfilm: MnCH proj. no. 579

1178 Breviarium divini officii juxta modum monasterii Mellicensis. MS. Benediktinerabtei Melk, Austria, codex 1573. 423 f. Duodecimo. Saec. 16(1593).
Microfilm: MnCH proj. no. 1972

1179 Breviarium divini officii secundum modum monasterii Mellicensis. MS. Benediktinerabtei Melk, Austria, codex 718. 223 f. Folio. Saec. 16.
Microfilm: MnCH proj. no. 1572

1180 Breviarium benedictinum secundum usum St. Peter Salisburgi. MS. Benediktinerabtei St. Peter, Salzburg, codex b.VII.11. 464 f. Quarto. Saec. 16.
Microfilm: MnCH proj. no. 10,521

1181 Breviarium San-Blasianum. MS. Benediktinerabtei St. Paul, Austria, codex 15/2. 1142 p. Folio. Saec. 16(1572).
Microfilm: MnCH proj. no. 11,742

1182 Breviarium nigrorum monachorum de observantia patrum Mellicensium. MS. Benediktinerabtei Melk, Austria, codex 1270. 816 p. Duodecimo. Saec. 16.
Microfilm: MnCH proj. no. 1895

1183 Breviarium monasticum Lunaelacense. MS. Vienna, Nationalbibliothek, codex 1918. 438 f. Octavo. Saec. 16.
Microfilm: MnCH proj. no. 15,233

1184 Breviarium monasticum, ex variis fragmentis consarcinatum. MS. Vienna, Nationalbibliothek, codex 3582. 388 f. Octavo. Saec. 16.
Microfilm: MnCH proj. no. 20,392

1185 Breviarium, pro parte majori impressum, sed opera diversarum manuum usui monasterii Lunaelacensis accomodatum intercalatis multis notis et pagellis integris manu scriptis. MS. Vienna, Nationalbibliothek, codex 3834. 195 f. Quarto. Saec. 16.
Microfilm: MnCH proj. no. 17,043

1186 Breviarium in usum monasterii Lunaelacensis, cum notis marginalibus Leonardi Schilling. MS. Vienna, Nationalbibliothek, codex 4060. 610 f. Octavo. Saec. 16.
Microfilm: MnCH proj. no. 17,242

1187 Breviarium festivum S. Blasii in Silva Nigra. MS. Benediktinerabtei St. Paul im Lavantthal, Austria, codex 81/6. 745 p. Octavo. Saec. 18(1783).
Microfilm: MnCH proj. no. 12,622

2. Printed Editions

1188 Breviarium secundum consuetudinem Congregationis Sanctae Iustinae, sive Ordinis Sancti Benedicti ordinatum summa cura ac diligentia maxima. Venice, Erhard Ratdolt, pridie calen. Maii, 1483.
430 leaves.
MnCS (microfilm); PLatS (microfilm)
Hain 3803

1189 Breviarium Fratrum Coelestinorum. Naples, Matthias von Olmütz, 1488.
400 leaves.
MnCS(microfilm); PLatS(microfilm)
Gesamtkatalog der Wiegendrucke 4210

1190 Breviarium Vallumbrosanum. Venice, Johann Emerich, 1493.
426 leaves.
PLatS (microfilm)
Gesamtkatalog der Wiegendrucke 5239

1191 Breviarium benedictinum ex romano restitutum, Pauli quinti pont. max. auctoritate approbatum. A mendis quae in editionem venetam, romanam, &c irrepserunt expurgatum. Rorschachii, Ioannes Röslerus, 1614.
[52], 871, cxlv p. 36 cm.
KAS

1192 Breviarium monasticum summorum pontificum cura recognitum pro omnibus sub Regula s.p. Benedicti militantibus jussu Abbatis Primatis editum. Taurini, Marietti [1963].
2 v. 17 cm.
KAS; InStme; MnCS; NcBe; PLatS

3. Supplements

1193 Supplementum Breviarii monastici; sive Officia propria sanctorum omnia . . . Summis Pontificibus ab anno 1640 usque 1692 concessa in usum omnium sub Regula s. p. Benedicti militantium . . . Salisburgi, Joan. Bapt. Mayr, 1692.
518 p.
NcBe

1194 Additamenta ad Breviarium monastico-benedictinum Einsidlense, usibus monasteriorum Brevnoviensis et Braunensis in Bohemia. Pragae, typis, Caroli Bellmann, 1876.
242, [16] p. 21 cm.
MnCS

1195 Supplementum ad Breviarium monasticum, continens officia nova. [Collegeville, Minn.] typis Abbatiae S. Joannis-Bapt. 1892.
132 p. 17 cm.
MnCS

1196 Supplementum ad Ordinem, continens Calendarium O.S.B. necnon textus novos pro Divino Officio explendo. Collegeville, Minn., typis Abbatiae Sancti Baptistae, 1962.
xvi, 76 p. 15 cm.
MnCS; PLatS

4. Selections

1197 Versiculi, responsoria, invitatoria et cetera officium acolythi concernentia per circulum anni secundum consuetudinem monasterii Mellicensis. MS. Benediktin-erabtei Melk, Austria, codex 1115.
vii, 79 f. Octavo. Saec. 14.
Microfilm: MnCH proj. no. 1859

1198 Versiculi, responsoria brevia, invitatoria et cetera officium accoliti concernentia per circulum anni secundum consuetudinem monasterii Mellicensis. MS. Benediktinerabtei Melk, Austria, codex 1479. 62 f. Sextodecimo. Saec. 16.
Microfilm: MnCH proj. no. 1947

h. Breviarium: Dutch, English, German, Gothic

1199 Middelnederlandse Brevierteksten. [Compiled by a Benedictine very questionably identified as Joseph de Bovy in 1949]. Handwritten.
214 p. 22 cm.
MnCS (facsimile)

1200 The Benedictine Office; an Old English text edited by James M. Ure. Edinburgh, University Press, 1957.
ix, 141 p. 23 cm. (Edinburgh University publications; language and literature, no. 1).
NcBe; OkShG

1201 Das Benediktiner-Offizium; ein altenglisches Brevier aus dem 11. Jahrhundert. Ein Beitrag zur Wulfstanfrage, von Emil Feiler. Heidelberg, C. Winter's Universitätsbuchhandlung, 1901; Amsterdam, Sweta & Zeitlinger, 1966.
81 p. 23 cm. (Anglistische Forschungen, Heft 4)
PLatS

1202 The Monastic Breviary, according to the Holy Rule of our most holy father Benedict. For private instruction and benefit of the Benedictine Sisters of Perpetual Adoration, Clyde, Mo., 1940–42.
5 v. 22 cm.
ILSP

1203 The proper and the common of the saints of the Monastic Breviary according to the Holy Rule of our most holy father Benedict. For private instruction and benefit of the Benedictine Sisters of Perpetual Adoration, Clyde, Mo., 1942.
604, 215 p. 22 cm.
Multigraphed.
MnCS

1204 Benet Lake Breviary manuals. [Benet Lake, Wis., 195–?–].
v. 29 cm.
Multigraphed.
WBenS

1205 The English matins of the Monastic Breviary according to the Holy Rule of

our most holy father Benedict. For
private use of the Benedictine Sisters of
Villa St. Scholastica, Duluth, Minn.,
1959.
4 v. 22 cm.
MnCS; MnDuS

1206 Deutsches Brevier. Winterteil. MS.
Universitätsbibliothek Graz, Austria,
codex 354. 284. f. Folio. Saec. 15.
Microfilm: MnCH proj. no. 26,263

1207 Breviarium monasticum, un usum collegii
cujusdam virginum. Germanice. MS.
Vienna, Nationalbibliothek, codex 2781.
233 f. Folio. Saec. 15.
Microfilm: MnCH proj. no. 16,037

1208 Breviarium benedictinum, cum calendario.
Germanice. Vienna, Nationalbibliothek,
codex 2972. 444 f. Quarto. Saec.
15(1454).
Microfilm: MnCH proj. no. 16,197

1209 Officium divinum parvum; bearb. und
hrsg. im Auftrag des Liturgischen
Referates der Fuldaer Bischofskon-
ferenz von P. Hildebrand Fleischmann,
O.S.B. Freiburg, Herder, 1951.
567 p. 16 cm. Text in Latin and German.
KAS

1210 El "Breviarium Gothicum" de Silos
(Archivo monastico, ms. 6) por Ismael
Fernández de la Cuesta, O.S.B. Madrid-
Barcelona, 1965.
126 p. 26 cm. (Monumenta Hispaniae
sacra, Serie liturgica, v. 8)
PLatS(facsim.)

i. Calendars

1211 Calendarium romanum et benedictinum.
MS. Benediktinerabtei St. Paul im
Lavantthal, Austria, codex 909/0,
pars III. Octavo. Saec. 17-18.

j. Cantatorium

1212 Cantatorium, IXe siècle, no. 359 de la
Bibliothèque de Saint-Gall. [Tournay
(Belgique), Desclèe & cie, 1924].
23 p. facsim. 33 cm. (Paléographie
musicale . . . Deuxième série [monumen-
tale] II)
KAS

1213 Cantus ecclesiastici ad usum in choro. MS.
Benediktinerinnenabtei Nonnberg, Salz-
burg, codex 23 C 6. 122 f. Quarto.
Saec. 17(1619).
Microfilm: MnCH proj. no. 10,849

k. Compline

1214 Prime and Compline of the Monastic
Breviary. Printed as manuscript for the
use of the Benedictine Brothers of St.
Benedict's Abbey, Atchison, Kans.
[Atchison, Kans., Abbey Student Press]
1960.
44 p. 24 cm.
KAS

l. Customaries

1. Manuscripts

(arranged alphabetically by title)

1215 Codex traditionum monasterii Lunaelacensis, Ordinis S. Benedicti. Ms. Vienna,
Haus-, Hof- und Staatsarchiv, codex B
70. 136 p. Quarto. Saec. 10–13.
Microfilm: MnCH proj. no. 23,502

1216 Consuetudines Hirsaugienses. MS. Benediktinerabtei Admont, Austria, codex
518. 136 f. Quarto. Saec. 12.
Microfilm: MnCH proj. no. 9563

1217 Consuetudines monasticae. MS. Benedictinerabtei Lambach, Austria, codex
chart. 325, f.31r-36r. Saec. 15.
Microfilm: MnCH proj. no. 701

1218 Consuetudines von Subiaco-Melk 1427-
1428 (Lambacher Abschrift). MS. Benediktinerabtei Kremsmünster, Austria,
codex 246. 398 p. Saec. 16.
Microfilm: MnCH proj. no. 428

1219 Diarien St. Blasianischer Gebräuche in und
ausser dem Chor. MS. Benediktinerabtei
St. Paul im Lavantthal, Austria, codex
90/6. 49 f. Folio. Saec. 19(1803).
Microfilm: MnCH proj. no. 12,681

1220 Divini cultus consuetudines monachales.
MS. Hereford, England, Cathedral
Library, codex P 5 i, f.1-26. Quarto.
Saec. 12.
Microfilm: MnCH

1221 Eckhardt, Karl August, ed.
Studia Corbeiensis: bibliotheca rerum
historicarum Corbeiensis; traditiones Corbeienses . . . Aalen, Scientia Verlag, 1970.
MnCS

1222 Fiecht, Austria (Benedictine abbey)
Gerbäuche bei Tisch und im Chor in St.
Georgenberg-Fiecht. MS. Benediktinerab-
tei Fiecht, Austria, codex 15a. 4 f. Quarto.
Saec. 15.
Microfilm: MnCH proj. no. 28,828

1223 Kremsmünster, Austria (Benedictine
abbey)
Liber de ordinatione officiorum
monasticorum tam in choro quam in
monasterio. MS. Benediktinerabtei

Kremsmünster, Austria, codex 321a. 83 f.
Saec. 14.
Microfilm: MnCH proj. no. 431

1224 Martinus, Abbot of Schottenstift, Vienna.
Caeremonialia. MS. Vienna, National-
bibliothek, codex 4970, f.8v-18v. Quarto.
Saec. 15.
Microfilm: MnCH proj. no. 18,143

1225 Melk, Austria, (Benedictine abbey).
Breviarium caeremoniarium monasterii
Mellicensis. MS. Benediktinerabtei Fiecht,
Austria, codex 184. Quarto. Saec. 15.
Microfilm: MnCH proj. no. 28,828

1226 Melk, Austria, (Benedictine abbey).
Prologus in breviarium caeremoniarum
Mellicensium ducatus Austriae. MS.
Benediktinerabtei Fiecht, codex 60. 101 f.
Folio. Saec. 15.
Microfilm: MnCH proj. no. 28,833

1227 Ordinarium (consuetudines) Ordinis S.
Benedicti. MS. Vienna, Nationalbibliothek, codex 12856. 168 f. Quarto. Saec.
16.
Microfilm: MnCH proj. no. 25,203

1228 Ordinarium divinorum nigrorum monachorum de observantia Bursfeldensi. MS.
Vienna, Schottenstift, codex 578, f.124r-
185r. Octavo. Saec. 16.
Microfilm: MnCH proj. no. 4272

1229 Peterborough Consuetudinary, part III.
MS. Lambeth Palace Library, London,
codex 198b. 293 f. Quarto. Saec. 14.
Microfilm: MnCH

1230 St. Paul im Lavantthal, Austria (Benedictine abbey).
Directorium cultus divini et disciplinae
monasticae in monasterio S. Pauli . . . auctore Hieronymo abbate. MS. Benediktinerabtei St. Paul im Lavantthal, Austria,
codex 28/0. 359 p. Folio. Saec. 17.
Microfilm: MnCH proj. no. 12,640

1231 Verbrüderungsbuch oder Traditionscodex
M. MS. Benediktinerabtei St. Paul,
Salzburg, Archivium Hs. A.1. 56 f. Folio.
Saec. 8-13.
Microfilm: MnCH proj. no. 10,021

2. Printed Editions

1232 Angerer, Joachim, O.S.B.
Die Bräuche der Abtei Tegernsee unter
Abt Kaspar Ayndorffer (1426-1461) verbunden mit einer textkritischen Edition
der Consuetudines Tegernseenses. Ottobeuren, Kommissionsverlag Winfried-
Werk, 1968.
xv, 362 p. 24 cm.
InStme

1233 Bec, France (Benedictine abbey).
Consuetudines Beccenses. Edidit Marie
Pascal Dickson. Siegburg, F. Schmitt,
1967.
xc, 419 p. 25 cm. (Corpus consuetudinum
monasticarum, 4)
InStme; KAS; PLatS

1234 Bury St. Edmunds Abbey, England.
The Customary of the Benedictine Abbey
of Bury St. Edmunds in Suffolk (from
Harleian MS. 1005 in the British Museum).
Edited by Antonia Grandsen, Chichester,
The Regnum Press, 1973.
xli, 142 p. 24 cm. (Henry Bradshaw
Society, [Publications] v. 99)
MnCS; PLatS

1235 Consuetudines Benedictinae variae (saec.
XI-XIV). Publici juris fecit Giles Constable. Siegburg, apud Franciscum
Schmitt, 1975.
395 p. 26 cm. (Corpus consuetudinum
monasticarum, t. 6)
PLatS

1235a Consuetudines Corbeinses. The customs of
Corbie. A translation by Charles W.
Jones of The Directives of Adalhard of
Corbie (753-826).
(In Horn, Walter W. The plan of St. Gall
. . . vol. III, p. 91-128)
MnCS; PLatS; InStme

1236 Corpus consuetudinum monasticarum. t. 1-
Siegburg, F. Schmitt, 1963-
v. 26 cm.
AStb; InStme; KAS; MnCS; MoCo;
PLatS

1237 Eynsham Abbey, England.
The Customary of the Benedictine Abbey
of Eynsham in Oxfordshire, edited by Antonia Grandsen. Siegburg, F. Schmitt,
1963.
245 p. 26 cm. (Corpus consuetudinum
monasticarum, t. 2)
InStme; KAS; NdRi; PLatS

1238 Fosbrooke, T. D.
British monachism; manners & customs
of the monks and nuns of England. New
ed. London, Nichols, 1817.
560 p. plates
AStb

1239 Göttweig, Austria (Benedictine Abbey).
Die Traditionsbücher des Benediktiner-
stiftes Göttweig, bearb. von Dr. Adalbert
Fr. Fuchs. Wien und Leipzig, Hölder-
Pichler-Tempsky, 1931.
x, 704 p. facsims. 24 cm.
MnCS

1240 Gougaud, Louis, O.S.B.
Anciennes coutumes claustrales. A.
Etudes générales. Ligugé, France, Abbaye
Saint-Martin, 1930.

121 p. 20 cm.
CaQStB; ILSP; InStme; KAS; MnCS; MoCo

1241 Initia consuetudinis benedictinae; consuetudines saeculi octavi et noni. Cooperantibus D. Petro Becher, O.S.B. [et al.]. Publici iuris fecit Kassius Hallinger, O.S.B. Siegburg, F. Schmitt, 1963.
cxxiii, 626 p. 26 cm. (Corpus consuetudinum monasticarum, t. 1)
InStme; PLatS

1242 Nuremberg, Germany. S. Aegidius (Benedictine abbey).
Excerpta consuetudinum observantiae regularis monasterii Nurnbergensis conventus Ordinis S. Benedicti. MS. Benediktinerabtei Melk, Austria, codex 639, f.247r-249v. Quarto. Saec. 15.
Microfilm: MnCH proj. no. 1524

1243 Saint-Benoît-sur-Loire, France (Benedictine abbey).
Consuetudines Floriacenses saeculi tertii. Siegburg, F. Schmitt, 1976.
lxxxix, 507 p. facsim. 26 cm. (Corpus consuetudinum monasticarum, t. 9)
InStme; MnCS; PLatS

1244 Trier, Germany. St. Matthias (Benedictine abbey).
Consuetudines et observantiae monasteriorum Sancti Matthiae et Sancti Maximi Treverensium ab Johanne Rode abbate conscriptae. Edidit Petrus Becker. Siegburg, F. Schmitt, 1968.
lxx, 320 p. 26 cm. (Corpus consuetudinum monasticarum, t. 5)
InStme; KAS; PLatS

m. Directorium Chori

1245 Directorium liturgicum benedictinum ad horas canonicas et Missam ad usum monasterii S. Lamberti. MS. Universitätsbibliothek Graz, Austria, codex 798. 166 f. Quarto. Saec. 13.
Microfilm: MnCH proj. no. 26,876

1246 Directorium liturgicum benedictinum. Breviarium chori S. Lamberti. MS. Universitätsbibliothek Graz, Austria, codex 193, f.2r-131r. Quarto. Saec. 14.
Microfilm: MnCH proj. no. 26,128

1247 Liber de choro monastico. MS. Pamplona, Spain, Archivo General de Navarra, codex 12. 287 f. Octavo. Saec. 14.
Microfilm: MnCH proj. no. 34,856

1248 Directorium liturgicum benedictinum. MS. Universitätsbibliothek Graz, Austria, codex 722. 99 f. Folio. Saec. 14.
Microfilm: MnCH proj. no. 26,819

1249 Liber choralis cum notis musicis. MS. Benediktinerabtei St. Paul im Lavantthal, Austria, codex 63/1. 30 f. Folio. Saec. 15.
Microfilm: MnCH proj. no. 11,715

1250 Festa abbatis, prioris, et hebdomadarii, quibus annexa sunt Agenda pro defunctis, in monasterio Mellicensi. MS. Benediktinerabtei Seitenstetten, Austria, codex 88, f. 200r-209v. Octavo. Saec. 15.
Microfilm: MnCH proj. no. 897

1251 Ordinationes quaedam divinum officium O.S.B. spectantes. MS. Benediktinerabtei Kremsmünster, Austria, codex 20, f.12-172. Saec. 15.
Microfilm: MnCH proj. no. 20

1252 Chorbuch, cum calendario. Latine. MS. Benediktinerinnenabtei Nonnberg, Salzburg, codex 23 B 5. 360 f. Quarto. Saec. 16(1558).
Microfilm: MnCH proj. no. 10,828

1253 Chorbuch für Festtage: Festa solemnia welche eine Frau Abbtissin durch das gantze Jahr zu verichten hat . . . MS. Benediktinerinnenabtei Nonnberg, Salzburg, codex 28 D 10. 143 f. Folio. Saec. 18.
Microfilm: MnCH proj. no. 10,958

n. Diurnale
1. Latin
a. Manuscripts
(arranged by century)

1254 Diurnale monasticum. MS. Benediktinerabtei Melk, Austria, codex 626. 186 f. Quarto. Saec. 13.
Microfilm: MnCH proj. no. 1520

1255 Diurnum monasticum. MS. Subiaco, Italy (Benedictine abbey), codex 281. 106 f. Saec. 13-14.
Microfilm: MnCS

1256 Diurnale monastico-benedictinum Gottwicense. MS. Benediktinerabtei Göttweig, Austria, codex 124. 162 f. Folio. Saec. 14.
Microfilm: MnCH proj. no. 3828

1257 Diurnale Lunaelacense (Mondsee), cum calendario praemisso. MS. Vienna, Nationalbibliothek, codex 3580. 274 f. Octavo. Saec. 14 et 16. Fol. 159a-169a sunt impressa. Opus priscum in membranaceo saec. 14, resarcinatum est in chartaceo saec. 16(1522) a variis manibus.
Microfilm: MnCH proj. no. 16,801

1258 Diurnale monasticum. MS. Cava, Italy Benedictine abbey), codex 63. 154 f. Quarto. Saec. 15-16.
Microfilm: MnCH

1259   Diurnale pro monialibus Ordinis Sancti Benedicti. MS. Benediktinerabtei Göttweig, Austria, codex 443. 245 f. Octavo. Saec. 15.
Microfilm: MnCH proj. no. 3706

1260   Diurnale. Benediktinerabtei Kremsmünster, Austria, codex 398. 157 f. Saec. 15.
Microfilm: MnCH proj. no. 388

1261   Diurnale Mellicense. MS. Benediktinerabtei Melk, Austria, codex 187. 149 f. Octavo. Saec. 15.
Microfilm: MnCH proj. no. 1231

1262   Diurnale Mellicense. MS. Benediktinerabtei Melk, Austria, codex 279. 314 f. Duodecimo. Saec. 15.
Microfilm: MnCH proj. no. 1303

1263   Diurnale monasticum. MS. Benediktinerabtei Melk, Austria, codex 757. 187 f. Octavo. Saec. 15.
Microfilm: MnCH proj. no. 1604

1264   Diurnale secundum consuetudinem monasterii Mellicensis. MS. Benediktinerabtei Melk, Austria, codex 1275. 403 f. Sextodecimo. Saec. 15.
Microfilm: MnCH proj. no. 1903

1265   Diurnale monasticum. MS. Monasterio benedictino de Montserrat, Spain, codex 51. 158 f. Octavo. Saec. 15.
Microfilm: MnCH proj. no. 29,994

1266   Diurnale. MS. Benediktinerinnenabtei Nonnberg, Salzburg, codex 23 A 31. 199 f. Duodecimo. Saec. 15.
Microfilm: MnCH proj. no. 10,820

1267   Diurnale breviarii. MS. Benediktinerabtei St. Peter, Salzburg, codex a.I.7., f.1r-97r. Duodecimo. Saec. 15.
Microfilm: MnCH proj. no. 9883

1268   Diurnale privatum pro monialibus. MS. Augustinerchorherrenstift St. Florian, Austria, codex XI,451. 191 f. Sextodecimo. Saec. 15 & 16.
Microfilm: MnCH proj. no. 2663

1269   Diurnale breviarii. MS. Benediktinerabtei St. Paul im Lavantthal, Austria, codex 103/3. 124 f. Duodecimo. Saec. 15.
Microfilm: MnCH proj. no. 12,220

1270   Diurnale officii ecclesiastici, in usum monasterii Lunaelacensis (Mondsee). MS. Vienna, Nationalbibliothek, codex 1916. 130 f. Octavo. Saec. 15.
Microfilm: MnCH proj. no. 15,241

1271   Diurnale monasticum Lunaelacense. MS. Vienna, Nationalbibliothek, codex 1972. 170 f. Octavo. Saec. 15.
Microfilm: MnCH proj. no. 15,265

1272   Diurnale benedictinum. MS. Vienna, Nationalbibliothek, codex 1990. 474 f. Octavo. Saec. 15(1482).
Microfilm: MnCH proj. no. 15,308

1273   Diurnale monasticum Lunaelacense. MS. Vienna, Nationalbibliothek, codex 1991. 356 f. Sextodecimo. Saec. 15.
Microfilm: MnCH proj. no. 15,290

1274   Diurnale monasticum Lunaelacense juxta ritum antiquum. MS. Vienna, Nationalbibliothek, codex 1996. 246 f. Sextodecimo. Saec. 15.
Microfilm: MnCH proj. no. 15,314

1275   Diurnale monasticum, praevio Officio Beatae Mariae Virginis secundum consuetudinem monasterii Sublacensis et Sacri Specus. MS. Vienna, Nationalbibliothek, codex 2031. 134 f. Sextodecimo. Saec. 15(1481).
Microfilm: MnCH proj. no. 15,345

1276   Diurnale monasticum, cum indice praemisso et hymnis perpaucis subnexis, quos scriptor notis musicis exornavit. MS. Vienna, Nationalbibliothek, codex 4896. 106 f. Quarto. Saec. 15.
Microfilm: MnCH proj. no. 18,078

1277   Diurnale monasticum. MS. Vienna, Schottenstift, codex 253. 290 f. Octavo. Saec. 15.
Microfilm: MnCH proj. no. 3998

1278   Diurnale secundum ritum monasterii Wiblingani. Benediktinerabtei Kremsmünster, Austria, codex 272. 210 f. Saec. 16.
Microfilm: MnCH proj. no. 256

1279   Diurnale Mellicense. MS. Benediktinerabtei Melk, Austria, codex 1215. 317 f. Sextodecimo. Saec. 16.
Microfilm: MnCH proj. no. 1860

1280   Diurnale breviarii secundum consuetudinem monasterii S. Petri. MS. Benediktinerabtei St. Peter, Salzburg, codex b.VII.7. 538 f. Octavo. Saec. 16.
Microfilm: MnCH proj. no. 10,582

1281   Horae Beatae Mariae Virginis secundum usum sacri monasterii Sancti Petri Larigniacensis (Lagny-sur-Marne). MS. Vienna, Nationalbibliothek, codex 1961. 117 f. Octavo. Saec. 16.
Microfilm: MnCH proj. no. 15,270

1282   Diurnale Lunaelacense. MS. Vienna, Nationalbibliothek, codex 3553. 210 f. Octavo. Saec. 16(1526).
Microfilm: MnCH proj. no. 16,771

1283   Diurnale monasticum. MS. Vienna, Schottenstift, codex 734. 194 f. Duodecimo. Saec. 16(1576).
Microfilm: MnCH proj. no. 4283

b. Printed Editions

1284 Diurnum monasticum Ordinis S. Benedicti de observantia Congregationis Otten-purranae SS. Martyrum Alexandri et Theodori patronor. [n.p.] 1594.
various pagings, illus. 17 cm.
PLatS

1285 Horae diurnae breviarii monastici, Pauli V. et Urbani VIII. ss. pontificum auctoritate recogniti, pro omnibus sub Regula ss. p. n. Benedicti militantibus, aucti officiis novissime praeceptis vel concessis per SS. Pont. et juxta sancitas leges revisi, sub moderamine Reverendissimi Abbatis Praesidis Generalis Congregationis Angliae O.S.B. Mechliniae, H. Dessain, 1906.
xix, 486, 304, 8 p. 21 cm.
InStme; MnCS

1286 Horae diurnale breviarii monastici Pauli pp. V jusu editi, ad mentem bullae "Divino afflatu" Pii pp. X auctoritate Benedicti pp. XV reformati. Pro omnibus congregationibus confoederatis sub Regula ss. patris nostri Benedicti militantibus. Mechliniae, H. Dessain, 1928.
xxxi, 774, 270, 14 p. 15 cm.
KAS; PLatS

1287 Livre d'heures, latin-français. Dourgne-Tarn, Editions de l'Abbaye d'Encalcat, 1952.
xlvii, 1487 p. 18 cm.
CaQStB; MnCS

2. English

1288 The Monastic Diurnal; or, The Day Hours of the Monastic Breviary . . . compiled by monks of St. John's Abbey, Collegeville, Minn. 3rd ed. Mechlin, H. Dessain, 1955.
1 v. (various pagings) 16 cm.
KAS

1289 – –5th ed. Mechlin, H. Dessain, 1963.
xxx, 487, 269, 385, 243, 59 p. 16 cm.
InFer; KAS

1290 The Monastic Diurnal noted. Adapted from the Benedictine plainsong by the Rev. Winfred Douglas. Kenosha, Wis., St. Mary's Convent, 1960-
2 v.
NcBe
This is an edition by the Protestant Episcopal Church in the U.S.A.

1291 The Day Hours of the Divine Office, with the proper of the season. Compiled and edited by the Benedictine Sisters of Perpetual Adoration in accord with the "Breviarium Monasticum" edition of the Abbot Primate, 1963. [n.p.] 1964.

294 p. 22 cm.
"For private use of the Congregation of Benedictine Sisters of Perpetual Adoration."
PLatS

1292 Lauds, Vespers, Compline, in English. Reprinted from the Hours of the Divine Office in English and Latin . . . prepared by the staff of The Liturgical Press, Collegeville, Minn., The Liturgical Press [c 1965].
6, 882 p. 18 cm.
KAS

3. French

1293 Livre d'heures, latin-français. Dourgne-Tarn, Editions de l'Abbaye d'Encalcat, 1952.
xlvii, 1487 p. 18 cm.
CaQStB; MnCS

4. German

1294 Diurnale, cum calendario. Germanice. MS. Benediktinerinnenabtei Nonnberg, Salzburg, codex 23 A 33. 218 f. Duodecimo. Saec. 15.
Microfilm: MnCH proj. no. 10,823

1295 Das Tagzeitenbuch des monastischen Breviers (Diurnale monasticum) im Anschluss an die Mess-Bücher von Anselm Schott, O.S.B. . . . 2. Aufl. Regensburg, F. Pustet, 1949.
36, 1670 p. 16 cm.
Latin and German in parallel columns.
First published 1934.
MnCS

o. Epistolarium

1296 Epistolarium in usum monasterii S. Chrysogoni Jaderae Ordinis Sancti Benedicti. MS. Vienna, Nationalbibliothek, codex 1807. 98 f. Folio. Saec. 15(1479).
Microfilm: MnCH proj. no. 15,125

1297 Liber epistolarum et evangeliorum monasterii Mellicensis. MS. Benediktinerabtei Melk, Austria, codex 8. 139 f. Folio. Saec. 15.
Microfilm: MnCH proj. no. 1133

p. Evangeliarium

1298 Codex millenarius maior: Evangelium quadruplex sive Plenarium I. MS. Benediktinerabtei Kremsmünster, Austria, codex Schatzkasten 1. [9], 348, [22] f. Folio. Saec. 8(ca. 800).
Microfilm: MnCH proj. no. 2324

1299 Liber evangeliorum per circulum anni. MS. Benediktinerabtei St. Paul im Lavantthal, Austria, codex 21/1. 47 f. Quarto. Saec. 11-12.
Microfilm: MnCH proj. no. 11,679

1300 Evangelistarium in usum monasterii S. Chrysogoni Jaderae Ordinis Sancti Benedicti, scriptum ab Alberto Borgondiensi. MS. Vienna. Nationalbibliothek, codex 1806. 123 f. Folio. Saec. 15(1479-1489).
Microfilm: MnCH proj. no. 15,126

1301 Plenarium idiomate germanico, seu, Liber in quo evangelia et epistolae plenaria continentur. MS. Benedictinerabtei Seitenstetten, Austria, codex 159. 360 f. Folio. Saec. 14 vel 15.
Microfilm: MnCH proj. no. 964

q. Exequiae

1302 Exequiae fratrum et sororum. MS. Benediktinerabtei St. Peter, Salzburg, codex a.V.30, f.1r-7r. Octavo. Saec. 14.
Microfilm: MnCH proj. no. 10,051

r. Feasts

1. Apostles

1303 Christ's twelve. [Benet Lake, Wis., Holy Family Convent, n.d.].
various pagings, 29 cm. (Benet Lake breviary manuals)
Multigraphed.
MnCS; WBenH

2. Benedict, Saint

1304 Feasts of our holy father St. Benedict: Matins. [Benet Lake, Wis., Holy Family Convent, n.d.].
50 p. 29 cm. (Benet Lake breviary manuals)
Multigraphed.
MnCS; OkTB; WBenH

1305 Missa in festo S. Benedicti abbatis, patroni principalis Europae, cum cantu. Editio typica. Typis Polyglottis Vaticanis [1966].
7 p. music. 21 cm.
MnCS

1306 S. p. n. Benedicti Regula et vita. Una cum officio & litaniis ejusdem s. p. & s. Scholasticae . . . Viennae, typis & sumptibus Ignatii Goldhann, anno MDCCXCV.
280 p. 14 cm.
PLatS

1307 Officium s. Benedicti. Metrice. Incipit: Benedictus opifex hora matutina. MS. Vienna, Nationalbibliothek, codex 4117, f.26v-27r. Sextodecimo. Saec. 16.
Microfilm: MnCH proj. no. 17,296

1308 Officium s. Benedicti; Litaniae. MS. Benediktinerabtei St. Peter, Salzburg, codex a.IV.41, f.80r-111r. Octavo. Saec. 17(1665).
Microfilm: MnCH proj. no. 10,028

3. Christmas

1309 Matins [for Christmas]. [Benet Lake, Wis., Holy Family Convent, 196-].
unpaged. 28 cm. (Benet Lake breviary manuals)
Multigraphed.
MnCS; WBenH

4. Gertrude, Saint

1310 Novena a santa Gertrudis la magna. Nueva edicion por un padre de Sto. Domingo de Silos. Burgos, Centro Católico, 1912.
39 p. 14 cm.
InStme; MnCS

1311 Novena en honor del glorioso patriarca San Benito, sequida de un triduo en honor de Santa Escolsstica y de Santa Gertrudis. 5. ed. Buenos Aires, Padres Benedictinos, 1945.
76 p. ports. 14 cm.

5. Gregory I, Saint

1312 On the feast of Saint Gregory the Great, bishop, confessor, and doctor of the church, apostle of England. March twelfth. The order of the music at evensong. New York, Cathedral of Saint John the Divine, n.d.
26 p. music, 21 cm.
MnCS

6. Holy Week

1313 Office and ceremonies for Holy Saturday and the Easter vigil according to the newly-restored rite. Plainsong with the rhythmic signs of the Benedictines of Solesmes. Paris, Desclée, 1962.
44 p. music. 19 cm.
KAS

1314 Ordo hebdomadae sanctae iuxta ritum monasticum. Editio cum cantu gregoriano cura et studio monachorum Solesmensium. Parisiis, Desclée et Socii, 1961.
498 p. 21 cm.
InStme

7. Mary, Blessed Virgin

1315 Cursus (Officium) Beatae Mariae Virginis.
MS. Benediktinerinnenabtei Nonnberg,
Salzburg, codex 23 A 18. Duodecimo.
Saec. 17(1620).
Microfilm: MnCH proj. no. 10,813

1316 Cursus Marianus secundum consuetu-
dinem Ordinis S. Benedicti, cum multis
aliis precibus. Praecedit calendarium.
MS. Augustinerchorherrenstift St.
Florian, Austria, codex XI,444. 157 f.
Duodecimo. Saec. 16(1575).
Microfilm: MnCH proj. no. 2657

1317 Mary, "our tainted nature's solitary boast."
[Benet Lake, Wis., Holy Family Con-
vent, 196-].
various pagings. 28 cm. (Benet Lake
breviary manuals)
Multigraphed.
MnCS; WBenH

1318 Office of Our Lady. [Compiled by the
Benedictine monks of Encalcat, France.
Translated from the French]. London,
Darton, Longman & Todd [1962].
v. 17 cm.
PLatS(v. 1, Winter; v. 2,Summer)

1319 Officium de S. Maria, quod Cursus
appellatur secundum consuetudinem
monachorum Petri Domus (Petrus-
hausen) et Sacri Specus Ordinis S. Benedicti. MS. Benediktinerabtei Melk,
Austria, codex 1392. 190 f. Duodecimo.
Saec. 15.
Microfilm: MnCH proj. no. 1914

8. Scholastica, Saint

1320 Novena en honor del glorioso patriarca
San Benito. Seguida de un triduo en
honor de Santa Escolástica. 6. ed.
Burgos, Abadia Benedictina de Santo
Domingo de Silos, 1944.
46 p. plates, 14 cm.
MnCS

1321 Novena en honor del glorioso patriarca
San Benito, sequida de un triduo en
honor de Santa Escolastica . . . 5. ed.
Buenos Aires, Padres Benedictinos,
1945.
76 p. ports. 14 cm.
MnCS

1322 Grégoire, Reginald, O.S.B.
Prières liturgiques médiévales en l'honneur de Saint Benoît, de Sainte Scholastique et de Saint Maur.
(*In* Analecta monastica, 7 sér. 1965.
p. 1-85)
PLatS

s. Graduale

1. Manuscripts

1323 Graduale. MS. Benediktinerabtei Melk,
Austria, codex 109. 163 f. Folio. Saec.
14.
Microfilm: MnCH proj. no. 2115

1324 Antiphonarium et Graduale ad usum
monasterii Ordinis Sancti Benedicti in
Domo Petri (Petershausen). MS. Benediktinerabtei Göttweig, Austria, codex
7-8. 2 vols. Folio. Saec. 15.
Microfilm: MnCH proj. no. 3313 & 3315

1325 Graduale. Benediktinerabtei Göttweig,
Austria, codex 235. 161 f. Folio. Saec.
15.
Microfilm: MnCH proj. no. 3832

1326 Graduale per totum annum por monasterio
Lambacensi, cum notis. Benediktinerabtei Lambach, Austria, codex chart. 60,
231 f. Saec. 15.
Microfilm: MnCH proj. no. 482

1327 Graduale. Incompletum, incipit a Dominica
Resurrectionis. Eleganter scriptum, cum
pulchris initialibus. MS. Benediktiner-
abtei Seitenstetten, Austria, codex 306.
Folio. Saec. 15.
Microfilm: MnCH proj. no. 1118

1328 Graduale, per totum notis musicis instruc-
tum, cum tabulis duabus officiorum
praemissis. MS. Vienna, Nationalbibliothek, codex 3787. 188 f. Folio. Saec. 15.
Microfilm: MnCH proj. no. 16,998

1329 Graduale. Commune Missarum sanctorum. MS. Barcelona, Spain, Sant Pere
de les Puel-les, Cantoral, 1. 268 f. Folio.
Saec. 16(1598).
Microfilm: MnCH proj. no. 34,666

1330 Graduale benedictinum ad usum monasterii S. Lamberti. MS. Universitätsbibliothek Graz, Austria, codex 557.
130 f. Folio. Saec. 16.
Microfilm: MnCH proj. no. 26,714

1331 Liber gradualis cum notis musicis. MS.
Benediktinerabtei St. Paul im Lavant-
thal, Austria, codex 67/1. 243 f. Folio.
Saec. 16.
Microfilm: MnCH proj. no. 11,732

2. Printed Editions

1332 Missae propriae Ordinis Sancti Benedicti.
Tornaci, Desclée, 1951.
43 p. 19 cm.
MnCS

1333 A ring-bindered edition [Graduale] of the
music used at Mass at St. Meinrad Archabbey, St. Meinrad, Ind. [1971].

1 vol. 22 cm.
InStme

1334   Gradual: English text fitted to Gregorian chant by Sister Cecile Gertken, O.S.B. Huntsville, Ut., Holy Trinity Abbey, 1977.
Issued in parts.
MnStj

t. Hebdomedarium

1335   Ein nutz puechel der wochnerin (Hebdomedarin) in chor zu preim, complet und zum Cursus (Officium). Cum notis musicis apud finem. MS. Benediktinerinnenabtei Nonnberg, Austria, Salzburg, codex 23 E 2. 54 f. Octavo. Saec. 16.
Microfilm: MnCH proj. no. 10,913

u. Hymnarium

1336   Hymni vel cantici secundum Regulam s. Benedicti. MS. Torino, Italy, Biblioteca Nazionale Universitaria, codex G.VII.18. Saec. 14?
Microfilm: MnCH

1337   Liber hymnorum per totum circulum anni. MS. Benediktinerinnenabtei Nonnberg, Salzburg, codex 23 C 19. 119 f. Quarto. Saec. 16(1558).
Microfilm: MnCH proj. no. 10,861

v. Invitatorium

1338   Invitatoria pro festis. Hymni ad matutinum et laudes. MS. Benediktinerinnenabtei Nonnberg, Austria, codex 23 C 25. 90 f. Quarto. Saec. 18(1774).
Microfilm: MnCH proj. no. 10,867

w. Kyriale

1339   Kyriale: Masses I, X, XV, XVI, XVII. English text. Organ accompaniment by Sister Cecile Gertken, O.S.B. St. Joseph, Minn., Sisters of Benedict, 1978.
MnStj

x. Lectionarium

1340   Lectionarium. MS. Cava, Italy (Benedictine abbey), codex 5. 120 f. Quarto. Saec. 12.
Microfilm: MnCH

1341   Lectiones Breviarii benedictini. Pars hiemalis et aestivalis. MS. Universitätsbibliothek Graz, Austria, codex 56. 2 vols. Folio. Saec. 12.
Microfilm: MnCH proj. no. 25,979

1342   Lectionarium. MS. Klagenfurt, Austria Kärntner Landesarchiv, codex GV 6/16 246 f. Octavo. Saec. 12.
Microfilm: MnCH proj. no. 12,825

1343   Lectionarium (fragmentum). MS. Benedik tinerabtei Kremsmünster, Austria codex 246 f.183r-214v. Saec. 12.
Microfilm: MnCH proj. no. 233

1344   Lectionarium. MS. Benediktinerabte Melk, Austria, codex 1891. 58 f. Folio Saec. 12.
Microfilm: MnCH proj. no. 2183

1345   Lectionarium cum calendario. MS. Bene diktinerabtei St. Peter, Salzburg, codex a.I.8. 192 f. Duodecimo. Saec. 12.
Microfilm: MnCH proj. no. 9879

1346   Epistolae et evangelia de tempore. MS Benediktinerabtei Melk, Austria, codex 242. Folio. Saec. 13.
Microfilm: MnCH proj. no. 1276

1347   Lectionarium. MS. Benediktinerabtei Kremsmünster, Austria, codex 132, f.97v-213r. Saec. 14.
Microfilm: MnCH proj. no. 148

1348   Lectionarium secundum Ord. Fratrum S. Mariae Montis Oliveti. Subiaco, Italy (Benedictine abbey), codex 300. 43 et 80 f. Octavo. Saec. 14.
Microfilm MnCH

1349   Lectiones ad tres nocturnos pro festis sanctorum. MS. Vienna, Schottenstift, codex 348. 411 f. Folio. Saec. 14.
Microfilm: MnCH proj. no. 4198

1350   Lectionarium Mellicense. MS. Benediktinerabtei Melk, Austria, codex 1597. xii, 570 f. Duodecimo. Saec. 15(1487).
Microfilm: MnCH proj. no. 1993

1351   Lectionarium pro festis sanctorum. MS. Benediktinerabtei St. Paul im Lavantthal, Austria, codex 65/1. 163 f. Folio. Saec. 15.
Microfilm: MnCH proj. no. 11,799

1352   Calendarium, orationes, capitula et lectiones per annum. MS. Benediktinerabtei St. Paul im Lavantthal, Austria, codex 70/1. 135 f. Folio. Saec. 15.
Microfilm: MnCH proj. no. 11,730

1353   Lectiones et homiliae ad Matutinam. 2. Theil. MS. Benediktinerinnenabtei Nonnberg, Salzburg, codex 23 E 21. 315 f. Octavo. Saec. 15.
Microfilm: MnCH proj. no. 10,923

1354   Lectionarium cum responsoriis secundum modum Breviariorum Mellicensium. MS. Benediktinerabtei Melk, Austria, codex 1222. 414 f. Sextodecimo. Saec. 16.
Microfilm: MnCH proj. no. 1871

1355 Epistolae et Evangelia totius anni. MS. Benediktinerabtei Michaelbeuern, Austria, codex cart. 112. 185 f. Quarto. Saec. 16.
Microfilm: MnCH proj. no. 11,608

1356 Lectionarium de tempore Breviarii benedictini. MS. Benediktinerabtei, St. Peter, Salzburg, codex b.VIII.8. 183 f. Folio. Saec. 16.
Microfilm: MnCH proj. no. 10,538

1357 Liber ad usum in choro "vor die Frau Abbtissin" (lectiones breves, orationes). MS. Benediktinerinnenabtei Nonnberg, Salzburg, codex 23 D 24. 23 f. Saec. 17-18.
Microfilm: MnCH proj. no. 10,891

1358 Liturgical readings; the lessons of the temporal cycle and the principal feasts of the sanctoral cycle according to the monastic Breviary. Originally compiled and adapted for the office of the Brothers of St. Meinrad's Abbey. St. Meinrad, Ind., A Grail Publication [1954].
568 p. 20 cm.
MnCS

1359 Missale et Lectionarium in linguam germanicam translatum. MS. Vienna, Nationalbibliothek, codex 2714. 172 f. Quarto. Saec. 14.
Microfilm: MnCH proj. no. 15,991

y. Liturgia Horarum

1360 Thesaurus Liturgiae horarum monasticae. Romae [Secretariatus Abbatis Primatis, O.S.B., Badia Primeziale Sant'Anselmo] 1977.
viii, 562 p. 30 cm.
Praefatio by Rembertus Weakland, O.S.B., Abbas Primas.
InStme; MnSC; MoCo

1360a The Book of Hours. Conception Abbey, Conception, Mo., 1974-76.
4 v.
Contents: v. 1: Per annum; v. 2: Advent and Christmas; v. 3: Lent and Easter; v. 4: Festive days.
MoCo

1361 The Liturgy of the Hours . . . St. Meinrad, Ind., St. Meinrad Archabbey [1974].
5 v. music, 23 cm.
InStme

1362 Psalter/Breviary. St. John's Abbey, Collegeville, Minn., [197-].
3 parts, music. 24 cm.
Contents: Pt. 1, Morning prayer; Pt. 2, Midday prayer; Pt. 3, Evening prayer.
MnCS

1363 Divine Office: English text fitted to Gregorian chant by Sister Cecile Gertken, O.S.B. Huntsville, Ut., Holy Trinity Abbey, 1977-78.
Issued in parts.
MnStj

z. Martyrologium

1364 Martyrologium. MS. Klagenfurt, Austria, Kärntner Landesarchiv, codex GV 6/36, f.1r-49v. Quarto. Saec. 12.
Microfilm: MnCH proj. no. 12,835

1365 Martyrologium. MS. Benediktinerabtei Lambach, Austria, codex membr. 131, f.2r-96r. Quarto. Saec. 12.
Microfilm: MnCH proj. no. 816

1366 Martyrologium (continens 39 vitae et passiones). MS. Benediktinerabtei St. Paul im Lavantthal, Austria, codex 23/1. 242 f. Folio. Saec. 12.
Microfilm: MnCH proj. no. 11,683

1367 Martyrologium romanum monasticum ad novam kalendarii rationem et ecclesiasticae historiae veritatem restitutum. MS. Monasterio benedictino de Montserrat, Spain, codex 16. 220 f. Quarto. Saec. 17(1695).
Microfilm: MnCH proj. no. 29,983

1368 Le martyrologe d'Usuard; texte et commentaire par Jacques Dubois [O.S.B.]. Bruxelles, Société des Bollandistes, 1965.
443 p. 24 cm. (Subsidia hagiographica, no. 40)
MnCS

aa. Matutinale

1369 Matutinalis secunda pars, quae intitulatur Laus Mariae. MS. Benediktinerabtei St. Paul im Lavantthal, Austria, codex 89/3. 133 f. Quarto. Saec. 14.
Microfilm: MnCH proj. no. 12,185

1370 Matins. [Benet Lake, Wis., Holy Family Convent, 196-].
341 p. 22 cm. (Benet Lake breviary manuals)
Multigraphed.
MnCS; WBenH

bb. Missale
1. Latin
a. Manuscripts
(arranged by century)

1371 Missale. MS. Benediktinerabtei St. Paul im Lavantthal, Austria, codex 14/1. 328 f. Quarto. Saec. 11-12.
Microfilm: MnCH proj. no. 12,519

1372 Missale secundum institutionem s. Benedicti (fragmenta). MS. Vienna, Nationalbibliothek, codex 15437. 12 f. Quarto. Saec. 11.
Microfilm: MnCH proj. no. 20,493

1373 Missale monasticum. MS. Benediktinerabtei Admont, Austria, codex 786. 131 f. Quarto. Saec. 12-14.
Microfilm: MnCH proj. no. 9822

1374 Missale monasticum. MS. Cava, Italy (Benedictine abbey), codex 38. 202 f. Quarto. Saec. 12.
Microfilm: MnCH

1375 Missale benedictinum. MS. Universitätsbibliothek Graz, Austria, codex 761. 196 f. Quarto. Saec. 12.
Microfilm: MnCH proj. no. 26,869

1376 Missale. MS. Benediktinerabtei Melk, Austria, codex 709. 161 f. Folio. Saec. 12.
Microfilm: MnCH proj. no. 1564

1377 Missale cum neumis, probabiliter monasterii S. Blasii in Nigra Silva. MS. Vienna, Nationalbibliothek, codex 1909. 209 f. Quarto. Saec. 12-13.
Microfilm: MnCH proj. no. 15,228

1378 Missale San-Blasianum. MS. Benediktinerabtei St. Paul im Lavantthal, Austria, codex 60/1. 266 f. Folio. Saec. 12.
Microfilm: MnCH proj. no. 11,718

1379 Missale monastico-benedictinum. Cum neumis. MS. Benediktinerabtei Göttweig, Austria, codex 58. 189 f. Folio. Saec. 13.
Microfilm: MnCH proj. no. 3834

1380 Missale monasticum. MS. Subiaco, Italy (Benedictine abbey), codex 18. 171 f. Saec. 13.
Microfilm: MnCH

1381 Missale benedictinum ad usum monasterii S. Lamberti. MS. Universitätsbibliothek Graz, Austria, codex 393. Folio. Saec. 14(1358).
Microfilm: MnCH proj. no. 26,569

1382 Missale benedictinum ad usum monasterii S. Lamberti. MS. Universitätsbibliothek Graz, Austria, codex 395. 623 f. Folio. Saec. 14(1336).
Microfilm: MnCH proj. no. 26,565

1383 Missale monasticum. MS. Benediktinerabtei Göttweig, Austria, codex 189. 78 f. Duodecimo. Saec. 14.
Microfilm: MnCH proj. no. 3470

1384 Missale (monastico-benedictinum?). MS. Benediktinerabtei Göttweig, Austria, codex 188. 326 f. Quarto. Saec. 14.
Microfilm: MnCH proj. no. 3459

1385 Missale in usum ecclesiae Cremifanensis, cum calendario et nonnullis picturis. MS. Benediktinerabtei Kremsmünster, Austria, codex 368. 144 f. Saec. 14.
Microfilm: MnCH proj. no. 330

1386 Missale secundum usum ecclesiae Cremifanensis. Benediktinerabtei Kremsmünster, Austria, codex 378. 259 f. Saec. 14.
Microfilm: MnCH proj. no. 357

1387 Missale parvum. MS. Benediktinerabtei St. Paul im Lavantthal, Austria, codex 42/1. 65 f. Duodecimo. Saec. 14-15.
Microfilm: MnCH proj. no. 11,700

1388 Missale. MS. Benediktinerabtei St. Paul im Lavantthal, Austria, codex 151/6. 321 f. Folio. Saec. 14.
Microfilm: MnCH proj. no. 12,630

1389 Missale (forsan Ordinis S. Benedicti cuiusdam monasterii Germaniae meriodionalis vel adiacentis partis Bohemiae). MS. Prämonstratenserabtei Schlägl, Austria, codex 23. 273 f. Folio. Saec. 14.
Microfilm: MnCH proj. no. 2963

1390 Missale monasticum. MS. Subiaco, Italy (Benedictine abbey), codex 32. 241 f. Folio. Saec. 14.
Microfilm: MnCH

1391 Missale monasticum. MS. Subiaco, Italy (Benedictine abbey), codex 133. 72 f. Quarto. Saec. 14.
Microfilm: MnCH

1392 Missale in usum monasterii dioecesis Salisburgensis. MS. Vienna, Nationalbibliothek, codex 1777. 328 f. Folio. Saec. 14.
Microfilm: MnCH proj. no. 20,311

1393 Missale dioecesis Salisburgensis, in usum monasterii Lunaelacensis scriptum. MS. Vienna, Nationalbibliothek, codex 1913. 190 f. Octavo. Saec. 14.
Microfilm: MnCH proj. no. 15,208

1394 Missale in usum monasterii Lunaelacensis. MS. Vienna, Nationalbibliothek, codex 3641. 183 f. Octavo. Saec. 14 et 15.
Microfilm: MnCH proj. no. 16,867

1395 Missale. MS. Benediktinerabtei Admont, Austria, codex 692. 155 f. Octavo. Saec. 15.
Microfilm: MnCH proj. no. 9723

1396 Missale benedictinum ad usum monasterii S. Lamberti. MS. Universitätsbibliothek Graz, Austria, codex 115. 420 f. Folio. Saec. 15.
Microfilm: MnCH proj. no. 26,048

1397 Missale benedictinum. MS. Universitätsbibliothek Graz, Austria, codex 122. 321 f. Folio. Saec. 15(1426).
Microfilm: MnCH proj. no. 26,039

1398 Missale secundum usum ecclesiae Cremifanensis. MS. Benediktinerabtei Kremsmünster, Austria, codex 339, f.1v-130v.
Saec. 15.
Microfilm: MnCH proj. no. 339

1399 Missale Lambacense, cum calendario. MS.
Benediktinerabtei Lambach, Austria,
codex chart. 164. Saec. 15.
Microfilm: MnCH proj. no. 580

1400 Missale Lambacense. MS. Benediktinerabtei Lambach, Austria, codex chart. 316.
343 f. Saec. 15.
Microfilm: MnCH proj. no. 688

1401 Missale Mellicense. Praecedit kalendarium.
MS. Benediktinerabtei Melk, Austria,
codex 1784. 402 f. Duodecimo. Saec. 15.
Microfilm: MnCH proj. no. 2095

1402 Missale Mellicense. Scriptor fuit Joannes
de Weilhaim 1454. MS. Benediktinerabtei Melk, Austria, codex 747. 378 f.
Quarto. Saec. 15.
Microfilm: MnCH proj. no. 1596

1403 Missale pro via de tempore et de sanctis, a
mense Septembri usque ad adventum
Domini, cum aliis missis specialibus. MS.
Benediktinerabtei Melk, Austria, codex
925. 94 f. Quarto. Saec. 15.
Microfilm: MnCH proj. no. 1741

1404 Missale secundum rubricam Curiae
Romanae ad consuetudinem monasterii
Mellicensis. MS. Benediktinerabtei Melk,
Austria, codex 1049. 183 f. Quarto.
Saec. 15.
Microfilm: MnCH proj. no. 1821

1405 Missale et Graduale cum notis musicis. MS.
Benediktinerabtei St. Paul im Lavant-
thal, Austria, codex 49/3. 147 f. Folio.
Saec. 15.
Microfilm: MnCH proj. no. 12,156

1406 Missale San-Blasianum. MS. Benediktinerabtei St. Paul im Lavantthal, Austria,
codex 59/1. 196 f. Quarto. Saec. 15.
Microfilm: MnCH proj. no. 11,704

1407 Missale San-Blasianum. MS. Benediktinerabtei St. Paul im Lavantthal, Austria,
codex 64/1. 275 f. Folio. Saec. 15(1491).
Microfilm: MnCH proj. no. 11,797

1408 Missale monasticum. MS. Benediktinerabtei Seitenstetten, Austria, codex 119.
134 f. Folio. Saec. 15(1493).
Microfilm: MnCH proj. no. 931

1409 Missale monasticum. MS. Subiaco, Italy
(Benedictine abbey), codex 43. 338 f.
Folio. Saec. 15.
Microfilm: MnCH

1410 Missale un usum ecclesiae Lunaelacensis
1488 destinatum. MS. Vienna, National-

bibliothek, codex 1785. 248 f. Folio.
Saec. 15.
Microfilm: MnCH proj. no. 15,089

1411 Missale romanum in usum monasterii
Lunaelacensis. MS. Vienna, National-
bibliothek, codex 1797. 325 f. Folio.
Saec. 15(1472).
Microfilm: MnCH proj. no. 15,115

1412 Missale aediculae S. Udalrici, parochialis
ecclesiae in Coenobio Lunaelacensi filiali,
dicatum. MS. Vienna, Nationalbibliothek, codex 1899. 162 f. Quarto. Saec.
15(1453).
Microfilm: MnCH proj. no. 15,214

b. Printed Editions

1413 Missale novum monasticum Pauli V. pont.
maximi auctoritate recognitum. Pro
omnibus sub Regula s. p. Benedicti
militantibus, in quo Missae propriae de
sanctis, ac festis novissimis a Summis
Pontificibus ab anno 1640 usq. ad 1679
tum de praecepto, tum ad libitum cele-
brari concessae, omnes suis locis, pro
celebrantium commoditate, ad longum
extensae, & appositae sunt. Campoduni,
per Rudolphum Dreher, 1679.
various pagings, 32 cm.
MnCS

1414 The Leofric Missal as used in the cathedral
of Exeter during the episcopate of its
first bishop, A.D. 1050-1072. Together
with some account of the Red book of
Derby, the Missal of Robert of Jumièges,
and a few other early manuscript service
books of the English Church. Edited,
with introduction and notes, by F. E.
Warren. Oxford, The Clarendon Press,
1883.
lxvi, 344 p. facsims. 29 cm.
InStme

1415 The Missal of the New Minster, Win-
chester. (Le Havre, Bibliothèque
Municipale, Ms. 330). Edited by D. H.
Turner. [London] 1962.
xxviii, 238 p. facsim. 24 cm. (Henry
Bradshaw Society Publications, v. 93)
MnCS; PLatS

1416 The Bec Missal. Edited by Anselm Hughes.
[London] 1963.
xv, 302 p. 23 cm. (Henry Bradshaw
Society Publications, v. 94)
KAS; MnCS; PLatS

2. German

1417 Missale et Lectionarium in linguam germanicam translata, adjectis expositioni-
bus item germanicis per circulum anni.

MS. Vienna, Nationalbibliothek, codex
3063. 275 f. Folio. Saec. 15(1457).
Microfilm: MnCH proj. no. 16,329

1418 Missale et Lectionarium in linguam ger-
manicam translatum. MS. Vienna,
Nationalbibliothek, codex 2714. 172 f.
Quarto. Saec. 14.
Microfilm: MnCH proj. no. 15,991

1419 Missale et Lectionarium. Pars hiemalis.
Germanice. Prologus incipit: Meyn
anevechten hat ir. Opus ipsum incipit:
Myn got ich habe myne sele. MS. Vienna,
Nationalbibliothek, codex 2845. 258 f.
Folio. Saec. 15.
Microfilm: MnCH proj. no. 16,115

cc. Missae Propriae

1420 Missae propriae Ordinis s. patris Benedicti.
Ratisbon, F. Pustet, 1921. 39 p.
MnCS

1421 Missae propriae totius Ordinis Sancti
Benedicti. New York, Benziger Brothers,
1923.
38 p.
MnCS

1422 Proprio de la Orden de San Benito.
Contiene el Oficio monástico en latín y
castellano desde Prima hasta Completas,
así como las Misas proprias del calendario benedictino. Versión de la 2da
edición francesa por Lorenzo M. Moli-
nero, O.S.B. Buenos Aires, Centro de
Apostolado Litúrgico [1941].
xxiv, 567, 92 p. 16 cm.
MnCS

1423 Missae propiae et kalendarium totius
Ordinis s. p. n. Benedicti. Neo Eboraci,
Benziger Brothers [1944].
vi, 56 p. 30 cm.
InStme; MnCS

1424 The Proper of the Masses for the Order of
our holy father Benedict. n.p., 1967.
70 p. music. 30 cm.
MnCS

dd. Nocturnale

1425 Nocturnale. MS. Vienna, Nationalbibliothek, codex 1964. 395 f. Octavo. Saec.
15(1460).
Microfilm: MnCH proj. no. 15,253

ee. Officia Propria

1426 Officia propria Ordinis S. Benedicti. MS.
Benediktinerabtei Altenburg, Austria,
codex AB 13 F 28. 66 p. Saec. 17.
Microfilm: MnCH proj. no. 6533

ff. Officium pro Defunctis

1427 Officium defunctorum. MS. Benediktinerinnenabtei Nonnberg, Salzburg, codex
23 A 13. Duodecimo. Saec. 16.
Microfilm: MnCH proj. no. 10,810

1428 Officium defunctorum cum notis musicis.
MS. Benediktinerabtei St. Peter, Salz-
burg, codex a.I.2. 71 f. Duodecimo.
Saec. 16.
Microfilm: MnCH proj. no. 9876

1429 Obsequiale et Benedictionale reformatum
juxta Romanum et Constantiense
novum, ritibus ac caeremoniis monasterii
S. Blasii conforme. MS. Benediktinerabtei St. Paul im Lavantthal, Austria,
codex 255/2. 201 f. Folio. Saec. 18.
Microfilm: MnCH proj. no. 12,082

gg. Orationale

1430 Orationale. Incipit: In nativitate Christi ad
summam missam. MS. Klagenfurt, Aus-
tria, Kärntner Landesarchiv, codex GV
6/3. 65 f. Octavo. Saec. 15.
Microfilm: MnCH proj. no. 12,815

1431 Orationale. Praecedit kalendarium. MS.
Benediktinerabtei Melk, Austria, codex
1927. 83 f. Octavo. Saec. 15.
Microfilm: MnCH proj. no. 2207

1432 Orationale secundum consuetudinem
Monialium Sancti Petri in Salzburg. MS.
Benediktinerabtei St. Peter, Salzburg,
codex a.II.39, f.52r-114r. Octavo. Saec.
15.
Microfilm: MnCH proj. no. 9927

1433 Orationale. Latine et germanice. MS.
Benediktinerabtei St. Peter, Salzburg,
codex b.I.9. 146 f. Octavo. Saec. 15.
Microfilm: MnCH proj. no. 10,284

1434 Orationale S. Petri Salisburgi. MS. Benediktinerabtei St. Peter, Salzburg, codex
b.II.25. 205 f. Octavo. Saec. 15-16.
Microfilm: MnCH proj. no. 10,332

1435 Capitula et orationes per annum et
benedictio mensae. MS. Benediktinerabtei St. Paul im Lavantthal, Austria,
codex 62/1. 144 f. Folio. Saec. 15.
Microfilm: MnCH proj. no. 11,721

1436 Orationale et Diurnale Lunaelacense, cum
calendario et multis in marginibus
conscriptis notabilibus opera diversarum
manuum. MS. Vienna, Nationalbibliothek, codex 3643. 310 f. Octavo. Saec. 15.
Microfilm: MnCH proj. no. 16,855

1437 Orationale, cum calendario. Latine et
germanice. MS. Klagenfurt, Austria,
Kärntner Landesarchiv, codex GV 5/35.
219 f. Octavo. Saec. 16(1520).
Microfilm: MnCH proj. no. 12,809

1438 Orationale secundum consuetudinem
monachorum S. Petri in Salzburg, cum
calendario. MS. Benediktinerabtei St.
Peter, Salzburg, codex b.I.21. 255 f.
Octavo. Saec. 16.
Microfilm: MnCH proj. no. 10,293

hh. Ordinarium

1439 Der älteste Liber Ordinarius der Trierer
Domkirche (London, British Museum,
Harley 2958, Anfang 14. Jh.); ein
Beitrag zur Liturgeschichte der deuts-
chen Ortskirchen, hrsg. und bearb. von
Adalbert Kurzeja, O.S.B. Münster i.W.,
Aschendorff [1970].
xxi, 626 p. 24 cm. (Liturgiewissenschaft-
liche Quellen und Forschungen, Heft 52)
PLatS

ii. Ordo Abbatis

1440 Ordo abbatis. MS. Benediktinerabtei
Kremsmünster, Austria, codex novus
109, f.1r-50r. Saec. 16.
Microfilm: MnCH proj. no. 396

jj. Ordo Divini Officii

1441 **Directorium Admontense.** MS. Benediktinerabtei Admont, Austria, codex
790. 76 f. Quarto. Saec. 15.
Microfilm: MnCH proj. no. 9819

1442 **Directorium ad Officium divinum monasticum.** MS. Benediktinerabtei Altenburg, Austria, codex AB 13 B 13.
119 f. Quarto. Saec. 15.
Microfilm: MnCH proj. no. 6455

1443 **Directorium Divini officii Admontense.**
MS. Benediktinerabtei Admont, Austria,
codex 474. 201 f. Folio. Saec. 16.
Microfilm: MnCH proj. no. 9527

1444 **Ordo operis Dei saeculis XIV., XV. et
XVI.** in S. Blasio usitatus. Praecedunt
calendarium, regulae quaedam de
influxu siderum et de festis mobilibus.
MS. Benediktinerabtei St. Paul im
Lavantthal, Austria, codex 66/1. 201 f.
Folio. Saec. 16(1573).
Microfilm: MnCH proj. no. 11,723

1445 **Calendarium abbatialis** et exemptae
ecclesiae Gottwicensis et Proprium
sanctorum dioeceseos Passaviensis. MS.
Vienna, Dominikanerkloster, codex 561.
202 p. Octavo. Saec. 17.
Microfilm: MnCH proj. no. 8847

1446 **Benedictine Congregation of the Annun-
ciation.**
Ordo Congregationis Annuntiationis
B.M.V., O.S.B. Mechlin [Belgique], H. Des-
sain.
MnCS

1447 **American Cassinese Congregation.**
Supplementum ad Ordinem, continens
Calendarium O.S.B. necnon textus novos
pro Divino Officio explendo. Collegeville,
Minn., typis Abbatiae Sancti Joannis Bap-
tistae, 1962.
xvi, 76 p. 15 cm.
MnCS; PLatS

1448 **Cucujaes, Portugal.**
Ordo operis Dei persolvendi sacrique
peragendi ritu monastico pro monachis
O.S.Benedicti . . . S. Martini, prioris jussu
editus pro anno Dñi 1881. Portucale, typ.
da "Palavra", 1881.
51 p. 18 cm.
PLatS

1449 **English Congregation.**
Directorium, formularium, et ritualis
compendium Congregationis Anglicanae
O.S.B Anneci, typis J. Nierat, 1901.
95 p. 22 cm.
KAS

1450 **English Congregation.**
Ordo divini officii recitandi sacrique
peragendi ad usum monachorum Congregationis Angliae O.S.B.
MnCS

1451 **Mariastein, Switzerland (Benedictine
abbey).**
Directorium monasterii Beinwilensis ad
Petram, vulgo Mariastein.
MnCS

1452 **Rome (City). S. Priscilla (abbey of
Benedictine nuns).**
Ordo divini officii recitandi sacrique
peragendi iuxta calendarium Ordinis S.
Benedicti. Typis Sororum S. Benedicti ad
Priscillam.
MnCS

kk. Passionale

1453 Passional (fragmentum). Germanice.
Benediktinerabtei Melk, Austria, codex
401. 9 f. Folio. Saec. 13-14.
Microfilm: MnCH proj. no. 1594

II. Pontificale

1454 Pontificale continens benedictionem
clericorum minorum ordinem. MS.
Benediktinerabtei St. Paul im Lavant-
thal, Austria, codex 87/1. 18 f. Folio.
Saec. 14.
Microfilm: MnCH proj. no. 11,726

1455 Pontificale ecclesiae Admontensis. MS.
Benediktinerabtei Admont, Austria,
codex 86. 76 f. Folio. Saec. 15.
Microfilm: MnCH proj. no. 9180

mm. Prime

1456 Prime and Compline of the Monastic
Breviary. Printed as manuscript for the
use of the Benedictine brothers of St.
Benedict's Abbey, Atchison, Kans.
[Atchison, Kans., Abbey Student Press]
1960.
44 p. 24 cm.
KAS

nn. Processionale

1457 Processionale. MS. Benediktinerabtei
Melk, Austria, codex 931. 120 f. Quarto.
Saec. 15.
Microfilm: MnCH proj. no. 1742

1458 Processionarius, cum notis musicis. Finis
deest. MS. Vienna, Nationalbibliothek,
codex 1894. 101 f. Quarto. Saec. 15.
Microfilm: MnCH proj. no. 15,196

1459 Processionale monasterii Sitticensis
(Saint-Bertin). MS. Benediktinerabtei
Admont, Austria, codex 747. 69 f.
Saec. 16.
Microfilm: MnCH proj. no. 9792

1460 Processionale, cum cantu. MS. Benediktinerinnenabtei Nonnberg, Salzburg, codex
23 E 7. 37 f. Quarto. Saec. 16(1535).
Microfilm: MnCH proj. no. 10,914

1461 Processionale novissimum monasterii S.
Blasii in Silva Nigra. MS. Benediktinerabtei St. Paul im Lavantthal, Austria,
codex 131/6. 299 p. Duodecimo. Saec.
17(1678).
Microfilm: MnCH proj. no. 12,637

1462 Processionale, sive Responsorium pro
choro monasterii S. Blasii. MS. Benedik-
tinerabtei St. Paul im Lavantthal,
Austria, codex 24/2. 189 f. Quarto.
Saec. 18.
Microfilm: MnCH proj. no. 11,762

1463 Responsorium processionale pro choro
monasterii S. Blasii. MS. Benediktinerabtei St. Paul im Lavantthal, Austria,
codex 74/6. 130 f. Sextodecimo. Saec.
18(1729).
Microfilm: MnCH proj. no. 12,618

1464 Processionale San-Blasianum. MS.
Benediktinerabtei St. Paul im Lavant-
thal, Austria, codex 124/6. 297 p. Octavo.
Saec. 18(1784).
Microfilm: MnCH proj. no. 12,625

1465 Processionale pro choro monasterii S.
Blasii in Silva Nigra. MS. Benediktinerabtei St. Paul im Lavantthal, Austria,
codex 130/6. 177 f. Octavo. Saec.
18(1778).
Microfilm: MnCH proj. no. 12,624

oo. Proprium Sanctorum

1466 Proprium sanctorum, cum cantu. MS.
Benediktinerinnenabtei Nonnberg, Salz-
burg, codex 23 C 7. 130 f. Quarto.
Saec. 17.
Microfilm: MnCH proj. no. 10,850

1467 Proprium Mettense, sive Supplementum
Breviarii benedictino-monastici pro
choro Mettenensi. Editum jussu et
auctoritate Gregorii I., abbatis Monasterii Metten. Landishuti, typis Jos.
Thomann, 1856.
240 p. 19 cm.
MnCS

pp. Prosarium

1468 Prosarium Leemovicense. Die Prosen der
Abtei St. Martial zu Limoges. Hrsg. von
Guido Maria Dreves, S.J. New York and
London, Johnson Reprint Corporation,
1961.
282 p. 21 cm. (Analecta hymnica Medii
Aevi, 7)
Reprint of Leipzig edition of 1889.
PLatS

qq. Psalterium

1. Latin

a. Manuscripts

(arranged by century)

1469 Psalterium Ivonis. MS. Lambeth Palace
Library, London, codex 540. 101 f.
Octavo. Saec. 12.
Microfilm: MnCH

1470 Psalterium, cum glossa et sequentia cum
neumis. MS. Vienna, Nationalbibliothek,
codex 1107. 112 f. Quarto. Saec. 12.
Microfilm: MnCH proj. no. 14,416

1471 Psalterium, cum solitis litaniis, precibus
et cantionibus. MS. Vienna, Nationalbibliothek, codex 1129. 143 f. Quarto.
Saec. 12.
Microfilm: MnCH proj. no. 14,508

1472 Psalterium . . . Cantica in dominicas . . . in
usum coenobii cujusdam Ordinis S.
Benedicti concinnata. MS. Vienna,
Nationalbibliothek, codex 1826, f.35r-
186v. Quarto. Saec. 12.
Microfilm: MnCH proj. no. 15,164

1473 Psalterium, praecedente calendario, in
usum monasterii Siegebergensis dioecesis Coloniensis. MS. Vienna, Nationalbibliothek, codex 1879. 186 f. Octavo.
Saec. 12.
Microfilm: MnCH proj. no. 15,170

1474 Psalterium, cum canticis, symbolis Apostolorum et Athanasii, et Litania maiori. MS. Benediktinerabtei St. Paul im Lavantthal, Austria, codex 26/1. 204 f. Quarto. Saec. 12.
Microfilm: MnCH proj. no. 11,674

1475 Psalterium Davidis: psalmi, cantica, litaniae, orationes latinae et germanicae. MS. Benediktinerabtei St. Peter, Salzburg, codex a.I.26. 190 f. Octavo. Saec. 12.
Microfilm: MnCH proj. no. 9898

1476 Psalterium, cum canticis, litaniis omnium sanctorum et officio defunctorum. MS. Benediktinerabtei Göttweig, Austria, codex 118. 128 f. Octavo. Saec. 13.
Microfilm: MnCH proj. no. 3397

1477 Psalterium et cantica officii monastici. MS. Benediktinerabtei Lambach, Austria, codex membr. 103. 141 f. Quarto. Saec. 13.
Microfilm: MnCH proj. no. 805

1478 Liber precum (Psalterium). MS. Benediktinerabtei Lambach, Austria, codex membr. 156. 60 f. Quarto. Saec. 13.
Microfilm: MnCH proj. no. 830

1479 Psalterium (St. Neot's Priory, Eynesbury, England). MS. Lambeth Palace Library, London, codex 563. 159 f. Duodecimo. Saec. 13.
Microfilm: MnCH

1480 Psalterium (Norwich Priory, England). MS. Lambeth Palace Library, London, codex 368. 139 f. Quarto. Saec. 13.
Microfilm: MnCH

1481 Psalterium (Christ Church Priory, Canterbury). MS. Lambeth Palace Library, London, codex 558. 286 f. Octavo. Saec. 13.
Microfilm: MnCH

1482 Psalterium Mellicense. MS. Benediktinerabtei Melk, Austria, codex 1439. 143 f. Saec. 13.
Microfilm: MnCH proj. no. 1931

1483 Psalterium breviarii. MS. Benediktinerabtei St. Peter, Salzburg, codex a.V.31. 181 f. Octavo. Saec. 13.
Microfilm: MnCH proj. no. 10,060

1484 Psalterium, ex Abbatia Ramsey in Anglia. Cum miniaturis et initialibus. MS. Benediktinerabtei St. Paul im Lavantthal, Austria, codex 58/1. 173 f. Quarto. Saec. 13.
Microfilm: MnCH proj. no. 12,667

1485 Psalterium benedictinum feriatum et Hymnarium. MS. Universitätsbibliothek Graz, Austria, codex 387. 280 f. Folio. Saec. 14.
Microfilm: MnCH proj. no. 26,363

1486 Psalterium cum canticis. MS. Benediktinerabtei Kremsmünster, Austria, codex 388, v.2r-399v. Saec. 14.
Microfilm: MnCH proj. no. 412

1487 Psalterium. Praecedit kalendarium. MS. Benediktinerabtei Melk, Austria, codex 1693. 267 f. Octavo. Saec. 14.
Microfilm. MnCH proj. no. 2024

1488 Psalterium. Cum multis tabulis pictis et litteris initialibus. MS. Benediktinerabtei Melk, Austria, codex 1903. Quarto. Saec. 14.
Microfilm: MnCH proj. no. 2092

1489 Psalterium Davidis, cum canticis, Te Deum, Magnificat, Benedictus, Symbolo et Litaniis (incompletum). MS. Benediktinerabtei St. Peter, Salzburg, codex a.I.4. 304 f. Duodecimo. Saec. 14.
Microfilm: MnCH proj. no. 9874

1490 Psalterium, cum Canticis et Litania majori et calendario. MS. Benediktinerabtei St. Paul im Lavantthal, Austria, codex 52/1. 326 f. Quarto. Saec. 14-15.
Microfilm: MnCH proj. no. 11,707

1491 Psalterium, cum glossa interlineari et marginali. MS. Benediktinerabtei Seitenstetten, Austria, codex 231, f.9v-236v. Quarto. Saec. 14-15.
Microfilm: MnCH proj. no. 1038

1492 Psalterium monasticum chorale. In fine mutilum. MS. Vienna, Nationalbibliothek, codex 1774. 236 f. Folio. Saec. 14.
Microfilm: MnCH proj. no. 20,304

1493 Psalterium chori et Missale. MS. Klagenfurt, Austria, Kärntner Landesarchiv, codex GV 8/14. 210 f. Folio. Saec. 15(1456).
Microfilm: MnCH proj. no. 12,053

1494 Psalterium ordinarium secundum consuetudinem monasterii Mellicensis. MS. Benediktinerabtei Melk, Austria, codex 1216, f.1-95. Sextodecimo. Saec. 15.

1495 Psalterium secundum consuetudinem monasterii Mellicensis. MS. Benediktinerabtei Melk, Austria, codex 1579, f.1-126. Octavo. Saec. 15.
Microfilm: MnCH proj. no. 1978

1496 Psalterium secundum modum monasterii Mellicensis. MS. Benediktinerabtei Melk, Austria, codex 153. 214 f. Folio. Saec. 15.
Microfilm: MnCH proj. no. 1212

1497 Psalterium secundum Regulam Ord. S. Benedicti ad modum sacri loci Specus. Praecedit kalendarium cum numero aureo ab 1499 usque 1560. MS. Benediktinerabtei Melk, Austria, codex 277. 474 f. Duodecimo. Saec. 15.
Microfilm: MnCH proj. no. 1300

1498 Psalterium, cum calendario. MS. Benedik-
      tinerinnenabtei Nonnberg, Salzburg,
      codex 23 A 2. Duodecimo. Saec. 15.
      Microfilm: MnCH proj. no. 10,801

1499 Psalterium pro horis, Officium parvum
      Beatae Mariae Virginis, Psalmi poeniten-
      tiales, Officium defunctorum. MS.
      Benediktinerinnenabtei Nonnberg, Salz-
      burg, codex 23 A 7. Duodecimo. Saec. 16.
      Microfilm: MnCH proj. no. 10,804

1500 Psalterium latine et germanice (Pater
      noster germanice). MS. Benediktiner-
      abtei St. Paul im Lavantthal, Austria,
      codex 2/4. 325 f. Folio. Saec. 15.
      Microfilm: MnCH proj. no. 12,233

1501 Psalterium Gallicanum correctum cum
      glossa. MS. Benediktinerabtei St. Paul
      im Lavantthal, Austria, codex 7/4. 395 f.
      Folio. Saec. 15.
      Microfilm: MnCH proj. no. 12,237

1502 Psalterium cum antiphonis, canticis et
      hymnis. Cum notis musicis. MS. Bene-
      diktinerabtei St. Paul im Lavantthal,
      Austria, codex 10/3. 190 f. Folio.
      Saec. 15-16.
      Microfilm: MnCH proj. no. 12,002

1503 Psalterium, cum glossa. MS. Benediktin-
      erabtei Seitenstetten, Austria, codex
      307. 202 f. Folio. Saec. 15.
      Microfilm: MnCH proj. no. 1081

1504 Psalterium secundum ritum Salisburgen-
      sem antiquum, cum calendario prae-
      misso. MS. Vienna, Nationalbibliothek,
      codex 3826. 415 f. Quarto. Saec. 15.
      Microfilm: MnCH proj. no. 3826

1505 Psalterium, cum notis interlinearibus et
      marginalibus. MS. Vienna, National-
      bibliothek, codex 4033, f.1r-159r.
      Quarto. Saec. 15.
      Microfilm: MnCH proj. no. 17,217

1506 Psalterium, cantica, hymnus Ambrosianus,
      symbolum Athanasianum, cum glossa
      interlineari. MS. Vienna, Schottenstift,
      codex 105, f.17r-116v. Folio. Saec. 15.
      Microfilm: MnCH proj. no. 3963

1507 Psalterium: psalmi, cantica, symbola,
      litaniae, Officium defunctorum. MS.
      Benediktinerabtei St. Peter, Salzburg,
      codex a.I.17. 234 f. Duodecimo. Saec. 15.
      Microfilm: MnCH proj. no. 9886

1508 Psalterium benedictinum cum notis
      musicis. MS. Benediktinerabtei St.
      Peter, Salzburg, codex a.XII.24. 231 f.
      Folio. Saec. 15.
      Microfilm: MnCH proj. no. 10,754

1509 Psalterium et Proprium de tempore. MS.
      Benediktinerabtei St. Peter, Salzburg,
      codex b.I.15. 198 f. Octavo. Saec. 16.
      Microfilm: MnCH proj. no. 10,287

1510 Psalterium benedictinum. MS. Vienna,
      Nationalbibliothek, codex 1823. 122 f.
      Folio. Saec. 16.
      Microfilm: MnCH proj. no. 15,150

1511 Psalterium benedictinum ad usum mona-
      sterii S. Lamberti. MS. Universitäts-
      bibliothek Graz, Austria, codex 3. 179 f.
      Folio. Saec. 17(1663).
      Microfilm: MnCH proj. no. 26,005

b. Printed Editions

1512 Psalterium Davidis, carmine redditum per
      Robanum Heffum . . . Egenolphum
      [Germany] 1537.
      423 p.
      NcBe

1513 Psalterium monasticum: pro omnibus sub
      Regula s. p. n. Benedicti militantibus.
      Cui addita sunt propria ss. festa, pro
      Austria superiori, & inferiori, necnon pro
      exempto Conventu Mellicensi in Austria,
      atq. pro Bohemia, & Hispania, a S. Sede
      Apostolica approbata. Editio nova, a
      mendis nitide, ac sedulo expurgata. Neo-
      Pragae, J. Mattis, 1698.
      [12], 252 p. 20 cm.
      InStme

1514 Psalterium monasticum ad experimentum
      novo ordine dispositum. Elmira, N.Y.,
      Mount Saviour Monastery [196-].
      172 p. 21 cm.
      Manuscripti instar.
      InStme; MnCS; PLatS

1515 Psalterium monasticum per quatuor
      hebdomadas distributum. [Elmira, N.Y.,
      Mount Saviour Monastery, 196-].
      151 p. 21 cm.
      Manuscripti instar.
      PLatS

1516 Dewick, Edward Samuel.
      On a ms. Psalter formerly belonging to
      the Abbey of Bury Saint Edmunds. – On a
      ms. Pontifical of a bishop of Metz of the
      fourteenth century . . . Westminster,
      printed by Nichols and Sons, 1895.
      12, 14 p. facsims. 29x12 cm.
      MnCS

1517 Marböck, Johann.
      Das Eindringen der Versio Gallicana des
      Psalteriums in die Psalterien der Benedik-
      tinerklöster Oberösterreichs. Wien, Verlag
      Notring, 1970.
      1 vol. (various pagings)
      A revised version of the author's thesis,
      Universität Graz, 1960.
      MnCS

2. Anglo-Saxon, English, German, Icelandic

1518 Psalterium glossatum anglo-sax. MS. Lambeth Palace Library, London, codex 427. 213 f. Quarto. Saec. 10-11. Microfilm: MnCH

1519 The Psalms (English) arranged for recitation and chant by Sister Cecile Gertken, O.S.B. St. Joseph, Minn., Sisters of St. Benedict, 1977. unpaged, 20 cm. MnStj

1520 Deutscher Psalter mit ausführlichem Kalender. MS. Universitätsbibliothek Graz, Austria, codex 1631. 206 f. Octavo. Saec. 14. Microfilm: MnCH proj. no. 26,559

1521 Psalterium Davidicum. Versio germanica. Finis deest. MS. Vienna, Nationalbibliothek, codex 2756. 203 f. Duodecimo. Saec. 14. Microfilm: MnCH proj. no. 16,031

1522 Psalterium. Lateinisch und Deutsch. MS. Universitätsbibliothek Graz, Austria, codex 1398. 174 f. Octavo. Saec. 15. Microfilm: MnCH proj. no. 26,386

1523 Deutsches gereimtes Psalterium. MS. Universitätsbibliothek Graz, Austria, codex 1593, f.12v-319v. Octavo. Saec. 15. Microfilm: MnCH proj. no. 26,501

1524 Psalterium germanicum. MS. Benediktinerabtei Melk, Austrai, codex 112. 383 f. Folio. Saec. 15. Microfilm: MnCH proj. no. 1189

1525 Psalterium germanicum. Incipit: Selig ist der man. MS. Benediktinerabtei Melk, Austria, codex 808, f.1r-92v. Quarto. Saec. 15. Microfilm: MnCH proj. no. 1644

1526 Psalterium. Germanice. MS. Benediktinerabtei St. Paul im Lavantthal, Austria, codex 210/4, pars I. Quarto. Saec. 15. Microfilm: MnCH proj. no. 12,445

1527 Psalterium. Germanice. MS. Vienna, Nationalbibliothek, codex 2940. 107 f. Quarto. Saec. 15. Microfilm: MnCH proj. no. 16,247

1528 Psalterium, cum notis musicis. Germanice. MS. Vienna, Nationalbibliothek, codex 3079, f.1r-164v. Folio. Saec. 15(1477). Microfilm: MnCH proj. no. 16,327

1529 Deutsches psalterium für Sonntage und Wochentage des Kirchenjahres. Zusammengestellt von Georg Braulik, O.S.B., Notker Güglister, O.S.B., Michael Prinz, O.S.B., Godhard Joppich, O.S.B. [Vier-Türme-Verlag, Abtei Münsterschwarzach, 1969]. 430 p. 18 cm.

Als Manuskript gedruckt. MnCS

1530 Psalterium latinum, et quidem XVI,8 usque CIII,6 cum translatione interlineari in linguam islandicam manu saeculi 14 scripta. MS. Vienna, Nationalbibliothek, codex 2713. 68 f. Quarto. Saec. 12(pars latina). Microfilm: MnCH proj. no. 16,065

rr. Responsorium

1531 Responsoriale pro processionibus ad usum monasterii S. Lamperti. MS. Universitätsbibliothek Graz, Austria, codex 1123. Octavo. Saec. 14. Microfilm: MnCH proj. no. 26,948

1532 Responsoria et antiphonae. MS. Benediktinerinnenabtei Nonnberg, Salzburg, codex 23 C 22. 60 f. Quarto. Saec. 16. Microfilm: MnCH proj. no. 10,863

1533 Liturgisches Responsenbuch mit Text u. Noten, der Stiftsfrau Katharina von Rost von Sonnenburg, MS. Innsbruck, Austria, Tiroler Landesarchiv, codex 2374. 121 f. Quarto. Saec. 17. Microfilm: MnCH proj. no. 29,176

1534 Responsoria brevia . . . pro choro S. Blasii in Silva Nigra. MS. Benediktinerabtei St. Paul im Lavantthal, Austria, codex 80/6. 82 f. Folio. Saec. 18(1781). Microfilm: MnCH proj. no. 12,632

1535 Pharetra: in welchem begriffen werden all kurze Responsotir zu den baiden Vesperas und Laudes, dessgleichen alle Versiculi zu allen Horas . . . nach dem reformirten Breviarium des ehrwürdigsten Klosters . . . auf dem Nunnenberg. Cum notis musicis. MS. Benediktinerinnenabtei Nonnberg, Salzburg, codex 23 E 35. 257 p. Octavo. Saec. 17(1625). Microfilm: MnCH proj. no. 10,907

ss. Rituale

1. Latin

a. Manuscripts

(arranged by centuries)

1536 **Rituale (Ceremoniale) Lambacense.** MS. Benediktinerabtei Lambach, Austria, codex membr. 73. 89 f. Quarto. Saec. 12–13. Microfilm: MnCH proj. no. 792

1537 **Rituale (Ceremoniale) Lambacense.** MS. Benediktinerabtei Lambach, Austria, codex membr. 73a. 78 f. Quarto. Saec. 12. Microfilm: MnCH proj. no. 793

1538 **Caeremoniale abbatis neumatum,** in usum monasterii Lunaelacensis. MS. Vienna, Nationalbibliothek, codex 1827. 78 f. Quarto. Saec. 13.
Microfilm: MnCH proj. no. 15,158

1539 **Ceremoniae regularis observantiae** Ordinis Sancti Benedicti, quae in s. monasterio Sublacensi et Specu practicantur. MS. Benediktinerabtei Melk, Austria, codex 952, f.1r-71r. Quarto. Saec. 14-15.
Microfilm: MnCH proj. no. 1751

1540 **Rituale in usum Lunaelacensis** et praesertim benedictiones continens. MS. Vienna, Nationalbibliothek, codex 3633. 102 f. Quarto. Saec. 14.
Microfilm: MnCH proj. no. 16,847

1541 **Rituale, cum notis musicis.** MS. Vienna, Schottenstift, codex 180. 103 f. Octavo. Saec. 14-15.
Microfilm: MnCH proj. no. 4082

1542 **Ceremonial monastico.** MS. Silos, Spain, Archivo del Monasterio de Sto. Domingo, MS. 14. 150 f. Quarto. Saec. 15.
Microfilm: MnCH proj. no. 33,696

1543 **Caeremonialia ab abbate Scotorum** relicta. Caeremonialia secundum modum Scotorum Viennae. MS. Vienna, Nationalbibliothek, codex 3548, f.29r-40v. et 137r-155v. Octavo. Saec. 15.
Microfilm: MnCH proj. no. 16,770

1544 **Caeremoniae regularis S. Benedicti,** quae hodie in monasterio suo Sublacensi et Specu practicantur. MS. Vienna, Nationalbibliothek, codex 3548, f.41r-86r. Octavo. Saec. 15.
Microfilm: MnCH proj. no. 16,770

1545 **Breviarium caeremoniarum monasterii** Mellicensis . . . anno 1415 per venerabiles patres monasteriorum Sublacensis et Sacri Specus auctoritate domini papae V reformatum. Vienna, Nationalbibliothek, codex 3805, f.1r-46v. Quarto. Saec. 15.
Microfilm: MnCH proj. no. 17,030

1546 **Caeremoniae regularis observantiae** Ordinis S. Benedicti. MS. Benediktinerabtei Altenburg, Austria, codex AB 13 A 10, f.1r-33r. Quarto. Saec. 15.
Microfilm: MnCH proj. no. 6401

1547 **Memoriale rituum monasticum,** cum neumis. Benediktinerabtei Kremsmünster, Austria, codex 239a. 123 f. Saec. 15.
Microfilm: MnCH proj. no. 228

1548 **Ceremoniae nigrorum monachorum** Ordinis Sancti Benedicti de observantia Bursfeldensi. MS. Benediktinerabtei Kremsmünster, Austria, codex 295, f.3r-104v. Saec. 15.
Microfilm: MnCH proj. no. 280

1549 **Ceremoniae regularis observancie** Ordinis sanctissimi patris nostri Benedicti ex ipsius Regula sumpte secundum quod hodie in sacro monasterio suo Sublacensi et Specu practicantur. MS. Benediktinerabtei Lambach, Austria, codex chart. 310. 122 f. Saec. 15.
Microfilm: MnCH proj. no. 685

1550 **Breviarium Caeremoniarum monasterii** Mellicensis . . . 1418. MS. Benediktinerabtei Melk, Austria, codex 662, f.1v-11v. Quarto. Saec. 15.
Microfilm: MnCH proj. no. 1532

1551 **Ceremoniae regularis observantiae** Ordinis S. Benedicti, ex ipsius Regula sumptae, secundum quod hodie in sacro monasterio suo Sublacensi et Specu practicantur. MS. Benediktinerabtei Melk, Austria, codex 1398, f.1r-128v. Duodecimo. Saec. 15.
Microfilm: MnCH proj. no. 1920

1552 **Breviarium ceremoniarum monasterii** Mellicensis, et aliae res ceremoniales et monasticae. MS. Benediktinerabtei Melk, Austria, codex 1603. 453 p. Duodecimo. Saec. 15.
Microfilm: MnCH proj. no. 1990

1553 **Ceremoniae regularis observantiae** Ordinis Sancti Benedicti ex ipsius Regula sumpta. MS. Benediktinerabtei St. Peter, Salzburg, codex b.II.14, f.1r-62r. Octavo. Saec. 15.
Microfilm: MnCH proj. no. 10,310

1554 **Ceremoniae regularis observantiae** Ordinis S. Benedicti ex ipsius Regula sumptae secundum quod hodie in sacro monasterio suo Sublacensi et Specu practicantur. MS. Vienna, Schottenstift, codex 240, f.97r-132v. Quarto. Saec. 15.
Microfilm: MnCH proj. no. 4152

1555 **Breviarium coeremoniarum monasterii Melicensis.** Benediktinerabtei Kremsmünster, Austria, codex 403. 118 f. Saec. 16.
Microfilm: MnCH proj. no. 402

1556 **Rubricae Cremifanenses.** Rubrica continens in se dispositionem fratrum chori Chremiphanensis monasterii quatenus ea concernit libris a maioribus nobis relictis 1594. MS. Benediktinerabtei Kremsmünster, Austria, codex 103. 177 f. Saec. 16.
Microfilm: MnCH proj. no. 96

1557 **Breviarium ceremoniarum monasterii Mellicensis.** MS. Benediktinerabtei Melk, Austria, codex 1748. 123 f. Duodecimo. Saec. 16.
Microfilm: MnCH proj. no. 2056

1558 **Ceremonial de Montserrat.** MS. Monasterio benedictino de Montserrat, Spain, codex 46 & 74. 242 f. Octavo. Saec. 16. Microfilm: MnCH proj. no. 29,991

1559 **Breviarium ceremonarium monasterii Mellicensis** . . . anno 1418 (Melker Reform-Statuten). MS. Benediktinerabtei St. Peter, Salzburg, codex a.IX.35, f.132r-184r. Folio. Saec. 16. Microfilm: MnCH proj. no. 10,231

1560 **Annotatio eorum quae in divinis officiis** vel in aliis fratrum actibus observanda sunt. MS. Benediktinerabtei St. Peter, Salzburg, codex a.III.26. 48 f. Octavo. Saec. 16. Microfilm: MnCH proj. no. 9973

1561 **Caeremoniae nigrorum monachorum** Ordinis Sancti Benedicti de observantia Bursfeldensi. MS. Vienna, Schottenstift, codex 578, f.41r-121v. Octavo. Saec. 16. Microfilm: MnCH proj. no. 4272

1562 **Caeremoniae regularis observantiae** Ordinis sanctissimi patris nostri Benedicti, ex ipsius Regula desumptae, in quod hodie in sacro monasterio suo Sublacensi et Specu practicantur. MS. Benediktinerabtei Altenburg, Austria, codex AB 13 F 13. 94 f. Octavo. Saec. 17 (1602-03). Microfilm: MnCH proj. no. 6493

1563 **Breviarium caeremoniarum monasterii** Mellicensis ducatus Austriae Pataviensis diocesis, anno Domini 1415 per venerabiles patres monasteriorum Sublacensis et S. Specus auctoritate D. Papae Martini V reformati. Tria ultima capitula desunt. MS. Benediktinerabtei Melk, Austria, codex 1051. 88 f. Quarto. Saec. 17. Microfilm: MnCH proj. no. 1824

1564 **Rubrica divini officii,** juxta ritum et consuetudinem monasterii Mellicensis Ordinis S. Benedicti de tempore et sanctis. MS. Benediktinerabtei Melk, Austria, codex 980. 276 f. Quarto. Saec. 17. Microfilm: MnCH proj. no. 1772

1565 **Caeremoniale in usum monasterii** S. Blasii. MS. Benediktinerabtei St. Paul im Lavantthal, Austria, codex 312/4. 86 f. Quarto. Saec. 17. Microfilm: MnCH proj. no. 12,557

b. Printed Editions

1566 **Biburg, Bavaria (Benedictine abbey).** Das Klosterrituale von Biburg (Budapest, cod. lat. m.ae. Nr. 330, 12 Jh.). Hrsg. von Walter von Arx. Freiburg, Schweiz, Universitätsverlag, 1970. xxviii, 357 p. 25 cm. PLatS

1567 **Rituale monasticum,** justorumque infirmantibus moribundis, necnon vita functis persolvendorum ratio, ex optimis quibusque, Romano praecipue & antiquiori Benedictino usibus deprompta. Tulli Leucorum, A. Laurent, 1681. 215 p. music. 16 cm. KAS

1568 **Subiaco Congregation. English Province.** Choir ceremonial of the English Province of the Cassinese Congregation P.O. Ramsgate, England, Monastery Press, 1949. 86 p. NdRi

1569 **Valladolid Congregation.** Ceremonial monastico, conforme al Breviario y Misal que la santidad de Paulo V. concedió à todos los que militan debajo de la Santa Regla du nuestro gloriosisimo padre . . . San Benito. Con los usos y costumbres loables de la Congregacion de España. Nuevamente dispuestro por el capitulo general . . . 1633 . . . Reimpresso . . . Madrid, Imprenta de Pedro Marin, 1774. [15], 900 p. music. 22 cm. KAS

2. German, Spanish

1570 Regulae quaedam liturgicae idiomate allemanico. MS. Benediktinerabtei St. Paul im Lavantthal, Austria, codex 50/1 (apud finem). Quarto. Saec. 14-15. Microfilm: MnCH proj. no. 11,712

1571 Ceremonial monastico. Lingua Castellana (Spanish). MS. Silos, Spain, Archivo del Monasterio de St. Domingo, ms. 15. 158 f. Octavo. Saec. 15. Microfilm: MnCH proj. no. 33,697

1572 Ceremonial monastico. Lingua Castellana. MS. Silos, Spain, Archivo del Monasterio de Sto. Domingo, ms. 43. 92 f. Octavo. Saec. 16. Microfilm: MnCH proj. no. 33,699

tt. Sacramentarium

1573 Liber sacramentorum de circulo anni expositum a S. Gregorio papa. MS. Benediktinerabtei St. Paul im Lavantthal, Austria, codex 20/1. 278 f. Saec. 10-11. Microfilm: MnCH proj. no. 12,528

1574　Liber sacramentorum. MS. Benediktiner-
　　　abtei Melk, Austria, codex 1792. 155 f.
　　　Saec. 12.

uu. Sequentiae

1575　Sequentiae pro diversis festivitatibus. MS.
　　　Subiaco, Italy (Benedictine abbey),
　　　codex 168. 30 f. Saec. 15.
　　　Microfilm: MnCH

vv. Table Prayers

1576　Benedictio mensae. Latine et germanice.
　　　MS. Benediktinerabtei St. Peter, Salz-
　　　burg, codex a.VI.21, f.1r-30v. Octavo.
　　　Saec. 16(1502).
　　　Microfilm: MnCH proj. no. 10,103

1577　Monastic table prayers, Convent of Saint
　　　Benedict, [Saint Joseph, Minn., St.
　　　Benedict's Press] 1955.
　　　58 p. 12 cm.
　　　MnStj(Archives)

ww. Troparium

1578　Daux, Camille.
　　　Deux livres choraux monastiques des Xe
et XIe siècles; étude historique, analytique
et musicale. Paris, A. Picard, 1899.
　　　xiv, 150 p. 29 cm.
　　　Partial contents: Le tropaire-prosier de
l'Abbeye Saint-Martin de Montauriol.
　　　KAS; PLatS

1579　Liturgica cum neumis. Troparium Cremi-
　　　fanense. MS. Benediktinerabtei Krems-
　　　münster, Austria, codex 309, f.169r-
　　　243v.
　　　Microfilm: MnCH proj. no. 293

xx. Vesperale

1580　Benedictine vespers in Latin and English
　　　for all Sundays and festivals with terce
　　　and compline and benediction. Ample-
　　　forth Abbey, York, 1910.
　　　189 p.
　　　NcBe

1581　Vesperal monastico de Montserrat. Texto
　　　Latino-Castellano, introducción y notas
　　　por F. S., O.S.B. Monasterio de Mont-
　　　serrat, 1947.
　　　728 p. illus. 17 cm.
　　　MnCS

VII. SPECIAL TOPICS

1. BENEDICTINES AND AGRICULTURE

1582 **La Bonifica Benedettina.** Roma, Istituto della Enciclopedia Italiana [1963?].
199 p. plates (part col.) 36 cm.
PLatS

1583 **Grand, Roger.**
L'agriculture au moyen age de la fin de l'Empire Romain au XVIe siècle, par Roger Grand avec la collaboration de Raymond Delatouche. Paris, E. De Boccard, 1950.
740 p. 28 cm.
PLatS

1584 **Olinda, Brazil. Sao Bento (Benedictine abbey).**
As escolas superiores de agricultura e medicina-veterinaria, Sao Bento, Pernambuco, 1913-1923. [Friburgo em Brisgau (Allemanha)], Tipographia de Herder [1923].
[5] p. 20 plates, 32 cm.
PLatS

1585 **Platt, Colin.**
The monastic grange in medieval England. New York, Fordham University Press, 1969.
272 p. illus. 23 cm.
MnCS; PLatS

1586 **Waites, Bryan.**
Moorland and vale-land farming in north-east Yorkshire: the monastic contribution in the thirteenth and fourteenth centuries. York, St. Anthony's Press, 1967.
35 p. maps, 22 cm. (University of York; Borthwick Institute of Historical Research, Borthwick papers, 32)
MnCS

2. BENEDICTINES AND ARCHITECTURE

1587 **Architectura Benedettina.**
(*In* Dizionario degli Istituti di Perfezione. Roma, 1973. vol. 1, col. 1197–1222)
MnCS

1587a **Braunfels, Wolfgang.**
Monasteries of western Europe: the architecture of the Orders. Princeton, N.J., Princeton University Press, 1972.
263 p. illus. 30 cm.
MnCS

1588 **Christe, Yves.**
Cluny et le Clunisois. Texte de Yves Christe. Photographie de Chislain Arens, Cluny. Geneve, Institut d'histoire de l'art du moyen age [1967].
78 p. illus. 24 cm.
MnCS

1589 **Conant, Kenneth John.**
Cluny; les églises et la maison du chef l'ordre. Macon, Protat Freres, 1968.
169 p. illus. 38 cm.
MnCS

1590 **Cranage, David H. S.**
The home of the monk; an account of English monastic life and buildings in the Middle Ages. 2d ed. Cambridge [England], University Press, 1926.
xv, 122 p. illus. 20 cm.
MnCS

1590a **Duby, Georges.**
Le temps des cathedrales; l'art et la société 980-1420. [Paris], Gallimard, [1976].
386 p. plates, 23 cm.
p. 9-111: Le monastère, 980-1130.
MnCS

1591 **Eschapasse, Maurice.**
L'architecture bénédictine en Europe. Paris, Editions des Deux-Mondes [1963].
231 p. illus., maps, plans. 27 cm.
InStme

1592 **Evans, Joan.**
Monastic architecture in France, from the Renaissance to the Revolution. Cambridge [England] University Press, 1964.
xlii, 186 p. 827 illus. (incl. plans) 29 cm.
NcBe; PLatS

1592a **Horn, Walter.**
The plan of St. Gall; a study of the architecture & economy of, & life in, a paradigmatic Carolingian monastery, by Walter Horn and Ernest Born . . . Berkeley, University of California Press, 1979.
3 v. illus. (part col.), plans. 37 cm. (California studies in the history of art, XIX)
MnCS; PLatS

1593 **Niebling, Howard V.**
Modern Benedictine churches; monastic churches erected by American Benedictines since World War II.
449 leaves, 28 cm.
Thesis (Ph.D.)–Columbia University, 1973.
Typescript.
PLatS

1594 **Palmer, Roger Liddesdale.**
English monasteries in the Middle Ages; an outline of monastic architecture and custom from the conquest to the suppression. London, Constable & Co., 1930.

xv, 232 p. illus. 26 cm.
MnCS

1595 **Rockwell, Anne F.**
Glass, stones & crown; the Abbé Suger
and the building of St. Denis. London,
Macmillan, 1968.
81 p. illus. 25 cm.
MnCS

1596 **Taylor, Harold McCarter.**
The architectural interest of
Aethelwulf's De abbatibus.
(*In* Anglo-Saxon England 3. Edited by
Peter Clemoes. Cambridge, England.
1974. p. 163–173)
PLatS

1597 **Die Vorarlberger Barockbaumeister;**
Ausstellung in Einsiedeln und Bregenz
zum 250. Todestag von Br. Caspar
Moosbrugger. Mai-September 1973.
Hrsg. von Werner Oechslin. Einsiedeln,
1973.
xvi, 298 p. plates (276 illus.) 24 cm.
MnCS

1598 **Zürcher, Richard.**
Zwiefalten; die Kirche der ehemaligen
Benediktinerabtei, ein Gesamtwerk der
süddeutschen Rokoko. Konstanz, Jan
Thorbeshe Verlag [1967].
72 p. 53 plates. 30 cm.
MnCS

3. BENEDICTINES AND ART

a. General Works

1599 **L'Abbaye de Saint-Vaast;** monographie
historique, archéologique et littéraire de
ce monastère. Arras, Typ. d'A. Brissy,
1865–68.
3 v. 28x23 cm.
KAS

1600 **Cantor, Norman F.**
The medieval world: 300-1300. New
York, Macmillan, 1968.
339 p.
InFer

1601 **Caravita, Andrea, O.S.B.**
I codici e le arti a Monte Cassino. Monte
Cassino, pei Tipi della Badia, 1870.
3 v.
MoCo

1602 **Genge, Hans Joachim.**
Die liturgiegeschichtlichen Voraussetzungen des Lambacher Freskenzyklus.
Münsterschwarzach, Vier-Türme-Verlag,
1972.
xx, 144 p. 21 cm.
MnCS

1603 **Fischer, Pius, O.S.B.**
Der Barokmaler, Johann Jakob Zeiller
und sein Ettaler Werk. München, Verlag
Herold [1964].
135 p. illus., plates (col.) 30 cm.
PLatS

1604 **Haacke, Rhagan, O.S.B.**
Programme zur bildenden Kunst in den
Schriften Ruperts von Deutz. Siegburg,
Respublica-Verlag, 1974.
63 p. 23 plates, 24 cm.
MnCS

1605 **Hartig, Michael.**
Bayerns Klöster und ihre Kunstschätze,
von der Einführung des Christentums bis
zur Säkularisation zu Beginn des 19.
Jahrhunderts. Ein Bilderbuch für alle
Freunde bayerischer Kunst. Diessen vor
München, J.C. Huber, 1913-
v. 24 cm.
NcBe(v.1)

1606 **Hess, Ignaz, O.S.B.**
Die Kunst im Kloster Engelberg.
Schriften zur Heimatkunde von
Engelberg, 1946.
136 p. illus.
MoCo

1607 **Indice artistico de Montserrat.** Abadia de
Montserrat, 1956.
45 p. 21 cm.
MnCS; CaQStB

1608 **Jameson, Mrs. Anna Brownell (Murphy).**
Legends of the monastic orders as
represented in the fine arts, forming the
second series of sacred and legendary art.
Corrected and enl. ed. Boston and New
York, Houghton, Mifflin and Co., 1894.
489 p.
NcBe

1609 **Krüger, Ekkehard.**
Die Schreib- und Malwerkstatt der Abtei
Helmarshausen bis in die Zeit Heinrichs
des Löwen. Darmstadt, Selbstverlag der
Hessischen Historischen Kommission,
1972.
3 v. 103 plates, diagrs. 22 cm.
MnCS

1610 **Kunst und Kultur im Weserraum,**
800-1600; Ausstellung des Landes
Nordrheim-Westfalen, Corvey, 1966.
4. Aufl. Münster, Aschendorff, 1967.
2 v. (xxiv, 931 p.) illus., plates (part col.)
24 cm.
MnCS

1611 **Linage Conde, Antonio.**
El monacato y el arte barroco.
(*In* his El monacato en Espana e
Hispanoamerica. Salamanca, 1977. p. 661-
694)
MnCS

1612 **Martindale, Andrew.**
The rise of the artist in the Middle Ages and early Renaissance. London, Thames and Hudson, [1972]
144 p. illus. (part col.) 21 cm.
vid. p. 65-78: The artist in the cloister.
MnCS

1613 **Monte Cassino, Italy (Benedictine abbey).**
La paleografia artistica nei codici Cassinesi applicata ai lavori industriali. Litografie di Montecassino, 1910.
[2] p. 20 plates in portfolio. 34 cm.
MnCS

1614 **Novelli, Leandro, O.S.B.**
Il coro intagliato della Basilica di S. Maria del Monte di Cesena. Cesena, Edizioni Badia S. Maria del Monte [n.d.].
43 p. plates, 32 cm.
MnCS

1615 **Novelli, Leandro, O.S.B.**
Ex voto del Santuario della Madonna del Monte di Cesena. Presentazione del Prof. Mario Salmi. [Forli, Santa Maria del Monte Cesena, 1961]
187 p. cxcii plates (part col.) 32 cm.
MnCS

1616 **Paleografia artistica di Montecassino.**
Montecassino. Litografia di Montecassino, 1876-84.
7 pts. in 1 vol., plates, facsims. 38 cm.
MnCS

1617 **Plossmann, Gerhard.**
Stift Melk und seine Kunstschätze. St. Pölten, Wien, Verlag Niederösterr. Pressehaus, 1976.
78 p. 32 plates, 28 cm.
MnCS

1618 **Rösch, Ernest Gerhard**
Tuotilo, Mönch und Künstler; Quellen zur Geschichte der Inklusen in der Stadt St. Gallen. St. Gallen, Fehr, 1953.
89 p. plates, 23 cm.
MnCS

1619 **Saint-Benoît-sur-Loire, France (Benedict abbey).**
Dialogues de saint Grégoire et Règle de saint Benoît. Extraits traduits par E. de Solms. La Pierre-qui-Vire, Zodiaque, 1965.
199 p., 72 plates (part col.) 26 cm.
MnCS

1620 **St. John's University, Collegeville, Minn.**
Encounter with artists, #10: selected works of the joint art faculty of St. John's University/College of Saint Benedict. [St. Paul, Minn.] Minnesota Museum of Art, 1973.
16 p. illus. 18x26 cm.
MnCS

1621 **Schapiro, Mayer.**
The Parma Ildefunsus; a romanesque illuminated manuscript from Cluny and related works. New York, College Art Association of America, 1964.
85, [38] p. illus., facsims. 32 cm.
(Monographs on archaeology and fine arts, 11)
MnCS

1622 **Sommer, Johannes.**
Das Deckenbild der Michaelskirche in Hildesheim. Hildesheim, Gerstenberg, 1966.
195 p. 87 plates (part col.) 31 cm.
MnCS

1623 **Springer, Anton Heinrich.**
Commentatio de artificibus monachis et laicis Medii Aevi. Bonnae, Carolus Georgus, 1861.
44 p. 27 cm.
CaQStB; MnCS

1624 **Stoddard, Whitney S.**
Monastery and cathedral in France; medieval architecture, sculpture, stained glass, manuscripts, the art of the church treasures. Middletown, Conn., Wesleyan University Press [1966].
xxi, 412 p. illus. 29 cm.
MnCS

1625 **Toubert, Hélène.**
Rome et le Mont-Cassin; nouvelles remarques sur les fresques de l'eglise inferieure de Saint-Clément de Rome.
(*In* Dumbarton Oaks papers, no. 309, 1976), p. 1–34)
MnCS

1626 **Venice, Italy San Lazzaro (Mechitarist Benedictine abbey).**
Armenian miniature paintings of the monastic library at San Lazzaro [by Mesrop Janashian, English version of the text by Bernard Grebanier]. Venice, Armenian Press, San Lazzaro, 1966-

1627 **Verheyen, Egon.**
Das goldene Evangelienbuch von Echternach. München, Prestel Verlag [1963].
95 p. illus., col. plates, 20 cm.
MnCS

1628 **Vienna, Austria. Mechitaristen-Congregation.**
Die illuminierten armenischen Handschriften der Mechitaristen-Congregation in Wien. Wien, 1976.
250 p. incl. 80 col. plates, 30 cm.
At head of title: Heide & Helmut Buschhausen unter Mithilfe von Eva Zimmermann.
MnCS

v. chiefly col. facsims. 46 cm.
PLatS

1629 **Weisbach, Werner.**
Religiöse Reform und mittelalterliche
Kunst. Mit 48 Bildern auf 17 Tafeln. Ein-
siedeln/Zürich, Benziger & Co. [1945].
230 p. plates, 25 cm.
MnCS

1630 **Wibiral, Norbert.**
Die Wandmalereien des XI. Jahrhun-
derts im ehemaligen Westchor der
Klosterkirche von Lambach.
(*In* Oberösterreich, Heft 3/4 [1967–68])
PLatS

1631 **Zarnecki, George.**
The monastic achievement. New York,
McGraw-Hill [1972].
144 p. illus. 22 cm. (Library of medieval
civilization)
MnCS

1632 **Zürcher, Richard.**
Zwiefalten, die Kirche der ehemaligen
Benediktinerabtei. Konstanz, J.
Thorbecke, 1967.
72 p. 53 plates, 24 cm.
MnCS

b. Beuronese Art

1633 **Aus dem Leben unserer lieben Frau;**
siebzehn Kunstblätter nach den Origin-
alcartons der Malerschule von Beuron zu
den Wandgemelden der Klosterkirche zu
Emaus-Prag. 2. Aufl. [n.p.] Druck und
Verlag der B.Kühlen'schen Kunstanstalt,
1896
1 vol.(unpaged) illus., xvii plates,
35x43 cm.
MnCS; MoCo

1634 **Beuron, Germany (Benedictine abbey).**
Muster Beuroner Bilder, ein- und
mehrfarbig. Beuron, Verlag der Beuroner
Kunstschule [n.d.].
39 p. mounted col. pictures, 18 cm.
MnCS

1635 **Dreher, Ansgar, O.S.B.**
Zur Beuroner Kunst.
(*In* Beuron, 1863-1963; Festschtift . . .
Beuron, 1963. p. 358-394)
PLatS

1636 **Janssens, Laurent, O.S.B.**
L'arte della scuola benedettina di
Beuron. Milano, Società dell'Arte Chris-
tiana [1913].
25 p. illus. 39 cm.
AStb; MnCS

1637 **Mayer, Heinrich Suso, O.S.B.**
Beuroner Bibliographie; Schriftsteller
und Künstler während der ersten hundert

Jahre des Benediktinerklosters Beuron,
1863-1963.
196 p. 24 cm.
MnCS

4. BENEDICTINES AND CHURCH MUSIC

1638 **Angerer, Joachim, O.S.B.**
Die Begriffe "Discantus, organa" und
"scolares" in reformgeschichtlichen
Urkunden des 15. Jahrhunderts. Ein
Beitrag zur Pflege d. Mehrstimmigkeit in
den Benediktinerklöstern des
österr.-süddeutschen Raumes. Wien,
Verlag der Oesterreichischen Akademie
der Wissenschaften, 1973.
147-170 p. 7 facsims. 24 cm.
Offprint from: Mitteilungen der Kommission für Musikforschung, Nr. 22.
MnCS

1638a **Die liturgisch-musikalische Erneurung**
der Melker Reform; Studien zur Erforschung der Musikpraxis in den Benediktinerklöstern des 15. Jahrhunderts.
Wien, Verlag der Oesterreichischen
Akademie der Wissenschaften, 1974.
176 p. fold. map, 24 cm.
MnCS

1639 **Gindele, Corbinian, O.S.B.**
Beurons Choralgesang.
(*In* Beuron, 1863-1963; Festschrift . . .
Beuron, 1963. p. 308-336)
PLatS

1640 **Korhammer, Michael.**
Die monastischen cantica im Mittelalter
und ihre altenglischen Interlinearver-
sionen; Studien und Textausgabe. München, Wilhelm Fink Verlag [1976].
xxi, 401 p. 24 cm.
MnCS

1641 **Monte Cassino, Italy (Benedictine**
abbey).
L'apostolato della musica sacra nel
secolo XX; visione nel XIII centenario di
San Gregorio Magno del 12 Marze al 12
Aprile 1904, per un solitario. Montecassino, 1904.
14 p. 24 cm.
MnCS

1642 **Orgelmusik in Benediktinerklöstern,**
hrsg. von Eberhard Kraus. Regensburg,
Verlag F. Pustet, 1959-
v. 22x32 cm.
InStme (v. 1-4)
Lists works in use in the Benedictine
monasteries at Kremsmünster, Prüfening,
Augsburg, St. Lambrecht, Mariazell,
Neresheim, Montecassino, Ottobeuern . . .

1643 **Riedel, Friedrich.**
Die Kirchenmusik im Benediktinerstift Göttweig. Wien, Mechitharistendruckerei, 1966.
8 p. 28 cm.
Sonderdruck aus "Singende Kirche," Heft 4, 1966.
MnCS

1643a **Schäfer, Gerhard M.**
Untersuchungen zur deutschsprachigen Marienlyrik des 12. und 13. Jahrhunderts. Göppingen, Verlag Alfred Kümmerle, 1971.
iv, 161 p. 20 cm. (Göppinger Arbeiten zur Germanistik, Nr. 48)
Includes chapters on Benedictine abbeys: Das Melker Marienlied; Die Mariensequenz aus St. Lambrecht; Die Mariensequenz aus Muri.
MnCS

1644 **Schubiger, Anselm, O.S.B.**
Die Sängerschule St. Gallens vom achten bis zwölften Jahrhundert; ein Beitrag zur Gesanggeschichte des Mittelalters. Einsiedeln, Gebrüder Benziger, 1858.
MnCS

1645 **Söhner, Leo.**
Die Geschichte der Begleitung des gregorianischen Chorals in Deutschland, vornehmlich im 18. Jahrhundert. Augsburg, B. Filser, 1931.
xvi, 213 p. illus. (music) 25 cm.
ILSP

1646 **Solesmes. France. Saint-Pierre (Benedictine abbey).**
La notation musicale des chants liturgiques latins. Présenté par les moines de Solesmes. [Solesmes, Abbaye de Saint-Pierre, 1963].
[38] p. 32 cm.
MnCS; PLatS

1647 **Solesmes, France. Saint-Pierre (Benedictine abbey).**
Paléographie musicale; les principaux manuscrits de chant grégorien, ambrosien, mozarabe, gallican, publié en facsimilés phototypique par les Bénédictins de Solesmes. Tournay, Desclée. v. 1-   1889-
CaQStB; InStme; MnCS; PLatS

1648 **Solesmes, France. Saint-Pierre (Benedictine abbey)**
Rules for psalmody. Adapted from the revised edition of Petit traité de psalmodie by the Benedictines of Solesmes. Rome, Desclée, Lefebvre & Co., 1904.
32 p. 17 cm.
InStme

5. BENEDICTINES AND CULTURE

1649 **Ambroise, Georges.**
Les moines du Moyen Age; leur influence intellectuelle et politique en France. 2. éd. Paris, A. Picard, 1945.
248 p. illus. 1945.
First published 1942.
MnCS; MoCo

1650 **Bertelli, Carlo.**
Testi figurativi per il lavoro monastico. (*In* La bonifica benedettina, p. 173-179)
PLatS

1651 **Brunhölzl, Franz.**
Zum Problem der Casinenser Klassikerüberlieferung. München, Fink, 1971.
39 p. 26 cm. (Abhandlungen der Marburger Gelehrten Gesellschaft, Jg. 1971, Nr. 3)
MnCS

1652 **Décarreux, John.**
Monks and civilization, from the barbarian invasions to the reign of Charlemagne. Translated by Charlotte Haldane. Garden City, N.Y., Doubleday, 1964.
377 p. maps, 22 cm.
MnCS; NcBe; PLatS

1653 **Leclercq, Jean, O.S.B.**
The love of learning and the desire for God; a study of monastic culture. [2d rev. ed.]. Translated by Catharine Misrahi. New York, Fordham University Press [1977].
viii, 397 p. 20 cm.
MnCS

1654 **Mabillon, Jean, O.S.B.**
Science et sainteté; l'étude dans la vie monastique. Textes recueillis et presentés par René Jean Hesbert. Paris, Editions Alsatia, 1958.
xxiii, 134 p. 19 cm. (Spirituels bénédictins du grand siècle)
CaQStB; InStme; KAS; MnCS; PLatS

1655 **Vidmar, Constantin Johannes.**
St. Benedikts Leben und die kulturelle Tätigkeit seines Orden. Berlin, Buchverlag Germania, 1933.
88 p.
NcBe

6. BENEDICTINES AND DRAMA

1656 **Dolan, Diane.**
Le drame liturgique de Pâques en Normandie et en Angleterre au Moyen Age. Paris, Presses Universitaires de France, 1975.
237 p. music, plates, 2 maps, 24 cm.
MnCS

1656a **Haider, Johann.**
Die Geschichte des Theaterwesens im Benediktinerstift Seitenstetten in Barock und Aufklärung. Wien, Verlag der Oesterreichischen Akademie der Wissenschaften, 1973.
226 p. illus. 24 cm.
MnCS

1657 **Womisch, Othmar.**
Die Theaterkultur des Stiftes St. Lambrecht. Graz, Historischer Verein für Staiermark, 1957.
75 p. 24 cm.
MnCS

7. BENEDICTINES AND ECUMENISM

1658 **Bouyer, Louis, C.Orat.**
Dom Lambert Beauduin, un homme d'Eglise. [Paris] Casterman, 1964.
185 p. illus. 20 cm. (Eglise vivente)
CaQStB; InStme; MnCS; MoCo; PLatS

1659 **Christians in conversation** [papers], with a preface by Peter W. Bartholome. Westminster, Md., Newman Press, 1962.
x, 112 p. 21 cm.
"A colloquy between American Catholics and Protestants . . . held at St. John's Abbey, Collegeville, Minnesota, on 1, 2, 3 December, 1960. Organized by the American Benedictine Academy."
MnCS; OkShG

1660 **The Ecumenical Institute, Belmont, N.C., 1975.**
Seminar on abortion. The proceedings of a dialogue between Catholics and Baptists sponsored by the Bishops' Committee for Ecumenical and Inter-religious Affairs and the Ecumenical Institute of Wake Forest University and Belmont Abbey College, November 10–12, 1975. Edited by Claude U. Broach. [Belmont, N.C., Belmont Abbey, 1975].
85 p.
NcBe

1660a **The Ecumenical Institute, Belmont, N.C., 1976.**
Issues of Church and State. The proceedings of a dialogue between Catholics and Baptists sponsored by the Bishops' Committee for Ecumenical and Inter-religious Affairs and the Ecumenical Institute of Wake Forest University and Belmont Abbey College, November 3-5, 1976. Edited by Claude U. Broach. [Belmont, N.C., Belmont Abbey, 1976].
96 p.
NcBe

1660b **Eins in Christus:** Altabt Emmanuel M. Heufelder zum 80. Geburtstag, 30. März 1978. Hrsg. von der Abtei Niederaltaich [1978].
97 p. plates, ports. 22 cm.
MnCS

1660c **Heufelder, Emmanuel Maria, O.S.B.**
In the hope of His coming; studies in Christian unity. Translated by Otto M. Knab. Notre Dame, Ind., Fides Publisher [1964].
261 p. 21 cm.
InFer; InStme; KAS; MnCS; MoCo; PLatS

1660d **Hören sein Wort;** Festgabe für Abt Emmanuel M. Heufelder zum 70. Geburtstag. Hrsg. von der Abtei Niederaltaich. Niederaltaich, Dreiberg-Verlag, 1968.
188 p. port. 23 cm.
PLatS

1660e **Institute for Ecumenical and Cultural Research, Collegeville, Minn.**
Annual Report, 1968-
The Institute has also produced the following Occasional Papers:
No. 1: Confessing faith in God today, by Patrick Henry and Thomas Stransky. December, 1976.
No. 2: Compassion: the cure of spiritual leadership. March, 1977.
No. 3: Confessing faith in God today, by Robert S. Bilheimer. November, 1977.
No. 4: Ministry: dilemmas and opportunities, by John S. Damm and Philip J. Murnion. February, 1978.
No. 5: A song of worshiping pilgrims, by Patrick Henry. March, 1978.
No. 6: Black theologians confess their faith in God, by J. Deotis Roberts and Thomas Hoyt, Jr. November, 1978.
No. 7: A confession of Christ the King, by Godfrey Diekmann, O.S.B. January, 1979.
No. 8: The workgroup on constructive Christian theology, by Julian N. Hartt. March, 1979.

1660f **International Ecumenical Colloquium, Sant'Anselmo, Rome, 1974.**
Unitatis redintegration, 1964-1974; impact of the decree on ecumenism. Edited by Gerard Békés, O.S.B., and Volmos Fajta. Roma, Editrice Anselmiane, 1977.
176 p. 25 cm. (Studia Anselmiana, 71)
PLatS

1660g **Irénikon,** v.1- 1926- Quarterly. Monastère Bénédictin, Chevetogne, Belgique.
CaQStB; InStme; MnCS; PLatS

1660h Journées oecuméniques, Chevetogne, Belgium, 1961.
L'infaillibilité de l'Eglise . . . Editions de Chevetogne [1963].
266 p. 22 cm.
InStme

1660i Louvain, Belgium. Abbaye du Mont-Cesar.
Une oeuvre monastique pour l'union des Eglises. Louvain, Abbaye du Mont-Cesar [n.d.].
32 p. 18 cm.
KAS

1660j Quitslund, Sonya A.
Beauduin, a prophet vindicated. New York, Newman Press [1973].
xvii, 366 p. illus. 24 cm.
KAS; MoCo; PLatS

1661 Una Sancta; Zeitschrift für ökumenische Begegnung. Jahrg. 1- 1946-
Meitingen-Reising. Quarterly.
Published under the direction of the Benedictines of Niederaltaich.
InStme; KAS; MnCS

1661b Veilleur avant l'aurore; colloque Lambert Beauduin [par] J. J. von Allmen [et al.].
Editions de Chevetogne, 1978.
296 p. 22 cm.
MnCS

8. BENEDICTINES AND EDUCATION

1662 Axtman, Boniface Joseph, O.S.B.
Educational work of the Benedictine Order in the Philippines.
226 leaves. 28 cm.
Thesis (M.A.)–University of Santo Tomas, Manila, 1941.
Typescript.
MnCS(Archives)

1663 Baumgartner, Alexander, S.J.
Literatur an den Klosterschulen: Fulda, Reichenau, St. Gallen.
(*In* his Weltliteratur. 1887–95. v. 4, p. 302-316)
AStb

1664 Botz, Paschal Robert, O.S.B.
Characteristics of Benedictine education.
(*In* The National Benedictine Education Association: Bulletin, v. 22(1939), p. 54-63)
MnCS

1665 Doris, Sebastian Thomas, O.S.B.
Belmont Abbey; its history and educational influence.
68 p. 28 cm.
Thesis (M.A.)–Catholic University of America, Washington, D.C., 1933.
NcBe

1666 Dworschak, Baldwin Wilfred, O.S.B.
Benedictine education.
15 p. 23 cm. (College of Saint Benedict, Saint Joseph, Minn. Mother Benedicta Riepp memorial lectureship. First annual lecture, 1963)
MnCS; MnStj(Archives)

1667 Governing boards of Benedictine colleges in the United States; a workshop held at St. Benedict's College, Atchison, Kansas, January 3 and 4, 1968.
44 leaves, 28 cm.
Includes text of lectures and discussions.
Mimeographed.
KAS

1668 Hausmann, Daniei, Sister, O.S.B.
Role of the president in American four-year liberal arts colleges conducted by the Benedictine Sisters.
199 p. tables, 28 cm.
Typescript, 1963.
MnStj

1669 Highbaugh, Assunta, Sister, O.S.B.
An analysis of the teacher-education programs of the Benedictine Sisters in the United States. Washington, Catholic University of America, 1961.
xi, 189 p. map, tables. 23 cm.
Thesis–Catholic University of America, Washington, D.C., 1961.
InStme; KAS; MnCS; PLatS

1670 Houtman, Mary Immaculata, Sister, O.S.B.
A study of some of the concepts applicable to business education in St. Benedict's Rule for monasteries.
117 p. 28 cm.
Thesis (M.A.)–Catholic University of America, Washington, D.C., 1962.
Typescript.
MdRi

1671 Lur, Henricus.
Tractatus epistolaris de gymnasio et studio generali in germanicis Ordinis Benedictini monasteriis erigendo. MS. Benediktinerabtei Melk, Austria, codex 1793, f.1r-8v. Quarto. Saec. 15.
Microfilm: MnCH proj. no. 2100

1672 Metten, Germany (Benedictine abbey).
Jahresbericht St. Michaels-Gymnasium der Benediktiner in Metten . . .
PLatS

1672a Murphy, James J.
Rhetoric in the Middle Ages; a history of rhetorical theory from Saint Augustine to the Renaissance. Berkeley, Calif., University of California Press, 1974.
395 p.

Includes Alberic of Monte Cassino, Alcuin and Hrabanus Maurus.
MnCS

1673 **Parry, David, O.S.B.**
Scholastic century: St. Augustine's Abbey School, Ramsgate (1865-1965). [Tenbury Wells, Worcestershire] Fowler Wright [1965].
101 p. plates, tables. 23 cm.
PLatS

1674 **Riché, Pierre.**
Education and culture in the barbarian West, sixth through eighth centuries. Translated from the 3rd French edition by John J.Contreni. Columbia, Union of South Carolina Press, 1976.
xxxvii, 557 p. 24 cm.
MnCS

1675 **Rome (City). Collegio di Sant'Anselmo.**
Statuta in Internationali Benedictinorum Collegio Sancti Anselmi de Urbe observanda. Manuscripti instar. Sublaci, Typis Proto-Coenobii, 1920.
78 p. 18 cm.
MnCS

1676 – – **Sublaci, Typis Proto-Coenobii**, 1939.
78 p. 18 cm.
MnCS

1677 **St. Augustine's Abbey, Ramsgate, England.**
University education under the guidance of the Church; or, Monastic studies. By a monk of St. Augustine's, Ramsgate. London, R. Washbourne, 1873.
120 p. 21 cm.
KAS; MnCS; PLatS

1678 **Seitenstetten, Austria, (Benedictine abbey)**
Oeffentliches Stiftsgymnasium Steitenstetten, 1814-1964. [Im Selbstverlag des Stiftes, n.d.]
63 p. ports., illus., maps. 21 cm.
PLatS

1679 **Semana de Estudios Monasticos,** 4th, Poblet, 1963.
Los monjes y los estudios. Poblet, Abadia de Poblet, 1963.
501 p. 25 cm.
In Spanish, French and English.
KAS

1680 **Volk, Paulus, O.S.B.**
Die Studien in der Bursfelder Kongregation.
(*In* Heutger, Nicolaus. Bursfeld und seine Reformklöster. Hildesheim, 1975. p. 99-111)
MnCS

1681 **West, Andrew Fleming.**
Alcuin and the rise of the Christian schools. New York, C. Scribner's Sons, 1892.
205 p. (The great educators, v. 2)
NcBe

1682 **Wilson, Debora, Sister, O.S.B.**
Benedictine higher education and the development of American higher education.
xvi, 335 p. 22 cm.
Thesis (Ph.D.)–University of Michigan, 1969.
Xeroxed by University Microfilms, Ann Arbor, Mich.
InStme; PLatS

1683 **Zimmer, Kathryn, Sister, O.S.B.**
Role of American Benedictine institutions of higher education for women.
5 leaves, 28 cm.
Summary of a doctoral dissertation, Catholic University of America, 1962.
NdBiA; PLatS

9. BENEDICTINES AND LITERATURE

1684 **Diemer, Joseph.**
Deutsche Gedichte des XI. und XII. Jahrhunderts . . . Wien, Wilhelm Braunmüller, 1849.
lxii, 384, 117 p. 26 cm.
Frau Ava, a Benedictine nun, was the author of a number of these early German poems.
MnCS

1685 **Scöverffy, Josef.**
St. Galler Dichter am Ende des 9. Jahrhunderts: Tropen und Anfänge der Sequenzendichtung.
(*In* his Die Annalen der lateinischen Hymnendichtung. Berlin, 1964. v.1, p. 262-312)
PLatS

10. BENEDICTINES AND MEDICINE

1686 **Duft, Johannes.**
Notker der Arzt; Klostermedizin und Mönchsarzt im frühmittel-alterlichen St. Gallen. St. Gallen, Verlag der Buchdruckerei Ostschweiz, 1972.
68 p. illus.
MoCo

1687 **Schipperges, Heinrich.**
Die Benediktiner in der Medizin des frühen Mittelalters. Leipzig, St. Benno-Verlag [1964].
62 p. 20 cm. (Erfurter theologische Schriften, 7)
PLatS

1687a **Stoffler, Hans-Dieter.**
Der Hortulus des Walahfrid Strabo; aus dem Kräutergarten des Klosters Reichenau . . . Sigmaringen, Jan Thorbecke Verlag, 1978.
102 p. illus. 20 cm.
MnCS

11. BENEDICTINES AND MISSIONARY WORK

1688 **Barry, Colman James, O.S.B.**
Upon these rocks; Catholics in the Bahamas. Collegeville, Minn., St. John's Abbey Press [1973].
ix, 582 p. illus. 24 cm.
AStb; InStme; MnCS; OkShG; PLatS

1688a **Beaver, Pierce.**
Benedictines and Indian missions.
(*In* his: The native American Christian community. Monrovia, Calif., 1979. p. 192–93, 163, etc.)

1688b **Dammertz, Victor, O.S.B.**
Benedictine presence in the Third World. Offprint from: The American Benedictine Review, v. 32(1981), p. 14–37.
MnCS

1689 **Demm, Eberhard.**
Reformmönchtum und Slawemission in 12. Jahrhundert. Lübeck & Hamburg, Matthiesen, 1970.
214 p. 24 cm. (Historische Studien, 41)
MnCS

1690 **Kansas monks in Brazil (periodical).**
v. 1–4, 1962–1971. Atchison, Kans., St. Benedict's Abbey.
KAS

1691 **Kasper, Adelhard, O.S.B.**
Hwan Gab; 60 Jahre Benediktinermission in Korea und in der Mandschurei [von] A. Kasper [und] P. Berger. Münsterschwarzach, Vier-Türme-Verlag, 1973.
xi, 368 p. map, plates. 21 cm.
MnCS

1692 **Kent, Mark Leo.**
The glory of Christ; a pageant of two hundred missionary lives from apostolic times to the present age, by Mark L. Kent and Mary Just. Milwaukee, Bruce Pub. Co., 1955.
285 p. 23 cm.
Part II (p. 31-65) is devoted almost entirely to Benedictine missionary saints.
InFer

1693 **Koch, Mary Imelda, Sister, O.S.B.**
By the power of the vine; history of the Missionary Benedictine Sisters in the United States, 1922-1952.
118 p. illus.

Thesis (M.A.)–St. John's University, Collegeville, Minn., 1964.
MnCS

1694 **Missionary Benedictine Sisters.**
Sixtieth anniversary of the Congregation of the Benedictine Missionary Sisters [1885-1945].
32 p. illus. 20 cm.
MnCS

1695 **The missionary work of the Benedictines.** Stratford-on-Avon, St. Gregory's Press, 1881.
41 p.
NcBe

1696 **Plautius, Caspar, abbot of Seitenstetten, fl. 1621.**
Nova typis transacta navigatio. Novi Orbis Indiae Occidentalis admodum reverendissimorum pp. ac ff. reverendissimi ac illustrissimi domini dn. Buellii Cataloni abbatis Montis Serrati, & in universam Americam, sive Novum Orbem Sacrae Sedis Apostolica Romanae a latere legati, vicarij, ac patriarchae: sociorumq monachorum ex Ordine s.p.n. Benedicti ad supradicti Novi Mundi barbaras gentes Christi s. evangelium praedicandi gratia delegatorum sacerdotum dimissi par S. D. D. Papam Alexandrum VI, anno Christi 1492. Nunc primu e varijs scriptoribus in unum collects, & figuris ornata. Authore venerandi fr. don Honorio Philopono Ordinis S. Benedicti monacho. [n.p.] 1621.
3, 101 p. 18 cm. plates (part fold.) 29 cm.
KAS

1697 **Roettger, Gregory John, O.S.B.**
Benedictine missionary method.
(*In* Social justice review, v. 43 (1950), p. 149-153)
PLatS

1698 **U.S. Catholic overseas missionary personnel** . . . Washington, Mission Secretariat.
v. tables. 22 cm.
PLatS

1699 **Watrin, Benno, O.S.B.**
St. Benedict's Mission, White Earth, Minn., 1878-1978. [White Earth, Minn., 1978].
[28] p. illus., ports. 20 cm.
MnCS

12. BENEDICTINES AND MYSTICISM

1700 **L'amour du Coeur de Jésus** contemplé avec les saints et les mystiques de l'Ordre de Saint Benoît; textes recueillis et traduits par les moniales de Ste Croix de Poitiers. 2. éd. Abbaye de Maredsous, 1936.

xvi, 235 p. 18 cm. (Collection "Pax", XXVI)
KAS

13. BENEDICTINES AND PASTORAL WORK

1701 **Benedictines. English Congregation.**
Regulae ab omnibus Congregationis Anglo-Benedictinae in missione laborantibus observandae. Stanbrook, Wigorniae, typis B. Mariae de Consolatione, 1879.
44, [4], 58 p. 16 cm.
KAS

1702 **Doppelfeld, Basilius, O.S.B.**
Mönchtum und kirchlicher Heilsdienst; Enstehung und Entwicklung des nordamerikanischen Benediktinertums im 19. Jahrhundert. Münsterschwarzach, Vier-Türme-Verlag, 1975.
xx, 381 p. 21 cm.
MnCS; PLatS

14. BENEDICTINES AND POPULAR DEVOTIONS

1703 **Barré, Henri.**
Prières anciennes de l'occident à la Mère du Sauveur, des origines à saint Anselme. Paris, P. Lethielleux [1963].
360 p. 26 cm.
PLatS

1704 **Leclercq, Jean, O.S.B.**
Le Secré-Coeur dans la tradition bénédictine au Moyen Age.
(*In* Cor Jesu; commentationes in . . . "Haurietis aquae." Roma, 1959. v. 2, p. 1-28)
PLatS

1705 **Maria Luise di S. Pietro, O.S.B.Cam.**
Esercizio di divozione da pratticarsi nelle dodici domeniche precedente la festa del glorioso patriarca e padre San Benedetto, composto e dedicato all monache dell' Ordine Benedettino. Roma, Francesco Bourlie, 1817.
297 p. 17 cm.
MnCS

15. BENEDICTINES AND PRINTING

1706 **Andreotti, Stanislaus, O.S.B.**
Subiaco, culla dell'Ordine Benedettino, sede della prima tipografia italiana. Subiaco, 1965.
108 p. illus.
MoCo

1707 **Carosi, G. F.**
La stampa da Magonza a Subiaco. Subiaco, Edizioni S. Scolastica, 1976.

139 p. plates, facsims. 24 cm.
MnCS

1708 **Dreyfus, J. G.**
An exhibit of productions from Stanbrook Abbey Press, 1876-1966. Printed in England, 1966.
8 p.
Accompanied exhibit at Margaret I. King Library-Rare Book Room, University of Kentucky, Lexington.
InFer

16. BENEDICTINES AND SCHOLARSHIP

1709 **Duckett, Eleanor Shipley.**
Anglo-Saxon saints and scholars. New York, Macmillan Company, 1947.
x, 488 p. 22cm.
Contents: Aldhelm of Malmesbury; Wilfrid of York; Bede of Jarrow; Boniface of Devon.
ILSH; NcBe; WaOSM

1710 **Knowles, David, O.S.B.**
Saints and scholars; twenty-five medieval portraits. Cambridge [England], University Press, 1962.
207 p. illus. 21 cm.
KAS; NdRi; PLatS

1710a **Kristeller, Paul Oscar.**
Humanists and scholars of the religious orders.
(*In* his Medieval aspects and renaissance learning. Durham, N.C., 1974. p. 126-158)
MnCS; PLatS

1711 **Lindner, Pirmin, O.S.B.**
Kurzer Umriss der literarischen Thätigkeit der Benediktiner in Bayern im achtzehnten Jahrhundert.
(*In* his: Die Schriftsteller . . . des Benediktiner-Ordens in . . . Bayern. Regensburg, 1880. v. 1, p. 14-37)
MnCS

1712 **Lutz, Cora E.**
Schoolmasters of the tenth century [Hamden, Conn.] Archon Books, 1977.
xi, 202 p. 20 cm.
Most of the scholars were Benedictine, with special attention to Dunstan, Abbo of Fleury, Aelfric of Eynsham, Notker III, Wolfgang of Regensburg, Bernward of Hildesheim, Pope Sylvester II.
MnCS

1712a **Scriptores Ordinis S. Benedicti** qui 1750-1880 fuerunt in Imperio Austriaco-Hungarico. Vindobonae, Leon. Woerl, 1881.
cxix, 601 p. 28 cm.
vid. p. lxxix-cxix: De litterarum studiis.
MnCS

1712b **Szczygielski, Stanislas, O.S.B.**
Doctina & studium literarum veterum
Benedictinorum.
(*In* his: Aquila Polono-Benedictina.
Crocoviae, 1663. p. 158-213)
KAS; MnCS

17. BENEDICTINES AND SCIENCE

1713 **Castelli, Benedetto, O.S.B.**
Della misura dell'acque correnti. Roma,
nella Stamparia Camerale, 1628.
3 leaves, 59 p. diagrs. 22 cm.
Benedetto Castelli, a pupil of Galileo, is
the founder of engineering hydraulics.
Locations: John Crerar Library,
Chicago; Massachusetts Institute of
Technology.

1714 **Castelli, Benedetto, O.S.B.**
Risposta alle oppositzioni del s. Lodovico
delle Colombe e del s. Vinzensio di Grazia,
contro trattati del sig. Galileo Galilei, delle
cose che stanno su l'acque, o che in quelle si
muovono. Firenze, appresso Cisimo Giunti,
MDCXV.
319 (i.e. 335) p. 23 cm.
Library of Congress; University of
Michigan

1715 **Richard of Wallingford, Abbot.**
An edition of his writings with introductions, English translation and commentary
by J. D. North. Oxford, Clarendon Press,
1976.
3 v. diagrs. 24 cm.
MnCS

18. BENEDICTINES AND SOCIAL WORK

1716 **Battaglia, Dante, conte.**
S. Benedetto di Norcia; l'apostolo sociale
e i suoi discepoli. Subiaco, Tipografia dei
Monasteri, 1928.
134 p. plates, 21 cm.
MnCS

1717 **Blazovich, Augustin.**
Soziologie des Mönchtums und der
Benediktinerregel. Wien, Herder, 1954.
167 p. 21 cm.
MnCS

1718 **Lentini, Anselmo, O.S.B.**
Vita e missione sociale di S. Benedetto.
(*In* La bonifica benedettine, p. 195-199)
PLatS

19. BENEDICTINES AND THEOLOGY

1719 **Gatch, Milton M.**
Preaching and theology in Anglo-Saxon
England: Aelfric and Wulfstan. Toronto,
University of Toronto Press, 1977.
266 p. 22 cm.

MnCS; InStme

1719a **Mahoney, Edward Joseph.**
The theological position of Gregory
Sayrus, O.S.B., 1560-1602. Ware
(England), Jennings & Bewley, 1922.
152 p. 21 cm.
Doctoral thesis, Fribourg.
MnCS

1719b **La part des moines;** théologie vivante
dans le monachisme français: Solesmes,
Ligugé, Saint-Benoît-sur-Loire, La
Pierre qui Vire, Timadeuc. Introduction
de Pierre Miquel, abbé de Ligugé, postface de Gustave Martelet, S.J. Paris,
Editions Beauchesne [1978].
204 p. 22 cm. (Le Point théologique, 28)
MnCS

1720 **Vandenbroucke, François, O.S.B.**
La morale monastique du XIe au XVe
siècle; pour l'histoire de la théologie
morale. Louvain, Editions Nauwelaerts,
1966.
209 p. 25 cm.
PLatS

20. BENEDICTINES AND WARS
a. Spanish Civil War, 1936-1939

1721 **Los martires de Montserrat;** trabajos
premios y resena de la fiesta celebrada
con motivo del concurso Montserratino
Regina martyrum. Barcelona, La
Hormiga de Oro, 1952.
94 p. illus. 17 cm.

1722   MnCS
Solà, Ferran M., O.S.B.
Gloria nostra; oda als martirs de Mont-
serrat. Barcelona, Libreria La Hormiga de
Oro, 1959.
52 p. illus. 21 cm.
MnCS

1723 **Xifra i Riera, Narcis.**
El 19 de juliol de 1936 al monestir de
Montserrat. Barcelona, Editorial Portic,
1973.
289 p. 19 cm.
MnCS

b. World War II, 1939-1945

See also: Monte Cassino, Italy. Siege,
1944, n. 3025-41.

1724 **Hundstorfer, Rudolf, O.S.B.**
Das Stift unterm Hakenkreuz. Wels,
Druck- und Verlaganstalt Welsermühl
[1961?].
93 p. plates, 24 cm.
Story of Kremsmünster Abbey, Austria,
and the Nazis.
MnCS

1725 **Roth, Benno, O.S.B.**
Beschlagnahme und Enteignung der
Benediktinerabtei Seckau in Obersteier-
mark am 8 April 1940 durch die Gestapo.
[Seckau] 1965.
106 p. 21 cm.
PLatS

21. BENEDICTINES AND WORK

1726 **St. John's Abbey, Collegeville, Minn.**
Symposium three: on work. [Collegeville,
Minn., St. John's Abbey, 1973?].
81 p. 28 cm.
By and for the members of St. John's
Abbey.
Multigraphed.
MnCS

22. HERALDRY, BENEDICTINE

1727 **Müller, Walter.**
Ein Auflassungs- und Investitursymbol
des Klosters St. Gallen: die schwarze
Kappe. Zürich, Juris Druck Verlag, 1972.
55 p. 20 cm. (Rechtshistorische Arbeiten,
Bd. 10)
MnCS

1728 **Zelenka, Ales.**
Die Wappen der Wiener Schotten [von]
Ales Zelenka [und] Walter Sauer, O.S.B.
Wien, Schottenstift, 1971.
40 p. illus. 20 cm.
MnCS

23. LIBRARIES, BENEDICTINE

See also: Manuscripts, Benedictine,
n. 1771-1861.

a. General Works

1729 **Kristeller, Paul Oscar.**
Libraries of religious orders.
(*In* his Medieval aspects of renaissance
learning. Durham, N.C., 1974. p. 121-125)
MnCS; PLatS

1730 **Lesne, Emile.**
Les livres, "scriptoria" et bibliothèque du
commencement du VIII. a la fin du XI. siècle. Lille, Facultés Catholiques (New York,
Johnson Reprint Corp., 1964).
849 p. 26 cm.
MnCS

1730a **Oxford, England. University. Bodleian
Library.**
The Benedictines and the book; an exhibition to commemorate the fifteenth
centenary of the birth of St. Benedict,
A.D., 480-1980. Bodleian Library, Oxford
[1980].

viii, 68 p. 20 cm.
MnCS

1731 **Putnam, George Haven.**
Books and their makers during the Middle Ages; a study of the conditions of the
production and distribution of literature
from the fall of the Roman Empire to the
close of the seventeenth century. New
York, Hillary House Publishers, 1962.
2 vols.
InFer

1732 **Tijurunga; an Australasian Benedictine
review.**
No. 12(1976) is in part dedicated to
libraries, and includes accounts of nine
Benedictine libraries in various countries
and continents.
MnCS

b. By Country

Austria

1733 **Altenburg, Austria (Benedictine abbey).**
Catalogus bibliothecae monasterii Altenburgensis noviter erectae sub auspiciis Rmi
Dni Mauri abbatis, continens libros tam in
cellis quam in bibliotheca existentes. Anno
1679. Auch einige spätere Nachträge. MS.
Benediktinerabtei Altenburg, Austria,
codex AB 5 Bd 89. 57 f. Quarto. Saec.
17(1679).
Microfilm: MnCH proj. no. 6574

1734 **Fiecht, Austria, (Benedictine abbey).**
Verzeichnis der Bibliothek des Stiftes
Fiecht im Jahre 1817 zurückgegebenen
Bücher und Landkarten. MS. Universitäts-
bibliothek Innsbruck, Austria, codex 983.
Folio. Saec. 17.
Verzeichnis eines Theiles der Bibliothek
des Klosters Fiecht. MS. Universitäts-
bibliothek Innsbruck, Austria, codex 983b.
156 f. Quarto. Saec. 18.
Microfilm: MnCH proj. no. 28,736

1735 **Krause, Adalbert, O.S.B.**
Die Stiftsbibliothek in Admont. 7. verb.
Aufl. Linz, Oberösterreichischer
Landesverlag [1969].
43, [3] p. illus. 17 cm.
MnCS

1736 **Kropff, Martinus, O.S.B.**
Bibliotheca Mellicensis; seu, Vitae et
scripta inde a sexcentis et eo amplius annis
Benedictinorum Mellicensium auctore
Martino Kropff, qui etiam catalogum selectorum nonnullorum manuscriptorum addidit, et hic primum ex bibliotheca mss.
Mellicensi publicae luci comisit. [Vin-
dobonae, sumptibus Ioannis Pauli Kraus]
1747.

24, 683, [14], 20 cm.
ILSP; MnCH

1737 **Melk, Austria (Benedictine abbey).**
Aeltester Bibliothekskatalog (15. Jahrhundert). MS. Benediktinerabtei Melk, Austria, codex 1898. 2 vols. Folio. Saec. 15.
Microfilm: MnCH proj. no. 2222

1738 **Melk, Austria (Benedictine abbey)**
Catalogus Mellicensium anno 1487 exaratus a F. Gregorio Gmayner. MS. Benediktinerabtei Seitenstetten, Austria, codex 94, f.201r-280r. Duodecimo. Saec. 15.
Microfilm: MnCH proj. no. 905

1739 **Melk, Austria (Benedictine abbey).**
Ichonographia de bene ordinanda ornandaque bibliotheca Mellicensi ac praecipue conficiendo duplici catalogo . . . 1751. MS. Benediktinerabtei Melk, Austria, codex 1906. 15 f. Quarto. Saec. 18.
Microfilm: MnCH proj. no. 2223

1740 **Melk, Austria (Benedictine abbey).**
Registrum omnium librorum Bibliothecae Mellicensis, et quidem triplex, primo opera auctorum nomina inotuerunt, secundo materiae quarum authores ignorantur, tertio singulorum voluminum. MS. Benediktinerabtei Melk, Austria, codex 874. 227 f. Quarto. Saec. 15(1483).
Microfilm: MnCH proj. no. 1692

1741 **Mittelalterliche Bibliothekskataloge Oesterreichs.** Wien, Verlag der Oesterreichischen Akademie der Wissenschaften, 1915-
v. 28 cm.
MnCS (v. 1-5, 1915-1975)

1742 **Petrus de Arbona, monk of Admont.**
Catalogus librorum bibliothecae Admontensis. MS. Benediktinerabtei Admont, Austria, codex 589. 30 f. Quarto. Saec. 14(1370).
Microfilm: MnCH proj. no. 9619

1743 **Pfaff, Carl.**
Scriptorium und Bibliothek des Klosters Mondsee im hohen Mittelalter. Wien, Böhlau in Kommission, 1967.
118 p. xxiv p. of illus., 24 cm.
MnCS

1743a **Pichler, Theodorich, O.S.B.**
Die Stiftsbibliothek.
(*In* Kremsmünster; 1200 Jahre Benediktinerstift. Linz, 1977. p. 215-225)
MnCS

1744 **Salzburg, Austria (Benedictine abbey).**
Catalogus librorum editorum ab anno 1500-1600 in bibliotheca antiqua et quidem secundum materias (18 divisiones) institutus. MS. Benediktinerabtei St. Peter,

Salzburg, codex b.XIV.1. 607 p. Folio. Saec. 18.
Microfilm: MnCH proj. no. 10,672

1745 **Sankt Georgen am Langsee, Austria (abbey of Benedictine nuns).**
Verzeichnis der für die Hofbibliothek ausgewählten Urkunden des Stiftes St. Georgen am Langsee. MS. Klagenfurt, Austria, Kärntner Landesarchiv, codex GV 9/36. 22 f. Folio. Saec. 19.
Microfilm: MnCH proj. no. 12,869

1746 **Sankt Paul im Lavantthal, Austria, (Benedictine abbey).**
Catalogus librorum in bibliotheca monasterii S. Pauli. MS. Benediktinerabtei St. Paul im Lavantthal, Austria, codex 18/0. 51 f. Folio. Saec. 17(1684).
Microfilm: MnCH proj. no. 12,654

1747 **Vienna, Austria, Schottenstift.**
Catalogus bibliothecae monasterii Scotensis. Pertinet usque ad annum fere 1750. MS. Vienna, Schottenstift, codex 531. 640 f. Folio. Saec. 18.
Microfilm: MnCH proj. no. 4287

1748 **Wenin, Lambert, O.S.B.**
Catalogus librorum bibliothecae monasterii ad S. Lambertum Altenburgi. MS. Benediktinerabtei Altenburg, Austria, codex AB 15 A 2/i. 297 p. Folio. Saec. 19(1864).
Microfilm: MnCH proj. no. 6591

1749 **Wenin, Lambert, O.S.B.**
Personal-Catalog der Stiftsbibliothek zu Altenburg. MS. Benediktinerabtei Altenburg, Austria, codex AB 15 A 2/2. 297 p. Folio. Saec. 19(1864).
Microfilm: MnCH proj. no. 6592

England

1750 **Ker, Neil Ripley.**
Medieval libraries of Great Britain; a list of surviving books. 2d ed. London, Offices of the Royal Historical Society, 1964.
xxxii, 424 p. 25 cm.
PLatS

1750a **Stockdale, Rachel.**
Benedictine libraries and writers.
(*In* The Benedictines in Britain. London, British Library, 1980, p. 62-81)
MnCS

1751 **Wormald, Francis**
The monastic library.
(*In* his The English library before 1700. London, 1958)
MnCS

France

1752 **Nortier, Geneviève.**
Les bibliothèques mediévales des abbayes bénédictins de Normandie: Fecamp,

Le Bec, Le Mont-Michel, Saint-Evroul, Lyre, Jumiéges, Saint-Wandrille, Saint-Ouen. Nouvelle éd. Paris, P. Lethielleux, 1971.
[4], 252 p. facsims, tables.
KAS; MnCS

Germany

1753 **Akademie der Wissenschaften, Munich.**
Mittelalterliche Bibliothekskataloge Deutschlands und der Schweiz. München, Beck, 1918-
v. 29 cm.
PLatS (v. 1-3)

1753a **Brall, Arthur, ed.**
Von der Klosterbibliothek zur Landes-bibliothek; Beiträge zum zweihundert-jährigen Bestehen der Hessischen Landes-bibliothek Fulda. Stuttgart, Anton Hiersemann, 1978.
xi, 503 p. illus. 23 cm. (Bibliothek des Buchwesens, Bd. 6)
The Klosterbibliothek in question is the library of the famous Benedictine abbey in Fulda.
MnCS

1754 **Engelmann, Ursmar, O.S.B.**
Hundert Jahre Bibliothek Beuron.
(*In* Beuron, 1863-1963: Festschrift . . . Beuron, 1963. p. 395-440)
PLatS

1754a **Die illuminierten Handschriften** der Hessischen Landesbibliothek Fulda. Stuttgart, Anton Hierseman, 1976-
vol. 1: 6. bis 13. Jahrhundert.
This library was the former library of the famous Benedictine abbey in Fulda.
MnCS

1755 **Lehmann, E.**
Die Bibliotheksräume der deutschen Klöster im Mittelalter. Berlin, 1957.
50 p. 64 illus.
MnCS

1756 **Mittler, Elmer.**
Die Bibliothek des Klosters S. Peter (auf dem Schwarzwald). Bühl, Baden, Verlag Konkordia, 1972.
280 p. 23 cm.
MnCS

1757 **Piendl, Max.**
Die Bibliotheken zu St. Emmeram in Regensburg, Kallmünz, M. Lassleben, 1971. viii, 101 p. 32 plates, 24 cm.
MnCS

1758 **Sankt Blasien im Schwarzwald, Germany (Benedictine abbey).**
Monumenta typographica in bibliotheca San-Blasiana. MS. Benediktinerabtei St.

Paul im Lavantthal, Austria, codex 122/6. 261 f. Folio. Saec. 18.
Microfilm: MnCH proj. no. 12,621

1759 **Schillmann, Fritz.**
Wolfgang Trefler und die Bibliothek des Jakobklosters zu Mainz . . . Leipzig, O. Harrassowitz, 1913; Nendeln, Kraus reprint, 1968.
vi, 226 p. 23 cm.
Catalog of the library compiled by Wolfgang Trefler in 1513, p. 17-213.
PLatS

Italy

1760 **O'Gorman, James F.**
The architecture of the monastic library in Italy, 1300-1600. Catalogue with introductory essay. New York, Published by New York University Press for the College Association of America, 1972.
xvi, 81 p., 31 p. of illus. 29 cm.
PLatS

1761 **Il patrimonio bibliografico** delle abbazie in Italia. Roma, Istituto Poligrafico dello Stato, 1974.
31 p. illus., map, facsims. 25 cm.
Estratto da: Vita Italiana, n. 11, novembre 1974.
InStme

Switzerland

1762 **Akademie der Wissenschaften, Munich.**
Mittelalterliche Bibliothekskataloge Deutschlands und der Schweiz. München, Beck, 1918-
v. 29 cm.
PLatS (v. 1-3)

1762a **Clark, J. M.**
The abbey of St. Gall as a centre of literature & art. Cambridge, University Press, 1926.
322 p. 20 cm.
vid. p. 273–284: The abbey library and its manuscripts.
MnCS

1763 **Duft, Johannes, ed.**
Die Stiftsbibliothek Sankt Gallen: der Barocksaal und seine Putten. Konstanz, Jan Thorbecke [1961].
95 p. illus., plates. 23 cm.
MnCS

1763a **Weidmann, Franz.**
Geschichte der Bibliothek von St. Gallen, seit ihrer Gründung um das Jahr 830 bis auf 1841. St. Gallen, 1841.
493 p. 20 cm.
Library of Congress; New York Public Library.

United States of America

1764 Dewig, Mary Boniface, Sister, O.S.B.
Study of the Benedictine convent libraries in the United States in view of establishing a library for a newly-founded Benedictine convent.
58 p. map, tables.
Thesis (M.A.)—Rosary College, Chicago, 1959.
InFer

1765 Mount St. Scholastica College, Atchison, Kans.
Dedication of Feeney Memorial Library, Mount St. Scholastica, Atchison, Kans., November 17, 1962.
[18] p. 23 cm.
PLatS

1766 The Off-campus Record, Spring, 1966.
Library dedication issue. Collegeville, Minn., St. John's University, 1966.
[27] p. illus. 28 cm.
PLatS

1767 St. Meinrad Archabbey, St. Meinrad, Ind.
Handbook, Archabbey Library, St. Meinrad, Indiana [1964].
[15] p. 22 cm.
PLatS

1768 St. Vincent Archabbey, Latrobe, Pa. Library.
[Catalogue]
18 v. in 28. 32 cm.
This is a classified subject catalog in book form, begun about 1900 and continued to about 1940. The entries are all in longhand. There is a corresponding author catalog an cards, first in longhand, later typed. The author cards and the books on the shelves carry the call numbers assigned to each book in the classified catalog. The call numbers were devised according to a threefold distinction, namely: first, the broad class indicated by a Roman number; then the breakdown by size (F for folios, Q for quartos, O for octavos, D for duodecimos); then arabic numbers were assigned consecutively as books were under the second breakdown. Example: VIII, F, 1374.

1769 Shoniker, Fintan Raymond, O.S.B.
A study of the Abbey Library, St. Benedict's College, Atchison, Kansas. Made on the occasion of a visit, February 21-23, 1968.
25 leaves, 28 cm.
Typescript.
PLatS

1770 Steiner, Urban James, O.S.B.
Benedictine libraries yesterday and today.
42 leaves. 29 cm.
Thesis (M.A.)—University of Illinois. Graduate School of Library Science, 1960. Multigraphed.
MnCS

24. MANUSCRIPTS, BENEDICTINE

Here are entered catalogs of and works about manuscript collections in Benedictine monasteries. Such collections are preserved as separate collections from the main library.

a. General Works

1771 Hill, Lawrence H., O.S.B.
A history of manuscript production in medieval monasteries. Latrobe, Pa., 1967.
11 leaves. 28 cm.
Typescript.
PLatS

1772 Kristeller, Paul Oscar.
Latin manuscript books before 1600; a list of the printed catalogs and unpublished inventories of extant collections. 3rd ed. New York, Fordham University Press, 1965.
xxvi, 284 p. 25 cm.

b. By Country

Austria

1773 Admont, Austria, (Benedictine abbey).
[Catalog of manuscripts in Stift Admont, Austria].
396 p. 29 cm.
Apud finem: "Deo gratias, Sept. 1888. P. Jacobus."
Handwritten.
Xeroxed copy prepared by University Microfilms, Ann Arbor, Michigan, 1968.
MnCS

1774 Akademie der Wissenschaften, Vienna.
Mittelalterliche Bibliothekskataloge Oesterreichs. Wien, A. Holzhausen, 1915-
v. facsims. 26 cm.
MnCS (v. 1-5, 1915-71)

1775 Catalogs of manuscripts in Austrian monasteries. Published for Monastic Manuscript Microfilm Library, St. John's University, Collegeville, Minnesota [by] University Microfilms, Ann Arbor, Mich., 1972.
6 p. 20 cm.
MnCH

1776 **Checklist of manuscripts** microfilmed for the Hill Monastic Manuscript Library. vol. I: Austria. Pt. 1(1967), 52 p.; Pt. 2(1974), 296 p. Compiled by Julian G. Plante. Hill Monastic Manuscript Library, St. John's Abbey and University, Collegeville, Minn., 1969-72.
MnCH

1777 **Dashian, Jacobus.**
Catalog der Armenischen Handschriften in der Mechitharisten-Bibliothek zu Wien, von P. Jacobus Dashian und P. Hamazasp Oskian. Wien, Mechitharisten-Buchdruckerei, 1895-1965.
2 v. 30 cm.
The entries are listed in Armenian and German.
MnCS

1778 **Fiecht, Tyrol (Benedictine abbey).**
[Catalog (handwritten) of manuscripts in St. Georgen-Fiecht].
unpaged. 25 cm.
Xeroxed by University Microfilms, Ann Arbor, Mich., 1973.
MnCS

1779 **Göttweig, Austria, (Benedictine abbey).**
Manuscripten-Catalog der Stiftsbibliothek zu Göttweig. [n.d.]
3 v. 27 cm.
Handwritten.
Xeroxed by University Microfilms, Ann Arbor, Mich., 1968.
MnCS

1780 **Heimling, Leander, O.S.B.**
Catalogus manuscriptorum bibliothecae Altenburgensis, anno 1924. MS. Benediktinerabtei Altenburg, Austria, codex AB 5 Bb 79. 50 p. Quarto. Saec. 20(1924).
Microfilm: MnCH proj. no. 6576

1780a **Holter, Kurt.**
Die Bibliothek: Handschriften und Inkunabeln.
(*In* Die Kunstdenkmäler des Benediktinerstiftes Kremsmünster. II. Teil, p. 134-220. Wien, 1977)
MnCS

1781 **Kapsner, Oliver Leonard, O.S.B.**
Monastic manuscript microfilm project; progress reports I-V, 1964-68. Collegeville, Minn., St. John's Abbey and University.
Multigraphed.
InStme; KAS; MnCS; PLatS

1782 **Kremsmünster, Austria, (Benedictine abbey).**
Catalogus librorum manuscriptorum antiquorum qui inventi fuerunt in Bibliotheca Cremifanensi. Anno 1631 (geschrieben von P. Matthias Pierbaumer). MS. Benediktin-erabtei Kremsmünster, Austria, codex novus 421. 64 p. Saec. 17.
Microfilm: MnCH proj. no. 403

1783 **Kremsmünster, Austria (Benedictine abbey).**
Catalogus codicum manuscriptorum in Bibliotheca Cremifanensi . . . asservatorum. In memoriam anni a fundato monasterio MC iubilaei edidit P. Hugo Schmid. Lintii, prostat in Libraria Ebenhoechiana, 1877.
2 v. 24 cm. (only the first 100 p. of vol. 1 are printed, the rest is handwritten).
Xeroxed by University Microfilms, Ann Arbor, Mich., 1966.
MnCS

1784 **Kremsmünster, Austria, (Benedictine abbey).**
Catalogus codicum manuscriptorum. Auszug aus dem Katalog des P. Hugo Schmid. Neue codices 1-1361.
2 v. 29 & 25 cm.
Handwritten.
Xeroxed by University Microfilms, Ann Arbor, Mich., 1966.
MnCS

1785 **Kremsmünster, Austria (Benedictine abbey).**
Codices im Schatzkasten [Compilation traced to P. Hugo Schmid].
unpaged. 28 cm.
Handwritten.
Xeroxed by University Microfilms, Ann Arbor, Mich., 1966.
MnCS

1786 **Kropff, Martinus, O.S.B.**
Bibliotheca Mellicensis . . . etiam catalogus selectorum nonnullorum manuscriptorum . . . Vindobonae, sumptibus Ioannis Pauli Kraus, 1747.
24, 683 p. 24 cm.
Xeroxed by University Microfilms, Ann Arbor, Mich., 1978.
ILSP; MnCS (Xerox copy)

1787 **Lambach, Austria (Benedictine abbey).**
Handschriften-Katalog Lambach.
2 v. 28 cm.
Handwritten. Compiled by Petrus Resch, late 18th century.
Xeroxed by University Microfilms, Ann Arbor, Mich., 1966.
MnCS

1788 **Mazal, Otto, ed.**
Handschriftenbeschreibung in Oesterreich; Referate, Beratungen und Ergebnisse der Arbeitstagungen. Wien, Verlag der Oesterreichischen Akademie der Wissenschaften, 1975-

v. 28 cm.
MnCS

1789 Melk, Austria (Benedictine abbey).
Codices manuscripti Bibliothecae Mellicensis. Collegit Frater Stephanus Burckhardus anno Domini 1517.
3 v. 28 cm.
Handwritten.
Xeroxed by University Microfilms, Ann Arbor, Mich., 1966.
Contents: v. 1, Shelflist which gives full contents of the collection (many volumes contain several items, sometimes even many); v. 2, Subject part, alphabetical; v. 3, Author part, alphabetical.
MnCS

1790 Melk, Austria (Benedictine abbey).
Catalogus condicum manu scriptorum qui in Bibliotheca Monasterii Mellicensis O.S.B. servantur. In memoriam anni ab introductis in hoc monasterium Benedictinis octingentesimi a Monasterio Mellicensi editus. Vindobonae, Alfredi Hielder, 1889.
3 v., 6 suppl. 21, 27 cm.
Xeroxed by University Microfilms, Ann Arbor, Mich., 1966.
MnCS

1791 Michaelbeuren, Austria (Benedictine abbey).
Catalogus manuscriptorum qui in bibliotheca Monasterii Burae ad S. Michaelem asservantur. P. Werigand Mayr, O.S.B., 1950.
unpaged. 22 cm.
Xeroxed by University Microfilms, Ann Arbor, Mich., 1968.
MnCS

1792 Mondsee, Austria (Benedictine abbey).
Mantissa chronici Lunae-lacensis bipartita . . . Monach. O. Pedepontani, sumptibus Joannis Gastl, 1749.
[8], 416 p. 20 cm.
"Catalogum manuscriptorum Lunaelacensium, ab aerae christianae saeculo IX. ad XVI. proponit." p. 350–416.
KAS; PLatS

1793 Neumüller, Willibrord, O.S.B.
Die mittelalterlichen Bibliotheksverzeichnisse des Stiftes Kremsmünster, von P. Willibrord Neumüller und Kurt Holter. Linz, Verlag des Amtes der o.-ö. Landesregierung, 1950.
69 p. 26 cm.
MnCS

1794 Salzburg, Austria. St. Peter (Benedictine abbey).
Catalogus manuscriptorum cartaceorum in bibliotheca monasterii ad S. Petrum Salisburgi extantium (443 codices). MS.

Benediktinerabtei St. Peter, Salzburg, codex b.XIV.38. 116, 50 p. Folio. Saec. 18.
Microfilm: MnCH proj. no. 10,668

1795 Salzburg, Austria. St. Peter (Benedictine abbey).
Catalogus manuscriptorum membraneorum in bibliotheca monasterii ad S. Petrum extantium (453 codices). MS. Benediktinerabtei St. Peter, Salzburg, codex b.XIV.39. 168, 46 p. Folio. Saec. 18.
Microfilm: MnCH proj. no. 10,666

1796 Salzburg, Austria. St. Peter (Benedictine abbey).
Catalogus codicum manu scriptorum Bibliothecae Regiae Monacensis: Codices n.15951-15965 Salisburgenses S. Petri. Monachii, sumptibus Bibliothecae Regiae, 1878. Unveränderter Nachdruck, Otto Harrassowitz, Wiesbaden 1969.
These are the manuscripts which were transferred from Salzburg to Munich during the Napoleonic era about 1805.
MnCS

1797 Salzburg, Austria. St. Peter (Benedictine abbey).
[Catalog of manuscripts in Stift St. Peter, Salzburg, Austria. n.d.]
5 v. 19 cm.
Handwritten.
Supplement: Handschriften die im Archiv sind. 1891. 28 cm.
Xeroxed by University Microfilms, Ann Arbor, Mich., 1968.
MnCS

1798 Schweighofer, Gregor, O.S.B.
Die Handschriften des Stiftes Altenburg (Sonderkatalog Nr. 1). 1956.
129 p. 28 cm.
Typescript.
Xeroxed by University Microfilms, Ann Arbor, Mich., 1966.
MnCS

1799 Seitenstetten, Austria (Benedictine abbey).
Catalogus codicum manuscriptorum bibliothecae Seitenstettensis. [n.d.]
2 v. 28 cm.
Handwritten.
Xeroxed by University Microfilms, Ann Arbor, Mich., 1966.
MnCS

1799a Unterkircher, Franz.
Die datierten Handschriften der Oesterreichischen Nationalbibliothek von 1451 bis 1600. Wien, Oesterreichische Akademie der Wissenschaften, 1974-1977.
4 v. 28 cm.
About 200 of the manuscripts belonged to the Benedictine abbey of Mondsee.
MnCS

1800 **Vienna, Austria. Mechitaristen-Kongregation.**
Catalog der Armenischen Handschriften in der Mechitharisten-Bibliothek zu Wien, von P. Jacobus Dashian und P. Hamazasp Oskian. Wien, Mechitharisten-Buchdruckerei, 1895-1963.
2 vols. 30 cm.
The entries are listed in Armenian and German.
MnCS

1801 **Vienna, Austria. Mechitaristen-Congregation.**
Die illuminierten Armenischen Handschriften der Mechitaristen Congregation in Wien. Wien, 1976.
250 p. incl. 80 col. plates. 30 cm.
At head of title: Heide & Helmut Buschhausen unter Mithilfe von Eva Zimmermann.
MnCS

1802 **Vienna, Austria, Schottenstift (Benedictine abbey).**
Catalogus codicum manu scriptorum qui in bibliotheca monasterii B.M.V. ad Scotos Vindobonae servantur. Ex mandato Ernesti Hauswirth edidit Albertus Hüble, O.S.B. Wiesbaden, Martin Sändig [1970].
x, 609 p. 21 cm.
First published 1899.
PLatS

1803 **Wagner, Benedikt, O.S.B.**
Der Religionsfonds versteigert eine alte Stiftsbibliothek.
(*In* Translatio studii . . . Collegeville, Minn., 1973. p. 235-243)
MnCS; PLatS

Bavaria

1804 **Andechs, Bavaria (Benedictine abbey).**
Catalogus codicum manu scriptorum Bibliothecae Regiae Monacensis n. 3001-3132 ex coenobio S. Nicolai in monte sancto Andechs. Monachii, sumptibus Bibliothecae Regiae, 1894.
MnCS

1805 **Aspach, Bavaria (Benedictine abbey).**
Catalogus codicum manu scriptorum Bibliothecae Regiae Monacensis, num. 3201-3261 ex coenobio Ordinis S. Benedicti Aspacensi. Monachii, sumptibus Bibliothecae Regiae, 1894.
MnCS

1806 **Attel, Bavaria (Benedictine abbey).**
Catalogus codicum manu scriptorum Bibliothecae Regiae Monacensis, num. 3301-3348 ex bibliothecae monasterii Ordinis S. Benedicti in Attel. Monachii, sumptibus Bibliothecae Regiae, 1894.
MnCS

1807 **Augsburg, Bavaria. St. Ulrich und Afra (Benedictine abbey).**
Catalogus codicum manu scriptorum Bibliothecae Regiae Monacensis, num. 4301-4432 ex bibliotheca monasterii S. Ulrici Augustae Vindelicorum. Monachii, sumptibus Bibliothecae Regiae, 1894.
MnCS

1808 **Augsburg, Bavaria. St. Ulrich u. Afra (Benedictine abbey).**
Notitia historica-literaria de codicibus manuscriptis in bibliotheca liberi ac imperialis monasterii Ordinis S. Benedicti ad SS. Udalricum et Afram Augustae extantibus. Congessit P. Placidus Braun . . . Augustae Vindelicorum, Petrus Veith, 1791-96.
2 v. in 6 parts.
PLatS(microfilm)

1809 **Benediktbeuern, Bavaria (Benedictine abbey).**
Catalogus codicum manu scriptorum Bibliothecae Regiae Monacensis, n.4510-5046 ex bibl. Benedictoburana. Monachii, sumptibus Bibliothecae Regiae, 1894.
MnCS

1809a **Die Benediktregel in Bayern:** Ausstellung der Bayerischen Staatsbibliothek, 29. November 1980 – 10. Januar 1981. München, Bayerische Staatsbibliothek, 1980.
79 p. 16 plates (part col.) 22 cm.
The exhibit consists of some 80 select precious manuscripts now in the Bayerische Staatsbibliothek, which were collected from the 49 Benedictine abbeys which were dissolved in Bavaria in 1803.
MnCS

1810 **Ebersberg, Bavaria (Benedictine abbey).**
Catalogus codicum manu scriptorum Bibliothecae Regiae Monacensis: Codices Ebersbergenses num. 5801-6059. Monachii, sumptibus Bibliothecae Regiae, 1873. Univeränderter Nachdruck, Otto Harrassowitz, Wiesbaden, 1968.
MnCS

1811 **Freising, Bavaria. S. Maria (Benedictine abbey).**
Catalogus codicum manu scriptorum Bibliothecae Regiae Monacensis: Codices Freisingenses num. 6201-6832. Monachii, sumptibus Bibliothecae Regiae, 1873. Unveränderter Nachdruck, Otto Harrassowitz, Wiesbaden, 1968.
MnCS

1811a **Die Handschriften der Universitätsbibliothek Würzburg.** 2. Bd: Handschriften aus benediktinischen Provien-

zen, bearb. von Hans Thurm. Wiesbaden, Harrassowitz, 1976.
MnCS

1812 **Hauke, Hermann.**
Die mittelalterlichen Handschriften in der Abtei Ottobeuren: Kurzverzeichnis . . . Erstellt im Auftr. d. Generaldirektion d. Bayer. Staalt Bibliotheken. Wiesbaden, O. Harrassowitz, 1974.
122 p. 28 cm.
MnCS

1813 **Mallersdorf, Bavaria (Benedictine abbey).**
Catalogus codicum manu scriptorum Bibliothecae Regiae Monacensis: Codices n.8121-8160 ex bibliotheca monasterii Ord. S. Benedicti in Mallersdorf. Monachii, sumptibus Bibliothecae Regiae, 1874. Unveränderter Nachdruck, Otto Harrassowitz, Wiesbaden, 1968.
MnCS

1814 **Metten, Bavaria (Benedictine abbey).**
Catalogus codicum manu scriptorum Bibliothecae Regiae Monacensis: Codices n.8201-8258 ex monasterio Ord. S. Benedicti in Metten. Monachii, sumptibus Bibliothecae Regiae, 1874. Unveränderter Nachdruck, Otto Harrassowitz, Wiesbaden, 1968.
MnCS

1815 **Munich, Germany. Bayerische Staatsbibliothek.**
Catalogus codicum manu scriptorum Bibliothecae Monacensis, t.V: Codices germanici. Wiesbaden, Otto Harrassowitz, 1920-
v. 24 cm.
The provenance (origin) of German manuscripts, namely, monasteries, etc., is indicated at the end of each volume under "Alte Signaturen."
MnCS (pt. 1-6, 1920-1973)

1816 **Niederaltaich, Bavaria (Benedictine abbey).**
Catalogus codicum manu scriptorum Bibliothecae Regiae Monacensis: Codices n.9475-9493 ex monasterio Niederaltaich. Monachii, sumptibus Bibliothecae Regiae, 1874. Unveränderter Nachdruck, Otto Harrassowitz, Wiesbaden, 1968.
MnCH

1817 **Oberaltaich, Bavaria (Benedictine abbey).**
Catalogus codicum manu scriptorum Bibliothecae Regiae Monacensis: Codices n.9501-9841 ex mon. Oberaltaich. Monachii, sumptibus Bibliothecae Regiae, 1874. Unveränderter Nachdruck, Otto Harrassowitz, Wiesbaden, 1968.
MnCS

1818 **Prüfening, Bavaria (Benedictine abbey).**
Catalogus codicum manu scriptorum Bibliothecae Regiae Monacensis: Codices n.12004-12054 ex monasterio in Prüfening sive Prüfling. Monachii, sumptibus Bibliothecae Reaiae, 1876. Unveränderter Nachdruck, Otto Harrassowitz, Wiesbaden, 1968.
MnCH

1819 **Regensburg, Bavaria. Sankt Emmeram (Benedictine abbey).**
Catalogus codicum manu scriptorum Bibliothecae Regiae Monacensis: Codices n. 14000-15028 ex bibliotheca monasterii Ord. S. Benedicti ad S. Emmeramum Ratisonensis. Monachii, sumptibus Bibliothecae Regiae, 1876. Unveränderter Nachdruck, Otto Harrassowitz, Wiesbaden, 1968.
MnCS

1820 **Rott am Inn, Bavaria (Benedictine abbey).**
Catalogus codicum manu scriptorum Bibliothecae Regiae Monacensis: Codices n. 15501-16633 monasterii Ord. S. Benedicti in Rot ad Oenum. Monachii, sumptibus Bibliothecae Regiae, 1878. Unveränderter Nachdruck, Otto Harrassowitz, Wiesbaden, 1969.
MnCS

1821 **Schäftlarn, Bavaria (Benedictine abbey).**
Catalogus codicum manu scriptorum Bibliothecae Regiae Monacensis: Codices n. 17001-17320 ex monasterio in Scheftlern. Monachii, sumptibus Bibliothecae Regiae, 1878. Unveränderter Nachdruck, Otto Harrassowitz, Wiesbaden, 1969.
MnCS

1822 **Scheyern, Bavaria (Benedictine abbey).**
Catalogus codicum manu scriptorum Bibliothecae Regiae Monacensis: Codices n. 17401-17524 monasterii Schirensis (B. Mariae in comitatu Scheyern). Monachii, sumptibus Bibliothecae Regiae, 1878. Unveränderter Nachdruck Otto Harrassowitz, Wiesbaden, 1969.
MnCS

1823 **Seeon, Bavaria (Benedictine abbey).**
Catalogus codicum manu scriptorum Bibliothecae Regiae Monacensis: Codices n. 17701-17730 ex monasterio in Seon. Monachii, sumptibus Bibliothecae Regiae, 1878. Unveränderter Nachdruck Otto Harrassowitz, Wiesbaden, 1969.
MnCS

1824 **Tegernsee, Bavaria (Benedictine abbey).**
Catalogus codicum manu scriptorum Bibliothecae Regiae Monacensis: Codices n. 18001-20212 ex monasterio in Tegern-

see. Monachii, sumptibus Bibliothecae Regiae, 1878. Unveränderter Nachdruck Otto Harrassowitz, Wiesbaden, 1969.
MnCS

1825 **Thierhaupten, Bavaria (Benedictine abbey).**
Catalogus codicum manu scriptorum Bibliothecae Regiae Monacensis: Codices n. 21001-21121 ex monasterio in Thierhaupten. Monachii, sumptibus Bibliothecae Regiae, 1878. Unveränderter Nachdruck Otto Harrassowitz, Wiesbaden, 1969.
MnCS

1826 **Weihenstephan, Bavaria (Benedictine abbey).**
Catalogus codicum manu scriptorum Bibliothecae Regiae Monacensis: Codices n. 21501-21725 ex bibliotheca monasterii in Weihenstephan. Monachii, sumptibus Bibliothecae Regiae, 1871. Unveränderter Nachdruck Otto Harrassowitz, Wiesbaden, 1969.
MnCS

1827 **Wessobrun, Bavaria (Benedictine abbey).**
Catalogus codicum manu scriptorum Bibliothecae Regiae Monacensis: Codices 22001-22129 ex monasterio S. Benedicti in Wessobrun. Monachii, sumptibus Bibliothecae Regiae, 1871. Unveränderter Nachdruck Otto Harrassowitz, Wiesbaden, 1969.
MnCS

England

1828 **James, Nontague Rhodes.**
Lists of manuscripts formerly in Peterborough Abbey library, with preface and identifications by M. R. James. Oxford, Printed at the Oxford University Press for the Bibliographical Society, 1926.
104 p. 22x18 cm.
MnCS

1829 **Luffield Priory, England.**
Luffield Priory charters . . . Edited, with an introduction, by G. R. Elvey. Jordens [Bucks.], Buckinghamshire Record Society; Oxford Northamptonshire Record Society, 1968-
v. facsims. 25 cm.
MnCS

1830 **Worcester Cathedral, England.**
Catalogue of manuscripts preserved in the chapter library of Worcester Cathedral, compiled by the Rev. John Kestell Floyer . . . and edited and revised throughout by Sidney Graves Hamilton. Oxford, Printed for the Worcestershire Historical Society, by James Parker and Co., 1906.

xviii, 196 p. illus., facsims. 29 cm.
MnCS

France

1831 **Achery, Luc d', O.S.B.**
Veterum aliquot scriptorum, qui in Galliae bibliothecis, maxime Benedictinorum, latuerunt. Parisiis, apud Carolum Savreux, 1665-77.
13 v.
CaQStB; MoCo

1831a **Hesbert, René Jean, O.S.B.**
Les manuscrits musicaux de Jumièges. Macon, Protat Frères, 1954.
102 p. 100 plates (facsims.) 33 cm. (Monumenta musicae sacrae, 2)
InStme; PLatS

1832 **Manuscrits du Mont Saint Michel.**
(*In* Art de Bassee-Normandie, no. 40, p. 17–63)
MnCS

1832a **Montfaucon, Bernard de, O.S.B.**
Bibliotheca bibliothecarum manuscriptorum nova . . . Parisiis, apud Briasson, 1739.
2 v. 40 cm.
In vol. 2 are listed the various Benedictine abbeys in France with the collections of their manuscripts.
MnCS

1832b **Paris. Bibliothèque Nationale.**
Catalogue général de manuscrits latin. Paris, Bibliothèque Nationale, 1939-
v. 24 cm.
Many manuscripts were acquired from dissolved monasteries.
MnCS

1833 **Samaran, Charles.**
Catalogue des manuscrits en écriture latine, portant des indications de date, de lieu ou de copiste. Paris, Centre National de la Recherche Scientifique, 1959-
v. 24 cm.
MnCS

1833a **Stoddard, Whitney S.**
Monastery and cathedral in France: medieval architecture, sculpture, stained glass, manuscripts . . . Middletown, Conn., Wesleyan University Press, [1966].
xxi, 412 p. illus. 29 cm.

Germany

See also Bavaria

1834 **Bischoff, Bernhard.**
Lorsch im Spiegel seiner Handschriften. München, Arben-Gesellschaft, 1974.
128 p. facsims. 24 cm.
MnCS

1835 **Bischoff, Bernhard.**
Die südostdeutschen Schreibschulen und
Bibliotheken in der Karolingerzeit. 2. Aufl.
Wiesbaden, Otto Harrassowitz, 1960-
v. facsims. 25 cm.
MnCS; PLatS

1835a **Houben, Hubert.**
St. Blasianer Handschriften des 11. und
12. Jahrhunderts. München, Arbeo-
Gesellschaft, 1979.
xiii, 220 p. 20 cm. (Münchener Beiträge
zur Mediävistik und Renaissance-
Forschung, 30)
MnCS

1835b **Mittelalterliche Bibliothekskataloge
Deutschlands und der Schweiz.** Hrsg.
von der Bayerischen Akademie der
Wissenschaften in München. München,
C. H. Beck, 1918-
v. 28 cm.
MnCS

1836 **Sankt Blasien im Schwarzwald, Ger-
many (Benedictine abbey).**
Catalogus codicum manuscriptorum ex
monasteriis S. Blassi in Nigra Silva et
Hospitalis ad Pyrhum Montem in Austria
nunc in monast. S. Pauli in Carinthia.
[113], 30 p. 29 cm.
Handwritten. Nachtrag typewritten.
Xeroxed by University Microfilms, Ann
Arbor, Mich., 1967.
MnCS

1837 **Weingarten, Germany (Benedictine
abbey).**
Die Handschriften des Klosters Weingarten, von Karl Löffler. Unter Beihilfe
von Dr. Scherer-Fulda. Leipzig, O. Harrassowitz, 1912; Nendeln, Kraus Reprint,
1968.
iv, 185 p. 24 cm.
PLatS

Italy

1838 **Allodi, Leone, O.S.B.**
Inventario dei manascritti della biblio-
theca di Subiaco. Forli, Casa editrice Luigi
Berlandini, 1891.
74 p. 29 cm.
MnCS

1839 **Caravita, Andrea, O.S.B.**
I codici e le arti a Monte Cassino. Monte
Cassino, pei tipi della Badia, 1870.
3 v.
MoCo

1840 **Mattei-Cerasoli, Leone, O.S.B.**
Codices Cavenses descripsit D. Leo
Mattei-Cerasoli, O.S.B. [Arpino, Società
Tipografica Arpinate] 1935-

v. 30 cm.
Only Pars I was published: Codices mem-
branacei.
MnCS (v. 1)

1841 **Mongelli,Giovanni, O.S.B.**
I codici dell'Abbazia di Montevergine.
Montevergine, Edizioni del Santuario
[1959].
53 p. 24 cm.
MnCS

1842 **Monte Cassino, Italy (Benedictine
abbey).**
Codicum Casinensium manuscriptorum
catalogus, cura et studio monachorum S.
Benedicti archicoenobii Montis Casini . . .
Montis Casini; Romae, ex Typographia
Pontificia Instituti Pii IX, 1915-1941.
3 v. 31 cm.
InStme; MnCS; NcBe

1843 **Monte Cassino, Italy (Benedictine
abbey).**
Paleografia artistica di Montecassino.
Montecassino, Litografia di Montecassino,
1874-1884.
7 pts. in 1 vol., plates, facsims. 38 cm.
MnCS

1844 **Monte Cassino, Italy (Benedictine
abbey).**
La paleografia artistica nei codici
Cassinesi applicata ai lavori industriali.
Litografia di Montecassino, 1910.
[2] p. 20 plates in portfolio, 34 cm.
MnCS

1845 **Montevergine, Italy (Benedictine abbey).**
Regesto delle pergamene. A cura di
Giovanni Mongelli. Roma, 1956-58.
6 v. facsims. 26 cm.
MnCS

1846 **Ruysschaert, José.**
Les manuscrits de l'Abbaye de Nonantola; table de concordance annotée et index
des manuscrits. Città del Vaticano,
Bibliotheca Apostolica Vaticana, 1955.
xxviii, 539 p. 26 cm. (Studi e testi, 182)
PLatS

1847 **Turin, Italy. Biblioteca nazionale.**
Codici bobbiesi nella Bibliotheca na-
zionale di Torino, indicati e descritti da
Giuseppe Ottino. Torino-Palermo, C.
Clausen, 1890.
viii, 72 p. 25x18 cm.
MnCS

1848 **Tosti, Luigi, O.S.B.**
Scritti vari. Roma, Tip. della Camera dei
deputati, 1886-90.
2 v. 22 cm.
KAS

1849 **Venice, Italy. San Lazzaro (Mechitarist Benedictine abbey).**
Armenian miniature paintings of the monastic library at San Lazzaro [by] Mesrop Janashian. English version of the text by Bernard Grebanier. Venice, Armenian Press, San Lazzaro, 1966-
  v. chiefly col. facsims. 46 cm.
PLatS

Spain

1850 **Checklist of manuscripts** microfilmed for the Hill Monastic Manuscript Library. Vol. II: Spain, pt. 1. Compiled by Julian G. Plante, with a comprehensive index by Donald Yates. Collegeville, Minn., St. John's University, Hill Monastic Manuscript Library, 1978.
  v, 295 p. 28 cm.
MnCH

1851 **Montserrat, Spain (Benedictine abbey).**
[Catalog of manuscripts].
  3 vols. 29 cm.
  Handwritten.
  Xeroxed by University Microfilms, Ann Arbor, Mich., 1974.
MnCS

1852 **Olivar, Alexandre, O.S.B.**
Catalog dels manuscrits de la bibliotheca del monestir de Montserrat. Monestir de Montserrat, 1977.
  xxiv, 562 p. 25 cm.
InStme; MnCS

1853 **Olivar, Alexandre, O.S.B.**
Els manuscrits litúrgics de la biblioteca de Montserrat. Monestir de Montserrat, 1969.
  211 p. 25 cm.
MnCS

1854 **Santo Domingo de Silos, Spain (Benedictine abbey).**
Los manuscritos del real monasterio de Santo Domingo de Silos, por Walter Muir Whitehill, jr., & Justo Pérez de Urbel, O.S.B. Madrid, Tipografia de la "Rivista de archivos," 1930.
  85 p. xi facsims. 24 cm.
MnCS (Xerox)

Switzerland

1855 **Bouveret, Switzerland. Saint-Benoît de Port-Valais (Benedictine abbey).**
Colophons de manuscrits occidentaux des origines au XV. siècle [par les] Bénédictins du Bouveret. Fribourg, Suisse, Editions Universitaires, 1965-
  v. 22 cm. (Spicilegii Friburgensis Subsidia, v. 2-
MnCS (V. 1-5, A-O, 1965-76)

1856 **Duft, Johannes.**
Hochfeste im Gallus-Kloster: die Miniaturen im Sacramentarium Codex 341, 11. Jahrhundert, mit Texten aus der Stiftsbibliothek Sankt Gallen. Beuron, Kunstverlag, 1963.
  80 p. illus. 23 cm.
MnCS; PLatS

1857 **Duft, Johannes.**
Irische Handschriften in der Stiftsbibliothek zu St. Gallen.
  (*In* Killer, Peter. Das Irland der Mönche. Zurich, 1970. p. 29-43)
MnCS

1858 **Einsiedeln, Switzerland (Benedictine abbey).**
Handschriften aus schweizerischen Benediktinerklöstern, 8.–18. Jahrhundert; Ausstellung (Stiftsbibliothek Einsiedeln), Juni–November, 1971.
  unpaged, 21 cm.
MnCS

1859 **St. Gall, Switzerland (Benedictine abbey).**
Verzeichniss der Handschriften der Stiftsbibliothek von St. Gallen. Hrsg. auf Veranstaltung und mit Unterstützung des Kath. Administrationsrathes des Kantons St. Gallen. Halle, Verlag der Buchhandlung des Waisenhauses, 1875.
  xii, 650 p. 24 cm.
MnCS

1860 **Scherer, Gustav.**
St. Gallische Handschriften. In Auszügen hrsg. von Gustav Scherer. St. Gallen, Huber und Comp., 1859.
  92 p.
PLatS (microfilm)

United States

1861 **Ecker, Gerald Robert, O.S.B.**
A descriptive catalog of the Carolingian manuscripts in Conception Abbey Library.
  67 p. 29 cm.
  Thesis (M.A.L.S.) – Rosary College, River Forest, Ill., 1955.
  Typescript.
MnCS; MoCo

25. MEDAL OF ST. BENEDICT

1862 **M., H. W. comp.**
A short explanation & history of the Medal or Cross of Saint Benedict, with a list of indulgences and conditions for gaining them, and the form for blessing the Medal. London, R. & T. Washbourne, 1907.
  15 p.
NcBe

1863 **McCann, Justin, O.S.B.**
The early history of the Benedictine Medal.
Offprint: Ampleforth journal, v. 38(1933), p. 83–94
NcBe

1864 **Regla del gran patriarcha S. Benito.**
Madrid, Antonio Sanz, 1746.
Partial contents: 4. Benedictio numismatis.
MnCS

1865 **Satan and the Medal of St. Benedict.**
(*In* Janvier, Abbé. The holy man of Tours. Baltimore, 1884. p. 185–203)
AStb

26. POSTAGE STAMPS

1866 **Yochum, Lucy, Sister, O.S.B.**
St. Benedict and the Benedictines on postage stamps. [Ferdinand, Ind., Convent of the Immaculate Conception]
[10] p. illus. 30 cm.
The article appeared in The Cross Chronicle, vols. 13–14, 1961–62.
Available on slides.
InFer; PLatS (slides)

27. SCAPULAR OF ST. BENEDICT

1867 **The second booke of the dialogues of S. Gregorie the Greate** . . . and A short treatise touching the Confraternitie of the Scapular of St. Benedicts Order.
Ilkley [England], Scolar Press, 1976.
Facsimile reprint of the 1639 edition.
MnCS; PLatS

28. SCRIPTORIA

1868 **Bick, Josef.**
Die Schreiber der Wiener griechischen Handschriften. Wien, Museion, 1920.
126 p. facsims. 36 cm.
MnCS

1869 **Bischoff, Bernhard.**
Libri Sancti Kyliani: die Würzburger Schreibschule und die Dombibliothek im 8. und 9. Jahrhundert. Würzburg, F. Schöningh, 1952.
200 p. facsims. 22 cm.
MnCS

1870 **Bourgeois-Lechaftier, Michel.**
Le Scriptorium de Mont Saint-Michel. Paris, P. Lethielleux, 1967.
72 p. illus. 24 cm.
MnCS

1871 **Bradley, John William.**
A dictionary of miniaturists, illuminators, calligraphers, and copyists, with reference to their works, and notice of their patrons, from the establishment of Christianity to the eighteenth century. London, B. Quaritsch, 1887–89; New York, Burt Franklin [n.d.].
3 v. 24 cm.
MnCS

1872 **Bruckner, Albert Theophil.**
Scriptoria medii aevi helvetica; Denkmäler schweizerischer Schreibkunst des Mittalalters. Genf, Roto-Sadag, 1935–
v. facsims. 40 cm.
MnCS (v. 3–13)

1873 **Erklärung über die Schreibkunst** der Bücher Georgs aus Sis und Aristakes. MS. Mechitaristenkongregation, Vienna, codex 593, f.317r–325v. Octavo. Saec. 15(1414).
Microfilm: MnCH proj. no. 8148

1874 **Forstner, Karl.**
Die Anfänge des Salzburger Schriftwesen.
(*In* Handschriftenbeschreibung in Oesterreich, hrsg. von Otto Mazel. Wien, 1975. p. 13–20)
MnCS

1875 **Gasquet, Francis Aidan, O.S.B.**
Sketches of mediaeval monastic life: III, the scriptorium. Yeovil [England], Printed by the Western Chronicle Co. [1892].
12 p. 22 cm.
The article also appeared in: Downside review, v. 11(1892), p. 3–10)
KAS

1876 **Hill, Lawrence, O.S.B.**
A history of manuscript production in medieval monasteries. Latrobe, Pa., 1967.
11 leaves, 28 cm.
Typescript.
PLatS

1877 **Holter, Kurt.**
Buchmalerei und Federzeichnungsinitialen im hochmittelalterlichen Skriptorium von Kremsmünster.
(*In* Handschriftenbeschreibung in Oesterreich, hrsg. von Otto Mazal. Wien, 1975. p. 41–50)
MnCS

1878 **Jones, L. W.**
The script of Cologne, from Hildebald to Hermann. Cambridge, Mass., Medieval Academy of America, 1932.
xi, 98 p. facsims. 39 cm.
MnCS

1879 **Klose, Josef.**
Das Urkundenwesen Abt Hermann von Niederaltaich (1242–1273), seine Kanzlei und Schreibschule. Kallmünz, M. Lassleben, 1967.

xi, 167 p. 25 cm.
MnCS

1880 **Krüger, Ekkehard.**
Die Schreib- und Malwerkstatt der Abtei
Helmarshausen bis in die Zeit Heinrichs
des Löwen. Darmstadt und Marburg,
Selbstverlag der Hessischen Historis-
chen Kommission, 1972.
3 v. 103 plates, diagrs. 22 cm.
MnCS

1881 **Lesne, Emile.**
Les livres, "scriptoria" et bibliothèques
du commencement du VIII. a la fin du XI.
siècle. Lille, Facultés Catholiques, 1938;
New York, Johnson Reprint Corp., 1964).
849 p. 26 cm.
MnCS

1882 **Lowe, Elias Avery.**
The Beneventan script; a history of the
South Italian minuscule. Oxford, Claren-
don Press, 1914.
xix, 384 p. facsims. 26 cm.
MnCS

1882a **Mateu Ibars, Josefina.**
Bibliografia paleografica. Barcelona,
Universidad de Barcelona, 1974.
xxviii, 932 p. illus. 24 cm.
Special mention of Bobbio, Corbie, Lux-
euil, Nonantola and Saint Gall.
MnCS

1883 **Melk, Austria (Benedictine abbey).**
A fifteenth-century modus scribendi
from the Abbey of Melk. Cambridge,
Printed at the University Press, 1940.
xxiv, 31 p. front. 23 cm.
MnCS

1884 **Natale, Alfio Rosario.**
Influenze merovingiche e studi
calligrafici nello scriptorium di Bobbio
(secoli VII–IX). Milano, Biblioteca Ambro-
siana [n.d.].
40 p. facsims. 30 cm.
Estratto dai Fontes Ambrosiani, XXVI;
miscellanea G. Galbiati, v. II, 1951.
MnCS

1885 **Pfaff, Carl.**
Scriptorium und Bibliothek des Klosters
Mondsee im hohen Mittelalter. Wien,
Böhlau in Kommission, 1967.
118 p. xxiv p. of illus., 24 cm.
MnCS; PLatS

1886 **Newton, Francis.**
The Desiderian scriptorium at Monte
Cassino; the chronicle and some surviving
manuscripts.
(*In* Dumbarton Oaks papers, no. 30(1967),
p. 35–54)
MnCS

1887 **Rand, Edward Kennard.**
A survey of the manuscripts of Tours.
Cambridge, Mass., Medieval Academy of
America, 1929.
2 v. facsims. 32 cm. (Studies in the script
of Tours, I)
MnCS

1888 **Rössl, Joachim.**
Entstehung und Entwicklung des Zwet-
tler Skriptoriums im 12. Jahrhundert.
(*In* Handschriftenbeschreibung im
Oesterreich, von Otto Mazal. Wien, 1975.
p. 91–104)
MnCS

1889 **Scriptorum opus;** Schreiber-Mönche am
Werk. Prof. Dr. Meyer zum 65. Geburt-
stag am 21. September 1971. Wiesbaden,
L. Reichert [1971].
31 p. illus. 33 cm.
MnCS

1890 **Staerkle, Paul.**
Der Schreiberstand.
(*In* his Die Rückermerke der älteren St.
Galler Urkunden. St. Gallen, 1966.
p. 40–47)
MnCS

1891 **Stiennon, Jacques.**
Paléographie du Moyen Age. Paris, A.
Colin, 1973.
352 p. illus. 23 cm.
MnCS

1892 **Stoddard, Whitney S.**
Illuminated manuscripts.
(*In* his Monastery and cathedral in
France. Middleton, Conn., 1966. p. 343–
354)
MnCS

1893 **Trithemius, Johannes, O.S.B.**
In praise of scribes. De laude scrip-
torium. Edited with introduction by Klaus
Arnold. Translated by Roland Behrendt,
O.S.B. Lawrence, Kans., Coronado Press,
1974.
viii, 111 p. illus. 22 cm.
KAS; MnCS; PLatS

1894 **Vezin, Jean.**
Les scriptoria d'Angers au XIe siècle.
Paris, H. Champion, 1974.
xiii, 347, 53 p. illus. 30 cm.
MnCS

1895 **Vogel, Marie.**
Die griechischen Schreiber des Mittelalters und der Renaissance.
xiv, 508 p. 24 cm.
MnCS

1896 **Walliser, Franz.**
Cistercienser Buchkunst; Heiligenkreuzer Skriptorium in seinem ersten

Jahrhundert, 1133–1230. Heiligenkreuz,
Wien, Heiligenkreuzer Verlag, 1969.
  44 p. 44 leaves of illus. 28 cm.
  MnCS

1897 **Wattenbach, Wilhelm.**
  Das Schriftwesen im Mittelalter. 4.
verm. Aufl. Graz, Akademiische Druck u.
Verlagsanstalt, 1958.
  670 p. 23 cm.
  MnCS

VIII. BENEDICTINE HISTORY

1. GENERAL WORKS

1898 **Belloc, J. T. de.**
La postérité de saint Benoît. Paris, Lamulle et Poisson, 1900.
xxxiv, 274 p. plates, 22 cm.
InStme

1899 **Bérengier, Théophile, O.S.B.**
Historical sketch of western monachism.
various pagings 28 cm.
Translation and adaptation made by Rev. Basil Stegmann, O.S.B.
Typescript.
MnCS

1900 **Bracco, Leone, O.S.B.**
Histoire de l'Ordre de S. Benoît.
(*In* Analecta juris pontificii, vol. V(1876), p. 513–546, 641–654)
AStb

1901 **Daly, Lowrie John, S.J.**
Benedictine monasticism, its formation and development through the 12th century. New York, Sheed and Ward [1965].
xv, 375 p. 22 cm.
ILSP; MnCS; PLatS

1902 **Frank, Karl Suso.**
Grundzüge der Geschichte des christlichen Mönchtums. Darmstadt, Wissenschaftliche Buchgesellschaft, 1975.
208 p. 21 cm.
MnCS

1903 **Gasquet, Francis Aiden, O.S.B.**
Saggio storico della constituzione monastica. Versione dell'inglese. Roma, Tipografica Vaticana, 1896.
72 p. 21 cm.
KAS

1903a **Hostie, Raymond.**
Vie et mort des ordres religieux; approches psychosociologiques. Paris, Desclée de Brouwer [1972].
381 p. maps, 24 cm.
See index under Benedictines and under names of Benedictine abbeys and congregations.
MnCS

1904 **Hunkeler, Leodegar, O.S.B.**
The historical development of Benedictine monasticism. [Mt. Angel, Or., 1951].
122 p. 28 cm.
A translation from the German.
Mimeographed.
KAS; WaOSM

1905 **Hunkeler, Leodegar, O.S.B.**
Uebersicht über die geschichtliche Entwicklung des benediktinschen Mönchtums. [Abtei Engelberg, Switzerland, 1946].
200 p.
Class lectures for novices, privately printed.
MoCo

1906 **Laporte, Jean, O.S.B.**
Histoire et vie monastiques. Paris, P. Lethielleux, 1966.
820 p. illus. 24 cm.
MnCS; PLatS

1907 **Leroy, Alfred.**
Quinze siècles de vie monastique: Comment ont-ils vécu? Comment vivent-ils? Bénédictins, Trappistes, Chartreux Franciscains, Augustins, Carmes, Dominicains. [Paris] Spes [1965].
235, [30] p. 19 cm.
PLatS

1908 **Frank, Karl Suso.**
Grundzüge der Geschichte des christlichen Mönchtums. Darmstadt, Wissenschaftliche Buchgesellschaft, 1975.
x, 208 p. 19 cm.
MnCS

1909 **Masoliver, Alejandro Maria.**
Historia del monaquisme cristia. Barcelona, Abadia de Montserrat, 1978–
v.
MnCS

1910 **Mège, Antoine Joseph, O.S.B.**
La vie de saint Benoît par s. Grégoire le Grand; avec une explication des endoits les plus importans, et un abrégé de l'histoire de son Ordre. Paris, Charles Robustel, 1690.
[48], 617 p.
CaQStB

1911 **Mohler, James A.**
The heresy of monasticism; the Christian monks: types and anti-types, an historical survey. Staten Island, N.Y., Alba House [1971].
xviii, 263 p. illus., maps. 22 cm.
InStme; NcBe

1912 **Toynbee, Arnold Joseph.**
Man at work in the light of history.
(*In* Protestant Episcopal Church in the U.S.A. Diocese of Albany. Man at work in God's world. New York, 1956. p. 3–41)
KAS

1913 **Wion, Arnold, O.S.B.**
Brieve dechiaratione dell'arbore monastico benedittino, intitolato Legno della vita causta da i cinque libri dechiarativi di detto arbore. Venetia, G. Angelieri, 1594.
144, 8 p. 15 cm.
KAS

1914 **Wishart, Alfred Wesley.**
A short history of monks and
monasteries. Trenton, N.J., Albert Brandt
Publisher, 1902.
462 p.
InFer

1915 **Yepes, Antonio de, O.S.B.**
Chronicon generale Ordinis S. Benedicti
patriarchae monachorum. Hispanice conditum, a Thoma Weiss lingua romana
donavit auxitq. Coloniae, Constantin
Münich, 1648.
2 v. 31 cm.
The first two volumes of the seven-
volume Spanish work published
1609–1621.
KAS

1916 **Yepes, Antonio de, O.S.B.**
Crónica general de la Orden de San
Benito. Estudio preliminar y edición por
Fray Justo Pérez de Urbel, O.S.B. Madrid,
Ediciones Atlas, 1959–60.
3 v. 25 cm.
MnCS; PLatS

2. EARLY PERIOD

1917 **Angenandt, Arnold E.**
Monachi peregrini; Studien zu Pirmin
und den monastischen Vorstellungen des
frühen Mittelalters. München, W. Fink,
1972.
269 p. 28 cm.
MnCS

1918 **Chronica Ordinis S. Benedicti.** Tomus
secundus: centuria secunda. MS. Vienna,
Schottenstift, codex 613. 22 f. Quarto.
Saec. 17.
Microfilm: MnCH proj. no. 4269

1919 **Décarreaux, John.**
Die Mönche und die abendländische
Zivilisation. [Aus dem Französischen über-
tragen von Leopold Voelker]. Wiesbaden
Rheinische Verlags-Anstalt [1964].
399 p. maps. 22 cm.
MnCS

1920 **Décarreaux, Jean.**
Monks and civilization, from the bar-
barian invasions to the reign of
Charlemagne. Translated by Charlotte
Haldane. Garden City, N.Y., Doubleday,
1964.
397 p. 22 cm.
InFer; KAS; MnCS; MoCo

1921 **Deseille, Placide, O.C.S.O.**
L'Evangile au dessert; des premiers
moines à Saint Bernard. Paris, Les Editions du Cerf [1965].
320 p.
MoCo

1922 **Duckett, Eleanor.**
Gateway to the Middle Ages:
monasticism. Ann Arbor, University of
Michigan Press, 1971.
262 p.
InFer

1923 **Frühes Mönchtum im Abendland:** ausgewählte Texte, eingeleitet, übersetzt
und erklärt von Karl Suso Frank. Zürich
und München, Artemis Verlag, 1975.
2 v. 18 cm.
MnCS

1924 **Hedley, John Cuthbert, O.S.B.**
The monasticism of St. Gregory the
Great.
(*In* The Centenary of St. Gregory the
Great at Downside. Downside, 1890.
p. 29–40)
PLatS

1925 **Initia consuetudinis Benedictinae;** consuetudines saeculi octavi et noni. Cooperantibus D. Petro Becker, O.S.B., [et al.]
publici iuris fecit Kassius Hallinger,
O.S.B. Siegburg, F. Schmitt, 1963.
cxxiii, 626 p. 26 cm. (Corpus consuetudinum monasticarum, t. 1)
InStme; PLatS

1925a **Laske, Walther.**
Das Problem der Mönchung in der
Völkerwanderungszeit. Zürich, Juris
Verlag, 1973.
134 p. 21 cm. (Rechtshistorische
Arbeiten, Bd. 11)
MnCS

1926 **Monumenta Germaniae historica** inde ab
anno Christi quingentesimo usque ad
annum millesimum et quingentesimum.
MnCS; PLatS

1927 **Prinz, Friedrich.**
Frühes Mönchtum im Frankenreich;
Kultur und Gesellschaft in Gallien, den
Rheinlanden und Bayern am Beispiel der
monastischen Entwicklung (4. bis. 8.
Jahrhundert). Wien, Oldenbourg, 1965.
633 p. maps (in pocket) 24 cm.
KAS

1928 **Smith, Isaac Gregory.**
Christian monasticism, from the fourth
to the ninth centuries of the Christian era.
London, A. D. Innes and Co., 1892.
351 p.
NcBe

1929 **Willmes, Peter.**
Der Herrscher 'Adventus' im Kloster des
Frühmittelalters. München, Wilhelm Fink
Verlag, 1976.
205 p. 24 cm.
MnCS

3. MIDDLE AGES

1930 **Ambroise, Georges.**
Les moines du moyen age; leur influence intellectuelle et politique en France. [2. éd.] Paris, A. Picard, 1946.
First published 1942.
KAS; MnCS

1931 **Berlière, Ursmer, O.S.B.**
Les origines de Cîteaux et l'Ordre bénédictin au XIIe siècle. Louvain, C. Peeters, 1901.
64 p. 25 cm.
KAS; MnCS

1932 **Blecker, Michael, O.S.B.**
The two laws and Benedictine monasticism; a study in Benedictine government, 1198–1216.
327 p. 28 cm.
Thesis (Ph.D.)–University of Wisconsin, 1964.
Xeroxed by University Microfilms, Ann Arbor, Mich.
MnCS; NcBe

1933 **Brooke, Christopher N. L.**
Die grosse Zeit der Klöster, 1000–1300. Basel, Herder, 1976.
272 p. plates (part col.), maps, plans. 32 cm.
InStme

1934 **Brooke, Christopher N. L.**
The monastic world, 1000–1300. New York, Random House; London, Elek [1974].
272 p. illus. 32 cm.
MnCS; MoCo

1935 **Centro italiano di studi sull'alto Medioevo.**
Il monachesimo nell'alto Medioevo e la formazione della civiltà occidentale [settimana di studi] 8–14 aprile, 1946. Spoleto, 1957.
625 p. plates, facsims. 21 cm.
Contributions in Italian, French or German.
InStme

1936 **Constable, Giles.**
Medieval monasticism; a select bibliography. Toronto, University of Toronto Press, 1976.
xx, 171 p. 23 cm. (Toronto medieval bibliographies, 6)
InStme; MnCS

1937 **Constable, Giles.**
Monastic tithes, from their origins to the twelfth century. Cambridge [England], University Press, 1964.
346 p.
MnCS; NcBe

1938 **Consuetudines Benedictinae variae**
(saec. XI–XIV). Publici juris fecit Giles Constable. Siegburg, F. Schmitt success., 1975.
395 p. 26 cm. (Corpus consuetudinum monasticarum, t. 6)
PLatS

1939 **Coulton, George Gordon.**
Five centuries of religion. Cambridge [England], University Press, 1923–50.
4 v. illus. 23 cm.
Vol. 4: The last days of medieval monachism.
MnCS

1939a **Dal Pino, Franco Andrea.**
Rinnovamento monastico-clericale e movimenti religiosi evangelici nei secoli X–XIII. Roma, Istituto Storico O.S.M., 1977.
274 p. 24 cm.
See index under Benedettini & under Regola di S. Benedetto.
MnCS

1940 **Daly, Lowrie John, S.J.**
Benedictine monasticism, its formation and deveolpment through the 12th century. New York, Sheed and Ward [1965].
xv, 375 p. 22 cm.
CaMWiSb; InStme; AStb; KAS; MnCS; MnStj; MdRi; PLatS; ViBris

1941 **Demm, Eberhard.**
Reformmönchtum und Slawemission im 12. Jahrhundert. Lübeck & Hamburg, Matthiesen, 1970.
214 p. 24 cm.
MnCS

1942 **Digby, Kenelm Henry.**
Studien über die Klöster des Mittelalters. Aus dem Englischen übersetzt von A. Kobler. Regensburg, New York, F. Pustet, 1867.
viii, 680 p. 24 cm.
Translation of Book X of his Mores catholici.
KAS

1943 **Hourlier, Jacques, O.S.B.**
L'âge classique, 1140–1378: les religieux. [Paris], Editions Cujas [1974].
567 p.
NcBe

1944 **Kastner, Jörg.**
Historiae fundationum monasteriorum; Frühformen monastischer Institutionsgeschichtsschreibung im Mittelalter. München, Arben-Gesellschaft, 1974.
vii, 193 p. 20 cm.
MnCS

1945 **Leclercq, Jean, O.S.B.**
Textes sur la vocation et la formation des moines au moyen âge.
(*In* Corona gratiarum; miscellanea patristica . . . Eligio Dekkers, O.S.B. . . . oblata. Brugge, 1975. v. 2, p. 169–194)
PLatS

1945a **Löwe, Heinz.**
Von Cassiodor zu Dante; ausgewählte Aufsätze zur Geschichtschreibung und politischen Ideenwelt des Mittelalters. Berlin, New York, Walter de Gruyter, 1973.
342 p. 25 cm.
Includes articles on: Notker von St. Gallen, Regino von Prüm, Petrus Damianus.
MnCS

1946 **Lunardi, Giovanni.**
L'ideale monastico nelle polemiche del secolo XII sulla vita religiosa. Noci, Edizioni "La Scala," 1970.
189 p. 23 cm.
KAS

1947 **Lynch, Joseph H.**
Simoniacal entry into religious life from 1000 to 1260; a social, economic and legal study. Columbus, Ohio State University Press, 1976.
xix, 266 p. 23 cm.
MnCS

1948 **Magrassi Mariano, O.S.B.**
La spiritualità del secolo XII benedettino attraverso gli studi degli ultimi tempi.
(*In* Problemi e orientamenti di spiritualità monastica . . . p. 235–293)
PLatS

1949 **Il monachesimo e la riforma ecclesiastica** (1049–1122); atti della quarta Settimana internazionale di studio, Mendola, 23–29 agosto 1968. Milano, Editrice Vita e pensiero [1971].
540 p. 24 cm.
MoCo; PLatS

1950 **Monumenta Germaniae historica** inde ab anno Christi quingentesimo usque ad annum millesimum et quingentesimum (500–1500).
MnCS; PLatS

1951 **Neumüller, Willibrord, O.S.B.**
Zur Benediktinerreform des heiligen Altmann.
(*In* Der heilige Altmann, Bischof von Passau. Göttweig, 1965. p. 16–22)
PLatS

1952 **Prinz, Friedrich, ed.**
Mönchtum und Gesellschaft im Frühmittelalter. Darmstadt, Wissenschaftlichen Buchgesellschaft, 1976.

459 p. (Wege der Forschung, 312)
MnCS

1952a **Riche, Pierre.**
La vie quotidienne dans l'Empire Carolingien. [Paris], Hachette, [1973].
380 p. 20 cm.
MnCS

1953 **Taylor, H. O.**
Mental aspects of eleventh-century France.
(*In* his The medieval mind. 1919. v. 1, p. 282–307)
AStb

1954 **Werner, Ernst.**
Die gesellschaftlichen Grundlagen der Klosterreform im 11. Jahrhundert. Berlin, Deutscher Verlag der Wissenschaften, 1953.
128 p. 21 cm.
MnCS

1955 **Zarnecki, George.**
The monastic achievement. New York, McGraw-Hill [1972].
144 p. illus. (Library of medieval civilization)
MoCo; NcBe

1956 **Zimmermann, Gerd.**
Ordensleben und Lebensstandard; die cura corporis in den Ordensschriften des abendländischen Hochmittelalters. Münster, Aschendorff [1973].
2 v. in 1, 23 cm. 23 cm.
PLatS

4. MODERN PERIOD

1957 **Freytas, Miguel Joaquim.**
Notas da analysis benedictina descubertas por Miguel Joachino de Freytas. Madrid, B. Peralta, 1734.
6 leaves, 192 p. 30 cm.
KAS

1958 **Freytas, Miguel Joaquim.**
Novas notas da analysis benedictina descubertas pelo Francisco de Santa Maria . . . dadas a luz por Miguel Joachino de Freytas. Madrid, B. Peralta, 1734.
99 p. 30 cm.
KAS

5. 18TH CENTURY

1959 **Santos, Manuel dos.**
Analysis benedictina. Conclue por documentos e razoens verdadeiras, que a sagrada, e augusta Ordem de S. Bento he a princeza das religions e a mais antiga com precedencia a todas: e defende as sentencas . . . Madrid, por la viuda de Francisco del Hierro, 1732.

[16], 234, 16 p. 30 cm.
KAS

6. 19TH CENTURY

1960 **Doppelfeld, Basilius, O.S.B.**
Mönchtum und kirchlicher Heilsdienst;
Enstehung und Entwicklung des nor-
damerikanischen Benediktinertums im 19.
Jahrhundert. Münsterschwarzach, Vier-
Türme-Verlag, 1974.
xx, 381 p. 21 cm.
InStme; MnCS; PLatS

1961 **Lemcke, Peter Henry, O.S.B.**
Haudegen Gottes: das Leben des P. H.
Lemke, 1796–1882, vom ihm selbst
erzählt. Kommentiert und hrsg. von
Willibald Mathäser. Würzburg, Kommis-
sionsverlag Echter, 1971.
305 p. 21 cm.
InStme; PLatS

7. 20TH CENTURY

1962 **Meeting of the Monastic Superiors** in the
Far East, Bangkok, Thailand, 1968.
A new charter for monasticism; pro-
ceedings. Edited, and with an introduction,
by John Moffitt. Foreword by George N.
Shuster. Notre Dame, University of Notre
Dame Press, 1970.
xv, 335 p. 24 cm.
InFer

1963 **Secretariat de l'aide à l'implantation
monastique.**
Monastic growth: Africa, Asia, Latin
America, Oceania. Paris, Editions Notre
Dame de la Trinité, 1970.
86 p. illus.
MoCo

IX. BENEDICTINE HISTORY: BY LOCALITY

AFRICA

1964 **Rathe, Gerard.**
Mud and mosaics; an African missionary journey from the Niger to the Copper Belt. Westminster, Md., Newman Press, 1960.
191 p.
InFer

AQUITAINE

1965 **Callahan, Daniel Francis.**
Benedictine monasticism in Aquitaine, 935–1030.
198 p.
Thesis (Ph.D.)–University of Wisconsin, 1968.
Xeroxed by University Microfilms, Ann Arbor, Mich.
NcBe

ARKANSAS

1966 **Assenmacher, High, O.S.B.**
A place called Subiaco; a history of the Benedictine monks in Arkansas. Little Rock [Ark.], Rose Publishing Company, 1977.
486 p. illus. 23 cm.
InStme; MnCS; MoCo; ArSu

1966a **Gallagher, Mary Maude.**
100 years of St. Mary's Church, Altus, and its mission, St. Matthew's, Coal Hill [Ark.]. Fort Smith, Ark., Von der Heide Printing and Litho, 1979.
211 p. illus.
ArSu

1967 **Voth, Agnes, Sister, O.S.B.**
Green olive branch. Chicago, Franciscan Herald Press [1973].
351 p.
KAS; MoCo

1968 **Weibel, Johann Eugen.**
The Catholic missions of north-east Arkansas, 1867–1893. Translated from the German by M. Agnes Voth. Edited by Lee A. Dew. [State College?], Printed by Arkansas State University Press, 1967.
109 p. 23 cm.
InFer; KAS; ArJH

1969 **Weibel, Johann Eugen.**
Forty years missionary in Arkansas. Translation [by] Sister M. Agnes. [Jonesboro, Ark., Holy Angels Convent] 1968.
252 p. illus. 23 cm.
ArJH; InStme; KAS; MoCo

ASIA

1970 **Gariador, Benedict.**
Les anciens monastères bénédictins en orient. [Paris] Desclée, De Brouwer [1912].
OkShG

AUSTRALIA

1971 **Hammerstein, L. von, S.J.**
Benediktiner-Gründung: Gründung von Neo-Norcia; Protestanten gegenüber Neo-Norcia; Erfolge in Neo-Norcia.
(*In* his Winfrid. 1895. p. 318–331)
AStb

1972 **Perez, Eugene, O.S.B.**
Kalumburu: the Benedictine Mission and the aborigines, 1908–1975. Kalumburu, West Australia, Kalumburu Benedictine Mission, 1977.
173 p. 8 plates, illus. 23 cm.
KAS

1972a **Shanahan, Mary Margaret.**
Out of time, out of place; Henry Gregory and the Benedictine Order in colonial Australia. Canberra, Australian National University Press, 1970.
xvi, 187 p. 23 cm.
InStme; KAS; MoCo

1973 **Tjurunga;** an Australasian Benedictine review. Published twice yearly for the Benedictines of Australasia. 1– 1971– Benedictine Abbey, New Norcia, Australia.
MnCS; KAS

AUSTRIA

1974 **Akademie der Wissenschaften, Vienna. Historische Kommission.**
Fontes rerum Austriacarum. Oesterreichische Geschichts-Quellen. Wien, K. K. Hof- und Staats-Druckerei, 1849– Graz, Akademische Druck- und Verlagsanstalt, 1964–
v. 20 cm.
PLatS

1975 **Acta visitationis et reformationis** monasteriorum O.S.B. provinciae Salisburgensis sub subscriptione Thomae Herlinger. MS. Vienna, Nationalbibliothek, codex 4969, f.110r–28v. Quarto. Saec. 15.
Microfilm: MnCH proj. no. 18,141

1976 **Catalogi monachorum et monialium O.S.B.:** S. Petri Salzburg, S. Michaelis

547

Burae, Lambach, Nonnberg i Salzburg, Säben i Tyrol. a.d. 1930.
45 p.
AStb

1977 **Copia chartae monasteriis visitatis** in visitatione generali anno Domini 1452. MS. Benediktinerabtei Melk, Austria, codex 916, f.97v–102v. Quarto. Saec. 15.
Microfilm: MnCH proj. no. 1734

1978 **De origine status monastici tractatus.** Cui additur in appendice brevis delucidatio epistolae nuperrime directae ad monasteria O.S.B. in Austria. Auctore quodam benedictino-professo in Austria. Augustae Vindel., M. Huttler, 1889.
24 p. 23 cm.
PLatS

1979 **Differentia cuisdam fratris** de Specu Sancti Benedicti de Austria de Sancto Lamberto. MS. Vienna, Schottenstift, codex 152, f.214r–217r. Octavo. Saec. 15.
Microfilm: MnCH proj. no. 4071

1980 **Epistolae abbatum** (Mellicensis, Lambacensis, etc.) et episcoporum, formae, intimationes, resolutiones, supplicationes, commendationes, petitiones monasticae. MS. Benediktinerabtei Melk, Austria, codex 778, f.48v–302v. Quarto. Saec. 15.
Microfilm: MnCH proj. no. 1618

1981 **Göttweig, Austria (Benedictine abbey).** Das Saal-Buch des Benedictiner-Stiftes Göttweig. Mit Erläuterungen und einem diplomatischen Anhange von Wilhelm Karlin. Wien, Hof- und Staatsdruckerei, 1855. Unveränderter Nachdruck, Graz, 1964.
xii, 440 p. 23 cm. (Fontes rerum Austriacarum)
MnCS

1982 **Klöster im Landt ob der Enss:** Urkunden zur Geschichte der oberösterreichischen Klöster (Kremsmünster, Lambach, Mondsee). MS. Vienna, Nationalbibliothek, codex series nova 3006. 309 f. Folio. Saec. 17.
Microfilm: MnCH proj. no. 20,802

1983 **Klöster in Oberösterreich.** [Linz, 1968].
102 p. illus. 30 cm. (Oberösterreich, Heft 3/4, 1967–68)
PLatS

1984 **Martinus, abbot of Schottenstift, Vienna.** Sermo in visitatione monasteriorum O.S.B. in provincia Salisburgensi. MS. Vienna, Nationalbibliothek, codex 4969, f.103r–108v. Quarto. Saec. 15.
Microfilm: MnCH proj. no. 18,141

1985 **Nicolaus, presbyter cardinal, Apostolicae Sedis legatus per Alemaniam.** Epistola ad religiosas personas provinciae Salisburgensis de visitatione. MS. Benediktinerabtei Melk, Austria, codex 1093, f.417–421. Duodecimo. Saec. 15.
Microfilm: MnCH proj. no. 1846

1986 **Nicolaus de Cusa.** Epistola encyclica ad abbates et abbatissas O.S.B. in provincia Salzburgensi . . . 1451. MS. Vienna, Nationalbibliothek, codex 4975, f.1r–2r. Quarto. Saec. 15.
Microfilm: MnCH proj. no. 18,124

1987 **Patzelt, Erna.** La colonizzazione benedettina in Austria. (*In* La bonifica benedettina, p. 153–171)
PLatS

1988 **Rizelius, Bertholdus, O.S.B.** Sancta et beata Austria; seu, Acta et vitae sanctorum eorum qui . . . eam quam nunc appellamus Austriam regionem olim illustrarunt. Edidit Bertholdus Mellicensis . . . Accessere tres dissertationes . . . Augustae Vindel., Joan. Daniel Hertz, 1750.
[40], 234, [18] p. engraved plates, 34 cm.
Dedication signed: Bertholdus Rizelius.
KAS

1988a **Schineköper, Berent.** Klosteraufhebungen als Folge von Reformation und Bauernkrieg im habsburgischen Vorderöstereich. (*In* Festschrift Friedrich Hausmann, hrsg. von Herwig Ebner. Graz, 1977. p. 489–504)
MnCS

1988b **Scriptores Ordinis S. Benedicti** qui 1750–1880 fuerunt in Imperio Austriaco-Hungarico. Vindobonae, Leon. Woerl, 1881.
cxix, 600 p. 28 cm.
vid. p. v–lxxviii: Ordinis Imperii Austriaco-Hungarii brevis historia.
MnCS

BAHAMAS

1989 **The Bahama Benedictine.** 1947–
MnCS

1990 **Barry, Colman James, O.S.B.** Upon these rocks; Catholics in the Bahamas. Collegeville, Minn., St. John's Abbey Press [1973].
ix, 582 p. illus. 24 cm.
MnCS; PLatS

BAVARIA

1991 **Bavaria benedictina.** Sonderausgabe der Zeitschrift "Bayerland." München [1961?].

68 p. illus. 30 cm.
PLatS

1992 **Hartig, Michael.**
Bayerns Klöster und ihre Kunstschätze,
von der Einführung des Christentums bis
zur Säkularisation zu Beginn des 19.
Jahrhunderts. Ein Bilderbuch für alle
Freunde bayerischer Kunst. Diessen vor
München, J. C. Huber, 1913–
v.
NcBe (v. 1)

1993 **Hemmerle, Josef.**
Die Benediktinerklöster in Bayern.
Augsburg, Kommissionsverlag Winfried-
Werk [1970].
415 p. coats of arms, maps (in pocket)
25 cm. (Germania benedictina, 2).
KAS; MnCS

1994 **Lohmeier, Georg.**
Liberalitas Bavariae von der guten und
weniger guten alten Zeit in Bayern. [Mün-
chen], Ehrenwith, [1971].
344 p. 23 cm.
PLatS

1995 **Rösermüller, Rudolf.**
Die bayerischen Benediktinerklöster in
Wort und Bild. Augsburg, Benno Filser
Verlag, 1929.
9 v. illus.
NcBe (v. 1)

1996 **Walcher, Bernhard.**
Beiträge zur Geschichte der bayerischen
Abtswahlen mit besonderer Berücksich-
tigung der Benediktinerklöster. München,
Kommissionsverlag R. Oldenbourg, 1930.
xi, 79 p. 23 cm.
KAS

BELGIUM

1997 **Delmelle, Joseph.**
Abbayes et beguinages de Belgique. Il-
lustré de 58 photographies. 2. éd. Bruxelles, Rossel Edition [1973].
143 p. illus. 20 cm.
MnCS

1997a **Le Mire, Aubert.**
Origines coenobiorvm benedictinorvm in
Belgio, quibus antiquae religionis ortus
progressusque deducitur. Antverpiae,
apud Hieronymum Verdussim, 1606.
[20], 199, [8] p. 16 cm.
KAS; PLatS

1997b **Monasticon Belge.** Liège, Centre de
Recherches d'Histoire Religieuse, 1955–
Contents: Tome I: Namur, 1961-62. 2 v.
Tome II: Liège, 1955-62. 3 v.
Tome III: Flandre Occidentale,
1960-78. 4 v.

Tome IV: Brabant, 1964-72.
6 v.
Tome V: Luxembourg, 1975.
1 v.
Tome VI: Limbourg, 1976. 1 v.
Tome VII: Flandre Orientale,
1977-79. 3 v.
MnCS

1998 **Moreau, E. de, S.J.**
Les abbayes de Belgique (VIIe–XIIe
siècles). Bruxelles, La Renaissance du livre
[1952].
164 p.
CaQStB; MoCo

BRAZIL

1999 **The Benedictines in Brazil. Translated
by Alexius Hoffman, O.S.B.**
Translation of: L'Ordre de S. Benoît au
Brésil, in Revue bénédictin, v. 15(1898),
p. 414-425.
Typescript.
MnCS (Archives)

2000 **Endres, José Lohr, O.S.B.**
Catalogo dos bispos, gerais, provinciais,
abades e mais cargos de Ordem de São
Bento do Brasil, 1582-1975. Salvador,
Bahia, Editor Beneditina, 1976.
510 p. plate, 32 cm.
MnCS

2001 **Endres, José Lohr, O.S.B.**
Primeiras constituições da Ordem de São
Bento na Província do Brasil, 1596.
Salvador, Bahia [Brasil], 1977.
[22] p. 21 cm.
Offprint from: Universitas, no. 17, 1977,
p. 105-126.
MnCS

2002 **Kansas monks in Brazil (periodical).**
v. 1-4, 1962-1971.
KAS

2003 **Kapsner, Oliver Leonard, O.S.B.**
The Benedictines in Brazil [review article
of José Lohr Endres, O.S.B., Catalogo dos
bispos, gerais . . . da Ordem de S. Bento do
Brasil, 1582-1975].
Offprint from: The American Benedic-
tine review, v. 28(1977), p. 113-132)
MnCS; PLatS

2004 **Olinda, Brazil. São Bento (Benedictine
abbey).**
As escolas superiores de agricultura e
medicina-veterinaria, São Bento, Pernambuco, 1913-1923. [Friburgo em Brisgau
(Allemanha)], Tipographia de Herder &
Cia, 1923.
[5] p. 20 plates, 32 cm.

2005 **Restauration de l'Ordre S. Benoît au
Brésil:** vie monastique-apostolat–appel
aux vocations. [Bruges] Desclée, De
Brouwer, 1895.
15 p. 22 cm.
KAS

CANADA

2006 **Saint-Benoît-du-Lac, Canada (Benedic-
tine abbey).**
Les Bénédictins et leurs oeuvres. [The
Abbey, 1919?].
45 p. 21 cm.
MnCS

CATALONIA

2007 **Catalonia monastica;** recuil de documents
i estudis refertens a monestirs catalans
. . . Monestir de Montserrat, 1927–
v. facsims. 29 cm.
MnCS

2008 **Verges Mundo, O.**
L'abat Oliba. Els primers Catalans.
Barcelona, 1976.
108 p.
MnCS

CEYLON

2008a **Barsenbach, Dunstan, O.S.B.**
The coolie bishop; the life story of Dom
Bernard Regno, O.S.B., bishop of Kandy,
Sri Lanka. [Kandy, Sri Lanka (Ceylon),
Bravi Press, 1979].
90 p. plates. 22 cm.
MnCS

CHINA

2009 **Catholic University of Peking.**
From provisional to final registration.
(*In* Catholic University of Peking.
Bulletin, no. 8(1931), p. 103–130)
PLatS

2009a **Muehlenbein, Wibora, Sister, O.S.B.**
Benedictine mission to China. St.
Joseph, Minn., St. Benedict's Convent,
1980.
36 p. illus. 22 cm.
MnCS; MnStj

CROATIA

2010 **Ostojić, Ivan.**
Benediktinci u Hrvatoskoj; i ostalim
nasim Krajevima. Split, Tkon (Benediktinski priorat), 1963–65.
3 v. illus., maps, 24 cm.

Latin half-title: Benedictini in Croatia et
regionibus finitimis.
InStme; MnCS; PLatS

DAKOTA TERRITORY

2011 **Aberle, George P.**
From the steppes to the prairies; the
story of the Germans settling in Russia on
the Volga and Ukraine . . . also their resettlement in the Americas . . . Dickinson,
N.D. [1963].
213 p. 24 cm.
KAS

DALMATIA

2012 **Ostojie, Ivan.**
Benediktinci u Dalmaciji.
(*In* his: Benediktinci u Hrvatslij i ostalim
nasim krajevima, v. 2)
InStme; KAS; PLatS

EASTERN EUROPE

2013 **Szeptyckyj, Andreas, Abp.**
La restauration du monachisme slave.
Lophem-lez-Bruges, Abbaye de St-André
[1923?].
14 p.
NcBe

ENGLAND

2014 **Aveling, Hugh.**
The handle and the axe: the Catholic
recusants in England from Reformation to
emancipation. London, Blond and Briggs,
1976.
384 p. 23 cm.
MnCS

2015 **Baker, Augustin, O.S.B.**
Apostolatus Benedictinorum in Anglia,
sive Disceptatio historica, de antiquitate
ordinis congregationisque monachorum
nigrorum s. Benedicti in regno Angliae . . .
edita opera et industria R. P. Clementis
Reyneri. Duaci, ex officina Laurentii
Kellami, 1626.
22, [2], 248, 222, [4] 254 p.
PLatS (microfilm)

2016 **Benedictines. English Congregation.**
The Benedictine almanac and guide to
abbeys, parishes, monks, nuns of the
English Congregation of the Order of St.
Benedict. Edited by Rev. E. R. Croft,
O.S.B. Exeter, The Catholic Records Press
[1965].
99 p. 18 cm.
PLatS

2017 **Braun, Hugh.**
English abbeys. London, Faber & Faber [1971].
299 p. 32 plates, plans. 22 cm.
InStme

2018 **Chaussy, Yves, O.S.B.**
Les Bénédictins anglais réfugiés en France au XVIIe siècle (1611–1669). Paris, P. Lethielleux, 1967.
xxiv, 255 p. illus. 24 cm.
InStme;KAS; MnCS; PLatS

2019 **Cook, George Henry, ed.**
Letters to Cromwell on the suppression of the monasteries. London, J. Baker [1965].
viii, 272 p. 22 cm.
PLatS

2020 **Cranage, David Herbert Somerset.**
The home of the monk; an account of English monastic life and buildings in the Middle Ages. [2d. ed.]. Cambridge [England], University Press, 1926.
xv, 122 p. illus. 20 cm.
MnCS; NcBe; WaOSM

2021 **Deanesly, Margaret.**
Augustine of Canterbury. [London], Nelson, [1964].
167 p. 22 cm.
PLatS

2022 **Dickinson, John Compton.**
Monastic life in medieval England, with fifty-seven photographs and six plans. New York, Barnes & Noble [1961].
xiii, 160 p. plates, plans.
MnCS; MoCo

2023 **Directory of religious orders,** congregations and societies of Great Britain and Ireland. Glasgow, J. S. Burns & Sons.
v. 19 cm. biennial.
KAS

2024 **Essex, England. Record Office.**
Essex monasteries; a brief pictorial record of religious houses during the Middle Ages. Chelmsford, The Essex County Council, 1964.
[28] p. illus. 25 cm.
PLatS

2024a **Farmer, David Hugh, ed.**
Benedict's disciples. Leominster, Herefordshire, Fowler Wright, 1980.
xii, 354 p. illus. 23 cm.
Consists of 25 biographies, from St. Benedict to Archbishop Ullathorne, by various writers.
KAS

2025 **Fosbrooke, T. D.**
British monachism; manners & customs of the monks and nuns of England. New ed. London, Nichols, 1817.
560 p. illus.
AStb

2026 **Graham, Rose.**
Monasticism.
(*In* Barnard, F. P., comp. Mediaeval England. 1924. p. 344–380)
AStb

2027 **Haigh, Christopher.**
The last days of the Lancashire monasteries and the Pilgrimage of Grace. Manchester, Published for the Chetham Society by the Manchester University Press, 1969.
x, 172 p. 2 maps, 22 cm.
PLatS

2028 **John, Eric.**
Orbis Britanniae, and other studies. Leicester, U. P., 1966.
xii, 303 p. 23 cm. (Studies in early English history, 4)
MnCS

2029 **Knowles, David, O.S.B.**
Medieval religious houses, England and Wales, by David Knowles and R. Neville Hadcock. New York, St. Martin's Press [1972].
xv, 565 p. fold. maps, 24 cm.
". . . substantially a new edition of the work published under the same title in 1953."
PLatS

2030 **Koenig, Clara.**
Englisches Klosterleben im 12. Jahrhundert, auf Grund der Chronik des Jocelins de Brakelonda. Jena, Frommannsche Buchhandlung, 1928.
vii, 98 p. 23 cm.
MnCS

2031 **Lamb, John William.**
The archbishopric of Lichfield (787–803). London, Faith Press [1964].
71 p. map. 22 cm.
PLatS

2032 **Lamb, John William.**
The archbishopric of York: the early years. London, Faith Press, 1967.
156 p. map. 19 cm.
PLatS

2032a **Lingard, John.**
The antiquities of the Anglo-Saxon Church. First American, from the second London edition. Philadelphia, M. Fifthian [1841].
324 p. illus., fold. map. 23 cm.
PLatS

2032b **London, England. British Library.**
The Benedictines in Britain. [London] The British Library [1980].

111 p. 60 illus. (mostly facsims.), 4 col. plates, 23 cm. (British Library series no. 3)
MnCS

2032c **Lunn, David.**
The English Benedictines, 1540–1688, from reformation to revolution. Foreword by Cardinal Basil Hume, O.S.B. London, Burns & Oates; New York, Barnes & Noble, c 1980.
xiv, 282 p. illus. 24 cm.
KAS

2033 **Milliken, Ernest Kenneth.**
English monasticism yesterday and today. London, Toronto, Harrap [1967].
123 p. illus., plans, diagrs. 23 cm.
KAS; MoCo; PLatS

2034 **Moorman, John Richard Humpidge.**
Church life in England in the thirteenth century. Cambridge, 1945.
Part II, p. 242–[401]: monasteries.
MnCS

2035 **Nashdom Abbey, Burnham, England.**
The jubilee book of the Benedictines of Nashdom, 1914–1964. London, Faith Press [1964].
886 p. illus. 22 cm.

2036 **Nichols, John, comp.**
Some account of the alien priories, and of such lands as they are known to have possessed in England and Wales. London, J. Nichols, MDCCLXXIX.
2 v. map, plates. 19 cm.
KAS

2037 **Platt, Colin.**
The monastic grange in medieval England; a reassessment. New York, Fordham University Press, 1969.
272 p. illus., maps. 23 cm.
MnCS; PLatS

2038 **Rudolph, Father, O.S.F.C.**
The monks of Old Chester; four lectures. Chester, England [Blayney] 1907.
72 p.
MoCo

2039 **Smith, Henry Percival.**
Learning and labour: from Alfred the Great to Aelfric of Eynsham. [Oxford, England, H. P. Smith] 1962.
47 p.
PLatS

2040 **Stuckert, Howard W.**
Corrodies in the English monasteries; a study in English social history of the Middle Ages. Philadelphia, 1923.
54 p. 24 cm.
MnCS

2041 **Waites, Bryan.**
Moorland and vale-land farming in northeast Yorkshire: the monastic contribution in the thirteenth and fourteenth centuries. York, St. Anthony's Press, 1967.
35 p. maps. 22 cm.
MnCS

2042 **Walsh, James, ed.**
Pre-Reformation English spirituality. New York, Fordham University Press, 1965.
xiii, 287 p. 23 cm.
20 articles on writers from Bede to Augustine Baker.
MnCS

2043 **Wood, Susan M.**
English monasteries and their patrons in the thirteenth century. London, Oxford Union Press, 1955.
viii, 191 p. 23 cm. (Oxford historical series)
MnCS

2044 **Woodward, G. W. O.**
The dissolution of the monasteries. London, Blandford Press, 1966.
186 p. illus.
MoCo

EUROPE

2045 **Eschapasse, Maurice.**
L'architecture bénédictine en Europe. Paris, Editions des Deux-Mondes [1963].
231 p. illus., maps, plans. 27 cm.
InStme

2046 **Le Mire, Aubert.**
Origines benedictinae; sive, Illustrium coenobiorum Ord. S. Benedicti, nigrorum monachorum, per Italiam, Hispaniam, Galliam, Germaniam, Poloniam, Belgium, Britanniam, aliasque provincias. Coloniae Agrippinae, Bernardus Gualther, 1614.
[18], 368, [10] p. 16 cm.
KAS

2047 **Richards, Ian.**
Abbeys of Europe. Feltham, Hamlyn, 1968.
189 p. illus. 22 cm.
PLatS

2048 **Schneider, Edouard.**
Cellules et couvents bénédictins. [Paris], P. Amiot [1958].
229 p. illus. 22 cm.
MnCS; PLatS

2049 **Some European Benedictine abbeys** as seen by one American monk. Saint Leo, Fla., Saint Leo Abbey Press, 1964.
92 p. 24 cm.
MoCo; PLatS

FINLAND

2050 **Leinberg, Karl Gabriel.**
De finska Klostrens historia. Helsing-fors, Tidnings, 1890.
viii, 509 p. 23 cm.
KAS

2051 **Oppermann, Charles James August.**
The English missionaries in Sweden and Finland. London, Macmillan Co., 1937.
xxii, 221 p. 22 cm.
MnCS

FLORIDA

2052 **Pilz, Gerard, O.S.B.**
Die katholische Colonie San Antonio, Pasco County, Florida. San Antonio, Fla., Imigrations-Gesellschaft und Land Agen-tur, 188–?
9 p.
FStL

FRANCE

2053 **Ambroise, Georges.**
Les moines du moyen age; leur influence intellectuelle et politique en France. 2. éd. Paris, A. Picard, 1946.
248 p. illus. 22 cm.
First published 1942.
MnCS; MoCo

2054 **Beaunier, Benedictine monk.**
Recueil historique, chronologique, et topographique, des archevêches, évêches, abbayes et prieures de France, tant d'hom-mes, que de filles . . . par ordre alpha-betique. Par Dom Beaunier. Paris, A.X.R. Mesnier, 1726.
2 v. illus., maps, 26 cm.
CtBeR; KAS; MnCS; PLatS

2055 **Bulst, Neithard.**
Untersuchungen zu den Kloster-reformen Wilhelms von Dijon (962–1031). Bonn, Ludwig Röhrscheid Verlag, 1973.
330 p.
MnCS

2056 **Chaussy, Yves, O.S.B.**
Les Bénédictins anglais réfugiés en France au XVIIe siècle (1611–1669). Paris, P. Lethielleux, 1967.
xxiv, 255 p. plates. 24 cm.
InStme; KAS; MnCS; MoCo; PLatS

2057 **Delisle, Leopold Victor.**
Enquête sur la fortune des établisse-ments de l'Ordre de Saint-Benoît en 1338. Paris, Imprimerie nationale, 1910.
54 p. 28 cm.
InStme

2058 **Denifle, Heinrich, O.P.**
La desolation des églises, monastères & hôpitaux en France pendent la Guerre de Cent Ans.
v. 25 cm.
PLatS

2059 **Denis, Paul, O.S.B.**
Le Cardinal de Richelieu et la réforme des monastères bénédictins. Paris, H. Champion, 1913.
xv, 510 p. 25 cm.
InStme

2060 **Gallia monastica:** tableaux et cartes de dépendances monastiques, publiés sous la direction de J. F. Lemarignier. Paris, A. Picard, 1974–
v. maps. 28 cm.
KAS; MnCS

2061 **Kessler, Verona, Sister, O.S.B.**
The effects of the laic laws of 1901 and 1904 on the Benedictines in France.
428 p.
Thesis (Ph.D.)–University of Notre Dame.
SdYa

2062 **Kessler, Verona, Sister, O.S.B.**
The suppression of the Benedictine Order in France during the Revolution.
184 p.
Thesis (M.A.)–Creighton University, Omaha, Nebr., 1957.
SdYa

2063 **Lot, Ferdinand, ed.**
Histoire des institutions françaises au Moyen Age. Paris, Presses universitaires de France, 1957–
v. 24 cm.
PLatS

2064 **Misonne, Daniel, O.S.B.**
Chapitres séculiers dépendant d'abbayes bénédictines au Moyen Age dans l'ancien diocèse de Liège.
(*In* La vita comme del clero nei secoli XI e XII. 1962. v. 1, p. 412–432)
PLatS

2064a **Oexle, Otto Gerard.**
Forschungen zu monastischen und geist-lichen Gemeinschaften im westfränkischen Bereich. München, Wilhelm, Fink Verlag, 1978.
208 p. plates, 24 cm.
Includes such Benedictine abbeys as: Saint-Germain-du-Prés, Saint-Denis, Saint-Martin (Tours).
MnCS

2065 **La part des moines;** théologie vivante dans le monachisme française: Solesmes, Ligugé, Saint-Benoit-sur-Loire, La

Pierre qui Vire, Timadeuc. Introduction
S.J. Paris, Editions Beauchesne [1978].
204 p. 22 cm. (Le Point théologique, 28)
MnCS

2065a **Pez, Bernard, O.S.B.**
Bibliotheca Benedictino-Mauriana. Seu,
De ortu, vitis, et scriptis patrum Benedic-
tinorum et celeberrima congregatione S.
Mauri in Francia . . . Augustae Vindel.,
Philippus Veith, 1716.
40, 492, [6] p. 17 cm.
ILSP; MnCS; NdRi; PLatS

2066 **Piolin, Paul Leo, O.S.B.**
Histoire de l'église du Mans. Paris, Julien
Lanier, 1851–63.
6 v. 23 cm.
KAS

2067 **Plongeron, Bernard.**
Les réguliers de Paris devant le serment
constitutionnel; sens et conséquences d'une
option 1789–1801. Paris, J. Vrin, 1964.
488 p. 25 cm.
PLatS

2068 **Poirier-Coutansais, Françoise.**
Les abbayes bénédictines du diocèse de
Reims. Paris, A. et J. Picard, 1974.
xv, 554 p. plates. 28 cm. (Gallia monas-
tica, 1)
KAS; MnCS

2069 **Prinz, Friedrich.**
Frühes Mönchtum im Frankenreich;
Kultur und Gesellschaft in Gallien, den
Rheinlanden und Bayern am Beispiel der
monastischen Entwicklung (4. bis 8. Jahrhundert). München-Wien, R. Oldenbourg,
1965.
633 p. maps. 24 cm.
MnCS; MoCo

2070 **Schmitz, Karl.**
Ursprung und Geschichte der Devotions-
formeln, bis zu ihrer Aufnahme in die
frankische Königsurkunde. Stuttgart, Ferdinand Enke, 1913; Amsterdam, P. Schippers, 1965.
xviii, 192 p. 23 cm.
PLatS

2070a **Thirion, Joseph.**
En exil; les congrégations francaises
hors de France. Paris, Librairie des Saints-
Peres, 1903.
xv, 123 p. 17 cm.
KAS

2071 **Ueding, Leo, S.J.**
Geschichte der Klostergründungen der
frühen Merowingerzeit. Berlin, Verlag
Emil Ebering, 1935.
vii, 288 p. 25 cm.
MnCS

2072 **Voight, Karl.**
Die karolingische Klosterpolitik und der
Niedergang des westfränkischen König-
tums, Laienäbte und Klosterinhaber
Stuttgart, Ferdinand Enke, 1917; Amster-
dam, P. Schippers, 1965.
xiv, 265 p. 23 cm.
PLatS

FRANCONIA

2073 **Dilworth, Mark, O.S.B.**
The Scots in Franconia; a century of
monastic life. Totowa, N.J., Rowman and
Littlefield [1974].
301 p. illus. 23 cm.
MnCS

2074 **Lohmeier, Georg.**
Franconia benedictina; geistlich-
weltliche Spaziergang durch Franken von
Georg Lohmeier und bebildert von Georg
Hetzelein. Nürnberg, Glock and Lutz,
1969.
46 p. illus. 12 x 19 cm.
MnCS

2075 **Prinz, Friedrich.**
Frühes Mönchtum im Frankenreich . . .
(4.-8. Jahrhundert). Wien, Oldenbourg,
1965.
633 p. maps, 24 cm.
MnCS

GEORGIA

2076 **Oetgen, Jerome.**
The origins of the Benedictine Order in
Georgia.
(*In* The Georgia historical quarterly, v.
53(1969), p. 165–183)
PLatS

GERMANY

See also Benedictines – Bavaria; Benedictines – Franconia; Benedictines – Saxony;
Benedictines – Silesia; Benedictines –
Swabia; Benedictines – Thuringia; Benedictines – Württemberg.

2077 **Brinkmann, Bernhard.**
Der Ordensgedanke und die katholischen
Klöster in Deutschland. Gotha, L. Klotz,
1936.
95 p. 23 cm.
MnCS

2078 **Bühler, Johannes.**
Die Benediktiner und Zisterzienser.
(*In* his: Klosterleben im deutschen Mit-
telalter. Leipzig, 1921. p. 1–279)
KAS; NcBe; PLatS

2079 **Feierabend, Hans.**
Die politische Stellung der deutschen
Reichsbteien während des Investitur-
streites. Breslau, 1913.
231 p. 22 cm.
MnCS

2080 **Germania monastica.** Klosterverzeichnis
der deutschen Benediktiner und Cisterzienser. Neu hrsg. von der Bayerischen Benediktiner-Akademie. (Unveränderter Nachdruck der Ausgabe
Salzburg, 1917). Augsburg, Verlag Winfried-Werk in Kommission, 1967.
185 p. 21 cm.
KAS; PLatS

2080a **Hellriegel, Ludwig.**
Benediktiner als Seelsorger im
linksrheinischen Gebiet des ehemaligen
Erzbistums Mainz vom Ende des 17. bis
zum Anfang des 19. Jahrhunderts . . .
Münster, Westfalen, Aschendorffsche
Verlagsbuchhandlung, 1980.
viii, 185 p. 22 cm. (Beiträge zur
Geschichte des alten Mönchtums und des
Benediktinerordens, 34)
MnCS

2081 **Homann, Johan Baptist.**
Atlas Germaniae specialis . . . Norimbergae, prostat in Officina Homaniana,
1761?
131 col. maps on double leaves. 55 cm.
The fourth map has title: Germania
benedictina.
KAS

2082 **Landers, Ernst.**
Die deutschen Klöster vom Ausgang
Karls des Grossen bis zum Wormser Kon-
kordat und ihr Verhältnis zu den
Reformen. Berlin, Emil Ebering, 1938.
81 p. 25 cm.
MnCS

2083 **Legipont, Oliver, O.S.B.**
Monasticon Moguntiacum . . . [Pragae],
typis Joannis Julii Gerzabek, 1746.
[32], 80 p. 16 cm.
KAS

2084 **Monumenta Niederaltacensia.**
(*In* Monumenta Boica, vol. 11, p. 1–340)
PLatS

2085 **Schamel, Johann Martin.**
Entwurff eines Closter-Lexici, worinnen
ethliche hundert in- und ausser Teutschland gelegene Closter, mit ihren Namen,
Orden Lage und Dioces anzeigen wollen
. . . Eisenach, Michael Gottlieb Griessbach, 1733.
[4] p. 56. columns, 22 cm.
KAS

2086 **Schorn, Carl.**
Eiflia sacra; oder, Geschichte der Klöster
und geistlichen Stiftungen der Eifel . . .
Bonn, P. Hanstein, 1888–89.
2 v. 23 cm.
_____ Register, nebst einigen Nachträ-
gen. Bonn, 1892.
84 p.
KAS

2087 **Schrader, Franz.**
Ringen, Untergang und Ueberleben der
katholischen Klöster in den Hochstiften
Magdeburg und Halberstadt von der
Reformation bis zum Westfälischen
Frieden. Münster, Aschendorff, 1977.
104 p. 22 cm.
MnCS

2088 **Schreiner, Klaus.**
Sozial- und Standesgeschichtliche Untersuchungen zu den Benediktinerkonventen
im östlichen Schwarzwald. Stuttgart, W.
Kohlhammer, 1964.
xxxv, 331 p.
MnCS

2089 **Schunder, Friedrich, ed.**
Die oberhessischen Klöster: Regesten
und Urkunden. Marburg, N. G. Elwert,
1961–
v. 24 cm.
PLatS

2090 **Sinnigen, Ansgar.**
Katholische Männerorden Deutschlands
(ausserhalb der Superioren-Vereinigung)
. . . 2. Aufl. Düsseldorf, Rhenania-Verlag
[1934].
ix, 174 p. illus. 30 cm.
InStme

2091 **Stengel, Karl, O.S.B.**
Monasteriologia in qua insignium aliquot
monasteriorum familiae S. Benedicti in
Germania origines, fundatores, clarique
viri ex eis oriundi describuntur . . .
Augustae Vindelicorum, 1619.
KAS (microfilm); PLatS (microfilm)

HOHENZOLLERN

2092 **Schefold, Max.**
Kirchen und Klöster in Württemberg
und Hohenzollern, nach alten Vorlagen.
Frankfurt am Main, W. Weidlich, 1961.
255 p. illus. 19 cm.
PLatS

HUNGARY

2093 **Fuxhoffer, Damian, O.S.B.**
Monasteriologiae regni Hungariae libri
duo, totidem tomis comprehensi. Recognovit, ad fidem fontium revocavit et auxit

Maurus Czinár. Vindobonae & Strigonii, Carolus Sartori, 1869.
2 v. 29 cm.
KAS

2094 **Juhasz, Koloman.**
Benediktiner-Abteien.
(*In* his: Stifte der Tschanader Diözese im Mittelalter. 1927. p. 21–72)
AStb; PLatS

2095 **Ostojić, Ivan.**
Benediktinci u Hrvatoskoj; i ostalim nasim Krajevima. Split, Tkon, Benediktinski Priorat, 1963–
v. illus., maps. 24 cm.
InStme; MnCS; PLatS

IDAHO

2096 **Elsensohn, Afreda, Sister, O.S.B.**
Sixty-six years of service, 1884–1950; a short historical sketch of the Sisters of St. Gertrude's Community. Cottonwood, Id. [Cottonwood Chronicle Print, 1950].
15 p. illus. 25 cm.
KAS

ILLINOIS

2097 **Blue Island, Ill.** St. Benedict Parish.
A memento of the founding of St. Benedict Parish, Blue Island, Ill., Oct. 25, 1936; a history of the parish.
unpaged, illus.
AStb

2098 **O'Rourke, Alice, Sister, O.P.**
The good work begun; centennial history of Peoria Diocese. [n.p.] The Lakeside Press, 1977.
xiv, 208 p. map. 25 cm.
PLatS

INDIA

2099 **Acharya, Francis, ed.**
Kurismuala; a symposium of Ashram life. Kerala, India, Kurisumala Ashram, 1974.
173 p. illus.
MoCo

2100 **Monchanin, Jules, S.A.M.**
A Benedictine Ashram, by J. Monchanin and Henri Le Saux. [Rev. ed.]. Douglas [Isle of Man], Times Press [1964].
91 p. ports., plates. 23 cm.
KAS; NcBe

2101 **Monchanin, Jules, S.A.M.**
Ermites du Saccidananda; un essai d'intégration chrétienne de la tradition monastique de l'Inde. [Par] J. Monchanin, S.A.M. [et] Henri Le Saux, O.S.B. 2. éd. Tournai, Casterman, 1957.

204 p. 22 cm. (Eglise vivante)
Translation of: An Indian Benedictine Ashram.
PLatS

INDIANA

See also St. Meinrad Archabbey, St. Meinrad, Ind.; Convent of the Immaculate Conception, Ferdinand, Ind.

2102 **Werner, Raymond.**
A history of St. Benedict Parish, Evansville, Ind., 1912–1978.
90 p. illus., ports.
InFer

IRELAND

2103 **Archdell, Mervyn.**
Monasticon hibernicum; or, A history of the abbeys, priories and other religious houses in Ireland. London, G.G.J. Robinson, 1786.
xxiii, 820 p. illus. 27 cm.
MnCS

2104 **Bradshaw, Brendan.**
The dissolution of the religious orders in Ireland under Henry VIII. [London, New York], Cambridge University Press [1974].
viii, 276 p. illus. 23 cm.
InStme

2105 **Gwynn, Aubrey Osborne, S.J.**
Medieval religious houses: Ireland . . . With a foreword by David Knowles. Harlow, Longman, 1970.
xli, 479 p. 23 cm.
MnCS

2105a **Mould, Daphne D.C.P.**
The monasteries of Ireland; an introduction. London, B. T. Batsford, 1976.
188 p. 12 plates. 23 cm.
InStme; PLatS

ISTRIA

2106 **Ostojić, Ivan.**
Benediktinci u Panonskij Hrvatskoj i Istre.
(*In* his: Benediktinci u Hravatoskou. vol. 3)
MnCS

ITALY

2107 **Armellini, Mariano, O.S.B.**
Catalogi tres episcoporum, reformatorum, et virorum sanctitate illustrium e Congregatione Casinensi alias S. Justinae Patavinae. Assisii, A. Sgariglia, 1733–34.

3 v.
PLatS (microfilm)

2108   **Benedettini nelle valli del Maceratese.**
Atti del II Convegno del Centro di studi
storici Maceratesi (9 ottobre 1966).
Ravenna, A. Longo, 1967.
281 p. plates, 25 cm.
MnCS

2109   **Cacciamani, Giuseppe, C.O.S.B.**
Atlante storico-geografico dei Benedet-
tini d'Italia, con 15 tavole. [Roma], Ed.
Paoline [1967].
284 p. maps. 18 cm.
MnCS

2110   **Décarreaux, Jean.**
Les Normands et les moines latins.
(*In* his: Normands, papes et moines.
Paris, 1974. p. 47–70)
MnCS

2111   **Lubin, Augustin.**
Abbatiarum Italiae brevis notitia . . .
Romae, Jo. Jacobus Komarek, 1693.
[12], 436 p. 23 cm.

_____ Additiones et corrections . . .
Romae, 1895. 87 p.
KAS

2112   **Penco, Gregorio, O.S.B.**
Storia del monachesimo in Italia, delle
origini alla fine del Medio Evo. [Roma],
Edizione Paoline, [1961].
601 p. illus. 21 cm.
PLatS

2113   **Penco, Gregorio, O.S.B.**
Storia del monachesimo in Italia
nell'epoca moderna. Roma, Edizioni
Paoline, 1969.
429 p. plates, 22 cm.
KAS; MoCo

2114   **Tosti, Luigi, O.S.B.**
S. Benedetto al Parlamento Nazionale.
Napoli, Gaetano Gioja, 1861.
30 p. 25 cm.
KAS; PLatS

KANSAS

See also Mount St. Scholastica Convent,
Atchison, Kans.; St. Benedict's Abbey, Atchison, Kans.

2115   **Burbach, Jude, O.S.B.**
The centennial of St. Patrick's Church,
1866–1966. Atchison, Kans. [1966].
21 p. illus. 22 cm.
KAS

2116   **Theis, Lawrence, O.S.B.**
Historical sketch of St. Charles Church,
Troy, Kansas, on the occasion of the
golden jubilee, 1881–1931.

28 p. ports. 23 cm.
KAS

KENTUCKY

2117   **Covington, Ky.** St. Joseph's Church.
Centennial souvenir, 1856–1956, of St.
Joseph's Church, Covington, Kentucky.
80 p. illus., ports. 23 cm.
PLatS

2118   **Covington, Ky.** St. Joseph's Church.
Souvenir of the golden jubilee celebration in commemoration of the fiftieth anniversary of the erection of the Boys' School,
Covington, Kentucky, 1870–1920.
56 p. illus., ports. 23 cm.
PLatS

KOREA

2119   **Kim, Joseph Chang-mun, ed.**
Catholic Korea, yesterday and today.
Seoul, Catholic Korea Pub. Co., 1964.
966 p. illus., tables.
InFer

2120   **O'Meara, Shaun, Sister, O.S.B.**
Benedictine meeting in Korea, April,
1970.
10 p. 28 cm.
Mimeographed.
MnStj (Archives)

LATIN AMERICA

2121   **Guarda Geywitz, Gabriel, O.S.B.**
La implantación del monacato en His-
panoamérica, siglos XV–XIV. Santiago,
Universidad Católica de Chile, 1973.
103 p. illus. 25 cm.
MnCS

LORRAINE

2122   **Calmet, Augustin, O.S.B.**
Histoire ecclésiastique et civile de Lorraine . . . Nancy, J. B. Cusson, 1728.
3 v., plates, maps. 39 cm.
KAS

MALTA

2123   **Notizie intorno ai monaci ed alle
monache dell'Ordine di San Benedetto
in Malta.** MS. Monastero di San Pietro,
Notabile (Mdina), Malta. 41 f. 30 cm.
Microfilm: MnCH proj. no. Malta 302

MEXICO

2124   **Una escuela de servicio del Señor.** Cuernavaca, Monasterio de Nuestra Señora
de la Resurrección [1951].

61 p. illus.
MxCu; NcBe

MINNESOTA

See also St. John's Abbey; St. Benedict's Convent; St. Scholastica Priory; St. Paul's Priory.

2125 **Ahern, Patrick H.**
Catholic heritage in Minnesota, North Dakota, South Dakota. St. Paul, 1964.
225 p. illus., maps.
InFer

2126 **Assumption Parish [St. Paul, Minn.];**
a German Catholic congregation which is the pride of the Church, grand work of the zealous Benedictine Fathers in Minnesota.
Copy from: Northwest Chronicle, St. Paul, Nov. 19, 1897, p. 7–12.
MnCS (Archives)

2127 **Avon, Minn.** St. Benedict's Church.
St. Benedict's Church of Avon: 100 years centennial celebration, June 15, 1969. [Sauk Rapids, Minn., Sentinel Publishing Co., 1969].
112 p.
MnSt (Archives)

2128 **Butkowski, George H.**
The mill in the woods, by George H. Butkowski and Vincent A. Yzermans. Saint Rose, Minn., Millwood Township Historical Association, 1973.
102 p. illus. 30 cm.
MnCS

2129 **Cold Spring, Minn.** St. Boniface Church.
Amid hills of granite – a spring of faith: a history of Saint Boniface Parish, Cold Spring, Minnesota, 1878–1978. [Cold Spring, Minn., Cold Spring Record, 1978].
117, [15] p.
MnStj (Archives)

2130 **Collegeville, Minn.** St. John the Baptist Parish.
Parish centennial: pictorial directory [1975].
unpaged (ca. 50 p.) illus., 30 cm.
MnCS

2131 **Farming, Minn.** St. Catherine's Church.
St. Catherine's Catholic Church, Farming, Minnesota [centennial, 1879–1979. History collected and written by Marilyn Brinkman and Marcelline Schleper. Printed by Weber Printing, Albany, Minn., 1979].
171 p. illus., ports. 20 cm.
MnCS

2131a **Farming, Minn.** St. Catherine's Parish.
The silver jubilee of Adalbert Unruhe, 1914–1939, Farming, Minn., and the 60th anniversary of the organization of the Parish of St. Catherine, 1879–1939, Farming, Stearns County, Minn., August 13, 1939. [St. Cloud, 1939].
MnStj (Archives); MnCS

2131b **Freeport, Minn.** Sacred Heart Parish.
Centennial 1881–1981; "heritage of faith."
[132] p. illus., ports., map, plates (part col.), 28 cm.
MnCS

2132 **Fruth, Alban, O.S.B.**
Church of St. Martin, St. Martin, Minnesota, 1973. [Chicago, C. D. Stampley Enterprise, 1973].
unpaged, ports. 28 cm.
MnCS

2133 **Minneapolis, Minn.** St. Joseph Church.
St. Joseph's of North Minneapolis, 1870–1970.
31 p. illus. 28 cm.
MnCS

2134 **One hundred years:** Seven Dolors Parish.
[A history of the parish Church of the Seven Dolors, Albany, Minn., 1968].
136 p. (p. 82–136 advertisements) illus., ports. 24 cm.
KAS

2135 **St. Cloud, Minn. (diocese).**
A century of living with Christ: pastoral letter and brief historical sketch. Diocese of St. Cloud, Minnesota, 1852–1952. [St. Cloud, Minn., 1952].
71 p. ports., tables. 22 cm.
KAS

2136 **St. Joseph, Minn.** St. Joseph's Church.
[Album of] St. Joseph's Parish, St. Joseph, Minn., 1977.
[30] leaves, col. plates, 21 cm.
MnCS

2137 **St. Martin, Minn.** St. Martin's Church.
Dedication and blessing of the Church of St. Martin, St. Martin, Minn., July 11, 1971.
36 p. illus.
MnStj (Archives)

2138 **St. Paul, Minn.** St. Bernard Church.
Gedenkblatt der 25-jährigen Jubelfeier der St. Bernard's Gemeinde in St. Paul, Minnesota, 1915.
32 p. illus. 28 cm.
MnCS

2139 **Schreifels, Ferdinand, O.S.B.**
History of St. Joseph's Church, Moorhead, Minn. [Moorhead, 1954].

unpaged. illus. 25 cm.
KAS; MnCS

2140 **Stones and hills**—Steine und Hügel: reflections, St. John the Baptist Parish, 1875–1975. Collegeville, Minn., St. John the Baptist Parish, 1975.
v, 180 p. illus. 23 cm.
MnCS

2141 **Watrin, Benno, O.S.B.**
St. Benedict's Mission, White Earth, Minn., 1878–1978. [White Earth, Minn., 1978].
[28] p. illus., ports. 20 cm.

MISSOURI

2142 **Malone, Edward E., O.S.B.**
An offering to God and the Catholic Church; the centennial history of St. Mary's Parish, Carrollton, Missouri. Marceline, Mo., Walsworth Publishing Co., 1972.
96 p. illus.
MoCo

NEBRASKA

2143 **Casper, Henry W., S.J.**
History of the Catholic Church in Nebraska, 1838–1874. Milwaukee, Bruce Pub. Co., 1960.
344 p. illus.
InFer

NETHERLANDS

2144 **Damen, Cornelius, O.S.B.**
Geschiedenis van de Benediktijenkloosters in de provincie Groningen. Assen, Van Gorcum [1972].
256 p. maps. 24 cm.
MnCS

2145 **Suur, Hemmo.**
Geschichte der ehemaligen Klöster in der Provinz Ostfriesland. Emden, T. Hahn, 1838.
vi, 188 p. fold. maps. 23 cm.
KAS

NEW JERSEY

2146 **Newark, N.J.** St. Mary's Church.
Andenken an das goldene Jubiläum der Sankt Marien Kirche, Newark, New Jersey, 1907.
56 p. 26 cm.
PLatS

2147 **Newark, N.J.** St. Mary's Church.
Official souvenir of St. Mary's Parish for the golden jubilee. [Newark, N.J.] Lawler Printing Co. [1907].

[18] p. 23 cm.
PLatS

NORMANDY

2148 **Baudot, Marcel.**
Normandie bénédictine. Preface de Régine Pernoud. Illustrations de Gerard Ambroselli et du Frère Raphael, O.S.B. Bec-Hellouin, Association Les Amis du Bec-Hellouin, 1979.
187 p. illus. 24 cm.
MnCS

2148a **Goyau, Georges.**
La Normandie bénédictine; pirates, vikings et moines normands. Paris, Plon [1940].
v, 242 p. 19 cm.
CaQStB; InStme

2149 **Le Conte, René.**
Curiositéz normandes comparées. Etudes historiques et archéologiques sur les abbayes de Bénédictins en général et sur celle de Hamby en particulier. Bernay, Misulle-Duval, 1890.
xvi, 556 p. plates. 19 cm.
KAS

2150 **Matthew, Donald.**
The Norman monasteries and their English possessions. Oxford University Press [1962].
200 p.
MoCo

2151 **La Normandie bénédictine au temps de Guillaume le Conquèrant**, XI. siècle. [Lille], Facultés Catholique de Lille, 1967.
576 p. 24 cm.
English or French.
InStme; MnCS

2152 **Nortier, Geneviève.**
Les bibliothèques mediévales des abbayes bénédictines de Normandia . . . Nouvelle éd. Paris, P. Lethielleux, 1971.
[4], 252 p. plates, tables.
KAS; MnCS

NORTH AMERICA

2153 **St. John's Abbey, Collegeville, Minn.**
American Benedictine foundations (portfolio) [Collegeville, Minn., The Scriptorium, 1960].
44 x 29 cm.
Includes abbeys and convents.
MnCS

NORTH DAKOTA

2154 **Aberle, George P.**
From the steppes to the prairies; the story of the Germans settling in Russia on

the Volga and Ukraine . . . their resettlement in the Americas . . . Dickinson, N.D. [1963].
213 p. 24 cm.
KAS

2155 **Clements, David J., O.S.B.**
"Built on a firm foundation"; Standing Rock centenary, 1873–1973. Fort Yates, N.D., Catholic Indian Mission, 1973.
96 p. illus.
MoCo

OKLAHOMA

2156 **In memoriam: Rev. Father Vincent Jolly, O.S.B.**, late apostolic missionary and pastor of Purcell, Indian Territory. Purcell, Ind. Terr., Register Job Printing Rooms, 1895.
14 p. illus. 23 cm.
KAS

2157 **Murphy, Joseph Francis, O.S.B.**
Historic Sacred Heart Mission. [n.d.]
[20] p. illus. 23 cm.
PLatS

2158 **Murphy, Joseph Francis, O.S.B.**
The monastic centers of the Order of St. Benedict in Oklahoma. Shawnee, Okla., Benedictine Color Press, 1968.
iv, 65 p. 28 cm.
Thesis – University of Oklahoma Graduate School.
OkShG

2159 **Murphy, Joseph Francis, O.S.B.**
Tenacious monks, the Oklahoma Benedictines, 1875–1975: Indian missionaries, Catholic founders, educators, agriculturists. Shawnee, Okla., Benedictine Color Press [1974].
x, 465 p. illus. 25 cm.
InStme; PLatS

OREGON

2160 **O'Hara, Edwin V.**
Pioneer Catholic history of Oregon. Paterson, N.J., St. Anthony Guild Press, 1939.
234 p. illus.
InFer

PENNSYLVANIA

See also St. Vincent Archabbey; St. Benedict's Convent.

2161 **Allegheny, Pa.** St. Mary's Church.
St. Marien Gemeinde; Gedenkblätter aus Vergangenheit & Gegenwart. Pittsburgh, Beobachter, 1898.
194 p. illus.
AStb

2162 **Brehm, Albert G.**
History . . . St. Mary's Church [St. Marys, Pa.]. St. Marys, Pa., Lenze Associated Enterprises, Inc., 1960.
89 p. illus. 26 cm.
PLatS

2163 **Debes, Dunstan William, O.S.B.**
St. Mary's Church, Bolivar, Pennsylvania, 1850–1961.
24 p. illus. 31 cm.
PLatS

2164 **Kmetz, Rosemarie.**
Solemn blessing and dedication of the new St. Boniface Church (Chestnut Ridge), Latrobe, Pennsylvania. Feast of St. Boniface, June 5, 1971.
16 p. illus. 22 cm.
PLatS

2165 **Kornides, Marcian, O.S.B.**
Sacred Heart Church, Jeannette, Pennsylvania: golden jubilee, 1924–1974. Parish founded, 1889. Present church erected, 1924.
unpaged, chiefly illus. 24 cm.
PLatS

2166 **Pfiester, Emeric James, O.S.B.**
Saint Bede Church, Bovard, Pa., 1915–1965.
36 p. illus., ports. 22 cm.
PLatS

2167 **South Greensburg, Pa.** St. Bruno's Church.
St. Bruno Church dedication, May 27, 1962.
103 p. illus. 28 cm.
PLatS

2168 **Stevens, Cyril R.**
Our Catholic heritage . . . the renewal: 125th jubilee [of] St. Benedict Catholic Church, Carrolltown, Pennsylvania, December 25, 1975.
[23] p. chiefly illus. 27 cm.
PLatS

2169 **Szarnicki, Henry A.**
Bishop O'Connor and the German Catholics.
(*In* his: Michael O'Connor, first Catholic bishop of Pittsburgh. Pittsburgh, 1975. p. 74–112)
MnCS; PLatS

2170 **Watson, Alfred M.**
St. Mary's Parish [Erie, Pa.]; a brief history. 1972.
35 p. illus. 28 cm.
PLatS

2171 **Whitney, Pa.** St. Cecilia Church.
Diamond jubilee [of] St. Cecilia Parish, Whitney, Pennsylvania, November 20, 1966.

[32] p. illus. 23 cm.
PLatS

2171a **Youngstown, Pa.** Sacred Heart Church.
Sacred Heart Church, 1875-1975. [Irene
Bisi and Pauline Schott, editors].
90 p. chiefly illus. 29 cm.
PLatS

2172 **Youngwood, Pa.** Holy Cross Church.
Holy Cross Church dedication, April 21,
1963.
63 p. illus., ports. 29 cm.
PLatS

PHILIPPINES

2173 **Axtman, Boniface Joseph, O.S.B.**
Educational work of the Benedictine
Order in the Philippines.
226 leaves. 28 cm.
Thesis (M.A.) – University of Santo
Tomas, Manila, 1941.
Typescript.
MnCS (Archives)

POLAND

2173a **Szczygielski, Stanislas, O.S.B.**
Aquila polono-benedictina in qua,
beatorum & illustrium virorum elogia,
caenobiorum, ac rerum memorabilium
synopsis, exordia quoq. & progressus Ordinis p. Benedicti per Poloniam & eius
sceptris subjectas provincias breviter describuntur . . . Cracoviae, in Officina
Vidua & Haeredum Francisci Casari, 1663.
[8], 367, [20] p. 19 cm.
KAS; MnCS

PORTUGAL

2174 **Cocheril, Maur, O.Cist.**
Etudes sur le monachisme en Espagne et
au Portugal. Paris, Lisbon, 1966.
437 p. 23 cm.
MnCS; PLatS

2175 **Leao de Santo Thomas.**
Benedictina lusitana. Em Coimbra,
1644-51.
2 v. 30 cm.
KAS

2176 **Lenage Conde, Antonio.**
Los origenes del monacato benedictino
en la Peninsula Iberica. Leon, 1973.
3 v. 25 cm.
Tesis – Salamanca, 1970.
InStme; KAS; MnCS; PLatS

ROME

2177 **Bachofen, Charles Augustine, O.S.B.**
Der Mons Aventinus zu Rom und die
Benediktinerklöster auf demselben.

53 p. 21 cm.
Offprint from Studien und Mittheilungen
aus dem Benediktinerorden, Jahrg. 18 &
19 (1897-98).
KAS

2178 **Ferrari, Guy, O.S.B.**
Early Roman monasteries; an historical
and topographical study of the monasteries
and convents at Rome from the V through
the X century. Rome, 1956.
3 v. 29 cm.
Typescript.
Contents: v. 1, Text; v. 2, Notes, v. 3,
Plans.
InStme

2179 **Ferrari, Guy, O.S.B.**
Early Roman monasteries; notes for the
history of the monasteries and convents at
Rome from the V through the X century.
Città del Vaticano, Pontificio Istituto de
Archeologia Christiana, 1957.
xxxvii, 455 p. plans. 26 cm. (Studi di an-
tichità christiana, 23)
InStme; MoCo

SARDINIA

2180 **Studi sui Vittorini [benedettini] in
Sardigna,** a cura di F. Artizzu [et al.].
Padova, CEDAM, 1963.
88 p. 25 cm.
KAS; MnCS

SAXONY

2181 **Borgolte, Claudia.**
Studien zur Klosterreform in Sachsen im
Mittelalter.
297 p.
Diss. – Universität Braunschweig, 1976.
MnCS

2182 **Hasse, Hermann Gustav.**
Geschichte der Sächsischen Klöster in
der Mark Meissen und Oberlausitz. Gotha,
F. A. Perthes, 1888.
viii, 317 p. 22 cm.
KAS

SICILY

2183 **White, Lynn Townsend.**
Latin monasticism in Norman Sicily.
Cambridge, Mass., Mediaeval Academy of
America, 1938.
xiii, 335 p. 26 cm.
InStme; PLatS

SILESIA

2184 **Fragmente aus der Geschichte der
Klöster und Stiftungen Schlesiens**

von ihrer Enstehung bis zur Zeit ihrer
Aufhebung im November 1810. Breslau,
Grasz und Barth [1811].
[8], 646 p. illus. 19 cm.
KAS

2185 **Kastner, August.**
Archiv für die Geschichte des Bisthums
Breslau. Neisse, 1859–63.
3 v. 21 cm.
KAS

SOUTH AMERICA

2186 **Linage Conde, Antonio.**
El monacato en España e Hispano-
america. Salamanca, 1977.
Partial contents: El monacato en Hispa-
noamerica, p. 619–660.
MnCS

SPAIN

2187 **Byne, Mildred.**
Forgotten shrines of Spain. Philadelphia
and London, J. B. Lippincott Co., 1926.
311 p. illus., plates, map. 23 cm.
InStme

2188 **Cocheril, Meur, O.Cist.**
Etudes sur le monachisme en Espagne et
su Portugal. Paris, Lisbon, 1966.
437 p. 23 cm.
MnCS; PLatS

2189 **Lacarra, José M.**
La colonizzazione benettina in Spagna.
(*In* La bonfica benedettina, p. 127–152)
PLatS

2190 **Leão de Santo Thomas.**
Benedictina lusitana. Em Coimbra,
1644–51.
2 v. 30 cm.
KAS

2191 **Linage Conde, Antonio.**
El monacato en España e Hispanoamerica. Salamanca, 1977.
778 p. 24 cm.
MnCS

2192 **Linage Conde, Antonio.**
Los origenes del monacato benedictino
en la Peninsula Ibérica. León, Centro de
Estudios e Investigagión San Isidoro,
1973.
3 v. 25 cm.
Tesis–Salamanca, 1970.
InStme; KAS; MnCS; PLatS

2193 **Perez de Urbel, Justo, O.S.B.**
El compromiso monastico en la España
de la reconquista.
(*In* Semana de Estudios monasticos,
14th, Silos, 1973. p. 57–73)
PLatS

2194 **Santoa Deiz, José Luis.**
La encomienda de monasterios en la
Corona de Castille, siglos X–XV. Roma-
Madrid [1961].
238 p. illus. 24 cm.
MnCS

2195 **Yepes, Antonio de, O.S.B.**
La coronica general de la Orden de San
Benito . . . en que se trata de muchos san-
tos, y varones illustres . . . y de los
monasterios . . . Valladolid, Francisco
Fernandez de Cordova, 1609–1621.
7 v. 30 cm.
MnCS; PLatS (microfilm)

2196 **Yepes, Antonio de, O.S.B.**
Crónica general de la Orden de San
Benito. Estudio preliminar y edición por
Justo Pérez de Urbel. Madrid, Ediciones
Atlas, 1959–60.
3 v. 26 cm.
MnCS

SWABIA

2197 **Schwarzmaier, Hansmartin.**
Königtum, Adel und Klöster im Gebiet
zwischen oberer Illier und Lech. Augsburg, Verlag der Schäbischen Forschungs-
gemeinschaft, 1961.
viii, 196 p. 24 cm.
MnCS

2198 **Zapf, Georg Wilhelm.**
Reisen in einige Klöster Schwabens,
durch den Schwarzwald und in die
Schweiz, im Jahr 1781. Erlangen, J. J.
Palm, 1786.
6, 260 p. plates. 25 cm.
KAS

SWEDEN

2199 **Oppermann, Charles James August.**
The English missionaries in Sweden and
Finland. London, Macmillan Co., 1937.
xxii, 221 p. 22 cm.
MnCS

SWITZERLAND

2200 **Kuhn, Konrad.**
Thurgovia Sacra; Geschichte der katholischen kirchlichen Stiftungen des Kantons
Thurgau. Frauenfeld, J. Gromann, 1876–
1883.
3 v. in 2. 21 cm.
KAS

2201 **Walter, Silja (Sr. M. Hedwig).**
Das Kloster am Rande der Stadt. Zürich,
Verlag der Arche [1971].
86 p. illus. 20 cm.
MnCS

THURINGIA

2202 **Otto, Heinrich Friedrich.**
Thuringia sacra; sive, Historia monasteriorum quae olim in Thuringia floruerunt . . . Francofurti, ex Officina Weidmanniana, 1737.
[10], 956, [18] p. illus., plates, coats of arms, seals. 36 cm.
KAS

UNITED STATES OF AMERICA

2203 **Cada, Joseph.**
Czech-American Catholics, 1850–1920. Chicago, Benedictine Abbey Press [1964].
124 p. 19 cm.
PLatS

2204 **Doppelfeld, Basilius, O.S.B.**
Mönchtum und kirchlicher Heilsdienst; Entstehung und Entwicklung des nordamerikanischen Benediktinertums im 19. Jahrhundert. Münsterschwarzach, Vier-Türme-Verlag, 1974.
xx, 381 p. 21 cm.
InStme; MnCS; PLatS

2205 **Lemcke, Peter Henry, O.S.B.**
Haudegen Gottes: das Leben des P. H. Lemke, 1796–1882, von ihm selbst erzählt, kommentirt und hrsg. von Willibald Mathäser. Würzburg, Kommissionsverlag Echter, 1971.
305 p. 21 cm.
InStme; PLatS

2205a **Neuman, Matthias, O.S.B.**
A directory of Benedictine resource personnel for North America. [St. Meinrad, Ind., St. Meinrad Archabbey, 1981].
[x, 200 leaves] 21 cm. (American Benedictine Academy. Research studies, 1)
InStme; MnCS

2206 **Rippinger, Joel, O.S.B.**
Some historical determinants of American Benedictine monasticism: 1846–1900.
38 p. 28 cm.
Thesis–Pontificium Athenaeum Anselmianum, Rome, 1974.
Typescript.
MoCo

2207 **Winston, Colleen, Sister, O.S.B.**
A journey in the spirit: Benedictines in the Americas. Slide-tape program commissioned by the Presidents of the American Benedictine Federations of North America, 1979.
KyCovS

VIRGINIA

2208 **Brennan, Robert John, O.S.B.**
Golden jubilee, Benedictine High School, 1911–1961. Centennial, Benedictine Fathers in Richmond, Va., 1861–1961.
[10] p. 28 cm.
NcBe; PLatS

2209 **Kollar, Edmund, O.S.B.**
Our parish school and convent dedication, January 17, 1965, St. Gregory the Great [Church, Virginia Beach, Va.].
[44] p. illus., ports. 23 cm.
PLatS

2210 **Richmond, Va.** St. Benedict's Parish.
Saint Benedict's Parish, golden jubilee, 1911–1961.
34 p.
NcBe

WALES

2211 **Cowley, F. G.**
The monastic order in South Wales, 1066–1349. Cardiff, Univ. of Wales Press, 1977.
xii, 317 p. plates. 22 cm.
MnCS

2212 **Knowles, David, O.S.B.**
Medieval religious houses, England and Wales. New York, St. Martin's Press [1972].
xv, 565 p. 24 cm.
PLatS

2213 **Nichols, John, comp.**
Some account of the alien priories, and of such lands as they are known to have possessed in England and Wales. London, J. Nichols, MDCCLXXIX.
2 v. plates. 19 cm.
KAS

WÜRTTEMBERG

2214 **Erzberger, Matthias.**
Die Säkularisation in Württemberg von 1802–1810; ihr Verlauf und ihre Nachwirkungen. Stuttgart, Verlag der Aktien-Gesellschaft "Deutsches Volksblatt," 1902.
vii, 448 p. 23 cm.
KAS

2215 **Rothenhäusler, Konrad.**
Die Abteien und Stifte des Herzogthums Württemberg im Zeitalter der Reformation. Stuttgart, "Deutsches Volksblatt," 1886.
xvi, 268 p. 23 cm.
KAS

2216 **Sattler, Christian Friedrich.**
Historische Beschreibung des Herzogthums Würtemberg und aller desselben

Städte, Klöster und darzu gehörigen
Aemter. Stuttgart, J. N. Stoll, 1752.

[20], 208, 292, [23] p. illus. 21 cm.

KAS

2217 **Sauter, Franz.**

Die Klöster Württembergs. Alphabe-
tische Uebersicht der Abteien, Chorherrenstifte, Probsteien, etc. Stuttgart, G.
Lemppenau, 1879.

64 p. 24 cm.

KAS

2218 **Schefold, Max.**

Kirchen und Klöster in Württemberg
und Hohenzollern, nach alten Vorlagen.
Frankfurt am Main, W. Weidlich, 1961.

255 p. illus. 19 cm.

PLatS

ZULULAND

2218a **Sieber, Gottfried.**

Der Aufbau der katholischen Kirche im
Zululand, von den Anfängen bis zur Gegen-
wart. Münsterschwarzach, Vier-Türme-
Verlag, 1976.

316 p. illus. 21 cm. (Münsterschwarzacher Studien, Bd. 21)

p. 57–89: Die Anfänge der Benediktiner-
mission im Zululand.

MnCS

X. BENEDICTINE HISTORY: CONGREGATIONS

1. GENERAL WORKS

2219 **Dammertz, Viktor, O.S.B.**
Das Verfassungsrecht der benediktinschen Mönchskongregationen in Geschichte und Gegenwart. Erzabtei St. Ottilien, Eos Verlag, 1963.
xxiv, 276 p. 25 cm.
KAS; MnCS; PLatS

2219a **Szczygielski, Stanislas, O.S.B.**
Diversae congregationes in Ordine et sub
Regula s.p. Benedicti.
(*In* his: Aquila Polono-Benedictina.
Cracoviae, 1663. p. 248–362)
KAS; MnCS

2. INDIVIDUAL CONGREGATIONS

American-Cassinese

2220 **Album monasteriorum,** collegiorum,
paroeciarum nec non scholarum parochialium quae a Congregationis Americano-Cassinensis patribus O.S.B.
administrantur, 1892–93. [Beatty, Pa.],
Typis Abbatiae St. Vincentii [1893].
70 p. 23 cm.
InStme; KAS; PLatS

2221 **Catalogus monachorum** Ord. S. B. Benedicti Congregationis-Casinensis, 1873–
1917. Typis Abbatiae S. Vincentii in
Pennsylvania.
vols., size varies (22 cm. & 14 cm.)
The first issues were called Congregationis Americae-Bavaricae Cassinensi af-
fliliatae.
The issues for 1873, 1874, 1878 and 1879
were published at St. Vincent Abbey,
Latrobe, Pa.; the issues for 1893–1917
were published at St. John's Abbey, Collegeville, Minn.
Since 1918 the catalogus or directory of
members is included in the Ordo Divini Officii for the Amercian Cassinese Congregation.
PLatS

2222 **Renew and create;** a statement of the
American-Cassinese Benedictine
monastic life, thirty–sixth general
chapter, second session, June, 1969.
78 p. 18 cm.
AStb; KAS; MnCS

2223 **Sause, Bernard Austin, O.S.B.**
How the general Decree (March 23,
1955) of the Sacred Congregation of Rites
on the simplification of rubrics affects the
Benedictines of the American Cassinese
Congregation. Complete text translated,

with brief commentary. [Atchison, Kans.,
1955].
34 leaves. 28 cm.
KAS

Annunciation B.V.M.

2224 **Ordo Congregationis Annunciationis
B.V.M., O.S.B.** Mechlin, H. Dessain.
v. 17 cm.
MnCS

Bavarian

2225 **Necrologium Congregationis Benedictinae Bavaricae,** 1836–1950. Monachii,
1950.
110 p.
AStb

2226 **Statuta Congregationis Benedictino-
Bavaricae.** Deggendorfii, Typis J.
Nothhaft, 1905.
59 p. 19 cm.
KAS; KySu

Beuronese

2227 **Helmecke, Drutmar, O.S.B.**
Die theologische Schule der Beuroner
Kongregation.
(*In* Beuron, 1863–1963; Festschrift . . .
Beuron, 1963. p. 441–472)
PLatS

2228 **Schäfer, Bernhard, O.S.B.**
Beuroner Benedictiner-Congregation,
50. jähriges Jubiläum. Hechingen, Press-
Verein, 1913.
19 p.
AStb

Brazilian

2229 **Endres, José Lohr, O.S.B.**
Catalogo dos bispos, gerais, provinciais,
abades e mais cargos da Ordem de Sao
Bento do Brasil, 1582–1975. Salvador,
Bahia, Editor Benedictina, 1976.
510 p. 32 cm.
MnCS

2230 **Luna, Joaquim Grangeiro de, O.S.B.**
The Benedictine Congregation of Brazil
in general. Translated by Otho Sullivan,
O.S.B.
43 leaves. 28 cm.
Typescript, 1966.
KAM

Bursfeld

2231 **Charmans, Bruno, O.S.B.**
Enchiridion pietatis benedictinae, in quo exhibentur duodecim exercitia monastica, ad Regulam, caeremonias, statuta, & observantias Ordinis S. Benedicti Congreg. Bursfeld, digesta. Coloniae, apud Constantinum Münich, 1661.
[24], 577 p. 13 cm.
KAS; MnCS

2232 **Frank, Barbara.**
Das Erfurter Peterskloster im 15. Jahrhundert; Studien zur Geschichte des Klosterreform und der Bursfelder Union. Göttingen, Vandenhoeck und Ruprecht, 1973.
465 p. fold. map. 25 cm.
MnCS

2233 **Heutger, Nicolaus C.**
Bursfeld und seine Reformklöster in Niedersachsen. 2. erweiterte Aufl. Hildesheim, A. Lax, 1975.
xxvii, 147 p. 20 plates. 23 cm.
MnCS

2234 **Volk, Paulus, O.S.B.**
Die Generalkapitels-Rezesse der Bursfelder Kongregation. Siegburg, Respublica-Verlag, 1955–1959.
3 v. 25 cm.
InStme; KAS; MnCS; PLatS

2235 **Volk, Paulus, O.S.B.**
Zur Geschichte des Bursfelder Breviers. [Beuron? 1928].
97 p. 21 cm.
MoCo; PLatS

2236 **Ziegler, Walter.**
Die Bursfelder Kongregation in der Reformationszeit, dargestellt an Hand der Generalkapitelsrezesse der Bursfelder Kongregation. Münster, Aschendorff [1968].
156 p. fold. map. 26 cm.
InStme; MnCS; PLatS

Cassinese

2237 **Barbo, Ludovico, O.S.B.**
De initiis Congregationis Cassinensis historia brevis. MS. Subiaco, Italy (Benedictine abbey), codex 159. 42 f. Octavo. Saec. 15.
Microfilm: MnCH

2238 **Bastien, Pierre, O.S.B.**
Compendium privilegiorum Congregationis Cassinensis.
115 p. 25 cm.
Xerox copy.
PLatS

2239 **Constitutiones vel Actus summorum pontificum,** ex quibus privilegia enarrata desumpta sunt. Monasterii Guestfalorum, Aschendorff, 1918.
14 p. 28 cm.
PLatS

2240 **De privilegiis Cassinensium brevis relatio.** Monasterii Guestafalorum, Aschendorff, 1917.
v, 44 p. 28 cm.
PLatS

Cassinese Congregation of the Primitive Observance. *See* Subiaco Congregation.

English

2241 **Allanson, Peter, O.S.B.**
A history of the English Benedictine Congregation, 1558–1850. Microfiche edition. Biscester, Oxon, OMP and Micromedia Ltd., c 1978.
2 v. (98 fiches. 148x105 mm.) 17 cm.
The original edition of 14 volumes is in copperplate script.
PLatS

2241a **Bishop, Edmund.**
Bishop Hedley and Dom U. Berlière on the history of the English Benedictines; a letter to a friend by Edmund Bishop. [n.p., 1897].
40 p.
NcBe

2242 **Chaussy, Yves, O.S.B.**
Les Bénédictins anglais réfugiés en France au XVIIe siècle (1611–1669). Paris, P. Lethielleux, 1967.
xxiv, 255 p. 24 cm.
InStme; KAS; MnCS; PLatS

2243 **Ford, Hugh Edmund, O.S.B.**
Notes on the origin and early development of the restored English Benedictine Congregation, 1600–1661, from contemporary documents. [Downside, 1887].
[16], 78 p. 24 cm.
NdRi; PLatS

2244 **Ford, Hugh Edmund, O.S.B.**
Some remarks on the question: To whom belongs what is required by the religious missionary in England? Yeovil, Printed by the Western Chronicle Company [1888].
12 p. 23 cm.
PLatS

2245 **Snow, Terence Benedict, O.S.B.**
Obit book of the English Benedictines from 1600 to 1912; being the necrology of the English Congregation of the Order of St. Benedict from 1600 to 1883, comp. by Abbot Snow, rev., enl. and continued by Dom Henry Hobert Birt. Privately printed

by J. C. Thomson at the Mercat Press,
1913. Westmead, England, Gregg, 1970.
xli, 414 p. 23 cm.
PLatS

Federation of the Americas. *See* Swiss-
American Congregation.

French Congregation. *See* Solesmes Congregation.

Montevergine

2246 **Mongelli, Giovanni, O.S.B.**
Storia di Montevergine e della Congregazione Verginiana. [Napoli, Administrazione provinciale di Avellino, 1965.
2 v. 25 cm.
KAS

St. Justina

2247 **Pitigliani, Riccardo.**
Il ven. Ludovico Barbo e la diffusione
dell'Imitazione di Cristo per opera della
Congregazione di S. Giustina. Padova,
Badia S. Giustina, 1943.
xxxi, 196 p. illus., plates. 25 cm.
MnCS; PLatS

2248 **Tassi, Ildefonso, O.S.B.**
Ludovico Barbo (1381–1443). Roma,
Storia e letteratura, 1952.
xvi, 179 p. 26 cm.
InStme; MnCS

St. Maur

2249 **Besse, Jean Martial Léon, O.S.B.**
Les fondateurs de la Congrégation de
Saint-Maur. Lille, H. Morel, 1902.
36 p.
Extrait de la Revue des sciences
ecclésiatiques.
NcBe

2250 **Chaussy, Yves, O.S.B.**
Matricula monachorum professorum
Congregationis S. Mauri in Gallia Ordinis
Sancti Patris Benedicti ab initio eiusdem
Congregationis usque ad annum 1789.
Paris, Librairie Perrée, 1959.
xx, 255 p. 25 cm.
PLatS; InStme; KAS; MnCS

2251 **Dantier, Alphonse.**
Rapports sur la correspondance inédite
des Bénédictins de Saint-Maur, addressés
à . . . le Ministre de l'Instruction Publique
et des Cultes. Paris, Imprimerie Impériale,
1858.
262 p. 24 cm.
Text of correspondence: p. 66–262.
MnCS

2252 **Dosh, Terence Leonard,** 1930–
The growth of the Congregation of Saint
Maur, 1618–1672.
253 p. 28 cm.
Thesis (Ph.D.) – University of Minnesota,
1971.
Xeroxed by University Microfilms, Ann
Arbor, Mich.
MnCS

2253 **Histoire littéraire de la Congrégation de
Saint-Maur,** Ordre de S. Benoît . . .
Bruxelles, Paris, chez Humblot, 1770.
xxviii, 800, [28] p. 26x20 cm.
KAS; MnCS

2254 **Nécrologe de la Congrégation de Saint-
Maur.** Publié avec introduction, supplé-
ments et appendices par m. l'abbé J-B.
Vanel. Paris, H. Champion, 1896.
lxiii, 412 p. 29 cm.
MnCS

2255 **Réjalot, Thierry, O.S.B.**
Inventaire des lettres publiées des
Bénédictins de la Congrégation de Saint-
Maur. [Liguge, France, Abbaye Saint Mar-
tin, 1933–43].
344 p. 25 cm.
KAS

2256 **Robert, Ulysse Léonard Léon.**
Supplément à l'Histoire littéraire de la
Congregation de Saint Maur [par R. P.
Tassin] par Ulysse Robert. Paris, A.
Picard, 1881.
98 p. 22x28 cm.
InStme

2257 **Rousseau, François.**
Moines bénédictins martyrs et con-
fesseurs de la foi pendant la Révolution.
Paris, Desclée, De Brouwer, 1926.
xiii, 390 p. 19 cm.
KAS

2257a **Tassin, René Prosper, O.S.B.**
Histoire littéraire de la Congrégation de
Saint-Maur . . . Bruxelles, Paris, chez
Humblot, 1770.
xxviii, 800 p.
KAS(microfilm); PLatS(microfilm);
MnCS

St. Ottilien

2258 **Hugger, Pirmin, O.S.B.**
Die Missionsgeschichte der Benediktinerkongregation von St. Ottilien.
(*In* Die Benediktinerabtei Münsterschwarzach. Vier-Thürme-Verlag, 1965.
p. 88–117)
PLatS

St. Vanne and St. Hydulphe

2259 **Cherest, Gilbert.**
Supplément à la Bibliothèque des Bénédictins de la Congrégation de Saint-Vanne et Saint-Hydulphe. [n.p., n.d.].
121 p. illus. 25 cm.
InStme

2260 **Matricula religiosorum professorum** clericorum et sacerdotum Congregationis Sanctorum Vitoni et Hydulphi (1604–1789). Nouvelle édition revue et traduite par Gilbert Chérest. Paris, P. Lethielleux, 1963.
xvi, 76 p. 25 cm.
InStme; KAS; MnCS; PLatS

Sankt Jakob zu Regensburg

2261 **Dilworth, Mark, O.S.B.**
The Scots in Franconia; a century of monastic life. Totowa, N.J., Rowman and Littlefield [1974].
301 p. illus., plan. 23 cm.
InStme; KAS; PLatS

Solesmes

2262 **Bibliographie des Bénédictins** de la Congrégation de France par des pêres de la meme Congrégation. Nouv. ed. entièrement refondue . . . Paris, H. Champion, 1906.
179 p. 25 cm.
CaQStB; KAS; MnCS; NcBe

2263 **Des Pilliers, Pierre-Marie-Raphaël.**
Les Bénédictins de la Congrégation de France. Mémoires . . . Bruxelles, P.J.D. DeSomer, 1868–69.
2 v. 24 cm.
KAS

Subiaco

2264 **Cisneros, Juan de, O.S.B.**
Origen de la Congregacion de la Observancia de S. Benito de Espana y sus monasterios captitulares. MS. Monasterio benedictino de Montserrat, Spain, codex 846. 135 f. Saec. 17(1645).
Microfilm: MnCH proj. no. 30,098

2265 **I monasteri italiani della Congregatione Sublacense** (1843–1972); saggi storici nel primo centenario della Congregazione. Parma, Scuola tipografica benedettina, 1972.
616 p. illus., ports., tables. 24 cm.
KAS

2266 **Pietro Casaretto e gli inizi della Congregazione Sublacense** (1810–1880).
Montserrat, Publicacions de l'Abadia de Montserrat, 1972.
Estratto dal vol. XIV(1972) di Studia monastica, p. 349–525.
InStme

Swiss

2267 **Benediktinische Lebensform;** Satzungen der Schweizerischen Benedictinerkongregation. Approbiert ad experimentum vom Kongregationskapitel, 1970.
92 p.
MoCo

Terracona

2268 **Tobella, Antonius M., O.S.B.**
Cronologia dels capítols de la Congregació Claustral Tarraconense i Cesaraugustana (primera part: 1219–1661).
(*In* Analecta Montserratensis, v. 10, p. 221–338)
PLatS

2269 **Tobella, Antonius M., O.S.B.**
Documents del primer segle de la Congregació Claustral Tarraconense.
(*In* Analecta Montserratensia, v. 10, p. 339–455)
PLatS

Valladolid

2270 **Aplec de plàtiques predicades en diferents monastirs,** explicitats, de la Congregació de San Benito el Real de Valladolid. MS. Monasterio benedictino de Montserrat, Spain, codex 709. 556 p. Quarto. Saec. 18. Lingua Castellà.
Microfilm: MnCH proj. no. 30,035

2271 **Colombás, García, O.S.B.**
Documentos sobre la sujeción del monasterio de Montserrat al de San Benito de Valladolid. Abadia de Montserrat, 1954–55.
Reprint from: Analecta Montserratensia, v. 8, p. 93–124.
MnCS

2272 **Colombás, García, O.S.B.**
La primera edición de las constituciones de la Congregación de Valladolid. Abadia de Montserrat, 1960.
8 p. facsims. 28 cm.
MnCS

2273 **Foyo, Bernardo, O.S.B.**
Catecismo benedictino, en donde se explican por menor los exercicios en que se debe compar un monge de la Congregación de San Benito de Valladolid. MS.

Monasterio benedictino de Montserrat, Spain, codex 23. 350 p. Quarto. Saec. 18(1793).

Microfilm: MnCH proj. no. 29,986

2274 **Serna, Clemente de la, O.S.B.**

El voto de clausura en la Congregación de Valladolid.

(*In* Semana de estudios monasticos, 14th, Silos, 1973. p. 149–182)

PLatS

2275 **Varous ilustres benedictinos** de la Congregación de Hespana llamada de San Benito de Valladolid. MS. Monasterio benedictino de Montserrat, Spain, codex 784. 166 f. Saec. 18(1788).

Microfilm: MnCH proj. no. 30,062

2276 **Zaragoza Pascual, Ernesto.**

Los generales de la Congregación de San Benito de Valladolid. Silos, 1973–

v. 24 cm.

InStme; KAS; MnCS; PLatS

1. GENERAL WORKS

2277 **Blume, Karl.**
Abbatia; ein Beitrag zur Geschichte der kirchlichen Rechtssprache. Stuttgart, F. Enke, 1914; Amsterdam, P. Schippers, 1965.
xiv, 118 p. 23 cm.
PLatS

2278 **Digby, Kenelm Henry.**
Studien über die Klöster des Mittelalters. Aus dem Englischen übersetzt von A. Kobler. Regensburg, New York, F. Pustet, 1967.
viii, 680 p. 24 cm.
Translation of Book X of Mores catholici by K. H. Digby.
KAS

2279 **Hettinger, Franz.**
Aus Welt und Kirche; Bilder & Skizzen. 3. Aufl. Freiburg, Herder, 1893.
2 v. illus.
Includes accounts of a number of Benedictine abbeys in various countries.
AStb

2280 **James, Montague Rhodes.**
Abbeys. With an additional chapter on "Monastic life and buildings" by A. Hamilton Thompson . . . With one hundred illustrations by photographic reproduction, fifty-six drawings, thirteen plans, seven colour plates and map. London, The Great Western Railway, 1926.
x, 153 p. illus. 23 cm.
NcBe; OrStb

2281 **Müller, Joannes, O.S.B.**
Atlas O.S.B.: Benedictinorum per orbem praesentia / Benedictines throughout the world. 1. ed. Romae, Editiones Anselmianae, 1973.
2 v. maps. 22–32 cm.
Contents: I. Index monasteriorum; II. Tabulae Geographicae.
MnCS

2. BY COUNTRY

Here are entered collective works only. For individual abbeys see chapter XII.

Austria

2282 **Bucelin, Gabriel, jr., O.S.B.**
Uebersicht der Mönchsabteien des Benediktinerordens in Deutschland, Oesterreich, der Schweiz bis zum Anfange dieses Jahrhunderts [saec. XX].

(*In* Archivalische Zeitschrift. Neue Folge, 2. Bd., p. 188–288)
KAS; MnCS

2283 **Röhrig, Floridus, C.R.S.A.**
Alte Stifte in Oesterreich. Wien, Schrollverlag, 1966–67.
2 v. plates. 24 cm.
Includes 17 Benedictine abbeys.
MnCS

2284 **Verzeichnisse der in Ländern** der westlichen Hälfte der Oesterreicheschen Monarchie von Kaiser Joseph II, 1782–1790 aufgehobenen Klöster. Gesammelt von P. P.
(*In* Archivalische Zeitschrift, hrsg. durch das Bayerische Allgemeine Reichsarchiv in München. Neue Folge, 5. Bd. (1894), p. 234–275; 6. Bd.(1895), p. 229–279; 7. Bd.(1897), p. 46–172).
This covers the area of present (1979) Austria and Czechoslovakia.
KAS; MnCS

2285 **Zarbel, J. B.**
Reise durch einige Abteien in Oesterreich. Ratisbon, F. Pustet, 1831.
298 p.
AStb

Baden

2286 **Die Benediktinerklöster in Baden-Württemberg,** bearb. von Franz Quarthal [und andere] . . . Augsburg, Verlag Winfried-Werk, 1975.
845 p. illus. maps. 25 cm. (Germania benedictina, Bd. 5)
MnCS; KAS

Bavaria

2287 **Hemmerle, Josef.**
Die Benediktinerklöster in Bayern. München, 1951.
150 p. 21 cm. (Bayerische Heimatforschung, Heft 4)
MnCS

2288 **Hemmerle, Josef.**
Die Benediktinerklöster in Bayern. Augsburg, Kommissionsverlag Winfried-Werk [1970].
415 p. coats of arms, maps. 25 cm. (Germania benedictina, Heft 2)
KAS; MnCS

2288a **Lindner, Pirmin, O.S.B.**
Die Schriftsteller und die um Wissenschaft und Kunst verdienten Mitglieder des Benediktiner Ordens im heutigen

Königreich Bayern vom Jahre 1750 bis zur Gegenwart. Regensburg, G. J. Manz, 1880.
2 v. 24 cm.
Arranged by abbeys.
InStme; KAS; MnCS; PLatS

2288b **Wild, Joachim.**
Beiträge zur Registerführung der Bayerischen Klöster und Hochstifte im Mittelalter. Kallmünz, Oberpfalz, Verlag Michael Lassleben, 1973.
119 p. 25 cm. (Münchener Historische Studien. Abteilung Hilfswissen-schaften, Bd XII)
MnCS

Belgium

2289 **Michel, Edouard.**
Abbayes et monastères de Belgique; leur importance et leur rôle dans le développement du pays. Bruxelles, Librairie Nationale d'art et d'histoire, 1923.
CaQStM; MoCo

England

2290 **Aedilvulfus, O.S.B.,** fl. 803.
De abbatibus [by] Aethelwulf. Edited by A. Campbell. Oxford, Clarendon Press, 1967.
xlix, 72 p. 19 cm.
PLatS

2291 **The Benedictine yearbook,** 1974; a guide to the abbeys, priories, parishes, monks and nuns of the English Congregations of the Order of Saint Benedict. Edited by Rev. Gordon Beattie, O.S.B. Warrington, St. Alban's Priory (1974).
155 p.
KAS; NcBe

2292 **Braun, Hugh.**
English abbeys. London, Faber and Faber Ltd. [1971].
299 p. 32 plates plans. 23 cm.
KAS

2293 **Cox, John Charles.**
The sanctuaries and sanctuary seekers of mediaeval England. London, G. Allen & Sons, 1911.
xx, 347 p. illus., plates, 23 cm.
PLatS

2294 **Crossley, Frederick Herbert.**
The English abbey. London, Batsford [1962].
192 p.
AStb;NcBe

2295 **Fosbrooke, Thomas Dudley.**
British monachism; or, manners & customs of the monks and nuns of England

. . . A new edition, very much enlarged. London, J. Nichols, 1817.
560 p. illus.
MoCo

2296 **Gilyard-Beer, R.**
Abbeys; an introduction to the religious houses of England and Wales. London, H. M. Stationery Office, 1958.
v, 89 p. illus., plans. 19 cm.
InStme

2297 **Harnett, Cynthia.**
Monasteries & monks. London, B. T. Batsford [1963].
176 p. illus., map, plans. 22 cm.
PLatS

2298 **Hearne, Thomas.**
Antiquities of Great Britain, illustrated in views of monasteries, castles, and churches, now existing. Engraved from drawings made by Thomas Hearne. London, T. Hearne, 1786–1807.
2 vols.
PLatS (microfilm)

2299 **Kelly, J. Thomas.**
Thorns on the Tudor rose: monks, rogues, vagabonds, and sturdy beggars. Jackson, University Press of Mississippi, 1977.
xii, 204 p. 24 cm.
InStme

2300 **Knowles, David, O.S.B.**
Bare ruined choirs: the dissolution of the English monasteries. Cambridge [England], New York, Cambridge University Press, 1976.
329 p. illus. 25 cm.
Abridged edition of: The religious orders in England, v. 3: The Tudor age, first published in 1959.
InStme

2301 **Knowles, David, O.S.B.**
The heads of religious houses, England and Wales, 940–1216. Edited by David Knowles, C.N.L. Brooke [and] Vera C.M. London. Cambridge [England], University Press, 1972.
xlviii, 277 p. 24 cm.
MnCS

2302 **Knowles, David, O.S.B.**
The monastic buildings of England.
(*In* his: The historian character, and other essays. Cambridge, 1963. p. 179–212)
PLatS

2302a **Kominiak, Benedict, O.S.B.**
Loci ubi Deus quaeritur . . . the Benedictine abbeys of the entire world . . . Erzabtei St. Ottilien, EOS Verlag [1980].

527 p. illus. 28 cm.
MnCS

2302b **Le Strange, Richard.**
Monasteries of Norfolk. [King's Lynn, Norfolk], Yates [1973].
139 p. 21 cm.
MnCS; PLatS

2302c **Morris, Richard.**
Cathedrals and abbeys of England and Wales; the building church, 600–1540. New York, W. W. Norton & Co., 1979.
294 p. illus., plates. 26 cm.
MnCS

2303 **Nichols, John.**
Some account of the alien priories, and of such lands as they are known to have possessed in England and Wales. London, Printed by and for J. Nichols, MDCCLX-XIX.
2 v. plates. 19 cm.
KAS

2304 **Oliver, George.**
Monasticon Dioecesis Exoniensis, being a collection of records and instruments illustrating the ancient conventual, collegiate and eleemosynary foundations . . . Exeter, P. A. Hannaford, 1846.
xxiv, 493 p. plates. 40 cm.
KAS

2305 **Palmer, Roger Liddesdale.**
English monasteries in the Middle Ages; an outline of monastic architecture and custom from the conquest to the suppression. London, Constable & Co., 1930.
xv, 232 p. illus. 26 cm.
MnCS

2306 **Ryan, Alice Mary.**
A map of old English monasteries and related ecclesiastical foundations, A.D. 400–1066. Ithaca, N.Y., Cornell University Press, 1939.
vi, 33 p. 23 cm.
MnCS; NcBe

2307 **Wood, Susan M.**
English monasteries and their patrons in the thirteenth century. London, Oxford University Press, 1955.
viii, 191 p. 23 cm.
MnCS

Europe

2308 **Braunfels, Wolfgang.**
Monasteries of Western Europe: thé architecture of the Orders. [Translated from the German by Alastair Laing]. London, Thames and Hudson [1972].
263 p. illus., plans. 29 cm.
KAS; MnCS; NcBe

2309 **David, Lucien, O.S.B.**
Les grandes abbayes d'Occident. Lille, Desclée [1907?].
473 p. illus. 30 cm.
CaQStB; MnCS

2310 **Kastner, Jörg.**
Historiae fundationum monasteriorum; Frühformen monastischer Institutionsgeschichts-schreibung im Mittelalter. München, Arben-Gesellschaft, 1974.
vii, 193 p. 20 cm.
MnCS

2311 **Monasteriologia:** documenta et excerpta ad historiam variorum monasteriorum. MS. Benediktinerabtei St. Paul im Lavantthal, Austria, codex 249/2. 456 f. Folio. Saec. 18.
Microfilm: MnCH proj. no. 12,100

2312 **Numerus monasteriorum** Ordinis S. Benedicti et religiones sub Regula ejusdem militantes. MS. Benediktinerabtei Melk, Austria, codex 525, f.272v. Folio. Saec. 15.
Microfilm: MnCH proj. no. 1472

2313 **Richards, Ian.**
Abbeys of Europe. Paul Hamlyn [1968].
187 p.
MoCo

2314 **Schamel, Johann Martin.**
Entwurff eines Closter-Lexici, worinnen etliche hundert in- und ausser Teutschland gelegene Closter, mit ihren Namen, Orden Lage und Dioces . . . . Eisenach und Naumburg, Michael Gottlieb Griessbach, 1733.
[4] p. 56 colums. 22 cm.
KAS

France

See also Normandy.

2315 **Anger, Pierre, O.S.B.**
Les dépendances de l'Abbaye de Saint-Germain-des-Prés. Paris, Veuve C. Poussielgue, 1906–09.
3 v. 25 cm.
MnCS

2316 **Beaunier, Benedictine monk.**
Recueil historique, chronologique, et topographique, des archevechez, evechez, abbayes et prieurez de France, tant d'hommes, que de filles . . . par ordre alphabetique . . . Par Dom Beaunier. Paris, A.X.R. Mesnier, 1726.
2 v. illus., maps. 26 cm.
CtBeR; KAS; MnCS; PLatS

2317 **Becquet, Jean, O.S.B.**
Abbayes et prieures de l'ancienne France; recueil historique des archevéches,

evéches, abbayes et prieures de France. Ligugé, Abbaye Saint-Martin [1970–75].
535 p. illus.
MoCo

2318 **France. Direction des archives.**
Etat général par fonds des archives départementales. Ancien régime et période révolutionnaire. Paris, A. Picard, 1903.
xii, 806 col., [809]-946 p. 33 cm.
KAS

2318a **Leclercq, Jean, O.S.B.**
Monks and love in twelfth-century France; psycho-historical essays. Oxford, Clarendon Press; New York, Oxford University Press, 1979.
x, 146 p. 23 cm.
InStme

2319 **Martene, Edmond.**
Voyage litteraire de deux religieux Bénédictins de la Congrégation de Saint-Maur, ou l'on trouvera. Westmead, England, Gregg International Publishers, 1969.
2 v. 27 cm.
Photocopy of 1717 edition published by Floretin Delaulne, Paris.
MnCS

Germany

2320 **Brouwer, Christoph.**
Metropolis Ecclesiae Trevericae . . . abbatiarum et monasteriorum ortus progressusque per Archdiocesin Trevirensem complectitur. Confluentibus [Koblenz], sumptibus Rudolphi Friderici Hergt, 1855–56.
2 v. 23 cm.
KAS

2321 **Bruschius, Caspar.**
Supplementum Bruschiaum . . . monasteriorum et episcopatuum Germaniae . . . chronicon. Vindobonae, J. J. Mann, 1692.
[6], 238 p. 21 cm.
KAS

2322 **Bucelin, Gabriel, jr.,O.S.B.**
Uebersicht der Mönchsabteien des Benediktinerordens in Deutschland, Oesterreich, der Schweiz bis zum Anfange dieses Jahrhunderts (saec. XX).
(*In* Archivalische Zeitschrift. Neuw Folge, 2. Bd., p. 188–288)
KAS; MnCS (photocopy)

2323 **Dumont, Karl Theodor.**
Descriptio omnium Archidioecesis Coloniensis ecclesiarum parochialium, collegiatarum, abbatiarum . . . ordine alphabetico circa annum 1800 digesta . . . mit einem Nachtrage . . . Köln, J. & W. Boisserée, 1879.

[8], 56 p. fold. map. 30 cm.
KAS

2324 **Germania monastica.** Klosterverzeichnis der deutschen Benediktiner und Cisterzienser. Neu hrsg. von der Bayerischen Benediktiner-Akademie. Augsburg, Verlag Winfried-Werk in Kommission, 1967.
185 p. 21 cm.
KAS; PLatS

2325 **Haunstinger, Nepomuk, O.S.B.**
Süddeutsche Klöster vor hundert Jahren; Reisetagebuch des . . . Bibliothekar von St. Gallen. Hrsg. mit einer Einleitung und Anmerkungen von P. Gabriel Meier. Köln, M. P. Bachem, 1889.
xv, 114 p. 22 cm.
KAS; MnCS; PLatS

2326 **Landers, Ernst.**
Die deutschen Klöster vom Ausgang Karls des Grossen bis zum Wormser Konkordat und ihr Verhältnis zu den Reformen. Berlin, Verlag Emil Ebering, 1938.
81 p. 25 cm.
PLatS

2327 **Legipont, Oliver, O.S.B.**
Monasticon Moguntiacum; sive, Succincta veterum monasteriorum in Archiepiscopatu Moguntio, vicinisque locis, partim extantium, partim suppressorum. [Pragae], typis Joannis Julii Gerzabek, 1746.
[32], 80 p. 16 cm.
KAS

2328 **Lindner, Pirmin, O.S.B.**
Verzeichnis der deutschen Benediktiner-Abteien vom 7.-20. Jahrhundert.
(*In* Germania monastica, Augsburg, 1967. p. 1–50)
PLatS

2329 **Schreiner, Klaus.**
Social- und Standesgeschichtliche Untersuchungen zu den Benediktinerkonventen im östlichen Schwarzwald. Stuttgart, W. Kohlhammer, 1964.
xxxv, 331 p.
MnCS

Great Britain

See also England; Scotland; Wales

2330 **Dixon, H. Claiborne.**
The abbeys of Great Britain. London, T. W. Laurie [1908].
204 p.
NcBe

2331 **Langdon-Davies, John.**
Henry VIII and the dissolution of the
monasteries; a collection of contemporary
documents. London, J. Cape [1966].
13 pieces, illus. 23x25 cm.
Issued in portfolio.
PLatS

2332 **Great Britain. Ordnance survey.**
Map of monastic Britain. 2d ed. Chess-
ington, Surrey, Director-General of the
Ordnance Survey, 1954–
v. folded col. map. 22 cm.
Map of v. 1 is 79 x 102 cm. folded to 22 x
16. Scale: 1:625,000.
InStme

2333 **Tanner, Thomas.**
Notitia monastica; or, An account of all
the abbies, priories and houses of friers,
formerly in England and Wales . . . now
reprinted with many additions by James
Nasmith. Cambridge, J. Archdeacon, 1787.
794 p.
KAS; PLatS(microfilm)

2334 **Taylor, Richard Cowling.**
Index monasticus; or, The abbeys and
other monasteries . . . of East Anglia,
systematically arranged and briefly
described . . . London, Printed for the
author by R. and A. Taylor, 1821.
6, xxxii, 132 p. illus., plates, maps.
50x35 cm.
KAS

2335 **Willis, Brown.**
A survey of the cathedrals of York,
Durham . . . containing an history of their
foundations . . . London, Printed for T.
Osborne in Gray's Inn, 1742.
3 v. illus., plates, plans. 26 cm.
KAS (v. 3)

Hohenzollern

2336 **Schefold, Max.**
Kirchen und Klöster in Württemberg
und Hohenzollern, nach alten Vorlagen.
Frankfurt am Main, V. Weidlich, 1961.
255 p. illus. 19 cm.
PLatS

Hungary

2337 **Fuxhoffer, Damian, O.S.B.**
Monasteriologiae regni Hungariae . . .
t. 1: Monasteria Ord. S. Benedicti. Vindobonae & Strigonii, Carolus Sartori,
1869.
KAS

Ireland

2338 **Mould, Daphne.**
The monasteries of Ireland; an introduction. London, B. T. Batsford, 1976.
188 p. 12 leaves of plates. 23 cm.
InStme

Netherlands

2339 **Damen, Cornelius Ignatius, O.S.B.**
Geschiedenes van den Benediktijnen-
klosters in de Provincie Gronigen. Asen,
Van Gorcum, 1972.
256 p. 24 cm.
MnCS

Normandy

2340 **Du Monstier, Arthur.**
Neustria pia; seu, De omnibus et singulis
abbatiis et prioratiis totius Normaniae . . .
Rothomagi, apud Ioannem Berthelin,
1663.
936 p. 38 cm.
KAS

2341 **Musset, Lucien.**
Les actes de Guillaume le Conquérant et
de la Reine Mathilde pour les abbayes
Caennaises. Caen, Société des antiquaires
de Normandie, 1967.
179 p. 26 cm.
MnCS

2342 **La Normandie bénédictine** au temps de
Guillaume le Conquérant, XI. siècle.
Lille, Facultés Catholiques de Lille,
1967.
567 p. 24 cm.
The 32 articles are mostly on individual
monasteries.
French or English.
InStme; MnCS

Portugal

2343 **Bronseval, Claude de.**
Peregrinatio hispanica; voyage de Dom
Edme de Saulieu, abbé de Clairvaux, en
Espagne et au Portugal, 1531-1533 . . .
Paris, Presses Universitaires de France,
1970.
2 v. facsims., maps. 25 cm.
Text in Latin and French.
KAS

2344 **Leão de Santo Thomas.**
Benedictina lusitana. Em Coimbra,
1644-51.
2 v. 30 cm.
KAS

Rome

2345 **Bachofen, Charles Augustine, O.S.B.**
Der Mons Aventinus zu Rom und die
Benediktiner Klöster auf demselben.
(*In* Studien und Mittheilungen aus dem
Benediktinerorden. Jahrg. 18(1897),
p. 663–669; 19(1898), p. 69–78, 303–310,
460–476, 648–661)
KAS

Saxony

2346 **Hasse, Hermann Gustav.**
Geschichte der sächsischen Klöster in
der Mark Meissen und Oberlausitz. Gotha,
F. A. Perthes, 1888.
viii, 317 p. 22 cm.
KAS

2347 **Heutger, Nicolaus C.**
Bursfeld und seine Reformklöster in
Niedersachsen. 2. erweiterte Aufl.
Hildesheim, A. Lax. 1975.
xxvii, 147 p. 20 plates. 23 cm.
MnCS

2348 **Stille, Ulrich.**
Dome, Kirchen und Klöster in Niedersachsen. Nach alten Vorlagen. Frankfurt
am Mein, W. Weidlich, 1963.
279 p. illus. 19 cm.
PLatS

Scotland

2349 **Eesson, David Edward.**
Medieval religious houses: Scotland.
London, New York, Longmans, Green,
[1957].
xxxvi, 204 p. maps. 23 cm.
MnCS

2350 **Gordon, James Frederick Skinner.**
Monasticon: an account of all the abbeys,
priories, collegiate churches and hospitals
in Scotland at the Reformation.
(*In* his: Ecclesiastical chronicle of
Scotland, vol. 3. Glasgow, 1867)
KAS

Sicily

2351 **Barberi, Giovanni Luca.**
Beneficia ecclesiastica. Palermo, U.
Manfredi, [1962–63].
2 v. 24 cm.
Contents: v. 1: Vescovadi e abbazie.
PLatS

Spain

2352 **Argaiz, Gregorio de, O.S.B.**
La soledad laureada, por San Benito y
sue hijos, en las iglesias de Espana y teatro
monastico de la provincia Cartaginense.
Madrid, por Bernardo de Herbada, 1675.
7 v. 29 cm.
MnCS (v. 1)

2353 **Bronseval, Claude.**
Peregrinatio hispanica; voyage de Dom
Edme de Saulieu, abbé de Clairvaux, en
Espagne et au Portugal, 1531–1533. Paris,
Presses Universitaires de France, 1970.
2 v. 25 cm.
Text in Latin and French.
KAS

2354 **Compilatio constitutionum monaster-
iorum in Navarra et Aragona.** MS.
Monasterio benedictino de Montserrat,
Spain, codex 995. 137 f. Folio. Saec. 15.
Microfilm: MnCH proj. no. 995

2355 **Martinez, Marcos G.**
Monasterios medievales Asturianos
(siglos VIII–XII). Salinas, Asturias [1977].
158 p. illus. 18 cm.
MnCS

2356 **Rahlves, Friedrich.**
Cathedrals and monasteries of Spain.
Translated [from the French] by James C.
Palmes. London, Kaye, 1966.
310 p. 167 illus., map, diagrs. 24 cm.
PLatS

Switzerland

2357 **Brevis historia monasteriorum** Congregationis Helveto Benedictinae. Codex
impressum, 1703. Cistercienserabtei
Mehrerau, Austria, codex SSS 104 ie.
63 f. Folio.
Microfilm: MnCH proj. no. 29,891

2358 **Bucelin, Gabriel, jr., O.S.B.**
Uebersicht der Mönchsabteien des
Benediktinerordens in Deutschland,
Oesterreich, der Schweiz bis zum Anfange
dieses Jahrhunderts [saec. XX].
(*In* Archivalische Zeitschrift. Neue
Folge, 2. Bd., p. 188–288)
KAS; MnCS(photocopy)

2359 **Die Vorarlberger Barockbaumeister;**
Austellung, Mai–September 1973, in
Einsiedeln und Bregenz zum 250.
Todestag von Br. Caspar Moosbrugger.
xvi, 298 p. plates (276 illus.) 24 cm.
MnCS

Thuringia

2360 **Otto, Heinrich Friedrich.**
Thuringia sacra; sive, Historia
monasteriorum quae olim in Thuringia
floruerunt . . . Francofurti, ex Officina
Weidmanniana, 1737.

[10], 956, [18] p. illus., plates, 36 cm.
KAS

Tirol

2361 **Tirolisches Landesgesetz,** dass die Klöster keine liegenden Güter erwerben dürfen, erlassen durch K. Leopold I. MS. Innsbruck, Austria, Tiroler Landesarchiv, codex 5039. 8 f. Folio. Saec. 17. Microfilm: MnCH proj. no. 29,221

2362 **Verzeichnis der seit** 1780 aufgehobenen Klöster und Bruderschaften in Südtirol. 45 f. Liste aller im röm. Reiche saecularisierten Bistüme, Stiften und Klöster ca. 1803. 13 f. MS. Innsbruck, Austria, Tiroler Landesarchiv, codex 2781 & 2803. Folio. Saec. 18 & 19. Microfilm: MnCH proj. no. 29,177

United States of America

2363 **St. John's Abbey, Collegeville, Minn.** American Benedictine foundations [portfolio]. [Collegeville, Minn., The Scriptorium, 1960]. 44 x 29 cm. MnCS

Wales

2364 **Cowley, Frederick George.** The monastic order in South Wales, 1066–1349. Cardiff, University of Wales Press, 1977. xii, 317 p. plates map. 23 cm. InStme

2365 **Knowles, David, O.S.B.** The heads of religious houses, England and Wales, 940–1216. Edited by David Knowles, C.N.L. Brooke [and] C. M. London. Cambridge [England], University Press, 1972. xlviii, 277 p. 24 cm. MnCS

2366 **Pritchard, Emily M.** The history of St. Dogmaels Abbey, together with her cells, Pill, Caldey and Glascareg, and the mother abbey of Tiron. London, Blades, East & Blades, 1907. 241 p. illus. CaBMi; MnCS; MoCo

Württemberg

2367 **Die Benediktinerklöster in Baden-Württemberg,** bearb. von Franz Quarthal [u.andere]. Augsburg, Verlag Winfried-Werk, 1975. 845 p. illus., maps. 25 cm. (Germania benedictina, Bd. 5) MnCS; KAS

2368 **Bericht über die Würtembergischen** und auch anderen Klöster, 1636–1639. MS. Innsbruck, Austria, Tiroler Landesarchiv, codex 383. 314 f. Folio. Saec. 17. Microfilm: MnCH proj. no. 29,553

2369 **Besold, Christoph.** Documenta rediviva monasteriorum praecipuorum in ducatu Wirtembergico sitorum . . . Tübingen, apud Philibertum Brunn, 1636. [4], 98, 980, 92 p. 20 cm.

2370 **Besold, Christoph.** Prodromus vindiciarum ecclesiasticarum Wirtembergicarum, sive succincta & in compendium redacta demonstratio, quod monasteria in Wirtembergia, quae aug. imperator noster D. Ferdinandus II, jure & armis deo & ecclesiae restituit, sint libera, & ducem jurisdictine immunis. Tubingae, apud Philibertum, 1636. [56], 260 p. 20 cm. KAS

2371 **Rothenhäusler, Konrad.** Die Abrteien und Stifte des Herzogthums Württemberg im Zeitalter der Reformation. Stuttgart, "Deutsches Volksblatt," 1886. xvi, 268 p. 23 cm. KAS

2372 **Sattler, Christian Friedrich.** Historische Beschreibung des Herzogthums Württemberg und aller desselben Städte, Klöster und darzu gehörigen Aemter. Stuttgart, J. N. Stoll, 1752. [20], 208, 292, [23] p. fold. illus. 21 cm. KAS

2373 **Schefold, Max.** Kirchen und Klöster in Württemberg und Hohenzollern, nach alten Vorlagen. Frankfurt am Main, W. Weidlich, 1961. 255 p. illus. 19 cm. PLatS

Abingdon Abbey, England

2374 **Lambrick, Gabrielle Margaret.**
Business affairs at Abingdon Abbey in
mediaeval times. Abingdon [Berks.],
Friends of Abingdon [1966].
31 p. plan. 22 cm.
PLatS

Admont, Austria (Benedictine abbey)

2375 **Album Admontense,** seu catalogus
religiosorum Ordinis S. P. Benedicti in
Abbatia Admontense anno jubilaeo 1874
viventium et ab anno 1674 pie defunctorum. Typis mandavit P. Florianus C.
Kinnast, O.S.B. Graecii, sumptibus
Abbatiae Admont, 1874.
161 p. 23 cm.
InStme; PLatS

2376 **Album Admontense,** seu catalogus
religiosorum Ordinis S.P.N. Benedicti in
Abbatia Admontensi, Congregationis
Austiaco-Benedictinae sub invocatione
B.M.V. sine labe originali conceptae . . .
anno domini 1901 viventium et ab anno
1891 pie defunctorum. Graecii, Abbatia
Admont, 1901.
81 p. 23 cm.
MnCS

2377 **[Catalog of manuscripts in Stift Admont,
Austria].**
396 p. 29 cm.
"Deo Gratias, Sept. 1888. P. Jacobus."
Handwritten.
Xeroxed by University Microfilms, Ann
Arbor, Mich., 1969.
MnCS

2378 **Decreta visitationis monasterii** Admont-
tensis et ecclesiarum suarum annis
1617–40 peractae. MS. Benedictiner-
abtei Admont, Austria, codex 829a,
f.1r–18v. Quarto. Saec. 17.
Microfilm: MnCH proj. no. 9858

2379 **Processus in electione . . .** futuri abbatis
Admontensis (a. 1568). MS. Cistercien-
serabtei Rein, codex 31, f.38v–45r.
Quarto. Saec. 16.
Microfilm: MnCH proj. no. 11,257

2380 **Schematismus der Benediktiner von
Admont.** [Admont, Benediktinerstift]
1900–
v. 23 cm.
InStme(1954); MnCS

2381 **Krause, Adalbert, O.S.B.**
Admont und das Gesäuse in Geschichte
und Sage. Mit 29 Textillustrationen von
Gerhard Hirnschrodt. 2. Aufl. [Linz,
Oberösterreichischer Landesverlag [1965].
144 p. illus. 21 cm.
MnCS

2382 **Krause, Adalbert, O.S.B.**
Das Blasiusmünster in Admont. Linz,
Oberösterreichischer Landesverlag [n.d.].
40, [12] p. 22 plates. 17 cm.
PLatS

2383 **Krause, Adalbert, O.S.B.**
Die Krippenkunst des Steirischen
Bildhauers Josef Thaddäus Stammel im
Stifte Admont. [Wien, Oesterreichische
Staatsdruckerei] 1962.
27 p. illus. (part col.) 17 cm.
PLatS

2384 **Krause, Adalbert, O.S.B.**
St. Hemma. Mödling bei Wien, Missionsdruckerei St. Gabriel, 1948.
47 p. illus., plates. 21 cm.
St. Hemma is the founder of Stift Admont.
MnCS

2385 **Krause, Adalbert, O.S.B.**
Die Stiftsbibliothek in Admont. 7. verb.
Aufl. Linz, Oberösterreichischer Landes-
verlag [1969].
45, [3] p. illus. 17 cm.
MnCS

2386 **List, Rudolf.**
Stift Admont, 1074–1974. Festschrift
zur Neunhundertjahrfeier. (Illustriert:
Conrad Fankhauser [u.a.]). Ried im
Innkreis, Oberösterreichischer Landes-
verlag, 1974.
xxiii, 559 p. illus. (part col.) 25 cm.
InStme; KAS; PLatS

2387 **Roth, F. W. E.**
Die Buchdruckerei des Jakob Köbel . . .
Zwei Bücherverzeichnisse des 14.
Jahrhunderts in der Admonter Stifts-
bibliothek von P. J. Wichner. Leipzig, O.
Harrassowitz, 1968.
36, 36 p.
MnCS

2388 **Rudbertus de Salzburg.**
Collatio in visitatione monasterii Ad-
montensis anno 1462. MS. Vienna, Na-
tionalbibliothek, codex 4969, f.74r–81v.
Quarto. Saec. 15.
Microfilm: MnCH proj. no. 18,141

2389 **Stift Admont.** Urkunden Abschriften.
MS. Vienna, Haus-, Hof- und Staat-
sarchiv, codex W 987/1. 118 f. Saec. 17.
Microfilm: MnCH proj. no. 23,610

2390 **Waagen, P. H.**
Der Stiftsherr von Admont; historischer
Roman. Regensburg, 1928.
NcBe

2391 **Wichner, Jakob, O.S.B.**
Geschichte des Benediktiner-Stiftes Admont. Graz, Im Selbstverlage des Verfassers, 1874–1880.
4 v. 24 cm.
InStme

Affligem, Belgium (Benedictine abbey)

2392 **Roy, Albertus, O.S.B.**
Affligem, roem van ons land. Leuven,
Davidsfonds, 1953.
228 p.
MoCo

Allerheiligen, Au, Switzerland
see
Au, Switzerland (Benedictine convent)

Almeneches, France (abbey of Benedictine nuns)

2393 **Chaussy, Yves, O.S.B.**
L'Abbaye d'Almenèches-Argentan. Et
Sainte Opportune, sa vie et son culte.
Paris, Lethielleux, 1970.
480 p. 24 cm.
MnCS; PLatS

Alpirsbach, Germany (Benedictine abbey)

2394 **Glatz, Karl Jordan.**
Geschichte des Klosters Alpirsbach auf
dem Schwarzwalde. Strassburg, K. J.
Trübner, 1877.
ix, 442 p. 23 cm.
KAS

2395 **Mettler, Adolf.**
Kloster Alpirsbach. Augsburg, Filser,
1927.
31 p.
AStb

Altdorf, Switzerland (Benedictine abbey)

2396 **Sattler, Magnus, O.S.B.**
Kurze Geschichte der Benedictiner-Abtei
von Altdorf. Strassburg, E. Bauer, 1887.
280 p. illus. 22 cm.
InStme

Altenburg, Austria (Benedictine abbey)

2397 **Heimling, Leander, O.S.B.**
Catalogus manuscriptorum bibliotecae
Altenburgensis, anno 1924. MS. Benedik-
tinerabtei Altenburg, Austria, codex AB 5
Bb 79. 50 p. Quarto. Saec. 20(1924).
Microfilm: MnCH proj. no. 6576

2398 **Necrologium monasterii Altenburgen-
sis.** MS. Benediktinerabtei Altenburg,
Austria, codex AB 6 G 5, f. 182r–208r.
Quarto. Saec. 15(1411).
Microfilm: MnCH proj. no. 6396

2399 **Schweighofer, Gregor, O.S.B.**
Die Handschriften des Stiftes Altenburg
(Sonderkatalog Nr. 1). 1956.
129 p. 28 cm.
Typescript.
Xeroxed by University Microfilms, Ann
Arbor, Mich., 1966.
MnCS

Ambronay, France (Benedictine abbey)

2400 **Bérnard, Alexandre.**
L'Abbaye d'Ambronay. Bourg, V.
Authier, 1888.
165 p. map. 22 cm.
KAS

Amorbach, Bavaria (Benedictine abbey)

2401 **Eisentraut, Engelhard.**
Die Amorbacher Kirchen. Amorbach, G.
Vookhardtschen Druckerei, 1922.
47 p. 19 cm.
KAS

Ampleforth Abbey, England

2402 **McCann, Justin, O.S.B.**
Ampleforth Abbey and College; a short
history. 4th ed. [York, England], Ampleforth Abbey, 1964.
24 p. 19 cm.
PLatS

Andechs, Bavaria (Benedictine abbey)

2403 **Bauerreis, Romuald, O.S.B.**
Der heilige Berg Andechs. 2. Aufl. München, Schnell und Steiner, 1972.
47 p. illus. 22 cm.
MnCS

2404 **Catalogus germanicus paramentorum** et
reliquiarum Montis Sancti Andecensis.
Epistola et tractatus ad principes
Bavariae de origine et veritate sacramenti mirabilis in Monte Andecensi
(auctore Johanne de Eugubio). Chronicon Andecense germanicum. MS.
Vienna, Nationalbibliothek, codex 2676.
26 f. Folio. Saec. 15(1457).
Microfilm: MnCH proj. no. 15,950

2405 **Chronicon Andecense.** MS. Vienna, Nationalbibliothek, codex 2672, f.85v–91r. Folio. Saec. 15(1453).
Microfilm: MnCH proj. no. 15,941

2406 **De sacro Monte Andecensi.** Germanice. MS. Vienna, Nationalbibliothek, codex 2012, f.1r–33r. Octavo. Saec. 15(1458).
Microfilm: MnCH proj. no. 16,280

2407 **Historia Montis Andechs.** Incipit: In dem namen der heiligen. MS. Vienna, Nationalbibliothek, codex 2862, f.97r–105r. Folio. Saec. 15.
Microfilm: MnCH proj. no. 16,157

2408 **Heindl, Emmeram, O.S.B.**
Der heilige Berg Andechs in seiner Geschichte, seinen Merkwürdigkeiten und Heiligthümern. München, Lentner, 1895.
xv, 196 p. illus. 24 cm.
AStb; InStme

2409 **Munich, Germany. Bayerisches Nationalmuseum.**
Der Schatz vom Heiligen Berg Andechs. [Katalogbearbeitung: Reiner Rückert et al.]. Kloster Andechs, 1967.
95, [62] p. illus., plates, facsims. 25 cm.
PLatS

2410 **Wünnenberg, Rolf.**
Andechser Votiv-Kerzen. Die Kunst des Einfachen auf Wachs, ein alter religiöser Volksbrauch in Bayern. [Augsburg], Multi-Druck Verlag für Gedruckte Besonderheiten, 1966.
123 p. (p. 77–123 illus.) 25 cm.
MnCS

Aniane, France (Benedictine abbey)

2411 **Morgand, Claude, O.S.B.**
Monumenta aevi Anianensis (saec. VIII. fin. - IX. med.).
(*In* Corpus consuetudineum monasticarum. Siegburg, 1963. t. 1, p. 176–422)
MnCS; PLatS

Annunciation Priory, Bismarck, N.D.

2412 **Annunciation Priory,** Sisters of Saint Benedict, Bismarck, N.D. St. Paul, Minn., North Central Publishing Co., 1964.
unpaged. illus.
MnStj(Archives); NdBiA

Argentan, France (abbey of Benedictine nuns)

2413 **Chaussy, Yves, O.S.B.**
L'Abbaye d'Almenèches-Argentan . . . Paris, Lethielleux, 1970.
480 p. 24 cm.
PLatS

2414 **Tissot, Gabriel, O.S.B.**
L'Abbaye Notre-Dame d'Argentan de 1830 à nos jours.
(*In* Chaussy, Yves. L'Abbaye d'Almenèches-Argentan. Paris, 1970. p. 173–217)
PLatS

Arnoldstein, Austria, (Benedictine abbey)

2415 **Beschreibung des Stiftes Arnoldstein.** MS. Klagenfurt, Austria, Kärntner Landesarchiv, codex GV 2/33. 134 f. Folio. Saec. 18.
Microfilm: MnCH proj. no. 12,748

Arras, France. Saint-Vaast (Benedictine abbey)

2416 **Cardevacque, Adolphe de.**
L'abbaye de Saint-Vaast; monographie historique, archéologique et littéraire de ce monastère. Arras, Typ. d'A. Brissy, 1865–88.
3 v. 23 cm.
KAS

Arvert, France. Notre-Dame de la Garde (Benedictine priory)

2417 **Grasilier, Th.**
Cartulaires inédits de la Saintonge. Niort, L. Clouzot, 1871.
2 v. 29 cm.
MnCH

Assumption Abbey, Richardton, N.D.

2418 **Fournier, Denis, O.S.B.**
Assumption Abbey, Richardton, N.D. 1965?
32 p. illus. 23 cm.
PLatS; NdRiA

Atchison, Kans. St. Benedict's Abbey
see
St. Benedict's Abbey, Atichson, Kans.

Atchison, Kans. Mount St. Scholastica Convent
see
Mount St. Scholastica Convent, Atchison, Kans.

Au, Switzerland (Benedictine convent)

2419 **Ringholz, Odilo, O.S.B.**
Geschichte des Benediktinerinnenklosters zu Allen Heiligen in der Au bei Einsiedeln. Einsiedeln, New York, Benziger, 1909.
142 p. 19 cm.

Auchy-les-Moines, Hesdin, France
see
Hesdin, France. Auchy-les-Moines

Augia Dives
see
Reichenau

Augia Major
see
Mehrerau

Augia Minor
see
Weissenau

Augia Rhenia
see
Rheinau

Augsburg, Germany. St. Stephan (Benedictine abbey)

2420 **Ad Sanctum Stephanum** 969–1969;
Festgabe zur Tausendjahr-Feier von St.
Stephan in Augsburg. [Hrsg. von Egino
Weidenhiller, O.S.B.] Wemding, G.
Appl, 1969.
[4], 322 p. illus., plates, plans. 24x23 cm.
InStme; KAS; PLatS

2421 **Weisshaar, Bernhard, O.S.B.**
Nova et vetera. [Augsburg] 1966.
32 p. illus. 21 cm.
Sonderdruck aus der Stephania, 39
(1966).
PLatS

Augsburg, Germany. SS. Ulrich und Afra (Benedictine abbey)

2422 **Braun, Placidus Ignatius, O.S.B.**
Notitia historico-literaria de codicibus
manuscriptis in bibliotheca liberi ac imperialis monasterii Ordinis S. Benedicti ad
SS. Udalricum et Afram Augustae extantibus. Augustae Vindelicorum, Fratres
Veith, 1791–96.
2 v. in 6 parts
PLatS(microfilm)

2422a **Werner, Joachim, ed.**
Die Ausgrabungen in St. Ulrich und Afra
in Augsburg, 1961–1968. München, C. H.
Beck'sche Verlagsbuchhandlung [1977].
2 v. illus. 30 cm. (Münchner Beiträge zur
Vor- und Frühgeschichte, Bd. 23).
MnCS

Aruillac, France (Benedictine abbey)

2423 **Bouange, Guillaume Marie Frédéric.**
Histoire de l'Abbaye d'Aurillac, précédés
et suivi de notes et pièces justificatives.
Paris, A. Fontemoing, 1899.
2 v. 24 cm.
MnCS

2424 **Bouange, Guillaume Marie Frédéric.**
Saint Géraud d'Aurillac et son illustre abbaye. Aurillac, L. Bonnet-Picut, 1881.
2 v. 22 cm.
KAS

Avignon, France. Saint-Martial (Benedictine priory)

2425 **Clément, Eusèbe.**
Le monastère-collège de Saint-Martial
d'Avignon; les moines et les étudiants
d'autrefois. Avignon, Seguin Frères, 1893.
x, 354 p. plates, plan. 22 cm.
KAS

Banz, Bavaria (Benedictine abbey)

2426 **Hess, Sales, O.S.B.**
Das Kloster Banz in seinen Beziehungen
zu den Hochstiften Bamberg und Würzburg unter Abt Johannes Burckhard . . .
St. Ottilien, Missionsdruckerei, 1935.
xii, 101 p. 23 cm.
KAS

Barcelona, Spain. S. Pedro de las Puellas (Benedictine abbey)

2427 **Pauli Melendez, Antonio.**
El real monasterio de San Pedro de las
Puellas de Barcelona. [Barcelona?] 1945.
205 p. illus. 17 cm.
MnCS

Barking Abbey, England

2428 **O'Leary, John Gerard.**
The book of Dagenham. Borough of
Dagenham, 1949.
86 p. illus.
InFer

Bath Abbey, England

2428a **Britton, John.**
The history and antiquities of Bath Abbey church; including biographical anec-
dotes of the most distinguished persons in-
terred in that edifice, with an essay on
epitaphs . . . London, Longman and Co.,
1825.
xvi, 220 p. 8 plates, 22 cm.
MnCS

Battle Abbey, England

2429 **Chronicon Monasterii de Bello.** Nunc primum typis mandatum . . . Londini, impensis Societatis, 1846.
xi, 203 p. 23 cm. (Anglia christiana)
InStme; KAS

2429a **The Chronicle of Battle Abbey.** Edited and translated by Eleanor Searle. Oxford, Clarendon Press, 1980.
357 p. (Oxford medieval texts)
NcBe

2430 **Searle, Eleanor.**
Lordship and community; Battle Abbey and its banlieu, 1066–1538. Toronto, Pontifical Institute of Mediaeval Studies, 1974.
479 p. 26 cm.
InStme; PLatS

2431 **Walcott, Mackenzie.**
Battle Abbey: with notices of the parish church and town. Battle, F. W. Ticehurst, 1866.
90 p. illus., plates, plan. 18 cm.
KAS

Bec, France (Benedictine abbey)

2432 **Abbaye du Bec-Hellouin;** journées Anselmiennes, 7–12 juillet, 1959, retour du bienheureux Herluin. [Beauvais, l'Imprimerie Centrale Adminstrative, 1960].
68 p. illus.
MoCo

2433 **Bourget, Jean, O.S.B.**
The history of the royal abbey of Bec near Rouen in Normandy. Translated from the French by [J. Nichols]. London, J. Nichola, 1779.
viii, 140 p. 2 fold. plates. 18 cm.
KAM; KAS

2434 **Chibnall, Marjorie.**
The English lands of the Abbey of Bec. Oxford, Clarendon Press [1968].
164 p.
First published 1946.
MnCS; NcBe

2435 **Consuetudines Beccenses.** Edidit Marie Pascal Dickson, O.S.B. Siegburg, F. Schmitt, 1967.
xc, 419 p. 25 cm. (Corpus consuetudinum monasticarum, 4)
InStme; KAS; PLatS

2436 **La Varende, Jean de.**
L'Abbaye du Bec-Hellouin. 24 photos. de Jean-Marie Marcel. Paris, Plon [1951].
37 p. illus. 23 cm.
KAS; MoCo; PLatS

2437 **Porée, Adolphe André.**
Chronique de Bec et chronique de François Carré. Rouen, Librairie de société de l'histoire de Normandie, 1883.
287 p.
MoCo

2438 **Porée, Adolphe André.**
Histoire de l'Abbaye du Bec. Evreux, C. Hérissey, 1901.
2 v. 23 cm.
KAS

2439 **Spicilegium Beccense;** ouvrage publié avec le concours du Centre National de la Recherche Scientifique. Paris, J. Vrin, 1959–
v. 25 cm.
CaQStB; MnCS; MoCo; PLatS

Beinwil, Switzerland (Benedictine abbey)

2440 **Schenker, Lukas, O.S.B.**
Das Benediktinerkloster Beinwil im 12. und 13. Jahrhundert . . . Solothurn, Gassmann, 1973.
157 p. 23 cm.
MnCS

Belloc, France (Benedictine abbey)

2441 **Darricau, Ildefonse, O.S.B.**
L'Abbaye de Belloc, 1875–1955. Urt, Editions Ezkila [1957].
viii, 104 p. plates. 23 cm.
KAS

Belmont Abbey, Belmont, N.C.

2442 **Baumstein, Paschal, O.S.B.**
A full life, an integrated life: the Benedictine monks of Belmont Abbey. [Gastonia, N.C., Commercial Printers, 1978].
16 p.
NcBe

2443 **Bradley, John P.**
The first hundred years; Belmont Abbey College, 1876–1976 [a centennial commemoration]. Belmont, N.C., Belmont Abbey College, 1976.
76 p.
NcBe

2444 **Doris, Sebastian Thomas, O.S.B.**
Belmont Abbey; its history and educational influence.
68 p.
Thesis (M.A.)–Catholic University of America, Washington, D.C., 1933.
NcBe

2445 **Doris, Sebastian Thomas, O.S.B.**
Belmont Abbey; its origin, development and present state.
112 p. 28 cm.
Typescript. 1971.
NcBe

2446 **Keefe, Ambrose John, O.S.B.**
A critical evaluation of the indexing of
the religious periodical literature of Bel-
mont Abbey College Library, Belmont,
N.C.
A research paper for M.S. Library
Science at University of North Carolina,
Chapel Hill.
NcBe

2447 **St. Mary's College, Gaston County, N.C.**
Catalogue of the officers and students of
St. Mary's College, Gaston County, N.C.
Wheeling, W. Va., James F. Carroll, 1879–
v. 20 cm.
St. Mary's College, Gaston County, N.C.,
later changed name to Belmont Abbey Col-
lege, Belmont, N.C.
NcBe (1879–1913)

**Benedictine Convent of Perpetual Adoration,
San Diego, Calif.**

2448 **Angela, Sister, O.S.B.**
God and a mouse; a festival of reflective
jubilation. San Diego, Calif., Benedictine
Sisters [1972].
12 p. illus. 16 cm.
CaMWiSb; CSan

Benedictine Institute, Kansas City, Mo.

2449 **Secular Benedictine Institute:** Constitution. [Kansas City, Mo., Benedictine
Institute Press, 1968].
36 p. 23 cm.
KAS

Benediktbeuern, Bavaria (Benedictine abbey)

2449a **Carmina Burana;** die Gedichte des Codex
Buranus, lateinisch und deutsch. Uebertragen von Carl Fischer. Uebersetzung
der mittelhochdeutschen Texte von
Hugo Kuhn. Anmerkungen und Nachwort von Günter Bernt. Zürich und
München, Artemis Verlag [1974].
996 p. 20 cm.
MnCS

Benet Hill Priory, Colorado Springs, Colo.

2450 **Hays, Alice Marie, Sister, O.S.B.**
A song in the pines. Erie, Pa., Benet
Press, 1976.
KAM; MnDu; CoCsB

Berau, Germany (abbey of Benedictine nuns)

2451 **Historische Beschreibung** des Ursprungs der Propstei und Frauenkloster
zu Berau. MS. Benediktinerabtei St.

Paul, Austria, codex 21/6. 119 f. Folio.
Saec. 18.
Microfilm: MnCH proj. no. 12,587

**Bergen bei Magdeburg, Germany (Benedictine
abbey)**

2452 **Meibom, Heinrich.**
Fasciculus opusculorum historicorum
selectius in quo exhibentur, I. H. Meibomii
Chronicon Bergense . . . Continuatum a S.
F. Habnio . . . Francofurti ad Moenum, ex
Officina Christiani Genschii [1721?].
[12], 160 p. illus. 33 cm.
KAS

**Besancon, France. St. Vincent (Benedictine
abbey)**

2453 **Realreportorium über** die in der Abtei
St. Vincent zu Besancon vorhandenen
Granvellischen Manuscripte. MS. Vien-
na, Haus-, Hof-und Staatsarchiv, codex
W 557. 284 f. Folio. Saec. 17.
Microfilm: MnCH proj. no. 23,593

Beuron, Germany (Benedictine abbey)

2454 **Beuron:** 1863–1963. Festschrift zum 100-
jährigen Bestehen der Erzabtei St.
Martin. Beuron (Hohenzollern), Beuroner Kunstverlag [1963].
566 p. plates (part col.), fold. map. 24 cm.
MnCS; PLatS

2455 **Brechter, Heinrich Suso, O.S.B.**
Beurons Beitrag zur Gründung von St.
Ottilien.
(*In* Beuron, 1863–1963. Festschrift . . .
Beuron, 1963. p. 231–267)
PLatS; MnCS

2456 **Engelmann, Ursmar, O.S.B.**
Hundert Jahre Bibliothek Beuron.
(*In* Beuron, 1863–1963. Festschrift . . .
Beuron, 1963. p. 395–440)
PLatS; MnCS

2457 **Erzabtei Beuron:** Kloster, Kirche,
Umgebung. 2. Aufl. Beuron, Beuroner
Kunstverlag, 1973.
59 p. 17 cm.
First published 1968.
MnCS

2458 **Fischer, Bonifatius, O.S.B.**
Vetus Latina Institut der Erzabtei
Beuron. Bericht 3. Beuron/Hohenzollern,
1969.
31 p. 21 cm.
MnCS

2459 **Gindele, Corbinian, O.S.B.**
Beurons Choralgesang.
(*In* Beuron, 1863–1963. Festschrift . . .
Beuron, 1963. p. 308–336)
PLatS

2460 **Kreitmaier, Josef.**
Beuroner Kunst; eine Ausdrucksform
der christlichen Mystik. 4. und 5. erw.
Aufl. Freiburg im Breisgau, Herder, 1923.
xviii, 130 p. illus., plates. 25 cm.
InStme; KAS

2461 **Maurus Wolter** dem Gründer Beurons
zum 100. Geburtstag; Erinnerungen und
Studien, 1825–1925. Beuron, Verlag der
Beuroner Kunstschule, 1925.
vii, 192 p. plates, ports. 24 cm.
KAS

2462 **Mayer, Heinrich Suso, O.S.B.**
Beuroner Bibliographie; Schriftsteller
und Künstler während der ersten hundert
Jahre des Benediktinerklosters Beuron,
1863–1963. Beuron, Hohenzollern, 1963.
196 p. 23 cm.
KAS; MnCS; NdRi; OkShG; PLatS

2463 **Merkle, Coelestin, O.S.B.**
Das hundertste Jahr; zur Hundertjahr-
feier der Benediktiner in Beuron, 1963.
Hrsg. von der Erzabtei St. Martin. Zusam-
mengestellt von P. Coelestin Merkle.
[Beuron], Beuroner Kunstverlag [1962].
159 p. illus., plates, ports. 20x21 cm.
MnCS

2464 **Oesterle, Gerard, O.S.B.**
Beuron und die Anfänge des Studien-
kollegs St. Anselm in Rom.
(*In* Beuron, 1863–1963; Festschrift . . .
Beuron, 1963. p. 268–280)
PLatS; MnCS

2465 **Wenzel, Paul.**
Der Freundeskreis um Anton Günther
und die Grüdung Beurons. Essen,
Ludgerus-Verlag, 1965.
xvi, 531 p. 22 cm.
MnCS

2466 **Zähringer, Damasus, O.S.B.**
Der Beitrag Beurons zur liturgischen
Erneuring.
(*In* Beuron, 1863–1963; Festschrift . . .
Beuron, 1963. p. 337–357)
PLatS; MnCS

Biburg, Bavaria (Benedictine abbey)

2467 **Arx, Walter von.**
Das Klosterrituale von Biburg
(Budapest, Cod. lat. m. ae. Nr. 330, 12.
Jh.). Freiburg/Schweiz, Univer-
sitätsverlag, 1970.
xxviii, 357 p. 26 cm.
MnCS; PLatS

Blois, France. Saint-Lomer (Benedictine abbey)

2468 **Mars, Noël, O.S.B.**
Histoire de royal momastère de Sainct-
Lomer de Blois de l'Ordre de Sainct-

Benoist . . . Blois, Imprimerie J.
Marchand,1869.
472 p. 27 cm.
MnCS

Blue Cloud Abbey, Marvin, S.D.

2469 **A Benedictine beginning in Dakota;**
the Blue Cloud Community's twenty-
fifth year. Marvin, S.D., Blue Cloud
Mission Press, 1975.
unpaged. illus.
MoCo; SdMar

2470 **Shidler, Stephen, O.S.B.**
In the beginning it was something like
this at Blue Cloud Abbey; or, The Blue
Cloud blues. [The Author] 1978.
251 p. illus. 28 cm.
InStme; SdMar

Bobbio, Italy (Benedictine abbey)

2471 **Bakker, Adolphine Henriëtte Annette.**
A study of Codex. Evang. Bobbiensis (k)
. . . Amsterdam, N.V. Noord-Hollandsche
Uitgevermaatschappij, 1933.
84 p. facsim. 24 cm.
Thesis–University of Amsterdam, 1933.
MnCS

2472 **Natale, Alfio Rosario.**
Influenze merovingiche e studi
calligrafici nello scriptorium di Bobbio
(secoli VII–IX). Milano, Biblioteca Ambro-
siana [1951].
44 p. facsims. 30 cm.
MnCS

2473 **Natale, Alfio Rosario.**
Studi paleografici; arte e imitazione della
scrittura insulare in codici Bobbiesi.
Milano, Edizioni del Capricorno [1950].
90 p. 13 facsims. 23 cm.
MnCS

2474 **Turin, Italy. Biblioteca nazionale.**
Codici Bobbiesi nella Biblioteca nazionale
di Torino, indicati e descritti da Giuseppe
Ottino. Torino-Palermo, C. Clausen, 1890.
viii, 72 p. 25x18 cm.
MnCS

Bologna, Italy. San Stefano (Benedictine abbey)

2475 **Petracchi, Celestino, O.S.B.**
Della insigne abbaziala basilica di S.
Stefano di Bologna libri due . . . Bologna,
Stamperia di Domenico Guidotti, 1747.
MnCS

Bonneval, France. Saint-Florentin (Benedictine abbey)

2476 **Thiroux, Jean Evangéliste, O.S.B.**
Histoire abrégée de l'Abbaye de Saint-
Florentin de Bonneval . . . continuée par

Beaupère et Lejeune. Chateaudun, H.
Lecesne, 1875.
clxxi, 258 p. 25 cm.
KAS; MnCS

Boscherville, France. Saint-Georges (Benedictine abbey)

2477 **Besnard, Paul.**
Monographie de l'église et l'abbaye Saint-
Georges de Boscherville (Seine-Inférieure).
Paris, Librairie Emile Lechevalier, 1899.
v, 168, cxiv, 57 p. illus., plates (part col.)
28 cm.
MnCS

Bourbourg, France. Notre-Dame (Benedictine abbey)

2478 **Un cartulaire de l'Abbaye de N.-D.** de
Bourbourg, recueilli et dressé par Ignace
de Coussemaker. Lille, Impr. V. Ducoulombier, 1882–91.
3 v. 26 cm.
KAS

Brevnov, Czechoslovakia (Benedictine abbey)

2479 **Catalogus religiosorum** sub Regula s. p.
Benedicti in archisterio Brevnoviensi et
monasterio Braunaviensi atque extra
eadem militantium, anno domini MDC-
CCLXXX . . . [Pragae, 1885].
23 p. 23 cm.
KAS

Brogne, Belgium (Benedictine abbey)

2480 **Berlière, Ursmer, O.S.B.**
Les terres & seigneuries de Maredsous
et de Maharenne. Maredsous, Abbaye de
Saint Benoît, 1920.
142 p. plates, plans. 26 cm.
MnCS

2481 **Del Marmol, Eugène.**
L'Abbaye de Brogne ou de Saint Bérard.
Namur, A. Wesmael-Legros, 1858.
139 p. illus. 25 cm.
KAS

Bruges, Belgium. Abbaye de Saint-André

2482 **Abbaye de Saint-André.** [n.d.]
35 p. chiefly illus. 18 cm.
PLatS

2483 **Les cahiers de Saint-André . . .** chroniques trimestrielles de l'Abbaye et des ses
oeuvres. v. 1- 192-
MnCS

2484 **Huyghebaert, Nicolas, O.S.B.**
Stella Maris; notes sur la dévotion
mariala à l'Abbaye de Saint-André. 1955.

51 p. illus. 22 cm.
InStme

Buckfast Abbey, England

2485 **Stephan, John, O.S.B.**
Historical guide to Buckfast Abbey. New
and revised. Devon, Buckfast Abbey
[1955].
48 p. illus.
MoCo

2486 **Stephan, John, O.S.B.**
A history of Buckfast Abbey, from
1018–1968. Bristol, Burleigh Press [1970].
ix, 372 p. illus., plates, fold. diagr. 22 cm.
KAS; PLatS

Buenos Aires, Argentina. San Benito (Benedictine abbey)

2487 **La Abadia de San Benito,** Buenos Aires,
1915–1965. Buenos Aires [1965?].
109 p. illus. 28 cm.
PLatS

Bürgel, Germany (Benedictine abbey)

2488 **Gleichenstein, Johann Basilius von.**
Burgelinensis abbatiae primitiae; oder,
Kurze historische Beschreibung der vor-
mahligen berühmten Abtey- und Closter-
Burgelin . . . Jena, J. R. Crökern, 1729.
200, 200 p. 17 cm.
KAS

Bursfeld, Germany (Benedictine abbey)

2489 **Excerpta ex ceremoniis** patrum de
observatione Bursfeldensi. MS. Benediktinerabtei Melk, Austria, codex 1418,
f.116r–129v. Duodecimo. Saec. 15.
Microfilm: MnCH proj. no. 1937

2490 **Heutger, Nicolaus C.**
Bursfeld und seine Reformklöster in
Niedersachsen. 2. erw. Aufl. Hildesheim,
A. Lax, 1975.
xxvii, 147 p. 20 plates. 23 cm.
MnCS

2491 **Ziegler, Walter.**
Die Bursfelder Kongregation in der
Reformationszeit, dargestellt an Hand der
Generalkapitelsrezesse der Bursfelder
Kongregation. Münster, Aschendorff,
[1968].
156 p. fold. map. 26 cm.
PLatS

Burton-on-Trent, England (Benedictine abbey)

2491a **Sawyer, P. H., ed.**
Charters of Burton Abbey. Oxford
University Press, 1979.

lv, 93 p. facsims., map, 25 cm. (Anglo-
Saxon charters, 11)
MnCS

Burtscheid, Germany (Benedictine abbey)

2492 **Quix, Christian.**
Geschichte der ehemaligen Reichs-Abtei
Burtscheid, von ihrer Gründung im 7ten
Jahrhunderte bis 1400 . . . mit 192
Urkunden. Aachen, in Commission J. A.
Mayer, 1834.
vii, 446 p. 17 cm.
KAS

Bury St. Edmunds Abbey, England

2493 **Apuleius Barbarus.**
The herbal of Apuleius Barbarus. From
the early twelfth-century manuscript
formerly in the abbey of Bury St. Edmunds
(Ms. Bodley 130). Described by Robert T.
Gunther. Oxford, The Roxburghe Club,
1925.
xxxvi p. plates (facsims.) 28 cm.
MnCS

2494 **Barker, H. R.**
West Suffolk illustrated. F. G. Pawsey &
Co., 1907.
411 p. illus.
InFer

2495 **The chronicle of Bury St. Edmunds,**
1212–1301. Edited with introduction,
notes, and translation by Antonia
Grandsen. [London, Camden, N.J.]
Nelson [1964].
xlv, 164, 164, [165]-187 p. 23 cm.
(Medieval texts)
InStme

2496 **The Customary of the Benedictine Abbey**
of Bury St. Edmunds in Suffolk (from
Harleian MS. 1005 in the British
Museum), edited by Antonia Grandsen.
[London], Henry Bradshaw Society,
1973.
xlii, 142 p. 23 cm.
KAS; PLatS

2497 **Electio Hugonis.**
The chronicle of the election of Hugh, abbot of Bury St. Edmunds and later bishop
of Ely. Edited and translated by R. M.
Thomson. Oxford, Clarendon Press, 1974.
li, 208 p. 23 cm. (Oxford medieval texts)
MnCS; PLatS

2498 **Jocelin de Brakelond.**
The chronicle of Jocelin of Brakelond
concerning the acts of Samson, abbot of
the monastery of St. Edmund. Translated
from the Latin with introduction, notes
and appendices by H. E. Butler. London,
Thomas Nelson, 1949.

xxviii, 167 [i.e., 334] p. 22 cm.
Latin and English texts on opposite
pages.
For other editions of this work *see*
Jocelin de Brakelond in the Author Part.
MnCS

2499 **Koenig, Clara.**
Englisches Klosterleben im 12.
Jahrhundert, auf Grund der Chronik des
Jocelinus de Brakelonda. Jena, Fromann-
sche Buchhandlung, 1928.
vii, 98 p. 23 cm.
MnCS

2500 **Tymms, Samuel, ed.**
Wills and inventories from the registers
of the commissary of Bury St. Edmunds
and the archdeacon of Sudbury. [London]
1850.
[Camden Society, Publications, no. 49]
ILSP

2501 **Whittingham, Arthur Bensely.**
Bury St. Edmunds Abbey, Suffolk. London, H.M.S.O., 1971.
31 p. 2 fold. plates, illus., plans. 22 cm.
MnCS

2502 **William of Hoo, O.S.B.**
The letter-book of William of Hoo,
sacrist of Bury St. Edmunds, 1280–1294.
Edited by Antonia Grandsen. [Ipswich]
Suffolk Records Society, 1963.
166 p. 25 cm.
Entries in Latin, summaries in English.
PLatS

Cagliari, Sardinia. San Saturno (Benedictine abbey)

2503 **Studi sui vittorini in Sardegna,** a cura di
F. Artizzu [et al.]. Padova, CEDAM,
1963.
88 p. 25 cm.
KAS

Calatayud, Spain. San Benito (Benedictine abbey)

2504 **Copia de la institucion** del monasterio de
San Benito de la ciudad de Calatayud.
MS. Perelada, Spain, Palacio de
Perelada, codex 41205. 14 v. Octavo.
Saec. 16.
Microfilm: MnCH proj. no. 34,705

Caldey Abbey, England

2505 **Camm, Bede, O.S.B.**
Caldey and St. Bride's.
(Catholic mind, no. 7, 1913)
AStb

2506 **Howells, Roscoe.**
      Total community: the monks of Caldey
      Island. Tenby, H. G. Walters (Publishers)
      [1975].
          224 p.
          NcBe

2506a **Mostyn, Francis, bp. of Menevia.**
      The Caldey Benedictines. [n.p., 1915?].
          4 p. 28 cm.
          An appeal for funds, signed by Francis,
      bishop of Menevia, and E. Cuthbert Butler,
      abbot of Downside.
          KAS

2507 **Pritchard, Emily M.**
      The history of St. Dogmaels Abbey,
      together with her cells, Pill, Caldey and
      Glascareg, and the mother abbey of Tiron .
      . . London, Blades, East & Blades, 1917.
          241 p. illus, plates, fold. map. 26 cm.
          MnCS

2508 **Shepherd, William Richard, ed.**
      The Benedictines of Caldey Island
      (formerly of Painsthorpe, York). Contain-
      ing the history, purpose, method, and sum-
      mary of the rule of the Benedictines of the
      Isle of Caldey, S. Wales . . . Caldey, The
      Abbey, 1907.
          xvi, 111 p. plates, ports., fold. map.
      23 cm.
          MnCS

Canterbury, England. St. Augustine's Abbey
see
St. Augustine's Abbey, Canterbury, England

Canterbury Cathedral, England

2509 **Blake, Philip Haslewood.**
      Christ Church gate, Canterbury
      Cathedral. [Canterbury (Kent)],
      Phillimore, 1965.
          xii, 51 p. plates. 21 cm.
          PLatS

2510 **Lanfranc, abp. of Canterbury.**
      Decreta Lanfranci monachis Cantuarien-
      sibus transmissa. Edidit David Knowles.
      Siegburg, apud Franciscum Schmitt, 1967.
          xlii, 149 p. 26 cm. (Corpus con-
      suetudinum monasticarum, 3)
          PLatS

2511 **Vitae sanctorum Cantuariensium.** MS.
      Lambeth Palace Library, London, codex
      159. 286 f. Quarto. Saec. 16(1507).
          Microfilm: MnCH

Cardeña, Spain. San Pedro (Benedictine abbey)

2512 **Chacón, Alfonso, O.P.**
      De martyrio ducentorum monachorum
      S. Petria Cardegna, Ordinis S. Benedicti

Hispaniarum Brugensis diocensis commentarius. Augustae, typis Chrysostomi
Dabertzhoseri [1594].
    138, 29 p. 13 cm.
    MnCS

2513 **Moreta Valayos, Salustiano.**
      El monasterio de San Pedro de Cardeña;
      historia de un dominio monástico
      Castellano (902-1338). Salamanca, Univer-
      sidad, 1971.
          302 p. plates, maps.
          Tesis – Salamanca.
          MnCS

2514 **Pedrosa, Juan de, O.S.B.**
      Responsio ad doctissimas et pruden-
      tissimas Sacrosanctae Congr. Sacorum
      Rituum oppositiones contra processum
      fulminatum super martyrio 200
      monachorum, qui in persecutione arabica
      apud Caradignam passi sunt. [n.p., 16th
      cent.]
          29 p. 13 cm.
          MnCS

Cardigan Priory, Wales

2515 **Pritchard, Emily M.**
      Cardigan Priory in the olden days. Lon-
      don, William Heinemann, 1904.
          xiii, 168 p. plates, fold. map. 26 cm.
          CaBMi; MnCS

Carrara, Italy. San Stefano (Benedictine abbey)

2516 **Ceoldo, Pietro.**
      Memorie della chiesa ed abbazia di S.
      Stefano di Carrara nella diocesi di Padova.
      Venezia, Antonio Zatta, 1802.
          209 p. illus., plan. 33 cm.
          MnCS

Catholic University of Peking

2517 **Healy, Sylvester, O.S.B.**
      The plans of the new university building.
      (*In* Catholic University of Peking.
      Bulletin, no. 6(1929), p. 3–12).
          PLatS

2518 **Pail, Leander, O.S.B.**
      History of the foundation of the Catholic
      University of Peking.
          unpaged, 20 cm.
          Entirely in Chinese.
          MnCS

2519 **Popes,** 1922-1939 (Pius XI).
      To our beloved son Aurelius Stehle,
      O.S.B. Given in Rome, at St. Peters, on the
      twentieth day of the month of August, in
      the year 1929 . . . [Latrobe, Pa., 1929]
          [4] p. 22 cm.
          KAS

Caunes, France (Benedictine abbey)

2520 **Bèziat, Louis.**
Histoire de l'Abbaye de Caunes, Ordre de
Saint-Benoît . . . Paris, A. Claudin, 1880.
xvi, 244 p. plates. 19 cm.
KAS

Cava, Italy (Benedictine abbey)

2521 **La Badia della SS.** Trinità di Cava; cenni
storici. Badia di Cava, 1942.
90 p. plates. 22 cm.
MnCS

2522 **Guillaume, Paul.**
Le navi Cavensi nel Mediterraneo
durante il Medio Evo . . . Cava dei Tirreni,
Badia della SS. Trinità, 1876.
56 p. 22 cm.
KAS

2523 **Mattei-Cerasoli, Leone, O.S.B.**
Codices Cavenses descripsit . . . [Arpino,
Società Tipografica Arpinate] 1935–
v. 30 cm.
Only Pars I, Codices membranacei, was
published.
MnCS

2524 **Morcaldi, Michael, O.S.B.**
Synopsis historico-diplomatica monsterii
et tabularii Cavensis. Neapoli, Petrus Piazzi, 1873.
75 p. 32 cm.
InStme

2525 **Il nono centenario della Badia di Cava,**
1011–1911. Napoli, D'Auria, 1912.
62 p. illus.
AStb

2526 **S. Congregatio Sacrorum Rituum.**
Nullius seu Caven. confirmationis cultus
ab immemorabili tempore praestiti servis
Dei Alpherio, Leoni, Petro et Constabili ab-
batibus Ordinis S. Benedicti sanctis nun-
cupatis. Positio super cultu immemorabili.
Romae, ex Typographia Artificum a S.
Joseph, 1893.
210, 17, 37 p. 30 cm.
MnCS

2527 **Ugo, abbot of Venosa.**
Vitae ss. Alferii, Leonis, Petri et Con-
stabilis, abbatum Cavensium. MS. Cava,
Italy (Benedictine abbey), codex 24. 37 f.
Folio. Saec. 13(1295).
Microfilm: MnCH

Cesana, Italy. Badia di S. Maria del Monte

2528 **Novelli, Leandro, O.S.B.**
Il coro intagliato della Basilica di S.
Maria del Monte di Cesena. Cesena, Edi-
zioni Badia di S. Maria del Monte [n.d.].

43 p. plates. 32 cm.
MnCS

2529 **Novelli, Leandro, O.S.B.**
Ex voto del Santuario della Madonna del
Monte di Cesena . . . [Forli, Società
Tipografica Forlivese, 1961].
187 p. 212 plates (20 col.) 32 cm.
MnCS; PLatS

Chaise-Dieu, France (Benedictine abbey)

2530 **Gaussin, Pierre Roger.**
L'Abbaye de la Chaise-Dieu (1043–1518).
Paris, Editions Cujas, 1962.
760 p. plates, tables, fold. maps. 25 cm.
KAS; MnCS; PLatS

Chamonix, France (Benedictine priory)

2531 **Perrin, André.**
Histoire de la vallée et du Prieuré de
Chamonix du Xe au XVIIIe siècle. Paris,
Fischbacher, 1887.
253 p. illus., fold. map. 25 cm.
KAS

Chester, England. St. Werburgh's Abbey

2532 **Annales Cestrienses;** or, Chronicle of the
Abbey of St. Werburgh at Chester.
Edited with an introduction, translation,
and notes by Richard Copley Christie.
[London], Printed for the Record
Society, 1887.
xxxii, 152 p. 22 cm. (The Record Society
for the Publication of Original Documents
Relating to Lancashire and Cheshire, XIV)
PLatS

2533 **Burne, R.V.H.**
The monks of Chester; the history of St.
Werburgh's Abbey. London, S.P.C.K.,
1962.
xix, 235 p. illus. 23 cm.
InStme; MoCo

Chevetogne, Belgium (Benedictine priory)

2534 **Le Monastére de Chevetogne;** notice
historique et informations. 2. éd.
Chevetogne [1962]
65 p. 17 cm.
KAS

2535 **Van der Heijden, Joannes B., O.S.B.**
L'Eglise orientale de Chevetogne: ar-
chitecture, décoration, symbolisme. Les
Editions de Chevetogne, 1962.
64 p. illus. 14 cm.
KAS

Chicago, Ill. St. Scholastica Priory
see
St. Scholastica Priory, Chicago, Ill.

Cismar, Germany. St. Johannes (Benedictine abbey)

2536 **Rumohr, Henning von.**
Dome, Kirchen und Klöster in Schleswig-Holstein und Hamburg, nach alten Vorlagen. Frankfurt am Main, W. Weidlich, 1962.
307 p. illus. 19 cm.
PLatS

Civate, Italy (Benedictine abbey)

2537 **Bognetti, Gian Piero.**
L'abbazia benedettina di Civate; note di storia e di arte. Civate, Amici della Casa del Cieco, 1957.
231 p. illus. (part col.), plans. 30 cm.
InStme

Claro, Switzerland. Santa Maria (Benedictine convent)

2538 **Schmid, Gabriel, O.S.B.**
Das Kloster Santa Maria in Claro, Tessin. [n.p., n.d.]
ll p. 15 p.
PLatS

Cleveland, Ohio. St. Andrew's Abbey
see
St. Andrew's Abbey, Cleveland, Ohio

Cluny, France (Benedictine abbey)

2539 **Anger, Pierre, O.S.B.**
Le Collège de Cluny, fondé à Paris dans le voisinage de la Sorbonne et dans le ressort de l'Université. Paris, A. Picard, 1916.
129 p.
NcBe; PLatS

2540 **Chaumont, Louis M. J.**
Histoire de Cluny depuis les origines jusqu'à la ruine de l'Abbaye. 2. éd., considerablement augmentée. Paris, J. De Gigord, 1911.
260 p. plates, plans. 22 cm.
PLatS (Xerox copy)

2541 **Cluny et le Clunisois.** Genève, Institut d'histoire de l'art du Moyen Age, 1967.
89 p. illus. 19 cm.
MnCS

2542 **Conant, Kenneth John.**
Cluny: les églises et la maison du chef d'Ordre. Mâcon, Protat Frères, 1968.
169 p. illus. (part col.), plans. 38 cm.
(Mediaeval Academy of America. Publication no. 77)
KAS; MnCS; MoCo; PLatS

2543 **Côte, Léon.**
Un moine de l'an mille, saint Odilon, abbé de Cluny de 994 à 1049. Moulins, Crépin-Leblond, 1949.
163 p. plates. 23 cm.
KAS

2544 **Davis, Cyprian, O.S.B.**
The familia at Cluny, 900–1350.
2 v. 27 cm.
Thesis (Ph.D.) – Université Catholique de Louvain, 1977.
Xeroxed copy from typescript.
InStme

2545 **Duckett, Sir George Floyd.**
Record-evidences, among archives of the ancient abbey of Cluny, from 1077 to 1534, illustrative of the history of some of our early kings, and many of its English affiliated foundations . . . Lewes, for the author, 1886.
64 p. 26 cm.
MnCS

2546 **L'Esprit de Cluny;** testes clunisiens. [La Pierre-qui-Vire (Yonne)], Zodiaque, 1963.
195 p. illus., col. plates. 26 cm.
KAS; MnCS

2547 **Fechter, Johannes.**
Cluny, Adel und Volk; Studien über das Verhältnis des Klosters zu den Ständen, 910–1156. [Stuttgart, Druck: Buchdr. Schwednter] 1966.
132 p. genal. table. 21 cm.
Inaug. Diss. – Tübingen.
MnCS

2548 **Gregoire, Reginald, O.S.B.**
La pratique des conseils évangeliques à Cluny.
(*In* Semana de Estudios monasticos, 14th, Silos, 1973. p. 75–101)
PLatS

2549 **Hallinger, Kassius, O.S.B.**
Zur geistigen Welt der Anfänge Klunys.
(*In* Richter, Helmut. Cluny; Beiträge zu Gestalt und Wirkung der Cluniezensischen Reform. Darmstadt, 1975. p. 91–124)
MnCS

2550 **Heath, Robert George.**
Crux imperatorium philosophia; imperial horizons of the Cluniac Confraternitas, 964–1109. Pittsburgh, Pickwick Press, 1976.
xx, 260 p. illus. 22 cm.
InStme

2551 **Hourlier, Jacques, O.S.B.**
Das Kloster des hl. Odilo. Cluny und der Begriff des religiösen Ordens.

(*In* Richter, Helmut. Cluny; Beiträge zu Gestalt und Wirkung der Cluniazensischen Reform. Darmstadt, 1975. p. 1–21, 50–59)
MnCS

2552 **Hunt, Noreen, ed.**
Cluniac monasticism in the central Middle Ages; readings in medieval and European history. [London] Macmillan [1971].
x, 248 p. 22 cm.
InStme; PLatS

2553 **Hunt, Noreen.**
Cluny under Saint Hugh, 1049–1109. London, Edward Arnold, 1967.
xii, 228 p. plates, map. 24 cm.
InFer; InStme; KAS; MnCS; MoCo; PLatS

2554 **Leclercq, Jean, O.S.B.**
Spiritualité et culture à Cluny.
(*In* Spiritualitè cluniacense. Todi, 1960. p. 101–152)
PLatS

2555 **Leclercq, Jean, O.S.B.**
Zur Geschichte des Lebens in Cluny.
(*In* Richter, Helmut. Cluny; Beiträge zu Gestalt und Wirkung der Cluniazensischen Reform. Darmstadt, 1975. p. 254–318)
MnCS

2556 **Oursel, Raymond.**
Les saints abbés de Cluny; textes choisis, traduits et présentés par Raymond Oursel. Namur, Belgique, Les Editions de Soleil Levant [1960].
100 p. 17 cm.
PLatS

2557 **Pierre Abélard,** Pierre le Vénérable: les courants philosophiques, littéraires et artistiques en Occident au milieu du XIIe siècle [actes et mémoires du colloque international, Abbaye de Cluny, 2 au 9 juillet 1972]. Paris, Editions du Centre national de la recherche scientifique, 1975.
782 p. plates (some col.) 25 cm.
MnCS

2558 **Richter, Helmut, ed.**
Cluny; Beiträge zu Gestalt und Wirkung der Cluniazensischen Reform. Darmstadt, Wissenschaftliche Buchgesellschaft, 1975.
xi, 414 p. 20 cm.
MnCS

2559 **Schapiro, Meyer.**
The Parma Ildefonsus; a romanesque illuminated manuscript from Cluny and related works. New York, College Art Association of America, 1964.
85, [38], illus., facsims. 32 cm.
MnCS

2560 **Schmitz, Philibert, O.S.B.**
La liturgie de Cluny.

(*In* Spiritualitè cluniacense. Todi, 1960. p. 83–100)
PLatS

2561 **Schnack, Ingeborg.**
Richard von Cluny; seine Chronik und sein Kloster in den Anfängen der Kirchenspaltung von 1159 . . . Berlin, 1921; Vaduz, Kraus Reprint, 1965.
173 p. 23 cm.
PLatS

2562 **Spiritualità Cluniacense,** 12–15 Ottobre, 1958. Todi, Presso l'Accademia Tudertina, 1960.
349 p.
MnCS

2563 **Tellenbach, Gerd.**
Neue Forschungen über Cluny und die Cluniacenser. Freiburg, Herder, 1959.
463 p. maps. 23 cm.
MnCS

2564 **Valous, Guy de.**
Le domaine de l'Abbaye de Cluny aux Xe et XIe siècles. Formation-organisation-administration. Paris, Librairie Ancienne Edouard Champion, 1923.
190 p.
NcBe

2565 **Valous, Guy de.**
Le monachisme clunisien des origines au XVe siècle; vie intérieure des monastères et organisation de l'Ordre. 2. éd. augm. Paris, A. et J. Picard, 1970.
2 v. 25 cm.
AStb; InStme; MnCS

2566 **Verlet, Pierre.**
Le Musée de Cluny [par] Pierre Verlet [et] Francis Salet. Paris, Editions des Musées nationaux, 1965.
194 p. illus.
MoCo

2567 **Wollasch, Joachim, ed.**
Cluny im 10. und 11. Jahrhundert . . . Göttingen, Vandenhoeck & Ruprecht [1967].
73 p. 20 cm.
MnCS; MoCo

Coldingham Priory, England

2568 **Carr, Alexander Allan.**
A history of Coldingham Priory; containing a survey of the civil and ecclesiastical history of the eastern portion of Berwickshire, anciently termed Coldinghamshire, with a sketch of its geological structure . . . Edinburgh, Adam Black, 1836.
vii, 328 p. illus., plates. 24 cm.
KAS

2569 **The correspondence,** inventories, account
rolls, and law proceedings of the Priory
of Coldingham. London, J. B. Nichols
and Son [1841].
xvii, 259, cxxxvi p. illus. 23 cm.
MnCS

Collegeville, Minn. St. John's Abbey
see
St. John's Abbey, Collegeville, Minn.

**Cologne, Germany. Gross St. Martin
(Benedictine abbey)**

2570 **Kessel, Johann Hubert.**
Antiquitates monasterii S. Martini ma-
joris Coloniensis . . . Coloniae, J. M.
Heberle, 1862.
xxvi, 441 p. 22 cm.
KAS

Colorado Springs, Colo. Benet Hill Priory
see
Benet Hill Priory, Colorado Springs, Colo.

Comburg, Württemberg (Benedictine abbey)

2571 **Joos, Rainer.**
Kloster Komburg im Mittelalter; Studien
zur Verfassungs-, Besitz- und Social-
geschichte einer fränkischen Benediktinerabtei. Schwäbisch Hall, Eppinger [1971].
241 p. maps. 21 cm.
PLatS

Conception Abbey, Conception, Mo.

2572 **Conception, Abbey, Conception, Mo.**
Centennial photo album, 1873–1973.
Conception, Mo., 1974.
4 v. illus.

2573 **Ecker, Gerald Robert, O.S.B.**
A descriptive catalog of the Carolingian
manuscripts in Conception Abbey Library.
67 p. 29 cm.
Thesis (M.A.L.S.) – Rosary College,
River Forest, Ill., 1955.
Typescript.
MoCo; MnCS

2574 **Malone, Edward Eugene, O.S.B.**
Conception: a history of the first century
of Conception colony, 1858–1958; a history
of the first century of Conception Abbey,
1873–1973; a history of New Engelberg
College, Conception College, and the Immaculate Conception Seminary, 1886–
1971. Omaha, Nebr., Interstate Printing Co. [1971].
223 p. illus. 29 cm.
InStme; MnCS

2575 **Rippinger, Joel.**
From old world to new; the origins and
development of St. Meinrad and Conception abbeys in the nineteenth century.
73 p. 28 cm.
Typescript, 1976.
MoCo

2576 **Schieber, Joachim, O.S.B.**
Father James Power and the Reading
Colony from Reading, Pennsylvania, to
Conception, Missouri.
v, 87 p. 28 cm.
Thesis – Catholic University of America,
Washington, D.C., 1953.
Typescript.
MoCo

**Convent of the Immaculate Conception,
Ferdinand, Ind.**

2577 **Century of Service:** 1867–1967. Souvenir
edition, supplement to the Ferdinand
News, July 27, 1967. Dedicated to the
Sisters of St. Benedict in Ferdinand on
the celebration of their centennial, July
20–August 6, 1967.
12 p. illus. tabloid size.
InFer

2578 **Christ, yesterday, today, forever.** Centennial: Sisters of St. Benedict, Convent
of the Immaculate Conception, Ferdinand, Indiana, 1867–1967.
unpaged, chiefly illus. 28 cm.
InFer; InStme; PLatS

2579 **Clauss, Benedicta, Sister, O.S.B.**
The first one-hundred years; commemorative pageant for the centennial of
the Sisters of St. Benedict, Ferdinand, Indiana, 1967.
27 p. illus.
InFer

2580 **Dudine, M. Frederica, Sister, O.S.B.**
The castle on the hill; centennial history
of the Convent of the Immaculate Concep-
tion, Ferdinand, Indiana, 1867–1967.
Milwaukee, Bruce Pub. Co., 1967.
xvi, 330 p. illus., ports., maps. 24 cm.
(American Benedictine Academy.
Historical studies, no. 5)
InFer; InStme; KAS; MoCo; PLatS

2581 **Scheesele, Mary Kenneth, Sister, O.S.B.**
A handbook of archival policies and pro-
cedures, brief history, and listing of major
collections of the Archives of the Sisters of
St. Benedict, Convent of the Immaculate
Conception, Ferdinand, Indiana. 1979.
25 p.
Typescript.
InFer(Archives)

Corbie, France (Benedictine abbey)

2582 **Amis du vieux Corbie.**
Le tresors de l'abbaye royale Saint-Pierre de Corbie. Amiens, Muses de Picardie, 1962.
51 p. plates, 20 cm.
MnCS

2583 **Corbie, abbaye royale,** volume du XIIIe centenaire. Lille, Facultés Catholique, 1963.
444 p. illus. 24 cm.
InStme; MnCS

2584 **Eckhardt, Karl August, ed.**
Studia Corbeiensia: bibliotheca rerum historicarum Corbeiensia; traditiones Corbeiensis; rotula Corbeiensis; chronicon Corbeiense et fasti Corbeienses. Aalen, Scientia Verlag, 1970.
MnCS

Corvey, Germany (Benedictine abbey)

2585 **Annales Corbeienses** a. 658–1148.
(*In* Monumenta Germaniae historica. Scriptores. Stuttgart, 1963, t. 3, p. 1–18)
MnCS; PLatS

2586 **Effmann, Wilhelm.**
Die Kirche der Abtei Corvey. Paderborn, Bonifacius-Druckerei, 1929.
159 p. 48 illus.
MoCo

2587 **Hüffer, Georg.**
Korveier Studien; quellenkritische Untersuchungen zur Karolinger-Geschichte. Münster, Aschendorff, 1898.
x, 232 p. 25 cm.
KAS

2588 **Kaminsky, Hans Heinrich.**
Studien zur Reichsabtei Corvey in der Salizeit. Köln, Graz, Böhlau, 1972.
304 p. 24 cm.
MnCS

2589 **Kreusch, Felix.**
Beobachtungen un der Westanlage der Klosterkirche zu Corvey . . . Köln, Böhlau, 1963.
vii, 73 p. illus.
MnCS; PLatS

2590 **Kunst und Kultur im Weserrarum,** 800–1600; Ausstellung des Landes Nordrhein-Westfalen, Corvey, 1966. 4. Aufl. Münster, Aschendorff, 1967.
2 v. illus., facsims., plates, maps, plans. 24 cm.
MnCS

2591 **Wigand, Paul.**
Geschichte der gefürsteten Reichs-abtei Corvey und der Städte Corvey und Höxter. Höxter, H. L. Bohn, 1819.

2 v. 19 cm.
KAS

Cottonwood, Id. St. Gertrude's Convent
see
St. Gertrude's Convent, Cottonwood, Id.

Crookston, Minn. Mount St. Benedict Priory
see
Mount St. Benedict Priory, Crookston, Minn.

Crossraguel Abbey, Scotland

2592 **Radford, Courtnay Arthur Raleigh.**
The Cluniac abbey of Crossraguel. Edinburgh, H.N.S.O., 1970.
20 p. plates, illus., plan. 21 cm.
MnCS

Cucujaes, Portugal (Benedictine abbey)

2593 **Ordo operis Dei persolvendi** sacrique peragendi ritu monastico pro monachis O.S. Benedicti . . . Portucale, typ. da "Palavra", 1881.
51 p. 18 cm.
PLatS

Cuxa, France (Benedictine abbey)

2594 **Barral i Aitet, Xavier.**
Els mosaica medievals de Ripoli i de Cuxa. Publet, Espana, Abadia de Poblet, 1971.
57 p.
MnCS

2595 **Saint Michel de Cuxa** . . . Photos F. Tur. Cuxa, Abbaye de Saint Michel, 1967.
54 p. illus., plates. 21 cm.
MnCS

Davington, England. St. Mary Magdalene Priory

2596 **An account of the church** and priory of Saint Mary Magdalene, Davington, in the County of Kent. Faversham, Frederick W. Monk, 1852.
24 p. 22 cm.
KAS

Deutz, Germany (Benedictine abbey)

2597 **Müller, Heribert.**
Heribert, Kanzler Ottos III. und Erzbischof von Köln. Köln, Verlag der Buchhandlung Dr. H. Wamper, 1977.
384 p. 24 cm. (Veröffentlichungen des Kölnischen Geschichtsvereins e.V., 33)
See index under Deutz.
MnCS

Dijon, France. St-Benigne (Benedictine abbey)

2598 **Bulst, Neithard.**
Untersuchungen zu den Kloster-
reformen Wilhelms von Dijon (962-1031).
Bonn, Ludwig Röhrscheid Verlag, 1973.
330 p. 23 cm.
MnCS

Dikninge, Netherlands (Benedictine abbey)

2599 **Arts, Antonius Johannes Maria.**
Het dubbelklooster Dikninge. Assen,
Van Gorcum & Comp. [1945].
285 p. plates. 24 cm.
MnCS

2600 **Joosting, J. G. C.**
Het archief der abdij te Dikninge.
Leiden, E. J. Brill, 1906.
349 p. 24 cm.
MnCS

Disentis, Switzerland (Benedictine abbey)

2601 **Müller, Iso, O.S.B.**
Die Fürstabtei Disentis im ausgehenden
18. Jahrhundert. Münster, Aschendorff,
1963.
viii, 247 p. 25 cm.
InStme; KAS; PLatS

2602 **Müller, Iso, O.S.B.**
Geschichte der Abtei Disentis von den
Anfängen bis zur Gegenwart. Einsiedeln,
Zürich, Köln, Benziger [1971].
276 p. maps, plates. 25 cm.
KAS

**Donauwerth, Germany. Heilige Kreuz
(Benedictine abbey)**

2603 **Königsdorfer, Cölestin, O.S.B.**
Geschichte des Klosters zum Heil.
Kreutz in Donauwörth. Donauwörth,
Sebastian Sedlmayr, 1819-29.
3 v. 22 cm.
KAS

Dormition Abbey, Jerusalem
see
Jerusalem. Dormition Abbey

Dowside Abbey, England

2604 **The centenary of St. Gregory the Great**
at Downside, with the three sermons
preached on the occasion. Downside, St.
Gregory's Monastery, 1890.
56 p. 23 cm.
PLatS

2605 **Connolly, Richard Hugh, O.S.B.**
Some dates and documents for the early
history of our house [Downside Abbey]. I.

Our establishment as a community at
Douay. Printed for private circulation,
1930.
69 p. 26 cm.
No more published.
PLatS

2606 **Downside review:** centenary number,
edited by the abbot of Downside. 1914.
233 p. illus.
AStb

2607 **A guide to the church** of Saint Gregory
the Great, Downside Abbey near Bath.
11th ed. Bath, Downside Abbey [1960].
27 p. plates, fold. plan. 18 cm.
KAS; MnCS

2608 **James, Augustine, O.S.B.**
The story of Downside Abbey church.
Stratton on the Fosse, Downside Abbey
[1961?].
115 p. illus., plan. 23 cm.
InStme; KAS; MoCo; PLatS

2609 **Murphy, Martin.**
Saint Oliver Plunkett and Downside.
Stratton on the Fosse, Downside Abbey,
1975.
12 p. illus. 21 cm.
MnCS

Drübech, Germany (abbey of Benedictine nuns)

2610 **Jacobs, Eduard.**
Das Kloster Drübeck; ein tausend-
jahriger geschichtlicher Rückblick und
Beschreibung der Klosterkirche. Wernigerode, 1877.
iv, 90 p. 25 cm.
KAS

Duluth, Minn. St. Scholastica Priory
see
St. Scholastica Priory, Duluth, Minn.

Duraton, Spain. San Frutos (Benedictine priory)

2611 **Martin Postigo, Maria de la Soterrana.**
San Frutos del Duratón; historia de un
priorato benedictino. Segovia, 1970.
306 p. plates. 24 cm.
MnCS

Durham Abbey, England

2612 **Boyd, Anne.**
The monks of Durham; life in a fifteenth-
century monastery. Cambridge [England],
Cambridge University Press [1975].
48 p. illus. 18x22 cm.
MnCS; MoCo

2613 **Dobson, Richard Barrie.**
Durham Priory, 1400-1450. Cambridge
[England], University Press, 1973.

xiii, 428 p. illus. 23 cm.
MnCS; MoCo; NcBe; PLatS

2614 **Liber vitae Ecclesiae Dunelmensis.** A collotype facsimile of the original manuscript, with introductory essays and notes . . . Durham, 1923.
v. facsims. 23 cm. (Publications of the Surtees Society . . . vol. CXXXVI)
MnCS

2615 **Raine, James, ed.**
The obituary roll of William Ebchester and John Burnby, priors of Durham, with notices of similar records preserved at Durham, from the year 1233 downwards, letters of fraternity, &c. Durham, 1856.
xxxv, 135 p. illus. 23 cm. (Publications of the Surtees Society . . . vol. XXXI)
MnCS

Eberbach, Germany (Benedictine abbey)

2616 **Bär, Hermann.**
Diplomatische Geschichte der Abtei Eberbach im Rheingau . . . Wiesbaden, 1855–58.
2 v. plates. 22 cm.
KAS

Echternach, Luxemburg (Benedictine abbey)

2617 **Metz, Peter.**
The Golden Gospels of Echternach: Codex aureus Epternacensis. Text based on the German by Peter Metz. New York, Praeger, [1957].
96 p. 106 facsims. (12 col.) 34 cm.
PLatS

2618 **Thiele, Augustinus, O.S.B.**
Echternach und Himmerod; Beispiele benediktinischer und zisterziensicher Wirtschaftsführung im 12. und 13. Jahrhundert. Stuttgart, G. Fischer, 1964.
186 p. facsims., map. 24 cm.
MnCS; PLatS

2619 **Verheyen, Egon.**
Das goldene Evangelienbuch von Echternach. München, Prestel Verlag [1963].
95 p. illus., col. plates. 20 cm.
MnCS

2620 **Wampach, Camillus.**
Geschichte der Grundherrschaft Echternach im Frühmittelalter . . . Luxemburg, 1930.
2 v.
AStb

Egmond, Netherlands (Benedictine abbey)

2621 **Johannes a Leydis.**
Kronyk van Egmond, of Jaarboeken der vorstelyke abten van Egmond. In't latyn

beschreeven door Broeder Jan van Leyden, vertaald door Kornelis van Herk, overgezien, vervolgt, en met de vertaalinge der fraffschriften verryky, door Gerard Kempher. Alkmaar, S. van Hoolwerf, 1732.
[36], 283 p. plates. 20 cm.
KAS

Egremont, England. St. Bees Priory

2622 **The life and miracles of Sancta Bega,** patroness of the Priory of St. Bees . . . written by a monkish historian [i.e., "probably" (Introduction, p. viii)], to which are appended a list of the Saint Bees priors and some explanatory notes, by G. C. Tomlinson. Carlisle, S. Jefferson, 1842.
xii, 80 p. 20 cm.
MnCS

2623 **The register of the Priory of St. Bees.** Durham, 1915.
xxxix, 661 p. 23 cm. (Publications of the Surtees Society . . . vol. CXXVI)
MnCS

Ebersberg, Germany (Benedictine abbey)

2624 **Paulhuber, Franz Xaver.**
Geschichte von Ebersberg und dessen Umgegend in Oberbayern. Burghausen, F. Lutzenberger, 1847.
xii, 704 p. illus. 20 cm.
KAS

Eichstätt, Germany. Abtei St. Walburg.

2625 **Benediktinerinnen-Abtei St. Walburg,** Eichstätt. Wasserburg am Inn, Joseph Käser.
[n.d. – post 1914].
unpaged. views. 9x15 cm.
MnCS

2626 **Joannes, bishop of Eichstätt.**
Epistola exhortatoria ad abbatissam et moniales monasterii S. Walburgae (1451). MS. Benediktinerabtei Melk, Austria, codex 751,2, f.296r–301r. Quarto. Saec. 15.
Microfilm: MnCH proj. no. 1603

Einsiedeln, Switzerland (Benedictine abbey)

2627 **Betschart, Ildefons, O.S.B.**
Salzburg und Einsiedeln; das Kraftespiel zweier Kulturzentren. Einsiedeln, J. & K. Eberle, 1951.
100 p. plates. 21 cm.
InStme

2628 **Bonstetten, Albertus von, O.S.B.**
Gesta monasterii Einsiedelensis. MS.
Benediktinerabtei St. Paul im Lavantthal,
Austria, codex 8/2, part II. Folio. Saec. 16.
Microfilm: MnCH proj. no. 11,741

2629 **Brandes, Karl, O.S.B.**
Leben und Wirken des heiligen Meinrad
für seine Zeit und für die Nachwelt; eine
Festschrift zur tausendjährigen Jubelfeier
des Benediktiner-Klosters Maria-
Einsiedeln. Einsiedeln, New York, K. u. N.
Benziger, 1861.
xx, 244 p. plates. 23 cm.
InStme; MoCo; NdRi; PLatS

2630 **Bugmann, Kuno, O.S.B.**
Einsiedeln; die Stiftskirche. 2. Ausgabe.
München, Verlag Schnell & Steiner, 1971.
22 p. illus. 17 cm.
MnCS

2631 **Catalogus religiosorum monast. B.V.M.**
Einsidlensis Ordinis S. Benedicti . . .
Einsidlae, typis Salesii Benziger.
v. 16 cm.
PLatS

2632 **Dreyfacher Ehrenkranz St. Meinradi;**
das ist, Einsidlische in drey Theil
verfasste Chronick. Worinnen entworfen
wird, Erstlich der Ursprung und
Aufnam der von Christo dem Herrn
eigenhädig eingeweyhten U. L. Frauen
Capellen. Zweytens der Anfang und
Wachsthum dess Einsidlischen unmittel-
bar unter den h. Apostolischen-Stuhl
gehörigen Fürstlichen Benediktiner
Gotteshauses Einsidlen. Drittens 405
bewehrteste und auserlesenste Wunder-
werck welche hin und wieder in gantz
Europa durch die Einsidlische Gnaden-
Mutter geschehen seynd. Einsidlen,
Meinrad Eberlin, 1728.
2 v. illus. 17 cm.
InStme

2633 **– –Neue Aufl. Einsiedlen, Johann
Eberhard Kälin, 1752.**
673 p. illus. 18 cm.
InStme; NdRi

2634 **Henggeler, Rudolf, O.S.B.**
Die Rosenkranz-Bruderschaft in Ein-
siedeln.
(*In* Sträter, Paul, S.J. Katholische
Marienkunde, v. 3(1962), p. 226–246)
PLatS

2635 **Henggeler, Rudolf, O.S.B.**
Das Stift Einsiedeln und die französische
Revolution . . . Einsiedeln, Einsiedler
Anzeiger, 1924.
160 p. 21 cm.
KAS

2636 **Huber, Albert, O.S.B.**
1000 Jahre Pferdezucht Kloster Einsiedeln . . . 2. Aufl. Einsiedeln, EDE-
Verlag [1963].
39 p. plates (part col.) 24 cm.
InStme

2637 **Keller, Hagen.**
Kloster Einsiedeln im ottonischen
Schwaben. Freiburg i.B., E. Albert, 1964.
189 p. facsims. 23 cm.
KAS; MnCS; NcBe; PLatS

2638 **Meier, Gabriel, O.S.B.**
Catalogus codicum manu scriptorum qui
in bibliotheca Monasterii Einsidlensis
O.S.B. servantur. Einsidlae, Sumptibus
Monasterii, 1899–
v. 28 cm.
Contents: t. 1: Complectens centurias
quinque priores.
MnCS

2639 **Meier, Gabriel, O.S.B.**
Heinrich von Ligerz, Bibliothekar von
Einsiedeln im 14. Jahrhundert. Leipzig,
Harrassowitz, 1968.
68 p. 24 cm.
MnCS; PLatS

2640 **Meinrad, Saint. Legend.**
Das Blockbuch von Sankt Meinrad und
seinen Mördern und vom Ursprung von
Einsiedeln. Farbige Faksimile-Ausgabe
zum elften Zentenar des Heiligen,
861–1961, mit einer Einleitung von Leo
Helbling. Einsiedeln, Benziger Verlag,
1961.
35, [64] p. col. illus. 19 cm.
Issued in portfolio.
InStme; MnCS; PLatS

2641 **Morel, Gall, O.S.B.**
Die Regesten der Benediktiner-Abtei
Einsiedeln. Chur, G. Hitz, 1848.
[10], 98 p. 30 cm.
KAS

2642 **Räber, Ludwig, O.S.B.**
Images d'Einsiedeln. 8. éd., rev. et corr.
Einsiedeln, Benziger [1966].
33 p. text, 64 plates. 17 cm.
Traduction française: Dom Germain
Varin.
MnCS

2643 **Ringholz, Odilo Emil Adolf, O.S.B.**
Anshelm von Schwanden, Abt des
Stiftes U.L.F. zu Einsiedeln. Mit
urkundlichen und artistischen Beilagen.
[n.p., n.d.].
100–148 p. 23 cm.
InStme

2644 **Salzgeber, Joachim, O.S.B.**
Die Klöster Einsiedeln und St. Gallen im
Barockzeitalter; historisch-soziologische

Studie. Münster, Aschendorff [1967].
xix, 232 p. 26 cm.
InStme; KAS; MnCS; PLatS

2645 **Scheiwiller, Otmar.**
Das "reiche" Kloster Einsiedeln; ein offenes Wort ans Schweizervolk. Einsiedeln, Meinrad-Verlag, 1949.
48 p. 21 cm.
MnCS

2646 **Schmid, Alfred Andreas.**
Corolla heremitana; neue Beiträge zur Kunst und Geschichte Einsiedelns und der Innerschweiz . . . Olten, im Breisgau, Walter-Verlag, 1964.
458 p. illus., port. 24 cm.
InStme

2647 **Das Totenbuch des Klosters Einsiedeln:**
861–1973. Einsiedeln, 1973.
158 p. 30 cm.
InStme

2648 **Zingg, Thaddäus.**
Die erneuerte Einsiedler Barockfassade . . . Einsiedeln, Benziger Verlag, 1957.
79, viii, 16 p. illus., plates. 22 cm.
InStme

Elizabeth, N.J. St. Walburga's Convent
see
St. Walburga's Convent, Elizabeth, N.J.

Ellwangen, Germany (Benedictine abbey)

2649 **Seckler, Aloys.**
Vollstädige Beschreibung der gefürsteten Reichs-Propstei Ellwangen. Stuttgart, A. Koch, 1864.
iv, 164 p. 19 cm.
KAS

2649a **Seiler, Alois.**
Das Schriftgut von Kloster und Stift Ellwangen im Staatsarchiv Ludwigsburg; eine Beständebericht. [Stuttgart, Hauptstaatsarchiv] 1976.
ii, 83 p. 23 cm.
MnCS

Engelberg, Switzerland (Benedictine abbey)

2650 **Heer, Gall, O.S.B.**
Aus der Vergangenheit von Kloster und Tal Engelberg, 1120–1970. Verlag Benediktinerkloster Engelberg [1975].
554 p.
MoCo

2651 **Hess, Ignaz, O.S.B.**
Die Kunst im Kloster Engelberg. Schriften zur Heimatkunde von Engelberg, 1946.
136 p. illus.
MoCo

2652 **Hess, Leopold.**
Engelberg: Kloster, Tal und Leute. [Engelberg, F. Hess, 1959?].
109 p. illus. 22 cm.
InStme; MoCo

2653 **Hunkeler, Leodegar, O.S.B.**
Benediktinerstift Engelberg. 3. Aufl. München, Verlag Schnell & Steiner, 1968.
14 p. illus. 17 cm.
MnCS

2654 **Versuch einer urkundlichen** Darstellung des reichsfreien Stiftes Engelberg, St. Benediktein-Ordens in der Schweiz, zwölftes und dreizehntes Jahrhundert. Luzern, Gebrüder Räber, 1846.
156 p. illus., facsims., geneal. table. 25 cm.
KAS

Erfurt, Germany. St. Peter (Benedictine abbey)

2655 **Frank, Barbara.**
Das Erfurter Peterskloster im 15. Jahrhundert; Studien zur Geschichte der Klosterreform und der Bursfelder Union. Göttingen, Vandenhoeck und Ruprecht, 1973.
465 p. fold. map. 25 cm.
MnCS

2656 **Holder-Egger, Oswald, ed.**
Monumenta Erphesfurtensia, saec. XII, XIII, XIV. Hannoverae et Lipsiae, impensis bibliopolii Hahniani, 1899.
viii, 919 p. illus. 22 cm.
MnCS

2657 **Muth, Placidus, O.S.B.**
Ueber den Einfluss des königlichen Benedictiner Stiftes auf dem Petersberge zu Erfurt auf die erste Urbarmachung der hiesigen Gegenden durch Ackerbau und Viehzucht . . . Erfurt, bey Beyer und Maring, 1798.
165–208 p. 22 cm.
Separate from: Akademie nützlicher Wissenschaften zu Erfurt, 2. November, 1797.
KAS

Erie, Pa. St. Benedict's Convent
see
St. Benedict's Convent, Erie, Pa.

Erla, Austria (abbey of Benedictine nuns)

2658 **Urbar des dem Orden** der Benedictinerinnen gehörigen Erlaklosters (1503). MS. Vienna, Haus-, Hof- und Staatsarchiv, codex B 501. 36 f. Folio. Saec. 16.
Microfilm: MnCH proj. no. 23,554

2659　**Urbarbuch des Klosters** der Benediktin-
erinnen zu Erla in Oesterreich unter der
Emms. MS. Vienna, Haus-, Hof- und
Staatsarchiv, codex W 651. 272 f. Folio.
Saec. 16.
Microfilm: MnCH proj. no. 23,560

2660　**Zehentbuch des Benedictinnerinnen**
Stiftes Erlakloster in Oesterreich unter
der Enns, später dem Königskloster
der Klarissinnen in Wien gehörig (1550–
1557). MS. Vienna, Haus-, Hof- und
Staatsarchiv, codex R 158. 153 f. Quarto.
Saec. 16.
Microfilm: MnCH proj. no. 23,574

Erstein, Alsace (Benedictine abbey)

2661　**Bernhard, Joseph.**
Histoire de l'Abbaye et de la ville d'Er-
stein. Rixheim, A. Sutter, 1883.
viii, 200 p. 23 cm.
KAS

Ettal, Bavaria (Benedictine abbey)

2662　**Acta reformationis monasterii** Beatae
Mariae Virginis in Ettal. MS. Vienna,
Nationalbibliothek, codex 3637, f.397v–
413v. Octavo. Saec. 16.
Microfilm: MnCH proj. no. 16,860

2663　**De fundatione monasterii Etal.** MS.
Benediktinerabtei Melk, Austria, codex
1653, f.177r. Sextodecimo. Saec. 15.
Microfilm: MnCH proj. no. 2011

2664　**Dussler, Georg, O.S.B.**
Geschichte der Ettaler Bergstrasse. 3.
Aufl.
(*In* Ettaler Mandl . . . Jahrg 51 (1971–
72), p. 73–170)
KAS

2665　**Eberl, Martin, O.S.B.**
Wallfahrt Ettal. Ettal, Kunstverlag Ettal [1941].
44 p. plates. 16 cm.
MnCS

2666　**Ettal.** [Ettal, Benediktinerabtei, 1975].
31 p. illus. 16 cm.
Text in English.
MnCS

2667　**Festschrift zum** 600 jährigen Weihejubi-
läum der Klosterkirche Ettal. (Red.:
Rupert Sarach u. Athanasius Kalff.)
Ettal, Buch-Kunstverlag, 1970.
251 p. illus. 24 cm.
MnCS

2668　**Fischer, Pius, O.S.B.**
Der Barokmaler, Johann Jakob Zeiller
und sein Ettaler Werk. München, Verlag
Herold [1964].
135 p. illus., plates (col.) 30 cm.
PLatS

2669　**Haiss, Emmanuel, O.S.B.**
Cathedral of Our Lady of Ettal. Ettal
Abbey [n.d.].
31 p. illus. 17 cm.
PLatS

2670　**Stift Ettal:** Urbarregister über Güter im
Ger. Kufstein, 1747–1761. MS. Inns-
bruck, Austria, Tiroler Landesarchiv,
codex Urbar 130/1. 257 p. Folio.
Saec. 18.
Microfilm: MnCH proj. no. 29,305

2671　**Wellnhofer, Simon, O.S.B.**
Ettal; seine Entstehung, Geschichte und
Kunst. Buch-Kunstverlag Ettal [n.d.].
80 p. plates. 17 cm.
MnCS; MnStj

Evesham Abbey, England

2672　**Tindal, William.**
The history and antiquities of the abbey
and borough of Evesham, comp. chiefly
from mss. in the British Museum.
Evesham, J. Agg, 1794.
viii, 363 p. plates. 27 cm.
KAS

Eynsham Abbey, England

2673　**The customary of the Benedictine abbey**
of Eynsham in Oxfordshire, edited by
Antonia Grandsen. Siegburg, F.
Schmitt, 1963.
245 p. 26 cm. (Corpus consuetudinum
monasticarum, t. 2)
InStme; KAS; NdRi; PLatS

Faenza, Italy (abbey of Vallumbrosian nuns)

2674　**Nel settimo centenario** della fondazione
del monastero Faentino de Santa
Umilta, 1266–1966. Miscellanea storico-
religiosa. [Faenza, 1966].
76 p. illus. 24 cm.
PLatS

Fahr, Switzerland (abbey of Benedictine nuns)

2675　**Walter, Silja.**
Das Kloster am Rande der Stadt; ein Tag
der Benediktinischen Nonne. Zürich,
Verlag die Arche, 1971.
87 p. illus. 20 cm.
MnCS

Farfa, Italy (Benedictine abbey)

2676　**Ring, Richard Raymond.**
The lands of Farfa; studies in Lombard
and Carolingian Italy.
276 leaves. 29 cm.

Thesis (Ph.D.) – University of Wisconsin, 1972.
Typescript.
MnCS(microfilm)

Faversham Abbey, England

2676a **Gregorio di Catino, monk of Farfa, fl. 1000.**
Il regesto di Farfa di Gregorio di Catino, pubblicato da I. Giorgi e U. Balzani. Roma, Presso la Società, 1878–83, 1914 (reprint).
5 v. 36 cm. (Biblioteca della R. Società Romana di storia patria)
MnCS

2677 **Telfer, W.**
Faversham Abbey and its last abbot, John Caslock . . . With a brief report by Brian Philp on the excavations at Faversham Abbey undertaken in January – February 1965. 3d ed. Faversham, Kent, Faversham Society, 1968.
21 p. illus. 26 cm.
PLatS

Fécamp, France (Benedictine abbey)

2678 **L'Abbaye bénédictine de Fécamp;**
ouvrage scientifique du XIIIe centenaire, 658–1958. Fécamp, L. Durand, 1959–61.
3 v. illus., plates, maps. 25 cm.
_____Addenda & errata, index & tables. [Fécamp, L. Durand, 1963].
165 p. 25 cm.
CaQStB; KAS; MnCS; MoCo; NcBe; PLatS

2679 **Laporte, Jean, O.S.B.**
Quelques documents sur Fécamp au temps d'Henri de Sully (1140–1189).
(*In* Analecta monastica, 6. dér., 1962, p. 23–33)
PLatS

Ferdinand, Ind. Convent of the Immaculate Conception
see
Convent of the Immaculate Conception, Ferdinand, Ind.

▶Ferrières-Gatinais, France (Benedictine abbey)

2680 **Lupus Servatus, abbot of Ferrières.**
The letters of Lupus of Ferrières. Translated, with an introduction and notes by Graydon W. Regenos. The Hague, M. Nijhoff, 1966.
xii, 160 p. 24 cm.
InStme

Fiecht, Austria, (Benedictine abbey)

2681 **Abschrift eines versecretierten Libels Transumpt** . . . zusammengestellt aus Urkunden des Stiftes Georgenberg (Fiecht) von 1331 bis 1497. 30 f.
Kopien von vorwiegend Landesfürst-lichen Urkunden für das Kloster Georgen-berg von 1097. bis 1507. 56 f. Saec. 16.
MS. Innsbruck, Austria, Tiroler Landes-archiv, codex 3825 & 3826.
Microfilm: MnCH proj. no. 29,205

2682 **Album der Schutzengel-Kongregation** auf Georgenberg, 1699–1784. MS. Innsbruck, Austria, Tiroler Landesarchiv, codex 671. 157 f. Folio. Saec. 17/18.
Microfilm: MnCH proj. no. 29,565

2683 **Das Benediktinerstift Fiecht** (St. Georgenberg), 1785. 122 p. & 31 f. Saec. 18. Ergänzungsinventar des Benediktiner-stiftes Fiecht, 1789. 32 p. Saec. 18.
MS. Innsbruck, Austria, Tirolerlandes-archiv, codex Klöster B 9/2 & B 9/3. Folio.
Microfilm: MnCH proj. no. 29,316

2684 **Domanig, Karl.**
Der Abt von Fiecht; eine poetische Erzählung. 6. Aufl. Kempten, Kösel, 1912.
72 p.
AStb

2685 **Kramer, Maurus, O.S.B.**
Abteikirche Fiecht, Tirol. [Salzburg, Rupertuswerk, 1959].
[23] p. illus. 17 cm.
MnCS; PLatS

2686 **Kramer, Maurus, O.S.B.**
Geschichte der Benediktinerabtei St. Georgenberg-Fiecht bei Schwaz in Tirol . . . Fiecht, Benediktinerabtei, 1954.
67 p. illus. 19 cm.
MnCS; PLatS

2687 **Die Wallfahrt zu St. Georgenberg** mit der Anweisung wie die Heiligtümer jährlich dem Volke zu zeigen sind. MS. Innsbruck, Austria, Tiroler Landes-archiv, codex Klöster B 9/1b. 66 f. Quarto. Saec. 16(1594).
Microfilm: MnCH proj. no. 29,321

Fifield, Wis. King of Martyrs Priory
see
King of Martyrs Priory, Fifield, Wis.

Flavigny-sur-Moselle, France. Abbaye de Saint-Eustase

2688 **Histoire de l'Abbaye bénédictine** de Saint-Eustase (966–1924) . . . par les religieuses de la Communauté. Nancy,

Société d'impressios typographiques, 1924.
xvi, 175 p.
KAS

Fleury, France. Saint-Benoît-sur-Loire.
see
Saint-Benoît-sur-Loire

Florence, Italy. S. Maria (Benedictine abbey)

2689 **Blum, Rudolf.**
La biblioteca della badia Fiorentina e i codici di Antonio Corbinelli. Città del Vaticano, Biblioteca Apostolica Vaticana, 1951.
xii, 190 p. 25 cm. (Studi e testi, v. 155)
MnCS

Fontanella, Italy. S. Egidio (Cluniac monastery)

2690 **Tagliabue, Mario.**
Il priorato di S. Egidio dei Benedettini Cluniacensi in Fontanella del Monte (1080–1473). Storia et documenti. Bergamo, Edizioni "Monumenta Bergomensia," 1960.
227 p. maps, plates. 25 cm.
MnCS; PLatS

Fontenelle, France. Saint-Wandrille
see
Saint-Wandrille, France

Fort Augustus, Scotland. St. Benedict's Abbey
see
St. Benedict's Abbey, Fort Augustus, Scotland

Frauenalb, Germany (abbey of Benedictine nuns)

2691 **Thoma, Albrecht.**
Geschichte des Klosters Frauenalb; ein Beitrag zur Kulturgeschichte von 7 Jahrhunderten. Freiburg i.B., Verlag von Paul Wastzel, 1898.
[4], 104 p. 20 cm.
KAS

Frauenmünster, Zurich, Switzerland
see
Zürich, Switzerland. Frauenmünster

Frauenzell, Bavaria (Benedictine abbey)

2692 **Sächerl, Joseph.**
Chronik des Benediktiner-Klosters Frauenzell . . . Regensburg, 1853.
257–466 p. 24 cm.
KAS

Fruttaria, France (Benedictine abbey)

2693 **Constitutiones benedictinae monasterii Fructuariensis.** MS. Benediktinerabtei Göttweig, Austria, codex 53b. 165 p. Quarto. Saec. 12.
Microfilm: MnCH proj. no. 3341

Fulda, Germany (Benedictine abbey)

2694 **Annales Fuldenses,** a.680–901.
(*In* Monumenta Germaniae historica. Scriptores. Stuttgart, 1963. t. 1, p. 337–415)
MnCS; PLatS

2695 **Annales Fuldenses antiqui,** a.651–838.
(*In* Monumenta Germaniae historica. Scriptores. Stuttgart, 1963. t. 3, p. 116–117)
MnCS; PLatS

2695a **Brall, Artur, ed.**
Von der Klosterbibliothek zur Landesbibliothek; Beiträge zum zweihundertjährigen Bestehen der Hessischen Landesbibliothek Fulda. Stuttgart, Anton Hiersemann, 1978.
xi, 503 p. illus. 23 cm. (Bibliothek des Buchwesens, Bd. 6)
The Klosterbibliothek in question is the library of the famous Benedictine abbey in Fulda.
MnCS

2696 **Christ, Karl.**
Die Bibliothek des Klosters Fulda im 16. Jahrhundert: die Handschriften-Verzeichnisse. Leipzig, Harrassowitz, 1933; Nendeln, Kraus Reprint, 1968.
xiv, 343 p. 23 cm.
PLatS

2696a **Chronica Fuldensis;** die Darmstädter Fragmente der Fuldaer Chronik, bearb. von Walter Heinemeyer. Köln u. Wien, Böhlau Verlag, 1976.
173 p. 24 cm. (Archiv für Diplomatik . . . Beiheft 1)
MnCS

2697 **Cornelius, F.**
Breviarium Fuldensi, in quo omnium archimandritarum ortus, potiora facta et obitus, usque ad MCCCCLXXIX breviter narrantur . . .
(*In* Paullini, C. F. Rerum et antiquitatum Germanarum syntagma. Francofurti, 1698. p. 421–466)
KAS

2698 **Fabricius, Eberhard.**
Abbatiae Ordinis Benedictini potentissimae, id est, Vitae et res gestae reverendissimorum et illustrissimorum ab-

batum Fuldensium . . . Giessae, Typis Chemlinianis, 1655.
[16], 104 p. 16 cm.
KAS

2699 **Falk, Franz.**
Beiträge zur Rekonstruktion der alten Bibliotheca Fuldensis und Bibliotheca Laureshamensis. Mit einer Beilage: der Fuldaer Handschriften-Katalog aus dem 16. Jahrhundert. Neu hrsg. und eingeleitet von Carl Scherer. Leipzig, Harrassowitz, 1902; Nendeln, Kraus Reprint, 1968.
112 p. 23 cm.
PLatS

2700 **Geuenich, Dieter.**
Die Personennamen der Klostergemeinschaft von Fulda im früheren Mittelalter. München, Wilhelm Fink, 1976.
300 p. (Münstersche Mittelalter-Schriften, 5)
MnCS

2701 **Hilpisch, Stephanus, O.S.B.**
Die Feier der Karwoche in der Abtei Fulda zu Beginn des 17. Jahrhunderts.
(*In* Perennitas; Beiträge . . . P. Thomas Michels, O.S.B. zum 70. Geburtstag. Münster, 1963. p. 189–196)
PLatS

2701a **Die illuminierten Handschriften** der Hessischen Landesbibliothek Fulda. Stuttgart, Anton Hiersemann, 1976–
vol. 1: 6. bis 13. Jahrhundert.
The library was the former library of the famous Benedictine abbey in Fulda.
MnCS

2702 **Lehmann, Paul Joachim Georg.**
Fuldaer Studien. München, Verlag der Bayerischen Akademie der Wissenschaften, 1925–
v. illus. 23 cm.
InStme

2703 **Leinweber, Josef.**
Das Hochstift Fulda vor der Reformation. Fulda, Parzeller, 1972.
352 p. illus. 23 cm.
PLatS

2704 **Looshorn, Johann.**
Gründung und I. Jahrhundert des Bisthums Bamberg . . . München, P. Zipperer, 1886.
viii, 544 p. 23 cm.
KAS; PLatS

2705 **Pralle, Ludwig.**
Die Wiederentdeckung des Tacitus; ein Beitrag zur Geistesgeschichte Fuldas und zur Biographie des jungen Cusanus. Fulda, Verlag Parzeller, 1952.
105 p. 24 cm.
MnCS

2706 **Traditiones et antiquitates Fuldenses.**
Hrsg. [von] Ernst Friedr. Joh. Dronke. Mit einem Steindruck. Neudruck der Ausg. 1844. Osnabrück, Zeller, 1966.
xvi, 244 p. 27 cm.
KAS; PLatS

2707 **Urkundenbuch des Klosters Fulda.**
Bearbeitet von Edmund E. Stengel. Marburg, N. G., Elwert Verlag, 1958–
v. 24 cm.
PLatS

2708 **Witzel, Friedrich-Wilhelm.**
Die Reichsbtei Fulda und ihre Hochvögte die Grafen von Ziegenhain im 12. und 13. Jahrhundert. Fulda, Parzeller, 1963.
67 p. 24 cm.
PLatS

Fulda, Germany. S. Maria (abbey of Benedictine nuns)

2709 **Troxler, Johann Baptist, O.S.B.**
Exil und Asyl der Klöster Maria-Stein u. Rathhausen in der Schweiz und St. Maria zu Fulda in Preussen . . . Solothurn, B. Schwendimann, 1879.
136 p. plates, ports. 22 cm.
MnCS; MoCo

Fürstenfeld, Germany (Benedictine abbey)

2710 **Fugger, Eberhard.**
Kloster Fürstenfeld, eine Wittelsbacher Stiftung, und deren Schicksale von 1258–1803. 2. Aufl. München, F. Metzner, 1885.
vi, 155 p.
KAS

Füssen, Germany. St. Mang (Benedictine abbey)

2711 **Mertin, Paul.**
Das vormalige Benediktinerstift St. Mang zu Füssen im ersten Jahrtausend seines Bestehens. Füssen, Verlag der Stadt, 1965.
xii, 163 p. 30 cm.
MnCS

Gandersheim, Germany (abbey of Benedictine nuns)

2712 **Boehmer, Heinrich.**
Willigis von Mainz; ein Beitrag zur Geschichte des Deutschen Reichs und der Deutschen Kirche in der sächsischen Kaiserzeit. Leipzig, Verlag von Duncker & Humblot, 1895.
viii, 206 p. 23 cm.
PLatS

2712a **Härtel, Helmar.**
Die Handschriften der Stiftsbibliothek zu Gandersheim, beschrieben von Helmar Härtel. Wiesbaden, Otto Harrassowitz, 1978.
83 p. 24 cm.
MnCS

Garsten, Austria (Benedictine abbey)

2713 **Banntaiding des Klosters Garsten** zu Wilhelmsburg, Lehenszinsbuch zu Krems und anderen Orden. Germanice. MS. Vienna, Nationalbibliothek, codex series nova 3282. 114 f. Quarto. Saec. 15(1495).
Microfilm: MnCH proj. no. 20,803

2714 **Beschreibung des Lebens des hl.** Bertold. Beschreibung des Ursprungs des Klosters Garsten. MS. Linz, Austria, Oberösterreichisches Landesarchiv. Stiftsarchiv Garsten, Hs. 63. 117 f. Saec. 17(1608).
Microfilm: MnCH proj. no. 27,613

2715 **Markstein des Klosters Garsten.** MS. Linz, Austria, Oberösterreichisches Landesarchiv. Stiftsarchiv Garsten, Hs. 6. 93 f. Saec. 16.
Microfilm: MnCH proj. no. 27,617

2716 **Nekrologium des Stiftes Garsten.** MS. Linz, Austria, Oberösterreichisches Landesarchiv. Stiftsarchiv Garsten, Hs. 2. 224 f. Saec. 18.
Microfilm: MnCH proj. no. 27,616

2717 **Traditions-Codex des Klosters Garsten** aus dem 12.-13. Jhdt. MS. Linz, Austria, Oberösterreichisches Landesarchiv. Stiftsarchiv. Garsten, Hs. 1. 58 f. Saec. 12-13.
Microfilm: MnCH proj. no. 27,614

Gegenbach, Germany (Benedictine abbey)

2718 **Franck, Wilhelm.**
Zur Geschichte der Benediktinerabtei und der Reichstadt Gegenbach (1525-1539).
(*In* Freiburger Diözesan-Archiv, v. 6, p. 1-26)
InStme

Geisenfeld, Germany (abbey of Benedictine nuns)

2719 **Monumenta Geisenfeldensia.**
(*In* Monumenta Boica. Monachii, 1763-1829. v. 14, p. 171-310)
KAS

Gembloux, France (Benedictine abbey)

2720 **Diplomata duo,** primum fundationis, alterum confirmationis papalis monasterii Gemblacensis. MS. Vienna, Nationalbibliothek, codex 3469, f.16v-20v. Quarto. Saec. 15.
Microfilm: MnCH proj. no. 20,398

2721 **Guibertus, abbot of Gembloux.**
Destructio vel potius combustio monasterii Gemblacensis, a.1037. Vienna, Nationalbibliothek, codex 3469, f.21r-24v. Quarto. Saec. 15.
Microfilm: MnCH proj. no. 20,398

Gerona, Spain. St. Daniel (Benedictine abbey)

2722 **Batlle i Prats, Lluis.**
La casa de Montserrat a Girona.
(*In* Analecta Montserratensia, v. 10, p. 65-70)

Ghent, Belgium. Saint-Bavon (Benedictine abbey)

2723 **Lokeren, Auguste van.**
Histoire de l'Abbaye de Saint-Bavon et de la crypte de Saint-Jean à Gand. Gand, L. Hebbelynck, 1855.
xvi, 257 p. 28 cm.
KAS; PLatS

Ghent, Belgium. Saint-Pierre (Benedictine abbey)

2724 **Huyghebaert, Nicolas, O.S.B.**
La consécration de l'église abbatiale de Saint-Pierre de Gand (975) et les reliques de Saint Bertulfe de Renty).
(*In* Corona gratiarum; miscellanea patristica . . . Eligio Dekkers . . . oblata. Brugge, 1975. v. 2, p. 129-141)
PLatS

Glascareg, Wales (Benedictine priory)

2725 **Pritchard, Emily M.**
The history of St. Dogmaels Abbey, together with her cells, Pill, Caldey and Glascareg, and the mother abbey of Tiron . . . London, Blades, East & Blades, 1907.
241 p. illus., plates, map. 26 cm.
MnCS

Glastonbury Abbey, England

2726 **Crake, Augustine David.**
The last abbot of Glastonbury; a tale of the dissolution of the monasteries. Oxford, A. R. Mowbray & Co. [1975].
xvi, 250 p. plates. 19 cm.
MnCS

2727 **Glastonbury:** a study in patterns. Editor: Mary Williams. London, Research into Lost Knowledge Organization, 1969.
37 p. illus. 28 cm.
MnCS

2728 **Greswell, William H. P.**
Chapters on the early history of Glastonbury Abbey. Taunton, Barnicott & Pearce, 1909.
155 p. illus.
MoCo

2728a **Horne, Ethelbert, O.S.B.**
Guide to Glastonbury Abbey. London, Catholic Truth Society, 1934.
32 p. illus., plans, 19 cm.
KAS

2729 **Kenawell, William W.**
The quest of Glastonbury; a biographical study of Frederick Bligh Bond. New York, Helix Press, 1965.
xi, 318 p. illus. 24 cm.
MnCS

2730 **Lewis, Lionel Smithett.**
Glastonbury, "the mother of saints"; her saints, a.d. 37–1539. 2d ed. London, Mowbray, 1927.
xviii, 89 p.
MoCo

2731 **Radford, Courtenay Arthur Ralegh.**
The pictorial history of Glastonbury Abbey. [London], Pitkin Pictorials, 1969.
24 p. illus. 23 cm.
PLatS

2732 **Robinson, Joseph Armitage.**
Somerset historical essays. London, Oxford University Press, 1921.
vii, 159 p. 26 cm.
PLatS

2733 **Ross, Williamson Hugh.**
The flowering hawthorn. New York, Hawthorn [1962].
102 p. illus.
MoCo; PLatS

2734 **Snow, Terence Benedict, O.S.B.**
Glastonbury. Yeovil, Printed by the Western Chronicle Company [n.d.].
27 p. illus. 23 cm.
"Reprinted from the Downside review."
PLatS

2735 **Warner, Richard.**
An history of the abbey of Glaston; end of the town of Glastonbury. Bath, Printed by R. Cruttwell, 1826.
vi, cxviii, [149]-280 p., ciii p. illus. 32 cm.
MnCS

2736 **William of Malmsbury, O.S.B.**
On the antiquity of Glastonbury.

(*In* Robinson, Joseph. Somerset historical essays. London, 1921)
PLatS

2737 **Willis, Robert.**
The architectural history of Glastonbury abbey. Cambridge, Deighton, Bell and Co., 1866.
vii, 91 p. illus., plates. 23 cm.
PLatS

Gloucester Abbey, England

2738 **An ecclesiastical miscellany,** containing a register of the churches of the Monastery of St. Peter's, Gloucester, a survey of the diocese of Gloucester, 1603, Wesleyan membership in Bristol, 1783.
ix, 159 p. 22 cm.
MnCS

Godstow, England (abbey of Benedictine nuns)

2739 **The English register of Godstow nunnery,** near Oxford, written about 1450. Edited, with an introduction, by Andrew Clark. London, K. Paul, Trench, Trübner & Co., 1911.
cxiv, 722 p. 23 cm. (Early English Text Society, Original series, 129–130, 142)
PLatS

Göss, Austria (abbey of Benedictine nuns)

2740 **Bracher, Karl.**
Beiträge zur mittelalterlichen Geschichte des Stiftes Göss. Graz, Historischer Verein für Steiermark, 1945.
96 p. illus. 23 cm.
MnCS

2741 **Pichler, Virgil, abbot of St. Peter, Salzburg.**
Schreiben an das Benediktiner Kloster Göss, 1497, und an das Benediktiner Kloster St. Georgen am Langsee, 1496.
MS. Benediktinerabtei St. Peter, Salzburg, codex b.V.20, f.52r–61r. Quarto. Saec. 15.
Microfilm: MnCH proj. no. 10,453

Gottesthal, Germany (Benedictine abbey)

2742 **Chronicon coenobii virginum Otterbergensis,** ad Netham, congregationis quondam Cisterciensis, nunc in Valle Dei, familiae Benedictinae, variis bullis & literis pontificum, principum . . . illustratum.
(*In* Paullini, Christian Franz. Rerum et antiquitatum Germanicarum syntagma. Francofurti ad Moenum, 1698. p. 169–260)
KAS

Göttweig, Austria (Benedictine abbey)

2743 **Göttweig, Austria (Benedictine abbey).**
Ausstellung [1. bis   ] des graphischen
Kabinettes des Stiftes. Leitung und
Gestaltung, P. Emmeram Ritter, O.S.B.
[Vienna, das Stift, 1960–   ]
v. plates. 21 cm.
MnCS

2744 **Göttweig, Austria (Benedictine abbey).**
Manuscripten-Catalog der Stifts-
bibliothek zu Göttweig.
3 v. 27 cm.
Handwritten.
Xeroxed by University Microfilms, Ann
Arbor, Mich., 1967.
MnCS

2745 **Koller, Ludwig, O.S.B.**
Stift Göttweig, Benediktinerabtei in
Niederösterreich. 5. neubearb. Aufl. München, Verlag Schnell & Steiner, 1967.
15 p. illus. 17 cm. (Kunstführer Nr. 645
von 1956)
PLatS

2746 **Modus visitationis monasterii Gottwicensis.** MS. Vienna, Nationalbibliothek, codex 4970, f.32r–35r. Quarto.
Saec. 15.
Microfilm: MnCH proj. no. 18,143

2746a **Lechner, Gregor M.**
Stift Göttweig und seine Kunstschätze.
Bilddokumentation Herbert Fasching. St.
Pölten, Wien, Verlag Niederösterreich-
isches Pressehaus [1977].
104 p. [32] leaves of plates (78 illus.),
28 cm.
MnCS

2747 **Riedel, Friedrich.**
Die Kirchenmusik im Benediktinerstift
Göttweig. Wien, Mechitharistendruckerei,
1966.
8 p. 28 cm.
Sonderdruck aus "Singende Kirche,"
Heft 4, 1966.
MnCS

2748 **Riedel, Friederich W.**
Das Musikalienrepertoire des Benedik-
tinerstiftes Göttweig um die Mitte des 17.
Jahrhunderts.
(*In* Translatio studii; manuscript and
library studies honoring Oliver L. Kapsner.
Collegeville, Minn., 1973. p. 149–155)
MnCS; PLatS

2749 **Schlitpacher, Johann.**
Articuli propositi tempore tentatae
reformationis monasterii Gottwicensis, anno 1450. Cointelligentia monasterii Gottwicensis cum reformatoribus in tantum in
quantum. MS. Benediktinerabtei Gött-

weig, Austria, codex 496b. 16 f. Quarto.
Saec. 15.
Microfilm: MnCH proj. no. 3748

2750 **Stift Göttweig.** Urkundenabschriften.
MS. Vienna, Haus-, Hof- und Staats-
archiv, codex W 987/3.
Microfilm: MnCH proj. no. 23,629

2751 **Zedinek, Wilhelm Felix, O.S.B.**
Das alte Göttweig.
(*In* Der heilige Altmann, Bischof von
Passau. 1965. p. 58–84)
PLatS

2752 **Zedinek, Wilhelm Felix, O.S.B.**
Die Göttweiger Stiftsbibliothek, ihr
Werden und Wachsen, ihre Kostbarkeiten.
9 p.
A lecture delivered March 23, 1964, in
Passau.
MnCH (microfilm)

Göttweig, Austria (abbey of Benedictine nuns)

2753 **Necrologium des Frauenklosters zu
Göttweig.** MS. Benediktinerabtei
Altenburg, Austria, codex AB 6 C 6,
f.94r–118r. Folio. Saec. 16. "Dies Puech
ist auss geschriben . . . in das Frawn
Chloster zw Göttweich . . . 1505."
Microfilm: MnCH proj. no. 6500

Grande-Sauve, France. Notre-Dame (abbey of Benedictine nuns)

2754 **Cirot de la Ville, abbé.**
Histoire de l'abbaye et congrégation de
Notre-Dame de la Grande-Sauve, Ordre de
Saint Benoît, en Guienne. Paris, Mé-
quignon junior, 1844.
2 v. plates, plan. 21 cm.
KAS

Grandmont, France (Benedictine abbey)

2755 **Becquet, Jean, O.S.B.**
Scriptores Ordinis Grandimontensis.
Turnholti, Brepols, 1968.
xiii, 628 p. 26 cm. (Corpus Chris-
tianorum. Continuatio mediaevalis, 8)
PLatS

Gries, Italy
see
Muri-Gries, Italy

Gross St. Martin, Cologne, Germany
see
Cologne, Germany. Gross St. Martin

Grossburschla, Germany (Benedictine abbey)

2756 **Kohlstedt, Georg.**
Die Benediktinerpropstei und das spätere Kollegiatstift Grossburschla an der Werra (9. Jahrhundert bis 1650). Leipzig, St. Benno-Verlag, 1965.
139 p. 22 cm.
KAS; PLatS

Grüssau, Silesia (Benedictine abbey)

2757 **Lutterotti, Nikolaus von, O.S.B.**
Abtei Grüssau; ein Führer. Grüssau in Schlesien, Verlag für Liturgik, 1930.
67 p. plates. 18 cm.
MnCS

2758 **Lutterotti, Nikolaus von, O.S.B.**
Altgrüssauer Klostergeschichten, Breslau, Verlag des Katholischen Sonntagsblattes, 1927.
59 p. 19 cm.
InStme

2759 **Rose, Ambrosius, O.S.B., ed.**
Grüssauer Gedenkbuch, in Verbindung mit Freunden und Mönchen der Abtei Grüssau hrsg. Stuttgart, Brentanoverlag [1949].
199 p. plates. 21 cm.
MnCS

Guixols, Spain
see
San Felix de Guixol

Guzule, Sardinia. San Nicola (Benedictine priory)

2760 **Studi sui vittorini in Sardegna,** a cura di F. Artizzu [et al.]. Padova, CEDAM, 1963.
88 p. 25 cm.
KAS

Hambye, Normandy (Benedictine abbey)

2761 **Le Conte, René.**
Curiosités normandes comparées; études historiques et archéologiques sur les abbayes de Bénédictins en général et sur celle de Hambye en particulier. Bernay, Miaulle Duval, 1890.
xvi, 556 p. plates. 19 cm.
KAS

Heilige Kreuz, Donauwerth, Germany
see
Donauwerth, Germany. Heilige Kreuz

Helmarshausen, Germany (Benedictine abbey)

2762 **Krüger, Ekkehard.**
Die Schreib und Malwerkstatt der Abtei Helmarshausen bis in die Zeit Heinrichs des Löwen. Darmstadt, Selbstverlag der Hessischen Historischen Kommission, 1972.
3 v. 103 plates, diagrs. 22 cm.
MnCS

Hersfeld, Germany (Benedictine abbey)

2763 **Demme, Louis, ed.**
Nachrichten und Urkunden zur Chronik von Hersfeld gesammelt und verzeichnet. Hersfeld, H. Schmidt, 1891–1900.
3 v. 24 cm.
KAS

2764 **Vigelius, J. C.**
Denkwürdigkeiten von Hersfeld . . . Hersfeld, Verlag von Hans Schmidt, 1888.
222 p. plates, 23 cm.
MnCS

Hesdin, France. Auchy-les-Moines (Benedictine abbey)

2765 **Cardevacque, Adolphe de.**
Histoire de l'Abbaye d'Auchy-les-Moines. Arras. Sueur-Charruey, 1875.
225 p. plan, coat of arms. 25 cm.
KAS

Hildesheim, Germany. St. Godehard (Benedictine abbey)

2766 **Hase, Conrad Wilhelm.**
Die Kirche des Klosters St. Godehardi in Hildesheim. Hannover, Gebr. Jäncke [1850?].
16 col. 2 plates (drawings) 35 cm.
KAS

Hildesheim, Germany. St. Michael (Benedictine abbey)

2767 **Sommer, Johannes.**
Das Deckenbild der Michaelskirche in Hildesheim. Hildesheim, Gerstenberg, 1966.
195 p. 87 plates (part col.) 31 cm.
MnCS

Hill Monastic Manuscript Library
see
St. John's University, Collegeville, Minn. Hill Monastic Manuscript Library.

Hirache, Spain
see
Irache, Spain

Hirsau, Germany (Benedictine abbey)

2768 **Guilielmus, abbot of Hirsau.**
Constitutiones Hirsaugienses. MS. Vienna, Schottenstift, codex 194. 134 f. Folio. Saec. 15.
Microfilm: MnCH proj. no. 4061

2769 **Scheck, Hanns.**
Hirsau, der Eulerturm. München-Grünwald, Selbstverlag, 1971.
76 p. illus. 24 cm.
MnCS

2770 **Schmid, Karl.**
Kloster Hirsau und seine Stifter. Freiburg i.B., Herder, 1959.
153 p. 22 cm.
MnCS

Holme Eden, England. St. Scholastica Abbey

2771 **Johannes de Oxenedes.**
Chronica Johannis de Oxenedes. Edited by Sir Henry Ellis . . . London, 1859.
(Gt. Brit. Public Record Office. Rerum britannicarum medii aevi scriptores, or Chronicles and memorials of Great Britain and Ireland during the Middle Ages, no. 13)
ILSP; PLatS

Holy Angels' Convent, Jonesboro, Ark.

2772 **Voth, Ages, Sister, O.S.B.**
Green olive branch. Chicago, Franciscan Herald Press [1973].
351 p.
MoCo; ArJH

Homburg, Germany (Benedictine abbey)

2773 **Historische Nachrichten von der ersten Stiftung,** Verbesserung und gänzlichen Aufhebung des ehemaligen Klosters Homburg bey Langensalza. Langensalza, bey Charlotte Magdalene Heergart, 1773.
[8], 51 p. 20 cm.
KAS

Ilsenburg, Germany (Benedictine abbey)

2774 **Urkundenbuch des in der Grafschaft** Wernigerode belegenen Klosters Ilsenburg . . . Bearb. im Auftrage Sr. Erlaucht des regierenden Grafen Otto zu Stolberg-Wernigerode, von Dr. Ed. Jacobs. Halle, Verlag der Buchhandlung des Waisenhauses, 1875–77.
2 v. col. plates, facsims. 23 cm.
KAS

Immaculata Convent, Norfolk, Nebr.

2775 **Koch, Mary Imelda, Sister, O.S.B.**
By the power of the vine; history of the Missionary Benedictine Sisters in the United States, 1922–1952. Collegeville, Minn., St. John's University Press, 1964.
118 p. illus.
Thesis (M.A.)–St. John's University, Collegeville, Minn.
MnStj (Archives); MoCo; NbNo

2776 **Dedication. Norfolk, Nebr., Immaculata Convent,** 1966.
unpaged. illus.
InFer; MnStj (Archives); NbNo

Innsbruck, Austria. Benediktinerpriorat für den Verein der Kinderfreunde

2777 **P. Edmund Hager,** der "Don Bosco Oesterreichs"; Lebensskizze eines Erziehers . . . von einem Mitgliede seiner Kongregation. Innsbruck, Kinderfreund-Anstalt [n.d.].
138 p. illus.
AStb

Irache, Spain (Benedictine abbey)

2778 **Lacarra, José Maria.**
Colección diplomática de Irache. Zaragoza, Consejo Superior de Investigaciones Cientificas, 1965–
v. 25 cm.
MnCS

2779 **Roca Laymon, Jaime.**
Irache. 3. ed. Pamplona, Diputación Foral de Navarra, 1975.
31 p. illus. 22 cm.
MnCS

Iranzu, Spain (Benedictine abbey)

2780 **Jimeno Jurío, José Maria.**
Iranzu. Pamplona, Duputacción Foral de Navarra, 1972.
31 p. illus. 22 cm.
MnCS

Irrsee, Bavaria (Benedictine abbey)

2781 **Pötzl, Walter.**
Geschichte des Klosters Irsee von der Gründung bis zum Beginn der Neuzeit 1182–1501. Ottobeuren, Kommissionsverlag Winfried-Werk, 1969.
264 p. illus. 26 cm.
MnCS; PLatS

Jarrow Abbey, England

2782 **The Saint Paul's Jarrow Project** for the restoration and protection of the

monastic site, home of the Venerable Bede . . . Newcastle upon Tyne, R. Ward & Sons [1971?].
10 p. illus. 21 cm.
PLatS

2783 **Vita s. Cuthberti,** auctore anonymo . . . Historia translationis s. Cuthberti . . . Historia abbatum Gyrensium . . . Sermo in natale s. Benedicti abbatis.
(*In* Bede the Venerable. Opera historica minora, p. 259–338)
PLatS

Jerusalem. Notre Dame de Josaphat (Benedictine abbey)

2784 **Kohler, Charles.**
Chartes de l'Abbaye de N.-D. de la Vallée de Josaphat; analyses et extraits. Paris, E. Leroux, 1900.
115 p. 25 cm.
KAS

Johannisberg im Rheingau, Germany (Benedictine abbey)

2784a **Struck, Wolf-Heino.**
Johannisberg im Rheingau; eine Kloster-, Dorf-, Schloss- und Weinchronik. Frankfurt a.M., Verlag Waldemar Kramer, 1977.
viii, 374 p. plates, 24 cm.
p. 5–92: Das Benediktinerkloster Johannisberg und die Benediktinerinnenklause St. Georg.
MnCS

Jonesboro, Ark. Holy Angels' Convent
see
Holy Angels' Convent, Jonesboro, Ark.

Jouarre, France (abbey of Benedictine nuns)

2785 **Abbaye de Notre-Dame de Jouarre.**
Les fêtes du XIIIe centenaire, 7–9 octobre 1930. Meaux, Imprimerie André-Pouyé, 1930.
50 p. illus.
AStb

2786 **Anciens documents inédits** sur l'Abbaye de Jouarre . . . Introduction et notes d'une moniale de l'abbaye. 1933–35.
128 p.
AStb

2787 **Chaussy, Y.**
L'Abbaye royale Notre-Dame de Jouarre. Paris, G. Victor, 1961.
x, 403 p. illus., plates, 1961.
InStme

2788 **Maillé, Geneviève Aliette.**
Les cryptes de Jouarre. Paris, A. & J. Picard, 1971.
309 p. illus., fold. plates. 33 cm.
KAS

Kaufungen, Germany (Benedictine abbey)

2789 **Urkundenbuch des Klosters Kaufungen** in Hessen. Im Auftrage des Historischen Vereines der Diocese Fulda bearb. u. hrsg. von Herman von Rogues. Cassel, Drewfs & Schönhoven, 1900–1902.
2 v. tables, maps. 25 cm.
KAS; MnCS

Kempten, Germany (Benedictine abbey)

2790 **Baumann, Franz Ludwig.**
Forschungen zur Schwäbischen Geschichte. Kempten, Jos. Kösel, 1899.
vii, 625 p. 23 cm.
Pages 1–151 pertain to the Benedictine abbey of Kempten.
KAS

King of Martyrs Priory, Fifield, Wis.

2791 **Sorg, Rembert, O.S.B.**
Religion at King of Martyrs: Credo in Spiritum Sanctum. Fifield, Wis., King of Martyrs Priory, 1963. (Private manuscript).
30 p. 23 cm.
MnCS; WFif

Kleinmariazell, Austria (Benedictine abbey)

2792 **Necrologium Mariae-Cellense.** MS. Benediktinerabtei Melk, Austria, codex 836, f.113r–138v. Quarto. Saec. 13.
Microfilm: MnCH proj. no. 1664

2793 **Wonisch, Othmar, O.S.B.**
Mariazell. München, Verlag Schnell & Steiner [1957].
46 p illus. 24 cm. (Kunstführer, Grosse Ausgabe, v. 21)
PLatS

Königslutter, Germany (Benedictine abbey)

2793a **Denkwürdigkeiten aus der Geschichte** des Stiftes Königslutter und Stifter desselben.
Detached from Braunschweigische Magazin, 1822, cols. 194–272.
KAS

Kremsmünster, Austria (Benedictine abbey)

2794 **Bernardus Noricus.**
De kathologo abbatum. Narracio de ecclesia Chremsmünster. Decretales pro ec-

clesia Chremsmuenster in causa Manegoldi abbatis. Epistola de cessione abbatis. MS. Benediktinerabtei Kremsmünster, Austria, Schatzkasten codex 3. Saec. 13 & 14.
Microfilm: MnCH proj. no. 382

2795 **Catalogus abbatum Cremifanensium,** usque ad 1298. MS. Vienna, National-bibliothek, codex 610, f.91–95r. Octavo. Saec. 14.
Microfilm: MnCH proj. no. 13,959

2796 **Catalogus religiosorum Ordinis S. P.** Benedicti in monasterio Cremifanensis vulgo Kremsmünster Superioris Austriae viventium . . .
v. 22 cm.
PLatS

2797 **Fill, Hauke.**
Bericht über den Stand der Handschriftenkatalogisierung in Kremsmünster.
(*In* Handschriftenbeschreibung in Oesterreich, von Otto Mazal. Wien, 1975. p. 105–108)
MnCS

2798 **Flotzinger, Rudolf.**
Die Lautentabulaturen des Stiftes Kremsmünster; thematischer Katalog. Wien, Böhlau, 1965.
274 p. music. 24 cm.

2798a **Haider, Siegfried, ed.**
Die Anfänge des Klosters Kremsmünster; Symposium 15.-18.Mai 1977. Linz, Oberösterreichisches Landesarchiv, 1978.
198 p. plates (42 illus.) 24 cm. (Ergänzungsband zu den Mitteilungen des Oberösterreichischen Landesarchivs, 2)
MnCS

2799 **Historia Cremifanensis.** MS. Universitätsbibliothek Graz, Austria, codex 536, f.116r–124v. Folio. Saec. 14.
Microfilm: MnCH proj. no. 26,675

2800 **Historia de b.** Thassilone duce Bavariae fundatoris monasterii Kremsmünster. MS. Benediktinerabtei Melk, Austria, codex 1842, p. 382–388. Duodecimo. Saec. 16.
Microfilm: MnCH proj. no. 2152

2801 **Heyrenbach, Josephus Benedictus.**
Collectanea ad historiam et seriem abbatum Cremifanensis. MS. Vienna, Nationalbibliothek, codex 7974. 14 f. Folio. Saec. 17.
Microfilm: MnCH proj. no. 18,961

2802 **Holter, Kurt.**
Buchmalerei und Federzeichnungsinitialen im hochmittelalterlichen Skriptorium von Kremsmünster.

(*In* Handschriftenbeschreibung in Oesterreich, hrsg. von Otto Mazal. Wien, 1975. p. 41–50)
MnCS

2802a **Holter, Kurt.**
Die Bibliothek: Handschriften und Inkunabeln.
(*In* Die Kunstdenkmäler des Benediktinerstiftes Kremsmünster. II. Teil, p. 134–220. Wien, 1977)
MnCS

2803 **Honorius III, Pope.**
Epistola ad abbates Salzburgenses, Garsten, Seitenstetten . . . inquirens electionem Manegaldi abbatis Cremifanensis. MS. Benediktinerabtei St. Peter, Salzburg, codex a.VIII.18, f. 88v. Quarto. Saec. 12.
Microfilm: MnCH proj. no. 10,186

2804 **Hundstorfer, Rudolf, O.S.B.**
Das Stift unterm Hakenkreuz. Wels, Druck- und Verlagsanstalt Welsermühl [1961?].
93 p. plates (facsims.) 24 cm.
MnCS

2805 **Kellner, Altman, O.S.B.**
Professbuch des Stiftes Kremsmünster. [Klagenfurt, St. Josef Vereines, 1968].
598 p. 25 cm.
MnCS

2806 **Kellner, Altman, O.S.B.**
Professbuch des Stiftes Kremsmünster. Sumptibus Monasterii Cremifanensis, 1968.
629 p. 25 cm.
InStme

2807 **Kellner, Altman, O.S.B.**
Stift Kremsmünster, Benediktinerabtei in Oberösterreich. 3. Aufl. München, Verlag Schnell & Steiner, 1967.
[23] p. plates, 17 cm. (Kunstführer Nr. 650 von 1957)
PLatS

2808 **Kremsmünster—heute.** Text: Patres von Kremsmünster. Fotos: Erich Widder.
13 p. illus. 30 cm.
PLatS

2808a **Kremsmünster:** 1200 Jahre Benediktinerstift. Schriftleitung, Rudolf Walter Litschel. 3. Aufl. Linz, Oberösterreichischer Landesverlag, 1977.
401 p. [103] leaves of plates, facsims. 27 cm.
MnCS

2808b **Cremifanum** 777–1977; Festschrift für die 1200–Jahr–Feier des Stiftes Kremsmünster. Linz, Oberösterreichisches Landesarchiv, 1977.
212 p. illus., 24 cm.
MnCS

2808c **1200 Jahre Kremsmünster:** Stiftsführer, Geschichte, Kunstsammlungen, Sternwarte. Schriftleitung, Otto Mutzel. Farb-Aufnahme, Elfriede Majohar. Amt d. Oestr. Landesregierung, Abt. Kultur. Kremsmünster, Benediktinerstift, 1977.
326 p. plates (part col.) 17 cm.
InStme

2808d **Festschrift zum** 1200-Jahr-Jubiläum des Stiftes Kremsmünster. Marktgemeinde Kremsmünster, 1977.
202 p. 22 cm.
MnCS

2808e **Die Kunstdenkmäler des Benediktinerstiftes Kremsmünster.** Hrsg. vom Institut für österreichische Kunstforschung des Bundesdenkmalamtes mit Unterstützung des Landes Oberösterreich. [Zum 1200. jährigen Bestehen des Stiftes Kremsmünster]. Wien, Verlag Anton Schroll, 1977.
2 v. illus., plates, 27 cm. (Oesterreichische Kunsttopographie, Bd. 43)
MnCS

2809 **Neumüller, Willibrord, O.S.B.**
Bernardus Noricus von Kremsmünster. Wels, Verlagsanstalt Welsermühl [1947?].
167 p. 24 cm.
MnCS

2810 **Neumüller, Willibrord, O.S.B.**
Der Codex Millenarius, von Willibrord Neumüller und Kurt Holter. Graz, In Kommission bei H. Böhlaus Nachf., 1959.
195 p. illus., col. plates, 31 cm. (Forschungen zur Geschichte Oberösterreichs, 6)
MnCS

2810a **Neumüller, Willibrord, O.S.B.**
Codex Millenarius Maior. Faksimile-Ausgabe im Originalformat des Codex cremifanensis cim. 1 des Benediktinerstifts Kremsmünster. Kommentar von Willibrord Neumüller u. Kurt Holter. Graz, Akademische Verlagsanstalt, 1974.
39, vi p. [398] leaves (facsims.), 34 cm. (Codices selecti phototypice impressi, 45)
The codex dates from about the year 800.
Both the text and the commentary contain illustrations in color.
MnCS

2810b **Neumüller, Willibrord, O.S.B.**
Das Gründungsjahr Kremsmünster.
(*In* Cremifanum 777–1977; Festschrift . . . Linz, 1977, p. 7–15)
MnCS

2811 **Neumüller, Wilibrord, O.S.B.**
Markus und der Löwe; die Evangelisten und ihre Symbole im Codex Millenarius.

Graz, Akademische Druck- u. Verlagsanstalt, 1977.
[15] p. 8 col. plates (facsims.) 30 cm.
MnCS; PLatS

2812 **Neumüller, Willibrord, O.S.B.**
Die mittelalterlichen Bibliotheksverzeichnisse des Stiftes Kremsmünster, von P. Willibrord Neumüller und Kurt Holter. Linz, Verlag des Amtes der o.-ö. Landesregierung, 1950.
69 p. 26 cm.
MnCS

2813 **Rechnungsbuch des Stiftes Kremsmünster** (fragmenta annorum 1494, 1495, 1514). Germanice. MS. Vienna, Nationalbibliothek, codex 80. 26 f. Octavo. Saec. 15–16.
Microfilm: MnCH proj. no. 20,551.

2813a **Pitschmann, Benedikt, O.S.B.**
Bemühungen der Eidgenossen um den Kardinalshut für Abt Alexander a Lacu von Kremsmünster (1601–1613).
(*In* Cremifanum 777–1977; Festschrift . . . Linz, 1977, p. 49–75)
MnCS

2814 **Schematismus der Benediktiner** von Kremsmünster, 1965. [Wels, O.O. Landesverlag].
56 p. 21 cm.
MnCS

2815 **Stollenmayer, Pankraz, O.S.B.**
Das Grab Herzog Tassilos III, von Bayern. [n.p., n.d.].
66 p. illus. 24 cm.
MnCS

2816 **Stollenmayer, Pankraz, O.S.B.**
Der Tassilokelch. Wels, Druck der Buch und Kunstdruckerei "Welsermühl" [1949?].
109 p. illus. 24 cm.
MnCS

2817 **Stollenmayer, Pankraz, O.S.B.**
Tassilo-Leuchter – Tassilo-Zepter. Wels, Druck- und Verlagsanstalt "Welsermühl" [1959?].
72 p. illus. 24 cm.
MnCS

2818 **Die Wiegendrucke des Stiftes Kremsmünster.** Hrsg. von der Stifsbibliothek. Linz/Donau, H. Muck, 1947.
279 p. plates. 24 cm.
Vorwort signed: Dr. P. Willibrord Neumüller, Stiftsbibliothekar.
MnCS

2819 **Zarbl, J. B.**
Reise durch einige Abteien in Oesterreich. Ratisbon, Pustet, 1831.
298 p.
AStb

Kreuzberg, Germany. St. Peter
(Benedictine abbey)

2820 **Craemer, Johannes, comp.**
Parva chronica monasterii S. Petri in
Monte Crucis ad Werram, Ordinis S.
Benedicti.
(*In* Paullini, C. F. Rerum et antiquitatum
germanicarum syntagma. 1698. p. 289–
324)
KAS; PLatS

Kübach, Germany (abbey of Benedictine nuns)

2821 **Monumenta Kuebacensia.**
(*In* Monumenta Boica. Monachii, 1763–
1829. v. 11, p. 519–550)
KAS

Kylemore Abbey, Connemara, Ireland

2821a **[Souvenir of] Kylemore Abbey,** Connemara, Ireland. [1979].
53 p. illus. 12 x 18 cm.
MnCS

Lambach, Austria (Benedictine abbey)

2822 **De institutione coenobii Lambacensis**
et vita Adalberonis. Series abbatum
Lambacensium. MS. Benediktinerabtei
Lambach, Austria, codex chart. 183,
p. 1–23. Saec. 15.
Microfilm: MnCH proj. no. 591

2823 **De institucione et consecracione** monasterij Lambacensis. MS. Benediktinerabtei Lambach, Austria, codex chart.
325, f.43r–71r. Saec. 15.
Microfilm: MnCH proj. no. 701

2824 **De institutione Lambacensis coenobii.**
De vita Adalberonis episopi. Benediktinerabtei Göttweig, Austria, codex 324,
f.1r–11r. Octavo. Saec. 15.
Microfilm: MnCH proj. no. 3723

2825 **Genge, Hans Joachim.**
Die liturgiegeschichtlichen Voraussat-
zungen des Lambacher Freskenzyklus.
Münsterschwarzach, Vier-Türme-Verlag,
1972.
xx, 144 p. 21 cm.
MnCS

2826 **Hainisch, Erwin.**
Die Kunstdenkmäler des Gerichtsbe-
zirkes Lambach.
(Oesterreichische Kunsttopographie,
v. 34)
MnCS

2827 **Luger, Walter.**
Die Benediktiner-Abtei Lambach . . . 2.,
verb.Aufl. [Linz, Oberösterreichischer
Landesverlag, 1966.

37 p. illus. 17 cm.
PLatS

2828 **900 Jahre Lambach;** eine Festgabe.
[Lambach, Benediktinern des Stiftes,
1956].
31 p. 37 plates, ports. 19 cm.
MnCS; NdRi; PLatS

2829 **Tenor cedulae,** cujus singula puncta d.
Iohannes abbas Lambacensis promisit se
adimpleturum ante reformationem. MS.
Benediktinerabtei Melk, Austria, codex
1094, f.276v–279v. Duodecimo. Saec. 15.
Microfilm: MnCH proj. no. 1847

2830 **Wibiral, Norbert.**
Die Wandmalereien des XI. Jahrhun-
derts im ehemaligen Westchor der Kloster-
kirche von Lambach.
(*In* Oberösterreich. Heft 3/4, 1967/68)
PLatS

Landévennec, France (Benedictine abbey)

2831 **De la Haye, Pierre.**
Abbaye de Landévennac. Chateaulin,
Editions d'art Jos le Doaré [1958].
40 p. plates, music, plans. 22 cm.
MnCS

Latrobe, Pa. St. Vincent Archabbey
see
St. Vincent Archabbey, Latrobe, Pa.

Lenó, Italy (Benedictine abbey)

2832 **Zaccaria, Francesco Antonio, S.J.**
Dell'antichissima Badia di Leno.
Venezia, Pietro Marcuzzi, 1767.
328 p. 28 cm.
MnCS

Leon, Spain. Monsterio de Santiago

2833 **Yanez Cifuentes, Maria del Pilar.**
El Monasterio de Santiago del León.
León, Centro de Estudios e Investigaceón
"San Isidoro," 1972.
320 p. fold. map. 26 cm.
MnCS

Le Puy, France. Saint-Pierre
(Benedictine abbey)

2834 **Cartulaire de l'Abbaye** de St.-Chaffre
du Monastier, Ordre de Saint-Benoît,
suivi de la chronique de Saint-Pierre
du Puy . . . Paris, A. Picard, 1884.
liv, 244 p. 25 cm.
KAS

Lérins, France (Benedictine abbey)

2835 **Allies, L.**
Histoire du monastère de Lérins. Paris,
A. Bray, 1862.
2 v. 26 cm.
PLatS

2836 **Cooper-Marsdin, Arthur Cooper.**
The school of Lérins. Rochester, Journal
Company [1905?].
123 p.
ILSP

2837 **Gouilloud, André, S.J.**
Saint Eucher, Lérins et l'église de Lyon.
au Ve siècle. Lyon, Librairie Briday, 1881.
x, 564 p. 22 cm.
PLatS

2838 **L'Ile et l'Abbaye de Lérins.** Récits et
description par un moine de Lérins. 2.
éd. Lérins, Imprimerie de l'Abbaye
[1909].
xii, 313 p. illus., plates, ports. 20 cm.
MnCS

2839 **L'Abbaye de Lérins;** histoire et monuments . . . Paris, Plon-Nourrit, 1909.
429 p.
MoCo

Liebenthal, Germany (abbey of Benedictine nuns)

2840 **Görlich, Franz Xavier.**
Das Benediktiner-Jungfrauenkloster
Liebenthal an der lausitz-böhmischen
Grenze in Niederschlesien. Breslau,
Selbstverlag, 1864.
xi, 281 p. 21 cm.
KAS

Liége, Belgium. Saint-Laurent (Benedictine abbey)

2841 **Exposition du millénaire** de Saint-
Laurent de Liège: église, abbaye,
hopital militaire . . . 23 septembre - 23
octobre 1968, Liège. [Liège, Belgique,
Cathédrale, 1968].
58 p. plates (part col.) 26 cm.
MnCS

2842 **Saint-Laurent de Liège:** église, abbaye et
hopital militaire – mille ans d'histoire.
Edition et introduction par Rita Lejeune.
Liège, Soledi [1968].
335 p. illus., 31 cm.
MnCS

Ligugé, France (Benedictine abbey)

2843 **L'Abbaye de Ligugé.** [Paris, Sadag, n.d.].
30 p. illus. 19 cm.
PLatS

2844 **Lettre de Ligugé.** 1–   1947–
v. 22 cm. 6 issues a year.
KAS

2845 **Mémorial de l'année martinienne,** M.DC-
CCC.LX - M.DCCCC.LXI: seizième
centenaire de l'Abbaye de Ligugé,
centenaire de la découverte du tombeau de Saint Martin à Tour. Paris,
J. Vrin, 1962.
xiv, 234 p. 25 cm.
MnCS

Limoges, France. Saint-Martial (Benedictine abbey)

2846 **Duplès-Agier, Henri.**
Chroniques de Saint-Martial de Limoges
. . . Paris, J. Renouard, 1874.
lxxii, 429 p. 24 cm.
KAS

2847 **Gaborit-Chopin, D.**
Le décoration des manuscrits à Saint-
Martial de Limoges et en Limousin du IXe
au XIIe siècle. Paris-Genève, Librairie
Droz, 1969.
239 p. 234 plates (facsims) 23 cm.
MnCS

Lindisfarne Abbey, Scotland

2848 **Dunleavy, Gareth W.**
Colum's other island: the Irish at Lindisfarne. Madison, University of Wisconsin, 1960.
x, 149 p. illus., map. 23 cm.
InStme

Lisle, Ill. St. Procopius Abbey
see
St. Procopius Abbey, Lisle, Ill.

Llavaneres, Spain. Capella de Santa Maria de Montserrat

2849 **Ferrer i Clariana, Lluís.**
La Capella de Santa Maria de Montser-
rat de Llavaneres.
(*In* Analecta Montserratensia, v. 10,
p. 71–75)
PLatS

Lobbes, Belgium (Benedictine abbey)

2850 **Vos, Joachim Joseph.**
Lobbes, son abbaye et son chapitre . . .
Louvain, Ch. Peeters, 1865.
2 v. plates, fold. plan. 22 cm.
KAS

Longueville, France. Sainte Foi (Cluniac priory)

2851 **Chartes du prieuré de Longueville,** de
l'Ordre de Cluny, au diocèse du Rouen,

antérieures à 1204 . . . Paris, A. Picard, 1934.
xxvii, 137 p. 25 cm.
MnCS

Lophem-lez Bruges, Belgium.
Abbaye de Saint-André
see
Bruges, Belgium. Abbaye de Saint-André

Lorsch, Germany (Benedictine abbey)

2852 **Bischoff, Bernhard.**
Lorsch im Spiegel seiner Handschriften. München, Arben-Gesellschaft, 1974.
128 p. plates, facsims. 24 cm.
MnCS

2853 **Büttner, Heinrich.**
Lorsch und St. Gallen in der Frühzeit; 2 Vorträge von Heinrich Büttner und Johannes Duft. Konstanz, Suttgart, Thorbecke [1965].
45 p. 21 cm.
MnCS; PLatS

2854 **Codex principis olim Laureshamensis** abbatiae diplomaticus ex aevo maxime Carolingico diu multumque desideratus. Mannhemii, Typis academicis, 1768–70.
3 v. 23 cm.
Edited by A. Lamey.
KAS

2855 **Falk, Franz.**
Beiträge zur Rekonstruktion der alten Bibliotheca Fuldensis und Bibliotheca Laureshamensis . . . Leipzig, Harrassowitz, 1902; Nendeln, Kraus Reprint, 1968.
112 p. 23 cm.
PLatS

2856 **Hülsen, Friedrich.**
Die Besitzungen des Klosters Lorsch in der Karolingerzeit . . . Berlin, 1913; Vaduz, Kraus Reprint, 1965.
150 p. maps. 23 cm.
PLatS

2857 **Pfaff, Christoph Matthäus.**
Oratio de fundatione, fatis, antiquitate & reformatione Monasterii Laureacensis, Tubingae d. xii Maji, a. 1728 . . . Tubingae, Georgius Fridericus Pflicke, 1728.
24 p. 18 cm.
KAS

2858 **Wehlt, Hans Peter.**
Reichsabtei und König . . . Göttingen, Vandenhoeck und Ruprecht, 1970.
393 p. fold. map. 25 cm.
MnCS

2859 **Weissenberger, Paul, O.S.B.**
Die Anfänge des Hohenstaufenklosters Lorch bei Schwäbisch-Gmünd.

(*In* Perennitas; Beiträge . . . P. Thomas Michels O.S.B. zum 70. Geburtstag. Münster, 1963. p. 246–273)
PLatS

Lublin, Poland. Benedictine abbey

2859a **Perzanowski, Zbigniew.**
Opactwo Benediyktynskie w Lubiniu; studia nad fandacia i rozwojem. Wroclaw, Ossolinskich, 1978.
154 p. 24 cm.
MnCS

Luffield Priory, England

2860 **Luffield Priory charters** . . . Edited, with an introduction, by G. R. Elvey. Jordens, Buckinghamshire Record Society, 1968–75.
2 v. plates, facsims. 25 cm.
MnCS

Lüneberg, Germany. St. Michael (Benedictine abbey)

2861 **Gebhardi, Ludwig Albrecht.**
Kurze Geschichte des Klosters St. Michaelis in Lüneberg. Celle, Capaun-Karlowa'sche Buchhandlung, 1857.
xii, 111 p. 24 cm.
KAS

Lyons, France. Saint-Pierre (Benedictine abbey)

2862 **Picot, Joseph.**
L'Abbaye de Saint-Pierre de Lyon. Paris, Société d'édition Les Belles Lettres [1970?].
vi, 264 p. maps, plates. 24 cm.
InStme

Lyre, France (Benedictine abbey)

2863 **Guéry, Ch.**
Histoire de l'Abbaye de Lyre. Evreux, Impr. de l'Eure, 1917.
664 p. plates, plans. 26 cm.
MnCS

Madonna del Monte, Cesena, Italy
see
Cesena, Italy. Maria del Monte.

Magdeburg, Prussia. Stötterlingenburg (Benedictine abbey)

2864 **Schmidt-Phiseldeck, Carl von.**
Die Urkunden des Klosters Stötterlingenburg . . . Halle, Verlag der Buchhandlung des Weisenhauses, 1874.
xx, 280 p. plates.
KAS

Mainz, Germany. St. Alban (Benedictine abbey)

2865 **Schum, Wilhelm.**
Die Jahrbücher des Sanct-Albans-
Klosters zu Mainz. Göttingen, W. F.
Kaestner, 1872.
130 p. 21 cm.
Inaug.-Diss. – Göttingen.
KAS

Mainz, Germany. St. Jakob (Benedictine abbey)

2866 **Wolfgang Trefler** und die Bibliothek des
Jakobklosters zu Mainz . . . Leipzig, O.
Harrassowitz, 1913; Hendeln, Kraus
Reprint, 1968.
vi, 226 p. 23 cm.
PLatS

Malmedy, Belgium (Benedictine abbey)

2867 **Recueil des chartes** de l'Abbaye de
Stavelot-Malmedy, publié par Jos. Jalkin
et C. G. Roland. Bruxelles, Kiessling et
Cie, 1909–30.
2 v. 31 cm.
MnCS

Malmesbury Abbey, England

2868 **Beaghen, A.**
Malmesbury Abbey. Feltham, Middx,
Caxton Press, 1951.
38 p. illus., plates. 19 cm.
MnCS

**Malvern, England. Great Malvern
(Benedictine priory)**

2869 **Nott, James.**
Some of the antiquities of "Moche
Malverne" (Great Malvern) including a
history of the ancient church and
monastery . . . Malvern, John Thompson,
1885.
202 p. plates, diagrs. 22 cm.
MnCS

Manchester, N.H. St. Anselm's Abbey
see
St. Anselm's Abbey, Manchester, N.H.

**Mandragone, Italy. S. Anna de Rocca
(Benedictine abbey)**

2870 **Littera Concilii Constantiensis** ad Nico-
laum, priorem Monasterii S. Annae de
Roccha, Mandragonis, Ord. S. Benedicti.
MS. Benediktinerabtei Melk, Austria,
codex 993, v.277v–278r. Quarto.
Saec. 15.
Microfilm: MnCH proj. no. 1807

Maredsous, Belgium (Benedictine abbey)

2871 **L'Abbaye de Maredsous;** guide illustrè.
[Maredsous, Belgique] 1923.
96 p. illus.
MoCo

2872 **Berlière, Ursmer, O.S.B.**
Les terres & seigneuries de Maredsous
et de Maharenne. Maredsous, Abbaye de
Saint Benoît, 1920.
142 p. plates, plans. 26 cm.
MnCS

2872a **Maredsous:** le monument, l'institution.
Bruges, Desclée de Brouwer, 1911.
44 p. 25 cm.
KAS

2873 **Du Roy, Olivier, O.S.B.**
Moines aujourd'hui; une experience de
réforme institutionnelle. Paris, Epi [1972].
403 p. 24 cm.

Maria del Monte, Cesana, Italy
see
Cesana, Italy. Maria del Monte

Maria Laach, Germany (Benedictine abbey)

2874 **Bogler, Theodor, O.S.B.**
Maria Laach; Vergangenheit und Gegen-
wart der Abtei am Laacher See. 4.,
neubearb. Aufl. München, Schnell &
Steiner, 1961.
48 p. illus., plan. 24 cm. (Die Grossen
Kunstführer, Bd. 12)
PLatS

2875 — —9. Aufl. München, Schnell & Steiner,
1975. 26 p.
MnCS

2876 **Bogler, Theodor, O.S.B.**
Maria Laach Abbey. English translation
by Margaret Senft-Howie and Radbert
Kohlhaas. 4th ed. Munich, Verlag Schnell
& Steiner, 1970.
PLatS

2877 **Cremer, Drutmar.**
Maria Laach: Landschaft, Baukunst,
Plastik. Würzburg, Echter Verlag [1971].
66 p. illus. 31 cm.
MnCS

2878 **Cremer, Drutmar.**
Zur Deutung eines Laacher Meisters.
Fotos: Dr. Kettenberger. Würzburg,
Echter Verlag, 1969.
36 p. illus. 36 cm.
MnCS

2878a **Hassling, Angelus A., O.S.B.**
Das Buch der Benediktregel in der Abtei
Maria Laach; eine kleine Ausstellung im
Benediktus-Jahr 1980. Maria Laach, 1980.

43 p. 21 cm.
Als Manuskript gedruckt.
MnCH

2879 **Hilpisch, Stephanus, O.S.B.**
Klosterleben, Mönchsleben. 3. neu bearb.
Aufl. Maria Laach, Ars Liturgica [1963].
55 p. illus. 17 cm.
KAS

Maria Rickenbach, Switzerland (Benedictine convent)

2880 **Jäger, Moritz, O.S.B.**
Schwester Gertrud Leupi, 1825–1904,
Gründerin der drei Benediktinerinnen-
klöster: Maria Rickenbach, Yankton
[U.S.A.], Marienburg. [Freiburg Schweiz,
Kanisius Verlag, 1974.
200 p. plates, ports. 19 cm.
MnCS

Mariastein, Switzerland (Benedictine abbey)

2881 **Beerli, Willibald, O.S.B.**
Mariastein: seine Geschichte, sein
Heiligtum, seine Gäste, seine Ablässe und
Gottesdienste. [Mariastein] Im
Selbstverlag, 1935.
63 p. plates. 18 cm.
InStme

2882 **Boell, Adolf.**
Kurze Geschichte des Klosters und der
Wallfahrt zu Maria Stein. Einsiedeln, Karl
und Nicolaus Benziger, 1871.
152 p. illus.
MoCo

2883 **Directorium monasterii Beinwilensis** ad
Petram, vulgo Mariastein . . .
v. 17 cm.
MnCS

2884 **Eschle, Laurentius, O.S.B.**
Unsere Liebe Frau im Stein, in Wort,
und Bild; Geschichte der Wallfahrt und des
Klosters Mariastein. Solothurn [Schweiz],
Verlag der Buch und Kunstdruckerei
Union, 1896.
204 p. illus. 19 cm.
IdCoS; KAS; NdRi

Maria Taferl, Austria (Benedictine abbey)

2885 **Weichselbaum, Josef.**
Maria Taferl; Wallfahrtsbasilika zur
Schmerzhaften Muttergottes, Niederöster-
reich, Bezirk Melk. [München, Verlag
Schnell & Steiner, 1965].
15 p. illus. 17 cm.
PLatS

Mariazell, Austria (Benedictine abbey)
see
Kleinmariazell, Austria .

Maria Zell, Austria (shrine)

2886 **Historia Beatae Virginis Cellensis** in
Styria concinnata ex archivo. MS.
Vienna, Schottenstift, codex 736. 53 f.
Quarto. Saec. 16(1600).
Microfilm: MnCH proj. no. 4290

2887 **Wonisch, Othmar, O.S.B.**
Erinnerungsblätter an die Jubiläums-
und Krönungsfeierlichkeiten in Mariazell
in den Jahren 1907 und 1908. St. Lambrecht, Selbstverlag des Benediktiner-
stiftes St. Lambrecht, 1909.
119 p. illus. 23 cm.
MnCS

Marienberg, Tirol (Benedictine abbey)

2888 **Urbarregister für die Güter in Ischgl u.**
Galtür, Stift Marienberg, O.S.B. MS.
Innsbruck, Austria, Tiroler Landes-
archiv, codex Urbar 97/3. 39 f. Folio.
Saec. 19(1806).
Microfilm: MnCH proj. no. 29,257

Marienburg, Switzerland (Benedictine abbey)

2889 **Jäger, Moritz, O.S.B.**
Schwester Gertrud Leupi, 1825–1904,
Gründerin der drei Benediktinerinnen-
klöster: Maria Rickenbach, Yankton
[U.S.A.], Marienburg. [Freiburg, Schweiz],
Kanisius Verlag [1974].
200 p. plates, ports. 19 cm.
MnCS

Marienmünster, Germany (Benedictine abbey)

2890 **Regesten und Urkunden** zur Geschichte
der ehemaligen Benediktiner-Abtei
Marienmünster unter Berücksichtigung
der früher incorporierten Pfarreien.
Erster Teil: Von der Gründung bis zum
Tode des Abts Georg I (1128–1518).
Gesammelt von Fr. X. Schrader. Mün-
ster, B. Theissing, 1887.
276 p. 21 cm.
KAS

Marmoutier, France (Benedictine abbey)

2891 **Cartulairte de Marmoutier** pour le
Vendormois, publié sous les auspices de
la Société archéologique du Vendomois
par M. le Trémault. Paris, A. Picard,
1893.
xxxii, 509 p. illus. 25 cm.
KAS

2892 **Marchegay, Paul Alexandre.**
Les prieurés de Marmoutier in Anjou; inventaire des titres et supplément aux

chartes des XIe et XIIe siècle. Angers, Cornilleau et Maige, 1846.
xlviii, 88 p. 23 cm.
KAS

Marseille, France. Saint-Victor (Benedictine abbey)

2893 **Studi sui Vittorini in Sardegna,** a cura di F. Artizzu [et al.]. Padova, CEDAM, 1963.
88 p. 25 cm.
KAS

Marty, S.D. St. Paul's Indian Mission
see
St. Paul's Indian Mission, Marty, S.D.

Marvin, S.D. Blue Cloud Abbey
see
Blue Cloud Abbey, Marvin, S.D.

Mas-d'Azil, France (Benedictine abbey)

2894 **Cau-Durban, D.**
Abbaye du Mas-d'Azil: monographie et cartulaire, 817–1774. Foix, Typ. veuve Pomiès, 1896.
210 p. facsim. 25 cm.
KAS

Mdina, Malta. St. Peter (abbey of Benedictine nuns)

2895 **Libro per la fabrica del monastero** di S. Pietro fatto l'anno 1719. MS. Mdina, Malta, Cathedral Museum, codex CEM. 157 f. 30 cm.
Microfilm: MnCH proj. no. Malta 545

2896 **Notizie intorno ai monaci** ed alle monache dell'Ordine de San Benedetto in Malta. MS. Monastero di San Pietro, Notabile (Mdina), Malta. 41 f. 30 cm.
Microfilm: MnCH proj. no. Malta 302

2897 **Scritture del ven.** monastero di S. Pietro dell'Ordine di San Benedetto, eretto nella Città Notabile (Mdina). MS. Mdina, Malta, Cathedral Museum, codex CEM. 120 f. 32 cm.
Microfilm: MnCH proj. no. Malta 544

2898 **Ven. monastero di S. Pietro** dell'Ordine di San Benedetto, eretto nella Città Notabile (Mdina) 1678–1682. MS. Mdina, Malta, Cathedral Museum, codex CEM. 48 f. 31 cm.
Microfilm: MnCH proj. no. Malta 543

Mehrerau, Austria (Benedictine abbey)

2899 **Chartular des Benedictinerstiftes** Mehrerau in Vorarlberg. MS. Vienna, Haus-,

Hof- und Staatsarchiv, codex B 355. 293 f. Folio. Saec. 15.
Microfilm: MnCH proj. no. 23,511

2900 **Materialien für die Geschichte** des Klosters Mehrerau nebst vielen Kopien alter merkwürdiger Urkunden, gesammelt aus Original-Closter-Akten, 1815. MS. Voralberger Landesarchiv, codex 49. 244 p. Folio. Saec. 19.
Microfilm: MnCH proj. no. 29,916

2901 **Necrologium Augiae Majoris** Brigantinae Ord. S. Benedicti. MS. Abtei Mehrerau, Tirol, codex 63. 42 f. Folio. Saec. 18(1768).
Microfilm: MnCH proj. no. 29,887

2902 **Ordo novitiorum secundum ritum** monasterii Brigentini. Ordo professionis. Ordo caeremoniarum. Statuta qualiter praelatus monasterii Mererow prope Brigantium tractare debeat erga conventum et conventus erga praelatum (germanice). Catalogus abbatum monasterii Augiae Majoris Brigantinae. Fundatio et origo monasterii Augiae Majoris Brigantinae. MS. Veinna, Nationalbibliothek, codex 12853. 60 f. Quarto. Saec. 16(1566).
Microfilm: MnCH proj. no. 20,021

Meissen, Germany (Benedictine abbey)

2903 **Registratur aller Brief des Stifts** Meissen vollendet im Jahr 1581, cum registro locorum alphabetico et duobus methodis denarios et modios veterum diplomatum metiendi et comparandi cum novis a Petro Albino. MS. Vienna, Nationalbibliothek, codex 9258. 300 f. Folio. Saec. 16.
Microfilm: MnCH proj. no. 19,257

Melk, Austria (Benedictine abbey)

2904 **Anonymus Mellicensis.**
De fundatoribus nostri monasterii Mellicensis. MS. Benediktinerabtei Melk, Austria, codex 937, f.143–146. Folio. Saec. 15.
Microfilm: MnCH proj. no. 1744

2904a **Angerer, Joachim, O.Praem.**
Die liturgisch-musikalische Erneurung der Melker Reform; Studium zur Erforschung der Musikpraxis in den Benediktinerklöstern des 15. Jahrhunderts. Wien, Verlag der Oesterreichischen Akademie der Wisseschaften, 1974.
176 p. fold. map, 24 cm.
MnCS

2905 **Brevis historia reformationis** monasterii Mellicensis, anno 1418 factae. MS.

Benediktinerabtei Melk, Austria, codex 46, f.318–323. Folio. Saec. 15.
Microfilm: MnCH proj. no. 1149

2906 **Casus in monasterio** Mellicensi reservati abbati. MS. Benediktinerabtei Melk, Austria, codex 1094, f.318v–319r. Duodecimo. Saec. 15.
Microfilm: MnCH proj. no. 1847

2907 **Catalogus religiosorum** . . . in Monasterio Mellicensi Inferioris Austriae anno jubilaeo 1889 viventium et ab anno 1789 defunctorum. Melk, Stift Melk, 1889.
99 p. 25 cm.
MnCS

2908 **Ceremoniae ecclesiae in confirmatione abbatis.** MS. Benediktinerabtei Melk, Austria, codex 1398, f.250r–257v. Duodecimo. Saec. 15.
Microfilm: MnCH proj. no. 1920

2909 **Chronicon Mellicense,** prima manu scriptum anno 1125 (teste pagina 125), varie glossatum et recentiorum manibus interpolatum, deinde glossatum usque ad annum 1564. MS. Benediktinerabtei Melk, Austria, codex 391, p. 45–166. Folio. Saec. 12–16.
Microfilm: MnCH proj. no. 2009

2910 **Chronicon Mellicense seu annales** Monasterii Mellicensis, utrumque statum . . . deinde exempti Monasterii Mellicensis . . . Authore P. Anselmo Schramb . . . Viennae Austriae, typis Joannis Georgii Schlegel, 1702.
[16], 980, [26] p. illus., fold plans. 32 cm.
InStme

2911 **Conradus, abbot of Obernburg.**
Tractatus de indulgentiis, maxime monasterio Mellicensi et capellae ad S. Georgium prope Weiteneck concessis a papis, archiepiscopis et episcopis. MS. Benediktinerabtei Melk, Austria, codex 1381, f.661–681. Duodecimo. Saec. 15.
Microfilm: MnCH proj. no. 1904

2912 **De fulminato tecto turris** monasterii Mellicensis anno 1516, et inscriptiones sex novarum campanarum. MS. Benediktinerabtei Melk, Austria, codex 1398, f.133v–134v. Duodecimo. Saec. 16.
Microfilm: MnCH proj. no. 1920

2913 **De fundatoribus hujus nostri** monasterii Mellicensis. MS. Benediktinerabtei Melk, Austria, codex 1398, f.236v–247r. Duodecimo. Saec. 15.
Microfilm: MnCH proj. no. 1920

2914 **De fundatoribus nostris.** Epitaphium Marchionum. Epitaphium Marchionissarum hic sepultarum. Officium et miracula S. Colomanni. MS. Benedik-

tinerabtei Melk, Austria, codex 278, p. 67–92. Duodecimo. Saec. 15.
Microfilm: MnCH proj. no. 2110

2915 **De indulgentiis ecclesiae Mellicensis.** MS. Benediktinerabtei Melk, Austria, codex 652, f.317r–326v. Quarto. Saec. 15.
Microfilm: MnCH proj. no. 1542

2916 **De portione ligni sanctissimae crucis,** quae in monasterio Mellicensi . . . asservatur. MS. Benediktinerabtei Melk, Austria, codex 1842, p. 399–412. Duodecimo. Saec. 16.
Microfilm: MnCH proj. no. 2152

2917 **Facultas priori Mellicensi concessa.** Facultas subprioris Mellicensis. MS. Benediktinerabtei Melk, Austria, codex 1399, f.136r–139v. Duodecimo. Saec. 15.
Microfilm: MnCH proj. no. 1920

2918 **De reformatione monasterii Mellicensis** sub abbate Nicolao de Matzen, et fatis sub ejus successoribus usque ad annum 1535. MS. Benediktinerabtei Melk, Austria, codex 391, p. 172–182. Folio. Saec. 16.
Microfilm: MnCH proj. no. 2009

2919 **A fifteenth-century modus scribendi** from the Abbey of Melk. Cambridge, Printed at the University Press, 1940.
xxiv, 31 p. front. 23 cm.
MnCS

2920 **Flossmann, Gerhard.**
Stift Melk und seine Kunstschätze. St. Pölten, Wien, Veralg Niederösterr. Pressehaus, 1976.
78 p. 32 leaves of plates. 28 cm.
MnCS

2921 **Hueber, Philibert.**
Farrago memorandorum monasterii Mellicensis ex variis antiquis manuscriptis in hunc librum congesta, anno 1594. MS. Benediktinerabtei Melk, Austria, codex 1362. 711 p. Quarto. Saec. 17.
Microfilm: MnCH proj. no. 1900

2922 **Indulgentiae monasterio Mellicensi** a Summo Pontificibus . . . archiepiscopis misericorditer concessae. MS. Benediktinerabtei Melk, Austria, codex 1564, f.54r–62r. Duodecimo. Saec. 15.
Microfilm: MnCH proj. no. 1964

2923 **Indulgentiae monasterio Mellicensi concessae.** MS. Benediktinerabtei Melk, Austria, codex 1088, f.413–419. Duodecimo. Saec. 15.
Microfilm: MnCH proj. no. 1850

2924 **Keiblinger, Ignaz Franz, O.S.B.**
Geschichte des Benedictiner-Stiftes Melk in Niederösterreich, seiner Besitzungen

und Umgebungen. Wien, Fr. Beck, 1851–1869.
2 v. plates. 24 cm.
KAS (v. 1)

2925 **Kropff, Martinus, O.S.B.**
Bibliotheca Mellicensis; seu, Vitae et scripta inde a sexcentis et eo amplius annis Benediktinorum Mellicensium . . . [Vindobonae, sumptibus Ioannis Pauli Kraus, 1747].
24, 683, [14], 14 p. 20 cm.
ILSP; MnCS (Xerox copy)

2926 **Kropff, Martinus, O.S.B.**
Dissertatio brevis historica de origine usus mitrae Mellicensium abbatum.
(*In* his: Bibliotheca Mellicensis . . . [appendix]. 14 p. Vindobonae, 1747)
ILSP; MnCS (Xerox copy)

2927 **Liber caeremoniarum:** statuta pro reformatione monasterii Mellicensis. MS. Benediktinerabtei St. Peter, Salzburg, b.III.84. 46 f. Quarto. Saec. 15.
Microfilm: MnCH proj. no. 10,447

2928 **Modus confitendi sacramentaliter** in monasterio Mellicensi saeculo XV usitatus. MS. Benediktinerabtei Melk, Austria, codex 1783, f.1r–2r. Duodecimo. Saec. 15.
Microfilm: MnCH proj. no. 2090

2929 **Ordo et series abbatum** monasterii Mellicensis usque ad Casparum Hoffmann inclusive. MS. Benediktinerabtei Melk, Austria, codex 1842, p. 389–391. Duodecimo. Saec. 16.
Microfilm: MnCH proj. no. 2152

2930 **Quaedam excerpta ex** memorialibus monasterii Mellicensis circa 1418. MS. Benediktinerabtei Melk, Austria, codex 1842, p. 243–292. Index rerum, p. 304–315. Duodecimo. Saec. 16.
Microfilm: MnCH proj. no. 2152

2931 **Schlitpacher, Johannes, O.S.B.**
De reformatione monasterii Mellecensi anno 1418. MS. Benediktinerabtei Melk, Austria, codex 91, f.311–312. Duodecimo. Saec. 15.
Microfilm: MnCH proj. no. 1170

2932 **Series abbatum Mellicensium scripta** 1504, et continuata usque 1739. MS. Benediktinerabtei Melk, Austria, codex 391, p. 185–186. Folio. Saec. 16–18.
Microfilm: MnCH proj. no. 2009

2933 **Statuta quaecam concernentia** infirmariam et infirmos in eadem morantes per dominum Ludwicum abbatem hujus monasterii Mellicensis. MS. Benediktinerabtei Melk, Austria, codex 1754, f.175–187. Duodecimo. Saec. 15.
Microfilm: MnCH proj. no. 2066

2934 **Zupancic, Reginald, O.S.B.**
Stift Melk, Benediktinerabtei in Niederösterreich. München, Verlag Schnell & Steiner, 1966.
15 p. illus. 17 cm. (Kunstführer Nr. 654 von 1957)

Memmingen, Germany (Benedictine abbey)

2935 **Quomodo monasterium** S. Nicolai Memmingae in Suevia fundatum est. Vienna, Nationalbibliothek, codex 3347, f.26r–34v. Folio. Saec. 15.
Microfilm: MnCH proj. no. 16,617

Memleben, Thuringia (Benedictine abbey)

2936 **Schamel, Johann Martin.**
Historische Beschreibung des vormahls berühmten Benedictiner-Klosters zu Memleben in Thüringen . . . Naumburg, Johann Christian Martini, 1739.
[93] -188 p. 21 cm.
KAS

Metten, Germany (Benedictine abbey)

2937 **Alt und jung Metten** (periodical). 1926–
Metten, Abtei Metten.
v. illus., ports. 20 cm.
MnCS; PLatS

2938 **Fink, Wilhelm, O.S.B.**
Kloster Metten. 2. neubearb. Aufl. München, Schnell & Steiner, 1957.
17 p. illus. 17 cm.
MnCS

2939 **Lohmeier, Georg.**
Liberalitas Bavariae von der guten und weniger guten alten Zeit in Bayern. [München], Ehrenwirth [1971].
344 p. 23 cm.
PLatS

2940 **Monumenta Mettensia.**
(*In* Monumenta Boica. Edidit Acad. Scientiar. Elect. Boica. Monachii, 1771. v. 11, p. 341–518)
KAS; PLatS

Michaelbeuern, Austria (Benedictine abbey)

2941 **De origine et fundatione ecclesiae** S. Michaelis in Peurn nec non nomina omnium abbatum qui praefuerunt huic monasterio usque in praesentem annum domini MLXXXIII. MS. Benediktinerabtei Michaelbeuern, Austria, codex cart. 113, f.206r–212v. Octavo. Saec. 16.
Microfilm: MnCH proj. no. 11,612

2942 **Mayr, Werigand, O.S.B.**
Benediktinerabtei Michaelbeuern bei Salzburg. München, Schnell & Steiner, 1958.

15 p. illus. 17 cm. (Kunstführer Nr. 660)
PLatS

2943 **Pichler, Franz de Paula.**
Chronicon Buranum, oder Jahres-
schriften des Stiftes Michelbeuern in dem
Erzstift Salzburg, nebst Beilager aller
Urkunden. MS. Benediktinerabtei St.
Peter, Salzburg, codex b.XIII.1. 605 f.
Folio. Saec. 18(1780).
Microfilm: MnCH proj. no. 10,729

Michaelfeld, Germany (Benedictine abbey)

2944 **Prechtl, Maximilianus.**
Succincta historia monasterii Michael-
feldensis. MS. Benediktinerabtei St. Paul
im Lavantthal, Austria, codex 373/4. 97 f.
Quarto. Saec. 18.
Microfilm: MnCH proj. no. 12,549

Michaelsberg, Germany (Benedictine abbey)

2945 **Diplomata ad historiam** monasterii
Montis Monachorum (Mönchsberg) et
documenta Stirensia. MS. Benediktinerabtei St. Paul im Lavantthal, Austria,
codex 248/2. 288 f. Folio. Saec. 18.
Microfilm: MnCSh proj. no. 12,091

2946 **Fasciculus abbatum monasterii** S.
Michaelis prope Bamberg, quem con-
scripsit Andreas in ordine abbatum
hujus monasterii 37 anno MCCCCXCIV.
MS. Benediktinerabtei St. Paul im
Lavantthal, Austria, codex 283/2. 97 f.
Quarto. Saec. 18.
Microfilm: MnCH proj. no. 12,122

2947 **Weber, Wunibald, O.S.B.**
Michaelsberg; Geschichte einer 900
jährigen Abtei. Siegburg, im Selbstverlag
der Abtei, 1953.
64 p. 21 cm.
KAS; NdRi

2948 **Wahrhafter, gruendlich-summarischer**
Entwurff der kayserlichen Stifftung
Michelsberg, ob Bamberg, Ordinis S.
Benedicti, sambt Ursachen, wodurch
jetziger Praelat Anselmus Bernhardus
Homodeus Mayer, 1741.
52 p. 32 cm.
KAS

Millstatt, Austria (Benedictine abbey)

2949 **Weinzierl-Fischer, Erika.**
Geschichte des Benediktinerklosters
Millstatt in Kärnten. Klagenfurt, Ferd.
Kleinmayr, 1951.
144 p. plates. 24 cm.
MnCS

Milton Abbey, England

2949a **Traskey, J.P.**
Milton Abbey; a Dorset monastery in the
Middle Ages. [Tisbury, Wiltshire, Eng-
land], Compton Press, [1978].
xi, 268 p. illus., map, 24 cm.
MnCS

Minster Abbey, Thanet, England

2950 **The Benedictine of Thanet,** 1856–1931.
Ramsgate, Monastery Press, 1931.
66 p. plates. 22 cm.
KAS; MoCo; NdRi; KAM

2951 **Van Zeller, Hubert, O.S.B.**
Benedictine life at Minster Abbey. [Ex-
eter, Catholic Records Press, n.d.].
23 p. plates. 12 cm.
MnCS

**Moissac, France. Saint-Pierre
(Benedictine abbey)**

2952 **Daux, Camille.**
Deux livres choraux monastiques des Xe
et XIe siècles . . . Paris, A. Picard, 1899.
xiv, 150 p. 29 cm.
Partial contents: L'hymnaire de l'Abbaye
Saint-Pierre de Moissac.
KAS; PLatS

Monastic Manuscript Microfilm Library
see
St. John's University, Collegeville, Minn.
Hill Monastic Manuscript Library

**Monastier, Le, France. Saint-Chaffre
(Benedictine abbey)**

2953 **Cartulaire de l'Abbaye de St.-Chaffre du
Monastier,** Ordre de Saint-Benoît.
Paris, A. Picard, 1884.
liv, 244 p. 25 cm.
KAS

Mönchsberg, Germany
see
Michaelsberg, Germany

Mondsee, Austria (Benedictine abbey)

2954 **Acta primae visitationis** monasterii
Lunaelacensis . . . 1435. MS. Vienna,
Nationalbibliothek, codex 4970, f.37r–
43r. Quarto. Saec. 15.
Microfilm: MnCH proj. no. 18,143

2955 **Acta reformationis monasterii Monseensis.** MS. Vienna, Nationalbibliothek,
codex 3637, f.138r–267v. Octavo.
Saec. 16.
Microfilm: MnCH proj. no. 16,860

2956 **Acta secundae visitationis monasterii Mondsee . . .** 1451. MS. Vienna, Nationalbibliothek, codex 4970, f.2r–8r. Quarto. Saec. 15.
Microfilm: MnCH proj. no. 18,143

2957 **Carta visitationis in Monsee,** 1451. Carta primae visitationis in Monsee, 1435. MS. Vienna, Nationalbibliothek, Vienna, codex 3548, f.3r–28r. Octavo. Saec. 15.
Microfilm: MnCH proj. no. 16,770

2958 **Catalogus abbatum Lunaelacensi cenobii.** MS. Benediktinerabtei Michaelbeuern, Austria, codex cart. 113, f.214r–226v. Octavo. Saec. 16.
Microfilm: MnCH proj. no. 11,612

2959 **Catalogus pontificum et abbatum** Lunaelacensium synchronorum ab Oportuno primo abbate usque ad Symonem post Johannem dictum Trenbeck. MS. Vienna, Nationalbibliothek, codex 3745, f.217v–218r. Folio. Saec. 15.
Microfilm: MnCH proj. no. 16,957

2960 **Chronologia monasterii Lunaelacensis** usque ad Simonem abbatem anno 1464. Repertorium documentorum ad monasterium Lunaelacense pertinentium ordine alphabetico dispositum. MS. Vienna, Nationalbibliothek, codex 11609, f.1r–35v. Quarto. Saec. 16.
Microfilm: MnCH proj. no. 19,872

2961 **Codex traditionum monasterii Lunaelacensis,** Ordinis S. Benedicti, MS. Vienna, Haus-, Hof- und Staatsarchiv, codex B 70. 136 p. Quarto. Saec. 10–13.
Microfilm: MnCH proj. no. 23,502

2962 **Collatio habita per quemdam virum religiosum,** in 30. depositionis die, venerabilis patris ac Domini Domini Simonis, abbatis Lunaelacensis monasterii. Epitaphium sepulchri Domini Abbatis Simonis. MS. Benediktinerabtei Melk, Austria, codex 1869, f.305v–308v. Folio. Saec. 15.
Microfilm: MnCH proj. no. 2166

2963 **Fundatores monasterii S. Michaelis Lunaelaci,** hexametris leojinis enumerati. Successio abbatum monasterii Lunaelacensis. Preces in monasterio Lunaelacensi dici solitae. MS. Vienna, Nationalbibliothek, codex 11698, f.5r–55v. Octavo. Saec. 17.
Microfilm: MnCH proj. no. 19,856

2964 **Luitholdus, monk of Mondsee.**
Epitaphia tria in Chunradum abbatem Lunaelacensem anno 1145 interfectum. MS. Vienna, Nationalbibliothek, codex 849, f. 132v. Quarto. Saec. 12.
Microfilm: MnCH proj. no. 14,168

2965 **Mantissa chronici Lunae-lacensis** bipartita . . . Monach. O. Pedepontani, sumptibus Joannis Gastl, 1749.
[8], 416 p. 20 cm.
KAS; PLatS

2965a **Mondsee-Wiener Liederhandschrift** aus codex Vindobonensis 2856. Wissenschaftlicher Kommentar Hedwig Heger. Graz, Akademische Druck- u. Verlagsanstalt, 1968.
44 p. facsim. 128 leaves (f. 166–284). 32 cm. (Codices selecti phototypice impressi, v. 19)
MnCS

2966 **Normann, Johannes.**
Catalogus generalis omnium librorum Monseensis bibliothecae renovatus anno 1632. MS. Vienna, Nationalbibliothek, codex 3766, f.163r–178r. Folio. Saec. 15 et 17.
Microfilm: MnCH proj. no. 16,995

2967 **Nota historica de pluribus professis** in monasterio S. Michaelis O.S.B. in Mansee (Mondsee), qui in Universitate Viennensi promoti sunt. MS. Vienna, Nationalbibliothek, codex 5161, f.117v. Quarto. Saec. 16.
Microfilm: MnCH proj. no. 18,318

2968 **Pfaff, Carl.**
Scriptorium und Bibliothek des Klosters Mondsee im hohen Mittelalter. Wien, Böhlau in Kommission, 1967.
118 p. xxiv p. of illus., 24 cm. (Schriften des Dr. Franz Josef Mayer-Gunthof-Fonds, Nr. 5)
MnCS; PLatS

2969 **Rudenberger, Stephanus.**
Collationes ad monachos in coenobio S. Michaelis Lunaelacensi. MS. Vienna, Nationalbibliothek, codex 4969, f.212r–276v. Quarto. Saec. 15.
Microfilm: MnCH proj. no. 18,141

2969a **Unterkircher, Franz.**
Die datierten Handschriften der Oesterreichischen Nationalbibliothek von 1451 bis 1600. Wien, Oesterreichische Akademie der Wissenschaften, 1974–1977.
4 v. 24 cm.
About 200 of the manuscripts came from Mondsee.
MnCS

Mont-Laurier, Canada (Quebec). Abbaye du Mont-de-la-Rédemption

2970 **Les Moniales bénédictines de Mont-Laurier.** Mont-Laurier, Abbaye du Mont-de-la-Rédemption [1977].
46 p. front. (map), illus. 32 cm.
CaQMo; MnCS

Mont-Saint-Michel, France (Benedictine abbey)

2971   **Alexander, Jonathan James Graham.**
Norman illumination of Mont-St. Michel,
966–1100. Oxford, Clarendon Press, 1970.
xxiv, 263 p. illus., facsims. 28 cm.
InStme

2972   **Baudot, Marcel, ed.**
Culte de Saint Michel et pèlerinages au
Mont. Paris, Bibliothèque d'histoire et d'ar-
cheologie chrétiennes, 1971.
526 p. 48 pages of plates, illus. 24 cm.
(Millenaire monastique de Mont-Saint-
Michel, 3)
PLatS

2972a **Bely, Lucien.**
Le Mont-Saint-Michel, monastere et
citadelle. Rennes, Ouest-France [1978].
235 p. illus. (some col.) 24 cm.
MnCS

2973   **Bourgeois-Lechaftier, Michel.**
Le scriptorium de Mont-Saint-Michel.
Paris, P. Lethielleux, 1967.
72 p.
MnCS

2974   **Foreville, Raymonde, ed.**
Vie montoise et rayonnement intellectuel
du Mont-Saint-Michel. Paris, Bibliothèque
d'histoire et d'archeologie chrétienne,
1967.
497 p. illus. 24 cm. (Millenaire monastique du Mont-Saint-Michel, t. II)
PLatS

2974a **Gout, Paul.**
Le Mont-Saint-Michel: histoire de l'abbaye et de la ville, étude archéologique et
architecturale des monuments. Paris,
Librairie Armand Colin [1910].
2 v. illus., plates. 28 cm.
MnCS

2975   **Horae eruditae ad codices Sancti**
Michaelis de Periculo Maris. Steen-
brugge, Abbatia Sancti Petri Alden-
burgensis, 1961–
v. 25 cm.
PLatS

2976   **Laporte, Jean, O.S.B.**
Histoire et vie monastiques. Paris, P.
Lethielleux, 1966.
820 p. illus. 24 cm. (Millénaire monasti-
que du Mont Saint-Michel, tome I)
PLatS

2977   **Manuscrits de Mont-Saint-Michel.**
(*In* Art de Basse-Normandie, no. 40,
p. 17–63)
MnCS

2978   **Millénaire monastique** du Mont-Saint-
Michel . . . [mélanges commémoratifs].
Paris, P. Lethielleux, 1966–

v. 24 cm.
InStme; KAS; MnCS (v. 1–6); PLatS

2979   **Miré, Georges de.**
Le Mont-Saint-Michel au péril de la mer
. . . [Paris], Hachette [1953].
186 p. illus., plans, map. 32 cm.
KAS; MnCS

2980   **Nortier, Michel.**
Bibliographie générale et sources [de]
Mont-Saint-Michel . . . Nogent-sur-
Marne, Société Parisienne d'histoire et
d'archeologie Normandes, 1967.
272 p. 24 cm. (Millénaire monastique du
Mont-Saint-Michel, tome IV)
MnCS

2981   **Percheron, René.**
Visiting Mont-St. Michel with René Percheron. [Paris], Lethielleux, 1955.
24 p. illus., 16 plates, plans. 18 cm.
KAS

2982   **René, Jacques.**
Mont-Saint-Michel. Paris, Bibliothèque
des arts, 1963.
61 p. col. illus.
NcBe

2983   **Riquet, Michel.**
Le Mont-Saint-Michel; mille ans au péril
de l'histoire. [Paris] Hachette [1965].
272 p. illus. 20 cm.
MnCS

2984   **Sérant, Paul.**
Le Mont-Saint-Michel; ou, L'archange
pour tous les temps. Paris, Editions S.O.S.
[1974].
239 p. illus. 22 cm.
MnCS

2985   **Voisin, H.**
Le Mont-St. Michel; 24 vues principales
avec notice historique. [Versailles, A.
Bourdier] n.d.
4 p. 24 plates. 22x30 cm.
MnCS

Monte Amiata, Italy (Benedictine abbey)

2986   **Calisse, Carlo.**
Documenti del monastero di San
Salvatore sul Monte Amiata, riguardanti il
territorio Romano (secoli VIII–XII). Roma,
R. Società Romana di storia patria, 1894.
161 p. 25 cm.
MnCS

Monte Cassino, Itlay (Benedictine abbey)

2987   **The Abbey of Monte Cassino;** an illustrated guide. [Printed in Itlay by
Alterocca-Terni, 196?].
44 p. chiefly col. illus. 21 cm.
MnCS; PLatS

2987a **Annigoni a Montecassino:** testi di Martino Matronola, Tommaso Leccisotti, Angelo Pantoni, Bernardo d'Onorio, Giovanni Fallani, Ferruccio Ulivi, Anselmo Lentino. Roma, Edizioni "La Gradiva" [1979].
111 p. illus. (part col.) 33 cm.
Pietro Annigoni was engaged to paint the rebuilt basilica at Montecassino.
MnCS

2988 **Bartolini, Domenico.**
Ancient Cassino and the primitive monastery of Saint Benedict. Translated by Walter P. Keeley. 1958.
36 p. illus.
MoCo

2989 **Bégule, Lucien.**
Le Mont-Cassin et ses travaux d'art. Lyon, Impr. A. Rey, 1908.
61 p. illus. 28 cm.
PLatS

2990 **Bloch, Herbert.**
Monte Cassino, Byzantium, and the West in the earlier Middle Ages.
(*In* Dumbarton Oaks papers, no. 3(1946), p. 163–224)
MnCS

2991 **Böhmler, Rudolf.**
Monte Cassino. Trans. from the German by R. H. Stevens. London, Cassell [1964].
314 p.
NcBe

2991a **Bond, Harold L.**
Return to Cassino; a memoir of the fight for Rome. Garden City, N.Y., Doubleday, 1964.
207 p. 22 cm.
PLatS; NcBe

2992 **Brunhölzl, Franz.**
Zum Problem der Casinenser Klassikerüberlieferung. München, Fink, 1971.
39 p. 26 cm.
MnCS

2993 **Caravita, Andrea, O.S.B.**
I codici e le arti a Monte Cassino. Monte Cassino, pei Tipi della Badia, 1870.
3 v.
MoCo

2994 **Descrizione storico-artistica** di Montecassino. Monte Cassino, 1901.
162 p.
NcBe

2994a **Dormeier, Heinrich.**
Montecassino und die Laien im 11. und 12. Jahrhundert / von Heinrich Dormeier, mit einem einleitenden Beitrag zur Geschichte Montecassinos im 11. und 12. Jahrhundert / von Hartmut Hoffmann. Stuttgart, A. Hiersemann, 1979.

xxxvii, 296 p. 24 cm. (Schriften der Monumenta Germaniae Historicae, Bd. 27)
PLatS

2995 **Ducoin, Felix.**
Souvenirs d'un voyage en Italie; l'Abbaye du Mont-Cassin. Marseille, Marius Olive, 1874.
72 p. 25 cm.
MnCS

2996 **Erzabtei Monte Cassino;** ein historischer Abriss. Aus dem Italienischen übersetzt von Constantin Joh. Vidmar, O.S.B. Donauwörth, Ludwig Auer [1928].
96 p. 20 cm.
Translation of: Montecassino; sunto storico.
MnCS

2997 **Fabiani, Luigi.**
La terra di S. Benedetto; studio storico-giuridico sull'Abbazia di Montecassino dall'VIII al XIII secolo. Montecassino, 1950.
1 vol. illus. 26 cm. (Miscellanea cassinese, 26)
InStme; MnCS

2998 — —**Badia di Montecassino,** 1968.
2 v. plates. 26 cm. (Miscellanea cassinese, 33–34)
KAS; PLatS

2999 **Un giorno nella casa di S. Benedetto.**
2. ed. Badia di Montecassino, 1938.
158 p. illus. 19 cm.
MnCS

3000 **Hoffmann, Hartmut.**
Stilistische Tradition in der Klosterchronik von Montecassino.
(*In* Monumenta Germaniae historica. Mittelalterliche Textüberlieferungen und ihre kritische Aufarbeitung. München, 1976. p. 29–41)
MnCS

3001 **Ianetta, Sabatino.**
Triumph of life; destruction and restoration of Montecassino. [Arpino, La tipografica Arpinate, 1963].
57 p. illus. 24 cm.
MnCS

3002 **Kenny, Thomas, J.**
Glimpses of Latin Europe. Baltimore, John Murphy Co., 1913.
390 p. illus.
InFer

3003 **Leccisotti, Tommaso Domenico, O.S.B.**
Casinensium Ordines antiquiores (saec. VIII med. - IX).
(*In* Corpus consuetudinum monasticarum. Siegburg, 1963. t. 1, p. 83–175)
PLatS

3004 **Leccisotti, Tommaso Domenico, O.S.B.**
Montecassino. 7. ed. Badia di
Montecassino, 1975.
346 p. plates. 22 cm.
MnCS

3005 **Leccisotti, Tommaso Domenico, O.S.B.**
S. Tommaso d'Aquino e Montecassino.
Badia di Montecassino, 1965.
[60] p. facsims. 27 cm. (Miscellanea
cassinense . . . 32)
PLatS

3006 **Leo Marsicanus, bp. of Ostia.**
Chronica sacri monsterii Casinensis . . .
continuatore Petro Diacono . . . ex
manuscriptis codicibus summa cura, et
fide, quarta hac editione, notis illustrata,
primus evulgat D. Angelus de Nuce
Neapolitanus . . . Lutetiae Parisiorum,
Ludovicus Billaine, 1668.
[38], 577, 72 p. 35 cm.
ILSP; InStme

3007 **Mancone, Ambrogio, O.S.B.**
L'Abazia di Montecassino.
(*In* La bonifica benedettina, p. 85–94)
PLatS

3008 **Mélanges,** publiés par les abbayes bénédictines de la Congrégation Belge la
fondation du Mont-Cassin, 529–1929.
Louvain, Abbaye de Maredsous, 1929.
270 p. plates. 26 cm.
KAS

3009 **Monte Cassino, Italy (Benedictine
abbey).**
Pacis nuntius: Paolo VI a Montecassino,
24 ottobre 1964. Abbazzia di Montecassino
[1965].
143 p. plates, 29 cm.
InStme; KAS; MnCS; PLatS

3010 **Monumeta litterarum ad consecrationem**
turris sanctissimi p. Benedicti pertinentia et ad conventum renovorum dd.
abbatum in archi-coenobio Montis Casini
habitum sacro Pentecostesfesto MCC-
CCLXXX. Typis Montis Casini [n.d.].
[24], 8 p. 23 cm.
PLatS

3011 **Nuovo cammino sull'antica scia;** ordina-
zione episcopale di S.Ecc. Rev. Martino
Matronola, Abate Ordinario di Montecassino, 1977.
135 p. (Bolletino diocesano, 2)
MoCo

3012 **Pantoni, Angelo, O.S.B.**
Una venduta Vaticana di Montecassino
nei suoi rapporti con le raffigurazioni e
descrizioni coeve delle'abbazia.
(*In* Mélanges Eugène Tisserant, v. 5,
p. 171–182)
PLatS

3013 **Pantoni, Angelo, O.S.B.**
La vicende delle basilica di Montecassino
attraverso la documentazione archeologica. Montecassino [1973].
225 p. plates (part col.) diagrs.
26 cm. (Miscellanea . . . 36)
MnCS

3014 **Paul VI, Pope.**
The address of His Holiness, Paul VI, at
the Abbey of Montecassino: Brief pro-
claiming St. Benedict patron of Europe . . .
Montecassino down the centuries.
(*In* Pax; the quarterly review of the
Benedictines of Prinknash. v. 54, p. 151–
180)
PLatS

3015 **Paul VI, Pope.**
Beata pacis visio; Paolo VI a
Montecassino consacra la basilica cat-
tedrale e proclama S. Benedetto principale
patrono dell'Europa. [Cassino], Bollettino
diocesano, 1964.
CaMWiSb

3016 **Paul VI, Pope.**
Discorso di S.S. Paolo VI, dal Cenobio di
Montecassino, in occasione della consecra-
zione della ricostruita basilica, e proclama-
zione di S. Benedetto a patrono di Europa.
[Roma, Tip. Scopel, 1964].
[9] p. 20 cm.
KAS

3017 **Petrus Diaconus, monk of Monte
Cassino.**
Petri Diaconi Ortus et vita iustorum
Cenobii Casinensis. Edited from the
autograph ms. and with a commentary, by
R. H. Rodgers. Berkeley, University of
California Press, 1972.
lx, 216 p. facsims. 24 cm.
A revision of the editor's thesis, Har-
vard, 1970.
InStme; KAS, MnCS

3018 **Rickenbach, Heinrich, O.S.B.**
The sanctuary of the Tower of S.
Benedict. Translated, revised, and com-
pleted by Dom Bede Camm, O.S.B. Monte
Cassino, Abbey Press, 1895.
67 p. illus. 18 cm.
MnCS

3019 **Rusconi, Arturo Jahn.**
Monte Cassino; con 143 illustrazioni e 2
tavole. Bergamo, Istituto italiano d'arti
grafiche [1929].
132 p. illus. 26 cm.
MnCS

3020 **Theodomar, monk of Monte Cassino.**
Epistola ad Carolum Magnum de observantia monasterii sui. MS. Benediktin-

erabtei Admont, Austria, codex 860, f.1r–11r. Octavo. Saec. 17.

For other manuscript copies of this work see under Theodomar in Author Part.

Microfilm: MnCH proj. no. 9872

3021 **Thomas, abbot of Monte Cassino.**
Regesto di Tommaso Decano, o Cartolaria del convento cassinese (1178–1280) pubblicato a cura de' monaci di Montecassino. Badia di Montcassino, 1915.
lvii, 359 p. facsims. 26 cm.
MnCS

3022 **Toubert, Hélène.**
Rome et le Mont-Cassin: nouvelles remarques sur les fresques de l'eglise inferieure de Saint-Clement de Rome.
(*In* Dumbarton Oaks papers, no. 30(1976), p. 1–34)
MnCS

3023 **Willard, Henry M.**
Abbot Desiderius and the ties between Montecassino and Amalfi in the eleventh century. Montecassino, Badia di Montecassino, 1973.
64 p. illus. 26 cm. (Miscellanea cassinese, 37)
KAS; MnCS; PLatS

3024 **Willard, Henry M.**
The Staurotheca of Romanus at Monte Cassino.
(*In* Dumbarton Oaks papers, no. 30(1976), p. 55–64)
MnCS

Monte Cassino, Italy. Siege, 1944

3025 **Bloch, Herbert.**
The bombardment of Monte Cassino (February 14–16, 1944). Montecassino, 1976.
46 p. illus. 24 cm.
MnCS

3026 **Böhmler, Rudolf.**
Monte Cassino. Darmstadt, Mittler, 1956.
496 p. illus., plates. 23 cm.
MnCS

3027 **Böhmler, Rudolf.**
Monte Cassino. Translated from the German by Lt. Col. R. H. Stevens. London, Cassell, [1964].
314 p. illus., plates, map. 26 cm.
NcBe; PLatS

3028 **Connell, Charles.**
Monte Cassino; the historic battle. London, Elek Books, 1963.
206 p. illus. 22 cm.
Library of Congress.

3029 **Czerkawski, Andrzej.**
Monte Cassino, 1944 rok. Warsawa, Spor i Turystyta, 1972.
27 p. illus. 20 cm.
Summary in English, French, German and Russian.
Library of Congress.

3030 **La distruzione de Montecassino;** documenti e testimonanze. Montecassino, 1950.
135 p. illus., maps. 22 cm.
MoCo; PLatS

3031 **Graham, Dominick.**
Cassino. New York, Ballantine Books, 1971.
158 p. illus. 21 cm.
Library of Congress.

3032 **Hassel, Sven.**
Gli sporchi dannati di Cassino; l'operazione segreta "Colletto da prete" nella battaglia di Cassino. Traduzione di Maria Marini. [3. ed.]. Milano, Longanesi [1971].
382 p. 20 cm.
MnCS

3033 **Lutter, Horst.**
Das war Monte Cassino; die Schlacht der Grünen Teufel. 2. Aufl. Stuttgart, E. Wancura, 1958.
250 p. illus. 21 cm.
Library of Congress.

3034 **Majdalany, Fred.**
The monastery. London, J. Lane [1945].
115 p. 19 cm.
"Reprinted 1950."
KAS

3035 **Majdalany, Fred.**
The monastery. Boston, Houghton Mifflin Co., 1946.
ix, 148 p. illus. 19 cm.
PLatS

3036 **Mrowiec, Alfons.**
Przez Monte Cassino do Polski, 1944–1946. Wydawn, "Slask", 1959.
228 p. illus. 24 cm.
Library of Congress.

3037 **Smith, E. D.**
The battles for Cassino. New York, Scribner, 1975.
192 p. illus. 23 cm.
InStme

3038 **Terlecki, Olgierd.**
Monte Cassino, 1944. Warszawa, Wydawn Ministerstwa Obrony Narodowej, 1970.
180 p. 16 cm.
Library of Congress.

3039 **Wankowicz, Melchior.**
Bitwa o Monte Cassino. Rome, 1947.

385 p. illus. 25 cm.
CaMWiSb

3040 **Wankowicz, Melchior.**
Monte Cassino. Wydanic rozszerzone.
[Warzawa], Institut Wydawniczy Pax,
1978.
678 p. 100 plates. 22 cm.
MnCS

3041 **Wankowicz, Melchior.**
Skice spod Monte Cassino. Warzawa,
Eiedza Ponszechna, 1978.
172 p. map. 18 cm.
MnCS

Monte Oliveto Maggiore, Italy
(Benedictine abbey)

3042 **Antonius Bargensis,** d. 1452.
Chronicon Montis Oliveti (1313–1450).
Edidit Placidus M. Lugano. Florentiae,
Abbatia Septimnianensi prope Florentiam,
1901–1903.
2 v. 25 cm.
InStme; MnCS (v. 1)

3043 **Capra, Ramiro M., O.S.B.Oliv.**
Monte Oliveto Maggiore. Seregno
(Milano), Maschile S. Giuseppe, 1954.
143 p. plates. 21 cm.
InStme; MnCS

3044 **Carli, Enzo.**
L'Abbazia di Monteoliveto. [Milano,
Electa editrice, 1962].
185 p., incl. 98 plates (part col.) 30 cm.
MnCS

3045 **Clausse, Gustave.**
Les origines bénédictines: Subiaco–
Mont-Cassin–Monte-Oliveto. Paris, Ernest
Leroux, 1899.
238 p. plates. 28 cm.
MnCS

Montevergine, Italy (Benedictine abbey)

3046 **Mongelli, Giovanni, O.S.B.**
L'archivio dell'Abbazia di Montevergine.
Roma, ["La Galluzza"], 1962.
181 p. 24 cm.
PLatS

3047 **Mongelli, Giovanni, O.S.B.**
I codici dell'Abbazia di Montevergine.
Montevergine, Edizioni del Santuario,
1959.
53 p. 24 cm.
MnCS

3048 **Mongelli, Giovanni, O.S.B.**
Storia di Montevergine e della Congregazione Verginiana. [Napoli], Adminstra-
zione provinciale di Avellino, 1965.
2 v. 25 cm.
KAS

3049 **La prodigiosa imagine di Maria SS.**
di Montevergine; tradizioni e memorie.
Roma, Desclée, 1904.
58 p. illus.
AStb

3050 **Tranfaglia, Anselmo, O.S.B.**
Montevergine e la Congregazione Verginiana. 2. ed. riveduta e aggiornata.
Montevergine, Edizioni del Santuario,
1960.
[72] p. 23 cm.
PLatS

Montoire, France. Saint-Gilles
(Benedictine priory)

3051 **Everlange, Pierre Emile d'.**
Histoire de Saint Gilles; sa vie, son abbaye, sa basilique, sa ville, son pèlerinage,
sa crypte et son tombeau. 10. éd. Avignon,
Seguin Frères, 1885.
xxx, 302 p. plates. 25 cm.
KAS

Montserrat, Spain (Benedictine abbey)

3052 **Albareda, Anselmo, O.S.B.**
Historia de Montserrat. 6. ed., revisada i
ampliada per Josep Massot y Muntaner.
[Montserrat], Publicacions de l'Abadia de
Montserrat, 1977.
331 p. col. plates, 24 cm.
MnCS

3053 **Albareda, Anselmo, O.S.B.**
Sant Ignasi a Montserrat. Monestir de
Montserrat, 1935.
248 p. 24 cm.
MnCS

3054 **Album de Montserrat;** amb text intro-
ductiu a sis llegües. 164 vistes. Abadia
de Montserrat [n.d.].
MnCS

3055 **Amades, Joan.**
Llegendes i tradicions de Montserrat.
Amb illustracions d' E. C. Ricart.
Barcelona, Editorial Selecta [1959].
255 p. 18 cm.
MnCS

3056 **Aramon i Serra.**
Els cants en vulgar del Llibre Vermell de
Montserrat. (Assaig d'edició crítica).
(*In* Analecta Montserratensia, v. 10,
p. 9–54)
PLatS

3057 **Baldona Alós, Juan.**
Montserrat, montana santa. [Barcelona],
Editorial Borrás [1945].
332 p. illus., plates, music. 34 cm.
MnCS

3058 **Basté, Andreu.**
Montserrat, pedra i homes. Fotografies
d'Andreu Basté i Pere Ferrer Sauqué . . .
Montserrat, Publicacions de l'Abadia de
Montserrat [1967].
xix, 279 p. 444 illus. 35 cm.
MnCS

3059 **The Black Virgin of Montserrat.**
7 p. 28 cm.
Offprint from Scriptorium (St. John's
Abbey), 1953.
MnCS

3060 **Bofill Suris, Francese.**
A journey through the history of Mont-
serrat . . . [Translated by Kenneth Lyons].
Montserrat, Publicacions de l'Abadia de
Montserrat [1975].
[40] p. col. illus. 24x34 cm.
PLatS

3061 **Cisneros, Garcias de, O.S.B.**
Constituciones et los Monges Her-
mitanos de la Montana de Montserrat. MS.
Monasterio benedictino de Montserrat,
Spain, codex 835, f.121–159. Quarto.
Saec. 17(1627).
Microfilm: MnCH proj. no. 30,092

3062 **Cisneros, Garcias de, O.S.B.**
Constituciones de los Padres Hermitanos
de la Montana de Monserrate. MS.
Monasterio benedictino de Montserrat,
Spain, codex 55. 80 f. Quarto. Saec. 18.
Microfilm: MnCH proj. no. 29,998

3063 **Colombás, García, O.S.B.**
La confirmació de la confreria de la Mare
de Déu de Montserrat per Garsias de
Cisneros i els seus monjos.
(*In* Analecta Montserratensia, v. 10,
p. 55–63)
PLatS

3064 **Corona literaria oferta** a la Mare de Déu
de Montserrat. Abadia de Montserrat,
1957.
361 p. 22 cm. (Biblioteca Montserrat, 2)
MnCS

3065 **Crusellas, Francisco de, O.S.B.**
Nueva historia del santuario y monasterio de Nuestra Senora de Montserrat.
MS. Monasterio benedictino de Montserrat, Spain, codex 843. 265 p. Folio. Saec.
19.
Microfilm: MnCH proj. no. 30,030

3066 **De Reus a Montserrat;** guía itineraria.
Publicacio de "Revista del Centro de
Lectura" de Reus [1966].
55 p. 3 fold. maps. 17 cm.
MnCS

3067 **Exercicios que se practican** en la santo
noviciado de Nuestra Senora de Montserrat. MS. Monasterio benedictino de

Montserrat, codex 292. 26 f. Octavo.
Saec. 18.
Microfilm: MnCH proj. no. 30,018

3068 **Eucologi de Montserrat;** llibre dels
confrares i dels devots Montserratins.
Abadia de Montserrat, Biblioteca Popular Liturgica, 1935.
213 p. 16 cm.
MnCS

3069 **Figuerás, Caesarius, O.S.B.**
De impedimentis admissionis in
religionem usque ad decretum Gratiani. In
Abbatia Montserrati, 1957.
xxv, 184 p. 25 cm. (Scripta et documenta,
9)
KAS

3070 **Guía de Montserrat.** 2. ed. Monasterio
de Montserrat, 1950.
342 p. fold. map, plates. 17 cm.
KAS

3071 **Indice artistico de Montserrat.** Abadia
de Montserrat, 1956.
45 p. 21 cm.
MnCS

3072 **Ledesma, Martin de.**
La Virgen de Monserrate (drama). MS.
Monasterio benedictino de Montserrat,
Spain, codex 47. 109 f. Octavo. Saec.
17(1632).
Microfilm: MnCH proj. no. 29,992

3073 **Leonard, Jacques.**
Montserrat: Fotos [per] Jacques
Leonard. La muntanya [per] Rossend
Llates. El monestir [per] Manuel Vigil. Els
monjos [per] Josep Tar-in-Iglesias. Traduc-
ció catalana [per] Joan Triadu. Barcelona,
Editorial Barna [1958].
154 p. illus. 24 cm.
MnCS

3074 **"Llibre vermell";** liber miraculorum
sanctae Mariae de Montserrato. MS.
Monasterio benedictino de Montserrat,
Spain, codex 1. 137 f. Folio. Saec. 14–15.
Microfilm: MnCH proj. no. 29,976

3075 **Miscellània Anselm M. Albareda.** Abadia
de Montserrat, 1962–
v. plates. 25 cm. (Analecta Montserratensia, v. 9   )
MnCS

3076 **Missa in honorem B.M.V. de Montserrato,** patronae principalis Cathalauniae
principatus (cum Vésperis et canticis ad
processionem). Monasterio Montiserrati,
1946.
46 p. music. 17 cm.
MnCS

3077 **Montserrat:** carpeta de varios documentos. 3 vols. MS. Barcelona, Spain,

Archivo Diocesano, Religios, codex 7d, 8a, 8b. Folio. Saec. 19.
Microfilm: MnCH proj. no. 32,543–32,545

3078   **Montserrat:** Oblats seglars benedictons de Montserrat. MS. Barcelona, Spain, Archivo Diocesano, Religiosos, codex 9. 200 f. Folio. Saec. 19.
Microfilm: MnCH proj. no. 32,546

3079   **Montserrat:** Patronato de la virgen y coronacion. MS. Barcelona, Spain, Archivo Diocesano, Religiosos, codex 7a. 160 f. Saec. 19.
Microfilm: MnCH proj. no. 32,540

3080   **Montserrat:** Varios documentos. MS. Barcelona, Spain, Archivo Diocesano, Religiosos, codex 7c. 219 f. Quarto. Saec. 18–19.
Microfilm: MnCH proj. no. 32,542

3081   **Montserrat, Spain (Benedictine abbey).**
La liturgia en Montserrat. Abadia de Montserrat, 1957.
57 p. plates. 20 cm.
MnCS

3082   **Montserrat, Spain (Benedictine abbey).**
Los mártires de Montserrat; trabajos premiados y resena de la fiesta celebrada con motivo del concurso Montserratino Regina martyrum. Barcelona, La Hormiga de Oro, 1952.
94 p. illus., plates. 17 cm.
MnCS

3083   **Montserrat, Spain (Benedictine abbey).**
Vettla de santa Maria. Abadia de Montserrat, 1956.
93 p. music, 17 cm.
MnCS

3084   **Montserrat, Spain (Benedictine abbey).**
Visioni attuali sulla vita monastica. Montserrat, 1966.
315 p. 19 cm.
MnCS

3085   **Montserrat, Spain (Benedictine abbey).**
What Montserrat is. 6th ed. [English translation by Roderic Bright]. Montserrat Abbey, 1967.
74 p. plates, 20 cm.
MnCS; PLatS

3086   **Montserrat, Spain (Benedictine abbey).**
Ordo divini officii recitandi sacrique peragendi pro Abbatia Montisserrati anno Domini mcmliii; ad normam Congregationis Sublacensis. Typis Abbatiae Montisserrati.
MnCS

3087   **Puig, Pere M.**
Preséncia de Sta. Maria a Montserrat. Abadia de Montserrat [1970].

139 p. illus. 19 cm.
MnCS

3088   **Puig, Ignacio, S.J.**
San Ignacio en Montserrat; la vela de las armas. Barcelona, Impr. Revista "Iberica," 1956.
142 p. plates. 17 cm.
MnCS

3089   **Sagarra, Jose Maria di.**
El poema de Montserrat. Barcelona, 1956.
505 p. 24 cm.
MnCS

3090   **Solà, Ferran M., O.S.B.**
Gloria nostra; oda als martirs de Montserrat. Barcelona, Libreria La Hormiga de Oro, 1959.
52 p. illus. 21 cm.
MnCS

3091   **Udina Martorell, Federico.**
José Tarín-Iglesias–Barcelona y Montserrat. Barcelona, 1961.
44 p. 22 cm.
MnCS

3092   **La vida monàstica i sacerdotal a Montserrat.** Abadia de Montserrat, 1956.
32 p. illus. 20 cm.
MnCS

3093   **Voici Montserrat:** une montagne, un sanctuaire, un monastère. Traduction française: Françoise Courtiade de Ferrer-Solvervicens. 5. éd. Publications de l'Abadia de Montserrat, 1967.
74 p. plates. 20 cm.
PLatS

3093a   **Warhafftige und gründliche historia/** vom ursprung/auch zunemung/des hochheiligen Spannischen Gotteshaus Montis Serrati, und wie daselbsten die Bildtnusz der Mutter Gottes Mariae wunderbarlich erfunden worden. Insonderheit auch von dem Leben/desz seligen Bruders und Einsidlers Ioannis Garlini/ wie und was er an disem ort durch anstifftung desz Teufels begangen . . . auf Hispanischer sprach durch einen Catholischen Patricium Augustanum in hochteutsche gebracht. Gedruck zu München bey Adam Berg anno 1588.
[46] p. 19 cm.
KAS

3094   **What Montserrat is:** a mountain, a shrine, a monastery . . . Translation: Kenneth Lyons. 6th ed. Publicacions de l'Abadia de Montserrat, 1967.
74 p. plates. 20 cm.
PLatS

3095 **Xifra i Riera, Narcis.**
El 19 de juliol de 1936 al Monestir de
Montserrat. Barcelona, Editorial Portic,
1973.
289 p. 19 cm.
MnCS

Montserrat, Spain (Benedictine abbey) Biblioteca.

3096 **Albareda, Anselmo, O.S.B.**
Bibbie manoscritte e bibbie stampate nel
quattrocento dell'antica biblioteca di
Monserrato, note bibliografiche.
(*In* Studi di bibliografia e di storia in
onore di T. De Marinis. p. 1–16)
PLatS

3097 **Olivar, Alexandre M., O.S.B.**
Catàleg dels incunables de la Biblioteca
de Montserrat. [Abadia de Montserrat]
1955.
xviii, 122 p. 12 facsims. 26 cm.
MnCS

3098 **Olivar, Alexandre M., O.S.B.**
Catàleg dels manuscrits de la Biblioteca
del Monestir de Montserrat, Monestir de
Montserrat, 1977.
xxiv, 562 p. 25 cm.
InStme

3099 **Olivar, Alexandre M., O.S.B.**
Els manuscrits litúrgics de la Biblioteca
de Montserrat. Monestir de Montserrat,
1969.
211 p. 25 cm.
InStme; MnCS

Moosburg, Germany. St. Castulus (Benedictine abbey)

3100 **Braun, Max.**
Geschichte der Stadt Moosburg.
Moosburg, G. Senftl, 1902.
130 p. illus., port. 21 cm.
InStme

Morristown, N.J. St. Mary's Abbey
see
St. Mary's Abbey, Morristown, N.J.

Mosteiro Sao Jose, Mineiros, Goias, Brazil

3101 **Kansas monks in Brazil** (periodical).
v. 1–4, 1962–1971.
KAS

Mount Angel Abbey, St. Benedict, Or.

3102 **Duerr, Gregory, O.S.B.**
Mount Angel Abbey. St. Benedict,
Or., 1973.
64 p. illus. 28 cm.
PLatS; OrStb

3103 **Turck, Blaise, O.S.B.**
Mount Angel Seminary, 1889–1964. [St.
Benedict, Or., 1964].
unpaged. illus., ports. 28 cm.
MnCS; OrStb

3104 **Villiger, Anselm, O.S.B.**
The foundation of Mount Angel Abbey as
recorded in the diary of the founding abbot
Anselm Villiger of Engelberg, January,
1881, to December, 1900.
57 p. 28 cm.
Translated from the German by Am-
brose Zenner, O.S.B., and Luke Eberle,
O.S.B.
Typescript.
MoCo

Mount St. Benedict Priory, Crookston, Minn.

3105 **With gladdened hearts we celebrate our
first fifty years,** 1919–1969: Sisters of
St. Benedict of Crookston, Mount St.
Benedict Priory, Crookston, Minnesota.
[St. Paul, Minn., North Central Pub-
lishing Co., 1970?].
60 p. illus. 22x28 cm.
InFer; AStb; KAS; MnCS; MnCrM;
PLatS

Mount Saint Mary Convent, Pittsburgh, Pa.

3106 **Benedictine Sisters of Pittsburgh,** 1870–
1970. [Pittsburgh, Pa., 1970].
45 p. chiefly illus. 28 cm.
MdRi; MnCS; MnStj(Archives); PLatS;
PPiSM

Mount St. Scholastica Convent, Atchison, Kans.

3107 **Schuster, Mary Faith, Sister, O.S.B.**
The meaning of the mountain; a history
of the first century of Mount St.
Scholastica. Baltimore, Helicon [1963].
329 p. illus., ports 23 cm. (Benedictine
studies, 6)
AStb; ILSP; InStme; KAM; KAS;
MnCS; MoCo; PLatS

Moyenmoutier, France (Benedictine abbey)

3108 **Belhomme, Hubert, O.S.B.**
Historia Mediani in monte Vosago
monasterii Ordinis Sancti Benedicti ex congregatione sanctorum Vitoni et Hidulfi.
Argenterati, J. R. Dulssecker, 1724.
[6], 467 p. 26 cm.
KAS

München-Gladbach, Germany (Benedictine abbey)

3109   **Eckertz, Gottfried.**
Das Verbrüderungs- und Todtenbuch der Abtei Galdbach. Aachen, F. N. Palm, 1881.
[x], 113 p. facsim. 23 cm.
At head of title: Necrologium Gladbacense.
KAS

3109a   **Petry, Manfred.**
Die Gründungsgeschichte der Abtei St. Vitus zu Mönchengladbach. Hrsg. und übersetzt von Manfred Petry. Mönchengladbach, [Stadtarchiv], 1974.
73 p. 5 facsims. 24 cm.
MnCS

3110   **Ropertz, Peter, ed.**
Quellen und Beiträge zur Geschichte der Benediktiner-Abtei des hl. Vitus in M. Gladbach. M. Gladbach, Franz van Oberger, 1877.
[6], 378 p. 22 cm.
KAS

Münchsmünster, Bavaria (Benedictine abbey)

3111   **Thiel, Matthias, O.S.B.**
Die Traditionen, Urkunden und Urbare des Klosters Münchsmünster. München, Beck, 1961.
73, 442 p. 25 cm.
PLatS

Muenster, Sask., Canada. St. Peter's Abbey
see
St. Peter's Abbey, Muenster, Sask., Canada

Münsterlingen, Switzerland (Benedictine convent)

3112   **Kuhn, Konrad.**
Thurgovia sacra. Geschichte der katholischen kirchlichen Stiftungen des Kantons Thurgau. Frauenfeld, J. Gromann, 1876–1883.
3 v. 21 cm.
KAS

Münsterschwarzach, Germany (Benedictine abbey)

3113   **Die Benediktinerabtei Münsterschwarzach.** Mit Beiträgen von Lambert Dörr [et al.]. Münsterschwarzach, Vier-Türme-Verlag [1965].
117 p. illus., facsims., maps. 19 cm.
PLatS

3114   **Kaspar, Adelhard, O.S.B.**
Die Quellen zur Geschichte der Abtei Münsterschwarzach am Main . . . München, Kommissionsverlag R. Oldenbourg, 1930.
xii, 86 p. 23 cm.
KAS

3115   **Studia suarzacensia;** Beiträge zur Geschichte der Abtei Münsterschwarzach anlässlich des 50. Jahrestages ihrer Wiederbesiedlung. Münsterschwarzach, Vier-Türme-Verlag [1963].
320 p. plates, ports., map. 25 cm.
MnCS

3116   **Vogt, Gabriel, O.S.B.**
Der selige Egbert, Abt von Münsterschwarzach, 1047–1077; Persönlichkeit und Werk des Reformabtes . . . [Münsterschwarzach, Vier-Türme-Verlag, 1976].
83 p. illus. 20 cm.
MnCS

Muri-Gries, Italy (Benedictine abbey)

3117   **Catalogus monachorum O.S.B.** Benedicti exempti monasterii Muro-Griesensis Congregationis Helveticae . . . Bulsani, A. Auer, 1904.
27 p. plates. 22 cm.
MnCS

3118   **Gesta et fundatio** monasterii Murensis in Pago Argowa a comitibus Vindovissensibus, nuncupatis de Altenburg, postinorum de Habesburg, constructum. MS. Benediktinerabtei St. Paul im Lavantthal, Austria, codex 77/2, 48 f. Folio. Saec. 18.
Microfilm: MnCH proj. no. 11,851

3119   **Kiem, Martin, O.S.B.**
Das Benediktinerstift Muri-Gries 1845–1895; ein Gedenkblatt zum fünfzigjährigen Bestande nebst Katalog der lebenden und verstorbenen Mitglieder. Sarnen, J. Müller, 1895.
47 p. 23 cm.
KAS

3120   **Kopp, Fridolin, O.S.B.**
Acta fundationis Murensis monasterij. [Typis Monasterij Murensis, 1750].
98 p. 25 cm.
KAS

3121   **Origines Murensis monasterii** in Helvetiis atque adeo Europa universa celeberrimi Ordinis S. Benedicti . . . Spirembergii, in Bibliopolio Brucknausenio, 1618.
[6], 65, [5] p. fold. chart. 24 cm.
KAS

3122   **Schilter, J.**
Die Benediktinerabtei Muri; Führer durch Schicksale und Bauten. Muri, Gebr. Steinmann [1947].

40 p. plates. 20 cm.
MnCS

3123 **Schmidfeld, Hugo, O.S.B.**
Acta Murensia integrae fidei restituta, sive Gesta et fundatio monasterii Murensis, a scriniis monasterii Engelbergensis . . . MS. Benediktinerabtei St. Paul im Lavantthal, Austria, codex 76/2. 2 vols. Saec. 18.
Microfilm: MnCH proj. no. 11,852 & 11,858

3124 **Strebel, Kurt.**
Die Benediktinerabtei Muri in nachreformatorischer Zeit 1549–1596, vom Tode des Abtes Laurenz von Heidegg bis zur Wahl von Abt Johann Jodok Singisen. Winterthur, Schellenberg, 1967.
xiv, 189 p. 23 cm.

3125 **Trafojer, Ambrose, O.S.B.**
Das Kloster Gries (Bolzano). Bolzano, Vogelweiser, 1927.
269 p. illus.
MoCo

3126 **Tschudi, Aegidius, O.S.B.**
Fundatio et acta monasterii Murensis. MS. Benediktinerabtei St. Paul im Lavantthal, Austria, codex 8/2, pt. III. Folio. Saec. 16.
Microfilm: MnCH proj. no. 11,741

**Müstair, Switzerland
(abbey of Benedictine nuns)**

3126a **Müller, Iso, O.S.B.**
Geschichte des Klosters Müstair, von den Anfängen bis zur Gegenwart. Disentis, Disentina-Verlag, 1978.
228 p. plates (part col.) 24 cm.
MnCS

**Nashdom, England
(Anglican Benedictine abbey)**

3127 **The Jubilee book of the Benedictines of Nashdom,** 1914–1964. London, The Faith Press [1964].
86 p. port., plates. 21 cm.
MnCS; MoCo; PLatS

Nauvoo, Ill. St. Mary's Priory
see
St. Mary's Priory, Nauvoo, Ill.

**Naumberg, Germany. St. Georgen
(Benedictine abbey)**

3128 **Schamel, Johann Martin.**
Historische Beschreibung von dem ehemahls berühmten Benediktiner-Kloster zu St. Georgen vor der Stadt Naumberg an der Saale . . . [Naumberg], Johann Christian Martin, 1728.
[10], 104 p. illus. 21 cm.
KAS

Neresheim, Germany (Benedictine abbey)

3129 **Engelhardt, Ottmar.**
Neresheim und das Härtsfeld. Stuttgart, Konrad Theis Verlag [1977].
120 p. chiefly illus. (part col.) 21 x 22 cm.
MnCS

3130 **Lang, Anselm.**
Kurze Geschichte des ehemaligen Klosters und Reichsstiftes Neresheim . . . Nördlingen, Verlag der C. H. Bech'schen Buchhandlung, 1839.
iv, 112 p. illus. 19 cm.
InStme

3130a **Nack, Karl Alois, O.S.B.**
Reichsstift Neresheim; eine kurze Geschichte dieser Benediktinerabtei in Schwaben, und Beschreibung ihrer im 1792 eingeweihten neuen Kirche . . . Neresheim, Bernard Kaelin, 1792.
144 p. 20 cm.
KAS

Neu-Corvey, Germany
see
Corvey, Germany

Neuss, Germany (priory of Benedictine nuns)

3131 **Effmann, Wilhelm.**
Die St. Quirinus-Kirche zu Neuss . . . mit 30 Abbildungen. Düsseldorf, L. Schwann, 1890.
[4], 46 p. illus. 29 cm.
KAS

Neuweiler, Germany (Benedictine abbey)

3132 **Fischer, Dagobert.**
Abtei und Stadt Neuweiler, historisch und archäologisch dargestellt. Zabern, H. Fuchs, 1876.
147 p. illus., plans. 19 cm.
InStme

New Norcia, Australia (Benedictine abbey)

3133 **Hammerstein, L. von, S.J.**
Benediktiner-Gründung (Neo-Norcia).
(*In* his: Winfrid. 1895. p. 318–331)
AStb

3134 **Hugo-Brunt, Michael.**
The Benedictine abbey of New Norcia, Western Australia; a bibliography. Monticello, Ill., Vance Bibliographies, 1978.

20 p. 28 cm.
KAS

3135 **Perez, Eugene, O.S.B.**
Benedictine items, featuring articles on
St. Benedict . . Monte Cassino . . . Benedictine foundations in Western Australia.
New Norcia, The Abbey Press, 1953.
76 p. illus., plates. 18 cm.
MnCS

New Subiaco Abbey, Subiaco, Ark.

3136 **Assenmacher, Hugo, O.S.B.**
A place called Subiaco; a history of the
Benedictine monks in Arkansas. Little
Rock, Rose Publishing Company, 1977.
486 p. illus. 23 cm.
InStme; KAS; MnCS; MoCo; NcBe

3137 **"A new Benedictine settlement in
Arkansas":** St. Benedict Priory, 1878–
1892; New Subiaco Abbey, 1892–1978.
Subiaco Abbey, 1978.
36 p. illus.
InFer

Niederaltaich, Bavaria (Benedictine abbey)

3138 **Hermannus, abbas,** 13th cent.
Subscripta de institutione monasterii
Altahensis inferioris Hermannus Abbas ex
vita S. Godehardi et ex chronicis ac
privilegiis compilavit. MS. Vienna, Nationalbibliothek, codex 9378. 3 f. Quarto.
Saec. 16.
Microfilm: MnCH proj. no. 19,266

3139 **Heufelder, Emmanuel Maria, O.S.B.**
Niederalteich, Benediktinerabtei und
Basilika. 10. erweiterte Farbausgabe.
München, Schnell & Steiner, 1972.
18 p. illus., col. plates. 17 cm.
MnCS

3140 **Klose, Josef.**
Das Urkundenwesen Abt Hermanns von
Niederaltaich (1242–1273), seine Kanzlei
und Schreibschule. Kallmünz, M.
Lassleben, 1967.
xi, 167 p. 25 cm.
MnCS

3141 **Kloster Niederaltaich.** Urkunden Abschriften. MS. Vienna, Haus-, Hof- und
Staatsarchiv, codex W 987/1. 118 f.
Saec. 17.
Microfilm: MnCH proj. no. 23,610

3142 **Stadtmüller, Georg.**
Geschichte der Abtei Niederaltaich 741–
1971 . . . Ottobeuren, Bayerische Benediktinerakademie, 1972.
516 p. illus. 25 cm.
InStme; KAS; MnCS; MoCo; NcBe

3143 **Urkunden-** und Notizen-Sammlung des
Abtes Hermann von Niederaltaich und
mehrere seiner Nachfolger, 1242 bis
circa 1300. MS. Vienna, Haus-, Hofund Staatsarchiv, codex R 83. 266 f.
Quarto. Saec. 13–14.
Microfilm: MnCH proj. no. 23,516

3144 **Zwei Visitationsrecesse** von 1452 und
1466, Niederaltaich betreffend. MS.
Cistercienserabtei Wilhering, Austria,
codex IX,14, f.52r–62v. Folio. Saec. 15.
Microfilm: MnCH proj. no. 2791

**Nivelles, Belgium. Sainte-Gertrude
(abbey of Benedictine nuns)**

3145 **Cartulaire de Nivelles.** Extrait des
archives communales de Nivelles transcrit et annoté par Joseph Buisseret et
Edgar de Prelle de la Nieppe. Nivelles,
Ch. Guignardé, 1892.
119 p. 25 cm.
KAS

**Nogent-le-Retrou, France. Saint-Denis
(Benedictine abbey)**

3146 **Saint Denis de Nogent-le-Rotrou,** 1031–
1789. Vannes, Lafolye, 1895.
cxxiv, 345 p. illus., plates, plan. 25 cm.
KAS

Nonantola, Italy (Benedictine abbey)

3147 **Fasoli, Gina.**
Le Abazia di Nonantola e di Pomposa.
(*In* La bonnifica benedettina, p. 95–105)
PLatS

3148 **Moderini, Ave.**
La notazione neumatica di Nonantola.
Cremona, Athenaeum Cremonense, 1970.
2 v. 25 cm.
Contents: v. 1. Testo; v. 2. Tavole ed
esempi.
PLatS

Nonnberg, Salzburg, Austria
see
Salzburg, Austria. Nonnberg

**Norcia, Italy. San Benedetto
(Benedictine abbey)**

3149 **La cripta di S. Benedetto in Norcia.**
[Valle di Pompei, Scuola tipografica
pontificia pei figli dei carcerati fondata
da Bartolo Longo, 1913].
23 p. illus. 31 cm.
InStme

3150 **Leccisotti, Tommaso, O.S.B.**
Documenti par la storia del Monastero di
S. Benedetto in Norcia.

(*In* Analecta monastica, 7. ser., 1965. p. 175–228)
PLatS

Norfolk, Nebr. Immaculata Convent
see
Immaculata Convent, Norfolk, Nebr.

Norwich Priory, England

3151 **Stone, Eric.**
Profit-and-loss accountancy at Norwich Cathedral Priory.
(*In* Royal Historical Society, London. Transactions. 5th ser., v. 12(1962) p. 25–48)
KAS

Notre-Dame, Bourbourg, France
see
Bourbourg, France. Notre-Dame

Notre-Dame, Grande-Sauve, France
see
Grande-Sauve, France. Notre-Dame

Notre-Dame de Josaphat, Jerusalem
see
Jerusalem. Notre-Dame de Josaphat

Notre-Dame de la Garde, Arvert, France
see
Arvert, France. Notre-Dame de la Garde

Nüremberg, Germany. Sankt Aegid (Benedictine abbey)

3152 **Schlitpacher, Johannes, O.S.B.**
Descriptio summorum pontificum, cardinalium, patriarcharum, archiepiscoporum, episcoporum, canonistorum, qui in conventu Nürnbergensi ad S. Egidium depicti sunt. MS. Benediktinerabtei Melk, Austria, codex 1763, f.211r–220v. Duodecimo. Saec. 15.
Microfilm: MnCH proj. no. 2072

Nütschau, Germany. Sankt Ansgar (Benedictine abbey)

3153 **Houben, Hubert.**
St. Blasianer Handschriften des 11. und 12. Jahrhunderts. München, Arbeo-Gesellschaft, 1979.
xiii, 220 p. 20 cm.
MnCS

3153a **Kloster Nütschau:** Benediktiner Priorat Sankt Ansgar. [n.p.] 1975.
12 p. 24 cm.
MnCS

Olinda, Brazil. Sao Bento (Benedictine abbey)

3154 **Restauration de l'Ordre de S. Benoît au Brésil:** vie monastique, apostolat, appel aux vocations. [Bruges], Société de St. Augustin, Desclée, 1895.
15 p. 22 cm.
KAS

Olympia, Wash. St. Martin's Abbey
see
St. Martin's Abbey, Olympia, Wash.

Oña, Spain. San Salvador (Benedictine abbey)

3155 **Alamo, Juan del.**
Colección diplomática de San Salvador de Oña (822–1284). Madrid, 1950.
2 v. illus., col. maps. 26 cm.
MnCS

Orval, Belgium (Benedictine abbey)

3156 **Aureavallis;** mélanges historiques reunis à l'occasion du neuvième centenaire de l'Abbaye d'Orval. Liège, Editions Soledi, 1975.
515 p. illus., plates. 26 cm.
MnCS

3157 **Jeantin, M.**
Les ruines et chroniques de l'Abbaye d'Orval; esquisse morale, religieuse et chevaleresque de l'ancien Comté de Chiny. 2. éd., corrigée et considerablement augmentée. Paris, Jules Tardieu, 1857.
456, 23 p. illus. 21 cm.
MnCS

Ossiach, Austria (Benedictine abbey)

3158 **Diploma historiam monasterii** Ossiacensis illustrans. MS. Vienna, Nationalbibliothek, codex 554. f.88v. Octavo. Saec. 11.
Microfilm: MnCH proj. no. 13,888

Otterberg, Germany (abbey of Benedictine nuns)

3159 **Chronicon coenobii virginum Otterbergensis,** ad Netham, congregationis quondam Cisterciensis, nunc in Valle Dei, familiae Benedictinae, variis bullis & literis pontificum, principum . . . illustratum.
(*In* Paullini, Chr. F. Rerum et antiquitatum Germanicarum syntagma. Francofurti ad Moenum, 1698. p. 169–260)
KAS

Ottobeuren, Germany (Benedictine abbey)

3160 **Hauke, Hermann.**
Die mittelalterlichen Handschriften in
der Abtei Ottobeuren: Kurzverzeichnis.
Erstellt im Auftrag der Generaldirektion
der Bayer. Stattl. Bibliotheken.
Wiesbaden, O. Harrassowita, 1974.
122 p. 28 cm.
MnCS

3161 **Hubay, Liona.**
Incunabula aus der staatlichen
Bibliothek Neuburg/Donau [und] in der
Benediktinerabtei Ottobeuren. Wiesbaden,
O. Harrassowitz, 1970.
xx, 271 p. plates (part col.) 28 cm. (In-
kunabelkataloge beyerischer Bibliotheken)
MnCS

3162 **Kolb, Aegidius, O.S.B., ed.**
Ottobeuren; Festschrift zur 1200-
Jahrfeier der Abtei. Augsburg, Verlag
Winfried-Werk, 1964.
viii, 416 p. 24 cm.
KAS; MnCS

3163 **Ottobeuren,** 764–1964; Beiträge zur
Geschichte der Abtei. Augsburg, Kommissionsverlag Winfried-Werk, 1964.
319 p. plates. 1964.
KAS

3164 **Schmidt-Glassner, Helga.**
Ottobeuren. Aufnahmen von Helga
Schmidt-Galssner. Einführender Text von
Johannes Beer. Königstein im Taunus,
Langewiesche-Bücherei [n.d.].
47 p. illus., plates. 20 cm.
InStme; MnCS

3165 **Schnell, Hugo.**
Ottobeuren: Kloster und Kirche. 6.,
überarbeitete u. verm. Aufl. München,
Schnell & Steiner [1971].
46 p. illus. 24 cm.
MnCS

3166 **Uttinburra** 764–1964; 1200 Jahre Benediktinerabtei Ottobeuren. [n.p., 1964].
portfolio. plates (part col.) 55 cm.
MnCS

Oudenbourg, Flanders (Benedictine abbey)

3167 **Chronique de monastère** d'Oudenbourg
de l'Ordre de S. Benoît, publiée pour la
première fois d'après un manuscrit du
XVe siècle, par l'abbé F. van de Putte.
Gand, Impr. de C. Amoot-Braeckman,
1843.
6, xi, 133 p. 31 cm.
KAS

Our Lady of Grace Convent, Beech Grove, Ind.

3168 **Encounter** (10 years anniversary edition,
1957–1967). Beech Grove, Ind., Our
Lady of Grace Convent, 1967.
40 p. illus.
InFer; MnStj (Archives)

**Oviedo, Spain. San Vicente
(Benedictine abbey)**

3169 **Colección diplomática des Monasterio**
de San Vicente de Oviedo (años 781–
1200). Estudio y transcripciòn por Pedro
Floriano Llorente. Oviedo, Instituto de
estudios asturianos, 1968–
v. 24 cm.
MnCS

**Padua, Italy. Santa Giustina
(Benedictine abbey)**

3170 **Pepi, Ruperto, O.S.B.**
L'Abbazia di Santa Giustina in Padova;
storia e arte. Pavoda, Edizioni Monaci
Benedettini, 1966.
203 p. illus. (part col.) 17 cm.
InStme; MnCS; PLatS

Pannonhalma, Hungary (Benedictine abbey)

3171 **Alapfy, Attila.**
Pannonhalma. [Introduced by Katalin
David, translated by Elisabeth Hoch].
Budapest, Corvina [1968].
chiefly illus. 24 cm.
PLatS

3172 **Levárdy, Ferenc.**
Pannonhalma. [Translated by Eva Rácz.
Translation revised by Bertha Gaster].
[Gyoma, Kner Printing House, 1968].
41, 40 p. plates, fold. plan. 17 cm.
At head of title: Corvina
MnCS; PLatS

3173 **A Pannonhalmi szent Benedik-rend**
névtára az 1907–1908 tanévre. Györ,
Gyöegyhazmegye Könyvsajtoja, 1907.
98 p. illus. 23 cm.
MnCS

**Paris, France. Saint-Germain-des-Prés
(Benedictine abbey)**

3174 **France. Archives Nationales.**
Saint-Germain-des-Prés, 558–1958.
[Montreuil] Hotel de Rohan [1958?].
60 p. 22 cm.
InStme; MnCS

3175 **Leroy, Jules.**
Saint-Germain-des-Prés, capitale des lettres. 2. éd. Paris, Nouvelles éditions latines
[1973].

251 p. plates. 20 cm.
MnCS

3176 Nécrologe de la Congrégation de Saint-Maur décédé à l'Abbaye de Saint-Germain-des-Prés. Publié avec introduction, suppléments et appendices par m. l'abbé J. B. Vanel. Paris, H. Champion, 1896.
lxiii, 412 p. 29 cm.
MnCS

3177 Vanel, Jean-Baptiste.
Les Bénédictins de Saint-Germain-des-Prés et les savants Lyonnais d'après leur correspondance inédite. Paris, A. Picard, 1894.
x, 379 p. 25 cm.
CaQStB; KAS; PLatS

Paris, France. Saint-Louis-du-Temple (abbey of Benedictine nuns)

3178 Les Moniales. Préface de Jean Guitton; introduction de Louis Chaigne. [Paris], Desclée de Brouwer [1966].
various pagings. illus. 23x27 cm.
Contents: L'Album de Mère Geneviève Gallois (1888–1962), présenté par Marcelle Auclair. Chronique de Saint-Louis-du-Temple, rédigée par Carmen Bernos de Gasztold avec la collaboration de René Rancoeur.
MnStj

Paris, France. Saint-Martin-des-Champs (Cluniac priory)

3179 Marrier, Martin.
Monasterii regalis S. Martini de Campis Paris ordinis cluniacensis historia. Libris sex partita. Parisiis, apud Sebastianum Cramoisy, 1637.
[14], 576 p. illus. 23 cm.
KAS

3180 Recueil de chartes et documents de Saint-Martin-des-Champs, monastère parisien, par J. Depoin. Paris, Jouve et cie, 1912–
v. 25 cm. (Archives de la France monastique, vols. 13, 16, 18, 20, 21)
MnCS

Paris, France. Saint-Maur-des-Fossés (Benedictine abbey)

3181 Piérart, Z. J.
Histoire de Saint-Maur-des-Fossés; de son abbaye, de sa péninsule, et des communes des cantons de Charenton, Vincennes et Boissy-Saint-Légar. Paris, Claudin, 1876.

2 v. illus., maps. 25 cm.
KAS

3182 Terroine, Anne.
Un abbé de Saint-Maur au XIII siècle, Pierre de Chevry, 1256–1285, avec l'édition plus anciens cas de justice de Saint-Maur-des-Fossés. Paris, C. Klincksieck, 1968.
238 p. map. 24 cm.
MnCS

Paris, France. Val-de-Grâce (abbey of Benedictine nuns)

3183 Delsart, H. M. pseud.
Marguerite d'Arbouze, abbesse du Val-de-Grâce, 1580–1626. Paris. P. Lethuelleux, 1923.
xii, 347 p. 19 cm.
KAS

Paulinzelle, Germany (Benedictine abbey)

3184 Hesse, Ludwig Friedrich.
Geschichte des Klosters Paulinzelle. Rudolstadt, gedruckt in der Froebelschen Hofbuchdruckerei, 1815.
45 p. illus. 39 cm.
KAS

Pegau, Saxony (Benedictine abbey)

3185 Necrologium monasterii Bigaviensis, nunc Pegau prope Lipsiam (fragmentum). MS. Vienna, Nationalbibliothek, codex 135. f.1r–2v. Folio. Saec. 12. Microfilm: MnCH proj. no. 13,494

Peña, La, Spain. San Juan (Benedictine abbey)

3186 Cronica de San Juan de la Peña. Versión latina e indices preparados por Antonio Ubieto Arteta. Valencia [Gráficas Bautista] 1961.
277 p. 17 cm. (Textos medievales, 4)
PLatS

3187 Valenzuela Foved, Virgilio.
Los monasterios de San Juan de la Peña y Santa Cruz de la Serós; guía del visitante. Huesca, 1959.
149 p. illus. 17 cm.
PLatS

Pendorada, Portugal. Entre-Douro-e-Minho (Benedictine abbey)

3188 Matoso, José, O.S.B.
L'Abbaye de Pendorada des origines à 1160. Coimbra, 1962.
xv, 194 p. maps. 25 cm.
InStme

Perugia, Italy. San Pietro (Benedictine abbey)

3189 **Millenario della basilica benedettina** di
S. Pietro in Perugia, 966–1966. Padri
benedettini di S. Pietro. [n.p., n.d.].
[32] p. illus. 22 cm.
PLatS

Peterborough Abbey, England

3190 **Britton, John.**
The history and antiquities of the abbey,
and cathedral church of Peterborough; illustrated by a series of engravings of
views, elevations. . . London, Longman,
Rees, Orme, Brown, and Green, 1828.
viii, 88 p. illus., plates, plan. 28 cm.
KAS

3191 **Carte nativorum;** a Peterborough Abbey
cartulary of the fourteenth century.
Edited by C.N.L. Brooks and M. M.
Postan. Oxford, University Press, 1960.
lxv, 261 p. 26 cm.
KAS

3192 **Chronicon Angliae Petriburgense.**
Iterum post Sparkium cum cod. msto
contulit J. A. Giles. New York, B.
Franklin [1967].
xiii, 180 p. 23 cm. (Publications of the
Caxton Society, 2)
PLatS

3193 **Chronicon Petroburgense.** Nunc primum
typis mandatum, curante Thomâ
Stapleton. Londini, 1849. [Camden
Society. Publications, 47].
ILSP

3194 **James, Montague Rhodes.**
Lists of manuscripts formerly in Peterborough Abbey library, with preface and
identifications by M. R. James. Oxford,
University Press, 1926.
104 p. 22x18 cm.
MnCS

3195 **King, Edmund.**
Peterborough Abbey, 1086–1310; a
study in the land market. Cambridge
[England], University Press, 1973.
xii, 208 p. 23 cm.
KAS; MnCS; PLatS

3196 **Mellows, William Thomas, ed.**
The foundation of Peterborough
Cathedral, A.D. 1541. [Kettering, Nor-
thamptonshire, 1941 [1967].
lxxxiii, 140 p. plates. 25 cm.
PLatS

Petershausen, Germany (Benedictine abbey)

3197 **De monasterio Petrushusano libri sex.**
MS. Benediktinerabtei St. Paul im

Lavantthal, Austria, codex 282/2. 231 p.
Quarto. Saec. 18.
Microfilm: MnCH proj. no. 12,114

Pfäfers, Switzerland (Benedictine abbey)

3198 **Vogler, Werner.**
Das Ringen um die Reform und
Restauration der Fürstabtei Pfävers 1549–
1637. 2. Aufl. Sarganerländische
Buchdruckerei AG Mels, 1973.
xxi, 149 p. facsims. 24 cm.
Originally presented as the author's
thesis, Fribourg.
InStme

3199 **Wegelin, Karl, ed.**
Die Regesten der Benediktiner-Abtei
Pfävers und der Landschaft Sargans.
Chur, G. Hitz, 1850.
[4], 108 p. 29 cm.
KAS

Pfalzel, Germany (abbey of Benedictine nuns)

3200 **Heyen, Franz Josef.**
Untersuchungen zur Geschichte des
Benediktinerinnenklosters Pfalzl bei Trier,
ca. 700 bis 1016. Göttingen, Vandenhoeck
& Ruprecht, 1966.
75 p. 25 cm.
KAS; PLatS

Pierre-qui-Vire, France (Benedictine abbey)

3201 **Dangar, Anne G.**
Lettres à la Pierre-qui-Vire. Saint-
Leger-Vauban, Zodiaque, 1972.
192 p. illus. 22 cm.
MnCS

3202 **Ordo operis divini persolvendi** sacrique
peragendi ad usum monachorum Sanc-
tae Mariae de Petra Gyrante. Exaratus
ad instar manuscripti.
v. 18 cm.
MnCS

Pill, Wales (Benedictine priory)

3203 **Pritchard, Emily M.**
The history of St. Dogmaels Abbey,
together with her cells, Pill, Caldey and
Glascareg, and the mother abbey of Tiron
. . . London, Blades, East & Blades, 1907.
241 p. illus., plates, map. 26 cm.
MnCS

Pirmil pres Nantes, France (Benedictine priory)

3204 **Saint-Sébastien d'Aignes prés Nantes,**
par l'abbé A. R. [Vannes, Imprimerie
Lafolye, 1897].

131 p. 25 cm.
KAS

Pittsburgh, Pa. Mount Saint Mary Convent
see
Mount Saint Mary Convent, Pittsburgh, Pa.

Plankstetten, Bavaria (Benedictine abbey)

3205   **Bauer, Petrus, O.S.B.**
Die Benediktinerabtei Plankstetten in
Geschichte und Gegenwart. Plankstetten/
Oberpfalz, Benediktinerabtei, 1979.
139 p. 80 plates (part col.), folded map,
23 cm.
MnCS

3205a **Götz, Franz Sales, O.S.B.**
Maurus Xaverius Herbst, Abt von Plankstetten; ein Lebensbild aus dem 18. Jahrhundert. 2., verb. Aufl., hrsg. von Bonifatius M. Schumacher, O.S.B. Würzburg,
Echter-Verlag, [1957].
87 p. illus. 19 cm.
PLatS

3206   **Rösermüller, Rudolf.**
Abtei Plankstetten. Augsburg, Benno
Filser Verlag, 1929.
(Die bayerischen Benediktinerklöster in
Wort und Bild. Erste Folge)
NcBe

Pluscarden Priory, Scotland

3207   **Skinner, Basil Chisholm.**
Pluscarden Priory near Elgin, Moray,
Scotland; the story of a XIIIth-century
monastery and how Benedictines of the
XXth-century returned to restore it.
[Derby, Pilgrim Press, 1964].
[20] p. illus., plates, diagrs. 13 x 20 cm.
PLatS

Polirone, Italy (Benedictine abbey)

3208   **Bacchini, Benedetto, O.S.B.**
Dell'istoria del monastero di S. Bene-
detto di Polirone nello stato di Mantua,
Modina, Capponi, 1696.
[28], 244, [11], 110, [5] p. 22 cm.
MnCS

3208a **Piva, Paolo.**
Per la storia di un complesso edilizio
monastico: San Benedetto di Polirone.
Roma, Abbazia di S. Paolo fuori le Mura,
1977.
122 p. illus. 24 cm.
PLatS

**Pomposa, Italy. Santa Maria
(Benedictine abbey)**

3209   **Convengo Internazionale di Studi
Storici Pomposiana, Codigoro, 1964.**

Analecta Pomposiana; atti del primo con-
vengno . . . 6–7 maggio 1964. A cura di
Antoni Samaritani. Codigoro, Giari, 1965.
xxxi, 516 p. 25 cm.
KAS

3210   **Fasoli, Gina.**
Le abbazia di Nonatola e di Pomposa.
(*In* La bonifica benedettina, p. 95–105)
PLatS

3211   **Salmi, Mario.**
The Abbey of Pomposa (43 illustrations).
2d ed. [Roma], Istituto poligrafico dello
stato [1965].
46 p. plates. 19 cm. (Guide-books to the
museums, galleries and monuments of
Italy, 62)
MnCS

3212   **Salmi, Mario.**
L'Abbazia di Pomposa. Roma, La
Libreria dello Stato, 1936.
279 p. illus. 41 cm., *and* Atlas of 45
plates, 45 cm.
MnCS

3213   **Salmi, Mario.**
L'Abbazia di Pomposa. 4. ed. Roma,
Libreria dello Stato [1957].
41 p. (p. 13–40 illus.) 19 cm. (Itinerari dei
musei e monumenti d'Italia, n. 62)
PLatS

**Pontoise, France. Saint-Martin
(Benedictine abbey)**

3214   **Tables du cartulaire de l'Abbaye Saint-
Martin de Pontoise.** Pontoise, Bureaux
de la Société historique, 1969.
55 p. tables. 24 cm.
MnCS

Portsmouth Abbey, Portsmouth, R.I.

3215   **Portsmouth Abbey School,** fiftieth anniversary, 1926–1976. Portsmouth, R.I.,
1976.
96 p. illus.
MoCo

Praglia, Italy (Benedictine abbey)

3216   **Tell, Isidoro, O.S.B.**
Praglia. 1960.
[32] p. illus. 17 cm.

**Prague, Czechoslovakia. Emmaus
(Benedictine abbey)**

3217   **Aus dem Leben unserer lieben Frau;**
siebzehn Kunstblätter nach den Ori-
ginalcartons der Malerschule von Beuron
zu den Wandgemälden der Klosterkirche zu Emaus-Prag. Mit siebzehn

Sonnetten von P. Fritz Esser, S.J. 2. Aufl. [n.p.] Druck und Verlag der B. Kühlen'schen Kunstanstalt, 1896. unpaged. illus., 17 plates. 35 x 43 cm. MnCS

Prinknash Abbey, England

3218 **The Benedictines of Caldey Island.** 2d ed. rev. The Abbey, Isle of Caldey, 1912.
xx, 152 p. illus., plates. 22 cm.
KAS

3219 **Prinknash Abbey.** [Gloucester, Prinknash Abbey, 1956?].
unpaged. illus. 17 cm.
Latin translation over each English section.
MnCS

3220 **Prinknash Abbey golden jubilee, 1928–1978.**
40 p. illus. 20 cm.
A separate print of Pax, spring–summer, 1978, no. 340.
MnCS

Prufening, Germany (Benedictine abbey)

3221 **Weixer, Melchior, O.S.B.**
Fontilegium sacrum sive fundatio . . . monasterii S. Georgii, Ord. D. Benedicti vulgo Prifling. dicti prope Ratisponam . . . Item privilegia, donationes . . . Ingolstadii, Gregorius Haenlinus, 1627.
[16], 312 p. 28 cm.
KAS

Prüm, Germany (Benedictine abbey)

3222 **De Reginone Prumiensi monacho et abbate.** Chronica Reginonis abbatis Prumiensis. MS. Benediktinerabtei St. Paul im Lavantthal, Austria, codex 80/2. 253 f. Folio. Saec. 18.
Microfilm: MnCH proj. no. 11,844

3222a **Haubrichs, Wolfgang.**
Die Kultur der Abtei Prüm zur Karolingerzeit; Studien zur Heimat des althochdeutschen Georgslied. Bonn, Ludwig Röhrscheid Verlag, 1979.
203 p. 3 maps, 23 cm. (Rheinisches Archiv, 105)
MnCS

3222b **Kuchenbuch, Ludolf.**
Bäuerliche Gesellschaft und Klosterherrschaft im 9. Jahrhundert; Studien zur Sozialstruktur der Familia der Abtei Prüm. Wiesbaden, Franz Steiner Verlag, 1978.
xv, 443 p. facsim., maps, 23 cm.
MnCS

3223 **Marx, J.**
Sie Salvatorkirche zu Prüm in ihrer Vergangenheit und in ihrer Gegenwart; eine Festschrift zur Feier des eilfhundertjährigen Jubiläums der Stiftung jener Kirche, in den Tagen vom 4. bis 11. Oktober, 1963. Prüm, im Selbstverlage der Salvatorkirche [1863].
vi, 69 p. 24 cm.
KAS

3224 **Regino, abbot of Prüm.**
Libri duo de synodalibus causis et disciplinis ecclesiasticis, ex diversis sanctorum patrum conciliis atque decretis collecti. Ad optimum codd. fidem recensuit adnotationem duplicem adjecit F.G.A. Wasserschleben. Lipsiae, Guil. Engelmann, 1840; Graz, Akademische Druck- u. Verlagsanstalt, 1964.
xxvi, 526 p. 19 cm.
PLatS

Puy, Le, France
see
Le Puy, France

Quedlinburg, Germany (Benedictine convent)

3225 **Kettner, Friedrich Ernst.**
Antiquitates Quedlinburgenses; oder, Keyserliche diplomata, Päbstliche Bullen . . . von dem Stiffte Quedlinburg. Leipzig, Joh. Christ. König, 1712.
[14], 702, [54] p. plates, engr. seals. 22 cm.
KAS

Ramsgate, England. St. Augustine's Abbey
see
St. Augustine's Abbey, Ramsgate, England

Rapid City, S.D. St. Martin's Convent
see
St. Martin's Convent, Rapid City, S.D.

Reading Abbey, England

3226 **Hurry, Jameson Boyd.**
In honor of Hugh de Boves and Hugh Cook Farrington, first and last abbots of Reading. [Reading], E. Poynder and Son, 1911.
33 p. 21 cm.
KAS

Redon, France. Saint-Saveur (Benedictine abbey)

3227 **Cartulaire de l'Abbaye de Redon en Bretagne,** publié per M. Aurélien de

Courson. Paris, Imprimerie impériale, 1863.
cccxcv, 760 p. 30 cm.
KAS

Regensburg, Germany. St. Emmeram
(Benedictine abbey)

3228 **Coelestinus, abbot of St. Emmeram.**
Ratisbona monastica. Klösterliches Regenspurg, erster Theil. Oder Mausoleum, herrliches Grab des bayrischen Apostels und Blutzeugen S. Ammerami nebst der Histori . . . dieses Klosters . . . so biss 1650, dann . . . verfasset anno 1680 von Coelestino [Vogl] . . . nunmehro vermehret und biss auf das Jahr 1752 fortgesetzet durch Joannem Baptistam [Kraus]. 4. Aufl . . . Regensburg, J. V. Rädlmayer, 1752.
[24], 620, [16] p. illus. 22 cm.
KAS

3229 **Grill, Maria Regis, Schwester, O.S.B.**
Coelestin Steiglehner, letzter Fürstabt von St. Emmeramm zu Regensburg. München, Selbstverlag der Bayerischen Benediktinerakademie, 1937.
xiv, 131 p. port. 25 cm.
KAS

3230 **Kraus, Andreas.**
Die translatio S. Dionysii Areopagitae von St. Emmeram in Regensburg. München, Verlag der Bayerischen Akademie der Wissenschaften, 1971.
70 p. 22 cm.
MnCS

3231 **Kraus, Johann Baptist, O.S.B.**
Liber probationum; sive, Bullae summorum pontificum, diplomata imperatorum et regum . . . quae ad historiam . . . S. Emmerami Ratisbonae maxime spectant. Ratisbonae, J. V. Raedlmayer, 1752.
[28], 563, [16] p. 22 cm.
KAS

3232 **Piendl, Max.**
Die Bibliotheken zu St. Emmeram in Regensburg. Kallmünz, M. Lassleben, 1971.
viii, 101 p. 32 plates, 24 cm.
MnCS

3233 **Piendl, Max.**
St. Emmeram zu Regensburg, ehemalige Benediktinerabtei. 5. neubearb. Aufl. München, Schnell und Steiner, 1975.
22 p. illus. 17 cm.

3234 **Ziegler, Walter.**
Das Benediktinerkloster St. Emmeram zu Regensburg in der Reformationszeit. Kallmünz, M. Lassleben, 1970.

264 p. 24 cm.
MnCS

Regensburg, Germany. St. Jakob
(Benedictine abbey)

3234a **Mai, Paul.**
Das Schottenkloster St. Jakob zu Regensburg im Wandel der Zeiten.
(*In* his: 100 Jahre Priesterseminar in St. Jakob zu Regensburg, 1872–1972. Regensburg, 1972. p. 6–36)
MnCS

Regensburg, Germany. Weih St. Peter
(Benedictine abbey)

3235 **Breatnach, P. A.**
Die Regensburger Schottenlegende. München, Arbeo-Gesellschaft, 1977.
324 p. (Münchener Beiträge, 27)
MnCS

3235a **Quomodo monasterium S. Petri apud Ratisbonam fundatum est.** MS. Vienna, Nationalbibliothek, codex 3347, f.1r–26r. Folio. Saec. 15.
Microfilm: MnCH proj. no. 16,617

Reichenau, Germany (Benedictine abbey)

3236 **Das alte necrologium von Reichenau im facsimile,** hrsg. und mit einem Commentar versehen von Dr. Ferdinand Keller. Zürich, Meyer Zeiler, 1848.
[37]–68 p. 26 cm. facsims. 29 cm. (Antiquarische Gesellschaft in Zürich. Mitteilungen, Bd. 6, Heft 2)
KAS

3236a **Berno von Reichenau.**
Die Briefe des Abtes Bern von Reichenau [von] Franz-Josef Schmale. Stuttgart, W. Kohlhammer [1961].
vii, 78 p. 24 cm.
German or Latin
MnCS

3237 **Beyrle, Konrad, ed.**
Die Kultur der Abtei Reichenau. München, Mucher, 1925.
2 v. illus.
MnCS; MoCo

3238 **Brambach, Wilhelm.**
Die Reichenauer Sängerschule; Beiträge zur Geschichte der Gelehrsamkeit und zur Kenntniss mittelalterlicher Musikhandschriften. Leipzig, O. Harrassowitz, 1888; Nendeln, Kraus Reprint, 1968.
43 p. facsim. 23 cm.
PLatS

3239 **Classen, Peter, ed.**
Die Gründungsurkunden der Reichenau. Sigmaringen, Jan Thorbecke Verlag, 1977.

88 p. 24 cm.
MnCS

3240 **Dodwell, Charles Reginald.**
Reichenau reconsidered; a reassessment
of the place of Reichenau in Ottonian art.
London, Warburg Institute, 1965.
x, 108 p. 12 plates. 25 cm.
NcBe; PLatS

3241 **Knoepfli, Albert.**
Kunstgeschichte des Bodenseeraumes.
Konstanz, J. Thorbecke, 1961–
v. illus., plates (part col.) 24 cm.
InStme

3242 **Maurer, Helmut.**
Die Abtei Reichenau: neue Beitr. z.
Geschichte u. Kultur d. Inselkloster . . .
Sigmaringen, Thorbecke [1974].
622 p. 112 illus., graphs. 24 cm.
MnCS

3243 **Ohem, Gallus, O.S.B.**
Chronik des Klosters Reichenau. Mit
colorirten Wappen. MS. Benediktinerabtei
St. Paul im Lavantthal, Austria, codex
11/2. 254 f. Quarto. Saec. 15.
Microfilm: MnCH proj. no. 11,746

3244 **Ohem, Gallus, O.S.B.**
Chronicon Augiae divitis (Reichenau).
MS. Benediktinerabtei St. Paul im Lavant-
thal, Austria, codex 8/2, part I. Folio. Saec.
16.
Microfilm: MnCH proj. no. 11,741

Reichenbach, Germany (Benedictine abbey)

3245 **De Reichenbacensis monasterii in Nigra
Silva** fundatione et donationibus. MS.
Benediktinerabtei St. Paul im Lavant-
thal, Austria, codex 15/1. 18 f. Quarto.
Saec. 12.
Microfilm: MnCH proj. no. 11,676

3246 **Excerpta e libro traditionum monasterii
Reichenbacensis.** Saec. xii.
(*In* Monumenta Boica. Monachii, 1763–
1829. v. 14, p. 406–428)
PLatS

3247 **Liber ordinationis et reformationis con-
suetudinum regularium** in monasterio
Reichenbachensi S. Mariae Virginis
O.S.B. Ratisponensis dioeceis. MS.
Vienna, Nationalbibliothek, codex 12832,
f.1r–30v. Quarto. Saec. 15.
Microfilm: MnCH proj. no. 20,024

Reinhardsbrunn, Saxony (Benedictine abbey)

3248 **Möller, Johann Heinrich.**
Urkundliche Geschichte des Klosters
Reinhardsbrunn . . . Gotha, J. G. Müller,
1843.

vi, 240 p. 23 cm.
KAS

Rejhrad, Czechoslovakia (Benedictine abbey)

3249 **Dukik, Beda Franziskus, O.S.B.**
Geschichte des Benediktiner-Stiftes Ray-
gern im Markgrafthum Mähren . . .
Brünn, Carl Winiker, 1849–1868.
2 v. illus., tables. 23 cm.
KAS

Remiremont, France (Benedictine abbey)

3250 **Hlawitschka, Eduard.**
Studien zur Aebtissennenreihe von Remiremont (7.-13. Jah.). Saarbrücken, 1963.
181 p. illus. 24 cm.
PLatS

3251 **Liber memorialis von Remiremont,**
bearb. von Eduard Hlawitschka, Karl
Schmid, und Gerd Tellenbach. Dublin,
Weidmann, 1970.
2 v. facsims. 30 cm.
Text in Latin. Introd. and notes in Ger-
man.
InStme

Rheinau, Switzerland (Benedictine abbey)

3252 **Dissertatio de Welfis monasterii Rhe-
naugiensis fundatoribus,** cum eorum
iconibus, ex veteri manuscripto Wingar-
tensi. MS. Benediktinerabtei St. Paul im
Lavantthal, Austria, codex 78/2. 246 f.
Folio. Saec. 18.
Microfilm: MnCH proj. no. 11,842

3253 **Erb, August.**
Das Kloster Rheinau und die helvetische
Revolution (1798–1803 resp. 1809). Zürich,
Keller & Müller [1895].
xii, 248 p. plan. 24 cm.
KAS

3254 **Fietz, Hermann.**
Kloster Rheinau. [Zürich] 1932.
47 p. illus. 29 cm.
InStme

3255 **Muos, Beatus, O.S.B.**
De jure advocatiae tutelaris antiquissimi,
liberi ac exempti monasterii Rhenoviensis
Beatae Mariae in Coelum Assumptae Ordinis s.p.n. Benedicti Constantiensis
dioecesis in Helvetia tractatus historico-
juridicus . . . publicae discussioni expo-
suerunt praeside P. Beato Muos . . . p.p.
Januarius Dangel, Benedictus Kahé,
Maurus Werner, Sebastianus Greutter
O.S.B. Lucernae, typis H. I. N. Hautt,
1748.
[10], 134, [22] p. 21 cm.
PLatS

Ribemont, France. St. Nicolas de Prés (Benedictine abbey)

3256 **Stein, Henri.**
Cartulaire de l'ancienna Abbaye de Saint Nicolas des Prés sous Ribemont . . . Saint-Quentin, C. Poette, 1884.
231 p. 25 cm.
KAS

Richardton, N.D. Assumption Abbey
see
Assumption Abbey, Richardton, N.D.

Rio de Janeiro, Brazil. Mosteiro de Sao Bento

3257 **Silva-Nigra, Clemente Maria da, O.S.B.**
Frei Bernardo de Sao Bento, o arquiteto seiscentista do Rio de Janeiro. Salvador, Bahia, Tip. Beneditina, 1950.
120, 27 p. illus. 50 plates, 33 cm.
MnCS

Ripoll, Spain. S. Juan de les Abadeses (abbey of Benedictine nuns)

3258 **Consueta de l'esglesia i monestir de Sant Joan de les Abadesses, II.** MS. Vich, Spain, codex 212. 284 f. Quarto. Saec. 15.
Microfilm: MnCH proj. no. 31,290

Ripoll, Spain. S. Maria (Benedictine abbey)

3259 **Rico, Francisco.**
Signos e indicios en la portada de Ripoll. Olibae abbatis carmina quae exstant de rebus monasterii Rivipullensis edidit A.M. Mundo . . . Barcelona, Fundación Juan March, 1976.
68 p. plates. 22 cm.
MnCS

Romainmotier, Switzerland (Benedictine abbey)

3260 **Liber cartularis S. Petri principis apostolorum Monasterii Romanensis.** Bibliothèque cantonale et universitaire Lausanne ms. 5011. Einleitung von Albert Brukner. Amsterdam, North-Holland Publishing Company, 1962.
xx, 29 p. plates (facsims.) 31 cm.
MnCS

Rome, Italy. Collegio di Sant'Anselmo

3261 **Bachofen, Charles Augustine, O.S.B.**
Der Mons Aventinus zu Rom und die Benediktiner Klöster auf demselben.
(*In* Studien und Mittheilungen aus dem Benediktinerorden. Jahrg. 18(1897), p. 663–669; 19(1898), p. 69–78, 303–310, 460–476, 648–661)

Offprint.
53 p. 21 cm.
KAS; OrStB

3262 **Marra, Luigi Taddeo della, O.S.B.**
Il Collegio Sant'Anselmo in Roma e il Cardinale Dusmet. Catania, C. Galatola, 1901.
107 p. 29 cm.
MnCS

3263 **Oesterle, Gerard, O.S.B.**
Beuron und die Anfänge des Studienkollegs St. Anselm in Rom.
(*In* Beuron, 1863–1963; Festschrift . . . Beuron, 1963. p. 268–328)
PLatS

Rome, Italy. San Bonifacio (Benedictine abbey)

3264 **Nerinus, Felice Maria.**
De templo et coenobio sanctorum Bonifacii et Alexii historica monumenta. Romae, Typographia Apollinea, 1752.
xxxi, [11], 600 p. illus. 30 cm.
San Bonifacio was first a Benedictine abbey, then became Saint'Alessio, Premonstratensian, then a Hieronymite abbey.
KAS

Rome, Italy. San Gregorio (Benedictine abbey)

3265 **Gibelli, Alberto.**
Dell'antichissima chiesa abbaziale dei SS. Andrea e Gregorio. Roma, 1878.
MoCo

3265a **Léonard, Emile J.**
Deux lettres de Dom Costantino Gaietani, fondateur du premier collège Bénédictin de Rome, a Richeleu et a Mazarin. Ligugé, E. Aubin, 1924.
9 p. 26 cm.
"Extrait de la Revue Mabillon, janvier, 1924."
KAS

Rome, Italy. San Paolo fuori le Mura (Benedictine abbey)

3266 **Kalendarium sacrosanctae patriarchalis basilicae Sancti Pauli** via Ostiensi ritu monastico . . . Romae.
v. 20 cm.
PLatS (1855, 1870)

3267 **Martinez-Fazio, L.M., S.J.**
La segunda basilica de San Pablo extramuros; estudios sobre su fundación. Roma, Università Gregoriana editrice, 1972.
xx, 395 p. 25 cm.
PLatS

3268 **Ordo peragendi opus Dei in sacrosancta patriarchali basilica Sancti Pauli de**

Urbe et adnexis ecclesiis et oratoriis ritu monastico . . . Sublaci, Typis Proto-Coenobii.
v. 16 cm.
MnCS

3269 **Ridolfini, Cecilia Pericoli.**
St. Paul's outside the walls, Rome. Bologna, Poligrafici il Resto del Carlino, 1967.
31 p. illus., plates (part col.) 31 cm.
MnCS

Rott am Inn, Bavaria (Benedictine abbey)

3270 **Geiss, Ernest.**
Urkunden zur Geschichte des Klosters Rott in Regesten gebracht und mitgetheilt. München, C. Wolf'schen, 1852.
105 p. 24 cm.
KAS

Rouen, France. Saint-Ouen (Benedictine abbey)

3271 **Chronique des Abbés de Saint-Ouen de Rouen** publiée pour la première fois . . . par Francisque Michel. Rouen, E. Frère, 1840.
vii, 98 p. 22 cm.
KAS

3272 **Daoust, Joseph.**
L'Abbaye royal de Saint-Ouen. [Rouen], Imro–Editions [1966].
[38] p. illus. 24 cm.

Ruinen, Netherlands (Benedictine abbey)

3273 **Arts, Antonius Johannes Maria.**
Die stichting te Ruinen.
(*In* his: Het dubbelklooster Dikninge. Assen, 1945. p. 24–35)
MnCS

Saalfeld, Germany (Benedictine abbey)

3274 **Schamel, Johann Martin.**
Historische Beschreibung . . . Memleben . . . [und] Historische Beschreibung der vornehmen Abtei und Benediktiner-Klosters auf dem Peters-Berge zu Salfeld. Naumberg, Johann Christian Martini, 1729.
[93]–188 p. 21 cm.
KAS

3275 **Thun, Georg, O.S.B.**
Das Lehenbuch des Abtes Georgius Thun zu Saalfeld, 1497–1526. Hrsg. von Ernst Koch. Jena, Gustav Fischer, 1913.
lxxx, 335 p. 22 cm.
MnCS

Säben, Italy (abbey of Benedictine nuns)

3276 **Hagemeyer, Oda, O.S.B.**
Säben, ein stiller Blickwinkel europäischer Geschichte. Bozen, Verlagsanstalt Athesia [1968].
86 p. illus. 20 cm.
PLatS

Säckingen, Germany (Benedictine abbey)

3277 **Schaubinger, Klemens.**
Geschichte des Stiftes Säckingen und seines Begründers, des heiligen Fridolin. Einsiedeln, Karl und Nikolaus Benziger, 1852.
vi, 183 p. 23 cm.
PLatS

Sacred Heart Convent, Yankton, S.D.

3278 **Duratschek, Claudia, Sister, O.S.B.**
Under the shadow of his wings; history of the Sacred Heart Convent of Benedictine Sisters, Yankton, South Dakota, 1880–1970. [Aberdeen, S.D., North Plains Press, 1971].
368 p. illus., ports. 24 cm.
InStme; MnCS; MoCo; SdYa

3279 **Jäger, Moritz, O.S.B.**
Schwester Gertrud Leupi, 1825–1904, Gründerin der drei Benediktinerinnen-klöster: Maria Rickenbach, Yankton, Marienburg. [Freiburg, Schweiz], Kanisius Verlag [1974].
200 p. plates, ports. 19 cm.
MnCS; SdYa

3280 **Ranek, Jeanne, Sister, O.S.B.**
Research report of the 1972–73 Sacred Heart Convent survey team. Yankton, S.D., Sacred Heart Convent, 1974.
63 p.
SdYa

Sacro Speco, Subiaco, Italy
see
Subiaco, Italy. Sacro Speco

Sahagun, Spain (Benedictine abbey)

3281 **Gonzalez Garcia, Manuel.**
Aspectos de la vida del monasterio de Sahagun hast el año 1100. León, Centro de Estudios e investigacion "San Isidoro," 1968.
103 p. fold. map. 25 cm.
MnCS

3282 **Minguez Fernandez, José Maria.**
Colección diplomatica del monasterio de Sahagun (siglos IX y X). León, Centro de

Estudios e Investigación "San Isidoro," 1976.
505 p. 25 cm.
MnCS

St. Alban's Abbey, England

3283 **Amundesham, Johannes, O.S.B.**
Annales Monasterii S. Albani, a Johanne Amundesham, monacho, ut videtur, conscripti (A.D. 1421–1440). Quibus praefigitur Chronicon rerum gestarum in Monasterio S. Albani (A.D. 1422–1431) a quodam auctore ignoto compilatum. Ed. by Henry Thomas Riley. London, Longmans, Green and Co., 1870–71.
2 v. 25 cm.
ILSP; InStme; PLatS

3284 **Carr, J. W.**
The abbey church of St. Alban's. London, Seeley, Jackson & Halliday, 1877.
45 p. illus. 32 cm.
WBenS

3285 **Gasquet, Francis Aidan, O.S.B.**
Abbot Wallingford; an enquiry into the charges made against him and his monks. London, Sands & Co. [1912?].
79 p. plates, plan. 18 cm.
PLatS

3286 **Gasquet, Francis Aidan, O.S.B.**
The making of St. Alban's shrine. [n.p., n.d.]
8 p. illus. 21 cm.
A paper read before the Guild of SS. Gregory and Luke at St. Alban's.
KAS; PLatS

3287 **Gasquet, Francis Aidan, O.S.B.**
Monastic life in the Middle Ages . . . London, G. Bell and Sons, 1922.
vii, 342 p. 20 cm.
PLatS

3288 **Jenkins, Claude.**
The monastic chronicler and the early school of St. Alban's. London, Society for Promoting Christian Knowledge; New York, Macmillan Co., 1922.
98 p. 20 cm.
InStme; MnCS; NdRi

3289 **Jessopp, Augustus.**
Studies by a recluse, in cloister, town, and country. London, T. F. Unwin, 1893.
xix, 281 p.
ILSP

3290 **Levett, Ada Elisabeth.**
Studies in manorial history. Edited by H. M. Cam, M. Coate [and] L. S. Sutherland. [London] Oxford University Press [1963].
xviii, 399 p. fold. map, tables. 23 cm.
First published 1938.
MnCS; PLatS

3291 **Liddell, Edward.**
St. Alban's Abbey . . . illustrated by F. G. Kitton. London, Isbister & Co., 1897.
58 p. illus., plates. 18 cm.
MnCS

3292 **Neale, James.**
The abbey church of Saint Alban, Hertfordshire. London [1877].
xii, 36 p. 60 plates. 57 cm.
MnCS

3293 **Newcome, Peter.**
The history of the ancient and royal foundation, called the Abbey of St. Alban, in the county of Hertford, from the founding thereof, in 793, to its dissolution, in 1539 . . . London, Printed for the author by J. Nichols, sold by Messrs. White, 1795.
xiii, 547 p. plates, fold. map, 2 fold. plans. 28 x 22 cm.
CaBMi; KAS; MnCS

3294 **Paris, Matthew, O.S.B.**
Matthaei Parisiensis, monachi Sancti Albani, Chronica majora. Edited by Henry Richards Luard . . . London, Longman & Co., 1872–83.
7 v. 26 cm. (Great Britain. Public Record Office. Rerum britannicarum medii aevi scriptores . . . no. 57).
ILSP; MnCS; PLatS

3295 **Paris, Matthew, O.S.B.**
Ex libro de gestis abbatum S. Albani.
(*In* Monumenta Germaniae historica. Scriptores. Hannoverae. 1888. t. 28, p. 434–440)
MnCS

3296 **Rishanger, William, O.S.B.**
Willelmi Rishanger, quondam monachi S. Albani, et quorundam anonymorum, chronica et annales, regnantibus Henrico Tertio et Edwardo Primo. Edited by Henry Thomas Riley . . . London, Longman, Green, Longman, Roberts, and Green, 1865.
xlii, 571 p. 26 cm.
ILSP; PLatS

3297 **Walsingham, Thomas, O.S.B.**
Gesta abbatum monaterii Sancti Albani, a Thoma Walsingham, regnante Ricardo Secundo, ejusdem ecclesiae praecentore, compilata. Edited by Henry Thomas Riley. London, Longmans, Green, and Co., 1867–69.
3 v. 25 cm.
ILSP; InStme; PLatS

3298 **Walsingham, Thomas, O.S.B.**
The St. Alban's chronicle 1406–1420, edited from Bodley ms. 462 by V. H. Galbraith. Oxford, The Clarendon Press, 1937.

lxxv, 164 p. 4 facsims. 23 cm.
"Life of Thomas Walsingham": p. xxxvi–
xlv.
PLatS

3299 **Williams, Laurence Frederic Rush-
brook.**
History of the Abbey of St. Alban. London, New York, Longmans, Green and Co.,
1917.
xiii, 251 p. plans. 23 cm.
KAS; MnCS; NdRi; WBens

Saint-Alire, Clermont, France
see
Clermont, France. Saint-Alire

Saint-Amand, Rouen, France
see
Rouen, France. Saint-Amand

**Saint-Amand-les-Eaux, France
(Benedictine abbey)**

3300 **Catalogus abbatum S. Amandi Elnonen-
sis.**
(*In* Monumenta Germaniae historica.
Scriptores. Hannoverae, 1881. t. 13, p.
386–388)
MnCS; PLatS

3301 **Gislebertus, monk of Saint-Amand-les-
Eaux.**
Carmen de incendio S. Amandi Elnonen-
sis, edente L. C. Bethmann.
(*In* Monumenta Germaniae historica.
Scriptores. Hannoverae, 1854. t. 11, p.
409–432)
MnCS; PLatS

3302 **Platelle, Henri.**
La justice seigneuriale de l'Abbaye de
Saint Amand; son organisation judiciare,
se procé dure et sa compétence du XIe au
XVIe siècle. Paris, Editions Béatrice-
Nauwelaerts, 1965.
462 p. fold. maps. 24 cm.
InStme

3303 **Platelle, Henri.**
Le temporel de l'Abbaye de Saint-Amand
des origines à 1340. Paris, Librairie
d'Argences, 1962.
350 p. fold. maps. 25 cm.
PLatS

Saint-André, Bruges, Belgium
see
Bruges, Belgium. Abbaye de Saint-André

Saint-André-le Haut, Vienne, France
see
Vienne, France. Saint-André-le-Haut

St. Andrew's Abbey, Cleveland, Ohio

3304 **Hruovský, Frantiek.**
Benediktínske Opátstvo sv. Andreja-
Svorada v Clevelande. Cleveland, Ohio,
Vydalo Opsátstvo sv. Andreja-Svorada,
1955.
105 p. illus., ports. 22 cm.
PLatS; OCLSta

3305 **The blessing of Jerome M. Koval,** coadjutor abbot of Saint Andrew Abbey at
the celebration of the Eucharist in the
Church of Saint Benedict, Cleveland,
Ohio, June 28, 1966.
unpaged. illus.(ports) 21 cm.
PLatS; OCLSta

**Saint Andrew's Convent,
Uniontown, Wash.**

3306 **Catalog des Benedictinerinnen-Klosters
St. Andreas in Sarnen** (Obwalden) und
seiner Filiale in America. Sarnen, Druck
von Jos. Müller, 1888.
12 p. 16 cm.
PLatS

Saint Andrew's Priory, Valyermo, Calif.

3307 **Armitage, Merle.**
Saint Andrew's Priory at Valyermo.
Photographs by Isabelle Armitage. [Yucca
Valley, Calif.], Manzanita Press, 1961.
[24] p. illus. 29 cm.
PLatS

3308 **O'Brien, Janice.**
Saint Andrew's Priory, Valyermo,
California. [Valyermo, Calif., St. Andrew's
Priory, 1966].
71 p. illus. 22 x 29 cm.
PLatS

**Saint Anselm's Abbey,
Manchester, N.H.**

3309 **History of the Catholic Church in the
New England States,** by Very Rev.
Wm. Bryne, Wm. A. Leahy [and others].
Boston, Hurd & Everts Co., 1899.
2 v. illus. 27 cm.
PLatS

3310 **Pfisterer, Raphael, O.S.B.**
Christian education; reveries on the
mural decorations of St. Anselm's College
chapel. Manchester, N.H. [n.p., n.d.].
unpaged. illus. 23 cm.
MnCS

3311 **Pfisterer, Raphael, O.S.B.**
Studio of Christian art. Manchester,
N.H., St. Anselm's College [192-?].
MnCS

St. Anselm's Abbey, Washington, D.C.

3312 **The Benedictine foundation at the Catholic University of America** in Washington. [n.p., 1923?].
11 p. illus. 24 cm.
Relates to the origins of St. Anselm's Abbey, Washington, D.C.
KAS

3313 **Ellis, John Tracy.**
You are the light of the world; sermon preached . . . at the solemn blessing of Right Reverend Alban Boultwood as first abbot of St. Anselm's Abbey, Washington, D.C. [in the] National Shrine of the Immaculate Conception, December 30, 1961.
8 leaves. 28 cm.
Reproduced from typed copy.
PLatS

Saint-Arnould, Metz, France
see
Metz, France. Saint-Arnould

Saint-Auban, Alsace (Benedictine priory)

3314 **Gilomen, Hans-Jörg.**
Die Grundherrschaft des Basler Cluniazenser-Priorates St. Alban im Mittelalter; ein Beitrag zur Wirtschaftsgeschichte am Oberrhein. Basel, Kommissionsverlag Friedrich Reeinhardt, 1977.
427 p. maps. 25 cm.
Diss.—Universität Basel, 1975.
MnCS

Saint-Aubin d'Angers
see
Angers, France. Saint-Aubin

Saint-Augustin, Limoges, France
see
Limoges, France. Saint-Augustin

St. Augustine's Abbey, Aurora, Ill.
see
Marmion Abbey, Aurora, Ill.

St. Augustine's Abbey, Canterbury, England

3315 **Boggis, Robert James Edmund.**
A history of St. Augustine's Monastery, Canterbury. Canterbury, Cross & Jackman, 1901.
196 p. fold. plan, facsims. 19 cm.
MnCS; MoCo; NdRi; PLatS

3316 **Emden, Alfred Brotherston.**
Donors of books to S. Augustine's Abbey, Canterbury. Oxford, Oxford Bibliographical Society, 1968.

viii, 46 p. 5 facsims. 25 cm.
MnCS

3317 **Gasquet, Francis Aidan, O.S.B.**
Monastic life in the Middle Ages . . . London, G. Bell and Sons, 1922.
vii, 342 p. 20 cm.
PLatS

3318 **James, Montague Rhodes.**
The ancient libraries of Canterbury and Dover. The catalogues of the libraries of Christ Church Priory and St. Augustine's Abbey of Canterbury . . . Now first collected and published with an introduction and identifications of the extant remains, by Montague Rhodes James. Cambridge, University Press, 1903.
xcv, 552 p. facsims. 22 cm.
InStme; MnCS; PLatS

3319 **Lincoln, Edward Frank.**
The story of Canterbury. London, Staples Press [1955].
160 p. illus. 21 cm.
PLatS

3320 **MacLear, G. F.**
St. Augustine's Canterbury. London, Wells, Gardner, Darton & Co., 1888.
86 p.
NdRi

3321 **Thomas of Elmham, O.S.B.**
Historia Monasterii S. Augustini Cantuariensis, by Thomas of Elmham, formerly monk and treasurer of that foundation. Ed. by Charles Hardwick . . . London, Longmans, Brown, Green, Longmans, and Roberts, 1858.
xxxv, 541 p. fold. facsim. 25 cm.
ILSP; InStme; PLatS

3322 **Thorne, William.**
William Thorne's Chronicle of Saint Augustine's Abbey, Canterbury, now rendered into English by A. H. Davis, with a preface by Professor A. Hamilton Thompson. Oxford, B. Blackwell, 1934.
lxii, 740 p. illus., fold. map. 24 cm.
InStme; KAS

St. Augustine's Abbey, Ramsgate, England

3323 **Parry, David, O.S.B.**
Benedictine heritage. Ramsgate, The Monastery Press, 1961.
44 p. 19 cm.
Chapter 7 is on St. Augustine's Abbey, Ramsgate.
MnCS; NdRi; PLatS

3324 **Parry, David, O.S.B.**
Monastic century: St. Augustine's Abbey, Ramsgate (1861–1961). [Tenbury Wells], Fowler Wright Books [1965].

142 p. 22 cm.
InStme; MnCS; NcBe; PLatS

3325 **Parry, David, O.S.B.**
Scholastic century; St. Augustine's Abbey School, Ramsgate, 1865–1965. [Tenbury Wells], Fowler Wright Books [1965].
101 p. illus. 23 cm.
InStme; KAS; MnCS; PLatS

St. Bees Priory, Egremont, England
see
Egremont, England. St. Bees Priory

St. Benedict, Or. Mount Angel Abbey
see
Mount Angel Abbey, St. Benedict, Or.

**St. Benedict Priory, Winnipeg, Man.,
Canada**

3326 **Hubicz, Edward M.**
The Benedictine Sisters.
(*In* his: Polish churches in Manitoba, London, 1960. p. 43–49)
PLatS

St. Benedict's Abbey, Atchison, Kans.

3327 **Heinz, Gerard, O.S.B.**
St. Benedict's Parish, Atchison, Kansas; an historical sketch, 1858–1908. Atchison, Kans., Abbey Student Press, St. Benedict's College [1908?].
[38] leaves. illus., ports. 26 cm.
KAM; KAS

3328 **Pusch, Edmung, O.S.B.**
A history of the Benedictines in Atchison, Atchison, Kans. [1951].
[7], 297 leaves. 29 cm.
Typescript
KAS

3329 **St. Benedict's Abbey, Atchison, Kans.**
Christ has a family in Atchison. [Atchison, Kans., Abbey Student Press, 1961?].
[14] p. chiefly illus. 27 cm.
KAS

3330 **St. Benedict's Abbey, Atchison, Kans.**
Latin and English of the monastic community prayers. Printed as manuscript for the use of the monks of St. Benedict's Abbey, Atchison, Kans. Atchison, Kans. Student Press, 1955.
79 p. 12 cm.
Cover title: Community prayers.
KAS

3331 **St. Benedict's Abbey, Atchison, Kans.**
A new monastery, St. Benedict's Abbey, Atchison, Kansas [1927].
19 p. illus. 18 cm.

Contains artist's conception of monastery and church.
KAS

St. Benedict's Abbey, Fort Augustus, Scotland

3332 **Fort Augustus Abbey,** past and present.
5th ed. Fort Augustus, Abbey Press, 1963.
24 p. illus. 19 cm.
PLatS

3333 **Hedley, John Cuthbert, O.S.B.**
New work and old ways; a sermon preached at the opening of the monastery and college of St. Benedict, at Fort Augustus, on August 26th, 1880, by the Right Rev. Bishop Hedley, O.S.B. London, Burns & Oates, 1880.
32 p. 23 cm.
KAS

St. Benedict's College, Atchison, Kans.

3334 **Hanson, Terance Maurice.**
A history of intercollegiate basketball at Saint Benedict's College from its initiation in 1919 through 1969.
[4], 150 p. 29 cm.
Photocopy of typescript.
Thesis (M.A.) – Southeast Missouri State College.
KAS

St. Benedict's Convent, Erie, Pa.

3335 **Sisters of Saint Benedict,** Erie, Pennsylvania, 1856–1931.
36 p. illus., ports. 32 cm.
PLatS; PErS

Saint-Benigne, Dijon, France
see
Dijon, France. Saint-Benigne

Saint-Benoît-du-Lac, Quebec, Canada

3336 **L'Abbaye de Saint-Benoît-du-Lac.**
[1953?].
[24] p. illus., 2 maps. 23 cm.
CaQStB; PLatS

3337 **L'Abbaye de Saint-Benoît-du-Lac.** 1962.
63 p. illus., plates, ports., map, plan. 22 cm.
KAS; MnCS; PLatS

3338 **Cérémonie de la bénédiction abbatiale du** . . . Odule Sylvain, O.S.B., abbé de Saint-Benoît-du-Lac . . . le 18 octobre, 1952. [Montréal, Presses de Pierre des Marais, 1952?]
54 p. 23 cm.

Liturgical text in Latin and French.
MnCS

Saint-Benoît-sur-Loire, France (Benedictine abbey)

3339 **Aubert, Marcel.**
L'église de Saint-Benoît-sur-Loire. Paris, Société générale d'imprimerie et d'édition, 1931.
90 p. illus., plates, fold. plan. 23 cm.
KAS

3340 **Bailey, Terence, ed.**
The Fleury play of Herod. Toronto, Pontifical Institute of Mediaeval Studies, 1965.
72 p. music (score) 22 cm.
Latin text produced twice, first with music, second with English translation on facing page.
Written ca. 1200 and used at Saint-Benoît-sur-Loire in Fleury.
Taken from ms. 201 in the Orleans municipal library.
PLatS

3340a **Barker-Benfield, B.C.**
A ninth-century manuscript from Fleury: Cato De senectute cum Macrobio.
(*In* Medieval learning and literature; essays presented to Richard W. Hunt. Oxford, 1976. p. 145–165)
MnCS

3341 **Brettes, Ferdinand.**
Catena Floriacensis de existentia corporis Sancti Benedicti in Galliis, connexa a Brettes et Cuissard. Paris, Victor Palmé, 1880.
284 p. fold. plate. 24 cm.
MnCS

3342 **Christophe, Jacques.**
Saint Benoît par monts et par vaux. Paris, Spes, 1969.
160 p.
MnCS

3343 **Consuetudines Floriacenses saeculi tertii decimii,** edidit Anselmus Davril. Sieburg, F. Schmitt, 1976.
lxxxix, 507 p. illus., facsim. 25 cm. (Corpus consuetudinum monasticarum, t. 9)
InStme; MnCS; PLatS

3344 **Courcelle, Pierre.**
Fragments patristiques de Fleury-sur-Loire.
(*In* Mélanges dédiés à mémoire de Félix Grat. Paris, 1949. v. 2, p. 145–158)
PLatS

3345 **Donnat, Lin.**
Saint-Benoît-sur-Loire et ses tresors. Paris, Publications d'art et d'histoire, 1966.
93 p.
MnCS

3346 **Leccisotti, Tommaso Domenico, O.S.B.**
Le réliquie di Fleury.
(*In* Il sepolcro di S. Benedetto. Montecassino, 1951. p. 215–224)
PLatS

3347 **Leclercq, Henri, O.S.B.**
Saint-Benoît-sur-Loire: les reliques, le monastère, l'eglise. Paris, Letouzey, 1925.
159 p. illus. 19 cm.
MnCS

3348 **Vidier, Alexandre Charles Philippe.**
L'historiographie à Saint-Benoît-sur-Loire et les miracles de saint Benoît. Ouvrage posthume revu et annoté par les soins des moines de l'Abbaye de Saint-Benoît de Fleury. Paris, Editions A. et J. Picard, 1965.
313 p. facsims. 25 cm.
"Thèse . . . soutenue . . . à l'Ecole des Chartes en 1898."
InStme; MnCS

Saint-Bertin, France (Benedictine abbey)

3349 **Dehaisnes, Chrétien César Auguste.**
Les annales de Saint-Bertin et de Saint-Vaast, suivies de fragments d'une chronique inédite . . . Paris, Mme. Va J. Renouard, 1871.
xviii, 472 p. 24 cm.
KAS

3350 **Ganshof, François L.**
Notes critiques sur les Annales Bertiiniani.
(*In* Mélanges dédiés à la mèmoire de Félix Grat. Paris, 1949. v. 2, p. 159–174)
PLatS

3351 **Morand, François.**
Appendice au cartulaire de l'Abbaye de Saint-Bertin. Paris, Imprimerie Impériale, 1867.
xviii, 111 p. 29 cm.
KAS

Saint-Chaffre, Monastier, France
see
Monastier, France. Saint-Chaffre

Saint-Denis, France (Benedictine abbey)

3352 **L'armure et les lettres de Jeanne d'Arc;** documents conservés à l'Abbaye de Saint-Denis et aux archives de la famille d'Arc du Lys. Annotés par Charles Roessler. Paris, A. Picard & Fils, 1910.
42 p. facsims. 23 cm.
MnCS

3353   **Ayzac, Félicie Marie Emilie d'.**
Histoire de l'Abbaye de Saint-Denis en
France. Paris, Imprimerie Impériale,
1860–61.
2 v. 24 cm.
InStme; PLatS

3354   **Crosby, Sumner McKnight.**
The apostle bas-relief at Saint-Denis.
New Haven, Yale University Press, 1972.
xvi, 116 p. 86 p. of illus. 26 cm.
MnCS

3355   **François, Michel.**
Les rois de France et les traditions de
l'Abbaye de Saint-Denis à la fin du XVe
siècle.
(*In* Mélanges dédiés à la mémoire de
Félix Grat. Paris, 1946. v. 1, p. 368–384)
PLatS

3356   **Lebel, Germaine Marie Léonie.**
Histoire administrative, économique et
financière de l'Abbaye de Saint-Denis . . .
Paris, Imprimerie Administrative Cen-
trale, 1935.
vii, 431 p. tables. 25 cm.
Thèse – Univ. de Paris.
MnCS

3357   **Levavesseur, Fernand.**
La basilique de Saint-Denys; guide du
visiteur. 2. éd. [Paris], J. Mersch, 1962.
vi, 111 p. illus. 18 cm.
MnCS

3358   **Montesquiou-Fezensac, Blaise.**
Le trésor de Saint-Denis: inventaire de
1634. Paris, A. et J. Picard, 1973.
333 p. 29 cm.
MnCS

3359   **Panofsky, Erwin.**
Architecture gothique et pensée scholastique . . . Traduction et postface de Pierre
Bourdieu. [Paris] Editions de Minuit
[1967].
217 p. illus. 22 cm.
PLatS

3360   **Rockwell, Anne F.**
Glass, stones & crown: the Abbé Suger
and the building of St. Denis. London,
Macmillan, 1968.
81 p. illus. 25 cm.
InFer; MnCS

Saint-Denis, Nogent-le-Rotrou, France
see
Nogent-le-Retrou, France. Saint-Denis

St. Dogmaels Abbey, Wales
3361   **Pritchard, Emily M.**
The history of St. Dogmaels Abbey, together with her cells, Pill, Caldey and Glas-

careg, and the mother abbey of Tiron . . .
London, Blades, East & Blades, 1907.
241 p. illus., plates, fold. map. 26 cm.
CaBMi; MnCS; MoCo

St. Edmundsbury, England
see
Bury St. Edmunds Abbey, England

Saint-Étienne, Vaux, France
see
Vaux, France. Saint-Étienne

Saint-Eustace, Flavingy-sur-Moselle, France
see
Flavingy-sur-Moselle, France. Saint-Eustace

Saint-Evroult-d'Ouche (Benedictine abbey)
3362   **Wolter, Hans.**
Ordericus Vitalis; ein Beitrag zur
kluniazensischen Geschichtsschreibung.
Wiesbaden, F. Steiner, 1955.
viii, 252 p. 25 cm.
MnCS; PLatS

**Saint-Fiacre-en-Erie, France
(Benedictine abbey)**
3363   **Dubois, Jacques, O.S.B.**
Une sanctuaire monastique en moyen-
age: Saint-Fiacre-en-Brie. Genève,
Librairie Droz, 1976.
371 p. 22 cm.
MnCS

Saint-Florentin, Bonneval, France
see
Bonneval, France. Saint-Florentin

St. Gall, Switzerland (Benedictine abbey)
3364   **Bauer, Hermann.**
Die Stiftskirche St. Gallen . . . St.
Gallen, Verlag der Leobuchhandlung
[1967].
unpaged. chiefly illus. 23 cm.
Text in English.
PLatS

3365   **Büttner, Heinrich.**
Lorsch und St. Gallen in der Frühzeit; 2
Vorträge von Heinrich Büttner und Johan-
nes Duft . . . Konstanz, Thorbecke [1965].
45 p. 21 cm.
MnCS; PLatS

3366   **Conradus de Fabaria,** 13th cent.
Casuum S. Galli continuatio III.
(*In* Monumenta Germaniae historica.
Scriptores. Stuttgart, 1963. t. 2, p. 163–
183)
PLatS

3367 **De viris illustribus monasterii S. Galli libri tres.** Anno Domini 1606. MS. Vienna, Schottenstift, codex 616. 177 f. Quarto. Saec. 17.
Microfilm: MnCH proj. no. 4276

3368 **Duft, Johannes.**
Hochfeste im Gallus-Kloster; die Miniaturen im Sacramentarium Codex 341 (11. Jahrhundert), mit Texten aus der Stiftsbibliothek Sankt Gallen. Beuron, Beuroner Kunstverlag [1963].
81 p. plates (facsims) 23 cm.
MnCS; PLatS

3369 **Duft, Johannes.**
Notker der Arzt; Klostermedizin und Mönchsarzt im frühmittel-alterlichen St. Gallen. St. Gallen, Verlag der Buchdruckerei Ostschweiz, 1972.
68 p. illus.
MoCo

3370 **Duft, Johannes, ed.**
Studien zum St. Galler Klosterplan. St. Gallen, Fehr, 1962.
302 p. illus., map, plans, 24 cm.
InStme; PLatS

3371 **Greith, Carl Johann.**
Geschichte der altirischen Kirche und ihrer Verbindung mit Rom, Gallien und Alemannien (von 430–630) als Einleitung in die Geschichte des Stifts St. Gallen. Freiburg im Breisgau, Herder, 1867.
462 p.
MoCo

3372 **Hafner, Wolfgang, O.S.B.**
Der St. Galler Klosterplan im Lichte von Hildemars Regelkommentar.
(*In* Duft, Johannes. Studien zum St. Galler Klosterplan. 1962. p. 177–192)
PLatS

3373 **Hallinger, Kassius, O.S.B.**
Die römischen Ordines von Lorsch, Murbach und St. Gallen.
(*In* Universitas . . . Festschrift für Bischof Albert Stohr. Mainz, 1960. v. 1, p. 466–477)
PLatS

3374 **Henggeler, Rudolf, O.S.B.**
Monasticon-benedictinum Helvetiae. Zug, Eberhard Kalt-Zehnder, 1929–
v. 32 cm.
InStme; MnCS; PLatS

3375 **Horn, Walter.**
The plan of St. Gall; a study of the architecture & economy of, & life in a paradigmatic Carolingian monastery, by Walter Horn and Ernest Born. With a foreword by Wolfgang Braunfels, a translation into English by Charles W. Jones of the directives of Adelhard, 753–826, the ninth abbot of Corbie, and with a note by A. Hunter Dupree on the significance of the Plan of St. Gall in the history of measurement. Berkeley, University of California Press, 1979. (California studies in the history of art, 19).
3 v. illus., plans. 37 cm.
MnCS; PLatS; InStme

3376 **Der karolingische Klosterplan von St. Gallen (Schweiz).** The Carolingian plan of St. Gall Abbey (Switzerland). Facsimile-Wiedergabe in acht Farben, mit einer Monographie: Der St. Galler Klosterplan, von Hans Reinhardt. [Mit Beiträgen von Dietrich Schwarz, Johannes Duft und Hans Bessler . . . und zehn Bildzeichungen von Hans Bühler]. St. Gallen, Kommissionsverlag der Fehr'schen Buchhandlung, 1952.
41 p. illus. and portfolio (folded col. plan, 116 x 81 cm.) 31 cm.
PLatS; MnCS

3377 **Keller, Ferdinand.**
Bauriss des Klosters St. Gallen, vom Jahr 820. Im Facsimile hrsg. und erläutert von Ferdinand Keller. Zürich, Meier & Zeller, 1844.
41 p. 30 cm. Plan inserted, 67 x 89 cm., folded to 29 x 23 cm.
Issued in folder.
MnCS; PLatS

3378 **Knoepfli, Albert.**
Kunstgeschichte des Bodenseeraumes. Konstanz, J. Thorbecke, 1961–
v. illus., plates (part col.) 24 cm.
InStme

3378a **Leclercq, Henri, O.S.B.**
Saint Gall.
168 cols. illus., facsims. 28 cm.
(*In* Dictionnaire d'archéologie chrétienne et liturgie, t. 6, col. 80–248)
Includes: Le plan de Saint Gall [with folded illus. of plan]., col. 86–106.
MnCS; PLatS

3379 **Mietlich, Karl.**
Festschrift zum Jubiläum der ersten Erwähnung Elggs in einer Schenkungsurkunde des Klosters St. Gallen vom 20. August 760. 2. verb. Aufl. Elgg, Volksverlag Elgg, 1960.
96 p. illus. 18 x 24 cm.
MnCS

3380 **Mocquereau, André, O.S.B.**
De la clivis épisématique dans les manuscrits de Saint-Gall.
(*In* Mélanges offerts à M. Emile Chatelain. Paris, 1910. p. 508–530)
PLatS

3381 **Müller, Iso, O.S.B.**
Die Altar-tituli des Klosterplanes.
(*In* Duft, Johannes. Studien zum St.
Galler Klosterplan. 1962. p. 129–176)
PLatS

3382 **Müller, Walter.**
Die Abgaben von Todes wegen in der
Abtei St. Gallen. Köln, Böhlau, 1961.
vii, 111 p. 23 cm.
MnCS

3383 **Müller, Walter.**
Ein Auflassungs- und Investitursymbol
des Klosters St. Gallen: die schwarze
Kappe. Zürich, Juris Druck Verlag, 1972.
55 p. 20 cm.
MnCS

3384 **Müller, Walter.**
Landsatzung und Landmandat der
Fürstabtei St. Gallen . . . 15. bis 18. Jahr-
hundert. St. Gallen, Fehr, 1971.
xx, 340 p. 23 cm.
MnCS

3385 **Munding, Emmanuel, O.S.B.**
Das Verzeichnis der St. Galler Heiligen-
leben und ihrer Handschriften in Codex
sang. 566 . . . Leipzig, O. Harrassowitz,
1918.
xvi, 184 p. 23 cm.
MnCS

3386 **Ratpert, monk of St. Gall.**
Casus S. Galli.
(*In* Monumenta Germaniae historica.
Scriptores. Stuttgart, 1963. t. 2, p. 59–74)
PLatS; MnCS

3387 **Rüsch, Ernst Gerhard.**
Tuotilo, Mönch und Künstler; Quellen
zur Geschichte der Inklusen in der Stadt
St. Gallen. St. Gallen, Fehr, 1953.
89 p. plates. 23 cm.
MnCS

3388 **Salzgeber, Joachim, O.S.B.**
Die Klöster Einsiedeln und St. Gallen im
Barockzeitalter; historisch-soziologische
Studie. Münster in Westfalen, Aschendorff
[1967].
xix, 232 p. 25 cm.
InStme; PLatS

3389 **Scöverffy, Josef.**
St. Galler Dichter am Ende des 9. Jahr-
hunderts: Tropen und Anfänge der
Sequenzendichtung.
(*In* his: Die Annalen der lateinischen
Hymnendichtung. Berlin, 1964. v. 1, p.
262–312)
PLatS

3390 **Sonderegger, Stefan.**
Althochdeutsch in St. Gallen; Ergebnisse
und Probleme der althochdeutschen
Sprachüberlieferung in St. Gallen vom 8.

bis ins 12. Jahrhundert. St. Gallen, Verlag
Ostschweiz [1970].
184 p. facsims. 23 cm.
PLatS

3391 **Spillman, Kurt.**
Zwingli und die zürcherische Politik
gegenüber der Abtei St. Gallen. St. Gallen,
Fehr, 1965.
122 p. 23 cm.
MnCS

3392 **Staerkle, Paul.**
Die Rückermerke der älteren St. Galler
Urkunden. St. Gallen, Fehr, 1966.
83 p. 3 maps. 24 cm.
MnCS

3393 **Steiger, Karl.**
Der sog. Rorschacherhandel zwischen
Stift St. Gallen und Stadt Wil im Jahre
1733. St. Gallen, "Ostschweiz," 1933.
96 p. 20 cm.
MnCS

3394 **Url, Eberhard.**
Das mittelalterliche Geschichtswerk
"Casus sancti Galli." St. Gallen, Fehr,
1969.
79 p. facsims. 32 cm.
MnCS

St. Gall, Switzerland. Stiftsbibliothek

3395 **Bennett, Melba Berry.**
The abbey library of St. Gall, Switzer-
land. Privately printed. Palm Springs,
Calif., Welwood Murray Memorial
Library, 1965.
8 p. 23 cm.
KAS

3396 **Duft, Johannes.**
Irische Handschriften in der Stiftsbiblio-
thek zu St. Gallen.
(*In* Killer, Peter. Das Irland der Mönche.
Zurich, 1970. p. 29–43)
MnCS

3397 **Duft, Johannes, ed.**
Die Stiftsbibliothek Sankt Gallen: der
Barocksaal und seine Putten . . . Aufnah-
men von Siegfried Lauterwasser.
Konstanz, Jan Thorbecke [1961].
95 p. illus., plates. 23 cm.
MnCS; PLatS

3398 **Duft, Johannes.**
Stiftsbibliothek St. Gallen: Geschichte,
Barocksaal, Manuskripte. Uznach, Verlag
der Buchdr. Gebr. Oberholzer, 1967.
27 p. 4 plates. 20 cm.
PLatS

3399 **Heiligenkreuz, Austria (Cistercian
abbey).**
Der Bibliothekskatalog des Stiftes Heiligenkreuz vom Jahre 1374. Aus der Hand-

schrift von St. Gallen. Hrsg. von P. Gabriel Meier, O.S.B. Wien, Carl Gerold's Sohn, 1901.
17 p. 24 cm.
MnCS

3400 **St. Gallische Handschriften.** In Auszügen hrsg. von Gustav Scherer . . . St. Gallen, Huber und Comp., 1859.
92 p.
PLatS (microfilm)

St. Gall, Switzerland. Stiftsbibliothek. MS 193

3401 **Codex Sangallensis 193,** continens fragmenta plurium Prophetarum secundum translationem S. Hieronymi. Beuronae, Lipsae, prostat apud O. Harrassowitz, 1913.
14 p. plates. 40 cm. (Spicilegium palimpsestorum, arte photographica paratum per S. Benedicti monachos Archiabbatiae Beuronensis, vol. I)
MnCS

St. Gall, Switzerland. Stiftsbibliothek. MS 393

3402 **Ekkehardus IV, monk of St. Gall.**
Der Liber benedictionum Ekkeharts IV., nebst den kleinen Dichtungen aus dem Codex Sangallensis 393. Zum ersten Mal vollständig hrsg. und erläutert von Johannes Egli. St. Gallen, Fehrische Buchhandlung, 1909.
li, 439 p. facsims. 24 cm.
MnCS

St. Gall, Switzerland. Stiftsbibliothek. Mss. 919

3402a **Das mittelrheinische Passionsspiel der St. Galler Handschrift 919.** Neu hrsg. von Rudolf Schützeichel . . . Tübingen, Max Niemayer Verlag, 1978.
x, 351 p. facsims. 23 cm.
Text, p. 99–157. Facsimile, p. 331–351.
MnCS

Saint-Georges, Boscherville, France
see
Boscherville, France. Saint-Georges

Saint-Germain-des-Prés, Paris, France
see
Paris, France. Saint-Germain-des-Prés

St. Gertrude's Convent, Cottonwood, Id.

3403 **Elsensohn, Alfreda, Sister, O.S.B.**
History of St. Gertrude's Convent, Cottonwood, Idaho; a short historical sketch – 78 years of service, 1884–1962, 53 years at

Cottonwood, 1909–1962. [Cottonwood, Id., Cottonwood Chronicle Print, 1962].
22 p. illus.
MnStj (Archives); IdCoS

3404 **Nuxoll, M. Ildephonse, Sister, O.S.B.**
Idaho Benedictine; St. Gertrude's Convent, Cottonwood, Idaho. [Cottonwood, Id., St. Gertrude's Convent, 1974].
71 p.
MoCo

St. Gertrude's Convent, Shakopee, Minn.

3405 **Coller, Julius A.**
The Shakopee story. [Shakopee, Minn., North Star Pictures, Inc., c 1960].
xvi, 772 p. illus., ports. 24 cm.
See index under Schools: St. Gertrude's Convent.
MnCS

3406 **Lynch, Claire, Sister, O.S.B.**
The Shakopee story; episodes in oppression.
(*In* Benedictines (periodical), vol. 31, p. 6–15, 35–37, 58–63)
MnSSP

3407 **Lynch, Claire, Sister, O.S.B.**
The story of St. Gertrude's Convent, Shakopee, Minnesota, 1862–1880.
32 p.
Privately printed, 1977.
MnSSP; MnStj (Archives)

3407a **Lynch, Claire, Sister, O.S.B.**
The leaven. St. Paul, Minn., Saint Paul's Priory [1980].
71 p. ports., facsims. 22 cm.
MnSSP; MnStj

Saint-Gilles, Montoire, France
see
Montoire, France. Saint-Gilles

St. Gregory's Abbey, Downside, England
see
Downside Abbey, England

St. Gregory's Abbey, Shawnee, Okla.

3408 **Murphy, Joseph Francis, O.S.B.**
Historic Sacred Heart mission. [n.p.] Crash Inc. [n.d.]
[20] p. illus. 23 cm.
PLatS

3409 **Murphy, Joseph Francis, O.S.B.**
The monastic centers of the Order of St. Benedict in Oklahoma. Shawnee, Okla., Benedictine Color Press, 1968.
iv, 65 p. 28 cm.

Thesis – University of Oklahoma Graduate School
OkShg

3410 **Murphy, Joseph Francis, O.S.B.**
Tenacious monks: the Oklahoma Benedictines, 1875–1975 – Indian missionaries, Catholic founders, educators, agriculturists. Shawnee, Okla., Benedictine Color Press [1974].
x, 465 p. illus. 24 cm.
InStme; MnCS; OkShg

St. John's Abbey, Collegeville, Minn.

3410a **Barry, Colman James, O.S.B.**
Worship and work; Saint John's Abbey and University, 1856–1980. Collegeville, Minn., The Liturgical Press, 1980.
526 p. plates, maps, 24 cm. (American Benedictine Academy. Historical studies [abbeys and convents], no. 2)
p. 343–413: Epilogue, 1956–1980.
MnCS

3411 **The Benedictine life: the price of peace.**
Collegeville, Minn., St. John's Abbey [1955?].
unpaged, illus. (ports) 15 x 19 cm.
MnCS

3412 **The Benedictines: the liberal tradition**
[Motion picture]. New York, Columbia Broadcasting System, Inc., CBS News [n.d.].
1 motion picture sd bw 16mm (Look up and live)
Narrated by Charles Kuralt.
Television film about St. John's in the 1960s.
MnCS

3413 **Biographical sketches [of St. John's Abbey].**
135 p. illus. 30 cm.
This is vol. 51, no. 1, 1956, of The Scriptorium. It consists of short biographies of the 241 members of St. John's Abbey who died during the first century, 1856–1956.
MnCS

3414 **Deegan, Paul J.**
The monastery; life in a religious community. Mankato, Minn., Creative Educational Society, 1970.
79 p. illus.
MnCS

3415 **Deutsch, Alfred Henry, O.S.B.**
Bruised reeds and other stories. Collegeville, Minn.; St. John's University Press [1971].
213 p. illus. 22 cm.
InStme; KAS; MnCS; NcBe; PLatS

3415a **Edelbrock, Alexius, O.S.B.**
Die Benediktiner in Minnesota [1856–1867].
96 leaves, 32 cm.
Manuscript. Written 1882.
MnCS (Archives)

3415b **Edelbrock, Alexius, O.S.B.**
The Benedictines in Minnesota [1856–1867]. [Translated from the German by Eugene Bode, O.S.B.].
97 leaves, 32 cm.
Manuscript.
MnCS (Archives)

3416 **Ellis, John Tracy.**
Saint John's: a living tradition.
(*In* his: Perspectives in American Catholicism. Baltimore, 1963. p. 271–287).
PLatS

3417 **Fratres nostri in pace dormientes.** Prepared by the novices of 1954, 1955 and 1956.
229 p. ports. 28 cm.
Typescript.
MnCS (Archives)

3418 **Hoffmann, Alexius, O.S.B.**
Literarische Tätigkeit der Patres der St. Joannes Abtei zu Collegeville in Minnesota, U.S.A. Prepared for the Catholic Exposition in Cologne, 1928.
9 p. 30 cm.
Typescript.
MnCS (Archives)

3418a **Hoffmann, Alexius, O.S.B.**
Natural history of Collegeville, Minn.
124 p. 24 cm.
Manuscript. Written 1926.
MnCS (Archives)

3419 **The monks of St. John's.** [Collegeville, Minn., St. John's Abbey, 1970].
103 p. illus., ports. 23 x 30 cm.
Multigraphed.
MnCS

3420 **Riss, Bruno, O.S.B.**
First beginnings of St. John's Abbey.
(Monthly installations in: The St. John's University Record, v. 2 (1889–90) and v. 3 (1890–91).
MnCS

3420a **St. John's Abbey, Collegeville, Minn.:**
[a photographic directory of the monks of Saint John's Abbey, comprising the monastic community of January 1, 1980 . . . Published by the Saint John's Abbey Archives, Fr. Vincent Tegeder, O.S.B., archivist].
106 p. illus., ports. 22 x 28 cm.
MnCS

3420b **Saint John's directory.** Prepared by Roman Paur, O.S.B. [and others]. Collegeville, Minn., St. John's University, Center for Human Resources, 1980.

49 p. ports. 28 cm.

Contents: Monks and employees of Saint John's Abbey, St. John's University, Saint John's Preparatory School; Photographs of Administration, Service, Support personnel; Chronology of Saint John's buildings and sites; Corporate structure; Parishes, missions, chaplaincies.

MnCS

3421 **Stones and hills** — Steine und Huegel; reflections, St. John the Baptist Parish, 1875–1975. Collegeville, Minn., 1975.

v, 1980 p. illus. 23 cm.

MnCS

3421a **Symposium on the apostolates of St. John's:** the parish apostolate, the University apostolate, the Preparatory School apostolate, The Liturgical Press apostolate, the mission apostolate, the chaplaincy, manual labor.

(*In* The Scriptorium [St. John's Abbey], vol. 22(1980), p. 62–97)

MnCS

3421b **Theisen, Wilfred, O.S.B.**

Sacred art at St. John's Abbey. Editors: Wilfred Theisen, O.S.B., Mark Twomey. [Collegeville, Minn., The Liturgical Press, 1980].

[32] p. illus. 26 cm.

MnCS

3421c **Wimmer, Simplicius, O.S.B.**

Kurze Geschichte der Benedictiner-Abtei St. Ludwig am See, jetzt St. John's — Abtei in Minnesota (Nord-Amerika).

(*In* Studien und Mitteilungen aus dem Benediktiner-Orden, II. Jahrg. (1881), 2. Bd., p. 266–281, III. Jahrg. (1882), 1. Bd., p. 42–65)

MnCS; PLatS

St. John's Abbey, Collegeville, Minn. Archives

3422 **Tegeder, Vincent George, O.S.B.**

Guide to the holdings [of] the archives, Saint John's Abbey and University, Collegeville, Minnesota, December 1, 1980.

10 p. 22 cm.

MnCS

St. John's Abbey, Collegeville, Minn. Carpenter Shop

3423 **Lavine, Marcia.**

Saint John's furniture 1874–1974. [Display at St. John's Abbey, Collegeville, Minn., October 9–30, 1974].

20 p. illus., ports. 21 cm.

Introduction by Marcia Lavine [&] Thomas Williams, O.S.B.

Includes: A history of the St. John's Carpentry Shop by Dietrich Reinhart, O.S.B.

MnCS

St. John's Abbey, Collegeville, Minn. Church

3424 **Benediction of the chime of the five bells at the abbey church.**

2 p. 28 cm.

Typescript copy from: St. Cloud Times, May 18, 1897.

MnCS (Archives)

3425 **Beyer, Rita Marie.**

Modern and traditional elements in St. John's Abbey and University Church, Collegeville, Minnesota.

51 p. 28 cm.

Thesis (M.A.) — University of Iowa, 1963. Typescript.

MnCS

3426 **Ceremony of consecration of Saint John's Abbey Church,** Collegeville, Minnesota, by . . . Most Reverend Peter W. Bartholome . . . Bishop of St. Cloud, Thursday, August 24, 1961.

MnCS

3427 **A martyred saint in New York;** the body of Saint Peregrinus, with jewelled crown and vestments and a phial of his life-blood, now in the Church of St. Anselm [New York], most valuable holy relic ever brought to America. (The relics of this saint are now, since 1926, in St. John's Abbey Church). ·

9 leaves, 30 cm.

Typescript copy from: New York World, May 26, 1895, p. 380 ff.

MnCS (Archives)

3428 **Roloff, Ronald William, O.S.B.,** 1922–

Abbey and university church of Saint John the Baptist, Collegeville, Minnesota. [Text by the Reverend Fathers Ronald Roloff and Brice Howard, O.S.B. Photography by Mr. Shin Koyama. Collegeville, Minn., St. John's Abbey, 1961].

[40] p. illus., diagrs, 31 cm.

Church dedication brochure, August 24, 1961.

CaQStB; KAS; MnCS; PLatS

3429 **Stein, Benjamin John, O.S.B.**

Microfilm record for a time capsule to be placed above the cornerstone of the abbey church. Filmed by Recordak Corporation, February 16, 1959.

Positive (Reduction 12–1). Negative in Abbey Archives.

Contents: 1. The Community at St. John's: Worship and work, by Colman J. Barry, O.S.B.; Ordo – title page and pages 141–156 (list of St. John's Abbey members, 1958); St. John's University student directory 1958–59; The Holy Rule.

2. Plans for the future: Adventure in architecture, by Whitney S. Stoddard; Minutes of the church committee; Plans for the new church; To praise the living God; List of donors (from St. John's Record); Progress thus far; Day book of construction; Photographs of the construction.

3430 **To praise the living God** [brochure about the new abbey church, St. John's Abbey, Collegeville, Minn., 1956].
[16] p. illus., plans. 30 cm.
MnCS; PLatS

St. John's Abbey, Collegeville, Minn.
Horticultural Trial Station

3431 **Katzner, John, O.S.B.**
Articles in: The Minnesota Horticulturist, vols. 35–46 (1907–1918).
For complete list of articles see under Katzner, John, in Author Part.
MnCS (Archives)

St. John's Preparatory, Collegeville, Minn.

3432 **Saint John's Preparatory, Collegeville, Minnesota,** conducted by the Benedictines of Saint John's Abbey. Collegeville, Minn., St. John's Preparatory [1965].
unpaged. illus. 23 x 24 cm.
MnCS

St. John's University, Collegeville, Minn.

3433 **Tucker, Dunstan, O.S.B.**
Scoreboard; a history of athletics of Saint John's University, Collegeville, Minnesota. Written and compiled by Dunstan Tucker, O.S.B., and Martin Schirber, O.S.B. Collegeville, Minn., St. John's University Press [c 1979].
xii, 444 p. illus. 22 cm.
MnCS

3434 **Wakin, Edward.**
St. John's, Collegeville: living life whole.
(*In* his: The Catholic campus. New York, 1963. p. 113–132)
PLatS

St. John's University, Collegeville, Minn.
Archives

3434a **Tegeder, Vincent George, O.S.B.**
Guide to the holdings [of] the archives, Saint John's Abbey and University, Collegeville, Minnesota, December 1, 1980.

10 p. 22 cm.
MnCS

St. John's University, Collegeville, Minn.
Benedictine Institute of Sacred Theology

3435 **Morran, Audrey, Sister, O.S.B.**
Origin of the Benedictine Institute of Sacred Theology. 1959.
20 p. 28 cm.
Typescript.
MnStj (Archives)

St. John's University, Collegeville, Minn.
Hill Monastic Manuscript Library

3436 **Archive of published articles and references** relating to the Hill Monastic Manuscript Library, 1965–
All separately analyzed and cataloged.
MnCH

3437 **Behrendt, Roland, O.S.B.**
Monastic Manuscript Library.
(*In* Tjurunga; an Australasian Benedictine review, October, 1976, p. 61–65)
MnCS

3437a **Jeffery, Peter.**
A bibliography for medieval and renaissance musical manuscript research; secondary materials at the Alcuin Library and Hill Monastic Manuscript Library at St. John's University, Collegeville, Minnesota. Collegeville, Minn., St. John's University Press, 1980.
68 p. 20 cm.
MnCH

3437b **Kapsner, Oliver Leonard, O.S.B.**
History of the Microfilm Project. Collegeville, Minn., 1977.
9 p. 28 cm.
Photocopy of typescript.
MnCH

3438 **Plante, Julian G.**
The Monastic Manuscript Microfilm Library; its purpose and progress. Text by Julian G. Plante. Designed by Frank Kacmarcik. Collegeville, Minn., Monastic Manuscript Microfilm Library, 1970.
[24] p. illus. (part col.) 23 x 28 cm.
MnCS

3438a **Plante, Julian G.**
The Hill Monastic Manuscript Library as a source for musicologists and musicians.
(*In* Sacred music, vol. 105 (1978), p. 7–11)
MnCS

3438b **Plante, Julian G.**
The Hill Monastic Manuscript Library; its origins, microfilmed collections, and activities.

(*In* Res publica litterarum; studies in the classical tradition. University of Kansas. II (1979), p. 251–261)
MnCH

3439 **Transatio studii;** manuscript and library studies honoring Oliver L. Kapsner. Edited by Julian G. Plante. Published for the Monastic Manuscript Microfilm Library by St. John's University Press, 1973.
288 p. illus. 25 cm.
Articles in English, German, French, or Spanish
InStme; KAS; MnCS; PLatS

3439a **Conservation et reproduction des manuscrits et imprimés;** colloque international organisé par la Bibliothèque à l'occasion de son V. centenaire, 21–24 octobre 1975. Citta del Vaticano, Biblioteca Apostolica Vaticana, 1976.
367 p. 26 cm. (Studi e testi, 276)
Includes several references to the Monastic Manuscript Microfilm Library.
MnCH

St. Joseph's Convent, St. Marys, Pa.

3440 **St. Joseph's Convent, St. Marys, Pa., 1977.**
50 slides, 2 x 2" color.
Photography by Sister Mary Kenneth Scheessele, O.S.B., on the occasion of the 125th annivarsary of St. Joseph's Convent and arrival of Benedictine Sisters in the U.S.A.
InFer (Archives)

Saint-Laurent, Liège, Belgium
see
Liège, Belgium. Saint-Laurent

Saint-Leger-Vauban, France. Le Pierre-qui-Vire
see
Pierre-qui-Vire, France

St. Leo Abbey, St. Leo, Fla.

3441 **St. Leo's Military College** [annual catalog]. Chartered June 4th, 1889. First year, 1890. Jacksonville, Fla., H. Drew & Bro., 1889.
NcBe (1889–1901, 1919)

St. Lomer, Blois, France
see
Blois, France. St. Lomer

St. Louis Priory, Creve Coeur, Mo.

3442 **A School in praise of God:** Saint Louis Priory School, Creve Coeur, Missouri.

[6] p. illus. 30 cm.
Offprint from Architectural Forum, November, 1957, p. 122–127.
PLatS

St. Martial, Avignon, France
see
Avignon, France. St. Martial

Saint-Martial, Limoges, France
see
Limoges, France. Saint-Martial

Saint-Martin, Ligugè, France
see
Ligugè, France. Saint-Martin

Saint-Martin, Moissac, France
see
Moissac, France. Saint-Martin

Saint-Martin, Montauban, France
see
Montauban, France. Saint-Martin

Saint-Martin, Pontoise, France
see
Pontoise, France. Saint-Martin

Saint-Martin, Tournai, Belgium
see
Tournai, Belgium. Saint-Martin

Saint-Martin-des-Champs, Paris, France
see
Paris, France. Saint-Martin-des-Champs

St. Martin's Abbey, Olympia, Wash.

3443 **The Ranger crossbow** [student yearbook]. Golden jubilee edition. Lacey, Wash., St. Martin's High School, 1945.
unpaged. illus. 28 cm.
KAS

St. Martin's Priory of the Black Hills, Rapid City, S.D.

3444 **Commemorating the dedication and diamond jubilee,** St. Martin's Convent and Academy, Rapid City, South Dakota, conducted by the Sisters of St. Benedict. Dedicated May 8, 1963.
unpaged. illus.
MnStj (Archives); MnCS

St. Mary Magdalen Priory, Davington, England
see
Davington, England. St. Mary Magdalene Priory

St. Mary's Abbey, Morristown, N.J.

3445 **Blessing of Saint Mary's Abbey,** Morristown, N.J., and Mass of thanksgiving, July 16, 1966.
unpaged. illus. 27 cm.
PLatS; NjMoS

3446 **Saint Mary's Abbey Church.** [Printed by Monastery of Our Lady of the Rosary, Summit. N.J., 1970].
7 p. illus. 27 cm.

St. Mary's Abbey, Winchester, England
see
Winchester, England. St. Mary's Abbey

St. Mary's Abbey, York, England
see
York, England. St. Mary's Abbey

St. Mary's Priory, Nauvoo, Ill.

3447 **Fallon, Clarisse, Sister, O.S.B.**
Share our joy, 1874–1974. Nauvoo, Ill., Benedictine Sisters, St. Mary's Priory, 1974.
48 p. illus. 22 cm.
MnStj (Archives); MoCo; ViBris

3448 **Gallivan, Ricarda, Sister, O.S.B.**
Shades in the fabric; excerpts from the Nauvoo Benedictine story. Nauvoo, Ill., 1970.
96 p. 28 cm.
Mimeographed.
ICSS; MnStj; MoCo

Saint-Maur-des-Fossés, Paris, France
see
Paris, France. Saint-Maur-des-Fossés

St. Meinrad Archabbey, St. Meinrad, Ind.

3449 **Barthel, Dominic, O.S.B.**
Manuale alumnorum; a collection of prayers, devotions and formulas used at the theological and preparatory seminaries of St. Meinrad. St. Meinrad Abbey Print, 1898.
151 p. 13 cm.
InStme

3450 **Behrman, Peter, O.S.B.**
The story of St. Meinrad Abbey; an historical sketch.
Offprint from The Grail, v. 10 (1929), p. 487–516 & 522.
PLatS

3451 **Doppelfeld, Basilius, O.S.B.**
Mönchtum und kirchlicher Heilsdienst; Entstehung und Entwicklung des nordamerikanischen Benediktinertums im 19.

Jahrhundert. Münsterschwarzach, Vier-Türme-Verlag, 1974.
xx, 381 p. 21 cm.
InStme; MnCS; PLatS

3452 **Essays on the priesthood** [offered to St. Meinrad Archabbey on the occasion of its centenary (1854–1954) by members of the alumni]. St. Meinrad, Ind., St. Meinrad Seminary, 1954.
100 p. (St. Meinrad essays, v. 11, no. 1)
InStme; NcBe

3453 **Gruwe, Luke, O.S.B.**
Gründungs- und Entwicklungsgeschichte der St. Meinrads-Abtei in Nordamerika. Salzburg, A. Pustet [1915?].
32 p. 23 cm.
InStme; KAS; MnCS; PLatS

3454 **Rippinger, Joel, O.S.B.**
From old world to new; the origins and development of St. Meinrad and Conception abbeys in the nineteenth century.
75 p. 28 cm.
Typescript, 1976.
MoCo

Saint-Michel, Cuxa, France
see
Cuxa, France. Saint-Michel

Saint-Michel, Treport, France
see
Treport, France. Saint-Michel

Saint-Mihiel, France (Benedictine abbey)

3455 **Raugel, Felix.**
Les orgues de l'Abbaye de Saint-Mihiel, anciennes orgues de la region Meusienne. Paris, L'Echo musical, 1919.
xv, 94 p. 10 plates. 26 cm.
PLatS

Saint-Nicolas de Prés, Ribemont, France
see
Ribemont, France. Saint-Nicolas de Prés

Saint-Ourn, Rouen, France
see
Rouen, France. Saint-Ouen

St. Paul's Indian Mission, Marty, S.D.

3456 **Hatai, Thomas.**
The Marty story. [Marty, S.D., St. Paul's Indian Mission, 1957].
First published in 1954.
KAS

St. Paul's Priory, St. Paul, Minn.

3457 Meagher, Luanne, Sister, O.S.B.
Beginning anew – St. Paul's Priory,
1948–1973. [St. Paul, North Central Publishing Co., 1973].
12 p. illus., plates, ports. 23 cm.
MnCS; MnStj (Archives); MnSSP

St. Peter's Abbey, Muenster, Sask., Canada

3458 Souvenir of the Silver Jubilee of St.
Peter's Colony, 1903–1928. Zum Andenken an das silberne Jubiläum der St.
Peter's Kolonie. [Muenster, Sask., St.
Peter's Press, 1929].
[48] p. illus. 28 cm.
CaSmu; NcBe; PLatS

Saint-Pierre, Ghent, Belgium
see
Ghent, Belgium. Saint-Pierre

Saint-Pierre, Le Puy, France
see
Le Puy, France. Saint-Pierre

Saint-Pierre, Lyons, France
see
Lyons, France. Saint-Pierre

Saint-Pierre, Moissac, France
see
Moissac, France. Saint-Pierre

St. Placid Priory, Olympia, Wash.

3459 Saint Placid's, 1952 to 1977.
(32) p. illus.
MnStj (Archives)

Saint-Pons, France (Benedictine abbey)

3460 Chartrier de l'Abbaye de Saint-Pons hors
les murs de Nice . . . [Monaco], Impr.
de Monaco, 1903.
xxxii, 549 p. 29 cm.
427 documents, dated from 999 to 1749.
MnCS

St. Procopius Abbey, Lisle, Ill.

3461 Blessing and dedication of St. Procopius
Abbey church and monastery, June 10,
1970.
62 p.
ILSP

3462 Abbey organ dedication, May 21, 1973
[St. Procopius Abbey, Lisle, Ill.].
6 p.
ILSP

3463 Proceedings of the first Unionistic
Congress, Sept. 28, 1956, to Sept. 30,
1956. Lisle, Ill., St. Procopius Abbey.
100 p. 23 cm.
MnCS

St. Procopius College, Lisle, Ill.

3464 C.-S. student life. No. 1–122, 1908–1931.
[St. Procopius College, Lisle, Ill.].
21 v. illus., ports. 23 cm.
ILSP; KAS

Saint-Riquier, France (Benedictine abbey)

3465 Angilbertus, Saint, abbot of St. Riquier.
Angilbert's ritual order for Saint-Riquier
[with Latin text].
(*In* Bishop, Edmund. Liturgica historica.
Oxford, 1918. p. 314–332)
PLatS

3466 Brunel, Clovis.
Saint-Riquier; études concernant l'abbaye depuis le huitième siècle jusqu'a la
Révolution. Somme, Abbaye de Saint-Riquier 1958–
MoCo; PLatS

3467 Cousin, Patrice, O.S.B.
Les moines de St-Riquier sous la réforme
mauriste et devant la Révolution.
(*In* Saint-Riquier; études . . . Abbaye de
Saint-Riquier, 1962. v. 1, p. 175–196)
PLatS

3468 Laporte, Jean, O.S.B.
Compléments à l'étude chronologique de
la liste abbatiale de St-Riquier.
(*In* Saint-Riquier; études . . . Abbaye de
Saint-Riquier, 1962. v. 1, p. 197–200)
PLatS

3469 Vanmackelberg, Maurice, O.S.B.
L'orgue de l'église abbatiale de St-Riquier.
(*In* Saint-Riquier; études . . . Abbaye de
Saint-Riquier, 1962. v. 1, p. 155–174)
PLatS

Saint-Sauveur, Ename, Belgium
see
Ename, Belgium. Saint-Sauveur

Saint-Sauveur, Redon, France
see
Redon, France. Saint-Sauveur

St. Scholastica Convent, Fort Smith, Ark.

3470 A brief history of the Sisters of St.
Benedict in Arkansas. Fort Smith,
1947.
74 p. illus.
InFer

3470a **Sharum, Elizabeth Louise, O.S.B.**
Write the vision down; a history of St.
Scholastica Convent, Fort Smith, Arkan-
sas, 1879–1979. Fort Smith, American
Print. & Lithographing Co., 1979.
xii, 175 p. illus. 23 cm.
InStme

St. Scholastica Priory, Chicago, Ill.

3471 **Harrison, Genevieve, Sister, O.S.B.**
Where there was need; a history of the
Chicago Benedictine Sisters from 1861 to
1965.
234 p. illus., maps. 29 cm.
Xeroxed from typescript, 1965.
ICSS

St. Scholastica Priory, Duluth, Minn.

3472 **Swinger of birches,** 1892–1967; rejoice
with us in peace and love . . . as we
celebrate the 75th jubilee of the Benedictine Sisters of Scholastica Priory . . .
unpaged, illus.
MnDu; MnStj (Archives)

Saint-Thierry, France (Benedictine abbey)

3472a **Saint-Thierry,** une abbaye du VIe au
XXe siècle: actes du Colloque interna-
tional d'Histoire Monastique Reims-
Saint-Thierry, 11 au 14 octobre, 1976,
reunis par Michel Bur. Saint-Thierry,
Association des Amis de l'Abbaye de
Saint-Thierry, 1979.
xviii, 643 p. 11 plates., map. 28 cm.
PLatS; MnCS

Saint-Trond, Belgium (Benedictine abbey)

3473 **Fagnant, Ivan.**
Le tribunal des XXII et l'abbé de Saint-
Trond devant le conseil aulique . . . Liège,
1967.
235 p. 28 cm.
MnCS

Saint-Vanne, Verdun, France
see
Verdun, France. Saint-Vanne

Saint-Victor, Marseille, France
see
Marseille, France. Saint-Victor

Saint-Vincent, Besancon, France
see
Besancon, France. Saint-Vincent

St. Vincent Archabbey, Latrobe, Pa.

3474 **Albert, George Dallas, ed.**
History of the County of Westmoreland,
Pennsylvania, with biographical sketches
of many of its pioneers and prominent
men. Philadelphia, L. H. Everts, 1882.
[Facsimile reprint. Evansville, Ind., Uni-
graphic, Inc., 1975].
727 p. illus. 28 cm.
An index is added to the reprint.
PLatS

3475 **Christ-Johner, Victor.**
A preliminary report on the master plan:
Saint Vincent Archabbey, Saint Vincent
Seminary, Saint Vincent College, [and]
Saint Vincent Preparatory School,
Latrobe, Pennsylvania. New Canaan,
Conn., Victor Christ-Jahner and
Associates, architect [1964?].
unpaged. illus. 23 x 26 cm.
PLatS

3476 **Cicognani, Amleto Giovanni.**
The spirit of Montecassino; an address
delivered in Latrobe, Pennsylvania,
September 2, 1946, on the occasion of the
Centenary of St. Vincent Archabbey.
(*In* his: Addresses and sermons, 1942–
51. Paterson, N.J., 1952. p. 98–102)
PLatS

3477 **Debuyst, Frederic, O.S.B.**
Benedictins pas morts.
(*In* Art d'Eglise, no. 142 (Janvier-fevrier-
mars, 1968), p. 129–131)
PLatS

3478 **Doppelfeld, Basilius, O.S.B.**
Mönchtum und kirchlicher Heilsdienst;
Entstehung und Entwicklung des nor-
damerikanischen Benediktinertums im 19.
Jahrhundert. Münsterschwarzach, Vier-
Türme-Verlag, 1974.
xx, 381 p. 21 cm.
MnCS; PLatS

3479 **Jeffcoat, Derris, O.S.B.**
St. Vincent Gristmill dates to 1854.
(Photocopied from The Latrobe Bulle-
tin, vol. 74, June 25, 1976, p. 42)
PLatS

3480 **Katselas, Tasso.**
L'Abbaye Saint-Vincent à Latrobe
(Pennsylvania).
(*In* Art d'Eglise, no. 142, 1968, p. 132–
137)
PLatS

3481 **Kline, Omer Urban, O.S.B.**
St. Vincent Brewery once center of con-
troversy.
(Photocopied from: The Latrobe Bulle-
tin, vol. 74, no. 159, June 25, 1976, p. 36)
PLatS

3482 **Latrobe Bulletin.**
[Bicentennial and historical observance].
60 p. illus., ports. 57 cm.
Issued as vol. 74, no. 159 (June 25, 1976).
Contains articles of historical interest of
the Latrobe area.
PLatS

3483 **Mathäser, Willibald, O.S.B.**
König Ludwig I von Bayern und die
Gründung der ersten bayerischen Benedik-
tinerabtei in Nordamerika.
(*In* Studien und Mitteilungen zur
Geschichte des Benediktiner-Ordens, Bd.
43 (1925), p. 123–182)
MnCS; PLatS

3484 **Moleck, Fred.**
Nineteenth-century musical activity at
St. Vincent Archabbey, Latrobe, Pa.
117 p. (plus unpaged appendix) 29 cm.
(appendix 38 x 28 cm.)
Thesis (Ph.D.)–University of Pitts-
burgh, 1970.
Typescript.
PLatS

3485 **Moleck, Fred.**
Nineteenth-century musical practices at
St. Vincent Archabbey, Latrobe, Pa.
25 leaves. 28 cm.
Paper presented at the American Musi-
cological Society Meeting, November 7,
1976, Washington, D.C.
Typescript.
PLatS

3486 **National Catholic Laymen's Retreat
Conference.**
Fourth National Conference of the
Laymen's Retreat Movement, 1931, St.
Vincent Archabbey, Latrobe, Pa.
[50] p. illus., ports. 30 cm.
Offprint from: St. Vincent College Jour-
nal, v. 40 (1931), p. 129–179.
PLatS

3487 **Oetgen, Jerome.**
An American abbot, Boniface Wimmer,
O.S.B., 1809–1887. Latrobe, Pa., Arch-
abbey Press, c 1976.
xi, 344 p. illus. 24 cm.
InStme; KAM; KAS; MnCS; MoCo;
PLatS

3487a **Rupprecht, Melvin Clarence, O.S.B.**
Saint Vincent Archabbey Church.
63 leaves. 28 cm.
Thesis (B.A.), Saint Vincent College,
Latrobe, Pa., 1938.
PLatS

3488 **St. Vincent Archabbey, Latrobe, Pa.**
The archabbey directory. Latrobe, Pa.,
1964.
13 p. 23 cm.

Mimeographed.
PLatS

3489 **Sportman's Hall and St. Vincent Abbey.**
(Serial in St. Vincent College Journal,
vol. 1 (1891), p. 73–80, 105–113, 138–147,
186–191, 218–223, 249, 253, 282–286,
370–376, 418–424)
PLatS

3490 **St. Vincents Abtei und College (Latrobe,
Westmoreland County, Pa.).**
(*In* Deutscher katholischer Marien-
Kalender von Amerika. Cincinnati. 1. Jahr-
gang, 1963, p. 41–43)
PLatS

3491 **Selle, Paulinus Jerome, O.S.B.**
Building construction at St. Vincent
[1789–1936].
vi, 84 leaves. 29 cm.
Thesis (B.A.)–St. Vincent College,
Latrobe, Pa., 1936.
Typescript.
PLatS

3492 **Swetnam, George.**
The ghost in St. Vincent Archabbey.
(Photocopied from: The Latrobe
Bulletin, vol. 74, June 25, 1976, p. 49)
PLatS

3493 **Szarnicki, Henry A.**
Michael O'Connor, first Catholic bishop
of Pittsburgh . . . 1843–1860; a story of
the Catholic pioneers of Pittsburgh and
western Pennsylvania. Pittsburgh,
Wolfson Pub. Co. [1975].
ix, 233 p. illus. 24 cm.
MnCS; PLatS

3494 **Tasch, Alcuin William, O.S.B.**
Formal organization of the Benedictine
Society of Westmoreland County and the
St. Vincent College, Latrobe, Penn-
sylvania. [Latrobe, Pa., St. Vincent Col-
lege, 1950].
v, 123 leaves. 28 cm.
Mimeographed.
PLatS

3495 **Verostko, Roman Joseph, O.S.B.**
Saint Vincent monastery. Latrobe, Pa.,
Archabbey Press, 1967.
[16] leaves. illus., plates, plan. 24 cm.
PLatS

3496 **Verostko, Roman Joseph, O.S.B.**
Sculptures de ciment, monastère de
Saint-Vincent.
(*In* Art d' Eglise, no. 142 (1968), p. 139–
141)
PLatS

3497 **Weakland, Rembert George, O.S.B.**
Mass of the Holy Spirit & closing of the
cloister, St. Vincent Archabbey, July 20,
1967. Music composed by: Archabbot

Rembert Weakland, O.S.B., Ildephonse Wortman, O.S.B. [and] Ralph Bailey, O.S.B. Archabbey Press, 1967.
13 leaves. 23 cm.
PLatS

St. Vincent College, Latrobe, Pa.

3498 **Gallia, Michael J.**
Student perceptions and use of counseling and consultative services available at Saint Vincent College.
v. 94 leaves. 28 cm.
Thesis (M.A.)–Indiana University of Pennsylvania, 1973.
Typescript.
PLatS

3499 **Stillwagon, Richard A.**
A study of the reasons which underlie the choice of an academic calendar by St. Vincent College students.
iv, 24 leaves. 28 cm.
Thesis (B.A.)–St. Vincent College, Latrobe, Pa., 1969.
Typescript.
PLatS

3500 **Wilson, Debora, Sister, O.S.B.**
Benedictine higher education and the development of American higher education.
xvi, 335 p. 22 cm.
Thesis (Ph.D.)–University of Michigan, 1969.
Typescript.
PLatS

3501 **World's record bed-push,** November 3–13, 1974, Saint Vincent College, Latrobe, Pa.
unpaged. illus. 28 cm.
Xeroxed.
Contents: Letters from Guinness Superlatives Limited, Letters from the Administration, Newspaper clippings, etc.
PLatS

St. Vincent College, Latrobe, Pa. Library

3502 **Cassady, Virginia Louise.**
A descriptive catalog of the incunabula in St. Vincent College and Archabbey Library. Graduate School of Library and Information Sciences, University of Pittsburgh [1976].
xviii, 74 p. 29 cm.
PLatS

3503 **Rare books;** St. Vincent's Archabbey preserves some unusual medieval documents.

(*In* Jubilee; a magazine of the Church and her people, v. 9 (1961), p. 20–21)
PLatS

3504 **Shoniker, Fintan Raymond, O.S.B.**
St. Vincent College Library.
(*In* Library Buildings and Equipment Institute, University of Maryland, Guidelines for library planners. 1960. p. 50–53)
PLatS

3505 **Shoniker, Fintan Raymond, O.S.B.**
Statement on the library, January, 1963.
4 p. 28 cm.
Reproduced from typed page.
PLatS

St. Walburg Convent, Covington, Ky.

3506 **Harmeling, Deborah, Sister, O.S.B.**
The story of Covington's Monte Cassino Chapel. Thomas More College, 1969.
51 p. 8 x 11 cm.
Typescript.
KyCovS

3507 **His holy will;** a pageant. Centenary, St. Walburg Convent, Covington, Ky. (phonodisc).
4 s 12" 33⅓ rpm
KyCovS

3508 **Wolking, Teresa, Sister, O.S.B.**
Archive holdings of St. Walburg Convent of the Benedictine Sisters of Covington, Kentucky.
Typescript, 1979.
KyCovS

St. Walburga's Convent, Elizabeth, N.J.

3509 **Campbell, Stephanie, Sister, O.S.B.**
Chosen for peace; the history of the Benedictine Sisters of Elizabeth, New Jersey. [Patterson, N.J., St. Anthony Guild Press, 1968].
246 p. illus. 24 cm.

Saint-Wandrille, France (Benedictine abbey)

3510 **L'Abbaye S. Wandrille de Fontenelle.**
No. 1–   1951–
Fontenelle, Editions de Fontenelle.
v. illus. 23 cm. annual
MnCS

3511 **Besse, Jean Martial Léon, O.S.B.**
Saint Wandrille (VIe–VIIe s.). Paris, V. Lecoffre, 1904.
v. 181 p. 19 cm.
InStme

3512 **Gesta abbatum Fontanellensium usque ad a.833.** Appendix annorum 834–850.

(*In* Monumenta Germaniae historica. Scriptores. Stuttgart, 1963. t. 2, p. 270–304)

PLatS

3513 **Simon, G. A., O.S.B.**
L'Abbaye de Saint-Wandrille. Grenoble, B. Arthaud [1937].
95 p. illus. 20 cm.
InStme

St. Werburgh's Abbey, Chester, England
see
Chester, England. St. Werburgh's Abbey

Sainte-Colombe-les-Sens, France (Benedictine abbey)

3514 **Prou, Maurice.**
Le privilège de Charles le Chauve pour Saint-Columbe de Sens du 5 decembre 847.
(*In* Mélanges d'histoire du Moyen Age, offerts à M. Ferdinand Lot. Paris, 1925. p. 677–690)
PLatS

Sainte Foi, Longueville, France
see
Longueville, France. Sainte Foi

Sainte-Gertrude, Nivelles, Belgium
see
Nivelles, Belgium. Sainte-Gertrude

Sainte-Marie, Paris, France
see
Paris, France. Abbaye Sainte-Marie

Sainte-Trinité, Tiron, France
see
Tiron, France. Sainte-Trinité

Salfeld, Germany
see
Saalfeld, Germany

Salinoves, Spain. Sant Cristofol (Benedictine abbey)

3515 **Riu i Riu, Manuel.**
El monestir de Sant Cristòfol de Salinoves.
(*In* Analecta Montserratensia, v. 10, p. 177–189)
PLatS

Salzburg, Austria. Nonnberg (abbey of Benedictine nuns)

3516 **Donationbrief Kaiser Heinrich II oder** der Heiligen an das Kloster Nonnberg

vom Jahre 1003. Auch Kopien und deutsche Uebersetzung. MS. Benediktinerinnenabtei Nonnberg, Archivium, Urkunde A 1.
Microfilm: MnCH proj. no. 10,965

3517 **Nonnberger Faltstuhl und Hirtenstab vom Jahre 1242.** Hrsg. von der Benediktinerinnenabtei Nonnberg in Salzburg. Salzburg, Anton Pustet [n.d.].
32 p. illus. 21 cm.
PLatS

3517a **Schmiedbauer, A.**
Stift Nonnberg/Salzburg. [Salzburg, 1970?].
A collection of colored slides with introductory comments.
Contents: Romanische Wandmalereien in der Stiftskirche, 6 slides; Gotische Glassfenster von 1480, 6 slides; Flügelaltar der Johanneskapelle, 12 slides; Kruzifixe und Kreuzgang, 12 slides; Alte Pontifikalien der Abtissen, 6 slides.
MnCS

3518 **Stift Nonnberg zu Salzburg im Wandel der Zeiten,** nach Aufzeichnungen der langjährigen Archivarin Frau M. Regintrudis Reichlin von Meldegg, gest. 1943. Salzburg, Anton Pustet [1953].
88 p. plates. 21 cm.
MnCS

Salzburg, Austria. St. Peter (Benedictine abbey)

3519 **Das Benediktiner-Stift St. Peter;** kurze Geschichte und Beschreibung des Stiftes und seiner Sehensürdigkeiten, von einem Mitglied des Stiftes. Salzburg, im Selbstverlage des Stiftes, 1908.
38 p. plates. 17 cm.
KAS

3520 **Betschart, Ildefons, O.S.B.**
Salzburg und Einsiedeln; das Kräftespiel zweier Kulturzentren. Einsiedeln, K. Eberle, 1951.
100 p. plates. 21 cm.
InStme

3521 **Catalogus abbatum monasterii S. Petri Salisburgae usque 1466** et ab alia manu continuatus usque ad 1518. MS. Vienna, Nationalbibliothek, codex 3402, f.184v–188v. Folio. Saec. 15 & 16.
Microfilm: MnCH proj. no. 16,624

3522 **Catalogus abbatum monasterii S. Petri a S. Ruperto**—1615. MS. Benediktinerabtei St. Peter, Salzburg, codex b.I.42. 58 p. Saec. 15 & 17.
Microfilm: MnCH proj. no. 10,330

3523 **Catalogus abbatum monasterii S. Petri Salzburgi.** MS. Benediktinerabtei St.

Peter, Salzburg, codex b.VI.51, f.131v–133v. Quarto. Saec. 16.
Microfilm: MnCH proj. no. 10,505

3524 **Codex traditionum monasterii S. Petri Salisburgensis** saec. 12 inclinante scriptus. MS. Vienna, Nationalbibliothek, codex 9271. 102 f. Folio. Saec. 18.
Microfilm: MnCH proj. no. 19,235

3525 **Forstner, Karl.**
Die Anfänge des Salzburger Schriftwesen.
(*In* Handschriftenbeschreibung in Oesterreich, hrsg. von Otto Mazal. Wien, 1975. p. 13–20)
MnCS

3526 **Goff, Frederic R.**
Incunabula in the Library of Congress, formerly in the Benedictine monastery of St. Peter in Salzburg. Wien, 1971.
21–36 p.
Library of Congress.

3527 **Hermann, Friedrich, O.S.B.**
St. Peter, Salzburg; geschichtlicher Ueberblick. 8. Aufl. Salzburg, Verlag St. Peter, 1967.
23 p. 27 cm.
PLatS

3528 **Hermannus Custos.**
Codex diplomaticus monasterii S. Petri Salisburgensis. MS. Vienna, Nationalbibliothek, codex 9271. 184 f. (loco secundo). Folio. Saec. 18.
Microfilm: MnCH proj. no. 19,235

3529 **Hintler, Anselm, O.S.B.**
Chronicon novissimum monasterii ad S. Petrum Salisburgi, ab anno 582 usque ad 1782. Anselm Hintler, O.S.B., et Beda Seeauer, O.S.B. MS. Benediktinerabtei St. Peter, Salzburg, codex b.XII.17. 20, 756, 490 p. Folio. Saec. 18.
Microfilm: MnCH proj. no. 10,691

3530 **Lind, Karl.**
Ein Antiphonarium mit Bilderschmuck aus der Zeit des XI. und XII. Jahrhunderts im Stifte St. Peter zu Salzburg befindlich. Beschrieben und hrsg. von Karl Lind. Wien, A. Prandel, 1870.
45 p. illus. (woodcuts), 45 plates. 31 cm.
PLatS; AStb

3531 **Salzburg, Austria. Sankt Peter (Benedictine abbey).**
Auszug der neuesten Chronick des alten Benediktiner Klosters zu St. Peter in Salzburg . . . Salzburg, Joh. Jos. Mayer, 1782.
2 v. illus. (woodcuts) 20 cm.
KAS

3532 **Salzburg, Austria. Sankt Peter (Benedictine abbey).**

Catalogus religiosorum Ordinis S. P. Benedicti in antiquissimo monasterio ad S. Petrum Salisburgi viventium . . .
v. size varies.
PLatS

3533 **Salzburg, Austria. Sankt Peter (Benedictine abbey).**
Novissimum chronicon antiqui monasterii ad sanctum Petrum Salisburgi . . . exhibens ordinem chronologicum episcoporum, archiepiscoporum et abbatum, qui per XII saecula ab anno 582 usque ad annum respective 1782 monasterio ad sanctum Petrum praefuerunt . . . praemissa disquisitione historico-chronica de adventu, fundatione et obitu sancti Ruperti. Augustae Vindelic., Josephus Wolff, 1772.
20, 683, 20 p. illus., ports. 35 cm.
MnCS; PLatS (microfilm)

3534 **Schlitpacher, Johannes, O.S.B.**
Carta visitatorum monasterii S. Petri. MS. Benediktinerabtei St. Peter, Augsburg, codex b.XI.19, f.30r–36v. Folio. Saec. 15.
Microfilm: MnCH proj. no. 10,671

3535 **Schnell, Hugo.**
St. Peter/Salzburg. [München, Verlag Schnell & Steiner, 1941].
22 p. illus. 18 cm.
InStme

3536 **Seeauer, Beda, O.S.B.**
Liber professionis in monasterio ad S. Petrum Salisburgi ab anno 1419–1817. MS. Benediktinerabtei St. Peter, Salzburg, Archivum Hs. A 98. 900 p. Folio. Saec. 18–19.
Microfilm: MnCH proj. no. 10,755

3537 **Series abbatum monasterii O.S.B.** ad S. Petrum Salisburgi a Friderico vicesimo primo abbate usque ad abbatem Martinum Huttinger 1584 electum. Germanice. MS. Vienna, Nationalbibliothek, codex 7330, f.76v–92r. Quarto. Saec. 17.
Microfilm: MnCH proj. no. 18,778

3538 **Sinhuber, Edmundus.**
Annotationes super episcopos, archiepiscopos et abbates S. Petri et ecclesiae Salisburgensis. MS. Benediktinerabtei St. Peter, Salzburg, Archivium HS. A 18. 306 p. Folio. Saec. 17 (1673).
Microfilm: MnCH proj. no. 10,758

3539 **Das Verbrüderungsbuch von St. Peter in Salzburg;** vollständige Faksimile-Ausgabe im Originalformat der Handschrift A 1 aus dem Archiv von St. Peter in Salzburg. Einführung: Karl Forstner. Graz, Akademische Druck- u. Verlagsanstalt, 1974.

36 p. 39 leaves (facsim.) 40 cm. (Codices selecti phototypice impressi, LI)
MnCS

3539a **Verzeichnis aller und jeder des alten** Klosters zu Sankt Peter in der Stadt Salzburg Aebten und Vorsteher (560–1615), mit zahlreichen Wappen. MS. Benediktinerabtei St. Peter, Salzburg, codex a.V.15. 50 f. Octavo. Saec. 17.
Microfilm: MnCH proj. no. 10,041

Salzburg, Austria. St. Peter (abbey of Benedictine nuns)

3540 **Betbüechl für Petersfrauen (Salzburg)** geschrieben von Bruder Stephan Aichperg, peichtvater der hochgepreisten Klosterfrawn zu Sankt Peter. MS. Benediktinerinnenabtei Nonnberg, Salzburg, codex 23 E 30, f.208r–270v. Octavo. Saec. 16(1520).
Microfilm: MnCH proj. no. 10,903

Salzburg, Austria. Universität

3541 **Acta de erectione confoederatione et visitatione academiae et universitatis Salisburgensis.** MS. Linz, Austria, Oberösterreichies Landesarchiv. Stiftsarchiv Mondsee, Hs. 7. 811 f. Saec. 17–18.
Microfilm: MnCH proj. no. 27,595

3541a **Sattler, Magnus, O.S.B.**
Collectanean-Blätter zur Geschichte der ehemaligen Benedictiner-Universität Salzburg, Kempten, J. Kösel, 1890.
vii, 710 p. 23 cm.
MnCS; NcBe; PLatS

Salzinnes, Belgium (Benedictine abbey)

3542 **Brouette, Emile, comp.**
Recueil des chartes et documents du l'Abbaye du Val-Saint-Georges à Salzinnes (Namur), 1196–1300. Achel, Abbaye cistercienne, 1971.
xlvi, 289 p. 24 cm.
KAS

Samos, Spain (Benedictine abbey)

3543 **Arias, Maximino.**
Un abadologico inedito del monasteri de Samos; presentación, transcripción y notas por el P. Maximino Arias. Leòn, 1968.
72 p. 26 cm.
MnCS

San Benedetto, Norcia, Italy
see
Norcia, Italy. San Benedetto

San Benito, Calatayud, Spain
see
Calatayud, Spain. San Benito

San Benito, Valladolid, Spain
see
Valladolid, Spain. San Benito

San Benito, Buenos Aires, Argentina
see
Buenos Aires, Argentina. San Benito

San Cugat del Valles, Spain
see
Valles, Spain. San Cugat

San Daniel, Gerona, Spain
see
Gerona, Spain. San Daniel

San Feliu de Guixols, Spain (Benedictine abbey)

3544 **Batlle y Prats, Luis.**
La biblioteca del monasterio de San Feliu de Guixols. Gerona, Maso, 1971.
178 p. 25 cm.
MnCS

3545 **Cano, Alfonso.**
Discurso general de este antiquissimo castillo y monasterio de Sant Feliu de Guixols. MS. Monasterio benedictino Montserrat, Spain, codex 6. 277 f. Folio. Saec. 17 (1606).
Microfilm: MnCH proj. no. 29,979

San Frutos, Duraton, Spain
see
Duraton, Spain. San Frutos

San Gregorio, Rome, Italy
see
Rome, Italy. San Gregorio

San Juan de la Pena, Spain
see
Pena, La, Spain. San Juan

San Juan de las Abadesses, Ripoll, Spain
see
Ripoll, Spain. San Juan de las Abadesses

San Millan de la Cogolla, Spain (Benedictine abbey)

3546 **Gaiffier d'Hestroy, Baudoin de.**
Les sources de la translation sancti Aemiliani (San Millán de la Cogolla).
(*In* Mélanges dédiés à la mémoire de Félix Grat. Paris, 1946. v. 1, p. 153–168)
PLatS

3547 **Garcia de Cortazar y Ruiz de Aguirre, Jose Angel.**
El dominio del Monasterio de San Millán de la Cogola (siglos X a XIII) . . . Salamanca, Universidad de Salamanca, 1969.
371 p. illus. 25 cm.
MnCS

San Nicola, Guzule, Sardinia
see
Guzule, Sardinia. San Nicola

San Paolo fuori le Mura, Rome, Italy
see
Rome, Italy. San Paolo fuori le Mura

San Pedro, Cardena, Spain
see
Cardena, Spain. San Pedro

San Pedro de la Dueñas, Spain
(Benedictine abbey)
3548 **Fernandez Caton, José Maria.**
Catalogo del archivo del monasterio de S. Pedro las Dueñas. León, 1977.
187 p. 26 cm.
MnCS

San Pedro de las Puellas, Barcelona, Spain
see
Barcelona, Spain. San Pedro de las Puellas

San Pedro de Montes, Spain
(Benedictine abbey)
3549 **Quintana Prieto, Augusto.**
Tumbo viejo de San Pedro de Montes, León, Centro de Estudios a Investigación "San Isidoro," 1971.
657 p. 25 cm.
MnCS

San Pietro, Perugia, Italy
see
Perugia, Italy. San Pietro

San Salvador, Oña, Spain
see
Oña, Spain. San Salvador

San Saturno, Cagliari, Sardinia
see
Cagliari, Sardinia. San Saturno

San Stefano, Bologna, Italy
see
Bologna, Italy. San Stefano

San Stefano, Carrara, Italy
see
Carrara, Italy. San Stefano

San Vicente, Oviedo, Spain
see
Oviedo, Spain. San Vicente

San Vincenzo al Volturno, Italy
(Benedictine abbey)
3550 **Treppo, Mario del.**
"Terra sancti Vincensii"; l'Abbazia di S. Vincenzo al Volturno nell'alto medioevo. Napoli, Libreria scientifica editrice [1968].
82 p. 28 cm.

Sankt Alban, Elsass
see
Saint Auban, Alsace

Sankt Alban, Mainz, Germany
see
Mainz, Germany. Sankt Alban

Sankt Andreas, Sarnen, Switzerland
see
Sarnen, Switzerland. Sankt Andreas

Sankt Ansgar, Nütschau, Germany
see
Nütschau, Germany. Sankt Ansgar

Sankt Blasien im Schwarzwald, Germany
(Benedictine abbey)
3551 **Abtei St. Blasien im Schwarzwald:** excerpta varia historica, prout in epistolis aliisque literis archivi San-Blasiani occurrebant. MS. Benediktinerabtei St. Paul im Lavantthal, Austria, codex 26/2. 52 f. Quarto. Saec. 18.
Microfilm: MnCH proj. no. 11,759

3552 **Acta betreffend des Herrn Abtes Caspar II Election und Benediction** sammt hierin begriffenen Merkwürdigkeiten de annis 1571–1696. Acta betreffend den Sterbfall Caspari II und die Election Martini I abbatis S. Blasii 1596. Acta die Election domini Blasii betreffend . . .1625. MS. Benediktinerabtei St. Paul im Lavantthal, Austria, codex 126/2. 406 f. Folio. Saec. 17.
Microfilm: MnCH proj. no. 11,893

3553 **Acta über die Auflösung des Stiftes St. Blasien im Schwarzwald.** MS. Benediktinerabtei St. Paul im Lavantthal, Austria, codex 35/6. 454 f. Folio. Saec. 19(1803–1808).
Microfilm: MnCH proj. no. 12,676

3553a **Adamek, Josef.**
St. Blasien im Schwarzwald, Benediktinerkloster und Jesuitenkolleg: Geschichte, Bedeutung, Gestalt. München, Schnell & Steiner [1978].
48 p. illus. 24 cm. (Die Grossen Kunstführer)
MnCS

3554 **Bober, Harry.**
The St. Blasien psalter. New York, H. P. Kraus, 1963.
78 p. mounted col. illus., 24 plates, map. 36 cm. (Rare books monographs series, v. 3)
PLatS

3555 **Caspar I, abbot of St. Blasien im Schwarzwald.**
Liber originum monasterii S. Blasii Hercyneae Silvae. MS. Benediktinerabtei St. Paul im Lavantthal, Austria, codex 98/2. 475 p. Folio. Saec. 16.
Microfilm: MnCH proj. no. 11,884

3556 **Caspar I, abbot of St. Blasien im Schwarzwald.**
Relatio de prima inhabitatione Silvae Nigrae et aedificatione monasterii S. Blasii. MS. Benediktinerabtei St. Paul im Lavantthal, Austria, codex 74/1. Folio. Saec. 16.
Microfilm: MnCH proj. no. 11,731

3557 **Catalogus über die von St. Blasien im Schwarzwalde** nach St. Paul im Lavantthale übertragenen Urkunden. [n.p., n.d. – 19th cent.]
unpaged, tables. 28 cm. (Archiv von St. Paul)
Xeroxed by University Microfilms, Ann Arbor, Mich., 1968.
MnCS

3558 **Corona gloriae et certum exultationis e variis abbatum S. Blasii** floribus connexum et D. Francisco praesuli anno 1643 feriis natilitiis impositum a studiosa juventute. MS. Benediktinerabtei St. Paul im Lavantthal, Austria, codex 27/2. 45 f. Quarto. Saec. 17.
Microfilm: MnCH proj. no. 11,763

3559 **Gumpp, Ignatius, O.S.B.**
Compendium discursus canonici de mensa privilegiata abbatis et conventus monasterii S. Blasii. MS. Benediktinerabtei St. Paul im Lavantthal, Austria, codex 260/2. 180 p. Folio. Saec. 18.
Microfilm: MnCH proj. no. 12,094

3560 **Herrgott, Marquard, O.S.B.**
Ad historiam S. Blasii. MS. Benediktinerabtei St. Paul im Lavantthal, Austria, codex 195/2. 2 vols. Folio. Saec. 18.
Microfilm: MnCH proj. no. 12,013 & 12,015

3561 **Herrgott, Marquard, O.S.B.**
Diplomata monasterii S. Blasii concernantis ab annis 1093–1236. MS. Benediktinerabtei St. Paul im Lavantthal, Austria, codex 60/2. 396 f. Folio. Saec. 18.
Microfilm: MnCH proj. no. 11,812

3562 **Herrgott, Marquard, O.S.B.**
Monasticon San-Blasianum. MS. Benediktinerabtei St. Paul im Lavantthal, Austria, codex 196/2. 361 f. Folio. Saec. 18.
Microfilm: MnCH proj. no. 12,028

3563 **Hilger, Franz M.**
Kirche und Kolleg St. Blasien. 22. überarbeitete Aufl. München, Schnell und Steiner, 1977.
22 p. illus. 17 cm.
MnCS

3564 **Hilger, Franz M.**
Martin Gerbert, Fürst und Abt von St. Blasien. Festschrift zur 250. Wiederker seines Geburtstages. Konstanz, Rosgarten Verlag, 1970.
87 p. plates. 22 cm.
MnCS

3564a **Houben, Hubert.**
St. Blasianer Handschriften des 11. und 12. Jahrhunderts. München, Arbeo-Gesellschaft, 1979.
xiii, 220 p. 20 cm. (Münchener Beiträge zur Mediävistik und Renaissance-Forschung, 30)
MnCS

3565 **Innocentius XII, Pope.**
Bulla confirmans omnia privilegia monasterii S. Blasii, Romae, 25. Junii, 1698. MS. Benediktinerabtei St. Paul im Lavantthal, Austria, Urkunden St. Blasien 174. 38 f. Folio. Saec. 17.
Microfilm: MnCH proj. no. 12,668

3566 **Jakobs, Hermann.**
Der Adel in der Klosterreform von St. Blasien. Köln, Böhlau, 1968.
xvi, 336 p. geneal. tables, map. 24 cm.
MnCS

3567 **Jura San-Blasiana secundum alphabetum.** MS. Benediktinerabtei St. Paul im Lavantthal, Austria, codex 23/2. 131 f. Octavo. Saec. 18.
Microfilm: MnCH proj. no. 11,760

3568 **Kettenaker, Paul, O.S.B.**
Kurze Nachrichten de scriptoribus San-Blasianis, de fatis bibliothecae San-Blasianae, de sacris reliquiis ad S. Blasianum, de bibliotheca ad S. Paulum. MS. Benediktinerabtei St. Paul im Lavantthal, Austria, codex 86/6. 129 f. Folio. Saec. 18.
Microfilm: MnCH proj. no. 12,628

3569 **Kopp, Ignatius, O.S.B.**
Breve chronicon monasterii S. Blasii.
MS. Benediktinerabtei St. Paul im Lavant-
thal, Austria, codex 32/6. 22 f. Folio. Saec.
17.
Microfilm: MnCH proj. no. 12,692

3570 **Mannhart, Johannes Baptist, O.S.B.**
Geschichtliche Darstellung der Auflösung von St. Blasien. MS. Benediktinerabtei St. Paul im Lavantthal, Austria, codex
34/6. 118 f. Folio. Saec. 18(1797–1807).
Microfilm: MnCH proj. no. 12,594

3571 **Nomina patrum,** fratrum et convsersorum
congregationis S. Blasii sub regimine
abbatis Augustini. Series abbatum
monasterii S. Blasii. Abbates postulati
ex gremio San-Blasiano. MS. Benediktinerabtei St. Paul im Lavantthal,
Austria, codex 30/2. 57 f. Octavo. Saec.
17(1695).
Microfilm: MnCH proj. no. 11,768

3572 **Otto, Hugo.**
Studien zur Geschichte des Klosters St.
Blasien im hohen und späten Mittelalter.
Stuttgart, W. Kohlhammer, 1963.
xix, 136 p. 24 cm.
MnCS; PLatS

3573 **Pelagius, Voester, O.S.B.**
Vinculum charitatis, seu Designatio
historica monasteriorum et collegiorum,
quae cum monasterio S. Blasii confoederata sunt et fuerunt. MS. Benediktinerabtei St. Paul im Lavantthal, Austria,
codex 200/2. 139 p. Folio. Saec. 18.
Microfilm: MnCH proj. no. 12,032

3574 **Relatio seu narratio** de prima inhabita-
tione hujus solitudinis et aedificatione
hujus monasterii, scilicet S. Blasii
(Abschrift des "Liber constructionis").
MS. Benediktinerabtei St. Paul im
Lavantthal, Austria, codex 122/2. 63 f.
Folio. Saec. 18.
Microfilm: MnCH proj. no. 11,895

3575 **Rettenacher, Paul, O.S.B.**
Geschichte von St. Blasien. MS. Bene-
diktinerabtei St. Paul im Lavantthal,
Austria, codex 34/2. 215 p. Quarto. Saec.
18.
Microfilm: MnCH proj. no. 11,756

3576 **Rettenacher, Paulus, O.S.B.**
Tractatus de disciplina monastica San-
Blasiens. MS. Benediktinerabtei St. Paul
im Lavantthal, Austria, codex 224/2. 3
vols. Folio. Saec. 18.
Microfilm: MnCH 12,052–53 & 12,075

3577 **Rösch, Johannes, O.S.B.**
Acta et res praeclare gestae, item electio
et confirmatio abbatis Caspari II, 157.

1592. MS. Benediktinerabtei St. Paul im
Lavantthal, Austria, codex 125/2. 289 p.
Folio. Saec. 16.
Microfilm: MnCH proj. no. 11,892

3578 **Sammelband,** enthaltend Einiges in Beziehung zur Auflösung von St. Blasien.
MS. Benediktinerabtei St. Paul, Austria,
codex 36/6. 154 f. Folio. Saec. 18.
Microfilm: MnCH proj. no. 12,592

3579 **Schmidfeld, Hugo, O.S.B.**
Conspectus diatribae de duobus Regin-
bertis, fundatoribus monasterii S. Blasii.
MS. Benediktinerabtei St. Paul im Lavant-
thal, Austria, codex 25/2. 74 f. Quarto.
Saec. 18.
Microfilm: MnCH proj. no. 11,755

3580 **Tractatus varii de juribus monasterii S.
Blasii.** MS. Benediktinerabtei St. Paul
im Lavantthal, Austria, codex 201/2.
122 f. Folio. Saec. 18.
Microfilm: MnCH proj. no. 12,030

3581 **Vellus aureum gemmis Blasianae virtu-
tis variegatum,** D. Francisci praesulis
collo injectum a studiosa juventute. MS.
Benediktinerabtei St. Paul im Lavantthal, Austria, codex 28/2. 27 f. Quarto.
Saec. 17.
Microfilm: MnCH proj. no. 11,765

3582 **Via crucis Salvatoris nostri,** Iesu Christi,
in XIV. stationes partita . . . pro usu
specialiter religiosi Ord. S. Benedicti
. . . Typis Prin. Monast. S. Blasii, 1767.
64 p. 17 cm.
KAS

3583 **Weiss, Johannes Baptist, O.S.B.**
Monatbuch der Congregation des heil.
Blasius auf dem Schwarzwalde, in
welchem die Lebensgeschichten der Heiligen und berühmten Mönche, die diesen Ort
durch ihre Reden und Thaten erhöhet, en-
thalten sind. MS. Benediktinerabtei St.
Paul im Lavantthal, Austria, codex 32/2.
157 p. Quarto. Saec. 18.
Microfilm: MnCH proj. no. 11,766

3584 **Wülberz, Stanislaus, O.S.B.**
Analecta ad historiam Blasianam. MS.
Benediktinerabtei St. Paul im Lavantthal,
Austria, codex 192/2. 8 vols. Folio. Saec.
18.
Microfilm: MnCH proj. no. 11,980–

3585 **Wülberz, Stanislaus, O.S.B.**
Analecta San-Blasiana. MS. Benediktinerabtei St. Paul im Lavantthal, Austria,
codex 187/2. 111 f. Folio. Saec. 18.
Microfilm: MnCH proj. no. 11,983

3586 **Wülzberg, Stanislaus, O.S.B.**
Codex probationum ad historiam Blasianum. MS. Benediktinerabtei St. Paul im

Lavantthal, Austria, codex 191/2. 4 vols.
Folio. Saec. 18.
Microfilm: MnCH proj. no. 11,977–

3587 Wülberg, Stanislaus, O.S.B.
Epitome omnium rerum, quae ad notitiam domesticam monasterii S. Blasii facere possunt usque ad annum 1749. MS. Benediktinerabtei St. Paul im Lavantthal, Austria, codex 186/2. 2 vols. Folio. Saec. 18.
Microfilm: MnCH proj. no. 11,969 & 11,971

Sankt Burkard, Wurzburg, Germany
see
Würzburg, Germany. Sankt Burkard

Sankt Castulus, Moosburg, Germany
see
Moosburg, Germany. Sankt Castulus

Sankt Emmeram, Regensburg, Germany
see
Regensburg, Germany. Sankt Emmeram

Sankt Gallen, Switzerland
see
Saint Gall, Switzerland

Sankt Georgen, Naumberg, Germany
see
Naumberg, Germany. Sankt Georgen

Sankt Georgen, Stein am Rhein, Switzerland
see
Stein am Rhein, Switzerland. Sankt Georgen

Sankt Georgen am Langsee, Austria (abbey of Benedictine nuns)

3588 Pichler, Virgil, abbot of St. Peter, Salzburg.
Schreiben an das Benediktiner Kloster Göss, 1497, und an das Benediktiner Kloster St. Georgen am Langsee, 1496. MS. Benediktinerabtei St. Paul im Lavantthal, Austria, codex b.V.20, f.52r–61r. Quarto. Saec. 15.
Microfilm: MnCH proj. no. 10,453

Sankt Georgen im Schwarzwald, Germany (Benedictine abbey)

3589 Stockburger, Erich.
S. Georgen: Chronik des Klosters und der Stadt. St. Georgen im Schwarzwald, 1972.
182 p. 23 cm.
MnCS

3590 Wollasch, Hans Josef.
Die Anfänge des Klosters St. Georgen im Schwarzwald. Freiburg i.B., Herder, 1964.
189 p. 22 cm.
MnCS

Sankt Georgenberg, Austria
see
Fiecht, Austria

Sankt Godehard, Hildesheim, Germany
see
Hildesheim, Germany. Sankt Godehard

Sankt Jakob, Mainz, Germany
see
Mainz, Germany. Sankt Jakob

Sankt Jakob, Wurzburg, Germany
see
Würzburg, Germany. Sankt Jakob

Sankt Lambert, Altenburg, Austria
see
Altenburg, Austria (Benedictine abbey)

Sankt Lambrecht, Austria (Benedictine abbey)

3591 Die beiden ältesten Todenbücher des Benedictinerstiftes St. Lambrecht in Obersteier. Mitgetheilt von Mathias Pangerl. Wien, Kaiserlich-Königliche Hof- und Staatsdruckerei, 1969.
345 p. 24 cm.
KAS

3592 Benedicta Virgo Cellensis . . . liberi et exempti monasterii Ordinis D. Benedicti ad S. Lambertum abbatiae, denuo in lucem edita, aucta, et illustrata. Graetii, Typis Widmanstadianis, 1645.
416 p. plates. 16 cm.
MnCS

3593 Catalogus religiosorum Ordinis S. P. Benedicti abb. Congregationis Immaculatae Conceptionis B.M.V. in antiquissimo monasterio ad S. Lambertum in Styria Sup. Styriae, Typographiae C. R. Universitatis.
v. 17 cm.
MnCS (1869–1901); PLatS

3594 Copiale monasterii Sancti Lamberti in Carinthia quod fundationis diploma anni 1069 continet, et papales confirmationes anni 1109, 1126, etc. . . . atque imperatorum diplomata anni 1103, 1104, etc. MS. Vienna, Nationalbibliothek, codex 14971. 13 f. Folio. Saec. 15.
Microfilm: MnCH proj. no. 20,290

3595 **Documenta monasterii S. Lamberti in Stiria et alia varia excerpta.** MS. Benediktinerabtei St. Paul im Lavantthal, Austria, codex 250/2. 285 f. Folio. Saec. 18.
Microfilm: MnCH proj. no. 12,096

3596 **Donationes et privilegie monasterii S. Lamberti in Styria.** MS. Vienna, Nationalbibliothek, codex 331. 107 f. Folio. Saec. 15.
Microfilm: MnCH proj. no. 13,669

3597 **Gotik in der Steiermark,** Stift St. Lambrecht, 28. Mai bis 8. Oktober 1978. Landesausstellung veranstaltet vom Kulturreferat der Steiermäfkischen Landesregierung. [Graz, Universitäts-Buchdruckerei, 1978].
344 p. 112 plates(part col.) 24 cm.
MnCS

3598 **Kloster St. Lambrecht.** Urkundenabschriften. MS. Vienna, Haus-, Hof- und Staatsarchiv, codex 987/3.
Microfilm: MnCH proj. no. 23,629

3599 **Lesky, Grete.**
Die Bibliotheksembleme der Benediktinerabtei St. Lambrecht in Steiermark . . . Graz, Imago-Verl. [1970].
96 p. 38 p. of illus. 28 cm.
MnCS

Plank, Benedikt, O.S.B.
3600 Benediktinerabtei St. Lambrecht/ Steiermark, . . . München, Schnell & Steiner, 1970.
105 p. illus. 17 cm.
MnCS

3600a **Plank, Benedikt, O.S.B.**
Geschichte der Abtei St. Lambrecht; Festschrift zur 900. Wiederkehr des Todestages des Gründers Markward v. Eppenstein, 1076–1976. St. Lambrecht, Stift St. Lambrecht, 1976.
107 p. 10 leaves of plates (part col.) 23 cm.
InStme

3601 **Reliquiae quae continentur in altaribus monasterii S. Lamberti.** MS. Universitätsbibliothek Graz, Austria, codex 193, f.132r–133v. Quarto. Saec. 14.
Microfilm: MnCH proj. no. 26,128

3602 **Wonisch, Othmar.**
Die Theaterkultur des Stiftes St. Lambrecht. Graz, Historischer Verein für Steiermark, 1957.
75 p. 24 cm.
MnCS

Sankt Leodegar im Hof, Lucerne, Switzerland
see
Lucerne, Switzerland. Sankt Leodegar im Hof

Sankt Mang, Füssen, Germany
see
Füssen, Germany. Sankt Mang

Sankt Maria, Fulda, Germany
see
Fulda, Germany. Sankt Maria

Sankt Matthias, Trier, Germany
see
Trier, Germany. Sankt Matthias

Sankt Mauritius, Tholey, Germany
see
Tholey, Germany. St. Mauritius

Sankt Maximin, Trier, Germany
see
Trier, Germany. Sankt Maximin

Sankt Michael, Hildesheim, Germany
see
Hildesheim, Germany. Sankt Michael

Sankt Michael, Lüneberg, Germany
see
Lüneberg, Germany. Sankt Michael

Sankt Michael, Siegburg, Germany
see
Siegburg, Germany. Sankt Michael

Sankt Ottilien, Bavaria (Benedictine abbey)

3603 **Bornemann, Fritz, S.V.D.**
Ein Briefwechsel zur Vorgeschichte von St. Ottilien. [Siegburg], Steyler Verlag, 1965.
90 p. 23 cm.
MnCS

3604 **Brechter, Heinrich Suso, O.S.B.**
Beurons Beitrag zur Gründung von St. Ottilien.
(*In* Beuron, 1863–1963; Festschrift . . . Beuron, 1963. p. 231–267)
PLatS

3605 **Renner, Frumentius, O.S.B.**
Der fünfarmige Leuchter; Beitr. z. Werden u. Wirken d. Benediktinerkongregation von St. Ottilien. Hrsg. von Frumentius Renner. Sankt Ottilien, Eos-Verlag, 1971.
2 v. illus. 25 cm.
MnCS

3606 **Renner, Frumentius, O.S.B.**
Sankt Ottilien – sein Werden und Wirken. Auszug und Sonderabdruck aus "Der fünfarmige Leuchter." 2. Aufl. St. Ottilien, Eos-Verlag [1972].

120 p. illus., ports. 23 cm.
InStme

3607 **Wehrmeister, Cyril, O.S.B.**
Die Benediktinermissionäre von St. Ottilien. 2te, stark erweiterte Aufl. Missionsverlag St. Ottilien, 1928.
108 p. illus., plates, maps. 23 cm.
MnCS

Sankt Paul im Lavantthal, Austria
(Benedictine abbey)

3608 **Catalogus codicum manuscriptorum** ex monasteriis S. Blasii in Nigra Silva et Hospitalis ad Pyrhum montem in Austria, nunc in monast. S. Pauli in Carinthia. [1868?]
[113] p. 30 p. 29 cm.
Handwritten. Nachtrag typescript.
Xeroxed by University Microfilms, Ann Arbor, Mich., 1968.
MnCS

3609 **Catalogus d. d. religiosorum Ordinis S. Benedicti** monasterii ad S. Paulum in dioecesi Gurcensi et valle Lavantina Carinthiae.
v. 22 cm.
PLatS

3610 **Disciplina regularis reformata in monasterio S. Pauli** . . . compilata opera et studio Alberti abbatis. MS. Benediktinerabtei St. Paul im Lavantthal, Austria, codex 33/0. 317 f. Folio. Saec. 17(1682).
Microfilm: MnCH proj. no. 12,677

3611 **Fresacher, Walther.**
Die mittelalterlichen Urbare des Benediktinerstiftes St. Paul in Kärnten, 1289–1371. Graz, Böhlau, 1968.
cviii, 354 p. maps. 24 cm.
MnCS

3612 **Ginhart, Karl.**
Das Stift St. Paul im Lavantthal. [6. erweiterte und korrigierte Aufl.]. Im Selbstverlag des Stiftes St. Paul, 1968].
47 p. illus. 17 cm.
MnCS; PLatS

3613 **Graz, Austria. Steiermärkische Landesarchiv.**
Catalogus der Urkunden, Abtei St. Paul und Stift Eberndorf.
116, 13 p. 29 cm.
Concordance of codex numbers in Abtei St. Paul, Austria. Unpaged.
Xeroxed by University Microfilms, Ann Arbor, Mich., 1968.
MnCS

3614 **Hieronymus, abbas S. Pauli.**
De fundatione rerum, statu, prospero, adverso, vita et morte fundatorum, bene-

factorum et abbatum et monachorum monasterii S. Pauli Vallis Lavantinae. MS. Benediktinerabtei St. Paul im Lavantthal, Austria, codex 1/0. f.1–110. Folio. Saec. 17(1619).
Microfilm: MnCH proj. no. 12,636

3615 **Lobreden auf die Aebte von St. Paul.**
MS. Benediktinerabtei St. Paul im Lavantthal, Austria, codex 42/0. 227 p. Quarto. Saec. 18.
Microfilm: MnCH proj. no. 12,644

3616 **Moro, Gotbert, ed.**
Festgabe zur 150-Jahr-Feier der Wiederbesiedlung des Benediktinerstiftes St. Paul im Lavantthal durch die Mönche von St. Blasien im Schwarzwald. Klagenfurt, Verlag des Geschichtsvereines für Kärnten, 1959.
607 p. plates, 24 cm.
MnCS

3617 **Oeffentliches Gymnasium des Benediktinerstiftes St. Paul.**
Jahresbericht über das Schuljahr 1967–1968 (159. Bestandsjahr). Hrsg. von der Anstaltsleitung Selbstverlag des Stiftsgymnasiums St. Paul, 1968.
51 p. illus. 24 cm.
MnCS

3618 **St. Paul, 1091, 1805, 1959.** [Festschrift zum 150. Jahresgedenktag der Wiederbesiedlung des Stiftes St. Paul . . . St. Paul im Lavantthal, 1959].
188 p. illus. 24 cm.
PLatS; KAS

3619 **Schroll, Beda, O.S.B.**
Necrologium des Benediktinerstiftes St. Paul im Lavantthale.
(*In* Archiv für vaterländische Geschichte. Klagenfurt, 10. Jahrg., 1866. p. 33–240)
KAS

3620 **Schroll, Beda, O.S.B.**
Regesten aus Leben-Urkunden des Benediktinerstiftes St. Paul vom XVI bis XVIII Jahrhunderts.
(*In* Archiv für vaterländische Geschichte. Klagenfurt. 12. Jahrg. (1972), p. 71–137)
KAS

3621 **Schroll, Beda, O.S.B., ed.**
Urkundenbuch des Benedictiner-Stiftes St. Paul in Kärnten. Wien, Karl Gerold's Sohn, 1876.
594 p. 23 cm. (Fontes rerum austriarcarum, 39)
MnCS

Sankt Peter, Erfurt, Germany
see
Erfurt, Germany. Sankt Peter

Sankt Peter, Kreuzberg, Germany
see
Kreuzberg, Germany. Sankt Peter

Sankt Peter, Salzburg, Austria
see
Salzburg, Austria. Sankt Peter

Sankt Peter auf dem Schwarzwald, Germany
(Benedictine abbey)

3622   **Mittler, Elmer.**
Die Bibliothek des Klosters S. Peter.
Bühl, Baden, Verlag Kondordia, 1972.
280 p. 23 cm.
MnCS

3622a **Mühleisen, Hans Otto.**
St. Peter im Schwarzwald. [2. Aufl.].
München, Verlag Schnell & Steiner [1976].
48 p. illus. 24 cm. (Die Grossen Kunst-
führer)
MnCS

3622b **Mühleisen, Hans Otto.**
St. Peter im   Schwarzwald; kultur-
geschichtliche und historische Beiträge
anlässlich der 250-Jahrfeier der Einweihung der Klosterkirche. München, Verlag
Schnell & Steiner, 1977.
263 p. illus. 24 cm.
MnCS

Sankt Stephan, Augsburg, Germany
see
Augsburg, Germany. Sankt Stephan

Sankt Ulrich und Afra, Augsburg, Germany
see
Augsburg, Austria. Sankt Ulrich und Afra

Sankt Veit, Germany (Benedictine abbey)

3623   **Hör, Hellmut.**
Die Urkunden des Klosters St. Veit,
1121–1450. München, Beck, 1960.
36, 340 p. 25 cm.
MnCS

3624   **Lechner, Martin.**
Die Pfarr- und ehemalige Benediktiner-
kirche Neumarkt-St-Veit. München,
Schnell und Steiner, 1973.
30 p. illus. 17 cm.
MnCS

Sankt Walburg, Eichstätt, Germany
see
Eichstätt, Germany. Sankt Walburg

Sant'Anselmo, Rome, Italy
see
Rome, Italy. Collegio di Sant'Anselmo

Sant Cristofil, Salinoves, Spain
see
Salinoves, Spain. Sant Cristofil

Sant Cugat, Valles, Spain
see
Valles, Spain. Sant Cugat

Sant Egidio, Fontanella, Italy
see
Fontanella, Italy. Sant Egidio

Sant'Eutizio (Benedictine abbey)
near Norcia, Italy

3625   **Pirri, Pietro**
L'Abbazia di Sant'Eutizio in Val
Castoriana presso Norcia e la chiese dipen-
denti. Romae, Herder, 1960.
vi, 376 p. illus. 25 cm. (Studia Anselmiana, 45)
InStme; PLatS

Sant Pau del Camp, Spain (Benedictine abbey)

3626   **Vigue, Jerdi.**
El monestir romànic de Sant Pau del
Camp . . . Barcelona, Arestudi edicions
[1974].
242 p. illus.(part col.) 20 cm.
MnCS

Santa Anna de Rocca, Mandragone, Italy
see
Madragone, Italy. Santa Anna de Rocca

Santa Cruz de la Seros, Spain
(Benedictine convent)

3627   **Valenzuela Foved, Virgilio.**
Los monasterios de San Juan de la Peña
y Santa Cruz de la Serós; guia del visitante. Huesca, 1959.
149 p. illus. 17 cm.
PLatS

Santa Cruz del Valle de los Caidos, Spain
(Benedictine abbey)

3628   **Monumento nacional de Santa Cruz** dell
Valle de Los Caidos; guia turistica.
4. ed. corregida y aumentada. Madrid,
Patrimonio Nacional.
128 p. illus. (part col.) 17 cm.
PLatS

Santa Giustina, Padua, Italy
see
Padua, Italy. Santa Giustina

Santa Maria, Claro, Switzerland
see
Claro, Switzerland. Santa Maria

Santa Maria, Pomposa, Italy
see
Pomposa, Italy. Santa Maria

Santa Maria, Ripoll, Spain
see
Ripoll, Spain. Santa Maria

Santa Maria del Monte, Cesana, Italy
see
Cesana, Italy. Santa Maria del Monte

Santa Maria in Sylvis, Sesto al Reghena, Italy
see
Sesto al Reghena, Italy. Santa Maria in Sylvis

Santa Scholastica, Subiaco, Italy
see
Subiaco, Italy (Benedictine abbey)

Santi Pietro e Paolo, Brugora, Italy
see
Brugora, Italy. SS. Pietro e Paolo

Santiago Monasterio, Leon, Spain
see
Leon, Spain. Santiago Monasterio

Santo Domingo, Silos, Spain
see
Silos, Spain. Santo Domingo

Sao Bento, Olinda, Brazil
see
Olinda, Brazil. Sao Bento

Sao Bento, Rio de Janeiro, Brazil
see
Rio de Janeiro, Brazil. Sao Bento

Sao Paulo, Brazil. Mosteir de S. Bento
3629 **Scherer, Michael Emilio, O.S.B.**
Ein grosser Benediktiner: Abt Michael
Kruse von Sao Paulo (1864–1929). München, Verlag der Bayer. Benediktinerabtei,
1963.
180 p. plates. 24 cm.
PLatS

Sarnen, Switzerland. St. Andreas
(Benedictine convent)
3630 **Catalog des Benedictinerinnen-Klosters
St. Andreas** in Sarnen (Obwalden) und

seiner Filiale in Amerika. Sarnen,
Druck von Jos. Müller, 1888.
12 p. 16 cm.
PLatS

Sassovivo, Italy (Benedictine abbey)
3631 **Concetti, Georgio.**
Le carte dell'Abbazia di S. Croce de
Sassovivo. Firenze, Leo S. Olschki, 1973–
v. 25 cm.
MnCS (v. 1, 2 & 4)

Savigny, France (Benedictine abbey)
3632 **Guique, Georges.**
Les Bénédictines chez les Bénédictins:
profession de religieuses à l'Abbaye de
Savigny en Lyonnais (XVe siècle). Paris,
Imprimerie Nationale, 1902.
24 p. 25 cm.
KAS

Schäftlarn, Bavaria (Benedictine abbey)
3633 **Mitterer, Sigisbert, O.S.B., ed.**
1200 Jahre Kloster Schäftlarn, 762–
1962; Blätter zum Gedächtnis. Schäftlarn,
Selbstverlag der Abtei, 1962.
171 p. illus., facsims. 24 cm.
InStme; MnCS; MoCo; NdRi; PLatS

Scheyern, Bavaria (Benedictine abbey)
3634 **Chronicon Schyrense.** MS. Vienna, Nationalbibliothek, codex 2672, f.91r–140r.
Folio. Saec. 15(1453).
Microfilm: MnCH proj. no. 15,941
3635 **Kreuzer, Ildefons, O.S.B.**
Die Wiedererrichtung der Benediktinerabtei Scheyern; ein Beitrag zur
Geschichte der Klosterpolitik König Lud-
wigs I. von Bayern. [n.p.] 1961.
175 leaves. illus. 30 cm.
Mimeographed.
KAS

Schottenstift, Vienna, Austria
see
Vienna, Austria. Schottenstift

Shawnee, Okla. St. Gregory's Abbey
see
St. Gregory's Abbey, Shawnee, Okla.

**Schwarzach am Rhein, Germany
(Benedictine abbey)**
3636 **Tschira, Arnold.**
Die ehemalige Benediktinerabtei
Schwarzach. 2. veränderte und erweiterte

Aufl. Institut für Baugeschichte an der Universität Karlsruhe, 1977.
viii, 102 p. 123 illus. 26 cm.
MnCS

Seckau, Austria (Benedictine abbey)

3637 **Roth, Benno, O.S.B.**
Benediktinee-Abtei Seckau [3. wesentlich umgerbeitete, neubebilderte Aufl.].
München, Schnell & Steiner [1965].
47 p. illus. 24 cm.
PLatS

3638 **Roth, Benno, O.S.B.**
Beschlagnahme und Enteignung der Benediktinerabtei Seckau in Obersteiermark am 8. April durch die Gestapo.
[Seckau] 1965.
106 p. port. 21 cm.
PLatS

3639 **Roth, Benno, O.S.B.**
Seckau; Erbe und Auftrag. Ein Gang durch seine Geschichte, Kunst und Kultur.
Wien, Bergland Verlag [1960].
78 p. illus. 18 cm.
KAS

Seitenstetten, Austria (Benedictine abbey)

3640 **Decker, Aegid, O.S.B.**
Stift Seitenstetten, Benediktinerabtei.
München, Schnell & Steiner, 1957.
15 p. 17 cm.
PLatS

3641 **Directorium seu Ordo opus Dei celebrandi** in usum monasterii Seitenstettensis O.S.B. . . .
v. 19 cm.
MnCS

3641a **Flossmann, Gerhard, ed.**
Die mittelalterlichen Urbare des Benediktinerstiftes Seitenstetten, 1292/98 und 1286/98. Wien, Verlag der Oesterreichischen Akademie der Wissenschaften, 1977.
cix, 300 p. illus. 25 cm.
MnCS

3642 **Gundackerus, abbot of Seitenstetten.**
Memoriale fundationis. MS. Benediktinerabtei Seitenstetten, Austria, codex 208, f.267r–269v. Folio. Saec. 15.
Microfilm: MnCH proj. no. 1013

3643 **Haider, Johann.**
Die Geschichte des Theaterwesens im Benediktinerstift Seitenstetten in Barock und Aufklärung. Wien, Verlag der Oesterreichischen Akademie der Wissenschaft, 1973.
226 p. illus. 24 cm.
MnCS

3644 **Raab, Isidor.**
Urkundenbuch des Benedictiner-Stiftes Seitenstetten. Wien, A. Holzhausen, 1870.
v, 421 p. 24 cm.
KAS

3645 **Stift Seitenstetten.** Urkundenabschriften. MS. Vienna, Haus- Hof- und Stattsarchiv, codex W. 987/5. Saec. 17.
Microfilm: MnCH proj. no. 23,614

3646 **Wagner, Benedikt, O.S.B.**
Der Religionsfonds versteigert eine alte Stiftsbibliothek.
(*In* Translatio studii; manuscript and library studies honoring Oliver L. Kapsner. Collegeville, Minn., 1973. p. 235–243)
MnCS; PLatS

Selby Abbey, England

3647 **Moody, Charles Harry.**
Selby Abbey; a resumé, 1069–1908. London, E. Stock, 1908.
114 p. illus. 22 cm.
CaBMi; KAS

Seligenstadt, Germany (Benedictine abbey)

3648 **Weinckens, Johannes, O.S.B.**
Navarchia Seligenstadiana, seu Fundatio antiquissimae & regalis abbatiae Seligenstadiensis . . . Francofurti ad Moenum, Joan. Ph. Andreas, 1714.
[12], 140 p. 33 cm.
KAS

Senones, France (Benedictine abbey)

3649 **Calmet, Augustin, O.S.B.**
Histoire de l'Abbaye de Senones. Manuscrit inédit de Dom Calmet, publié . . . avec une préface, des notes . . . par F. Dinago. Saint-Dié, L. Humbert [1879].
439 p. illus.
CaQStB

Seeon, Bavaria (Benedictine abbey)

3650 **Wiest, Veneranda, Schwester, O.S.B.**
Honorat Kolb, Abt von Seon, 1603–1670. München, Selbstverlag der Bayerischen Benediktinerabtei, 1937.
xx, 139 p. plates. port. 25 cm.
KAS

Sens, France. Sainte-Colombe

see

Sainte-Colombe-les-Sens, France

Sesto al Reghena, Italy. S. Maria in Sylvis (Vallumbrosian abbey)

3651 **Gerometta, Tommaso.**
L'abbazia benedettina di S. Maria in Sylvis in Sesto al Reghena; guida storico-

artistica corredata di 85 illus. [Portogruaro], 1957.
223 p. illus. 21 cm.
PLatS

Shaftesbury Abbey, England

3652 **Shaftesbury and its abbey.** Lingfield, Oakwood Press [1959].
132 p. illus., plates. 23 cm.
PLatS

Shakopee, Minn. St. Gertrude's Convent
see
St. Gertrude's Convent, Shakopee, Minn.

Shawnee, Okla. St. Gregory's Abbey
see
St. Gregory's Abbey, Shawnee, Okla.

Siegburg, Germany (Benedictine abbey)

3653 **Monumenta Annonis**—Köln und Siegburg; Weltbild und Kunst im hohen Mittelalter. Eine Ausstellung des Schütgen-Museums der Stadt Köln in der Cäcilienkirche vom 30. April bis zum 27. Juli 1975. Köln, 1975.
248 p. illus., plates (part col.) 30 cm.
MnCS

3654 **Weber, Wunibald, O.S.B.**
Die Benediktiner-Abtei auf dem Michaelsberg zu Siegburg. Siegburg, Verlag Michaelsberg [n.d.].
20 p. illus. 20 cm.
MnCS

3654a **Wisplinghoff, Erich.**
Die Benediktinerabtei Siegburg. Köln, Erzbistum Köln, 1975.
(Germania sacra. Neue Folge)
MnCS

Silos, Spain. Santo Domingo (Benedictine abbey)

3655 **Fernandez, Ismael, O.S.B.**
El "Breviarium gothicum" de Silos; Archivo monástico, MS. 6. Madrid, 1965.
126 p. 25 cm.
MnCS

3656 **Magarinos, Santiago.**
El libro de Silos. [Madrid, Santander] n.d.
119 p. illus., plates. 24 cm.
MnCS

3657 **Palacios, Mariano, O.S.B.**
Il monasterio de Santo Domingo de Silos.
2. ed. Madrid, Editorial Everest [1977].
64 p. illus. 26 cm.

3658 **Ruiz, Agustin, O.S.B.**
Abadía de Santo Domingo de Silos: el abad santo, el claustro románico, la vida benedictina. [Burgos, 1960].
102 p. plates, ports. map. 24 cm.
MnCS

3659 **Ruiz, Agustin S., O.S.B.**
Los exclaustrados de Silos, una "communidad" fuera de su monasterio.
(*In* Semana de estudios monasticos, 14th, Silos, Spain, 1973. p. 247–277)
PLatS

Solesmes, France. Abbaye Saint-Pierre

3660 **L'Abbaye Saint-Pierre de Solesmes.** Solesmes, 1969.
64 p. illus.
MoCo

3661 **Bouvilliers, Adelard, O.S.B.**
An outlook on the sixty years of the Solesmes School of Music. Washington, D.C., Benedictine Foundation.
Offprint from The Placidian, p. 151–161.
NcBe

3662 **Des Pilliers, Pierre-Marie-Raphaël.**
Les Bénédictins de la Congrégation de France. Bruxelles, PlJ.D. DeSomer, 1868–69.
2 v. 24 cm.
Contents: pt.1: L'Abbaye de Solesmes.
KAS

3663 **Gajard, Joseph, O.S.B.**
Les débuts de la restauration grégorienne à Solesmes. Roma, Associazione italiana Santa Cecilia [195-?].
32 p. 24 cm.
MnCS

3664 **Murray, Gregory, O.S.B.**
Plainsong rhythm; the editorial methods of Solesmes. [Exeter, Printed at Catholic Records Press, 1956].
18 p. illus.(music) 22 cm.
PLatS

3665 **Soltner, Louis, O.S.B.**
Solesmes & Dom Guéranger, 1805–1975. Saint-Pierre de Solesmes, 1974.
177 p. 48 leaves of plates & illus. 24 cm.
InStme

3666 **Weakland, Rembert George, O.S.B.**
The lesson of Solesmes.
Offprint from The Catholic choirmaster, v. 38(1952), p. 6.
PLatS

Sonnenburg, Austria (abbey of Benedictine nuns)

3667 **Handlung und Vertragsausspruch zwischen dem Stift Brixen** und

Gotshaus Sonnenburg wegen den Holz-
nutzung in den Wäldern Sare u. Stares
zn der Grenze zwischen Enneberg und
Sonnenburg, 1599. MS. Innsbruck,
Austria, Tiroler Landesarchiv, codex
2351. 95 f. Folio. Saec. 16.
Microfilm: MnCH proj. no. 29,172

3668 **Liturgischer Kalender für den Kirchen-
dienst im Stift Sonnenburg.** 14 f.
·Saec. 18. Form und Weis der Auffnem-
mung, Einklaidung und Profess der
Novizinnen des fürstl. Stifts zu Sonnen-
burg (Ceremonien und Gesänge). 108 p.
Saec. 17. MS. Innsbruck, Austria,
Tiroler Landesarchiv, codex 3863 &
3864.
Microfilm: MnCH proj. no. 29,200

3669 **Missivbuch des Stiftes Sonnenburg,**
1564–1568. MS. Innsbruck, Austria,
Tiroler Landesarchiv, codex 2339. 253
f. Folio. Saec. 16.
Microfilm: MnCH proj. no. 29,161

3670 **Prozess der Aebtissin Clara von Sonnenburg mit dem o.ö. Kammerprokurator**
wegen der Wälder im Tale Mühlwald,
Lopach und Weissenbach, 1542–1548.
MS. Innsbruck, Austria, Tiroler Landesarchiv, codex 1429. 98 f. Folio. Saec. 16.
Microfilm: MnCH proj. no. 29,141

3671 **Regeln oder Satzungen für die Laien-
schwestern im Stift Sonnenburg,**
bestätigt von Bischof Leopold von
Brixen, 1752. MS. Innsbruck, Austria,
Tiroler Landesarchiv, codex 2375. 16 f.
Quarto. Saec. 18.
Microfilm: MnCH proj. no. 29,176

3672 **Register über die Urkunden und Akten**
des Archivs des Stiftes Sonnenburg
(Repertorium) 1665 angelegt. MS. Innsbruck, Austria, Tiroler Landesarchiv,
codex 2770. 219 f. Folio. Saec. 17.
Microfilm: MnCH proj. no. 29,180

3673 **Wolfsgruber, Karl, ed.**
Die ältesten Urbare des Benediktinerin-
nenstiftes Sonnenburg im Pustertal. Wien,
Böhlau, 1968.
lxxix, 147 p. 25 cm.
Register of land titles in Latin and Mid-
dle High German.
MnCS

Sponheim, Germany (Benedictine abbey)

3674 **Trithemius, Johannes, O.S.B.**
Des Abtes Johannes Trithemius Chronik
des Klosters Sponheim. Wortgetreue
Uebersetzung nach den in Würzburg und
Madrid vorliegenden Handschriften, unter
Benützung der jüngeren Druckausgabe

von Freher, Frankfurt, 1601. (Chronicon
Spanheimense) Deutsch, 1024–1509. Bad
Kreuznach, Selbstverlag Carl Velten
[Herausgeber] 1969.
263 p. illus. 24 cm.
MnCS

Stams, Austria (Benedictine abbey)

3675 **Geschichte der Gründung und Weihe
des Klosters Stams.** MS. Universitätsbibliothek Innsbruck, Austria, codex 42,
f.191r–192r. Folio. Saec. 13.
Microfilm: MnCH proj. no. 28,131

Stanbrook Abbey, England

3676 **The Stanbrook Abbey Press;** ninety-two
years of its history written and illustrated by the Benedictines of Stanbrook.
Worcester, Stanbrook Abbey Press,
1970.
xiv, 180 p. illus. 23 cm.
MnCS; PLatS

Stavelot, Belgium (Benedictine abbey)

3677 **Recueil des chartes de l'Abbaye de
Stavelot-Malmedy,** publié par Jos.
Halkin et C. G. Roland. Bruxelles, Kiess-
ling et cie, 1909–30.
2 v. fold. map. 31 cm.
MnCS

**Stein am Rhein, Switzerland
(Benedictine abbey)**

3678 **Schmid, Heinrich Alfred.**
Die Wandgemälde im Festsaal des
Klosters St. Georgen in Stein am Rhein
aus den Jahren 1515–16. 3., unveränderte
Aufl. [Bern]
72 p. illus. 25 cm.
PLatS

Subiaco, Ark. New Subiaco Abbey
see
New Subiaco Abbey, Subiaco, Ark.

Subiaco, Italy (Benedictine abbey)

3679 **Allodi, Leone, O.S.B.**
Inventario dei manoscritti della biblio-
teca di Subiaco. Forli, Casaeditrice Luigi
Bordandini, 1891.
74 p. 29 cm.
MnCS

3680 **Andreotti, Stanislao, O.S.B.**
Subiaco, culla dell'Ordine Benedettino,
sede della prima tipografia italiana.
Subiaco, 1965.

108 p. illus.
MoCo

3681 **Andreotti, Stanislao, O.S.B.**
Subiaco nella seconda metà del sette-
cento. Subiaco, Tipografia editrice S.
Scolastica, 1975.
239, 10 p. plates. 24 cm.
MnCS

3682 **Carosi, G. P.**
La stampa da Magonza a Subiaco.
Subiaco, Edizioni S. Scolastica, 1976.
139 p. plates, facsims. 24 cm.
MnCS

3683 **Catalogo dei beni del mon. di S. Scolastica.** MS. Subiaco, Italy (Benedictine
abbey), codex 377. Saec. 18(1727).
Microfilm: MnCH

3684 **Copie di privilegi a favore del mon.
Sublacense di Nicolo V, 1449;** Sisto IV,
1474; Urbano VI; Callisto II, 1457;
Eugenio IV, 1432; Pio II; Eugenio IV,
1444; Nicolo V, 1447. MS. Subiaco,
Italy (Benedictine abbey), codex 383.
43 f. Saec. 15.
Microfilm: MnCH

3685 **Cum ad monasterium Sublacense.** MS.
Benediktinerabtei Melk, Austria, codex
1214, f. 73r–74v. Sextodecimo. Saec. 15.
Microfilm: MnCH proj. no. 1865

3686 **Drinkwater, Geneva Halliday.**
History of the monastery of Subiaco to
1500.
iv, 191 leaves. 29 cm.
Thesis – University of Chicago, 1931.
Typescript.
MnCS; Library of Congress

3687 **Epistola quaedam totum processum con-
versationis monasterii Sublacensis
continens.** MS. Benediktinerabtei Melk,
Austria, codex 979, f.1r–2v. Quarto.
Saec. 15.
Microfilm: MnCH proj. no. 1790

3688 **Expositio capituli:** Cum ad monasterium
Sublacense. De statu monachorum. Expositio domini hostiensis. MS. Benediktinerabtei Melk, Austria, codex 793,
351r–376v.
Microfilm: MnCH proj. no. 1634

3689 **Federici, Domenico.**
Abbrivi benedettini in val d'Aniene.
Frascati, 1957.
73 p. 24 cm.
PLatS

3690 **Pierantonio da Trevi.**
Compendio della storia dell'Abbazia di
Subiaco. MS. Subiaco, Italy (Benedictine
abbey), codex 335. Saec. 17.
Microfilm: MnCH

3691 **Protocollo d'istrumenti, 1656–86,** relativi
al monasterio de S. Scolastica. MS.
Subiaco, Italy (Benedictine abbey), codex
380. Saec. 17.
Microfilm: MnCH

3692 **Regestrum insigne veterum monumen-
torum** (in tutti, 216) monasterii S.
Scolasticae Sublaci: il primo del 3 agosto
369, l'ultimo dell'aprile 1192. MS. Subiaco, Italy (Benedictine abbey), codex
381. 220 f. Folio. Saec. 11.
Microfilm: MnCH

3693 **Reggiani, Ferrucio.**
Les voies de la paix. Subiaco, Abbaye
Bénédictine, 1971.
116 p. illus. 20 cm.
MnCS

3694 **Il Sacro Speco e il Monastero di S.
Scolastica.** Benedittini di Subiaco, 1966.
71 p. illus., plates (col.) 17 cm.
MnCS

3695 **St. Scholastica's Abbey;** an historical
and artistic guide, edited by Benedictine
Fathers. Roma, Casa editrice Lozzi
[1971].
46 p. illus. (part col.), plans. 18 cm.
MnCS

Subiaco, Italy. Sacro Speco

3696 **Gasdia, Vincenzo Eduardo.**
San Benedetto cavernicola nel Sacro
Speco di Subiaco. [Verona], Ghidini &
Fiorini, 1958.
45 p. 25 cm.
PLatS

3697 **Il Sacro Speco di Subiaco:** 32 tavole.
Terni, Stab. Alterocca [n.d.].
32 plates. 20 x 26 cm.
MnCS; PLatS

3698 **Sacro Speco, Subiaco.** Benedettini di
Subiaco, 1968.
71 p. illus., plates (col). 17 cm.
French and English.
MnCS

3699 **Il Sacro Speco e il Monastero di S. Scolastica.** Benedettini di Subiaco, 1966.
71 p. illus., plates (col.). 17 cm.
MnCS

3700 **Il Sacro Speco di Subiaco.** LII vedute.
Ediz. del Monastero del Sacro Speco
[n.d.].
52 plates. 26 x 20 cm.
MnCS

Susteren, Netherlands
(abbey of Benedictine nuns)

3701 **Roozen, N., C.M.**
Rondom de grafzerken in der voormalige
abdijkerk te Susteren. [Harreveld,

Grafische Vakschool en Drukkerij "St. Joseph"], 1958.
127 p. plates. 21 cm.

Tarragone, Spain (Benedictine abbey)

3702   **Tobella, Antonius M., O.S.B.**
Cronologia dels capítols de la congregació claustral Tarraconense i Cesaraugustana (primera parte: 1219–1661).
(*In* Analecta Montserratensia, v. 10, p. 221–398)
PLatS

3703   **Tobella, Antonius M., O.S.B.**
Documents del primer segle de la congregació claustral Tarraconense.
(*In* Analecta Montserratensia, v. 10, p. 139–455)
PLatS

Tegernsee, Bavaria (Benedictine abbey)

3704   **Angerer, Joachim, O.S.B.**
Die Bräuche der Abtei Tegernsee unter Abt Ayndorffer (1426–1461), verbunden mit einer textkritischen Edition der Consuetudines Tegernseensees. Ottobeuren, Kommissionsverlag Winfried-Werk, 1968.
xv, 362 p. 25 cm.
InStme; KAS; MnCS; PLatS

3705   **Behrendt, Roland, O.S.B.**
Fifteenth-century Tegernsee revisited.
Sonderdruck aus: Regulae Benedicti studia, v. 3–4(1974–75), p. 125–131.
The essay is a review article of: Tegernsee und die deutsche Geistesgeschichte im 15. Jahrhundert, von P. Virgil Redlich O.S.B. (München, 1931. Reprint: Allen, 1974)
MnCS

3705a   **Eder, Christine Elisabeth.**
Die Schule des Klosters Tegernsee im frühen Mittelalter im Spiegel der Tegernseen Handschriften. München, Arbeo Gesellschaft, 1972.
155 p. 24 cm.
"Sonderdruck aus Studien und Mitteilungen des Benediktinerordens, Bd. 83(1972), p. 6–155."
MnCS

3706   **Lindner, Pirmin, O.S.B.**
Die Aebte und Mönche der Benediktiner-Abtei Tegernsee von den ältesten Zeiten bis zu ihrem Aussterben (1861) und ihr literarischer Nachlass. München, Histor. Vereins von Oberbayern, 1897–98.
2 v. 25 cm.
KAS

3707   **Redlich, Virgil, O.S.B.**
Tegernsee und die deutsche Geistesgeschichte im 15. Jahrhundert. Aalen, Scientia Verlag, 1974.
268 p. 23 cm.
MnCS

3707a   **Ruodlieb. Mittellateinisch und deutsch.**
Uebertragung, Kommentar und Nachwort von Fritz Peter Knapp. Stuttgart, Philipp Reclam Jun. [1977].
252 p. 15 cm.
Written in Tegernsee about 1050.
MnCS

3708   **Velthuis, Hendrik Jacob.**
De Tegernseeër Glossen op Vergilius. Groningen, J.B. Wolters, 1892.
116 p. 25 cm.
MnCS

3709   **Von dem erwürdigen Closter zu Tegernsee wie es erst gepauet ward,** und wie der heilig martrer sant Quirein ward gepracht von Rom her gen Tegernsee.
MS. Vienna, Nationalbibliothek, codex series nov 12,801. 40 f. Folio. Saec. 15. Microfilm: MnCH proj. no. 25,166

Tewkesbury Abbey, England

3710   **Spence-Jones, Henry Donald Maurice.**
Tewkesbury.
(*In* his: Cloister life in the days of Coeur de Lion. London, 1892. p. 82–139)
PLatS

Thanet, England. Minster Abbey
see
Minster Abbey, Thanet, England

Tholey, Germany (Benedictine abbey)

3711   **Abteikirche und Pfarrkirche St. Mauritius, Tholey.** Hrsg. von der Abtei St. Mauritius, Tholey-Saar. St. Wendel-Saar, St. Wendler Buchdruckerei und Verlag [1961].
74 p. illus., plates. 21 x 20 cm.
MnCS; KAS

3712   **Reichert, Franz Josef.**
Die Baugeschichte der Benediktiner-Abteikirche Tholey. Saarbrücken, Institut für Landeskunde des Saarlandes [1961].
312 p. (incl. 56 plates), 5 fold. diagrs. 24 cm.
PLatS

Tinley Park, Ill.
Our Lady of Sorrows Convent.
see
Our Lady of Sorrows Convent, Tinley Park, Ill.

Tiron, France. Sainte-Trinite (Benedictine abbey)

3713 **Pritchard, Emoly M.**
The history of St. Dogmaels Abbey, together with her cells, Pill, Caldey and Glascareg, and the mother abbey of Tiron . . . London, Blades, East & Blades, 1907.
241 p. illus., plates, fold. map. 26 cm.
MnCS

Tournai, Belgium. Saint-Martin (Benedictine abbey)

3714 **Boutemy, A.**
Odon d'Orleans et les origines de la bibliothèque de l'Abbaye de Saint-Martin de Tournai.
(*In* Mélanges dédiés à la mémoire de Fêlix Grat. Paris, 1949. v. 2, p. 179–222)
PLatS

3715 **Haenens, Albert d'.**
L'Abbaye Saint-Martin de Tournai de 1290 à 1350: origines, évolution et dénouement d'une crise. Louvain, Publications universitaites, 1961.
321 p. 25 cm.
MoCo; PLatS

3716 **Haenens, Albert d'.**
Comptes et documents de l'Abbaye de Saint-Martin de Tournai sous l'administration des gardiens toyaus (1312–1366). Bruxelles, Palais des Académies, 1962.
882 p. 22 cm.
KAS

3717 **Herbomez, Armand Auguste d'.**
Chartes de l'Abbaye de Saint-Martin de Tournai . . . Bruxelles, Hayes, impr., 1898–1901.
2 v. 31 cm.
KAS(v.1)

Treport, Le, France. Saint-Michel (Benedictine abbey)

3718 **Cartulaire de l'Abbaye de Saint-Michel du Tréport** (Ordre de Saint Benoît), par P. Laffleur de Kermaingant. Paris, Firmin-Didot, 1880.
clix, 425 p. 29 cm.
KAS

Trier, Germany. Sankt Matthias (Benedictine abbey)

3719 **Becker, Peter, O.S.B.**
Das monastische Reformprogramm des Johannes Rode, Abtes von St. Matthias in Trier; ein darstellender Kommentar zu seinen Consuetudines. Münster, Aschendorff [1970].

xix, 218 p. 25 cm.
PLatS

3720 **Consuetudines et observatiae monasteriorum Sancti Matthiae** et Sancti Maximi Treverensium ab Johanne Rode abbate conscriptae. Edidit Petrus Becker. Siegburg, F. Schmitt, 1968.
lxx, 320 p. 26 cm. (Corpus consuetudinum monasticarum, 5)
InStme; KAS; PLatS

3721 **Führer durch die Basilika des hl. Apostels Matthias zu Trier.** Trier, Druck der Paulinus-Druckerei [n.d.].
64 p. illus. 11x14 cm.
MnCS

3722 **Hau, Johannes.**
Die Erzbruderschaft des hl. Matthias in Geschichte und Gegenwart; ein Beitrag zur Wegbereitung der katholischen Aktion . . . Trier, Paulinus-Druckerei [1936].
50 p. 23 cm.
MnCS

Trier, Germany. Sankt Maximin (Benedictine abbey)

3723 **Eisplinghoff, Erich.**
Untersuchungen zur frühen Geschichte der Abtei S. Maximin bei Trier von den Anfängen bis etwa 1150. Mainz, Gessellschaft für Mittelrheinische Kirchengeschichte, 1970.
xvi, 224 p. plates. 24 cm.
MnCS

Troia, Italy (Benedictine abbey)

3724 **Leccisotti, Tommaso Domenico, O.S.B.**
Le colonie Cassinesi in Capitanata. Montecassino, 1937–1940.
4 v. plates. 26 cm.
Contents: v. 4: Troia.
MnCS; PLatS

Tyniec, Poland (Benedictine abbey)

3725 **Codex diplomaticus monasterii Tynecensis.** Kodeks dyplomatyczny Klasztoru Tynieckiego . . . Wydali Dr. Wojciech Ketryznski i Dr. Stanislaw Smolka. we Lwowie, 1875.
2 v. 29 cm.
KAS

Uniontown, Wash. St. Andrew's Convent
see
St. Andrew's Convent, Uniontown, Wash.

Unsere Liebe Frau zu den Schotten, Vienna, Austria
see
Vienna, Austria. Schottenstift

Urspring, Germany (abbey of Benedictine nuns)

3726 **Abbates Bernardus Hirsaugiensis,**
Joannes Wiblingensis, Ulricus Balburen-
sis de visitatione monasterii Urspringen-
sis anno 1474 facta referunt. MS. Vienna, Schottenstift, codex 232, f.1r–17v.
Quarto. Saec. 15.
Microfilm: MnCH proj. no. 4158

Val-de-Grace, Paris, France
see
Paris, France. Val-de-Grace

**Valladolid, Spain. San Benito
(Benedictine abbey)**

3727 **Serna, Clemente de la, O.S.B.**
El voto de clausura en la Congregación
de Valladolid.
(*In* Semana de Estudios Monasticos,
14th, Silos, 1973. p. 149–182)
PLatS

Valles, Spain. Sant Cugat (Benedictine abbey)

3728 **Ainaud, Joan.**
L'abat Donadeu de Sant Cugat, restau-
rador d'eglésies.
(*In* Miscellània Anselm M. Albareda. v.
1(1962), p. 239–244)
PLatS

3729 **Carpetas de documentos varios.** 14 vols.
MS. Barcelona, Spain, Archivo Dioce-
sana, St. Cugat, codex 1a–14a. Folio.
Saec. 19.
Microfilm: MnCH proj. no. 32,547–
32,563

3730 **Coll i Alentorn, Miguel.**
El cronicó de Sant Cugat.
(*In* Miscellània Anselm M. Albareda. v.
1(1962), p. 245–259)
PLatS

3731 **Compte, Efrem M., O.S.B.**
Els necrologis antics de Sant Cugat del
Valles.
(*In* Analecta Montserratensia, v. 10, p.
131–164)
PLatS

3732 **Vives, Josep.**
Sèrie de "benedictiones lectionum" en un
manuscrit de Sant Cugat.
(*In* Miscellània Anselm M. Albareda. v.
1(1962), p. 261–264)
PLatS

Vallombrosa, Italy (Benedictine abbey)

3733 **L'Abbazia di Vallombrosa nel pensiero
contemporaneo;** a cura della casa
generalizia dei monaci benedettini Vallombrosani. Pref. di Piero Bargellino.
Edizioni "Vallombrosa" [1953–   ].
v. illus., plates. 21 cm.
KAS

3734 **Kovacevich, Carlo A.**
L'Abbazia di Vallombrosa. Roma,
Liberia dello Stato, 1951.
43 p. illus. 19 cm.
PLatS

3734a **Vallombrosa nel IX centenario** della
morte del fondatore Giovanni Gualberto 12 luglio 1073. Firenze, Giorgi &
Gambi, 1973.
179 p. 27 plates, 24 cm.
KAS

Valvanera, Spain (Benedictine abbey)

3734b **Perez Alonso, Alexjandro.**
Historia de la Real Abadia-Santuario de
Nuestra Señora de Valvanera en la Rioja.
Gijon, 1971.
524 p. plates (part col.) 25 cm.
MnCS

Valyermo, Calif. St. Andrew's Priory
see
St. Andrew's Priory, Valyermo, Calif.

Varensell, Germany (Benedictine abbey)

3735 **Von Raczeck, Eucharis, O.S.B.**
Im Heiligthum unserer Lieben Frau von
Varensell. Paderborn, Bonifacius-
Druckerei, [1956?].
72 p. illus. 21 cm.
MnCS

**Vaux, France. Saint-Etienne
(Benedictine abbey)**

3736 **Grasilier, Th., ed.**
Cartulaires inédits de la Saintonge.
Niort, L. Clouzot, 1871.
2 v. 29 cm.
MnCS

**Verdun, France. Saint-Vanne
(Benedictine abbey)**

3737 **Souplet, Maxime.**
Abbaye Saint-Vanne de Verdun, fondée
en 981. Troisièmes journées Vannistes: 5–6
octobre, 1968, année sacerdotale jubilaire.
40 p. illus. 22 cm.
MnCS

Verein der Kinderfreunde, Innsbruck, Austria
see
Innsbruck, Austria. Verein der Kinderfreunde

Vezelay, France (Benedictine abbey)

3738 **Defarges, Beninge, O.S.B.**
Histoire petite chronique de Vezelay.
(*In* Bourgogne romane . . . 4. éd. La
Pierre-qui-Vire, 1962. p. 209–211)
PLatS

3739 **Hugo Pictavinus,** 12th cent.
Histoire du Monastère de la Madeleine
par Hugues de Poitiers, moine et
secrétaire de l'abbé de Vézelay. Traduit du
latin en français par François Guizot,
présenté et annoté par François Vogade.
La Charité-sur-Loire, Imprimerie Bernadat, 1969.
273 p. 19 cm.
PLatS

3740 **Monumenta Vizeliacensia;** textes relatifs
à l'histoire de l'Abbaye de Vézelay.
Edités par R.B.C. Huygens. Turnholti,
Brepols, 1976.
xli, 686 p. facsims., maps. 26 cm. (Corpus
christianorum. Continuatio mediaevalis,
42)
InStme; MnCS; PLatS

Vienna, Austria. Schottenstift

3741 **Berger, Willibald, O.S.B.**
Die Wiener Schotten. Wien, Bergland
Verlag [1962].
71 p. illus. 18 cm.
MnCS

3742 **Catalogus religiosorum Ordinis S. P.**
Benedicti in monasterio B.M.V. ad
Scotos Viennae et S. Stephani, regis
apost. de Telky in Hungaria, viventium.
v. 23 cm.
PLatS

3743 **Directorium seu Ordo divinum officium**
persolvendi et Missas celebrandi juxta
ritum Romano-monastico-benedic-
tinum usui Monasterii B.M.V. ad
Scotos Vindobonae Ord. S. P. Benedicti.
v. 19 cm.
MnCS

3744 **Hübl, Albert, O.S.B.**
Catalogus codicum manu scriptorum qui
in bibliotheca Monasterii B.M.V. ad Scotos
Vindobonae servantur. Wiesbaden, Martin
Sändig, [1970].
x, 609 p. 21 cm.
Reprint of 1899 edition.
PLatS

3744a **Kramreiter, Robert.**
Die Schottengruft in Wien: Grabstätte
Heinrich Jasomirgotts und des Grafen
Rüdiger von Starhemberg. [Wien], Selbst-
verlag Wiener Schottenstift [1962].
62 p. illus. 20 x 22 cm.
MnCS

3745 **Modus reformationis Monasterii Scotorum Viennensis.** MS. Vienna, Nationalbibliothek, codex 4970, f.23r–32r.
Quarto. Saec. 15.
Microfilm: MnCH proj. no. 18,143

3746 **Monasterii Scotorum fundatio.** MS.
Benediktinerabtei Michaelbeuern,
Austria, codex cart. 113, f.230r–235v.
Octavo. Saec. 16.
Microfilm: MnCH proj. no. 11,612

3746a **Perger, Richard.**
Die mittelalterlichen Kirchen und Klöster Wiens. Wien, Paul Zsolnay Verlag
[1977].
335 p. illus. 22 cm.
p. 95–122: Das Schottenkloster.
MnCS

3747 **Rapf, Cölestin Roman, O.S.B.**
Die Bibliothek der Benediktinerabtei
Unserer Lieben Frau zu den Schotten in
Wien.
(*In* Translatio studii; manuscript and
library studies honoring Oliver L. Kapsner.
Collegeville, Minn., 1973. p. 4–35)
PLatS

3747a **Sauer, Walter.**
Studien zur Geschichte des Schotten-
stiftes in Wien, 1800–1850. Wien, Selbstverlag, 1973.
67 p. illus. 22 cm.
MnCS

3748 **Schottenblatt;** Konveninterner Rund-
brief für die Benediktiner des Schotten-
stiftes im Stift und auf den Pfarren.
v. 1– [1960?–].
v. illus. 30 cm.
KAS

3749 **Scotensia.** MS. Vienna, Schottenstift,
codex 151, f.200v–211r. Octavo. Saec.
15.
Microfilm: MnCH proj. no. 4077

3750 **Zelenku, Ales.**
Die Wappen der Wiener Schottenäbte.
Von Ales Zelenku und Walter Sauer. Wien,
Schottenstift, 1971.
39 p. illus. 20 cm.
MnCS

Vittoriosa, Malta. St. Scholastica (abbey of Benedictine nuns)

3751 **Notizie intorno ai monaci ed alle
monache dell'Ordine de San Benedetto
in Malta.** MS. Monastero di San Pietro,
Notabile (Mdina), Malta. 41 f. 30 cm.
Microfilm: MnCH proj. no. Malta 302

Walsdorf, Germany (Benedictine abbey)

3752 **Deissmann, Adolf.**
Geschichte des Benediktinerklosters
Walsdorf . . . Wiesbaden, W. Roth, 1863.
iv, 103 p. plates. 22 cm.
KAS

Washington, D.C. St. Anselm's Abbey
see
St. Anselm's Abbey, Washington, D.C.

Weih Sankt Peter, Regensburg, Germany
see
Regensburg, Germany. Weih Sankt Peter

Weihenstephan, Bavaria (Benedictine abbey)

3753 **Carta visitationis monasterii Weihen-**
stephan anno 1426. Consuetudines et
ceremoniae regulares, quas domini visitatores imitandas monasterio in Weihenstephan sanciverunt. MS. Benediktinerabtei Admont, Austria, codex 581,
f.35r–82v. Quarto. Saec. 15.
Microfilm: MnCH proj. no. 9632

Weingarten, Germany (Benedictine abbey)

3754 **Schmidt-Glassner, Helga.**
Weingarten. Aufnahmen von Helga
Schmidt-Glassner; einführender Text von
Richard Schmidt. Königstein im Taunus,
Landewische [1955].
47 p. illus. 21 cm.
InStme

3755 **Schnell, Hugo.**
Weingarten. 4. Aufl. München, Schnell &
Steiner [1972].
47 p. plates, plans. 24 cm.
MnCS

3755a **Spahr, Gebhard.**
Die Basilika Weingarten; ein Barock-
juwel in Oberschwaben. Sigmaringen, Jan
Thorbecke Verlag [1974].
233 p. 152 illus.(part col.) 24 cm.
MnCS

3756 **Streitschriften des Klosters Weingarten**
gegen Gemeinde und Unterthanen der
Herrschaft Blumenegg, 1637–1638.
MS. Innsbruck, Austria, Tiroler Lande-
sarchiv, codex 170. 90 & 61 f. Folio.
Saec. 17.
Microfilm: MnCH proj. no. 29,031

3757 **Zeugenverhör im Prozess Weingarten**
contra Einsiedeln, 1624. MS. Voralberger Landesarchiv, Austria. HS. Rh.
Blumenegg 167. 55 f. Folio. Saec. 17.
Microfilm: MnCH proj. no. 29,905

Weissenau, Germany (Benedictine abbey)

3758 **Historia monasterii Weissenoensis**
Ordinis Sancti Benedicti dioecesis
Bambergensis. MS. Benediktinerabtei
St. Paul im Lavantthal, Austria, codex
20/6. 30 f. Folio. Saec. 18.
Microfilm: MnCH proj. no. 12,642

Wells, England
(Benedictine Priory Cathedral)

3759 **Robinson, Joseph Armitage.**
Somerset historical essays. London, Ox-
ford University Press, 1921.
vii, 159 p. 26 cm.
Appendix B: The first deans of Wells.
Appendix D: Jocelin of Wells and members
of his family.
PLatS

Weltenburg, Bavaria (Benedictine abbey)

3760 **Riess, Otmar.**
Die Abtei Weltenburg zwischen Dreissig-
jährigem Krieg und Säkularisation (1626–
1803). Regensburg, Verlag des Vereins für
Regensburger Bistumgeschichte, 1975.
514 p. 24 cm.
MnCS

3760a **Thiel, Matthias, O.S.B.**
Die Traditionen, Urkunden und Urbara
des Klosters Weltenburg. München, Beck,
1958.
64, 443 p. plates. 25 cm.
PLatS

Werden, Germany (Benedictine abbey)

3761 **Verhoeff, Karl Edward.**
Das Cartularium Werthinense.
Geschichte der Stiftung der ehemaligen
Benediktiner-Abtei in Werden an der Ruhr
im 8. und 9. Jahrhundert. Münster, F.
Regensberg, 1948.
iv, 100 p. map. 23 cm.
KAS

Weremouth, England (Benedictine abbey)

3762 **Bede, the Venerable, Saint.**
Historia ecclesiastica gentis Anglorum,
Historia abbatum et Epistola ad Ecberc-
tum . . . Cura Georgii H. Moberly. Oxonii,
e Typographeo Clarendoniano, 1881.
xxviii, 442 p. 20 cm.
For other editions of this work see under
Bede, the Venerable, in Author Part.
PLatS

Wessobrunn, Bavaria (Benedictine abbey)

3763 Dischinger, Gabriele.
Johann und Joseph Schmuzer, zwei Wessobrunner Barockbaumeister. Sigmaringen, Jan Thorbecke Verlag [1977].
193 p. illus., plates, 24 cm.
MnCS

3763a Fugger, Eberhard.
Kloster Wessobrunn, ein Stück Kulturgeschichte unseres engeren Vaterlandes. München, G. Messner, 1885.
v, 125 p. 24 cm.
KAS

3764 Wessobrunner Gebet. [Facsimile of early ninth-century compendium from Kloster Wessobrun, Oberbayern]. München, Kurt Wolff, 1922.
100 facsim. leaves. 20 cm.
A full facsimile of Ms. Munich, Bayerische Staatsbibliothek clm 22053.
Contents: Pt. 1, On measuring and geography; Pt. 2, On grammar; Pt. 3, On arithmetic.
MnCS

Westminster Abbey, England

3765 Aveling, Hugh, O.S.B.
Westminster Abbey – the beginning to 1474.
(*In* Carpenter, E. F. ed. A house of kings. 1966. p. 3–84)
PLatS

3766 Carpenter, Edward Frederick, ed.
A house of kings: the history of Westminster Abbey. London, Baker, 1966.
xix, 491 p. plates, tables. 26 cm.
KAS; PLatS

3767 Harvey, Barbara F., ed.
Documents illustrating the rule of Walter de Wenlok, abbot of Westminster, 1283–1307. London, Royal Historical Society, 1965.
vii, 285 p. 23 cm.
PLatS

3768 Lethaby, William Richard.
Westminster Abbey & the kings' craftsmen; a study of mediaeval building. New York, B. Blom, 1971.
xvi, 382 p. illus. 22 cm.
Reprint of the 1906 edition.
PLatS

3769 Pearce, Ernest Harold.
The monks of Westminster; being a register of the brethren of the convent from the time of the Confessor to the dissolution, with lists of the obedientiaries and an introduction . . . Cambridge, University Press, 1916.

236 p.
NcBe

3770 Smith, Emily Tennyson.
Westminster Abbey; its story and association. London, Cassell and Co., 1906.
384 p. plates. 20 cm.
MnCS; NcBe

3771 Westminster Abbey, England.
The glory of Westminster Abbey. Norwich, Published by Jarrold for the Dean and Chapter of Westminster, 1966.
48 p. illus. 26 cm.
PLatS

Westminster Abbey, Mission City, B.C., Canada

3772 The Benedictines. By a monk of Westminster Abbey. Mission City, B.C. [1957].
13 p. 15 cm.
On cover: The Benedictines of Westminster Abbey.
KAS; CaBMi

Whitby Abbey, England

3773 Cartularium abbathiae de Whiteby, Ordinis s. Benedicti, fundatae anno MLXXVIII. Durham, 1879–81.
2 v. 23 cm. (Publications of the Surtees Society, v. LXIX, LXXII)
MnCS

Wimmelburg, Germany (Benedictine abbey)

3773a Medem, L. B. von.
Beiträge zur Geschichte des Klosters Wimmelburg.
95–102 p. 21 cm.
Section of an unidentified book or periodical.
KAS

Winchester, England. St. Mary's Abbey

3774 Birch, Walter de Gray, ed.
An ancient manuscript of the eighth or ninth century, formerly belonging to St. Mary's Abbey, or Nunnaminster, Winchester. London, Simpkin & Marshall, 1899.
162 p. 23 cm.
MnCS (xerox copy)

Winnipeg, Canada. St. Benedict's Priory
see
St. Benedict's Priory, Winnipeg, Canada

Wissembourg, Alsace (Benedictine abbey)

3775 Rheinwald, J.
L'abbaye et la ville de Wissembourg . . . Wissembourg, Fr. Wentzel fils, 1863.

xix, 509 p. 22 cm.
KAS

Worcester Priory, England

3776 **Catalogue of manuscripts preserved in the chapter library of Worcester Cathedral,** compiled by the Rev. John Kestell Floyer . . . and edited and revised throughout by Sidney Graves Hamilton. Oxford, Printed for the Worcestershire Historical Society, by James Parker and Co., 1906.
xviii, 196 p. illus., plates. 29 cm.
MnCS

3777 **Compotus rolls of the priory of Worcester of the XIVth and XVth centuries** transcribed and edited by Sidney Graves Hamilton. Oxford, James Parker and Co., 1910.
xxv, 93, 49–64 p. 28 cm.
MnCS

3778 **The protiforium of Saint Wulstan** (Corpus Christi College, Cambridge, Ms. 391). Edited by Dom Anselm Hughes. Leighton Buzzard, England, Henry Bradshaw Society, 1958–1960.
2 v. 23 cm.
MnCS

Würzburg, Germany. Sankt Burkard (Benedictine abbey)

3779 **Wieland, Michael.**
Historische Darstellung des Stiftes St. Burkard zu Würzburg.
(*In* Historischer Verein von Unterfranken . . . Würzburg, Archiv. 15. Bd(1860), p. 43–114; 2. Heft(1861, p. 1–259)
KAS

Würzburg, Germany. Sankt Jacob (Benedictine abbey)

3780 **Dilworth, Mark, O.S.B.**
The Scots in Franconia: a century of monastic life. Totowa, N.J., Rowman and Littlefield, 1974.
301 p. illus. 23 cm.
Instme; KAS; MnCS; PLatS

Yankton, S.D. Sacred Heart Convent
see
Sacred Heart Convent, Yankton, S.D.

York, England. St. Mary's Abbey

3781 **The chronicle of St. Mary's Abbey, York,** from Bodley ms. 39, edited by H.H.E. Craster and M. E. Thornton. London, B. Quaritch, 1934.

xiii, 154 p. 23 cm.
MnCS

3782 **Richardson, Harold.**
The Bootham fair of the abbot of St. Mary's Abbey.
(*In* his: The medieval fairs and markets of York. York, 1961. p. 7–11)
PLatS

3783 **Wellbeloved, Charles.**
Account of the ancient and present state of the Abbey of St. Mary, York, and of the discoveries made in the recent excavations conducted by the Yorkshire Philosophical Society . . . London, Society of Antiquaries, 1829.
17 p. plates LI–LX, plan. 54 cm.
KAS

Zevenkerken, Belgium. Abbey de Saint-André
see
Bruges, Belgium. Abbaye de Saint-André

Zurich, Switzerland. Frauenmunster

3784 **Wyss, Georg von.**
Geschichte der Abtei Zürich. Beilagen. Urkunden nebst zwei Siegeltafeln. Zürich, in Commission bei Meyer und Zeller, 1851–58.
112, 38, xii, 504 p. plates, plan, seals. 29 cm.
"Beilagen": 504 p. at the end.
KAS

Zurzach, Switzerland (Benedictine abbey)

3785 **Huber, Johann.**
Des Stiftes Zurzach Schicksale; Festschrift zur Erinnerung an did 600jährige Gründungsfeier des Collegiatstiftes zur heil. Verona in Zurzach im Jahre 1879. Luzern, Gebrüder Räber, 1879.
iv, 90 p. 24 cm.
KAS

Zwiefalten, Germany (Benedictine abbey)

3786 **Holzherr, Karl.**
Geschichte der ehemaligan Benediktiner- und Reichs-Abtei Zwiefalten in Oberschwaben. Stuttgart, W. Kohlhammer, 1887.
viii, 182 p. 21 cm.
InStme; KAS

3787 **Zürcher, Richard.**
Zwiefalten; die Kirche der ehemaligen Benediktinerabtei, ein Gesamtwerk der süddeutschen Rokoko. Konstanz-Stuttgart, Jan Thorbecke Verlag [1967].
72 p. 53 plates. 30 cm.
MnCS

XIII. BENEDICTINE HISTORY: COLLECTIVE BIOGRAPHY

1. GENERAL WORKS

3788 **Farmer, David Hugh, ed.**
Benedict's disciples. Leominster, Herefordshire, Fowler Wright, c 1980.
xii, 354 p. illus. 23 cm.
Consists of 25 biographies, from St. Benedict to Archbishop Ullathorne, by various writers.
KAS

3788a **Die Grossen Deutschen;** deutsche Biographie. Ullstein Berlin, Propyläen-Verlag, 1956–57.
5 v. 24 cm.
Vol. 5, p. 9–47: Bonifatius, Hrabanus Maurus, Notker der Dichter, Hildegard von Bingen.
MnCS

3788b **Neumann, Matthias, O.S.B.**
A directory of Benedictine resource personnel for North America. [St. Meinrad, Ind., St. Meinrad Archabbey, 1981].
[x, 200 leaves] 21 cm. (American Benedictine Academy. Research studies, 1)
InStme; MnCS

3788c **Nigg, Walter.**
Mit Mönchen beten; Gebete, die auch uns zu Gott führen. Unter Mitarbeit von St. M. Lucia, O.C.D. München, Rex-Verlag [1976].
135 p. 20 cm.
p. 36–42, Benediktiner: Benedikt von Nursia, Rabanus Maurus, Hermann der Lahme, Anselm von Canterbury, Hildegard von Bingen, Gertrud die Grosse, Elisabeth von Schönau, Columba Marmion.
MnCS

3788d **Schöppner, A.**
Charakterbilder der allgemeinen Geschichte. Schaffhausen, Hurter, 1871–73.
3 v. 24 cm.
Vol. 2, Das Mittelalter, includes: Benedikt von Nursia und die Benediktiner; Gregor der Grosse; Bekehrung der Angelsachsen; Kloster Fulda; Adalbert, Apostel der Preussen; Lanfrank's Bekehrung; Cluny; Gregor VII und Heinrich IV; Schottenklöster in Deutschland; Bernhard von Clairvaux.
AStb; MnCS

3788e **Szczygielski, Stanislas, O.S.B.**
Aquila polono-benedictina in qua, beatorum & illustrium virorum elogia . . . exordia & progressus Ordinis d. p. Benedicti per Poloniam . . . describuntur.

Cracoviae, Haeredes Francisci Casari, 1663.
[8], 367, [20] p. 22 cm.
KAS; MnCS

3789 **Wion, Arnold, O.S.B.**
Lignum vitae, continens fundatoris s.p. Benedicti, dilatorum et restauratorum ac aliorum insignium virorum nomina et gesta. MS. Benediktinerabtei St. Peter, Salzburg, codex a.III.16. 92 f. Octavo. Saec. 17(1645).
Microfilm: MnCH proj. no. 9961

2. ABBESSES

3790 **Tamburini de Marradio, Ascanio, O.S.B.**
De iure abbatissarum et monialium; sive, Praxis gubernandi moniales . . . cui accedunt Sacrae Rotae Romanae decisiones . . . Editio emendata & aucta. Lugduini, sumptibus Laurentii Anisson, 1668.
[16], 220, [31], 80, 36 p. 37 cm.
KAS

Blessing of an Abbess
see Chapter VI, 2, d

3. ABBOTS

a. General Works

3791 **Abbas;** la figura dell'abate nel pensiero di S. Bendetto. Sorrento, Monasterio di S. Paolo [1960?].
49 p. 23 cm.
PLatS

3792 **Aliqui casus in quibus praelatus monsterii est deponendus.** MS. Benediktinerabtei Melk, Austria, codex 1754, f.187–191. Duodecimo. Saec. 15.
Microfilm: MnCH proj. no. 2066

3793 **Blume, Karl.**
Abbatia; ein Beitrag zur Geschichte der kirchlichen Rechtssprache. Stuttgart, F. Enke, 1914; Amsterdam, P. Schippers, 1965.
xiv, 118 p. tables. 23 cm.
MnCS; PLatS

3794 **Caeremoniae abbatis per circulum anni.** MS. Benediktinerabtei Michaelbeuern, Austria, codex cart. 86, f.225r–234v. Quarto. Saec. 15.
Microfilm: MnCH proj. no. 11,578

3795 **Caeremoniae regularis observantiae O.S.B. abbatis.** MS. Benediktinerabtei St. Peter, Salzburg, codex b.VI.6, f.1r–15v. Quarto. Saec. 15.
Microfilm: MnCH proj. no. 10,483

3796 **Casus abbatis in monasterio.** MS. Benediktinerabtei Melk, Austria, codex 979, f.295r. Quarto. Saec. 15. Microfilm: MnCH proj. no. 1790

3797 **De potestate absolvendi quam habet abbas in suos.** Tractatus de electione abbatis. MS. Benediktinerabtei Lambach, Austria, codex chart. 437, f.119v–120r, 127r–130v. Saec. 15. Microfilm: MnCH proj. no. 726

3798 **Hildemar.** Nota ex tractatu et expositione Regulae s. Benedicti in capitulo de abbate. MS. Vienna, Schottenstift, codex 177, f.344r–369v. Octavo. Saec. 15. Microfilm: MnCH proj. no. 3910

3799 **Leclercq, Jean, O.S.B.** Un traité sur la "Profession des abbés" au XIIe siècle. (*In* Analecta monastica, 6. ser., 1962, p. 177–191) PLatS

3800 **Missae et officia ad Abbatem pertinentes.** MS. Benediktinerabtei Melk, Austria, codex 1766, f.177r. Duodecimo. Saec. 15. Microfilm: MnCH proj. no. 2076

3801 **Salmon, Pierre, O.S.B.** L'abbé dans la tradition monastique; contribution à l'histoire de caractère perpétual des supérieurs religieux en Occident. [Paris], Sirey, 1962. ix, 168 p. KAS; MnCS; PLatS

3802 **Salmon, Pierre, O.S.B.** The abbot in monastic tradition; a contribution to the history of the perpetual character of the office of religious superiors in the West. Translated by Claire Lavoie. Washington, Cistercian Publications, 1972. xv, 160 p. 23 cm. (Cistercian studies series, no. 14) InStme; KAS; MnCS; MoCo; PLatS

3803 **Schlitpacher, Johannes, O.S.B.** Tractatus de casibus, in quibus prelatus monasticus esset deponendus. MS. Benediktinerabtei Melk, Austria, codex 959, f.189r–189v. Quarto. Saec. 15. Microfilm: MnCH proj. no. 1762

3804 **Stark, Matthew, O.S.B.** The office of abbot. (*In* Monastic studies, v. 10, p. 165–179) PLatS

3805 **Tractatus bonus de regimine abbatis** et modo se habendi circa patres et fratres. MS. Benediktinerabtei Melk, Austria, codex 1468, f.122r–136r. Duodecimo. Saec. 15. Microfilm: MnCH proj. no. 1940

3806 **Vogüé, Adalbert de, O.S.B.** La communauté et l'abbé dans la Règle de saint Benoît. Préface du Louis Bouyer. [Bruges], Desclée, De Brouwer [1961]. 559 p. 20 cm. KAS; MnCS; PLatS

3806a **Vogüé, Adalbert de, O.S.B.** Community and abbot in the Rule of Saint Benedict. Translated by Charles Philippi, O.S.B. Kalamazoo, Mich., Cistercian Publications, 1978– v. 23 cm. (Cistercian studies series, no. 5/1) MnCS; PLatS

3807 **Weakland, Rembert George, O.S.B.** L'abate in una società democratica. (*In* Vita monastica, n. 99(1969), p. 206–214)

3808 **Weakland, Rembert George, O.S.B.** The abbot as spiritual father. Offprint from: Cistercian studies, n. 2 & 3 (1974), p. 231–238. PLatS

3809 **Weakland, Rembert, George, O.S.B.** The abbot in a democratic society. Offprint from: Cistercian studies, n. 4(1969), p. 95–100. PLatS

Blessing of an Abbot
see chapter VI, 2, e

b. Biography

3810 **Duchesne, André.** Historiae Normannorum scriptores antiqui, res ab illis per Galliam, Angliam, Apuliam, Capuae principatum, Siciliam & Orientem gestas explicantes . . . Insertae sunt . . . series episcoporum ac abbatum. Lutetiae Parisiorum, 1619. 6, 1104, 14 p. KAS(microfilm)

3811 **Glatz, Karl Jordan.** Geschichte des Klosters Alpirsbach auf dem Schwarzwalde, nach Urkunden bearbeitet . . . Strassburg, K. J. Trübner, 1877. ix, 442 p. 23 cm. KAS

3812 **Series abbatum monasterii O.S.B. ad S. Petrum Salisburgi.** [Salzburg], Ex typographia aulica Duyleana [1856?]. 32 p. 22 cm. MnCS

c. Canon Law

3813 **Casus in quibus abbas de iure communi potest cum suis monachis dispensare.**
Casus in quibus abbas auctoritate Regulae potest dispensare. MS. Benediktinerabtei Melk, Austria, codex 1088, f.521–526. Duodecimo. Saec. 15.
Microfilm: MnCH proj. no. 1850

3814 **De potestate abbatis ex jure regulari.**
MS. Benediktinerabtei St. Peter, Salzburg, codex a.VII.18, f.185v–188r. Quarto. Saec. 15.
Microfilm: MnCH proj. no. 10,142

3815 **Hegglin, Benno, O.S.B.**
Der benediktinische Abt in rechtsgeschichtlicher Entwicklung und geltenden Kirchenrecht. Eos Verlag der Erzabtei St. Ottilien [Bavaria], 1961.
xxiv, 227 p. 25 cm.
MnCS; PLatS

3816 **Oesterle, Gerard, O.S.B.**
De potestate abbatum dispensandi ab irregularitatibus.
(*In* Liturgica: Cardinal I. A. Schuster in memoriam. 1958. v. 2, p. 465–481)
PLatS

3817 **Toner, Jerome Lorraine, O.S.B.**
Abbatial power. Washington, D.C., Catholic University of America, 1962.
Reprinted from The Jurist, v. 22 (1962), p. 81–89.
NcBe

d. Election

3818 **De abbate eligendo.** MS. Vienna, Schottenstift, codex 356, f.370r–372v. Folio. Saec. 15.
Microfilm: MnCH proj. no. 4206

3819 **Hallinger, Kassius, O.S.B.**
Regula Benedicti 64 und die Wahlgewohnheiten des 6.-12. Jahrhunderts.
(*In* Latinität und alte Kirche; Festschrift für Rudolf Hanslik zum 70. Geburtstag. Wien, 1977. p. 109–130)
MnCS

3820 **Schlitpacher, Johannes, O.S.B.**
Tractatus de triplici modo eligendi abbatum. MS. Benediktinerabtei Melk, Austria, codex 959, f.186r–189v. Quarto. Saec. 15.
Microfilm: MnCH proj. no. 1762

e. Insignia

3821 **Blättler, Aloysius.**
Die kirchlichen Insignien eines Abtes; Predigt bei der feierlichen Benediktion des Hochwürdigsten Gnädigen Herrn Basilius Oberholzer, Abt des Benediktiner-Stiftes Maria Einsiedeln, den 9. Mai 1875 in der Stiftskirche zu Einsiedeln. Einsiedeln, Marianus Benziger u. Soh, 1875.
13 p. 23 cm.
PLatS

3822 **Hanser, Laurentius, O.S.B.**
Colloquia liturgica de pontificalibus abbatum. Romae, Typis Vaticanis, 1900.
xv, 160 p. 24 cm.
KAS

3823 **Hofmeister, Philipp, O.S.B.**
Mitra und Stab der wirklichen Prälaten ohne bischöflichen Charakter. Stuttgart, F. Enke, 1928; Amsterdam, P. Schippers, 1962.
x, 132 p. 23 cm.
ILSP; MnCS; PLatS

3824 **Kropff, Martin, O.S.B.**
Dissertatio brevis historica de origine usus mitrae Mellicensium abbatum.
(*In* his Bibliotheca Mellicenses. Vienna, 1747. Appendix. 14 p.)
MnCS

3825 **Salmon, Pierre, O.S.B.**
Etude sur les insignes du pontife dans le rit roman; histoire et liturgie. Roma, Officium Libri Catholici, 1955.
102 p. 22 cm.
CaQStB; InStme; MnCS; PLatS

4. ABBOT PRIMATE

3826 **Modus procedendi in deliberationibus R. morum DD.** Abbatum in electione Abbatis Primatis. Roma, Campitelli, 1925.
7 p.
AStb

3827 **Vincenzo, Amando di, O.S.B.**
De Abbate Primate confoederationis Benedictinae excerpta. Romae, apud Custodiam Librariem Pontificii Instituti Utriusque Juris [1952].
80 p.
Thesis ad lauream.
MnCS; MoCo; NcBe

5. ABBOT NULLIUS

3828 **Myers, Russell W.**
Abbot Nullius and canon 215, 2 (Book II, part 1, and Book V).
30 p. 28 cm.
Thesis (M.A.)–St. Vincent College, Latrobe, Pa., 1945.
PLatS

6. MARTYRS, BENEDICTINE

3829 **Chacon, Alfonso, O.P.**
De martyrio ducentorum monachorum
S. Petria Cardegne, Ordinis S. Benedicti
Hispaniarum Burgensis dioecesis commen-
tarius. Augustae, typis Chrysostomi
Dabertzhoseri [1594].
138, 29 p. 13 cm.
MnCS

3830 **Pedrosa, Juan de, O.S.B.**
Responsio ad doctissimas et prudentissimas sacrosanctae Congr. Sacrorum
Rituum oppositiones contra processum
fulminatum super martyrio 200
monachorum, qui in persecutione arabica,
apud Caradignam passi sint. [n.p., n.d.]
29 p. 13 cm.
MnCS

7. POPES, BENEDICTINE

3831 **Beekman, Andreas, O.S.B.**
Pausen – Benedictijn.
(*In* his: Het leven van de heilige Bene-
dictus. Deutekom, 1950. p. 205)
Lists 24 popes as Benedictine.
PLatS

3832 **Historias y vidas de los papas que fueron
benedictinos.** Vol. II: de Sant Gregori
VII a Urban II. MS. Monasterio benedictino de Montserrat, Spain, codex 11.
575 f. Folio. Saec. 18.
Microfilm: MnCH proj. no. 29,980

3833 **Summi Pontifices Romani assumpti** ex
Ordine S. Benedicti saec. VI–XVI. MS.
Benediktinerabtei St. Paul im Lavant-
thal, Austria, codex 46/2. 173 f. Folio.
Saec. 17.
Microfilm: MnCH proj. no. 11,777

3833a **Szczygielski, Stanislas, O.S.B.**
Summi pontifici, qui ex Ordine Sanctis-
simi Patriarchae Benedicti prodierunt.
(*In* his: Aquila polono-benedictina.
Cracoviae, 1663. p. 18–19)
Listed are 55 Benedictines as popes,
based on book by Gabriel Bucelin.
KAS; MnCS

8. SAINTS, BENEDICTINE

3834 **Albertson, Clinton, ed.**
Anglo-Saxon saints and heroes. [New
York], Fordham University Press [1967].
347 p.
NcBe

3835 **Andreas, abbot of Michelsberg.**
Der Catalogus sanctorum Ordinis Sancti
Benedicti des Abtes Andreas von Michels-

berg [hrsg.] von Joseph Fassbinder. Bonn,
Carl Georgi, 1910.
136 p. 22 cm.
Diss. – Rheinische Friedrich-Wilhelms-
Universität zu Bonn.
InStme; MnCS

3836 **Duckett, Eleanor Shipley.**
Anglo-Saxon saints and scholars. New
York, Macmillan, 1947.
x, 488 p. 22 cm.
ILSH; NcBe; WaOSM

3837 **Gaetano, Constantino, O.S.B.**
Sanctor/ trium episcopor/ relig.is
bened.ae luminum, Isidori Hispalens., Ildefonsi Tolet., Gregorii card. Ost. vitae, et
actiones . . . Romae, apud Jacobum Mascardum, 1606.
156 p. 24 cm.
MnCS

3838 **Jacobi, Andrea, O.S.B.Sylv.**
The saints of the Benedictine Order of
Montefano. Clifton, N.J., Holy Face
Monastery [1972].
268 p. illus. 21 cm.
Translations of Latin mss. by Francis
Fattorini.
InStme; KAS; MnCS; MoCo; NcBe

3839 **Kent, Mark Leo.**
The glory of Christ; a pageant of two
hundred missionary lives from apostolic
times to the present age. Milwaukee,
Bruce Pub. Co., 1955.
285 p. 23 cm.
Part II (p. 31–65) is devoted almost entirely to Benedictine missionary saints.
InFer

3840 **Knowles, David, O.S.B.**
Saints and scholars; twenty-five
medieval portraits. Cambridge [Eng-
land]. University Press, 1962.
207 p. illus. 21 cm.
PLatS

3841 **Oursel, Raymond.**
Les saints abbés de Cluny. Textes
choisis, traduits et présentés par Raymond
Oursel. Namur, Belgique, Les Editions du
Soleil Levant [1960].
100 p. 17 cm.
PLatS

3842 **Un Pensiero dei santi benedettini**
per ciascun giorno dell'anno. Traduzione dal francese. Prato, Tip. Contrucci & comp., 1887.
128 p. 12 cm.
PLatS

3843 **Portraits of Benedictine saints.** Biographical sketch under each engraving
[n.p., n.d.].
273 leaves of engravings. 20 cm.

Lacks title page.
Portraits in alphabetical sequence.
PLatS

3844 **Propria sanctorum pro Cathedrali Ecclesia SS Trinitatis Cava Tyrrenorum.**
[Cava dei Tirreni, Stab. Tip. del Popolo, n.d.].
95 p. 19 cm.
Published ca. 1800.
PLatS

3845 **Stengel, Carl, O.S.B.**
Imagines sanctorum Ordinis S. Benedicti tabellis aereis expressae, cum eulogiis eorundem vitis. [Augsburg, Mon. SS. Udalricae & Afrae], 1625.
180, [3] p., incl. 86 full-page engravings. 20 cm.
MnCS

3846 **Versus de canonizatis Ordinis S. Benedicti.** MS. Benediktinerabtei Melk, Austria, codex 1842, p. 381–382. Duodecimo. Saec. 16.
Microfilm: MnCH proj. no. 2152

9. WRITERS, BENEDICTINE

3847 **Armellini, Mariano, O.S.B.**
Appendix de quibusdam aliis per Italiam Ordinis S. Benedicti Congregationem scriptoribus, episcopis, virisque sanctitate illustribus. Fulginei, typis Pompeii Campana Impressoris Cameralis, 1736.
76 p. 21 cm.
Includes: Camaldulese, Celestines, Cistercians, Olivetans, Sylvestrines, Vallumbrosians.
MnCS

3848 **François, Jean, O.S.B.**
Bibliothèque générale des écrivains de l'Ordre de Saint Benoît. Reproduction anastatique accompagnée d'une note liminaire sur les bibliographies bénédictines. Louvain-Héverlé, Bibliothèque S.J., 1961.
4 v. 27 cm.
Reprint of Bouillon edition of 1777–78.
CaStB; InStme; ILSP; MoCo; NdRi; PLatS

3849 **Gillow, Joseph.**
A literary and biographical history, or bibliographical dictionary of the English Catholics, from the breach with Rome, in 1534, to the present time. London, Burns & Oates; New York, Catholic Pub. Soc. Co., 1885–1903.
5 v. 23 cm.
PLatS

3850 **Hautecombe, France. Saint Pierre-du-Curtille (Benedictine abbey).**
Saint Benoît et ses fils; textes bénédictins traduits par les moines d'Hautecombe. Introduction et notes par Dom M. F. Lacan. Préface de Daniel-Rops . . . Paris, Fayard [1961].
412 p. 18 cm.
MnCS

3851 **Kapsner, Oliver L., O.S.B.**
A Benedictine bibliography; an author-subject list. Compiled for the Library Science Section of the American Benedictine Academy. 2d. ed. Collegeville, Minn., St. John's Abbey Press, 1962.
2 v. 27 cm. (American Benedictine Academy. Library science studies, no. 1)
Acu., etc.

3852 **Kristeller, Paul Oskar.**
The contribution of religious orders to renaissance thought and learning.
55 p. 26 cm.
Offprint from: American Benedictine review, v. 21(1970), p. 1–55.
KAS

3853 **Kropff, Martinus, O.S.B.**
Breviarium de vitis et scriptis Benedictinorum Mellicensis monasterii.
(*In* his: Bibliotheca Mellicensis. Vindobonae, 1747. p. 91–682)
ILSP; MnCS

3854 **Lecomte, Maurice.**
Les Bénédictins et l'histoire des provinces aux XVIIe et XVIIIe siècles. Abbaye Saint-Martin de Ligugé, 1928.
81 p. 25 cm.
MnCS

3855 **Mayer, Heinrich Suso, O.S.B.**
Beuroner Bibliographie; Schriftsteller und Künstler während der ersten hundert Jahre des Benediktinerklosters Beuron, 1863–1963. Beuron, Hohenzollern, 1963.
196 p. 24 cm.
MnCS; PLatS

3855a **Pastore Stocchi, Manlio.**
Esempi di prosa latina medievale per esertazioni universitairie. Padova, Liviana Editrice, 1975.
147 p. 20 cm.
Includes: Gregory the Great, Paul the Deacon, Eginhard, Peter Abelard.
MnCS

3856 **Spirituels bénédictins du grand siècle;** collection de textes publiée sous la direction de Domm. R. J. Hesbert. 1958(?)– Paris, Editions Alsatia.
PLatS

3856a **Stockdale, Rachel.**
Benedictine libraries and writers.
(*In* The Benedictines in Britain. London, British Library, 1980, p. 62–81)
MnCS

3857 **Tassin, René Prosper, O.S.B.**
Histoire littéraire de la Congregation de Saint-Maur, Ordre de S. Benoît . . . Bruxelles, Paris, chez Humblot, 1770.

xxviii, 800 p. 28x20 cm.
KAS; MnCH

3857a **Walsh, James, ed.**
Pre-Reformation English spirituality. New York, Fordham University Press, 1965.
MnCS

XIV. BENEDICTINE HISTORY: INDIVIDUAL BIOGRAPHY

Abélard, Pierre, 1079-1142

3858 **Adams, Henry.**
Abélard.
(*In* his: Mont Saint Michel and Chartres. Boston, 1904. p. 285–319)
PLatS

3859 **Dronke, Peter.**
Abelard and Heloise in medieval testimonies; the twenty-sixth W. F. Ker memorial lecture delivered in the University of Glasgow, 29th October, 1976. [Glasgow], University of Glasgow Press, 1976.
63 p. 24 cm.
MnCS

3860 **Gerhohus de Reichersperg.**
Epistola ad Petrum Abaelard. MS. Augustinerchorherrenstift Klosterneuburg, Austria, codex 762, f.1r–1v. Quarto. Saec. 12.
Microfilm: MnCH proj. no. 762

3861 **Klibansky, Raymond.**
Peter Abailard and Bernard of Clairvaux.
(*In* Mediaeval and renaissance studies, v. 5, p. 1–27)
PLatS

3862 **Knowles, David, O.S.B.**
The humanism of the twelfth century.
(*In* his: The historian and character, and other essays. Cambridge, 1963. p.16–30)
PLatS

3863 **Knowles, David, O.S.B.**
Peter Abelard.
(*In* his: The evolution of medieval thought. Baltimore, 1962. p. 116–130)
PLatS

3864 **Meadows, Denis.**
A saint and a half; a new interpretation of Abelard and St. Bernard of Clairvaux. New York, Devin-Adair [1963].
xi, 209 p. 21 cm.
NcBe; PLatS

3865 **Murray, A. Victor.**
Abelard and St. Bernard; a study of twelfth-century "modernism." Manchester University Press; New York, Barnes & Noble [1967].
viii, 168 p. 22 cm.
PLatS

3866 **Nigg, Walter.**
Peter Abelard.
(*In* his: The heretics. New York, 1962, p. 159–176)
PLatS

3867 **Oursel, Raymond.**
La dispute et la grâce; essai sur la rédemption d'Abélard. Paris, Société Les Belles Lettres, 1959.
94 p. 25 cm.
PLatS

Achery, Luc d', 1609-1685

3868 **Fohlen, Jeannine.**
Dom Luc d'Achery (1609–1685) et les debuts de l'erudition Mauriste. Besancon, Imprimerie Neo-typo, 1968.
156 p.
Extrait de la Revue Mabillon, 1965–67.
MoCo

Adalard, Saint, abbot of Corbie, 751-826

3869 **Lesne, E.**
L'économie domestique d'un monastère au IXe siècle d'aprés les statuts d'Adalhard, abbé de Corbie.
(*In* Mélanges d'histoire du Moyen Age, offerts à M. Ferdinand Lot. Paris, 1925. p. 385–420)
PLatS

3870 **Paschasius Radbertus, Saint.**
Charlemagne's cousins; contemporary lives of Adalard and Wala. Translated, with introductory notes, by Allen Cabaniss. [Syracuse, N.Y.], Syracuse University Press, 1967.
vii, 266 p. 24 cm.
Translation of Vita sancti Adalhardi and Vita Walae.
InStme; PLatS

3871 **Paschasius Radbertus, Saint.**
Ex Paschasii Radberti vita s. Adalhardi abbatis Corbeiensis et vita Walae abbatis Corbeiensis.
(*In* Monumenta Germaniae historica. Scriptores. Stuttgart, 1963. t. 2, p. 524–569)
MnCS; PLatS

Adalbero, Saint, bishop of Würzburg, 1010-1090

3872 **De institutione Lambacensis coenobii.**
De vita Adalberonis episcopi. Epitaphium Adalberonis. Micrologus de signis et miraculis beati Adalberonis episcopi. MS. Benediktinerabtei Göttweig, Austria, codex 324. 30 f. Octavo. Saec. 15.
Microfilm: MnCH proj. no. 3723

3873 **De signis et miraculis beati Adalberonis.**
MS. Benediktinerabtei Lambach,
Austria, codex chart. 183, p. 23–55.
Saec. 15.
Microfilm: MnCH proj. no. 591

3874 **Sermo in anniversario beati Adalberonis
(1463).** MS. Benediktinerabtei Lambach,
Austria, codex cart. 223, 273r–277r.
Saec. 15.
Microfilm: MnCH proj. no. 612

3875 **Vita et miraculis Adalberonis.** MS.
Benediktinerabtei Lambach, Austria,
codex membr. 54. 44 f. Folio. Saec. 12.
Microfilm: MnCH proj. no. 785

Adalbert, Saint, bishop of Prague, 956–997

3876 **Bzowski, Abraham, O.P.**
Silvester II. Adiuncta est vita s. Adalberti m. ab eodem Silvestro edita, studio
eiusdem Bzouij auctori suo vindicata, et
notis illustrata. Romae, Typis Vaticanis,
1629.
KAS(microfilm)

3877 **Joannes Canaparius.**
Vita s. Adalberti episcopi.
(*In* Monumenta Germaniae historica.
Scriptores. Stuttgart, 1963. t. 4, p. 581–
595)
PLatS

3878 **Karwasińska, Jadwiga.**
Les trois rédactions de "Vita I" de s.
Adalbert. Roma, A. Signorelli [1960].
28 p. 25 cm.
PLatS

Adam of Eynsham, fl. 1196–1232

3879 **Visio monachi de Eynsham.**
[The revelation to the monk of Evesham.
London, W. de Machlinia, 1485].
MnCS(microfilm)

Adelaide, Saint, 931–999

3880 **Legenda de b. Adalheida.** Germanice.
MS. Vienna, Schottenstift, codex 234,
f.120r–169r. Quarto. Saec. 15.
Microfilm: MnCH proj. no. 4155

3881 **Vita s. Adelheidis imperatricis,** Ottonis
I. imperatoris coniugis, quae cum marito
praecipua fundatrix monasterii nostri
extitit. Ex ms. codice biblioth. nostrae
Heremitanae.
(*In* Hartmann, Christopher. Annales
Heremi Dei Parae Mastris monasterii in
Helvetia. Friburgi Brisg., 1612. 30 p. apud
finem)
PLatS

Aedilvulfus, Abbot, f. 803

3882 **Taylor, Harold McCarter.**
The architectural interest of Aethel-
wulf's De abbatibus.
(*In* Anglo-Saxon England 3. Edited by
Peter Clemoes. Cambridge, 1974. p.
163–173)
PLatS

Aegidius, Saint, d. ca. 750

3883 **Vita s. Aegydii abbatis.** MS. Benediktinerabtei Melk, Austria, codex 1248,
f.57r–64r. Quarto. Saec. 12.
Microfilm: MnCH proj. no. 1879

3884 **Vita s. Aegidii abbatis.** MS. Cistercienserabtei Rein, Austria, codex 44, f.190r–
198r. Quarto. Saec. 12.
Microfilm: MnCH proj. no. 7441

3885 **Vita s. Aegidii confessoris.** MS. Vienna,
Nationalbibliothek, codex 503, f.126r–
131v. Quarto. Saec. 12.
Microfilm: MnCH proj. no. 13,844

3886 **Vita s. Aegidii et s. Johannis evangelistae.** MS. Linz, Austria, Studienbibliothek, codex 190, f.105v–133v. Octavo.
Saec. 13.
Microfilm: MnCH proj. no. 27,841

Aelfric, abbot of Eynsham, ca. 955–1025

3887 **Cross, James E.**
Aelfric and the mediaeval homiliary –
objection and contribution. Lund, Gleerup,
[1963].
34 p. 24 cm.
PLatS

3887a **Gatch, Milton.**
Preaching and theology in Anglo-Saxon
England: Aelfric and Wulfstan. Toronto;
Buffalo: University of Toronto Press,
1977.
xiii, 266 p. 24 cm.
InStme; MnCS

3888 **Smith, Henry Percival, ed.**
Learning and labour: from Alfred the
Great to Aelfric of Eynsham. [Oxford,
H. P. Smith] 1962.
47 p.
PLatS

3889 **Stanbrook Abbey, England.**
Aelfric of Eynsham, by a Benedictine of
Stanbrook Abbey (D.S.H.).
(*In* Davis, Charles. English spiritual
writers. New York, 1961. p. 1–17)
PLatS

3889a **White, Caroline Louisa.**
Aelfric: a new study of his life and
writings. With a supplementary classified

bibliography, prepared by Malcom R. Godden [Hamden, Conn.], Archon Books, 1974 [c 1898].
244 p. 22 cm.
PLatS

Aethelwold, Saint, bishop of Winchester, 908-984

3890   **Winterbottom, Michael, comp.**
Three lives of English saints. Toronto, Published for the Centre for Medieval Studies by the Pontifical Institute of Mediaeval Studies [1972].
94 p. 22 cm.
Texts in Latin.
PLatS

Agius, monk of Corvey, fl. 9th cent.

3891   **Hüffer, Georg.**
Korveier Studien; quellenkritische Untersuchungen zur Karolinger-Geschichte. Münster i. W., Aschendorff, 1898.
x, 232 p. 25 cm.
KAS

Aimoin, monk of St. Germain-des-Prés, d.ca.896

3892   **Winterfeld, Paul Karl Rudolf von.**
De vita et miraculis et de translatione sancti Germani.
(*In* Poetae latini aevi carolini . . . Recensuit Paulus de Winterfeld . . . Berolini. t. IV, fasc. I(1899), p. 123-140)
KAS

Albareda, Anselmo Maria, 1892-1966

3893   **Collectanea Vaticana in honorem Anselmi M. Card.** Albareda a Bibliotheca Apostolica edita. Città del Vaticano, Biblioteca Apostolica Vaticana, 1962.
2 v. illus., facsims. 25 cm. (Studi e testi, 219-220)
ILSP; InStme; PLatS

3894   **Miscellania Anselm M. Albareda.** Abadia di Montserrat, 1962-
v. plates. 25 cm. (Analecta Montserratensis, v.9-   )
PLatS

3895   **Prete, Sesto, ed.**
Didascaliae; studies in honor of Anselm M. Albareda, prefect of the Vatican Library, presented by a group of American scholars. New York, B. M. Rosenthal [1961].
xiv, 530 p. illus., plates, facsims. 25 cm.
InStme; KAS; MnCS; MoCo; PLatS

Albert, Saint, bishop of Liege, d. 1192

3896   **Del Marmol, B.**
St. Albert de Louvain, évêque de Liége et martyr (1192). Paris, J. Gabalda, 1922.
xxix, 168 p. 19 cm.
KAS

Albert, abbot of Oberaltaich, 1239-1311

3897   **Sturm, Angelus.**
Albert von Oberaltaich.
(*In* Bayerische Benediktinerakademie. Jahresbericht, 4. Bd., 1925)
AStb; MnCS

Alcuin, 735-804

3898   **Carolus Magnus, rex Francorum.**
Epistola ad Alcuinum. MS. Vienna, Nationalbibliothek, codex 795, f.200r-203v. Quarto. Saec. 10.
Microfilm: MnCH proj. no. 14,139

3899   **Carolus Magnus, rex Francorum.**
Epistola ad Alcuinum. MS. Vienna, Nationalbibliothek, codex 966, f. 26v-27r. Folio. Saec. 10.
Microfilm: MnCH proj. no. 14,277

3900   **Carolus Magnus, rex Francorum.**
Epistola ad Albinum. Augustinerchorherrenstift Klosterneuburg, Austria, codex 1023, f.66v-67r. Quarto. Saec. 13.
Microfilm: MnCH proj. no. 6022

3901   **Gaskoin, Charles Jacinth Bellairs.**
Alcuin; his life and his work. New York, Russell & Russell, 1966.
xxii, 275 p. 23 cm.
First published in 1904.
InStme; NcBe; PLatS

3902   **Glunz, Hans Hermann.**
History of the Vulgate in England from Alcuin to Roger Bacon; being an inquiry into the text of some English manuscripts of the Vulgate Gospels. Cambridge [England], University Press, 1933.
xx, 383 p. 23 cm.
PLatS

3903   **Kuhar, Aloysius L.**
Alcuin and the Carolingian missions.
(*In* his Slovene medieval history. New York, 1962. p. 67-84)
PLatS

3904   **Monnier, François.**
Alcuin et Charlemagne avec des fragments d'un commentaire inédit d'Alcuin sur Saint Matthieu . . . 2. éd. augm. Paris, Henri Plon, 1863.
376 p. 13 cm.
MnCS

3905 **Wilmart, André, O.S.B.**
Le Lectionnaire d'Alcuin. Roma,
Ephemerides liturgicae, 1937.
Excerptum ex Ephemerides liturgicae,
1937, p. 137–197.
InStme

Altmann, Blessed, bishop of Passau, d. 1091

3906 **Der heilige Altmann, Bischof von
Passau;** sein Leben und sein Werk.
Festschrift zur 900-Jahr-Feier 1965.
[Hrsg. und Verleger Abtei Göttweig,
Austria, 1965].
168, [48] p. illus. 30 cm.
PLatS

Alto, Saint, fl. 759–763

3907 **Festschrift** zum zwölfhundert-jährigen
Sankt Alto-Jubiläum. Von einem Verehrer des hl. Alto. München, Salesianer
[1930].
152 p. illus.
AStb

Amandus, Saint, bishop of Maastricht, d. 675

3908 **Duckett, Eleanor Shipley.**
Saint Amand and Saint Willibrord; Belgium and the Netherlands in the seventh
century.
(*In* her: The wandering saints of the
early Middle Ages. New York, 1959. p.
140–164)
PLatS

Angilbertus, Saint, abbot of St-Riquier, d. 814

3909 **Fural, Edmond.**
Le poème d'Engelbert sur la bataille de
Fontenoy. [n.p., n.d.]
86–98 p. 24 cm.
MnCS

Anno, Saint, abp. of Cologne, d. 1075

3910 **Libellus de translatione Sancti Annonis
archiepiscopi,** et miracula Sancti Annonis. Liber primus et secundus. Hrsg.
von Mauritius Mittler. Siegburg,
Respuclica, 1966–
v. 24 cm.
Latin and German.
KAS

3910a **Monumenta Annonis**—Köln und Siegburg; Weltbild und Kunst im hohen
Mittelalter. Eine Ausstellung des
Schütgen-Museums der Stadt Köln in
der Cäcilienkirche vom 30. April bis
zum 27. Juli 1975. Köln, 1975.
248 p. illus., plates (part col.) 30 cm.
MnCS

**Anselm, Saint, abp. of Canterbury,
1033–1109**

3911 **Analecta Anselmiana.** Untersuchungen
über Person und Werk Anselms von
Canterbury. In Verbindung mit K.
Flasch, B. Geyer . . . hrsg. von F. S.
Schmitt. Frankfurt/Main, Minerva
GMBH, 1969–
v. 24 cm.
InStme

3912 **Barré, Henri.**
Prières anciennes de l'occident à la Mère
du Sauveur, des origines à saint Anselme.
Paris, P. Lethielleux [1963].
360 p. 26 cm.
PLatS

3913 **Barth, Karl.**
Anselm: Fides quaerens intellectum;
Anselm's proof of the existence of God in
the context of his theological scheme.
[Translated by Ian W. Robertson from the
German]. Richmond, Va., John Knox Press
[1960].
173 p. 23 cm.
InStme; NcBe; PLatS

3914 **Beckaert, A.**
Une justification platonicienne de l'argu-
ment a priori.
(*In* Spicilegium Beccense. 1959. v. 1,
185–190)
PLatS

3915 **Bouillard, Henri, S.J.**
La preuve de Dieu dans le Proslogion et
son interprétation par Karl Barth.
(*In* Spicilegium Beccense. 1959. v. 1, p.
191–208)
PLatS

3916 **Bouvier, Michel.**
La pensée du Révérend Pére Thomas-
André Audet, O.P., sur la théologie du
"Cur Deus homo" de saint Anselme.
(*In* Spicilegium Beccense. 1959. v. 1, p.
313–326)
PLatS

3917 **Bultot, Robert.**
Christianisme et valeurs humaines. A: la
doctrine du mépris du monde, en Occident,
de S. Ambroise à Innocent III. Louvain,
Nauwelaerts, 1963–
6 v. in 11. 21 cm.
KAS

3918 **Bütler, Anselm, O.S.B.**
Die Seinslehre des h. Anselm von
Canterbury. Ingenbohl [Switzerland],
Theodosius Druckerei, 1959.
112 p. 21 cm.
Thesis—Universität Fribourg (Schweiz).
MnCS; PLatS

3919   **Chatillon, Jean.**
De Guillaume d'Auxerre à saint Thomas d'Aquin. L'argument de saint Anselme chez les premiers scolastiques du XIIIe siècle.
(*In* Spicilegium Beccense. 1959. v. 1, p. 209-232)
PLatS

3920   **Chibnall, Mrs. Marjorie.**
The relations of St. Anselm with the English dependencies of the Abbey of Bec, 1079-1093.
(*In* Spicilegium Beccense. 1959. v. 1, p. 521-530)
PLatS

3921   **Congar, Marie Joseph, O.P.**
L'Eglise chez saint Anselme.
(*In* Spicilegium Beccense. 1959. v. 1, p. 371-400)
PLatS

3922   **Cruz Hernandez, Miguel.**
Les caractères fondamentaus de la pensée de saint Anselme.
(*In* Spicilegium Beccense. 1959. v. 1, p. 9-18)
PLatS

3923   **Danoust, Joseph.**
Le janséniste Dom Gerberon, éditeur de saint Anselme (1675).
(*In* Spicilegium Beccense. 1959. v. 1, p. 531-540)
PLatS

3924   **Delhaye, Philippe.**
Quelques aspects de la morale de saint Anselme.
(*In* Spicilegium Beccense. 1959. v. 1, p. 401-422)
PLatS

3925   **Dickinson, John C.**
Saint Anselm and the first Regular Canons in England.
(*In* Spicilegium Beccense. 1959. v. 1, p. 541-546)
PLatS

3926   **Domet de Vorges, Edmond C.E.**
Saint Anselme. Paris, F. Alcan, 1901.
vi, 334 p. 23 cm. (Les grands philosophes)
InStme

3927   **Eadmer, prior of Canterbury.**
Vita beati Anselmi, archiepiscopi Cantuariensis. MS. Vienna, Nationalbibliothek, codex 1869, f. 166r-191v. Folio. Saec. 15.
Microfilm: MnCH proj. no. 2166

3928   **Eadmer, prior of Canterbury.**
The life of St. Anselm, archbishop of Canterbury. Edited with introduction, notes, and translation by R. W. Southern. London, New York, T. Nelson, 1962.
xxxvi, 171, 171, 172-179 p. 23 cm.
Latin and English on opposite pages.
ILSP; InStme; MnCS; NcBe; NdRi; PLatS

3929   **Evdokomov, Paul.**
L'aspect apophatique de l'argument de saint Anselme.
(*In* Spicilegium Beccense. 1959. v. 1, p. 233-258)
PLatS

3930   **Fairweather, Eugene R.**
"Iustitia Dei" as "ratio" of the Incarnation.
(*In* Spicilegium Beccense. 1959. v. 1, p. 327-336)
PLatS

3931   **Finance, Joseph de, S.J.**
Position anselmienne et démarche cartésienne.
(*In* Spicilegium Beccense. 1959. v. 1, p. 259-272)
PLatS

3932   **Forest, Aimé.**
L'argument de saint Anselme dans la philosophie réflexive.
(*In* Spicilegium Beccense. 1959. v. 1, p. 273-294)
PLatS

3933   **Foreville, Raymonde.**
L'ultime "ratio" de la morale politique de saint Anselme: "rectitudo voluntatis propter se servata."
(*In* Spicilegium Beccense. 1959. v. 1, p. 423-438)
PLatS

3934   **Glorieux, Palamon.**
Quelques aspects de la Christologie de saint Anselme.
(*In* Spicilegium Beccense. 1959. v. 1, p. 337-348)
PLatS

3935   **Gogacz, Mieczyslaw.**
Problem istnienia Boga u Anzelma z Canterbury i problem prawdy u Henryka z Gandawy. Lublin, Tow. Naukowe Katolickiego Uniwersytetu Lubelskiego, 1961.
121 p. 25 cm.
PLatS

3936   **Hartshorne, Charles.**
Anselm's discovery: re-examination of the ontological proof for God's existence. La Salle, Ill., Open Court [1965].
xvi, 333 p. 21 cm.
PLatS

3937   **Hasse, Friedrich Rudolf.**
Anselm von Canterbury. Frankfurt a. M., Minerva, 1966.

2 v. 22 cm.
Unveränderter Nachdruck of Leipzig
edition of 1843–52.
PLatS

3938   **Hayen, A. S., S.J.**
Saint Anselme et saint Thomas; la vrai
nature de la théologie et sa portée apostolique.
(*In* Spicilegium Beccense. 1959. v. 1, p.
45–86)
PLatS

3939   **Henry, Desmond Paul.**
The logic of Saint Anselm. Oxford,
Clarendon Press, 1967.
viii, 258 p. 23 cm.
InStme; PLatS

3940   **Henry, Desmond Paul.**
Remarks of Saint Anselm's treatment of
possibility.
(*In* Spicilegium Beccense. 1959. f. 1, p.
19–22)
PLatS

3941   **Hick, John, comp.**
The many-faced argument; recent
studies on the ontological argument for the
existence of God, edited by John Hick and
Arthur G. McGill. New York, Macmillan
[1967].
vii, 373 p. 22 cm.
InStme

3942   **Hopkins, Jasper.**
A companion to the study of St. Anselm.
Minneapolis, University of Minnesota
Press [1972].
ix, 291 p. 24 cm.
InStme; KAS

3943   **John of Salisbury, bp. of Chartres.**
Vita Anselmi archiepiscopi.
(*In* his Opera omnia. Oxonii, 1848. vol. 5)
MnCS

3944   **Knox, Ronald Arbuthnott.**
St. Anselm (preached at St. Anselm and
St. Cecilia's, Kingway).
(*In* his Captive flames; a collection of
panegyrics. London, 1941. p. 28–34)
PLatS

3945   **Laporte, Jean, O.S.B.**
Saint Anselme et l'ordre monastique.
(*In* Spicilegium Beccense. 1959. v. 1, p.
455–476)
PLatS

3946   **Lefèvre, Yves.**
Saint Anselme et l'enseignement systé-
matique de la doctrine.
(*In* Spicilegium Beccense. 1959. v. 1, p.
87–94)
PLatS

3947   **Le Rohellec, Joseph, C.S.Sp.**
Origine augustinienne et plotinienne de
l'argument ontologique de saint Anselme.
(*In* his: Problèmes philosophiques. Paris,
1932. p. 346–360)
PLatS

3948   **Lubac, Henri de, S.J.**
Sur le chapitre XIVe du Proslogion.
(*In* Spicilegium Beccense. 1959. v. 1, p.
295–312)
PLatS

3949   **McIntyre, John.**
Premises and conclusions in the systems
of St. Anselm's theology.
(*In* Spicilegium Beccense. 1959. v. 1, p.
95–102)
PLatS

3950   **Mason, J.F.A.**
St. Anselm's relations with laymen:
selected letters.
(*In* Spicilegium Beccense. 1959. v. 1, p.
547–560)
PLatS

3951   **Merton, Louis, O.C.S.O.**
Reflections on some recent studies of St.
Anselm.
(*In* Monastic studies, v. 3, p. 221–236)
PLatS

3952   **Michaud-Quantin, Pierre.**
Notes sur le vocabulaire psychologique
de saint Anselme.
(*In* Spicilegium Beccense. 1959. v. 1, p.
23–30)
PLatS

3953   **Nedoncelle, Maurice.**
La notion de personne dans l'oeuvre de
saint Anselme.
(*In* Spicilegium Beccense. 1959. v. 1, p.
31–44)
PLatS

3954   **Plagnieux, Jean.**
Le binôme "iustitia-potentia" dans la
sotériologie augustinienne et anselmienne.
(*In* Spicilegium Beccense. 1959. v. 1, p.
141–154)
PLatS

3955   **Pouchet, Jean Marie, O.S.B.**
La componction de l'humilité et de la
piété chez saint Anselme d'après des "Orationes sive Meditations."
(*In* Spicilegium Beccense. 1959. v. 1, p.
489–508)
PLatS

3956   **Pouchet, Robert, O.S.B.**
La rectitudo chez saint Anselme; un
itinéraire augustinien de l'ame à Dieu.
Paris, Etudes Augustiniennes, 1964.
330 p. 25 cm.
InStme; MnCS; PLatS

3957 **Rondet, Henri, S.J.**
Grâce et péché; l'augustinisme de saint Anselme.
(*In* Spicilegium Beccense. 1959. v. 1, p. 155–170)
PLatS

3958 **Saenz de Aguirre, José.**
Auctoritas infallibilis et summa Cathedrae S. Petri extras et supra concilia quaelibet . . . Salmanticae, Lucas Perez, 1683.
xxxii, 544, clx, 28 p.
Partial contents: Tractatus appendix, in quo ostenditur S. Anselmum fuisse eximium defensorem cathedrae S. Petri adversus rebelles, praesertim Graecos, & longe contraria praedictae declarationi tradidisse.
PLatS (microfilm)

3959 **Salmon, Pierre, O.S.B.**
L'ascèse monastique dans les lettres de saint Anselme de Canterbury.
(*In* Spicilegium Beccense. 1959. v. 1, p. 509–520)
PLatS

3960 **Schmitt, Franciscus Salesius, O.S.B.**
Die wissenschaftliche Methode in "Cur Deus homo."
(*In* Spicilegium Beccense. 1959. v. 1, p. 349–370)
PLatS

3961 **Secret, Bernard.**
Saint Anselme, burguignon d'Aoste.
(*In* Spicilegium Beccense. 1959. v. 1, p. 561–570)
PLatS

3962 **Sola ratione;** Anselm-Studien für Pater Dr. h. c. Franciscus Salesius Schmitt, O.S.B., zum 75. Geburtstag zm 20. Dez. 1969 (In Verbindung mit B. Geyer und A. Hufnagel hrsg. von Helmut K. Kohlenberger). Stuttgart-Bad-Cannstatt, Frommann, 1970.
236 p. 22 cm.
French, German, or Italian.
MnCS

3963 **Southern, Richard William.**
St. Anselm and Gilbert Crispin, abbot of Westminster.
(*In* Mediaeval and renaissance studies, v. 3, p. 78–115)
PLatS

3964 **Southern, Richard William.**
Saint Anselm and his biographer; a study of monastic life and thought, 1069–1130. Cambridge [England], University Press, 1963.
xvi, 389 p. 23 cm.
ILSP; InFer; InStme; MnCS; NcBe; PLatS

3965 **Southern, Richard William.**
St. Anselm and his English pupils.
(*In* Mediaeval and renaissance studies, v. 1, no. 1, p. 3–34)
PLatS

3966 **Spicilegium Beccense;** ouvrage publié avec le concours de Centre National de la Recherche Scientifique. Paris, J. Vrin, 1959–
v. 25 cm.
MnCS; MoCo; PLatS; CaQStB

3967 **Steinen, Wolfram von den.**
Von heiligen Geist des Mittelalters: Anselm von Canterbury, Bernhard von Clairvaux. [2., unveränderte Aufl.]. Darmstedt, Wissenschaftliche Buchgesellschaft, 1968.
x, 307 p. 23 cm.
Reprint of 1926 edition.
InStme

3968 **Thonnard, François Joseph.**
Caractère augustinien de la méthode philosophique de saint Anselme.
(*In* Spicilegium Beccense. 1959. v. 1, p. 171–184)
PLatS

3969 **Urry, William G.**
Saint Anselm and his cult at Canterbury.
(*In* Spicilegium Beccense. 1959. v. 1, p. 571–594)
PLatS

3970 **Vagaggini, Cyprian, O.S.B.**
La hantise des "rationes necessariae" de saint Anselme dans la théologie des processions trinitaires de saint Thomas.
(*In* Spicilegium Beccense. 1959. v. 1, p. 103–140)
PLatS

3971 **Vitae s. Bernardi et s. Anselmi.** MS. Lambeth Palace Library, London, codex 163. 100 f. Quarto. Saec. 13.
Microfilm: MnCH

3972 **Warnach, Viktor, O.S.B.**
Wort und Wirklichkeit bei Anselm von Canterbury.
(*In* Festschrift für Albert Auer, O.S.B. [Salzburger Jahrbuch für Philosophie, Bd. 5–6, 1961–62], p. 157–176)
PLatS

Ansgar, Saint, archbishop of Hamburg and Bremen, 801–865

3973 **Duckett, Eleanor Shipley.**
Saint Anskar: Denmark and Sweden in the ninth century.
(*In* her: The wandering saints in the early Middle Ages. New York, 1959. p. 249–272)
PLatS

3974 **Rembert, Saint.**
Rimberti vita Anskari. Rimbert, Ansgars Leben.
(*In* Quellen des 9. und 11. Jahrhunderts zur Geschichte der hamburgischen Kirche und des Reiches, p. 613–707)
Latin and German.
PLatS

3975 **Senger, Basilius, O.S.B.**
Ansgar, Mönch und Apostels des Nordens. Dülmen i.W., A. Laumann [1964].
80 p. plates. 19 cm.
MnCS

3976 **Vita s. Anscharii primi archiepiscopi Hamburgensis,** conscripta a s. Rimberto ejus successore, ex codice olim monasterii Corbeiensis, nunc vero S. Germani Pratensis. MS. Vienna, Nationalbibliothek, codex 9372, f.1r–51v. Quarto. Saec. 17.
Microfilm: MnCH proj. no. 19,305

3977 **Vita s. Anscharii a Gualdone monacho Corbeiensi composita,** ex codice olim monasterii Corbeiensis, nunc vero S. Germani Pratensis. MS. Vienna, Nationalbibliothek, codex 9372a, f.53r–94r. Quarto. Saec. 17.
Microfilm: MnCH proj. no. 19,305

3978 **Vita s. Anscarii,** dialecto vulgari Germaniae inferioris conscripta. Initium deest. Incipit: lerynge bekert to deme thelouen. Vienna, Nationalbibliothek, codex 2673. 6 f. Folio. Saec. 15.
Microfilm: MnCH proj. no. 15,977

Aribo Scholasticus, 11th cent.

3979 **Rawski, Conrad H.**
Notes on Aribo Scholasticus.
(*In* Natalicia musicologica. Hafniae, 1962. p. 19–29)
PLatS

Auer, Albert, 1891–

3980 **Festschrift für Albert Auer, O.S.B.**
Hrsg. von den Professoren des Philosophischen Instituts in Salzburg. München-Salzburg, Verlag Anton Pustet, 1961.
488 p. 24 cm.
PLatS

Augustine, Saint, archbishop of Canterbury, d. 604

3981 **Browne, George Forrest.**
Augustine and his companions. Four lectures delivered at St. Paul's in January, 1895. Published under the direction of the Tract Committee. London, Society for Promoting Christian Knowledge; New York, R. Young, 1895.
201 p. 17 cm.
KAS

3982 **Deanesly, Margaret.**
Augustine of Canterbury. London; Camden, N.J., Nelson, 1964.
vii, 167 p. illus., map. 23 cm.
InStme; PLatS

3983 **Gasquet, Francis Aidan, O.S.B.**
The mission of St. Augustine; its import for Englishmen and Catholics today. London, Catholic Truth Society [1897].
32 p. 19 cm.
KAS

Ava, member of Gottweig Abbey of Benedictine nuns, d. 1127

3984 **Frau Ava.**
(*In* Wilpert, Gero von. Deutsches Dichterlexikon. 2., erw. Aufl. Stuttgart, 1976. p. 31)
MnCS

3985 **Langguth, Adolf.**
Untersuchungen über die Geschichte der Ava. Budapest, 1880.
133 p. 24 cm.
Harvard University; University of Chicago

Ayglier, Bernard, abbot of Monte Cassino, d. 1282

3986 **Bohier, Pierre.**
Commentarius in Speculum monachorum Bernardi Cassinensis ad Narbonensem episcopum. MS. Vienna, Nationalbibliothek, codex 5135, f.144r–191r. Folio. Saec. 15.
Microfilm: MnCH proj. no. 18,301

Ayndorffer, Kaspar, 1401–1461

3987 **Angerer, Joachim, O.S.B.**
Die Bräuche der Abtei Tegernsee unter Abt Kaspar Ayndorffer (1426–1461) . . . Ottobeuren, Kommissionsverlag Winfried-Werk, 1968.
xv, 362 p. 24 cm.
InStme

Baker, Augustine, 1575–1641

3988 **Hayner, Renée.**
Augustine Baker.
(*In* Walsh, James, S.J. Pre-Reformation English spirituality. New York, 1965. p. 252–264)
PLatS

3989 **Knowles, David, O.S.B.**
Father Augustine Baker.
(*In* Davis, Charles. English spiritual
writers. New York, 1961. p. 97–111)
PLatS

3990 **Low, Anthony.**
Augustine Baker. New York, Twayne
Publishers [1970].
170 p. 21 cm.
KAS; NcBe; PLatS

Bar, Catherine de
see
Mechtilde de Saint-Sacrement

Barbo, Ludovico, 1382–1443

3991 **Pesche, Luigi.**
Ludovico Barbo, vescovo de Treviso
(1437–1443): cura pastorale, riforma della
Chiesa, spiritualità. Padova, Editrice
Antenore, 1969.
2 v. 25 cm.
KAS; PLatS

3992 **Pitigliani, Riccardo.**
Il Ven. Ludovico Barbo e la diffusione
dell'Imitazione di Ciristo per opera della
Congregazione di S. Giustina. Padova,
Badia S. Giustina, 1943.
xxxi, 196 p. illus., plates. 25 cm.
InStme

3993 **Tassi, Ildefonso, O.S.B.**
Ludovico Barbo (1381–1443). Roma,
Storia e letteratura, 1952.
xvi, 179 p. 26 cm.
InStme; MnCS

Bavoz, Placide Therese, 1768–1838

3994 **Buenner, Denys, O.S.B.**
Madame de Bavoz, abbesse de Pradines
de l'Ordre de Saint Benoît . . . Paris, E.
Vitte [1961].
xxi, 572 p. plates. 26 cm.
CaQStB; MnCS; PLatS

Bayne, William Wilfried, 1893–

3995 **American Society of Heraldry.**
A presentation of the heraldic art of Rev.
Dom William Wilfried Bayne, O.S.B.,
Ch.L.J. [n.p.] Published by the Society for
private distribution in a limited edition,
1967.
39 p. illus. 28 cm.
PLatS

Beato de Liebana, O.S.B., d. 798

3995a **Romero de Lecea, Carlos.**
Trompetas y citaras en los codices de
Beato de Liebana. Discurso leido por

Carlos Romero de Lecea & contestacion de
Federico Sopena Ibanez. Madrid, Real
Academia de Bellas Artes de San Fer-
nando, 1977.
142 p. illus., col. plate, 24 cm.
MnCS

Beauduin, Lambert, 1873–1960

3996 **Bouyer, Louis, C.Orat.**
Dom Lambert Beauduin, un homme
d'Eglise. [Paris], Casterman, 1964.
185 p. illus. 20 cm.
CaQAtB; InStme; MnCS; MoCo; PLatS

3997 **Quitslund, Sonya A.**
Beauduin, a prophet vindicated. New
York, Newman Press [1973].
xvii, 366 p. illus. 24 cm.
KAS; MoCo; PLatS

3997a **Veilleur avant l'aurore;** colloque Lambert
Beauduin [par] J. J. von Allmen [&
others]. Editions de Chevetogne, 1978.
296 p. 22 cm.
MnCS

Bede the Venerable, Saint, 673–735

3998 **Anonymi commentarius** in Venerabilis
Bedae opus de natura rerum et temporum ratione. Incipit: Non est praeter-
mittendum cum dixit. MS. Benediktinerabtei Melk, Austria, codex 412, f.32–
38. Folio. Saec. 9.
Microfilm: MnCH proj. no. 1957

3999 **Bedae morientis cantus,** in lingua anglo-
saxonica. MS. Augustinerchorherren-
stift Klosterneuburg, Austria, codex
787, f.183r. Folio. Saec. 12.
Microfilm: MnCH proj. no. 5764

4000 **Blair, Peter Hunter, O.S.B.**
Bede's Ecclesiastical history of the
English nation and its importance today.
[Jarrow, Co. Durham, England, The
Rectory, 1959].
15 p. 22 cm. (Jarrow lecture, 1959)
PLatS

4001 **Blair, Peter Hunter, O.S.B.**
The world of Bede. London, Secker &
Warburg [1970].
x, 340 p. 23 cm.
InStme; KAS; NcBe; PLatS

4002 **Cuthbert, monk of Jarrow.**
Obitus S. Bedae Venerabilis. MS. Benediktinerabtei Göttweig, Austria, codex 54,
f.12r–12v. Folio. Saec. 12.
Microfilm: MnCH proj. no. 3342

4003 **Cuthbert, monk of Jarrow.**
De obitu Bedae Venerabilis presbiteri.
MS. Augustinerchorherrenstift Kloster-

neuburg, Austria, codex 787, f.182r–184v. Folio. Saec. 12.
Microfilm: MnCH proj. no. 5764

4004 **Cuthbert, monk of Jarrow.**
Epistola ad Chuninum de transitu Bedae Venerabilis. MS. Vienna, Nationalbibliothek, codex 12,761, f.122r–123r. Quarto. Saec. 15.
Microfilm: MnCH proj. no. 14,454

4005 **De Beda presbytero quare dicatur venerabilis.** MS. Vienna, Nationalbibliothek, codex 389, f.16r. Folio. Saec. 14.
Microfilm: MnCH proj. no. 13,725

4006 **Famulus Christi:** essays in commemoration of the thirteenth centenary of the birth of the Venerable Bede. Edited by Gerald Bonner. London, SPCK, 1976.
xii, 404 p. illus. 23 cm.
InStme; MnCS; PLatS

4007 **Meyvaert, Paul.**
Bede and Gregory the Great. [Printed by J. & P. Bealls, Newcastle upon Tyne, 1964].
26 p. 22 cm.
PLatS

4008 **Meyvaert, Paul.**
The Bede 'signature' in the Leningrad colophon. [Abbaye de Maredsous, Belgique, 1961].
Offprint from: Revue bénédictine, v. 71(1961), p. 274–286.
PLatS

4009 **Meyvaert, Paul.**
Benedict, Gregory, Bede and others. London, Variorum Reprints, 1977.
[388] p., in various pagings, illus. 24 cm.
Reprint of 16 articles published between 1955 and 1976.
InStme

4010 **Nicholl, Donald.**
St. Bede.
(*In* Walsh, James, S.J. Pre-Reformation English spirituality. New York, 1965. p. 1–14)
PLatS

4011 **Sweet, Henry, ed.**
The oldest English texts. Edited with introductions and a glossary by Henry Sweet. Oxford University Press [1966, 1885].
vii, 668 p. 23 cm. (The Early English Text Society. Original series, no. 83)
MnCS; PLatS

4012 **Wright, D. H.**
The date of the Leningrad Bede. [Abbaye de Maredsous, Belgique, 1961].
Offprint from Revue bénédictine, v. 71(1961), p. 265–273.
PLatS

Benedict, Saint, abbot of Monte Cassino, 480–547

For works about Saint Benedict *see* Chapter II.

Berliere, Ursmer, 1861–1932

4013 **Bishop, Edmund.**
Bishop Hedley and Dom U. Berlière on the history of the English Benedictines; a letter to a friend by Edmund Bishop. [n.p., 1897].
40 p.
NcBe; PLatS

Bernard Tolomei, Saint, 1272–1348

4014 **Marechaux, Bernard M., O.S.B.Oliv.**
Vita del beato Bernardo Tolomei, fondatore della Congregazione di N. S. di Monte Oliveto dell'Ordine di S. Benedetto. Traduzione e ristampa dal testo francese a cura dal P. Don Isidoro Maria Minucci . . . Robigo, Istituto Padano di Arti Graffiche, 1948.
360 p. 18 cm.
PLatS

Bernard von Baching

4015 **Schlitpacher, Johannes, O.S.B.**
Iudicium de tractatu Bernardi de Baching contra illicitum esum carnium. MS. Benediktinerabtei Melk, Austria, codex 960, f.405–406. Quarto. Saec. 15.
Microfilm: MnCH proj. no. 1775

Bernardus Noricus, fl. 1290–1326

4016 **Neumüller, Willibrord, O.S.B.**
Bernardus Noricus von Kremsmünster. Wels [Austria], Verlag "Weisermühl," 1947.
167 p. 24 cm.
MnCS; PLatS

Berno, abbot of Cluny, 850–927

4017 **Oursel, Raymond.**
Les saints abbés de Cluny. Textes choisis, traduits et présentés par Raymond Oursel. Namur, Belgique, Editions du Soleil Levant [1960].
100 p. 17 cm.
PLatS

Berno, abbot of Reichenau, d. 1048

4018 **Oesch, Hans.**
Berno und Hermann von Reichenau als Musiktheoretiker, mit einen Ueberblick über ihr Leben und die handschriftliche Ueberlieferung ihrer Werke . . . Bern, P. Haupt [1961].

251 p. 23 cm.
PLatS

Berthold, Blessed, abbot of Garsten,
ca.1090-1142

4019 **Legenda s. Berchtoldi Garstensis.** MS.
Benediktinerabtei Melk, Austria, codex
1469. 44 f. Duodecimo. Saec. 14.
Microfilm: MnCH proj. no. 1958

4020 **Vita s. Bertholdi abbatis.** MS. Benediktinerabtei Melk, Austria, codex 222,
f.87r–98r. Folio. Saec. 13.
Microfilm: MnCH proj. no. 1260

Bernward, Saint, bishop of Hildesheim,
ca.960-1022

4021 **Beissel, Stephan, S.J.**
Der heilige Bernward von Hildesheim als
Künstler und Förderer der deutschen
Kunst. Hildesheim, A. Lax, 1895.
viii, 74, xi p. illus., plates. 30 cm.
PLatS

4022 **Beissel, Stephan, S.J.**
Des hl. Bernward Evangelienbuch im
Dome zu Hildesheim. Mit Handschriften
des 10. und 11. Jahrhunderts in kunsthis-
torischer und liturgischer Hinsicht ver-
glichen. 2.Ausgabe mit V Tafeln, hrsg. von
G. Schrader und F. Koch. Hildesheim, A.
Lax, 1891.
vi, 71 p. xxvi facsims. 29 cm.
PLatS

4023 **Dibelius, Franz.**
Die Bernwardstür zu Hildesheim. Mit 3
Abbildungen im Text und 15 Tafeln.
Strassburg, Heitz & Mündel, 1907.
vi, 152 p. illus. 25 cm.
PLatS

4024 **Habicht, Victor Kurt.**
Des heiligen Bernward von Hildesheim
Kunstwerke (zum neunhandertjähr.
Todestag des hl. Bernward). Bremen,
Angelsachsen-Verlag, 1922.
42, 25 p. 23 cm.
PLatS

4025 **Miracula sancti Bernwardi.**
(*In* Monumenta Germaniae historica.
Scriptores. Stuttgart, 1963. t. 4, p.
782–786)
MnCS; PLatS

4026 **Pilz, Walter.**
Bernward: Bischof und Künstler. [Hilde-
sheim] Bernward Verlag [1962].
94 p. illus., map. 19 cm.
PLatS

Bogler, Theodor, 1897-1968

4027 **P. Theodor Bogler,** 1897–1968. [Abtei
Maria Laach, 1968]
15 p. port. 21 cm.
MnCS

Bohier, Pierre, bishop of Orvieto, 14th cent.

4028 **Huertebize, Benjamin.**
Pierre Bohier, bénédictin évêque d'Orvieto. Ligugé, Impr. E. Aubin, 1910.
19 p.
NcBe

Boniface, Saint, archbishop of Mainz,
680-1755

4029 **Briefe des Bonifatius . . .** nebst einigen
zeitgenössischen Dokumenten . . . Neu
bearb. von Reinhold Rau. Darmstadt,
Wissenschaftliche Buchgesellschaft,
1968.
535 p. 23 cm.
MnCS

4030 **Duckett, Eleanor Shipley.**
Saint Boniface, Saint Lull, Saint Leoba:
Germany in the eighth century.
(*In* her: The wandering saints in the
early Middle Ages. New York, 1959. p.
193–228)
PLatS

4030a **Finch, Margaret.**
St. Boniface and the Christmas tree.
London, Catholic Truth Society, 1975.
[10] p. illus. 19 cm. (Catholic Truth
Society publications, B470, [v. 6])
PLatS

4030b **The Greatest Englishman;** essays on St.
Boniface and the Church at Crediton,
edited by Timothy Reuter. Exeter,
Paternoster Press, c 1980.
140 p. 23 cm.
KAS

4031 **Lampen, Willibrord, O.F.M.**
Willibrord en Bonifatius. Amsterdam,
P. N. Van Kampen, 1939.
159 p. plates. 20 cm.
MnCS

4032 **Löwe, Heinz.**
Ein literarischer Wisersacher des Bonifatius, Virgil von Salzburg, und die Kosmographie des Aethicus Ister. Mainz, Akademie der Wissenschaften und der Literatur [1952].
90 p. 25 cm.
MnCS

4033 **Pfeiffer, Erwin.**
Bonifatius, sein Leben und Wirken. München, Max Hueber [1936].

119 p. 19 cm.
MnCS

4034 **Schürmann, M.**
Der heilige Bonifacius: Haupt-Momente
aus seinem Leben. Fulda, A. Maier, 1882.
vi, 23 p. 22 cm.
KAS

4035 **Treu zur Kirche!** Predigten über Glaube
und Kirche, gehalten im Dome zu Fulda
anlässlich der 1150 jährigen Iubelfeier
des Martyrtodes des Apostels der Deutschen. Fulda, Verlag der Fuldaer Ac-
tiendruckerei, 1907.
215 p. 20 cm.
Includes nine sermons on St. Boniface.
PLatS

4036 **Vita s. Bonifacii.** MS. Benediktinerabtei
Admont, Austria, codex 654, f. 183r–
186r. Quarto. Saec. 12.
Microfilm: MnCH proj. no. 9694

4037 **Vita sancti Bonifacii archiepiscopi.** MS.
Cistercienserabtei Zwettl, Austria,
codex 77, f. 124r–147r. Folio. Saec. 12.
Microfilm: MnCH proj. no. 6674

4038 **Willibald, Presbyter.**
Vita s. Bonifacii. MS. Benediktinerabtei
Admont, Austria, codex 654, f. 146r–
182v. Quarto. Saec. 12.
Microfilm: MnCH proj. no. 9694

4039 **Willibald, Presbyter.**
Vita s. Bonifacii. MS. Vienna, National-
bibliothek, codex 474, f.179r–210r. Folio.
Saec. 11.
Microfilm: MnCH proj. no. 13,819

Botte, Bernard, 1893–

4040 **Mélanges liturgiques offerts au R. P.**
Dom Bernard Botte, O.S.B., de l'Abbaye de Mont César à l'occasion du cin-
quantième anniversaire de son ordination sacerdotale (4 juin 1972). Louvain,
Abbaye du Mont César, 1972.
xxxii, 540 p. port. 25 cm.
KAS; PLatS

Boultwood, Alban, 1911–

4041 **Ellis, John Tracy.**
You are the light of the world; sermon
preached . . . at the solemn blessing of
Right Reverend Alban Boultwood as first
abbot of St. Anselm's Abbey, Washington,
D.C. [in the] National Shrine of the Imma-
culate Conception, December 30, 1961.
8 leaves. 28 cm.
Reproduced from typed copy.
PLatS

Boyer, Jacques

4042 **Journal de voyage de Dom Jacques**
Boyer, religieux bénédictin de la Con-
grégation de Saint-Maur . . . 1710–
1714. Publié et annoté par Antoine
Vernière. Clermont-Ferrand, F.
Thibaud, 1886.
537 p.
CaQStB

Braunmüller, Benedikt, 1825–1898

4043 **Fink, Wilhelm, O.S.B.**
Abt Benedikt Braunmüller von Metten.
(*In* Bayerische Benediktinerakademie.
Jahresbericht, 4. Bd., 1925)
AStb; MnCS

4044 **Götz, Wunibald, O.S.B.**
Abt Dr. Benedikt Braunmüller; ein
Lebensbild. [Landshut, Jos. Thomman,
1901].
38 p. 21 cm.
KAS

Bruno, Saint, bishop of Segni, 1041(ca.)–1123

4045 **Grégoire, Réginald, O.S.B.**
Bruno de Segni, exégète médiéval et
thélogien monastique. Spoleto, 1965.
445 p. 21 cm.
KAS; PLatS

4046 **Kamlah, Wilhelm.**
Apokalypse und Geschichtstheologie
. . . Berlin, Emil Ebering, 1935.
131 p. 25 cm.
Partial contents: Bruno von Segni und
die Glossentradition.
PLatS

Burckhard, Johannes, 1538–1598

4047 **Hess, Sales, O.S.B.**
Das Kloster Banz in seinen Beziehungen
zu den Hochstiften Bamberg und Würzburg unter Abt Johannes Burckhard. St.
Ottilien, Missionsdruckerei, 1935.
xii, 101 p.
KAS

Butler, Edward Cuthbert, 1858–1934

4048 **Knowles, David, O.S.B.**
Edward Cuthbert Butler, 1858–1934. I.
Abbot Butler: a memoir. II. The works and
thought of Abbot Butler.
(*In* his: The historian and character and
other essays. Cambridge, 1963. p.
264–362)
PLatS

Calmet, Augustin, 1672–1757

4049 **Seillière, Frédéric.**
Compte-rendu par M. Frédéric Seillière
des fouilles entreprises pour retrouver les
restes de Dom Augustin Calmet, abbé de
Senones. Saint-Dié, Imprimerie de Ed.
Trotot, 1868.
24 p.
CaQStB

4050 **Seillière, Frédéric.**
Rapport présenté à la Commission du
monument de Dom Calmet à Senones . . .
Saint-Dié, Typographie de L. Humbert,
1873.
104 p.
CaQStB

Casaretto, Pietro, 1810–1880

4051 **Lunardi, Giovanni.**
Pietro Casaretto e gli inizi della Congregatione Sublacense (1810–1880); saggio
storico nel I. centenario della Congregazione, 1872–1972. Publicacions de l'Abadia
Montserrat, 1972.
525 p. illus. (Subsidia monastica, 3)
MoCo

Casel, Odo, 1886–1948

4052 **Casel, Odo, O.S.B.**
Das christliche Opfermysterium . . .
Hrsg. von Viktor Warnach. Graz, Verlag
Styria, 1968.
lv, 719 p. 21 cm.
Bibliography of Odo Casel's works: p.
681–685.
KAS

4053 **Gozier, André.**
Dom Casel. Paris, Fleurus, 1968.
191 p. 18 cm.
KAS

4054 **Plooij, Jacob.**
De mysterie-leer van Odo Casel; een
bijdrage tot het oecumenisch gesprek der
kerken. Zwolle, W.E.J. Tjeenk Willink,
1964.
267 p. 23 cm.
MnCS

4055 **Plooij, Jacob.**
Die Mysterienlehre Odo Casel's; ein
Beitrag zum ökumenischen Gespräch der
Kirchen. Deutsche Ausgabe besorgt von
Oda Hagemeyer . . . Neustadt an der
Aisch, Verlag Ph. C. W. Schmidt, 1968.
222 p. 23 cm.
MnCS

Caslock, John

4056 **Telfer, W.**
Faversham Abbey and its last abbot,
John Caslock . . . 3d ed. Faversham,
Kent, Faversham Society, 1968.
21 p. illus. 26 cm.
PLatS

Castelli, Benedictus, 1577–1644

4057 **Armellini, Mariano, O.S.B.**
Benedictus Castelli [vita].
(*In* his Bibliotheca benedictino-
Casinensis, v. 1, p. 92–97)
MnCS; MoCo

Caspar, abbot of Tegernsee, d. 1461

4058 **Epistola de obitu Domini Caspari,** olim
abbatis in Tegernsee. MS. Benediktinerabtei Melk, Austria, codex 1086,
f.219–221. Duodecimo. Saec. 15.
Microfilm: MnCH proj. no. 1848

Celestine V, Saint, Pope, 1215(ca.)–1296

4059 **Spinelli, Vincenzo.**
Vita di s. Pietro del Morrone papa, detto
Celestino quinto. Roma, Fabio di Falco,
1664.
241 p.
PLatS(microfilm)

Chapman, John, 1865–1933

4060 **Butler, Basil Christopher, O.S.B.**
John Chapman.
(*In* Davis, Charles. English spiritual
writers. New York, 1961. p. 182–202)
PLatS

Christina, of Markyate, Saint 1096(ca.)–1160

4061 **Talbot, C.H.**
The life of Christina of Markyate, a
twelfth-century recluse. Edited and trans-
lated by C. H. Talbot. Oxford, Clarendon
Press, 1959.
ix, 193 p. map., facsim. 22 cm.
Text in Latin and English.
PLatS

Cisneros, Garcia de, 1455–1510

4062 **Albareda, Anselmo, O.S.B.**
Bibliografia dels monjos de Montserrat
(segle XVI). Monestir de Montserrat, 1928.
vid. p. 43–142: Garsias de Cisneros.
MnCS

4062a **Baraut, Cebrià, O.S.B.**
Les fonts franciscanes dels escrits de
Garsias de Cisneros.

(*In* Miscellania Anselm M. Albareda. v. 1(1962), p. 64–78)
PLatS

4063 **Colombás, García, O.S.B.**
La confirmació de la confraria de la Mare de Déu de Montserrat.
(*In* Analecta Montserratensia, v. 10, p. 55–63)
PLatS

4064 **La vida del ven. Garcia de Cisneros,** abad de Monserrate . . . por el padre maestre F. Lorenço de Ayala.
(*In* Regla del bienaventurado San Benito . . . Valladolid, 1599. n. 3)
MnCS

4065 **Vida del ven Garcia de Cisneros,** abad de Monserrate.
(*In* Leteras apostolicas de San Gregorio Papa. Barcelona, 1633. n. 9)
MnCS

Conrad, Frowin, 1833–1923

4066 **Fuenfzig Lieder zur Feier des goldenen Profess-Jubilaeums** . . . Frowin Conrad. Atchison, Kans., 1903.
82 p.
MoCo

Conrad, Ignatius, 1846–1926

4067 **Hess, Luke, O.S.B.**
New Subiaco Abbey; a retrospect on the occasion of the silver jubilee of Abbot Ignatius Conrad, O.S.B., 1917. With an appendix by Vincent Orth, O.S.B. [n.p., 1917?].
125 p. illus. 25 cm.
InStme

Conradus Hirsaugiensis, d. 1190

4068 **Bultot, Robert.**
Dialogus de mundi contemptu vel amore, attribué à Conrad d'Hirsau. Extraits de l'Allocutio ad Deum et du De veritatis inquisitione. Textes inédits introduits par R. Bultot. Louvain, Editions Nauwelaerts, 1966.
90 p. 24 cm.
Latin and French.
MnCS

Constabilis, Saint, abbot of Cava, 1066–1124

4069 **S. Congregatio Sacrorum Rituum.**
Nullius seu Caven. confirmationis cultus ab immemorabili tempore praestiti servis Dei Alpherio, Leoni, Petro et Constabili abbatibus Ordinis S. Benedicti sanctis nuncupatis. Positio super cultu immemorabili.

Romae, ex Typographia Artificum a S. Joseph, 1893.
210, 17, 37 p. 30 cm.
MnCS

Coppersmith, Anselm, 1908–

4070 **Ceremony of the blessing of the Rt. Rev. Anselm Coppersmith, O.S.B.,** fourth abbot of Conception Abbey. Conception Abbey Press, 1962.
70 p.
MoCo

Corbinian, Saint, bishop of Freising, d.ca.730

4071 **Vita et actus beati Corbiniani.** MS. Benediktinerabtei Kremsmünster, Austria, codex 7, f.137r–166v. Saec. 13.
Microfilm: MnCH proj. no. 7

4072 **Vita s. Corbiniani.** Vienna, Austria, Nationalbibliothek, codex 416, f.17r–45v. Folio. Saec. 13.
Microfilm: MnCH proj. no. 13,750

Corrêa de Souza, Bernardo de Sao Bento, 1624–1693

4073 **Silva-Nigra, Clemente Maria de, O.S.B.**
Frei Bernardo de Sao Bento, o arquiteto seiscentista do Rio de Janeiro. Salvador-Bahia, Tip. Beneditina, 1950.
120, 27 p. illus. 50 plates. 33 cm.
MnCS

Crispin, Gilbert
see
Gilbert, abbot of Westminster

Cuthbert, Saint, 635–687

4074 **Bede the Venerable, Saint.**
The life and miracles of Saint Cuthbert, bishop of Lindisfarne.
(*In* his: Ecclesiastical history of the English nation. New York, 1954. p. 349–365)
PLatS

4075 **Colgrave, Bertram, ed. and tr.**
Two lives of Saint Cuthbert; a life by an anonymous monk of Lindisfarne and Bede's prose life. Texts, translation, and notes by Bertram Colgrave. New York, Greenwood Press [1969].
xiii, 375 p. 23 cm.
Latin and English on opposite pages.
InStme; MoCo; NcBe

4076 **Duckett, Eleanor Shipley.**
Saint Oswald, Saint Aidan, Saint Cuthbert: northern England in the seventh century.

(*In* her: The wandering saints of the early Middle Ages. New York, 1959. p. 93–117)
PLatS

4077 **Simeon, of Durham.**
Symeonis Dunelmensis Opera et collectanea. Vol. I. Durham [Eng.], 1868.
lxxxi, 301 p. 23 cm. (The Publications of the Surtees Society, vol. LI)
MnCS

4078 **Vita s. Cuthberti,** auctore anonymo . . .
(*In* Venerabilis Bedae Opera historica minora, p. 259–338)
PLatS

Danzer, Jakob, 1743–1796

4079 **Peleman, Albert, O.S.B.**
Der Benediktiner, Simpert Schwarzhueber, Professor in Salzburg . . . seine Beziehungen . . . zum Salzburger Moraltheologen Jakob Danzer . . . Regensburg, Fr. Pustet, 1961.
196 p. 22 cm.
MnCS

Dekkers, Eligius

4080 **Corona gratiarum miscellanea patristica,** historica et liturgica Eligio Dekkers, O.S.B. XII lustra complenti oblata. Brugge, Sint Pietersabdej, 1975.
2 v. illus. 26 cm.
Dutch, English, French, German, Italian, or Spanish.
InStme; MnCS; PLatS

Delfin, Peter, 1444–1525

4081 **Schnitzer, Joseph.**
Peter Delfin, General des Camaldulenserorden (1444–1525); ein Beitrag der Kirchenreform Alexanders VI und Savonarolas. München, Ernst Reinhardt, 1926.
459 p. illus.
MnCS

Desiderius, abbot of Monte Cassino
see
Victor III, Pope

Deutsch, Alcuin Henry, 1877–1951

4082 **Deutsch, Alfred Henry, O.S.B.**
Bruised reeds and other stories. Collegeville, Minn., St. John's University Press, [1971].
213 p. illus. 22 cm.
InStme; KAS; MnCS; PLatS

Diekmann, Godfrey Leo, 1908–

4083 **McManus, Frederick Richard, ed.**
The revival of the liturgy. [New York] Herder and Herder [1963].
224 p. 21 cm.
Homage volume to Godfrey Diekmann, O.S.B., for his 25 years as editor of Worship.
ILSP; InStme; KAS; MnCS; PLatS

Doëns, Marguerite-Marie, 1841–1884

4084 **Misserey, E.**
Sous le signe de l'hostie: la Mère M.-M. Doëns, moniale bénédictine. Paris, Desclée, De Brouwer, 1934.
xv, 227 p. 19 cm.
CaQStM; InStme; WaOSM

Dominicus Loricatus, Saint, 995–1060

4085 **Peter Damian, Saint.**
La vita di S. Domenico, confessore, detto il Loricato, eremita benedettino di S. Croce del Fonte Avellano. Tratta dagli scritti di S. Pier-Damiano. Raccolta, ed illustrata da Ottavio Turchi. Roma, Stamperia di Antonio de' Rossi, 1749.
200 p. 25 cm.
MnCS

Dowdall, Joseph, 1927–

4086 **The abbatial blessing of the Right Reverend Joseph Dowdall, O.S.B.,** by His Grace, the Most Rev. Jeremiah Kinane . . . at St. Columba's Abbey, Glenstal, Co. Limerick [Ireland] on Saturday, 24th of June, 1957.
24 p. 19 cm.
PLatS

Dunlap, Fidelis, James, 1925–

4087 **The solemn blessing of the Right Reverend Fidelis J. Dunlap, O.S.B.,** abbot of Saint Leo Abbey at the celebration of the Eucharist in the William P. McDonald Center, Saint Leo, Florida, August 27, 1970.
28 p. ports. 29 cm.
PLatS

Dunstan, Saint, archbishop of Canterbury, d. 988

4088 **Saint Dunstan's classbook from Glastonbury:** Codex Biblioth. Bodleianae Oxon. Auct. F.4./32. Introduction by R. W. Hunt. Amsterdam, North Holland Publishing Company, 1961.

xvii, p. facsims. (47 leaves) 31 cm.
(Umbrae codicum occidentalium, 4)
PLatS

4088a **Stubbs, William, bp. of Oxford.**
Memorials of Saint Dunstan, archbishop
of Canterbury. Edited from various manu-
scripts by William Stubbs. London,
Longman & Co., 1874.
cxxii, 490 p. 24 cm.
Contents: Introduction; Seven different
Vitae sancti Dunstani; 41 Epistolae;
Ritualia de Dunstano (prayers, Mass, etc.).
MnCS

**Dusmet, Giuseppe Benedetto, Cardinal,
1818-1894**

4089 **Della Marra, Luigi Taddeo, O.S.B.**
Il Collegio Sant'Anselmo in Roma e il
Cardinale Dusmet. Catania, C. Galàtola,
1901.
107 p. 27 cm.
MnCS; PLatS

4089a **Leccisotti, Tomaso Domenico, O.S.B.**
Il cardinale Dusmet. Catania, O.V.E.,
1962.
xix, 684 p. 33 plates, 24 cm.
PLatS

Eadmer, 1060(ca.)-1124

4090 **Del Marmol, Boniface, O.S.B.**
Marie corédemptrice. Eadmer enseigna-
t-il que Marie rachetante fut rachetée?
(*In* Virgo Immaculata; actus Congressus
Mariologici-Mariani, 1954, v. 5, p. 194-201)
PLatS

4091 **Southern, Richard William.**
Saint Anselm and his biographer; a study
of monastic life and thought, 1059-1130.
Cambridge [England], University Press,
1963.
xvi, 389 p. 23 cm.
ILSP; InStme; MnCS; NcBe; PLatS

Ebel, Basilius, 1896-1968

4092 **Bogler, Theodor, O.S.B., ed.**
Leben aus der Taufe [Abt Basilius Ebel
zum 25. Jahrestag seiner äbtlichen Weihe
dargebracht]. Gesammelte Aufsätze, hrsg.
von P. Theodor Bogler, O.S.B. Maria
Laach, Verlag Ars Liturgica, 1963-64.
216 p. plates. 23 cm.
MnCS; PLatS

4093 **Bomm, Urban, O.S.B.**
Gottesdienstliches Wort bei den Exe-
quien für Vater Abt Basilius Ebel. Maria
Laach, 1968.
3 p. 21 cm.

On cover: Abt Basilius zum Gedächtnis.
MnCS

4094 **Maria Laach, Germany (Benedictine
abbey).**
Abt Basilius Ebel, 1896-1968.
17 p. port. 21 cm.
MnCS

**Edmund, Saint, archbishop of Canterbury,
d. 1240**

4095 **O'Brien, Elmer, S.J.**
Varieties of mystic experience; an an-
thology and interpretation. New York,
Holt, Rinehart and Winston [1964].
x, 321 p. 24 cm.
PLatS

Egbert, abbot of Münsterschwarzach, d. 1076

4096 **Vogt, Gabriel, O.S.B.**
Der selige Egbert, Abt von Münsterschwarzach, 1046-1076; Persönlichkeit
und Werk des fränkisches Reformabtes.
[Münsterschwarzach, Vier-Türme-Verlag,
1976].
83 p. illus. 20 cm.
MnCS

Eidenschink, John Albert, 1914-

4097 **The eucharistic liturgy;** the rite of bless-
ing an abbot. The blessing of John A.
Eidenschink, O.S.B., abbot of St. John's
Abbey, Collegeville, Minnesota . . .
October 15, 1971. [Collegeville, Minn.,
St. John's Abbey Press, 1971].
26 p. music 34 cm.
MnCS

Einhard, 770(ca.)-840

4098 **Weinckens, Johannes, O.S.B.**
Vir fama super aethera notus Eginhartus, quondam Caroli Magni cancellarius
. . . illustratus et contra quosdam
authores vindicatus . . . Francofurti ad
Moenum, impensis Joannis Philippi Andreae, 1714.
[16], 127 p. 33 cm.
KAS

Eizenhofer, Leo, 1907-

4099 **Manuale Casinense (Cod. Ottob. lat. 145)**
[hrsg. von] Klaus Gamber [und] Sieg-
hild Rehle. Regensburg, Kommissions
Verlag F. Pustet [1977].
172 p. 22 cm.
Bibliographie von Dr. P. Leo Eizenhofer, pp. 166-168.
PLatS

Ekkehardus, abbot of Aura, fl. 1100

4100 **Schum, Wilhelm.**
Die Jahrbücher des Sanct-Albans-Klosters zu Mainz. Göttingen, W. F. Kaestner, 1872.
130 p. 21 cm.
KAS

Elizabeth, Saint, of Schönau, 1128(ca.)–1164

4101 **Eckbert, abbot of Schönau.**
Visiones S. Elisabethae ancillae Christi in Sconaugia. De obitu S. Elisabethae Schönaugiensis. MS. Vienna, Nationalbibliothek, codex 488, f.47r–170r. Quarto. Saec. 13.
Microfilm: MnCH proj. no. 13,822

Emmeramus, Saint, bishop of Poitiers, 7th cent.

4102 **Babl, Karl.**
Emmeram von Regensburg: Legende und Kult. Kallmünz, Verlag Michael Lassleben, 1973.
310 p. 25 cm.
MnCS

4102a **Coelestinus, abbot of St. Emmeram.**
Ratisbona monastica. Klösterliches Regenspurg. Erster Theil. Oder, Mausoloem: herrliches Grab des bayrischen Apostels und Blutzeugen s. Emmerami. Regenspurg, J. V. Rädlmayer, 1752.
[24], 620, [163] p. 22 cm.
KAS

4103 **Passio s. Emmerami episcopi et martyris.** MS. Benediktinerabtei St. Peter, Salzburg, codex a.VI.46, f.90r–108r. Quarto. Saec. 15.
Microfilm: MnCH proj. no. 10,119

4104 **Vita beati Emmerami.** MS. Benediktinerabtei Kremsmünster, Austria, codex 7, f.166v–189v. Saec. 13.
Microfilm: MnCH proj. no. 7

Engelbert, abbot of Admont, 1250(ca.)–1311

4105 **Fowler, George Bingham.**
A medieval thinker confronts modern perplexities: Engelbert, abbot of Admont, O.S.B.
Extract from: The American Benedictine Review, v. 23(1972), p. 226–248.
PLatS

4106 **Fowler, George Bingham.**
Ven. Engelberti abbatis Admontensis Tractatus metricus De consilio vivendi.
(*In* Translatio studii; manuscript and library studies honoring Oliver L. Kapsner. Collegeville, Minn., 1973. p. 224–234)

Eric of Auxerre, Saint, 843?–876

4107 **Quadri, Riccardo, O.F.M.Cap.**
I collectanea di Erico di Auxerre. Freiburg, Schweiz, Edizione Universitaire, 1966.
xv, 172 p. 25 cm.
PLatS

Etlin, Lukas, 1864–1927

4108 **Kansas City-St. Joseph, Mo. (diocese).**
Ordinary informative process for the beatification and canonization of the servant of God, Father Lukas Etlin. Clyde, Mo., Benedictine Convent, 1960.
54 p.
MoCo

4109 **Luthold-Minder, Ida.**
Ein Apostel der Eucharistie, Pater Lukas Etlin, O.S.B. Einführung von Arnold Guillet, Nachwort von Kardinal Charles Journet. Aschaffenburg, Paul Pattloch-Verlag [1975].
215 p. illus.
MoCo

Eugene III, Pope, d. 1153

4110 **Delannes, Jean, O.Cist.**
Histoire du pontificat d'Eugène III. Nancy, Pierre Antoine, 1737.
274 p.
KAS(microfilm)

Eugster, Meinrad, Brother, 1848–1925

4111 **Beatificationis et canonizationis servi Dei Meinradi Eugster,** fratris conversi O.S.B. Einsidlensis. Positio super causae introductione. Romae, Guerra et Belli, 1946.
393, xiv, 483, 106, 32 p. 29 cm.
InStme

4112 **Die Heiligen sterben nicht aus;** aus dem Leben eines heiligmässigen Laienbruders, Br. Meinrad Eugster, O.S.B. 8. u. 9. verb. u. stark verm. Aufl. Einsiedeln, Im Selbstverlag des Klosters, 1942.
79 p. plates. 15 cm.
MnCS

4113 **Jüngt, Thomas Aquinas, O.S.B.**
Leben des Dieners Gottes, Bruder Meinrad Eugster, Benediktiner aus dem Stifte Maria-Einsiedeln. [3., neu durchgesehene Aufl.]. Einsiedeln, Benziger Verlag [1955].
207 p. illus. 20 cm.
InStme

4114 **Zürcher, Johannes Chrysostomus, O.S.B.**
Man of God – Brother Meinrad Eugster. Einsiedeln, Benziger [1976].

135 p. illus., ports., plates. 26 cm.
InStme

4115 **Zürcher, Johannes Chrysosomus, O.S.B.**
Mann Gottes, Bruder Meinrad Eugster,
Benediktiner von Maria-Einsiedeln. Photo-
graphien von Benedikt Rast. Einsiedeln,
Verlag des P. Vizepostulators [1965].
135 p. plates, ports. (part col.) 26 cm.
InStme; KAS; MnCS

Fabiani, Ignaz von, 18th cent.

4116 **Peleman, Albert, O.S.B.**
Der Benediktiner, Simpert Schwarzhue-
ber (1727–1795), Professor in Salzburg, als
Moraltheologe . . . seine Beziehungen
. . . zu Ignaz von Fabiani. Regensburg,
Fr. Pustet, 1961.
196 p. 22 cm.
MnCS

Faringdon, Hugh, Blessed, d. 1539

4117 **Hurry, Jameson Boyd.**
In honor of Hugh de Boves and Hugh
Cook Farrington, first and last abbots of
Reading. [Reading, England, E. Poynder
and Son] 1911.
33 p. 21 cm.
KAS

Feijoó y Montenegro, Benito Jerónimo, 1676–1764

4118 **McClelland, Ivy Lilian.**
Benito Jerónimo Feijóo. New York,
Twayne Publishers [1969].
x, 172 p. 22 cm.
KAM

Fink, Louis Mary, Bishop, 1834–1904

4119 **Aberle, George P.**
From the steppes to the prairies; the
story of the Germans settling in Russia on
the Volga and Ukraine; also . . . their resettlement in the Americas . . . Dickinson,
N.D. [1963].
213 p. 24 cm.
KAS

Foliot, Gilbert, Bp., d. 1187

4120 **Morey, Adrian, O.S.B.**
Gilbert Foliot and his letters. Cambridge
[England], University Press, 1965.
xv, 312 p. charts. 23 cm.
InStme; PLatS

Frances of Rome, Saint, 1384–1440

4121 **Berthem-Bontoux.**
Sainte Françoise romaine et son temps
(1384–1440). Paris, Bloud et Gay, 1931.

lx, 553 p.
CaQStB

4122 **Fullerton, Georgiana Charlotte.**
Vita di santa Francesca Romana. 2. ed.
italiana con 10 illustrazioni a cura del P. D.
Placido Lugano, O.S.B. Torino, Pietro
Marietti, 1924.
185 p. plates. 19 cm.
MnCS

4123 **Lugano, Placido, O.S.B., ed.**
I processi inediti per Francesca Bussa
dei Ponziani (Santa Francesca Romana
1440–1453). Città del Vaticano, Biblioteca
Apostolica Vaticana, 1945.
xl, 345 p. 3 facsims. 26 cm. (Studi e testi,
120)
CaQStB; MnCS; PLatS

4124 **Parente, Pascal Prospero.**
Angelic manifestations: Saint Frances of
Rome.
(*In* his: Beyond space. New York, 1961.
p. 135–138)

4125 **Rome, Italy. Tor de' Specchi (convent of
Benedictine sisters).**
Fatti memorabili della vita di Santa
Francesca Romana tratti delle pitture
murali del convento . . . 1440–1940.
[Roma, Tipografia Marviana, 1940?].
unpaged, illus. 21 cm.
MnCS

Frey, Maria Benedetta, 1836–1913

4126 **Aurelio della Passione, C.P.**
Martirio e sorriso; Donna Maria Benedetta Frey, O.S.B., modello di attacca-
mento al sommo pontefice. Venezia, Tipografia Emiliana [1949].
270 p. plates. 21 cm.
MnCS

Fructuosus, Saint, bishop of Braga, d.ca.665

4127 **Herwegen, Ildefons, O.S.B.**
Das Pactum des hl. Fruktuosus von
Braga; ein Beitrag zur Geschichte des
suevisch-westgothischen Mönchtums und
seines Rechtes. Stuttgart, F. Enke, 1907;
Amsterdam, P. Schippers, 1965.
x, 84 p. 23 cm.
PLatS

Fursey, Saint, abbot of Lagny-sur-Marne, d. 650

4128 **Duckett, Eleanor Shipley.**
Saint Ouen of Rouen and Saint Fursey:
France in the seventh century.
(*In* her: The wandering saints of the
early Middle Ages. New York, 1959. p.
140–164)
PLatS

Gaetano, Constantino, 1560–1650

4129 **Léonard, Emile J.**
Deux lettres de Dom Constantino Gaetani, fondateur du premier collège Bénédictin de Rome, a Richelieu et a Mazarin. Ligugé, E. Aubin, 1924.
9 p. 27 cm.
On cover: "Extrait de la Revue Mabillon, janvier, 1924."
KAS

4129a **Ruysschaert, José.**
Constantino Gaetano, O.S.B., chasseur de manuscrits; contribution à l'histoire de trois bibliothèques Romaines du XVIIe: S. l'Aniciana, l'Alessandrina et la Chigi.
(*In* Mélanges Eugène Tisserant, v. 7, p. 261–326)
PLatS

Gallus, Saint, 550(ca.)–627

4130 **Duckett, Eleanor Shipley.**
Saint Columban and Saint Gall: France, Switzerland, and Italy in the sixth and seventh centuries.
(*In* her: The wandering saints of the early Middle Ages. New York, 1959. p. 93–117)
PLatS

4131 **Walafrid Strabo.**
Vita s. Galli. MS. Vienna, Nationalbibliothek, codex 520, f.1v–77r. Quarto. Saec. 11.
Microfilm: MnCH proj. no. 13,858
For other manuscript copies of this work see Walafrid Strabo in the Author Part.

Gallus Anonymus

4132 **Zathey, Jerzy.**
Gallus l'Anonyme, l'auteur de la Chronique de Pologne. Tentative pour définir son milieu.
(*In* Spicilegium Beccense. 1959. v. 1, p. 595–597)
PLatS

Gasquet, Francis Aidan, 1846–1929

4133 **Knowles, David, O.S.B.**
Cardinal Gasquet as an historian.
(*In* his: The historian and character, and other essays. Cambridge, 1963. p. 240–263)
PLatS

Gauzlin, abbot of Fleury, 11th cent.

4134 **Andreas, monk of Fleury,** 11th cent.
Vie de Gauzlin, abbé de Fleury. Vita Gauzlini abbatis Floriacensis monasterii

[par] André de Fleury. Texte édité, traduit et annoté par Robert-Henri Bautier et Gillette Labory. Paris, Editions du Centre National de la Recherche Scientifique, 1969.
234 p. facsim., fold. maps. 25 cm.
InStme; MnCS; PLatS

Gebhard, Johann, 1676–1756

4135 **Wutzlhofer, Hans.**
Johann Gebhard von Prüfening, ein altbayerischer Maler aus der Barockzeit. Regensburg, Gebrüder Habbel, 1934.
120 p. plates. 24 cm.
KAS

Genestout, Augustin, 1888–

4136 **Jaspert, Bernd.**
Die Regula Benedicti, Regula Magistri, Kontroverse. Hildesheim, H. A. Gerstenberg, 1975.
xxii, 519 p. 22 cm. (Regulae Benedicti studia. Supplementa, Bd. 3)
MnCS

Gerald of Aurillac, Saint, 855(ca.)–1884

4137 **Bouange, Guillaume, M. F.**
Saint Géraud d'Aurillac et son illustre abbaye. Aurillac, L. Bonnet-Picut, 1881.
2 v. 22 cm.
KAS

Gerberon, Gabriel, 1628–1711

4138 **Daoust, Joseph.**
Le janséniste Dom Gerberon, éditeur de saint Anselme (1675).
(*In* Spicilegium Beccense. 1959. v. 1, p. 531–540)
PLatS

Gerbert, Martin, 1720–1793

4139 **Acten über den Tod des Fürsten-Abten Martin II und die Wahl Moriz I, 1793.**
MS. Benediktinerabtei St. Paul im Lavantthal, Austria, codex 152/2. 191 f. Folio. Saec. 18.
Microfilm: MnCH proj. no. 11,923

4140 **Deissler, Alfons.**
Fürstabt Martin Gerbert von St. Blasien und die theologische Methode . . . München, Neuer Filser-Verlag, 1940.
xxiv, 196 p. 24 cm.
KAS

4141 **Grandidier, Ph. And.**
Ad Martinum Gerbertum abbatem S. Blasii (ad hist. Nigrae Silvae). MS. Benediktinerabtei St. Paul im Lavantthal,

Austria, codex 94/2, pars IV. Folio. Saec. 18.

Microfilm: MnCH proj. no. 11,867

4142 **Hilger, Franz M.**
Martin Gerbert, Fürst und Abt von St. Blasien; Festschrift zur 250. Wiederkehr seines Geburtstages. Konstanz, Rusgarten Verlag, 1970.
87 p. plates. 22 cm.
MnCS

4143 **Pfeilschifter, Georg.**
Fürstabt Martin Gerbert von St. Blasien. (*In* Görres-Gesellschaft zur Pflege der Wissenschaft im katholischen Deutschland. 3. Vereinsschrift, 1912, p. 38–72)
PLatS

Gerrer, Gregory, 1867-1946

4144 **Brady, Teresa Anna.**
Father Gregory: artist-priest.
vii, 114 p. 29 cm.
Thesis (M.A.)–University of Oklahoma, 1942.
Typescript.
OkShg; OkTaB

Gersen, Giovanni, abbot of Vercelli, 14th cent.

4145 **Funk, Franz Xaver von.**
Kirchengeschichtliche Abhandlungen und Untersuchungen. Paderborn, Ferdinand Schöningh, 1897-1907.
3 v. 23 cm.
InStme

4146 **Maerz, Angelus, O.S.B.**
Angelus contra Michaelem; seu, Crisis apologetica adversus . . . Michaelis [i.e. Michael Kuen] praepositi Wengensis ulmae abatis Lateranensis &c. Joannem de Canabaco . . . in favorem Joannis Gersenii abbatis Vercellensis O.S.B. concepta. Frisingae, P. L. Böck, 1761.
79 p. 17 cm.
PLatS

Gertrude, Saint, the Great, 1256-1302

4147 **Castaniza, Juan de, O.S.B.**
Vida de la prodigiosa virgen Santa Gertrudis la Magna . . . sacada de los cinco libros intitulados: Insinuación de la piedad divina. Madrid, Blas Roman, 1782.
396 p. 21 cm.
MnCS

4148 **Clement, Laurentius, O.S.B.**
Insinuationes divinae pietatis . . . In quo praeter vitam s. virginis Gertrudis continentur revelationes, gratiae . . . Salisburgi, Joan. Bapt. Mayr, 1662.

63, 813 p. 16 cm.
MnCS

4149 **Ledos, Eugène Gabriel.**
Sainte Gertrude (1256?–1303). 8. éd. Paris, J. Gabalda, 1924.
iv, 217 p. 19 cm.
InStme

4150 **The love of the Sacred Heart** illustrated by St. Gertrude. With a preface by the Most Rev. Alban Goodier, S.J. New York, Benziger Brothers, 1921.
xiii, 223 p. 19 cm.
PLatS

4151 **Mary Jeremy, Sister, O.P.**
Scholars and mystics. Chicago, H. Regnery, 1962.
213 p. 22 cm.
Partial contents: The book of Helfta. The book of Gertrude.
InStme; KAS; PLatS

4152 **Vagaggini, Cipriano, O.S.B.**
La dévotion au Sacré-Coeur chez Sainte Mechtilde et Sainte Gertrude.
(*In* Cor Jesu; commentationes in . . . "Haurietis aquas." Roma, 1959. v. 2, p. 29–48)
PLatS

4153 **Von der seligen Truta (Gertrud).** Etliche Stück von ihren Töchtern. Orationes ad s. Gertrudem (germanice). MS. Vienna, Schottenstift, codex 234, f.44r–72v. Quarto. Saec. 15.
Microfilm: MnCH proj. no. 4155

4154 **Wieland, Otmar, O.S.B.**
Gertrud von Helfta, ein Botte der göttlichen Miltekeit. Ottobeuren, Kommissionsverlag Winfried-Werk, 1973.
xviii, 254 p. 24 cm.
MnCS; PLatS

Gertrude, Saint
see also Feasts–St. Gertrude, in ch. VI r

Gilbert, abbot of Westminster, d. 1114

4155 **Southern, Richard William.**
St. Anselm and Gilbert Crispin, abbot of Westminster.
(*In* Mediaeval and renaissance studies, v. 3, p. 78–115)
PLatS

Giles, Saint
see
Aegidius, Saint

Giovanni de Matera, Saint
see
John of Matera, Saint

Gislebertus, 12th cent.

4156 **Grivot, Denis.**
Gislebertus, sculptor of Autun, by Denis Grivot and George Zarnecki. [New York] Orion Press [1961].
180 p. illus., maps, plans. 32 cm.
MnCS

Giustiniani, Paolo, 1476-1528

4157 **Leclercq, Jean, O.S.B.**
Alone with God. [Translated by Elizabeth McCabe from the French]. New York, Farrar, Straus and Cudahy [1961].
xxvii, 209 p. 21 cm.
Translation of: Seul avec Dieu; la vie érémitique.
ILSP; KAS; MnCS; MoCo; NdRi; OKShg; PLatS

Goeltl, Maria

4158 **Scheller, LaVerne, Sister, O.S.B.**
Life in a German and American culture; a biographical sketch of Sister Maria Goeltl, O.S.B.
14 p. illus.
Graduate research paper – University of Evansville, Indiana, 1977.
Typescript.
InFer

Gomez Ferreira de Silva

4159 **Nunes, Eduardo.**
Dom Frey Gomez, abade de Florença, 1420–1440. Braga, Libraria editore Pax, 1963–
v. 26 cm.
KAS

Gottwald, Benedict, 1845-1908

4160 **A., P. C.**
P. Benedikt Gottwald, O.S.B., Konventual des Stiftes Engelberg, 1845–1908. Luzern, Räber, 1908.
8 p. 18 cm.
Separat-Abdruck aus: Vaterland, 26. Febr. 1908, mit einigen Zusätzen.
MnCS

Grasso, Carlo Gregorio, 1869-1929

4161 **Masi, Donato.**
Vita di Mons. Carlo Gregorio M. Grasso, O.S.B., arcivescovo primate de Salerno, amminstratore perpetuo di Acerno, già abate ordinario di Montevergine. [Salerno, Scuola arti grafiche, 1954].
x, 639 p. plates, ports. 25 cm.
PLatS

Gratianus, the Canonist, 12th cent.

4162 **Commentarius in decretum Gratiani.** Incipit: Quoniam in omnibus rebus adimadvertitur in esse perfectum. MS. Vienna, Nationalbibliothek, codex 570. 35 f. Quarto. Saec. 13.
Microfilm: MnCH proj. no. 13,908

4163 **Guido de Baysio.**
Commentarius in decretum Gratiani ("Rosarium"). MS. Universitätsbibliothek Salzburg, codex M III 2. 330 f. Folio. Saec. 14.
Microfilm: MnCH proj. no. 11,419

4164 **Guido de Baysio.**
Commentaria in Decretum Gratiani. MS. Vich, Spain, Archivo Capitular, codex 136. 317 f. Folio. Saec. 14.
Microfilm: MnCH proj. no. 31,115

4165 **Guido de Baysio.**
Rosarium seu apparatus in Gratiani decretum. MS. Universitätsbibliothek Graz, Austria, codex 53. 356 f. Folio. Saec. 14.
Microfilm: MnCH proj. no. 25,980

Gregory I, the Great, Saint, Pope, 540(ca.)-604

4166 **Benediktsson, Hreinn, ed.**
The life of St. Gregory and his dialogues; fragments of an Icelandic manuscript from the 13th century. Copenhagen, Minksgaard, 1963.
62 p. facsims.
PLatS

4167 **Bianchi-Giovini, Aurelio Angelo.**
Pontificato di san Gregorio il Grande. Milano, Stablimento Civelli E. C., 1844.
264 p.
PLatS (microfilm)

4168 **Butler, Edward Cuthbert, O.S.B.**
Western mysticism: the teaching of Augustine, Gregory and Bernard on contemplation and the contemplative life. 3rd ed., with Afterthoughts and a new foreword by Professor David Knowles. London, Constable, 1967.
lxxii, 242 p. 23 cm.
PLatS

4169 **Byrne, K. H.**
Developments under St. Leo I and St. Gregory I.
(*In* Lattey, Cuthbert, ed. The Church; papers from the Summer School of Catholic Studies held at Cambridge, 1927. p. 111–129)
PLatS

4170 **The Centenary of St. Gregory the Great at Downside,** with the three sermons preached on the occasion. Together with

an appendix giving some account of the Catholic churches in England dedicated to St. Gregory. Downside, St. Gregory's Monastery, 1890.
56 p. 23 cm.
PLatS

4171 **Conception Abbey, Conception, Mo.**
To the memory of the first Benedictine pope, St. Gregory the Great, on the occasion of the thirteenth centennial of his death, 604–1904. By a Benedictine of Conception Abbey. Conception, Mo. [1904?].
unpaged. 20 cm.
MnCS

4171a **Dagens, Claude.**
Saint Grégoire le Grand; culture et expérience chrétienne. Paris, Etudes augustiniennes, 1977.
475 p. 25 cm.
MnCS

4172 **De perditione** et inventione librorum moralium beatissimi Gergorii Papae Romae. MS. Benediktinerabtei Melk, Austria, codex 688, f.108v–109v. Quarto. Saec. 15.
Microfilm: MnCH proj. no. 1552

4173 **Dudden, Frederick Homes.**
Gregory the Great, his place in history and thought. New York, Russell & Russell [1967].
2 v. 22 cm.
Reprint of 1905 edition.
PLatS

4174 **Dufner, Georg.**
Die "Moralia" Gregors des Grossen in ihren italienischen Volgarizzamenti. Padova, Editrice Antenore, 1958.
200 p. 22 cm.
PLatS

4175 **The earliest life of Gregory the Great,** by an anonymous monk of Whitby. Text, translation & notes by Bertram Colgrave. Lawrence, University of Kansas Press, 1968.
ix, 180 p. 22 cm.
Latin and English on opposite pages.
InStme; KAS

4176 **Gillet, Robert, O.S.B.**
Spiritualité et place du moine dans l'Eglise selon Saint Grégoire le Grand.
(*In* Théologie de la vie monastique, p. 323–351)
PLatS

4177 **Halloran, Briant James, O.S.B.**
Saint Gregory I – a Benedictine.
45 leaves. 28 cm.
Typescript.
PLatS

4178 **Hedley, John Cuthbert.**
The monasticism of St. Gregory the Great.
(*In* The Centenary of St. Gregory the Great at Downside. Downside, 1890. p. 29–40)
PLatS

4179 **Honorii Sermo de S. Gregorio.** MS. Benediktinerabtei Melk, Austria, codex 61, f.294–295. Quarto. Saec. 15.
Microfilm: MnCH proj. no. 1147

4180 **Joannes Diaconus.**
Vita s. Gregorii Magni. MS. Benediktinerabtei Göttweig, Austria, codex 108, f.1r–130v. Quarto. Saec. 12.
Microfilm: MnCH proj. no. 9118
For other manuscript copies of this work see under Joannes Diaconus in the Author Part.

4181 **Knox, Ronald Arbuthnott.**
St. Gregory the Great (preached to schoolboys at St. Edmund's, Ware)
(*In* his: Captive flames; a collection of panegyrics. London, 1941. p. 13–18)
PLatS

4182 **Lathcen.**
Egologa quam scripsit Lathcen filius Baith De moralibus Job quas Gregorius fecit. Cura et studio M. Adriaen. Turnholti, Brepols, 1969.
x, 373 p. 26 cm. (Corpus Christianorum, series latina, 145)
PLatS

4183 **Libellus de laudibus s. Gregorii papae.** MS. Vienna, Nationalbibliothek, codex 1737, f. 11v–45r. Octavo. Saec. 14.
Micrcfilm: MnCH proj. no. 15,055

4184 **McCabe, Joseph.**
Gregory the Great, the first mediaeval pope.
(*In* his: Crises in the history of the papacy. New York, 1916. p. 55–77)
PLatS

4185 **Meyvaert, Paul.**
Bede and Gregory the Great. Newcastle upon Tyne, J. & P. Bealls, 1964.
26 p. 22 cm.
PLatS

4186 **Meyvaert, Paul.**
Benedict, Gregory, Bede and others. London, Variorum Reprints, 1977.
388 p. illus. 24 cm.
Reprint of 16 studies published between 1955 and 1976.
English or French.
InStme; MnCS

4187 **Narratio visionis et factae in ea patefactionis operum s. Gregorii moralium,** quae per negligentiam omissa erant. MS.

Benediktinerabtei Göttweig, Austria, codex 465a, f.83r. Quarto. Saec. 15.
Microfilm: MnCH proj. no. 3720

4188 **Pons, André.**
La réforme de Saint Grégoire le Grand; son application dans le monde occidental. St-Maurice (Suisse), Editions de l'Oeuvre St-Augustin [1959].
207 p. 24 cm.
PLatS

4189 **Quare beatus Gregorius appellatur organum Sancti Spiritus** et depingitur sedendo scribens et columba ad aures ejus. De humilitate beati Gregorii papae. MS. Benediktinerabtei Lambach, Austria, codex chart. 223, f.226v–227r. Saec. 15.
Microfilm: MnCH proj. no. 612

4190 **Roland, Donatien.**
Activisme ou pastorale? Le message de Saint Grégoire le Grand. Paris, Les Editions Ouvrières [1963].
101 p. 19 cm.
PLatS

4191 **Santi, Angelo de, S.J.**
S. Gregorio Magno, Leone XIII e il canto liturgico. Roma, A. Befani, 1891.
15 p. 23 cm.
PLatS

4192 **Schmirger, Gertrud.**
Gregory the Great, by Gerhart Ellert [pseud.]. Translated from the German by Richard and Clara Winston. New York, Harcourt, Brace & World [1963].
277 p. maps. 21 cm.
ILSP; PLatS

4193 **Sol, Hendrik Bastiaan.**
La vie du pape saint Grégoire; huit versions françaises médiévals de La Légende du bon pécheur. [Amsterdam], Rodopi, 1977.
xxxv, 470 p. facsims. 30 cm.
MnCS

4194 **Stuhlfath, Walter.**
Gregor I. der Grosse, sein Leben bis zu seiner Wahl zum Papste, nebst einer Untersuchung der ältesten Viten. Hadelberg, Carl Winter, 1913.
x, 112 p. table. 23 cm.
MnCS

4195 **Vita sancti Gregorii.** MS. Universitätsbibliothek Innsbruck, Austria, codex 357, f.64v–67r. Octavo. Saec. 12.
Microfilm: MnCH proj. no. 28,392

4196 **Vogüé, Adalbert de, O.S.B.**
Sur le texte des Dialogues de saint Grégoire le Grand; l'utilisation du manuscrit de Milan par les editeurs.

(*In* Latinität und alte Kirche; Festschrift für Rudolf Hanslik zum 70. Geburtstag. Wien, 1977. p. 326–335)
MnCS

4197 **Walsh, William Thomas.**
The revolution of Benedict and Gregory. (*In* his: Saints in action. Garden City, N.Y., 1961. p. 265–341)
PLatS

Gregory VII, Saint, Pope, 1015–1085

4198 **Bernheim, Ernst.**
Quellen zur Geschichte des Investiturstreites. Heft I: Zur Geschichte Gregors VII und Heinrichs IV. Leipzig, B. G. Teubner, 1907.
vi, 104 p. 21 cm.
PLatS

4199 **Gebehardus, abp. of Salzburg.**
Epistola ad Herimannum, Metensem episcopum, pro Gregorio VII, contra schismaticos. MS. Cistercienserabtei Rein, Austria, codex 23, f.45r–64v. Quarto. Saec. 12.
Microfilm: MnCH proj. no. 7420

4200 **Hübinger, Paul Egen.**
Die letzten Worte Papst Gregors VII. Opladen, Westdeutscher Verlag [1973].
112 p. 24 cm.
MnCS

4201 **Leclercq, Jean, O.S.B.**
Un témoignage sur l'influence de Grégoire VII dans la réforme canoniale. (*In* Borino, G. B. Studi gregoriani. Roma, 1959–61. v. 6, p. 173–228)
PLatS

4202 **McCabe, Joseph.**
Hildebrand. (*In* his: Crises in the history of the papacy. New York, 1916. p. 141–170)
PLatS

4203 **Williams, Schafer, ed.**
The Gregorian epoch: reformation, revolution, reaction? Boston, Heath [1964].
xiv, 110 p. 24 cm.
PLatS

Gregory, Saint, bishop of Ostia, c. 1257(ca.)

4204 **Gaetano, Constantino, O.S.B.**
Sanctor/ trium episcopor! relig.is bened.ae luminum: Isidori Hispalens., Ildefonsi Tolet., Gregorii card. Ost. vitae, et actiones. Formae, apud Jacobum Mascardum, 1606.
156 p. 24 cm.
MnCS

Gregory, Saint, bishop of Utrecht, 707–780?

4205 **Duckett, Eleanor Shipley.**
Saint Gregory of Utrecht, Saint Liudger, Saint Lebuin: the Netherlands in the eighth century.
(*In* her: The wandering saints in the early Middle Ages. New York, 1959. p. 229–248)
PLatS

Guéranger, Prosper, 1806–1875

4206 **Des Pilliers, Pierre-Marie-Raphaël.**
Les Bénédictins de la Congrégation de France.   Bruxelles, P.J.D. DeSomer, 1868–69.
2 v. 24 cm.
KAS

4207 **Freppel, Charles Emile.**
The monastic ideal; an address delivered . . . in the abbey church of Solesmes, at the anniversary observance of the death of Dom Prosper Guéranger, March 16, 1876. Translated by Bernard A. Sause, O.S.B. [Atchison, Kans., St. Benedict's Abbey, 1961].
22 p. 23 cm.
Offprint from: The Benedictine Review, January–July, 1961.
PLatS

4208 **Grénaud, Georges, O.S.B.**
Dom Guéranger et le project de bulle "Quemadmodum Ecclesia" pour la définition de l'Immaculée Conception.
(*In* Virgo Immaculata; acta Congressus Mariologici-Mariani, 1954, v. 2, p. 337–386)

4209 **Preville, Jacques, O.S.B.**
Dom Guéranger et les voeux monastiques.
(*In* Semana de Estudios Monasticos, 14th, Silos, 1973. p. 279–296)
PLatS

4210 **Soltner, Louis, O.S.B.**
Solesmes & Dom Guéranger, 1805–1875. Solesmes, Abbaye Saint-Pierre, 1974.
177 p. 48 leaves of plates. 24 cm.
InStme

Guibert, Saint, d. 962

4211 **Sigebertus, monk of Gembleux.**
Vitae s. Guiberti et Maclovii. MS. Vienna, Nationalbibliothek, codex 490, f.1v–30v. Quarto. Saec. 12.
Microfilm: MnCH proj. no. 13,827

4212 **Sigebertus, monk of Gembleux.**
Vita s. Wicberti. MS. Vienna, Nationalbibliothek, codex 3469, f.2r–14v. Quarto. Saec. 15.
Microfilm: MnCH proj. no. 20,398

Guibert de Nogent, 1053–1124?

4213 **Guth, Klaus.**
Guibert von Nogent und die hochmittelalterliche Kritik an der Reliquienverehrung. Ottobeuren, Kommissionsverlag Winfried-Werk, 1970.
xix, 154 p. 25 cm.

Guido d'Arezzo, d. 1050?

4214 **Brandi, Antonio, O.S.B.**
Guido Aretino, monaco di s. Benedetto; della sua vita, del suo tempo e dei suoi scritti . . . Firenze, Arte della Stampa, 1882.
480 p. illus.(music), fold. plan. 23 cm.
PLatS

4215 **Falchi, Michele.**
Studi su Guido monaco. Firenze, Tip. di G. Barbera, 1882.
112 p. 2 facsims. 27 cm.
MnCS

4215a **Smits van Waesberghe, Joseph, ed.**
Expositiones in Micrologum Guidonis Aretini. Amsterdam, North-Holland Publishing Company, 1957.
175 p. illus., facsims. 24 cm.
MnCS

4216 **Tractatus de Micrologo Guidonis de Aretio.** Incipit: Micros graece brevis, logos sermo. Inde Micrologus. MS. Vienna, Nationalbibliothek, codex 2502, f.1r–24r. Octavo. Saec. 12.
Microfilm: MnCH proj. no. 15,815

Guilelmus
see also
Guillaume
Wilhelmus
William

Guilelmus, monk of Jumiéges, fl. 1080

4217 **Marx, Jean.**
Guillaume de Poitiers et Guillaume de Jumiéges.
(*In* Mélanges d'histoire du Moyen Age, offerts à M. Ferdinand Lot. Paris, 1925. p. 543–548)
PLatS

Guillaume de Dijon, Saint
see
William, Saint, abbot of St. Bénigne, Dijon

Guillaume de Saint-Thierry, 1085(ca.)–1148?

4218 **Brooke, Odo, O.S.B.**
William of St. Thierry.

(*In* Walsh, James, S.J. Spirituality
through the centuries, p. 121–131)
PLatS

4218a **Brooke, Odo, O.S.B.**
Studies in monastic theology. Kalamazoo, Mich., Cistercian Publications, 1980.
xv, 274 p. 22 cm. (Cistercian studies
series, no. 37)
Mostly studies on William of St. Thierry.
InStme; KAS

4219 **Davy, Marie Magdeleine.**
Théologie et mystique de Guillaume de
Saint-Thierry. Paris, J. Vrin, 1954–
v. 25 cm.
PLatS

4220 **Déchanet, Jean Marie.**
William of St. Thierry; the man and his
work. Translated by Richard Strachan.
Spencer, Mass., Cistercian Publications,
1972.
x, 172 p. 23 cm.
KAS; PLatS

4220a **Honemann, Volker.**
Die "Epistola ad fratres de Monte Dei"
des Wilhelm von Saint-Thierry; lateinische
Ueberlieferung und mittelalterliche Ueber-
setzungen. Zürich und München, Artemis
Verlag, 1978.
xi, 483 p. fold. map, 24 cm.
MnCS

4221 **O'Brien, Elmer, S.J.**
Varieties of mystic experience; an an-
thology and interpretation. New York,
Holt, Rinehart and Winston [1964].
x, 321 p. 24 cm.
PLatS

4221a **Saint-Thierry, une abbaye du VIe au XXe
siècle:** actes du Culloque international
d'Histoire Monastique, Reims-Saint-
Thierry, 11 au 14 octobre, 1976, reunis
par Michel Bur. Saint-Thierry, Association des Amis de l'Abbaye de Saint-
Thierry, 1979.
xviii, 643 p. illus., plates, map, 28 cm.
PLatS; MnCS

4222 **Thomas, Robert, O.C.S.O.**
William of St. Thierry's Our life in the
Trinity.
(*In* Monastic studies, v. 3, p. 139–163)
Translated by a monk of New Melleray
Abbey.
PLatS

Guitmundus, archbishop of Aversa, d. 1095

4223 **Shaughnessy, Patrick, O.S.B.**
The eucharistic doctrine of Guitmond of
Aversa. Roma, Scuola Salesiana del Libro,
1939.

xi, 119 p. 23 cm.
Thesis – Collegio di Sant'Anselmo,
Rome.
InStme; MoCo

Gundulf, bishop of Rochester, 1024?–1108

4224 **The life of the venerable** man, Gundolf,
bishop of Rochester; translated into
English by the nuns of Malling Abbey.
[West Malling, Kent, printed at St.
Mary's Abbey, 1968].
[8], v, 76 p. 19 cm.
KAS

Hager, Edmund Leopold, 1829–1890

4225 **P. Edmund Hager,** der "Don Bosco
Oesterreichs"; Lebensskizze eines Er-
ziehers . . . von einem Mitgliede seiner
Kongregation. Innsbruck, Kinderfreund-
Anstalt [n.d.].
138 p. illus.
AStb

Haneberg, Daniel Bonifatius von, 1816–1876

4226 **Huth, Albert.**
Daniel Bonifaziius von Haneberg, Abt
von St. Bonifaz in München und Bischof
von Speyer; ein Lebensbild. Speyer,
Verlag der Dr. Jaegerschen Buchhandlung, 1927.
360 p. 19 cm.
InStme

4227 **Jud, Rupert, O.S.B.**
Erinnerungen an Daniel Bonifatius Dr.
von Haneberg . . . Beuron, Kunstverlag,
1922.
"Sonderabdruck aus der Benediktinischen Monatschrift, IV Jahrg., 1922."
KAS; PLatS

Hathumoda, abbess of Gandersheim, 840–874

4228 **Agius, monk of Corvey.**
Agii vita et obitus Hathumodae a. 840–
874.
(*In* Monumenta Germaniae historica.
Scriptores. Stuttgart, 1963. t. 4, p.
165–189)
PLatS

Havlik, Thomas, 1913–

4229 **The abbatial blessing of Rt. Rev.
Thomas Havlik,** 6th abbot of St. Pro-
copius Abbey, conferred by Most Rev.
Romeo Blanchette, June 1, 1971.
38 p.
ILSP

Hedley, John Cuthbert, 1837-1915

4230 **Bishop, Edmund.**
Bishop Hedley and Dom U. Berlière on
the history of the English Benedictines; a
letter to a friend by Edmund Bishop . . .
[n.p., 1897].
40 p.
NcBe; PLatS

Heloise, abbess of Le Paraclet, 1101-1164

4231 **Dronke, Peter.**
Abelard and Heloise in medieval testimonies; the twenty-sixth W. F. Ker
memorial lecture delivered in the University of Glasgow, 29th October, 1976. [Glas-
gow], University of Glasgow Press, 1976.
63 p. 24 cm.
MnCS

4232 **Hamilton, Elizabeth.**
Héloise. Garden City, N.Y., Doubleday,
1967.
234 p. 22 cm.
MnCS

Hemptinne, Pie de, 1880-1907

4233 **Hemptinne, Jean de.**
Dom Pie de Hemptinne, 1880-1907,
moine de l'Abbaye de Maredsous. 10. éd.
Editions de Maredsous [1963].
ix, 282 p. 18 cm.

4234 **Kramer, Herbert George, S.M.**
Mad lover of Jesus: Pius de Hemptinne.
(*In* his: Crucified with Christ. New York,
1949. p. 117-158)
PLatS; InFer

Herbst, Maurus Xaverius, 1701-1757

4235 **Götz, Franz Sales, O.S.B.**
Maurus Xaverius Herbst, Abt von Plankstetten; ein Lebensbild aus dem 18. Jahrhundert. 2., verb. Aufl. hrsg. von Bonifatius M. Schumacher, O.S.B. Würzburg,
Echter-Verlag [1957].
87 p. illus. 19 cm.
PLatS

Herrgott, Marquard, 1694-1762

4236 **Ortner, Josef Peter.**
Marquard Hergott (1694-1762); sein
Leben und Wirken als Historiker und
Diplomat. Wien, In Kommission bei Her-
mann Böhlaus Nachf., 1972.
103 p. 24 cm.
MnCS

Hermannus Contractus, 1013-1054

4237 **Bultot, Robert.**
Christianisme et valeurs humaines. A:
La doctrine du mépris du monde, en Occident, a S. Ambroise à Innocent III. Louvain, Nauwelaerts, 1963–
v. 21 cm.
KAS

4238 **Oesch, Hans.**
Berno und Hermann von Reichenau als
Musiktheoretiker, mit einen Ueberblick
über ihr Leben und die handschriftliche
Ueberlieferung ihrer Werke. Beigabe: Das
Geschichtswerk Hermanns des Lahmen in
seiner Ueberlieferung, von Arno Duch.
Bern, P. Haupt [1961].
251 p. 23 cm.
PLatS

4239 **Ziesche, Maria Calasanz.**
Die letzte Freiheit (Roman). Rheinbach
b. Bonn, Schwestern Unserer Lieben Frau
[1967].
337 p. plates. 20 cm.
MnCS

Herwegen, Ildefons, 1874-1946

4240 **Ehrengabe zur Feier des 25 jährigen
Abts-Jubiläums** dem Hochwürdigsten
Herrn D. Dr. Ildefons Herwegen Abte
von Maria Laach. Berlin, Liturgisches
Leben, 1939.
192 p. illus.
MoCo

4241 **Severus, Emmanuel von, O.S.B., ed.**
Was haltet ihr von der Kirche? Die Frage
des Abtes Ildefons Herwegen an seine und
unsere Zeit. Beiträge und Würdigungen
aus Anlass seines Geburtstages vor hundert Jahren am 27. November 1874 . . .
Münster, Aschendorff [1976].
36 p. 23 cm.
InStme; MnCS; PLatS

Heufelder, Emmanuel Maria, 1898-

4242 **Eins in Christus:** Altabt Emmanuel M.
Heufelder zum 80. Geburtstag, 30. März
1978. Hrsg. von der Abtei Niederaltaich
[1978].
97 p. plates, ports. 22 cm.
MnCS

4242a **Hören sein Wort;** Festgabe für Abt
Emmanuel M. Heufelder zum 70. Geburtstag. Hrsg. von der Abtei Niederaltaich. Niederaltaich, Dreiberg-Verlag,
1968.
188 p. port. 23 cm.
PLatS

Higden, Ranulph, d. 1364

4243 **Taylor, John.**
The universal chronicle of Ranulf Higden. Oxford, Clarendon Press, 1966.
xi, 198 p. map, tables. 22 cm.
"Writings by Higden and writings attributed to him": p. 182–184.
MnCS

Hildebertus, archbishop of Tours, 1056?–1133

4244 **Barth, Franz Xaver.**
Hildebert von Lavardin (1056–1133) und das kirchliche Stellenbesetzungsrecht. Stuttgart, F. Enke, 1906; Amsterdam, P. Schippers, 1965.
xx, 489 p. 23 cm.
PLatS

4245 **Johannes.**
Expositio in versus Hildeberti de Missa. MS. Universitätsbibliothek Graz, Austria, codex 423, f.167v–234r. Folio. Saec. 15.
Microfilm: MnCH proj. no. 26,652

Hildegard, Saint, 1098?–1179

4246 **Alessandro, Olga d'.**
Mistica e filosofia in Ildegarda di Bingen. Padova, CEDAM, 1966.
89 p. illus. 24 cm.
PLatS

4247 **Bendish, Frank J.**
The life and prophecies of St. Hildegard. New York, Carlton Press [1971].
117 p.
NcBe

4248 **Epistola monachorum claustri S. Martini Moguntiaci ad S. Hildegardim,** et hujus sanctae responsio visionis instar. MS. Vienna, Nationalbibliothek, codex 624, f.1r–7v. Octavo. Saec. 12.
Microfilm: MnCH proj. no. 13,958

4249 **Gebeno, prior of Everbach.**
Gebenonis Commentarius in prophetiam S. Hildegardis de Wiklefistis, ad moniales de S. Ruperto missus. MS. Benediktinerabtei Seitenstetten, Austria, codex 262, f.23v–29a. Folio. Saec. 15.
Microfilm: MnCH proj. no. 1065

4250 **Gebeno, prior of Everbach.**
Speculum futurorum temporum, seu Pentachordum S. Hildegardis virginis. MS. Vienna, Nationalbibliothek, codex 963, f.1v–42v. Folio. Saec. 13.
Microfilm: MnCH proj. no. 14,263

4251 **Gebeno, prior of Everbach.**
Speculum futurorum temporum, seu Pentachronum S. Hildegardis. MS. Bene-

diktinerabtei Kremsmünster, Austria, codex 94, f.1r–73v. Saec. 15.
Microfilm: MnCH proj. no. 87

4252 **Liebeschütz, Hans.**
Das allegorische Weltbild der heiligen Hildegard von Bingen. Mit einem Nachwort zum Neudruck. Darmstadt, Wissenschaftliche Buchgesellschaft, 1964.
ix, 188 p. 24 cm.
PLatS

4253 **Pitra, Jean Baptiste.**
Analecta sanctae Hildegardis opera spicilegio Solesmensi parata. Typis Sacri Montis Casinensis, 1882.
xxiii, 614 p. 28 cm.
PLatS

4254 **Singer, Charles Joseph.**
From magic to science; essays on the scientific twilight. New York, Dover Publications [1958].
253 p. illus. 21 cm.
MnCS

4255 **Theodoricus.**
Vita s. Hildegardis. Finis mutilus. MS. Vienna, Nationalbibliothek, codex 624, f.8v–87v. Octavo. Saec. 13.
Microfilm: MnCH proj. no. 13,958

Hincmar, archbishop of Reims, 806–882

4256 **Devisse, Jean.**
Hincmar, archevêque de Reims, 845–882. Genève, Librairie Droz, 1975.
3 v. 23 cm.
MnCS

4257 **Levillain, Léon.**
De quelques personnages nommés Bernard dans les Annales d'Hincmar.
(*In* Mélanges dédiés à la mémoire de Félix Grat. Paris, 1946. v. 1, p. 169–202)
PLatS

Hrabanus Maurus, 784?–856

4258 **Ernst, Joseph.**
Die Lehre des hl. Paschasius Radbertus von der Eucharistie. Mit besonderer Berücksichtigung der Stellung des hl. Rhabanus Maurus und des Ratramnus zu derselben. Freiburg i.B., Herder, 1896.
iv, 136 p. 23 cm.
Inaug.-Diss. – Würzburg.
InStme

4259 **Gassner, Gabriel, O.S.B.**
Rabanus Maurus; Vortrag gehalten 1956 in einer Feierstunde in Eltville, anlässlich der elfhundertsten Wiederkehr des Todestages des heiligen Rabanus Maurus. [Eltville, Druckerei Seb. Wolf, 1956].

16 p. 22 cm.
PLatS

4260 **Kohake, Cletus Paul, O.S.B.**
The life and educational writings of
Rabanus Maurus.
188, 183 leaves. illus. 27 cm.
Thesis – Cornell University, 1948.
Typescript.
KAS

Hrotsvit of Gandersheim, b. ca. 935

4261 **Haight, Anne (Lyon) ed.**
Hroswitha of Gandersheim; her life,
times, and works, and a comprehensive
bibliography. New York, Hroswitha Club,
1965.
xiv, 129 p. illus., facsims. geneal. table.
27 cm.
InStme; MnCS; PLatS

4262 **Nagel, Bert.**
Roswitha von Gandersheim. [Anhang zur
"Ruperto-Carola"]. Heidelberg (Universi-
tät) 1963.
40 p. illus., facsims. 24 cm.
MnCS

4263 **Nagel, Bert.**
Hrotsvit von Gandersheim. Stuttgart,
Metzler, 1965.
89 p. 19 cm.
MnCS

4264 **Schütze-Pflugk, Marianus.**
Herscher und Märtyrerauffassung der
Hrotsvit von Gandersheim. Wiesbaden,
Steiner Verlag, 1972.
129 p. 24 cm.
MnCS

4265 **Sebastian, Irmine, Sister, O.S.B.**
Hroswitha, tenth century nun-poetess.
14 p. 28 cm.
Thesis – University of Notre Dame, In-
diana, 1940.
Typescript.
InFer

Huber, Celestine, 1884–1974

4266 **Golden jubilee of the Reverend Celestine
Huber, O.S.B.**, 1912–1962. Sunday,
May the twentieth, Nineteen hundred
and sixty-two, St. Mary's Church, Pittsburgh, Pa., 1962.
[16] p. illus. 23 cm.
PLatS

4267 **This is your life, Father Celestine**
[Huber, O.S.B. Pittsburgh, Pa., St.
Mary's Church, 1962].
11 p. 22 cm.
PLatS

Hugeburg von Heidenheim, 8th cent.

4268 **Gottschaller, Eva.**
Hugeburg von Heidenheim; philologische
Untersuchungen zu den Heiligenbio-
graphien einer Nonne des achten Jahrhunderts. München, bei der Arbeo-Gesellschaft, 1973.
115 p. 22 cm.
MnCS

Hugh, abbot of Bury St. Edmunds
see
Northwold, Hugh

Hugh, abbot of Reading, d. 1164

4269 **Hurry, Jameson Boyd.**
In honor of Hugh de Boves and Hugh
Cook Farrington, first and last abbots of
Reading. [Reading, England, E. Poynder
and Son] 1911.
33 p. 21 cm.

Humbertus, Cardinal, d. 1061?

4270 **Hoesch, Henning.**
Die kanonischen Quellen im Werk Hum-
berts von Moyenmoutier; ein Beitrag zur
Geschichte der vorgregorianischen
Reform. Köln, Böhlau Verlag, 1970.
ix, 279 p. 24 cm.
PLatS

Ildephonsus, Saint, archbishop of Toledo, d. 667

4271 **Gaetano, Constantino, O.S.B.**
Sanctor/ trium episcopor/ relig.is
bened.ae liminum, Isidori Hispalens., Ildefonsi Tolet., Gregorii card. Ost. vitae, et
actiones . . . Romae, apud Jacobum
Mascardum, 1606.
156 p. 24 cm.
MnCS

Jackisch, Theresia Elisabeth, 1895–1972

4272 **Herstelle, Germany. Abtei vom Heiligen
Kreuz.**
Mutter Theresia Elisabeth Jackisch, Ab-
tissin der Abtei.
20 p. 21 cm. (Totenchronik aus der Abtei
Hl. Kreuz – Herstelle, 1972)
MnCS

Jean de Stavelot, 1388–1449

4273 **Delisle, Léopold Victor.**
Le livre de Jean de Stavelot sur Saint
Benoît. Paris, Impr. Nationale, 1908.
35 p. plate. 28 cm.
MnCS

Joannes de Spira, d.ca. 1456

4274 **Kropff, Martinus, O.S.B.**
Joannes de Spira.
(*In* his: Bibliotheca Mellicensis. Vindo-
bonae, J. P. Kraus, 1747, p. 256–297)
ILSP; MnCS

Jocelin de Brakelond, fl. 1200

4275 **Koenig, Clara.**
Englisches Klosterleben im 12. Jahrhundert, auf Grund der Chronik des Jocelinus
de Brakelonda. Jena, Frommannsche
Buchhandlung, 1928.
vii, 98 p. 23 cm.
MnCS

Johannes von Kastl, 15th cent.

4276 **Sudbrack, Josef.**
Die geistliche Theologie des Johannes
von Kastl; Studien zur Frömmigkeitsge-
schichte des Spätmittelalters. Münster,
Westf., Aschendorff, 1966–67.
2 v. 25 cm.
InStme

Johannes von Schwanden, d. 1327

4277 **Ringholz, Odilo, O.S.B.**
Geschichte des fürstlichen Benediktiner-
stiftes U.L.F. zu Einsiedeln unter Abt
Johannes I. von Schwanden, 1298–1327
. . . [n.p., 1890?].
[129]–394 p. 22 cm.
InStme

John Gualbert, Saint, d. 1073

4278 **Andrea, abate di Strumi.**
San Giovanni Gualberto [di] Andrea
abate di Strumi e discepolo anonimo. Traduzione di Enrico Baccetti. Siena, Cantagalli [1974].
126 p. ports. 20 cm.
MnCS

4279 **Martindale, Cyril Charlie, S.J.**
St. Christopher: breaker of men and
other stories. London, R. and T. Washbourne [1908].
158 p.
NcBe

John of Matera, Saint, 1070?-1139

4280 **Morelli, Marcello.**
Vita di s. Giovanni da Matera, abbate,
fondatore della congregazione benedettina
di Pulsano. Bari, De Robertis [1930].
220 p.
AStb

Johnston, Henry Joseph, d. 1723

4281 **Clagett, Nicholas, the younger.**
An answer to the representer's reflections upon the state and view of the controversy. With a reply to the vindicator's full
answer, showing, that the vindicator has
utterly ruined the new design of expound-
ing and representing popery. London,
Printed for Ric. Chiswell, MDCLXXXVIII.
130 p. 20 cm.
PLatS

4282 **Clagett, William.**
A discourse concerning the pretended
sacrament of Extreme Unction. With an
account of the occasions and beginnings of
it in the Western Church. With a letter to
the vindicator of the bishop of Condom.
London, Printed for Richard Chiswell,
MDCLXXXVII.
136 p. 20 cm.
PLatS

4283 **Wake, William, abp. of Canterbury.**
A defence of the exposition of the doctrine of the Church of England, against the
exceptions of Monsieur de Meaux, late
bishop of Condom, and his vindicator. London, Printed for Richard Chiswell,
MDCLXXXVI.
xxiv, 166 p. 20 cm.
PLatS

4284 **Wake, William, abp. of Canterbury.**
A second defence of the exposition of the
doctrine of the Church of England: against
the new exceptions of Monsieur de Meaux,
late bishop of Condom, and his vindicator.
London, Printed for Richard Chiswell,
MDCLXXXVII.
2 v. 20 cm.
PLatS

Jolly, Vincent Leo, 1860-1894

4285 **In memoriam:** Rev. Father Vincent Jolly,
O.S.B., late apostolic missionary and
pastor of Purcell, Indian Territory
[Okla.]. Purcell, Ind. Terr., Register Job
Printing Rooms, 1895.
14 p. illus. 23 cm.
KAS

Josep de Sant Benet, Brother, 1654-1723

4286 **Curiel, Fausto, O.S.B.**
Vida del Ven. H. José de San Benito,
religioso de Montserrat, Spain. MS.
Monasterio de Montserrat, codex 1178.
35 f. Octavo. Saec. 20.
Microfilm: MnCH proj. no. 30,157

4287 **Vida del v. fra Josep de Sant Benet,**
religiòs llec del real monestir de Santa
Maria de Montserrat de Catalunya, excrita de la seva pròpria mà. Monestir de
Montserrat, 1930.
186 p. port. 17 cm.
PLatS

Juliana of Norwich, 1343-1443

4288 **Graef, Hilda C.**
Women mystics: Catherine of Siena
[and] Julian of Norwich.
(*In* her: The light and the rainbow. Lon-
don, 1959. p. 242-277)
PLatS

4289 **O'Brien, Elmer, S.J.**
Varieties of mystic experience; an an-
thology and interpretation. New York,
Holt, Rinehart and Winston [1964].
x, 321 p. 24 cm.
PLatS

4290 **Reynolds, Anna Maria, Sister, O.P.**
Julian of Norwich.
(*In* Walsh, James, S.J. Pre-Reformation
English spirituality. New York, 1965. p.
198-209)
PLatS

4291 **Stanbrook Abbey, England.**
Dame Julian of Norwich, by a Benedic-
tine of Stanbrook (D.S.H.).
(*In* Davis, Charles. English spiritual
writers. New York, 1961. p. 51-65)
PLatS

Kapsner, Oliver Leonard, 1902-

4292 **Shoniker, Fintan Raymond, O.S.B.**
A Benedictine bibliography – now a
reality.
Reprint from American Benedictine
Review, v. 13(1962), p. 610-615.
PLatS

4293 **Translatio studii;** manuscript and library
studies honoring Oliver L. Kapsner,
O.S.B. Edited by Julian G. Plante. Col-
legeville, Minn., Published for the
Monastic Manuscript Microfilm Library
by St. John's University Press, 1973.
288 p. illus. 25 cm.
In English, German, French, or Spanish.
"Publications of Oliver L. Kapsner,
O.S.B.": p. 273-278.
InStme; KAS; MnCS; PLatS

Keck, Johannes, 1400-1450

4294 **Monachus Mellicensis.**
Responsio ad apologiam (Ecclesiasticum
unitor) Johannis Keck. MS. Vienna, Na-

tionalbibliothek, codex 4957, f. 95r-97v.
Quarto. Saec. 15.
Microfilm: MnCH proj. no. 18,139

4295 **Schlitpacher, Johannes, O.S.B.**
Epistola critica contra Apologiam uni-
toris ecclesiastici a Keckio editam. MS.
Benediktinerabtei Melk, Austria, codex
662, f.183v-184r. Quarto. Saec. 15.
Microfilm: MnCH proj. no. 1532

4296 **Schlitpacher, Johannes, O.S.B.**
Prima epistola adversus Ioannis Keckii
Tegernseensis Unitorem ecclesticum. MS.
Benediktinerabtei Melk, Austria, codex
662, f.181r. Quarto. Saec. 15.
Microfilm: MnCH proj. no. 1532

Kienle, Ambrosius, 1852-1905

4297 **Krutschek, Paul.**
Rechtes Mass und rechte Milde in kir-
chenmusikalischen Dingen; eine Antwort
auf P. Ambrosius Kienles "Mass und
Milde." Regensburg, New York, F. Pustet,
1901.
60 p. 21 cm.
PLatS

Knoebber, Mildred, Sister

4298 **Mount Saint Scholastica Convent,
Atchison, Kans.**
Special dedication in remembrance of the
golden jubilee of profession [of] Mother
Mildred Knoebber, O.S.B., 1918-1968.
[48] p.
MnStj(Archives)

Knowles, David, 1896-1974

4299 **Brooke, Christopher.**
A bibliography of the writings of Dom
David Knowles, 1919-1962.
(*In* Knowles, David. The historian and
character. Cambridge, 1963. p. 363-373)
PLatS

4300 **Egan, Keith J., O.Carm.**
Dom David Knowles, 1896-1974.
Offprint from The American Benedic-
tine Review, v. 27(1976), p. 235-246.
KAS; MnCS; PLatS

4300a **Morey, Adrian.**
Dàvid Knowles; a memoir. London,
Longman & Todd, 1979.
viii, 166 p. 23 cm.
KAS; InStme; MnCS

4301 **Pantin, William Abel.**
Curriculum vitae [of Dom David
Knowles].
(*In* Knowles, David. The historian and
character. Cambridge, 1963. p. xvii-xxviii)
PLatS

Kolb, Honorat, 1603-1670

4302   **Wiest, Veneranda, Sister, O.S.B.**
Honorat Kolb, Abt von Seon, 1603-1670.
München, Selbstverlag der Bayerischen
Benediktinerakademie, 1937.
xx, 139 p. port. 25 cm.
KAS

Königsperger, Marianus, 1708-1769

4303   **Zwickler, Friedhelm.**
Frater Marianus Königsperger, O.S.B.
(1708-1769); ein Beitrag zur süddeutschen
Kirchenmusik des 18. Jahrhunderts.
298 p. music. 21 cm.
Inaug.-Diss. – Johannes Gutenberg-
Universität zu Mainz, 1964.
PLatS

Krul, Leopold Joseph, 1918-

4303a   **Connare, William, bp. of Greensburg.**
Homily at the abbatial blessing of the
Right Reverend Leopold J. Krul, O.S.B.,
Saint Vincent Archabbey Basilica,
Latrobe, Pa., July 24, 1979.
3 p. 28 cm.
Multigraphed.
PLatS(archives); MnCS(archives)

4303b   **Testimonial honoring Rt. Rev. Leopold
J. Krul, O.S.B.,** archabbot, Saint Vin-
cent Archabbey, Latrobe, Pa., Sunday,
November 4, 1979.
[84] p. illus. 23 cm.
PLatS

Kruse, Michael, 1864-1929

4304   **Scherer, Michael Emilio, O.S.B.**
Ein grosser Benediktiner, Abt Michael
Kruse von Sao Paulo (1864-1929). Mün-
chen, Abtei St. Bonifaz, 1963.
180 p. plates. 24 cm.
MnCS; NdRi; PLatS

Kunigunde, Saint
see
Cunigund, Saint

Lambot, Cyrille, 1900-

4305   **Memorial Dom Cyrille Lambot.**
(*In* Revue bénédictine, v. 79(1969), p.
8-327)
KAS

Lanfranc, archbishop of Canterbury, ca.1005-1089

4306   **Gibson, Margaret.**
Lanfranc of Bec. Oxford, Clarendon
Press, 1978.

xii, 266 p. 23 cm.
MnCS

4307   **Gjerlow, Lilli.**
Adoratio crucis: the Regularis concordia
and the Decreta Lanfranci; manuscript
studies in the early medieval Church of
Norway. [Oslo, Boston], Norwegian Universities Press, 1961.
176 p. facsims. 25 cm.
InStme

4308   **Glunz, Hans Hermann.**
History of the Vulgate in England from
Alcuin to Roger Bacon; being an inquiry
into the text of some English manuscripts
of the Vulgate Gospels. Cambridge [Eng-
land], University Press, 1933.
xx, 383 p. 23 cm.
PLatS

4309   **Murrman, Warren Daniel, O.S.B.**
Lanfranc of Bec.
44 leaves. 28 cm.
Thesis (M.A.) – St. Vincent College,
Latrobe, Pa., 1966.
Typescript.

Langland, William, 1330?-1400?

4310   **Bloomfield, Morton W.**
Was William Langland a Benedictine
monk?
Offprint from Modern Language Quar-
terly, v. 4, p. 57-61.
PLatS

Laveyne, Jean Baptiste de, 1693-1719

4311   **Veuillot, François.**
Dom de Laveyne et la Congrégation des
Soeurs de la Charité et de l'Instruction
Chrêtienne. Paris, Editions Alsatia [1948].
251 p. plates. 19 cm.
MnCS

Lebuin, Saint, d. ca. 770

4312   **Duckett, Eleanor Shipley.**
Saint Gregory of Utrecht, Saint Liudger,
Saint Lebuin: the Netherlands in the
eighth century.
(*In* her: The wandering saints in the
early Middle Ages. New York, 1959. p.
229-248)
PLatS

4313   **Hucbald, monk of St. Amand.**
Ex vita s. Lebuini auctore Hucbaldo
Elnonensi.
(*In* Monumenta Germaniae historica.
Scriptores. Stuttgart, 1963. t. 2, p.
360-364)
MnCS; PLatS

Leccisotti, Tommaso Domenico, 1895–

4313a **Studi in onore di d. Tommaso Leccisotti** nel suo 50e di sacerdozio. Roma, Abbazia San Paolo.
3 v. (Benedictina; fascicoli di studi benedettini, anno XIX–XXI, 1972–74)
CaQStB; InStme; MnCS

Leclercq, Henri, 1869–1945

4313b **Klauser, Theodor.**
Henri Leclercq, 1869–1945: vom Autodidakton zum Kompilator grossen Stils. Münster, Westfalen, Aschendorffsche Verlagsbuchhandlung, 1977.
165 p. plates, 28 cm. (Jahrbuch für Antike und Christentum, 5)
MnCS

Leclercq, Jean, 1911–

4314 **Leloir, Louis, O.S.B.**
Bibliography of the works of Jean Leclercq.
(*In* Bernard of Clairvaux: studies presented to Dom Jean Leclercq. Cistercian studies series, no. 23 (1973), p. 217–264)
InStme; PLatS

Lemcke, Peter Henry, 1796–1882

4315 **Flick, Lawrence Francis.**
Biographical sketch of Rev. Peter Henry Lemke, O.S.B., 1796–1882.
Extract from Records of the American Catholic Historical Society, v. 9(1898), p. 129–192.
PLatS

4316 **Lemcke, Peter Henry, O.S.B.**
Haudegen Gottes; das Leben des P. H. Lemke, 1796–1882 von ihm selbst erzählt, kommentiert und hrsg. von Willibald Mathäser. [Würzburg], Kommissionsverlag Echter [1971].
305 p. illus. 21 cm.

Leo Marsicanus, bishop of Ostia, d. 1115?

4317 **Meyvaert, Paul, O.S.B.**
Autour de Léon d'Ostie et de sa "Translatio S. Clementis." Bruxelles, Société des Bollandistes, 1956.
Reprint from Analecta Bollandiana, t. 74 (1956), p. 189–240.
PLatS

Leupi, Gertrud, Sister, 1825–1904

4318 **Jäger, Moritz, O.S.B.**
Schwester Gertrud Leupi, 1825–1904, Gründerin der drei Benedictinerinnenklös-

ter: Maria Rickenbach, Yankton, Marienburg. [Freiburg, Schweiz], Kanisius Verlag [1974].
200 p. plates, ports. 19 cm.
MnCS

4319 **Jäger, Moritz, O.S.B.**
Sr. Gertrude Leupi, 1825–1904. Translated by Alexander J. Luetkemeyer.
188 p. 28 cm.
Typescript, 1974.
MoCo

Lioba, Saint, 8th cent.

4320 **Duckett, Eleanor Shipley.**
Saint Boniface, Saint Lull, Saint Leoba: Germany in the eighth century.
(*In* her: The wandering saints in the early Middle Ages. New York, 1959. p. 193–228)
PLatS

Liutwin, Saint, bishop of Treves, d. 713

4321 **Lampen, Willibrord, O.F.M.**
Thiofried van Echternach en zijn Vita S. Liutwini. 'S-Hertogenbosch, Teulings' Uitgevers-Maatschappij, 1936.
xxxvi, 57 p. 27 cm.
MnCS

Löhr, Aemiliana, Sister, 1896–1972

4322 **Herstelle, Germany.** Abtei vom Heiligen Kreuz.
Schw. Aemiliana Löhr.
16 p. 21 cm. (Totenchronik aus der Abtei Hl. Kreuz – Herstelle, 1972)
KAS

Ludger, Saint, bishop of Munster, 744–809

4323 **Duckett, Eleanor Shipley.**
Saint Gregory of Utrecht, Saint Liudger, Saint Lebuin: the Netherlands in the eighth century.
(*In* her: The wandering saints in the early Middle Ages. New York, 1959, p. 229–248)
PLatS

Lupus Servatus, abbot of Ferrieres, 9th cent.

4324 **Gariepy, Robert Joseph.**
Lupus of Ferrieres and the classics. Darien, Conn., Monographic Press, 1967.
viii, 110 p. 28 cm.
MnCS; PLatS

4325 **Snijders, Cherubine, Sister, O.S.F.**
Het latijn der brieven van Lupus van Ferrières, middeleeuws humanist. Amsterdam, Pordon & Zoon, 1943.

171 p. 24 cm.
MnCS

Lydgate, John, 1370?-1451?

4326 **Pearsall, Derek Albert.**
John Lydgate. London, Routledge & K.
Paul, 1970.
[10], 312 p. 3 plats, 3 illus. 23 cm. (Poets
of the later Middle Ages)
PLatS

4327 **Ringler, William A.**
Lydgate's Serpent of division, 1559, ed.
by John Stow.
(*In* Virginia. University. Studies in bib-
liography, v. 14(1961), p. 201-203)
PLatS

4328 **Schirmer, Walter Franz.**
John Lydgate; a study in the culture of
the XVth century. Translated by Ann E.
Keep. London, Methuen [1961].
xiii, 303 p. plates. 23 cm.
KAS; PLatS

Lyne, Joseph Leycester, 1837-1908

4329 **Bertouch, Beatrice de.**
The life of Father Ignatius, O.S.B., the
monk of Llanthony. New York, Dutton,
1905.
x, 607 p. plates. 23 cm.
KAS

Mabillon, Jean, 1632-1707

4330 **Butler, Edward Cuthbert, O.S.B.**
Mabillon.
Reprinted from Downside review, 1893,
p. 116-132.
PLatS

4331 **Didio, Henri.**
La querelle de Mabillon et de l'abbé de
Rancé. Amiens, Rousseau-Leroy, 1892.
xvii, 464 p. 23 cm.
MnCS

4332 **Jadart, Henri.**
Dom Jean Mabillon (1632-1707); étude
suivie de documents inédits sur sa vie, ses
oeuvres, sa mémoire. Reims, Deligne et
Renart, 1879.
268 p. illus. 23 cm.
InStme

4333 **Jadart, Henri.**
Dom Thierry Ruinart (1657-1709);
notice suivie de documents inédits sur sa
famille, sa vie, ses oeuvres, ses relations
avec D. Mabillon. Paris, H. Champion,
1886.
190 p. 22 cm.
MnCS

4334 **Knowles, David, O.S.B.**
Jean Mabillon.
(*In* his: The historian and character, and
other essays. Cambridge, 1963. p. 213-
239)
PLatS

4335 **La Barre, Louis François Joseph.**
Vita Joannis Mabillonii presbyteri et
monachi Ordinis S. Benedicti, Congrega-
tionis Sancti Mauri.
(*In* Mabillon, Jean. Vetera analecta.
Parisiis, 1723. Preliminary p. 1-43)
PLatS

4336 **Manning, Joseph Matthew, S.J.**
The contribution of Dom Jean Mabillon,
O.S.B. to the science of palaeography.
246 p. plates.
Thesis (Ph.D.)–Fordham University,
New York, 1950.
MnCS (Xeroxed typescript)

4337 **Monnoyeur, Jean Baptiste, O.S.B.**
L'argument de Mabillon contre Thomas à
Kempis, auteur de l'Imitation. 3. éd.
Ligugé, Abbaye Saint-Martin [n.d.].
46 p. 24 cm.
First published 1930.
PLatS

4338 **Ruinart, Thierry, O.S.B.**
Abregé de la vie de Dom Jean Mabillon,
prêtre & religieux bénédictin de la Congregation de Saint-Maur. Paris, chez la Veuve
François Muguet, 1709.
436 p. 17 cm.
InStme

Madelgisil, Saint, d. 685

4339 **Dekkers, Eligius, O.S.B.**
Un cas de critique historique à St-
Riquier; les reliques de St Mauguille.
(*In* Saint-Riquier; études . . . Abbaye de
Saint-Riquier, 1962. v. 1, p. 59-67)
PLatS

Malet, André, 1862-1936

4340 **Chenevière, Etienne.**
Toi seul me suffis: Dom André Malet,
1862-1936. Préface du Cardinal Garrone.
Abbaye de Westmalle [Belgique] 1971.
xv, 294 p. illus. 20 cm.
MnCS

Manuk, Peter
see
Mechitar of Sebaste

Marcet, Antoni Maria, 1878-1946

4341 **L'abat Marcet;** resum biogràfic fisonomia
espiritual; oracio fúnebre. Abadia de
Montserrat, 1951.
60 p. plates. 18 cm.
MnCS

Marmion, Columba, 1848-1923

4342 **Delforge, Thomas, O.S.B.**
Columba Marmion, serviteur de Dieu.
Turnhout, Brepols, 1963.
82 p. 18 cm.
MnCS; PLatS

4343 **Delforge, Thomas, O.S.B.**
Columba Marmion; servant of God.
Translated by Richard L. Stewart. St.
Louis, Herder, 1965.
viii, 71 p. 19 cm.
CaMWiSb; InStme; MnCS; PLatS

4344 **Marmion Abbey, Aurora, Ill.**
Abbot Columba Marmion, by the monks
of Marmion Abbey, Aurora, Illinois, on the
occasion of the centenary of [his] birth.
Benet Lake, Wis., Our Faith Press, 1958.
30 p. 12 cm.
KAS

4345 **Thibaut, Raymond, O.S.B.**
Un maitre de la vie spirituelle: Dom
Columba Marmion, abbé de Maredsous
(1858-1923). Edition entièrement revue.
Les Editions de Maredsous, 1953.
xi, 472 p. illus. 20 cm.
PLatS

Marty, Martin, 1834-1896

4346 **Fitzgerald, Mary Clement, Sister,
P.B.V.M.**
Bishop Marty and his Sioux missions,
1876-1896.
(*In* South Dakota Historical Collections,
v. 20(1940), p. 523-558)
Originally thesis (M.A.)–University of
Notre Dame, Ind., 1933.
MnCS

4346a **Karolevitz, Robert F.**
Bishop Martin Marty, "the black robe
lean chief." Mission Hill, S.D., The Home-
stead Publishers, 1980.
154 p. illus., ports, 23 cm.
MnCS

Matronola, Martino, 1903-

4347 **Eredità perenne:** D. Martino Matronola,
nuovo abate di Montecassino. [Stampato
dalla Industria Grafica Cassinate, 1971].
79 p. illus. (part col.) 24 cm. (Bollettino
diocesano. Numero speciale)
KAS; PLatS

4348 **Nuovo cammino sull'antica scia;** ordi-
nazione episcopale di S. Ecc. Rev. Martino Matronola, abate ordinario di
Montecassino, 1977.
135 p. (Bolletino diocesano, 2)
MoCo

Matzen, Nicolaus, d. 1425

4349 **Kropff, Martinus, O.S.B.**
Venerab. Nicolaus de Mazen, abbas
Mellicensis XXXII.
(*In* his: Bibliotheca Mellicensis. Vindo-
bonae, 1747, p. 135-199)
ILSP; MnCS

Maugille, Saint
see
Madelgisil, Saint

Maurus, Saint, d. ca. 584

4350 **Faustus, monk of Monte Cassino.**
Vita Mauri abbatis auctore Fausto monacho. MS. Benediktinerabtei Kremsmünster, Austria, codex 27, f.182r-202r. Saec.
14.
Microfilm: MnCH proj. no. 27

4351 **Faustus, monk of Monte Cassino.**
Vita s. Mauri Glannafolii. MS. Benediktinerabtei Melk, Austria, codex 909,
f.164r-183v. Quarto. Saec. 15.
Microfilm: MnCH proj. no. 1727

4352 **Faustus, monk of Monte Cassino.**
Vita s. Mauri abbatis. MS. Cistercienserabtei Rein, Austria, codex 85, f.156r-
187v. Folio. Saec. 12.
Microfilm: MnCH proj. no. 7486

4353 **Grégoire, Reginald, O.S.B.**
Prières liturgiques médiévales en l'honneur de Saint Benoît, de Sainte Scholastique et de Saint Maur.
(*In* Analecta monastica, 7. sér. (1965), p.
1-85)
PLatS

4354 **Leben des hl. Maurus.** MS. Benediktinerinnenabtei Nonnberg, Salzburg,
codex 23 C 3, f.381r-454r. Quarto.
Saec. 16.
Microfilm: MnCH proj. no. 10,844

4355 **Leben des hl. Maurus.** MS. Benediktinerabtei St. Peter, Salzburg, codex
b.VII.2, f.346r-422r. Quarto. Saec. 17.
Microfilm: MnCH proj. no. 10,511

4356 **Legenda de s. Mauro.** MS. Benediktinerabtei Melk, Austria, codex 652,
f.244r-267v. Quarto. Saec. 15.
Microfilm: MnCH proj. no. 1542

4357 **Vita s. Mauri.** MS. Cistercienserabtei Lilienfeld, Austria, codex 80, f.6r–37v. Quarto. Saec. 15.
Microfilm: MnCH proj. no. 4383

4358 **Vita s. Mauri abbatis.** MS. Augustiner-chorherrenstift Vorau, Austria, codex 264, f.24r–42v. Folio. Saec. 15.
Microfilm: MnCH proj. no. 7245

4359 **Vita s. Mauri abbatis, discipuli s. Benedicti.** MS. Benediktinerabtei Michaelbeuern, Austria, codex cart. 60, f.238r–248v. Folio. Saec. 15.
Microfilm: MnCH proj. no. 11,552

4360 **Vita s. Mauri discipuli s. Benedicti.** MS. Hereford, England, Cathedral Library, codex 0 6 xi, f.95–119. Quarto. Saec. 11.
Microfilm: MnCH

Mechitar of Sebaste, 1676–1749

4361 **Lebensgeschichte des Abtes Mechithar von Sebaste.** MS. Mechitaristenkongregation, Vienna, codex 1220. 57 f. Octavo. Saec. 19.
Microfilm: MnCH proj. no. 8743

4362 **Matthäus aus Eudokia.**
Biographie des Mechithar von Sebastia, Gründer der Mechitaristen-Congregation. MS. Mechitaristenkenkongregation, Vienna, codex 494. 66 f. Octavo. Saec. 19.
Microfilm: MnCH proj. no. 8065

4363 **Mechiter-Festschrift zum 200.** Todestage des gottseligen Abtes Mechitar, Stifters der Mechitharisten-Kongregation, 1749–1949. Wien, Mechitharisten-Buchdruckerein, 1949.
434 p. 30 cm.
MnCS

4364 **Nurikhan, Minas, A.B.A.**
The life and times (1660–1750) of the servant of God, Mechitar, founder of the Armenian Mechtarists of Venice (San Lazzaro). Historical and theological oriental questions. Venice, St. Lazarus' Island, 1915.
424 p. illus. 21 cm.
MnCS; NdRi

Mechtild of Magdeburg, ca.1212–ca.1282

4365 **Ancelet-Hustache, Jeanne.**
Mechtilde de Magdebourg (1207–1282); étude de psychologie religieuse. Paris, H. Champion, 1926.
402 p. 26 cm.
PLatS

4366 **Colledge, Edmund, O.S.A.**
Mechtild of Magdeburg.

(*In* Walsh, James, S.J. Spirituality through the centuries, p. 159–170)
PLatS

4367 **O'Brien, Elmer, S.J.**
Varieties of mystic experience; an anthology and interpretation. New York, Holt, Rinehart and Winston [1964].
x, 321 p. 24 cm.
PLatS

Mechtilde, Saint, 1241–1299

4368 **Mary Jeremy, Sister.**
Scholars and mystics. Chicago, H. Regnery, 1962.
213 p. 22 cm.
InStme

4369 **Mechthildenbuch.** Lingua germanica. MS. Linz, Austria, Studienbibliothek, codex 194, f.1r–94v. Octavo. Saec. 16.
Microfilm: MnCH proj. no. 27,831

4370 **Rome, Italy. S. Benedetto (abbey of Benedictine nuns).**
Life of St. Mechtildis. Printed at the Vatican Press, Rome, 1899.
295 p. 20 cm.

4371 **Vagaggini, Cipriano, O.S.B.**
La dévotion au Sacré-Coeur chez Sainte Mechtilde et Sainte Gertrude.
(*In* Cor Jesu; commentationes in . . . "Haurietis aquas." Roma, 1959. v. 2, p. 29–48)
PLatS

Meinrad, Saint, 797?–861

4372 **Berno, abbot of Reichenau.**
Vita s. Meginradi ex antiquissimis manuscriptis membranis nostrae bibliothecae sumta, anonymo quidem, sed, meo [i.e., C. Hartmann] iudicio, Bernone auctore.
[8] p. 31 cm.
(Issued with Hartmann, C. Annales Heremi . . . Friburgi, 1612)
InStme; PLatS

4373 **Brandes, Karl, O.S.B.**
Leben und Wirken des heiligen Meinrad für seine Zeit und für die Nachwelt; eine Festschrift zur tausendjährigen Jubelfeier des Benediktiner-Klosters Maria-Einsiedeln. Einsiedeln, New York, K. u. N. Benziger, 1861.
xx, 244 p. plates. 23 cm.
InStme; MoCo; NdRi; PLatS

4374 **Das Blockbuch von Sankt Meinrad und seinen Mördern und vom Ursprung von Einsiedeln;** farbige Faksimile-Ausgabe zum elften Zentenar des Heiligen, 861–961. Mit einer Einleitung von Leo Helbling, O.S.B. Einsiedeln, Benziger, 1961.

35 p. plates (facsims. col.) 19 cm.
MnCS

4375 **Einsiedeln, Switzerland (Benedictine abbey).**
Sankt Meinrad, zum elften Zentenarium seines Todes, 861-1961. Hrsg. von Benediktinern des Klosters Maria Einsiedeln. Einsiedeln, Benziger, 1961.
126 p. illus. (part col. mounted), facsims. 22 cm.
InStme; MoCo; PLatS

4376 **Vita ven. viri Meginradi heremite et eius passio.** MS. Linz, Austria, Studienbibliothek, codex 191, f.241r-246v. Octavo. Saec. 15.
Microfilm: MnCH proj. no. 27,993

Metellus von Tegernsee, fl. 1167

4377 **Jacobsen, Peter Christian.**
Die Quirinalien des Metellus von Tegernsee. Untersuchungen zur Dichtkunst und kritische Textausgabe. Leiden und Köln, E. J. Brill, 1965.
416 p. 25 cm.
PLatS

Michel, Virgil George, 1890-1938

4378 **Hall, Jeremy, Sister, O.S.B.**
The full stature of Christ; the ecclesiology of Virgil Michel. A golden anniversary edition, 1926-1976. Collegeville, Minn., The Liturgical Press, 1976.
xix, 234 p. 24 cm.
InStme; MnCS; MnStj

Michels, Thomas Aquinas, 1892-

4379 **Michels, Thomas Aquinas, O.S.B.**
Sarmenta: gesammelte Studien/von Thomas Michels. Anlässlich seines 80. Geburtstages hrsg. von Norbert Brox u. Ansgar Pau, O.S.B. Münster, Aschendorff [1972].
xii, 241 p. 13 illus. 25 cm.
English, French, German, or Latin.
Bibliography of the author's works: p. vii–xiii.
InStme

4380 **Rahner, Hugo, S.J., ed.**
Perennitas; Beiträge zur christlichen Archäologie und Kunst . . . P. Thomas Michels, O.S.B., zum 70. Geburtstag. Hrsg. von Hugo Rahner, S.J., und Emmanuel von Severus, O.S.B. Münster, Aschendorff [1963].
xxiii, 734 p. illus. 25 cm.
InStme; KAS; PLatS

Miller, Athanasius, 1881-

4381 **Duncker, P.G., O.P.**
Dom Atanasio Miller, O.S.B., segretario della Pontificia Commissione Biblica.
(*In* Mélanges Tisserant, v. 1, p. 197-208)
PLatS

Montfaucon, Bernard de, 1655-1741

4382 **Pélissier, L. G.**
Un collaborateur provencal de Montfaucon (dix lettres au président Thomassin Mazaugues le fils)
(*In* Mélanges offerts à M. Emile Chatelain. Paris, 1910. p. 429-439)
PLatS

4383 **Vatican. Biblioteca Vaticana.**
Les manuscrits de la reine de Suède au Vatican: réédition du catalogue de Montfaucon et cotes actuelles. Città del Vaticano, Biblioteca Apostolica Vaticana, 1964.
133 p. 26 cm. (Studi e testi, 238)
PLatS

Moosbrugger, Caspar, 1656-1723

4384 **Die Vorarlberger Barockbaumeister;** Ausstellung in Einsiedeln und Bregenz zum 250. Todestag von Br. Caspar Moosbrugger, Mai-September 1973. Hrsg. von Werner Oechslin. Einsiedeln, 1973.
xvi, 298 p. plates (276 illus.) 24 cm.
MnCS

Morcaldi, Michele, 1818-1894

4385 **Bonazzi, Benedetto, O.S.B.**
Poche parole pronunziate per la santa memoria di d. Michele Morcaldi, O.S.B., abate ordinario della SS. Trinità dei Tirreni . . . Napoli, Tipografia Francesco Giannini & Figli, 1894.
20 p. 20 cm.
PLatS

Müller, Jean Pierre, 1904-

4386 **Sapientiae procerum amore:** mélanges médiévistes offerts à Dom Jean-Pierre Müller, O.S.B., à l'occasion de son 70eme anniversaire. Edités par Theodor Wolfram Köhler. Roma, Editrice Anselmiana, 1975.
xvii, 514 p. 25 cm. (Studia Anselmiana philosophica theologica . . . fasc. 63)
MnCS; PLatS

Nectarius, abbot of Casole, 1155(ca.)-1235

4387 **Hoeck, Johannes, O.S.B.**
Nicolaos-Nektarios von Otranto, Abt von Casole; Beiträge zur Geschichte der ost-

westlichen Beziehungen unter Innozenz III. und Friedrich II . . . Ettal, Buch-Kunstverlag, 1965.
265 p. 26 cm.
PLatS

Neunheuser, Burkhard, 1903-

4387a **Eulogia miscellanea liturgica in onore di P. Burkhard Neunheuser, O.S.B.,** preside del Pontificio Istituto Liturgico. Roma, Editrice Anselmiana, 1979.
xvi, 632 p. 25 cm. (Studia Anselmiana, 68)
PLatS; InStme

Northwold, Hugh, d. 1254

4388 **The Chronicle of the election of Hugh,** abbot of Bury St. Edmunds and later bishop of Ely. Edited and translated by R. M. Thomson. Oxford, Clarendon Press, 1974.
li, 208 p. 23 cm. (Oxford medieval texts)
MnCS; PLatS

Notker Balbulus, 840(ca.)-912

4389 **Crocker, Richard L.**
The early medieval sequence. Berkeley, University of California Press, 1977.
x, 470 p. plates, facsims., music. 29 cm.
InStme

Notker Labeo, 950(ca.)-1022

4390 **Lloyd, Albert L.**
The manuscripts and fragments of Notker's Psalter. Giessen, Wilhelm Schmitz, 1958.
73 p. 21 cm.
PLatS

Oberholzer, Basilius, 1821-1895

4391 **Benziger, Bernard, O.S.B.**
Abt Basilius; ein Lebensbild für die Zöglinge und Freunde der Stiftsschule von Maria-Einsiedeln. Einsiedeln, Benziger & Co., 1896.
76 p. plates (ports.) 23 cm.
InStme; MnCS

4392 **Blättler, Aloysius.**
Die kirchlichen Insignien eines Abtes; Predigt bei der feierlichen Benediktion des Hochwürdigsten Gnädigen Herrn Basilius Oberholzer, Abt des Benediktiner-Stiftes Maria Einsiedeln, den 9. Mai 1875 in der Stiftskirche zu Einsiedeln. Einsiedeln, Marianus Benziger u. Sohn, 1875.
13 p. 23 cm.
PLatS

Odilia, Saint, 660(ca.)-720

4393 **Winterer, L.**
Sainte Odile. 4. éd. Mulhouse, F. Gangloff, 1894.
32 p. 19 cm.
PLatS

Odilo, Saint, abbot of Cluny 962(ca.)-1048

4394 **Hourlier, Jacques, O.S.B.**
Le monastère de saint Odilon.
(*In* Analecta monastica, 6. sér. 1962. p. 5-21)
PLatS

4395 **Hourlier, Jacques, O.S.B.**
Saint Odilon, abbé de Cluny. Louvain, Bibliothèque de l'Université, 1964.
234 p. 25 cm.
InStme; KAS; MnCS

Oliva, abbot of Montserrat, 971?-1046

4396 **Mundó, Anscari, O.S.B.**
Entorn de la carta de l'abat Oliba a Arnau Mir de Tost.
(*In* Miscel·lània Anselm M. Albareda. v. 1(1962), p. 207-216)
PLatS

Opportuna, Saint, d. 770

4397 **Chaussy, Yves, O.S.B.**
L'Abbaye d'Almenèches-Argentan; et Saint Opportune, sa vie et son culte. Paris, Lethielleux, 1970.
480 p. 24 cm.
MnCS; PLatS

Osbern, monk of Gloucester

4398 **Hunt, Richard W.**
The "Lost" preface to the Liber derivationum of Osbern of Gloucester.
(*In* Mediaeval and renaissance studies, v. 4, p. 267-282)
PLatS

Oswald, Saint, archbishop of York, d. 992

4399 **Carmen epicum de S. Oswaldo.** Germanice. MS. Vienna, Nationalbibliothek, codex 3007, f.205r-233r. Octavo. Saec. 15(1472).
Microfilm: MnCH proj. no. 16,234

4400 **Duckett, Eleanor Shipley.**
Saint Oswald, Saint Aidan, Saint Cuthbert: northern England in the seventh century.
(*In* her: The wandering saints of the early Middle Ages. New York, 1959. p. 93-117)
PLatS

4401 **Poema germanicum de vita s. Oswaldi.**
MS. Vienna, Nationalbibliothek, codex
12540. 58 f. Quarto. Saec. 15.
Microfilm: MnCH proj. no. 19,954

4402 **Vita s. Osvaldi.** MS. Vienna, National-
bibliothek, codex 1262, f.145r–151r.
Folio. Saec. 14.
Microfilm: MnCH proj. no. 14,601

Othmar, Saint, abbot of St. Gall, d.759

4403 **Iso, monk of St. Gall.**
Ysonis de miraculis s. Otmari libri II.
(*In* Monumenta Germaniae historica.
Scriptores. Stuttgart, 1963. t. 2, p. 47–54)
PLatS

4404 **Liber de virtutibus s. Othmari abbatis.**
MS. Cistercienserabtei Lilienfeld,
Austria, codex 104, f.99v–107r. Quarto.
Saec. 15.
Microfilm: MnCH proj. no. 4402

4405 **Rhythmi de s. Otmaro,** edente D. Ilde-
phonso ab Arx.
(*In* Monumenta Germaniae historica.
Scriptores. Stuttgart, 1963. t. 2, p. 54–58)
PLatS

4406 **Vita de s. Ottmaro, abbatis.** MS. Linz,
Austria, Studienbibliothek, codex 89,
f.106r–128v. Quarto. Saec. 12.
Microfilm: MnCH proj. no. 27,840

4407 **Vita s. Othmari.** MS. Cistercienserabtei
Lilienfeld, Austria, codex 134, f.111r–
112v. Folio. Saec. 13.
Microfilm: MnCH proj. no. 4429

4408 **Vita s. Othmari abbatis.** Vienna, Schot-
tenstift, codex 147, f.108r–115v. Folio.
Saec. 12–13.
Microfilm: MnCH proj. no. 4040

4409 **Walafrid Strabo.**
Vita s. Otmari. MS. Benediktinerabtei
Kremsmünster, Austria, codex 126,
f.325v–336v. Saec. 12.
Microfilm: MnCH proj. no. 119
For other manuscript copies of this work
see under Walafrid Strabo in Author Part.

Owen, Saint, bishop of Rouen, 609(ca.)–683(ca.)

4410 **Duckett, Eleanor Shipley.**
Saint Ouen of Rouen and Saint Fursey;
France in the seventh century.
(*In* her: The wandering saints of the
early Middle Ages. New York, 1959. p.
140–164)
PLatS

Paolucci, Placida Ida, Sister, 1908–1928

4411 **Novelli, Nazareno.**
Negli orti fioriti de S. Benedetto: Donna
Placida (Ida) Paolucci monaca benedettina.
Subiaco, Tipografia dei Monasteri [1928].
32 p. front.(port) 19 cm.
MnCS

Paschasius Radbertus, abbot of Corbie, d.ca.860

4412 **Ernst, Joseph.**
Die Lehre des hl. Paschasius Radbertus
von der Eucharistie. Mit besonderer
Berücksichtigung der Stellung des hl.
Rhabanus Maurus und des Ratramnus zu
derselben. Freiburg i.B., Herder, 1896.
iv, 136 p. 23 cm.
Inaug.-Diss. – Würzburg.
InStme

4413 **Ripberger, Albert.**
Der Pseuco-Hieronymus Brief IX
"Cogitis me"; ein erster Marianischer Traktat des Mittelalters von Paschasius Radbert. Freiburg, Schweiz, Universitätsverlag, 1962.
xiv, 150 p. 26 cm. (Spicilegium Friburgense, v. 9)
PLatS

Paul de Moll, 1824–1896

4414 **Speybrouck, Edouard van.**
Some characteristics from the life of
Father Paul of Moll, Benedictine. Trans-
lated from the French by P. Nolan, O.S.B.
3rd ed. [Port Louis, Mauritius, Catholic
Union of Port-Louis, 1907].
152 p. port. 18 cm.
KAS

Paulus Diaconus, 720(ca.)–797?

4415 **Engels, Lodewijk Josef.**
Observations sur le vocabulaire de Paul
Diacre. Nijmegen, Dekker & Van de Vegt,
1961.
vii, 290 p. 24 cm.
Issued also as thesis, Nijmegen.
PLatS

Peichl, Hermann, 1887–1966

4416 **Kisser, Josef, ed.**
Wissenschaft im Dienste des Glaubens;
Festschrift für Abt Dr. Hermann Peichl,
O.S.B., Präsident der Wiener Katholischen
Akademie, dargeboten zum 35. Abt-
jubiläum . . . Wien, Wiener Katholische
Akademie, 1965.

261 p. illus. 24 cm. (Studien der Wiener Katholischen Akademie, 4. Bd.)
InStme

Pérez de Urbel, Justo, 1895-

4417 **Homenaje a Fray Justo Pérez de Urbel, O.S.B.** [Prologo Fra Clemente de la Serna]. Burgos, Abadia de Silos, 1976.
2 v. diagrs., facsims. 25 cm.
MnCS; PLatS

Peter Damian, Saint, 1007?-1072

4418 **Foschini, Giulio.**
Letture dall'epistolario di S. Pier Damiani. Faenza, Fratella Lega [1960].
62 p. 22 cm.
PLatS

4419 **Laqua, Hans Peter.**
Traditionen und Leitbilder bei dem Ravennater Reformer Petrus Damiani, 1042-1052. München, Wilhelm Fink Verlag, 1976.
390 p. 24 cm.
MnCS

4420 **Leclercq, Jean, O.S.B.**
Saint Pierre Damien, ermite et homme d'Eglise. Roma, Edizioni di storia e letteratura, 1960.
283 p. 26 cm.
KAS; MnCS; PLatS

4421 **Miccioli, Giovanni.**
Théologie de la vie monastique chez Saint Pierre Damien.
(*In* Théologie de la vie monastique, p. 459-483)
PLatS

Peter the Venerable
see
Petrus Venerabilis

Petrus Atroensis, Saint, 773-837

4422 **Sabas, monk,** 9th cent.
La vita retractata et les miracles posthumes de saint Pierre d'Atroa. Texte grec édité, traduit et commenté par Vitalien Laurent. Bruxelles, Société des Bollandistes, 1958.
186 p. map. 25 cm.
MnCS

Petrus Diaconus of Montecassino, 12th cent.

4422a **Meyvaert, Paul.**
Peter the Deacon and the tomb of St. Benedict.
70 p. 23 cm.

(*In* his: Benedict, Gregory, Bede and others. London, Variorum Reprints, 1977)
Reprint from Revue bénédictine, 65(1955).
MnCS

Petrus Venerabilis, abbot of Cluny, 1092?-1156

4423 **Duparay, B.**
Pierre-le-Vénérable, abbé de Cluny: sa vie, ses oeuvres, et la société monastique au XIIe siècle. Chalon-sur-Saone, P. Mulcey, 1862.
172 p. 32 cm.
MnCS

4424 **Kritzeck, James.**
Peter the Venerable and Islam. Princeton, N.J., Princeton University Press, 1964.
xiv, 301 p. 24 cm. (Princeton Oriental studies, no. 23)
InStme; KAS; MnCS; PLatS

4425 **Pierre Abélard, Pierre le Vénérable:** les courants philosophiques, littéraires et artistiques en Occident au milieu du XIIe siècle [actes et mémoires du colloque international], Abbaye de Cluny, 2 au 9 juillet 1972. Paris, Editions du Centre national de la recherche scientifique, 1975.
782 p. 20 leaves of plates (part col.) 25 cm.
MnCS

4426 **Renner, Emmanuel, Sister, O.S.B.**
The relationship of Peter the Venerable and Bernard of Clairvaux.
47 p. 28 cm.
Research paper (M.A.)–University of Minnesota, 1955.
Typescript.
MnStj(Archives)

4427 **Simonson, Diane.**
An analysis of the letters between St. Bernard of Clairvaux and Peter the Venerable concerning disputed seating of the bishop of Langres, 1138 A.D.
33 p. 30 cm.
Typescript.
MnCS

4428 **Vinay, Gustave.**
Pietro il Venerabile.
(*In* Spiritualità cluniacense. Todi, 1960. p. 57-82)
PLatS

4429 **Wilkens, Cornelius August.**
Petrus der Ehrwürdige, Abt von Cluny; ein Mönchs-leben. Leipzig, Verlag von Breitkopf und Härtel, 1857.
xiv, 277 p. 18 cm.
KAS; InStme

Petrus de Chevriaco, d. 1285

4430 **Terroine, Anne.**
Un abbé de Saint-Maur au XIII siècle,
Pierre de Chevry, 1256–1285, avec l'édi-
tion des plus anciens cas de justice de
Saint-Maur-des-Fossés. Paris, C. Klinck-
sieck, 1968.
238 p. map. 24 cm.
MnCS

Petrus von Rosenheim, 1380(ca.)–1433

4431 **Kropff, Martinus, O.S.B.**
Petrus de Rosenheim, prior Mellicensis.
(*In* his: Bibliotheca Mellicensis. Vindo-
bonae, 1747. p. 206–217)
ILSP; MnCS

4432 **Thoma, Franz.**
Petrus von Rosenheim, O.S.B.
Sonderdruck aus . . . Das bayerische
Inn-Oberland, 32. Bd.(1962), p. 97–164)
MnCS

Pez, Bernhard, 1683–1735

4433 **Kropff, Martinus, O.S.B.**
P. Bernardus Pezius, bibliothecarius
Mellicensis.
(*In* his: Bibliotheca Mellicensis. Vindo-
bonae, 1747. p. 546–608)
ILSP; MnCS

Philibert, Saint, d. 684

4434 **Vita et miracula s. Filiberti abbatis.**
MS. Vienna, Nationalbibliothek, codex
484, f.25r–77r. Quarto. Saec. 11.
Microfilm: MnCH proj. no. 13,824

Pirmin, Saint, d. 753

4435 **Vita s. Pirminii.** MS. Vienna, National-
bibliothek, codex 520, f.103r–113v.
Quarto. Saec. 11.
Microfilm: MnCH proj. no. 13,858

Piscopia, Elena Lucrezia, 1646–1684

4436 **Celebrazioni centenaire in onore di
Elena Lucrezia Cornado Piscopia,**
prima donna laureata nel mondo, 1678.
Padova, Abbazia S. Giustina, 1978.
unpaged, illus.
InFer

Pius VII, Pope, 1742–1823

4437 **Browne-Olf, Lillian.**
Pius VII, 1800–1823.
(*In* her: Their name is Pius. Milwaukee,
1941. p. 59–130)
InFer; PLatS

4438 **Consalvi, Ercole.**
Memorie del cardinale Ercole Consalvi.
A cura di Mons. Mario Nasalli Rocca di
Corneliano. Roma, A. Signorelli, 1950.
xix, 424 p. illus., ports. 26 cm.
PLatS

4439 **Hales, Edward Elton Young.**
The emperor and the pope; the story of
Napoleon and Pius VII. Garden City, N.Y.,
Doubleday, 1961.
168 p. 22 cm.
PLatS

4440 **McCabe, Joseph.**
Pius VII and the revolution.
(*In* his: Crisis in the history of the
papacy. New York, 1916. p. 368–390)
PLatS

4441 **Pacca, Bartolomeo, Cardinal.**
Historische Denkwürdigkeiten . . . Aus
dem Italienischen . . . übersetzt. Augsburg, Karl Kollmann, 1832.
xiv, 215 p. 22 cm.
InStme

4442 _____ **2., durchaus verbesserte und
sehr vermehrte Auflage.** Augsburg,
Verlag der Kollmann'schen Buchhandlung, 1835.
3 v. 22 cm.
InStme

4443 **Pacca, Bartolomeo, Cardinal.**
Reise Sr. Heiligkeit des Papstes Pius VII
nach Genua, im Frühjahre 1815, als der
Kirchenstaat von den Neapolitanern unter
Mürat gewaltsam occupirt wurde, und
seine Rückkehr nach Rom . . . Nach dem
italienischen Originale (Orvieto 1833) in's
Deutsche übertragen. Augsburg, Verlag
der Karl Kollmann'schen Buchhandlung,
1834.
viii, 72 p. 22 cm.
InStme

4444 **Pacca, Bartolomeo, Cardinal.**
Memorie storiche dil ministero de' due
viaggi in Francia e della prigionia nel Forte
di S. Carlo in Fenestrelle . . . Napoli,
Stamperia del Genio Tipografico, 1830.
3 v. 18 cm.
PLatS

4445 **Pistolesi, Erasmo.**
Vita del sommo pontefice Pio VII. Roma,
Francesco Bourlié, 1824–30.
4 v. 20 cm.
PLatS; PLatS(microfilm)

4446 **Sala, Giuseppe Antonio, Cardinal.**
Piano di riforma umiliato a Pio VII.
(*In* his: Scritti. Roma, 1888. v. 4, p.
45–234)
PLatS

4447 **Welschinger, Henri.**
Le Pape et l'Empereur, 1804–1815. 2.
éd. Paris, Plon, 1905.
iv, 473 p. 25 cm.
PLatS

Placenti, Guglielmo, 1913-

4448 **Mocciaro, Bernardo, O.S.B.**
A d. Guglielmo Placenti, O.S.B., priore
conventuale di S. Martino delle Scale nel
suo primo giubileo sacerdotale. S. Martino
delle Scale, 1961.
80 p. plates, ports. 30 cm.
MnCS

Placidus, Saint, 515(ca.)–550(ca.)

4449 **Leben des hl. Placidus.** MS. Benediktinerinnenabtei Nonnberg, Salzburg,
codex 23 C 3, f.232r–378r. Quarto. Saec.
16.
Microfilm: MnCH proj. no. 10,844

Placidus, Saint, d. 720

4450 **Martin, Paul E.**
Les sources hagiographiques relatives
aux saints Placide et Sigebert et aux origines du monastère de Disentis.
(*In* Mélanges d'histoire du Moyen Age,
offerts à M. Ferdinand Lot. Paris, 1925. p.
515–541)
PLatS

Polding, John Bede, 1794–1877

4451 **Australian Catholic church history;** the
Polding era. Teachers resource book.
[Pennant Hills, N.S.W., Australia, Tju-
runga, 1978].
unpaged, plates, 30 cm.
Loose-leaf binding.
50 col. slides in pocket.
MnCS; PLatS

4452 **Compton, Margaret E.**
A life of John Bede Polding.
ix, 400 p. illus., ports. 26 cm.
Thesis (M.A.)–University of New
England, 1977.
Mimeographed.
InStme

4453 **Polding's sanctity; an appreciation.**
(*In* Polding, John Bede. The eye of faith.
Kilmore, Australia, 1978. p. 26–41)·
MnCS

4454 **A series of articles about Polding's work**
in: Tjurunga, an Australian Benedictine
review, nos. 13–16, 1977–1978.
MnCS

Procopius of Sazava, Saint, d. 1053

4455 **Ekert, Frantisek.**
St. Procopius, abbot of Sásava. [Chicago,
Benedictine Abbey Press, 1961].
22 p. illus. 17 cm.
"Adapted in translation from: Sv. Pro-
kop, opat sázavský, patron ceský."
ILSP; PLatS

4456 **Kadlec, Jaroslav.**
Saint Procopius, guardian of the Cyrolo-
Methodian legacy. Translated by Vitus
Buresh. [Cleveland, Micro Photo Division,
Bell & Howell Co.] 1964.
ILSP

Raitenau, Aegyd Everard von, 1605–1675

4457 **Schwab, Franz.**
P. Aegyd Everard von Raitenau,
1605–1675, Benediktiner von Krems-
münster, Mathematiker, Mechaniker und
Architekt . . . Salzburg, Buchdruckerei
Oberndorfer & Cie., 1898.
105 p. plans. 24 cm.
KAS

Ratramnus, monk of Corbie, d. ca. 868

4458 **Ernst, Joseph.**
Die Lehre des hl. Paschasius Radbertus
von der Eucharistie. Mit besonderer
Berücksichtigung der Stellung des hl.
Rhabanus Maurus und des Ratramnus zu
derselben. Freiburg i.B., Herder, 1896.
iv, 136 p. 23 cm.
Inaug.-Diss. – Würzburg.

4459 **Fahey, John F.**
The eucharistic teaching of Ratram of
Corbie. Mundelein, Ill., Saint Mary of
the Lake Seminary, 1951.
176 p. 22 cm. (Pontificia Facultas Theolo-
gica Seminarii Sanctae Mariae ad Lacum.
Dissertationes ad lauream, 22)
InStme

Rautenstrauch, Franz Stephan, 1734–1785

4460 **Menzel, Beda Franz, O.S.B.**
Abt Franz Stephan Rautenstrauch von
Brevnov-Braunau: Herkunft, Umwelt und
Wirkungskreis. Königstein/Ts., König-
steiner Institut für Kirchen- und Geistes-
geschichte der Sudetenländer, 1969.
284 p. illus. 24 cm.
KAS; MnCS

Rea, Ildefonso, 1896–1971

4461 **Recessit Pastor noster;** [in Memoria di
D. Ildefonso Rea, abate di Mcntecassino.
Montecassino, 1971].

35 p. port. 22 cm.
PLatS

Reding, Augustinus, 1625-1692

4462 **Helbling, Leo, O.S.B.**
Die "Exhortationes in Regulam sancti Benedicti" des Einsiedler Abtes Augustin Reding.
(*In* Studien aus dem Gebiete von Kirche und Kultur. Paderborn, 1930. p. 87-127)
PLatS

Reginald of Canterbury, f. 1112

4463 **Hunt, Richard W.**
Alberic of Monte Cassino and Reginald of Canterbury.
(*In* Mediaeval and renaissance studies, v. 1, p. 39-40)
PLatS

Regno, Bernard, Bishop, 1886-1977

4463a **Barsenbach, Dunstan, O.S.B.**
The coolie bishop; the life story of Dom Bernard Regno O.S.B., bishop of Kandy, Sri Lanka. [Kandy, Sri Lanka (Ceylon), Bravi Press, 1979].
90 p. plates, 22 cm.
MnCS

Rembert, Saint, archbishop of Hamburg and Bremen, d. 888

4464 **Meersseman, Gillis, O.P.**
Rembert van Torhout. Brugge, De Kinkhoren, 1943.
199 p. map. 20 cm.
PLatS

Reynolds, Bede, 1892-

4465 **Reynolds, Bede, O.S.B.**
A rebel from riches: the autobiography of an unpremidated monk / Bede Reynolds (né Kenyon L. Reynolds). Canfield, Ohio, Alba Books [1975].
150 p. illus. 18 cm.
KAS

Riccardi, Placido, 1844-1915

4466 **Gorla, Pietro.**
Il servo di Dio Don Placido Riccardi, monaco dell'Abbazia San Paolo fuori le Mura di Roma, 1844-1915. Torino, Società Editrice Internazionale [1936].
366 p. port., plates. 21 cm.
MnCS

Richard of Wallingford, 1232(ca.)-1336

4467 **North, J. D.**
The life of Richard of Wallingford.
(*In* Richard of Wallingford. An edition of his writings. Oxford, 1889. v. 2, p. 1-21)
MnCS

Richardus Pictaviensis, 12th cent.

4468 **Schnack, Ingeborg.**
Richard von Cluny, seine Chronik und sein Kloster in den Anfängen der Kirchenspaltung von 1159 . . . Berlin, 1921; Vaduz, Kraus Reprint, 1965.
173 p. 23 cm.
PLatS

Ricker, Anselm, 1824-1902

4469 **Kevacs, Elisabeth.**
Anselm Ricker und seine Pastoralpsychiatrie. Wien, Wiener-Dom-Verlag, 1973.
MnCS

Robert, Saint, abbot of Chaise-Dieu, c. 1067?

4470 **Gaussin, Pierre Roger.**
L'Abbaye de la Chaise-Dieu, 1043-1518. [Paris, Editions Cujas, 1962].
760 p. illus., maps. 25 cm.
InStme; MnCS

Rode, Johann, 1358?-1439

4471 **Becker, Peter, O.S.B.**
Das monastische Reformprogramm des Johannes Rode, Abtes von St. Matthias in Trier . . . Münster, Aschendorff, 1970.
xix, 218 p. 25 cm.
InStme; PLatS

Roger, of Caen, fl. 1090

4472 **Bultot, Robert.**
Christianisme et valeurs humaines. A: La doctrine du mépris du monde, en Occident, de S. Ambroise à Innocent III. Louvain, Nauwelaerts, 1963-
6 v. 21 cm.
KAS

Romuald, Saint, 952(ca.)-1027

4473 **Pagnani, Alberico.**
Vita di s. Romualdo, abbate fondatore dei Camaldolesi. 2. ed. completamente rifusa. Fabriano, Arti grafice "Gentile," 1927.
400 p. plates. 23 cm.
MnCS

4474 **Peter Damian, Saint.**
Ex Petri Damiani Vita s. Romualdi,
edente D. G. Waitz.
(*In* Monumenta Germaniae historica.
Scriptores. Stuttgart, 1963. t. 4, p.
846–854)
MnCS; PLatS

Rosa, Bernardus

4475 **Lutterotti, Nicolaus, O.S.B.**
Abt Bernardus von Grüssau. Nach Notizien P. Nikolaus v. Lutterotti bearb. u.
hrsg. durch Ambrosius Rosa, O.S.B. Stuttgart, Brentano Verlag, 1960.
128 p. ports. 22 cm.
MnCS; PLatS

Ruinart, Thierry, 1657–1709

4476 **Jadart, Henri.**
Dom Thierry Ruinart (1657–1709).
Notice suivis de documents inédits sur sa
famille, sa vie, ses oeuvres, ses relations
avec D. Mabillon. Paris, H. Champion,
1886.
190 p. 22 cm.
MnCS

Rupert, Saint, bishop of Salzburg, d.ca.718

4477 **Collectanea ex bullis pontificiis de vita
et monachatu s. Ruperti.** MS. Benediktinerabtei St. Peter, Salzburg, Archivium Hs. A 12. 97 p. Folio. Saec. 17
(1628).
Microfilm: MnCH proj. no. 10,771

4478 **De sancto Ruperto episcopo Salisburgensi.** Successores proximi s. Ruperti.
MS. Vienna, Nationalbibliothek, codex
546, f.2r–3r. Quarto. Saec. 12.
Microfilm: MnCH proj. no. 13,873

4479 **Hauthaler, Willibald, O.S.B.**
Die dem heiligen Rupertus, Apostel von
Bayern, geweihten Kirchen und Kapellen.
Salzburg, Verlag der Consistorial-Kanzlei,
1885.
31 p. fold. map. 20 cm.
KAS

4480 **Hildegard, Saint.**
Vita s. Ruperti confessoris. MS. Vienna,
Nationalbibliothek, codex 963,
f.151r–155r. Folio. Saec. 13.
Microfilm: MnCH proj. no. 14,263

4481 **Historia von St. Ruprecht,** St. Trudbert
und St. Erntraut, herausgegeben von
dem Petrischen Manuscripto. MS. Benediktinerabtei St. Peter, Salzburg, codex
b.V.24. 30 f. Quarto. Saec. 17.
Microfilm: MnCH proj. no. 10,467

4482 **Homilia in translatione s. Ruotperti.**
MS. Vienna, Nationalbibliothek, codex
520, f.91r–98v. Quarto. Saec. 11.
Microfilm: MnCH proj. no. 13,858

4483 **Leben des hl. Rupert und der hl. Eren-
trud,** herausgegeben von dem S. Petrischen Manuscripto LL. MS. Benediktinerabtei St. Peter, Salzburg, codex
bIII.41. 106 p. Quarto. Saec. 17.
Microfilm: MnCH proj. no. 10,385

4484 **Legenda de s. Ruperto per modum lectionum.** MS. Benediktinerabtei Seitenstetten, Austria, codex 215, f.3r–4r.
Folio. Saec. 14.
Microfilm: MnCH proj. no. 1027

4485 **Legendae de s. Ruperto et Virgilio.** MS.
Augustinerchorherrenstift Vorau,
Austria, codex 381, f.109r–114v. Quarto.
Saec. 15.
Microfilm: MnCH proj. no. 7352

4486 **Officium, genealogia et vita s. Rudberti et s. Erentrudis,** cum adnexis
orationibus. MS. Benediktinerabtei St.
Peter, Salzburg, codex b.VI.3, f.248v–
253v. Quarto. Saec. 16.
Microfilm: MnCH proj. no. 10,464

4487 **Sermo de ss. Ruperto,** Virgilio et Eren-
trudi. MS. Vienna, Nationalbibliothek,
codex 3825, f.195r–215r. Quarto. Saec.
15.
Microfilm: MnCH proj. no. 17,027

4488 **Steinhauser, Johann.**
Die Erhebung der Leiber des hl. Ru-
precht, Martin und anderer Heiligen in
Salzburg. MS. Benediktinerabtei St. Peter,
Salzburg, codex b.XIII.32, p. 1–18 (8. vice).
Microfilm: MnCH proj. no. 10,723

4489 **Steinhauser, Johann.**
Lebensbeschreibung des heyligsten
Christi Bekhenners s. Ruperti, aus allerley
Martyrologiis verfasset. MS. Benedikti-
nerabtei St. Peter, Salzburg, codex b.V.3.
150 f. Octavo. Saec. 17(1618).
Microfilm: MnCH proj. no. 10,441

4490 **Vita s. Rudberti et conversio Bajuvario-
rum et Carantanorum.** MS. Vienna,
Nationalbibliothek, codex 596, f.1v–17r.
Quarto. Saec. 11.
Microfilm: MnCH proj. no. 13,928

Rupert, abbot of Deutz, 1070(ca.)–1129

4491 **Beinert, Wolfgang.**
Die Kirche, Gottes Heil in der Welt; die
Lehre von der Kirche nach den Schriften
des Rupert von Deutz, Honorius Augusto-
dinensis und Gerhoch von Reichersberg.
Münster, Aschendorff, 1973.
461 p. 23 cm.
MnCS

4492 **Conflictus Herberti episc. cum Roud-berto de Deutz abbate.** MS. Universitätsbibliothek Graz, Austria, codex 795, f.149r–151r. Quarto. Saec. 12. Microfilm: MnCH proj. no. 26,887

4493 **Dinter, Peter.**
Rupert von Deutz, Vita Heriberti. Kritische Edition mit Kommentar und Untersuchungen von Peter Dinter. Bonn, Ludwig Röhrscheid Verlag, 1976.
146 p. 24 cm.
MnCS

4494 **Haacke, Rhaban, O.S.B.**
Programme zur bildenden Kunst in den Schriften Ruperts von Deutz. Siegburg, Respublica-Verlag, 1974.
63 p. 23 plates. 24 cm.
MnCS

4495 **Haacke, Rhaban, O.S.B.**
Rupert von Deutz zur Frage: Cur Deus homo?
(*In* Corona gratiarum . . . Eligio Dekkers, O.S.B. XII lustra complenti oblata. Brugge, 1975. v. 2, p. 143–159)
PLatS

4496 **Magrassi, Mariano, O.S.B.**
Teologia e storia nel pensiero di Ruperto di Deutz. Roma, apud Pontificium Universitatem Urbanianam de Propaganda Fide [1960].
290 p. 25 cm.
MnCS

4497 **Scheffczyk, L.**
Die heilsgeschichtliche Trinitätslehre des Rupert von Deutz und ihre dogmatische Bedeutung.
(*In* Betz, Johannes. Kirche und Ueberlieferung. Freiburg, 1960. p. 90–118)
PLatS

Rupertus Tuitiensis
see
Rupert, abbot of Deutz

Sadlier, Francis Rupert, 1889–1962

4498 **Staudacher, Rosemarian V.**
The priest of Carville.
(*In* her: Chaplains in action. New York, 1962. p. 117–130)
PLatS

Salomon III, bishop of Constance, d. 920

4499 **Zeller, Ulrich.**
Bischof Salom III von Konstanz, Abt von St. Gallen. Hildesheim, Gerstenberg, 1974.
xi, 107 p. 24 cm.
MnCS

Samson, abbot of Bury St. Edmunds, 1135–1211

4500 **Bury St. Edmunds Abbey, England.**
The kalendar of Abbot Samson of Bury St. Edmunds and related documents, edited for the Royal Historical Society by R.H.C. Davis. London, Offices of the Royal Historical Society, 1954.
ix, 200 p. maps. 22 cm. (Camden third series, v. 84)
MnCS

Sayrus, Gregory, 1560–1602

4501 **Mahoney, Edward Joseph.**
The theological position of Gregory Sayrus, O.S.B., 1560–1602. Ware [England], Jennings & Bewley, 1922.
152 p. 21 cm.
Thesis (S.T.D.) – Fribourg.
MnCS

Schenkl, Maurus von, 1749–1816

4502 **Schmeing, Clemens, O.S.B.**
Studien zur "Ethica christiana" Maurus von Schenkls, O.S.B., und zu ihren Quellen. Regensburg, Fr. Pustet, 1959.
172 p. 22 cm.
InStme: MnCS; PLatS

Schlitpacher, Joannes, 1403–1482

4503 **Epistolae duae Magistri Marquardi ad Magistrum Johannem Schlitpacher.** MS. Benediktinerabtei Melk, Austria, codex 662, f.184v–185v. Quarto. Saec. 15.
Microfilm: MnCH proj. no. 1532

4504 **Epistolae sex ad Ioannem Schlitpacher Mellicensem datae.** MS. Benediktinerabtei Melk, Austria, codex 91, f.82–86. Duodecimo. Saec. 15.
Microfilm: MnCH proj. no. 1170

4505 **Ioannes de Geissenfeld.**
Epistola ad Ioannem Schlitpacher. MS. Benediktinerabtei Melk, Austria, codex 662, f. 189r. Quarto. Saec. 15.
Microfilm: MnCH proj. no. 1532

4506 **Jodocus de Heilprunna.**
Epistolae quinque ad Ioannem Schlitpacher. MS. Benediktinerabtei Melk, Austria, codex 662, f.197r–200r. Quarto. Saec. 15.
Microfilm: MnCH proj. no. 1532

4507 **Kropff, Martinus, O.S.B.**
Joannes Schlitpacher, vulgo de Weilhaim, prior Mellicensis.
(*In* his: Bibliotheca Mellicensis. Vindobonae, 1747. p. 369–441)
ILSP; MnCS

4508 **Stephanus de Spanberg, abbot of Melk.**
Epistolae quatuor ad Johannem Schlitpacher. MS. Benediktinerabtei Melk, Austria, codex 662, f.186r–188r. Quarto. Saec. 15.
Microfilm: MnCH proj. no. 1532

Schmitt, Jerome Gerhard, 1857–1904

4509 **Suter, Walter R.**
The father of the Scmitt Box, [by] Walter R. Suter and the Rev. Jerome Rupprecht, O.S.B.
Extracted from: Entomological News, v. 85(1974), p. 298–300)
PLatS

Schneider, Hubert, 1902–

4510 **Reinhart, Dietrich, O.S.B.**
A history of the St. John's Carpentry Shop.
(*In* Saint John's furniture 1874–1974. Collegeville, Minn., 1974)
MnCS

Scholastica, Saint, 480(?)–547

4511 **Bertharius, abbot of Monte Cassino.**
Homilia in laudem s. Scholasticae. MS. Benediktinerabtei St. Peter, Salzburg, codex a.VI.46, f.78r–79r. Quarto. Saec. 15.
Microfilm: MnCH proj. no. 10,119

4512 **Bertharius, abbot of Monte Cassino.**
Sermo de sancta Scholastica. MS. Benediktinerabtei Melk, Austria, codex 1386, f.31v–59v. Duodecimo. Saec. 15.
Microfilm: MnCH proj. no. 1908

4513 **Historia de s. Scholastica virgine.** MS. Benediktinerabtei Melk, Austria, codex 1869, f.285v–288r. Folio. Saec. 15.
Microfilm: MnCH proj. no. 2166

4514 **Leben der hl. Scholastica.** MS. Benediktinerinnenabtei Nonnberg, Salzburg, codex 23 C 3, f.158r–224r. Quarto. Saec. 16.
Microfilm: MnCH proj. no. 10,844

4515 **Paulus Diaconus (?).**
Legenda de s. Scholastica virgine. MS. Benediktinerabtei St. Peter, Salzburg, codex z.VI.46, f.73r–78r. Quarto. Saec. 15.
Microfilm: MnCH proj. no. 10,119

4516 **Schuster, Ildefonso, O.S.B.**
More powerful than her brother.
(*In* his: Saint Benedict and his times. St. Louis, 1951, p. 338–349)
PLatS

4517 **Il sepolcro di s. Benedetto. Montecassino, 1951.**
245 p. plates, diagrs. 26 cm. (Miscellanea cassinese, 27)

Partial contents: II. Il recente rinvenimento delle reliquie de s. Benedetto e di s. Scolastica e la loro ricognizione.
MnCS; PLatS

4518 **Sermo de s. Scholastica.** MS. Benediktinerabtei Göttweig, Austria, codex 375, f.179r–180r. Folio. Saec. 15.
Microfilm: MnCH proj. no. 3643

Scholastica, Saint
see also Chapter 6 r: Feasts

Schuster, Ildefonso, 1880–1954

4519 **Baur, Benedikt, O.S.B.**
Kardinal Ildefons Schuster; ein Lebensbild, Mödling bei Wien, St. Gabriel-Verlag, 1961.
103 p. illus. 19 cm.
InStme

4520 **John XXIII, Pope.**
Orazione funebre [sul Cardinale Schuster] pronunciata dal patriarca di Venezia Cardinale Roncalli.
(*In* Schuster, Ildefonso. Scritti. Venegone Inferiore, 1959. p. 15–22)
PLatS

4520a **Leccisotti, Tomaso Domenico, O.S.B.**
Il Cardinale Schuster. Milano [Scuola Tipografica S. Benedetto] 1969.
2 v. plates, 24 cm.
MnCS

4521 **Terraneo, Ecclesio.**
Il servo di Dio card. Ildefonso Schuster, arcivescovo di Milano. Brevi cenni biografici. Milano, Pontificia editrice arcivescovile G. Daverio [1962].
173 p. illus. 21 cm.
PLatS

Schwarzhueber, Simpert, 1727–1795

4522 **Peleman, Albert, O.S.B.**
Der Benediktiner, Simpert Schwarzhueber (1727–1795), Professor in Salzburg, als Moraltheologe; seine Beziehungen zur Moraltheologie des Protestanten Gottfried Less, zum Salzburger Moraltheologen Jakob Danzer, und zu Ignaz von Fabiani. Regensburg, Friedrich Pustet, 1961.
196 p. 22 cm.
InStme; MnCS; PLatS

Seidel, Wolfgang, 1492–1562

4523 **Pöhlein, Hubert.**
Wolfgang Seidel, 1492–1562; Benediktiner aus Tegernsee, Prediger zu München –sein Leben und sein Werk. München, K. Zink, 1951.
xxviii, 274 p. illus. 23 cm.
InStme

Seldenbüren, Konrad von, d. 1126

4524 **Konrad von Seldenbüren;** Gedenkblätter zur 8. Jahrhundertfeier seines Todes, 1126–1926. Engelberg, 1926.
24 p.
AStb

Sigebertus, monk of Gembloux, d. 1112

4525 **Beumann, Jutta.**
Sigebert von Gembloux und der Traktat de investitura episcoporum. Sigmaringen, Jan Thorbecke Verlag [1976].
168 p. 20 cm.
MnCS

Sigisbert, Saint, 8th cent.

4526 **Martin, Paul E.**
Les sources hagiographiques relatives aux saints Placide et Sigebert et aux origines du monastère de Disentis.
(*In* Mélanges d'histoire du Moyen Age, offerts à M. Ferdinand Lot. Paris, 1925. p. 515–541)
PLatS

Silva, Domingos de Conseiçao da, 1669–1718

4527 **Silva-Nigra, Clemente Maria de, O.S.B.**
Frei Domingos de Conceiçao; o escultor seiscentista do Rio de Janeiro. Salvador, Bahia, Brazil, Tipografia Benedictina, 1950.
42, 20 p. 70 plates. 32 cm.
MnCS

Silvester Gozzolini, Saint, 1177–1267

4527a **Atti del Convegno di studi storici:** VIII centenario naschita S. Silvestro, 1177–1977. Monastero S. Silvestro (Fabriano) [1978].
236 p. illus. 24 cm.
MnCS

Smaragdus, abbot of Saint-Mihiel, fl. 809–819

4527b **Rädle, Fidel.**
Studien zu Smaragd von Saint-Mihiel. München, Wilhelm Fink Verlag, 1974.
252 p. 24 cm. (Medium Aevum – Philologische Studien, Bd. 29)
MnCS

Spindler, Antonius, d. 1648

4528 **Carmen ad Antonium Spindler abbatem Scotensem** (ab a.1642–1648). MS. Vienna, Schottenstift, codex 638, f.60v. Quarto. Saec. 17.
Microfilm: MnCH proj. no. 4280

Staupitz, Johannes von, d. 1524

4529 **Steinmetz, David Curtis.**
Misericordia Dei; the theology of Johannes von Staupitz in its late medieval setting. Leiden, E. J. Brill, 1968.
x, 198 p. 25 cm.
MnCS

Stehle, Aurelius, 1877–1930

4530 **Pius XI, Pope.**
To our beloved son Aurelius Stehle, O.S.B. . . . Given in Rome, at St. Peter's, on the twentieth day of the month of August, in the year 1929 . . . [Latrobe, Pa., 1929?].
[4] p. 22 cm.
KAS

Steiglehner, Coelestin, 1738–1819

4531 **Grill, Maria Regis, Sister, O.S.B.**
Coelestin Steiglehner, letzter Fürstabt von St. Emmeram zu Regensburg. München, Selbstverlag der Bayerischen Benediktinerakademie, 1937.
xiv, 131 p. port. 25 cm.
MnCS

Steinegger, Ambrosius, 1833–1913

4532 **Muri-Gries, Italy (Benedictine abbey).**
Gedenk-Blatt zum 50.jährigen Priesterjubiläum seiner Gnaden des Hochwst. Herrn Prälaten Abt Ambrosius II., 5. September 1906. [Bozen, Alois Auer] 1906.
14 p. port. 22 cm.
MnCS

Stengel, Carl, 1581–1663

4533 **Bishop, Edmund.**
Abbot Stengel.
(*In* his: Liturgica historica. Oxford, 1918. p. 453–461)
PLatS

Stephanus de Spanberg, abbot of Melk

4534 **Epitaphium Stephani de Spanberg, abbatis Mellicensis.** MS. Benediktinerabtei Melk, Austria, codex 1869, f.308v. Folio. Saec. 15.
Microfilm: MnCH proj. no. 2166

Stolz, Anselm, 1900–1942

4535 **Lipari, Anselmo, O.S.B.**
Dottrina spirituale teologico-symbolica in Anselm Stolz, O.S.B. Palermo, Edizioni o Theologos, 1975.
93 p. 25 cm.
PLatS

Strittmatter, Denis Omer, 1896-1971

4536 **McCarthy, Gerald, O.S.B.**
Homily of Abbot Gerald McCarthy at the funeral Mass of Archabbot Denis O. Strittmatter, O.S.B., Saint Vincent Archabbey, Latrobe, Pa., April 1, 1971.
5 leaves. 28 cm.
Typescript.
PLatS

Suger, abbot of Saint-Denis, 1081-1151

4537 **Cartellieri, Otto.**
Abt Suger von Saint-Denis, 1081-1151. Berlin, 1898; Vaduz, Kraus Reprint, 1965.
xv, 191 p. 23 cm.
MnCS; PLatS

4538 **Discours sur Suger,** et son siècle. Génève, 1779.
79 p. 21 cm.
InStme

4539 **Jumel, Jean Charles.**
Eloge de Suger, abbé de Saint-Denis, ministre d'Etat, & régent du Royaume sous le regne de Louis-le-Jeune . . . Bruxelles, chez Valade, 1779.
48 p. illus. 21 cm.
InStme

4540 **Panofsky, Erwin.**
Architecture gothique et pensée scholastique. Précéde de: L'Abbé Suger de Saint-Denis. Traduction et postface de Pierre Bourdieu. [Paris], Editions de Minuit [1967].
217 p. illus. 22 cm.
PLatS

4541 **Rockwell, Anne F.**
Glass, stones & crown; the Abbé Suger and the building of St. Denis. New York, Atheneum [1968]; London, Macmillan, 1968.
80 p. illus.
InFer; MnCS

4542 **Sahuget d'Espagnac, Marc René Marie.**
Réflexions sur l'Abbé Suger et son siècle. Londres, 1780.
83 p. 21 cm.
InStme

4543 **Suger, moine de Saint-Denis.** [n.p.] 1779.
88 p. 21 cm.
InStme

Sylvester II, Pope, 945(ca.)-1003

4544 **Hock, Karl Ferdinand.**
Gerbert, oder Papst Sylvester II. und sein Jahrhundert. Wien, F. Beck, 1837.
239 p.
NcBe

4545 **Lattin, Harriet (Pratt).**
The peasant boy who became pope; story of Gerbert. [New York, Henry Schuman, 1951].
xi, 179 p. plates. 19 cm.
A novel.
InFer; PLatS

Swyneshed, Roger, d. 1365

4546 **Weisheipl, James A., O.P.**
Roger Swyneshed, O.S.B., logician, natural philosopher and theologian.
Offprint from Oxford studies presented to Daniel Callus, Oxford Historical Society, n.s., 16(1964), p. 231-252.
MnCH

Tedeschi, Ercole, 1843-1919

4547 **D. Ercole Tedeschi, O.S.B.,** 1843-1919; cenni sulla vita, elogio funebre. [Palermo, Boccone del Povero, n.d.]
55 p.
AStb

Tedeschi, Niccolo, archbishop of Palermo, 1386-1445

4548 **Nörr, Knut Wolfgang.**
Kirche und Konzil bei Nicolaus de Tedeschis (Panormitanus). Köln, Böhlau, 1964.
vi, 192 p. 23 cm.
Originally a thesis, Munich, 1960.
PLatS

Theisen, Jerome, 1930-

4548a **Community celebration of the blessing of Abbot Jerome Theisen, O.S.B.,** St. John's Abbey [Collegeville, Minn.], October 19, 1979.
8 pages, music. 20 x 22 cm.
MnCS

Thiemo, Saint, archbishop of Salzburg

4549 **Heinricus, abbot of Breitenau, d. 1170.**
Des Abtes Heinrich zu Breitenau Passio s. Thimonis (inedita) . . . von Dr. Nolte. Wien, Karl Gerold's Sohn, 1876.
8 p. 23 cm.
MnCS

Thurstan, archbishop of York 1070(ca.)-1140

4550 **Nicholl, Donald.**
Thurstan, Archbishop of York (1114-1140). York [England], Stonegate Press, 1964.
277 p.
MoCo

Trithemius, Johannes, 1462-1516

4551 **Arnold, Klaus.**
Johannes Trithemius (1462-1516). Würzburg, F. Schöningh, 1971.
xi, 319 p. ports. 23 cm.
InStme; KAS; MnCS
Originally a thesis, Würzburg.

4552 **Arnold, Klaus.**
Johannes Trithemius und Bamberg: Oratio ad clerum Bambergensem, Otto Meyer zum 65. Geburtstag.
Sonderdruck aus: 107. Bericht des Historischen Vereins Bamberg, 1971, p. 161-189.
MnCS

4553 **Behrendt, Roland, O.S.B.**
Abbot John Trithemius, monk and humanist.
Reprint from Revue bénédictine, t. 84(1974), p. 212-229.
The essay is a review article of three recent books: Johannes Trithemius, von Arnold Klaus (Würzburg, 1971); Des Abtes Johannes Trithemius Chronik des Klosters Sponheim, von C. Velten (Kreuznach, 1969); Grandeur et adversité de Jean Trithème, par P. Chacornac (Paris, 1963).
MnCS

4554 **Chacornac, Paul.**
Grandeur et adversité de Jean Trithème . . . La vie, la légende, l'oeuvre. Paris, Editions Traditionelles, 1963.
187 p. plates. 23 cm.
MnCS

4555 **Gerwalin, Hans, ed.**
Fünfhundert-Jahrfeier Johannes Trithemius, 1462-1962, am 11. August 1962 in Trittenheim/Mosel. Herausgeber: Gemeinde Trittenheim a.d. Mosel.
88 p. ports. 21 cm.
MnCS

4556 **Lehmann, Paul Joachim Georg.**
Merkwürdigkeiten des Abtes Johannes Trithemius. München, Verlag der Bayerischen Akademie der Wissenschaften, 1961.
81 p. 23 cm.
KAS; PLatS

4557 **Lehmann-Haupt, Hellmut.**
Johannes Trithemius, father of bibliography. New York, H. P. Kraus, 1957.
7 p. 31 cm.
InStme

4558 **Müller, Herman.**
Quellen, welche der Abt Trithemius im ersten Theile seiner Hirsauer Annalen benutzt hat. Leipzig, Paul Frohberg, 1871.
59 p. 21 cm.
MnCS

4559 **Sharkey, Mary Giles, Sister, O.S.B.**
The De regimine claustralium of Abbot Johannes Trithemius; a study of his sources and method of composition.
73 p. 29 cm.
Thesis (M.A.) – Fordham University, New York, 1964.
Mimeographed.
MnCS

4560 **Thommen, Bonaventura, O.S.B.**
Die Prunkreden des Abtes Johannes Trithemius. Sarnen, Luis Ehrli, 1934.
2 v. 24 cm.
MnCS

4561 **Volk, Paulus, O.S.B.**
Abt Johannes Trithemius.
Sonderabdruck aus Rheinische Vierteljahrs-Blätter. Jahrg. 27(1962), p. 37-49.
KAS; MnCS

Ubach, Bonaventura, 1879-1960

4562 **Diaz, Romuald, O.S.B.**
Dom Bonaventura Ubach: l'home, el monjo, el biblista . . . Barcelona, Editorial Aedos [1962].
252 p. plates, ports. 22 cm.
MnCS

Ulric, Saint, bishop of Augsburg, 890-973

4563 **Berno, abbot of Reichenau.**
Vita s. Udalrici episcopi. MS. Cistercienserabtei Rein, Austria, codex 36, f.239r-255r. Quarto. Saec. 15.
Microfilm: MnCH proj. no. 7432
For other manuscript copies of this work see under Berno in the Author Part.

4564 **De vita s. Udalrici.** MS. Benediktinerabtei St. Peter, Salzburg, codex b.VIII.17, f.176r-204r. Folio. Saec. 15.
Microfilm: MnCH proj. no. 10,548

4565 **Garardus, of Augsburg,** 11th cent.
Libellus de signis Udalrici episcopi (excerpta). MS. Cistercienserabtei Rein, Austria, codex 36, f.255r-257v. Quarto. Saec. 15.
Microfilm: MnCH proj. no. 7432

4566 **Hymnus in laudem s. Ulrici,** versibus hexametris, cum neumis. Vienna, Nationalbibliothek, codex 573, f.19r-25r. Quarto. Saec. 12.
Microfilm: MnCH proj. no. 13,904

4567 **Legenda de s. Udalrico.** MS. Benediktinerabtei Admont, Austria, codex 771, f.116. Octavo. Saec. 14.
Microfilm: MnCH proj. no. 9804

4568 **Vita s. Udalrici.** MS. Vienna, Nationalbibliothek, codex 554, f.1r-88r. Octavo. Saec. 11.
Microfilm: MnCH proj. no. 13,888

4569 **Vita s. Udalrici.** MS. Benediktinerabtei Admont, Austria, codex 642, f.58v–61v. Quarto. Saec. 14.
Microfilm: MnCH proj. no. 9689

4570 **Vita sancti ac beatissimi Udalrici episcopi.** MS. Cistercienserabtei Lilienfeld, Austria, codex 104, f.107v–116r. Quarto. Saec. 15.
Microfilm: MnCH proj. no. 4402

4571 **Vita s. Udalrici episcopi.** MS. Cistercienserabtei Zwettl, Austria, codex 144, f.175v–185v. Folio. Saec. 12.
Microfilm: MnCH proj. no. 6735

4572 **Vita s. Udalrici episcopi.** MS. Vienna, Schottenstift, codex 147, f.125v–135v. Folio. Saec. 12–13.
Microfilm: MnCH proj. no. 4040

4573 **Vita s. Udalrici episcopi Augustani** (auctore Berno). Signa de veteri vita s. Udalrici (auctore Gerardo). Miracula s. Udalrici. De manifestatione et translatione corporis s. Udalrici. Qualiter canonizatus sit sanctus Udalricus. Officium s. Udalrici (cum notis musicis). Sequentia de sancto Udalrico (cum notis musicis). Hymnus de sancto Udalrico (cum notis musicis). Miracula sancti Udalrici. MS. Vienna, Schottenstift, codex 210. 110 f. Quarto. Saec. 14.
Microfilm: MnCH proj. no. 3907

Uria y Valdés, Benito, 1729-1810

4574 **Perez de Castro, José Luis.**
Fr. Benito de Uria y Valdés, O.S.B., 1729–1810; discurso leido por el autor en el acto de su solemne recepción academica, el die 9 de marz de 1970. Oviedo, 1970.
64 p. plates. 24 cm.
MnCS

Ursmar, Saint, abbot of Lobbes, d. 713

4575 **Ermin, Saint, abbot of Lobbes.**
La plus ancienne vie de s. Ursmer; poème acrostiche inédit de s. Ermin, son successeur [par] Dom Germain Morin, O.S.B. Bruxelles, Imprimerie Polleunis et Ceuterick, 1904.
Extrait des Analecta Bollandiana, t. 23, p. 315–319.
PLatS

4576 **Vos, Joachim Joseph.**
Lobbes, son abbaye et son chapitre; ou, Histoire compléte de Monastère de Saint-Pierre à Lobbes, et du chapitre de Saint-Ursmer à Lobes et à Binche. Louvain, Ch. Peeters, 1865.
2 v. plates, fold. plan. 22 cm.
KAS; MnCS

Usuard, monk of St. Germain-des-Prés, d.ca.875

4577 **Casas Homs, Josep M.**
Una grammàtica inédita d'Usuard.
(*In* Analecta Montserratensia, v. 10, p. 77–129)
PLatS

4578 **Dubois, Jacques, O.S.B.**
Le martyrologe d'Usuard; texte et commentaire. Bruxelles, Société des Bollandistes, 1965.
444 p. facsims. 25 cm.
InStme

Uthred of Boldon, b.ca.1320

4579 **Knowles, David, O.S.B.**
The censured opinions of Uthred of Boldon.
(*In* his: The historian and character, and other essays. Cambridge, 1963. p. 129–170)
PLatS

Vagaggini, Cipriano, 1909-

4580 **Peifer, Claude, O.S.B.**
Feature review of Problemi e orientamenti di spiritualità monastica, biblica e liturgica [di] C. Vagaggini, S. Bovo [et al.]
(*In* Monastic studies, no. 2(1964), p. 137–165)
PLatS

4580a **Lex orandi lex credendi:** miscellanea in onore di P. Cipriano Vagaggini, a cura di Gerardo J. Bekes e Giustino Farnedi. Roma, Editrice Anselmiana, 1980.
377 p. 25 cm. (Studia Anselmiana, 79)
KAS

Van Zeller, Hubert, 1905-

4581 **Van Zeller, Hubert, O.S.B.**
One foot in the cradle; an autobiography. New York, Holt, Rinehart and Winston, 1966.
xi, 282 p. illus., ports. 22 cm.
InStme; KAS; MnCS; MoCo; PLatS

Victor III, Pope, 1027-1087

4582 **Willard, Henry M.**
Abbot Desiderius and the ties between Montecassino and Amalfi in the eleventh century. Montecassino, Badia di Montecassino, 1973.
64 p. illus. 26 cm. (Miscellanea cassinese, 37)
MnCS; PLatS

Virgil, Saint, bishop of Salzburg, 700(ca.)-784

4583　**Hymni de s. Virgilio.** Legenda de s. Virgilio. MS. Vienna, Nationalbibliothek, codex 547, f.1r-56v. Quarto. Saec. 15. Microfilm: MnCH proj. no. 13,877

4584　**Löwe, Heinz.**
Ein literarischer Widersacher des Bonifatius, Virgil von Salzburg, und die Kosmographie des Aethicus Ister. Mainz, Akademie der Wissenschaften und der Literatur, [1952].
90 p. 25 cm.
MnCS

4585　**Vita s. Virgilii episcopi et confessoris.** MS. Benediktinerabtei St. Peter, Salzburg, incunabulum 240, f.49r-69v. Quarto. Saec. 13.
Microfilm: MnCH proj. no. 10,737

Viti, Maria Fortunata, 1827-1922

4586　**Sarra, Andrea.**
Potenza e carità di Dio: beata Maria Fortunata Viti, monaca benedettina. Milano, Editrice Ancora [1967].
390 p. ports., plates. 23 cm.
MnCS

4587　**Un'umile figlia di s. Benedetto;** la serva di Dio, suor Maria Fortunata Viti. Roma, Subiaco, 1935.
129 p.
MoCo

4588　**Veroli, Italy. S. Maria de' Franconi (abbey of Benedictine nuns).**
Suor M. Fortunata Viti, religiosa conversa nel monastero benedettino di S. Maria de' Franconi in Veroli. [n.p., 1928].
53 p. 20 cm.
MnCS

Volk, Paulus, 1889-

4589　**Bibliographie P. Paulus Volk.** [Siegburg, F. Schmitt, 1964?].
23 p. port. 20 cm.
MnCS

Vonier, Anscar, 1875-1938

4590　**Froehle, Charles.**
The idea of sacred sign according to Abbot Anscar Vonier. Rome, Catholic Book Agency, 1971.
vi, 161 p. 25 cm.
InStme; MnCS; MoCo; PLatS

4591　**In memoriam: Abbot Vonier,** 1875-1938. [Buckfast Abbey Publications, 1939].
56 p. illus. 25 cm.
Special number of Buckfast Abbey Chronicle, v. 9, no. 1, 1939.
InStme

Wala, Saint, abbot of Corbie, d. 836

4592　**Paschasius Radbertus.**
Charlemagne's cousins; contemporary lives of Adalard and Wala. Translated, with introductory notes by Allen Cabaniss. [Syracuse, N.Y.], Syracuse University Press [1967].
vii, 266 p. 24 cm.
InStme; PLatS

4593　**Paschasius Radbertus.**
Vita s. Adalhardi abbatis Corbeiensis et Vita Walae abbatis Corbeiensis.
(*In* Monumenta Germaniae historica. Scriptores. Stuttgart, 1963. t. 2, p. 524-569)
MnCS; PLatS

4594　**Weinrich, Lorenz.**
Wala, Graf, Mönch und Rebell; die Biographie eines Karolingers. Lübeck, Matthiesen, 1963.
105 p. geneal. table. 24 cm.
PLatS

Walahfried Strabo, 807-849

4594a　**Stoffler, Hans-Dieter.**
Der Hortulus des Walahfried Strabo; aus dem Kräutergarten des Klosters Reichenau . . . Sigmaringen, Jan Thorbecke Verlag, 1978.
120 p. illus. 24 cm.
MnCS

Walburga, Saint, 710(ca.)-780(ca.)

4595　**Belmont Abbey, Belmont, N.C.**
Saint Walburga's manual; prefaced by a short sketch of the saint's life, by a member of the Benedictine Order. Belmont, N.C., Belmont Abbey Press, 1913.
69 p.
NcBe

4596　**Vita s. Walpurgis virginis.** MS. Cistercienserabtei Lilienfeld, Austria, codex 134, f.113r-116v.
Microfilm: MnCH proj. no. 4429

4597　**Walafrid Strabo.**
Vita s. Walpurgis virginis. MS. Cistercienserabtei Heiligenkreuz, Austria, codex 282, f. 73r-82v. Quarto. Saec. 13.
Microfilm: MnCH proj. no. 4821

Walter, monk of Honnecourt, 11th cent.

4598　**Morin, Germain, O.S.B.**
Un écrivain inconnu du XIe siècle: Walter, moine de Nonnecourt, puis de Vézelay.
16 p. 25 cm.

Extrait de la Revue bénédictine, t.XXII (1905), p. 165–180.
PLatS

Wandrille, Saint, 600(ca.)–663

4599 **Müller-Marquardt, Fritz.**
Die Sprache der alten Vita Wandregiseli. Halle a.S., Verlag von Max Niemeyer, 1912.
xvi, 255 p. 23 cm.
MnCS

Weakland, Rembert George, 1927–

4600 **Catholic University of America, Washington, D.C.**
Convocation for the conferral of an honorary degree on the Most Reverend Rembert G. Weakland, O.S.B., Friday, September 26, 1975 . . . Washington, D.C.
3 p. 23 cm.
PLatS

4601 **Liturgy of the blessing of the Right Reverend Rembert G. Weakland, O.S.B.,** coadjutor archabbot of Saint Vincent, Saint Vincent Basilica, Latrobe, Pennsylvania, August 29, 1963. [Editors: Rev. Campion Gavaler, O.S.B., and Rev. Maurus Wallace, O.S.B. [Latrobe, Pa., Archabbey Press, 1963].
[38] p. music. 14 x 16 cm.
PLatS

4602 **Mitred musician;** [thumbnail sketch of Archabbot Rembert G. Weakland, O.S.B.].
Reprint from: The Priest, v. 19 (1963), p. 788–792
PLatS

Weinzaepfel, Roman, 1813–1895

4603 **Timmermeyer, William F.**
The Rev. Roman Weinzaepfel; an incident in American nativisim, 1841–1847.
148 p. 28 cm.
Thesis–Catholic University of America, Washington, D.C., 1973.
InStme

Wenlok, Walter de, d. 1307

4604 **Harvey, Barbara F., ed.**
Documents illustrating the rule of Walter de Wenlok, abbot of Westminster, 1283–1307. London, Royal Historical Society, 1965.
vii, 285 p. 23 cm.
PLatS

Whiting, Richard, d. 1539

4605 **Crake, Augustine David.**
The last abbot of Glastonbury; a tale of the dissolution of the monasteries. With nine illustrations by George E. Kruger. Oxford, A. R. Mowbray & Co. [1915].
xvi, 250 p. plates. 19 cm.
MnCS

Wilfrid, Saint, archbishop of York, 634–709

4606 **Eddius,** 8th cent.
Eddius Stephanus: Life of Wilfrid.
(*In* Webb, J. F., ed. Lives of the saints. Baltimore, 1965)
PLatS

Wilhelmus, abbot of Hirsau, d. 1091

4607 **Vita Wilhelmi, abbatis Hirsaugiensis.**
MS. Benediktinerabtei Admont, Austria, codex 712, f.136r–165v. Quarto. Saec. 12.
Microfilm: MnCH proj. no. 9751

William, Saint, abbot of St. Benigne, Dijon, 962–1031

4608 **Bulst, Neithard.**
Untersuchungen zu den Klosterreformen Wilhelms von Dijon (962–1031). Bonn, Ludwig Röhrscheid, Verlag, 1973.
330 p. 23 cm.
MnCS

4609 **Chevallier, Gustave.**
Le vénérable Guillaume, abbé de Saint-Bénigne de Dijon, réformateur de l'Ordre Bénédictin au XIe siècle . . . Paris, V. Palmé, 1875.
306 p. 22 cm.
InStme; MnCS

4610 **Rodulphus Glaber.**
Ex Rodulfi Glabri Vita s. Willelmi Divionensis.
(*In* Monumenta Germaniae historica. Scriptores. Stuttgart, 1963. t. 4, p. 655–658)
MnCS; PLatS

William, Saint, of Monte Vergine, 1085–1142

4611 **Mercuro, Celestino, O.S.B.**
Una leggenda medioevale di san Guglielmo da Vercelli. Roma, S. Maria Nova, 1907.
67 p.
AStb

4612 **Mercuro, Celestino, O.S.B.**
Vita di s. Guglielmo da Vercelli, fondatore della badia e della congregazione di

Montevergine, scritta dal suo discipulo s.
Giovanni da Nusco. Roma, Desclée, 1907.
94 p.
AStb

William de Colchester, 1338?-1420

4613 **Pearce, Ernest Harold.**
William de Colchester, abbot of Westminster. London, S.P.C.K., 1915.
92 p.
MoCo

Willibald, Saint 700-787?

4614 **Gretser, Jacob.**
Philippi ecclesiae Eystettensis XXXIX
episcopi de eiusdem ecclesiae divis tutelari-
bus s. Richardo, s. Willibaldo, s. Wuni-
baldo, s. Walpurga commentarius nunc
primum evulgatus . . . Ingolstadii, ex
Typographia Ederiana, 1617.
[37], 593, [57] p. 19 cm.
InStme

4615 **Laudes s. Willibaldi,** sive Cantica latina
in honorem beatissimi ejusdem praesulis
a decem abhinc saeculis collecta. [Eysta-
dii, Carolus Brönner, 1897]
17 p. 28 cm.
MnCS

Willibrord, Saint, bishop of Utrecht, d. 738

4616 **Duckett, Eleanor Shipley.**
Saint Amand and Saint Willibrord:
Belgium and the Netherlands in the
seventh century.
(*In* her: The wandering saints of the
early Middle Ages. New York, 1959. p.
140-164)
PLatS

4617 **Lampen, Willibrord, O.F.M.**
Willibrord en Bonifatius. Amsterdam,
P. N. Van Kampen, 1939.
159 p. plates. 20 cm.
MnCS

Wimmer, Boniface, 1809-1887

4618 **Barry, Colman James, O.S.B.**
Boniface Wimmer, pioneer of the
American Benedictines.
Offprint from: The Catholic Historical
Review, v. 41 (1955), p. 272-296.
MnCS

4619 **Bonifaz Wimmer und König Ludwig:
Briefe.** Copies of letters at St. Vincent
Archabbey. Archives from the following
sources:
Linz, Austria: Bischöfliches Ordinariats-
archiv.

München: Geheimes Hausarchiv.
München: Geheimes Staatsarchiv.
München: Archiv des Ludwig-Missions-
Vereines.
München: Stiftsarchiv St. Bonifaz.
Metten, Germany: Stiftsarchiv.
Scheyern, Germany: Stiftsarchiv.
St. Vincent Archabbey, Pa.: Archives.
Studien und Mitteilungen zur Geschichte
des Benediktinerordens und seiner
Zweige.
PLatS (Archives)

4620 **Doppelfeld, Basilius, O.S.B.**
Mönchtum und kirchlicher Heilsdienst;
Enstehung und Entwicklung des nordame-
rikanischen Benediktinertums im 19. Jahr-
hundert. Münsterschwarzach, Vier-Türme-
Verlag, 1975.
xx, 381 p. 21 cm. (Münsterschwarzacher
Studien, Bd. 22)
MnCS; PLatS

4621 **Goetz, Rhabanus, O.S.B.**
Archabbot Boniface Wimmer; catalog of
his letters to the abbots of Metten taken
from the collection-in-book-form Archives
of St. Vincent upon the following arrangement (as seems to be the best). NO: date,
place, person (to whom addressed). 1964.
19 leaves. 29 cm.
Typescript (Xeroxed).
PLatS

4622 **Hundt, Ferdinand.**
Seiner Gnaden dem Hochwürdigsten
Herrn Abt Bonifacius Wimmer, O.S.B.,
zur Feier seines goldenen Priester-
jubiläums, August 1, 1881.
[4] p. 22 cm.
A poem.
PLatS

4623 **Oetgen, Jerome.**
An American abbot, Boniface Wimmer,
O.S.B., 1809-1887. Latrobe, Pa., The
Archabbey Press [c 1976].
xi, 344 p. illus. 24 cm.
InStme; KAM; KAS; MnCS; MnStj;
MoCo; PLatS; ViBris

4624 **Rt. Rev. Boniface Wimmer, O.S.B.**
(*In* Gresham, John M. Biographical and
historical cyclopedia of Westmoreland
County, Pennsylvania. Philadelphia, 1890.
p. 525-528)
PLatS

4625 **Scherer, Michael Emilio, O.S.B.**
Ein grosser Benediktiner: Abt Michael
Kruse von Sao Paulo (1864-1929). München, Verlag der Bayer. Benediktinerakademie, Abtei St. Bonifaz, 1963.
180 p. plates. 24 cm.

Bonifaz Wimmer – passim.
PLatS

4626 **Szarnicki, Henry A.**
Bishop O'Connor and the German Catholics.
(*In* his: Michael O'Connor, first Catholic bishop of Pittsburgh. Pittsburgh, 1975. p. 74–112)
MnCS; PLatS

4627 **Wilson, Debora, Sister, O.S.B.**
Benedictine higher education and the development of American higher education.
xvi, 335 p. 28 cm.
Thesis (Ph.D.) – University of Michigan, 1969.
PLatS

Winefride, Saint, ca. 600–660

4628 **Robert, abbot of Shrewsbury.**
The admirable life of Saint VVenefride, virgin, martyr, abbesse. Written in Latin about 500 yeares ago, by Robert, monke and priour of Shrewsbury, of the Ven. Order of S. Benedict . . . now translated into English, out of a very ancient and authenticall manuscript, for the edification and comfort of Catholikes, by I. F. of the Society of Iesvs. [St. Omer?] 1635.
[32], 275, [11] p. 14 cm.
The translator is John Falconer, S.J.
PLatS

4629 _____ **London, The Scolar Press,** 1976.
[30], 275, [10] p. front. 20 cm. (English recusant literature, 1558–1640, v. 319)
Facsimile reprint of the 1635 edition.
PLatS

Winslow, Bede, 1888–1959

4630 **Armstrong, Arthur Hilary, ed.**
Rediscovering Eastern Christendom; essays in commemoration of Dom Bede Winslow. London, Darton Longman & Todd [1963].
xvi, 166 p. port. 22 cm.
ILSP; InStme; KAS; PLatS

Wirth, Augustine, 1828–1901

4631 **U.S. Supreme Court.**
The Order of St. Benedict of New Jersey, a corporation, plaintiff in error, vs. Albert Steinhauser, individually and as administrator of the goods, chattels and credits of Augustin Wirth, deceased, defendant in error. Brief in behalf of plaintiff in error upon review of decision of the United States Circuit Court of Appeals for the

Eighth District [by] Otto Kueffner [and] Albert Schaller. New York, Evening Post Job Print. Off. [n.d.].
66 p.
At head of title: In the Supreme Court of the United States. October term, 1913. No. 267.
NcBe; PLatS

Wirtner, Modestus, 1861–1948

4632 **Wheeler, A. G.**
Rev. Modestus Wirtner: biographical sketch and additions and corrections to the miridae in his 1904 list of Western Pennsylvania hemiptera [by] A. G. Wheeler, Jr., and Thomas J. Henry.
Extract from: The Great Lakes Entomologist, v. 10(1977), p. 145–157.
PLatS

Wolfgang, Saint, bishop of Regensburg, 924–994

4633 **Excerpta ex Legenda de S. Wolfgango.**
MS. Benediktinerabtei Melk, Austria, codex 1917, 1, f.76v–85v. Quarto. Saec. 15.
Microfilm: MnCH proj. no. 2202

4634 **Legenda s. Wolfgangi metrica,** cum glossis. MS. Vienna, Nationalbibliothek, codex 3604, f.1r–13v. Quarto. Saec. 15.
Microfilm: MnCH proj. no. 16,815

4635 **Legenda de s. Wolfgango,** Ratisponensi episcopo. Carmen de beato Wolfgango. Oratio de s. Wolfgango. MS. Benediktinerabtei Melk, Austria, codex 1869, f. 289v–305r. Folio. Saec. 15.
Microfilm: MnCH proj. no. 2166

4636 **Legende vom hl. Wolfgang.** MS. Benediktinerabtei St. Peter, Salzburg, codex b.IV.31, f.147v–163r. Quarto. Saec. 16.
Microfilm: MnCH proj. no. 10,417

4637 **Othlo, monk of St. Emmeram.**
Vita s. Wolfgangi. MS. Universitätsbibliothek Graz, Austria, codex 964, f.286r–294r. Quarto. Saec. 15.
Microfilm: MnCH proj. no. 27,027

4638 **Othlo, monk of St. Emmeram.**
Vita s. Wolfgangi episcopi. Finis deest. MS. Vienna, Nationalbibliothek, codex 818, f.107r–116v. Quarto. Saec. 12.
Microfilm: MnCH proj. no. 14,152

4639 **Vita s. Wolfgangi episcopi.** MS. Augustinerchorherrenstift Herzogenburg, Austria, codex 57, f.211r–222r. Folio. Saec. 15.
Microfilm: MnCH proj. no. 3210

4640 **Vita s. Wolfgangi.** MS. Benediktinerabtei Kremsmünster, Austria, codex 128,
f.96r–113v. Saec. 13.
Microfilm: MnCH proj. no. 118

4641 **Vita s. Wolfgangi Ratistonensis epis-
copi.** MS. Benediktinerabtei Lambach,
Austria, codex chart. 212, f.8r–22v.
Saec. 15.
Microfilm: MnCH proj. no. 603

4642 **Vita sancti Wolfgangi episcopi.** MS.
Benediktinerabtei Lambach, Austria,
codex chart. 441, f.5r–15v. Saec. 15.
Microfilm: MnCH proj. no. 730

4643 **Vita s. Wolfgangi,** cum commentario
Hieronymi de Werden. In fine mutila.
MS. Vienna, Nationalbibliothek, codex
3777. 33 f. Folio. Saec. 15.
Microfilm: MnCH proj. no. 17,000

4644 **Schindler, Joseph.**
Der heilige Wolfgang in seinem Leben
und Wirken quellenmässig dargestellt.
Prag, Rohlicek & Sievers, 1885.
viii, 204 p. 21 cm.
KAS

Wolfsgruber, Cölestin, 1848–1924

4645 **Braulik, Georg Peter, O.S.B.**
Cölestin Wolfsgruber, O.S.B., Hofprediger und Professor für Kirchengeschichte
(1848–1924). Wien, Herder [1968].
121 p. 23 cm. (Wiener Beiträge zur
Theologie, Bd. 19)

MnCS
Originally issued as thesis, Universität
Wien.

Wolter, Maurus, 1825–1890

4646 **Reetz, Benedikt, O.S.B.**
Die monastischen Grundprinzipien nach
Erzabt Dr. Maurus Wolter.
(*In* Beuron, 1863–1963; Festschrift zum
hundertjährigen Bestehen der Erzabtei
. . . Beuron, 1963. p. 19–38)
PLatS

Wulfstan, archbishop of York, d. 1023

4646a **Gatch, Milton M.**
Preaching and theology in Anglo-Saxon
England: Aelfric and Wulfstan. Toronto,
University of Toronto Press, 1977.
266 p. 22 cm.
InStme; MnCS

Wulfstan, Saint, archbishop of Worcester, 1012?–1095

4647 **The portiforium of Saint Wulstan** (Corpus Christi College, Cambridge, Ms.
391). Edited by Dom Anselm Hughes.
Leighton Buzzard, England, Henry
Bradshaw Society, 1958–1960.
2 v. 23 cm. (Henry Bradshaw Society, 89)
MnCS

XV. BENEDICTINE BROTHERS

1. GENERAL WORKS

4648 **Benedictines. Congregations. Bavarian.**
Satzungen der Bayerischen Benedik-tiner-Kongregation von dem hl. Schutzen-gelen . . . Auszug für Laienbrüder und Oblaten. Augsburg, Mühlberger, 1922.
56 p.
AStb; MnCS

4649 **Botz, Paschal Robert, O.S.B.**
The spiritual direction of professed brothers.
(*In* Report of the Benedictine Brother In-structors' Convention, St. Meinrad Abbey, St. Meinrad, Ind., June 9–11, 1942, p. 102–122)
MnCS

4650 **Davis, Cyprian, O.S.B.**
The familia at Cluny, 800–1350.
2 v. 27 cm.
Thesis (Ph.D.) – Université Catholique de Louvain, 1977.
Xeroxed typescript.
InStme

4651 **Eckardt, Maternus, O.S.B.**
Der Bruder im Beuroner Kloster.
(*In* Beuron, 1863–1963; Festschrift zum hundertjährigen Bestehen der Erzabtei . . . Beuron, 1963. p. 473–485)
PLatS

4652 **Ernest, Brother.**
Our Brothers. New York, Scott, Fores-man and Co., 1931.
171 p.
Benedictine brothers: p. 18–20.
InFer

4653 **Leonard, Ludger, O.S.B.**
The Benedictine lay brother; a manual of instruction and devotion for the use of brothers and sisters of the Order of St. Benedict. Adapted from the German by a monk of Fort Augustus. Fort Augustus [Scotland], Abbey Press, 1888.
iv, 319 p. 15 cm.
InStme; PSaS; WaOSM

4654 **Leonard, Ludger, O.S.B.**
Die klösterliche Tagesordnung; Anlei-tung für Ordensbrüder und Ordensschwes-tern, die täglichen Uebungen ihres hl. Standes im rechten Geist zu verrichten . . . 6. verm. u. verb. Aufl. Regensburg, J. Kösel, 1924.
viii, 586 p. 16 cm.
InStme

4655 **Ordinationes et doctrinae pro fratribus minoribus** (extractum de constitutione

Mellicensi). MS. Abtei Kremsmünster, Austria, codex 20, f.18r–29v. Saec. 15.
Microfilm: MnCH proj. no. 20

4656 **Mohr, Charles Henry, O.S.B.**
Supplement to the Handbuch für die Laienbrüder. St. Leo Abbey, Fla. [192-?].
15 p.
ArStb

4657 **Regel der Conversen.** MS. Benediktin-erabtei Admont, Austria, codex 757, f. 19v–30v. Octavo. Saec. 15.
Microfilm: MnCH proj. no. 9795

4658 **Regula fratrum conversorum Ordinis Sancti Benedicti.** Germanice. Incipit: Wie vol das ist das. MS. Vienna, Na-tionalbibliothek, codex 3021, f.176r–180r. Octavo. Saec. 15.
Microfilm: MnCH proj. no. 16,252

4659 **St. Meinrad Archabbey, St. Meinrad, Ind.**
The Benedictine junior brother. St. Meinrad, Ind. [1934].
unpaged. illus.
AStb

4660 **Springer, Anton Heinrich.**
Commentatio de artificibus monachis et laicis medii aevi. Bonnae, Carolus Georgus, 1861.
44 p. 27 cm.
MnCS

4661 **Statuta von den Laienbrüdern.** Incipit: Wann ein lay den orden versuchen. MS. Vienna, Nationalbibliothek, codex 2968, f.167v–173v. Quarto. Saec. 15.
Microfilm: MnCH proj. no. 16,212

2. INVESTITURE AND PROFESSION

4662 **Modus professionis pro conversis.** MS. Benediktinerabtei Lambach, Austria, codex chart. 435, f.108v, 205r–205v. Saec. 15.
Microfilm: MnCH proj. no. 725

4663 **Professio conversorum.** Germanice. In-cipit: In dem Namen . . . Ich brueder N. von Maennsee. MS. Vienna, National-bibliothek, codex 3348. f. 179r–184v. Saec. 15.
Microfilm: MnCH proj. no. 16,770

3. PRAYER BOOKS

4664 **Hie ist vermerkt was dye laypruder petten sullen.** MS. Vienna, National-bibliothek, codex 2731, f.54v–57v. Oc-tavo. Saec. 15.
Microfilm: MnCH proj. no. 16,032

4665 **Latin and English of the monastic com-munity prayers.** Printed as manuscript for the use of the brothers at St. Bene-dict's Abbey, Atchison, Kans. [Atchi-son, Kans., Abbey Student Press, 1953?] 68 p. 12 cm.
KAS

4666 **Prime and Compline of the monastic breviary.** Printed as manuscript for the use of the Benedictine brothers of St. Benedict's Abbey, Atchison, Kans. [Atchison, Kans., Abbey Student Press] 1960. 44 p. 24 cm.
MnCS

XVI. BENEDICTINE OBLATES

1. GENERAL WORKS

4667 **Angelis, Seraphinus de.**
De s. Benedicti oblatis.
(*In* his: De fidelium associationibus.
Neapoli, 1959. v. 1, p. 253–261)
PLatS

4668 **Azcárate, Andrés, O.S.B.**
Tesoro del oblato benedictino. Buenos
Aires, Padres Benedictinos, 1930.
209 p. 16 cm.
MnCS

4669 **Benedictines. Congregations. Bavarian.**
Satzungen der Bayerischen Benedik-
tiner-Kongregation von dem hl.
Schutzengel . . . Auszug für Laienbrüder
und Oblaten. Augsburg, Mühlberger, 1922.
56 p.
AStb; MnCS

4670 **Une Congrégation actuelle:** les Oblates
Régulières Bénédictines de Notre-Dame.
[Paris, Maison des Oblates de n.-D.
1938].
12 p. 21 cm.
KAS

4671 **Eiten, Robert B.**
A layman's way to perfection. St. Mein-
rad, Ind., A Grail Publication, 1953.
117 p.
Benedictine Oblates: p. 105 sq.
InFer

4672 **Feligonde, Jean, O.S.B.**
La paroisse de l'Hay les Roses et les
Oblats de Saint Benoît.
(*In* Paroisse et liturgie; collection de pas-
torale liturgique, n. 8, p. 7–16)
PLatS

4673 **Moretti, Emmanuella, Abbes, O.S.B.**
L'Oblato Benedettino; lineamenti di
spiritualità. [Parma, Scuola tipografica
benedettina, 1969].
30 p. plates. 22 cm.
MnCS

4674 **Reger, Ambrose, O.S.B.**
The Secular Oblates of St. Benedict. St.
Bernard Abbey, Ala. [1932].
38 p.
AStb

4675 **The Secular Institute of St. Benedict:
Constitution.** Conception, Mo., Benedictine Institute, 1968.
30 p.
AStb

2. HANDBOOKS

4676 **Daily companion for Oblates of St. Benedict.** [4th rev. ed.]. St. Meinrad, Ind.,
Abbey Press [1960].

96 p. 16 cm.
KAS

4677 **Daily companion for Secular Oblates of
St. Benedict.** St. Meinrad, Ind., Grail
Publications [1963].
100 p. 15 cm.
Originally published by Benedictine Con-
vent of Perpetual Adoration, Clyde, Mo.
MnCS

4678 **Daily companion for Oblates of St. Benedict.** 5th rev. ed. St. Meinrad, Ind.,
Abbey Press, 1974.
141 p. illus. 16 cm.
InStme

4679 **Joliette, Canada (Quebec).** Abbaye de
Notre-Dame-de-la-Paix.
Manuel des Oblats et Oblates de saint
Benoît de l'Abbaye de Notre-Dame-de-la-
Paix. Mont-Laurier, P.Q., Canada, Edi-
tions de Moniales Bénédictines [1977].
96 p. illus. 16 cm.
CaQJo

4680 **Mont-Laurier, Canada (Quebec).** Abbaye
de Mont-de-la-Rédemption.
Manuel des Oblats et Oblates de saint
Benoît de l'Abbaye du Mont-de-la-Rédemption du Mont-Laurier. Mont-Laurier, P.Q.,
Canada, Editions de Moniales Bénédictins
[1976].
96 p. illus. 16 cm.
CaQMo; MnCS

4681 **Oer, Sebastien von, O.S.B.**
Handbuch für Oblaten des hl. Vaters
Benediktus. Beuron, 1898.
v, 150 p. 16 cm.
InStme

4682 **Prinknash Abbey, England.**
The Benedictine Oblate's manual. Edited
by a monk of Prinknash Priory, Gloucester. [Gloucester, 1928].
240 p. 18 cm.
PLatS

4683 **St. John's Abbey, Collegeville, Minn.**
Manual for Oblates of St. Benedict, pre-
pared by monks of St. John's Abbey under
the direction of the National Conference of
Oblate Directors. [6th ed.]. Collegeville,
Minn., St. John's Abbey Press, 1961.
viii, 212 p. 16 cm.
InStme

4684 **Saint Placid Hall manual.** St. Meinrad,
Ind., St. Meinrad's Abbey, 1941.
38 p. 15 cm.
MnCS

4685 **St. Vincent Archabbey, Latrobe, Pa.**
Manual for Benedictine Oblates. Edited
by the monks of St. Vincent Archabbey.

[4th ed.]. Latrobe, Pa., Saint Vincent Archabbey Press [1962].
> 139 p. illus. 18 cm.
> InStme; MnCS; NcBe; PLatS

3. PERIODICALS

4686 **Messager des Oblats de la Congrégation
Bénédictine Belge.** Abbaye de Maredsous. no. 1–133 [19--?]–1953. Quarterly.
Continued as Revue monastique, no.
134–157, 1954–59. Continued as Lumière
du Christ, no. 158–   1960–
> KAS

4. READING LISTS

4687 **St. John's Abbey, Collegeville, Minn.**
Oblate library catalog, July, 1958. [Col-
legeville, Minn., St. John's Abbey].
> 70 p. 23 cm.
> MnCS

5. SPIRITUAL LIFE

4688 **Simon, George Abel.**
Commentary for Benedictine Oblates on
the Rule of St. Benedict. Translated from
the second French edition by Leonard
Doyle. Collegeville, Minn., St. John's Abbey Press, 1950.
> xxvi, 511 p. 20 cm.
> KAS; MnCS; NcBe

XVII. BENEDICTINE NUNS AND SISTERS

A. BENEDICTINE NUNS

1. General Works

4689 **Benedettine, Monache.**
(*In* Dizionario degli Istituti di Perfezione. Rome, 1973. vol. 1, col. 1222–1246)
MnCS

4689a **Bonanni, Philippo, S.J.**
Ordinum religiosorum in Ecclesia militanti catalogus, eorumque indumenta in iconibus expressa. Roma, De Rossi, 1706–41.
4 v.
v. 2: Virgines Deo dicatae.
AStb

4690 **Brussels, Belgium. Our Blessed Lady the Perpetual Virgin Mary (abbey of Benedictine nuns)**
Statutes compiled for the better observation of the Holy Rule of the Most Glorious Father and Patriarch S. Benedict . . . Gant, Printed by I. Dooms [1632].
3 parts.
MnCS(microfilm)

4691 **Diurnale privatum pro monialibus.** MS. Augustinerchorherrenstift St. Florian, Austria, codex XI, 451. 191 f. Sextodecimo. Saec. 15 & 16.
Microfilm: MnCH proj. no. 2663

4692 **Eckenstein, Lina.**
Women under monasticism; chapters on saint-lore and convent life between A.D. 500 and A.D. 1500. Cambridge [England], University Press, 1896.
xv, 496 p. 24 cm.
KAM; NcBe; NdRi; PLatS

4693 **Forma chartae vulgaris pro monialibus datae.** Germanice. Benediktinerabtei Melk, Austria, codex 959, f. 203r–205v. Quarto. Saec. 15.
Microfilm: MnCH proj. no. 1762

4694 **Hilpisch, Stephanus, O.S.B.**
Geschichte der Benediktinerinnen. St. Ottilien, Eos Verlag der Erzabtei, 1951.
v, 135 p. 21 cm.
MnCS

4695 **Jouarre, France (abbey of Benedictine nuns).**
La Règle du bienheureux père Saint Benoît et les Constitutions de l'Abbaye de Notre-Dame de Jouarre, approuvées par le Saint-Siège le 12 septembre 1884. La Chapelle-Montligeon, Imprimerie de Montligeon, 1949.
216 p. 22 cm.
CaQStB

4695a **Kemp-Welch, Alice.**
Of six mediaeval women . . . Williamstown, Mass., 1972.
xxix, 188 p. 20 cm.
Partial contents: p. 1–28, A tenth-century romance-writer, Roswitha the nun; p. 57–82, A thirteenth-century mystic and beguine, Mechtild of Magdeburg.
MnCS

4696 **Leclercq, Jean, O.S.B.**
Moines et moniales, ont-ils un avenir? Bruxelles, Editions Lumen Vitae, 1971.
263 p. 19 cm.
MnCS

4697 **Linage Conde, Antonio.**
Una regla monastica riojana feminina des siglo X: al "Libellus a Regula Sancti Benedicti Subtractatus." Salamanca, Universidad, 1973.
xiii, 142 p. facsims. 26 cm.
MnCS

4698 **Moniales et sorores vel oblatae regulares O.S.B.** Desumptum ex Catalogo familiarum confoederatarum O.S.B. [Romae] Published periodically.
KAS; MnCS; InStme; PLatS; ViBris

4699 **Müller, Joannes, O.S.B.**
Atlas O.S.B. Benedictinorum per orbem praesentia. Benedictines throughout the world . . . Romae, Editiones Anselmianae, 1973.
2 v. 22–32 cm.
Contents: I. Index monasteriorum. II. Tabulae geographicae.
Lists 300-plus abbeys of Benedictine nuns.
InStme; KAS; MnCS; PLatS

4700 **Rode, Joannes, O.S.B.**
Statuta pro monialibus Ordinis S. Benedicti. Germanice. MS. Benediktinerabtei Göttweig, Austria, codex 499, f. 1r–24v. Quarto. Saec. 15.
Microfilm: MnCH proj. no. 3754

4701 **Schlitpacher, Johannes, O.S.B.**
Copia chartae ejusmodi vulgaris pro monialibus Ord. S. Benedicti dandae. Germanice. MS. Benediktinerabtei Melk, Austria, codex 896, f.IVr. Quarto. Saec. 15.
Microfilm: MnCH proj. no. 1715

4702 **Schlitpacher, Johannes, O.S.B.**
Epistola ad Bernardum de Kreyburg de modo reformandi et dispensandi cum monialibus Ordinis S. Benedicti dioecesis Salisburgensis. MS. Benediktinerabtei

Melk, Austria, codex 896, f.196v. Quarto.
Saec. 15.
Microfilm: MnCH proj. no. 1715

4703 **Schneider, Edouard.**
Cellules et couvants bénédictins. Paris,
P. Amiot, 1958.
229 p.
MnCS

4703a **Schuller, Helga.**
Dos – praebenda – peculium [der
weiblichen Kongregationen des Mittel-
alters.]
(*In* Festschrift Friedrich Hausmann.
Graz, 1977. p. 453–487)
The article covers abbeys of nuns (Bene-
dictine, Cistercian, Augustinian and Pre-
monstratensian) in southern Germany,
Austria and Switzerland.
MnCS

4704 **Statuta pro monialibus Ordinis S. Benedicti, germanice.** Regula s. Benedicti,
germanice, pro monialibus. MS. Benediktinerabtei Göttweig, Austria, codex
499. 75 f. Quarto. Saec. 15.
Microfilm: MnCH proj. no. 2754

4705 **Tamburini, Ascanio, C.V.O.S.B.**
De iure abbatissarum et monialium; sive,
Praxis gubernandi moniales . . . cui accedunt Sacrae Rotae Romanae decisiones
. . . una cum formulario epistolarum
pastoralium . . . aliorumque agendorum
pro eisdem monialibus . . . Editio emendata & aucta. Lugduni, Laurentius Anisson, 1668.
[16], 220, [31], 80, 36 p. 37 cm.
KAS

4705a **Tornare alle fonti;** il primo convegno
della abbadesse e priore benedettine in
Italia, 24–29 ottobre 1966. [Sorrento,
Italia, Monsterio di S. Paolo, 1966.
283 p. 22 cm.
MnCS

4706 **Van Zeller, Hubert, O.S.B.**
Benedictine life at Münster Abbey. [Ex-
eter, Catholic Records Press] n.d.
23 p. plates. 12 cm.
MnCS

4707 **Van Zeller, Hubert, O.S.B.**
The Benedictine nun, her story and aim.
Baltimore, Helicon [1965].
271 p. 22 cm.
AStb; InStme; KAS; MnCS; MoCo

4708 **Viboldone, Italy (abbey of Benedictine
nuns).**
Galateo monastico. Viboldone, Scuola
tipografico San Benedetto [1960].
xv, 205 p. 19 cm.
PLatS

4709 **Walter, Silja (Sr. M. Hedwig).**
Der Tag der benediktinischen Nonne.
(*In* her: Das Kloster am Rande der Stadt.
Zürich, 1971. p. 13–52)
MnCS

4710 **Weakland, Rembert George, O.S.B.**
Conference de Pére Abbé Primat aux abbesses, jeudi matin, 2. mai [n.d.].
11 p. 30 cm.
PLatS

2. Investiture and Profession

4711 **Die Consecration oder Weihung der
Kloster Jungfrauen,** nach Inhalt des
Römischen Pontifical, und soll der ganze
Act, nach Anzeigung des Pontifical
gehalten werden, wie solches gegen-
wärtige aus dem Pontifical verteutschte
Rubr. anzeigen. MS. Benediktinerin-
nenabtei Nonnberg, Salzburg, codex 23
D 21. 72 f. Octavo. Saec. 18.
Microfilm: MnCH proj. no. 10,901

4712 **Form und Weiss wie eine Novizin** auf
die ihr vorgetragene Fragen vor der
heiligen Profession, oder auf Einklei-
dung antworten köne. MS. Benediktinerinnenabtei Nonnberg, Salzburg,
codex 23 D 27. 27 f. Octavo. Saec. 17.
Microfilm: MnCH proj. no. 10,899

4713 **Guique, Georges.**
Les Bénédictines chez les Bénédictins;
profession de religieuses à l'Abbaye de
Savigny en Lyonnais (XVe siècle). Paris,
Imprimerie Nationale, 1902.
24 p. 25 cm.
Offprint from Bulletin historique et
philologique, 1901.
KAS

4714 **Stegbuecher, Joachim, O.S.B.**
Vorbereitung auf die heilige Profess:
Geistliche Uebungen auf 6 Tag ausgethai-
let und einer geistlichen Braut zu mehrerer Vorbereitung auf ihre Weihe und of-
fentliche Vermählung mit Christo dem
Herrn. MS. Benediktinerinnenabtei Nonnberg, Salzburg, codex 23 E 33. 188 f. Octavo. Saec. 17(1604).
Microfilm: MnCH proj. no. 10,935

3. Other Nuns Following
the Rule of St. Benedict:

Cistercian Nuns

4715 **Demoulin, Louis.**
Le Jansénisme et l'Abbaye d'Orval.
Bruxelle, Institut historique belge de
Rome, 1976.
332 p. illus. 25 cm.
MnCS

4716 Du Taillis, O. Vergé.
Chroniques de l'Abbaye Royale de Maubuisson, 1236–1738. Paris, Librairie Académique Perrin, 1947.
252 p. illus. 20 cm.
MnCS

4717 Huemer, Blasius, O.S.B.
Verzeichnis der deutschen Cisterziensinerinnenklöster.
(*In* Germania monastica, Augsburg, 1967. p. 139–185)
PLatS

4718 Idung, of Prüfening.
Cistercians and Cluniacs; the case for Cîteaux. Translated by Jeremiah F. O'Sullivan . . . Kalamazoo, Cistercian Publications, 1977.
230 p. 23 cm.
Translation of Dialogus duorum monachorum, and De quatuor quaestionibus.
InStme

4719 Kastner, August.
Archiv für die Geschichte des Bisthums Breslau. Neisse, 1859–63.
3 v. 21 cm.
Partial contents: 2. Bd. Geschichte und Beschreibung des fürstlichen jungfräulichen Klosterstiftes Cistercienser Ordens in Trebnitz.
KAS

4720 Nichols, John A.
The history and cartulary of the Cistercian nuns of Marham Abbey, 1249–1536.
vi, 316 leaves. 29 cm.
Thesis – Kent State University, 1974.
MnCS(microfilm)

4721 Trouncer, Margaret (Lahey).
The reluctant abbess: Angelique Arnauld of Port-Royal (1591–1661). New York, Sheed and Ward [1957].
277 p. 22 cm.
MnCS

4722 Zeimet, Johannes.
Die Cistercienserinnenabtei St. Katharinen b. Linz a. Rh. Augsburg, Benno Filser Verlag, 1929.
242 p. illus. 23 cm.
MnCS

B. BENEDICTINE SISTERS

1. General Works

4723 Benedettine, Suore.
(*In* Dizionario degli Istituti di Perfezione. Roma, 1973. vol. 1, col. 1246–1283)
MnCS

4723a Climb along the cutting edge; an analysis of change in religious life [by] Joan

Chittister [et al.]. New York, Paulist Press, 1977.
xiv, 304 p. 23 cm.
MnCS; MoCo

4724 Jones, Susanna, Sister, O.S.B.
The American Benedictine Sister; a historical profile.
13 p. 28 cm.
Typescript.
InFer

4725 Listen; testament of the Federation of Saint Gertrude according to the Rule of St. Benedict. Richardton, N.D., Assumption Abbey, 1976.
47 p.
MoCo

4726 Monasteria monialium et sororum O.S.B.; appendix to SS. Patriarchae Benedicti Confoederatae. Rome, Sant' Anselmo, 1975.
Lists 300-plus abbeys of Benedictine nuns and 500-plus convents of Benedictine sisters.
InStme; KAS; MnCS; PLatS; ViBris

4727 Prager, Mirjam, O.S.B.
Die religiösen Frauenorden. Aschaffenburg, P. Pattloch, 1968.
164 p. 19 cm.
MnCS

4728 St. Benedict's Convent, St. Joseph, Minn.
Seekers of God. St. Joseph, Minn., Convent of St. Benedict [1957?].
[32] p. illus. 21 cm.
MnStj; PLatS

4729 Tate, Judith, Sister, O.S.B.
Sisters of the world. [New York], Herder and Herder [1966].
141 p. 21 cm.
ICSS; InStme; MnStj; MoCo; OKShG

2. Canon Law

4730 Fontette, Micheline de.
Les religieuses à l'age classique du droit canon; recherches sur les structures juridiques des branches féminines des ordres . . . Paris, J. Vrin, 1964.
170 p. 25 cm.
Revision of the author's thesis.
MnCS

3. Congregations

Grande-Sauve

4731 Cirot de la Ville, abbé.
Histoire de l'Abbaye et Congrégation de Notre-Dame de la Grande-Sauve, Ordre du

Saint Benoît, en Guienne. Paris, Méquig-
non junior, 1844.
2 v. plates, plan. 21 cm.
KAS

Maredsous

4732 **La Congrégation des Soeurs de Saint
Benoît de Maredsous** à la Maison
d'Emmaus. [Namur, 1941].
14 p.
CaQStB

St. Benedict

4733 **Declarations on the Rule of our holy
father Benedict** and constitutions of the
Congregation of St. Benedict. St.
Joseph, Minn., 1958.
107 p. 19 cm.
MnCS

St. Scholastica

4734 **Call to life,** Sisters of Saint Benedict,
constitutions of the Federation of Saint
Scholastica, according to the Rule of
Saint Benedict. [Erie, Pa., Benet Press,
1974].
73 p.
MoCo

4. Constitutions

4735 **St. Benedict's Convent, Erie, Pa.**
Constitutions of the Benedictine sisters,
Erie, Pa. Approved Dec. 7, 1880. Erie, Pa.,
St. Benedict's Convent, 1880.
114, [8] p. 13 cm.
PLatS

4736 **St. Walburg's Convent, Covington,
Ky.**
Constitutions of St. Walburg's Monas-
tery of Benedictine sisters of Covington.
Covington, Ky., 1890.
136 p. 15 cm.
PLatS

5. Directories

4737 **Catalogue of the nuns and convents of
the holy Order of St. Benedict** in the
United States. [Beatty, Pa.], St. Vincent's Abbey, 1879.
69 p. 22 cm.
PLatS

4738 **Sarnen, Switzerland. St. Andreas (Benedictine convent).**
Catalog des Benedictinerinnen-Klosters
St. Andreas in Sarnen (Obwalden) und
seiner Filiale in Amerika. Sarnen, Druck
von Jos. Müller, 1888.

12 p. 16 cm.
PLatS

6. Education

4739 **Highbaugh, Assunta, Sister, O.S.B.**
An analysis of the teacher-education pro-
grams of the Benedictine sisters in the
United States. Washington, Catholic Uni-
versity of America, 1961.
xi, 189 p. 23 cm.
Thesis – Catholic University of America,
Washington, D.C.
InStme; KAS; MnCS; PLatS

4740 **Zimmer, Kathryn, Sister, O.S.B.**
Role of American Benedictine institu-
tions of higher education for women. [Bis-
marck, N.D., Annunciation Priory, 1962].
5 leaves. 28 cm.
Summary of doctoral dissertation,
Catholic University of America, Washing-
ton, D.C.
Reproduced from typed copy.
PLatS

7. Investiture and Profession

4741 **Ceremony of profession of vows,** Our
Lady of Peace Chapel, St. Scholastica
Priory, Duluth, Minn. [1964?].
15 p. 21 cm.
MnCS

4742 **Ceremony of profession of vows,** the
Sisters of St. Benedict, adapted from
the Monastic Ritual of the American
Cassinese Congregation of the Order of
St. Benedict. St. Joseph, Minn., Sisters
of the Order of St. Benedict, 1953.
39 p. 16 cm.
MnCS

4743 **St. Benedict's Convent, St. Joseph,
Minn.**
Golden jubilee profession of vows accord-
ing to the rite used by the Sisters of Saint
Benedict. Adapted from the "Caeremoniale
monasticum" (1st ed., 1875) of the
American Cassinese Congregation of the
Order of Saint Benedict, St. Joseph, Minn.,
St. Benedict's Convent, 1937.
18 p. 15 cm.
MnStj(Archives)

4744 **St. Paul's Priory, St. Paul, Minn.**
Reception of novices according to the
rite used by the Sisters of St. Benedict,
adapted from the Caeremoniale Monasti-
cum, first edition, 1875, of the American
Cassinese Congregation of the Order of St.
Benedict. St. Paul, Minn., St. Paul's
Priory, 1953.

36 p. 16 cm.
MnCS

8. Missionary Work

4745 **Missionary Benedictine Sisters.**
Sixtieth anniversary of the Congregation
of the Benedictine Missionary Sisters
[1885–1945]. [n.p.], 1945.
32 p. illus. 20 cm.
MnCS

9. Obituaries

4746 **Necrology, Federation of St. Benedict.**
St. Joseph, Minn., 1976.
13 p. 22 cm.
MnStj(Archives)

10. Prayer Books

4747 **The Day Hours [Diurnale] of the Divine
Office,** with the proper of the season.
Compiled and edited by the Benedictine Sisters of Perpetual Adoration in
accord with the "Breviarium Monasticum" edition of the abbot primate, 1963.
[n.p.] 1964.
294 p. 22 cm.
PLatS

11. Retreats

4748 **Behrendt, Roland, O.S.B.**
The consecration of virgins; conferences
to Benedictine sisters. Collegeville, Minn.,
St. John's Abbey, 1964.
198 p. 28 cm.
Multigraphed.
MnCS

12. Spiritual Life

4749 **Mercier, James, O.S.B.**
Short spiritual treatises on some funda-
mental truths, written for the Sisters of St.
Gertrude's Community, Cottonwood,
Idaho. 1927 (1917).
138, 187 p. 23 cm.
MnCS

4750 **Romero, Mary Jane, Sister, O.S.B.**
Seeking; a paraphrase of the Rule of
Saint Benedict, with commentary. College-
ville, Minn., The Liturgical Press [1972].
xiv, 67 p. 20 cm.
KAS; MnCS

13. By Country (for nuns and sisters)

See also names of individual abbeys and
convents in chapter 12.

Austria

4751 **Catalogi monachorum et monianlium
O.S.B.:** S. Petri, Salzburg . . . Nonn-
berg i Salzburg, St. Hemma i Gurk,
Säben i Tirol. [n.p.] 1913.
113–165 p. 14 cm.
AStb; MnCS

4752 **Chronik des adeligen Benediktiner-
Frauen-Stiftes Nonnberg in Salzburg;**
vom Entstehen desselben [ca. 700]
bis zum Jahre 1840, aus den Quellen
bearbeitet von P. Franz Esterl, aus dem
Stifte St. Peter. Salzburg, Franz Xaver
Duyle, 1841.
xii, 267 p. 18 cm.
MnCS

4753 **Stift Nonnberg zu Salzburg im Wandel
der Zeiten,** nach Aufzeichnungen der
langjährigen Archivarin Frau M. Regintrudis Reichlin von Meldegg, gest. 1943.
Salzburg, Anton Pustet [1953].
88 p. plates, facsims. 21 cm.
MnCS

Canada

4754 **Hubicz, Edward M.**
The Benedictine Sisters.
(*In* his: Polish churches in Manitoba.
London, 1960. p. 43–49)
PLatS

England

4755 **Bennett, A. H.**
Through an Anglican sisterhood to
Rome, by A. H. Bennett, with a preface by
Sr. Scholastica M. Ewart . . . London,
New York, Longmans, Green and Co.,
1914.
xi, 203 p. plates. 20 cm.
KAS

4756 **Cook, George Henry.**
Mediaeval nunneries.
(*In* his: English monasteries in the Mid-
dle Ages. London, 1961. p. 220–232)
PLatS

4757 **Fosbrooke, T. D.**
British monachism; manners & customs
of the monks and nuns of England. New
ed. London, Nichols, 1817.
560 p. illus.
AStb; MnCS

4758 **Power, Eileen.**
Medieval English nunneries, ca.
1275–1535. New York, Biblo and Tannen,
1964.
xiv, 724 p. illus. 24 cm.
First published, Cambridge, 1922.
KAM; MnCS

France

4758a **Chaussy, Yves, O.S.B.**
Les Bénédictines et le réforme catholique en France au XVIIIe siècle. [Paris], Editions de la Source, 1975.
2 v. maps, 22 cm.
MnCS

Malta

4759 **Notabile, Malta. San Pietro (Benedictine monastery).**
Notitie intorno ai monaci ed alle monache dell'Ordine di San Benedetto in Malta. [n.d.]
41 leaves. 30x21 cm.
Microfilm: MnCH, Malta project no. 302

North America

4760 **St. John's Abbey, Collegeville, Minn.**
American Benedictine foundations (portfolio). [Collegeville, Minn., The Scriptorium, 1960].
44x29 cm.
Includes motherhouses of Benedictine sisters.
MnCS

Swabia

4761 **Horn, Adam.**
Dome, Kirchen und Klöster in Bayr. Schwaben. Nach alten Vorlagen. Frankfurt am Main, W. Weidlich, 1963.
247 p. illus., fold. map. 19 cm.
PLatS

United States

4762 **Federation of St. Benedict: a chronicle.**
[Bismarck, N.D., Annunciation Priory, 1975].
various pagings. 28 cm.
A compilation of the histories of each priory in the Federation.
MnStj(Archives)

4763 **Catalogue of the nuns and convents of the holy Order of St. Benedict in the United States.** Compiled from information furnished by each convent and arranged according to date of profession and year of erection respectively, by a member of St. Vincent's Abbey, Pa. [Beatty, Pa., Printed at St. Vincent's Abbey, 1879].
69 p. 22 cm.
KAS; PLatS

4764 **Conference of American Benedictine Prioresses,** Norfolk, Nebr., March 7, 1975.

Upon this tradition; a statement of monastic values in the lives of American Benedictine sisters. Erie, Pa., Benet Press, 1975.
[8] p.
MnStj

4765 **Conference of American Benedictine Prioresses,** Madison, Wisconsin, March 5, 1978.
Of time made holy; a statement on the Liturgy of the Hours in the lives of American Benedictine Sisters. Erie, Pa., Benet Arts, 1978.
[12] p. (Upon this tradition, II)
MnStj

4766 **Highbaugh, Assunta, Sister, O.S.B.**
An analysis of the teacher-education programs of the Benedictine Sisters in the United States. Washington, Catholic University of America, 1961.
xi, 189 p. map, tables. 23 cm.
Thesis – Catholic University of America, Washington, D.C.
InStme; KAS; MnCS; PLatS

4767 **Koch, Mary Imelda, Sister, O.S.B.**
By the power of the vine; history of the Missionary Benedictine Sisters in the United States, 1922–1952. Collegeville, Minn., St. John's University Press, 1964.
118 p. illus.
Thesis (M.A.)–St. John's University, Collegeville, Minn.
MoCo

4768 **St. John's Abbey, Collegeville, Minn.**
American Benedictine foundations (portfolio). [Collegeville, Minn., The Scriptorium, 1960].
44x29 cm.
Includes motherhouses of Benedictine Sisters.
MnCS

4769 **St. Joseph's Convent, St. Marys, Pa.**
Catalogue of the nuns and convents of the Order of St. Benedict in the United States. Compiled from information furnished by each convent and arranged according to date of profession and year of erection respectively. To which is added a sketch of their work in half a century. By the Sisters of St. Marys, Elk Co., Pa. St. Marys, Pa., Herald Printing House, 1903.
115, 20 p. plates. 24 cm.
PLatS

4770 **Zimmer, Kathryn, Sister, O.S.B.**
Role of American Benedictine institutions of higher education for women. [Bismarck, N.D., Annunciation Priory, 1962].
5 leaves. 28 cm.

Summary of a doctoral dissertation, Catholic University of America, Washington, D.C.

Reproduced from typed copy.

PLatS

14. Independent Benedictine Sisterhoods

Benedictine Servants of the Poor

4771 **La Congrégation des servantes des pauvres,** oblates Bénédictines. [Lyon, Lescuyer et fils, 1956].
77 p. illus., plates. 19 cm.
MnCS

Benedictine Sisters of Perpetual Adoration

4772 **100 years for you;** the story of the Benedictine Sisters of Perpetual Adoration. St. Louis, Mo., 1973.
MoCo

Benedictine Sisters of the Blessed Sacrament

4773 **Constitutions sur la Règle de Saint-Benoît,** pour les religieuses bénédictines de l'adoration perpétuelle de Très-Saint-Sacrement, confirmées et approuvées par N.S.P. le Pape Clément XI. Paris, Imprimerie de Le Normant, 1817.
177 p.
CaQStB

4774 **Mechtilde Saint-Sacrement, Mère.**
Lettres inédites. Rouen, Bénédictines du Saint-Sacrement, 1976.
428 p. illus. 22 cm.
MnCS

4775 **Priez sans cesse;** 300 ans de prière, Laudetur sacrosanctum sacramentum. Paris, Desclée, De Brouwer, 1953.
216, [11] p. illus., plates. 19 cm.
"Mélanges à l'occasion du tricentenaire de l'Institut des Bénédictines de l'Adoration Perpétuelle du Saint Sacrement."
KAM

Benedictine Sisters of the Most Pure Heart of Mary

4776 **Buenner, Denys, O.S.B.**
Madame de Bavox, abbesse de Pradines de l'Ordre de Saint-Benoît (1758-1838). Paris, E. Vitte [1961].
xxi, 573 p. plates. 26 cm.
PLatS

Cistercian Nuns

see above A.3

Missionary Benedictine Sisters

4777 **Koch, Imelda, Sister, O.S.B.**
By the power of the vine; history of the Missionary Benedictine Sisters in the United States, 1922-1952.
118 p.
Thesis (M.A.)–St. John's University, Collegeville, Minn., 1964.
MnStj(Archives); MoCo

4778 **Weibel, Johann Eugen, O.S.B.**
The Catholic missions of north-east Arkansas, 1867-1893. Translated by Sister M. Agnes Voth, O.S.B. Arkansas State University Press, 1967.
109 p.
InFer

Olivetan Benedictine Sisters

4779 **Voth, Agnes, Sister, O.S.B.**
Green olive branch, by M. Agnes Voth. Edited by M. Raymond. Illus. by M. Louise Frankenberger and M. Michelle Bullock. Chicago, Franciscan Herald Press [1973].
xii, 351 p. illus. 21 cm.
InStme; KAS

Sisters of St. Lioba

4780 **Die Kongregation der Benediktinerinnen von der heiligen Lioba.** München, Verlag Paulus Rehm, 1961.
[13] p. 21x12 cm.
MnCS

4781 **Michels, Charitas, Sister, O.S.B.**
Rückblick und Ausschau (1920-1962). Freiburg-Günterstal, St. Lioba, 1962.
23 p. 21 cm.
"Fastenkonferenz 1962 – Priorin Charitas Michels."
MnCS

15. Anglican and Episcopalian Benedictine Sisters

4782 **Mary Hilary, Sister, C.S.M.(Anglican).**
Ten decades of praise; the story of the Community of Saint Mary during its first century, 1865-1965. Racine, Wis., DeKoven Foundation, 1965.
226, [8] p. illus., ports., map. 22 cm.
MnCS

XVIII. OTHER ORDERS FOLLOWING THE RULE OF ST. BENEDICT

1. CAMALDOLESE

4783 **Acta Camaldulensium in Monte S. Josephi prope Vienniam.** MS. Vienna, Schottenstift, codex 540. 260 f. Folio. Saec. 17–18.
Microfilm: MnCH proj. no. 4305

4784 **Bede, Michael.**
The hermits of New Camaldoli. [Monterey, Calif., 1958].
16 p. illus. 23 cm.
KySu; PLatS

4785 **Cacciamani, Giuseppe, O.S.B.Cam.**
L'antica foresta di Camaldoli; storia e codice forestale con illustrazioni fuori testo. Edizioni Camaldoli, 1965.
75 p. 18 leaves of illus. 24 cm.
PLatS

4786 **Cacciamani, Giuseppe, O.S.B.Cam.**
La reclusione presso l'ordine Camaldolese. [Fano], Edizioni Camaldoli, 1960.
48 p. 25 cm.
PLatS

4786a **Giustiniani, Paolo, O.S.B.Cam.**
Trattati, lettere e frammenti dai manoscritti originali dell'Archivio dei Camaldolesi di Monte Corona nell'Eremo di Frascati. A cura di Eugenio Massa. Roma, Edizioni di Storia e Letteratura, 1967–
v. 35 cm.
MnCS

4787 **In Regulam divi patris Benedicti declarationes et constitutiones PP.** Ordinis Camaldulensis. Florentiae, apud Bartholomaeum Sermatellium, 1572.
[32], 334 p. 17 cm.
KAS

4788 **Landino, Cristoforo.**
Camaldolensische Gespräche. Aus dem Lateinischen übersetzt und eingeleitet von Eugen Wolf. [Jena, E. Diederichs] 1927.
xxviii, 135 p. 22 cm.
MnCS

4789 **Lugano, Placido, O.S.B.**
La Congregazione Camaldolese degli eremeti di Montecorona dall origini ai nostri tempi. [Roma, Santa Maria Nova]; Frascati, Sacra Eremo Tuscolano, 1908.
543 p. 26 cm.
KAS

4790 **Masetti, Francesco.**
Teatro storico del Sacro Eremo di Camaldoli, e degli insigni monasteri di S. Salvadore, di S. Maria degli Angioli, di S. Felice in Piazza, e di S. Benedetto di Firenze, tutti del Sacro Ordine Camaldolese. Lucca, Salvatore Marescandoki, 1723.

356 p. 21 cm.
– –Supplemento storico alla vita del beato Ambrogio Traversari, generali perpetuo di Camaldoli . . .
56 p. 21 cm.
InStme

4791 **Menologio Camaldolese.** Tivoli, De Rossi, 1950.
90 p. ports. 21 cm.
MnCS

4792 **Mittarelli, Giovanni Benedetto, O.S.B.Cam.**
Annales Camaldulenses Ordinis Sancti Benedicti, quibus plura interferuntur tum ceteras italico-monasticas res, tum historiam ecclesiasticam remque diplomaticam illustrantia . . . Venetiis, Jo. Bapt. Pasquali, 1755–73.
9 v. illus., plates (part fold.), ports., facsims., geogr. charts. 39 cm.
ILSP; KAS; MnCS; NdRi; PLatS

4793 **Pagnani, Alberico.**
Vita di s. Romualdo, abbate fondatore dei Camaldolesi. 2. ed. completamente rifusa. Fabriano, Arti grafiche "Gentile," 1967.
400 p. plates. 23 cm.
MnCS

4794 **Regula s. Benedicti,** cum constitutionibus Eremitarum s. Romualdi, Ordinis Camaldulensis. Venetiis, apud Matthaeum Valentinum, 1595.
[16], 285 p. 16 cm.
PLatS

4795 **Rodossány, Ladislaus, O.S.B.Cam.**
Epitome antiquarii tripartiti Sacri Ordinis Eremetico-Camaldolensis. Neostadij, Austria, typis Samuelis Müller, 1726.
468 p. 20 cm.
MnCS

4796 **Traversarius, Ambrosius, O.S.B.Cam.**
Ambrosii Traversarii generalis Camaldulensium aliorumque ad ipsum, et ad alios de eodem Ambrosio, latinae epistolae. Bologna, Forni editore, 1968.
2 v. 26 cm.
Includes title page of original edition of 1759.
MnCS

4797 **Ziegelbauer, Magnoald, O.S.B.**
Centifolium Camaldulense; sive, Notitia scriptorum Camaldulensium, quam ceu prodromum excepta est Bibliotheca patrum Camaldulensium. Venetiis, ex typogr. J. B. Albrizzi Hieronymi filii, 1750.
[8], 96 p. 40 cm.

The proposed Bibliotheca apparently was never published.

KAS

4798 _____Republished (in offset) by Gregg Press, Farnborough, England, 1967.
MnCS

2. CELESTINES

4799 **Statuta Ordinis Coelestinorum,** a capitulo 14 usque ad finem. MS. Vienna, Nationalbibliothek, codex 4554, f. 40r-86v. Octavo. Saec. 15.
Microfilm: MnCH proj. no. 17,731

3. CISTERCIANS
a. General Works

4800 **Armorial Cistercien.** Rochefort [Belgique], Abbaye N.-D. de S. Remy [n.d.] 18 col. coats of arms. 15x11 cm. (La Documentation Cistercienne. Serie I, 1–18) The coats of arms are for 18 different abbeys.
PLatS

4801 **Bélorgey, Godfroid, O.Cist.**
L'humilité bénédictine. Paris, Editions du Cerf, 1948.
316 p. 18 cm.
MnCS

4802 **Berlière, Ursmer, O.S.B.**
Les origines de Cîteaux et l'Ordre Bénédictin au XIIe siècle. Louvain, C. Peeters, 1901.
64 p. 25 cm.
KAS; MnCS

4803 **Bibliographie générale de l'Ordre Cistercien,** par H. Rochais . . . Rochefort, Belgique, Abbaye Notre-Dame de St-Remy, 1977–
v. 30 cm. (Documentation cistercienne, v. 21)
MnCS

4804 **Bock, Colomban, O.C.R.**
Les codifications du droit cistercien. Westmalle [Belgique], Imprimerie de l'Ordre [1956].
215 p.
MnCS

4805 **Boec van der ondercheit van den doerluchtighen maanen der Orden der Cistercien.** MS. Vienna, Nationalbibliothek, codex series nova, 12,844. 189 f. Quarto. Saec. 15.
Microfilm: MnCH proj. no. 25,189

4806 **Bühler, Johannes, comp.**
Klosterleben im deutschen Mittelalter, nach zeitgenössischen Aufzeichnungen. Leipzig, Insel-Verlag, 1921.

viii, 527 p.
p. 1–279: Die Benediktiner und Zisterzienser.
KAS

4807 **Carta caritatis Ordinis Cisterciensis.** MS. Cistercienserabtei Zwettl, Austria, codex 361, f.11r–13r. Quarto. Saec. 13.
Microfilm: MnCH proj. no. 6960

4808 **Catalogus personarum religiosarum sacri et exempti Ordinis Cisterciensis** anno a fundatione Cistercii saeculari octavo Deo militantium . . . Vindobonae, sumptibus Monasteriorum Visterciensium, 1898.
393 p. 25 cm.
MnCS

4809 **Charta caritatis.** MS. Cistercienserabtei Heiligenkreuz, Austria, codex 131, f.7v–10v. Folio. Saec. 13.
Microfilm: MnCH proj. no. 4675

4810 **Charta caritatis cum definitionibus Clementis IV papae super eandem.** MS. Cistercienserabtei Lilienfeld, Austria, codex 66, f.1r–56v. Quarto. Saec. 15.
Microfilm: MnCH proj. no. 4473

4811 **Charta caritatis Ordinis Cisterciensis.** MS. Linz, Austria, Studienbibliothek, codex 28, f.70r–164r. Octavo. Saec. 16.
Microfilm: MnCH proj. no. 27,821

4811a **Cistercensi.**
(*In* Dizionario degli Istituti di Perfezione. Rome, 1973. vol. 2, col. 1034–1106)
MnCS

4812 **The Cistercian Fathers;** or, Lives and legends of certain saints and blessed of the Order of Cîteaux. Translated by Henry Collins. Second series. London, Thomas Richardson and Son; New York, Henry H. Richardson, 1874.
vii, 315 p. 20 cm.
KAS

4813 **Cistercian ideals and reality.** Edited by John R. Sommerfeldt. Kalamazoo, Mich., Cistercian Publications, 1978.
vii, 351 p. 21 cm. (Cistercian studies series, 60)
KAS; NcBe

4814 **The Cistercian spirit;** a symposium in memory of Thomas Merton. Spencer, Mass., Cistercian Publications, 1970.
xv, 284 p. 22 cm. (Cistercian studies series, 3)
Edited by Basil M. Pennington.
KAS

4815 **Cistercian Studies Conference, 2nd, Kalamazoo, Mich., 1972.**
Studies in medieval Cistercian history, II. Edited by John R. Sommerfeldt. Kala-

mazoo, Mich., Cistercian Publications, 1976.

xiii, 207 p. 22 cm. (Cistercian studies series, 24)

MnCS

4816   Cocheril, Maur, O.Cist.
Dictionnaire des monastères cisterciens. Rochefort [Belgique], Abbaye Notre-Dame de St. Remy, 1976–

v. 30 cm. (La Documentation cistercienne, v. 18)

MnCS

4817   La codification Cistercienne de 1202 et son évolution ultérieure. (Etude et ed. du texte par] Bernard Lucet. Roma, Editiones Cistercienses, 1964.

189 p. 27 cm. (Bibliotheca cisterciensis, 2)

KAS; PLatS

4818   Les codifications Cisterciennes de 1237 et de 1257, par Bernard Lucet, 1977.

399 p. 25 cm. (Sources d'histoire médiévale)

MnCS

4819   Constitutiones.
Benedictus XII, papa. Constitutiones . . . datum Avinionis IV. nonas Julii, pontificatus nostri anno I. MS. Cistercienserabtei Lilienfeld, Austria, codex 66, f.82v–99v. Quarto. Saec. 15.

Microfilm: MnCH proj. no. 4473

4820   De egressu Cysterciensium monachorum de Molismo. De exordio Cysterciensis cenobii. Carta caritatis. De forma visitationis. Liber usuum Ordinis Cisterciensis. Liber usuum conversorum Cisterciensium. MS. Universitätsbibliothek Graz, Austria, codex 190.

113 f. Quarto. Saec. 14.

Microfilm: MnCH proj. no. 26,101

4821   Derksen, Johannes.
Im verschlossenen Garten; Mönch Ludeger von Altzella, 1162–1234. Leipzig, St. Benno-Verlag [1965].

699 p. 118 illus. 20 cm.

Benutzte Literatur: p. 648–650.

MnCS

4822   Deseilles, Placid.
Principles of monastic spirituality in the Cistercian tradition. Translated from the French by Bro. M. Cyprian Thibodeau. Abbey of Gethsemani, 1964.

80 p.

MoCo

4823   Dialogus duorum monachorum Cluniacensis et Cisterciensis. MS. Cistercienserabtei Zwettl, Austria, codex 380, f.78r–128r. Octavo. Saec. 12.

Microfilm: MnCH proj. no. 6977

4824   Dictionnaire des auteurs Cisterciens, sous la direction de Emile Brouette, Anselme Dimier et Eugène Manning. Rochefort [Belgique], Abbaye Notre-Dame de St-Remy, 1975–

v. 26 cm. (La Documentation cistercienne, v. 16

MnCS

4825   Dijon, France. Musée.
Saint Bernard et l'art des Cisterciens. Mudéd de Dijon, 1953.

80 p. 20 plates. 19 cm.

MnCS

4826   Donkin, R. A.
A check list of printed works relating to the Cistercian Order as a whole and to the houses of the British Isles in particular. [Rochefort, Belgique, Abbaye ND de S. Remy] 1969.

104, 8 p. 24 cm. (Documentation cistercienne, v. 2)

KAS

4827   Duo elenchi coenobiorum Ordinis Cisterciensis, prior chronologicus, alter alphabeticus. MS. Vienna, Nationalbibliothek, codex 4781, f.77r–87v. Octavo. Saec. 15.

Microfilm: MnCH proj. no. 17,946

4828   Evans, Joan.
Monastic architecture in France, from the Renaissance to the Revolution. Cambridge [England], University Press, 1964.

xlii, 186 p. 827 illus. 29 cm.

PLatS

4829   Gallus, abbas Cisterciensis.
Malogranatum, seu Dialogus de triplici statu religiosorum, cum prologo. MS. Vienna, Nationalbibliothek, codex 3712–13. 2 vols. Folio. Saec. 15(1420) & 1453).

Microfilm: MnCH proj. no. 16,918 & 16,934

4830   Guiguard, Philippe.
Les monuments primitifs de la régle Cistercienne, publiés d'après les manuscrits de l'Abbaye de Citeaux. [Dijon, J. E. Rabutot, 1878].

652 p. 22 cm.

MnCS

4831   Die Handschriften-Verzeichnisse der Cistercienser-Stifte Reun in Steiermark; Heiligenkreuz, Zwettl, Lilienfeld in Nieder-Oesterreich; Wilhering und Schlierbach in Ober-Oesterreich; Ossegg und Hohenfurt in Boehmen; Stams in Tirol. Wien, Alfred Hölder, 1891 (Xenia bernardina. Pars secunda)

MnCS

4832   Idea chrono-topographica congregat. cisterc. s. Bernardi per Superiorem Germaniam, in qua omnium congregationis ejusdem monasteriorum utriusque sexus nomina, dioeceses, provinciae, anni fundationum . . . exhibentur . . . [n.p.] 1720.

154 p.

KAS(microfilm)

4833 **Idung, of Prüfening.**
Cistercians and Cluniacs; the case for Cîteaux. Translated by Jeremiah F. O'Sullivan, Joseph Leahey, Grace Perigo. Kalamazoo [Mich.], Cistercian Publications, 1977.

230 p. 23 cm. (Cistercian Fathers series, v. 33)

InStme; NcBe

4834 **Institutiones Ordinis Cisterciensis.** MS. Cistercienserabtei Stams, Tirol, codex 21. 94 f. Quarto. Saec. 13–14.

Microfilm: MnCH proj. no. 29,870

4835 **Jungelincx, Gaspar, O.Cist.**
Notitia abbatiarum Ordinis Cisterciensis per orbem universum. Coloniae Aggrippinae, sumptibus auctoris, 1640.

723 p.

MnCS(microfilm)

4836 **Jungelincx, Gaspar, O.Cist.**
Purpura divi Bernardi, repraesentans elogia et insignia gentilitia, tum pontificum, tum cardinalium, nec non archiepiscoporum et episcoporum qui assumpti ex Ordine Cisterciensi in Sacra Romana Ecclesia floruerunt. Coloniae Agrippinae, H. Krafft, 1644.

129 p. illus.

KAS(microfilm)

4837 **Knowles, David, O.S.B.**
Great historical enterprises; problems in monastic history. London, New York, Nelson [1964, c1963].

viii, 231 p. 23 cm.

MnCS

4838 **Konrad von Eberbach, O.Cist.**
Exordium magnum Cisterciense; sive, Narratio de initio Cisterciensis Ordinis . . . Romae, Editiones Cistercienses, 1961.

382 p. 27 cm.

MnCS

4839 **Lackner, Bede K.**
The eleventh-century background of Cîteaux. Washington, Cistercian Publications, 1972.

309 p. (Cistercian studies series, no. 8)

NcBe

4840 **Le Bail, Anselme, O.S.B.**
L'Ordre de Cîteaux "La Trappe." Paris, Letouzy et Ané, 1924.

160 p. plates. 19 cm.

MnCS

4841 **Leclercq, Jean, O.S.B.**
Bernard of Clairvaux and the Cistercian spirit. Translated [from the French] by Claire Lavoie. Kalamazoo, Mich., Cistercian Publications, 1976.

163 [14] p. 23 cm. (Cistercian studies series, no. 16)

InStme; MnCS; MoCo; NcBe; PLatS

4842 **Leclercq, Jean, O.S.B.**
The intentions of the founders of the Cistercian Order.

(*In* The Cistercian spirit; a symposium in memory of Thomas Merton. 1970. p. 88–133)

PLatS

4843 **Leclercq, Jean, O.S.B.**
St. Bernard et l'esprit cistercien. Paris, Editions du Seuil, 1966.

192 p. illus. 18 cm.

MnCS; PLatS

4844 **Lekai, Louis Julius, O.C.S.O.**
The Cistercians; ideals and reality. [Kent, Ohio], Kent State University Press [1977].

x, 524 p. plates, 22 cm.

MnCS; MoCo; NcBe

4845 **Le Mire, Aubert.**
Chronicon Cisterciensis Ordinis . . . Aubertus Miraeus . . . publicabat. Coloniae, Agrippinae, sumptibus Bernardi Gualtheri, 1614.

326 p.

KAS(microfilm)

4846 **Libellus antiquarum definitionum et Statuta Ordinis Cisterciensis.** MS. Poblet, Spain, codex 20. 202 f. Quarto. Saec. 14/15.

Microfilm: MnCH proj. no. 30,540

4847 **Libellus definitionum Ordinis Cisterciensis.** MS. Universitätsbibliothek Graz, Austria, codex 1610. 156 f. Octavo. Saec. 14.

Microfilm: MnCH proj. no. 26,521

4848 **Libellus deffinitionum Ordinis Cisterciensis.** MS. Cistercienserabtei Stams, Tirol, codex 28. 155 f. Quarto. Saec. 14.

Microfilm: MnCH proj. no. 29,851

4849 **Libellus definitionum Ordinis Cisterciensis.** MS. Cistercienserabtei Wilhering, Austria, codex IX,154. 61 f. Duodecimo. Saec. 14.

Microfilm: MnCH proj. no. 2922

4850 **Libellus definitionum Ordinis Cisterciensis 1289.** Incipit Prologus in Chartum charitatis. MS. Cistercienserabtei Wilhering, Austria, codex VI,17. 81 f. Quarto. Saec. 16.

Microfilm: MnCH proj. no. 2928

4851 **Libellus statutorum Cisterciensis Ordinis.** MS. Cistercienserabtei Heiligenkreuz, Austria, codex 279, f.1r–158r. Quarto. Saec. 14.
Microfilm: MnCH proj. no. 4816

4852 **Libellus statutorum Cisterciensis Ordinis** . . . editus in capitulo generali anno 1317. MS. Cistercienserabtei Rein, Austria, codex 156, f.15r–87r. Quarto. Saec. 14.
Microfilm: MnCH proj. no. 7520

4853 **Manrique, Angel.**
Cisterciensium seu verius ecclesiasticorum annalium a condito Cistercio. Lugduni, G. Boissat, 1642–59.
4 v. 35 cm.
KAS(v. 1–2); MnCS

4854 **Meer, Frédéric van der.**
Atlas de l'Ordre Cistercien. Paris-Bruxelles, Editions Sequoia [1965].
308 p. plates, maps. 35 cm.
MnCS; PLatS

4855 **Merton, Thomas, O.C.S.O.**
An introduction to Cistercian theology; lectures given to the scholastics in the Cistercian abbey of Gethsemani. Collegeville, Minn., Bibliotheca Clericorum Abb. S. Ioannis Bapt. [n.d.].
79 p. 28 cm.
Mimeographed.
MnCS

4856 **Orthodox-Cistercian Conference, Oxford, 1973.**
Theology and prayer: essays on monastic themes presented at the Orthodox-Cistercian Conference, Oxford, 1973. Edited by A. M. Allchim. London, Fellowship of St. Alban and St. Sergius, 1975.
107 p. 22 cm. (Studies supplementary to Sobornost, no. 3)
MnCS

4857 **Orthodox-Cistercian Symposium, Oxford University, 1973.**
One yet two: monastic tradition, East and West. Orthodox-Cistercian Symposium, Oxford University, 26 August–1 September, 1973. Edited by M. Basil Pennington. Kalamazoo, Mich., Cistercian Publications, 1976.
509 p. 23 cm. (Cistercian studies series, no. 29)
InStme; MnCS

4858 **Ordo visitandi monasteria Ordinis Cisterciensis.** MS. Cistercienserabtei Rein, Austria, codex 31, f.95v–102r. Quarto. Saec. 16.
Microfilm: MnCH proj. no. 11,257

4859 **Les plus anciens textes de Cîteaux;** sources, textes, et notes historiques,

par Jean de la Croix Bouton et Jean Baptiste Van Damme. Achel, Abbaye Cistercienne, 1974.
152 p. 24 cm.
KAS

4860 **Regel für Laienbrüder (Cisterzienser).** Germanice. MS. Cistercienserabtei Zwettl, Austria, codex 129. 43 f. Saec. 15.
Microfilm: MnCH proj. no. 6720.

4861 **Schneider, Bruno, O.Cist.**
Cîteaux und die benediktinische Tradition.
(*In* Analecta Sacri Ordinis Cisterciensis. v. 17, p. 73–114)
PLatS

4862 **The spirit of simplicity characteristic of Cîteaux;** a report asked for and approved by the general chapter of 1925 of the Cistercians of the Strict Observance. [Trappist, Ky.], Abbey of Our Lady of Gethsemani, 1935].
56 p. 19 cm.
MnCS

4863 **Statuta Ordinis Cisterciensis.** MS. Cistercienserabtei Zwettl, Austria, codex 361, f.1r–42v. Quarto. Saec. 13.
Microfilm: MnCH proj. no. 6960

4864 **Statuta Ordinis Cisterciensis annorum 1258–1350.** MS. Vienna, Nationalbibliothek, codex 2234. 82 f. Quarto. Saec. 14.
Microfilm: MnCH proj. no. 15,522

4865 **Statuta Ordinis Cisterciensis.** MS. Cistercienserabtei Schlierbach, Austria, codex 34. 184 f. Quarto. Saec. 15.
Microfilm: MnCH proj. no. 28,095

4866 **Statuta Ordinis Cisterciensis.** MS. Cistercienserabtei Schlierbach, Austria, codex 90. 131 f. Duodecimo. Saec. 16.
Microfilm: MnCH proj. no. 28,083

4867 **Statuta et definitiones Ordinis Cisterciensis:** Instituta capituli generalis, Charta charitatis, Clementina, Benedictina, Novellae definitiones. MS. Cistercienserabtei Heiligenkreuz, Austria, codex 390. 168 f. Octavo. Saec. 17.
Microfilm: MnCH proj. no. 4903

4868 **Statuta et definitiones Sacri Ordinis Cisterciensis descripta 1634.** MS. Heiligenkreuz, Austria, codex 546. 194 f. Quarto. Saec. 17
Microfilm: MnCH proj. no. 4914

4869 **Statuta Ordinis Cisterciensis:** Charta charitatis, Clementina, Benedictina, Definitiones capituli generalis de annis 1431, 1456, 1492, 1548, 1550, 1601, etc. MS. Cistercienserabtei Heiligen-

kreuz, Austria, codex 531. 157 f. Quarto.
Saec. 17.
Microfilm: MnCH proj. no. 4922

4870 **Statuta congregationis Cisterciensis
Ordinis per superiorem Germaniam,**
revisa et correcta . . . anno 1654. MS.
Cistercienserabtei Rein, Austria, codex
144, f.1r–108r. Octavo. Saec. 17.
Microfilm: MnCH proj. no. 7515

4871 **Studies in medieval Cistercian history.**
v. 1–   Spencer, Mass., Cistercian
Publications, 1971–
MnCS (v.1–4, 1971–1980); NcBe (v.1–4)

4872 **Van Damme, Jean B., O.C.R.**
La Constitution Cistercienne de 1165.
(*In* Analecta Sacri Ordinis Cisterciensis,
annus 19, p. 51–104)
PLatS

4873 **Visch, Karl de, O.Cist.**
Bibliotheca scriptorum Sacri Ordinis Cisterciensis elogiis plurimorum maxime illustrium adornata . . . Editio secunda, ab
authore recognita, et notabiliter aucta . . .
Coloniae Agrippinae, apud Ioannem
Busaeum, 1656.
22, 432 p.
PLatS(microfilm)

4874 **Xenia Bernardina:** Sancta Bernardi primi
abbatis Claravaliensis octavos natales
saeculares pia mente celebrantes ediderunt antistites et conventus Cistercienses   provinciae   Austriaco-
Hungaricae. Vindobonae, in commisis
apud Alfredum Hölder, 1891.
6 v.
MnCS(v. 2 & 3 Xerographed)

b. Liturgy

1. General Works

4875 **Schneider, Bruno, O.Cist.**
Cîteaux und die Benediktinische Tradi-
tion; die Quellenfrage des Liber usuum im
Lichte der Consuetudines monasticae.
(*In* Analecta Sacri Ordinis Cistercien-
sis, v. 16(1960), p. 169–254)
PLatS

2. Liturgical Books

Arranged by title, and under each title by
date (century)

a. Antiphonarium

4876 **Antiphonarium Cisterciense.** MS. Cistercienserabtei Heiligenkreuz, Austria,
codex 20, f.1r–220r. Folio. Saec. 13.
Microfilm: MnCH proj. no. 4563

4877 **Antiphonarium Cisterciense.** MS. Cistercienserabtei Heiligenkreuz, Austria,
codex 65. 264 f. Folio. Saec. 13.
Microfilm: MnCH proj. no. 4605

4878 **Antifonario Cisterciense.** MS. Poblet,
Spain, Monasterio de Santa Maria, codex
5. 288 f. Folio. Saec. 13.
Microfilm: MnCH proj. no. 30,526

4879 **Antifonario Cisterciense.** MS. Poblet,
Spain, Monasterio de Santa Maria, codex
6. 151 f. Folio. Saec. 13.
Microfilm: MnCH proj. no. 30,527

4880 **Antifonario Cisterciense.** MS. Poblet,
Spain, Monasterio de Santa Maria, codex
9. 175 f. Folio. Saec. 13.
Microfilm: MnCH proj. no. 30,530

4881 **Antiphonarium ad usum Sacri Ordinis
Cisterciensis.** MS. Cistercienserabtei
Zwettl, Austria, codex 195. 189 f. Folio.
Saec. 13.
Microfilm: MnCH proj. no. 6782

4882 **Antiphonarium Cisterciense.** MS. Cistercienserabtei Zwettl, Austria, codex 203.
269 f. Quarto. Saec. 13.
Microfilm: MnCH proj. no. 6795

4883 **Antiphonale.** Cum pulchris initialibus.
MS. Cistercienserabtei Zwettl, Austria,
codex 401. 169 f. Folio. Saec. 13.
Microfilm: MnCH proj. no. 6987

4884 **Antiphonarium Cisterciense.** MS. Universitätsbibliothek Graz, Austria, codex
1471. 291 f. Octavo. Saec. 14.
Microfilm: MnCH proj. no. 26,433

4885 **Antiphonale Cisterciense.** MS. Augus-
tinerchorherrenstift Herzogenburg,
Austria, codex 97. 181 f. Folio. Saec. 14.
Microfilm: MnCH proj. no. 3299

4886 **Antiphonarium Cisterciense.** MS. Universitätsbibliothek Graz, Austria, codex
34. 300 f. Folio. Saec. 15.
Microfilm: MnCH proj. no. 25,964

4887 **Antifonario Cisterciense.** MS. Poblet,
Spain, Monasterio de Santa Maria, codex
12. 211 f. Folio. Saec. 15/16.
Microfilm: MnCH proj. no. 30,533

4888 **Antiphonale Cisterciense.** Pars aestivalis, a Pascha usque ad Adventum Domini.
MS. Cistercienserabtei Rein, Austria,
codex 100. 327 f. Folio. Saec. 15.
Microfilm: MnCH proj. no. 7549

4889 **Antiphonale Cisterciense.** MS. Cister-
cienserabtei Neukloster, Wiener-
Neustadt, Austria, codex C 9. 192 f.
Folio. Saec. 15.
Microfilm: MnCH proj. no. 4949

4890 **Antiphonale Cisterciense.** MS. Cister-
cienserabtei Wilhering, Austria, codex
IX,1,1–2. 2 vols. Folio. Saec. 15.
Microfilm: MnCH proj. no. 2782 & 2793

4891 **Antiphonale Cisterciense.** MS. Cistercienserabtei Wilhering, Austria, codex IX,3. 216 f. Folio. Saec. 15.
Microfilm: MnCH proj. no. 2783

4892 **Antiphonarium Cisterciense,** auctoritate Dominici Rogues editum. Westmalle [Belgique], Typographia Cisterciensium Strictioris Observantiae, 1947.
2 v. 53 cm.
MnCS

b. Breviarium

4893 **Breviarium Cisterciense.** MS. Cistercienserabtei Heiligenkreuz, Austria, codex 18. 249 f. Folio. Saec. 13.
Microfilm: MnCH proj. no. 4565

4894 **Breviarium Cisterciense.** MS. Cistercienserabtei Heiligenkreuz, Austria, codex 276. 339 f. Quarto. Saec. 13.
Microfilm: MnCH proj. no. 4820

4895 **Breviarium Cisterciense.** MS. Cistercienserabtei Heiligenkreuz, Austria, codex 309. 330 f. Quarto. Saec. 13–14.
Microfilm: MnCH proj. no. 4850

4896 **Breviarium Cisterciense.** MS. Tarragona, Spain, Archivo Historico Archidiocesano, codex sine numero. 447 f. Duodecimo. Saec. 13.
Microfilm: MnCH proj. no. 30,520

4897 **Breviario de coro.** MS. Vallbona de las Monjas, Spain, codex 18. Folio. Saec. 13.
Microfilm: MnCH proj. no. 30,563

4898 **Breviarium Cisterciense.** MS. Cistercienserabtei Wilhering, Austria, codex IX,114. 247 f. Octavo. Saec. 13 & 14.
Microfilm: MnCH proj. no. 2888

4899 **Breviarium Cisterciense.** MS. Universitätsbibliothek Graz, Austria, codex 1463. 268 f. Octavo. Saec. 14(1357).
Microfilm: MnCH proj. no. 26,430

4900 **Breviarium Cisterciense.** MS. Cistercienserabtei Heiligenkreuz, Austria, codex 336. 436 f. Octavo. Saec. 14.
Microfilm: MnCH proj. no. 4856

4901 **Breviarium Cisterciense.** Pars hiemalis et aestivalis. MS. Cistercienserabtei Heiligenkreuz, Austria, codex 280. 400 f. Quarto. Saec. 14.
Microfilm: MnCH proj. no. 4814

4902 **Breviarium Cisterciense.** MS. Augustinerchorherrenstift Herzogenburg, Austria, codex 80. 178 f. Octavo. Saec. 14–15.
Microfilm: MnCH proj. no. 3297

4903 **Breviarium: antiphonae, lectiones, collectae.** MS. Cistercienserabtei Lilienfeld, Austria, codex 1b. 348 f. Duodecimo. Saec. 14.
Microfilm: MnCH proj. no. 4317

4904 **Breviarium. Pars aestivalis.** Sine psalterio. MS. Cistercienserabtei Lilienfeld, Austria, codex 7. 194 f. Quarto. Saec. 14.
Microfilm: MnCH proj. no. 4322

4905 **Breviarium. Pars hiemalis.** Sine psalterio. MS. Cistercienserabtei Lilienfeld, Austria, codex 8. 266 f. Quarto. Saec. 14.
Microfilm: MnCH proj. no. 4511

4906 **Breviarium Cisterciense.** MS. Cistercienserabtei Zwettl, Austria, codex 114. 243 f. Octavo. Saec. 14.
Microfilm: MnCH proj. no. 6703

4907 **Breviarium Cisterciense.** MS. Cistercienserabtei Zwettl, Austria, codex 120. 378 f. Saec. 14.
Microfilm: MnCH proj. no. 6709

4908 **Breviario Cisterciense para uso de Poblet.** MS. Poblet, Spain, Monasterio de Santa Maria, codex 14. 444 f. Quarto. Saec. 14.
Microfilm: MnCH proj. no. 30,535

4909 **Breviarium Cisterciense.** MS. Cistercienserabtei Wilhering, Austria, codex IX,115. 286 f. Octavo. Saec. 14.
Microfilm: MnCH proj. no. 2890

4910 **Breviarium Cisterciense.** MS. Cistercienserabtei Wilhering, Austria, codex IX,144. 324 f. Duodecimo. Saec. 14.
Microfilm: MnCH proj. no. 2915

4911 **Breviarium Cisterciense ad usum monasterii in Neuberg.** Pars aestivalis. MS. Universitätsbibliothek Graz, codex 868 & 879. 2 vols. Quarto. Saec. 15.
Microfilm: MnCH proj. no. 26,911 & 26,962

4912 **Breviarium.** MS. Cistercienserabtei Lilienfeld, Austria, codex 9. 470 f. Quarto. Saec. 15.
Microfilm: MnCH proj. no. 4321

4913 **Breviarium Cisterciense.** MS. Cistercienserabtei Wilhering, Austria, codex IX,113. 507 f. Octavo. Saec. 15.
Microfilm: MnCH proj. no. 2894

4914 **Breviarium Cisterciense.** MS. Cistercienserabtei Wilhering, Austria, codex IX,146. 536 f. Duodecimo. Saec. 15.
Microfilm: MnCH proj. no. 2901

4915 **Breviarium Cisterciense.** MS. Cistercienserabtei Zwettl, Austria, codex 230. 317 f. Quarto. Saec. 15.
Microfilm: MnCH proj. no. 6824

4916 **Breviario Cisterciense.** MS. Poblet, Spain, Monasterio de Santa Maria, codex 17. 412 f. Quarto. Saec. 16.
Microfilm: MnCH proj. no. 30,538

c. Customary

4917 Consuetudines Cistercienses. MS. Cistercienserabtei Heiligenkreuz, Austria, codex 131, f.1r–7v. Folio. Saec. 13.
Microfilm: MnCH proj. no. 4675

4918 Liber usuum Cisterciensium. MS. Cistercienserabtei Heiligenkreuz, Austria, codex 131, f.14v–91v. Folio. Saec. 13.
Microfilm: MnCH proj. no. 4675

4919 Consuetudines seu leges Ordinis Cisterciensis, cum brevi historia originis huius ordinis. MS. Cistercienserabtei Lilienfeld, Austria, codex 108. 109 f. Quarto. Saec. 13.
Microfilm: MnCH proj. no. 4472

4920 Consuetudines Cistercienses. MS. Cistercienserabtei Lilienfeld, Austria, codex 64. 198 f. Octavo. Saec. 15.
Microfilm: MnCH proj. no. 4469

4921 Liber usuum S. Ordinis Cisterciensis. MS. Universitätsbibliothek Graz, Austria, codex 1573. 128 f. Octavo. Saec. 16.
Microfilm: MnCH proj. no. 26,507

4922 Liber usuum et constitutionum Cisterciensis Ordinis. MS. Cistercienserabtei Heiligenkreuz, Austria, codex 327. 175 f. Octavo. Saec. 17.
Microfilm: MnCH proj. no. 4872

4923 Liber usuum S. Ordinis Cisterciensis. MS. Cistercienserabtei Heiligenkreuz, Austria, codex 477, p. 315–569. Quarto. Saec. 17.
Microfilm: MnCH proj. no. 4886

4924 Usus S. Ordinis Cisterciensis. MS. Cistercienserabtei Heiligenkreuz, Austria, codex 493. f.1r–108v. Quarto. Saec. 17.

4925 Liber usuum Ordinis Cisterciensis. Anno 1630. Cum registro. MS. Cistercienserabtei Heiligenkreuz, Austria, codex 535. 158 f. Octavo. Saec. 17.
Microfilm: MnCH proj. no. 4892

4926 Liber usuum Ordinis Cisterciensis. MS. Cistercienserabtei Neukloster, Wiener-Neustadt, Austria, codex D 9. 49 f. Octavo. Saec. 17.
Microfilm: MnCH proj. no. 4973

4927 Liber usuum Sacri Ordinis Cisterciensis 1648. MS. Cistercienserabtei Rein, Austria, codex 147. 204 p. Octavo. Saec. 17.
Microfilm: MnCH proj. no. 7514

d. Diurnale

4928 Diurnale Cisterciense. MS. Universitätsbibliothek Graz, Austria, codex 1621. 351 f. Duodecimo. Saec. 14.
Microfilm: MnCH proj. no. 26,520

4929 Diurnale Cisterciense. MS. Universitätsbibliothek Graz, Austria, codex 1648. 158 f. Duodecimo. Saec. 15.
Microfilm: MnCH proj. no. 26,536

4930 Diurnale Cisterciense. MS. Cistercienserabtei Heiligenkreuz, Austria, codex 342. 106 f. Duodecimo. Saec. 15.
Microfilm: MnCH proj. no. 4883

e. Epistolarium

4931 Liber epistolarum et prophetarum ad usum Ordinis Cisterciensis. MS. Cistercienserabtei Zwettl, Austria, codex 208. 186 f. Quarto. Saec. 12.
Microfilm: MnCH proj. no. 6797

4932 Epistolario. MS. Vallbona de las Monjas, Spain, codex 14. 72 f. Quarto. Saec. 13.
Microfilm: MnCH proj. no. 30,559

f. Evangeliarium

4933 Liber evangeliorum secundum usum Sacri Ordinis Cisterciensis. MS. Cistercienserabtei Zwettl, Austria, codex 197. 406 f. Folio. Saec. 12.
Microfilm: MnCH proj. no. 6787

4934 Evangeliario. MS. Valbona de las Monjas, Spain, codex 1. 163 f. Quarto. Saec. 13.
Microfilm: MnCH proj. no. 30,546

g. Graduale

4935 Gradual Cisterciense. MS. Poblet, Spain, Monasterio de Santa Maria, codex 11. 132 f. Folio. Saec. 13.
Microfilm: MnCH proj. no. 30,532

4936 Graduale Cisterciense. MS. Cistercienserabtei Wilhering, Austria, codex IX,6. 124 f. (mancant f.48–56, 70, 87, 115–120). Folio. Saec. 13.
Microfilm: MnCH proj. no. 2786

4937 Graduale Cisterciense. MS. Cistercienserabtei Zwettl, Austria, codex 196. 161 f. Folio. Saec. 13.
Microfilm: MnCH proj. no. 6785

4938 Graduale Cisterciense. MS. Cistercienserabtei Zwettl, Austria, codex 199. 147 f. Saec. 13.
Microfilm: MnCH proj. no. 6788

4939 Graduale Cisterciense. MS. Cistercienserabtei Zwettl, Austria, codex 245. 160 f. Quarto. Saec. 13.
Microfilm: MnCH proj. no. 6848

4940 Graduale Cisterciense. MS. Universitätsbibliothek Graz, Austria, codex 10. 182 f. Folio. Saec. 15.
Microfilm: MnCH proj. no. 25,970

4941 **Graduale Cisterciense.** MS. Cistercienserabtei Wilhering, Austria, codex IX,2.
197 f. Folio. Saec. 15.
Microfilm: MnCH proj. no. 2796

h. Hymnarium

4942 **Hymnarium (Cisterciense?),** cum calendario (fragmentum). MS. Vienna, Nationalbibliothek, codex series nova 2456.
38 f. Octavo. Saec. 13.
Microfilm: MnCH proj. no. 20,696

4943 **Antiphonarium et hymnarium Cisterciense.** MS. Universitätsbibliothek Graz,
Austria, codex 114. 250 f. Folio. Saec.
15.
Microfilm: MnCH proj. no. 25,042

i. Lectionarium

4944 **Lectionarium a consuetudine Ordinis
Cisterciensis.** MS. Pamplona, Spain,
Archivo General de Navarra, codex 1.
110 f. Quarto. Saec. 13.
Microfilm: MnCH proj. no. 34,845

4945 **Leccionario.** MS. Vallbona de las Monjas,
Spain, codex 9. 214 f. Folio. Saec. 13.
Microfilm: MnCH proj. no. 30,554

j. Liber Choralis

4946 **Liber choralis Ordinis Cisterciensis.**
MS. Vienna, Nationalbibliothek, codex
1813. 234 f. Folio. Saec. 14.
Microfilm: MnCH proj. no. 15,128

4947 **Liber choralis.** MS. Cistercienserabtei
Zwettl, Austria, codex 407. 91 f. Folio.
Saec. 15.
Microfilm: MnCH proj. no. 6991

k. Liber Collectarium

4948 **Liber collectarium Cisterciense.** MS.
Cistercienserabtei Wilhering, Austria,
codex IX,48. 209 f. Quarto. Saec. 14.
Microfilm: MnCH proj. no. 2824

4949 **Liber collectarium.** MS. Cistercienserabtei Wilhering, Austria, codex IX, 49. 110
f. Quarto. Saec. 14.
Microfilm: MnCH proj. no. 2826

l. Martyrologium

4950 **Martyrologium.** MS. Cistercienserabtei
Zwettl, Austria, codex 84, f.10r–122v.
Folio. Saec. 12.
Microfilm: MnCH proj. no. 6803

m. Matutinale

4951 **Matutinale, Diurnale, Missale Ordinis
Cisterciensis.** MS. Cistercienserabtei
Stams, Tirol, codex 30. 465 f. Quarto.
Saec. 15.
Microfilm: MnCH proj. no. 29,850

n. Missale

4952 **Missale Cisterciense.** MS. Cistercienserabtei Heiligenkreuz, Austria, codex
127. 166 f. Folio. Saec. 13.
Microfilm: MnCH proj. no. 4667

4953 **Missale Cisterciense.** MS. Cistercienserabtei Zwettl, Austria, codex 194.
156 f. Folio. Saec. 12 & 13.
Microfilm: MnCH proj. no. 6806

4954 **Missale Cisterciense.** MS. Universitätsbibliothek Graz, Austria, codex 1534.
356 f. Octavo. Saec. 13–14.
Microfilm: MnCH proj. no. 26,500

4955 **Missale Cisterciense.** MS. Cistercienserabtei Heiligenkreuz, Austria, codex
99. 283 f. Folio. Saec. 13.
Microfilm: MnCH proj. no. 4643

4956 **Missale Cisterciense.** MS. Cistercienserabtei Heiligenkreuz, Austria, codex
275. 120 f. Quarto. Saec. 13.
Microfilm: MnCH proj. no. 4813

4957 **Missale Cisterciense.** MS. Cistercienserabtei Heiligenkreuz, Austria, codex
124. 278 f. Folio. Saec. 13.
Microfilm: MnCH proj. no. 4669

4958 **Missale.** MS. Cistercienserabtei Zwettl,
Austria, codex 198. 213 f. Folio. Saec.
13–14.
Microfilm: MnCH proj. no. 6789

4959 **Missale Cisterciense.** MS. Universitätsbibliothek Graz, Austria, codex 447.
237 f. Folio. Saec. 14.
Microfilm: MnCH proj. no. 26,610

4960 **Missale Cisterciense.** MS. Universitätsbibliothek Graz, Austria, codex 1289.
331 f. Octavo. Saec. 14(1315).
Microfilm: MnCH proj. no. 26,370

4961 **Missale Cisterciense.** MS. Cistercienserabtei Heiligenkreuz, Austria, codex
136. 235 f. Folio. Saec. 14–15.
Microfilm: MnCH proj. no. 4677

4962 **Missale Cisterciense.** MS. Cistercienserabtei Heiligenkreuz, Austria, codex
277. 177 f. Quarto. Saec. 14.
Microfilm: MnCH proj. no. 4815

4963 **Missale Cisterciense.** MS. Cistercienserabtei Heiligenkreuz, Austria, codex
328. 132 f. Quarto. Saec. 14.
Microfilm: MnCH proj. no. 4875

4964 **Missale.** MS. Cistercienserabtei Lilien-
feld, Austria, codex 13. Duodecimo.
Saec. 14.
Microfilm: MnCH proj. no. 4531

4965 **Missale Cisterciense.** MS. Cistercienserabtei Zwettl, Austria, codex 229. 190 f. Folio. Saec. 14–15.
Microfilm: MnCH proj. no. 6830

4966 **Missale ad usum monasterii Ruensis,** Ordinis Cisterciensis. MS. Cistercienserabtei Rein, Austria, codex 206. 285 f. Folio. Saec. 15.
Microfilm: MnCH proj. no. 9823

4967 **Missale Cisterciense.** MS. Cistercienserabtei Heiligenkreuz, Austria, codex 51. 310 f. Folio. Saec. 15.
Microfilm: MnCH proj. no. 4596

4968 **Missale Cisterciense.** MS. Cistercienserabtei Heiligenkreuz, Austria, codex 139. 128 f. Folio. Saec. 15.
Microfilm: MnCH proj. no. 4688

4969 **Missale.** MS. Cistercienserabtei Lilienfeld, Austria, codex 14. 214 f. Quarto. Saec. 15.
Microfilm: MnCH proj. no. 4323

o. Officia Propria

4970 **Proprium Cisterciense.** MS. Augustinerchorherrenstift Herzogenburg, Austria, codex 175. 186 f. Quarto. Saec. 16.
Microfilm: MnCH proj. no. 3291

p. Orationale

4971 **Preces in usum monachorum Ordinis Cisterciensis.** MS. Vienna, Nationalbibliothek, codex 4781, f.88r–159v. Octavo. Saec. 15.

q. Ordinarium

4972 **Ordinarium beate Marie Cisterciensis.** MS. Monasterio benedictino de Montserrat, Spain, codex 812. 122 f. Quarto. Saec. 15.
Microfilm: MnCH proj. no. 30,079

4973 **Ordinarium Cisterciense.** MS. Cistercienserabtei Zwettl, Austria, codex 351. 172 f. Quarto. Saec. 16.
Microfilm: MnCH proj. no. 6947

4974 **Ordinarium S. Ordinis Cisterciensis.** MS. Cistercienserabtei Heiligenkreuz, Austria, codex 477, p.1–314. Quarto. Saec. 17.
Microfilm: MnCH proj. no. 4886

4975 **Ordinarium Cisterciense.** MS. Cistercienserabtei Rein, Austria, codex 147. 173 p. Octavo. Saec. 17.
Microfilm: MnCH proj. no. 7514

r. Ordo Divini Officii

4976 **Rationale divinorum officiorum (libri octo).** Incipit: Quaecunque in ecclesiasticis officiis. MS. Cistercienserabtei Zwettl, Austria, codex 191. 527 f. Quarto. Saec. 15. (f.523v–425v: Tabellae calendarii pro annis 1462–1533).
Microfilm: MnCH proj. no. 6783

4977 **Directorium Officii Divini secundum usum S. Ordinis Cisterciensis . . .** anno 1635. MS. Cistercienserabtei Heiligenkreuz, Austria, codex 494. 111 p. Octavo. Saec. 17.
Microfilm: MnCH proj. no. 4908

4978 **Directorium chori secundum usum S. Ordinis Cisterciensis . . .** in monasterio Campililiorum renovatum anno 1642. MS. Cistercienserabtei Heiligenkreuz, Austria, codex 495. 39 f. Quarto. Saec. 17.
Microfilm: MnCH proj. no. 4919

s. Processionale

4979 **Processional Cisterciense.** MS. Poblet, Spain, Monasterio de Santa Maria, codex 18. 72 f. Quarto. Saec. 18.
Microfilm: MnCH proj. no. 30,539

t. Psalterium

4980 **Psalterium Cisterciense.** MS. Cistercienserabtei Heiligenkreuz, Austria, codex 66. 137 f. Folio. Saec. 13.
Microfilm: MnCH proj. no. 4606

4981 **Psalterium Cisterciense.** MS. Cistercienserabtei Zwettl, Austria, codex 202. 119 f. Quarto. Saec. 13.
Microfilm: MnCH proj. no. 6793

4982 **Psalterium.** Cum pulchris initialibus. MS. Cistercienserabtei Zwettl, Austria, codex 204. 240 f. Saec. 13.
Microfilm: MnCH proj. no. 6801

4983 **Psalterium, cantica, officium defunctorum.** MS. Cistercienserabtei Lilienfeld, Austria, codex 1a. 83 f. Duodecimo. Saec. 14.
Microfilm: MnCH proj. no. 4318

4983a **Salterio.** MS. Vallbona de las Monjas, Spain. Codex 8. 180 f. Folio. Saec. 14.
Microfilm: MnCH proj. no. 30,553

u. Rituale

4984 **Rituale Cisterciense.** MS. Cistercienserabtei Heiligenkreuz, Austria, codex 337. 152 f. Octavo. Saec. 15.
Microfilm: MnCH proj. no. 4862

4985 **Rituale Cisterciense.** MS. Cistercienserabtei Zwettl, Austria, codex 415. 100 f. Duodecimo. Saec. 15–17.
Microfilm: MnCH proj. no. 6999

4986 **Libellus Ordinis Cisterciensis,** seu Rituale Cisterciense. MS. Cistercienserabtei Heiligenkreuz, Austria, codex 338. 142 f. Octavo. Saec. 16.
Microfilm: MnCH proj. no. 4870

4987 **Rituale Cisterciense pro electione novi abbatis et visitatione monasteriorum.** MS. Cistercienserabtei Zwettl, Austria, codex 414. 64 f. Octavo. Saec. 16.
Microfilm: MnCH proj. no. 7000

4988 **Rituale Cisterciense ex libro usuum,** difinitionibus Ordinis, et caeremonali episcoporum collectum. Lirinae, H. Bernardi, 1892.
xxvi, 705, xv p., 23 cm.
KAS

v. Sacramentarium

4989 **Sacramentario Cisterciense.** MS. Vallbona de las Monjas, Spain, codex 7. 208 f. Folio. Saec. 13.
Microfilm: MnCH proj. no. 30,552

c. Obituaries

4990 **Necrologium antiquum Campililiense.** Coeptum primo monasterii saeculo, id est, saeculo XIII. Describens quaterno columnarum ordine praesules, monachos atque canonicos, conversos laicos ordinis fratres, familiares deum et seculares quoscunque beneficos atque merentes per nonas, idus, calendasque. Dolendum quod Ianuarii mensis folium primum atque Decembris omnia post diem 12um sunt avulsa. MS. Cistercienserabtei Lilienfeld, Austria, codex non numeratus. 146 f. Folio. Saec. 13–17.
Microfilm: MnCH proj. no. 4470

d. Periodicals

4991 **Analecta Cisterciensa.** v. 1–   1945–
Roma, Editiones Cistercienses. English, French, German, or Latin.
Vol. 1–20(1945–1964) have title: Analecta Sacri Ordinis Cisterciensis.
KAS; MnCS

4992 **Cistercian fathers series.** v. 1–   1971–
Spencer, Mass., Cistercian Publications.
Monograph series.
MnCS; MoCo

4993 **Cistercian studies.** 1–   1961–   Berryville, Va., Abbey of Our Lady of the Holy Cross.
PLatS

4994 **Cistercian studies;** a quarterly review dealing with monastic spirituality, published in collaboration with Collectanea Cisterciensia. v. 1–   1965–   Abbaye N.D. de-la-Pais, Chimay, Belgium.
MnCS; MoCo

4995 **Cistercian studies series.** v. 1–   1969–
Kalamazoo, Mich., Cistercian Publications.
Monograph series.
MnCS; MoCo; PLatS

4996 **Cistercium;** revista española de espiritualitad, historia y doctrina, publicada por los monjes Cistercienses. Año 1–   1949–
KAS; MnCS

4997 **Commentarii Cistercienses;** studia et documenta. v. 1–   1970(?)–
MnCS

4998 **Documentation Cistercienne.** v. 1–   1968–   Rochefort, Belgique, Abbaye ND de S. Remy.
Monograph series.
KAS; MnCS

4999 **Liturgy.** v. 1–   1966–   Gethsemani Abbey, Trappist, Ky.
MnCS; MoCo

5000 **Monastic studies.** no. 1–   1963–
Berryville, Va., Our Lady of Holy Cross Abbey.
CaMWiSb; KAS; MoCo; PLatS; ViBris

5001 **Monastic exchange.** v. 1–   1969–
Gethsemani Abbey, Trappist, Ky.
MoCo

5002 **Zisterzienser-Studien.** 1–   1975–
Berlin, Colloquium Verlag.
MnCS

e. History: General

5003 **Conradus, abbot of Eberbach,** 12th cent.
Exordium magnum Cisterciense; sive, Narratio de initio Cisterciensis Ordinis. Ad codicum fidem recensuit Bruno Griesser. Romae, Editiones Cistercienses, 1961.
382 p. 27 cm.
PLatS; MnCS

5004 **An epitome of Cistercian history;** from Cîteaux (12th cent.) to Roscrea (20th cent.) by a Cistercian. Roscrea, Mount St. Joseph Abbey [1925].
69 p.
NcBe

5005 **Festschrift zum 800-Jahrgedächtnis des Todes Bernhards von Clairvaux,** hrsg. von der Oesterreichischen Cistercienserkongregation vom Heiligsten Herzen Jesu. Wien, Verlag Herold [1953].
520 p. plates. 24 cm.
MnCS

5006 **Janauschek, Leopold, O.Cist.**
Originum Cisterciensium tomus I, in quo praemissis congregationum domiciliis adjectisque tabulis chronologico-genealogicis, veterum abbatiarum a monachis habitatarum fundationes ad fidem antiquissimorum fontium primus descripsit . . . Vindobonae, in commissis apud Alfredum Hoelder, 1877.
vii, lxxxii, 394 p. fold. chart. 32 cm.
No more published.
KAS

5007 _____Ridgewood, N.J., Gregg, 1964.
vii, lxxxii, 394 [19] p. 34 cm.
Reprint with addition: [Appendix]. Arbor genealogica abbatiarum Cisterciensium.
PLatS

5008 **Knowles, David, O.S.B.**
Great historical enterprises. Problems in monastic history. London, New York, Nelson [1964, c1963].
viii, 231 p. 23 cm.
KAS; MnCS; PLatS

f. History: By Country

Austria

5009 **Konrad, Nivard.**
Die Entstehung der Oesterreichisch-Ungarischen Zisterzienserkongregation (1849–1869). Roma, Editiones Cistercienses, 1967.
334 p. 27 cm. (Bibliotheca cisterciensis, 5)
PLatS

5010 **Krausen, Edgar.**
Die Zisterzienserabtei Raitenhaslach. Berlin, New York, Walter de Gruyter, 1977.
xii, 523 p.
MnCS

5011 **Kurze Geschichte des Stiftes Lilienfeld.** Breves notitiae in Campum Lilionum. MS. Cistercienserabtei Lilienfeld, Austria, codex Archivium VI, 81. 105 p. Quarto. Saec. 17.
Microfilm: MnCH proj. no. 4542

5012 **Mosler, Hans.**
Die Cistercienser Altenberg. Berlin, W. de Gruyter, 1965.
viii, 299 p. 26 cm.
KAS

5013 **Niemetz, Alois.**
800 Jahre Musikpflege in Heiligenkreutz. Heiligenkreuzer Verlag [Austria], 1977.
140 p. illus., music. 20 cm.
MnCS

5014 **Röhrig, Floridus, C.R.S.A.**
Alte Stifte in Oesterreich. Wien, Schrollverlag, 1966–67.
2 v. plates. 24 cm.
Includes nine Cistercian abbeys.
MnCS

5014a **Schwineköper, Berent.**
Klosteraufhebungen als Folge von Reformation und Bauernkrieg im habsburgischen Vorderöstereich.
(*In* Festschrift Friedrich Hausmann. Graz, 1977. p. 489–504)
MnCS

5015 **Das Stiftungen-Buch des Cistercienser-Klosters Zwettl.** Hrsg. von Johann von Frast [O. Cist.]. Wien, K. K. Hof- und Staatsdruckerei, 1851. [Graz, Akademische Druck-und-Verlagsanstalt, 1964].
xvi, 736 p. 20 cm. (Fontes rerum austriacarum, 4)
MnCS; PLatS

5016 **Zwettler Stiftungsbuch (Bärenhaut):** Stammbaum der Kuenringer vor 1350. MS. Cistercienserabtei Zwettl, Austria, codex in archivio. 198 f. Folio. Saec. 13–14.
Microfilm: MnCH proj. no. 6808

Belgium

5017 **Brouette, Emile, comp.**
Recueil des chartes et documents de l'Abbaye du Val-Saint-Georges à Salzinnes (Namur), 1196–1300. Achel, Abbaye Cistercienne, 1971.
xlvi, 289 p. 24 cm.
Texts in Latin, with critical matter in French.
KAS

5018 **Roisin, Simone.**
L'hagiographie cistercienne dans le diocèse de Liège au XIIIe siècle. Louvain, Bibliothèque de l'Université, 1947.
301 p. 25 cm.
MnCS

Bolivia

5019 **Reisinger, Amadeus, O.Cist.**
Die Zistercienser in Bolivien; Gründungsgeschichte der Zistercienser-Niederlassung in Bolivien. Wilhering [Austria], 1933.
63 p. plates. 23 cm.
MnCS

Denmark

5020 **McGuire, Brian Patrick.**
Conflict and continuity at Om Abbey; a Cistercian experience in medieval Den-

mark. Copenhagen, Museum Tusculanum, 1976.
151 p. plates. 23 cm. (Opuscula graeco-latina, v. 8)
MnCS

England

5021 **A concise history of the Cistercian Order,** with the lives of Ss. Robert, Alberic and Stephen. London, Thomas Richardson, 1852.
382 p.
MoCo

5022 **Donkin, R. A.**
A check list of printed works relating to the Cistercian Order as a whole and to the houses of the British Isles in particular. [Rochefort, Belgium, Abbaye ND de S. Remy, 1971?].
104, 8 p. 24 cm. (Documentation cistercienne, v. 2)
KAS

5023 **Donkin, R. A.**
The Cistercians: studies in the geography of medieval England and Wales. Toronto, Pontifical Institute of Mediaeval Studies, 1978.
241 p. plates, maps. 24 cm. (Studies and texts, 38)
MnCS

5024 **Hill, Bennett D.**
English Cistercian monasteries and their patrons in the twelfth century. Urbana [Ill.], University of Illinois Press, 1968.
xi, 188 p. illus. 22 cm.
MnCS; MoCo; PLatS

5025 **Hockey, Frederick, O.S.B.**
The account-book of Beaulieu Abbey. [London], Offices of the Royal Historical Society, University College London, 1975.
348 p. 24 cm.
MnCS

5026 **Hockey, Frederick, O.S.B.**
Beaulieu, King John's abbey; a history of Beaulieu Abbey, Hampshire, 1204-1538. Pioneer Publications Limited [1976].
xiv, 251 p. illus. 22 cm.
MnCS

5027 **Hockey, Frederick, O.S.B.**
Quarr Abbey and its lands, 1132-1631. Leicester, Leicester U.P., 1970.
xxii, 320 p. maps. 23 cm.
MnCS

5028 **Hodges, George.**
Fountains Abbey; the story of a medieval monastery. New York, Dutton, 1904.
129 p.
NcBe

5029 **O'Sullivan, Jeremiah Francis.**
Cistercian settlements in Wales and Monmouthshire, 1140-1540. New York, D. X. McMullen Co. [1947].
ix, 137 p. map. 22 cm.
MnCS

5030 **Talbot, Charles H., comp.**
Letters from the English abbots to the chapter of Cîteaux, 1442-1521. London, Offices of the Royal Historical Society, University College London, 1967.
282 p. 23 cm.

5031 **Williams, David H.**
White monks in Gwent and the border. In commemoration of the 750th anniversary of the foundation of Grace Dieu Abbey (1226-1976). Pontypool, Hughes and Son, 1976.
ix, 169 p. 24 cm.
MnCS

France

5032 **Berenguier, R.**
L'Abbaye du Thoronet. Paris, 1975.
62 p.
MnCS

5033 **Carré, Remi, O.S.B.**
Recueil curieux & édifiant, sur les cloches de l'église, avec les cérémonies de leur bénédiction, à l'occasion de celle qui fui faite à Paris le jeudi 3 juin 1756 à l'Abbaye de Penthemont, sous le gouvernement de Madame de Bethisy . . . Cologne, 1757.
104 p. 17 cm.
MnCS (Plante)

5034 **Dimier, M. Anselm, O.C.R.**
Amedé de Lausanne, disciple de Saint Bernard. Abbaye S. Wandrille, Editions de Fontenelle, 1949.
490 p.
MoCo

5035 **Ferras, Vincent, O.S.B.**
Sainte-Marie de Compagnes, première abbaye Cistercienne en pays d'Aude, sise en Montagne Noire (1145-1177). Société d'études scientifiques de l'Aude [1974].
55 p. plates. 20 cm.
MnCS

5036 **Gallagher, Philip Francis.**
The monastery of Mortemer-en-Lyons in the twelfth century; its history and its cartulary.
374 p.
Thesis (Ph.D.) – University of Notre Dame, Ind., 1976.
NcBe (Xerographic reprint)

5037 **Guignard, Philippe.**
Les monuments primitifs de la règle Cistercienne, publiés d'après les manuscrits de

l'Abbaye de Cîteaux. [Dijon, J.-E. Rabutot, 1878].
652 p. 22 cm.
MnCS

5038 **Le Hardy, Gaston.**
Etude sur la baronnie et l'abbaye d'Aunay-sur-Odon. Caen, H. Delesques, 1897.
438 p. 23 cm.
KAS

5039 **Lekai, Louis Julius, O.C.S.O.**
Moral and material status of French Cistercian abbeys in the seventeenth century.
(*In* Analecta Sacri Ordinis Cisterciensis, annus 19, p. 199–266)
PLatS

5040 **Marilier, Jean.**
Chartes et documents concernant l'Abbaye de Cîteaux, 1098–1182. Roma, Editiones Cistercienses, 1961.
viii, 251 p. 27 cm. (Bibliotheca Cisterciensis, 1)
PLatS

5041 **Poquet, Alexandre Eusèbe.**
Monographie de l'Abbaye de Longpont, son histoire, ses monuments, ses abbés, ses personnages célébres, ses sepultures, ses possessions territoriales. Paris, E. Didron, Dumoulin, 1869.
216 p. plates, fold. plan. 25 cm.
KAS

5042 **Rievaulx Abbey.**
Cartularium abbathiae de Rievalle, Ordinis Cisterciensis, fundatae anno MCXXXII. Durham [England], Pub. for the Surtees Society by Andrews & Co., 1889.
cxiii, 471, 18 p. 23 cm.
MnCS

Germany

5043 **Arnsburg, Germany (Cistercian abbey).**
Urkundenbuch des Klosters Arnsburg in der Wetterau, bearb. und hrsg. von Ludwig Baur. Darmstadt, Verlag des Historischen Vereins für das Grossherzogthum Hessen, 1849–51.
3 v. 23 cm.
KAS

5043a **Dicks, M.**
Die Abtei Camp am Niederrhein; Geschichte des ersten Cistercienserklosters in Deutschland (1123–1802). Moers, Steiger Verlag [1979].
xxiii, 709 p. illus. 24 cm.
MnCS

5044 **Germania monastica: Klosterverzeichnis der deutschen Benediktiner und Cis-**
terzienser. Neu hrsg. von der Bayerischen Benediktiner-Akademie. Augsburg, Winfried-Werk, 1967.
185 p. 21 cm.
Reprint of Klosterverzeichnis der deutschen Benediktiner und Cisterzienser. Salzburg, 1917.
KAS; PLatS

5044a **Grüger, Heinrich.**
Heinrichau; Geschichte eines schlesischen Zisterzienserklosters, 1227–1977. Köln, Böhlau Verlag, 1978.
xix, 323 p. illus., maps. 25 cm.
MnCS

5045 **Hees, Nikolaus.**
Manipulus rerum memorabilium claustri Hemenrodensis, Ordinis Cisterciensis in archidoecese Trevirensi. Coloniae, Joannes Henningham, 1641.
88 p. illus. 31 cm.
MnCS

5046 **Heutger, N.**
850 Jahre Kloster Walkenreid. Hildesheim, 1977.
166 p. 72 illus.
MnCS

5047 **Himmelstein, Franz Xaver.**
Das Frauenkloster Wechterswinkel.
(*In* Historischer Verein von Unterfranken und Aschaffenburg, Würzburg. Archiv. 15. Bd.(1860), p. 115–176)
KAS

5048 **Himmerod;** eine Festgabe zum 50. Jahrestag der kirchlichen Wiedererichtung des Klosters U.L. Frau, 15. Oktober 1972. Selbstverlag der Abtei Himmerod, 1972.
40 p. illus. 30 cm.
MnCS

5049 **Hoppe, Willy.**
Kloster Zinna; ein Beitrag zur Geschichte des ostdeutschen Koloniallandes und des Cistercienserordens. München, Duncker & Humblot, 1914.
xvi, 275 p. 2 maps. 23 cm.
KAS

5050 **Kloster Ichterhausen;** Urkundenbuch, Geschichte und bauliche Beschreibung . . . hrsg. von Dr. Wilhelm Rein. Weimar, H. Böhlau, 1863.
viii, 200 p. plan. 23 cm.
KAS

5051 **Magirius, Heinrich.**
Die Baugeschichte des Klosters Altzella. Berlin, Akademie-Verlag, 1962.
231 p. 83 plates. 28 cm.
MnCS

5052   **Mosler, Hans.**
Die Cistercienserabtei Altenberg. Berlin,
W. de Gruyter, 1965.
viii, 299 p. 26 cm. (Germania sacra, Neue
Folge, 2)
MnCS; KAS

5053   **Ribbe, Wolfgang.**
Das Landbuch des Klosters Zinna.
Berlin, Colloquium Verlag, 1976.
216 p. (Zisterzienser-Studien, 2. Studien
zur europäischen Geschichte, 12)
MnCS

5054   **Röckl, Karl Ad.**
Beschreibung von Fürstenfeld. München, Georg Franz, 1840.
viii, 88 p. 24 cm.
KAS

5055   **Schneider, Ambrosius, O.Cist.**
Himmerod; Geschichte und Sendung. Im
Selbstverlag der Abtei Himmerod, 1967.
64 p. illus. 22 cm.
MnCS

5056   **Stillfried, R.G.**
Kloster Heilsbronn. Berlin, C. Heymann,
1877.
xx, 398 p. illus., plates. 26 cm.
KAS

5057   **Wellstein, Gilbert, O.Cist.**
Die Cisterzienserabtei U.L. Frau von
Himmerod in der Eifel. Im Selbstverlag
des Klosters [1923?].
100 p. illus. 18 cm.
MnCS

Hungary

5058   **Vargha, Damiaan, O.Cist.**
Hongerije en de Cisterciënsers. 2. ed.
Hertogenbosch, O.L. Vrouw van
Onsenoort [1935].
252 p. plates. 23 cm.
MnCS

Ireland

5059   **Carville, Geraldine.**
The heritage of Holy Cross. Belfast,
Blackstaff Press, 1973.
175 p. illus., maps. 24 cm.
MnCS

5060   **O'Dwyer, Barry William.**
The conspiracy of Mallifont, 1216–1231;
an episode in the history of the Cistercian
Order in medieval Ireland. Published for
the Dublin Historical Association, 1970.
47 p. map. 22 cm.
MnCS

Italy

5061   **Agostini, Filippo P., O.Cist.**
La Congregazione delle Oblate Cister-
ciensi di Anagni.
(*In* Analecta Sacri Ordinis Cisterciensis,
annus 19, p. 267–274)
PLatS

5061a **Albergo, Vito.**
Eremo e abbazia di San Galgano. Die
Abtei San Galgano und die Rundkirche von
Monte Siepi. Pistoia, Libreria Editrice
Tellini [1980].
83 p. illus.(part col.) 21 x 20 cm.
MnCS

5062   **Bedini, Balduino Gustavo.**
Breve prospetto delle abazie cisterciensi
d'Italia, dalla fondazione di Citeaux (1098)
alla metà del secolo decimo-quarto.
[Romae? Tipografia di Casameri, 1964].
191 p. plates. 22 cm.
MnCS

Jugoslavia

5063   **Turkovic, Milan.**
Der Cistercienser Orden im Königreiche
Jugoslavien. Susak, Zavod, 1936.
107 p. illus. 23 cm.
MnCS

5064   **Turkovic, Milan.**
Povijest opatija reda Cistercita (Ordinis
Cisterciensis) u Hrvatskoj-Slavoniji i Dal-
maciji. Susak, Zavod, 1936.
93 p. illus. 24 cm.
MnCS

Netherlands

5065   **Joosting, J. G. C.**
Het archief der abtij te Assen. Leiden, E.
J. Brill, 1906.
139 p. 24 cm.
MnCS

Norway

5066   **Johnsen, Arne Odd.**
De norske Cistercienserklostre, 1146–
1264; sett i europeisk sammenheng. Oslo,
Universitetsforlaget, 1977.
96 p. 26 cm.
MnCS

Portugal

5067   **Gusmão, Artur de.**
A expansão de arquitectura borgonhesa
e os mosteiros de Cisterem Portugal.
Lisboa [Casa Pia de Lisboa] 1956.
377 p. plates. 23 cm.
MnCS

Silesia

5068 **Grundmann, Günther.**
Dome, Kirchen und Klöster in Schlesien. Nach alter Vorlagen. Frankfurt am Main, W. Weidlich, 1963.
267 p. illus., fold map. 19 cm.
PLatS

5069 **Kastner, August, ed.**
Archiv für die Geschichte des Bisthums Breslau. Neisse [The Author], 1859-63.
3 v. 21 cm.
2.Bd.: Geschichte und Beschreibung des fürstlichen jungfräulichen Klosterstiftes Cistercienser Ordens in Trebnitz.
KAS

Spain

5070 **L'Abadia de Poblet, Poblet, 1969.**
20 p. 18 col. plates. 18 cm.
MnCS

5071 **Linage Conde, Antonio.**
El monacato en España e Hispanoamerica. Salamanca, 1977.
778 p. 24 cm.
MnCS

5072 **Masoliver, Alejandro Maria.**
Origen y primeros años (1616-1634) de la Congregación Cisterciense de la Corona de Aragón. Poblet (Taragona), Abadia, 1973.
xii, 560 p. 25 cm.
MnCS

5073 **Necrologi dels monestirs cistercenos espanyols,** masculins i femenins. MS. Monasterio benedictino de Montserrat, Spain, codex 627. 356 f. Quarto. Saec. 18-19.
Microfilm: MnCH proj. no. 30,028

5073a **Torralba Seriano, Federico.**
Monasterios de Veruela, Rueda & Piedra. 2. ed. Lebon, Editorial Everest [1979].
63 p. illus. 25 cm.
MnCS

5074 **Vives i Miret, Josep.**
Restes precistercenques a Poblet.
(*In* Analecta Montserratensia, v. 10, p. 191-202)
PLatS

5075 **Yanez Neira, Damián.**
El monasterio de la Espina y sus abades. León, Centro e Investigación "San Isidoro," 1972.
149 p. 25 cm.
MnCS

Sweden

5076 **Curman, Sigurd.**
Bidrag till kännedomen om Cistercienserordens bygg nadskonst: I. Iyrkoplanen. Stockholm, Norstedt & Söner, 1912.
213 p. illus. 28 cm.
MnCS

Switzerland

5077 **Ducotterd, Georges.**
Les faverges en Lavaux; vignoble millenaire. Lausanne, Editions du Grand-Pont [1976].
160 p. plates (part col.) 25 cm.
MnCS

5078 **Junker, F.**
Sankt Urban; eine Monographie der ehemaligen Abtei. Lucerne, Raeber, 1975.
79 p. illus.
MnCS

5079 **Tschudi, Aegidius, O.S.B.**
Collectiones de monasterio Wetingense. MS. Benediktinerabtei St. Paul im Lavantthal, Austria, codex 28/6. 53 f. Folio. Saec. 18(1733).
Microfilm: MnCH proj. no. 12,699

5080 **Waeber-Antiglio, Catherine.**
Hauterive; la construction d'une abbaye cistercienne au Moyen Age. Freibourg, Ed. Universitaires, 1976.
255 p. illus. 24 x 18 cm.
MnCS

United States

5081 **Vision of peace** . . . Spencer, Mass., Saint Joseph's Abbey, Cistercian Monks of the Strict Observance [1960?].
95 p. chiefly illus., plan. 26 cm.
KAS

Wales

5082 **Hays, Rhys Williams.**
The history of the Abbey of Aberconway, 1186-1537. Cardiff, University of Wales Press, 1963.
xiii, 210 p. maps. 22 cm.
PLatS

5082a **Howells, Roscoe.**
Total community; the monks of Caldey Island. Tenby, H. G. Walters (Publishers) 1975.
224 p. illus. 23 cm.
MnCS; NcBe

5083 **Williams, David Henry.**
The Welsh Cistercians; aspects of their economic history. Pontypool (Mon.), Griffin P., 1969.

100 p.
NcBe

5084 **Williams, David Henry.**
White monks in Gwent and the border.
Pontypool, Hughes and Son, 1976.
xii, 169 p. illus. 26 cm.
MnCS

4. CLUNIACS

See also Cluny in chapter XII

5085 **Atlas des monastères de l'Ordre de Cluny au moyen-age.** Annexe au tome VI des Status, Chapitres Généraux et Visites de l'Ordre de Cluny. Paris, Editions E. de Boccard, 1977.
27, [4] p. 29 cm.
PLatS; InStme; KAS; MnCS

5085a **Brachmann, Albert.**
Zur politischen Bedeutung der kluniazensischen Bewegung. 2. unveränderte Aufl. Darmstadt, Wissenschaftliche Buchgesellschaft, 1958.
75 p. 19 cm.
KAS

5086 **Centro di Studi sulla Spiritualita Medievale.** Convegno, 2d, 1958. Spiritualità cluniacense. Todi, Accademia Tudertina, 1960.
349 p. plates. 23 cm.
MnCS

5087 **Charvin, Vedastus, O.S.B.**
Status chapitres generaux et vusties de l'Ordre de Cluny, avec un avant-propos et des notes par Dom V. Charvin. Paris, Editions E. de Boccard, 1965–
MnCS; MoCo

5088 **Christe, Yves.**
Cluny et le Clunisois. Genève, Institut d'histoire de l'art du Moyen Age [1967].
78 p. illus. 24 cm.
MnCS

5089 **Constable, Giles.**
Organization of monasteries, 7th–11th centuries [Phonotape cassette]. Recorded at St. John's University, July 24, 1973.
1 tape cassette.
MnCS

5090 **Cook, George Henry, ed.**
Letters to Cromwell on the suppression of the monasteries. London, J. Baker [1965].
viii, 272 p. 22 cm.
PLatS

5091 **Cowdrey, Herbert Edward John.**
The Cluniacs and the Gregorian reform. Oxford, Clarendon Press, 1970.
xxvii, 289 p. 23 cm.
MnCS; MoCo

5092 **Dialogus duorum monachorum Cluniacensis et Cisterciensis.** MS. Cistercienserabtei Zwettl, Austria, codex 380, f. 78r–128r. Octavo. Saec. 12.
Microfilm: MnCH proj. no. 6977

5093 **Duby, Georges.**
Cluny e l'economia rurale.
(*In* La bonifica benedettina, p. 107–117)
PLatS

5094 **L'Esprit de Cluny;** textes clunisiens. [La Pierre-qui-Vire (Yonne)] Zodiaque, 1963.
195 p. illus., col. plates. 26 cm.
InStme; MnCS; KAS; PLatS

5095 **Hunt, Noreen, comp.**
Cluniac monasticism in the Central Middle Ages. [London], Macmillan, [1971].
x, 248 p. 22 cm.
InStme; MnCS

5096 _____ [Hamden, Conn.], Archon Books, 1971.
x, 248 p. 23 cm.
MnCS; PLatS

5097 **Idung of Prüfening.**
Cistercians and Cluniacs; the case of Cîteaux. Translated by Jeremiah F. O'Sullivan . . . Kalamazoo, Mich., Cistercian Publications, 1977.
230 p. 23 cm.
InStme; NcBe

5098 **Knowles, David, O.S.B.**
The Cluniacs in England.
(*In* Williams, Schafer. The Gregorian epoch. Boston, 1964. p. 37–41)
PLatS

5099 **Lamma, Paolo.**
Momenti di storiografia cluniacense. Roma, 1961.
203 p. 26 cm.
InStme; PLatS

5100 **Leclercq, Jean, O.S.B.**
Le monachisme Clunisien.
(*In* Théologie de la vie monastique, p. 447–457)
PLatS

5101 **Longueville, France. Sainte Foi (Cluniac priory).**
Chartes du prieuré de Longueville . . . publiés avec introduction et notes . . . par Paul Le Chacheux. Rouen, A. Lestringant, 1934.
xxvii, 137 p. 25 cm.
MnCS

5102 **Mattoso, José.**
Le monachisme ibérique et Cluny . . . Louvain, Bibliothèque de l'Université, 1968.
xix, 437 p. illus. 26 cm.
KAS

5103 **Petrus Venerabilis, abbot of Cluny.**
Statuta suae congregationis. Forma visi-
tationis ecclesiae. MS. Benediktinerabtei
Admont, Austria, codex 497, f.111r–114v.
Folio. Saec. 12.
Microfilm: MnCH proj. no. 9547

5104 **Sackur, Ernst.**
Die Cluniacenser in ihrer kirchlichen und
algemeingeschichtlichen Wirkamsamkeit
bis zur Mitte des elften Jahrhunderts.
Darmstadt, Wissenschaftliche Buchgesellschaft, 1965.
2 v. 22 cm.
Reprint of Halle edition of 1892–94.
InStme; MnCS

5105 **Status, chapitres généraux et visites
de l'Ordre de Cluny.** Paris, E. de Boccard, 1965–
v. 28 cm.
French or Latin.
InStme; KAS; MnCS; PLatS

5106 **Tellenbach, Gerd, ed.**
Neue Forschungen über Cluny und die
Cluniacenser, von Joachim Wollasch [u.a.].
Freiburg, Herder, 1959.
463 p. maps. 23 cm.
KAS; MnCS; PLatS

5107 **Valous, Guy de.**
Le monachisme clunisien des origines au
XVe siècle. 2. éd. augm. Paris, A. et J.
Picard, 1970.
2 v. 24 cm.
InStme; MnCS

5108 **Werner, Ernst.**
Die gesellschaftlichen Grundlagen der
Klosterreform im 11. Jahrhundert. Berlin,
Deutscher Verlag der Wissenschaften,
1953.
128 p. map. 21 cm.
MnCS

5109 **Williams, Schafer, ed.**
The Gregorian epoch: reformation,
revolution, reaction? Boston, Heath [1964].
xiv, 110 p. 24 cm.
PLatS

5. GRANDMONT, ORDER OF

5110 **Becquet, Jean, O.S.B.**
Scriptores Ordinis Grandimontensis.
Turnholti, Brepols, 1968.
xiii, 628 p. (Corpus Christianorum. Con-
tinuatio mediaevalis, 8)
InStme; KAS; MnCS; PLatS

6. MECHITARISTS

a. General Works

See also Mechitar, of Sebaste, in Author
Part, n. 4862–4867 & Subject Part, n.
4361–4364.

5111 **Abriss der Geschichte der Wiener Mech-
itaristen-Congregation** und ihrer
Wirksamkeit aus Anlass des 50-jährigen
Jubiläums der Grundsteinlegung zu
ihrem neuen Kloster durch ihre Majes-
täten Kaiser Ferdinand und Kaiserin
Maria Anna. Wien, Mechitaristen-
Buchdruckerei, 1887.
43 p. 23 cm.
MnCS

5112 **Festschrift aus Anlass der Hundertjahrfeier des Neubaues** des Mutterhauses der Mechitaristen in Wien,
1837–1937. Wien. Mechitaristen-
Buchdruckerei, 1937.
8 p. [46] plates. 25 cm.
MnCS

5113 **Huschardzen;** Festschrift aus Anlass
des 100-jährigen Bestandes der Mechitaristen-Kongregation in Wien (1811–
1911) und des 25. Jahrgangs der philologischen Monatschrift "Handes amsorya" (1887–1911) . . . Wien, Mechitaristen-Kongregation, 1911 [i.e. 1912].
435 p. illus. 32 cm.
Edited by P. N. Akinian.
MnCS

5114 **Inglizian, Vahan.**
Hundertfünfzig Jahre Mechitaristen in
Wien (1811–1961). Wien, Verlag der
Mechitaristen-Kongregation, 1961.
198 p. plates. 24 cm.
MnCS

5115 **Kasper, Robert E.**
Hundertfünfzig Jahre Mechitaristen-
Buchdruckerei. [Wien, Druck der Mechitaristen-Buchdruckerei, 1961].
54 p. 22 x 22 cm. (on folded leaves), illus.
23 cm.
MnCS

5116 **Mechiter-Festschrift zum 200.** Todestage
des gottseligen Abtes Mechitar, Stifters
der Mechitaristen-Kongregation, 1749–
1949. Wien, Mechitaristen-Buchdruckerei, 1949 [i.e., 1950].
434 p. 30 cm.
MnCS

5117 **Neumann, Karl Friedrich.**
Versuch einer Geschichte der arme-
nischen Literatur, nach den Werken der
Mechitaristen frei bearbeitet. Leipzig,
Verlag von Johann Ambrosius Barth,
1836.
xii, 308 p. 22 cm.
MnCS

b. Liturgical Books

All liturgical books listed below are in the Armenian language, unless otherwise indicated.

1. Breviarium

5118   **Breviarium Armenium.** MS. Mechitaristenkongregation, Vienna, codex 416. 200 f. Duodecimo. Saec. 14–15.
Microfilm: MnCH proj. no. 8001

5119   **Breviarium Armenium.** MS. Mechitaristenkongregation, Vienna, codex 544. 155 f. Duodecimo. Saec. 14–15.
Microfilm: MnCH proj. no. 8112

5120   **Breviarium Armenium und Gebete der Armenischen Kirche in tatarischer Uebersetzung** (mit armenischen Lettern geschrieben). MS. Mechitaristenkongregation, Vienna, codex 143. 283 f. Octavo. Saec. 15–16.
Microfilm: MnCH proj. no. 7722

5121   **Breviarium Armenium und Liturgie der Armenischen Kirche.** MS. Mechitaristen-kongregation, Vienna, codex 1023. 149 f. Duodecimo. Saec. 16(1512).
Microfilm: MnCH proj. no. 8582

5122   **Breviarium Armenium,** Psalterium und Kalendarium. MS. Mechitaristenkongregation, Vienna, codex 1105. 156 f. Folio. Saec. 16(?).
Microfilm: MnCH proj. no. 8668

5123   **Breviarium Armenium und Liturgie der Armenischen Kirche.** MS. Mechitaristen-kongregation, Vienna, codex 1255. 172 f. Octavo. Saec. 16(1564).
Microfilm: MnCH proj. no. 8755

5124   **Breviarium Armenium.** MS. Mechitaristenkongregation, Vienna, codex 69, f.89r–143r. Quarto. Saec. 17(1662).
Microfilm: MnCH proj. no. 7670

5125   **Brevarium et Psalterium Armenium.** MS. Mechitaristenkongregation, Vienna, codex 270. 266 f. Quarto. Saec. 17(1653).
Microfilm: MnCH proj. no. 7855

5126   **Breviarium et Hymnarium Armenium.** MS. Mechitaristenkongregation, Vienna, codex 291. 558 f. Octavo. Saec. 17.
Microfilm: MnCH proj. no. 7862

5127   **Breviarium (Horologium) der Armeno-Römäer.** MS. Mechitaristenkongregation, Vienna, codex 942. 186 f. Octavo. Saec. 17–18.
Microfilm: MnCH proj. no. 8491

5128   **Liederbuch und Breviarium Armenium.** MS. Mechitaristenkongregation, Vienna, codex 1191. 206 f. Octavo. Saec. 18 (1723).
Microfilm: MnCH proj. no. 8716

5129   **Breviarium der Muttergottes und Gebetbuch.** MS. Mechitaristenkongregation, Vienna, codex 1268. 314 f. Octavo. Saec. 19(1854).
Microfilm: MnCH proj. no. 8762

2. Calendarium

5130   **Ewiges Kalendarium.** MS. Mechitaristenkongregation, Vienna, codex 1177. 155 f. Octavo. Saec. 19(1847).
Microfilm: MnCH proj. no. 8708

5131   **Kalendarium Armenium und Evangelienausweis.** MS. Mechitaristenkongregation, Vienna, codex 201. 196 f. Duodecimo. Saec. 16–17.
Microfilm: MnCH proj. no. 201

3. Catechism

5132   **Katechismus** (Erklärung des Katechismus). MS. Mechitaristenkongregation, Vienna, codex 1206. 5. f. & 195 p. Octavo. Saec. 19(1811).
Microfilm: MnCH proj. no. 8727

4. Confession

5133   **Das Buch der Beichtväter.** MS. Mechitaristenkongregation, Vienna, codex 1132. 119 f. Folio. Saec. 19.
Microfilm: MnCH proj. no. 8670

5. Evangeliarium

5134   **Evangelium und Psalterium türkisch-armenisch.** MS. Mechitaristenkongregation, Vienna, codex 23. 283 f. Quarto. Saec. 16–17.
Microfilm: MnCH proj. no. 7626

6. Holy Week

5135   **Die Karwoche:** Betrachtungen und Gebete. Neuarmenisch. MS. Mechitaristenkongregation, Vienna, codex 1180. 530 f. Octavo. Saec. 19(1862).
Microfilm: MnCH proj. no. 8745

7. Hymnarium

5136   **Hymnarium Armenium.** MS. Mechitaristenkongregation, Vienna, codex 145. 272 f. Octavo. Saec. 13(1269).
Microfilm: MnCH proj. no. 7737

5137   **Hymnarium Armenium (mancat initium).** Mechitaristenkongregation, Vienna, codex 161. 345 f. Duodecimo. Saec. 14 (1335).
Microfilm: MnCH proj. no. 7738

5138 **Hymnarium Armenium.** MS. Mechitaristenkongregation, Vienna, codex 173. 247 f. Duodecimo. Saec. 14(1343). Microfilm: MnCH proj. no. 7747

5139 **Hymnarium Armenium.** MS. Mechitaristenkongregation, Vienna, codex 180. 353 f. Duodecimo. Saec. 14(1329). Microfilm: MnCH proj. no. 7752

5140 **Hymnarium Armenium.** MS. Mechitaristenkongregation, Vienna, codex 163. 339 f. Octavo. Saec. 15(?). Microfilm: MnCH proj. no. 7733

5141 **Hymnarium Armenium.** MS. Mechitaristenkongregation, Vienna, codex 179. 293 f. Duodecimo. Saec. 15–16. Microfilm: MnCH proj. no. 7749

5142 **Hymnarium Armenium.** MS. Mechitaristenkongregation, Vienna, codex 150. 438 f. Duodecimo. Saec. 16(1560). Microfilm: MnCH proj. no. 7721

5143 **Hymnarium Armenium.** MS. Mechitaristenkongregation, Vienna, codex 142. 400 f. Octavo. Saec. 17(1625). Microfilm: MnCH proj. no. 7720

5144 **Hymnarium Armenium.** MS. Mechitaristenkongregation, Vienna, codex 155. 368 f. Duodecimo. Saec. 17(1652). Microfilm: MnCH proj. no. 7731

8. Lectionarium

5145 **Lectionarium.** MS. Mechitaristenkongregation, Vienna, codex 3. 256 f. Folio. Saec. 10–11. Microfilm: MnCH proj. no. 7616

5146 **Lectionarium Armenium (incompletum).** MS. Mechitaristenkongregation, Vienna, codex 60. 239 f. Quarto. Saec. 12–13. Microfilm: MnCH proj. no. 7675

5147 **Lectionarium Armenium (incompletum —usque ad Pentecosten).** MS. Mechitaristenkongregation, Vienna, codex 53. 218 f. Quarto. Saec. 13. Microfilm: MnCH proj. no. 7652

5148 **Lectionarium Armenium.** MS. Mechitaristenkongregation, Vienna, codex 241. 229 f. Quarto. Saec. 13–14. Microfilm: MnCH proj. no. 7816

5149 **Lectionarium Armenium.** MS. Mechitaristenkongregation, Vienna, codex 245. 462 f. Quarto. Saec. 13. Microfilm: MnCH proj. no. 7801

5150 **Lectionarium.** MS. Mechitaristenkongregation, Vienna, codex 5. 431 f. Folio. Saec. 13. Microfilm: MnCH proj. no. 7617

5151 **Lectionarium.** MS. Mechitaristenkongregation, Vienna, codex 9. 364 p. Folio. Saec. 16. Microfilm: MnCH proj. no. 7623

5152 **Lectionarium Armenium.** Mechitaristenkongregation, Vienna, codex 698. 429 f. Folio. Saec. 17(1643). Microfilm: MnCH proj. no. 8328

5153 **Lectionarium Armenium.** Mechitaristenkongregation, Vienna, codex 269. 346 f. Quarto. Saec. 18(1720). Microfilm: MnCH proj. no. 7842

9. Liturgia

5154 **Liturgie der Armenischen Kirche (Abschrift).** Mechitaristenkongregation, Vienna, codex 892. 50 f. Octavo. Saec. 14(1334). Microfilm: MnCH proj. no. 8470

5155 **Liturgie der Armenischen Kirche.** MS. Mechitaristenkongregation, Vienna, codex 690, f.99r–159v. Duodecimo. Saec. 15(1474). Microfilm: MnCH proj. no. 8250

5156 **Liturgie der Armenischen Kirche.** MS. Mechitaristenkongregation, Vienna, codex 435. 59 f. Folio. Saec. 17–18. Microfilm: MnCH proj. no. 8012

5157 **Messliturgia der Armenischen Kirche:** 1. Vom hl. Athanasius; 2. Vom hl. Chrysostomus; 3. Vom hl. Basilius. MS. Mechitaristenkongregation, Vienna, codex 1303. 140 f. Saec. 15(?) & 17(?). Microfilm: MnCH proj. no. 8785

5158 **Nerses, Lampronaci.** Erklärung der Gebete der Liturgie. MS. Mechitaristenkongregation, Vienna, codex 831. 218 f. Quarto. Saec. 18. Microfilm: MnCH proj. no. 8391

5159 **Nerses, Lampronaci.** Erklärung der Gebete der hl. Liturgie. MS. Mechitaristenkongregation, Vienna, codex 1122. 229 f. Octavo. Saec. 18(1788). Microfilm: MnCH proj. no. 8647

10. Martyrologium

5160 **Martyrologium Armenium.** MS. Mechitaristenkongregation, Vienna, codex 1048. 493 f. Folio. Saec. 14(1302). Microfilm: MnCH proj. no. 8608

5161 **Martyrologium.** MS. Mechitaristenkongregation, Vienna, codex 7. 607 f. Folio. Saec. 15(1439). Microfilm: MnCH proj. no. 7625

5162 **Martyrologium Armenium.** MS. Mechitaristenkongregation, Vienna, codex 213. 353 f. Folio. Saec. 15–16. Microfilm: MnCH proj. no. 7809

5163 **Martyrologium Armenium.** MS. Mechitaristenkongregation, Vienna, codex 219. 515 f. Folio. Saec. 16(1591). Microfilm: MnCH proj. no. 7799

5164 **Martyrologium.** MS. Mechitaristenkon-
gregation, Vienna, codex 10. 548 f.
Folio. Saec. 16.
Microfilm: MnCH proj. no. 7631

5165 **Martyrologium Armenium.** MS. Mechitaristenkongregation, Vienna, codex
1035. 561 f. Folio. Saec. 17(?).
Microfilm: MnCH proj. no. 8600

5166 **Martyrologium Armenium.** MS. Mechitaristenkongregation, Vienna, codex
1037. 604 f. Folio. Saec. 17(1628).
Microfilm: MnCH proj. no. 8605

11. Missale

5167 **Missale der Armenier in Polen.** MS.
Mechitaristenkongregation, Vienna,
codex 445. 55, 10, 10 f. Folio. Saec.
17.
Microfilm: MnCH proj. no. 8077

12. Ordo Ministrandi

5168 **Ordo ministrandi der hl. Messe (Liturgie).** MS. Mechitaristenkongregation,
Vienna, codex 411, f.75v–103v. Duodecimo. Saec. 17(1669).
Microfilm: MnCH proj. no. 7994

5169 **Ordo ministrandi & Missa.** MS. Mechitaristenkongregation, Vienna, codex
664, f.1r–55v. Octavo. Saec. 17(1646).
Microfilm: MnCH proj. no. 8252

5170 **Ordo ministrandi und Liederbuch.** MS.
Mechitaristenkongregation, Vienna,
codex 1284. 99 f. Duodecimo. Saec.
18–19.
Microfilm: MnCH proj. no. 8779

13. Psalterium

5171 **Psalterium Armenium.** MS. Mechitaristenkongregation, Vienna, codex 187.
201 f. Duodecimo. Saec. 15–16.
Microfilm: MnCH proj. no. 7768

5172 **Psalterium Armenium (incompletum).**
MS. Mechitaristenkongregation, Vienna,
codex 391. 271 f. Duodecimo. Saec. 15.
Microfilm: MnCH proj. no. 7956

5173 **Psalterium Armenium.** MS. Mechitaristenkongregation, Vienna, codex 410.
239 f. Duodecimo. Saec. 16(1596).
Microfilm: MnCH proj. no. 7971

5174 **Psalterium Armenium.** MS. Mechitaristenkongregation, Vienna, codex 69,
f.1r–88v. Quarto. Saec. 17(1662).
Microfilm: MnCH proj. no. 7670

5175 **Psalterium et Breviarium Armenium.**
MS. Mechitaristenkongregation, Vienna,
codex 333. 367 f. Octavo. Saec. 17.
(1618)
Microfilm: MnCH proj. no. 7891

5176 **Psalterium Armenium.** MS. Mechitaristenkongregation, Vienna, codex 141.
230 f. Octavo. Saec. 18(1735).
Microfilm: MnCH proj. no. 7717

5177 **Tomar, oder Kalendarium Armenium.**
Psalterium Armenium. Breviarium
Armenium. Die gewöhnliche Arme-
nische Liturgie. MS. Mechitaristenkon-
gregation, Vienna, codex 393. 271 f.
Duodecimo. Saec. 17(1690).
Microfilm: MnCH proj. no. 7950

14. Rituale

5178 **Rituale Armenium.** MS. Mechitaristenkongregation, Vienna, codex 240. 238
f. Quarto. Saec. 11–12.
Microfilm: MnCH proj. no. 7823

5179 **Rituale Armenium für Priesterbegräb-
niss,** Canones für acht Tage. MS.
Mechitaristenkongregation, Vienna,
codex 280, 223 f. Quarto. Saec. 13(1214).
Microfilm: MnCH proj. no. 7863

5180 **Rituale Armenium.** MS. Mechitaristen-
kongregation, Vienna, codex 264. 219 f.
Quarto. Saec. 14–15.
Microfilm: MnCH proj. no. 7852

5181 **Rituale Armenium.** MS. Mechitaristen-
kongregation, Vienna, codex 108. 188 f.
Octavo. Saec. 15(1418).
Microfilm: MnCH proj. no. 7691

5182 **Rituale Armenium.** MS. Mechitaristenkongregation, Vienna, codex 133, f.3r–
187r. Octavo. Saec. 15(1455).
Microfilm: MnCH proj. no. 7713

5183 **Rituale Armenium und Kirchenlieder.**
Weihe der Diakonissinnen. Kanon der
Fusswashung. MS. Mechitaristenkon-
gregation, Vienna, codex 600. 218 f.
Octavo. Saec. 15(1440).
Microfilm: MnCH proj. no. 8143

5184 **Rituale Armenium.** MS. Mechitaristen-
kongregation, Vienna, codex 68. 192 f.
Quarto. Saec. 16(1567).
Microfilm: MnCH proj. no. 7667

5185 **Rituale Armenium.** MS. Mechitaristen-
kongregation, Vienna, codex 138. 254 f.
Octavo. Saec. 16(1534).
Microfilm: MnCH proj. no. 7739

5186 **Rituale Armenium.** MS. Mechitaristen-
kongregation, Vienna, codex 123. 284 f.
Octavo. Saec. 16(1511).
Microfilm: MnCH proj. no. 7698

5187 **Rituale Armenium und "Klagelieder."**
MS. Mechitaristenkongregation, Vienna,
codex 148. 110 f. Duodecimo. Saec. 17
(1650).
Microfilm: MnCH proj. no. 7730

5188 **Rituale Armenium und "Klagelieder."** MS. Mechitaristenkongregation, Vienna, codex 149. 93 f. Octavo. Saec. 17–18. Microfilm: MnCH proj. no. 7716

5189 **Rituale Armenium und Kirchenlieder.** MS. Mechitaristenkongregation, Vienna, codex 415. 190 f. Duodecimo. Saec. 17–18. Microfilm: MnCH proj. no. 7970

5190 **Rituale Armenium und Buch der Sakramente.** MS. Mechitaristenkongregation, Vienna, codex 1073. 348 f. Octavo. Saec. 18–19. Microfilm: MnCH proj. no. 8621

5191 **Rituale Armenium.** 2 vols. MS. Mechitaristenkongregation, Vienna, codices 1077–78. Octavo. Saec. 19(1816). Microfilm: MnCH proj. no. 8629 & 8632

15. Rituale Ordinationis

5192 **Rituale ordinationis Armenium.** Das Buch der Handauflegung. MS. Mechitaristenkongregation, Vienna, codex 331. 78 f. Octavo. Saec. 14–15. Microfilm: MnCH proj. no. 7910

16. Stations of the Cross

5193 **Kreuzwegandachtsbuch.** MS. Mechitaristenkongregation, Vienna, codex 1269. 48 f. Octavo. Saec. 18(1774). Microfilm: MnCH proj. no. 8778

7. OLIVETANS

5194 **Acta Curiae Generalis.** Siena, Abbazia di Monteoliveto Maggiore, 1959– LLa

5195 **Antonius Bargensis, ed.** Chronicon Montis Oliveti (1313–1450). Florentiae, Abbatia Septimnianensi prope Florentiam, 1901–1903. 2 v. geneal. tables. 25 cm. (Spicilegium Montolivetense, 1–2) InStme

5196 **Capra, Ramiro M., O.S.B.Oliv.** Monte Oliveto Maggiore. [n.p., 1967]. 153 p. illus. (part col.) 16 cm. PLatS

5197 **Lancellotti, Secondo, O.S.B.Oliv.** Historiae Olivetanae. Venetiis, Typographia Guereliana, 1623. [24], 360 p. 22 cm.

5198 **Il Pilastrello (periodical).** Lendinara, Rovigo. 1916– LLa

5199 **Scarpini, Modesto.** I monaci benedettini di Monte Oliveto. Alessandria Edizione "L'Ulivo" [1952].

511 p. 25 cm. MnCS

5200 **L'Ulivo (periodical).** Abbazia di Monteoliveto Maggiore, Siena. 1974– LLa

5201 **La Vetta di Picciano (periodical).** Matera. 1974– LLa

8. PULSANO, ORDER OF

5202 **Morelli, Marcello.** Vita di s. Giovanni da Matera, abate fondatore della Congregazione Benedittina di Pulsano. Putiganano di Bari, De Robertis & figli [1930]. 220 p. 22 cm. KAS; NdRi; NcBe

9. SCOTTISH BENEDICTINES

5203 **Barry, Patrick J.** Irish Benedictines in Nuremberg; an examination of the Chronicle of the monastery of St. Aegidius in Nuremberg. (In Studies, v. 21(1932) p. 579–597; v. 22 (1933), p. 435–453) MnCS

5204 **Barry, Patrick J.** Die Zustände im Wiener Schottenkloster vor der Reform des Jahres 1418. Aichach, Lothar Schütte, 1927. 106 p. 23 cm. Inaug.-Diss.–München. MnCS

5205 **Berger, Willibald, O.S.B.** Die Wiener Schotten. Wien, Bergland Verlag [1962]. 71 p. illus. 18 cm. (Oesterreich-Reihe, Bd. 179/181) MnCS

5205a **Breatnach, P. A.** Die Regensburger Schottenlegende. München, Arbeo-Gesellschaft, 1977. 324 p. (Münchener Beiträge . . . 27) MnCS

5206 **Dilworth, Mark, O.S.B.** The Scots in Franconia; a century of monastic life. Totowa, N.J., Rowan and Littlefield [1974]. 301 p. illus. 23 cm. InStme; KAS; PLatS

5207 **Fuhrmann, Joseph Paul, O.S.B.** Irish medieval monasteries on the continent. [Washington, D.C.] 1927. xiii, 121 p. 23 cm. Thesis (Ph.D.)–Catholic University of America, Washington, D.C., 1927. AStb; MnCS; NcBe

5208 **Hübl, Albert, O.S.B.**
Baugeschichte des Stiftes Schotten in Wien. Wien, Gerold, 1914.
52 p. illus.
AStb

5208a **Lindner, Pirmin, O.S.B.**
Die Schriftsteller . . . des Benediktinerordens im heutigen Königreich Bayern vom Jahre 1750 bis zur Gegenwart. Regensburg, G. J. Manz, 1880.
vid. p. 232–241: Die Schottenstifte St. Jacob in Regensburg & St. Jacob in Würzburg.
MnCS

5208b **Mai, Paul.**
Das Schottenkloster St. Jakob zu Regensburg im Wandel der Zeiten.
(*In* his: 100 Jahre Priesterseminar in St. Jakob zu Regensburg, 1872–1972. Regensburg, 1972. p. 6–36).
MnCS

5209 **Nüremberg, Germany. St. Aegidius (Benedictine abbey).**
Excerpta consuetudinum observantiae regularis monasterii Nurnbergensis conventus Ordinis S. Benedicti. MS. Benediktinerabtei Melk, Austria, codex 639, f.247r–249v. Quarto. Saec. 15.
Microfilm: MnCH proj. no. 1524

5210 **Quomodo monasterium S. Nicolai Memmingae in Suevis fundatum est.** MS. Vienna, Nationalbibliothek, codex 3347, f.26r–34v. Folio. Saec. 15.
Microfilm: MnCH proj. no. 16,617

5211 **Quomodo monasterium S. Petri apud Ratisbonam fundatum est.** MS. Vienna, Nationalbibliothek, codex 3347, f.1r–26r. Folio. Saec. 15.
Microfilm: MnCH proj. no. 16,617

5211a **Schöppner, A.**
Schottenklöster in Deutschland.
(*In* his: Charakterbilder der allgemeinen Geschichte. Schaffhausen, 1871–73. vol. 2)
AStb; MnCS

5212 **Stiegler, A.**
St. Jakob in Regensburg. [Regensburg, Ratisbona-Kunstverlag]
15 p. illus. 19 cm.
NdRi

10. SYLVESTRINES

5213 **Atti del Convegno di studi storici:** VIII centenario naschita S. Silvestro, 1177–1977. Monastero S. Silvestro (Fabriano), [1978].
236 p. illus. 24 cm.
MnCS

5213a **Bibliotheca Montisfani (periodical).**
Fabriano. 1975–
MiOx

5214 **Inter fratres (periodical).** Detroit-Rome.
1950–
MiOx

5215 **Jacobi, Andrea, O.S.B.Syl.**
The saints of the Benedictine Order of Montefano. Clifton, N.J., Holy Face Monastery [1972].
268 p. illus. 22 cm.
InStme; PLatS

11. TRAPPISTS

a. General Works

5216 **Amedeus, Father, O.C.S.O.**
The Right Reverend Dom M. Edmond Obrecht, O.C.S.O., fourth abbot of Our Lady of Gethsemani (1852–1935). Trappist, Ky., Abbey of Our Lady of Gethsemani [1937].
335 p. plates. 23 cm.
MnCS

5217 **Barakat, Robert A.**
The Cistercian sign language; a study in non-verbal communication. Kalamazoo, Mich., Cistercian Publications, 1975.
220 p. illus. (Cistercian studies series, n. 11)
MoCo

5218 **Breve ragguaglio delle costituzioni delle badie della Trappa,** di Buonsollazo e di Casamari della stretta osservanza dell' Ordine Cisterciense, scritto dall'abate di Buonsollazo . . . Firenze, Tartini e Franchi, 1718.
256 p.
MnCS; KAS(microfilm)

5219 **Cistercian contemplatives;** monks of the strict observance at Our Lady of Gethsemani, Ky., Our Lady of the Holy Ghost, Ga., Our Lady of the Holy Trinity, Utah. A guide to Trappist life. [Trappist, Ky., Our Lady of Gethsemani, 1948].
62 p. illus. 24 cm.
KAS

5220 **The Cistercian life with the Strict Observance (Trappists).** Translated from the original French by a monk of the Abbey of Gethsemani. Trappist, Ky., Our Lady of Gethsemani [1953].
131 p.
NcBe

5221 **Constitutiones et acta capitulorum strictioris observantiae Cisterciensis** [1624–1687]. Editionem curavit Julius Donatus Leloczky. Roma, Ediciones Cistercienses, 1967.

255 p. 27 cm. (Bibliotheca Cisterciensis, 4)
KAS

5222 Constitutiones ac declarationes congregationis monachorum reformatorum S. Bernardi Ordinis Cisterciensis in Regulam sanctissimi patris nostri Benedicti abbatis a capitulis generalibus annis 1639 & 1696 recognitae & approbatae. Romae, ex Typographia Antonii de Rubeis, 1700.
216, [24] p.
KAS(microfilm)

5223 Constitutiones Ordinis Cisterciensium Strictioris Observantiae a Sancta Sede approbatae et confirmatae. Westmalle [Belgique], Typographia Ordinis Cisterciensium Strictioris Observantiae, MCMXXV.
48 p.
CaQStB

5224 Directoire spirituel à l'usage des Cisterciens réformés de la stricte observance. Abbaye de Notre-Dame de Grace, 1910.
563 p. 23 cm.
MnCS

5225 Hart, Brother Patrick.
Thomas Merton, monk: a monastic tribute. New York, Image Books, 1976.
232 p.
InFer

5226 Lancelot, Claude, O.S.B.
Narrative of a tour taken in the year 1667 to la Grande Chartreuse and Alet . . . including some account of Dom A. J. Le Bouthillier de Rancé . . . Cornhill [England], J. and A. Arch, 1813.
xxiv, 261 p. 22 cm.
KAS

5227 La Trappe: congrégation de moines de l'Ordre Bénédictino-Cistercien. Romae, Imprimerie Forense, 1864.
39 p. 23 cm.
PLatS

5228 Lekai, Louis Julius, O.C.S.O.
The rise of the Cistercian strict observance in seventeenth-century France. Washington, D.C. Catholic University of America Press [1968].
vii, 261 p. illus., map. 24 cm.
KAS; NcBe

5229 Louf, André.
The message of monastic spirituality, by André Louf and the staff of Collectanea OCR. Translated by Luke Stevens. New York, Desclée Co., 1964.
xv, 304 p. 22 cm.

A translation of the 1962 Bulletin de spiritualité monastique.
MnCS

5230 McGinley, Gerard, O.C.S.O.
A Trappist writes home; letters of Abbot Gerard McGinley, O.C.S.O., to his family. Introduction by Father Raymond. Milwaukee, Bruce Pub. Co., [1960].
175 p. illus. 22 cm.
KAS

5231 Nouwen, Henri J. M.
The Genesee diary; a report from a Trappist monastery. Garden City, N.Y., Doubleday [1976].
xvi, 199 p. 22 cm.
CaMWiSb

5232 Peeters, Michael.
Histoire des Trappistes du Val-Sainte-Marie, diocèse de Besançon, avec des notices interèssantes sur les autres monastères de La Trappe en France, en Belgique, en Angleterre, en Irlande, et sur plusieurs religieux Trappistes. 3. éd. considérablement augmentè . . . Bruxelles, J. J. Vanderborght, 1841.
520 p.
MnCS

5233 Raymond, Father, O.C.S.O.
The silent spire speaks. Milwaukee, Bruce Pub. Co. [1966].
vii, 194 p. 23 cm.
MnCS

5234 The spirit of simplicity characteristic of Cîteaux; a report asked for and approved by the General Chapter of 1925 of the Cistercians of the Strict Observance. [Trappist, Ky.], Abbey of Our Lady of Gethsemani, 1935.
56 p. 19 cm.
MnCS

5235 A Spiritual directory for religious; translated from the original French text "Directoire spirituel à l'usage des Cisterciens de la Stricte Observance" by a priest of New Melleray Abbey, Peosta, Ia. Trappist, Ky., Abbey of Our Lady of Gethsemani, 1946.
567 p.
NcBe

b. By Country

Africa

5236 Pfanner, Franz.
The Trappists in South Africa, by P. Francis . . . [Beatty, Pa.], St. Vincent Abbey Print., 1883.
16 p. 23 cm.

"Translated from the German, 3rd edition, 1881."
KAS

England

5237   **La Trappe in England;** chronicles of an
unknown monastery [Holy Cross Abbey,
Stapehill, Dorset]. London, Burns, Oates
& Washbourne, 1935.
224 p. illus.
MoCo

France

5238   **Zakar, Polycarpe.**
Histoire de la stricte observance de
l'Ordre Cistercien depuis ses débuts
jusqu'au généralat du cardinal de Richelieu
(1606–1635). Roma, Editiones Cistercienses, 1966.
338 p. 27 cm. (Bibliotheca Cisterciensis,
3)
KAS; PLatS

United States of America

5239   **Burden, Shirley.**
God is my life; the story of Our Lady of
Gethsemani. Photos by Shirley Burden, in-
troduction by Thomas Merton. New York,
Reynal [1960].
unpaged. illus. 29 cm.
InFer

12. VALLUMBROSIANS

5240   **Bullarium Vallumbrosanum;** sive, Tabula
chronologica in qua continentur bullae
illorum pontificum qui eumdem Ordinem
privilegiis decorarunt. Florentiae, typis
Dominici Ambrosii Verdi, 1729.
134, 8 p.
MnCS (microfilm); PLatS (microfilm)

5241   **Domenichetti, Basilio, C.V.U.O.S.B.**
Guida storica illustrata di Vallombrosa.
3. ed. Firenze "Faggio Vallombrosano,"
[1929].
208 p. illus. 16 cm.
MnCS

5242   **Giovanni Gualberto, Saint,** d. 1073.
Manuale precum sancti Joannis Gualberti, d. Alphonsi Salvini ejusdem congregationis alumni cura editum. Romae, Soc.
Sancti Pauli, 1933.
97 p. illus. 22 cm.
MnCS

5243   **Lucchesi, Emiliano, O.S.B.V.**
I monaci benedettini Vallombrosani nella
diocesi di Pistoia e Prato. Firenze, Fiorentina [1941].
407 p. illus. 20 cm.
MnCS

5244   **Sala, Torello, O.S.B.V.**
Dizionario storico biografico di scrittori,
letterati ed artisti del l'Ordine di Vallombrosa. Firenze, Tipografia dell'Istituto
Gualandi Sordomuti [1929].
2 v. 21 cm.
MnCS

13. WILLIAMITES

5245   **Silvius, Peter, O.S.B.**
Vita s. Guilelmi eremitae et confessoris
nec non primicerii Ordinis Guilielmitarum.
MS. Benediktinerabtei St. Paul im Lavant-
thal, Austria, codex 31/2. 138 f. Octavo.
Saec. 17.
Microfilm: MnCH proj. no. 11,757

14. ANGLICAN AND EPISCOPALIAN BENEDICTINES

5246   **Anson, Peter Frederick.**
Building up the waste places: the revival
of monastic life on medieval lines in the
post-Reformation Church of England.
Leighton Buzzard, Faith Press, 1973.
KAS

5247   **The Jubilee book of the Benedictines of
Nashdom,** 1914–1964. London, The
Faith Press [1964].
86 p. plates. 21 cm.
PLatS

5248   **St. Gregory's Abbey, Three Rivers,
Mich.**
Abbey letter (quarterly), 1954–
MnCS

AUTHOR INDEX

The Author Index lists (1) non-Benedictine writers and (2) anonymous titles which presumably are not of Benedictine origin but treat of some Benedictine topic. All Benedictine writers, personal and corporate (abbeys, convents, learned academies, congresses, etc.) are listed alphabetically in the Author Part.

The numerals refer to the numbered items in the Subject Part.

The Subject Index covers all the Benedictine topics, including individual biographies and individual abbeys, treated in this bibliography.

The numerals refer to the numbered items in the Subject Part.

THE AUTHOR

OLIVER L. KAPSNER, O.S.B., was professed a monk of St. John's Abbey, Collegeville, Minnesota, in 1923. For more than a half century since then, Father Oliver has served the international academic community as a scholar, librarian, author, and cataloguer. In 1925 he received a B.A. in philosophy from St. Vincent College and in 1927 an S.T.B. from The Catholic University of America. He is also the recipient of three honorary doctorates – St. Vincent College (1958), Belmont College (1961), and St. John's University (1966).

Apart from some years of study and military service, between 1932 and 1950 Father Oliver served as either the assistant librarian or the chief librarian at St. John's Abbey and University, where he also taught philosophy classes. From 1951 to 1958 he was a research cataloguer in the library of The Catholic University of America, as well as a consultant for cataloging Catholic literature for the Library of Congress. From 1958 to 1964 he was a research cataloguer in the library of St. Vincent Archabbey and College, where he completely reorganized the collection. From 1964 to 1971 Father Oliver directed the photographic operations in Europe for the Hill Monastic Manuscript Library of St. John's Abbey and University, where he supervised the microfilming of more than 25,000 manuscripts from more than 40 Austrian libraries. In the middle 1970s Father Oliver retired to St. John's Abbey but not from library work. A major focus of his retirement has been the publication of this Supplement to the second edition (1962) of *A Benedictine Bibliography*.

Besides this bibliographic work, Father Oliver is the author of various other titles, including *A Manual of Cataloging Practice for Catholic Author and Title Entries* (1953), *Catholic Religious Orders* (1957), and five editions of *Catholic Subject Headings* (between 1942 and 1963), as well as numerous pamphlets and articles, particularly for *The Catholic Library World* and *The New Catholic Encyclopedia*.